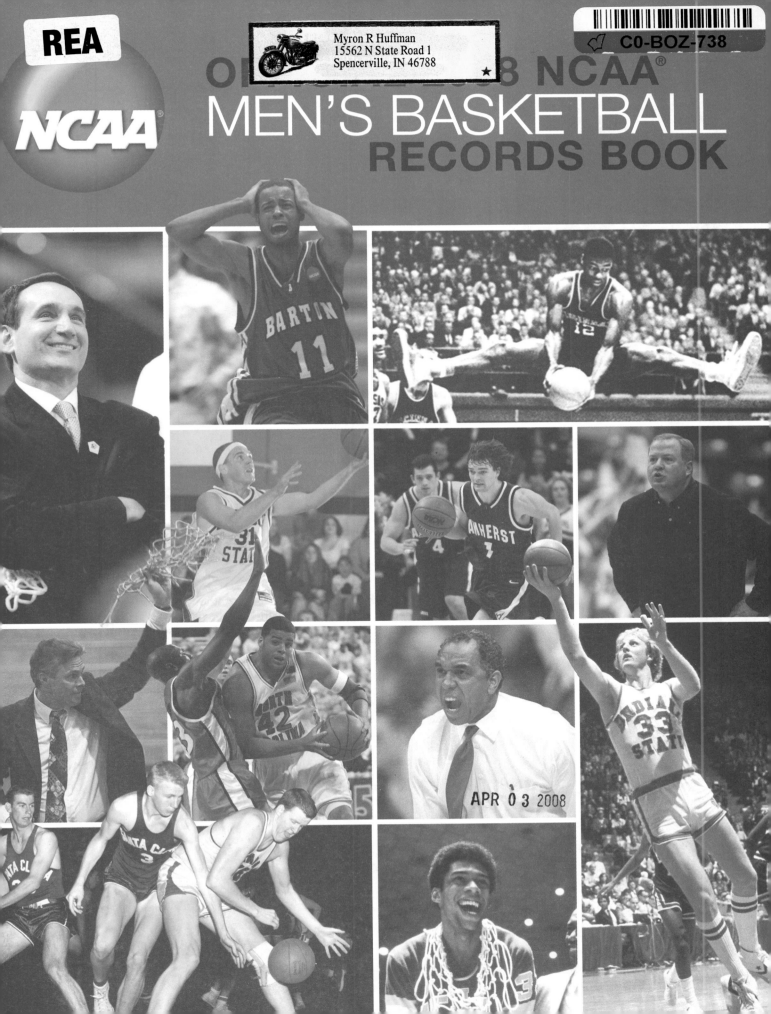

REA

NCAA

OFFICIAL 2008 NCAA
MEN'S BASKETBALL
RECORDS BOOK

THE NATIONAL COLLEGIATE ATHLETIC ASSOCIATION
P.O. Box 6222, Indianapolis, Indiana 46206-6222
317/917-6222
www.ncaa.org

October 2007

Compiled By:
Gary K. Johnson, *Associate Director of Statistics*.
Sean W. Straziscar, *Associate Director of Statistics*.
Bonnie Senappe, *Assistant Director of Statistics*.
Jeff Williams, *Assistant Director of Statistics*.
Kevin Buerge, *Statistics Assistant*.

SPECIAL THANKS TO:
Walt Meyer for his help through the years on career scoring.
William B. Johnson for his help on double-double and triple-double research.

ON THE COVER
Top row (left to right): Mike Krzyzewski, Duke; Anthony Atkinson, Barton; Oscar Robertson, Cincinnati. Second Row: Patrick Glover, Johnson State; Andrew Olson, Amherst; Mike Leaf, Winona State. Third Row: Bo Ryan, Wisconsin-Platteville; Sean May, North Carolina; Tubby Smith, Kentucky; Larry Bird, Indiana State. Bottom Row: Ken Sears (3) of Santa Clara & Clyde Lovellette of Kansas; Lew Alcindor (Kareem Abdul-Jabbar), UCLA.

Cover photos by Andres Alonso, Rich Clarkson, David Gonzales, John Hickey, Ryan McKee, Suzanne Ouellette and Chris Putman of NCAA Photos; and the Sports Information offices of Cincinnati and Johnson State.

Distributed to sports information directors and conference publicity directors.

ISSN 1089-5280
NCAA 61144-10/07

Contents

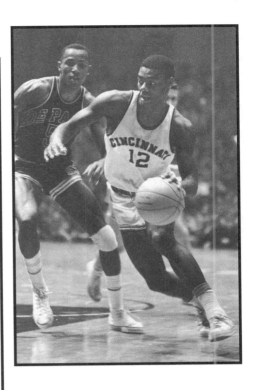

New To this Book

Division I Records

Award Winners

Championships

Attendance Records

Playing-Rules History

School Name-Change/Abbreviation Key

The following players changed their names after their collegiate careers ended. They are listed throughout the book by the names under which they played in college (those listed at the left). Their current names are listed below. In addition, various schools have changed their name. The current school name is listed along with other names by which the schools have been referred.

PLAYER name changes

Name as a collegian:	Changed to:
Lew Alcindor (UCLA)	Kareem Abdul-Jabbar
Walt Hazzard (UCLA)	Mahdi Abdul-Rahmad
Chris Jackson (LSU)	Mahmoud Abdul-Rauf
Akeem Olajuwon (Houston)	Hakeem Olajuwon
Don Smith (Iowa St.)	Zaid Abdul-Aziz
Keith Wilkes (UCLA)	Jamaal Wilkes
Jason Williams (Duke)	Jay Williams

SCHOOL name changes

Current school name:	Changed from:
Akron	Buchtel
Albertson	Col. of Idaho
Alcorn St.	Alcorn A&M
Alliant Int'l	U.S. Int'l; Cal Western
Arcadia	Beaver
Arizona St.	Tempe St.
Ark.-Pine Bluff	Arkansas AM&N
Armstrong Atlantic	Armstrong St.
Auburn	Alabama Poly
Augusta St.	Augusta
Benedictine (Ill.)	Ill. Benedictine
Bradley	Bradley Tech
UC Davis	California Aggies
Cal St. East Bay	Cal St. Hayward
Cal St. Fullerton	Orange County State College; Orange St.
Cal St. L.A.	Los Angeles St.
Cal St. Northridge	San Fernando Valley St.
Carnegie Mellon	Carnegie Tech
Case Reserve	Case Institute of Technology
Central Ark.	Conway St.
Central Conn. St.	New Haven St.
Central Mich.	Mt. Pleasant
Central Mo.	Central Mo. St.
Central Okla.	Central St. (Okla.)
Charleston So.	Baptist (S.C.)
Charleston (W.V.)	Morris Harvey
Cleveland St.	Fenn
Colorado St.	Colorado A&M
Colorado St.-Pueblo	Southern Colo.
Columbus St.	Columbus
Concordia (Cal.)	Christ College-Irvine
Concordia Chicago	Concordia (Ill.)
Concordia (Tex.)	Concordia-Austin
Connecticut	Connecticut Aggies
Crown (Minn.)	St. Paul Bible
Dayton	St. Mary's Institute
Delaware Valley	National Aggies
DeSales	Allentown
Detroit	Detroit Mercy; Detroit Tech
Dist. Columbia	Federal City
Dominican (Ill.)	Rosary
Drexel	Drexel Tech
Dubuque	Columbia Col.
Duke	Trinity (N.C.)
Eastern Conn. St.	Willimantic St.
Eastern Mich.	Michigan Normal
Eckerd	Fla. Presbyterian
Emporia St.	Kansas St. Normal
FDU-Florham	FDU-Madison
Fort Hays St.	Kansas St. Normal-Western
Fresno St.	Fresno Pacific
Idaho St.	Academy of Idaho; Idaho Tech. Inst.; Idaho-Southern
Ill.-Chicago	Ill.-Chicago Circle
Illinois St.	Illinois St. Normal; Illinois Normal
Indiana (Pa.)	Indiana St. (Pa.)
Indianapolis	Indiana Central
Iowa	State University of Iowa
Iowa St.	Ames
James Madison	Madison
Johnson C. Smith	Johnson Smith

Current school name:	Also known as:
Kansas St.	Kansas Aggies
Kean	Newark St.
Kent St.	Kent
La Sierra	Loma Linda
Lamar	Lamar Tech
Liberty	Lynchburg Baptist; Liberty Baptist
La.-Lafayette	Southwestern La.
La.-Monroe	Northeast La.
Loyola Marymount	St. Vincent; Loyola U. of L.A.
Lycoming	Williamsport Dickinson Seminary
Lynn	College of Boca Raton
Lyon	Arkansas Col.
Me.-Farmington	Western State Normal School
Maritime (N.Y.)	N.Y. Maritime
Marycrest Int'l	Teikyo Marycrest
Md.-East. Shore	Maryland St.
Massachusetts	Massachusetts St.; Massachusetts Agriculture Col.
Mass.-Dartmouth	Southeastern Mass.
Mass.-Lowell	Lowell; Lowell St.; Lowell Tech
McDaniel	Western Md.
Memphis	Memphis St.; West Tenn. St. Normal
Michigan Tech	Michigan Mines and Tech
Millersville	Millersville St.
Millikin	James Millikin
Minn. St. Mankato	Mankato St.
Minn. St. Moorhead	Moorhead St.
Mississippi Col.	Mississippi A&M
Mississippi Val.	Mississippi Vocational
Missouri St.	Southwest Mo. St.
Mo.-Rolla	Missouri School of Mines
Mont. St.-Billings	Eastern Montana
Montana St.-Northern	Northern Montana
Neb.-Kearney	Kearney St.
Neb.-Omaha	Omaha
New England U.	St. Francis (Me.)
New Jersey City	Jersey City St.
New Mexico St.	New Mexico A&M
New Orleans	Louisiana St. (N.O.)
North Ala.	Florence St.
N.C. Central	North Caro. College
UNC Pembroke	Pembroke St.
North Central Texas	Cooke County
North Texas	North Tex. St.
Northeastern St.	Northeastern Okla. St.
Northern Ariz.	Arizona St.-Flagstaff
Northern Colo.	Colorado St. Col.; State Teachers
Okla. Panhandle	Panhandle A&M; Panhandle St.
Oklahoma St.	Oklahoma A&M
Old Dominion	William & Mary (Norfolk)
Penn St.-Berks	Penn St. Berks-Lehigh Val.; Berks & Lehigh
Penn St.-Harrisburg	Penn St.-Capitol
Pepperdine	George Pepperdine
Phila. Sciences	Phila. Pharmacy
Philadelphia U.	Phila. Textile
Pittsburgh	Western Pennsylvania
Plymouth St.	Plymouth Normal; Plymouth Teachers
Polytechnic (N.Y.)	New York Poly; Brooklyn Poly
Portland St.	Vanport
Post	Teikyo Post
Randolph	Randolph-Macon Woman's
Rhodes	Southwestern (Tenn.)
Rice	Rice Institute
Richard Stockton	Stockton St.
Rochester Inst.	Mechanics Institute
Rose-Hulman	Rose Polytechnic Institute
Rowan	Glassboro St.
Salem Int'l	Salem-Teikyo; Salem
Samford	Howard Col.
S.C. Upstate	S.C.-Spartanburg
Southern Ark.	Magnolia A&M
Southern Conn. St.	New Britain St.
Southern Ind.	Indiana St.-Evansville
Southern Me.	Maine Portland-Gorham; Gorham St. (Me.)
Southern Miss.	Mississippi Southern Col.; Mississippi Normal
Southern N.H.	New Hamp. Col.
Southern U.	Southern B.R.
Southwest Minn. St.	Southwest St.
Stevens Institute	Stevens Tech
Taylor-Ft. Wayne	Summit Christian

Current school name:	Changed from:
Tex.-Pan American	Pan American
Texas St.	Southwest Tex. St.
Towson	Towson St.
Troy	Troy St.
Truman	Northeast Mo. St.; Truman St.
Tulsa	Henry Kendall
Washburn	Lincoln Col.
Washington-St. Louis	Washington (Mo.)
Washington St.	Washington Agricultural Col.
West Ala.	Livingston
West Tex. A&M	West Texas St.
Western N.M.	New Mexico Western
Western Ore.	Monmouth Normal; Oregon Tech; Oregon College of Education
Western St.	Colo. Western; Colorado Normal
Wichita St.	Fairmount
Widener	Pennsylvania Military Col.
Wm. Paterson	Paterson St.
Wis.-Superior	Superior Normal
Xavier	St. Xavier

In the early days of colleges and universities, many schools used the designation of Teachers College. Due to the high numbers of such schools, they are not listed here.

SCHOOLS also known as

Current school name:	Also known as:
A&M-Corpus Christi	Tex. A&M-Corp. Chris.
Air Force	U.S. Air Force Academy
Apprentice School	Newport News
Army	U.S. Military Academy; West Point
Baruch	Bernard M. Baruch
BYU	Brigham Young
Case Reserve	Case Western Reserve
Charlotte	UNC Charlotte
Chattanooga	Tenn.-Chatt.
CCNY	City College of New York
City Tech	New York City Tech (was NYCCT)
Coast Guard	U.S. Coast Guard Academy
GCSU	Georgia College & State
Green Bay	Wis.-Green Bay
Hawthorne	Nathaniel Hawthorne
IPFW	Indiana/Purdue-Ft. Wayne
IUPUI	Indiana/Purdue-Indianapolis
Lehman	Herbert H. Lehman
Lipscomb	David Lipscomb
Long Island	LIU-Brooklyn
LSU	Louisiana St.
Mass. Liberal Arts	Massachusetts College (was North Adams St.)
Merchant Marine	King's Point; U.S. Merchant Marine Academy
Milwaukee	Wis.-Milwaukee
MIT	Massachusetts Institute of Technology
Navy	U.S. Naval Academy
NJIT	Newark Engineering (was N.J. Inst. of Tech.)
NYIT	New York Institute of Technology; New York Tech
Rensselaer	RPI, Rensselaer Poly Inst.
Rochester Inst.	RIT
Sewanee	University of the South
SMU	Southern Methodist
Southampton	LIU-Southampton
SUNYIT	Utica/Rome
TCNJ	The College of New Jersey (was Trenton St.)
TCU	Texas Christian (was AddRan Christian)
UAB	Ala.-Birmingham
UCF	Central Fla. (was Florida Tech)
UCLA	University of California, Los Angeles
UMBC	Md.-Balt. County
UMKC	Mo.-Kansas City
UNI	Northern Iowa (was Iowa Normal; State Col. of Iowa)
UNLV	Nevada-Las Vegas (was Nevada Southern)
UTEP	Texas-El Paso (was Texas Western)
UTSA	Texas-San Antonio
VCU	Va. Commonwealth
VMI	Va. Military
WPI	Worcester Poly Inst.; Worcester Tech

SCHOOL MERGERS

Current school name:	Two Schools Merged & Year:
Case Reserve	Case Tech & Western Reserve; 1971-72
Martin Luther	Northwestern (Wis.) & Dr. Martin Luther, 1995-96
Mass.-Lowell	Lowell St. & Lowell Tech; 1975-76

Division I Records

Individual Records

Basketball records are confined to the "modern era," which began with the 1937-38 season, the first without the center jump after each goal scored. Except for the school's all-time won-lost record or coaches' records, only statistics achieved while an institution was an active member of the NCAA are included in team or individual categories. Official weekly statistics rankings in scoring and shooting began with the 1947-48 season; individual rebounds were added for the 1950-51 season, although team rebounds were not added until 1954-55. Individual assists were kept in 1950-51 and 1951-52, and permanently added in 1983-84. Blocked shots and steals were added in 1985-86 and three-point field goals were added in 1986-87. For Triple-Doubles and Double-Doubles, the individual has to reach double figures in two or more of the following categories: points, rebounds, assists, blocked shots or steals. Triple-Doubles and Double-Doubles include only the years in which each category was officially kept by the NCAA. Scoring, rebounding, assists, blocked shots and steals are ranked on total number and on per-game average; shooting, on percentage. In statistical rankings, the rounding of percentages and/or averages may indicate ties where none exist. In these cases, the numerical order of the rankings is accurate. In 1973, freshmen became eligible to compete on the varsity level.

Scoring

POINTS
Game
  100—Frank Selvy, Furman vs. Newberry, Feb. 13, 1954 (41 FGs, 18 FTs)
Season
  1,381—Pete Maravich, LSU, 1970 (522 FGs, 337 FTs, 31 games)
Career
  3,667—Pete Maravich, LSU, 1968-70 (1,387 FGs, 893 FTs, 83 games)

POINTS VS. DIVISION I OPPONENT
Game
  72—Kevin Bradshaw, U.S. Int'l vs. Loyola Marymount, Jan. 5, 1991

AVERAGE PER GAME
Season
  44.5—Pete Maravich, LSU, 1970 (1,381 in 31)
Career
  44.2—Pete Maravich, LSU, 1968-70 (3,667 in 83)

POINTS IN FIRST CAREER GAME
Game
  56—Lew Alcindor, UCLA vs. Southern California, Dec. 3, 1966

COMBINED POINTS, TWO TEAMMATES
Game
  125—Frank Selvy (100) and Darrell Floyd (25), Furman vs. Newberry, Feb. 13, 1954

COMBINED POINTS, TWO TEAMMATES VS. DIVISION I OPPONENT
Game
  92—Kevin Bradshaw (72) and Isaac Brown (20), U.S. Int'l vs. Loyola Marymount, Jan. 5, 1991

COMBINED POINTS, TWO OPPOSING PLAYERS ON DIVISION I TEAMS
Game
  115—Pete Maravich (64), LSU and Dan Issel (51), Kentucky, Feb. 21, 1970

GAMES SCORING AT LEAST 50 POINTS
Season
  10—Pete Maravich, LSU, 1970
Season—Consecutive Games
  3—Pete Maravich, LSU, Feb. 10 to Feb. 15, 1969
Career
  28—Pete Maravich, LSU, 1968-70

GAMES SCORING AT LEAST 40 POINTS
Career
  56—Pete Maravich, LSU, 1968-70

GAMES SCORING IN DOUBLE FIGURES
Career
  132—Danny Manning, Kansas, 1985-88

CONSECUTIVE GAMES SCORING IN DOUBLE FIGURES
Career
  115—Lionel Simmons, La Salle, 1987-90

Field Goals

FIELD GOALS
Game
  41—Frank Selvy, Furman vs. Newberry, Feb. 13, 1954 (66 attempts)
Season
  522—Pete Maravich, LSU, 1970 (1,168 attempts)
Career
  1,387—Pete Maravich, LSU, 1968-70 (3,166 attempts)

CONSECUTIVE FIELD GOALS
Game
  16—Doug Grayson, Kent St. vs. North Carolina, Dec. 6, 1967 (18 of 19)
Season
  25—Ray Voelkel, American, 1978 (during nine games, Nov. 24-Dec. 16)

FIELD-GOAL ATTEMPTS
Game
  71—Jay Handlan, Wash. & Lee vs. Furman, Feb. 17, 1951 (30 made)
Season
  1,168—Pete Maravich, LSU, 1970 (522 made)
Career
  3,166—Pete Maravich, LSU, 1968-70 (1,387 made)

FIELD-GOAL PERCENTAGE
Game
  (Min. 15 made) 100%—Clifford Rozier, Louisville vs. Eastern Ky., Dec. 11, 1993 (15 of 15)
  (Min. 20 made) 95.5%—Bill Walton, UCLA vs. Memphis, March 26, 1973 (21 of 22)
*Season
  74.6%—Steve Johnson, Oregon St., 1981 (235 of 315)

*Based on qualifiers for national championship.

Career
  (Min. 400 made and 4 made per game) 67.8%—Steve Johnson, Oregon St., 1976-81 (828 of 1,222)

Three-Point Field Goals

THREE-POINT FIELD GOALS
Game
  15—Keith Veney, Marshall vs. Morehead St., Dec. 14, 1996 (25 attempts)
Season
  158—Darrin Fitzgerald, Butler, 1987 (362 attempts)
Career
  457—J.J. Redick, Duke, 2003-06 (1,126 attempts)

THREE-POINT FIELD GOALS MADE PER GAME
Season
  5.6—Darrin Fitzgerald, Butler, 1987 (158 in 28)
Career
  (Min. 200 made) 4.6—Timothy Pollard, Mississippi Val., 1988-89 (256 in 56)

CONSECUTIVE THREE-POINT FIELD GOALS
Game
  11—Gary Bossert, Niagara vs. Siena, Jan. 7, 1987
Season
  15—Todd Leslie, Northwestern, 1990 (during four games, Dec. 15-28)

CONSECUTIVE GAMES MAKING A THREE-POINT FIELD GOAL
Season
  38—Steve Kerr, Arizona, Nov. 27, 1987, to April 2, 1988
Career
  88—Cory Bradford, Illinois, Nov. 10, 1998 to Feb. 10, 2001

THREE-POINT FIELD-GOAL ATTEMPTS
Game
  27—Bruce Seals, Manhattan vs. Canisius, Jan. 31, 2000 (9 made)
Season
  362—Darrin Fitzgerald, Butler, 1987 (158 made)
Career
  1,192—Keydren Clark, St. Peter's, 2003-06 (435 made)

THREE-POINT FIELD-GOAL ATTEMPTS PER GAME
Season
  12.9—Darrin Fitzgerald, Butler, 1987 (362 in 28)
  10.1—Keydren Clark, St. Peter's, 2003-06 (1,192 in 118)

THREE-POINT FIELD-GOAL PERCENTAGE
Game
  (Min. 9 made) 100%—Mark Poag, Old Dominion vs. VMI, Nov. 25, 1997 (9 of 9); Markus Wilson, Evansville vs. Tenn.-Martin, Nov. 18, 1998 (9 of 9); Donnie McGrath, Providence vs. Virginia, Feb. 2, 2005 (9 of 9)
  (Min. 12 made) 85.7%—Gary Bossert, Niagara vs. Siena, Jan. 7, 1987 (12 of 14)
Season
  (Min. 50 made) 63.4%—Glenn Tropf, Holy Cross, 1988 (52 of 82)
  (Min. 100 made) 57.3%—Steve Kerr, Arizona, 1988 (114 of 199)
Career
  (Min. 200 made and 2.0 made per game) 49.7%—Tony Bennett, Green Bay, 1989-92 (290 of 584)
  (Min. 300 made) 46.9%—Stephan Sir, San Diego St. & Northern Ariz., 2003-07 (323 of 689)

Free Throws

FREE THROWS
Game
  30—Pete Maravich, LSU vs. Oregon St., Dec. 22, 1969 (31 attempts)
Season
  355—Frank Selvy, Furman, 1954 (444 attempts)
Career
  (4 yrs.) 905—Dickie Hemric, Wake Forest, 1952-55 (1,359 attempts)
  (3 yrs.) 893—Pete Maravich, LSU, 1968-70 (1,152 attempts)

CONSECUTIVE FREE THROWS MADE
Game
  24—Arlen Clark, Oklahoma St. vs. Colorado, March 7, 1959 (24 of 24)
Season
  73—Gary Buchanan, Villanova, 2000-01 (during 21 games, Nov. 17-Feb. 12)
Career
  85—Darnell Archey, Butler, 2001-03 (during 57 games, Feb. 15, 2001-Jan. 18, 2003)

FREE THROWS ATTEMPTED
Game
  36—Ed Tooley, Brown vs. Amherst, Dec. 4, 1954 (23 made)
Season
  444—Frank Selvy, Furman, 1954 (355 made)
Career
  (4 yrs.) 1,359—Dickie Hemric, Wake Forest, 1952-55 (905 made)
  (3 yrs.) 1,152—Pete Maravich, LSU, 1968-70 (893 made)

FREE-THROW PERCENTAGE
Game
(Min. 24 made) 100% —Arlen Clark, Oklahoma St. vs. Colorado, March 7, 1959 (24 of 24)

*Season
97.5%—Blake Ahearn, Missouri St., 2004 (117 of 120)

*Based on qualifiers for national championship.

Career
(Min. 300 made and 2.5 made per game) 94.6%—Blake Ahearn, Missouri St., 2004-07 (435 of 460)
(Min. 600 made) 91.2%—J.J. Redick, Duke, 2003-06 (662 of 726)

Rebounds

REBOUNDS
Game
51—Bill Chambers, William & Mary vs. Virginia, Feb. 14, 1953
(Since 1973) 35—Larry Abney, Fresno St. vs. SMU, Feb. 17, 2000

Season
734—Walt Dukes, Seton Hall, 1953 (33 games)
(Since 1973) 597—Marvin Barnes, Providence, 1974 (32 games)

Career
(4 yrs.) 2,201—Tom Gola, La Salle, 1952-55 (118 games)
(3 yrs.) 1,751—Paul Silas, Creighton, 1962-64 (81 games)
(Since 1973) 1,570—Tim Duncan, Wake Forest, 1994-97 (128 games)

AVERAGE PER GAME
Season
25.6—Charlie Slack, Marshall, 1955 (538 in 21)
(Since 1973) 20.4—Kermit Washington, American, 1973 (511 in 25)

Career
(Min. 800) 22.7—Artis Gilmore, Jacksonville, 1970-71 (1,224 in 54)
(4 yrs.) 21.8—Charlie Slack, Marshall, 1953-56 (1,916 in 88)
(Since 1973) 15.2—Glenn Mosley, Seton Hall, 1974-77 (1,263 in 83)

Assists

ASSISTS
Game
22—Tony Fairley, Charleston So. vs. Armstrong Atlantic, Feb. 9, 1987; Avery Johnson, Southern U. vs. Texas Southern, Jan. 25, 1988; Sherman Douglas, Syracuse vs. Providence, Jan. 28, 1989

Season
406—Mark Wade, UNLV, 1987 (38 games)

Career
1,076—Bobby Hurley, Duke, 1990-93 (140 games)

AVERAGE PER GAME
Season
13.3—Avery Johnson, Southern U., 1988 (399 in 30)

Career
(Min. 600) 12.0—Avery Johnson, Southern U., 1987-88 (732 in 61)
(4 yrs.) 8.4—Chris Corchiani, North Carolina St., 1988-91 (1,038 in 124)

Blocked Shots

BLOCKED SHOTS
Game
16—Mickell Gladness, Alabama A&M vs. Texas Southern, Feb. 24, 2007

Season
207—David Robinson, Navy, 1986 (35 games)

Career
535—Wojciech Myrda, La.-Monroe, 1999-2002 (115 games)

AVERAGE PER GAME
Season
6.5—Shawn James, Northeastern, 2006 (196 in 30)

Career
(Min. 225) 5.9—Keith Closs, Central Conn. St., 1995-96 (317 in 54)
(4 yrs.) 4.7—Wojciech Myrda, La.-Monroe, 1999-2002 (535 in 115)

Steals

STEALS
Game
13—Mookie Blaylock, Oklahoma vs. Centenary (La.), Dec. 12, 1987; and vs. Loyola Marymount, Dec. 17, 1988

Season
160—Desmond Cambridge, Alabama A&M, 2002 (29 games)

Career
385—John Linehan, Providence, 1998-2002 (122 games)

AVERAGE PER GAME
Season
5.5—Desmond Cambridge, Alabama A&M, 2002 (160 in 29)

Career
(Min. 225) 3.9—Desmond Cambridge, Alabama A&M, 1999-2002 (330 in 84)
(4 yrs.) 3.2—Eric Murdock, Providence, 1988-91 (376 in 117)

Double-Doubles

TRIPLE-DOUBLES
Season
4—Michael Anderson, Drexel, 1986; Jason Kidd, California, 1994

Career
6—Michael Anderson, Drexel, 1985-88; Shaquille O'Neal, LSU, 1990-92

CONSECUTIVE GAMES MAKING A TRIPLE-DOUBLE
Season
2—Kevin Robertson, Vermont, Jan. 7-9, 1992; Shaquille O'Neal, LSU, Feb. 19-22, 1992; Anfernee Hardaway, Memphis, Jan. 4-6, 1993

DOUBLE-DOUBLES
Season
31—David Robinson, Navy, 1986

Career
87—Tim Duncan, Wake Forest, 1994-97

DOUBLE-DOUBLES BY A FRESHMAN
Season
22—Carmelo Anthony, Syracuse, 2003

CONSECUTIVE GAMES MAKING A DOUBLE-DOUBLE
Season
29—Mel Counts, Oregon St., Nov. 30, 1963-Mar. 10, 1964

Career
40—Billy Cunningham, North Carolina, Dec, 5, 1962-Feb. 22, 1964

Fouls

SHORTEST PLAYING TIME BEFORE BEING DISQUALIFIED
Game
1:11—Ben Wardrop, San Diego St. vs. Colorado St., Jan. 24, 2004

MOST GAMES NEVER FOULING OUT
Full Career
138—Ed Cota, North Carolina, 1997-2000

Games

GAMES PLAYED (SINCE 1947-48)
Season
40—Mark Alarie, Tommy Amaker, Johnny Dawkins, Danny Ferry and Billy King, Duke, 1986; Larry Johnson, UNLV, 1990; Anthony Epps, Jamaal Magloire, Ron Mercer and Wayne Turner, Kentucky, 1997

Career
151—Wayne Turner, Kentucky, 1996-99

General

ACHIEVED 2,000 POINTS AND 2,000 REBOUNDS
Career
Tom Gola, La Salle, 1952-55 (2,462 points and 2,201 rebounds)
Joe Holup, George Washington, 1953-56 (2,226 points and 2,030 rebounds)

AVERAGED 20 POINTS AND 20 REBOUNDS
Career
Bill Russell, San Francisco, 1954-56 (20.7 points and 20.3 rebounds)
Paul Silas, Creighton, 1962-64 (20.5 points and 21.6 rebounds)
Julius Erving, Massachusetts, 1970-71 (26.3 points and 20.2 rebounds)
Artis Gilmore, Jacksonville, 1970-71 (24.3 points and 22.7 rebounds)
Kermit Washington, American, 1971-73 (20.1 points and 20.2 rebounds)

Team Records

Note: Where records involve both teams, each team must be an NCAA Division I member institution.

SINGLE-GAME RECORDS

Scoring

POINTS
186—Loyola Marymount vs. U.S. Int'l (140), Jan. 5, 1991

POINTS BY LOSING TEAM
150—U.S. Int'l vs. Loyola Marymount (181), Jan. 31, 1989

POINTS, BOTH TEAMS
331—Loyola Marymount (181) vs. U.S. Int'l (150), Jan. 31, 1989

MARGIN OF VICTORY
117—Long Island (179) vs. Medgar Evers (62), Nov. 26, 1997

MARGIN OF VICTORY VS. DIVISION I OPPONENT
91—Tulsa (141) vs. Prairie View (50), Dec. 7, 1995

POINTS IN A HALF
98—Long Island vs. Medgar Evers, Nov. 26, 1997 (2nd)

POINTS IN A HALF VS. DIVISION I OPPONENT
97—Oklahoma vs. U.S. Int'l, Nov. 29, 1989 (1st)

POINTS IN A HALF, BOTH TEAMS
172—Loyola Marymount (86) vs. Gonzaga (86), Feb. 18, 1989 (2nd)

LEAD BEFORE OPPONENT SCORES AT START OF A GAME
34-0—Seton Hall vs. Kean, Nov. 29, 1998

LEAD BEFORE DIVISION I OPPONENT SCORES AT START OF A GAME
32-0—Connecticut vs. New Hampshire, Dec. 12, 1990

LARGEST SCORING RUN VS. A DIVISION I OPPONENT
37-0—Utah St. vs. Idaho, Feb. 15, 2006

DEFICIT OVERCOME TO WIN GAME
32—Duke (74) vs. Tulane (72), Dec. 30, 1950 (trailed 22-54 with 2:00 left in the first half)

SECOND-HALF DEFICIT OVERCOME TO WIN GAME
31—Duke (74) vs. Tulane (72), Dec. 30, 1950 (trailed 27-58 with 19:00 left in the second half); Kentucky (99) vs. LSU (95), Feb. 15, 1994 (trailed 37-68 with 15:34 left in the second half)

HALFTIME DEFICIT OVERCOME TO WIN GAME
29—Duke (74) vs. Tulane (72), Dec. 30, 1950 (trailed 27-56 at halftime)

DEFICIT OVERCOME BEFORE SCORING TO WIN GAME
28—New Mexico St. (117) vs. Bradley (109), Jan. 27, 1977 (trailed 0-28 with 13:49 left in first half)

Field Goals

FIELD GOALS
76—Long Island vs. Medgar Evers, Nov. 26, 1997 (124 attempts)

FIELD GOALS VS. DIVISION I OPPONENT
74—Houston vs. Valparaiso, Feb. 24, 1968 (112 attempts)

FIELD GOALS, BOTH TEAMS
130—Loyola Marymount (67) vs. U.S. Int'l (63), Jan. 31, 1989

FIELD GOALS IN A HALF
42—Oklahoma vs. U.S. Int'l, Nov. 29, 1989 (90 attempts) (1st half)

FIELD-GOAL ATTEMPTS
147—Oklahoma vs. U.S. Int'l, Nov. 29, 1989 (70 made)

FIELD-GOAL ATTEMPTS, BOTH TEAMS
245—Loyola Marymount (124) vs. U.S. Int'l (121), Jan. 7, 1989

FIELD-GOAL ATTEMPTS IN A HALF
90—Oklahoma vs. U.S. Int'l, Nov. 29, 1989 (42 made) (1st half)

FIELD-GOAL PERCENTAGE
(Min. 15 made) 83.3%—Maryland vs. South Carolina, Jan. 9, 1971 (15 of 18)
(Min. 30 made) 81.4%—New Mexico vs. Oregon St., Nov. 30, 1985 (35 of 43)

FIELD-GOAL PERCENTAGE, HALF
94.1%—North Carolina vs. Virginia, Jan. 7, 1978 (16 of 17) (2nd half)

Three-Point Field Goals

THREE-POINT FIELD GOALS
28—Troy vs. George Mason, Dec. 10, 1994 (74 attempts)

THREE-POINT FIELD GOALS, BOTH TEAMS
44—Troy (28) vs. George Mason (16), Dec. 10, 1994

CONSECUTIVE THREE-POINT FIELD GOALS MADE WITHOUT A MISS
11—Niagara vs. Siena, Jan. 7, 1987; Eastern Ky. vs. UNC Asheville, Jan. 14, 1987

THREE-POINT FIELD-GOAL ATTEMPTS WITHOUT MAKING ONE
22—Canisius vs. St. Bonaventure, Jan. 21, 1995

NUMBER OF DIFFERENT PLAYERS TO SCORE A THREE-POINT FIELD GOAL, ONE TEAM
9—Dartmouth vs. Boston College, Nov. 30, 1993

THREE-POINT FIELD-GOAL ATTEMPTS
74—Troy vs. George Mason, Dec. 10, 1994 (28 made)

THREE-POINT FIELD-GOAL ATTEMPTS, BOTH TEAMS
108—Troy (74) vs. George Mason (34), Dec. 10, 1994

THREE-POINT FIELD-GOAL PERCENTAGE
(Min. 10 made) 91.7%—Drexel vs. Delaware, Dec. 3, 2000 (11 of 12); Northern Ariz. vs. Willamette, Dec. 11, 2004 (11 of 12)
(Min. 15 made) 83.3%—Eastern Ky. vs. UNC Asheville, Jan. 14, 1987 (15 of 18)

THREE-POINT FIELD-GOAL PERCENTAGE, BOTH TEAMS
(Min. 10 made) 83.3%—Lafayette (7 of 8) vs. Marist (3 of 4), Dec. 6, 1986 (10 of 12)
(Min. 15 made) 76.2%—Florida (10 of 14) vs. California (6 of 7), Dec. 27, 1986 (16 of 21)
(Min. 20 made) 72.4%—Princeton (12 of 15) vs. Brown (9 of 14), Feb. 20, 1988 (21 of 29)

Free Throws

FREE THROWS MADE
56—TCU vs. Eastern Mich., Dec. 21, 1999 (70 attempts)

FREE THROWS MADE, BOTH TEAMS
88—Morehead St. (53) vs. Cincinnati (35), Feb. 11, 1956 (111 attempts)

FREE-THROW ATTEMPTS
79—Northern Ariz. vs. Arizona, Jan. 26, 1953 (46 made)

FREE THROWS, BOTH TEAMS
130—Northern Ariz. (79) vs. Arizona (51), Jan. 26, 1953 (78 made)

FREE-THROW PERCENTAGE
(Min. 32 made) 100.0%—UC Irvine vs. Pacific, Feb. 21, 1981 (34 of 34); Samford vs. UCF, Dec. 20, 1990 (34 of 34)
(Min. 35 made) 97.2%—Vanderbilt vs. Mississippi St., Feb. 26, 1986 (35 of 36); Butler vs. Dayton, Feb. 21, 1991 (35 of 36); Marquette vs. Memphis, Jan. 23, 1993 (35 of 36)
(Min. 40 made) 95.5%—UNLV vs. San Diego St., Dec. 11, 1976 (42 of 44)

FREE-THROW PERCENTAGE, BOTH TEAMS
100%—Purdue (25 of 25) vs. Wisconsin (22 of 22), Feb. 7, 1976 (47 of 47)

Rebounds

REBOUNDS
108—Kentucky vs. Mississippi, Feb. 8, 1964

REBOUNDS, BOTH TEAMS
152—Indiana (95) vs. Michigan (57), March 11, 1961

REBOUND MARGIN
84—Arizona (102) vs. Northern Ariz. (18), Jan. 6, 1951

Assists

ASSISTS (INCLUDING OVERTIMES)
44—Colorado vs. George Mason, Dec. 2, 1995 (ot)

ASSISTS (REGULATION)
43—TCU vs. Central Okla., Dec. 12, 1998.

ASSISTS, BOTH TEAMS (INCLUDING OVERTIMES)
67—Colorado (44) vs. George Mason (23), Dec. 2, 1995 (ot)

ASSISTS, BOTH TEAMS (REGULATION)
65—Dayton (34) vs. UCF (31), Dec. 3, 1988

Blocked Shots

BLOCKED SHOTS
21—Georgetown vs. Southern (N.O.), Dec. 1, 1993; Alabama A&M vs. Texas Southern, Feb. 24, 2007

BLOCKED SHOTS, BOTH TEAMS
29—Rider (17) vs. Fairleigh Dickinson (12), Jan. 9, 1989

Steals

STEALS
39—Long Island vs. Medgar Evers, Nov. 26, 1997

STEALS VS. DIVISION I OPPONENT
34—Oklahoma vs. Centenary (La.), Dec. 12, 1987

STEALS, BOTH TEAMS
44—Oklahoma (34) vs. Centenary (La.) (10), Dec. 12, 1987

Fouls

FOULS
50—Arizona vs. Northern Ariz., Jan. 26, 1953

FOULS, BOTH TEAMS
84—Arizona (50) vs. Northern Ariz. (34), Jan. 26, 1953

PLAYERS DISQUALIFIED
8—St. Joseph's vs. Xavier, Jan. 10, 1976

PLAYERS DISQUALIFIED, BOTH TEAMS
12—UNLV (6) vs. Hawaii (6), Jan. 19, 1979 (ot); Arizona (7) vs. West Tex. A&M (5), Feb. 14, 1952

Defense

FEWEST POINTS ALLOWED (Since 1938)
6—Tennessee (11) vs. Temple, Dec. 15, 1973; Kentucky (75) vs. Arkansas St., Jan. 8, 1945

FEWEST POINTS ALLOWED (Since 1986)
21—Coastal Caro. (61) vs. Ga. Southern, Jan. 2, 1997; Monmouth (41) vs. Princeton, Dec. 14, 2005

FEWEST POINTS, BOTH TEAMS
(Since 1938)
  17—Tennessee (11) vs. Temple (6), Dec. 15, 1973

FEWEST POINTS, BOTH TEAMS
(Since 1986)
  62—Monmouth (41) vs. Princeton (21), Dec. 14, 2005

FEWEST POINTS ALLOWED IN A HALF
(Since 1938)
  0—Duke (7) vs. North Carolina, Feb. 24, 1979 (1st)

FEWEST POINTS ALLOWED IN A HALF
(Since 1986)
  7—Ohio (35) vs. Central Mich., Jan. 14, 2006 (1st)

FEWEST POINTS, BOTH TEAMS IN A HALF
(Since 1938)
  7—Duke (7) vs. North Carolina, Feb. 24, 1979 (1st)

FEWEST POINTS, BOTH TEAMS IN A HALF
(Since 1986)
  28—Mississippi (15) vs. South Carolina (13), Jan. 8, 2003 (1st)

LONGEST TIME HOLDING THE OPPONENT SCORELESS
  20:48—Duke vs. North Carolina, Feb. 25, 1979 (UNC scored its first points of the game at 19:12 in the 2nd half)

LONGEST TIME HOLDING THE OPPONENT SCORELESS
(Since 1986)
  13:53—Utah St. vs. Idaho, Feb. 15, 2006 (last 7:49 of the 1st half and first 6:04 of the 2nd half)

FEWEST FIELD GOALS
(Since 1938)
  2—Duke vs. North Carolina St., March 8, 1968 (11 attempts); Arkansas St. vs. Kentucky, Jan. 8, 1945

FEWEST FIELD GOALS IN A HALF
(Since 1986)
  2—Central Mich. vs. Ohio, Jan. 14, 2006 (1st)

FEWEST FIELD-GOAL ATTEMPTS
(Since 1938)
  9—Pittsburgh vs. Penn St., March 1, 1952 (3 made)

LOWEST FIELD-GOAL PERCENTAGE
(Since 1986)
  13.3%—Miami (Ohio) vs. Dayton, Dec. 29, 2001 (8 of 60)

LOWEST FIELD-GOAL PERCENTAGE IN A HALF
  8.3%—Central Mich. vs. Ohio, Jan. 14, 2006 (2 of 24) (1st)

FEWEST THREE-POINT FIELD GOALS MADE
  0—Many teams

FEWEST THREE-POINT FIELD-GOAL ATTEMPTS
  0—Many teams

FEWEST FREE THROWS MADE
  0—Many teams

FEWEST FREE-THROW ATTEMPTS
  0—Many teams

Overtimes

OVERTIME PERIODS
  7—Cincinnati (75) vs. Bradley (73), Dec. 21, 1981

POINTS IN ONE OVERTIME PERIOD
  26—Vermont vs. Hartford, Jan. 24, 1998

POINTS IN ONE OVERTIME PERIOD, BOTH TEAMS
  45—VCU (23) vs. Texas A&M (22), Dec. 2, 2000

POINTS IN OVERTIME PERIODS
  49—Middle Tenn. vs. Tennessee Tech, Feb. 12, 2000 (4 ot)

POINTS IN OVERTIME PERIODS, BOTH TEAMS
  94—Middle Tenn. (49) vs. Tennessee Tech (45), Feb. 12, 2000 (4 ot)

WINNING MARGIN IN OVERTIME GAME
  21—Nicholls St. (86) vs. Sam Houston St. (65), Feb. 4, 1999 (23-2 in the ot)

SEASON RECORDS

Scoring

POINTS
  4,012—Oklahoma, 1988 (39 games)

POINTS PER GAME
  122.4—Loyola Marymount, 1990 (3,918 in 32)

SCORING MARGIN AVERAGE
  30.3—UCLA, 1972 (94.6 offense, 64.3 defense)

GAMES AT LEAST 100 POINTS
  28—Loyola Marymount, 1990

CONSECUTIVE GAMES AT LEAST 100 POINTS
  12—UNLV, 1977; Loyola Marymount, 1990

Field Goals

FIELD GOALS
  1,533—Oklahoma, 1988 (3,094 attempts)

FIELD GOALS PER GAME
  46.3—UNLV, 1976 (1,436 in 31)

FIELD-GOAL ATTEMPTS
  3,094—Oklahoma, 1988 (1,533 made)

FIELD-GOAL ATTEMPTS PER GAME
  98.5—Oral Roberts, 1973 (2,659 in 27)

FIELD-GOAL PERCENTAGE
  57.2%—Missouri, 1980 (936 of 1,635)

Three-Point Field Goals

THREE-POINT FIELD GOALS
  442—VMI, 2007 (1,383 attempts)

THREE-POINT FIELD GOALS PER GAME
  13.4—VMI, 2007 (442 in 33)

THREE-POINT FIELD-GOAL ATTEMPTS
  1,383—VMI, 2007 (442 made)

THREE-POINT FIELD-GOAL ATTEMPTS PER GAME
  41.9—VMI, 2007 (1,383 in 33)

THREE-POINT FIELD-GOAL PERCENTAGE
  (Min. 100 made) 50.8%—Indiana, 1987 (130 of 256)
  (Min. 150 made) 50.0%—Mississippi Val., 1987 (161 of 322)
  (Min. 200 made) 49.2%—Princeton, 1988 (211 of 429)

CONSECUTIVE GAMES SCORING A THREE-POINT FIELD GOAL
(Multiple Seasons)
  668—UNLV, Nov. 26, 1986, to present

Free Throws

FREE THROWS MADE
  888—Duke, 1990 (1,165 attempts)

FREE THROWS MADE PER GAME
  28.9—Morehead St., 1956 (838 in 29)

CONSECUTIVE FREE THROWS MADE
  50—Wake Forest, 2005 (during two games, Jan. 15-18)

FREE THROW ATTEMPTS
  1,263—Bradley, 1954 (865 made)

FREE-THROW ATTEMPTS PER GAME
  41.0—Bradley, 1953 (1,107 in 27)

FREE-THROW PERCENTAGE
  82.2%—Harvard, 1984 (535 of 651)

Rebounds

REBOUNDS
  2,109—Kentucky, 1951 (34 games)

REBOUNDS PER GAME
  70.0—Connecticut, 1955 (1,751 in 25)

REBOUND MARGIN AVERAGE
  25.0—Morehead St., 1957 (64.3 offense, 39.3 defense)
  (Since 1973) 18.5—Manhattan, 1973 (56.5, 38.0)

Assists

ASSISTS
  926—UNLV, 1990 (40 games)

ASSISTS PER GAME
  24.7—UNLV, 1991 (863 in 35)

Blocked Shots

BLOCKED SHOTS
  315—Connecticut, 2004 (39 games)

BLOCKED SHOTS PER GAME
  9.1—Georgetown, 1989 (309 in 34)

Steals

STEALS
  490—VMI, 2007 (33 games)

STEALS PER GAME
  14.9—Long Island, 1998 (478 in 32)

Fouls

FOULS
  966—Providence, 1987 (34 games)

FOULS PER GAME
  29.3—Indiana, 1952 (644 in 22)

FEWEST FOULS
  253—Air Force, 1962 (23 games)

FEWEST FOULS PER GAME
  11.0—Air Force, 1962 (253 in 23)

Defense

LOWEST SCORING AVERAGE PER GAME ALLOWED
(Since 1982)
  (Since 1938) 25.7—Oklahoma St., 1939 (693 in 27)
  (Since 1948) 32.5—Oklahoma St., 1948 (1,006 in 31)
  (Since 1965) 47.1—Fresno St., 1982 (1,412 in 30)

LOWEST FIELD-GOAL PERCENTAGE ALLOWED
  (Since 1978) 35.2—Stanford, 2000 (667 of 1,893)

Overtimes

OVERTIME GAMES
  8—Western Ky., 1978 (won 5, lost 3); Portland, 1984 (won 4, lost 4); Valparaiso, 1993 (won 4, lost 4)

CONSECUTIVE OVERTIME GAMES
  4—Jacksonville, 1982 (won 3, lost 1); Illinois St., 1985 (won 3, lost 1); Dayton, 1988 (won 1, lost 3)

OVERTIME WINS
  6—Chattanooga, 1989 (6-0); Wake Forest, 1984 (6-1)

OVERTIME HOME WINS
  5—Cincinnati, 1967 (5-0)

OVERTIME ROAD WINS

4—Delaware, 1973 (4-0); Arizona St., 1981 (4-0); Cal St. Fullerton, 1989 (4-0); New Mexico St., 1994 (4-0)

OVERTIME PERIODS

14—Bradley, 1982 (3-3)

CONSECUTIVE OVERTIME WINS—ALL-TIME

11—Louisville, Feb. 10, 1968-March 29, 1975; Massachusetts, March 21, 1991-Feb. 28, 1996; Virginia, Dec. 5, 1991-Feb. 8, 1996

General Records

GAMES IN A SEASON

45—Oregon, 1945 (30-15)

GAMES IN A SEASON (Since 1948)

40—Duke, 1986 (37-3); UNLV, 1990 (35-5); Kentucky, 1997 (35-5); Florida, 2007 (35-5)

VICTORIES IN A SEASON

37—Duke, 1986 (37-3) & 1999 (37-2); UNLV, 1987 (37-2); Illinois, 2005 (37-2)

VICTORIES IN A PERFECT SEASON

32—North Carolina, 1957; Indiana, 1976

VICTORIES IN FIRST SEASON IN DIVISION I

29—Seattle, 1953 (29-4)

WON-LOST PERCENTAGE IN FIRST SEASON IN DIVISION I

.931—Md.-East. Shore, 1974 (27-2)

MOST-IMPROVED TEAM FROM ONE SEASON TO THE NEXT

17 games—Mercer, 2003 (from 6-23 to 23-6); UTEP, 2004 (from 6-24 to 24-8)

CONSECUTIVE VICTORIES IN A SEASON

34—UNLV, 1991 (34-1)

CONSECUTIVE VICTORIES

88—UCLA, from Jan. 30, 1971, through Jan. 17, 1974 (ended Jan. 19, 1974, at Notre Dame, 71-70; last UCLA defeat before streak also came at Notre Dame, 89-82)

CONSECUTIVE REGULAR-SEASON VICTORIES (NATIONAL POSTSEASON TOURNAMENTS NOT INCLUDED)

76—UCLA, 1971-74

CONSECUTIVE HOME-COURT VICTORIES

129—Kentucky, from Jan. 4, 1943, to Jan. 8, 1955 (ended by Georgia Tech, 59-58)

CONSECUTIVE ROAD VICTORIES (OPPONENTS' HOME SITE ONLY)

35—Kansas, Feb. 20, 1924-Jan. 13, 1928 (ended by Oklahoma, 45-19)

CONSECUTIVE NON-HOME VICTORIES (ROAD AND NEUTRAL SITE GAMES ONLY)

39—UCLA, Feb. 6, 1971-Jan. 7, 1974 (ended by Notre Dame, 71-70)

DEFEATS IN A SEASON

30—Grambling, 2000 (1-30)

DEFEATS IN A WINLESS SEASON

28—Prairie View, 1992 (0-28); Savannah St., 2005 (0-28)

CONSECUTIVE DEFEATS IN A SEASON

28—Prairie View, 1992 (0-28); Savannah St., 2005 (0-28)

CONSECUTIVE DEFEATS

34—Sacramento St., from Dec. 22, 1997, to Jan. 27, 1999

CONSECUTIVE HOME-COURT DEFEATS

32—New Hampshire, from Feb. 9, 1988, to Feb. 2, 1991 (ended vs. Holy Cross, 72-56)

CONSECUTIVE ROAD DEFEATS (INCLUDING ONLY GAMES AT THE OPPONENTS' HOME SITES)

64—Tex.-Pan American, from Nov. 25, 1995, to Jan. 8, 2000 (ended vs. Oral Roberts, 79-62)

CONSECUTIVE NON-HOME DEFEATS (INCLUDING GAMES AT THE OPPONENTS' HOME SITES AND AT NEUTRAL SITES)

56—Sacramento St., from Nov. 22, 1991, to Jan. 5, 1995 [ended at Loyola (Ill.), 68-56]

CONSECUTIVE 30-WIN SEASONS

3—Kentucky, 1947-49 and 1996-98

CURRENT CONSECUTIVE 30-WIN SEASONS

2—Florida, Memphis & UCLA, 2006-07

CONSECUTIVE 25-WIN SEASONS

10—UCLA, 1967-76; UNLV, 1983-92

CURRENT CONSECUTIVE 25-WIN SEASONS

4—Nevada, 2004-07

CONSECUTIVE 20-WIN SEASONS

31—North Carolina, 1971-2001

CURRENT CONSECUTIVE 20-WIN SEASONS

20—Arizona, 1988-2007

CONSECUTIVE WINNING SEASONS

54—UCLA, 1949-2002

CURRENT CONSECUTIVE WINNING SEASONS

37—Syracuse, 1971-2007

CONSECUTIVE NON-LOSING SEASONS (INCLUDES .500 RECORD)

60—Kentucky, 1928-52, 54-88# (2 .500 seasons)

#Kentucky did not play basketball during the 1953 season.

CONSECUTIVE NON-LOSING SEASONS (INCLUDES .500 RECORD)-CURRENT

38—Syracuse, 1970-2007 (one .500 season)

UNBEATEN TEAMS (SINCE 1938; NUMBER OF VICTORIES IN PARENTHESES)

1939 Long Island (24)†
1940 Seton Hall (19)††
1944 Army (15)††
1954 Kentucky (25)††
1956 San Francisco (29)*
1957 North Carolina (32)*
1964 UCLA (30)*
1967 UCLA (30)*
1972 UCLA (30)*
1973 UCLA (30)*
1973 North Carolina St. (27)††
1976 Indiana (32)*

*NCAA champion; †NIT champion; ††not in either tournament

UNBEATEN IN REGULAR SEASON BUT LOST IN NCAA (*) OR NIT (†)

1939 Loyola (Ill.) (20; 21-1)†
1941 Seton Hall (19; 20-2)†
1951 Columbia (21; 21-1)*
1961 Ohio St. (24; 27-1)*
1968 Houston (28; 31-2)*
1968 St. Bonaventure (22; 23-2)*
1971 Marquette (26; 28-1)*
1971 Penn (26; 28-1)*
1975 Indiana (29; 31-1)*
1976 Rutgers (28; 31-2)*
1979 Indiana St. (27; 33-1)*
1979 Alcorn St. (25; 28-1)†
1991 UNLV (30; 34-1)*

30-GAME WINNERS (Since 1938)

37—Duke, 1986 & 1999; Illinois, 2005; UNLV, 1987.

36—Kentucky, 1948.

35—Arizona, 1988; Duke, 2001; Florida, 2007; Georgetown, 1985; Kansas, 1986 & 1998; Kentucky, 1997 & 1998; Massachusetts, 1996; UNLV, 1990; Ohio St., 2007; Oklahoma, 1988.

34—Arkansas, 1991; Connecticut, 1999; Duke, 1992; Georgetown, 1984; Kansas, 1997; Kentucky, 1947 & 1996; UNLV, 1991; North Carolina, 1993 & 1998.

33—Connecticut, 2004; Florida, 2006; Indiana St., 1979; Kansas, 2007; Louisville, 1980 & 2005; Memphis, 2006 & 2007; Michigan St., 1999; UNLV, 1986; North Carolina, 2005.

32—Arkansas, 1978 & 1995; Bradley, 1950, 1951 & 1986; Connecticut, 1996 & 1998; Duke, 1991, 1998 & 2006; Houston, 1984; Indiana, 1976; Iowa St., 2000; Kentucky, 1949, 1951, 1986 & 2003; Louisville, 1983 & 1986; Marshall, 1947; Maryland, 2002; Michigan St., 2000; North Carolina, 1957, 1982 & 1987; Temple, 1987 & 1988; Tulsa, 2000; UCLA, 2006.

31—Arkansas, 1994; Cincinnati, 2002; Connecticut, 1990; Duke, 2002 & 2004; Houston, 1968 & 1983; Illinois, 1989; Indiana, 1975 & 1993; LSU, 1981; Memphis, 1985; Michigan, 1993; Minnesota, 1997; North Carolina, 2007; Oklahoma, 1985 & 2002; Oklahoma St., 1946 & 2004; Pittsburgh, 2004; Rutgers, 1976; St. John's (N.Y.), 1985 & 1986; Seton Hall, 1953 & 1989; Stanford, 2001; Syracuse, 1987; UCLA, 1995; Wyoming, 1943.

30—Arizona, 1998 & 2005; Arkansas, 1990; California, 1946; Connecticut, 2006; Georgetown, 1982 & 2007; Indiana, 1987; Iowa, 1987; Kansas, 1990 & 2003; Kentucky, 1978 & 1993; La Salle, 1990; Massachusetts, 1992; Michigan, 1989; Navy, 1986; UNLV, 2007; North Carolina, 1946; North Carolina St., 1951 & 1974; Oklahoma, 1989; Oregon, 1945; St. Joseph's, 2004; Stanford 1998 & 2004; Syracuse, 1989 & 2003; Texas, 2006; Texas Tech, 1996; UCLA, 1964, 1967, 1972, 1973 & 2007; Utah, 1991 & 1998; Virginia, 1982; Western Ky., 1938, Wisconsin, 2007.

All-Time Individual Leaders

Single-Game Records

SCORING HIGHS VS. DIVISION I OPPONENT

Pts.	Player, Team vs. Opponent	Date
72	Kevin Bradshaw, U.S. Int'l vs. Loyola Marymount	Jan. 5, 1991
69	Pete Maravich, LSU vs. Alabama	Feb. 7, 1970
68	Calvin Murphy, Niagara vs. Syracuse	Dec. 7, 1968
66	Jay Handlan, Wash. & Lee vs. Furman	Feb. 17, 1951
66	Pete Maravich, LSU vs. Tulane	Feb. 10, 1969
66	Anthony Roberts, Oral Roberts vs. N.C. A&T	Feb. 19, 1977
65	Anthony Roberts, Oral Roberts vs. Oregon	Mar. 9, 1977
65	Scott Haffner, Evansville vs. Dayton	Feb. 18, 1989
64	Pete Maravich, LSU vs. Kentucky	Feb. 21, 1970
63	Johnny Neumann, Mississippi vs. LSU	Jan. 30, 1971
63	Hersey Hawkins, Bradley vs. Detroit	Feb. 22, 1988

Pts.	Player, Team vs. Opponent	Date
62	Darrell Floyd, Furman vs. Citadel	Jan. 14, 1956
62	Oscar Robertson, Cincinnati vs. North Texas	Feb. 6, 1960
62	Askia Jones, Kansas St. vs. Fresno St.	Mar. 24, 1994
61	Lew Alcindor, UCLA vs. Washington St.	Feb. 25, 1967
61	Pete Maravich, LSU vs. Vanderbilt	Dec. 11, 1969
61	Rick Mount, Purdue vs. Iowa	Feb. 28, 1970
61	Austin Carr, Notre Dame vs. Ohio	Mar. 7, 1970
61	Wayman Tisdale, Oklahoma vs. UTSA	Dec. 28, 1983
61	Eddie House, Arizona St. vs. California (2 ot)	Jan. 8, 2000
60	Elgin Baylor, Seattle vs. Portland	Jan. 30, 1958
60	Billy McGill, Utah vs. BYU	Feb. 24, 1962
60	John Mengelt, Auburn vs. Alabama	Feb. 14, 1970
60	Johnny Neumann, Mississippi vs. Baylor	Dec. 29, 1970
59	Pete Maravich, LSU vs. Alabama	Feb. 17, 1968
59	Ernie Fleming, Jacksonville vs. St. Peter's	Jan. 29, 1972
59	Kevin Bradshaw, U.S. Int'l vs. Florida Int'l	Jan. 14, 1991

SCORING HIGHS VS. NON-DIVISION I OPPONENT

Pts.	Player, Team vs. Opponent	Date
100	Frank Selvy, Furman vs. Newberry	Feb. 13, 1954
85	Paul Arizin, Villanova vs. Philadelphia NAMC	Feb. 12, 1949
81	Freeman Williams, Portland St. vs. Rocky Mountain	Feb. 3, 1978
73	Bill Mlkvy, Temple vs. Wilkes	Mar. 3, 1951
71	Freeman Williams, Portland St. vs. Southern Ore.	Feb. 9, 1977
67	Darrell Floyd, Furman vs. Morehead St.	Jan. 22, 1955
66	Freeman Williams, Portland St. vs. George Fox	Jan. 13, 1978
65	Bob Zawoluk, St. John's (N.Y.) vs. St. Peter's	Mar. 30, 1950
63	Sherman White, Long Island vs. John Marshall	Feb. 1950
63	Frank Selvy, Furman vs. Mercer	Feb. 11, 1953
62	Elvin Hayes, Houston vs. Valparaiso	Feb. 24, 1968
61	Matt Teahan, Denver vs. Neb. Wesleyan	Feb. 26, 1979
60	Bob Pettit, LSU vs. Louisiana College	Dec. 7, 1953
60	Harry Kelly, Texas Southern vs. Jarvis Christian	Feb. 23, 1983
60	Dave Jamerson, Ohio vs. Charleston (W.V.)	Dec. 21, 1989
59	Rick Barry, Miami (Fla.) vs. Rollins	Jan. 23, 1965
58	Frank Selvy, Furman vs. Wofford	Feb. 23, 1954
57	David Thompson, North Carolina St. vs. Buffalo St.	Dec. 5, 1974
57	Calvin Murphy, Niagara vs. Villa Madonna	Dec. 6, 1967
56	Stan Davis, Appalachian St. vs. Carson-Newman	Jan. 24, 1974
56	Tim Roberts, Southern U. vs. Faith Baptist	Dec. 12, 1994
55	Rick Barry, Miami (Fla.) vs. Tampa	Dec. 1, 1964
55	Elvin Hayes, Houston vs. Texas St.	Feb. 12, 1966
55	Wayman Tisdale, Oklahoma vs. Texas St.	Dec. 10, 1984
54	Rick Barry, Miami (Fla.) vs. Florida Southern	Jan. 13, 1965

FIELD-GOAL PERCENTAGE
(Minimum 12 field goals made)

Pct.	Player, Team vs. Opponent (FG-FGA)	Date
100	Clifford Rozier, Louisville vs. Eastern Ky. (15 of 15)	Dec. 11, 1993
100	Dan Henderson, Arkansas St. vs. Ga. Southern (14 of 14)	Feb. 26, 1976
100	Cornelius Holden, Louisville vs. Southern Miss. (14 of 14)	Mar. 3, 1990
100	Dana Jones, Pepperdine vs. Boise St. (14 of 14)	Nov. 30, 1991
100	Ted Guzek, Butler vs. Michigan (13 of 13)	Dec. 15, 1956
100	Rick Dean, Syracuse vs. Colgate (13 of 13)	Feb. 14, 1966
100	Gary Lechman, Gonzaga vs. Portland St. (13 of 13)	Jan. 21, 1967
100	Kevin King, Charlotte vs. South Ala. (13 of 13)	Feb. 20, 1978
100	Vernon Smith, Texas A&M vs. Alas. Anchorage (13 of 13)	Nov. 26, 1978
100	Steve Johnson, Oregon St. vs. Hawaii-Hilo (13 of 13)	Dec. 5, 1979
100	Antoine Carr, Wichita St. vs. Abilene Christian (13 of 13)	Nov. 28, 1980
100	Doug Hashley, Montana St. vs. Idaho St. (13 of 13)	Feb. 5, 1982
100	Brad Daugherty, North Carolina vs. UCLA (13 of 13)	Nov. 24, 1985
100	Ricky Butler, UC Irvine vs. Cal St. Fullerton (13 of 13)	Feb. 21, 1991
100	Rafael Solis, Brooklyn vs. Wagner (13 of 13)	Dec. 11, 1991
100	Ben Handlogten, Western Mich. vs. Toledo (13 of 13)	Jan. 27, 1996
100	Mate Milisa, Long Beach St. vs. Cal St. Monterey (13 of 13)	Dec. 22, 1999
100	Leon Roberts, Northern Ill. vs. Rockford (13 of 13)	Dec. 6, 2000
100	Calvin Ento, Montana St. vs. Dickinson St. (13 of 13)	Dec. 10, 2002
100	22 tied (12 of 12)	

THREE-POINT FIELD GOALS MADE

3FG	Player, Team vs. Opponent	Date
15	Keith Veney, Marshall vs. Morehead St.	Dec. 14, 1996
14	Dave Jamerson, Ohio vs. Col. of Charleston	Dec. 21, 1989
14	Askia Jones, Kansas St. vs. Fresno St.	Mar. 24, 1994
14	Ronald Blackshear, Marshall vs. Akron	Mar. 1, 2002
12	Gary Bossert, Niagara vs. Siena	Jan. 7, 1987
12	Darrin Fitzgerald, Butler vs. Detroit	Feb. 9, 1987
12	Alex Dillard, Arkansas vs. Delaware St.	Dec. 11, 1993
12	Mitch Taylor, Southern U. vs. La. Christian	Dec. 1, 1994
12	David McMahan, Winthrop vs. Coastal Caro.	Jan. 15, 1996
12	Clarence Gilbert, Missouri vs. Colorado	Feb. 23, 2002
12	Terrence Woods, Florida A&M vs. Coppin St.	Mar. 1, 2003
12	Michael Jenkins, Winthrop vs. North Greenville	Nov. 11, 2006
11	Jeff Hodson, Augusta St. vs. Armstrong Atlantic	Jan. 28, 1986
11	Dennis Scott, Georgia Tech vs. Houston	Dec. 28, 1988
11	Scott Haffner, Evansville vs. Dayton	Feb. 18, 1989
11	Bobby Phills, Southern U. vs. Alcorn St.	Feb. 3, 1990
11	Dave Jamerson, Ohio vs. Kent St.	Feb. 24, 1990
11	Jeff Fryer, Loyola Marymount vs. Michigan	Mar. 18, 1990
11	Doug Day, Radford vs. Central Conn. St.	Dec. 12, 1990
11	Brent Price, Oklahoma vs. Loyola Marymount	Dec. 15, 1990
11	Bobby Phills, Southern U. vs. Manhattan	Dec. 28, 1990
11	Terry Brown, Kansas vs. North Carolina St.	Jan. 5, 1991
11	Marc Rybczyk, Central Conn. St. vs. Long Island	Nov. 26, 1991
11	Mark Alberts, Akron vs. Wright St.	Feb. 8, 1992
11	Mike Alcorn, Youngstown St. vs. Pitt-Bradford	Feb. 24, 1992
11	Doug Day, Radford vs. Morgan St.	Dec. 9, 1992
11	Lindsey Hunter, Jackson St. vs. Kansas	Dec. 27, 1992
11	Keith Veney, Lamar vs. Prairie View	Feb. 2, 1993
11	Keith Veney, Lamar vs. Ark.-Little Rock	Feb. 11, 1993
11	Scott Neely, Campbell vs. Coastal Caro.	Jan. 29, 1994

3FG	Player, Team vs. Opponent	Date
11	Chris Brown, UC Irvine vs. New Mexico St.	Mar. 13, 1994
11	Randy Rutherford, Oklahoma St. vs. Kansas	Mar. 5, 1995
11	Troy Hudson, Southern Ill. vs. Hawaii-Hilo	Dec. 29, 1995
11	Seth Chadwick, Wofford vs. Mercer	Feb. 15, 1997
11	Cory Schwab, Northern Ariz. vs. Cal Poly	Dec. 2, 2000
11	Ron Williamson, Howard vs. Georgetown	Dec. 16, 2000
11	T.J. Sorrentine, Vermont vs. Northeastern	Jan. 17, 2002
11	Ron Williamson, Howard vs. N.C. A&T	Jan. 21, 2003
11	Terrence Woods, Florida A&M vs. N.C. A&T	Feb. 1, 2003
11	Kevin Bettencourt, Bucknell vs. St. Francis (Pa.)	Dec. 6, 2003
11	Earnest Crumbley, Fla. Atlantic vs. Campbell	Feb. 26, 2004
11	Elton Nesbitt, Ga. Southern vs. Chattanooga	Jan. 17, 2005
11	Bobby Brown, Cal St. Fullerton vs. Bethune-Cookman	Dec. 16, 2006
11	Eric Moore, Buffalo vs. Bowling Green	Jan. 7, 2007

THREE-POINT FIELD-GOAL PERCENTAGE
(Minimum 7 three-point field goals made)

Pct.	Player, Team vs. Opponent (3FG-FGA)	Date
100	Mark Poag, Old Dominion vs. VMI (9 of 9)	Nov. 25, 1997
100	Marcus Wilson, Evansville vs. Tenn.-Martin (9 of 9)	Nov. 18, 1998
100	Donnie McGrath, Providence vs. Virginia (9 of 9)	Dec. 2, 2005
100	Tomas Thompson, San Francisco vs. Loyola Marymount (8 of 8)	Mar. 7, 1992
100	Shawn Haughn, Dayton vs. St. Louis (8 of 8)	Feb. 13, 1994
100	James Singleton, Murray St. vs. Eastern Ill. (8 of 8)	Feb. 13, 2003
100	John Goldsberry, UNC Wilmington vs. Maryland (8 of 8)	Mar. 21, 2003
100	Doug D'Amore, Idaho St. vs. Montana (8 of 8)	Jan. 17, 2004
100	Kelvin Collins, La.-Monroe vs. Nevada (7 of 7)	Dec. 30, 1986
100	Wally Lancaster, Virginia Tech vs. San Fran. St. (7 of 7)	Jan. 3, 1987
100	Ramon Trice, St. Louis vs. Butler (7 of 7)	Feb. 16, 1987
100	Juan Sanchez, Temple vs. Rhode Island (7 of 7)	Feb. 16, 1997
100	DeMar Moore, Bowling Green vs. Western Mich. (7 of 7)	Jan. 3, 1998
100	Senque Carey, Washington vs. Old Dominion (7 of 7)	Dec. 4, 1999
100	Okechi Egbe, Tenn.-Martin vs. Bethel (7 of 7)	Nov. 20, 2000
100	Justin Brown, Montana St. vs. Western Ill. (7 of 7)	Dec. 6, 2000
100	Lionel Armstead, West Virginia vs. Ark.-Monticello (7 of 7)	Dec. 1, 2001
100	Bronski Dockery, St. Francis (N.Y.) vs. Central Conn. St. (7 of 7)	Dec. 3, 2001
100	Nick Moore, Toledo vs. Akron (7 of 7)	Feb. 13, 2002
100	Felton Freeman, Sam Houston St. vs. TCU (7 of 7)	Nov. 22, 2002
100	Matt Walsh, Florida vs. Miami (Fla.) (7 of 7)	Dec. 21, 2002
100	Ezra Williams, Georgia vs. LSU (7 of 7)	Jan. 5, 2003
100	Tyrone Green, N.C. A&T vs. N.C. Central (7 of 7)	Jan. 19, 2003
100	Avery Sheets, Butler vs. Loyola (Ill.) (7 of 7)	Feb. 3, 2005
100	Rashad Anderson, Connecticut vs. Morehead St. (7 of 7)	Dec. 23, 2005
100	Ricky Porter, UC Riverside vs. Pacific (7 of 7)	Jan. 7, 2006
100	Jawann McClellan, Arizona vs. New Mexico St. (7 of 7)	Nov. 19, 2006
100	Matt Lojeski, Hawaii vs. Boise St. (7 of 7)	Mar. 3, 2007
100	Bryce Taylor, Oregon vs. Southern California (7 of 7)	Mar. 10, 2007

FREE-THROW PERCENTAGE
(Minimum 18 free throws made)

Pct.	Player, Team vs. Opponent (FT-FTA)	Date
100	Arlen Clark, Oklahoma St. vs. Colorado (24 of 24)	Mar. 7, 1959
100	York Larese, North Carolina vs. Duke (21 of 21)	Dec. 29, 1959
100	Steve Nash, Santa Clara vs. St. Mary's (Cal.) (21 of 21)	Jan. 7, 1995
100	Paul Renfro, Texas-Arlington vs. Lafayette (20 of 20)	Feb. 11, 1979
100	Anthony Peeler, Missouri vs. Iowa St. (20 of 20)	Jan. 31, 1990
100	Donyell Marshall, Connecticut vs. St. John's (N.Y.) (20 of 20)	Jan 15, 1994
100	Jeron Roberts, Wyoming vs. UTEP (20 of 20)	Feb. 7, 1998
100	Dick Ricketts, Duquesne vs. Dayton (19 of 19)	Dec. 29, 1955
100	Skip Chappelle, Maine vs. Massachusetts (19 of 19)	1961
100	Gene Phillips, SMU vs. Texas A&M (19 of 19)	Feb. 2, 1971
100	Jim Kennedy, Missouri vs. Hawaii (19 of 19)	Dec. 22, 1975
100	Kevin Smith, Michigan St. vs. Indiana (19 of 19)	Jan. 7, 1982
100	Sidney Goodman, Coppin St. vs. N.C. A&T (19 of 19)	Feb. 18, 1995
100	Geno Ford, Ohio vs. Eastern Mich. (19 of 19)	Feb. 12, 1997
100	Eddie Benton, Vermont vs. New Hampshire (19 of 19)	Feb. 18, 1993
100	Tommy Boyer, Arkansas vs. Texas Tech (18 of 18)	Feb. 19, 1963
100	Ted Kitchel, Indiana vs. Illinois (18 of 18)	Jan. 10, 1981
100	Eric Rhodes, Stephen F. Austin vs. Texas St. (18 of 18)	Feb. 21, 1987
100	Todd Lichti, Stanford vs. UC Santa Barbara (18 of 18)	Dec. 28, 1987
100	Lionel Simmons, La Salle vs. American (18 of 18)	Feb. 2, 1988
100	Jeff Webster, Oklahoma vs. SMU (18 of 18)	Jan. 2, 1994
100	Anquell McCollum, Western Caro. vs. Marshall (18 of 18)	Feb. 5, 1996
100	Keith Van Horn, Utah vs. TCU (18 of 18)	Feb. 13, 1997
100	Edwin Young, Dayton vs. La.-Monroe (18 of 18)	Dec. 18, 1997
100	Rayford Young, Texas Tech vs. Kansas (18 of 18)	Feb 13, 1993
100	Lynn Greer, Temple vs. St. Joseph's (18 of 18)	Feb. 2, 2002
100	Gabe Martin, Liberty vs. Fla. Atlantic (18 of 18)	Dec. 20, 2002
100	Matt Freije, Vanderbilt vs. Indiana (18 of 18)	Nov. 24, 2003
100	Ron Lewis, Bowling Green vs. Eastern Mich. (18 of 18)	Mar. 6, 2004
100	James Shuler, Winthrop vs. High Point (18 of 18)	Feb. 23, 2006

REBOUNDS

Reb.	Player, Team vs. Opponent	Date
51	Bill Chambers, William & Mary vs. Virginia	Feb. 14, 1953
43	Charlie Slack, Marshall vs. Morris Harvey	Jan. 12, 1954
42	Tom Heinsohn, Holy Cross vs. Boston College	Mar. 1, 1955
40	Art Quimby, Connecticut vs. Boston U.	Jan. 11, 1955
40	John Tresvant, Seattle vs. Montana	Feb. 8, 1963
39	Maurice Stokes, St. Francis (Pa.) vs. John Carroll	Jan. 28, 1955
39	Dave DeBusschere, Detroit vs. Central Mich.	Jan. 30, 1960
39	Keith Swagerty, Pacific vs. UC Santa Barbara	Mar. 5, 1965
38	Jerry Koch, St. Louis vs. Bradley	Mar. 5, 1954
38	Charlie Tyra, Louisville vs. Canisius	Dec. 10, 1955
38	Steve Hamilton, Morehead St. vs. Florida St.	Jan. 2, 1957
38	Paul Silas, Creighton vs. Centenary (La.)	Feb. 19, 1962
38	Tommy Woods, East Tenn. St. vs. Middle Tenn.	Mar. 1, 1965
37	Elgin Baylor, Seattle vs. Pacific Lutheran	Feb. 28, 1958
36	Herb Neff, Tennessee vs. Georgia Tech	Jan. 26, 1952
36	Dickie Hemric, Wake Forest vs. Clemson	Feb. 4, 1955
36	Swede Halbrook, Oregon St. vs. Idaho	Feb. 15, 1955
36	Wilt Chamberlain, Kansas vs. Iowa St.	Feb. 15, 1958
36	Jim Barnes, UTEP vs. Western N.M.	Jan. 4, 1964
35	Don Lange, Navy vs. Loyola (Md.)	Feb. 18, 1953
35	Ronnie Shavlik, North Carolina St. vs. Villanova	Jan. 29, 1955
35	Bill Ebben, Detroit vs. BYU	Dec. 28, 1955
35	Larry Abney, Fresno St. vs. SMU	Feb. 17, 2000
34	Bob Burrow, Kentucky vs. Temple	Dec. 10, 1955
34	Ronnie Shavlik, North Carolina St. vs. South Carolina	Feb. 11, 1955
34	Fred Cohen, Temple vs. Connecticut	Mar. 16, 1956
34	Bailey Howell, Mississippi St. vs. LSU	Feb. 1, 1957
34	Cal Ramsey, New York U. vs. Boston College	Feb. 16, 1957
34	Artis Gilmore, Jacksonville vs. St. Peter's	Dec. 3, 1970
34	David Vaughn, Oral Roberts vs. Brandeis	Jan. 8, 1973

(Since 1973)

Reb.	Player, Team vs. Opponent	Date
35	Larry Abney, Fresno St. vs. SMU	Feb. 17, 2000
34	David Vaughn, Oral Roberts vs. Brandeis	Jan. 8, 1973
32	Durand Macklin, LSU vs. Tulane	Nov. 26, 1976
32	Jervaughn Scales, Southern U. vs. Grambling	Feb. 7, 1994
31	Jim Bradley, Northern Ill. vs. Milwaukee	Feb. 19, 1973
31	Calvin Natt, La.-Monroe vs. Ga. Southern	Dec. 29, 1976
30	Marvin Barnes, Providence vs. Assumption	Feb. 3, 1973
30	Brad Robinson, Kent St. vs. Central Mich.	Feb. 9, 1974
30	Monti Davis, Tennessee St. vs. Alabama St.	Feb. 8, 1979
30	Rashad Jones-Jennings, Ark.-Little Rock vs. Ark.-Pine Bluff	Dec. 13, 2005
29	Lionel Garrett, Southern U. vs. Bishop	Feb. 16, 1979
29	Donald Newman, Ark.-Little Rock vs. Centenary (La.)	Jan. 24, 1984
29	Hank Gathers, Loyola Marymount vs. U.S. Int'l	Jan. 31, 1989
28	Alvan Adams, Oklahoma vs. Indiana St.	Nov. 27, 1972
28	Cliff Robinson, Southern California vs. Portland St.	Jan. 20, 1978
28	Eric McArthur, UC Santa Barbara vs. New Mexico St.	Jan. 11, 1990
28	Marcus Mann, Mississippi Val. vs. Jackson St.	Mar. 9, 1996
28	David Bluthenthal, Southern California vs. Arizona St.	Jan. 20, 2000
28	Paul Millsap, Louisiana Tech vs. San Jose St.	Feb. 15, 2006
27	Andy Hopson, Oklahoma St. vs. Missouri	Jan. 30, 1973
27	Henry Ray, McNeese St. vs. Texas-Arlington	1974
27	Bill Walton, UCLA vs. Loyola (Ill.)	Jan. 25, 1973
27	Bill Walton, UCLA vs. Maryland	Dec. 1, 1973
27	Rick Kelley, Stanford vs. Kentucky	Dec. 22, 1974
27	Kerry Davis, Cal St. Fullerton vs. Central Mich.	Dec. 15, 1975
27	Hank Gathers, Loyola Marymount vs. U.S. Int'l	Dec. 7, 1989
27	Dikembe Mutombo, Georgetown vs. Connecticut	Mar. 8, 1991
27	Reginald Slater, Wyoming vs. Troy	Dec. 14, 1991
27	Ervin Johnson, New Orleans vs. Lamar	Feb. 18, 1993
27	Willie Fisher, Jacksonville vs. Louisiana Tech	Dec. 4, 1993
27	Kareem Carpenter, Eastern Mich. vs. Western Mich.	Feb. 8, 1995
27	Amien Hicks, Morris Brown vs. Clark Atlanta	Jan. 14, 2002
27	Andre Brown, DePaul vs. TCU	Feb. 6, 2002

ASSISTS

Ast.	Player, Team vs. Opponent	Date
22	Tony Fairley, Charleston So. vs. Armstrong Atlantic	Feb. 9, 1987
22	Avery Johnson, Southern U. vs. Texas Southern	Jan. 25, 1988
22	Sherman Douglas, Syracuse vs. Providence	Jan. 28, 1989
21	Mark Wade, UNLV vs. Navy	Dec. 29, 1986
21	Kelvin Scarborough, New Mexico vs. Hawaii	Feb. 13, 1987
21	Anthony Manuel, Bradley vs. UC Irvine	Dec. 19, 1987
21	Avery Johnson, Southern U. vs. Alabama St.	Jan. 16, 1988
20	Grayson Marshall, Clemson vs. Md.-East. Shore	Nov. 25, 1985
20	James Johnson, Middle Tenn. vs. Freed-Hardeman	Jan. 2, 1986
20	Avery Johnson, Southern U. vs. Texas Southern	Mar. 6, 1987
20	Avery Johnson, Southern U. vs. Mississippi Val.	Feb. 8, 1988
20	Howard Evans, Temple vs. Villanova	Feb. 10, 1988
20	Jasper Walker, St. Peter's vs. Holy Cross	Feb. 11, 1989

Ast.	Player, Team vs. Opponent	Date
20	Chris Corchiani, North Carolina St. vs. Maryland	Feb. 27, 1991
20	Drew Henderson, Fairfield vs. Loyola (Md.)	Jan. 25, 1992
20	Dana Harris, UMBC vs. St. Mary's	Dec. 12, 1992
20	Sam Crawford, New Mexico St. vs. Sam Houston St.	Dec. 21, 1992
20	Ray Washington, Nicholls St. vs. McNeese St.	Jan. 28, 1995
20	Mateen Cleaves, Michigan St. vs. Michigan	Mar. 4, 2000
19	Frank Nardi, Green Bay vs. UNI	Feb. 24, 1986
19	Avery Johnson, Southern U. vs. Tex. A&M-Kingsville	Dec. 6, 1986
19	Avery Johnson, Southern U. vs. Jackson St.	Jan. 16, 1987
19	Andre Van Drost, Wagner vs. Long Island	Feb. 25, 1987
19	Todd Lehmann, Drexel vs. Liberty	Feb. 5, 1990
19	Greg Anthony, UNLV vs. Pacific	Dec. 29, 1990
19	Keith Jennings, East Tenn. St. vs. Appalachian St.	Feb. 2, 1991
19	Nelson Haggerty, Baylor vs. Oral Roberts	Feb. 27, 1993
19	Andres Rodriguez, American vs. Navy	Jan. 14, 2004
19	Jason Richards, Davidson vs. Mt. St. Mary (N.Y.)	Dec. 15, 2006

BLOCKED SHOTS

Blk.	Player, Team vs. Opponent	Date
16	Mickell Gladness, Alabama A&M vs. Texas Southern	Feb. 24, 2007
14	David Robinson, Navy vs. UNC Wilmington	Jan. 4, 1986
14	Shawn Bradley, BYU vs. Eastern Ky.	Dec. 7, 1990
14	Roy Rogers, Alabama vs. Georgia	Feb. 10, 1996
14	Loren Woods, Arizona vs. Oregon	Feb. 3, 2000
13	Kevin Roberson, Vermont vs. New Hampshire	Jan. 9, 1992
13	Jim McIlvaine, Marquette vs. Northeastern Ill.	Dec. 9, 1992
13	Keith Closs, Central Conn. St. vs. St. Francis (Pa.)	Dec. 21, 1994
13	D'or Fischer, Northwestern St. vs. Texas St.	Jan. 22, 2001
13	Kyle Davis, Auburn vs. Miami (Fla.)	Mar. 14, 2001
13	Wojciech Myrda, La.-Monroe vs. UTSA	Jan. 17, 2002
13	Anthony King, Miami (Fla.) vs. Fla. Atlantic	Nov. 29, 2004
13	Deng Gai, Fairfield vs. Siena	Jan. 22, 2005
13	Sean Williams, Boston College vs. Duquesne	Dec. 28, 2006
13	Joel Anthony, UNLV vs. TCU	Feb. 7, 2007
12	David Robinson, Navy vs. James Madison	Jan. 9, 1986
12	Derrick Lewis, Maryland vs. James Madison	Jan. 28, 1987
12	Rodney Blake, St. Joseph's vs. Cleveland St.	Dec. 2, 1987
12	Walter Palmer, Dartmouth vs. Harvard	Jan. 9, 1988
12	Alan Ogg, UAB vs. Florida A&M	Dec. 16, 1988
12	Dikembe Mutombo, Georgetown vs. St. John's (N.Y.)	Jan. 23, 1989
12	Shaquille O'Neal, LSU vs. Loyola Marymount	Feb. 3, 1990
12	Cedric Lewis, Maryland vs. South Fla.	Jan. 19, 1991
12	Ervin Johnson, New Orleans vs. Texas A&M	Dec. 29, 1992
12	Kurt Thomas, TCU vs. Texas A&M	Feb. 25, 1995
12	Keith Closs, Central Conn. St. vs. Troy	Jan. 20, 1996
12	Adonal Foyle, Colgate vs. Fairfield	Nov. 26, 1996
12	Adonal Foyle, Colgate vs. Navy	Feb. 5, 1997
12	Tarvis Williams, Hampton vs. N.C. A&T	Jan. 9, 1999
12	Darrick Davenport, TCU vs. Alas. Fairbanks	Nov. 20, 1999
12	Tarvis Williams, Hampton vs. Delaware St.	Jan. 13, 2001
12	D'or Fischer, Northwestern St. vs. Siena	Nov. 21, 2001
12	Justin Williams, Wyoming vs. Utah	Mar. 10, 2006
12	Sean Williams, Boston College vs. Providence	Nov. 22, 2006
12	Brook Lopez, Stanford vs. Southern California	Jan. 25, 2007

STEALS

Stl.	Player, Team vs. Opponent	Date
13	Mookie Blaylock, Oklahoma vs. Centenary (La.)	Dec. 12, 1987
13	Mookie Blaylock, Oklahoma vs. Loyola Marymount	Dec. 17, 1988
12	Kenny Robertson, Cleveland St. vs. Wagner	Dec. 3, 1988
12	Terry Evans, Oklahoma vs. Florida A&M	Jan. 27, 1993
12	Richard Duncan, Middle Tenn. vs. Eastern Ky.	Feb. 20, 1999
12	Greedy Daniels, TCU vs. Ark.-Pine Bluff	Dec. 30, 2000
12	Jehiel Lewis, Navy vs. Bucknell	Jan. 12, 2002
12	Carldwell Johnson, UAB vs. South Carolina St.	Nov. 27, 2005
11	Darron Brittman, Chicago St. vs. McKendree	Jan. 24, 1986
11	Darron Brittman, Chicago St. vs. St. Xavier	Feb. 8, 1986
11	Marty Johnson, Towson vs. Bucknell	Feb. 17, 1988
11	Aldwin Ware, Florida A&M vs. Tuskegee	Feb. 24, 1988
11	Mark Macon, Temple vs. Notre Dame	Jan. 29, 1989
11	Carl Thomas, Eastern Mich. vs. Chicago St.	Feb. 20, 1991
11	Ron Arnold, St. Francis (N.Y.) vs. Mt. St. Mary's	Feb. 4, 1993
11	Tyus Edney, UCLA vs. George Mason	Dec. 22, 1995
11	Philip Huler, Fla. Atlantic vs. Campbell	Jan. 18, 1997
11	Ali Ton, Davidson vs. Tufts	Nov. 29, 1997
11	Chris Thomas, Notre Dame vs. New Hampshire	Nov. 16, 2001
11	Drew Schifino, West Virginia vs. Ark.-Monticello	Dec. 1, 2001
11	John Linehan, Providence vs. Rutgers	Jan. 22, 2002
11	Travis Demanby, Fresno St. vs. Oklahoma St.	Feb. 10, 2002
11	Travis Holmes, VMI vs. Bridgewater (Va.)	Jan. 18, 2007
10	37 tied	

Season Records

POINTS

Player, Team	Season	G	FG	3FG	FT	Pts.
Pete Maravich, LSU	†1970	31	522	—	337	1,381
Elvin Hayes, Houston	†1968	33	519	—	176	1,214
Frank Selvy, Furman	†1954	29	427	—	355	1,209
Pete Maravich, LSU	†1969	26	433	—	282	1,148
Pete Maravich, LSU	1968	26	432	—	274	1,138
Bo Kimble, Loyola Marymount	†1990	32	404	92	231	1,131
Hersey Hawkins, Bradley	†1988	31	377	87	284	1,125
Austin Carr, Notre Dame	1970	29	444	—	218	1,106
Austin Carr, Notre Dame	†1971	29	430	—	241	1,101
Otis Birdsong, Houston	†1977	36	452	—	186	1,090
Dwight Lamar, La.-Lafayette	†1972	29	429	—	196	1,054
Kevin Bradshaw, U.S. Int'l	†1991	28	358	60	278	1,054
Glenn Robinson, Purdue	†1994	34	368	79	215	1,030
Hank Gathers, Loyola Marymount	†1989	31	419	0	177	1,015
Oscar Robertson, Cincinnati	†1960	30	369	—	273	1,011
Freeman Williams, Portland St.	1977	26	417	—	176	1,010
Billy McGill, Utah	†1962	26	394	—	221	1,009
Rich Fuqua, Oral Roberts	1972	28	423	—	160	1,006
Oscar Robertson, Cincinnati	†1958	28	352	—	280	984
Oscar Robertson, Cincinnati	†1959	30	331	—	316	978
Rick Barry, Miami (Fla.)	†1965	26	340	—	293	973
Larry Bird, Indiana St.	†1979	34	376	—	221	973
Dennis Scott, Georgia Tech	1990	35	336	137	161	970
Freeman Williams, Portland St.	†1978	27	410	—	149	969
Chris Jackson, LSU	1989	32	359	84	163	965

†national leader

SCORING AVERAGE

Player, Team	Season	G	FG	3FG	FT	Pts.	Avg.
Pete Maravich, LSU	†1970	31	522	—	337	1,381	44.5
Pete Maravich, LSU	†1969	26	433	—	282	1,148	44.2
Pete Maravich, LSU	†1968	26	432	—	274	1,138	43.8
Frank Selvy, Furman	†1954	29	427	—	355	1,209	41.7
Johnny Neumann, Mississippi	†1971	23	366	—	191	923	40.1
Freeman Williams, Portland St.	†1977	26	417	—	176	1,010	38.8
Billy McGill, Utah	†1962	26	394	—	221	1,009	38.8
Calvin Murphy, Niagara	1968	24	337	—	242	916	38.2
Austin Carr, Notre Dame	1970	29	444	—	218	1,106	38.1
Austin Carr, Notre Dame	1971	29	430	—	241	1,101	38.0
Kevin Bradshaw, U.S. Int'l	†1991	28	358	60	278	1,054	37.6
Rick Barry, Miami (Fla.)	†1965	26	340	—	293	973	37.4
Elvin Hayes, Houston	1968	33	519	—	176	1,214	36.8
Marshall Rogers, Tex.-Pan American	†1976	25	361	—	197	919	36.8
Howard Komives, Bowling Green	†1964	23	292	—	260	844	36.7
Dwight Lamar, La.-Lafayette	†1972	29	429	—	196	1,054	36.3
Hersey Hawkins, Bradley	†1988	31	377	87	284	1,125	36.3
Darrell Floyd, Furman	†1955	25	344	—	209	897	35.9
Rich Fuqua, Oral Roberts	1972	28	423	—	160	1,006	35.9
Freeman Williams, Portland St.	†1978	27	410	—	149	969	35.9
Rick Mount, Purdue	1970	20	285	—	138	708	35.4
Bo Kimble, Loyola Marymount	†1990	32	404	92	231	1,131	35.3
Oscar Robertson, Cincinnati	†1958	28	352	—	280	984	35.1
Anthony Roberts, Oral Roberts	1977	28	402	—	147	951	34.0
Dan Issel, Kentucky	1970	28	369	—	210	948	33.9
William Averitt, Pepperdine	†1973	25	352	—	144	848	33.9

†national leader

FIELD-GOAL PERCENTAGE
(Based on qualifiers for annual championship)

Player, Team	Season	G	FG	FGA	Pct.
Steve Johnson, Oregon St.	†1981	28	235	315	74.6
Dwayne Davis, Florida	†1989	33	179	248	72.2
Keith Walker, Utica	†1985	27	154	216	71.3
Steve Johnson, Oregon St.	†1980	30	211	297	71.0
Adam Mark, Belmont	†2002	26	150	212	70.8
Oliver Miller, Arkansas	†1991	38	254	361	70.4
Alan Williams, Princeton	†1987	25	163	232	70.3
Mark McNamara, California	†1982	27	231	329	70.2
Warren Kidd, Middle Tenn.	1991	30	173	247	70.0
Pete Freeman, Akron	1991	28	175	250	70.0
Joe Senser, West Chester	†1977	25	130	186	69.9
Lee Campbell, Missouri St.	†1990	29	192	275	69.8
Stephen Scheffler, Purdue	1990	30	173	248	69.8
Brendan Haywood, North Carolina	†2000	36	191	274	69.7
Mike Atkinson, Long Beach St.	†1994	26	141	203	69.5
Lester James, St. Francis (N.Y.)	1991	29	149	215	69.3
Micheal Bradley, Villanova	†2001	31	254	367	69.2

(continued)

Player, Team	Season	G	FG	FGA	Pct.
Murray Brown, Florida St.	†1979	29	237	343	69.1
Joe Senser, West Chester	†1978	25	135	197	68.5
Charles Outlaw, Houston	†1992	31	156	228	68.4
Shane Kline-Ruminski, Bowling Green	†1995	26	181	265	68.3
Marcus Kennedy, Eastern Mich.	1991	33	240	352	68.2
Felton Spencer, Louisville	1990	35	188	276	68.1
Tyrone Howard, Eastern Ky.	1987	30	156	230	67.8
Nigel Dixon, Western Ky.	†2004	28	179	264	67.8
Mike Freeman, Hampton	†2007	30	162	239	67.8

†national leader

THREE-POINT FIELD GOALS MADE

Player, Team	Season	G	3FG
Darrin Fitzgerald, Butler	†1987	28	158
Freddie Banks, UNLV	1987	39	152
Randy Rutherford, Oklahoma St.	†1995	37	146
Terrence Woods, Florida A&M	†2004	31	140
Terrence Woods, Florida A&M	†2003	28	139
J.J. Redick, Duke	†2006	36	139
Dennis Scott, Georgia Tech	†1990	35	137
Demon Brown, Charlotte	2003	29	137
Will Whittington, Marist	†2007	30	137
Rashad Phillips, Detroit	†2001	35	136
Pat Carroll, St. Joseph's	†2005	35	135
Troy Hudson, Southern Ill.	†1997	30	134
Timothy Pollard, Mississippi Val.	†1988	28	132
Jason Williams, Duke	2001	39	132
Dave Jamerson, Ohio	1990	28	131
Sydney Grider, La.-Lafayette	1990	29	131
Keith Veney, Marshall	1997	29	130
Curtis Staples, Virginia	†1998	30	130
Kyle Korver, Creighton	2003	34	129
Lazelle Durden, Cincinnati	1995	34	127
Jeff Fryer, Loyola Marymount	†1989	31	126
Jack Leasure, Coastal Caro.	2006	30	125
Timothy Pollard, Mississippi Val.	1989	28	124
Shane Battier, Duke	2001	39	124
Stephen Sir, Northern Ariz.	2007	30	124

†national leader

THREE-POINT FIELD GOALS MADE PER GAME
(Based on qualifiers for annual championship)

Player, Team	Season	G	3FG	Avg.
Darrin Fitzgerald, Butler	†1987	28	158	5.64
Terrence Woods, Florida A&M	†2003	28	139	4.96
Demon Brown, Charlotte	2003	29	137	4.72
Timothy Pollard, Mississippi Val.	†1988	28	132	4.71
Chris Brown, UC Irvine	†1994	26	122	4.69
Dave Jamerson, Ohio	†1990	28	131	4.68
William Fourche, Southern U.	†1997	27	122	4.52
Sydney Grider, La.-Lafayette	1990	29	131	4.52
Terrence Woods, Florida A&M	†2004	31	140	4.52
Keith Veney, Marshall	1997	29	130	4.48
Troy Hudson, Southern Ill.	1997	30	134	4.47
Timothy Pollard, Mississippi Val.	†1989	28	124	4.43
Keke Hicks, Coastal Caro.	1994	26	115	4.42
Bobby Phills, Southern U.	†1991	28	123	4.39
Mitch Taylor, Southern U.	†1995	25	109	4.36
Mark Alberts, Akron	1990	28	122	4.36
Curtis Staples, Virginia	†1998	30	130	4.33
Jeff Fryer, Loyola Marymount	1990	28	121	4.32
Shawn Respert, Michigan St.	1995	28	119	4.25
Sydney Grider, La.-Lafayette	1989	29	122	4.21
Andre Collins, Loyola (Md.)	†2006	28	118	4.21
Bernard Haslett, Southern Miss.	†1993	26	109	4.19
Stevin Smith, Arizona St.	1993	27	113	4.19
Jack Leasure, Coastal Caro.	2006	30	125	4.17
Tim Roberts, Southern U.	1995	26	108	4.15

†national leader

THREE-POINT FIELD-GOAL PERCENTAGE
(Based on qualifiers for annual championship)

Player, Team	Season	G	3FG	3FGA	Pct.
Glenn Tropf, Holy Cross	†1988	29	52	82	63.4
Sean Wightman, Western Mich.	†1992	30	48	76	63.2
Keith Jennings, East Tenn. St.	†1991	33	84	142	59.2
Dave Calloway, Monmouth	†1989	28	48	82	58.5
Steve Kerr, Arizona	1988	38	114	199	57.3
Reginald Jones, Prairie View	†1987	28	64	112	57.1
Jim Cantamessa, Siena	†1998	29	66	117	56.4
Joel Tribelhorn, Colorado St.	1989	33	76	135	56.3

Player, Team	Season	G	3FG	3FGA	Pct.
Mike Joseph, Bucknell	1988	28	65	116	56.0
Brian Jackson, Evansville	†1995	27	53	95	55.8
Amory Sanders, Southeast Mo. St.	†2001	24	53	95	55.8
Christian Laettner, Duke	1992	35	54	97	55.7
Reginald Jones, Prairie View	1988	27	85	155	54.8
Eric Rhodes, Stephen F. Austin	1987	30	58	106	54.7
Dave Orlandini, Princeton	1988	26	60	110	54.5
David Falknor, Akron	2001	22	47	87	54.0
Mike Joseph, Bucknell	1989	31	62	115	53.9
John Bays, Towson	1989	29	71	132	53.8
Jeff Anderson, Kent St.	†1993	26	44	82	53.7
Jay Edwards, Indiana	1988	23	59	110	53.6
Anthony Davis, George Mason	1987	27	45	84	53.6
Mark Anglavar, Marquette	1989	28	53	99	53.5
Scot Dimak, Stephen F. Austin	1987	30	46	86	53.5
Matt Lapin, Princeton	†1990	27	71	133	53.4
Michael Charles, UAB	1988	28	63	118	53.4

†national leader

FREE-THROW PERCENTAGE
(Based on qualifiers for annual championship)

Player, Team	Season	G	FT	FTA	Pct.
Blake Ahearn, Missouri St.	†2004	33	117	120	97.5
Derek Raivio, Gonzaga	†2007	34	148	154	96.1
Craig Collins, Penn St.	†1985	27	94	98	95.9
J.J. Redick, Duke	2004	37	143	150	95.3
Steve Drabyn, Belmont	†2003	29	78	82	95.1
Rod Foster, UCLA	†1982	27	95	100	95.0
Clay McKnight, Pacific	†2000	24	74	78	94.9
Matt Logie, Lehigh	2003	28	91	96	94.8
A.J. Green, Butler	2007	35	145	153	94.8
Blake Ahearn, Missouri St.	†2005	32	90	95	94.7
Carlos Gibson, Marshall	†1978	28	84	89	94.4
Danny Basile, Marist	†1994	27	84	89	94.4
Jim Barton, Dartmouth	†1986	26	65	69	94.2
Gary Buchanon, Villanova	†2001	31	97	103	94.2
Jack Moore, Nebraska	1982	27	123	131	93.9
J.J. Redick, Duke	2005	33	196	209	93.8
Blake Ahearn, Missouri St.	†2006	31	117	125	93.6
Rob Robbins, New Mexico	†1990	34	101	108	93.5
Dandrea Evans, Troy	1994	27	72	77	93.5
Tommy Boyer, Arkansas	†1962	23	125	134	93.3
Jake Sullivan, Iowa St.	2003	33	83	89	93.3
Damon Goodwin, Dayton	1986	30	95	102	93.1
Brent Jolly, Tennesee Tech	2001	29	95	102	93.1
Ryan Mendez, Stanford	2001	34	94	101	93.1
Brian Magid, George Washington	†1980	26	79	85	92.9
Mike Joseph, Bucknell	1990	29	144	155	92.9
Hollis Price, Oklahoma	2003	34	130	140	92.9

†national leader

REBOUNDS

Player, Team	Ht.	Season	G	Reb.
Walt Dukes, Seton Hall	6-10	†1953	33	734
Leroy Wright, Pacific	6-8	†1959	26	652
Tom Gola, La Salle	6-6	†1954	30	652
Charlie Tyra, Louisville	6-8	†1956	29	645
Paul Silas, Creighton	6-7	†1964	29	631
Elvin Hayes, Houston	6-8	†1968	33	624
Artis Gilmore, Jacksonville	7-2	†1970	28	621
Tom Gola, La Salle	6-6	†1955	31	618
Ed Conlin, Fordham	6-5	1953	26	612
Art Quimby, Connecticut	6-5	1955	25	611
Bill Russell, San Francisco	6-9	1956	29	609
Jim Ware, Oklahoma City	6-8	†1966	29	607
Joe Holup, George Washington	6-6	1956	26	604
Artis Gilmore, Jacksonville	7-2	†1971	26	603
Elton Tuttle, Creighton	6-5	1954	30	601
Marvin Barnes, Providence	6-9	†1974	32	597
Bill Russell, San Francisco	6-9	1955	29	594
Art Quimby, Connecticut	6-5	1954	26	588
Ed Conlin, Fordham	6-5	1955	27	578
Marvin Barnes, Providence	6-9	†1973	30	571
Bill Spivey, Kentucky	7-0	†1951	33	567
Bob Pelkington, Xavier	6-7	1964	26	567
Paul Silas, Creighton	6-7	†1962	25	563
Elgin Baylor, Seattle	6-6	†1959	29	559
Paul Silas, Creighton	6-7	†1963	27	557

†national leader

(Since 1973)

Player, Team	Ht.	Season	G	Reb.
Marvin Barnes, Providence	6-9	†1974	32	597
Marvin Barnes, Providence	6-9	†1973	30	571
Kermit Washington, American	6-8	1973	25	511
Bill Walton, UCLA	6-11	1973	30	506
Larry Bird, Indiana St.	6-9	†1979	34	505
Larry Kenon, Memphis	6-9	†1973	30	501
Akeem Olajuwon, Houston	7-0	†1984	37	500
Glenn Mosley, Seton Hall	6-8	†1977	29	473
Popeye Jones, Murray St.	6-8	†1991	33	469
Pete Padgett, Nevada	6-8	†1973	26	462
Xavier McDaniel, Wichita St.	6-8	†1985	31	460
Larry Johnson, UNLV	6-7	1990	40	457
Tim Duncan, Wake Forest	6-11	†1997	31	457
Anthony Bonner, St. Louis	6-8	1990	33	456
Bill Cartwright, San Francisco	7-1	1979	29	455
David Robinson, Navy	6-11	†1986	35	455
Benoit Benjamin, Creighton	7-0	1985	32	451
Jerome Lane, Pittsburgh	6-6	†1987	33	444
Robert Elmore, Wichita St.	6-10	1977	28	441
John Irving, Hofstra	6-9	1977	27	440
Paul Millsap, Louisiana Tech	6-8	†2006	33	438
Lionel Garrett, Southern U.	6-9	1979	28	433
Popeye Jones, Murray St.	6-8	†1992	30	431
Andrew Bogut, Utah	7-0	†2005	35	427
Jim Bradley, Northern Ill.	6-10	1973	24	426
Hank Gathers, Loyola Marymount	6-7	†1989	31	426

†national leader

REBOUND AVERAGE

Player, Team	Ht.	Season	G	Reb.	Avg.
Charlie Slack, Marshall	6-5	†1955	21	538	25.6
Leroy Wright, Pacific	6-8	†1959	26	652	25.1
Art Quimby, Connecticut	6-5	1955	25	611	24.4
Charlie Slack, Marshall	6-5	1956	22	520	23.6
Ed Conlin, Fordham	6-5	†1953	26	612	23.5
Joe Holup, George Washington	6-6	††1956	26	604	23.2
Artis Gilmore, Jacksonville	7-2	†1971	26	603	23.2
Art Quimby, Connecticut	6-5	†1954	26	588	22.6
Paul Silas, Creighton	6-7	1962	25	563	22.5
Leroy Wright, Pacific	6-8	†1960	17	380	22.4
Walt Dukes, Seton Hall	6-10	1953	33	734	22.2
Charlie Tyra, Louisville	6-8	1956	29	645	22.2
Charlie Slack, Marshall	6-5	1954	21	466	22.2
Artis Gilmore, Jacksonville	7-2	†1970	28	621	22.2
Bill Chambers, William & Mary	6-4	1953	22	480	21.8
Bob Pelkington, Xavier	6-7	†1964	26	567	21.8
Dick Cunningham, Murray St.	6-10	†1967	22	479	21.8
Paul Silas, Creighton	6-7	1964	29	631	21.8
Tom Gola, La Salle	6-6	1954	30	652	21.7
Jerry Harper, Alabama	6-8	1956	24	517	21.5
Spencer Haywood, Detroit	6-8	†1969	22	472	21.5
Ed Conlin, Fordham	6-5	1955	27	578	21.4
Tom Heinsohn, Holy Cross	6-7	1956	26	549	21.1
Bill Russell, San Francisco	6-9	1956	29	609	21.0
Toby Kimball, Connecticut	6-8	†1965	23	483	21.0

†national leader; ††From 1956 through 1962, individual champions were determined by percentage of all recoveries; Holup led in percentage of recoveries and Slack led in average in 1956.

(Since 1973)

Player, Team	Ht.	Season	G	Reb.	Avg.
Kermit Washington, American	6-8	†1973	25	511	20.4
Marvin Barnes, Providence	6-9	1973	30	571	19.0
Marvin Barnes, Providence	6-9	†1974	32	597	18.7
Pete Padgett, Nevada	6-8	1973	26	462	17.8
Jim Bradley, Northern Ill.	6-10	1973	24	426	17.8
Bill Walton, UCLA	6-11	1973	30	506	16.9
Larry Kenon, Memphis	6-9	1973	30	501	16.7
Glenn Mosley, Seton Hall	6-8	†1977	29	473	16.3
John Irving, Hofstra	6-9	1977	27	440	16.3
Carlos McCullough, Tex.-Pan American	6-7	1974	22	358	16.3
Brad Robinson, Kent St.	6-7	1974	26	423	16.3
Monti Davis, Tennessee St.	6-7	†1979	26	421	16.2
Sam Pellom, Buffalo	6-8	†1976	26	420	16.2
Robert Elmore, Wichita St.	6-10	1977	28	441	15.8
Bill Cartwright, San Francisco	7-1	1979	29	455	15.7
Bill Champion, Manhattan	6-10	1973	26	402	15.5
Bill Champion, Manhattan	6-10	1974	27	419	15.5
Lionel Garrett, Southern U.	6-9	1979	28	433	15.5
Dwayne Barnett, Samford	6-6	1976	23	354	15.4
John Irving, Hofstra	6-9	†1975	21	323	15.4
Cornelius Cash, Bowling Green	6-8	1973	26	396	15.2
Pete Padgett, Nevada	6-8	1974	26	395	15.2

Player, Team	Ht.	Season	G	Reb.	Avg.
Jimmie Baker, UNLV	6-9	1973	28	424	15.1
Larry Smith, Alcorn St.	6-8	†1980	26	392	15.1
Charles McKinney, Baylor	6-6	1974	25	375	15.0
Lewis Lloyd, Drake	6-6	1980	27	406	15.0

†national leader

ASSISTS

Player, Team	Season	G	Ast.
Mark Wade, UNLV	†1987	38	406
Avery Johnson, Southern U.	†1988	30	399
Anthony Manuel, Bradley	1988	31	373
Avery Johnson, Southern U.	1987	31	333
Mark Jackson, St. John's (N.Y.)	†1986	32	328
Sherman Douglas, Syracuse	†1989	38	326
Greg Anthony, UNLV	†1991	35	310
Sam Crawford, New Mexico St.	†1993	34	310
Reid Gettys, Houston	†1984	37	309
Carl Golston, Loyola (Ill.)	†1985	33	305
Craig Neal, Georgia Tech	1988	32	303
Keith Jennings, East Tenn. St.	1991	33	301
Doug Gottlieb, Oklahoma St.	†1999	34	299
Chris Corchiani, North Carolina St.	1991	31	299
Keith Jennings, East Tenn. St.	†1990	34	297
Howard Evans, Temple	1988	34	294
Ahlon Lewis, Arizona St.	†1998	32	294
Doug Gottlieb, Oklahoma St.	†2000	34	293
Danny Tarkanian, UNLV	1984	34	289
Sherman Douglas, Syracuse	1987	38	289
Bobby Hurley, Duke	1991	39	289
Greg Anthony, UNLV	1990	39	289
Sherman Douglas, Syracuse	1988	35	288
Bobby Hurley, Duke	1990	38	288
Marcus Carr, Cal St. Northridge	†2001	32	286
Steve Blake, Maryland	†2002	36	286
Jared Jordan, Marist	†2007	33	286

†national leader

ASSIST AVERAGE

Player, Team	Season	G	Ast.	Avg.
Avery Johnson, Southern U.	†1988	30	399	13.30
Anthony Manuel, Bradley	1988	31	373	12.03
Avery Johnson, Southern U.	†1987	31	333	10.74
Mark Wade, UNLV	1987	38	406	10.68
Nelson Haggerty, Baylor	†1995	28	284	10.14
Glenn Williams, Holy Cross	†1989	28	278	9.92
Chris Corchiani, North Carolina St.	†1991	31	299	9.65
Tony Fairley, Charleston So.	1987	28	270	9.64
Tyrone Bogues, Wake Forest	1987	29	276	9.52
Ron Weingard, Hofstra	†1985	24	228	9.50
Craig Neal, Georgia Tech	1988	32	303	9.47
Craig Lathan, Ill.-Chicago	†1984	29	274	9.45
Curtis McCants, George Mason	1995	27	251	9.30
Andre Van Drost, Wagner	1987	28	260	9.29
Todd Lehmann, Drexel	†1990	28	260	9.29
Danny Tirado, Jacksonville	1991	28	259	9.25
Carl Golston, Loyola (Ill.)	1985	33	305	9.24
Ahlon Lewis, Arizona St.	†1998	32	294	9.19
Terrell Lowery, Loyola Marymount	1991	31	283	9.13
Keith Jennings, East Tenn. St.	1991	33	301	9.12
Sam Crawford, New Mexico St.	†1993	34	310	9.12
Mark Jackson, St. John's (N.Y.)	†1986	36	328	9.11
Aaron Mitchell, La.-Lafayette	1990	29	264	9.10
Jason Kidd, California	†1994	30	272	9.07
Mark Dickel, UNLV	†2000	31	280	9.03

†national leader

BLOCKED SHOTS

Player, Team	Season	G	Blk.
David Robinson, Navy	†1986	35	207
Shawn James, Northeastern	†2006	30	196
Mickell Gladness, Alabama A&M	†2007	30	188
Adonal Foyle, Colgate	†1997	28	180
Keith Closs, Central Conn. St.	†1996	28	178
Shawn Bradley, BYU	†1991	34	177
Wojciech Myrda, La.-Monroe	†2002	32	172
Alonzo Mourning, Georgetown	†1989	34	169
Stephane Lasme, Massachusetts	2007	33	168
Adonal Foyle, Colgate	1996	29	165
Deng Gai, Fairfield	†2005	30	165
Justin Williams, Wyoming	2006	30	163
Ken Johnson, Ohio St.	†2000	30	161

Player, Team	Season	G	Blk.
Alonzo Mourning, Georgetown	†1992	32	160
Shaquille O'Neal, LSU	1992	30	157
Roy Rogers, Alabama	1996	32	156
Emeka Okafor, Connecticut	†2003	33	156
Dikembe Mutombo, Georgetown	1991	32	151
Adonal Foyle, Colgate	†1995	30	147
Tarvis Williams, Hampton	†2001	32	147
Emeka Okafor, Connecticut	†2004	36	147
Theo Ratliff, Wyoming	1995	28	144
David Robinson, Navy	†1987	32	144
Wojciech Myrda, La.-Monroe	2000	28	144
Cedric Lewis, Maryland	1991	28	143

†national leader

BLOCKED-SHOT AVERAGE

Player, Team	Season	G	Blk.	Avg.
Shawn James, Northeastern	†2006	30	196	6.53
Adonal Foyle, Colgate	†1997	28	180	6.43
Keith Closs, Central Conn. St.	†1996	28	178	6.36
Mickell Gladness, Alabama A&M	†2007	30	188	6.27
David Robinson, Navy	†1986	35	207	5.91
Adonal Foyle, Colgate	1996	29	165	5.69
Deng Gai, Fairfield	†2005	30	165	5.50
Shawn James, Northeastern	2005	25	136	5.44
Justin Williams, Wyoming	2006	30	163	5.43
Wojciech Myrda, La.-Monroe	†2002	32	172	5.38
Ken Johnson, Ohio St.	†2000	30	161	5.37
Keith Closs, Central Conn. St.	†1995	26	139	5.35
Shaquille O'Neal, LSU	†1992	30	157	5.23
Shawn Bradley, BYU	†1991	34	177	5.21
Theo Ratliff, Wyoming	1995	28	144	5.14
Wojciech Myrda, La.-Monroe	2000	28	144	5.14
Cedric Lewis, Maryland	1991	28	143	5.11
Stephane Lasme, Massachusetts	2007	33	168	5.09
Shaquille O'Neal, LSU	1991	28	140	5.00
Alonzo Mourning, Georgetown	1992	32	160	5.00
Tarvis Williams, Hampton	†1999	27	135	5.00
Alonzo Mourning, Georgetown	†1989	34	169	4.97
Kevin Roberson, Vermont	1992	28	139	4.96
Adonal Foyle, Colgate	1995	30	147	4.90
Roy Rogers, Alabama	1996	32	156	4.88

†national leader

STEALS

Player, Team	Season	G	Stl.
Desmond Cambridge, Alabama A&M	†2002	29	160
Mookie Blaylock, Oklahoma	†1988	39	150
Aldwin Ware, Florida A&M	1988	29	142
Darron Brittman, Chicago St.	†1986	28	139
John Linehan, Providence	2002	31	139
Nadav Henefeld, Connecticut	†1990	37	138
Mookie Blaylock, Oklahoma	†1989	35	131
Ronn McMahon, Eastern Wash.	1990	29	130
Obie Trotter, Alabama A&M	†2005	32	125
Marty Johnson, Towson	1988	30	124
Allen Iverson, Georgetown	†1996	37	124
Eric Coley, Tulsa	†2000	37	123
Jim Paguaga, St. Francis (N.Y.)	1986	28	120
Shawn Griggs, La.-Lafayette	†1994	30	120
Pointer Williams, McNeese St.	1996	27	118
Tony Fairley, Charleston So.	†1987	28	114
Scott Burrell, Connecticut	†1991	31	112
Kenny Robertson, Cleveland St.	1989	28	111
Lance Blanks, Texas	1989	34	111
Eric Murdock, Providence	1991	32	111
Travis Holmes, VMI	†2007	33	111
Jason Kidd, California	†1993	29	110
Johnny Rhodes, Maryland	1996	30	110
Robert Dowdell, Coastal Caro.	1990	29	109
Keith Jennings, East Tenn. St.	1991	33	109
Mark Woods, Wright St.	1993	30	109
Gerald Walker, San Francisco	1994	28	109

†national leader

STEAL AVERAGE

Player, Team	Season	G	Stl.	Avg.
Desmond Cambridge, Alabama A&M	†2002	29	160	5.52
Darron Brittman, Chicago St.	†1986	28	139	4.96
Aldwin Ware, Florida A&M	†1988	29	142	4.90
John Linehan, Providence	2002	31	139	4.48
Ronn McMahon, Eastern Wash.	†1990	29	130	4.48

Player, Team	Season	G	Stl.	Avg.
Pointer Williams, McNeese St.	†1996	27	118	4.37
Greedy Daniels, TCU	†2001	25	108	4.32
Jim Paguaga, St. Francis (N.Y.)	1986	28	120	4.29
Marty Johnson, Towson	1988	30	124	4.13
Tony Fairley, Charleston So.	†1987	28	114	4.07
Shawn Griggs, La.-Lafayette	†1994	30	120	4.00
Kenny Robertson, Cleveland St.	†1989	28	111	3.96
Marques Green, St. Bonaventure	†2004	27	107	3.96
Alexis McMillan, Stetson	†2003	22	87	3.95
Obie Trotter, Alabama A&M	†2005	32	125	3.91
Gerald Walker, San Francisco	1994	28	109	3.89
Mookie Blaylock, Oklahoma	1988	39	150	3.85
Carl Williams, Liberty	†2000	28	107	3.82
Desmond Cambridge, Alabama A&M	2001	28	107	3.82
Jason Kidd, California	†1993	29	110	3.79
Jay Goodman, Utah St.	1993	27	102	3.78
Andre Cradle, Long Island	1994	21	79	3.76
Robert Dowdell, Coastal Caro.	1990	29	109	3.76
Mookie Blaylock, Oklahoma	1989	35	131	3.74
Johnny Rhodes, Maryland	1996	30	110	3.67

†national leader

TRIPLE-DOUBLES

Player, Team	Class	Season	3B-2Bs
Michael Anderson, Drexel	So.	1986	4
Brian Shaw, UC Santa Barbara	Sr.	1988	4
Jason Kidd, California	So.	1994	4
Stephane Lasme, Massachusetts	Sr.	2007	4
David Robinson, Navy	Jr.	1986	3
Shaquille O'Neal, LSU	Jr.	1992	3
Gerald Lewis, SMU	Sr.	1993	3
David Edwards, Texas A&M	Sr.	1994	3
Andre Iguodala, Arizona	So.	2004	3
Derrick Lewis, Maryland	Jr.	1987	2
Luc Longley, New Mexico	Jr.	1990	2
Shaquille O'Neal, LSU	Fr.	1990	2
Kevin Roberson, Vermont	So.	1990	2
Dave Barnett, Fresno St.	Sr.	1991	2
Kevin Roberson, Vermont	Sr.	1992	2
Anfernee Hardaway, Memphis	Jr.	1993	2
Sharone Wright, Clemson	So.	1993	2
Roy Rogers, Alabama	Sr.	1996	2
Keith Closs, Central Conn. St.	So.	1996	2
Adonal Foyle, Colgate	Jr.	1997	2
Jerome James, Florida A&M	Jr.	1997	2
Sean Kennedy, Marist	Sr.	2002	2
Wojciech Murda, La.-Monroe	Sr.	2002	2
David Harrison, Colorado	So.	2003	2
Damitrius Coleman, Mercer	Jr.	2005	2
Shawn James, Northeastern	Fr.	2005	2
Shawn James, Northeastern	So.	2006	2
Dominic McGuire, Fresno St.	Jr.	2007	2

CONSECUTIVE TRIPLE-DOUBLES

Player, Team	Class	Dates	3B-2Bs
Kevin Roberson, Vermont	Sr.	Jan. 7-9, 1992	2
Shaquille O'Neal, LSU	Jr.	Feb. 19-22, 1992	2
Anfernee Hardaway, Memphis	Jr.	Jan. 4-6, 1993	2
Gerald Lewis, SMU	Sr.	Mar. 3-6, 1993	2
David Edwards, Texas A&M	Sr.	Mar. 5-10, 1994	2

DOUBLE-DOUBLES

Player, Team	Class	Season	2B-2Bs
David Robinson, Navy	Jr.	1986	31
Jerry West, West Virginia	Sr.	1960	30
Mel Counts, Oregon St.	Sr.	1964	29
Rudy Hackett, Syracuse	Sr.	1975	29
Benoit Benjamin, Creighton	Jr.	1985	29
Derrick Coleman, Syracuse	Jr.	1989	29
Tim Duncan, Wake Forest	Sr.	1997	29
Oscar Robertson, Cincinnati	Jr.	1959	28
Lew Alcindor, UCLA	So.	1967	28
Larry Bird, Indiana St.	Sr.	1979	28
Oscar Robertson, Cincinnati	Jr.	1960	27
Mel Counts, Oregon St.	Jr.	1963	27
Paul Silas, Creighton	Sr.	1964	27
Lew Alcindor, UCLA	Jr.	1968	27
Artis Gilmore, Jacksonville	Jr.	1970	27
Bill Walton, UCLA	Jr.	1973	27
Willie Naulls, UCLA	Sr.	1956	26
Jerry Lucas, Ohio St.	So.	1960	26
Jerry Lucas, Ohio St.	Jr.	1961	26
Jerry Lucas, Ohio St.	Sr.	1962	26

Player, Team	Class	Season	2B-2Bs
Len Chappell, Wake Forest	Sr.	1962	26
Dan Issel, Kentucky	Sr.	1970	26
Jerome Lane, Pittsburgh	Jr.	1987	26
Brad Sellers, Ohio St.	Sr.	1986	26
Hank Gathers, Loyola Marymount	Jr.	1989	26
Andrew Bogut, Utah	So.	2005	26

DOUBLE-DOUBLES FOR A FRESHMAN

Player, Team	Season	2B-2Bs
Carmelo Anthony, Syracuse	2003	22
Ralph Sampson, Virginia	1980	21
Kenny Miller, Loyola (Ill.)	1988	21
Eddie Griffin, Seton Hall	2001	21
Gary Winton, Army	1975	20
Kevin Durant, Texas	2007	20
Wayman Tisdale, Oklahoma	1983	19
Rickey Brown, Mississippi St.	1977	18
Steve Stielper, James Madison	1977	18
Herb Williams, Ohio St.	1978	18
Alvan Adams, Oklahoma	1973	17
Malik Rose, Drexel	1993	15
Caleb Green, Oral Roberts	2004	15
Gene Banks, Duke	1978	14
Andrew Bogut, Utah	2004	14
Leon Powe, California	2004	14
Tyrus Thomas, LSU	2006	14
Greg Oden, Ohio St.	2007	14
Ron Baxter, Texas	1977	13
Vernon Butler, Navy	1983	13
Derrick Coleman, Syracuse	1987	13
Tim Duncan, Wake Forest	1994	13
Mike Gminski, Duke	1977	12
LaSalle Thompson, Texas	1980	12
Charles Barkley, Auburn	1982	12
Michael Harris, Rice	2002	12

CONSECUTIVE DOUBLE-DOUBLES

Player, Team	Class	Dates	2B-2Bs
Mel Counts, Oregon St.	Sr.	Nov. 30, 1963-Mar. 10, 1964	29
Benoit Benjamin, Creighton	Jr.	Nov. 24, 1984-Feb. 16, 1985	27
Lew Alcindor, UCLA	Jr.	Dec. 27, 1967-Mar. 23, 1968	26
Willie Naulls, UCLA	Sr.	Dec. 2, 1955-Mar. 9, 1956	25
Oscar Robertson, Cincinnati	Jr.	Dec. 31, 1958-Mar. 21, 1959	23
#Jerry Lucas, Ohio St.	Jr.	Dec. 1, 1960-Mar. 11, 1961	23
Jerry Lucas, Ohio St.	Sr.	Dec. 2, 1961-Feb. 24, 1962	21
Mike Lewis, Duke	Sr.	Dec. 1, 1967-Feb. 20, 1968	20
Jerry West, West Virginia	Sr.	Jan. 5-Mar. 12, 1960	20
Billy Cunningham, North Carolina	So.	Dec. 5, 1962-Mar. 1, 1963	20
Billy Cunningham, North Carolina	Jr.	Dec. 2, 1963-Feb. 22, 1964	20
Dave Gunther, Iowa	Sr.	Dec. 8, 1958-Feb. 21, 1959	19
Artis Gilmore, Jacksonville	Sr.	Dec. 1, 1970-Feb. 8 1971	18
Steve Smith, Loyola Marymount	Jr.	Jan. 4-Mar. 4, 1972	18
Jack Twyman, Cincinnati	Jr.	Dec. 17, 1953-Mar. 4, 1954	17
Artis Gilmore, Jacksonville	Jr.	Dec. 9, 1969-Feb. 13, 1970	17
Tim Duncan, Wake Forest	Sr.	Nov. 24, 1996-Jan. 28, 1997	17
Larry Bird, Indiana St.	Sr.	Dec. 9, 1978-Feb. 6, 1979	16
Len Chappell, Wake Forest	Sr.	Feb. 3-Mar. 24, 1962	16
Jerry Lucas, Ohio St.	So.	Jan. 23-Mar. 19, 1960	15
Bill Walton, UCLA	So.	Dec. 10, 1971-Jan. 28, 1972	15
Rickey Brown, Mississippi St.	Sr.	Nov. 30, 1979-Jan. 17, 1980	15
David Robinson, Navy	Jr.	Feb. 12-Nov. 29, 1986	15
Andre Moore, Loyola (Ill.)	Sr.	Jan. 12-Feb. 23, 1987	15
Spencer Dunkley, Delaware	Sr.	Dec. 10, 1992-Feb. 6, 1993	15

#Missed the Jan. 9, 1961, game because of injury.

Top Season Performances by Class

SCORING AVERAGE

Class	Player, Team	Season	G	FG	3FG	FT	Pts.	Avg.
Senior	Pete Maravich, LSU	1970	31	522	—	337	1,381	44.5
Junior	Pete Maravich, LSU	1969	26	433	—	282	1,148	44.2
Sophomore	Pete Maravich, LSU	1968	26	432	—	274	1,138	43.8
Freshman	Chris Jackson, LSU	1989	32	359	84	163	965	30.2

FIELD-GOAL PERCENTAGE

Class	Player, Team	Season	G	FG	FGA	Pct.
Senior	Steve Johnson, Oregon St.	1981	28	235	315	74.6
Junior	Steve Johnson, Oregon St.	1980	30	211	297	71.0
Sophomore	Dwayne Davis, Florida	1989	33	179	248	72.2

DIVISION I

Class	Player, Team	Season	G	FG	FGA	Pct.
Freshman	Mike Freeman, Hampton	2007	30	162	239	67.8

THREE-POINT FIELD GOALS MADE PER GAME

Class	Player, Team	Season	G	3FG	Avg.
Senior	Darrin Fitzgerald, Butler	1987	28	158	5.64
Junior	Terrence Woods, Florida A&M	2003	28	139	4.96
Sophomore	Mark Alberts, Akron	1990	28	122	4.36
Freshman	Keith Veney, Lamar	1993	27	106	3.93

THREE-POINT FIELD-GOAL PERCENTAGE

Class	Player, Team	Season	G	3FG	3FGA	Pct.
Senior	Keith Jennings, East Tenn. St.	1991	33	84	142	59.2
Junior	Glenn Tropf, Holy Cross	1988	29	52	82	63.4
Sophomore	Dave Calloway, Monmouth	1989	28	48	82	58.5
Freshman	Jay Edwards, Indiana	1988	23	59	110	53.6

FREE-THROW PERCENTAGE

Class	Player, Team	Season	G	FT	FTA	Pct.
Senior	Derek Raivio, Gonzaga	2007	34	148	154	96.1
Junior	Steve Drabyn, Belmont	2003	29	78	82	95.1
Sophomore	J.J. Redick, Duke	2004	37	143	150	95.3
Freshman	Blake Ahearn, Missouri St.	2004	33	117	120	97.5

REBOUND AVERAGE

Class	Player, Team	Season	G	Reb.	Avg.
Senior	Art Quimby, Connecticut	1955	25	611	24.4
Junior	Charlie Slack, Marshall	1955	21	538	25.6
Sophomore	Ed Conlin, Fordham	1953	26	612	23.5
Freshman	Pete Padgett, Nevada	1973	26	462	17.8

REBOUND AVERAGE
(Since 1973)

Class	Player, Team	Season	G	Reb.	Avg.
Senior	Kermit Washington, American	1973	22	439	20.0
Junior	Marvin Barnes, Providence	1973	30	571	19.0
Sophomore	Brad Robinson, Kent St.	1974	26	423	16.3
Freshman	Pete Padgett, Nevada	1973	26	462	17.8

ASSIST AVERAGE

Class	Player, Team	Season	G	Ast.	Avg.
Senior	Avery Johnson, Southern U.	1988	30	399	13.30
Junior	Anthony Manuel, Bradley	1988	31	373	12.03
Sophomore	Curtis McCants, George Mason	1995	27	251	9.30
Freshman	Omar Cook, St. John's (N.Y.)	2001	29	252	8.69

BLOCKED-SHOT AVERAGE

Class	Player, Team	Season	G	Blk.	Avg.
Senior	Deng Gai, Fairfield	2005	30	165	5.50
Junior	Adonal Foyle, Colgate	1997	28	180	6.43
Sophomore	Shawn James, Northeastern	2006	30	196	6.53
Freshman	Shawn James, Northeastern	2005	26	136	5.44

STEAL AVERAGE

Class	Player, Team	Season	G	Stl.	Avg.
Senior	Desmond Cambridge, Alabama A&M	2002	29	160	5.52
Junior	Kenny Robertson, Cleveland St.	1989	28	111	3.96
Sophomore	Gerald Walker, San Francisco	1994	28	109	3.89
Freshman	Jason Kidd, California	1993	29	110	3.79

Top Season Performances by a Freshman

POINTS

Player, Team	Season	G	FG	3FG	FT	Pts.
Chris Jackson, LSU	1989	32	359	84	163	965
Kevin Durant, Texas	2007	35	306	82	209	903
James Williams, Austin Peay	1973	29	360	—	134	854
Jason Conley, VMI	2002	28	285	79	171	820
Wayman Tisdale, Oklahoma	1983	33	338	—	134	810

SCORING AVERAGE

Player, Team	Season	G	FG	3FG	FT	Pts.	Avg.
Chris Jackson, LSU	1989	32	359	84	163	965	30.2
Alphonso Ford, Mississippi Val.	1990	27	289	104	126	808	29.9
James Williams, Austin Peay	1973	29	360	—	134	854	29.4
Jason Conley, VMI	2002	28	285	79	171	820	29.3
Harry Kelly, Texas Southern	1980	26	313	—	127	753	29.0

FIELD-GOAL PERCENTAGE

Player, Team	Season	G	FG	FGA	Pct.
Mike Freeman, Hampton	2007	30	162	239	67.8
Sidney Moncrief, Arkansas	1976	28	149	224	66.5
Gary Trent, Ohio	1993	27	194	298	65.1
Brandan Wright, North Carolina	2007	37	228	353	64.6
Ed Pinckney, Villanova	1982	32	169	264	64.0

THREE-POINT FIELD GOALS MADE

Player, Team	Season	G	3FG
Stephen Curry, Davidson	2007	34	122
Tajuan Porter, Oregon	2007	35	110
Keydren Clark, St. Peter's	2003	29	109
Keith Veney, Lamar	1993	27	106
Alphonso Ford, Mississippi Val.	1990	27	104
Tony Ross, San Diego St.	1987	28	104
Adam Leonard, Eastern Ky.	2007	33	104

THREE-POINT FIELD GOALS MADE PER GAME

Player, Team	Season	G	3FG	Avg.
Keith Veney, Lamar	1993	27	106	3.93
Alphonso Ford, Mississippi Val.	1990	27	104	3.85
Keydren Clark, St. Peter's	2003	29	109	3.76
Tony Ross, San Diego St.	1987	28	104	3.71
Donnie Carr, La Salle	1997	27	99	3.67

THREE-POINT FIELD-GOAL PERCENTAGE

Player, Team	Season	G	3FG	3FGA	Pct.
Jay Edwards, Indiana	1988	23	59	110	53.6
Ross Richardson, Loyola Marymount	1991	25	61	116	52.6
Lance Barker, Valparaiso	1992	26	61	117	52.1
Ed Peterson, Yale	1989	28	53	104	51.0
Ross Land, Northern Ariz.	1997	28	64	126	50.8
Willie Brand, Texas-Arlington	1988	29	65	128	50.8

FREE-THROW PERCENTAGE

Player, Team	Season	G	FT	FTA	Pct.
Blake Ahearn, Missouri St.	2004	33	117	120	97.5
Jim Barton, Dartmouth	1986	26	65	69	94.2
J.J. Redick, Duke	2003	33	102	111	91.9
David Kool, Western Mich.	2007	29	99	108	91.7
Steve Alford, Indiana	1984	31	137	150	91.3

REBOUNDS

Player, Team	Season	G	Reb.
Pete Padgett, Nevada	1973	26	462
Kenny Miller, Loyola (Ill.)	1988	29	395
Kevin Durant, Texas	2007	35	390
Shaquille O'Neal, LSU	1990	32	385
Ralph Sampson, Virginia	1980	34	381

REBOUND AVERAGE

Player, Team	Season	G	Reb.	Avg.
Pete Padgett, Nevada	1973	26	462	17.8
Glenn Mosley, Seton Hall	1974	21	299	14.2
Ira Terrell, SMU	1973	25	352	14.1
Kenny Miller, Loyola (Ill.)	1988	29	395	13.6
Bob Stephens, Drexel	1976	23	307	13.3

ASSISTS

Player, Team	Season	G	Ast.
Bobby Hurley, Duke	1990	38	288
Kenny Anderson, Georgia Tech	1990	35	285
T.J. Ford, Texas	2002	33	273
Andre LaFleur, Northeastern	1984	32	252
Omar Cook, St. John's (N.Y.)	2001	29	252
Chris Thomas, Notre Dame	2002	33	252

ASSIST AVERAGE

Player, Team	Season	G	Ast.	Avg.
Omar Cook, St. John's (N.Y.)	2001	29	252	8.69
T.J. Ford, Texas	2002	33	273	8.27
Orlando Smart, San Francisco	1991	29	237	8.17
Kenny Anderson, Georgia Tech	1990	35	285	8.14
Taurence Chisholm, Delaware	1985	28	224	8.00

BLOCKED SHOTS

Player, Team	Season	G	Blk.
Shawn Bradley, BYU	1991	34	177
Alonzo Mourning, Georgetown	1989	34	169
Adonal Foyle, Colgate	1995	30	147

Player, Team	Season	G	Blk.
Alvin Jones, Georgia Tech	1998	33	141
Keith Closs, Central Conn. St.	1995	26	139

BLOCKED-SHOT AVERAGE

Player, Team	Season	G	Blk.	Avg.
Shawn James, Northeastern	2005	25	136	5.44
Keith Closs, Central Conn. St.	1995	26	139	5.35
Shawn Bradley, BYU	1991	34	177	5.21
Alonzo Mourning, Georgetown	1989	34	169	4.97
Adonal Foyle, Colgate	1995	30	147	4.90

STEALS

Player, Team	Season	G	Stl.
Nadav Henefeld, Connecticut	1990	37	138
Jason Kidd, California	1993	29	110
Kellii Taylor, Pittsburgh	1997	32	101
Ben Larson, Cal Poly	1996	29	100
Five tied with 90			

STEAL AVERAGE

Player, Team	Season	G	Stl.	Avg.
Jason Kidd, California	1993	29	110	3.79
Nadav Henefeld, Connecticut	1990	37	138	3.73
Ben Larson, Cal Poly	1996	29	100	3.45
Eric Murdock, Providence	1988	28	90	3.21
Pat Baldwin, Northwestern	1991	28	90	3.21
Joel Hoover, Md.-East. Shore	1997	28	90	3.21

Career Records

POINTS

Player, Team	Ht.	Last Season	Yrs.	G	FG	3FG#	FT	Pts.
Pete Maravich, LSU	6-5	1970	3	83	1,387	—	893	3,667
Freeman Williams, Portland St.	6-4	1978	4	106	1,369	—	511	3,249
Lionel Simmons, La Salle	6-7	1990	4	131	1,244	56	673	3,217
Alphonso Ford, Mississippi Valley	6-2	1993	4	109	1,121	333	590	3,165
Harry Kelly, Texas Southern	6-7	1983	4	110	1,234	—	598	3,066
Keydren Clark, St. Peter's	5-9	2006	4	118	967	435	689	3,058
Hersey Hawkins, Bradley	6-3	1988	4	125	1,100	118	690	3,008
Oscar Robertson, Cincinnati	6-5	1960	3	88	1,052	—	869	2,973
Danny Manning, Kansas	6-10	1988	4	147	1,216	10	509	2,951
Alfredrick Hughes, Loyola (Ill.)	6-5	1985	4	120	1,226	—	462	2,914
Elvin Hayes, Houston	6-8	1968	3	93	1,215	—	454	2,884
Larry Bird, Indiana St.	6-9	1979	3	94	1,154	—	542	2,850
Otis Birdsong, Houston	6-4	1977	4	116	1,176	—	480	2,832
Kevin Bradshaw, Bethune-Cookman & U.S. Int'l	6-6	1991	4	111	1,027	132	618	2,804
Allan Houston, Tennessee	6-5	1993	4	128	902	346	651	2,801
J.J. Redick, Duke	6-4	2006	4	139	825	457	662	2,769
Hank Gathers, Southern Cal & Loyola Marymount	6-7	1990	4	117	1,127	0	469	2,723
Reggie Lewis, Northeastern	6-7	1987	4	122	1,043	30(1)	592	2,708
Daren Queenan, Lehigh	6-5	1988	4	118	1,024	29	626	2,703
Byron Larkin, Xavier	6-3	1988	4	121	1,022	51	601	2,696
David Robinson, Navy	7-1	1987	4	127	1,032	1	604	2,669
Wayman Tisdale, Oklahoma	6-9	1985	3	104	1,077	—	507	2,661
Troy Bell, Boston College	6-1	2003	4	122	761	300	810	2,632
Michael Brooks, La Salle	6-7	1980	4	114	1,064	—	500	2,628
Calbert Cheaney, Indiana	6-6	1993	4	132	1,018	148	429	2,613
Mark Macon, Temple	6-5	1991	4	126	980	246	403	2,609
Don MacLean, UCLA	6-10	1992	4	127	943	11	711	2,608
Joe Dumars, McNeese St.	6-3	1985	4	116	941	(5)	723	2,605
Henry Domercant, Eastern Ill.	6-4	2003	4	120	861	285	595	2,602
Terrance Bailey, Wagner	6-2	1987	4	110	985	42	579	2,591
Dickie Hemric, Wake Forest	6-6	1955	4	104	841	—	905	2,587
Calvin Natt, La.-Monroe	6-5	1979	4	108	1,017	—	547	2,581
Derrick Chievous, Missouri	6-7	1988	4	130	893	30	764	2,580
Skip Henderson, Marshall	6-2	1988	4	125	1,000	133	441	2,574
Austin Carr, Notre Dame	6-3	1971	3	74	1,017	—	526	2,560
Sean Elliott, Arizona	6-8	1989	4	133	896	140	623	2,555
Rodney Monroe, North Carolina St.	6-3	1991	4	124	885	322	459	2,551
Calvin Murphy, Niagara	5-10	1970	3	77	947	—	654	2,548
Keith Van Horn, Utah	6-9	1997	4	122	891	206	554	2,542
Frank Selvy, Furman	6-3	1954	3	78	922	—	694	2,538
Johnny Dawkins, Duke	6-2	1986	4	133	1,026	(19)	485	2,537

Player, Team	Ht.	Last Season	Yrs.	G	FG	3FG#	FT	Pts.
Willie Jackson, Centenary (La.)	6-6	1984	4	114	995	(18)	545	2,535
Steve Rogers, Alabama St.	6-5	1992	4	113	817	187	713	2,534
Steve Burtt, Iona	6-2	1984	4	121	1,003	—	528	2,534
Shawn Respert, Michigan St.	6-3	1995	4	118	866	331	468	2,531
Joe Jakubick, Akron	6-5	1984	4	108	973	(53)	584	2,530
Andrew Toney, La.-Lafayette	6-3	1980	4	107	996	—	534	2,526
Ron Perry, Holy Cross	6-2	1980	4	109	922	—	680	2,524
Ronnie McCollum, Centenary (La.)	6-4	2001	4	113	822	345	535	2,524
Mike Olliver, Lamar	6-1	1981	4	122	1,130	—	258	2,518
Bryant Stith, Virginia	6-5	1992	4	131	856	114	690	2,516
Bill Bradley, Princeton	6-5	1965	3	83	856	—	791	2,503
Caleb Green, Oral Roberts	6-8	2007	4	128	821	9	852	2,503
Jeff Grayer, Iowa St.	6-5	1988	4	125	974	27	527	2,502
Elgin Baylor, Albertson & Seattle	6-6	1958	3	80	956	—	588	2,500

#Listed is the number of three-pointers scored since it became the national rule in 1987; the number in the parenthesis is number scored before 1987—these counted as three points in the game but counted as two-pointers in the national rankings. The three-pointers in the parenthesis are not included in total points.

2,000-POINT SCORERS

A total of 434 players in Division I history have scored at least 2,000 points over their careers. The first was Jim Lacy, Loyola (Md.), with 2,154 over four seasons ending with 1949. The first to reach 2,000 in a three-season career was Furman's Frank Selvy, 2,538 through 1954. The 434 come from 214 different colleges. Duke leads with nine 2,000-pointers: Jim Spanarkel (last season was 1979), Mike Gminski (1980), Gene Banks (1981), Mark Alarie (1986), Johnny Dawkins (1986), Danny Ferry (1989), Christian Laettner (1992), Jason Williams (2002) and J.J. Redick (2006). Next are Boston College, Georgia Tech, La Salle, Notre Dame, Syracuse and Villanova with six, followed by Indiana, Michigan, Murray State, North Carolina, Oklahoma, Tennessee, Wake Forest and Xavier with five apiece.

SCORING AVERAGE
(Minimum 1,400 points)

Player, Team	Last Season	Yrs.	G	FG	3FG	FT	Pts.	Avg.
Pete Maravich, LSU	1970	3	83	1,387	—	893	3,667	44.2
Austin Carr, Notre Dame	1971	3	74	1,017	—	526	2,560	34.6
Oscar Robertson, Cincinnati	1960	3	88	1,052	—	869	2,973	33.8
Calvin Murphy, Niagara	1970	3	77	947	—	654	2,548	33.1
Dwight Lamar, La.-Lafayette	†1973	2	57	768	—	326	1,862	32.7
Frank Selvy, Furman	1954	3	78	922	—	694	2,538	32.5
Rick Mount, Purdue	1970	3	72	910	—	503	2,323	32.3
Darrell Floyd, Furman	1956	3	71	868	—	545	2,281	32.1
Nick Werkman, Seton Hall	1964	3	71	812	—	649	2,273	32.0
Willie Humes, Idaho St.	1971	2	48	565	—	380	1,510	31.5
William Averitt, Pepperdine	1973	2	49	615	—	311	1,541	31.4
Elgin Baylor, Albertson & Seattle	1958	3	80	956	—	588	2,500	31.3
Elvin Hayes, Houston	1968	3	93	1,215	—	454	2,884	31.0
Freeman Williams, Portland St.	1978	4	106	1,369	—	511	3,249	30.7
Larry Bird, Indiana St.	1979	3	94	1,154	—	542	2,850	30.3
Bill Bradley, Princeton	1965	3	83	856	—	791	2,503	30.2
Rich Fuqua, Oral Roberts	†1973	2	54	692	—	233	1,617	29.9
Wilt Chamberlain, Kansas	1958	2	48	503	—	427	1,433	29.9
Rick Barry, Miami (Fla.)	1965	3	77	816	—	666	2,298	29.8
Doug Collins, Illinois St.	1973	3	77	894	—	452	2,240	29.1
Alphonso Ford, Mississippi Val.	1993	4	109	1,121	333	590	3,165	29.0
Chris Jackson, LSU	1990	2	64	664	172	354	1,854	29.0
Dave Schellhase, Purdue	1966	3	74	746	—	582	2,074	28.8
Dick Wilkinson, Virginia	1955	3	78	783	—	665	2,233	28.6
James Williams, Austin Peay	1974	2	54	632	—	277	1,541	28.5

†Each played two years of non-Division I competition (Lamar—four years, 3,493 points and 31.2 average; Fuqua—four years, 3,004 points and 27.1 average).

FIELD-GOAL PERCENTAGE
(Minimum 400 field goals made and 4 field goals made per game)

Player, Team	Ht.	Last Season	Yrs.	G	FG	FGA	Pct.
Steve Johnson, Oregon St.	6-10	1981	4	116	828	1,222	67.8
Michael Bradley, Kentucky & Villanova	6-10	2001	3	100	441	651	67.7
Murray Brown, Florida St.	6-8	1980	4	106	566	847	66.8
Lee Campbell, Middle Tenn. & Missouri St.	6-7	1990	3	88	411	618	66.5
Warren Kidd, Middle Tenn.	6-9	1993	3	83	496	747	66.4
Todd MacCulloch, Washington	7-0	1999	4	115	702	1,058	66.4
Joe Senser, West Chester	6-5	1979	4	96	476	719	66.2
Kevin Magee, UC Irvine	6-8	1982	2	56	552	841	65.6
Orlando Phillips, Pepperdine	6-7	1983	2	56	404	618	65.4

Player, Team	Ht.	Last Season	Yrs.	G	FG	FGA	Pct.
Bill Walton, UCLA	6-11	1974	3	87	747	1,147	65.1
William Herndon, Massachusetts	6-3	1992	4	100	472	728	64.8
Larry Stewart, Coppin St.	6-8	1991	3	91	676	1,046	64.6
Adam Mark, Belmont	6-8	2004	4	112	656	1,018	64.4
Larry Johnson, UNLV	6-7	1991	2	75	612	952	64.3
Dwayne Davis, Florida	6-7	1991	4	124	572	892	64.1
Nate Harris, Utah St.	6-7	2006	5	126	588	918	64.1
Lew Alcindor, UCLA	7-2	1969	3	88	943	1,476	63.9
Akeem Olajuwon, Houston	7-0	1984	3	100	532	833	63.9
Oliver Miller, Arkansas	6-9	1992	4	137	680	1,069	63.6
Mike Coleman, Liberty	6-7	1992	4	105	421	663	63.5
Jeff Ruland, Iona	6-10	1980	3	89	717	1,130	63.5
Mark McNamara, California	6-10	1982	4	107	709	1,119	63.4
Dan McClintock, Northern Ariz.	7-0	2000	4	115	542	858	63.2
Cherokee Rhone, Centenary (La.)	6-8	1982	3	63	421	667	63.1
Carlos Boozer, Duke	6-9	2002	3	101	554	878	63.1
Bobby Lee Hunt, Alabama	6-9	1985	4	126	646	1,024	63.1

THREE-POINT FIELD GOALS

Player, Team	Ht.	Last Season	Yrs.	G	3FG
J.J. Redick, Duke	6-4	2006	4	139	457
Keydren Clark, St. Peter's	5-9	2006	4	118	435
Curtis Staples, Virginia	6-3	1998	4	122	413
Keith Veney, Lamar & Marshall	6-3	1997	4	111	409
Doug Day, Radford	6-1	1993	4	117	401
Gerry McNamara, Syracuse	6-2	2006	4	135	400
Michael Watson, UMKC	6-0	2004	4	117	391
Ronnie Schmitz, UMKC	6-3	1993	4	112	378
Mark Alberts, Akron	6-1	1993	4	107	375
Brett Blizzard, UNC Wilmington	6-4	2003	4	125	371
Kyle Korver, Creighton	6-7	2003	4	128	371
Pat Bradley, Arkansas	6-2	1999	4	132	366
Bryce Drew, Valparaiso	6-3	1998	4	121	364
Jeff Fryer, Loyola Marymount	6-2	1990	4	112	363
Will Whittington, Marist	6-3	2007	4	114	362
Taquan Dean, Louisville	6-3	2006	4	128	359
T.J. Sorrentine, Vermont	6-3	2005	4	120	354
Steve Novak, Marquette	6-10	2006	4	126	354
Terrence Woods, Florida A&M	6-3	2004	4	123	353
Dennis Scott, Georgia Tech	6-8	1990	3	99	351
Rashad Phillips, Detroit	5-10	2001	4	129	348
Allan Houston, Tennessee	6-5	1993	4	128	346
Jobey Thomas, Charlotte	6-4	2002	4	130	346
Ronnie McCollum, Centenary (La.)	6-4	2001	4	113	345
Brendan Plavich, Vanderbilt & Charlotte	6-2	2005	4	120	345

THREE-POINT FIELD GOALS PER GAME
(Minimum 200 three-point field goals made)

Player, Team	Ht.	Last Season	Yrs.	G	3FG	Avg.
Timothy Pollard, Mississippi Val.	6-3	1989	2	56	256	4.57
Sydney Grider, La.-Lafayette	6-3	1990	2	58	253	4.36
Brian Merriweather, Tex.-Pan American	6-3	2001	3	84	332	3.95
Josh Heard, Tennessee Tech	6-2	2000	2	55	210	3.82
Kareem Townes, La Salle	6-3	1995	3	81	300	3.70
Keydren Clark, St. Peter's	5-9	2006	4	118	435	3.69
Keith Veney, Lamar & Marshall	6-3	1997	4	111	409	3.68
Dave Mooney, Coastal Caro.	6-4	1988	2	56	202	3.61
Dennis Scott, Georgia Tech	6-8	1990	3	99	351	3.55
Mark Alberts, Akron	6-1	1993	4	107	375	3.50
Doug Day, Radford	6-1	1993	4	117	401	3.43
Curtis Staples, Virginia	6-3	1998	4	122	413	3.39
Ronnie Schmitz, UMKC	6-3	1993	4	112	378	3.38
Michael Watson, UMKC	6-0	2004	4	117	391	3.34
J.J. Redick, Duke	6-4	2006	4	139	457	3.29
Jeff Fryer, Loyola Marymount	6-2	1990	4	112	363	3.24
Keddric Mays, Chattanooga	6-0	2007	2	65	209	3.22
Dana Barros, Boston College	5-11	1989	3	91	291	3.20
Tony Ross, San Diego St.	6-3	1989	3	85	270	3.18
Will Whittington, Marist	6-3	2007	4	114	362	3.18
Randy Woods, La Salle	6-0	1992	3	88	278	3.16
Dominick Young, Fresno St.	5-10	1997	3	89	279	3.13
Wally Lancaster, Virginia Tech	6-5	1989	3	82	257	3.13
David Sivulich, St. Mary's (Cal.)	5-10	1998	3	76	238	3.13
Jim Barton, Dartmouth	6-4	1989	3	78	242	3.10

THREE-POINT FIELD-GOAL PERCENTAGE
(Minimum 200 three-point field goals made and 2.0 three-point field goals made per game)

Player, Team	Ht.	Last Season	Yrs.	G	3FG	3FGA	Pct.
Tony Bennett, Green Bay	6-0	1992	4	118	290	584	49.7
Stephen Sir, San Diego St. & Northern Ariz.	6-5	2007	5	111	323	689	46.9
David Olson, Eastern Ill.	6-4	1992	4	111	262	562	46.6
Ross Land, Northern Ariz.	6-5	2000	4	117	308	664	46.4
Dan Dickau, Washington & Gonzaga	6-0	2002	4	97	215	465	46.2
Steve Novak, Marquette	6-10	2006	4	126	354	768	46.1
Sean Jackson, Ohio & Princeton	5-11	1992	4	104	243	528	46.0
Barry Booker, Vanderbilt	6-3	1989	3	98	246	535	46.0
Kevin Booth, Mt. St. Mary's	6-0	1993	5	110	265	577	45.9
Dave Calloway, Monmouth	6-3	1991	4	115	260	567	45.9
Tony Ross, San Diego St.	6-3	1992	3	85	270	589	45.8
Salim Stoudamire, Arizona	6-1	2005	4	129	342	747	45.8
Jason Matthews, Pittsburgh	6-3	1991	4	123	259	567	45.7
Corey Reed, Radford	6-3	1998	4	104	232	510	45.5
Jim Barton, Dartmouth	6-4	1989	3	78	242	532	45.5
Shawn Respert, Michigan St.	6-3	1995	4	118	331	728	45.5
Kyle Korver, Creighton	6-7	2003	4	128	371	819	45.3
Carlton Becton, N.C. A&T	6-6	1989	3	84	209	462	45.2
Eric Channing, New Mexico St.	6-4	2002	4	124	283	627	45.1
Ray Allen, Connecticut	6-5	1996	3	101	233	520	44.8
Curtis Shelton, Southeast Mo. St.	5-9	1994	4	107	215	480	44.8
Jeff McCool, New Mexico St.	6-5	1989	3	92	201	450	44.7
Jason Kapono, UCLA	6-8	2003	4	127	317	710	44.6
Pat Carroll, St. Joseph's	6-5	2005	4	110	294	661	44.5
Lee Humphrey, Florida	6-2	2007	4	136	288	649	44.4

FREE-THROW PERCENTAGE
(Minimum 300 free throws made and 2.5 free throws made per game)

Player, Team	Ht.	Last Season	Yrs.	G	FT	FTA	Pct.
Blake Ahearn, Missouri St.	6-2	2007	4	129	435	460	94.6
Derek Raivio, Gonzaga	6-1	2007	4	127	343	370	92.7
Gary Buchanan, Villanova	6-3	2003	4	122	324	355	91.3
J.J. Redick, Duke	6-4	2006	4	139	662	726	91.2
Greg Starrick, Kentucky & Southern Ill.	6-2	1972	4	72	341	375	90.9
Jack Moore, Nebraska	5-9	1982	4	105	446	495	90.1
Steve Henson, Kansas St.	6-1	1990	4	127	361	401	90.0
Steve Alford, Indiana	6-2	1987	4	125	535	596	89.8
Bob Lloyd, Rutgers	6-1	1967	3	77	543	605	89.8
Jake Sullivan, Iowa St.	6-1	2004	4	123	354	395	89.6
Jim Barton, Dartmouth	6-4	1989	4	104	394	440	89.5
Tommy Boyer, Arkansas	6-6	1963	3	70	315	353	89.2
Gerry McNamara, Syracuse	6-2	2006	4	135	435	490	88.8
Brent Jolly, Tennessee Tech	6-6	2003	4	123	347	391	88.7
Marcus Wilson, Evansville	6-3	1999	4	119	455	513	88.7
Joe Crispin, Penn St.	6-1	2001	4	127	448	506	88.5
Ron Perry, Holy Cross	6-2	1980	4	109	680	768	88.5
Joe Dykstra, Western Ill.	6-6	1983	4	117	587	663	88.5
Mike Joseph, Bucknell	6-0	1990	4	115	397	449	88.4
Kyle Macy, Purdue & Kentucky	6-3	1980	5	125	416	471	88.3
Matt Hildebrand, Liberty	6-3	1994	4	117	398	451	88.2
Jimmy England, Tennessee	6-1	1971	3	81	319	362	88.1
Rod Foster, UCLA	6-1	1983	4	113	309	351	88.0
Michael Smith, BYU	6-10	1989	4	122	431	491	87.8
Jason Matthews, Pittsburgh	6-3	1991	4	123	481	548	87.8
Mike Iuzzolino, Penn St. & St. Francis (Pa.)	5-10	1991	4	112	402	458	87.8

REBOUNDS

Player, Team	Ht.	Last Season	Yrs.	G	Reb.
Tom Gola, La Salle	6-6	1955	4	118	2,201
Joe Holup, George Washington	6-6	1956	4	104	2,030
Charlie Slack, Marshall	6-5	1956	4	88	1,916
Ed Conlin, Fordham	6-5	1955	4	102	1,884
Dickie Hemric, Wake Forest	6-6	1955	4	104	1,802
Paul Silas, Creighton	6-7	1964	3	81	1,751
Art Quimby, Connecticut	6-5	1955	4	80	1,716
Jerry Harper, Alabama	6-8	1956	4	93	1,688
Jeff Cohen, William & Mary	6-7	1961	4	103	1,679
Steve Hamilton, Morehead St.	6-7	1958	4	102	1,675
Charlie Tyra, Louisville	6-8	1957	4	95	1,617
Bill Russell, San Francisco	6-9	1956	3	79	1,606
Elvin Hayes, Houston	6-8	1968	3	93	1,602
Ron Shavlik, North Carolina St.	6-8	1956	3	95	1,598

Player, Team	Ht.	Last Season	Yrs.	G	Reb.
Marvin Barnes, Providence	6-9	1974	3	89	1,592
Tim Duncan, Wake Forest	6-11	1997	4	128	1,570
Elgin Baylor, Albertson & Seattle	6-6	1958	3	80	1,559
Ernie Beck, Penn	6-4	1953	3	82	1,557
Dave DeBusschere, Detroit	6-5	1962	3	80	1,552
Wes Unseld, Louisville	6-8	1968	3	82	1,551
Derrick Coleman, Syracuse	6-9	1990	4	143	1,537
Malik Rose, Drexel	6-7	1996	4	120	1,514
Ralph Sampson, Virginia	7-4	1983	4	132	1,511
Chris Smith, Virginia Tech	6-6	1961	4	88	1,508
Keith Swagerty, Pacific	6-7	1967	3	82	1,505

(For careers beginning in 1973 or after)

Player, Team	Ht.	Last Season	Yrs.	G	Reb.
Tim Duncan, Wake Forest	6-11	1997	4	128	1,570
Derrick Coleman, Syracuse	6-9	1990	4	143	1,537
Malik Rose, Drexel	6-7	1996	4	120	1,514
Ralph Sampson, Virginia	7-4	1983	4	132	1,511
Pete Padgett, Nevada	6-8	1976	4	104	1,464
Lionel Simmons, La Salle	6-7	1990	4	131	1,429
Anthony Bonner, St. Louis	6-7	1990	4	133	1,424
Tyrone Hill, Xavier	6-9	1990	4	126	1,380
Popeye Jones, Murray St.	6-8	1992	4	123	1,374
Michael Brooks, La Salle	6-7	1980	4	114	1,372
Xavier McDaniel, Wichita St.	6-7	1985	4	117	1,359
John Irving, Arizona & Hofstra	6-9	1977	4	103	1,348
Sam Clancy, Pittsburgh	6-6	1981	4	116	1,342
Keith Lee, Memphis	6-10	1985	4	128	1,336
Larry Smith, Alcorn St.	6-8	1980	4	111	1,334
Clarence Weatherspoon, Southern Miss.	6-7	1992	4	117	1,320
Michael Cage, San Diego St.	6-9	1984	4	112	1,317
Bob Stephens, Drexel	6-7	1979	4	99	1,316
Patrick Ewing, Georgetown	7-0	1985	4	143	1,316
David Robinson, Navy	7-1	1987	4	127	1,314
Wayne Rollins, Clemson	7-1	1977	4	110	1,311
David West, Xavier	6-9	2003	4	126	1,309
Bob Warner, Maine	6-6	1976	4	96	1,304
Ervin Johnson, New Orleans	6-11	1993	4	123	1,287
Calvin Natt, La.-Monroe	6-5	1979	4	108	1,285

REBOUND AVERAGE
(Minimum 800 rebounds)

Player, Team	Ht.	Last Season	Yrs.	G	Reb.	Avg.
Artis Gilmore, Jacksonville	7-2	1971	2	54	1,224	22.7
Charlie Slack, Marshall	6-5	1956	4	88	1,916	21.8
Paul Silas, Creighton	6-7	1964	3	81	1,751	21.6
Leroy Wright, Pacific	6-8	1960	3	67	1,442	21.5
Art Quimby, Connecticut	6-5	1955	4	80	1,716	21.5
Walt Dukes, Seton Hall	6-10	1953	2	59	1,247	21.1
Bill Russell, San Francisco	6-9	1956	3	79	1,606	20.3
Kermit Washington, American	6-8	1973	3	73	1,478	20.2
Julius Erving, Massachusetts	6-6	1971	2	52	1,049	20.2
Joe Holup, George Washington	6-6	1956	4	104	2,030	19.5
Elgin Baylor, Albertson & Seattle	6-6	1958	3	80	1,559	19.5
Dave DeBusschere, Detroit	6-5	1962	3	80	1,552	19.4
Ernie Beck, Penn	6-4	1953	3	82	1,557	19.0
Wes Unseld, Louisville	6-8	1968	3	82	1,551	18.9
Tom Gola, La Salle	6-6	1955	4	118	2,201	18.7
Ed Conlin, Fordham	6-5	1955	4	102	1,884	18.5
Keith Swagerty, Pacific	6-7	1967	3	82	1,505	18.4
Wilt Chamberlain, Kansas	7-0	1958	2	48	877	18.3
Jerry Harper, Alabama	6-8	1956	4	93	1,688	18.2
Dick Cunningham, Murray St.	6-10	1968	3	71	1,292	18.2
Marvin Barnes, Providence	6-9	1974	3	89	1,592	17.9
Jim Barnes, UTEP	6-8	1964	2	54	965	17.9
Alex Ellis, Niagara	6-5	1958	3	77	1,376	17.9
Dickie Hemric, Wake Forest	6-6	1955	4	104	1,802	17.3
Elvin Hayes, Houston	6-8	1968	3	93	1,602	17.2

(For careers beginning in 1973 or after; minimum 800 rebounds)

Player, Team	Ht.	Last Season	Yrs.	G	Reb.	Avg.
Glenn Mosley, Seton Hall	6-8	1977	4	83	1,263	15.2
Bill Campion, Manhattan	6-10	1975	3	74	1,070	14.6
Pete Padgett, Nevada	6-8	1976	4	104	1,464	14.1
Bob Warner, Maine	6-6	1976	4	96	1,304	13.6
Shaquille O'Neal, LSU	7-1	1992	3	90	1,217	13.5
Cornelius Cash, Bowling Green	6-8	1975	3	79	1,068	13.5
Ira Terrell, SMU	6-8	1976	3	80	1,077	13.5
Bob Stephens, Drexel	6-7	1979	4	99	1,316	13.3
Larry Bird, Indiana St.	6-9	1979	3	94	1,247	13.3

Player, Team	Ht.	Last Season	Yrs.	G	Reb.	Avg.
Bernard King, Tennessee	6-7	1977	3	76	1,004	13.2
John Irving, Arizona & Hofstra	6-9	1977	4	103	1,348	13.1
Carey Scurry, Long Island	6-9	1985	3	79	1,013	12.8
Paul Millsap, Louisiana Tech	6-8	2006	3	92	1,172	12.7
Adonal Foyle, Colgate	6-10	1997	3	87	1,103	12.7
Warren Kidd, Middle Tenn.	6-6	1993	3	83	1,048	12.6
Malik Rose, Drexel	6-7	1996	4	120	1,514	12.5
Jervaughn Scales, Southern U.	6-6	1994	3	88	1,099	12.5
Tim Duncan, Wake Forest	6-11	1997	4	128	1,570	12.3
Michael Brooks, La Salle	6-7	1980	4	114	1,372	12.0
Larry Smith, Alcorn St.	6-8	1980	4	111	1,334	12.0
Wayne Rollins, Clemson	7-1	1977	4	110	1,311	11.9
Calvin Natt, La.-Monroe	6-5	1979	4	108	1,285	11.9
Ed Lawrence, McNeese St.	7-0	1976	4	102	1,212	11.9
Michael Cage, San Diego St.	6-9	1984	4	112	1,317	11.8
Xavier McDaniel, Wichita St.	6-7	1985	4	117	1,359	11.6
John Rudd, McNeese St.	6-6	1978	4	102	1,181	11.6
Sam Clancy, Pittsburgh	6-6	1981	4	116	1,342	11.6
Larry Stewart, Coppin St.	6-6	1991	3	91	1,052	11.6
Reggie Jackson, Nicholls St.	6-6	1995	4	110	1,271	11.6

ASSISTS

Player, Team	Ht.	Last Season	Yrs.	G	Ast.
Bobby Hurley, Duke	6-0	1993	4	140	1,076
Chris Corchiani, North Carolina St.	6-1	1991	4	124	1,038
Ed Cota, North Carolina	6-2	2000	4	138	1,030
Keith Jennings, East Tenn. St.	5-7	1991	4	127	983
Steve Blake, Maryland	6-3	2003	4	138	972
Sherman Douglas, Syracuse	6-0	1989	4	138	960
Tony Miller, Marquette	6-0	1995	4	123	956
Aaron Miles, Kansas	6-1	2005	4	138	954
Greg Anthony, Portland & UNLV	6-1	1991	4	138	950
Doug Gottlieb, Notre Dame & Oklahoma St.	6-1	2000	4	124	947
Gary Payton, Oregon St.	6-2	1990	4	120	939
Orlando Smart, San Francisco	6-0	1994	4	116	902
Andre LaFleur, Northeastern	6-3	1987	4	128	894
Chico Fletcher, Arkansas St.	5-6	2000	4	114	893
Jim Les, Bradley	5-11	1986	4	118	884
Frank Smith, Old Dominion	6-0	1988	4	120	883
Taurence Chisholm, Delaware	5-7	1988	4	110	877
Grayson Marshall, Clemson	6-2	1988	4	122	857
Anthony Manuel, Bradley	5-11	1989	4	108	855
Pooh Richardson, UCLA	6-1	1989	4	122	833
Chris Thomas, Notre Dame	6-1	2005	4	128	833
Butch Moore, SMU	5-10	1986	4	125	828
Chris Duhon, Duke	6-1	2004	4	144	819
Mateen Cleaves, Michigan St.	6-3	2000	4	123	816
Jared Jordan, Marist	6-2	2007	4	117	813

ASSIST AVERAGE
(Minimum 550 assists)

Player, Team	Ht.	Last Season	Yrs.	G	Ast.	Avg.
Avery Johnson, Southern U.	5-11	1988	2	61	732	12.00
Sam Crawford, New Mexico St.	5-8	1993	2	67	592	8.84
Mark Wade, Oklahoma & UNLV	6-0	1987	3	79	693	8.77
Chris Corchiani, North Carolina St.	6-1	1991	4	124	1,038	8.37
Taurence Chisholm, Delaware	5-7	1988	4	110	877	7.97
Van Usher, Tennessee Tech	6-0	1992	3	85	676	7.95
Anthony Manuel, Bradley	5-11	1989	4	108	855	7.92
Chico Fletcher, Arkansas St.	5-6	2000	4	114	893	7.83
Gary Payton, Oregon St.	6-2	1990	4	120	938	7.82
Orlando Smart, San Francisco	6-0	1994	4	116	902	7.78
Tony Miller, Marquette	6-0	1995	4	123	956	7.77
Keith Jennings, East Tenn. St.	5-7	1991	4	127	983	7.74
Bobby Hurley, Duke	6-0	1993	4	140	1,076	7.69
Doug Gottlieb, Notre Dame & Oklahoma St.	6-1	2000	4	124	947	7.63
Chuck Evans, Old Dominion & Mississippi St.	5-11	1993	3	85	648	7.62
Jim Les, Bradley	5-11	1986	4	118	884	7.49
Ed Cota, North Carolina	6-2	2000	4	138	1,030	7.46
Curtis McCants, George Mason	6-0	1998	3	81	598	7.38
Frank Smith, Old Dominion	6-0	1988	4	120	883	7.36
Doug Wojcik, Navy	6-1	1987	4	99	714	7.21
Mark Woods, Wright St.	6-1	1993	4	113	811	7.18
Nelson Haggerty, Baylor	6-0	1995	4	98	699	7.13
Steve Blake, Maryland	6-3	2003	4	138	972	7.04
Grayson Marshall, Clemson	6-2	1988	4	122	857	7.02
Drafton Davis, Marist	6-0	1988	4	115	804	6.99

BLOCKED SHOTS

Player, Team	Ht.	Last Season	Yrs.	G	Blk.
Wojciech Mydra, La.-Monroe	7-2	2002	4	115	535
Adonal Foyle, Colgate	6-10	1997	3	87	492
Tim Duncan, Wake Forest	6-11	1997	4	128	481
Alonzo Mourning, Georgetown	6-10	1992	4	120	453
Tarvis Williams, Hampton	6-9	2001	4	114	452
Ken Johnson, Ohio St.	6-11	2001	4	127	444
Deng Gai, Fairfield	6-9	2005	4	100	442
Emeka Okafor, Connecticut	6-9	2004	3	103	441
Lorenzo Coleman, Tennessee Tech	7-1	1997	4	113	437
Calvin Booth, Penn St.	6-11	1999	4	114	428
Theo Ratliff, Wyoming	6-10	1995	4	111	425
Troy Murphy, Notre Dame	6-9	2001	3	94	425
Etan Thomas, Syracuse	6-9	2000	4	122	424
Shelden Williams, Duke	6-9	2006	4	139	422
Rodney Blake, St. Joseph's	6-8	1988	4	116	419
Shaquille O'Neal, LSU	7-1	1992	3	90	412
Kevin Roberson, Vermont	6-7	1992	4	112	409
Jim McIlvaine, Marquette	7-1	1994	4	118	399
Stephane Lasme, Massachusetts	6-8	2007	4	118	399
Tim Perry, Temple	6-9	1988	4	130	392
D'or Fischer, Northwestern St. & West Virginia	6-11	2005	4	127	392
Jason Lawson, Villanova	6-11	1997	4	131	375
Pervis Ellison, Louisville	6-9	1989	4	136	374
Peter Aluma, Liberty	6-10	1997	4	119	366
Acie Earl, Iowa	6-10	1993	4	116	365

BLOCKED-SHOT AVERAGE
(Minimum 225 blocked shots)

Player, Team	Ht.	Last Season	Yrs.	G	Blk.	Avg.
Keith Closs, Central Conn. St.	7-2	1996	2	54	317	5.87
Adonal Foyle, Colgate	6-10	1997	3	87	492	5.66
David Robinson, Navy	6-11	1987	2	67	351	5.24
Wojciech Mydra, La.-Monroe	7-2	2002	4	115	535	4.65
Shaquille O'Neal, LSU	7-1	1992	3	90	412	4.58
Troy Murphy, Notre Dame	6-9	2001	3	94	425	4.52
Jerome James, Florida A&M	7-1	1998	3	81	363	4.48
Deng Gai, Fairfield	6-9	2005	4	100	442	4.42
Emeka Okafor, Connecticut	6-9	2004	3	103	441	4.28
Justin Williams, Wyoming	6-10	2006	2	58	244	4.21
Justin Rowe, Maine	7-0	2003	2	55	226	4.11
Tarvis Williams, Hampton	6-9	2001	4	114	452	3.96
Lorenzo Coleman, Tennessee Tech	7-1	1997	4	113	437	3.87
Theo Ratliff, Wyoming	6-10	1995	4	111	425	3.83
Alonzo Mourning, Georgetown	6-10	1992	4	120	453	3.78
Tim Duncan, Wake Forest	6-11	1997	4	128	481	3.76
Calvin Booth, Penn St.	6-11	1999	4	114	428	3.75
Lorenzo Williams, Stetson	6-9	1991	2	63	234	3.71
Dikembe Mutombo, Georgetown	7-2	1991	3	96	354	3.69
Marcus Camby, Massachusetts	6-11	1996	3	92	336	3.65
Kevin Roberson, Vermont	6-7	1992	4	112	409	3.65
Rodney Blake, St. Joseph's	6-8	1988	4	116	419	3.61
Ken Johnson, Ohio St.	6-11	2001	4	127	444	3.50
Etan Thomas, Syracuse	6-9	2000	4	122	424	3.48
Kelvin Cato, South Ala. & Iowa St.	6-11	1997	3	79	274	3.47

STEALS

Player, Team	Ht.	Last Season	Yrs.	G	Stl.
John Linehan, Providence	5-9	2002	5	122	385
Eric Murdock, Providence	6-2	1991	4	117	376
Pepe Sanchez, Temple	6-0	2000	4	116	365
Cookie Belcher, Nebraska	6-4	2001	5	131	353
Kevin Braswell, Georgetown	6-2	2002	4	128	349
Bonzi Wells, Ball St.	6-5	1998	4	116	347
Obie Trotter, Alabama A&M	6-1	2006	4	114	346
Gerald Walker, San Francisco	6-1	1996	4	111	344
Johnny Rhodes, Maryland	6-6	1996	4	122	344
Michael Anderson, Drexel	5-11	1988	4	115	341
Kenny Robertson, Cleveland St.	6-0	1990	4	119	341
Keith Jennings, East Tenn. St.	5-7	1991	4	127	334
Juan Dixon, Maryland	6-3	2002	4	141	333
Desmond Cambridge, Alabama A&M	6-1	2002	3	84	330
Greg Anthony, Portland & UNLV	6-1	1991	4	138	329
Jason Hart, Syracuse	6-3	2000	4	132	329
Chris Corchiani, North Carolina St.	6-1	1991	4	124	328
Marques Green, St. Bonaventure	5-7	2004	4	112	325
Gary Payton, Oregon St.	6-2	1990	4	120	321
Chris Garner, Memphis	5-10	1997	4	123	321
Tim Winn, St. Bonaventure	5-10	2000	4	108	319
Mark Woods, Wright St.	6-1	1993	4	113	314
Pointer Williams, Tulane & McNeese St.	6-0	1996	4	115	314
Tim Smith, East Tenn. St.	5-9	2006	4	114	313
Scott Burrell, Connecticut	6-7	1993	4	119	310
Clarence Ceasar, LSU	6-7	1995	4	112	310
Shawnta Rogers, George Washington	5-4	1999	4	114	310

STEAL AVERAGE
(Minimum 225 steals)

Player, Team	Ht.	Last Season	Yrs.	G	Stl.	Avg.
Desmond Cambridge, Alabama A&M	6-1	2002	3	84	330	3.93
Mookie Blaylock, Oklahoma	6-0	1989	2	74	281	3.80
Ronn McMahon, Eastern Wash.	5-9	1990	3	64	225	3.52
Eric Murdock, Providence	6-2	1991	4	117	376	3.21
Van Usher, Tennessee Tech	6-0	1992	3	85	270	3.18
John Linehan, Providence	5-9	2002	5	122	385	3.16
Pepe Sanchez, Temple	6-0	2000	4	116	365	3.15
Gerald Walker, San Francisco	6-1	1996	4	111	344	3.10
Obie Trotter, Alabama A&M	6-1	2006	4	114	346	3.04
Bonzi Wells, Ball St.	6-5	1998	4	116	347	2.99
Michael Anderson, Drexel	5-11	1988	4	115	341	2.97
Tim Winn, St. Bonaventure	5-10	2000	4	108	319	2.95
Haywoode Workman, Oral Roberts	6-3	1989	3	85	250	2.94
Shawn Griggs, LSU & La.-Lafayette	6-6	1994	3	89	260	2.92
Marques Green, St. Bonaventure	5-7	2004	4	112	325	2.90
Morris Scott, Florida A&M	6-0	2001	4	87	252	2.90
Kenny Robertson, Cleveland St.	6-0	1990	4	119	341	2.87
Jason Rowe, Loyola (Md.)	5-10	2000	4	95	272	2.86
Darnell Mee, Western Ky.	6-3	1993	3	91	259	2.85
Pat Baldwin, Northwestern	6-1	1994	4	96	272	2.83
Johnny Rhodes, Maryland	6-6	1996	4	122	344	2.82
Mark Woods, Wright St.	6-1	1993	4	113	314	2.78
Clarence Ceasar, LSU	6-7	1995	4	112	310	2.77
Louis Ford, Howard	5-6	2006	4	86	238	2.77
Aldwin Ware, Florida A&M	6-2	1988	4	110	301	2.74

2,000 POINTS & 1,000 REBOUNDS

Player, Team	Ht.	Last Season	Yrs.	G	Pts.	Reb.
Lionel Simmons, La Salle	6-7	1990	4	131	3,217	1,429
Harry Kelly, Texas Southern	6-7	1983	4	110	3,066	1,085
Oscar Robertson, Cincinnati	6-5	1960	3	88	2,973	1,338
Danny Manning, Kansas	6-10	1988	4	147	2,951	1,187
Elvin Hayes, Houston	6-8	1968	3	93	2,884	1,602
Larry Bird, Indiana St.	6-9	1979	3	94	2,850	1,247
Hank Gathers, Southern California & Loyola Marymount	6-7	1990	4	117	2,723	1,128
Daren Queenan, Lehigh	6-5	1988	4	118	2,703	1,013
David Robinson, Navy	7-1	1987	4	127	2,669	1,314
Wayman Tisdale, Oklahoma	6-9	1985	3	104	2,661	1,048
Michael Brooks, La Salle	6-7	1980	4	114	2,628	1,372
Dickie Hemric, Wake Forest	6-6	1955	4	104	2,587	1,802
Calvin Natt, La.-Monroe	6-5	1979	4	108	2,581	1,285
Keith Van Horn, Utah	6-9	1997	4	122	2,542	1,074
Willie Jackson, Centenary (La.)	6-6	1984	4	114	2,535	1,013
Caleb Green, Oral Roberts	6-8	2007	4	128	2,503	1,189
Bill Bradley, Princeton	6-5	1965	3	83	2,503	1,008
Elgin Baylor, Albertson & Seattle	6-6	1958	3	80	2,500	1,559
Nick Fazekas, Nevada	6-11	2007	4	131	2,464	1,254
Tom Gola, La Salle	6-6	1955	4	118	2,462	2,201
Christian Laettner, Duke	6-11	1992	4	148	2,460	1,149
Keith Lee, Memphis	6-11	1985	4	128	2,408	1,336
Phil Sellers, Rutgers	6-5	1976	4	114	2,399	1,115
Byron Houston, Oklahoma St.	6-7	1992	4	127	2,379	1,190
Ron Harper, Miami (Ohio)	6-6	1986	4	120	2,377	1,119
Bryant Reeves, Oklahoma St.	7-0	1995	4	136	2,367	1,152
Craig Smith, Boston College	6-7	2006	4	130	2,349	1,114
Lew Alcindor, UCLA	7-2	1969	3	88	2,325	1,367
Mike Gminski, Duke	6-11	1980	4	122	2,323	1,242
Billy McGill, Utah	6-9	1962	3	86	2,321	1,106
Adam Keefe, Stanford	6-9	1992	4	125	2,319	1,119
Jerry West, West Virginia	6-3	1960	3	93	2,309	1,240
Tunji Awojobi, Boston U.	6-5	1997	4	114	2,308	1,237
Jonathan Moore, Furman	6-8	1980	4	117	2,299	1,242
Rick Barry, Miami (Fla.)	6-7	1965	3	77	2,298	1,274
Gary Winton, Army	6-5	1978	4	105	2,296	1,168
Kenneth Lyons, North Texas	6-7	1983	4	111	2,291	1,020
Tom Davis, Delaware St.	6-6	1991	4	95	2,274	1,013
Nick Werkman, Seton Hall	6-3	1964	3	71	2,273	1,036
Jim McDaniels, Western Ky.	7-0	1971	3	81	2,238	1,118
Joe Holup, George Washington	6-6	1956	4	104	2,226	2,030
Ralph Sampson, Virginia	7-4	1983	4	132	2,225	1,511
Juan Mendez, Niagara	6-7	2005	4	123	2,210	1,053

DIVISION I

Player, Team	Ht.	Last Season	Yrs.	G	Pts.	Reb.
Patrick Ewing, Georgetown	7-0	1985	4	143	2,184	1,316
Doug Smith, Missouri	6-10	1991	4	128	2,184	1,054
Jenny Sanders, George Mason	6-5	1989	4	107	2,177	1,026
Joe Barry Carroll, Purdue	7-1	1980	4	123	2,175	1,148
Reggie King, Alabama	6-6	1979	4	118	2,168	1,279
Len Chappell, Wake Forest	6-8	1962	3	87	2,165	1,213
Danny Ferry, Duke	6-10	1989	4	143	2,155	1,003
Xavier McDaniel, Wichita St.	6-7	1985	4	117	2,152	1,359
Derrick Coleman, Syracuse	6-9	1990	4	143	2,143	1,537
Joe Binion, N.C. A&T	6-8	1984	4	116	2,143	1,194
Pervis Ellison, Louisville	6-9	1989	4	136	2,143	1,149
Dan Issel, Kentucky	6-9	1970	3	83	2,138	1,078
Jesse Arnelle, Penn St.	6-5	1955	4	102	2,138	1,238
Ryan Gomes, Providence	6-7	2005	4	116	2,138	1,028
Sam Perkins, North Carolina	6-10	1984	4	135	2,133	1,167
David West, Xavier	6-9	2003	4	126	2,132	1,309
Bob Elliott, Arizona	6-10	1977	4	114	2,131	1,083
Clarence Weatherspoon, Southern Miss.	6-7	1992	4	117	2,130	1,320
Reggie Jackson, Nicholls St.	6-6	1995	4	110	2,124	1,271
Greg Grant, Utah St.	6-7	1986	4	115	2,124	1,003
John Wallace, Syracuse	6-8	1996	4	127	2,119	1,065
Tim Duncan, Wake Forest	6-11	1997	4	128	2,117	1,570
Odell Hodge, Old Dominion	6-9	1997	5	128	2,117	1,086
Bill Cartwright, San Francisco	6-11	1979	4	111	2,116	1,137
Bob Harstad, Creighton	6-6	1991	4	128	2,110	1,126
Gary Trent, Ohio	6-8	1995	3	93	2,108	1,050
Nick Collison, Kansas	6-9	2003	4	142	2,097	1,143
B.B. Davis, Lamar	6-8	1981	4	119	2,084	1,122
Durand Macklin, LSU	6-7	1981	5	123	2,080	1,276
Ralph Crosthwaite, Western Ky.	6-9	1959	4	103	2,076	1,309
Hakim Warrick, Syracuse	6-8	2005	4	135	2,073	1,025
Sidney Green, UNLV	6-9	1983	4	119	2,069	1,276
Bob Lanier, St. Bonaventure	6-11	1970	3	75	2,067	1,180
Raef LaFrentz, Kansas	6-11	1998	4	131	2,066	1,186
Fred West, Texas Southern	6-9	1990	4	118	2,066	1,136
Sidney Moncrief, Arkansas	6-4	1979	4	122	2,066	1,015
Popeye Jones, Murray St.	6-8	1992	4	123	2,057	1,374
Danya Abrams, Boston College	6-7	1997	4	122	2,053	1,029
Mark Acres, Oral Roberts	6-11	1985	4	110	2,038	1,051
Fred Hetzel, Davidson	6-8	1965	3	79	2,032	1,094
Bailey Howell, Mississippi St.	6-7	1959	3	75	2,030	1,277
Malik Rose, Drexel	6-7	1996	4	120	2,024	1,514
Larry Krystkowiak, Montana	6-9	1986	4	120	2,017	1,105
Greg Kelser, Michigan St.	6-7	1979	4	115	2,014	1,092
Michael Harris, Rice	6-6	2005	4	121	2,014	1,111
Brandon Hunter, Ohio	6-7	2003	4	119	2,012	1,103
Herb Williams, Ohio St.	6-10	1981	4	114	2,011	1,111
Stacey Augmon, UNLV	6-8	1991	4	145	2,011	1,005
Jeff Cohen, William & Mary	6-7	1961	4	103	2,003	1,679
Tyrone Hill, Xavier	6-9	1990	4	126	2,003	1,380
Alonzo Mourning, Georgetown	6-10	1992	4	120	2,001	1,032
Josh Grant, Utah	6-9	1993	5	131	2,000	1,066

TRIPLE-DOUBLES

Player, Team	Last Season	Yrs.	3B-2Bs
Michael Anderson, Drexel	1988	4	6
Shaquille O'Neal, LSU	1992	3	6
Brian Shaw, UC Santa Barbara	1988	2	5
Kevin Roberson, Vermont	1992	4	5
David Robinson, Navy	1987	4	4
Jason Kidd, California	1994	3	4
David Edwards, Texas A&M	1994	4	4
Adonal Foyle, Colgate	1997	3	4
Shawn James, Northeastern	2006	2	4
Stephane Lasme, Massachusetts	2007	4	4
Gerald Lewis, SMU	1993	4	3
Trenton Hassell, Austin Peay	2001	3	3
Wojciech Murda, La.-Monroe	2002	3	3
Andre Iguodala, Arizona	2004	3	3
Derrick Lewis, Maryland	1988	4	2
Luc Longley, New Mexico	1991	4	2
Dave Barnett, Fresno St.	1991	2	2
Alonzo Mourning, Georgetown	1991	4	2
Stacey Augmon, UNLV	1991	4	2
Chris Mills, Kentucky & Arizona	1993	4	2
Anfernee Hardaway, Memphis	1993	3	2
Sharone Wright, Clemson	1994	3	2
Mark Davis, Texas Tech	1995	3	2
Keith Closs, Central Conn. St.	1996	2	2
Roy Rogers, Alabama	1996	4	2
Brian Skinner, Baylor	1998	4	2
Jerome James, Florida A&M	1998	4	2
Bonzi Wells, Ball St.	1998	4	2
Kenyon Martin, Cincinnati	2000	4	2
Loren Woods, Arizona	2001	2	2
D'or Fischer, Northwestern St. & West Virginia	2005	4	2
Sean Kennedy, Marist	2002	4	2
Luke Jackson, Oregon	2004	4	2
David Harrison, Colorado	2004	3	2
Damitrius Coleman, Mercer & Bethune-Cookman	2007	2	2
Dominic McGuire, California & Fresno St.	2007	3	2

DOUBLE-DOUBLES

Player, Team	Last Season	Yrs.	2B-2Bs
Tim Duncan, Wake Forest	1997	4	87
Ralph Sampson, Virginia	1983	4	84
Derrick Coleman, Syracuse	1990	4	83
Malik Rose, Drexel	1996	4	80
Oscar Robertson, Cincinnati	1960	3	79
Jerry Lucas, Ohio St.	1962	3	78
Mel Counts, Oregon St.	1964	3	78
Lew Alcindor, UCLA	1969	3	78
Keith Lee, Memphis	1985	4	74
David Robinson, Navy	1987	4	73
Don May, Dayton	1968	3	72
Bill Walton, UCLA	1974	3	72
Paul Silas, Creighton	1964	3	71
Gary Winton, Army	1978	4	71
Hank Finkel, Dayton	1966	3	69
Larry Bird, Indiana St.	1979	3	68
David West, Xavier	2003	4	68
Bob Stephens, Drexel	1979	4	67
Tyrone Hill, Xavier	1990	4	67
Len Chappell, Wake Forest	1962	3	66
Jim Haderlein, Loyola Marymount	1971	3	66
Sam Clancy, Pittsburgh	1981	4	66
Dan Issel, Kentucky	1970	3	64
Mike Gminski, Duke	1980	3	63
Jack Twyman, Cincinnati	1955	4	62
Dave Cowens, Florida St.	1970	3	62

CONSECUTIVE DOUBLE-DOUBLES

Player, Team	Dates	2B-2Bs
Billy Cunningham, North Carolina	Dec. 5, 1962-Feb. 22, 1964	40
#Jerry Lucas, Ohio St.	Jan. 23, 1960-Mar. 11, 1961	38
Oscar Robertson, Cincinnati	Dec. 31, 1958-Jan. 2, 1960	33
Mel Counts, Oregon St.	Mar. 23, 1963-Mar. 10, 1964	30
Lew Alcindor, UCLA	Dec. 27, 1967-Dec. 6, 1968	28
Benoit Benjamin, Creighton	Mar. 15, 1984-Feb. 16, 1985	28
Artis Gilmore, Jacksonville	Feb. 18, 1970-Feb. 8 1971	27
Willie Naulls, UCLA	Dec. 2, 1955-Mar. 9, 1956	25
Jerry Lucas, Ohio St.	Mar. 18, 1961-Feb. 24, 1962	24
Mike Lewis, Duke	Mar. 13, 1967-Feb. 20, 1968	21
Jack Twyman, Cincinnati	Dec. 17, 1953-Jan. 6, 1955	20
Jerry West, West Virginia	Jan. 5-Mar. 12, 1960	20
Jim Haderlein, Loyola Marymount	Feb. 21, 1969-Jan. 29, 1970	20
Steve Smith, Loyola Marymount	Jan. 4-Dec. 4, 1972	20
Dave Gunther, Iowa	Dec. 8, 1958-Feb. 21, 1959	19
Jerry West, West Virginia	Feb. 18-Dec. 29, 1959	17
Marvin Roberts, Utah St.	Feb. 26, 1970-Jan. 14, 1971	17
Artis Gilmore, Jacksonville	Dec. 9, 1969-Feb. 13, 1970	17
Tim Duncan, Wake Forest	Nov. 24, 1996-Jan. 28, 1997	17
Len Chappell, Wake Forest	1962	16
Larry Bird, Indiana St.	Dec. 9-Feb. 6, 1979	16
Rickey Brown, Mississippi St.	Mar. 8, 1979-Jan. 17, 1980	16
Shaun Vandiver, Colorado	Feb. 13-Dec. 12, 1990	16
Bill Walton, UCLA	Dec. 10, 1971-Jan. 28, 1972	15
David Robinson, Navy	Feb. 12-Nov. 29, 1986	15
Andre Moore, Loyola (Ill.)	Jan. 12-Feb. 23, 1987	15
Spencer Dunkley, Delaware	Dec. 10, 1992-Feb. 6, 1993	15

#Missed the Jan. 9, 1961, game because of injury.

Note: Triple-Doubles and Double-Doubles include only statistics from points, rebounds (since 1951), assists (since 1984), blocked shots (since 1986) or steals (since 1986).

GAMES PLAYED

Player, Team	Last Season	Yrs.	G
Wayne Turner, Kentucky	1999	4	151
Christian Laettner, Duke	1992	4	148
Danny Manning, Kansas	1988	4	147
Greg Koubek, Duke	1991	4	147

Player, Team	Last Season	Yrs.	G
Shane Battier, Duke	2001	4	146
Stacey Augmon, UNLV	1991	4	145
Jamaal Magloire, Kentucky	2000	4	145
Chris Duhon, Duke	2004	4	144
Patrick Ewing, Georgetown	1985	4	143
Danny Ferry, Duke	1989	4	143
Derrick Coleman, Syracuse	1990	4	143
Jared Prickett, Kentucky	1997	4	143
Ryan Robertson, Kansas	1999	4	142
Nick Collison, Kansas	2003	4	142
Brian Davis, Duke	1992	4	141
Thomas Hill, Duke	1993	4	141
Anthony Epps, Kentucky	1997	4	141
Brendan Haywood, North Carolina	2001	4	141
Juan Dixon, Maryland	2002	4	141

Player, Team	Last Season	Yrs.	G
Kirk Hinrich, Kansas	2003	4	141
Chris Richard, Duke	2007	4	141
Bobby Hurley, Duke	1993	4	140
Kevin Freeman, Connecticut	2000	4	140
Charlie Bell, Michigan St.	2001	4	140
Ralph Beard, Kentucky	1949	4	139
Lee Mayberry, Arkansas	1992	4	139
Kevin Pritchard, Kansas	1990	4	139
Ademola Okulaja, North Carolina	1999	4	139
Eric Chenowith, Kansas	2001	4	139
Dante Swanson, Tulsa	2003	4	139
J.J. Redick, Duke	2006	4	139
Shelden Williams, Duke	2006	4	139
Tony Young, Southern Ill.	2007	4	139

Top 10 Individual Scoring Leaders

Year-by-Year Top 10

1948
Rk.	Player, School	G	Pts.	Avg.
1.	Murray Wier, Iowa	19	399	21.0
2.	Tony Lavelli, Yale	27	554	20.5
3.	Frank Kudelka, St. Mary's	24	489	20.4
4.	Ernie Vandeweghe, Colgate	19	385	20.3
5.	Hal Haskins, Hamline	31	605	19.5
6.	George Kok, Arkansas	24	469	19.5
7.	Jim McIntyre, Minnesota	19	360	18.9
8.	William Hatchett, Rutgers	11	201	18.3
9.	Gene Berce, Marquette	22	390	17.7
10.	Duane Klueh, Indiana St.	34	597	17.6

1949
Rk.	Player, School	G	Pts.	Avg.
1.	Tony Lavelli, Yale	30	671	22.4
2.	Paul Arizin, Villanova	27	594	22.0
3.	Chet Giermak, William & Mary	34	740	21.8
4.	George Senesky, St. Joseph's	23	483	21.0
5.	Ernie Vandeweghe, Colgate	19	397	20.9
6.	Alex Groza, Kentucky	34	698	20.5
7.	Billy Goodwin, Rhode Island	22	433	19.7
8.	Joe Noertker, Virginia	23	442	19.2
9.	Vince Boryla, Denver	33	624	18.9
10.	Fred Schaus, West Virginia	24	442	18.4

1950
Rk.	Player, School	G	Pts.	Avg.
1.	Paul Arizin, Villanova	29	735	25.3
2.	George Senesky, St. Joseph's	24	537	22.4
3.	Sherm White, Long Island	25	551	22.0
4.	Clyde Lovellette, Kansas	25	545	21.8
5.	Bobby Lavoy, Western Ky.	31	671	21.6
6.	Dick Schnittker, Ohio St.	22	469	21.3
7.	Chet Giermak, William & Mary	31	646	20.8
8.	Jay Handlan, Wash. & Lee	20	406	20.3
9.	Bob Zawoluk, St. John's (N.Y.)	29	588	20.3
10.	Joe Noertker, Virginia	25	503	20.1

1951
Rk.	Player, School	G	Pts.	Avg.
1.	Bill Milkvy, Temple	25	731	29.2
2.	Jay Handlan, Wash. & Lee	25	656	26.2
3.	Mark Workman, West Virginia	27	705	26.1
4.	Dick Groat, Duke	33	831	25.2
5.	Clyde Lovellette, Kansas	24	548	22.8
6.	Fred Slaughter, South Carolina	25	569	22.8
7.	Larry Hennessey, Villanova	32	703	22.0
8.	Jim Ove, Valparaiso	22	469	21.3
9.	Bob Zawoluk, St. John's (N.Y.)	31	654	21.1
10.	Sam Ranzino, North Carolina St.	34	706	20.8

1952
Rk.	Player, School	G	Pts.	Avg.
1.	Clyde Lovellette, Kansas	28	795	28.4
2.	Dick Groat, Duke	30	780	26.0
3.	Bob Pettit, LSU	24	612	25.5
4.	Chuck Darling, Iowa	22	561	25.5
5.	Frank Selvy, Furman	24	591	24.6
6.	Mark Workman, West Virginia	25	577	23.1
7.	Dick Retherford, Baldwin-Wallace	21	457	21.8
8.	Dickie Hemric, Wake Forest	29	629	21.7
9.	Cliff Hagan, Kentucky	32	692	21.6
10.	John Clune, Navy	23	487	21.2

1953
Rk.	Player, School	G	Pts.	Avg.
1.	Frank Selvy, Furman	25	738	29.5
2.	Larry Hennessey, Villanova	15	438	29.2
3.	Johnny O'Brien, Seattle	31	884	28.5
4.	Walter Dukes, Seton Hall	33	861	26.1
5.	Ernie Beck, Penn	26	673	25.9
6.	Bob Houbregs, Washington	31	800	25.8
7.	Don Schlundt, Indiana	26	661	25.4
8.	Dickie Hemric, Wake Forest	25	623	24.9
9.	George Dalton, John Carroll	27	669	24.8
10.	Bob Pettit, LSU	21	519	24.7

1954
Rk.	Player, School	G	Pts.	Avg.
1.	Frank Selvy, Furman	29	1,209	41.7
2.	Bob Pettit, LSU	25	785	31.4
3.	Buzz Wilkinson, Virginia	27	814	30.1
4.	Arney Short, Oklahoma City	25	696	27.8
5.	Bob Schafer, Villanova	31	836	27.0
6.	Walt Walowac, Marshall	21	548	26.1
7.	Tom Marshall, Western Ky.	32	829	25.9
8.	John Kerr, Illinois	22	556	25.3
9.	Al Bianchi, Bowling Green	24	600	25.0
10.	Togo Palazzi, Holy Cross	27	670	24.8

1955
Rk.	Player, School	G	Pts.	Avg.
1.	Darrel Floyd, Furman	25	897	35.9
2.	Buzz Wilkinson, Virginia	28	898	32.1
3.	Robin Freeman, Ohio St.	13	409	31.5
4.	Bill Yarborough, Clemson	23	651	28.3
5.	Dick O'Neal, TCU	24	676	28.2
6.	Dickie Hemric, Wake Forest	27	746	27.6
7.	Bob Patterson, Tulsa	28	773	27.6
8.	Johnny Mahoney, William & Mary	24	656	27.3
9.	Denver Brackeen, Mississippi	22	599	27.2
10.	Jesse Arnelle, Penn St.	28	731	26.1

1956
Rk.	Player, School	G	Pts.	Avg.
1.	Darrel Floyd, Furman	28	946	33.8
2.	Robin Freeman, Ohio St.	23	723	32.9
3.	Dan Swartz, Morehead St.	29	828	28.6
4.	Tom Heinsohn, Holy Cross	27	740	27.4
5.	Julius McCoy, Michigan St.	22	600	27.3
6.	Len Rosenbluth, No. Carolina	23	614	26.7
7.	Rod Hundley, West Virginia	30	798	26.6
8.	Raymond Downs, Texas	22	580	26.4
9.	Jim Ray, Toledo	22	563	25.6
10.	Roger Sigler, LSU	20	501	25.1

1957
Rk.	Player, School	G	Pts.	Avg.
1.	Grady Wallace, South Carolina	29	906	31.2
2.	Joe Gibbon, Mississippi	21	631	30.0
3.	Elgin Baylor, Seattle	25	743	29.7
4.	Wilt Chamberlain, Kansas	27	800	29.6
5.	Chet Forte, Columbia	24	694	28.9
6.	Jim Ashmore, Mississippi St.	24	708	28.3
7.	Lennie Rosenbluth, North Carolina	32	895	28.0
8.	Bill Ebben, Detroit	26	724	27.8
9.	Bailey Howell, Mississippi St.	25	647	25.9
10.	Archie Dees, Indiana	22	550	25.0

1958
Rk.	Player, School	G	Pts.	Avg.
1.	Oscar Robertson, Cincinnati	28	984	35.1
2.	Elgin Baylor, Seattle	29	943	32.5
3.	Wilt Chamberlain, Kansas	21	633	30.1
4.	Bailey Howell, Mississippi St.	25	695	27.8
5.	Phil Murrell, Drake	25	668	26.7
6.	King Coleman, Ky. Wesleyan	24	639	26.6
7.	Don Hennon, Pittsburgh	25	651	26.0
8.	Hub Reed, Oklahoma City	26	666	25.6
9.	Archie Dees, Indiana	24	613	25.5
10.	Dom Flora, Wash. & Lee	25	634	25.4

1959
Rk.	Player, School	G	Pts.	Avg.
1.	Ocsar Robertson, Cincinnati	30	978	32.6
2.	Leo Byrd, Marshall	24	704	29.3
3.	Jim Hagan, Tennessee Tech	25	720	28.8
4.	Bailey Howell, Miss. St.	25	688	27.5
5.	Jerry West, West Virginia	34	903	26.6
6.	Bob Ayersman, Virginia Tech	21	556	26.5
7.	Don Hennon, Pittsburgh	24	617	25.7
8.	Bob Boozer, Kansas St.	27	691	25.6
9.	Tony Windis, Wyoming	19	463	24.4
10.	Tom Hawkins, Notre Dame	22	514	23.4

1960

Rk.	Player, School	G	Pts.	Avg.
1.	Oscar Robertson, Cincinnati	30	1,011	33.7
2.	Tom Stith, St. Bonaventure	26	819	31.5
3.	Jim Darrow, Bowling Green	24	705	29.4
4.	Jerry West, West Virginia	31	908	29.3
5.	Frank Burgess, Gonzaga	26	751	28.9
6.	Al Butler, Niagara	25	714	28.6
7.	Terry Dischinger, Purdue	23	605	26.3
8.	Jerry Lucas, Ohio St.	27	710	26.3
9.	Dave DeBusschere, Detroit	27	691	25.6
10.	Jim Mudd, North Texas	24	605	25.2

1961

Rk.	Player, School	G	Pts.	Avg.
1.	Frank Burgess, Gonzaga	26	842	32.4
2.	Tom Chilton, East Tennessee	24	771	32.1
3.	Tom Stith, St. Bonaventure	28	830	29.6
4.	Terry Dischinger, Purdue	23	648	28.2
5.	Billy McGill, Utah	31	862	27.8
6.	Len Chappell, Wake Forest	28	745	26.6
7.	Jack Foley, Holy Cross	26	688	26.5
8.	Chet Walker, Bradley	26	656	25.2
9.	Art Heyman, Duke	25	629	25.2
10.	Ronald Warner, Gettysburg	25	623	24.9

1962

Rk.	Player, School	G	Pts.	Avg.
1.	Bill McGill, Utah	26	1,009	38.8
2.	Jack Foley, Holy Cross	26	866	33.3
3.	Nick Werkman, Seton Hall	24	793	33.0
4.	Terry Dischinger, Purdue	24	726	30.3
5.	Len Chappell, Wake Forest	31	932	30.1
6.	Jimmy Rayl, Indiana	24	714	29.8
7.	Jerry Smith, Furman	27	728	27.0
8.	Dave DeBusschere, Detroit	26	696	26.8
9.	Bob Duffy, Colgate	23	611	26.6
10.	Chet Walker, Bradley	26	687	26.4

1963

Rk.	Player, School	G	Pts.	Avg.
1.	Nick Werkman, Seton Hall	22	650	29.5
2.	Berry Kramer, New York U.	23	675	29.3
3.	Bill Green, Colorado St.	23	649	28.2
4.	Gary Bradds, Ohio St.	24	672	28.0
5.	Bill Bradley, Princeton	25	682	27.3
6.	Flynn Robinson, Wyoming	26	682	26.2
7.	Eddie Miles, Seattle	27	697	25.8
8.	Jimmy Rayl, Indiana	24	608	25.8
9.	Art Heyman, Duke	30	747	24.9
10.	Art Crump, Idaho St.	24	595	24.8

1964

Rk.	Player, School	G	Pts.	Avg.
1.	Butch Komives, Bowling Green	23	844	36.7
2.	Nick Werkman, Seton Hall	25	830	33.2
3.	Manny Newsome, Western Mich.	20	653	32.7
4.	Bill Bradley, Princeton	29	936	32.3
5.	Rick Barry, Miami (Fla.)	27	870	32.2
6.	Gary Bradds, Ohio St.	24	735	30.6
7.	Steve Thomas, Xavier	26	779	30.0
8.	John Austin, Boston College	21	614	29.2
9.	Jim Barnes, Texas Western	28	816	29.1
10.	Wayne Estes, Utah St.	29	821	28.3

1965

Rk.	Player, School	G	Pts.	Avg.
1.	Rick Barry, Miami (Fla.)	26	973	37.4
2.	Wayne Estes, Utah St.	19	641	33.7
3.	Bill Bradley, Princeton	29	885	30.5
4.	Dave Schellhase, Purdue	24	704	29.3
5.	Steve Thomas, Xavier	14	405	28.9
6.	Flynn Robinson, Wyoming	26	701	27.0
7.	John Austin, Boston College	25	673	26.9
8.	Fred Hetzel, Davidson	26	689	26.5
9.	John Beasley, Texas A&M	24	619	25.8
10.	Cazzie Russell, Michigan	27	694	25.7

1966

Rk.	Player, School	G	Pts.	Avg.
1.	Dave Schellhase, Purdue	24	781	32.5
2.	Dave Wagnon, Idaho St.	26	845	32.5
3.	Cazzie Russell, Michigan	26	800	30.8
4.	Jerry Chambers, Utah	31	892	28.8
5.	Dave Bing, Syracuse	28	794	28.4
6.	Tom Kerwin, Centenary (La.)	26	726	27.9
7.	Don Freeman, Illinois	24	668	27.8
8.	John Beasley, Texas A&M	24	668	27.8
9.	Bill Melchionni, Villanova	29	801	27.6
10.	Bob Lewis, North Carolina	27	740	27.4

1967

Rk.	Player, School	G	Pts.	Avg.
1.	Jimmy Walker, Providence	28	851	30.4
2.	Lew Alcindor, UCLA	30	870	29.0
3.	Mal Graham, New York U.	24	688	28.7
4.	Elvin Hayes, Houston	31	881	28.4
5.	Wes Bialosuknia, Connecticut	24	673	28.0
6.	Bob Lloyd, Rutgers	29	809	27.9
7.	Gary Gray, Oklahoma City	26	715	27.5
8.	Cliff Anderson, St. Joseph's	26	690	26.5
9.	Bob Verga, Duke	27	705	26.1
10.	Jim Tillman, Loyola (Ill.)	22	553	25.1

1968

Rk.	Player, School	G	Pts.	Avg.
1.	Pete Maravich, LSU	26	1,138	43.8
2.	Calvin Murphy, Niagara	24	916	38.2
3.	Elvin Hayes, Houston	33	1,214	36.8
4.	Rich Travis, Oklahoma City	27	808	29.9
5.	Bob Portman, Creighton	25	738	29.5
6.	Rick Mount, Purdue	24	683	28.5
7.	Bobby Joe Hill, West Texas St.	21	573	27.3
8.	Shaler Halimon, Utah St.	25	671	26.8
9.	Fred Foster, Miami (Ohio)	23	617	26.8
10.	Neal Walk, Florida	25	663	26.5

1969

Rk.	Player, School	G	Pts.	Avg.
1.	Pete Maravich, LSU	26	1,148	44.2
2.	Rick Mount, Purdue	28	932	33.3
3.	Calvin Murphy, Niagara	24	778	32.4
4.	Spencer Haywood, Detroit	22	699	31.8
5.	Bob Tallent, George Washington	25	723	28.9
6.	Marv Roberts, Utah St.	26	718	27.6
7.	Don Curnutt, Miami (Fla.)	24	661	27.5
8.	Bob Lanier, St. Bonaventure	24	654	27.3
9.	Rich Travis, Oklahoma City	27	729	27.0
10.	Rex Morgan, Jacksonville	23	613	26.7

1970

Rk.	Player, School	G	Pts.	Avg.
1.	Pete Maravich, LSU	31	1,381	44.5
2.	Austin Carr, Notre Dame	29	1,106	38.1
3.	Rick Mount, Purdue	20	708	35.4
4.	Dan Issel, Kentucky	28	948	33.9
5.	Willie Humes, Idaho St.	24	733	30.5
6.	Rich Yunkus, Georgia Tech	27	814	30.1
7.	Rudy Tomjanovich, Michigan	24	722	30.1
8.	Calvin Murphy, Niagara	29	854	29.4
9.	Dod Lanier, St. Bonaventure	26	757	29.1
10.	Ralph Simpson, Michigan St.	23	667	29.0

1971

Rk.	Player, School	G	Pts.	Avg.
1.	Johnny Neumann, Mississippi	23	923	40.1
2.	Austin Carr, Notre Dame	29	1,101	38.0
3.	Willie Humes, Idaho St.	24	777	32.4
4.	George McGinnis, Indiana	24	719	30.0
5.	Jim McDaniels, Western Ky.	30	878	29.3
6.	Rich Rinaldi, St. Peter's	24	687	28.6
7.	John Mengelt, Auburn	26	738	28.4
8.	Gene Phillips, SMU	26	737	28.3
9.	Cliff Meely, Colorado	26	729	28.0
10.	Wiley Brown, Iowa	24	662	27.6

1972

Rk.	Player, School	G	Pts.	Avg.
1.	Bo Lamar, La.-Lafayette	29	1,054	36.3
2.	Richie Fuqua, Oral Roberts	28	1,006	35.9
3.	Doug Collins, Illinois St.	26	847	32.6
4.	Wil Robertson, West Virginia	24	706	29.4
5.	Bird Averitt, Pepperdine	24	693	28.9
6.	John Williamson, New Mexico St.	25	678	27.1
7.	Greg Kohls, Syracuse	28	748	26.7
8.	Tony Miller, Florida	19	507	26.7
9.	Les Taylor, Murray St.	21	538	25.6
10.	Ted Martiniuk, St. Peter's	24	611	25.5

1973

Rk.	Player, School	G	Pts.	Avg.
1.	Bird Averitt, Pepperdine	25	848	33.9
2.	Ray Lewis, LSU	24	789	32.9
3.	Willie Biles, Tulsa	26	788	30.3
4.	Aron Stewart, Richmond	19	574	30.2
5.	Fly Williams, Austin Peay	29	854	29.4
6.	Bo Lamar, La.-Lafayette	28	808	28.9
7.	Ozie Edwards, Oklahoma City	27	767	28.4
8.	Martin Terry, Arkansas	26	735	28.3
9.	John Williamson, New Mexico St.	18	490	27.2
10.	Doug Collins, Illinois St.	25	650	26.0

1974

Rk.	Player, School	G	Pts.	Avg.
1.	Larry Fogle, Canisius	25	835	33.4
2.	Bruce King, Tex.-Pan Americn	22	681	31.0
3.	Fly Williams, Austin Peay	25	687	27.5
4.	Aaron Stewart, Richmond	25	663	26.5
5.	David Thompson, North Caro. St.	31	805	26.0
6.	Larry Bullington, Ball St.	26	664	25.5
7.	Frank Oleynick, Seattle	26	653	25.1
8.	James Outlaw, N.C. A&T	26	647	24.9
9.	Willie Biles, Tulsa	26	641	24.7
10.	John Shumate, Notre Dame	29	703	24.2

1975

Rk.	Player, School	G	Pts.	Avg.
1.	Bob McCurdy, Richmond	26	855	32.9
2.	Adrien Dantley, Notre Dame	29	883	30.4
3.	David Thompson, North Caro. St.	28	838	29.9
4.	Luther Burden, Utah	26	747	28.7
5.	Hercle Ivy, Iowa St.	26	737	28.3
6.	Mike Coleman, Southern Miss.	20	564	28.2
7.	Frank Oleynick, Seattle	26	709	27.3
8.	Don Scaife, Arkansas St.	25	678	27.1
9.	Marshall Rogers, Tex.-Pan Am.	22	588	26.7
10.	Alvan Adams, Oklahoma	26	691	26.6

1976

Rk.	Player, School	G	Pts.	Avg.
1.	Marshall Rogers, Tex.-Pan Am.	25	919	36.8
2.	Freeman Williams, Portland St.	27	834	30.9
3.	Terry Furlow, Michigan St.	27	793	29.4
4.	Adrian Dantley, Notre Dame	29	829	28.6
5.	Kenny Carr, North Carolina St.	30	798	26.6
6.	Lee Dixon, Hard-Simmons	27	707	26.2
7.	Tracy Tripucka, Lafayette	26	679	26.1
8.	Otis Birdsong, Houston	28	730	26.1
9.	Ernie Grunfeld, Tennessee	27	683	25.3
10.	Willie Smith, Missouri	31	783	25.3

1977

Rk.	Player, School	G	Pts.	Avg.
1.	Freeman Williams, Portland St.	26	1,010	38.8
2.	Anthony Roberts, Oral Roberts	28	951	34.0
3.	Larry Bird, Indiana St.	28	918	32.8
4.	Otis Birdsong, Houston	36	1,090	30.3
5.	Rich Laurel, Hofstra	30	908	30.3
6.	Calvin Natt, La.-Monroe	27	782	29.0
7.	Mike McConathy, Louisiana Tech	26	716	27.5
8.	Roger Phegley, Bradley	27	739	27.4
9.	Billy Reynolds, Northwestern St.	26	686	26.4
10.	Tony Hanson, Connecticut	27	702	26.0

1978

Rk.	Player, School	G	Pts.	Avg.
1.	Freeman Williams, Portland St.	27	969	35.9
2.	Larry Bird, Indiana St.	32	959	30.0
3.	Purvis Short, Jackson St.	22	650	29.5
4.	Oliver Mack, East Carolina	25	699	28.0
5.	Roger Phegley, Bradley	24	663	27.6
6.	Frankie Sanders, Southern U.	27	740	27.4
7.	Ron Carter, VMI	28	736	26.3
8.	John Gerdy, Davidson	26	670	25.8
9.	Michael Brooks, La Salle	28	696	24.9
10.	Mike Mitchell, Auburn	27	671	24.9

1979

Rk.	Player, School	G	Pts.	Avg.
1.	Lawrence Butler, Idaho St.	27	812	30.1
2.	Larry Bird, Indiana St.	34	973	28.6
3.	Nick Galis, Seton Hall	27	743	27.5
4.	James Tillman, Eastern Ky.	29	780	26.9
5.	Paul Dawkins, Northern Ill.	26	695	26.7
6.	John Gerdy, Davidson	27	721	26.7
7.	Ernie Hill, Oklahoma City	29	771	26.6
8.	John Stroud, Mississippi	27	709	26.3
9.	John Manning, North Texas	27	699	25.9
10.	Steve Stielper, James Madison	26	668	25.7

1980

Rk.	Player, School	G	Pts.	Avg.
1.	Tony Murphy, Southern	29	932	32.1
2.	Lewis Lloyd, Drake	27	815	30.2
3.	Harry Kelly, Texas Southern	26	753	29.0
4.	Kenny Page, New Mexico	28	784	28.0
5.	James Tillman, Eastern Ky.	27	734	27.2
6.	Earl Belcher, St. Bonaventure	24	646	26.9
7.	Russel Bowers, American	27	726	26.9
8.	Carl Nicks, Indiana St.	27	723	26.8
9.	Mark Aguirre, DePaul	28	749	26.8
10.	Andrew Toney, La.-Lafayette	24	627	26.1

1981

Rk.	Player, School	G	Pts.	Avg.
1.	Zam Fredrick, South Carolina	27	781	28.9
2.	Mike Ferrara, Colgate	27	772	28.6
3.	Kevin Magee, UC Irvine	27	743	27.5
4.	Lewis Lloyd, Drake	29	762	26.3
5.	Rob Williams, Houston	30	749	25.0
6.	Rubin Jackson, Oklahoma City	29	719	24.8
7.	Frank Edwards, Cleveland St.	27	664	24.6
8.	Earl Belcher, St. Bonaventure	26	637	24.5
9.	Danny Ainge, BYU	32	787	24.4
10.	Mike McGee, Michigan	30	732	24.4

1982

Rk.	Player, School	G	Pts.	Avg.
1.	Harry Kelly, Texas Southern	29	862	29.7
2.	Ricky Pierce, Rice	30	805	26.8
3.	Dan Callandrillo, Seton Hall	27	698	25.9
4.	Kevin Magee, UC Irvine	29	732	25.2
5.	Quintin Dailey, San Francisco	30	755	25.2
6.	Willie Jackson, Centenary (La.)	29	693	23.9
7.	Mitchell Wiggins, Florida St.	22	523	23.8
8.	Perry Moss, Northeastern	30	710	23.7
9.	Melvin McLaughlin, Central Mich.	25	581	23.2
10.	Joe Jakubick, Akron	26	594	22.8

1983

Rk.	Player, School	G	Pts.	Avg.
1.	Harry Kelly, Texas Southern	29	835	28.8
2.	Jeff Malone, Mississippi St.	29	777	26.8
3.	Carlos Yates, George Mason	27	723	26.8
4.	Charlie Bradley, South Florida	32	855	26.7
5.	Joe Jakubick, Akron	29	774	26.7
6.	Greg Goorjian, Loyola Marymount	23	601	26.1
7.	Alfredrick Hughes, Loyola (Ill.)	29	744	25.7
8.	Wayman Tisdale, Oklahoma	33	810	24.5
9.	Kenneth Lyons, North Texas St.	30	728	24.3
10.	Willie Jackson, Centenary (La.)	29	697	24.0

1984

Rk.	Player, School	G	Pts.	Avg.
1.	Joe Jakublick, Akron	27	814	30.1
2.	Lewis Jackson, Alabama St.	28	812	29.0
3.	Devin Durrant, BYU	31	866	27.9
4.	Alfredrick Hughes, Loyola (Ill.)	29	800	27.6
5.	Wayman Tisdale, Oklahoma	34	919	27.0
6.	Joe Dumars, McNeese St.	31	817	26.4
7.	Brett Crawford, U.S. Int'l	25	614	24.6
8.	Michael Cage, San Diego St.	28	686	24.5
9.	Steve Burtt, Iona	31	749	24.2
10.	Leon Wood, Cal. St.-Fullerton	30	719	24.0

1985

Rk.	Player, School	G	Pts.	Avg.
1.	Xavier McDaniel, Wichita St.	31	844	27.2
2.	Alfredrick Hughes, Loyola (Ill.)	33	868	26.3
3.	Dan Palombizio, Ball St.	29	762	26.3
4.	Joe Dumars, McNeese St.	27	697	25.8
5.	Terry Catledge, South Ala.	28	718	25.6
6.	Derrick Gervin, Tex.-San Antonio	28	718	25.6
7.	Wayman Tisdale, Oklahoma	37	932	25.2
8.	Keith Smith, Loyola Marymount	27	678	25.1
9.	Sam Mitchell, Mercer	31	774	25.0
10.	Ron Harper, Miami (Ohio)	31	772	24.9

1986

Rk.	Player, School	G	Pts.	Avg.
1.	Terrance Bailey, Wagner	29	854	29.4
2.	Scott Skiles, Michigan St.	31	850	27.4
3.	Joe Yezback, U.S. Int'l	28	755	27.0
4.	Reggie Miller, UCLA	29	750	25.9
5.	Ron Harper, Miami (Ohio)	31	757	24.4
6.	Dell Curry, Virginia Tech	30	722	24.1
7.	Reggie Lewis, Northeastern	30	714	23.8
8.	Len Bias, Maryland	32	743	23.2
9.	Frank Ross, American	28	645	23.0
10.	Walter Berry, St. John's (N.Y.)	36	828	23.0

1987

Rk.	Player, School	G	Pts.	Avg.
1.	Kevin Houston, Army	29	953	32.9
2.	Dennis Hopson, Ohio St.	33	958	29.0
3.	Dave Robinson, Navy	32	903	28.2
4.	Terrance Bailey, Wagner	28	788	28.1
5.	Hersey Hawkins, Bradley	29	788	28.1
6.	Darrin Fitzgerald, Butler	28	734	26.2
7.	Gay Elmore, VMI	28	713	25.5
8.	Frank Ross, American	27	683	25.3
9.	Daren Queenan, Lehigh	29	720	24.8
10.	Byron Larkin, Xavier	32	792	24.7

1988

Rk.	Player, School	G	Pts.	Avg.
1.	Hershey Hawkins, Bradley	31	1,125	36.3
2.	Daren Queenan, Lehigh	31	882	28.5
3.	Anthony Mason, Tennessee St.	28	783	28.0
4.	Gerald Hayward, Loyola (Ill.)	29	756	26.1
5.	Jeff Martin, Murray St.	31	806	26.0
6.	Marty Simmons, Evansville	29	750	25.9
7.	Steve Middleton, Southern Ill.	28	711	25.4
8.	Jeff Grayer, Iowa St.	32	811	25.3
9.	Byron Larkin, Xavier	30	758	25.3
10.	Skip Henderson, Marshall	32	804	25.1

1989

Rk.	Player, School	G	Pts.	Avg.
1.	Hank Gathers, Loyola Marymount	31	1,015	32.7
2.	Chris Jackson, Louisiana St.	32	965	30.2
3.	Lionel Simmons, La Salle	32	908	28.4
4.	Gerald Glass, Mississippi	30	841	28.0
5.	Blue Edwards, East Caro.	29	773	26.7
6.	Raymond Dudley, Air Force	28	746	26.6
7.	Bimbo Coles, Virginia Tech	27	717	26.6
8.	Michael Smith, BYU	29	765	26.4
9.	Stacey King, Oklahoma	33	859	26.0
10.	John Taft, Marshall	27	701	26.0

1990

Rk.	Player, School	G	Pts.	Avg.
1.	Bo Kimble, Loyola Marymount	32	1,131	35.3
2.	Kevin Bradshaw, U.S. Int'l	28	875	31.3
3.	Dave Jamerson, Ohio	28	874	31.2
4.	Alphonzo Ford, Miss. Val.	27	808	29.9
5.	Steve Rogers, Alabama St.	28	831	29.7
6.	Hank Gathers, Loyola Marymount	26	754	29.0
7.	Darryl Brooks, Tennessee St.	24	690	28.8
8.	Chris Jackson, LSU	32	889	27.8
9.	Dennis Scott, Georgia Tech	35	970	27.7
10.	Mark Stevenson, Duquesne	29	788	27.2

1991

Rk.	Player, School	G	Pts.	Avg.
1.	Kevin Bradshaw, U.S. Int'l	28	1,054	37.6
2.	Alphonso Ford, Miss. Valley	28	915	32.7
3.	Von McDade, Milwaukee	28	830	29.6
4.	Steve Rogers, Alabama St.	29	852	29.4
5.	Terrell Lowery, Loyola Marymount	31	884	28.5
6.	Bibby Phills, Southern U.	28	795	28.4
7.	Shaquille O'Neal, LSU	28	774	27.6
8.	John Taft, Marshall	28	764	27.3
9.	Rodney Monroe, North Caro. St.	31	836	27.0
10.	Terrell Brandon, Oregon	28	745	26.6

1992

Rk.	Player, School	G	Pts.	Avg.
1.	Brett Roberts, Morehead St.	29	815	28.1
2.	Vin Baker, Hartford	27	745	27.6
3.	Alphonso Ford, Mississippi Val.	26	714	27.5
4.	Randy Woods, La Salle	31	847	27.3
5.	Steve Rogers, Alabama St.	28	764	27.3
6.	Walt Williams, Maryland	29	776	26.8
7.	Harold Miner, Southern California	30	789	26.3
8.	Terrell Lowery, Loyola Marymount	26	675	26.0
9.	Reggie Cunnigham, Beth.-Cook.	29	744	25.7
10.	Parrish Casebier, Evansville	25	634	25.4

1993

Rk.	Player, School	G	Pts.	Avg.
1.	Greg Guy, Tex.-Pan American	19	556	29.3
2.	J.R.Rider, UNLV	28	814	29.1
3.	John Best, Tennessee Tech	28	799	28.5
4.	Vin Baker, Hartford	28	792	28.3
5.	Lindsey Hunter, Jackson St.	34	907	26.7
6.	Alphonzo Ford, Mississippi Val.	28	728	26.0
7.	Bill Edwards, Wright St.	30	757	25.2
8.	Billy Ross, Appalachian St.	28	683	24.4
9.	Glenn Robinson, Purdue	28	676	24.1
10.	Kenneth Sykes, Grambling	27	644	23.9

1994

Rk.	Player, School	G	Pts.	Avg.
1.	Glenn Robinson, Purdue	34	1,030	30.3
2.	Rob Feaster, Holy Cross	28	785	28.0
3.	Jervaughn Scales, Southern U.	27	733	27.1
4.	Frankie King, Western Caro.	28	752	26.9
5.	Tucker Neale, Colgate	29	771	26.6
6.	Eddie Benton, Vermont	26	687	26.4
7.	Doremus Bennerman, Siena	33	858	26.0
8.	Tony Dumas, UMKC	29	753	26.0
9.	Otis Jones, Air Force	26	663	25.5
10.	Izett Buchanan, Marist	27	685	25.4

1995

Rk.	Player, School	G	Pts.	Avg.
1.	Kurt Thomas, TCU	27	781	28.9
2.	Frankie King, Western Caro.	28	743	26.5
3.	Kenny Sykes, Grambling	26	684	26.3
4.	Sherell Ford, Ill.-Chicago	27	707	26.2
5.	Tim Roberts, Southern U.	26	680	26.2
6.	Kareem Townes, La Salle	27	699	25.9
7.	Joe Griffin, Long Island	28	723	25.8
8.	Shawn Respert, Michigan St.	28	716	25.6
9.	Rob Feaster, Holy Cross	27	672	24.9
10.	Shannon Smith, Wis.-Milw.	27	661	24.5

1996

Rk.	Player, School	G	Pts.	Avg.
1.	Kevin Granger, Texas Southern	24	648	27.0
2.	Marcus Brown, Murray St.	29	767	26.4
3.	Bubba Wells, Austin Peay	30	789	26.3
4.	JaFonde Williams, Hampton	26	669	25.7
5.	Bonzi Wells, Ball St.	28	712	25.4
6.	Anquell McCollum, Western Caro.	30	751	25.0
7.	Allen Iverson, Georgetown	37	926	25.0
8.	Eddie Benton, Vermont	26	636	24.5
9.	Matt Alosa, New Hampshire	26	624	24.0
10.	Ray Allen, Connecticut	35	818	23.4

1997

Rk.	Player, School	G	Pts.	Avg.
1.	Charles Jones, Long Island	30	903	30.1
2.	Ed Gray, California	26	644	24.8
3.	Adonal Foyle, Colgate	28	682	24.4
4.	Raymond Tutt, UC Santa Barbara	27	649	24.0
5.	Antonio Daniels, Bowling Green	32	767	24.0
6.	Donnie Carr, La Salle	27	646	23.9
7.	Oliver Saint-Jean, San Jose St.	26	619	23.8
8.	James Cotton, Long Beach St.	27	634	23.5
9.	Roderick Blakney, South Caro. St.	28	655	23.4
10.	Cory Carr, Texas Tech	28	646	23.1

1998

Rk.	Player, School	G	Pts.	Avg.
1.	Charles Jones, Long Island	30	869	29.0
2.	Earl Boykins, Eastern Mich.	29	746	25.7
3.	Lee Nailon, TCU	32	796	24.9
4.	Brett Eppehimer, Lehigh	27	667	24.7
5.	Cory Carr, Texas Tech	27	628	23.3
6.	Pat Garrity, Notre Dame	27	627	23.2
7.	Mike Powell, Loyola (Md.)	28	647	23.1
8.	Bonzi Wells, Ball St.	29	662	22.8
9.	Xavier Singletary, Howard	23	514	22.3
10.	Michael Olowokandi, Pacific	33	734	22.2

1999

Rk.	Player, School	G	Pts.	Avg.
1.	Alvin Young, Niagara	29	728	25.1
2.	Ray Minlend, St. Francis (N.Y.)	28	680	24.3
3.	Wally Szczerbiak, Miami (Ohio)	32	775	24.2
4.	Brian Merriweather, Tex.-Pan Am.	27	641	23.7
5.	Damian Woolfolk, Norfolk St.	27	635	23.5
6.	Quincy Lewis, Minnesota	27	625	23.1
7.	Jason Hartman, Portland St.	28	639	22.8
8.	Lee Nailon, TCU	31	707	22.8
9.	Maurice Evans, Wichita St.	28	632	22.6
10.	Harold Arceneaux, Weber St.	32	713	22.3

2000

Rk.	Player, School	G	Pts.	Avg.
1.	Courtney Alexander, Fresno St.	27	669	24.8
2.	SirValiant Brown, Geo. Washington	30	738	24.6
3.	Ronnie McCollum, Centenary (La.)	28	667	23.8
4.	Eddie House, Arizona St.	32	736	23.0
5.	Harold Arceneaux, Weber St.	28	644	23.0
6.	Rashad Phillips, Detroit	32	735	23.0
7.	Demond Stewart, Niagara	29	665	22.9
8.	Marcus Fizer, Iowa St.	37	844	22.8
9.	Craig Claxton, Hofstra	31	706	22.8
10.	Troy Murphy, Notre Dame	37	839	22.7

2001

Rk.	Player, School	G	Pts.	Avg.
1.	Ronnie McCollum, Centenary (La.)	27	787	29.1
2.	Kyle Hill, Eastern Ill.	31	737	23.8
3.	DeWayne Jefferson, Miss. Val.	27	637	23.6
4.	Tarise Bryson, Illinois St.	30	685	22.8
5.	Henry Domercant, Eastern Ill.	31	706	22.8
6.	Rahsad Phillips, Detroit	35	785	22.4
7.	Brandon Wolfram, UTEP	32	714	22.3
8.	Rasual Butler, La Salle	29	641	22.1
9.	Brandon Armstrong, Pepperdine	31	684	22.1
10.	Marvin O'Connor, St. Joseph's	32	706	22.1

2002

Rk.	Player, School	G	Pts.	Avg.
1.	Jason Conley, VMI	28	820	29.3
2.	Henry Domercant, Eastern Ill.	31	817	26.4
3.	Mire Chatman, Tex.-Pan American	29	760	26.2
4.	Ernest Bremer, St. Bonaventure	30	738	24.6
5.	Melvin Ely, Fresno St.	28	653	23.3
6.	Lynn Greer, Temple	31	719	23.2
7.	Nick Stapleton, Austin Peay	32	742	23.2
8.	Keith McLeod, Bowling Green	33	755	22.9
9.	Chris Davis, North Texas	29	653	22.5
10.	Ricky Minard, Morehead St.	29	646	22.3

2003

Rk.	Player, School	G	Pts.	Avg.
1.	Ruben Douglas, New Mexico	28	783	28.0
2.	Henry Domercant, Eastern Ill.	29	810	27.9
3.	Mike Helms, Oakland	28	752	26.9
4.	Michael Watson, UMKC	29	740	25.5
5.	Troy Bell, Boston College	31	781	25.2
6.	Keydren Clark, St. Peter's	29	722	24.9
7.	Luis Flores, Manhattan	30	739	24.6
8.	Chris Williams, Ball St.	30	736	24.5
9.	Mike Sweetney, Georgetown	34	776	22.8
10.	Kevin Martin, Western Caro.	24	546	22.8

2004

Rk.	Player, School	G	Pts.	Avg.
1.	Keydren Clark, St. Peter's	29	775	26.7
2.	Kevin Martin, Western Caro.	27	673	24.9
3.	David Hawkins, Temple	29	709	24.4
4.	Taylor Coppenrath, Vermont	24	579	24.1
5.	Luis Flores, Manhattan	31	744	24.0
6.	Michael Watson, UMKC	29	680	23.4
7.	Mike Helms, Oakland	30	695	23.2
8.	Odell Bradley, IUPUI	29	671	23.1
9.	Ike Diogu, Arizona St.	27	615	22.8
10.	Derrick Tarver, Akron	27	612	22.7

2005

Rk.	Player, School	G	Pts.	Avg.
1.	Keydren Clark, St. Peter's	28	721	25.8
2.	Taylor Coppenrath, Vermont	31	777	25.1
3.	Juan Mendez, Niagara	30	705	23.5
4.	Rob Monroe, Quinnipiac	26	589	22.7
5.	Bo McCalebb, New Orleans	30	679	22.6
6.	Ike Diogu, Arizona St.	32	724	22.6
7.	Tim Smith, East Tenn. St.	29	645	22.2
8.	Jose Juan Barea, Northeastern	30	665	22.2
9.	J.J. Redick, Duke	33	721	21.8
10.	Ryan Gomes, Providence	31	670	21.6

2006

Rk.	Player, School	G	Pts.	Avg.
1.	Adam Morrison, Gonzaga	33	926	28.1
2.	J.J. Redick, Duke	36	964	26.8
3.	Keydren Clark, St. Peter's	32	840	26.3
4.	Andre Collins, Loyola (Md.)	28	731	26.1
5.	Brion Rush, Grambling	21	541	25.8
6.	Quincy Douby, Rutgers	33	839	25.4
7.	Steve Burtt, Iona	31	780	25.2
8.	Rodney Stuckey, Eastern Wash.	30	726	24.2
9.	Alan Daniels, Lamar	31	730	23.5
10.	Trey Johnson, Jackson St.	32	751	23.5

2007

Rk.	Player, School	G	Pts.	Avg.
1.	Reggie Williams, VMI	33	928	28.1
2.	Trey Johnson, Jackson St.	35	947	27.1
3.	Morris Almond, Rice	32	844	26.4
4.	Kevin Durant, Texas	35	903	25.8
5.	Gary Neal, Towson	32	810	25.3
6.	Bo McCalebb, New Orleans	31	776	25.0
7.	Rodney Stuckey, Eastern Wash.	29	712	24.6
8.	Gerald Brown, Loyola (Md.)	29	643	22.2
9.	Stephen Curry, Davidson	34	730	21.5
10.	Jaycee Carroll, Utah St.	35	746	21.3

Annual Individual Champions

Scoring Average

Season	Player, Team	Ht.	Cl.	G	FG	FT	Pts.	Avg.
1948	Murray Wier, Iowa	5-9	Sr.	19	152	95	399	21.0
1949	Tony Lavelli, Yale	6-3	Sr.	30	228	215	671	22.4
1950	Paul Arizin, Villanova	6-3	Sr.	29	260	215	735	25.3
1951	Bill Mlkvy, Temple	6-4	Sr.	25	303	125	731	29.2
1952	Clyde Lovellette, Kansas	6-9	Sr.	28	315	165	795	28.4
1953	Frank Selvy, Furman	6-3	Jr.	25	272	194	738	29.5
1954	Frank Selvy, Furman	6-3	Sr.	29	427	*355	1,209	41.7
1955	Darrell Floyd, Furman	6-1	Jr.	25	344	209	897	35.9
1956	Darrell Floyd, Furman	6-1	Sr.	28	339	268	946	33.8
1957	Grady Wallace, South Carolina	6-4	Sr.	29	336	234	906	31.2
1958	Oscar Robertson, Cincinnati	6-5	So.	28	352	280	984	35.1
1959	Oscar Robertson, Cincinnati	6-5	Jr.	30	331	316	978	32.6
1960	Oscar Robertson, Cincinnati	6-5	Sr.	30	369	273	1,011	33.7
1961	Frank Burgess, Gonzaga	6-1	Sr.	26	304	234	842	32.4
1962	Billy McGill, Utah	6-9	Sr.	26	394	221	1,009	38.8
1963	Nick Werkman, Seton Hall	6-3	Jr.	22	221	208	650	29.5
1964	Howard Komives, Bowling Green	6-1	Sr.	23	292	260	844	36.7
1965	Rick Barry, Miami (Fla.)	6-7	Sr.	26	340	293	973	37.4
1966	Dave Schellhase, Purdue	6-4	Sr.	24	284	213	781	32.5
1967	Jim Walker, Providence	6-3	Sr.	28	323	205	851	30.4
1968	Pete Maravich, LSU	6-5	So.	26	432	274	1,138	43.8
1969	Pete Maravich, LSU	6-5	Jr.	26	433	282	1,148	44.2
1970	Pete Maravich, LSU	6-5	Sr.	31	*522	337	*1,381	*44.5
1971	Johnny Neumann, Mississippi	6-6	So.	23	366	191	923	40.1
1972	Dwight Lamar, La.-Lafayette	6-1	Jr.	29	429	196	1,054	36.3
1973	William Averitt, Pepperdine	6-1	Sr.	25	352	144	848	33.9
1974	Larry Fogle, Canisius	6-5	So.	25	326	183	835	33.4
1975	Bob McCurdy, Richmond	6-7	Sr.	26	321	213	855	32.9
1976	Marshall Rodgers, Tex.-Pan American	6-2	Sr.	25	361	197	919	36.8
1977	Freeman Williams, Portland St.	6-4	Jr.	26	417	176	1,010	38.8
1978	Freeman Williams, Portland St.	6-4	Sr.	27	410	149	969	35.9
1979	Lawrence Butler, Idaho St.	6-3	Sr.	27	310	192	812	30.1
1980	Tony Murphy, Southern U.	6-3	Sr.	29	377	178	932	32.1
1981	Zam Fredrick, South Carolina	6-2	Sr.	27	300	181	781	28.9
1982	Harry Kelly, Texas Southern	6-7	Jr.	29	336	190	862	29.7
1983	Harry Kelly, Texas Southern	6-7	Sr.	29	333	169	835	28.8
1984	Joe Jakubick, Akron	6-5	Sr.	27	304	206	814	30.1
1985	Xavier McDaniel, Wichita St.	6-8	Sr.	31	351	142	844	27.2
1986	Terrance Bailey, Wagner	6-2	Jr.	29	321	212	854	29.4
1987	Kevin Houston, Army	5-11	Sr.	29	311	268	953	32.9
1988	Hersey Hawkins, Bradley	6-3	Sr.	31	377	87	1,125	36.3
1989	Hank Gathers, Loyola Marymount	6-7	Jr.	31	419	0	177	1,015	32.7
1990	Bo Kimble, Loyola Marymount	6-5	Sr.	32	404	92	231	1,131	35.3
1991	Kevin Bradshaw, U.S. Int'l	6-6	Sr.	28	358	60	278	1,054	37.6
1992	Brett Roberts, Morehead St.	6-8	Sr.	29	278	66	193	815	28.1
1993	Greg Guy, Tex.-Pan American	6-1	Jr.	19	189	67	111	556	29.3
1994	Glenn Robinson, Purdue	6-8	Jr.	34	368	79	215	1,030	30.3
1995	Kurt Thomas, TCU	6-9	Sr.	27	288	3	202	781	28.9
1996	Kevin Granger, Texas Southern	6-3	Sr.	24	194	30	230	648	27.0
1997	Charles Jones, Long Island	6-3	Jr.	30	338	109	118	903	30.1
1998	Charles Jones, Long Island	6-3	Sr.	30	326	116	101	869	29.0
1999	Alvin Young, Niagara	6-3	Sr.	29	253	65	157	728	25.1
2000	Courtney Alexander, Fresno St.	6-6	Sr.	27	252	58	107	669	24.8
2001	Ronnie McCollum, Centenary (La.)	6-4	Sr.	27	244	85	214	787	29.1
2002	Jason Conley, VMI	6-5	Fr.	28	285	79	171	820	29.3
2003	Ruben Douglas, New Mexico	6-5	Sr.	28	218	94	253	783	28.0
2004	Keydren Clark, St. Peter's	5-8	So.	29	233	112	197	775	26.7
2005	Keydren Clark, St. Peter's	5-9	Jr.	28	230	109	152	721	25.8
2006	Adam Morrison, Gonzaga	6-8	Jr.	33	306	74	240	926	28.1
2007	Reggie Williams, VMI	6-5	Jr.	33	338	76	176	928	28.1

*record

Field-Goal Percentage

Season	Player, Team	Cl.	G	FG	FGA	Pct.
1948	Alex Peterson, Oregon St.	Jr.	27	89	187	47.6
1949	Ed Macauley, St. Louis	Sr.	26	144	275	52.4
1950	Jim Moran, Niagara	Jr.	27	98	185	53.0
1951	Don Meineke, Dayton	Jr.	32	240	469	51.2
1952	Art Spoelstra, Western Ky.	So.	31	178	345	51.6
1953	Vernon Stokes, St. Francis (N.Y)	Sr.	24	147	247	59.5
1954	Joe Holup, George Washington	So.	26	179	313	57.2
1955	Ed O'Connor, Manhattan	Sr.	23	147	243	60.5
1956	Joe Holup, George Washington	Sr.	26	200	309	64.7
1957	Bailey Howell, Mississippi St.	So.	25	217	382	56.8
1958	Ralph Crosthwaite, Western Ky.	Jr.	25	202	331	61.0
1959	Ralph Crosthwaite, Western Ky.	Sr.	26	191	296	64.5
1960	Jerry Lucas, Ohio St.	So.	27	283	444	63.7
1961	Jerry Lucas, Ohio St.	Jr.	27	256	411	62.3
1962	Jerry Lucas, Ohio St.	Sr.	28	237	388	61.1
1963	Lyle Harger, Houston	Sr.	26	193	294	65.6
1964	Terry Holland, Davidson	Sr.	26	135	214	63.1
1965	Tim Kehoe, St. Peter's	Sr.	19	138	209	66.0
1966	Julian Hammond, Tulsa	Sr.	29	172	261	65.9
1967	Lew Alcindor, UCLA	So.	30	346	519	66.7
1968	Joe Allen, Bradley	Sr.	28	258	394	65.5
1969	Lew Alcindor, UCLA	Sr.	30	303	477	63.5
1970	Willie Williams, Florida St.	Sr.	26	185	291	63.6
1971	John Belcher, Arkansas St.	Jr.	24	174	275	63.3
1972	Kent Martens, Abilene Christian	Sr.	21	136	204	66.7
1973	Elton Hayes, Lamar	Sr.	24	146	222	65.8
1974	Al Fleming, Arizona	So.	26	136	204	66.7
1975	Bernard King, Tennessee	Fr.	25	273	439	62.2
1976	Sidney Moncrief, Arkansas	Fr.	28	149	224	66.5
1977	Joe Senser, West Chester	So.	25	130	186	69.9
1978	Joe Senser, West Chester	Jr.	25	135	197	68.5
1979	Murray Brown, Florida St.	Jr.	29	237	343	69.1
1980	Steve Johnson, Oregon St.	Jr.	30	211	297	71.0
1981	Steve Johnson, Oregon St.	Sr.	28	235	315	*74.6
1982	Mark McNamara, California	Sr.	27	231	329	70.2
1983	Troy Lee Mikel, East Tenn. St.	Sr.	29	197	292	67.5
1984	Akeem Olajuwon, Houston	Jr.	37	249	369	67.5
1985	Keith Walker, Utica	Sr.	27	154	216	71.3
1986	Brad Daugherty, North Carolina	Sr.	34	284	438	64.8
1987	Alan Williams, Princeton	Sr.	25	163	232	70.3
1988	Arnell Jones, Boise St.	Sr.	30	187	283	66.1
1989	Dwayne Davis, Florida	So.	33	179	248	72.2
1990	Lee Campbell, Missouri St.	Sr.	29	192	275	69.8
1991	Oliver Miller, Arkansas	Jr.	38	254	361	70.4
1992	Charles Outlaw, Houston	Jr.	31	156	228	68.4
1993	Charles Outlaw, Houston	Sr.	30	196	298	65.8
1994	Mike Atkinson, Long Beach St.	Jr.	26	141	203	69.5
1995	Shane Kline-Ruminski, Bowling Green	Sr.	26	181	265	68.3
1996	Quadre Lollis, Montana St.	Sr.	30	212	314	67.5
1997	Todd MacCulloch, Washington	So.	28	163	241	67.6
1998	Todd MacCulloch, Washington	Jr.	30	225	346	65.0
1999	Todd MacCulloch, Washington	Sr.	29	210	317	66.2
2000	Brendan Haywood, North Carolina	Jr.	36	191	274	69.7
2001	Michael Bradley, Villanova	Jr.	31	254	367	69.2
2002	Adam Mark, Belmont	So.	26	150	212	70.8
2003	Adam Mark, Belmont	Jr.	28	199	297	67.0
2004	Nigel Dixon, Western Ky.	Sr.	28	179	264	67.8
2005	Bruce Brown, Hampton	Jr.	30	178	269	66.2
2006	Randall Hanke, Providence	So.	27	149	220	67.7
2007	Mike Freeman, Hampton	Fr.	30	162	239	67.8

*record

Three-Point Field Goals Made Per Game

Season	Player, Team	Cl.	G	3FG	Avg.
1987	Darrin Fitzgerald, Butler	Sr.	28	158	*5.64
1988	Timothy Pollard, Mississippi Val.	Jr.	28	132	4.71
1989	Timothy Pollard, Mississippi Val.	Sr.	28	124	4.43
1990	Dave Jamerson, Ohio	Sr.	28	131	4.68
1991	Bobby Phills, Southern U.	Sr.	28	123	4.39
1992	Doug Day, Radford	Jr.	29	117	4.03
1993	Bernard Haslett, Southern Miss.	Jr.	26	109	4.19
1994	Chris Brown, UC Irvine	Jr.	26	122	4.69
1995	Mitch Taylor, Southern U.	Jr.	25	109	4.36
1996	Dominick Young, Fresno St.	Jr.	29	120	4.14

Season	Player, Team	Cl.	G	3FG	Avg.
1997	William Fourche, Southern U.	Sr.	27	122	4.52
1998	Curtis Staples, Virginia	Sr.	30	130	4.33
1999	Brian Merriweather, Tex.-Pan American	So.	27	110	4.07
2000	Brian Merriweather, Tex.-Pan American	Jr.	28	114	4.07
2001	DeWayne Jefferson, Mississippi Val.	Sr.	27	107	3.96
2002	Cain Doliboa, Wright St.	Sr.	28	104	3.71
2003	Terrence Woods, Florida A&M	Jr.	28	139	4.96
2004	Terrence Woods, Florida A&M	Sr.	31	140	4.52
2005	Brendan Plavich, Charlotte	Sr.	29	114	3.93
2006	Andre Collins, Loyola (Md.)	Sr.	28	118	4.21
2007	Stephen Sir, Northern Ariz.	Sr.	30	124	4.13

*record

Three-Point Field-Goal Percentage

Season	Player, Team	Cl.	G	3FG	3FGA	Pct.
1987	Reginald Jones, Prairie View	Jr.	28	64	112	57.1
1988	Glenn Tropf, Holy Cross	Jr.	29	52	82	*63.4
1989	Dave Calloway, Monmouth	So.	28	48	82	58.5
1990	Matt Lapin, Princeton	Sr.	27	71	133	53.4
1991	Keith Jennings, East Tenn. St.	Sr.	33	84	142	59.2
1992	Sean Wightman, Western Mich.	Jr.	30	48	76	63.2
1993	Jeff Anderson, Kent St.	Jr.	26	44	82	53.7
1994	Brent Kell, Evansville	So.	29	62	123	50.4
1995	Brian Jackson, Evansville	Jr.	27	53	95	55.8
1996	Joe Stafford, Western Caro.	Jr.	30	58	110	52.7
1997	Kent McCausland, Iowa	So.	29	70	134	52.2
1998	Jim Cantamessa, Siena	So.	29	66	117	56.4
1999	Rodney Thomas, IUPUI	Jr.	26	59	113	52.2
2000	Jonathan Whitworth, Middle Tenn.	Jr.	28	50	99	50.5
2001	Amory Sanders, Southeast Mo. St.	Sr.	24	53	95	55.8
2002	Dante Swanson, Tulsa	Jr.	33	73	149	49.0
2003	Jeff Schiffner, Penn	Jr.	28	74	150	49.3
2004	Brad Lechtenberg, San Diego	Sr.	23	71	139	51.1
2005	Salim Stoudamire, Arizona	Sr.	36	120	238	50.4
2006	Stephen Sir, Northern Ariz.	Sr.	32	93	190	48.9
2007	Josh Carter, Texas A&M	So.	34	86	172	50.0
	Jeremy Crouch, Bradley	Jr.	27	83	166	50.0

*record

Free-Throw Percentage

Season	Player, Team	Cl.	G	FT	FTA	Pct.
1948	Sam Urzetta, St. Bonaventure	So.	22	59	64	92.2
1949	Bill Schroer, Valparaiso	So.	24	59	68	86.8
1950	Sam Urzetta, St. Bonaventure	Sr.	22	54	61	88.5
1951	Jay Handlan, Wash. & Lee	Jr.	22	148	172	86.0
1952	Sy Chadroff, Miami (Fla.)	Sr.	22	99	123	80.5
1953	John Weber, Yale	Sr.	24	117	141	83.0
1954	Dick Daugherty, Arizona St.	Sr.	23	75	86	87.2
1955	Jim Scott, West Tex. A&M	Sr.	23	153	171	89.5
1956	Bill Von Weyhe, Rhode Island	Jr.	25	180	208	86.5
1957	Ernie Wiggins, Wake Forest	Sr.	28	93	106	87.7
1958	Semi Mintz, Davidson	Sr.	24	105	119	88.2
1959	Arlen Clark, Oklahoma St.	Sr.	25	201	236	85.2
1960	Jack Waters, Mississippi	Jr.	24	103	118	87.3
1961	Stew Sherard, Army	Jr.	24	135	154	87.7
1962	Tommy Boyer, Arkansas	Jr.	23	125	134	93.3
1963	Tommy Boyer, Arkansas	Sr.	24	147	161	91.3
1964	Rick Park, Tulsa	Jr.	25	121	134	90.3
1965	Bill Bradley, Princeton	Sr.	29	273	308	88.6
1966	Bill Blair, Providence	Sr.	27	101	112	90.2
1967	Bob Lloyd, Rutgers	Sr.	29	255	277	92.1
1968	Joe Heiser, Princeton	Sr.	26	117	130	90.0
1969	Bill Justus, Tennessee	Sr.	28	133	147	90.5
1970	Steve Kaplan, Rutgers	So.	23	102	110	92.7
1971	Greg Starrick, Southern Ill.	Jr.	23	119	132	90.2
1972	Greg Starrick, Southern Ill.	Sr.	26	148	160	92.5
1973	Don Smith, Dayton	Jr.	26	111	122	91.0
1974	Rickey Medlock, Arkansas	Jr.	26	87	95	91.6
1975	Frank Oleynick, Seattle	Sr.	26	135	152	88.8
1976	Tad Dufelmeier, Loyola (Ill.)	Jr.	25	71	80	88.8
1977	Robert Smith, UNLV	Sr.	32	98	106	92.5
1978	Carlos Gibson, Marshall	Jr.	28	84	89	94.4
1979	Darrell Mauldin, Campbell	Jr.	26	70	76	92.1
1980	Brian Magid, George Washington	Sr.	26	79	85	92.9
1981	Dave Hildahl, Portland St.	Sr.	21	76	82	92.7
1982	Rod Foster, UCLA	Jr.	27	95	100	95.0
1983	Rob Gonzalez, Colorado	Sr.	28	75	82	91.5

Season	Player, Team	Cl.	G	FT	FTA	Pct.
1984	Steve Alford, Indiana	Fr.	31	137	150	91.3
1985	Craig Collins, Penn St.	Sr.	27	94	98	95.9
1986	Jim Barton, Dartmouth	Fr.	26	65	69	94.2
1987	Kevin Houston, Army	Sr.	29	268	294	91.2
1988	Steve Henson, Kansas St.	So.	34	111	120	92.5
1989	Michael Smith, BYU	Sr.	29	160	173	92.5
1990	Rob Robbins, New Mexico	Jr.	34	101	108	93.5
1991	Darin Archbold, Butler	Jr.	29	187	205	91.2
1992	Don MacLean, UCLA	Sr.	32	197	214	92.1
1993	Josh Grant, Utah	Sr.	31	104	113	92.0
1994	Danny Basile, Marist	So.	27	84	89	94.4
1995	Greg Bibb, Tennessee Tech	Jr.	27	106	117	90.6
1996	Mike Dillard, Sam Houston St.	Jr.	25	63	68	92.6
1997	Aaron Zobrist, Bradley	Sr.	30	77	85	90.6
1998	Matt Sundblad, Lamar	Jr.	27	96	104	92.3
1999	Lonnie Cooper, Louisiana Tech	Sr.	25	70	76	92.1
2000	Clay McKnight, Pacific	Sr.	24	74	78	94.9
2001	Gary Buchanan, Villanova	So.	31	97	103	94.2
2002	Cary Cochran, Nebraska	Sr.	28	71	77	92.2
2003	Steve Drabyn, Belmont	Jr.	29	78	82	95.1
2004	Blake Ahearn, Missouri St.	Fr.	33	117	120	*97.5
2005	Blake Ahearn, Missouri St.	So.	32	90	95	94.7
2006	Blake Ahearn, Missouri St.	Jr.	31	117	125	93.6
2007	Derek Raivio, Gonzaga	Sr.	34	148	154	96.1

*record

Rebound Average

Season	Player, Team	Ht.	Cl.	G	Reb.	Avg.
1951	Ernie Beck, Penn	6-4	So.	27	556	20.6
1952	Bill Hannon, Army	6-3	So.	17	355	20.9
1953	Ed Conlin, Fordham	6-5	So.	26	612	23.5
1954	Art Quimby, Connecticut	6-5	Jr.	26	588	22.6
1955	Charlie Slack, Marshall	6-5	Jr.	21	538	*25.6
1956	Joe Holup, George Washington	6-6	Sr.	26	604	†.256
1957	Elgin Baylor, Seattle	6-6	Jr.	25	508	†.235
1958	Alex Ellis, Niagara	6-5	Sr.	25	536	†.262
1959	Leroy Wright, Pacific	6-8	Jr.	26	652	†.238
1960	Leroy Wright, Pacific	6-8	Sr.	17	380	†.234
1961	Jerry Lucas, Ohio St.	6-8	Jr.	27	470	†.198
1962	Jerry Lucas, Ohio St.	6-8	Sr.	28	499	†.211
1963	Paul Silas, Creighton	6-7	Sr.	27	557	20.6
1964	Bob Pelkington, Xavier	6-7	Sr.	26	567	21.8
1965	Toby Kimball, Connecticut	6-8	Sr.	23	483	21.0
1966	Jim Ware, Oklahoma City	6-8	Sr.	29	607	20.9
1967	Dick Cunningham, Murray St.	6-10	Jr.	22	479	21.8
1968	Neal Walk, Florida	6-10	Jr.	25	494	19.8
1969	Spencer Haywood, Detroit	6-8	So.	22	472	21.5
1970	Artis Gilmore, Jacksonville	7-2	Jr.	28	621	22.2
1971	Artis Gilmore, Jacksonville	7-2	Sr.	26	603	23.2
1972	Kermit Washington, American	6-8	Jr.	23	455	19.8
1973	Kermit Washington, American	6-8	Sr.	22	439	20.0
1974	Marvin Barnes, Providence	6-9	Sr.	32	597	18.7
1975	John Irving, Hofstra	6-9	So.	21	323	15.4
1976	Sam Pellom, Buffalo	6-8	So.	26	420	16.2
1977	Glenn Mosley, Seton Hall	6-8	Sr.	29	473	16.3
1978	Ken Williams, North Texas	6-7	Sr.	28	411	14.7
1979	Monti Davis, Tennessee St.	6-7	Jr.	26	421	16.2
1980	Larry Smith, Alcorn St.	6-8	Sr.	26	392	15.1
1981	Darryl Watson, Mississippi Val.	6-7	Sr.	27	379	14.0
1982	LaSalle Thompson, Texas	6-10	Jr.	27	365	13.5
1983	Xavier McDaniel, Wichita St.	6-7	So.	28	403	14.4
1984	Akeem Olajuwon, Houston	7-0	Jr.	37	500	13.5
1985	Xavier McDaniel, Wichita St.	6-8	Sr.	31	460	14.8
1986	David Robinson, Navy	6-11	Jr.	35	455	13.0
1987	Jerome Lane, Pittsburgh	6-6	So.	33	444	13.5
1988	Kenny Miller, Loyola (Ill.)	6-9	Fr.	29	395	13.6
1989	Hank Gathers, Loyola Marymount	6-7	Jr.	31	426	13.7
1990	Anthony Bonner, St. Louis	6-8	Sr.	33	456	13.8
1991	Shaquille O'Neal, LSU	7-1	So.	28	411	14.7
1992	Popeye Jones, Murray St.	6-8	Sr.	30	431	14.4
1993	Warren Kidd, Middle Tenn.	6-9	Sr.	26	386	14.8
1994	Jerome Lambert, Baylor	6-8	Jr.	24	355	14.8
1995	Kurt Thomas, TCU	6-9	Sr.	27	393	14.6
1996	Marcus Mann, Mississippi Val.	6-8	Sr.	29	394	13.6
1997	Tim Duncan, Wake Forest	6-11	Sr.	31	457	14.7
1998	Ryan Perryman, Dayton	6-7	Sr.	33	412	12.5
1999	Ian McGinnis, Dartmouth	6-8	So.	26	317	12.2
2000	Darren Phillip, Fairfield	6-7	Sr.	29	405	14.0
2001	Chris Marcus, Western Ky.	7-1	Jr.	31	374	12.1
2002	Jeremy Bishop, Quinnipiac	6-6	Jr.	29	347	12.0

Season	Player, Team	Ht.	Cl.	G	Reb.	Avg.
2003	Brandon Hunter, Ohio	6-7	Sr.	30	378	12.6
2004	Paul Millsap, Louisiana Tech	6-7	Fr.	30	374	12.5
2005	Paul Millsap, Louisiana Tech	6-8	So.	29	360	12.4
2006	Paul Millsap, Louisiana Tech	6-8	Jr.	33	438	13.3
2007	Rashad Jones-Jennings, Ark.-Little Rock	6-8	Sr.	30	392	13.1

*record; †From 1956 through 1962, championship was determined on highest individual recoveries out of total by both teams in all games.

Assist Average

Season	Player, Team	Cl.	G	Ast.	Avg.
1951	Bill Walker, Toledo	Sr.	29	210	7.24
1952	Tom O'Toole, Boston College	Sr.	27	213	7.89
1984	Craig Lathen, Ill.-Chicago	Jr.	29	274	9.45
1985	Rob Weingard, Hofstra	Sr.	24	228	9.50
1986	Mark Jackson, St. John's (N.Y.)	Jr.	36	328	9.11
1987	Avery Johnson, Southern U.	Jr.	31	333	10.74
1988	Avery Johnson, Southern U.	Sr.	30	399	*13.30
1989	Glenn Williams, Holy Cross	Sr.	28	278	9.93
1990	Todd Lehmann, Drexel	Sr.	28	260	9.29
1991	Chris Corchiani, North Carolina St.	Sr.	31	299	9.65
1992	Van Usher, Tennessee Tech	Sr.	29	254	8.76
1993	Sam Crawford, New Mexico St.	Sr.	34	310	9.12
1994	Jason Kidd, California	So.	30	272	9.07
1995	Nelson Haggerty, Baylor	Sr.	28	284	10.14
1996	Raimonds Miglinieks, UC Irvine	Sr.	27	230	8.52
1997	Kenny Mitchell, Dartmouth	Sr.	26	203	7.81
1998	Ahlon Lewis, Arizona St.	Sr.	32	294	9.19
1999	Doug Gottlieb, Oklahoma St.	Jr.	34	299	8.79
2000	Mark Dickel, UNLV	Sr.	31	280	9.03
2001	Markus Carr, Cal St. Northridge	Jr.	32	286	8.94
2002	T.J. Ford, Texas	Fr.	33	273	8.27
2003	Martell Bailey, Ill.-Chicago	Jr.	30	244	8.13
2004	Greg Davis, Troy.	Sr.	31	256	8.26
2005	Damitrius Coleman, Mercer.	Jr.	28	224	8.00
	Will Funn, Portland St.	Sr.	28	224	8.00
2006	Jared Jordan, Marist	Jr.	29	247	8.52
2007	Jared Jordan, Marist	Sr.	33	286	8.67

*record

Blocked-Shot Average

Season	Player, Team	Cl.	G	Blk.	Avg.
1986	David Robinson, Navy	Jr.	35	207	5.91
1987	David Robinson, Navy	Sr.	32	144	4.50
1988	Rodney Blake, St. Joseph's	Sr.	29	116	4.00

Season	Player, Team	Cl.	G	Blk.	Avg.
1989	Alonzo Mourning, Georgetown	Fr.	34	169	4.97
1990	Kenny Green, Rhode Island	Sr.	26	124	4.77
1991	Shawn Bradley, BYU	Fr.	34	177	5.21
1992	Shaquille O'Neal, LSU	Jr.	30	157	5.23
1993	Theo Ratliff, Wyoming	Jr.	28	124	4.43
1994	Grady Livingston, Howard	Jr.	26	115	4.42
1995	Keith Closs, Central Conn. St.	Fr.	26	139	5.35
1996	Keith Closs, Central Conn. St.	So.	28	178	6.36
1997	Adonal Foyle, Colgate	Jr.	28	180	*6.43
1998	Jerome James, Florida A&M	Sr.	27	125	4.63
1999	Tarvis Williams, Hampton	So.	27	135	5.00
2000	Ken Johnson, Ohio St.	Sr.	30	161	5.37
2001	Tarvis Williams, Hampton	Sr.	32	147	4.59
2002	Wojciech Myrda, La.-Monroe	Sr.	32	172	5.38
2003	Emeka Okafor, Connecticut	So.	33	156	4.73
2004	Anwar Ferguson, Houston	Sr.	27	111	4.11
2005	Deng Gai, Fairfield	Sr.	30	165	5.50
2006	Shawn James, Northeastern	So.	30	196	6.53
2007	Mickell Gladness, Alabama A&M	Jr.	30	188	6.27

*record

Steal Average

Season	Player, Team	Cl.	G	Stl.	Avg.
1986	Darron Brittman, Chicago St.	Sr.	28	139	4.96
1987	Tony Fairley, Charleston So.	Sr.	28	114	4.07
1988	Aldwin Ware, Florida A&M	Sr.	29	142	4.90
1989	Kenny Robertson, Cleveland St.	Jr.	28	111	3.96
1990	Ronn McMahon, Eastern Wash.	Sr.	29	130	4.48
1991	Van Usher, Tennessee Tech	Jr.	28	104	3.71
1992	Victor Snipes, Northeastern Ill.	So.	25	86	3.44
1993	Jason Kidd, California	Fr.	29	110	3.79
1994	Shawn Griggs, La.-Lafayette	Sr.	30	120	4.00
1995	Roderick Anderson, Texas	Sr.	30	101	3.37
1996	Pointer Williams, McNeese St.	Sr.	27	118	4.37
1997	Joel Hoover, Md.-East. Shore	Fr.	28	90	3.21
1998	Bonzi Wells, Ball St.	Sr.	29	103	3.55
1999	Shawnta Rogers, George Washington	Sr.	29	103	3.55
2000	Carl Williams, Liberty	Sr.	28	107	3.82
2001	Greedy Daniels, TCU	Jr.	25	108	4.32
2002	Desmond Cambridge, Alabama A&M	Sr.	29	160	*5.52
2003	Alexis McMillan, Stetson	Sr.	22	87	3.95
2004	Marques Green, St. Bonaventure	Sr.	27	107	3.96
2005	Obie Trotter, Alabama A&M	Jr.	32	125	3.91
2006	Tim Smith, East Tenn. St.	Sr.	28	95	3.39
2007	Travis Holmes, VMI	So.	33	111	3.36

*record

Miscellaneous Player Information

Declared Early for the NBA Draft

Year	4-Year College Underclassmen	Jr. Col.	High School	U.S.	Foreign Country	Declared	Drafted	Total W/drew#
1971	6	0	0	6	0	6	5	0
1972	6	2	0	8	0	8	3	2
1973	10	1	0	11	0	11	7	2
1974	18	2	1	21	0	21	11	7
1975	13	1	2	16	0	16	14	0
1976	12	1	0	13	0	13	7	0
1977	6	0	0	6	0	6	4	0
1978	4	1	0	5	0	5	4	0
1979	4	0	0	4	0	4	4	0
1980	6	1	0	7	0	7	4	0
1981	5	0	0	5	0	5	5	0
1982	13	0	0	13	0	13	9	1
1983	6	0	0	6	0	6	6	0
1984	9	0	0	9	0	9	8	0
1985	12	0	0	12	0	12	11	0
1986	9	0	0	9	0	9	7	0
1987	9	0	0	9	0	9	5	0
1988	12	0	0	12	0	12	8	0

Year	4-Year College Underclassmen	Jr. Col.	High School	U.S.	Foreign Country	Declared	Drafted	Total W/drew#
1989	10	3	0	13	1	14	6	0
1990	22	1	0	23	0	23	7	0
1991	11	0	0	11	1	12	6	0
1992	14	2	0	16	0	16	4	0
1993	13	5	0	18	1	19	7	0
1994	20	0	0	20	0	20	12	2
1995	14	2	1	17	0	17	13	3
1996	25	4	4	33	4	37	21	6
1997	19	0	1	20	0	20	12	6
1998	26	2	4	32	3	35	20	3
1999	18	3	2	23	4	27	15	12
2000	25	2	2	29	8	37	25	19
2001	34	7	6	47	8	55	37	23
2002	33	8	4	45	9	54	29	24
2003	22	3	5	30	21	51	35	29
2004	19	3	10	32	10	42	27	54
2005	35	4	11	50	10	60	37	65
2006	33	4	0	37	10	47	33	41
2007	43	2	0	45	12	57	32	15

#Those athletes who withdrew before the draft are not included in any of the other columns.

Foreign Players at NCAA Division I Schools

Players whose home towns on their schools' rosters were listed as being from a country other than the U.S.

Year	Div. I Schools	Foreign Players
1993	298	135
1994	301	—
1995	302	178
1996	305	212
1997	305	238

Year	Div. I Schools	Foreign Players
1998	306	268
1999	310	291
2000	318	285
2001	318	340
2002	321	366
2003	325	392
2004	326	392
2005	326	396
2006	326	402
2007	325	424

All-Time Team Leaders

Single-Game Records

SCORING HIGHS

Pts.	Team vs. Opponent (Opp. Pts.)	Date
186	Loyola Marymount vs. U.S. Int'l (140)	Jan. 5, 1991
181	Loyola Marymount vs. U.S. Int'l (150)	Jan. 31, 1989
179	Long Island vs. Medgar Evers (62)	Nov. 26, 1997
173	Oklahoma vs. U.S. Int'l (101)	Nov. 29, 1989
172	Oklahoma vs. Loyola Marymount (112)	Dec. 15, 1990
166	Arkansas vs. U.S. Int'l (101)	Dec. 9, 1989
164	UNLV vs. Hawaii-Hilo (111)	Feb. 19, 1976
164	Loyola Marymount vs. Azusa-Pacific (138)	Nov. 28, 1988
162	Loyola Marymount vs. U.S. Int'l (144)	Jan. 7, 1989
162	Loyola Marymount vs. Chaminade (129)	Nov. 25, 1990
162	Oklahoma vs. Angelo St. (99)	Dec. 1, 1990
162	Drake vs. Grinnell (110)	Dec. 11, 2002
159	Southern U. vs. Texas College (65)	Dec. 6, 1990
159	LSU vs. Northern Ariz. (86)	Dec. 28, 1991
159	Cal St. Northridge vs. Redlands (97)	Nov. 15, 2006
157	Loyola Marymount vs. San Francisco (115)	Feb. 5, 1990
156	Southern U. vs. Baptist Christian (91)	Dec. 14, 1992
156	South Ala. vs. Prairie View (114)	Dec. 2, 1994
156	VMI vs. Va. Intermont (95)	Nov. 15, 2006
155	Oral Roberts vs. Union (Tenn.) (113)	Feb. 24, 1972
155	Southern U. vs. Prairie View (91)	Feb. 22, 1993
154	Texas-Arlington vs. Huston-Tillotson (85)	Nov. 29, 1990
154	Southern U. vs. Patten (57)	Nov. 26, 1993
153	TCU vs. Tex.-Pan American (87)	Nov. 29, 1997
152	Jacksonville vs. St. Peter's (106)	Dec. 3, 1970
152	Oklahoma vs. Centenary (La.) (84)	Dec. 12, 1987
152	Oklahoma vs. Oral Roberts (122)	Dec. 10, 1988
152	Loyola Marymount vs. U.S. Int'l (137)	Dec. 7, 1989
152	Northeastern vs. Loyola Marymount (123)	Nov. 24, 1990

SCORING HIGHS BY LOSING TEAM

Pts.	Team vs. Opponent (Opp. Pts.)	Date
150	U.S. Int'l vs. Loyola Marymount (181)	Jan. 31, 1989
144	U.S. Int'l vs. Loyola Marymount (162)	Jan. 7, 1989
141	Loyola Marymount vs. LSU (148) (ot)	Feb. 3, 1990
140	Utah St. vs. UNLV (142) (3 ot)	Jan. 2, 1985
140	U.S. Int'l vs. Loyola Marymount (186)	Jan. 5, 1991
140	Long Island vs. St. Francis (N.Y.) (142) (2 ot)	Feb. 22, 2003
137	U.S. Int'l vs. Loyola Marymount (152)	Dec. 7, 1989
136	Gonzaga vs. Loyola Marymount (147)	Feb. 18, 1989
132	Troy vs. George Mason (148)	Dec. 10, 1994
130	Fairleigh Dickinson vs. Sacred Heart (133) (4 ot)	Dec. 1, 2001
127	Pepperdine vs. Loyola Marymount (142)	Feb. 20, 1988
127	Troy vs. George Mason (142)	Nov. 28, 1995
126	Western Mich. vs. Marshall (127)	Dec. 20, 1999
125	Nevada vs. Loyola Marymount (130)	Dec. 30, 1988
123	San Francisco vs. Loyola Marymount (137)	Feb. 9, 1990
123	Loyola Marymount vs. Pepperdine (148)	Feb. 17, 1990
123	Loyola Marymount vs. Northeastern (152)	Nov. 24, 1990
123	Sam Houston St. vs. Texas-Arlington (125)	Dec. 28, 1998
122	Oral Roberts vs. Oklahoma (152)	Dec. 10, 1988
121	Loyola Marymount vs. LSU (148) (ot)	Feb. 3, 1990
121	Loyola Marymount vs. Oklahoma (136)	Dec. 23, 1989
121	Central Mich. vs. Ohio (122) (2 ot)	Feb. 5, 1998

SCORING HIGHS BOTH TEAMS COMBINED

Pts.	Team (Pts.) vs. Team (Pts.)	Date
331	Loyola Marymount (181) vs. U.S. Int'l (150)	Jan. 31, 1989
326	Loyola Marymount (186) vs. U.S. Int'l (140)	Jan. 5, 1991
306	Loyola Marymount (162) vs. U.S. Int'l (144)	Jan. 7, 1989
289	Loyola Marymount (152) vs. U.S. Int'l (137)	Dec. 7, 1989
289	LSU (148) vs. Loyola Marymount (141) (ot)	Feb. 3, 1990
284	Oklahoma (172) vs. Loyola Marymount (112)	Dec. 15, 1990
283	Loyola Marymount (147) vs. Gonzaga (136)	Feb. 18, 1989
282	UNLV (142) vs. Utah St. (140) (3 ot)	Jan. 2, 1985
282	St. Francis (N.Y.) (142) vs. Long Island (140) (2 ot)	Feb. 22, 2003
280	George Mason (148) vs. Troy (132)	Dec. 10, 1994
275	Northeastern (152) vs. Loyola Marymount (123)	Nov. 24, 1990
274	Oklahoma (152) vs. Oral Roberts (122)	Dec. 10, 1988
274	Oklahoma (173) vs. U.S. Int'l (101)	Nov. 29, 1989
272	Loyola Marymount (157) vs. San Francisco (115)	Feb. 4, 1990
269	Loyola Marymount (142) vs. Pepperdine (127)	Feb. 20, 1988
269	Loyola Marymount (150) vs. St. Mary's (Cal.) (119)	Feb. 1, 1990
269	George Mason (142) vs. Troy (127)	Nov. 28, 1995

MARGIN OF VICTORY

Pts.	Team (Pts.) vs. Opponent (Opp. Pts.)	Date
117	Long Island (179) vs. Medgar Evers (62)	Nov. 26, 1997
101	Texas (102) vs. San Marcos Baptist (1)	Jan. 10, 1916
97	Southern U. (154) vs. Patten (57)	Nov. 26, 1993
97	Winthrop (130) vs. Johnson & Wales (33)	Dec. 7, 1996
96	Purdue (112) vs. Indiana St. (6)	Jan. 10, 1911
96	Western Ky. (103) vs. Adairville Independents (7)	Jan. 10, 1923
95	Oklahoma (146) vs. Northeastern Ill. (51)	Dec. 2, 1989
94	Southern U. (159) vs. Texas College (65)	Dec. 6, 1990
93	Washington (100) vs. Puget Sound (7)	Jan. 14, 1921
93	Furman (126) vs. Va. Intermont (33)	Dec. 29, 2004
92	Villanova (117) vs. Philadelphia NAMC (25)	Feb. 12, 1949
91	LSU (124) vs. Rhodes (33)	Dec. 8, 1952
91	Tennessee St. (148) vs. Fisk (57)	Dec. 6, 1993
91	Tulsa (141) vs. Prairie View (50)	Dec. 7, 1995
89	Northwestern La. vs. LeTourneau (51)	Jan. 20, 1992
89	Nicholls St. (140) vs. Faith Baptist (51)	Dec. 17, 1994
88	Southern U. (132) vs. Faith Baptist (44)	Dec. 12, 1994
88	Prairie View (129) vs. Okla. Baptist (41)	Jan. 21, 1997
87	Canisius (107) vs. St. Ann's (20)	Dec. 8, 1907
86	Ohio St. (88) vs. Ohio (2)	Feb. 6, 1903
84	Rhode Island (118) vs. Fort Varnum (34)	Nov. 20, 1943
83	Texas (89) vs. Texas St. (6)	Feb. 11, 1919
82	Navy (126) vs. McDaniel (44)	Dec. 3, 1952
82	Morehead St. (130) vs. Asbury (48)	Nov. 30, 1994
81	Rhode Island (119) vs. Mass. Maritime (38)	1945
81	Oklahoma (146) vs. Florida A&M (65)	Jan. 27, 1993
81	Davidson (125) vs. Wash. & Jeff. (44)	Dec. 21, 2002

MARGIN OF VICTORY VS. DIVISION I OPPONENT (SINCE 1938)

Pts.	Team (Pts.) vs. Opponent (Opp. Pts.)	Date
91	Tulsa (141) vs. Prairie View (50)	Dec. 7, 1995
81	Oklahoma (146) vs. Florida A&M (65)	Jan. 27, 1993
80	Minnesota (114) vs. Alabama St. (34)	Dec. 23, 1996
77	Kentucky (143) vs. Georgia (66)	Feb. 27, 1956
76	Duke (130) vs. Harvard (54)	Nov. 25, 1989
75	Maryland (132) vs. North Texas (57)	Dec. 23, 1998

Pts.	Team (Pts.) vs. Opponent (Opp. Pts.)	Date
75	LSU (112) vs. Grambling (37)	Nov. 20, 1999
75	Florida (125) vs. Florida A&M (50)	Dec. 10, 2000
74	Kentucky (124) vs. Tenn.-Martin (50)	Nov. 26, 1994
74	Texas A&M (101) vs. Grambling (27)	Dec. 28, 2006
73	LSU (159) vs. Northern Ariz. (86)	Dec. 28, 1991
72	Iowa (103) vs. Chicago (31)	Feb. 5, 1944
72	Oklahoma (173) vs. U.S. Int'l (101)	Nov. 29, 1989
72	Ohio St. (116) vs. Chicago St. (44)	Nov. 30, 1991
72	Missouri (117) vs. Chicago St. (45)	Dec. 2, 1995
72	Texas Tech (107) vs. Nicholls (35)	Dec. 7, 2002
71	Ohio St. (109) vs. Delaware (38)	Jan. 11, 1960
71	New Mexico (71) vs. Dartmouth (36)	Dec. 29, 1972
71	Dayton (109) vs. Bowling Green (38)	Dec. 11, 1954
70	Massachusetts (108) vs. Maine (38)	Feb. 23, 1974
70	Kansas (115) vs. Brown (45)	Jan. 3, 1989
70	Connecticut (116) vs. Central Conn. St. (46)	Jan. 23, 1996
70	Memphis (112) vs. Howard (42)	Jan. 3, 2001
69	Kentucky (98) vs. Vanderbilt (29)	Feb. 27, 1947
69	Lamar (126) vs. Sam Houston St. (57)	Dec. 30, 1991

SCORING HIGHS IN A HALF

Pts.	Team vs. Opponent (Half)	Date
98	Long Island vs. Medgar Evers (2nd)	Nov. 26, 1997
97	Oklahoma vs. U.S. Int'l (1st)	Nov. 29, 1989
96	Southern U. vs. Texas College (2nd)	Dec. 6, 1990
94	Loyola Marymount vs. U.S. Int'l (1st)	Jan. 31, 1989
94	Oklahoma vs. Northeastern Ill. (2nd)	Dec. 2, 1989
94	Loyola Marymount vs. U.S. Int'l (1st)	Jan. 5, 1991
93	Loyola Marymount vs. U.S. Int'l (1st)	Jan. 7, 1989
93	Oklahoma vs. Loyola Marymount (2nd)	Dec. 15, 1990
92	Loyola Marymount vs. U.S. Int'l (2nd)	Jan. 5, 1991
92	Alabama St. vs. Grambling (2nd)	Jan. 21, 1991
91	Oklahoma vs. Angelo St. (2nd)	Dec. 1, 1990
87	Oklahoma vs. Oral Roberts (2nd)	Dec. 10, 1988
87	Loyola Marymount vs. U.S. Int'l (2nd)	Jan. 31, 1989
86	Jacksonville vs. St. Peter's (2nd)	Dec. 3, 1970
86	Lamar vs. Portland (2nd)	Jan. 12, 1980
86	Loyola Marymount vs. Gonzaga (2nd)	Feb. 18, 1989
86	Gonzaga vs. Loyola Marymount (2nd)	Feb. 18, 1989
86	Kentucky vs. LSU (1st)	Jan. 16, 1996
86	Cal St. Northridge vs. Redlands (2nd)	Nov. 15, 2006

SCORING HIGHS IN A HALF BOTH TEAMS COMBINED

Pts.	Team (Pts.) vs. Team (Pts.) (Half)	Date
172	Loyola Marymount (86) vs. Gonzaga (86) (2nd)	Feb. 18, 1989
170	Loyola Marymount (94) vs. U.S. Int'l (76) (1st)	Jan. 31, 1989
164	Loyola Marymount (94) vs. U.S. Int'l (70) (1st)	Jan. 5, 1991
162	Loyola Marymount (92) vs. U.S. Int'l (70) (2nd)	Jan. 5, 1991
161	Loyola Marymount (93) vs. U.S. Int'l (68) (1st)	Jan. 7, 1989
161	Loyola Marymount (87) vs. U.S. Int'l (74) (2nd)	Jan. 31, 1989
160	Oklahoma (87) vs. Oral Roberts (73) (2nd)	Dec. 10, 1988

FEWEST POINTS SCORED IN A GAME SINCE 1938

Pts.	Team vs. Opponent (Opp. Pts.)	Date
6	Temple vs. Tennessee (11)	Dec. 15, 1974
9	Pittsburgh vs. Penn St. (24)	Mar. 1, 1952
10	Duke vs. North Carolina St. (12)	Mar. 8, 1968
11	Oklahoma vs. Oklahoma St. (14)	Feb. 19, 1944
11	Tennessee vs. Temple (6)	Dec. 15, 1974
11	Cincinnati vs. Kentucky (24)	Dec. 20, 1983
12	Marquette vs. Creighton (57)	Dec. 16, 1940
12	Pittsburgh vs. Penn St. (15)	Jan. 15, 1944
12	North Carolina St. vs. Duke (10)	Mar. 8, 1968
13	Pittsburgh vs. Penn St. (32)	Feb. 20, 1943
13	Illinois vs. Purdue (23)	Feb. 7, 1938
14	Virginia vs. Navy (36)	Jan. 12, 1938
14	Michigan St. vs. Michigan (42)	Dec. 7, 1940
14	Kansas St. vs. Missouri (38)	Mar. 4, 1944
14	Oklahoma St. vs. Oklahoma (11)	Feb. 19, 1944
14	Alabama vs. Tennessee (23)	Jan. 11, 1945
15	Alabama vs. Tennessee (37)	Jan. 9, 1942
15	Arkansas vs. Oklahoma St. (17)	Jan. 28, 1944
15	Penn St. vs. Pittsburgh (12)	Jan. 15, 1944
15	Creighton vs. Oklahoma (35)	Feb. 9, 1948
15	Charleston So. vs. Col. of Charleston (18)	Feb. 6, 1980
16	Vanderbilt vs. Tennessee Tech (21)	1938
16	Miami (Ohio) vs. Marshall (22)	Feb. 19, 1938
16	South Carolina vs. Clemson (38)	Feb. 10, 1939
16	South Carolina vs. Clemson (43)	Feb. 18, 1939
16	Stanford vs. Oregon St. (18)	Jan. 28, 1980

FEWEST POINTS SCORED IN A GAME SINCE 1986

Pts.	Team vs. Opponent (Opp. Pts.)	Date
21	Ga. Southern vs. Coastal Caro. (61)	Jan. 2, 1997
21	Princeton vs. Monmouth (41)	Dec. 14, 2005
22	Hartford vs. Boston U. (73)	Jan. 6, 2005
23	Miami (Ohio) vs. Dayton (60)	Dec. 29, 2001
23	Army vs. Bucknell (56)	Jan. 23, 2004
24	Nicholls St. vs. LSU (68)	Nov. 22, 2002
24	Ark.-Pine Bluff vs. Oklahoma (94)	Dec. 2, 2003
25	Texas-Pan American vs. North Carolina St. (75)	Jan. 7, 1997
25	Valparaiso vs. Green Bay (69)	Mar. 2, 1992
25	Army vs. Bucknell (75)	Feb. 22, 2004
26	Northwestern vs. Evansville (48)	Nov. 26, 1999
26	Bethune-Cookman vs. Nebraska (70)	Dec. 20, 2003
27	New Hampshire vs. Providence (56)	Dec. 5, 1992
27	Yale vs. Princeton (55)	Jan. 11, 1991
27	Bucknell vs. Princeton (68)	Dec. 9, 1998
27	Eastern Wash. vs. California (56)	Nov. 16, 2001
27	Southern U. vs. Florida (83)	Nov. 28, 2006
27	Grambling vs. Texas A&M (101)	Dec. 28, 2006
28	Dartmouth vs. Princeton (66)	Feb. 10, 1990
28	Wofford vs. North Carolina St. (57)	Dec. 3, 1996
28	Winthrop vs. North Carolina St. (57)	Dec. 3, 1996
28	Rice vs. Princeton (51)	Jan. 6, 2007
29	Long Beach St. vs. UNLV (49)	Mar. 9, 1991
29	Texas-Pan American vs. Iowa (85)	Dec. 4, 1992
29	Loyola (Ill.) vs. Wisconsin (66)	Nov. 14, 1998
29	Northwestern vs. Michigan St. (59)	Jan. 27, 2000
29	Washington St. vs. Fresno St. (46)	Dec. 22, 2003
29	New Hampshire vs. Boston U. (53)	Jan. 13, 2007

FEWEST POINTS SCORED BY BOTH TEAMS IN A GAME SINCE 1938

Pts.	Team vs. Opponent (Opp. Pts.)	Date
17	Tennessee (11) vs. Temple (6)	Dec. 15, 1974
22	North Carolina St. (12) vs. Duke (10)	Mar. 8, 1968
25	Oklahoma St. (14) vs. Oklahoma (11)	Feb. 19, 1944
27	Penn St. (15) vs. Pittsburgh (12)	Jan. 15, 1944
32	Oklahoma St. (17) vs. Arkansas (15)	Jan. 28, 1944
33	Penn St. (24) vs. Pittsburgh (9)	Mar. 1, 1952
33	Col. of Charleston (18) vs. Charleston So. (15)	Feb. 6, 1980
34	Oregon St. (18) vs. Stanford (16)	Jan. 28, 1980
35	Kentucky (24) vs. Cincinnati (11)	Dec. 20, 1983
36	Purdue (23) vs. Illinois (13)	Feb. 7, 1938
37	Tennessee (23) vs. Alabama (14)	Jan. 11, 1945
37	Tennessee Tech (21) vs. Vanderbilt (16)	1938
38	Marshall (22) vs. Miami (Ohio) (16)	Feb. 19, 1938

FEWEST POINTS SCORED BY BOTH TEAMS IN A GAME SINCE 1986

Pts.	Team vs. Opponent (Opp. Pts.)	Date
62	Monmouth (41) vs. Princeton (21)	Dec. 14, 2005
67	SMU (36) vs. Tex.-Arlington (31)	Dec. 16, 1989
67	Green Bay (46) vs. Northern Mich. (21)	Nov. 22, 1996
68	George Mason (35) vs. UNC Wilmington (33)	Mar. 4, 2001
72	Princeton (37) vs. Monmouth (35)	Nov. 20, 1999
72	Binghamton (38) vs. Charleston So. (34)	Nov. 30, 2003
72	Tex.-Pan American (37) vs. Air Force (35)	Feb. 16, 2004
74	Princeton (38) vs. North Carolina St. (36)	Nov. 12, 1997
74	Evansville (48) vs. Northwestern (26)	Nov. 26, 1999
75	Fresno St. (46) vs. Washington St. (29)	Dec. 22, 2003
75	Missouri St. (43) vs. Wisconsin (32)	Mar. 12, 1999
76	Princeton (43) vs. Colgate (33)	Nov. 30, 1988
76	Yale (39) vs. Princeton (37)	Jan. 12, 1990
76	Cornell (41) vs. Columbia (35)	Jan. 27, 2001
76	Utah (41) vs. St. Mary's (Cal.) (35)	Jan. 7, 2002
76	Alabama St. (43) vs. Ark.-Pine Bluff (33)	Jan. 11, 2003
77	Idaho (40) vs. UC Santa Barbara (37)	Feb. 2, 2002
78	UNLV (49) vs. Long Beach St. (29)	Mar. 9, 1991
78	Northern Ill. (48) vs. Akron (30)	Jan. 26, 1991
78	Auburn (43) vs. Tennessee (35)	Jan. 15, 1997
78	Richmond (41) vs. UNC Wilmington (37)	Jan. 17, 2001
78	Yale (43) vs. Princeton (35)	Feb. 2, 2007
79	Princeton (48) vs. Cornell (31)	Feb. 8, 1992
79	Butler (43) vs. La Salle (36)	Dec. 29, 1999
79	Bucknell (56) vs. Army (23)	Jan. 23, 2004
79	Northwestern (40) vs. Purdue (39)	Feb. 11, 2004
79	Princeton (51) vs. Rice (28)	Jan. 6, 2007

FIELD-GOAL PERCENTAGE

Pct.	Team (FG-FGA) vs. Opponent	Date
83.3	Maryland (15-18) vs. South Carolina	Jan. 9, 1971
81.4	New Mexico (35-43) vs. Oregon St.	Nov. 30, 1985
81.0	Fresno St. (34-42) vs. Portland St.	Dec. 3, 1977
81.0	St. Peter's (34-42) vs. Utica	Dec. 4, 1984
80.5	Fordham (33-41) vs. Fairfield	Feb. 27, 1984
80.0	Holy Cross (32-40) vs. Vermont	Nov. 30, 1981
80.0	Oklahoma St. (28-35) vs. Tulane	Mar. 22, 1992
80.0	Long Beach St. (56-70) vs. Cal St. Monterey Bay	Dec. 22, 1999
80.0	Utah (24-30) vs. Air Force	Jan. 24, 2005
79.4	Arkansas (27-34) vs. Texas Tech	Feb. 20, 1979
79.4	Columbia (27-34) vs. Dartmouth	Mar. 2, 1984
79.0	North Carolina (49-62) vs. Loyola Marymount	Mar. 19, 1988
78.6	Villanova (22-28) vs. Georgetown	Apr. 1, 1985
78.6	St. Peter's (22-28) vs. Army	Jan. 9, 1982
78.4	Western Ky. (29-37) vs. Dayton	Jan. 24, 1979
78.1	Army (25-32) vs. Manhattan	Jan. 20, 1971
78.0	Southern Utah (32-41) vs. Montana Tech	Dec. 19, 2002
77.8	Samford (35-45) vs. Loyola (La.)	Dec. 12, 1992
77.8	Utah St. (28-36) vs. UC Davis	Nov. 27, 2004
77.5	Nicholls St. (31-40) vs. Samford	Dec. 30, 1983
77.4	Richmond (24-31) vs. Citadel	Feb. 8, 1976
77.2	Stephen F. Austin (44-57) vs. LeTourneau	Nov. 26, 2002
77.0	Purdue (47-61) vs. Long Island	Nov. 14, 1997

THREE-POINT FIELD GOALS

3FG	Team vs. Opponent	Date
28	Troy vs. George Mason	Dec. 10, 1994
26	Troy vs. Oakwood	Nov. 24, 2003
24	Cincinnati vs. Oakland	Dec. 5, 1998
23	Lamar vs. Louisiana Tech	Feb. 28, 1993
23	Kansas St. vs. Fresno St.	Mar. 24, 1994
23	Troy vs. George Mason	Nov. 28, 1995
23	Samford vs. Troy	Jan. 13, 2001
22	Gonzaga vs. San Francisco	Feb. 23, 1995
22	Troy vs. Mercer	Jan. 31, 2005
22	Ga. Southern vs. Chattanooga	Jan. 17, 2005
22	VMI vs. Lees-McRae	Dec. 6, 2006
21	Kentucky vs. North Carolina	Dec. 27, 1989
21	Loyola Marymount vs. Michigan	Mar. 18, 1990
21	UNLV vs. Nevada	Dec. 8, 1990
21	Troy vs. Loyola (La.)	Dec. 22, 1993
21	Cal Poly vs. Cal Baptist	Dec. 3, 1996
21	Mississippi Val. vs. Troy	Dec. 6, 1996
21	Arkansas vs. Troy	Dec. 10, 1996
21	Long Island vs. Robert Morris	Feb. 3, 1997
21	Troy vs. Lipscomb	Jan. 10, 2004
21	Furman vs. Va. Intermont	Dec. 29, 2004
21	Pepperdine vs. Nicholls St.	Nov. 14, 2006
21	VMI vs. Va. Intermont	Nov. 15, 2006
21	Morgan St. vs. East Caro.	Dec. 18, 2006
21	N.C. A&T vs. Arizona St.	Dec. 21, 2006
21	VMI vs. Charleston So.	Jan. 13, 2007
21	Nicholls St. vs. A&M-Corpus Christi	Feb. 8, 2007

THREE-POINT FIELD GOALS ATTEMPTED

3FGA	Team vs. Opponent	Date
74	Troy vs. George Mason	Dec 10, 1994
67	Mississippi Val. vs. Troy	Dec. 6, 1996
61	VMI vs. Va. Intermont	Nov. 15, 2006
59	VMI vs. Southern Va.	Nov. 20, 2006
58	Cal Poly vs. Cal Baptist	Dec. 3, 1996
56	VMI vs. Charleston So.	Jan. 13, 2007
55	VMI vs. Bridgewater (Va.)	Jan. 18, 2007
54	VMI vs. Cornell	Dec. 1, 2006
54	VMI vs. Penn St.	Dec. 30, 2006
53	Kentucky vs. La.-Lafayette	Dec. 23, 1989
52	Troy vs. Oakwood	Nov. 24, 2003
51	Texas-Arlington vs. New Mexico	Nov. 23, 1990
51	Arizona St. vs. BYU	Dec. 1, 1992
50	Morehead St. vs. George Mason	Dec. 3, 1996
50	Cal Poly vs. Air Force	Dec. 5, 1997
50	VMI vs. Coastal Caro.	Jan. 15, 2007
49	VMI vs. Lees-McRae	Dec. 6, 2006
48	Kentucky vs. North Carolina	Dec. 27, 1989
48	Cincinnati vs. Oakland	Dec. 5, 1998
48	VMI vs. Mercer	Dec. 9, 2006
47	Kentucky vs. Furman	Dec. 19, 1989
47	Charleston So. vs. Clemson	Dec. 1, 1993
47	Centenary (La.) vs. UCF	Jan. 11, 1993
47	VMI vs. Ohio St.	Nov. 10, 2006
47	VMI vs. South Dakota St.	Nov. 12, 2006

THREE-POINT FIELD-GOAL PERCENTAGE
(Minimum 10 three-point field goals made)

Pct.	Team (3FG-3FGA) vs. Opponent	Date
91.7	Drexel (11-12) vs. Delaware	Dec. 3, 2000
91.7	Northern Ariz. (11-12) vs. Willamette	Dec. 11, 2004
90.9	Duke (10-11) vs. Clemson	Feb. 1, 1988
90.9	Hofstra (10-11) vs. Rhode Island	Jan. 16, 1993
87.5	Stetson (14-16) vs. Centenary (La.)	Jan. 13, 1996
85.7	Western Ill. (12-14) vs. Valparaiso	Jan. 13, 1992
84.6	Murray St. (11-13) vs. Southeast Mo. St.	Jan. 16, 1993
84.6	Clemson (11-13) vs. North Carolina	Jan. 31, 2004
83.3	Eastern Ky. (15-18) vs. UNC Asheville	Jan. 14, 1987
83.3	Princeton (10-12) vs. Penn	Jan. 6, 1990
83.3	Evansville (10-12) vs. Butler	Feb. 9, 1991
83.3	Southern Utah (10-12) vs. Cal St. Northridge	Mar. 1, 1991
83.3	Milwaukee (10-12) vs. Eastern Mich.	Feb. 19, 1992
83.3	Purdue (10-12) vs. Michigan	Feb. 7, 1993
83.3	UNLV (10-12) vs. William & Mary	Feb. 11, 1995
83.3	Evansville (10-12) vs. Southern Ill.	Feb. 24, 1996
83.3	Green Bay (10-12) vs. Miami (Ohio)	Dec. 5, 1998
81.3	Niagara (13-16) vs. Siena	Jan. 7, 1987
80.0	Marshall (12-15) vs. Wyoming	Dec. 7, 1991
80.0	Washington St. (12-15) vs. Princeton	Dec. 29, 1992
80.0	Princeton (12-15) vs. Columbia	Feb. 13, 1993
80.0	Niagara (12-15) vs. Iona	Feb. 17, 1995
80.0	Marquette (12-15) vs. Tulane	Jan. 27, 2001
80.0	Iona (12-15) vs. St. Peter's	Feb. 17, 2004
78.9	Ohio (15-19) vs. Col. of Charleston	Dec. 21, 1989
78.9	San Francisco (15-19) vs. Gonzaga	Feb. 9, 2001

FREE-THROW PERCENTAGE
(Minimum 30 free throws made)

Pct.	Team (FT-FTA) vs. Opponent	Date
100	UC Irvine (34-34) vs. Pacific	Feb. 21, 1981
100	Samford (34-34) vs. UCF	Dec. 20, 1990
100	Wake Forest (32-32) vs. North Carolina	Jan. 15, 2005
100	Marshall (31-31) vs. Davidson	Dec. 17, 1979
100	Indiana St. (31-31) vs. Wichita St.	Feb. 18, 1991
97.2	Vanderbilt (35-36) vs. Mississippi St.	Feb. 26, 1986
97.2	Butler (35-36) vs. Dayton	Feb. 21, 1991
97.2	Marquette (35-36) vs. Memphis	Jan. 23, 1993
97.1	Bowling Green (34-35) vs. Kent St.	Jan. 26, 2006
97.0	Miami (Fla.) (32-33) vs. Creighton	Feb. 10, 1964
97.0	Toledo (32-33) vs. Old Dominion	Dec. 9, 1995
97.0	Hawaii (32-33) vs. New Mexico	Feb. 24, 1996
96.8	Oregon St. (30-31) vs. Memphis	Dec. 19, 1990
96.8	Niagara (30-31) vs. Fairfield	Jan. 31, 1998
95.5	UNLV (42-44) vs. San Diego St.	Dec. 11, 1976
94.7	Missouri St. (36-38) vs. Evansville	Dec. 30, 2001
94.6	TCU (35-37) vs. Tex.-Arlington	Dec. 23, 1996
94.4	Eastern Mich. (34-36) vs. Jackson St.	Dec. 20, 1994
93.8	North Carolina St. (30-32) vs. North Carolina	Feb. 21, 1998
93.8	BYU (30-32) vs. Weber St.	Dec. 28, 2000
93.7	Mount St. Mary's (30-32) vs. Robert Morris	Feb. 6, 1990

REBOUNDS

Reb.	Team vs. Opponent	Date
108	Kentucky vs. Mississippi	Feb. 8, 1964
103	Holy Cross vs. Boston College	Mar. 1, 1956
102	Arizona vs. Northern Ariz.	Jan. 6, 1951
101	Weber St. vs. Idaho St.	Jan. 22, 1966
100	William & Mary vs. Virginia	Feb. 14, 1954
95	Indiana vs. Michigan	Mar. 11, 1961
95	Murray St. vs. MacMurray	Jan. 2, 1967
92	Santa Clara vs. St. Mary's (Cal.)	Feb. 15, 1971
92	Oral Roberts vs. Brandeis	Jan. 8, 1973
91	Notre Dame vs. St. Norbert	Dec. 7, 1965
91	Southern Miss. vs. Tex.-Pan American	Feb. 9, 1970
91	Houston vs. Rice	Mar. 7, 1974
90	Vanderbilt vs. Sewanee	Dec. 4, 1954

ASSISTS

Ast.	Team vs. Opponent	Date
44	Colorado vs. George Mason (ot)	Dec. 2, 1995
43	TCU vs. Central Okla.	Dec. 12, 1998
41	North Carolina vs. Manhattan	Dec. 27, 1985
41	Weber St. vs. Northern Ariz.	Mar. 2, 1991
40	New Mexico vs. Texas-Arlington	Nov. 23, 1990
40	Loyola Marymount vs. U.S. Int'l	Jan. 5, 1991
40	Southern Utah vs. Texas Wesleyan	Jan. 25, 1992
40	Lamar vs. Prairie View	Feb. 2, 1993
40	TCU vs. North Texas	Dec. 1, 1998

Ast.	Team vs. Opponent	Date
39	Southern Miss. vs. Virginia Tech	Jan. 16, 1988
39	UNLV vs. Pacific	Feb. 8, 1990
39	UNLV vs. Rutgers	Feb. 3, 1991
39	Davidson vs. Warren Wilson	Dec. 9, 1991
39	TCU vs. Midwestern St.	Nov. 30, 1994
39	Arizona St. vs. Delaware St.	Dec. 1, 1997
39	TCU vs. Central Okla.	Dec. 9, 2000
38	New Mexico vs. U.S. Int'l	Dec. 3, 1985
38	Pepperdine vs. U.S. Int'l	Jan. 7, 1986
38	UCLA vs. Loyola Marymount	Dec. 2, 1990
38	Arizona vs. Northern Ariz.	Dec. 18, 1991
38	Tex.-Pan American vs. Concordia Lutheran	Dec. 4, 1993
38	LSU vs. George Mason	Dec. 3, 1994
38	Arizona vs. Morgan St.	Nov. 20, 1997
38	TCU vs. Ark.-Pine Bluff	Dec. 30, 2000
37	15 tied	

BLOCKED SHOTS

Blk.	Team vs. Opponent	Date
21	Georgetown vs. Southern (N.O.)	Dec. 1, 1993
21	Alabama A&M vs. Texas Southern	Feb. 24, 2007
20	Iona vs. Northern Ill.	Jan. 7, 1989
20	Georgia vs. Bethune-Cookman	Dec. 7, 1993
20	Massachusetts vs. West Virginia	Jan. 3, 1995
19	Seton Hall vs. Norfolk St.	Dec. 4, 2000
19	Connecticut vs. Florida Int'l	Nov. 30, 2004
19	UNLV vs. TCU	Feb. 7, 2007
19	Stanford vs. Southern California	Jan. 25, 2007
18	North Carolina vs. Stanford	Dec. 20, 1985
18	Boston College vs. Duquesne	Dec. 28, 2006
17	Maryland vs. Md.-East. Shore	Feb. 27, 1987
17	Rider vs. Fairleigh Dickinson	Jan. 9, 1989
17	Georgetown vs. Providence	Feb. 22, 1989
17	Georgetown vs. Hawaii-Loa	Nov. 23, 1990
17	BYU vs. Eastern Ky.	Dec. 7, 1990
17	Northwestern St. vs. Ouachita Baptist	Nov. 30, 1991
17	New Orleans vs. Texas A&M	Dec. 29, 1992
17	Massachusetts vs. Hartford	Dec. 28, 1993
17	Louisville vs. Kentucky	Jan. 1, 1995
17	William & Mary vs. George Mason	Feb. 26, 1996
17	Miami (Fla.) vs. Hartford	Dec. 13, 1996
17	Fairleigh Dickinson vs. Hartford	Nov. 11, 1997
17	Kentucky vs. Morehead St.	Nov. 20, 1997
17	Duke vs. Virginia	Jan. 10, 1999
17	La.-Monroe vs. Lamar	Feb. 3, 2000
17	Georgetown vs. Southern-N.O.	Feb. 10, 2000
17	Connecticut vs. Quinnipiac	Dec. 30, 2004

STEALS

Stl.	Team vs. Opponent	Date
39	Long Island vs. Medgar Evers	Nov. 26, 1997
35	VMI vs. Va. Intermont	Nov. 15, 2006
34	Oklahoma vs. Centenary (La.)	Dec. 12, 1987
34	Northwestern St. vs. LeTourneau	Jan. 20, 1992
33	Connecticut vs. Pittsburgh	Jan. 6, 1990
32	Manhattan vs. Lehman	Dec. 14, 1987
32	Oklahoma vs. Angelo St.	Dec. 1, 1990
32	Long Island vs. Medgar Evers	Nov. 29, 1994
32	La.-Lafayette vs. Baptist Christian	Nov. 25, 1995
30	Southern U. vs. Baptist Christian	Dec. 14, 1992
30	Cal Poly vs. Notre Dame (Cal.)	Nov. 25, 1995
30	TCU vs. Ark.-Pine Bluff	Dec. 30, 2000
29	Cleveland St. vs. Canisius	Dec. 28, 1986
29	Oklahoma vs. U.S. Int'l	Nov. 19, 1989
29	Centenary (La.) vs. East Texas Baptist	Dec. 12, 1992
29	TCU vs. Delaware St.	Dec. 3, 1997
28	Oklahoma vs. Morgan St.	Dec. 21, 1991
28	Memphis vs. Southeastern La.	Jan. 11, 1993
28	Oklahoma vs. Florida A&M	Jan. 27, 1993
28	VMI vs. Southern Va.	Nov. 20, 2006
27	Oregon St. vs. Hawaii-Loa	Dec. 22, 1985
27	Cal St. Fullerton vs. Lamar	Nov. 24, 1989
27	UTSA vs. Samford	Jan. 19, 1991
27	Iowa St. vs. Bethune-Cookman	Dec. 31, 1992
27	San Francisco vs. Delaware St.	Nov. 27, 1993
27	Charleston So. vs. Warner Southern	Dec. 11, 1993
27	Georgetown vs. Southern (N.O.)	Feb. 13, 1999
27	TCU vs. Alabama St.	Nov. 20, 2000

Season Records

VICTORIES

Team	Season	Won	Lost	Pct.
UNLV	†1987	37	2	.949
Duke	†1999	37	2	.949
Illinois	†2005	37	2	.949
Duke	†1986	37	3	.925
Kentucky	†1948	36	3	.923
Massachusetts	†1996	35	2	.946
Georgetown	†1985	35	3	.921
Arizona	†1988	35	3	.921
Kansas	1986	35	4	.897
Oklahoma	†1988	35	4	.897
Kansas	†1998	35	4	.897
Kentucky	†1998	35	4	.897
Duke	†2001	35	4	.897
Ohio St.	†2007	35	4	.897
UNLV	†1990	35	5	.875
Kentucky	†1997	35	5	.875
Florida	2007	35	5	.875
UNLV	†1991	34	1	.971
Duke	†1992	34	2	.944
Kentucky	1996	34	2	.944
Kansas	1997	34	2	.944
Connecticut	1999	34	2	.944
Kentucky	†1947	34	3	.919
Georgetown	†1984	34	3	.919
Arkansas	†1991	34	4	.895
North Carolina	†1993	34	4	.895
North Carolina	1998	34	4	.895

†national leader

VICTORIES IN FIRST SEASON IN DIVISION I

Team	Season	Won	Lost	Pct.
Seattle#	1953	29	4	.879
Md.-East. Shore	1974	27	2	.931
Oral Roberts	1972	26	2	.929
Old Dominion	1977	25	4	.862
Long Beach St.#	1970	24	5	.828
La.-Lafayette#	1972	23	3	.885
Southern U.	1978	23	5	.821
Hawaii	1971	23	5	.821
Alabama St.	1983	22	6	.786
Alcorn St.	1978	22	7	.759
Stephen F. Austin	1987	22	8	.733
Idaho St.#	1959	21	7	.750
McNeese St.	1974	20	5	.800
Memphis#	1956	20	7	.741
Birmingham So.	2004	20	7	.741
Loyola (La.)	1952	20	14	.588
Jackson St.	1978	19	5	.792
Northeastern	1973	19	7	.731
Ga. Southern	1974	19	7	.731
Miami (Fla.)	1949	19	8	.704
Col. of Charleston	1992	19	8	.704
Morehead St.#	1956	19	10	.655
New Mexico St.	1951	19	14	.576
New Orleans	1976	18	8	.692
Florida A&M	1979	18	9	.667
Alabama A&M	2000	18	10	.643

#appeared in NCAA tournament

WON-LOST PERCENTAGE

Team	Season	Won	Lost	Pct.
North Carolina	†1957	32	0	1.000
Indiana	†1976	32	0	1.000
UCLA	†1964	30	0	1.000
UCLA	†1967	30	0	1.000
UCLA	†1972	30	0	1.000
UCLA	†1973	30	0	1.000
San Francisco	†1956	29	0	1.000
North Carolina St.	1973	27	0	1.000
Kentucky	†1954	25	0	1.000
Long Island	†1939	24	0	1.000
Seton Hall	†1940	19	0	1.000
Army	†1944	15	0	1.000
UNLV	†1991	34	1	.971
Indiana St.	†1979	33	1	.971
Indiana	†1975	31	1	.969

DIVISION I

Team	Season	Won	Lost	Pct.
North Carolina St.	†1974	30	1	.968
UCLA	†1968	29	1	.967
UCLA	†1969	29	1	.967
UCLA	†1971	29	1	.967
San Francisco	†1955	28	1	.966
UTEP	†1966	28	1	.966
Marquette	1971	28	1	.966
Penn	1971	28	1	.966
Alcorn St.	1979	28	1	.966
Ohio St.	†1961	27	1	.964

†national leader

WON-LOST PERCENTAGE IN FIRST SEASON IN DIVISION I

Team	Season	Won	Lost	Pct.
Md.-East. Shore	1974	27	2	.931
Oral Roberts	1972	26	2	.929
Seattle#	1953	29	4	.879
La.-Lafayette#	1972	25	4	.862
Old Dominion	1977	25	4	.862
Long Beach St.#	1970	24	5	.828
Southern U.	1978	23	5	.821
Hawaii	1971	23	5	.821
McNeese St.	1974	20	5	.800
Jackson St.	1978	19	5	.792
Alabama St.	1983	22	6	.786
Alcorn St.	1978	22	7	.759
Idaho St.#	1959	21	7	.750
Memphis#	1956	20	7	.741
Birmingham So.	2004	20	7	.741
Air Force	1958	17	6	.739
Stephen F. Austin	1987	22	8	.733
Northeastern	1973	19	7	.731
Ga. Southern	1974	19	7	.731
VCU	1974	17	7	.708
Miami (Fla.)	1949	19	8	.704
Col. of Charleston	1992	19	8	.704
New Orleans	1976	18	8	.692
Weber St.	1964	17	8	.680
George Mason	1979	17	8	.680
Florida A&M	1979	18	9	.667
Mercer	1974	16	8	.667
Tennessee Tech	1956	14	7	.667
American	1967	16	8	.667
Fairfield	1965	14	7	.667

#appeared in NCAA tournament

MOST-IMPROVED TEAMS (Since 1974)

Team	Season	W-L Record	Previous Yr. W-L	Games Imp.
Mercer	†2003	23-6	6-23	17
UTEP	†2004	24-8	6-24	17
N.C. A&T	†1978	20-8	3-24	16½
Murray St.	†1980	23-8	4-22	16½
Liberty	†1992	22-7	5-23	16½
North Texas	†1976	22-4	6-20	16
Ohio State	†1999	27-9	8-22	16
Tulsa	†1981	26-7	8-19	15
Utah St.	†1983	20-9	4-23	15
Radford	†1991	22-7	7-22	15
Boston College	†2001	27-5	11-19	15
Western Mich.	1992	21-9	5-22	14½
Tennessee St.	†1993	19-10	4-24	14½
Central Mich.	2001	20-8	6-23	14½
Fresno St.	1978	21-6	7-20	14
James Madison	†1987	20-10	5-23	14
Loyola Marymount	†1988	28-4	12-16	14
Cal Poly	†1996	16-13	1-26	14
Northern Ariz.	†1997	21-7	6-20	14
McNeese St.	2001	22-9	6-21	14
Central Mich.	2003	25-7	9-19	14
Michigan St.	1978	25-5	10-17	13½
Loyola (Md.)	†1994	17-13	2-25	13½
UTSA	†1998	16-11	3-25	13½
Iowa St.	†2000	32-5	15-15	13½
Ark.-Little Rock	2001	18-11	4-23	13½

†national leader

POINTS

Team	Season	G	Pts.
Oklahoma	†1988	39	4,012
Loyola Marymount	†1990	32	3,918
Arkansas	†1991	38	3,783

Team	Season	G	Pts.
UNLV	1990	40	3,739
Oklahoma	†1989	36	3,680
UNLV	†1987	39	3,612
Duke	†1999	39	3,581
Duke	†2001	39	3,538
Loyola Marymount	1988	32	3,528
Loyola Marymount	1989	31	3,486
Houston	†1977	37	3,482
UNLV	†1976	31	3,426
UNLV	1977	32	3,426
Duke	1991	39	3,421
UNLV	1991	35	3,420
Arkansas	†1995	39	3,416
Syracuse	1989	38	3,410
Michigan	1989	37	3,393
Duke	1990	38	3,386
Kansas	†2002	37	3,365
Oklahoma	1991	35	3,363
Arkansas	1990	35	3,345
North Carolina	1989	37	3,331
VMI	†2007	33	3,331
Oklahoma	†1985	37	3,328

†national leader

SCORING OFFENSE

Team	Season	G	Pts.	Avg.
Loyola Marymount	†1990	32	3,918	122.4
Loyola Marymount	†1989	31	3,486	112.5
UNLV	†1976	31	3,426	110.5
Loyola Marymount	†1988	32	3,528	110.3
UNLV	1977	32	3,426	107.1
Oral Roberts	†1972	28	2,943	105.1
Southern U.	†1991	28	2,924	104.4
Loyola Marymount	1991	31	3,211	103.6
Oklahoma	1988	39	4,012	102.9
Oklahoma	1989	36	3,680	102.2
Oklahoma	1990	32	3,243	101.3
Southern U.	†1994	27	2,727	101.0
VMI	†2007	33	3,331	100.9
Jacksonville	†1970	28	2,809	100.3
Jacksonville	†1971	26	2,598	99.9
Arkansas	1991	38	3,783	99.6
Southern U.	1990	31	3,078	99.3
Syracuse	†1966	28	2,773	99.0
Iowa	1970	25	2,467	98.7
Miami (Fla.)	†1965	26	2,558	98.4
Houston	1966	29	2,845	98.1
La.-Lafayette	1972	29	2,840	97.9
U.S. Int'l	1990	28	2,738	97.8
Houston	†1968	33	3,226	97.8
UNLV	1991	35	3,420	97.7

†national leader

SCORING DEFENSE

Team	Season	G	Pts.	Avg.
Oklahoma St.	†1948	31	1,006	32.5
Oklahoma St.	†1949	28	985	35.2
Oklahoma St.	†1950	27	1,059	39.2
Alabama	1948	27	1,070	39.6
Creighton	1948	23	925	40.2
Wyoming	1948	27	1,101	40.8
Wyoming	1950	36	1,491	41.4
Siena	1948	28	1,161	41.5
St. Bonaventure	1948	22	921	41.9
Siena	1949	29	1,215	41.9
Tulane	1948	26	1,102	42.4
Wyoming	1949	35	1,509	43.1
Texas	1948	25	1,079	43.2
Utah	1948	20	868	43.4
Minnesota	1949	21	912	43.4
Washington-St. Louis	1948	21	915	43.6
St. Bonaventure	1949	26	1,137	43.7
St. Louis	1948	27	1,183	43.8
Kentucky	1949	34	1,492	43.9
Washington St.	1949	30	1,317	43.9
Texas A&M	†1951	29	1,275	44.0
Kentucky	1948	39	1,730	44.4
Baylor	1949	24	1,068	44.5
Tulsa	1950	23	1,027	44.7
Hamline	1948	31	1,389	44.8

†national leader

(Since 1965)

Team	Season	G	Pts.	Avg.
Fresno St.	†1982	30	1,412	47.1
Princeton	†1992	28	1,349	48.2
Princeton	†1991	27	1,320	48.9
North Carolina St.	1982	32	1,570	49.1
Princeton	1982	26	1,277	49.1
Princeton	†1984	28	1,403	50.1
St. Peter's	†1980	31	1,563	50.4
Fresno St.	†1981	29	1,470	50.7
Air Force	†2004	29	1,475	50.9
Princeton	†1990	27	1,378	51.0
Princeton	1981	28	1,438	51.4
Princeton	†1998	29	1,491	51.4
St. Peter's	1981	26	1,338	51.5
Wyoming	1982	30	1,545	51.5
Princeton	†1977	26	1,343	51.7
Princeton	†1996	29	1,498	51.7
Princeton	†1983	29	1,507	52.0
James Madison	1982	30	1,559	52.0
Fresno St.	†1978	27	1,417	52.5
Princeton	†1999	30	1,581	52.7
Princeton	†1976	27	1,427	52.9
Columbia	1982	26	1,375	52.9
Princeton	†1989	27	1,430	53.0
Fresno St.	†1985	32	1,696	53.0
Princeton	†2007	28	1,493	53.3

†national leader

SCORING MARGIN

Team	Season	Off.	Def.	Mar.
UCLA	†1972	94.6	64.3	30.3
North Carolina St.	†1948	75.3	47.2	28.1
Kentucky	†1954	87.5	60.3	27.2
Kentucky	†1952	82.3	55.4	26.9
UNLV	†1991	97.7	71.0	26.7
UCLA	†1968	93.4	67.2	26.2
UCLA	†1967	89.6	63.7	25.9
Houston	1968	97.8	72.5	25.3
Duke	†1999	91.8	67.2	24.7
Kentucky	1948	69.0	44.4	24.6
Kentucky	†1949	68.2	43.9	24.3
Bowling Green	1948	70.5	46.7	23.8
Loyola (Ill.)	†1963	91.8	68.1	23.7
Charlotte	†1975	88.9	65.2	23.7
Arizona St.	†1962	90.1	67.6	22.5
St. Bonaventure	†1970	88.4	65.9	22.5
Kentucky	†1951	74.7	52.5	22.2
Indiana	1975	88.0	65.9	22.1
Kentucky	†1996	91.4	69.4	22.1
Cincinnati	†1960	86.7	64.7	22.0
Oklahoma	†1988	102.9	81.0	21.9
North Carolina St.	†1973	92.9	71.1	21.8
Jacksonville	1970	100.3	78.5	21.8
UNLV	†1976	110.5	89.0	21.5
Duke	†1998	85.6	64.1	21.5

†national leader

FIELD-GOAL PERCENTAGE

Team	Season	FG	FGA	Pct.
Missouri	†1980	936	1,635	57.2
Michigan	†1989	1,325	2,341	56.6
Oregon St.	†1981	862	1,528	56.4
UC Irvine	†1982	920	1,639	56.1
Michigan St.	†1986	1,043	1,860	56.1
North Carolina	1986	1,197	2,140	55.9
Kansas	1986	1,260	2,266	55.6
Kentucky	†1983	869	1,564	55.6
Notre Dame	1981	824	1,492	55.2
Houston Baptist	†1984	797	1,445	55.2
Maryland	1980	985	1,789	55.1
Idaho	1981	816	1,484	55.0
UC Irvine	1981	934	1,703	54.8
Navy	†1985	946	1,726	54.8
Stanford	1983	752	1,373	54.8
Maryland	†1975	1,049	1,918	54.7
New Orleans	1983	937	1,714	54.7
Georgia Tech	1986	1,008	1,846	54.6
Arkansas	†1978	1,060	1,943	54.6
Michigan	†1988	1,198	2,196	54.6
New Mexico	1989	992	1,819	54.5
Southern U.	1978	1,107	2,031	54.5
Arkansas	†1977	849	1,558	54.5

Team	Season	FG	FGA	Pct.
Arizona	1988	1,147	2,106	54.5
Pepperdine	1983	900	1,653	54.4
Oregon St.	1980	943	1,732	54.4
Ohio St.	†1970	831	1,527	54.4
UNC Wilmington	1977	816	1,500	54.4
Davidson	†1964	894	1,644	54.4

†national leader

FIELD-GOAL PERCENTAGE DEFENSE (Since 1978)

Team	Season	FG	FGA	Pct.
Stanford	†2000	667	1,893	35.2
Marquette	†1994	750	2,097	35.8
Marquette	†1997	628	1,735	36.2
Temple	2000	633	1,747	36.2
Wake Forest	1997	667	1,832	36.4
UNLV	†1992	628	1,723	36.5
Green Bay	1997	499	1,368	36.5
Georgetown	†1991	680	1,847	36.8
Temple	†1994	621	1,686	36.8
Connecticut	†2004	924	2,502	36.9
Kansas	†2006	702	1,896	37.0
Princeton	2000	577	1,558	37.0
Connecticut	†2007	677	1,824	37.1
Boston U.	†2005	588	1,584	37.1
Kansas St.	†1999	729	1,963	37.1
St. Joseph's	†2003	609	1,639	37.2
Detroit	1999	590	1,583	37.3
Northwestern	1999	577	1,548	37.3
Texas St.	1999	597	1,601	37.3
Cincinnati	2005	749	2,008	37.3
Green Bay	1994	664	1,777	37.4
VCU	†2002	767	2,052	37.4
Cincinnati	2002	761	2,035	37.4
Texas A&M	2007	672	1,793	37.5
Syracuse	2007	834	2,223	37.5

†national leader

THREE-POINT FIELD GOALS MADE

Team	Season	G	3FG
VMI	†2007	33	442
Duke	†2001	39	407
West Virginia	2007	36	371
Troy	†2004	31	364
Arkansas	†1995	39	361
Louisville	†2005	38	361
Oregon	2007	37	350
Bradley	2007	35	349
Illinois	2005	39	344
Troy	†2006	29	344
Kentucky	†1993	34	340
West Virginia	2006	33	337
Houston	2007	33	330
Davidson	2007	34	328
Tennessee	2007	35	327
Missouri	†2002	36	326
Butler	2007	36	321
Kentucky	†1992	36	317
Vanderbilt	2007	34	317
Air Force	2007	35	316
St. Bonaventure	2002	30	314
Samford	†2000	32	313
St. Joseph's	2004	32	313
Troy	†2003	32	312
Marist	2007	34	312

†national leader

THREE-POINT FIELD GOALS MADE PER GAME

Team	Season	G	3FG	Avg.
VMI	†2007	33	442	13.39
Troy	†2006	29	344	11.86
Troy	†2004	31	364	11.74
Troy	†2005	30	338	11.27
Troy	†1996	27	300	11.11
Mississippi Val.	†1997	29	309	10.66
Troy	†1995	27	287	10.63
St. Bonaventure	†2002	30	314	10.47
Duke	†2001	39	407	10.44
Samford	1995	27	279	10.33
Mississippi Val.	†2003	29	299	10.31
West Virginia	2007	36	371	10.31
Belmont	2001	28	288	10.29
West Virginia	2006	33	337	10.21

Team	Season	G	3FG	Avg.
Marshall	1996	28	284	10.14
Lamar	†1993	27	271	10.04
St. Bonaventure	2003	27	271	10.04
Kentucky	†1990	28	281	10.04
Long Island	1997	30	301	10.03
Kentucky	1993	34	340	10.00
Houston	2007	35	330	10.00
Bradley	2007	28	349	9.97
Tennessee Tech	†2000	28	279	9.96
Davidson	2003	27	269	9.96
Vermont	1995	27	268	9.93

†national leader

THREE-POINT FIELD-GOAL PERCENTAGE
(Minimum 100 three-point field goals made)

Team	Season	G	3FG	3FGA	Pct.
Indiana	†1987	34	130	256	50.8
Mississippi Val.	1987	28	161	322	50.0
Stephen F. Austin	1987	30	120	241	49.8
Princeton	†1988	26	211	429	49.2
Prairie View	1988	27	129	266	48.5
Kansas St.	1988	34	179	370	48.4
Arizona	1988	38	254	526	48.3
Indiana	†1989	35	121	256	47.3
Bucknell	1988	28	154	328	47.0
Holy Cross	1988	29	158	337	46.9
Michigan	1989	37	196	419	46.8
Green Bay	†1992	30	204	437	46.7
Citadel	1989	28	153	328	46.6
Niagara	1987	31	128	275	46.5
Eastern Mich.	1987	29	144	310	46.5
Green Bay	†1991	31	189	407	46.4
Colorado St.	1989	33	141	305	46.2
Bucknell	1989	31	160	347	46.1
Illinois	1987	31	112	243	46.1
Illinois St.	1987	32	110	240	45.8
Jacksonville	1987	30	188	412	45.6
Rider	1987	28	151	331	45.6
Davidson	1987	30	138	303	45.5
New Mexico St.	1988	32	143	314	45.5
Gonzaga	1989	28	119	262	45.4
Indiana	†1994	30	182	401	45.4

†national leader

FREE-THROW PERCENTAGE

Team	Season	FT	FTA	Pct.
Harvard	†1984	535	651	82.2
BYU	†1989	527	647	81.5
Harvard	†1985	450	555	81.1
Ohio St.	†1970	452	559	80.9
Siena	†1998	574	715	80.3
Vanderbilt	†1974	477	595	80.2
Michigan St.	†1986	490	613	79.9
St. Joseph's	†2006	525	657	79.9
North Carolina St.	†2004	481	602	79.9
Butler	†1988	413	517	79.9
Miami (Fla.)	†1965	642	807	79.6
Tulane	†1963	390	492	79.3
Tennessee	†1971	538	679	79.2
UTEP	†2005	606	765	79.2
Auburn	†1966	476	601	79.2
Oklahoma St.	†1958	488	617	79.1
Duke	†1978	665	841	79.1
Utah	†1993	476	602	79.1
Gonzaga	1989	485	614	79.0
Western Ky.	†1997	342	433	79.0
Montana St.	†2000	481	609	79.0
Oral Roberts	†1980	481	610	78.9
Marshall	1958	479	608	78.8
Bucknell	1989	590	749	78.8
Manhattan	†2003	560	711	78.8

†national leader

REBOUNDS

Team	Season	G	Reb.
Kentucky	†1951	34	2,109
North Carolina St.	1951	37	2,091
Houston	†1968	33	2,074
Columbia	†1957	24	2,016
Fordham	†1953	27	1,879
North Carolina St.	†1955	32	1,864

Team	Season	G	Reb.
Houston	†1967	31	1,862
Fordham	†1952	29	1,859
Kentucky	1952	32	1,817
West Virginia	†1959	34	1,810
Western Ky.	†1954	32	1,810
Creighton	†1964	29	1,803
North Carolina St.	1952	34	1,782
Connecticut	†2004	39	1,742
Dayton	1955	29	1,738
North Carolina St.	1954	35	1,735
Notre Dame	†1965	27	1,722
Dayton	†1956	29	1,713
New Mexico St.	1970	31	1,713
Seton Hall	1953	33	1,706
La Salle	1955	31	1,697
LSU	†1970	32	1,691
Middle Tenn.	†1969	26	1,685
Kansas	†1998	39	1,682
Kentucky	1955	26	1,680

†national leader

REBOUND MARGIN
(Since 1973)

Team	Season	Off.	Def.	Mar.
Manhattan	†1973	56.5	38.0	18.5
American	1973	56.7	40.3	16.4
Alcorn St.	†1978	52.3	36.0	16.3
Oral Roberts	1973	66.9	50.3	15.6
Alcorn St.	†1980	49.2	33.8	15.4
Michigan St.	†2001	42.5	27.1	15.4
UCLA	1973	49.0	33.9	15.1
Houston	1973	54.7	40.8	13.9
Massachusetts	†1974	44.5	30.7	13.8
Alcorn St.	†1979	50.1	36.3	13.8
Minnesota	1973	49.0	36.0	13.0
VCU	1974	55.1	42.1	13.0
Northeastern	†1981	44.9	32.0	12.9
Stetson	†1975	47.1	34.7	12.4
Notre Dame	†1976	46.3	34.1	12.2
Harvard	1973	53.5	41.3	12.2
Tennessee St.	1980	46.5	34.3	12.2
Tennessee St.	1979	49.7	37.9	11.8
Buffalo	1976	51.5	39.7	11.8
Southern U.	1978	43.1	31.4	11.7
Wyoming	1981	42.0	30.3	11.7
Michigan St.	†2000	39.0	27.3	11.7
Alabama	1973	50.9	39.3	11.6
Mississippi Val.	†1996	48.3	36.8	11.6
Iowa	†1987	43.1	31.5	11.5

†national leader

ASSISTS

Team	Season	G	Ast.
UNLV	†1990	40	926
UNLV	†1991	35	863
Oklahoma	†1988	39	862
UNLV	†1987	39	853
Oklahoma	†1985	37	828
Arkansas	1991	38	819
Kansas	†1986	39	814
North Carolina	1986	34	800
North Carolina	†1989	37	788
SMU	1988	35	786
Kentucky	†1996	36	783
North Carolina	1987	36	782
Kentucky	†1997	40	776
Kansas	†2002	37	767
Loyola Marymount	1990	32	763
Kansas	1990	35	762
Kansas	†1998	39	746
Oklahoma	1989	36	743
Illinois	†2005	39	727
Arkansas	†1995	39	721
Maryland	2002	36	714
North Carolina	2005	37	706
Duke	†2001	39	701
North Carolina	1991	35	699
North Carolina	1998	38	699

†national leader

ASSISTS PER GAME

Team	Season	G	Ast.	Avg.
UNLV	†1991	35	863	24.7
Loyola Marymount	†1990	32	762	23.8
North Carolina	†1986	34	800	23.5
UNLV	1990	40	926	23.2
SMU	†1987	29	655	22.6
SMU	†1988	35	786	22.5
Oklahoma	†1985	37	828	22.4
Oklahoma	1988	39	862	22.1
Northwestern St.	†1993	26	570	21.9
UNLV	1987	39	853	21.9
Kansas	1990	35	763	21.8
Kentucky	1996	36	783	21.8
North Carolina	1987	36	782	21.7
Iowa St.	1988	32	694	21.7
Arkansas	1991	38	819	21.6
North Carolina	†1989	37	788	21.3
Georgia Tech	1988	32	680	21.3
Montana St.	1996	30	627	20.9
Montana St.	†1995	29	606	20.9
Montana St.	†1998	30	624	20.8
Kansas	†2002	37	767	20.7
VMI	†2007	33	681	20.6
TCU	†1999	32	650	20.3
Arkansas	†1994	34	687	20.2
Fresno St.	1998	34	685	20.2

†national leader

BLOCKED SHOTS

Team	Season	G	Blk.
Connecticut	†2004	39	315
Georgetown	†1989	34	309
Connecticut	†2006	34	298
Connecticut	†2005	31	275
Massachusetts	†1995	34	273
UNLV	†1991	35	266
Connecticut	†2007	31	264
Connecticut	†2003	33	253
Syracuse	2007	35	250
Old Dominion	†1999	34	248
Syracuse	2003	35	247
BYU	1991	34	246
Massachusetts	2007	33	246
Kansas	2007	38	246
Duke	1999	39	245
Kentucky	†1998	39	240
Duke	2004	37	240
Northeastern	2006	30	240
Seton Hall	†2001	31	236
Connecticut	†2002	34	236
LSU	2006	36	236
Alabama A&M	2007	30	236
Clemson	†1990	35	235
Georgetown	1991	32	235
Central Conn. St.	†1996	28	235
Maryland	†2000	35	235
Memphis	2006	37	235

†national leader

BLOCKED SHOTS PER GAME

Team	Season	G	Blk.	Avg.
Georgetown	†1989	34	309	9.09
Connecticut	†2005	31	275	8.87
Connecticut	†2006	34	298	8.76
Connecticut	†2007	31	264	8.52
Central Conn. St.	†1996	28	235	8.39
Connecticut	†2004	39	315	8.08
Massachusetts	†1995	34	273	8.03
Northeastern	2006	30	240	8.00
Alabama A&M	2007	30	236	7.87
Colgate	†1997	28	217	7.75
Connecticut	†2003	33	253	7.67
Seton Hall	†2001	31	236	7.61
UNLV	†1991	35	266	7.60
Georgetown	†1990	31	233	7.52
Central Conn. St.	1995	26	194	7.46
Massachusetts	2007	33	246	7.45
La.-Monroe	†2000	28	207	7.39
Georgetown	1991	32	235	7.34
Florida A&M	1996	27	198	7.33
Iona	†1999	30	220	7.33
Old Dominion	1999	34	248	7.29

Team	Season	G	Blk.	Avg.
BYU	1991	34	246	7.24
Massachusetts	2006	28	202	7.21
Syracuse	2007	35	250	7.14
Old Dominion	1997	33	233	7.06
Syracuse	2003	35	247	7.06

†national leader

STEALS

Team	Season	G	Stl.
VMI	†2007	33	490
Oklahoma	†1988	39	486
Connecticut	†1990	37	484
Kentucky	†1997	40	480
Long Island	†1998	32	478
Cleveland St.	†1987	33	473
Arkansas	†1991	38	467
Texas	†1994	34	453
Loyola Marymount	1990	32	450
Arkansas	†1995	39	445
Cleveland St.	†1986	33	436
Kentucky	1996	36	435
Tulsa	†2000	37	433
Georgetown	1996	37	431
Maryland	†1999	34	431
UTSA	1991	29	430
Duke	†2001	39	411
West Virginia	1998	33	407
Oklahoma	†1993	32	405
UNLV	1991	35	399
Long Island	1997	30	396
Florida A&M	1988	30	395
Alabama A&M	†2002	27	395
Kentucky	1994	34	394
Syracuse	2002	36	394
UAB	†2003	34	394

†national leader

STEALS PER GAME

Team	Season	G	Stl.	Avg.
Long Island	†1998	32	478	14.94
VMI	†2007	33	490	14.85
UTSA	†1991	29	430	14.83
Cleveland St.	†1987	33	473	14.33
Centenary (La.)	†1993	27	380	14.07
Loyola Marymount	†1990	32	450	14.06
Alabama A&M	†2002	27	395	13.62
Liberty	†2000	28	376	13.43
Texas	†1994	34	453	13.32
Cleveland St.	†1986	33	436	13.21
Long Island	†1997	30	396	13.20
Florida A&M	†1988	30	395	13.17
Connecticut	1990	37	484	13.08
Alabama A&M	2000	28	366	13.07
Charlotte	1991	28	363	12.96
Northeastern Ill.	†1992	28	358	12.79
Maryland	†1999	34	431	12.68
Oklahoma	1993	32	405	12.66
Southern U.	1991	28	352	12.57
Cleveland St.	1988	30	376	12.53
Nicholls St.	†1995	30	376	12.53
Tulane	1992	31	388	12.52
Southern U.	1993	31	387	12.48
Drake	1994	27	337	12.48
Houston	†2006	31	385	12.42

†national leader

MOST GAMES PLAYED
(Since 1947-48)

Team	Season	W	L	G
Duke	†1986	37	3	40
UNLV	†1990	35	5	40
Kentucky	†1997	35	5	40
Florida	†2007	35	5	40
Kentucky	†1948	36	3	39
Kansas	†1986	35	4	39
Louisville	†1986	32	7	39
UNLV	†1987	37	2	39
LSU	†1987	24	15	39
Oklahoma	†1988	35	4	39
Duke	†1991	32	7	39
Arkansas	†1995	32	7	39

Team	Season	W	L	G
Kansas	†1998	35	4	39
Kentucky	†1998	35	4	39
Duke	†1999	37	2	39
Michigan St.	†2000	32	7	39
Duke	†2001	35	4	39
Duke	†2004	33	6	39
Illinois	†2005	37	2	39
Florida	†2006	33	6	39
UCLA	†2006	32	7	39
Ohio St.	2007	35	4	39
Georgetown	†1985	35	3	38
UNLV	1986	33	5	38
LSU	1986	26	12	38
Syracuse	1987	31	7	38
Western Ky.	1987	29	9	38
Kansas	1988	27	11	38

Team	Season	W	L	G
Arizona	1988	35	3	38
Seton Hall	†1989	31	7	38
Syracuse	†1989	30	8	38
Duke	1990	29	9	38
Arkansas	1991	34	4	38
North Carolina	†1993	34	4	38
Syracuse	†1996	29	9	38
North Carolina	1998	34	4	38
Michigan St.	1999	33	5	38
Kansas	†2003	30	8	38
Louisville	2005	33	5	38
South Carolina	2006	23	15	38
Kansas	2007	33	5	38
North Carolina	2007	31	7	38

†national leader

Annual Team Champions

Won-Lost Percentage

Season	Team	Won	Lost	Pct.
1948	Western Ky.	28	2	.933
1949	Kentucky	32	2	.941
1950	Holy Cross	27	4	.871
1951	Columbia	21	1	.956
1952	Kansas	26	2	.929
1953	Seton Hall	31	2	.939
1954	Kentucky	25	0	1.000
1955	San Francisco	28	1	.966
1956	San Francisco	29	0	1.000
1957	North Carolina	32	0	1.000
1958	West Virginia	26	2	.929
1959	Mississippi St.	24	1	.960
1960	California	28	2	.933
	Cincinnati	28	2	.933
1961	Ohio St.	27	1	.964
1962	Mississippi St.	24	1	.960
1963	Loyola (Ill.)	29	2	.935
1964	UCLA	30	0	1.000
1965	UCLA	28	2	.933
1966	UTEP	28	1	.966
1967	UCLA	30	0	1.000
1968	UCLA	29	1	.967
1969	UCLA	29	1	.967
1970	UCLA	28	2	.933
1971	UCLA	29	1	.967
1972	UCLA	30	0	1.000
1973	UCLA	30	0	1.000
	North Carolina St.	27	0	1.000
1974	North Carolina St.	30	1	.968
1975	Indiana	31	1	.969
1976	Indiana	32	0	1.000
1977	San Francisco	29	2	.935
1978	Kentucky	30	2	.938
1979	Indiana St.	33	1	.971
1980	Alcorn St.	28	2	.933
1981	DePaul	27	2	.931
1982	North Carolina	32	2	.941
1983	Houston	31	3	.912
1984	Georgetown	34	3	.919
1985	Georgetown	35	3	.921
1986	Duke	37	3	.925
1987	UNLV	37	2	.949
1988	Temple	32	2	.941
1989	Ball St.	29	3	.906
1990	La Salle	30	2	.938
1991	UNLV	34	1	.971
1992	Duke	34	2	.944
1993	North Carolina	34	4	.895
1994	Arkansas	31	3	.912
1995	UCLA	31	2	.939
1996	Massachusetts	35	2	.946
1997	Kansas	34	2	.944
1998	Princeton	27	2	.931
1999	Duke	37	2	.949
2000	Cincinnnati	29	4	.879
2001	Stanford	31	3	.912
2002	Kansas	33	4	.892
2003	Kentucky	32	4	.889
2004	St. Joseph's	30	2	.938
	Stanford	30	2	.938
2005	Illinois	37	2	.949
2006	George Washington	27	3	.900
2007	Ohio St.	35	4	.897

Most-Improved Teams

Season	Team	W-L Record	Previous Yr. W-L	Games Imp.
1974	Kansas	23-7	8-18	13
1975	Holy Cross	20-8	8-18	11
1976	North Texas	22-4	6-20	16
1977	La.-Lafayette	21-8	7-19	12½
1978	N.C. A&T	20-8	3-24	16½
1979	Wagner	21-7	7-19	13
1980	Murray St.	23-8	4-22	16½
1981	Tulsa	26-7	8-19	15
1982	Cal St. Fullerton	18-14	4-23	11½
1983	Utah St.	20-9	4-23	15
1984	Northeastern	27-5	13-15	12
	Loyola (Md.)	16-12	4-24	12
1985	Cincinnati	17-14	3-25	12½
1986	Bradley	32-3	17-13	12½
1987	James Madison	20-10	5-23	14
1988	Loyola Marymount	28-4	12-16	14
1989	Ball St.	29-3	14-14	13
1990	South Fla.	20-11	7-21	11½
	George Washington	14-17	1-27	11½
1991	Radford	22-7	7-22	15
1992	Liberty	22-7	5-23	16½
1993	Tennessee St.	19-10	4-24	14½
1994	Loyola (Md.)	17-13	2-25	13½
1995	Western Ill.	20-8	7-20	12½
1996	Cal Poly	16-13	1-26	14
1997	Northern Ariz.	21-7	6-20	14
1998	UTSA	16-11	3-25	13½
1999	Ohio St.	27-9	8-22	16
2000	Iowa St.	32-5	15-15	13½
2001	Boston College	27-5	11-19	15
2002	Fla. Atlantic	19-12	7-24	12
	Texas Tech	23-9	9-19	12
2003	Mercer	23-6	6-23	17
2004	UTEP	24-8	6-24	17
2005	Texas A&M	21-10	7-21	12½
	San Diego	16-13	4-26	12½
2006	South Ala.	24-7	10-18	12½
2007	Jacksonville	15-14	1-26	13

DIVISION I

Scoring Offense

Season	Team	G	W-L	Pts.	Avg.
1948	Rhode Island	23	17-6	1,755	76.3
1949	Rhode Island	22	16-6	1,575	71.6
1950	Villanova	29	25-4	2,111	72.8
1951	Cincinnati	22	18-4	1,694	77.0
1952	Kentucky	32	29-3	2,635	82.3
1953	Furman	27	21-6	2,435	90.2
1954	Furman	29	20-9	2,658	91.7
1955	Furman	27	17-10	2,572	95.3
1956	Morehead St.	29	19-10	2,782	95.9
1957	Connecticut	25	17-8	2,183	87.3
1958	Marshall	24	17-7	2,113	88.0
1959	Miami (Fla.)	25	18-7	2,190	87.6
1960	Ohio St.	28	25-3	2,532	90.4
1961	St. Bonaventure	28	24-4	2,479	88.5
1962	Loyola (Ill.)	27	23-4	2,436	90.2
1963	Loyola (Ill.)	31	29-2	2,847	91.8
1964	Detroit	25	14-11	2,402	96.1
1965	Miami (Fla.)	26	22-4	2,558	98.4
1966	Syracuse	28	22-6	2,773	99.0
1967	Oklahoma City	26	16-10	2,496	96.0
1968	Houston	33	31-2	3,226	97.8
1969	Purdue	28	23-5	2,605	93.0
1970	Jacksonville	28	26-2	2,809	100.3
1971	Jacksonville	26	22-4	2,598	99.9
1972	Oral Roberts	28	26-2	2,943	105.1
1973	Oral Roberts	27	21-6	2,626	97.3
1974	Md.-East. Shore	29	27-2	2,831	97.6
1975	South Ala.	26	19-7	2,412	92.8
1976	UNLV	31	29-2	3,426	110.5
1977	UNLV	32	29-3	3,426	107.1
1978	New Mexico	28	24-4	2,731	97.5
1979	UNLV	29	21-9	2,700	93.1
1980	Alcorn St.	30	28-2	2,729	92.0
1981	UC Irvine	27	17-10	2,332	86.4
1982	Long Island	30	20-10	2,605	86.8
1983	Boston College	32	25-7	2,697	84.3
1984	Tulsa	31	27-4	2,816	90.8
1985	Oklahoma	37	31-6	3,328	89.9
1986	U.S. Int'l	28	8-20	2,542	90.8
1987	UNLV	39	37-2	3,612	92.6
1988	Loyola Marymount	32	28-4	3,528	110.3
1989	Loyola Marymount	31	20-11	3,486	112.5
1990	Loyola Marymount	32	26-6	3,918	*122.4
1991	Southern U.	28	19-9	2,924	104.4
1992	Northwestern St.	28	15-13	2,660	95.0
1993	Southern U.	31	21-10	3,011	97.1
1994	Southern U.	27	16-11	2,727	101.0
1995	TCU	27	16-11	2,529	93.7
1996	Troy	27	11-16	2,551	94.5
1997	Long Island	30	21-9	2,746	91.5
1998	TCU	33	27-6	3,209	97.2
1999	Duke	39	37-2	3,581	91.8
2000	Duke	34	29-5	2,992	88.0
2001	TCU	31	20-11	2,902	93.6
2002	Kansas	37	33-4	3,365	90.9
2003	Arizona	32	28-4	2,725	85.2
2004	Arizona	30	20-10	2,614	87.1
2005	North Carolina	37	33-4	3,257	88.0
2006	Long Beach St.	30	18-12	2,498	83.3
2007	VMI	33	14-19	3,331	100.9

*record

Scoring Defense

Season	Team	G	W-L	Pts.	Avg.
1948	Oklahoma St.	31	27-4	1,006	*32.5
1949	Oklahoma St.	28	23-5	985	35.2
1950	Oklahoma St.	27	18-9	1,059	39.2
1951	Texas A&M	29	17-12	1,275	44.0
1952	Oklahoma St.	27	19-8	1,228	45.5
1953	Oklahoma St.	30	23-7	1,614	53.8
1954	Oklahoma St.	29	24-5	1,539	53.1
1955	San Francisco	29	28-1	1,511	52.1
1956	San Francisco	29	29-0	1,514	52.2
1957	Oklahoma St.	26	17-9	1,420	54.6
1958	San Francisco	27	25-2	1,363	50.5
1959	California	29	25-4	1,480	51.0
1960	California	30	28-2	1,486	49.5

Season	Team	G	W-L	Pts.	Avg.
1961	Santa Clara	27	18-9	1,314	48.7
1962	Santa Clara	25	19-6	1,302	52.1
1963	Cincinnati	28	26-2	1,480	52.9
1964	San Jose St.	24	14-10	1,307	54.5
1965	Tennessee	25	20-5	1,391	55.6
1966	Oregon St.	28	21-7	1,527	54.5
1967	Tennessee	28	21-7	1,511	54.0
1968	Army	25	20-5	1,448	57.9
1969	Army	28	18-10	1,498	53.5
1970	Army	28	22-6	1,515	54.1
1971	Fairleigh Dickinson	23	16-7	1,236	53.7
1972	Minnesota	25	18-7	1,451	58.0
1973	UTEP	26	16-10	1,460	56.2
1974	UTEP	25	18-7	1,413	56.5
1975	UTEP	26	20-6	1,491	57.3
1976	Princeton	27	22-5	1,427	52.9
1977	Princeton	26	21-5	1,343	51.7
1978	Fresno St.	27	21-6	1,417	52.5
1979	Princeton	26	14-12	1,452	55.8
1980	St. Peter's	31	22-9	1,563	50.4
1981	Fresno St.	29	25-4	1,470	50.7
1982	Fresno St.	30	27-3	1,412	47.1
1983	Princeton	29	20-9	1,507	52.0
1984	Princeton	28	18-10	1,403	50.1
1985	Fresno St.	32	23-9	1,696	53.0
1986	Princeton	26	13-13	1,429	55.0
1987	Missouri St.	34	28-6	1,958	57.6
1988	Ga. Southern	31	24-7	1,725	55.6
1989	Princeton	27	19-8	1,430	53.0
1990	Princeton	27	20-7	1,378	51.0
1991	Princeton	27	24-3	1,320	48.9
1992	Princeton	28	22-6	1,349	48.2
1993	Princeton	26	15-11	1,421	54.7
1994	Princeton	26	18-8	1,361	52.3
1995	Princeton	26	16-10	1,501	57.7
1996	Princeton	29	22-7	1,498	51.7
1997	Princeton	28	24-4	1,496	53.4
1998	Princeton	29	27-2	1,491	51.4
1999	Princeton	30	22-8	1,581	52.7
2000	Princeton	30	19-11	1,637	54.6
2001	Wisconsin	29	18-11	1,641	56.6
2002	Columbia	28	11-17	1,596	57.0
2003	Air Force	28	12-16	1,596	57.0
2004	Air Force	29	22-7	1,475	50.9
2005	Air Force	30	18-12	1,629	54.3
2006	Air Force	31	24-7	1,695	54.7
2007	Princeton	28	11-17	1,493	53.3

*record

Scoring Margin

Season	Team	G	Off.	Def.	Mar.
1949	Kentucky	34	68.2	43.9	24.3
1950	Holy Cross	31	72.6	55.4	17.2
1951	Kentucky	34	74.7	52.5	22.2
1952	Kentucky	32	82.3	55.4	26.9
1953	La Salle	28	80.1	61.8	18.3
1954	Kentucky	25	87.5	60.3	27.2
1955	Utah	28	79.0	59.9	19.1
1956	San Francisco	29	72.2	52.2	20.0
1957	Kentucky	28	84.2	69.4	14.8
1958	Cincinnati	28	86.5	65.9	20.6
1959	Idaho St.	28	74.2	53.7	20.5
1960	Cincinnati	30	86.7	64.7	22.0
1961	Memphis	23	85.0	64.2	20.8
1962	Arizona St.	27	90.1	67.6	22.5
1963	Loyola (Ill.)	31	91.8	68.1	23.7
1964	Davidson	26	89.3	70.5	18.8
1965	Connecticut	26	85.1	66.5	18.6
1966	Loyola (Ill.)	25	97.5	76.6	20.9
1967	UCLA	30	89.6	63.7	25.9
1968	UCLA	30	93.4	67.2	26.2
1969	UCLA	30	84.7	63.8	20.9
1970	St. Bonaventure	28	88.4	65.9	22.5
1971	Jacksonville	26	99.9	79.0	20.9
1972	UCLA	30	94.6	64.3	*30.3
1973	North Carolina St.	27	92.9	71.1	21.8
1974	Charlotte	26	90.2	69.4	20.8
1975	Charlotte	26	88.9	65.2	23.7
1976	UNLV	31	110.5	89.0	21.5
1977	UNLV	32	107.1	87.7	19.4

Season	Team	G	Off.	Def.	Mar.
1978	UCLA	28	85.3	67.4	17.9
1979	Syracuse	30	88.7	71.5	17.2
1980	Alcorn St.	30	91.0	73.6	17.4
1981	Wyoming	30	73.6	57.5	16.1
1982	Oregon St.	27	69.6	55.0	14.6
1983	Houston	34	82.4	64.9	17.4
1984	Georgetown	37	74.3	57.9	16.4
1985	Georgetown	38	74.3	57.3	17.1
1986	Cleveland St.	33	88.9	69.6	19.3
1987	UNLV	39	92.6	75.5	17.1
1988	Oklahoma	39	102.9	81.0	21.9
1989	St. Mary's (Cal.)	30	76.1	57.6	18.5
1990	Oklahoma	32	101.3	80.4	21.0
1991	UNLV	35	97.7	71.0	26.7
1992	Indiana	34	83.4	65.8	17.6
1993	North Carolina	38	86.1	68.3	17.8
1994	Arkansas	34	93.4	75.6	17.9
1995	Kentucky	33	87.4	69.0	18.4
1996	Kentucky	36	91.4	69.4	22.1
1997	Kentucky	40	83.1	62.8	20.3
1998	Duke	36	85.6	64.1	21.5
1999	Duke	39	91.8	67.2	24.7
2000	Stanford	31	78.9	59.7	19.3
2001	Duke	39	90.7	70.5	20.2
2002	Duke	35	88.9	69.2	19.7
2003	Kansas	38	82.7	66.9	15.8
2004	Gonzaga	31	81.8	66.2	15.6
2005	North Carolina	37	88.0	70.3	17.8
2006	A&M-Corpus Christi	28	82.4	67.4	15.0
2007	Florida	40	79.8	62.6	17.2

*record

Field-Goal Percentage

Season	Team	FG	FGA	Pct.
1948	Oregon St.	668	1,818	36.7
1949	Muhlenberg	593	1,512	39.2
1950	TCU	476	1,191	40.0
1951	Maryland	481	1,210	39.8
1952	Boston College	787	1,893	41.6
1953	Furman	936	2,106	44.4
1954	George Washington	744	1,632	45.6
1955	George Washington	867	1,822	47.6
1956	George Washington	725	1,451	50.0
1957	Manhattan	679	1,489	45.6
1958	Fordham	693	1,440	48.1
1959	Auburn	593	1,216	48.8
1960	Auburn	532	1,022	52.1
1961	Ohio St.	939	1,886	49.8
1962	Florida St.	709	1,386	51.2
1963	Duke	984	1,926	51.1
1964	Davidson	894	1,644	54.4
1965	St. Peter's	579	1,089	53.2
1966	North Carolina	838	1,620	51.7
1967	UCLA	1,082	2,081	52.0
1968	Bradley	927	1,768	52.4
1969	UCLA	1,027	1,999	51.4
1970	Ohio St.	831	1,527	54.4
1971	Jacksonville	1,077	2,008	53.6
1972	North Carolina	1,031	1,954	52.8
1973	North Carolina	1,150	2,181	52.7
1974	Notre Dame	1,056	1,992	53.0
1975	Maryland	1,049	1,918	54.7
1976	Maryland	996	1,854	53.7
1977	Arkansas	849	1,558	54.5
1978	Arkansas	1,060	1,943	54.6
1979	UCLA	1,053	1,897	55.5
1980	Missouri	936	1,635	*57.2
1981	Oregon St.	862	1,528	56.4
1982	UC Irvine	920	1,639	56.1
1983	Kentucky	869	1,564	55.6
1984	Houston Baptist	797	1,445	55.2
1985	Navy	946	1,726	54.8
1986	Michigan St.	1,043	1,860	56.1
1987	Princeton	601	1,111	54.1
1988	Michigan	1,198	2,196	54.6
1989	Michigan	1,325	2,341	56.6
1990	Kansas	1,204	2,258	53.3
1991	UNLV	1,305	2,441	53.5
1992	Duke	1,108	2,069	53.6
1993	Indiana	1,076	2,062	52.2
1994	Auburn	854	1,689	50.6
1995	Washington St.	902	1,743	51.7
1996	UCLA	897	1,698	52.8
1997	UCLA	932	1,791	52.0
1998	North Carolina	1,131	2,184	51.8
1999	Northern Ariz.	783	1,497	52.3
2000	Samford	825	1,649	50.0
2001	Stanford	953	1,865	51.1
2002	Kansas	1,259	2,487	50.6
2003	Morehead St.	854	1,674	51.0
2004	Oklahoma St.	1,002	1,953	51.3
2005	Utah St.	851	1,621	52.5
2006	A&M-Corpus Christi	837	1,671	50.1
2007	Florida	1,125	2,138	52.6

*record

Field-Goal Percentage Defense

Season	Team	FG	FGA	Pct.
1977	Minnesota	766	1,886	40.6
1978	Delaware St.	733	1,802	40.7
1979	Illinois	738	1,828	40.4
1980	Penn St.	543	1,309	41.5
1981	Wyoming	637	1,589	40.1
1982	Wyoming	584	1,470	39.7
1983	Wyoming	599	1,441	41.6
1984	Georgetown	799	2,025	39.5
1985	Georgetown	833	2,064	40.4
1986	St. Peter's	574	1,395	41.1
1987	San Diego	660	1,645	40.1
1988	Temple	777	1,981	39.2
1989	Georgetown	795	1,993	39.9
1990	Georgetown	713	1,929	37.0
1991	Georgetown	680	1,847	36.8
1992	UNLV	628	1,723	36.4
1993	Marquette	634	1,613	39.3
1994	Marquette	750	2,097	35.8
1995	Alabama	771	2,048	37.6
1996	Temple	670	1,741	38.5
1997	Marquette	628	1,735	36.2
1998	Miami (Fla.)	634	1,672	37.9
1999	Kansas St.	729	1,963	37.1
2000	Stanford	667	1,893	*35.2
2001	Kansas	782	2,069	37.8
2002	VCU	767	2,052	37.4
2003	St. Joseph's	609	1,639	37.2
2004	Connecticut	924	2,502	36.9
2005	Boston U.	588	1,584	37.1
2006	Kansas	702	1,896	37.0
2007	Connecticut	677	1,824	37.1

*record

Three-Point Field Goals Made Per Game

Season	Team	G	3FG	Avg.
1987	Providence	34	280	8.24
1988	Princeton	26	211	8.12
1989	Loyola Marymount	31	287	9.26
1990	Kentucky	28	281	10.04
1991	Texas-Arlington	29	265	9.14
1992	La Salle	31	294	9.48
1993	Lamar	27	271	10.04
1994	Troy	27	262	9.70
1995	Troy	27	287	10.63
1996	Troy	27	300	11.11
1997	Mississippi Val.	29	309	10.66
1998	Florida	29	285	9.83
1999	Cal Poly	27	255	9.44
2000	Tennessee Tech	28	279	9.96
2001	Duke	39	407	10.44
2002	St. Bonaventure	30	314	10.47
2003	Mississippi Val.	29	299	10.31
2004	Troy	31	364	11.74
2005	Troy	30	338	11.27
2006	Troy	29	344	11.86
2007	VMI	33	442	*13.39

*record

Three-Point Field-Goal Percentage

Season	Team	G	3FG	3FGA	Pct.
1987	Indiana	34	130	256	*50.8
1988	Princeton	26	211	429	49.2
1989	Indiana	35	121	256	47.3
1990	Princeton	27	208	460	45.2
1991	Green Bay	31	189	407	46.4
1992	Green Bay	30	204	437	46.7
1993	Valparaiso	28	214	500	42.8
1994	Indiana	30	182	401	45.4
1995	Southern Utah	28	244	571	42.7
1996	Weber St.	30	245	577	42.5
1997	Northern Ariz.	28	221	527	41.9
1998	Northern Ariz.	29	254	591	43.0
1999	Northern Ariz.	29	243	546	44.5
2000	Colorado St.	30	255	579	44.0
2001	Akron	28	189	436	43.3
2002	Marshall	30	252	595	42.4
2003	Illinois St.	29	188	427	44.0
2004	Birmingham-So.	27	243	565	43.0
2005	Oklahoma St.	33	240	564	42.6
2006	Southern Utah	30	226	527	42.9
2007	Northern Ariz.	30	229	537	42.7

*record

Free-Throw Percentage

Season	Team	FT	FTA	Pct.
1948	Texas	351	481	73.0
1949	Davidson	347	489	71.0
1950	Temple	342	483	70.8
1951	Minnesota	287	401	71.6
1952	Kansas	491	707	69.4
1953	George Washington	502	696	72.1
1954	Wake Forest	734	1,010	72.7
1955	Wake Forest	709	938	75.6
1956	SMU	701	917	76.4
1957	Oklahoma St.	569	752	75.7
1958	Oklahoma St.	488	617	79.1
1959	Tulsa	446	586	76.1
1960	Auburn	424	549	77.2
1961	Tulane	459	604	76.0
1962	Arkansas	647	502	77.6
1963	Tulane	390	492	79.3
1964	Miami (Fla.)	593	780	76.0
1965	Miami (Fla.)	642	807	79.6
1966	Auburn	476	601	79.2
1967	West Tex. A&M	400	518	77.2
1968	Vanderbilt	527	684	77.0
1969	Jacksonville	574	733	78.3
1970	Ohio St.	452	559	80.9
1971	Tennessee	538	679	79.2
1972	Lafayette	656	844	77.7
1973	Duke	496	632	78.5
1974	Vanderbilt	477	595	80.2
1975	Vanderbilt	530	692	76.6
1976	Morehead St.	452	577	78.3
1977	Utah	499	638	78.2
1978	Duke	665	841	79.1
1979	St. Francis (Pa.)	350	446	78.5
1980	Oral Roberts	481	610	78.9
1981	Connecticut	487	623	78.2
1982	Western Ill.	447	569	78.6
1983	Western Ill.	526	679	77.5
1984	Harvard	535	651	*82.2
1985	Harvard	450	555	81.1
1986	Michigan St.	490	613	79.9
1987	Alabama	521	662	78.7
1988	Butler	413	517	79.9
1989	BYU	527	647	81.5
1990	Lafayette	461	588	78.4
1991	Butler	725	922	78.6
1992	Northwestern	497	651	76.3
1993	Utah	476	602	79.1
1994	Colgate	511	665	76.8
1995	BYU	617	798	77.3
1996	Utah	649	828	78.4
1997	Western Ky.	342	433	79.0
1998	Siena	574	715	80.3
1999	Siena	672	854	78.7
2000	Montana St.	481	609	79.0
2001	BYU	651	835	78.0
2002	Morehead St.	485	619	78.4
2003	Manhattan	560	711	78.8
2004	North Carolina St.	481	602	79.9
2005	UTEP	606	765	79.2
2006	St. Joseph's	525	657	79.9
2007	Villanova	594	761	78.1

*record

Rebounding

Season	Team	G	Reb.	Pct.
1955	Niagara	26	1,507	.624
1956	George Washington	26	1,451	.616
1957	Morehead St.	27	1,735	.621
1958	Manhattan	26	1,437	.591
1959	Mississippi St.	25	1,012	.589
1960	Iona	18	1,054	.607
1961	Bradley	26	1,330	.592
1962	Cornell	25	1,463	.590
1963	UTEP	26	1,167	.591
1964	Iona	20	1,071	.640
1965	Iona	23	1,191	.628
1966	UTEP	29	1,430	.577
1967	Florida	25	1,275	.600

Season	Team	G	Reb.	Avg.
1968	Houston	33	2,074	62.8
1969	Middle Tenn.	26	1,685	64.8
1970	Florida St.	26	1,451	55.8
1971	Pacific	28	1,643	58.7
1972	Oral Roberts	28	1,686	60.2

Season	Team	G	Off.	Def.	Pct.
1973	Manhattan	26	56.5	38.0	*18.5
1974	Massachusetts	26	44.5	30.7	13.8
1975	Stetson	26	47.1	34.7	12.4
1976	Notre Dame	29	46.3	34.1	12.2
1977	Notre Dame	29	42.4	31.6	10.8
1978	Alcorn St.	29	52.3	36.0	16.3
1979	Alcorn St.	29	50.1	36.3	13.8
1980	Alcorn St.	30	49.2	33.8	15.4
1981	Northeastern	30	44.9	32.0	12.9
1982	Northeastern	30	41.2	30.8	10.4
1983	Wichita St.	28	42.4	33.6	8.8
1984	Northeastern	32	40.1	30.3	9.8
1985	Georgetown	38	39.6	30.5	9.1
1986	Notre Dame	29	36.4	27.8	8.6
1987	Iowa	35	43.1	31.5	11.5
1988	Notre Dame	29	36.0	26.2	9.9
1989	Iowa	33	41.4	31.8	9.6
1990	Georgetown	31	44.8	34.0	10.8
1991	New Orleans	31	41.7	32.4	9.3
1992	Delaware	31	42.1	33.8	8.3
1993	Massachusetts	31	43.9	32.8	11.2
1994	Utah St.	27	38.4	29.8	8.6
1995	Navy	29	40.6	29.6	11.0
1996	Mississippi Val.	29	48.3	36.8	11.6
1997	Utah St.	29	37.4	26.6	10.9
1998	Utah	34	37.0	27.1	10.0
1999	Navy	27	43.6	33.7	10.0
2000	Michigan St.	39	39.0	27.3	11.7
2001	Michigan St.	33	42.5	27.1	15.4
2002	Gonzaga	33	41.5	32.6	8.9
2003	Wake Forest	31	41.7	32.0	9.6
2004	Connecticut	39	44.7	34.9	9.7
2005	Connecticut	31	45.5	34.3	11.3
2006	Texas	37	40.5	29.9	10.6
2007	Vermont	33	40.7	31.1	9.6

Note: From 1955 through 1967, the rebounding champion was determined by highest team recoveries out of the total by both teams in all games. From 1968 through 1972, the champion was determined by rebound average per game. Beginning with the 1973 season, the champion is determined by rebounding margin.

*record

Assists

Season	Team	G	Ast.	Avg.
1984	Clemson	28	571	20.4
1985	Oklahoma	37	828	22.4
1986	North Carolina	34	800	23.5
1987	SMU	29	655	22.6
1988	SMU	35	786	22.5
1989	North Carolina	37	788	21.3
1990	Loyola Marymount	32	762	23.8
1991	UNLV	35	863	*24.7
1992	Arkansas	34	674	19.8
1993	Northwestern St.	26	570	21.9
1994	Arkansas	34	687	20.2
1995	Montana St.	29	606	20.9
1996	Kentucky	36	783	21.8
1997	Kentucky	40	776	19.4
1998	Montana St.	30	624	20.8
1999	TCU	32	650	20.3
2000	UNLV	31	623	20.1
2001	Kansas	33	641	19.4
2002	Kansas	37	767	20.7
2003	Maryland	31	573	18.5
2004	Sam Houston St.	28	530	18.9
2005	North Carolina	37	706	19.1
2006	A&M-Corpus Christi	28	550	19.6
2007	VMI	33	681	20.6

*record

Blocked Shots

Season	Team	G	Blk.	Avg.
1986	Navy	35	233	6.66
1987	Siena	29	188	6.48
1988	Siena	29	193	6.66
1989	Georgetown	34	309	*9.09
1990	Georgetown	31	233	7.52
1991	UNLV	35	266	7.60
1992	Vermont	29	198	6.83
1993	Wyoming	28	184	6.57
1994	Howard	27	179	6.63
1995	Massachusetts	34	273	8.03

Season	Team	G	Blk.	Avg.
1996	Central Conn. St.	28	235	8.39
1997	Colgate	28	217	7.75
1998	Texas	31	203	6.55
1999	Iona	30	220	7.33
2000	La.-Monroe	28	207	7.39
2001	Seton Hall	31	236	7.61
2002	Connecticut	34	236	6.94
2003	Connecticut	33	253	7.67
2004	Connecticut	39	315	8.08
2005	Connecticut	31	275	8.87
2006	Connecticut	34	298	8.76
2007	Connecticut	31	264	8.52

*record

Steals

Season	Team	G	Stl.	Avg.
1986	Cleveland St.	33	436	13.2
1987	Cleveland St.	33	473	14.3
1988	Florida A&M	30	395	13.2
1989	Arkansas	32	372	11.6
1990	Loyola Marymount	32	450	14.1
1991	UTSA	29	430	14.8
1992	Northeastern Ill.	28	358	12.8
1993	Centenary (La.)	27	380	14.1
1994	Texas	34	453	13.3
1995	Nicholls St.	30	376	12.5
1996	McNeese St.	27	330	12.2
1997	Long Island	30	396	13.2
1998	Long Island	32	478	*14.9
1999	Maryland	34	431	12.7
2000	Liberty	28	376	13.4
2001	Alabama A&M	28	339	12.1
2002	Alabama A&M	29	395	13.6
2003	UAB	34	394	11.6
2004	UAB	32	371	11.6
2005	UAB	33	382	11.6
2006	Houston	31	385	12.4
2007	VMI	33	490	14.8

*record

Statistical Trends

Year	Teams	Games	FG Made	FG Att.	Pct.	FT Made	FT Att.	Pct.	PF	Pts.
1948	160	24.7	20.3	69.4	29.3	12.7	21.1	59.8	18.5	53.3
1949	148	25.3	20.7	67.4	30.8	13.4	21.7	61.6	19.4	54.8
1950	145	25.2	21.6	68.4	31.6	14.4	23.3	61.8	19.5	57.6
1951	153	26.0	22.8	68.9	33.1	15.1	24.1	62.8	21.4	60.7
1952	156	25.7	23.8	*70.3	33.7	15.8	25.3	62.6	*22.5	63.3
1953	158	23.8	24.0	69.1	34.7	21.1	*32.9	64.0	21.3	69.1
1954	160	24.6	24.4	67.8	35.4	21.0	32.2	65.2	21.0	69.0
1955	162	23.6	25.6	69.3	36.9	*21.6	32.4	66.5	19.0	72.7
1956	166	24.7	26.1	69.5	37.5	21.2	31.7	66.8	18.9	73.3
1957	167	24.6	25.8	67.6	38.2	20.4	30.3	67.3	18.3	72.0
1958	173	24.0	25.8	67.1	38.4	16.8	25.3	66.4	18.2	68.4
1959	174	24.3	25.9	66.2	39.1	17.0	25.4	67.1	18.2	68.7
1960	175	24.5	26.3	66.2	39.8	17.4	25.8	67.4	18.4	70.0
1961	173	24.5	26.7	65.6	40.7	17.4	25.5	68.2	18.2	70.7
1962	178	24.4	27.0	67.3	40.2	16.5	24.3	67.9	18.1	70.5
1963	178	23.5	26.6	63.8	41.7	16.3	23.9	68.2	18.2	69.5
1964	179	24.3	28.7	67.4	42.5	17.1	25.1	68.3	19.1	74.4
1965	182	24.8	29.2	67.7	43.1	17.4	25.2	69.0	19.3	75.7
1966	182	21.9	30.0	68.8	43.6	17.5	25.3	69.2	19.2	77.5
1967	185	24.9	28.9	66.0	43.8	17.2	24.9	69.0	19.2	74.9
1968	189	25.1	29.1	66.6	43.7	17.4	25.1	69.1	19.0	75.5
1969	193	25.3	29.1	66.4	43.8	17.4	25.4	68.4	19.0	75.6
1970	196	25.4	30.0	67.8	44.2	17.7	25.7	68.7	19.3	77.6
1971	203	25.8	30.1	67.8	44.4	17.5	25.7	68.1	19.3	*77.7
1972	210	25.7	30.1	67.2	44.8	17.5	25.6	68.6	19.2	*77.7
1973	216	25.8	31.2	69.6	44.8	13.1	19.2	68.4	19.2	75.5
1974	233	26.0	31.0	68.3	45.4	12.8	18.7	68.4	19.2	74.8
1975	235	26.2	*31.5	68.4	46.0	13.7	19.9	69.0	20.2	76.6
1976	235	26.6	31.0	66.3	46.7	13.8	19.9	69.2	20.2	75.7
1977	245	27.2	30.4	64.9	46.7	14.2	20.5	69.4	20.1	74.9
1978	254	27.2	30.1	63.6	47.3	14.3	20.7	69.2	20.2	74.5
1979	257	27.7	29.6	62.1	47.7	14.8	21.1	*69.7	20.6	74.0
1980	261	28.0	28.6	59.7	47.9	14.9	21.3	69.6	20.2	72.0
1981	264	28.1	27.8	58.0	48.0	14.5	21.0	68.9	20.1	70.1
1982	273	28.0	26.7	55.6	47.9	14.3	20.8	68.6	19.4	67.6
1983	274	29.0	27.2	57.0	47.7	14.5	21.2	68.5	19.9	69.3
1984	276	29.1	26.7	55.6	*48.1	14.8	21.4	68.9	20.0	68.2
1985	282	29.3	27.3	57.0	47.9	14.7	21.3	68.9	19.7	69.2
1986	283	29.5	27.4	57.3	47.7	14.7	21.3	69.1	19.6	69.4

Year	Teams	Games	FG Made	FG Att.	Pct.	3FG Made	3FG Att.	Pct.	FT Made	FT Att.	Pct.	PF	Pts.
1987	290	29.6	27.2	58.7	46.4	3.5	9.2	*38.4	14.9	21.5	69.1	19.7	72.8
1988	290	29.6	27.6	58.4	47.3	4.0	10.4	38.3	15.2	22.0	68.9	19.7	74.4
1989	293	29.6	28.1	59.4	47.3	4.4	11.8	37.8	15.6	22.6	69.1	20.1	76.2
1990	292	29.6	27.5	59.5	46.2	4.7	12.8	36.8	15.6	22.6	68.9	19.8	75.3
1991	295	29.6	27.9	60.6	46.1	5.0	13.8	36.2	15.9	23.2	68.6	19.6	76.7
1992	298	29.5	26.7	58.4	45.7	5.0	14.0	35.6	15.9	23.3	68.1	20.0	74.2
1993	298	28.6	26.5	58.6	45.2	5.3	14.9	35.4	15.4	22.8	67.7	19.6	73.6
1994	301	28.7	26.8	60.6	44.3	5.7	16.5	34.5	15.6	23.2	67.1	19.9	75.0
1995	302	28.7	26.5	59.7	44.4	5.9	17.2	34.5	15.3	22.6	67.6	19.7	74.2
1996	305	28.7	25.8	58.5	44.1	5.9	17.1	34.3	15.1	22.4	67.4	19.4	72.5
1997	305	28.8	25.0	57.3	43.7	5.8	17.1	34.1	14.8	21.9	67.4	19.3	70.6
1998	306	29.1	25.3	57.7	43.9	6.0	17.4	34.4	14.9	22.0	67.5	19.4	71.4
1999	310	29.1	24.8	57.0	43.6	5.9	17.4	34.2	14.7	21.6	67.8	19.0	70.3
2000	318	30.0	25.0	57.4	43.5	6.1	17.7	34.4	14.5	21.2	68.1	18.9	70.5
2001	318	29.8	25.0	56.8	44.0	6.1	17.7	34.6	15.4	22.4	68.5	19.9	71.4
2002	321	30.2	25.1	57.2	43.8	6.3	18.3	34.6	14.8	21.5	69.0	19.2	71.3
2003	325	29.7	24.8	56.4	44.0	6.3	18.1	34.8	14.4	20.7	69.4	19.1	70.2
2004	*326	29.7	24.5	55.9	43.8	6.3	18.3	34.6	14.3	20.7	68.8	19.0	69.6
2005	*326	29.9	24.4	55.7	43.9	6.4	18.3	34.7	14.0	20.4	68.7	18.6	69.2
2006	*326	30.1	24.4	55.6	43.9	6.4	18.4	35.0	13.9	20.1	69.1	18.4	69.2
2007	325	*31.7	24.4	55.2	44.3	*6.6	*18.9	35.0	14.0	20.3	69.0	18.7	69.5

Year	Teams	Games	Reb.	Ast.	Blk.	St.	TO
1993	298	28.6	36.1	*14.5	3.2	7.6	15.8
1994	301	28.7	*37.8	*14.5	3.3	*7.8	15.9
1995	302	28.7	37.2	*14.5	3.3	7.5	15.8
1996	305	28.7	36.7	14.1	3.2	7.4	15.6
1997	305	28.8	36.1	13.9	3.2	7.5	15.7
1998	306	29.1	36.4	14.0	3.2	7.6	15.9
1999	310	29.1	36.1	13.9	*3.4	*7.8	*16.0
2000	318	30.0	36.3	14.0	*3.4	7.6	15.8
2001	318	29.8	35.9	13.9	3.3	7.1	15.2
2002	321	30.2	35.9	13.9	*3.4	7.3	15.1
2003	325	29.7	35.1	13.8	3.3	7.2	14.9
2004	*326	29.7	35.1	13.7	3.2	7.2	14.9
2005	*326	29.9	34.9	13.7	3.3	7.2	14.7
2006	*326	30.1	34.7	13.7	3.3	7.1	14.7
2007	325	*31.7	34.4	13.6	3.3	6.8	14.5

*all-time high

All-Time Winningest Teams

By Victories

(Minimum 25 years in Division I)

No.	Team	First Season	Yrs.	Won	Lost	Tied	Pct.
1.	Kentucky	1903	104	1,948	608	1	.762
2.	North Carolina	1911	97	1,914	696	0	.733
3.	Kansas	1899	109	1,906	782	0	.709
4.	Duke	1906	102	1,818	802	0	.694
5.	Syracuse	1901	106	1,704	782	0	.685
6.	Temple	1895	111	1,668	935	0	.641
7.	St. John's (N.Y.)	1908	100	1,659	831	0	.666
8.	Penn	1897	107	1,634	913	2	.641
9.	UCLA	1920	88	1,611	713	0	.693
10.	Indiana	1901	107	1,610	876	0	.648
11.	Notre Dame	1898	102	1,605	885	1	.645
12.	Utah	1909	99	1,595	833	0	.657
13.	Oregon St.	1902	106	1,570	1,137	0	.580
14.	Illinois	1906	102	1,569	824	0	.656
15.	Western Ky.	1915	88	1,548	764	0	.670
15.	Washington	1896	105	1,548	1,021	0	.603
17.	Princeton	1901	107	1,533	949	0	.618
18.	Texas	1906	101	1,532	926	0	.623
19.	Louisville	1912	93	1,529	816	0	.652
20.	Arizona	1905	102	1,528	829	1	.648
21.	BYU	1903	105	1,526	978	0	.609
22.	Cincinnati	1902	106	1,522	882	0	.633
23.	Purdue	1897	109	1,513	908	0	.625
24.	North Carolina St.	1913	95	1,503	894	0	.627
25.	West Virginia	1904	98	1,501	949	0	.613
26.	Bradley	1903	103	1,495	974	0	.606
27.	Missouri St.	1909	95	1,470	797	0	.648
28.	Villanova	1921	87	1,453	829	0	.637
29.	Arkansas	1924	84	1,450	794	0	.646
30.	Alabama	1913	94	1,447	868	1	.625
31.	Oklahoma	1908	100	1,446	922	0	.611
32.	Connecticut	1901	104	1,444	825	0	.636
33.	St. Joseph's	1910	98	1,439	938	0	.605
34.	Iowa	1902	106	1,438	970	0	.597
35.	Oklahoma St.	1908	98	1,435	1,002	0	.589
36.	Georgetown	1907	99	1,432	903	0	.613
37.	Fordham	1903	104	1,420	1,148	0	.553
38.	Southern California	1907	101	1,414	1,017	0	.582
38.	Washington St.	1902	106	1,414	1,316	0	.518
40.	Montana St.	1902	105	1,412	1,116	0	.559
41.	Missouri	1907	101	1,406	994	0	.586
42.	Oregon	1903	102	1,392	1,213	0	.534
43.	Michigan St.	1899	108	1,391	979	0	.587
43.	Illinois St.	1899	109	1,391	1,016	0	.578
45.	Tennessee	1909	98	1,390	901	2	.607
45.	Ohio St.	1899	106	1,390	957	0	.592
47.	Kansas St.	1903	103	1,386	1,012	0	.578
48.	Southern Ill.	1914	93	1,384	920	0	.601
49.	Vanderbilt	1901	105	1,378	995	0	.581
50.	Minnesota	1896	112	1,377	1,052	2	.567

By Percentage

(Minimum 25 years in Division I)

No.	Team	First Season	Yrs.	Won	Lost	Tied	Pct.
1.	Kentucky	1903	104	1,948	608	1	.762
2.	North Carolina	1911	97	1,914	696	0	.733
3.	UNLV	1959	49	1,010	410	0	.711
4.	Kansas	1899	109	1,906	782	0	.709
5.	Duke	1906	102	1,818	802	0	.694
6.	UCLA	1920	88	1,611	713	0	.693
7.	Syracuse	1901	106	1,704	782	0	.685
8.	Western Ky.	1915	88	1,548	764	0	.670
9.	St. John's (N.Y.)	1908	100	1,659	831	0	.666
10.	Utah	1909	99	1,595	833	0	.657
11.	Illinois	1906	102	1,569	824	0	.656
12.	Louisville	1912	93	1,529	816	0	.652
13.	Missouri St.	1909	95	1,470	797	0	.648
14.	Arizona	1905	102	1,528	829	1	.648
15.	Indiana	1901	107	1,610	876	0	.648
16.	Arkansas	1924	84	1,450	794	0	.646
17.	Notre Dame	1898	102	1,605	885	1	.645
18.	Penn	1897	107	1,634	913	2	.641
19.	Temple	1895	111	1,668	935	0	.641
20.	Villanova	1921	87	1,453	829	0	.637

No.	Team	First Season	Yrs.	Won	Lost	Tied	Pct.
21.	Connecticut	1901	104	1,444	825	0	.636
22.	Murray St.	1926	82	1,360	781	0	.635
23.	DePaul	1924	84	1,332	766	0	.635
24.	Weber St.	1963	45	815	472	0	.633
25.	Cincinnati	1902	106	1,522	882	0	.633
26.	North Carolina St.	1913	95	1,503	894	0	.627
27.	Alabama	1913	94	1,447	868	1	.625
28.	Purdue	1897	109	1,513	908	0	.625
29.	UAB	1979	29	572	344	0	.624
30.	Texas	1906	101	1,532	926	0	.623
31.	VCU	1971	37	659	400	0	.622
32.	Jackson St.	1951	56	970	596	0	.619
33.	Memphis	1921	86	1,298	799	0	.619
34.	Princeton	1901	107	1,533	949	0	.618
35.	Old Dominion	1951	57	911	568	0	.616
36.	Marquette	1917	90	1,374	857	0	.616
37.	Georgetown	1907	99	1,432	903	0	.613
38.	West Virginia	1904	98	1,501	949	0	.613
39.	Oklahoma	1908	100	1,446	922	0	.611
40.	Holy Cross	1901	88	1,247	799	0	.609
41.	BYU	1903	105	1,526	978	0	.609
42.	Tennessee	1909	98	1,390	901	2	.607
43.	Bradley	1903	103	1,495	974	0	.606
44.	St. Joseph's	1910	98	1,439	938	0	.605
45.	Tennessee St.	1945	63	1,034	680	0	.603
46.	Providence	1921	82	1,240	817	0	.603
47.	Washington	1896	105	1,548	1,021	0	.603
48.	Green Bay	1970	38	667	441	0	.602
49.	Akron	1902	106	1,340	886	0	.602
50.	Southern Ill.	1914	93	1,384	920	0	.601

All-Time Won-Lost Records

(Alphabetical Listing; No Minimum Seasons of Competition)

Team	First Season	Yrs.	Won	Lost	Tied	Pct.
Air Force	1957	51	593	748	0	.442
Akron	1902	106	1,340	886	0	.602
Alabama	1913	94	1,447	868	1	.625
Alabama A&M	1951	50	733	582	0	.557
Alabama St.	1935	68	1,041	708	0	.595
UAB	1979	29	572	344	0	.624
Albany (N.Y.)	1910	94	1,057	768	0	.579
Alcorn St.	1945	62	1,065	747	0	.588
American	1935	73	937	895	0	.511
Appalachian St.	1920	82	1,064	922	0	.536
Arizona	1905	102	1,528	829	1	.648
Arizona St.	1912	95	1,161	1,057	0	.523
Arkansas	1924	84	1,450	794	0	.646
Arkansas St.	1927	79	1,011	954	0	.515
Ark.-Little Rock	1968	40	600	518	0	.537
Ark.-Pine Bluff	1957	39	485	538	0	.474
Army	1903	105	1,069	1,049	0	.505
Auburn	1906	101	1,162	1,011	1	.535
Austin Peay	1930	76	1,015	888	0	.533
Ball St.	1921	86	1,059	939	1	.530
Baylor	1907	101	1,068	1,234	0	.464
Belmont	1953	55	852	718	0	.543
Bethune-Cookman	1962	46	562	691	0	.449
Binghamton	1947	61	567	776	0	.422
Boise St.	1969	39	595	507	0	.540
Boston College	1905	74	1,031	783	0	.568
Boston U.	1902	98	972	956	0	.504
Bowling Green	1916	92	1,199	986	0	.549
Bradley	1903	103	1,495	974	0	.606
BYU	1903	105	1,526	978	0	.609
Brown	1901	101	893	1,328	0	.402
Bucknell	1896	112	1,212	1,071	0	.531
Buffalo	1916	90	967	963	0	.501
Butler	1897	109	1,306	1,016	0	.562
Cal Poly	1922	76	929	874	0	.515
California	1908	98	1,354	1,032	0	.567
UC Davis	1911	95	933	1,108	0	.457
UC Irvine	1966	42	581	597	0	.493
UC Riverside	1955	53	771	600	0	.562
UC Santa Barbara	1922	82	1,010	962	0	.512
Cal St. Fullerton	1961	47	593	692	0	.461
Cal St. Northridge	1959	49	640	691	0	.481
Campbell	1962	46	593	676	0	.467
Canisius	1904	103	1,128	1,059	0	.516

Team	First Season	Yrs.	Won	Lost	Tied	Pct.
Centenary (La.)	1922	81	1,030	1,051	0	.495
Central Conn. St.	1935	71	972	724	0	.573
UCF	1970	38	595	451	0	.569
Central Mich.	1905	103	1,131	1,050	1	.519
Col. of Charleston	1899	97	1,022	844	0	.548
Charleston So.	1966	42	478	659	0	.420
Charlotte	1966	42	674	525	0	.562
Chattanooga	1916	86	1,105	871	0	.559
Chicago St.	1967	41	468	676	0	.409
Cincinnati	1902	106	1,522	882	0	.633
Citadel	1913	95	868	1,117	0	.437
Clemson	1912	96	1,092	1,145	2	.488
Cleveland St.	1930	76	692	1,002	0	.409
Coastal Caro.	1975	33	447	491	0	.477
Colgate	1901	107	1,122	1,184	0	.487
Colorado	1902	104	1,092	1,031	0	.514
Colorado St.	1902	103	1,061	1,083	0	.495
Columbia	1901	107	1,125	1,127	0	.500
Connecticut	1901	104	1,444	825	0	.636
Coppin St.	1965	43	656	502	0	.566
Cornell	1899	109	1,096	1,253	0	.467
Creighton	1912	90	1,319	903	0	.594
Dartmouth	1901	106	1,181	1,284	0	.479
Davidson	1909	98	1,195	1,085	0	.524
Dayton	1904	102	1,374	981	0	.583
Delaware	1906	102	1,016	1,102	2	.480
Delaware St.	1957	50	570	734	0	.437
Denver	1904	103	1,111	1,141	0	.493
DePaul	1924	84	1,332	766	0	.635
Detroit	1906	100	1,256	1,014	0	.553
Drake	1907	101	1,059	1,276	0	.454
Drexel	1921	86	1,028	841	0	.550
Duke	1906	102	1,818	802	0	.694
Duquesne	1914	91	1,218	928	0	.568
East Caro.	1932	75	914	935	0	.494
East Tenn. St.	1922	78	1,048	848	0	.553
Eastern Ill.	1909	96	1,157	1,048	0	.525
Eastern Ky.	1910	95	1,062	999	1	.515
Eastern Mich.	1904	100	1,055	1,068	0	.497
Eastern Wash.	1904	99	1,246	1,030	0	.547
Elon	1911	95	1,241	1,102	0	.530
Evansville	1920	88	1,195	900	0	.570
Fairfield	1949	59	758	775	0	.494
Fairleigh Dickinson	1950	58	821	698	0	.540
Florida	1916	88	1,141	984	0	.537
Florida A&M	1951	57	864	684	0	.558
Fla. Atlantic	1989	19	192	343	0	.359
Florida Int'l	1982	26	310	422	0	.423
Florida St.	1948	60	950	709	0	.573
Fordham	1903	104	1,420	1,148	0	.553
Fresno St.	1922	85	1,143	943	0	.548
Furman	1909	94	1,077	1,071	0	.501
Gardner-Webb	1970	26	471	276	0	.631
George Mason	1967	41	569	585	0	.493
George Washington	1907	93	1,168	978	0	.544
Georgetown	1907	99	1,432	903	0	.613
Georgia	1906	102	1,218	1,120	0	.521
Ga. Southern	1927	75	1,101	786	0	.583
Georgia St.	1964	44	417	760	0	.354
Georgia Tech	1906	92	1,190	1,038	0	.534
Gonzaga	1908	99	1,311	1,028	0	.560
Grambling	1957	51	792	654	0	.548
Green Bay	1970	38	667	441	0	.602
Hampton	1953	55	799	662	0	.547
Hartford	1963	45	570	615	0	.481
Harvard	1901	96	923	1,197	0	.435
Hawaii	1938	64	634	764	0	.454
High Point	1928	80	1,224	883	0	.581
Hofstra	1937	69	1,050	771	0	.577
Holy Cross	1901	88	1,247	799	0	.609
Houston	1946	62	1,041	702	0	.597
Howard	1902	93	987	1,063	0	.481
Idaho	1906	102	1,163	1,300	0	.472
Idaho St.	1927	80	1,046	978	0	.517
Illinois	1906	102	1,569	824	0	.656
Illinois St.	1899	109	1,391	1,016	0	.578
Ill.-Chicago	1948	60	717	740	0	.492
Indiana	1901	107	1,610	876	0	.648
Indiana St.	1900	108	1,305	1,093	0	.544
IPFW	1974	34	374	554	0	.403
IUPUI	1972	36	508	526	0	.491
Iona	1941	64	946	709	0	.572

Team	First Season	Yrs.	Won	Lost	Tied	Pct.
Iowa	1902	106	1,438	970	0	.597
Iowa St.	1908	100	1,134	1,160	0	.494
Jackson St.	1951	56	970	596	0	.619
Jacksonville	1949	59	817	734	0	.527
Jacksonville St.	1926	64	1,010	615	0	.622
James Madison	1970	38	579	478	0	.548
Kansas	1899	109	1,906	782	0	.709
Kansas St.	1903	103	1,386	1,012	0	.578
Kent St.	1914	91	978	1,091	0	.473
Kentucky	1903	104	1,948	608	1	.762
La Salle	1932	76	1,189	794	0	.600
Lafayette	1901	97	1,180	1,049	0	.529
Lamar	1952	56	831	692	0	.546
Lehigh	1902	106	889	1,257	0	.414
Liberty	1973	35	485	527	0	.479
Lipscomb	1937	57	1,029	514	0	.667
Long Beach St.	1951	57	813	719	0	.531
Long Island	1929	73	1,065	791	2	.574
Longwood	1977	31	418	428	0	.494
LSU	1909	99	1,346	1,010	0	.571
Louisiana Tech	1926	80	1,127	873	0	.564
La.-Lafayette	1912	91	1,206	920	0	.567
La.-Monroe	1952	56	854	664	0	.563
Louisville	1912	93	1,529	816	0	.652
Loyola (Ill.)	1914	91	1,145	982	0	.538
Loyola (Md.)	1908	97	1,105	1,119	0	.497
Loyola Marymount	1924	79	895	1,053	0	.459
Maine	1902	92	892	965	0	.480
Manhattan	1905	101	1,193	1,039	0	.534
Marist	1967	41	573	556	0	.508
Marquette	1917	90	1,374	857	0	.616
Marshall	1907	95	1,288	933	2	.580
Maryland	1905	88	1,303	921	0	.586
UMBC	1971	37	420	589	0	.416
Md.-East. Shore	1955	46	546	637	0	.462
Massachusetts	1900	98	1,088	977	0	.527
McNeese St.	1941	65	924	754	0	.551
Memphis	1921	86	1,298	799	0	.619
Mercer	1909	90	1,034	1,011	0	.506
Miami (Fla.)	1928	55	765	616	0	.554
Miami (Ohio)	1906	102	1,218	983	0	.553
Michigan	1909	91	1,223	893	0	.578
Michigan St.	1899	108	1,391	979	0	.587
Middle Tenn.	1914	84	984	925	0	.515
Milwaukee	1897	111	1,175	1,079	1	.521
Minnesota	1896	112	1,377	1,052	2	.567
Mississippi	1909	97	1,067	1,154	0	.480
Mississippi St.	1909	95	1,202	1,020	0	.541
Mississippi Val.	1962	39	507	581	0	.466
Missouri	1907	101	1,406	994	0	.586
Missouri St.	1909	95	1,470	797	0	.648
UMKC	1970	37	528	520	0	.504
Monmouth	1957	51	814	571	0	.588
Montana	1906	99	1,253	1,107	0	.531
Montana St.	1902	105	1,412	1,116	0	.559
Morehead St.	1930	78	956	931	0	.507
Morgan St.	1948	60	640	894	0	.417
Mt. St. Mary's	1955	53	871	600	0	.592
Murray St.	1926	82	1,360	781	0	.635
Navy	1907	101	1,236	854	0	.591
Nebraska	1897	111	1,314	1,175	0	.528
Nevada	1913	94	1,106	1,032	0	.517
UNLV	1959	49	1,010	410	0	.711
New Hampshire	1903	103	781	1,268	0	.381
New Mexico	1900	104	1,262	996	0	.559
New Mexico St.	1905	98	1,253	961	2	.566
New Orleans	1970	38	655	436	0	.600
Niagara	1906	101	1,302	1,030	1	.558
Nicholls St.	1964	42	489	632	0	.436
Norfolk St.	1963	44	863	393	0	.687
North Carolina	1911	97	1,914	696	0	.733
N.C. A&T	1953	55	873	625	0	.583
UNC Asheville	1965	43	603	631	0	.489
UNC Greensboro	1968	40	465	562	0	.453
North Carolina St.	1913	95	1,503	894	0	.627
UNC Wilmington	1964	44	616	594	0	.509
North Texas	1915	90	962	1,136	0	.459
Northeastern	1921	87	1,018	948	0	.518
Northern Ariz.	1910	95	1,011	1,032	0	.495
Northern Colo.	1902	103	971	1,077	0	.474
Northern Ill.	1955	50	606	696	0	.465
UNI	1901	102	1,068	996	0	.517
Northwestern	1905	102	892	1,324	1	.403

Team	First Season	Yrs.	Won	Lost	Tied	Pct.
Northwestern St.	1966	42	530	630	0	.457
Notre Dame	1898	102	1,605	885	1	.645
Oakland	1968	40	558	546	0	.505
Ohio	1908	100	1,296	986	0	.568
Ohio St.	1899	106	1,390	957	0	.592
Oklahoma	1908	100	1,446	922	0	.611
Oklahoma St.	1908	98	1,435	1,002	0	.589
Old Dominion	1951	57	911	568	0	.616
Oral Roberts	1970	34	578	400	0	.591
Oregon	1903	102	1,392	1,213	0	.534
Oregon St.	1902	106	1,570	1,137	0	.580
Pacific	1911	97	1,098	1,075	0	.505
Penn	1897	107	1,634	913	2	.641
Penn St.	1897	111	1,277	985	1	.565
Pepperdine	1939	69	1,091	858	0	.560
Pittsburgh	1906	100	1,353	1,018	0	.571
Portland	1923	82	1,021	1,096	0	.482
Portland St.	1947	46	598	592	0	.503
Prairie View	1957	47	458	800	0	.364
Princeton	1901	107	1,533	949	0	.618
Providence	1921	82	1,240	817	0	.603
Purdue	1897	109	1,513	908	0	.625
Quinnipiac	1952	56	769	706	0	.521
Radford	1975	33	512	412	0	.554
Rhode Island	1904	101	1,285	968	0	.570
Rice	1915	93	957	1,174	0	.449
Richmond	1913	95	1,144	1,035	0	.525
Rider	1928	77	986	881	0	.528
Robert Morris	1977	31	388	484	0	.445
Rutgers	1907	95	1,089	996	0	.522
Sacramento St.	1949	59	654	911	0	.418
Sacred Heart	1966	42	685	512	0	.572
St. Bonaventure	1920	87	1,140	870	0	.567
St. Francis (N.Y.)	1902	88	1,067	1,070	0	.499
St. Francis (Pa.)	1919	81	978	935	2	.511
St. John's (N.Y.)	1908	100	1,659	831	0	.666
St. Joseph's	1910	98	1,439	938	0	.605
St. Louis	1916	91	1,207	1,042	0	.537
St. Mary's (Cal.)	1910	84	1,029	1,095	0	.484
St. Peter's	1931	74	930	868	0	.517
Sam Houston St.	1918	85	1,074	977	0	.524
Samford	1902	91	963	1,138	0	.458
San Diego	1956	52	729	688	0	.514
San Diego St.	1922	86	1,160	999	0	.537
San Francisco	1924	80	1,188	821	0	.591
San Jose St.	1910	93	1,026	1,139	0	.474
Santa Clara	1905	100	1,307	904	0	.591
Savannah St.	1965	43	491	659	0	.427
Seton Hall	1904	95	1,294	915	2	.586
Siena	1939	66	918	770	0	.544
South Ala.	1969	39	629	471	0	.572
South Carolina	1909	99	1,223	1,068	1	.534
South Carolina St.	1956	52	830	605	0	.578
South Fla.	1972	36	490	531	0	.480
Southeast Mo. St.	1953	49	737	533	0	.580
Southeastern La.	1948	59	673	853	0	.441
Southern California	1907	101	1,414	1,017	0	.582
Southern Ill.	1914	93	1,384	920	0	.601
SMU	1917	91	1,114	1,053	0	.514
Southern Miss.	1913	88	1,043	898	1	.537
Southern U.	1950	45	744	528	0	.585
Southern Utah	1969	39	576	480	0	.545
Stanford	1914	92	1,296	988	0	.567
Stephen F. Austin	1925	81	1,209	827	0	.594
Stetson	1901	91	1,101	927	0	.543
Stony Brook	1961	47	582	569	0	.506
Syracuse	1901	106	1,704	782	0	.685
Temple	1895	111	1,668	935	0	.641
Tennessee	1909	98	1,390	901	2	.607
Tennessee St.	1945	63	1,034	680	0	.603
Tennessee Tech	1925	83	958	917	1	.511
Tenn.-Martin	1952	56	622	770	0	.447
Texas	1906	101	1,532	926	0	.623
Texas A&M	1913	95	1,176	1,119	0	.512
A&M-Corpus Chris	2000	8	134	91	0	.596
TCU	1909	96	1,036	1,185	0	.466
Texas Southern	1950	57	933	703	0	.570
Texas St.	1921	86	1,131	964	0	.540
Texas Tech	1926	82	1,221	915	0	.572
Texas-Arlington	1960	48	519	776	0	.401
UTEP	1915	86	1,161	897	0	.564
Tex.-Pan American	1953	55	706	761	0	.481

Team	First Season	Yrs.	Won	Lost	Tied	Pct.
UTSA	1982	26	386	354	0	.522
Toledo	1916	92	1,267	879	0	.590
Towson	1959	49	550	711	0	.436
Troy	1951	57	905	678	0	.572
Tulane	1906	97	1,064	1,073	0	.498
Tulsa	1908	96	1,212	1,001	0	.548
UCLA	1920	88	1,611	713	0	.693
Utah	1909	99	1,595	833	0	.657
Utah St.	1904	101	1,332	970	0	.579
Utah Valley St.	2004	4	77	37	0	.675
Valparaiso	1918	90	1,126	1,064	0	.514
Vanderbilt	1901	105	1,378	995	0	.581
Vermont	1901	93	985	1,000	0	.496
Villanova	1921	87	1,453	829	0	.637
Virginia	1906	102	1,351	1,045	1	.564
VCU	1971	37	659	400	0	.622
VMI	1909	99	732	1,326	0	.356
Virginia Tech	1909	99	1,239	1,043	0	.543
Wagner	1923	70	866	897	0	.491
Wake Forest	1906	101	1,349	1,029	0	.567
Washington	1896	105	1,548	1,021	0	.603
Washington St.	1902	106	1,414	1,316	0	.518
Weber St.	1963	45	815	472	0	.633
West Virginia	1904	98	1,501	949	0	.613
Western Caro.	1929	79	1,051	1,001	0	.512
Western Ill.	1948	60	840	790	0	.515
Western Ky.	1915	88	1,548	764	0	.670
Western Mich.	1914	94	1,134	1,019	0	.527
Wichita St.	1906	100	1,278	1,090	0	.540
William & Mary	1906	102	1,043	1,212	0	.463
Winthrop	1979	29	479	394	0	.549
Wisconsin	1899	109	1,314	1,089	0	.547
Wofford	1916	83	1,037	1,033	0	.501
Wright St.	1971	37	613	420	0	.593
Wyoming	1905	102	1,337	989	0	.575
Xavier	1920	86	1,199	877	0	.578
Yale	1896	112	1,270	1,324	1	.490
Youngstown St.	1928	77	956	934	0	.506

Note: Records are adjusted with vacated and forfeited games.

Schools in the process of becoming Division I

Team	First Season	Yrs.	Won	Lost	Tied	Pct.
Cal St. Bakersfield	1972	36	730	307	0	.704
Central Ark.	1921	85	1,357	842	1	.617
Fla. Gulf Coast	2003	5	114	39	0	.745
Kennesaw St.	1986	22	365	281	0	.565
NJIT	1924	76	799	654	0	.550
N.C. Central	1928	74	1,026	804	0	.561
North Dakota St.	1898	108	1,387	987	0	.584
North Fla.	1993	15	161	255	0	.387
Presbyterian	1952	43	712	527	0	.575
S.C. Upstate	1975	33	567	382	0	.597
South Dakota St.	1906	99	1,277	879	1	.592
Utah Valley St.	2004	4	77	37	0	.675
Winston-Salem	1947	61	1,056	622	0	.629

Vacated and Forfeited Games

Teams	Coach	Year	Actual W-L	Adjusted W-L	Games Affected*
Alabama	Wimp Sanderson	1987	28-5	26-4	V: Tr 2-1
Arizona	Lute Olson	1999	22-7	22-6	V: Tr 0-1
Arizona St.	Bill Freider	1995	24-9	22-8	V: Tr 2-1
Austin Peay	Lake Kelly	1973	22-7	21-5	V: Tr 1-2
California	Todd Bozeman	1995	13-14	0-27	F: RS 13 wins
California	Todd Bozeman	1996	17-11	2-25	F: RS 15 wins; V: 0-1
Clemson	Cliff Ellis	1990	26-9	24-8	V: Tr 2-1
Connecticut	Jim Calhoun	1996	32-3	30-2	V: Tr 2-1
DePaul	Joey Meyer	1986	18-13	16-12	V: Tr 2-1
DePaul	Joey Meyer	1987	28-3	26-2	V: Tr 2-1
DePaul	Joey Meyer	1988	22-8	21-7	V: Tr 1-1
DePaul	Joey Meyer	1989	21-12	20-11	V: Tr 1-1
Florida	Norm Sloan	1987	23-11	21-10	V: Tr 2-1
Florida	Norm Sloan	1988	23-12	22-11	V: Tr 1-1
Fresno St.	Jerry Tarkanian	1999	21-12	1-12	V: RS 20 wins
Fresno St.	Jerry Tarkanian	2000	24-10	12-9	V: RS 12 wins, Tr 0-1
Fresno St.	Jerry Tarkanian	2001	26-7	9-7	V: RS 17 wins
Georgia	Hugh Durham	1985	22-9	21-8	V: Tr 1-1
Georgia	Jim Harrick	2002	22-10	21-9	V: Tr 1-1
Iona	Jim Valvano	1980	29-5	28-4	V: Tr 1-1
Kentucky	Eddie Sutton	1988	27-6	25-5	V: Tr 2-1
Long Beach St.	Jerry Tarkanian	1971	24-5	22-4	V: Tr 2-1
Long Beach St.	Jerry Tarkanian	1972	25-4	23-3	V: Tr 2-1
Long Beach St.	Jerry Tarkanian	1973	26-3	24-2	V: Tr 2-1
La.-Lafayette	Berly Shipley	1972	25-4	23-3	V: Tr 2-1
La.-Lafayette	Berly Shipley	1973	24-5	23-3	V: Tr 1-2
La.-Lafayette	Jessie Evans	2004	20-9	6-8	V: RS 14 wins, Tr 0-1
La.-Lafayette	Robert Lee	2005	20-11	3-10	V: RS 17 wins, Tr 0-1
Loyola Marymount	Ron Jacobs	1980	14-14	14-13	V: Tr 0-1
Marshall	Ricky Huckabay	1987	25-6	25-5	V: Tr 0-1
Maryland	Bob Wade	1988	18-13	17-12	V: Tr 1-1
Massachusetts	John Calipari	996	35-2	31-1	V: Tr 4-1
Memphis	Dana Kirk	1982	24-5	23-4	V: Tr 1-1
Memphis	Dana Kirk	1983	23-8	22-7	V: Tr 1-1
Memphis	Dana Kirk	1984	26-7	24-6	V: Tr 2-1
Memphis	Dana Kirk	1985	31-4	27-3	V: Tr 4-1
Memphis	Dana Kirk	1986	28-6	27-5	V: Tr 1-1
Miami (Ohio)	Jerry Pierson	1989	13-15	5-23	F: RS 8 wins
Michigan	Steve Fisher	1992	25-9	20-8	V: Tr 5-1
Michigan	Steve Fisher	1993	31-5	0-5	V: RS 26 wins, Tr 5-1
Michigan	Steve Fisher	1996	21-11	0-11	V: RS 21 wins, Tr 0-1
Michigan	Steve Fisher	1997	24-11	0-11	V: RS 24 wins
Michigan	Brian Ellerbe	1998	25-9	0-9	V: RS 24 wins, Tr 1-1
Michigan	Brian Ellerbe	1999	12-19	0-19	V: RS 12 wins
Minnesota	Bill Musselman	1972	18-7	17-6	V: Tr 1-1
Minnesota	Jim Dutcher	1977	24-3	0-27	F: RS 24 wins
Minnesota	Clem Haskins	1994	22-13	21-12	V: Tr 1-1
Minnesota	Clem Haskins	1995	19-13	19-12	V: Tr 0-1
Minnesota	Clem Haskins	1996	19-13	18-12	V: NIT 1-1
Minnesota	Clem Haskins	1997	35-5	31-4	V: Tr 4-1
Minnesota	Clem Haskins	1998	20-15	15-15	V: NIT 5-0
Missouri	Norm Stewart	1994	28-4	25-3	V: Tr 3-1
New Mexico St.	Neil McCarthy	1992	25-8	23-7	V: Tr 2-1
New Mexico St.	Neil McCarthy	1993	26-8	25-7	V: Tr 1-1
New Mexico St.	Neil McCarthy	1994	23-8	23-7	V: Tr 0-1
New Mexico St.	Neil McCarthy	1997	19-9	0-0	V: RS 19 wins
New Mexico St.	Lou Henson	1998	18-12	0-0	V: RS 18 wins
North Carolina St.	Jim Valvano	1987	20-14	20-13	V: Tr 0-1
North Carolina St.	Jim Valvano	1988	24-7	24-6	V: Tr 0-1
Ohio St.	Jim O'Brien	1999	27-9	1-1	V: RS 22-7, Tr 4-1
Ohio St.	Jim O'Brien	2000	23-7	11-3	V: RS 11-3, Tr 1-1
Ohio St.	Jim O'Brien	2001	20-11	0-0	V: RS 20-10, Tr 0-1
Ohio St.	Jim O'Brien	2002	24-8	0-0	V: RS 23-7, Tr 1-1
Oregon St.	Ralph Miller	1976	18-9	3-24	F: RS 15 wins
Oregon St.	Ralph Miller	1980	26-4	26-3	V: Tr 0-1
Oregon St.	Ralph Miller	1981	26-2	26-1	V: Tr 0-1
Oregon St.	Ralph Miller	1982	25-5	23-4	V: Tr 2-1
Purdue	Gene Keady	1996	26-6	7-23	F: RS 18 wins; V: Tr 1-1
St. Bonaventure	Jan van Breda Kolff	2002	13-14	1-14	V: RS 12 wins
St. John's (N.Y.)	Mike Jarvis	2001	14-15	5-15	V: RS 9 wins
St. John's (N.Y.)	Mike Jarvis	2002	20-12	7-11	V: RS 13 wins, Tr 0-1
St. John's (N.Y.)	Mike Jarvis	2003	21-13	1-13	V: RS 20 wins
St. John's (N.Y.)	Mike Jarvis	2004	6-21	2-21	V: RS 4 wins
St. Joseph's	Jack Ramsay	1961	25-5	22-4	V: Tr 3-1
Texas Tech	James Dickey	1996	30-2	28-1	V: Tr 2-1
UCLA	Larry Brown	1980	22-10	17-9	V: Tr 5-1
UCLA	Steve Lavin	1999	22-9	22-8	V: Tr 0-1
Villanova	Jack Kraft	1971	27-7	23-6	V: Tr 4-1
Western Ky.	Johnny Oldham	1971	24-6	20-5	V: Tr 4-1

*F=Forfeited, V=Vacated.
*NIT=National Invitational Tournament, RS=Regular Season, Tr=NCAA Tournament.

Winningest Teams by Decade

1930-39

Rk.	Team	Won	Lost	Pct.
1.	Long Island	198	38	.839
2.	Kentucky	162	34	.827
3.	St. John's (N.Y.)	181	40	.819
4.	Kansas	153	37	.805
5.	Syracuse	143	37	.794
6.	Purdue	148	39	.791
7.	Western Ky.	197	52	.791
8.	Rhode Island	142	39	.785
9.	Notre Dame	170	49	.776
10.	CCNY	120	35	.774
11.	Washington	206	63	.766
12.	DePaul	142	44	.763
13.	Arkansas	167	57	.746
14.	Duquesne	143	50	.741
15.	Wyoming	147	52	.739
16.	Navy	108	40	.730
17.	North Carolina	163	61	.728
18.	George Washington	129	50	.721
19.	New York U.	124	49	.717
20.	Western Mich.	123	50	.711

1940-49

Rk.	Team	Won	Lost	Pct.
1.	Kentucky	239	42	.851
2.	Oklahoma St.	237	55	.812
3.	Rhode Island	178	44	.802
4.	Eastern Ky.	145	40	.784
5.	Western Ky.	222	66	.771
6.	Tennessee	152	46	.768
7.	Bowling Green	204	66	.756
8.	Notre Dame	162	55	.747
9.	Toledo	176	65	.730
10.	St. John's (N.Y.)	162	60	.730
11.	North Carolina	196	75	.723
12.	West Virginia	157	59	.727
13.	Illinois	150	57	.725
14.	DePaul	180	69	.723
15.	Bradley	144	56	.720
16.	New York U.	150	60	.714
17.	Utah	159	68	.700
18.	Wyoming	163	70	.700
19.	Texas	168	73	.697
20.	CCNY	133	62	.682
Played only seven seasons:				
	Seton Hall	128	22	.853
	Duquesne	118	32	.787
	George Washington	117	47	.713

1950-59

Rk.	Team	Won	Lost	Pct.
1.	Kentucky	224	33	.872
2.	North Carolina St.	240	65	.787
3.	Seattle	233	69	.772
4.	La Salle	209	65	.763
5.	Dayton	228	71	.763
6.	Holy Cross	199	65	.754
7.	Kansas St.	179	63	.740
8.	Connecticut	187	67	.736
9.	West Virginia	205	74	.735
10.	Louisville	202	77	.724
11.	Illinois	165	64	.721
12.	Western Ky.	205	82	.714
13.	UCLA	193	78	.712
14.	Duquesne	187	76	.711
15.	Kansas	171	74	.698
16.	St. John's (N.Y.)	176	77	.696
17.	Cincinnati	175	80	.686
18.	Oklahoma St.	192	88	.686
19.	Lafayette	171	81	.679
20.	St. Louis	185	88	.678

1960-69

Rk.	Team	Won	Lost	Pct.
1.	UCLA	234	52	.818
2.	Cincinnati	214	63	.773
3.	Providence	204	64	.761
4.	Duke	213	67	.761
5.	Kentucky	197	69	.741
6.	Ohio St.	188	69	.732
7.	St. Joseph's	201	74	.731
8.	Dayton	207	77	.729
9.	Bradley	197	74	.727
10.	Princeton	188	71	.726
11.	Vanderbilt	182	69	.725
12.	North Carolina	184	72	.719
13.	St. Bonaventure	172	69	.714
14.	Villanova	193	79	.710
15.	Houston	198	82	.707
16.	St. John's (N.Y.)	185	79	.701
17.	Miami (Fla.)	183	82	.691
18.	West Virginia	197	89	.689
19.	Temple	183	83	.688
20.	UTEP	177	81	.686
Played only seven seasons:				
	Weber St.	147	36	.803

1970-79

Rk.	Team	Won	Lost	Pct.
1.	UCLA	273	27	.910
2.	Marquette	251	41	.860
3.	Penn	223	56	.799
4.	North Carolina	239	65	.786
5.	Kentucky	223	69	.764
6.	Louisville	224	70	.762
7.	Syracuse	213	69	.755
8.	Long Beach St.	209	71	.746
9.	Indiana	208	75	.735
10.	Florida St.	201	74	.731
11.	UNLV	203	78	.722
12.	North Carolina St.	208	80	.722
13.	San Francisco	202	79	.719
14.	Houston	210	84	.714
15.	Providence	209	84	.713
16.	South Carolina	198	80	.712
17.	St. John's (N.Y.)	205	85	.707
18.	Maryland	199	85	.701
19.	Rutgers	193	84	.697
20.	Notre Dame	202	89	.694
Played only eight seasons:				
	Oral Roberts	161	59	.732

1980-89

Rk.	Team	Won	Lost	Pct.
1.	North Carolina	281	63	.817
2.	UNLV	271	65	.807
3.	Georgetown	269	69	.796
4.	DePaul	235	67	.778
5.	Temple	225	78	.743
6.	Syracuse	243	87	.736
7.	UTEP	227	82	.735
8.	Oklahoma	245	90	.731
9.	Kentucky	233	86	.730
10.	St. John's (N.Y.)	228	85	.728
11.	Indiana	228	86	.726
12.	Oregon St.	212	80	.726
13.	Louisville	250	96	.723
14.	Illinois	233	90	.721
15.	Memphis	225	89	.717
16.	Northeastern	213	86	.712
17.	Chattanooga	215	89	.707
18.	Arkansas	218	92	.703
19.	Missouri	227	99	.696
20.	West Virginia	217	95	.696

DIVISION I

1990-99

Rk.	Team	Won	Lost	Pct.
1.	Kansas	286	60	.827
2.	Kentucky	282	63	.817
3.	Arizona	256	67	.793
4.	Duke	271	78	.777
5.	North Carolina	270	78	.776
6.	Connecticut	259	75	.775
7.	Utah	250	76	.767
8.	Princeton	210	66	.761
9.	Arkansas	260	83	.758
10.	UCLA	240	79	.752
11.	Cincinnati	246	83	.748
12.	Xavier	217	86	.716
13.	Syracuse	232	92	.716
14.	Massachusetts	237	94	.716
15.	Murray St.	219	88	.713
16.	Indiana	229	94	.709
17.	New Mexico St.	219	91	.706
18.	Green Bay	211	90	.701
19.	Purdue	222	96	.698
20.	New Mexico	224	97	.698

Played only eight seasons:

	Col. of Charleston	191	42	.820

2000-07

Rk.	Team	Won	Lost	Pct.
1.	Duke	233	47	.832
2.	Gonzaga	211	52	.802
3.	Kansas	218	58	.790
4.	Florida	212	62	.774
5.	Illinois	212	62	.774
6.	Utah St.	198	62	.762
7.	Kentucky	200	70	.741
8.	Syracuse	201	71	.739
9.	Arizona	197	70	.738
10.	Connecticut	198	71	.736
11.	Oklahoma	192	69	.736
12.	Pittsburgh	194	70	.735
13.	Stanford	184	68	.730
14.	Texas	197	73	.730
15.	Southern Ill.	191	73	.723
16.	Creighton	184	73	.716
17.	Memphis	196	79	.713
18.	Oklahoma St.	188	76	.712
19.	Kent St.	186	76	.710
20.	Xavier	183	75	.709

Winningest Teams Over Periods of Time

Victories Over a Two-Year Period

Team	First Year	Last Year	Won	Lost
Montana St.	1928	1929	72	4
Kentucky	1947	1948	70	6
UNLV	1986	1987	70	7
Kentucky	1997	1998	70	9
Georgetown	1984	1985	69	6
UNLV	1990	1991	69	6
Kansas	1997	1998	69	6
Duke	1998	1999	69	6
Kentucky	1996	1997	69	7
Kentucky	1948	1949	68	5
Florida	2006	2007	68	11
Connecticut	1998	1999	66	7
Duke	1999	2000	66	7
Duke	2001	2002	66	8
Memphis	2006	2007	66	8
Montana St.	1927	1928	66	9
Duke	1991	1992	66	9
Oklahoma	1988	1989	65	10
Michigan St.	1999	2000	65	12
UNLV	1987	1988	65	8
Temple	1987	1988	64	6
Arizona	1988	1989	64	7
Massachusetts	1995	1996	64	7
Arkansas	1990	1991	64	9
Duke	2000	2001	64	9
Bradley	1950	1951	64	11
UNLV	1989	1990	64	13

Victories Over a Three-Year Period

Team	First Year	Last Year	Won	Lost
Kentucky	1996	1998	104	11
Kentucky	1947	1949	102	8
Montana St.	1927	1929	102	11
Duke	1999	2001	101	11
Kentucky	1946	1948	98	8
Kansas	1996	1998	98	11
Duke	1998	2000	98	11
UNLV	1985	1987	98	11
UNLV	1986	1988	98	13
UNLV	1989	1991	98	14
Kentucky	1997	1999	98	18

Team	First Year	Last Year	Won	Lost
Kentucky	1995	1997	97	12
UNLV	1990	1992	95	8
Duke	2000	2002	95	13
Duke	1990	1992	95	18
UNLV	1987	1989	94	16
Kentucky	1948	1950	93	10
Montana St.	1928	1930	93	14
Georgetown	1984	1986	93	14
Duke	1997	1999	93	15
Michigan St.	1999	2001	93	17
Massachusetts	1994	1996	92	14
Oklahoma	1988	1990	92	15
Duke	2001	2003	92	15
Kansas	1997	1999	92	16
UNLV	1988	1990	92	19
Florida	2005	2007	92	19

Victories Over a Four-Year Period

Team	First Year	Last Year	Won	Lost
Duke	1998	2001	133	15
Duke	1999	2002	132	15
Kentucky	1995	1998	132	16
Kentucky	1996	1999	132	20
Kentucky	1946	1949	130	10
UNLV	1987	1990	129	21
Kentucky	1947	1950	127	13
UNLV	1984	1987	127	17
UNLV	1986	1989	127	21
UNLV	1985	1988	126	17
UNLV	1988	1991	126	20
Kentucky	1948	1951	125	12
UNLV	1989	1992	124	16
Kentucky	1994	1997	124	19
Kansas	1995	1998	123	17
Montana St.	1927	1930	123	21
Duke	2001	2004	123	21
Duke	1989	1992	123	26
Georgetown	1984	1987	122	19
Duke	1997	2000	122	20
Montana St.	1926	1929	122	23
Duke	2000	2003	121	20
Kansas	1996	1999	121	21
Georgetown	1982	1985	121	23
Kentucky	1997	2000	121	28

Winning Percentage Over a Two-Year Period

(Minimum 40 games)

Team	First Year	Last Year	Won	Lost	Pct.
UCLA	1972	1973	60	0	1.000
Indiana	1975	1976	63	1	.984
UCLA	1967	1968	59	1	.983
UCLA	1971	1972	59	1	.983
North Carolina St.	1973	1974	57	1	.983
North Carolina	1923	1924	41	1	.976
UCLA	1964	1965	58	2	.967
UCLA	1968	1969	58	2	.967
Long Island	1935	1936	49	2	.961
St. John's (N.Y.)	1930	1931	46	2	.958
UNLV	1991	1992	60	3	.952
Seton Hall	1940	1941	39	2	.951
Arkansas	1928	1929	38	2	.950
Notre Dame	1926	1927	38	2	.950
UCLA	1969	1970	57	3	.950
UCLA	1970	1971	57	3	.950
Alcorn St.	1978	1979	56	3	.949
Montana St.	1928	1929	72	4	.947
Long Island	1936	1937	53	3	.946
Penn	1970	1971	53	3	.946
Ohio St.	1961	1962	53	3	.946
Long Island	1934	1935	50	3	.943
Kentucky	1954	1955	48	3	.941
St. John's (N.Y.)	1929	1930	46	3	.939
Penn	1920	1921	43	3	.935

Winning Percentage Over a Three-Year Period

(Minimum 60 games)

Team	First Year	Last Year	Won	Lost	Pct.
UCLA	1971	1973	89	1	.989
UCLA	1967	1969	88	2	.978
UCLA	1970	1972	87	3	.967
Long Island	1934	1936	75	3	.962
UCLA	1968	1970	86	4	.956
UCLA	1969	1971	86	4	.956
UCLA	1972	1974	86	4	.956
St. John's (N.Y.)	1929	1931	67	4	.944
Long Island	1935	1937	77	5	.939
Penn	1919	1921	58	4	.935
Indiana	1974	1976	86	6	.935
Ohio St.	1960	1962	78	6	.929

Team	First Year	Last Year	Won	Lost	Pct.
Penn	1970	1972	78	6	.929
Kentucky	1947	1949	102	8	.927
Kentucky	1946	1948	98	8	.925
Kentucky	1951	1953	61	5	.924
Cincinnati	1960	1962	84	7	.923
UCLA	1973	1975	84	7	.923
UNLV	1990	1992	95	8	.922
Cincinnati	1961	1963	82	7	.921
North Carolina St.	1973	1975	79	7	.919
DePaul	1980	1982	79	7	.917
Arkansas	1926	1928	56	5	.918
Penn	1920	1922	67	6	.918
St. John's (N.Y.)	1930	1932	66	6	.917
Seton Hall	1940	1942	55	5	.917
Kentucky	1949	1951	89	9	.908
Marquette	1970	1972	79	8	.908
Kentucky	1996	1998	104	11	.904
Kentucky	1945	1947	84	9	.903

Winning Percentage Over a Four-Year Period

(Minimum 80 games)

Team	First Year	Last Year	Won	Lost	Pct.
UCLA	1970	1973	117	3	.975
UCLA	1967	1970	116	4	.967
UCLA	1969	1972	116	4	.967
UCLA	1968	1971	115	5	.958
UCLA	1971	1974	115	5	.958
Kentucky	1951	1954	86	5	.945
Long Island	1934	1937	103	6	.945
UCLA	1972	1975	114	7	.942
Kentucky	1946	1949	130	10	.929
Kentucky	1952	1955	77	6	.928
Penn	1918	1921	76	6	.927
Arkansas	1926	1929	75	6	.929
Long Island	1936	1939	99	8	.925
Cincinnati	1960	1963	110	9	.924
Penn	1919	1922	82	7	.921
St. John's (N.Y.)	1929	1932	89	8	.918
St. John's (N.Y.)	1928	1931	85	8	.914
UCLA	1964	1967	106	10	.914
UCLA	1966	1969	106	10	.914
Kentucky	1948	1951	125	12	.912
Long Island	1939	1942	92	9	.911
UCLA	1973	1976	112	11	.911
Long Island	1935	1938	100	10	.909
Kentucky	1945	1948	120	12	.909
Cincinnati	1959	1962	110	11	.909

Winning Streaks

Full Season

Wins	Team	Seasons	Ended By	Score
88	UCLA	1971-74	Notre Dame	71-70
60	San Francisco	1955-57	Illinois	62-33
47	UCLA	1966-68	Houston	71-69
45	UNLV	1990-91	Duke	79-77
44	Texas	1913-17	Rice	24-18
43	Seton Hall	1939-41	Long Island	49-26
43	Long Island	1935-37	Stanford	45-31
41	UCLA	1968-69	Southern California	46-44
39	Marquette	1970-71	Ohio St.	60-59
37	Cincinnati	1962-63	Wichita St.	65-64
37	North Carolina	1957-58	West Virginia	75-64
36	North Carolina St.	1974-75	Wake Forest	83-78
35	Arkansas	1927-29	Texas	26-25

Regular Season

(Does not include national postseason tournaments)

Wins	Team	Seasons	Ended By	Score
76	UCLA	1971-74	Notre Dame	71-70
57	Indiana	1975-77	Toledo	59-57
56	Marquette	1970-72	Detroit	70-49
54	Kentucky	1952-55	Georgia Tech	59-58
51	San Francisco	1955-57	Illinois	62-33
48	Penn	1970-72	Temple	57-52
47	Ohio St.	1960-62	Wisconsin	86-67
44	Texas	1913-17	Rice	24-18
43	UCLA	1966-68	Houston	71-69
43	Long Island	1935-37	Stanford	45-31
42	Seton Hall	1939-41	Long Island	49-26

Home Court

Wins	Team	Seasons	Ended By	Score
129	Kentucky	1943-55	Georgia Tech	59-58
99	St. Bonaventure	1948-61	Niagara	87-77
98	UCLA	1970-76	Oregon	65-45
86	Cincinnati	1957-64	Bradley	87-77
81	Arizona	1945-51	Kansas St.	76-57
81	Marquette	1967-73	Notre Dame	71-69
80	Lamar	1978-84	Louisiana Tech	68-65
75	Long Beach St.	1968-74	San Francisco	94-84
72	UNLV	1974-78	New Mexico	102-98
71	Arizona	1987-92	UCLA	89-87
68	Cincinnati	1972-78	Georgia Tech	59-56
67	Western Ky.	1949-55	Xavier	(ot) 82-80

Current Home Court

Wins	Team	Wins	Team
32	Memphis	17	UNLV
31	BYU	16	Tennessee
25	Ohio St.	14	La.-Monroe
23	Winthrop	14	Southern Ill.
22	Wisconsin	12	Nevada
20	Notre Dame	11	Central Conn. St.
20	UCLA	10	Akron
19	Florida		
19	Holy Cross		
17	Indiana		

Rivalries

Consecutive Years

Years	Opponents	First Year	Last Year
106	Columbia vs. Yale	1902	2007
106	Princeton vs. Yale	1902	2007
105	Penn vs. Princeton	1903	2007
104	Columbia vs. Penn	1904	2007
104	Cornell vs. Penn	1904	2007
103	Maine vs. New Hampshire	1905	2007
102	Idaho vs. Washington St.	1906	2007
101	Kansas vs. Kansas St.	1907	2007
101	Kansas vs. Missouri	1907	2007
100	Kansas St. vs. Nebraska	1908	2007

Games Played

Games	Opponents	First Year	Last Year
327	Oregon vs. Oregon St.	1903	2007
280	Oregon vs. Washington	1904	2007
279	Oregon St. vs. Washington	1904	2007
274	Oregon St. vs. Washington St.	1907	2007
270	Oregon vs. Washington St.	1908	2007
263	Washington vs. Washington St.	1910	2007
262	Kansas vs. Kansas St.	1907	2007
256	Kansas vs. Missouri	1907	2007
249	California vs. Stanford	1912	2007
242	BYU vs. Utah	1909	2007

Victories for One Opponent

W-L	Opponents	First Year	Last Year
180-147	Oregon St. vs. Oregon	1903	2007
179-101	Washington vs. Oregon	1904	2007
173-89	Kansas vs. Kansas St.	1907	2007
167-96	Washington vs. Washington St.	1910	2007
164-93	Kansas vs. Missouri	1907	2007
162-58	Kansas vs. Iowa St.	1908	2007
161-71	Kansas vs. Nebraska	1900	2007
161-113	Oregon St. vs. Washington St.	1909	2007
154-107	Washington St. vs. Idaho	1906	2007
154-116	Oregon vs. Washington St.	1908	2007

Consecutive Victories

Won	Opponents	First Year	Last Year
52	UCLA vs. California	1961	1985
41	Southern California vs. UCLA	1932	1943
41	Syracuse vs. Colgate	1963	†2007
39	Kentucky vs. Mississippi	1929	1972
39	Rhode Island vs. Maine	1924	1952
38	Arizona vs. Washington St.	1986	2004
38	Providence vs. Brown	1959	1978
35	Connecticut vs. New Hampshire	1939	1961
35	South Carolina vs. Citadel	1945	1988
34	Marquette vs. Milwaukee	1917	†1999

†active streak

Current Consecutive Victories

Won	Opponents	First Year	Last Year
41	Syracuse vs. Colgate	1963	2007
34	Marquette vs. Milwaukee	1917	1999
33	North Carolina vs. VMI	1922	1997
29	Pittsburgh vs. St. Francis (Pa.)	1973	2005
29	Syracuse vs. Cornell	1969	2006
25	Kentucky vs. Xavier	1942	1968
21	Duke vs. Clemson	1997	2007
20	Duke vs. Davidson	1982	2007
20	Duke vs. East Caro.	1969	1991

Consecutive Home Victories

Won	Opponents	First Year	Last Year
52	Princeton vs. Brown	1929	2002
52	North Carolina vs. Clemson	1926	†2006
47	UCLA vs. Washington St.	1950	2003
41	Kentucky vs. Mississippi	1929	1996
37	Southern California vs. UCLA	1932	1944
34	Kentucky vs. Georgia	1930	1984
33	Rhode Island vs. Northeastern	1917	1988
33	Indiana vs. Northwestern	1969	†2006
32	Rhode Island vs. New Hampshire	1937	1973
32	UCLA vs. California	1961	1989

†active streak

Current Consecutive Home Victories

Won	Opponents	First Year	Last Year
52	North Carolina vs. Clemson	1926	2006
33	Indiana vs. Northwestern	1969	2006
31	Marquette vs. Milwaukee	1920	1999
29	Syracuse vs. Colgate	1963	2007
25	Syracuse vs. Cornell	1966	2006
20	Oklahoma St. vs. Drake	1931	1958
19	Pittsburgh vs. St. Francis (Pa.)	1973	2005
19	Duke vs. East Caro.	1969	1991
16	Duke vs. William & Mary	1925	2000
14	Syracuse vs. Canisius	1970	2004

Victories for One Opponent in One Year

W-L	Opponents	Year
5-0	Kansas vs. Nebraska	1909
5-0	Kansas vs. Kansas St.	1935
4-0	by many	

Associated Press (A.P.) Poll Records

Full Season at No. 1

1956, San Francisco, 14 weeks
1960, Cincinnati, 12 weeks
1961, Ohio St., 13 weeks
1962, Ohio St., 14 weeks
1963, Cincinnati, 16 weeks

1967, UCLA, 15 weeks
1969, UCLA, 15 weeks
1972, UCLA, 16 weeks
1973, UCLA, 16 weeks
1976, Indiana, 17 weeks

1991, UNLV, 17 weeks
1992, Duke, 18 weeks

Most Consecutive Weeks at No. 1

46, UCLA, Feb. 9, 1971 to Jan. 15, 1974
27, Ohio St., Dec. 13, 1960 to March 13, 1962
23, UCLA, Preseason Nov. 1966 to Jan. 16, 1968
19, San Francisco, Feb. 8, 1955 to March 6, 1956
18, Duke, Preseason Nov. 1991 to March 16, 1992

17, Indiana, Preseason Nov. 1975 to March 16, 1976
17, UNLV, Preseason Nov. 1990 to March 12, 1991
16, Cincinnati, Preseason Nov. 1962 to March 12, 1963
15, UCLA, Preseason Nov. 1968 to March 4, 1969
15, North Carolina, Dec. 6, 1983 to March 13, 1984

15, Kansas, Dec. 3, 1996 to March 11, 1997
15, Illinois, Dec. 7, 2004 to March 15, 2005

Preseason No. 1 to not Ranked No. 1 the Rest of the Season

1970, South Carolina
1978, North Carolina
1981, Kentucky
1986, Georgia Tech
1988, Syracuse

1990, UNLV
2000, Connecticut

Biggest Jump to No. 1 from Previous Week

8th, West Virginia, Dec. 17 to Dec. 24, 1957
6th, Duke, Dec. 7 to Dec. 14, 1965
6th, Kansas, Nov. 25 to Dec. 2, 2003
5th, Holy Cross, Jan. 10 to Jan. 17, 1950
5th, Kansas St., Dec. 23 to Dec. 30, 1952

5th, Indiana, Dec. 21 to Dec. 28, 1982
5th, UCLA, Jan. 11 to Jan. 18, 1983
5th, Temple, Feb. 2 to Feb. 9, 1988
5th, Oklahoma, Feb. 7 to Feb. 14, 1989
5th, Oklahoma, Feb. 27 to March 6, 1990

5th, Illinois, Nov. 30 to Dec. 7, 2004
5th, UCLA, Nov. 21 to Nov. 28, 2006

Biggest Jump from Not Ranked the Previous Week

(at least 20 ranked)
4th, Kansas, Preseason to Nov. 27, 1989
5th, St. Louis, Dec. 26, 1950 to Jan. 3, 1951
5th, Cincinnati, Jan. 31 to Feb. 7, 1961
6th, Notre Dame, Jan. 12 to Jan. 19, 1954
6th, Missouri, Dec. 7 to Dec. 14, 1954

6th, Maryland, Dec. 10 to Dec. 17, 1957
6th, Oklahoma St., Jan. 21 to Jan. 28, 1958
7th, Bradley, March 9 to March 23, 1954
7th, Oklahoma City, Jan. 14 to Jan. 21, 1958
7th, Iowa, Dec. 27, 1960, to Jan. 3, 1961

7th, Wake Forest, Jan. 30 to Feb. 6, 1976
7th, North Carolina St., Preseason to Nov. 29, 1983

Biggest Jump from Not Ranked the Previous Week

(at least 25 ranked)
4th, Kansas, Preseason to Nov. 27, 1989
8th, Arizona, Preseason to Nov. 20, 2001
10th, Notre Dame, Dec. 3 to Dec. 10, 2002
12th, Arizona St., Nov. 21 to Nov. 28, 1994
12th, Duke, Nov. 20 to Nov. 27, 1995

12th, North Carolina, Nov. 26 to Dec. 3, 2002
13th, Wake Forest, Jan. 25 to Feb. 1, 1993
13th, Oregon, Jan. 29 to Feb. 5, 2002
13th, Georgia Tech, Nov. 25 to Dec. 2, 2003
14th, Iowa, Jan. 9 to Jan. 16, 2001

14th, Pittsburgh, Feb. 5 to Feb. 12, 2002
14th, Florida, Nov. 15 to Nov. 22, 2005

Biggest Drop from No. 1 from Previous Week

15th, Florida, Dec. 9 to Dec. 15, 2003
9th, UNLV, Feb. 22 to March 1, 1983
8th, UCLA, Dec. 7 to Dec. 14, 1965
8th, South Carolina, Preseason Nov. to Dec. 9, 1969
8th, Duke, Jan. 17 to Jan. 24, 1989

8th, Connecticut, Preseason Nov. to Nov. 16, 1999
7th, St. John (N.Y.), Dec. 18 to Dec. 26, 1951
7th, UCLA, Jan. 25 to Feb. 1, 1983
7th, Cincinnati, March 7 to March 14, 2000
6th, Michigan St., Jan. 9 to Jan. 16, 1979

6th, Memphis, Jan. 11 to Jan. 18, 1983
6th, UNLV, Preseason Nov. 1989 to Nov. 27, 1989
6th, Syracuse, Jan. 2 to Jan. 9, 1990
6th, Michigan, Nov. 30 to Dec. 7, 1992
6th, Kentucky, Nov. 29 to Dec. 6, 1993

6th, Wake Forest, Nov. 30 to Dec. 7, 2004

Biggest Drop to Not Ranked from the Previous Week

(at least 20 ranked)
2nd, Louisville, Preseason to Dec. 2, 1986
4th, Indiana, Dec. 27, 1960, to Jan. 3, 1961
5th, Kansas, Dec. 8 to Dec. 15, 1953
6th, Iowa, Dec. 27, 1955, to Jan. 3, 1956
6th, Louisville, Preseason to Nov. 29, 1983

7th, Indiana, Dec. 14 to Dec. 21, 1954
7th, Missouri, Dec. 21 to Dec. 28, 1954
7th, Utah, Dec. 27, 1955, to Jan. 3, 1956
7th, Kansas, Dec. 9 to Dec. 16, 1958
7th, Duquesne, Dec. 9 to Dec. 16, 1969

7th, Ohio St., Dec. 16 to Dec. 23, 1980

Biggest Drop to Not Ranked from the Previous Week

(at least 25 ranked)
11th, Indiana, Dec. 21 to Dec. 28, 1994
13th, Stanford, Nov. 13 to Nov. 22, 2005
13th, West Virginia, Nov. 22 to Nov. 29, 2005
14th, UCLA, Nov. 26 to Dec. 3, 2002
15th, St. John's (N.Y.), Nov. 15 to Nov. 23, 1999

15th, UCLA, Nov. 21 to Nov. 28, 2000
15th, St. Joseph's, Dec. 18 to Dec. 25, 2001
15th, Marquette, Jan. 2 to Jan. 9, 2007
16th, Oklahoma, Feb. 1 to Feb. 8, 1993
16th, Duke, Jan. 9 to Jan. 16, 1995

16th, Minnesota, Dec. 19 to Dec. 26, 1994
16th, Arkansas, Preseason to Nov. 20, 1995
16th, Temple, Dec. 8 to Dec. 15, 1998
16th, Wichita St., Dec. 26 to Jan. 2, 2007
16th, Virginia Tech, Jan. 30 to Feb. 6, 2007

16th, Duke, Feb. 6 to Feb. 13, 2007

Lowest Ranking to Rise to No. 1 during the Season

(does not include 1962-69 when only 10 ranked)
NR, Indiana St., Dec. 5, 1978 to Feb. 13, 1979 (only 20 ranked)
21st, Stanford, Dec. 2, 2003 to Feb. 17, 2004
20th, UNLV, Preseason Nov. 1982 to Feb. 15, 1983
20th, Kentucky, Dec. 31, 2002 to March 18, 2003
19th, Indiana, Dec. 16, 1952 to March 3, 1953

19th, Houston, Jan. 4 to March 1, 1983
19th, Connecticut, Preseason Nov. 1994 to Feb. 13, 1995
18th, North Carolina, Jan. 4 to Feb. 1, 1983
18th, Duke, Nov. 16, 1999 to March 14, 2000
17th, San Francisco, Dec. 21, 1954 to Feb. 8, 1955

17th, Arizona, Preseason Nov. to Dec. 22, 1987
17th, Oklahoma, Nov. 27, 1989 to March 6, 1990
17th, UCLA, Jan. 24 to March 17, 1994
17th, St. Joseph's, Preseason Nov. 2003 to March 9, 2004

Lowest Ranking to Drop from No. 1 during the Season

(does not include 1962-69 when only 10 ranked)
NR, St. John's (N.Y.), Dec. 18, 1951 to Jan. 15, 1952 (only 20 ranked)
NR, Duke, Jan. 8 to Feb. 26, 1980 (only 20 ranked)
NR, Alabama, Dec. 31, 2002 to Feb. 11, 2003
NR, Florida, Dec. 9, 2003 to Feb. 17, 2004
24th, Connecticut, Preseason Nov. 1999 to Feb, 29, 2000

21st, Arizona, Nov. 21, 2000 to Jan. 9, 2001
21st, Kansas, Dec. 2, 2003 to Feb. 17, 2004
20th, Indiana, Dec. 11, 1979 to Feb. 5, 1980
17th, Memphis, Jan. 11 to March 1, 1983
17th, Syracuse, Preseason Nov. 1987 to Jan. 26, 1988

Most Teams at No. 1 in One Season

7, 1983 Houston, Indiana, Memphis, UNLV, North Carolina, UCLA and Virginia
6, 1993 Duke, Indiana, Kansas, Kentucky, Michigan and North Carolina
6, 1994 Arkansas, Duke, Kansas, Kentucky, North Carolina and UCLA
6, 1995 Arkansas, Connecticut, Kansas, Massachusetts, North Carolina and UCLA
6, 2004 Connecticut, Duke, Florida, Kansas, St. Joseph's and Stanford

5, 1979 Duke, Indiana, Michigan St., Notre Dame and UCLA
5, 1990 Kansas, Missouri, UNLV, Oklahoma and Syracuse
5, 2001 Arizona, Duke, Michigan St., North Carolina and Stanford
5, 2003 Alabama, Arizona, Duke, Florida and Kentucky
5, 2007 Florida, North Carolina, Ohio St., UCLA and Wisconsin

Most Consecutive Weeks with a Different No. 1

7, Jan. 3 to Feb. 14, 1994 (in order: Arkansas, North Carolina, Kansas, UCLA, Duke, North Carolina and Arkansas)
5, Jan. 17 to Feb. 14, 1989 (in order: Duke, Illinois, Oklahoma, Arizona and Oklahoma)
5, Feb. 6 to March 6, 1990 (in order: Missouri, Kansas, Missouri, Kansas and Oklahoma)
5, Jan. 30 to Feb. 27, 1995 (in order: Massachusetts, North Carolina, Connecticut, Kansas and UCLA)
4, Dec. 11, 1951 to Jan. 2, 1952 [in order: Kentucky, St. John's (N.Y.), Kentucky and Kansas]

4, Feb. 17 to March 10, 1970 (in order: UCLA, Kentucky, UCLA and Kentucky)
4, Feb. 7 to Feb. 28, 1978 (in order: Kentucky, Arkansas, Marquette and Kentucky)
4, Feb. 6 to Feb. 27, 1979 (in order: Notre Dame, Indiana St., UCLA and Indiana St.)
4, Jan. 13 to Feb. 3, 1987 (in order: UNLV, Iowa, North Carolina and UNLV)
4, Nov. 25 to Dec. 16, 2003 (in order: Connecticut, Kansas, Florida and Connecticut)

Most Times No. 1 Defeated in a Season

10, 1993-94
9, 2003-04
8, 1978-79
8, 1982-83
8, 1989-90

7, 1987-88
7, 1988-89
7, 1992-93
7, 1997-98

7, 1999-2000
7, 2002-03
7, 2006-07

Largest Point Margin in Defeating No. 1

41, No. 2 Kentucky (81) vs. No. 1 St. John's (N.Y.), Lexington, KY, Dec. 17, 1951
32, No. 2 UCLA (101) vs. No. 1 Houston (69), Los Angeles (NSF), March 22, 1968
24, No. 3 Massachusetts (104) vs. No. 1 Arkansas (80), Springfield, MA, Nov. 25, 1994
24, No. 2 North Carolina (97) vs. No. 1 Duke (73), Chapel Hill, NC, Feb. 5, 1998
23, No. 15 Villanova (96) vs. No. 1 Connecticut (73), Storrs, CT, Feb. 18, 1995
22, Tied No. 5 Oklahoma (100) vs. No. 1 Kansas (78), Norman, OK, Feb. 27, 1990
20, No. 5 Arizona St. (87) vs. No. 1 Oregon St. (67), Corvallis, OR, March 7, 1981
20, No. 13 North Carolina (91) vs. No. 1 Duke (71), Durham, NC, Jan. 18, 1989
20, No. 17 Georgia Tech (89) vs. No. 1 North Carolina (69), Atlanta, Jan. 12, 1994
20, NR Xavier (87) vs. No. 1 St. Joseph's (67), Dayton, OH, March 11, 2004

Largest Point Margin for an Unranked Opponent Defeating No. 1

20, Xavier (87) vs. St. Joseph's (67), Dayton, OH, March 11, 2004
19, Wisconsin (86) vs. Ohio St. (67), Madison, WI, March 3, 1962
19, Villanova (93) vs. Syracuse (74), Syracuse, NY, Jan. 6, 1970
18, Maryland (69) vs. North Carolina (51), College Park, MD, Feb. 21, 1959
16, Alabama (78) vs. Kentucky (62), Tuscaloosa, AL, Jan. 23, 1978

16, Nebraska (67) vs. Missouri (51), Columbia, MO, Feb. 6, 1982
16, Georgia Tech (77) vs. Connecticut (61), New York, Nov. 26, 2003
15, Vanderbilt (101) vs. Kentucky (86), Nashville, TN, Jan. 13, 1993
15, Long Beach St. (64) vs. Kansas (49), Lawrence, KS, Jan. 25, 1993
15, California (85) vs. UCLA (70), Oakland, CA, Jan. 30, 1994

Most Weeks at No. 1- All-Time

(Complete List)

Weeks	Team	Years
134	UCLA	1964-2007
110	Duke	1966-2006
85	North Carolina	1957-2007
80	Kentucky	1949-2003
45	Cincinnati	1959-2000
44	Indiana	1953-93
42	Kansas	1952-2005
32	UNLV	1983-91
30	Ohio St.	1961-2007
29	Arizona	1988-2003
28	San Francisco	1955-77
24	Connecticut	1995-2006
21	Michigan	1965-93
17	Illinois	1952-2005
16	Kansas St.	1952-59
16	Stanford	2000-04
15	DePaul	1980-81
15	Massachusetts	1995-96
13	North Carolina St.	1975
12	Arkansas	1978-95
12	Georgetown	1985
12	Virginia	1981-83
11	Houston	1968-83
10	Florida	2003-07
8	St. John's (N.Y.)	1950-85
8	West Virginia	1958
7	Syracuse	1988-90
6	Missouri	1982-90
6	Seton Hall	1953
6	Temple	1988
5	Bradley	1950-51
5	Holy Cross	1950
5	Notre Dame	1974-79
5	Oklahoma	1989-90
5	Oregon St.	1981
4	Indiana St.	1979
4	La Salle	1953-55
4	Loyola (Ill.)	1964
4	Michigan St.	1979-2001
3	Marquette	1971-78
2	Alabama	2003
2	Duquesne	1954
2	St. Louis	1949
2	Wake Forest	2005
1	Georgia Tech	1986
1	Iowa	1987
1	Memphis	1983
1	Oklahoma St.	1951

1 ....St. Joseph's........................2004
1 ....South Carolina................1970
1 ....Wichita St...........................1965
1 ....Wisconsin 2007

Most Times Defeating No. 1

(Complete List)

12 ....North Carolina...............1959-2006
10 ....UCLA....................................1965-2003
9 ....Maryland 1959-2004
8 ....Duke.....................................1958-97
8 ....Georgia Tech 1955-2004
8 ....Ohio St..................................1965-2007
7 ....Notre Dame......................1971-87
7 ....Oklahoma..........................1951-2002
6 ....Kansas.................................1953-2007
6 ....Kentucky............................1951-2003
6 ....Vanderbilt..........................1951-2007
5 ....Cincinnati 1954-98
5 ....Indiana................................1984-2002
5 ....North Carolina St. 1983-2004
5 ....St. John's (N.Y.)................1951-85
5 ....Villanova 1983-2006
4 ....Alabama.............................1978-2004
4 ....Arizona...............................1987-2001
4 ....Missouri..............................1989-97
4 ....Stanford 1988-2003
4 ....Wake Forest 1975-92
3 ....DePaul..................................1950-52
3 ....Georgetown 1963-2006
3 ....Louisville 1953-2004
3 ....Massachusetts................1993-95
3 ....Minnesota 1951-89
3 ....Nebraska.............................1958-82
3 ....Oregon................................1970-2007
3 ....St. Louis 1951-2000
3 ....Syracuse 1985-2006
3 ....Utah......................................1954-2002
3 ....West Virginia 1957-83
3 ....Xavier 1996-2004
2 ....California.............................1960-94
2 ....CCNY....................................1950
2 ....Clemson...............................1980-2001
2 ....Dayton.................................1953-54
2 ....Florida 2000-07
2 ....Florida St..............................2002-06
2 ....George Washington.....1995-96
2 ....Houston 1968-78
2 ....Illinois 1979-2005
2 ....Iowa 1965-99
2 ....Kansas St..............................1990-94
2 ....Loyola (Ill.) 1949-63
2 ....LSU 1978-2002
2 ....Michigan.............................1964-97
2 ....Michigan St........................1979-2007
2 ....Mississippi St...................1959-96
2 ....Oklahoma St. 1949-89
2 ....Oregon St..........................1953-74
2 ....Purdue 1979-2000
2 ....Southern California.......1969-70
2 ....Temple 1995-2000
2 ....Virginia Tech 1983-2007
2 ....Washington 1979-2004
1 ....Arizona St............................1981
1 ....Arkansas..............................1984
1 ....Auburn 1988
1 ....Boston College...............1994
1 ....Bradley 1960
1 ....Cal St. Fullerton..............1983
1 ....Chaminade 1982
1 ....Charlotte 1977
1 ....Connecticut 1999
1 ....Detroit 1951
1 ....Iowa St..................................1957
1 ....Jacksonville 1970
1 ....Long Beach St..................1993
1 ....Manhattan 1958
1 ....Marquette 2003
1 ....New Mexico........................1988
1 ....Old Dominion...................1981
1 ....Providence 1976
1 ....St. Joseph's.........................1981
1 ....Tennessee...........................1969
1 ....UNLV 1989
1 ....UTEP 1966
1 ....Virginia 1986
1 ....Wichita St.............................1963
1 ....Wisconsin 1962

Notes About No. 1

No. 1 has been defeated 240 times.
No. 1 has been defeated 11 times in overtime.
No. 1 has been defeated 34 times by one point.
No. 1 has been defeated 121 times by a non-ranked opponent.
Chaminade is the only non-Division I team to upset the nation's top team. It happened in Honolulu December 24, 1982, when Chaminade defeated No. 1 Virginia, 77-72.
California, CCNY, Louisville, Maryland, UTEP and Villanova have never been ranked No. 1 despite winning the NCAA championship.
The following men's and women's programs from the same school have been ranked No. 1 at the same time:
Connecticut, Feb. 13, 1995
Connecticut, Nov. 30, 1998
Duke, Jan. 7-14, 2003
Connecticut, Preseason 2003 to Nov. 25, 2003
Duke, Feb. 21, 2006

No. 1 vs. No. 2

Date	No. 1, Score	W-L	No. 2, Score	Site
Mar. 26, 1949	Kentucky 46	W	Oklahoma St. 36	Seattle (CH)
Dec. 17, 1951	St. John's (N.Y.) 40	L	Kentucky 81	Lexington, KY
Dec. 21, 1954	Kentucky 70	W	Utah 65	Lexington, KY
Mar. 23, 1957	North Carolina 54	W	Kansas 53	Kansas City, MO (CH)
Mar. 18, 1960	Cincinnati 69	L	California 77	San Francisco (NSF)
Mar. 25, 1961	Ohio St. 65	L (ot)	Cincinnati 70	Kansas City, MO (CH)
Mar. 24, 1962	Ohio St. 59	L	Cincinnati 71	Louisville, KY (CH)
Dec. 14, 1964	Wichita St. 85	L	Michigan 87	Detroit
Mar. 20, 1965	Michigan 80	L	UCLA 91	Portland, OR (CH)
Mar. 18, 1966	Kentucky 83	W	Duke 79	College Park, MD (NSF)
Jan. 20, 1968	UCLA 69	L	Houston 71	Houston
Mar. 22, 1968	Houston 69	L	UCLA 101	Los Angeles (NSF)
Dec. 15, 1973	UCLA 84	W	North Carolina St. 66	St. Louis
Jan. 19, 1974	UCLA 70	L	Notre Dame 71	South Bend, IN
Jan. 26, 1974	Notre Dame 75	L	UCLA 94	Los Angeles
Mar. 25, 1974	North Carolina St. 80	W	UCLA 77	Greensboro, NC (NSF)
Mar. 31, 1975	UCLA 92	W	Kentucky 85	San Diego (CH)
Nov. 29, 1975	Indiana 84	W	UCLA 64	St. Louis
Mar. 22, 1976	Indiana 65	W	Marquette 56	Baton Rouge, LA
Dec. 26, 1981	North Carolina 82	W	Kentucky 69	East Rutherford, NJ
Jan. 9, 1982	North Carolina 65	W	Virginia 60	Chapel Hill, NC
April 2, 1983	Houston 94	W	Louisville 81	Albuquerque, NM (NSF)

Date	No. 1, Score	W-L	No. 2, Score	Site
Dec. 15, 1984	Georgetown 77	W	DePaul 57	Landover, MD
Jan. 26, 1985	Georgetown 65	L	St. John's (N.Y.) 66	Washington, DC
Feb. 27, 1985	St. John's (N.Y.) 69	L	Georgetown 85	New York
Mar. 9, 1985	Georgetown 92	W	St. John's (N.Y.) 80	New York
Feb. 4, 1986	North Carolina 78	W (ot)	Georgia Tech 77	Atlanta
Mar. 29, 1986	Duke 71	W	Kansas 67	Dallas (NSF)
Feb. 13, 1990	Kansas 71	L	Missouri 77	Lawrence, KS
Mar. 10, 1990	Oklahoma 95	W	Kansas 77	Kansas City, MO
Feb. 10, 1991	UNLV 112	W	Arkansas 105	Fayetteville, AR
Feb. 3, 1994	Duke 78	L	North Carolina 89	Chapel Hill, NC
Mar. 30, 1996	Massachusetts 74	L	Kentucky 81	East Rutherford, NJ (NSF)
Feb. 5, 1998	Duke 73	L	North Carolina 97	Chapel Hill, NC
April 4, 2005	Illinois 70	L	North Carolina 75	St. Louis (CH)
Dec. 10, 2005	Duke 97	W	Texas 66	East Rutherford, NJ
Feb. 25, 2007	Wisconsin 48	L	Ohio State 49	Columbus, OH

Schools Defeating No. 1

Date	Rank	School	No. 1 Team	Score	Site
Jan. 20, 1949	3	Oklahoma St.	St. Louis	29-27	Stillwater, OK
Mar. 14, 1949	16	Loyola (Ill.)	Kentucky	67-56	New York
Jan. 17, 1950	NR	DePaul	St. John's (N.Y.)	74-68	New York
Mar. 18, 1950	NR	CCNY	Bradley	69-61	New York
Mar. 28, 1950	NR	CCNY	Bradley	71-68	New York (CH)
Dec. 29, 1950	NR	St. Louis	Kentucky	43-42	New Orleans
Jan. 11, 1951	11	St. John's (N.Y.)	Bradley	68-59	New York
Jan. 15, 1951	NR	Detroit	Bradley	70-65	Peoria, IL
Jan. 20, 1951	NR	Oklahoma	Oklahoma St.	44-40	Norman, OK
Mar. 3, 1951	NR	Vanderbilt	Kentucky	61-57	Louisville, KY
Dec. 13, 1951	NR	Minnesota	Kentucky	61-57	Minneapolis
Dec. 17, 1951	2	Kentucky	St. John's (N.Y.)	81-40	Lexington, KY
Dec. 29, 1951	12	St. Louis	Kentucky	61-60	New Orleans
Jan. 28, 1952	NR	DePaul	Illinois	69-65	Chicago
Mar. 22, 1952	10	St. John's (N.Y.)	Kentucky	64-57	Raleigh, NC (RF)
Dec. 27, 1952	NR	DePaul	La Salle	63-61	Chicago
Jan. 17, 1953	15	Kansas	Kansas St.	80-66	Lawrence, KS
Mar. 1, 1953	NR	Dayton	Seton Hall	70-65	Dayton, OH
Mar. 2, 1953	18	Louisville	Seton Hall	73-67	Louisville, KY
Mar. 7, 1953	NR	Minnesota	Indiana	65-63	Minneapolis
Dec. 22, 1953	12	Oregon St.	Indiana	67-51	Eugene, OR
Feb. 25, 1954	NR	Cincinnati	Duquesne	66-52	Cincinnati
Feb. 27, 1954	16	Dayton	Duquesne	64-54	Dayton, OH
Dec. 18, 1954	15	Utah	La Salle	79-69	New York
Jan. 8, 1955	NR	Georgia Tech	Kentucky	59-58	Lexington, KY
Jan. 31, 1955	NR	Georgia Tech	Kentucky	65-59	Atlanta
Jan. 14, 1957	9	Iowa St.	Kansas	39-37	Ames, IA
Dec. 21, 1957	8	West Virginia	North Carolina	75-64	Lexington, KY
Jan. 27, 1958	NR	Duke	West Virginia	72-68	Durham, NC
Mar. 3, 1958	NR	Nebraska	Kansas St.	55-48	Lincoln, NE
Mar. 8, 1958	10	Kansas	Kansas St.	61-44	Manhattan, KS
Mar. 11, 1958	NR	Manhattan	West Virginia	89-84	New York
Jan. 6, 1959	NR	Vanderbilt	Kentucky	75-66	Nashville, TN
Jan. 14, 1959	3	North Carolina	North Carolina St.	72-68	Raleigh, NC
Feb. 9, 1959	10	Mississippi St.	Kentucky	66-58	Mississippi State, MS
Feb. 21, 1959	NR	Maryland	North Carolina	69-51	College Park, MD
Mar. 14, 1959	5	Cincinnati	Kansas St.	85-75	Lawrence, KS (RF)
Jan. 16, 1960	4	Bradley	Cincinnati	91-90	Peoria, IL
Mar. 18, 1960	2	California	Cincinnati	77-69	San Francisco (NSF)
Mar. 25, 1961	2	Cincinnati	Ohio St.	70-65 (ot)	Kansas City, MO (CH)
Mar. 3, 1962	NR	Wisconsin	Ohio St.	86-67	Madison, WI
Mar. 24, 1962	2	Cincinnati	Ohio St.	71-59	Louisville, KY (CH)
Feb. 16, 1963	NR	Wichita St.	Cincinnati	65-64	Wichita, KS
Mar. 23, 1963	3	Loyola (Ill.)	Cincinnati	60-58	Louisville, KY
Dec. 28, 1963	NR	Georgetown	Loyola (Ill.)	69-58	Philadelphia
Jan. 4, 1964	NR	Georgia Tech	Kentucky	76-67	Atlanta
Jan. 6, 1964	6	Vanderbilt	Kentucky	85-83	Nashville, TN
Dec. 12, 1964	NR	Nebraska	Michigan	74-73	Lincoln, NE
Dec. 14, 1964	2	Michigan	Wichita St.	87-85	Detroit
Jan. 2, 1965	NR	St. John's (N.Y.)	Michigan	75-74	New York
Jan. 29, 1965	NR	Iowa	UCLA	87-82	Chicago
Mar. 8, 1965	NR	Ohio St.	Michigan	93-85	Columbus, OH
Mar. 20, 1965	2	UCLA	Michigan	91-80	Portland, OR (CH)
Dec. 10, 1965	6	Duke	UCLA	82-66	Durham, NC
Dec. 11, 1965	6	Duke	UCLA	94-75	Charlotte, NC
Feb. 7, 1966	NR	West Virginia	Duke	94-90	Morgantown, WV
Mar. 19, 1966	3	UTEP	Kentucky	72-65	College Park, MD (CH)
Jan. 20, 1968	2	Houston	UCLA	71-69	Houston
Mar. 22, 1968	2	UCLA	Houston	101-69	Los Angeles (NSF)

Date	Rank	School	No. 1 Team	Score	Site
Mar. 23, 1968	NR	Ohio St.	Houston	89-85	Los Angeles (N3rd)
Mar. 8, 1969	NR	Southern California	UCLA	46-44	Los Angeles
Dec. 6, 1969	NR	Tennessee	South Carolina	55-54	Columbia, SC
Feb. 21, 1970	NR	Oregon	UCLA	78-65	Eugene, OR
Mar. 6, 1970	NR	Southern California	UCLA	87-86	Los Angeles
Mar. 14, 1970	4	Jacksonville	Kentucky	106-100	Columbus, OH (RF)
Jan. 23, 1971	9	Notre Dame	UCLA	89-82	South Bend, IN
Jan. 19, 1974	2	North Dame	UCLA	71-70	South Bend, IN
Jan. 26, 1974	2	UCLA	Notre Dame	94-75	Los Angeles
Feb. 15, 1974	NR	Oregon St.	UCLA	61-57	Corvallis, OR
Feb. 16, 1974	NR	Oregon	UCLA	56-51	Eugene, OR
Jan. 3, 1975	NR	Wake Forest	North Carolina St.	83-78	Greensboro, NC
Mar. 22, 1975	5	Kentucky	Indiana	92-90	Dayton, OH (RF)
Dec. 29, 1976	NR	Providence	Michigan	82-81 (2ot)	Providence, RI
Mar. 1, 1977		Notre Dame	San Francisco	93-82	South Bend, IN
Mar. 19, 1977	17	Charlotte	Michigan	75-68	Lexington, KY (RF)
Jan. 23, 1978	NR	Alabama	Kentucky	78-62	Tuscaloosa, AL
Feb. 11, 1978	NR	LSU	Kentucky	95-94	Baton Rouge, LA
Feb. 18, 1978	NR	Houston	Arkansas	84-75	Houston
Feb. 26, 1978	9	Notre Dame	Marquette	65-59	South Bend, IN
Dec. 29, 1978	NR	Ohio St.	Duke	90-84	New York
Dec. 30, 1978	NR	St. John's (N.Y.)	Duke	69-66	New York
Jan. 11, 1979	4	Illinois	Michigan St.	57-55	Champaign, IL
Jan. 13, 1979		Purdue	Michigan St.	52-50	West Lafayette, IN
Jan. 27, 1979	NR	Maryland	Notre Dame	67-66	College Park, MD
Feb. 11, 1979	4	UCLA	Notre Dame	56-52	South Bend, IN
Feb. 22, 1979	NR	Washington	UCLA	69-68	Seattle
Mar. 26, 1979	3	Michigan St.	Indiana St.	75-64	Salt Lake City
Dec. 18, 1979	5	Kentucky	Indiana	69-58	Lexington, KY
Jan. 9, 1980	18	Clemson	Duke	87-82	Clemson, SC
Jan. 12, 1980	15	North Carolina	Duke	82-67	Durham, NC
Feb. 27, 1980	14	Notre Dame	DePaul	76-74 (2 ot)	South Bend, IN
Mar. 9, 1980	NR	UCLA	DePaul	77-71	Tempe, AZ (2nd)
Jan. 10, 1981	NR	Old Dominion	DePaul	63-62	Chicago
Feb. 22, 1981	11	Notre Dame	Virginia	57-56	Chicago
Mar. 7, 1981	5	Arizona St.	Oregon St.	87-67	Corvallis, OR
Mar. 14, 1981	NR	St. Joseph's	DePaul	49-48	Dayton, OH (1st)
Jan. 21, 1982	NR	Wake Forest	North Carolina	55-48	Chapel Hill, NC
Feb. 6, 1982	NR	Nebraska	Missouri	67-51	Columbia, MO
Feb. 27, 1982	NR	Maryland	Virginia	47-46 (ot)	College Park, MD
Dec. 24, 1982	NR	Chaminade	Virginia	77-72	Honolulu
Jan. 8, 1983	NR	Ohio St.	Indiana	70-67	Columbus, OH
Jan. 10, 1983	NR	Virginia Tech	Memphis	64-56	Blacksburg, VA
Jan. 28, 1983	NR	Alabama	UCLA	70-67	Los Angeles
Feb.13, 1983	12	Villanova	North Carolina	56-53	Chapel Hill, NC
Feb. 24, 1983	NR	Cal St. Fullerton	UNLV	86-78	Fullerton, CA
Feb. 27, 1983	NR	West Virginia	UNLV	87-78	Morgantown, WV
Apr. 4, 1983	16	North Carolina St.	Houston	54-52	Albuquerque, NM (CH)
Feb. 12, 1984	NR	Arkansas	North Carolina	65-64	Pine Bluff, NC
Mar. 10, 1984	16	Duke	North Carolina	77-75	Greensboro, NC
Mar. 22, 1984	NR	Indiana	North Carolina	72-68	Atlanta (RSF)
Jan. 26, 1985	2	St. John's (N.Y.)	Georgetown	66-65	Washington, DC
Jan. 28, 1985	11	Syracuse	Georgetown	65-63	Syracuse, NY
Feb. 27, 1985	2	Georgetown	St. John's (N.Y.)	85-69	New York
Apr. 1, 1985	NR	Villanova	Georgetown	66-64	Lexington, KY
Jan. 30, 1986	NR	Virginia	North Carolina	86-73	Charlottesville, VA
Feb. 20, 1986	NR	Maryland	North Carolina	77-72	Chapel Hill, NC
Feb. 23, 1986	20	North Carolina St.	North Carolina	76-65	Raleigh, NC
Mar. 31, 1986	7	Louisville	Duke	72-69	Dallas (CH)
Dec. 1, 1986	NR	UCLA	North Carolina	89-84	Los Angeles
Jan. 17, 1987	16	Oklahoma	UNLV	89-88	Norman, OK
Jan. 24, 1987	NR	Ohio St.	Iowa	80-76	Iowa City, IA
Feb. 1, 1987	NR	Notre Dame	North Carolina	60-58	South Bend, IN
Mar. 28, 1987	3	Indiana	UNLV	97-93	New Orleans (NSF)
Nov. 21, 1987	3	North Carolina	Syracuse	96-93	Springfield, MA
Nov. 30, 1987	17	Arizona	Syracuse	80-69	Anchorage, AK
Dec. 5, 1987	NR	Vanderbilt	North Carolina	78-76	Nashville, TN
Jan. 2, 1988	NR	New Mexico	Arizona	61-59	Albuquerque, NM
Jan. 9, 1988	NR	Auburn	Kentucky	53-52	Lexington, KY
Feb. 4, 1988	NR	Stanford	Arizona	82-74	Palo Alto, CA
Mar. 26, 1988 (RF)	5	Duke	Temple	63-53	East Rutherford, NJ
Jan. 18, 1989	13	North Carolina	Duke	91-71	Durham, NC
Jan. 21, 1989	NR	Wake Forest	Duke	75-71	Winston-Salem, NC
Jan. 26, 1989	NR	Minnesota	Illinois	69-62	Minneapolis
Feb. 4, 1989	NR	Oklahoma St.	Oklahoma	77-73	Stillwater, OK
Feb. 12, 1989	5	Oklahoma	Arizona	82-80	Norman, OK
Feb. 25, 1989	7	Missouri	Oklahoma	97-84	Columbia, MO
Mar. 23, 1989	15	UNLV	Arizona	68-67	Denver (RSF)
Nov. 22, 1989	NR	Kansas	UNLV	91-77	New York
Jan. 6, 1990	NR	Villanova	Syracuse	93-74	Greensboro, NC
Jan. 20, 1990	4	Missouri	Kansas	95-87	Columbia, MO
Feb. 8, 1990	NR	Kansas St.	Missouri	65-58	Manhattan, KS

Date	Rank	School	No. 1 Team	Score	Site
Feb. 13, 1990	2	Missouri	Kansas	77-71	Lawrence, KS
Feb. 25, 1990	10	Oklahoma	Missouri	107-90	Norman, OK
Feb. 27, 1990	T5	Oklahoma	Kansas	100-78	Norman, OK
Mar. 17, 1990	NR	North Carolina	Oklahoma	79-77	Austin, TX (2nd)
Mar. 30, 1991	6	Duke	UNLV	79-77	Indianapolis (NSF)
Feb. 5, 1992	9	North Carolina	Duke	75-73	Chapel Hill, NC
Feb. 23, 1992	NR	Wake Forest	Duke	72-68	Winston-Salem, NC
Dec. 5, 1992	4	Duke	Michigan	79-68	Durham, NC
Jan. 10, 1993	10	Georgia Tech	Duke	80-79	Atlanta
Jan. 13, 1993	NR	Vanderbilt	Kentucky	101-86	Nashville, TN
Jan. 25, 1993	NR	Long Beach St.	Kansas	64-49	Lawrence, KS
Feb. 23, 1993	NR	Ohio St.	Indiana	81-77 (ot)	Columbus, OH
Mar. 14, 1993	NR	Georgia Tech	North Carolina	77-75	Charlotte, NC
Mar. 27, 1993	9	Kansas	Indiana	83-77	St. Louis (RF)
Nov. 24, 1993	18	Massachusetts	North Carolina	91-86 (ot)	New York
Dec. 4, 1993	21	Indiana	Kentucky	96-84	Indianapolis
Jan. 8, 1994	NR	Alabama	Arkansas	66-64	Tuscaloosa, AL
Jan. 12, 1994	17	Georgia Tech	North Carolina	89-69	Atlanta
Jan. 17, 1994	NR	Kansas St.	Kansas	68-64	Lawrence, KS
Jan. 30, 1994	NR	California	UCLA	85-70	Oakland, CA
Feb. 3, 1994	2	North Carolina	Duke	89-78	Chapel Hill, NC
Feb. 12, 1994	NR	Georgia Tech	North Carolina	96-89	Chapel Hill, NC
Mar. 12, 1994	10	Kentucky	Arkansas	90-78	Memphis, TN
Mar. 20, 1994	NR	Boston College	North Carolina	75-72	Landover, MD (2nd)
Nov. 25, 1994	3	Massachusetts	Arkansas	104-80	Springfield, MA
Dec. 3, 1994	7	Kansas	Massachusetts	81-75	New York
Jan. 4, 1995	NR	North Carolina St.	North Carolina	80-70	Raleigh, NC
Feb. 4, 1995	NR	George Washington	Massachusetts	78-75	Washington, DC
Feb. 7, 1995	8	Maryland	North Carolina	86-73	College Park, MD
Feb. 18, 1995	15	Villanova	Connecticut	96-73	Storrs, CT
Feb. 20, 1995	25	Oklahoma	Kansas	76-73	Norman, OK
Nov. 28, 1995	5	Massachusetts	Kentucky	92-82	Auburn Hills, MI
Dec. 22, 1995	NR	Temple	Kansas	75-66	East Rutherford, NJ
Feb. 24, 1996	NR	George Washington	Massachusetts	86-76	Amherst, MA
Mar. 10, 1996	NR	Mississippi St.	Kentucky	84-73	New Orleans
Mar. 30, 1996	2	Kentucky	Massachusetts	81-74	East Rutherford, NJ (NSF)
Nov. 26, 1996	NR	Xavier	Cincinnati	71-69	Cincinnati
Feb. 4, 1997	NR	Missouri	Kansas	96-94	Columbia, MO
Mar. 21, 1997	15	Arizona	Kansas	85-82	Birmingham, AL (RSF)
Nov. 26, 1997	3	Duke	Arizona	95-87	Lahaina, HI
Dec. 13, 1997	NR	Michigan	Duke	81-73	Ann Arbor, MI
Jan. 14, 1998	NR	Maryland	North Carolina	89-83 (ot)	College Park, MD
Feb. 5, 1998	2	North Carolina	Duke	97-73	Chapel Hill, NC
Feb. 21, 1998	NR	North Carolina St.	North Carolina	86-72	Chapel Hill, NC
Mar. 8, 1998	4	North Carolina	Duke	83-68	Greensboro, NC
Mar. 28, 1998	7	Utah	North Carolina	65-59	San Antonio, TX (NSF)
Nov. 28, 1998	15	Cincinnati	Duke	77-75	Anchorage, AK
Feb. 1, 1999	17	Syracuse	Connecticut	59-42	Hartford, CT
Mar. 29, 1999	3	Connecticut	Duke	77-74	St. Petersburg, FL (CH)
Nov. 11, 1999	NR	Iowa	Connecticut	70-68	New York
Nov. 18, 1999	NR	Xavier	Cincinnati	66-64	Cincinnati
Jan. 8, 2000	5	Arizona	Stanford	68-65	Palo Alto, CA
Feb. 12, 2000	15	Temple	Cincinnati	77-69	Cincinnati
Mar. 4, 2000	NR	UCLA	Stanford	94-93 (ot)	Palo Alto, CA
Mar. 9, 2000	NR	St. Louis	Cincinnati	68-58	Memphis, TN
Mar. 24, 2000	11	Florida	Duke	87-78	Syracuse, NY (RSF)
Nov. 25, 2000	NR	Purdue	Arizona	72-69	Indianapolis
Dec. 21, 2000	3	Stanford	Duke	84-83	Oakland, CA
Jan. 7, 2001	NR	Indiana	Michigan St.	59-58	Bloomington, IN
Feb. 3, 2001	NR	UCLA	Stanford	79-73	Palo Alto, CA
Feb. 18, 2001	NR	Clemson	North Carolina	75-65	Clemson, SC
Mar. 8, 2001	8	Arizona	Stanford	76-75	Palo Alto, CA
Jan. 6, 2002	NR	Florida St.	Duke	77-76	Tallahassee, FL
Jan. 12, 2002	11	UCLA	Kansas	87-77	Los Angeles
Feb. 17, 2002	3	Maryland	Duke	87-73	College Park, MD
Mar. 10, 2002	4	Oklahoma	Kansas	64-55	Kansas City, MO
Mar. 21, 2002	NR	Indiana	Duke	74-73	Lexington, KY (RSF)
Dec. 21, 2002	NR	LSU	Arizona	66-65	Baton Rouge, LA
Dec. 30, 2002	NR	Utah	Alabama	51-49	Salt Lake City
Jan. 18, 2003	17	Maryland	Duke	87-72	College Park, MD
Jan. 30, 2003	24	Stanford	Arizona	82-77	Tucson, AZ
Feb. 4, 2003	6	Kentucky	Florida	70-55	Lexington, KY
Mar. 13, 2003	NR	UCLA	Arizona	96-89 (ot)	Los Angeles
Mar. 29, 2003	9	Marquette	Kentucky	83-69	Minneapolis (RF)
Nov. 26, 2003	NR	Georgia Tech	Connecticut	77-61	New York
Dec. 6, 2003	21	Stanford	Kansas	64-58	Los Angeles
Dec. 10, 2003	NR	Maryland	Florida	69-68 (ot)	Gainesville, FL
Dec. 13, 2003	NR	Louisville	Florida	73-65	Louisville, KY
Jan. 17, 2004	11	North Carolina	Connecticut	86-83	Chapel Hill, NC
Feb. 15, 2004	21	North Carolina St.	Duke	78-74	Raleigh, NC
Mar. 6, 2004	NR	Washington	Stanford	75-62	Seattle
Mar. 11, 2004	NR	Xavier	St. Joseph's	87-67	Dayton, OH

Date	Rank	School	No. 1 Team	Score	Site
Mar. 20, 2004	NR	Alabama	Stanford	70-67	Seattle, (2nd)
Dec. 1, 2004	5	Illinois	Wake Forest	91-73	Champaign, IL
Mar. 6, 2005	NR	Ohio St.	Illinois	65-64	Columbus, OH
Apr. 4, 2005	2	North Carolina	Illinois	75-70	St. Louis (CH)
Jan. 21, 2006	NR	Georgetown	Duke	87-84	Washington
Feb. 13, 2006	4	Villanova	Connecticut	69-64	Philadelphia
Mar. 1, 2006	NR	Florida St.	Duke	79-74	Tallahassee, FL
Mar. 4, 2006	15	North Carolina	Duke	83-76	Durham, NC
Mar. 9, 2006	NR	Syracuse	Connecticut	86-84	New York
Nov. 26, 2006	10	Kansas	Florida	82-80 (ot)	Las Vegas
Jan. 6, 2007	17	Oregon	UCLA	68-66	Eugene, OR
Jan. 13, 2007	NR	Virginia Tech	North Carolina	94-88	Blacksburg, VA
Feb. 17, 2007	NR	Vanderbilt	Florida	83-70	Nashville, TN
Feb. 20, 2007	NR	Michigan St.	Wisconsin	64-55	East Lansing, MI
Feb. 25, 2007	2	Ohio St.	Wisconsin	49-48	Columbus, OH
Apr. 2, 2007	3	Florida	Ohio St.	84-75	Atlanta, GA (NCAA Final)

NR=Not Rated
NCAA Tournament Abbreviations After Site:
NF=National Final or Championship Game
NSF=National Semifinal
N3rd= NCAA National Consolation Game
RF=Regional Final
RSF=Regional Semifinal
2nd=Second-Round Game
1st=First-Round Game

Week-by-Week A.P. Polls

REGULAR-SEASON POLLS

The Associated Press began its basketball poll on January 20, 1949. The following are those polls, year by year and week by week. Starting in the 1961-62 season, A.P. provided a preseason (PS) poll. A.P. did a post-tournament poll in 1953, 1954, 1974 and 1975.

1948-49

	Jan 18	Jan 25	Feb 1	Feb 8	Feb 15	Feb 22	Mar 1	Mar 8
Arkansas	-	-	-	-	-	-	20	-
Baylor	-	18	-	-	-	-	-	-
Bowling Green	15	-	14	14	10	9	9	10
Bradley	16	19	18	-	12	10	10	7
Butler	19	17	16	16	11	11	11	18
Cincinnati	13	-	-	-	-	-	-	-
DePaul	-	16	-	-	17	-	-	-
Duquesne	-	-	-	20	20	17	-	-
Eastern Ky.	-	-	20	-	-	-	-	-
Hamline	8	7	8	5	9	15	16	19
Holy Cross	14	20	19	15	-	-	-	-
Illinois	7	6	4	4	4	4	4	4
Kentucky	2	2	1	1	1	1	1	1
Loyola (Ill.)	12	13	13	11	13	12	14	16
Minnesota	4	5	5	7	6	5	5	6
North Carolina St.	-	15	17	-	18	-	15	13
New York U.	20	-	15	-	-	-	-	-
Ohio St.	-	-	-	18	-	18	19	20
Oklahoma	-	-	-	-	16	-	-	-
Oklahoma St.	5	3	3	3	3	3	2	2
St. Louis	1	1	2	2	2	2	3	3
San Francisco	6	9	10	9	8	8	8	8
Southern California	-	-	-	-	-	19	-	-
Stanford	17	11	9	10	20	-	-	-
Texas	-	-	-	-	-	20	-	-
Tulane	11	12	11	8	5	6	7	9
UCLA	-	-	-	-	-	-	-	15
Utah	10	10	12	12	14	16	13	12
Villanova	9	8	7	13	15	-	17	14
Western Ky.	3	4	6	6	7	7	6	5
Washington St.	18	14	-	17	-	-	-	-
Wyoming	-	-	-	19	19	14	12	17
Yale	-	-	-	-	20	13	18	11

1949-50

	Jan 5	Jan 10	Jan 17	Jan 24	Jan 31	Feb 7	Feb 14	Feb 21	Feb 28	Mar 7
Arizona	-	-	-	-	-	18	17	19	15	15
Bowling Green	19	-	-	-	-	-	-	-	-	-
Bradley	3	6	4	6	3	2	2	1	1	1
CCNY	14	7	7	8	10	14	13	20	-	-
Cincinnati	-	12	20	-	-	-	-	-	-	-
Duquesne	8	8	6	2	2	3	7	4	5	6

	Jan 5	Jan 10	Jan 17	Jan 24	Jan 31	Feb 7	Feb 14	Feb 21	Feb 28	Mar 7
Hamline	-	-	-	-	-	20	-	-	-	-
Holy Cross	6	5	1	1	1	1	1	2	3	4
Illinois	16	-	-	20	-	-	-	-	-	-
Indiana	5	4	8	9	12	16	-	17	-	20
Kansas	-	-	-	-	-	-	-	-	-	19
Kansas St.	20	-	13	12	11	10	14	13	12	14
Kentucky	2	2	5	4	6	7	5	5	4	3
La Salle	18	13	10	7	8	9	11	12	9	10
Long Island	4	3	3	3	4	6	6	10	14	13
Louisville	-	-	19	-	15	13	-	-	-	-
Minnesota	10	11	16	18	-	-	-	-	-	-
Missouri	12	16	-	-	-	-	-	-	-	-
Nebraska	-	-	-	-	-	-	-	-	16	-
North Carolina St.	7	9	12	10	9	8	8	9	8	5
Notre Dame	-	-	-	-	16	-	-	-	-	-
Ohio St.	-	15	11	13	7	4	3	3	2	2
Oklahoma	17	19	-	-	-	-	-	-	-	-
Oklahoma St.	-	-	-	-	19	-	-	-	-	-
St. John's (N.Y.)	1	1	2	5	5	4	4	6	10	9
St. Louis	11	-	-	-	-	19	18	15	-	-
San Francisco	-	-	-	-	-	15	12	11	13	12
San Jose St.	-	-	-	-	-	-	-	18	19	17
Siena	-	-	18	-	-	-	-	-	-	-
Southern California	-	-	-	-	-	-	-	19	16	-
Tennessee	-	-	17	-	-	-	-	-	-	-
Toledo	-	-	-	-	-	-	-	14	17	-
Tulane	-	-	15	-	-	-	-	-	-	-
UCLA	9	10	9	11	13	12	10	7	6	7
Vanderbilt	-	-	-	-	18	-	20	-	20	-
Villanova	13	17	18	19	-	-	15	-	11	11
Washington	-	20	-	16	-	-	-	-	-	-
Washington St.	-	-	-	-	-	17	16	-	-	18
Western Ky.	-	14	14	17	14	11	9	8	7	8
Wisconsin	15	-	-	15	17	-	-	-	-	16
Wyoming	-	-	-	14	20	-	-	-	18	-

1950-51

	Dec 19	Dec 26	Jan 3	Jan 9	Jan 16	Jan 23	Jan 30	Feb 6	Feb 13	Feb 20	Feb 27	Mar 7
Arizona	-	-	16	-	-	14	15	13	16	11	12	12
Beloit	-	-	-	-	-	-	-	18	20	16	-	-
Bradley	2	2	1	1	3	4	5	5	8	7	5	6
BYU	15	-	-	-	19	12	14	12	14	11	11	11

	December 19	26	January 3	9	16	23	30	February 6	13	20	27	Mar. 7
CCNY	6	11	-	-	-	-	-	-	-	-	-	-
Cincinnati	17	17	17	-	16	15	16	11	15	18	-	17
Columbia	-	8	14	8	7	7	6	6	4	3	3	3
Cornell	19	18	14	-	-	-	-	-	-	-	-	-
Dayton	-	-	-	-	-	-	18	17	14	14	-	13
Duquesne	-	-	13	15	20	-	-	-	-	-	-	-
Illinois	-	20	-	14	14	16	14	16	11	10	6	5
Indiana	4	5	6	6	6	5	3	3	6	4	7	7
Kansas	11	10	20	17	-	-	17	20	-	-	-	-
Kansas St.	20	-	9	9	10	9	7	4	3	5	4	4
Kentucky	1	1	3	3	2	1	1	1	1	1	1	1
La Salle	-	16	-	19	-	17	-	-	-	-	-	-
Long Island	7	4	4	4	4	2	4	12	19	16	-	-
Louisville	-	-	-	-	-	-	-	17	14	-	-	-
Missouri	8	9	-	-	-	-	-	-	-	-	-	-
Murray St.	-	-	-	-	-	-	-	-	-	-	20	16
North Carolina St.	3	6	7	7	9	8	8	10	9	9	8	8
Notre Dame	14	-	-	-	-	-	-	-	-	-	-	-
Oklahoma	16	-	-	-	-	18	18	-	-	17	-	-
Oklahoma St.	5	3	2	2	1	3	2	2	2	2	2	2
Princeton	-	-	18	20	-	-	-	-	-	-	-	-
St. Bonaventure	-	-	-	-	17	-	-	-	-	-	-	-
St. John's (N.Y.)	13	12	11	11	5	6	9	7	7	8	9	9
St. Louis	-	-	5	5	8	10	10	8	5	6	10	10
Seattle	-	-	-	-	-	-	-	20	-	-	-	-
Siena	-	-	-	-	18	13	-	19	-	-	-	18
Southern California	-	-	-	13	19	12	13	15	13	13	18	19
Toledo	10	13	19	18	12	-	20	-	-	-	13	14
UCLA	9	-	-	-	-	-	19	-	-	-	17	-
Villanova	18	7	8	16	11	11	11	9	10	15	15	20
Washington	12	15	12	12	15	-	-	-	-	19	19	15
West Virginia	-	19	-	-	-	-	-	-	-	-	-	-
Wyoming	-	14	10	10	13	20	-	-	-	-	-	-

1951-52

	December 10	17	25	January 1	8	15	22	29	February 5	12	19	26	March 4
Dayton	-	-	-	-	20	19	16	14	11	11	11	11	11
DePaul	-	-	-	-	-	-	19	-	18	-	-	15	12
Duke	12	19	-	-	-	-	-	-	-	-	-	-	-
Duquesne	-	-	-	-	16	7	10	7	5	3	3	4	4
Eastern Ky.	19	-	-	-	-	-	-	-	-	-	-	-	-
Fordham	-	-	-	-	-	-	-	20	-	-	-	-	-
Holy Cross	-	17	-	-	-	20	11	17	-	19	17	17	13
Illinois	3	3	2	2	2	2	1	3	3	6	5	2	2
Indiana	11	6	5	5	4	14	20	13	18	20	-	-	-
Iowa	-	-	-	12	10	4	4	8	9	5	4	7	7
Kansas	8	7	4	1	1	2	4	6	9	7	8	8	8
Kansas St.	5	5	8	9	7	9	7	2	2	2	2	3	3
Kentucky	1	2	1	4	3	3	3	1	1	1	1	1	1
La Salle	9	12	17	13	-	15	18	-	19	-	20	-	17
Louisville	17	-	-	-	15	13	14	12	13	15	15	13	17
Michigan St.	-	-	-	20	19	-	-	-	-	-	-	-	-
Minnesota	-	15	-	-	-	-	-	-	-	-	-	-	-
Murray St.	-	-	18	16	-	-	-	-	-	-	-	-	-
North Carolina St.	10	9	19	17	-	17	-	-	-	-	-	-	-
Notre Dame	14	20	9	14	-	-	-	-	-	-	-	-	-
New York U.	20	11	6	6	13	-	-	-	-	-	-	-	-
Oklahoma City	-	-	-	15	18	18	-	16	15	13	-	-	-
Oklahoma St.	13	13	-	-	-	-	-	-	16	-	-	-	-
Penn St.	-	-	-	-	-	-	-	-	14	17	13	-	-
St. Bonaventure	-	-	-	10	8	6	5	5	4	4	10	12	15
St. John's (N.Y.)	2	1	7	8	12	-	15	15	10	10	8	9	10
St. Louis	4	4	12	7	5	5	8	6	7	7	9	5	5
Seattle	-	-	-	-	-	-	-	-	-	-	16	-	18
Seton Hall	7	10	10	11	9	12	13	11	17	12	14	14	14
Siena	-	-	-	-	17	11	19	18	-	16	18	20	-
Stanford	16	-	13	-	-	-	-	-	-	-	-	-	-
Texas St.	-	-	-	-	-	-	-	-	-	-	-	-	20
Syracuse	-	-	20	19	14	-	-	-	-	-	-	-	-
TCU	-	-	-	-	-	15	12	-	-	-	-	-	-
UCLA	-	-	16	-	-	-	-	-	-	-	-	-	19
Utah	-	-	15	18	-	17	-	-	-	-	-	-	-
Vanderbilt	18	-	-	-	-	-	-	-	-	-	-	-	-
Villanova	15	18	14	-	-	-	-	-	-	-	-	19	-
Washington	6	8	3	3	6	8	6	9	8	8	6	6	6
West Virginia	-	-	-	-	11	10	9	10	12	14	12	10	9
Western Ky.	-	16	11	-	-	-	-	-	20	-	-	18	-
Wyoming	-	14	-	-	-	-	-	-	-	-	19	16	16

1952-53

	December 16	23	30	January 6	13	20	27	February 3	10	17	24	March 3	10	24
California	18	-	-	20	-	14	-	14	19	19	-	-	-	-
Colorado	-	18	-	-	-	-	-	-	-	-	-	-	-	-
DePaul	-	-	14	-	-	-	10	7	7	14	15	-	-	19
Duke	-	-	-	-	-	-	-	-	18	-	-	-	-	-
Duquesne	-	-	-	-	-	-	-	-	-	-	19	18	11	9
Eastern Ky.	-	-	-	-	18	15	-	-	-	20	-	17	-	-
Fordham	-	-	-	8	7	10	7	13	16	-	-	-	-	-
Georgetown	-	-	-	-	20	-	-	-	-	-	-	-	-	-
Holy Cross	8	4	6	14	17	-	-	17	-	-	-	20	-	13
Idaho	-	20	-	18	-	-	-	-	-	-	-	-	-	-
Illinois	3	2	4	4	4	6	6	6	5	5	10	10	13	11
Indiana	19	15	12	7	6	2	2	2	2	2	2	1	1	1
Kansas	20	-	-	-	15	9	14	18	14	10	5	6	5	3
Kansas St.	2	5	1	1	1	4	5	5	10	8	9	8	8	12
La Salle	1	1	3	3	3	5	4	4	4	4	4	2	3	6
LSU	10	8	17	11	14	14	11	10	8	6	6	5	7	5
Louisville	-	-	-	-	-	-	-	17	16	18	-	14	14	-
Manhattan	-	-	-	-	20	19	-	19	15	13	16	-	20	-
Miami (Ohio)	-	-	-	-	-	-	-	-	-	-	12	16	-	-
Minnesota	16	17	9	19	-	19	-	-	-	-	-	-	-	-
Missouri St.	-	-	-	-	-	-	-	-	-	-	-	-	-	20
Murray St.	-	-	-	-	-	-	-	-	17	-	-	-	-	-
Navy	20	13	-	15	-	16	-	-	-	-	-	18	19	-
Niagara	-	-	-	-	-	-	-	20	17	-	-	-	-	-
North Carolina	-	-	-	-	-	18	12	-	-	-	-	-	-	-
North Carolina St.	6	6	11	9	8	8	12	15	12	15	13	12	18	18
Notre Dame	7	11	19	13	11	16	17	-	-	17	-	13	17	10
Oklahoma City	13	19	16	-	18	17	-	16	13	12	11	11	10	-
Oklahoma St.	5	9	7	5	9	7	8	9	6	7	7	7	6	8
St. Bonaventure	14	12	15	-	-	-	-	-	-	-	-	-	-	-
St. John's (N.Y.)	-	-	-	-	-	-	-	-	-	-	-	-	20	7
St. Louis	17	-	-	-	-	-	-	-	-	-	-	-	-	-
Santa Clara	-	-	-	-	-	-	-	-	-	-	-	-	-	16
Seattle	-	15	13	16	16	13	13	11	11	11	14	15	14	14
Seton Hall	4	3	2	2	2	1	1	1	1	1	1	3	4	2
Southern California	-	-	-	12	12	-	-	-	-	-	-	-	-	-
Toledo	-	-	18	-	-	-	-	-	-	-	-	-	-	-
Tulsa	15	14	8	17	13	11	20	-	19	-	-	-	-	-
UCLA	12	20	-	-	19	-	-	-	-	-	-	-	-	-
Villanova	-	-	-	-	-	-	-	-	-	19	-	-	-	-
Wake Forest	-	-	-	-	-	-	-	-	-	-	-	-	12	15
Washington	9	7	5	6	5	3	3	3	3	3	3	4	2	4
Wayne St. (Mich.)	-	-	20	-	-	-	-	-	-	-	-	-	-	-
Western Ky.	11	10	10	10	10	12	9	8	9	9	8	9	9	17
Wyoming	-	-	-	-	-	-	-	-	-	-	-	-	16	-

1953-54

	December 8	15	22	29	January 5	12	19	26	February 2	9	16	23	March 2	9	23
Bradley	-	-	-	-	-	-	-	-	18	-	-	-	-	-	7
BYU	-	-	-	19	-	-	-	-	-	-	-	-	-	-	-
California	17	15	-	-	-	15	14	-	15	14	-	-	-	-	-
Colorado A&M	-	-	-	-	-	18	-	-	-	-	19	18	-	19	-
Connecticut	-	-	-	-	-	-	-	18	-	-	-	-	19	-	-
Dayton	15	-	16	-	14	17	-	18	-	-	17	16	14	15	-
Duke	-	13	-	-	8	9	13	20	8	15	14	10	11	18	15
Duquesne	3	3	3	2	2	2	2	2	2	1	1	-	4	3	5
Fordham	-	9	7	10	-	-	-	-	-	-	-	-	-	-	-
George Washington	-	-	-	-	12	7	10	10	11	10	8	8	9	7	12
Holy Cross	19	14	10	12	7	6	8	7	9	9	7	-	13	9	3
Idaho	-	-	20	17	-	20	-	-	-	-	-	-	-	-	-
Illinois	9	4	4	8	15	19	20	-	-	-	-	20	-	-	19
Indiana	1	1	1	3	3	3	3	3	3	3	3	3	2	2	4
Iowa	-	-	-	-	-	-	-	-	-	10	20	16	16	13	-
Kansas	5	-	-	-	16	11	17	17	19	20	-	17	15	13	18
Kansas St.	8	-	-	-	-	-	-	-	-	-	-	-	-	-	-
Kentucky	2	2	2	1	1	1	1	1	1	1	2	2	1	1	1
La Salle	6	20	16	13	-	-	19	12	9	7	12	13	8	12	2
LSU	10	5	14	18	-	16	12	14	17	13	12	-	7	8	14
Louisville	-	-	-	-	-	-	-	-	20	-	-	20	-	-	-
Maryland	-	-	-	-	-	-	14	13	13	11	11	11	17	14	20
Minnesota	12	6	8	6	6	10	9	8	12	12	18	-	-	-	-
Navy	-	-	-	-	-	18	-	-	16	20	-	-	-	-	-
Niagara	-	18	-	-	12	13	18	-	-	-	-	-	-	-	16
North Carolina St.	7	8	9	9	20	-	-	-	-	-	19	-	18	10	-
Notre Dame	-	16	19	-	-	-	6	6	7	6	6	6	5	6	6
Oklahoma City	19	12	15	5	-	9	8	7	9	16	13	16	15	-	-
Oklahoma St.	4	7	5	5	4	4	5	4	5	4	5	5	6	5	10
Oregon St.	13	11	12	4	10	-	-	-	-	-	-	-	-	16	-
Penn St.	-	-	-	-	-	-	-	-	-	-	-	-	-	-	9
Rice	-	-	11	16	11	15	-	-	-	-	-	-	-	-	-

	Dec 8	15	22	29	Jan 5	12	19	26	Feb 2	9	16	23	Mar 2	9	23
St. Louis	18	-	-	-	-	-	-	-	-	-	-	-	-	-	-
Santa Clara	16	-	-	-	-	-	-	-	-	-	-	-	-	-	-
Seattle	-	-	-	15	16	14	16	11	6	8	7	9	10	11	17
Siena	-	19	-	-	-	-	-	-	-	-	-	-	-	-	-
Southern California	-	-	-	-	-	-	-	-	-	-	-	-	-	-	11
UCLA	-	17	13	14	-	-	-	-	-	-	-	19	-	-	-
Vanderbilt	-	-	20	20	19	-	-	-	-	-	-	-	-	-	-
Western Ky.	11	10	6	7	5	5	4	4	4	5	4	4	3	4	8
Wichita St.	-	-	-	-	-	11	11	16	14	18	15	14	12	20	-
Wisconsin	-	-	18	-	-	-	-	-	-	-	-	-	-	-	-
Wyoming	14	-	-	20	-	-	-	-	-	-	-	-	-	-	-

1954-55

	Dec 7	14	21	28	Jan 4	11	18	25	Feb 1	8	15	22	Mar 1	8
Alabama	-	-	19	12	20	16	12	14	13	13	17	12	11	12
Auburn	-	-	-	-	-	20	-	-	-	-	-	-	-	-
Cincinnati	-	-	-	-	-	-	-	-	-	17	12	17	-	-
Colorado	-	-	-	-	-	-	-	-	-	-	-	-	-	15
Dayton	7	5	6	4	10	12	18	15	15	16	13	11	10	9
Duke	17	-	-	18	17	-	-	-	-	-	-	-	-	-
Duquesne	3	9	9	8	2	3	5	4	4	4	4	4	8	6
George Washington	-	11	8	9	6	8	9	6	7	6	5	10	13	14
Holy Cross	5	19	-	-	-	-	16	13	14	-	-	-	-	-
Illinois	14	3	3	6	12	7	7	10	10	10	14	13	17	18
Indiana	6	7	-	-	-	-	-	-	-	-	-	-	-	-
Iowa	4	13	20	19	14	19	19	19	-	15	15	16	12	5
Kansas	-	-	20	16	-	-	-	-	-	-	-	-	-	-
Kentucky	2	2	1	1	1	1	1	1	1	2	2	2	2	2
La Salle	1	1	4	3	4	4	4	5	3	3	3	3	3	3
Louisville	-	12	14	13	16	20	-	-	-	-	-	-	-	-
Marquette	-	-	-	-	-	-	15	11	9	9	6	5	4	8
Maryland	-	-	-	-	11	11	6	8	12	11	11	17	18	-
Memphis	-	-	-	-	-	-	-	-	-	-	-	15	19	-
Minnesota	-	-	-	11	13	14	14	-	11	12	8	7	6	11
Missouri	-	6	7	-	9	6	8	12	17	14	-	20	20	-
Niagara	8	10	10	10	15	15	20	20	16	-	-	-	-	-
North Carolina St.	10	4	5	2	3	2	2	3	6	7	7	6	5	4
Northwestern	-	-	-	-	-	-	-	16	-	-	-	-	-	-
Notre Dame	9	20	-	-	20	-	-	-	-	-	-	-	-	-
Ohio St.	-	14	11	20	-	-	-	-	-	-	-	-	-	-
Oklahoma St.	11	-	-	-	-	-	-	-	-	-	-	-	-	-
Oregon St.	-	-	-	-	-	-	-	-	19	18	16	-	14	10
Penn	-	-	16	17	19	-	-	-	-	-	-	-	-	-
Penn St.	19	-	-	-	-	-	-	-	-	-	-	-	-	-
Purdue	-	-	-	-	-	17	-	-	-	-	-	-	-	-
Richmond	-	-	-	-	-	13	13	17	-	-	-	-	-	-
St. John's (N.Y.)	-	16	-	-	-	-	-	-	-	-	-	-	-	-
St. Louis	12	-	-	-	-	-	-	-	-	-	-	-	-	20
San Francisco	-	-	17	5	5	5	3	2	2	1	1	1	1	1
Seton Hall	-	-	-	-	-	20	-	-	-	-	-	-	-	-
Southern California	-	-	13	14	-	18	-	-	-	-	-	-	-	-
Tennessee	-	-	-	-	-	-	-	-	-	-	18	-	-	-
TCU	-	-	-	-	-	-	20	-	-	-	-	-	-	-
Tulsa	-	-	-	-	-	-	-	-	-	-	19	19	15	16
UCLA	13	8	17	15	7	10	10	9	8	8	9	9	9	13
Utah	16	15	2	7	8	9	10	7	5	5	10	8	7	7
Vanderbilt	-	-	-	-	-	-	17	18	20	20	20	14	16	17
Villanova	-	-	-	-	17	-	-	-	17	19	-	-	-	-
Wake Forest	17	17	-	-	-	-	-	-	-	-	-	-	-	-
West Virginia	-	-	12	-	-	-	-	-	-	-	-	-	-	19
Western Ky.	20	-	-	-	-	-	-	-	-	-	-	-	-	-
Wichita St.	15	17	14	-	-	-	-	-	-	-	-	-	-	-

1955-56

	Dec 6	13	20	27	Jan 3	10	17	24	31	Feb 7	14	21	28	Mar 6
Alabama	6	5	16	19	17	19	13	12	12	10	8	7	4	4
BYU	10	8	5	20	-	-	-	-	-	-	-	-	-	-
Cincinnati	-	14	-	-	20	-	14	-	-	20	-	-	-	-
Dayton	7	7	4	2	3	2	2	2	2	2	2	4	3	3
Duke	-	-	14	8	11	6	7	10	10	8	11	11	11	19
Duquesne	9	6	20	-	-	-	-	-	-	-	-	-	-	-
George Washington	13	13	11	12	7	14	-	-	-	-	19	-	19	-
Holy Cross	11	10	7	14	14	11	12	11	14	13	16	17	15	12
Houston	-	-	-	-	-	-	-	-	-	-	18	14	18	17
Illinois	8	-	17	9	9	8	5	6	6	9	3	2	2	7
Indiana	-	19	18	-	13	12	-	-	-	-	-	-	-	-
Iowa	4	4	10	6	-	-	20	13	19	17	15	13	10	5
Iowa St.	-	-	-	-	8	15	-	-	-	-	-	20	-	-
Kansas	-	18	-	-	-	-	-	-	-	-	-	-	-	-
Kansas St.	-	-	-	-	-	-	-	-	17	-	-	-	-	-
Kentucky	2	12	9	13	6	5	4	3	8	7	7	8	12	9
La Salle	18	-	-	-	-	-	-	-	-	-	-	-	-	-
Louisville	-	-	-	11	-	13	10	9	5	5	4	3	6	6
Marquette	14	-	13	-	-	-	-	-	-	-	-	-	-	-
Marshall	-	-	-	-	-	-	-	-	18	-	-	-	-	-
Memphis	-	-	18	-	12	17	15	19	16	-	19	-	-	-
Michigan St.	-	-	-	16	20	-	-	-	-	-	-	-	-	-
Minnesota	20	-	-	-	-	-	-	-	-	-	-	-	-	-
North Carolina	-	16	6	4	5	9	9	8	9	12	10	9	8	15
North Carolina St.	3	2	2	3	2	3	3	4	4	4	5	6	5	2
Ohio St.	16	-	15	-	10	7	11	-	-	-	-	-	-	-
Oklahoma City	12	20	15	10	-	16	14	16	16	14	14	18	16	16
Oklahoma St.	-	-	-	-	-	20	-	20	-	-	-	-	-	-
Rice	-	-	17	-	18	-	-	-	-	-	-	-	-	-
St. Francis (N.Y.)	-	-	-	-	-	-	-	15	13	16	13	16	-	-
St. Louis	-	17	-	-	-	17	17	11	11	17	-	19	-	-
San Francisco	1	1	1	1	1	1	1	1	1	1	1	1	1	1
SMU	-	-	-	-	-	19	18	17	15	12	12	9	-	8
Stanford	19	-	-	-	-	-	-	-	-	-	-	-	-	-
Temple	-	11	12	17	16	10	8	6	7	9	9	10	14	13
Tulsa	-	-	-	-	-	15	-	-	-	-	-	-	-	-
UCLA	16	-	-	-	-	18	-	-	20	18	20	15	13	10
Utah	5	3	3	7	-	20	16	-	-	-	-	-	-	20
Vanderbilt	-	9	8	5	4	4	5	7	3	3	6	5	7	11
Wake Forest	-	-	-	-	-	18	-	-	-	-	-	-	20	18
West Virginia	14	15	-	-	19	-	-	-	-	-	-	-	-	14

1956-57

	Dec 11	18	26	Jan 2	8	15	22	29	Feb 5	12	19	26	Mar 5	12
Alabama	9	17	-	-	-	-	-	-	-	-	-	-	-	-
Bradley	-	-	-	-	12	10	10	8	5	7	7	-	13	19
California	-	-	-	-	19	19	19	19	12	15	-	-	14	13
Canisius	10	18	17	15	14	14	14	12	14	14	-	-	-	20
Dayton	15	-	-	-	-	-	-	-	-	-	-	-	-	-
Duke	-	13	9	-	15	16	15	19	-	17	16	-	-	-
Idaho St.	-	-	20	-	-	-	-	17	20	-	-	15	15	16
Illinois	7	5	6	5	10	8	9	7	15	16	-	-	-	-
Indiana	-	-	-	-	-	-	-	-	-	18	11	10	-	-
Iowa St.	17	14	14	7	7	9	3	8	9	9	9	16	17	-
Kansas	1	1	1	1	1	1	2	2	2	2	2	2	2	2
Kansas St.	14	10	-	-	-	-	-	-	-	-	17	12	-	-
Kentucky	3	7	3	3	3	4	5	4	3	3	3	3	3	3
Louisville	4	6	8	6	5	5	4	3	6	8	7	8	6	6
Manhattan	-	-	-	13	-	-	-	-	-	-	-	-	-	-
Memphis	-	-	20	-	-	-	-	-	16	-	20	19	19	12
Michigan St.	-	-	-	-	16	-	-	-	-	-	-	-	8	11
Minnesota	-	-	-	-	-	19	-	-	-	-	-	-	-	-
Mississippi St.	-	-	-	-	-	-	-	-	-	19	20	-	18	15
Niagara	16	-	-	-	-	-	-	-	-	-	-	-	-	-
North Carolina	6	3	2	2	2	1	1	1	1	1	1	1	1	1
North Carolina St.	8	19	-	-	-	-	-	-	-	-	-	-	-	17
Notre Dame	-	-	-	-	-	-	-	-	-	-	-	-	-	17
Ohio St.	11	11	-	-	17	12	11	12	-	-	-	-	-	-
Oklahoma City	18	15	11	17	11	13	16	16	13	13	13	18	10	9
Oklahoma St.	19	12	10	11	-	20	-	-	-	-	17	-	16	20
Purdue	-	-	-	-	-	-	-	-	17	-	-	-	-	-
St. John's (N.Y.)	-	15	-	-	-	-	-	-	-	-	-	-	-	-
St. Louis	-	9	5	16	17	-	-	-	-	20	-	14	12	10
San Francisco	2	2	19	-	-	-	-	-	-	-	-	-	-	-
Seattle	20	-	18	10	9	7	8	9	7	4	4	5	5	5
SMU	5	4	7	4	4	3	6	6	4	6	6	4	4	4
Tennessee	-	-	-	-	12	16	-	-	-	-	-	-	-	-
Tulane	-	-	-	-	16	-	-	-	-	18	14	-	-	-
UCLA	-	-	-	-	-	8	6	7	5	7	8	6	7	14
Vanderbilt	-	-	12	9	6	10	13	-	18	18	10	9	9	8
Wake Forest	-	-	-	-	18	13	11	13	10	11	12	13	20	18
West Virginia	13	8	4	19	18	15	17	18	11	10	14	11	11	7
West Va. Tech	-	-	-	-	-	-	-	-	-	15	18	-	-	-
Western Ky.	12	20	15	14	20	18	20	-	-	-	-	-	-	-

1957-58

	Dec 10	17	24	31	Jan 7	14	21	28	Feb 4	11	18	25	Mar 4	11
Arkansas	-	-	-	-	-	-	20	17	18	-	-	-	-	-
Auburn	-	-	-	-	-	-	-	-	-	-	-	20	16	16
Bradley	4	11	11	12	10	10	10	12	11	13	15	14	11	14
California	-	-	-	19	-	-	-	-	-	-	-	19	-	-
Cincinnati	19	4	5	5	7	5	4	3	3	2	3	3	8	5
Dartmouth	-	-	-	-	-	19	18	19	20	-	19	-	-	-
Dayton	-	-	-	-	-	-	17	16	14	14	11	10	8	11

DIVISION I

	December				January				February				March	
	10	17	24	31	7	14	21	28	4	11	18	25	4	11
Duke	-	-	-	-	-	-	-	-	13	8	7	6	6	10
Georgia Tech	-	-	-	-	-	-	-	-	19	-	-	-	-	-
Illinois	-	-	-	-	17	-	-	-	-	-	-	-	-	-
Indiana	-	-	-	-	-	-	-	-	-	-	-	-	-	12
Iowa St.	-	-	20	-	-	-	-	-	-	-	-	-	-	-
Kansas	2	2	2	2	2	3	2	2	2	4	4	7	10	7
Kansas St.	5	3	3	3	4	2	3	4	4	1	1	1	1	3
Kentucky	3	5	9	10	9	9	9	8	12	12	13	12	9	9
La Salle	-	-	-	20	-	-	-	-	-	-	-	-	-	-
Maryland	-	6	6	7	11	8	6	9	8	9	14	17	17	6
Memphis	20	-	-	-	18	-	-	-	-	-	-	-	-	-
Michigan St.	7	9	8	8	14	18	15	15	15	19	12	15	12	17
Minnesota	11	10	-	-	-	-	-	-	-	-	-	-	-	-
Mississippi St.	-	18	10	9	5	11	14	14	17	18	18	16	15	15
North Carolina	1	1	4	4	3	6	8	7	7	11	16	9	13	13
North Carolina St.	12	20	13	11	13	20	12	10	9	10	9	11	14	20
Notre Dame	15	-	-	-	-	-	-	-	-	17	10	8	7	8
Oklahoma	-	-	-	-	-	14	-	-	-	20	-	-	-	-
Oklahoma St.	18	16	14	14	8	7	7	6	6	6	8	13	18	19
Oregon St.	-	17	-	18	15	16	-	20	-	-	-	-	-	-
Rice	16	14	-	-	-	-	-	-	-	-	-	-	-	-
Richmond	-	19	17	-	-	-	-	-	-	-	-	-	-	-
St. Bonaventure	-	-	-	-	-	-	-	-	-	-	-	-	20	-
St. John's (N.Y.)	-	-	19	17	16	15	13	13	-	-	-	-	-	-
St. Louis	9	-	18	-	-	-	-	-	-	-	-	-	-	-
San Francisco	6	7	7	6	6	4	5	5	5	5	5	4	4	4
Seattle	14	12	15	-	20	-	-	-	16	16	17	18	19	18
Syracuse	17	-	-	-	-	-	-	-	-	-	-	-	-	-
Temple	10	-	-	13	12	12	11	11	10	7	6	5	5	5
Tennessee	-	-	-	-	-	13	16	-	-	15	20	-	-	-
TCU	-	-	-	16	-	-	-	-	-	-	-	-	-	-
UCLA	13	13	-	-	-	-	-	-	-	-	-	-	-	-
Utah	-	15	12	15	19	-	-	-	-	-	-	-	-	-
West Virginia	8	8	1	1	1	1	1	1	1	2	3	2	2	1
Western Ky.	-	-	16	-	-	-	-	-	-	-	-	-	-	-
Wichita St.	-	-	-	-	20	17	19	18	-	-	-	-	-	-

1958-59

	December				January				February				March	
	9	16	23	30	6	13	20	27	3	10	17	24	2	9
Auburn	12	13	8	9	6	5	5	4	4	4	2	6	7	8
Bradley	-	11	13	10	9	7	9	9	8	7	10	9	9	4
California	-	15	14	20	-	20	-	20	19	18	15	12	11	11
Cincinnati	1	1	2	2	7	6	6	5	5	5	6	4	3	5
Dayton	-	-	20	-	-	-	-	-	-	-	-	-	-	-
Illinois	-	-	-	-	20	-	-	18	-	-	-	-	-	-
Indiana	19	-	-	-	-	19	-	-	-	15	19	-	-	-
Kansas	7	-	-	-	-	-	-	-	-	-	-	-	-	-
Kansas St.	3	3	4	3	4	4	3	3	3	3	4	2	2	1
Kentucky	2	2	1	1	1	2	1	1	1	1	3	1	1	2
Louisville	-	-	-	-	-	-	-	17	-	-	-	-	-	-
Marquette	17	-	17	15	15	13	12	12	12	11	13	13	13	20
Memphis	-	-	18	-	-	-	-	-	-	-	-	-	-	-
Michigan St.	15	11	9	7	5	8	8	8	7	12	9	8	6	7
Mississippi St.	8	8	7	8	12	12	11	11	11	10	5	5	4	3
North Carolina	13	10	3	4	3	3	2	2	2	2	1	3	5	9
North Carolina St.	5	4	6	5	2	1	4	6	6	6	6	7	10	6
Northwestern	10	6	12	6	8	11	18	-	-	-	-	-	-	-
Notre Dame	11	-	-	-	-	-	-	-	-	-	-	-	-	-
Oklahoma City	-	-	-	17	13	17	15	14	13	14	18	15	14	17
Oklahoma St.	20	-	-	-	-	-	-	-	-	-	-	-	-	-
Pittsburgh	-	18	-	-	-	-	-	-	-	-	-	-	-	-
Portland	-	-	-	-	-	18	17	-	-	-	-	19	-	-
Purdue	-	-	-	18	-	14	13	16	18	-	14	18	19	19
St. Bonaventure	-	-	-	-	-	-	-	-	-	-	-	-	-	-
St. John's (N.Y.)	20	-	-	13	10	9	7	7	15	19	-	17	18	-
St. Joseph's	-	14	-	12	-	-	-	-	20	-	-	-	20	14
St. Louis	9	17	16	16	14	15	14	15	9	8	8	11	12	12
St. Mary's (Cal.)	14	-	-	-	-	-	-	-	-	-	-	20	17	15
Seattle	-	16	-	-	16	16	16	13	14	13	12	16	-	13
SMU	18	20	-	-	-	-	-	-	-	-	-	-	-	-
Tennessee	6	5	11	14	17	-	-	-	-	-	-	-	-	-
Texas A&M	-	-	-	-	19	-	-	-	-	-	-	-	-	-
TCU	-	-	-	19	-	-	-	19	17	16	16	14	15	16
UCLA	-	19	-	-	-	-	-	-	-	-	-	-	-	-
Utah	-	-	-	-	-	20	-	-	16	17	17	-	16	18
Villanova	-	-	15	-	18	-	19	-	-	-	-	-	-	-
Washington	-	-	19	-	-	-	-	-	-	-	-	-	-	-
West Virginia	4	7	5	11	11	10	10	10	10	9	11	10	8	10
Xavier	16	9	10	-	-	-	-	-	-	-	-	-	-	-

1959-60

	December		January				February				March	
	22	29	5	12	19	26	2	9	16	23	1	8
Auburn	-	-	-	-	-	-	-	17	17	13	11	11
Bradley	5	9	4	4	2	2	2	2	2	3	4	4
California	4	3	2	2	3	3	3	3	3	4	3	2
Cincinnati	1	1	1	1	1	1	1	1	1	1	1	1
Dayton	-	-	-	-	19	19	13	15	-	-	-	-
DePaul	-	20	-	-	-	-	-	-	-	-	-	-
Detroit	17	11	15	20	20	14	14	19	-	-	-	-
Duke	16	18	-	-	-	-	-	-	-	-	-	18
Georgia Tech	8	10	6	6	6	6	6	6	6	6	7	13
Holy Cross	-	-	-	-	-	-	-	16	13	17	20	16
Illinois	10	8	9	14	13	-	19	20	20	-	-	-
Indiana	9	7	11	-	-	-	-	-	-	20	12	7
Iowa	19	14	-	-	15	-	-	-	-	-	-	-
Kansas St.	-	-	-	-	-	-	15	-	-	-	-	-
Kentucky	13	13	-	17	16	15	-	-	-	-	-	-
La Salle	14	-	-	19	-	-	-	-	-	-	-	-
Miami (Fla.)	-	15	14	15	11	11	11	10	10	9	8	10
Michigan St.	11	-	-	-	-	-	-	-	-	-	-	-
New York U.	12	12	-	-	-	-	-	-	-	14	14	12
North Carolina	-	-	19	16	12	12	17	13	19	-	16	-
Ohio	-	-	-	-	-	-	-	-	18	-	-	-
Ohio St.	3	5	7	5	5	5	4	4	2	2	2	3
Providence	-	-	-	-	-	20	16	14	16	15	15	14
St. Bonaventure	-	-	-	-	-	-	19	-	14	10	9	9
St. John's (N.Y.)	-	-	-	-	-	-	-	15	11	-	19	20
St. Louis	7	6	12	11	18	16	18	18	-	16	13	15
Southern California	20	-	10	10	14	18	-	-	-	-	-	-
Texas A&M	18	-	13	8	10	10	10	12	11	18	-	-
Toledo	-	16	20	18	17	13	12	11	12	19	-	-
Utah	6	4	5	7	7	7	7	9	8	5	6	6
Utah St.	-	-	17	12	9	9	9	7	7	8	10	8
Villanova	15	17	16	9	8	8	8	8	9	12	17	17
Virginia Tech	-	-	-	-	-	17	-	-	-	-	-	-
Wake Forest	-	19	8	13	-	20	-	-	-	-	18	19
West Virginia	2	2	3	3	4	4	5	5	5	7	5	5
Western Ky.	-	-	18	-	-	-	-	-	-	-	-	-

1960-61

	December			January					February				March
	13	20	27	3	10	17	24	31	7	14	21	28	7
Auburn	11	9	9	10	-	-	-	-	-	-	-	-	-
Bradley	2	2	2	2	2	3	3	3	4	5	4	4	6
Cincinnati	-	-	-	-	-	-	-	-	5	4	3	3	2
Colorado	-	15	-	-	-	-	-	-	-	-	-	-	-
Dayton	20	-	-	-	-	-	-	-	-	-	-	-	-
DePaul	-	-	-	-	7	-	-	-	-	-	-	-	-
Detroit	3	8	13	-	-	-	-	-	-	-	-	-	-
Drake	-	20	14	-	-	-	-	-	-	-	-	-	-
Duke	8	7	6	8	8	8	5	4	3	6	9	-	10
Georgia Tech	15	-	-	-	-	-	-	-	-	-	-	-	-
Illinois	19	-	-	-	-	-	-	-	-	-	-	-	-
Indiana	4	4	4	-	-	-	-	-	-	-	-	-	-
Iowa	-	-	-	7	6	4	6	6	9	9	5	6	8
Kansas	16	20	-	-	-	-	-	-	-	-	-	-	-
Kansas St.	20	12	12	-	9	10	-	10	7	6	8	7	4
Kentucky	20	-	19	-	-	-	-	-	-	-	-	-	-
Louisville	9	5	5	4	4	5	8	8	10	-	-	-	-
Maryland	12	-	-	-	-	-	-	-	-	-	-	-	-
Memphis	-	-	19	-	-	-	-	-	-	-	-	-	-
North Carolina	5	10	11	6	7	4	5	-	6	7	5	5	-
North Carolina St.	10	10	10	-	-	-	-	-	-	-	-	-	-
Ohio St.	1	1	1	1	1	1	1	1	1	1	1	1	1
Providence	-	13	15	-	-	-	-	10	-	-	-	-	-
Purdue	-	-	-	-	-	-	10	-	-	-	-	-	-
St. Bonaventure	6	3	3	3	3	2	2	2	2	2	2	2	3
St. John's (N.Y.)	7	6	7	5	5	9	7	7	-	-	-	-	-
St. Louis	-	16	8	-	-	-	-	-	-	-	-	-	-
Southern California	-	-	-	-	-	-	-	9	9	8	10	10	7
UCLA	13	14	16	9	10	-	-	-	-	-	-	-	-
Utah	18	18	-	-	-	-	-	-	-	-	-	-	-
Utah St.	14	-	-	-	-	-	-	-	-	-	-	-	-
Vanderbilt	-	17	16	-	-	-	-	-	-	-	-	-	-
Wake Forest	-	19	-	-	-	-	-	-	-	-	-	-	-
West Virginia	-	-	-	-	-	-	-	-	-	10	9	8	9
Wichita St.	16	-	18	-	-	-	-	-	-	-	-	-	-

1961-62

		December		January					February				March	
	PS	19	26	2	9	16	23	30	6	13	20	27	6	13
Arizona St.	-	10	-	-	-	-	-	-	-	-	-	-	-	-
Bowling Green	-	-	-	10	9	8	8	8	8	10	7	7	8	8
Bradley	-	-	-	-	9	9	9	7	5	6	6	6	-	5
Cincinnati	2	2	2	2	3	3	3	3	3	2	2	2	2	2
Colorado	-	-	-	-	-	-	-	-	-	-	9	9	-	9
Duke	7	-	10	8	10	7	7	6	5	7	8	8	9	10
Duquesne	-	7	3	7	8	5	6	7	6	9	-	-	-	-
Kansas St.	8	4	5	4	5	4	4	4	4	4	4	3	3	6
Kentucky	-	-	6	3	3	2	2	2	2	2	3	4	4	3
Loyola (Ill.)	-	-	-	-	-	-	-	-	-	-	-	-	10	-
Mississippi St.	-	-	-	9	7	10	10	10	9	8	5	5	5	4
Ohio St.	1	1	1	1	1	1	1	1	1	1	1	1	1	1
Oregon St.	-	-	-	-	-	-	-	10	6	10	-	-	-	-
Providence	5	3	-	-	-	-	-	-	-	-	-	-	-	-
Purdue	6	8	9	-	-	-	-	-	-	-	-	-	-	-
St. Bonaventure	-	9	-	-	-	-	-	-	-	-	-	-	-	-
St. John's (N.Y.)	9	-	-	-	-	-	-	-	-	-	-	-	-	-
Seattle	10	10	-	-	-	-	-	-	-	-	-	-	-	-
Southern California	4	6	4	6	4	6	5	5	-	-	-	-	-	-
Utah	-	-	-	-	-	-	-	-	-	-	-	10	7	7
Villanova	-	-	-	5	6	-	-	-	-	-	-	-	-	-
Wake Forest	3	-	-	-	-	-	-	-	-	-	-	-	-	-
West Virginia	-	5	7	-	-	-	-	-	-	-	-	-	-	-
Wichita St.	-	-	8	-	-	-	-	-	-	-	-	-	-	-

1962-63

		December				January					February				March	
	PS	4	11	18	25	1	8	15	22	29	5	12	19	26	5	12
Arizona St.	-	-	-	-	6	4	3	4	5	5	5	5	4	4	4	4
Auburn	-	-	-	-	-	10	-	-	-	-	-	9	-	-	-	-
Cincinnati	1	1	1	1	1	1	1	1	1	1	1	1	1	1	1	1
Colorado	-	-	8	6	-	-	-	-	8	7	7	-	-	-	-	10
Duke	2	2	2	2	8	7	6	5	4	3	3	3	2	2	2	2
Georgia Tech	-	-	-	-	-	7	6	7	6	6	10	-	10	-	-	-
Illinois	8	-	10	8	4	3	5	3	3	4	4	4	6	6	8	8
Indiana	8	-	-	-	-	-	-	-	-	-	-	-	-	-	-	-
Kentucky	3	9	-	9	5	6	-	-	-	-	-	-	-	-	-	-
Loyola (Ill.)	4	4	4	4	3	2	2	2	2	2	2	2	3	3	5	3
Mississippi St.	6	5	5	5	10	-	-	9	9	-	8	6	8	7	7	6
New York U.	-	-	-	-	-	-	-	-	-	-	-	-	10	9	-	9
North Carolina	-	-	-	-	-	-	10	-	-	-	-	-	-	-	-	-
Ohio St.	-	-	3	3	2	5	4	8	-	-	9	5	5	3	7	-
Oregon St.	7	7	9	-	-	-	-	10	-	9	-	-	-	-	-	-
Providence	-	-	-	-	-	-	-	-	-	-	-	-	-	-	10	-
St. Bonaventure	9	-	-	-	-	-	-	-	-	-	-	-	-	-	-	-
Seattle	-	-	-	10	-	-	-	-	-	-	-	-	-	-	-	-
Southern California	-	-	-	-	-	-	7	-	-	-	-	-	-	-	-	-
Stanford	-	-	-	-	9	-	-	10	7	10	8	-	9	-	-	-
UCLA	-	-	-	-	-	9	-	-	-	-	-	-	-	-	-	-
West Virginia	5	3	6	7	-	9	-	6	-	-	-	-	-	-	-	-
Wichita St.	-	10	-	-	8	8	7	8	10	9	-	7	8	6	5	-
Wisconsin	10	6	7	-	-	-	-	-	-	-	-	-	-	-	-	-

1963-64

		December				January				February				March	
	PS	10	17	24	31	7	14	21	28	4	11	18	25	3	10
Arizona St.	6	4	-	-	-	-	-	-	-	-	-	-	-	-	-
Cincinnati	3	6	4	5	4	8	8	-	-	-	-	-	-	-	-
Davidson	-	-	10	7	7	5	5	4	3	5	4	8	7	10	10
DePaul	-	-	-	-	-	-	-	9	9	10	10	9	9	8	9
Drake	-	-	-	-	-	-	-	-	-	10	-	-	-	-	-
Duke	4	3	5	8	9	9	10	8	8	7	5	4	4	4	3
Kansas	-	10	-	-	-	-	-	-	-	-	-	-	-	-	-
Kentucky	9	5	2	2	1	2	4	5	4	3	3	3	2	3	4
Loyola (Ill.)	1	1	1	1	3	3	2	3	10	9	-	-	10	9	8
Michigan	8	7	3	3	5	4	3	2	2	4	2	2	2	2	2
New York U.	2	7	10	-	-	-	-	-	-	-	-	-	-	-	-
Ohio St.	7	8	-	-	-	-	-	-	-	-	-	-	-	-	-
Oregon St.	10	9	-	9	8	6	7	10	-	9	7	6	6	6	-
Toledo	-	9	-	-	-	-	-	-	-	-	-	-	-	-	-
UCLA	-	6	4	2	1	1	1	1	1	1	1	1	1	1	1
Vanderbilt	-	8	6	6	7	6	6	5	8	7	-	-	-	-	-
Villanova	-	-	-	10	10	9	7	6	6	8	5	8	7	7	-
Wichita St.	5	-	-	-	-	-	-	-	10	7	4	6	6	5	5

1964-65

		December				January				February				March	
	PS	8	15	22	29	5	12	19	26	2	9	16	23	2	9
Bradley	14	-	-	-	-	-	-	-	-	-	-	-	-	-	-
BYU	19	-	-	-	-	-	-	-	-	-	-	-	-	-	-
Davidson	4	-	10	-	-	10	8	7	6	5	5	5	6	7	6
DePaul	20	-	-	-	-	-	-	-	-	-	-	-	-	-	-
Duke	5	8	6	6	8	6	10	10	10	6	6	6	5	8	10
Illinois	-	-	-	7	6	-	-	-	-	-	10	-	-	-	-
Indiana	-	-	8	7	2	5	5	9	7	8	7	7	-	-	-
Kansas	18	-	-	-	-	-	-	-	-	-	-	-	-	-	-
Kansas St.	8	-	-	-	-	-	-	-	-	-	-	-	-	-	-
Kentucky	11	9	8	-	-	-	-	-	-	-	-	-	-	-	-
Michigan	1	1	2	1	1	3	2	2	2	1	1	1	1	1	1
Minnesota	11	6	4	3	3	-	-	-	-	-	-	9	8	6	7
New Mexico	-	-	-	-	-	-	-	-	-	-	10	-	-	-	-
North Carolina	13	-	-	-	-	-	-	-	-	-	-	-	-	-	-
Notre Dame	17	-	-	-	-	-	-	-	-	-	-	-	-	-	-
Providence	-	-	-	-	-	9	6	6	4	4	4	4	4	4	4
St. John's (N.Y.)	10	10	7	-	-	7	7	8	7	-	-	-	-	-	-
St. Joseph's	-	-	-	-	10	4	4	3	3	3	3	3	3	3	3
St. Louis	-	4	10	9	9	8	9	9	8	10	-	-	-	-	-
San Francisco	9	5	3	5	5	-	-	-	-	-	-	-	-	-	-
Seattle	15	-	-	-	-	-	-	-	-	-	-	-	-	-	-
Syracuse	7	-	-	-	-	-	-	-	-	-	-	-	-	-	-
Tennessee	-	-	-	-	-	-	-	-	-	-	8	-	-	-	-
UCLA	2	7	5	4	4	1	1	1	1	2	2	2	2	2	2
Vanderbilt	6	3	9	-	-	-	-	-	-	9	7	-	9	5	5
Villanova	16	-	-	-	-	-	-	-	-	-	-	-	-	-	-
Wichita St.	3	2	1	2	2	5	3	4	5	8	9	10	-	9	8

1965-66

		December				January				February				March	
	PS	7	14	21	28	4	11	18	25	1	8	15	22	1	8
Bradley	9	9	9	5	3	5	5	7	-	-	-	-	-	-	-
BYU	-	-	-	-	6	8	7	-	-	-	-	-	-	-	-
Cincinnati	-	-	-	-	-	-	-	8	10	-	-	-	-	10	7
Duke	3	6	1	1	1	1	1	1	1	1	2	2	2	3	2
Iowa	-	-	9	4	7	-	-	-	-	-	-	-	-	-	-
Kansas	8	7	4	-	-	10	6	9	-	7	7	7	6	6	4
Kansas St.	10	-	-	-	-	-	-	-	-	-	-	-	-	-	-
Kentucky	-	-	-	10	5	2	2	2	2	2	1	1	1	1	1
Loyola (Ill.)	-	-	-	-	-	-	-	9	7	5	3	4	4	6	9
Michigan	2	3	3	3	7	-	-	-	-	-	9	10	10	10	-
Minnesota	7	5	6	6	9	-	-	-	-	-	-	-	-	-	-
Nebraska	-	-	-	-	-	-	-	-	-	-	9	9	8	9	-
Providence	6	8	7	7	10	6	6	4	3	4	6	6	9	8	-
St. Joseph's	4	3	2	2	8	4	4	3	5	5	5	5	5	5	8
South Carolina	-	10	-	-	-	-	-	-	-	-	-	-	-	-	-
UTEP	-	-	-	-	-	9	8	8	6	4	6	4	3	2	2
UCLA	1	1	8	-	-	10	9	10	10	-	-	-	-	-	-
Vanderbilt	5	4	5	4	2	3	3	5	4	3	5	5	5	5	8
Western Ky.	-	-	-	-	-	-	-	-	-	-	-	-	-	-	10
Wichita St.	-	-	10	8	-	-	-	-	-	-	-	-	-	-	-

1966-67

		December				January					February				March
	PS	6	13	20	27	3	10	17	24	31	7	14	21	28	7
Boston College	-	-	-	-	-	-	-	-	-	-	10	-	-	10	9
Bradley	-	-	-	-	-	-	-	-	10	-	-	-	-	-	-
BYU	-	9	7	-	-	-	-	-	-	-	-	-	-	-	-
Cincinnati	10	10	10	7	7	8	-	-	-	-	-	-	-	-	-
Duke	4	7	-	-	-	-	-	-	-	-	-	-	-	-	-
Florida	-	-	-	-	-	-	10	8	-	-	-	-	-	-	-
Houston	7	5	9	8	6	5	4	3	6	5	7	7	7	7	7
Kansas	-	-	9	-	9	8	7	7	7	6	4	4	4	3	3
Kentucky	3	3	4	-	-	-	-	-	-	-	-	-	-	-	-
Louisville	5	4	3	2	2	2	2	4	3	2	2	2	2	2	2
Michigan St.	-	-	8	5	10	-	-	-	-	-	-	-	-	-	-
Mississippi St.	-	-	-	-	-	-	-	10	-	-	-	-	-	-	-
New Mexico	6	6	5	3	3	-	9	-	-	-	-	-	-	-	-
North Carolina	9	8	6	3	3	3	5	4	2	2	4	5	3	4	4
Princeton	-	-	-	-	-	-	7	5	5	5	4	3	6	5	5
Providence	-	-	-	-	-	-	7	9	10	10	10	9	-	-	-
St. John's (N.Y.)	-	-	-	-	-	-	-	8	-	-	-	-	-	-	-
Syracuse	-	-	-	-	-	-	-	-	-	-	-	10	8	-	-
Tennessee	-	-	-	-	-	-	-	-	-	-	-	-	9	8	8
UTEP	2	2	2	4	4	6	6	6	4	8	8	10	9	-	10
UCLA	1	1	1	1	1	1	1	1	1	1	1	1	1	1	1
Vanderbilt	8	-	-	-	-	10	9	-	9	9	-	-	-	6	6
Western Ky.	8	-	-	-	-	-	-	-	-	8	8	6	5	3	6

1967-68

		December				January					February				March	
	PS	5	12	19	26	2	9	16	23	30	6	13	20	27	5	12
Boston College	7	10	6	8	10	-	-	-	-	-	-	-	-	-	-	-
Bradley	-	-	-	10	-	-	-	-	-	-	-	-	-	-	-	-
Columbia	-	-	-	-	-	-	10	10	8	8	7	6	6	6	8	7
Davidson	10	-	8	6	8	-	-	-	-	-	-	-	-	-	10	8
Dayton	6	6	-	-	-	-	-	-	-	-	-	-	-	-	-	-
Duke	-	-	-	-	-	-	-	-	-	9	-	10	8	10	6	10
Houston	2	2	2	2	2	2	2	2	1	1	1	1	1	1	1	1
Indiana	-	-	9	5	3	-	-	-	-	-	-	-	-	-	-	-
BKansas	5	4	-	-	-	-	-	-	-	-	-	-	-	-	-	-
Kentucky	-	9	4	7	6	5	4	8	9	10	8	8	5	5	4	5
Louisville	3	3	5	-	-	-	-	-	-	-	-	-	-	9	9	9
Marquette	-	-	-	-	-	-	-	-	-	-	-	-	10	8	-	-
New Mexico	-	-	-	-	-	10	9	6	4	4	6	5	7	7	7	6
New Mexico St.	-	-	-	-	-	-	-	-	-	-	10	-	-	-	-	-
North Carolina	4	5	7	4	5	3	3	3	3	3	3	3	3	3	5	4
Oklahoma City	-	-	-	-	-	8	-	-	-	-	-	-	-	-	-	-
Princeton	8	-	10	-	-	-	-	-	-	-	-	-	-	-	-	-
Purdue	-	7	-	-	-	-	-	-	-	-	-	-	-	-	-	-
St. Bonaventure	-	-	-	-	-	9	7	7	5	5	4	4	4	4	3	3
Tennessee	-	-	-	9	4	6	5	4	6	6	5	7	-	-	-	-
UCLA	1	1	1	1	1	1	1	1	2	2	2	2	2	2	2	2
Utah	-	-	-	-	7	7	6	5	10	-	-	-	-	-	-	-
Vanderbilt	9	8	3	3	9	4	8	9	7	7	9	9	9	-	-	-

1968-69

		December					January				February				March
	PS	3	10	17	24	31	7	14	21	28	4	11	18	25	4
Baylor	-	-	-	-	-	-	-	18	-	-	-	19	-	-	-
Boston College	-	-	-	-	-	-	-	-	-	-	-	-	-	20	16
California	-	19	18	15	-	-	-	-	-	-	-	-	-	-	-
Cincinnati	14	9	6	6	10	10	19	19	-	-	-	-	-	-	-
Colorado	-	-	-	-	-	-	-	20	17	17	20	14	18	-	18
Columbia	-	-	-	-	-	-	-	-	19	18	14	-	-	-	-
Davidson	6	6	3	3	3	2	6	4	4	4	6	6	5	5	5
Dayton	-	-	-	-	-	-	-	-	20	20	19	17	-	-	-
Detroit	18	15	14	13	11	7	13	-	-	-	-	-	-	-	-
Drake	-	-	-	-	-	-	18	-	-	-	-	-	-	-	11
Duke	17	16	9	-	-	-	-	-	-	-	-	-	-	-	-
Duquesne	-	-	-	-	-	15	15	12	10	11	15	13	8	10	9
Florida	19	-	-	-	-	-	-	-	-	-	-	-	-	-	-
Houston	8	6	12	20	-	-	-	-	-	-	-	-	-	-	-
Illinois	-	-	-	-	12	8	4	8	8	7	10	10	19	15	20
Iowa	-	20	19	-	-	-	-	-	-	-	-	-	-	-	-
Kansas	5	4	11	11	8	5	5	10	13	15	13	12	16	13	19
Kentucky	3	3	4	4	4	3	7	5	5	5	4	4	6	6	7
La Salle	-	-	20	16	17	11	11	11	9	9	7	5	4	3	2
Louisville	-	-	-	19	14	14	14	-	-	-	-	20	13	11	15
Marquette	15	20	-	-	-	-	20	15	16	16	17	18	20	18	14
New Mexico	9	8	5	5	6	18	-	-	-	-	18	-	-	-	-
New Mexico St.	-	-	-	14	15	12	10	7	7	8	16	15	15	16	12
North Carolina	2	2	2	2	2	4	2	2	2	2	2	2	3	2	4
Northwestern	-	-	-	-	-	19	12	17	-	-	-	-	-	-	-
Notre Dame	4	5	7	7	7	16	17	16	15	-	-	-	-	-	17
Ohio St.	12	13	17	17	16	13	16	13	12	12	12	16	10	14	-
Purdue	10	14	13	12	18	-	-	-	18	14	9	8	9	9	6
St. Bonaventure	7	11	10	9	13	20	-	-	-	-	-	-	-	-	-
St. John's (N.Y.)	-	-	-	-	-	17	8	6	6	6	5	9	7	7	8
Santa Clara	-	18	16	10	9	6	3	3	3	3	3	3	2	4	3
South Carolina	-	-	-	-	-	-	-	-	-	19	-	-	12	8	13
Tennessee	20	20	-	-	20	-	-	-	-	-	-	-	17	17	-
Tulsa	-	-	-	-	-	-	-	14	14	13	11	7	14	19	-
UCLA	1	1	1	1	1	1	1	1	1	1	1	1	1	1	1
Vanderbilt	13	12	-	-	-	-	-	-	-	-	-	-	-	-	-
Villanova	11	10	8	8	5	9	9	9	11	10	8	11	11	12	10
Western Ky.	16	17	15	18	-	-	-	-	-	-	-	-	-	-	-
Wyoming	-	-	-	-	19	-	-	-	-	-	-	-	-	-	-

1969-70

		December				January				February				March	
	PS	9	16	23	30	6	13	20	27	3	10	17	24	3	10
Cincinnati	-	-	-	-	-	-	-	-	-	-	-	-	-	19	-
Colorado	10	17	16	-	20	-	-	-	-	-	-	-	-	-	-
Columbia	-	-	-	-	15	17	13	-	17	17	19	-	18	-	-
Davidson	5	4	4	9	11	8	8	11	11	15	13	9	11	10	15
Drake	19	-	-	-	-	-	-	-	16	13	11	17	16	14	14
Duke	-	-	-	-	-	19	19	16	-	-	-	-	-	-	-
Duquesne	11	7	-	-	-	-	-	-	-	-	-	-	-	-	-
Florida St.	-	-	-	-	-	-	-	-	18	12	9	8	10	11	11
Georgia	-	-	-	-	-	-	-	-	-	-	20	-	-	-	-
Houston	20	-	19	8	8	11	9	7	12	16	15	15	15	13	12
Illinois	-	-	-	15	-	-	17	12	10	14	-	-	-	-	-
Iowa	-	-	-	-	-	-	-	18	20	20	14	11	9	8	7
Jacksonville	-	18	18	13	10	7	6	6	6	8	7	6	6	6	4
Kansas	-	-	-	16	-	-	-	-	-	-	-	-	-	-	-
Kansas St.	-	-	-	-	-	-	-	17	19	18	-	18	17	16	-
Kentucky	2	1	1	1	1	2	2	2	2	3	3	2	1	2	1
Long Beach St.	-	-	-	-	-	-	-	-	-	-	-	-	-	-	19
LSU	-	-	15	-	-	-	-	-	-	-	-	-	-	-	-
Louisville	15	11	14	14	-	20	18	18	-	-	-	19	-	-	-
Marquette	8	12	17	-	18	13	10	8	7	9	12	10	8	9	8
New Mexico St.	6	3	3	7	7	6	5	5	5	6	6	5	5	5	5
Niagara	-	-	-	-	-	15	12	-	-	-	-	-	-	-	17
North Carolina	7	5	7	4	4	4	7	9	9	7	10	13	19	-	-
North Carolina St.	-	-	-	-	15	10	11	10	8	5	5	12	14	19	10
Notre Dame	13	10	6	11	13	-	-	20	-	-	16	14	13	15	9
Ohio	-	19	10	5	5	9	14	13	13	-	-	-	-	17	-
Ohio St.	18	16	-	-	-	-	-	-	-	-	-	-	-	-	-
Oklahoma	-	-	-	-	-	16	-	-	-	-	-	-	-	-	-
Penn	-	-	-	17	14	18	15	14	14	10	8	7	7	7	13
Purdue	3	14	12	18	17	-	-	-	-	-	-	-	-	-	-
St. Bonaventure	17	20	-	19	12	5	4	4	3	4	4	3	3	4	3
St. John's (N.Y.)	14	-	-	-	-	-	-	-	-	-	-	-	-	-	-
Santa Clara	12	15	11	-	-	-	-	-	-	-	-	20	-	-	-
South Carolina	1	8	5	3	3	3	3	3	4	2	2	4	4	3	6
Southern California	16	6	13	12	19	-	20	15	15	11	18	-	-	-	20
Tennessee	-	9	8	6	6	12	-	-	-	-	-	-	-	-	-
UCLA	4	2	2	2	2	1	1	1	1	1	1	1	2	1	2
Utah St.	-	-	-	-	-	-	-	-	-	-	-	-	20	18	16
Villanova	9	12	9	20	-	-	-	-	-	19	-	-	-	-	-
Washington	-	-	20	10	9	14	15	-	-	-	-	-	-	-	-
Western Ky.	-	-	-	-	-	-	-	-	-	-	17	16	12	12	18

1970-71

		December				January				February				March		
	PS	8	15	22	29	5	12	19	26	2	9	16	23	2	9	16
Army	-	14	-	-	-	-	-	-	-	-	-	-	-	-	-	-
BYU	-	-	-	-	-	-	-	-	-	-	-	-	-	-	-	20
Drake	10	7	9	9	7	16	-	-	-	-	-	-	-	-	-	18
Duke	13	-	-	-	-	-	-	-	-	-	-	-	-	-	19	-
Duquesne	-	-	-	-	-	-	-	-	17	14	12	10	8	11	11	15
Florida St.	-	-	17	-	-	-	-	-	-	-	-	-	-	-	-	-
Fordham	-	-	-	-	-	18	14	17	-	-	20	18	11	10	10	9
Houston	17	-	-	-	-	-	-	-	-	18	15	-	-	15	18	14
Illinois	-	-	-	-	-	-	-	-	18	15	-	-	-	-	-	-
Indiana	16	11	13	11	14	12	11	18	-	-	-	-	-	18	-	-
Jacksonville	4	3	5	4	9	7	7	6	6	6	6	6	6	9	9	11
Kansas	14	11	12	8	12	8	8	5	5	5	5	5	5	4	5	4
Kentucky	3	5	3	7	8	11	10	12	11	8	8	12	10	8	8	8
La Salle	-	-	-	-	-	-	-	15	14	10	13	11	14	19	-	-
Long Beach St.	18	-	-	-	-	-	-	-	-	-	-	-	20	17	17	16
LSU	-	-	-	-	18	-	-	-	-	-	-	-	-	-	-	-
Louisville	-	20	-	-	17	13	16	-	-	-	-	19	15	-	-	-
Marquette	6	4	4	3	3	3	2	2	1	1	2	2	2	2	2	2
Memphis	-	-	-	-	-	-	19	-	-	-	-	-	-	-	-	-
Miami (Ohio)	-	-	-	-	-	-	-	-	-	-	-	-	-	-	20	-
Michigan	-	-	-	-	-	-	-	-	-	20	16	16	12	-	-	-
Murray St.	-	-	-	-	-	-	-	-	19	19	17	17	-	-	-	-
New Mexico St.	15	15	17	20	-	-	-	-	-	-	-	-	-	-	-	-
North Carolina	-	-	20	17	-	20	15	20	20	16	11	8	13	12	13	13
North Caro. St.	19	-	-	-	-	-	-	-	-	-	-	-	-	-	-	-
Notre Dame	5	6	7	14	15	9	9	9	7	12	9	14	19	16	14	12
Ohio St.	-	-	-	-	-	-	-	-	-	-	-	20	18	13	12	10
Oregon	-	18	16	17	16	-	-	16	13	-	-	-	-	-	-	-
Oregon St.	-	-	-	-	-	-	20	-	-	-	-	-	-	-	-	-
Penn	11	8	6	5	6	5	4	4	4	4	4	4	4	5	4	3
Purdue	-	-	-	16	20	19	-	-	-	-	-	-	-	-	-	-
St. Bonaventure	-	19	19	15	13	10	12	10	-	-	-	-	-	-	-	-
St. John's (N.Y.)	-	-	-	19	-	-	-	-	-	-	-	-	-	-	-	-
South Carolina	2	2	2	2	2	2	6	11	10	7	10	7	7	6	6	6
Southern California	7	9	8	6	4	4	3	3	3	2	3	3	3	3	3	5
Tennessee	-	17	14	12	10	17	18	8	8	11	14	13	17	14	15	17
UCLA	1	1	1	1	1	1	1	1	2	3	1	1	1	1	1	1
Utah St.	12	16	15	-	19	15	17	12	9	13	19	15	16	20	16	-
Villanova	8	10	10	13	11	14	13	14	16	17	18	-	-	-	-	19
Virginia	-	-	-	-	-	-	-	19	15	-	-	-	-	-	-	-
Western Ky.	9	13	11	10	5	6	5	7	12	9	7	9	9	7	7	7

1971-72

		December				January					February				March	
	PS	7	14	21	28	4	11	18	25	1	8	15	22	29	7	14
Arizona St.	-	17	-	-	-	-	-	-	-	-	-	-	-	-	-	-
BYU	19	15	6	7	8	18	14	13	13	10	10	11	7	7	8	9
Duquesne	-	-	-	-	-	-	-	-	-	-	20	-	-	-	-	-

		December				January					February				March	
	PS	7	14	21	28	4	11	18	25	1	8	15	22	29	7	14
Florida St.	-	18	9	14	-	20	12	11	10	12	14	14	11	10	14	10
Hawaii	-	-	-	-	18	16	19	18	15	14	18	16	17	15	12	-
Houston	7	12	20	-	-	-	-	-	-	-	-	-	16	13	19	-
Illinois	-	-	-	-	-	-	16	-	-	-	-	-	-	-	-	-
Indiana	-	-	12	8	7	5	17	-	-	-	-	-	-	-	20	17
Jacksonville	11	8	14	16	-	-	-	-	-	17	16	-	-	-	-	-
Kansas	14	-	-	-	-	-	-	-	-	-	-	-	-	-	-	-
Kentucky	10	7	7	11	12	19	15	-	-	-	-	17	18	-	-	18
Long Beach St.	8	6	13	9	10	8	7	4	5	5	8	9	6	6	5	5
La.-Lafayette	-	-	16	12	13	15	13	12	12	13	13	12	10	11	9	8
Louisville	9	16	17	19	15	7	5	6	4	3	4	4	3	2	4	4
Marquette	4	2	2	2	2	2	2	2	2	2	2	2	2	5	7	7
Marshall	-	-	-	20	17	13	20	16	14	11	11	10	8	9	10	12
Maryland	6	5	15	15	16	12	-	-	18	-	-	19	12	18	13	14
Memphis	-	-	-	-	-	-	-	-	-	-	15	18	19	20	11	13
Michigan	13	9	-	-	-	-	-	-	-	20	-	-	-	16	-	-
Minnesota	-	-	-	-	-	-	-	17	16	19	19	-	-	-	16	11
Missouri	-	-	-	-	-	-	18	-	20	15	17	15	14	19	18	-
New Mexico	16	-	-	-	-	-	-	-	-	-	-	-	-	-	-	-
North Carolina	2	3	4	4	4	3	3	3	3	4	3	3	5	3	3	2
North Caro. St.	-	20	-	-	-	-	-	-	-	-	-	-	-	-	-	-
Northern Ill.	-	-	-	-	-	-	-	20	19	-	-	-	-	-	-	-
Ohio	-	-	-	17	-	-	-	-	-	-	-	-	-	-	-	-
Ohio St.	5	4	10	6	6	10	9	7	6	9	7	8	15	14	-	19
Oklahoma	20	-	-	-	-	-	-	-	-	-	-	-	-	-	-	-
Oral Roberts	-	-	-	-	-	-	-	-	-	-	-	-	20	17	17	16
Penn	15	10	5	13	14	6	6	10	9	6	5	5	4	4	2	3
Princeton	-	-	18	-	-	-	-	14	17	-	-	-	-	-	-	-
Providence	-	-	-	-	-	-	-	-	-	16	12	13	-	-	-	-
St. John's (N.Y.)	17	14	8	10	9	17	-	-	-	-	-	-	-	-	-	-
South Carolina	12	11	3	3	3	4	4	5	11	8	9	7	9	8	6	6
Southern California	3	13	10	5	5	11	10	8	7	18	-	-	-	-	-	-
Tennessee	-	-	-	-	20	-	-	19	-	-	-	20	-	-	-	-
UCLA	1	1	1	1	1	1	1	1	1	1	1	1	1	1	1	1
Villanova	18	18	-	-	-	14	11	15	-	-	-	-	-	-	-	15
Virginia	-	-	19	18	11	9	8	9	8	7	6	6	13	12	15	20
West Virginia	-	-	-	-	19	-	-	-	-	-	-	-	-	-	-	-

1972-73

		December				January					February				March	
	PS	5	12	19	26	2	9	16	23	30	6	13	20	27	6	13
Alabama	-	-	-	-	18	14	14	11	9	6	10	17	18	-	-	-
Arizona St.	-	-	-	-	-	-	-	-	-	-	-	-	-	-	-	16
Austin Peay	-	-	-	-	-	-	-	-	-	-	-	-	-	-	-	19
BYU	12	-	17	15	14	15	-	-	-	-	-	20	-	-	-	-
Florida St.	2	2	2	7	12	19	18	19	-	-	-	-	-	-	-	-
Houston	15	20	16	14	13	10	10	12	11	11	11	7	9	8	7	13
Indiana	-	-	15	9	15	20	16	16	6	5	4	11	10	12	9	6
Jacksonville	-	-	-	-	-	-	15	15	13	15	16	13	20	18	16	-
Kansas St.	17	16	20	17	16	18	17	14	18	18	18	15	13	16	11	9
Kentucky	13	8	-	-	-	-	-	-	-	-	-	-	-	-	19	17
Long Beach St.	6	7	7	6	6	5	6	5	5	4	3	3	3	4	4	3
La.-Lafayette	7	10	8	8	9	8	13	13	12	13	13	14	12	11	14	7
Louisville	20	-	-	-	-	-	20	20	-	-	-	-	-	-	-	-
Marquette	5	5	4	3	3	3	4	7	10	10	7	5	5	5	6	5
Maryland	3	3	3	2	2	2	2	3	4	3	9	10	8	9	10	8
Memphis	11	11	19	-	-	-	-	-	17	17	15	16	14	10	15	12
Michigan	19	18	18	-	-	-	-	-	-	-	-	-	-	-	-	-
Minnesota	4	4	5	5	5	6	8	6	8	9	5	4	4	3	3	10
Missouri	-	-	12	10	7	7	5	8	7	7	8	12	16	13	12	15
New Mexico	-	-	-	-	-	16	-	-	19	-	20	18	15	15	-	-
North Carolina	-	13	11	13	11	9	7	4	3	8	6	6	6	7	8	11
North Carolina St.	8	6	6	4	4	4	3	2	2	2	2	2	2	2	2	2
Ohio St.	10	15	-	-	-	-	-	-	-	-	-	-	-	-	-	-
Oklahoma	-	-	-	19	19	-	-	-	-	-	-	-	-	-	-	-
Oral Roberts	18	12	10	16	-	-	-	-	-	19	19	-	-	-	-	-
Penn	9	9	9	11	8	17	-	-	-	-	-	-	-	-	-	18
Providence	-	19	14	18	17	13	11	9	14	12	12	8	7	6	5	4
Purdue	-	-	-	-	-	-	-	-	20	-	-	-	17	20	-	-
St. John's (N.Y.)	-	-	-	-	-	-	18	17	15	14	14	9	11	17	17	-
St. Joseph's	-	-	-	-	-	-	-	-	-	-	-	-	-	-	18	-
San Francisco	-	-	-	-	20	12	12	10	16	16	17	-	-	-	19	20
Santa Clara	-	-	-	20	-	-	-	-	-	-	-	-	-	-	-	-
South Carolina	16	-	-	-	-	-	-	-	-	-	-	-	-	19	-	-
Southern California	20	17	-	-	-	-	-	-	-	20	-	-	-	-	-	-
Syracuse	-	-	-	-	-	-	-	-	-	-	-	-	-	14	13	14
Tennessee	14	14	-	-	-	-	-	-	-	-	-	-	-	-	-	-
UCLA	1	1	1	1	1	1	1	1	1	1	1	1	1	1	1	1
Vanderbilt	-	-	13	12	10	11	9	18	-	-	-	-	-	-	-	-
Virginia Tech	-	-	-	-	-	-	-	-	-	-	-	19	19	-	-	-

1973-74

		December				January					February				March			
	PS	4	11	18	25	2	8	15	22	29	5	12	19	26	5	12	19	27
Alabama	18	18	13	10	13	7	12	10	9	8	8	8	8	7	12	11	13	14
Arizona	15	15	14	14	12	15	-	-	-	-	-	20	-	18	-	-	-	-
Arizona St.	-	-	-	-	-	-	-	-	20	-	-	-	-	-	-	-	-	-
Austin Peay	-	-	-	-	20	20	-	-	-	-	-	-	-	-	-	-	-	-
Centenary (La.)	-	-	-	-	-	-	-	-	18	-	-	-	-	-	-	-	-	-
Cincinnati	-	-	-	20	-	-	-	20	-	-	-	-	-	-	-	-	-	-
Creighton	-	-	-	-	-	-	-	-	-	-	-	17	15	16	19	19	-	-
Dayton	-	-	-	-	-	-	-	-	-	-	-	-	-	-	-	20	16	20
Hawaii	-	-	-	-	-	-	20	-	-	-	-	-	-	-	-	-	-	-
Houston	14	14	-	-	-	-	-	-	-	-	-	-	-	-	-	-	-	-
Indiana	3	3	3	7	7	8	13	12	11	12	12	12	10	9	13	10	11	9
Jacksonville	17	17	19	19	-	-	-	-	-	-	-	-	-	-	-	-	-	-
Kansas	13	-	-	-	-	-	-	-	-	18	17	16	16	15	15	14	6	7
Kansas St.	-	13	15	13	18	-	-	-	-	-	-	-	18	-	-	-	-	-
Kentucky	10	10	-	-	-	-	-	-	-	-	-	-	-	-	-	-	-	-
Long Beach St.	12	12	12	11	10	9	9	9	10	10	9	10	13	13	9	9	9	10
Louisville	9	9	9	8	8	13	11	16	14	15	15	18	20	20	18	16	-	-
Marquette	7	7	7	6	6	6	7	6	6	5	6	9	9	8	11	7	3	3
Maryland	4	4	4	2	2	3	3	4	5	6	7	6	5	5	4	4	4	4
Md.-East. Shore	-	-	-	-	-	-	-	-	-	-	20	-	-	-	-	-	-	-
Memphis	20	10	12	16	18	19	-	-	-	-	-	-	-	-	-	-	-	-
Michigan	-	-	-	-	-	-	18	14	15	20	16	15	19	17	16	12	7	6
Missouri	-	-	-	-	-	-	-	18	-	-	-	-	-	-	-	-	-	-
UNLV	19	19	-	-	19	15	16	-	-	-	-	-	-	-	-	-	-	-
New Mexico	-	-	-	-	17	12	8	15	19	17	-	-	-	19	17	17	20	-
North Carolina	5	5	5	4	4	4	5	5	4	4	4	4	6	4	6	8	10	12
North Carolina St.	2	2	2	5	5	5	4	3	3	2	2	2	1	1	1	1	1	1
Notre Dame	8	8	6	3	3	2	2	2	1	3	3	3	2	2	2	3	5	5
Oral Roberts	-	-	-	-	-	-	-	-	-	19	19	-	-	-	20	-	18	18
Penn	16	16	11	-	-	-	-	-	-	-	-	-	-	-	-	-	-	-
Pittsburgh	-	-	-	-	-	-	-	17	16	13	10	7	7	11	14	13	15	16
Providence	6	6	8	9	9	14	10	7	8	9	11	11	11	12	8	5	8	8
Purdue	-	-	-	-	-	-	-	-	-	-	-	-	-	-	-	-	18	11
San Francisco	11	11	17	-	-	-	-	-	-	-	-	-	-	-	-	-	-	-
South Carolina	-	-	16	15	-	-	15	11	13	14	13	14	14	14	10	18	17	19
Southern California	-	-	20	16	14	11	17	13	12	11	14	13	12	10	7	15	14	17
Syracuse	-	-	18	18	15	19	-	-	-	-	-	-	-	-	-	-	-	-
UTEP	-	-	-	-	-	-	-	-	18	-	-	-	-	-	-	-	-	-
UCLA	1	1	1	1	1	1	1	1	2	1	1	1	3	3	3	2	2	2
Utah	-	-	-	-	-	-	-	-	-	-	-	19	17	-	-	-	-	15
Vanderbilt	-	-	-	17	11	10	6	8	7	7	5	5	4	6	5	6	11	13
Wisconsin	-	-	-	-	-	17	13	19	17	16	-	-	-	-	-	-	-	-

1974-75

		December					January				February				March				Apr.
	PS	3	10	17	24	31	7	14	21	28	4	11	18	25	4	11	18	25	2
Alabama	9	11	10	8	7	6	8	7	6	9	7	7	5	8	7	10	11	11	10
Arizona	19	18	17	13	10	14	10	13	13	15	17	19	15	19	19	-	-	-	-
Arizona St.	-	-	-	-	-	16	12	9	10	12	10	8	8	9	9	8	7	7	8
Auburn	-	-	-	-	-	-	-	-	20	14	-	-	-	-	-	-	-	-	-
Centenary (La.)	-	-	-	-	-	-	-	-	-	-	-	-	18	-	-	17	19	18	-
Cincinnati	-	-	-	-	-	-	-	-	-	-	-	-	-	-	-	17	12	12	13
Clemson	-	-	-	-	-	-	-	-	-	-	16	18	16	11	14	14	-	-	-
Creighton	-	-	-	-	-	-	-	-	-	-	18	20	14	13	13	-	-	-	-
Drake	-	-	-	-	-	-	-	-	-	-	-	-	-	-	-	-	14	16	16
Houston	-	20	-	-	-	-	-	-	-	-	-	-	-	-	-	-	-	-	-
Indiana	3	3	3	2	2	2	1	1	1	1	1	1	1	1	1	1	1	3	3
Kansas	6	7	9	18	-	-	-	-	18	20	-	-	-	-	-	-	-	-	-
Kansas St.	-	-	-	-	-	-	-	-	-	-	-	-	-	-	-	-	17	15	15
Kentucky	16	15	-	20	17	9	7	10	11	5	5	4	7	4	6	6	5	2	2
La Salle	-	-	-	-	-	-	14	11	9	7	13	12	17	-	-	-	-	-	-
Louisville	8	6	4	4	4	4	3	3	2	3	3	6	6	3	3	3	3	4	4
Marquette	5	8	7	6	14	13	13	12	12	13	11	9	9	6	5	5	10	10	11
Maryland	4	4	5	5	5	7	5	5	3	8	4	3	3	2	2	4	4	5	5
Memphis	15	16	14	11	16	19	-	-	-	-	-	-	-	-	-	-	-	-	-
Michigan	17	19	16	-	-	17	11	19	-	-	-	-	-	-	-	-	-	19	19
Minnesota	18	-	-	-	-	-	17	16	17	-	-	-	-	-	-	-	-	-	-
UNLV	-	-	-	-	-	-	-	-	-	-	-	-	-	-	-	-	16	20	17
North Carolina	11	9	8	10	8	8	15	14	14	10	12	11	13	14	12	7	6	9	9
North Caro. St.	1	1	1	1	1	1	4	4	5	2	6	5	4	7	8	9	8	8	7
Notre Dame	12	13	11	12	13	19	-	-	-	16	14	16	11	16	16	12	9	14	14
Oklahoma	-	-	19	17	18	-	-	-	-	-	-	-	-	-	-	-	-	-	-
Oregon	-	-	18	19	19	11	9	8	8	11	9	13	-	-	-	-	-	-	-
Oregon St.	-	-	-	-	-	-	-	-	-	-	-	17	20	17	15	15	13	-	18
Penn	20	14	12	9	9	12	-	-	-	-	20	14	12	10	10	11	15	17	-
Princeton	-	-	-	-	-	-	-	-	-	-	-	-	-	-	-	-	-	13	12
Providence	14	17	20	16	12	10	19	15	16	-	-	-	-	-	-	-	-	-	20
Purdue	13	12	15	15	15	18	-	-	20	-	-	-	-	-	-	-	-	-	-
Rutgers	-	-	-	-	20	-	-	17	19	-	19	-	-	-	20	16	-	-	-
South Carolina	7	5	13	14	11	15	16	20	-	19	-	-	-	-	-	-	-	-	-
Southern California	10	10	6	7	6	5	6	6	7	6	8	10	10	12	11	13	18	-	-

	December						January				February				March				Apr.
	PS	3	10	17	24	31	7	14	21	28	4	11	18	25	4	11	18	25	2
Stanford	-	-	-	-	-	-	-	-	15	17	-	-	-	-	-	-	20	6	6
Syracuse	-	-	-	-	-	18	18	-	18	15	-	-	-	-	-	-	-	-	-
Tennessee	-	-	-	-	-	-	-	-	-	-	-	-	-	15	18	17	-	-	-
UTEP	-	-	-	-	-	-	-	-	-	-	-	-	15	18	17	-	-	-	-
Tex.-Pan American	-	-	-	-	-	-	-	-	-	-	-	15	19	18	17	20	-	-	-
UCLA	2	2	3	3	3	2	2	4	4	4	2	2	2	5	4	2	2	1	1
Wake Forest	-	-	-	-	-	19	-	-	-	-	-	-	-	-	-	-	-	-	-
Washington	-	-	-	-	-	-	-	-	-	-	-	-	20	-	-	-	-	-	-

1975-76

	December						January				February				March		
	PS	2	9	16	23	30	6	13	20	27	3	10	17	24	2	9	16
Alabama	12	14	11	8	8	8	10	11	12	11	14	11	10	7	16	8	6
Arizona	11	11	10	-	-	-	-	-	-	-	-	-	-	-	-	18	15
Arizona St.	18	19	19	19	-	-	-	-	-	-	-	-	-	-	-	-	-
Auburn	-	17	17	17	-	-	-	-	-	-	-	-	-	-	-	-	-
Centenary (La.)	-	-	-	-	19	18	-	18	-	19	18	19	20	19	20	20	19
Charlotte	19	-	-	-	-	-	-	-	-	-	-	-	-	-	-	18	17
Cincinnati	10	10	9	7	6	7	15	14	16	18	16	13	13	18	13	15	12
DePaul	-	-	-	-	-	-	-	-	-	-	-	-	-	-	-	18	17
Florida St.	-	-	-	-	-	-	-	-	-	-	-	-	-	-	-	-	-
Indiana	1	1	1	1	1	1	1	1	1	1	1	1	1	1	1	1	1
Kansas St.	14	18	-	-	-	-	-	-	-	-	-	-	-	-	-	-	-
Kentucky	6	7	14	20	18	-	-	-	-	-	-	-	-	-	-	-	-
La Salle	-	-	-	-	-	20	-	-	-	-	-	-	19	-	-	-	-
Louisville	8	6	6	10	11	11	16	-	-	-	-	19	-	-	-	-	-
Marquette	4	3	3	3	7	6	4	3	3	2	2	2	2	2	2	2	2
Maryland	3	2	2	2	2	2	2	2	7	5	4	7	10	-	9	12	11
Memphis	19	-	-	-	-	-	-	-	-	-	-	-	-	-	-	-	-
Michigan	16	16	18	16	16	17	19	16	17	15	16	16	15	13	11	14	9
Minnesota	-	-	-	20	16	17	-	-	-	-	-	-	-	-	-	-	-
Missouri	-	-	20	-	-	-	20	-	13	-	13	14	14	12	15	10	14
UNLV	-	-	16	13	12	10	5	4	4	3	3	7	6	5	5	4	3
North Carolina	5	4	4	4	3	3	6	7	5	4	4	3	3	4	4	5	8
North Carolina St.	13	13	13	9	9	9	11	13	11	8	10	12	12	15	17	-	-
North Texas	-	-	-	-	-	-	-	-	-	-	20	20	-	-	-	-	-
Notre Dame	7	9	8	5	5	5	13	15	15	10	11	10	8	6	8	7	7
Oregon	-	-	-	-	-	-	-	-	-	-	-	-	-	-	17	-	-
Oregon St.	-	-	-	-	-	-	17	13	16	-	-	-	-	-	-	-	-
Pepperdine	-	-	-	-	-	-	-	-	-	-	-	-	-	-	-	-	20
Princeton	-	-	-	-	-	-	-	-	17	-	15	-	-	-	-	-	-
Providence	17	15	-	-	-	-	-	-	-	-	-	-	-	-	-	-	-
Rutgers	-	-	-	15	15	14	12	10	7	5	7	5	4	3	3	3	4
St. John's (N.Y.)	-	-	-	18	17	15	14	12	9	14	12	17	16	14	16	17	-
San Francisco	15	12	12	14	14	19	20	-	-	-	-	-	-	-	-	-	-
Southern California	-	-	-	-	-	-	-	-	18	-	-	-	-	-	-	-	-
Syracuse	20	-	-	-	-	-	-	-	-	-	-	-	-	-	-	-	-
Tennessee	9	8	7	11	10	12	9	-	9	10	9	8	8	9	11	12	9 13
Texas A&M	-	-	-	-	-	-	-	-	-	-	-	-	-	20	19	-	-
Texas Tech	-	-	-	-	-	-	-	-	-	-	-	-	-	-	-	19	16
UCLA	2	5	5	6	4	4	3	8	6	12	9	6	5	9	7	6	5
Virginia	-	-	-	-	-	-	-	-	-	-	-	-	-	-	-	13	18
Virginia Tech	-	-	-	-	-	-	-	-	-	-	19	18	18	-	-	-	-
VMI	-	-	-	-	-	-	-	-	20	-	-	-	-	-	-	-	-
Wake Forest	-	-	-	-	-	-	7	5	14	-	-	-	-	-	-	-	-
Washington	-	20	15	12	13	13	8	6	8	6	6	9	11	8	10	11	-
West Tex. A&M	-	-	-	-	-	-	19	19	20	-	-	-	-	-	-	-	-
Western Mich.	-	-	-	-	-	-	-	-	-	-	17	15	17	16	14	16	10
Wisconsin	-	-	-	-	-	-	-	18	-	-	-	-	-	-	-	-	-

1976-77

	Nov.	December				January				February				March		
	PS	30	7	14	21	28	4	11	18	25	1	8	15	22	1	8	15
Alabama	13	13	10	7	5	4	4	4	3	3	8	7	4	8	12	12	11
Arizona	10	11	9	8	14	13	11	10	16	16	19	18	17	20	17	20	-
Arkansas	-	-	-	19	18	17	18	16	17	15	14	13	11	6	7	8	18
Auburn	-	-	-	-	20	-	-	-	-	-	-	-	-	-	-	-	-
Charlotte	19	-	-	-	-	-	-	-	-	-	-	-	-	-	-	18	17
Cincinnati	12	12	8	6	4	5	2	3	2	12	12	12	10	14	14	11	-
Clemson	-	-	16	13	11	10	16	17	-	19	16	15	18	19	18	-	-
DePaul	18	18	19	-	-	-	-	-	-	-	-	-	-	-	-	-	-
Detroit	-	-	-	-	-	-	-	-	-	20	19	15	16	15	17	12	-
Indiana	5	4	13	16	-	-	-	-	-	-	-	-	-	-	-	-	16
Kansas St.	-	-	-	-	-	-	-	-	-	-	-	-	-	-	-	-	-
Kentucky	6	5	4	3	7	6	3	2	6	6	3	3	2	2	2	6	3
Louisville	9	7	14	17	13	14	14	13	12	11	9	6	8	10	10	14	19
Marquette	2	2	2	6	2	12	12	11	8	9	6	9	18	19	16	7	-
Maryland	8	16	17	14	15	16	15	14	13	-	-	-	-	-	-	-	-
Memphis	-	-	-	-	-	20	18	18	20	-	-	-	-	-	-	-	-
Michigan	1	1	1	1	1	1	5	5	7	5	7	7	5	5	3	1	1
Minnesota	-	-	-	20	15	13	9	11	13	10	8	12	13	9	9	13	-
Missouri	20	-	-	-	-	-	-	-	-	-	-	-	-	-	-	-	-
UNLV	7	6	5	12	12	11	9	8	7	5	4	10	6	4	5	5	4

	Nov.	December				January				February				March		
	PS	30	7	14	21	28	4	11	18	25	1	8	15	22	1	8	15
North Carolina	3	9	12	11	10	9	6	5	4	4	13	14	13	9	6	4	5
North Carolina St.	15	-	-	-	-	-	-	-	-	-	-	-	-	-	-	-	-
Notre Dame	14	8	7	4	2	2	8	19	-	-	-	-	-	-	-	-	-
Oregon	-	-	-	-	-	-	-	20	-	-	-	-	-	17	-	-	-
Providence	-	-	-	-	-	-	17	15	15	14	15	16	16	12	8	13	-
Purdue	-	-	-	-	-	-	-	-	19	18	18	-	-	-	-	-	-
Rutgers	17	19	-	-	-	-	-	-	-	-	-	-	-	-	-	-	-
St. John's (N.Y.)	-	-	20	-	-	-	-	-	-	-	-	-	-	-	-	-	-
San Francisco	11	10	6	5	3	3	1	1	1	1	1	1	1	1	1	3	8
Southern Ill.	-	17	18	18	-	-	-	-	-	-	-	-	-	-	-	-	-
Syracuse	-	20	15	17	18	19	-	20	17	17	17	20	15	13	10	6	-
Tennessee	16	15	15	-	19	-	-	14	7	11	11	14	7	11	7	15	-
UCLA	4	3	3	9	8	8	7	12	10	8	2	2	3	5	4	2	2
Utah	-	-	-	16	19	-	-	-	-	-	-	-	-	-	20	19	14
VMI	-	-	-	-	-	-	-	-	-	-	-	-	20	19	-	-	20
Wake Forest	-	14	11	10	9	7	10	7	9	10	5	4	7	11	16	-	9

1977-78

	Nov.	December				January					February				March	
	PS	29	6	13	20	27	3	10	17	24	31	7	14	21	28	6	13
Alabama	15	15	-	18	-	-	-	-	-	-	-	-	-	-	-	-	-
Arkansas	7	7	6	4	3	3	6	4	2	1	4	4	2	1	4	7	5
Cincinnati	9	8	7	6	12	11	12	19	-	-	-	-	-	-	-	-	-
DePaul	-	-	-	-	-	20	18	19	13	11	8	7	6	4	3	-	-
Detroit	19	19	17	16	15	20	-	-	-	-	-	17	19	16	15	19	18
Duke	-	-	-	-	-	-	17	11	17	-	20	13	15	8	13	15	-
Florida St.	-	-	-	18	-	-	17	15	16	14	12	11	13	15	-	-	-
Georgetown	-	-	-	-	-	20	17	19	16	14	-	18	18	17	-	-	-
Holy Cross	18	17	15	13	12	16	13	14	-	-	-	-	-	-	-	14	-
Houston	-	-	-	-	-	-	-	-	-	-	-	-	14	-	-	-	-
Illinois St.	-	-	-	-	-	20	19	15	15	15	13	17	-	-	-	-	13
Indiana	-	-	-	-	-	15	11	18	-	-	-	-	-	-	-	-	13
Indiana St.	-	11	7	6	6	6	4	13	-	8	8	6	6	5	-	9	10
Kansas	-	19	20	16	17	14	10	8	-	-	-	-	-	-	-	9	10
Kansas St.	-	-	19	-	-	-	-	-	-	-	-	-	-	-	-	-	-
Kentucky	2	1	1	1	1	1	1	1	1	1	1	1	3	2	1	1	1
Louisville	10	9	16	10	8	7	10	9	9	12	9	9	9	20	20	12	9
Marquette	3	4	4	3	2	5	4	4	2	2	3	2	1	3	3	3	8
Maryland	14	14	12	18	20	14	15	-	-	-	-	-	-	-	-	-	19
Miami (Ohio)	-	-	-	-	-	-	-	-	-	-	-	-	-	-	-	-	19
Michigan	13	13	9	15	-	-	-	-	-	-	-	-	-	-	-	-	-
Michigan St.	-	-	-	-	-	-	18	12	10	7	7	10	10	10	9	6	4
Minnesota	16	-	-	-	-	-	-	-	-	-	-	-	19	-	-	-	-
Nebraska	8	10	10	9	9	11	16	-	-	-	-	-	-	-	-	-	-
New Mexico	-	-	-	-	-	-	20	14	10	6	5	5	8	5	12	-	-
North Carolina	1	2	2	5	3	2	2	5	3	6	7	11	8	10	11	16	-
North Caro. St.	-	-	-	-	-	-	-	16	-	-	-	-	-	-	-	-	-
Notre Dame	4	3	3	2	5	4	4	7	7	9	7	7	9	7	10	6	-
Penn	-	-	-	-	-	-	-	-	-	-	-	-	-	-	-	-	20
Providence	-	-	20	14	14	13	17	14	12	9	16	20	13	11	18	-	-
Purdue	12	11	-	17	-	-	-	-	-	-	-	-	-	-	-	-	-
St. John's (N.Y.)	20	16	13	-	-	-	-	-	-	-	-	-	-	-	-	-	-
San Francisco	5	5	8	11	11	19	19	-	-	20	-	-	-	20	11	-	-
Syracuse	11	12	-	18	12	10	10	8	11	10	18	18	16	17	14	18	-
Texas	-	-	-	-	-	-	-	15	15	12	12	12	14	12	16	17	-
UCLA	6	6	5	8	7	8	7	7	3	6	5	4	4	3	2	2	2
Utah	-	20	14	-	17	-	-	-	-	-	-	-	-	19	15	14	-
Virginia	-	-	-	-	19	16	13	15	13	11	13	17	-	-	-	-	-
Wake Forest	17	18	-	-	-	-	-	-	-	-	-	-	14	-	-	-	-

1978-79

	Nov.	December				January					February				March	
	PS	28	5	12	19	26	3	9	16	23	30	6	13	20	27	6	13
Alabama	19	-	-	-	-	-	-	-	18	18	15	16	20	-	-	-	-
Arkansas	-	-	-	-	-	20	14	10	11	15	14	11	10	9	7	7	5
DePaul	-	-	-	-	-	-	-	-	-	-	-	20	15	8	6	-	-
Detroit	-	-	-	-	-	-	-	-	18	16	18	17	-	-	-	-	-
Duke	1	1	1	1	1	1	5	7	8	7	3	5	6	5	6	-	11
Georgetown	-	-	20	16	14	15	12	14	10	11	17	18	16	17	16	11	-
Illinois	-	-	-	-	-	18	15	6	4	4	4	8	19	20	-	-	-
Indiana	10	20	-	-	-	-	-	-	-	-	-	-	-	-	-	-	-
Indiana St.	-	-	-	-	-	20	16	11	10	4	3	2	1	2	1	1	1
Iowa	-	-	-	-	-	-	-	-	-	-	18	15	14	12	11	14	20
Kansas	5	4	5	8	7	18	19	15	20	-	-	-	-	-	-	-	-
Kentucky	11	10	10	6	11	13	9	17	-	-	-	-	-	-	-	-	-
Long Beach St.	-	-	-	-	-	-	-	17	15	19	-	-	-	-	-	-	-
LSU	14	11	12	11	10	7	9	8	6	5	8	9	7	-	-	-	-
Louisville	4	5	7	4	12	10	16	12	9	5	13	13	18	13	-	-	-
Marquette	18	17	16	14	13	18	17	13	11	13	9	10	12	10	-	-	-
Maryland	19	19	-	20	19	-	-	-	-	-	-	-	-	-	-	-	-
Michigan	8	6	9	9	8	13	16	-	-	-	-	-	-	-	-	-	-
Michigan St.	7	7	4	3	5	4	10	8	7	4	4	3	-	-	-	-	-

	PS	Nov. 28	December 5	12	19	26	January 3	9	16	23	30	February 6	13	20	27	March 6	13
Mississippi St.	-	-	-	-	-	-	18	-	-	-	-	-	-	-	-	-	-
UNLV	20	18	15	15	18	14	-	-	-	-	-	-	-	-	-	-	-
North Carolina	16	14	14	13	6	5	3	3	2	2	7	6	4	4	7	3	9
North Caro. St.	12	6	8	7	4	9	8	8	14	20	-	-	-	-	-	-	-
Notre Dame	3	3	3	2	2	2	2	2	1	1	1	1	3	3	2	5	4
Ohio St.	-	-	-	-	-	-	-	-	16	10	13	13	17	14	17	-	-
Oklahoma	-	-	-	-	-	-	-	-	-	-	-	-	-	-	-	-	16
Penn	-	-	-	-	-	-	-	-	-	-	-	-	-	-	-	-	14
Purdue	-	-	-	-	-	-	-	-	-	-	-	-	13	18	19	16	15
Rutgers	15	16	18	-	-	-	-	-	-	-	-	-	-	-	-	-	18
St. John's (N.Y.)	-	-	-	-	-	-	-	-	-	-	-	-	-	-	-	-	17
San Francisco	17	15	17	19	-	-	-	-	-	-	-	-	-	-	20	19	12
Southern Cal	13	12	11	12	20	-	-	-	-	-	-	-	-	-	-	-	-
Syracuse	9	9	9	10	8	19	-	20	12	12	8	7	7	8	6	10	8
Temple	-	-	-	-	-	-	-	18	17	16	20	19	15	15	12	13	-
Tennessee	-	-	-	-	-	-	-	-	-	-	-	-	-	-	-	20	-
Texas	6	13	13	17	19	-	-	-	-	17	11	12	12	11	14	15	-
Texas A&M	-	-	-	-	17	12	10	11	15	14	12	11	-	-	-	-	-
Toledo	-	-	-	-	-	-	-	-	-	-	-	-	-	-	-	-	19
UCLA	2	2	2	5	3	3	6	6	3	6	6	4	2	1	3	2	2
Vanderbilt	-	-	-	-	-	-	-	-	-	19	16	17	19	19	-	-	-

1979-80

	PS	December 4	11	18	26	January 2	8	15	22	29	February 5	12	19	26	March 4
Arizona St.	-	-	-	-	-	-	-	-	-	-	19	18	18	15	18
Arkansas	-	-	20	20	19	-	-	-	-	-	-	-	-	-	-
BYU	15	18	18	18	20	19	17	18	20	19	14	13	14	12	12
Clemson	-	-	-	-	-	-	18	17	12	16	16	10	12	17	-
DePaul	9	10	11	6	4	3	2	1	1	1	1	1	1	1	1
Duke	3	2	2	1	1	1	1	5	3	5	10	16	17	-	14
Georgetown	19	17	16	17	17	18	20	-	-	-	-	-	-	20	11
Illinois	-	-	-	-	-	20	-	-	-	-	-	-	-	-	-
Indiana	1	1	1	5	10	11	19	19	16	18	20	-	19	13	7
Iona	-	-	-	-	-	-	-	-	-	-	-	-	-	-	19
Iowa	-	20	17	13	11	10	12	13	-	-	-	20	-	-	-
Kansas	20	19	-	-	-	-	-	-	-	-	-	-	-	-	-
Kansas St.	-	-	-	-	-	-	-	-	-	20	-	19	-	-	-
Kentucky	2	5	5	3	2	2	4	6	5	3	6	5	3	2	4
LSU	7	6	6	7	5	4	6	14	11	10	7	6	5	5	3
Louisville	10	14	12	11	12	15	11	7	7	7	3	3	2	4	2
Marquette	18	16	-	-	-	-	-	-	-	-	-	-	-	-	-
Maryland	-	-	-	-	-	-	-	-	15	12	5	8	9	7	8
Missouri	-	-	19	16	13	12	13	15	10	14	15	14	13	11	16
North Carolina	6	8	8	8	6	6	15	9	13	11	11	11	8	10	15
North Caro. St.	-	-	-	-	-	-	-	16	-	-	-	-	-	19	-
Notre Dame	5	4	4	4	3	7	7	8	8	8	9	12	10	14	9
Ohio St.	4	3	3	2	7	5	3	2	4	6	13	9	11	9	10
Oregon St.	17	15	14	19	18	14	9	4	2	2	4	4	6	6	5
Purdue	11	12	9	9	8	8	10	11	14	17	12	15	15	18	20
St. John's (N.Y.)	16	9	15	15	15	17	14	10	9	9	8	7	7	8	13
Syracuse	12	11	10	10	9	9	5	3	6	4	2	2	4	3	6
Tennessee	-	-	-	-	-	-	-	20	19	-	-	-	-	-	-
Texas A&M	14	-	-	-	-	-	-	-	-	-	-	-	-	-	-
UCLA	8	7	7	14	16	16	16	-	-	-	-	-	-	-	-
Virginia	13	13	13	12	14	13	8	12	17	13	18	-	-	-	-
Washington St.	-	-	-	-	-	-	-	-	-	-	-	-	20	-	-
Weber St.	-	-	-	-	-	-	-	-	18	15	17	17	16	16	17

1980-81

	PS	December 2	9	16	23	30	January 6	13	20	27	February 3	10	17	24	March 3	10
Arizona St.	-	-	15	14	11	13	14	12	7	5	5	5	7	5	5	3
Arkansas	20	11	17	19	17	-	-	-	-	-	-	-	-	18	15	20
BYU	18	19	19	18	20	19	17	15	18	15	16	15	17	15	18	16
Clemson	-	-	-	-	-	-	20	19	19	-	-	-	-	-	-	-
Connecticut	-	-	-	-	-	-	-	-	20	20	-	-	-	-	-	-
DePaul	2	1	1	1	1	1	1	4	T3	3	3	3	3	4	2	1
Georgetown	16	19	-	-	-	-	-	-	-	-	-	-	-	-	-	-
Illinois	-	-	-	17	18	16	12	18	15	-	18	17	15	14	16	19
Indiana	5	5	7	11	15	15	-	-	-	-	17	20	16	16	14	9
Iowa	14	12	16	16	14	14	11	14	9	13	15	14	12	8	8	13
Kansas	-	-	-	-	-	-	-	-	-	18	-	-	-	-	-	-
Kentucky	1	2	2	2	2	5	4	3	6	7	6	11	10	9	7	8
Lamar	-	-	-	-	-	-	-	-	-	-	-	-	19	-	-	-
LSU	12	15	11	10	10	10	9	6	5	4	4	4	4	2	3	4
Louisville	3	8	-	20	-	-	-	-	-	-	-	-	-	20	17	12
Maryland	4	4	4	9	9	9	8	10	10	14	13	19	20	17	20	18
Michigan	-	-	18	15	13	12	10	9	16	17	14	13	18	-	-	-
Minnesota	-	-	-	-	-	-	19	20	-	19	-	-	-	-	-	-
Missouri	11	17	14	-	-	-	-	-	-	-	-	-	-	-	-	-
North Carolina	13	10	10	8	6	6	16	17	17	12	11	10	13	11	12	6
Notre Dame	10	13	9	6	8	4	5	7	13	8	9	12	11	6	6	7
Ohio St.	9	9	8	7	-	-	-	-	-	-	-	-	-	-	-	-
Oregon St.	7	6	5	4	4	2	2	1	1	T1	2	2	2	1	1	2
St. John's (N.Y.)	17	16	-	-	-	-	-	-	-	-	-	-	-	-	-	-
South Ala.	-	-	-	-	16	17	15	13	11	16	20	18	-	-	-	-
Syracuse	19	18	20	-	-	-	-	-	-	-	-	-	-	-	-	-
Tennessee	-	-	-	-	-	18	13	11	8	11	10	9	8	10	10	15
Texas A&M	15	14	12	13	12	11	-	-	-	-	-	-	-	-	-	-
UCLA	6	3	3	3	3	7	7	8	12	10	12	8	6	13	13	10
Utah	-	-	-	-	19	20	18	16	14	9	7	6	9	7	9	14
Virginia	8	7	6	5	5	3	3	2	2	T1	1	1	1	3	4	5
Wake Forest	-	-	13	12	7	8	6	5	T3	6	8	7	5	12	11	11
Wichita St.	-	-	-	-	-	-	-	-	-	-	19	16	14	19	-	-
Wyoming	-	-	-	-	-	-	-	-	-	-	-	-	-	-	19	17

1981-82

	PS	December 1	8	15	22	29	January 5	12	19	26	February 2	9	16	23	March 2	9
Alabama	20	17	16	14	12	12	16	13	16	13	8	10	19	17	18	13
UAB	14	11	9	16	19	-	-	-	-	-	-	-	-	-	20	17
Arkansas	18	13	11	9	6	5	11	9	15	12	14	8	17	15	14	12
BYU	-	15	-	-	-	-	-	-	-	-	-	-	-	-	-	-
DePaul	8	7	7	7	13	8	5	4	4	4	4	3	3	3	2	2
Fresno St.	-	-	-	-	-	-	-	-	-	19	17	18	15	14	12	11
Georgetown	5	20	20	19	17	17	13	8	13	-	-	20	13	12	8	6
Georgia	16	-	-	-	-	-	-	-	-	-	-	-	-	-	-	-
Houston	-	-	-	-	18	18	14	10	19	-	-	-	-	-	-	-
Idaho	-	-	-	-	-	-	18	14	8	11	15	13	11	9	6	8
Indiana	12	12	10	13	11	11	-	-	-	-	-	-	20	-	-	-
Iowa	9	6	6	6	10	10	7	5	6	6	5	5	7	11	11	16
Kansas St.	-	-	-	-	-	-	-	-	18	14	T19	15	18	-	17	-
Kentucky	3	2	2	2	2	4	3	6	9	7	9	12	10	7	15	15
La.-Lafayette	-	-	18	15	-	-	-	-	-	-	-	-	-	-	-	-
LSU	17	-	-	-	-	-	-	-	-	-	-	-	-	-	-	-
Louisville	4	3	3	3	8	14	12	17	17	-	-	-	-	-	-	20
Memphis	-	-	-	-	-	-	-	-	-	-	T19	14	12	10	13	9
Minnesota	10	10	8	8	5	9	6	11	5	10	6	9	8	13	7	7
Missouri	15	16	13	11	9	7	4	2	2	1	1	4	4	5	5	5
UNLV	-	18	15	-	-	-	-	-	-	-	-	-	-	-	-	-
North Carolina	1	1	1	1	1	1	1	1	1	2	2	2	2	2	1	1
North Caro. St.	-	-	-	-	-	20	15	12	14	17	-	-	-	-	-	-
Notre Dame	19	-	-	-	-	-	-	-	-	-	-	-	-	-	-	-
Oregon St.	-	-	19	20	16	15	17	15	12	8	10	6	5	4	4	4
St. John's (N.Y.)	-	-	-	-	-	-	20	-	-	-	-	-	-	-	-	-
San Francisco	-	14	12	10	7	6	8	7	11	9	7	17	16	16	-	-
Tennessee	-	-	-	-	-	-	-	-	20	15	16	-	-	19	-	-
Texas	-	-	-	-	-	-	-	19	7	5	12	-	-	-	-	-
Tulsa	11	9	14	12	14	13	10	18	10	16	11	7	6	8	10	10
UCLA	2	8	17	17	15	16	19	-	-	-	-	-	-	20	19	19
Villanova	-	-	-	18	20	19	-	-	-	20	-	-	-	-	-	-
Virginia	7	5	5	5	4	3	2	3	3	3	3	1	1	1	3	3
Virginia Tech	-	-	-	-	-	-	-	20	-	-	-	-	-	-	-	-
Wake Forest	13	-	-	-	-	-	-	-	-	18	13	16	14	18	16	18
Washington	-	-	-	-	-	-	-	-	-	-	-	19	-	-	-	-
West Virginia	-	-	-	-	-	-	-	-	-	-	18	11	9	6	9	14
Wichita St.	6	4	4	4	3	2	9	16	-	-	-	-	-	-	-	-

1982-83

	PS	Nov. 30	December 7	14	21	28	January 4	11	18	25	February 1	8	15	22	March 1	8	15
Alabama	12	13	11	10	8	6	5	10	-	-	-	-	-	-	-	-	-
Arkansas	17	16	15	13	12	11	10	7	4	12	9	8	7	6	5	6	9
Auburn	-	-	-	-	-	-	-	-	20	-	-	-	-	-	-	-	-
Boston College	-	-	-	-	-	-	-	-	-	-	-	-	18	19	15	14	11
Chattanooga	-	-	-	-	-	-	-	-	-	-	-	-	-	-	19	18	15
Georgetown	2	2	3	T5	11	10	17	-	19	15	14	14	14	18	16	15	20
Georgia	-	-	-	-	-	-	-	-	-	-	19	-	-	-	-	-	18
Houston	14	11	9	14	19	18	19	16	14	9	8	6	4	2	1	1	1
Illinois St.	-	-	-	-	-	-	-	-	-	17	16	17	-	-	-	-	-
Indiana	9	8	6	T5	5	1	1	4	2	2	6	4	2	4	11	7	5
Iowa	11	10	7	7	10	9	8	12	10	14	13	20	16	17	-	-	-
Kentucky	4	3	2	2	2	3	3	6	11	10	15	13	11	10	7	10	12
Louisville	8	7	13	12	14	13	13	9	9	8	12	11	9	5	3	3	2
Marquette	18	17	16	-	-	-	-	-	-	-	-	-	-	-	-	-	-
Memphis	6	5	4	3	4	2	2	1	6	5	4	9	13	14	17	17	17
Minnesota	-	-	-	-	-	-	-	17	16	16	17	19	-	-	-	-	-
Missouri	15	9	8	8	6	12	15	14	12	13	10	10	12	T15	13	12	10
UNLV	T20	19	18	18	17	15	11	8	5	4	2	2	1	1	9	9	6
North Carolina	3	15	17	17	-	-	18	11	3	3	1	1	3	11	8	5	8
North Caro. St.	16	18	18	15	15	17	16	19	-	-	-	-	-	-	-	-	16
Ohio St.	-	-	-	-	-	-	-	20	-	-	-	-	20	T15	14	16	-
Oklahoma	T20	-	-	-	-	-	-	-	-	-	-	-	19	-	-	19	-
Oklahoma St.	-	-	-	-	-	-	-	-	18	20	-	-	-	-	-	-	19

		Nov.	December				January				February				March		
	PS	30	7	14	21	28	4	11	18	25	1	8	15	22	1	8	15
Oregon St.	10	19	-	-	-	-	-	-	-	-	-	-	-	-	-	-	-
Purdue	-	-	20	-	-	-	20	-	-	-	-	18	-	-	20	-	-
St. John's (N.Y.)	19	12	12	9	7	7	7	3	8	7	5	7	6	9	10	8	3
Syracuse	-	-	-	16	13	14	9	13	15	18	20	15	17	13	18	20	-
Tennessee	13	14	14	11	9	8	12	18	-	-	-	-	-	20	-	-	-
Tulsa	-	-	-	-	20	19	-	-	-	-	-	-	-	-	-	-	-
UCLA	7	6	5	4	3	5	6	5	1	1	7	5	10	8	6	4	7
Villanova	5	4	10	19	18	16	14	15	13	11	11	12	8	7	4	13	13
Virginia	1	1	1	1	1	4	4	2	7	6	3	3	5	3	2	2	4
Virginia Tech	-	-	-	-	-	-	-	-	17	-	-	-	-	-	-	-	-
Wake Forest	-	-	-	-	-	-	-	-	-	19	-	-	-	-	-	-	-
Washington St.	-	-	-	-	-	-	-	-	-	-	18	-	-	-	-	-	-
West Virginia	-	-	-	20	16	20	-	-	-	-	-	-	-	-	-	-	-
Wichita St.	-	-	-	-	-	-	-	-	-	-	-	16	15	12	12	11	14

1983-84

		Nov.	December				January					February				March	
	PS	29	6	13	20	27	3	10	17	24	31	7	14	21	28	6	13
Arkansas	14	14	15	-	-	-	-	-	-	16	-	-	14	11	12	8	8
Auburn	-	-	-	-	-	-	-	-	-	-	19	16	-	19	-	-	-
Boston College	15	15	12	8	6	12	17	18	16	-	-	-	-	-	-	-	-
DePaul	18	16	13	4	4	4	3	3	2	2	2	2	3	5	5	4	4
Duke	-	-	-	-	-	-	-	-	-	-	-	-	19	14	15	16	14
Fresno St.	13	17	20	-	-	-	16	13	17	-	-	-	-	-	-	-	-
Georgetown	4	3	3	5	5	5	4	4	6	4	4	3	2	2	4	2	2
Georgia	16	13	10	12	14	11	11	15	-	18	-	-	-	-	-	-	-
Georgia Tech	-	-	-	-	-	-	-	-	-	-	18	18	-	-	-	-	-
Houston	3	8	6	3	3	3	7	7	4	7	6	5	4	3	2	5	5
Illinois	-	-	-	-	-	20	14	9	10	9	8	8	7	6	10	7	6
Indiana	19	-	-	-	-	-	-	-	-	-	-	-	T17	-	-	-	-
Iowa	7	5	5	18	19	-	-	-	-	-	-	-	-	-	-	-	-
Kansas	17	-	-	-	-	-	-	-	-	-	-	-	-	-	-	-	-
Kentucky	2	1	2	2	2	2	2	2	3	3	3	6	6	4	3	3	3
LSU	11	12	9	10	11	9	9	11	15	10	14	20	T17	-	-	-	-
Louisville	6	-	-	16	10	14	-	-	-	14	17	15	-	-	-	18	-
Maryland	8	6	11	9	8	6	5	5	7	5	10	13	-	-	19	14	11
Memphis	5	4	4	T6	16	17	19	19	18	13	9	9	8	12	14	17	16
Michigan	-	-	-	-	20	15	-	-	-	-	-	-	-	-	-	-	-
Michigan St.	12	11	17	17	-	-	-	-	-	-	-	-	-	-	-	-	-
UNLV	-	-	-	-	-	-	18	14	8	6	5	4	5	7	7	10	13
North Carolina	1	2	1	1	1	1	1	1	1	1	1	1	1	1	1	1	1
North Caro. St.	-	7	8	T6	13	13	12	-	-	-	-	-	-	-	-	-	-
Oklahoma	20	-	-	-	-	-	-	17	20	11	12	10	9	8	6	6	7
Oregon St.	10	10	18	14	15	19	15	16	11	-	-	-	-	20	20	20	17
Purdue	-	-	19	11	7	18	-	-	19	-	16	11	11	13	11	11	10
St. John's (N.Y.)	-	19	16	13	12	8	13	10	14	-	-	-	-	-	-	-	-
Syracuse	-	-	-	-	-	-	-	-	-	20	13	19	16	16	16	-	18
Temple	-	-	-	-	-	-	-	-	-	-	-	-	20	17	18	15	20
UTEP	-	-	-	20	18	16	10	8	5	8	7	7	10	9	8	9	9
Tulsa	-	-	-	-	-	-	-	20	13	12	11	12	12	10	9	12	12
UCLA	9	9	7	15	9	7	6	6	9	15	20	-	-	-	-	-	-
Virginia	-	-	-	-	-	-	20	-	-	19	-	-	-	-	-	-	-
Va. C'wealth	-	20	-	-	-	-	-	-	-	-	-	-	-	-	-	-	-
Wake Forest	-	-	-	19	17	10	8	12	12	17	15	14	13	15	17	19	19
Washington	-	-	-	-	-	-	-	-	-	-	-	17	15	18	13	13	15
Wichita St.	-	18	14	-	-	-	-	-	-	-	-	-	-	-	-	-	-

1984-85

		Nov.	December				January					February				March	
	PS	27	4	11	18	25	1	8	15	22	29	5	12	19	26	5	12
UAB	-	13	18	17	-	-	-	-	-	-	20	-	19	-	-	-	-
Arizona	-	-	-	-	-	-	-	-	-	-	-	-	-	-	19	-	-
Arkansas	16	17	-	-	-	-	-	-	-	-	-	-	-	-	-	-	-
Boston College	-	-	-	-	-	-	-	12	15	-	-	-	-	20	-	-	-
DePaul	3	2	2	2	5	9	10	13	10	7	13	18	-	-	-	-	-
Duke	6	4	4	3	2	2	2	2	2	5	6	5	7	6	5	7	10
Georgetown	1	1	1	1	1	1	1	1	1	1	2	2	2	2	2	1	1
Georgia	-	-	-	-	-	-	-	-	-	-	-	-	-	18	14	17	19
Georgia Tech	20	18	15	12	13	10	8	9	17	16	8	10	6	8	10	9	6
Illinois	2	7	7	6	4	8	6	15	11	6	5	9	17	16	18	14	12
Indiana	4	12	11	16	16	15	12	11	8	13	-	-	-	-	-	-	-
Iowa	-	-	-	-	-	-	-	19	-	-	-	12	11	14	-	-	-
Kansas	19	t20	19	18	15	12	11	10	9	15	19	13	10	15	11	10	13
Kentucky	18	-	-	-	-	-	-	-	-	-	-	-	-	-	-	-	-
LSU	14	16	13	19	19	18	14	-	-	-	-	-	-	-	-	19	20
Louisiana Tech	-	-	-	-	20	19	18	14	12	12	15	14	12	10	7	8	8
Louisville	17	6	6	14	12	20	-	-	-	-	-	-	-	-	-	-	-
Loyola (Ill.)	-	-	-	-	-	-	-	-	-	-	-	-	-	-	20	16	14
Maryland	-	-	-	-	-	-	19	-	-	-	17	20	20	-	-	-	-
Memphis	8	5	5	5	3	3	3	6	5	4	3	3	5	4	4	5	5
Michigan	-	-	-	20	18	13	16	-	-	18	10	8	3	3	3	3	2
Michigan St.	-	-	-	-	-	-	-	17	19	-	-	-	-	-	-	-	-
UNLV	11	t20	20	-	-	-	-	-	-	20	16	11	14	11	9	11	9
North Carolina	-	19	16	13	10	7	9	5	6	8	11	15	13	13	8	6	7
North Caro. St.	13	11	10	9	14	14	17	-	-	-	-	-	-	-	16	18	16
Oklahoma	5	10	17	15	11	17	13	8	13	9	7	7	4	5	6	4	4
Oregon St.	-	-	-	-	-	-	-	20	14	10	14	16	18	19	-	-	-
St. John's (N.Y.)	7	3	3	4	8	5	4	3	4	2	1	1	1	1	1	2	3
SMU	-	10	9	8	7	6	4	7	4	3	2	4	4	9	9	13	20
Syracuse	12	14	12	10	9	6	5	7	7	11	9	6	8	7	12	13	15
Texas Tech	-	-	-	-	-	-	-	-	-	-	-	-	-	-	-	-	17
Tulsa	-	-	-	-	-	-	-	-	20	17	12	17	15	12	15	15	18
VCU	-	-	-	-	-	-	20	18	16	19	-	-	-	17	17	12	11
Virginia Tech	15	15	14	11	17	16	-	-	-	-	-	-	-	-	-	-	-
Villanova	-	-	-	-	-	-	-	16	18	14	18	19	16	-	-	-	-
Washington	9	8	9	8	7	11	15	-	-	-	-	-	-	-		-	-

1985-86

		Nov.	December					January				February				March	
	PS	26	3	10	17	24	31	7	14	21	28	4	11	18	25	4	11
Alabama	-	-	-	-	-	-	-	-	-	-	-	20	18	-	-	-	-
UAB	16	20	17	16	14	14	16	14	12	18	-	-	-	-	-	-	-
Auburn	10	19	t19	-	-	-	-	-	-	-	-	-	-	-	-	-	-
Bradley	-	-	-	-	-	-	-	-	20	17	13	13	13	12	11	9	14
DePaul	-	-	19	18	20	-	-	-		-	-	-	-	-	-	-	-
Duke	6	6	3	3	3	3	3	3	3	2	5	4	2	2	1	1	1
Georgetown	8	8	6	t5	5	5	11	13	15	12	12	11	9	13	15	14	13
Georgia Tech	1	2	5	t5	7	7	6	5	5	4	3	2	5	5	4	6	6
Illinois	7	7	12	10	15	16	14	18	-	-	-	-	-	-	-	19	19
Indiana	-	-	t19	18	17	17	15	-	-	-	15	18	16	15	16	16	16
Iowa	-	-	18	-	-	-	-	-	-	-	-	-	-	-	-	-	-
Kansas	5	5	7	7	6	6	5	9	8	7	4	6	3	3	2	2	2
Kentucky	11	10	9	9	13	13	12	11	11	11	8	12	11	8	5	3	3
LSU	14	12	11	11	9	9	8	8	14	14	17	-	-	-	-	-	-
Louisville	9	9	16	15	16	15	18	17	18	13	18	16	19	16	13	11	7
Maryland	t19	17	-	-	-	-	-	-	-	-	-	-	-	-	-	-	-
Memphis	15	14	13	12	10	10	9	6	6	3	2	3	4	4	7	10	12
Michigan	3	3	2	2	2	2	2	2	2	6	9	7	10	7	10	7	5
Michigan St.	-	-	-	-	-	-	-	-	-	-	-	-	-	19	17	17	18
Navy	t19	-	-	-	-	-	-	-	-	-	-	-	-	17	19	18	17
UNLV	18	16	14	13	12	12	13	12	10	10	10	9	6	11	9	13	11
North Carolina	2	1	1	1	1	1	1	1	1	1	1	1	1	1	3	4	8
North Caro. St.	17	15	-	-	-	-	-	-	-	-	-	-	17	20	18	20	-
Notre Dame	12	11	10	17	19	18	17	16	13	16	14	14	14	14	12	12	10
Ohio St.	-	-	-	20	-	-	-	-	-	-	-	-	-	-	-	-	-
Oklahoma	13	13	8	8	8	8	7	7	7	5	6	5	8	10	14	15	15
Purdue	-	-	-	-	-	-	-	20	19	15	-	-	-	-	20	-	-
Richmond	-	-	-	-	-	-	-	-	-	-	20	-	-	-	-	-	-
St. John's (N.Y.)	-	18	15	14	11	11	10	10	9	8	7	10	7	6	8	5	4
Syracuse	4	4	4	4	4	4	4	4	4	9	11	8	12	9	6	8	9
UTEP	-	-	-	-	-	-	19	15	17	19	19	17	15	-	-	-	20
Virginia Tech	-	-	-	-	20	19	20	19	16	20	16	15	20	18	-	-	-
Western Ky.	-	-	-	-	-	-	-	-	-	-	-	19	-	-	-	-	-

1986-87

		December					January				February				March	
	PS	2	9	16	23	30	6	13	20	27	3	10	17	24	3	10
Alabama	13	8	18	-	-	-	-	15	13	9	9	14	12	10	9	9
Arizona	19	20	-	-	-	-	-	-	-	-	-	-	-	-	-	-
Arkansas	-	-	20	-	-	-	-	-	-	-	-	-	-	-	-	-
Auburn	12	7	7	6	5	5	13	10	17	18	20	-	-	-	-	-
Clemson	-	-	-	-	-	-	20	12	10	14	12	12	10	13	13	13
Cleveland St.	20	-	-	-	-	-	-	-	-	-	-	-	-	-	-	-
DePaul	-	-	-	19	17	15	7	7	6	8	5	5	4	4	5	5
Duke	-	-	-	-	-	20	17	14	12	13	16	15	17	17	14	17
Florida	-	-	-	-	20	-	-	-	-	19	-	19	18	18	-	-
Georgetown	18	16	13	10	10	8	16	9	15	11	10	13	11	8	7	4
Georgia Tech	6	15	16	16	19	18	-	-	-	-	-	-	-	-	-	-
Illinois	14	9	6	5	9	16	12	8	9	12	14	11	14	14	12	11
Indiana	3	3	2	8	8	6	4	4	3	t4	2	2	2	3	4	3
Iowa	10	5	4	3	3	3	2	2	1	2	4	4	7	7	6	6
Kansas	8	6	14	13	13	12	19	20	-	20	18	17	15	16	-	20
Kentucky	11	13	19	18	18	11	9	-	-	-	-	-	-	-	-	-
Louisville	2	-	-	-	-	-	-	-	-	-	-	-	-	-	-	-
Missouri	-	-	-	-	-	-	-	-	-	-	-	-	-	-	19	14
Navy	9	10	10	11	12	9	15	19	18	-	-	-	-	-	-	-
UNLV	5	2	1	1	1	1	1	1	4	3	1	1	1	1	1	1
New Orleans	-	-	-	-	-	-	-	-	-	-	-	-	-	19	16	16
North Carolina	1	1	5	4	4	4	3	3	2	1	3	3	3	2	2	2
North Caro. St.	17	18	15	12	11	19	18	17	20	-	-	-	-	-	-	-
Northeastern	-	19	-	-	-	-	-	-	-	-	-	-	-	-	-	-
Notre Dame	-	-	-	-	-	-	-	-	-	-	-	-	-	-	20	18
Oklahoma	7	11	9	7	6	13	11	16	11	10	8	8	13	12	17	-
Pittsburgh	16	12	17	14	14	17	14	18	16	17	13	10	8	9	11	12

		December					January				February				March	
	PS	2	9	16	23	30	6	13	20	27	3	10	17	24	3	10
Providence	-	-	-	-	-	-	-	-	-	-	17	20	19	20	-	-
Purdue	4	4	3	2	2	2	6	6	5	t4	7	7	6	6	3	7
St. John's (N.Y.)	-	-	-	15	15	10	10	13	14	15	19	16	20	-	-	-
Syracuse	15	17	12	9	7	7	5	5	7	6	11	9	9	11	10	10
Temple	-	-	-	20	16	14	8	11	8	7	6	6	5	5	8	8
TCU	-	-	-	-	-	-	-	-	19	16	15	18	16	15	15	19
UCLA	-	-	11	17	-	-	-	-	-	-	-	-	-	-	18	15
Western Ky.	-	14	8	-	-	-	-	-	-	-	-	-	-	-	-	-

1987-88

		December					January				February				March		
	PS	1	8	15	22	29	5	12	19	26	2	9	16	23	1	8	15
Arizona	17	9	4	2	1	1	3	1	1	1	1	3	3	3	3	3	2
Auburn	-	-	-	-	-	-	-	19	-	-	-	-	-	-	-	-	-
Bradley	-	-	-	-	-	-	-	-	-	-	18	15	17	14	14	12	11
BYU	-	-	-	-	-	-	-	-	12	7	4	t8	7	11	15	17	19
DePaul	20	-	-	-	-	-	-	-	-	-	-	-	-	-	-	-	-
Duke	15	13	10	10	9	9	9	7	9	5	3	t8	6	5	9	8	5
Florida	14	7	12	11	8	8	15	-	-	14	19	-	-	-	-	-	-
Georgia Tech	18	-	-	-	-	-	-	-	-	-	-	-	-	20	13	18	-
Georgetown	16	17	14	18	19	18	14	11	15	15	14	-	-	-	-	-	-
Illinois	-	-	-	-	-	-	19	20	13	13	17	-	-	-	-	19	16
Indiana	6	5	6	5	13	13	12	15	-	-	-	19	-	-	-	-	-
Iowa	11	6	3	7	14	14	16	17	19	16	13	13	13	13	11	15	17
Iowa St.	-	-	-	20	16	16	17	14	10	12	16	-	-	-	-	-	-
Kansas	7	16	18	17	18	17	18	16	16	-	-	-	-	-	-	-	-
Kansas St.	-	-	-	-	-	-	-	-	-	-	-	14	-	-	-	-	20
Kentucky	5	2	1	1	2	2	1	5	4	9	10	10	9	12	8	6	6
Louisville	13	14	-	-	-	20	-	-	-	-	-	-	-	-	-	-	-
Loyola Marymnt.	-	-	-	-	-	-	-	-	-	-	-	-	20	19	18	16	15
Memphis	-	20	20	19	20	19	-	-	-	-	-	-	-	-	-	-	-
Michigan	9	15	15	13	11	12	11	10	7	8	11	12	10	7	10	10	10
Missouri	8	8	9	16	17	-	-	-	-	-	-	-	15	15	-	-	-
UNLV	-	19	17	15	15	15	13	13	8	4	2	7	11	8	5	7	12
New Mexico	-	-	-	-	-	-	-	18	-	-	-	-	-	-	-	-	-
North Carolina	3	1	5	4	4	4	4	2	2	3	8	6	5	9	6	9	7
North Caro. St.	-	-	-	-	-	-	-	20	-	-	-	-	-	16	11	14	
Notre Dame	-	-	19	-	-	-	-	-	-	-	-	-	-	-	-	-	-
Oklahoma	19	18	16	14	12	10	8	3	11	10	7	4	4	4	4	4	4
Pittsburgh	4	4	2	3	3	3	2	6	6	11	9	5	8	6	7	5	8
Purdue	2	11	13	12	10	11	10	8	5	2	6	2	2	2	2	2	3
St. John's (N.Y.)	-	-	-	-	-	-	20	-	-	-	20	-	-	-	-	-	-
Southern Miss.	-	-	-	-	-	-	-	-	-	20	-	16	14	18	-	-	-
Syracuse	1	3	8	9	7	7	7	9	14	17	12	11	12	10	12	13	9
Temple	12	12	11	8	6	6	6	4	3	6	5	1	1	1	1	1	1
UTEP	-	-	-	-	-	-	-	-	18	18	-	-	-	-	-	-	-
Vanderbilt	-	-	-	-	-	-	-	-	-	-	15	17	16	17	19	-	-
Villanova	-	-	-	-	-	-	-	-	-	19	-	20	-	-	-	-	-
Wyoming	10	10	7	6	5	5	5	12	17	-	-	18	19	16	17	14	13
Xavier	-	-	-	-	-	-	-	-	-	-	-	-	-	-	20	20	18

1988-89

		Nov.		December				January					February				March	
	PS	22	29	6	13	20	27	3	10	17	24	31	7	14	21	28	7	14
Alabama	-	-	-	-	-	-	-	-	-	-	-	-	-	-	-	-	-	20
Arizona	11	10	11	10	9	9	8	8	12	9	6	4	1	2	2	1	1	1
Ball St.	-	-	-	-	-	-	-	-	-	-	-	-	-	-	20	19	19	18
Connecticut	-	-	-	-	18	-	-	-	-	-	-	-	-	-	-	-	-	-
Duke	1	1	1	1	1	1	1	1	1	1	8	12	14	11	9	9	7	9
Florida	15	15	19	-	-	-	-	-	-	-	-	-	-	-	-	-	-	-
Florida St.	16	17	14	13	12	11	10	15	14	14	11	8	12	7	12	16	14	16
Georgetown	2	2	3	4	5	6	5	5	7	3	2	6	2	4	3	2	3	2
Georgia	-	-	-	-	-	-	-	-	20	-	-	-	-	-	-	-	-	-
Georgia Tech	13	14	12	12	11	16	17	19	19	-	-	-	20	-	-	-	-	-
Illinois	9	9	7	7	6	5	4	3	2	2	1	2	7	5	10	8	4	3
Indiana	-	20	-	-	-	-	-	-	-	19	16	17	13	9	4	3	6	8
Iowa	7	7	6	5	4	4	9	9	5	7	12	9	8	15	14	11	15	14
Kansas	-	-	-	-	-	-	20	20	18	16	17	18	-	-	-	-	-	-
LSU	-	-	-	-	-	-	-	-	-	-	-	-	19	-	20	-	-	-
Louisville	4	12	13	15	15	14	14	13	9	4	3	7	4	10	8	14	16	12
Michigan	3	3	2	2	2	2	2	7	6	6	10	11	10	13	13	10	8	10
Missouri	14	13	8	11	10	10	11	11	10	8	5	5	3	3	7	7	10	6
UNLV	10	8	9	9	13	13	12	12	11	10	13	16	19	18	18	18	18	15
North Carolina	6	5	10	8	8	8	7	6	8	13	7	3	6	8	5	5	9	5
North Caro. St.	18	18	16	19	18	17	18	16	15	15	15	13	17	19	17	20	17	19
Notre Dame	-	-	-	-	-	19	-	-	-	-	-	-	-	-	-	-	-	-
Ohio St.	17	16	15	14	14	12	15	14	18	16	17	17	16	16	-	-	-	-
Oklahoma	5	4	5	6	7	7	6	4	3	5	4	1	5	1	1	4	2	4
Providence	-	-	-	-	-	-	-	-	-	20	-	20	-	-	-	-	-	-
St. Mary's (Cal.)	-	-	-	-	-	-	-	-	-	-	-	-	-	-	-	19	17	20
Seton Hall	-	-	-	20	17	15	13	10	13	12	9	10	11	12	15	12	11	11
South Carolina	-	-	-	-	-	-	18	16	-	-	-	-	-	-	-	-	-	-
Stanford	20	-	-	-	-	-	-	-	-	20	19	20	18	17	16	13	12	13
Syracuse	8	6	4	3	3	3	3	2	4	11	14	14	9	6	6	6	5	7
Temple	19	19	17	-	-	-	-	-	-	-	-	-	-	-	-	-	-	-
Tennessee	-	-	-	20	16	16	19	19	17	17	18	-	-	-	-	-	-	-
UCLA	-	-	-	-	-	20	-	-	-	-	-	-	-	-	-	-	-	-
Villanova	12	11	18	17	-	-	-	-	-	-	-	-	-	-	-	-	-	-
West Virginia	-	-	-	-	-	-	-	-	-	-	-	18	15	14	11	15	13	17

1989-90

		Nov.	December				January					February				March	
	PS	27	5	12	19	26	2	9	16	23	30	6	13	20	27	6	13
Alabama	-	-	21	19	20	22	22	24	25	24	-	-	-	-	-	-	23
Arizona	6	2	20	20	22	21	19	18	23	19	24	22	20	21	23	15	14
Arkansas	9	11	10	7	10	11	14	12	12	6	3	3	8	13	12	9	7
Clemson	-	-	-	-	-	-	-	-	-	-	-	-	-	23	20	17	17
Connecticut	-	-	-	-	-	-	-	-	-	20	13	8	10	6	4	8	4
Duke	10	7	6	12	12	13	13	10	8	8	5	4	6	3	t5	12	15
Florida	23	24	25	24	-	-	-	-	-	-	-	-	-	-	-	-	-
Georgetown	5	3	3	3	3	3	3	2	2	3	6	5	3	5	7	5	8
Georgia	-	-	-	-	-	-	-	-	-	-	-	-	-	-	25	25	-
Georgia Tech	22	21	18	15	14	14	12	9	11	13	17	16	13	8	11	14	9
Illinois	8	8	7	5	5	4	4	8	7	10	11	12	15	t19	18	20	18
Indiana	14	14	14	11	11	10	9	13	14	12	22	25	-	25	-	-	-
Iowa	-	-	-	21	16	18	20	-	-	-	-	-	-	-	-	-	-
Kansas	-	4	2	2	2	2	2	1	1	2	2	2	1	2	1	2	5
La Salle	-	-	-	-	23	20	17	21	17	18	15	14	14	14	13	11	12
LSU	2	9	9	9	8	9	11	14	13	16	14	11	9	12	15	16	19
Louisville	12	13	11	10	9	8	8	11	10	4	10	15	18	16	21	18	16
Loyola Marymount.	-	-	-	-	-	-	25	23	21	22	20	20	19	22	22	21	21
Memphis	24	22	16	17	17	15	21	20	-	-	-	-	-	-	-	-	-
Michigan	4	10	8	6	6	5	5	3	6	7	4	7	5	7	8	13	13
Michigan St.	-	-	-	25	25	-	-	-	-	-	-	23	21	15	14	7	3
Minnesota	20	-	-	-	-	25	24	16	22	21	19	17	17	18	17	19	20
Missouri	11	5	4	4	4	7	7	5	4	1	1	1	2	1	3	6	11
UNLV	1	6	5	14	13	12	10	7	9	5	12	9	7	4	2	3	2
New Mexico St.	-	-	-	-	-	-	-	-	-	-	-	-	25	24	24	23	24
North Carolina	7	12	17	-	-	24	-	-	-	-	25	-	-	-	-	-	-
North Caro. St.	19	25	19	16	15	19	18	17	19	-	-	-	-	-	-	-	-
Notre Dame	17	19	-	-	-	-	-	-	-	-	-	-	-	-	-	-	-
Oklahoma	16	17	12	8	7	6	6	4	3	9	9	13	11	10	t5	1	1
Oklahoma St.	21	23	-	22	24	-	-	-	-	-	-	-	-	-	-	-	-
Oregon St.	-	-	24	23	21	23	23	22	18	17	21	18	16	17	16	22	22
Pittsburgh	18	18	22	-	-	-	-	-	-	-	-	-	-	-	-	-	-
Purdue	-	-	-	-	-	-	-	-	24	13	8	10	12	9	9	10	10
St. John's (N.Y.)	25	20	15	18	19	17	16	15	15	15	18	24	24	-	-	-	-
Syracuse	3	1	1	1	1	1	1	6	5	11	7	6	4	11	10	4	6
Temple	15	16	23	-	-	-	-	-	-	-	-	-	-	-	-	-	-
UCLA	13	15	13	13	18	16	15	19	16	23	16	19	23	-	-	-	-
Xavier	-	-	-	-	-	-	-	25	20	25	23	21	22	t19	19	24	25

1990-91

		Nov.	December				January					February				March	
	PS	27	4	11	18	25	1	8	15	22	29	5	12	19	26	5	12
Alabama	7	6	12	20	-	-	-	-	-	-	-	-	-	24	-	24	19
Arizona	3	2	2	4	4	4	4	6	6	5	6	5	6	9	7	9	8
Arkansas	2	3	3	2	2	2	2	2	2	2	2	2	3	3	3	5	2
Connecticut	17	15	14	16	15	13	12	9	13	19	-	-	-	-	-	-	-
DePaul	-	-	-	-	-	-	-	-	-	-	-	-	-	-	-	25	24
Duke	6	8	5	10	9	8	8	14	12	9	7	6	5	7	8	6	6
East Tenn. St.	-	-	-	24	21	20	17	16	15	12	16	13	10	13	19	15	17
Georgetown	9	9	6	5	12	16	15	15	19	21	18	20	18	25	-	-	-
Georgia	21	17	13	11	17	17	-	-	-	-	-	-	-	-	-	-	-
Georgia Tech	16	14	20	23	-	-	24	24	-	-	23	-	-	-	-	-	-
Indiana	8	10	7	7	6	5	5	3	3	3	4	4	4	4	5	3	3
Iowa	-	-	-	-	-	23	22	22	24	-	-	-	-	-	-	-	-
Kansas	-	-	-	-	-	-	-	-	-	-	24	18	11	8	10	12	12
Kentucky	-	-	25	18	18	18	16	11	9	8	10	10	16	12	13	10	9
LSU	14	20	18	12	10	15	14	20	20	16	14	19	20	19	18	16	22
Louisville	23	25	-	-	-	-	-	-	-	-	-	-	-	-	-	-	-
Michigan St.	4	5	19	21	24	25	25	-	-	22	-	25	-	-	-	-	-
Mississippi St.	-	-	-	-	-	-	-	-	-	-	-	-	23	21	23	18	21
Missouri	20	23	-	-	-	-	-	-	-	-	-	-	-	-	-	-	-
Nebraska	-	-	-	-	22	22	19	18	17	14	11	15	17	14	15	13	11
UNLV	1	1	1	1	1	1	1	1	1	1	1	1	1	1	1	1	1
New Mexico St.	-	-	-	-	-	24	23	23	21	23	20	16	12	15	11	11	15
New Orleans	-	-	-	-	-	-	-	-	-	24	22	21	-	-	-	-	-
North Carolina	5	4	10	9	8	7	7	5	5	7	9	9	8	6	4	7	4
Ohio St.	10	11	9	8	7	6	6	4	4	4	3	3	2	2	2	2	5
Oklahoma	15	18	16	13	11	14	13	12	11	13	21	23	-	-	-	-	-
Oklahoma St.	-	-	-	-	-	-	-	-	-	-	-	22	21	16	12	12	14
Pittsburgh	12	13	11	15	14	11	11	17	16	17	19	24	22	23	22	-	-
Princeton	-	-	-	-	25	-	-	-	-	-	-	-	25	23	21	19	18
St. John's (N.Y.)	25	21	17	14	13	9	9	10	10	10	5	8	13	18	17	20	20

		Nov.	December				January					February				March	
	PS	27	4	11	18	25	1	8	15	22	29	5	12	19	26	5	12
Seton Hall	-	-	-	-	-	-	-	-	25	-	25	-	-	24	20	21	13
South Carolina	-	-	t21	17	16	12	20	21	22	25	-	-	-	-	-	-	-
Southern Miss.	24	19	15	22	20	21	21	19	18	15	17	12	9	11	14	22	25
Syracuse	13	7	4	3	3	3	3	8	8	6	8	7	7	5	6	4	7
Temple	19	-	24	-	-	-	-	-	-	-	-	-	-	-	-	-	-
Texas	22	22	23	25	23	-	-	-	-	-	-	-	24	-	-	23	23
UTEP	-	-	-	-	-	-	-	25	-	-	-	-	-	-	-	-	-
UCLA	11	12	8	6	5	10	10	7	7	11	12	14	15	17	16	17	16
Utah	-	-	-	-	-	-	-	-	23	20	13	17	14	10	9	8	10
Villanova	-	24	-	-	-	-	-	-	-	-	-	-	-	-	-	-	-
Virginia	18	16	t21	19	19	19	18	13	14	18	15	11	19	20	25	-	-

1991-92

		Nov.	December					January				February				March		
	PS	25	2	9	16	23	30	6	13	20	27	3	10	17	24	2	9	16
Alabama	17	16	15	20	20	20	19	16	9	15	22	18	16	14	16	20	17	13
Arizona	5	3	3	2	2	6	6	6	7	11	9	7	7	5	5	4	2	10
Arizona St.	24	25	-	-	-	-	-	-	-	-	-	-	-	-	-	-	-	-
Arkansas	3	2	11	19	19	15	16	13	12	9	7	5	11	10	9	7	6	9
Charlotte	-	-	-	24	24	25	21	22	18	19	17	20	22	-	-	-	-	-
Cincinnati	-	-	-	-	-	-	-	-	-	-	-	-	24	19	19	14	12	12
Connecticut	15	15	12	8	7	5	5	5	8	7	6	10	18	21	24	-	-	-
DePaul	18	20	20	-	-	-	-	-	-	-	-	-	-	-	21	15	19	24
Duke	1	1	1	1	1	1	1	1	1	1	1	1	1	1	1	1	1	1
Florida St.	-	-	-	-	-	-	-	-	-	-	23	23	23	16	22	19	18	20
Georgetown	16	17	18	23	23	24	22	-	22	-	-	-	-	25	18	17	21	22
Georgia Tech	23	18	17	t13	13	13	15	14	16	18	20	24	-	-	-	-	-	-
Indiana	2	10	9	t13	14	10	10	10	5	4	4	6	4	7	2	2	4	5
Iowa	21	21	21	16	22	23	-	-	-	-	-	-	-	-	-	-	-	-
Iowa St.	-	-	-	-	-	-	-	-	24	-	-	-	-	23	-	-	-	-
Kansas	12	12	10	7	6	4	4	4	6	5	5	3	4	3	3	3	3	2
Kentucky	4	13	14	9	8	17	17	15	10	8	14	19	19	13	11	10	9	6
LSU	6	9	16	25	-	-	-	-	-	-	-	22	20	-	-	23	23	25
Louisville	25	-	-	-	25	21	24	-	25	20	24	-	-	-	-	-	-	-
Massachusetts	-	-	-	-	-	-	-	25	-	-	-	-	-	-	-	25	22	17
Michigan	20	23	25	18	15	11	11	11	15	16	15	15	17	20	17	18	14	15
Michigan St.	-	-	22	t13	12	9	9	9	11	14	13	11	12	11	12	13	16	14
Missouri	-	-	-	21	17	16	13	12	13	12	8	12	9	9	6	11	13	16
Nebraska	-	-	-	-	-	-	-	-	-	-	-	-	-	-	25	-	-	-
UNLV	-	-	24	-	-	-	-	-	-	25	21	17	15	12	7	6	7	7
North Carolina	8	6	5	5	9	8	8	8	14	10	11	9	6	4	10	16	20	18
Ohio St.	7	5	4	4	4	7	7	7	4	6	10	8	8	6	8	5	5	3
Oklahoma	19	19	19	17	16	14	14	21	23	17	18	21	-	-	-	-	24	23
Oklahoma St.	13	11	8	6	5	3	3	3	3	3	3	2	2	8	14	12	11	11
Pittsburgh	-	24	-	-	-	-	-	-	-	-	-	-	-	-	-	-	-	-
St. John's (N.Y.)	10	8	7	11	10	18	18	17	17	22	-	-	-	24	20	-	25	-
Seton Hall	9	7	6	12	11	12	12	18	21	-	-	-	25	22	-	22	15	19
Southern Cal.	-	-	-	-	-	-	25	23	-	-	25	16	13	15	13	8	10	8
Stanford	-	-	-	-	-	-	-	-	-	24	-	-	-	-	-	-	-	-
Syracuse	-	-	-	-	-	-	23	20	20	13	12	13	10	17	22	24	-	21
UTEP	-	-	-	-	-	-	-	-	-	23	19	25	21	-	-	-	-	-
Tulane	-	-	-	-	-	-	-	24	19	21	16	14	14	18	15	21	-	-
UCLA	11	4	2	3	3	2	2	2	2	2	2	4	3	2	4	9	8	4
Utah	14	14	13	10	18	19	-	-	-	-	-	-	-	-	-	-	-	-
Wake Forest	22	22	23	22	21	22	20	19	-	-	-	-	-	-	-	-	-	-

1992-93

		Nov.		December				January				February				March		
	PS	23	30	7	14	21	28	4	11	18	25	1	8	15	22	1	8	15
Arizona	10	10	9	14	15	14	22	20	12	11	8	8	5	4	4	3	6	5
Arkansas	-	-	-	16	12	10	9	13	9	8	16	17	14	13	15	13	14	12
Boston College	-	-	-	-	-	-	-	-	22	-	-	-	21	-	-	-	-	-
BYU	-	-	-	-	-	-	25	-	-	-	-	-	-	-	23	21	25	-
California	-	-	-	-	25	21	19	-	-	-	-	-	-	-	-	-	-	-
Cincinnati	21	23	22	19	19	23	21	16	11	9	6	4	8	8	10	12	11	7
Connecticut	16	16	25	-	24	22	23	19	15	17	22	-	-	-	-	-	-	-
Duke	3	3	4	1	1	1	1	1	3	6	7	5	3	7	9	6	8	10
Florida St.	9	7	11	10	10	18	18	23	-	-	19	12	10	9	6	11	10	11
Georgetown	12	13	14	t11	11	11	10	17	20	18	21	23	-	-	-	-	-	-
Georgia Tech	14	14	13	17	17	16	14	10	8	16	18	22	-	-	-	-	-	18
Houston	-	-	-	-	-	-	-	-	-	-	25	-	-	-	-	-	-	-
Indiana	4	4	2	4	4	4	4	5	6	2	2	1	1	1	1	2	2	1
Iowa	11	11	10	8	8	8	8	8	13	14	11	9	13	20	18	15	17	13
Iowa St.	19	24	-	-	-	-	-	-	-	-	-	-	-	-	-	-	-	-
Kansas	2	2	3	2	2	2	2	4	4	1	1	3	7	6	7	8	7	9
Kansas St.	-	-	-	-	-	-	-	-	-	-	-	-	23	-	-	-	-	-
Kentucky	5	5	5	3	3	3	3	2	1	4	4	2	2	2	2	5	4	2
Long Beach St.	-	-	-	-	-	-	-	-	-	25	-	-	-	-	-	-	-	-
Louisville	13	12	12	9	21	-	-	-	-	-	-	-	-	22	-	22	16	15
Marquette	-	-	-	-	-	-	-	-	-	-	24	20	15	24	20	-	-	-
Massachusetts	23	20	19	23	-	-	-	22	-	-	-	-	22	19	21	23	20	14
Memphis	8	9	8	21	-	-	-	-	-	-	-	-	-	-	-	-	-	-
Michigan	1	1	1	6	6	6	6	3	2	5	5	7	4	5	5	4	3	3
Michigan St.	20	18	18	24	23	20	17	14	23	21	-	25	-	-	-	-	-	-
Minnesota	-	-	-	-	-	-	-	-	19	-	-	-	-	-	-	-	-	-
Nebraska	25	25	-	25	20	17	20	-	-	-	-	-	-	-	-	-	-	-
UNLV	22	22	23	22	22	19	16	12	18	15	10	10	12	15	13	16	19	25
New Mexico	-	-	-	-	-	-	-	-	-	-	-	-	-	-	-	-	-	21
New Mexico St.	-	-	21	-	-	-	-	-	-	-	-	-	-	-	-	-	24	24
New Orleans	-	-	-	-	-	-	-	-	-	-	-	-	25	21	19	17	13	17
North Carolina	7	8	7	5	5	5	5	6	5	3	3	6	6	3	3	1	1	4
Ohio St.	-	-	-	-	-	-	-	-	21	24	-	-	-	-	-	-	-	-
Oklahoma	15	15	15	t11	9	9	15	11	10	12	20	16	-	-	-	-	-	-
Oklahoma St.	-	-	-	-	-	-	-	-	-	-	-	-	-	-	-	19	21	23
Pittsburgh	-	-	-	-	-	-	-	24	-	20	13	15	17	17	25	-	-	-
Purdue	-	-	24	18	16	15	13	9	17	13	14	19	18	14	17	24	18	22
St. John's (N.Y.)	-	-	-	-	-	-	-	-	-	-	-	-	-	25	-	25	-	-
Seton Hall	6	6	6	7	7	7	7	7	7	10	9	14	19	16	14	10	9	6
Syracuse	18	17	17	15	14	13	12	21	24	-	-	-	-	-	-	-	-	-
Tulane	17	19	20	20	18	24	-	-	-	-	23	18	20	18	16	20	23	-
UCLA	24	21	16	13	13	12	11	15	16	23	-	-	-	-	-	-	-	-
Utah	-	-	-	-	-	-	-	-	25	22	17	21	16	12	11	9	15	19
Vanderbilt	-	-	-	-	-	25	24	18	-	19	11	11	11	11	8	7	5	8
Virginia	-	-	-	-	-	-	-	25	14	7	15	24	24	23	22	-	-	-
Wake Forest	-	-	-	-	-	-	-	-	-	-	-	13	9	10	12	14	12	16
Western Ky.	-	-	-	-	-	-	-	-	-	-	-	-	-	-	-	-	-	20
Xavier	-	-	-	-	-	-	-	-	-	-	-	-	-	-	24	18	22	-

1993-94

		Nov.		December				January					February				March	
	PS	22	29	6	13	20	27	3	10	17	24	31	7	14	21	28	7	14
UAB	-	-	-	-	-	-	-	-	22	18	20	17	19	21	-	24	22	-
Arizona	18	19	19	14	13	13	12	9	6	9	13	12	16	15	9	8	7	9
Arkansas	3	3	2	1	1	1	1	1	4	3	5	6	3	1	1	1	1	2
Boston College	-	-	-	-	20	18	23	20	20	-	-	-	-	-	21	23	-	-
California	6	12	13	25	-	-	-	24	19	21	-	19	18	19	17	20	16	16
Cincinnati	19	22	23	20	17	20	18	17	21	19	-	25	-	23	-	-	-	25
Connecticut	-	-	-	21	16	15	14	16	14	10	6	5	6	3	5	4	2	4
Duke	4	4	6	4	3	3	3	3	2	5	2	1	2	6	2	2	5	6
Florida	-	-	-	-	-	-	-	-	-	-	-	24	20	17	16	19	17	14
Florida St.	25	-	-	-	-	-	-	-	-	-	-	-	-	-	-	-	-	-
Geo. Washington	24	23	22	24	23	23	21	23	-	-	-	-	-	-	-	-	-	-
Georgetown	15	15	25	-	-	-	-	-	-	-	-	-	-	-	-	-	-	-
Georgia Tech	14	13	17	18	14	14	15	12	17	17	21	-	-	25	23	-	-	-
Illinois	17	17	16	16	19	19	22	21	-	-	-	-	24	-	-	-	-	-
Indiana	12	11	21	12	12	12	13	14	11	8	11	14	12	16	12	17	18	18
Kansas	9	6	3	7	6	6	6	5	3	1	3	3	5	4	10	13	11	13
Kentucky	2	2	1	6	5	5	5	4	8	7	9	7	4	11	7	7	10	7
LSU	-	-	-	-	25	-	-	-	-	-	-	-	-	-	-	-	-	-
Louisville	7	7	11	10	10	11	11	11	15	13	12	9	7	5	13	10	14	10
Marquette	-	-	-	-	-	24	24	25	-	-	22	-	22	22	22	22	19	21
Maryland	-	-	-	-	-	-	-	-	-	25	18	21	-	-	-	-	-	-
Massachusetts	22	18	9	8	8	8	9	8	7	6	8	11	13	10	11	11	9	8
Michigan	5	5	5	3	7	7	7	13	10	15	15	13	11	7	3	3	8	11
Minnesota	10	9	15	17	15	16	16	19	18	20	17	22	23	20	20	18	20	23
Missouri	-	-	-	-	-	-	-	-	t25	-	24	20	15	12	6	6	3	5
Nebraska	-	-	-	-	-	-	-	-	-	-	-	-	-	-	-	-	-	22
New Mexico St.	-	-	-	-	-	-	-	-	-	-	25	23	-	-	25	-	-	-
North Carolina	1	1	4	2	2	2	2	2	1	4	4	2	1	2	4	5	4	1
Oklahoma St.	11	10	8	15	22	22	20	-	-	-	-	-	-	-	24	21	23	19
Penn	-	-	-	-	-	-	-	-	-	-	-	-	-	-	25	24	-	
Purdue	21	21	14	11	11	10	10	10	9	12	7	8	10	9	14	9	6	3
St. Louis	-	-	-	-	-	-	-	-	-	23	23	18	17	18	19	16	21	24
Syracuse	20	20	18	13	21	21	19	18	16	16	14	15	14	14	18	14	13	15
Temple	8	8	7	5	4	4	4	7	13	11	10	10	8	13	8	12	12	12
Texas	-	-	-	-	-	-	-	-	-	-	-	-	-	-	-	-	25	20
UCLA	13	14	10	9	9	9	8	6	5	2	1	4	9	8	15	15	15	17
Vanderbilt	23	24	20	23	24	-	-	22	24	-	-	-	-	-				
Virginia	16	16	12	22	-	-	-	-	-	-	-	-	-	-	-	-	-	-
West Virginia	-	-	-	-	-	-	-	-	23	24	19	-	-	-	-	-	-	-
Western Ky.	-	-	-	-	-	25	25	-	-	-	-	-	-	-	-	-	-	-
Wisconsin	-	25	24	19	18	17	17	15	12	14	16	16	21	24	-	-	-	-
Xavier	-	-	-	-	-	-	-	-	t25	22	-	-	25	-	-	-	-	-

1994-95

		Nov.		December				January					February				March	
	PS	21	28	5	12	19	26	2	9	16	23	30	6	13	20	27	6	13
Alabama	18	25	-	-	-	-	-	-	-	-	-	20	23	18	20	21	20	20
Arizona	5	5	9	8	7	6	10	9	13	11	12	12	9	12	13	12	12	15
Arizona St.	-	-	12	16	13	15	16	15	12	13	13	16	14	13	15	15	18	16
Arkansas	1	1	4	3	4	3	3	3	5	9	9	8	12	10	8	7	5	6
California	-	-	-	-	-	24	14	17	20	-	-	-	-	-	-	-	-	-
Cincinnati	13	12	10	13	17	13	20	-	-	23	19	23	-	-	-	-	-	-
Clemson	-	-	-	-	-	-	-	-	18	-	-	-	-	-	-	-	-	-
Connecticut	19	16	16	10	10	10	8	6	2	2	2	4	3	1	4	4	6	8

		Nov.		December				January					February				March	
	PS	21	28	5	12	19	26	2	9	16	23	30	6	13	20	27	6	13
Duke	8	8	6	9	9	9	7	11	16	-	-	-	-	-	-	-	-	-
Florida	10	10	8	6	8	8	13	13	15	24	23	25	-	-	-	-	-	-
Georgetown	15	14	19	18	15	12	12	12	10	10	14	13	20	-	-	23	24	22
Georgia Tech	23	22	20	17	14	18	17	24	22	22	21	21	18	20	24	-	-	-
Illinois	25	-	-	-	-	23	-	-	-	20	-	-	-	-	-	-	-	-
Indiana	9	11	-	-	-	-	24	21	-	-	-	-	-	-	-	-	-	-
Iowa	-	-	-	-	-	-	-	22	19	-	-	-	-	-	-	-	-	-
Iowa St.	-	-	-	-	-	25	21	16	23	14	11	11	19	21	23	24	-	24
Kansas	11	9	7	4	3	7	6	5	3	7	7	3	2	3	1	3	2	5
Kentucky	4	4	3	7	6	5	5	8	7	5	5	6	5	4	6	5	3	2
Maryland	7	7	11	11	12	11	9	7	9	8	8	5	8	7	7	6	10	10
Massachusetts	3	3	1	5	5	4	4	4	1	1	1	1	4	5	5	8	8	7
Michigan	16	13	17	23	25	-	-	-	-	-	-	-	-	-	-	-	-	-
Michigan St.	20	17	18	15	18	17	15	14	11	12	10	9	7	8	12	10	9	11
Minnesota	-	-	15	12	11	16	-	-	-	-	-	-	-	24	22	-	-	-
Mississippi St.	-	-	-	-	-	-	-	-	-	-	-	-	21	23	16	14	15	18
Missouri	-	-	-	-	-	-	-	-	17	16	20	18	13	9	14	19	17	23
Nebraska	-	-	-	-	-	-	23	19	-	-	-	-	-	-	-	-	-	-
New Mexico St.	-	-	25	22	24	21	22	20	24	19	24	-	-	-	-	-	-	-
North Carolina	2	2	2	1	1	1	1	1	4	3	3	2	1	2	3	2	4	4
Ohio	-	23	14	21	19	-	-	-	-	-	-	-	-	-	-	-	-	-
Oklahoma	-	-	-	-	-	-	-	-	-	-	25	24	-	-	25	16	16	17
Oklahoma St.	21	19	-	-	-	-	-	-	-	-	-	-	24	22	18	18	19	14
Oregon	-	-	-	-	-	-	-	-	25	17	18	22	22	19	-	-	25	-
Penn	-	-	-	-	-	-	-	25	21	25	-	-	-	-	-	-	-	-
Purdue	-	-	-	-	-	-	-	-	-	-	-	-	25	25	21	17	14	12
St. John's (N.Y.)	-	-	-	-	-	-	25	-	-	-	-	-	-	-	-	-	-	-
Stanford	-	-	-	-	-	-	-	23	-	21	17	17	15	17	19	20	-	-
Syracuse	12	18	22	19	16	14	11	10	8	6	6	10	10	11	17	22	21	25
UCLA	6	6	5	2	2	2	2	2	6	4	4	7	6	6	2	1	1	1
Utah	-	-	-	-	-	-	-	-	-	-	-	-	-	-	-	-	22	19
Villanova	22	21	24	24	22	-	-	-	-	-	22	19	16	15	9	11	13	9
Virginia	14	20	23	20	23	22	-	-	-	18	15	15	17	16	11	13	11	13
Wake Forest	24	24	21	25	21	19	18	18	14	15	16	14	11	14	10	9	7	3
Western Ky.	-	-	-	-	-	-	-	-	-	-	-	-	-	-	-	-	23	21
Wisconsin	17	15	13	14	20	20	19	-	-	-	-	-	-	-	-	-	-	-
Xavier	-	-	-	-	-	-	-	-	-	-	-	-	-	-	-	25	-	-

1995-96

		Nov.		December				January					February				March	
	PS	20	27	4	11	18	26	2	8	15	22	29	5	12	19	26	5	12
Arizona	19	4	4	4	3	9	9	18	18	13	14	16	13	13	13	11	11	11
Arkansas	16	-	25	-	-	-	-	-	-	-	-	-	-	-	-	-	-	-
Auburn	-	-	-	-	-	-	-	-	-	23	21	22	-	-	-	-	-	-
Boston College	-	-	-	-	-	-	-	24	-	24	20	21	22	21	20	-	-	-
California	25	-	-	-	-	24	-	-	-	-	25	-	-	-	-	-	-	-
Cincinnati	21	21	21	17	12	9	5	5	4	3	5	5	5	6	6	7	8	7
Clemson	-	-	-	-	-	-	24	22	16	19	18	24	-	-	-	-	-	-
Connecticut	6	6	9	9	8	8	7	7	6	5	4	4	4	3	3	4	3	3
Duke	-	-	12	18	21	20	20	19	-	-	-	-	-	-	-	-	-	-
Eastern Mich.	-	-	-	-	-	-	-	-	-	-	-	23	24	23	-	-	-	-
Geo. Washington	-	-	-	-	-	-	-	-	-	-	-	-	-	-	-	24	-	-
Georgetown	5	5	6	6	7	6	6	6	5	8	6	9	8	14	11	8	6	4
Georgia	-	-	-	-	-	18	16	14	19	22	-	-	-	-	-	-	-	-
Georgia Tech	-	25	20	16	19	21	-	-	-	-	-	25	-	-	23	18	18	13
Green Bay	-	-	-	-	-	-	-	-	-	-	-	-	-	-	25	22	24	-
Illinois	-	-	-	21	16	14	12	13	21	-	-	-	-	-	-	-	-	-
Indiana	23	23	-	-	-	-	-	-	-	-	-	-	-	-	-	-	-	-
Iowa	8	10	11	12	9	10	10	10	11	16	T22	16	19	19	18	20	19	21
Iowa St.	-	-	-	-	-	-	-	-	-	-	-	-	21	22	22	23	23	17
Kansas	2	2	2	1	1	1	4	4	3	4	3	3	3	5	5	3	5	6
Kentucky	1	1	1	5	5	4	2	2	2	2	2	2	2	2	2	1	1	2
Louisville	12	13	18	23	20	25	-	-	-	-	-	-	20	24	21	21	22	24
Marquette	-	-	-	-	-	-	-	-	-	-	24	-	-	-	-	-	21	20
Maryland	15	14	19	20	-	-	-	-	-	-	-	-	-	-	-	-	-	-
Massachusetts	7	7	5	3	3	2	1	1	1	1	1	1	1	1	1	2	2	1
Memphis	13	12	7	7	6	5	3	3	9	9	12	11	15	15	19	14	14	16
Michigan	17	16	24	22	18	17	19	21	23	20	16	20	23	-	-	-	-	-
Mississippi St.	9	9	8	8	15	16	17	17	12	21	-	-	-	25	-	-	-	-
Missouri	14	15	13	11	14	15	18	-	-	-	-	-	-	-	-	-	-	-
New Mexico	-	-	-	-	-	-	-	25	25	-	-	-	-	-	-	-	-	23
North Carolina	20	20	17	13	10	11	11	16	10	10	11	8	12	17	17	19	20	25
Penn St.	-	-	-	-	-	-	-	-	20	14	14	10	10	9	14	12	16	18
Purdue	24	24	-	-	-	-	-	-	22	17	19	17	14	11	7	5	4	5
Santa Clara	-	-	-	25	22	-	-	-	-	-	-	-	-	-	-	-	-	-
Stanford	18	18	16	24	-	-	-	-	24	-	-	-	25	20	24	25	-	-
Syracuse	-	-	-	-	25	19	13	11	14	12	17	18	18	16	15	15	13	15
Texas	-	-	-	-	-	-	-	23	-	-	-	-	-	-	-	-	-	-
Texas Tech	-	-	-	-	-	-	-	-	-	25	T22	15	13	12	9	9	7	8
Tulsa	-	-	-	-	-	-	25	-	-	-	-	-	-	-	-	-	-	-
UCLA	4	4	23	-	24	-	23	20	17	13	15	19	17	18	16	17	17	14
Utah	10	8	14	14	13	13	15	15	13	15	10	7	7	7	8	10	10	12
Villanova	3	3	3	2	2	7	8	8	7	7	7	6	6	4	4	6	9	10
Virginia	19	17	15	15	23	23	22	-	-	-	-	-	-	-	-	-	-	-
Virginia Tech	22	22	22	19	17	22	21	18	15	11	8	13	11	10	12	16	15	22
Wake Forest	11	11	10	10	11	12	14	12	8	6	9	12	9	8	10	13	12	9

1996-97

		Nov.		December					January				February				March	
	PS	19	26	3	10	17	24	31	7	14	21	28	4	11	18	25	4	11
Alabama	-	-	-	-	24	20	19	-	-	-	-	-	-	-	-	-	-	-
Arizona	19	19	11	15	8	6	9	9	7	6	11	10	14	11	13	15	12	15
Arkansas	13	16	16	22	20	19	22	22	-	-	-	-	-	-	-	-	-	-
Boston College	21	21	23	20	25	-	25	25	23	19	22	-	-	-	-	-	-	23
California	-	-	-	-	-	-	-	-	-	-	-	-	-	-	25	-	-	-
Col. of Charleston	-	-	-	-	-	-	-	-	-	-	-	-	-	25	22	20	17	16
Cincinnati	1	1	1	4	7	7	7	6	6	4	9	8	12	8	11	9	10	10
Clemson	20	12	10	12	10	8	6	5	5	3	2	7	10	7	8	12	13	14
Colorado	-	-	-	-	-	-	-	-	-	-	18	18	15	15	21	19	18	24
Duke	10	10	6	10	14	11	12	13	10	13	10	12	8	6	6	7	7	8
Fresno St.	14	14	15	13	16	21	-	-	-	-	-	-	-	-	-	-	-	-
Geo. Washington	24	24	25	-	-	-	-	-	-	-	-	-	-	-	-	-	-	-
Georgia	-	-	-	-	-	-	-	-	24	21	-	-	-	-	-	-	24	17
Illinois	-	-	-	-	-	-	-	24	25	-	-	-	-	20	23	21	15	19
Indiana	-	22	20	8	12	13	13	12	15	17	21	17	24	-	24	22	25	-
Iowa	23	25	-	-	-	-	-	-	-	-	-	-	25	-	-	-	-	-
Iowa St.	11	11	9	9	6	5	5	4	4	8	14	11	6	9	7	13	16	18
Kansas	2	2	2	1	1	1	1	1	1	1	1	1	1	1	1	1	1	1
Kentucky	3	8	8	6	3	3	3	3	3	5	3	3	3	4	3	3	6	5
Louisville	-	-	-	-	22	18	16	14	14	10	6	9	11	17	15	17	20	25
Marquette	25	-	-	-	-	-	-	-	-	-	25	24	-	-	-	-	-	-
Maryland	-	-	-	-	-	25	21	19	19	11	7	5	7	10	14	16	22	22
Massachusetts	15	15	17	-	-	-	-	-	-	-	-	-	-	-	-	-	-	-
Michigan	9	9	7	7	5	4	4	8	16	18	13	16	13	14	18	24	-	-
Minnesota	22	23	24	16	17	16	15	15	11	7	8	6	4	3	2	2	2	3
Mississippi	-	-	-	-	-	-	-	-	-	20	-	-	-	-	-	-	-	-
New Mexico	17	18	19	11	15	15	14	16	18	12	15	13	9	13	10	11	14	11
North Carolina	8	7	14	14	11	12	11	11	13	22	19	19	20	16	12	8	5	4
Oregon	-	-	-	-	-	-	24	20	17	24	-	-	-	-	-	-	-	-
St. Joseph's	-	-	-	-	-	-	-	-	-	-	-	-	-	-	-	23	19	12
South Carolina	-	-	-	-	-	-	-	-	-	-	-	25	19	12	9	6	4	6
Stanford	18	20	21	24	21	22	23	21	21	15	17	15	18	22	20	25	23	21
Syracuse	12	13	12	19	-	-	-	-	-	-	-	-	-	-	-	-	-	-
Texas	16	17	18	18	13	14	18	18	22	23	23	23	-	-	-	-	-	-
Texas Tech	-	-	-	-	18	23	-	23	20	25	20	22	23	21	-	-	-	-
Tulane	-	-	-	-	-	-	-	-	-	-	-	-	21	23	-	-	-	-
Tulsa	-	-	22	21	-	-	-	-	-	-	24	21	22	-	-	-	-	-
UCLA	5	5	13	17	23	24	-	-	-	-	-	-	-	24	17	10	9	7
Utah	6	4	4	3	9	9	8	7	9	9	5	4	5	5	5	4	3	2
Villanova	7	6	5	5	4	10	10	10	8	16	12	14	16	18	19	18	21	20
Virginia	-	-	-	25	-	-	-	-	-	-	-	-	-	-	-	-	-	-
Wake Forest	4	3	3	2	2	2	2	2	2	2	4	2	2	2	4	5	8	9
Xavier	-	-	-	23	19	17	17	17	12	14	16	20	17	19	16	14	11	13

1997-98

		Nov.		December					January				February				March	
	PS	18	25	2	9	16	23	30	6	13	20	27	3	10	17	24	3	10
Arizona	1	1	1	4	6	5	5	8	5	5	6	6	4	3	3	2	2	4
Arkansas	-	-	-	18	15	13	12	23	22	22	18	15	14	12	16	12	16	17
Charlotte	18	17	25	-	-	-	-	-	-	-	-	-	-	-	-	-	-	-
Cincinnati	-	-	-	-	-	-	-	-	-	-	21	18	20	19	17	17	14	9
Clemson	5	5	13	17	17	-	21	21	24	-	25	-	-	-	-	-	-	-
Connecticut	12	12	11	13	13	12	11	10	8	10	8	9	7	6	7	6	6	6
Duke	3	3	3	1	1	3	3	3	2	2	1	1	1	2	2	1	1	3
Florida St.	-	-	-	19	16	17	17	15	13	17	20	-	-	-	-	-	-	-
Fresno St.	13	13	12	16	18	-	-	-	-	-	-	-	-	-	-	-	-	-
Geo. Washington	-	-	-	-	-	-	-	-	-	-	-	-	22	17	24	-	-	-
Georgia	19	25	22	21	23	20	-	-	-	-	-	-	-	-	-	-	-	-
Georgia Tech	-	-	-	22	24	-	-	-	-	-	-	-	-	-	-	-	-	-
Hawaii	-	-	-	-	-	-	-	-	21	24	24	-	-	-	-	-	-	-
Illinois	-	-	-	-	-	-	-	-	-	-	-	-	-	-	23	22	18	22
Illinois St.	-	24	-	-	-	-	-	-	-	-	-	-	-	-	-	-	-	-
Indiana	17	23	21	-	-	-	-	-	-	-	-	25	-	-	-	-	-	-
Iowa	15	14	14	10	10	15	15	14	11	13	10	16	24	-	-	-	-	-
Kansas	2	2	2	2	3	2	2	2	4	3	3	5	3	4	4	4	4	2
Kentucky	8	9	8	7	4	4	4	6	6	6	7	7	8	7	8	7	7	5
Louisville	25	22	19	-	-	-	-	-	-	-	-	-	-	-	-	-	-	-
Marquette	-	-	-	-	-	-	-	25	20	23	-	-	-	-	-	-	-	-
Maryland	-	-	24	23	19	22	20	20	-	-	-	23	25	24	25	-	21	20
Massachusetts	-	-	-	-	-	-	-	-	-	-	-	-	23	20	18	20	-	-
Michigan	-	-	-	-	-	21	-	18	17	19	16	19	18	21	22	21	17	12
Michigan St.	-	-	-	-	-	-	-	-	-	-	-	22	16	13	14	10	12	16
Mississippi	23	21	17	14	21	18	16	16	14	11	13	12	17	18	15	13	10	13
Murray St.	-	-	-	-	-	-	-	-	-	-	-	-	-	-	-	-	-	25
New Mexico	11	11	10	8	14	14	14	12	12	T15	17	14	12	11	11	16	20	18

		Nov.		December					January				February				March	
	PS	18	25	2	9	16	23	30	6	13	20	27	3	10	17	24	3	10
North Carolina	4	4	4	3	2	1	1	1	1	1	2	2	2	1	1	3	4	1
Oklahoma	20	19	18	-	-	-	-	-	-	-	-	-	-	-	-	-	-	-
Oklahoma St.	-	-	-	-	-	-	-	-	-	25	-	-	-	-	-	25	25	-
Princeton	-	-	-	25	22	19	18	17	15	12	11	11	11	10	9	9	8	8
Purdue	9	8	6	6	8	8	7	5	9	9	12	10	10	8	5	11	9	11
Rhode Island	21	20	23	-	-	-	22	24	23	20	22	21	-	25	-	-	-	-
South Carolina	7	6	5	5	5	6	10	11	16	14	14	13	13	15	13	14	15	14
Stanford	14	15	15	12	11	9	8	7	7	7	5	4	9	14	10	8	11	10
Syracuse	-	-	-	-	-	25	19	19	18	T15	15	20	19	23	21	23	22	21
Temple	24	18	20	20	20	16	24	-	-	-	-	-	-	-	-	24	24	24
Texas	22	-	-	-	-	-	-	-	-	-	-	-	-	-	-	-	-	-
TCU	-	-	-	-	-	24	25	-	-	-	-	-	-	22	19	15	13	15
UCLA	6	7	7	15	12	11	9	9	10	8	9	8	6	9	12	18	19	19
Utah	16	16	16	11	9	7	6	4	3	4	4	3	5	5	6	5	5	7
Wake Forest	-	-	-	24	25	23	-	-	-	-	-	-	-	-	-	-	-	-
West Virginia	-	-	-	-	-	-	23	22	25	21	23	17	15	16	20	19	23	-
Xavier	10	10	9	9	7	10	13	13	19	18	19	24	21	-	-	-	-	23

1998-99

		Nov.		December					January				February				March	
	PS	17	24	1	8	15	22	29	5	12	19	26	2	9	16	23	2	9
Arizona	18	12	11	13	8	t8	8	6	11	7	9	13	10	10	8	7	13	12
Arkansas	19	19	21	19	23	20	19	20	18	24	22	21	23	-	-	-	22	17
Auburn	-	-	-	-	-	19	18	17	14	8	6	7	6	3	3	2	4	4
Charlotte	-	-	-	-	-	-	-	-	-	-	-	-	-	-	-	-	-	24
Col. of Charleston	-	-	-	-	-	-	-	-	-	-	-	-	22	20	18	17	16	16
Cincinnati	15	17	15	6	4	4	4	3	3	3	5	5	3	4	9	9	7	11
Clemson	-	24	22	24	17	16	16	14	20	25	-	-	-	-	-	-	-	-
Connecticut	2	2	2	1	1	1	1	1	1	1	1	1	1	2	2	4	3	3
Duke	1	1	1	4	3	2	2	2	2	2	2	2	2	1	1	1	1	1
Florida	-	-	-	-	-	-	-	-	-	-	-	25	-	23	23	19	21	23
Indiana	22	21	17	16	11	10	10	8	13	23	18	20	21	17	19	20	17	19
Iowa	-	-	-	-	-	25	21	21	19	12	14	16	14	19	20	18	20	21
Kansas	8	8	8	7	10	13	13	18	16	15	19	22	-	24	-	-	-	22
Kentucky	4	4	4	8	5	3	3	7	5	6	7	6	5	8	6	13	14	8
Louisville	-	-	-	-	-	-	-	-	-	-	24	-	-	-	-	-	-	-
Maryland	6	6	5	2	2	5	5	4	6	5	4	4	7	7	5	5	5	5
Massachusetts	24	23	-	-	-	-	-	-	-	-	-	-	-	-	-	-	-	-
Miami (Fla.)	-	-	-	-	-	-	-	-	-	-	25	23	25	16	15	11	9	10
Miami (Ohio)	-	-	24	22	-	-	-	-	-	-	-	-	-	-	25	-	-	-
Michigan St.	5	5	7	9	14	14	15	13	12	14	11	8	8	5	4	3	2	2
Minnesota	-	-	-	-	24	17	17	16	17	19	17	19t	18	22	-	-	23	-
Missouri	-	-	-	-	-	-	-	-	-	-	-	-	24	-	22	-	24	-
New Mexico	t20	20	20	17	12	11	11	15	15	16	12	18	17	25	24	21	25	25
North Carolina	11	10	9	3	7	7	7	9	10	9	10	10	12	12	14	14	15	13
Ohio St.	-	-	-	-	-	-	-	-	25	21	-	15	15	13	11	10	11	14
Oklahoma	-	-	-	-	-	24	23	-	-	-	-	-	-	-	-	-	-	-
Oklahoma St.	13	13	12	11	19	18	25	25	22	22	23	-	-	-	-	-	-	-
Pittsburgh	-	-	-	20	20	22	24	23	-	-	-	-	-	-	-	-	-	-
Purdue	16	15	14	14	9	t8	9	11	7	13	16	14t	18	21	17	23	-	-
Rhode Island	23	25	-	-	-	-	-	-	-	-	-	-	-	-	-	-	-	-
St. John's (N.Y.)	-	-	23	25	18	15	14	12	9	11	8	9	9	11	10	8	10	9
Stanford	3	3	3	5	6	6	6	5	4	4	3	3	4	6	7	6	6	7
Syracuse	t20	22	19	12	13	21	22	22	21	18	20	17	16	18	21	t24	-	-
Temple	7	7	6	10	16	-	-	-	-	-	-	-	-	-	-	t24	-	-
Tennessee	9	18	25	-	21	-	-	-	-	-	-	-	-	-	-	-	18	20
Texas	-	-	-	-	-	-	-	-	-	-	-	-	-	-	-	22	-	-
TCU	25	-	-	-	-	-	-	24	24	20	21	24	-	-	-	-	-	-
UCLA	12	11	10	18	15	12	12	10	8	10	13	11	13	9	16	15	12	15
Utah	10	9	18	21	25	-	-	-	-	-	-	-	20	14	12	12	8	6
Washington	14	14	16	15	22	-	-	-	-	-	-	-	-	-	-	-	-	-
Wisconsin	-	-	-	-	-	23	20	19	23	17	15	12	11	15	13	16	19	18
Xavier	17	16	13	23	-	-	-	-	-	-	-	-	-	-	-	-	-	-

1999-2000

		Nov.			December				January				February					March	
	PS	16	23	30	7	14	21	28	4	11	18	25	1	8	15	22	29	7	14
Arizona	9	10	8	4	2	4	3	5	5	2	2	5	9	7	4	4	3	9	4
Auburn	4	3	2	7	8	6	7	4	4	4	4	7	10	9	12	11	19	-	24
Cincinnati	2	1	1	1	1	1	4	3	3	1	1	1	1	1	1	3	2	1	7
Connecticut	1	8	7	5	6	3	2	2	2	5	8	6	7	13	18	22	24	21	20
DePaul	20	20	18	22	20	19	24	24	23	21	23	-	-	-	-	-	-	-	-
Duke	10	18	16	17	14	11	10	9	8	6	5	3	3	3	3	2	4	3	1
Florida	8	7	6	11	9	9	8	6	6	10	9	10	12	12	11	9	8	11	13
Gonzaga	24	25	25	25	24	22	22	-	-	-	-	-	-	-	-	-	-	-	-
Illinois	16	17	15	16	22	20	15	20	19	22	-	-	-	-	-	-	25	25	21
Indiana	-	-	-	23	15	21	20	12	10	9	11	14	11	10	10	16	14	18	22
Iowa	-	22	23	-	-	-	-	-	-	-	-	-	-	-	-	-	-	-	-
Iowa St.	-	-	-	-	-	-	-	-	-	-	-	-	20	17	14	17	10	7	6
Kansas	11	11	10	6	5	8	12	10	9	8	7	12	15	20	24	23	23	24	-
Kentucky	14	14	11	13	23	-	-	-	25	20	18	16	14	11	19	18	22	16	19
LSU	-	-	-	-	-	-	-	-	21	24	-	-	22	25	16	15	12	10	10
Louisville	-	-	-	-	-	-	-	-	-	25	-	-	-	-	-	-	-	-	-
Maryland	-	-	24	24	21	16	17	14	12	18	24	22	25	23	22	19	17	20	17
Miami (Fla.)	25	-	-	-	-	-	-	-	-	-	-	-	-	-	-	-	-	23	23
Michigan St.	3	2	3	8	4	5	5	8	11	11	10	9	8	6	6	5	7	5	2
North Carolina	6	5	4	2	7	7	6	13	14	13	21	-	-	-	-	-	-	-	-
North Caro. St.	-	-	-	-	-	25	-	-	-	-	21	-	-	-	-	-	-	-	
Ohio St.	5	4	12	15	13	12	16	15	13	17	13	8	5	5	7	6	6	4	8
Oklahoma	-	-	-	-	-	23	21	22	20	16	17	18	18	16	20	20	21	15	12
Oklahoma St.	22	23	21	21	17	14	13	11	16	14	12	15	13	14	8	10	13	17	14
Oregon	-	-	-	-	-	-	-	-	-	-	-	-	23	24	-	-	-	-	-
Purdue	23	24	22	19	25	24	-	-	-	-	-	-	-	-	25	21	20	22	25
St. John's (N.Y.)	18	15	-	-	-	-	-	-	-	-	19	25	-	-	-	-	18	19	9
Seton Hall	-	-	-	-	-	-	-	-	-	-	-	-	-	-	23	-	-	-	-
Southern Cal.	-	-	-	-	-	-	-	-	-	-	-	23	-	-	-	-	-	-	-
Stanford	13	9	9	3	3	2	1	1	1	3	3	2	2	2	2	1	1	2	3
Syracuse	17	13	14	14	12	10	9	7	7	7	6	4	4	4	9	13	9	12	16
Temple	7	6	5	10	19	17	19	17	-	23	-	23	21	19	15	8	5	6	5
Tennessee	19	19	17	18	16	13	11	16	15	12	16	11	6	8	5	7	11	8	11
Texas	21	21	20	9	10	15	14	18	17	15	14	17	16	18	17	14	16	13	15
Tulsa	-	-	-	-	-	-	-	25	22	19	15	13	17	15	13	12	15	14	18
UCLA	12	12	13	12	11	18	18	23	24	-	25	-	-	-	-	-	-	-	-
Utah	15	16	19	20	-	-	-	21	18	-	22	19	19	21	21	25	-	-	-
Vanderbilt	-	-	-	-	-	-	-	-	-	-	20	20	24	22	-	24	-	-	-
Wake Forest	-	-	-	-	18	25	23	19	-	-	-	-	-	-	-	-	-	-	-

2000-01

		Nov.			December				January					February				March	
	PS	14	21	28	5	12	19	26	2	9	16	23	30	6	13	20	27	6	13
Alabama	-	-	-	-	23	18	17	20	18	16	t15	18	17	18	21	14	20	-	-
Arizona	1	1	1	5	5	7	10	12	16	21	17	12	7	11	8	8	9	8	5
Arkansas	t15	15	24	25	21	25	25	-	-	-	-	-	-	-	-	-	-	-	-
Boston College	-	-	-	-	-	-	-	-	-	24	25	23	20	17	9	10	11	10	7
Cincinnati	18	17	16	22	18	17	22	19	25	-	-	-	-	-	-	-	-	-	-
Connecticut	14	13	12	16	15	11	11	10	10	13	t15	24	-	-	-	-	-	-	-
Dayton	-	-	-	24	-	-	-	-	-	-	-	-	-	-	-	-	-	-	-
DePaul	21	22	21	-	-	-	-	-	-	-	-	-	-	-	-	-	-	-	-
Duke	2	2	2	1	1	1	1	3	3	2	2	2	2	3	3	4	2	3	1
Florida	11	11	11	10	8	8	7	5	5	8	7	14	13	8	11	7	6	5	8
Fresno St.	-	-	-	-	-	-	-	-	-	-	-	22	19	23	20	-	-	25	-
Georgetown	-	-	-	-	-	24	23	21	19	12	9	10	14	15	18	21	21	18	21
Georgia	-	-	-	-	-	-	-	-	-	-	-	-	25	-	-	-	-	-	-
Illinois	8	8	8	9	9	5	5	9	9	7	11	7	6	7	4	3	5	4	4
Indiana	-	-	-	-	-	-	-	-	-	-	-	-	-	-	-	-	-	-	20
Iowa	-	-	-	-	-	22	19	23	-	-	14	21	18	14	25	-	-	-	24
Iowa St.	25	-	-	-	25	-	-	25	23	18	23	17	15	12	7	6	8	7	10
Kansas	7	4	3	2	3	10	9	7	7	5	5	4	3	5	6	11	10	9	12
Kentucky	12	20	22	-	-	-	-	-	-	-	-	-	-	-	22	13	15	15	9
Maryland	5	6	6	13	19	20	20	18	17	14	12	8	9	13	17	20	16	11	11
Michigan St.	3	3	4	3	2	2	2	1	1	3	3	3	5	4	5	5	3	2	3
Mississippi	-	-	-	-	-	23	24	24	22	20	21	19	-	25	16	12	14	14	14
Missouri	-	-	-	-	-	-	-	-	-	-	20	-	-	-	-	-	-	-	-
No. Carolina	6	7	7	6	14	15	15	14	13	9	6	5	4	1	1	2	4	6	6
Notre Dame	t15	16	14	11	10	21	21	22	21	25	-	-	23	20	14	18	13	19	19
Ohio St.	-	-	-	-	-	-	-	-	-	-	-	-	-	-	-	-	-	24	-
Oklahoma	22	21	19	14	20	19	18	17	15	22	22	-	24	21	13	16	17	16	13
Providence	-	-	-	-	-	-	-	-	-	-	-	-	-	-	-	25	-	-	-
St. John's (N.Y.)	24	23	19	24	-	-	-	-	-	-	-	-	-	-	-	-	-	-	
St. Joseph's	-	-	-	-	-	-	-	-	-	-	-	-	-	-	-	23	18	21	22
Seton Hall	10	10	10	8	7	9	8	11	11	15	18	16	22	-	-	-	-	-	-
Southern Cal	23	23	20	15	12	13	13	16	20	19	24	25	21	22	-	-	-	-	-
Stanford	4	5	5	4	4	3	3	2	2	1	1	1	1	2	2	1	1	1	2
Syracuse	-	-	-	20	13	12	12	15	14	11	8	11	12	9	10	17	19	17	17
Temple	-	-	-	17	-	-	-	-	-	-	-	-	-	-	-	-	-	-	-
Tennessee	9	9	9	7	6	4	4	6	6	4	4	6	8	10	15	22	-	-	-
Texas	-	-	-	-	-	-	-	-	24	23	-	20	-	-	-	-	24	20	18
UCLA	17	14	15	-	-	-	-	-	-	-	-	-	-	-	24	15	12	13	15
Utah	13	12	13	18	22	-	-	-	-	-	-	-	-	-	-	-	-	-	-
Virginia	24	25	25	21	16	14	14	8	8	10	13	13	11	6	12	9	7	12	16
Wake Forest	20	18	17	12	11	6	6	4	4	6	10	9	16	19	23	24	23	22	23
Wisconsin	19	19	18	23	17	16	16	13	12	17	19	15	10	16	19	19	22	23	25
Xavier	-	-	-	-	-	-	-	-	-	-	-	-	-	24	-	-	25	-	-

2001-02

		Nov.		December				January					February				March	
	PS	20	27	4	11	18	25	1	8	15	22	29	5	12	19	26	5	12
Alabama	24	22	21	16	22	23	21	18	t14	16	14	7	5	7	5	6	8	8
Arizona	-	8	4	7	6	11	14	15	20	15	10	19	11	9	14	14	15	7
Ball St.	-	-	16	15	20	21	-	-	-	-	-	-	-	-	-	-	-	-
Boston College	17	17	15	13	11	10	11	11	16	22	-	-	-	-	-	-	-	-
Butler	-	-	-	-	-	-	23	20	24	-	-	-	-	-	-	-	-	-
California	-	-	-	-	-	-	-	-	-	-	-	-	-	-	-	21	25	-
Cincinnati	-	-	-	-	-	25	17	13	10	7	4	4	6	5	4	4	5	5
Connecticut	-	-	-	-	-	-	-	-	-	-	25	17	-	-	-	23	19	10

		Nov.		December				January					February				March	
	PS	20	27	4	11	18	25	1	8	15	22	29	5	12	19	26	5	12
Duke	1	1	1	1	1	1	1	1	2	1	1	1	1	1	3	3	3	1
Florida	6	7	6	6	5	4	3	3	3	2	5	5	8	6	8	8	11	15
Fresno St.	-	23	24	21	-	-	-	-	-	-	-	-	-	-	-	-	-	-
Georgetown	14	16	18	19	18	16	20	24	-	-	-	-	-	-	-	-	-	-
Georgia	-	-	-	-	-	-	-	-	-	20	15	16	17	21	18	16	17	23
Gonzaga	-	-	-	-	25	24	22	22	18	13	16	11	9	8	7	7	6	6
Hawaii	-	-	-	-	-	-	-	-	-	-	-	-	-	-	-	-	-	25
Illinois	3	2	2	5	10	9	7	7	9	11	9	12	21	18	16	15	10	13
Indiana	22	20	-	-	21	-	-	-	-	25	-	-	-	22	23	25	23	-
Iowa	9	9	7	12	15	12	9	9	13	17	-	-	-	-	-	-	-	-
Kansas	7	4	8	4	4	3	2	2	1	4	2	2	2	2	1	1	1	2
Kentucky	4	10	13	11	9	7	6	6	8	12	8	10	7	10	12	11	12	16
Marquette	-	-	23	17	14	14	19	25	-	-	-	-	18	11	9	9	13	12
Maryland	2	6	5	3	3	2	8	8	4	3	3	3	3	3	2	2	2	4
Memphis	12	12	20	22	-	-	-	-	-	-	-	-	-	-	-	-	-	-
Miami (Fla.)	-	-	-	-	-	-	24	21	21	24	22	15	12	13	17	22	20	21
Michigan St.	15	13	22	24	23	17	13	19	25	-	-	-	-	-	-	-	-	-
Mississippi St.	-	-	-	-	-	-	-	-	22	-	-	-	-	-	-	-	-	17
Missouri	8	5	3	2	2	8	10	17	17	21	18	22	22	-	-	-	-	-
North Carolina	19	-	-	-	-	-	-	-	-	-	-	-	-	-	-	-	-	-
North Caro. St.	-	-	-	-	-	-	-	-	-	-	-	-	24	-	-	-	-	
Ohio St.	-	-	-	-	-	-	-	-	-	-	20	25	16	23	19	18	21	14
Oklahoma	25	-	-	-	24	22	12	10	5	5	6	6	4	4	6	5	4	3
Oklahoma St.	18	15	14	10	8	6	5	5	6	6	11	9	14	16	13	12	14	20
Oregon	-	-	-	-	-	-	-	-	-	23	19	-	13	17	15	13	9	11
Pittsburgh	-	-	-	-	-	-	-	-	23	-	-	21	-	14	11	10	7	9
St. Joseph's	10	19	19	18	16	15	-	-	-	-	-	-	-	-	-	-	-	-
Southern Cal	20	24	-	-	-	-	-	-	-	18	23	23	25	25	t20	19	22	18
Stanford	13	14	11	14	12	13	16	12	t14	19	17	18	20	12	10	17	16	24
Syracuse	21	18	12	9	13	18	18	16	12	8	12	14	23	-	-	-	-	-
Temple	16	25	-	-	-	-	-	-	-	-	-	-	-	-	-	-	-	-
Texas	23	-	-	-	-	-	-	-	-	-	24	-	-	-	-	-	-	-
Texas Tech	-	-	-	-	-	-	-	-	-	-	-	20	24	-	-	-	-	-
UCLA	5	3	10	20	17	19	15	14	11	9	13	13	15	20	25	-	-	-
Virginia	11	11	9	8	7	5	4	4	7	10	7	8	10	15	22	-	-	-
Wake Forest	-	-	25	23	19	20	25	23	19	14	21	24	19	19	t20	24	-	-
Western Ky.	-	21	17	25	-	-	-	-	-	-	-	-	-	-	24	20	18	19
Xavier	-	-	-	-	-	-	-	-	-	-	-	-	-	-	-	-	24	22

2002-03

		Nov.		December					January				February				March		
	PS	19	26	3	10	17	24	31	7	14	21	28	4	11	18	25	4	11	18
Alabama	8	4	4	3	2	2	1	1	4	9	15	23	22	-	-	-	-	-	-
Arizona	1	1	1	1	1	1	4	4	2	2	1	1	2	1	1	1	1	1	2
Auburn	-	-	-	-	-	-	-	-	-	-	24	-	-	-	-	-	-	-	-
California	-	-	-	-	-	-	-	-	-	-	25	20	-	22	18	23	22	24	-
Col. of Charleston	-	-	-	-	25	-	-	-	-	-	-	-	-	-	-	-	-	-	-
Cincinnati	23	23	21	-	23	-	-	-	-	-	-	-	-	-	-	-	-	-	-
Connecticut	15	14	12	11	9	8	6	5	3	t6	11	14	18	23	-	-	-	-	23
Creighton	-	-	-	-	-	20	18	15	16	13	10	16	13	12	17	17	19	19	15
Dayton	-	-	-	-	-	-	-	-	-	-	-	-	-	-	25	25	21	22	16
Duke	6	6	6	4	3	3	3	3	1	1	3	5	9	8	8	6	10	12	7
Florida	7	8	7	8	14	13	12	12	11	t6	5	4	1	4	7	4	3	7	10
Georgia	16	18	17	-	-	-	-	-	20	20	19	15	17	20	22	21	25	21	25
Gonzaga	22	21	20	-	-	-	-	-	-	-	-	-	-	-	-	-	-	-	-
Illinois	-	-	-	25	15	12	7	11	10	8	18	13	16	14	20	18	14	13	11
Indiana	21	22	19	10	7	6	10	17	15	18	14	19	-	-	-	-	-	-	-
Kansas	2	2	2	14	20	19	19	18	14	12	6	12	12	9	6	7	6	4	6
Kentucky	17	17	15	18	12	18	14	20	18	16	8	7	6	3	2	2	2	2	1
LSU	-	-	-	-	-	-	24	21	-	23	-	-	-	-	-	-	-	-	-
Louisville	-	-	-	-	-	-	-	24	19	15	9	8	5	2	4	11	15	20	14
Marquette	18	16	13	13	16	14	13	13	24	21	20	18	15	11	11	10	8	8	9
Maryland	13	t12	11	9	18	24	23	22	t21	17	12	10	8	16	13	14	13	14	17
Memphis	-	-	-	-	-	-	-	-	-	-	-	-	-	-	-	24	18	16	19
Michigan St.	9	9	9	21	21	15	15	14	25	-	-	-	-	-	-	-	-	-	-
Minnesota	24	24	24	20	-	25	-	-	-	-	-	-	-	-	-	-	-	-	-
Mississippi St.	12	t12	23	24	24	16	16	8	7	14	22	21	23	19	19	20	23	-	20
Missouri	19	20	18	15	11	11	17	16	13	11	21	25	21	21	-	-	-	-	24
North Carolina	-	-	-	12	22	23	22	-	-	-	-	-	-	-	-	-	-	-	-
Notre Dame	-	-	-	-	10	9	8	6	5	10	16	11	10	10	12	9	16	17	22
Oklahoma	3	7	8	6	6	7	5	10	9	5	7	6	7	5	5	3	5	6	3
Oklahoma St.	-	-	-	-	-	-	-	-	-	24	13	9	11	13	16	16	20	23	-
Oregon	11	10	10	7	5	5	11	9	12	22	23	22	-	-	-	-	-	-	-
Pittsburgh	5	5	5	5	4	4	2	2	6	3	2	2	4	7	9	8	7	5	4
Purdue	-	-	-	-	-	-	-	-	-	-	-	-	24	-	24	-	-	-	-
St. Joseph's	-	-	-	-	-	-	-	-	-	-	-	-	-	25	-	-	-	25	-
Stanford	-	-	-	17	19	17	-	-	-	-	-	-	25	24	21	19	17	15	18
Syracuse	-	-	-	-	-	-	-	-	-	25	-	24	19	17	15	15	12	11	13
Texas	4	3	3	2	8	10	9	7	8	4	4	3	3	6	3	5	4	3	5
Texas Tech	-	-	-	-	-	-	-	25	23	-	-	-	-	-	-	-	-	-	-
Tulsa	25	25	22	19	17	22	20	-	-	-	-	-	-	-	-	-	-	-	-
UCLA	14	15	14	-	-	-	-	-	-	-	-	-	-	-	-	-	-	-	-
Utah	-	-	-	-	-	-	-	-	-	-	-	-	-	-	23	22	-	-	-
Virginia	-	-	-	22	-	-	-	-	-	-	-	-	-	-	-	-	-	-	-
Wake Forest	-	-	-	-	-	-	25	23	17	19	17	17	14	15	10	12	9	9	8
Western Ky.	20	19	-	-	-	-	-	-	-	-	-	-	-	-	-	-	-	-	-
Wisconsin	-	-	25	23	-	-	-	-	-	-	-	-	-	-	-	-	24	18	21
Xavier	10	11	16	16	13	21	21	19	t21	-	-	-	20	18	14	13	11	10	12

2003-04

		Nov.	December					January				February				March		
	PS	25	2	9	16	23	31	6	13	20	27	3	10	17	24	2	9	16
Air Force	-	-	-	-	-	-	-	-	-	-	-	-	-	-	-	-	25	-
Arizona	4	4	7	9	7	5	4	3	7	14	9	12	16	14	17	22	21	22
Boston College	-	-	-	-	-	-	-	-	-	-	-	-	-	-	-	-	-	t25
Cincinnati	18	19	19	18	16	14	12	11	10	6	8	10	13	17	15	13	13	11
Connecticut	1	1	3	2	1	1	1	1	1	4	6	5	5	8	8	7	9	7
Creighton	-	-	-	-	-	-	-	-	24	-	-	-	-	-	-	-	-	-
Dayton	-	-	-	25	24	23	-	-	-	-	-	-	-	-	-	-	-	-
Duke	2	2	6	4	3	3	2	2	2	1	1	1	1	3	5	3	5	6
Florida	8	8	2	1	15	13	14	14	15	17	22	21	22	-	-	-	-	-
Georgia Tech	-	-	13	10	5	4	3	8	12	11	14	15	15	18	18	19	14	14
Gonzaga	10	16	17	17	13	15	16	16	16	15	10	8	7	6	4	4	3	3
Illinois	13	12	11	14	21	21	20	19	25	-	-	-	-	-	23	18	12	13
Iowa	-	-	-	24	-	-	-	-	-	-	-	-	-	-	-	-	-	-
Kansas	6	6	1	5	6	12	13	13	14	12	15	20	12	21	20	21	18	16
Kentucky	11	10	9	8	2	2	8	7	5	9	5	9	8	9	9	9	8	2
LSU	-	-	-	-	-	-	-	-	-	-	-	-	-	24	-	-	-	-
Louisville	16	17	-	-	20	20	11	10	8	5	4	6	9	10	21	25	-	-
Marquette	23	23	24	22	23	-	25	23	21	-	-	-	-	-	-	-	-	-
Maryland	-	-	-	-	25	24	-	-	-	-	-	-	-	-	-	-	-	19
Memphis	-	-	-	-	-	-	-	-	-	-	-	-	-	23	19	20	23	24
Michigan St.	3	3	5	21	-	-	-	-	-	-	-	-	-	-	-	-	-	-
Mississippi St.	-	-	-	-	-	-	24	22	20	19	11	7	6	4	7	5	4	8
Missouri	5	5	4	3	10	11	23	-	-	-	-	-	-	-	-	-	-	-
North Carolina	9	9	10	7	4	9	9	12	9	7	12	17	14	16	12	14	16	18
North Caro. St.	24	25	-	-	-	-	-	-	-	-	-	-	21	13	14	16	17	15
Notre Dame	21	21	23	-	-	-	-	-	-	-	-	-	-	-	-	-	-	-
Oklahoma	14	14	14	11	8	7	7	6	11	20	25	22	-	-	-	-	-	-
Oklahoma St.	25	24	25	-	-	-	-	-	-	24	18	13	10	7	6	8	7	4
Pittsburgh	22	22	22	20	18	16	15	15	13	8	7	4	4	5	3	6	6	9
Providence	-	-	-	-	-	-	-	25	-	-	23	23	24	19	13	12	20	21
Purdue	-	-	20	16	17	22	21	24	-	23	21	-	-	-	-	-	-	-
St. Joseph's	17	13	12	12	t11	10	10	9	6	3	3	3	3	2	2	2	1	5
South Carolina	-	-	-	-	-	-	-	-	-	25	24	25	25	25	-	-	-	23
Southern Ill.	-	-	-	-	-	-	-	-	-	-	-	-	23	20	16	15	24	-
Stanford	19	20	21	13	9	6	5	4	3	2	2	2	2	1	1	1	2	1
Syracuse	7	7	16	19	19	17	17	17	17	13	20	18	-	-	-	24	19	20
Texas	12	11	8	6	t11	18	19	18	18	16	16	11	11	11	10	10	11	12
Texas Tech	-	-	-	-	-	-	-	-	22	18	13	19	18	22	25	-	-	-
Utah St.	-	-	-	-	-	-	-	-	-	-	-	24	19	-	24	23	22	t25
Vanderbilt	-	-	-	-	-	25	22	20	23	22	-	-	-	-	-	-	-	-
Wake Forest	20	18	18	15	14	8	6	5	4	10	19	16	20	15	11	11	15	17
Wisconsin	15	15	15	23	22	19	18	21	19	21	17	14	17	12	22	17	10	10

2004-05

		Nov.			December				January				February				March		
	PS	16	23	30	7	14	21	28	4	11	18	25	1	8	15	22	1	8	15
Alabama	18	18	19	22	18	17	19	18	19	23	22	14	11	17	16	16	21	20	21
Arizona	10	10	18	21	15	15	14	14	13	17	13	11	14	12	10	9	11	8	9
Boston College	-	-	-	-	-	-	-	-	25	13	9	8	5	4	6	3	5	7	14
Charlotte	-	-	-	-	-	-	-	-	-	-	-	-	-	-	23	21	18	25	-
Cincinnati	-	-	-	-	-	25	22	22	23	18	20	21	18	21	24	24	22	21	23
Connecticut	8	8	7	7	7	11	11	11	10	12	16	19	23	19	18	17	15	12	13
Duke	11	11	9	10	9	7	6	6	5	5	4	2	4	7	7	7	6	5	3
Florida	23	23	23	19	-	-	-	-	-	-	-	-	-	-	-	-	-	-	16
Geo. Washington	-	-	-	-	21	19	20	20	24	21	-	-	-	-	-	-	-	-	-
Georgia Tech	3	3	3	4	3	3	9	9	9	8	12	22	25	-	-	-	-	-	25
Gonzaga	25	25	24	-	25	22	13	12	11	16	11	17	17	14	13	12	12	11	10
Illinois	5	6	5	5	1	1	1	1	1	1	1	1	1	1	1	1	1	1	1
Iowa	-	-	-	23	17	16	17	16	14	24	23	23	-	-	-	-	-	-	-
Kansas	1	1	2	2	2	2	2	2	2	2	2	6	3	3	2	8	7	9	12
Kentucky	9	9	8	8	10	9	8	8	8	9	8	7	6	5	3	5	3	4	7
Louisville	14	14	12	17	13	13	18	19	17	19	14	12	9	9	12	11	9	6	4
Marquette	-	-	-	-	-	-	-	-	-	22	25	-	-	-	-	-	-	-	-
Maryland	15	15	13	12	23	23	24	24	22	-	-	-	22	-	22	-	-	-	-
Memphis	24	24	25	-	-	-	-	-	-	-	-	-	-	-	-	-	-	-	-
Michigan St.	13	13	10	11	20	21	23	23	20	15	19	15	12	13	11	10	14	13	15
Mississippi St.	12	12	14	15	22	20	21	21	18	11	17	24	-	-	-	-	-	-	-
Nevada	-	-	-	-	-	-	-	-	-	-	-	-	-	-	-	25	25	24	-
North Carolina	4	4	11	9	8	5	4	4	3	3	6	3	2	2	4	2	2	2	2
North Caro. St.	19	19	17	16	12	12	16	17	-	-	-	-	-	-	-	-	-	-	-
Notre Dame	20	20	21	20	-	-	-	-	-	-	-	-	-	-	-	-	-	-	-

(2004-05, continued)

Team	PS	Nov 16	23	30	Dec 7	14	21	28	Jan 4	11	18	25	Feb 1	8	15	22	Mar 1	8	15
Oklahoma	-	-	-	-	-	-	-	-	25	18	13	-	15	16	21	22	20	17	17
Oklahoma St.	7	7	6	6	5	4	3	3	7	6	5	9	10	10	8	4	8	10	6
Pacific	-	-	-	-	-	-	-	-	-	-	-	-	-	24	19	19	17	18	22
Pittsburgh	17	17	16	13	11	10	10	10	16	20	21	20	16	18	17	18	24	22	-
Syracuse	6	5	4	3	4	8	7	7	6	7	7	4	8	8	9	15	13	16	11
Texas	16	16	15	18	14	14	15	15	15	10	15	16	20	23	-	-	-	-	-
Texas Tech	-	-	-	-	-	-	-	-	-	-	-	-	25	-	-	-	-	-	24
Utah	-	-	-	-	-	-	-	-	-	-	-	25	21	15	14	13	16	15	18
Villanova	-	-	-	-	-	-	-	-	-	-	-	-	24	22	25	23	19	19	19
Virginia	-	-	24	19	24	25	25	-	-	-	-	-	-	-	-	-	-	-	-
Wake Forest	2	2	1	1	6	6	5	5	4	4	3	5	7	6	5	6	4	3	5
Washington	22	22	22	14	16	18	12	13	12	14	10	10	13	11	15	14	10	14	8
West Virginia	-	-	-	-	-	-	-	-	21	-	-	-	-	-	-	-	-	-	-
Wisconsin	21	21	20	25	24	-	-	-	-	-	24	18	19	20	20	20	23	23	20

2005-06

Team	PS	Nov 15	22	29	Dec 6	13	20	27	Jan 3	10	17	24	31	Feb 7	14	21	28	Mar 7	14
Alabama	15	15	19	21	22	-	-	-	-	-	-	-	-	-	-	-	-	-	-
UAB	-	-	-	-	-	-	-	-	-	-	-	-	-	-	-	-	-	24	25
Arizona	10	10	9	15	24	24	-	21	24	-	-	-	-	-	-	-	-	-	-
Boston College	11	11	10	8	6	13	14	13	11	15	21	20	15	17	13	11	12	11	t7
Bucknell	-	-	-	-	-	-	-	-	-	-	-	-	-	24	-	-	-	-	-
Cincinnati	-	-	-	-	-	-	-	-	25	-	-	-	-	-	-	-	-	-	-
Connecticut	3	3	3	3	2	2	2	4	3	1	1	1	3	2	1	2			
Duke	1	1	1	1	1	1	1	1	1	1	2	2	2	2	1	1	3	1	
Florida	-	-	14	11	10	7	5	5	5	2	2	5	8	7	10	12	17	16	11
Geo. Washington	21	21	21	19	19	15	13	12	20	17	16	14	10	8	7	6	7	6	14
Georgetown	-	-	-	-	-	-	-	-	-	-	-	21	17	15	17	23	20	23	23
Gonzaga	8	9	8	6	9	10	8	8	8	6	6	7	5	5	5	5	5	4	5
Houston	-	-	-	-	-	-	25	-	-	-	-	-	-	-	-	-	-	-	-
Illinois	17	17	15	12	11	9	6	6	6	7	7	8	6	8	10	14	8	10	13
Indiana	24	23	20	17	18	18	18	17	16	9	13	13	22	24	-	-	-	-	-
Iowa	20	20	18	14	12	22	25	-	-	23	-	23	18	18	20	23	20	15	-
Iowa St.	25	25	-	-	-	-	-	-	-	-	-	-	-	-	-	-	-	-	-
Kansas	-	-	-	-	-	-	-	-	-	-	-	-	-	-	22	16	18	17	12
Kentucky	9	8	7	10	15	23	19	18	19	-	-	-	-	-	24	-	25	24	21
LSU	-	-	25	-	-	-	-	-	-	-	-	-	24	-	25	24	21	18	19
Louisville	7	7	6	7	5	4	11	10	9	10	17	22	-	-	-	-	-	-	-
Maryland	23	24	23	23	21	17	16	16	14	23	22	18	-	-	-	-	-	-	-
Memphis	12	12	11	9	7	5	4	4	4	5	4	3	3	3	4	3	5	4	
Michigan	-	-	-	-	-	-	-	-	-	-	-	-	-	21	22	-	-	-	-
Michigan St.	4	4	12	13	14	12	10	9	7	14	11	11	12	12	16	18	25	-	-
Nevada	22	22	22	20	17	20	20	20	-	-	-	-	-	-	-	t25	24	21	20
North Carolina	-	-	-	23	19	17	23	25	20	24	-	-	23	23	21	13	10	10	10
North Caro. St.	-	-	24	25	21	21	19	13	18	14	15	18	16	21	15	22	25	-	-
UNI	-	-	-	-	-	-	-	-	-	-	-	-	25	25	t25	-	-	-	-
Ohio St.	-	-	-	-	-	-	24	21	18	19	19	16	20	19	12	13	9	7	6
Oklahoma	6	6	5	5	8	8	7	14	12	22	25	24	19	20	19	22	19	22	24
Pittsburgh	-	-	-	-	-	-	-	-	22	12	9	12	9	14	9	9	8	15	16
Stanford	13	13	-	-	-	-	-	-	-	-	-	-	-	-	-	-	-	-	-
Syracuse	16	16	17	-	-	-	-	-	-	-	20	25	-	-	-	-	-	-	21
Tennessee	-	-	-	-	-	-	-	23	-	-	-	19	13	11	8	10	11	14	18
Texas	2	2	2	2	2	6	15	15	15	8	5	4	7	6	6	8	9	-	-
UCLA	19	18	16	16	16	14	12	11	17	11	18	17	14	13	15	19	15	13	t7
Villanova	5	5	4	4	4	3	3	3	3	8	6	4	4	4	2	4	2	3	
Wake Forest	18	19	24	22	20	16	22	22	23	-	-	-	-	-	-	-	-	-	-
Washington	-	-	25	18	13	11	9	7	10	13	10	10	16	21	20	17	14	12	17
West Virginia	14	14	13	-	-	-	25	24	16	12	9	11	9	11	14	16	19	22	-
Wisconsin	-	-	-	-	-	-	-	24	-	21	15	23	-	-	-	-	-	-	-

2006-07

Team	PS	Nov 14	21	28	Dec 5	12	19	26	Jan 2	9	16	23	30	Feb 6	13	20	27	Mar 6	13
Air Force	-	-	-	-	24	24	23	20	18	13	16	17	15	17	14	25	-	-	-
Alabama	11	10	8	6	4	9	10	8	8	14	10	12	19	18	25	25	-	-	-
Arizona	10	15	15	16	14	10	9	7	7	10	11	17	20	24	19	-	-	-	-
Boston College	15	14	23	-	-	-	-	-	-	-	-	-	-	21	-	-	-	-	-
BYU	-	-	-	-	-	-	-	-	-	-	-	-	-	-	-	21	-	23	24
Butler	-	-	-	19	15	18	16	15	13	12	18	14	13	10	13	15	18	19	21
Clemson	-	-	-	-	-	25	23	17	19	19	25	-	-	-	-	-	-	-	-
Connecticut	18	21	18	20	19	14	14	12	18	24	-	-	-	-	-	-	-	-	-
Creighton	19	20	-	-	-	-	-	22	18	16	22	-	-	-	-	-	-	-	-
Duke	12	11	9	11	t7	6	6	5	5	11	14	10	8	16	-	18	14	21	-
Florida	1	1	1	4	t7	5	5	3	3	2	1	1	1	1	1	3	5	6	3
Georgetown	8	8	14	18	-	-	-	-	-	-	-	-	-	22	14	12	9	9	8
Georgia Tech	23	23	19	21	25	-	-	-	-	-	-	-	23	-	24	-	-	-	-
Gonzaga	-	-	-	22	18	16	22	-	-	-	-	-	-	23	-	24	-	-	-
Indiana	-	-	-	-	-	-	-	-	-	-	-	-	25	-	20	20	-	-	-
Kansas	3	3	10	5	12	11	11	9	9	6	5	8	6	9	9	6	3	2	2
Kentucky	22	22	20	-	-	-	-	-	25	-	20	20	-	-	-	-	-	-	-
LSU	5	7	6	10	9	12	12	17	14	13	16	21	-	-	-	-	-	-	-
Louisville	-	-	-	-	-	-	-	-	-	-	-	-	-	-	20	16	12	16	
Marquette	16	16	13	8	17	20	19	18	15	-	24	15	14	11	12	16	20	18	20
Maryland	-	-	25	23	23	-	-	-	-	-	-	-	-	-	-	-	24	17	18
Memphis	14	13	12	14	16	19	18	22	22	20	17	11	11	8	8	7	6	5	5
Nevada	24	24	21	24	20	25	25	24	21	19	15	18	15	12	11	11	10	10	15
UNLV	-	-	-	-	-	-	-	-	-	-	-	-	-	-	-	-	-	25	19
North Carolina	2	2	7	3	3	2	2	2	1	4	4	3	5	4	5	8	8	4	
Notre Dame	-	-	-	-	21	20	19	17	22	20	22	21	-	-	22	20	17	-	-
Ohio St.	7	5	4	3	5	4	3	6	6	5	7	5	4	3	2	2	1	1	1
Oklahoma St.	-	-	-	-	22	15	13	12	9	12	13	12	17	18	-	-	-	-	-
Oregon	-	-	-	22	21	20	16	15	9	7	9	13	15	23	17	16	10	-	-
Pittsburgh	4	4	3	2	2	2	7	10	10	7	6	9	7	7	7	10	12	13	12
Southern Cal	-	-	-	-	-	-	-	-	-	-	25	-	19	22	-	23	-	-	23
Southern Ill.	-	-	-	-	-	-	-	-	-	-	-	-	-	21	16	13	11	14	14
Syracuse	20	18	17	15	21	23	23	-	-	-	-	-	-	-	-	-	-	-	-
Stanford	-	-	-	-	-	-	-	-	-	-	-	-	-	23	25	-	-	-	-
Tennessee	25	25	22	-	-	-	21	19	16	22	-	-	-	-	-	-	-	22	25
Texas	21	19	-	-	-	-	-	-	25	21	-	22	-	-	19	15	15	11	
Texas A&M	13	12	11	9	6	13	13	11	11	8	8	6	10	6	6	8	7	7	9
UCLA	6	6	5	1	1	1	1	1	1	4	3	3	5	2	5	4	2	4	7
Vanderbilt	-	-	-	-	-	-	-	-	-	-	24	23	-	17	19	-	-	-	-
Virginia	-	-	-	25	-	-	-	-	-	-	-	23	24	16	-	-	21	-	-
Virginia Tech	-	-	-	-	-	-	-	-	23	24	16	-	-	-	21	-	-	-	-
Washington	17	17	16	13	13	17	17	14	24	-	-	-	-	-	-	-	-	-	-
Washington St.	-	-	-	-	-	-	-	-	-	23	-	20	18	14	10	9	13	11	13
West Virginia	-	-	-	-	-	-	-	-	-	25	21	-	-	-	23	22	-	-	-
Wichita St.	-	-	24	17	10	8	8	16	-	-	-	-	-	-	-	-	-	-	-
Winthrop	-	-	-	-	-	-	-	-	-	-	-	-	-	-	-	-	-	24	22
Wisconsin	9	9	7	12	11	7	4	4	4	3	2	2	2	4	3	1	4	3	6

(Note: AP does not do a post-tournament poll.)

Final Season Polls

Final Regular-Season Polls

The Helms Foundation of Los Angeles selected the national college men's basketball champions from 1942-82 and researched retroactive picks from 1901-41. The Helms winners are listed in this section to the time The Associated Press (AP) poll started in 1949. The AP is the writers' poll, while the UPI and USA Today/CNN and USA Today/NABC polls are the coaches' polls.

HELMS

1901	Yale
1902	Minnesota
1903	Yale
1904	Columbia
1905	Columbia
1906	Dartmouth
1907	Chicago
1908	Chicago
1909	Chicago
1910	Columbia
1911	St. John's (N.Y.)
1912	Wisconsin
1913	Navy
1914	Wisconsin
1915	Illinois
1916	Wisconsin
1917	Washington St.
1918	Syracuse
1919	Minnesota
1920	Penn
1921	Penn
1922	Kansas
1923	Kansas
1924	North Carolina
1925	Princeton
1926	Syracuse
1927	Notre Dame
1928	Pittsburgh
1929	Montana St.
1930	Pittsburgh
1931	Northwestern
1932	Purdue
1933	Kentucky
1934	Wyoming
1935	New York U.
1936	Notre Dame
1937	Stanford
1938	Temple
1939	Long Island
1940	Southern Cal.
1941	Wisconsin
1942	Stanford
1943	Wyoming
1944	Army
1945	Oklahoma St.
1946	Oklahoma St.
1947	Holy Cross
1948	Kentucky

1949
AP
1. Kentucky
2. Oklahoma St.
3. St. Louis
4. Illinois
5. Western Ky.
6. Minnesota
7. Bradley
8. San Francisco
9. Tulane
10. Bowling Green
11. Yale
12. Utah
13. North Carolina St.
14. Villanova
15. UCLA
16. Loyola (Ill.)
17. Wyoming
18. Butler
19. Hamline
20. Ohio St.

1950
AP
1. Bradley
2. Ohio St.
3. Kentucky
4. Holy Cross
5. North Carolina St.
6. Duquesne
7. UCLA
8. Western Ky.
9. St. John's (N.Y.)
10. La Salle
11. Villanova
12. San Francisco
13. Long Island
14. Kansas St.
15. Arizona
16. Wisconsin
17. San Jose St.
18. Washington St.
19. Kansas
20. Indiana

1951
AP
1. Kentucky
2. Oklahoma St.
3. Columbia
4. Kansas St.
5. Illinois
6. Bradley
7. Indiana
8. North Carolina St.
9. St. John's (N.Y.)
10. St. Louis
11. BYU
12. Arizona
13. Dayton
14. Toledo
15. Washington
16. Murray St.
17. Cincinnati
18. Siena
19. Southern California
20. Villanova

UPI
1. Kentucky
2. Oklahoma St.
3. Kansas St.
4. Illinois
5. Columbia
6. Bradley
7. North Carolina St.
8. Indiana
9. St. John's (N.Y.)
10. BYU
11. St. Louis
12. Arizona
13. Washington
14. Beloit
14. Villanova
16. UCLA
17. Cincinnati
18. Dayton
18. St. Bonaventure
18. Seton Hall
18. Texas A&M

1952
AP
1. Kentucky
2. Illinois
3. Kansas St.
4. Duquesne
5. St. Louis
6. Washington
7. Iowa
8. Kansas
9. West Virginia
10. St. John's (N.Y.)
11. Dayton
12. Duke
13. Holy Cross
14. Seton Hall
15. St. Bonaventure
16. Wyoming
17. Louisville
18. Seattle
19. UCLA
20. Texas St.

UPI
1. Kentucky
2. Illinois
3. Kansas
4. Duquesne
5. Washington
6. Kansas St.
7. St. Louis
8. Iowa
9. St. John's (N.Y.)
10. Wyoming
11. St. Bonaventure
12. Seton Hall
13. TCU
14. West Virginia
15. Holy Cross
16. Western Ky.
17. La Salle
18. Dayton
19. Louisville
20. Indiana

1953
AP
1. Indiana
2. Seton Hall
3. Kansas
4. Washington
5. LSU
6. La Salle
7. St. John's (N.Y.)
8. Oklahoma St.
9. Duquesne
10. Notre Dame
11. Illinois
12. Kansas St.
13. Holy Cross
14. Seattle
15. Wake Forest
16. Santa Clara
17. Western Ky.
18. North Carolina St.
19. DePaul
20. Missouri St.

UPI
1. Indiana
2. Seton Hall
3. Washington
4. La Salle
5. Kansas
6. LSU
7. Oklahoma St.
8. North Carolina St.
9. Kansas St.
10. Illinois
11. Western Ky.
12. California
13. Notre Dame
14. DePaul
14. Wyoming
16. St. Louis
17. Holy Cross
18. Oklahoma City
19. BYU
20. Duquesne

1954
AP
1. Kentucky
2. La Salle
3. Holy Cross
4. Indiana
5. Duquesne
6. Notre Dame
7. Bradley
8. Western Ky.
9. Penn St.
10. Oklahoma St.
11. Southern California
12. George Washington
13. Iowa
14. LSU
15. Duke
16. Niagara
17. Seattle
18. Kansas
19. Illinois
20. Maryland

UPI
1. Indiana
2. Kentucky
3. Duquesne
4. Oklahoma St.
5. Notre Dame
6. Western Ky.
7. Kansas
8. LSU
9. Holy Cross
10. Iowa
11. La Salle
12. Illinois
13. Colorado St.
14. North Carolina St.
14. Southern California
16. Oregon St.
17. Seattle
17. Dayton
19. Rice
20. Duke

1955
AP
1. San Francisco
2. Kentucky
3. La Salle
4. North Carolina St.
5. Iowa
6. Duquesne
7. Utah
8. Marquette
9. Dayton
10. Oregon St.
11. Minnesota
12. Alabama
13. UCLA
14. George Washington
15. Colorado
16. Tulsa
17. Vanderbilt
18. Illinois
19. West Virginia
20. St. Louis

UPI
1. San Francisco
2. Kentucky
3. La Salle
4. Utah
5. Iowa
6. North Carolina St.
7. Duquesne
8. Oregon St.
9. Marquette
10. Dayton
11. Colorado
12. UCLA
13. Minnesota
14. Tulsa
15. George Washington
16. Illinois
17. Niagara
18. St. Louis
19. Holy Cross
20. Cincinnati

1956
AP
1. San Francisco
2. North Carolina St.
3. Dayton
4. Iowa
5. Alabama
...

3. Duquesne
4. Oklahoma St.
5. Notre Dame
6. Western Ky.
7. Kansas
8. LSU
9. Holy Cross
10. Iowa
11. La Salle
12. Illinois
13. Colorado St.
14. North Carolina
14. Southern California
16. Oregon St.
17. Seattle
17. Dayton
19. Rice
20. Duke

UPI
1. San Francisco
2. North Carolina St.
3. Dayton
4. Iowa
5. Alabama
6. SMU
7. Louisville
8. Illinois
9. UCLA
10. Vanderbilt
11. North Carolina
12. Kentucky
13. Utah
14. Temple
15. Holy Cross
16. Oklahoma St.
16. St. Louis
18. Seattle
18. Duke
18. Canisius

1957
AP
1. North Carolina
2. Kansas
3. Kentucky
4. SMU
5. Seattle
6. Louisville
7. West Virginia
8. Vanderbilt
9. Oklahoma City
10. St. Louis
11. Michigan St.
12. Memphis
13. California
14. UCLA
15. Mississippi St.
16. Idaho St.
17. Notre Dame
18. Wake Forest
19. Canisius
19. Oklahoma St.

UPI
1. North Carolina
2. Kansas
3. Kentucky
4. SMU
5. Seattle
6. California
7. Michigan St.
8. Louisville
9. UCLA
9. St. Louis

6. Louisville
7. SMU
8. UCLA
9. Kentucky
10. Illinois
11. Oklahoma City
12. Vanderbilt
13. North Carolina
14. Holy Cross
15. Temple
16. Wake Forest
17. Duke
18. Utah
19. Oklahoma St.
20. West Virginia

UPI
1. San Francisco
2. North Carolina St.
3. Dayton
4. Iowa
5. Alabama
6. SMU
7. Louisville
8. Illinois
9. UCLA
10. Vanderbilt
11. North Carolina
12. Kentucky
13. Utah
14. Temple
15. Holy Cross
16. Oklahoma St.
16. St. Louis
18. Seattle
18. Duke
18. Canisius

1958
AP
1. West Virginia
2. Cincinnati
3. Kansas St.
4. San Francisco
5. Temple
6. Maryland
7. Kansas
8. Notre Dame
9. Kentucky
10. Duke
11. Dayton
12. Indiana
13. North Carolina
14. Bradley
15. Mississippi St.
16. Auburn
17. Michigan St.
18. Seattle
19. Oklahoma St.
20. North Carolina St.

UPI
1. West Virginia
2. Cincinnati
3. San Francisco
4. Kansas St.
5. Temple
6. Maryland
7. Notre Dame
8. Kansas
9. Dayton
10. Indiana
11. Bradley
12. North Carolina
13. Duke
14. Kentucky
15. Oklahoma St.
16. Oregon St.
16. North Carolina St.
18. St. Bonaventure
19. Michigan St.
19. Wyoming
19. Seattle

1959
AP
1. Kansas St.
2. Kentucky
3. Mississippi St.
4. Bradley
5. Cincinnati
6. North Carolina St.
7. Michigan St.
8. Auburn
9. North Carolina
10. West Virginia
11. California
12. St. Louis

1959 (cont.)
11. West Virginia
12. Dayton
13. Bradley
14. BYU
15. Indiana
16. Vanderbilt
16. Xavier
16. Oklahoma City
19. Notre Dame
20. Kansas St.

13. Seattle
14. St. Joseph's
15. St. Mary's (Cal.)
16. TCU
17. Oklahoma City
18. Utah
19. St. Bonaventure
20. Marquette

UPI
1. Kansas St.
2. Kentucky
3. Michigan St.
4. Cincinnati
5. North Carolina St.
6. North Carolina
7. Mississippi St.
8. Bradley
9. California
10. Auburn
11. West Virginia
12. TCU
13. St. Louis
14. Utah
15. Marquette
16. Tennessee Tech
17. St. John's (N.Y.)
18. Navy
18. St. Mary's (Cal.)
20. St. Joseph's

1960

AP
1. Cincinnati
2. California
3. Ohio St.
4. Bradley
5. West Virginia
6. Utah
7. Indiana
8. Utah St.
9. St. Bonaventure
10. Miami (Fla.)
11. Auburn
12. New York U.
13. Georgia Tech
14. Providence
15. St. Louis
16. Holy Cross
17. Villanova
18. Duke
19. Wake Forest
20. St. John's (N.Y.)

UPI
1. California
2. Cincinnati
3. Ohio St.
4. Bradley
5. Utah
6. West Virginia
7. Utah St.
8. Georgia Tech
9. Villanova
10. Indiana
11. St. Bonaventure
12. New York U.
13. Texas
14. North Carolina
15. Duke
16. Kansas St.
17. Auburn
18. Providence
19. St. Louis
20. Dayton

1961

AP
1. Ohio St.
2. Cincinnati
3. St. Bonaventure
4. Kansas St.
5. North Carolina
6. Bradley
7. Southern California
8. Iowa
9. West Virginia
10. Duke
11. Utah
12. Texas Tech
13. Niagara

14. Memphis
15. Wake Forest
16. St. John's (N.Y.)
17. St. Joseph's
18. Drake
19. Holy Cross
20. Kentucky

UPI
1. Ohio St.
2. Cincinnati
3. St. Bonaventure
4. Kansas St.
5. Southern California
6. North Carolina
7. Bradley
8. St. John's (N.Y.)
9. Duke
10. Wake Forest
11. Iowa
12. West Virginia
13. Utah
14. St. Louis
15. Louisville
16. St. Joseph's
17. Dayton
18. Kentucky
19. Texas Tech
20. Memphis

1962

AP
1. Ohio St.
2. Cincinnati
3. Kentucky
4. Mississippi St.
5. Bradley
6. Kansas St.
7. Utah
8. Bowling Green
9. Colorado
10. Duke
11. Loyola (Ill.)
12. St. John's (N.Y.)
13. Wake Forest
14. Oregon St.
15. West Virginia
16. Arizona St.
17. Duquesne
18. Utah St.
19. UCLA
20. Villanova

UPI
1. Ohio St.
2. Cincinnati
3. Kentucky
4. Mississippi St.
5. Kansas St.
6. Bradley
7. Wake Forest
8. Colorado
9. Bowling Green
10. Utah
11. Oregon St.
12. St. John's (N.Y.)
13. Duke
14. Loyola (Ill.)
15. Arizona St.
16. West Virginia
17. UCLA
18. Duquesne
19. Utah St.
20. Villanova

1963

AP
1. Cincinnati
2. Duke
3. Loyola (Ill.)
4. Arizona St.
5. Wichita St.
6. Mississippi St.
7. Ohio St.
8. Illinois
9. New York U.
10. Colorado

UPI
1. Cincinnati
2. Duke

3. Arizona St.
4. Loyola (Ill.)
5. Illinois
6. Wichita St.
7. Mississippi St.
8. Ohio St.
9. Colorado
10. Stanford
11. New York U.
12. Texas
13. Providence
14. Oregon St.
15. UCLA
16. St. Joseph's
17. West Virginia
18. Bowling Green
19. Kansas St.
19. Seattle

1964

AP
1. UCLA
2. Michigan
3. Duke
4. Kentucky
5. Wichita St.
6. Oregon St.
7. Villanova
8. Loyola (Ill.)
9. DePaul
10. Davidson

UPI
1. UCLA
2. Michigan
3. Kentucky
4. Duke
5. Oregon St.
6. Wichita St.
7. Villanova
8. Loyola (Ill.)
9. UTEP
10. Davidson
11. DePaul
12. Kansas St.
13. Drake
13. San Francisco
15. Utah St.
16. Ohio St.
16. New Mexico
18. Texas A&M
19. Arizona St.
19. Providence

1965

AP
1. Michigan
2. UCLA
3. St. Joseph's
4. Providence
5. Vanderbilt
6. Davidson
7. Minnesota
8. Villanova
9. BYU
10. Duke

UPI
1. Michigan
2. UCLA
3. St. Joseph's
4. Providence
5. Vanderbilt
6. BYU
7. Davidson
8. Minnesota
9. Duke
10. San Francisco
11. Villanova
12. North Carolina St.
13. Oklahoma St.
14. Wichita St.
15. Connecticut
16. Illinois
17. Tennessee
18. Indiana
19. Miami (Fla.)
20. Dayton

1966

AP
1. Kentucky
2. Duke
3. UTEP
4. Kansas
5. St. Joseph's
6. Loyola (Ill.)
7. Cincinnati
8. Vanderbilt
9. Michigan
10. Western Ky.

UPI
1. Kentucky
2. Duke
3. UTEP
4. Kansas
5. Loyola (Ill.)
6. St. Joseph's
7. Michigan
8. Vanderbilt
9. Cincinnati
10. Providence
11. Nebraska
12. Utah
13. Oklahoma City
14. Houston
15. Oregon St.
16. Syracuse
17. Pacific
18. Davidson
19. BYU
19. Dayton

1967

AP
1. UCLA
2. Louisville
3. Kansas
4. North Carolina
5. Princeton
6. Western Ky.
7. Houston
8. Tennessee
9. Boston College
10. UTEP

UPI
1. UCLA
2. Louisville
3. North Carolina
4. Kansas
5. Princeton
6. Houston
7. Western Ky.
8. UTEP
9. Tennessee
10. Boston College
11. Toledo
12. St. John's (N.Y.)
13. Tulsa
14. Vanderbilt
14. Utah St.
16. Pacific
17. Providence
18. New Mexico
19. Duke
20. Florida

1968

AP
1. Houston
2. UCLA
3. St. Bonaventure
4. North Carolina
5. Kentucky
6. New Mexico
7. Columbia
8. Davidson
9. Louisville
10. Duke

UPI
1. Houston
2. UCLA
3. St. Bonaventure
4. North Carolina
5. Kentucky
6. Columbia

7. New Mexico
8. Louisville
9. Davidson
10. Marquette
11. Duke
12. New Mexico St.
13. Vanderbilt
14. Kansas St.
15. Princeton
16. Army
17. Santa Clara
18. Utah
19. Bradley
20. Iowa

1969

AP
1. UCLA
2. La Salle
3. Santa Clara
4. North Carolina
5. Davidson
6. Purdue
7. Kentucky
8. St. John's (N.Y.)
9. Duquesne
10. Villanova
11. Drake
12. New Mexico St.
13. South Carolina
14. Marquette
15. Louisville
16. Boston College
17. Notre Dame
18. Colorado
19. Kansas
20. Illinois

UPI
1. UCLA
2. North Carolina
3. Davidson
4. Santa Clara
5. Kentucky
6. La Salle
7. Purdue
8. St. John's (N.Y.)
9. New Mexico St.
10. Duquesne
11. Drake
12. Colorado
13. Louisville
14. Marquette
15. Villanova
15. Boston College
17. Weber St.
17. Wyoming
19. Colorado St.
20. South Carolina
20. Kansas

1970

AP
1. Kentucky
2. UCLA
3. St. Bonaventure
4. Jacksonville
5. New Mexico St.
6. South Carolina
7. Iowa
8. Marquette
9. Notre Dame
10. North Carolina St.
11. Florida St.
12. Houston
13. Penn
14. Drake
15. Davidson
16. Utah St.
17. Niagara
18. Western Ky.
19. Long Beach St.
20. Southern California

UPI
1. Kentucky
2. UCLA
3. St. Bonaventure
4. New Mexico St.
5. Jacksonville

6. South Carolina
7. Iowa
8. Notre Dame
9. Drake
10. Marquette
11. Houston
12. North Carolina St.
13. Penn
14. Florida St.
15. Villanova
16. Long Beach St.
17. Western Ky.
17. Utah St.
17. Niagara
20. Cincinnati
20. UTEP

1971

AP
1. UCLA
2. Marquette
3. Penn
4. Kansas
5. Southern California
6. South Carolina
7. Western Ky.
8. Kentucky
9. Fordham
10. Ohio St.
11. Jacksonville
12. Notre Dame
13. North Carolina
14. Houston
15. Duquesne
16. Long Beach St.
17. Tennessee
18. Villanova
19. Drake
20. BYU

UPI
1. UCLA
2. Marquette
3. Penn
4. Kansas
5. Southern California
6. South Carolina
7. Western Ky.
8. Kentucky
9. Fordham
10. Ohio St.
11. Jacksonville
11. BYU
13. North Carolina
14. Notre Dame
14. Long Beach St.
16. Drake
17. Villanova
18. Duquesne
18. Houston
20. Weber St.

1972

AP
1. UCLA
2. North Carolina
3. Penn
4. Louisville
5. Long Beach St.
6. South Carolina
7. Marquette
8. La.-Lafayette
9. BYU
10. Florida St.
11. Minnesota
12. Marshall
13. Memphis
14. Maryland
15. Villanova
16. Oral Roberts
17. Indiana
18. Kentucky
19. Ohio St.
20. Virginia

UPI
1. UCLA
2. North Carolina
3. Penn
4. Louisville
5. South Carolina

6. Long Beach St.
7. Marquette
8. La.-Lafayette
9. BYU
10. Florida St.
11. Maryland
12. Minnesota
13. Memphis
14. Kentucky
15. Villanova
16. Kansas St.
17. UTEP
18. Marshall
19. Missouri
19. Weber St.

1973

AP
1. UCLA
2. North Carolina St.
3. Long Beach St.
4. Providence
5. Marquette
6. Indiana
7. La.-Lafayette
8. Maryland
9. Kansas St.
10. Minnesota
11. North Carolina
12. Memphis
13. Houston
14. Syracuse
15. Missouri
16. Arizona St.
17. Kentucky
18. Penn
19. Austin Peay
20. San Francisco

UPI
1. UCLA
2. North Carolina St.
3. Long Beach St.
4. Marquette
5. Providence
6. Indiana
7. La.-Lafayette
8. Kansas St.
9. Minnesota
10. Maryland
11. Memphis
12. North Carolina
13. Arizona St.
14. Syracuse
15. Kentucky
16. South Carolina
17. Missouri
18. Weber St.
18. Houston
20. Penn

1974

AP
1. North Carolina St.
2. UCLA
3. Marquette
4. Maryland
5. Notre Dame
6. Michigan
7. Kansas
8. Providence
9. Indiana
10. Long Beach St.
11. Purdue
12. North Carolina
13. Vanderbilt
14. Alabama
15. Utah
16. Pittsburgh
17. Southern California
18. Oral Roberts
19. South Carolina
20. Dayton

UPI
1. North Carolina St.
2. UCLA
3. Notre Dame
4. Maryland
5. Marquette
6. Providence

7. Vanderbilt
8. North Carolina
9. Indiana
10. Kansas
11. Long Beach St.
12. Michigan
13. Southern California
14. Pittsburgh
15. Louisville
16. South Carolina
17. Creighton
18. New Mexico
19. Alabama
19. Dayton

1975

AP
1. UCLA
2. Kentucky
3. Indiana
4. Louisville
5. Maryland
6. Syracuse
7. North Carolina St.
8. Arizona St.
9. North Carolina
10. Alabama
11. Marquette
12. Princeton
13. Cincinnati
14. Notre Dame
15. Kansas St.
16. Drake
17. UNLV
18. Oregon St.
19. Michigan
20. Penn

UPI
1. Indiana
2. UCLA
3. Louisville
4. Kentucky
5. Maryland
6. Marquette
7. Arizona St.
8. Alabama
9. North Carolina St.
10. North Carolina
11. Penn
12. Southern California
13. Utah St.
14. UNLV
14. Notre Dame
16. Creighton
17. Arizona
18. New Mexico St.
19. Clemson
20. UTEP

1976

AP
1. Indiana
2. Marquette
3. UNLV
4. Rutgers
5. UCLA
6. Alabama
7. Notre Dame
8. North Carolina
9. Michigan
10. Western Mich.
11. Maryland
12. Cincinnati
13. Tennessee
14. Missouri
15. Arizona
16. Texas Tech
17. DePaul
18. Virginia
19. Centenary (La.)
20. Pepperdine

UPI
1. Indiana
2. Marquette
3. Rutgers
4. UNLV
5. UCLA
6. North Carolina
7. Alabama

8. Notre Dame
9. Michigan
10. Washington
11. Missouri
12. Arizona
13. Maryland
14. Tennessee
15. Virginia
16. Cincinnati
16. Florida St.
18. St. John's (N.Y.)
19. Western Mich.
19. Princeton

1977

AP
1. Michigan
2. UCLA
3. Kentucky
4. UNLV
5. North Carolina
6. Syracuse
7. Marquette
8. San Francisco
9. Wake Forest
10. Notre Dame
11. Alabama
12. Detroit
13. Minnesota
14. Utah
15. Tennessee
16. Kansas St.
17. Charlotte
18. Arkansas
19. Louisville
20. VMI

UPI
1. Michigan
2. San Francisco
3. North Carolina
4. UCLA
5. Kentucky
6. UNLV
7. Arkansas
8. Tennessee
9. Syracuse
10. Utah
11. Kansas St.
12. Cincinnati
13. Louisville
14. Marquette
15. Providence
16. Indiana St.
17. Minnesota
18. Alabama
19. Detroit
20. Purdue

1978

AP
1. Kentucky
2. UCLA
3. DePaul
4. Michigan St.
5. Arkansas
6. Notre Dame
7. Duke
8. Marquette
9. Louisville
10. Kansas
11. San Francisco
12. New Mexico
13. Indiana
14. Utah
15. Florida St.
16. North Carolina
17. Texas
18. Detroit
19. Miami (Ohio)
20. Penn

UPI
1. Kentucky
2. UCLA
3. Marquette
4. New Mexico
5. Michigan St.
6. Arkansas
7. DePaul
8. Kansas

9. Duke
10. North Carolina
11. Notre Dame
12. Florida St.
13. San Francisco
14. Louisville
15. Indiana
16. Houston
17. Utah St.
18. Utah
19. Texas
20. Georgetown

1979

AP
1. Indiana St.
2. UCLA
3. Michigan St.
4. Notre Dame
5. Arkansas
6. DePaul
7. LSU
8. Syracuse
9. North Carolina
10. Marquette
11. Duke
12. San Francisco
13. Louisville
14. Penn
15. Purdue
16. Oklahoma
17. St. John's (N.Y.)
18. Rutgers
19. Toledo
20. Iowa

UPI
1. Indiana St.
2. UCLA
3. North Carolina
4. Michigan St.
5. Notre Dame
6. Arkansas
7. Duke
8. DePaul
9. LSU
10. Syracuse
11. Iowa
12. Georgetown
13. Marquette
14. Purdue
15. Texas
16. Temple
17. San Francisco
18. Tennessee
19. Louisville
20. Detroit

1980

AP
1. DePaul
2. Louisville
3. LSU
4. Kentucky
5. Oregon St.
6. Syracuse
7. Indiana
8. Maryland
9. Notre Dame
10. Ohio St.
11. Georgetown
12. BYU
13. St. John's (N.Y.)
14. Duke
15. North Carolina
16. Missouri
17. Weber St.
18. Arizona St.
19. Iona
20. Purdue

UPI
1. DePaul
2. LSU
3. Kentucky
4. Louisville
5. Oregon St.
6. Syracuse
7. Indiana
8. Maryland
9. Ohio St.

10. Georgetown
11. Notre Dame
12. BYU
13. St. John's (N.Y.)
14. Missouri
15. North Carolina
16. Duke
17. Weber St.
18. Texas A&M
19. Arizona St.
20. Kansas St.

1981

AP
1. DePaul
2. Oregon St.
3. Arizona St.
4. LSU
5. Virginia
6. North Carolina
7. Notre Dame
8. Kentucky
9. Indiana
10. UCLA
11. Wake Forest
12. Louisville
13. Iowa
14. Utah
15. Tennessee
16. BYU
17. Wyoming
18. Maryland
19. Illinois
20. Arkansas

UPI
1. DePaul
2. Oregon St.
3. Virginia
4. LSU
5. Arizona St.
6. North Carolina
7. Indiana
8. Kentucky
9. Notre Dame
10. Utah
11. UCLA
12. Iowa
13. Louisville
14. Wake Forest
15. Tennessee
16. Wyoming
17. BYU
18. Illinois
19. Kansas
20. Maryland

1982

AP
1. North Carolina
2. DePaul
3. Virginia
4. Oregon St.
5. Missouri
6. Georgetown
7. Minnesota
8. Idaho
9. Memphis
10. Tulsa
11. Fresno St.
12. Arkansas
13. Alabama
14. West Virginia
15. Kentucky
16. Iowa
17. UAB
18. Wake Forest
19. UCLA
20. Louisville

UPI
1. North Carolina
2. DePaul
3. Virginia
4. Oregon St.
5. Missouri
6. Minnesota
7. Georgetown
8. Idaho
9. Memphis
10. Fresno St.

11. Tulsa
12. Alabama
13. Arkansas
14. Kentucky
15. Wyoming
16. Iowa
17. West Virginia
18. Kansas St.
19. Wake Forest
20. Louisville

1983

AP
1. Houston
2. Louisville
3. St. John's (N.Y.)
4. Virginia
5. Indiana
6. UNLV
7. UCLA
8. North Carolina
9. Arkansas
10. Missouri
11. Boston College
12. Kentucky
13. Villanova
14. Wichita St.
15. Chattanooga
16. North Carolina St.
17. Memphis
18. Georgia
19. Oklahoma St.
20. Georgetown

UPI
1. Houston
2. Louisville
3. St. John's (N.Y.)
4. Virginia
5. Indiana
6. UNLV
7. UCLA
8. North Carolina
9. Arkansas
10. Kentucky
11. Villanova
12. Missouri
13. Boston College
14. North Carolina St.
15. Georgia
16. Chattanooga
17. Memphis
18. Illinois St.
19. Oklahoma St.
20. Georgetown

1984

AP
1. North Carolina
2. Georgetown
3. Kentucky
4. DePaul
5. Houston
6. Illinois
7. Oklahoma
8. Arkansas
9. UTEP
10. Purdue
11. Maryland
12. Tulsa
13. UNLV
14. Duke
15. Washington
16. Memphis
17. Oregon St.
18. Syracuse
19. Wake Forest
20. Temple

UPI
1. North Carolina
2. Georgetown
3. Kentucky
4. DePaul
5. Houston
6. Illinois
7. Arkansas
8. Oklahoma
9. UTEP
10. Maryland
11. Purdue

12. Tulsa
13. UNLV
14. Duke
15. Washington
16. Memphis
16. Syracuse
18. Indiana
19. Auburn
20. Oregon St.

1985
AP
1. Georgetown
2. Michigan
3. St. John's (N.Y.)
4. Oklahoma
5. Memphis
6. Georgia Tech
7. North Carolina
8. Louisiana Tech
9. UNLV
10. Duke
11. VCU
12. Illinois
13. Kansas
14. Loyola (Ill.)
15. Syracuse
16. North Carolina St.
17. Texas Tech
18. Tulsa
19. Georgia
20. LSU

UPI
1. Georgetown
2. Michigan
3. St. John's (N.Y.)
4. Memphis
5. Oklahoma
6. Georgia Tech
7. North Carolina
8. Louisiana Tech
9. UNLV
10. Illinois
11. VCU
12. Duke
13. Kansas
14. Tulsa
15. Syracuse
16. Texas Tech
17. Loyola (Ill.)
18. North Carolina St.
19. LSU
20. Michigan St.

1986
AP
1. Duke
2. Kansas
3. Kentucky
4. St. John's (N.Y.)
5. Michigan
6. Georgia Tech
7. Louisville
8. North Carolina
9. Syracuse
10. Notre Dame
11. UNLV
12. Memphis
13. Georgetown
14. Bradley
15. Oklahoma
16. Indiana
17. Navy
18. Michigan St.
19. Illinois
20. UTEP

UPI
1. Duke
2. Kansas
3. St. John's (N.Y.)
4. Kentucky
5. Michigan
6. Georgia Tech
7. Louisville
8. North Carolina
9. Syracuse
10. UNLV
11. Notre Dame
12. Memphis

13. Bradley
14. Indiana
15. Georgetown
16. UTEP
17. Oklahoma
18. Michigan St.
19. Alabama
20. Illinois

1987
AP
1. UNLV
2. North Carolina
3. Indiana
4. Georgetown
5. DePaul
6. Iowa
7. Purdue
8. Temple
9. Alabama
10. Syracuse
11. Illinois
12. Pittsburgh
13. Clemson
14. Missouri
15. UCLA
16. New Orleans
17. Duke
18. Notre Dame
19. TCU
20. Kansas

UPI
1. UNLV
2. Indiana
3. North Carolina
4. Georgetown
5. DePaul
6. Purdue
7. Iowa
8. Temple
9. Alabama
10. Syracuse
11. Illinois
12. Pittsburgh
13. UCLA
14. Missouri
15. Clemson
16. TCU
17. Wyoming
18. Notre Dame
19. New Orleans
19. Oklahoma
19. UTEP

1988
AP
1. Temple
2. Arizona
3. Purdue
4. Oklahoma
5. Duke
6. Kentucky
7. North Carolina
8. Pittsburgh
9. Syracuse
10. Michigan
11. Bradley
12. UNLV
13. Wyoming
14. North Carolina St.
15. Loyola Marymount
16. Illinois
17. Iowa
18. Xavier
19. BYU
20. Kansas St.

UPI
1. Temple
2. Arizona
3. Purdue
4. Oklahoma
5. Duke
6. Kentucky
7. Pittsburgh
8. North Carolina
9. Syracuse
10. Michigan
11. UNLV
12. Bradley

13. North Carolina St.
14. Wyoming
15. Illinois
16. Loyola Marymount
17. BYU
18. Iowa
19. Indiana
20. Kansas St.

1989
AP
1. Arizona
2. Georgetown
3. Illinois
4. Oklahoma
5. North Carolina
6. Missouri
7. Syracuse
8. Indiana
9. Duke
10. Michigan
11. Seton Hall
12. Louisville
13. Stanford
14. Iowa
15. UNLV
16. Florida St.
17. West Virginia
18. Ball St.
19. North Carolina St.
20. Alabama

UPI
1. Arizona
2. Georgetown
3. Illinois
4. North Carolina
5. Oklahoma
6. Indiana
7. Duke
8. Missouri
9. Syracuse
10. Michigan
11. Seton Hall
12. Stanford
13. Louisville
14. UNLV
15. Iowa
16. Florida St.
17. Arkansas
18. North Carolina St.
19. West Virginia
20. Alabama

1990
AP
1. Oklahoma
2. UNLV
3. Connecticut
4. Michigan St.
5. Kansas
6. Syracuse
7. Arkansas
8. Georgetown
9. Georgia Tech
10. Purdue
11. Missouri
12. La Salle
13. Michigan
14. Arizona
15. Duke
16. Louisville
17. Clemson
18. Illinois
19. LSU
20. Minnesota
21. Loyola Marymount
22. Oregon St.
23. Alabama
24. New Mexico St.
25. Xavier

UPI
1. Oklahoma
2. UNLV
3. Connecticut
4. Michigan St.
5. Kansas
6. Syracuse
7. Georgia Tech
8. Arkansas

9. Georgetown
10. Purdue
11. Missouri
12. Arizona
13. La Salle
14. Duke
15. Michigan
16. Louisville
17. Clemson
18. Illinois
19. Alabama
20. New Mexico St.

1991
AP
1. UNLV
2. Arkansas
3. Indiana
4. North Carolina
5. Ohio St.
6. Duke
7. Syracuse
8. Arizona
9. Kentucky
10. Utah
11. Nebraska
12. Kansas
13. Seton Hall
14. Oklahoma St.
15. New Mexico St.
16. UCLA
17. East Tenn. St.
18. Princeton
19. Alabama
20. St. John's (N.Y.)
21. Mississippi St.
22. LSU
23. Texas
24. DePaul
25. Southern Miss.

UPI
1. UNLV
2. Arkansas
3. Indiana
4. North Carolina
5. Ohio St.
6. Duke
7. Arizona
8. Syracuse
9. Nebraska
10. Utah
11. Seton Hall
12. Kansas
13. Oklahoma St.
14. UCLA
15. East Tenn. St.
16. Alabama
17. New Mexico St.
18. Mississippi St.
19. St. John's (N.Y.)
20. Princeton
21. LSU
22. Michigan St.
23. Georgetown
24. North Carolina St.
25. Texas

1992
AP
1. Duke
2. Kansas
3. Ohio St.
4. UCLA
5. Indiana
6. Kentucky
7. UNLV
8. Southern California
9. Arkansas
10. Arizona
11. Oklahoma St.
12. Cincinnati
13. Alabama
14. Michigan St.
15. Michigan
16. Missouri
17. Massachusetts
18. North Carolina
19. Seton Hall
20. Florida St.

21. Syracuse
22. Georgetown
23. Oklahoma
24. DePaul
25. LSU

UPI
1. Duke
2. Kansas
3. UCLA
4. Ohio St.
5. Arizona
6. Indiana
7. Southern California
8. Arkansas
9. Kentucky
10. Oklahoma St.
11. Michigan St.
12. Missouri
13. Alabama
14. Cincinnati
15. North Carolina
16. Florida St.
17. Michigan
18. Seton Hall
19. Georgetown
20. Syracuse
21. Massachusetts
22. Oklahoma
23. DePaul
24. St. John's (N.Y.)
25. Tulane

1993
AP
1. Indiana
2. Kentucky
3. Michigan
4. North Carolina
5. Arizona
6. Seton Hall
7. Cincinnati
8. Vanderbilt
9. Kansas
10. Duke
11. Florida St.
12. Arkansas
13. Iowa
14. Massachusetts
15. Louisville
16. Wake Forest
17. New Orleans
18. Georgia Tech
19. Utah
20. Western Ky.
21. New Mexico
22. Purdue
23. Oklahoma St.
24. New Mexico St.
25. UNLV

USA TODAY/CNN
1. Indiana
2. North Carolina
3. Kentucky
4. Michigan
5. Arizona
6. Seton Hall
7. Cincinnati
8. Kansas
9. Vanderbilt
10. Duke
11. Florida St.
12. Arkansas
13. Iowa
14. Louisville
15. Wake Forest
16. Utah
17. Massachusetts
18. New Orleans
19. UNLV
20. Georgia Tech
21. Purdue
22. Virginia
23. Oklahoma St.
24. New Mexico St.
25. Western Ky.

1994
AP
1. North Carolina

2. Arkansas
3. Purdue
4. Connecticut
5. Missouri
6. Duke
7. Kentucky
8. Massachusetts
9. Arizona
10. Louisville
11. Michigan
12. Temple
13. Kansas
14. Florida
15. Syracuse
16. California
17. UCLA
18. Indiana
19. Oklahoma St.
20. Texas
21. Marquette
22. Nebraska
23. Minnesota
24. St. Louis
25. Cincinnati

USA TODAY/CNN
1. Arkansas
2. North Carolina
3. Connecticut
4. Purdue
5. Missouri
6. Duke
7. Massachusetts
8. Kentucky
9. Louisville
10. Arizona
11. Michigan
12. Temple
13. Kansas
14. Syracuse
15. Florida
16. UCLA
17. California
18. Indiana
19. Oklahoma St.
20. Minnesota
21. St. Louis
22. Marquette
23. UAB
24. Texas
25. Cincinnati

1995
AP
1. UCLA
2. Kentucky
3. Wake Forest
4. North Carolina
5. Kansas
6. Arkansas
7. Massachusetts
8. Connecticut
9. Villanova
10. Maryland
11. Michigan St.
12. Purdue
13. Virginia
14. Oklahoma St.
15. Arizona
16. Arizona St.
17. Oklahoma
18. Mississippi St.
19. Utah
20. Alabama
21. Western Ky.
22. Georgetown
23. Missouri
24. Iowa St.
25. Syracuse

USA TODAY/NABC
1. UCLA
2. Kentucky
3. Wake Forest
4. Kansas
5. North Carolina
6. Arkansas
7. Massachusetts
8. Connecticut
9. Michigan St.
10. Maryland
11. Purdue

DIVISION I

12. Villanova
13. Arizona
14. Oklahoma St.
15. Virginia
16. Arizona St.
17. Utah
18. Iowa St.
19. Mississippi St.
20. Oklahoma
21. Alabama
22. Syracuse
23. Missouri
24. Oregon
25. Stanford

1996
AP
1. Massachusetts
2. Kentucky
3. Connecticut
4. Georgetown
4. Kansas
6. Purdue
7. Cincinnati
8. Texas Tech
9. Wake Forest
10. Villanova
11. Arizona
12. Utah
13. Georgia Tech
14. UCLA
15. Syracuse
16. Memphis
17. Iowa St.
18. Penn St.
19. Mississippi St.
20. Marquette
21. Iowa
22. Virginia Tech
23. New Mexico
24. Louisville
25. North Carolina

USA TODAY/NABC
1. Massachusetts
2. Kentucky
3. Connecticut
4. Purdue
5. Georgetown
6. Cincinnati
7. Texas Tech
8. Kansas
9. Wake Forest
10. Utah
11. Arizona
12. Villanova
13. UCLA
14. Syracuse
15. Georgia Tech
16. Iowa St.
17. Memphis
18. Penn St.
19. Iowa
20. Mississippi St.
21. Virginia Tech
22. Marquette
23. Louisville
24. North Carolina
25. Stanford

1997
AP
1. Kansas
2. Utah
3. Minnesota
4. North Carolina
5. Kentucky
6. South Carolina
7. UCLA
8. Duke
9. Wake Forest
10. Cincinnati
11. New Mexico
12. St. Joseph's
13. Xavier
14. Clemson
15. Arizona
16. Col. of Charleston
17. Georgia
18. Iowa St.
19. Illinois
20. Villanova
21. Stanford
22. Maryland
23. Boston College
24. Colorado
25. Louisville

USA TODAY/NABC
1. Kansas
2. Utah
3. Minnesota
4. Kentucky
5. North Carolina
6. South Carolina
7. UCLA
8. Duke
9. Wake Forest
10. Cincinnati
11. New Mexico
12. Clemson
13. Arizona
14. Xavier
15. St. Joseph's
16. Villanova
17. Iowa St.
18. Col. of Charleston
19. Maryland
20. Boston College
21. Stanford
22. Georgia
23. Colorado
24. Illinois
25. Louisville

1998
AP
1. North Carolina
2. Kansas
3. Duke
4. Arizona
5. Kentucky
6. Connecticut
7. Utah
8. Princeton
9. Cincinnati
10. Stanford
11. Purdue
12. Michigan
13. Mississippi
14. South Carolina
15. TCU
16. Michigan St.
17. Arkansas
18. New Mexico
19. UCLA
20. Maryland
21. Syracuse
22. Illinois
23. Xavier
24. Temple
25. Murray St.

USA TODAY/NABC
1. North Carolina
2. Kansas
3. Duke
4. Arizona
5. Connecticut
6. Kentucky
7. Utah
8. Princeton
9. Purdue
10. Stanford
11. Cincinnati
12. Michigan
13. South Carolina
14. Mississippi
15. Michigan St.
16. TCU
17. Arkansas
18. New Mexico
19. Syracuse
20. UCLA
21. Xavier
22. Maryland
23. Illinois
24. Temple
25. Oklahoma

1999
AP
1. Duke
2. Michigan St.
3. Connecticut
4. Auburn
5. Maryland
6. Utah
7. Stanford
8. Kentucky
9. St. John's (N.Y.)
10. Miami (Fla.)
11. Cincinnati
12. Arizona
13. North Carolina
14. Ohio St.
15. UCLA
16. Col. of Charleston
17. Arkansas
18. Wisconson
19. Indiana
20. Texas
21. Iowa
22. Kansas
23. Florida
24. Charlotte
25. New Mexico

USA TODAY/NABC
1. Duke
2. Michigan St.
3. Connecticut
4. Auburn
5. Maryland
6. Utah
7. Stanford
8. St. John's (N.Y.)
9. Cincinnati
10. Arizona
11. Kentucky
12. Miami (Fla.)
13. North Carolina
14. Ohio St.
15. UCLA
16. Col. of Charleston
17. Wisconsin
18. Indiana
19. Arkansas
20. Iowa
21. Syracuse
22. Kansas
23. Texas
24. New Mexico
25. Florida

2000
AP
1. Duke
2. Michigan St.
3. Stanford
4. Arizona
5. Temple
6. Iowa St.
7. Cincinnati
8. Ohio St.
9. St. John's (N.Y.)
10. LSU
11. Tennessee
12. Oklahoma
13. Florida
14. Oklahoma St.
15. Texas
16. Syracuse
17. Maryland
18. Tulsa
19. Kentucky
20. Connecticut
21. Illinois
22. Indiana
23. Miami (Fla.)
24. Auburn
25. Purdue

USA TODAY/NABC
1. Duke
2. Michigan St.
3. Stanford
4. Arizona
5. Temple
6. Cincinnati
7. Iowa St.
8. Ohio St.
9. LSU
10. Tennessee
11. Florida
12. St. John's (N.Y.)
13. Oklahoma
14. Syracuse
15. Oklahoma St.
16. Maryland
17. Indiana
18. Texas
19. Tulsa
20. Kentucky
21. Connecticut
22. Auburn
23. Illinois
24. Purdue
25. Miami (Fla.)

2001
AP
1. Duke
2. Stanford
3. Michigan St.
4. Illinois
5. Arizona
6. North Carolina
7. Boston College
8. Florida
9. Kentucky
10. Iowa St.
11. Maryland
12. Kansas
13. Oklahoma
14. Mississippi
15. UCLA
16. Virginia
17. Syracuse
18. Texas
19. Notre Dame
20. Indiana
21. Georgetown
22. St. Joseph's
23. Wake Forest
24. Iowa
25. Wisconsin

USA TODAY/NABC
1. Duke
2. Stanford
3. Michigan St.
4. Arizona
5. North Carolina
6. Illinois
7. Boston College
8. Florida
9. Iowa St.
10. Kentucky
11. Maryland
12. Kansas
13. Mississippi
14. Oklahoma
15. Virginia
16. Syracuse
17. Texas
18. UCLA
19. Notre Dame
20. Georgetown
21. Indiana
22. Wake Forest
23. St. Joseph's
24. Wisconsin
25. Iowa

2002
AP
1. Duke
2. Kansas
3. Oklahoma
4. Maryland
5. Cincinnati
6. Gonzaga
7. Arizona
8. Alabama
9. Pittsburgh
10. Connecticut
11. Oregon
12. Marquette
13. Illinois
14. Ohio St.
15. Florida
16. Kentucky
17. Mississippi St.
18. Southern California
19. Western Ky.
20. Oklahoma St.
21. Miami (Fla.)
22. Xavier
23. Georgia
24. Stanford
25. Hawaii

USA TODAY/ESPN
1. Duke
2. Kansas
3. Oklahoma
4. Maryland
5. Cincinnati
6. Gonzaga
7. Pittsburgh
8. Alabama
9. Arizona
10. Marquette
11. Oregon
12. Ohio St.
13. Connecticut
14. Florida
15. Kentucky
16. Illinois
17. Southern California
18. Mississippi St.
19. Xavier
20. Western Ky.
21. Miami (Fla.)
22. Oklahoma St.
23. Stanford
24. Hawaii
25. North Carolina St.

2003
AP
1. Kentucky
2. Arizona
3. Oklahoma
4. Pittsburgh
5. Texas
6. Kansas
7. Duke
8. Wake Forest
9. Marquette
10. Florida
11. Illinois
12. Xavier
13. Syracuse
14. Louisville
15. Creighton
16. Dayton
17. Maryland
18. Stanford
19. Memphis
20. Mississippi St.
21. Wisconsin
22. Notre Dame
23. Connecticut
24. Missouri
25. Georgia

USA TODAY/ESPN
1. Kentucky
2. Arizona
3. Oklahoma
4. Pittsburgh
5. Texas
6. Kansas
7. Duke
8. Florida
9. Wake Forest
10. Illinois
11. Marquette
12. Syracuse
13. Louisville
14. Xavier
15. Creighton
16. Stanford
17. Maryland
18. Dayton
19. Wisconsin
20. Notre Dame
21. Mississippi St.
22. Memphis
23. Oklahoma St.
24. Connecticut
25. Missouri

2004
AP
1. Stanford
2. Kentucky
3. Gonzaga
4. Oklahoma St.
5. St. Joseph's
6. Duke
7. Connecticut
8. Mississippi St.
9. Pittsburgh
10. Wisconsin
11. Cincinnati
12. Texas
13. Illinois
14. Georgia Tech
15. North Carolina St.
16. Kansas
17. Wake Forest
18. North Carolina
19. Maryland
20. Syracuse
21. Providence
22. Arizona
23. South Carolina
24. Memphis
25. Boston College
    Utah St.

USA TODAY/ESPN
1. Stanford
2. Gonzaga
3. Oklahoma St.
4. Kentucky
5. St. Joseph's
6. Duke
7. Connecticut
8. Pittsburgh
9. Mississippi St.
10. Wisconsin
11. Texas
12. Cincinnati
13. Illinois
14. Kansas
15. Georgia Tech
16. Wake Forest
17. North Carolina St.
18. Arizona
19. Providence
20. North Carolina
21. Maryland
22. Utah St.
23. Southern Ill.
24. Syracuse
25. Michigan St.

2005
AP
1. Illinois
2. North Carolina
3. Duke
4. Louisville
5. Wake Forest
6. Oklahoma St.
7. Kentucky
8. Washington
9. Arizona
10. Gonzaga
11. Syracuse
12. Kansas
13. Connecticut
14. Boston College
15. Michigan St.
16. Florida
17. Oklahoma
18. Utah
19. Villanova
20. Wisconsin
21. Alabama
22. Pacific
23. Cincinnati
24. Texas Tech
25. Georgia Tech

USA TODAY/ESPN
1. Illinois
2. Duke
3. North Carolina
4. Louisville

5. Kentucky
6. Wake Forest
7. Washington
8. Oklahoma St.
9. Arizona
10. Kansas
11. Gonzaga
12. Boston College
13. Syracuse
14. Connecticut
15. Michigan St.
16. Oklahoma
17. Utah
18. Florida
19. Wisconsin
20. Pacific
21. Alabama
22. Villanova
23. Cincinnati
24. Texas Tech
25. Georgia Tech

2006
AP
1. Duke
2. Connecticut
3. Villanova
4. Memphis
5. Gonzaga
6. Ohio St.
7. Boston College
   UCLA
9. Texas
10. North Carolina
11. Florida
12. Kansas
13. Illinois
14. George Washington
15. Iowa
16. Pittsburgh
17. Washington
18. Tennessee
19. LSU
20. Nevada
21. Syracuse
22. West Virginia
23. Georgetown
24. Oklahoma
25. UAB

USA TODAY/ESPN
1. Duke
2. Connecticut
3. Memphis
4. Villanova
5. Gonzaga
6. Ohio St.
7. Boston College
8. UCLA
9. Texas
10. Florida
11. George Washington
12. North Carolina
13. Kansas
14. Illinois
15. Iowa
16. Pittsburgh
17. Washington
18. LSU
19. Tennessee
20. Oklahoma
21. Nevada
22. Syracuse
23. West Virginia
24. Georgetown
25. UAB

2007
AP
1. Ohio St.
2. Kansas
3. Florida
4. North Carolina
5. Memphis
6. Wisconsin
7. UCLA
8. Georgetown
9. Texas A&M
10. Oregon
11. Texas

12. Pittsburgh
13. Washington St.
14. Southern Ill.
15. Nevada
16. Louisville
17. Notre Dame
18. Maryland
19. UNLV
20. Marquette
21. Butler
22. Winthrop
23. Southern California
24. BYU
25. Tennessee

USA TODAY/ESPN
1. Ohio St.
2. Kansas
3. Florida
4. North Carolina
5. Memphis
6. UCLA
7. Wisconsin
8. Georgetown
9. Texas A&M
10. Pittsburgh
11. Texas
12. Oregon
13. Nevada
    Washington St.
15. Southern Ill.
16. Louisville
17. Notre Dame
18. UNLV
19. Butler
20. Marquette
21. Winthrop
22. Maryland
23. BYU
24. Creighton
25. Southern California

Final Post-Tournament Polls

1994
USA TODAY/CNN
1. Arkansas
2. Duke
3. Arizona
4. Florida
5. Purdue
6. Missouri
7. Connecticut
8. Michigan
9. North Carolina
10. Louisville
11. Boston College
12. Kansas
13. Kentucky
14. Syracuse
15. Massachusetts
16. Indiana
17. Marquette
18. Temple
19. Tulsa
20. Maryland
21. Oklahoma St.
22. UCLA
23. Minnesota
24. Texas
25. Penn

1995
USA TODAY/NABC
1. UCLA
2. Arkansas
3. North Carolina
4. Oklahoma St.
5. Kentucky
6. Connecticut
7. Massachusetts
8. Virginia
9. Wake Forest
10. Kansas

11. Maryland
12. Mississippi St.
13. Arizona St.
14. Memphis
15. Tulsa
16. Georgetown
17. Syracuse
18. Missouri
19. Purdue
20. Michigan St.
21. Alabama
22. Utah
23. Villanova
24. Texas
25. Arizona

1996
USA TODAY/NABC
1. Kentucky
2. Massachusetts
3. Syracuse
4. Mississippi St.
5. Kansas
6. Cincinnati
7. Georgetown
8. Connecticut
9. Wake Forest
10. Texas Tech
11. Arizona
12. Utah
13. Georgia Tech
14. Louisville
15. Purdue
16. Georgia
17. Villanova
18. Arkansas
19. UCLA
20. Iowa St.
21. Virginia Tech
22. Iowa
23. Marquette
24. North Carolina
25. New Mexico

1997
USA TODAY/NABC
1. Arizona
2. Kentucky
3. Minnesota
4. North Carolina
5. Kansas
6. Utah
7. UCLA
8. Clemson
9. Wake Forest
10. Louisville
11. Duke
12. Stanford
13. Iowa St.
14. South Carolina
15. Providence
16. Cincinnati
17. St. Joseph's
18. California
19. New Mexico
20. Texas
21. Col. of Charleston
22. Xavier
23. Boston College
24. Michigan
25. Colorado

1998
USA TODAY/NABC
1. Kentucky
2. Utah
3. North Carolina
4. Stanford
5. Duke
6. Arizona
7. Connecticut
8. Kansas
9. Purdue
10. Michigan St.
11. Rhode Island
12. UCLA
13. Syracuse
14. Cincinnati
15. Maryland

16. Princeton
17. Michigan
18. West Virginia
19. South Carolina
20. Mississippi
21. New Mexico
22. Arkansas
23. Valparaiso
24. Washington
25. TCU

1999
USA TODAY/NABC
1. Connecticut
2. Duke
3. Michigan St.
4. Ohio St.
5. Kentucky
5. St. John's (N.Y.)
7. Auburn
8. Maryland
9. Stanford
10. Utah
11. Cincinnati
12. Gonzaga
12. Miami (Fla.)
14. Temple
15. Iowa
16. Arizona
17. Florida
18. North Carolina
19. Oklahoma
20. Miami (Ohio)
21. UCLA
22. Purdue
23. Kansas
24. Missouri St.
25. Arkansas

2000
USA TODAY/NABC
1. Michigan St.
2. Florida
3. Iowa St.
4. Duke
5. Stanford
6. Oklahoma St.
7. Cincinnati
8. Arizona
9. Tulsa
10. Temple
11. North Carolina
12. Syracuse
12. LSU
14. Tennessee
15. Purdue
16. Wisconsin
17. Ohio St.
18. St. John's (N.Y.)
19. Oklahoma
20. Miami (Fla.)
21. Texas
22. Kentucky
23. UCLA
24. Gonzaga
25. Maryland

2001
USA TODAY/NABC
1. Duke
2. Arizona
3. Michigan St.
4. Maryland
5. Stanford
6. Illinois
7. Kansas
8. Kentucky
9. Mississippi
10. North Carolina
11. Boston College
12. UCLA
13. Florida
14. Southern California
15. Iowa St.
16. Temple
17. Georgetown
18. Syracuse
19. Oklahoma
20. Gonzaga

21. Virginia
22. Cincinnati
23. Notre Dame
24. St. Joseph's
25. Penn St.

2002
USA/ESPN
1. Maryland
2. Kansas
3. Indiana
4. Oklahoma
5. Duke
6. Connecticut
7. Oregon
8. Cincinnati
9. Pittsburgh
10. Arizona
11. Illinois
12. Kent St.
13. Kentucky
14. Alabama
15. Missouri
16. Gonzaga
17. Ohio St.
18. Marquette
19. Texas
20. UCLA
21. Mississippi St.
22. Southern Ill.
23. Florida
24. Xavier
25. North Carolina St.

2003
USA/ESPN
1. Syracuse
2. Kansas
3. Texas
4. Kentucky
5. Arizona
6. Marquette
7. Oklahoma
8. Pittsburgh
9. Duke
10. Maryland
11. Connecticut
12. Wake Forest
13. Illinois
13. Wisconsin
15. Notre Dame
16. Florida
17. Xavier
18. Michigan St.
19. Louisville
20. Stanford
21. Butler
22. Missouri
23. Creighton
24. Oklahoma St.
25. Dayton

2004
USA/ESPN
1. Connecticut
2. Duke
3. Georgia Tech
4. Oklahoma St.
5. St. Joseph's
6. Stanford
7. Pittsburgh
8. Kentucky
9. Kansas
10. Texas
11. Illinois
12. Gonzaga
13. Mississippi St.
14. Xavier
15. Wake Forest
16. Wisconsin
17. Alabama
18. Cincinnati
19. Syracuse
20. North Carolina St.
21. Nevada
22. North Carolina
23. UAB
24. Maryland
25. Vanderbilt

2005
USA/ESPN
1. North Carolina
2. Illinois
3. Louisville
4. Michigan St.
5. Kentucky
6. Arizona
7. Duke
8. Oklahoma St.
9. Washington
10. Wisconsin
11. Wake Forest
12. West Virginia
13. Syracuse
14. Utah
15. Kansas
16. Texas Tech
17. Connecticut
18. Gonzaga
19. Boston College
20. Oklahoma
21. Syracuse
22. North Carolina St.
23. Milwaukee
24. Florida
25. Cincinnati

2006
USA/ESPN
1. Florida
2. UCLA
3. LSU
4. Connecticut
5. Villanova
6. Memphis
7. Duke
8. George Mason
9. Texas
10. Gonzaga
11. Boston College
12. Washington
13. Ohio St.
14. North Carolina
15. West Virginia
16. Georgetown
17. Illinois
18. Pittsburgh
19. George Washington
20. Tennessee
21. Wichita St.
22. Kansas
23. Iowa
24. Bradley
25. Bucknell

2007
USA/ESPN
1. Florida
2. Ohio St.
3. UCLA
4. Georgetown
5. Kansas
   North Carolina
7. Memphis
8. Oregon
9. Texas A&M
10. Pittsburgh
11. Southern Ill.
    Wisconsin
13. Butler
14. UNLV
15. Southern California
16. Texas
17. Washington St.
18. Tennessee
19. Vanderbilt
20. Louisville
21. Nevada
22. Winthrop
23. Maryland
24. Virginia
25. Virginia Tech

American Sports Wire Poll

The following poll ranks the top historically black institutions of the NCAA as selected by American Sports Wire and compiled by Dick Simpson.

Year	Team	Coach	Won	Lost
1992	Howard	Butch Beard	17	14
1993	Jackson St.	Andy Stoglin	25	9
1994	Texas Southern	Robert Moreland	19	11
1995	Texas Southern	Robert Moreland	22	7
1996	South Carolina St.	Cy Alexander	22	8
1997	Coppin St.	Fang Mitchell	22	9
1998	South Carolina St.	Cy Alexander	22	8
1999	Alcorn St.	Davey L. Whitney	23	7
2000	South Carolina St.	Cy Alexander	20	14
2001	Hampton	Steve Merfeld	25	7
2002	Hampton	Steve Merfeld	25	7
2003	South Carolina St.	Cy Alexander	20	11
2004	Florida A&M	Michael Gillespie	15	17
2005	Delaware St.	Greg Jackson	19	14
2006	Delaware St.	Greg Jackson	21	14
2007	Delaware St.	Greg Jackson	21	13

Division II
Records

Individual Records

Basketball records are confined to the "modern era," which began with the 1937-38 season, the first without the center jump after each goal scored. Official weekly statistics rankings in scoring and shooting began with the 1947-48 season. Individual rebounds were added for the 1950-51 season, while team rebounds were added for the 1959-60 season. Assists were added for the 1988-89 season. Blocked shots and steals were added for the 1992-93 season. Scoring and rebounding are ranked on per-game average; shooting, on percentage. Beginning with the 1967-68 season, Division II rankings were limited only to NCAA members. The 1973-74 season was the first under a three-division reorganization plan adopted by the special NCAA Convention of August 1973. In statistical rankings, the rounding of percentages and/or averages may indicate ties where none exist. In these cases, the numerical order of the rankings is accurate.

Scoring

POINTS
Game
113—Clarence "Bevo" Francis, Rio Grande vs. Hillsdale, Feb. 2, 1954
Season
1,329—Earl Monroe, Winston-Salem, 1967 (32 games)
Career
4,045—Travis Grant, Kentucky St., 1969-72 (121 games)

AVERAGE PER GAME
Season
†46.5—Clarence "Bevo" Francis, Rio Grande, 1954 (1,255 in 27)
Career
(Min. 1,400) 33.4—Travis Grant, Kentucky St., 1969-72 (4,045 in 121)

†Season and career figures for Francis limited only to his 39 games (27 in 1954) against four-year colleges.

GAMES SCORING AT LEAST 50 POINTS
Season
†8—Clarence "Bevo" Francis, Rio Grande, 1954
Career
†14—Clarence "Bevo" Francis, Rio Grande, 1953-54

†Season and career figures for Francis limited only to his 39 games (27 in 1954) against four-year colleges.

MOST GAMES SCORING IN DOUBLE FIGURES
Career
130—Lambert Shell, Bridgeport, 1989-92

POINTS SCORED IN OVERTIME
18—John Green, Barton vs. St. Andrews, Feb. 5, 2004 (team scored 19)

Field Goals

FIELD GOALS
Game
38—Clarence "Bevo" Francis, Rio Grande vs. Alliance, Jan. 16, 1954 (71 attempts) and vs. Hillsdale, Feb. 2, 1954 (70 attempts)
Season
539—Travis Grant, Kentucky St., 1972 (869 attempts)
Career
1,760—Travis Grant, Kentucky St., 1969-72 (2,759 attempts)

CONSECUTIVE FIELD GOALS
Game
20—Lance Berwald, North Dakota St. vs. Augustana (S.D.), Feb. 17, 1984
Season
28—Don McAllister, Hartwick, 1980 (during six games, Jan. 26-Feb. 9); Lance Berwald, North Dakota St., 1984 (during three games, Feb. 13-18)

FIELD-GOAL ATTEMPTS
Game
71—Clarence "Bevo" Francis, Rio Grande vs. Alliance, Jan. 16, 1954 (38 made)
Season
925—Jim Toombs, Stillman, 1965 (388 made)
Career
3,309—Bob Hopkins, Grambling, 1953-56 (1,403 made)

FIELD-GOAL PERCENTAGE
Game
(Min. 20 made) 100%—Lance Berwald, North Dakota St. vs. Augustana (S.D.), Feb. 17, 1984 (20 of 20)
*Season
75.2%—Todd Linder, Tampa, 1987 (282 of 375)

*based on qualifiers for annual championship
Career
(Min. 400 made) 70.8%—Todd Linder, Tampa, 1984-87 (909 of 1,284)

Three-Point Field Goals

THREE-POINT FIELD GOALS
Game
16—Thomas Vincent, Emporia St. vs. Southwest Baptist, Feb. 28, 2004 (23 attempts); Markus Hallgrimson, Mont. St.-Billings vs. Western N.M., Feb. 12, 2000 (28 attempts)
Season
167—Alex Williams, Sacramento St., 1988 (369 attempts)
Career
451—Cameron Munoz, Mont. St.-Billings, 2003-06 (1,042 attempts)

THREE-POINT FIELD GOALS MADE PER GAME
Season
6.2—Markus Hallgrimson, Mont. St.-Billings, 2000 (160 in 26)
Career
4.7—Antonio Harris, LeMoyne-Owen, 1998-99 (245 in 52)

CONSECUTIVE THREE-POINT FIELD GOALS
Game
10—Duane Huddleston, Mo.-Rolla vs. Truman, Jan. 23, 1988
Season
18—Dan Drews, Le Moyne (during 11 games, Dec. 11, 1993 to Feb. 2, 1994)

CONSECUTIVE GAMES MAKING A THREE-POINT FIELD GOAL
Season
35—Tarvoris Uzoigwe, Henderson St., Nov. 15, 2002 to March 17, 2003 (one season)
Career
93—Daniel Parke, Rollins, Jan. 26, 1994, to Feb. 28, 1997

THREE-POINT FIELD-GOAL ATTEMPTS
Game
34—Markus Hallgrimson, Mont. St.-Billings vs. Western N.M., Feb. 26, 2000 (13 made)
Season
382—Markus Hallgrimson, Mont. St.-Billings, 2000 (160 made)
Career
1,047—Tony Smith, Pfeiffer, 1989-92 (431 made)

THREE-POINT FIELD-GOAL ATTEMPTS PER GAME
Season
14.7—Markus Hallgrimson, Mont. St.-Billings, 2000 (382 in 26)
Career
11.3—Markus Hallgrimson, Mont. St.-Billings, 1997-00 (927 in 82)

THREE-POINT FIELD-GOAL PERCENTAGE
Game
(Min. 10 made) 100%—Rodney Edgerson, Ky. Wesleyan vs. Wis.-Parkside, Jan. 25, 2007 (10 of 10)
*Season
(Min. 35 made) 65.0%—Ray Lee, Hampton, 1988 (39 of 60)
(Min. 50 made) 60.3%—Aaron Fehler, Oakland City, 1995 (73 of 121)

(Min. 100 made) 56.7%—Scott Martin, Rollins, 1991 (114 of 201)
(Min. 150 made) 45.3%—Alex Williams, Sacramento St., 1988 (167 of 369)

*based on qualifiers for annual championship
Career
(Min. 200 made) 51.3%—Scott Martin, Rollins, 1988-91 (236 of 460)

Free Throws

FREE THROWS
Game
37—Clarence "Bevo" Francis, Rio Grande vs. Hillsdale, Feb. 2, 1954 (45 attempts)
Season
401—Joe Miller, Alderson-Broaddus, 1957 (496 attempts)
Career
1,130—Joe Miller, Alderson-Broaddus, 1954-57 (1,460 attempts)

CONSECUTIVE FREE THROWS
Game
26—Jim Moore, St. Anselm vs. St. Rose, Feb. 18, 2006
Season
94—Paul Cluxton, Northern Ky., 1997 (during 34 games, Nov. 8-Mar. 20)

FREE-THROW ATTEMPTS
Game
45—Clarence "Bevo" Francis, Rio Grande vs. Hillsdale, Feb. 2, 1954 (37 made)
Season
†510—Clarence "Bevo" Francis, Rio Grande, 1954 (367 made)
Career
1,460—Joe Miller, Alderson-Broaddus, 1954-57 (1,130 made)

†Season figure for Francis limited to 27 games against four-year colleges.

FREE-THROW PERCENTAGE
Game
(Min. 20 made) 100%—Milosh Pujo, Lewis vs. Mt. St. Clare, Dec. 30, 1997 (20 of 20); Forrest "Butch" Meyeraan, Minn. St. Mankato vs. Wis.-River Falls, Feb. 21, 1961 (20 of 20)
*Season
100%—Paul Cluxton, Northern Ky., 1997 (94 of 94)

*based on qualifiers for annual championship
Career
(Min. 250 made) 93.5%—Paul Cluxton, Northern Ky., 1994-97 (272 of 291)
(Min. 500 made) 87.9%—Steve Nisenson, Hofstra, 1963-65 (602 of 685)

Rebounds

REBOUNDS
Game
46—Tom Hart, Middlebury vs. Trinity (Conn.), Feb. 5, 1955, and vs. Clarkson, Feb. 12, 1955
Season
799—Elmore Smith, Kentucky St., 1971 (33 games)
Career
2,334—Jim Smith, Steubenville, 1955-58 (112 games)

AVERAGE PER GAME
Season
29.5—Tom Hart, Middlebury, 1956 (620 in 21)
Career
(Min. 900) 27.6—Tom Hart, Middlebury, 1953, 55-56 (1,738 in 63)

Assists

ASSISTS
Game
25—Ali Baaqar, Morris Brown vs. Albany St. (Ga.), Jan. 26, 1991; Adrian Hutt, Metro St. vs. Sacramento St., Feb. 9, 1991
Season
400—Steve Ray, Bridgeport, 1989 (32 games)
Career
1,044—Demetri Beekman, Assumption, 1990-93 (119 games)
AVERAGE PER GAME
Season
12.5—Steve Ray, Bridgeport, 1989 (400 in 32)
Career
(Min. 550) 12.1—Steve Ray, Bridgeport, 1989-90 (785 in 65)

Blocked Shots

BLOCKED SHOTS
Game
15—Mark Hensel, Pitt.-Johnstown vs. Slippery Rock, Jan. 22, 1994

Season
157—James Doyle, Concord, 1998 (30 games)
Career
416—James Doyle, Concord, 1995-98 (120 games)
AVERAGE PER GAME
Season
5.3—Antonio Harvey, Pfeiffer, 1993 (155 in 29)
Career
4.00—Derek Moore, S.C.-Aiken, 1996-99 (408 in 102)

Steals

STEALS
Game
17—Antonio Walls, Alabama A&M vs. Albany St. (Ga.), Jan. 5, 1998
Season
139—J.R. Gamble, Queens (N.C.), 2001 (32 games)
Career
383—Eddin Santiago, Mo. Southern St., 1999-02, (117 games)
AVERAGE PER GAME
Season
5.0—Wayne Copeland, Lynn, 2000 (129 in 26)

Career
4.46—Wayne Copeland, Lynn, 1999-00 (254 in 57)

Games

GAMES PLAYED
Season
38—Terrence Hill, Rey Luque, Reggie McCoy, Kevin McDonald, Cardale Talley, Justin Thompson, Tommy Thompson, Kennesaw St., 2004
Career
133—Gino Bartolone, Ky. Wesleyan, 1998-01; Pat Morris, Bridgeport, 1989-92

Team Records

Note: Where records involve both teams, each team must be an NCAA Division II member institution.

SINGLE-GAME RECORDS

Scoring

POINTS
258—Troy vs. DeVry (Ga.) (141), Jan. 12, 1992
POINTS VS. DIVISION II TEAM
169—Stillman vs. Miles (123), Feb. 17, 1966
POINTS BY LOSING TEAM
146—Mississippi Col. vs. West Ala. (160), Dec. 2, 1969
POINTS, BOTH TEAMS
306—West Ala. (160) and Mississippi Col. (146), Dec. 2, 1969
POINTS IN A HALF
135—Troy vs. DeVry (Ga.), Jan. 12, 1992
FEWEST POINTS ALLOWED (SINCE 1938)
4—Albion (76) vs. Adrian, Dec. 12, 1938; Tennessee St. (7) vs. Oglethorpe, Feb. 16, 1971
FEWEST POINTS, BOTH TEAMS (SINCE 1938)
11—Tennessee St. (7) and Oglethorpe (4), Feb. 16, 1971
WIDEST MARGIN OF VICTORY
118—Mississippi Col. (168) vs. Dallas Bible (50), Dec. 9, 1971

Field Goals

FIELD GOALS
102—Troy vs. DeVry (Ga.), Jan. 12, 1992 (190 attempts)
FIELD-GOAL ATTEMPTS
190—Troy vs. DeVry (Ga.), Jan. 12, 1992 (102 made)
FEWEST FIELD GOALS (SINCE 1938)
0—Adrian vs. Albion, Dec. 12, 1938 (28 attempts)
FEWEST FIELD-GOAL ATTEMPTS
7—Mansfield vs. West Chester, Dec. 8, 1984 (4 made)
FIELD-GOAL PERCENTAGE
81.6%—Youngstown St. vs. UNI, Jan. 26, 1980 (31 of 38)
FIELD-GOAL PERCENTAGE, HALF
95.0%—Abilene Christian vs. Cameron, Jan. 21, 1989 (19 of 20)

Three-Point Field Goals

THREE-POINT FIELD GOALS
51—Troy vs. DeVry (Ga.), Jan. 12, 1992 (109 attempts)
THREE-POINT FIELD GOALS, BOTH TEAMS
39—Columbus St. (22) vs. Troy (17), Feb. 14, 1991
CONSECUTIVE THREE-POINT FIELD GOALS MADE WITHOUT A MISS
12—Southwest St. vs. Bemidji St., Jan. 22, 2000; Catawba vs. Wingate, Feb. 28, 1998; Pace vs. Medgar Evers, Nov. 27, 1991
NUMBER OF DIFFERENT PLAYERS TO SCORE A THREE-POINT FIELD GOAL, ONE TEAM
10—Troy vs. DeVry (Ga.), Jan. 12, 1992
THREE-POINT FIELD-GOAL ATTEMPTS
109—Troy vs. DeVry (Ga.), Jan. 12, 1992 (51 made)
THREE-POINT FIELD-GOAL ATTEMPTS, BOTH TEAMS
95—Columbus St. (52) vs. Troy (43), Feb. 14, 1991
THREE-POINT FIELD-GOAL PERCENTAGE
(Min. 10 made) 100%—LeMooyne-Owen vs. Delta St., Nov. 25, 2006 (10 of 10)
HIGHEST THREE-POINT FIELD-GOAL PERCENTAGE, BOTH TEAMS
(Min. 10 made) 83.3%—Tampa (9 of 10) vs. St. Leo (1 of 2), Jan. 21, 1987 (10 of 12)
(Min. 20 made) 77.8%—LeMoyne-Owen (10 of 10) vs. Delta St. (11 of 17), Nov. 25, 2006 (21 of 27)

Free Throws

FREE THROWS MADE
64—Wayne St. (Mich.) vs. Grand Valley St., Feb. 13, 1993 (79 attempts); Baltimore vs. Washington (Md.), Feb. 9, 1955 (84 attempts)
FREE THROWS MADE, BOTH TEAMS
89—Southern Ind. (50) vs. Northern St. (39), Nov. 15, 1997 (3ot); Baltimore (64) and Washington (Md.) (25), Feb. 9,1955
CONSECUTIVE FREE THROWS MADE
37—Southern Ind., January 23-30, 2003 (three games)
FREE-THROW ATTEMPTS
84—Baltimore vs. Washington (Md.), Feb. 9, 1955 (64 made)

FREE-THROW ATTEMPTS, BOTH TEAMS
142—Southern Ind. (80) vs. Northern St. (62), Nov. 15, 1997 (3 ot) (89 made)
FREE-THROW PERCENTAGE
(Min. 31 made) 100%—Dowling vs. Southampton, Feb. 6, 1985 (31 of 31)
FREE-THROW PERCENTAGE, BOTH TEAMS
(Min. 30 made) 97.0%—Hartford (17 of 17) vs. Bentley (15 of 16), Feb. 22, 1983 (32 of 33)

Rebounds

REBOUNDS
111—Central Mich. vs. Alma, Dec. 7, 1963
REBOUNDS, BOTH TEAMS
141—Loyola (Md.) (75) vs. McDaniel (66), Dec. 6, 1961; Concordia (Ill.) (72) vs. Concordia (Neb.) (69), Feb. 26, 1965
REBOUND MARGIN
65—Moravian (100) vs. Drew (35), Feb. 18, 1969

Assists

ASSISTS
65—Troy vs. DeVry (Ga.), Jan. 12, 1992
ASSISTS, BOTH TEAMS
65—Central Okla. (34) vs. Stonehill (31), Dec. 29, 1990

Personal Fouls

PERSONAL FOULS
51—Northern St. vs. Southern Ind., Nov. 15, 1997 (3 ot)
PERSONAL FOULS, BOTH TEAMS (Including Overtimes)
91—Northern St. (51) vs. Southern Ind. (40), Nov. 15, 1997 (3 ot)
PERSONAL FOULS, BOTH TEAMS (Regulation Time)
78—Cal St. Chico (41) vs. Cal St. San B'dino (37), Feb. 12, 2005 (85 total personal fouls including overtime)

DIVISION II

PLAYERS DISQUALIFIED

7—Northern St. vs. Southern Ind., Nov. 15, 1997 (3 ot); Illinois Col. vs. Illinois Tech, Dec. 13, 1952; Steubenville vs. West Liberty, 1952; Washington (Md.) vs. Baltimore, Feb. 9, 1955; Colorado St.-Pueblo vs. Air Force, Jan. 12, 1972; Edinboro vs. California (Pa.) (5 ot), Feb. 4, 1989

PLAYERS DISQUALIFIED, BOTH TEAMS

12—Alfred (6) and Rensselaer (6), Jan. 9, 1971

Overtimes

OVERTIME PERIODS

7—Yankton (79) vs. Black Hills (80), Feb. 18, 1956

POINTS IN ONE OVERTIME PERIOD

27—Southern Ind. vs. Central Mo., Jan. 5, 1985

POINTS IN ONE OVERTIME PERIOD, BOTH TEAMS

46—North Dakota St. (25) vs. St. Cloud St. (21), Jan. 16, 1999; North Dakota St. (25) vs. South Dakota (21), Jan. 9, 1999

POINTS IN OVERTIME PERIODS

60—California (Pa.) vs. Edinboro (5 ot), Feb. 4, 1989

POINTS IN OVERTIME PERIODS, BOTH TEAMS

114—California (Pa.) (60) vs. Edinboro (54) (5 ot), Feb. 4, 1989

WINNING MARGIN IN OVERTIME GAME

22—Pfeiffer (72) vs. Belmont Abbey (50), Dec. 8, 1960

SEASON RECORDS

Scoring

POINTS

3,566—Troy, 1993 (32 games); Central Okla., 1992 (32 games)

AVERAGE PER GAME

121.1—Troy, 1992 (3,513 in 29)

AVERAGE SCORING MARGIN

31.4—Bryan, 1961 (93.8 offense, 62.4 defense)

GAMES AT LEAST 100 POINTS

25—Troy, 1993 (32-game season)

CONSECUTIVE GAMES AT LEAST 100 POINTS

17—Norfolk St., 1970

Field Goals

FIELD GOALS

1,455—Kentucky St., 1971 (2,605 attempts)

FIELD GOALS PER GAME

46.9—Lincoln (Mo.), 1967 (1,267 in 27)

FIELD-GOAL ATTEMPTS

2,853—Ark.-Pine Bluff, 1967 (1,306 made)

FIELD-GOAL ATTEMPTS PER GAME

108.2—Stillman, 1968 (2,814 in 26)

FIELD-GOAL PERCENTAGE

62.4%—Kentucky St., 1976 (1,093 of 1,753)

Three-Point Field Goals

THREE-POINT FIELD GOALS

444—Troy, 1992 (1,303 attempts)

THREE-POINT FIELD GOALS PER GAME

15.3—Troy, 1992 (444 in 29)

THREE-POINT FIELD-GOAL ATTEMPTS

1,303—Troy, 1992 (444 made)

THREE-POINT FIELD-GOAL ATTEMPTS PER GAME

44.9—Troy, 1992 (1,303 in 29)

THREE-POINT FIELD-GOAL PERCENTAGE

(Min. 90 made) 53.8%—Winston-Salem, 1988 (98 of 182)
(Min. 200 made) 50.2%—Oakland City, 1992 (244 of 486)

CONSECUTIVE GAMES SCORING A THREE-POINT FIELD GOAL (Multiple Seasons)

567—Ky. Wesleyan, Nov. 22, 1986-Present

Free Throws

FREE THROWS MADE

896—Ouachita Baptist, 1965 (1,226 attempts)

FREE THROWS MADE PER GAME

36.1—Baltimore, 1955 (686 in 19)

FREE-THROW ATTEMPTS

1,226—Ouachita Baptist, 1965 (896 made)

FREE-THROW ATTEMPTS PER GAME

49.6—Baltimore, 1955 (943 in 19)

FREE-THROW PERCENTAGE

82.5%—Gannon, 1998 (473 of 573)

Rebounds

REBOUNDS

1,667—Norfolk St., 1973 (31 games)

AVERAGE PER GAME

65.8—Bentley, 1964 (1,513 in 23)

AVERAGE REBOUND MARGIN

24.4—Mississippi Val., 1976 (63.9 offense, 39.5 defense)

Assists

ASSISTS

736—Southern N.H., 1993 (33 games)

AVERAGE PER GAME

25.6—Quincy, 1994 (716 in 28)

Personal Fouls

PERSONAL FOULS

947—Seattle, 1952 (37 games)

PERSONAL FOULS PER GAME

29.9—Shaw, 1987 (748 in 25)

FEWEST PERSONAL FOULS

184—Sewanee, 1962 (17 games)

FEWEST PERSONAL FOULS PER GAME

10.0—Ashland, 1969 (301 in 30)

Defense

LOWEST POINTS PER GAME ALLOWED

20.2—Alcorn St., 1941 (323 in 16)

LOWEST POINTS PER GAME ALLOWED (Since 1948)

29.1—Miss. Industrial, 1948 (436 in 15)

LOWEST FIELD-GOAL PERCENTAGE ALLOWED (Since 1978)

35.8—Tarleton St., 2002 (657 of 1,837)

Overtimes

MOST OVERTIME GAMES

8—Barton, 2007 (won 8, lost 0); Belmont Abbey, 1983 (won 4, lost 4)

MOST CONSECUTIVE OVERTIME GAMES

3—10 times, most recent: Pace, 1996 (won 3, lost 0)

MOST OVERTIME WINS

8—Barton, 2007 (won 8, lost 0)

MOST MULTIPLE-OVERTIME GAMES

5—Cal St. Dom. Hills, 1987 (four 2 ot, one 3 ot; won 2, lost 3)

General Records

GAMES IN A SEASON

39—Kennesaw St., 2004 (35-4); Regis (Colo.), 1949 (36-3)

VICTORIES IN A SEASON

36—Regis (Colo.), 1949 (36-3)

VICTORIES IN A PERFECT SEASON

34—Fort Hays St., 1996

CONSECUTIVE VICTORIES

57—Winona St. (from Jan. 13, 2006-March 22, 2007)

CONSECUTIVE 30-WIN SEASONS

4—Ky. Wesleyan, 1998 (30); 1999 (35); 2000 (31); 2001 (31)

CONSECUTIVE HOME-COURT VICTORIES

80—Philadelphia U. (from Jan. 8, 1991 to Nov. 21, 1995)

CONSECUTIVE REGULAR-SEASON VICTORIES (postseason tournaments not included)

52—Langston (from 1943-44 opener through fifth game of 1945-46 season)

CONSECUTIVE VICTORIES AGAINST AN OPPONENT

43—Fla. Southern vs. St. Leo, Feb. 11, 1985-current

DEFEATS IN A SEASON

28—UNC Pembroke, 2003 (0-28)

CONSECUTIVE DEFEATS IN A SEASON

28—UNC Pembroke, 2003 (0-28)

CONSECUTIVE DEFEATS

46—Olivet, Feb. 21, 1959, to Dec. 4, 1961; Southwest Minn. St., Dec. 11, 1971, to Dec. 1, 1973

CONSECUTIVE WINNING SEASONS

35—Norfolk St., 1963-97

CONSECUTIVE NON-LOSING SEASONS

35—Norfolk St., 1963-97

††UNBEATEN TEAMS (Since 1938; Number of Victories in Parentheses)

1938 Glenville St. (28)
1941 Milwaukee St. (16)
1942 Indianapolis (16)
1942 Rochester (16)
1944 Langston (23)
1945 Langston (24)
1948 West Virginia St. (23)
1949 Tennessee St. (24)
1956 Rochester Inst. (17)
1959 Grand Canyon (20)
1961 Calvin (20)
1964 Bethany (W.V.) (18)
1965 Central St. (Ohio) (30)
1965 Evansville (29)#
1993 Cal St. Bakersfield (33)#
1996 Fort Hays St. (34)#

††at least 15 victories; #NCAA Division II champion

All-Time Individual Leaders

Single-Game Records

SCORING HIGHS

Pts.	Player, Team vs. Opponent	Season
113	Clarence "Bevo" Francis, Rio Grande vs. Hillsdale	1954
84	Clarence "Bevo" Francis, Rio Grande vs. Alliance	1954
82	Clarence "Bevo" Francis, Rio Grande vs. Bluffton	1954
80	Paul Crissman, Southern California Col. vs. Pacific Christian	1966
77	William English, Winston-Salem vs. Fayetteville St.	1968
75	Travis Grant, Kentucky St. vs. Northwood (Mich.)	1970
72	Nate DeLong, Wis.-River Falls vs. Winona St.	1948
72	Lloyd Brown, Aquinas vs. Cleary	1953
72	Clarence "Bevo" Francis, Rio Grande vs. California (Pa.)	1953
72	John McElroy, Youngstown St. vs. Wayne St. (Mich.)	1969
71	Clayborn Jones, L.A. Pacific vs. L.A. Baptist	1965
70	Paul Wilcox, Davis & Elkins vs. Glenville St.	1959
70	Bo Clark, UCF vs. Fla. Memorial	1977

Season Records

SCORING AVERAGE

Player, Team	Season	G	FG	FT	Pts.	Avg.
Clarence "Bevo" Francis, Rio Grande	†1954	27	444	367	1,255	*46.5
Earl Glass, Miss. Industrial	†1963	19	322	171	815	42.9
Earl Monroe, Winston-Salem	†1967	32	509	311	*1,329	41.5
John Rinka, Kenyon	†1970	23	354	234	942	41.0
Willie Shaw, Lane	†1964	18	303	121	727	40.4
Travis Grant, Kentucky St.	†1972	33	*539	226	1,304	39.5
Thales McReynolds, Miles	†1965	18	294	118	706	39.2
Bob Johnson, Fitchburg St.	1963	18	213	277	703	39.1
Roger Kuss, Wis.-River Falls	†1953	21	291	235	817	38.9
Florindo Vieira, Quinnipiac	1954	14	191	138	520	37.1

†national champion; *record

FIELD-GOAL PERCENTAGE
(Based on qualifiers for annual championship)

Player, Team	Season	G	FG	FGA	Pct.
Todd Linder, Tampa	†1987	32	282	375	*75.2
Maurice Stafford, North Ala.	†1984	34	198	264	75.0
Matthew Cornegay, Tuskegee	†1982	29	208	278	74.8
Callistus Eziukwu, Grand Valley St.	†2005	28	157	213	73.7
Brian Moten, West Ga.	†1992	26	141	192	73.4
Ed Phillips, Alabama A&M	†1968	22	154	210	73.3
Ray Strozier, Central Mo.	†1980	28	142	195	72.8
Harold Booker, Cheyney	†1965	24	144	198	72.7
Chad Scott, California (Pa.)	†1994	30	178	245	72.7
Tom Schurfranz, Bellarmine	†1991	30	245	339	72.3
Marv Lewis, Southampton	†1969	24	271	375	72.3
Louis Newsome, North Ala.	†1988	29	192	266	72.2
Ed Phillips, Alabama A&M	†1971	24	159	221	71.9
Gregg Northington, Alabama St.	1971	26	324	451	71.8

†national champion; *record

THREE-POINT FIELD GOALS

Player, Team	Season	G	3FG
Alex Williams, Sacramento St.	1988	30	167
Markus Hallgrimson, Mont. St.-Billings	2000	26	160
Yandel Brown, Columbus St.	2005	32	148
Eric Kline, Northern St.	1995	30	148
Eric Kline, Northern St.	1994	33	148
Cameron Munoz, Mont. St.-Billings	2006	28	147
Mike Taylor, West Virginia St.	2004	32	140
Shawn Pughsley, Central Okla.	1998	32	139
Jed Bedford, Columbus St.	2003	32	135
Reece Gliko, Mont. St.-Billings	1997	28	135
Ray Gutierrez, California (Pa.)	1993	27	135
Jason Garrow, Augustana (S.D.)	1992	27	135
Markus Hallgrimson, Mont. St.-Billings	1999	28	133
Stephen Dye, Alderson-Broaddus	2004	34	129
Shawn Williams, Central Okla.	1991	29	129
Tarvoris Uzoigwe, Henderson St.	2003	35	128
Robert Martin, Sacramento St.	1988	30	128
Steve Brown, West Ala.	2000	26	126
Antonio Harris, LeMoyne-Owen	1999	26	126
Tommie Spearman, Columbus	1995	29	126

Player, Team	Season	G	3FG
Kwame Morton, Clarion	1994	26	126

THREE-POINT FIELD GOALS PER GAME

Player, Team	Season	G	3FG	Avg.
Markus Hallgrimson, Mont. St.-Billings	†2000	26	160	*6.2
Alex Williams, Sacramento St.	†1988	30	*167	5.6
Cameron Munoz, Mont. St.-Billings	†2006	28	147	5.3
Jason Garrow, Augustana (S.D.)	†1992	27	135	5.0
Eric Kline, Northern St.	†1995	30	148	4.9
Ray Gutierrez, California (Pa.)	†1993	29	142	4.9
Steve Brown, West Ala.	2000	26	126	4.8
Antonio Harris, LeMoyne-Owen	†1999	26	126	4.8
Kwame Morton, Clarion	1994	26	126	4.8
Reece Gliko, Mont. St.-Billings	†1997	28	135	4.8
Markus Hallgrimson, Mont. St.-Billings	1999	28	133	4.8
John Boyd, LeMoyne-Owen	1992	26	123	4.7
Duane Huddleston, Mo.-Rolla	1988	25	118	4.7
Yandel Brown, Columbus St.	†2005	32	148	4.6
Antonio Harris, LeMoyne-Owen	†1998	26	119	4.6
Ricardo Watkins, Tuskegee	2000	24	110	4.6
Eric Kline, Northern St.	1994	33	148	4.5
Robbie Waldrop, Lees-McRae	2001	25	112	4.5
Damien Blair, West Chester	1994	28	125	4.5
Eric Carpenter, Cal St. San B'dino	1994	26	116	4.5

†national champion; *record

THREE-POINT FIELD-GOAL PERCENTAGE
(Based on qualifiers for annual championship)

Player, Team	Season	G	3FG	3FGA	Pct.
Ray Lee, Hampton	†1988	24	39	60	*65.0
Steve Hood, Winston-Salem	1988	28	42	67	62.7
Mark Willey, Fort Hays St.	†1990	29	49	81	60.5
Aaron Fehler, Oakland City	†1995	26	73	121	60.3
Aaron Baker, Mississippi Col.	†1989	27	69	117	59.0
Walter Hurd, Johnson C. Smith	1989	27	49	84	58.3
Matt Hopson, Oakland City	†1996	31	84	145	57.9
Jon Bryant, St. Cloud St.	1996	27	54	94	57.4
Adam Harness, Oakland City	†1997	26	39	68	57.4
Scott Martin, Rollins	†1991	28	114	201	56.7
Charles Byrd, West Tex. A&M	†1987	31	95	168	56.5
Aaron Buckoski, Michigan Tech	1997	26	39	69	56.5
Jay Nolan, Bowie St.	1987	27	70	124	56.5
Kris Kidwell, Oakland City	1996	28	44	78	56.4
Tony Harris, Dist. Columbia	1987	30	79	141	56.0
Rickey Barrett, Ala.-Huntsville	1987	26	63	113	55.8
Quinn Murphy, Drury	1995	27	45	81	55.6
Erik Fisher, San Fran. St.	1991	28	80	144	55.6
Mike Doyle, Philadelphia U.	1988	30	82	149	55.0

†national champion; *record

FREE-THROW PERCENTAGE
(Based on qualifiers for annual championship)

Player, Team	Season	G	FT	FTA	Pct.
Paul Cluxton, Northern Ky.	†1997	35	94	94	*100.0
Tomas Rimkus, Pace	1997	25	65	68	95.6
C. J. Cowgill, Chaminade	†2001	22	113	119	95.0
Billy Newton, Morgan St.	†1976	28	85	90	94.4
Kent Andrews, McNeese St.	†1968	24	85	90	94.4
Mike Sanders, Northern Colo.	†1987	28	82	87	94.3
Curtis Small, Southampton	†2002	29	109	116	94.0
Brent Mason, St. Joseph's (Ind.)	2001	31	125	133	94.0
Aaron Farley, Harding	†2003	30	137	146	93.8
Marcus Martinez, Cal St. Stanislaus	†2006	27	75	80	93.8
Travis Starns, Colorado Mines	†1999	26	87	93	93.5
Jay Harrie, Mont. St.-Billings	†1994	26	86	92	93.5
Joe Cullen, Hartwick	†1969	18	96	103	93.2
Dan Shanks, Coker	1997	27	119	128	93.0
Charles Byrd, West Tex. A&M	†1988	29	92	99	92.9
Jeremy Kudera, South Dakota	2001	28	78	84	92.9
Brian Koephick, Minn. St. Mankato	1988	28	104	112	92.9
Lance Den Boer, Central Wash.	2006	28	155	167	92.8
Jon Hagen, Minn. St. Mankato	†1963	25	76	82	92.7
Paul Cluxton, Northern Ky.	†1996	32	100	108	92.6

†national champion; *record

REBOUNDS (SINCE 1973)

Player, Team	Season	G	Reb.
Marvin Webster, Morgan St.	1974	33	740
Major Jones, Albany St. (Ga.)	1975	27	608

Player, Team	Season	G	Reb.
Earl Williams, Winston-Salem	1974	26	553
Antonio Garcia, Ky. Wesleyan	1999	37	540
Charles Oakley, Virginia Union	1985	31	535
Larry Johnson, Prairie View	1974	23	519
Andre Means, Sacred Heart	1977	32	516
Major Jones, Albany St. (Ga.)	1975	25	513
Harvey Jones, Alabama St.	1974	28	503
Andre Means, Sacred Heart	1978	30	493
Colin Duchacme, Longwood	2001	31	490
Rick Mahorn, Hampton	1980	31	490
Rob Roesch, Staten Island	1989	31	482
Leonard Robinson, Tennessee St.	1974	28	478
Major Jones, Albany St. (Ga.)	1976	24	475

REBOUND AVERAGE

Player, Team	Season	G	Reb.	Avg.
Tom Hart, Middlebury	†1956	21	620	*29.5
Tom Hart, Middlebury	†1955	22	649	29.5
Frank Stronczek, American Int'l	†1966	26	717	27.6
R.C. Owens, Albertson	†1954	25	677	27.1
Maurice Stokes, St. Francis (Pa.)	1954	26	689	26.5
Roman Turmon, Clark Atlanta	1954	23	602	26.2
Pat Callahan, Lewis	1955	20	523	26.2
Hank Brown, Mass.-Lowell	1966	19	496	26.1
Maurice Stokes, St. Francis (Pa.)	1955	28	726	25.9

†national champion; *record

(Since 1973)

Player, Team	Season	G	Reb.	Avg.
Larry Johnson, Prairie View	1974	23	519	22.6
Major Jones, Albany St. (Ga.)	1975	27	608	22.5
Marvin Webster, Morgan St.	1974	33	740	22.4
Earl Williams, Winston-Salem	1974	26	553	21.3
Major Jones, Albany St. (Ga.)	1974	25	513	20.5
Larry Gooding, St. Augustine's	1974	22	443	20.1
Major Jones, Albany St. (Ga.)	1976	24	475	19.8
Calvin Robinson, Mississippi Valley	1976	23	432	18.8
Scott Mountz, California (Pa.)	1978	24	431	18.0
Howard Shockley, Salisbury	1975	23	406	17.7
Charles Oakley, Virginia Union	1985	31	535	17.3
Marvin Webster, Morgan St.	1975	27	458	17.0
Larry Johnson, Ark.-Little Rock	1976	24	402	16.8
Keith Smith, Shaw	1979	20	329	16.5
Andre Means, Sacred Heart	1978	30	493	16.4
Donnie Roberts, St. Paul's	1975	25	406	16.2
Andre Means, Sacred Heart	1977	32	516	16.1
Dan Donahue, SIU Edwardsville	1975	26	419	16.1
Lorenzo Poole, Albany St. (Ga.)	1995	26	417	16.0
David Binion, N.C. Central	1983	25	400	16.0

ASSISTS

Player, Team	Season	G	Ast.
Steve Ray, Bridgeport	†1989	32	*400
Steve Ray, Bridgeport	†1990	33	385
Tony Smith, Pfeiffer	†1992	35	349
Rob Paternostro, Southern N.H.	1995	33	309
Jim Ferrer, Bentley	1989	31	309
Brian Gregory, Oakland	1989	28	300
Charles Jordan, Erskine	1992	34	298
Ernest Jenkins, N.M. Highlands	†1995	27	291
Pat Chambers, Philadelphia U.	1994	30	290
Zack Whiting, Chaminade	†2007	27	289
Craig Lottie, Alabama A&M	1995	32	287
Adrian Hutt, Metro St.	†1991	28	285
Javar Cheatham, Gannon	†2001	30	283
Patrick Boen, Stonehill	1989	32	278
Ernest Jenkins, N.M. Highlands	†1994	27	277
Clayton Smith, Metro St.	†2003	33	274
Adam Kaufman, Edinboro	1998	34	273
Darnell White, California (Pa.)	1994	30	273
Demetri Beekman, Assumption	1992	32	271
Tyrone Tate, Southern Ind.	1994	32	270

†national champion; *record

ASSIST AVERAGE

Player, Team	Season	G	Ast.	Avg.
Steve Ray, Bridgeport	†1989	32	*400	*12.5
Steve Ray, Bridgeport	†1990	33	385	11.7
Demetri Beekman, Assumption	†1993	23	264	11.5
Ernest Jenkins, N.M. Highlands	†1995	27	291	10.8
Brian Gregory, Oakland	1989	28	300	10.7
Zack Whiting, Chaminade	†2007	27	289	10.7
Brent Schremp, Slippery Rock	1995	25	259	10.4
Ernest Jenkins, N.M. Highlands	†1994	27	277	10.3

Player, Team	Season	G	Ast.	Avg.
Adrian Hutt, Metro St.	†1991	28	285	10.2
Tony Smith, Pfeiffer	†1992	35	349	10.0
Jim Ferrer, Bentley	1989	31	309	10.0
Ryan Nelson, Grand Canyon	†2006	27	263	9.7
Todd Chappell, Texas Wesleyan	†2000	27	263	9.7
Pat Chambers, Philadelphia U.	1994	30	290	9.7
Marcus Talbert, Colo. Christian	1994	27	261	9.7
Carlin Hughes, Mont. St.-Billings	2006	28	269	9.6
Paul Beaty, Miles	1992	26	248	9.5
Lawrence Jordan, IPFW	1990	28	266	9.5
Hal Chambers, Columbus St.	1993	24	227	9.5
Javar Cheatham, Gannon	†2001	30	283	9.4
Rob Paternostro, Southern N.H.	1995	33	309	9.4

†national champion; *record

BLOCKED SHOTS

Player, Team	Season	G	Blk.
James Doyle, Concord	†1998	30	*157
Antonio Harvey, Pfeiffer	†1993	29	155
Bryan Grier, Wingate	†2006	31	151
Ramel Allen, Bridgeport	†2005	30	146
Kenyon Gamble, Tuskegee	†2004	28	142
John Burke, Southampton	†1996	28	142
Vonzell McGrew, Mo. Western St.	†1995	31	132
Colin Ducharme, Longwood	2001	31	130
Corey Johnson, Pace	1995	30	130
Derek Moore, S.C.-Aiken	1998	30	129
John Smith, Winona St.	2006	36	127
Johnny Tyson, Central Okla.	†1994	27	126
Garth Joseph, St. Rose	†1997	34	124
Kino Outlaw, Mount Olive	1995	28	124
Bryan Grier, Wingate	2007	34	119
Kobby Acquah, Clark Atlanta	2005	28	118
Sean McKeon, Kutztown	†2007	28	117
Kino Outlaw, Mount Olive	1996	27	117
Moustapha Diouf, Queens (N.C.)	2003	33	116
Callistus Eziukwu, Grand Valley St.	2005	28	114
Ben Wallace, Virginia Union	1996	31	114

†national champion; *record

BLOCKED-SHOT AVERAGE

Player, Team	Season	G	Blk.	Avg.
Antonio Harvey, Pfeiffer	†1993	29	155	*5.34
James Doyle, Concord	†1998	30	*157	5.23
Kenyon Gamble, Tuskegee	†2004	28	142	5.07
John Burke, Southampton	†1996	28	142	5.07
Bryan Grier, Wingate	†2006	31	151	4.87
Ramel Allen, Bridgeport	†2005	30	146	4.86
Johnny Tyson, Central Okla.	†1994	27	126	4.66
Kino Outlaw, Mount Olive	†1995	28	124	4.43
Kino Outlaw, Mount Olive	1996	27	117	4.33
Corey Johnson, Pace	1995	30	130	4.33
Derek Moore, S.C.-Aiken	1998	30	129	4.30
Vonzell McGrew, Mo. Western St.	1995	31	132	4.26
Jason Roseto, Edinboro	†2001	23	97	4.22
Kobby Acquah, Clark Atlanta	2005	28	118	4.21
Colin Ducharme, Longwood	2001	31	130	4.19
Mark Hensel, Pitt.-Johnstown	1994	27	113	4.19
Sean McKeon, Kutztown	†2007	28	117	4.18
Aaron Davis, Southern Conn. St.	†2003	25	103	4.12
Callistus Eziukwu, Grand Valley St.	2005	28	114	4.07
Victorius Payne, Lane	1996	25	101	4.04

†national champion; *record

STEALS

Player, Team	Season	G	Stl.
J.R. Gamble, Queens (N.C.)	†2001	32	*139
Wayne Copeland, Lynn	†2000	26	129
Japhet McNeil, Bridgeport	†2007	31	125
Wayne Copeland, Lynn	†1999	31	125
Terrance Gist, S.C. Upstate	†1998	29	122
Devlin Herring, Pitt.-Johnstown	†1997	27	122
Oronn Brown, Clarion	1997	29	120
Devlin Herring, Pitt.-Johnstown	1998	29	118
David Clark, Bluefield St.	†1996	31	118
Tyrone McDaniel, Lenoir-Rhyne	†1993	32	116
Ken Francis, Molloy	†1994	27	116
Darnell White, California (Pa.)	1994	30	115
Drew Williamson, Metro St.	†2006	31	114
Jayson Williams, Lane	2005	32	114
Luke Kendall, Metro St.	2004	34	114
Eddin Santiago, Mo. Southern St.	2001	30	114

Player, Team	Season	G	Stl.
Tracy Gross, High Point	1997	29	114
Robert Campbell, Armstrong Atlantic	2001	33	113
Shaun McKie, Salem Int'l	†2005	31	111
Joe Newton, Central Okla.	1993	32	110
Peron Austin, Colorado St.-Pueblo	1997	28	110
Marcus Stubblefield, Queens (N.C.)	1993	28	110
Shannon Holmes, NYIT	†1995	30	110

†national champion; *record

STEAL AVERAGE

Player, Team	Season	G	Stl.	Avg.
Wayne Copeland, Lynn	†2000	26	129	*4.96
John Morris, Bluefield St.	1994	23	104	4.52
Devlin Herring, Pitt.-Johnstown	†1997	27	122	4.52
J.R. Gamble, Queens (N.C.)	†2001	32	*139	4.34
Ken Francis, Molloy	†1994	27	116	4.29
Terrance Gist, S.C. Upstate	†1998	29	122	4.21
Oronn Brown, Clarion	1997	29	120	4.14
Devlin Herring, Pitt.-Johnstown	1998	29	118	4.07
Michael Dean, Cal St. East Bay	1998	26	105	4.04
Terryl Woolery, Cal Poly Pomona	1997	27	109	4.04
Japhet McNeil, Bridgeport	†2007	31	125	4.03
Wayne Copeland, Lynn	†1999	31	125	4.03
Kevin Nichols, Bemidji St.	1994	26	104	4.00
Tracy Gross, High Point	1997	29	114	3.93
Peron Austin, Colorado St.-Pueblo	1997	28	110	3.93
Marcus Stubblefield, Queens (N.C.)	1993	28	110	3.93
Demetri Beekman, Assumption	1993	23	89	3.87
Darnell White, California (Pa.)	1994	30	115	3.83
J.R. Gamble, Queens (N.C.)	2000	28	107	3.82
David Clark, Bluefield St.	†1996	31	118	3.81

†national champion; *record

Career Records

POINTS

Player, Team	Seasons	Pts.
Travis Grant, Kentucky St.	1969-72	*4,045
Bob Hopkins, Grambling	1953-56	3,759
Tony Smith, Pfeiffer	1989-92	3,350
Earnest Lee, Clark Atlanta	1984-87	3,298
Joe Miller, Alderson-Broaddus	1954-57	3,294
Henry Logan, Western Caro.	1965-68	3,290
John Rinka, Kenyon	1967-70	3,251
Dick Barnett, Tennessee St.	1956-59	3,209
Willie Scott, Alabama St.	1966-69	3,155
Johnnie Allen, Bethune-Cookman	1966-69	3,058
Bennie Swain, Texas Southern	1955-58	3,008
Lambert Shell, Bridgeport	1989-92	3,001
Carl Hartman, Alderson-Broaddus	1952-55	2,959
Earl Monroe, Winston-Salem	1964-67	2,935

*record

SCORING AVERAGE
(Minimum 1,400 points)

Player, Team	Seasons	G	FG	3FG	FT	Pts.	Avg.
Travis Grant, Kentucky St.	1969-72	121	*1,760	—	525	*4,045	*33.4
John Rinka, Kenyon	1967-70	99	1,261	—	729	3,251	32.8
Florindo Vieira, Quinnipiac	1954-57	69	761	—	741	2,263	32.8
Willie Shaw, Lane	1961-64	76	960	—	459	2,379	31.3
Mike Davis, Virginia Union	1966-69	89	1,014	—	730	2,758	31.0
Henry Logan, Western Caro.	1965-68	107	1,263	—	764	3,290	30.7
Willie Scott, Alabama St.	1966-69	103	1,277	—	601	3,155	30.6
Carlos Knox, IUPUI	1995-98	85	832	208	684	2,556	30.1
George Gilmore, Chaminade	1991-92	51	485	174	387	1,531	30.0
Brett Beeson, Minn. St. Moorhead	1995-96	54	551	92	421	1,615	29.9
Bob Hopkins, Grambling	1953-56	126	1,403	—	953	3,759	29.8
Rod Butler, Western New Eng.	1968-70	59	697	—	331	1,725	29.2
Gregg Northington, Alabama St.	1970-72	75	894	—	403	2,191	29.2
Isaiah Wilson, Baltimore	1969-71	67	731	—	471	1,933	28.9

*record

FIELD-GOAL PERCENTAGE
(Minimum 400 field goals made)

Player, Team	Seasons	G	FG	FGA	Pct.
Todd Linder, Tampa	1984-87	122	909	1,284	*70.8
Tom Schurfranz, Bellarmine	1987-88, 91-92	112	742	1,057	70.2
Chad Scott, California (Pa.)	1991-94	115	465	664	70.0
Ed Phillips, Alabama A&M	1968-71	95	610	885	68.9

Player, Team	Seasons	G	FG	FGA	Pct.
Ulysses Hackett, S.C. Upstate	1990-92	90	824	1,213	67.9
Larry Tucker, Lewis	1981-83	84	677	999	67.8
Otis Evans, Wayne St. (Mich.)	1989-92	106	472	697	67.7
Matthew Cornegay, Tuskegee	1979-82	105	524	783	66.9
Ray Strozier, Central Mo.	1978-81	110	563	843	66.8
Dennis Edwards, Fort Hays St.	1994-95	59	666	998	66.7
James Morris, Central Okla.	1990-93	76	532	798	66.7
Lance Berwald, North Dakota St.	1983-84	58	475	717	66.2
Harold Booker, Cheyney	1965-67, 69	108	662	1,002	66.1

*record

THREE-POINT FIELD GOALS MADE

Player, Team	Seasons	G	3FG
Cameron Munoz, Mont. St.-Billings	2003-06	99	*451
Stephen Dye, Alderson-Broaddus	2002-05	121	443
Steve Moyer, Gannon	1996-99	112	442
Tony Smith, Pfeiffer	1989-92	126	431
Kwame Morton, Clarion	1991-94	105	411
Tarvoris Uzoigwe, Henderson St.	2002-05	119	404
Gary Duda, Merrimack	1989-92	122	389
Mike Taylor, West Virginia St.	2001-04	116	378
Markus Hallgrimson, Mont. St.-Billings	1998-00	82	371
Nate Newell, Ark.-Monticello	2004-07	112	355
Columbus Parker, Johnson C. Smith	1990-93	115	354
Gary Paul, Indianapolis	1987-90	111	354
Jared Hembree, West Ala.	2004-07	108	353
Matt Miller, Drury	1999-02	106	351
Travis Tuttle, North Dakota	1994-97	108	350
Mike Ziegler, Colorado Mines	1987-90	118	344
Chris Brown, Tuskegee	1993-96	104	339
Stephen Hamrick, Eastern N.M.	1993-96	107	339
Jason Marcotte, Michigan Tech	2002-05	120	335
Mike Kuhens, Queens (N.Y.)	1995-98	104	334
Jesse Ogden, Edinboro	1995-98	110	334
Brent Welton, Philadelphia U.	2002-05	119	329
Brent Kincaid, California (Pa.)	1993-96	115	325
John Williams, Bryant	2003-06	103	323
Jason Stampley, Southeastern Okla.	2004-07	115	322

*record

THREE-POINT FIELD GOALS MADE PER GAME
(Minimum 200 three-point field goals made)

Player, Team	Seasons	G	3FG	Avg.
Antonio Harris, LeMoyne-Owen	1998-99	52	245	*4.71
Cameron Munoz, Mont. St.-Billings	2003-06	99	*451	4.56
Markus Hallgrimson, Mont. St.-Billings	1998-00	82	371	4.52
Alex Williams, Sacramento St.	1987-88	58	247	4.26
Yandel Brown, Columbus St.	2004-05	63	264	4.19
Tommie Spearman, Columbus St.	1994-95	56	233	4.16
Reece Gliko, Mont. St.-Billings	1996-97	56	231	4.13
Danny Phillips, Mont. St.-Billings	2001-02	55	222	4.03
Steve Moyer, Gannon	1996-99	112	442	3.95
Kwame Morton, Clarion	1991-94	105	411	3.91
Zoderick Green, Central Okla.	1993-95	57	212	3.72
Shawn Williams, Central Okla.	1989-91	57	212	3.72
Stephen Dye, Alderson-Broaddus	2002-05	121	*443	3.66
Mike Sinclair, Bowie St.	1987-89	82	299	3.65
Tai Crutchfield, Philadelphia U.	2000-01	58	210	3.62
Nate Allen, Western St.	1996-97	57	205	3.60
Robert Martin, Sacramento St.	1987-89	85	294	3.46
Tony Smith, Pfeiffer	1989-92	126	431	3.42
Tarvoris Uzoigwe, Henderson St.	2002-05	119	404	3.39
Michael Shue, Lock Haven	1994-97	92	308	3.35
Matt Miller, Drury	1999-02	106	351	3.31
Jared Hembree, West Ala.	2004-07	108	353	3.27
Chris Brown, Tuskegee	1993-96	104	339	3.26
Mike Taylor, West Virginia St.	2001-04	116	378	3.26
Travis Tuttle, North Dakota	1994-97	108	350	3.24

*record

THREE-POINT FIELD-GOAL PERCENTAGE
(Minimum 200 three-point field goals made)

Player, Team	Seasons	G	3FG	3FGA	Pct.
Scott Martin, Rollins	1988-91	104	236	460	*51.3
Todd Woelfle, Oakland City	1995-98	103	210	412	51.0
Matt Markle, Shippensburg	1989-92	101	202	408	49.5
Paul Cluxton, Northern Ky.	1994-97	122	303	619	48.9
Lance Gelnett, Millersville	1989-92	109	266	547	48.6
Antonio Harris, LeMoyne-Owen	1998-99	52	245	510	48.0
Mark Willey, Fort Hays St.	1989-92	117	224	478	46.9
Todd Bowden, Randolph-Macon	1987-89	84	229	491	46.6

Player, Team	Seasons	G	3FG	3FGA	Pct.
Gary Paul, Indianapolis	1987-90	111	354	768	46.1
Ben Nemmers, North Dakota St.	2001-04	110	257	558	46.1
Brad Oleson, Alas. Fairbanks	2003-05	87	229	499	45.9
Matt Ripaldi, Southern N.H.	1993-96	123	277	604	45.9
Chad Miller, Oakland City	2004-07	113	315	688	45.8
Alex Williams, Sacramento St.	1987-88	58	247	541	45.7
Benjamin Chasten, Johnson C. Smith	2002-05	92	202	448	45.1
Jason Bullock, Indiana (Pa.)	1993-96	119	287	637	45.1
Boyd Printy, Truman	1990-92	77	201	447	45.0
Lance Luitjens, Northern St.	1994-96	95	275	614	44.8
Buck Williams, North Ala.	1987-89	84	238	535	44.5

*record

FREE-THROW PERCENTAGE
(Minimum 250 free throws made)

Player, Team	Seasons	G	FT	FTA	Pct.
Paul Cluxton, Northern Ky.	1994-97	122	272	291	*93.5
Kent Andrews, McNeese St.	1967-69	67	252	275	91.6
Jon Hagen, Minn. St. Mankato	1963-65	73	252	280	90.0
Lance Den Boer, Central Wash.	2005-07	80	386	432	89.4
Dave Reynolds, Davis & Elkins	1986-89	107	383	429	89.3
Michael Shue, Lock Haven	1994-97	92	354	400	88.5
Tony Budzik, Mansfield	1989-92	107	367	416	88.2
Terry Gill, New Orleans	1972-74	79	261	296	88.2
Bryan Vacca, Randolph-Macon	1980-83	94	262	298	87.9
Steve Nisenson, Hofstra	1963-65	83	602	685	87.9
Jeff Gore, St. Rose	1991-93	91	333	379	87.9
Jack Sparks, Bentley	1976-80	99	253	288	87.8
Dan Shanks, Coker	1994-97	102	467	533	87.6
Troy Nesmith, Gannon	1997-98	54	274	313	87.5
Wayne Profitt, Lynchburg	1965-67	57	482	551	87.5
Clyde Briley, McNeese St.	1962-65	101	561	642	87.4
Jason Sempsrott, South Dakota St.	1994-97	110	462	529	87.3
Foy Ballance, Armstrong Atlantic	1978-81	108	351	402	87.3
Jehu Brabham, Mississippi Col.	1969-71	72	452	518	87.3
Pete Chambers, West Chester	1966-68	67	267	306	87.3

*record

REBOUNDS
(For careers beginning in 1973 or after)

Player, Team	Seasons	G	Reb.
Major Jones, Albany St. (Ga.)	1973-76	105	2,052
Clemon Johnson, Florida A&M	1975-78	109	1,494
Wayne Robertson, Southern N.H.	1991-94	127	1,487
Carlos Terry, Winston-Salem	1975-78	117	1,467
James Hector, American Int'l	1991-94	115	1,446
Jeff Covington, Youngstown St.	1975-78	106	1,381
John Ebeling, Fla. Southern	1979-82	127	1,362
Damon Reed, St. Rose	1997-00	128	1,280
Kelvin Hicks, NYIT	1977-80	94	1,258
Jonathan Roberts, East Stroudsburg	1987-90	112	1,247
John Edwards, Fla. Southern	1973-76	94	1,214
John Fox, Millersville	1984-87	118	1,214
Dave Vonesh, North Dakota	1988-91	122	1,207
Marvin Webster, Morgan St.	1975-76	60	1,198
Ramzee Stanton, West Chester	2000-03	111	1,142
Mark Tetzlaff, South Dakota St.	1982-85	118	1,132
Chris Bowles, Southern Ind.	1991-94	114	1,129
Jakim Donaldson, Edinboro	2002-05	109	1,100
Steve O'Neill, American Int'l	1977-81	108	1,093
Garth Joseph, St. Rose	1995-97	89	1,072
Bob Stanley, Mo.-Rolla	1974-77	95	1,049
Ernie DeWitt, Bryant	1978-81	107	1,036
Gerald Lavender, North Ala.	1977-80	118	1,033
Brian Robinson, Assumption	2002-05	115	1,027
Todd Orlando, Bentley	1981-84	108	1,024
Walt Whitakere, Minn. St. Moorhead	1979-82	107	1,017
Andre Means, Sacred Heart	1977-78	62	1,009
John Smith, Winona St.	2005-07	107	1,007
Leo Parent, Mass.-Lowell	1987-89	92	1,001
Mario Elie, American Int'l	1982-85	120	1,001

#active player

REBOUND AVERAGE
(Minimum 800 rebounds)

Player, Team	Seasons	G	Reb.	Avg.
Tom Hart, Middlebury	1953, 55-56	63	1,738	*27.6
Maurice Stokes, St. Francis (Pa.)	1953-55	72	1,812	25.2
Frank Stronczek, American Int'l	1965-67	62	1,549	25.0
Bill Thieben, Hofstra	1954-56	76	1,837	24.2
Hank Brown, Mass.-Lowell	1965-67	49	1,129	23.0

Player, Team	Seasons	G	Reb.	Avg.
Elmore Smith, Kentucky St.	1969-71	85	1,917	22.6
Charles Wrinn, Trinity (Conn.)	1951-53	53	1,176	22.2
Roman Turmon, Clark Atlanta	1952-54	60	1,312	21.9
Tony Missere, Pratt	1966-68	62	1,348	21.7
Ron Horton, Delaware St.	1966-68	64	1,384	21.6

*record

(For careers beginning in 1973 or after; minimum 800 rebounds)

Player, Team	Seasons	G	Reb.	Avg.
Marvin Webster, Morgan St.	1975-76	60	1,198	20.0
Major Jones, Albany St. (Ga.)	1973-76	105	2,052	19.5
Howard Shockley, Salisbury	1975-76	49	817	16.7
Andre Means, Sacred Heart	1977-78	62	1,009	16.3
Antonio Garcia, Ky. Wesleyan	1998-99	70	997	14.2
Clemon Johnson, Florida A&M	1975-78	109	1,494	13.7
Larry Johnson, Ark.-Little Rock	1976-78	69	944	13.7
Kelvin Hicks, NYIT	1977-80	94	1,258	13.4
John Edwards, Fla. Southern	1973-76	94	1,214	12.9
James Hector, American Int'l	1991-94	115	1,446	12.6
Garth Joseph, St. Rose	1995-97	89	1,072	12.0
Wayne Robertson, Southern N.H.	1991-94	127	1,487	11.7
Wayne Armstrong, Southern Atlantic	1975-79	78	897	11.5
Jonathan Roberts, East Stroudsburg	1987-90	112	1,247	11.1
Bob Stanley, Mo.-Rolla	1974-77	95	1,049	11.0
Leo Parent, Mass.-Lowell	1987-89	92	1,011	11.0

ASSISTS

Player, Team	Seasons	G	Ast.
Demetri Beekman, Assumption	1990-93	119	*1,044
Adam Kaufman, Edinboro	1998-01	116	936
Rob Paternostro, Southern N.H.	1992-95	129	919
Tony Smith, Pfeiffer	1989-92	126	828
Jamie Stevens, Mont. St.-Billings	1996-99	110	805
Josh Mueller, South Dakota	2002-05	120	801
Steve Ray, Bridgeport	1989-90	65	785
Dan Ward, St. Cloud St.	1992-95	100	774
Chris Dunn, West Virginia St.	2003-06	123	769
Jordan Canfield, Washburn	1994-97	126	756
Charles Jordan, Erskine	1989-92	119	727
Jamie Holden, St. Joseph's (Ind.)	2001-04	110	723
Donald Johnson, Franklin Pierce	1998-01	114	722
Dennis Springs, Ferris St.	2003-06	115	713
Patrick Chambers, Philadelphia U.	1991-94	123	709
Lamont Jones, Bridgeport	1992-95	119	708
Zack Whiting, Chaminade	2004-07	86	703
Ernest Jenkins, N.M. Highlands	1992-95	84	699
Antoine Campbell, Ashland	1995-98	113	697
Pat Madden, Jacksonville St.	1989-91	88	688
Nate Tibbetts, South Dakota	1998-01	112	678
Candice Pickens, California (Pa.)	1993-96	121	675
Mark Benson, Tex. A&M-Kingsville	1989-91	86	674
Craig Lottie, Alabama A&M	1992-95	93	673

*record

ASSIST AVERAGE
(Minimum 550 assists)

Player, Team	Seasons	G	Ast.	Avg.
Steve Ray, Bridgeport	1989-90	65	785	*12.1
Demetri Beekman, Assumption	1990-93	119	*1,044	8.8
Ernest Jenkins, N.M. Highlands	1992-95	84	699	8.3
Zack Whiting, Chaminade	2004-07	86	703	8.2
Adam Kaufman, Edinboro	1998-01	116	936	8.1
Mark Benson, Tex. A&M-Kingsville	1989-91	86	674	7.8
Pat Madden, Jacksonville St.	1989-91	88	688	7.8
Dan Ward, St. Cloud St.	1992-95	100	774	7.7
Mark Borders, Tampa	2004-06	86	649	7.5
Jamie Stevens, Mont. St.-Billings	1996-99	110	805	7.3
Craig Lottie, Alabama A&M	1992-95	93	673	7.2
Rob Paternostro, Southern N.H.	1992-95	129	919	7.1
Eddin Santiago, Mo. Southern St.	1999-02	117	804	6.9
Josh Mueller, South Dakota	2002-05	120	801	6.7
Jamie Holden, St. Joseph's (Ind.)	2001-04	110	723	6.6
Tony Smith, Pfeiffer	1989-92	126	828	6.6
Donald Johnson, Franklin Pierce	1998-01	114	722	6.3
Mike Buscetto, Quinnipiac	1990-93	99	624	6.3
Chris Dunn, West Virginia St.	2003-06	123	769	6.3
Patrick Herron, Winston-Salem	1992-95	97	604	6.2
Dennis Springs, Ferris St.	2003-06	115	713	6.2
Pat Delaney, St. Anselm	1999-02	118	731	6.2
Antoine Campbell, Ashland	1995-98	113	697	6.2
Charles Jordan, Erskine	1989-92	119	727	6.1
Nate Tibbetts, South Dakota	1998-01	112	678	6.1

*record

BLOCKED SHOTS

Player, Team	Seasons	G	Blk.
James Doyle, Concord	1995-98	120	*416
Bilal Salaam, Kutztown	2002-05	109	408
Derek Moore, S.C.-Aiken	1996-99	102	408
Avis Wyatt, Virginia St.	2003-05, 07	113	350
Bryan Grier, Wingate#	2005-07	93	335
John Smith, Winona St.#	2005-07	107	317
Rich Edwards, Adelphi	1999-02	123	305
Kino Outlaw, Mount Olive	1994-96	81	305
Mike Williams, Bryant	2001-05	129	301
Garth Joseph, St. Rose	1995-97	89	300
Kenyon Gamble, Florida Tech/Tuskegee	2001-02, 04-05	103	297
Sylvere Bryan, Tampa	1999-02	116	294
Kerwin Thompson, Eckerd	1993-96	116	284
Aaron Davis, Southern Conn. St.	2000-03	94	269
Jeff Weirsma, Erskine	2000-03	109	268
Eugene Haith, Philadelphia U.	1993-95	86	267
John Tomsich, Le Moyne	1996-99	114	264
Chandar Bingham, Virginia Union	1997-00	106	261
Coata Malone, Alabama A&M	1994-96	90	243
Alonzo Goldston, Fort Hays St.	1995-97	96	240
Damon Reed, St. Rose	1997-00	128	236
Brian Robinson, Assumption	2002-05	115	234
Ben Wallace, Virginia Union	1995-96	62	225
Chris Whitfield, Minn. St. Mankato	2003-06	106	224
Antwain Smith, St. Paul's	1996-99	105	222

*record. #Active player

BLOCKED-SHOT AVERAGE
(Minimum 175 blocked shots)

Player, Team	Seasons	G	Blk.	Avg.
Derek Moore, S.C.-Aiken	1996-99	102	408	4.00
John Burke, Southampton	1995-96	54	205	3.80
Kino Outlaw, Mount Olive	1994-96	81	305	3.77
Bilal Salaam, Kutztown	2002-05	109	408	3.74
Vonzell McGrew, Mo. Western St.	1993-95	57	211	3.70
Tihomir Juric, Wis.-Parkside	1993-94	53	193	3.64
Ben Wallace, Virginia Union	1995-96	62	225	3.63
Corey Johnson, Pace	1993-95	58	210	3.62
James Doyle, Concord	1995-98	120	*416	3.47
Mark Hensel, Pitt.-Johnstown	1993-94	53	180	3.40
Garth Joseph, St. Rose	1995-97	89	300	3.37
Moustapha Diouf, Queens (N.C.)	2003-04	61	201	3.30
Eugene Haith, Philadelphia U.	1993-95	86	267	3.10
Avis Wyatt, Virginia St.	2003-05, 07	113	350	3.10
Kenyon Gamble, Florida Tech/Tuskegee	2001-02, 04-05	103	297	2.88
Aaron Davis, Southern Conn. St.	2000-03	94	269	2.86
Coata Malone, Alabama A&M	1994-96	90	243	2.70
Sylvere Bryan, Tampa	1999-02	116	294	2.53
Alonzo Goldston, Fort Hays St.	1995-97	96	240	2.50
Rich Edwards, Adelphi	1999-02	123	305	2.48
Chandar Bingham, Virginia Union	1997-00	106	261	2.46
Jeff Weirsma, Erskine	2000-03	109	268	2.46
Kerwin Thompson, Eckerd	1993-96	116	284	2.45
Merriel Jenkins, Hawaii-Hilo	1997-99	77	188	2.44
Mike Williams, Bryant	2001-05	129	301	2.33

*record

STEALS

Player, Team	Seasons	G	Stl.
Eddin Santiago, Mo. Southern St.	1999-02	117	*383
Oronn Brown, Clarion	1994-97	106	361
Robert Campbell, Armstrong Atlantic	1998-01	118	357
Marcus Best, Winston-Salem	1999-02	119	345
Shaun McKie, Salem Int'l	2004-07	113	340
Devlin Herring, Pitt.-Johnstown	1995-98	106	333
Dustin Pfeifer, Findlay	2003-06	127	328
Luqman Jaaber, Virginia St./Virginia Union	2000, 03-05	114	316
Rolondo Hall, Davis & Elkins	1998-01	106	314
John Baiano, Southern N.H.	2003-06	122	304
Jonte Flowers, Winona St.#	2005-07	105	293
Andre Dabney, Bloomfield	2004-07	120	283
Terrence Baxter, Pfeiffer	1998-01	108	281
David Clark, Bluefield St.	1994-96	83	278
Terrance Gist, S.C. Upstate	1994-97	112	276
Jeremy Byrd, S.C. Upstate#	2005-07	88	274
Omar Kasi, Molloy	1997-00	109	272
DeMarcos Anzures, Metro St.	1997-00	125	271
Mike Hancock, Neb.-Kearney	1995-98	121	271
Carlton Epps, Ferris St.	2002-05	109	270
Lorinza Harrington, Wingate	1999-02	121	263
Patrick Herron, Winston-Salem	1993-95	78	263
Ken Francis, Molloy	1993-95	81	260
Eddie Peterson, Indiana (Pa.)	2003-06	119	259
Brandon Hughes, Newberry	1997-00	88	259

*record #Active player

STEAL AVERAGE
(Minimum 150 steals)

Player, Team	Seasons	G	Stl.	Avg.
Wayne Copeland, Lynn	1999-00	57	254	4.46
J.R. Gamble, Queens (N.C.)	2000-01	60	246	4.10
John Morris, Bluefield St.	1994-95	50	185	3.70
Oronn Brown, Clarion	1994-97	106	361	3.41
Patrick Herron, Winston-Salem	1993-95	78	263	3.37
David Clark, Bluefield St.	1994-96	83	278	3.35
Peron Austin, Colorado St.-Pueblo	1997-98	58	190	3.28
Eddin Santiago, Mo. Southern St.	1999-02	117	*383	3.27
Gallagher Driscoll, St. Rose	1991-92	59	192	3.25
Darnell White, California (Pa.)	1993-94	59	192	3.25
Rudy Berry, Cal St. Stanislaus	1993-94	51	164	3.21
Ken Francis, Molloy	1993-95	81	260	3.21
Bob Cunningham, NYIT	1995-96	55	175	3.18
Devlin Herring, Pitt.-Johnstown	1995-98	106	333	3.14
Craig Fergeson, Columbus St.	1995-96	61	191	3.13
Ron Harris, Caldwell	2004-05	59	181	3.07
Bryan Heaps, Abilene Christian	1993-94	56	171	3.05
Lamont Jones, Bridgeport	1993-95	84	256	3.05
Shaun McKie, Salem Int'l	2004-07	113	340	3.01
Kelly Mann, Concord	1997-98	62	185	2.98
Javar Cheatham, Gannon	2000-01	58	172	2.97
Rolondo Hall, Davis & Elkins	1998-01	106	314	2.96
Rickey Gibson, Stillman	2005-06	58	171	2.95
Brandon Hughes, Newberry	1997-00	88	259	2.94
Malcolm Turner, Sonoma St.	1995-96	52	152	2.92

*record

Annual Individual Champions

Scoring Average

Season	Player, Team	G	FG	FT	Pts.	Avg.
1948	Nate DeLong, Wis.-River Falls	22	206	206	618	28.1
1949	George King, Charleston (W.V.)	26	289	179	757	29.1
1950	George King, Charleston (W.V.)	31	354	259	967	31.2
1951	Scott Seagall, Millikin	31	314	260	888	28.6
1952	Harold Wolfe, Findlay	22	285	101	671	30.5
1953	Roger Kuss, Wis.-River Falls	21	291	235	817	38.9
1954	Clarence "Bevo" Francis, Rio Grande	27	444	367	1,255	*46.5
1955	Bill Warden, North Central (Ill.)	13	162	127	451	34.7
1956	Bill Reigel, McNeese St.	36	425	370	1,220	33.9
1957	Ken Hammond, West Va. Tech	27	334	274	942	34.9
1958	John Lee Butcher, Pikeville	27	330	210	870	32.2
1959	Paul Wilcox, Davis & Elkins	23	289	195	773	33.6
1960	Don Perrelli, Southern Conn. St.	22	263	168	694	31.5
1961	Lebron Bell, Bryant	14	174	114	462	33.0
1962	Willie Shaw, Lane	18	239	115	593	32.9

Season	Player, Team	G	FG	FT	Pts.	Avg.
1963	Earl Glass, Miss. Industrial	19	322	171	815	42.9
1964	Willie Shaw, Lane	18	303	121	727	40.4
1965	Thales McReynolds, Miles	18	294	118	706	39.2
1966	Paul Crissman, Vanguard	23	373	90	836	36.3
1967	Earl Monroe, Winston-Salem	32	509	311	*1,329	41.5
1968	Mike Davis, Virginia Union	25	351	206	908	36.3
1969	John Rinka, Kenyon	26	340	202	882	33.9
1970	John Rinka, Kenyon	23	354	234	942	41.0
1971	Bo Lamar, La.-Lafayette	29	424	196	1,044	36.0
1972	Travis Grant, Kentucky St.	33	*539	226	1,304	39.5
1973	Claude White, Elmhurst	18	248	101	597	33.2
1974	Aaron James, Grambling	27	366	137	869	32.2
1975	Ron Barrow, Southern U.	23	296	115	707	30.7
1976	Ron Barrow, Southern U.	27	318	136	772	28.6
1977	Ed Murphy, Merrimack	28	369	158	896	32.0
1978	Harold Robertson, Lincoln (Mo.)	28	408	149	965	34.5
1979	Bo Clark, UCF	23	315	97	727	31.6
1980	Bill Fennelly, Central Mo.	28	337	189	863	30.8

Season	Player, Team	G	FG	FT	Pts.	Avg.
1981	Gregory Jackson, St. Paul's	26	267	183	717	27.6
1982	John Ebeling, Fla. Southern	32	286	284	856	26.8
1983	Danny Dixon, Alabama A&M	27	379	152	910	33.7
1984	Earl Jones, Dist. Columbia	22	215	200	630	28.6
1985	Earnest Lee, Clark Atlanta	29	380	230	990	34.1
1986	Earnest Lee, Clark Atlanta	28	314	191	819	29.3

Season	Player, Team	G	FG	3FG	FT	Pts.	Avg.
1987	Earnest Lee, Clark Atlanta	29	326	35	174	861	29.7
1988	Daryl Cambrelen, Southampton	25	242	32	170	686	27.4
1989	Steve deLaveaga, Cal Lutheran	28	278	79	151	786	28.1
1990	A.J. English, Virginia Union	30	333	65	270	1,001	33.4
1991	Gary Mattison, St. Augustine's	26	277	53	159	766	29.5
1992	George Gilmore, Chaminade	28	280	82	238	880	31.4
1993	Darrin Robinson, Sacred Heart	26	313	75	130	831	32.0
1994	Kwame Mortin, Clarion	26	264	126	191	845	32.5
1995	Carlos Knox, IUPUI	29	284	39	218	825	28.4
1996	Brett Beeson, Minn. St. Moorhead	27	305	58	232	900	33.3
1997	Dan Sancomb, Wheeling Jesuit	27	295	11	125	726	26.9
1998	Carlos Knox, IUPUI	26	238	96	209	781	30.0
1999	Eddie Robinson, Central Okla.	26	305	24	95	729	28.0
2000	David Evans, BYU-Hawaii	28	300	48	134	782	27.9
2001	Marlon Dawson, Central Okla.	26	206	101	155	668	25.7
2002	Angel Figueroa, Dowling	25	216	79	143	654	26.2
2003	Ron Christy, Post	29	295	64	134	788	27.2
2004	Lewis Muse, Concord	26	308	0	125	741	28.5
2005	David Logan, Indianapolis	29	291	121	126	829	28.6
2006	Tayron Thomas, Philadelphia U.	31	298	42	260	898	29.0
2007	Ted Scott, West Virginia St.	33	315	125	137	892	27.0

*record

Field-Goal Percentage

Season	Player, Team	G	FG	FGA	Pct.
1949	Vern Mikkelson, Hamline	30	203	377	53.8
1950	Nate DeLong, Wis.-River Falls	29	287	492	58.3
1951	Johnny O'Brien, Seattle	33	248	434	57.1
1952	Forrest Hamilton, Missouri St.	30	147	246	59.8
1953	Bob Buis, Carleton	21	149	246	60.6
1954	Paul Lauritzen, Augustana (Ill.)	19	158	251	62.9
1955	Jim O'Hara, UC Santa Barb.	24	140	214	65.4
1956	Logan Gipe, Ky. Wesleyan	22	134	224	59.8
1957	John Wilfred, Winston-Salem	30	229	381	60.1
1958	Bennie Swain, Texas Southern	35	363	587	61.8
1959	Dick O'Meara, Babson	18	144	225	64.0
1960	Edwin Cox, Howard Payne	26	126	194	64.9
1961	Tony Solomon, St. Paul's	20	94	149	63.1
1962	Tom Morris, St. Paul's	17	108	168	64.3
1963	Howard Trice, Howard Payne	26	168	237	70.9
1964	Robert Springer, Howard Payne	24	119	174	68.4
1965	Harold Booker, Cheyney	24	144	198	72.7
1966	Harold Booker, Cheyney	27	170	240	70.8
1967	John Dickson, Arkansas St.	24	214	308	69.5
1968	Edward Phillips, Alabama A&M	22	154	210	73.3
1969	Marvin Lewis, Southampton	24	271	375	72.3
1970	Travis Grant, Kentucky St.	31	482	688	70.1
1971	Edward Phillips, Alabama A&M	24	159	221	71.9
1972	Don Manley, Otterbein	23	146	207	70.5
1973	Glynn Berry, Southampton	26	191	302	63.2
1974	Kirby Thurston, Western Caro.	25	242	367	65.9
1975	Gerald Cunningham, Kentucky St.	29	280	411	68.1
1976	Thomas Blue, Elizabeth City St.	24	270	388	69.6
1977	Kelvin Hicks, NYIT	24	161	232	69.4
1978	Ron Ripley, Green Bay	32	162	239	67.8
1979	Carl Bailey, Tuskegee	27	210	307	68.4
1980	Ray Strozier, Central Mo.	28	142	195	72.8
1981	Matthew Cornegay, Tuskegee	26	177	247	71.7
1982	Matthew Cornegay, Tuskegee	29	208	278	74.8
1983	Rudy Burton, Elizabeth City St.	24	142	201	70.6
1984	Maurice Stafford, North Ala.	34	198	264	75.0
1985	Todd Linder, Tampa	31	219	306	71.6
1986	Todd Linder, Tampa	28	204	291	70.1
1987	Todd Linder, Tampa	32	282	375	*75.2
1988	Louis Newsome, North Ala.	29	192	266	72.2
1989	Tom Schurfranz, Bellarmine	28	164	240	68.2
1990	Ulysses Hackett, S.C. Upstate	32	301	426	70.7
1991	Tom Schurfranz, Bellarmine	30	245	339	72.3
1992	Brian Moten, West Ga.	26	141	192	73.4
1993	Chad Scott, California (Pa.)	28	173	245	70.6
1994	Chad Scott, California (Pa.)	30	178	245	72.7
1995	John Pruett, SIU Edwardsville	26	138	193	71.5
1996	Kyle Kirby, IPFW	26	133	195	68.2

Season	Player, Team	G	FG	FGA	Pct
1997	Andy Robertson, Fla. Southern	32	183	269	68.0
1998	Anthony Russell, West Fla.	28	191	284	67.3
1999	DaVonn Harp, Kutztown	27	140	205	68.3
2000	Shaun Bass, Drury	28	156	237	65.8
2001	Charles Ward, St. Augustine's	27	159	243	65.4
2002	Brett Barnard, Le Moyne	27	141	211	66.8
2003	Anthony Greenup, Shaw	30	172	242	71.1
2004	Anthony Greenup, Shaw	24	210	296	70.9
2005	Callistus Eziukwu, Grand Valley St.	28	157	213	73.7
2006	Chris Gilliam, Pitt.-Johnstown	27	199	290	68.6
2007	Garret Siler, Augusta St.	31	166	241	68.9

*record

Three-Point Field Goals Made Per Game

Season	Player, Team	G	3FG	Avg.
1987	Bill Harris, Northern Mich.	27	117	4.3
1988	Alex Williams, Sacramento St.	30	*167	5.6
1989	Robert Martin, Sacramento St.	28	118	4.2
1990	Gary Paul, Indianapolis	28	110	3.9
1991	Shawn Williams, Central Okla.	29	129	4.4
1992	Jason Garrow, Augustana (S.D.)	27	135	5.0
1993	Ray Gutierrez, California (Pa.)	29	142	4.9
1994	Kwame Morton, Clarion	26	126	4.8
1995	Eric Kline, Northern St.	30	148	4.9
1996	Daren Alix, Merrimack	28	114	4.1
1997	Reece Gliko, Mont. St.-Billings	28	135	4.8
1998	Antonio Harris, LeMoyne-Owen	26	119	4.6
1999	Antonio Harris, LeMoyne-Owen	26	126	4.8
2000	Markus Hallgrimson, Mont. St.-Billings	26	160	*6.2
2001	Blake Johnson, Edinboro	28	111	4.0
2002	Danny Phillips, Mont. St.-Billings	28	120	4.2
2003	Jed Bedford, Columbus St.	32	135	4.2
2004	Mike Taylor, West Virginia St.	32	140	4.4
2005	Yandel Brown, Columbus St.	32	148	4.6
2006	Cameron Munoz, Mont. St.-Billings	28	147	5.3
2007	Brett Rector, Davis & Elkins	24	99	4.1

*record

Three-Point Field-Goal Percentage

Season	Player, Team	G	3FG	3FGA	Pct
1987	Charles Byrd, West Tex. A&M	31	95	168	56.5
1988	Ray Lee, Hampton	24	39	60	*65.0
1989	Aaron Baker, Mississippi Col.	27	69	117	59.0
1990	Mark Willey, Fort Hays St.	29	49	81	60.5
1991	Scott Martin, Rollins	28	114	201	56.7
1992	Jeff Duvall, Oakland City	30	49	91	53.8
1993	Greg Wilkinson, Oakland City	32	82	152	53.9
1994	Todd Jones, Southern Ind.	29	56	105	53.3
1995	Aaron Fehler, Oakland City	26	73	121	†60.3
1996	Matt Hopson, Oakland City	31	84	145	57.9
1997	Adam Harness, Oakland City	26	39	68	57.4
1998	Todd Woelfe, Oakland City	27	87	162	53.7
1999	John Cabanilla, Oakland City	29	46	85	54.1
2000	Jasen Gast, Incarnate Word	26	39	72	54.2
2001	Bobby Hoegh, Southwest Baptist	23	72	147	49.0
2002	Jared Ramirez, Northern Colo.	27	60	115	52.2
2003	Ben Nemmers, North Dakota St.	30	83	159	52.2
2004	Derek Archer, Wayne St. (Neb.)	28	77	142	54.2
	Shawn Opunui, BYU-Hawaii	29	77	142	54.2
2005	Justin Belcastro, Fairmont St.	27	69	134	51.5
2006	Rich Davis, Grand Canyon	27	107	210	51.0
2007	Michael Bahl, Metro St.	32	105	202	52.0

*record for minimum 35 made; †record for minimum 50 made

Free-Throw Percentage

Season	Player, Team	G	FT	FTA	Pct.
1948	Frank Cochran, Delta St.	22	36	43	83.7
1949	Jim Walsh, Spring Hill	25	62	75	82.7
1950	Dean Ehlers, Central Methodist	33	186	213	87.3
1951	Jim Hoverder, Central Mo.	23	75	85	88.2
1952	Jim Fenton, Akron	24	104	121	86.0
1953	Dick Parfitt, Central Mich.	22	93	105	88.6
1954	Bill Parrott, David Lipscomb	24	174	198	87.9

Season	Player, Team	G	FT	FTA	Pct.
1955	Pete Kovacs, Monmouth (Ill.)	20	175	199	87.9
1956	Fred May, Loras	22	127	146	87.0
1957	Jim Sutton, South Dakota St.	22	127	138	92.0
1958	Arnold Smith, Allen	22	103	113	91.2
1959	Bill Reece, Lenoir-Rhyne	27	84	92	91.3
1960	Ron Slaymaker, Emporia St.	20	80	88	90.9
1961	Harvey Rosen, Wilkes	22	105	115	91.3
1962	Wayne Mahone, Stephen F. Austin	26	76	84	90.5
1963	Jon Hagen, Minn. St. Mankato	25	76	82	92.7
1964	Steve Nisenson, Hofstra	28	230	252	91.3
1965	Jon Hagen, Minn. St. Mankato	23	103	112	92.0
1966	Jack Cryan, Rider	25	182	198	91.9
1967	Kent Andrews, McNeese St.	22	101	110	91.8
1968	Kent Andrews, McNeese St.	24	85	90	94.4
1969	Joe Cullen, Hartwick	18	96	103	93.2
1970	John Rinka, Kenyon	23	234	263	89.0
1971	Ed Roeth, Defiance	26	138	152	90.8
1972	Jeff Kuntz, St. Norbert	25	142	155	91.6
1973	Bob Kronisch, Brooklyn	30	93	105	88.6
1974	Terry Gill, New Orleans	30	97	105	92.4
1975	Clarence Rand, Alabama St.	29	91	101	90.1
1976	Billy Newton, Morgan St.	28	85	90	94.4
1977	Emery Sammons, Philadelphia U.	28	145	157	92.4
1978	Dana Skinner, Merrimack	28	142	154	92.2
1979	Jack Sparks, Bentley	28	76	84	90.5
1980	Grey Giovanine, Central Mo.	28	75	83	90.4
1981	Ted Smith, SIU Edwardsville	26	67	73	91.8
1982	Carl Gonder, Augustana (S.D.)	27	86	93	92.5
1983	Joe Sclafani, New Haven	28	86	98	87.8
1984	Darrell Johnston, Southern N.H.	29	74	81	91.4
1985	Tom McDonald, South Dakota St.	33	88	97	90.7
1986	Todd Mezzulo, Alas. Fairbanks	27	114	125	91.2
1987	Mike Sanders, Northern Colo.	28	82	87	94.3
1988	Charles Byrd, West Tex. A&M	29	92	99	92.8
1989	Mike Boschee, North Dakota	28	71	77	92.2
1990	Mike Morris, Ala.-Huntsville	28	114	125	91.2
1991	Ryun Williams, South Dakota	30	114	125	91.2
1992	Hal McManus, Lander	28	110	119	92.4
1993	Jason Williams, New Haven	27	115	125	92.0
1994	Jay Harrie, Mont. St.-Billings	26	86	92	93.5
1995	Jim Borodawka, Mass.-Lowell	27	74	80	92.5
1996	Paul Cluxton, Northern Ky.	32	100	108	92.6
1997	Paul Cluxton, Northern Ky.	35	94	94	*100.0
1998	Troy Nesmith, Gannon	27	146	158	92.4
1999	Travis Starns, Colorado Mines	26	87	93	93.5
2000	Jason Kreider, Michigan Tech	31	84	91	92.3
2001	C.J. Cowgill, Chaminade	22	113	119	95.0
2002	Curtis Small, Southampton	29	109	116	94.0
2003	Aaron Farley, Harding	30	137	146	93.8
2004	Ralph Steele, Seattle Pacific	27	82	90	91.1
2005	Luqman Jaaber, Virginia Union	34	125	139	89.9
2006	Marcus Martinez, Cal St. Stanislaus	27	75	80	93.8
2007	Richard Stone, St. Andrews	28	101	110	91.8

*record

Rebound Average

Season	Player, Team	G	Reb.	Avg.
1951	Walter Lenz, Frank. & Marsh.	17	338	19.9
1952	Charley Wrinn, Trinity (Conn.)	19	486	25.6
1953	Ellerbe Neal, Wofford	23	609	26.5
1954	R.C. Owens, Albertson	25	677	27.1
1955	Tom Hart, Middlebury	22	649	29.5
1956	Tom Hart, Middlebury	21	620	*29.5
1957	Jim Smith, Steubenville	26	651	25.0
1958	Marv Becker, Widener	18	450	25.0
1959	Jim Davis, King's (Pa.)	17	384	22.6
1960	Jackie Jackson, Virginia Union	19	424	†.241
1961	Jackie Jackson, Virginia Union	26	641	24.7
1962	Jim Ahrens, Buena Vista	28	682	24.4
1963	Gerry Govan, St. Mary's (Kan.)	18	445	24.7
1964	Ernie Brock, Virginia St.	24	597	24.9
1965	Dean Sandifer, Lakeland	23	592	25.7
1966	Frank Stronczek, American Int'l	26	717	27.6
1967	Frank Stronczek, American Int'l	25	602	24.1
1968	Ron Horton, Delaware St.	23	543	23.6
1969	Wilbert Jones, Albany St. (Ga.)	28	670	23.9
1970	Russell Jackson, Southern U.	22	544	24.7
1971	Tony Williams, St. Francis (Me.)	24	599	25.0
1972	No rankings			
1973	No rankings			
1974	Larry Johnson, Prairie View	23	519	22.6
1975	Major Jones, Albany St. (Ga.)	27	608	22.5
1976	Major Jones, Albany St. (Ga.)	24	475	19.8
1977	Andre Means, Sacred Heart	32	516	16.1
1978	Scott Mountz, California (Pa.)	24	431	18.0
1979	Keith Smith, Shaw	20	329	16.5
1980	Ricky Mahorn, Hampton	31	490	15.8
1981	Earl Jones, Dist. Columbia	25	333	13.3
1982	Donnie Carter, Tuskegee	29	372	12.8
1983	David Binion, N.C. Central	25	400	16.0
1984	Jerome Kersey, Longwood	27	383	14.2
1985	Charles Oakley, Virginia Union	31	535	17.3
1986	Raheem Muhammad, Wayne St. (Mich.)	31	428	13.8
1987	Andre Porter, Southampton	23	309	13.4
1988	Anthony Ikeobi, Clark Atlanta	27	380	14.1
1989	Toby Barber, Winston-Salem	24	327	13.6
1990	Leroy Gasque, Morris Brown	24	375	15.6
1991	Sheldon Owens, Shaw	27	325	12.0
1992	David Allen, Wayne St. (Neb.)	28	362	12.9
1993	James Hector, American Int'l	28	389	13.9
1994	Pat Armour, Jacksonville St.	25	363	14.5
1995	Lorenzo Poole, Albany St. (Ga.)	26	417	16.0
1996	J.J. Sims, West Ga.	28	374	13.4
1997	Kebu Stewart, Cal St. Bakersfield	33	442	13.4
1998	Antonio Garcia, Ky. Wesleyan	33	457	13.8
1999	Antonio Garcia, Ky. Wesleyan	37	540	14.6
2000	Howard Jackson, Lincoln Memorial	24	321	13.4
2001	Colin Duchacme, Longwood	31	490	15.8
2002	Danny Jones, Tarleton St.	33	416	13.0
2003	Billy McDaniel, Ark.-Monticello	27	345	12.8
2004	Jack Bain, UC-Colo. Spgs.	27	336	12.4
2005	Ramel Allen, Bridgeport	30	423	14.1
2006	Raheim Lowery, Dowling	27	342	12.7
2007	Eric Dawson, Midwestern St.	30	341	11.4

*record; †Championship determined by highest individual recoveries out of total by both teams in all games.

Assist Average

Season	Player, Team	G	Ast.	Avg.
1989	Steve Ray, Bridgeport	32	*400	*12.5
1990	Steve Ray, Bridgeport	33	385	11.7
1991	Adrian Hutt, Metro St.	28	285	10.2
1992	Tony Smith, Pfeiffer	35	349	10.0
1993	Demetri Beekman, Assumption	23	264	11.5
1994	Ernest Jenkins, N.M. Highlands	27	277	10.3
1995	Ernest Jenkins, N.M. Highlands	27	291	10.8
1996	Bobby Banks, Metro St.	27	244	9.0
1997	Emanuel Richardson, Pitt.-Johnstown	27	235	8.7
1998	Emanuel Richardson, Pitt.-Johnstown	29	260	9.0
1999	Shawn Brown, Merrimack	27	223	8.3
2000	Todd Chappell, Texas Wesleyan	27	263	9.7
2001	Javar Cheatham, Gannon	30	283	9.4
2002	Pat Delany, St. Anselm	30	234	7.8
2003	Clayton Smith, Metro St.	33	274	8.3
2004	Deshawn Bowman, Columbus St.	27	220	8.1
2005	Darnell Miller, West Ga.	28	219	7.8
2006	Ryan Nelson, Grand Canyon	27	263	9.7
2007	Zack Whiting, Chaminade	27	289	10.7

*record

Blocked-Shot Average

Season	Player, Team	G	Blk.	Avg.
1993	Antonio Harvey, Pfeiffer	29	155	*5.3
1994	Johnny Tyson, Central Okla.	27	126	4.7
1995	Kino Outlaw, Mount Olive	28	124	4.4
1996	John Burke, Southampton	28	142	5.1
1997	Garth Joseph, St. Rose	34	124	3.6
1998	James Doyle, Concord	30	*157	5.2
1999	Chandar Bingham, Virginia Union	27	95	3.5
2000	Josh Stanhiser, Columbia Union	25	87	3.5
2001	Jason Roseto, Edinboro	23	97	4.2
2002	George Bailey, Lock Haven	20	79	4.0
2003	Aaron Davis, Southern Conn. St.	25	103	4.1
2004	Kenyon Gamble, Tuskegee	28	142	5.1
2005	Ramel Allen, Bridgeport	30	146	4.9
2006	Bryan Grier, Wingate	31	151	4.9
2007	Sean McKeon, Kutztown	28	117	4.2

*record

DIVISION II

Steal Average

Season	Player, Team	G	Stl.	Avg.
1993	Marcus Stubblefield, Queens (N.C.)	28	110	3.9
1994	Ken Francis, Molloy	27	116	4.3
1995	Shannon Holmes, NYIT	30	110	3.7
1996	David Clark, Bluefield St.	31	118	3.8
1997	Devlin Herring, Pitt.-Johnstown	27	122	4.5
1998	Terrance Gist, S.C. Upstate	29	122	4.2
1999	Wayne Copeland, Lynn	31	125	4.0

Season	Player, Team	G	Stl.	Avg.
2000	Wayne Copeland, Lynn	26	129	*5.0
2001	J.R. Gamble, Queens (N.C.)	32	*139	4.3
2002	Shahar Golan, Assumption	30	106	3.5
2003	Gerry McNair, C.W. Post	30	103	3.4
2004	Luqman Jaaber, Virginia Union	30	103	3.4
2005	Shaun McKie, Salem Int'l	31	111	3.6
2006	Drew Williamson, Metro St.	31	114	3.7
2007	Japhet McNeil, Bridgeport	31	125	4.0

*record

Annual Team Champions

Won-Lost Percentage

Season	Team	Won	Lost	Pct.
1968	Monmouth	27	2	.931
1969	Alcorn St.	26	1	.963
1970	Central Wash.	31	2	.939
1971	Kentucky St.	31	2	.939
1972	Olivet	22	1	.957
1973	Coe	24	1	.960
1974	West Ga.	29	4	.879
1975	Bentley	23	2	.920
1976	Philadelphia U.	25	3	.893
1977	Clarion	27	3	.900
	Kentucky St.	27	3	.900
	Towson	27	3	.900
1978	Green Bay	30	2	.938
1979	Roanoke	25	3	.893
1980	Alabama St.	32	2	.941
1981	Mt. St. Mary's	28	3	.903
1982	Cheyney	28	3	.903
1983	Dist. Columbia	29	3	.906
1984	Norfolk St.	29	2	.935
1985	Jacksonville St.	31	1	.969
	Virginia Union	31	1	.969
1986	Wright St.	28	3	.903
1987	Norfolk St.	28	3	.903
1988	Fla. Southern	31	3	.912
1989	UC Riverside	30	4	.882
1990	Ky. Wesleyan	31	2	.939
1991	Southwest Baptist	29	3	.906
1992	California (Pa.)	31	2	.939
1993	Cal St. Bakersfield	33	0	1.000
1994	Philadelphia U.	29	2	.935
1995	Jacksonville St.	24	1	.960
1996	Fort Hays St.	34	0	1.000
1997	Fort Hays St.	29	2	.935
1998	UC Davis	31	2	.939
1999	Ky. Wesleyan	35	2	.946
2000	Fla. Southern	32	2	.941
2001	Adelphi	31	1	.969
2002	Cal St. San B'dino	28	2	.933
	Northeastern St.	28	2	.933
2003	Northeastern St.	32	3	.914
2004	Metro St.	32	3	.914
2005	Virginia Union	30	4	.882
	Findlay	30	4	.882
2006	Delta St.	30	2	.938
2007	Winona St.	35	1	.972

Season	Team	G	W-L	Pts.	Avg.
1961	Lawrence Tech	25	19-6	2,409	96.4
1962	Troy	25	20-5	2,402	96.1
1963	Miles	21	17-4	2,011	95.8
1964	Benedict	27	19-8	2,730	101.1
1965	Ark.-Pine Bluff	26	22-4	2,655	102.1
1966	Southern Cal College	23	15-8	2,480	107.8
1967	Lincoln (Mo.)	27	24-3	2,925	108.3
1968	Stillman	26	17-9	2,898	111.5
1969	Norfolk St.	25	21-4	2,653	106.1
1970	Norfolk St.	26	19-7	2,796	107.5
1971	Savannah St.	29	18-11	3,051	105.2
1972	Florida A&M	28	18-10	2,869	102.5
1973	Md.-East. Shore	31	26-5	2,974	95.9
1974	Texas Southern	28	15-13	2,884	103.0
1975	Prairie View	26	16-10	2,774	106.7
1976	Southern U.	27	13-14	2,637	97.7
1977	Virginia Union	30	25-5	2,966	98.9
1978	Merrimack	28	22-6	2,606	93.1
1979	Armstrong Atlantic	27	21-6	2,626	97.3
1980	Ashland	27	11-16	2,514	93.1
1981	Virginia St.	31	20-11	2,761	89.1
1982	Alabama St.	28	22-6	2,429	86.8
1983	Virginia St.	29	19-10	2,802	96.6
1984	Southern N.H.	29	18-11	2,564	88.4
1985	Alabama A&M	31	21-10	2,881	92.9
1986	Alabama A&M	32	23-9	2,897	90.5
1987	Alabama A&M	30	23-7	2,826	94.2
1988	Oakland	28	19-9	2,685	95.9
1989	Stonehill	32	23-9	3,244	101.4
1990	Jacksonville St.	29	24-5	2,872	99.0
1991	Troy	30	22-8	3,259	108.6
1992	Troy	29	23-6	3,513	*121.1
1993	Central Okla.	29	23-6	3,293	113.6
1994	Central Okla.	27	17-10	2,782	103.0
1995	Central Okla.	30	23-7	3,219	107.3
1996	Central Okla.	29	19-10	2,933	101.1
1997	Mont. St.-Billings	28	22-6	2,904	103.7
1998	Mont. St.-Billings	28	21-7	2,945	105.2
1999	Central Okla.	27	16-11	2,657	98.4
2000	Mont. St.-Billings	26	17-9	2,460	94.6
2001	Mont. St.-Billings	27	18-9	2,648	98.1
2002	Mont. St.-Billings	28	21-7	2,559	91.4
2003	Pfeiffer	31	22-9	2,926	94.4
2004	Pfeiffer	34	31-3	3,278	96.4
2005	Pfeiffer	32	27-5	3,042	95.1
2006	West Liberty St.	29	21-8	2,841	98.0
2007	West Liberty St.	30	25-5	2,962	98.7

*record

Scoring Offense

Season	Team	G	W-L	Pts.	Avg.
1948	St. Anselm	19	12-7	1,329	69.9
1949	Charleston (W.V.)	26	18-8	2,023	77.8
1950	Charleston (W.V.)	31	22-9	2,477	79.9
1951	Beloit	23	18-5	1,961	85.3
1952	Lambuth	22	17-5	1,985	90.2
1953	Arkansas Tech	21	20-1	1,976	94.1
1954	Montclair St.	22	18-4	2,128	96.7
1955	West Va. Tech	20	15-5	2,150	107.5
1956	West Va. Tech	22	16-6	2,210	100.5
1957	West Va. Tech	29	26-3	2,976	102.6
1958	West Va. Tech	29	24-5	2,941	101.4
1959	Grambling	29	28-1	2,764	95.3
1960	Mississippi Col.	19	15-4	2,169	114.2

Scoring Defense

Season	Team	G	W-L	Pts.	Avg.
1948	Miss. Industrial	15	13-2	436	‡29.1
1949	Gordon	20	16-4	655	32.8
1950	Tex. A&M-Corp. Chris.	26	25-1	1,030	39.6
1951	St. Martin's	24	11-13	1,137	47.4
1952	Truman	19	12-7	876	46.1
1953	Sacramento St.	26	18-8	1,381	53.1
1954	Sacramento St.	18	9-9	883	49.1
1955	Amherst	22	16-6	1,233	56.0
1956	Amherst	22	16-6	1,277	58.0
1957	Stephen F. Austin	26	23-3	1,337	51.4
1958	McNeese St.	23	19-4	1,068	46.4
1959	Humboldt St.	23	14-9	1,166	50.7
1960	Wittenberg	24	22-2	1,122	46.8

Season	Team	G	W-L	Pts.	Avg.
1961	Wittenberg	29	25-4	1,270	43.8
1962	Wittenberg	26	21-5	1,089	41.9
1963	Wittenberg	28	26-2	1,285	45.9
1964	Wittenberg	23	18-5	1,186	51.6
1965	Cheyney	25	24-1	1,393	55.7
1966	Chicago	16	12-4	894	55.9
1967	Ashland	24	21-3	1,025	42.7
1968	Ashland	30	23-7	1,164	38.8
1969	Ashland	30	26-4	1,017	33.9
1970	Ashland	27	23-4	1,118	41.4
1971	Ashland	28	25-3	1,523	54.4
1972	Chicago	20	16-4	1,132	56.6
1973	Steubenville	29	22-7	1,271	43.8
1974	Steubenville	26	14-12	1,336	51.4
1975	Cal Poly	26	15-11	1,590	61.2
1976	Green Bay	29	21-8	1,768	61.0
1977	Green Bay	29	26-3	1,682	58.0
1978	Green Bay	32	30-2	1,682	52.6
1979	Green Bay	32	24-8	1,612	50.4
1980	Green Bay	27	15-12	1,577	58.4
1981	San Fran. St.	26	17-9	1,463	56.3
1982	Cal Poly	29	23-6	1,537	53.0
1983	Cal Poly	28	18-10	1,553	55.5
1984	Cal Poly	28	20-8	1,458	52.1
1985	Cal Poly	27	16-11	1,430	53.0
1986	Lewis	30	24-6	1,702	56.7
1987	Denver	29	20-9	1,844	63.6
1988	N.C. Central	29	26-3	1,683	58.0
1989	N.C. Central	32	28-4	1,791	56.0
1990	Humboldt St.	31	20-11	1,831	59.1
1991	Minn. Duluth	32	27-5	1,899	59.3
1992	Pace	30	23-7	1,517	50.6
1993	Philadelphia U.	32	30-2	1,898	59.3
1994	Pace	29	19-10	1,715	59.1
1995	Armstrong Atlantic	31	20-11	1,929	62.2
1996	Coker	26	16-10	1,592	61.2
1997	Fort Hays St.	31	29-2	1,837	59.3
1998	Presbyterian	28	16-12	1,704	60.9
1999	Incarnate Word	30	28-2	1,727	57.6
2000	Wingate	30	26-4	1,775	59.2
2001	Henderson St.	32	22-10	1,919	60.0
2002	Tusculum	28	15-13	1,600	57.1
2003	Barry	28	18-10	1,490	53.2
2004	Valdosta St.	29	25-4	1,514	52.2
2005	Adelphi	29	22-7	1,609	55.5
2006	Adelphi	32	27-5	1,749	54.7
2007	Bentley	33	32-1	1,898	57.5

‡record since 1948

Season	Team	Off.	Def.	Mar.
1979	Roanoke	77.8	60.8	17.0
1980	UCF	91.7	72.1	19.6
1981	West Ga.	88.5	70.2	18.3
1982	Minn. Duluth	81.7	64.8	16.9
1983	Minn. Duluth	84.8	69.8	15.0
1984	Chicago St.	85.9	70.2	15.7
1985	Virginia Union	87.6	67.8	19.8
1986	Mt. St. Mary's	80.0	65.7	14.3
1987	Ky. Wesleyan	92.4	72.9	19.8
1988	Fla. Southern	89.6	70.5	19.1
1989	Virginia Union	88.2	69.6	18.6
1990	Ky. Wesleyan	97.3	76.8	20.5
1991	Ashland	99.8	78.2	21.6
1992	Oakland City	99.5	77.1	22.4
1993	Philadelphia U.	78.8	59.3	19.4
1994	Oakland City	87.8	65.5	22.3
1995	Jacksonville St.	101.2	77.6	23.6
1996	Fort Hays St.	92.1	70.2	21.9
1997	Fort Hays St.	84.1	59.3	24.8
1998	Oakland City	85.8	64.1	21.7
1999	Incarnate Word	78.5	57.6	21.0
2000	Metro St.	87.0	67.9	19.1
2001	Adelphi	85.3	65.7	19.7
2002	Ky. Wesleyan	91.3	72.7	18.6
2003	Ky. Wesleyan	88.9	72.7	16.3
2004	Metro St.	93.4	65.3	28.1
2005	Oakland City	83.5	63.2	20.3
2006	Pitt.-Johnstown	80.1	62.9	17.2
2007	Winona St.	85.6	66.5	19.1

*record

Scoring Margin

Season	Team	Off.	Def.	Mar.
1950	Montana	77.4	57.7	19.7
1951	Eastern Ill.	84.7	57.9	26.8
1952	Texas St.	77.4	48.9	28.5
1953	Arkansas Tech	94.7	74.3	20.4
1954	Texas Southern	89.2	63.3	25.9
1955	Mt. St. Mary's	95.2	73.3	21.9
1956	Western Ill.	92.5	72.1	20.4
1957	West Va. Tech	102.6	77.2	25.4
1958	Tennessee St.	88.7	64.1	24.6
1959	Grambling	95.3	73.3	22.0
1960	Mississippi Col.	114.2	92.9	21.3
1961	Bryan	93.8	62.4	*31.4
1962	Mansfield	87.6	64.7	22.9
1963	Gorham St.	94.7	69.7	25.0
1964	Central Conn. St.	94.5	67.7	26.8
1965	Cheyney	80.7	55.7	25.0
1966	Cheyney	90.0	64.4	25.6
1967	Lincoln (Mo.)	108.3	82.2	26.1
1968	Western New Eng.	104.7	76.8	27.9
1969	Indiana (Pa.)	88.6	64.5	24.1
1970	Husson	106.1	79.0	27.1
1971	Kentucky St.	103.5	78.2	25.3
1972	Brockport St.	93.8	70.3	23.5
1973	Green Bay	71.2	52.1	19.1
1974	Alcorn St.	96.9	79.8	17.1
1975	Bentley	95.2	78.7	16.5
1976	UCF	94.8	78.4	16.4
1977	Texas Southern	88.4	71.9	16.5
1978	Green Bay	68.8	52.6	16.2

Field-Goal Percentage

Season	Team	FG	FGA	Pct.
1948	Tex. A&M-Commerce	445	1,119	39.8
1949	Missouri St.	482	1,106	43.6
1950	Tex. A&M-Corp. Chris.	555	1,290	43.0
1951	Beloit	773	1,734	44.6
1952	Missouri St.	890	1,903	46.8
1953	Lebanon Valley	637	1,349	47.2
1954	San Diego St.	675	1,502	44.9
1955	UC Santa Barb.	672	1,383	48.6
1956	UC Santa Barb.	552	1,142	48.3
1957	Alderson-Broaddus	1,006	2,094	48.0
1958	N.C. A&T	552	1,072	51.5
1959	Grambling	1,111	2,205	50.4
1960	William Carey	708	1,372	51.6
1961	Virginia Union	908	1,735	52.3
1962	West Va. Tech	871	1,575	55.3
1963	Lenoir-Rhyne	869	1,647	52.8
1964	LeMoyne-Owen	844	1,520	55.5
1965	Southern U.	1,036	1,915	54.1
1966	Howard Payne	932	1,710	54.5
1967	Alabama St.	874	1,555	56.2
1968	South Carolina St.	588	1,010	58.2
1969	Southampton	846	1,588	53.3
1970	Savannah St.	1,145	1,969	58.2
1971	Alabama St.	1,196	2,100	57.0
1972	Florida A&M	1,194	2,143	55.7
1973	Green Bay	929	1,700	54.6
1974	Kentucky St.	1,252	2,266	55.3
1975	Kentucky St.	1,121	1,979	56.6
1976	Kentucky St.	1,093	1,753	*62.4
1977	Merrimack	1,120	2,008	55.8
1978	Green Bay	840	1,509	55.7
1979	Morris Brown	980	1,763	55.6
1980	UNC Pembroke	849	1,544	55.0
1981	Bellarmine	851	1,561	54.5
1982	Fla. Southern	943	1,644	57.4
1983	Lewis	807	1,448	55.7
1984	Lewis	851	1,494	57.0
1985	Virginia Union	1,132	1,967	57.5
1986	Tampa	856	1,546	55.4
1987	Johnson Smith	995	1,817	54.8
1988	Fla. Southern	1,118	2,026	55.2
1989	Millersville	1,119	2,079	53.8
1990	S.C. Upstate	954	1,745	54.7
1991	S.C. Upstate	923	1,631	56.6
1992	S.C. Upstate	898	1,664	54.0
1993	Cal St. Bakersfield	1,002	1,849	54.2
1994	Southern Ind.	1,171	2,142	54.7

Season	Team	FG	FGA	Pct.
1995	High Point	862	1,603	53.8
1996	Fort Hays St.	1,158	2,145	54.0
1997	Oakland City	961	1,821	52.8
1998	West Tex. A&M	953	1,841	51.8
1999	South Dakota	835	1,631	51.2
2000	Mo. Western St.	845	1,621	52.1
2001	Southern Ind.	1,014	1,937	52.3
2002	Neb.-Kearney	899	1,762	51.0
2003	Michigan Tech	920	1,740	52.9
2004	BYU-Hawaii	824	1,573	52.4
2005	Colo. Christian	859	1,642	52.3
2006	Southern Ind.	1,042	1,974	52.8
2007	Winona St.	1,128	2,162	52.2

*record

Field-Goal Percentage Defense

Season	Team	FG	FGA	Pct.
1978	Green Bay	681	1,830	37.2
1979	Green Bay	639	1,709	37.4
1980	Wis.-Parkside	688	1,666	41.3
1981	Central St. (Ohio)	675	1,724	39.2
1982	Minn. St. Mankato	699	1,735	40.3
1983	Central Mo.	746	1,838	40.6
1984	Norfolk St.	812	1,910	42.5
1985	Central Mo.	683	1,660	41.1
1986	Norfolk St.	782	1,925	40.6
1987	Denver	691	1,709	40.4
1988	Minn. Duluth	702	1,691	41.5
1989	N.C. Central	633	1,642	38.6
1990	Central Mo.	696	1,757	39.6
1991	Southwest Baptist	758	1,942	39.0
1992	Virginia Union	766	2,069	37.0
1993	Pfeiffer	767	2,028	37.8
1994	Virginia Union	705	1,966	35.9
1995	Virginia Union	723	1,973	36.6
1996	Virginia Union	718	1,944	36.9
1997	St. Rose	887	2,409	36.8
1998	Delta St.	705	1,930	36.5
1999	Delta St.	610	1,652	36.9
2000	Fla. Southern	702	1,887	37.2
2001	Tampa	631	1,723	36.6
2002	Tarleton St.	657	1,837	*35.8
2003	Tarleton St.	655	1,757	37.3
2004	Central Ark.	624	1,699	36.7
2005	Adelphi	539	1,432	37.6
2006	Adelphi	546	1,524	35.8
2007	Grand Valley St.	677	1,831	37.0

*record

Three-Point Field Goals Made Per Game

Season	Team	G	3FG	Avg.
1987	Northern Mich.	27	187	6.9
1988	Sacramento St.	30	303	10.1
1989	Central Okla.	27	280	10.4
1990	Stonehill	27	259	9.6
1991	Hillsdale	27	318	11.8
1992	Troy	29	*444	*15.3
1993	Hillsdale	28	366	13.1
1994	Hillsdale	25	315	12.6
1995	Hillsdale	29	330	11.4
1996	Mont. St.-Billings	28	304	10.9
1997	Mont. St.-Billings	28	394	14.1
1998	Mont. St.-Billings	28	375	13.4
1999	Mont. St.-Billings	28	355	12.7
2000	Mont. St.-Billings	26	294	11.3
2001	Mont. St.-Billings	27	284	10.5
2002	St. Anselm	30	301	10.0
2003	Bemidji St.	29	338	11.7
2004	Mont. St.-Billings	27	334	12.4
2005	Oakland City	31	394	12.7
2006	Mont. St.-Billings	28	360	12.9
2007	Fairmont St.	28	296	10.6

*record

Three-Point Field-Goal Percentage

Season	Team	G	3FG	3FGA	Pct.
1987	St. Anselm	30	97	189	51.3
1988	Winston-Salem	28	98	182	*53.8
1989	Mississippi Col.	27	144	276	52.2
1990	Shaw	27	74	143	51.7
1991	Rollins	28	278	585	47.5
1992	Oakland City	30	244	486	50.2
1993	Oakland City	32	215	465	46.2
1994	Oakland City	28	225	495	45.5
1995	Oakland City	30	256	561	45.6
1996	Oakland City	31	260	537	48.4
1997	Oakland City	30	311	651	47.8
1998	Michigan Tech	31	267	613	43.6
1999	South Dakota	29	258	577	44.7
2000	Eckerd	28	156	366	42.6
2001	Mesa St.	27	152	346	43.9
2002	Michigan Tech	30	216	499	43.3
2003	Michigan Tech	32	252	581	43.4
2004	Alas. Anchorage	30	280	612	45.8
2005	Colo. Christian	28	220	493	44.6
2006	Grand Canyon	27	286	640	44.7
2007	Metro St.	32	298	675	44.1

*record

Free-Throw Percentage

Season	Team	FT	FTA	Pct.
1948	Charleston (W.V.)	446	659	67.7
1949	Linfield	276	402	68.7
1950	Jacksonville St.	452	613	73.7
1951	Millikin	603	846	71.3
1952	Eastern Ill.	521	688	75.7
1953	Upsala	513	69	74.0
1954	Central Mich.	376	509	73.9
1955	Mississippi Col.	559	733	76.3
1956	Wheaton (Ill.)	625	842	74.2
1957	Wheaton (Ill.)	689	936	73.6
1958	Wheaton (Ill.)	517	689	75.0
1959	Wabash	418	545	76.7
1960	Allen	225	297	75.8
1961	Missouri St.	453	605	74.9
1962	Lenoir-Rhyne	477	599	79.6
1963	Hampden-Sydney	442	559	79.1
1964	Western Caro.	492	621	79.2
1965	Mississippi Col.	529	663	79.8
1966	Athens St.	631	802	78.7
1967	Northwestern St.	528	678	77.9
1968	Kenyon	684	858	79.7
1969	Kenyon	583	727	80.2
1970	Wooster	571	714	80.0
1971	South Ala.	422	518	81.5
1972	Clark Atlanta	409	520	78.7
1973	Rockford (Ill.)	367	481	76.3
1974	New Orleans	537	701	76.6
1975	Alabama St.	456	565	80.7
1976	Alabama St.	451	576	78.3
1977	Puget Sound	495	637	77.7
1978	Merrimack	508	636	79.9
1979	Bentley	506	652	77.6
1980	Philadelphia U.	436	549	79.4
1981	Coppin St.	401	514	78.0
1982	Fla. Southern	726	936	77.6
1983	Transylvania	463	606	76.4
1984	Transylvania	491	639	76.8
1985	Minn. St. Mankato	349	445	78.4
1986	Southern N.H.	507	672	75.4
1987	Columbus St.	339	433	78.3
1988	Rollins	631	795	79.4
1989	Rollins	477	607	78.6
1990	Rollins	449	582	77.1
1991	Lenoir-Rhyne	441	564	78.2
1992	Adams St.	397	512	77.5
1993	Philadelphia U.	491	630	77.9
1994	West Liberty St.	473	602	78.0
1995	Western St.	469	603	77.8
1996	South Dakota	501	648	77.3
1997	Hawaii-Hilo	471	606	77.7
1998	Gannon	473	573	*82.5
1999	Minn. Duluth	430	547	78.6

Season	Team	FT	FTA	Pct.
2000	Bemidji St.	386	492	78.5
2001	Morningside	383	485	79.0
2002	St. Cloud St.	461	587	78.5
2003	South Dakota	452	566	79.9
2004	Seattle Pacific	455	573	79.4
2005	St. Anselm	549	676	81.2
2006	Western Wash.	590	751	78.6
2007	Northwest Nazarene	384	473	81.2

*record

Rebound Margin

Season	Team	Off.	Def.	Mar.
1976	Mississippi Val.	63.9	39.5	*24.4
1977	Philadelphia U.	38.7	24.1	14.6
1978	Mass.-Lowell	49.0	37.5	11.5
1979	Dowling	48.2	32.6	15.6
1980	Ark.-Pine Bluff	40.3	25.9	14.4
1981	Green Bay	40.6	26.5	14.1
1982	Central St. (Ohio)	48.0	37.2	10.8
1983	Hampton	50.2	38.5	11.8
1984	California (Pa.)	46.4	33.1	13.3

Season	Team	Off.	Def.	Mar.
1985	Virginia Union	44.1	32.0	12.1
1986	Tampa	39.9	28.0	11.8
1987	Millersville	44.7	33.8	10.9
1988	Clark Atlanta	44.7	32.5	12.1
1989	Hampton	46.7	36.3	10.3
1990	Fla. Atlantic	41.0	29.4	11.6
1991	California (Pa.)	44.6	32.0	12.6
1992	Oakland City	43.4	31.8	11.6
1993	Metro St.	45.5	32.0	13.5
1994	Oakland City	44.0	33.7	10.3
1995	Jacksonville St.	47.7	35.2	12.5
1996	Virginia Union	48.0	36.1	11.9
1997	Southern Conn. St.	41.6	32.3	9.3
1998	South Dakota St.	46.5	35.9	10.6
1999	Ky. Wesleyan	44.8	32.6	12.2
2000	Salem Int'l	44.2	32.1	12.1
2001	Salem Int'l	42.6	31.3	11.1
2002	Tarleton St.	43.0	32.0	11.1
2003	South Dakota St.	44.1	32.5	11.6
2004	Washburn	42.5	30.7	11.8
2005	Fla. Gulf Coast	41.5	31.3	10.2
2006	Gannon	38.8	27.5	11.3
2007	Fla. Gulf Coast	44.5	33.7	10.8

*record

2007 Most-Improved Teams

	School (Coach)	2007	2006	*Games Improved
1.	Dist. Columbia (Julius Smith)	20-9	1-22	16
2.	Millersville (Fred Thompson)	28-5	10-17	15
3.	NYIT (Sal Lagano)	20-9	5-22	14
4.	Virginia St. (Tony Collins)	20-8	9-20	11½
5.	UC-Colo. Spgs. (Russ Caton)	16-12	5-22	10½
5.	Lander (Bruce Evans)	17-11	9-21	10½
7.	Cal St. San B'dino (Jeff Oliver)	26-6	13-13	10
8.	Bentley (Jay Lawson)	32-1	21-9	9½
8.	Indianapolis (Todd Sturgeon)	13-13	4-23	9½
10.	Incarnate Word (Ken Burmeister)	18-11	8-19	9
11.	Southwestern Okla. (Todd Thurman)	17-10	9-19	8½

	School (Coach)	2007	2006	*Games Improved
12.	Barry (Cesar Odio)	23-7	15-15	8
12.	Lock Haven (John Wilson)	12-15	4-23	8
14.	Augusta St. (Darren Metress)	24-7	15-13	7½
14.	Bluefield St. (Donald Jones)	10-19	2-26	7½
14.	Fla. Gulf South (Dave Balza)	27-6	18-12	7½
14.	Humboldt St. (Tom Wood)	26-4	17-10	7½
14.	Pittsburg St. (Gene Iba)	18-13	9-19	7½
19.	Bloomsburg (John Sanow)	13-14	6-21	7
19.	Southeastern Okla. (Tony Robinson)	27-5	18-10	7

*To determine games improved, add the difference in victories between the two seasons to the difference in losses, then divide by two.

All-Time Winningest Teams

Includes records as a senior college only; minimum 10 seasons of competition. Postseason games are included.

By Percentage

	Team	Yrs.	Won	Lost	Pct.
1.	Metro St.	23	487	204	.705
2.	Philadelphia U.	72	1,207	527	.696
3.	Lynn	14	280	126	.690
4.	Virginia Union	82	1,359	615	.688
5.	Southern N.H.	44	832	413	.668
6.	Cheyney	44	810	403	.668
7.	Southern Ind.	38	719	367	.662
8.	St. Rose	33	621	327	.655
9.	Ky. Wesleyan	93	1,343	709	.654
10.	Central Wash.	100	1,545	825	.652
11.	St. Mary's (Tex.)	53	968	519	.651
12.	Bentley	44	766	426	.643
13.	Gannon	63	1,044	597	.636
14.	Northern St.	104	1,430	820	.636
15.	LeMoyne-Owen	49	841	483	.635
16.	Mesa St.	32	565	330	.631
17.	Fairmont St.	82	1,352	794	.630
18.	Drury	99	1,365	816	.626
19.	Fort Hays St.	98	1,346	809	.625
20.	Central Mo.	102	1,451	873	.624
21.	Carson-Newman	49	919	554	.624
22.	Cal St. San B'dino	23	388	236	.622
23.	Millersville	106	1,271	780	.620
24.	Incarnate Word	24	426	263	.618
25.	North Dakota	102	1,407	872	.617
26.	Grand Canyon	58	962	597	.617
27.	St. Cloud St.	82	1,146	712	.617
28.	Indiana (Pa.)	78	1,083	677	.615

By Victories

	Team	Yrs.	Won	Lost	Pct.
29.	Fla. Southern	80	1,165	731	.614
30.	Alas. Anchorage	30	535	336	.614

	Team	Yrs.	Won	Lost	Pct.
1.	Central Wash.	100	1,545	825	.652
2.	Central Mo.	102	1,451	873	.624
3.	Northern St.	104	1,430	820	.636
4.	North Dakota	102	1,407	872	.617
5.	Drury	99	1,365	816	.626
6.	Virginia Union	82	1,359	615	.688
7.	Fairmont St.	82	1,352	794	.630
8.	Fort Hays St.	98	1,346	809	.625
9.	Ky. Wesleyan	93	1,343	709	.654
10.	Washburn	101	1,336	925	.591
11.	West Tex. A&M	86	1,329	862	.607
12.	Pittsburg St.	98	1,273	1,021	.555
13.	Millersville	106	1,271	780	.620
14.	Emporia St.	101	1,245	1,010	.552
15.	Neb.-Kearney	100	1,242	853	.593
16.	Western Wash.	105	1,234	930	.570
17.	Rockhurst	86	1,208	934	.564
	West Chester	107	1,208	963	.556
19.	Philadelphia U.	72	1,207	527	.696
	Lenoir-Rhyne	86	1,207	945	.561
21.	Northwest Mo. St.	91	1,204	874	.579
22.	Cal St. Chico	94	1,193	1,051	.532
23.	Bloomsburg	102	1,184	780	.603
24.	Tex. A&M-Commerce	90	1,173	951	.552
25.	Fla. Southern	80	1,165	731	.614
26.	East Central	80	1,156	804	.590

Team	Yrs.	Won	Lost	Pct.
Indianapolis	83	1,156	816	.586
28. St. Cloud St.	82	1,146	712	.617
Catawba	81	1,146	954	.546
30. Northern Mich.	97	1,143	787	.592

Winningest Teams of the 2000s

BY PERCENTAGE

(Minimum 5 seasons as NCAA member)

	Team	Yrs.	Won	Lost	Pct.
1.	Metro St.	8	223	43	.838
2.	Findlay	7	174	41	.809
3.	Southern Ind.	8	209	50	.807
4.	Cal St. San B'dino	8	184	47	.797
5.	Neb.-Kearney	8	190	54	.779
6.	Northwest Mo. St.	8	192	59	.765
7.	Adelphi	8	186	58	.762
8.	Virginia Union	8	178	58	.754
9.	Salem Int'l	8	184	61	.751
10.	Tarleton St.	8	182	64	.740
11.	Pfeiffer	8	177	63	.738
12.	South Dakota	8	174	62	.737
13.	Alderson-Broaddus	8	179	65	.734
14.	Ky. Wesleyan	8	176	65	.730
15.	Eckerd	8	176	68	.721
16.	Seattle Pacific	8	166	65	.719
17.	St. Cloud St.	8	167	68	.711
18.	California (Pa.)	8	166	69	.706
19.	Bentley	8	173	73	.703
20.	Charleston (W.V.)	8	170	72	.702
21.	Humboldt St.	8	161	69	.700
22.	Rollins	8	170	73	.700
23.	Cal Poly Pomona	8	158	68	.699
24.	Henderson St.	8	170	74	.697
25.	Cal St. Bakersfield	8	158	69	.696
26.	Fort Hays St.	8	160	70	.696
27.	Winona St.	8	173	76	.695
28.	Washburn	8	167	74	.693
29.	Mass.-Lowell	8	169	75	.693
30.	Delta St.	8	162	72	.692

BY VICTORIES

	Team	Yrs.	Won	Lost	Pct.
1.	Metro St.	8	223	43	.838
2.	Southern Ind.	8	209	50	.807
3.	Northwest Mo. St.	8	192	59	.765
4.	Neb.-Kearney	8	190	54	.779
5.	Adelphi	8	186	58	.762
6.	Cal St. San B'dino	8	184	47	.797
	Salem Int'l	8	184	61	.751
8.	Tarleton St.	8	182	64	.740
9.	Alderson-Broaddus	8	179	65	.734
10.	Virginia Union	8	178	58	.754
11.	Pfeiffer	8	177	63	.738
12.	Ky. Wesleyan	8	176	65	.730
	Eckerd	8	176	68	.721
14.	Findlay	7	174	41	.809
	South Dakota	8	174	62	.737
16.	Bentley	8	173	73	.703
	Winona St.	8	173	76	.695
18.	Charleston (W.V.)	8	170	72	.702
	Rollins	8	170	73	.700
	Henderson St.	8	170	74	.697
21.	Mass.-Lowell	8	169	75	.693
22.	Columbus St.	8	168	76	.689
	Northern Ky.	8	168	78	.683
24.	St. Cloud St.	8	167	68	.711
	Washburn	8	167	74	.693
26.	Seattle Pacific	8	166	65	.719
	California (Pa.)	8	166	69	.706
28.	Fla. Southern	8	165	74	.690
29.	Bowie St.	8	163	75	.685
29.	Philadelphia U.	8	163	76	.682

All-Time Won-Lost Records

(Alphabetical Listing; No Minimum Seasons of Competition)

Team	First Year	Yrs.	Won	Lost	Pct.
Abilene Christian	1920	86	1,015	953	.516
Adams St.	1947	43	534	598	.472
Adelphi	1947	61	930	675	.579
Ala.-Huntsville	1974	34	480	490	.495
Alas. Anchorage	1978	30	535	336	.614
Alas. Fairbanks	1953	51	557	632	.468
Albany St. (Ga.)	1961	47	744	585	.560
Alderson-Broaddus	1935	70	1,086	867	.556
American Int'l	1934	73	864	890	.493
Angelo St.	1966	42	566	574	.496
Ark.-Monticello	1946	62	712	886	.446
Arkansas Tech	1915	84	1,084	905	.545
Armstrong Atlantic	1967	41	634	516	.551
Ashland	1921	87	1,028	875	.540
Assumption	1924	80	991	815	.549
Augusta St.	1966	42	636	535	.543
Augustana (S.D.)	1922	81	830	924	.473
Barry	1985	23	320	320	.500
Bellarmine	1951	57	744	728	.505
Belmont Abbey	1954	54	824	663	.554
Bemidji St.	1922	85	866	979	.469
Bentley	1964	44	766	426	.643
Bloomsburg	1902	102	1,184	780	.603
Bridgeport	1948	60	862	733	.540
Bryant	1964	44	604	587	.507
BYU-Hawaii	1978	30	518	349	.597
C.W. Post	1957	51	812	514	.612
UC San Diego	1966	42	535	548	.494
Cal Poly Pomona	1948	60	836	766	.522
Cal St. Chico	1914	94	1,193	1,051	.532
Cal St. Dom. Hills	1978	30	384	419	.478
Cal St. L.A.	1949	59	721	802	.473
Cal St. San B'dino	1985	23	388	236	.622
Cal St. Stanislaus	1967	41	504	587	.462
Carson-Newman	1959	49	919	554	.624
Catawba	1927	81	1,146	954	.546
Central Mo.	1906	102	1,451	873	.624
Central Okla.	1922	81	1,095	874	.556
Central Wash.	1902	100	1,545	825	.652
Chadron St.	1922	83	971	958	.503
Chaminade	1978	30	464	371	.556
Cheyney	1964	44	810	403	.668
Christian Bros.	1955	53	773	724	.516
Clark Atlanta	1950	58	815	718	.532
Clayton St.	1991	17	263	226	.538
UC-Colo. Spgs.	1988	20	130	405	.243
Colo. Christian	1991	17	192	271	.415
Colorado Mines	1912	95	704	1,231	.364
Colorado St.-Pueblo	1964	44	729	484	.601
Columbus St.	1968	40	655	441	.598
Delta St.	1928	76	1,108	725	.604
Dowling	1967	41	620	522	.543
Drury	1909	99	1,365	816	.626
East Central	1928	80	1,156	804	.590
East Stroudsburg	1927	80	861	910	.486
Eastern N.M.	1935	71	891	956	.482
Eckerd	1964	44	643	468	.579
Edinboro	1929	77	975	695	.584
Elizabeth City St.	1950	58	826	692	.544
Emporia St.	1902	101	1,245	1,010	.552
Erskine	1914	82	994	911	.522
Fairmont St.	1917	82	1,352	794	.630
Fayetteville St.	1937	64	807	823	.495
Ferris St.	1926	79	943	875	.519
Findlay	1911	85	1,096	709	.607
Fla. Southern	1924	80	1,165	731	.614
Florida Tech	1965	43	449	678	.398
Fort Hays St.	1908	98	1,346	809	.625
Fort Lewis	1964	44	560	599	.483
Francis Marion	1971	37	492	538	.478
Franklin Pierce	1964	44	680	470	.591
Gannon	1945	63	1,044	597	.636
GCSU	1971	37	528	510	.509
Glenville St.	1909	88	1,140	951	.545
Grand Canyon	1950	58	962	597	.617
Grand Valley St.	1967	41	691	452	.605
Harding	1958	50	658	722	.477
Hawaii Pacific	1979	29	505	362	.582

Team	First Year	Yrs.	Won	Lost	Pct.
Hawaii-Hilo	1977	31	524	379	.580
Henderson St.	1913	92	1,139	861	.570
Hillsdale	1900	104	982	1,146	.461
Humboldt St.	1924	84	832	928	.473
Incarnate Word	1981	24	426	263	.618
Indiana (Pa.)	1928	78	1,083	677	.615
Indianapolis	1923	83	1,156	816	.586
Johnson C. Smith	1929	67	906	691	.567
Ky. Wesleyan	1908	93	1,343	709	.654
Lake Superior St.	1947	61	774	694	.527
Lander	1969	39	637	521	.550
Le Moyne	1949	59	822	640	.562
LeMoyne-Owen	1959	49	841	483	.635
Lenoir-Rhyne	1920	86	1,207	945	.561
Lewis	1949	59	937	631	.598
Lincoln Memorial	1923	85	1,116	928	.546
Lock Haven	1919	83	629	987	.389
Lynn	1994	14	280	126	.690
Mansfield	1918	84	892	785	.532
Mars Hill	1964	44	510	715	.416
Mass.-Lowell	1967	41	550	545	.502
Mercyhurst	1972	36	495	465	.516
Merrimack	1950	58	732	743	.496
Mesa St.	1976	32	565	330	.631
Metro St.	1985	23	487	204	.705
Michigan Tech	1918	87	781	917	.460
Midwestern St.	1947	61	1,116	736	.603
Miles	1971	47	472	524	.474
Millersville	1900	106	1,271	780	.620
Minn. St. Mankato	1921	83	1,079	796	.575
Minn.-Duluth	1931	74	1,067	685	.609
Mo. Southern St.	1969	39	601	528	.532
Mo. Western St.	1970	38	660	451	.594
Mo.-Rolla	1910	95	761	1,159	.396
Mo.-St. Louis	1967	41	507	568	.472
Molloy	1993	15	142	267	.347
Mont. St.-Billings	1928	77	982	842	.538
Montevallo	1965	43	656	570	.535
Morehouse	1911	96	1,058	948	.527
UNC-Pembroke	1940	68	831	847	.495
N.C. Central	1928	73	1,016	788	.563
NJIT	1924	76	799	654	.550
N.M. Highlands	1924	81	829	982	.458
Neb.-Kearney	1907	100	1,242	853	.593
Neb.-Omaha	1913	90	979	993	.496
NYIT	1971	36	505	444	.532
Newberry	1913	92	926	1,182	.439
North Ala.	1932	73	941	765	.552
North Dakota	1905	102	1,407	872	.617
Northeastern St.	1925	71	948	852	.527
Northern Ky.	1972	36	604	418	.591
Northern Mich.	1907	97	1,143	787	.592
Northern St.	1903	104	1,430	820	.636
Northwest Mo. St.	1917	91	1,204	874	.579
Northwood (Mich.)	1961	47	543	667	.449
Nova Southeastern	1983	25	283	423	.401
Oakland City	1923	66	825	726	.532
Ouachita Baptist	1921	81	1,025	860	.544
Pace	1948	60	754	730	.508

Team	First Year	Yrs.	Won	Lost	Pct.
Philadelphia U.	1921	72	1,207	527	.696
Philadelphia Sciences	1902	99	1,120	821	.577
Pittsburg St.	1909	98	1,273	1,021	.555
Pitt.-Johnstown	1970	38	469	499	.485
Quincy	1941	63	1,006	759	.570
Regis (Colo.)	1946	60	840	738	.532
Rockhurst	1922	86	1,208	934	.564
Rollins	1951	57	812	679	.545
Saginaw Valley	1970	38	531	517	.507
St. Andrews	1975	33	421	464	.476
St. Anselm	1935	70	953	703	.575
St. Cloud St.	1923	82	1,146	712	.617
St. Joseph's (Ind.)	1906	91	1,022	935	.522
St. Leo	1966	42	432	657	.397
St. Mary's (Tex.)	1955	53	968	519	.651
St. Michael's	1920	87	996	926	.518
St. Rose	1974	33	621	327	.655
San Fran. St.	1930	76	962	977	.496
Seattle	1946	62	911	823	.525
Seattle Pacific	1944	64	1,018	750	.576
Shepherd	1907	100	1,110	1,054	.513
Slippery Rock	1910	96	1,034	966	.517
Sonoma St.	1964	38	427	538	.442
S.C.-Aiken	1970	38	504	601	.456
S.C. Upstate	1968	40	629	454	.581
South Dakota	1909	97	1,117	931	.545
Southern Conn. St.	1960	48	558	701	.443
SIU-Edwardsville	1968	39	531	505	.513
Southern Ind.	1970	38	719	367	.662
Southern N.H.	1964	44	832	413	.668
Southwest Baptist	1966	42	610	530	.535
Southwest Minn. St.	1968	40	449	631	.416
Stonehill	1950	58	821	665	.552
Tampa	1951	45	713	520	.578
Tarleton St.	1962	46	571	678	.457
Tex. A&M-Commerce	1917	90	1,173	951	.552
Tex. A&M-Kingsville	1926	73	800	915	.466
Truman	1920	87	1,046	934	.528
Tuskegee	1909	78	1,025	971	.514
Upper Iowa	1916	92	817	959	.460
Valdosta St.	1955	53	819	541	.602
Virginia Union	1926	82	1,359	615	.688
Washburn	1906	101	1,336	925	.591
Wayne St. (Mich.)	1918	89	1,074	891	.547
Wayne St. (Neb.)	1913	93	1,112	961	.536
West Ala.	1957	51	589	710	.453
West Chester	1898	107	1,208	963	.556
West Fla.	1968	23	336	273	.552
West Ga.	1958	50	765	549	.582
West Liberty St.	1924	84	810	877	.480
West Tex. A&M	1921	86	1,329	862	.607
West Va. St.	1945	63	903	757	.544
Western Ore.	1921	83	1,018	986	.508
Western	1924	81	726	1,135	.390
Western Wash.	1903	105	1,234	930	.570
Wheeling Jesuit	1958	50	661	661	.500
Winona St.	1916	91	953	1,023	.482
Wis.-Parkside	1970	38	518	543	.488

Division III Records

Individual Records

Division III men's basketball records are based on the performances of Division III teams since the three-division reorganization plan was adopted by the special NCAA Convention in August 1973. Assists were added for the 1988-89 season; blocked shots and steals were added for the 1992-93 season. In statistical rankings, the rounding of percentages and/or averages may indicate ties where none exist. In these cases, the numerical order of the rankings is accurate.

Scoring

POINTS
Game
77—Jeff Clement, Grinnell vs. Illinois Col., Feb. 18, 1998
Season
1,044—Greg Grant, TCNJ, 1989 (32 games)
Career
2,940—Andre Foreman, Salisbury, 1988-89, 91-92 (109 games)

AVERAGE PER GAME
Season
37.3—Steve Diekmann, Grinnell, 1995 (745 in 20)
Career
(Min. 1,400) 32.8—Dwain Govan, Bishop, 1974-75 (1,805 in 55)

POINTS SCORED WITH NO TIME ELAPSING
Game
24—Rob Rittgers, UC San Diego vs. Menlo, Jan. 16, 1988 (made 24 consecutive free throws due to 12 bench technical fouls)

CONSECUTIVE POINTS SCORED
Game
25—Andy Panko, Lebanon Valley vs. Frank. & Marsh., Jan. 19, 1998

GAMES SCORING AT LEAST 50 POINTS
Season
4—Mike Hoyt, Mt. St. Mary (N.Y.), 2007
Career
4—Mike Hoyt, Mt. St. Mary (N.Y.), 2004-07; Jeff Clement, Grinnell, 1996-99; Steve Diekmann, Grinnell, 1993-95

GAMES SCORING IN DOUBLE FIGURES
Career
116—Lamont Strothers, Chris. Newport, 1988-91

CONSECUTIVE GAMES SCORING IN DOUBLE FIGURES
Career
116—Lamont Strothers, Chris. Newport, from Nov. 20, 1987, to March 8, 1991

Field Goals

FIELD GOALS
Game
29—Ryan Hodges, Cal Lutheran vs. Redlands, Jan. 15, 2005 (31 attempts); Shannon Lilly, Bishop vs. Southwest Assembly of God, Jan. 31, 1983 (36 attempts)
Season
394—Dave Russell, Shepherd, 1975 (687 attempts)
Career
1,140—Andre Foreman, Salisbury, 1988-89, 91-92 (2,125 attempts)

CONSECUTIVE FIELD GOALS
Game
18—Franklyn Beckford, Lake Forest vs. Grinnell, Feb. 14, 2004; Jason Light, Emory & Henry vs. King (Tenn.), Dec. 2, 1995
Season
24—Todd Richards, Mount Union, 2000 (during five games)

FIELD-GOAL ATTEMPTS
Game
68—Jeff Clement, Grinnell vs. Illinois Col., Feb. 18, 1998 (26 made)
Season
742—Greg Grant, TCNJ, 1989 (387 made)
Career
2,149—Lamont Strothers, Chris. Newport, 1988-91 (1,016 made)

FIELD-GOAL PERCENTAGE
Game
(Min. 18 made) 100%— Franklyn Beckford, Lake Forest vs. Grinnell, Feb. 14, 2004 (18 of 18); Jason Light, Emory & Henry vs. King (Tenn.), Dec. 2, 1995 (18 of 18)
*Season
76.6—Travis Weiss, St. John's (Minn.), 1994 (160 of 209)
*Based on qualifiers for annual championship.
Career
(Min. 400 made) 73.6—Tony Rychlec, Mass. Maritime, 1981-83 (509 of 692)

Three-Point Field Goals

THREE-POINT FIELD GOALS
Game
21—Sami Wylie, Lincoln (Pa.) vs. Ohio St.-Marion, Dec. 2, 2006
Season
186—Jeff Clement, Grinnell, 1998 (511 attempts)
Career
516—Jeff Clement, Grinnell, 1996-99 (1,532 attempts)

THREE-POINT FIELD GOALS MADE PER GAME
Season
8.5—Jeff Clement, Grinnell, 1998 (186 in 22)
Career
5.7—Jeff Clement, Grinnell, 1996-99 (516 in 91)

CONSECUTIVE THREE-POINT FIELD GOALS
Game
11—Joe Goldin, Randolph-Macon vs. Emory & Henry, Feb. 16, 1997
Season
16—John Richards, Sewanee (during five games, Feb. 10 to Feb. 25, 1990)

CONSECUTIVE GAMES MAKING A THREE-POINT FIELD GOAL
Season
31—Troy Greenlee, DePauw, Nov. 17, 1989, to March 17, 1990
Career
75—Chris Carideo, Widener, 1992-95

THREE-POINT FIELD-GOAL ATTEMPTS
Game
52—Jeff Clement, Grinnell vs. Illinois Col., Feb. 18, 1998 (19 made)
Season
511—Jeff Clement, Grinnell, 1998 (186 made)
Career
1,532—Jeff Clement, Grinnell, 1996-99 (516 made)

THREE-POINT FIELD-GOAL ATTEMPTS PER GAME
Season
23.2—Jeff Clement, Grinnell, 1998 (511 in 22)
Career
16.8—Jeff Clement, Grinnell, 1996-99 (1,532 in 91)

THREE-POINT FIELD-GOAL PERCENTAGE
Game
(Min. 11 made) 100%—Joe Goldin, Randolph-Macon vs. Emory & Henry, Feb. 16, 1997 (11 of 11)
Season
(Min. 40 made) 67.0%—Reggie James, NJIT, 1989 (59 of 88)
(Min. 90 made) 56.9%—Eric Harris, Bishop, 1987 (91 of 160)
Career
(Min. 200 made) 51.3%—Jeff Seifriz, Wis.-Whitewater, 1987-89 (217 of 432)

Free Throws

FREE THROWS
Game
30—Rob Rittgers, UC San Diego vs. Menlo, Jan. 16, 1988 (30 attempts)
Season
249—Dave Russell, Shepherd, 1975 (293 attempts)
Career
792—Matt Hancock, Colby, 1987-90 (928 attempts)

CONSECUTIVE FREE THROWS MADE
Game
30—Rob Rittgers, UC San Diego vs. Menlo, Jan. 16, 1988
Season
59—Mike Michelson, Coast Guard (during 13 games, Jan. 16 to Feb. 27, 1990)
Career
84—Dirk Rhinehart, Kalamazoo (16 games, Jan. 3, 2001 to Dec. 17, 2001)

FREE THROWS ATTEMPTED
Game
30—Rob Rittgers, UC San Diego vs. Menlo, Jan. 16, 1988 (30 made)
Season
326—Moses Jean-Pierre, Plymouth St., 1994 (243 made)
Career
928—Matt Hancock, Colby, 1987-90 (792 made)

FREE-THROW PERCENTAGE
Game
(Min. 30 made) 100%—Rob Rittgers, UC San Diego vs. Menlo, Jan. 16, 1988 (30 of 30)
*Season
96.3%—Korey Coon, Ill. Wesleyan, 2000 (157 of 163)
*based on qualifiers for annual championship
Career
(Min. 250 made) 92.5%—Andy Enfield, Johns Hopkins, 1988-91 (431 of 466)
(Min. 500 made) 86.2%—Brad Clark, Wis.-Oshkosh, 1997-00 (535 of 621)

Rebounds

REBOUNDS
Game
36—Mark Veenstra, Calvin vs. Colorado St.-Pueblo., Feb. 3, 1976; Clinton Montford, Methodist vs. Warren Wilson, Jan. 21, 1989
Season
579—Joe Manley, Bowie St., 1976 (29 games)
Career
1,628—Michael Smith, Hamilton, 1989-92 (107 games)

AVERAGE PER GAME
Season
19.97—Joe Manley, Bowie St., 1976 (579 in 29)
Career
(Min. 900) 17.4—Larry Parker, Plattsburgh St., 1975-78 (1,482 in 85)

Assists

ASSISTS
Game
26—Robert James, Kean vs. NJIT, March 11, 1989
Season
391—Robert James, Kean, 1989 (29 games)
Career
917—Tennyson Whitted, Ramapo, 2000-03 (108 games)

AVERAGE PER GAME
Season
13.5—Robert James, Kean, 1989 (391 in 29)
Career
(Min. 550) 8.6—Phil Dixon, Shenandoah, 1993-96 (889 in 103)

Blocked Shots

BLOCKED SHOTS
Game
18—John Bunch, Lincoln (Pa.) vs. New Jersey City, Jan. 19, 2004; John Bunch, Lincoln (Pa.) vs. Valley Forge, Dec. 13, 2003
Season
198—Tory Black, NJIT, 1997 (26 games)
Career
576—Ira Nicholson, Mt. St. Vincent, 1994-97 (100 games)

AVERAGE PER GAME
Season
7.6—Tory Black, NJIT, 1997 (198 in 26)
Career
6.1—Neil Edwards, York (N.Y.), 1998-00 (337 in 55)

Steals

STEALS
Game
17—Matt Newton, Principia vs. Harris-Stowe, Jan. 4, 1994
Season
189—Moses Jean-Pierre, Plymouth St., 1994 (30 games)
Career
448—Tennyson Whitted, Ramapo, 2000-03 (108 games)

AVERAGE PER GAME
Season
6.3—Moses Jean-Pierre, Plymouth St., 1994 (189 in 30)
Career
5.5—Moses Jean-Pierre, Plymouth St., 1993-94 (303 in 55 games)

Games

GAMES PLAYED
Season
34—Nick Bennett, Kyle Grusczynski, Jason Kaslow, Neal Krajnik, Eric Maus and Tamaris Releford, Wis.-Stevens Point, 2004; Thane Anderson, Matt Benedict, Tim Blair, Lanse Carter, Mike Johnson, Todd Oehrlein, Mike Prasher and Derrick Shelton, Wis.-Eau Claire, 1990
Career
123—Kyle Witucky, Wooster, 2003-06

Team Records

Note: Where records involve both teams, each team must be an NCAA Division III member institution.

SINGLE-GAME RECORDS

Scoring

POINTS
201—Lincoln (Pa.) vs. Ohio St.-Marion (78), Dec. 2, 2006
POINTS BY LOSING TEAM
153—Redlands vs. Cal Baptist, Dec. 10, 2004; Chapman vs. Redlands, December 4, 2003 (3ot)
POINTS, BOTH TEAMS
315—Simpson (167) vs. Grinnell (148), Nov. 19, 1994
POINTS IN A HALF
104—Lincoln (Pa.) vs. Ohio St.-Marion (78), Dec. 2, 2006 (second half)
POINTS SCORED WITH NO TIME ELAPSING OFF OF THE CLOCK
24—UC San Diego vs. Menlo, Jan. 16, 1988 (made 24 consecutive free throws due to 12 bench technical fouls)
FEWEST POINTS ALLOWED
6—Dickinson (15) vs. Muhlenberg, Feb. 3, 1982
FEWEST POINTS ALLOWED IN A HALF
0—Dickinson (2) vs. Muhlenberg (first), Feb. 3, 1982
FEWEST POINTS, BOTH TEAMS
21—Dickinson (15) vs. Muhlenberg (6), Feb. 3, 1982
FEWEST POINTS, HALF, BOTH TEAMS
2—Dickinson (2) vs. Muhlenberg (0) (first), Feb. 3, 1982
MARGIN OF VICTORY
123—Lincoln (Pa.) (201) vs. Ohio St.-Marion (78), Dec. 2, 2006

Field Goals

FIELD GOALS
79—Lincoln (Pa.) vs. Ohio St.-Marion, Dec. 2, 2006 (141 attempts)
FIELD-GOAL ATTEMPTS
141—Lincoln (Pa.) vs. Ohio St.-Marion, Dec. 2, 2006 (made 79)
FEWEST FIELD GOALS
3—Muhlenberg vs. Dickinson, Feb. 3, 1982 (11 attempts)
FEWEST FIELD-GOAL ATTEMPTS
11—Muhlenberg vs. Dickinson, Feb. 3, 1982 (3 made)

FIELD-GOAL PERCENTAGE
89.8%—St. Norbert vs. Grinnell, Jan. 28, 2000
FIELD-GOAL PERCENTAGE, HALF
95.7—Beloit vs. Grinnell, Jan. 27, 2001 (22 of 23)

Three-Point Field Goals

THREE-POINT FIELD GOALS
37—Redlands vs. La Sierra, Dec. 13, 2003 (97 attempts)
THREE-POINT FIELD GOALS, BOTH TEAMS
47—Redlands (35) vs. Whittier (12), Feb. 21, 2004
CONSECUTIVE THREE-POINT FIELD GOALS MADE WITHOUT A MISS
11—Willamette vs. Western Baptist, Jan. 8, 1987
NUMBER OF DIFFERENT PLAYERS TO SCORE A THREE-POINT FIELD GOAL, ONE TEAM
14—Redlands vs. Caltech, Jan. 29, 2005
THREE-POINT FIELD-GOAL ATTEMPTS
106—Redlands vs. La Sierra, Jan. 6, 2005 (35 made)
THREE-POINT FIELD-GOAL ATTEMPTS, BOTH TEAMS
119—Redlands (82) vs. Chapman (37), Dec. 5, 2003
THREE-POINT FIELD-GOAL PERCENTAGE
(Min. 10 made) 100%—Willamette vs. Western Baptist, Jan. 8, 1987 (11 of 11); Kean vs. Ramapo, Feb. 11, 1987 (10 of 10)
(Min. 15 made) 89.5%—Simpson vs. Dubuque, Feb. 22, 2003 (17 of 19)
THREE-POINT FIELD-GOAL PERCENTAGE, BOTH TEAMS
(Min. 10 made) 92.9%—Luther (8 of 8) vs. Wartburg (5 of 6), Feb. 14, 1987 (13 of 14)
(Min. 15 made) 75.0%—Anna Maria (4 of 6) vs. Nichols (11 of 14), Feb. 10, 1987 (15 of 20)
(Min. 20 made) 62.9%—Simpson (17 of 19) vs. Dubuque (5 of 16), Feb. 22, 2003 (22 of 35)

Free Throws

FREE THROWS MADE
53—UC San Diego vs. Menlo, Jan. 16, 1988 (59 attempts)
FREE THROWS MADE, BOTH TEAMS
93—Grinnell (50) vs. Beloit (43), Jan. 10, 1998
FREE THROWS ATTEMPTED
71—Earlham vs. Oberlin, Dec. 5, 1992 (46 made)
FREE THROWS ATTEMPTED, BOTH TEAMS
105—Earlham (71) vs. Oberlin (34), Dec. 5, 1992

FEWEST FREE THROWS MADE
0—Many teams
FEWEST FREE-THROW ATTEMPTS
0—Many teams
FREE-THROW PERCENTAGE
(Min. 28 made) 10.0%—Aibany (N.Y.) vs. Potsdam St., Feb. 19, 1994 (28 of 28)
(Min. 30 made) 97.2%—Ill. Wesleyan vs. North Park, Feb. 19, 2003 (35 of 36)
(Min. 45 made) 92.6%—Grinnell vs. Beloit, Jan. 10, 1998 (50 of 54)
FREE-THROW PERCENTAGE, BOTH TEAMS
(Min. 20 made) 100%—Bethel (Minn.) (15 of 15) vs. Carleton (5 of 5), Feb. 24, 2004
(Min. 30 made) 94.9%—Muskingum (30 of 31) vs. Ohio Wesleyan (7 of 8), Jan. 10, 1981 (37 of 39)

Rebounds

REBOUNDS
98—Alma vs. Marion, Dec. 28, 1973
REBOUNDS, BOTH TEAMS
124—Chapman (65) vs. Redlands (59), Dec. 5, 2003; Ill. Wesleyan (62) vs. North Central (Ill.) (62), Feb. 8, 1977; Rochester Inst. (72) vs. Thiel (52), Nov. 18, 1988
REBOUND MARGIN
56—MIT (74) vs. Emerson-MCA (18), Feb. 21, 1990

Assists

ASSISTS
53—Simpson vs. Grinnell, Nov. 25, 1995
ASSISTS, BOTH TEAMS
79—Simpson (53) vs. Grinnell (26), Nov. 25, 1995

Personal Fouls

PERSONAL FOULS
47—Concordia Chicago vs. Trinity Christian, Feb. 26, 1988
PERSONAL FOULS, BOTH TEAMS
80—Grinnell (46) vs. St. Norbert (34), Jan. 28, 2000
PLAYERS DISQUALIFIED
6—Thomas More vs. Franklin, Feb. 2, 2002; Union (N.Y.) vs. Rochester, Feb. 15, 1985; Haverford vs. Drew, Jan. 10, 1990; Manhattanville vs. Drew, Jan. 11, 1992; Roger Williams vs Curry, Jan. 14, 1995
PLAYERS DISQUALIFIED, BOTH TEAMS
11—Union (N.Y.) (6) vs. Rochester (5), Feb. 15, 1985

DIVISION III

Overtimes

OVERTIME PERIODS

5—Babson (115) vs. Wheaton (Mass.) (107), Feb. 18, 1999; Capital (86) vs. Muskingum (89), Jan. 5, 1980; Carnegie Mellon (81) vs. Allegheny (76), Feb. 12, 1983; Rochester (99) vs. Union (N.Y.) (98), Feb. 15, 1985

POINTS IN ONE OVERTIME PERIOD

31—Marymount (Va.) vs. Catholic, Jan. 30, 1999

POINTS IN ONE OVERTIME PERIOD, BOTH TEAMS

51—Wash. & Lee (28) vs. Mary Washington (23), Jan. 9, 1995

POINTS IN OVERTIME PERIODS

50—Babson (50) vs. Wheaton (Mass.) (5 ot), Feb. 18, 1999

POINTS IN OVERTIME PERIODS, BOTH TEAMS

92—Babson (50) vs. Wheaton (Mass.) (42) (5 ot), Feb. 18, 1999

SEASON RECORDS

Scoring

POINTS

3,310—Redlands, 2005 (25 games)

AVERAGE PER GAME

132.4—Redlands, 2005 (3,310 in 25)

AVERAGE SCORING MARGIN

31.1—Husson, 1976 (98.7 offense, 67.6 defense)

GAMES AT LEAST 100 POINTS

23—Redlands, 2005 (25-game season); Grinnell, 2002 (24-game season)

CONSECUTIVE GAMES AT LEAST 100 POINTS

19—Grinnell, from Nov. 23, 2002, to Feb. 8, 2003

CONSECUTIVE GAMES AT LEAST 100 POINTS (Multiple Seasons)

28—Grinnell, from Jan. 25, 2002, to Feb. 8, 2003

Field Goals

FIELD GOALS

1,323—Shepherd, 1975 (2,644 attempts)

FIELD GOALS PER GAME

44.6—Redlands, 2005 (1,116 in 25)

FIELD-GOAL ATTEMPTS

2,757—Redlands, 2005 (1,116 made)

FIELD-GOAL ATTEMPTS PER GAME

110.3—Redlands, 2005 (2,757 in 25)

FIELD-GOAL PERCENTAGE

60.0—Stony Brook, 1978 (1,033 of 1,721)

Three-Point Field Goals

THREE-POINT FIELD GOALS

595—Redlands, 2005 (1,813 attempts)

THREE-POINT FIELD GOALS PER GAME

23.8—Redlands, 2005 (595 in 25)

THREE-POINT FIELD-GOAL ATTEMPTS

1,813—Redlands, 2005 (595 made)

THREE-POINT FIELD-GOAL ATTEMPTS PER GAME

72.5—Redlands, 2005 (1,813 in 25)

THREE-POINT FIELD-GOAL PERCENTAGE

(Min. 100 made) 62.0%—NJIT, 1989 (124 of 200)

(Min. 150 made) 49.1%—Eureka, 1994 (317 of 646)

CONSECUTIVE GAMES SCORING A THREE-POINT FIELD GOAL

474—Salisbury, Nov. 25, 1986-Present

Free Throws

FREE THROWS MADE

698—Ohio Wesleyan, 1988 (888 attempts)

FREE THROWS MADE PER GAME

23.7—Grinnell, 1995 (498 in 21)

FREE-THROW ATTEMPTS

930—Queens (N.Y.), 1981 (636 made)

FREE-THROW ATTEMPTS PER GAME

33.2—Grinnell, 1995 (698 in 21)

FREE-THROW PERCENTAGE

81.8%—Wis.-Oshkosh, 1998 (516 of 631)

Rebounds

REBOUNDS

1,616—Keene St., 1976 (29 games)

AVERAGE PER GAME

56.3—Mercy, 1977 (1,408 in 25)

AVERAGE REBOUND MARGIN

17.0—Hamilton, 1991 (49.6 offense, 32.5 defense)

Assists

ASSISTS

861—Salisbury, 1991 (29 games)

AVERAGE PER GAME

31.2—Me.-Farmington, 1991 (748 in 24)

Fouls

FOULS

801—McMurry, 2001 (28 games)

FOULS PER GAME

3.9—Grinnell, 1998 (679 in 22)

FEWEST FOULS

177—Caltech, 1997 (20 games)

FEWEST FOULS PER GAME

8.9—Caltech, 1997 (177 in 20)

Defense

FEWEST POINTS PER GAME ALLOWED

47.5—Wis.-Platteville, 1997 (1,283 in 27)

LOWEST FIELD-GOAL PERCENTAGE ALLOWED (Since 1978)

35.4—New York U., 2007 (552 of 1,560)

Overtimes

OVERTIME GAMES

7—McMurry, 2003 (won 7, lost 0); Albany (N.Y.), 1981 (won 5, lost 2); TCNJ, 1982 (won 6, lost 1); St. John's (Minn.), 1983 (won 4, lost 3); New Jersey City, 1994 (won 4, lost 3)

CONSECUTIVE OVERTIME GAMES

3—McMurry, 2003 (won 3, lost 0); Albright, 1997 (won 3, lost 0); Buffalo St., 1997 (won 2, lost 1); Ferrum, 1997 (won 1, lost 2); Ithaca, 1987 (won 3, lost 0); Cortland St., 1989 (won 1, lost 2); Oberlin, 1989 (won 1, lost 2); Susquehanna, 1989 (won 3, lost 0)

OVERTIME WINS

7—McMurry, 2003 (7-0)

OVERTIME HOME WINS

5—McMurry, 2003 (5-0)

General Records

GAMES PLAYED IN A SEASON

34—Wis.-Stevens Point, 2004 (29-5); Wis.-Eau Claire, 1990 (30-4); LeMoyne-Owen, 1980 (26-8)

VICTORIES IN A SEASON

32—Potsdam St., 1986 (32-0)

CONSECUTIVE VICTORIES

60—Potsdam St. (from first game of 1985-86 season to March 14, 1987)

CONSECUTIVE HOME-COURT VICTORIES

62—North Park (from Feb. 8, 1984, to Feb. 3, 1988)

CONSECUTIVE REGULAR-SEASON VICTORIES

59—Potsdam St. (from Nov. 22, 1985, to Dec. 12, 1987)

DEFEATS IN A SEASON

26—Otterbein, 1988 (1-26); Maryville (Mo.), 1991 (0-26)

CONSECUTIVE DEFEATS IN A SEASON

26—Maryville (Mo.), 1991 (0-26)

CONSECUTIVE DEFEATS

117—Rutgers-Camden (from Jan. 22, 1992, to Jan. 3, 1997; ended with 77-72 win vs. Bloomfield on Jan. 7, 1997)

CONSECUTIVE WINNING SEASONS

37—Wittenberg, 1969-05 (current)

CONSECUTIVE NON-LOSING SEASONS

49—Wittenberg, 1957-05 (current)

UNBEATEN TEAMS (Number of victories in parentheses)

Potsdam St., 1986 (32); Wis.-Platteville, 1995 (31); Wis.-Platteville, 1998 (30)

All-Time Individual Leaders

Single-Game Records

SCORING HIGHS

Pts.	Player, Team vs. Opponent	Season
77	Jeff Clement, Grinnell vs. Illinois Col.	1998
69	Sami Wylie, Lincoln (Pa.) vs. Ohio St.-Marion	2007
69	Steve Diekmann, Grinnell vs. Simpson	1995
64	Tim Russell, Albertus Magnus vs. Mitchell	2005
63	Ryan Hodges, Cal Lutheran vs. Redlands	2005
63	Joe DeRoche, Thomas vs. St. Joseph's (Me.)	1988
62	Kyle Myrick, Lincoln (Pa.) vs. Penn St.-Abington	2006
62	Nick Pelotte, Plymouth St. vs. Western Conn. St.	2005
62	Shannon Lilly, Bishop vs. Southwest Assembly of God	1983
61	Josh Metzger, Wis.-Lutheran vs. Grinnell	2001
61	Steve Honderd, Calvin vs. Kalamazoo	1993
61	Dana Wilson, Husson vs. Ricker	1974
60	Ed Brands, Grinnell vs. Ripon	1996
60	Steve Diekmann, Grinnell vs. Coe	1994
59	Ben Strong, Guilford vs. Lincoln (Pa.)	2007
59	Mike Hoyt, Mt. St. Mary (N.Y.) vs. Farmingdale	2007
59	Ed Brands, Grinnell vs. Chicago	1996
59	Steve Diekmann, Grinnell vs. Monmouth (Ill.)	1995
58	Andy Panko, Lebanon Valley vs. Juniata	1999
58	Jeff Clement, Grinnell vs. Clarke	1998

Season Records

SCORING AVERAGE

Player, Team	Season	G	FG	3FG	FT	Pts.	Avg.
Steve Diekmann, Grinnell	†1995	20	223	137	162	745	*37.3
Rickey Sutton, Lyndon St.	†1976	14	207	—	93	507	36.2
Shannon Lilly, Bishop	†1983	26	345	—	218	908	34.9
Dana Wilson, Husson	†1974	20	288	—	122	698	34.9
Rickey Sutton, Lyndon St.	†1977	16	223	—	112	558	34.9
Mike Hoyt, Mt. St. Mary (N.Y.)	†2007	26	274	121	229	898	34.5
Steve Diekmann, Grinnell	†1994	21	250	117	106	723	34.4
Ed Brands, Grinnell	†1996	24	260	158	136	814	33.9
Jeff Clement, Grinnell	†1998	22	238	*186	84	746	33.9
Kyle Myrick, Lincoln (Pa.)	†2006	30	387	59	177	1,010	33.7
Dwain Govan, Bishop	†1975	29	392	—	179	963	33.2
Clarence Caldwell, Greensboro	1976	22	306	—	111	723	32.8
Jeff Clement, Grinnell	†1999	22	217	166	121	721	32.8
Tim Russell, Albertus Magnus	†2005	25	292	74	161	819	32.8
Greg Grant, TCNJ	†1989	32	387	76	194	*1,044	32.6
Dennis Stanton, Ursinus	†2004	27	261	140	217	879	32.6
Dave Russell, Shepherd	1975	32	*394	—	*249	1,037	32.4
Dwain Govan, Bishop	1974	26	358	—	126	842	32.4
Ron Stewart, Otterbein	1983	24	297	—	166	760	31.7

†national champion; *record

FIELD-GOAL PERCENTAGE
(Based on qualifiers for annual championship)

Player, Team	Season	G	FG	FGA	Pct.
Travis Weiss, St. John's (Minn.)	†1994	26	160	209	*76.6
Brian Schmitting, Ripon	†2006	21	122	160	76.3
Pete Metzelaars, Wabash	†1982	28	271	360	75.3
Tony Rychlec, Mass. Maritime	†1981	25	233	311	74.9
Tony Rychlec, Mass. Maritime	1982	20	193	264	73.1
Russ Newnan, Menlo	1991	26	130	178	73.0
Ed Owens, Hampden-Sydney	†1979	24	140	192	72.9
Scott Baxter, Capital	†1991	26	164	226	72.6
Maurice Woods, Potsdam St.	1982	30	203	280	72.5
Earl Keith, Stony Brook	1979	24	164	227	72.2
Pete Metzelaars, Wabash	1981	25	204	283	72.1
Brandon King, Rowan	†2005	26	141	196	71.9
Jon Rosner, Yeshiva	1991	22	141	196	71.9
Pete Metzelaars, Wabash	1979	24	122	170	71.8
Anthony Farley, Miles	1982	26	168	235	71.5

†national champion; *record

THREE-POINT FIELD GOALS MADE

Player, Team	Season	G	3FG
Jeff Clement, Grinnell	1998	22	*186
Jeff Clement, Grinnell	1999	22	166
Ed Brands, Grinnell	1996	24	158
Billy Shivers, Redlands	2004	25	153
Chris Peterson, Eureka	1994	31	145
Amir Mazarei, Redlands	2007	23	143
Dennis Stanton, Ursinus	2004	27	140
Amir Mazarei, Redlands	2006	24	138
Steve Nordlund, Grinnell	2002	24	137
Steve Diekmann, Grinnell	1995	20	137
Chris Jans, Loras	1991	25	133
Eric Burdette, Wis.-Whitewater	1996	28	130
Ed Brands, Grinnell	1995	20	129
Sami Wylie, Lincoln (Pa.)	2006	30	128
Kyle Seyboth, Elms	2005	29	125
Tommy Doyle, Salem St.	1996	28	124
Everett Foxx, Ferrum	1992	29	124
Kirk Anderson, Augustana (Ill.)	1993	30	123
Jeff deLaveaga, Cal Lutheran	1992	28	122
Mike Hoyt, Mt. St. Mary (N.Y.)	2007	26	121

*record

THREE-POINT FIELD GOALS MADE PER GAME

Player, Team	Season	G	3FG	Avg.
Jeff Clement, Grinnell	†1998	22	*186	*8.5
Jeff Clement, Grinnell	†1999	22	166	7.5
Steve Diekmann, Grinnell	†1995	20	137	6.9
Ed Brands, Grinnell	†1996	24	158	6.6
Ed Brands, Grinnell	1995	29	129	6.5
Amir Mazarei, Redlands	†2007	23	143	6.2
Billy Shivers, Redlands	†2004	25	153	6.1
Amir Mazarei, Redlands	†2006	24	138	5.8
Steve Nordlund, Grinnell	†2002	24	137	5.7
Steve Diekmann, Grinnell	†1994	21	117	5.6
Chris Jans, Loras	†1991	25	133	5.3
Woody Piirto, Grinnell	1999	22	117	5.3
John Grotberg, Grinnell	2006	23	120	5.2
Dennis Stanton, Ursinus	2004	27	140	5.2
Jeff Clement, Grinnell	†1997	22	113	5.1
Mark Bedell, Fisk	1997	19	97	5.1
David Bailey, Concordia Chicago	1994	24	120	5.0
Jarett Kearse, Lincoln (Pa.)	†2005	22	105	4.8
Steve Nordlund, Grinnell	†2003	25	119	4.8
Steve Nordlund, Grinnell	2004	24	114	4.8

†national champion; *record

THREE-POINT FIELD-GOAL PERCENTAGE
(Based on qualifiers for annual championship)

Player, Team	Season	G	3FG	3FGA	Pct.
Reggie James, NJIT	†1989	29	59	88	*67.0
Chris Miles, NJIT	†1987	26	41	65	63.1
Chris Miles, NJIT	1989	29	46	75	61.3
Matt Miota, Lawrence	†1990	22	33	54	61.1
Mike Bachman, Alma	†1991	26	46	76	60.5
Ray Magee, Richard Stockton	†1988	26	41	71	57.7
Keith Orchard, Whitman	1988	26	42	73	57.5
Brian O'Donnell, Rutgers-Camden	1988	24	65	114	57.0
Erick Hunt, Methodist	1989	27	45	79	57.0
Eric Harris, Bishop	1987	26	91	160	56.9
Rick Brown, Muskingum	1988	30	71	125	56.8
Jamie Eichel, Fredonia St.	1989	24	51	90	56.7

†national champion; *record

FREE-THROW PERCENTAGE
(Based on qualifiers for annual championship)

Player, Team	Season	G	FT	FTA	Pct.
Korey Coon, Ill. Wesleyan	†2000	25	157	163	*96.3
Nick Wilkins, Coe	†2003	26	66	69	95.7
Chanse Young, Manchester	†1998	25	65	68	95.6
Andy Enfield, Johns Hopkins	†1991	29	123	129	95.3
Chris Carideo, Widener	†1992	26	80	84	95.2
Yudi Teichman, Yeshiva	†1989	21	119	125	95.2
Joseph Chatman, Lesley	†2007	27	126	133	94.7
Brett Davis, Wis.-Oshkosh	1998	27	72	76	94.7
Joe Bueckers, Concordia-M'head	†2004	26	71	75	94.7
Mark Giovino, Babson	†1997	28	86	91	94.5
Aaron Faulkner, St. Norbert	2004	23	64	68	94.1
Mike Scheib, Susquehanna	†1977	22	80	85	94.1
Jason Prenevost, Middlebury	†1994	22	60	64	93.8
Derrick Rogers, Averett	†2001	27	72	77	93.5
Hans Hoeg, Wis.-River Falls	†2005	25	113	121	93.4

DIVISION III

Player, Team	Season	G	FT	FTA	Pct.
Jerry Prestier, Baldwin-Wallace	†1978	25	125	134	93.3
Charlie Nanick, Scranton	†1996	25	96	103	93.2
Jeff Bowers, Southern Me.	†1988	29	95	102	93.1
Eric Jacobs, Scranton	1986	29	81	87	93.1
Casey Taggatz, Wis.-La Crosse	2004	25	67	72	93.1
Jim Durrell, Colby-Sawyer	†1993	25	67	72	93.1

*†national champion; *record*

REBOUND AVERAGE

Player, Team	Season	G	Reb.	Avg.
Joe Manley, Bowie St.	†1976	29	*579	*19.97
Fred Petty, Southern N.H.	†1974	22	436	19.8
Larry Williams, Pratt	†1977	24	457	19.0
Charles Greer, Thomas	1977	17	318	18.7
Larry Parker, Plattsburgh St.	†1975	23	430	18.7
John Jordan, Southern Me.	†1978	29	536	18.5
Keith Woolfolk, Upper Iowa	1978	26	479	18.4
Michael Stubbs, Trinity (Conn.)	†1990	22	398	18.1
Mike Taylor, Pratt	1978	23	414	18.0
Walt Edwards, Husson	1976	26	467	18.0
Dave Kufeld, Yeshiva	†1979	20	355	17.8

*†national champion; *record*

ASSISTS

Player, Team	Season	G	Ast.
Robert James, Kean	†1989	29	*391
Tennyson Whitted, Ramapo	†2002	29	319
Ricky Spicer, Wis.-Whitewater	1989	31	295
Joe Marcotte, NJIT	†1995	30	292
Andre Bolton, Chris. Newport	†1996	30	289
Ron Torgalski, Hamilton	1989	26	275
Albert Kirchner, Mt. St. Vincent	†1990	24	267
Steve Artis, Chris. Newport	1991	29	262
Phil Dixon, Shenandoah	1996	27	258
Tennyson Whitted, Ramapo	†2003	30	253
Phil Dixon, Shenandoah	†1994	26	253
Steve Artis, Chris. Newport	1990	28	251
Michael Crotty, Williams	†2004	32	249
David Genovese, Mt. St. Vincent	1994	27	248
Russell Springman, Salisbury	1990	27	246
John Ancrum, Elms	†2005	29	245
Michael Crotty, Williams	2003	32	245
Tom Genco, Manhattanville	1990	26	244
Andrew Olson, Amherst	†2007	32	243
Andre Bolton, Chris. Newport	1995	28	243

*†national champion; *record*

ASSIST AVERAGE

Player, Team	Season	G	Ast.	Avg.
Robert James, Kean	†1989	29	*391	*13.5
Albert Kirchner, Mt. St. Vincent	†1990	24	267	11.1
Tennyson Whitted, Ramapo	†2002	29	319	11.0
Ron Torgalski, Hamilton	1989	26	275	10.6
Louis Adams, Rust	1989	22	227	10.3
Eric Johnson, Coe	†1991	24	238	9.9
Joe Marcotte, NJIT	†1995	30	292	9.7
Phil Dixon, Shenandoah	†1994	26	253	9.7
Mark Cottom, Ferrum	1991	25	242	9.7
Andre Bolton, Chris. Newport	†1996	30	289	9.6
Phil Dixon, Shenandoah	1996	27	258	9.6
Ricky Spicer, Wis.-Whitewater	1989	31	295	9.5
David Rubin, Hobart	†1998	25	237	9.5
Pat Heldman, Maryville (Tenn.)	1989	25	236	9.4
Deshone Bond, Stillman	†1997	25	235	9.4
Tom Genco, Manhattanville	1990	26	244	9.4
Justin Culhane, Suffolk	1992	24	225	9.4

*†national champion; *record*

BLOCKED SHOTS

Player, Team	Season	G	Blk.
Tory Black, NJIT	†1997	26	*198
Neil Edwards, York (N.Y.)	†2000	26	193
Ira Nicholson, Mt. St. Vincent	†1995	28	188
John Bunch, Lincoln (Pa.)	†2004	25	173
Shacun Malave, City Tech	2004	28	167
Ira Nicholson, Mt. St. Vincent	†1996	27	163
Ira Nicholson, Mt. St. Vincent	1997	24	151
Antoine Hyman, Keuka	1997	26	148
Matt Cusano, Scranton	†1993	29	145
Neil Edwards, York (N.Y.)	†1999	26	144
Johnny Woods, Wesley	2000	24	132
Badou Gaye, Gwynedd-Mercy	2004	29	131
Antoine Hyman, Keuka	1996	25	131
Ifesinachi Anosike, Salem St.	†2005	29	129
Andrew South, NJIT	†1994	27	128
Mike Mientus, Allentown	1995	27	118
Roy Woods, Fontbonne	1995	25	117
Eric Lidecis, Maritime (N.Y.)	1994	26	116
Steve Juskin, Frank. & Marsh.	2004	30	114
Antonio Ramos, Clarke	2001	25	114

*†national champion; *record*

BLOCKED-SHOT AVERAGE

Player, Team	Season	G	Blk.	Avg.
Tory Black, NJIT	†1997	26	*198	*7.62
Neil Edwards, York (N.Y.)	†2000	26	193	7.42
John Bunch, Lincoln (Pa.)	†2004	25	173	6.92
Ira Nicholson, Mt. St. Vincent	†1995	28	188	6.71
Ira Nicholson, Mt. St. Vincent	1997	24	151	6.29
Ira Nicholson, Mt. St. Vincent	†1996	27	163	6.04
Shacun Malave, City Tech	2004	28	167	5.96
Antoine Hyman, Keuka	1997	26	148	5.69
Neil Edwards, York (N.Y.)	†1999	26	144	5.54
Johnny Woods, Wesley	2000	24	132	5.50
Antoine Hyman, Keuka	1996	25	131	5.24
Joe Henderson, Hunter	1999	22	112	5.09
Matt Cusano, Scranton	†1993	29	145	5.00
Drew Cohen, Colby	†2006	23	111	4.83
Andrew South, NJIT	†1994	27	128	4.74
Roy Woods, Fontbonne	1995	25	117	4.68
Johnny Woods, Wesley	†2001	22	101	4.59
Antonio Ramos, Clarke	2001	25	114	4.56
Badou Gaye, Gwynedd-Mercy	2004	29	131	4.52
Erik Lidecis, Maritime (N.Y.)	1994	26	116	4.46

*†national champion; *record*

STEALS

Player, Team	Season	G	Stl.
Moses Jean-Pierre, Plymouth St.	†1994	30	*189
Daniel Martinez, McMurry	†2000	29	178
Purvis Presha, Stillman	†1996	25	144
Tennyson Whitted, Ramapo	†2002	29	138
Matt Newton, Principia	1994	25	138
John Gallogly, Salve Regina	†1997	24	137
Elbie Murphy, St. Joseph's (Me.)	†2007	30	126
Greg Dean, Concordia-M'head	1997	23	126
Scott Clarke, Utica	†1995	24	126
Deron Black, Allegheny	1996	27	123
David Brown, Westfield St.	1994	25	122
Ricky Hollis, Brockport St.	2000	27	121
John Gallogly, Salve Regina	†1998	23	121
Barry Aranoff, Yeshiva	1995	22	121
Horace Jenkins, Wm. Paterson	2001	31	120
Brian Meehan, Salve Regina	1995	28	120
Tennyson Whitted, Ramapo	†2003	30	118
Scott Clarke, Utica	1996	26	118
Quameir Harding, Ramapo	†2006	29	116
Benny West, Howard Payne	†2004	25	116

*†national champion; *record*

STEAL AVERAGE

Player, Team	Season	G	Stl.	Avg.
Moses Jean-Pierre, Plymouth St.	†1994	30	*189	*6.30
Daniel Martinez, McMurry	†2000	29	178	6.14
Purvis Presha, Stillman	†1996	25	144	5.76
John Gallogly, Salve Regina	†1997	24	137	5.71
Matt Newton, Principia	1994	25	138	5.52
Barry Aranoff, Yeshiva	†1995	22	121	5.50
Greg Dean, Concordia-M'head	1997	23	126	5.48
John Gallogly, Salve Regina	†1998	23	121	5.26
Scott Clarke, Utica	1995	24	126	5.25
Joel Heckendorf, Martin Luther	1996	17	84	4.94
David Brown, Westfield St.	1994	25	122	4.88
Ivo Moyano, Polytechnic (N.Y.)	1994	19	91	4.78
Tennyson Whitted, Ramapo	†2002	29	138	4.76
Mario Thompson, Occidental	†1999	24	114	4.75
Benny West, Howard Payne	†2004	25	116	4.64
Keith Darden, Concordia (Tex.)	†2001	24	111	4.63
Moses Jean-Pierre, Plymouth St.	†1993	25	114	4.56
Deron Black, Allegheny	1996	27	123	4.55
Scott Clarke, Utica	1996	26	118	4.54
Ricky Hollis, Brockport St.	2000	27	121	4.48

*†national champion; *record*

Career Records

POINTS

Player, Team	Seasons	Pts.
Andre Foreman, Salisbury	1988-89, 91-92	*2,940
Willie Chandler, Misericordia	2000-03	2,898
Lamont Strothers, Chris. Newport	1988-91	2,709
Matt Hancock, Colby	1987-90	2,678
Scott Fitch, Geneseo St.	1990-91, 93-94	2,634
Greg Grant, TCNJ	1987-89	2,611
Rick Hughes, Thomas More	1993-96	2,605
Mike Hoyt, Mt. St. Mary (N.Y.)	2004-07	2,586
Wil Peterson, St. Andrews	1980-83	2,553
Ron Stewart, Otterbein	1980-83	2,549
Andy Panko, Lebanon Valley	1996-99	2,515
Scott Tedder, Ohio Wesleyan	1985-88	2,501
Moses Jean-Pierre, Plymouth St.	1991-94	2,483
Steve Honderd, Calvin	1990-93	2,469
Herman Alston, Kean	1988-91	2,457
Dick Hempy, Otterbein	1984-87	2,439
John Patraitis, Anna Maria	1995-98	2,434
Kevin Moran, Curry	1983-86	2,415
Alex Butler, Rhode Island Col.	1994-97	2,398
Steve Wood, Grinnell	2001-04	2,381
Rickey Sutton, Lyndon St.	1976-79	2,379
Frank Wachlarowicz, St. John's (Minn.)	1975-79	2,357
Henry Shannon, Maryville (Mo.)	1996-99	2,352
Cedric Oliver, Hamilton	1976-79	2,349
Dana Janssen, Neb. Wesleyan	1983-86	2,333

*record

SCORING AVERAGE
(Minimum 1,400 points)

Player, Team	Seasons	G	FG	3FG	FT	Pts.	Avg.
Dwain Govan, Bishop	1974-75	55	750	—	305	1,805	*32.8
Dave Russell, Shepherd	1974-75	60	710	—	413	1,833	30.6
Kyle Myrick, Lincoln (Pa.)	2005-06	57	667	78	309	1,721	30.2
Rickey Sutton, Lyndon St.	1976-79	80	960	—	459	2,379	29.7
John Atkins, Knoxville	1976-78	70	845	—	322	2,012	28.7
Steve Peknik, Windham	1974-77	76	816	—	467	2,099	27.6
Clarence Caldwell, Greensboro	1975-77	70	802	—	299	1,903	27.2
Andre Foreman, Salisbury	1988-89, 91-92	109	*1,140	68	592	*2,940	27.0
Darrel Lewis, Lincoln (Pa.)	1996-99	86	796	265	409	2,267	26.4
Willie Chandler, Misericordia	2000-03		1,005	346	542	2,898	26.3
Matt Hancock, Colby	1987-90	102	844	198	*792	2,678	26.3
Terrence Dupree, Polytechnic (N.Y.)	1990-92	70	700	22	407	1,829	26.1
Steve Diekmann, Grinnell	1992-95	85	741	371	365	2,218	26.1
Rick Hughes, Thomas More	1993-96	101	1,039	13	514	2,605	25.8
Mark Veenstra, Calvin	1974-77	89	960	—	341	2,261	25.4
Ron Swartz, Hiram	1984-87	90	883	78	408	2,252	25.0
Clarence Caldwell, Greensboro	1974-77	93	971	—	363	2,309	24.8
James Rehnquist, Amherst	1975-77	61	614	—	284	1,512	24.8

*record

FIELD-GOAL PERCENTAGE
(Minimum 400 field goals made)

Player, Team	Seasons	G	FG	FGA	Pct.
Tony Rychlec, Mass. Maritime	1981-83	55	509	692	*73.6
Pete Metzelaars, Wabash	1979-82	103	784	1,083	72.4
Brian Schmitting, Ripon	2004-07	78	418	602	69.4
Maurice Woods, Potsdam St.	1980-82	93	559	829	67.4
Earl Keith, Stony Brook	1975-76, 78-79	94	777	1,161	66.9
Dan Rush, Bridgewater (Va.)	1992-95	102	712	1,069	66.6
Ryan Hodges, Cal Lutheran	2001, 03-05	94	518	787	65.8
Wade Gugino, Hope	1989-92	97	664	1,010	65.7
David Otte, Simpson	1992-95	76	549	840	65.4
Rick Batt, UC San Diego	1989-92	106	558	855	65.2
Kevin Ryan, TCNJ	1987-90	102	619	955	64.8
Greg Kemp, Aurora	1991-94	102	680	1,051	64.7
Scott Baxter, Capital	1988-91	104	505	782	64.6
Pat Fitzsimmons, Amherst	2000-03	101	452	700	64.6
Paul Rich, Geneseo St.	1978-81	88	452	700	64.6
Nate Thomas, Neb. Wesleyan	1995-98	98	497	772	64.4
Tod Hart, Ithaca	1980-83	97	726	1,133	64.1
Tony Seay, Averett	1989-90	55	465	726	64.0
John Ellenwood, Wooster	1997-00	98	442	692	63.9
Jon Konzelman, Baptist Bible (Pa.)	2004-06	84	469	735	63.8
Jeff Gibbs, Otterbein	1999-02	109	758	1,188	63.8
Dick Hempy, Otterbein	1984-87	112	923	1,447	63.8
John Wassenbergh, St. Joseph's (Me.)	1993-96	108	815	1,281	63.6
Jason Boone, New York U.	2004-07	104	496	780	63.6
Jason Nickerson, Va. Wesleyan	1996-99	79	614	967	63.5

*record

THREE-POINT FIELD GOALS MADE

Player, Team	Seasons	G	3FG
Jeff Clement, Grinnell	1996-99	91	*516
Amir Mazarei, Redlands	2004-07	97	470
Steve Nordlund, Grinnell	2001-04	97	449
Chris Carideo, Widener	1992-95	103	402
Mike Hoyt, Mt. St. Mary (N.Y.)	2004-07	105	376
Steve Diekmann, Grinnell	1992-95	85	371
Greg Cole, Western Conn. St.	2002, 04-06	110	367
Brendan Twomey, Mt. St. Mary (N.Y.)/Oneonta St.	2000, 02-04	109	362
Matt Garvey, Bates	1994-97	95	361
Ray Wilson, UC Santa Cruz	1989-92	100	354
Ed Brands, Grinnell	1993-96	78	347
Willie Chandler, Misericordia	2000-03	110	346
Robert Hennigan, Emerson	2001-04	105	342
Steve Matthews, Emerson/Wentworth Inst.	1998-00	81	334
Chris Hamilton, Blackburn	1988-91	101	334
Scott Fitch, Geneseo St.	1990-91, 93-94	109	332
Billy Collins, Nichols	1992-95	92	331
John Estelle, Wabash	1997-00	109	328
Tony Barros, Mass.-Boston	2004-07	101	326
Mike Lee, Mary Washington	2004-07	106	323
Mark Bedell, Fisk	1994-97	94	321
James Mooney, Mt. St. Vincent	2003-06	102	318
Jason Valant, Colorado Col.	1990-93	103	315
Everett Foxx, Ferrum	1989-92	104	315
Derek Johnson, St. Scholastica	2004-07	106	313
Bryan Schnettler, St. Thomas (Minn.)/Wis.-Superior	2004-07	108	313
Nevada Smith, Bethany (W.V.)	1999-02	105	313
Aaron Lee, Mass.-Dartmouth	1992-95	115	313

*record

THREE-POINT FIELD GOALS MADE PER GAME
(Minimum 200 three-point field goals made)

Player, Team	Season	G	3FG	Avg.
Jeff Clement, Grinnell	1996-99	91	*516	*5.67
Amir Mazarei, Redlands	2004-07	97	470	4.85
Steve Nordlund, Grinnell	2001-04	97	449	4.63
Ed Brands, Grinnell	1993-96	78	347	4.45
Steve Diekmann, Grinnell	1992-95	85	371	4.36
Steve Matthews, Emerson/Wentworth Inst.	1998-00	81	334	4.12
Chris Carideo, Widener	1992-95	103	402	3.90
Matt Garvey, Bates	1994-97	95	361	3.80
Sami Wylie, Lincoln (Pa.)	2006-07	58	220	3.79
Rohan Russell, Johnson & Wales (R.I.)	2003-04	54	202	3.74
Billy Collins, Nichols	1992-95	92	331	3.60
Mike Hoyt, Mt. St. Mary (N.Y.)	2004-07	105	376	3.58
Ray Wilson, UC Santa Cruz	1989-92	100	354	3.54
Chris Geruschat, Bethany (W.V.)	1989-92	89	307	3.45
Mark Bedell, Fisk	1994-97	94	321	3.41
Greg Cole, Western Conn. St.	2002, 04-06	110	367	3.34
Brendan Twomey, Mt. St. Mary (N.Y.)/Oneonta St.	2000, 02-04	109	362	3.32
Chris Hamilton, Blackburn	1988-91	101	334	3.31
Jeff Jones, Lycoming	1987-89	71	232	3.27
Robert Hennigan, Emerson	2001-04	105	342	3.26
Willie Chandler, Misericordia	2000-03	110	346	3.15
James Mooney, Mt. St. Vincent	2003-06	102	318	3.12
Darrel Lewis, Lincoln (Pa.)	1996-99	86	265	3.08
Jim Durrell, Colby-Sawyer	1991-94	100	308	3.08
Jason Valant, Colorado Col.	1990-93	103	315	3.06

*record

THREE-POINT FIELD-GOAL PERCENTAGE
(Minimum 200 three-point field goals made)

Player, Team	Season	G	3FG	3FGA	Pct.
Jeff Seifriz, Wis.-Whitewater	1987-89	85	217	423	*51.3
Chris Peterson, Eureka	1991-94	78	215	421	51.1
Everett Foxx, Ferrum	1989-92	104	315	630	50.0
Brad Alberts, Ripon	1989-92	95	277	563	49.2
Jeff Jones, Lycoming	1987-89	71	232	472	49.2
Troy Greenlee, DePauw	1988-91	106	232	473	49.0
David Todd, Pomona-Pitzer	1987-90	84	212	439	48.3
Al Callejas, Scranton	1998-01	90	225	466	48.3

*record

DIVISION III

FREE-THROW PERCENTAGE
(Minimum 250 free throws made)

Player, Team	Season	G	FT	FTA	Pct.
Andy Enfield, Johns Hopkins	1988-91	108	431	466	*92.5
Korey Coon, Ill. Wesleyan	1997-00	109	449	492	91.3
Ryan Knuppel, Elmhurst	1998-01	102	288	317	90.9
Doug Brown, Elizabethtown	1976-80	96	252	279	90.3
Al Callejas, Scranton	1998-01	90	333	372	89.5
Tim McGraw, Hartwick	1985-88	107	330	371	88.9
Eric Jacobs, Wilkes/Scranton	1984-87	106	303	343	88.3
John Luisi, Suffolk	1999-02	105	265	300	88.3
Charles Nenick, Scranton	1994-97	98	259	294	88.1
Kevin Guyden, Mary Hardin-Baylor	2004-07	94	277	315	87.9
Todd Reinhardt, Wartburg	1988-91	105	283	322	87.9
Jeff Thomas, King's (Pa.)	1989-92	110	466	532	87.6
Brian Andrews, Alfred	1984-87	101	306	350	87.4
Matt Freesemann, Wartburg	1994-96	73	297	340	87.4
Dave Jannuzzi, Wilkes	1997-99, 2001	112	425	487	87.3
Nick Bennett, Wis.-Stevens Point	2002-05	117	322	369	87.3
Ryan Cain, WPI	2004-07	109	525	602	87.2
Sean O'Brien, St. John Fisher	2003-06	96	305	350	87.1
Eric Elliott, Hope	1988-91	103	350	403	86.8
Chad Onofrio, Tufts	1993-96	100	329	379	86.8
Pat Pruitt, Albright	1989-92	87	261	301	86.7
Ryan Billet, Elizabethtown	1995-98	98	434	501	86.6
Mike Johnson, Wis.-Eau Claire	1989-92	89	421	486	86.6
Sean Fleming, Clark (Mass.)	2000-03	109	371	429	86.6
Ron Barczak, Kalamazoo	1988-91	98	360	416	86.5

*record

REBOUND AVERAGE
(Minimum 900 rebounds)

Player, Team	Season	G	Reb.	Avg.
Larry Parker, Plattsburgh St.	1975-78	85	1,482	*17.4
Charles Greer, Thomas	1975-77	58	926	16.0
Willie Parr, LeMoyne-Owen	1974-76	76	1,182	15.6
Michael Smith, Hamilton	1989-92	107	*1,628	15.2
Dave Kufeld, Yeshiva	1977-80	81	1,222	15.1
Ed Owens, Hampden-Sydney	1977-80	77	1,160	15.1
Kevin Clark, Clark (Mass.)	1978-81	101	1,450	14.4
Mark Veenstra, Calvin	1974-77	89	1,260	14.2
Anthony Fitzgerald, Villa Julie	2003-06	107	1,496	14.0

*record

ASSISTS

Player, Team	Seasons	G	Ast.
Tennyson Whitted, Ramapo	2000-03	108	*917
Steve Artis, Chris. Newport	1990-93	112	909
Phil Dixon, Shenandoah	1993-96	103	889
Michael Crotty, Williams	2001-04	*122	819
David Genovese, Mt. St. Vincent	1992-95	107	800
Mike McGarvey, Ursinus	2003-06	111	754
Andre Bolton, Chris. Newport	1993-96	109	737
Tim Gaspar, Mass.-Dartmouth	2000-03	97	690
Matt Lucero, Austin	1998-01	99	677
Brian Nigro, Mt. St. Vincent	1997-00	99	674
Greg Dunne, Nazareth	1996-99	106	671
Moses Jean-Pierre, Plymouth St.	1991-94	109	669
Mike Rhoades, Lebanon Valley	1992-95	114	668
Lance Andrews, NJIT	1990-93	113	664
Dennis Jacobi, Bowdoin	1989-92	93	662
Tim Lawrence, Maryville (Tenn.)	1989-92	106	660
Pat Skerry, Tufts	1989-92	95	650
Eric Prendeville, Salisbury	1996-99	107	641
Eric Johnson, Coe	1989-92	90	637
John Snyder, King's (Pa.)	1989-92	107	631
Jason Saurbaugh, York (Pa.)	1997-00	101	624
Sammy Briggs, Catholic	1994-97	103	621
Anthony Robinson, Wittenberg	1993-96	117	618
Jerry Dennis, Otterbein	1989-92	118	613
Alex Morrison, Daniel Webster	1997-00	100	613

*record

ASSIST AVERAGE
(Minimum 550 assists)

Player, Team	Season	G	Ast.	Avg.
Phil Dixon, Shenandoah	1993-96	103	889	*8.6
Tennyson Whitted, Ramapo	2000-03	108	*917	8.5
Steve Artis, Chris. Newport	1990-93	112	909	8.1
David Genovese, Mt. St. Vincent	1992-95	107	800	7.5
Kevin Root, Eureka	1989-91	81	579	7.1
Dennis Jacobi, Bowdoin	1989-92	93	662	7.1
Tim Gaspar, Mass.-Dartmouth	2000-03	97	690	7.1
Eric Johnson, Coe	1989-92	90	637	7.1
Nathan Reeves, York (N.Y.)	1994-97	81	572	7.1
Pat Skerry, Tufts	1989-92	95	650	6.8
Matt Lucero, Austin	1998-01	99	677	6.8
Brian Nigro, Mt. St. Vincent	1997-00	99	674	6.8
Mike McGarvey, Ursinus	2003-06	111	754	6.8
Andre Bolton, Chris. Newport	1993-96	109	737	6.8
Michael Crotty, Williams	2001-04	*122	819	6.7
Tony Wyzzard, Emerson-MCA	1992-95	90	604	6.7
Greg Dunne, Nazareth	1996-99	106	671	6.3
Tim Lawrence, Maryville (Tenn.)	1989-92	106	660	6.2
Jason Saurbaugh, York (Pa.)	1997-00	101	624	6.2
Kevin Clipperton, Upper Iowa	1994-97	99	610	6.2
Moses Jean-Pierre, Plymouth St.	1991-94	109	669	6.1
Paul Ferrell, Guilford	1991-94	99	607	6.1
Alex Morrison, Daniel Webster	1997-00	100	613	6.1
Eric Prendeville, Salisbury	1996-99	107	641	6.0
Sammy Briggs, Catholic	1994-97	103	621	6.0

*record

BLOCKED SHOTS

Player, Team	Seasons	G	Blk.
Ira Nicholson, Mt. St. Vincent	1994-97	100	*576
Antoine Hyman, Keuka	1994-97	101	440
Kerry Gibson, Wis.-Oshkosh	2004-07	107	351
Andrew South, NJIT	1993-95	80	344
Badou Gaye, Gwynedd-Mercy	2002-05	104	340
Neil Edwards, York (N.Y.)	1998-00	55	337
Steve Juskin, Frank. & Marsh.	2001-04	114	330
Sean Devins, Trinity (Tex.)	2002-05	107	329
Mike Mientus, DeSales	1994-97	87	324
Arthur Hatch, Methodist	2001-04	97	321
Johnny Woods, Wesley	1999-02	78	319
Antonio Ramos, Clarke	2001-03	77	318
Terry Gray, Chris. Newport	2000-03	104	300
Jacob Nonemacher, Wis.-Stout	2004-07	100	292
Drew Cohen, Colby	2004-07	84	285
Jarriott Rook, Washington-St. Louis	2000-03	107	285
Jason Alexander, Catholic	1995-98	107	283
Jeremy Putman, Dubuque	1993-96	99	274
Matt Hilleary, Catholic	2000-03	118	273
Shacun Malave, City Tech	2004-05	53	272
Terry Thomas, Chris. Newport	1993-96	113	271
Ken LaFlamme, Emerson-MCA	1994-97	91	269
David Apple, Averett	1998-00	76	268
John Bunch, Lincoln (Pa.)	2003-04	48	265
Don Overbeek, Hope	2000-03	100	264

*record

BLOCKED-SHOT AVERAGE
(Minimum 175 blocked shots)

Player, Team	Seasons	G	Blk.	Avg.
Neil Edwards, York (N.Y.)	1998-00	55	337	*6.13
Ira Nicholson, Mt. St. Vincent	1994-97	100	*576	5.76
John Bunch, Lincoln (Pa.)	2003-04	48	265	5.52
Shacun Malave, City Tech	2004-05	53	272	5.13
Tory Black, NJIT	1995-96	53	261	4.92
Antoine Hyman, Keuka	1994-97	101	440	4.36
Andrew South, NJIT	1993-95	80	344	4.30
Antonio Ramos, Clarke	2001-03	77	318	4.13
Johnny Woods, Wesley	1999-02	78	319	4.09
Ifesinachi Anosike, Salem St.	2004-05	56	221	3.95
Mike Mientus, DeSales	1994-97	87	324	3.72
Steve Butler, Chris. Newport	1997-98	55	196	3.56
David Apple, Averett	1998-00	76	268	3.53
Drew Cohen, Colby	2004-07	84	285	3.39
Arthur Hatch, Methodist	2001-04	97	321	3.31
Kerry Gibson, Wis.-Oshkosh	2004-07	107	351	3.28
Badou Gaye, Gwynedd-Mercy	2002-05	104	340	3.27
Sean Devins, Trinity (Tex.)	2002-05	107	329	3.07
Ken LaFlamme, Emerson-MCA	1994-97	91	269	2.96
Jacob Nonemacher, Wis.-Stout	2004-07	100	292	2.92
Steve Juskin, Frank. & Marsh.	2001-04	114	330	2.89
Terry Gray, Chris. Newport	2000-03	104	300	2.88
Jeremy Putman, Dubuque	1993-96	99	274	2.77
Mike Brown, Clark (Mass.)	1997-00	71	195	2.75
Jarriott Rook, Washington-St. Louis	2000-03	107	285	2.66

*record

STEALS

Player, Team	Seasons	G	Stl.
Tennyson Whitted, Ramapo	2000-03	108	*448
John Gallogly, Salve Regina	1995-98	98	413
Daniel Martinez, McMurry	1998-00	76	380
Ivo Moyano, Polytechnic (N.Y.)	1994-97	87	368
Benny West, Howard Payne	2001-04	98	363
Eric Bell, New Paltz St.	1993-96	94	355
Keith Darden, Concordia (Tex.)	2001-02, 04-05	90	348
Scott Clarke, Utica	1993-96	96	346
Jeff Mikos, Milwaukee Engr.	2003-06	105	340
Ricky Hollis, Brockport St.	1999-02	90	322
Adam Harper, Amherst	2001-04	111	321
Greg Dean, Concordia-M'head	1995-97	75	307
Tom Roeder, St. Joseph's (L.I.)	1999-02	98	303
Moses Jean-Pierre, Plymouth St.	1993-94	55	303
Joel Holstege, Hope	1995-98	118	301
Mike McGarvey, Ursinus	2003-06	111	300
Mario Thompson, Occidental	1999-01	71	300
Darrell Lewis, Lincoln (Pa.)	1996-99	86	298
Henry Shannon, Maryville (Mo.)	1996-99	106	292
Alex Morrison, Daniel Webster	1997-00	100	289
B.J. Reilly, Montclair St.	1997-00	101	287
Damien Hunter, Alvernia	1995-98	110	287
Keith Poppor, Amherst	1993-96	98	283
Carl Cochran, Richard Stockton	1994-97	113	281
Kevin Weakly, Otterbein	1996-99	104	277
Terrence Stewart, Rowan	1993-96	113	277

*record

STEAL AVERAGE
(Minimum 175 steals)

Player, Team	Seasons	G	Stl.	Avg.
Moses Jean-Pierre, Plymouth St.	1993-94	55	303	*5.51
Daniel Martinez, McMurry	1998-00	76	380	5.00
Ivo Moyano, Polytechnic (N.Y.)	1994-97	87	368	4.23
Mario Thompson, Occidental	1999-01	71	300	4.23
John Gallogly, Salve Regina	1995-98	98	413	4.21
Tennyson Whitted, Ramapo	2000-03	108	*448	4.15
Greg Dean, Concordia-M'head	1995-97	75	307	4.09
Keith Darden, Concordia (Tex.)	2001-02, 04-05	90	348	3.87
Rodney Lusain, UC San Diego	1993-94	50	193	3.86
Eric Bell, New Paltz St.	1993-96	94	355	3.78
Benny West, Howard Payne	2001-04	98	363	3.70
David Brown, Westfield St.	1993-95	53	193	3.64
Scott Clarke, Utica	1993-96	96	346	3.60
Ricky Hollis, Brockport St.	1999-02	90	322	3.58
Gerald Garlic, Goucher	1993-95	70	244	3.49
Darrel Lewis, Lincoln (Pa.)	1996-99	86	298	3.47
Shuron Woodyard, Villa Julie	1995-97	73	238	3.26
Jeff Mikos, Milwaukee Engr.	2003-06	105	340	3.24
Shawn McCarthy, Hunter	1993-95	81	261	3.22
Carl Small, Cornell College	1993-95	69	222	3.22
Horace Jenkins, Wm. Paterson	1998-01	82	263	3.21
Tom Roeder, St. Joseph's (L.I.)	1999-02	98	303	3.09
Deron Black, Allegheny	1993-96	78	240	3.08
Reuben Reyes, Salve Regina	1993-95	74	226	3.05
Ernie Peavy, Wis.-Platteville	1993-95	87	264	3.03

*record

Annual Individual Champions

Scoring Average

Season	Player, Team	G	FG	FT	Pts.	Avg.
1974	Dana Wilson, Husson	20	288	122	698	34.9
1975	Dwain Govan, Bishop	29	392	179	963	33.2
1976	Rickey Sutton, Lyndon St.	14	207	93	507	36.2
1977	Rickey Sutton, Lyndon St.	16	223	112	558	34.9
1978	John Atkins, Knoxville	25	340	103	783	31.3
1979	Scott Rogers, Kenyon	24	289	109	687	28.6
1980	Ray Buckland, Mass.-Boston	25	271	153	695	27.8
1981	Gerald Reece, William Penn	27	306	145	757	28.0
1982	Ashley Cooper, Ripon	22	256	89	601	27.3
1983	Shannon Lilly, Bishop	26	345	218	908	34.9
1984	Mark Van Valkenburg, Framingham St.	25	312	133	757	30.3
1985	Adam St. John, Maine Maritime	18	193	135	521	28.9
1986	John Saintignon, UC Santa Cruz	22	291	104	686	31.2

Season	Player, Team	G	FG	3FG	FT	Pts.	Avg.
1987	Rod Swartz, Hiram	23	232	78	133	675	29.3
1988	Matt Hancock, Colby	27	275	56	247	853	31.6
1989	Greg Grant, TCNJ	32	387	76	194	*1,044	32.6
1990	Grant Glover, Rust	23	235	1	164	635	27.6
1991	Andre Foreman, Salisbury	29	350	39	175	914	31.5
1992	Jeff deLaveaga, Cal Lutheran	28	258	122	187	825	29.5
1993	Dave Shaw, Drew	23	210	74	169	663	28.8
1994	Steve Diekmann, Grinnell	21	250	117	106	723	34.4
1995	Steve Diekmann, Grinnell	20	223	137	162	745	*37.3
1996	Ed Brands, Grinnell	24	260	158	136	814	33.9
1997	Mark Bedell, Fisk	19	177	97	88	539	28.4
1998	Jeff Clement, Grinnell	22	238	*186	84	746	33.9
1999	Jeff Clement, Grinnell	22	217	166	121	721	32.8
2000	Willie Chandler, Misericordia	27	249	92	114	704	26.1
2001	Willie Chandler, Misericordia	26	271	96	125	763	29.3
2002	Patrick Glover, Johnson St.	24	237	28	147	649	27.0
2003	Patrick Glover, Johnson St.	26	269	37	188	763	29.3
2004	Dennis Stanton, Ursinus	27	261	140	217	879	32.6
2005	Tim Russell, Albertus Magnus	25	292	74	161	819	32.8
2006	Kyle Myrick, Lincoln (Pa.)	30	387	59	177	1,010	33.7
2007	Mike Hoyt, Mt. St. Mary (N.Y.)	26	274	121	229	898	34.5

*record

Field-Goal Percentage

Season	Player, Team	G	FG	FGA	Pct.
1974	Fred Waldstein, Wartburg	28	163	248	65.7
1975	Dan Woodard, Elizabethtown	23	190	299	63.5
1976	Paul Merlis, Yeshiva	21	145	217	66.8
1977	Brent Cawelti, Trinity (Conn.)	20	107	164	65.2
1978	Earl Keith, Stony Brook	29	228	322	70.8
1979	Ed Owens, Hampden-Sydney	24	140	192	72.9
1980	E.D. Schechterley, Lynchburg	25	184	259	71.0
1981	Tony Rychlec, Mass. Maritime	25	233	311	74.9
1982	Pete Metzelaars, Wabash	28	271	360	75.3
1983	Mike Johnson, Drew	23	138	205	67.3
1984	Mark Van Valkenburg, Framingham St.	25	312	467	66.8
1985	Reinout Brugman, Muhlenberg	26	176	266	66.2
1986	Oliver Kyler, Frostburg St.	28	183	266	68.8
1987	Tim Ervin, Albion	21	127	194	65.5
1988	Matt Strong, Hope	27	163	232	70.3
1989	Kevin Ryan, TCNJ	32	246	345	71.3
1990	Bill Triplett, NJIT	28	169	237	71.3
1991	Scott Baxter, Capital	26	164	226	72.6
1992	Brett Grebing, Redlands	23	125	176	71.0
1993	Jim Leibel, St. Thomas (Minn.)	28	141	202	69.8
1994	Travis Weiss, St. John's (Minn.)	26	160	209	*76.6
1995	Justin Wilkins, Neb. Wesleyan	28	163	237	68.8
1996	Jason Light, Emory & Henry	25	207	294	70.4
1997	Jason Hayes, Marietta	25	184	271	67.9
1998	Lonnie Walker, Alvernia	27	165	237	69.6
1999	Jason Nickerson, Va. Wesleyan	26	242	363	66.7
2000	Jack Jirak, Hampden-Sydney	28	147	220	66.8
2001	John Thomas, Fontbonne	22	157	223	70.4
2002	Omar Warthen, Neumann	27	135	202	66.8
2003	Aaron Marshall, St. Lawrence	27	206	305	67.5
2004	Jon Konzelman, Baptist Bible (Pa.)	26	144	212	67.9
2005	Brandon King, Rowan	26	141	196	71.9
2006	Brian Schmitting, Ripon	21	122	160	76.3
2007	Brandon Adair, Va. Wesleyan	32	246	356	69.1

*record

DIVISION III

Three-Point Field Goals Made Per Game

Season	Player, Team	G	3FG	Avg.
1987	Scott Fearrin, MacMurray	25	96	3.8
1988	Jeff Jones, Lycoming	23	97	4.2
1989	Brad Block, Aurora	26	112	4.3
1990	Chris Hamilton, Blackburn	24	109	4.5
1991	Chris Jans, Loras	25	133	5.3
1992	Jeff deLaveaga, Cal Lutheran	28	122	4.4
1993	Mike Connelly, Catholic	27	111	4.1
1994	Steve Diekmann, Grinnell	21	117	5.6
1995	Steve Diekmann, Grinnell	20	137	6.8
1996	Ed Brands, Grinnell	24	158	6.6
1997	Jeff Clement, Grinnell	22	113	5.1
1998	Jeff Clement, Grinnell	22	*186	*8.5
1999	Jeff Clement, Grinnell	22	166	7.5
2000	Woody Piirto, Grinnell	20	87	4.3
2001	Nevada Smith, Bethany (W.V.)	26	101	3.9
2002	Steve Nordlund, Grinnell	24	137	5.7
2003	Steve Nordlund, Grinnell	28	119	4.8
2004	Billy Shivers, Redlands	25	153	6.1
2005	Jarett Kearse, Lincoln (Pa.)	22	105	4.8
2006	Amir Mazarei, Redlands	24	138	5.8
2007	Amir Mazarei, Redlands	23	143	6.2

*record

Three-Point Field-Goal Percentage

Season	Player, Team	G	3FG	3FGA	Pct.
1987	Chris Miles, NJIT	26	41	65	63.1
1988	Ray Magee, Richard Stockton	26	41	71	57.7
1989	Reggie James, NJIT	29	59	88	*67.0
1990	Matt Miota, Lawrence	22	33	54	61.1
1991	Mike Bachman, Alma	26	46	76	60.5
1992	John Kmack, Plattsburgh St.	26	44	84	52.4
1993	Brad Apple, Greensboro	26	49	91	53.8
1994	Trever George, Coast Guard	23	38	72	52.8
1995	Tony Frieden, Manchester	32	58	107	54.2
1996	Joey Bigler, John Carroll	27	54	111	48.6
1997	Andy Strommen, Chicago	27	49	93	52.7
1998	Pat Maloney, Catholic	29	59	114	51.8
1999	Al Callejas, Scranton	26	66	122	54.1
2000	Brett Lively, Mary Washington	20	40	78	51.3
2001	Bryan Bertola, Lake Forest	23	58	110	52.7
2002	Doug Schneider, Pitt.-Bradford	28	78	143	54.5
2003	Jeremy Currier, Endicott	28	74	144	51.4
2004	Landon Lewis, Chapman	24	84	159	52.8
2005	John McAllen, Rivier	26	68	135	50.4
2006	Peter Lipka, Farmingdale	26	67	121	55.4
2007	Nate Stahl, Capital	28	74	146	50.7

*record

Free-Throw Percentage

Season	Player, Team	G	FT	FTA	Pct.
1974	Bruce Johnson, Plymouth St.	17	73	81	90.1
1975	Harold Howard, Austin	24	83	92	90.2
1976	Tim Mieure, Hamline	25	88	95	92.6
1977	Mike Scheib, Susquehanna	22	80	85	94.1
1978	Jerry Prestier, Baldwin-Wallace	25	125	134	93.3
1979	Joe Purcell, King's (Pa.)	26	66	71	93.0
1980	David Whiteside, UNC Greensboro	28	120	132	90.9
1981	Jim Cooney, Elmhurst	26	65	72	90.3
1982	Shannon Lilly, Bishop	22	142	153	92.8
1983	Mike Sain, Eureka	26	66	72	91.7
1984	Chris Genian, Redlands	24	71	78	91.0
1985	Bob Possehl, Coe	22	59	65	90.8
1986	Eric Jacobs, Scranton	29	81	87	93.1
1987	Chris Miles, NJIT	26	70	76	92.1
1988	Jeff Bowers, Southern Me.	29	95	102	93.1
1989	Yudi Teichman, Yeshiva	21	119	125	95.2
1990	Todd Reinhardt, Wartburg	26	91	98	92.9
1991	Andy Enfield, Johns Hopkins	29	123	129	95.3
1992	Chris Carideo, Widener	26	80	84	95.2
1993	Jim Durrell, Colby-Sawyer	25	67	72	93.1
1994	Jason Prenevost, Middlebury	22	60	64	93.8
1995	Matt Freesemann, Wartburg	24	128	138	92.8
1996	Charlie Nanick, Scranton	25	96	103	93.2

Season	Player, Team	G	FT	FTA	Pct.
1997	Mark Giovino, Babson	28	86	91	94.5
1998	Chanse Young, Manchester	25	65	68	95.6
1999	Ryan Eklund, Wis.-La Crosse	26	80	87	92.0
2000	Korey Coon, Ill. Wesleyan	25	157	163	*96.3
2001	Derrick Rogers, Averett	27	72	77	93.5
2002	Jason Luisi, Suffolk	28	87	94	92.6
2003	Nick Wilkins, Coe	26	66	69	95.7
2004	Joe Bueckers, Concordia-M'head	26	71	75	94.7
2005	Hans Hoeg, Wis.-River Falls	25	113	121	93.4
2006	Tony Bollier, Wheaton (Ill.)	25	104	112	92.9
2006	Matt Secrease, Hendrix	24	65	70	92.9
2007	Joseph Chatman, Lesley	27	126	133	94.7

*record

Rebound Average

Season	Player, Team	G	Reb.	Avg.
1974	Fred Petty, Southern N.H.	22	436	19.8
1975	Larry Parker, Plattsburgh St.	23	430	18.7
1976	Joe Manley, Bowie St.	29	*579	*19.97
1977	Larry Williams, Pratt	24	457	19.0
1978	John Jordan, Southern Me.	29	536	18.5
1979	Dave Kufeld, Yeshiva	20	355	17.8
1980	Dave Kufeld, Yeshiva	20	353	17.7
1981	Kevin Clark, Clark (Mass.)	27	465	17.2
1982	Len Washington, Mass.-Boston	23	361	15.7
1983	Luis Frias, Anna Maria	23	320	13.9
1984	Joe Weber, Aurora	27	370	13.7
1985	Albert Wells, Rust	22	326	14.8
1986	Russell Thompson, Westfield St.	22	338	15.4
1987	Randy Gorniak, Penn St.-Behrend	25	410	16.4
1988	Mike Nelson, Hamilton	26	349	13.4
1989	Clinton Montford, Methodist	27	459	17.0
1990	Michael Stubbs, Trinity (Conn.)	22	398	18.1
1991	Mike Smith, Hamilton	27	435	16.1
1992	Jeff Black, Fitchburg St.	22	363	16.5
1993	Steve Lemmer, Hamilton	27	404	15.0
1994	Chris Sullivan, St. John Fisher	23	319	13.9
1995	Scott Suhr, Milwaukee Engr.	25	349	14.0
1996	Craig Jones, Rochester Inst.	26	363	14.0
1997	Lonnie Walker, Alvernia	32	430	13.4
1998	Adam Doll, Simpson	25	366	14.6
1999	Anthony Peeples, Montclair St.	24	345	14.4
2000	Jeff Gibbs, Otterbein	23	307	13.3
2001	Jeff Gibbs, Otterbein	25	390	15.6
2002	Jeff Gibbs, Otterbein	32	523	16.3
2003	Jed Johnson, Maine Maritime	25	414	16.6
2004	Matt Clement, Maine Maritime	19	303	15.9
2005	Jeremy Coleman, Phila. Bible	28	391	14.0
2006	Anthony Fitzgerald, Villa Julie	29	416	14.3
2007	Nick Harrington, Southern Vt.	21	281	13.4

*record

Assist Average

Season	Player, Team	G	Ast.	Avg.
1989	Robert James, Kean	27	*391	*13.5
1990	Albert Kirchner, Mt. St. Vincent	24	267	11.1
1991	Eric Johnson, Coe	24	238	9.9
1992	Edgar Loera, La Verne	23	202	8.8
1993	David Genovese, Mt. St. Vincent	27	237	8.8
1994	Phil Dixon, Shenandoah	26	253	9.7
1995	Joe Marcotte, N.J. Inst. of Tech	30	292	9.7
1996	Andre Bolton, Chris. Newport	30	289	9.6
1997	Deshone Bond, Stillman	25	235	9.4
1998	David Rubin, Hobart	25	237	9.5
1999	Tim Kelly, Pacific Lutheran	25	214	8.6
2000	Daniel Martinez, McMurry	29	229	7.9
2001	Jimmy Driggs, Hamilton	25	213	8.5
2002	Tennyson Whitted, Ramapo	29	319	11.0
2003	Tennyson Whitted, Ramapo	30	253	8.4
2004	Michael Crotty, Williams	32	249	7.8
2005	John Ancrum, Elms	29	245	8.4
2006	David Arseneault, Grinnell	23	198	8.6
2007	David Arseneault, Grinnell	24	203	8.5

*record

Blocked-Shot Average

Season	Player, Team	G	Stl.	Avg.
1993	Matt Cusano, Scranton	29	145	5.0
1994	Andrew South, NJIT	27	128	4.7
1995	Ira Nicholson, Mt. St. Vincent	28	188	6.7
1996	Ira Nicholson, Mt. St. Vincent	27	163	6.0
1997	Tory Black, NJIT	26	*198	*7.6
1998	Tony Seehase, Upper Iowa	23	89	3.9
1999	Neil Edwards, York (N.Y.)	26	144	5.5
2000	Neil Edwards, York (N.Y.)	26	193	7.4
2001	Johnny Woods, Wesley	22	101	4.6
2002	Kyle McNamar, Curry	25	107	4.3
2003	John Bunch, Lincoln (Pa.)	23	92	4.0
2004	John Bunch, Lincoln (Pa.)	25	173	6.9
2005	Ifesinachi Anosike, Salem St.	29	129	4.4
2006	Drew Cohen, Colby	23	111	4.8
2007	Kerry Gibson, Wis.-Oshkosh	27	103	3.8

*record

Steal Average

Season	Player, Team	G	Stl.	Avg.
1993	Moses Jean-Pierre, Plymouth St.	25	114	4.6
1994	Moses Jean-Pierre, Plymouth St.	30	*189	*6.3
1995	Barry Aranoff, Yeshiva	22	121	5.5
1996	Purvis Presha, Stillman	25	144	5.8
1997	John Gallogly, Salve Regina	24	137	5.7
1998	John Gallogly, Salve Regina	23	121	5.3
1999	Mario Thompson, Occidental	24	114	4.8
2000	Daniel Martinez, McMurry	29	178	6.1
2001	Keith Darden, Concordia (Tex.)	24	111	4.6
2002	Tennyson Whitted, Ramapo	29	138	4.8
2003	Benny West, Howard Payne	24	99	4.1
2004	Benny West, Howard Payne	25	116	4.6
2005	Keith Darden, Concordia (Tex.)	25	96	3.8
2006	Quameir Harding, Ramapo	29	116	4.0
2007	Elbie Murphy, St. Joseph's (Me.)	30	126	4.2

*record

Annual Team Champions

Won-Lost Percentage

Season	Team	Won	Lost	Pct.
1974	Calvin	21	2	.913
1975	Calvin	22	1	.957
1976	Husson	25	1	.961
1977	Mass.-Boston	25	3	.893
1978	North Park	29	2	.935
1979	Stony Brook	24	3	.889
1980	Franklin Pierce	29	2	.935
1981	Potsdam St.	30	2	.938
1982	St. Andrews	27	3	.900
1983	Roanoke	31	2	.939
1984	Roanoke	27	2	.931
1985	Colby	22	3	.880
1986	Potsdam St.	32	0	1.000
1987	Potsdam St.	28	1	.966
1988	Scranton	29	3	.906
1989	TCNJ	30	2	.938
1990	Colby	26	1	.963
1991	Hamilton	26	1	.963
1992	Calvin	31	1	.969
1993	Rowan	29	2	.935
1994	Wittenberg	30	2	.938
1995	Wis.-Platteville	31	0	1.000
1996	Wilkes	28	2	.933
1997	Ill. Wesleyan	29	2	.935
1998	Wis.-Platteville	30	0	1.000
1999	Connecticut Col.	28	1	.966
2000	Calvin	30	2	.938
2001	Mass.-Dartmouth	25	3	.893
2002	Carthage	28	2	.933
2003	Williams	31	1	.969
2004	Williams	30	2	.938
2005	St. John Fisher	28	1	.966
2006	Lawrence	25	1	.962
2007	Amherst	30	2	.938

Scoring Offense

Season	Team	G	W-L	Pts.	Avg.
1974	Bishop	26	14-12	2,527	97.2
1975	Bishop	29	25-4	2,932	101.1
1976	Husson	26	25-1	2,567	98.7
1977	Mercy	25	16-9	2,587	103.5
1978	Mercy	26	16-10	2,602	10.1
1979	Ashland	25	14-11	2,375	95.0
1980	Franklin Pierce	31	29-2	3,073	99.1
1981	Husson	23	20-3	2,173	94.5
1982	Husson	26	19-7	2,279	87.7
1983	Bishop	26	18-8	2,529	97.3
1984	St. Joseph's (Me.)	29	24-5	2,666	91.9
1985	St. Joseph's (Me.)	30	22-8	2,752	91.7

Season	Team	G	W-L	Pts.	Avg.
1986	St. Joseph's (Me.)	30	26-4	2,837	94.6
1987	Bishop	26	13-13	2,534	97.5
1988	St. Joseph's (Me.)	29	20-9	2,785	96.0
1989	Redlands	25	15-10	2,507	10.3
1990	Salisbury	27	14-13	2,822	104.5
1991	Redlands	26	15-11	2,726	104.8
1992	Redlands	25	18-7	2,510	10.4
1993	Salisbury	26	18-8	2,551	98.1
1994	Grinnell	21	13-8	2,297	109.4
1995	Grinnell	21	14-7	2,422	115.3
1996	Grinnell	25	17-8	2,587	103.5
1997	Grinnell	22	10-12	2,254	102.5
1998	Grinnell	22	10-12	2,434	11.6
1999	Grinnell	22	11-11	2,509	114.0
2000	Grinnell	21	6-15	2,175	103.6
2001	Grinnell	24	16-8	2,837	118.2
2002	Grinnell	24	12-12	2,997	124.9
2003	Grinnell	25	19-6	3,119	124.8
2004	Grinnell	24	18-6	3,029	126.2
2005	Redlands	25	14-11	*3,310	*132.4
2006	Grinnell	23	14-9	2,699	117.3
2007	Redlands	24	17-7	2,810	117.1

*record

Scoring Defense

Season	Team	G	W-L	Pts.	Avg.
1974	Fredonia St.	22	13-9	1,049	47.7
1975	Chicago	15	9-6	790	52.7
1976	Fredonia St.	23	10-13	1,223	53.2
1977	Hamline	30	22-8	1,560	52.0
1978	Widener	31	26-5	1,693	54.6
1979	Coast Guard	24	21-3	1,160	48.3
1980	John Jay	27	10-17	1,411	52.3
1981	Wis.-Stevens Point	26	19-7	1,394	53.6
1982	Wis.-Stevens Point	28	22-6	1,491	53.3
1983	Ohio Northern	26	18-8	1,379	53.0
1984	Wis.-Stevens Point	32	28-4	1,559	48.7
1985	Wis.-Stevens Point	30	25-3	1,438	47.9
1986	Widener	27	15-12	1,356	50.2
1987	Muskingum	27	16-11	1,454	53.9
1988	Ohio Northern	30	21-9	1,734	57.8
1989	Wooster	28	21-7	1,600	57.1
1990	Randolph-Macon	29	24-5	1,646	56.8
1991	Ohio Northern	27	14-13	1,508	55.9
1992	Wittenberg	29	23-6	1,651	56.9
1993	St. Thomas (Minn.)	28	19-9	1,599	57.1
1994	Yeshiva	22	12-10	1,308	59.5
1995	Johnson St.	26	15-11	1,559	60.0
1996	Upper Iowa	26	21-5	1,500	57.7
1997	Wis.-Platteville	27	24-3	1,283	*47.5
1998	Wis.-Platteville	30	30-0	1,552	51.7
1999	Rowan	27	25-2	1,549	57.4

DIVISION III

Season	Team	G	W-L	Pts.	Avg.
2000	Baruch	28	19-9	1,639	58.5
2001	Cortland St.	28	21-7	1,678	59.9
2002	Babson	30	25-5	1,693	56.4
2003	Randolph-Macon	30	28-2	1,599	53.3
2004	Penn St.-Behrend	26	22-4	1,366	52.5
2005	Wittenberg	29	25-4	1,613	55.6
2006	Wittenberg	34	30-4	1,857	54.6
2007	Mississippi Col.	30	27-3	1,711	57.0

*record

Scoring Margin

Season	Team	Off.	Def.	Mar.
1974	Fisk	83.3	65.7	17.6
1975	Monmouth (Ill.)	83.9	66.0	17.9
1976	Husson	98.7	67.6	*31.1
1977	Husson	101.2	78.6	22.6
1978	Stony Brook	86.6	68.7	17.9
1979	North Park	84.4	67.3	17.1
1980	Franklin Pierce	99.1	76.5	22.6
1981	Husson	94.5	70.1	24.4
1982	Hope	83.9	70.0	13.8
1983	Trinity (Conn.)	79.8	61.4	18.4
1984	Wis.-Stevens Point	68.4	48.7	19.7
1985	Hope	85.4	66.0	19.4
1986	Potsdam St.	81.5	57.3	24.2
1987	NJIT	90.8	63.9	26.9
1988	Cal St. San B'dino	89.4	69.4	20.0
1989	TCNJ	92.3	68.5	23.8
1990	Colby	94.7	71.9	22.8
1991	Hamilton	89.8	66.2	23.6
1992	NJIT	95.0	73.4	21.6
1993	NJIT	90.4	65.7	24.7
1994	Rowan	89.6	64.4	25.3
1995	Colby-Sawyer	94.4	71.7	22.6
1996	Cabrini	89.4	67.6	21.8
1997	Williams	83.6	62.5	21.0
1998	Wis.-Platteville	73.9	51.7	22.2
1999	Hampden-Sydney	84.2	62.3	21.9
2000	Hampden-Sydney	88.2	66.4	21.8
2001	Chapman	81.2	63.4	17.9
2002	Brockport St.	84.5	64.9	19.6
2003	Williams	83.1	62.4	20.7
2004	Amherst	87.1	66.3	20.8
2005	Wittenberg	74.2	55.6	18.6
2006	Wooster	98.2	76.6	21.5
2007	Amherst	81.4	60.8	20.6

*record

Field-Goal Percentage

Season	Team	FG	FGA	Pct.
1974	Muskingum	560	1,056	53.0
1975	Savannah St.	1,072	1,978	54.2
1976	Stony Brook	778	1,401	55.5
1977	Stony Brook	842	1,455	57.9
1978	Stony Brook	1,033	1,721	*60.0
1979	Stony Brook	980	1,651	59.4
1980	Framingham St.	924	1,613	57.3
1981	Averett	845	1,447	58.4
1982	Lebanon Valley	608	1,098	55.4
1983	Bishop	1,037	1,775	58.4
1984	Framingham St.	849	1,446	58.7
1985	Me.-Farmington	751	1,347	55.8
1986	Frostburg St.	971	1,747	55.6
1987	NJIT	969	1,799	53.9
1988	Rust	878	1,493	58.8
1989	Bridgewater (Va.)	650	1,181	55.0
1990	Wartburg	792	1,474	53.7
1991	Otterbein	1,104	2,050	53.9
1992	Bridgewater (Va.)	706	1,315	53.7
1993	St. John's (Minn.)	744	1,415	52.6
1994	Oglethorpe	774	1,491	51.9
1995	Simpson	892	1,627	54.8
1996	Simpson	946	1,749	54.1
1997	Neb. Wesleyan	968	1,834	52.8
1998	Ill. Wesleyan	843	1,546	54.5
1999	Lebanon Valley	751	1,445	52.0
2000	Franklin	814	1,577	51.6

Season	Team	FG	FGA	Pct.
2001	St. John's (Minn.)	772	1,471	52.5
2002	Wis.-Oshkosh	784	1,500	52.3
2003	Wis.-Oshkosh	849	1,600	53.1
2004	Chapman	648	1,266	51.2
2005	Cal Lutheran	659	1,251	52.7
2006	Baldwin-Wallace	933	1,743	53.5
2007	Mississippi Col.	789	1,504	52.5

*record

Field-Goal Percentage Defense

Season	Team	FG	FGA	Pct.
1978	Grove City	589	1,477	39.9
1979	Coast Guard	464	1,172	39.6
1980	Calvin	552	1,364	40.5
1981	Wittenberg	670	1,651	40.6
1982	Tufts	622	1,505	41.3
1983	Trinity (Conn.)	580	1,408	41.2
1984	Widener	617	1,557	39.6
1985	Colby	679	1,712	39.7
1986	Widener	531	1,344	39.5
1987	Widener	608	1,636	37.2
1988	Rust	603	1,499	40.2
1989	Wooster	595	1,563	38.1
1990	Rochester	760	1,990	38.2
1991	Hamilton	679	1,771	38.3
1992	Scranton	589	1,547	38.1
1993	Scranton	659	1,806	36.5
1994	Lebanon Valley	708	1,925	36.8
1995	New Jersey City	702	1,897	37.0
1996	Bowdoin	569	1,482	38.4
1997	NJIT	572	1,565	36.5
1998	Rhodes	552	1,488	37.1
1999	Grove City	533	1,469	36.3
2000	Baruch	608	1,689	36.0
2001	Endicott	575	1,569	36.6
2002	Rowan	503	1,377	36.5
2003	Trinity (Tex.)	589	1,587	37.1
2004	Kean	517	1,398	37.0
2005	Lebanon Valley	576	1,595	36.1
2006	Huntingdon	568	1,604	*35.4
2007	New York U.	552	1,560	*35.4

*record

Three-Point Field Goals Made Per Game

Season	Team	G	3FG	Avg.
1987	Grinnell	22	166	7.5
1988	Southern Me.	29	233	8.0
1989	Redlands	25	261	10.4
1990	Augsburg	25	266	10.6
1991	Redlands	26	307	11.8
1992	Catholic	26	335	12.9
1993	Anna Maria	27	302	11.2
1994	Grinnell	21	297	14.1
1995	Grinnell	21	368	17.5
1996	Grinnell	25	415	16.6
1997	Grinnell	22	367	16.7
1998	Grinnell	22	406	18.5
1999	Grinnell	22	436	19.8
2000	Grinnell	21	353	16.8
2001	Grinnell	24	443	18.5
2002	Grinnell	24	490	20.4
2003	Grinnell	25	522	20.9
2004	Redlands	25	585	23.4
2005	Redlands	25	*595	*23.8
2006	Redlands	24	507	21.1
2007	Redlands	24	440	18.3

*record

Three-Point Field-Goal Percentage

Season	Team	G	3FG	3FGA	Pct.
1987	Mass.-Dartmouth	28	102	198	51.5
1988	Richard Stockton	26	122	211	57.8
1989	NJIT	29	124	200	*62.0
1990	Western New Eng.	26	85	167	50.9

Season	Team	G	3FG	3FGA	Pct.
1991	Ripon	26	154	331	46.5
1992	Dickinson	27	126	267	47.2
1993	DePauw	26	191	419	45.6
1994	Eureka	31	317	646	49.1
1995	Manchester	32	222	487	45.6
1996	John Carroll	27	169	388	43.6
1997	Williams	30	235	507	46.4
1998	Franklin	29	168	390	43.1
1999	Union (N.Y.)	25	233	512	45.5
2000	Franklin	28	195	467	41.8
2001	Albion	25	192	417	46.0
2002	Gordon	27	262	590	44.4
2003	Wis.-Oshkosh	32	229	532	43.0
2004	Ill. Wesleyan	28	201	458	43.9
2005	Concordia-M'head	25	140	322	43.5
2006	Potsdam St.	28	210	485	43.3
2007	Augustana (Ill.)	28	159	361	44.0

*record

Free-Throw Percentage

Season	Team	FT	FTA	Pct.
1974	Lake Superior St.	369	461	80.0
1975	Muskingum	298	379	78.6
1976	Case Reserve	266	343	77.6
1977	Hamilton	491	640	76.7
1978	Case Reserve	278	351	79.2
1979	Marietta	364	460	79.1
1980	Denison	377	478	78.9
1981	Ripon	378	494	76.5
1982	Otterbein	458	589	77.8
1983	DePauw	368	475	77.5
1984	Redlands	426	534	79.8
1985	Wis.-Stevens Point	363	455	79.8
1986	Heidelberg	375	489	76.7
1987	Denison	442	560	78.9
1988	Capital	377	473	79.7
1989	Colby	464	585	79.3
1990	Colby	485	605	80.2
1991	Wartburg	565	711	79.5
1992	Thiel	393	491	80.0
1993	Colby	391	506	77.3
1994	Wheaton (Ill.)	455	572	79.5
1995	Baldwin-Wallace	454	582	78.0
1996	Anderson	454	592	76.7
1997	Ill. Wesleyan	616	790	78.0
1998	Wis.-Oshkosh	516	631	*81.8

Season	Team	FT	FTA	Pct.
1999	Carleton	423	540	78.3
2000	Ill. Wesleyan	426	543	78.5
2001	Franklin	570	713	79.9
2002	Moravian	407	512	79.5
2003	Wooster	543	685	79.3
2004	St. Norbert	307	377	81.4
2005	Louisiana Col.	358	455	78.7
2006	Wis.-Stevens Point	419	529	79.2
2007	Wis.-Stevens Point	339	412	82.3

*record

Rebound Margin

Season	Team	Off.	Def.	Mar.
1976	Bowie St.	54.0	37.5	16.5
1977	Husson	51.6	35.0	16.7
1978	Gallaudet	46.3	33.0	13.3
1979	St. Lawrence	43.2	28.7	14.5
1980	Elmira	41.4	28.7	12.7
1981	Clark (Mass.)	40.0	25.0	15.0
1982	Maryville (Mo.)	41.0	26.7	14.4
1983	Framingham St.	38.0	22.2	15.8
1984	New England Col.	43.3	29.3	14.0
1985	Bethel (Minn.)	45.0	32.2	12.8
1986	St. Joseph's (Me.)	43.7	29.5	14.2
1987	Elmira	40.6	29.3	11.3
1988	Cal St. San B'dino	46.6	29.7	16.9
1989	Yeshiva	49.8	34.6	15.2
1990	Bethel (Minn.)	42.2	30.3	12.0
1991	Hamilton	49.6	32.5	*17.0
1992	Bethel (Minn.)	42.3	31.0	11.3
1993	Eureka	33.9	22.2	11.7
1994	Maritime (N.Y.)	46.3	32.3	14.1
1995	Wittenberg	43.1	29.2	13.9
1996	Cabrini	47.9	34.7	13.1
1997	Rochester Inst.	42.8	31.9	10.8
1998	Chris. Newport	47.5	33.7	13.9
1999	Rensselaer	41.5	29.8	11.7
2000	Albright	41.3	29.6	11.7
2001	Wittenberg	44.7	30.7	14.0
2002	Wittenberg	42.5	30.1	12.4
2003	Williams	43.7	31.1	12.6
2004	Wooster	40.6	27.8	12.8
2005	Norwich	45.1	32.6	12.5
2006	Coast Guard	40.6	29.5	11.1
2007	New York U.	39.9	29.4	10.5

*record

2007 Most-Improved Teams

School (Coach)	2007	2006	*Games Improved
1. Eureka (Jay Bruer)	16-10	4-22	12
2. FDU-Florham (Peter Marion)	17-10	6-19	10
2. Guilford (Tom Palombo)	24-5	13-14	10
4. LaGrange (Warren Haynes)	18-9	8-18	9½
5. Brockport St. (Nelson Whitmore)	26-6	15-13	9
5. North Park (Paul Brenegan)	13-12	4-21	9
7. Aurora (James Lancaster)	25-3	16-11	8½
7. Clarkson (Adam Stockwell)	14-12	5-20	8½
7. Hunter (Nick Plevritis)	12-14	3-22	8½
10. Chestnut Hill (Jesse Balcer)	19-9	10-16	8
10. Redlands (Gary Smith)	17-7	9-15	8
10. St. Lawrence (Chris Downs)	23-6	13-12	8
10. Wis.-Stevens Point (Bob Semling)	26-3	17-10	8
14. Defiance (Jonathon Miller)	17-9	9-16	7½
14. Rivier (Dave Morissette)	20-9	11-15	7½
14. Rowan (Joe Cassidy)	20-6	12-13	7½
17. Babson (Steve Brennan)	16-10	9-17	7
17. Cal Lutheran (Rich Rider)	17-8	10-15	7
17. DePauw (Bill Fenlon)	22-6	15-13	7
17. Greensboro (Bryan Galuski)	20-7	12-13	7
17. Lake Forest (Chris Conger)	15-10	7-16	7
17. LeTourneau (Robert Davis)	15-10	8-17	7
17. Lewis & Clark (Bob Galliard)	19-7	11-13	7
17. MacMurray (Steve Hettinga)	16-9	9-16	7
17. Medaille (Mike MacDonald)	11-14	4-21	7
17. Rhode Island Col. (Bob Walsh)	27-4	19-10	7
17. Texas-Dallas (Terry Butterfield)	18-8	11-15	7
17. Westminster (Pa.) (Larry Ondako)	18-9	11-16	7

*To determine games improved, add the difference in victories between the two seasons to the difference in losses, then divide by two.

All-Time Winningest Teams

Includes records as a senior college only; minimum 10 seasons of competition. Postseason games are included.

By Percentage

	Team	Yrs.	Won	Lost	Pct.
1.	Wittenberg	96	1,559	618	.716
2.	Colby-Sawyer	17	306	148	.674
3.	Calvin	88	1,220	591	.674
4.	Cabrini	27	497	250	.665
5.	Hope	102	1,380	700	.663
6.	Wooster	107	1,449	745	.660
7.	St. Joseph's (Me.)	36	628	328	.657
8.	Chris. Newport	40	692	362	.657
9.	Williams	106	1,284	679	.654
10.	Staten Island	29	524	285	.648
11.	Richard Stockton	35	606	330	.647
12.	Wis.-Eau Claire	91	1,281	703	*.646
13.	Ill. Wesleyan	98	1,431	807	.639
14.	St. John Fisher	45	702	399	.638
15.	New Jersey City	65	975	556	.637
16.	St. Thomas (Minn.)	98	1,397	803	.635
17.	New York U.	89	1,157	666	.635
18.	Wis.-Stevens Point	109	1,253	745	.627
19.	Roanoke	94	1,242	742	.626
20.	Wartburg	72	1,055	643	.621
21.	Mass.-Dartmouth	41	650	415	.610
22.	Defiance	98	1,247	806	.607
23.	Amherst	106	1,059	686	.607
24.	Randolph-Macon	94	1,288	844	.604
25.	Springfield	98	1,300	854	.604
26.	Augustana (Ill.)	102	1,276	842	.602
27.	Scranton	90	1,267	846	.600
28.	Colby	67	933	630	.597
29.	Capital	101	1,183	799	.597
30.	Buffalo St.	78	998	680	.595

*includes one tie

By Victories

	Team	Yrs.	Won	Lost	Pct.
1.	Wittenberg	96	1,559	618	.716
2.	Wooster	107	1,449	745	.660
3.	Ill. Wesleyan	98	1,431	807	.639
4.	St. Thomas (Minn.)	98	1,397	803	.635
5.	Hope	102	1,380	700	.663
6.	Neb. Wesleyan	102	1,311	907	.591
7.	Springfield	98	1,300	854	.604
8.	Randolph-Macon	94	1,288	844	.604
9.	Williams	106	1,284	679	.654
10.	Gust. Adolphus	98	1,284	885	.592
11.	Wis.-Eau Claire	91	1,281	703	.646
12.	Augustana (Ill.)	102	1,276	842	.602
13.	Scranton	90	1,267	846	.600
14.	Wis.-Stevens Point	109	1,253	745	.627
15.	Defiance	98	1,247	806	.607
16.	Wheaton (Ill.)	106	1,244	961	.564
17.	Roanoke	94	1,242	742	.626
18.	Calvin	88	1,220	591	.674
19.	Willamette	83	1,205	900	.572
20.	Loras	99	1,202	926	.565
21.	Muskingum	105	1,196	896	.572
22.	Rochester (N.Y.)	106	1,189	847	.584
23.	Capital	101	1,183	799	.597
24.	DePauw	101	1,174	910	.563
25.	Hamline	97	1,174	918	.561
26.	Hampden-Sydney	96	1,169	870	.573
27.	Frank. & Marsh.	104	1,166	821	.587
28.	Mount Union	110	1,166	996	.539
29.	Ohio Wesleyan	102	1,158	1,035	.528
30.	New York U.	89	1,157	666	.635

*Includes one tie.

Winningest Teams of the 2000s

BY PERCENTAGE
(Minimum five seasons as NCAA member)

	Team	Yrs.	Won	Lost	Pct.
1.	Wooster	8	209	33	.864
2.	Amherst	8	198	37	.843
3.	Wittenberg	8	189	40	.825
4.	Wis.-Stevens Point	8	189	43	.815
5.	Mississippi Col.	8	181	42	.812
6.	Salem St.	8	184	44	.807
7.	Catholic	8	190	47	.802
8.	Washington-St. Louis	8	166	44	.790
9.	Maryville (Tenn.)	8	181	48	.790
10.	Buena Vista	8	180	50	.783
11.	Williams	8	173	49	.779
12.	Hampden-Sydney	8	180	51	.779
13.	Hanover	8	168	49	.774
14.	St. John Fisher	8	169	53	.761
15.	Calvin	8	177	58	.753
16.	Chris. Newport	8	165	55	.750
17.	Rochester (N.Y.)	8	161	54	.749
18.	St. Thomas (Minn.)	8	161	56	.742
19.	McMurry	8	159	56	.740
20.	Chapman	8	149	53	.738
21.	Trinity (Conn.)	8	146	52	.737
22.	Hope	8	165	60	.733
23.	Trinity (Tex.)	8	161	59	.732
24.	Aurora	8	158	58	.731
25.	Gust. Adolphus	8	163	61	.728
26.	Va. Wesleyan	8	165	63	.724
27.	Alvernia	8	163	63	.721
28.	Penn St.-Behrend	8	160	62	.721
29.	Frank. & Marsh.	8	162	64	.717
30.	Keene St.	8	162	65	.714

BY VICTORIES
(Minimum five seasons as NCAA member)

	Team	Yrs.	Won	Lost	Pct.
1.	Wooster	8	209	33	.864
2.	Amherst	8	198	37	.843
3.	Catholic	8	190	47	.802
4.	Wittenberg	8	189	40	.825
	Wis.-Stevens Point	8	189	43	.815
6.	Salem St.	8	184	44	.807
7.	Mississippi Col.	8	181	42	.812
	Maryville (Tenn.)	8	181	48	.790
9.	Buena Vista	8	180	50	.783
	Hampden-Sydney	8	180	51	.779
11.	Calvin	8	177	58	.753
12.	Williams	8	173	49	.779
13.	St. John Fisher	8	169	53	.761
14.	Hanover	8	168	49	.774
	Brockport St.	8	168	68	.712
16.	Washington-St. Louis	8	166	44	.790
17.	Chris. Newport	8	165	55	.750
	Hope	8	165	60	.733
	Va. Wesleyan	8	165	63	.724
20.	Gust. Adolphus	8	163	61	.728
	Alvernia	8	163	63	.721
22.	Frank. & Marsh.	8	162	64	.717
	Keene St.	8	162	65	.714
24.	Rochester (N.Y.)	8	161	54	.749
	St. Thomas (Minn.)	8	161	56	.742
	Trinity (Tex.)	8	161	59	.732
27.	Penn St.-Behrend	8	160	62	.721
28.	McMurry	8	159	56	.740
	Ramapo	8	159	66	.707
30.	Aurora	8	158	58	.731

All-Time Won-Lost Records

(Alphabetical Listing; No Minimum Seasons of Competition)

Team	First Year	Yrs.	Won	Lost	Pct.
Adrian	1903	96	749	1,204	.384
Albion	1898	96	1,020	866	.541
Albright	1901	100	1,155	1,011	.533
Alfred	1908	90	761	999	.432
Allegheny	1896	112	1,089	921	.542
Alma	1912	94	887	1,052	.457
Alvernia	1975	33	526	361	.593
Amherst	1902	106	1,059	686	.607
Anderson (Ind.)	1932	75	909	914	.499
Anna Maria	1983	25	292	349	.456
Augustana (Ill.)	1902	102	1,276	842	.602
Aurora	1913	91	889	894	.499
Austin	1912	77	550	1,024	.349
Babson	1931	67	734	684	.518
Baldwin-Wallace	1904	102	1,082	1,002	.519
Bates	1901	78	673	866	.437
Beloit	1906	97	1,099	759	.591
Benedictine (Ill.)	1966	42	580	489	.543
Bethany (W.Va.)	1906	99	882	1,046	.457
Bethel (Minn.)	1947	61	707	716	.497
Bluffton	1915	92	793	1,103	.418
Bowdoin	1942	66	605	738	.450
Bridgewater (Va.)	1903	86	808	963	.456
Bridgewater St.	1906	87	838	854	.495
Brockport St.	1929	75	869	709	.551
Buena Vista	1917	88	835	1,002	.455
Buffalo St.	1927	78	998	680	.595
Cabrini	1981	27	497	250	.665
Cal Lutheran	1962	46	568	668	.460
Cal St. East Bay	1962	46	517	705	.423
Caltech	1919	88	288	1,246	.188
Calvin	1920	88	1,220	591	.674
Capital	1907	101	1,183	799	.597
Carleton	1910	98	1,110	859	.564
Carnegie Mellon	1907	99	827	1,194	.409
Carroll (Wis.)	1949	59	576	787	.423
Carthage	1907	100	969	1,082	.472
Case Reserve	1902	106	1,082	936	.536
Castleton	1952	56	593	689	.463
Catholic	1912	95	1,110	971	.533
CCNY	1906	102	1,007	974	.508
Central (Iowa)	1910	97	932	967	.491
Centre	1953	55	654	658	.498
Chapman	1923	82	1,106	841	.568
Chicago	1896	106	1,070	1,035	.508
Chris. Newport	1968	40	692	362	.657
Claremont-M-S	1958	49	650	573	.531
Clark (Mass.)	1921	85	862	833	.509
Clarke	1986	22	211	376	.359
Clarkson	1930	78	608	964	.387
Coast Guard	1926	81	682	898	.432
Coe	1901	107	967	975	.498
Colby	1938	67	933	630	.597
Colby-Sawyer	1991	17	306	148	.674
Colorado Col.	1915	93	822	1,058	.437
Concordia (Ill.)	1924	84	789	987	.444
Concordia (Wis.)	1916	92	944	869	.521
Concordia-Austin	1959	40	333	657	.336
Concordia-M'head	1923	85	857	1,083	.442
Connecticut Col.	1970	37	376	388	.492
Cornell College	1910	98	886	990	.472
Cortland St.	1924	82	876	768	.533
Curry	1942	66	791	808	.495
Dallas	1917	34	224	484	.316
Daniel Webster	1991	17	108	310	.258
Defiance	1905	98	1,247	806	.607
Delaware Valley	1927	78	552	944	.369
Denison	1900	105	968	1,080	.473
DePauw	1905	101	1,174	910	.563
DeSales	1969	39	467	492	.487
Dickinson	1901	97	831	994	.455
Drew	1930	76	545	927	.370
Dubuque	1916	90	856	970	.469
East. Mennonite	1967	40	334	677	.330
Eastern Conn. St.	1942	63	722	702	.507
Eastern Nazarene	1957	51	673	596	.530
Edgewood	1972	32	466	339	.579
Elizabethtown	1929	79	885	867	.505
Elmhurst	1922	83	775	999	.437
Elmira	1972	36	448	477	.484
Elms	1999	9	110	125	.468
Emory	1987	21	240	286	.456
Emory & Henry	1921	83	920	944	.494
Endicott	1995	13	202	145	.582
Eureka	1920	86	968	877	.525
FDU-Florham	1961	47	546	580	.485
Ferrum	1986	22	240	323	.426
Fitchburg St.	1968	38	318	618	.340
Framingham St.	1968	40	437	528	.453
Frank. & Marsh.	1900	104	1,166	821	.587
Franklin	1907	100	1,112	955	.538
Fredonia St.	1935	69	650	777	.456
Frostburg St.	1937	65	719	772	.482
Gallaudet	1904	104	547	1,344	.289
Geneseo St.	1915	89	784	817	.490
Gettysburg	1901	104	1,112	996	.528
Goucher	1991	17	228	212	.518
Greensboro	1967	41	481	557	.463
Grinnell	1901	105	837	1,119	.428
Grove City	1899	103	1,096	889	.552
Guilford	1906	93	857	994	.463
Gust. Adolphus	1904	98	1,284	885	.592
Gwynedd-Mercy	1994	14	214	158	.575
Hamilton	1901	95	986	725	.576
Hamline	1910	97	1,174	918	.561
Hampden-Sydney	1909	96	1,169	870	.573
Hanover	1901	102	1,112	886	.557
Hardin-Simmons	1908	98	1,053	1,067	.497
Hartwick	1929	77	961	710	.575
Haverford	1920	87	541	1,053	.339
Heidelberg	1903	101	871	1,069	.449
Hendrix	1908	84	960	818	.540
Hiram	1894	109	770	1,203	.390
Hobart	1902	97	679	1,022	.399
Hope	1902	102	1,380	700	.663
Howard Payne	1913	90	1,071	912	.540
Hunter	1953	53	626	634	.497
Ill. Wesleyan	1910	98	1,431	807	.639
Immaculata	2006	2	16	36	.308
Ithaca	1930	77	953	713	.572
John Carroll	1920	86	910	884	.507
Johns Hopkins	1920	82	784	887	.469
Johnson & Wales (R.I.)	1996	11	119	146	.449
Juniata	1905	103	783	1,144	.406
Kalamazoo	1908	100	1,038	931	.527
Kean	1931	67	726	819	.470
Keene St.	1925	71	752	841	.472
Kenyon	1900	105	698	1,210	.366
Keuka	1986	22	253	291	.465
King's (Pa.)	1947	61	794	656	.548
Knox	1908	98	906	909	.499
LaGrange	1955	53	636	804	.442
Lake Erie	1988	20	157	353	.308
Lake Forest	1905	97	739	1,093	.403
Lakeland	1934	74	1,097	825	.571
Lawrence	1904	104	841	941	.472
Lebanon Valley	1904	104	972	928	.512
LeTourneau	1955	53	457	779	.370
Lewis & Clark	1946	62	909	747	.549
Loras	1909	99	1,202	926	.565
Luther	1904	104	1,030	1,008	.505
Lycoming	1949	59	660	681	.492
Lynchburg	1957	51	513	757	.404
Manhattanville	1975	33	461	406	.532
Marian (Wis.)	1973	35	468	446	.512
Marietta	1902	103	930	1,093	.460
Mary Washington	1975	33	365	470	.437
Marymount (Va.)	1988	20	239	279	.461
Maryville (Mo.)	1977	31	340	469	.420
Maryville (Tenn.)	1903	104	1,124	883	.560
Marywood	1994	14	68	267	.203
Mass.-Boston	1981	27	280	413	.404
Mass.-Dartmouth	1967	41	650	415	.610
McDaniel	1922	85	687	1,128	.379
McMurry	1924	82	984	904	.521
Menlo	1987	20	286	258	.526
Merchant Marine	1946	62	661	779	.459
Messiah	1962	46	516	551	.484
Methodist	1964	44	481	602	.444
Middlebury	1918	90	679	1,042	.395

DIVISION III

Team	First Year	Yrs.	Won	Lost	Pct.
Millikin	1904	101	1,135	975	.538
Millsaps	1912	95	806	1,156	.411
Misericordia	1991	17	205	236	.465
Mississippi Col.	1909	95	1,111	878	.559
MIT	1953	55	527	716	.424
Monmouth (Ill.)	1900	107	1,111	879	.558
Montclair St.	1929	79	1,010	788	.562
Moravian	1936	66	773	768	.502
Mount Union	1896	110	1,166	996	.539
Mt. St. Vincent	1982	26	372	294	.559
Muhlenberg	1901	100	1,132	998	.531
Muskingum	1903	105	1,196	896	.572
N.C. Wesleyan	1964	44	513	564	.476
Nazareth	1978	30	437	331	.569
Neb. Wesleyan	1906	102	1,311	907	.591
New Jersey City	1932	65	975	556	.637
New York U.	1907	89	1,157	666	.635
Nichols	1959	49	443	682	.394
North Central (Ill.)	1948	59	579	840	.408
North Park	1959	49	706	531	.571
Oberlin	1903	105	767	1,212	.388
Occidental	1955	52	697	587	.543
Ohio Northern	1911	96	1,152	852	.575
Ohio Wesleyan	1906	102	1,158	1,035	.528
Olivet	1899	95	679	1,165	.368
Otterbein	1903	105	1,105	885	.555
Ozarks (Ark.)	1948	60	668	873	.433
Pacific (Ore.)	1912	92	860	1,243	.409
Pacific Lutheran	1939	67	966	768	.557
Pitt.-Bradford	1980	28	375	368	.505
Plattsburgh St.	1926	78	675	668	.503
Plymouth St.	1948	60	774	595	.565
Randolph-Macon	1910	94	1,288	844	.604
Redlands	1918	90	967	872	.526
Rensselaer	1904	104	897	936	.489
Rhode Island Col.	1959	49	664	578	.535
Richard Stockton	1973	35	606	330	.647
Ripon	1898	109	1,089	825	.569
Roanoke	1912	94	1,242	742	.626
Rochester (N.Y.)	1902	106	1,189	847	.584
Rochester Inst.	1916	86	946	830	.533
Roger Williams	1970	33	414	431	.490
Rose-Hulman	1898	100	948	956	.498
Rowan	1923	65	907	621	.594
Salisbury	1963	45	540	577	.483
Salve Regina	1975	32	319	409	.438
Scranton	1917	90	1,267	846	.600
Sewanee	1909	82	687	921	.427
Shenandoah	1975	33	371	470	.441
Simpson	1902	106	1,101	1,061	.509
Southern Me.	1923	80	793	717	.525
Springfield	1906	98	1,300	854	.604
St. John Fisher	1963	45	702	399	.638
St. John's (Minn.)	1903	105	1,029	1,026	.501
St. Joseph's (Me.)	1972	36	628	328	.657
St. Mary's (Md.)	1967	41	444	593	.428
St. Norbert	1917	89	864	809	.516
St. Olaf	1907	101	961	1,026	.484
St. Thomas (Minn.)	1905	98	1,397	803	.635
Staten Island	1979	29	524	285	.648
Stevens Tech	1917	91	719	797	.474
Susquehanna	1902	104	892	1,073	.454
Swarthmore	1902	106	768	1,149	.401
Thiel	1917	87	534	1,148	.317
Thomas More	1948	57	595	848	.412
Transylvania	1903	86	1,077	796	.575
Trinity (Conn.)	1906	94	1,007	712	.586
Tufts	1905	96	1,004	911	.524
Ursinus	1915	93	791	1,026	.435
Vassar	1970	36	280	473	.372
Wabash	1897	111	1,131	1,022	.525
Wartburg	1936	72	1,055	643	.621
Wash. & Jeff.	1913	92	882	854	.508
Wash. & Lee	1907	99	1,034	1,050	.496
Washington (Md.)	1913	95	997	929	.518
Washington-St. Louis	1905	92	1,049	870	.547
Wentworth Inst.	1985	23	215	359	.375
Wesleyan (Conn.)	1902	106	982	908	.520
Western Conn. St.	1947	61	708	660	.518
Western New Eng.	1967	41	490	532	.479
Westfield St.	1951	57	652	668	.494
Westminster (Mo.)	1909	92	907	1,005	.474
Wheaton (Ill.)	1902	106	1,244	961	.564
Wheaton (Mass.)	1990	18	243	230	.514
Widener	1906	99	1,106	802	.580
Wilkes	1947	61	738	692	.516
Willamette	1925	83	1,205	900	.572
Williams	1901	106	1,284	679	.654
Wilmington (Ohio)	1917	90	804	1,098	.423
Wis.-Eau Claire	1917	91	1,281	703	*.646
Wis.-La Crosse	1911	97	1,016	863	.541
Wis.-Oshkosh	1899	109	1,084	930	.538
Wis.-Platteville	1909	85	1,015	724	.584
Wis.-River Falls	1912	96	937	993	.485
Wis.-Stevens Point	1898	109	1,253	745	.627
Wis.-Stout	1907	98	907	965	.485
Wis.-Whitewater	1902	97	1,061	829	.561
Wittenberg	1912	96	1,559	618	.716
Wm. Paterson	1939	66	850	756	.529
Wooster	1901	107	1,449	745	.660
Worcester St.	1951	57	642	683	.485
WPI	1903	97	850	938	.475
Yeshiva	1936	72	647	805	.446
York (Pa.)	1970	38	474	504	.485

*Includes one tie.

Individual Collegiate Records

Individual Collegiate Records

Individual collegiate leaders are determined by comparing the best records in all three divisions in equivalent categories. Included are players whose careers were split between two divisions (e.g., Dwight Lamar of Louisiana-Lafayette or Howard Shockley of Salisbury).

Single-Game Records

POINTS

Pts.	Div.	Player, Team vs. Opponent	Date
113	II	Clarence "Bevo" Francis, Rio Grande vs. Hillsdale	Feb. 2, 1954
100	I	Frank Selvy, Furman vs. Newberry	Feb. 13, 1954
85	I	Paul Arizin, Villanova vs. Philadelphia NAMC	Feb. 12, 1949
84	II	Clarence "Bevo" Francis, Rio Grande vs. Alliance	1954
82	II	Clarence "Bevo" Francis, Rio Grande vs. Bluffton	1954
81	I	Freeman Williams, Portland St. vs. Rocky Mountain	Feb. 3, 1978
80	II	Paul Crissman, Southern Cal Col. vs. Pacific Christian	Feb. 18, 1966
77	III	Jeff Clement, Grinnell vs. Illinois Col.	Feb. 18, 1998
77	II	William English, Winston-Salem vs. Fayetteville St.	Feb. 19, 1968
75	II	Travis Grant, Kentucky St. vs. Northwood (Mich.)	1970
73	I	Bill Mlkvy, Temple vs. Wilkes	Mar. 3, 1951
72	II	Nate DeLong, Wis.-River Falls vs. Winona St.	Feb. 24, 1948
72	II	Lloyd Brown, Aquinas vs. Cleary	1953
72	II	Clarence "Bevo" Francis, Rio Grande vs. California (Pa.)	1953
72	II	John McElroy, Youngstown St. vs. Wayne St. (Mich.)	Feb. 26, 1969
72	I	Kevin Bradshaw, Alliant Int'l vs. Loyola Marymount	Jan. 5, 1991
71	II	Clayborn Jones, L.A. Pacific vs. L.A. Baptist	Jan. 30, 1965
71	I	Freeman Williams, Portland St. vs. Southern Ore.	Feb. 9, 1977
70	II	Paul Wilcox, Davis & Elkins vs. Glenville St.	1959
70	II	Bo Clark, UCF vs. Fla. Memorial	Jan. 31, 1977
69	II	Clarence "Bevo" Francis, Rio Grande vs. Wilberforce	1953
69	II	Clarence Burks, St. Augustine's vs. St. Paul's	1955
69	I	Pete Maravich, LSU vs. Alabama	Feb. 7, 1970
69	II	John Rinka, Kenyon vs. Wooster	Dec. 9, 1969
69	III	Steve Diekmann, Grinnell vs. Simpson	Nov. 19, 1994
68	II	Florindo Vieira, Quinnipiac vs. Brooklyn Poly	Feb. 13, 1957
68	II	Wayne Proffitt, Lynchburg vs. Charlotte	Feb. 5, 1966
68	II	Earl Monroe, Winston-Salem vs. Fayetteville St.	Jan. 6, 1967
68	I	Calvin Murphy, Niagara vs. Syracuse	Dec. 7, 1968

FIELD-GOAL PERCENTAGE
(Minimum 13 field goals made)

Pct.	Div.	Player, Team vs. Opponent (FG-FGA)	Date
100	II	Lance Berwald, North Dakota St. vs. Augustana (S.D.) (20 of 20)	Feb. 17, 1984
100	III	Franklyn Beckford, Lake Forest vs. Grinnell (18 of 18)	Feb. 14, 2004
100	III	Jason Light, Emory & Henry vs. King (Tenn.) (18 of 18)	Dec. 2, 1995
100	II	Patrick Hannaway, UC-Colo. Springs vs. Carroll (Wis.) (15 of 15)	Nov. 25, 2006
100	I	Clifford Rozier, Louisville vs. Eastern Ky. (15 of 15)	Dec. 11, 1993
100	II	Kyle Boast, Central Wash. vs. Alas. Anchorage (14 of 14)	Feb. 12, 2005
100	II	Derrick Scott, California (Pa.) vs. Columbia Union (14 of 14)	Dec. 6, 1995
100	I	Dan Henderson, Arkansas St. vs. Ga. Southern (14 of 14)	Feb. 26, 1976
100	I	Cornelius Holden, Louisville vs. Southern Miss. (14 of 14)	Mar. 3, 1990
100	I	Dana Jones, Pepperdine vs. Boise St. (14 of 14)	Nov. 30, 1991
100	III	Waverly Yates, Clark (Mass.) vs. Suffolk (14 of 14)	Feb. 10, 1993
100	III	Esmir Guzonjic, North Ala. vs. West Fla. (13 of 13)	Feb. 3, 2007
100	III	Dee Dee Drake, Henderson St. vs. Rhema (13 of 13)	Dec. 4, 2006
100	III	Dallin Wilson, Occidental vs. Redlands (13 of 13)	Feb. 18, 2004
100	II	Derrick Freeman, Indiana (Pa.) vs. Clarion (13 of 13)	Feb. 17, 1996
100	I	Ben Handlogten, Western Mich. vs. Toledo (13 of 13)	Jan. 27, 1996
100	II	Ralfs Jansons, St. Rose vs. Concordia (N.Y.) (13 of 13)	Jan. 13, 1996
100	I	Ted Guzek, Butler vs. Michigan (13 of 13)	Dec. 15, 1956
100	I	Rick Dean, Syracuse vs. Colgate (13 of 13)	Feb. 14, 1966
100	I	Gary Lechman, Gonzaga vs. Portland St. (13 of 13)	Jan. 21, 1967
100	I	Kevin King, Charlotte vs. South Ala. (13 of 13)	Feb. 20, 1978
100	I	Vernon Smith, Texas A&M vs. Alas. Anchorage (13 of 13)	Nov. 26, 1978
100	I	Steve Johnson, Oregon St. vs. Hawaii-Hilo (13 of 13)	Dec. 5, 1979
100	I	Antoine Carr, Wichita St. vs. Abilene Christian (13 of 13)	Nov. 28, 1980
100	III	Rich Lengieza, Nichols vs. Mass.-Dartmouth (13 of 13)	Feb. 22, 1981
100	I	Doug Hashley, Montana St. vs. Idaho St. (13 of 13)	Feb. 5, 1982
100	I	Brad Daugherty, North Carolina vs. UCLA (13 of 13)	Nov. 24, 1985
100	III	Bruce Merklinger, Susquehanna vs. Drew (13 of 13)	Jan. 22, 1986

Pct.	Div.	Player, Team vs. Opponent (FG-FGA)	Date
100	III	Antonio Randolph, Averett vs. Methodist (13 of 13)	Jan. 26, 1991
100	III	Pat Holland, Randolph-Macon vs. East. Mennonite (13 of 13)	Feb. 9, 1991
100	I	Ricky Butler, UC Irvine vs. Cal St. Fullerton (13 of 13)	Feb. 21, 1991
100	I	Rafael Solis, Brooklyn vs. Wagner (13 of 13)	Dec. 11, 1991
100	III	Todd Seifferlein, DePauw vs. Franklin (13 of 13)	Jan. 18, 1992
100	I	Mate Milisa, Long Beach St. vs. Cal St. Monterey Bay (13 of 13)	Dec. 22, 1999
100	I	Nathan Blessen, South Dakota vs. Neb.-Omaha (13 of 13)	Jan. 9, 2000

THREE-POINT FIELD GOALS MADE

3FG	Div.	Player, Team vs. Opponent	Date
19	III	Jeff Clement, Grinnell vs. Illinois Col.	Feb. 18, 1998
17	III	Billy Shivers, Redlands vs. Whittier	Feb. 21, 2004
17	III	Jeff Clement, Grinnell vs. Clarke	Dec. 3, 1997
16	II	Thomas Vincent, Emporia St. vs. Southwest Baptist	Feb. 28, 2004
16	II	Markus Hallgrimson, Mont. St.-Billings vs. Western N.M.	Feb. 9, 2000
16	III	Jeff Clement, Grinnell vs. Lawrence	Feb. 21, 1998
16	III	Jeff Clement, Grinnell vs. Monmouth (Ill.)	Feb. 8, 1997
15	I	Keith Veney, Marshall vs. Morehead St.	Dec. 14, 1996
14	III	Scott Stone, Washington-St. Louis vs. Fontbonne	Dec. 17, 2005
14	II	Taylor Patterson, Kennesaw St. vs. Carver Bible	Dec. 15, 2003
14	I	Ronald Blackshear, Marshall vs. Akron	Mar. 1, 2002
14	II	Antonio Harris, LeMoyne-Owen vs. Savannah St.	Feb. 6, 1999
14	III	Ed Brands, Grinnell vs. Ripon	Feb. 24, 1996
14	I	Dave Jamerson, Ohio vs. Col. of Charleston	Dec. 21, 1989
14	I	Askia Jones, Kansas St. vs. Fresno St.	Mar. 24, 1994
14	II	Andy Schmidtmann, Wis.-Parkside vs. Lakeland	Feb. 14, 1989
14	III	Steve Diekmann, Grinnell vs. Illinois Col.	Feb. 18, 1994
14	III	Steve Diekmann, Grinnell vs. Simpson	Nov. 19, 1994
13	III	Sami Wylie, Lincoln (Pa.) vs. Delaware Valley	Feb. 2, 2006
13	II	Bobby Ewing, Tusculum vs. Augusta St.	Dec. 30, 2004
13	II	Markus Hallgrimson, Mont. St.-Billings vs. Western N.M.	Feb. 26, 2000
13	II	Markus Hallgrimson, Mont. St.-Billings vs. Chaminade	Feb. 5, 2000
13	II	Rodney Thomas, IUPUI vs. Wilberforce	Feb. 24, 1997
13	II	Danny Lewis, Wayne St. (Mich.) vs. Michigan Tech	Feb. 20, 1993
13	III	Eric Ochel, Sewanee vs. Emory	Feb. 22, 1995

REBOUNDS

Reb.	Div.	Player, Team vs. Opponent	Date
51	I	Bill Chambers, William & Mary vs. Virginia	Feb. 14, 1953
46	II	Tom Hart, Middlebury vs. Trinity (Conn.)	Feb. 5, 1955
46	II	Tom Hart, Middlebury vs. Clarkson	Feb. 12, 1955
45	II	William Henrikson, Windham vs. New England Col.	Feb. 4, 1970
44	II	Charles McCullough, Loyola (Md.) vs. McDaniel	Feb. 17, 1955
44	II	Norman Rokeach, Long Island vs. Brooklyn Poly	Dec. 28, 1963
43	I	Charlie Slack, Marshall vs. Morris Harvey	Jan. 12, 1954
43	II	Bob Bessoir, Scranton vs. King's (Pa.)	Mar. 5, 1955
42	I	Tom Heinsohn, Holy Cross vs. Boston College	Mar. 1, 1955
42	II	Larry Gooding, St. Augustine's vs. Shaw	Jan. 12, 1974
41	II	Richard Kross, American Int'l vs. Springfield	Feb. 19, 1958
40	II	Ellerbe Neal, Wofford vs. Presbyterian	Jan. 3, 1953
40	I	Art Quimby, Connecticut vs. Boston U.	Jan. 11, 1955
40	II	Donnie Fowler, Wofford vs. Mercer	Jan. 22, 1955
40	II	Charlie Harrison, N.C. A&T vs. Johnson C. Smith	Feb. 8, 1958
40	II	Anthony Romano, Willimantic St. vs. Fitchburg St.	Jan. 5, 1963
40	II	Ed Halicki, Monmouth vs. Southeastern	Dec. 4, 1970
39	II	Maurice Stokes, St. Francis (Pa.) vs. John Carroll	Jan. 28, 1955
39	II	Roger Lotchin, Millikin vs. Lake Forest	Feb. 11, 1956
39	II	Joe Cole, Texas St. vs. Texas Lutheran	Dec. 10, 1956
39	I	Dave DeBusschere, Detroit vs. Central Mich.	Jan. 30, 1960
39	I	Keith Swagerty, Pacific vs. UC Santa Barb.	Mar. 5, 1965
39	II	Curtis Pritchett, St. Augustine vs. St. Paul's	Jan. 24, 1970
38		14 tied	

(Since 1973)

Reb.	Div.	Player, Team vs. Opponent	Date
42	II	Larry Gooding, St. Augustine's vs. Shaw	Jan. 12, 1974
36	III	Josh Hinz, Beloit vs. Grinnell	Feb. 4, 2006
36	III	Mark Veenstra, Calvin vs. Colorado St.-Pueblo	Feb. 3, 1976
36	III	Clinton Montford, Methodist vs. Warren Wilson	Jan. 21, 1989
35	I	Larry Abney, Fresno St. vs. SMU	Feb. 17, 2000
35	III	Ayal Hod, Yeshiva vs. Vassar	Feb. 22, 1989
34	I	David Vaughn, Oral Roberts vs. Brandeis	Jan. 8, 1973
34	II	Major Jones, Albany St. (Ga.) vs. Valdosta St.	Jan. 23, 1975
34	II	Herman Harris, Mississippi Val. vs. Texas Southern	Jan. 12, 1976
34	III	Walt Edwards, Husson vs. Me.-Farmington	Feb. 24, 1976
33	II	Joe Dombrowski, St. Anselm vs. New Hampshire	Dec. 8, 1974

Reb.	Div.	Player, Team vs. Opponent	Date
33	II	Lee Roy Williams, Cal Poly Pomona vs. Wheaton (Ill.)	Dec. 15, 1973
33	III	Willie Parr, LeMoyne-Owen vs. Southern U.	Jan. 10, 1976
33	III	Larry Williams, Pratt vs. Mercy	Jan. 22, 1977
32	II	Marvin Webster, Morgan St. vs. South Carolina St.	Dec. 8, 1973
32	II	Earl Williams, Winston-Salem vs. N.C. Central	Dec. 13, 1973
32	III	Fred Petty, Southern N.H. vs. Curry	Jan. 28, 1974
32	II	George Wilson, Union (Ky.) vs. Southwestern	1974
32	II	Tony DuCros, Regis vs. Neb. Wesleyan	Feb. 28, 1975
32	I	Durand Macklin, LSU vs. Tulane	Nov. 26, 1976
32	II	Robert Clements, Jacksonville vs. Shorter	Jan. 12, 1977
32	I	Jervaughn Scales, Southern U. vs. Grambling	Feb. 7, 1994
31	II	Pete Harris, Stephen F. Austin vs. Texas A&M	Jan. 22, 1973
31	I	Jim Bradley, Northern Ill. vs. Milwaukee	Feb. 19, 1973
31	III	John Humphrie, Swarthmore vs. Ursinus	Dec. 8, 1973
31	II	Roy Smith, Kentucky St. vs. Union (Ky.)	Feb. 10, 1975
31	III	Larry Parker, Plattsburgh St. vs. Clarkson	Jan. 19, 1976
31	I	Calvin Natt, La.-Monroe vs. Ga. Southern	Dec. 29, 1976
31	II	Charles Wode, Mississippi Val. vs. Miss. Industrial	Dec. 10, 1977
31	III	Jon Ford, Norwich vs. Johnson St.	Feb. 16, 1982

ASSISTS

Ast.	Div.	Player, Team vs. Opponent	Date
26	III	Robert James, Kean vs. NJIT	Mar. 11, 1989
25	II	Ali Baaqar, Morris Brown vs. Albany St. (Ga.)	Jan. 26, 1991
25	II	Adrian Hutt, Metro St. vs. Sacramento St.	Feb. 9, 1991
24	II	Steve Ray, Bridgeport vs. Sacred Heart	Jan. 25, 1989
24	II	Steve Ray, Bridgeport vs. New Haven	Feb. 8, 1989
24	III	Adam Dzierzynski, Chapman vs. Amer. Indian Bible	Feb. 9, 1995
23	II	Todd Chappell, Texas Wesleyan vs. Texas Lutheran	Feb. 12, 2000
23	II	Steve Ray, Bridgeport vs. St. Anselm	Nov. 26, 1989
23	II	Jeff Duvall, Oakland City vs. St. Meinrad	Dec. 3, 1991
22	I	Tony Fairley, Charleston So. vs. Armstrong Atlantic	Feb. 9, 1987
22	I	Avery Johnson, Southern U. vs. Texas Southern	Jan. 25, 1988
22	I	Sherman Douglas, Syracuse vs. Providence	Jan. 28, 1989
22	II	Antonio Whitley, St. Augustine's vs. Shaw	Feb. 1, 1992
22	II	Ernest Jenkins, N.M. Highlands vs. Panhandle St.	Jan. 29, 1994
21	I	Mark Wade, UNLV vs. Navy	Dec. 29, 1986
21	I	Kelvin Scarborough, New Mexico vs. Hawaii	Feb. 13, 1987
21	I	Anthony Manuel, Bradley vs. UC Irvine	Dec. 19, 1987
21	I	Avery Johnson, Southern U. vs. Alabama St.	Jan. 16, 1988
21	III	Ron Torgalski, Hamilton vs. Vassar	Jan. 28, 1989
21	III	Mark Cottom, Ferrum vs. Concord	Dec. 15, 1990
21	II	Candice Pickens, California (Pa.) vs. Slippery Rock	Feb. 8, 1995

BLOCKED SHOTS

Blk.	Div.	Player, Team vs. Opponent	Date
18	III	John Bunch, Lincoln (Pa.) vs. New Jersey City	Jan. 19, 2004
18	III	John Bunch, Lincoln (Pa.) vs. Valley Forge Christian	Dec. 13, 2003
16	I	Mickell Gladness, Alabama A&M vs. Texas Southern	Feb. 24, 2007
16	III	Tory Black, NJIT vs. Polytechnic (N.Y.)	Feb. 5, 1997
15	III	Johnny Woods, Wesley vs. Salisbury	Feb. 14, 2000
15	III	Antoine Hyman, Keuka vs. Hobart	Feb. 21, 1996
15	III	Erick Lidecis, Maritime (N.Y.) vs. Stevens Institute	Nov. 30, 1993
15	II	Mark Hensel, Pitt.-Johnstown vs. Slippery Rock	Jan. 22, 1994
15	III	Roy Woods, Fontbonne vs. MacMurray	Jan. 26, 1995
15	III	Ira Nicholson, Mt. St. Vincent vs. Stevens Institute	Nov. 27, 1994
14	III	Johnny Woods, Wesley vs. Eastern	Jan. 17, 2001
14	III	Neil Edwards, York (N.Y.) vs. Lehman	Feb. 12, 2000
14	I	Loren Woods, Arizona vs. Oregon	Feb. 3, 2000
14	I	Roy Rogers, Alabama vs. Georgia	Feb. 10, 1996
14	II	Victorlus Payne, Lane vs. Talladega	Jan. 26, 1996
14	I	David Robinson, Navy vs. UNC Wilmington	Jan. 4, 1986
14	I	Shawn Bradley, BYU vs. Eastern Ky.	Dec. 7, 1990
14	II	Maurice Barnett, Elizabeth City St. vs. Bowie St.	Feb. 3, 1994
14	III	Andrew South, NJIT vs. Stevens Institute	Feb. 14, 1994
13	I	Joel Anthony, UNLV vs. TCU	Feb. 7, 2007
13	I	Sean Williams, Boston College vs. Duquesne	Dec. 28, 2006
13	II	Mervyn Clarke, Oakland City vs. Ind.-East	Nov. 15, 2006
13	II	Callistus Eziukwu, Grand Valley St. vs. Ferris St.	Feb. 7, 2005
13	I	Deng Gai, Fairfield vs. Siena	Jan. 22, 2005
13	I	Anthony King, Miami (Fla.) vs. Fla. Atlantic	Nov. 29, 2004
13	I	Wojciech Myrda, La.-Monroe vs. UTSA	Jan. 17, 2002
13	I	Kyle Davis, Auburn vs. Miami (Fla.)	Mar. 14, 2001
13	I	D'or Fischer, Northwestern St. vs. Texas St.	Jan. 22, 2001
13	I	Neil Edwards, York (N.Y.) vs. Brooklyn	Feb. 22, 2000
13	III	Antoine Hyman, Keuka vs. Hobart	Jan. 8, 1997
13	III	Damon Avinger, CCNY vs. St. Joseph's (N.Y.)	Jan. 7, 1996
13	I	Kevin Roberson, Vermont vs. New Hampshire	Jan. 9, 1992
13	I	Jim McIlvaine, Marquette vs. Northeastern Ill.	Dec. 9, 1992
13	II	Mark Hensel, Pitt.-Johnstown vs. Wheeling Jesuit	Jan. 31, 1994
13	I	Keith Closs, Central Conn. St. vs. St. Francis (Pa.)	Dec. 21, 1994

STEALS

Stl.	Div.	Player, Team vs. Opponent	Date
17	II	Antonio Walls, Alabama A&M vs. Albany St. (Ga.)	Jan. 5, 1998
17	III	Matt Newton, Principia vs. Harris-Stowe	Jan. 4, 1994
15	II	David Clark, Delta St. vs. LeMoyne-Owen	Nov. 25, 2006
14	III	Moses Jean-Pierre, Plymouth St. vs. Rivier	Dec. 7, 1993
13	III	Daniel Martinez, McMurry vs. Concordia (Tex.)	Feb. 3, 2000
13	III	Todd Lange, Pomona-Pitzer vs. LaSierra	Jan. 7, 1999
13	III	John Gallogly, Salve Regina vs. Roger Williams	Feb. 10, 1997
13	I	Mookie Blaylock, Oklahoma vs. Centenary (La.)	Dec. 12, 1987
13	I	Mookie Blaylock, Oklahoma vs. Loyola Marymount	Dec. 17, 1988
13	I	Carldwell Johnson, UAB vs. South Carolina St.	Nov. 27, 2005
12	III	Curtis Miller, Albertus Magnus vs. Emmanuel (Mass.)	Jan. 22, 2004
12	III	Benny West, Howard Payne vs. Sul Ross St.	Dec. 13, 2003
12	I	Jehiel Lewis, Navy vs. Bucknell	Jan. 12, 2002
12	I	Greedy Daniels, TCU vs. Ark.-Pine Bluff	Dec. 30, 2000
12	II	Terrence Baxter, Pfeiffer vs. Livingstone	Nov. 22, 2000
12	III	Greg Brown, Albertus Magnus vs. Rivier	Feb. 3, 2000
12	III	Daniel Martinez, McMurry vs. Ozarks (Ark.)	Dec. 2, 1999
12	I	Richard Duncan, Middle Tenn. vs. Eastern Ky.	Feb. 20, 1999
12	III	Derrick Brown, Davis & Elkins vs. Ohio Valley	Feb. 9, 1999
12	II	Marche' Bearad, Ark.-Monticello vs. Christian Bros.	Feb. 8, 1999
12	II	Freddy Conyers, Mass.-Boston vs.Westfield St.	Dec. 10, 1998
12	III	Mario Thompson, Occidental vs. LIFE Bible	Nov. 21, 1998
12	III	Deron Black, Allegheny vs. Case Reserve	Jan. 17, 1996
12	III	Jamal Elliott, Haverford vs. Gwynedd-Mercy	Jan. 15, 1996
12	I	Kenny Robertson, Cleveland St. vs. Wagner	Dec. 3, 1988
12	III	Moses Jean-Pierre, Plymouth St. vs. Rhode Island Col.	Jan. 23, 1993
12	I	Terry Evans, Oklahoma vs. Florida A&M	Jan. 27, 1993
12	III	David Brown, Westfield St. vs. Albertus Magnus	Jan. 8, 1994
12	III	Barry Aranoff, Yeshiva vs. Purchase	Feb. 13, 1995

Season Records

(Based on qualifiers for annual statistical championship)

POINTS

Player, Team (Division)	Season	G	FG	3FG	FT	Pts.
Pete Maravich, LSU (I)	1970	31	522	—	337	1,381
Earl Monroe, Winston-Salem (II)	1967	32	509	—	311	1,329
Travis Grant, Kentucky St. (II)	1972	33	539	—	226	1,304
Clarence "Bevo" Francis, Rio Grande (II)	1954	27	444	—	367	1,255
Bill Reigel, McNeese St. (II)	1956	36	425	—	370	1,220
Elvin Hayes, Houston (I)	1968	33	519	—	176	1,214
Frank Selvy, Furman (I)	1954	29	427	—	355	1,209
Pete Maravich, LSU (I)	1969	26	433	—	282	1,148
Pete Maravich, LSU (I)	1968	26	432	—	274	1,138
Bo Kimble, Loyola Marymount (I)	1990	32	404	92	231	1,131
Hersey Hawkins, Bradley (I)	1988	31	377	87	284	1,125
Austin Carr, Notre Dame (I)	1970	29	444	—	218	1,106
Austin Carr, Notre Dame (I)	1971	29	430	—	241	1,101
Otis Birdsong, Houston (I)	1977	36	452	—	186	1,090
Dwight Lamar, La.-Lafayette (I)	1972	29	429	—	196	1,054
Kevin Bradshaw, Alliant Int'l (I)	1991	28	358	60	278	1,054
Dwight Lamar, La.-Lafayette (II)	1971	29	424	—	196	1,044
Greg Grant, TCNJ (III)	1989	32	387	76	194	1,044
Dave Russell, Shepherd (III)	1975	32	394	—	249	1,037
Glenn Robinson, Purdue (I)	1994	34	368	79	215	1,030
Kyle Myrick, Lincoln (Pa.) (III)	2006	30	387	59	177	1,010
Oscar Robertson, Cincinnati (I)	1958	28	352	—	280	984
Oscar Robertson, Cincinnati (I)	1959	30	331	—	316	978
Rick Barry, Miami (Fla.) (I)	1965	26	340	—	221	973
Larry Bird, Indiana St. (I)	1979	34	376	—	221	973
Dennis Scott, Georgia Tech (I)	1990	35	336	137	161	970

SCORING AVERAGE

Player, Team (Division)	Season	G	FG	3FG	FT	Pts.	Avg.
Clarence "Bevo" Francis, Rio Grande (II)	1954	27	444	—	367	1,255	46.5
Pete Maravich, LSU (I)	1970	31	522	—	337	1,381	44.5
Pete Maravich, LSU (I)	1969	26	433	—	282	1,148	44.2
Pete Maravich, LSU (I)	1968	26	432	—	274	1,138	43.8
Earl Glass, Miss. Industrial (II)	1963	19	322	—	171	815	42.9
Frank Selvy, Furman (I)	1954	29	427	—	355	1,209	41.7
Earl Monroe, Winston-Salem (II)	1967	32	509	—	311	1,329	41.5
John Rinka, Kenyon (II)	1970	23	354	—	234	942	41.0
Willie Shaw, Lane (II)	1964	18	303	—	121	727	40.4
Johnny Neumann, Mississippi (I)	1971	23	366	—	191	923	40.1
Travis Grant, Kentucky St. (II)	1972	33	539	—	226	1,304	39.5
Thales McReynolds, Miles (II)	1965	18	294	—	118	706	39.2
Bob Johnson, Fitchburg St. (II)	1963	18	213	—	277	703	39.1
Roger Kuss, Wis.-River Falls (II)	1953	21	291	—	235	817	38.9

Player, Team (Division)	Season	G	FG	3FG	FT	Pts.	Avg.
Freeman Williams, Portland St. (I)	1977	26	417	—	176	1,010	38.8
Billy McGill, Utah (I)	1962	26	394	—	221	1,009	38.8
Calvin Murphy, Niagara (I)	1968	24	337	—	242	916	38.2
Austin Carr, Notre Dame (I)	1970	29	444	—	218	1,106	38.1
Austin Carr, Notre Dame (I)	1971	29	430	—	241	1,101	38.0
Kevin Bradshaw, Alliant Int'l (I)	1991	28	358	60	278	1,054	37.6
Rick Barry, Miami (Fla.) (I)	1965	26	340	—	221	973	37.4
Steve Diekmann, Grinnell (III)	1995	20	223	137	162	745	37.3
Florindo Vieira, Quinnipiac (II)	1954	14	191	—	138	520	37.1
Elvin Hayes, Houston (I)	1968	33	519	—	176	1,214	36.8
Marshall Rogers, Tex.-Pan American (I)	1976	25	361	—	197	919	36.8

FIELD-GOAL PERCENTAGE

Player, Team (Division)	Season	G	FG	FGA	Pct.
Travis Weiss, St. John's (Minn.) (III)	1994	26	160	209	76.6
Brian Schmitting, Ripon (III)	2006	21	122	160	76.3
Pete Metzelaars, Wabash (III)	1982	28	271	360	75.3
Todd Linder, Tampa (II)	1987	32	282	375	75.2
Maurice Stafford, North Ala. (II)	1984	34	198	264	75.0
Tony Rychlec, Mass. Maritime (III)	1981	25	233	311	74.9
Matthew Cornegay, Tuskegee (II)	1982	29	208	278	74.8
Steve Johnson, Oregon St. (I)	1981	28	235	315	74.6
Callistus Eziukwu, Grand Valley St. (II)	2005	28	157	213	73.7
Brian Moten, West Ga. (II)	1992	26	141	192	73.4
Ed Phillips, Alabama A&M (II)	1968	22	154	210	73.3
Tony Rychlec, Mass. Maritime (III)	1982	20	193	264	73.1
Russ Newman, Menlo (III)	1991	26	130	178	73.0
Ed Owens, Hampden-Sydney (III)	1979	24	140	192	72.9
Ray Strozier, Central Mo. St. (II)	1980	28	142	195	72.8
Harold Booker, Cheyney (II)	1965	24	144	198	72.7
Chad Scott, California (Pa.) (II)	1994	30	178	245	72.7
Scott Baxter, Capital (III)	1991	26	164	226	72.6
Maurice Woods, Potsdam St. (III)	1982	30	203	280	72.5
Tom Schurfranz, Bellarmine (II)	1991	30	245	339	72.3
Marv Lewis, Southampton (II)	1969	24	271	375	72.3
Earl Keith, Stony Brook (III)	1979	24	164	227	72.2
Louis Newsome, North Ala. (II)	1988	29	192	266	72.2
Pete Metzelaars, Wabash (III)	1981	25	204	283	72.1
Ed Phillips, Alabama A&M (II)	1971	24	159	221	71.9
Brandon King, Rowan (III)	2005	26	141	196	71.9
Jon Rosner, Yeshiva (III)	1991	22	141	196	71.9

THREE-POINT FIELD GOALS MADE

Player, Team (Division)	Season	G	3FG
Jeff Clement, Grinnell (III)	1998	22	186
Alex Williams, Sacramento St. (II)	1988	30	167
Jeff Clement, Grinnell (III)	1999	22	166
Markus Hallgrimson, Mont. St.-Billings (II)	2000	26	160
Ed Brands, Grinnell (III)	1996	24	158
Darrin Fitzgerald, Butler (I)	1987	28	158
Billy Shivers, Redlands (III)	2004	25	153
Freddie Banks, UNLV (I)	1987	39	152
Yandel Brown, Columbus St. (II)	2005	32	148
Eric Kline, Northern St. (II)	1994	33	148
Eric Kline, Northern St. (II)	1995	30	148
Cameron Munoz, Mont. St.-Billings (II)	2006	28	147
Randy Rutherford, Oklahoma St. (I)	1995	37	146
Chris Peterson, Eureka (III)	1994	31	145
Amir Mazarei, Redlands (III)	2007	23	143
Dennis Stanton, Ursinus (III)	2004	27	140
Terrence Woods, Florida A&M (I)	2004	31	140
Mike Taylor, West Virginia St. (II)	2004	32	140
J.J. Redick, Duke (I)	2006	36	139
Terrence Woods, Florida A&M (I)	2003	28	139
Shawn Pughsley, Central Okla. (II)	1998	32	139
Amir Mazarei, Redlands (III)	2006	24	138
Will Whittington, Marist (I)	2007	34	137
Demon Brown, Charlotte (I)	2003	29	137
Dennis Scott, Georgia Tech (I)	1990	35	137
Steve Diekmann, Grinnell (III)	1995	20	137
Steve Nordlund, Grinnell (III)	2002	24	137

THREE-POINT FIELD GOALS MADE PER GAME

Player, Team (Division)	Season	G	3FG	Avg.
Jeff Clement, Grinnell (III)	1998	22	186	8.45
Jeff Clement, Grinnell (III)	1999	22	166	7.55
Steve Diekmann, Grinnell (III)	1995	20	137	6.85
Ed Brands, Grinnell (III)	1996	24	158	6.58
Ed Brands, Grinnell (III)	1995	20	129	6.45
Amir Mazarei, Redlands (III)	2007	23	143	6.22
Markus Hallgrimson, Mont. St.-Billings (II)	2000	26	160	6.15
Billy Shivers, Redlands (III)	2004	25	153	6.12
Amir Mazarei, Redlands (III)	2006	24	138	5.75
Steve Nordlund, Grinnell (III)	2002	24	137	5.71
Darrin Fitzgerald, Butler (I)	1987	28	158	5.64
Steve Diekmann, Grinnell (III)	1994	21	117	5.57
Alex Williams, Sacramento St. (II)	1988	30	167	5.57
Chris Jans, Loras (III)	1991	25	133	5.32
Woody Piirto, Grinnell (III)	1999	22	117	5.32
Cameron Munoz, Mont. St.-Billings (II)	2006	28	147	5.25
John Grotberg, Grinnell (III)	2006	23	120	5.22
Dennis Stanton, Ursinus (III)	2004	27	140	5.19
Jeff Clement, Grinnell (III)	1997	22	113	5.14
Mark Bedell, Fisk (III)	1997	19	97	5.11
Jason Garrow, Augustana (S.D.) (II)	1992	27	135	5.00
David Bailey, Concordia Chicago (III)	1994	24	120	5.00
Terrence Woods, Florida A&M (I)	2003	28	139	4.96
Eric Kline, Northern St. (II)	1995	30	148	4.93
Ray Gutierrez, California (Pa.) (II)	1993	29	142	4.90

THREE-POINT FIELD-GOAL PERCENTAGE

Player, Team (Division)	Season	G	3FG	3FGA	Pct.
Reggie James, NJIT (III)	1989	29	59	88	67.0
Ray Lee, Hampton (II)	1988	24	39	60	65.0
Glenn Tropf, Holy Cross (I)	1988	29	52	82	63.4
Sean Wightman, Western Mich. (I)	1992	30	48	76	63.2
Chris Miles, NJIT (III)	1987	26	41	65	63.1
Steve Hood, Winston-Salem (II)	1988	28	42	67	62.7
Chris Miles, NJIT (III)	1989	26	46	75	61.3
Matt Miota, Lawrence (III)	1990	22	33	54	61.1
Mike Bachman, Alma (III)	1991	26	46	76	60.5
Mark Wiley, Fort Hays St. (II)	1990	29	49	81	60.5
Aaron Fehler, Oakland City (II)	1995	26	73	121	60.3
Keith Jennings, East Tenn. St. (I)	1991	33	84	142	59.2
Aaron Baker, Mississippi Col. (II)	1989	27	69	117	59.0
Dave Calloway, Monmouth (I)	1989	28	48	82	58.5
Walter Hurd, Johnson C. Smith (II)	1989	27	49	84	58.3
Matt Hopson, Oakland City (II)	1996	31	84	145	57.9
Ray Magee, Richard Stockton (III)	1988	26	41	71	57.7
Keith Orchard, Whitman (III)	1988	26	42	73	57.5
Jon Bryant, St. Cloud St. (II)	1996	27	54	94	57.4
Adam Harness, Oakland City (II)	1997	26	39	68	57.4
Steve Kerr, Arizona (I)	1988	38	114	199	57.3
Reginald Jones, Prairie View (I)	1987	28	64	112	57.1
Brian O'Donnell, Rutgers-Camden (III)	1988	24	65	114	57.0
Erick Hunt, Methodist (III)	1989	27	45	79	57.0
Eric Harris, Bishop (III)	1987	26	91	160	56.9

FREE-THROW PERCENTAGE

Player, Team (Division)	Season	G	FT	FTA	Pct.
Paul Cluxton, Northern Ky. (II)	1997	35	94	94	100.0
Blake Ahearn, Missouri St. (I)	2004	33	117	120	97.5
Korey Coon, Ill. Wesleyan (III)	2000	25	157	163	96.3
Derek Raivio, Gonzaga (I)	2007	34	148	154	96.1
Craig Collins, Penn St. (I)	1985	27	94	98	95.9
Nick Wilkins, Coe (III)	2003	26	66	69	95.7
Chanse Young, Manchester (III)	1998	25	65	68	95.6
Tomas Rimkus, Pace (II)	1997	25	65	68	95.6
Andy Enfield, Johns Hopkins (III)	1991	29	123	129	95.3
J.J. Redick, Duke (I)	2004	37	143	150	95.3
Chris Carideo, Eureka (III)	1992	26	80	84	95.2
Yudi Teichman, Yeshiva (III)	1989	21	119	125	95.2
Steve Drabyn, Belmont (I)	2003	29	78	82	95.1
Rod Foster, UCLA (I)	1982	27	95	100	95.0
C.J. Cowgill, Chaminade (II)	2001	22	113	119	95.0
Clay McKnight, Pacific (I)	2000	24	74	78	94.9
Matt Logie, Lehigh (I)	2003	28	91	96	94.8
A.J. Graves, Butler (I)	2007	35	145	153	94.8
Joseph Chatman, Lesley (III)	2007	27	126	133	94.7
Blake Ahearn, Missouri St. (I)	2005	32	90	95	94.7
Brett Davis, Wis.-Oshkosh (III)	1998	27	72	76	94.7
Joe Bueckers, Concordia-M'head (III)	2004	26	71	75	94.7
Mark Giovino, Babson (III)	1997	28	86	91	94.5
Kent Andrews, McNeese St. (II)	1968	24	85	90	94.4
Billy Newton, Morgan St. (II)	1976	28	85	90	94.4
Carlos Gibson, Marshall (I)	1978	28	84	89	94.4
Danny Basile, Marist (I)	1994	27	84	89	94.4

REBOUNDS

Player, Team (Division)	Season	G	Reb.
Elmore Smith, Kentucky St. (II)	1972	33	799
Marvin Webster, Morgan St. (II)	1974	33	740
Walt Dukes, Seton Hall (I)	1953	33	734
Maurice Stokes, St. Francis (Pa.) (II)	1955	28	726

Player, Team (Division)	Season	G	Reb.
Frank Stronczek, American Int'l (II)	1966	26	717
Maurice Stokes, St. Francis (Pa.) (II)	1954	26	689
Jim Ahrens, Buena Vista (II)	1962	28	682
Elmore Smith, Kentucky St. (II)	1970	30	682
R.C. Owens, Albertson (II)	1954	25	677
Wilbert Jones, Albany St. (Ga.) (II)	1969	28	670
Leroy Wright, Pacific (I)	1959	26	652
Tom Gola, La Salle (I)	1954	30	652
Jim Smith, Steubenville (II)	1957	26	651
Marvin Webster, Morgan St. (II)	1973	28	650
Tom Hart, Middlebury (II)	1955	22	649
Charlie Tyra, Louisville (I)	1956	29	645
Jackie Jackson, Virginia Union (II)	1961	26	641
Vincent White, Savannah St. (II)	1972	29	633
Paul Silas, Creighton (I)	1964	29	631
Bill Thieben, Hofstra (II)	1955	26	627
Lucious Jackson, Tex.-Pan American (II)	1963	32	626
Elvin Hayes, Houston (I)	1968	33	624
Vincent White, Savannah St. (II)	1970	27	624
Artis Gilmore, Jacksonville (I)	1970	28	621
Bill Thieben, Hofstra (I)	1954	24	620
Tom Hart, Middlebury (II)	1956	21	620

(Since 1973)

Player, Team (Division)	Season	G	Reb.
Marvin Webster, Morgan St. (II)	1974	33	740
Marvin Webster, Morgan St. (II)	1973	28	650
Major Jones, Albany St. (Ga.) (II)	1975	27	608
Marvin Barnes, Providence (I)	1974	32	597
Joe Manley, Bowie St. (III)	1976	29	579
Marvin Barnes, Providence (I)	1973	30	571
Earl Williams, Winston-Salem (II)	1974	26	553
John Jordan, Southern Me. (II)	1978	29	536
Charles Oakley, Virginia Union (III)	1985	31	535
Lawrence Johnson, Prairie View (II)	1974	23	519
Andre Means, Sacred Heart (II)	1977	32	516
Major Jones, Albany St. (Ga.) (II)	1975	25	513
Kermit Washington, American (I)	1973	25	511
Bill Walton, UCLA (I)	1973	30	506
Larry Bird, Indiana St. (I)	1979	34	505
Harvey Jones, Alabama St. (II)	1974	28	503
Larry Kenon, Memphis (I)	1973	30	501
Akeem Olajuwon, Houston (I)	1984	37	500
Andre Means, Sacred Heart (II)	1978	30	493
Ricky Mahorn, Hampton (II)	1980	31	490
Rob Roesch, Staten Island (II)	1989	31	482
Howard Shockley, Salisbury (III)	1974	27	482
Keith Woolfolk, Upper Iowa (III)	1978	26	479
Leonard Robinson, Tennessee St. (II)	1974	28	478
Major Jones, Albany St. (Ga.) (II)	1976	24	475

REBOUND AVERAGE

Player, Team (Division)	Season	G	Reb.	Avg.
Tom Hart, Middlebury (II)	1956	21	620	29.5
Tom Hart, Middlebury (II)	1955	22	649	29.5
Frank Stronczek, American Int'l (II)	1966	26	717	27.6
R.C. Owens, Albertson (II)	1954	25	677	27.1
Maurice Stokes, St. Francis (Pa.) (II)	1954	26	689	26.5
Ellerbe Neal, Wofford (II)	1953	23	609	26.5
Roman Turmon, Clark Atlanta (II)	1954	23	602	26.2
Pat Callahan, Lewis (II)	1955	20	523	26.2
Hank Brown, Mass.-Lowell (II)	1966	19	496	26.1
Maurice Stokes, St. Francis (Pa.) (II)	1955	28	726	25.9
Bill Thieben, Hofstra (II)	1954	24	620	25.8
Dean Sandifer, Lakeland (II)	1965	23	592	25.7
Charlie Slack, Marshall (II)	1955	21	538	25.6
Charles Wrinn, Trinity (Conn.) (II)	1952	19	486	25.6
Leroy Wright, Pacific (I)	1959	26	652	25.1
Jim Smith, Steubenville (II)	1957	26	651	25.0
Marv Becker, Widener (II)	1958	18	450	25.0
Tony Williams, St. Francis (Me.) (II)	1971	24	599	25.0
Ernie Brock, Virginia St. (II)	1964	24	597	24.9
Russell Jackson, Southern U. (II)	1970	22	544	24.7
Gerry Govan, St. Mary's (Kan.) (II)	1963	18	445	24.7
Merv Shorr, CCNY (II)	1954	18	444	24.7
Art Quimby, Connecticut (I)	1955	25	611	24.4
Charlie Slack, Marshall (I)	1956	22	520	23.6
Ed Conlin, Fordham (I)	1953	26	612	23.5

(Since 1973)

Player, Team (Division)	Season	G	Reb.	Avg.
Marvin Webster, Morgan St. (II)	1973	28	650	23.2
Lawrence Johnson, Prairie View (II)	1974	23	519	22.6
Major Jones, Albany St. (Ga.) (II)	1975	27	608	22.5
Marvin Webster, Morgan St. (II)	1974	33	740	22.4
Earl Williams, Winston-Salem (II)	1974	26	553	21.3

Player, Team (Division)	Season	G	Reb.	Avg.
Major Jones, Albany St. (Ga.) (II)	1975	25	513	20.5
Kermit Washington, American (I)	1973	25	511	20.4
Larry Gooding, St. Augustine's (II)	1974	22	443	20.1
Joe Manley, Bowie St. (III)	1976	29	579	20.0
Fred Petty, Southern N.H. (III)	1974	22	436	19.8
Major Jones, Albany St. (Ga.) (II)	1976	24	475	19.8
Larry Williams, Pratt (III)	1977	24	457	19.0
Marvin Barnes, Providence (I)	1973	30	571	19.0
Calvin Robinson, Mississippi Val. (II)	1976	23	432	18.8
Larry Williams, Pratt (III)	1977	17	318	18.7
Larry Parker, Plattsburgh St. (III)	1975	23	430	18.7
Marvin Barnes, Providence (I)	1974	32	597	18.7
Charles Greer, Thomas (III)	1977	17	318	18.7
John Jordan, Southern Me. (III)	1978	29	536	18.5
Keith Woolfolk, Upper Iowa (III)	1978	26	479	18.4
Michael Stubbs, Trinity (Conn.) (III)	1990	22	398	18.1
Mike Taylor, Pratt (III)	1978	23	414	18.0
Harvey Jones, Alabama St. (II)	1974	28	503	18.0
Walt Edwards, Husson (III)	1976	26	467	18.0
Scott Mountz, California (Pa.) (II)	1978	24	431	18.0

ASSISTS

Player, Team (Division)	Season	G	Ast.
Mark Wade, UNLV (I)	1987	38	406
Steve Ray, Bridgeport (II)	1989	32	400
Avery Johnson, Southern U. (I)	1988	30	399
Robert James, Kean (III)	1989	29	391
Steve Ray, Bridgeport (II)	1990	33	385
Anthony Manuel, Bradley (I)	1988	31	373
Tony Smith, Pfeiffer (II)	1992	35	349
Avery Johnson, Southern U. (I)	1987	31	333
Mark Jackson, St. John's (N.Y.) (I)	1986	32	328
Sherman Douglas, Syracuse (I)	1989	38	326
Tennyson Whitted, Ramapo (III)	2002	29	319
Greg Anthony, UNLV (I)	1991	35	310
Sam Crawford, New Mexico St. (I)	1993	34	310
Reid Gettys, Houston (I)	1984	37	309
Jim Ferrer, Bentley (II)	1989	31	309
Rob Paternostro, Southern N.H. (II)	1995	33	309
Carl Golson, Loyola (Ill.) (I)	1985	33	305
Craig Neal, Georgia Tech (I)	1988	32	303
Keith Jennings, East Tenn. St. (I)	1991	33	301
Brian Gregory, Oakland (II)	1989	28	300
Doug Gottlieb, Oklahoma St. (I)	1999	34	299
Chris Corchiani, North Carolina St. (I)	1991	31	299
Charles Jordan, Erskine (II)	1992	34	298
Keith Jennings, East Tenn. St. (I)	1990	34	297
Ricky Spicer, Wis.-Whitewater (III)	1989	31	295

ASSIST AVERAGE

Player, Team (Division)	Season	G	Ast.	Avg.
Robert James, Kean (III)	1989	29	391	13.48
Avery Johnson, Southern U. (I)	1988	30	399	13.30
Steve Ray, Bridgeport (II)	1989	32	400	12.50
Anthony Manuel, Bradley (I)	1988	31	373	12.03
Steve Ray, Bridgeport (II)	1990	33	385	11.66
Demetri Beekman, Assumption (II)	1993	23	264	11.47
Albert Kirchner, Mt. St. Vincent (III)	1990	24	267	11.12
Tennyson Whitted, Ramapo (III)	2002	29	319	11.00
Ernest Jenkins, N.M. Highlands (II)	1995	27	291	10.78
Avery Johnson, Southern U. (I)	1987	31	333	10.74
Brian Gregory, Oakland (II)	1989	28	300	10.71
Zack Whiting, Chaminade (II)	2007	27	289	10.70
Mark Wade, UNLV (I)	1987	38	406	10.68
Ron Torgalski, Hamilton (III)	1989	26	275	10.57
Brent Schremp, Slippery Rock (II)	1995	25	259	10.36
Louis Adams, Rust (III)	1989	22	227	10.31
Ernest Jenkins, N.M. Highlands (II)	1994	27	277	10.31
Adrian Hutt, Metro St. (II)	1991	28	285	10.17
Nelson Haggerty, Baylor (I)	1995	28	284	10.14
Tony Smith, Pfeiffer (II)	1992	35	349	9.97
Jim Ferrer, Bentley (II)	1989	31	309	9.96
Glenn Williams, Holy Cross (I)	1989	28	278	9.92
Eric Johnson, Coe (III)	1991	24	238	9.91
Ryan Nelson, Grand Canyon (II)	2006	27	263	9.74
Todd Chappell, Texas Wesleyan (II)	2000	27	263	9.74

BLOCKED SHOTS

Player, Team (Division)	Season	G	Blk.
David Robinson, Navy (I)	1986	35	207
Tory Black, NJIT (III)	1997	26	198
Shawn James, Northeastern (I)	2006	30	196
Neil Edwards, York (N.Y.) (III)	2000	26	193

Player, Team (Division)	Season	G	Blk.
Mickell Gladness, Alabama A&M (I)	2007	30	188
Ira Nicholson, Mt. St. Vincent (III)	1995	28	188
Adonal Foyle, Colgate (I)	1997	28	180
Keith Closs, Central Conn. St. (I)	1996	28	178
Shawn Bradley, BYU (I)	1991	34	177
John Bunch, Lincoln (Pa.) (III)	2004	25	173
Wojciech Mydra, La.-Monroe (I)	2002	32	172
Alonzo Mourning, Georgetown (I)	1989	34	169
Stephane Lasme, Massachusetts (I)	2007	33	168
Shacun Malave, City Tech (III)	2004	28	167
Deng Gai, Fairfield (I)	2005	30	165
Adonal Foyle, Colgate (I)	1996	29	165
Justin Williams, Wyoming (I)	2006	30	163
Ira Nicholson, Mt. St. Vincent (III)	1996	27	163
Ken Johnson, Ohio St. (I)	2000	30	161
Alonzo Mourning, Georgetown (I)	1992	32	160
James Doyle, Concord (II)	1998	30	157
Shaquille O'Neal, LSU (I)	1992	30	157
Emeka Okafor, Connecticut (I)	2003	33	156
Roy Rogers, Alabama (I)	1996	32	156
Antonio Harvey, Pfeiffer (II)	1993	29	155

BLOCKED-SHOT AVERAGE

Player, Team (Division)	Season	G	Blk.	Avg.
Tory Black, NJIT (III)	1997	26	198	7.62
Neil Edwards, York (N.Y.) (III)	2000	26	193	7.42
John Bunch, Lincoln (Pa.) (III)	2004	25	173	6.92
Ira Nicholson, Mt. St. Vincent (III)	1995	28	188	6.71
Shawn James, Northeastern (I)	2006	30	196	6.53
Adonal Foyle, Colgate (I)	1997	28	180	6.43
Keith Closs, Central Conn. St. (I)	1996	28	178	6.36
Ira Nicholson, Mt. St. Vincent (III)	1997	24	151	6.29
Ira Nicholson, Mt. St. Vincent (III)	1996	27	163	6.04
Shacun Malave, City Tech (III)	2004	28	167	5.96
David Robinson, Navy (I)	1986	35	207	5.91
Antoine Hyman, Keuka (III)	1997	26	148	5.69
Adonal Foyle, Colgate (I)	1996	29	165	5.69
Neil Edwards, York (N.Y.) (III)	1999	26	144	5.54
Deng Gai, Fairfield (I)	2005	30	165	5.50
Johnny Woods, Wesley (II)	2000	24	132	5.50
Shawn James, Northeastern (I)	2005	25	136	5.44
Justin Williams, Wyoming (I)	2006	30	163	5.43
Wojciech Mydra, La.-Monroe (I)	2002	32	172	5.38
Ken Johnson, Ohio St. (I)	2000	30	161	5.37
Keith Closs, Central Conn. St. (I)	1995	26	139	5.35
Antonio Harvey, Pfeiffer (II)	1993	29	155	5.34
Antoine Hyman, Keuka (III)	1996	25	131	5.24
James Doyle, Concord (II)	1998	30	157	5.23
Shaquille O'Neal, LSU (I)	1992	30	157	5.23

STEALS

Player, Team (Division)	Season	G	Stl.
Moses Jean-Pierre, Plymouth St. (III)	1994	30	189
Daniel Martinez, McMurry (III)	2000	29	178
Desmond Cambridge, Alabama A&M (I)	2002	29	160
Mookie Blaylock, Oklahoma (I)	1988	39	150
Purvis Presha, Stillman (III)	1996	25	144
Aldwin Ware, Florida A&M (I)	1988	29	142
John Linehan, Providence (I)	2002	31	139
J.R. Gamble, Queens (N.C.) (II)	2001	32	139
Darron Brittman, Chicago St. (I)	1986	28	139
Tennyson Whitted, Ramapo (III)	2002	29	138
Nadav Henefeld, Connecticut (I)	1990	37	138
Matt Newton, Principia (III)	1994	25	138
John Gallogly, Salve Regina (III)	1997	24	137
Mookie Blaylock, Oklahoma (I)	1989	35	131
Ronn McMahon, Eastern Wash. (I)	1990	29	130
Wayne Copeland, Lynn (II)	2000	26	129
Elbie Murphy, St. Joseph's (Me.) (III)	2007	30	126
Greg Dean, Concordia-M'head (III)	1997	23	126
Scott Clarke, Utica (III)	1995	24	126
Japhet McNeil, Bridgeport (II)	2007	31	125
Obie Trotter, Alabama A&M (I)	2005	32	125
Wayne Copeland, Lynn (II)	1999	31	125
Allen Iverson, Georgetown (I)	1996	37	124
Marty Johnson, Towson (I)	1988	30	124
Eric Coley, Tulsa (I)	2000	37	123
Deron Black, Allegheny (III)	1996	27	123

STEAL AVERAGE

Player, Team (Division)	Season	G	Stl.	Avg.
Moses Jean-Pierre, Plymouth St. (III)	1994	30	189	6.30
Daniel Martinez, McMurry (III)	2000	29	178	6.14
Purvis Presha, Stillman (III)	1996	25	144	5.76
John Gallogly, Salve Regina (III)	1997	24	137	5.71
Matt Newton, Principia (III)	1994	25	138	5.52
Desmond Cambridge, Alabama A&M (I)	2002	29	160	5.52
Barry Aranoff, Yeshiva (III)	1995	22	121	5.50
Greg Dean, Concordia-M'head (III)	1997	23	126	5.48
John Gallogly, Salve Regina (III)	1998	23	121	5.26
Scott Clarke, Utica (III)	1995	24	126	5.25
Darron Brittman, Chicago St. (I)	1986	28	139	4.96
Wayne Copeland, Lynn (II)	2000	26	129	4.96
Joel Heckendorf, Martin Luther (III)	1996	17	84	4.94
Aldwin Ware, Florida A&M (I)	1988	29	142	4.90
David Brown, Westfield St. (III)	1994	25	122	4.88
Ivo Moyano, Polytechnic (N.Y.) (III)	1994	19	91	4.78
Tennyson Whitted, Ramapo (III)	2002	29	138	4.76
Mario Thompson, Occidental (III)	1999	24	114	4.75
Benny West, Howard Payne (III)	2004	25	116	4.64
Keith Darden, Concordia (Tex.) (III)	2001	24	111	4.63
Moses Jean-Pierre, Plymouth St. (III)	1993	25	114	4.56
Deron Black, Allegheny (III)	1996	27	123	4.56
Scott Clark, Utica (III)	1996	26	118	4.54
John Morris, Bluefield St. (II)	1994	23	104	4.52
Devlin Herring, Pitt.-Johnstown (II)	1997	27	122	4.52

Career Records

POINTS

Player, Team (Division)	Last Season	Yrs.	G	FG	3FG	FT	Pts.
Travis Grant, Kentucky St. (II)	1972	4	121	1,760	—	525	4,045
Bob Hopkins, Grambling (II)	1956	4	126	1,403	—	953	3,759
Pete Maravich, LSU (I)	1970	3	83	1,387	—	893	3,667
Dwight Lamar, La.-Lafayette (II & I)	1973	4	112	1,445	—	603	3,493
Tony Smith, Pfeiffer (II)	1992	4	126	1,150	431	619	3,350
Earnest Lee, Clark Atlanta (II)	1987	4	115	1,270	35	723	3,298
Joe Miller, Alderson-Broaddus (II)	1957	4	129	1,082	—	1,130	3,294
John Rinka, Kenyon (II)	1970	4	99	1,261	—	729	3,251
Freeman Williams, Portland St. (I)	1978	4	106	1,369	—	511	3,249
Lionel Simmons, La Salle (I)	1990	4	131	1,244	56	673	3,217
Dick Barnett, Tennessee St. (II)	1959	4	136	1,312	—	585	3,209
Alphonso Ford, Mississippi Val. (I)	1993	4	109	1,121	333	590	3,165
Willie Scott, Alabama St. (II)	1969	4	103	1,277	—	601	3,155
Harry Kelly, Texas Southern (I)	1983	4	110	1,234	—	598	3,066
Keydren Clark, St. Peter's (I)	2006	4	118	967	435	689	3,058
Johnnie Allen, Bethune-Cookman (II)	1969	4	111	1,306	—	446	3,058
Bennie Swain, Texas Southern (II)	1958	4	137	1,157	—	694	3,008
Hersey Hawkins, Bradley (I)	1988	4	125	1,100	118	690	3,008
Rich Fuqua, Oral Roberts (II & I)	1973	4	111	1,273	—	458	3,004
Lambert Shell, Bridgeport (II)	1992	4	132	1,102	22	775	3,001
Oscar Robertson, Cincinnati (I)	1960	3	88	1,052	—	869	2,973
Carl Hartman, Alderson-Broaddus (II)	1955	4	118	1,124	—	711	2,959
Danny Manning, Kansas (I)	1988	4	147	1,216	10	509	2,951
Andre Foreman, Salisbury (III)	1992	5	109	1,141	68	592	2,940
Earl Monroe, Winston-Salem (II)	1967	4	110	1,158	—	619	2,935
Alfredrick Hughes, Loyola (Ill.) (I)	1985	4	120	1,226	—	462	2,914

SCORING AVERAGE
(Minimum 1,500 points)

Player, Team (Division)	Last Season	Yrs.	G	FG	3FG	FT	Pts.	Avg.
Pete Maravich, LSU (I)	1970	3	83	1,387	—	893	3,667	44.2
Austin Carr, Notre Dame (I)	1971	3	74	1,017	—	526	2,560	34.6
Oscar Robertson, Cincinnati (I)	1960	3	88	1,052	—	869	2,973	33.8
Travis Grant, Kentucky St. (II)	1972	4	121	1,760	—	525	4,045	33.4
Calvin Murphy, Niagara (I)	1970	3	77	947	—	654	2,548	33.1
John Rinka, Kenyon (II)	1970	4	99	1,261	—	729	3,251	32.8
Dwain Govan, Bishop (II)	1975	2	55	750	—	305	1,805	32.8
Florindo Vieira, Quinnipiac (II)	1957	4	69	761	—	741	2,263	32.8
Dwight Lamar, La.-Lafayette (I)	1973	2	57	768	—	326	1,862	32.7
Frank Selvy, Furman (I)	1954	3	78	922	—	694	2,538	32.5
Rick Mount, Purdue (I)	1970	3	72	910	—	503	2,323	32.3
Darrell Floyd, Furman (I)	1956	3	71	868	—	545	2,281	32.1
Nick Werkman, Seton Hall (I)	1964	3	71	812	—	649	2,273	32.0
Willie Humes, Idaho St. (I)	1971	2	48	565	—	380	1,510	31.5
William Averitt, Pepperdine (I)	1973	2	48	615	—	311	1,541	31.4
Elgin Baylor, Albertson/Seattle (I)	1958	3	80	956	—	588	2,500	31.3
Willie Shaw, Lane (II)	1964	4	76	960	—	459	2,379	31.3

Player, Team (Division)	Last Season	Yrs.	G	FG	3FG	FT	Pts.	Avg.
Mike Davis, Virginia Union (II)	1969	4	89	1,014	—	730	2,758	31.0
Elvin Hayes, Houston (I)	1968	3	93	1,215	—	454	2,884	31.0
Freeman Williams, Portland St. (I)	1978	4	106	1,369	—	511	3,249	30.7
Willie Scott, Alabama St. (II)	1969	4	103	1,277	—	601	3,155	30.6
Dave Russell, Shepherd (III)	1975	2	60	710	—	413	1,833	30.6
Larry Bird, Indiana St. (I)	1979	3	94	1,154	—	542	2,850	30.3
Kyle Myrick, Lincoln (Pa.) (III)	2006	2	57	667	78	309	1,721	30.2
Carlos Knox, IUPUI (II)	1998	4	85	832	208	684	2,556	30.1
George Gilmore, Chaminade (II)	1992	2	51	485	174	387	1,531	30.0

FIELD-GOAL PERCENTAGE
(Minimum 400 field goals)

Player, Team (Division)	Last Season	Yrs.	G	FG	FGA	Pct.
Tony Rychlec, Mass. Maritime (III)	1983	3	55	509	692	73.6
Pete Metzelaars, Wabash (III)	1982	4	103	784	1,083	72.4
Todd Linder, Tampa (II)	1987	4	122	909	1,284	70.8
Tom Schurfranz, Bellarmine (II)	1992	4	112	742	1,057	70.2
Chad Scott, California (Pa.) (II)	1994	4	115	465	664	70.0
Brian Schmitting, Ripon (III)	2007	4	78	418	602	69.4
Ricky Nedd, Appalachian St. (I)	1994	4	113	412	597	69.0
Ed Phillips, Alabama A&M (II)	1971	4	95	610	885	68.9
Stephen Scheffler, Purdue (I)	1990	4	110	408	596	68.5
Ulysses Hackett, S.C. Upstate (II)	1992	3	90	824	1,213	67.9
Larry Tucker, Lewis (II)	1983	3	84	677	994	67.8
Steve Johnson, Oregon St. (I)	1981	4	116	828	1,222	67.8
Michael Bradley, Kentucky/Villanova (I)	2001	4	100	441	651	67.7
Otis Evans, Wayne St. (Mich.) (II)	1992	4	106	472	697	67.7
Maurice Woods, Potsdam St. (III)	1982	3	93	559	829	67.4
Matthew Cornegay, Tuskegee (II)	1982	4	105	524	783	66.9
Earl Keith, Stony Brook (III)	1979	4	94	777	1,161	66.9
Murray Brown, Florida St. (I)	1980	4	106	566	847	66.8
Ray Strozier, Central Mo. St. (II)	1981	4	110	563	843	66.8
Dennis Edwards, Fort Hays St. (II)	1995	2	59	666	998	66.7
James Morris, Central Okla. (II)	1993	4	76	532	798	66.7
Dan Rush, Bridgewater (Va.) (III)	1995	4	102	712	1,069	66.6
Lee Campbell, Middle Tenn./Missouri St. (I)	1990	3	88	411	618	66.5
Warren Kidd, Middle Tenn. (I)	1993	3	83	496	747	66.4
Todd MacCulloch, Washington (I)	1999	4	115	702	1,058	66.4
Joe Senser, West Chester (I)	1979	4	96	476	719	66.2
Lance Berwald, North Dakota St. (II)	1984	2	58	475	717	66.2

THREE-POINT FIELD GOALS

Player, Team (Division)	Last Season	Yrs.	G	3FG
Jeff Clement, Grinnell (III)	1999	4	91	516
Amir Mazarei, Redlands (III)	2007	4	97	470
J.J. Redick, Duke (I)	2006	4	139	457
Cameron Munoz, Mont. St.-Billings (II)	2006	4	99	451
Steve Nordlund, Grinnell (III)	2004	4	97	449
Stephen Dye, Alderson-Broaddus (II)	2005	4	121	443
Steve Moyer, Gannon (II)	1999	4	112	442
Keydren Clark, St. Peter's (I)	2006	4	118	435
Tony Smith, Pfeiffer (II)	1992	4	126	431
Curtis Staples, Virginia (I)	1998	4	122	413
Kwame Morton, Clarion (II)	1994	4	105	411
Keith Veney, Lamar/Marshall (I)	1997	4	111	409
Tarvoris Uzoigwe, Henderson St. (II)	2005	4	119	404
Chris Carideo, Widener (III)	1995	4	103	402
Doug Day, Radford (I)	1993	4	117	401
Gerry McNamara, Syracuse (I)	2006	4	135	400
Michael Watson, UMKC (I)	2004	4	117	391
Gary Duda, Merrimack (II)	1992	4	122	389
Mike Taylor, West Virginia St. (II)	2004	4	116	378
Ronnie Schmitz, UMKC (I)	1993	4	112	378
Mike Hoyt, Mt. St. Mary (N.Y.) (III)	2007	4	105	376
Mark Alberts, Akron (I)	1993	4	107	375
Brett Blizzard, UNC Wilmington (I)	2003	4	125	371
Kyle Korver, Creighton (I)	2003	4	128	371
Markus Hallgrimson, Mont. St.-Billings (II)	2000	3	82	371
Steve Diekmann, Grinnell (III)	1995	4	85	371
Greg Cole, Western Conn. St. (III)	2006	4	110	367
Pat Bradley, Arkansas (I)	1999	4	132	366
Bryce Drew, Valparaiso (I)	1998	4	121	364
Jeff Fryer, Loyola Marymount (I)	1990	4	112	363

THREE-POINT FIELD GOALS PER GAME
(Minimum 200 three-point field goals)

Player, Team (Division)	Last Season	Yrs.	G	3FG	Avg.
Jeff Clement, Grinnell (III)	1999	4	91	516	5.67

Player, Team (Division)	Last Season	Yrs.	G	3FG	Avg.
Amir Mazarei, Redlands (III)	2007	4	97	470	4.85
Antonio Harris, LeMoyne-Owen (II)	1999	2	52	245	4.71
Steve Nordlund, Grinnell (III)	2004	4	97	449	4.63
Timothy Pollard, Mississippi Val. (I)	1989	2	56	256	4.57
Cameron Munoz, Mont. St.-Billings (II)	2006	4	99	451	4.56
Markus Hallgrimson, Mont. St.-Billings (II)	2000	3	82	371	4.52
Ed Brands, Grinnell (III)	1996	4	78	347	4.45
Steve Diekmann, Grinnell (III)	1995	4	85	371	4.36
Sydney Grider, La.-Lafayette (I)	1990	2	58	253	4.36
Alex Williams, Sacramento St. (II)	1988	2	58	247	4.26
Yandel Brown, Columbus St. (II)	2005	2	63	264	4.19
Tommie Spearman, Columbus St. (II)	1995	2	56	233	4.16
Reece Gliko, Mont. St.-Billings (II)	1997	2	56	231	4.13
Steve Matthews, Emerson/Wentworth Inst. (III)	2000	3	81	334	4.12
Danny Phillips, Mont. St.-Billings (II)	2002	2	55	222	4.03
Brian Merriweather, Tex.-Pan American (I)	2001	3	84	332	3.95
Steve Moyer, Gannon (II)	1999	4	112	442	3.95
Kwame Morton, Clarion (II)	1994	4	105	411	3.91
Chris Carideo, Widener (III)	1995	4	103	402	3.90
Josh Heard, Tennessee Tech (I)	2000	2	55	210	3.82
Matt Garvey, Bates (III)	1997	4	95	361	3.80
Sami Wylie, Lincoln (Pa.) (III)	2007	2	58	220	3.79
Shawn Williams, Central Okla. (II)	1991	3	57	212	3.72
Zoderick Green, Central Okla. (II)	1995	3	57	212	3.72
Kareem Townes, La Salle (I)	1995	3	81	300	3.70
Keydren Clark, St. Peter's (I)	2006	4	118	435	3.69
Keith Veney, Lamar/Marshall (I)	1997	4	111	409	3.68
Stephen Dye, Alderson-Broaddus (II)	2005	4	121	443	3.66
Mike Sinclair, Bowie St. (II)	1989	3	82	299	3.65

THREE-POINT FIELD-GOAL PERCENTAGE
(Minimum 200 three-point field goals)

Player, Team (Division)	Last Season	Yrs.	G	3FG	3FGA	Pct.
Scott Martin, Rollins (II)	1991	4	104	236	460	51.3
Jeff Seifriz, Wis.-Whitewater (III)	1989	3	85	217	423	51.3
Chris Peterson, Eureka (III)	1994	4	78	215	421	51.1
Todd Woelfle, Oakland City (II)	1998	4	103	210	412	51.0
Everett Foxx, Ferrum (III)	1992	4	104	315	630	50.0
Tony Bennett, Green Bay (I)	1992	4	118	290	584	49.7
Matt Markle, Shippensburg (II)	1992	4	101	202	408	49.5
Keith Jennings, East Tenn. St. (I)	1991	4	127	223	452	49.3
Brad Alberts, Ripon (III)	1992	4	95	277	563	49.2
Jeff Jones, Lycoming (III)	1989	3	71	232	472	49.2
Troy Greenlee, DePauw (III)	1991	4	106	232	473	49.0
Paul Cluxton, Northern Ky. (II)	1997	4	122	303	619	48.9
Lance Gelnett, Millersville (II)	1992	4	109	266	547	48.6
David Todd, Pomona-Pitzer (III)	1990	4	84	212	439	48.3
Al Callejas, Scranton (III)	2001	4	90	225	466	48.3
Antonio Harris, LeMoyne-Owen (II)	1999	2	52	245	510	48.0
Jason Bullock, Indiana (Pa.) (II)	1995	4	88	235	491	47.9
Matt Ripaldi, Southern N.H. (II)	1995	4	95	205	431	47.6
Kirk Manns, Michigan St. (I)	1990	4	120	212	446	47.5
Tim Locum, Wisconsin (I)	1991	4	118	227	481	47.2
Stephen Sir, San Diego St./ Northern Ariz. (I)	2007	5	111	323	689	46.9
Mark Willey, Fort Hays St. (II)	1992	4	117	224	478	46.9
David Olson, Eastern Ill. (I)	1992	4	111	262	562	46.6
Todd Bowden, Randolph-Macon (II)	1989	3	84	229	491	46.6
Ross Land, Northern Ariz. (I)	2000	4	117	308	664	46.4
Dan Dickau, Washington/Gonzaga (I)	2002	4	97	215	465	46.2

FREE-THROW PERCENTAGE
(Minimum 300 free throws made)

Player, Team (Division)	Last Season	Yrs.	G	FT	FTA	Pct.
Blake Ahearn, Missouri St. (I)	2007	4	129	435	460	94.6
Derek Raivio, Gonzaga (I)	2007	4	127	343	370	92.7
Andy Enfield, Johns Hopkins (III)	1991	4	108	431	466	92.5
Gary Buchanan, Villanova (I)	2003	4	122	324	355	91.3
Korey Coon, Ill. Wesleyan (III)	2000	4	109	449	492	91.3
J.J. Redick, Duke (I)	2006	4	139	662	726	91.2
Greg Starrick, Kentucky/Southern Ill. (I)	1972	4	72	341	375	90.9
Ryan Knuppel, Elmhurst (III)	2001	4	102	288	317	90.9
Jack Moore, Nebraska (I)	1982	4	105	446	495	90.1
Steve Henson, Kansas St. (I)	1990	4	127	361	401	90.0
Steve Alford, Indiana (I)	1987	4	125	535	596	89.8
Bob Lloyd, Rutgers (I)	1967	3	77	543	605	89.8
Jake Sullivan, Iowa St. (I)	2004	4	123	354	395	89.6
Jim Barton, Dartmouth (I)	1989	4	104	394	440	89.5
Al Callejas, Scranton (III)	2001	4	90	333	372	89.5

INDIVIDUAL COLLEGIATE

Player, Team (Division)	Last Season	Yrs.	G	FT	FTA	Pct.
Dave Reynolds, Davis & Elkins (II)	1989	4	107	383	429	89.3
Tommy Boyer, Arkansas (I)	1963	3	70	315	353	89.2
Kyle Korver, Creighton (I)	2003	4	128	312	350	89.1
Lance Den Boer, Central Wash. (II)/ Washington St. (I)	2007	4	94	391	439	89.1
Tim McGraw, Hartwick (III)	1988	4	107	330	371	88.9
Rob Robbins, New Mexico (I)	1991	4	133	309	348	88.8
Gerry McNamara, Syracuse (I)	2006	4	135	435	490	88.8
Brent Jolly, Tennessee Tech (I)	2003	4	123	347	391	88.7
Marcus Wilson, Evansville (I)	1999	4	119	455	513	88.7
Sean Miller, Pittsburgh (I)	1992	4	128	317	358	88.5
Ron Perry, Holy Cross (I)	1980	4	109	680	768	88.5
Joe Crispin, Penn St. (I)	2001	4	127	448	506	88.5
Joe Dykstra, Western Ill. (I)	1983	4	117	587	663	88.5
Michael Shue, Lock Haven (II)	1997	4	92	354	400	88.5
Mike Joseph, Bucknell (I)	1990	4	115	397	449	88.4

REBOUNDS

Player, Team (Division)	Last Season	Yrs.	G	Reb.
Jim Smith, Steubenville (II)	1958	4	112	2,334
Marvin Webster, Morgan St. (II)	1975	4	114	2,267
Tom Gola, La Salle (I)	1955	4	118	2,201
Major Jones, Albany St. (Ga.) (II)	1976	4	105	2,052
Joe Holup, George Washington (I)	1956	4	104	2,030
Charles Hardnett, Grambling (II)	1962	4	117	1,983
Jim Ahrens, Buena Vista (II)	1962	4	95	1,977
Elmore Smith, Kentucky St. (II)	1971	3	85	1,917
Charlie Slack, Marshall (I)	1956	4	88	1,916
Zelmo Beaty, Prairie View (II)	1962	4	97	1,916
Ed Conlin, Fordham (I)	1955	4	102	1,884
Hal Booker, Cheyney (II)	1969	4	103	1,882
Bill Thieben, Hofstra (II)	1956	3	76	1,837
Maurice Stokes, St. Francis (Pa.) (II)	1955	3	72	1,812
Dickie Hemric, Wake Forest (I)	1955	4	104	1,802
Paul Silas, Creighton (I)	1964	3	81	1,751
James Morgan, Md.-East. Shore (II)	1970	4	95	1,747
Tom Hart, Middlebury (II)	1956	3	63	1,738
Joe Casey, Boston St. (II)	1969	4	102	1,733
Art Quimby, Connecticut (I)	1955	4	80	1,716
Jerry Harper, Alabama (I)	1956	4	93	1,688
Jeff Cohen, William & Mary (I)	1961	4	103	1,679
Steve Hamilton, Morehead St. (I)	1958	4	102	1,675
Herb Lake, Youngstown St. (I)	1959	4	95	1,638
Jim Fay, St. Ambrose (II)	1953	4	95	1,633

(For careers beginning in 1973 or after)

Player, Team (Division)	Last Season	Yrs.	G	Reb.
Major Jones, Albany St. (Ga.) (II)	1976	4	105	2,052
Michael Smith, Hamilton (III)	1992	4	107	1,628
Tim Duncan, Wake Forest (I)	1997	4	128	1,570
Derrick Coleman, Syracuse (I)	1990	4	143	1,537
Malik Rose, Drexel (I)	1996	4	120	1,514
Ralph Sampson, Virginia (I)	1983	4	132	1,511
John Jordan, Southern Me. (III)	1981	4	105	1,504
Clemon Johnson, Florida A&M (II)	1978	4	109	1,494
Wayne Robertson, Southern N.H. (II)	1994	4	127	1,487
Larry Parker, Plattsburgh St. (II)	1978	4	85	1,482
Carlos Terry, Winston-Salem (II)	1978	4	117	1,467
Pete Padgett, Nevada (I)	1976	4	104	1,464
Kevin Clark, Clark (Mass.) (III)	1981	4	101	1,450
James Hector, American Int'l (II)	1994	4	115	1,446
Lionel Simmons, La Salle (I)	1990	4	131	1,429
Anthony Bonner, St. Louis (I)	1990	4	133	1,424
E.D. Schecterly, Lynchburg (III)	1980	4	104	1,404
Jeff Covington, Youngstown St. (II)	1978	4	106	1,381
Tyrone Hill, Xavier (I)	1990	4	126	1,380
Larry Sheets, East. Mennonite (III)	1983	4	105	1,378
Popeye Jones, Murray St. (I)	1992	4	123	1,374
Michael Brooks, La Salle (I)	1980	4	114	1,372
John Ebeling, Fla. Southern (II)	1982	4	127	1,362
Xavier McDaniel, Wichita St. (I)	1985	4	117	1,359
John Irving, Arizona/Hofstra (I)	1977	4	103	1,348

REBOUND AVERAGE
(Minimum 800 rebounds)

Player, Team (Division)	Last Season	Yrs.	G	Reb.	Avg.
Tom Hart, Middlebury (II)	1956	3	63	1,738	27.6
Maurice Stokes, St. Francis (Pa.) (II)	1955	3	72	1,812	25.2
Frank Stronczek, American Int'l (II)	1967	3	62	1,549	25.0
Bill Thieben, Hofstra (II)	1956	3	76	1,837	24.2
Hank Brown, Mass.-Lowell (II)	1967	3	49	1,129	23.0
Artis Gilmore, Jacksonville (I)	1970	2	54	1,224	22.7
Elmore Smith, Kentucky St. (II)	1971	3	85	1,917	22.6

Player, Team (Division)	Last Season	Yrs.	G	Reb.	Avg.
Charles Wrinn, Trinity (Conn.) (II)	1953	3	53	1,176	22.2
Roman Turmon, Clark Atlanta (II)	1954	3	60	1,312	21.9
Charlie Slack, Marshall (I)	1956	4	88	1,916	21.8
Tony Missere, Pratt (II)	1968	3	62	1,348	21.7
Ron Horton, Delaware St. (II)	1968	3	64	1,384	21.6
Paul Silas, Creighton (I)	1964	3	81	1,751	21.6
Leroy Wright, Pacific (I)	1960	3	67	1,442	21.5
Art Quimby, Connecticut (I)	1955	4	80	1,716	21.5
Walt Dukes, Seton Hall (I)	1953	2	59	1,247	21.1
Jim Smith, Steubenville (II)	1958	4	112	2,334	20.8
Jim Ahrens, Buena Vista (II)	1962	4	95	1,977	20.8
Bob Brandes, Upsala (II)	1962	3	74	1,520	20.5
Jackie Jackson, Virginia Union (II)	1961	3	66	1,351	20.5
Bill Russell, San Francisco (I)	1956	3	79	1,606	20.3
Kermit Washington, American (I)	1973	3	73	1,478	20.2
Julius Erving, Massachusetts (I)	1971	2	52	1,049	20.2
Frank Hunter, Northland (II)	1962	4	79	1,581	20.0
Marvin Webster, Morgan St. (II)	1975	4	114	2,267	19.9

(For careers beginning in 1973 or after)

Player, Team (Division)	Last Season	Yrs.	G	Reb.	Avg.
Major Jones, Albany St. (Ga.) (II)	1976	4	105	2,052	19.5
Larry Parker, Plattsburgh St. (II)	1978	4	85	1,482	17.4
Howard Shockley, Salisbury (III & II)	1976	3	76	1,299	17.1
Andre Means, Sacred Heart (II)	1978	2	62	1,009	16.3
Charles Greer, Thomas (I)	1977	3	58	926	16.0
Willie Parr, LeMoyne-Owen (III)	1976	3	76	1,182	15.6
Glenn Mosley, Seton Hall (I)	1977	4	83	1,263	15.2
Michael Smith, Hamilton (III)	1992	4	107	1,628	15.2
Dave Kufeld, Yeshiva (III)	1980	4	81	1,222	15.1
Ed Owens, Hampden-Sydney (III)	1980	4	77	1,160	15.1
Tony Rychlec, Mass. Maritime (III)	1983	3	55	812	14.8
Bill Campion, Manhattan (I)	1975	3	74	1,070	14.5
John Jordan, Southern Me. (III)	1981	4	105	1,504	14.4
Kevin Clark, Clark (Mass.) (III)	1981	4	101	1,450	14.4
Antonio Garcia, Ky. Wesleyan (II)	1999	2	70	997	14.2
Mark Veenstra, Calvin (III)	1977	4	89	1,260	14.2
Pete Padgett, Nevada (I)	1976	4	104	1,464	14.1
Anthony Fitzgerald, Villa Julie (III)	2006	4	107	1,496	14.0
Rob Roesch, Staten Island (III)	1989	2	61	850	13.9
Clemon Johnson, Florida A&M (II)	1978	4	109	1,494	13.7
Larry Johnson, Ark.-Little Rock (I)	1978	3	69	944	13.7
Carlo DeTommaso, Rhode Island Col. (III)	1976	3	72	984	13.7
Bob Warner, Maine (I)	1976	4	96	1,304	13.6
Shaquille O'Neal, LSU (I)	1992	3	90	1,217	13.5
Cornelius Cash, Bowling Green (I)	1975	3	79	1,068	13.5
E.D. Schecterly, Lynchburg (III)	1980	4	104	1,404	13.5
Ira Terrell, SMU (I)	1976	3	80	1,077	13.5

ASSISTS

Player, Team (Division)	Last Season	Yrs.	G	Ast.
Bobby Hurley, Duke (I)	1993	4	140	1,076
Demetri Beekman, Assumption (II)	1993	4	119	1,044
Chris Corchiani, North Carolina St. (I)	1991	4	124	1,038
Ed Cota, North Carolina (I)	2000	4	138	1,030
Keith Jennings, East Tenn. St. (I)	1991	4	127	983
Steve Blake, Maryland (I)	2003	4	138	972
Sherman Douglas, Syracuse (I)	1989	4	138	960
Tony Miller, Marquette (I)	1995	4	123	956
Aaron Miles, Kansas (I)	2005	4	138	954
Greg Anthony, Portland/UNLV (I)	1991	4	138	950
Doug Gottlieb, Notre Dame/Oklahoma St. (I)	2000	4	124	947
Gary Payton, Oregon St. (I)	1990	4	120	938
Adam Kaufman, Edinboro (II)	2001	4	116	936
Rob Paternostro, Southern N.H. (II)	1995	4	129	919
Tennyson Whitted, Ramapo (III)	2003	4	108	917
Steve Artis, Chris. Newport (III)	1993	4	112	909
Orlando Smart, San Francisco (I)	1994	4	116	902
Andre LaFleur, Northeastern (I)	1987	4	128	894
Chico Fletcher, Arkansas St. (I)	2000	4	114	893
Phil Dixon, Shenandoah (III)	1996	4	103	889
Jim Les, Bradley (I)	1986	4	118	884
Frank Smith, Old Dominion (I)	1988	4	120	883
Taurence Chisholm, Delaware (I)	1988	4	110	877
Grayson Marshall, Clemson (I)	1988	4	122	857
Anthony Manuel, Bradley (I)	1989	4	108	855

ASSIST AVERAGE
(Minimum 550 assists)

Player, Team (Division)	Last Season	Yrs.	G	Ast.	Avg.
Steve Ray, Bridgeport (II)	1990	2	65	785	12.08
Avery Johnson, Southern U. (I)	1988	2	61	732	12.00

Player, Team (Division)	Last Season	Yrs.	G	Ast.	Avg.
Sam Crawford, New Mexico St. (I)	1993	2	67	592	8.84
Mark Wade, Oklahoma/UNLV (I)	1987	3	79	693	8.77
Demetri Beekman, Assumption (II)	1993	4	119	1,044	8.77
Phil Dixon, Shenandoah (III)	1996	4	103	889	8.63
Tennyson Whitted, Ramapo (III)	2003	4	108	917	8.49
Chris Corchiani, North Carolina St. (I)	1991	4	124	1,038	8.37
Ernest Jenkins, N.M. Highlands (II)	1995	4	84	699	8.32
Zack Whiting, Chaminade (II)	2007	4	86	703	8.17
Steve Artis, Chris. Newport (III)	1993	4	112	909	8.12
Adam Kaufman, Edinboro (II)	2001	4	116	936	8.07
Taurence Chisholm, Delaware (I)	1988	4	110	877	7.97
Van Usher, Tennessee Tech (I)	1992	3	85	676	7.95
Anthony Manuel, Bradley (I)	1989	4	108	855	7.92
Mark Benson, Tex. A&M-Kingsville (II)	1991	3	86	674	7.84
Chico Fletcher, Arkansas St. (I)	2000	4	114	893	7.83
Pat Madden, Jacksonville St. (II)	1991	3	88	688	7.82
Gary Payton, Oregon St. (I)	1990	4	120	938	7.82
Orlando Smart, San Francisco (I)	1994	4	116	902	7.78
Tony Miller, Marquette (I)	1995	4	123	956	7.77
Keith Jennings, East Tenn. St. (I)	1991	4	127	983	7.74
Dan Ward, St. Cloud St. (II)	1995	4	100	774	7.74
Bobby Hurley, Duke (I)	1993	4	140	1,076	7.69
Doug Gottlieb, Notre Dame/Oklahoma St. (I)	2000	4	124	947	7.63
Chuck Evans, Old Dominion/Mississippi St. (I)	1993	3	85	648	7.62

BLOCKED SHOTS

Player, Team (Division)	Last Season	Yrs.	G	Blk.
Ira Nicholson, Mt. St. Vincent (III)	1997	4	100	576
Wojciech Mydra, La.-Monroe (I)	2002	4	115	535
Adonal Foyle, Colgate (I)	1997	3	87	492
Tim Duncan, Wake Forest (I)	1997	4	128	481
Alonzo Mourning, Georgetown (I)	1992	4	120	453
Tarvis Williams, Hampton (II)	2001	4	114	452
Ken Johnson, Ohio St. (I)	2001	4	127	444
Deng Gai, Fairfield (I)	2005	4	100	442
Emeka Okafor, Connecticut (I)	2004	3	103	441
Antoine Hyman, Keuka (III)	1997	4	101	440
Lorenzo Coleman, Tennessee Tech (I)	1997	4	113	437
Calvin Booth, Penn St. (I)	1999	4	114	428
Troy Murphy, Notre Dame (I)	2001	3	94	425
Theo Ratliff, Wyoming (I)	1995	4	111	425
Etan Thomas, Syracuse (I)	2000	4	122	424
Shelden Williams, Duke (I)	2006	4	139	422
Rodney Blake, St. Joseph's (I)	1988	4	116	419
James Doyle, Concord (II)	1998	4	120	416
Shaquille O'Neal, LSU (I)	1992	3	90	412
Kevin Roberson, Vermont (I)	1992	4	112	409
Bilal Salaam, Kutztown (II)	2005	4	109	408
Derek Moore, S.C.-Aiken (II)	1999	4	102	408
Stephane Lasme, Massachusetts (I)	2007	4	118	399
Jim McIlvaine, Marquette (I)	1994	4	118	399
D'or Fischer, Northwestern St./West Virginia (I)	2005	4	127	392
Tim Perry, Temple (I)	1988	4	130	392
Jason Lawson, Villanova (I)	1997	4	131	375
Pervis Ellison, Louisville (I)	1989	4	136	374
Peter Aluma, Liberty (I)	1997	4	119	366
Acie Earl, Iowa (I)	1993	3	116	365

BLOCKED-SHOT AVERAGE
(Minimum 200 blocked shots)

Player, Team (Division)	Last Season	Yrs.	G	Blk.	Avg.
Neil Edwards, York (N.Y.) (III)	2000	3	55	337	6.13
Ira Nicholson, Mt. St. Vincent (III)	1997	4	100	576	5.76
Adonal Foyle, Colgate (I)	1997	3	87	492	5.66
John Bunch, Lincoln (Pa.) (III)	2004	2	48	265	5.52
David Robinson, Navy (I)	1987	2	67	351	5.24
Shacun Malave, City Tech (III)	2005	2	53	272	5.13
Wojciech Mydra, La.-Monroe (I)	2002	4	115	535	4.65
Shaquille O'Neal, LSU (I)	1992	3	90	412	4.58
Troy Murphy, Notre Dame (I)	2001	3	94	425	4.52
Jerome James, Florida A&M (I)	1998	3	81	363	4.48
Deng Gai, Fairfield (I)	2005	4	100	442	4.42
Antoine Hyman, Keuka (III)	1997	4	101	440	4.36
Andrew South, NJIT (III)	1995	3	80	344	4.30
Emeka Okafor, Connecticut (I)	2004	3	103	441	4.28
Justin Williams, Wyoming (I)	2006	2	58	244	4.21
Antonio Ramos, Clarke (III)	2003	3	77	318	4.13
Justin Rowe, Maine (I)	2003	2	55	226	4.11
Johnny Woods, Wesley (III)	2002	4	78	319	4.09
Derek Moore, S.C.-Aiken (II)	1999	4	102	408	4.00

Player, Team (Division)	Last Season	Yrs.	G	Blk.	Avg.
Tarvis Williams, Hampton (I)	2001	4	114	452	3.96
Ifesinachi Anosike, Salem St. (III)	2005	2	56	221	3.95
Lorenzo Coleman, Tennessee Tech (I)	1997	4	113	437	3.87
Theo Ratliff, Wyoming (I)	1995	4	111	425	3.83
John Burke, Southampton (II)	1996	2	54	205	3.80
Alonzo Mourning, Georgetown (I)	1992	4	120	453	3.78
Kino Outlaw, Mount Olive (II)	1996	3	81	305	3.77
Calvin Booth, Penn St. (I)	1999	4	114	428	3.75
Bilal Salaam, Kutztown (II)	2005	4	109	408	3.74
Mike Mientus, Allentown (III)	1997	4	87	324	3.72
Tarvis Williams, Hampton (I)	2000	3	82	305	3.72

STEALS

Player, Team (Division)	Last Season	Yrs.	G	Stl.
Tennyson Whitted, Ramapo (III)	2003	4	108	448
John Gallogly, Salve Regina (III)	1998	4	98	413
John Linehan, Providence (I)	2002	5	122	385
Eddin Santiago, Mo. Southern St. (II)	2002	4	117	383
Daniel Martinez, McMurry (III)	2000	3	76	380
Eric Murdock, Providence (I)	1991	4	117	376
Ivo Moyano, Polytechnic (N.Y.) (III)	1997	4	87	368
Pepe Sanchez, Temple (I)	2000	4	116	365
Benny West, Howard Payne (III)	2004	4	98	363
Oronn Brown, Clarion (II)	1997	4	106	361
Robert Campbell, Armstrong Atlantic (II)	2001	4	118	357
Eric Bell, New Paltz St. (III)	1996	4	94	355
Cookie Belcher, Nebraska (I)	2001	5	131	353
Kevin Braswell, Georgetown (I)	2002	4	128	349
Keith Darden, Concordia (Tex.) (III)	2005	4	90	348
Bonzi Wells, Ball St. (I)	1998	4	116	347
Obie Trotter, Alabama A&M (I)	2006	4	114	346
Scott Clarke, Utica (III)	1996	4	96	346
Marcus Best, Winston-Salem (II)	2002	4	119	345
Gerald Walker, San Francisco (I)	1996	4	111	344
Johnny Rhodes, Maryland (I)	1996	4	122	344
Michael Anderson, Drexel (I)	1988	4	115	341
Kenny Robertson, Cleveland St. (I)	1990	4	119	341
Shaun McKie, Salem Int'l (II)	2007	4	113	340
Jeff Mikos, Milwaukee Engr. (III)	2006	4	105	340
Keith Jennings, East Tenn. St. (I)	1991	4	127	334
Juan Dixon, Maryland (I)	2002	4	141	333
Devlin Herring, Pitt.-Johnstown (II)	1998	4	106	333
Desmond Cambridge, Alabama A&M (I)	2002	3	84	330
Jason Hart, Syracuse (I)	2000	4	132	329
Greg Anthony, Portland/UNLV (I)	1991	4	138	329

STEAL AVERAGE
(Minimum 200 steals)

Player, Team (Division)	Last Season	Yrs.	G	Stl.	Avg.
Moses Jean-Pierre, Plymouth St. (III)	1994	2	55	303	5.51
Daniel Martinez, McMurry (III)	2000	3	76	380	5.00
Wayne Copeland, Lynn (II)	2000	2	57	254	4.46
Ivo Moyano, Polytechnic (N.Y.) (III)	1997	4	87	368	4.23
Mario Thompson, Occidental (III)	2001	3	71	300	4.23
John Gallogly, Salve Regina (III)	1998	4	98	413	4.21
Tennyson Whitted, Ramapo (III)	2003	4	108	448	4.15
Greg Dean, Concordia-M'head (III)	1997	3	75	307	4.09
Desmond Cambridge, Alabama A&M (I)	2002	3	84	330	3.93
Keith Darden, Concordia (Tex.) (III)	2005	4	90	348	3.87
Mookie Blaylock, Oklahoma (I)	1989	2	74	281	3.80
Eric Bell, New Paltz St. (III)	1996	4	94	355	3.78
Benny West, Howard Payne (III)	2004	4	98	363	3.70
Scott Clarke, Utica (III)	1996	4	96	346	3.60
Ricky Hollis, Brockport St. (III)	2002	4	90	322	3.58
Ronn McMahon, Eastern Wash. (I)	1990	3	64	225	3.52
Gerald Garlic, Goucher (III)	1995	3	70	244	3.49
Darrel Lewis, Lincoln (Pa.) (III)	1999	4	86	298	3.47
Oronn Brown, Clarion (II)	1997	4	106	361	3.41
Patrick Herron, Winston-Salem (II)	1995	3	78	263	3.37
David Clark, Bluefield St. (II)	1996	3	83	278	3.35
Eddin Santiago, Mo. Southern St. (II)	2002	4	117	383	3.27
Shuron Woodyard, Villa Julie (III)	1997	3	73	238	3.26
Jeff Mikos, Milwaukee Engr. (III)	2006	4	105	340	3.24
Shawn McCartney, Hunter (III)	1995	3	81	261	3.22
Carl Small, Cornell College (III)	1995	3	69	222	3.22
Eric Murdock, Providence (I)	1991	4	117	376	3.21
Ken Francis, Molloy (II)	1995	3	81	260	3.21

Award Winners

Division I Consensus All-American Selections

By Season

1929
Charley Hyatt, Pittsburgh; Joe Schaaf, Penn; Charles Murphy, Purdue; Vern Corbin, California; Thomas Churchill, Oklahoma; John Thompson, Montana St.

1930
Charley Hyatt, Pittsburgh; Charles Murphy, Purdue; Branch McCracken, Indiana; John Thompson, Montana St.; Frank Ward, Montana St.; John Wooden, Purdue.

1931
John Wooden, Purdue; Joe Reiff, Northwestern; George Gregory, Columbia; Wes Fesler, Ohio St.; Elwood Romney, BYU.

1932
Forest Sale, Kentucky; Ed Krause, Notre Dame; John Wooden, Purdue; Louis Berger, Maryland; Les Witte, Wyoming.

1933
Forest Sale, Kentucky; Don Smith, Pittsburgh; Elliott Loughlin, Navy; Joe Reiff, Northwestern; Ed Krause, Notre Dame; Jerry Nemer, Southern California

1934
Claire Cribbs, Pittsburgh; Ed Krause, Notre Dame; Les Witte, Wyoming; Hal Lee, Washington; Norman Cottom, Purdue.

1935
Jack Gray, Texas; Lee Guttero, Southern California; Claire Cribbs, Pittsburgh; Bud Browning, Oklahoma; Leroy Edwards, Kentucky.

1936
Bob Kessler, Purdue; Paul Nowak, Notre Dame; Hank Luisetti, Stanford; Vern Huffman, Indiana; John Moir, Notre Dame; Ike Poole, Arkansas; Bill Kinner, Utah.

1937
Hank Luisetti, Stanford; Paul Nowak, Notre Dame; Jules Bender, Long Island; John Moir, Notre Dame; Jewell Young, Purdue.

1938
Hank Luisetti, Stanford; John Moir, Notre Dame; Fred Pralle, Kansas; Jewell Young, Purdue; Paul Nowak, Notre Dame; Meyer Bloom, Temple.

1939
First Team—Irving Torgoff, Long Island; Urgel Wintermute, Oregon; Chet Jaworski, Rhode Island; Ernie Andres, Indiana; Jimmy Hull, Ohio St.
Second Team—Bob Calihan, Detroit; Michael Novak, Loyola (Ill.); Bernard Opper, Kentucky; Robert Anet, Oregon; Bob Hassmiller, Fordham.

1940
First Team—Ralph Vaughn, Southern California; John Dick, Oregon; Bill Hapac, Illinois; George Glamack, North Carolina; Gus Broberg, Dartmouth.
Second Team—Jack Harvey, Colorado; Marvin Huffman, Indiana; James McNatt, Oklahoma; Jesse Renick, Oklahoma St.

1941
First Team—Gus Broberg, Dartmouth; John Adams, Arkansas; Howard Engleman, Kansas; George Glamack, North Carolina; Gene Englund, Wisconsin.
Second Team—Frank Baumholtz, Ohio; Paul Lindeman, Washington St.; Oscar Schechtman, Long Island; Robert Kinney, Rice; Stan Modzelewski, Rhode Island.

1942
First Team—John Kotz, Wisconsin; Price Brookfield, West Tex. A&M; Bob Kinney, Rice; Andrew Phillip, Illinois; Robert Davies, Seton Hall.
Second Team—Robert Doll, Colorado; Wilfred Doerner, Evansville; Donald Burness, Stanford; George Munroe, Dartmouth; Stan Modzelewski, Rhode Island; John Mandic, Oregon St.

1943
First Team—Andrew Phillip, Illinois; George Senesky, St. Joseph's; Ken Sailors, Wyoming; Harry Boykoff, St. John's (N.Y.); Charles Black, Kansas; Ed Beisser, Creighton; William Closs, Rice.

Second Team—Gerald Tucker, Oklahoma; Bob Rensberger, Notre Dame; Gene Rock, Southern California; John Kotz, Wisconsin; Otto Graham, Northwestern; Gale Bishop, Washington St.

1944
First Team—George Mikan, DePaul; Audley Brindley, Dartmouth; Otto Graham, Northwestern; Robert Brannum, Kentucky; Alva Paine, Oklahoma; Robert Kurland, Oklahoma St.; Leo Klier, Notre Dame.
Second Team—Arnold Ferrin, Utah; Dale Hall, Army; Don Grate, Ohio St.; Bob Dille, Valparaiso; William Henry, Rice; Dick Triptow, DePaul.

1945
First Team—George Mikan, DePaul; Robert Kurland, Oklahoma St.; Arnold Ferrin, Utah; Walton Kirk, Illinois; William Hassett, Notre Dame; William Henry, Rice; Howard Dallmar, Penn; Wyndol Gray, Bowling Green.
Second Team—Richard Ives, Iowa; Vince Hanson, Washington St.; Dale Hall, Army; Max Norris, Northwestern; Don Grate, Ohio St.; Herb Wilkinson, Iowa.

1946
First Team—George Mikan, DePaul; Robert Kurland, Oklahoma St.; Leo Klier, Notre Dame; Max Norris, Northwestern; Sid Tanenbaum, New York U.
Second Team—Jack Parkinson, Kentucky; John Dillon, North Carolina; Ken Sailors, Wyoming; Charles Black, Kansas; Tony Lavelli, Yale; William Hassett, Notre Dame.

1947
First Team—Ralph Beard, Kentucky; Gerald Tucker, Oklahoma; Alex Groza, Kentucky; Sid Tanenbaum, New York U.; Ralph Hamilton, Indiana.
Second Team—George Kaftan, Holy Cross; John Hargis, Texas; Don Barksdale, UCLA; Arnold Ferrin, Utah; Andrew Phillip, Illinois; Ed Koffenberger, Duke; Vern Gardner, Utah.

1948
First Team—Murray Wier, Iowa, 5-9, Muscatine, IA; Ed Macauley, St. Louis, 6-8, St. Louis; Jim McIntyre, Minnesota, 6-10, Minneapolis; Kevin O'Shea, Notre Dame, 6-1, San Francisco; Ralph Beard, Kentucky, 5-10, Louisville, KY.
Second Team—Dick Dickey, North Carolina St.; Arnold Ferrin, Utah; Alex Groza, Kentucky; Harold Haskins, Hamline; George Kaftan, Holy Cross; Duane Klueh, Indiana St.; Tony Lavelli, Yale; Jack Nichols, Washington; Andy Wolfe, California.

1949
First Team—Tony Lavelli, Yale, 6-3, Somerville, MA; Vince Boryla, Denver, 6-5, East Chicago, IN; Ed Macauley, St. Louis, 6-8, St. Louis; Alex Groza, Kentucky, 6-7, Martin's Ferry, OH; Ralph Beard, Kentucky, 5-10, Louisville, KY.
Second Team—Bill Erickson, Illinois; Vern Gardner, Utah; Wallace Jones, Kentucky; Jim McIntyre, Minnesota; Ernie Vandeweghe, Colgate.

1950
First Team—Dick Schnittker, Ohio St., 6-5, Sandusky, OH; Bob Cousy, Holy Cross, 6-1, St. Albans, NY; Paul Arizin, Villanova, 6-3, Philadelphia; Paul Unruh, Bradley, 6-4, Toulon, IL; Bill Sharman, Southern California, 6-2, Porterville, CA.
Second Team—Charles Cooper, Duquesne; Don Lofgran, San Francisco; Kevin O'Shea, Notre Dame; Don Rehfeldt, Wisconsin; Sherman White, Long Island.

1951
First Team—Bill Mlkvy, Temple, 6-4, Palmerton, PA; Sam Ranzino, North Carolina St., 6-1, Gary, IN; Bill Spivey, Kentucky, 7-0, Macon, GA; Clyde Lovellette, Kansas, 6-9, Terre Haute, IN; Gene Melchiorre, Bradley, 5-8, Highland Park, IL.
Second Team—Ernie Barrett, Kansas St.; Bill Garrett, Indiana; Dick Groat, Duke; Mel Hutchins, BYU; Gale McArthur, Oklahoma St.

1952
First Team—Cliff Hagan, Kentucky, 6-4, Owensboro, KY; Rod Fletcher, Illinois, 6-4, Champaign, IL; Chuck Darling, Iowa, 6-8, Denver; Clyde Lovellette, Kansas, 6-9, Terre Haute, IN; Dick Groat, Duke, 6-0, Swissvale, PA.
Second Team—Bob Houbregs, Washington; Don Meineke, Dayton; Johnny O'Brien, Seattle; Mark Workman, West Virginia; Bob Zawoluk, St. John's (N.Y.).

1953
First Team—Ernie Beck, Penn, 6-4, Philadelphia; Bob Houbregs, Washington, 6-7, Seattle; Walt Dukes, Seton Hall, 6-11, Rochester, NY; Tom Gola, La Salle, 6-6, Philadelphia; Johnny O'Brien, Seattle, 5-8, South Amboy, NJ.
Second Team—Dick Knostman, Kansas St.; Bob Pettit, LSU; Joe Richey, BYU; Don Schlundt, Indiana; Frank Selvy, Furman.

1954
First Team—Frank Selvy, Furman, 6-3, Corbin, KY; Tom Gola, La Salle, 6-6, Philadelphia; Don Schlundt, Indiana, 6-10, South Bend, IN; Bob Pettit, LSU, 6-9, Baton Rouge, LA; Cliff Hagan, Kentucky, 6-4, Owensboro, KY.
Second Team—Bob Leonard, Indiana; Tom Marshall, Western Ky.; Bob Mattick, Oklahoma St.; Frank Ramsey, Kentucky; Dick Ricketts, Duquesne.

1955
First Team—Tom Gola, La Salle, 6-6, Philadelphia; Dick Ricketts, Duquesne, 6-8, Pottstown, PA; Bill Russell, San Francisco, 6-9, Oakland, CA; Si Green, Duquesne, 6-3, Brooklyn, NY; Dick Garmaker, Minnesota, 6-3, Hibbing, MN.
Second Team—Darrell Floyd, Furman; Robin Freeman, Ohio St.; Dickie Hemric, Wake Forest; Don Schlundt, Indiana; Ron Shavlik, North Carolina St.

1956
First Team—Tom Heinsohn, Holy Cross, 6-7, Union City, NJ; Ron Shavlik, North Carolina St., 6-9, Denver; Bill Russell, San Francisco, 6-9, Oakland, CA; Si Green, Duquesne, 6-3, Brooklyn, NY; Robin Freeman, Ohio St., 5-11, Cincinnati.
Second Team—Bob Burrow, Kentucky; Darrell Floyd, Furman; Rod Hundley, West Virginia; K.C. Jones, San Francisco; Willie Naulls, UCLA; Bill Uhl, Dayton.

1957
First Team—Rod Hundley, West Virginia, 6-4, Charleston, WV; Lenny Rosenbluth, North Carolina, 6-5, New York; Jim Krebs, SMU, 6-8, Webster Groves, MO; Wilt Chamberlain, Kansas, 7-0, Philadelphia; Charlie Tyra, Louisville, 6-8, Louisville, KY; Chet Forte, Columbia, 5-9, Hackensack, NJ.
Second Team—Elgin Baylor, Seattle; Frank Howard, Ohio St.; Guy Rodgers, Temple; Gary Thompson, Iowa St.; Grady Wallace, South Carolina

1958
First Team—Bob Boozer, Kansas St., 6-8, Omaha, NE; Elgin Baylor, Seattle, 6-6, Washington, DC; Wilt Chamberlain, Kansas, 7-0, Philadelphia; Oscar Robertson, Cincinnati, 6-5, Indianapolis; Guy Rodgers, Temple, 6-0, Philadelphia; Don Hennon, Pittsburgh, 5-9, Wampum, PA.
Second Team—Pete Brennan, North Carolina; Archie Dees, Indiana; Dave Gambee, Oregon St.; Mike Farmer, San Francisco; Bailey Howell, Mississippi St.

1959
First Team—Bailey Howell, Mississippi St., 6-7, Middleton, TN; Bob Boozer, Kansas St., 6-8, Omaha, NE; Oscar Robertson, Cincinnati, 6-5, Indianapolis; Jerry West, West Virginia, 6-3, Cabin Creek, WV; Johnny Cox, Kentucky, 6-4, Hazard, KY.
Second Team—Leo Byrd, Marshall; Johnny Green, Michigan St.; Tom Hawkins, Notre Dame; Don Hennon, Pittsburgh; Alan Seiden, St. John's (N.Y.).

1960
First Team—Oscar Robertson, Cincinnati, 6-5, Indianapolis; Jerry West, West Virginia, 6-3, Cabin Creek, WV; Jerry Lucas, Ohio St., 6-8, Middletown, OH; Darrall Imhoff, California, 6-10, Alhambra, CA; Tom Stith, St. Bonaventure, 6-5, Brooklyn, NY.
Second Team—Terry Dischinger, Purdue; Tony Jackson, St. John's (N.Y.); Roger Kaiser, Georgia Tech; Lee Shaffer, North Carolina; Len Wilkens, Providence.

1961
First Team—Jerry Lucas, Ohio St., 6-8, Middletown, OH; Tom Stith, St. Bonaventure, 6-5, Brooklyn, NY; Terry Dischinger, Purdue, 6-7, Terre Haute, IN; Roger Kaiser, Georgia Tech, 6-1, Dale, IN; Chet Walker, Bradley, 6-6, Benton Harbor, MI.
Second Team—Walt Bellamy, Indiana; Frank Burgess, Gonzaga; Tony Jackson, St. John's (N.Y.); Billy McGill, Utah; Larry Siegfried, Ohio St.

1962
First Team—Jerry Lucas, Ohio St., 6-8, Middletown, OH; Len Chappell, Wake Forest, 6-8, Portage Area, PA; Billy McGill, Utah, 6-9, Los Angeles; Terry Dischinger, Purdue, 6-7, Terre Haute, IN; Chet Walker, Bradley, 6-6, Benton Harbor, MI.

Second Team—Jack Foley, Holy Cross; John Havlicek, Ohio St.; Art Heyman, Duke; Cotton Nash, Kentucky; John Rudometkin, Southern California; Rod Thorn, West Virginia.

1963
First Team—Art Heyman, Duke, 6-5, Rockville Center, NY; Ron Bonham, Cincinnati, 6-5, Muncie, IN; Barry Kramer, New York U., 6-4, Schenectady, NY; Jerry Harkness, Loyola (Ill.), 6-3, New York; Tom Thacker, Cincinnati, 6-2, Covington, KY.

Second Team—Gary Bradds, Ohio St.; Bill Green, Colorado St.; Cotton Nash, Kentucky; Rod Thorn, West Virginia; Nate Thurmond, Bowling Green.

1964
First Team—Bill Bradley, Princeton, 6-5, Crystal City, MO; Dave Stallworth, Wichita St., 6-7, Dallas; Gary Bradds, Ohio St., 6-8, Jamestown, OH; Walt Hazzard, UCLA, 6-2, Philadelphia; Cotton Nash, Kentucky, 6-5, Leominster, MA.

Second Team—Ron Bonham, Cincinnati; Mel Counts, Oregon St.; Fred Hetzel, Davidson; Jeff Mullins, Duke; Cazzie Russell, Michigan.

1965
First Team—Bill Bradley, Princeton, 6-5, Crystal City, MO; Rick Barry, Miami (Fla.), 6-7, Roselle Park, NJ; Fred Hetzel, Davidson, 6-8, Washington, DC; Cazzie Russell, Michigan, 6-5, Chicago; Gail Goodrich, UCLA, 6-1, North Hollywood, CA.

Second Team—Bill Buntin, Michigan; Wayne Estes, Utah St.; Clyde Lee, Vanderbilt; Dave Schellhase, Purdue; Dave Stallworth, Wichita St.

1966
First Team—Dave Bing, Syracuse, 6-3, Washington, DC; Dave Schellhase, Purdue, 6-4, Evansville, IN; Clyde Lee, Vanderbilt, 6-9, Nashville, TN; Cazzie Russell, Michigan, 6-5, Chicago; Jim Walker, Providence, 6-3, Boston.

Second Team—Lou Dampier, Kentucky; Matt Guokas, St. Joseph's; Jack Marin, Duke; Dick Snyder, Davidson; Bob Verga, Duke; Walt Wesley, Kansas.

1967
First Team—Lew Alcindor, UCLA, 7-2, New York; Elvin Hayes, Houston, 6-8, Rayville, LA; Wes Unseld, Louisville, 6-8, Louisville, KY; Jim Walker, Providence, 6-3, Boston; Clem Haskins, Western Ky., 6-3, Campbellsville, KY; Bob Lloyd, Rutgers, 6-1, Upper Darby, PA; Bob Verga, Duke, 6-0, Sea Girt, NJ.

Second Team—Mel Daniels, New Mexico; Sonny Dove, St. John's (N.Y.); Larry Miller, North Carolina; Don May, Dayton; Lou Dampier, Kentucky.

1968
First Team—Wes Unseld, Louisville, 6-8, Louisville, KY; Elvin Hayes, Houston, 6-8, Rayville, LA; Lew Alcindor, UCLA, 7-2, New York; Pete Maravich, LSU, 6-5, Raleigh, NC; Larry Miller, North Carolina, 6-4, Catasaqua, PA.

Second Team—Lucius Allen, UCLA; Bob Lanier, St. Bonaventure; Don May, Dayton; Calvin Murphy, Niagara; Jo Jo White, Kansas.

1969
First Team—Lew Alcindor, UCLA, 7-2, New York; Spencer Haywood, Detroit, 6-8, Detroit; Pete Maravich, LSU, 6-5, Raleigh, NC; Rick Mount, Purdue, 6-4, Lebanon, IN; Calvin Murphy, Niagara, 5-10, Norwalk, CT.

Second Team—Dan Issel, Kentucky; Mike Maloy, Davidson; Bud Ogden, Santa Clara; Charlie Scott, North Carolina; Jo Jo White, Kansas.

1970
First Team—Pete Maravich, LSU, 6-5, Raleigh, NC; Rick Mount, Purdue, 6-4, Lebanon, IN; Bob Lanier, St. Bonaventure, 6-11, Buffalo, NY; Dan Issel, Kentucky, 6-9, Batavia, IL; Calvin Murphy, Niagara, 5-10, Norwalk, CT.

Second Team—Austin Carr, Notre Dame; Jim Collins, New Mexico St.; John Roche, South Carolina; Charlie Scott, North Carolina; Sidney Wicks, UCLA.

1971
First Team—Austin Carr, Notre Dame, 6-3, Washington, DC; Sidney Wicks, UCLA, 6-8, Los Angeles; Artis Gilmore, Jacksonville, 7-2, Dothan, AL; Dean Meminger, Marquette, 6-1, New York; Jim McDaniels, Western Ky., 7-0, Scottsville, KY.

Second Team—John Roche, South Carolina; Johnny Neumann, Mississippi; Ken Durrett, La Salle; Howard Porter, Villanova; Curtis Rowe, UCLA.

1972
First Team—Bill Walton, UCLA, 6-11, La Mesa, CA; Dwight Lamar, La.-Lafayette, 6-1, Columbus, OH; Ed Ratleff, Long Beach St., 6-6, Columbus, OH; Bob McAdoo, North Carolina, 6-8, Greensboro, NC; Tom Riker, South Carolina, 6-10, Oyster Bay, NY; Jim Chones, Marquette, 6-11, Racine, WI; Henry Bibby, UCLA, 6-1, Franklinton, NC.

Second Team—Barry Parkhill, Virginia; Jim Price, Louisville; Bud Stallworth, Kansas; Henry Willmore, Michigan; Rich Fuqua, Oral Roberts.

1973
First Team—Doug Collins, Illinois St., 6-6, Benton, IL; Ed Ratleff, Long Beach St., 6-6, Columbus, OH; Dwight Lamar, La.-Lafayette, 6-1, Columbus, OH; Bill Walton, UCLA, 6-11, La Mesa, CA; Ernie DiGregorio, Providence, 6-0, North Providence, RI; David Thompson, North Carolina St., 6-4, Shelby, NC; Keith Wilkes, UCLA, 6-6, Santa Barbara, CA.

Second Team—Jim Brewer, Minnesota; Kevin Joyce, South Carolina; Kermit Washington, American; Tom Burleson, North Carolina St.; Larry Finch, Memphis; Tom McMillen, Maryland.

1974
First Team—Keith Wilkes, UCLA, 6-6, Santa Barbara, CA; John Shumate, Notre Dame, 6-9, Elizabeth, NJ; Bill Walton, UCLA, 6-11, La Mesa, CA; David Thompson, North Carolina St., 6-4, Shelby, NC; Marvin Barnes, Providence, 6-9, Providence, RI.

Second Team—Len Elmore, Maryland; Bobby Jones, North Carolina; Bill Knight, Pittsburgh; Larry Fogle, Canisius; Campy Russell, Michigan.

1975
First Team—David Thompson, North Carolina St., 6-4, Shelby, NC; Adrian Dantley, Notre Dame, 6-5, Washington, DC; Scott May, Indiana, 6-7, Sandusky, OH; John Lucas, Maryland, 6-4, Durham, NC; Dave Meyers, UCLA, 6-8, La Habra, CA.

Second Team—Luther Burden, Utah; Kevin Grevey, Kentucky; Leon Douglas, Alabama; Gus Williams, Southern California; Ron Lee, Oregon.

1976
First Team—Scott May, Indiana, 6-7, Sandusky, OH; Richard Washington, UCLA, 6-10, Portland, OR; John Lucas, Maryland, 6-4, Durham, NC; Kent Benson, Indiana, 6-11, New Castle, IN; Adrian Dantley, Notre Dame, 6-5, Washington, DC.

Second Team—Mitch Kupchak, North Carolina; Phil Sellers, Rutgers; Phil Ford, North Carolina; Earl Tatum, Marquette; Bernard King, Tennessee.

1977
First Team—Otis Birdsong, Houston, 6-4, Winter Haven, FL; Marques Johnson, UCLA, 6-7, Los Angeles; Kent Benson, Indiana, 6-11, New Castle, IN; Rickey Green, Michigan, 6-2, Chicago; Phil Ford, North Carolina, 6-2, Rocky Mount, NC; Bernard King, Tennessee, 6-7, Brooklyn, NY.

Second Team—Phil Hubbard, Michigan; Mychal Thompson, Minnesota; Ernie Grunfeld, Tennessee; Greg Ballard, Oregon; Rod Griffin, Wake Forest; Butch Lee, Marquette; Bill Cartwright, San Francisco.

1978
First Team—Phil Ford, North Carolina, 6-2, Rocky Mount, NC; Butch Lee, Marquette, 6-2, Bronx, NY; David Greenwood, UCLA, 6-9, Los Angeles; Mychal Thompson, Minnesota, 6-10, Nassau, Bahamas; Larry Bird, Indiana St., 6-9, French Lick, IN.

Second Team—Jack Givens, Kentucky; Freeman Williams, Portland St.; Rick Robey, Kentucky; Ron Brewer, Arkansas; Rod Griffin, Wake Forest.

1979
First Team—Larry Bird, Indiana St., 6-9, French Lick, IN; David Greenwood, UCLA, 6-9, Los Angeles; Earvin Johnson, Michigan St., 6-8, Lansing, MI; Sidney Moncrief, Arkansas, 6-4, Little Rock, AR; Mike Gminski, Duke, 6-11, Monroe, CT.

Second Team—Bill Cartwright, San Francisco; Calvin Natt, La.-Monroe; Kelly Tripucka, Notre Dame; Mike O'Koren, North Carolina; Jim Spanarkel, Duke; Jim Paxson, Dayton; Sly Williams, Rhode Island.

1980
First Team—Mark Aguirre, DePaul, 6-7, Chicago; Michael Brooks, La Salle, 6-7, Philadelphia; Joe Barry Carroll, Purdue, 7-1, Denver; Kyle Macy, Kentucky, 6-3, Peru, IN; Darrell Griffith, Louisville, 6-4, Louisville, KY.

Second Team—Albert King, Maryland; Mike Gminski, Duke; Mike O'Koren, North Carolina; Sam Worthen, Marquette; Kelvin Ransey, Ohio St.

1981
First Team—Mark Aguirre, DePaul, 6-7, Chicago; Danny Ainge, BYU, 6-5, Eugene, OR; Steve Johnson, Oregon St., 6-11, San Bernardino, CA; Ralph Sampson, Virginia, 7-4, Harrisonburg, VA; Isiah Thomas, Indiana, 6-1, Chicago.

Second Team—Sam Bowie, Kentucky; Jeff Lamp, Virginia; Durand Macklin, LSU; Kelly Tripucka, Notre Dame; Danny Vranes, Utah; Al Wood, North Carolina.

1982
First Team—Terry Cummings, DePaul, 6-9, Chicago; Quintin Dailey, San Francisco, 6-4, Baltimore; Eric Floyd, Georgetown, 6-3, Gastonia, NC; Ralph Sampson, Virginia, 7-4, Harrisonburg, VA; James Worthy, North Carolina, 6-9, Gastonia, NC.

Second Team—Dale Ellis, Tennessee; Kevin Magee, UC Irvine; John Paxson, Notre Dame; Sam Perkins, North Carolina; Paul Pressey, Tulsa.

1983
First Team—Dale Ellis, Tennessee, 6-7, Marietta, GA; Patrick Ewing, Georgetown, 7-0, Cambridge, MA; Michael Jordan, North Carolina, 6-6, Wilmington, NC; Sam Perkins, North Carolina, 6-9, Latham, NY; Ralph Sampson, Virginia, 7-4, Harrisonburg, VA; Wayman Tisdale, Oklahoma, 6-9, Tulsa, OK; Keith Lee, Memphis, 6-9, West Memphis, AR.

Second Team—Clyde Drexler, Houston; John Paxson, Notre Dame; Steve Stipanovich, Missouri; Jon Sundvold, Missouri; Darrell Walker, Arkansas; Sidney Green, UNLV; Randy Wittman, Indiana.

1984
First Team—Wayman Tisdale, Oklahoma, 6-9, Tulsa, OK; Sam Perkins, North Carolina, 6-10, Latham, NY; Patrick Ewing, Georgetown, 7-0, Cambridge, MA; Akeem Olajuwon, Houston, 7-0, Lagos, Nigeria; Michael Jordan, North Carolina, 6-5, Wilmington, NC.

Second Team—Chris Mullin, St. John's (N.Y.); Devin Durrant, BYU; Leon Wood, Cal St. Fullerton; Keith Lee, Memphis; Melvin Turpin, Kentucky; Michael Cage, San Diego St.

1985
First Team—Wayman Tisdale, Oklahoma, 6-9, Tulsa, OK; Patrick Ewing, Georgetown, 7-0, Cambridge, MA; Keith Lee, Memphis, 6-10, West Memphis, AR; Chris Mullin, St. John's (N.Y.), 6-6, Brooklyn, NY; Xavier McDaniel, Wichita St., 6-7, Columbia, SC; Johnny Dawkins, Duke, 6-2, Washington, DC.

Second Team—Kenny Walker, Kentucky; Jon Koncak, SMU; Len Bias, Maryland; Mark Price, Georgia Tech; Dwayne Washington, Syracuse.

1986
First Team—Len Bias, Maryland, 6-8, Landover, MD; Kenny Walker, Kentucky, 6-8, Roberta, GA; Walter Berry, St. John's (N.Y.), 6-8, Bronx, NY; Johnny Dawkins, Duke, 6-2, Washington, DC; Steve Alford, Indiana, 6-2, New Castle, IN.

Second Team—Dell Curry, Virginia Tech; Brad Daugherty, North Carolina; Danny Manning, Kansas; Ron Harper, Miami (Ohio); Scott Skiles, Michigan St.; David Robinson, Navy.

1987
First Team—David Robinson, Navy, 7-1, Woodbridge, VA; Danny Manning, Kansas, 6-11, Lawrence, KS; Reggie Williams, Georgetown, 6-7, Baltimore; Steve Alford, Indiana, 6-2, New Castle, IN; Kenny Smith, North Carolina, 6-3, Queens, NY.

Second Team—Armon Gilliam, UNLV; Dennis Hopson, Ohio St.; Mark Jackson, St. John's (N.Y.); Ken Norman, Illinois; Horace Grant, Clemson.

1988

First Team—Gary Grant, Michigan, 6-3, Canton, OH; Hersey Hawkins, Bradley, 6-3, Chicago; J.R. Reid, North Carolina, 6-9, Virginia Beach, VA; Sean Elliott, Arizona, 6-8, Tucson, AZ; Danny Manning, Kansas, 6-11, Lawrence, KS.

Second Team—Mark Macon, Temple; Rony Seikaly, Syracuse; Danny Ferry, Duke; Jerome Lane, Pittsburgh; Mitch Richmond, Kansas St.; Michael Smith, BYU.

1989

First Team—Sean Elliott, Arizona, 6-8, Sr., Tucson, AZ; Pervis Ellison, Louisville, 6-9, Sr., Savannah, GA; Danny Ferry, Duke, 6-10, Sr., Bowie, MD; Chris Jackson, LSU, 6-1, Fr., Gulfport, MS; Stacey King, Oklahoma, 6-11, Sr., Lawton, OK.

Second Team—Mookie Blaylock, Oklahoma, 6-1, Sr.; Sherman Douglas, Syracuse, 6-0, Sr.; Jay Edwards, Indiana, 6-4, So.; Todd Lichti, Stanford, 6-4, Sr.; Glen Rice, Michigan, 6-7, Sr.; Lionel Simmons, La Salle, 6-6, Jr.

1990

First Team—Derrick Coleman, Syracuse, 6-10, Sr., Detroit; Chris Jackson, LSU, 6-1, So., Gulfport, MS; Larry Johnson, UNLV, 6-7, Jr., Dallas; Gary Payton, Oregon St., 6-3, Sr., Oakland, CA; Lionel Simmons, La Salle, 6-6, Sr., Philadelphia.

Second Team—Hank Gathers, Loyola Marymount, 6-7, Sr.; Kendall Gill, Illinois, 6-5, Sr.; Bo Kimble, Loyola Marymount, 6-5, Sr.; Alonzo Mourning, Georgetown, 6-10, So.; Rumeal Robinson, Michigan, 6-2, Sr.; Dennis Scott, Georgia Tech, 6-8, Jr.; Doug Smith, Missouri, 6-10, Jr.

1991

First Team—Kenny Anderson, Georgia Tech, 6-2, So., Rego Park, NY; Jim Jackson, Ohio St., 6-6, So., Toledo, OH; Larry Johnson, UNLV, 6-7, Sr., Dallas; Shaquille O'Neal, LSU, 7-1, So., San Antonio; Billy Owens, Syracuse, 6-9, Jr., Carlisle, PA.

Second Team—Stacey Augmon, UNLV, 6-8, Sr.; Keith Jennings, East Tenn. St., 5-7, Sr.; Christian Laettner, Duke, 6-11, Jr.; Eric Murdock, Providence, 6-2, Sr.; Steve Smith, Michigan St., 6-6, Sr.

1992

First Team—Jim Jackson, Ohio St., 6-6, Jr., Toledo, OH; Christian Laettner, Duke, 6-11, Sr., Angola, NY; Harold Miner, Southern California, 6-5, Jr., Inglewood, CA; Alonzo Mourning, Georgetown, 6-10, Sr., Chesapeake, VA; Shaquille O'Neal, LSU, 7-1, Jr., San Antonio.

Second Team—Byron Houston, Oklahoma St., 6-7, Sr.; Don MacLean, UCLA, 6-10, Sr.; Anthony Peeler, Missouri, 6-4, Sr.; Malik Sealy, St. John's (N.Y.), 6-7, Sr.; Walt Williams, Maryland, 6-8, Sr.

1993

First Team—Calbert Cheaney, Indiana, 6-7, Sr., Evansville, IN; Anfernee Hardaway, Memphis, 6-7, Jr., Memphis, TN; Bobby Hurley, Duke, 6-0, Sr., Jersey City, NJ; Jamal Mashburn, Kentucky, 6-8, Jr., New York; Chris Webber, Michigan, 6-9, So., Detroit.

Second Team—Terry Dehere, Seton Hall, 6-3, Sr.; Grant Hill, Duke, 6-7, Jr.; Billy McCaffrey, Vanderbilt, 6-3, Jr.; Eric Montross, North Carolina, 7-0, Jr.; J.R. Rider, UNLV, 6-7, Sr.; Glenn Robinson, Purdue, 6-9, So.; Rodney Rogers, Wake Forest, 6-8, Jr.

1994

First Team—Grant Hill, Duke, 6-8, Sr., Reston, VA; Jason Kidd, California, 6-4, So., Oakland, CA; Donyell Marshall, Connecticut, 6-9, Jr., Reading, PA; Glenn Robinson, Purdue, 6-8, Jr., Gary, IN; Clifford Rozier, Louisville, 6-9, Jr., Bradenton, FL.

Second Team—Melvin Booker, Missouri, 6-2, Sr.; Eric Montross, North Carolina, 7-0, Sr.; Lamond Murray, California, 6-7, Jr.; Khalid Reeves, Arizona, 6-2, Sr.; Jalen Rose, Michigan, 6-8, Jr.; Corliss Williamson, Arkansas, 6-7, So.

1995

First Team—Ed O'Bannon, UCLA, 6-8, Sr., Lakewood, CA; Shawn Respert, Michigan St., 6-3, Sr., Detroit; Joe Smith, Maryland, 6-10, So., Norfolk, VA; Jerry Stackhouse, North Carolina, 6-6, So., Kingston, NC; Damon Stoudamire, Arizona, 6-10, Sr., Portland, OR.

Second Team—Randolph Childress, Wake Forest, 6-2, Sr.; Kerry Kittles, Villanova, 6-5, Jr.; Lou Roe, Massachusetts, 6-7, Sr.; Rasheed Wallace, North Carolina, 6-10, So.; Corliss Williamson, Arkansas, 6-7, Jr.

1996

First Team—Ray Allen, Connecticut, 6-5, Jr., Dalzell, SC; Marcus Camby, Massachusetts, 6-11, Jr., Hartford, CT; Tony Delk, Kentucky, 6-1, Sr., Brownsville, TN; Tim Duncan, Wake Forest, 6-10, Jr., St. Croix, Virgin Islands; Allen Iverson, Georgetown, 6-1, So., Hampton, VA; Kerry Kittles, Villanova, 6-5, Sr., New Orleans.

Second Team—Danny Fortson, Cincinnati, 6-7, So.; Keith Van Horn, Utah, 6-9, Jr.; Jacque Vaughn, Kansas, 6-1, Jr.; John Wallace, Syracuse, 6-8, Sr.; Lorenzen Wright, Memphis, 6-11, So.

1997

First Team—Tim Duncan, Wake Forest, 6-10, Sr., St. Croix, Virgin Islands; Danny Fortson, Cincinnati, 6-7, Jr., Pittsburgh; Raef LaFrentz, Kansas, 6-11, Jr., Monona, IA; Ron Mercer, Kentucky, 6-7, So., Nashville, TN; Keith Van Horn, Utah, 6-9, Sr., Diamond Bar, CA.

Second Team—Chauncey Billups, Colorado, 6-3, So.; Bobby Jackson, Minnesota, 6-1, Sr.; Antawn Jamison, North Carolina, 6-9, So.; Brevin Knight, Stanford, 5-10, Sr.; Jacque Vaughn, Kansas, 6-1, Sr.

1998

First Team—Mike Bibby, Arizona, 6-2, So., Phoenix, AZ; Antawn Jamison, North Carolina, 6-9, Jr., Charlotte, NC; Raef LaFrentz, Kansas, 6-11, Sr., Monona, IA; Paul Pierce, Kansas, 6-7, Jr., Inglewood, CA; Miles Simon, Arizona, 6-5, Sr., Fullerton, CA.

Second Team—Vince Carter, North Carolina, 6-6, Jr.; Mateen Cleaves, Michigan St., 6-2, So.; Pat Garrity, Notre Dame, 6-9, Sr.; Richard Hamilton, Connecticut, 6-6, So.; Ansu Sesay, Mississippi, 6-9, Sr.

1999

First Team—Elton Brand, Duke, 6-8, So., Peekskill, NY; Mateen Cleaves, Michigan St., 6-2, Jr., Flint, MI; Richard Hamilton, Connecticut, 6-6, Jr., Coatesville, PA; Andre Miller, Utah, 6-2, Sr., Los Angeles; Jason Terry, Arizona, 6-2, Sr., Seattle.

Second Team—Evan Eschmeyer, Northwestern, 6-11, Sr.; Steve Francis, Maryland, 6-3, Jr.; Trajan Langdon, Duke, 6-3, Sr.; Chris Porter, Auburn, 6-7, Jr.; Wally Szczerbiak, Miami (Ohio), 6-8, Sr.

2000

First Team—Chris Carrawell, Duke, 6-6, Sr., St. Louis; Marcus Fizer, Iowa St., 6-8, Jr., Arcadia, LA; A.J. Guyton, Indiana, 6-1, Sr., Peoria, IL; Kenyon Martin, Cincinnati, 6-9, Sr., Dallas; Chris Mihm, Texas, 7-0, Jr., Austin, TX; Troy Murphy, Notre Dame, 6-10, So., Morristown, NJ.

Second Team—Courtney Alexander, Fresno St., 6-6, Sr.; Shane Battier, Duke, 6-8, Jr.; Mateen Cleaves, Michigan St., 6-2, Sr.; Scoonie Penn, Ohio St., 5-10, Sr.; Morrison Peterson, Michigan St., 6-6, Sr.; Stromile Swift, LSU, 6-9, So.

2001

First Team—Shane Battier, Duke, 6-8, Sr., Birmingham, MI; Joseph Forte, North Carolina, 6-4, So., Greenbelt, MD; Casey Jacobsen, Stanford, 6-6, So., Glendora, CA; Troy Murphy, Notre Dame, 6-10, Jr., Morristown, NJ; Jason Williams, Duke, 6-2, So., Plainfield, NJ.

Second Team—Troy Bell, Boston College, 6-1, So.; Michael Bradley, Villanova, 6-10, Jr.; Tayshaun Prince, Kentucky, 6-9, Jr.; Jason Richardson, Michigan St., 6-6, So.; Jamaal Tinsley, Iowa St., 6-3, Sr.

2002

First Team—Juan Dixon, Maryland, 6-3, Sr., Baltimore; Dan Dickau, Gonzaga, 6-1, Sr., Vancouver, WA; Drew Gooden, Kansas, 6-10, Jr., Richmond, CA; Steve Logan, Cincinnati, 6-1, Sr., Cleveland; Jason Williams, Duke, 6-2, Jr., Plainfield, NJ.

Second Team—Sam Clancy, Southern California, 6-7, Sr.; Mike Dunleavy, Duke, 6-9, Jr.; Casey Jacobsen, Stanford, 6-6, Jr.; Jared Jeffries, Indiana, 6-10, So.; David West, Xavier, 6-8, Jr.

2003

First Team—Nick Collison, Kansas, 6-9, Sr., Iowa Falls, IA; T.J. Ford, Texas, 5-10, So., Houston; Josh Howard, Wake Forest, 6-6, Sr., Winston-Salem, NC; Dwyane Wade, Marquette, 6-4, Jr., Robbins, IL; David West, Xavier, 6-9, Sr., Garner, NC.

Second Team—Carmelo Anthony, Syracuse, 6-8, Fr.; Troy Bell, Boston College, 6-1, Sr.; Jason Gardner, Arizona, 5-10, Sr.; Kyle Korver, Creighton, 6-7, Sr.; Hollis Price, Oklahoma, 6-1, Sr.

2004

First Team—Andre Emmett, Texas Tech, 6-5, Sr., Dallas; Ryan Gomes, Providence, 6-7, Jr., Waterbury, CT; Jameer Nelson, St. Joseph's, 6-0, Sr., Chester, PA; Emeka Okafor, Connecticut, 6-10, Jr., Houston; Lawrence Roberts, Mississippi St., 6-9, Jr., Houston.

Second Team—Josh Childress, Stanford, 6-8, Jr.; Devin Harris, Wisconsin, 6-3, Jr.; Julius Hodge, North Carolina St., 6-6, Jr.; Luke Jackson, Oregon, 6-7, Sr.; Blake Stepp, Gonzaga, 6-4, Sr.

2005

First Team—Andrew Bogut, Utah, 7-0, So., Melbourne, Australia; Dee Brown, Illinois, 6-0, Jr., Maywood, IL; Chris Paul, Wake Forest, 6-0, So., Lewisville, NC; J.J. Redick, Duke, 6-4, Jr., Roanoke, VA; Wayne Simien, Kansas, 6-9, Sr., Leavenworth, KS; Hakim Warrick, Syracuse, 6-9, Sr., Philadelphia.

Second Team—Ike Diogu, Arizona St., 6-8, Jr.; Luther Head, Illinois, 6-3, Sr.; Sean May, North Carolina, 6-9, Jr.; Salim Stoudamire, Arizona, 6-1, Sr.; Deron Williams, Illinois, 6-3, Jr.

2006

First Team—Randy Foye, Villanova, 6-4, Sr., Newark, NJ; Adam Morrison, Gonzaga, 6-8, Jr., Spokane, WA; J.J. Redick, Duke, 6-4, Sr., Roanoke, VA; Brandon Roy, Washington, 6-6, Sr., Seattle; Shelden Williams, Duke, 6-9, Sr., Forest Park, OK.

Second Team—Dee Brown, Illinois, 6-0, Sr.; Rodney Carney, Memphis, 6-7, Sr.; Rudy Gay, Connecticut, 6-9, So.; Tyler Hansbrough, North Carolina, 6-9, Fr.; Leon Powe, California, 6-8, So.; Allan Ray, Villanova, 6-2, Sr.; P.J. Tucker, Texas, 6-5, Jr.

2007

First Team—Arron Afflalo, UCLA, 6-5, Jr., Compton, CA; Kevin Durant, Texas, 6-9, Fr., Suitland, MD; Tyler Hansbrough, North Carolina, 6-9, So., Poplar Bluff, MO; Acie Law IV, Texas A&M, 6-3, Sr., Dallas; Alando Tucker, Wisconsin, 6-6, Sr., Lockport, IL.

Second Team—Jared Dudley, Boston College, 6-7, Sr.; Nick Fazekas, Nevada, 6-11, Sr.; Chris Lofton, Tennessee, 6-2, Jr.; Joakim Noah, Florida, 6-11, Jr.; Greg Oden, Ohio St., 7-0, Fr.

Teams used for consensus selections:

Helms Foundation—1929-48
Converse Yearbook—1932-48
College Humor Magazine—1929-33, 1936
Christy Walsh Syndicate—1929-30
Literary Digest Magazine—1934
Madison Square Garden—1937-42
Omaha World Newspaper—1937
Newspaper Enterprises Assn.—1938, 1953-63
Colliers (Basketball Coaches)—1939, 1949-56
Pic Magazine—1942-44
Argosy Magazine—1945
True Magazine—1946-47
International News Service—1950-58
Look Magazine—1949-63
United Press International—1949-96
Sporting News—1943-46, 1997-2007
The Associated Press—1948-2007
National Assoc. of Basketball Coaches—1957-2007
U.S. Basketball Writers Association—1960-2007

Consensus First-Team All-Americans By Team

ARIZONA
1988—Sean Elliott
1989—Sean Elliott
1995—Damon Stoudamire
1998—Mike Bibby
Miles Simon
1999—Jason Terry

ARKANSAS
1936—Ike Poole
1941—John Adams
1979—Sidney Moncrief

BOWLING GREEN
1945—Wyndol Gray

BRADLEY
1950—Paul Unruh
1951—Gene Melchiorre
1961—Chet Walker
1962—Chet Walker
1988—Hersey Hawkins

BYU
1931—Elwood Romney
1981—Danny Ainge

CALIFORNIA
1929—Vern Corbin
1960—Darrall Imhoff
1994—Jason Kidd

CINCINNATI
1958—Oscar Robertson
1959—Oscar Robertson
1960—Oscar Robertson
1963—Ron Bonham
Tom Thacker
1997—Danny Fortson
2000—Kenyon Martin
2002—Steve Logan

COLUMBIA
1931—George Gregory
1957—Chet Forte

CONNECTICUT
1994—Donyell Marshall
1996—Ray Allen
1999—Richard Hamilton
2004—Emeka Okafor

CREIGHTON
1943—Ed Beisser

DARTMOUTH
1940—Gus Broberg
1941—Gus Broberg
1944—Audley Brindley

DAVIDSON
1965—Fred Hetzel

DENVER
1949—Vince Boryla

DePAUL
1944—George Mikan
1945—George Mikan
1946—George Mikan
1980—Mark Aguirre
1981—Mark Aguirre
1982—Terry Cummings

DETROIT
1969—Spencer Haywood

DUKE
1952—Dick Groat
1963—Art Heyman
1967—Bob Verga
1979—Mike Gminski
1985—Johnny Dawkins
1986—Johnny Dawkins
1989—Danny Ferry
1992—Christian Laettner
1993—Bobby Hurley
1994—Grant Hill
1999—Elton Brand

2000—Chris Carrawell
2001—Shane Battier
Jason Williams
2002—Jason Williams
2005—J.J. Redick
2006—J.J. Redick
Shelden Williams

DUQUESNE
1955—Dick Ricketts
Si Green
1956—Si Green

FURMAN
1954—Frank Selvy

GEORGETOWN
1982—Eric Floyd
1983—Patrick Ewing
1984—Patrick Ewing
1985—Patrick Ewing
1987—Reggie Williams
1992—Alonzo Mourning
1996—Allen Iverson

GEORGIA TECH
1961—Roger Kaiser
1991—Kenny Anderson

GONZAGA
2002—Dan Dickau
2006—Adam Morrison

HOLY CROSS
1950—Bob Cousy
1956—Tom Heinsohn

HOUSTON
1967—Elvin Hayes
1968—Elvin Hayes
1977—Otis Birdsong
1984—Akeem Olajuwon

ILLINOIS
1940—Bill Hapac
1942—Andrew Phillip
1943—Andrew Phillip
1945—Walton Kirk
1952—Rod Fletcher
2005—Dee Brown

ILLINOIS ST.
1973—Doug Collins

INDIANA
1930—Branch McCracken
1936—Vern Huffman
1939—Ernie Andres
1947—Ralph Hamilton
1954—Don Schlundt
1975—Scott May
1976—Scott May
Kent Benson
1977—Kent Benson
1981—Isiah Thomas
1986—Steve Alford
1987—Steve Alford
1993—Calbert Cheaney
2000—A.J. Guyton

INDIANA ST.
1978—Larry Bird
1979—Larry Bird

IOWA
1948—Murray Wier
1952—Chuck Darling

IOWA ST.
2000—Marcus Fizer

JACKSONVILLE
1971—Artis Gilmore

KANSAS
1938—Fred Pralle
1941—Howard Engleman
1943—Charles Black
1951—Clyde Lovellette
1952—Clyde Lovellette
1957—Wilt Chamberlain
1958—Wilt Chamberlain
1987—Danny Manning
1988—Danny Manning
1997—Raef LaFrentz
1998—Raef LaFrentz
Paul Pierce
2002—Drew Gooden

2003—Nick Collison
2005—Wayne Simien

KANSAS ST.
1958—Bob Boozer
1959—Bob Boozer

KENTUCKY
1932—Forest Sale
1933—Forest Sale
1935—Leroy Edwards
1944—Robert Brannum
1947—Ralph Beard
Alex Groza
1948—Ralph Beard
1949—Ralph Beard
Alex Groza
1951—Bill Spivey
1952—Cliff Hagan
1954—Cliff Hagan
1959—Johnny Cox
1964—Cotton Nash
1970—Dan Issel
1980—Kyle Macy
1986—Kenny Walker
1993—Jamal Mashburn
1996—Tony Delk
1997—Ron Mercer

LA SALLE
1953—Tom Gola
1954—Tom Gola
1955—Tom Gola
1980—Michael Brooks
1990—Lionel Simmons

LONG BEACH ST.
1972—Ed Ratleff
1973—Ed Ratleff

LONG ISLAND
1937—Jules Bender
1939—Irving Torgoff

LA.-LAFAYETTE
1972—Dwight Lamar
1973—Dwight Lamar

LSU
1954—Bob Pettit
1968—Pete Maravich
1969—Pete Maravich
1970—Pete Maravich
1989—Chris Jackson
1990—Chris Jackson
1991—Shaquille O'Neal
1992—Shaquille O'Neal

LOUISVILLE
1957—Charlie Tyra
1967—Wes Unseld
1968—Wes Unseld
1980—Darrell Griffith
1989—Pervis Ellison
1994—Clifford Rozier

LOYOLA (ILL.)
1963—Jerry Harkness

MARQUETTE
1971—Dean Meminger
1972—Jim Chones
1978—Butch Lee
2003—Dwyane Wade

MARYLAND
1932—Louis Berger
1975—John Lucas
1976—John Lucas
1986—Len Bias
1995—Joe Smith
2002—Juan Dixon

MASSACHUSETTS
1996—Marcus Camby

MEMPHIS
1983—Keith Lee
1985—Keith Lee
1993—Anfernee Hardaway

MIAMI (FLA.)
1965—Rick Barry

MICHIGAN
1965—Cazzie Russell
1966—Cazzie Russell
1977—Rickey Green

1988—Gary Grant
1993—Chris Webber

MICHIGAN ST.
1979—Earvin Johnson
1995—Shawn Respert
1999—Mateen Cleaves

MINNESOTA
1948—Jim McIntyre
1955—Dick Garmaker
1978—Mychal Thompson

MISSISSIPPI ST.
1959—Bailey Howell
2004—Lawrence Roberts

MONTANA ST.
1929—John Thompson
1930—John Thompson
Frank Ward

NAVY
1933—Elliott Loughlin
1987—David Robinson

UNLV
1990—Larry Johnson
1991—Larry Johnson

NEW YORK U.
1946—Sid Tanenbaum
1947—Sid Tanenbaum
1963—Barry Kramer

NIAGARA
1969—Calvin Murphy
1970—Calvin Murphy

NORTH CAROLINA
1940—George Glamack
1941—George Glamack
1957—Lenny Rosenbluth
1968—Larry Miller
1972—Bob McAdoo
1977—Phil Ford
1978—Phil Ford
1982—James Worthy
1983—Michael Jordan
Sam Perkins
1984—Michael Jordan
Sam Perkins
1987—Kenny Smith
1988—J.R. Reid
1995—Jerry Stackhouse
1998—Antawn Jamison
2001—Joseph Forte
2007—Tyler Hansbrough

NORTH CAROLINA ST.
1951—Sam Ranzino
1956—Ron Shavlik
1973—David Thompson
1974—David Thompson
1975—David Thompson

NORTHWESTERN
1931—Joe Reiff
1933—Joe Reiff
1944—Otto Graham
1946—Max Norris

NOTRE DAME
1932—Ed Krause
1933—Ed Krause
1934—Ed Krause
1936—Paul Nowak
John Moir
1937—Paul Nowak
John Moir
1938—Paul Nowak
John Moir
1944—Leo Klier
1945—William Hassett
1946—Leo Klier
1948—Kevin O'Shea
1971—Austin Carr
1974—John Shumate
1975—Adrian Dantley
1976—Adrian Dantley
2000—Troy Murphy
2001—Troy Murphy

OHIO ST.
1931—Wes Fesler
1939—Jimmy Hull
1950—Dick Schnittker

1956—Robin Freeman
1960—Jerry Lucas
1961—Jerry Lucas
1962—Jerry Lucas
1964—Gary Bradds
1991—Jim Jackson
1992—Jim Jackson

OKLAHOMA
1929—Thomas Churchill
1935—Bud Browning
1944—Alva Paine
1947—Gerald Tucker
1983—Wayman Tisdale
1984—Wayman Tisdale
1985—Wayman Tisdale
1989—Stacey King

OKLAHOMA ST.
1944—Robert Kurland
1945—Robert Kurland
1946—Robert Kurland

OREGON
1939—Urgel Wintermute
1940—John Dick

OREGON ST.
1981—Steve Johnson
1990—Gary Payton

PENN
1929—Joe Schaaf
1945—Howard Dallmar
1953—Ernie Beck

PITTSBURGH
1929—Charley Hyatt
1930—Charley Hyatt
1933—Don Smith
1934—Claire Cribbs
1935—Claire Cribbs
1958—Don Hennon

PRINCETON
1964—Bill Bradley
1965—Bill Bradley

PROVIDENCE
1966—Jim Walker
1967—Jim Walker
1973—Ernie DiGregorio
1974—Marvin Barnes
2004—Ryan Gomes

PURDUE
1929—Charles Murphy
1930—Charles Murphy
John Wooden
1931—John Wooden
1932—John Wooden
1934—Norman Cottom
1936—Bob Kessler
1937—Jewell Young
1938—Jewell Young
1961—Terry Dischinger
1962—Terry Dischinger
1966—Dave Schellhase
1969—Rick Mount
1970—Rick Mount
1980—Joe Barry Carroll
1994—Glenn Robinson

RHODE ISLAND
1939—Chet Jaworski

RICE
1942—Bob Kinney
1943—William Closs
1945—William Henry

RUTGERS
1967—Bob Lloyd

ST. BONAVENTURE
1960—Tom Stith
1961—Tom Stith
1970—Bob Lanier

ST. JOHN'S (N.Y.)
1943—Harry Boykoff
1985—Chris Mullin
1986—Walter Berry

ST. JOSEPH'S
1943—George Senesky
2004—Jameer Nelson

ST. LOUIS
1948—Ed Macauley
1949—Ed Macauley

SAN FRANCISCO
1955—Bill Russell
1956—Bill Russell
1982—Quintin Dailey

SEATTLE
1953—Johnny O'Brien
1958—Elgin Baylor

SETON HALL
1942—Robert Davies
1953—Walt Dukes

SOUTH CAROLINA
1972—Tom Riker

SOUTHERN CALIFORNIA
1933—Jerry Nemer
1935—Lee Guttero
1940—Ralph Vaughn
1950—Bill Sharman
1992—Harold Miner

SMU
1957—Jim Krebs

STANFORD
1936—Hank Luisetti
1937—Hank Luisetti
1938—Hank Luisetti
2001—Casey Jacobsen

SYRACUSE
1966—Dave Bing
1990—Derrick Coleman
1991—Billy Owens
2005—Hakim Warrick

TEMPLE
1938—Meyer Bloom
1951—Bill Mlkvy
1958—Guy Rodgers

TENNESSEE
1977—Bernard King
1983—Dale Ellis

TEXAS
1935—Jack Gray
2000—Chris Mihm
2003—T.J. Ford
2007—Kevin Durant

TEXAS A&M
2007—Acie Law IV

TEXAS TECH
2004—Andre Emmett

UCLA
1964—Walt Hazzard
1965—Gail Goodrich
1967—Lew Alcindor
1968—Lew Alcindor
1969—Lew Alcindor
1971—Sidney Wicks
1972—Bill Walton
        Henry Bibby
1973—Bill Walton
        Keith Wilkes
1974—Bill Walton
        Keith Wilkes
1975—Dave Meyers
1976—Richard Washington
1977—Marques Johnson
1978—David Greenwood
1979—David Greenwood
1995—Ed O'Bannon
2007—Arron Afflalo

UTAH
1936—Bill Kinner
1945—Arnold Ferrin
1962—Billy McGill

1997—Keith Van Horn
1999—Andre Miller
2005—Andre Bogut

VANDERBILT
1966—Clyde Lee

VILLANOVA
1950—Paul Arizin
1996—Kerry Kittles
2006—Randy Foye

VIRGINIA
1981—Ralph Sampson
1982—Ralph Sampson
1983—Ralph Sampson

WAKE FOREST
1962—Len Chappell
1996—Tim Duncan
1997—Tim Duncan
2003—Josh Howard
2005—Chris Paul

WASHINGTON
1934—Hal Lee
1953—Bob Houbregs
2006—Brandon Roy

WEST TEX. A&M
1942—Price Brookfield

WEST VIRGINIA
1957—Rod Hundley
1959—Jerry West
1960—Jerry West

WESTERN KY.
1967—Clem Haskins
1971—Jim McDaniels

WICHITA ST.
1964—Dave Stallworth
1985—Xavier McDaniel

WISCONSIN
1941—Gene Englund
1942—John Kotz
2007—Alando Tucker

WYOMING
1932—Les Witte
1934—Les Witte
1943—Ken Sailors

XAVIER
2003—David West

YALE
1949—Tony Lavelli

Team Leaders in Consensus First-Team All-Americans

(Ranked on total number of selections)

Team	No.	Players
Kentucky	20	15
UCLA	19	13
Notre Dame	19	10
Duke	18	14
North Carolina	18	14
Purdue	16	10
Kansas	15	11
Indiana	14	11
Ohio St.	10	7
Cincinnati	8	6
Oklahoma	8	6
LSU	8	4
Georgetown	7	5

Team	No.	Players
Utah	6	6
Arizona	6	5
Illinois	6	5
Louisville	6	5
Maryland	6	5
Pittsburgh	6	4
DePaul	6	3
Southern California	5	5
Bradley	5	4
Providence	5	4
Wake Forest	5	4
La Salle	5	3
Michigan	5	3
North Carolina St.	5	3

Division I Academic All-Americans by Team

AIR FORCE
1968—Cliff Parsons
1970—Jim Cooper
1978—Tom Schneeberger

AMERICAN
1972—Kermit Washington
1973—Kermit Washington
1987—Patrick Witting

ARIZONA
1976—Bob Elliott
1977—Bob Elliott

ARIZONA ST.
1964—Art Becker
1999—Bobby Lazor

ARKANSAS
1978—Jim Counce

ARMY
1964—Mike Silliman

BALL ST.
2002—Patrick Jackson

BAYLOR
1996—Doug Brandt
1997—Doug Brandt

BELMONT
2002—Wes Burtner
2003—Adam Mark
2004—Adam Mark

BOSTON COLLEGE
1968—Terry Driscoll

BYU
1980—Danny Ainge
1981—Danny Ainge
1983—Devin Durrant
1984—Devin Durrant
1987—Michael Smith
1988—Michael Smith
1989—Michael Smith
1990—Andy Toolson

BROWN
1986—Jim Turner

BUCKNELL
1999—Valter Karavanic

BUTLER
2007—A.J. Graves

CALIFORNIA
1987—David Butler

CENTRAL MICH.
1993—Sander Scott

COL. OF CHARLESTON
2000—Jody Lumpkin
2001—Jody Lumpkin

CINCINNATI
1967—Mike Rolf

CLEVELAND ST.
1973—Pat Lyons

COLGATE
1997—Adonal Foyle

CONNECTICUT
1967—Wes Bialosuknia
2003—Emeka Okafor
2004—Emeka Okafor

CORNELL
2007—Graham Dow

CREIGHTON
1964—Paul Silas
1978—Rick Apke

DARTMOUTH
1984—Paul Anderson
1996—Seamus Lonergan

DAVIDSON
1988—Derek Rucker

DAYTON
1979—Jim Paxson
1981—Mike Kanieski
1982—Mike Kanieski

DENVER
2003—Brett Starkey

DePAUL
1991—Stephen Howard

1992—Stephen Howard

DUKE
1963—Jay Buckley
1964—Jay Buckley
1971—Dick DeVenzio
1972—Gary Melchionni
1975—Bob Fleischer
1978—Mike Gminski
        Jim Spanarkel
1979—Mike Gminski
        Jim Spanarkel
1980—Mike Gminski
2000—Shane Battier
2001—Shane Battier

DUQUESNE
1969—Bill Zopf
1970—Bill Zopf

EVANSVILLE
1989—Scott Haffner
2003—Clint Cuffle

FAIRLEIGH DICKINSON
1978—John Jorgensen

FLORIDA
2002—Matt Bonner
2003—Matt Bonner
2007—Lee Humphrey

FORDHAM
1975—Darryl Brown

GEORGE WASHINGTON
1976—Pat Tallent
1986—Steve Frick

GEORGIA
1988—Alec Kessler
1989—Alec Kessler
1990—Alec Kessler

GEORGIA TECH
1964—Jim Caldwell
1969—Rich Yunkus
1970—Rich Yunkus
1971—Rich Yunkus
1998—Matt Harpring

GONZAGA
1984—Bryce McPhee
        John Stockton
1985—Bryce McPhee
1992—Jarrod Davis
1993—Jeff Brown
1994—Jeff Brown
2002—Dan Dickau

GREEN BAY
1992—Tony Bennett

HARVARD
1985—Joe Carrabino
1987—Arne Duncan

HAWAII
2004—Michael Kuebler

HOLY CROSS
1969—Ed Siudut
1978—Ronnie Perry
1979—Ronnie Perry
1980—Ronnie Perry
1991—Jim Nairus

ILLINOIS
1968—Dave Scholz
1969—Dave Scholz
1971—Rich Howatt
1974—Rick Schmidt
1975—Rick Schmidt

ILLINOIS ST.
1973—Doug Collins

INDIANA
1964—Dick Van Arsdale
1965—Dick Van Arsdale
1965—Tom Van Arsdale
1973—John Ritter
1974—Steve Green
1975—Steve Green
1976—Kent Benson
1977—Kent Benson
1978—Wayne Radford
1982—Randy Wittman
1983—Randy Wittman
1985—Uwe Blab
1989—Joe Hillman

IOWA
2007—Adam Haluska

IOWA ST.
1995—Fred Hoiberg

JACKSONVILLE
1971—Vaughan Wedeking
1983—Maurice Roulhac

KANSAS
1971—Bud Stallworth
1974—Tom Kivisto
1977—Ken Koenigs
　　　Chris Barnthouse
1978—Ken Koenigs
1979—Darnell Valentine
1980—Darnell Valentine
1981—Darnell Valentine
1982—David Magley
1996—Jacque Vaughn
1997—Jerod Haase
　　　Jacque Vaughn
1999—Ryan Robertson

KANSAS ST.
1968—Earl Seyfert
1982—Tim Jankovich
　　　Ed Nealy

KENTUCKY
1966—Lou Dampier
1967—Lou Dampier
1969—Larry Conley
1970—Dan Issel
　　　Mike Pratt
1971—Mike Casey
1975—Bob Guyette
　　　Jimmy Dan Conner
1979—Kyle Macy

LA SALLE
1977—Tony DiLeo
1988—Tim Legler
1992—Jack Hurd

LAMAR
1999—Matt Sundblad

LEWIS
1989—Jamie Martin

LOUISVILLE
1976—Phil Bond

LOYOLA MARYMOUNT
1973—Steve Smith

MANHATTAN
1990—Peter Runge

MARQUETTE
1982—Marc Marotta
1983—Marc Marotta
1984—Marc Marotta

MARSHALL
1972—Mike D'Antoni
1973—Mike D'Antoni

MARYLAND
1972—Tom McMillen
1973—Tom McMillen
1974—Tom McMillen
1991—Matt Roe

MERCER
2005—Will Emerson
2006—Will Emerson

MIAMI (OHIO)
1993—Craig Michaelis

MICHIGAN
1976—Steve Grote
1981—Marty Bodnar

MICHIGAN ST.
1970—Ralph Simpson
1979—Greg Kelser
2004—Chris Hill
2005—Chris Hill

MISSISSIPPI
1975—Dave Shepherd

MISSOURI
1983—Steve Stipanovich

MONTANA
1981—Craig Zanon
1985—Larry Krystkowiak
1986—Larry Krystkowiak

MURRAY ST.
1985—Mike Lahm

NEBRASKA
1984—John Matzke

UNLV
1983—Danny Tarkanian
1984—Danny Tarkanian

NEW MEXICO
1969—Ron Becker
1970—Ron Becker

NEW MEXICO ST.
2001—Eric Channing
2002—Eric Channing

NORTH CAROLINA
1965—Billy Cunningham
1970—Charlie Scott
1972—Dennis Wuycik
　　　Steve Previs
1976—Tommy LaGarde

1986—Steve Hale
1994—Eric Montross

UNC GREENSBORO
2001—Nathan Jameson

NORTH CAROLINA ST.
1984—Terry Gannon
1985—Terry Gannon
1995—Todd Fuller
1996—Todd Fuller

NORTHEASTERN
1977—David Caligaris
1978—David Caligaris

NORTHERN ILL.
1984—Tim Dillion
1998—T.J. Lux
2000—T.J. Lux

UNI
1984—Randy Kraayenbrink

NORTHWESTERN
1967—Jim Burns
1980—Mike Campbell
1987—Shon Morris
1988—Shon Morris

NOTRE DAME
1967—Bob Arnzen
1968—Bob Arnzen
1969—Bob Arnzen
1974—Gary Novak
1979—Kelly Tripucka
1980—Rich Branning
1982—John Paxson
1983—John Paxson
1997—Pat Garrity
1998—Pat Garrity
2005—Chris Quinn

OHIO
1971—Craig Love
1977—Steve Skaggs
1990—Dave Jamerson

OHIO ST.
1968—Bill Hosket

OKLAHOMA
1974—Alvan Adams
1975—Alvan Adams
1980—Terry Stotts

OKLAHOMA ST.
1964—Gary Hassmann
1969—Joe Smith

PACIFIC
1967—Keith Swagerty

PENN
1972—Robert Morse

PENN ST.
1994—John Amaechi
1995—John Amaechi

PRINCETON
1965—Bill Bradley
1991—Kit Mueller

PURDUE
1965—Dave Schellhase
1966—Dave Schellhase
1972—Robert Ford
1981—Brian Walker
1982—Keith Edmonson

1983—Steve Reid
1985—Steve Reid

RADFORD
1998—Corey Reed

RICE
1994—Adam Peakes

SACRED HEART
2006—Kibwe Trim

ST. FRANCIS (PA.)
1990—Michael Iuzzolino
1991—Michael Iuzzolino

ST. LOUIS
1968—Rich Niemann
1994—Scott Highmark
1995—Scott Highmark

SAN DIEGO ST.
1976—Steve Copp

SANTA CLARA
1968—Dennis Awtrey
1969—Dennis Awtrey
1970—Dennis Awtrey

SIENA
1985—Doug Peotzch
1992—Bruce Schroeder

SOUTH CAROLINA
1970—John Roche
1971—John Roche

SOUTHEAST MO. ST.
2005—Derek Winans

SOUTHERN ILL.
1976—Mike Glenn
1977—Mike Glenn

SMU
1977—Pete Lodwick
2005—Eric Castro

STANFORD
2000—Mark Madsen
2006—Dan Grunfeld

SYRACUSE
1981—Dan Schayes

TENNESSEE
1968—Bill Justus
1993—Lang Wiseman

TEXAS
1979—Jim Krivacs

UTEP
2000—Brandon Wolfram
2001—Brandon Wolfram

TEXAS A&M
1964—Bill Robinette

TULSA
1999—Michael Ruffin

UCLA
1967—Mike Warren
1969—Kenny Heitz
1971—Sidney Wicks
1972—Bill Walton
　　　Keith Wilkes
　　　Greg Lee
1973—Bill Walton
　　　Keith Wilkes
　　　Greg Lee

1974—Bill Walton
　　　Keith Wilkes
　　　Greg Lee
1975—Ralph Drollinger
1977—Marques Johnson
1979—Kiki Vandeweghe
1980—Kiki Vandeweghe
1995—George Zidek

UTAH
1970—Mike Newlin
1971—Mike Newlin
1977—Jeff Jonas
1998—Michael Doleac

UTAH ST.
1964—Gary Watts
1980—Dean Hunger
1982—Larry Bergeson
1996—Eric Franson

VANDERBILT
1975—Jeff Fosnes
1976—Jeff Fosnes
1993—Bruce Elder

VILLANOVA
1973—Tom Inglesby
1982—John Pinone
1983—John Pinone
1986—Harold Jensen
1987—Harold Jensen

VIRGINIA
1976—Wally Walker
1981—Jeff Lamp
　　　Lee Raker

VMI
1980—Andy Kolesar
1981—Andy Kolesar

WASHINGTON
1982—Dave Henley

WASHINGTON ST.
1989—Brian Quinnett

WEBER ST.
1985—Randy Worster

WEST VIRGINIA
2005—Johannes Herber
2006—Johannes Herber

WESTERN MICH.
2007—Joe Reitz

WICHITA ST.
1967—Jamie Thompson
1969—Ron Mendell

WILLIAM & MARY
1985—Keith Cieplicki
2004—Adam Hess

WISCONSIN
1974—Dan Anderson

Division I Player of the Year

Season	United Press International	The Associated Press	Oscar Robertson Trophy (USBWA)	Wooden Award	Nat'l Assn. of Basketball Coaches	Naismith Award	Adolph Rupp Trophy
1955	Tom Gola La Salle						
1956	Bill Russell San Francisco						
1957	Chet Forte Columbia						
1958	Oscar Robertson Cincinnati						
1959	Oscar Robertson Cincinnati		Oscar Robertson Cincinnati				
1960	Oscar Robertson Cincinnati		Oscar Robertson Cincinnati				
1961	Jerry Lucas Ohio St.	Jerry Lucas Ohio St.	Jerry Lucas Ohio St.				
1962	Jerry Lucas Ohio St.	Jerry Lucas Ohio St.	Jerry Lucas Ohio St.				
1963	Art Heyman Duke	Art Heyman Duke	Art Heyman Duke				
1964	Gary Bradds Ohio St.	Gary Bradds Ohio St.	Walt Hazzard UCLA				
1965	Bill Bradley Princeton	Bill Bradley Princeton	Bill Bradley Princeton				
1966	Cazzie Russell Michigan	Cazzie Russell Michigan	Cazzie Russell Michigan				
1967	Lew Alcindor UCLA	Lew Alcindor UCLA	Lew Alcindor UCLA				
1968	Elvin Hayes Houston	Elvin Hayes Houston	Elvin Hayes Houston				
1969	Lew Alcindor UCLA	Lew Alcindor UCLA	Lew Alcindor UCLA			Lew Alcindor UCLA	
1970	Pete Maravich LSU	Pete Maravich LSU	Pete Maravich LSU			Pete Maravich LSU	
1971	Austin Carr Notre Dame	Austin Carr Notre Dame	Sidney Wicks UCLA			Austin Carr Notre Dame	
1972	Bill Walton UCLA	Bill Walton UCLA	Bill Walton UCLA			Bill Walton UCLA	Bill Walton UCLA
1973	Bill Walton UCLA	Bill Walton UCLA	Bill Walton UCLA			Bill Walton UCLA	Bill Walton UCLA
1974	Bill Walton UCLA	David Thompson North Carolina St.	Bill Walton UCLA			Bill Walton UCLA	Bill Walton UCLA
1975	David Thompson North Carolina St.	David Thompson North Carolina St.	David Thompson North Carolina St.		David Thompson North Carolina St.	David Thompson North Carolina St.	David Thompson North Carolina St.
1976	Scott May Indiana	Scott May Indiana	Adrian Dantley Notre Dame		Scott May Indiana	Scott May Indiana	Scott May Indiana
1977	Marques Johnson UCLA	Marques Johnson UCLA	Marques Johnson UCLA	Marques Johnson UCLA	Marques Johnson UCLA	Marques Johnson UCLA	Marques Johnson UCLA
1978	Butch Lee Marquette	Butch Lee Marquette	Phil Ford North Carolina	Phil Ford North Carolina	Phil Ford North Carolina	Butch Lee Marquette	Butch Lee Marquette
1979	Larry Bird Indiana St.	Larry Bird Indiana St.	Larry Bird Indiana St.	Larry Bird Indiana St.	Larry Bird Indiana St.	Larry Bird Indiana St.	Larry Bird Indiana St.
1980	Mark Aguirre DePaul	Mark Aguirre DePaul	Mark Aguirre DePaul	Darrell Griffith Louisville	Michael Brooks La Salle	Mark Aguirre DePaul	Mark Aguirre DePaul
1981	Ralph Sampson Virginia	Ralph Sampson Virginia	Ralph Sampson Virginia	Danny Ainge BYU	Danny Ainge BYU	Ralph Sampson Virginia	Ralph Sampson Virginia
1982	Ralph Sampson Virginia	Ralph Sampson Virginia	Ralph Sampson Virginia	Ralph Sampson Virginia	Ralph Sampson Virginia	Ralph Sampson Virginia	Ralph Sampson Virginia
1983	Ralph Sampson Virginia	Ralph Sampson Virginia	Ralph Sampson Virginia	Ralph Sampson Virginia	Ralph Sampson Virginia	Ralph Sampson Virginia	Ralph Sampson Virginia
1984	Michael Jordan North Carolina	Michael Jordan North Carolina	Michael Jordan North Carolina	Michael Jordan North Carolina	Michael Jordan North Carolina	Michael Jordan North Carolina	Michael Jordan North Carolina
1985	Chris Mullin St. John's (N.Y.)	Patrick Ewing Georgetown	Chris Mullin St. John's (N.Y.)	Chris Mullin St. John's (N.Y.)	Patrick Ewing Georgetown	Patrick Ewing Georgetown	Patrick Ewing Georgetown
1986	Walter Berry St. John's (N.Y.)	Walter Berry St. John's (N.Y.)	Walter Berry St. John's (N.Y.)	Walter Berry St. John's (N.Y.)	Walter Berry St. John's (N.Y.)	Johnny Dawkins Duke	Walter Berry St. John's (N.Y.)
1987	David Robinson Navy	David Robinson Navy	David Robinson Navy	David Robinson Navy	David Robinson Navy	David Robinson Navy	David Robinson Navy
1988	Hersey Hawkins Bradley	Hersey Hawkins Bradley	Hersey Hawkins Bradley	Danny Manning Kansas	Danny Manning Kansas	Danny Manning Kansas	Hersey Hawkins Bradley
1989	Danny Ferry Duke	Sean Elliott Arizona	Danny Ferry Duke	Sean Elliott Arizona	Sean Elliott Arizona	Danny Ferry Duke	Sean Elliott Arizona
1990	Lionel Simmons La Salle	Lionel Simmons La Salle	Lionel Simmons La Salle	Lionel Simmons La Salle	Lionel Simmons La Salle	Lionel Simmons La Salle	Lionel Simmons La Salle

Season	United Press International	The Associated Press	Oscar Robertson Trophy (USBWA)	Wooden Award	Nat'l Assn. of Basketball Coaches	Naismith Award	Adolph Rupp Trophy
1991	Shaquille O'Neal LSU	Shaquille O'Neal LSU	Larry Johnson UNLV	Larry Johnson UNLV	Larry Johnson UNLV	Larry Johnson UNLV	Shaquille O'Neal LSU
1992	Jim Jackson Ohio St.	Christian Laettner Duke	Christian Laettner Duke	Christian Laettner Duke	Christian Laettner Duke	Christian Laettner Duke	Christian Laettner Duke
1993	Calbert Cheaney Indiana	Calbert Cheaney Indiana	Calbert Cheaney Indiana	Calbert Cheaney Indiana	Calbert Cheaney Indiana	Calbert Cheaney Indiana	Calbert Cheaney Indiana
1994	Glenn Robinson Purdue	Glenn Robinson Purdue	Glenn Robinson Purdue	Glenn Robinson Purdue	Glenn Robinson Purdue	Glenn Robinson Purdue	Glenn Robinson Purdue
1995	Joe Smith Maryland	Joe Smith Maryland	Ed O'Bannon UCLA	Ed O'Bannon UCLA	Shawn Respert Michigan St.	Joe Smith Maryland	Joe Smith Maryland
1996	Marcus Camby Massachusetts	Marcus Camby Massachusetts	Marcus Camby Massachusetts	Marcus Camby Massachusetts	Marcus Camby Massachusetts	Marcus Camby Massachusetts	Marcus Camby Massachusetts
1997		Tim Duncan Wake Forest	Tim Duncan Wake Forest	Tim Duncan Wake Forest	Tim Duncan Wake Forest	Tim Duncan Wake Forest	Tim Duncan Wake Forest
1998	Antawn Jamison North Carolina	Antawn Jamison North Carolina	Antawn Jamison North Carolina	Antawn Jamison North Carolina	Antawn Jamison North Carolina	Antawn Jamison North Carolina	Antawn Jamison North Carolina
1999	Elton Brand Duke	Elton Brand Duke	Elton Brand Duke	Elton Brand Duke	Elton Brand Duke	Elton Brand Duke	Elton Brand Duke
2000	Kenyon Martin Cincinnati	Kenyon Martin Cincinnati	Kenyon Martin Cincinnati	Kenyon Martin Cincinnati	Kenyon Martin Cincinnati	Kenyon Martin Cincinnati	Kenyon Martin Cincinnati
2001	Shane Battier Duke	Shane Battier Duke	Shane Battier Duke	Jason Williams Duke	Shane Battier Duke	Shane Battier Duke	Shane Battier Duke
2002	Jason Williams Duke	Jason Williams Duke	Jason Williams Duke	Jason Williams Duke Drew Gooden Kansas	Jason Williams Duke	Jason Williams Duke	Jason Williams Duke
2003	David West Xavier	David West Xavier	T.J. Ford Texas	Nick Collison Kansas	T.J. Ford Texas	David West Xavier
2004	Jameer Nelson St. Joseph's	Jameer Nelson St. Joseph's	Jameer Nelson St. Joseph's	Jameer Nelson St. Joseph's Emeka Okafor Connecticut	Jameer Nelson St. Joseph's	Jameer Nelson St. Joseph's
2005	Andrew Bogut Utah	Andrew Bogut Utah	Andrew Bogut Utah	Andrew Bogut Utah	Andrew Bogut Utah	J.J. Redick Duke
2006	J.J. Redick Duke	J.J. Redick Duke	J.J. Redick Duke Adam Morrison Gonzaga	J.J. Redick Duke	J.J. Redick Duke Adam Morrison Gonzaga	J.J. Redick Duke
2007	Kevin Durant Texas	Kevin Durant Texas	Kevin Durant Texas	Kevin Durant Texas	Kevin Durant Texas	Kevin Durant Texas

Basketball Times Player of the Year: 1982-Ralph Sampson, Virginia; 1983-Ralph Sampson, Virginia; 1984-Akeem Olajuwon, Houston; 1985-Patrick Ewing, Georgetown; 1986-Scott Skiles, Michigan St.; 1987-Kenny Smith, North Carolina; 1988-Hersey Hawkins, Bradley; 1989-Sean Elliot, Arizona; 1990-Derrick Coleman, Syracuse; 1991-Larry Johnson, UNLV; 1992-Christian Laettner, Duke; 1993-Jamaal Mashburn, Kentucky; 1994-Glenn Robinson, Purdue; 1995-Ed O'Bannon, UCLA; 1996-Marcus Camby, Massachusetts; 1997-Tim Duncan, Wake Forest; 1998-Antawn Jamison, North Carolina; 1999-Jason Terry, Arizona; 2000-Kenyon Martin, Cincinnati; 2001-Shane Battier, Duke; 2002-Jason Williams, Duke; 2003-David West, Xavier; 2004-Jameer Nelson, St. Joseph's; 2005-Andrew Bogut, Utah; 2006-J.J. Redick, Duke, & Adam Morrison, Gonzaga; 2007-Kevin Durant, Texas.

The Sporting News Player of the Year (no selection made in missing years): 1943-Andy Phillips, Illinois; 1944-Dale Hall, Army; 1945-George Mikan, DePaul; 1946-Bob Kurland, Oklahoma St.; 1950-Paul Arizin, Villanova; 1951-Sherman White, Long Island; 1958-Oscar Robertson, Cincinnati; 1959-Oscar Robertson, Cincinnati; 1960-Oscar Robertson, Cincinnati; 1961-Jerry Lucas, Ohio St.; 1962-Jerry Lucas, Ohio St.; 1963-Art Heyman, Duke; 1964-Bill Bradley, Princeton; 1965-Bill Bradley, Princeton; 1966-Cazzie Russell, Michigan; 1967-Lew Alcindor, UCLA; 1968-Elvin Hayes, Houston; 1969-Lew Alcindor, UCLA; 1970-Pete Maravich, LSU; 1971-Sidney Wicks, UCLA; 1972-Bill Walton, UCLA; 1973-Bill Walton, UCLA; 1974-Bill Walton, UCLA; 1975-David Thompson, North Carolina St.; 1976-Scott May, Indiana; 1977-Marques Johnson, UCLA; 1978-Phil Ford, North Carolina; 1979-Larry Bird, Indiana St.; 1980-Darrell Griffith, Louisville; 1981-Mark Aguirre, DePaul; 1982-Ralph Sampson, Virginia; 1983-Michael Jordan, North Carolina; 1984-Michael Jordan, North Carolina; 1985-Patrick Ewing, Georgetown; 1986-Walter Berry, St. John's (N.Y.); 1987-David Robinson, Navy; 1988-Hersey Hawkins, Bradley; 1989-Stacey King, Oklahoma; 1990-Dennis Scott, Georgia Tech; 1991-Larry Johnson, UNLV; 1992-Christian Laettner, Duke; 1993-Calbert Cheaney, Indiana; 1994-Glenn Robinson, Purdue; 1995-Shawn Respert, Michigan St.; 1996-Marcus Camby, Massachusetts; 1997-Tim Duncan, Wake Forest; 1998-Antawn Jamison, North Carolina; 1999-Elton Brand, Duke; 2000-Kenyon Martin, Cincinnati; 2001-Shane Battier, Duke; 2002-Jason Williams, Duke; 2003-T.J. Ford, Texas; 2004-Jameer Nelson, St. Joseph's; 2005-Dee Brown, Illinois; 2006-J.J. Redick, Duke; 2007-Kevin Durant, Texas.

Frances Pomeroy Naismith Award (Most Outstanding Player who stands 6-foot tall or under): 1969-Billy Keller, Purdue; 1970-John Rinka, Kenyon; 1971- Charlie Johnson, California; 1972-Scott Martin, Oklahoma; 1973-Bobby Sherwin, Army; 1974-Mike Robinson, Michigan St.; 1975-Monty Towe, North Carolina St.; 1976-Frank Algia, St. John's (N.Y.); 1977-Jeff Jonas, Utah; 1978-Mike Scheib, Susquehanna; 1979-Alton Byrd, Columbia; 1980-Jim Sweeney, Boston College; 1981-Terry Adolph, West Texas A&M; 1982-Jack Moore, Nebraska; 1983-Ray McCallum, Ball St.; 1984-Ricky Stokes, Virginia; 1985-Bubba Jennings, Texas Tech; 1986-Jim Les, Bradley; 1987-Muggsy Bogues, Wake Forest; 1988-Jerry Johnson, Fla. Southern; 1989-Tim Hardaway, UTEP; 1990-Boo Harvey, St. John's (N.Y.); 1991-Keith Jennings, East Tenn. St.; 1992-Tony Bennett, Green Bay; 1993-Sam Crawford, New Mexico St.; 1994-Greg Brown, Evansville; 1995-Tyus Edney, UCLA; 1996-Eddie Benton, Vermont; 1997-Kent McCausland, Iowa; 1998-Earl Boykins, Eastern Mich.; 1999-Shawnta Rogers, George Washington; 2000-Scoonie Penn, Ohio St.; 2001-Rashad Phillips, Detroit; 2002-Steve Logan, Cincinnati; 2003-Jason Gardner, Arizona; 2004-Jameer Nelson, St. Joseph's; 2005-Nate Robinson, Washington; 2006-Dee Brown, Illinois; 2007-Tre' Kelly, South Carolina.

Defensive Player of the Year: 1987-Tommy Amaker, Duke; 1988-Billy King, Duke; 1989-Stacey Augmon, UNLV; 1990-Stacey Augmon, UNLV; 1991-Stacey Augmon, UNLV; 1992-Alonzo Mourning, Georgetown; 1993-Grant Hill, Duke; 1994-Jim McIlvaine, Marquette; 1995-Tim Duncan, Wake Forest; 1996-Tim Duncan, Wake Forest; 1997-Tim Duncan, Wake Forest; 1998-Steve Wojciechowski, Duke; 1999-Shane Battier, Duke; 2000-Kenyon Martin, Cincinnatti & Shane Battier, Duke; 2001-Shane Battier, Duke; 2002-John Linehan, Providence; 2003-Emeka Okafor, Connecticut; 2004-Emeka Okafor, Connecticut; 2005-Shelden Williams, Duke; 2006-Shelden Williams, Duke; 2007-Greg Oden, Ohio St.

Bob Cousy Award (top point guard): 2004-Jameer Nelson, St. Joseph's; 2005-Raymond Felton, North Carolina; 2006-Dee Brown, Illinois; 2007-Acie Law IV, Texas A&M.

Divisions II & III Player Of The Year

The Divisions II and III Player of the Year are chosen by the National Association of Basketball Coaches (NABC).

	Division II	**Division III**
1983	Earl Jones, Dist. of Columbia	Leroy Witherspoon, Potsdam St.
1984	Earl Jones, Dist. of Columbia	Leroy Witherspoon, Potsdam St.
1985	Charles Oakley, Virginia Union	Tim Casey, Wittenberg
1986	Todd Linder, Tampa	Dick Hempy, Otterbein
1987	Ralph Talley, Norfolk St.	Brendan Mitchell, Potsdam St.
1988	Jerry Johnson, Fla. Southern	Scott Tedder, Ohio Wesleyan
1989	Kris Kearney, Fla. Southern	Greg Grant, TCNJ
1990	A.J. English, Virginia Union	Matt Hancock, Colby
1991	Corey Crowder, Ky. Wesleyan	Brad Baldridge, Wittenberg
1992	Eric Manuel, Oklahoma City	Andre Foreman, Salisbury
1993	Alex Wright, Central Okla.	Steve Hondred, Calvin
1994	Derrick Johnson, Virginia Union	Scott Fitch, Geneseo St.
1995	Stan Gourard, Southern Ind.	D'Artis Jones, Ohio Northern
1996	Stan Gourard, Southern Ind.	David Benter, Hanover
1997	Kebu Stewart, Cal St. Bakersfield	Bryan Crabtree, Ill. Wesleyan
1998	Joe Newton, Central Okla.	Mike Nogelo, Williams
1999	Antonio Garica, Ky. Wesleyan	Merrill Berunson, Wis.-Platteville
2000	Ajumu Gaines, Charleston (W.V.)	Aaron Winkle, Calvin
2001	Colin Ducharme, Longwood	Horace Jenkins, Wm. Paterson
2002	Ronald Murray, Shaw	Jeff Gibbs, Otterbein
2003	Marlon Parmer, Ky. Wesleyan	Bryan Nelson, Williams
2004	Elad Inbar, Mass.-Lowell	Richard Melzer, Wis.-River Falls
2005	Mark Worthington, Metro St.	Jason Kalsow, Wis.-Stevens Point
2006	Daruis Hargrove, Virginia Union	Brandon Adair, Va. Wesleyan
	Turner Trofholz, South Dakota	
2007	John Smith, Winona St.	Andrew Olson, Amherst
		Ben Strong, Guilford

Divisions II and III First-Team All-Americans by Team

Current Division I member denoted by (*). Non-NCAA member denoted by (†).

ABILENE CHRISTIAN
1968—John Godfrey

ADELPHI
2001—Ryan McCormack

AKRON*
1967—Bill Turner
1972—Len Paul

ALA.-HUNTSVILLE
1978—Tony Vann
2006—Jason Smith

ALAS. ANCHORAGE
1987—Jesse Jackson
1987—Hansi Gnad
1989—Michael Johnson
1990—Todd Fisher
2005—Brad Oleson

ALBANY ST. (GA.)
1975—Major Jones

ALBION
2005—Travis Dupree
2006—Brandon Crawford

ALCORN ST.*
1976—John McGill

ALFRED
2001—Devon Downing

AMERICAN*
1960—Willie Jones

AMERICAN INT'L
1969—Greg Hill
1970—Greg Hill
2002—Malik Moore

AMHERST
1970—Dave Auten
1971—James Rehnquist
2003—Steve Zieja
2005—Andrew Schiel
2007—Andrew Olson

ARK.-MONTICELLO
2004—Billy McDaniel

ARKANSAS ST.*
1965—Jerry Rook

ARMSTRONG ATLANTIC
1975—Ike Williams

ASSUMPTION
1970—Jake Jones
1971—Jake Jones
1973—Mike Boylan
1974—John Grochowalski
1975—John Grochowalski
1976—Bill Wurm

AUGUSTA ST.
2007—A.J. Bowman

AUGUSTANA (ILL.)
1973—John Laing

BABSON
1992—Jim Pierrakos

BARTON
2007—Anthony Atkinson

BEMIDJI ST.
2004—Charles Hanks

BENTLEY
1974—Brian Hammel
1975—Brian Hammel
2005—Tim Forbes

BISHOP
1983—Shannon Lilly

BOWIE ST.
2005—Letheal Cook
2007—Gail Goodrich

BRIDGEPORT
1969—Gary Baum
1976—Lee Hollerbach
1985—Manute Bol
1991—Lambert Shell
1992—Lambert Shell
1995—Lamont Jones

BRIDGEWATER (VA.)
1995—Dan Rush

2002—Kyle Williford

BYU-HAWAII
2000—David Evans

BROCKPORT ST.
2002—Mike Medbury

BRYANT
1981—Ernie DeWitt
2004—Romuald Augustin

UC RIVERSIDE*
1989—Maurice Pullum

CAL POLY POMONA
2005—Jeff Bonds

CAL ST. BAKERSFIELD
1996—Kebu Stewart
1997—Kebu Stewart

CAL ST. SAN B'DINO
2004—Jonathan Levy

CALIFORNIA (PA.)
1993—Ray Gutierrez

CALVIN
1993—Steve Honderd
2000—Aaron Winkle

CAMERON
1974—Jerry Davenport

CARLETON
1993—Gerrick Monroe

CARTHAGE
2002—Antoine McDaniel

CENTENARY (LA.)*
1957—Milt Williams

CENTRAL CONN. ST.*
1969—Howie Dickenman

UCF*
1979—Bo Clark
1980—Bo Clark

CENTRAL MO. ST.
1981—Bill Fennelly

1985—Ron Nunnelly
1991—Armando Becker
2006—Michael Hicks

CENTRAL OKLA.
1993—Alex Wright
1997—Tyrone Hopkins
1998—Joe Newton
1999—Eddie Robinson

CENTRAL WASH.
1967—Mel Cox

CHARLESTON (W.V.)
2000—Ajamu Gaines

CHATTANOOGA*
1977—Wayne Golden

CHEYNEY
1979—Andrew Fields
1981—George Melton
1982—George Melton

CHICAGO
2003—Derek Reich

CHRIS. NEWPORT
1991—Lamont Strothers
2001—Antoine Sinclair

CLAREMONT-M-S
1992—Chris Greene

CLARION
1994—Kwame Morton

CLARK (MASS.)
1980—Kevin Clark
1981—Kevin Clark
1988—Kermit Sharp

COLBY
1977—Paul Harvey
1978—Paul Harvey
1989—Matt Hancock
1990—Matt Hancock

COLUMBUS ST.
2004—Yandel Brown
2005—Yandel Brown

CONCORD
2004—Lewis Muse

CORTLAND ST.
2000—Tom Williams

DAVIS & ELKINS
1959—Paul Wilcox

DELTA ST.
1969—Sammy Little
2006—Jasper Johnson

DePAUW
1987—David Galle

DIST. COLUMBIA
1982—Earl Jones
1983—Earl Jones
        Michael Britt
1984—Earl Jones

EASTERN MICH.*
1971—Ken McIntosh
1972—George Gervin

EDINBORO
1996—Tyrone Mason
2002—Kenny Tate
2005—Jakim Donaldson

ELMHURST
2001—Ryan Knuppel

EMORY
1990—Tim Garrett

EMORY & HENRY
2004—Justin Call

EVANSVILLE*
1959—Hugh Ahlering
1960—Ed Smallwood
1965—Jerry Sloan
        Larry Humes
1966—Larry Humes

FINDLAY
2006—Dustin Pfeiffer
2007—Frank Phillips

FLA. SOUTHERN
1981—John Ebeling
1982—John Ebeling
1988—Jerry Johnson
        Kris Kearney
1989—Kris Kearney
1990—Donolly Tyrell

FORT HAYS ST.
1997—Alonzo Goldston

FRAMINGHAM ST.
1984—Mark Van Valkenburg

FRANKLIN
1999—Jason Sibley

FRANK. & MARSH.
1992—Will Lasky
1996—Jeremiah Henry
2000—Alex Kraft

GANNON
1985—Butch Warner
1998—Troy Nesmith

GENESEO ST.
1994—Scott Fitch

GEORGETOWN (KY.)†
1964—Cecil Tuttle

GRAMBLING*
1961—Charles Hardnett
1962—Charles Hardnett
1964—Willis Reed
1966—Johnny Comeaux
1976—Larry Wright

GRAND CANYON
1976—Bayard Forest

GRAND VALLEY ST.
1997—Joe Modderman

GREEN BAY*
1978—Tom Anderson
1979—Ron Ripley

GUILFORD
1968—Bob Kauffman
1975—Lloyd Free
2007—Ben Strong

HAMILTON
1977—Cedric Oliver
1978—Cedric Oliver
1979—Cedric Oliver
1987—John Cavanaugh
1998—Mike Schantz
1999—Michael Schantz
2003—Joe Finley

HAMPDEN-SYDNEY
1992—Russell Turner
2000—T.J. Grimes

HANOVER
1996—David Benter

HARTFORD*
1979—Mark Noon

HARTWICK
1977—Dana Gahres
1983—Tim O'Brien

HAVERFORD
1977—Dick Vioth

HENDERSON ST.
2002—Niki Arinze
2004—Tarvoris Uzoique

HOPE
1984—Chip Henry
1998—Joel Holstege

HUMBOLDT ST.
2004—Austin Nichols
2007—Kevin Johnson

ILLINOIS ST.*
1968—Jerry McGreal

ILL. WESLEYAN
1977—Jack Sikma
1989—Jeff Kuehl
1995—Chris Simich
1997—Bryan Crabtree
1998—Brent Niebrugge
2000—Korey Coon

2004—Keelan Amelianovich
2005—Adam Dauksas

INDIANA (PA.)
1995—Derrick Freeman

IUPUI*
1996—Carlos Knox

INDIANA ST.*
1968—Jerry Newsome

INDIANAPOLIS
2005—David Logan

ITHACA
2000—Pat Britton

JACKSON ST.*
1974—Eugene Short
1975—Eugene Short
1977—Purvis Short

JACKSONVILLE*
1962—Roger Strickland
1963—Roger Strickland

JOHNSON C. SMITH
2001—Wiyle Perry

KEAN
1993—Fred Drains

KEENE ST.
2001—Chris Coates

KENNESAW ST.
2004—Terrence Hill

KENTUCKY ST.
1971—Travis Grant
        Elmore Smith
1972—Travis Grant
1975—Gerald Cunningham
1977—Gerald Cunningham

KY. WESLEYAN
1957—Mason Cope
1967—Sam Smith
1968—Dallas Thornton
1969—George Tinsley
1984—Rod Drake
        Dwight Higgs
1988—J.B. Brown
1990—Corey Crowder
1991—Corey Crowder
1995—Willis Cheaney
1998—Antonio Garcia
1999—Antonio Garcia
        Dana Williams
2000—LeRoy John
2001—Lorico Duncan
2002—Ronald Evans

KENYON
1969—John Rinka
1970—John Rinka
1979—Scott Rogers
1980—Scott Rogers

LAWRENCE
2006—Chris Braier

LEBANON VALLEY
1995—Mike Rhodes
1997—Andy Panko
1998—Andy Panko
1999—Andy Panko
2005—J.D. Byers

LEWIS
2004—Monta McGhee

LEWIS & CLARK
1963—Jim Boutin
1964—Jim Boutin
1999—Andy Panko

LINCOLN (MO.)
1978—Harold Robertson

LIPSCOMB*
1988—Phillip Hutcheson
1989—Phillip Hutcheson
1990—Phillip Hutcheson
1992—John Pierce

LONG ISLAND*
1968—Luther Green
        Larry Newbold

LONGWOOD*
1984—Jerome Kersey
2001—Colin Ducharme

LA.-LAFAYETTE*
1965—Dean Church
1970—Marvin Winkler
1971—Dwight Lamar

LOUISIANA COL.
1979—Paul Poe

LOUISIANA TECH*
1973—Mike Green

MAINE*
1961—Tom Chappelle

MASS.-DARTMOUTH
1993—Steve Haynes

MASS.-LOWELL
1989—Leo Parent
2004—Elad Inbar
2005—Stacey Moragne
2006—Stacey Moragne

MERCHANT MARINE
1990—Kevin D'Arcy

MERRIMACK
1977—Ed Murphy
1978—Ed Murphy
        Dana Skinner
1983—Joe Dickson

METHODIST
1997—Jason Childers

METRO ST.
2005—Mark Worthington

MICHIGAN TECH
2003—Matt Cameron
2004—Josh Buettner
2005—Josh Buettner

MINN. DULUTH
1977—Bob Bone

MINN. ST. MANKATO
2005—Jamel Staten
2006—Luke Anderson
2007—Luke Anderson

MISERICORDIA
2003—Willie Chandler

MO.-ST. LOUIS
1977—Bob Bone

MONTCLAIR ST.
1999—Anthony Peoples
2006—Gian Paul Gonzalez

MONTEVALLO
2005—James Hall
2007—Greg Brown
        Marcus Kennedy

MORGAN ST.*
1974—Marvin Webster
1975—Marvin Webster
1999—Tim West

MT. ST. MARY'S*
1957—Jack Sullivan

MOUNT UNION
1997—Aaron Shipp

MUHLENBERG
2002—Mark Lesko

MUSKINGUM
1992—Andy Moore

NEB.-OMAHA
1992—Phil Cartwright

NEB. WESLEYAN
1986—Dana Janssen

NEW HAVEN
1988—Herb Watkins

CNJ
1988—Greg Grant
1989—Greg Grant

NEW JERSEY CITY
1979—Brett Wyatt
2004—Samar Battle

N.J. INST. OF TECH.
1996—Clarence Pierce

NEW ORLEANS*
1971—Xavier Webster

NYIT
1980—Kelvin Hicks

NICHOLLS ST.*
1978—Larry Wilson

NORFOLK ST.*
1979—Ken Evans
1984—David Pope
1987—Ralph Talley
1995—Corey Williams

NORTH ALA.
1980—Otis Boddie

N.C. WESLEYAN
1999—Marquis McDougald

NORTH DAKOTA
1966—Phil Jackson
1967—Phil Jackson
1991—Dave Vonesh
1993—Scott Guldseth
2003—Jerome Beasley

NORTH DAKOTA ST.*
1960—Marvin Bachmeier

NORTH PARK
1979—Mike Harper
1980—Mike Harper
1981—Mike Thomas

NORTHEASTERN ST.
2003—Jon Shepherd
2004—Darnell Hinson

NORTHERN MICH.
1987—Bill Harris
2000—Cory Brathol
2007—Ricky Volcy

NORTHWOOD
1973—Fred Smile

OHIO NORTHERN
1982—Stan Mories
1995—D'Artis Jones
2001—Kris Oberdick
2004—Jim Conrad

OHIO WESLEYAN
1987—Scott Tedder
1988—Scott Tedder

OKLAHOMA CITY†
1992—Eric Manuel

OLD DOMINION*
1972—Dave Twardzik
1974—Joel Copeland
1976—Wilson Washington

OTTERBEIN
1966—Don Carlos
1982—Ron Stewart
1983—Ron Stewart
1985—Dick Hempy
1986—Dick Hempy
1987—Dick Hempy
1991—James Bradley
1994—Nick Gutman
1999—Kevin Weakley
2002—Jeff Gibbs

PACIFIC LUTHERAN
1959—Chuck Curtis

PFEIFFER
1992—Tony Smith
2005—Rico Grier
2006—DeMario Grier

PHILADELPHIA U.
1976—Emory Sammons
1977—Emory Sammons
2006—Tayron Thomas
2007—Christian Burns

PITTSBURG ST.
2005—Eddie Jackson

PLYMOUTH ST.
1994—Moses Jean-Pierre
1999—Adam DeChristopher

POTSDAM ST.
1980—Derrick Rowland
1981—Derrick Rowland
1982—Maurice Woods
1983—Leroy Witherspoon
1984—Leroy Witherspoon
1986—Roosevelt Bullock
1986—Brendan Mitchell
1987—Brendan Mitchell
1988—Steve Babiarz
1989—Steve Babiarz

PRAIRIE VIEW*
1962—Zelmo Beaty

PUGET SOUND
1979—Joe Leonard

QUEENS (N.C.)
1998—Soce Faye

RAMAPO
2003—Charles Ransom
2005—Amin Wright

RANDOLPH-MACON
1983—Bryan Vacca
2003—Jared Mills
2005—Justin Wansley

RICHARD STOCKTON
1997—Carl Cochrane

ROANOKE
1972—Hal Johnston
1973—Jay Piccola
1974—Jay Piccola
1983—Gerald Holmes
1984—Reggie Thomas
1985—Reggie Thomas
1994—Hilliary Scott

ROCHESTER
1991—Chris Fite
1992—Chris Fite
2004—Seth Hauben
2005—Seth Hauben

ROCHESTER INST.
1996—Craig Jones
1997—Craig Jones

ROWAN
1998—Rob Scott
2007—Thomas Baker

RUTGERS-CAMDEN
2002—Brian Turner

SACRED HEART*
1972—Ed Czernota
1978—Hector Olivencia
        Andre Means
1982—Keith Bennett
1983—Keith Bennett
1986—Roger Younger
1993—Darrin Robinson

ST. CLOUD ST.
1957—Vern Baggenstoss
1986—Kevin Catron

ST. JOHN FISHER
2006—Sean O'Brien

ST. JOSEPH'S (IND.)
1960—Bobby Williams
2006—Sullivan Sykes

ST. MICHAEL'S
1965—Richie Tarrant

ST. NORBERT
1963—Mike Wisneski

ST. ROSE
2007—Steve Dagostino

ST. THOMAS
2006—Isaac Rosefelt
2007—Isaac Rosefelt

SALEM INT'L
1976—Archie Talley
2006—Shaun McKie

SALEM ST.
2000—Tishaun Jenkins

SALISBURY
1991—Andre Foreman
1992—Andre Foreman

SAM HOUSTON ST.*
1973—James Lister

SCRANTON
1963—Bill Witaconis
1977—Irvin Johnson
1978—Irvin Johnson
1984—Bill Bessoir
1985—Bill Bessoir
1993—Matt Cusano

SEATTLE PACIFIC
2006—Tony Binetti
2007—Dustin Bremerman

SEWANEE
1998—Ryan Harrigan

SHAW
2002—Ronald Murray

SHENANDOAH
1996—Phil Dixon

SLIPPERY ROCK
1991—Myron Brown

SOUTH DAKOTA
1958—Jim Daniels
2004—Tommie King
2006—Turner Trofholz

SOUTH DAKOTA ST.*
1961—Don Jacobsen
1964—Tom Black
2005—Turner Trofholz

SOUTHEASTERN OKLA.
1957—Jim Spivey
2007—Eric Babers

SOUTHERN ILL.*
1966—George McNeil
1967—Walt Frazier

SOUTHERN IND.
1995—Stan Gouard
1996—Stan Gouard

SOUTHERN N.H.
2003—Sotirios Karapostolou

SOUTHWEST BAPTIST
2006—Sheldon Pace

SPRINGFIELD
1970—Dennis Clark
1986—Ivan Olivares

STEPHEN F. AUSTIN*
1970—Surry Oliver

STETSON*
1970—Ernie Killum

STEUBENVILLE†
1958—Jim Smith

STONEHILL
1979—Bill Zolga
1980—Bill Zolga
1982—Bob Reitz

STONY BROOK*
1979—Earl Keith

SUSQUEHANNA
1986—Dan Harnum

TAMPA
1985—Todd Linder
1986—Todd Linder
1987—Todd Linder
1994—DeCarlo Deveaux

TARLETON ST.
2004—Tim Burnette

TENNESSEE ST.*
1958—Dick Barnett
1959—Dick Barnett
1971—Ted McClain
1972—Lloyd Neal
1974—Leonard Robinson

TEX.-PAN AMERICAN*
1964—Lucious Jackson
1968—Otto Moore

TEXAS SOUTHERN*
1958—Bennie Swain
1977—Alonzo Bradley

TEXAS ST.*
1959—Charles Sharp
1960—Charles Sharp

THOMAS MORE
1996—Rick Hughes

TRINITY (CONN.)
2006—Tyler Rhoten

TRINITY (TEX.)
1968—Larry Jeffries
1969—Larry Jeffries
2002—Colin Tabb

TROY*
1993—Terry McCord

TUFTS
1995—Chris McMahon

UPSALA
1981—Steve Keenan
1982—Steve Keenan

URSINUS
2004—Dennis Stanton

UTICA
2007—Ray Bryant

VIRGINIA UNION
1985—Charles Oakley
1990—A.J. English
1994—Derrick Johnson
　　　　Warren Peebles
1996—Ben Wallace
1998—Marquise Newbie
2006—Duane Crockett
　　　　Darius Hargrove

VA. WESLEYAN
2006—Brandon Adair

WABASH
1982—Pete Metzelaars

WASHBURN
1994—Clarence Tyson
1997—Dan Buie
2001—Ewan Auguste
2005—Travis Robbins

WASH. & LEE
1978—Pat Dennis

WAYNE ST. (NEB.)
1999—Tyler Johnson

WEST CHESTER
2003—Ramzee Stanton

WEST GA.
1974—Clarence Walker

WEST TEXAS A&M
2007—Damien Lolar

WEST VIRGINIA ST.
2004—Mike Taylor
2007—Ted Scott

WESTERN CARO.*
1968—Henry Logan

WESTERN WASH.
2006—Grant Dykstra

WESTMINSTER (PA.)
1962—Ron Galbreath

WESTMINSTER (UTAH)†
1969—Ken Hall

WHEATON (ILL.)
1958—Mel Peterson
2007—Kent Raymond

WIDENER
1978—Dennis James
1988—Lou Stevens
2006—Kristian Clarkson

WILKES
2001—Dave Jannuzzi

WM. PATERSON
2000—Horace Jenkins
2001—Horace Jenkins

WILLIAMS
1961—Bob Mahland
1962—Bob Mahland
1996—Mike Nogelo
1997—Mike Nogelo
1998—Mike Nogelo
2004—Ben Coffin

WINONA ST.
2007—John Smith

WINSTON-SALEM*
1967—Earl Monroe
1980—Reginald Gaines

WIS.-EAU CLAIRE
1972—Mike Ratliff

WIS.-OSHKOSH
1996—Dennis Ruedinger
2002—Tim Dworak

WIS.-PARKSIDE
1976—Gary Cole

WIS.-PLATTEVILLE
1992—T.J. Van Wie
1998—Ben Hoffmann
1999—Merrill Brunson

WIS.-RIVER FALLS
2003—Richard Melzer
2004—Richard Melzer

WIS.-STEVENS POINT
1985—Terry Porter
2000—Brant Bailey
2005—Jason Kalsow

WIS.-SUPERIOR
2001—Vince Thomas

WIS.-WHITEWATER
1990—Ricky Spicer
1994—Ty Evans
1997—James Stewart

WITTENBERG
1961—George Fisher
1963—Al Thrasher
1980—Brian Agler
1981—Tyrone Curtis
1985—Tim Casey
1989—Steve Allison
1990—Brad Baldridge
1991—Brad Baldridge

WOOSTER
2003—Bryan Nelson
2007—Tom Port

WRIGHT ST.*
1981—Rodney Benson
1986—Mark Vest

XAVIER (LA.)†
1973—Bruce Seals

YORK (PA.)
2007—Chad McGowan

YOUNGSTOWN ST.*
1977—Jeff Covington
1978—Jeff Covington

Teams used for selections:
AP Little All-America—
　　1957-79
NABC College Division—
　　1967-76
NABC Divisions II, III—
　　1977-2006

Divisions II and III Academic All-Americans by Team

ABILENE CHRISTIAN
1999—Jared Mosley

AKRON
1972—Wil Schwarzinger

ALBANY (N.Y.)
1988—John Carmello

ALBION
1979—John Nibert

ALDERSON-BROADDUS
2002—Kevyn McBride

ARKANSAS TECH
1990—Gray Townsend
1994—David Bevis
1995—David Bevis

ASHLAND
1967—Jim Basista
1970—Jay Franson

ASSUMPTION
1967—George Ridick

AUGUSTANA (ILL.)
1973—Bruce Hamming
1974—Bruce Hamming
1975—Bruce Hamming
1979—Glen Heiden

AUGUSTANA (S.D.)
1974—John Ritterbusch
1975—John Ritterbusch

BALDWIN-WALLACE
1985—Bob Scelza

BARRINGTON
1982—Shawn Smith

BATES
1983—Herb Taylor
1984—Herb Taylor

BEMIDJI ST.
1976—Steve Vogel
1977—Steve Vogel
1978—Steve Vogel
2003—Royce Bryan

BENTLEY
1980—Joe Betley

BETHANY (W.V.)
2006—Matt Drahos

BETHEL (MINN.)
1994—Jason Mekelburg

BLOOMSBURG
1978—Steve Bright

BRANDEIS
1978—John Martin

BRIAR CLIFF
1989—Chad Neubrand

BRIDGEWATER (VA.)
1985—Sean O'Connell

BRYAN
1981—Dean Ropp

C.W. POST
1973—Ed Fields

CALIFORNIA (PA.)
1993—Raymond Guttierez

UC DAVIS
1970—Tom Cupps
1983—Preston Neumayr

UC RIVERSIDE
1971—Kirby Gordon

CAL LUTHERAN
1983—Bill Burgess

CALVIN
1992—Steve Honderd
1993—Steve Honderd
1994—Chris Knoester

CAPITAL
1973—Charles Gashill

CARNEGIE MELLON
1973—Mike Wegener
1979—Larry Hufnagel
1980—Larry Hufnagel

CASE RESERVE
1996—Jim Fox
1997—Jim Fox

CASTLETON ST.
1985—Bryan DeLoatch

CATHOLIC
1997—Jeremy Borys

UCF
1982—Jimmie Farrell

CENTRAL MICH.
1967—John Berends
1971—Mike Hackett

CENTRAL ST. (OHIO)
1971—Sterling Quant

CHADRON ST.
1992—Josh Robinson

CHAPMAN
2006—Zach Wheatley

CLAREMONT-M-S
2002—Bob Donlan

COAST GUARD
1971—Ken Bicknell

COLBY-SAWYER
2006—Andrew St. Clair

COLORADO MINES
1991—Daniel McKeon
1991—Hank Prey

UC-COLO. SPRINGS
2007—Patrick Hannaway

COLORADO ST.-PUEBLO
1972—Jim Von Loh

CORNELL COLLEGE
1974—Randy Kuhlman
1977—Dick Grant
1978—Robert Wisco
1979—Robert Wisco
1987—Jeff Fleming

DAVID LIPSCOMB
1989—Phil Hutcheson
1990—Phil Hutcheson
1992—Jerry Meyer

DELTA ST.
1972—Larry MaGee

DENISON
1967—Bill Druckemiller
1970—Charles Claggett
1987—Kevin Locke
1988—Kevin Locke
1997—Casey Chroust

DENVER
1987—Joe Fisher

DePAUW
1970—Richard Tharp
1973—Gordon Pittenger
1987—David Galle

DICKINSON
1971—Lloyd Bonner
1981—David Freysinger
1982—David Freysinger

DREXEL
1967—Joe Hertrich

ELMHURST
2001—Ryan Knuppel

ELON
1988—Brian Branson
1988—Steve Page
1998—Christopher Kiger

EMBRY-RIDDLE
2001—Kyle Mas

EMORY
2000—Neil Bhutta
2005—Chase Fawsett

EMORY & HENRY
2004—Justin Call

FLA. GULF COAST
2007—Beau Bauer

FORT HAYS ST.
1978—Mike Pauls

FORT LEWIS
1998—Ryan Ostrom

FRANK. & MARSH.
2000—Jerome Maiatico

GANNON
2007—Aurimas Truskauskas

GETTYSBURG
1975—Jeffrey Clark

GREEN BAY
1974—Tom Jones

GRINNELL
1976—John Haigh
1994—Steve Diekmann
1995—Steve Diekmann
1996—Ed Brands

GROVE CITY
1979—Mike Donahoe
1984—Curt Silverling
1985—Curt Silverling

GUST. ADOLPHUS
1983—Mark Hanson

HAMILTON
1978—John Klauberg

HAMLINE
1986—Paul Westling
1989—John Banovetz

HAMPDEN-SYDNEY
1992—Russell Turner

HARDING
1985—Kenneth Collins
1986—Kenneth Collins

HOWARD PAYNE
1973—Garland Bullock
1974—Garland Bullock

ILL. WESLEYAN
1972—Dean Gravlin
1973—Dean Gravlin
1975—Jack Sikma
       Bob Spear
1976—Jack Sikma
       Bob Spear
1977—Jack Sikma
       Bob Spear
1979—Al Black
1981—Greg Yess
1982—Greg Yess
1987—Brian Coderre
1999—Korey Coon
2000—Korey Coon
2006—Keelan Amelianovich

INCARNATE WORD
1993—Randy Henderson

JAMES MADISON
1976—Sherman Dillard

JAMESTOWN
1980—Pete Anderson
1981—Pete Anderson

JOHN CARROLL
1999—Mark Heidorf

JOHNS HOPKINS
1991—Andy Enfield

KENYON
1970—John Rinka
1977—Tim Appleton
1985—Chris Coe Russell

LaGRANGE
1980—Todd Whitsitt

LEBANON VALLEY
2005—J.D. Byers

LIBERTY
1980—Karl Hess

LUTHER
1981—Doug Kintzinger
1982—Doug Kintzinger

MacMURRAY
1970—Tom Peters

MARIAN (WIS.)
2002—Scott Jaeger

MARIETTA
1982—Rick Clark
1983—Rick Clark

MARYVILLE (MO.)
2003—Kevin Bartow

MASS.-LOWELL
1970—Alfred Spinell
1984—John Paganetti

MIT
1980—Ray Nagem
1991—David Tomlinson

McDANIEL
1983—Douglas Pinto
1985—David Malin

McGILL
1983—Willie Hinz

McNEESE ST.
1972—David Wallace

MERRIMACK
1983—Joseph Dickson
1984—Joseph Dickson

MICHIGAN TECH
1981—Russ VanDuine
1985—Wayne Helmila
2003—J.T. Luginski

MILLIKIN
1977—Roy Mosser
       Dale Wills
1978—Gregg Finigan
1979—Rich Rames
       Gary Jackson
1980—Gary Jackson
1981—Gary Jackson
1989—Brian Horst

MILWAUKEE ENGR.
1983—Jeffrey Brezovar

MINN. ST. MANKATO
1997—David Kruse

MINN. ST. MOORHEAD
1996—Brett Beeson

MO.-ROLLA
1984—Todd Wentz
2004—Brian Westre

MO.-ST. LOUIS
1975—Bobby Bone
1976—Bobby Bone
1977—Bobby Bone

MONMOUTH (ILL.)
1990—S. Juan Mitchell

MONT. ST.-BILLINGS
2004—Jerett Skrifvars

MOUNT UNION
1971—Jim Howell

MUHLENBERG
1979—Greg Campisi
1981—Dan Barletta

NEB.-KEARNEY
1974—Tom Kropp
1975—Tom Kropp
2004—Nick Branting
2006—Dusty Jura

NEB.-OMAHA
1981—Jim Gregory

NEB. WESLEYAN
1984—Kevin Cook
1986—Kevin Cook
1995—Justin Wilkins
1997—Kipp Kissinger
1998—Kipp Kissinger

UNC ASHEVILLE
1974—Randy Pallas

NORTHERN COLO.
1967—Dennis Colson

NORTHWESTERN (MINN.)
2005—Jeff VerSteeg

OBERLIN
1971—Vic Guerrieri
1972—Vic Guerrieri

OHIO NORTHERN
2001—Kris Oberdick

OHIO WESLEYAN
1990—Mark Slayman

1998—John Camillus

OLD DOMINION
1974—Gray Eubank
1975—Gray Eubank

OTTERBEIN
1980—Mike Cochran

PACIFIC LUTHERAN
1967—Doug Leeland

POINT PARK
1986—Richard Condo

RIPON
1999—Bret Van Dyken

ROCHESTER
1984—Joe Augustine

ROCKFORD
1976—John Morrissey
1977—John Morrissey

ROSE-HULMAN
2002—Christopher Unton

ST. JOHN'S (MINN.)
1995—Joe Deignan

ST. JOSEPH'S (IND.)
1975—James Thordsen

ST. LEO
1977—Ralph Nelson

ST. ROSE
2007—Steve Dagostino

ST. THOMAS (FLA.)
1976—Arthur Collins
1977—Mike LaPrete

ST. THOMAS (MINN.)
1967—Dan Hansard
1978—Terry Fleming

SCRANTON
1983—Michael Banas
1984—Michael Banas
1985—Dan Polacheck
1993—Matt Cusano

SHIPPENSBURG
1979—John Whitmer
1981—Brian Cozzens
1982—Brian Cozzens

SIMPSON
2002—Jesse Harris
2003—Jesse Harris

SLIPPERY ROCK
1971—Robert Wiegand
1979—Mike Hardy
1983—John Samsa
1995—Mark Metzka

SOUTH DAKOTA
1970—Bill Hamer
1975—Rick Nissen
1976—Rick Nissen
1978—Jeff Nannen
1980—Jeff Nannen
1985—Rob Swanhorst

SOUTH DAKOTA ST.
1971—Jim Higgins
1972—Jim Higgins

SOUTHERN N.H.
2003—Brian Larrabee

SUSQUEHANNA
1986—Donald Harnum
1994—Tres Wolf

TENNESSEE TEMPLE
1977—Dan Smith
1978—Dan Smith

TEXAS LUTHERAN
2005—Tommy Stolhandske

TRINITY (CONN.)
1996—Keith Wolff

TRUMAN
1984—Mark Campbell
1999—Jason Reinberg
2000—Jason Reinberg

UNION (N.Y.)
1970—Jim Tedisco

URSINUS
2004—Dennis Stanton

VIRGINIA TECH
1968—Ted Ware

WABASH
1973—Joe Haklin

WARTBURG
1971—Dave Platte
1972—Dave Platte
1974—Fred Waldstein
1990—Dan Nettleton
1991—Dan Nettleton

WASHBURN
2001—Ewan Auguste

WASHINGTON-ST. LOUIS
1988—Paul Jackson
2007—Troy Ruths

WASH. & JEFF.
1980—David Damico

WENTWORTH INST.
2000—Kevin Hanlon

WESLEYAN (CONN.)
1972—James Akin
1974—Rich Fairbrother
1982—Steven Maizes

WESTERN ST.
1970—Michael Adams
1973—Rod Smith

WESTMINSTER (PA.)
1967—John Fontanella

WILKES
2001—Dave Jannuzzi

WM. PATERSON
2001—Horace Jenkins

WIS.-EAU CLAIRE
1972—Steven Johnson
1975—Ken Kaiser
1976—Ken Kaiser

WIS.-OSHKOSH
1998—Joe Imhoff

WIS.-PLATTEVILLE
1992—T.J. Van Wie
1993—T.J. Van Wie

WIS.-SUPERIOR
2001—Vince Thomas

WITTENBERG
1967—Jim Appleby

WOOSTER
2005—Matt Schlingman

WPI
1996—James Naughton

NCAA Postgraduate Scholarship Winners by Team

ABILENE CHRISTIAN
1999—Jared Mosley

AIR FORCE
1970—James Cooper
1973—Thomas Blase
1974—Richard Nickelson
1978—Thomas Schneeberger
1992—Brent Roberts
1993—Brad Boyer

UAB
1999—Damon Cobb

ALBANY (N.Y.)
1988—John Carmello

ALLEGHENY
1976—Robert Del Greco

ALMA
1976—Stuart TenHoor

AMERICAN
1973—Kermit Washington
1998—Nathan Smith

ARIZONA
1988—Steve Kerr
1991—Matt Muehlebach

ARIZONA ST.
1965—Dennis Dairman

ARKANSAS ST.
1975—J.H. Williams

ARMY
1965—John Ritch III
1972—Edward Mueller
1973—Robert Sherwin Jr.
1985—Randall Cozzens
1994—David Ardayfio

ASSUMPTION
1975—Paul Brennan
1977—William Wurm
2004—Shahar Golan

AUBURN
1976—Gary Redding

AUGUSTANA (ILL.)
1975—Bruce Hamming

AUGUSTANA (S.D.)
1975—Neil Klutman
1992—Jason Garrow

BALL ST.
1989—Richard Hall

BATES
1984—Herbert Taylor

BAYLOR
1997—Doug Brandt

BELLARMINE
1992—Tom Schurfranz
2001—Ronald Brooks

BELMONT
2004—Adam Mark

BENTLEY
1980—Joseph Betley

BOSTON COLLEGE
1967—William Wolters
1970—Thomas Veronneau
1972—James Phelan
1980—James Sweeney
1995—Marc Molinsky

BOWDOIN
1966—Howard Pease

BOWLING GREEN
1965—Robert Dwors

BRANDEIS
1972—Donald Fishman
1978—John Martin

BRIDGEWATER (VA.)
1970—Frederick Wampler

BYU
1966—Richard Nemelka
1983—Gregory Kite

1984—Devin Durrant
1987—Brent Stephenson
1989—Michael Smith
1990—Andy Toolson
1991—Steve Schreiner

BYU-HAWAII
2000—David Evans

BROWN
1972—Arnold Berman
1997—Jade Newburn

BUENA VISTA
2000—Landon Roth

BUTLER
1977—Wayne Burris
1991—John Karaffa

CALIFORNIA
1987—David Butler

UC DAVIS
1970—Thomas Cupps
1977—Mark Ford
1983—Preston Neumayr
1991—Matt Cordova

UC IRVINE
1975—Carl Baker

UC RIVERSIDE
1975—Randy Burnett

UC SAN DIEGO
1997—Matt Aune

UC SANTA BARBARA
1973—Robert Schachter
1993—Michael Meyer

CAL POLY POMONA
1978—Thomas Ispas

CAL ST. DOM. HILLS
1987—John Nojima

CAL ST. STANISLAUS
1983—Richard Thompson

CALIFORNIA (PA.)
1984—William Belko

CALTECH
1966—Alden Holford
1967—James Pearson
1968—James Stanley
1971—Thomas Heinz

CALVIN
1977—Mark Veenstra
1993—Steve Honderd

CARLETON
1969—Thomas Weaver
1982—James Tolf
1999—Joshua Wilhelm

CARNEGIE MELLON
1980—Lawrence Hufnagel

CASE RESERVE
1971—Mark Estes

CATHOLIC
1972—Joseph Good
1997—Jeremy Borys

CENTRAL (IOWA)
1973—Dana Snoap
1980—Jeffrey Verhoef

CENTRAL MICH.
1993—Sander Scott

CENTRE
1985—Thomas Cowens

CHAPMAN
1970—Anthony Mason

CHICAGO
1969—Dennis Waldon
1974—Gerald Clark
1985—Keith Libert

CINCINNATI
1977—Gary Yoder

CLAREMONT-M-S
1972—Jeffrey Naslund

CLARION
1973—Joseph Sebestyen

CLEMSON
1967—James Sutherland
1980—Robert Conrad Jr.
1999—Tom Wideman

COE
1965—Gary Schlarbaum

COLBY
1972—Matthew Zweig

COLGATE
1999—Ben Wandtke

COLORADO
1966—Charles Gardner
1985—Alex Stivrins

COLORADO MINES
1991—Hank Prey
1994—Todd Kenyon

UC-COLO. SPRINGS
2007—Patrick Hannaway

COLORADO ST.
1986—Richard Strong Jr.

COLUMBIA
1968—William Ames

CORNELL COLLEGE
1967—David Crow
1979—Robert Wisco
1981—Eric Reitan
1987—Jefferson Fleming
1994—Abram Tubbs
      Chad Reed

CREIGHTON
1971—Dennis Bresnahan Jr.
1978—Richard Apke

DARTMOUTH
1968—Joseph Colgan
1976—William Healey
1984—Paul Anderson
1997—Sea Lonergan

DAVIDSON
1969—Wayne Huckel
1983—Clifford Tribus

DAYTON
1979—Jim Paxson
1985—Larry Schellenberg

DELAWARE
1978—Brian Downie

DENISON
1968—William Druckemiller Jr.
1988—Kevin Locke
1993—Kevin Frye
1997—Casey Chroust
1999—John Rusnak

DENVER
1968—Richard Callahan
2000—Tyler Church
2004—Brett Starkey

DePAUL
1992—Stephen Howard

DePAUW
1969—Thomas McCormick
1970—Richard Tharp
1973—Gordon Pittenger
1986—Phillip Wendel

DeSALES
1985—George Bilicic Jr.

DICKINSON
1982—David Freysinger
1987—Michael Erdos

DREW
1989—Joe Novak

DUKE
1975—Robert Fleischer

EASTERN WASH.
2000—Ryan Hansen

ELON
1998—Christopher Kiger

EMORY
1993—Kevin Felner
1999—Lewis Satterwhite
2000—Neil Bhutta

EVANSVILLE
1989—Scott Haffner

FAIRLEIGH DICKINSON
1978—John Jorgensen
1993—Kevin Conway

FLORIDA
1970—Andrew Owens Jr.
1973—Anthony Miller
2003—Matthew Bonner
2007—Lee Humphrey

FLA. SOUTHERN
1969—Richard Lewis
1979—Larry Tucker
1989—Kris Kearney

FORT LEWIS
1998—Ryan Ostrom

FRANKLIN
1994—David Dunkle

FRANK. & MARSH.
2000—Jerome Maiatico

GEORGE WASHINGTON
1976—Pat Tallent
1987—Steve Frick

GEORGETOWN
1968—Bruce Stinebrickner

GEORGIA
1965—McCarthy Crenshaw Jr.
1987—Chad Kessler
1990—Alec Kessler

GEORGIA TECH
1998—Matt Harping

GONZAGA
1992—Jarrod Davis
1994—Jeff Brown
1996—Jon Kinloch

GRAMBLING
1983—William Hobdy

GRINNELL
1968—James Schwartz
1976—John Haigh

HAMILTON
1969—Brooks McCuen
1978—John Klauberg

HAMLINE
1989—John Banovetz

HAMPDEN-SYDNEY
1983—Christopher Kelly
1999—David Hobbs

HARVARD
1979—Glenn Fine

HAVERFORD
1966—Hunter Rawlings III
1967—Michael Bratman
1977—Richard Voith

HIRAM
1977—Edwin Niehaus

HOLY CROSS
1969—Edward Siudut
1977—William Doran Jr.
1979—John O'Connor
1980—Ronnie Perry

HOUSTON BAPTIST
1985—Albert Almanza

IDAHO
1967—Michael Wicks

IDAHO ST.
1993—Corey Bruce

ILLINOIS
1971—Rich Howat

ILLINOIS ST.
1988—Jeffrey Harris
1998—Dan Muller

ILLINOIS TECH
1969—Eric Wilson

ILL. WESLEYAN
1988—Brian Coderre
2000—Korey Coon
2006—Adam Dauksas

INDIANA
1975—Steven Green
1982—Randy Wittman
1985—Uwe Blab

INDIANA ST.
1972—Danny Bush
1981—Steven Reed

IOWA
1966—Dennis Pauling
1976—G. Scott Thompson
1981—Steven Waite
1998—Jess Settles

IOWA ST.
1989—Marc Urquhart

ITHACA
1973—David Hollowell

JACKSONVILLE
1971—Vaughn Wedeking
1983—Maurice Roulhac
1986—Thomas Terrell

JAMES MADISON
1978—Sherman Dillard

JAMESTOWN
1981—Peter Anderson

JOHNS HOPKINS
1965—Robert Smith
1975—Andrew Schreiber
1991—Andy Enfield
1992—Jay Gangemi
1997—Matt Gorman
1998—Greg Roehrig

KALAMAZOO
1965—Thomas Nicolai
1973—James Van Sweden
1979—David Dame
1982—John Schelske
1996—Jeremy Cole

KANSAS
1974—Thomas Kivisto
1978—Kenneth Koenigs
1997—Jerod Haase
1999—Ryan Robertson
      T.J. Pugh

KANSAS ST.
1968—Earl Seyfert

KENT ST.
1994—Rodney Koch
2002—Demetric Shaw

KENTUCKY
1975—Robert Guyette
1996—Mark Pope

KENYON
1995—Jamie Harless

KING'S (PA.)
1981—James Shea

KNOX
1965—James Jepson

LA SALLE
1992—John Hurd

LA VERNE
2001—Kevin Gustafson

LAFAYETTE
1972—Joseph Mottola
1980—Robert Falconiero
1991—Bruce Stankavage
1994—Keith Brazzo

LAKE FOREST
1968—Frederick Broda

LAMAR
1970—James Nicholson
1999—Matt Sundblad

LEWIS
1989—James Martin

LONG BEACH ST.
1990—Tyrone Mitchell

LORAS
1971—Patrick Lillis
1972—John Buri

LOUISVILLE
1977—Phillip Bond

LOYOLA (MD.)
1979—John Vogt

LOYOLA MARYMOUNT
1973—Stephen Smith

LUTHER
1968—David Mueller
1974—Timothy O'Neill
1982—Douglas Kintzinger
1986—Scott Sawyer

MAINE
1990—Dean Smith

MARQUETTE
1984—Marc Marotta

MARSHALL
1973—Michael D'Antoni
1997—John Brannen

MARYLAND
1974—Tom McMillen
1981—Gregory Manning
1991—Matt Roe

MARYVILLE (MO.)
2003—Kevin Bartow

MASS.-LOWELL
1970—Alfred Spinell Jr.

MIT
1966—John Mazola
1967—Robert Hardt
1968—David Jansson
1971—Bruce Wheeler
1991—David Tomlinson

McDANIEL
1983—Douglas Pinto

McNEESE ST.
1978—John Rudd

MERCER
2006—Will Emerson

MIAMI (OHIO)
1982—George Sweigert

MICHIGAN
1981—Martin Bodnar
1993—Rob Pelinka

MICHIGAN ST.
2005—Chris Hill

MICHIGAN TECH
1978—Michael Trewhella
1981—Russell Van Duine

MIDDLEBURY
1975—David Pentkowski
1982—Paul Righi

MINNESOTA
1970—Michael Regenfuss

MINN. MORRIS
1997—Todd Hanson

MINN. ST. MANKATO
1997—David Kruse

MINN. ST. MOORHEAD
1980—Kevin Mulder
1996—Brett Beeson

MISSISSIPPI ST.
1976—Richard Knarr

MISSOURI
1972—Gregory Flaker

MO.-ROLLA
1977—Ross Klie

MO.-ST. LOUIS
1977—Robert Bone

MISSOURI ST.
1971—Tillman Williams

MONMOUTH (ILL.)
1992—Steve Swanson

MONTANA
1968—Gregory Hanson
1981—Craig Zanon
1986—Larry Krystkowiak
1992—Daren Engellant
1995—Jeremy Lake

MONTANA ST.
1988—Ray Willis Jr.
1996—Nico Harrison
2004—Jason Erikson

MONT. ST.-BILLINGS
2007—Jonathan Wiley

MORNINGSIDE
1986—John Kelzenberg

MT. ST. MARY'S
1976—Richard Kidwell

MUHLENBERG
1976—Glenn Salo

MUSKINGUM
1974—Gary Ferber
1983—Myron Dulkoski Jr.

NAVY
1979—Kevin Sinnett
1984—Clifford Maurer
1995—Wesley Cooper

NEBRASKA
1972—Alan Nissen
1986—John Matzke
1987—William Jackman
1991—Beau Reid
2006—Bronsen Schliep

NEB.-KEARNEY
2004—Nicholas Branting

NEB.-OMAHA
1981—James Gregory

NEB. WESLEYAN
1995—Justin Wilkins
1998—Kipp Kissinger

UNLV
1984—Danny Tarkanian

NEW MEXICO
1973—Breck Roberts

NEW YORK U.
1996—Greg Belinfanti

NORTH CAROLINA
1966—Robert Bennett Jr.
1974—John O'Donnell
1977—Bruce Buckley
1986—Steve Hale
1995—Pearce Landry

UNC GREENSBORO
2001—Nathan Jameson

UNC WILMINGTON
1997—Bill Mayew

NORTH CAROLINA ST.
1966—Peter Coker
1985—Terrence Gannon
1996—Todd Fuller

NORTH DAKOTA ST.
1981—Brady Lipp
1989—Joe Regnier
2000—Jason Retzlaff

NORTHEASTERN
1978—David Caligaris

NORTHERN ARIZ.
1979—Troy Hudson
2006—Kelly Golob

NORTHERN COLO.
1968—Dennis Colson
1990—Toby Moser

NORTHERN ILL.
1984—Timothy Dillion
2000—A.J. Lux

UNI
1979—Michael Kemp

NORTHERN KY.
2000—Kevin Listerman

NORTHWEST MO. ST.
1989—Robert Sundell

NORTHWESTERN
1973—Richard Sund
1980—Michael Campbell
1990—Walker Lambiotte
1994—Kevin Rankin

NORTHWOOD
1999—Jeremy Piggott

NOTRE DAME
1969—Robert Arnzen
1974—Gary Novak
1983—John Paxson
1998—Pat Garrity

OAKLAND
1990—Brian Gregory

OBERLIN
1972—Victor Guerrieri

OCCIDENTAL
1973—Douglas McAdam
1981—Miles Glidden
1996—John Pike

OGLETHORPE
1992—David Fischer

OHIO
1967—John Hamilton
1968—Wayne Young
1979—Steven Skaggs

OHIO ST.
1968—Wilmer Hosket

OHIO WESLEYAN
2007—Benjamin Chojnacki

OKLAHOMA
1972—Scott Martin
1975—Robert Pritchard
1980—Terry Stotts
1988—Dave Sieger

OKLAHOMA CITY
1967—Gary Gray

OKLAHOMA ST.
1965—Gary Hassmann
1969—Joseph Smith

OLD DOMINION
1975—Gray Eubank

OLIVET
1999—Jeff Bell

OREGON
1971—William Drozdiak
1988—Keith Balderston
2000—Adrian Smith

OREGON ST.
1967—Edward Fredenburg

PACIFIC
1967—Bruce Parsons Jr.
1979—Terence Carney
1986—Richard Anema
1992—Delano Demps

PENN
1972—Robert Morse

PENN ST.
1982—Michael Edelman
1995—John Amaechi

PITTSBURGH
1976—Thomas Richards
1986—Joseph David
1992—Darren Morningstar

POMONA-PITZER
1966—Gordon Schloming
1970—Douglas Covey
1986—David Di Cesaris

PORTLAND ST.
1966—John Nelson

POTSDAM ST.
2005—Christian Turner

POLYTECHNIC (N.Y.)
1968—Charles Privalsky

PRINCETON
1969—Christopher Thomforde
1997—Sydney Johnson

PRINCIPIA
1979—William Kelsey

PUGET SOUND
1974—Richard Brown

PURDUE
1971—George Faerber
1981—Brian Walker

RADFORD
1998—Corey Reed

REDLANDS
1990—Robert Stone

REGIS (COLO.)
1988—John Nilles
1994—Pat Holloway

RENSSELAER
1967—Kurt Hollasch

RHODES
1994—Greg Gonda
1996—Scott Brown

RICE
1995—Adam Peakes
2001—Michael Wilks

RICHMOND
1986—John Davis Jr.

RIPON
1978—Ludwig Wurtz
1999—Bret Van Dyken

ROANOKE
2000—Paris Butler

ROLLINS
1993—David Wolf

RUTGERS
1985—Stephen Perry

ST. ANSELM
1980—Sean Canning

ST. FRANCIS (PA.)
1997—Eric Shaner

ST. JOHN FISHER
1997—Eric Shaner

ST. JOHN'S (N.Y.)
1981—Frank Gilroy

ST. JOSEPH'S (IND.)
1975—James Thordsen

ST. JOSEPH'S
1966—Charles McKenna

ST. LAWRENCE
1969—Philip McWhorter

ST. LEO
1981—Kevin McDonald

ST. LOUIS
1967—John Kilo
1995—Scott Highmark

ST. MARY'S (CAL.)
1980—Calvin Wood
1999—Eric Schraeder

ST. NORBERT
1987—Andris Arians

ST. OLAF
1966—Eric Grimsrud
1971—David Finholt

ST. THOMAS (MINN.)
1967—Daniel Hansard
1995—John Tauer

SAN DIEGO
1978—Michael Strode

SAN DIEGO ST.
1976—Steven Copp

SAN FRANCISCO
1990—Joel DeBortoli

SANTA CLARA
1994—Peter Eisenrich

SCRANTON
1974—Joseph Cantafio
1984—Michael Banas
1985—Daniel Polacheck
1988—John Andrejko
1993—Matt Cusano

SEATTLE PACIFIC
1997—Geoffrey Ping
2006—Michael Binetti

SETON HALL
1969—John Suminski

SEWANEE
1967—Thomas Ward Jr.
1976—Henry Hoffman Jr.
1982—James Sherman
1998—Ryan Harrigan

SIENA
1992—Bruce Schroeder

SIMPSON
1980—John Hines
1995—David Otte
2003—Jesse Harris

SLIPPERY ROCK
1975—Clyde Long

SOUTH ALA.
1998—Toby Madison

SOUTH DAKOTA
1976—Rick Nissen
2001—Jeremy Kudera

SOUTH DAKOTA ST.
1973—David Thomas
1997—Jason Sempsrott
2000—Casey Estling

SOUTH FLA.
1992—Radenko Dobras

SOUTHERN CALIFORNIA
1974—Daniel Anderson
1975—John Lambert

SOUTHERN ILL.
1977—Michael Glenn

SMU
1977—Peter Lodwick

SOUTHERN UTAH
1991—Peter Johnson
1993—Richard Barton

STANFORD
1976—Edward Schweitzer
1980—Kimberly Belton
2000—Mark Madsen

SUSQUEHANNA
1986—Donald Harnum
1994—Lloyd Wolf

SWARTHMORE
1965—Cavin Wright
1987—Michael Dell

SYRACUSE
1981—Dan Schayes
1998—Marius Janulis

TENNESSEE
1993—Lang Wiseman

TENN.-MARTIN
1976—Michael Baker

TEXAS
1974—Harry Larrabee
1979—Jim Krivacs

TEXAS-ARLINGTON
1980—Paul Renfor

TEX.-PAN AMERICAN
1976—Jesus Guerra Jr.

TEXAS A&M
1970—James Heitmann

TCU
1970—Jeffrey Harp
1981—Larry Frevert

TEXAS TECH
1985—Brooks Jennings Jr.
1986—Tobin Doda

TOLEDO
1967—William Backensto
1980—Timothy Selgo

TRANSYLVANIA
1972—Robert Jobe Jr.
1980—Lawrence Kopczyk

TRINITY (CONN.)
1971—Howard Greenblatt
1996—Keith Wolff

TRINITY (TEX.)
1975—Phillip Miller

TRUMAN
2000—Jason Reinberg

TUFTS
1981—Scott Brown

TULSA
1999—Michael Ruffin

UCLA
1969—Kenneth Heitz
1971—George Schofield
1980—Kiki Vandeweghe
1995—George Zidek

UTAH
1968—Lyndon MacKay
1971—Michael Newlin
1977—Jeffrey Jonas
1998—Drew Hansen

UTAH ST.
1996—Eric Franson

VANDERBILT
1976—Jeffrey Fosnes

VILLANOVA
1983—John Pinone

VIRGINIA
1973—James Hobgood

VMI
1969—John Mitchell
1971—Jan Essenburg
1977—William Bynum III
1981—Andrew Kolesar
1987—Gay Elmore Jr.
1996—Bobby Prince

VIRGINIA TECH
1972—Robert McNeer

WABASH
1976—Len Fulkerson

WAKE FOREST
1969—Jerry Montgomery
1994—Marcus Blucas
1996—Rusty LaRue

WARTBURG
1972—David Platte
1974—Fred Waldstein
1991—Dan Nettleton

WASHINGTON
1970—Vincent Stone
1974—Raymond Price
1987—Rodney Ripley

WASHINGTON (MD.)
1979—Joseph Wilson
1990—Tim Keehan
1998—Bradd Burkhart

WASHINGTON-ST. LOUIS
1991—Jed Bargen

WASH. & JEFF.
1970—Terry Evans
1981—David Damico

WASH. & LEE
1983—Brian Hanson
1984—John Graves

WEBER ST.
1980—Mark Mattos
1985—Kent Hagan

WESLEYAN (CONN.)
1973—Brad Rogers
1974—Richard Fairbrother
1977—Steve Malinowski
1982—Steven Maizes
1985—Gregory Porydzy

WEST VIRGINIA
2006—Johannes Herber

WESTERN CARO.
1982—Gregory Dennis
1987—Richard Rogers

WESTERN ILL.
1984—Todd Hutcheson

WESTMINSTER (PA.)
1967—John Fontanella

WHEATON (ILL.)
1995—Nathan Frank

WHITTIER
1977—Rodney Snook

WICHITA ST.
1969—Ronald Mendell
1991—Paul Guffrovich

WIDENER
1983—Louis DeRogatis

WILLIAM & MARY
1985—Keith Cieplicki
2004—Adam Hess

WILLIAMS
1965—Edgar Coolidge III
1986—Timothy Walsh

WISCONSIN
1987—Rodney Ripley

WIS.-OSHKOSH
1998—Joe Imhoff

WIS.-PLATTEVILLE
1993—T.J. Van Wie

WIS.-STEVENS POINT
1983—John Mack

WITTENBERG
1984—Jay Ferguson
1996—Scott Schwartz

WOOSTER
1995—Scott Meech
2005—Matt Schlingman
2006—Kyle Witucky

WRIGHT ST.
1978—Alan McGee

XAVIER
1975—Peter Accetta
1981—Gary Massa

YALE
1967—Richard Johnson
1968—Robert McCallum Jr.

YORK (PA.)
2006—Brandon Bushey

Coaching Records

All-Divisions Coaching Records

Some of the won-lost records included in this coaches section have been adjusted because of action by the NCAA Council or the NCAA Executive Committee to forfeit particular regular-season games or vacate particular NCAA tournament games.

Coaches with at Least 500 Career Wins

(This list includes all coaches who have won at least 500 games regardless of classification with a minimum 10 head coaching seasons at NCAA schools.)

Coach (Alma Mater), Teams Coached, Tenure	Yrs.	Won	Lost	Pct.
1. Bob Knight (Ohio St. 1962) Army 1966-71, Indiana 72-2000, Texas Tech 02-07*	41	890	363	.710
2. Dean Smith (Kansas 1953) North Carolina 1962-97	36	879	254	.776
3. Adolph Rupp (Kansas 1923) Kentucky 1931-52, 54-72	41	876	190	.822
4. Don Meyer (Northern Colo. 1967) Hamline 1973-75, Lipscomb 76-99, Northern St. 2000-07*	35	862	295	.745
5. Herb Magee (Philadelphia U. 1963) Philadelphia U. 1968-2007*	40	833	327	.718
6. Jim Phelan (La Salle 1951) Mt. St. Mary's 1955-2003	49	830	524	.613
7. Clarence "Big House" Gaines (Morgan St. 1945) Winston-Salem 1947-93	47	828	447	.649
8. Jerry Johnson (Fayetteville St. 1951) LeMoyne-Owen 1959-2005	47	821	447	.647
9. Eddie Sutton (Oklahoma St. 1958) Creighton 1970-74, Arkansas 75-85, Kentucky 86-89, Oklahoma St. 91-2006	36	798	315	.717
10. Lefty Driesell (Duke 1954) Davidson 1961-69, Maryland 70-86, James Madison 89-97, Georgia St. 98-2003	41	786	394	.666
11. Lute Olson (Augsburg 1956) Long Beach St. 1974, Iowa 75-83, Arizona 84-2007*	34	780	280	.736
12. Lou Henson (New Mexico St. 1955) Hardin-Simmons 1963-66, Illinois 76-96, New Mexico St. 67-75, 98-2005	41	779	412	.654
13. Mike Krzyzewski (Army 1969) Army 1976-80, Duke 81-2007*	32	775	261	.748
14. Henry Iba [Westminster (Mo.) 1928] Northwest Mo. St. 1930-33, Colorado 34, Oklahoma St. 35-70	41	764	339	.693
15. Ed Diddle (Centre 1921) Western Ky. 1923-64	42	759	302	.715
16. Jim Boeheim (Syracuse 1966) Syracuse 1977-2007*	31	750	264	.740
16. Jim Calhoun (American Int'l 1968) Northeastern 1973-86, Connecticut 87-2007*	35	750	328	.696
18. Phog Allen (Kansas 1906) Baker 1906-08, Haskell 09, Central Mo. St. 13-19, Kansas 08-09, 20-56	48	746	264	.739
19. John Chaney (Bethune-Cookman 1955) Cheyney 1973-82, Temple 83-2006	34	741	312	.704
20. Jerry Tarkanian (Fresno St. 1955) Long Beach St. 1969-73, UNLV 74-92, Fresno St. 96-2002	31	729	201	.784
21. Norm Stewart (Missouri 1956) UNI 1962-67, Missouri 68-99	38	728	374	.661
22. Ray Meyer (Notre Dame 1938) DePaul 1943-84	42	724	354	.672
23. Don Haskins (Oklahoma St. 1952) UTEP 1962-99	38	719	353	.671
24. Glenn Robinson (West Chester 1967) Frank. & Marsh. 1972-2007*	36	718	271	.726
25. Dick Sauers (Slippery Rock 1951) Albany (N.Y.) 1956-87, 89-97	41	702	330	.680
26. Dave Robbins (Catawba 1966) Virginia Union 1979-2007*	29	691	186	.788
27. Denny Crum (UCLA 1958) Louisville 1972-2001	30	675	295	.696
28. Jim Smith (Marquette 1956) St. John's (Minn.) 1965-2007*	43	671	463	.592
29. Dennis Bridges (Ill. Wesleyan 1961) Ill. Wesleyan 1966-2001	36	666	320	.675
30. John Wooden (Purdue 1932) Indiana St. 1947-48, UCLA 49-75	29	664	162	.804
31. Ralph Miller (Kansas 1942) Wichita St. 1952-64, Iowa 65-70, Oregon St. 71-89	38	657	382	.632
32. Gene Bartow (Truman 1953) Central Mo. St. 1962-64, Valparaiso 65-70, Memphis 71-74, Illinois 75, UCLA 76-77, UAB 79-96	34	647	353	.647
33. Billy Tubbs (Lamar 1958) Southwestern (Tex.) 1972-73, Oklahoma 81-94, TCU 95-2002, Lamar 1977-80, 2004-06	31	641	340	.653
34. Marv Harshman (Pacific Lutheran 1942) Pacific Lutheran 1946-58, Washington St. 59-71, Washington 72-85	40	637	443	.590
35. Tom Murphy (Springfield 1960) Hamilton 1971-2004, SUNYIT 06–07*	36	635	286	.689
36. Hugh Durham (Florida St. 1959) Florida St. 1967-78, Georgia 79-95, Jacksonville 98-2005	37	633	429	.596
37. John Lance (Pittsburg St. 1918) Southwestern Okla. 1919-22, Pittsburg St. 23-34, 36-63	44	632	340	.650
38. Ken Anderson (Wis.-Eau Claire 1955) Wis.-Eau Claire 1969-95	27	631	152	.806
39. Cam Henderson (Salem 1917) Muskingum 1920-23, Davis & Elkins 24-35, Marshall 36-55	36	630	243	.722
39. Ed Messbarger (Northwest Mo. St. 1956) Benedictine Hts. 1958-60, Dallas 61-63, St. Mary's (Tex.) 64-78, Angelo St. 79-98	41	630	518	.549
41. Bob Chipman (Kansas St. 1973) Washburn 1980-2007*	28	628	240	.724
42. Norm Sloan (North Carolina St. 1951) Presbyterian 1952-55, Citadel 57-60, Florida 61-66, North Carolina St. 67-80, Florida 81-89	37	624	393	.614
43. Dean Nicholson (Central Wash. 1950) Central Wash. 1965-90	26	620	199	.757
44. Ed Adams (Tuskegee 1934) N.C. Central 1935-36, Tuskegee 37-49, Texas Southern 50-58	24	612	150	.803
45. Dick Reynolds (Otterbein 1965) Otterbein 1973-2007*	35	611	341	.642
46. Jerry Steele (Wake Forest 1961) Guilford 1963-70, High Point 73-2003	39	609	486	.556
47. Jerry Slocum [King's (N.Y.) 1975] Nyack 1976-87, Geneva 1988-96, Gannon 97-2005, Youngstown St. 06-07*	32	601	363	.623
48. Slats Gill (Oregon St. 1924) Oregon St. 1929-64	36	599	393	.604
49. Tom Davis (Wis.-Platteville 1960) Lafayette 1972-77, Boston College 78-82, Stanford 83-86, Iowa 87-99, Drake 2004-07	32	598	355	.627
50. Abe Lemons (Oklahoma City 1949) Tex.-Pan American 1974-76, Texas 77-82, Oklahoma City 56-73, 84-90	34	597	344	.634
51. John Thompson (Providence 1964) Georgetown 1973-99	27	596	239	.714
52. Guy Lewis (Houston 1947) Houston 1957-86	30	592	279	.680
53. Joe Hutton (Carleton 1924) Hamline 1932-65	34	591	207	.741
54. Glenn Van Wieren (Hope 1964) Hope 1978-2007*	30	590	199	.748
54. Bob Huggins (West Virginia 1977) Walsh 1981-83, Akron 85-89, Cincinnati 90-2005, Kansas St. 07, West Virginia*	25	590	211	.737
54. Dom Rosselli (Geneva 1939) Youngstown St. 1941-42, 47-82	38	590	387	.604
57. Gary Williams (Maryland 1968) American 1979-82, Boston College 83-86, Ohio St. 87-89, Maryland 90-2007*	29	585	328	.641
58. Tom Penders (Connecticut 1967) Tufts 1972-74, Columbia 75-78, Fordham 79-86, Rhode Island 87-88, Texas 89-98, George Washington 99-2001, Houston 05-07*	33	584	400	.593
59. Dan McCarrell (North Park 1961) North Park 1968-84, Minn. St. Mankato 85-2001	34	579	347	.625
60. Dick Whitmore (Bowdoin 1965) Colby 1971-2001, 03-07*	36	577	302	.656
61. Fred Hobdy (Grambling 1949) Grambling 1957-86	30	571	287	.666
61. Homer Drew (William Jewell 1966) Bethel (Ind.) 1977-87, Ind.-South Bend 88, Valparaiso 89-2002, 04-07*	30	571	362	.612
63. Eldon Miller (Wittenberg 1961) Wittenberg 1963-70, Western Mich. 71-76, Ohio St. 77-86, UNI 87-98	36	568	419	.575
64. Davey Whitney (Kentucky St. 1953) Texas Southern 1965-69, Alcorn St. 70-89, 97-2003	32	566	356	.614
65. Gale Catlett (West Virginia 1963) Cincinnati 1973-78, West Virginia 79-2002	30	565	325	.635
66. Rudy Marisa (Penn St. 1956) Waynesburg 1970-2003	34	563	300	.652
66. Gary Colson (Lipscomb 1956) Valdosta St. 1959-68, Pepperdine 69-79, New Mexico 81-88, Fresno St. 91-95	34	563	385	.594
68. John Kresse [St. John's (N.Y.) 1964] Col. of Charleston 1980-2002	23	560	143	.797
69. Charles Chronister (East Stroudsburg 1963) Bloomsburg 1972-2002	31	559	288	.660
70. Tony Hinkle (Chicago 1921) Butler 1927-42, 46-70	41	558	392	.587
71. Ed Douma (Calvin 1973) Alma 1974, Lake Superior St. 75-78, Kent St. 79-82, UNC Greensboro 83-84, Calvin 85-96, Hillsdale 99-2007	32	555	302	.648
71. Bill Knapton (Wis.-La Crosse 1952) Beloit 1958-97	40	555	344	.617
73. Steve Moore (Wittenberg 1974) Muhlenberg 1982-87, Wooster 88-2007*	26	554	173	.762
73. Bob Bessoir (Scranton 1955) Scranton 1973-2001	29	554	263	.678
75. Glenn Wilkes (Mercer 1950) Stetson 1958-93	36	551	436	.558
76. David Hixon (Amherst 1975) Amherst 1978-2007*	30	550	222	.712
77. Frank McGuire [St. John's (N.Y.) 1936] St. John's (N.Y.) 1948-52, North Carolina 53-61, South Carolina 65-80	30	549	236	.699

Coach (Alma Mater), Teams Coached, Tenure	Yrs.	Won	Lost	Pct.
77. Bruce Webster (Rutgers 1959) Bridgeport 1966-99	34	549	405	.575
79. Mike Montgomery (Long Beach St. 1968) Montana 1979-86, Stanford 87-2004	26	547	244	.692
80. Tom Smith (Valparaiso 1967) Central Mo. St. 1976-80, Valparaiso 81-88, Mo. Western St. 89-2007*	32	546	367	.598
80. Sam Moir (Appalachian St. 1950) Catawba 1961-94	34	546	399	.578
82. Jim Burson (Muskingum 1963) Muskingum 1968-2005	38	543	425	.561
83. Chet Kammerer [Grace (Ind.) 1964] Grace (Ind.) 1966-75, Westmont 76-92	27	542	261	.675
84. Ben Braun (Wisconsin 1975) Siena Heights 1978-85, Eastern Mich. 86-96, California 97-2007*	30	539	381	.586
85. Bob Davis [Georgetown (Ky.) 1950] High Point 1951-53, Georgetown (Ky.) 54-73, Auburn 74-78	28	538	277	.660
86. C. Alan Rowe (Villanova 1953) Widener 1966-98	33	536	324	.623
86. Harry Miller (Eastern N.M. 1951) Western St. 1953-58, Fresno St. 61-65, Eastern N.M. 66-70, North Texas 71, Wichita St. 72-78, Stephen F. Austin 79-88	34	536	375	.588
88. Cliff Ellis (Florida St. 1968) South Ala. 1976-84, Clemson 85-94, Auburn 95-2004	29	534	337	.613
89. Larry Hunter (Ohio 1971) Wittenberg 1977-89, Ohio 90-2001, Western Caro. 06-07*	27	533	261	.671
89. Bill C. Foster (Carson-Newman 1958) Shorter 1963-67, Charlotte 71-75, Clemson 76-84, Miami (Fla.) 86-90, Virginia Tech 92-97	30	532	325	.621
91. Gene Keady (Kansas St. 1958) Western Ky. 1979-80, Purdue 81-2005	27	531	306	.634
92. Pat Douglass (Pacific 1972) Mont. St.-Billings 1982-87, Cal St. Bakersfield 88-97, UC Irvine 98-2007*	26	529	257	.673
93. Richard Schmidt (Western Ky. 1964) Vanderbilt 1980-81, Tampa 84-2007*	26	527	236	.691
94. Lou Carnesecca [St. John's (N.Y.) 1946] St. John's (N.Y.) 1966-70, 74-92	24	526	200	.725
94. Dave Bliss (Cornell 1965) Oklahoma 1976-80, Southern Methodist 81-88, New Mexico 89-99, Baylor 2000-03	28	526	328	.616
96. Bo Ryan (Wilkes 1969) Wis.-Platteville 1985-99, Milwaukee 2000-01, Wisconsin 02-07*	23	525	158	.769
96. Pete Carril (Lafayette 1952) Lehigh 1967, Princeton 68-96	30	525	273	.658
96. Gene Mehaffey (Southern Methodist 1954) Carson-Newman 1968-78, Ohio Wesleyan 80-99	31	525	384	.578
99. Roy Williams (North Carolina 1972) Kansas 1989-2003, North Carolina 04-07*	19	524	131	.800
99. Tom Young (Maryland 1958) Catholic 1959-67, American 70-73, Rutgers 74-85, Old Dominion 86-91	31	524	328	.615
99. Ben Jobe (Fisk 1956) Talladega 1965-67, Alabama St. 68, South Carolina St. 69-73, Denver 79-80, Alabama A&M 83-86, Tuskegee 97-2000, Southern U. 1987-96, 2002-03	31	524	333	.611

Coach (Alma Mater), Teams Coached, Tenure	Yrs.	Won	Lost	Pct.
102. Fred Enke (Minnesota 1921) Louisville 1924-25, Arizona 26-61	38	523	344	.603
103. Arthur McAfee (Wichita St. 1951) Lane 1961, Mississippi Val. 62, Lincoln (Mo.) 63, Bishop 64-65, Morehouse 66-2000	40	516	510	.503
104. Rollie Massimino (Vermont 1956) Stony Brook 1970-71, Villanova 74-92, UNLV 93-94, Cleveland St. 97-2003	30	515	391	.568
105. Arad McCutchan (Evansville 1934) Evansville 1947-77	31	514	314	.621
105. Jim Gudger (Western Caro. 1942) Western Caro. 1951-69, Tex. A&M-Commerce 70-83	33	514	415	.553
107. Don DeVoe (Ohio St. 1964) Virginia Tech 1972-76, Wyoming 77-78, Tennessee 79-89, Florida 90, Navy 93-2004	31	512	387	.568
108. Paul Webb (William & Mary 1951) Randolph-Macon 1957-75, Old Dominion 76-85	29	511	257	.665
109. Buzz Levick (Drake 1950) Wartburg 1966-93	28	510	225	.694
109. Herbert Greene (Auburn 1967) Aub.-Montgomery 1976-77, Columbus St. 82-2006	27	510	270	.654
109. Aubrey Bonham (UNI 1927) Whittier 1938-43, 46-68	29	510	285	.642
109. Mike Neer (Wash. & Lee 1970) Rochester 1977-2007*	31	510	301	.629
113. Nolan Richardson (UTEP 1965) Tulsa 1981-85, Arkansas 86-2002	22	509	207	.711
113. Don Lane [Union (Ky.) 1965] Transylvania 1976-2001	26	509	241	.679
113. C.M. Newton (Kentucky 1952) Transylvania 1956-64, 66-68, Alabama 69-80, Vanderbilt 82-89	32	509	375	.576
116. Hec Edmundson (Idaho 1909) Idaho 1917-18, Washington 21-47	29	508	204	.713
116. Mike Turner (Albion 1969) Albion 1975-2007*	33	508	313	.619
118. Leo Nicholson (Washington 1925) Central Wash. 1930-43, 46-64	33	505	281	.642
118. Gerald Stockton (Oklahoma St. 1953) Sul Ross St. 1967-68, Midwestern St. 71-94	26	505	363	.582
120. Harold Anderson (Otterbein 1924) Toledo 1935-42, Bowling Green 43-63	29	504	226	.690
121. Jerry Welsh (Ithaca 1958) Potsdam St. 1969, 71-91, Iona 92-95	26	502	205	.710
122. David Boots (Augsburg 1979) Augsburg 1983-88, South Dakota 89-2007*	25	501	212	.703
122. Randy Lambert (Maryville (Tenn.) 1976) Maryville (Tenn.) 1981-2007*	27	501	222	.693
122. Ed Martin (N.C. A&T 1951) South Carolina St. 1956-68, Tennessee St. 69-85	30	501	254	.664
122. Bobby Vaughan (Virginia St. 1948) Elizabeth City St. 1952-66, 68-86	34	501	363	.580
126. Cal Luther (Valparaiso 1951) DePauw 1955-58, Murray St. 59-74, Longwood 82-90, Tenn.-Martin 91-99, Bethel (Tenn.) 2000	39	500	489	.506

*active

COACHING RECORDS

Division I Coaching Records

Winningest Active Coaches

(Minimum five years as a Division I head coach; includes record at four-year U.S. colleges only.)

BY PERCENTAGE

No.	Coach	Team	Yrs.	Won	Lost	Pct.
1.	Mark Few	Gonzaga	8	211	52	.802
2.	Roy Williams	North Carolina	19	524	131	.800
3.	Bruce Pearl	Tennessee	15	363	103	.779
4.	Thad Matta	Ohio St.	7	183	53	.775
5.	Bo Ryan	Wisconsin	23	525	158	.769
6.	Mike Krzyzewski	Duke	32	775	261	.748
7.	Rick Majerus	St. Louis	20	422	147	.742
8.	Jim Boeheim	Syracuse	31	750	264	.740
9.	Bob Huggins	West Virginia	25	590	211	.737
10.	Lute Olson	Arizona	34	780	280	.736
11.	John Calipari	Memphis	15	370	133	.736
12.	Rick Pitino	Louisville	21	494	182	.731
13.	Tubby Smith	Minnesota	16	387	145	.727
14.	Bruce Weber	Illinois	9	215	82	.724
15.	Bob Knight	Texas Tech	41	890	363	.710
16.	Billy Donovan	Florida	13	296	123	.706

No.	Coach	Team	Yrs.	Won	Lost	Pct.
17.	Gregg Marshall	Wichita St.	9	194	83	.700
18.	Bill Self	Kansas	14	312	134	.700
19.	Danny Kaspar	Stephen F. Austin	16	327	142	.697
20.	Tom Izzo	Michigan St.	12	278	121	.697
21.	Jim Calhoun	Connecticut	35	750	328	.696
22.	Todd Lickliter	Iowa	6	131	61	.682
23.	Roger Reid	Southern Utah	7	151	71	.680
24.	Brad Brownell	Wright St.	5	106	50	.679
25.	Jim Christian	Kent St.	5	109	52	.677
26.	Pat Douglass	UC Irvine	26	529	257	.673
27.	Larry Hunter	Western Caro.	27	533	261	.671
28.	Stew Morrill	Utah St.	21	431	213	.669
29.	Mike Anderson	Missouri	5	107	53	.669
30.	John Thompson III	Georgetown	7	140	72	.660
31.	Blaine Taylor	Old Dominion	13	259	134	.659
32.	Tom Crean	Marquette	8	165	86	.657
33.	Mark Gottfried	Alabama	12	250	131	.656
34.	L. Vann Pettaway	Alabama A&M	21	407	214	.655
35.	Rick Barnes	Texas	20	418	220	.655
36.	Jeff Price	Ga. Southern	14	271	143	.655
37.	Mike Brey	Notre Dame	12	241	130	.650
38.	Ben Howland	UCLA	13	259	140	.649
39.	Tim Floyd	Southern California	14	285	155	.648
40.	Keith Dambrot	Akron	9	176	97	.645

No.	Coach	Team	Yrs.	Won	Lost	Pct.
41.	Kelvin Sampson	Indiana	24	477	267	.641
42.	Gary Williams	Maryland	29	585	328	.641
43.	Fran Dunphy	Temple	18	322	181	.640
44.	Rick Stansbury	Mississippi St.	9	185	104	.640
45.	Rick Byrd	Belmont	26	516	294	.637
46.	Karl Hobbs	George Washington	6	114	65	.637
47.	Mack McCarthy	East Caro.	16	309	177	.636
48.	Bobby Lutz	Charlotte	18	348	201	.634
49.	John Beilein	Michigan	25	476	275	.634
50.	Phil Martelli	St. Joseph's	12	240	139	.633
51.	Billy Gillispie	Kentucky	5	100	58	.633
52.	Jeff Capel III	Oklahoma	5	95	56	.629
53.	Steve Alford	New Mexico	16	308	183	.627
54.	John Giannini	La Salle	18	331	198	.626
55.	Greg McDermott	Iowa St.	13	236	143	.623
56.	Dana Altman	Creighton	18	343	208	.623
57.	Greg Jackson	Delaware St.	16	281	173	.619
58.	Jay Wright	Villanova	13	248	155	.615
59.	Cliff Ellis	Coastal Caro.	29	534	337	.613
60.	Paul Hewitt	Georgia Tech	10	193	122	.613

No.	Coach	Team	Yrs.	Won	Lost	Pct.
61.	Homer Drew	Valparaiso	30	571	362	.612
62.	Kevin Stallings	Vanderbilt	14	267	171	.610
63.	Pat Flannery	Bucknell	18	315	203	.608
64.	Larry Eustachy	Southern Miss.	16	301	194	.608
65.	Bob Marlin	Sam Houston St.	9	159	103	.607
66.	Bobby Gonzalez	Seton Hall	8	142	93	.604
67.	Barry Hinson	Missouri St.	10	188	124	.603
68.	Dave Odom	South Carolina	21	391	261	.600

(Coaches with fewer than five years as a Division I head coach; includes record at four-year U.S. colleges only.)

No.	Coach	Team	Yrs.	Won	Lost	Pct.
1.	Mike Lonergan	Vermont	14	289	113	.719
2.	Bart Lundy	High Point	9	185	92	.668
3.	Tony Shaver	William & Mary	21	396	198	.667
4.	Ken Bone	Portland	15	288	147	.662
5.	Jim Yarbrough	Southeastern La.	7	129	68	.655
6.	Jerry Slocum	Youngstown St.	32	601	363	.623
7.	Tim Miles	Colorado St.	12	212	132	.616

BY VICTORIES

No.	Coach, Team	Won
1.	Bob Knight, Texas Tech	890
2.	Lute Olson, Arizona	780
3.	Mike Krzyzewski, Duke	775
4.	Jim Boeheim, Syracuse	750
4.	Jim Calhoun, Connecticut	750
6.	Bob Huggins, West Virginia	590
7.	Gary Williams, Maryland	585
8.	Tom Penders, Houston	584
9.	Homer Drew, Valparaiso	571
10.	Ben Braun, California	539
11.	Cliff Ellis, Coastal Caro.	534
12.	Larry Hunter, Western Caro.	533
13.	Pat Douglass, UC Irvine	529
14.	Bo Ryan, Wisconsin	525
15.	Roy Williams, North Carolina	524
16.	Rick Byrd, Belmont	516
17.	Rick Pitino, Louisville	494
18.	Kelvin Sampson, Indiana	477
19.	John Beilein, Michigan	476
19.	Bobby Cremins, Col. of Charleston	476
21.	Pat Kennedy, Towson	448
22.	Dave Bike, Sacred Heart	445
23.	Stew Morrill, Utah St.	431
24.	Rick Majerus, St. Louis	422
25.	Don Maestri, Troy	421
26.	Rick Barnes, Texas	418
27.	L. Vann Pettaway, Alabama A&M	407

No.	Coach, Team	Won
28.	Mike Deane, Wagner	392
28.	Tom Green, Fairleigh Dickinson	392
30.	Dave Odom, South Carolina	391
31.	Tubby Smith, Minnesota	387
32.	Lon Kruger, UNLV	382
33.	Jim Larranaga, George Mason	381
34.	Greg Kampe, Oakland	377
35.	Bob Thomason, Pacific	375
36.	John Calipari, Memphis	370
37.	Bruce Pearl, Tennessee	363
38.	Rick Scruggs, Gardner-Webb	362
39.	Dave Loos, Austin Peay	353
40.	Bobby Lutz, Charlotte	348
41.	Dana Altman, Creighton	343
42.	Fang Mitchell, Coppin St.	342
43.	Al Skinner, Boston College	334
44.	Rob Spivery, Southern U.	333
45.	John Giannini, La Salle	331
46.	Jim Crews, Army	328
47.	Danny Kaspar, Stephen F. Austin	327
48.	Oliver Purnell, Clemson	326
49.	Bob Williams, UC Santa Barbara	325
50.	Fran Dunphy, Temple	322
50.	Cy Alexander, Tennessee St.	322
52.	Pat Flannery, Bucknell	315
53.	Bill Self, Kansas	312
54.	Bob McKillop, Davidson	311
54.	Jim Wooldridge, UC Riverside	311

No.	Coach, Team	Won
56.	Steve Alford, New Mexico	308
57.	Ralph Willard, Holy Cross	303
58.	Larry Eustachy, Southern Miss.	301
59.	Billy Donovan, Florida	296
60.	Jim Baron, Rhode Island	292
61.	Mike Dement, UNC Greensboro	290
62.	Leonard Hamilton, Florida St.	287
63.	Tim Floyd, Southern California	285
63.	Charlie Coles, Miami (Ohio)	285
65.	Ernie Kent, Oregon	283
66.	Greg Jackson, Delaware St.	281
67.	Seth Greenberg, Virginia Tech	280
68.	Tom Izzo, Michigan St.	278
69.	John Brady, LSU	273
70.	Jeff Price, Ga. Southern	271
71.	Kevin Stallings, Vanderbilt	267
72.	Herb Sendek, Arizona St.	262
73.	Blaine Taylor, Old Dominion	259
73.	Ben Howland, UCLA	259
73.	Bill Herrion, New Hampshire	259
76.	Perry Watson, Detroit	254
77.	Mark Gottfried, Alabama	250
77.	Perry Clark, A&M-Corpus Christi	250
79.	Jeff Jones, American	249
80.	Jay Wright, Villanova	248
80.	Ronnie Arrow, South Ala.	248
82.	Dennis Wolff, Boston U.	246
83.	Mike Brey, Notre Dame	241

No.	Coach, Team	Won
84.	Phil Martelli, St. Joseph's	240
85.	Greg McDermott, Iowa St.	236
85.	Steve Fisher, San Diego St.	236
87.	Al Walker, Binghamton	234
88.	Kirk Speraw, UCF	231
89.	Jerry Wainwright, DePaul	217
90.	Bruce Weber, Illinois	215
90.	Tim Welsh, Providence	215
90.	Willis Wilson, Rice	215
93.	Mark Few, Gonzaga	211
94.	Glen Miller, Penn	210
95.	Ron Hunter, IUPUI	206

(Coaches with fewer than five years as a Division I head coach; includes record at four-year U.S. colleges only.)

No.	Coach, Team	Won
1.	Jerry Slocum, Youngstown St.	601
2.	Tony Shaver, William & Mary	396
3.	Jim Whitesell, Loyola (Ill.)	331
4.	George Pfeifer, Idaho	300
5.	Mike Lonergan, Vermont	289
6.	Ken Bone, Portland St.	288
7.	Steve Hawkins, Western Mich.	213
8.	Tim Miles, Colorado St.	212

Winningest Coaches All-Time

(Minimum 10 head coaching seasons in Division I)

BY PERCENTAGE

Coach, team coached & tenure	Yrs.	Won	Lost	Pct.
1. Clair Bee, Rider 1929-31, Long Island 1932-43, 46-51	21	412	87	.826
2. Adolph Rupp, Kentucky 1931-52, 54-72	41	876	190	.822
3. John Wooden, Indiana St. 1947-48, UCLA 49-75	29	664	162	.804
4. Roy Williams, Kansas 1989-2003, North Carolina 04-07*	19	524	131	.800
5. John Kresse, Col. of Charleston 1980-02	23	560	143	.797
6. Jerry Tarkanian, Long Beach St. 1969-73, UNLV 74-92, Fresno St. 96-2002	31	729	201	.784
7. Francis Schmidt, Tulsa 1916-17, 19-22, Arkansas 24-29, TCU 30-34	17	258	72	.782
8. Dean Smith, North Carolina 1962-97	36	879	254	.776
9. George Keogan, Wis.-Superior 1913-14, St. Louis 16, St. Thomas (Minn.) 18, Allegheny 19, Valparaiso 20-21, Notre Dame 24-43 #	27	414	127	.765
10. Jack Ramsay, St. Joseph's 1956-66	11	231	71	.765
11. Frank Keaney, Rhode Island 1921-48	28	401	124	.764
12. Vic Bubas, Duke 1960-69	10	213	67	.761
13. Harry Fisher, Fordham 1905, Columbia 1907-16, St. John's (N.Y.) 1910, Army 07, 22-23, 25	16	189	60	.759
14. Mike Krzyzewski, Army 1976-80, Duke 81-2007*	32	775	261	.748
15. Fred Bennion, BYU 1909-10, Utah 11-14, Montana St. 15-19	11	95	32	.748
16. Chick Davies, Duquesne 1925-43, 47-48	21	314	106	.748
17. Ray Mears, Wittenberg 1957-62, Tennessee 63-77	21	399	135	.747
18. Edward McNichol, Pennsylvania 1921-30	10	186	63	.747
19. Rick Majerus, Marquette 1984-86, Ball St. 88-89, Utah 1990-2004, St. Louis*	20	422	147	.742
20. Al McGuire, Belmont Abbey 1958-64, Marquette 65-77	20	406	142	.741
21. Jim Boeheim, Syracuse 1977-2007*	31	750	264	.740
22. Phog Allen, Baker 1906-08, Haskell 09, Central Mo. St. 13-19, Kansas 08-09, 20-56	50	746	264	.739
23. Everett Case, North Carolina St. 1947-65	19	377	134	.738
24. Bob Huggins, Walsh 1981-83, Akron 85-89, Cincinnati 90-2005, Kansas St. 07, West Virginia*	25	590	211	.737
25. Lute Olson, Long Beach St. 1974, Iowa 75-83, Arizona 84-2007*	34	780	280	.736
26. Arthur Schabinger, Ottawa 1917-20, Emporia St. 21-22, Creighton 23-35	19	245	88	.736
27. John Calipari, Massachusetts 1989-96, Memphis 2001-07*	15	370	133	.736
28. G. Ott Romney, Montana St. 1923-28, BYU 29-35	13	283	102	.735

Coach, team coached & tenure	Yrs.	Won	Lost	Pct.
29. Doc Meanwell, Wisconsin 1912-17, Missouri 18, Wisconsin 21-34	22	280	101	.735
30. Rick Pitino, Boston U. 1979-83, Providence 86-87, Kentucky 90-97, Louisville 2002-07*	21	494	182	.731
31. Henry Lannigan, Virginia 1906-29 #	24	254	95	.727
32. Tubby Smith, Tulsa 1992-95, Georgia 96-97, Kentucky 98-2007, Minnesota*	16	387	145	.727
33. Lew Andreas, Syracuse 1925-50	25	358	135	.726
34. Lou Carnesecca, St. John's (N.Y.) 1966-70, 74-92	24	526	200	.725
35. Fred Schaus, West Virginia 1955-60, Purdue 1973-78	12	251	96	.723
36. James Usilton, Temple 1927-39	13	205	79	.722
37. Cam Henderson, Muskingum 1920-23, Davis & Elkins 24-35, Marshall 36-55	36	630	243	.722
38. Joe Lapchick, St. John's (N.Y.) 1937-47, 57-65	20	334	130	.720
39. Edmund Dollard, Syracuse 1912-24	13	151	59	.719
40. Hugh Greer, Connecticut 1947-63	17	286	112	.719
41. Eddie Sutton, Creighton 1970-74, Arkansas 75-85, Kentucky 86-89, Oklahoma St. 91-2006	36	798	315	.717
42. Dudey Moore, Duquesne 1949-58, La Salle 59-63	15	270	107	.716
43. Ed Diddle, Western Ky. 1923-64	42	759	302	.715
44. Tom Blackburn, Dayton 1948-64	17	352	141	.714
45. John Lawther, Westminster (Pa.) 1927-36, Penn St. 37-49	23	317	127	.714
46. John Thompson, Georgetown 1973-99	27	596	239	.714
47. Lee Rose, Transylvania 1965-66, 69-75, Charlotte 76-78, Purdue 79-80, South Fla. 81-86	19	384	154	.714
48. Hec Edmundson, Idaho 1917-18, Washington 21-47	29	508	204	.713
49. Nolan Richardson, Tulsa 1981-85, Arkansas 86-2002	22	509	207	.711
50. Edward Kelleher, St. John's (N.Y.) 1922, Fordham 23-34, 39-43, Army 44-45	19	258	105	.711
51. Bob Knight, Army 1966-71, Indiana 72-2000, Texas Tech 02-07*	41	890	363	.710
52. Piggy Lambert, Purdue 1917-17, 19-46	29	371	152	.709
53. Pat Page, Chicago 1912-20, Butler 21-26	15	257	106	.708
54. Peck Hickman, Louisville 1945-67	23	443	183	.708
55. Billy Donovan, Marshall 1995-96, Florida 97-2007*	13	296	123	.706
56. Joe B. Hall, Regis (Colo.) 1960-64, Central Mo. St. 65, Kentucky 73-85	19	373	156	.705
57. John Chaney, Cheyney 1973-82, Temple 83-2006	34	741	312	.704
58. Harlan Dykes, Santa Clara 1927-35, St. Mary's (Cal.) 38-39	11	147	63	.700
59. Bill Self, Oral Roberts 1994-97, Tulsa 98-2000, Illinois 01-03, Kansas 04-07*	14	312	134	.700
60. Frank McGuire, St. John's (N.Y.) 1948-52, North Carolina 53-61, South Carolina 65-80	30	549	236	.699
61. Bennie Owen, Oklahoma 1909-21	13	113	49	.698
62. Tom Izzo, Michigan St. 1996-2007*	12	278	121	.697
63. E.C. Hayes, Mississippi St. 1912-24	12	124	54	.697
64. Boyd Grant, Fresno St. 1978-86, Colorado St. 88-91	13	275	120	.696
65. Denny Crum, Louisville 1972-01	30	675	295	.696
66. Douglas R. Mills, Illinois 1937-47	11	151	66	.696
67. Jim Calhoun, Northeastern 1973-86, Connecticut 87-2007*	35	750	328	.696
68. Honey Russell, Seton Hall 1937-43, Manhattan 46, Seton Hall 50-60	19	310	137	.694
69. Henry Iba, Northwest Mo. St. 1930-33, Colorado 34, Oklahoma St. 35-70	41	764	339	.693
70. Eddie M. Cameron, Wash. & Lee 1925, Duke 29-42	15	234	104	.692
71. Larry Weise, St. Bonaventure 1962-73	12	202	90	.692
72. Mike Montgomery, Montana 1979-86, Stanford 87-04	26	547	244	.692
73. Gene Smithson, Illinois St. 1976-78, Wichita St. 79-86	11	221	99	.691
74. Zora Clevenger, Indiana 1905-06, Tennessee 12-16, Kansas St. 17-20	11	116	52	.690
75. Harold Anderson, Toledo 1935-42, Bowling Green 43-63	29	504	226	.690
76. Nat Holman, CCNY 1920-52, 55-56, 59-60	37	423	190	.690
77. Ralph R. Jones, Butler 1904, Wabash 05-09, Purdue 10-12, Illinois 13-20, Lake Forest 34-39, 46	24	232	106	.686
78. John R. Wilson, Navy 1927-46	20	204	94	.685
79. Herman Stegeman, Georgia 1920-31	12	170	79	.683
80. Dana Kirk, Tampa 1967-71, Va. Commonwealth 77-79, Memphis 80-86	15	281	131	.682
81. Guy Lewis, Houston 1957-86	30	592	279	.680
82. John Oldham, Tennessee Tech 1956-64, Western Ky. 65-71	16	260	123	.679
83. Harry Combes, Illinois 1948-67	20	316	150	.678
84. Digger Phelps, Fordham 1971, Notre Dame 72-91	21	419	200	.677
85. Bob King, New Mexico 1963-72, Indiana St. 76-78	13	236	113	.676
86. Buck Read, Western Mich. 1922-49	28	358	173	.674
87. Jack Gardner, Kansas St. 1940-42, 47-53, Utah 54-71	28	486	235	.674
88. Leo Novak, Army 1927-39	13	126	61	.674
89. J.R. Crozier, Wake Forest 1916-17	12	95	46	.674
90. Roy Skinner, Vanderbilt 1959-59, 62-76	16	278	135	.673
91. Pat Douglass, Mont. St.-Billings 1982-87, Cal St. Bakersfield 88-97, UC Irvine 98-2007*	26	529	257	.673
92. Thomas Haggerty, DePaul 1937-40, Loyola (Ill.) 46-50, Loyola (La.) 51-53	12	224	109	.673
93. Alex Severence, Villanova 1937-61	25	413	201	.673

Coach, team coached & tenure	Yrs.	Won	Lost	Pct.
94. Ray Meyer, DePaul 1943-84	42	724	354	.672
95. Larry Hunter, Wittenberg 1977-89, Ohio 90-2001, Western Caro. 06-07*	27	533	261	.671
96. Don Haskins, UTEP 1962-99	38	719	353	.671
97. Dutch Hermann, Penn St. 1916-17, 20-32	15	148	73	.670
98. Don Corbett, Lincoln (Mo.) 1972-79, N.C. A&T 80-93	22	413	204	.669
99. Ozzie Cowles, Carleton 1925-30, Wis.-River Falls 33-36, Dartmouth 37-43, 45-46, Michigan 47-48, Minnesota 49-59	32	421	208	.669
100. Stew Morrill, Montana 1987-91, Colorado St. 92-98, Utah St. 99-2007*	21	431	213	.669
101. Jim Harrick, Pepperdine 1980-88, UCLA 89-96, Rhode Island 98-99, Georgia 2000-03	23	470	233	.669
102. Neil Cohalan, Manhattan 1930-42	13	165	82	.668
103. Charles Moir, Roanoke 1968-73, Tulane 74-76, Virginia Tech 77-87	20	392	196	.667
103. Jack Gray, Texas 1937-42, 46-51	12	194	97	.667
105. Neil McCarthy, Weber St. 1975-85, New Mexico St. 86-97	22	431	216	.666
106. Lefty Driesell, Davidson 1961-69, Maryland 70-86, James Madison 89-97, Georgia St. 98-2003	41	786	394	.666
107. Harold Bradley, Hartwick 1948-50, Duke 51-59, Texas 60-67	20	337	169	.666
108. Skip Prosser, Loyola (Md.) 1994, Xavier 95-2001, Wake Forest 02-07	14	291	146	.666
109. Wimp Sanderson, Alabama 1981-92, Ark.-Little Rock 95-99	17	350	176	.665
110. Hank Crisp, Alabama 1924-42, 46-46	20	264	133	.665
111. Edward J. Stewart, Mount Union 1908, Purdue 09, Oregon St. 12-16, Nebraska 17-19, Texas 24-27, UTEP 28	15	193	98	.663
112. Branch McCracken, Ball St. 1931-38, Indiana 39-43, 47-65	32	450	231	.661
113. Norm Stewart, Northern Iowa 1962-67, Missouri 68-99	38	728	374	.661
114. W.O. Hamilton, William Jewell 1899-1900, 07-08, Kansas 10-19	14	144	74	.661
115. Dave Gavitt, Dartmouth 1968-69, Providence 70-79	12	227	117	.660
116. Terry Holland, Davidson 1970-74, Virginia 75-90	21	418	216	.659
117. Blaine Taylor, Montana 1992-98, Old Dominion 2002-07*	13	259	134	.659
118. Harry Litwack, Temple 1953-73	21	373	193	.659
119. Pete Carril, Lehigh 1967, Princeton 68-96	30	525	273	.658
120. Mike Gottfried, Murray St. 1996-98, Alabama 99-2007*	12	250	131	.656
121. Louis Cooke, Minnesota 1898-1924 #	27	242	127	.655
122. Pete Newell, San Francisco 1947-50, Michigan St. 51-54, California 55-60	14	234	123	.655
123. Rick Barnes, George Mason 1988, Providence 89-94, Clemson 95-98, Texas 99-2007*	20	418	220	.655
124. Dick Tarrant, Richmond 1982-93	12	239	126	.655
125. Lou Henson, Hardin-Simmons 1963-66, Illinois 76-96, New Mexico St. 67-75, 1998-2005	41	779	412	.654
126. Billy Tubbs, Southwestern (Tex.) 1972-73, Lamar 77-80, Oklahoma 81-94, TCU 95-2002, Lamar 04-06	31	641	340	.653
127. Fred Taylor, Ohio St. 1959-76	18	297	158	.653
128. Jack Hartman, Southern Ill. 1963-70, Kansas St. 71-86	24	437	233	.652
129. Paul Evans, St. Lawrence 1974-80, Navy 81-86, Pittsburgh 87-94	21	390	208	.652
130. Eddie Hickey, Creighton 1936-43, 47, St. Louis 48-58, Marquette 59-64	26	433	231	.652
131. George King, Charleston (W.Va.) 1957, West Virginia 61-65, Purdue 66-72	13	223	119	.652
132. Leonard Palmer, CCNY 1907-16	10	71	38	.651
133. J. Craig Ruby, Missouri 1921-22, Illinois 23-36	16	181	97	.651
134. John Kraft, Villanova 1962-73, Rhode Island 74-81	20	341	183	.651
135. Mike Brey, Delaware 1996-2000, Notre Dame 01-07*	12	241	130	.650

*active; # ties included in calculating the winning percentages for: George Keogan 3 ties, Henry Lannigan 1 and Louis Cooke 1.

BY VICTORIES
(Minimum 10 head coaching seasons in Division I)

Coach	Wins
1. Bob Knight*	890
2. Dean Smith	879
3. Adolph Rupp	876
4. Jim Phelan, Mt. St. Mary's 1955-2003	830
5. Eddie Sutton	798
6. Lefty Driesell	786
7. Lute Olson*	780
8. Lou Henson	779
9. Mike Krzyzewski*	775
10. Henry Iba	764
11. Ed Diddle	759
12. Jim Boeheim*	750
12. Jim Calhoun*	750
14. Phog Allen	746
15. John Chaney	741
16. Jerry Tarkanian	729

COACHING RECORDS

Coach	Wins
17. Norm Stewart	728
18. Ray Meyer	724
19. Don Haskins	719
20. Denny Crum	675
21. John Wooden	664
22. Ralph Miller, Wichita St. 1952-64, Iowa 65-70, Oregon St. 71-89	657
23. Gene Bartow, Central Mo. St. 1962-64, Valparaiso 65-70, Memphis 71-74, Illinois 75, UCLA 76-77, UAB 79-96	647
24. Billy Tubbs	641
25. Marv Harshman, Pacific Lutheran 1946-58, Washington St. 59-71, Washington 72-85	637
26. Hugh Durham, Florida St. 1967-78, Georgia 79-95, Jacksonville 98-2005	633
27. Cam Henderson	630
28. Norm Sloan, Presbyterian 1952-55, Citadel 57-60, Florida 61-66, North Carolina St. 67-80, Florida 81-89	624
29. Slats Gill, Oregon St. 1929-64	599
30. Tom Davis, Lafayette 1972-77, Boston College 78-82, Stanford 83-86, Iowa 87-99, Drake 2004-07	598
31. Abe Lemons, Tex.-Pan American 1974-76, Texas 77-82, Oklahoma City 56-73, 84-90	597
32. John Thompson	596
33. Guy Lewis	592
34. Bob Huggins*	590
35. Gary Williams, American 1979-82, Boston College 83-86, Ohio St. 87-89, Maryland 90-2007*	585
36. Tom Penders, Tufts 1972-74, Columbia 75-78, Fordham 79-86, Rhode Island 87-88, Texas 89-98, George Washington 99-2001, Houston 05-07*	584
37. Homer Drew, Bethel (Ind.) 1977-87, Ind.-South Bend 88, Valparaiso 89-2002, 04-07*	571
38. Eldon Miller, Wittenberg 1963-70, Western Mich. 71-76, Ohio St. 77-86, Northern Iowa 87-98	568
39. Davey L. Whitney, Texas Southern 1965-69, Alcorn St. 70-89, 97-2003	566
40. Gale Catlett, Cincinnati 1973-78, West Virginia 79-2002	565
41. Gary Colson, Valdosta St. 1959-68, Pepperdine 69-79, New Mexico 81-88, Fresno St. 91-95	563
42. John Kresse	560
43. Tony Hinkle, Butler 1927-42, 46-70	558
44. Glenn Wilkes, Stetson 1958-93	551
45. Frank McGuire	549
46. Mike Montgomery	547
47. Ben Braun, Siena Heights 1978-85, Eastern Mich. 86-96, California 97-2007*	539
48. Cliff Ellis, South Ala. 1976-84, Clemson 85-94, Auburn 95-2004, Coastal Caro.*	534
48. Harry Miller, Western St. 1953-58, Fresno St. 61-65, Eastern N.M. 66-70, North Texas 71, Wichita St. 72-78, Stephen F. Austin 79-88	534
50. Larry Hunter*	533
51. Bill C. Foster, Shorter 1963-67, Charlotte 71-75, Clemson 76-84, Miami (Fla.) 86-90, Virginia Tech 92-97	532
52. Gene Keady, Western Ky. 1979-80, Purdue 81-2005	531
53. Pat Douglass*	529
54. Dave Bliss, Oklahoma 1976-80, Southern Methodist 81-88, New Mexico 89-99, Baylor 2000-03	526
54. Lou Carnesecca	526
56. Pete Carril	525
57. Ben Jobe, Talladega 1965-67, Alabama St. 68, South Carolina St. 69-73, Denver 79-80, Alabama A&M 83-86, Southern U. 87-96, Tuskegee 97-2000, Southern U. 02-03	524
57. Roy Williams*	524
57. Tom Young, Catholic 1959-67, American 70-73, Rutgers 74-85, Old Dominion 86-91	524
60. Fred Enke, Louisville 1924-25, Arizona 26-61	523
61. Rollie Massimino, Stony Brook 1970-71, Villanova 74-92, UNLV 93-94, Cleveland St. 97-2003	515
62. Don DeVoe, Virginia Tech 1972-76, Wyoming 77-78, Tennessee 79-89, Florida 90, Navy 93-2004	512
63. C.M. Newton, Transylvania 1956-64, 66-68, Alabama 69-80, Vanderbilt 82-89	509
63. Nolan Richardson	509
65. Hec Edmundson	508
66. Harold Anderson	504
67. Cal Luther, DePauw 1955-58, Murray St. 59-74, Longwood 82-90, Tenn.-Martin 91-99, Bethel (Tenn.) 2000	500
68. Bill Reinhart, Oregon 1924-35, George Washington 36-42, 50-66	499
69. Jack Friel, Washington St. 1929-58	495
69. Everett Shelton, Phillips (Okla.) 1924-26, Wyoming 40-43, 45-59, Sacramento St. 60-68	495
69. Ned Wulk, Xavier 1952-57, Arizona St. 58-82	495
72. Rick Pitino*	494
73. Dick Bennett, Wis.-Stevens Point 1977-85, Green Bay 86-95, Wisconsin 96-2001, Washington St. 04-07*	490
74. Jack Gardner	486
75. Bob Hallberg, St. Xavier 1972-77, Chicago St. 78-87, Ill.-Chicago 88-96	485
76. Butch van Breda Kolff, Princeton 1963-67, New Orleans 78-79, Lafayette 52-55, 85-88, Hofstra 56-62, 89-94	482

Coach	Wins
77. Kelvin Sampson, Montana Tech 1982-85, Washington St. 88-94, Oklahoma 95-2006, Indiana 07*	477
78. John Beilein, Nazareth 1983, Le Moyne 84-92, Canisius 93-97, Richmond 98-2002, West Virginia 03-07, Michigan*	476
78. Bobby Cremins, Appalachian St. 1976-81, Georgia Tech 82-2000, Col. of Charleston 07*	476
80. Jim Harrick	470
81. Bill E. Foster, Bloomsburg 1961-63, Rutgers 64-71, Utah 72-74, Duke 75-80, South Carolina 81-86, Northwestern 87-93	467
82. Johnny Orr, Massachusetts 1964-66, Michigan 69-80, Iowa St. 81-94	466
83. Taps Gallagher, Niagara 1932-43, 47-65	465
84. George Blaney, Stonehill 1968-69, Dartmouth 70-72, Holy Cross 73-94, Seton Hall 95-97	460
85. Tex Winter, Marquette 1952-53, Kansas St. 54-68, Washington 69-71, Northwestern 74-78, Long Beach St. 79-83	453
86. Gene Iba, Houston Baptist 1978-85, Baylor 86-92, Pittsburg St. 96-2007*	450
86. Branch McCracken	450
88. Nibs Price, California 1925-54	449
89. Dale Brown, LSU 1973-97	448
89. Pat Kennedy, Iona 1981-86, Florida St. 87-97, DePaul 98-2002, Montana 03-04, Towson 05-07*	448
91. Peck Hickman	443
91. Shelby Metcalf, Texas A&M 1964-90	443
93. Don Donoher, Dayton 1965-89	437
93. Jack Hartman	437
95. Eddie S. Hickey	433
96. Neil McCarthy	431
96. Stew Morrill*	431
98. Nat Holman	423
99. Rick Majerus*	422
100. Ozzie Cowles	421
100. Don Maestri, Troy 1983-2007*	421
102. Murray Arnold, Birmingham-So. 1971-78, Chattanooga 80-85, Western Ky. 87-90, Stetson 98-2001	420
103. Digger Phelps	419
104. Rick Barnes*	418
104. Sam Barry, Knox 1919-22, Iowa 23-29, Southern California 30-50	418
104. Jud Heathcote, Montana 1972-76, Michigan St. 77-95	418
104. Terry Holland	418
108. Frank J. Hill, Seton Hall 1912-18, 20-36, Rutgers 1916-43	415
109. George Keogan	414
110. Don Corbett	413
110. Alex Severence	413
112. Clair Bee	412
113. Howard Cann, New York U. 1924-58	409
113. Danny Nee, Ohio 1981-86, Nebraska 87-2000, Robert Morris 01, Duquesne 02-07*	409
115. Al McGuire	406
116. Howard Hobson, Southern Ore. 1933-35, Oregon 36-44, 46-47, Yale 48-56	401
116. Frank Keaney	401
116. Mike Vining, La.-Monroe 1982-2005	401

*active.

Division I Active Coaches Listed by School

Coach	School	Yrs.	Won	Lost	Pct.
Perry Clark	A&M-Corpus Chris.	15	250	199	.557
Jeff Reynolds	Air Force	4	82	34	.707
Keith Dambrot	Akron	9	176	97	.645
Mark Gottfried	Alabama	12	250	131	.656
L. Vann Pettaway	Alabama A&M	21	407	214	.655
Lewis Jackson	Alabama St.	2	22	38	.367
Will Brown	Albany (N.Y.)	6	76	93	.450
Samuel West	Alcorn St.	4	37	79	.319
Jeff Jones	American	15	249	206	.547
Houston Fancher	Appalachian St.	7	106	105	.502
Lute Olson	Arizona	34	780	280	.736
Herb Sendek	Arizona St.	14	262	180	.593
Steve Shields	Ark.-Little Rock	4	62	54	.534
Van Holt	Ark.-Pine Bluff	5	37	106	.259
John Pelphrey	Arkansas	5	80	67	.544
Dickey Nutt	Arkansas St.	12	180	170	.514
Jim Crews	Army	22	328	314	.511
Jeff Lebo	Auburn	9	158	111	.587
Dave Loos	Austin Peay	21	353	289	.550
Billy Taylor	Ball St.	5	81	69	.540
Scott Drew	Baylor	5	56	80	.412
Rick Byrd	Belmont	26	516	294	.637

Coach	School	Yrs.	Won	Lost	Pct.
Clifford Reed	Bethune-Cookman	6	59	100	.371
Al Walker	Binghamton	19	234	279	.456
Greg Graham	Boise St.	6	101	78	.564
Al Skinner	Boston College	19	334	246	.576
Dennis Wolff	Boston U.	15	246	185	.571
Louis Orr	Bowling Green	6	100	80	.556
Jim Les	Bradley	5	84	73	.535
Craig Robinson	Brown	1	11	18	.379
Pat Flannery	Bucknell	18	315	203	.608
Reggie Witherspoon	Buffalo	8	95	139	.406
Brad Stevens	Butler	0	0	0	.000
Dave Rose	BYU	2	45	18	.714
Kevin Bromley	Cal Poly	7	80	106	.430
Bob Burton	Cal St. Fullerton	4	68	51	.571
Bobby Braswell	Cal St. Northridge	11	168	157	.517
Ben Braun	California	30	539	381	.586
Robbie Laing	Campbell	4	29	84	.257
Tom Parrotta	Canisius	1	12	19	.387
Rob Flaska	Centenary (La.)	2	14	44	.241
Howie Dickenman	Central Conn. St.	11	178	145	.551
Ernie Zeigler	Central Mich.	1	13	18	.419
Barclay Radebaugh	Charleston So.	3	42	46	.477
Bobby Lutz	Charlotte	18	348	201	.634
John Shulman	Chattanooga	3	54	42	.563
Benjy Taylor	Chicago St.	3	28	46	.378
Mick Cronin	Cincinnati	4	80	43	.650
Ed Conroy	Citadel	4	48	63	.432
Oliver Purnell	Clemson	19	326	249	.567
Gary Waters	Cleveland St.	11	181	156	.537
Cliff Ellis	Coastal Caro.	29	534	337	.613
Bobby Cremins	Col. of Charleston	26	476	318	.599
Emmett Davis	Colgate	9	118	138	.461
Jeff Bzdelik	Colorado	4	75	47	.615
Tim Miles	Colorado St.	12	212	132	.616
Joe Jones	Columbia	4	49	60	.450
Jim Calhoun	Connecticut	35	750	328	.696
Fang Mitchell	Coppin St.	21	342	281	.549
Steve Donahue	Cornell	7	74	117	.387
Dana Altman	Creighton	18	343	208	.623
Terry Dunn	Dartmouth	3	25	56	.309
Bob McKillop	Davidson	18	311	218	.588
Brian Gregory	Dayton	4	75	49	.605
Monte Ross	Delaware	1	5	26	.161
Greg Jackson	Delaware St.	16	281	173	.619
Joe Scott	Denver	7	89	108	.452
Jerry Wainwright	DePaul	13	217	174	.555
Perry Watson	Detroit	14	254	175	.592
Keno Davis	Drake	0	0	0	.000
Bruiser Flint	Drexel	11	192	146	.568
Mike Krzyzewski	Duke	32	775	261	.748
Ron Everhart	Duquesne	13	184	191	.491
Mack McCarthy	East Caro.	16	309	177	.636
Murry Bartow	East Tenn. St.	10	179	131	.577
Mike Miller	Eastern Ill.	8	103	120	.462
Jeff Neubauer	Eastern Ky.	2	35	28	.556
Charles Ramsey	Eastern Mich.	2	20	40	.333
Kirk Earlywine	Eastern Wash.	1	21	8	.724
Ernie Nestor	Elon	9	110	159	.409
Marty Simmons	Evansville	6	99	72	.579
Ed Cooley	Fairfield	1	13	19	.406
Tom Green	Fairleigh Dickinson	24	392	308	.560
Rex Walters	Fla. Atlantic	1	16	15	.516
Billy Donovan	Florida	13	296	123	.706
Eugene Harris	Florida A&M	0	0	0	.000
Sergio Rouco	Florida Int'l	3	33	54	.379
Leonard Hamilton	Florida St.	19	287	281	.505
Dereck Whittenburg	Fordham	8	120	116	.508
Steve Cleveland	Fresno St.	10	175	131	.572
Jeff Jackson	Furman	4	36	76	.321
Jeff Price	Ga. Southern	14	271	143	.655
Rick Scruggs	Gardner-Webb	21	362	277	.567
Jim Larranaga	George Mason	23	381	290	.568
Karl Hobbs	George Washington	6	114	65	.637
John Thompson III	Georgetown	7	140	72	.660
Dennis Felton	Georgia	9	158	117	.575
Rod Barnes	Georgia St.	8	141	109	.564
Paul Hewitt	Georgia Tech	10	193	122	.613
Mark Few	Gonzaga	8	211	52	.802
Larry Wright	Grambling	8	81	142	.363
Kevin Nickelberry	Hampton	1	15	16	.484
Dan Leibovitz	Hartford	1	13	18	.419
Tommy Amaker	Harvard	10	176	139	.559
Bob Nash	Hawaii	0	0	0	.000

Coach	School	Yrs.	Won	Lost	Pct.
Bart Lundy	High Point	9	185	92	.668
Tom Pecora	Hofstra	6	103	82	.557
Ralph Willard	Holy Cross	17	303	213	.587
Tom Penders	Houston	33	584	400	.593
Gil Jackson	Howard	2	16	44	.267
George Pfeifer	Idaho	17	300	233	.563
Joe O'Brien	Idaho St.	1	13	17	.433
Jimmy Collins	Ill.-Chicago	11	176	156	.530
Bruce Weber	Illinois	9	215	82	.724
Tim Jankovich	Illinois St.	4	53	57	.482
Kelvin Sampson	Indiana	24	477	267	.641
Kevin McKenna	Indiana St.	4	89	33	.730
Kevin Willard	Iona	0	0	0	.000
Todd Lickliter	Iowa	6	131	61	.682
Greg McDermott	Iowa St.	13	236	143	.623
Dane Fife	IPFW	2	22	35	.386
Ron Hunter	IUPUI	13	206	173	.544
Tevester Anderson	Jackson St.	9	166	117	.587
Cliff Warren	Jacksonville	2	16	40	.286
Mike LaPlante	Jacksonville St.	7	88	115	.433
Dean Keener	James Madison	3	18	68	.209
Bill Self	Kansas	14	312	134	.700
Frank Martin	Kansas St.	0	0	0	.000
Jim Christian	Kent St.	5	109	52	.677
Billy Gillispie	Kentucky	5	100	58	.633
John Giannini	La Salle	18	331	198	.626
Robert Lee	La.-Lafayette	3	25	47	.347
Orlando Early	La.-Monroe	2	28	32	.467
Fran O'Hanlon	Lafayette	12	170	174	.494
Steve Roccaforte	Lamar	1	15	17	.469
Brett Reed	Lehigh	0	0	0	.000
Ritchie McKay	Liberty	11	165	158	.511
Scott Sanderson	Lipscomb	7	97	105	.480
Dan Monson	Long Beach St.	10	170	123	.580
Jim Ferry	Long Island	9	157	107	.595
Mike Gillian	Longwood	4	25	94	.210
Kerry Rupp	Louisiana Tech	1	9	4	.692
Rick Pitino	Louisville	21	494	182	.731
Jim Whitesell	Loyola (Ill.)	20	331	233	.587
Jimmy Patsos	Loyola (Md.)	3	39	48	.448
Rodney Tention	Loyola Marymount	4	39	74	.345
John Brady	LSU	16	273	203	.574
Ted Woodward	Maine	3	38	49	.437
Barry Rohrssen	Manhattan	1	13	17	.433
Matt Brady	Marist	3	55	36	.604
Tom Crean	Marquette	8	165	86	.657
Donnie Jones	Marshall	0	0	0	.000
Gary Williams	Maryland	29	585	328	.641
Travis Ford	Massachusetts	10	156	144	.520
Dave Simmons	McNeese St.	1	15	17	.469
Meredith Smith	Md.-East. Shore	0	0	0	.000
John Calipari	Memphis	15	370	133	.736
Mark Slonaker	Mercer	11	118	194	.378
Frank Haith	Miami (Fla.)	3	46	49	.484
Charlie Coles	Miami (Ohio)	17	285	225	.559
John Beilein	Michigan	25	476	275	.634
Tom Izzo	Michigan St.	12	278	121	.697
Kermit Davis Jr.	Middle Tenn.	9	154	117	.568
Tubby Smith	Minnesota	16	387	145	.727
Andy Kennedy	Mississippi	2	42	26	.618
Rick Stansbury	Mississippi St.	9	185	104	.640
James Green	Mississippi Val.	10	150	146	.507
Mike Anderson	Missouri	5	107	53	.669
Barry Hinson	Missouri St.	10	188	124	.603
Dave Calloway	Monmouth	9	139	130	.517
Wayne Tinkle	Montana	1	17	15	.531
Brad Huse	Montana St.	1	11	19	.367
Donnie Tyndall	Morehead St.	1	12	18	.400
Todd Bozeman	Morgan St.	5	48	80	.375
Milan Brown	Mt. St. Mary's	4	41	76	.350
Billy Kennedy	Murray St.	9	120	140	.462
Jerry Eaves	N.C. A&T	4	30	89	.252
Billy Lange	Navy	5	72	72	.500
Doc Sadler	Nebraska	3	65	32	.670
Mark Fox	Nevada	3	81	18	.818
Bill Herrion	New Hampshire	16	259	206	.557
Steve Alford	New Mexico	16	308	183	.627
Marvin Menzies	New Mexico St.	0	0	0	.000
Joe Pasternack	New Orleans	0	0	0	.000
Joe Mihalich	Niagara	9	160	113	.586
J.P. Piper	Nicholls St.	3	23	61	.274
Anthony Evans	Norfolk St.	0	0	0	.000
Roy Williams	North Carolina	19	524	131	.800
Sidney Lowe	North Carolina St.	1	20	16	.556

Coach	School	Yrs.	Won	Lost	Pct.
Johnny Jones	North Texas	7	101	105	.490
Bill Coen	Northeastern	1	13	19	.406
Mike Adras	Northern Ariz.	8	129	106	.549
Tad Boyle	Northern Colo.	1	4	24	.143
Ricardo Patton	Northern Ill.	12	184	160	.535
Bill Carmody	Northwestern	11	187	138	.575
Mike McConathy	Northwestern St.	8	130	117	.526
Mike Brey	Notre Dame	12	241	130	.650
Greg Kampe	Oakland	23	377	290	.565
Tim O'Shea	Ohio	6	100	82	.549
Thad Matta	Ohio St.	7	183	53	.775
Jeff Capel III	Oklahoma	5	95	56	.629
Sean Sutton	Oklahoma St.	1	22	13	.629
Blaine Taylor	Old Dominion	13	259	134	.659
Scott Sutton	Oral Roberts	8	144	102	.585
Ernie Kent	Oregon	16	283	200	.586
Jay John	Oregon St.	5	66	85	.437
Bob Thomason	Pacific	22	375	266	.585
Glen Miller	Penn	14	210	166	.559
Ed DeChellis	Penn St.	11	147	169	.465
Vance Walberg	Pepperdine	1	8	23	.258
Jamie Dixon	Pittsburgh	4	105	30	.778
Eric Reveno	Portland	1	9	23	.281
Ken Bone	Portland St.	15	288	147	.662
Byron Rimm II	Prairie View	4	55	61	.474
Sydney Johnson	Princeton	0	0	0	.000
Tim Welsh	Providence	12	215	149	.591
Matt Painter	Purdue	3	56	36	.609
Tom Moore	Quinnipiac	5	76	59	.563
Brad Greenberg	Radford	0	0	0	.000
Jim Baron	Rhode Island	20	292	298	.495
Willis Wilson	Rice	15	215	220	.494
Chris Mooney	Richmond	5	63	78	.447
Tommy Dempsey	Rider	2	24	35	.407
Mike Rice	Robert Morris	0	0	0	.000
Fred Jr. Hill	Rutgers	1	10	19	.345
Jerome Jenkins	Sacramento St.	7	76	123	.382
Dave Bike	Sacred Heart	29	445	401	.526
Bob Marlin	Sam Houston St.	9	159	103	.607
Jimmy Tillette	Samford	10	165	129	.561
Bill Grier	San Diego	0	0	0	.000
Steve Fisher	San Diego St.	17	236	197	.545
Jessie Evans	San Francisco	10	159	129	.552
George Nessman	San Jose St.	2	11	50	.180
Kerry Keating	Santa Clara	0	0	0	.000
Horace Broadnax	Savannah St.	7	56	135	.293
Bobby Gonzalez	Seton Hall	8	142	93	.604
Fran McCaffery	Siena	11	174	151	.535
Matt Doherty	SMU	6	104	88	.542
Ronnie Arrow	South Ala.	16	248	184	.574
Dave Odom	South Carolina	21	391	261	.600
Tim Carter	South Carolina St.	12	171	168	.504
Stan Heath	South Fla.	6	112	77	.593
Scott Edgar	Southeast Mo. St.	8	119	115	.509
Jim Yarbrough	Southeastern La.	7	129	68	.655
Tim Floyd	Southern California	14	285	155	.648
Chris Lowery	Southern Ill.	3	78	26	.750
Larry Eustachy	Southern Miss.	16	301	194	.608
Rob Spivery	Southern U.	22	333	314	.515
Roger Reid	Southern Utah	7	151	71	.680
Mark Schmidt	St. Bonaventure	6	82	90	.477
Brian Nash	St. Francis (N.Y.)	2	19	39	.328
Bobby Jones	St. Francis (Pa.)	8	79	144	.354
Norm Roberts	St. John's (N.Y.)	7	61	132	.316
Phil Martelli	St. Joseph's	12	240	139	.633
Rick Majerus	St. Louis	20	422	147	.742
Randy Bennett	St. Mary's (Cal.)	6	102	83	.551
John Dunne	St. Peter's	1	5	25	.167
Trent Johnson	Stanford	8	131	114	.535
Danny Kaspar	Stephen F. Austin	16	327	142	.697
Derek Waugh	Stetson	7	77	114	.403
Steve Pikiell	Stony Brook	3	18	62	.225
Jim Boeheim	Syracuse	31	750	264	.740
Neil Dougherty	TCU	5	61	92	.399
Fran Dunphy	Temple	18	322	181	.640
Bret Campbell	Tenn.-Martin	8	86	142	.377
Bruce Pearl	Tennessee	15	363	103	.779
Cy Alexander	Tennessee St.	20	322	273	.541
Mike Sutton	Tennessee Tech.	5	89	63	.586
Tom Schuberth	Tex.-Pan American	1	14	15	.483
Rick Barnes	Texas	20	418	220	.655
Mark Turgeon	Texas A&M	9	153	119	.563
to be named	Texas Southern	0	0	0	.000

Coach	School	Yrs.	Won	Lost	Pct.
Doug Davalos	Texas St.	5	81	55	.596
Bob Knight	Texas Tech	41	890	363	.710
Scott Cross	Texas-Arlington	1	13	17	.433
Stan Joplin	Toledo	11	191	137	.582
Pat Kennedy	Towson	27	448	368	.549
Don Maestri	Troy	25	421	297	.586
Dave Dickerson	Tulane	2	29	30	.492
Doug Wojcik	Tulsa	2	31	28	.525
Mike Davis	UAB	7	130	95	.578
Gary Stewart	UC Davis	14	184	188	.495
Pat Douglass	UC Irvine	26	529	257	.673
Jim Wooldridge	UC Riverside	19	311	238	.566
Bob Williams	UC Santa Barb.	19	325	223	.593
Kirk Speraw	UCF	14	231	187	.553
Ben Howland	UCLA	13	259	140	.649
Randy Monroe	UMBC	3	33	56	.371
Matt Brown	UMKC	0	0	0	.000
Eddie Biedenbach	UNC Asheville	14	172	227	.431
Mike Dement	UNC Greensboro	20	290	279	.510
Benny Moss	UNC Wilmington	1	7	22	.241
Ben Jacobson	UNI	1	18	13	.581
Lon Kruger	UNLV	21	382	267	.589
Jim Boylen	Utah	0	0	0	.000
Stew Morrill	Utah St.	21	431	213	.669
Tony Barbee	UTEP	1	14	17	.452
Brooks Thompson	UTSA	1	7	22	.241
Homer Drew	Valparaiso	30	571	362	.612
Kevin Stallings	Vanderbilt	14	267	171	.610
Anthony Grant	VCU	1	28	7	.800
Mike Lonergan	Vermont	14	289	113	.719
Jay Wright	Villanova	13	248	155	.615
Dave Leitao	Virginia	7	116	95	.550
Seth Greenberg	Virginia Tech	17	280	226	.553
Duggar Baucom	VMI	4	58	58	.500
Mike Deane	Wagner	23	392	286	.578
Dino Gaudio	Wake Forest	7	68	124	.354
Lorenzo Romar	Washington	11	196	143	.578
Tony Bennett	Washington St.	1	26	8	.765
Randy Rahe	Weber St.	1	20	12	.625
Bob Huggins	West Virginia	25	590	211	.737
Larry Hunter	Western Caro.	27	533	261	.671
Derek Thomas	Western Ill.	4	28	86	.246
Darrin Horn	Western Ky.	4	82	41	.667
Steve Hawkins	Western Mich.	13	213	162	.568
Gregg Marshall	Wichita St.	9	194	83	.700
Tony Shaver	William & Mary	21	396	198	.667
Randy Peele	Winthrop	4	46	69	.400
Tod Kowalczyk	Wis.-Green Bay	5	77	73	.513
Rob Jeter	Wis.-Milwaukee	2	31	31	.500
Bo Ryan	Wisconsin	23	525	158	.769
Mike Young	Wofford	5	58	87	.400
Brad Brownell	Wright St.	5	106	50	.679
Heath Schroyer	Wyoming	3	35	47	.427
Sean Miller	Xavier	3	63	32	.663
James Jones	Yale	8	104	119	.466
Jerry Slocum	Youngstown St.	32	601	363	.623

Fastest To Milestone Wins

(Head coaches with at least half their seasons at Division I.)

FASTEST TO 100 WINS

Rk. Name, School	G	W	L	Pct.	Yr.	Season
1. Doc Meanwell, Wisconsin & Missouri	109	100	9	.917	7th	1918
2. Buck Freeman, St. John's (N.Y.)	110	100	10	.909	5th	1932
3. Adolph Rupp, Kentucky	116	100	16	.862	6th	1936
4. Jim Boeheim, Syracuse	117	100	17	.855	4th	1980
4. Jerry Tarkanian, Long Beach St.	117	100	17	.855	5th	1973
6. Everett Case, North Carolina St.	120	100	20	.833	4th	1950
6. Fred Taylor, Ohio St.	120	100	20	.833	5th	1963
7. Lew Andreas, Syracuse	122	100	22	.820	7th	1931
7. Denny Crum, Louisville	122	100	22	.820	5th	1976
7. Everett Dean, Carleton & Indiana	122	100	22	.820	7th	1929
11. Clair Bee, Rider & Long Island	123	100	23	.813	5th	1934
12. Don Haskins, UTEP	125	100	25	.800	5th	1966
12. Nat Holman, CCNY	125	100	25	.800	10th	1929
12. Buster Sheary, Holy Cross	125	100	25	.800	5th	1953
15. Jamie Dixon, Pittsburgh	126	100	26	.794	4th	2007
15. Mark Few, Gonzaga	126	100	26	.794	4th	2003
15. Tony Hinkle, Butler	126	100	26	.794	7th	1933

Rk.	Name, School	G	W	L	Pct.	Yr.	Season
15.	Ray Meyer, DePaul	126	100	26	.794	6th	1948
19.	Harry Combes, Illinois	127	100	27	.787	6th	1953
19.	Peck Hickman, Louisville	127	100	27	.787	5th	1949
21.	Vic Bubas, Duke	128	100	28	.781	5th	1964
22.	Hugh Greer, Connecticut	129	100	29	.775	6th	1952
22.	Roy Williams, Kansas	129	100	29	.775	4th	1992
24.	Speedy Morris, La Salle	130	100	30	.769	4th	1990
24.	Fred Schaus, West Virginia	130	100	30	.769	5th	1959
24.	Clifford Wells, Tulane	130	100	30	.769	6th	1951
24.	Thad Matta, Butler & Xavier	130	100	30	.769	4th	2004
28.	Harry Fisher, Columbia	131	100	31	.763	10th	1916
28.	Joseph Lapchick, St. John's (N.Y.)	131	100	31	.763	7th	1943
28.	Nolan Richardson, Tulsa	131	100	31	.763	5th	1985

FASTEST TO 200 WINS

Rk.	Name, School	G	W	L	Pct.	Yr.	Season
1.	Clair Bee, Rider & Long Island	231	200	31	.866	12th	1938
2.	Jerry Tarkanian, Long Beach St. & UNLV	234	200	34	.855	9th	1977
3.	Mark Few, Gonzaga	247	200	47	.810	8th	2007
4.	Everett Case, North Carolina St.	250	200	50	.800	9th	1954
5.	Harold Anderson, Toledo & Bowling Green	251	200	51	.797	10th	1945
5.	Lew Andreas, Syracuse	251	200	51	.797	14th	1939
5.	Nat Holman, CCNY	251	200	51	.797	18th	1937
5.	Adolph Rupp, Kentucky	251	200	51	.797	13th	1943
9.	Roy Williams, Kansas	252	200	52	.794	8th	1996
10.	Vic Bubas, Duke	254	200	54	.787	10th	1969
10.	Denny Crum, Louisville	254	200	54	.787	9th	1980
10.	Henry Iba, Northwest Mo. St., Colorado & Oklahoma St.	254	200	54	.787	11th	1940
10.	Doc Meanwell, Missouri & Wisconsin	254	200	54	.787	15th	1927
14.	Hec Edmundson, Washington	261	200	61	.766	13th	1931
14.	Hugh Greer, Connecticut	261	200	61	.766	11th	1957
16.	George Keogan, Wis.-Superior, St. Louis, St. Thomas (Minn.), Allegheny, Valparaiso & Notre Dame	263	200	63	.760	14th	1930
16.	Joseph Lapchick, St. John's (N.Y.)	263	200	63	.760	13th	1958
18.	Jack Ramsay, St. Joseph's	264	200	64	.758	10th	1965
19.	Peck Hickman, Louisville	265	200	65	.755	10th	1954
20.	Jim Boeheim, Syracuse	266	200	66	.752	9th	1985
20.	Fred Schaus, West Virginia & Purdue	266	200	66	.752	10th	1976
22.	Don Haskins, UTEP	269	200	69	.743	11th	1972
23.	Bob Knight, Army & Indiana	270	200	70	.741	11th	1976
24.	Lou Carnesecca, St. John's (N.Y.)	271	200	71	.738	10th	1978
24.	Harry Combes, Illinois	271	200	71	.738	12th	1959
24.	Arthur Schabinger, Ottawa, Emporia St. & Creighton	271	200	71	.738	16th	1932
27.	Dudey Moore, Duquesne	272	200	72	.735	11th	1959
27.	Bruce Weber, Southern Ill. & Illinois	272	200	72	.735	9th	2007
29.	Pete Gillen, Xavier	273	200	73	.733	9th	1994
30.	Tom Blackburn, Dayton	274	200	74	.730	10th	1957

FASTEST TO 300 WINS

Rk.	Name, School	G	W	L	Pct.	Yr.	Season
1.	Clair Bee, Rider & Long Island	344	300	44	.872	15th	1943
2.	Adolph Rupp, Kentucky	366	300	66	.820	17th	1947
3.	Jerry Tarkanian, Long Beach St. & UNLV	370	300	70	.811	13th	1982
3.	Roy Williams, Kansas	370	300	70	.811	11th	1999
5.	Everett Case, North Carolina St.	377	300	77	.796	13th	1959
6.	Harold Anderson, Toledo & Bowling Green	378	300	78	.794	14th	1949
7.	Denny Crum, Louisville	382	300	82	.785	13th	1984
7.	Henry Iba, Northwest Mo. St., Colorado & Oklahoma St.	382	300	82	.785	15th	1944
9.	Hec Edmundson, Washington	392	300	92	.765	18th	1936
10.	Jim Boeheim, Syracuse	393	300	93	.763	13th	1989
10.	Frank Keaney, Rhode Island	393	300	93	.763	24th	1944
12.	George Keogan, Wis.-Superior, St. Louis, St. Thomas (Minn.), Allegheny, Valparaiso & Notre Dame	394	300	94	.761	20th	1936
13.	Ray Mears, Wittenberg & Tennessee	395	300	95	.759	16th	1972
14.	Piggy Lambert, Purdue	397	300	97	.756	23rd	1940
15.	Lew Andreas, Syracuse	400	300	100	.750	23rd	1947
15.	Chick Davies, Duquesne	400	300	100	.750	21st	1948
17.	John Lawther, Westminster (Pa.) & Penn St.	402	300	102	.746	21st	1947
18.	Nolan Richardson, Tulsa & Arkansas	404	300	104	.743	13th	1993
19.	Peck Hickman, Louisville	405	300	105	.741	15th	1959
20.	Dean Smith, North Carolina	406	300	106	.739	15th	1976
20.	Eddie Sutton, Creighton & Arkansas	406	300	106	.739	15th	1984
22.	Bob Knight, Army & Indiana	407	300	107	.737	15th	1980
22.	John Thompson, Georgetown	407	300	107	.737	14th	1986
24.	Nat Holman, CCNY	408	300	108	.735	27th	1946
25.	Rick Majerus, Marquette, Ball St. & Utah	409	300	109	.733	14th	1998

FASTEST TO 400 WINS

Rk.	Name, School	G	W	L	Pct.	Yr.	Season
1.	Adolph Rupp, Kentucky	477	400	77	.839	20th	1950
2.	Clair Bee, Rider & Long Island	483	400	83	.828	21st	1951
3.	Jerry Tarkanian, Long Beach St. & UNLV	492	400	92	.813	17th	1985
4.	Roy Williams, Kansas	496	400	96	.806	15th	2003
5.	Henry Iba, Northwest Mo. St., Colorado & Oklahoma St.	500	400	100	.800	19th	1948
6.	Frank Keaney, Rhode Island	521	400	121	.768	28th	1948
7.	Phog Allen, Baker, Haskell, Central Mo. St. & Kansas	522	400	122	.766	29th	1935
7.	George Keogan, Wis.-Superior, St. Louis, St. Thomas (Minn.), Allegheny, Valparaiso & Notre Dame	522	400	122	.766	26th	1942
9.	Jim Boeheim, Syracuse	527	400	127	.759	17th	1993
10.	Dean Smith, North Carolina	531	400	131	.753	19th	1980
11.	Lou Carnesecca, St. John's (N.Y.)	535	400	135	.748	18th	1986
11.	John Thompson, Georgetown	535	400	135	.748	18th	1990
13.	Denny Crum, Louisville	536	400	136	.746	17th	1988
13.	Ed Diddle, Western Ky.	536	400	136	.746	24th	1946
13.	Nolan Richardson, Tulsa & Arkansas	536	400	136	.746	17th	1997
16.	Rick Majerus, Marquette, Ball St. & Utah	538	400	138	.743	19th	2003
17.	Nat Holman, CCNY	539	400	139	.742	32nd	1952
18.	Eddie Sutton, Creighton, Arkansas & Kentucky	541	400	141	.739	19th	1988
19.	Al McGuire, Belmont Abbey & Marquette	542	400	142	.738	20th	1977
20.	Bob Knight, Army & Indiana	545	400	145	.734	20th	1985
20.	Rick Pitino, Boston U., Providence, Kentucky & Louisville	545	400	145	.734	18th	2004
22.	Bob Huggins, Walsh, Akron & Cincinnati	548	400	148	.730	19th	1999
22.	John Wooden, Indiana St. & UCLA	548	400	148	.730	20th	1966

FASTEST TO 500 WINS

Rk.	Name, School	G	W	L	Pct.	Yr.	Season
1.	Adolph Rupp, Kentucky	583	500	83	.858	23rd	1955
2.	Jerry Tarkanian, Long Beach St. & UNLV	604	500	104	.828	20th	1988
3.	Roy Williams, Kansas & North Carolina	627	500	127	.797	19th	2007
4.	Henry Iba, Northwest Mo. St., Colorado & Oklahoma St.	631	500	131	.792	23rd	1952
5.	Phog Allen, Baker, Haskell, Central Mo. St. & Kansas	646	500	146	.774	34th	1940
6.	John Wooden, Indiana St. & UCLA	652	500	152	.767	24th	1970
7.	Dean Smith, North Carolina	653	500	153	.766	23rd	1984
8.	John Chaney, Cheyney & Temple	662	500	162	.755	22nd	1994
9.	Ed Diddle, Western Ky.	667	500	167	.750	28th	1950
10.	Jim Boeheim, Syracuse	669	500	169	.747	21st	1997
11.	Bob Huggins, Walsh, Akron & Cincinnati	671	500	171	.745	21st	2002
12.	Lou Carnesecca, St. John's (N.Y.)	683	500	183	.732	23rd	1991
12.	Bob Knight, Army & Indiana	683	500	183	.732	24th	1989
14.	Eddie Sutton, Creighton, Arkansas, Kentucky & Oklahoma St.	685	500	185	.730	23rd	1993
14.	John Thompson, Georgetown	685	500	185	.730	22nd	1994
16.	Denny Crum, Louisville	687	500	187	.728	22nd	1993
17.	Lute Olson, Long Beach St., Iowa & Arizona	690	500	190	.725	23rd	1996
18.	Nolan Richardson, Tulsa & Arkansas	695	500	195	.719	22nd	2002
19.	Frank McGuire, St. John's (N.Y.)	699	500	199	.715	27th	1977
20.	Mike Krzyzewski, Army & Duke	710	500	210	.704	23rd	1998
21.	Harold Anderson, Toledo & Bowling Green	724	500	224	.691	29th	1963

FASTEST TO 600 WINS

Rk. Name, School	G	W	L	Pct.	Yr.	Season
1. Adolph Rupp, Kentucky	704	600	104	.852	27th	1959
2. Jerry Tarkanian, Long Beach St. & UNLV	720	600	120	.833	24th	1992
3. John Wooden, Indiana St. & UCLA	755	600	155	.795	27th	1973
4. Dean Smith, North Carolina	773	600	173	.776	26th	1987
5. Henry Iba, Northwest Mo. St., Colorado & Oklahoma St.	775	600	175	.774	29th	1958
6. Phog Allen, Baker, Haskell, Central Mo. St. & Kansas	780	600	180	.769	41st	1947
7. Ed Diddle, Western Ky.	790	600	190	.759	32nd	1954
8. Jim Boeheim, Syracuse	807	600	207	.743	25th	2001
9. Bob Knight, Army & Indiana	812	600	212	.739	27th	1993
10. Lute Olson, Long Beach St., Iowa & Arizona	815	600	215	.736	27th	2000
11. John Chaney, Cheyney & Temple	816	600	216	.735	27th	1999
12. Mike Krzyzewski, Army & Duke	823	600	223	.729	26th	2001
13. Denny Crum, Louisville	825	600	225	.727	26th	1997
14. Cam Henderson, Muskingum, Davis & Elkins, & Marshall	830	600	230	.723	34th	1953
15. Eddie Sutton, Creighton, Arkansas, Kentucky & Oklahoma St.	837	600	237	.717	28th	1998
16. Don Haskins, UTEP	861	600	261	.697	31st	1992
17. Lefty Driesell, Davidson, Maryland & James Madison	868	600	268	.691	30th	1992
18. Jim Calhoun, Northeastern & Connecticut	879	600	279	.683	30th	2001
19. Guy Lewis, Houston	882	600	282	.680	31st	1987
20. Lou Henson, Hardin-Simmons, New Mexico St. & Illinois	887	600	287	.676	32nd	1993

FASTEST TO 700 WINS

Rk. Name, School	G	W	L	Pct.	Yr.	Season
1. Adolph Rupp, Kentucky	836	700	136	.837	32nd	1964
2. Jerry Tarkanian, Long Beach St., UNLV & Fresno St.	876	700	176	.799	29th	2000
3. Dean Smith, North Carolina	904	700	204	.774	30th	1991
4. Phog Allen, Baker, Haskell, Central Mo. St. & Kansas	938	700	238	.746	47th	1953
5. Jim Boeheim, Syracuse	939	700	239	.745	29th	2005
6. Mike Krzyzewski, Army & Duke	940	700	240	.745	30th	2005
6. Lute Olson, Long Beach St., Iowa & Arizona	940	700	240	.745	31st	2004
8. Ed Diddle, Western Ky.	946	700	246	.740	28th	1960
9. Henry Iba, Northwest Mo. St., Colorado & Oklahoma St.	953	700	253	.735	36th	1965
10. Bob Knight, Army & Indiana	956	700	256	.732	32nd	1997
11. Eddie Sutton, Creighton, Arkansas, Kentucky & Oklahoma St.	975	700	275	.718	32nd	2002
12. John Chaney, Cheyney & Temple	978	700	278	.716	32nd	2004
13. Jim Calhoun, Northeastern & Connecticut	1,008	700	308	.694	33rd	2005
14. Don Haskins, UTEP	1,029	700	329	.680	37th	1998
15. Lou Henson, Hardin-Simmons, Illinois & New Mexico St.	1,046	700	346	.669	36th	2000
16. Lefty Driesell, Davidson, Maryland, James Madison & Georgia St.	1,048	700	348	.668	37th	1999
17. Ray Meyer, DePaul	1,051	700	351	.666	52nd	1984
18. Norm Stewart, UNI & Missouri	1,055	700	355	.664	36th	1998

FASTEST TO 800 WINS

Rk. Name, School	G	W	L	Pct.	Yr.	Season
1. Adolph Rupp, Kentucky	972	800	172	.823	37th	1969
2. Dean Smith, North Carolina	1,029	800	229	.777	33rd	1994
3. Bob Knight, Army, Indiana & Texas Tech	1,102	800	302	.726	37th	2003

Top 10 Best Career Starts By Percentage

(Head coaches with at least half of their seasons at Division I)

1 SEASON

Coach, Team	Season	W	L	Pct.
Norman Shepard, North Carolina	1924	23	0	1.000
Bill Hodges, Indiana St.	1979	33	1	.970
Tom Gola, La Salle	1969	23	1	.958
Lou Rossini, Columbia	1951	21	1	.955
Earl Brown, Dartmouth	1944	19	2	.905
Phil Johnson, Weber St.	1969	27	3	.900
Bill Guthridge, North Carolina	1998	34	4	.895
Gary Cunningham, UCLA	1978	25	3	.893
Bob Davies, Seton Hall	1947	24	3	.889
Jerry Tarkanian, Long Beach St.	1969	23	3	.885

2 SEASONS

Coach, Team	Seasons	W	L	Pct.
Lew Andreas, Syracuse	1925-26	33	3	.917
Bill Carmody, Princeton	1997-98	51	6	.895
Everett Case, North Carolina St.	1947-48	55	8	.873
Buck Freeman, St. John's (N.Y.)	1928-29	41	6	.872
Gary Cunningham, UCLA	1978-79	50	8	.862
Nibs Price, California	1925-26	25	4	.862
Denny Crum, Louisville	1972-73	49	8	.860
Adolph Rupp, Kentucky	1931-32	30	5	.857
Jerry Tarkanian, Long Beach St.	1969-70	47	8	.855
John Castellani, Seattle	1957-58	45	9	.833

3 SEASONS

Coach, Team	Seasons	W	L	Pct.
Nibs Price, California	1925-27	38	4	.905
Buck Freeman, St. John's (N.Y.)	1928-30	64	7	.901
Lew Andreas, Syracuse	1925-27	48	7	.873
Adolph Rupp, Kentucky	1931-33	51	8	.864
Jerry Tarkanian, Long Beach St.	1969-71	69	12	.852
Jim Boeheim, Syracuse	1977-79	74	14	.841
Bill Carmody, Princeton	1997-99	73	14	.841
Everett Case, North Carolina St.	1947-49	80	16	.833
Ben Carnevale, North Carolina & Navy	1945-47	68	14	.829
Mark Fox, Nevada	2005-07	81	18	.818

4 SEASONS

Coach, Team	Seasons	W	L	Pct.
Buck Freeman, St. John's (N.Y.)	1928-31	85	8	.914
Adolph Rupp, Kentucky	1931-34	67	9	.882
Jerry Tarkanian, Long Beach St.	1969-72	92	15	.860
Jim Boeheim, Syracuse	1977-80	100	18	.847
Fred Taylor, Ohio St.	1959-62	89	17	.840
Everett Case, North Carolina St.	1947-50	107	22	.829
Nibs Price, California	1925-28	47	10	.825
Nat Holman, CCNY	1920-23	46	10	.821
Denny Crum, Louisville	1972-75	98	22	.817
Lew Andreas, Syracuse	1925-28	58	13	.817

5 SEASONS

Coach, Team	Seasons	W	L	Pct.
Buck Freeman, St. John's (N.Y.)	1928-32	107	12	.899
Adolph Rupp, Kentucky	1931-35	86	11	.887
Jerry Tarkanian, Long Beach St. & UNLV	1969-73	116	17	.872
Nat Holman, CCNY	1920-24	58	11	.841
Fred Taylor, Ohio St.	1959-63	109	21	.838
Nibs Price, California	1925-29	64	13	.831
Everett Case, North Carolina St.	1947-51	137	29	.825
Charles Orsborn, Bradley	1957-61	115	25	.821
Mark Few, Gonzaga	2000-04	133	32	.806
Buster Sheary, Holy Cross	1949-53	110	27	.803
Jim Boeheim, Syracuse	1977-81	122	30	.803

6 SEASONS

Coach, Team	Seasons	W	L	Pct.
Buck Freeman, St. John's (N.Y.)	1928-33	130	16	.890
Adolph Rupp, Kentucky	1931-36	101	17	.856
Jerry Tarkanian, Long Beach St. & UNLV	1969-74	136	23	.855
Nat Holman, CCNY	1920-25	70	13	.843
Buster Sheary, Holy Cross	1949-54	136	29	.824
Lew Andreas, Syracuse	1925-30	87	19	.821
Everett Dean, Carleton & Indiana	1922-27	82	18	.820
Clair Bee, Rider & Long Island	1929-34	101	23	.815
Fred Taylor, Ohio St.	1959-64	125	29	.812
Mark Few, Gonzaga	2000-05	159	37	.811

7 SEASONS

Coach, Team	Seasons	W	L	Pct.
Buck Freeman, St. John's (N.Y.)	1928-34	146	19	.885
Jerry Tarkanian, Long Beach St. & UNLV	1969-75	160	28	.851
Adolph Rupp, Kentucky	1931-37	118	22	.843
Clair Bee, Rider & Long Island	1929-35	125	25	.833
Everett Dean, Carleton & Indiana	1922-28	97	20	.829
Mark Few, Gonzaga	2000-06	188	41	.821
Lew Andreas, Syracuse	1925-31	103	23	.817
Nat Holman, CCNY	1920-26	79	18	.814
Buster Sheary, Holy Cross	1949-55	155	36	.812
Everett Case, North Carolina St.	1947-53	187	45	.806

8 SEASONS

Coach, Team	Seasons	W	L	Pct.
Jerry Tarkanian, Long Beach St. & UNLV	1969-76	189	30	.863
Clair Bee, Rider & Long Island	1929-36	150	25	.857

Coach, Team	Seasons	W	L	Pct.
Buck Freeman, St. John's (N.Y.)	1928-35	159	27	.855
Adolph Rupp, Kentucky	1931-38	131	27	.829
Nat Holman, CCNY	1920-27	88	21	.807
Everett Case, North Carolina St.	1947-54	213	52	.804
Mark Few, Gonzaga	2000-07	211	52	.802
Hugh Greer, Connecticut	1947-54	151	38	.799
Lew Andreas, Syracuse	1925-32	116	30	.795
Roy Williams, Kansas	1989-96	213	56	.792

9 SEASONS

Coach, Team	Seasons	W	L	Pct.
Jerry Tarkanian, Long Beach St. & UNLV	1969-77	218	33	.869
Clair Bee, Rider & Long Island	1929-37	177	28	.863
Buck Freeman, St. John's (N.Y.)	1928-36	177	31	.851
Adolph Rupp, Kentucky	1931-39	147	31	.826
Everett Case, North Carolina St.	1947-55	241	56	.811
Roy Williams, Kansas	1989-97	247	58	.810
Lew Andreas, Syracuse	1925-33	130	32	.802
Henry Iba, Northwest Mo. St., Colorado & Oklahoma St.	1930-38	180	45	.800
Denny Crum, Louisville	1972-80	219	55	.799
Hugh Greer, Connecticut	1947-55	171	43	.799

10 SEASONS

Coach, Team	Seasons	W	L	Pct.
Clair Bee, Rider & Long Island	1929-38	200	32	.862
Jerry Tarkanian, Long Beach St. & UNLV	1969-78	238	41	.853
Roy Williams, Kansas	1989-98	282	62	.820
Everett Case, North Carolina St.	1947-56	265	60	.815
Adolph Rupp, Kentucky	1931-40	162	37	.814
Lew Andreas, Syracuse	1925-34	145	34	.810
Henry Iba, Northwest Mo. St., Colorado & Oklahoma St.	1930-39	199	53	.790
Denny Crum, Louisville	1972-81	240	64	.789
Harold Anderson, Toledo & Bowling Green	1935-44	182	50	.784
Nat Holman, CCNY	1920-29	108	30	.783

11 SEASONS

Coach, Team	Seasons	W	L	Pct.
Clair Bee, Rider & Long Island	1929-39	223	32	.875
Jerry Tarkanian, Long Beach St. & UNLV	1969-79	259	49	.841
Lew Andreas, Syracuse	1925-35	160	36	.816
Roy Williams, Kansas	1989-99	305	72	.809
Henry Iba, Northwest Mo. St., Colorado & Oklahoma St.	1930-40	225	56	.801
Adolph Rupp, Kentucky	1931-41	179	45	.799
Everett Case, North Carolina St.	1947-57	280	71	.798
Harold Anderson, Toledo & Bowling Green	1935-45	206	54	.792
Nat Holman, CCNY	1920-30	119	33	.783
Denny Crum, Louisville	1972-82	263	74	.780

12 SEASONS

Coach, Team	Seasons	W	L	Pct.
Clair Bee, Rider & Long Island	1929-40	242	36	.871
Jerry Tarkanian, Long Beach St. & UNLV	1969-80	282	58	.829
Lew Andreas, Syracuse	1925-36	172	41	.806
Roy Williams, Kansas	1989-2000	329	82	.800
Harold Anderson, Toledo & Bowling Green	1935-46	233	59	.798
Adolph Rupp, Kentucky	1931-42	198	51	.795
Everett Case, North Carolina St.	1947-58	298	77	.795
Henry Iba, Northwest Mo. St., Colorado & Oklahoma St.	1930-41	243	63	.794
Denny Crum, Louisville	1972-83	295	78	.791
Joe Mullaney, Norwich & Providence	1955-66	243	68	.781

13 SEASONS

Coach, Team	Seasons	W	L	Pct.
Clair Bee, Rider & Long Island	1929-41	267	38	.875
Jerry Tarkanian, Long Beach St. & UNLV	1969-81	298	70	.810
Lew Andreas, Syracuse	1925-37	185	45	.804
Roy Williams, Kansas	1989-2001	355	89	.800
Harold Anderson, Toledo & Bowling Green	1935-47	261	66	.798
Everett Case, North Carolina St.	1947-59	320	81	.798
Nat Holman, CCNY	1920-32	147	38	.795
Henry Iba, Northwest Mo. St., Colorado & Oklahoma St.	1930-42	263	69	.792
Adolph Rupp, Kentucky	1931-43	215	57	.790
Denny Crum, Louisville	1972-84	319	89	.782

14 SEASONS

Coach, Team	Seasons	W	L	Pct.
Clair Bee, Rider & Long Island	1929-42	291	41	.877
Roy Williams, Kansas	1989-2002	388	93	.807
Nat Holman, CCNY	1920-33	160	39	.804
Harold Anderson, Toledo & Bowling Green	1935-48	288	72	.800
Jerry Tarkanian, Long Beach St. & UNLV	1969-82	318	80	.799
Adolph Rupp, Kentucky	1931-44	234	59	.799
Lew Andreas, Syracuse	1925-38	198	50	.798
Henry Iba, Northwest Mo. St., Colorado & Oklahoma St.	1930-43	277	79	.778
Everett Case, North Carolina St.	1947-60	331	96	.775
Jim Boeheim, Syracuse	1977-90	343	108	.761

15 SEASONS

Coach, Team	Seasons	W	L	Pct.
Clair Bee, Rider & Long Island	1929-43	304	47	.866
Nat Holman, CCNY	1920-34	174	40	.813
Jerry Tarkanian, Long Beach St. & UNLV	1969-83	346	83	.807
Roy Williams, Kansas	1989-2003	418	101	.805
Adolph Rupp, Kentucky	1931-45	256	63	.803
Harold Anderson, Toledo & Bowling Green	1935-49	312	79	.798
Lew Andreas, Syracuse	1925-39	212	54	.797
Henry Iba, Northwest Mo. St., Colorado & Oklahoma St.	1930-44	304	85	.781
Everett Case, North Carolina St.	1947-61	347	105	.768
Denny Crum, Louisville	1972-86	370	114	.764
Jim Boeheim, Syracuse	1977-91	369	114	.764

16 SEASONS

Coach, Team	Seasons	W	L	Pct.
Clair Bee, Rider & Long Island	1929-43, 46	318	56	.850
Adolph Rupp, Kentucky	1931-46	284	65	.814
Jerry Tarkanian, Long Beach St. & UNLV	1969-84	375	89	.808
Nat Holman, CCNY	1920-35	184	46	.800
Roy Williams, Kansas & North Carolina	1989-2004	437	112	.796
Henry Iba, Northwest Mo. St., Colorado & Oklahoma St.	1930-45	331	89	.788
Harold Anderson, Toledo & Bowling Green	1935-50	331	90	.786
Lew Andreas, Syracuse	1925-40	222	62	.782
Everett Case, North Carolina St.	1947-62	358	111	.763
Ray Mears, Wittenberg & Tennessee	1957-72	306	97	.759
Jim Boeheim, Syracuse	1977-92	391	124	.759

17 SEASONS

Coach, Team	Seasons	W	L	Pct.
Clair Bee, Rider & Long Island	1929-43, 46-47	335	61	.850
Adolph Rupp, Kentucky	1931-47	318	68	.824
Jerry Tarkanian, Long Beach St. & UNLV	1969-85	403	93	.813
Roy Williams, Kansas & North Carolina	1989-2005	470	116	.802
Henry Iba, Northwest Mo. St., Colorado & Oklahoma St.	1930-46	362	91	.799
Nat Holman, CCNY	1920-36	194	50	.795
Harold Anderson, Toledo & Bowling Green	1935-51	341	94	.784
Lew Andreas, Syracuse	1925-41	236	67	.779
Jim Boeheim, Syracuse	1977-93	411	133	.756
Joseph Lapchick, St. John's (N.Y.)	1937-47, 57-62	291	95	.754

18 SEASONS

Coach, Team	Seasons	W	L	Pct.
Clair Bee, Rider & Long Island	1929-43, 46-48	352	65	.844
Adolph Rupp, Kentucky	1931-48	354	71	.833
Jerry Tarkanian, Long Beach St. & UNLV	1969-86	436	98	.816
Roy Williams, Kansas & North Carolina	1989-2006	493	124	.799
Henry Iba, Northwest Mo. St., Colorado & Oklahoma St.	1930-47	386	99	.796
Nat Holman, CCNY	1920-37	204	56	.785
Harold Anderson, Toledo & Bowling Green	1935-52	358	104	.775
Lew Andreas, Syracuse	1925-42	251	73	.775
Jim Boeheim, Syracuse	1977-94	434	140	.756
Dean Smith, North Carolina	1962-79	386	127	.752

19 SEASONS

Coach, Team	Seasons	W	L	Pct.
Adolph Rupp, Kentucky	1931-49	386	73	.841
Clair Bee, Rider & Long Island	1929-43, 46-49	370	77	.828
Jerry Tarkanian, Long Beach St. & UNLV	1969-87	473	100	.825
Henry Iba, Northwest Mo. St., Colorado & Oklahoma St.	1930-48	413	103	.800
Roy Williams, Kansas & North Carolina	1989-2007	524	131	.800
Nat Holman, CCNY	1920-38	217	59	.786
Lew Andreas, Syracuse	1925-43	259	83	.757
Harold Anderson, Toledo & Bowling Green	1935-53	370	119	.757
Jim Boeheim, Syracuse	1977-95	454	150	.752
Dean Smith, North Carolina	1962-80	407	135	.751

COACHING RECORDS

20 SEASONS

Coach, Team	Seasons	W	L	Pct.
Adolph Rupp, Kentucky	1931-50	411	78	.840
Clair Bee, Rider & Long Island	1929-43, 46-50	390	82	.826
Jerry Tarkanian, Long Beach St. & UNLV	1969-88	501	106	.825
Henry Iba, Northwest Mo. St., Colorado & Oklahoma St.	1930-49	436	108	.801
Phog Allen, Baker, Kansas, Haskell, Central Mo. St. & Kansas	1906-09, 13-28	325	89	.785
Nat Holman, CCNY	1920-39	228	65	.778
John Chaney, Cheyney & Temple	1973-92	458	143	.762
Frank Keaney, Rhode Island	1922-41	265	86	.755
Harold Anderson, Toledo & Bowling Green	1935-54	387	126	.754
Dean Smith, North Carolina	1962-81	436	143	.753

21 SEASONS

Coach, Team	Seasons	W	L	Pct.
Adolph Rupp, Kentucky	1931-51	443	80	.847
Clair Bee, Rider & Long Island	1929-43, 46-51	410	86	.827
Jerry Tarkanian, Long Beach St. & UNLV	1969-89	530	114	.823
Henry Iba, Northwest Mo. St., Colorado & Oklahoma St.	1930-50	454	117	.795
Nat Holman, CCNY	1920-40	236	73	.764
Dean Smith, North Carolina	1962-82	468	145	.763
Phog Allen, Baker, Kansas, Haskell, Central Mo. St. & Kansas	1906-09, 13-29	328	104	.759
Frank Keaney, Rhode Island	1922-42	283	90	.759
John Chaney, Cheyney & Temple	1973-93	478	156	.754
Chick Davies, Duquesne	1925-40, 47-48	314	106	.748

22 SEASONS

Coach, Team	Seasons	W	L	Pct.
Adolph Rupp, Kentucky	1931-52	472	83	.850
Jerry Tarkanian, Long Beach St. & UNLV	1969-90	565	119	.826
Henry Iba, Northwest Mo. St., Colorado & Oklahoma St.	1930-51	483	123	.797
Nat Holman, CCNY	1920-41	253	78	.764
Dean Smith, North Carolina	1962-83	496	153	.764
Frank Keaney, Rhode Island	1922-43	299	93	.763
Phog Allen, Baker, Kansas, Haskell, Central Mo. St. & Kansas	1906-09, 13-30	342	108	.760
John Wooden, Indiana St. & UCLA	1947-68	464	151	.754
John Chaney, Cheyney & Temple	1973-94	501	164	.753
Lew Andreas, Syracuse	1925-47	308	105	.746

23 SEASONS

Coach, Team	Seasons	W	L	Pct.
Adolph Rupp, Kentucky	1931-52, 54	497	83	.857
Jerry Tarkanian, Long Beach St. & UNLV	1969-91	599	120	.833
Henry Iba, Northwest Mo. St., Colorado & Oklahoma St.	1930-52	502	131	.793
Dean Smith, North Carolina	1962-84	524	156	.771
Nat Holman, CCNY	1920-42	269	81	.769
John Wooden, Indiana St. & UCLA	1947-69	493	152	.764
Phog Allen, Baker, Kansas, Haskell, Central Mo. St. & Kansas	1906-09, 13-31	357	111	.763
Frank Keaney, Rhode Island	1922-44	313	99	.760
John Chaney, Cheyney & Temple	1973-95	520	175	.748
Ed Diddle, Western Ky.	1923-45	395	134	.747

24 SEASONS

Coach, Team	Seasons	W	L	Pct.
Adolph Rupp, Kentucky	1931-52, 54-55	520	86	.858
Jerry Tarkanian, Long Beach St. & UNLV	1969-92	625	122	.837
Henry Iba, Northwest Mo. St., Colorado & Oklahoma St.	1930-53	525	138	.792
John Wooden, Indiana St. & UCLA	1947-70	521	154	.772
Dean Smith, North Carolina	1962-85	551	165	.770
Frank Keaney, Rhode Island	1922-45	333	104	.762
Phog Allen, Baker, Kansas, Haskell, Central Mo. St. & Kansas	1906-09, 13-32	370	116	.761
Nat Holman, CCNY	1920-43	277	91	.753
Jim Boeheim, Syracuse	1977-2000	575	199	.743
Bob Huggins, Walsh, Akron & Cincinnati	1981-2005	567	199	.740

25 SEASONS

Coach, Team	Seasons	W	L	Pct.
Adolph Rupp, Kentucky	1931-52, 54-56	540	92	.854
Jerry Tarkanian, Long Beach St., UNLV & Fresno St.	1969-92, 96	647	133	.829
Henry Iba, Northwest Mo. St., Colorado & Oklahoma St.	1930-54	549	143	.793
John Wooden, Indiana St. & UCLA	1947-71	550	155	.780
Dean Smith, North Carolina	1962-86	579	171	.772

Coach, Team	Seasons	W	L	Pct.
Frank Keaney, Rhode Island	1922-46	354	107	.768
Phog Allen, Baker, Kansas, Haskell, Central Mo. St. & Kansas	1906-09, 13-33	383	120	.761
Jim Boeheim, Syracuse	1977-2001	600	208	.743
John Chaney, Cheyney & Temple	1973-97	560	199	.738
Bob Huggins, Walsh, Akron, Cincinnati & Kansas St.	1981-2005, 07	590	211	.737

26 SEASONS

Coach, Team	Seasons	W	L	Pct.
Adolph Rupp, Kentucky	1931-52, 54-57	563	97	.853
Jerry Tarkanian, Long Beach St., UNLV & Fresno St.	1969-92, 96-97	667	145	.821
John Wooden, Indiana St. & UCLA	1947-72	580	155	.789
Henry Iba, Northwest Mo. St., Colorado & Oklahoma St.	1930-55	561	156	.782
Dean Smith, North Carolina	1962-87	611	175	.777
Frank Keaney, Rhode Island	1922-47	371	110	.771
Phog Allen, Baker, Kansas, Haskell, Central Mo. St. & Kansas	1906-09, 13-34	399	121	.767
Ed Diddle, Western Ky.	1923-48	463	159	.744
Jim Boeheim, Syracuse	1977-2002	623	221	.738
John Chaney, Cheyney & Temple	1973-98	581	208	.736
Nat Holman, CCNY	1920-45	295	106	.736

27 SEASONS

Coach, Team	Seasons	W	L	Pct.
Adolph Rupp, Kentucky	1931-52, 54-58	586	103	.851
Jerry Tarkanian, Long Beach St., UNLV & Fresno St.	1969-92, 96-98	688	158	.813
John Wooden, Indiana St. & UCLA	1947-73	610	155	.797
Henry Iba, Northwest Mo. St., Colorado & Oklahoma St.	1930-56	579	165	.778
Dean Smith, North Carolina	1962-88	638	182	.778
Frank Keaney, Rhode Island	1922-48	387	117	.768
Phog Allen, Baker, Kansas, Haskell, Central Mo. St. & Kansas	1906-09, 13-35	414	126	.767
Ed Diddle, Western Ky.	1923-49	488	163	.750
Jim Boeheim, Syracuse	1977-2003	653	226	.743
Nat Holman, CCNY	1920-46	309	110	.737
Bob Knight, Army & Indiana	1966-92	588	210	.737

28 SEASONS

Coach, Team	Seasons	W	L	Pct.
Adolph Rupp, Kentucky	1931-52, 54-59	610	106	.852
Jerry Tarkanian, Long Beach St., UNLV & Fresno St.	1969-92, 96-99	689	170	.802
John Wooden, Indiana St. & UCLA	1947-74	636	159	.800
Dean Smith, North Carolina	1962-89	667	190	.778
Henry Iba, Northwest Mo. St., Colorado & Oklahoma St.	1930-57	596	174	.774
Phog Allen, Baker, Kansas, Haskell, Central Mo. St. & Kansas	1906-09, 13-36	435	128	.773
Ed Diddle, Western Ky.	1923-50	513	169	.752
Bob Knight, Army & Indiana	1966-93	619	214	.743
Jim Boeheim, Syracuse	1977-2004	676	234	.743
Mike Krzyzewski, Army & Duke	1976-2003	663	234	.739

29 SEASONS

Coach, Team	Seasons	W	L	Pct.
Adolph Rupp, Kentucky	1931-52, 54-60	628	113	.848
John Wooden, Indiana St. & UCLA	1947-75	664	162	.804
Jerry Tarkanian, Long Beach St., UNLV & Fresno St.	1969-92, 96-2000	701	179	.797
Phog Allen, Baker, Kansas, Haskell, Central Mo. St. & Kansas	1906-09, 13-37	450	132	.773
Henry Iba, Northwest Mo. St., Colorado & Oklahoma St.	1930-58	617	182	.772
Dean Smith, North Carolina	1962-90	688	203	.772
Ed Diddle, Western Ky.	1923-51	532	179	.748
Jim Boeheim, Syracuse	1977-2005	703	241	.745
Mike Krzyzewski, Army & Duke	1976-2004	694	240	.743
Nat Holman, CCNY	1920-48	344	119	.743

30 SEASONS

Coach, Team	Seasons	W	L	Pct.
Adolph Rupp, Kentucky	1931-52, 54-61	647	122	.841
Jerry Tarkanian, Long Beach St., UNLV & Fresno St.	1969-92, 96-2001	710	186	.792
Phog Allen, Baker, Kansas, Haskell, Central Mo. St. & Kansas	1906-09, 13-38	468	134	.777
Dean Smith, North Carolina	1962-91	717	209	.774

Coach, Team	Seasons	W	L	Pct.
Henry Iba, Northwest Mo. St., Colorado & Oklahoma St.	1930-59	628	196	.762
Ed Diddle, Western Ky.	1923-52	558	184	.752
Mike Krzyzewski, Army & Duke	1976-2005	721	246	.746
Lute Olson, Long Beach St., Iowa & Arizona	1974-2003	690	240	.742
Jim Boeheim, Syracuse	1977-2006	726	253	.742
Nat Holman, CCNY	1920-49	361	127	.740

31 SEASONS

Coach, Team	Seasons	W	L	Pct.
Adolph Rupp, Kentucky	1931-52, 54-62	670	125	.843
Jerry Tarkanian, Long Beach St., UNLV & Fresno St.	1969-92, 96-2000	729	201	.784
Phog Allen, Baker, Kansas, Haskell, Central Mo. St. & Kansas	1906-09, 13-39	481	141	.773
Dean Smith, North Carolina	1962-92	740	219	.772
Ed Diddle, Western Ky.	1923-53	583	190	.754
Henry Iba, Northwest Mo. St., Colorado & Oklahoma St.	1930-60	638	211	.751
Mike Krzyzewski, Army & Duke	1976-2006	753	250	.751
Nat Holman, CCNY	1920-50	385	132	.745
Lute Olson, Long Beach St., Iowa & Arizona	1974-2004	710	249	.740
Jim Boeheim, Syracuse	1977-2007	750	264	.740

32 SEASONS

Coach, Team	Seasons	W	L	Pct.
Adolph Rupp, Kentucky	1931-52, 54-63	686	134	.837
Dean Smith, North Carolina	1962-93	774	223	.776
Phog Allen, Baker, Kansas, Haskell, Central Mo. St. & Kansas	1906-09, 13-40	500	147	.773
Ed Diddle, Western Ky.	1923-54	612	193	.760
Mike Krzyzewski, Army & Duke	1976-2007	775	261	.748
Henry Iba, Northwest Mo. St., Colorado & Oklahoma St.	1930-61	652	222	.746
Lute Olson, Long Beach St., Iowa & Arizona	1974-2005	740	256	.743
Nat Holman, CCNY	1920-51	397	139	.741
Bob Knight, Army & Indiana	1966-97	700	258	.731
Eddie Sutton, Creighton, Arkansas, Kentucky & Oklahoma St.	1970-89, 91-2002	702	278	.716

33 SEASONS

Coach, Team	Seasons	W	L	Pct.
Adolph Rupp, Kentucky	1931-52, 54-64	707	140	.835
Dean Smith, North Carolina	1962-94	802	230	.777
Phog Allen, Baker, Kansas, Haskell, Central Mo. St. & Kansas	1906-09, 13-41	512	153	.770
Ed Diddle, Western Ky.	1923-55	630	203	.756
Henry Iba, Northwest Mo. St., Colorado & Oklahoma St.	1930-62	666	233	.741
Lute Olson, Long Beach St., Iowa & Arizona	1974-2006	760	269	.739
Nat Holman, CCNY	1920-52	405	150	.730
Bob Knight, Army & Indiana	1966-98	720	270	.727
Eddie Sutton, Creighton, Arkansas, Kentucky & Oklahoma St.	1970-89, 91-2003	724	288	.715
John Chaney, Cheyney & Temple	1973-2005	724	297	.709

34 SEASONS

Coach, Team	Seasons	W	L	Pct.
Adolph Rupp, Kentucky	1931-52, 54-65	722	150	.828
Dean Smith, North Carolina	1962-95	830	236	.779
Phog Allen, Baker, Kansas, Haskell, Central Mo. St. & Kansas	1906-09, 13-42	529	158	.770
Ed Diddle, Western Ky.	1923-56	646	215	.750
Henry Iba, Northwest Mo. St., Colorado & Oklahoma St.	1930-63	682	242	.738
Lute Olson, Long Beach St., Iowa & Arizona	1974-2007	780	280	.736
Bob Knight, Army & Indiana	1966-99	743	281	.726
Eddie Sutton, Creighton, Arkansas, Kentucky & Oklahoma St.	1970-89, 91-2004	755	292	.721
Nat Holman, CCNY	1920-52, 55	413	160	.721
John Chaney, Cheyney & Temple	1973-2006	741	312	.704

35 SEASONS

Coach, Team	Seasons	W	L	Pct.
Adolph Rupp, Kentucky	1931-52, 54-66	749	152	.831
Dean Smith, North Carolina	1962-96	851	247	.775
Phog Allen, Baker, Kansas, Haskell, Central Mo. St. & Kansas	1906-09, 13-43	551	164	.771
Ed Diddle, Western Ky.	1923-57	663	224	.747
Henry Iba, Northwest Mo. St., Colorado & Oklahoma St.	1930-64	697	252	.734
Bob Knight, Army & Indiana	1966-2000	764	289	.726
Eddie Sutton, Creighton, Arkansas, Kentucky & Oklahoma St.	1970-89, 91-2005	781	299	.723
Nat Holman, CCNY	1920-52, 55-56	417	174	.706
Jim Calhoun, Northeastern & Connecticut	1973-2007	750	328	.696
Don Haskins, UTEP	1962-96	678	313	.684

36 SEASONS

Coach, Team	Seasons	W	L	Pct.
Adolph Rupp, Kentucky	1931-52, 54-67	762	165	.822
Dean Smith, North Carolina	1962-97	879	254	.776
Phog Allen, Baker, Kansas, Haskell, Central Mo. St. & Kansas	1906-09, 13-44	568	173	.767
Ed Diddle, Western Ky.	1923-58	677	235	.742
Henry Iba, Northwest Mo. St., Colorado & Oklahoma St.	1930-65	717	259	.735
Bob Knight, Army, Indiana & Texas Tech	1966-2000, 02	787	298	.725
Eddie Sutton, Creighton, Arkansas, Kentucky & Oklahoma St.	1970-89, 91-2006	798	315	.717
Nat Holman, CCNY	1920-52, 55-56, 59	423	186	.695
Don Haskins, UTEP	1962-97	691	351	.679
Lou Henson, Hardin-Simmons, New Mexico St., Illinois & New Mexico St.	1963-96, 99-2000	708	351	.669

37 SEASONS

Coach, Team	Seasons	W	L	Pct.
Adolph Rupp, Kentucky	1931-52, 54-68	784	170	.822
Phog Allen, Baker, Kansas, Haskell, Central Mo. St. & Kansas	1906-09, 13-45	580	178	.765
Ed Diddle, Western Ky.	1923-59	693	245	.739
Bob Knight, Army, Indiana & Texas Tech	1966-2000, 02-03	809	311	.722
Henry Iba, Northwest Mo. St., Colorado & Oklahoma St.	1930-66	721	280	.720
Nat Holman, CCNY	1920-52, 55-56, 59-60	423	190	.690
Don Haskins, UTEP	1962-98	703	341	.673
Lefty Driesell, Davidson, Maryland, James Madison & Georgia St.	1961-86, 89-99	716	360	.665
Lou Henson, Hardin-Simmons, New Mexico St., Illinois & New Mexico St.	1963-96, 99-2001	722	365	.664
Norm Stewart, UNI & Missouri	1962-98	711	366	.660

38 SEASONS

Coach, Team	Seasons	W	L	Pct.
Adolph Rupp, Kentucky	1931-52, 54-69	807	175	.822
Phog Allen, Baker, Kansas, Haskell, Central Mo. St. & Kansas	1906-09, 13-46	599	180	.769
Ed Diddle, Western Ky.	1923-60	714	252	.739
Bob Knight, Army, Indiana & Texas Tech	1966-2000, 02-04	832	322	.721
Henry Iba, Northwest Mo. St., Colorado & Oklahoma St.	1930-67	728	298	.710
Don Haskins, UTEP	1962-99	719	353	.671
Lefty Driesell, Davidson, Maryland, James Madison & Georgia St.	1961-86, 89-2000	733	372	.663
Lou Henson, Hardin-Simmons, New Mexico St., Illinois & New Mexico St.	1963-96, 99-2002	742	377	.663
Norm Stewart, UNI & Missouri	1962-99	731	375	.661
Ray Meyer, DePaul	1943-80	623	335	.650

39 SEASONS

Coach, Team	Seasons	W	L	Pct.
Adolph Rupp, Kentucky	1931-52, 54-70	833	177	.825
Phog Allen, Baker, Kansas, Haskell, Central Mo. St. & Kansas	1906-09, 13-47	607	185	.766
Ed Diddle, Western Ky.	1923-61	732	260	.740
Bob Knight, Army, Indiana & Texas Tech	1966-2000, 02-05	854	333	.719
Henry Iba, Northwest Mo. St., Colorado & Oklahoma St.	1930-68	738	314	.702
Lefty Driesell, Davidson, Maryland, James Madison & Georgia St.	1961-86, 89-2001	762	377	.669
Ray Meyer, DePaul	1943-81	650	337	.659
Lou Henson, Hardin-Simmons, New Mexico St., Illinois & New Mexico St.	1963-96, 99-2003	762	386	.664
Tony Hinkle, Butler	1927-42, 46-68	531	367	.591
Marv Harshman, Pacific Lutheran, Washington St. & Washington	1946-84	632	439	.590

40 SEASONS

Coach, Team	Seasons	W	L	Pct.
Adolph Rupp, Kentucky	1931-52, 54-71	855	183	.824
Phog Allen, Baker, Kansas, Haskell, Central Mo. St. & Kansas	1906-09, 13-48	616	200	.755
Ed Diddle, Western Ky.	1923-62	749	270	.735
Bob Knight, Army, Indiana & Texas Tech	1966-2000, 02-06	869	350	.713
Henry Iba, Northwest Mo. St., Colorado & Oklahoma St.	1930-69	750	327	.696

COACHING RECORDS

Coach, Team	Seasons	W	L	Pct.
Lefty Driesell, Davidson, Maryland, James Madison & Georgia St.	1961-86, 89-2002	782	388	.668
Ray Meyer, DePaul	1943-82	676	339	.666
Lou Henson, Hardin-Simmons, New Mexico St., Illinois & New Mexico St.	1963-96, 99-2004	775	400	.660
Marv Harshman, Pacific Lutheran, Washington St. & Washington	1946-85	654	449	.593
Tony Hinkle, Butler	1927-42, 46-69	542	382	.587

41 SEASONS

Coach, Team	Seasons	W	L	Pct.
Adolph Rupp, Kentucky	1931-52, 54-72	876	190	.822
Phog Allen, Baker, Kansas, Haskell, Central Mo. St. & Kansas	1906-09, 13-49	628	212	.748
Ed Diddle, Western Ky.	1923-63	754	286	.725
Bob Knight, Army, Indiana & Texas Tech	1966-2000, 02-07	890	363	.710
Henry Iba, Northwest Mo. St., Colorado & Oklahoma	1930-70	764	339	.693
Ray Meyer, DePaul	1943-83	697	351	.665
Lefty Driesell, Davidson, Maryland, James Madison & Georgia St.	1961-86, 89-2003	800	409	.662
Lou Henson, Hardin-Simmons, New Mexico St., Illinois & New Mexico St.	1963-96, 99-2005	779	412	.654
Tony Hinkle, Butler	1927-42, 46-70	557	393	.586

42 SEASONS

Coach, Team	Seasons	W	L	Pct.
Phog Allen, Baker, Kansas, Haskell, Central Mo. St. & Kansas	1906-09, 13-50	642	223	.742
Ed Diddle, Western Ky.	1923-64	759	302	.715
Ray Meyer, DePaul	1943-84	724	354	.672

Top 10 Best Career Starts By Wins

(Head coaches with at least half their seasons at Division I)

1 SEASON

Coach, Team	Season	W	L	Pct.
Bill Guthridge, North Carolina	1998	34	4	.895
Bill Hodges, Indiana St.	1979	33	1	.970
Jamie Dixon, Pittsburgh	2004	31	5	.861
Stan Heath, Kent St.	2002	30	6	.833
John Warren, Oregon	1945	30	13	.698
Mick Cronin, Murray St.	2004	28	6	.824
Anthony Grant, VCU	2007	28	7	.800
Phil Johnson, Weber St.	1969	27	3	.900
Blaine Taylor, Montana	1992	27	4	.871
Tevester Anderson, Murray St.	1999	27	6	.818
John Phillips, Tulsa	2002	27	7	.794
Chris Lowery, Southern Ill.	2005	27	8	.771
Doc Sadler, UTEP	2005	27	8	.771

2 SEASONS

Coach, Team	Seasons	W	L	Pct.
Bill Guthridge, North Carolina	1998-99	58	14	.806
Everett Case, North Carolina St.	1947-48	55	8	.873
Todd Lickliter, Butler	2002-03	53	12	.815
Ben Carnevale, North Carolina	1945-46	52	11	.825
Mark Fox, Nevada	2005-06	52	13	.800
Mark Few, Gonzaga	2000-01	52	16	.765
Don Monson, Gonzaga	1998-99	52	17	.754
Bill Carmody, Princeton	1997-98	51	6	.895
Jamie Dixon, Pittsburgh	2004-05	51	14	.785
Gary Cunningham, UCLA	1978-79	50	8	.862
Kermit Davis Jr., Idaho	1989-90	50	12	.806
Nolan Richardson, Tulsa	1981-82	50	13	.794
Thad Matta, Butler & Xavier	2001-02	50	14	.781
Tevester Anderson, Murray St.	1999-2000	50	15	.769
John Phillips, Tulsa	2002-03	50	17	.746
Stan Watts, BYU	1950-51	50	21	.704

3 SEASONS

Coach, Team	Seasons	W	L	Pct.
Mark Fox, Nevada	2005-07	81	18	.818
Mark Few, Gonzaga	2000-02	81	20	.802
Everett Case, North Carolina St.	1947-49	80	16	.833
Bill Guthridge, North Carolina	1998-2000	80	28	.741
Chris Lowery, Southern Ill.	2005-07	78	26	.750
Thad Matta, Butler & Xavier	2001-03	76	20	.792
Jamie Dixon, Pittsburgh	2004-06	76	22	.776
Roy Williams, Kansas	1989-91	76	25	.752

Coach, Team	Seasons	W	L	Pct.
Jim Boeheim, Syracuse	1977-79	74	14	.841
Bill Carmody, Princeton	1997-99	73	14	.839

4 SEASONS

Coach, Team	Seasons	W	L	Pct.
Everett Case, North Carolina St.	1947-50	107	22	.829
Mark Few, Gonzaga	2000-03	105	29	.784
Jamie Dixon, Pittsburgh	2004-07	105	30	.778
Bruce Stewart, West Va. Wesleyan & Middle Tenn.	1983-86	104	34	.754
Roy Williams, Kansas	1989-92	103	30	.774
Thad Matta, Butler & Xavier	2001-04	102	31	.767
Jim Boeheim, Syracuse	1977-80	100	18	.847
Speedy Morris, La Salle	1987-90	100	31	.763
Paul Westphal, Grand Canyon & Pepperdine	1987-88, 2002-03	100	40	.714
Denny Crum, Louisville	1972-75	98	22	.817

5 SEASONS

Coach, Team	Seasons	W	L	Pct.
Everett Case, North Carolina St.	1947-51	137	29	.825
Mark Few, Gonzaga	2000-04	133	32	.806
Roy Williams, Kansas	1989-93	132	37	.781
Bruce Stewart, West Va. Wesleyan & Middle Tenn.	1983-87	126	41	.754
Forddy Anderson, Drake & Bradley	1947-51	123	42	.745
Jerry Tarkanian, Long Beach St. & UNLV	1969-73	122	20	.859
Jim Boeheim, Syracuse	1977-81	122	30	.803
Thad Matta, Butler, Xavier & Ohio St.	2001-05	122	43	.739
Fred Schaus, West Virginia	1955-59	120	32	.789
Larry Brown, UCLA & Kansas	1980-81, 84-86	120	38	.759
Tom Izzo, Michigan St.	1996-2000	120	48	.714

6 SEASONS

Coach, Team	Seasons	W	L	Pct.
Everett Case, North Carolina St.	1947-52	161	39	.805
Roy Williams, Kansas	1989-94	159	45	.779
Mark Few, Gonzaga	2000-05	159	37	.811
Bruce Stewart, West Va. Wesleyan & Middle Tenn.	1983-88	149	52	.741
Thad Matta, Butler, Xavier & Ohio St.	2001-06	148	49	.751
Tom Izzo, Michigan St.	1996-2001	148	53	.736
Fred Schaus, West Virginia	1955-60	146	37	.798
Larry Brown, UCLA & Kansas	1980-81, 84-87	145	49	.747
Pete Gillen, Xavier	1986-91	141	49	.742
Forddy Anderson, Drake & Bradley	1947-52	140	54	.722

7 SEASONS

Coach, Team	Seasons	W	L	Pct.
Mark Few, Gonzaga	2000-06	188	41	.821
Everett Case, North Carolina St.	1947-53	187	45	.806
Roy Williams, Kansas	1989-95	184	51	.783
Thad Matta, Butler, Xavier & Ohio St.	2001-07	183	53	.775
Larry Brown, UCLA & Kansas	1980-81, 84-88	172	60	.741
Bruce Stewart, West Va. Wesleyan & Middle Tenn.	1983-89	172	60	.741
Tom Izzo, Michigan St.	1996-2002	167	65	.720
Bruce Weber, Southern Ill. & Illinois	1999-2005	166	63	.725
Jerry Tarkanian, Long Beach St. & UNLV	1969-75	160	28	.851
Denny Crum, Louisville	1972-78	162	44	.786
Howard Hobson, Southern Ore. & Oregon	1933-39	162	48	.771

8 SEASONS

Coach, Team	Seasons	W	L	Pct.
Everett Case, North Carolina St.	1947-54	213	52	.804
Roy Williams, Kansas	1989-96	213	56	.792
Mark Few, Gonzaga	2000-07	211	52	.802
Bruce Weber, Southern Ill. & Illinois	1999-2006	192	70	.733
Jerry Tarkanian, Long Beach St. & UNLV	1969-76	189	30	.863
John Calipari, Massachusetts	1989-96	189	70	.730
Tom Izzo, Michigan St.	1996-2003	189	78	.708
Tubby Smith, Tulsa, Georgia & Kentucky	1992-99	187	75	.714
Denny Crum, Louisville	1972-79	186	52	.782
Bruce Stewart, West Va. Wesleyan & Middle Tenn.	1983-90	184	75	.710
Fred Schaus, West Virginia & Purdue	1955-60, 73-74	182	55	.768
Jim Boeheim, Syracuse	1977-84	182	62	.745

9 SEASONS

Coach, Team	Seasons	W	L	Pct.
Roy Williams, Kansas	1989-97	247	58	.810
Everett Case, North Carolina St.	1947-55	241	56	.811
Denny Crum, Louisville	1972-80	219	55	.799
Jerry Tarkanian, Long Beach St. & UNLV	1969-77	218	33	.869
Bruce Weber, Southern Ill. & Illinois	1999-2007	215	82	.724

Coach, Team	Seasons	W	L	Pct.
John Calipari, Massachusetts & Memphis	1989-96, 2001	210	85	.712
Tubby Smith, Tulsa, Georgia & Kentucky	1992-2000	210	85	.712
Tom Izzo, Michigan St.	1996-2004	207	90	.697
Jim Boeheim, Syracuse	1977-85	204	71	.742
Fred Schaus, West Virginia & Purdue	1955-60, 73-75	199	66	.751
Howard Hobson, Southern Ore. & Oregon	1933-41	199	78	.718

10 SEASONS

Coach, Team	Seasons	W	L	Pct.
Roy Williams, Kansas	1989-98	282	62	.820
Everett Case, North Carolina St.	1947-56	265	60	.815
Denny Crum, Louisville	1972-81	240	64	.789
Jerry Tarkanian, Long Beach St. & UNLV	1969-78	238	41	.853
John Calipari, Massachusetts & Memphis	1989-96, 2001-02	237	94	.716
Tubby Smith, Tulsa, Georgia & Kentucky	1992-2001	234	95	.711
Tom Izzo, Michigan St.	1996-2005	233	97	.706
Jim Boeheim, Syracuse	1977-86	230	77	.749
Nolan Richardson, Tulsa & Arkansas	1981-90	226	88	.720
Pete Gillen, Xavier & Providence	1986-95	219	88	.713

11 SEASONS

Coach, Team	Seasons	W	L	Pct.
Roy Williams, Kansas	1989-99	305	72	.809
Everett Case, North Carolina St.	1947-57	280	71	.798
Denny Crum, Louisville	1972-82	263	74	.780
Jim Boeheim, Syracuse	1977-87	261	84	.757
Nolan Richardson, Tulsa & Arkansas	1981-91	260	92	.739
John Calipari, Massachusetts & Memphis	1989-96, 2001-03	260	101	.720
Jerry Tarkanian, Long Beach St. & UNLV	1969-79	259	49	.841
Tubby Smith, Tulsa, Georgia & Kentucky	1992-2002	256	105	.709
Tom Izzo, Michigan St.	1996-2006	255	109	.701
Tom Blackburn, Dayton	1948-58	242	87	.736

12 SEASONS

Coach, Team	Seasons	W	L	Pct.
Roy Williams, Kansas	1989-2000	329	82	.800
Everett Case, North Carolina St.	1947-58	298	77	.795
Denny Crum, Louisville	1972-83	295	78	.791
Tubby Smith, Tulsa, Georgia & Kentucky	1992-2003	288	109	.725
Jim Boeheim, Syracuse	1977-88	287	93	.755
Nolan Richardson, Tulsa & Arkansas	1981-92	286	100	.741
Jerry Tarkanian, Long Beach St. & UNLV	1969-80	282	58	.829
John Calipari, Massachusetts & Memphis	1989-96, 2001-04	282	109	.721
Tom Izzo, Michigan St.	1996-2007	278	121	.697
Wimp Sanderson, Alabama	1981-92	265	118	.692

13 SEASONS

Coach, Team	Seasons	W	L	Pct.
Roy Williams, Kansas	1989-2001	355	89	.800
Everett Case, North Carolina St.	1947-59	320	81	.798
Denny Crum, Louisville	1972-84	319	89	.782
Jim Boeheim, Syracuse	1977-89	317	101	.758
Tubby Smith, Tulsa, Georgia & Kentucky	1992-2004	315	114	.734
Nolan Richardson, Tulsa & Arkansas	1981-93	308	109	.739
John Calipari, Massachusetts & Memphis	1989-96, 2001-05	304	125	.709
Jerry Tarkanian, Long Beach St. & UNLV	1969-81	298	70	.810
John Thompson, Georgetown	1973-85	297	107	.735
Billy Donovan, Marshall & Florida	1995-2007	296	123	.706
Bob Huggins, Walsh, Akron & Cincinnati	1981-1994	284	118	.706

14 SEASONS

Coach, Team	Seasons	W	L	Pct.
Roy Williams, Kansas	1989-2002	388	93	.807
Jim Boeheim, Syracuse	1977-90	343	108	.761
Tubby Smith, Tulsa, Georgia & Kentucky	1992-2005	343	120	.741
Nolan Richardson, Tulsa & Arkansas	1981-94	339	112	.752
Denny Crum, Louisville	1972-85	338	107	.760
John Calipari, Massachusetts & Memphis	1989-96, 2001-06	337	129	.723
Everett Case, North Carolina St.	1947-60	331	96	.775
John Thompson, Georgetown	1973-86	321	115	.736
Jerry Tarkanian, Long Beach St. & UNLV	1969-82	318	80	.799
Rick Pitino, Boston U., Providence & Kentucky	1979-83, 86-87, 90-96	317	119	.727

15 SEASONS

Coach, Team	Seasons	W	L	Pct.
Roy Williams, Kansas	1989-2003	418	101	.805
Nolan Richardson, Tulsa & Arkansas	1981-95	371	119	.757
Denny Crum, Louisville	1972-86	370	114	.764
John Calipari, Massachusetts & Memphis	1989-96, 2001-07	370	133	.736
Jim Boeheim, Syracuse	1977-91	369	114	.764
Tubby Smith, Tulsa, Georgia & Kentucky	1992-2006	365	133	.733
Rick Pitino, Boston U., Providence & Kentucky	1979-83, 86-87, 90--97	352	124	.739
John Thompson, Georgetown	1973-87	350	120	.745
Everett Case, North Carolina St.	1947-61	347	105	.768
Jerry Tarkanian, Long Beach St. & UNLV	1969-83	346	83	.807

16 SEASONS

Coach, Team	Seasons	W	L	Pct.
Roy Williams, Kansas & North Carolina	1989-2004	437	112	.796
Jim Boeheim, Syracuse	1977-92	391	124	.759
Nolan Richardson, Tulsa & Arkansas	1981-96	391	132	.748
Denny Crum, Louisville	1972-87	388	128	.752
Tubby Smith, Tulsa, Georgia & Kentucky	1992-2007	387	145	.727
Jerry Tarkanian, Long Beach St. & UNLV	1969-84	375	89	.808
Rick Pitino, Boston U., Providence, Kentucky & Louisville	1979-83, 86-87, 90-97, 2002	371	137	.730
John Thompson, Georgetown	1973-88	370	130	.740
Billy Tubbs, Texas St., Lamar & Oklahoma	1972-73, 77-90	363	153	.703
Bob Huggins, Walsh, Akron & Cincinnati	1981-97	361	142	.718

17 SEASONS

Coach, Team	Seasons	W	L	Pct.
Roy Williams, Kansas & North Carolina	1989-2005	470	116	.802
Denny Crum, Louisville	1972-88	412	139	.748
Jim Boeheim, Syracuse	1977-93	411	133	.756
Nolan Richardson, Tulsa & Arkansas	1981-97	409	146	.737
Jerry Tarkanian, Long Beach St. & UNLV	1969-85	403	93	.813
John Thompson, Georgetown	1973-89	399	135	.747
Rick Pitino, Boston U., Providence, Kentucky & Louisville	1979-83, 86-87, 90-97, 2002-03	396	144	.733
Bob Huggins, Walsh, Akron & Cincinnati	1981-98	388	148	.724
Billy Tubbs, Texas St., Lamar & Oklahoma	1972-73, 77-91	383	168	.695
Eddie Sutton, Creighton, Arkansas & Kentucky	1970-86	374	129	.744

18 SEASONS

Coach, Team	Seasons	W	L	Pct.
Roy Williams, Kansas & North Carolina	1989-2006	493	124	.799
Jerry Tarkanian, Long Beach St. & UNLV	1969-86	436	98	.816
Denny Crum, Louisville	1972-89	436	148	.747
Jim Boeheim, Syracuse	1977-94	434	140	.756
Nolan Richardson, Tulsa & Arkansas	1981-98	433	155	.736
John Thompson, Georgetown	1973-90	423	142	.749
Rick Pitino, Boston U., Providence, Kentucky & Louisville	1979-83, 86-87, 90-97, 2002-04	416	154	.730
Bob Huggins, Walsh, Akron & Cincinnati	1981-99	415	154	.729
Billy Tubbs, Texas St., Lamar & Oklahoma	1972-73, 77-92	404	177	.695
Lou Carnesecca, St. John's (N.Y.)	1966-70, 74-86	402	136	.747

19 SEASONS

Coach, Team	Seasons	W	L	Pct.
Roy Williams, Kansas & North Carolina	1989-2007	524	131	.800
Jerry Tarkanian, Long Beach St. & UNLV	1969-87	473	100	.825
Denny Crum, Louisville	1972-90	463	156	.748
Nolan Richardson, Tulsa & Arkansas	1981-99	456	166	.733
Jim Boeheim, Syracuse	1977-95	454	150	.752
Rick Pitino, Boston U., Providence, Kentucky & Louisville	1979-83, 86-87, 90-97, 2002-05	449	159	.738
Bob Huggins, Walsh, Akron & Cincinnati	1981-2000	444	158	.738
John Thompson, Georgetown	1973-91	442	155	.740
Billy Tubbs, Texas St., Lamar & Oklahoma	1972-73, 77-93	424	189	.692
Lou Carnesecca, St. John's (N.Y.)	1966-70, 74-87	423	145	.745

20 SEASONS

Coach, Team	Seasons	W	L	Pct.
Jerry Tarkanian, Long Beach St. & UNLV	1969-88	501	106	.825
Jim Boeheim, Syracuse	1977-96	483	159	.752
Denny Crum, Louisville	1972-91	477	172	.735
Nolan Richardson, Tulsa & Arkansas	1981-2000	475	181	.724
Rick Pitino, Boston U., Providence, Kentucky & Louisville	1979-83, 86-87, 90-97, 2002-06	470	172	.732
Bob Huggins, Walsh, Akron & Cincinnati	1981-2001	469	168	.736
John Thompson, Georgetown	1973-92	464	165	.738
John Chaney, Cheyney & Temple	1973-92	458	143	.762
Lou Carnesecca, St. John's (N.Y.)	1966-70, 74-88	440	157	.737
Billy Tubbs, Texas St., Lamar & Oklahoma	1972-73, 77-94	439	202	.685
Henry Iba, Northwest Mo. St., Colorado & Oklahoma St.	1930-49	436	108	.801
Dean Smith, North Carolina	1962-81	436	143	.753

21 SEASONS

Coach, Team	Seasons	W	L	Pct.
Jerry Tarkanian, Long Beach St. & UNLV	1969-89	530	114	.823

Coach, Team	Seasons	W	L	Pct.
Jim Boeheim, Syracuse	1977-97	502	172	.745
Bob Huggins, Walsh, Akron & Cincinnati	1981-2002	500	172	.744
Denny Crum, Louisville	1972-92	496	183	.730
Nolan Richardson, Tulsa & Arkansas	1981-2001	495	192	.721
Rick Pitino, Boston U., Providence, Kentucky & Louisville	1979-83, 86-87, 90-97, 2002-07	494	182	.731
John Thompson, Georgetown	1973-93	484	178	.731
John Chaney, Cheyney & Temple	1973-93	478	156	.754
Dean Smith, North Carolina	1962-82	468	145	.763
Lou Carnesecca, St. John's (N.Y.)	1966-70, 74-89	460	170	.730

22 SEASONS

Coach, Team	Seasons	W	L	Pct.
Jerry Tarkanian, Long Beach St. & UNLV	1969-90	565	119	.826
Jim Boeheim, Syracuse	1977-98	528	181	.745
Denny Crum, Louisville	1972-93	518	192	.730
Bob Huggins, Walsh, Akron & Cincinnati	1981-2003	517	184	.738
John Thompson, Georgetown	1973-94	503	190	.726
John Chaney, Cheyney & Temple	1973-94	501	164	.753
Dean Smith, North Carolina	1962-83	496	153	.764
Lou Carnesecca, St. John's (N.Y.)	1966-70, 74-90	484	180	.729
Henry Iba, Northwest Mo. St., Colorado & Oklahoma St.	1930-51	483	123	.797
Eddie Sutton, Creighton, Arkansas, Kentucky & Oklahoma St.	1970-89, 91-92	482	180	.728
Lute Olson, Long Beach St., Iowa & Arizona	1974-95	482	186	.722

23 SEASONS

Coach, Team	Seasons	W	L	Pct.
Jerry Tarkanian, Long Beach St. & UNLV	1969-91	599	120	.833
Jim Boeheim, Syracuse	1977-99	549	193	.740
Denny Crum, Louisville	1972-94	546	198	.734
Bob Huggins, Walsh, Akron & Cincinnati	1981-2004	542	191	.739
Dean Smith, North Carolina	1962-84	524	156	.771
John Thompson, Georgetown	1973-95	524	200	.724
John Chaney, Cheyney & Temple	1973-95	520	175	.748
Lute Olson, Long Beach St., Iowa & Arizona	1974-96	509	192	.726
Lou Carnesecca, St. John's (N.Y.)	1966-70, 74-91	507	189	.728
Mike Krzyzewski, Army & Duke	1976-98	505	212	.704

24 SEASONS

Coach, Team	Seasons	W	L	Pct.
Jerry Tarkanian, Long Beach St. & UNLV	1969-92	625	122	.837
Jim Boeheim, Syracuse	1977-2000	575	199	.743
Bob Huggins, Walsh, Akron & Cincinnati	1981-2005	567	199	.740
Denny Crum, Louisville	1972-95	565	212	.727
John Thompson, Georgetown	1973-96	553	208	.727
Dean Smith, North Carolina	1962-85	551	165	.770
Mike Krzyzewski, Army & Duke	1976-99	542	214	.717
John Chaney, Cheyney & Temple	1973-96	540	188	.742
Lute Olson, Long Beach St., Iowa & Arizona	1974-97	534	201	.718
Eddie Sutton, Creighton, Arkansas, Kentucky & Oklahoma St.	1970-89, 91-94	526	199	.726
Lou Carnesecca, St. John's (N.Y.)	1966-70, 74-92	526	200	.725

25 SEASONS

Coach, Team	Seasons	W	L	Pct.
Jerry Tarkanian, Long Beach St., UNLV & Fresno St.	1969-92, 96	647	133	.829
Jim Boeheim, Syracuse	1977-2001	600	208	.743
Bob Huggins, Walsh, Akron, Cincinnati & Kansas St.	1981-2005, 07	590	211	.737
Denny Crum, Louisville	1972-96	587	224	.724
Dean Smith, North Carolina	1962-86	579	171	.772
John Thompson, Georgetown	1973-97	573	218	.724
Mike Krzyzewski, Army & Duke	1976-2000	571	219	.723
Lute Olson, Long Beach St., Iowa & Arizona	1974-98	564	206	.732
John Chaney, Cheyney & Temple	1973-97	560	199	.738
Eddie Sutton, Creighton, Arkansas, Kentucky & Oklahoma St.	1970-89, 91-95	553	209	.726

26 SEASONS

Coach, Team	Seasons	W	L	Pct.
Jerry Tarkanian, Long Beach St., UNLV & Fresno St.	1969-92, 96-97	667	145	.821
Jim Boeheim, Syracuse	1977-2002	623	221	.738
Denny Crum, Louisville	1972-97	613	233	.725
Dean Smith, North Carolina	1962-87	611	175	.777
Mike Krzyzewski, Army & Duke	1976-2001	606	223	.731
John Thompson, Georgetown	1973-98	589	233	.717
Lute Olson, Long Beach St., Iowa & Arizona	1974-99	586	213	.733
John Chaney, Cheyney & Temple	1973-98	581	208	.736
John Wooden, Indiana St. & UCLA	1947-72	580	155	.789
Eddie Sutton, Creighton, Arkansas, Kentucky & Oklahoma St.	1970-89, 91-96	570	219	.722

27 SEASONS

Coach, Team	Seasons	W	L	Pct.
Jerry Tarkanian, Long Beach St., UNLV & Fresno St.	1969-92, 96-98	688	158	.813
Jim Boeheim, Syracuse	1977-2003	653	226	.743
Dean Smith, North Carolina	1962-88	638	182	.778
Mike Krzyzewski, Army & Duke	1976-2002	637	227	.737
Denny Crum, Louisville	1972-98	625	253	.712
Lute Olson, Long Beach St., Iowa & Arizona	1974-2000	613	220	.736
John Wooden, Indiana St. & UCLA	1947-73	610	155	.797
John Chaney, Cheyney & Temple	1973-99	605	219	.734
John Thompson, Georgetown	1973-99	596	239	.714
Bob Knight, Army & Indiana	1966-92	588	210	.737

28 SEASONS

Coach, Team	Seasons	W	L	Pct.
Jerry Tarkanian, Long Beach St., UNLV & Fresno St.	1969-92, 96-99	689	170	.802
Jim Boeheim, Syracuse	1977-2004	676	234	.743
Dean Smith, North Carolina	1962-89	667	190	.778
Mike Krzyzewski, Army & Duke	1976-2003	663	234	.739
Denny Crum, Louisville	1972-99	644	264	.709
Lute Olson, Long Beach St., Iowa & Arizona	1974-2001	638	226	.738
John Wooden, Indiana St. & UCLA	1947-74	636	159	.800
John Chaney, Cheyney & Temple	1973-2000	632	225	.737
Bob Knight, Army & Indiana	1966-93	619	214	.743
Adolph Rupp, Kentucky	1931-52, 54-59	610	106	.852

29 SEASONS

Coach, Team	Seasons	W	L	Pct.
Jim Boeheim, Syracuse	1977-2005	703	241	.745
Jerry Tarkanian, Long Beach St., UNLV & Fresno St.	1969-92, 96-2000	701	179	.797
Mike Krzyzewski, Army & Duke	1976-2004	694	240	.743
Dean Smith, North Carolina	1962-90	688	203	.772
John Wooden, Indiana St. & UCLA	1947-75	664	162	.804
Denny Crum, Louisville	1972-2000	663	276	.706
Lute Olson, Long Beach St., Iowa & Arizona	1974-2002	662	236	.737
John Chaney, Cheyney & Temple	1973-2001	656	238	.734
Bob Knight, Army & Indiana	1966-94	640	223	.742
Eddie Sutton, Creighton, Arkansas, Kentucky & Oklahoma St.	1970-89, 91-99	632	252	.715

30 SEASONS

Coach, Team	Seasons	W	L	Pct.
Jim Boeheim, Syracuse	1977-2006	726	253	.742
Mike Krzyzewski, Army & Duke	1976-2005	721	246	.746
Dean Smith, North Carolina	1962-91	717	209	.774
Jerry Tarkanian, Long Beach St., UNLV & Fresno St.	1969-92, 96-2001	710	186	.792
Lute Olson, Long Beach St., Iowa & Arizona	1974-2003	690	240	.742
John Chaney, Cheyney & Temple	1973-2002	675	253	.727
Denny Crum, Louisville	1972-2001	675	295	.696
Bob Knight, Army & Indiana	1966-95	659	235	.737
Eddie Sutton, Creighton, Arkansas, Kentucky & Oklahoma St.	1970-89, 91-2000	659	259	.718
Adolph Rupp, Kentucky	1931-52, 54-61	647	122	.841

31 SEASONS

Coach, Team	Seasons	W	L	Pct.
Mike Krzyzewski, Army & Duke	1976-2006	753	250	.751
Jim Boeheim, Syracuse	1977-2007	750	264	.740
Dean Smith, North Carolina	1962-92	740	219	.772
Jerry Tarkanian, Long Beach St., UNLV & Fresno St.	1969-92, 96-2002	729	201	.784
Lute Olson, Long Beach St., Iowa & Arizona	1974-2004	710	249	.740
John Chaney, Cheyney & Temple	1973-2003	693	269	.720
Bob Knight, Army & Indiana	1966-96	679	246	.734
Eddie Sutton, Creighton, Arkansas, Kentucky & Oklahoma St.	1970-89, 91-2001	679	269	.716
Adolph Rupp, Kentucky	1931-52, 54-62	670	125	.843
Jim Calhoun, Northeastern & Connecticut	1973-2003	647	296	.686

32 SEASONS

Coach, Team	Seasons	W	L	Pct.
Mike Krzyzewski, Army & Duke	1976-2007	775	261	.748
Dean Smith, North Carolina	1962-93	774	223	.776
Lute Olson, Long Beach St., Iowa & Arizona	1974-2005	740	256	.743
John Chaney, Cheyney & Temple	1973-2004	708	283	.714
Eddie Sutton, Creighton, Arkansas, Kentucky & Oklahoma St.	1970-89, 91-2002	702	278	.716
Bob Knight, Army & Indiana	1966-97	701	257	.732
Adolph Rupp, Kentucky	1931-52, 54-63	686	134	.837
Jim Calhoun, Northeastern & Connecticut	1973-2004	680	302	.692

Coach, Team	Seasons	W	L	Pct.
Henry Iba, Northwest Mo. St., Colorado & Oklahoma St.	1930-61	652	221	.746
Lefty Driesell, Davidson, Maryland & James Madison	1961-86, 89-94	641	289	.689

33 SEASONS

Coach, Team	Seasons	W	L	Pct.
Dean Smith, North Carolina	1962-94	802	230	.777
Lute Olson, Long Beach St., Iowa & Arizona	1974-2006	760	269	.739
Eddie Sutton, Creighton, Arkansas, Kentucky & Oklahoma St.	1970-89, 91-2003	724	288	.715
John Chaney, Cheyney & Temple	1973-2005	724	297	.709
Bob Knight, Army & Indiana	1966-98	721	269	.728
Adolph Rupp, Kentucky	1931-52, 54-64	707	140	.835
Jim Calhoun, Northeastern & Connecticut	1973-2005	703	310	.694
Henry Iba, Northwest Mo. St., Colorado & Oklahoma St.	1930-62	666	233	.741
Lefty Driesell, Davidson, Maryland & James Madison	1961-86, 89-95	657	302	.685
Don Haskins, UTEP	1962-94	645	288	.691
Lou Henson, Hardin-Simmons, New Mexico St. & Illinois	1963-95	645	318	.670

34 SEASONS

Coach, Team	Seasons	W	L	Pct.
Dean Smith, North Carolina	1962-95	830	236	.779
Lute Olson, Long Beach St., Iowa & Arizona	1974-2007	780	280	.736
Eddie Sutton, Creighton, Arkansas, Kentucky & Oklahoma St.	1970-89, 91-2004	755	292	.721
Bob Knight, Army & Indiana	1966-99	744	280	.727
John Chaney, Cheyney & Temple	1973-2006	741	312	.704
Jim Calhoun, Northeastern & Connecticut	1973-2006	733	314	.700
Adolph Rupp, Kentucky	1931-52, 54-65	722	150	.828
Henry Iba, Northwest Mo. St., Colorado & Oklahoma St.	1930-63	682	242	.738
Lefty Driesell, Davidson, Maryland & James Madison	1961-86, 89-96	667	322	.674
Don Haskins, UTEP	1962-95	665	298	.691

35 SEASONS

Coach, Team	Seasons	W	L	Pct.
Dean Smith, North Carolina	1962-96	851	247	.775
Eddie Sutton, Creighton, Arkansas, Kentucky & Oklahoma St.	1970-89, 91-2005	781	299	.723
Bob Knight, Army & Indiana	1966-2000	764	289	.726
Jim Calhoun, Northeastern & Connecticut	1973-2007	750	328	.696
Adolph Rupp, Kentucky	1931-52, 54-66	749	152	.831
Henry Iba, Northwest Mo. St., Colorado & Oklahoma St.	1930-64	697	252	.734
Lou Henson, Hardin-Simmons, New Mexico St., Illinois & New Mexico St.	1963-96, 99	686	341	.668
Lefty Driesell, Davidson, Maryland & James Madison	1961-86, 89-97	683	335	.671
Don Haskins, UTEP	1962-96	678	313	.684
Norm Stewart, UNI & Missouri	1962-96	678	334	.670

36 SEASONS

Coach, Team	Seasons	W	L	Pct.
Dean Smith, North Carolina	1962-97	879	254	.776
Eddie Sutton, Creighton, Arkansas, Kentucky & Oklahoma St.	1970-89, 91-2006	798	315	.717
Bob Knight, Army, Indiana & Texas Tech	1966-2000, 02	787	298	.725
Adolph Rupp, Kentucky	1931-52, 54-67	762	165	.822
Henry Iba, Northwest Mo. St., Colorado & Oklahoma St.	1930-65	717	259	.735
Lou Henson, Hardin-Simmons, New Mexico St., Illinois & New Mexico St.	1963-96, 99-2000	708	351	.669
Lefty Driesell, Davidson, Maryland, James Madison & Georgia St.	1961-86, 89-98	699	347	.668
Norm Stewart, UNI & Missouri	1962-97	694	351	.664
Don Haskins, UTEP	1962-97	691	327	.679
Ed Diddle, Western Ky.	1923-58	677	235	.742

37 SEASONS

Coach, Team	Seasons	W	L	Pct.
Bob Knight, Army, Indiana & Texas Tech	1966-2000, 02-03	809	311	.722
Adolph Rupp, Kentucky	1931-52, 54-68	784	170	.822
Lou Henson, Hardin-Simmons, New Mexico St., Illinois & New Mexico St.	1963-96, 99-2001	722	365	.664
Henry Iba, Northwest Mo. St., Colorado & Oklahoma St.	1930-66	721	280	.720
Lefty Driesell, Davidson, Maryland, James Madison & Georgia St.	1961-86, 89-99	716	360	.665
Norm Stewart, UNI & Missouri	1962-98	711	366	.660

Coach, Team	Seasons	W	L	Pct.
Don Haskins, UTEP	1962-98	703	341	.673
Ed Diddle, Western Ky.	1923-59	693	245	.739
Ralph Miller, Wichita St., Iowa & Oregon St.	1952-88	635	374	.629
Hugh Durham, Florida St., Georgia & Jacksonville	1967-95, 98-2005	633	429	.596

38 SEASONS

Coach, Team	Seasons	W	L	Pct.
Bob Knight, Army, Indiana & Texas Tech	1966-2000, 02-04	832	322	.721
Adolph Rupp, Kentucky	1931-52, 54-69	807	175	.822
Lou Henson, Hardin-Simmons, New Mexico St., Illinois & New Mexico St.	1963-96, 99-2002	742	377	.663
Lefty Driesell, Davidson, Maryland, James Madison & Georgia St.	1961-86, 89-2000	733	372	.663
Norm Stewart, UNI & Missouri	1962-99	731	375	.661
Henry Iba, Northwest Mo. St., Colorado & Oklahoma St.	1930-67	728	298	.710
Don Haskins, UTEP	1962-99	719	353	.671
Ed Diddle, Western Ky.	1923-60	714	252	.739
Ralph Miller, Wichita St., Iowa & Oregon St.	1952-89	657	382	.632
Ray Meyer, DePaul	1943-80	623	335	.650

39 SEASONS

Coach, Team	Seasons	W	L	Pct.
Bob Knight, Army, Indiana & Texas Tech	1966-2000, 02-05	854	333	.719
Adolph Rupp, Kentucky	1931-52, 54-70	833	177	.825
Lefty Driesell, Davidson, Maryland, James Madison & Georgia St.	1961-86, 89-2001	762	377	.669
Lou Henson, Hardin-Simmons, New Mexico St., Illinois & New Mexico St.	1963-96, 99-2003	762	386	.664
Henry Iba, Northwest Mo. St., Colorado & Oklahoma St.	1930-68	738	314	.702
Ed Diddle, Western Ky.	1923-61	732	260	.740
Ray Meyer, DePaul	1943-81	650	337	.659
Marv Harshman, Pacific Lutheran, Washington St. & Washington	1946-84	632	439	.590
Phog Allen, Baker, Kansas, Haskell, Central Mo. St. & Kansas	1906-09, 13-47	607	185	.766
Tony Hinkle, Butler	1927-42, 46-68	531	367	.591

40 SEASONS

Coach, Team	Seasons	W	L	Pct.
Bob Knight, Army, Indiana & Texas Tech	1966-2000, 02-06	869	350	.713
Adolph Rupp, Kentucky	1931-52, 54-71	855	183	.824
Lefty Driesell, Davidson, Maryland, James Madison & Georgia St.	1961-86, 89-2002	782	388	.668
Lou Henson, Hardin-Simmons, New Mexico St., Illinois & New Mexico St.	1963-96, 99-2004	775	400	.660
Henry Iba, Northwest Mo. St., Colorado & Oklahoma St.	1930-69	750	327	.696
Ed Diddle, Western Ky.	1923-62	749	270	.735
Ray Meyer, DePaul	1943-82	676	339	.666
Marv Harshman, Pacific Lutheran, Washington St. & Washington	1946-85	654	449	.593
Phog Allen, Baker, Kansas, Haskell, Central Mo. St. & Kansas	1906-09, 13-40	616	200	.755
Tony Hinkle, Butler	1927-42, 46-69	542	382	.587

41 SEASONS

Coach, Team	Seasons	W	L	Pct.
Bob Knight, Army, Indiana & Texas Tech	1966-2000, 02-07	890	363	.710
Adolph Rupp, Kentucky	1931-52, 54-72	876	190	.822
Lefty Driesell, Davidson, Maryland, James Madison & Georgia St.	1961-86, 89-2003	800	409	.662
Lou Henson, Hardin-Simmons, New Mexico St., Illinois & New Mexico St.	1963-96, 99-2005	779	412	.654
Henry Iba, Northwest Mo. St., Colorado & Oklahoma St.	1930-70	764	339	.693
Ed Diddle, Western Ky.	1923-63	754	286	.725
Ray Meyer, DePaul	1943-83	697	351	.665
Phog Allen, Baker, Kansas, Haskell, Central Mo. St. & Kansas	1906-09, 13-49	628	212	.748
Tony Hinkle, Butler	1927-42, 46-70	557	393	.586

42 SEASONS

Coach, Team	Seasons	W	L	Pct.
Ed Diddle, Western Ky.	1923-64	759	302	.715
Ray Meyer, DePaul	1943-84	724	354	.672
Phog Allen, Baker, Kansas, Haskell, Central Mo. St. & Kansas	1906-09, 13-50	642	223	.742

COACHING RECORDS

Active Coaching Longevity Records

(Minimum five years as a Division I head coach)

MOST GAMES

No.	Coach, Team and Seasons
1,253	Bob Knight, Army 1966-71, Indiana 72-2000, Texas Tech 02-07
1,078	Jim Calhoun, Northeastern 1973-86, Connecticut 87-2007
1,060	Lute Olson, Long Beach St. 1974, Iowa 75-83, Arizona 84-2007
1,036	Mike Krzyzewski, Army 1976-80, Duke 81-2007
1,014	Jim Boeheim, Syracuse 1977-2007
984	Tom Penders, Tufts 1972-74, Columbia 75-78, Fordham 79-86, Rhode Island 87-88, Texas 89-98, George Washington 99-2001, Houston 05-07
933	Homer Drew, Bethel (Ind.) 1977-87, Ind.-South Bend 88, Valparaiso 89-2002, 04-07
920	Ben Braun, Siena Heights 1978-85, Eastern Mich. 86-96, California 97-2007
913	Gary Williams, American 1979-82, Boston College 83-86, Ohio St. 87-89, Maryland 90-2007
846	Dave Bike, Sacred Heart 1979-2007
816	Pat Kennedy, Iona 1981-86, Florida St. 87-97, DePaul 98-2002, Montana 03-04, Towson 05-07
810	Rick Byrd, Maryville (Tenn.) 1979-80, Lincoln Memorial 84-86, Belmont 87-2007
801	Bob Huggins, Walsh 1981-83, Akron 85-89, Cincinnati 90-2005, Kansas St. 07, West Virginia
794	Larry Hunter, Wittenberg 1977-89, Ohio 90-2001, Western Caro. 06-07
794	Bobby Cremins, Appalachian St. 1976-81, Georgia Tech 82-2000, Col. of Charleston 07
786	Pat Douglass, Mont. St.-Billings 1982-87, Cal St. Bakersfield 88-97, UC Irvine 98-2007
751	John Beilein, Nazareth 1983, Le Moyne 84-92, Canisius 93-97, Richmond 98-2002, West Virginia 03-07, Michigan
744	Kelvin Sampson, Montana Tech 1982-85, Washington St. 88-94, Oklahoma 95-2007, Indiana 07
718	Don Maestri, Troy 1983-2007
700	Tom Green, Fairleigh Dickinson 1984-2007

MOST SEASONS

No.	Coach, Team and Seasons
41	Bob Knight, Army 1966-71, Indiana 72-2000, Texas Tech 02-07
35	Jim Calhoun, Northeastern 1973-86, Connecticut 87-2007
34	Lute Olson, Long Beach St. 1974, Iowa 75-83, Arizona 84-2007
33	Tom Penders, Tufts 1972-74, Columbia 75-78, Fordham 79-86, Rhode Island 87-88, Texas 89-98, George Washington 99-2001, Houston 05-07
32	Mike Krzyzewski, Army 1976-80, Duke 81-2007
31	Jim Boeheim, Syracuse 1977-2007
30	Ben Braun, Siena Heights 1978-85, Eastern Mich. 86-96, California 97-2007
30	Homer Drew, Bethel (Ind.) 1977-87, Ind.-South Bend 88, Valparaiso 89-2002, 04-07
29	Dave Bike, Sacred Heart 1979-2007
29	Cliff Ellis, South Ala. 1976-84, Clemson 85-94, Auburn 95-2004 Coastal Caro.
29	Gary Williams, American 1979-82, Boston College 83-86, Ohio St. 87-89, Maryland 90-2007
27	Larry Hunter, Wittenberg 1977-89, Ohio 90-2001, Western Caro. 06-07
27	Pat Kennedy, Iona 1981-86, Florida St. 87-97, DePaul 98-2002, Montana 03-04, Towson 05-07
26	Rick Byrd, Maryville (Tenn.) 1979-80, Lincoln Memorial 84-86, Belmont 87-2007
26	Bobby Cremins, Appalachian St. 1976-81, Georgia Tech 82-2000, Col. of Charleston 07
26	Pat Douglass, Mont. St.-Billings 1982-87, Cal St. Bakersfield 88-97, UC Irvine 98-2007
25	Bob Huggins, Walsh 1981-83, Akron 85-89, Cincinnati 90-2005, Kansas St. 07, West Virginia
25	John Beilein, Nazareth 1983, Le Moyne 84-92, Canisius 93-97, Richmond 98-2002, West Virginia 03-07, Michigan
25	Don Maestri, Troy 1983-2007
24	Kelvin Sampson, Montana Tech 1982-85, Washington St. 88-94, Oklahoma 95-2006, Indiana 07
24	Tom Green, Fairleigh Dickinson 1984-2007

MOST SEASONS WITH CURRENT SCHOOL

No.	Coach, Team and Seasons
31	Jim Boeheim, #Syracuse 1977-2007
29	Dave Bike, #Sacred Heart 1979-2007
27	Mike Krzyzewski, Duke 1981-2007
25	Don Maestri, #Troy 1983-2007
24	Tom Green, #Fairleigh Dickinson 1984-2007
24	Lute Olson, Arizona 1984-2007
23	Greg Kampe, #Oakland 1985-2007
21	Rick Byrd, Belmont 1987-2007

No.	Coach, Team and Seasons
21	Jim Calhoun, Connecticut 1987-2007
21	Fang Mitchell, #Coppin St. 1987-2007
21	L. Vann Pettaway, #Alabama A&M 1987-2007
19	Bob Thomason, Pacific 1989-2007
18	Homer Drew, Valparaiso 1989-2002, 04-07
18	Bob McKillop, #Davidson 1990-2007
18	Gary Williams, Maryland 1990-2007
17	Dave Loos, Austin Peay 1991-2007
15	Willis Wilson, #Rice 1993-2007
14	Kirk Speraw, #UCF 1994-2007
14	Perry Watson, #Detroit 1994-2007
13	Dana Altman, Creighton 1995-2007
13	Pat Flannery, Bucknell 1995-2007
13	Ron Hunter, #IUPUI 1995-2007
13	Dennis Wolff, Boston U. 1995-2007

#has coached only at this school

MOST DIVISION I 20-WIN SEASONS

No.	Coach, Team and Seasons
29	Jim Boeheim, Syracuse 1977-2007
29	Bob Knight, Army 1966-71, Indiana 72-2000, Texas Tech 02-07
29	Lute Olson, Long Beach St. 1974, Iowa 75-83, Arizona 84-2007
23	Mike Krzyzewski, Army 1976-80, Duke 81-2007
21	Jim Calhoun, Northeastern 1973-86, Connecticut 87-2007
19	Bob Huggins, Walsh 1981-83, Akron 85-89, Cincinnati 90-2005, Kansas St. 07, West Virginia
17	Roy Williams, Kansas 1989-2003, North Carolina 04-07
16	Gary Williams, American 1979-82, Boston College 83-86, Ohio St. 87-89, Maryland 90-2007
15	Rick Pitino, Boston U. 1979-83, Providence 86-87, Kentucky 90-97, Louisville 2002-05
14	Tubby Smith, Tulsa 1992-95, Georgia 96-97, Kentucky 98-2007, Minnesota
13	John Calipari, Massachusetts 1989-96, Memphis 2001-07
13	Kelvin Sampson, Montana Tech 1982-85, Washington St. 88-94, Oklahoma 95-2007, Indiana 07
12	Rick Barnes, George Mason 1988, Providence 89-94, Clemson 95-98, Texas 99-2007
12	Rick Byrd, Maryville (Tenn.) 1979-80, Lincoln Memorial 84-86, Belmont 87-2007
12	Stew Morrill, Montana 1987-91, Colorado St. 92-98, Utah St. 1999-2007
11	Tom Penders, Tufts 1972-74, Columbia 75-78, Fordham 79-86, Rhode Island 87-88, Texas 89-98, George Washington 99-2001, Houston 05-07
10	Ben Braun, Siena Heights 1978-85, Eastern Mich. 86-96, California 97-2007
10	Pat Kennedy, Iona 1981-86, Florida St. 87-97, DePaul 98-2002, Montana 03-04, Towson 05-07
10	Dave Odom, East Caro. 1980-82, Wake Forest 90-2001, South Carolina 02-2007
9	Cliff Ellis, South Ala. 1976-84, Clemson 85-94, Auburn 95-2004 Coastal Caro.

MOST CONSECUTIVE DIVISION I 20-WIN SEASONS

No.	Coach, Team and Seasons
20	Lute Olson, Arizona 1988-2007
14	Jim Boeheim, Syracuse 1983-96
14	Tubby Smith, Tulsa 1994-95, Georgia 96-97, Kentucky 98-2007, Minnesota
14	Roy Williams, Kansas 1990-2003
11	Mike Krzyzewski, Duke 1984-94
11	Mike Krzyzewski, Duke 1997-2007
10	Jim Boeheim, Syracuse 1998-2007
10	Kelvin Sampson, Oklahoma 1998-2007
9	Dana Altman, Creighton 1999-2007
9	Jim Calhoun, Connecticut 1998-2007
9	Billy Donovan, Florida 1999-2007
9	Bill Self, Tulsa 1999-2000, Illinois 01-03, Kansas 04-07
8	Rick Barnes, Texas 2000-07
8	Mark Few, Gonzaga 2000-07
8	Stew Morrill, Utah St. 2000-07
8	Gary Williams, Maryland 1997-2004
7	John Calipari, Memphis 2001-07
7	Thad Matta, Butler 2001, Xavier 02-04, Ohio St. 05-07
7	Rick Pitino, Kentucky 1991-97
6	Mike Brey, Delaware 1998-2000, Notre Dame 01-03
6	John Calipari, Massachusetts 1991-96
6	Homer Drew, Valparaiso 1994-99
6	Tom Penders, Rhode Island 1987-88, Texas 89-92
6	Bruce Weber, Southern Ill. 2002-03, Illinois 04-07

CURRENT MOST CONSECUTIVE DIVISION I 20-WIN SEASONS

No.	Coach, Team and Seasons
20	Lute Olson, Arizona 1988-2007
14	Tubby Smith, Tulsa 1994-95, Georgia 96-97, Kentucky 98-2007, Minnesota
11	Mike Krzyzewski, Duke 1997-2007
10	Jim Boeheim, Syracuse 1998-2007
10	Kelvin Sampson, Oklahoma 1998-2006, Indiana 07
9	Dana Altman, Creighton 1999-2007
9	Billy Donovan, Florida 1999-2007
9	Bill Self, Tulsa 1999-2000, Illinois 01-03, Kansas 04-07
8	Rick Barnes, Texas 2000-07
8	Mark Few, Gonzaga 2000-07
8	Stew Morrill, Utah St. 2000-07
7	John Calipari, Memphis 2001-07
7	Thad Matta, Butler 2001, Xavier 02-04, Ohio St. 05-07
6	Bruce Weber, Southern Ill. 2002-03, Illinois 04-07
5	Jim Christian, Kent St. 2003-07
5	Bruce Pearl, Milwaukee 2003-05, Tennessee 06-07
5	Rick Pitino, Louisville 2003-07
4	Al Skinner, Boston College 2004-07
3	13 coaches tied

MOST DIVISION I 30-WIN SEASONS

No.	Coach, Team and Seasons
9	Mike Krzyzewski, Army 1976-80, Duke 81-2007
7	Roy Williams, Kansas 1989-2003, North Carolina 04-07
6	Jim Calhoun, Northeastern 1973-86, Connecticut 1987-2007
4	John Calipari, Massachusetts 1989-96, Memphis 2001-07
4	Bob Knight, Army 1966-71, Indiana 1972-2000, Texas Tech 02-07
4	Rick Pitino, Boston U. 1979-83, Providence 86-87, Kentucky 1990-97, Louisville 2002-07
3	Jim Boeheim, Syracuse 1977-2007
3	Lute Olson, Long Beach St. 1974, Iowa 75-83, Arizona 1984-2007
2	Billy Donovan, Marshall 1995-96, Florida 97-2007
2	Ben Howland, Northern Ariz. 1995-99, Pittsburgh 2000-03, UCLA 04-07
2	Tom Izzo, Michigan St. 1996-2007
2	Bill Self, Oral Roberts 1994-97, Tulsa 98-2000, Illinois 01-03, Kansas 04-07
2	Tubby Smith, Tulsa 1992-95, Georgia 96-97, Kentucky 1998-2007, Minnesota

MOST TEAMS

No.	Coach, Team and Seasons
7	Tom Penders, Tufts 1972-74, Columbia 75-78, Fordham 79-86, Rhode Island 87-88, Texas 89-98, George Washington 99-2001, Houston 05-07
6	John Beilein, Nazareth 1983, Le Moyne 84-92, Canisius 93-97, Richmond 98-2002, West Virginia 03-07, Michigan
5	Mike Deane, Oswego St. 1981-82, Siena 87-94, Marquette 95-99, Lamar 2000-03, Wagner 04-07
5	Bob Huggins, Walsh 1981-83, Akron 85-89, Cincinnati 90-2005, Kansas St. 07, West Virginia
5	Pat Kennedy, Iona 1981-86, Florida St. 87-97, DePaul 98-2002, Montana 03-04, Towson 05-07
5	Lon Kruger, Tex.-Pan American 1983-86, Kansas St. 87-90, Florida 91-92, 94-96, Illinois 97-2000, UNLV 05-07
5	Ritchie McKay, Portland St. 1997-98, Colorado St. 99-2000, Oregon St. 01-02, New Mexico 03-07, Liberty
5	Rick Scruggs, North Greenville 1987-89, Belmont Abbey 90-91, Pikeville 92-94, Milligan 95, Gardner-Webb 96-2007
5	Jim Wooldrige, Central Mo. 1986-91, Texas St. 92-94, Louisana Tech 95-98, Kansas St. 2001-06, UC Riverside
4	Steve Alford, Manchester 1992-95, Missouri St. 96-99, Iowa 2000-07, New Mexico
4	Rick Barnes, George Mason 1988, Providence 89-94, Clemson 95-98, Texas 99-2007
4	Keith Dambrot, Tiffin 1985-86, Ashland 90-91, Central Mich. 92-93, Akron 05-07
4	Matt Doherty, Notre Dame 2000, North Carolina 01-03, Fla. Atlantic 06, SMU 07
4	Cliff Ellis, South Ala. 1976-84, Clemson 85-94, Auburn 95-2004, Coastal Caro.
4	Larry Eustachy, Idaho 1991-93, Utah St. 94-98, Iowa St. 99-2003, Southern Miss. 05-07
4	Tim Floyd, Idaho 1987-88, New Orleans 89-94, Iowa St. 95-98, Southern California 2006-07
4	Rick Majerus, Marquette 1984-86, Ball St. 88-89, Utah 90-2004, St. Louis
4	Greg McDermott, Wayne St. (Neb.) 1995-2000, North Dakota St. 01, UNI 02-06, Iowa St. 07
4	Buzz Peterson, Appalachian St. 1997-2000, Tulsa 01, Tennessee 02-05, Coastal Caro. 06
4	Rick Pitino, Boston U. 1979-83, Providence 86-87, Kentucky 90-97, Louisville 2002-07
4	Oliver Purnell, Radford 1989-91, Old Dominion 92-94, Dayton 95-2003, Clemson 04-07

No.	Coach, Team and Seasons
4	Kelvin Sampson, Montana Tech 1982-85, Washington St. 88-94, Oklahoma 95-2006, Indiana 07
4	Bill Self, Oral Roberts 1994-97, Tulsa 98-2000, Illinois 01-03, Kansas 04-07
4	Tubby Smith, Tulsa 1992-95, Georgia 96-97, Kentucky 98-2007, Minnesota
4	Rob Spivery, Montevallo 1986-95, Ashland 96, Alabama St. 97-2005, Southern U. 06
4	Al Walker, Colorado Col. 1989-93, Cornell 94-96, Chaminade 97-2000, Binghamton 01-07
4	Gary Williams, American 1979-82, Boston College 83-86, Ohio St. 87-89, Maryland 90-2007

All-Time Coaching Longevity Records

(Minimum 10 years as a Division I head coach)

MOST GAMES

No.	Coach, Team and Seasons
1,354	Jim Phelan, Mt. St. Mary's 1955-03
1,253	Bob Knight, Army 1966-71, Indiana 72-2000, Texas Tech 02-07*
1,191	Lou Henson, Hardin-Simmons 1963-66, Illinois 76-96, New Mexico St. 67-75, 98-2005
1,180	Lefty Driesell, Davidson 1961-69, Maryland 70-86, James Madison 89-97, Georgia St. 1998-2003
1,133	Dean Smith, North Carolina 1962-97
1,113	Eddie Sutton, Creighton 1970-74, Arkansas 75-85, Kentucky 86-89, Oklahoma St. 91-2006
1,103	Henry Iba, Northwest Mo. St. 1930-33, Colorado 34, Oklahoma St. 35-70
1,102	Norm Stewart, UNI 1962-67, Missouri 68-99
1,080	Marv Harshman, Pacific Lutheran 1946-58, Washington St. 59-71, Washington 72-85
1,078	Jim Calhoun, Northeastern 1973-86, Connecticut 87-2007*
1,078	Ray Meyer, DePaul 1943-84
1,072	Don Haskins, UTEP 1962-99
1,066	Adolph Rupp, Kentucky 1931-52, 54-72
1,062	Hugh Durham, Florida St. 1967-78, Georgia 79-95, Jacksonville 98-2005
1,061	Ed Diddle, Western Ky. 1923-64
1,060	Lute Olson, Long Beach St. 1974, Iowa 75-83, Arizona 84-2007*
1,053	John Chaney, Cheyney 1973-82, Temple 83-2006
1,039	Ralph Miller, Wichita St. 1952-64, Iowa 65-70, Oregon St. 71-89
1,036	Mike Krzyzewski, Army 1976-80, Duke 81-2007
1,017	Norm Sloan, Presbyterian 1952-55, Citadel 57-60, North Carolina St. 67-80, Florida 61-66, 81-89

*active

MOST SEASONS

No.	Coach, Team and Seasons
50	Phog Allen, Baker 1906-08, Haskell 09, Central Mo. St. 13-19, Kansas 08-09, 20-56
49	Jim Phelan, Mt. St. Mary's 1955-03
46	Frank J. Hill, Seton Hall 1912-18, 20-30, Rutgers 16-43
42	Ed Diddle, Western Ky. 1923-64
42	Ray Meyer, DePaul 1943-84
41	Lefty Driesell, Davidson 1961-69, Maryland 70-86, James Madison 89-97, Georgia St. 98-2003
41	Lou Henson, Hardin-Simmons 1963-66, Illinois 76-96, New Mexico St. 67-75, 98-2005
41	Tony Hinkle, Butler 1927-42, 46-70
41	Henry Iba, Northwest Mo. St. 1930-33, Colorado 34, Oklahoma St. 35-70
41	Bob Knight, Army 1966-71, Indiana 72-2000, Texas Tech 02-07*
41	Adolph Rupp, Kentucky 1931-52, 54-72
40	Marv Harshman, Pacific Lutheran 1946-58, Washington St. 59-71, Washington 72-85
39	Cal Luther, DePauw 1955-58, Murray St. 59-74, Longwood 82-90, Tenn.-Martin 91-99, Bethel (Tenn.) 2000
38	Fred Enke, Louisville 1924-25, Arizona 26-61
38	Don Haskins, UTEP 1962-99
38	Ralph Miller, Wichita St. 1952-64, Iowa 65-70, Oregon St. 71-89
38	Norm Stewart, UNI 1962-67, Missouri 68-99
37	Hugh Durham, Florida St. 1967-78, Georgia 79-95, Jacksonville 98-2005
37	Nat Holman, CCNY 1920-52, 55-56, 59-60
37	Norm Sloan, Presbyterian 1952-55, Citadel 57-60, North Carolina St. 67-80, Florida 61-66, 81-89

*active

MOST SEASONS AT ONE SCHOOL

No.	Coach, Team and Seasons
49	James Phelan, #Mt. St. Mary's 1955-2003
42	Ed Diddle, #Western Ky. 1923-64
42	Ray Meyer, #DePaul 1943-84

No.	Coach, Team and Seasons
41	Tony Hinkle, #Butler 1927-42, 46-70
41	Adolph Rupp, #Kentucky 1931-52, 54-72
39	Phog Allen, Kansas 1908-09, 20-56
38	Don Haskins, #UTEP 1962-99
37	Nat Holman, #CCNY 1920-52, 55-56, 59-60
36	Fred Enke, Arizona 1926-61
36	Slats Gill, #Oregon St. 1929-64
36	Henry Iba, Oklahoma St. 1935-70
36	Dean Smith, #North Carolina 1962-97
36	Glenn Wilkes, #Stetson 1958-93
35	Howard Cann, #New York U. 1924-58
34	Nelson Norgren, #Chicago 1922-42, 45-57
32	Norm Stewart, Missouri 1968-99
31	Jim Boeheim, #Syracuse 1977-2007*
31	Doc Carlson, #Pittsburgh 1923-53
31	Taps Gallagher, #Niagara 1932-43, 47-65
31	Cy McClairen, #Bethune-Cookman 1962-66, 68-93

*active; #has coached only at this school

COACHES WITH 100 OR MORE WINS AT FOUR DIVISION I SCHOOLS

Coach, Total Wins (Schools, Wins)

Lefty Driesell, 786 wins, 1961-86, 89-2003 (Davidson 176, Maryland 348, James Madison 159, Georgia St. 103)

COACHES WITH 100 OR MORE WINS AT THREE DIVISION I SCHOOLS

Coach, Total Wins (Schools, Wins)

Tom Davis, 581 wins, 1972-99, 2004-06 (Lafayette 116, Boston College 100, Iowa 270)
Hugh Durham, 633 wins, 1967-95, 98-2005 (Florida St. 230, Georgia 297, Jacksonville 106)
Cliff Ellis, 534 wins, 1976-2004 (South Ala. 171, Clemson 177, Auburn 186)
Mike Jarvis, 369 wins, 1986-2004 [Boston U. 101, George Washington 152, St. John's (N.Y.) 116]
Bob Knight, 869 wins, 1966-2000, 02-07 (Army 102, Indiana 662, Texas Tech 126)*
Frank McGuire, 549 wins [St. John's (N.Y.) 102, North Carolina 164, South Carolina 283]
Jerry Tarkanian, 729 wins (Long Beach St. 116, UNLV 509, Fresno St. 104)
Billy Tubbs, 641 wins (Oklahoma 333, TCU 156, Lamar 121)
Butch van Breda Kolff, 482 wins (Lafayette 132, Hofstra 215, Princeton 103)

*active.

COACHES WITH 200 OR MORE WINS AT TWO DIVISION I SCHOOLS

Coach, Total Wins (Schools, Wins)

Jim Calhoun, 733 wins (Northeastern 248, Connecticut 502)*
Hugh Durham, 633 wins (Florida St. 230, Georgia 297)
Lou Henson, 779 wins (Illinois 423, New Mexico St. 289)
Neil McCarthy, 431 wins (Weber St. 205, New Mexico St. 226)
Ralph Miller, 657 wins (Wichita St. 220, Oregon St. 342)
Johnny Orr, 466 wins (Michigan 248, Iowa St. 218)
Norm Sloan, 624 wins (Florida 232, North Carolina St. 266)
Eddie Sutton, 798 wins (Arkansas 260, Oklahoma 368)

*active.

MOST DIVISION I 20-WIN SEASONS

No.	Coach, Team and Seasons
30	Dean Smith, North Carolina 1962-97
29	Jim Boeheim, Syracuse 1977-2007*
29	Bob Knight, Army 1966-71, Indiana 72-2000, Texas Tech 02-07*
29	Lute Olson, Long Beach St. 1974, Iowa 75-83, Arizona 84-2007*
25	Eddie Sutton, Creighton 1970-74, Arkansas 75-85, Kentucky 86-89, Oklahoma St. 91-2007*
25	Jerry Tarkanian, Long Beach St. 1969-73, UNLV 74-92, Fresno St. 96-2002
23	Mike Krzyzewski, Army 1976-80, Duke 81-2007*
23	Adolph Rupp, Kentucky 1931-52, 54-72
22	Lefty Driesell, Davidson 1961-69, Maryland 70-86, James Madison 89-97, Georgia St. 1998-2003
21	Jim Calhoun, Northeastern 1973-86, Connecticut 87-2007*
21	Denny Crum, Louisville 1972-2001
20	Lou Henson, Hardin-Simmons 1963-66, Illinois 76-96, New Mexico St. 67-75, 99-2005
19	Bob Huggins, Walsh 1981-83, Akron 1985-89, Cincinnati 90-2005, Kansas St. 07, West Virginia*
19	John Thompson, Georgetown 1973-99
18	Lou Carnesecca, St. John's (N.Y.) 1966-92
18	Ed Diddle, Western Ky. 1923-64
18	Billy Tubbs, Southwestern (Tex.) 1972-73, Oklahoma 81-94, TCU 95-2002, Lamar 1977-80, 2004-06
18	John Wooden, Indiana St. 1947-48, UCLA 49-75
17	Don Haskins, UTEP 1962-99
17	Mike Montgomery, Montana 1979-86, Stanford 87-2004
17	Norm Stewart, UNI 1962-67, Missouri 1968-99
17	Roy Williams, Kansas 1989-2003, North Carolina 04-2007*

*active

MOST CONSECUTIVE DIVISION I 20-WIN SEASONS

No.	Coach, Team and Seasons
27	Dean Smith, North Carolina 1971-97
20	Lute Olson, Arizona 1988-2007*
14	Jim Boeheim, Syracuse 1983-96*
14	Tubby Smith, Tulsa 1994-95, Georgia 96-97, Kentucky 98-2007, Minnesota*
14	Roy Williams, Kansas 1990-2003*
13	Denny Crum, Louisville 1972-84
13	John Thompson, Georgetown 1978-90
12	Billy Tubbs, Oklahoma 1982-93
11	Bob Huggins, Cincinnati 1992-2002
11	Mike Krzyzewski, Duke 1997-2007*
11	Mike Krzyzewski, Duke 1984-94*
11	Al McGuire, Marquette 1967-77
11	Jerry Tarkanian, Long Beach St. 1970-73, UNLV 74-80
11	Jerry Tarkanian, UNLV 1982-92
10	Jim Boeheim, Syracuse 1998-2007*
10	Everett Case, North Carolina St. 1947-56
10	Mike Montgomery, Stanford 1995-2004
10	G. Ott Romney, Montana St. 1924-28, BYU 29-33
10	Kelvin Sampson, Oklahoma 1998-2006, Indiana 07*
10	Eddie Sutton, Arkansas 1977-85, Kentucky 86

*active

MOST DIVISION I 30-WIN SEASONS

No.	Coach, Team and Seasons
9	Mike Krzyzewski, Army 1976-80, Duke 1981-2007*
7	Roy Williams, Kansas 1989-2003, North Carolina 2004-07*
6	Jim Calhoun, Northeastern 1973-86, Connecticut 87-2007*
4	John Calipari, Massachusetts 1989-96, Memphis 2001-07*
4	Bob Knight, Army 1966-71, Indiana 1972-2000, Texas Tech 02-07*
4	Rick Pitino, Boston U. 1979-83, Providence 86-87, Kentucky 1990-97, Louisville 2002-07*
4	Nolan Richardson, Tulsa 1981-85, Arkansas 1986-2002
4	Adolph Rupp, Kentucky 1931-52, 54-72
4	Jerry Tarkanian, Long Beach St. 1969-73, UNLV 1974-92, Fresno St. 96-2002
4	John Wooden, Indiana St. 1947-48, UCLA 1949-1975
3	Jim Boeheim, Syracuse 1977-2007*
3	Denny Crum, Louisville 1972-2001
3	Guy Lewis, Houston 1957-86
3	Mike Montgomery, Montana 1979-86, Stanford 1987-2004
3	Lute Olson, Long Beach St. 1974, Iowa 75-83, Arizona 1984-2007*
3	Dean Smith, North Carolina 1962-97
3	Eddie Sutton, Creighton 1970-74, Arkansas 1975-85, Kentucky 86-89, Oklahoma St. 91-2006
3	John Thompson, Georgetown 1973-99
3	Billy Tubbs, Southwestern (Tex.) 1972-73, Oklahoma 1981-94, TCU 95-2002, Lamar 1977-80, 2004-06
2	Forddy Anderson, Drake 1947-48, Bradley 1949-54, Michigan St, 55-65, Hiram Scott 66-70
2	Lou Carnesecca, St. John's (N.Y.) 1966-92
2	John Chaney, Cheyney 1973-82, Temple 1983-2006
2	Billy Donovan, Marshall 1995-96, Florida 97-2007*
2	Ben Howland, Northern Ariz. 1995-99, Pittsburgh 2000-03, UCLA 04-07*
2	Tom Izzo, Michigan St. 1996-2007*
2	Rick Majerus, Marquette 1984-86, Ball St. 88-89, Utah 1990-2004
2	G. Ott Romney, Montana St. 1923-28, BYU 29-35
2	Bill Self, Oral Roberts 1994-97, Tulsa 98-2000, Illinois 01-03, Kansas 04-07*
2	Tubby Smith, Tulsa 1992-95, Georgia 96-97, Kentucky 1998-2007, Minnostota*

*active

MOST TEAMS

No.	Coach, Team and Seasons
7	Ben Jobe, Talladega 1965-67, Alabama St. 68, South Carolina St. 69-73, Denver 79-80, Alabama A&M 83-86, Tuskegee 97-2000, Southern U. 1987-96, 2002-03
7	Tom Penders, Tufts 1972-74, Columbia 75-78, Fordham 79-86, Rhode Island 87-88, Texas 89-98, George Washington 99-2001, Houston 05-07*
7	Elmer Ripley, Wagner 1923-25, Georgetown 28-29, 39-43, 47-49, Yale 30-35, Columbia 44-45, Notre Dame 46, John Carroll 50-51, Army 52-53

No.	Coach, Team and Seasons
7	Bob Vanatta, Central Methodist 1943, 48-50, Missouri St. 51-53, Army 54, Bradley 55-56, Memphis 57-62, Missouri 63-67, Delta St. 73
6	J.D. Barnett, Lenoir Rhyne 1970, High Point 71, Louisiana Tech 78-79, Va. Commonwealth 80-85, Tulsa 86-91, Northwestern St. 95-99
6	Gene Bartow, Central Mo. St. 1962-64, Valparaiso 65-70, Memphis 71-74, Illinois 75, UCLA 76-77, UAB 79-96
6	John Beilein, Nazareth 1983, Le Moyne 84-92, Canisius 93-97, Richmond 99-2002, West Virginia 03-07, Michigan*
6	Bill E. Foster, Bloomsburg 1961-63, Rutgers 64-71, Utah 72-74, Duke 75-80, South Carolina 81-86, Northwestern 87-93
6	George Keogan, Wis.-Superior 1913-14, St. Louis 16, St. Thomas (Minn.)18, Allegheny 19, Valparaiso 20-21, Notre Dame 24-43
6	Press Maravich, West Va. Wesleyan 1950, Davis & Elkins 51-52, Clemson 57-62, North Carolina St. 65-66, LSU 67-72, Appalachian St. 73-75
6	Harry Miller, Western St. 1953-58, Fresno St. 61-65, Eastern N.M. 66-70, North Texas 71, Wichita St. 72-78, Stephen F. Austin 79-88
6	Hal Wissel, TCNJ 1965-67, Lafayette 68-71, Fordham 72-76, Fla. Southern 78-82, Charlotte 83-85, Springfield 87-90
5	Ozzie Cowles, Carleton 1925-30, Wis.-River Falls 34-36, Dartmouth 37-43, 45-46, Michigan 47-48, Minnesota 49-59
5	Tom Davis, Lafayette 1972-77, Boston College 78-82, Stanford 83-86, Iowa 87-99, Drake 2004-07
5	Mike Deane, Oswego St. 1981-82, Siena 87-94, Marquette 95-99, Lamar 2000-03, Wagner 04-07*
5	Don DeVoe, Virginia Tech 1972-76, Wyoming 77-78, Tennessee 79-89, Florida 90, Navy 93-2004
5	Bill C. Foster, Shorter 1963-67, Charlotte 71-75, Clemson 76-84, Miami (Fla.) 86-90, Virginia Tech 92-97

No.	Coach, Team and Seasons
5	Ron Greene, Loyola (La.) 1968-69, New Orleans 70-77, Mississippi St. 78, Murray St. 79-85, Indiana St. 86-89
5	Blair Gullion, Earlham 1928-35, Tennessee 36-38, Cornell 39-42, Connecticut 46-47, Washington-St. Louis 48-52, 54-59
5	Bob Huggins, Walsh 1981-83, Akron 85-89, Cincinnati 90-2005, Kansas St. 07, West Virginia*
5	Pat Kennedy, Iona 1981-86, Florida St. 87-97, DePaul 98-2002, Montana 03-04, Towson 05-07*
5	Lon Kruger, Tex.-Pan American 1983-86, Kansas St. 87-90, Florida 91-92, Illinois 97-2000, UNLV 05-07*
5	Tates Locke, Army 1964-65, Miami (Ohio) 67-70, Clemson 71-75, Jacksonville 79-81, Indiana St. 90-94
5	Ken Loeffler, Geneva 1929-35, Yale 36-42, Denver 46, La Salle 50-55, Texas A&M 56-57
5	Cal Luther, DePauw 1955-58, Murray St. 59-74, Longwood 82-90, Tenn.-Martin 91-99, Bethel (Tenn.) 2000
5	John Mauer, Kentucky 1928-30, Miami (Ohio) 31-38, Tennessee 39-43, 45-47, Army 48-51, Florida 52-60
5	Lynn Nance, Iowa St. 1977-80, Central Mo. St. 81-85, St. Mary's (Cal.) 87-89, Washington 90-93, Southwest Baptist 97-99
5	Norm Shepard, North Carolina 1924, Guilford 29, Randolph-Macon 30-36, Davidson 38-49, Harvard 50-54
5	Gordon Stauffer, Washburn 1967, Indiana St. 68-75, IPFW 76-79, Geneva 80-81, Nicholls 82-90
5	E.J. Stewart, Purdue 1909, Oregon St. 12-16, Nebraska 17-19, Texas 24-27, UTEP 28
5	Tex Winter, Marquette 1952-53, Kansas St. 54-68, Washington 69-71, Northwestern 74-78, Long Beach St. 79-83
5	Jim Wooldrige, Central Mo. 1986-91, Texas St. 92-94, Louisana Tech 95-98, Kansas St. 2001-06, UC Riverside*

active

Division I Head Coaching Changes

Year	Teams	Chngs.	Pct.	1st Yr.	Year	Teams	Chngs.	Pct.	1st Yr.
1950	145	22	15.2	11	1963	178	24	13.5	15
1951	153	28	18.3	15	1964	179	23	12.8	17
1952	156	23	14.7	18	1965	182	15	8.2	8
1953	158	20	12.7	13	1966	182	24	13.2	20
1954	160	12	7.5	7	1967	185	33	17.8	18
1955	162	21	13.0	9	1968	189	26	13.8	16
1956	166	18	10.8	12	1969	193	29	15.0	19
1957	167	18	10.8	9	1970	196	29	14.8	17
1958	173	14	8.1	8	1971	203	30	14.8	17
1959	174	20	11.5	10	1972	210	37	17.6	21
1960	175	23	13.1	15	1973	216	38	17.6	24
1961	173	15	8.7	11	1974	233	41	17.6	23
1962	178	15	8.4	14					

Year	Teams	Chngs.	Pct.	1st Yr.	Year	Teams	Chngs.	Pct.	1st Yr.
1975	235	44	18.7	30	1992	298	39	13.1	15
1976	235	34	14.5	20	1993	298	34	11.4	15
1977	245	39	15.9	21	1994	301	33	11.0	17
1978	254	39	15.4	24	1995	302	58	19.2	28
1979	257	53	20.6	28	1996	305	42	13.8	31
1980	261	43	16.5	23	1997	305	52	17.0	29
1981	264	42	15.9	21	1998	306	63	20.6	31
1982	273	37	13.6	20	1999	310	45	14.5	30
1983	274	37	13.5	18	2000	318	55	17.3	27
1984	276	38	13.8	21	2001	318	53	16.7	31
1985	282	26	9.2	15	2002	321	47	14.6	22
1986	283	56	19.8	21	2003	325	44	13.5	29
1987	290	66	22.8	35	2004	326	46	14.1	20
1988	290	39	13.4	16	2005	326	40	12.3	25
1989	293	42	14.3	24	2006	326	47	14.4	25
1990	292	54	18.5	29	2007	325	61	18.8	35
1991	295	41	13.9	16					

Division I Coach of the Year

Season	United Press International	The Associated Press	U.S. Basketball Writers Assn.	National Assn. of Basketball Coaches	Naismith	The Sporting News	CBS/Chevrolet
1955	Phil Woolpert, San Francisco						
1956	Phil Woolpert, San Francisco						
1957	Frank McGuire, North Carolina						
1958	Tex Winter, Kansas St.						
1959	Adolph Rupp, Kentucky		Eddie Hickey, Marquette				
1960	Pete Newell, California		Pete Newell, California				
1961	Fred Taylor, Ohio St.		Fred Taylor, Ohio St.				
1962	Fred Taylor, Ohio St.		Fred Taylor, Ohio St.				
1963	Ed Jucker, Cincinnati		Ed Jucker, Cincinnati				
1964	John Wooden, UCLA		John Wooden, UCLA			John Wooden, UCLA	
1965	Dave Strack, Michigan		Bill van Breda Kolff, Princeton				
1966	Adolph Rupp, Kentucky		Adolph Rupp, Kentucky			Adolph Rupp, Kentucky	
1967	John Wooden, UCLA	John Wooden, UCLA	John Wooden, UCLA			Jack Hartman, Southern Ill.	
1968	Guy Lewis, Houston	Guy Lewis, Houston	Guy Lewis, Houston			Guy Lewis, Houston	
1969	John Wooden, UCLA	John Wooden, UCLA	Maury John, Drake	John Wooden, UCLA		John Wooden, UCLA	
1970	John Wooden, UCLA	John Wooden, UCLA	John Wooden, UCLA	John Wooden, UCLA		Adolph Rupp, Kentucky	
1971	Al McGuire, Marquette	Al McGuire, Marquette	Al McGuire, Marquette	Jack Kraft, Villanova		Al McGuire, Marquette	
1972	John Wooden, UCLA	John Wooden, UCLA	John Wooden, UCLA	John Wooden, UCLA		John Wooden, UCLA	
1973	John Wooden, UCLA	John Wooden, UCLA	John Wooden, UCLA	Gene Bartow, Memphis		John Wooden, UCLA	
1974	Digger Phelps, Notre Dame	Norm Sloan, North Carolina St.	Norm Sloan, North Carolina St.	Al McGuire, Marquette		Digger Phelps, Notre Dame	
1975	Bob Knight, Indiana	Bob Knight, Indiana	Bob Knight, Indiana	Bob Knight, Indiana		Bob Knight, Indiana	
1976	Tom Young, Rutgers	Bob Knight, Indiana	Bob Knight, Indiana	Johnny Orr, Michigan		Tom Young, Rutgers	
1977	Bob Gaillard, San Francisco	Bob Gaillard, San Francisco	Eddie Sutton, Arkansas	Dean Smith, North Carolina		Lee Rose, Charlotte	
1978	Eddie Sutton, Arkansas	Eddie Sutton, Arkansas	Ray Meyer, DePaul	Bill Foster, Duke; Abe Lemons, Texas		Bill Foster, Duke	
1979	Bill Hodges, Indiana St.	Bill Hodges, Indiana St.	Dean Smith, North Carolina	Ray Meyer, DePaul		Bill Hodges, Indiana St.	
1980	Ray Meyer, DePaul	Ray Meyer, DePaul	Ray Meyer, DePaul	Lute Olson, Iowa		Lute Olson, Iowa	
1981	Ralph Miller, Oregon St.	Ralph Miller, Oregon St.	Ralph Miller, Oregon St.	Ralph Miller, Oregon St.; Jack Hartman, Kansas St.		Dale Brown, LSU	Dale Brown, LSU
1982	Norm Stewart, Missouri	Ralph Miller, Oregon St.	John Thompson, Georgetown	Don Monson, Idaho		Ralph Miller, Oregon St.	Gene Keady, Purdue
1983	Jerry Tarkanian, UNLV	Guy Lewis, Houston	Lou Carnesecca, St. John's (N.Y.)	Lou Carnesecca, St. John's (N.Y.)		Denny Crum, Louisville	Lou Carnesecca, St. John's (N.Y)
1984	Ray Meyer, DePaul	Ray Meyer, DePaul	Gene Keady, Purdue	Marv Harshman, Washington		John Thompson, Georgetown	Gene Keady, Purdue
1985	Lou Carnesecca, St. John's (N.Y.)	Bill Frieder, Michigan	Lou Carnesecca, St. John's (N.Y.)	John Thompson, Georgetown		Lou Carnesecca, St. John's (N.Y.)	Dale Brown, LSU
1986	Mike Krzyzewski, Duke	Eddie Sutton, Kentucky	Dick Versace, Bradley	Eddie Sutton, Kentucky		Denny Crum, Louisville	Mike Krzyzewski, Duke
1987	John Thompson, Georgetown	Tom Davis, Iowa	John Chaney, Temple	Rick Pitino, Providence	Bob Knight, Indiana	Rick Pitino, Providence	Joey Meyer, DePaul
1988	John Chaney, Temple	John Chaney, Temple	John Chaney, Temple	John Chaney, Temple	Larry Brown, Kansas	John Chaney, Temple	John Chaney, Temple
1989	Bob Knight, Indiana	Bob Knight, Indiana	Bob Knight, Indiana	P.J. Carlesimo, Seton Hall	Mike Krzyzewski, Duke	P.J. Carlesimo, Seton Hall	Lute Olson, Arizona
1990	Jim Calhoun, Connecticut	Jim Calhoun, Connecticut	Roy Williams, Kansas	Jud Heathcote, Michigan St.	Bobby Cremins, Georgia Tech	Jim Calhoun, Connecticut	Jim Calhoun, Connecticut
1991	Rick Majerus, Utah	Randy Ayers, Ohio St.	Randy Ayers, Ohio St.	Mike Krzyzewski, Duke	Randy Ayers, Ohio St.	Rick Pitino, Kentucky	Randy Ayers, Ohio St.
1992	Perry Clark, Tulane	Roy Williams, Kansas	Perry Clark, Tulane	George Raveling, Southern California	Mike Krzyzewski, Duke	Mike Krzyzewski, Duke	George Raveling, Southern California
1993	Eddie Fogler, Vanderbilt	Eddie Fogler, Vanderbilt	Eddie Fogler, Vanderbilt	Eddie Fogler, Vanderbilt	Dean Smith, North Carolina	Eddie Fogler, Vanderbilt	Eddie Fogler, Vanderbilt

Season	United Press International	The Associated Press	U.S. Basketball Writers Assn.	National Assn. of Basketball Coaches	Naismith	The Sporting News	CBS/Chevrolet
1994	Norm Stewart Missouri	Norm Stewart Missouri	Charlie Spoonhour St. Louis	Nolan Richardson Arkansas Gene Keady Purdue	Nolan Richardson Arkansas	Norm Stewart Missouri	Nolan Richardson Arkansas
1995	Leonard Hamilton Miami (Fla.)	Kelvin Sampson Oklahoma	Kelvin Sampson Oklahoma	Jim Harrick UCLA	Jim Harrick UCLA	Jud Heathcote Michigan St.	Gene Keady Purdue
1996	Gene Keady Purdue	Gene Keady Purdue	Gene Keady Purdue	John Calipari Massachusetts	John Calipari Massachusetts	John Calipari Massachusetts	Gene Keady Purdue
1997		Clem Haskins Minnesota	Clem Haskins Minnesota	Clem Haskins Minnesota	Roy Williams Kansas	Roy Williams Kansas	Clem Haskins Minnesota
1998		Tom Izzo Michigan St.	Tom Izzo Michigan St.	Bill Guthridge North Carolina	Bill Guthridge North Carolina	Bill Guthridge North Carolina	Bill Guthridge North Carolina
1999		Cliff Ellis Auburn	Cliff Ellis Auburn	Mike Krzyzewski Duke	Mike Krzyzewski Duke	Cliff Ellis Auburn	Cliff Ellis Auburn
2000		Larry Eustachy Iowa St.	Larry Eustachy Iowa St.	Gene Keady Purdue	Mike Montgomery Stanford	Bob Huggins Cincinnati Bill Self Tulsa	Mike Krzyzewski Duke
2001		Matt Doherty North Carolina	Al Skinner Boston College	Tom Izzo Michigan St.	Rod Barnes Mississippi	Al Skinner Boston College	Al Skinner Boston College
2002		Ben Howland Pittsburgh	Ben Howland Pittsburgh	Kelvin Sampson Oklahoma	Ben Howland Pittsburgh	Ben Howland Pittsburgh	Kelvin Sampson Oklahoma
2003		Tubby Smith Kentucky	Tubby Smith Kentucky	Tubby Smith Kentucky	Tubby Smith Kentucky	Tubby Smith Kentucky	Tubby Smith Kentucky
2004		Phil Martelli St. Joseph's	Phil Martelli St. Joseph's	Phil Martelli St. Joseph's Mike Montgomery Stanford	Phil Martelli St. Joseph's	Mike Montgomery Stanford	Phil Martelli St. Joseph's
2005		Bruce Weber Illinois	Bruce Weber Illinois	Bruce Weber Illinois	Bruce Weber Illinois	Bruce Weber Illinois	Bruce Weber Illinois
2006		Roy Williams North Carolina	Roy Williams North Carolina	Jay Wright Villanova	Jay Wright Villanova	Bruce Pearl Tennessee	Jay Wright Villanova
2007		Tony Bennett Washington St.	Tony Bennett Washington St.	Todd Lickliter Butler	Tony Bennett Washington St.	Tony Bennett Washington St.	Tony Bennett Washington St.

Adolph Rupp Cup: 2004-Phil Martelli, St. Joseph's; 2005-Bruce Weber, Illinois; 2006-Roy Williams, North Carolina; 2007-Bo Ryan, Wisconsin.

Basketball Times **Coach of the Year:** 1982-Gale Catlett, West Virginia; 1983-Lou Carnesecca, St. John's (N.Y.); 1984-Jerry Tarkanian, UNLV; 1985-Bobby Cremins, Georgia Tech; 1986-Mike Krzyzewski, Duke; 1987-Wimp Sanderson, Alabama; 1988-Lute Olson, Arizona; 1989-Bob Knight, Indiana; 1990-Rick Pitino, Kentucky; 1991-Rick Majerus, Utah; 1992-Steve Fisher, Michigan; 1993-Dean Smith, North Carolina; 1994-Norm Stewart, Missouri; 1995-Eddie Sutton, Oklahoma St.; 1996-John Calipari, Massachusetts; 1997-Mike Krzyzewski, Duke; 1998-Bob Huggins, Cincinnati; 1999-Tom Izzo, Michigan St.; 2000-Mike Montgomery, Stanford; 2001-Al Skinner, Boston College; 2002-Bob Knight, Texas Tech; 2003-Tubby Smith, Kentucky; 2004-Mike Montgomery, Stanford; 2005-Bruce Weber, Illinois; 2006-Bruce Pearl; 2007-Tony Bennett, Washington St.

Jim Phelan Award: 2003-Mark Slonaker, Mercer; 2004-Phil Martelli, St. Joseph's; 2005-Tubby Smith, Kentucky; 2006-Ben Howland, UCLA; 2007- Tony Bennett, Washington St.

Legends of Coaching Award: 1999-Dean Smith, North Carolina; 2000-Mike Krzyzewski, Duke; 2001-Lute Olson, Arizona; 2002-Denny Crum, Louisville; 2003-Roy Williams, Kansas; 2004-Mike Montgomery, Stanford; 2005-Jim Calhoun, Connecticut; 2006-Jim Boeheim, Syracuse; 2007- Gene Keady, Purdue.

Division II Coaching Records

Winningest Active Coaches

(Minimum five years as a head coach; includes record at four-year colleges only.)

BY PERCENTAGE

Coach, Team	Years	Won	Lost	Pct.
1. Danny Young, Montevallo	6	157	39	.801
2. Rick Herdes, Southern Ind.	6	158	40	.798
3. Dave Robbins, Virginia Union	29	691	186	.788
4. Greg Zimmerman, Alderson-Broaddus	6	146	42	.777
5. Jeff Oliver, Cal St. San B'dino	5	109	35	.757
6. Don Meyer, Northern St.	35	862	295	.745
7. Ron Niekamp, Findlay	22	477	169	.738
8. Tom Kropp, Neb.-Kearney	17	373	135	.734
9. Bob Chipman, Washburn	28	628	240	.724
10. Gordon Gibbons, Clayton St.	17	373	143	.723
11. Brian Beaury, St. Rose	21	467	181	.721
12. Herb Magee, Philadelphia U.	40	833	327	.718
13. Kim Anderson, Central Mo.	5	109	45	.708
14. Greg Kamansky, Cal Poly Pomona	7	140	59	.704
15. Rick Cooper, West Tex. A&M	20	426	180	.703
16. David Boots, South Dakota	25	501	212	.703
17. Richard Schmidt, Tampa	26	527	236	.691
18. Stan Spirou, Southern N.H.	22	454	207	.687
19. Luke D'Alessio, Bowie St.	8	163	75	.685
20. Lonn Reisman, Tarleton St.	19	391	180	.685
21. Mark Johnson, Fort Hays St.	6	119	55	.684
22. Ken Barer, Mass.-Lowell	6	124	58	.681
23. Mike Leaf, Winona St.	9	188	88	.681
24. Steve Tappmeyer, Northwest Mo. St.	19	371	185	.667
25. Ken Wagner, BYU-Hawaii	17	323	163	.665
26. Matt Margenthaler, Minn. St. Mankato	6	118	60	.663
27. Kevin Schlagel, St. Cloud St.	11	199	102	.661
28. Jeff Hironaka, Seattle Pacific	5	94	49	.657
29. Greg Walcavich, Edinboro	26	485	253	.657
30. Tom Ryan, Eckerd	11	213	112	.655
31. Jeff Ray, Midwestern St.	10	192	101	.655
32. Kevin Luke, Michigan Tech	13	247	131	.653
33. Keith Dickson, St. Anselm	21	407	217	.652
34. Jay Lawson, Bentley	16	304	163	.651
35. Jim Baker, Catawba	13	243	133	.646
36. Jeff Guiot, Southwest Baptist	6	113	63	.642
37. Jim Heaps, Mesa St.	11	195	109	.641
38. Craig Carse, Mont. St.-Billings	16	289	162	.641
39. Grady Brewer, Morehouse	7	128	72	.640
40. Dick DeLaney, West Chester	20	355	201	.638
41. Fred Thompson, Millersville	9	161	94	.631
42. Dave Balza, Fla. Gulf Coast	8	149	87	.631
43. Brad Jackson, Western Wash.	22	409	239	.631
44. Jeff Burkhamer, Armstrong Atlantic	5	94	55	.631
45. Dave Davis, Pfeiffer	16	288	170	.629
46. Mike Ruane, Bridgeport	7	132	78	.629
47. Tom Klusman, Rollins	27	483	287	.627
48. James Cosgrove, Adelphi	10	177	107	.623
49. Steve Joyner, Johnson C. Smith	20	358	217	.623
50. Bill Brown, California (Pa.)	21	355	218	.620

COACHING RECORDS

Coach, Team	Years	Won	Lost	Pct.
51. Bill Clingan, Mount Olive	17	301	188	.616
52. Terry Evans, Central Okla.	5	89	56	.614
53. Gregg Nibert, Presbyterian	18	327	206	.614
54. Mark Corino, Caldwell	24	429	274	.610
55. Mike Sandifar, Oakland City	25	435	279	.609
56. Darren Metress, Augusta St.	11	192	124	.608
57. Parker Laketa, Wingate	7	129	84	.606
58. Bryan Poore, West Virginia St.	9	161	105	.605
59. Jeff Morgan, Harding	15	253	167	.602
60. Tom Smith, Mo. Western St.	32	546	367	.598
61. Ron Righter, Clarion	21	334	226	.596
62. Larry Gipson, Northeastern St.	15	254	175	.592
63. Terry Sellers, GC&SU	14	234	162	.591
64. Cesar Odio, Barry	13	217	153	.586
65. David Moe, Emporia St.	6	100	71	.585
66. Greg Sparling, Central Wash.	13	199	142	.584
67. Gary Edwards, Francis Marion	23	392	281	.582
68. Ron Spry, Paine	27	440	317	.581
69. Art Luptowski, American Int'l	18	301	217	.581
70. Stu Engen, Minn. St. Moorhead	15	229	166	.580

BY VICTORIES

(Minimum five years as a head coach; includes record at four-year colleges only.)

Coach, Team	Years	Won	Lost	Pct.
1. Don Meyer, Northern St.	35	862	295	.745
2. Herb Magee, Philadelphia U.	40	833	327	.718
3. Dave Robbins, Virginia Union	29	691	186	.788
4. Bob Chipman, Washburn	28	628	240	.724
5. Tom Smith, Mo. Western St.	32	546	367	.598
6. Richard Schmidt, Tampa	26	527	236	.691
7. Dave Boots, South Dakota	25	501	212	.703
8. Greg Walcavich, Edinboro	26	485	253	.657
9. Tom Klusman, Rollins	27	483	287	.627
10. Ron Niekamp, Findlay	22	477	169	.738
11. Lonnie Porter, Regis (Colo.)	30	476	353	.574
12. Brian Beaury, St. Rose	21	467	181	.721
13. Tim Hills, Northwest Nazarene	28	461	426	.520
14. Stan Spirou, Southern N.H.	22	454	207	.687
15. Gene Iba, Pittsburg St.	27	450	329	.578
16. Ron Spry, Paine	27	440	317	.581
17. Mike Sandifar, Oakland City	25	435	279	.609
18. Mark Corino, Caldwell	24	429	274	.610
19. Rick Cooper, West Tex. A&M	20	426	180	.703
20. Brad Jackson, Western Wash.	22	409	239	.631
21. Keith Dickson, St. Anselm	21	407	217	.652
22. Tom Wood, Humboldt St.	26	401	322	.555
23. Gary Edwards, Indiana (Pa.)	23	392	281	.582
24. Lonn Reisman, Tarleton St.	19	391	180	.685
25. Bert Hammel, Merrimack	27	387	379	.505
26. John Lentz, Lenoir-Rhyne	24	379	294	.563
27. Tom Kropp, Neb.-Kearney	17	373	135	.734
Gordon Gibbons, Clayton St.	17	373	143	.723
29. Steve Tappmeyer, Northwest Mo. St.	19	371	185	.667
30. Mike Nienaber, Christian Bros.	24	363	382	.487
31. Billy Lee, St. Andrews	27	360	407	.469
32. Steve Joyner, Johnson C. Smith	20	358	217	.623
33. Dick DeLaney, West Chester	20	355	201	.638
Bill Brown, California (Pa.)	21	355	218	.620
35. Jim Boone, Tusculum	21	347	263	.569
36. Gary Tuell, Nova Southeastern	19	346	252	.579
37. Dean Ellis, Northern Mich.	21	339	253	.573
38. Ron Righter, Clarion	21	334	226	.596
39. Gregg Nibert, Presbyterian	18	327	206	.614
40. Eddie Payne, S.C. Upstate	21	325	282	.535
41. Ken Wagner, BYU-Hawaii	17	323	163	.665
42. Bob Hofman, Fort Lewis	19	311	227	.578
43. Greg White, Charleston (W.V.)	21	307	281	.522
44. Jay Lawson, Bentley	16	304	163	.651
45. Bill Clingan, Mount Olive	17	301	188	.616
Art Luptowski, American Int'l	18	301	217	.581
47. Serge DeBari, Assumption	21	300	244	.551
48. Steve Cox, Concord	18	291	230	.559
49. Craig Carse, Mont. St.-Billings	16	289	162	.641
50. Dave Davis, Pfeiffer	16	288	170	.629
51. Lennie Acuff, Ala.-Huntsville	17	286	222	.563
52. Prescott Smith, Cal St. Chico	20	280	275	.505
53. Bob Rukavina, Pitt.-Johnstown	18	279	204	.578
54. Dale Clayton, Carson-Newman	19	277	259	.517
55. Rick Reedy, West Ala.	23	275	340	.447
56. Dennis O'Donnell, St. Thomas Aquinas	16	274	203	.574
57. Robert Corn, Mo. Southern St.	18	273	237	.535
58. Ron Lievense, Barton	19	269	252	.516

Coach, Team	Years	Won	Lost	Pct.
59. Dan Schmotzer, Coker	20	262	277	.486
60. Larry Gipson, Northeastern St.	15	254	175	.592
61. Jeff Morgan, Harding	15	253	167	.602
62. Larry Epperly, Limestone	20	251	309	.448
63. Mike Newell, Ark.-Monticello	15	250	195	.562
64. Kevin Luke, Michigan Tech	13	247	131	.653
65. Jim Baker, Catawba	13	243	133	.646
66. Tony Robinson, Southeastern Okla.	16	239	208	.535
67. Joe Clinton, Dominican (N.Y.)	16	236	241	.495

Winningest Coaches All-Time

(Minimum 10 head coaching seasons in Division II)

BY PERCENTAGE

Coach (Team coached, tenure)	Years	Won	Lost	Pct.
1. Walter Harris (Philadelphia U. 1954-65, 67)	13	240	56	.811
2. Dolph Stanley (Beloit 1946-57)	12	238	56	.810
3. Ed Adams (N.C. Central 1936-37, Tuskegee 37-49, Texas Southern 50-58)	24	612	150	.803
4. Dave Robbins (Virginia Union 1979-07)*	29	691	186	.788
5. Charles Christian (Norfolk St. 1974-78, 82-90)	14	318	95	.770
6. Lucias Mitchell (Alabama St. 1964-67, Kentucky St. 68-75, Norfolk St. 79-81)	15	325	103	.759
7. Mike Dunlap (Cal Lutheran 1990-94, Metro St. 98-06)	14	328	105	.758
8. Dean Nicholson (Central Wash. 1965-90)	26	620	199	.757
9. John Kochan (Millersville 1984-96)	13	285	96	.748
10. Joe Hutton (Hamline 1932-65)	34	591	207	.741
11. Ed Oglesby (Florida A&M 1951-70, 72)	21	386	138	.737
12. John McLendon (N.C. Central 1941-52, Hampton 53-54, Tennessee St. 55-59, Kentucky St. 64-66, Cleveland St. 67-69)	25	496	179	.735
13. Moco Mercer (Dubuque 1941-50)	10	119	43	.735
14. Tom Kropp (Neb.-Kearney 1991-07)*	17	373	135	.734
15. Calvin Irvin (Johnson C. Smith 1948-51, N.C. A&T 55-72)	22	397	144	.734
16. Garland Pinholster (Oglethorpe 1957-66)	10	180	68	.726
17. Bob Chipman (Washburn 1980-07)*	28	628	240	.724
18. Gordon Gibbons (South Fla. 1980; Fla. Southern 91-00, Clayton St. 2002-07)*	17	373	143	.723
19. Brian Beaury (St. Rose 1987-07)*	21	467	181	.721
20. Albert Muyskens (Calvin 1936-45)	10	118	46	.720
21. Herb Magee (Philadelphia U. 1968-07)*	40	833	327	.718
22. Fred Sefton (Akron 1916-24, 26-27)	11	103	42	.710
23. Butch Haswell (Fairmont St. 1994-04)	11	226	93	.708
24. Andrew Laska (Assumption 1952-67)	16	224	93	.707
25. Al Shields (Bentley 1964-78)	15	257	107	.706
26. Lou D'Allesandro (Southern N.H. 1964-70, 73-75)	10	183	77	.704
27. Bill Boylan (Monmouth 1957-77)	21	368	155	.704
28. Rick Cooper (Wayland Baptist 1988-93; West Tex. A&M 94-07)*	20	426	180	.703
29. Dave Boots (Augsburg 1983-88, South Dakota 89-07)*	25	501	212	.703
30. Beryl Shipley (La.-Lafayette 1958-73)	16	293	126	.699
31. Edwin Nihiser (Brockport St. 1929-34, 36-39, 41-42)	12	104	45	.698
32. Ernest Hole (Wooster 1927-58)	32	412	181	.695
33. Sam Cozen (Drexel 1953-68)	16	213	94	.694
34. Barney Steen (Calvin 1954-66)	13	189	84	.692
35. Richard Schmidt (Vanderbilt 1980-81, Tampa 84-07)*	26	527	236	.691
36. Ed Jucker (Merchant Marine 1946-47, Rensselaer 49-53, Cincinnati 61-65, Rollins 73-77)	17	266	109	.709
37. Stan Spirou (Southern N.H. 1986-07)*	22	454	207	.687
38. Lonn Reisman (Tarleton St. 1989-07)*	19	391	180	.685
39. Robert Rainey (Albany St. [Ga.] 1961-72)	12	243	112	.685
40. Dick Sauers (Albany [N.Y.] 1956-87, 89-97)	41	702	330	.680
41. Clem Leitch (North Dakota 1926-43)	18	224	106	.679
42. Bill E. Jones (Florence St. 1973, North Ala. 74, Jacksonville St. 75-98)	26	477	226	.679
43. Rutherford Baker (Albany [N.Y.] 1925-35)	11	63	30	.677
44. Danny Rose (Central Mich. 1938-43, 47-54)	14	176	84	.677
45. Albin Schneidler (St. Joseph's [Ind.] 1912-25)	14	111	54	.673
46. Dale Race (Milton 1976-79, Minn. Duluth 85-98)	18	363	177	.672
47. Russell Beichly (Akron 1941-59)	19	288	141	.671
48. Steve Rives (Louisiana Col. 1986, Delta St. 87-06)	21	402	200	.668
49. William Lucas (Central St. 1961-74)	14	241	120	.668
50. Steve Tappmeyer (Northwest Mo. St. 1989-07)*	19	371	185	.667
51. Fred Hobdy (Grambling 1957-86)	30	571	287	.666
52. Paul Webb (Randolph-Macon 1957-75, Old Dominion 76-85)	29	511	257	.666
53. Ed Martin (South Carolina St. 1956-68, Tennessee St. 69-85)	30	501	253	.664

Coach (Team coached, tenure)	Years	Won	Lost	Pct.
54. Marlowe Severson (St. Cloud St. 1959-69, Minn. St. Mankato 70-73)	15	250	127	.663
55. Don Zech (Puget Sound 1969-89)	21	386	197	.662
56. Ken Bone (Cal St. Stanislaus 1985, Seattle Pacific 91-02, Portland St.07)*	15	288	147	.662
57. Dave Buss (Green Bay 1970-82, Long Beach St. 84, St. Olaf 88-94)	21	381	195	.661
58. Kevin Schlagel (St. Cloud St. 1984, 98-07)*	11	199	102	.661
59. Scott Nagy (South Dakota St. 1996-07)*	12	235	121	.660
60. Charles Chronister (Bloomsburg 1972-02)	31	559	288	.660
61. Wayne Boultinghouse (Southern Ind. 1975-81; Ky. Wesleyan 91-96)	13	240	124	.659
62. Donald Feeley (Sacred Heart 1966-78, Fairleigh Dickinson 81-83)	16	285	148	.658
63. Greg Walcavich (Birmingham-So. 1979-83, Rice 87, West Va. Wesleyan 88-89, Edinboro 90-07)*	26	485	253	.657
64. L. Vann Pettaway (Alabama A&M 1987-07)*	21	407	214	.655
65. Tom Ryan (Eckerd 1997-07)*	11	213	112	.655
66. Roger Kaiser (West Ga. 1970-90)	21	387	204	.655
67. Boyd King (Truman 1947-71)	25	377	199	.655
68. Ernie Wheeler (Cal Poly 1973-86; Mont. St.-Billings 89-91)	17	314	166	.654
69. Jim McDonald (Edinboro 1963-71, 73-75)	12	174	92	.654
70. Herbert Greene (Aub.-Montgomery 1976-77; Columbus St. 82-06)	27	510	270	.654

*Active coaches

BY VICTORIES
(Minimum 10 head coaching seasons in Division II)

Coach (Team coached, tenure)	Years	Won	Lost	Pct.
1. Herb Magee (Philadelphia U. 1968-07)*	40	833	327	.718
2. Clarence Gaines (Winston-Salem 1947-93)	47	828	447	.649
3. Jerry Johnson (LeMoyne-Owen 1959-05)	47	821	447	.647
4. Dick Sauers (Albany [N.Y.] 1956-87, 89-97)	41	702	330	.680
5. Dave Robbins (Virginia Union 1979-07)*	29	691	186	.788
6. John Lance (Southwestern Okla. 1919-22, Pittsburg St. 23-34, 36-63)	44	632	340	.650
7. Ed Messbarger (Benedictine Hts. 1958-60, Dallas 61-63, St. Mary's [Tex.] 64-78, Angelo St. 79-98)	41	630	518	.549
8. Bob Chipman (Washburn 1980-07)*	28	628	240	.724
9. Dean Nicholson (Central Wash. 1965-90)	26	620	199	.757
10. Ed Adams (N.C. Central 1936-37, Tuskegee 37-49, Texas Southern 50-58)	24	612	150	.803
11. Joe Hutton (Hamline 1932-65)	34	591	207	.741
12. Dom Rosselli (Youngstown St. 1941-42, 47-82)	38	590	387	.604
13. Dan McCarrell (North Park 1968-84, Minn. St. Mankato 85-01)	34	579	347	.625
14. Fred Hobdy (Grambling 1957-86)	30	571	287	.666
15. Charles Chronister (Bloomsburg 1972-02)	31	559	288	.660
16. Ed Douma (Alma 1974, Lake Superior St. 75-78, Kent St. 79-82, UNC Greensboro 83-84, Calvin 85-96, Hillsdale 99-07)	32	555	302	.648
Bill Knapton (Beloit 1958-97)	40	555	344	.617
18. Bruce Webster (Bridgeport 1966-99)	34	549	405	.575
19. Tom Smith (Central Mo. St. 1976-80, Valparaiso 81-88, Mo. Western St. 89-07)*	32	546	367	.598
20. Richard Schmidt (Vanderbilt 1980-81, Tampa 84-07)*	26	527	236	.691
21. Arthur McAfee (Lane 1961, Mississippi Val. 62, Lincoln [Mo.] 63, Bishop 64-65, Morehouse 66-2000)	40	516	510	.503
22. Arad McCutchan (Evansville 1947-77)	31	514	314	.621
Jim Gudger (Western Caro. 1951-69, Tex. A&M-Commerce 70-83)	33	514	415	.553
24. Paul Webb (Randolph-Macon 1957-75, Old Dominion 76-85)	29	511	257	.665
25. Herbert Greene (Aub.-Montgomery 1976-77, Columbus St. 82-06)	27	510	270	.654
Aubrey Bonham (Whittier 1938-43, 46-68)	29	510	285	.642
27. Leo Nicholson (Central Wash. 1930-64)	33	505	281	.642

Coach (Team coached, tenure)	Years	Won	Lost	Pct.
28. Ed Martin (South Carolina St. 1956-68, Tennessee St. 69-85)	30	501	253	.664
Dave Boots (Augsburg 1983-88, South Dakota 89-07)*	25	501	212	.703
Bobby Vaughan (Elizabeth City St. 1952-66, 68-86)	34	501	363	.580
31. Will Renken (Bloomfield 1948-52, Albright 56-88)	38	497	466	.516
32. John McLendon (N.C. Central 1941-52, Hampton 53-54, Tennessee St. 55-59, Kentucky St. 64-66, Cleveland St. 67-69)	25	496	179	.735
33. Ed Murphy (West Ala. 1979-83, Delta St. 84-86, Mississippi 87-92, West Ga. 94-07)	28	493	309	.615
34. Rich Glas (Minn.-Morris 1975-79, Willamette 80-84, North Dakota 89-06)	28	490	302	.619
35. Greg Walcavich (Birmingham-So. 1979-83, Rice 87, West Va. Wesleyan 88-89, Edinboro 90-07)*	26	485	253	.657
36. Tom Klusman (Rollins 1981-07)*	27	483	287	.627
37. Angus Nicoson (Indianapolis 1948-76)	29	482	274	.638
38. Hamlet Peterson (Luther 1923-65)	43	481	356	.575
39. Bill Detrick (Central Conn. St. 1960-87, Coast Guard 90)	30	479	278	.633
40. Bill E. Jones (Florence St. 1973, North Ala. 74, Jacksonville St. 75-98)	26	477	226	.679
41. Dave Gunther (Wayne St. [Neb.] 1968-70, North Dakota 71-88, Buena Vista 94-95, Bemidji St. 96-01)	29	476	328	.592
Lonnie Porter (Regis [Colo.] 1978-07)*	30	476	353	.574
43. Brian Beaury (St. Rose 1987-07)*	21	467	181	.721
Tom Galeazzi (C.W. Post 1982-06)	25	467	259	.643
45. John Masi (UC Riverside 1980-05)	26	462	269	.632
46. Burt Kahn (Quinnipiac 1962-91)	30	459	355	.564
Richard Meckfessel (Charleston [W.V.] 1966-79, Mo.-St. Louis 83-99)	31	459	420	.522
Oliver Jones (Albany St. [Ga.] 1973-00, Tuskegee 01-04)	32	459	424	.520
49. Stan Spirou (Southern N.H. 1986-07)*	22	454	207	.687
Jim Seward (Wayne St. [Neb.] 1975-78, Ashland 79-83, Kansas Newman 84-87, Central Okla. 88-02)	28	454	339	.573
51. Gene Iba (Houston Baptist 1978-85, Baylor 86-92, Pittsburg St. 96-07)*	27	450	329	.578
52. Butch Raymond (Augsburg 1971-73, Minn. St. Mankato 74-84, St. Cloud St. 85-97)	27	447	302	.597
J.B. Scearce (North Ga. 1942-43, Cumberland 47, Ga. Southern 48-79)	26	447	244	.647
54. Ron Shumate (Chattanooga 1973-79, Southeast Mo. St. 82-97)	23	445	232	.657
Dave Bike (Sacred Heart 1979-07)*	29	445	401	.526
56. Ron Spry (Paine 1981-07)*	27	440	317	.581
57. Tom Villemure (Detroit Business 1967, Grand Valley St. 73-96)	25	437	268	.620
58. James Dominey (Valdosta St. 1972-00)	29	436	343	.560
59. Mike Sandifar (Averett 1979-81, Southwestern [Kan.] 82-87, Oakland City 88-99, 04-07)*	25	435	279	.609
60. Hal Nunnally (Randolph-Macon 1976-99)	24	431	232	.650
Leonidas Epps (Clark Atlanta 1950-78)	29	431	291	.597
62. Ollie Gelston (New Jersey City 1960-67, Montclair St. 68-91)	32	429	347	.553
63. Rick Cooper (Wayland Baptist 1988-93, West Tex. A&M 94-07)*	20	426	180	.703
64. Jim Harley (Eckerd 1964-96)	32	420	349	.546
65. Irvin Peterson (Neb. Wesleyan 1949-51, 54-80)	30	419	314	.572
66. Tom Feely (St. Thomas [Minn.] 1955-80)	26	417	269	.608
67. Don P. Smith (Elizabethtown 1955-64, Bucknell 65-72, Elizabethtown 73-88)	34	413	381	.520
68. Ernest Hole (Wooster 1927-58)	32	412	181	.695
69. L. Vann Pettaway (Alabama A&M 1987-07)*	21	407	214	.655
Keith Dickson (St. Anselm 1987-07)*	21	407	217	.652

*Active coaches

Division III Coaching Records

Winningest Active Coaches

(Minimum five years as a head coach; includes record at four-year colleges only.)

BY PERCENTAGE

Coach, Team	Years	Won	Lost	Pct.
1. Rob Kornaker, St. John Fisher	6	134	36	.788
2. Steve Moore, Wooster	26	554	173	.762
3. Mike Jones, Mississippi Col.	15	311	98	.760
4. Brian VanHaaften, Buena Vista	11	232	75	.756
5. David Macedo, Va. Wesleyan	7	152	50	.752
6. Glenn Van Wieren, Hope	30	590	199	.748
7. Chris Harvey, Salem St.	5	104	36	.743
8. Pat Miller, Wis.-Whitewater	6	122	44	.735
9. Jerry Rickrode, Wilkes	15	290	107	.730
10. Glenn Robinson, Frank. & Marsh.	36	718	271	.726
11. Joe Cassidy, Rowan	11	212	81	.724
12. Mark Hanson, Gust. Adolphus	17	339	131	.721
13. J.P. Andrejko, King's (Pa.)	6	118	47	.715
14. C.J. Woollum, Chris. Newport	23	459	183	.715
15. Stan Ogrodnik, Trinity (Conn.)	26	448	179	.715
16. Brian Meehan, Brandeis	11	215	86	.714
17. Rob Colbert, Keene St.	8	162	65	.714
18. David Hixon, Amherst	30	550	222	.712
19. Bob Campbell, Western Conn. St.	23	448	181	.712
20. Mike Rhoades, Randolph-Macon	8	157	64	.710
21. Bill Foti, Colby-Sawyer	15	287	117	.710
22. Jim Hayford, Whitworth	8	156	66	.703
23. Warren Caruso, Husson	5	94	40	.701
24. James Lancaster, Aurora	13	239	103	.699
25. Gerry Matthews, Richard Stockton	21	405	179	.693
26. Aaron Huffman, Bethany (W.V.)	5	95	42	.693
27. Bob Gillespie, Ripon	27	445	197	.693
28. Randy Lambert, Maryville (Tenn.)	27	501	222	.693
29. Bill Brown, Wittenberg	20	387	174	.690
30. Tom Murphy, SUNYIT	36	635	286	.689
31. Charles Brown, New Jersey City	25	483	218	.689
32. Bosko Djurickovic, Carthage	21	385	175	.688
33. Brian Baptiste, Mass.-Dartmouth	24	451	206	.686
34. Joe Nesci, New York U.	19	337	154	.686
35. David Paulsen, Williams	13	245	112	.686
36. Chuck McBreen, Ramapo	9	170	79	.683
37. Todd Raridon, North Central (Ill.)	18	322	151	.681
38. Dave Niland, Penn St.-Behrend	13	240	113	.680
39. Greg Mason, Centre	8	143	68	.678
40. Nelson Whitmore, Brockport St.	9	176	84	.677
41. Steve Fritz, St. Thomas (Minn.)	27	486	235	.674
42. Bill Harris, Wheaton (Ill.)	22	399	197	.669
43. Jose Rebimas, Wm. Paterson	13	234	116	.669
44. Mark Edwards, Washington-St. Louis	26	451	228	.664
45. Bob Gaillard, Lewis & Clark	26	470	238	.664
46. Kevin Van de Streek, Calvin	17	322	164	.663
47. Mike Bokosky, Chapman	15	247	127	.660
48. Ron Holmes, McMurry	17	299	154	.660
49. Dick Peth, Wartburg	22	402	209	.658
50. Ted Van Dellen, Wis.-Oshkosh	17	299	156	.657
51. Dick Whitmore, Colby	36	577	302	.656
52. Mike Moran, John Carroll	15	272	144	.654
53. Mike McGrath, Chicago	8	134	72	.650
54. Mike Beitzel, Hanover	27	481	262	.647
55. Bill Nelson, Johns Hopkins	27	456	249	.647
56. Page Moir, Roanoke	18	314	172	.646
57. John Baron, Gwynedd-Mercy	5	88	49	.642
58. Dick Reynolds, Otterbein	35	611	341	.642
59. Ken Scalmanini, Claremont-M-S	9	142	81	.637
60. Chris Bartley, WPI	6	101	58	.635
61. Scott Coval, DeSales	14	235	138	.630
62. Bill Fenlon, DePauw	22	357	210	.630
63. Mike Neer, Rochester	31	510	301	.629
64. Carl Danzig, Scranton	6	101	60	.627
65. Paul Phillips, Clark (Mass.)	19	317	190	.625
66. Brad McAlester, Lebanon Valley	13	220	132	.625
67. Mark Scherer, Elmhurst	11	175	105	.625
68. David Schultz, Carroll (Wis.)	5	78	47	.624
69. Kevin Small, Ursinus	7	116	70	.624
70. Gordie James, Willamette	20	334	204	.621

BY VICTORIES

(Minimum five years as a head coach; includes record at four-year colleges only.)

Coach, Team	Years	Won	Lost	Pct.
1. Glenn Robinson, Frank. & Marsh.	36	718	271	.726
2. Jim Smith, St. John's (Minn.)	43	671	463	.592
3. Tom Murphy, SUNYIT	36	635	286	.689
4. Dick Reynolds, Otterbein	35	611	341	.642
5. Glenn Van Wieren, Hope	30	590	199	.748
6. Dick Whitmore, Colby	36	577	302	.656
7. Steve Moore, Wooster	26	554	173	.762
8. David Hixon, Amherst	30	550	222	.712
9. Mike Neer, Rochester	31	510	301	.629
10. Mike Turner, Albion	33	508	313	.619
11. Randy Lambert, Maryville (Tenn.)	27	501	222	.693
12. Jon Davison, Clarke	38	499	478	.511
13. Steve Fritz, St. Thomas (Minn.)	27	486	235	.674
14. Charles Brown, New Jersey City	25	483	218	.689
15. Mike Beitzel, Hanover	27	481	262	.647
16. Mac Petty, Wabash	34	474	380	.555
17. Bob Gaillard, Lewis & Clark	26	470	238	.664
18. Lee McKinney, Fontbonne	29	465	347	.573
19. C.J. Woollum, Chris. Newport	23	459	183	.715
20. Bill Nelson, Johns Hopkins	27	456	249	.647
21. Brian Baptiste, Mass.-Dartmouth	24	451	206	.686
Mark Edwards, Washington-St. Louis	26	451	228	.664
23. Stan Ogrodnik, Trinity (Conn.)	26	448	179	.715
Bob Campbell, Western Conn. St.	23	448	181	.712
25. Bob Gillespie, Ripon	27	445	197	.693
26. Herb Hilgeman, Rhodes	31	444	313	.587
27. Bob McVean, Rochester Inst.	29	424	315	.574
28. Jeff Gamber, York (Pa.)	30	411	371	.526
29. Steve Bankston, Baldwin-Wallace	27	407	314	.564
30. Gerry Matthews, Richard Stockton	21	405	179	.693
31. Dick Peth, Wartburg	22	402	209	.658
32. Bill Harris, Wheaton (Ill.)	22	399	197	.669
33. Kerry Prather, Franklin	24	390	258	.602
34. Bill Brown, Wittenberg	20	387	174	.690
35. Bosko Djurickovic, Carthage	21	385	175	.688
36. Peter Barry, Coast Guard	25	377	295	.561
37. Bob Johnson, Emory & Henry	27	370	333	.526
Charlie Brock, Springfield	27	370	334	.526
39. Jim Walker, Moravian	28	368	336	.523
40. Bill Fenlon, DePauw	22	357	210	.630
41. Jonathon Halpert, Yeshiva	35	356	430	.453
42. Ed Andrist, Wis.-Stout	18	351	269	.566
43. Mike Griffin, Rensselaer	30	349	405	.463
44. Rich Rider, Cal Lutheran	22	344	220	.610
45. Mark Hanson, Gust. Adolphus	17	339	131	.721
46. Joe Nesci, New York U.	19	337	154	.686
47. Gordie James, Willamette	20	334	204	.621
48. Ray Rankis, Baruch	24	331	309	.517
49. Todd Raridon, North Central (Ill.)	18	322	151	.681
Kevin Van de Streek, Calvin	17	322	164	.663
Bill Leatherman, Bridgewater (Va.)	22	322	249	.564
52. Bruce Wilson, Simpson	22	321	250	.562
53. Paul Phillips, Clark (Mass.)	19	317	190	.625
54. Page Moir, Roanoke	18	314	172	.646
55. Charles Katsiaficas, Pomona-Pitzer	20	313	199	.611
Pat Cunningham, Trinity (Tex.)	20	313	225	.582
57. Mike Jones, Mississippi Col.	15	311	98	.760
58. Guy Kalland, Carleton	23	310	274	.531
59. Ron Holmes, McMurry	17	299	154	.660
Ted Van Dellen, Wis.-Oshkosh	17	299	156	.657
61. Tim Gilbride, Bowdoin	22	298	235	.559
62. Jerry Rickrode, Wilkes	15	290	107	.730
63. Ted Fiore, Montclair St.	18	289	202	.589
64. Robert Sheldon, Tufts	19	288	190	.603
65. Bill Foti, Colby-Sawyer	15	287	117	.710
66. Dave Madeira, Muhlenburg	20	285	221	.563
67. Mike Daley, Nazareth	21	284	261	.521
68. Brian Newhall, Occidental	19	280	196	.588
69. Dick Meader, Me.-Farmington	26	277	332	.455
70. Anthony Petosa, Staten Island	17	275	190	.591

Winningest Coaches All-Time

(Minimum 10 head coaching seasons in Division III)

BY PERCENTAGE

	Coach (Team coached, tenure)	Years	Won	Lost	Pct.
1.	Bo Ryan (Wis.-Platteville 1985-99, Milwaukee 00-01, Wisconsin 02-07)*	23	525	158	.769
2.	Steve Moore (Muhlenberg 1982-87, Wooster 88-07)*	26	554	173	.762
3.	Jim Borcherding (Augustana [Ill.] 1970-84)	15	313	100	.758
4.	Harry Sheehy (Williams 1984-00)	17	324	104	.757
5.	Brian VanHaaften (Buena Vista 1997-07)*	11	232	75	.756
6.	Glenn Van Wieren (Hope 1978-07)*	30	590	199	.748
7.	Jerry Rickrode (Wilkes 1993-07)*	15	290	107	.730
8.	Glenn Robinson (Frank. & Marsh. 1972-07)*	36	718	271	.726
9.	Rick Simonds (St. Joseph's [Me.] 1980-03)	23	463	176	.725
10.	Joe Cassidy (Rowan 1997-07)*	11	212	81	.724
11.	Mark Hanson (Gust. Adolphus 1991-07)*	17	339	131	.721
12.	Mike Lonergan (Catholic 1992-03, Vermont 06-07)*	14	289	113	.719
13.	Dave Darnall (Eureka 1975-94)	20	383	150	.719
14.	Joe Campoli (Ohio Northern 1993-05)	13	254	101	.715
15.	C.J. Woollum (Chris. Newport 85-07)*	23	459	183	.715
16.	Stan Ogrodnik (Trinity [Conn.] 1982-07)*	26	448	179	.715
17.	Brian Meehan (Salem St. 1997-03, Brandeis 04-07)*	11	215	86	.714
18.	David Hixon (Amherst 1978-07)*	30	550	222	.712
19.	Bob Campbell (Western Conn. St. 1985-07)*	23	448	181	.712
20.	Bob Ward (St. John Fisher 1988-01)	14	261	106	.711
21.	Bill Foti (Colby-Sawyer 1993-07)*	15	287	117	.710
22.	James Catalano (NJIT 1980-01)	22	431	176	.710
23.	Jerry Welsh (Potsdam St. 1969, 71-91, Iona 92-95)	26	502	205	.710
24.	Dave Vander Meulen (Wis.-Whitewater 1979-01)	23	440	182	.707
25.	James Lancaster (Aurora 1995-07)*	13	239	103	.699
26.	John Reynders (Allegheny 1980-89)	10	180	78	.698
27.	Lewis Levick (Wartburg 1966-93)	28	510	225	.694
28.	Gerry Mathews (Richard Stockton 1986-94, 96-07)*	21	405	179	.693
29.	Bob Gillespie (Ripon 1981-07)*	27	445	197	.693
30.	Randy Lambert (Maryville [Tenn.] 1981-07)*	27	501	222	.693
31.	John Dzik (Cabrini 1981-05)	25	481	216	.690
32.	Jim Todd (Fitchburg St. 1978-79, Salem St. 88-96)	11	207	93	.690
33.	Bill Brown (Wooster 1983, Kenyon 84-88, Wittenberg 94-07)*	20	387	174	.690
34.	Tom Murphy (Hamilton 1971-04, SUNYIT 06-07)*	36	635	286	.689
35.	Charles Brown (New Jersey City 1983-07)*	25	483	218	.689
36.	Bosko Djurickovic (North Park 1985-94, Carthage 97-07)*	21	385	175	.688
37.	Brian Baptiste (Mass.-Dartmouth 1984-07)*	24	451	206	.686
38.	Joe Nesci (New York U. 1989-07)*	19	337	154	.686
39.	David Paulsen (St. Lawrence 1995-97, Le Moyne 98-00, Williams 01-07)*	13	245	112	.686
40.	Todd Raridon (Neb. Wesleyan 1990-04, North Central [Ill.] 05-07)*	18	322	151	.681
41.	Richard Bihr (Buffalo St. 1980-99, 01-05)	25	449	211	.680
42.	Dave Niland (Penn St.-Behrend 1995-07)*	13	240	113	.680
43.	Bob Bessoir (Scranton 1973-01)	29	554	263	.678
44.	Dennie Bridges (Ill. Wesleyan 1966-01)	36	666	320	.675
45.	Steve Fritz (St. Thomas [Minn.] 1981-07)*	27	486	235	.674
46.	John McCloskey (Alvernia 1992-97, 99-04)	12	227	111	.672
47.	Bill Harris (King's [N.Y.] 1986-91, Wheaton [Ill.] 92-07)*	22	399	197	.669
48.	Jose Rebimbas (Montclair St. 1995, Wm. Paterson 96-07)*	13	234	116	.669
49.	Tony Shaver (Hampden-Sydney 1987-03, William & Mary 04-07)*	21	396	198	.667
50.	Naylond Hayes (Rust 1970-88)	18	338	169	.667
51.	Mark Edwards (Washington-St. Louis 1982-07)*	26	451	228	.664
52.	Kevin Van de Streek (Sioux Falls 1991-96, Calvin 97-07)*	17	322	164	.663
53.	Mike Bokosky (Chapman 1993-07)*	15	247	127	.660
54.	Ron Holmes (McMurry 1991-07)*	17	299	154	.660
55.	Ted Van Dellen (Wis.-Oshkosh 1991-07)*	17	299	156	.657
56.	Dick Whitmore (Colby 1971-01, 03-07)*	36	577	302	.656
57.	Mike Moran (John Carroll 1993-07)*	15	272	144	.654
58.	John Tharp (Lawrence 1995-07)*	13	203	108	.653
59.	Rudy Marisa (Waynesburg 1970-03)	34	563	300	.652
60.	Nick Lambros (Hartwick 1978-98)	21	352	191	.648
61.	Mike Beitzel (Northern Ky. 1981-88, Hanover 89-07)*	27	481	262	.647
62.	Bill Nelson (Rochester Inst. 1981-83, Nazareth 84-86, Johns Hopkins 87-07)*	27	456	249	.647
63.	Page Moir (Roanoke 1990-07)*	18	314	172	.646
64.	Dick Reynolds (Otterbein 1973-07)*	35	611	341	.642
65.	Doug Riley (St. Andrews 1978-86, Plattsburgh St. 87, Armstrong Atlantic 88-92)	15	245	139	.638
66.	Scott Coval (DeSales 1994-07)*	14	235	138	.630
67.	Bill Fenlon (Sewanee 1986-88, Rose-Hulman 89-91, Southwestern [Tex.] 92, DePauw 93-07)*	22	357	210	.630
68.	Mike Neer (Rochester 1977-07)*	31	510	301	.629
69.	Steve Larson (Edgewood 1987-06)	20	362	216	.626
70.	Raymond Amalbert (Hunter 1989-94, City Tech 02-05)	10	169	101	.626

*Active coaches

BY VICTORIES

(Minimum 10 head coaching seasons in Division III)

	Coach (Team coached, tenure)	Years	Won	Lost	Pct.
1.	Glenn Robinson (Frank. & Marsh. 1972-07)*	36	718	271	.726
2.	Jim Smith (St. John's [Minn.] 1965-07)*	43	671	463	.592
3.	Dennie Bridges (Ill. Wesleyan 1966-01)	36	666	320	.675
4.	Tom Murphy (Hamilton 1971-04, SUNYIT 06-07)*	36	635	286	.689
5.	Dick Reynolds (Otterbein 73-07)*	35	611	341	.642
6.	Glenn Van Wieren (Hope 1978-07)*	30	590	199	.748
7.	Dick Whitmore (Colby 1971-01, 03-07)*	36	577	302	.656
8.	Rudy Marisa (Waynesburg 1970-03)	34	563	300	.652
9.	Steve Moore (Muhlenberg 1982-87, Wooster 88-07)*	26	554	173	.762
	Bob Bessoir (Scranton 1973-01)	29	554	263	.678
11.	David Hixon (Amherst 1978-07)*	30	550	222	.712
12.	Jim Burson (Muskingum 1968-05)	38	543	425	.561
13.	C. Alan Rowe (Widener 1966-98)	33	536	324	.623
14.	Bo Ryan (Wis.-Platteville 1985-99, Milwaukee 00-01, Wisconsin 02-07)*	23	525	158	.769
	Gene Mehaffey (Carson-Newman 1968-78, Ohio Wesleyan 80-99)	31	525	384	.578
16.	Lewis Levick (Wartburg 1966-93)	28	510	225	.694
	Mike Neer (Rochester 1977-07)*	31	510	301	.629
18.	Mike Turner (Albion 1975-07)*	33	508	313	.619
19.	Jerry Welsh (Potsdam St. 1969, 71-91, Iona 92-95)	26	502	205	.710
20.	Randy Lambert (Maryville [Tenn.] 1981-07)*	27	501	222	.693
21.	Jon Davison (Dubuque 1967-93, Clarke 97-07)*	38	499	478	.511
22.	Steve Fritz (St. Thomas [Minn.] 1981-07)*	27	486	235	.674
23.	Charles Brown (New Jersey City 1983-07)*	25	483	218	.689
24.	John Dzik (Cabrini 1981-05)	25	481	216	.690
	Mike Beitzel (Northern Ky. 1981-88, Hanover 89-07)*	27	481	262	.647
26.	Mac Petty (Sewanee 1974-76, Wabash 77-07)*	34	474	380	.555
27.	Terry Glasgow (Monmouth [Ill.] 1973-07)	35	469	313	.600
28.	Lee McKinney (Mo. Baptist 1979-88, Fontbonne 89-07)*	29	465	347	.573
29.	Rick Simonds (St. Joseph's [Me.] 1980-03)	23	463	176	.725
	Cliff Garrison (Hendrix 1973-03)	31	463	376	.552
31.	Verne Canfield (Wash. & Lee 1965-95)	31	460	337	.577
32.	C.J. Woollum (Chris. Newport 1985-07)*	23	459	183	.715
33.	Bill Nelson (Rochester Inst. 1981-83, Nazareth 84-86, Johns Hopkins 87-07)*	27	456	249	.647
34.	Brian Baptiste (Mass.-Dartmouth 1984-07)*	24	451	206	.686
	Mark Edwards (Washington-St. Louis 1982-07)*	26	451	228	.664
36.	Gary Smith (Redlands 1972-07)	36	450	467	.491
37.	Richard Bihr (Buffalo St. 1980-99, 01-05)	25	449	211	.680
38.	Stan Ogrodnik (Trinity [Conn.] 1982-07)*	26	448	179	.715
	Bob Campbell (Western Conn. St. 1985-07)*	23	448	181	.712
40.	Bob Gillespie (Ripon 1981-07)*	27	445	197	.693
41.	Herb Hilgeman (Rhodes 1977-07)*	31	444	313	.587
42.	Dave Vander Meulen (Wis.-Whitewater 1979-01)	23	440	182	.707
43.	James Catalano (N.J. Inst. of Tech. 1980-01)	22	431	176	.710
44.	Ollie Gelston (New Jersey City 1960-67, Montclair St. 68-91)	32	429	347	.553
45.	Bob McVean (Eisenhower 1979-83, Rochester Inst. 84-07)*	29	424	315	.574
46.	Leon Richardson (Ozarks [Ark.] 1956, Dubuque 58-59, Drury 60-65, William Penn 75-02)	37	422	459	.479
47.	Don Smith (Elizabethtown 1955-64, Bucknell 65-72, Elizabethtown 73-88)	34	413	381	.520
48.	Jeff Gamber (York [Pa.] 1978-07)*	30	411	371	.526
49.	Steve Bankston (Baldwin-Wallace 1981-07)*	27	407	314	.564
50.	Gerry Mathews (Richard Stockton 1986-94, 96-07)*	21	405	179	.693

* Active coaches.

COACHING RECORDS

Championships

Division I Championship

2007 Results

OPENING ROUND
Niagara 77, Florida A&M 69.

FIRST ROUND
Florida 112, Jackson St. 69
Purdue 72, Arizona 63
Butler 57, Old Dominion 46
Maryland 82, Davidson 70
Winthrop 84, Notre Dame 74
Oregon 58, Miami (Ohio) 56
UNLV 67, Ga. Tech 63
Wisconsin 76, A&M-Corpus Christi 63
Kansas 107, Niagara 67
Kentucky 67, Villanova 58
Va. Tech 54, Illinois 52
Southern Ill. 61, Holy Cross 51
VCU 79, Duke 77
Pittsburgh 79, Wright St. 58
Indiana 70, Gonzaga 57
UCLA 70, Weber St. 42
North Carolina 88, Eastern Ky. 65
Michigan St. 61, Marquette 49
Southern California 77, Arkansas 60
Texas 79, New Mexico St. 67
Vanderbilt 77, George Washington 44
Washington St. 70, Oral Roberts 54
Boston College 84, Texas Tech 75
Georgetown 80, Belmont 55
Ohio St. 78, Central Conn. St. 57
Xavier 79, BYU 77
Tennessee 121, Long Beach St. 86
Virginia 84, Albany (N.Y.) 57
Louisville 78, Stanford 58
Texas A&M 68, Penn 52
Nevada 77, Creighton 71 (ot)
Memphis 73, North Texas 58

SECOND ROUND
Florida 74, Purdue 67
Butler 62, Maryland 59
Oregon 75, Winthrop 61
UNLV 74, Wisconsin 68
Kansas 88, Kentucky 76
Southern Ill. 63, Va. Tech 48
Pittsburgh 84, VCU 79, (ot)
UCLA 54, Indiana 49
North Carolina 81, Michigan St. 67
Southern California 87, Texas 68
Vanderbilt 78, Washington St. 74, (2 ot)
Georgetown 62, Boston College 55
Ohio St. 78, Xavier 71 (ot)
Tennessee 77, Virginia 74
Texas A&M 72, Louisville 69
Memphis 78, Nevada 58

REGIONAL SEMIFINALS
Florida 65, Butler 57
Oregon 76, UNLV 72
Kansas 61, Southern Ill. 58
UCLA 64, Pittsburgh 55
North Carolina 74, Southern California 64
Georgetown 66, Vanderbilt 65
Ohio St. 85, Tennessee 84
Memphis 65, Texas A&M 64

REGIONAL FINALS
Florida 85, Oregon 77
UCLA 68, Kansas 55
Georgetown 96, North Carolina 84 (ot)
Ohio St. 92, Memphis 76

SEMIFINALS
Florida 76, UCLA 66
Ohio St. 67, Georgetown 60

CHAMPIONSHIP
Florida 84, Ohio St. 75

Final Four Box Scores

SEMIFINALS
MARCH 31 IN ATLANTA

Ohio St. 67, Georgetown 60

Georgetown	FG-FGA	FTM-FTA	RB	PF	TP
DaJuan Summers*	1-10	1-2	3	0	3
Jeff Green*	4-5	1-2	12	4	9
Roy Hibbert*	9-13	1-4	6	4	19
Jonathan Wallace*	7-12	0-0	1	1	19
Jessie Sapp*	4-9	0-0	2	2	10
Vernon Macklin	0-0	0-0	2	0	0
Jeremiah Rivers	0-0	0-0	1	1	0
Tyler Crawford	0-0	0-0	0	0	0
Patrick Ewing Jr.	0-2	0-0	2	3	0
Team			1		
TOTALS	25-51	3-8	30	15	60

Ohio St.	FG-FGA	FTM-FTA	RB	PF	TP
Ivan Harris*	3-7	2-4	7	0	9
Greg Oden*	6-11	1-4	9	4	13
Mike Conley Jr.*	7-12	0-0	5	1	15
Ron Lewis*	1-8	7-8	5	0	9
Jamar Butler*	4-9	0-0	0	1	10
David Lighty	2-3	1-1	3	2	5
Daequan Cook	0-4	2-2	0	0	2
Matt Terwilliger	1-1	0-0	3	1	2
Othello Hunter	1-2	0-0	4	1	2
Team			1		
TOTALS	25-57	13-19	37	10	67

Halftime: Ohio St. 27, Georgetown 23. Three-point field goals: Georgetown 7-21 (Summers 0-4, Wallace 5-9, Sapp 2-7, Ewing 0-1); Ohio St. 4-14 (Harris 1-1, Conley 1-3, Lewis 0-3, Butler 2-6, Cook 0-1). Turnovers: Georgetown 14, Ohio St. 8. Officials: Ted Valentine, Richard Cartmell, Mike Kitts. Attendance: 53,510.

FLORIDA 76, UCLA 66

UCLA	FG-FGA	FTM-FTA	RB	PF	TP
Josh Shipp*	7-14	4-4	4	2	18
Luc Richard Mbah A Moute*	2-4	0-0	5	5	4
Lorenzo Mata*	3-6	0-0	2	5	6
Darren Collison*	3-14	2-2	0	1	9
Arron Afflalo*	5-14	4-4	3	5	17
Russell Westbrook	1-2	0-0	0	1	2
Ryan Wright	0-0	0-0	1	0	0
Alfred Aboya	2-4	1-2	3	4	5
James Keefe	1-1	0-1	6	3	2
Michael Roll	1-5	0-0	1	0	3
Team			1		
TOTALS	25-64	11-13	26	26	66

Florida	FG-FGA	FTM-FTA	RB	PF	TP
Corey Brewer*	5-7	5-6	2	3	19
Joakim Noah*	3-7	2-7	11	2	8
Al Horford*	2-3	5-9	17	4	9
Taurean Green*	2-9	5-6	4	2	10
Lee Humphrey*	5-9	0-1	2	1	14
Walter Hodge	0-2	0-0	2	3	0
Dan Werner	0-1	0-0	0	0	0
Chris Richard	7-7	2-2	4	2	16
Team			1		
TOTALS	24-45	19-31	43	17	76

Halftime: Florida 29, UCLA 23. Three-point field goals: UCLA 5-23 (Shipp 0-4, Collison 1-6, Afflalo 3-9, Roll 1-4); Florida 9-22 (Brewer 4-5, Green 1-7, Humphrey 4-8, Hodge 0-1, Werner 0-1). Turnovers: UCLA 3, Florida 16. Officials: Tom O'Neill, Verne Harris, Curtis Shaw. Attendance: 53,510.

NATIONAL CHAMPIONSHIP
APRIL 2 IN ATLANTA

Florida 84, Ohio St. 75

Ohio St.	FG-FGA	FTM-FTA	RB	PF	TP
Ivan Harris*	2-8	1-2	5	2	7
Greg Oden*	10-15	5-8	12	4	25
Mike Conley Jr.*	7-13	5-6	3	3	20
Ron Lewis*	6-13	0-1	3	3	12
Jamar Butler*	1-7	0-0	2	3	3
David Lighty	2-3	0-0	0	1	4
Daequan Cook	1-2	0-0	0	1	2
Matt Terwilliger	1-1	0-0	0	1	2
Othello Hunter	0-2	0-0	2	2	0
Team			1		
TOTALS	30-64	11-17	28	20	75

Florida	FG-FGA	FTM-FTA	RB	PF	TP
Corey Brewer*	4-12	2-2	8	2	13
Joakim Noah*	1-3	6-6	3	4	8
Al Horford*	6-15	6-8	12	3	18
Taurean Green*	4-6	5-5	3	0	16
Lee Humphrey*	5-8	0-0	1	1	14
Walter Hodge	2-2	1-1	1	1	5
Chris Richard	3-5	2-3	8	5	8
Marreese Speights	1-2	0-0	2	3	2
Team			0		
TOTALS	26-53	22-25	38	19	84

Halftime: Florida 40, Ohio St. 29. Three-point field goals: Ohio St. 4-23 (Harris 2-8, Conley 1-3, Lewis 0-4, Butler 1-6, Lighty 0-1, Cook 0-1); Florida 10-18 (Brewer 3-8, Green 3-3, Humphrey 4-7). Turnovers: Ohio St. 7, Florida 15. Officials: Karl Hess, Edward Corbett, Tony Greene. Attendance: 51,458.

Year-by-Year Results

Season	Champion (record)	Score	Runner-Up	Third Place	Fourth Place	Championship Game Attendance	Championship Total Attendance
1939	Oregon (29-5)	46-33	Ohio St.	+ Oklahoma	+ Villanova	5,500	15,025
1940	Indiana (20-3)	60-42	Kansas	+ Duquesne	+ Southern California	10,000	36,880
1941	Wisconsin (20-3)	39-34	Washington St.	+ Pittsburgh	+ Arkansas	7,219	48,055
1942	Stanford (28-4)	53-38	Dartmouth	+ Colorado	+ Kentucky	6,500	24,372
1943	Wyoming (31-2)	46-34	Georgetown	+ Texas	+ DePaul	13,300	56,876
1944	Utah (21-4)	42-40 (ot)	Dartmouth	+ Iowa St.	+ Ohio St.	15,000	59,369
1945	Oklahoma St. (27-4)	49-45	New York U.	+ Arkansas	+ Ohio St.	18,035	67,780
1946	Oklahoma St. (31-2)	43-40	North Carolina	Ohio St.	California	18,479	73,116
1947	Holy Cross (27-3)	58-47	Oklahoma	Texas	CCNY	18,445	72,959
1948	Kentucky (36-3)	58-42	Baylor	Holy Cross	Kansas St.	16,174	72,523
1949	Kentucky (32-2)	46-36	Oklahoma St.	Illinois	Oregon St.	10,600	66,077
1950	CCNY (24-5)	71-68	Bradley	North Carolina St.	Baylor	18,142	75,464
1951	Kentucky (32-2)	68-58	Kansas St.	Illinois	Oklahoma St.	15,348	110,645
1952	Kansas (28-3)	80-63	St. John's (N.Y.)	Illinois	Santa Clara	10,700	115,712
1953	Indiana (23-3)	69-68	Kansas	Washington	LSU	10,500	127,149
1954	La Salle (26-4)	92-76	Bradley	Penn St.	Southern California	10,500	115,391
1955	San Francisco (28-1)	77-63	La Salle	Colorado	Iowa	10,500	116,983
1956	San Francisco (29-0)	83-71	Iowa	Temple	SMU	10,600	132,513
1957	North Carolina (32-0)	54-53 (3ot)	Kansas	San Francisco	Michigan St.	10,500	108,891
1958	Kentucky (23-6)	84-72	Seattle	Temple	Kansas St.	18,803	176,878
1959	California (25-4)	71-70	West Virginia	Cincinnati	Louisville	18,498	161,809
1960	Ohio St. (25-3)	75-55	California	Cincinnati	New York U.	14,500	155,491
1961	Cincinnati (27-3)	70-65 (ot)	Ohio St.	* St. Joseph's	Utah	10,700	169,520
1962	Cincinnati (29-2)	71-59	Ohio St.	Wake Forest	UCLA	18,469	177,469
1963	Loyola (Ill.) (29-2)	60-58 (ot)	Cincinnati	Duke	Oregon St.	19,153	153,065
1964	UCLA (30-0)	98-83	Duke	Michigan	Kansas St.	10,864	140,790
1965	UCLA (28-2)	91-80	Michigan	Princeton	Wichita St.	13,204	140,673
1966	UTEP (28-1)	72-65	Kentucky	Duke	Utah	14,253	140,925
1967	UCLA (30-0)	79-64	Dayton	Houston	North Carolina	18,892	159,570
1968	UCLA (29-1)	78-55	North Carolina	Ohio St.	Houston	14,438	160,888
1969	UCLA (29-1)	92-72	Purdue	Drake	North Carolina	18,669	165,712
1970	UCLA (28-2)	80-69	Jacksonville	New Mexico St.	St. Bonaventure	14,380	146,794
1971	UCLA (29-1)	68-62	* Villanova	* Western Ky.	Kansas	31,765	207,200
1972	UCLA (30-0)	81-76	Florida St.	North Carolina	Louisville	15,063	147,304
1973	UCLA (30-0)	87-66	Memphis	Indiana	Providence	19,301	163,160
1974	North Carolina St. (30-1)	76-64	Marquette	UCLA	Kansas	15,742	154,112
1975	UCLA (28-3)	92-85	Kentucky	Louisville	Syracuse	15,151	183,857
1976	Indiana (32-0)	86-68	Michigan	UCLA	Rutgers	17,540	202,502
1977	Marquette (25-7)	67-59	North Carolina	UNLV	Charlotte	16,086	241,610
1978	Kentucky (30-2)	94-88	Duke	Arkansas	Notre Dame	18,721	227,149
1979	Michigan St. (26-6)	75-64	Indiana St.	DePaul	Penn	15,410	262,101
1980	Louisville (33-3)	59-54	* UCLA	Purdue	Iowa	16,637	321,260
1981	Indiana (26-9)	63-50	North Carolina	Virginia	LSU	18,276	347,414
1982	North Carolina (32-2)	63-62	Georgetown	+ Houston	+ Louisville	61,612	427,251
1983	North Carolina St. (26-10)	54-52	Houston	+ Georgia	+ Louisville	17,327	364,356
1984	Georgetown (34-3)	84-75	Houston	+ Kentucky	+ Virginia	38,471	397,481
1985	Villanova (25-10)	66-64	Georgetown	+ St. John's (N.Y.)	+* Memphis	23,124	422,519
1986	Louisville (32-7)	72-69	Duke	+ Kansas	+ LSU	16,493	499,704
1987	Indiana (30-4)	74-73	Syracuse	+ UNLV	+ Providence	64,959	654,744
1988	Kansas (27-11)	83-79	Oklahoma	+ Arizona	+ Duke	16,392	558,998
1989	Michigan (30-7)	80-79 (ot)	Seton Hall	+ Duke	+ Illinois	39,187	613,242
1990	UNLV (35-5)	103-73	Duke	+ Arkansas	+ Georgia Tech	17,765	537,138
1991	Duke (32-7)	72-65	Kansas	+ UNLV	+ North Carolina	47,100	665,707
1992	Duke (34-2)	71-51	Michigan	+ Cincinnati	+ Indiana	50,379	580,462
1993	North Carolina (34-4)	77-71	Michigan	+ Kansas	+ Kentucky	64,151	707,719
1994	Arkansas (31-3)	76-72	Duke	+ Arizona	+ Florida	23,674	578,007
1995	UCLA (31-2)	89-78	Arkansas	+ North Carolina	+ Oklahoma St.	38,540	540,101
1996	Kentucky (34-2)	76-67	Syracuse	+ Massachusetts	+ Mississippi St.	19,229	631,834
1997	Arizona (25-9)	84-79 (ot)	Kentucky	+ Minnesota	+ North Carolina	47,028	646,531
1998	Kentucky (35-4)	78-69	Utah	+ North Carolina	+ Stanford	40,509	663,876
1999	Connecticut (34-2)	77-74	Duke	+ Michigan St.	+ Ohio St.	41,340	720,685
2000	Michigan St. (32-7)	89-76	Florida	+ North Carolina	+ Wisconsin	43,116	624,777
2001	Duke (35-4)	82-72	Arizona	+ Maryland	+ Michigan St.	45,994	612,089
2002	Maryland (32-4)	64-52	Indiana	+ Kansas	+ Oklahoma	52,647	720,433
2003	Syracuse (30-5)	81-78	Kansas	+ Marquette	+ Texas	54,524	715,080
2004	Connecticut (33-6)	82-73	Georgia Tech	+ Duke	+ Oklahoma St.	44,468	716,899
2005	North Carolina (33-4)	75-70	Illinois	+ Louisville	+ Michigan St.	47,262	689,317
2006	Florida (33-6)	73-57	UCLA	+ George Mason	+ LSU	43,168	670,254
2007	Florida (35-5)	84-75	Ohio St.	+ Georgetown	+ UCLA	51,458	696,992

+tied for third place; *later vacated

Season	Site of Finals	Coach of Champion	Outstanding Player Award
1939	Evanston, Ill.	Howard Hobson, Oregon	Jimmy Hull, Ohio St.
1940	Kansas City, Mo.	Branch McCracken, Indiana	Marvin Huffman, Indiana
1941	Kansas City, Mo.	Harold Foster, Wisconsin	John Kotz, Wisconsin
1942	Kansas City, Mo.	Everett Dean, Stanford	Howard Dallmar, Stanford
1943	New York City	Everett Shelton, Wyoming	Ken Sailors, Wyoming
1944	New York City	Vadal Peterson, Utah	Arnold Ferrin, Utah
1945	New York City	Hank Iba, Oklahoma St.	Bob Kurland, Oklahoma St.

CHAMPIONSHIPS

Season	Site of Finals	Coach of Champion	Outstanding Player Award
1946	New York City	Hank Iba, Oklahoma St.	Bob Kurland, Oklahoma St.
1947	New York City	Alvin Julian, Holy Cross	George Kaftan, Holy Cross
1948	New York City	Adolph Rupp, Kentucky	Alex Groza, Kentucky
1949	Seattle	Adolph Rupp, Kentucky	Alex Groza, Kentucky
1950	New York City	Nat Holman, CCNY	Irwin Dambrot, CCNY
1951	Minneapolis	Adolph Rupp, Kentucky	Bill Spivey, Kentucky
1952	Seattle	Forrest Allen, Kansas	Clyde Lovellette, Kansas
1953	Kansas City, Mo.	Branch McCracken, Indiana	B.H. Born, Kansas
1954	Kansas City, Mo.	Kenneth Loeffler, La Salle	Tom Gola, La Salle
1955	Kansas City, Mo.	Phil Woolpert, San Francisco	Bill Russell, San Francisco
1956	Evanston, Ill.	Phil Woolpert, San Francisco	Hal Lear, Temple
1957	Kansas City, Mo.	Frank McGuire, North Carolina	Wilt Chamberlain, Kansas
1958	Louisville, Ky.	Adolph Rupp, Kentucky	Elgin Baylor, Seattle
1959	Louisville, Ky.	Pete Newell, California	Jerry West, West Virginia
1960	San Francisco	Fred Taylor, Ohio St.	Jerry Lucas, Ohio St.
1961	Kansas City, Mo.	Edwin Jucker, Cincinnati	Jerry Lucas, Ohio St.
1962	Louisville, Ky.	Edwin Jucker, Cincinnati	Paul Hogue, Cincinnati
1963	Louisville, Ky.	George Ireland, Loyola (Ill.)	Art Heyman, Duke
1964	Kansas City, Mo.	John Wooden, UCLA	Walt Hazzard, UCLA
1965	Portland, Ore.	John Wooden, UCLA	Bill Bradley, Princeton
1966	College Park, Md.	Don Haskins, UTEP	Jerry Chambers, Utah
1967	Louisville, Ky.	John Wooden, UCLA	Lew Alcindor, UCLA
1968	Los Angeles	John Wooden, UCLA	Lew Alcindor, UCLA
1969	Louisville, Ky.	John Wooden, UCLA	Lew Alcindor, UCLA
1970	College Park, Md.	John Wooden, UCLA	Sidney Wicks, UCLA
1971	Houston	John Wooden, UCLA	*Howard Porter, Villanova
1972	Los Angeles	John Wooden, UCLA	Bill Walton, UCLA
1973	St. Louis	John Wooden, UCLA	Bill Walton, UCLA
1974	Greensboro, N.C.	Norm Sloan, North Carolina St.	David Thompson, North Carolina St.
1975	San Diego	John Wooden, UCLA	Richard Washington, UCLA
1976	Philadelphia	Bob Knight, Indiana	Kent Benson, Indiana
1977	Atlanta	Al McGuire, Marquette	Butch Lee, Marquette
1978	St. Louis	Joe B. Hall, Kentucky	Jack Givens, Kentucky
1979	Salt Lake City	Jud Heathcote, Michigan St.	Earvin Johnson, Michigan St.
1980	Indianapolis	Denny Crum, Louisville	Darrell Griffith, Louisville
1981	Philadelphia	Bob Knight, Indiana	Isiah Thomas, Indiana
1982	New Orleans	Dean Smith, North Carolina	James Worthy, North Carolina
1983	Albuquerque, N.M.	Jim Valvano, North Carolina St.	Akeem Olajuwon, Houston
1984	Seattle	John Thompson, Georgetown	Patrick Ewing, Georgetown
1985	Lexington, Ky.	Rollie Massimino, Villanova	Ed Pinckney, Villanova
1986	Dallas	Denny Crum, Louisville	Pervis Ellison, Louisville
1987	New Orleans	Bob Knight, Indiana	Keith Smart, Indiana
1988	Kansas City, Mo.	Larry Brown, Kansas	Danny Manning, Kansas
1989	Seattle	Steve Fisher, Michigan	Glen Rice, Michigan
1990	Denver	Jerry Tarkanian, UNLV	Anderson Hunt, UNLV
1991	Indianapolis	Mike Krzyzewski, Duke	Christian Laettner, Duke
1992	Minneapolis	Mike Krzyzewski, Duke	Bobby Hurley, Duke
1993	New Orleans	Dean Smith, North Carolina	Donald Williams, North Carolina
1994	Charlotte, N.C.	Nolan Richardson, Arkansas	Corliss Williamson, Arkansas
1995	Seattle	Jim Harrick, UCLA	Ed O'Bannon, UCLA
1996	East Rutherford, N.J.	Rick Pitino, Kentucky	Tony Delk, Kentucky
1997	Indianapolis	Lute Olson, Arizona	Miles Simon, Arizona
1998	San Antonio	Tubby Smith, Kentucky	Jeff Sheppard, Kentucky
1999	St. Petersburg, Fla.	Jim Calhoun, Connecticut	Richard Hamilton, Connecticut
2000	Indianapolis	Tom Izzo, Michigan St.	Mateen Cleaves, Michigan St.
2001	Minneapolis	Mike Krzyzewski, Duke	Shane Battier, Duke
2002	Atlanta	Gary Williams, Maryland	Juan Dixon, Maryland
2003	New Orleans	Jim Boeheim, Syracuse	Carmelo Anthony, Syracuse
2004	San Antonio	Jim Calhoun, Connecticut	Emeka Okafor, Connecticut
2005	St. Louis	Roy Williams, North Carolina	Sean May, North Carolina
2006	Indianapolis	Billy Donovan, Florida	Joakim Noah, Florida
2007	Atlanta	Billy Donovan, Florida	Corey Brewer, Florida

*Record later vacated

Individual Leaders Year-by-Year

MOST POINTS

Note: On all percentages of the year-by-year leaders, a player must have played in at least 50 percent of the maximum tournament games. Thus, there is a two-game minimum from 1939-52 and a three-game minimum from 1953 to present.

Season	Player, Team	G	FG	FTM	Pts.	Avg.
1939	Jim Hull, Ohio St.	3	22	14	58	19.3
1940	Howard Engleman, Kansas	3	18	3	39	13.0
1941	John Adams, Arkansas	2	21	6	48	24.0
1942	Jim Pollard, Stanford	2	19	5	43	21.5
	Chet Palmer, Rice	2	20	3	43	21.5
1943	John Hargis, Texas	2	21	17	59	29.5
1944	Aud Brindley, Dartmouth	3	24	4	52	17.3
1945	Bob Kurland, Oklahoma St.	3	30	5	65	21.7

Season	Player, Team	G	FG	FTM	Pts.	Avg.
1946	Bob Kurland, Oklahoma St.	3	28	16	72	24.0
1947	George Kaftan, Holy Cross	3	25	13	63	21.0
1948	Alex Groza, Kentucky	3	23	8	54	18.0
1949	Alex Groza, Kentucky	3	31	20	82	27.3
1950	Sam Ranzino, North Carolina St.	3	25	25	75	25.0
1951	Don Sunderlage, Illinois	4	28	27	83	20.8
1952	Clyde Lovellette, Kansas	4	53	35	141	35.3
1953	Bob Houbregs, Washington	4	57	25	139	34.8
1954	Tom Gola, La Salle	5	38	38	114	22.8
1955	Bill Russell, San Francisco	5	49	20	118	23.6
1956	Hal Lear, Temple	5	63	34	160	32.0
1957	Len Rosenbluth, North Carolina	5	53	34	140	28.0
1958	Elgin Baylor, Seattle	5	48	39	135	27.0
1959	Jerry West, West Virginia	5	57	46	160	32.0
1960	Oscar Robertson, Cincinnati	4	47	28	122	30.5
1961	Billy McGill, Utah	4	49	21	119	29.8
1962	Len Chappell, Wake Forest	5	45	44	134	26.8

Season	Player, Team	G	FG	FTM	Pts.	Avg.
1963	Mel Counts, Oregon St.	5	50	23	123	24.6
1964	Jeff Mullins, Duke	4	50	16	116	29.0
1965	Bill Bradley, Princeton	5	65	47	177	35.4
1966	Jerry Chambers, Utah	4	55	33	143	35.8
1967	Elvin Hayes, Houston	5	57	14	128	25.6
1968	Elvin Hayes, Houston	5	70	27	167	33.4
1969	Rick Mount, Purdue	4	49	24	122	30.5
1970	Austin Carr, Notre Dame	3	68	22	158	52.7
1971	*Jim McDaniels, Western Ky.	5	61	25	147	29.4
	Austin Carr, Notre Dame	3	48	29	125	41.7
1972	Jim Price, Louisville	4	41	21	103	25.8
1973	Ernie DiGregorio, Providence	5	59	10	128	25.6
1974	David Thompson, North Carolina St.	4	38	21	97	24.3
1975	Jim Lee, Syracuse	5	51	17	119	23.8
1976	Scott May, Indiana	5	45	23	113	22.6
1977	Cedric Maxwell, Charlotte	5	39	45	123	24.6
1978	Mike Gminski, Duke	5	45	19	109	21.8
1979	Tony Price, Penn	6	58	26	142	23.7
1980	Joe Barry Carroll, Purdue	6	63	32	158	26.3
1981	Al Wood, North Carolina	5	44	21	109	21.8
1982	Rob Williams, Houston	5	30	28	88	17.6
1983	Dereck Whittenburg, North Carolina St.	6	47	26	120	20.0
1984	Roosevelt Chapman, Dayton	4	35	35	105	26.3
1985	Chris Mullin, St. John's (N.Y.)	5	39	32	110	22.0
1986	Johnny Dawkins, Duke	6	66	21	153	25.5

Season	Player, Team	G	FG	3FG	FTM	Pts.	Avg.
1987	Steve Alford, Indiana	6	42	21	33	138	23.0
	Rony Seikaly, Syracuse	6	87	0	32	138	23.0
1988	Danny Manning, Kansas	6	69	2	23	163	27.2
1989	Glen Rice, Michigan	6	75	27	7	184	30.7
1990	Dennis Scott, Georgia Tech	5	51	24	27	153	30.6
1991	Christian Laettner, Duke	6	37	2	49	125	20.8
1992	Christian Laettner, Duke	6	39	7	30	115	19.2
1993	Donald Williams, North Carolina	6	40	22	16	118	19.7
1994	Khalid Reeves, Arizona	5	45	8	39	137	27.4
1995	Corliss Williamson, Arkansas	6	49	0	27	125	20.8
1996	John Wallace, Syracuse	6	47	7	30	131	21.8
1997	Miles Simon, Arizona	6	42	10	38	132	22.0
1998	Michael Doleac, Utah	6	34	2	45	115	19.2
1999	Richard Hamilton, Connecticut	6	56	7	26	145	24.2
2000	Morris Peterson, Michigan St.	6	35	15	20	105	17.5
2001	Jason Williams, Duke	6	52	23	27	154	25.7
2002	Juan Dixon, Maryland	6	52	22	29	155	25.8
2003	Carmelo Anthony, Syracuse	6	47	10	17	121	20.2
2004	Ben Gordon, Connecticut	6	37	14	39	127	21.2
2005	Sean May, North Carolina	6	52	0	30	134	22.3
2006	Glen Davis, LSU	5	33	1	30	97	19.4
	Joakim Noah, Florida	6	33	0	31	97	16.2
2007	Ron Lewis, Ohio St.	6	34	12	38	108	18.0

*later vacated

HIGHEST SCORING AVERAGE

Season	Player, Team	G	FG	FTM	Pts.	Avg.
1939	Jim Hull, Ohio St.	3	22	14	58	19.3
1940	Howard Engleman, Kansas	3	18	3	39	13.0
	Bob Kinney, Rice	2	12	2	26	13.0
1941	John Adams, Arkansas	2	21	6	48	24.0
1942	Chet Palmer, Rice	2	19	5	43	21.5
	Jim Pollard, Stanford	2	20	3	43	21.5
1943	John Hargis, Texas	2	21	17	59	29.5
1944	Nick Bozolich, Pepperdine	2	17	11	45	22.5
1945	Dick Wilkins, Oregon	2	19	6	44	22.0
1946	Bob Kurland, Oklahoma St.	3	28	16	72	24.0
1947	George Kaftan, Holy Cross	3	25	13	63	21.0
1948	Jack Nichols, Washington	2	13	13	39	19.5
1949	Alex Groza, Kentucky	3	31	20	82	27.3
1950	Sam Ranzino, North Carolina St.	3	25	25	75	25.0
1951	William Kukoy, North Carolina St.	3	25	19	69	23.0
1952	Clyde Lovellette, Kansas	4	53	35	141	35.3
1953	Bob Houbregs, Washington	4	57	25	139	34.8
1954	John Clune, Navy	3	30	19	79	26.3
1955	Terry Rand, Marquette	3	31	11	73	24.3
1956	Hal Lear, Temple	5	63	34	160	32.0
1957	Wilt Chamberlain, Kansas	4	40	41	121	30.3
1958	Wayne Embry, Miami (Ohio)	3	32	19	83	27.7
1959	Jerry West, West Virginia	5	57	46	160	32.0
1960	Jerry West, West Virginia	3	35	35	105	35.0
1961	Billy McGill, Utah	4	49	21	119	29.8
1962	Len Chappell, Wake Forest	5	45	44	134	26.8
1963	Barry Kramer, New York U.	3	31	28	100	33.3
1964	Jeff Mullins, Duke	4	50	16	116	29.0
1965	Bill Bradley, Princeton	5	65	47	147	35.4
1966	Jerry Chambers, Utah	4	55	33	143	35.8

Season	Player, Team	G	FG	FTM	Pts.	Avg.
1967	Lew Alcindor, UCLA	4	39	28	106	26.5
1968	Elvin Hayes, Houston	5	70	27	167	33.4
1969	Rick Mount, Purdue	4	49	24	122	30.5
1970	Austin Carr, Notre Dame	3	68	22	158	52.7
1971	Austin Carr, Notre Dame	3	48	29	125	41.7
1972	*Dwight Lamar, La.-Lafayette	4	41	18	100	33.3
	Jim Price, Louisville	4	41	21	103	25.8
1973	Larry Finch, Memphis	4	34	39	107	26.8
1974	John Shumate, Notre Dame	3	35	16	86	28.7
1975	Adrian Dantley, Notre Dame	3	29	34	92	30.7
1976	Willie Smith, Missouri	3	38	18	94	31.3
1977	Cedric Maxwell, Charlotte	5	39	45	123	24.6
1978	Dave Corzine, DePaul	3	33	16	82	27.3
1979	Larry Bird, Indiana St.	5	52	32	136	27.2
1980	Joe Barry Carroll, Purdue	6	63	32	158	26.3
1981	Al Wood, North Carolina	5	44	21	109	21.8
1982	Oliver Robinson, UAB	3	27	12	66	22.0
1983	Greg Stokes, Iowa	3	24	13	61	20.3
1984	Roosevelt Chapman, Dayton	4	35	35	105	26.3
1985	Kenny Walker, Kentucky	3	28	19	75	25.0
1986	David Robinson, Navy	4	35	40	110	27.5

Season	Player, Team	G	FG	3FG	FTM	Pts.	Avg.
1987	Fennis Dembo, Wyoming	3	25	11	23	84	28.0
1988	Danny Manning, Kansas	6	69	2	23	163	27.2
1989	Glen Rice, Michigan	6	75	27	7	184	30.7
1990	Bo Kimble, Loyola Marymount	4	51	15	26	143	35.8
1991	Terry Dehere, Seton Hall	4	34	12	17	97	24.3
1992	Jamal Mashburn, Kentucky	4	34	6	22	96	24.0
1993	Calbert Cheaney, Indiana	4	40	3	23	106	26.5
1994	Gary Collier, Tulsa	3	30	13	21	94	31.3
1995	Darryl Wilson, Mississippi St.	3	21	9	22	73	24.3
1996	Allen Iverson, Georgetown	4	38	12	23	111	27.8
1997	Dedric Willoughby, Iowa St.	3	24	14	12	74	24.7
1998	Khalid El-Amin, Connecticut	4	30	10	23	93	23.3
1999	Wally Szczerbiak, Miami (Ohio)	3	32	11	15	90	30.0
2000	Marcus Fizer, Iowa St.	3	32	2	14	80	20.0
2001	Jason Williams, Duke	6	52	23	27	154	25.7
2002	Caron Butler, Connecticut	4	32	8	34	106	26.5
2003	Dahntay Jones, Duke	3	25	8	16	74	24.7
2004	Gerry McNamara, Syracuse	3	19	15	27	80	26.7
2005	Joah Tucker, Milwaukee	3	25	6	20	76	25.3
2006	Adam Morrison, Gonzaga	3	26	5	15	73	24.3
2007	Chris Lofton, Tennessee	3	22	13	12	69	23.0

*later vacated

MOST REBOUNDS

Season	Player, Team	G	Reb.	Avg.
1951	Bill Spivey, Kentucky	4	65	16.3
1957	John Green, Michigan St.	4	77	19.3
1958	Elgin Baylor, Seattle	5	91	18.2
1959	Jerry West, West Virginia	5	73	14.6
1960	Tom Sanders, New York U.	5	83	16.6
1961	Jerry Lucas, Ohio St.	4	73	18.3
1962	Len Chappell, Wake Forest	5	86	17.2
1963	Nate Thurmond, Bowling Green	3	70	23.3
	Vic Rouse, Loyola (Ill.)	5	70	14.0
1964	Paul Silas, Creighton	3	57	19.0
1965	Bill Bradley, Princeton	5	57	11.4
1966	Jerry Chambers, Utah	4	56	14.0
1967	Don May, Dayton	5	82	16.4
1968	Elvin Hayes, Houston	5	97	19.4
1969	Lew Alcindor, UCLA	4	64	16.0
1970	Artis Gilmore, Jacksonville	5	93	18.6
1971	*Clarence Glover, Western Ky.	5	89	17.8
	Sidney Wicks, UCLA	4	52	13.0
1972	Bill Walton, UCLA	4	64	16.0
1973	Bill Walton, UCLA	4	58	14.5
1974	Tom Burleson, North Carolina St.	4	61	15.3
1975	Richard Washington, UCLA	5	60	12.0
1976	Phil Hubbard, Michigan	5	61	12.2
1977	Cedric Maxwell, Charlotte	5	64	12.8
1978	Eugene Banks, Duke	5	50	10.0
1979	Larry Bird, Indiana St.	5	67	13.4
1980	*Mike Sanders, UCLA	6	60	10.0
1981	Cliff Levingston, Wichita St.	4	53	13.3
1982	Clyde Drexler, Houston	5	42	8.4
1983	Akeem Olajuwon, Houston	5	65	13.0
1984	Akeem Olajuwon, Houston	5	57	11.4
1985	Ed Pinckney, Villanova	6	48	8.0
1986	Pervis Ellison, Louisville	6	57	9.5
1987	Derrick Coleman, Syracuse	6	73	12.2
1988	Danny Manning, Kansas	6	56	9.3

Season	Player, Team	G	Reb.	Avg.
1989	Daryll Walker, Seton Hall	6	58	9.7
1990	Larry Johnson, UNLV	6	75	12.5
1991	Larry Johnson, UNLV	5	51	10.2
1992	*Chris Webber, Michigan	6	58	9.7
1993	*Chris Webber, Michigan	6	68	11.3
1994	Cherokee Parks, Duke	6	55	9.2
1995	Ed O'Bannon, UCLA	6	54	9.0
1996	Tim Duncan, Wake Forest	4	52	13.0
1997	A.J. Bramlett, Arizona	6	62	10.3
1998	Antawn Jamison, North Carolina	5	63	12.6
1999	Elton Brand, Duke	6	55	9.2
2000	Brendan Haywood, North Carolina	5	48	9.6
2001	Shane Battier, Duke	6	61	10.2
2002	Drew Gooden, Kansas	5	61	12.2
2003	Nick Collison, Kansas	6	81	13.5
2004	Emeka Okafor, Connecticut	6	68	11.3
2005	Sean May, North Carolina	6	64	10.7
2006	Al Horford, Florida	6	60	10.0
2007	Al Horford, Florida	6	68	11.3

*later vacated

HIGHEST REBOUNDING AVERAGE

Season	Player, Team	G	Reb.	Avg.
1951	Bill Spivey, Kentucky	4	65	16.3
1957	John Green, Michigan St.	4	77	19.3
1958	Elgin Baylor, Seattle	5	91	18.2
1959	Oscar Robertson, Cincinnati	4	63	15.8
1960	Howard Jolliff, Ohio	3	64	21.3
1961	Jerry Lucas, Ohio St.	4	73	18.3
1962	Mel Counts, Oregon St.	3	53	17.7
1963	Nate Thurmond, Bowling Green	3	70	23.3
1964	Paul Silas, Creighton	3	57	19.0
1965	James Ware, Oklahoma City	3	55	18.3
1966	Elvin Hayes, Houston	3	50	16.7
1967	Don May, Dayton	5	82	16.4
1968	Elvin Hayes, Houston	5	97	19.4
1969	Lew Alcindor, UCLA	4	64	16.0
1970	Artis Gilmore, Jacksonville	5	93	18.6
1971	*Clarence Glover, Western Ky.	5	89	17.8
	Collis Jones, Notre Dame	3	49	16.3
1972	Bill Walton, UCLA	4	64	16.0
1973	Bill Walton, UCLA	4	58	14.5
1974	Marvin Barnes, Providence	3	51	17.0
1975	Mike Franklin, Cincinnati	3	49	16.3
1976	Al Fleming, Arizona	3	39	13.0
1977	Phil Hubbard, Michigan	3	45	15.0
1978	Greg Kelser, Michigan St.	3	37	12.3
1979	Larry Bird, Indiana St.	5	67	13.4
1980	Durand Macklin, LSU	3	31	10.3
1981	Cliff Levingston, Wichita St.	4	53	13.3
1982	Ed Pinckney, Villanova	3	30	10.0
1983	Akeem Olajuwon, Houston	5	65	13.0
1984	*Keith Lee, Memphis	3	37	12.3
	Akeem Olajuwon, Houston	5	57	11.4
1985	Karl Malone, Louisiana Tech	3	40	13.3
1986	David Robinson, Navy	4	47	11.8
1987	Derrick Coleman, Syracuse	6	73	12.2
1988	Pervis Ellison, Louisville	3	33	11.0
1989	Pervis Ellison, Louisville	3	31	10.3
	Stacey King, Oklahoma	3	31	10.3
1990	Dale Davis, Clemson	3	44	14.7
1991	Byron Houston, Oklahoma St.	3	36	12.0
1992	Doug Edwards, Florida St.	3	32	10.7
1993	*Chris Webber, Michigan	6	68	11.3
1994	*Juwan Howard, Michigan	6	51	12.8
1995	Tim Duncan, Wake Forest	3	43	14.3
1996	Tim Duncan, Wake Forest	4	52	13.0
1997	Paul Pierce, Kansas	3	36	12.0
1998	Antawn Jamison, North Carolina	5	63	12.6
1999	Eduardo Najera, Oklahoma	3	35	11.7
2000	Eric Coley, Tulsa	4	43	10.8
2001	Dan Gadzuric, UCLA	3	36	12.0
2002	Drew Gooden, Kansas	5	61	12.2
2003	Nick Collison, Kansas	6	81	13.5
2004	Emeka Okafor, Connecticut	6	68	11.3
2005	Paul Davis, Michigan St.	5	58	11.6
2006	P.J. Tucker, Texas	4	50	12.5
2007	Al Horford, Florida	6	68	11.3
	Taj Gibson, Southern California	3	34	11.3

*later vacated

TOP 10 INDIVIDUAL LEADERS

Single-Game

POINTS
61, Austin Carr, Notre Dame vs. Ohio, 1st R, 3-7-1970
58, Bill Bradley, Princeton vs. Wichita St., N3d, 3-20-1965
56, Oscar Robertson, Cincinnati vs. Arkansas, R3d, 3-15-1958
52, Austin Carr, Notre Dame vs. Kentucky, RSF, 3-12-1970
52, Austin Carr, Notre Dame vs. TCU, 1st R, 3-13-1971
50, David Robinson, Navy vs. Michigan, 1st R, 3-12-1987
49, Elvin Hayes, Houston vs. Loyola (Ill.), 1st R, 3-9-1968
48, Hal Lear, Temple vs. SMU, N3d, 3-23-1956
47, Austin Carr, Notre Dame vs. Houston, R3d, 3-20-1971
46, Dave Corzine, DePaul vs. Louisville, RSF, 3-17-1978 (2 ot)

REBOUNDS
34, Fred Cohen, Temple vs. Connecticut, RSF, 3-16-1956
31, Nate Thurmond, Bowling Green vs. Mississippi St., R3d, 3-16-1963
30, Jerry Lucas, Ohio St. vs. Kentucky, RF, 3-18-1961
29, Toby Kimball, Connecticut vs. St. Joseph's, 1st R, 3-8-1965
28, Elvin Hayes, Houston vs. Pacific, R3d, 3-12-1966
27, Bill Russell, San Francisco vs. Iowa, CH, 3-19-1956
27, John Green, Michigan St. vs. Notre Dame, RSF, 3-15-1957
27, Paul Silas, Creighton vs. Oklahoma City, 1st R, 3-9-1964
27, Elvin Hayes, Houston vs. Loyola (Ill.), 1st R, 3-9-1968
26, Howard Jolliff, Ohio vs. Georgia Tech, RSF, 3-11-1960
26, Phil Hubbard, Michigan vs. Detroit, RSF, 3-17-1977

REBOUNDS SINCE 1973
26, Phil Hubbard, Michigan vs. Detroit, RSF, 3-17-1977
24, Tom Burleson, North Carolina St. vs. Providence, RSF, 3-14-1974
23, Kent Benson, Indiana vs. UCLA, RF, 3-22-1975
22, Larry Kenon, Memphis vs. Providence, NSF, 3-26-1973
22, Akeem Olajuwon, Houston vs. Louisville, NSF, 1983
22, Tim Duncan, Wake Forest vs. Oklahoma St., RSF, 3-24-1995
22, Tim Duncan, Wake Forest vs. St. Mary's (Cal.), 1st R, 3-14-1997
21, Marvin Barnes, Providence vs. Furman, R3d, 3-16-1974
21, Leon Douglas, Alabama vs. Arizona St., 1st R, 3-15-1975
21, Ralph Sampson, Virginia vs. UAB, RSF, 3-18-1982
21, Loy Vaught, Michigan vs. Illinois St., 1st R, 3-16-1990
21, Joy Smith, Maryland vs. Texas, 2nd R, 3-18-1995
21, Nick Collison, Kansas vs. Syracuse, CH, 4-7-2003

Series

POINTS
184, Glen Rice, Michigan, 1989 (6 games)
177, Bill Bradley, Princeton, 1965 (5)
167, Elvin Hayes, Houston, 1968 (5)
163, Danny Manning, Kansas, 1988 (6)
160, Hal Lear, Temple, 1956 (5)
160, Jerry West, West Virginia, 1959 (5)
158, Austin Carr, Notre Dame, 1970 (3)
158, Joe Barry Carroll, Purdue, 1980 (6)
155, Juan Dixon, Maryland, 2002 (6)
154, Jason Williams, Duke, 2001 (6)

SCORING AVERAGE
52.7 (158 points in 3 games), Austin Carr, Notre Dame, 1970
41.7 (125 in 3), Austin Carr, Notre Dame, 1971
35.8 (143 in 4), Jerry Chambers, Utah, 1966
35.8 (143 in 4), Bo Kimble, Loyola Marymount, 1990
35.4 (177 in 5), Bill Bradley, Princeton, 1965
35.3 (141 in 4), Clyde Lovellette, Kansas, 1952
35.0 (140 in 4), Gail Goodrich, UCLA, 1965
35.0 (105 in 3), Jerry West, West Virginia, 1960
34.8 (139 in 4), Bob Houbregs, Washington, 1953
33.4 (167 in 5), Elvin Hayes, Houston, 1968

REBOUNDS
97, Elvin Hayes, Houston, 1968 (5 games)
93, Artis Gilmore, Jacksonville, 1970 (5)
91, Elgin Baylor, Seattle, 1958 (5)
90, Sam Lacey, New Mexico St., 1970 (5)
89, *Clarence Glover, Western Ky., 1971 (5)
86, Len Chappell, Wake Forest, 1962 (5)
83, Tom Sanders, New York U., 1960 (5)
82, Don May, Dayton, 1967 (5)
81, Nick Collison, Kansas, 2003 (6)
77, John Green, Michigan St., 1957 (4)

REBOUNDS SINCE 1973

81, Nick Collison, Kansas, 2003 (6 games)
75, Larry Johnson, UNLV, 1990 (6)
73, Derrick Coleman, Syracuse, 1987 (6)
68, *Chris Webber, Michigan, 1993 (6)
68, Emeka Okafor, Connecticut, 2004 (6)
67, Larry Bird, Indiana St., 1979 (5)
65, Akeem Olajuwon, Houston, 1983 (5)
64, Cedric Maxwell, Charlotte, 1977 (5)
64, Sean May, North Carolina, 2005 (6)
63, Antawn Jamison, North Carolina, 1998 (5)

REBOUND AVERAGE (MIN. 3 GAMES)

23.3 (70 rebounds in 3 games), Nate Thurmond, Bowling Green, 1963
21.3 (64 in 3), Howard Jolliff, Ohio, 1960
19.4 (97 in 5), Elvin Hayes, Houston, 1968
19.3 (77 in 4), John Green, Michigan St., 1957
19.0 (57 in 3), Paul Silas, Creighton, 1964
18.8 (75 in 4), Lew Alcindor, UCLA, 1968
18.6 (93 in 5), Artis Gilmore, Jacksonville, 1970
18.3 (55 in 3), James Ware, Oklahoma City, 1965
18.3 (73 in 4), Jerry Lucas, Ohio St., 1961
18.2 (91 in 5), Elgin Baylor, Seattle, 1958

REBOUND AVERAGE SINCE 1973 (MIN. 3 GAMES)

17.0 (51 rebounds in 3 games), Marvin Barnes, Providence, 1974
16.3 (49 in 3), Mike Franklin, Cincinnati, 1975
15.3 (61 in 4), Tom Burleson, North Carolina St., 1974
15.0 (45 in 3), Phil Hubbard, Michigan, 1977
14.7 (44 in 3), Dale Davis, Clemson, 1990
14.5 (58 in 4), Bill Walton, UCLA, 1973
14.3 (57 in 4), Larry Kenon, Memphis, 1973
14.3 (43 in 3), Tim Duncan, Wake Forest, 1995
14.0 (56 in 4), Ronnie Robinson, Memphis, 1973
14.0 (42 in 3), Kent Benson, Indiana, 1975

Career

POINTS

407, Christian Laettner, Duke, 1989-92 (23 games)
358, Elvin Hayes, Houston, 1966-68 (13)
328, Danny Manning, Kansas, 1985-88 (16)
324, Oscar Robertson, Cincinnati, 1958-60 (10)
308, Glen Rice, Michigan, 1986-89 (13)
304, Lew Alcindor, UCLA, 1967-69 (12)
303, Bill Bradley, Princeton, 1963-65 (9)
303, Corliss Williamson, Arkansas, 1993-95 (15)
294, Juan Dixon, Maryland, 1999-2002 (16)
289, Austin Carr, Notre Dame, 1969-71 (7)

SCORING AVERAGE (MIN. 6 GAMES)

41.3 (289 points in 7 games), Austin Carr, Notre Dame, 1969-71
33.7 (303 in 9), Bill Bradley, Princeton, 1963-65
32.4 (324 in 10), Oscar Robertson, Cincinnati, 1958-60
30.6 (275 in 9), Jerry West, West Virginia, 1958-60
30.5 (183 in 6), Bob Pettit, LSU, 1953-54
29.3 (176 in 6), Dan Issel, Kentucky, 1968-70
29.3 (176 in 6), *Jim McDaniels, Western Ky., 1970-71
29.2 (175 in 6), Dwight Lamar, La.-Lafayette, 1972-73
29.1 (204 in 7), Bo Kimble, Loyola Marymount, 1988-90
28.6 (200 in 7), David Robinson, Navy, 1985-87

REBOUNDS

222, Elvin Hayes, Houston, 1966-68 (13 games)
201, Lew Alcindor, UCLA, 1967-69 (12)
197, Jerry Lucas, Ohio St., 1960-62 (12)
181, Nick Collison, Kansas, 2000-03 (16)
176, Bill Walton, UCLA, 1972-74 (12)
169, Christian Laettner, Duke, 1989-92 (23)
165, Tim Duncan, Wake Forest, 1994-97 (11)
160, Paul Hogue, Cincinnati, 1960-62 (12)
157, Sam Lacey, New Mexico St., 1968-70 (11)
155, Derrick Coleman, Syracuse, 1987-90 (14)

REBOUNDS SINCE 1973

181, Nick Collison, Kansas, 2000-03 (16 games)
169, Christian Laettner, Duke, 1989-92 (23)
165, Tim Duncan, Wake Forest, 1994-97 (11)
155, Derrick Coleman, Syracuse, 1987-90 (14)
153, Akeem Olajuwon, Houston, 1982-84 (15)
144, Patrick Ewing, Georgetown, 1982-85 (18)
141, Emeka Okafor, Connecticut, 2002-04 (13)
138, Marques Johnson, UCLA, 1974-77 (16)
138, George Lynch, North Carolina, 1990-93 (17)
137, Lonny Baxter, Maryland, 1999-2002 (16)
137, Al Horford, Florida, 2004-07 (14)

REBOUNDING AVERAGE (MIN. 6 GAMES)

19.7 (118 rebounds in 6 games), John Green, Michigan St., 1957-59
19.2 (115 in 6), Artis Gilmore, Jacksonville, 1970-71
18.5 (111 in 6), Paul Silas, Creighton, 1962-64
17.1 (137 in 8), Len Chappell, Wake Forest, 1961-62
17.1 (222 in 13), Elvin Hayes, Houston, 1966-68
16.8 (201 in 12), Lew Alcindor, UCLA, 1967-69
16.4 (197 in 12), Jerry Lucas, Ohio St., 1960-62
15.0 (165 in 11), Tim Duncan, Wake Forest, 1994-97
14.7 (176 in 12), Bill Walton, UCLA, 1972-74
14.3 (157 in 11), Sam Lacey, New Mexico St., 1968-70

REBOUNDING AVERAGE SINCE 1973 (MIN. 7 GAMES)

15.0 (165 in 11), Tim Duncan, Wake Forest, 1994-97
14.1 (99 in 7), Marvin Barnes, Providence, 1973-74
14.0 (112 in 8), Bill Walton, UCLA, 1973-74
13.3 (106 in 8), Phil Hubbard, Michigan, 1976-77
12.3 (86 in 7), David Robinson, Navy, 1985-87
12.0 (96 in 8), Maurice Lucas, Marquette, 1973-74
11.5 (126 in 11), Larry Johnson, UNLV, 1990-91
11.4 (114 in 10), Shelden Williams, Duke, 2004-07
11.3 (181 in 16), Nick Collison, Kansas, 2000-03
11.3 (113 in 10), Ralph Sampson, Virginia, 1981-83
11.3 (90 in 8), Greg Kelser, Michigan St., 1978-79

CH-National Championship Game
NSF-National Semifinal Game
N3d-National Third Place Game
RF-Regional Final Game
RSF-Regional Semifinal Game
R3d-Regional Third Place Game
2nd R-Second Round Game
1st R-First Round Game
OR-Opening Round Game

*-Record later vacated

INDIVIDUAL RECORDS

Single Game

POINTS
61—Austin Carr, Notre Dame vs. Ohio, 1st R, 3-7-1970

POINTS BY TWO TEAMMATES
85—Austin Carr (61) and Collis Jones (24), Notre Dame vs. Ohio, 1st R, 3-7-1970

POINTS BY TWO OPPOSING PLAYERS
96—Austin Carr (52), Notre Dame, and Dan Issel (44), Kentucky, RSF, 3-12-1970

FIELD GOALS
25—Austin Carr, Notre Dame vs. Ohio, 1st R, 3-7-1970

FIELD GOALS ATTEMPTED
44—Austin Carr, Notre Dame vs. Ohio, 1st R, 3-7-1970

FIELD-GOAL PERCENTAGE
(Minimum 11 FGM)
100% (11-11)—Kenny Walker, Kentucky vs. Western Ky., 2nd R, 3-16-1986; Marcus Williams, Connecticut vs. Washington, RSF, 3-24-2006 (ot)

THREE-POINT FIELD GOALS
11—Jeff Fryer, Loyola Marymount vs. Michigan, 2nd R, 3-18-1990

THREE-POINT FIELD GOALS ATTEMPTED
22—Jeff Fryer, Loyola Marymount vs. Arkansas, 1st R, 3-16-1989

THREE-POINT FIELD-GOAL PERCENTAGE
(Minimum 8 3FGM)
100% (8-8)—John Goldsberry, UNC Wilmington vs. Maryland, 1st R, 3-21-2003

FREE THROWS
23—Bob Carney, Bradley vs. Colorado, RSF, 3-12-1954; Travis Mays, Texas vs. Georgia, 1st R, 3-17-1990

FREE THROWS ATTEMPTED
27—David Robinson, Navy vs. Syracuse, 2nd R, 3-16-1986; Travis Mays, Texas vs. Georgia, 1st R, 3-17-1990

FREE-THROW PERCENTAGE
(Minimum 16 FTM)
100% (16-16)—Bill Bradley, Princeton vs. St. Joseph's, 1st R, 3-11-1963; Fennis Dembo, Wyoming vs. UCLA, 2nd R, 3-14-1987

REBOUNDS
34—Fred Cohen, Temple vs. Connecticut, RSF, 3-16-1956

REBOUNDS SINCE 1973
26—Phil Hubbard, Michigan vs. Detroit, RSF, 3-17-1977

ASSISTS
18—Mark Wade, UNLV vs. Indiana, NSF, 3-28-1987

BLOCKED SHOTS
11—Shaquille O'Neal, LSU vs. BYU, 1st R, 3-19-1992

STEALS
8—Darrell Hawkins, Arkansas vs. Holy Cross, 1st R, 3-18-1993; Grant Hill, Duke vs. California, 2nd R, 3-20-1993; Duane Clemens, Ball St. vs. UCLA, 1st R, 3-16-2000

Series

(Three-game minimum for averages and percentages)

POINTS
184—Glen Rice, Michigan, 1989 (6 games)

SCORING AVERAGE
52.7 (158 points in 3 games)—Austin Carr, Notre Dame, 1970

FIELD GOALS
75—Glen Rice, Michigan, 1989 (6 games)

FIELD GOALS ATTEMPTED
138—*Jim McDaniels, Western Ky., 1971 (5 games)
137—Elvin Hayes, Houston, 1968 (5)

FIELD-GOAL PERCENTAGE
(Minimum 5 FGM per game)
78.8% (26-33)—Christian Laettner, Duke, 1989 (5 games)

THREE-POINT FIELD GOALS
27—Glen Rice, Michigan, 1989 (6 games)

THREE-POINT FIELD GOALS ATTEMPTED
66—Jason Williams, Duke, 2001 (6 games)

THREE-POINT FIELD-GOAL PERCENTAGE
(Minimum 1.5 3FGM per game, 2.0 3FGM Since 2001)
100% (6-6)—Ranzino Smith, North Carolina, 1987 (4 games)

FREE THROWS
55—Bob Carney, Bradley, 1954 (5 games)

FREE THROWS ATTEMPTED
71—Jerry West, West Virginia, 1959 (5 games)

PERFECT FREE-THROW PERCENTAGE
(Minimum 2.5 FTM per game)
100% (35-35)—Arthur Lee, Stanford, 1998 (5 games)

REBOUNDS
97—Elvin Hayes, Houston, 1968 (5 games)

REBOUNDS SINCE 1973
81—Nick Collison, Kansas, 2003 (6 games)

REBOUND AVERAGE
23.3 (70 rebounds in 3 games)—Nate Thurmond, Bowling Green, 1963

REBOUND AVERAGE SINCE 1973
17.0 (51 rebounds in 3 games)—Marvin Barnes, Providence, 1974

ASSISTS
61—Mark Wade, UNLV, 1987 (5 games)

BLOCKED SHOTS
29—Joakim Noah, Florida, 2006 (6 games)

STEALS
23—Mookie Blaylock, Oklahoma, 1988 (6 games)

Career

(Two-year minimum for averages and percentages)

POINTS
407—Christian Laettner, Duke, 1989-92 (23 games)

SCORING AVERAGE
(Minimum 6 games)
41.3—Austin Carr, Notre Dame, 1969-71 (289 points in 7 games)

FIELD GOALS
152—Elvin Hayes, Houston, 1966-68

FIELD GOALS ATTEMPTED
310—Elvin Hayes, Houston, 1966-68

FIELD-GOAL PERCENTAGE
(Minimum 70 made)
68.6% (109-159)—Bill Walton, UCLA, 1972-74

THREE-POINT FIELD GOALS
47—Lee Humphrey, Florida, 2004-07 (15 games)

THREE-POINT FIELD GOALS ATTEMPTED
115—J.J. Redick, Duke, 2003-06 (14 games)

THREE-POINT FIELD-GOAL PERCENTAGE
(Minimum 30 made)
56.5% (35-62)—Glen Rice, Michigan, 1986-89 (13 games)
(Minimum 20 made)
65.0% (26-40)—William Scott, Kansas St., 1987-88 (5 games)

FREE THROWS MADE
142—Christian Laettner, Duke, 1989-92 (23 games)

FREE THROWS ATTEMPTED
167—Christian Laettner, Duke, 1989-92 (23 games)

FREE-THROW PERCENTAGE
(Minimum 50 made)
93.5% (58-62)—Arthur Lee, Stanford, 1996-99 (12 games)
(Minimum 30 made)
97.7% (42-43)—Keith Van Horn, Utah, 1995-97 (8 games)

REBOUNDS
222—Elvin Hayes, Houston, 1966-68 (13 games)

REBOUNDS SINCE 1973
181—Nick Collison, Kansas, 2000-03 (16 games)

REBOUNDING AVERAGE
(Minimum 6 games)
19.7—John Green, Michigan St., 1957-59 (118 rebounds in 6 games)

REBOUNDING AVERAGE SINCE 1973
(Minimum 6 games)
15.0—Tim Duncan, Wake Forest, 1994-97 (165 rebounds in 11 games)

ASSISTS
145—Bobby Hurley, Duke, 1990-93 (20 games)

BLOCKED SHOTS
50—Tim Duncan, Wake Forest, 1994-97 (11 games)

STEALS
39—Grant Hill, Duke, 1991-94 (20 games)

GAMES PLAYED
23—Christian Laettner, Duke, 1989--92

TEAM RECORDS

Single Game

POINTS
149—Loyola Marymount vs. Michigan (115), 2nd R, 3-18-1990

FEWEST POINTS
20—North Carolina vs. Pittsburgh (26), RF, 3-21-1941

WINNING MARGIN
69—Loyola (Ill.) (111) vs. Tennessee Tech (42), 1st R, 3-11-1963

SMALLEST WINNING MARGIN
1—167 tied (most recent: three in 2007)

POINTS SCORED BY LOSING TEAM
120—Utah vs. *St. Joseph's (127), N3d, 3-25-1961 (4 ot)

FIELD GOALS
52—Iowa vs. Notre Dame, R3d, 3-14-1970

FEWEST FIELD GOALS
8—Springfield vs. Indiana, RF, 3-20-1940

FIELD GOALS ATTEMPTED
112—Marshall vs. La.-Lafayette, 1st R, 3-11-1972

FIELD-GOAL PERCENTAGE
80.0% (28-35)—Oklahoma St. vs. Tulane, 2nd R, 3-22-1992

LOWEST FIELD-GOAL PERCENTAGE
12.7% (8-63)—Springfield vs. Indiana, RF, 3-20-1940

THREE-POINT FIELD GOALS
21—Loyola Marymount vs. Michigan, 2nd R, 3-18-1990

THREE-POINT FIELD GOALS ATTEMPTED
43—St. Joseph's vs. Boston College, 2nd R, 3-15-1997 (ot)

THREE-POINT FIELD-GOAL PERCENTAGE
(Minimum 7 3FGM)
88.9% (8-9)—Kansas St. vs. Georgia, 1st R, 3-12-1987

FREE THROWS
43—Arizona vs. Illinois, RF, 3-25-2001

FREE THROWS ATTEMPTED
56—Arizona vs. Illinois, RF, 3-25-2001

FREE-THROW PERCENTAGE
(Minimum 22 FTM)
100% (22-22)—Fordham vs. South Carolina, R3d, 3-20-1971

REBOUNDS
86—Notre Dame vs. Tennessee Tech, 1st R, 3-11-1958

REBOUND MARGIN
42—Notre Dame (86) vs. Tennessee Tech (44), 1st R, 3-11-1958

ASSISTS
36—North Carolina vs. Loyola Marymount, 2nd R, 3-19-1988

BLOCKED SHOTS
14—Kentucky vs. UCLA, RSF, 3-20-1998

STEALS
19—Providence vs. Austin Peay, 2nd R, 3-14-1987; Connecticut vs. Boston U., 1st R, 3-15-1990; Washington vs. Connecticut, RSF, 3-24-2006

PERSONAL FOULS
41—Dayton vs. Illinois, RSF, 3-21-1952

PLAYERS DISQUALIFIED
6—Kansas vs. Notre Dame, 1st R, 3-15-1975; Illinois vs. Arizona, RF, 3-25-2001

Single Game, Both Teams

POINTS
264—Loyola Marymount (149) vs. Michigan (115), 2nd R, 3-18-1990

FEWEST POINTS
46—Pittsburgh (26) vs. North Carolina (20), RF, 3-21-1941

FIELD GOALS
97—Iowa (52) vs. Notre Dame (45), R3d, 3-14-1970

FIELD GOALS ATTEMPTED
204—Utah (103) vs. *St. Joseph's (101), N3d, 3-25-1961 (4 ot)

THREE-POINT FIELD GOALS
29—West Virginia (18) vs. Louisville (11), RF, 3-26-2005

THREE-POINT FIELD GOALS ATTEMPTED
66—UCLA (36) vs. Cincinnati (30), 2nd R, 3-17-2002

FREE THROWS
69—Morehead St. (37) vs. Pittsburgh (32), 1st R, 3-11-1957

FREE THROWS ATTEMPTED
105—Morehead St. (53) vs. Iowa (52), RSF, 3-16-1956

REBOUNDS
134—Marshall (68) vs. *La.-Lafayette (66), 1st R, 3-11-1972
132—Pacific (67) vs. Houston (65), R3d, 3-12-1966

ASSISTS
58—UNLV (35) vs. Loyola Marymount (23), RF, 3-25-1990

BLOCKED SHOTS
20—Kentucky (14) vs. UCLA (6), RSF, 3-20-1998

STEALS
32—Kansas (17) vs. UCLA (15), RF, 3-24-2007

PERSONAL FOULS
68—Iowa (35) vs. Morehead St. (33), RSF, 3-16-1956

Series

(Three-game minimum for averages and percentages)

POINTS
571—UNLV, 1990 (6 games)

SCORING AVERAGE
105.8—Loyola Marymount, 1990 (423 points in 4 games)

SCORING MARGIN
23.75—UCLA, 1967 (4 games)

FIELD GOALS
218,-UNLV—1977 (5 games)

FIELD GOALS ATTEMPTED
442—*Western Ky., 1971 (5 games)
441—UNLV, 1977 (5)

FIELD-GOAL PERCENTAGE
60.4% (113-187)—North Carolina, 1975 (3 games)

THREE-POINT FIELD GOALS
60—Arkansas, 1995 (6 games); Duke, 2001 (6)

THREE-POINT FIELD GOALS ATTEMPTED
175—Duke, 2001 (6 games)

THREE-POINT FIELD-GOAL PERCENTAGE
(Minimum 12 3FGM)
60.9% (14-23)—Indiana, 1989 (3 games)
(Minimum 30 3FGM)
51.9% (40-77)—Kansas, 1993 (5 games)

FREE THROWS
146—Bradley, 1954 (5 games)

FREE THROWS ATTEMPTED
194—Bradley, 1954 (5 games)

FREE-THROW PERCENTAGE
(Minimum 30 FTM)
87.0% (47-54)—St. John's (N.Y.), 1969 (3 games)

REBOUNDS
306—Houston, 1968 (5 games)

ASSISTS
143—Kentucky, 1996 (6 games)

BLOCKED SHOTS
48—Kentucky, 1998 (6 games)

STEALS
72—Oklahoma, 1988 (6 games)

PERSONAL FOULS
150—Penn, 1979 (6 games)

CH—National Championship Game
NSF—National Semifinal Game
N3d—National Third Place Game
RF—Regional Final Game
RSF—Regional Semifinal Game
R3d—Regional Third Place Game
2nd R—Second Round Game
1st R—First Round Game
OR—Opening Round Game

Record later vacated

All-Time Division I Tournament Records

RECORD OF EACH TEAM COACH BY COACH
(296 Teams)

	Yrs.	W	L	CH	2D	3d%	4th	RR
AIR FORCE								
Bob Spear (DePauw 1941) 1960, 62	2	0	2	0	0	0	0	0
Joe Scott (Princeton 1987) 2004	1	0	1	0	0	0	0	0
Jeff Bzdelik (Ill.-Chicago 1976) 2006	1	0	1	0	0	0	0	0
TOTAL	4	0	4	0	0	0	0	0
AKRON								
Bob Huggins (West Virginia 1977) 1986	1	0	1	0	0	0	0	0
TOTAL	1	0	1	0	0	0	0	0
ALABAMA*								
C.M. Newton (Kentucky 1952) 1975, 76	2	1	2	0	0	0	0	0
Wimp Sanderson (North Ala. 1959) 1982, 83,84, 85, 86, 87*, 89, 90, 91, 92	10	12	10	0	0	0	0	0
David Hobbs (VCU 1971) 1994,95	2	2	2	0	0	0	0	0
Mark Gottfried (Alabama 1987) 2002, 03, 04RR, 05, 06	5	5	5	0	0	0	0	1
TOTAL	19	20	19	0	0	0	0	1
ALABAMA A&M								
L. Vann Pettaway (Alabama A&M 1980) 2005	1	0	1	0	0	0	0	0
TOTAL	1	0	1	0	0	0	0	0
ALABAMA ST.								
Rob Spivery (Ashland 1972) 2001, 04	2	0	2	0	0	0	0	0
TOTAL	2	0	2	0	0	0	0	0
UAB								
Gene Bartow (Truman 1953) 1981, 82RR, 83,84, 85, 86, 87, 90, 94	9	6	9	0	0	0	0	1
Murry Bartow (UAB 1985) 1999	1	0	1	0	0	0	0	0
Mike Anderson (Tulsa 1982) 2004, 05, 06	3	3	3	0	0	0	0	0
TOTAL	13	9	13	0	0	0	0	1
ALBANY (N.Y.)								
Will Brown (Dowling 1995) 2006, 07	2	0	2	0	0	0	0	0
TOTAL	2	0	2	0	0	0	0	0
ALCORN ST.								
Davey L. Whitney (Kentucky St. 1953) 1980, 82, 83, 84, 99, 2002	6	3	6	0	0	0	0	0
TOTAL	6	3	6	0	0	0	0	0
APPALACHIAN ST.								
Bobby Cremins (South Carolina 1970) 1979	1	0	1	0	0	0	0	0
Buzz Peterson (North Carolina 1986) 2000	1	0	1	0	0	0	0	0
TOTAL	2	0	2	0	0	0	0	0
ARIZONA*								
Fred Enke (Minnesota 1921) 1951	1	0	1	0	0	0	0	0
Fred Snowden [Wayne St. (Mich.) 1958] 1976RR, 77	2	2	2	0	0	0	0	1
Lute Olson (Augsburg 1957) 1985, 86, 87, 88-T3d, 89, 90, 91, 92, 93, 94-T3d, 95, 96, 97-CH, 98RR, 99*, 2000, 01-2d, 02, 03RR, 04, 05RR, 06, 07	23	39	22	1	1	2	0	3
TOTAL	26	41	25	1	1	2	0	4
ARIZONA ST.*								
Ned Wulk (Wis.-La Crosse 1942) 1958, 61RR, 62, 63RR, 64, 73, 75RR, 80, 81	9	8	10	0	0	0	0	3
Bill Frieder (Michigan 1964) 1991, 95*	2	3	2	0	0	0	0	0
Rob Evans (New Mexico St. 1968) 2003	1	1	1	0	0	0	0	0
TOTAL	12	12	13	0	0	0	0	3
ARKANSAS								
Eugene Lambert (Arkansas 1929) 1945-T3d, 49RR	2	2	2	0	0	1	0	1
Glen Rose (Arkansas 1928) 1941-T3d, 58	2	1	3	0	0	1	0	0
Eddie Sutton (Oklahoma St. 1958) 1977, 78-3d, 79RR,80, 81, 82, 83, 84, 85	9	10	9	0	0	1	0	1
Nolan Richardson (UTEP 1965) 1988, 89, 90-T3d, 91RR, 92, 93, 94-CH, 95-2d, 96, 98, 99, 2000, 01	13	26	12	1	1	1	0	1
Stan Heath (Eastern Mich. 1988) 2006, 07.	2	0	2	0	0	0	0	0
TOTAL	28	39	28	1	1	4	0	3
ARKANSAS ST.								
Dickey Nutt (Oklahoma St. 1982) 1999	1	0	1	0	0	0	0	0
TOTAL	1	0	1	0	0	0	0	0
ARK.-LITTLE ROCK								
Mike Newell (Sam Houston St. 1973) 1986, 89, 90	3	1	3	0	0	0	0	0
TOTAL	3	1	3	0	0	0	0	0
AUBURN								
Sonny Smith (Milligan 1958) 1984, 85, 86RR, 87, 88	5	7	5	0	0	0	0	1
Cliff Ellis (Florida St. 1968) 1999, 2000, 03	3	5	3	0	0	0	0	0
TOTAL	8	12	8	0	0	0	0	1
AUSTIN PEAY*								
Lake Kelly (Ga. Tech 1956) 1973*, 74, 87	3	2	4	0	0	0	0	0
Dave Loos (Memphis 1970) 1996, 2003	2	0	2	0	0	0	0	0
TOTAL	5	2	6	0	0	0	0	0
BALL ST.								
Steve Yoder (Ill. Wesleyan 1962) 1981	1	0	1	0	0	0	0	0
Al Brown (Purdue 1964) 1986	1	0	1	0	0	0	0	0
Rick Majerus (Marquette 1970) 1989	1	1	1	0	0	0	0	0
Dick Hunsaker (Weber St. 1977) 1990, 93	2	2	2	0	0	0	0	0

CHAMPIONSHIPS

	Yrs.	W	L	CH	2D	3d%	4th	RR
Ray McCallum (Ball St. 1983) 1995, 2000....	2	0	2	0	0	0	0	0
TOTAL	7	3	7	0	0	0	0	0

BAYLOR

	Yrs.	W	L	CH	2D	3d%	4th	RR
R.E. "Bill" Henderson (Howard Payne 1925) 1946RR, 48-2d, 50-4th....	3	3	5	0	1	0	1	1
Gene Iba (Tulsa 1963) 1988	1	0	1	0	0	0	0	0
TOTAL	4	3	6	0	1	0	1	1

BELMONT

	Yrs.	W	L	CH	2D	3d%	4th	RR
Rick Byrd (Tennessee 1976) 2006, 07	2	0	2	0	0	0	0	0
TOTAL	2	0	2	0	0	0	0	0

BOISE ST.

	Yrs.	W	L	CH	2D	3d%	4th	RR
Doran "Bus" Connor (Idaho St. 1955) 1976	1	0	1	0	0	0	0	0
Bob Dye (Idaho St. 1962) 1988, 93, 94	3	0	3	0	0	0	0	0
TOTAL	4	0	4	0	0	0	0	0

BOSTON COLLEGE

	Yrs.	W	L	CH	2D	3d%	4th	RR
Donald Martin (Georgetown 1941) 1958...	1	0	1	0	0	0	0	0
Bob Cousy (Holy Cross 1948) 1967RR, 68	2	2	2	0	0	0	0	1
Bob Zuffelato (Central Conn. St. 1959) 1975	1	1	2	0	0	0	0	0
Tom Davis (Wis.-Platteville 1960) 1981, 82RR	2	5	2	0	0	0	0	1
Gary Williams (Maryland 1967) 1983, 85	2	3	2	0	0	0	0	0
Jim O'Brien (Boston College 1971) 1994RR, 96, 97	3	5	3	0	0	0	0	1
Al Skinner (Massachusetts 1974) 2001, 02, 04, 05, 06, 07	6	6	6	0	0	0	0	0
TOTAL	17	22	18	0	0	0	0	3

BOSTON U.

	Yrs.	W	L	CH	2D	3d%	4th	RR
Matt Zunic (George Washington 1942) 1959RR	1	2	1	0	0	0	0	1
Rick Pitino (Massachusetts 1974) 1983	1	0	1	0	0	0	0	0
Mike Jarvis (Northeastern 1968) 1988, 90	2	0	2	0	0	0	0	0
Dennis Wolff (Connecticut 1978) 1997, 2002	2	0	2	0	0	0	0	0
TOTAL	6	2	6	0	0	0	0	1

BOWLING GREEN

	Yrs.	W	L	CH	2D	3d%	4th	RR
Harold Anderson (Otterbein 1924) 1959, 62, 63	3	1	4	0	0	0	0	0
Bill Fitch (Coe 1954) 1968	1	0	1	0	0	0	0	0
TOTAL	4	1	5	0	0	0	0	0

BRADLEY

	Yrs.	W	L	CH	2D	3d%	4th	RR
Forrest "Forddy" Anderson (Stanford 1942) 1950-2d, 54-2d	2	6	2	0	2	0	0	0
Bob Vanatta (Central Methodist 1945) 1955RR	1	2	1	0	0	0	0	1
Dick Versace (Wisconsin 1964) 1980, 86	2	1	2	0	0	0	0	0
Stan Albeck (Bradley 1955) 1988	1	0	1	0	0	0	0	0
Jim Molinari (Ill. Wesleyan 1977) 1996	1	0	1	0	0	0	0	0
Jim Les (Bradley 1986) 2006	1	2	1	0	0	0	0	0
TOTAL	8	11	8	0	2	0	0	1

BYU

	Yrs.	W	L	CH	2D	3d%	4th	RR
Stan Watts (BYU 1938) 1950RR, 51RR, 57, 65, 69, 71, 72	7	4	10	0	0	0	0	2
Frank Arnold (Idaho St. 1956) 1979, 80, 81RR	3	3	3	0	0	0	0	1
Ladell Andersen (Utah St. 1951) 1984, 87, 88	3	2	3	0	0	0	0	0
Roger Reid (Weber St. 1967) 1990, 91, 92, 93, 95	5	2	5	0	0	0	0	0
Steve Cleveland (UC Irvine 1976) 2001, 03, 04	3	0	3	0	0	0	0	0
Dave Rose (Houston 1984) 2007	1	0	1	0	0	0	0	0
TOTAL	22	11	25	0	0	0	0	3

BROWN

	Yrs.	W	L	CH	2D	3d%	4th	RR
George Allen (West Virginia 1935) 1939RR	1	0	1	0	0	0	0	1
Mike Cingiser (Brown 1962) 1986	1	0	1	0	0	0	0	0
TOTAL	2	0	2	0	0	0	0	1

BUCKNELL

	Yrs.	W	L	CH	2D	3d%	4th	RR
Charles Woollum (William & Mary 1962) 1987, 89	2	0	2	0	0	0	0	0
Pat Flannery (Bucknell 1980) 2005, 06	2	2	2	0	0	0	0	0
TOTAL	4	2	4	0	0	0	0	0

BUTLER

	Yrs.	W	L	CH	2D	3d%	4th	RR
Paul "Tony" Hinkle (Chicago 1921) 1962	1	2	1	0	0	0	0	0
Barry Collier (Butler 1976) 1997, 98, 2000	3	0	3	0	0	0	0	0
Thad Matta (Butler 1990) 2001	1	1	1	0	0	0	0	0
Todd Lickliter (Butler 1979) 2003, 07	2	4	2	0	0	0	0	0
TOTAL	7	7	7	0	0	0	0	0

CALIFORNIA*

	Yrs.	W	L	CH	2D	3d%	4th	RR
Clarence "Nibs" Price (California 1914) 1946-4th.	1	1	2	0	0	0	1	0
Pete Newell (Loyola Marymount 1940) 1957RR, 58RR, 59-CH, 60-2d	4	10	3	1	1	0	0	2
Lou Campanelli (Montclair St. 1960) 1990	1	1	1	0	0	0	0	0
Todd Bozeman (Rhode Island 1986) 1993, 94, 96*	3	2	3	0	0	0	0	0
Ben Braun (Wisconsin 1975) 1997, 2001, 02, 03, 06	5	4	5	0	0	0	0	0
TOTAL	14	18	14	1	1	0	1	2

UC SANTA BARBARA

	Yrs.	W	L	CH	2D	3d%	4th	RR
Jerry Pimm (Southern California 1961) 1988, 90	2	1	2	0	0	0	0	0
Bob Williams (San Jose St. 1975) 2002	1	0	1	0	0	0	0	0
TOTAL	3	1	3	0	0	0	0	0

CAL ST. FULLERTON

	Yrs.	W	L	CH	2D	3d%	4th	RR
Bob Dye (Idaho St. 1962) 1978RR	1	2	1	0	0	0	0	1
TOTAL	1	2	1	0	0	0	0	1

CAL ST. L.A.

	Yrs.	W	L	CH	2D	3d%	4th	RR
Bob Miller (Occidental 1953) 1974	1	0	1	0	0	0	0	0
TOTAL	1	0	1	0	0	0	0	0

CAL ST. NORTHRIDGE

	Yrs.	W	L	CH	2D	3d%	4th	RR
Bobby Braswell (Cal St. Northridge 1984) 2001	1	0	1	0	0	0	0	0
TOTAL	1	0	1	0	0	0	0	0

CAMPBELL

	Yrs.	W	L	CH	2D	3d%	4th	RR
Billy Lee (Barton 1971) 1992	1	0	1	0	0	0	0	0
TOTAL	1	0	1	0	0	0	0	0

CANISIUS

	Yrs.	W	L	CH	2D	3d%	4th	RR
Joseph Curran (Canisius 1943) 1955RR, 56RR, 57	3	6	3	0	0	0	0	2
John Beilein (Wheeling Jesuit 1975) 1996	1	0	1	0	0	0	0	0
TOTAL	4	6	4	0	0	0	0	2

CATHOLIC

	Yrs.	W	L	CH	2D	3d%	4th	RR
John Long (Catholic 1928) 1944RR	1	0	2	0	0	0	0	1
TOTAL	1	0	2	0	0	0	0	1

CENTRAL CONN. ST.

	Yrs.	W	L	CH	2D	3d%	4th	RR
Howie Dickenmann (Central Conn. St. 1970) 2000, 02, 07	3	0	3	0	0	0	0	0
TOTAL	3	0	3	0	0	0	0	0

UCF

	Yrs.	W	L	CH	2D	3d%	4th	RR
Kirk Speraw (Iowa 1980) 1994, 96, 2004, 05	4	0	4	0	0	0	0	0
TOTAL	4	0	4	0	0	0	0	0

CENTRAL MICH.

	Yrs.	W	L	CH	2D	3d%	4th	RR
Dick Parfitt (Central Mich. 1953) 1975, 77..	2	2	2	0	0	0	0	0
Charlie Coles [Miami (Ohio) 1965] 1987	1	0	1	0	0	0	0	0
Jay Smith (Saginaw Valley 1984) 2003	1	1	1	0	0	0	0	0
TOTAL	4	3	4	0	0	0	0	0

COL. OF CHARLESTON

	Yrs.	W	L	CH	2D	3d%	4th	RR
John Kresse [St. John's (N.Y.) 1964] 1994, 97, 98, 99	4	1	4	0	0	0	0	0
TOTAL	4	1	4	0	0	0	0	0

CHARLESTON SO.

	Yrs.	W	L	CH	2D	3d%	4th	RR
Tom Conrad (Old Dominion 1979) 1997	1	0	1	0	0	0	0	0
TOTAL	1	0	1	0	0	0	0	0

CHARLOTTE

	Yrs.	W	L	CH	2D	3d%	4th	RR
Lee Rose (Transylvania 1958) 1977-4th	1	3	2	0	0	0	1	0
Jeff Mullins (Duke 1964) 1988, 92, 95	3	0	3	0	0	0	0	0
Melvin Watkins (Charlotte 1977) 1997, 98.	2	2	2	0	0	0	0	0
Bob Lutz (Charlotte 1980) 1999, 2001, 02, 04, 05.	5	2	5	0	0	0	0	0
TOTAL	11	7	12	0	0	0	1	0

CHATTANOOGA

	Yrs.	W	L	CH	2D	3d%	4th	RR
Murray Arnold (American 1960) 1981, 82, 83	3	1	3	0	0	0	0	0
Mack McCarthy (Virginia Tech 1974) 1988, 93, 94, 95, 97	5	2	5	0	0	0	0	0
John Shulman (East Tenn. St. 1989) 2005 ..	1	0	1	0	0	0	0	0
TOTAL	9	3	9	0	0	0	0	0

CINCINNATI

	Yrs.	W	L	CH	2D	3d%	4th	RR
George Smith (Cincinnati 1935) 1958, 59-3d, 60-3d	3	7	3	0	0	2	0	0
Ed Jucker (Cincinnati 1940) 1961-CH, 62-CH, 63-2d	3	11	1	2	1	0	0	0
Tay Baker (Cincinnati 1950) 1966	1	0	2	0	0	0	0	0

	Yrs.	W	L	CH	2D	3d%	4th	RR
Gale Catlett (West Virginia 1963) 1975, 76, 77	3	2	3	0	0	0	0	0
Bob Huggins (West Virginia 1977) 1992-T3d, 93RR, 94, 95,96RR, 97, 98, 99, 2000, 01, 02, 03, 04, 05	14	20	14	0	0	1	0	2
TOTAL	24	40	23	2	1	3	0	2
CCNY								
Nat Holman (Savage School of Phys. Ed. 1917) 1947-4th, 50-CH	2	4	2	1	0	0	1	0
TOTAL	2	4	2	1	0	0	1	0
CLEMSON*								
Bill C. Foster (Carson-Newman 1958) 1980RR	1	3	1	0	0	0	0	1
Cliff Ellis (Florida St. 1968) 1987, 89, 90*	3	3	3	0	0	0	0	0
Rick Barnes (Lenoir-Rhyne 1977) 1996, 97, 98	3	2	3	0	0	0	0	0
TOTAL	7	8	7	0	0	0	0	1
CLEVELAND ST.								
Kevin Mackey (St. Anselm 1967) 1986	1	2	1	0	0	0	0	0
TOTAL	1	2	1	0	0	0	0	0
COASTAL CARO.								
Russ Bergman (LSU 1970) 1991, 93	2	0	2	0	0	0	0	0
TOTAL	2	0	2	0	0	0	0	0
COLGATE								
Jack Bruen (Catholic 1972) 1995, 96	2	0	2	0	0	0	0	0
TOTAL	2	0	2	0	0	0	0	0
COLORADO								
Forrest "Frosty" Cox (Kansas 1930) 1940RR, 42-T3d, 46RR	3	2	4	0	0	1	0	2
Horace "Bebe" Lee (Stanford 1938) 1954, 55-3d	2	3	3	0	0	1	0	0
Russell "Sox" Walseth (Colorado 1948) 1962RR, 63RR, 69	3	3	3	0	0	0	0	2
Ricardo Patton (Belmont 1980) 1997, 2003	2	1	2	0	0	0	0	0
TOTAL	10	9	12	0	0	2	0	4
COLORADO ST.								
Bill Strannigan (Wyoming 1941) 1954	1	0	2	0	0	0	0	0
Jim Williams (Utah St. 1947) 1963, 65, 66, 69RR	4	2	4	0	0	0	0	1
Boyd Grant (Colorado St. 1957) 1989, 90	2	1	2	0	0	0	0	0
Dale Layer (Eckerd 1979) 2003	1	0	1	0	0	0	0	0
TOTAL	8	3	9	0	0	0	0	1
COLUMBIA								
Gordon Ridings (Oregon 1929) 1948RR	1	0	2	0	0	0	0	1
Lou Rossini (Columbia 1948) 1951	1	0	1	0	0	0	0	0
John "Jack" Rohan (Columbia 1953) 1968	1	2	1	0	0	0	0	0
TOTAL	3	2	4	0	0	0	0	1
CONNECTICUT*								
Hugh Greer (Connecticut 1926) 1951, 54, 56, 57, 58, 59, 60	7	1	8	0	0	0	0	0
George Wigton (Ohio St. 1956) 1963	1	0	1	0	0	0	0	0
Fred Shabel (Duke 1954) 1964RR, 65, 67	3	2	3	0	0	0	0	1
Donald "Dee" Rowe (Middlebury 1952) 1976	1	1	1	0	0	0	0	0
Dom Perno (Connecticut 1964) 1979	1	0	1	0	0	0	0	0
Jim Calhoun (American Int'l 1968) 1990RR, 91, 92, 94,95RR, 96*, 98RR, 99-CH, 2000, 02RR, 03, 04-CH, 05, 06RR	14	38	12	2	0	0	0	5
TOTAL	27	42	26	2	0	0	0	6
COPPIN ST.								
Ron Mitchell (Edison 1984) 1990, 93, 97	3	1	3	0	0	0	0	0
TOTAL	3	1	3	0	0	0	0	0
CORNELL								
Royner Greene (Illinois 1929) 1954	1	0	2	0	0	0	0	0
Mike Dement (East Caro. 1976) 1988	1	0	1	0	0	0	0	0
TOTAL	2	0	3	0	0	0	0	0
CREIGHTON								
Eddie Hickey (Creighton 1927) 1941RR	1	1	1	0	0	0	0	1
John "Red" McManus (St. Ambrose 1949) 1962, 64	2	3	3	0	0	0	0	0
Eddie Sutton (Oklahoma St. 1958) 1974	1	2	1	0	0	0	0	0
Tom Apke (Creighton 1965) 1975, 78, 81	3	0	3	0	0	0	0	0
Tony Barone (Duke 1968) 1989, 91	2	1	2	0	0	0	0	0
Dana Altman (Eastern N.M. 1980) 1999, 2000, 01, 02, 03, 05, 07	7	2	7	0	0	0	0	0
TOTAL	16	9	17	0	0	0	0	1
DARTMOUTH								
Osborne "Ozzie" Cowles (Carleton 1922) 1941RR, 42-2d, 43RR	3	4	3	0	1	0	0	2

	Yrs.	W	L	CH	2D	3d%	4th	RR
Earl Brown (Notre Dame 1939) 1944-2d	1	2	1	0	1	0	0	0
Alvin "Doggie" Julian (Bucknell 1923) 1956, 58RR, 59	3	4	3	0	0	0	0	1
TOTAL	7	10	7	0	2	0	0	3
DAVIDSON								
Charles "Lefty" Driesell (Duke 1954) 1966, 68RR, 69RR	3	5	4	0	0	0	0	2
Terry Holland (Davidson 1964) 1970	1	0	1	0	0	0	0	0
Bobby Hussey (Appalachian St. 1962) 1986	1	0	1	0	0	0	0	0
Bob McKillop (Hofstra 1972) 1998, 2002, 06, 07	4	0	4	0	0	0	0	0
TOTAL	9	5	10	0	0	0	0	2
DAYTON								
Tom Blackburn [Wilmington (Ohio) 1931] 1952	1	1	1	0	0	0	0	0
Don Donoher (Dayton 1954) 1965, 66, 67-2d, 69, 70, 74, 84RR, 85	8	11	10	0	1	0	0	1
Jim O'Brien (St. Joseph's 1974) 1990	1	1	1	0	0	0	0	0
Oliver Purnell (Old Dominion 1975) 2000, 03	2	0	2	0	0	0	0	0
Brian Gregory (Oakland 1990) 2004	1	0	1	0	0	0	0	0
TOTAL	13	13	15	0	1	0	0	1
DELAWARE								
Steve Steinwedel (Mississippi St. 1975) 1992, 93	2	0	2	0	0	0	0	0
Mike Brey (George Washington 1982) 1998, 99	2	0	2	0	0	0	0	0
TOTAL	4	0	4	0	0	0	0	0
DELAWARE ST.								
Greg Jackson (St. Paul's 1982) 2005	1	0	1	0	0	0	0	0
TOTAL	1	0	1	0	0	0	0	0
DePAUL*								
Ray Meyer (Notre Dame 1938) 1943-T3d, 53, 56, 59, 60, 65, 76, 78RR, 79-3d, 80, 81, 82, 84	13	14	16	0	0	2	0	1
Joey Meyer (DePaul 1971) 1985, 86*, 87*, 88*, 89*, 91, 92	7	6	7	0	0	0	0	0
Pat Kennedy [King's (Pa.) 1976] 2000	1	0	1	0	0	0	0	0
Dave Leitao (Northeastern 1983) 2004	1	1	1	0	0	0	0	0
TOTAL	22	21	25	0	0	2	0	1
DETROIT								
Robert Calihan (Detroit 1940) 1962	1	0	1	0	0	0	0	0
Dick Vitale (Seton Hall 1962) 1977	1	1	1	0	0	0	0	0
Dave "Smokey" Gaines (LeMoyne-Owen 1963) 1979	1	0	1	0	0	0	0	0
Perry Watson (Eastern Mich. 1972) 1998, 99	2	2	2	0	0	0	0	0
TOTAL	5	3	5	0	0	0	0	0
DRAKE								
Maurice John (Central Mo. St. 1941) 1969-3d, 70RR, 71RR	3	5	3	0	0	1	0	2
TOTAL	3	5	3	0	0	1	0	2
DREXEL								
Eddie Burke (La Salle 1967) 1986	1	0	1	0	0	0	0	0
Bill Herrion (Merrimack 1981) 1994, 95, 96	3	1	3	0	0	0	0	0
TOTAL	4	1	4	0	0	0	0	0
DUKE								
Harold Bradley (Hartwick 1934) 1955	1	0	1	0	0	0	0	0
Vic Bubas (North Carolina St. 1951) 1960RR, 63-3d, 64-2d, 66-3d	4	11	4	0	1	2	0	1
W.E. "Bill" Foster (Elizabethtown 1954) 1978-2d, 79, 80RR	3	6	3	0	1	0	0	1
Mike Krzyzewski (Army 1969) 1984, 85, 86-2d, 87, 88-T3d, 89-T3d, 90-2d, 91-CH, 92-CH, 93, 94-2d, 96, 97, 98RR, 99-2d, 2000, 01-CH, 02, 03, 04-T3d, 05, 06, 07	23	68	20	3	4	3	0	1
TOTAL	31	85	28	3	6	5	0	3
DUQUESNE								
Charles "Chick" Davies (Duquesne 1934) 1940-T3d	1	1	1	0	0	1	0	0
Donald "Dudey" Moore (Duquesne 1934) 1952RR	1	1	1	0	0	0	0	1
John "Red" Manning (Duquesne 1951) 1969, 71	2	2	2	0	0	0	0	0
John Cinicola (Duquesne 1955) 1977	1	0	1	0	0	0	0	0
TOTAL	5	4	5	0	0	1	0	1
EAST CARO.								
Tom Quinn (Marshall 1954) 1972	1	0	1	0	0	0	0	0
Eddie Payne (Wake Forest 1973) 1993	1	0	1	0	0	0	0	0
TOTAL	2	0	2	0	0	0	0	0

	Yrs.	W	L	CH	2D	3d%	4th	RR
EAST TENN. ST.								
J. Madison Brooks (Louisiana Tech 1937) 1968	1	1	2	0	0	0	0	0
Les Robinson (North Carolina St. 1964) 1989, 90	2	0	2	0	0	0	0	0
Alan LeForce (Cumberland 1957) 1991, 92	2	1	2	0	0	0	0	0
Ed DeChellis (Penn St. 1982) 2003	1	0	1	0	0	0	0	0
Murry Bartow (UAB 1985) 2004	1	0	1	0	0	0	0	0
TOTAL	7	2	8	0	0	0	0	0
EASTERN ILL.								
Rick Samuels (Chadron St. 1971) 1992, 2001	2	0	2	0	0	0	0	0
TOTAL	2	0	2	0	0	0	0	0
EASTERN KY.								
Paul McBrayer (Kentucky 1930) 1953, 59	2	0	2	0	0	0	0	0
Jim Baechtold (Eastern Ky. 1952) 1965	1	0	1	0	0	0	0	0
Guy Strong (Eastern Ky. 1955) 1972	1	0	1	0	0	0	0	0
Ed Byhre [Augustana (S.D.) 1966] 1979	1	0	1	0	0	0	0	0
Travis Ford (Kentucky 1994) 2005	1	0	1	0	0	0	0	0
Jeff Neubauer (La Salle 1993) 2007	1	0	1	0	0	0	0	0
TOTAL	7	0	7	0	0	0	0	0
EASTERN MICH.								
Ben Braun (Wisconsin 1975) 1988, 91, 96	3	3	3	0	0	0	0	0
Milton Barnes (Albion 1979) 1998	1	0	1	0	0	0	0	0
TOTAL	4	3	4	0	0	0	0	0
EASTERN WASH.								
Ray Giacoletti (Minot St. 1984) 2004	1	0	1	0	0	0	0	0
TOTAL	1	0	1	0	0	0	0	0
EVANSVILLE								
Dick Walters (Illinois St. 1969) 1982	1	0	1	0	0	0	0	0
Jim Crews (Indiana 1976) 1989, 92, 93, 99	4	1	4	0	0	0	0	0
TOTAL	5	1	5	0	0	0	0	0
FAIRFIELD								
Mitch Buonaguro (Boston College 1975) 1986, 87	2	0	2	0	0	0	0	0
Paul Cormier (New Hampshire 1973) 1997	1	0	1	0	0	0	0	0
TOTAL	3	0	3	0	0	0	0	0
FAIRLEIGH DICKINSON								
Tom Green (Syracuse 1971) 1985, 88, 98, 2005	4	0	4	0	0	0	0	0
TOTAL	4	0	4	0	0	0	0	0
FLORIDA*								
Norm Sloan (North Carolina St. 1951) 1987*, 88*, 89	3	3	3	0	0	0	0	0
Lon Kruger (Kansas St. 1974) 1994-T3d, 95	2	4	2	0	0	1	0	0
Billy Donovan (Providence 1987) 1999, 2000-2d, 01, 02, 03, 04, 05, 06-CH, 07-CH	9	22	7	2	1	0	0	0
TOTAL	14	29	12	2	1	1	0	0
FLORIDA A&M								
Mickey Clayton (Florida A&M 1975) 1999	1	0	1	0	0	0	0	0
Mike Gillespie (DePaul 1974) 2004, 07	2	1	2	0	0	0	0	0
TOTAL	3	1	3	0	0	0	0	0
FLA. ATLANTIC								
Sydney Green (UNLV 1983), 2002	1	0	1	0	0	0	0	0
TOTAL	1	0	1	0	0	0	0	0
FLORIDA INT'L								
Bob Weltlich (Ohio St. 1967) 1995	1	0	1	0	0	0	0	0
TOTAL	1	0	1	0	0	0	0	0
FLORIDA ST.								
Hugh Durham (Florida St. 1959) 1968, 72-2d, 78	3	4	3	0	1	0	0	0
Joe Williams (SMU 1956) 1980	1	1	1	0	0	0	0	0
Pat Kennedy [King's (Pa.) 1976] 1988, 89, 91, 92, 93RR	5	6	5	0	0	0	0	1
Steve Robinson (Radford 1981) 1998	1	1	1	0	0	0	0	0
TOTAL	10	12	10	0	1	0	0	1
FORDHAM								
John Bach (Fordham 1948) 1953, 54	2	0	2	0	0	0	0	0
Richard "Digger" Phelps (Rider 1963) 1971	1	2	1	0	0	0	0	0
Nick Macarchuk (Fairfield 1963) 1992	1	0	1	0	0	0	0	0
TOTAL	4	2	4	0	0	0	0	0
FRESNO ST.*								
Boyd Grant (Colorado St. 1961) 1981, 82, 84	3	1	3	0	0	0	0	0
Jerry Tarkanian (Fresno St. 1956) 2000*, 01	2	1	2	0	0	0	0	0
TOTAL	5	2	5	0	0	0	0	0
FURMAN								
Joe Williams (SMU 1956) 1971, 73, 74, 75, 78	5	1	6	0	0	0	0	0
Eddie Holbrook (Lenoir-Rhyne 1962) 1980	1	0	1	0	0	0	0	0
TOTAL	6	1	7	0	0	0	0	0
GEORGE MASON								
Ernie Nestor (Alderson-Broaddus 1968) 1989	1	0	1	0	0	0	0	0
Jim Larranaga (Providence 1971) 1999, 2001, 06-T3d	3	4	3	0	0	1	0	0
TOTAL	4	4	4	0	0	1	0	0
GEORGE WASHINGTON								
Bill Reinhart (Oregon 1923) 1954, 61	2	0	2	0	0	0	0	0
Mike Jarvis (Northeastern 1968) 1993, 94, 96, 98	4	3	4	0	0	0	0	0
Tom Penders (Connecticut 1967) 1999	1	0	1	0	0	0	0	0
Karl Hobbs (Connecticut 1985) 2005, 06, 07	3	1	3	0	0	0	0	0
TOTAL	10	4	10	0	0	0	0	0
GEORGETOWN								
Elmer Ripley (No college) 1943-2d	1	2	1	0	1	0	0	0
John Thompson (Providence 1964) 1975, 76, 79, 80RR, 81, 82-2d, 83, 84-CH, 85-2d, 86, 87RR, 88, 89RR, 90, 91, 92, 94, 95, 96RR, 97	20	34	19	1	2	0	0	4
Craig Esherick (Georgetown 1978) 2001	1	2	1	0	0	0	0	0
John Thompson III (Princeton 1988) 2006, 07-T3d	2	6	2	0	0	1	0	0
TOTAL	24	44	23	1	3	1	0	4
GEORGIA*								
Hugh Durham (Florida St. 1959) 1983-T3d, 85*, 87, 90, 91	5	4	5	0	0	1	0	0
Tubby Smith (High Point 1973) 1996, 97	2	2	2	0	0	0	0	0
Jim Harrick [Charleston (W.V.) 1960] 2001, 02*	2	1	2	0	0	0	0	0
TOTAL	9	7	9	0	0	1	0	0
GA. SOUTHERN								
Frank Kerns (Alabama 1957) 1983, 87, 92	3	0	3	0	0	0	0	0
TOTAL	3	0	3	0	0	0	0	0
GEORGIA ST.								
Bob Reinhart (Indiana 1961) 1991	1	0	1	0	0	0	0	0
Charles "Lefty" Driesell (Duke 1954) 2001	1	1	1	0	0	0	0	0
TOTAL	2	1	2	0	0	0	0	0
GEORGIA TECH								
John "Whack" Hyder (Georgia Tech 1937) 1960RR	1	1	1	0	0	0	0	1
Bobby Cremins (South Carolina 1970) 1985RR, 86, 87, 88, 89, 90-T3d, 91, 92, 93, 96	10	15	10	0	0	1	0	1
Paul Hewitt (St. John Fisher 1985) 2001, 04-2d, 05, 07	4	5	4	0	1	0	0	0
TOTAL	15	21	15	0	1	1	0	2
GONZAGA								
Dan Fitzgerald (Cal St. L.A. 1965) 1995	1	0	1	0	0	0	0	0
Dan Monson (Idaho 1985) 1999RR	1	3	1	0	0	0	0	1
Mark Few (Oregon 1987) 2000, 01, 02, 03, 04, 05, 06, 07	8	9	8	0	0	0	0	0
TOTAL	10	12	10	0	0	0	0	1
GREEN BAY								
Dick Bennett (Ripon 1965) 1991, 94, 95	3	1	3	0	0	0	0	0
Mike Heideman (Wis.-La Crosse 1971) 1996	1	0	1	0	0	0	0	0
TOTAL	4	1	4	0	0	0	0	0
HAMPTON								
Steve Merfeld (Wis.-La Crosse 1984) 2001, 02	2	1	2	0	0	0	0	0
Bobby Collins (Eastern Ky. 1991) 2006	1	0	1	0	0	0	0	0
TOTAL	3	1	3	0	0	0	0	0
HARDIN-SIMMONS								
Bill Scott (Hardin-Simmons 1947) 1953, 57	2	0	2	0	0	0	0	0
TOTAL	2	0	2	0	0	0	0	0
HARVARD								
Floyd Stahl (Illinois 1926) 1946RR	1	0	2	0	0	0	1	1
TOTAL	1	0	2	0	0	0	1	1

HAWAII

	Yrs.	W	L	CH	2D	3d%	4th	RR
Ephraim "Red" Rocha (Oregon St. 1950) 1972	1	0	1	0	0	0	0	0
Riley Wallace [Centenary (La.) 1964] 1994, 2001, 02	3	0	3	0	0	0	0	0
TOTAL	4	0	4	0	0	0	0	0

HOFSTRA

	Yrs.	W	L	CH	2D	3d%	4th	RR
Roger Gaeckler (Gettysburg 1965) 1976, 77	2	0	2	0	0	0	0	0
Jay Wright (Bucknell 1983) 2000, 01	2	0	2	0	0	0	0	0
TOTAL	4	0	4	0	0	0	0	0

HOLY CROSS

	Yrs.	W	L	CH	2D	3d%	4th	RR
Alvin "Doggie" Julian (Bucknell 1923) 1947-CH, 48-3d	2	5	1	1	0	1	0	0
Lester "Buster" Sheary (Catholic 1933) 1950RR, 53RR	2	2	3	0	0	0	0	2
Roy Leenig [Trinity (Conn.) 1942] 1956	1	0	1	0	0	0	0	0
George Blaney (Holy Cross 1961) 1977, 80, 93	3	0	3	0	0	0	0	0
Ralph Willard (Holy Cross 1967) 2001, 02, 03, 07	4	0	4	0	0	0	0	0
TOTAL	12	7	12	1	0	1	0	2

HOUSTON

	Yrs.	W	L	CH	2D	3d%	4th	RR
Alden Pasche (Rice 1932) 1956	1	0	2	0	0	0	0	0
Guy Lewis (Houston 1947) 1961, 65, 66, 67-3d, 68-4th, 70, 71, 72, 73, 78, 81, 82-T3d, 83-2d, 84-2d	14	26	18	0	2	2	1	0
Pat Foster (Arkansas 1961) 1987, 90, 92	3	0	3	0	0	0	0	0
TOTAL	18	26	23	0	2	2	1	0

HOUSTON BAPTIST

	Yrs.	W	L	CH	2D	3d%	4th	RR
Gene Iba (Tulsa 1963) 1984	1	0	1	0	0	0	0	0
TOTAL	1	0	1	0	0	0	0	0

HOWARD

	Yrs.	W	L	CH	2D	3d%	4th	RR
A.B. Williamson (N.C. A&T 1968) 1981	1	0	1	0	0	0	0	0
Alfred "Butch" Beard (Louisville 1972) 1992	1	0	1	0	0	0	0	0
TOTAL	2	0	2	0	0	0	0	0

IDAHO

	Yrs.	W	L	CH	2D	3d%	4th	RR
Don Monson (Idaho 1955) 1981, 82	2	1	2	0	0	0	0	0
Kermit Davis Jr. (Mississippi St. 1982) 1989, 90	2	0	2	0	0	0	0	0
TOTAL	4	1	4	0	0	0	0	0

IDAHO ST.

	Yrs.	W	L	CH	2D	3d%	4th	RR
Steve Belko (Idaho 1939) 1953, 54, 55, 56	4	2	4	0	0	0	0	0
John Grayson (Oklahoma 1938) 1957, 58, 59	3	4	5	0	0	0	0	0
John Evans (Idaho 1948) 1960	1	0	1	0	0	0	0	0
Jim Killingsworth (Northeastern Okla. St. 1948) 1974, 77RR	2	2	2	0	0	0	0	1
Jim Boutin (Lewis & Clark 1964) 1987	1	0	1	0	0	0	0	0
TOTAL	11	8	13	0	0	0	0	1

ILLINOIS

	Yrs.	W	L	CH	2D	3d%	4th	RR
Doug Mills (Illinois 1930) 1942RR	1	0	2	0	0	0	0	1
Harry Combes (Illinois 1937) 1949-3d, 51-3d, 52-3d, 63RR	4	9	4	0	0	3	0	1
Lou Henson (New Mexico St. 1955) 1981, 83, 84RR, 85, 86, 87, 88, 89-T3d, 90, 93, 94, 95	12	12	12	0	0	1	0	1
Lon Kruger (Kansas St. 1974) 1997, 98, 2000	3	3	3	0	0	0	0	0
Bill Self (Oklahoma St. 1985) 2001RR, 02, 03	3	6	3	0	0	0	0	1
Bruce Weber (Milwaukee 1978) 2004, 05-2d, 06, 07	4	8	4	0	1	0	0	0
TOTAL	27	38	28	0	1	4	0	4

ILLINOIS ST.

	Yrs.	W	L	CH	2D	3d%	4th	RR
Bob Donewald (Hanover 1964) 1983, 84, 85	3	2	3	0	0	0	0	0
Bob Bender (Duke 1980) 1990	1	0	1	0	0	0	0	0
Kevin Stallings (Purdue 1982) 1997, 98	2	1	2	0	0	0	0	0
TOTAL	6	3	6	0	0	0	0	0

ILL.-CHICAGO

	Yrs.	W	L	CH	2D	3d%	4th	RR
Jimmy Collins (New Mexico St. 1970) 1998, 2002, 04	3	0	3	0	0	0	0	0
TOTAL	3	0	3	0	0	0	0	0

INDIANA

	Yrs.	W	L	CH	2D	3d%	4th	RR
Branch McCracken (Indiana 1930) 1940-CH, 53-CH, 54, 58	4	9	2	2	0	0	0	0
Lou Watson (Indiana 1950) 1967	1	1	1	0	0	0	0	0
Bob Knight (Ohio St. 1962) 1973-3d, 75RR, 76-CH, 78, 80, 81-CH, 82, 83, 84RR, 86, 87-CH, 88, 89, 90, 91, 92-T3d, 93RR, 94, 95, 96, 97, 98, 99, 2000	24	42	21	3	0	2	0	3
Mike Davis (Alabama 1983) 2001, 02-2d, 03, 06	4	7	4	0	1	0	0	0
Kelvin Sampson (UNC Pembroke 1978) 2007	1	1	1	0	0	0	0	1
TOTAL	34	60	29	5	1	2	0	3

IUPUI

	Yrs.	W	L	CH	2D	3d%	4th	RR
Ron Hunter [Miami (Ohio) 1986] 2003	1	0	1	0	0	0	0	0
TOTAL	1	0	1	0	0	0	0	0

INDIANA ST.

	Yrs.	W	L	CH	2D	3d%	4th	RR
Bill Hodges (Marian 1970) 1979-2d	1	4	1	0	1	0	0	0
Royce Waltman (Slippery Rock 1964) 2000, 01	2	1	2	0	0	0	0	0
TOTAL	3	5	3	0	1	0	0	0

IONA*

	Yrs.	W	L	CH	2D	3d%	4th	RR
Jim Valvano (Rutgers 1967) 1979, 80*	2	1	2	0	0	0	0	0
Pat Kennedy [King's (Pa.) 1976] 1984, 85	2	0	2	0	0	0	0	0
Tim Welsh (Potsdam St. 1984) 1998	1	0	1	0	0	0	0	0
Jeff Ruland (Iona 1991) 2000, 01, 06	3	0	3	0	0	0	0	0
TOTAL	8	1	8	0	0	0	0	0

IOWA

	Yrs.	W	L	CH	2D	3d%	4th	RR
Frank "Bucky" O'Connor (Drake 1938) 1955-4th, 56-2d	2	5	3	0	1	0	1	0
Ralph Miller (Kansas 1942) 1970	1	1	1	0	0	0	0	0
Lute Olson (Augsburg 1957) 1979, 80-4th, 81, 82, 83	5	7	6	0	0	0	1	0
George Raveling (Villanova 1960) 1985, 86	2	0	2	0	0	0	0	0
Tom Davis (Wis.-Platteville 1960) 1987RR, 88, 89, 91, 92, 93, 96, 97, 99	9	13	9	0	0	0	0	1
Steve Alford (Indiana 1987) 2001, 05, 06	3	1	3	0	0	0	0	0
TOTAL	22	27	24	0	1	0	2	1

IOWA ST.

	Yrs.	W	L	CH	2D	3d%	4th	RR
Louis Menze (Central Mo. St. 1928) 1944-T3d	1	1	1	0	0	1	0	0
Johnny Orr (Beloit 1949) 1985, 86, 88, 89, 92, 93	6	3	6	0	0	0	0	0
Tim Floyd (Louisiana Tech 1977) 1995, 96, 97	3	4	3	0	0	0	0	0
Larry Eustachy (Long Beach St. 1979) 2000RR, 01	2	3	2	0	0	0	0	1
Wayne Morgan (St. Lawrence 1973) 2005	1	1	1	0	0	0	0	0
TOTAL	13	12	13	0	0	1	0	1

JACKSON ST.

	Yrs.	W	L	CH	2D	3d%	4th	RR
Andy Stoglin (UTEP 1965) 1997, 2000	2	0	2	0	0	0	0	0
Tevester Anderson (Ark.-Pine Bluff 1962) 2007	1	0	1	0	0	0	0	1
TOTAL	3	0	3	0	0	0	0	1

JACKSONVILLE

	Yrs.	W	L	CH	2D	3d%	4th	RR
Joe Williams (SMU 1956) 1970-2d	1	4	1	0	1	0	0	0
Tom Wasdin (Florida 1957) 1971, 73	2	0	2	0	0	0	0	0
Tates Locke (Ohio Wesleyan 1959) 1979	1	0	1	0	0	0	0	0
Bob Wenzel (Rutgers 1971) 1986	1	0	1	0	0	0	0	0
TOTAL	5	4	5	0	1	0	0	0

JAMES MADISON

	Yrs.	W	L	CH	2D	3d%	4th	RR
Lou Campanelli (Montclair St. 1960) 1981, 82, 83	3	3	3	0	0	0	0	0
Charles "Lefty" Driesell (Duke 1954) 1994	1	0	1	0	0	0	0	0
TOTAL	4	3	4	0	0	0	0	0

KANSAS

	Yrs.	W	L	CH	2D	3d%	4th	RR
Forrest C. "Phog" Allen (Kansas 1906) 1940-2d, 42RR, 52-CH, 53-2d	4	10	3	1	2	0	0	1
Dick Harp (Kansas 1940) 1957-2d, 60RR	2	4	2	0	1	0	0	1
Ted Owens (Oklahoma 1951) 1966RR, 67, 71-4th, 74-4th, 75, 78, 81	7	8	9	0	0	0	2	1
Larry Brown (North Carolina 1963) 1984, 85, 86-T3d, 87, 88-CH	5	14	4	1	0	1	0	0
Roy Williams (North Carolina 1972) 1990, 91-2d, 92, 93-T3d, 94, 95, 96RR, 97, 98, 99, 2000, 01, 02-T3d, 03-2d	14	34	14	0	2	2	0	1
Bill Self (Oklahoma St. 1985) 2004RR, 05, 06, 07RR	4	6	4	0	0	0	0	2
TOTAL	36	76	36	2	5	3	2	6

KANSAS ST.

	Yrs.	W	L	CH	2D	3d%	4th	RR
Jack Gardner (Southern California 1932) 1948-4th, 51-2d	2	4	3	0	1	0	1	0
Fred "Tex" Winter (Southern California 1947) 1956, 58-4th, 59RR, 61RR, 64-4th, 68	6	7	9	0	0	0	2	2
Lowell "Cotton" Fitzsimmons (Midwestern St. 1955) 1970	1	1	1	0	0	0	0	0
Jack Hartman (Oklahoma St. 1949) 1972RR, 73RR, 75RR, 77, 80, 81RR, 82	7	11	7	0	0	0	0	4

	Yrs.	W	L	CH	2D	3d%	4th	RR
Lon Kruger (Kansas St. 1974) 1987, 88RR, 89, 90	4	4	4	0	0	0	0	1
Dana Altman (Eastern N.M. 1980) 1993	1	0	1	0	0	0	0	0
Tom Asbury (Wyoming 1967) 1996	1	0	1	0	0	0	0	0
TOTAL	22	27	26	0	1	0	3	7

KENT ST.

	Yrs.	W	L	CH	2D	3d%	4th	RR
Gary Waters (Ferris St. 1975) 1999, 2001	2	1	2	0	0	0	0	0
Stan Heath (Eastern Mich. 1988) 2002RR	1	3	1	0	0	0	0	1
Jim Christian (Rhode Island 1988) 2006	1	0	1	0	0	0	0	0
TOTAL	4	4	4	0	0	0	0	1

KENTUCKY*

	Yrs.	W	L	CH	2D	3d%	4th	RR
Adolph Rupp (Kansas 1923) 1942-T3d, 45RR, 48-CH,49-CH, 51-CH, 52RR, 55, 56RR, 57RR, 58-CH, 59,61RR, 62RR, 64, 66-2d, 68RR, 69, 70RR, 71, 72RR	20	30	18	4	1	1	0	9
Joe B. Hall (Sewanee 1951) 1973RR, 75-2d, 77RR, 78-CH, 80, 81, 82, 83RR, 84-T3d, 85	10	20	9	1	1	1	0	3
Eddie Sutton (Oklahoma St. 1958) 1986RR, 87, 88*	3	5	3	0	0	0	1	1
Rick Pitino (Massachusetts 1974) 1992RR, 93-T3d, 94, 95RR 96-CH, 97-2d	6	22	5	1	1	1	0	2
Tubby Smith (High Point 1973) 1998-CH, 99RR, 2000, 01, 02, 03RR, 04, 05RR, 06 07	10	23	9	1	0	0	0	3
TOTAL	49	100	44	7	3	3	0	18

LA SALLE

	Yrs.	W	L	CH	2D	3d%	4th	RR
Ken Loeffler (Penn St. 1924) 1954-CH, 55-2d	2	9	1	1	1	0	0	0
Jim Harding (Iowa 1949) 1968	1	0	1	0	0	0	0	0
Paul Westhead (St. Joseph's 1961) 1975, 78	2	0	2	0	0	0	0	0
Dave "Lefty" Ervin (La Salle 1968) 1980, 83	2	1	2	0	0	0	0	0
Bill "Speedy" Morris (St. Joseph's 1973) 1988, 89, 90, 92	4	1	4	0	0	0	0	0
TOTAL	11	11	10	1	1	0	0	0

LAFAYETTE

	Yrs.	W	L	CH	2D	3d%	4th	RR
George Davidson (Lafayette 1951) 1957	1	0	2	0	0	0	0	0
Fran O'Hanlon (Villanova 1970) 1999, 2000	2	0	2	0	0	0	0	0
TOTAL	3	0	4	0	0	0	0	0

LAMAR

	Yrs.	W	L	CH	2D	3d%	4th	RR
Billy Tubbs (Lamar 1958) 1979, 80	2	3	2	0	0	0	0	0
Pat Foster (Arkansas 1961) 1981, 83	2	2	2	0	0	0	0	0
Mike Deane (Potsdam St. 1974) 2000	1	0	1	0	0	0	0	0
TOTAL	5	5	5	0	0	0	0	0

LEBANON VALLEY

	Yrs.	W	L	CH	2D	3d%	4th	RR
George "Rinso" Marquette (Lebanon Valley 1948) 1953	1	1	2	0	0	0	0	0
TOTAL	1	1	2	0	0	0	0	0

LEHIGH

	Yrs.	W	L	CH	2D	3d%	4th	RR
Tom Schneider (Bucknell 1969) 1985	1	0	1	0	0	0	0	0
Fran McCaffery (Penn 1982) 1988	1	0	1	0	0	0	0	0
Billy Taylor (Notre Dame 1995) 2004	1	0	1	0	0	0	0	0
TOTAL	3	0	3	0	0	0	0	0

LIBERTY

	Yrs.	W	L	CH	2D	3d%	4th	RR
Jeff Meyer (Taylor 1976) 1994	1	0	1	0	0	0	0	0
Randy Dunton [Baptist Bible (Mo.) 1984] 2004	1	0	1	0	0	0	0	0
TOTAL	2	0	2	0	0	0	0	0

LONG BEACH ST.*

	Yrs.	W	L	CH	2D	3d%	4th	RR
Jerry Tarkanian (Fresno St. 1956) 1970, 71RR*, 72RR*, 73*	4	7	5	0	0	0	0	2
Dwight Jones (Pepperdine 1965) 1977	1	0	1	0	0	0	0	0
Seth Greenberg (Fairleigh Dickinson 1978) 1993, 95	2	0	2	0	0	0	0	0
Larry Reynolds (UC Riverside 1976) 2007	1	0	1	0	0	0	0	1
TOTAL	8	7	9	0	0	0	0	2

LONG ISLAND

	Yrs.	W	L	CH	2D	3d%	4th	RR
Paul Lizzo (Northwest Mo. St. 1963) 1981, 84	2	0	2	0	0	0	0	0
Ray Haskins (Shaw 1972) 1997	1	0	1	0	0	0	0	0
TOTAL	3	0	3	0	0	0	0	0

LA.-LAFAYETTE*

	Yrs.	W	L	CH	2D	3d%	4th	RR
Beryl Shipley (Delta St. 1951) 1972*, 73*	2	3	3	0	0	0	0	0
Bobby Paschal (Stetson 1964) 1982, 83	2	0	2	0	0	0	0	0
Marty Fletcher (Maryland 1973) 1992, 94	2	1	2	0	0	0	0	0
Jessie Evans (Eastern Mich. 1972) 2000, 04	2	0	2	0	0	0	0	0
Robert Lee (Nicholls St. 1991) 2005	1	0	1	0	0	0	0	0
TOTAL	9	4	10	0	0	0	0	0

LA.-MONROE

	Yrs.	W	L	CH	2D	3d%	4th	RR
Mike Vining (La.-Monroe 1967) 1982, 86, 90, 91, 92, 93, 96	7	0	7	0	0	0	0	0
TOTAL	7	0	7	0	0	0	0	0

LSU

	Yrs.	W	L	CH	2D	3d%	4th	RR
Harry Rabenhorst (Wake Forest 1921) 1953-4th, 54	2	2	4	0	0	0	1	0
Dale Brown (Minot St. 1957) 1979, 80RR, 81-4th, 84, 85, 86-T3d, 87RR, 88, 89, 90, 91, 92, 93	13	15	14	0	0	1	1	2
John Brady (Belhaven 1976) 2000, 03, 05, 06-T3d	4	6	4	0	0	1	0	0
TOTAL	19	24	22	0	0	2	2	2

LOUISIANA TECH

	Yrs.	W	L	CH	2D	3d%	4th	RR
Andy Russo (Lake Forest 1970) 1984, 85	2	3	2	0	0	0	0	0
Tommy Joe Eagles (Louisiana Tech 1971) 1987, 89	2	1	2	0	0	0	0	0
Jerry Loyd (LeTourneau 1976) 1991	1	0	1	0	0	0	0	0
TOTAL	5	4	5	0	0	0	0	0

LOUISVILLE

	Yrs.	W	L	CH	2D	3d%	4th	RR
Bernard "Peck" Hickman (Western Ky. 1935) 1951, 59-4th, 61, 64, 67	5	5	7	0	0	0	1	0
John Dromo (John Carroll 1939) 1968	1	1	1	0	0	0	0	0
Denny Crum (UCLA 1959) 1972-4th, 74, 75-3d, 77, 78, 79, 80-CH, 81, 82-T3d, 83-T3d, 84, 86-CH, 88, 89, 90, 92, 93, 94, 95, 96, 97RR, 99, 2000	23	42	23	2	0	3	1	1
Rick Pitino (Massachusetts 1974) 2003, 04, 05-T3d, 07	4	6	4	0	0	1	0	0
TOTAL	33	54	35	2	0	4	2	1

LOYOLA MARYMOUNT*

	Yrs.	W	L	CH	2D	3d%	4th	RR
William Donovan (Loyola Marymount 1950) 1961	1	1	1	0	0	0	0	0
Ron Jacobs (Southern California 1964) 1980*	1	0	1	0	0	0	0	0
Paul Westhead (St. Joseph's 1961) 1988, 89, 90RR	3	4	3	0	0	0	0	1
TOTAL	5	5	5	0	0	0	0	1

LOYOLA (ILL.)

	Yrs.	W	L	CH	2D	3d%	4th	RR
George Ireland (Notre Dame 1936) 1963-CH, 64, 66, 68	4	7	3	1	0	0	0	0
Gene Sullivan (Notre Dame 1953) 1985	1	2	1	0	0	0	0	0
TOTAL	5	9	4	1	0	0	0	0

LOYOLA (LA.)

	Yrs.	W	L	CH	2D	3d%	4th	RR
Jim McCafferty [Loyola (La.) 1942] 1954, 57	2	0	2	0	0	0	0	0
Jim Harding (Iowa 1949) 1958	1	0	1	0	0	0	0	0
TOTAL	3	0	3	0	0	0	0	0

LOYOLA (MD.)

	Yrs.	W	L	CH	2D	3d%	4th	RR
Skip Prosser (Merchant Marine 1972) 1994	1	0	1	0	0	0	0	0
TOTAL	1	0	1	0	0	0	0	0

MANHATTAN

	Yrs.	W	L	CH	2D	3d%	4th	RR
Ken Norton (Long Island 1939) 1956, 58	2	1	3	0	0	0	0	0
Fran Fraschilla (Brooklyn 1980) 1993, 95	2	1	2	0	0	0	0	0
Bobby Gonzalez (Buffalo St. 1986) 2003, 04	2	1	2	0	0	0	0	0
TOTAL	6	3	7	0	0	0	0	0

MARIST

	Yrs.	W	L	CH	2D	3d%	4th	RR
Matt Furjanic (Point Park 1973) 1986	1	0	1	0	0	0	0	0
Dave Magarity [St. Francis (Pa.) 1974] 1987	1	0	1	0	0	0	0	0
TOTAL	2	0	2	0	0	0	0	0

MARQUETTE

	Yrs.	W	L	CH	2D	3d%	4th	RR
Jack Nagle (Marquette 1940) 1955RR	1	2	1	0	0	0	0	1
Eddie Hickey (Creighton 1927) 1959, 61	2	1	3	0	0	0	0	0
Al McGuire [St. John's (N.Y.) 1951] 1968, 69RR, 71, 72, 73, 74-2d, 75, 76RR, 77-CH	9	20	9	1	1	0	0	2
Hank Raymonds (St. Louis 1948) 1978, 79, 80, 82, 83	5	2	5	0	0	0	0	0
Kevin O'Neill (McGill 1979) 1993, 94	2	2	2	0	0	0	0	0
Mike Deane (Potsdam St. 1974) 1996, 97	2	1	2	0	0	0	0	0
Tom Crean (Central Mich. 1989) 2002, 03-T3d, 06, 07	4	4	4	0	0	1	0	0
TOTAL	25	32	26	1	1	1	0	3

MARSHALL*

	Yrs.	W	L	CH	2D	3d%	4th	RR
Jule Rivlin (Marshall 1940) 1956	1	0	1	0	0	0	0	0
Carl Tacy (Davis & Elkins 1956) 1972	1	0	1	0	0	0	0	0
Rick Huckabay (Louisiana Tech 1967) 1984, 85, 87*	3	0	3	0	0	0	0	0
TOTAL	5	0	5	0	0	0	0	0

	Yrs.	W	L	CH	2D	3d%	4th	RR
MARYLAND*								
H.A. "Bud" Millikan (Oklahoma St. 1942) 1958	1	2	1	0	0	0	0	0
Charles "Lefty" Driesell (Duke 1954) 1973RR, 75RR, 80, 81, 83, 84, 85, 86	8	10	8	0	0	0	0	2
Bob Wade (Morgan St. 1967) 1988*	1	1	1	0	0	0	0	0
Gary Williams (Maryland 1967) 1994, 95, 96, 97, 98, 99, 2000, 01-T3d, 02-CH, 03, 04, 07	12	23	11	1	0	1	0	0
TOTAL	22	36	21	1	0	1	0	2
MASSACHUSETTS*								
Matt Zunic (George Washington 1942) 1962	1	0	1	0	0	0	0	0
John Calipari (Clarion 1982) 1992, 93, 94, 95RR, 96-T3d*	5	11	5	0	0	1	0	1
James Flint (St. Joseph's 1987) 1997, 98	2	0	2	0	0	0	0	0
TOTAL	8	11	8	0	0	1	0	1
McNEESE ST.								
Steve Welch (Southeastern La. 1971) 1989	1	0	1	0	0	0	0	0
Tic Price (Virginia Tech 1979) 2002	1	0	1	0	0	0	0	0
TOTAL	2	0	2	0	0	0	0	0
MEMPHIS*								
Eugene Lambert (Arkansas 1929) 1955, 56	2	0	2	0	0	0	0	0
Bob Vanatta (Central Methodist 1945) 1962	1	0	1	0	0	0	0	0
Gene Bartow (Truman 1953) 1973-2d	1	3	1	0	1	0	0	0
Wayne Yates (Memphis 1961) 1976	1	0	1	0	0	0	0	0
Dana Kirk (Marshall 1960) 1982*, 83*, 84*, 85-T3d*, 86*	5	9	5	0	0	1	0	0
Larry Finch (Memphis 1973) 1988, 89, 92RR, 93, 95, 96	6	6	6	0	0	0	0	1
John Calipari (Clarion 1982) 2003, 04, 06RR, 07RR	4	7	4	0	0	0	0	2
TOTAL	20	25	20	0	1	1	0	3
MERCER								
Bill Bibb (Ky. Wesleyan 1957) 1981, 85	2	0	2	0	0	0	0	0
TOTAL	2	0	2	0	0	0	0	0
MIAMI (FLA.)								
Bruce Hale (Santa Clara 1941) 1960	1	0	1	0	0	0	0	0
Leonard Hamilton (Tenn.-Martin 1971) 1998, 99, 2000, 02	4	3	4	0	0	0	0	0
TOTAL	5	3	5	0	0	0	0	0
MIAMI (OHIO)								
Bill Rohr (Ohio Wesleyan 1940) 1953, 55, 57	3	0	3	0	0	0	0	0
Dick Shrider (Ohio 1948) 1958, 66	2	1	3	0	0	0	0	0
Tates Locke (Ohio Wesleyan 1959) 1969	1	1	2	0	0	0	0	0
Darrell Hedric [Miami (Ohio) 1955] 1971, 73, 78, 84	4	1	4	0	0	0	0	0
Jerry Peirson [Miami (Ohio) 1966] 1985, 86	2	0	2	0	0	0	0	0
Joby Wright (Indiana 1972) 1992	1	0	1	0	0	0	0	0
Herb Sendek (Carnegie Mellon 1985) 1995	1	1	1	0	0	0	0	0
Charlie Coles [Miami (Ohio) 1965] 1997, 99, 2007	3	2	3	0	0	0	0	0
TOTAL	17	6	19	0	0	0	0	0
MICHIGAN#*								
Osborne "Ozzie" Cowles (Carleton 1922) 1948RR	1	1	1	0	0	0	0	1
Dave Strack (Michigan 1946) 1964-3d, 65-2d, 66RR	3	7	3	0	1	1	0	1
Johnny Orr (Beloit 1949) 1974RR, 75, 76-2d, 77RR	4	7	4	0	1	0	0	2
Bill Frieder (Michigan 1964) 1985, 86, 87, 88	4	5	4	0	0	0	0	0
Steve Fisher (Illinois St. 1967) 1989-CH, 90, 92-2d*, 93-2d*, 94RR, 95, 96*	7	20	6	1	2	0	0	1
Brian Ellerbe (Rutgers 1985) 1998*	1	1	1	0	0	0	0	0
TOTAL	20	41	19	1	4	1	0	5
MICHIGAN ST.								
Forrest "Forddy" Anderson (Stanford 1942) 1957-4th, 59RR	2	3	3	0	0	0	1	1
George "Jud" Heathcote (Washington St. 1950) 1978RR, 79-CH, 85, 86, 90, 91, 92, 94, 95	9	14	8	1	0	0	0	1
Tom Izzo (Northern Mich. 1977) 1998, 99-T3d, 2000-CH, 01-T3d, 02, 03RR, 04, 05-T3d, 06, 07	10	24	9	1	0	3	0	1
TOTAL	21	41	20	2	0	3	1	3
MIDDLE TENN.								
Jimmy Earle (Middle Tenn. 1959) 1975, 77	2	0	2	0	0	0	0	0

	Yrs.	W	L	CH	2D	3d%	4th	RR
Stan Simpson (Ga. Southern 1961) 1982	1	1	1	0	0	0	0	0
Bruce Stewart (Jacksonville St. 1975) 1985, 87, 89	3	1	3	0	0	0	0	0
TOTAL	6	2	6	0	0	0	0	0
MILWAUKEE								
Bruce Pearl (Boston College 1982) 2003, 05	2	2	2	0	0	0	0	0
Rob Jeter (Wis.-Platteville 1991) 2006	1	1	1	0	0	0	0	0
TOTAL	3	3	3	0	0	0	0	0
MINNESOTA*								
Bill Musselman (Wittenberg 1961) 1972*	1	1	1	0	0	0	0	0
Jim Dutcher (Michigan 1955) 1982	1	1	1	0	0	0	0	0
Clem Haskins (Western Ky. 1967) 1989, 90RR, 94*, 95*, 97-T3d*, 99	6	10	6	0	0	1	0	1
Dan Monson (Idaho 1985) 2005	1	0	1	0	0	0	0	0
TOTAL	9	12	9	0	0	1	0	1
MISSISSIPPI								
Bob Weltlich (Ohio St. 1967) 1981	1	0	1	0	0	0	0	0
Rob Evans (New Mexico St. 1968) 1997, 98	2	0	2	0	0	0	0	0
Rod Barnes (Mississippi 1988) 1999, 2001, 02	3	3	3	0	0	0	0	0
TOTAL	6	3	6	0	0	0	0	0
MISSISSIPPI ST.								
James "Babe" McCarthy (Mississippi St. 1949) 1963	1	1	1	0	0	0	0	0
Richard Williams (Mississippi St. 1967) 1991, 95, 96-T3d	3	6	3	0	0	1	0	0
Rick Stansbury (Campbellsville 1982) 2002, 03, 04, 05	4	3	4	0	0	0	0	0
TOTAL	8	10	8	0	0	1	0	0
MISSISSIPPI VAL.								
Lafayette Stribling (Miss. Industrial 1957) 1986, 92, 96	3	0	3	0	0	0	0	0
TOTAL	3	0	3	0	0	0	0	0
MISSOURI#*								
George Edwards (Missouri 1913) 1944RR	1	1	1	0	0	0	0	1
Norm Stewart (Missouri 1956) 1976RR, 78, 80, 81, 82 83, 86, 87, 88, 89, 90, 92, 93, 94RR*, 95, 99	16	12	16	0	0	0	0	2
Quin Snyder (Duke 1989) 2000, 01, 02RR, 03	4	5	4	0	0	0	0	1
TOTAL	21	18	21	0	0	0	0	4
MISSOURI ST.								
Charlie Spoonhour (School of Ozarks 1961) 1987, 88, 89, 90, 92	5	1	5	0	0	0	0	0
Steve Alford (Indiana 1987) 1999	1	2	1	0	0	0	0	0
TOTAL	6	3	6	0	0	0	0	0
MONMOUTH								
Wayne Szoke (Maryland 1963) 1996	1	0	1	0	0	0	0	0
Dave Calloway (Monmouth 1991) 2001, 04, 06	3	1	3	0	0	0	0	0
TOTAL	4	1	4	0	0	0	0	0
MONTANA								
George "Jud" Heathcote (Washington St. 1950) 1975	1	1	2	0	0	0	0	0
Stew Morrill (Gonzaga 1974) 1991	1	0	1	0	0	0	0	0
Blaine Taylor (Montana 1982) 1992, 97	2	0	2	0	0	0	0	0
Don Holst (Northern Mont. 1975) 2002	1	0	1	0	0	0	0	0
Larry Krystkowiak (Montana 1996) 2005, 06	2	1	2	0	0	0	0	0
TOTAL	7	2	8	0	0	0	0	0
MONTANA ST.								
John Breeden (Montana St. 1929) 1951	1	0	1	0	0	0	0	0
Stu Starner (Minn.-Morris 1965) 1986	1	0	1	0	0	0	0	0
Mike Durham (Montana St. 1979) 1996	1	0	1	0	0	0	0	0
TOTAL	3	0	3	0	0	0	0	0
MOREHEAD ST.								
Robert Laughlin (Morehead St. 1937) 1956, 57, 61	3	3	4	0	0	0	0	0
Wayne Martin (Morehead St. 1968) 1983, 84	2	1	2	0	0	0	0	0
TOTAL	5	4	6	0	0	0	0	0
MT. ST. MARY'S								
James Phelan (La Salle 1951) 1995, 99	2	0	2	0	0	0	0	0
TOTAL	2	0	2	0	0	0	0	0
MURRAY ST.								
Cal Luther (Valparaiso 1951) 1964, 69	2	0	2	0	0	0	0	0
Steve Newton (Indiana St. 1963) 1988, 90, 91	3	1	3	0	0	0	0	0

	Yrs.	W	L	CH	2D	3d%	4th	RR
Scott Edgar (Pitt.-Johnstown 1978) 1992, 95	2	0	2	0	0	0	0	0
Mark Gottfried (Alabama 1987) 1997, 98	2	0	2	0	0	0	0	0
Tevester Anderson (Ark.-Pine Bluff 1962) 1999, 2002	2	0	2	0	0	0	0	0
Mick Cronin (Cincinnati 1997) 2004, 06	2	0	2	0	0	0	0	0
TOTAL	13	1	13	0	0	0	0	0
NAVY								
Ben Carnevale (New York U. 1938) 1947RR, 53, 54RR, 59, 60	5	4	6	0	0	0	0	2
Paul Evans (Ithaca 1967) 1985, 86RR	2	4	2	0	0	0	0	1
Pete Herrmann (Geneseo St. 1970) 1987	1	0	1	0	0	0	0	0
Don DeVoe (Ohio St. 1964) 1994, 97, 98	3	0	3	0	0	0	0	0
TOTAL	11	8	12	0	0	0	0	3
NEBRASKA								
Moe Iba (Oklahoma St. 1962) 1986	1	0	1	0	0	0	0	0
Danny Nee (St. Marys of the Plains 1971) 1991, 92, 93, 94, 98	5	0	5	0	0	0	0	0
TOTAL	6	0	6	0	0	0	0	0
NEVADA								
Sonny Allen (Marshall 1959) 1984, 85	2	0	2	0	0	0	0	0
Trent Johnson (Boise St. 1983) 2004	1	2	1	0	0	0	0	0
Mark Fox (Eastern N.M. 1991) 2005, 06, 07	3	2	3	0	0	0	0	0
TOTAL	6	4	6	0	0	0	0	0
UNLV								
Jerry Tarkanian (Fresno St. 1956) 1975, 76, 77-3d, 83, 84, 85, 86, 87-T3d, 88, 89RR, 90-CH, 91-T3d	12	30	11	1	0	3	0	1
Bill Bayno (Sacred Heart 1985) 1998, 2000	2	0	2	0	0	0	0	0
Lon Kruger (Kansas St. 1974) 2007	1	2	1	0	0	0	0	0
TOTAL	15	32	14	1	0	3	0	1
NEW MEXICO								
Bob King (Iowa 1947) 1968	1	0	2	0	0	0	0	0
Norm Ellenberger (Butler 1955) 1974, 78	2	2	2	0	0	0	0	0
Dave Bliss (Cornell 1965) 1991, 93, 94, 96, 97, 98, 99	7	4	7	0	0	0	0	0
Ritchie McKay (Seattle Pacific 1987) 2005	1	0	1	0	0	0	0	0
TOTAL	11	6	12	0	0	0	0	0
NEW MEXICO ST.*								
George McCarty (New Mexico St. 1950) 1952	1	0	2	0	0	0	0	0
Presley Askew (Southeastern Okla. 1930) 1959, 60	2	0	2	0	0	0	0	0
Ken Hayes (Northeastern St. 1956) 1979	1	0	1	0	0	0	0	0
Neil McCarthy (Sacramento St. 1965) 1990, 91, 92*, 93*, 94*	5	3	5	0	0	0	0	0
Lou Henson (New Mexico St. 1955) 1967, 68, 69, 70-3d, 71, 75, 99	7	7	8	0	0	1	0	0
Reggie Theus (UNLV 2002) 2007	1	0	1	0	0	0	0	0
TOTAL	17	10	19	0	0	1	0	0
NEW ORLEANS								
Benny Dees (Wyoming 1958) 1987	1	1	1	0	0	0	0	0
Tim Floyd (Louisiana Tech 1977) 1991, 93	2	0	2	0	0	0	0	0
Tic Price (Virginia Tech 1979) 1996	1	0	1	0	0	0	0	0
TOTAL	4	1	4	0	0	0	0	0
NEW YORK U.								
Howard Cann (New York U. 1920) 1943RR, 45-2d, 46RR	3	3	4	0	1	0	0	2
Lou Rossini (Columbia 1948) 1960-4th, 62, 63	3	6	5	0	0	0	1	0
TOTAL	6	9	9	0	1	0	1	2
NIAGARA								
Frank Layden (Niagara 1955) 1970	1	1	2	0	0	0	0	0
Joe Mihalich (La Salle 1978) 2005, 07	2	1	2	0	0	0	0	0
TOTAL	3	2	4	0	0	0	0	0
NICHOLLS ST.								
Rickey Broussard (La.-Lafayette 1970) 1995, 98	2	0	2	0	0	0	0	0
TOTAL	2	0	2	0	0	0	0	0
NORTH CAROLINA								
Bill Lange (Wittenberg 1921) 1941RR	1	0	2	0	0	0	0	1
Ben Carnevale (New York U. 1938) 1946-2d	1	2	1	0	1	0	0	0
Frank McGuire [St. John's (N.Y.) 1936] 1957-CH, 59	2	5	1	1	0	0	0	0
Dean Smith (Kansas 1953) 1967-4th, 68-2d, 69-4th, 72-3d, 75 76, 77-2d, 78, 79, 80, 81-2d, 82-CH, 83RR, 84, 85RR, 86, 87RR, 88RR, 89, 90, 91-T3d, 92, 93-CH, 94, 95-T3d, 96, 97-T3d	27	65	27	2	3	4	2	4
Bill Guthridge (Kansas St. 1963) 1998-T3d, 99, 2000-T3d	3	8	3	0	0	2	0	0
Matt Doherty (North Carolina 1984) 2001	1	1	1	0	0	0	0	0
Roy Williams (North Carolina 1972) 2004, 05-CH, 06, 07RR	4	11	3	1	0	0	0	1
TOTAL	39	92	38	4	4	6	2	6
UNC ASHEVILLE								
Eddie Biedenback (North Carolina St. 1968) 2003	1	1	1	0	0	0	0	0
TOTAL	1	1	1	0	0	0	0	0
UNC GREENSBORO								
Randy Peele (Va. Wesleyan 1980) 1996	1	0	1	0	0	0	0	0
Fran McCaffery (Penn 1982) 2001	1	0	1	0	0	0	0	0
TOTAL	2	0	2	0	0	0	0	0
UNC WILMINGTON								
Jerry Wainwright (Colorado Col. 1968) 2000, 02	2	1	2	0	0	0	0	0
Brad Brownell (DePauw 1991) 2003, 06	2	0	2	0	0	0	0	0
TOTAL	4	1	4	0	0	0	0	0
N.C. A&T								
Don Corbett [Lincoln (Mo.) 1965] 1982, 83, 84, 85, 86, 87, 88	7	0	7	0	0	0	0	0
Jeff Capel (Fayetteville St. 1977) 1994	1	0	1	0	0	0	0	0
Roy Thomas (Baylor 1974) 1995	1	0	1	0	0	0	0	0
TOTAL	9	0	9	0	0	0	0	0
NORTH CAROLINA ST.*								
Everett Case (Wisconsin 1923) 1950-3d, 51RR, 52, 54, 56	5	6	6	0	0	1	0	1
Press Maravich (Davis & Elkins 1941) 1965	1	1	1	0	0	0	0	0
Norm Sloan (North Carolina St. 1951) 1970, 74-CH, 80	3	5	2	1	0	0	0	0
Jim Valvano (Rutgers 1967) 1982, 83-CH, 85RR, 86RR 87*, 88*, 89	7	14	6	1	0	0	0	2
Les Robinson (North Carolina St. 1964) 1991	1	1	1	0	0	0	0	0
Herb Sendek (Carnegie Mellon 1985) 2002, 03, 04, 05, 06	5	5	5	0	0	0	0	0
TOTAL	22	32	21	2	0	1	0	3
NORTH TEXAS								
Jimmy Gales (Alcorn St. 1963) 1988	1	0	1	0	0	0	0	0
Johnny Jones (LSU 1985) 2007	1	0	1	0	0	0	0	1
TOTAL	2	0	2	0	0	0	0	0
NORTHEASTERN								
Jim Calhoun (American Int'l 1966) 1981, 82, 84, 85, 86	5	3	5	0	0	0	0	0
Karl Fogel (Colby 1968) 1987, 91	2	0	2	0	0	0	0	0
TOTAL	7	3	7	0	0	0	0	0
NORTHERN ARIZ.								
Ben Howland (Weber St. 1980) 1998	1	0	1	0	0	0	0	0
Mike Adras (UC Santa Barbara 1983) 2000	1	0	1	0	0	0	0	0
TOTAL	2	0	2	0	0	0	0	0
NORTHERN ILL.								
John McDougal (Evansville 1950) 1982	1	0	1	0	0	0	0	0
Jim Molinari (Ill. Wesleyan 1977) 1991	1	0	1	0	0	0	0	0
Brian Hammel (Bentley 1975) 1996	1	0	1	0	0	0	0	0
TOTAL	3	0	3	0	0	0	0	0
UNI								
Eldon Miller (Wittenberg 1961) 1990	1	1	1	0	0	0	0	0
Greg McDermott (UNI 1988) 2004, 05, 06	3	0	3	0	0	0	0	0
TOTAL	4	1	4	0	0	0	0	0
NORTHWESTERN ST.								
Mike McConathy (Louisiana Tech 1977) 2001, 06	2	2	2	0	0	0	0	0
TOTAL	2	2	2	0	0	0	0	0
NOTRE DAME								
John Jordan (Notre Dame 1935) 1953RR, 54RR, 57, 58RR, 60, 63	6	8	6	0	0	0	0	3
Johnny Dee (Notre Dame 1946) 1965, 69, 70, 71	4	2	6	0	0	0	0	0
Richard "Digger" Phelps (Rider 1963) 1974,75, 76, 77, 78-4th, 79RR, 80, 81, 85, 86, 87, 88, 89, 90	14	15	16	0	0	0	1	1
Mike Brey (George Washington 1982) 2001, 02, 03, 07	4	4	4	0	0	0	0	0
TOTAL	28	29	32	0	0	0	1	4
OAKLAND								
Greg Kampe (Bowling Green 1978) 2005	1	1	1	0	0	0	0	0
TOTAL	1	1	1	0	0	0	0	0

OHIO

	Yrs.	W	L	CH	2D	3d%	4th	RR
James Snyder (Ohio 1941) 1960, 61, 64RR, 65, 70, 72, 74	7	3	8	0	0	0	0	1
Danny Nee (St. Mary of the Plains 1971) 1983, 85	2	1	2	0	0	0	0	0
Larry Hunter (Ohio 1971) 1994	1	0	1	0	0	0	0	0
Tim O'Shea (Boston College 1984) 2005	1	0	1	0	0	0	0	0
TOTAL	11	4	12	0	0	0	0	1

OHIO ST.*

	Yrs.	W	L	CH	2D	3d%	4th	RR
Harold Olsen (Wisconsin 1917) 1939-2d, 44-T3d, 45-T3d, 46-3d	4	6	4	0	1	3	0	0
William "Tippy" Dye (Ohio St. 1937) 1950RR	1	1	1	0	0	0	0	1
Fred Taylor (Ohio St. 1950) 1960-CH, 61-2d, 62-2d, 68-3d, 71RR	5	14	4	1	2	1	0	1
Eldon Miller (Wittenberg 1961) 1980, 82, 83, 85	4	3	4	0	0	0	0	0
Gary Williams (Maryland 1967) 1987	1	1	1	0	0	0	0	0
Randy Ayers [Miami (Ohio) 1978] 1990, 91, 92RR	3	6	3	0	0	0	0	1
Jim O'Brien (Boston College 1971) 1999-T3d*, 2000*, 01*, 02*	4	6	4	0	0	1	0	0
Thad Matta (Butler 1990) 2006, 07-2d	2	6	2	0	1	0	0	0
TOTAL	24	43	23	1	4	5	0	3

OKLAHOMA

	Yrs.	W	L	CH	2D	3d%	4th	RR
Bruce Drake (Oklahoma 1929) 1939-T3d, 43RR, 47-2d	3	4	3	0	1	1	0	1
Dave Bliss (Cornell 1965) 1979	1	1	1	0	0	0	0	0
Billy Tubbs (Lamar 1958) 1983, 84, 85RR, 86, 87, 88-2d, 89, 90, 92	9	15	9	0	1	0	0	1
Kelvin Sampson (UNC Pembroke 1978) 1995, 96, 97, 98, 99, 2000, 01, 02-T3d, 03RR, 05, 06	11	11	11	0	0	1	0	1
TOTAL	24	31	24	0	2	2	0	3

OKLAHOMA CITY

	Yrs.	W	L	CH	2D	3d%	4th	RR
Doyle Parrack (Oklahoma St. 1945) 1952, 53, 54, 55	4	1	5	0	0	0	0	0
A.E. "Abe" Lemons (Oklahoma City 1949) 1956RR, 57RR, 63, 64, 65, 66, 73	7	7	8	0	0	0	0	2
TOTAL	11	8	13	0	0	0	0	2

OKLAHOMA ST.

	Yrs.	W	L	CH	2D	3d%	4th	RR
Hank Iba [Westminster (Mo.) 1928] 1945-CH, 46-CH, 49-2d, 51-4th, 53-RR, 54-RR, 58RR, 65RR	8	15	7	2	1	0	1	4
Paul Hansen (Oklahoma City 1950) 1983	1	0	1	0	0	0	0	0
Eddie Sutton (Oklahoma St. 1958) 1991, 92, 93, 94, 95-T3d, 98, 99, 2000RR, 01, 02, 03, 04-T3d, 05	13	22	13	0	0	2	0	1
TOTAL	22	37	21	2	1	2	1	5

OLD DOMINION

	Yrs.	W	L	CH	2D	3d%	4th	RR
Paul Webb (William & Mary 1951) 1980, 82, 85	3	0	3	0	0	0	0	0
Tom Young (Maryland 1958) 1986	1	1	1	0	0	0	0	0
Oliver Purnell (Old Dominion 1975) 1992	1	0	1	0	0	0	0	0
Jeff Capel (Fayetteville St. 1977) 1995, 97	2	1	2	0	0	0	0	0
Blaine Taylor (Montana 1982) 2005, 07	2	0	2	0	0	0	0	0
TOTAL	9	2	9	0	0	0	0	0

ORAL ROBERTS

	Yrs.	W	L	CH	2D	3d%	4th	RR
Ken Trickey (Middle Tenn. 1954) 1974RR	1	2	1	0	0	0	0	1
Dick Acres (UC Santa Barbara) 1984	1	0	1	0	0	0	0	0
Scott Sutton (Oklahoma St. 1994) 2006, 07	2	0	2	0	0	0	0	0
TOTAL	4	2	4	0	0	0	0	1

OREGON

	Yrs.	W	L	CH	2D	3d%	4th	RR
Howard Hobson (Oregon 1926) 1939-CH	1	3	0	1	0	0	0	0
John Warren (Oregon 1928) 1945RR	1	1	1	0	0	0	0	1
Steve Belko (Idaho 1939) 1960RR, 61	2	2	2	0	0	0	0	1
Jerry Green (Appalachian St. 1968) 1995	1	0	1	0	0	0	0	0
Ernie Kent (Oregon 1977) 2000, 02RR, 03, 07RR	4	6	4	0	0	0	0	2
TOTAL	9	12	8	1	0	0	0	4

OREGON ST.*

	Yrs.	W	L	CH	2D	3d%	4th	RR
Amory "Slats" Gill (Oregon St. 1925) 1947RR, 49-4th, 55RR, 62RR, 63-4th, 64	6	8	8	0	0	0	2	3
Paul Valenti (Oregon St. 1942) 1966RR	1	1	1	0	0	0	0	1
Ralph Miller (Kansas 1942) 1975, 80*, 81*, 82RR*, 84, 85, 88, 89	8	3	9	0	0	0	0	1
Jim Anderson (Oregon St. 1959) 1990	1	0	1	0	0	0	0	0
TOTAL	16	12	19	0	0	0	2	5

PACIFIC

	Yrs.	W	L	CH	2D	3d%	4th	RR
Dick Edwards (Culver-Stockton 1952) 1966, 67RR, 71	3	2	4	0	0	0	0	1
Stan Morrison (California 1962) 1979	1	0	1	0	0	0	0	0
Bob Thomason (Pacific 1971) 1997, 2004, 05, 06	4	2	4	0	0	0	0	0
TOTAL	8	4	9	0	0	0	0	1

PENN

	Yrs.	W	L	CH	2D	3d%	4th	RR
Howard "Howie" Dallmar (Stanford 1948) 1953	1	1	1	0	0	0	0	0
Dick Harter (Penn 1953) 1970, 71RR	2	2	2	0	0	0	0	1
Chuck Daly (Bloomsburg 1953) 1972RR, 73, 74, 75	4	3	5	0	0	0	0	1
Bob Weinhauer (Cortland St. 1961) 1978, 79-4th, 80, 82	4	6	5	0	0	0	1	0
Craig Littlepage (Penn 1973) 1985	1	0	1	0	0	0	0	0
Tom Schneider (Bucknell 1969) 1987	1	0	1	0	0	0	0	0
Fran Dunphy (La Salle 1970) 1993, 94, 95, 99, 2000, 02, 03, 05, 06	9	1	9	0	0	0	0	0
Glen Miller (Connecticut 1986) 2007	1	0	1	0	0	0	0	0
TOTAL	23	13	25	0	0	0	1	2

PENN ST.

	Yrs.	W	L	CH	2D	3d%	4th	RR
John Lawther [Westminster (Pa.) 1919] 1942RR	1	1	1	0	0	0	0	1
Elmer Gross (Penn St. 1942) 1952, 54-3d	2	4	3	0	0	1	0	0
John Egli (Penn St. 1947) 1955, 65	2	1	3	0	0	0	0	0
Bruce Parkhill (Lock Haven 1971) 1991	1	1	1	0	0	0	0	0
Jerry Dunn (George Mason 1980) 1996, 2001	2	2	2	0	0	0	0	0
TOTAL	8	9	10	0	0	1	0	1

PEPPERDINE

	Yrs.	W	L	CH	2D	3d%	4th	RR
Al Duer (Emporia St. 1929) 1944RR	1	0	2	0	0	0	0	1
R.L. "Duck" Dowell (Northwest Mo. St. 1933) 1962	1	1	1	0	0	0	0	0
Gary Colson (David Lipscomb 1956) 1976, 79	2	2	2	0	0	0	0	0
Jim Harrick [Charleston (W.V.) 1960] 1982, 83, 85, 86	4	1	4	0	0	0	0	0
Tom Asbury (Wyoming 1967) 1991, 92, 94	3	0	3	0	0	0	0	0
Jan van Breda Kolff (Vanderbilt 1974) 2000	1	1	1	0	0	0	0	0
Paul Westphal (Southern California 1972) 2002	1	0	1	0	0	0	0	0
TOTAL	13	5	14	0	0	0	0	1

PITTSBURGH

	Yrs.	W	L	CH	2D	3d%	4th	RR
Henry Carlson (Pittsburgh 1917) 1941-T3d	1	1	1	0	0	1	0	0
Bob Timmons (Pittsburgh 1933) 1957, 58, 63	3	1	4	0	0	0	0	0
Charles "Buzz" Ridl [Westminster (Pa.) 1942] 1974RR	1	2	1	0	0	0	0	1
Roy Chipman (Maine 1961) 1981, 82, 85	3	1	3	0	0	0	0	0
Paul Evans (Ithaca 1967) 1987, 88, 89, 91, 93	5	3	5	0	0	0	0	0
Ben Howland (Weber St. 1980) 2002, 03	2	4	2	0	0	0	0	0
Jamie Dixon (TCU 1987) 2004, 05, 06, 07	4	5	4	0	0	0	0	0
TOTAL	19	17	20	0	0	1	0	1

PORTLAND

	Yrs.	W	L	CH	2D	3d%	4th	RR
Al Negratti (Seton Hall 1943) 1959	1	0	1	0	0	0	0	0
Rob Chavez (Mesa St. 1980) 1996	1	0	1	0	0	0	0	0
TOTAL	2	0	2	0	0	0	0	0

PRAIRIE VIEW

	Yrs.	W	L	CH	2D	3d%	4th	RR
Elwood Plummer (Jackson St. 1966) 1998	1	0	1	0	0	0	0	0
TOTAL	1	0	1	0	0	0	0	0

PRINCETON#

	Yrs.	W	L	CH	2D	3d%	4th	RR
Franklin Cappon (Michigan 1924) 1952, 55, 60	3	0	5	0	0	0	0	0
J.L. "Jake" McCandless (Princeton 1951) 1961	1	1	2	0	0	0	0	0
Butch van Breda Kolff (Princeton 1947) 1963, 64, 65-3d, 67	4	7	5	0	0	1	0	0
Pete Carril (Lafayette 1952) 1969, 76, 77, 81, 83, 84, 89, 90, 91, 92, 96	11	4	11	0	0	0	0	0
Bill Carmody [Union (N.Y.) 1975] 1997, 98	2	1	2	0	0	0	0	0
John Thompson III (Princeton 1989) 2001, 04	2	0	2	0	0	0	0	0
TOTAL	23	13	27	0	0	1	0	0

PROVIDENCE

	Yrs.	W	L	CH	2D	3d%	4th	RR
Joe Mullaney (Holy Cross 1949) 1964, 65RR, 66	3	2	3	0	0	0	0	1
Dave Gavitt (Dartmouth 1959) 1972, 73-4th, 74, 77, 78	5	5	6	0	0	0	1	0
Rick Pitino (Massachusetts 1974) 1987 tie-3d	1	4	1	0	0	1	0	0
Rick Barnes (Lenior-Rhyne 1977) 1989, 90, 94	3	0	3	0	0	0	0	0
Pete Gillen (Fairfield 1968) 1997RR	1	3	1	0	0	0	0	1

	Yrs.	W	L	CH	2D	3d%	4th	RR
Tim Welsh (Potsdam St. 1984) 2001, 04	2	0	2	0	0	0	0	0
TOTAL	15	14	16	0	0	1	1	2
PURDUE*								
George King [Charleston (W.V.) 1950] 1969-2d	1	3	1	0	1	0	0	0
Fred Schaus (West Virginia 1949) 1977	1	0	1	0	0	0	0	0
Lee Rose (Transylvania 1958) 1980-3d	1	5	1	0	0	1	0	0
Gene Keady (Kansas St. 1958) 1983, 84, 85, 86, 87, 88, 90, 91, 93, 94RR, 95, 96*, 97, 98, 99, 2000RR, 03	17	19	17	0	0	0	0	2
Matt Painter (Purdue 1993) 2007	1	1	1	0	0	0	0	0
TOTAL	21	28	21	0	1	1	0	2
RADFORD								
Ron Bradley (Eastern Nazarene 1973) 1998	1	0	1	0	0	0	0	0
TOTAL	1	0	1	0	0	0	0	0
RHODE ISLAND								
Ernie Calverley (Rhode Island 1946) 1961, 66	2	0	2	0	0	0	0	0
Jack Kraft (St. Joseph's 1942) 1978	1	0	1	0	0	0	0	0
Tom Penders (Connecticut 1967) 1988	1	2	1	0	0	0	0	0
Al Skinner (Massachusetts 1974) 1993, 97	2	1	2	0	0	0	0	0
Jim Harrick [Charleston (W.V.) 1960] 1998RR, 99	2	3	2	0	0	0	0	1
TOTAL	8	6	8	0	0	0	0	1
RICE								
Byron "Buster" Brannon (TCU 1933) 1940RR, 42RR	2	1	3	0	0	0	0	2
Don Suman (Rice 1944) 1954	1	1	1	0	0	0	0	0
Don Knodel [Miami (Ohio) 1953] 1970	1	0	1	0	0	0	0	0
TOTAL	4	2	5	0	0	0	0	2
RICHMOND								
Dick Tarrant (Fordham 1951) 1984, 86, 88, 90, 91	5	5	5	0	0	0	0	0
John Beilein (Wheeling Jesuit 1975) 1998	1	1	1	0	0	0	0	0
Jerry Wainwright (Colorado Col. 1968) 2004	1	0	1	0	0	0	0	0
TOTAL	7	6	7	0	0	0	0	0
RIDER								
John Carpenter (Penn St. 1958) 1984	1	0	1	0	0	0	0	0
Kevin Bannon (St. Peter's 1979) 1993, 94	2	0	2	0	0	0	0	0
TOTAL	3	0	3	0	0	0	0	0
ROBERT MORRIS								
Matt Furjanic (Point Park 1973) 1982, 83	2	1	2	0	0	0	0	0
Jarrett Durham (Duquesne 1971) 1989, 90, 92	3	0	3	0	0	0	0	0
TOTAL	5	1	5	0	0	0	0	0
RUTGERS								
Tom Young (Maryland 1958) 1975, 76-4th, 79, 83	4	5	5	0	0	0	1	0
Bob Wenzel (Rutgers 1971) 1989, 91	2	0	2	0	0	0	0	0
TOTAL	6	5	7	0	0	0	1	0
ST. BONAVENTURE								
Eddie Donovan (St. Bonaventure 1950) 1961	1	2	1	0	0	0	0	0
Larry Weise (St. Bonaventure 1958) 1968, 70-4th	2	4	4	0	0	0	1	0
Jim Satalin (St. Bonaventure 1969) 1978	1	0	1	0	0	0	0	0
Jim Baron (St. Bonaventure 1977) 2000	1	0	1	0	0	0	0	0
TOTAL	5	6	7	0	0	0	1	0
ST. FRANCIS (PA.)								
Jim Baron (St. Bonaventure 1977) 1991	1	0	1	0	0	0	0	0
TOTAL	1	0	1	0	0	0	0	0
ST. JOHN'S (N.Y.)*								
Frank McGuire [St. John's (N.Y.) 1936] 1951RR, 52-2d	2	5	2	0	1	0	0	1
Joe Lapchick (No college) 1961	1	0	1	0	0	0	0	0
Frank Mulzoff [St. John's (N.Y.) 1951] 1973	1	0	1	0	0	0	0	0
Lou Carnesecca [St. John's (N.Y.) 1946] 1967, 68, 69, 76, 77, 78, 79RR, 80, 82, 83, 84, 85-T3d, 86, 87, 88, 90, 91RR, 92	18	17	20	0	0	1	0	2
Brian Mahoney (Manhattan 1971) 1993	1	1	1	0	0	0	0	0
Fran Fraschilla (Brooklyn 1980) 1998	1	0	1	0	0	0	0	0
Mike Jarvis (Northeastern 1968) 1999RR, 2000, 02*	3	4	3	0	0	0	0	1
TOTAL	27	27	29	0	1	1	0	4
ST. JOSEPH'S*								
John "Jack" Ramsay (St. Joseph's 1949) 1959, 60, 61-3d*, 62, 63RR, 65, 66	7	8	11	0	0	1	0	1
John "Jack" McKinney (St. Joseph's 1957) 1969, 71, 73, 74	4	0	4	0	0	0	0	0

	Yrs.	W	L	CH	2D	3d%	4th	RR
Jim Lynam (St. Joseph's 1964) 1981RR	1	3	1	0	0	0	0	1
Jim Boyle (St. Joseph's 1964) 1982, 86	2	1	2	0	0	0	0	0
Phil Martelli (Widener 1976) 1997, 2001, 03, 04RR	4	6	4	0	0	0	0	1
TOTAL	18	18	22	0	0	1	0	3
ST. LOUIS								
Eddie Hickey (Creighton 1927) 1952RR, 57	2	1	3	0	0	0	0	1
Charlie Spoonhour (School of Ozarks 1961) 1994, 95, 98	3	2	3	0	0	0	0	0
Lorenzo Romar (Washington 1980) 2000	1	0	1	0	0	0	0	0
TOTAL	6	3	7	0	0	0	0	1
ST. MARY'S (CAL.)								
James Weaver (DePaul 1947) 1959RR	1	1	1	0	0	0	0	1
Lynn Nance (Washington 1965) 1989	1	0	1	0	0	0	0	0
Ernie Kent (Oregon 1977) 1997	1	0	1	0	0	0	0	0
Randy Bennett (UC San Diego 1986) 2005	1	0	1	0	0	0	0	0
TOTAL	4	1	4	0	0	0	0	1
ST. PETER'S								
Ted Fiore (Seton Hall 1962) 1991, 95	2	0	2	0	0	0	0	0
TOTAL	2	0	2	0	0	0	0	0
SAM HOUSTON ST.								
Bob Marlin (Mississippi St. 1981) 2003	1	0	1	0	0	0	0	0
TOTAL	1	0	1	0	0	0	0	0
SAMFORD								
Jimmy Tillette (Our Lady of Holy Cross 1975) 1999, 2000	2	0	2	0	0	0	0	0
TOTAL	2	0	2	0	0	0	0	0
SAN DIEGO								
Jim Brovelli (San Francisco 1964) 1984	1	0	1	0	0	0	0	0
Hank Egan (Navy 1960) 1987	1	0	1	0	0	0	0	0
Brad Holland (UCLA 1979) 2003	1	0	1	0	0	0	0	0
TOTAL	3	0	3	0	0	0	0	0
SAN DIEGO ST.								
Tim Vezie (Denver 1967) 1975, 76	2	0	2	0	0	0	0	0
Dave "Smokey" Gaines (LeMoyne-Owen 1963) 1985	1	0	1	0	0	0	0	0
Steve Fisher (Illinois St. 1967) 2002, 06	2	0	2	0	0	0	0	0
TOTAL	5	0	5	0	0	0	0	0
SAN FRANCISCO								
Phil Woolpert (Loyola Marymount 1940) 1955-CH, 56-CH, 57-3d, 58	4	13	2	2	0	1	0	0
Peter Peletta (Sacramento St. 1950) 1963, 64RR, 65RR	3	3	3	0	0	0	0	2
Bob Gaillard (San Francisco 1962) 1972, 73RR, 74RR, 77, 78	5	4	5	0	0	0	0	2
Dan Belluomini (San Francisco 1964) 1979	1	1	1	0	0	0	0	0
Peter Barry (San Francisco 1970) 1981, 82	2	0	2	0	0	0	0	0
Phil Mathews (UC Irvine 1972) 1998	1	0	1	0	0	0	0	0
TOTAL	16	21	14	2	0	1	0	4
SAN JOSE ST.								
Walter McPherson (San Jose St. 1940) 1951	1	0	1	0	0	0	0	0
Bill Berry (Michigan St. 1965) 1980	1	0	1	0	0	0	0	0
Stan Morrison (California 1962) 1996	1	0	1	0	0	0	0	0
TOTAL	3	0	3	0	0	0	0	0
SANTA CLARA								
Bob Feerick (Santa Clara 1941) 1952-4th, 53RR, 54RR, 60	4	6	6	0	0	0	1	2
Dick Garibaldi (Santa Clara 1957) 1968RR, 69RR, 70	3	3	3	0	0	0	0	2
Carroll Williams (San Jose St. 1955) 1987	1	0	1	0	0	0	0	0
Dick Davey (Pacific 1964) 1993, 95, 96	3	2	3	0	0	0	0	0
TOTAL	11	11	13	0	0	0	1	4
SEATTLE#								
Al Brightman [Charleston (W.V.)] 1953, 54, 55, 56	4	4	6	0	0	0	0	0
John Castellani (Notre Dame 1952) 1958-2d	1	4	1	0	1	0	0	0
Vince Cazzetta (Arnold 1950) 1961, 62	2	0	2	0	0	0	0	0
Clair Markey (Seattle 1963) 1963	1	0	1	0	0	0	0	0
Bob Boyd (Southern California 1953) 1964	1	2	1	0	0	0	0	0
Lionel Purcell (UC Santa Barbara 1952) 1967	1	0	1	0	0	0	0	0
Morris Buckwalter (Utah 1956) 1969	1	0	1	0	0	0	0	0
TOTAL	11	10	13	0	1	0	0	0
SETON HALL								
P. J. Carlesimo (Fordham 1971) 1988, 89-2d, 91RR, 92, 93, 94	6	12	6	0	1	0	0	1

	Yrs.	W	L	CH	2D	3d%	4th	RR
Tommy Amaker (Duke 1987) 2000	1	2	1	0	0	0	0	0
Louis Orr (Syracuse 1980) 2004, 06	2	1	2	0	0	0	0	0
TOTAL	9	15	9	0	1	0	0	1

SIENA

	Yrs.	W	L	CH	2D	3d%	4th	RR
Mike Deane (Potsdam St. 1974) 1989	1	1	1	0	0	0	0	0
Paul Hewitt (St. John Fisher 1985) 1999	1	0	1	0	0	0	0	0
Rob Lanier (St. Bonaventure 1990) 2002	1	1	1	0	0	0	0	0
TOTAL	3	2	3	0	0	0	0	0

SOUTH ALA.

	Yrs.	W	L	CH	2D	3d%	4th	RR
Cliff Ellis (Florida St. 1968) 1979, 80	2	0	2	0	0	0	0	0
Ronnie Arrow (Texas St. 1969) 1989, 91	2	1	2	0	0	0	0	0
Bill Musselman (Wittenberg 1962) 1997	1	0	1	0	0	0	0	0
Bob Weltlich (Ohio St. 1967) 1998	1	0	1	0	0	0	0	0
John Pelphrey (Kentucky 1992) 2006	1	0	1	0	0	0	0	0
TOTAL	7	1	7	0	0	0	0	0

SOUTH CAROLINA

	Yrs.	W	L	CH	2D	3d%	4th	RR
Frank McGuire [St. John's (N.Y.) 1936] 1971, 72, 73, 74	4	4	5	0	0	0	0	0
George Felton (South Carolina 1975) 1989	1	0	1	0	0	0	0	0
Eddie Fogler (North Carolina 1970) 1997, 98	2	0	2	0	0	0	0	0
Dave Odom (Guilford 1965) 2004	1	0	1	0	0	0	0	0
TOTAL	8	4	9	0	0	0	0	0

SOUTH CAROLINA ST.

	Yrs.	W	L	CH	2D	3d%	4th	RR
Cy Alexander (Catawba 1975) 1989, 96, 98, 2000, 03	5	0	5	0	0	0	0	0
TOTAL	5	0	5	0	0	0	0	0

SOUTH FLA.

	Yrs.	W	L	CH	2D	3d%	4th	RR
Bobby Paschal (Stetson 1964) 1990, 92	2	0	2	0	0	0	0	0
TOTAL	2	0	2	0	0	0	0	0

SOUTHEAST MO. ST.

	Yrs.	W	L	CH	2D	3d%	4th	RR
Gary Garner (Missouri 1965) 2000	1	0	1	0	0	0	0	0
TOTAL	1	0	1	0	0	0	0	0

SOUTHEASTERN LA.

	Yrs.	W	L	CH	2D	3d%	4th	RR
Billy Kennedy (Southeastern La. 1986) 2005	1	0	1	0	0	0	0	0
TOTAL	1	0	1	0	0	0	0	0

SOUTHERN U.

	Yrs.	W	L	CH	2D	3d%	4th	RR
Carl Stewart (Grambling 1954) 1981	1	0	1	0	0	0	0	0
Robert Hopkins (Grambling 1956) 1985	1	0	1	0	0	0	0	0
Ben Jobe (Fisk 1956) 1987, 88, 89, 93	4	1	4	0	0	0	0	0
Rob Spivery (Ashland 1972) 2006	1	0	1	0	0	0	0	0
TOTAL	7	1	7	0	0	0	0	0

SOUTHERN CALIFORNIA

	Yrs.	W	L	CH	2D	3d%	4th	RR
Justin "Sam" Barry (Lawrence 13) 1940-T3d	1	1	1	0	0	1	0	0
Forrest Twogood (Iowa 1929) 1954-4th, 60, 61	3	3	5	0	0	0	1	0
Bob Boyd (Southern California 1953) 1979	1	1	1	0	0	0	0	0
Stan Morrison (California 1962) 1982, 85	2	0	2	0	0	0	0	0
George Raveling (Villanova 1960) 1991, 92	2	1	2	0	0	0	0	0
Henry Bibby (UCLA 1972) 1997, 2001RR, 02	3	3	3	0	0	0	0	1
Tim Floyd (Louisiana Tech 1977) 2007	1	2	1	0	0	0	0	0
TOTAL	13	11	15	0	0	1	1	1

SOUTHERN ILL.

	Yrs.	W	L	CH	2D	3d%	4th	RR
Paul Lambert (William Jewell 1956) 1977	1	1	1	0	0	0	0	0
Rich Herrin (McKendree 1956) 1993, 94, 95	3	0	3	0	0	0	0	0
Bruce Weber (Milwaukee 1978) 2002, 03	2	2	2	0	0	0	0	0
Matt Painter (Purdue 1994) 2004	1	0	1	0	0	0	0	0
Chris Lowery (Southern Ill. 1995) 2005, 06, 07	3	3	3	0	0	0	0	0
TOTAL	10	6	10	0	0	0	0	0

SMU

	Yrs.	W	L	CH	2D	3d%	4th	RR
E.O. "Doc" Hayes (North Texas 1927) 1955, 56-4th, 57, 65, 66, 67RR	6	7	8	0	0	0	1	1
Dave Bliss (Cornell 1965) 1984, 85, 88	3	3	3	0	0	0	0	0
John Shumate (Notre Dame 1974) 1993	1	0	1	0	0	0	0	0
TOTAL	10	10	12	0	0	0	1	1

SOUTHERN MISS.

	Yrs.	W	L	CH	2D	3d%	4th	RR
M.K. Turk (Livingston 1964) 1990, 91	2	0	2	0	0	0	0	0
TOTAL	2	0	2	0	0	0	0	0

SOUTHERN UTAH

	Yrs.	W	L	CH	2D	3d%	4th	RR
Bill Evans (Southern Utah 1972) 2001	1	0	1	0	0	0	0	0
TOTAL	1	0	1	0	0	0	0	0

SPRINGFIELD

	Yrs.	W	L	CH	2D	3d%	4th	RR
Ed Hickox (Ohio Wesleyan 1905) 1940RR	1	0	1	0	0	0	0	1
TOTAL	1	0	1	0	0	0	0	1

STANFORD

	Yrs.	W	L	CH	2D	3d%	4th	RR
Everett Dean (Indiana 1921) 1942-CH	1	3	0	1	0	0	0	0
Mike Montgomery (Long Beach St. 1968) 1989, 92, 95, 96, 97, 98-T3d, 99, 2000, 01RR, 02, 03, 04	12	16	12	0	0	1	0	1
Trent Johnson (Boise St. 1983) 2005, 07	2	0	2	0	0	0	0	0
TOTAL	15	19	14	1	0	1	0	1

SYRACUSE

	Yrs.	W	L	CH	2D	3d%	4th	RR
Marc Guley (Syracuse 1936) 1957RR	1	2	1	0	0	0	0	1
Fred Lewis (Eastern Ky. 1946) 1966RR	1	1	1	0	0	0	0	1
Roy Danforth (Southern Miss. 1962) 1973, 74, 75-4th, 76	4	5	5	0	0	0	1	0
Jim Boeheim (Syracuse 1966) 1977, 78, 79, 80, 83, 84, 85, 86, 87-2d, 88, 89RR, 90, 91, 92, 94, 95, 96-2d, 98, 99, 2000, 01, 03-CH, 04, 05, 06	25	40	24	1	2	0	0	1
TOTAL	31	48	31	1	2	0	1	3

TEMPLE

	Yrs.	W	L	CH	2D	3d%	4th	RR
Josh Cody (Vanderbilt 1920) 1944RR	1	1	1	0	0	0	0	1
Harry Litwack (Temple 1930) 1956-3d, 58-3d, 64, 67, 70, 72	6	7	6	0	0	2	0	0
Don Casey (Temple 1970) 1979	1	0	1	0	0	0	0	0
John Chaney (Bethune-Cookman 1955) 1984, 85, 86, 87, 88RR, 90, 91RR, 92, 93RR, 94, 95, 96, 97, 98, 99RR, 2000, 01RR	17	23	17	0	0	0	0	5
TOTAL	25	31	25	0	0	2	0	6

TENNESSEE

	Yrs.	W	L	CH	2D	3d%	4th	RR
Ramon "Ray" Mears [Miami (Ohio) 1949] 1967, 76, 77	3	0	4	0	0	0	0	0
Don DeVoe (Ohio St. 1964) 1979, 80, 81, 82, 83, 89	6	5	6	0	0	0	0	0
Jerry Green (Appalachian St. 1968) 1998, 99, 2000, 01	4	3	4	0	0	0	0	0
Bruce Pearl (Boston College 1982) 2006, 07	2	3	2	0	0	0	0	0
TOTAL	15	11	16	0	0	0	0	0

TENNESSEE ST.

	Yrs.	W	L	CH	2D	3d%	4th	RR
Frankie Allen (Roanoke 1971) 1993, 94	2	0	2	0	0	0	0	0
TOTAL	2	0	2	0	0	0	0	0

TENNESSEE TECH

	Yrs.	W	L	CH	2D	3d%	4th	RR
Johnny Oldham (Western Ky. 1948) 1958, 63	2	0	2	0	0	0	0	0
TOTAL	2	0	2	0	0	0	0	0

TEXAS

	Yrs.	W	L	CH	2D	3d%	4th	RR
H.C. "Bully" Gilstrap (Texas 1922) 1943-T3d	1	1	1	0	0	1	0	0
Jack Gray (Texas 1935) 1939RR, 47-3d	2	2	3	0	0	1	0	1
Harold Bradley (Hartwick 1934) 1960, 63	2	2	3	0	0	0	0	0
Leon Black (Texas 1953) 1972, 74	2	1	3	0	0	0	0	0
A.E. "Abe" Lemons (Oklahoma City 1949) 1979	1	0	1	0	0	0	0	0
Tom Penders (Connecticut 1967) 1989, 90RR, 91, 92, 94, 95, 96, 97	8	10	8	0	0	0	0	1
Rick Barnes (Lenior-Rhyne 1977) 1999, 2000, 01, 02, 03-T3d, 04, 05, 06RR, 07	9	13	9	0	0	1	0	1
TOTAL	25	29	28	0	0	3	0	3

UTSA

	Yrs.	W	L	CH	2D	3d%	4th	RR
Ken Burmeister [St. Mary's (Tex.) 1971] 1988	1	0	1	0	0	0	0	0
Tim Carter (Kansas 1979) 1999, 2004	2	0	2	0	0	0	0	0
TOTAL	3	0	3	0	0	0	0	0

TEXAS A&M

	Yrs.	W	L	CH	2D	3d%	4th	RR
John Floyd (Oklahoma St. 1941) 1951	1	0	1	0	0	0	0	0
Shelby Metcalf (Tex. A&M-Commerce 1953) 1964, 69, 75, 80, 87	5	3	6	0	0	0	0	0
Billy Gillispie (Texas St. 1983) 2006, 07	2	3	2	0	0	0	0	0
TOTAL	8	6	9	0	0	0	0	0

A&M-CORPUS CHRISTI

	Yrs.	W	L	CH	2D	3d%	4th	RR
Ronnie Arrow (Texas St. 1969) 2007	1	0	1	0	0	0	0	0
TOTAL	1	0	1	0	0	0	0	0

TCU

	Yrs.	W	L	CH	2D	3d%	4th	RR
Byron "Buster" Brannon (TCU 1933) 1952, 53, 59	3	3	3	0	0	0	0	0
Johnny Swaim (TCU 1953) 1968RR, 71	2	1	2	0	0	0	0	1
Jim Killingsworth (Northeastern Okla. St. 1948) 1987	1	1	1	0	0	0	0	0
Billy Tubbs (Lamar 1958) 1998	1	0	1	0	0	0	0	0
TOTAL	7	5	7	0	0	0	0	1

TEXAS SOUTHERN

	Yrs.	W	L	CH	2D	3d%	4th	RR
Robert Moreland (Tougaloo 1962) 1990, 94, 95	3	0	3	0	0	0	0	0
Ronnie Courtney (McMurry 1981) 2003	1	0	1	0	0	0	0	0
TOTAL	4	0	4	0	0	0	0	0

TEXAS ST.

	Yrs.	W	L	CH	2D	3d%	4th	RR
Jim Wooldridge (Louisiana Tech 1977) 1994	1	0	1					
Mike Miller (Tex. A&M-Commerce 1987) 1997	1	0	1	0	0	0	0	0
TOTAL	2	0	2	0	0	0	0	0

TEXAS TECH*

	Yrs.	W	L	CH	2D	3d%	4th	RR
Polk Robison (Texas Tech 1935) 1954, 56, 61	3	1	3	0	0	0	0	0
Gene Gibson (Texas Tech 1950) 1962	1	1	2	0	0	0	0	0
Gerald Myers (Texas Tech 1959) 1973, 76, 85, 86	4	1	4	0	0	0	0	0
James Dickey (Central Ark. 1976) 1993, 96*	2	2	2	0	0	0	0	0
Bob Knight (Ohio St. 1962) 2002, 04, 05, 07	4	3	4	0	0	0	0	0
TOTAL	14	8	15	0	0	0	0	0

TOLEDO

	Yrs.	W	L	CH	2D	3d%	4th	RR
Jerry Bush [St. John's (N.Y.) 1938] 1954	1	0	1	0	0	0	0	0
Bob Nichols (Toledo 1953) 1967, 79, 80	3	1	3	0	0	0	0	0
TOTAL	4	1	4	0	0	0	0	0

TOWSON

	Yrs.	W	L	CH	2D	3d%	4th	RR
Terry Truax (Maryland 1968) 1990, 91	2	0	2	0	0	0	0	0
TOTAL	2	0	2	0	0	0	0	0

TRINITY (TEX.)

	Yrs.	W	L	CH	2D	3d%	4th	RR
Bob Polk (Evansville 1939) 1969	1	0	1	0	0	0	0	0
TOTAL	1	0	1	0	0	0	0	0

TROY

	Yrs.	W	L	CH	2D	3d%	4th	RR
Don Maestri (Southern Miss. 1968) 2003	1	0	1	0	0	0	0	0
TOTAL	1	0	1	0	0	0	0	1

TUFTS

	Yrs.	W	L	CH	2D	3d%	4th	RR
Richard Cochran (Tufts 1934) 1945RR	1	0	2	0	0	0	0	1
TOTAL	1	0	2	0	0	0	0	1

TULANE

	Yrs.	W	L	CH	2D	3d%	4th	RR
Perry Clark (Gettysburg 1974) 1992, 93, 95	3	3	3	0	0	0	0	0
TOTAL	3	3	3	0	0	0	0	0

TULSA

	Yrs.	W	L	CH	2D	3d%	4th	RR
Clarence Iba (Panhandle St. 1936) 1955	1	1	1	0	0	0	0	0
Nolan Richardson (UTEP 1965) 1982, 84, 85	3	0	3	0	0	0	0	0
J.D. Barnett (Winona St. 1966) 1986, 87	2	0	2	0	0	0	0	0
Tubby Smith (High Point 1973) 1994, 95	2	4	2	0	0	0	0	0
Steve Robinson (Radford 1981) 1996, 97	2	1	2	0	0	0	0	0
Bill Self (Oklahoma St. 1985) 1999, 2000RR	2	4	2	0	0	0	0	1
John Phillips (Oklahoma St. 1973) 2002, 03	2	2	2	0	0	0	0	0
TOTAL	14	12	14	0	0	0	0	1

UCLA*

	Yrs.	W	L	CH	2D	3d%	4th	RR
John Wooden (Purdue 1932) 1950RR, 52, 56, 62-4th, 63, 64-CH, 65-CH, 67-CH, 68-CH, 69-CH, 70-CH, 71-CH, 72-CH, 73-CH, 74-3d, 75-CH	16	47	10	10	0	1	1	1
Gene Bartow (Truman 1953) 1976-3d, 77	2	5	2	0	0	1	0	0
Gary Cunningham (UCLA 1962) 1978, 79RR	2	3	2	0	0	0	0	1
Larry Brown (North Carolina 1963) 1980-2d*, 81	2	5	2	0	1	0	0	0
Larry Farmer (UCLA 1973) 1983	1	0	1	0	0	0	0	0
Walt Hazzard (UCLA 1964) 1987	1	1	1	0	0	0	0	0
Jim Harrick [Charleston (W.V.) 1960] 1989, 90, 91, 92RR, 93, 94, 95-CH, 96	8	13	7	1	0	0	0	1
Steve Lavin (Chapman 1988) 1997RR, 98, 99*, 2000, 01, 02	6	11	6	0	0	0	0	1
Ben Howland (Weber St. 1979) 2005, 06-2d, 07-T3d	3	9	3	0	1	1	0	0
TOTAL	41	94	34	11	2	3	1	4

UTAH

	Yrs.	W	L	CH	2D	3d%	4th	RR
Vadal Petersen (Utah 1920) 1944-CH, 45RR	2	3	2	1	0	0	0	1
Jack Gardner (Southern California 1932) 1955, 56RR, 59, 60, 61-4th, 66-4th	6	8	9	0	0	0	2	1
Jerry Pimm (Southern California 1960) 1977, 78, 79, 81, 83	5	5	5	0	0	0	0	0
Lynn Archibald (Fresno St. 1968) 1986	1	0	1	0	0	0	0	0
Rick Majerus (Marquette 1970) 1991, 93, 95, 96, 97RR, 98-2d, 99, 2000, 02, 03	10	17	10	0	1	0	0	1
Kerry Rupp (Southern Utah 1977) 2004	1	0	1	0	0	0	0	0
Ray Giacoletti (Minot St. 1985) 2005	1	2	1	0	0	0	0	0
TOTAL	26	35	29	1	1	0	2	3

UTAH ST.

	Yrs.	W	L	CH	2D	3d%	4th	RR
E.L. "Dick" Romney (Utah 1917) 1939RR	1	1	1	0	0	0	0	1
Ladell Andersen (Utah St. 1951) 1962, 63, 64, 70RR, 71	5	4	7	0	0	0	0	1
Gordon "Dutch" Belnap (Utah St. 1958) 1975, 79	2	0	2	0	0	0	0	0
Rod Tueller (Utah St. 1959) 1980, 83, 88	3	0	3	0	0	0	0	0
Larry Eustachy (Long Beach St. 1979) 1998	1	0	1	0	0	0	0	0
Steve Morrill (Gonzaga 1974) 2000, 01, 03, 05, 06	5	1	5	0	0	0	0	0
TOTAL	17	6	19	0	0	0	0	2

UTEP

	Yrs.	W	L	CH	2D	3d%	4th	RR
Don Haskins (Oklahoma St. 1953) 1963, 64, 66-CH, 67, 70, 75, 84, 85, 86, 87, 88, 89, 90, 92	14	14	13	1	0	0	0	0
Billy Gillispie (Texas St. 1983) 2004	1	0	1	0	0	0	0	0
Doc Sadler (Arkansas 1982) 2005	1	0	1	0	0	0	0	0
TOTAL	16	14	15	1	0	0	0	0

VALPARAISO

	Yrs.	W	L	CH	2D	3d%	4th	RR
Homer Drew (William Jewell 1966) 1996, 97, 98, 99, 2000, 02, 04	7	2	7	0	0	0	0	0
TOTAL	7	2	7	0	0	0	0	0

VANDERBILT

	Yrs.	W	L	CH	2D	3d%	4th	RR
Roy Skinner (Presbyterian 1952) 1965RR, 74	2	1	3	0	0	0	0	1
C.M. Newton (Kentucky 1952) 1988, 89	2	2	2	0	0	0	0	0
Eddie Fogler (North Carolina 1970) 1991, 93	2	2	2	0	0	0	0	0
Jan van Breda Kolff (Vanderbilt 1974) 1997	1	0	1	0	0	0	0	0
Kevin Stallings (Purdue 1982) 2004, 07	2	4	2	0	0	0	0	0
TOTAL	9	9	10	0	0	0	0	1

VERMONT

	Yrs.	W	L	CH	2D	3d%	4th	RR
Tom Brennan (Georgia 1971) 2003, 04, 05	3	1	3	0	0	0	0	0
TOTAL	3	1	3	0	0	0	0	0

VILLANOVA*

	Yrs.	W	L	CH	2D	3d%	4th	RR
Alex Severance (Villanova 1929) 1939-T3d, 49RR, 51, 55	4	4	4	0	0	1	0	1
Jack Kraft (St. Joseph's 1942) 1962RR, 64, 69, 70RR, 71-2d*, 72	6	11	7	0	1	0	0	2
Rollie Massimino (Vermont 1956) 1978RR, 80, 81, 82RR, 83RR, 84, 85-CH, 86, 88RR, 90, 91	11	20	10	1	0	0	0	4
Steve Lappas (CCNY 1977) 1995, 96, 97, 99	4	2	4	0	0	0	0	0
Jay Wright (Bucknell 1983) 2005, 06RR, 07	3	5	3	0	0	0	0	1
TOTAL	28	42	28	1	1	1	0	8

VIRGINIA

	Yrs.	W	L	CH	2D	3d%	4th	RR
Terry Holland (Davidson 1964) 1976, 81-3d, 82, 83RR, 84-T3d, 86, 87, 89RR, 90	9	15	9	0	0	2	0	2
Jeff Jones (Virginia 1982) 1991, 93, 94, 5RR, 95	5	6	5	0	0	0	0	1
Pete Gillen (Fairfield 1968) 2001	1	0	1	0	0	0	0	0
Dave Leitao (Northeastern 1983) 2007	1	1	1	0	0	0	0	0
TOTAL	16	22	16	0	0	2	0	3

VCU

	Yrs.	W	L	CH	2D	3d%	4th	RR
J.D. Barnett (Winona St. 1966) 1980, 81, 83, 84, 85	5	4	5	0	0	0	0	0
Sonny Smith (Milligan 1958) 1996	1	0	1	0	0	0	0	0
Jeff Capel III (Duke 1997) 2004	1	0	1	0	0	0	0	0
Anthony Grant (Dayton 1983) 2007	1	1	1	0	0	0	0	0
TOTAL	8	5	8	0	0	0	0	0

VMI

	Yrs.	W	L	CH	2D	3d%	4th	RR
Louis "Weenie" Miller (Richmond 1947) 1964	1	0	1	0	0	0	0	0
Bill Blair (VMI 1964) 1976RR	1	2	1	0	0	0	0	1
Charlie Schmaus (VMI 1966) 1977	1	1	1	0	0	0	0	0
TOTAL	3	3	3	0	0	0	0	1

VIRGINIA TECH

	Yrs.	W	L	CH	2D	3d%	4th	RR
Howard Shannon (Kansas St. 1948) 1967RR	1	2	1	0	0	0	0	1
Don DeVoe (Ohio St. 1964) 1976	1	0	1	0	0	0	0	0
Charles Moir (Appalachian St. 1952) 1979, 80, 85, 86	4	2	4	0	0	0	0	0
Bill C. Foster (Carson-Newman 1958) 1996	1	1	1	0	0	0	0	0

	Yrs.	W	L	CH	2D	3d%	4th	RR
Seth Greenberg (Fairleigh Dickinson 1978) 2007	1	1	1	0	0	0	0	0
TOTAL	8	6	8	0	0	0	0	1

WAGNER
	Yrs.	W	L	CH	2D	3d%	4th	RR
Derek Whittenburg (North Carolina St. 1984) 2003	1	0	1	0	0	0	0	0
TOTAL	1	0	1	0	0	0	0	0

WAKE FOREST
	Yrs.	W	L	CH	2D	3d%	4th	RR
Murray Greason (Wake Forest 1926) 1939RR, 53	2	1	2	0	0	0	0	1
Horace "Bones" McKinney (North Carolina 1946) 1961RR, 62-3d	2	6	2	0	0	1	0	1
Carl Tacy (Davis & Elkins 1956) 1977RR, 81, 82, 84RR	4	5	4	0	0	0	0	2
Dave Odom (Guilford 1965) 1991, 92, 93, 94, 95, 96RR, 97, 2001	8	10	8	0	0	0	0	1
Skip Prosser (Merchant Marine 1972) 2002, 03, 04, 05	4	5	4	0	0	0	0	0
TOTAL	20	27	20	0	0	1	0	5

WASHINGTON
	Yrs.	W	L	CH	2D	3d%	4th	RR
Clarence "Hec" Edmundson (Idaho 1909) 1943RR	1	0	2	0	0	0	0	1
Art McLarney (Washington St. 1932) 1948RR	1	1	1	0	0	0	0	1
William "Tippy" Dye (Ohio St. 1937) 1951RR, 53-3d	2	5	2	0	0	1	0	1
Marv Harshman (Pacific Lutheran 1942) 1976, 84, 85	3	2	3	0	0	0	0	0
Andy Russo (Lake Forest 1970) 1986	1	0	1	0	0	0	0	0
Bob Bender (Duke 1980) 1998, 99	2	2	2	0	0	0	0	0
Lorenzo Romar (Washington 1980) 2004, 05, 06	3	4	3	0	0	0	0	0
Tony Bennett (Green Bay 1992) 2007	1	1	1	0	0	0	0	0
TOTAL	14	15	15	0	0	1	0	3

WASHINGTON ST.
	Yrs.	W	L	CH	2D	3d%	4th	RR
Jack Friel (Washington St. 1923) 1941-2d	1	2	1	0	1	0	0	0
George Raveling (Villanova 1960) 1980, 83	2	1	2	0	0	0	0	0
Kelvin Sampson (UNC Pembroke 1978) 1994	1	0	1	0	0	0	0	0
TOTAL	4	3	4	0	1	0	0	0

WAYNE ST. (MICH.)
	Yrs.	W	L	CH	2D	3d%	4th	RR
Joel Mason (Western Mich. 1936) 1956	1	1	2	0	0	0	0	0
TOTAL	1	1	2	0	0	0	0	0

WEBER ST.
	Yrs.	W	L	CH	2D	3d%	4th	RR
Dick Motta (Utah St. 1953) 1968	1	0	1	0	0	0	0	0
Phil Johnson (Utah St. 1953) 1969, 70, 71	3	2	3	0	0	0	0	0
Gene Visscher (Weber St. 1966) 1972, 73	2	1	3	0	0	0	0	0
Neil McCarthy (Sacramento St. 1965) 1978, 79, 80, 83	4	1	4	0	0	0	0	0
Ron Abegglen (BYU 1962) 1995, 99	2	2	2	0	0	0	0	0
Joe Cravens (Tex.-Arlington 1977) 2003	1	0	1	0	0	0	0	0
Randy Rahe (Buena Vista 1982) 2007	1	0	1	0	0	0	0	0
TOTAL	14	6	15	0	0	0	0	0

WEST TEXAS A&M
	Yrs.	W	L	CH	2D	3d%	4th	RR
W.A. "Gus" Miller (West Texas A&M 1927) 1955	1	0	1	0	0	0	0	0
TOTAL	1	0	1	0	0	0	0	0

WEST VIRGINIA
	Yrs.	W	L	CH	2D	3d%	4th	RR
Fred Schaus (West Virginia 1949) 1955, 56, 57, 58, 59-2d, 60	6	6	6	0	1	0	0	0
George King [Charleston (W.V.) 1950] 1962, 63, 65	3	2	3	0	0	0	0	0
Raymond "Bucky" Waters (North Carolina St. 1957) 1967	1	0	1	0	0	0	0	0
Gale Catlett (West Virginia 1963) 1982, 83, 84, 86, 87, 89, 92, 98	8	5	8	0	0	0	0	0
John Beilein (Wheeling Jesuit 1975) 2005RR, 06	2	5	2	0	0	0	0	1
TOTAL	20	18	20	0	1	0	0	1

WESTERN CARO.
	Yrs.	W	L	CH	2D	3d%	4th	RR
Phil Hopkins (Gardner-Webb 1972) 1996	1	0	1	0	0	0	0	0
TOTAL	1	0	1	0	0	0	0	0

WESTERN KY.*
	Yrs.	W	L	CH	2D	3d%	4th	RR
Ed Diddle (Centre 1921) 1940RR, 60, 62	3	3	4	0	0	0	0	1
Johnny Oldham (Western Ky. 1948) 1966, 67, 70, 71-3d*	4	6	4	0	0	1	0	0
Jim Richards (Western Ky. 1959) 1976, 78	2	1	2	0	0	0	0	0
Gene Keady (Kansas St. 1958) 1980	1	0	1	0	0	0	0	0
Clem Haskins (Western Ky. 1967) 1981, 86	2	1	2	0	0	0	0	0
Murray Arnold (American 1960) 1987	1	1	1	0	0	0	0	0
Ralph Willard (Holy Cross 1967) 1993, 94	2	2	2	0	0	0	0	0

	Yrs.	W	L	CH	2D	3d%	4th	RR
Matt Kilcullen (Lehman 1976) 1995	1	1	1	0	0	0	0	0
Dennis Felton (Howard 1985) 2001, 02, 03	3	0	3	0	0	0	0	0
TOTAL	19	15	20	0	0	1	0	1

WESTERN MICH.
	Yrs.	W	L	CH	2D	3d%	4th	RR
Eldon Miller (Wittenberg 1961) 1976	1	1	1	0	0	0	0	0
Bob Donewald (Hanover 1964) 1998	1	1	1	0	0	0	0	0
Steve Hawkins (South Ala. 1987) 2004	1	0	1	0	0	0	0	0
TOTAL	3	2	3	0	0	0	0	0

WICHITA ST.
	Yrs.	W	L	CH	2D	3d%	4th	RR
Ralph Miller (Kansas 1942) 1964RR	1	1	1	0	0	0	0	1
Gary Thompson (Wichita St. 1954) 1965-4th	1	2	2	0	0	0	1	0
Harry Miller (Eastern N.M. 1951) 1976	1	0	1	0	0	0	0	0
Gene Smithson (North Central 1961) 1981RR, 85	2	3	2	0	0	0	0	1
Eddie Fogler (North Carolina 1970) 1987, 88	2	0	2	0	0	0	0	0
Mark Turgeon (Kansas 1987) 2006	1	2	1	0	0	0	0	0
TOTAL	8	8	9	0	0	0	1	2

WILLIAMS
	Yrs.	W	L	CH	2D	3d%	4th	RR
Alex Shaw (Michigan 1932) 1955	1	0	1	0	0	0	0	0
TOTAL	1	0	1	0	0	0	0	0

WINTHROP
	Yrs.	W	L	CH	2D	3d%	4th	RR
Gregg Marshall (Randolph-Macon 1985) 1999, 2000, 01, 02, 05, 06	6	0	6	0	0	0	0	0
TOTAL	6	0	6	0	0	0	0	0

WISCONSIN
	Yrs.	W	L	CH	2D	3d%	4th	RR
Harold "Bud" Foster (Wisconsin 1930) 1941-CH, 47RR	2	4	1	1	0	0	0	1
Stu Jackson (Seattle 1978) 1994	1	1	1	0	0	0	0	0
Dick Bennett (Ripon 1965) 1997, 99, 2000-T3d	3	4	3	0	0	1	0	0
Brad Soderberg (Wis.-Stevens Point 1985) 2001	1	0	1	0	0	0	0	0
Bo Ryan (Wilkes 1969) 2002, 03, 04, 05RR, 06, 07	6	8	6	0	0	0	0	1
TOTAL	13	17	12	1	0	1	0	2

WRIGHT ST.
	Yrs.	W	L	CH	2D	3d%	4th	RR
Ralph Underhill (Tennessee Tech 1964) 1993	1	0	1	0	0	0	0	0
Brad Brownell (DePauw 1991) 2007	1	0	1	0	0	0	0	0
TOTAL	2	0	2	0	0	0	0	0

WYOMING
	Yrs.	W	L	CH	2D	3d%	4th	RR
Everett Shelton (Phillips 1923) 1941RR, 43-CH, 47RR, 48RR, 49RR, 52RR, 53, 58	8	4	12	1	0	0	0	5
Bill Strannigan (Wyoming 1941) 1967	1	0	2	0	0	0	0	0
Jim Brandenburg (Colorado St. 1958) 1981, 82, 87	3	4	3	0	0	0	0	0
Benny Dees (Wyoming 1958) 1988	1	0	1	0	0	0	0	0
Steve McClain (Chadron St. 1984) 2002	1	1	1	0	0	0	0	0
TOTAL	14	9	19	1	0	0	0	5

XAVIER
	Yrs.	W	L	CH	2D	3d%	4th	RR
Jim McCafferty [Loyola (La.) 1942] 1961	1	0	1	0	0	0	0	0
Bob Staak (Connecticut 1971) 1983	1	0	1	0	0	0	0	0
Pete Gillen (Fairfield 1968) 1986, 87, 88, 89, 90, 91, 93	7	5	7	0	0	0	0	0
Skip Prosser (Merchant Marine 1972) 1995, 97, 98, 2001	4	1	4	0	0	0	0	0
Thad Matta (Butler 1990) 2002, 03, 04RR	3	5	3	0	0	0	0	1
Sean Miller (Pittsburgh 1992) 2006, 07	2	1	2	0	0	0	0	1
TOTAL	18	12	18	0	0	0	0	1

YALE
	Yrs.	W	L	CH	2D	3d%	4th	RR
Howard Hobson (Oregon 1926) 1949RR	1	0	2	0	0	0	0	1
Joe Vancisin (Dartmouth 1944) 1957, 62	2	0	2	0	0	0	0	0
TOTAL	3	0	4	0	0	0	0	1

National 3rd-place games did not start until 1946 and ended in 1981; in other years, two teams tied for third and both are listed in this column. RR-Regional runner-up, or one victory from Final Four, thus in the top eight.

NOTES ON TEAMS AND COACHES:
MICHIGAN: Steve Fisher coached Michigan in the 1989 tournament; Bill Freider was the coach during the regular season.

MISSOURI: Rich Daly coached Missouri in the 1989 tournament due to Norm Stewart's illness; Missouri credits the entire 1989 season to Stewart.

PRINCETON: J.L. McCandless coached Princeton in the 1961 tournament; Franklin Cappon suffered a heart attack 11 games into the season; Princeton credits the 1961 regular season to Cappon and the postseason to McCandless.

SEATTLE: Clair Markey coached Seattle in the 1963 tournament due to Vince Cazetta's resignation.

* TEAMS VACATING NCAA TOURNAMENT ACTION

Teams	Years	Record	Placing	Conference
Alabama	1987	2-1		Southeastern
Arizona	1999	0-1		Pacific-10
Arizona St.	1995	2-1		Pacific-10
Austin Peay	1973	1-2		Ohio Valley
California	1996	0-1		Pacific-10
Clemson	1990	2-1		Atlantic Coast
Connecticut	1996	2-1		Big East
DePaul	1986-89	6-4		Independent
Florida	1987-88	3-2		Southeastern
Fresno St.	2000	0-1		Western Athletic
Georgia	1985, 2002	2-2		Southeastern
Iona	1980	1-1		Independent
Kentucky	1988	2-1		Southeastern
Long Beach St.	1971-73	6-3	2 RR	Pacific Coast
La.-Lafayette	1972-73	3-3		Southland
Loyola Marymount	1980	0-1		West Coast
Marshall	1987	0-1		Southern
Maryland	1988	1-1		Atlantic Coast
Massachusetts	1996	4-1	3d	Atlantic 10
Memphis	1982-86	9-5	3d	Metro
Michigan	1992-93, 96, 98	10-4	2 2d	Big Ten
Minnesota	1972, 94-95, 97	6-4	3d	Big Ten
Missouri	1994	3-1	RR	Big Eight
New Mexico St.	1992-94	3-3		Big West
North Carolina St.	1987-88	0-2		Atlantic Coast
Ohio St.	1999-2002	6-4	3d	Big Ten
Oregon St.	1980-82	2-3	RR	Pacific-10
Purdue	1996	1-1		Big Ten
St. John's (N.Y.)	2002	0-1		Big East
St. Joseph's	1961	3-1	3d	Middle Atlantic
Texas Tech	1996	2-1		Southwest
UCLA	1980, 99	5-2	2d	Pacific-10
Villanova	1971	4-1	2d	Independent
Western Ky.	1971	4-1	3d	Ohio Valley
33 schools	61 years	92-63	4 2d, 6 3d, 4 RR	

Official NCAA Records

	Yrs	Won	Lost	CH	2d	3d	4th	RR
Alabama	18	18	18	0	0	0	0	0
Arizona	24	41	23	1	1	2	0	4
Arizona St.	11	10	12	0	0	0	0	3
Austin Peay	4	1	4	0	0	0	0	0
California	13	18	13	1	1	0	1	2
Clemson	6	6	6	0	0	0	0	1
Connecticut	26	40	25	1	0	0	0	6
DePaul	18	15	21	0	0	2	0	1
Florida	11	20	10	1	0	1	0	0
Fresno St.	4	2	4	0	0	0	0	0
Georgia	7	5	7	0	0	1	0	0
Iona	7	0	7	0	0	0	0	0
Kentucky	47	97	42	7	3	3	0	18
Long Beach St.	4	1	5	0	0	0	0	0
La.-Lafayette	7	1	7	0	0	0	0	0
Loyola Marymount	4	5	4	0	0	0	0	1
Marshall	4	0	4	0	0	0	0	0
Maryland	20	34	19	1	0	1	0	2
Massachusetts	7	7	7	0	0	0	0	1
Memphis	14	13	14	0	1	0	0	0
Michigan	16	31	15	1	2	1	0	5
Minnesota	5	6	5	0	0	0	0	1
Missouri	20	15	20	0	0	0	0	3
New Mexico St.	13	7	15	0	0	1	0	0
North Carolina St.	20	32	19	2	0	1	0	3
Ohio St.	19	32	18	1	3	4	0	3
Oregon St.	13	10	16	0	0	0	2	4
Purdue	19	26	19	0	1	1	0	2
St. John's (N.Y.)	26	27	28	0	1	1	0	4
St. Joseph's	17	15	21	0	0	0	0	2
Texas Tech	12	6	13	0	0	0	0	0
UCLA	38	85	31	11	1	2	1	4
Villanova	26	38	26	1	0	1	0	8
Western Ky.	18	11	19	0	0	0	0	1

Final Four All-Tournament Teams

(First player listed on each team was the outstanding player in the Final Four)

1939—Not chosen.

1940—Marvin Huffman, Indiana
Howard Engleman, Kansas
Bob Allen, Kansas
Jay McCreary, Indiana
William Menke, Indiana

1941-51— Not chosen.

1952—Clyde Lovellette, Kansas
Bob Zawoluk, St. John's (N.Y.)
John Kerr, Illinois
Ron MacGilvray, St. John's (N.Y.)
Dean Kelley, Kansas

1953—B.H. Born, Kansas
Bob Houbregs, Washington
Bob Leonard, Indiana
Dean Kelley, Kansas
Don Schlundt, Indiana

1954—Tom Gola, La Salle
Chuck Singley, La Salle
Jesse Arnelle, Penn St.
Roy Irvin, Southern California
Bob Carney, Bradley

1955—Bill Russell, San Francisco
Tom Gola, La Salle
K.C. Jones, San Francisco
Jim Ranglos, Colorado
Carl Cain, Iowa

1956—Hal Lear, Temple
Bill Russell, San Francisco
Carl Cain, Iowa
Hal Perry, San Francisco
Bill Logan, Iowa

1957—Wilt Chamberlain, Kansas
Len Rosenbluth, North Carolina
John Green, Michigan St.
Gene Brown, San Francisco
Pete Brennan, North Carolina

1958—Elgin Baylor, Seattle
John Cox, Kentucky
Guy Rodgers, Temple
Charley Brown, Seattle
Vern Hatton, Kentucky

1959—Jerry West, West Virginia
Oscar Robertson, Cincinnati
Darrall Imhoff, California
Don Goldstein, Louisville
Denny Fitzpatrick, California

1960—Jerry Lucas, Ohio St.
Oscar Robertson, Cincinnati
Mel Nowell, Ohio St.
Darrall Imhoff, California
Tom Sanders, New York U.

1961—Jerry Lucas, Ohio St.
Bob Wiesenhahn, Cincinnati
Larry Siegfried, Ohio St.
Carl Bouldin, Cincinnati
*Jack Egan, St. Joseph's

1962—Paul Hogue, Cincinnati
Jerry Lucas, Ohio St.
Tom Thacker, Cincinnati
John Havlicek, Ohio St.
Len Chappell, Wake Forest

1963—Art Heyman, Duke
Tom Thacker, Cincinnati
Les Hunter, Loyola (Ill.)
George Wilson, Cincinnati
Ron Bonham, Cincinnati

1964—Walt Hazzard, UCLA
Jeff Mullins, Duke
Bill Buntin, Michigan
Willie Murrell, Kansas St.
Gail Goodrich, UCLA

1965—Bill Bradley, Princeton
Gail Goodrich, UCLA
Cazzie Russell, Michigan
Edgar Lacey, UCLA
Kenny Washington, UCLA

1966—Jerry Chambers, Utah
Pat Riley, Kentucky
Jack Marin, Duke
Louie Dampier, Kentucky
Bobby Joe Hill, UTEP

1967—Lew Alcindor, UCLA
Don May, Dayton
Mike Warren, UCLA
Elvin Hayes, Houston
Lucius Allen, UCLA

1968—Lew Alcindor, UCLA
Lynn Shackelford, UCLA
Mike Warren, UCLA
Lucius Allen, UCLA
Larry Miller, North Carolina

1969—Lew Alcindor, UCLA
Rick Mount, Purdue
Charlie Scott, North Carolina
Willie McCarter, Drake
John Vallely, UCLA

1970—Sidney Wicks, UCLA
Jimmy Collins, New Mexico St.
John Vallely, UCLA
Artis Gilmore, Jacksonville
Curtis Rowe, UCLA

1971—*Howard Porter, Villanova
*Hank Siemjonkowski, Villanova
*Jim McDaniels, Western Ky.
Steve Patterson, UCLA
Sidney Wicks, UCLA

1972—Bill Walton, UCLA
Keith Wilkes, UCLA
Bob McAdoo, North Carolina
Jim Price, Louisville
Ron King, Florida St.

1973—Bill Walton, UCLA
Steve Downing, Indiana
Ernie DiGregorio, Providence
Larry Finch, Memphis
Larry Kenon, Memphis

1974—David Thompson, North Carolina St.
Bill Walton, UCLA
Tom Burleson, North Carolina St.
Monte Towe, North Carolina St.
Maurice Lucas, Marquette

1975—Richard Washington, UCLA
Kevin Grevey, Kentucky
Dave Myers, UCLA
Allen Murphy, Louisville
Jim Lee, Syracuse

1976—Kent Benson, Indiana
Scott May, Indiana
Rickey Green, Michigan
Marques Johnson, UCLA
Tom Abernethy, Indiana

1977—Butch Lee, Marquette
Mike O'Koren, North Carolina
Cedric Maxwell, Charlotte
Bo Ellis, Marquette
Walter Davis, North Carolina
Jerome Whitehead, Marquette

1978—Jack Givens, Kentucky
Ron Brewer, Arkansas
Mike Gminski, Duke
Rick Robey, Kentucky
Jim Spanarkel, Duke

1979—Earvin Johnson, Michigan St.
Greg Kelser, Michigan St.
Larry Bird, Indiana St.
Mark Aguirre, DePaul
Gary Garland, DePaul

1980—Darrell Griffith, Louisville
*Rod Foster, UCLA
Joe Barry Carroll, Purdue
*Kike Vandeweghe, UCLA
Rodney McCray, Louisville

1981—Isiah Thomas, Indiana
Jeff Lamp, Virginia
Jim Thomas, Indiana
Landon Turner, Indiana
Al Wood, North Carolina

1982—James Worthy, North Carolina
Patrick Ewing, Georgetown
Eric Floyd, Georgetown
Michael Jordan, North Carolina
Sam Perkins, North Carolina

1983—Akeem Olajuwon, Houston
Thurl Bailey, North Carolina St.
Sidney Lowe, North Carolina St.
Milt Wagner, Louisville
Dereck Whittenburg, North Carolina St.

1984—Patrick Ewing, Georgetown
Michael Graham, Georgetown
Akeem Olajuwon, Houston
Michael Young, Houston
Alvin Franklin, Houston

1985—Patrick Ewing, Georgetown
Ed Pinckney, Villanova
Dwayne McClain, Villanova
Harold Jensen, Villanova
Gary McLain, Villanova

1986—Pervis Ellison, Louisville
Billy Thompson, Louisville
Johnny Dawkins, Duke
Mark Alarie, Duke
Tommy Amaker, Duke

1987—Keith Smart, Indiana
Sherman Douglas, Syracuse
Derrick Coleman, Syracuse
Armon Gilliam, UNLV
Steve Alford, Indiana

1988—Danny Manning, Kansas
Milt Newton, Kansas
Stacey King, Oklahoma
Dave Sieger, Oklahoma
Sean Elliott, Arizona

1989—Glen Rice, Michigan
Rumeal Robinson, Michigan
Danny Ferry, Duke
Gerald Greene, Seton Hall
John Morton, Seton Hall

1990—Anderson Hunt, UNLV
Stacey Augmon, UNLV
Larry Johnson, UNLV
Phil Henderson, Duke
Dennis Scott, Georgia Tech

1991—Christian Laettner, Duke
Bobby Hurley, Duke
Bill McCaffrey, Duke
Mark Randall, Kansas
Anderson Hunt, UNLV

1992—Bobby Hurley, Duke
Grant Hill, Duke
Christian Laettner, Duke
Jalen Rose, Michigan
Chris Webber, Michigan

1993—Donald Williams, North Carolina
Eric Montross, North Carolina
George Lynch, North Carolina
Chris Webber, Michigan
Jamal Mashburn, Kentucky

1994—Corliss Williamson, Arkansas
Corey Beck, Arkansas
Scotty Thurman, Arkansas
Grant Hill, Duke
Antonio Lang, Duke

1995—Ed O'Bannon, UCLA
Toby Bailey, UCLA
Corliss Williamson, Arkansas
Clint McDaniel, Arkansas
Bryant Reeves, Oklahoma St.

1996—Tony Delk, Kentucky
Ron Mercer, Kentucky
Marcus Camby, Massachusetts
Todd Burgan, Syracuse
John Wallace, Syracuse

1997—Miles Simon, Arizona
Mike Bibby, Arizona
Ron Mercer, Kentucky
Scott Padgett, Kentucky
Bobby Jackson, Minnesota

1998—Jeff Sheppard, Kentucky
Scott Padgett, Kentucky
Arthur Lee, Stanford
Michael Doleac, Utah
Andre Miller, Utah

1999—Richard Hamilton, Connecticut
Khalid El-Amin, Connecticut
Ricky Moore, Connecticut
Elton Brand, Duke
Trajan Langdon, Duke

2000—Mateen Cleaves, Michigan St.
Udonis Haslem, Florida
Charlie Bell, Michigan St.
A.J. Granger, Michigan St.
Morris Peterson, Michigan St.

2001—Shane Battier, Duke
Mike Dunleavy, Duke
Richard Jefferson, Arizona
Jason Williams, Duke
Loren Woods, Arizona

2002—Juan Dixon, Maryland
Lonny Baxter, Maryland
Chris Wilcox, Maryland
Dane Fife, Indiana
Kyle Hornsby, Indiana

2003—Carmelo Anthony, Syracuse
Gerry McNamara, Syracuse
Nick Collison, Kansas
Kirk Hinrich, Kansas
Keith Langford, Kansas

2004—Emeka Okafor, Connecticut
Rashad Anderson, Connecticut
Ben Gordon, Connecticut
Will Bynum, Georgia Tech
Luke Schenscher, Georgia Tech

2005—Sean May, North Carolina
Luther Head, Illinois
Deron Williams, Illinois
Raymond Felton, North Carolina
Rashad McCants, North Carolina

2006—Joakim Noah, Florida
Corey Brewer, Florida
Taurean Green, Florida
Lee Humphrey, Florida
Jordan Farmar, UCLA

2007—Corey Brewer, Florida
Al Horford, Florida
Lee Humphrey, Florida
Mike Conley Jr., Ohio St.
Greg Oden, Ohio St.

*Record later vacated.

National Invitation Tournament Year-by-Year Results

Season	Champion	Score	Runner-Up	Third Place	Fourth Place
1938	Temple	60-36	Colorado	Oklahoma St.	New York U.
1939	Long Island	44-32	Loyola (Ill.)	Bradley	St. John's (N.Y.)
1940	Colorado	51-40	Duquesne	Oklahoma St.	DePaul
1941	Long Island	56-42	Ohio	CCNY	Seton Hall
1942	West Virginia	47-45	Western Ky.	Creighton	Toledo
1943	St. John's (N.Y.)	48-27	Toledo	Wash. & Jeff.	Fordham
1944	St. John's (N.Y.)	47-39	DePaul	Kentucky	Oklahoma St.
1945	DePaul	71-54	Bowling Green	St. John's (N.Y.)	Rhode Island
1946	Kentucky	46-45	Rhode Island	West Virginia	Muhlenberg
1947	Utah	49-45	Kentucky	North Carolina St.	West Virginia
1948	St. Louis	65-52	New York U.	Western Ky.	DePaul
1949	San Francisco	48-47	Loyola (Ill.)	Bowling Green	Bradley
1950	CCNY	69-61	Bradley	St. John's (N.Y.)	Duquesne
1951	BYU	62-43	Dayton	St. John's (N.Y.)	Seton Hall
1952	La Salle	75-64	Dayton	St. Bonaventure	Duquesne
1953	Seton Hall	58-46	St. John's (N.Y.)	Duquesne	Manhattan
1954	Holy Cross	71-62	Duquesne	Niagara	Western Ky.
1955	Duquesne	70-58	Dayton	Cincinnati	St. Francis (Pa.)
1956	Louisville	93-80	Dayton	St. Joseph's	St. Francis (N.Y.)
1957	Bradley	84-83	Memphis	Tampa	St. Bonaventure

Season	Champion	Score	Runner-Up	Third Place	Fourth Place
1958	Xavier	78-74 (ot)	Dayton	St. Bonaventure	St. John's (N.Y.)
1959	St. John's (N.Y.)	76-71 (ot)	Bradley	New York U.	Providence
1960	Bradley	88-72	Providence	Utah St.	St. Bonaventure
1961	Providence	62-59	St. Louis	Holy Cross	Dayton
1962	Dayton	73-67	St. John's (N.Y.)	Loyola (Ill.)	Duquesne
1963	Providence	81-66	Canisius	Marquette	Villanova
1964	Bradley	86-54	New Mexico	Army	New York U.
1965	St. John's (N.Y.)	55-51	Villanova	Army	New York U.
1966	BYU	97-84	New York U.	Villanova	Army
1967	Southern Ill.	71-56	Marquette	Rutgers	Marshall
1968	Dayton	61-48	Kansas	Notre Dame	St. Peter's
1969	Temple	89-76	Boston College	Tennessee	Army
1970	Marquette	65-53	St. John's (N.Y.)	Army	LSU
1971	North Carolina	84-66	Georgia Tech	St. Bonaventure	Duke
1972	Maryland	100-69	Niagara	Jacksonville	St. John's (N.Y.)
1973	Virginia Tech	92-91 (ot)	Notre Dame	North Carolina	Alabama
1974	Purdue	87-81	Utah	Boston College	Jacksonville
1975	Princeton	80-69	Providence	Oregon	St. John's (N.Y.)
1976	Kentucky	81-76	Charlotte	North Carolina St.	Providence
1977	St. Bonaventure	94-91	Houston	Villanova	Alabama
1978	Texas	101-93	North Carolina St.	Rutgers	Georgetown
1979	Indiana	53-52	Purdue	Alabama	Ohio St.
1980	Virginia	58-55	Minnesota	Illinois	UNLV
1981	Tulsa	86-84 (ot)	Syracuse	Purdue	West Virginia
1982	Bradley	67-58	Purdue	+ Georgia	+ Oklahoma
1983	Fresno St.	69-60	DePaul	+ Nebraska	+ Wake Forest
1984	Michigan	83-63	Notre Dame	Virginia Tech	La.-Lafayette
1985	UCLA	65-62	Indiana	Tennessee	Louisville
1986	Ohio St.	73-63	Wyoming	Louisiana Tech	Florida
1987	Southern Miss.	84-80	La Salle	Nebraska	Ark.-Little Rock
1988	Connecticut	72-67	Ohio St.	Colorado St.	Boston College
1989	St. John's (N.Y.)	73-65	St. Louis	UAB	Michigan St.
1990	Vanderbilt	74-72	St. Louis	Penn St.	New Mexico
1991	Stanford	78-72	Oklahoma	Colorado	Massachusetts
1992	Virginia	81-76	Notre Dame	Utah	Florida
1993	Minnesota	92-61	Georgetown	UAB	Providence
1994	Villanova	80-73	Vanderbilt	Siena	Kansas St.
1995	Virginia Tech	65-64 (ot)	Marquette	Penn St.	Canisius
1996	Nebraska	60-56	St. Joseph's	Tulane	Alabama
1997	Michigan	82-73	Florida St.	Connecticut	Arkansas
1998	Minnesota	79-72	Penn St.	Georgia	Fresno St.
1999	California	61-60	Clemson	Xavier	Oregon
2000	Wake Forest	71-61	Notre Dame	Penn St.	North Carolina St.
2001	Tulsa	79-60	Alabama	Memphis	Detroit
2002	Memphis	72-62	South Carolina	Syracuse	Temple
2003	St. John's (N.Y.)	70-67	Georgetown	Minnesota	Texas Tech
2004	Michigan	62-55	Rutgers	+ Iowa St.	+ Oregon
2005	South Carolina	60-57	St. Joseph's	+ Maryland	+ Memphis
2006	South Carolina	76-64	Michigan	+ Louisville	+ Old Dominion
2007	West Virginia	78-73	Clemson	+ Air Force	+ Mississippi St.

+tied for third place

POSTSEASON CHARITY GAME

During World War II, the American Red Cross sponsored a basketball game to raise money for the war effort. The game featured that year's NCAA champion versus the NIT champion.

Season	Winner	Score	Loser	Site
1943	Wyoming (NCAA champion)	52-47 (ot)	St. John's (N.Y.) (NIT champion)	New York
1944	Utah (NCAA champion)	43-36	St. John's (N.Y.) (NIT champion)	New York
1945	Oklahoma St. (NCAA champion)	52-44	DePaul (NIT champion)	New York

NABC All-Star Game Results

Season	Winner	Score	MVP	Winning Coach	Losing Coach	Attendance
1963	East	77-70	Art Heyman, Duke	Harold Anderson	Cliff Wells	9,000
1964	West	79-78	Willie Murrell, Kansas St.	Slats Gill	Jack Gardner	9,700
1965	West	87-74	Gail Goodrich, UCLA	Doggie Julian	Joe Lapchick	7,000
1966	East	126-99	Cazzie Russell, Michigan	Taps Gallagher	Forrest Twogood	8,000
1967	East	102-93	Sonny Dove, St. John's (N.Y.)	Ben Carnevale	Everest Shelton	7,300
1968	West	95-88	Pete Maravich, LSU	Phog Allen & Tex Winter	Art Schabinger & John Bach	14,500
1969	East	104-80	Neal Walk, Florida	Tony Hinkle	Branch McCracken	6,100
1970	East	116-102	Charlie Scott, North Carolina	Nat Holman	Bud Foster	14,756
1971	East	106-104 (ot)	Jim McDaniels, Western Ky.	Dutch Lonborg	Vadal Peterson	13,178
1972	East	96-91 (ot)	Billy Shepard, Butler	Howard Hobson	Hank Iba	7,856
1973	West	98-94	Jim Brewer, Minnesota	Stan Watts	Adolph Rupp	8,609
1974	East	105-85	Marvin Barnes, Providence	Harry Litwack	John Hyder	8,396
1975	West	110-89	Gus Williams, Southern California	Bruce Drake	Eddie Hickey	NA
1976	West	101-98	Chuckie Williams, Kansas St.	Marv Harshman	Dean Smith	5,951
1977	East	114-93	Ernie Grunfeld, Tennessee	Bob Knight	Johnny Orr	6,537
1978	East	93-87	Butch Lee, Marquette	Frank McGuire	Al McGuire	4,275
1979	East	114-109	Greg Deane, Utah	Joe B. Hall	Bill Foster	7,472
1980	East	88-79	Mike O'Koren, North Carolina	Bill Hodges	Jud Heathcote	7,600
1981	West	99-97	Danny Ainge, BYU	Larry Brown	Denny Crum	3,116
1982	West	102-68	Ricky Frazier, Missouri	Dale Brown	Bob Knight	3,965
1983	West	99-94	Darrell Walker, Arkansas	John Thompson	Dean Smith	4,178
1984	West	111-77	Fred Reynolds, UTEP	Marv Harshman	Jim Valvano	4,126
1985	West	97-90	Lorenzo Charles, North Carolina St.	Guy Lewis	Joe B. Hall	10,464
1986	West	94-92	David Wingate, Georgetown	Rollie Massimino	Lou Carnesecca	7,009
1987	West	92-91	David Robinson, Navy	Denny Crum	Mike Krzyzewski	8,041
1988	East	97-91	David Rivers, Notre Dame	Jim Boeheim	Jerry Tarkanian	8,528
1989	West	150-111	Tim Hardaway, UTEP	Lute Olson	Billy Tubbs	7,541
1990	East	127-126	Travis Mays, Texas	P.J. Carlesimo	Steve Fisher	7,161
1991	West	122-113	Jimmy Oliver, Purdue	Nolan Richardson	Bobby Cremins	8,000
1992	West	117-93	Doug Christie, Pepperdine	Roy Williams	Clem Haskins	10,344
1993	West	104-95	Ervin Johnson, New Orleans	Bob Huggins	Mike Krzyzewski	6,604
1994	East	77-73	Charlie Ward, Florida St.	Clarence "Bighouse" Gaines	Guy Lewis	6,500
1995	West	117-88	Fred Hoiberg, Iowa St.	Lute Olson	Lon Kruger	7,900
1996	East	99-92	Danetri Hill, Florida	Eddie Sutton	Jim Harrick	5,500
1997	East	105-94	James Collins, Florida St.	Jim Boeheim	Norm Stewart	6,019
1998	East	102-89	Felipe Lopez, St. John's (N.Y.)	Clem Haskins	Steve Lavin	8,998
1999	West	93-86	Doug Swenson, Creighton	Rick Majerus	Tubby Smith	6,753

Year	Score NABC-Opp.	NABC MVP	NABC Coach	Opponent	Attendance
2000	80-82	Kenyon Jones, San Francisco	Jim Calhoun	Harlem Globetrotters	8,000
2001	63-75	Kyle Hill, Eastern Mich.	Gene Keady	Harlem Globetrotters	15,253
2002	86-76	Tony Akins, Georgia Tech	Tom Izzo	Harlem Globetrotters	8,758
2003	85-87 (ot)	Dahntay Jones, Duke	Gary Williams	Harlem Globetrotters	14,844
2004	72-88	David Hawkins, Temple	Jim Boeheim	Harlem Globetrotters	11,637
2005	73-68	Chuck Hayes, Kentucky	Jim Calhoun	Harlem Globetrotters	13,000
2006	87-83	Bobby Jones, Washington	Bruce Weber	Harlem Globetrotters	10,921

Season	Winner	Score	American Team MVP	National Team MVP	American Coach	National Coach	Attendance
2007	National	128-100	Justin Doellman, Xavier	Torrell Martin, Winthrop	John Brady	Jim Larranaga	3,800

Game Sites: 1963-67—Lexington, Kentucky; 1968-70—Indianapolis, Indiana; 1971-74—Dayton, Ohio; 1975-77—Tulsa, Ok.; 1978-present—same city as the NCAA Final Four.

CHAMPIONSHIPS

All-Time Results

1939 First Round: Villanova 42, Brown 30; Ohio St. 64, Wake Forest 52; Oklahoma 50, Utah St. 39; Oregon 56, Texas 41. **Regional Third Place:** Utah St. 51, Texas 49. **Semifinals:** Ohio St. 53, Villanova 36; Oregon 55, Oklahoma 37. **Championship:** Oregon 46, Ohio St. 33.

1940 First Round: Kansas 50, Rice 44; Southern California 38, Colorado 32; Duquesne 30, Western Ky. 29; Indiana 48, Springfield 24. **Regional Third Place:** Rice 60, Colorado 56 (ot). **Semifinals:** Kansas 43, Southern California 42; Indiana 39, Duquesne 30. **Championship:** Indiana 60, Kansas 42.

1941 First Round: Wisconsin 51, Dartmouth 50; Pittsburgh 26, North Carolina 20; Washington St. 48, Creighton 39; Arkansas 52, Wyoming 40. **Regional Third Place:** Dartmouth 60, North Carolina 59; Creighton 45, Wyoming 44. **Semifinals:** Wisconsin 36, Pittsburgh 30; Washington St. 64, Arkansas 53. **Championship:** Wisconsin 39, Washington St. 34.

1942 First Round: Dartmouth 44, Penn St. 39; Kentucky 46, Illinois 44; Stanford 53, Rice 47; Colorado 46, Kansas 44. **Regional Third Place:** Penn St. 41, Illinois 34; Kansas 55, Rice 53. **Semifinals:** Dartmouth 47, Kentucky 28; Stanford 46, Colorado 35. **Championship:** Stanford 53, Dartmouth 38.

1943 First Round: Georgetown 55, New York U. 36; DePaul 46, Dartmouth 35; Texas 59, Washington 55; Wyoming 53, Oklahoma 50. **Regional Third Place:** Dartmouth 51, New York U. 49; Oklahoma 48, Washington 43. **Semifinals:** Georgetown 53, DePaul 49; Wyoming 58, Texas 54. **Championship:** Wyoming 46, Georgetown 34.

1944 First Round: Dartmouth 63, Catholic 38; Ohio St. 57, Temple 47; Iowa St. 44, Pepperdine 39; Utah 45, Missouri 35. **Regional Third Place:** Temple 55, Catholic 35; Missouri 61, Pepperdine 46. **Semifinals:** Dartmouth 60, Ohio St. 53; Utah 40, Iowa St. 31. **Championship:** Utah 42, Dartmouth 40 (ot).

1945 First Round: New York U. 59, Tufts 44; Ohio St. 45, Kentucky 37; Arkansas 79, Oregon 76; Oklahoma St. 62, Utah 37. **Regional Third Place:** Kentucky 66, Tufts 56; Oregon 69, Utah 66. **Semifinals:** New York U. 70, Ohio St. 65 (ot); Oklahoma St. 68, Arkansas 41. **Championship:** Oklahoma St. 49, New York U. 45.

1946 First Round: Ohio St. 46, Harvard 38; North Carolina 57, New York U. 49; Oklahoma St. 44, Baylor 29; California 50, Colorado 44. **Regional Third Place:** New York U. 67, Harvard 61; Colorado 59, Baylor 44. **Semifinals:** North Carolina 60, Ohio St. 57 (ot); Oklahoma St. 52, California 35. **Third Place:** Ohio St. 63, California 45. **Championship:** Oklahoma St. 43, North Carolina 40.

1947 First Round: Holy Cross 55, Navy 47; CCNY 70, Wisconsin 56; Texas 42, Wyoming 40; Oklahoma 56, Oregon St. 54. **Regional Third Place:** Wisconsin 50, Navy 49; Oregon St. 63, Wyoming 46. **Semifinals:** Holy Cross 60, CCNY 45; Oklahoma 55, Texas 54. **Third Place:** Texas 54, CCNY 50. **Championship:** Holy Cross 58, Oklahoma 47.

1948 First Round: Kentucky 76, Columbia 53; Holy Cross 63, Michigan 45; Kansas St. 58, Wyoming 48; Baylor 64, Washington 62. **Regional Third Place:** Michigan 66, Columbia 49; Washington 57, Wyoming 47. **Semifinals:** Kentucky 60, Holy Cross 52; Baylor 60, Kansas St. 52. **Third Place:** Holy Cross 60, Kansas St. 54. **Championship:** Kentucky 58, Baylor 42.

1949 First Round: Illinois 71, Yale 67; Kentucky 85, Villanova 72; Oklahoma St. 40, Wyoming 39; Oregon St. 56, Arkansas 38. **Regional Third Place:** Villanova 78, Yale 67; Arkansas 61, Wyoming 48. **Semifinals:** Kentucky 76, Illinois 47; Oklahoma St. 55, Oregon St. 30. **Third Place:** Illinois 57, Oregon St. 53. **Championship:** Kentucky 46, Oklahoma St. 36.

1950 First Round: CCNY 56, Ohio St. 55; North Carolina St. 87, Holy Cross 74; Baylor 56, BYU 55; Bradley 73, UCLA 59. **Regional Third** Place: Ohio St. 72, Holy Cross 52; BYU 83, UCLA 62. **Semifinals:** CCNY 78, North Carolina St. 73; Bradley 68, Baylor 66. **Third Place:** North Carolina St. 53, Baylor 41. **Championship:** CCNY 71, Bradley 68.

1951 First Round: North Carolina St. 67, Villanova 62; Illinois 79, Columbia 71; St. John's (N.Y.) 63, Connecticut 52; Kentucky 79, Louisville 68; Washington 62, Texas A&M 40; Oklahoma St. 50, Montana St. 46; BYU 68, San Jose St. 61; Kansas St. 61, Arizona 59. **Second Round:** Illinois 84, North Carolina St. 70; Kentucky 59, St. John's (N.Y.) 43; Oklahoma St. 61, Washington 57; Kansas St. 64, BYU 54. **Regional Third Place:** St. John's (N.Y.) 71, North Carolina St. 59; Washington 80, BYU 67. **Semifinals:** Kentucky 76, Illinois 74; Kansas St. 68, Oklahoma St. 44. **Third Place:** Illinois 61, Oklahoma St. 46. **Championship:** Kentucky 68, Kansas St. 58.

1952 First Round: Kentucky 82, Penn St. 54; St. John's (N.Y.) 60, North Carolina St. 49; Illinois 80, Dayton 61; Duquesne 60, Princeton 49; Kansas 68, TCU 64; St. Louis 62, New Mexico St. 53; Santa Clara 68, UCLA 59; Wyoming 54, Oklahoma City 48. **Regional Third Place:** North Carolina St. 69, Penn St. 60; Dayton 77, Princeton 61; TCU 61, New Mexico St. 44; Oklahoma City 55, UCLA 53. **Regional Championships:** St. John's (N.Y.) 64, Kentucky 57; Illinois 74, Duquesne 68; Kansas 74, St. Louis 55; Santa Clara 56, Wyoming 53. **Semifinals:** St. John's (N.Y.) 61, Illinois 59; Kansas 74, Santa Clara 55. **Third Place:** Illinois 67, Santa Clara 64. **Championship:** Kansas 80, St. John's (N.Y.) 63.

1953 First Round: Notre Dame 72, Eastern Ky. 57; DePaul 74, Miami (Ohio) 72; Holy Cross 87, Navy 74; Lebanon Valley 80, Fordham 67; Seattle 88, Idaho St. 77; Santa Clara 81, Hardin-Simmons 56. **Second Round:** Notre Dame 69, Penn 57; Indiana 82, DePaul 80; Holy Cross 79, Wake Forest 71; LSU 89, Lebanon Valley 76; Kansas 73, Oklahoma City 65; Oklahoma St. 71, TCU 54; Washington 92, Seattle 70; Santa Clara 67, Wyoming 52. **Regional Third Place:** Penn 90, DePaul 70; Wake Forest 91, Lebanon Valley 71; TCU 58, Oklahoma City 56; Seattle 80, Wyoming 64. **Regional Championships:** Indiana 79, Notre Dame 66; LSU 81, Holy Cross 73; Kansas 61, Oklahoma St. 55; Washington 74, Santa Clara 62. **Semifinals:** Indiana 80, LSU 67; Kansas 79, Washington 53. **Third Place:** Washington 88, LSU 69. **Championship:** Indiana 69, Kansas 68.

1954 First Round: La Salle 76, Fordham 74; North Carolina St. 75, George Washington 73; Navy 85, Connecticut 80; Notre Dame 80, Loyola (La.) 70; Penn St. 62, Toledo 50; Bradley 61, Oklahoma City 55; Idaho St. 77, Seattle 75 (ot); Santa Clara 73, Texas Tech 64. **Second Round:** La Salle 88, North Carolina St. 81; Navy 69, Cornell 67; Penn St. 78, LSU 70; Notre Dame 65, Indiana 64; Bradley 76, Colorado 64; Oklahoma St. 51, Rice 45; Southern California 73, Idaho St. 59; Santa Clara 73, Colorado St. 50. **Regional Third Place:** North Carolina St. 65, Cornell 54; Indiana 73, LSU 62; Rice 78, Colorado 55; Idaho St. 62, Colorado St. 57. **Regional Championships:** La Salle 64, Navy 48; Penn St. 71, Notre Dame 63; Bradley 71, Oklahoma St. 57; Southern California 66, Santa Clara 65 (2 ot). **Semifinals:** La Salle 69, Penn St. 54; Bradley 74, Southern California 72. **Third Place:** Penn St. 70, Southern California 61. **Championship:** La Salle 92, Bradley 76.

1955 First Round: Marquette 90, Miami (Ohio) 79; Penn St. 59, Memphis 55; La Salle 95, West Virginia 61; Villanova 74, Duke 73; Canisius 73, Williams 60; Bradley 69, Oklahoma City 65; Seattle 80, Idaho St. 63; San Francisco 89, West Tex. A&M 66. **Second Round:** Marquette 79, Kentucky 71; Iowa 82, Penn St. 53; La Salle 73, Princeton 46; Canisius 73, Villanova 71; Bradley 81, SMU 79; Colorado 69, Tulsa 59; Oregon St. 83, Seattle 71; San Francisco 78, Utah 59. **Regional Third Place:** Villanova 64, Princeton 57; Kentucky 84, Penn St. 59; Tulsa 68, SMU 67; Utah 108, Seattle 85. **Regional Championships:** La Salle 99, Canisius 64; Iowa 86, Marquette 81; Colorado 93, Bradley 81; San Francisco 57, Oregon St. 56. **Semifinals:** La Salle 76, Iowa 73; San Francisco 62, Colorado 50. **Third Place:** Colorado 75, Iowa 54. **Championship:** San Francisco 77, La Salle 63.

1956 First Round: Connecticut 84, Manhattan 75; Temple 74, Holy Cross 72; Dartmouth 61, West Virginia 59 (ot); Canisius 79, North Carolina St. 78 (4 ot); Wayne St. (Mich.) 72, DePaul 63; Morehead St. 107, Marshall 92; Seattle 68, Idaho St. 66; SMU 68, Texas Tech 67; Oklahoma City 97, Memphis 81. **Second Round:** Iowa 97, Morehead St. 83; Temple 65, Connecticut 59; Kentucky 84, Wayne St. (Mich.) 64; Canisius 66, Dartmouth 58; San Francisco 72, UCLA 61; Utah 81, Seattle 72; SMU 89, Houston 74; Oklahoma City 97, Kansas St. 93. **Regional Third Place:** Morehead St. 95, Wayne St. (Mich.) 84; Dartmouth 85, Connecticut 64; UCLA 94, Seattle 70; Kansas St. 89, Houston 70. **Regional Championships:** Temple 60, Canisius 58; Iowa 89, Kentucky 77; San Francisco 92, Utah 77; SMU 84, Oklahoma City 63. **Semifinals:** Iowa 83, Temple 76; San Francisco 86, SMU 68. **Third Place:** Temple 90, SMU 81. **Championship:** San Francisco 83, Iowa 71.

1957 First Round: Syracuse 82, Connecticut 76; Canisius 64, West Virginia 56; North Carolina 90, Yale 74; Pittsburgh 86, Morehead St. 85; Notre Dame 89, Miami (Ohio) 77; Oklahoma City 76, Loyola (La.) 55; Idaho St. 68, Hardin-Simmons 57. **Second Round:** Syracuse 75, Lafayette 71; North Carolina 87, Canisius 75; Kentucky 98, Pittsburgh 92; Michigan St. 85, Notre Dame 83; Kansas 73, SMU 65 (ot); Oklahoma City 75, St. Louis 66; San Francisco 66, Idaho St. 51; California 86, BYU 59. **Regional Third Place:** Canisius 82, Lafayette 76; Notre Dame 86, Pittsburgh 85; SMU 78, St. Louis 68; BYU 65, Idaho St. 54. **Regional Championships:** North Carolina 67, Syracuse 58; Michigan St. 80, Kentucky 68; Kansas 81, Oklahoma City 61; San Francisco 50, California 46. **Semifinals:** North Carolina 74, Michigan St. 70 (3 ot); Kansas 80, San Francisco 56. **Third Place:** San Francisco 67, Michigan St. 60. **Championship:** North Carolina 54, Kansas 53 (3 ot).

1958 First Round: Dartmouth 75, Connecticut 64; Manhattan 89, West Virginia 84; Maryland 86, Boston College 63; Miami (Ohio) 82, Pittsburgh 77; Notre Dame 94, Tennessee Tech 61; Oklahoma St. 59, Loyola (La.) 42; Idaho St. 72, Arizona St. 68; Seattle 88, Wyoming 51. **Second Round:** Dartmouth 79, Manhattan 62; Temple 71, Maryland 67; Notre Dame 94, Indiana 87; Kentucky 94, Miami (Ohio) 70; Oklahoma St. 65, Arkansas 40; Kansas St. 83, Cincinnati 80 (ot); California 54, Idaho St. 43; Seattle 69, San Francisco 67. **Regional Third Place:** Maryland 59, Manhattan 55; Indiana 98, Miami (Ohio) 91; Cincinnati 97, Arkansas 62; San Francisco 57, Idaho St. 51. **Regional Championships:** Temple 69, Dartmouth 50; Kentucky 89, Notre Dame 56; Kansas St. 69, Oklahoma St. 57; Seattle 66, California 62 (ot). **Semifinals:** Kentucky 61, Temple 60; Seattle 73, Kansas St. 51. **Third Place:** Temple 67, Kansas St. 57. **Championship:** Kentucky 84, Seattle 72.

1959 First Round: West Virginia 82, Dartmouth 68; Boston U. 60, Connecticut 58; Navy 76, North Carolina 63; Louisville 77, Eastern Ky. 63; Marquette 89, Bowling Green 71; DePaul 57, Portland 56; Idaho St. 62, New Mexico St. 61. **Second Round:** West Virginia 95, St. Joseph's 92; Boston U. 62, Navy 55; Louisville 76, Kentucky 61; Michigan St. 74, Marquette 69; Kansas St. 102, DePaul 70; Cincinnati 77, TCU 73; St. Mary's (Cal.) 80, Idaho St. 71; California 71, Utah 53. **Regional Third Place:** Kentucky 98, Marquette 69; Navy 70, St. Joseph's 56; TCU 71, DePaul 65; Idaho St. 71, Utah 65. **Regional Championships:** West Virginia 86, Boston U. 82; Louisville 88, Michigan St. 81; Cincinnati 85, Kansas St. 75; California 66, St. Mary's (Cal.) 46. **Semifinals:** West Virginia 94, Louisville 79; California 64, Cincinnati 58. **Third Place:** Cincinnati 98, Louisville 85. **Championship:** California 71, West Virginia 70.

1960 First Round: Duke 84, Princeton 60; West Virginia 94, Navy 86; New York U. 78, Connecticut 59; Ohio 74, Notre Dame 66; Western Ky. 107, Miami (Fla.) 84; California 71, Idaho St. 44; Oregon 68, New Mexico St. 60; Utah 80, Southern California 73; DePaul 69, Air Force 63. **Second Round:** Duke 58, St. Joseph's 56; New York U. 82, West Virginia 81 (ot); Georgia Tech 57, Ohio 54; Ohio St. 98, Western Ky. 79; Kansas 90, Texas 81; Cincinnati 99, DePaul 59; California 69, Santa Clara 49; Oregon 65, Utah 54. **Regional Third Place:** West Virginia 106, St. Joseph's 100; Western Ky. 97, Ohio 87; Utah 89, Santa Clara 81; DePaul 67, Texas 61. **Regional Championships:** New York U. 74, Duke 59; Ohio St. 86, Georgia Tech 69; Cincinnati 82, Kansas 71; California 70, Oregon 49. **Semifinals:** Ohio St. 76, New York U. 54; California 77, Cincinnati 69. **Third Place:** Cincinnati 95, New York U. 71. **Championship:** Ohio St. 75, California 55.

1961 First Round: Princeton 84, George Washington 67; St. Bonaventure 86, Rhode Island 76; Wake Forest 97, St. John's (N.Y.) 74; Louisville 76, Ohio 70; Morehead St. 71, Xavier 66; Houston 77, Marquette 61; Arizona St. 72, Seattle 70; Southern California 81, Oregon 79. **Second Round:** *St. Joseph's 72, Princeton 67; Wake Forest 78, St. Bonaventure 73; Ohio St. 56, Louisville 55; Kentucky 71, Morehead St. 64; Cincinnati 78, Texas Tech 55; Kansas St. 75, Houston 64; Utah 91, Loyola Marymount 75; Arizona St. 86, Southern California 71. **Regional Third Place:** St. Bonaventure 85, Princeton 67; Louisville 83, Morehead St. 61; Loyola Marymount 69, Southern California 67; Texas Tech 69, Houston 67. **Regional Championships:** *St. Joseph's 96, Wake Forest 86; Ohio St. 87, Kentucky 74; Cincinnati 69, Kansas St. 64; Utah 88, Arizona St. 80. **Semifinals:** Ohio St. 95, *St. Joseph's 69; Cincinnati 82, Utah 67. **Third Place:** *St. Joseph's 127, Utah 120 (4 ot). **Championship:** Cincinnati 70, Ohio St. 65 (ot).

**St. Joseph's participation in 1961 tournament vacated.*

1962 First Round: Wake Forest 92, Yale 82 (ot); New York U. 70, Massachusetts 50; Villanova 90, West Virginia 75; Butler 56, Bowling Green 55; Western Ky. 90, Detroit 81; Texas Tech 68, Air Force 66; Creighton 87, Memphis 83; Oregon St. 69, Seattle 65 (ot); Utah St. 78, Arizona St. 73. **Second Round:** Wake Forest 96, St. Joseph's 85 (ot); Villanova 79, New York U. 76; Kentucky 81, Butler 60; Ohio St. 93, Western Ky. 73; Colorado 67, Texas Tech 60; Cincinnati 66, Creighton 46; Oregon St. 69, Pepperdine 67; UCLA

73, Utah St. 62. **Regional Third Place:** New York U. 94, St. Joseph's 85; Butler 87, Western Ky. 86 (ot); Creighton 63, Texas Tech 61; Pepperdine 75, Utah St. 71. **Regional Championships:** Wake Forest 79, Villanova 69; Ohio St. 74, Kentucky 64; Cincinnati 73, Colorado 46; UCLA 88, Oregon St. 69. **Semifinals:** Ohio St. 84, Wake Forest 68; Cincinnati 72, UCLA 70. **Third Place:** Wake Forest 82, UCLA 80. **Championship:** Cincinnati 71, Ohio St. 59.

1963 First Round: New York U. 93, Pittsburgh 83; West Virginia 77, Connecticut 71; St. Joseph's 82, Princeton 81; Bowling Green 77, Notre Dame 72; Loyola (Ill.) 111, Tennessee Tech 42; Oklahoma City 70, Colorado St. 67; Texas 65, UTEP 47; Arizona St. 79, Utah St. 75 (ot); Oregon St. 70, Seattle 66. **Second Round:** Duke 81, New York U. 76; St. Joseph's 97, West Virginia 88; Illinois 70, Bowling Green 67; Loyola (Ill.) 61, Mississippi St. 51; Colorado 78, Oklahoma City 72; Cincinnati 73, Texas 68; Arizona St. 93, UCLA 79; Oregon St. 65, San Francisco 61. **Regional Third Place:** Mississippi St. 65, Bowling Green 60; West Virginia 83, New York U. 73; Texas 90, Oklahoma City 83; San Francisco 76, UCLA 75. **Regional Championships:** Duke 73, St. Joseph's 59; Loyola (Ill.) 79, Illinois 64; Cincinnati 67, Colorado 60; Oregon St. 83, Arizona St. 65. **Semifinals:** Loyola (Ill.) 94, Duke 75; Cincinnati 80, Oregon St. 46. **Third Place:** Duke 85, Oregon St. 63. **Championship:** Loyola (Ill.) 60, Cincinnati 58 (ot).

1964 First Round: Villanova 77, Providence 66; Connecticut 53, Temple 48; Princeton 86, VMI 60; Ohio 71, Louisville 69; Loyola (Ill.) 101, Murray St. 91; Creighton 89, Oklahoma City 78; UTEP 68, Texas A&M 62; Seattle 61, Oregon St. 57; Utah St. 92, Arizona St. 90. **Second Round:** Duke 87, Villanova 73; Connecticut 52, Princeton 50; Ohio 85, Kentucky 69; Michigan 84, Loyola (Ill.) 80; Wichita St. 84, Creighton 68; Kansas St. 64, UTEP 60; UCLA 95, Seattle 90; San Francisco 64, Utah St. 58. **Regional Third Place:** Villanova 74, Princeton 62; Loyola (Ill.) 100, Kentucky 91; UTEP 63, Creighton 52; Seattle 88, Utah St. 78. **Regional Championships:** Duke 101, Connecticut 54; Michigan 69, Ohio 57; Kansas St. 94, Wichita St. 86; UCLA 76, San Francisco 72. **Semifinals:** Duke 91, Michigan 80; UCLA 90, Kansas St. 84. **Third Place:** Michigan 100, Kansas St. 90. **Championship:** UCLA 98, Duke 83.

1965 First Round: Princeton 60, Penn St. 58; St. Joseph's 67, Connecticut 61; Providence 91, West Virginia 67; DePaul 99, Eastern Ky. 52; Dayton 66, Ohio 65; Houston 99, Notre Dame 98; Oklahoma City 70, Colorado St. 68. **Second Round:** Princeton 66, North Carolina St. 48; Providence 81, St. Joseph's 73 (ot); Vanderbilt 83, DePaul 78 (ot); Michigan 98, Dayton 71; Wichita St. 86, SMU 81; Oklahoma St. 75, Houston 60; UCLA 100, BYU 76; San Francisco 91, Oklahoma City 67. **Regional Third Place:** North Carolina St. 103, St. Joseph's 81; Dayton 75, DePaul 69; SMU 89, Houston 87; Oklahoma City 112, BYU 102. **Regional Championships:** Princeton 109, Providence 69; Michigan 87, Vanderbilt 85; Wichita St. 54, Oklahoma St. 46; UCLA 101, San Francisco 93. **Semifinals:** Michigan 93, Princeton 76; UCLA 108, Wichita St. 89. **Third Place:** Princeton 118, Wichita St. 82. **Championship:** UCLA 91, Michigan 80.

1966 First Round: St. Joseph's 65, Providence 48; Davidson 95, Rhode Island 65; Dayton 58, Miami (Ohio) 51; Western Ky. 105, Loyola (Ill.) 86; UTEP 89, Oklahoma City 74; Houston 82, Colorado St. 76. **Second Round:** Duke 76, St. Joseph's 74; Syracuse 94, Davidson 78; Kentucky 86, Dayton 79; Michigan 80, Western Ky. 79; UTEP 78, Cincinnati 76 (ot); Kansas 76, SMU 70; Oregon St. 63, Houston 60; Utah 83, Pacific 74. **Regional Third Place:** St. Joseph's 92, Davidson 76; Western Ky. 82, Dayton 62; SMU 89, Cincinnati 84; Houston 102, Pacific 91. **Regional Championships:** Duke 91, Syracuse 81; Kentucky 84, Michigan 77; UTEP 81, Kansas 80 (2 ot); Utah 70, Oregon St. 64. **Semifinals:** Kentucky 83, Duke 79; UTEP 85, Utah 78. **Third Place:** Duke 79, Utah 77. **Championship:** UTEP 72, Kentucky 65.

1967 First Round: Princeton 68, West Virginia 57; St. John's (N.Y.) 57, Temple 53; Boston College 48, Connecticut 42; Dayton 69, Western Ky. 67 (ot); Virginia Tech 82, Toledo 76; Houston 59, New Mexico St. 58; UTEP 62, Seattle 54. **Second Round:** North Carolina 78, Princeton 70 (ot); Boston College 63, St. John's (N.Y.) 62; Dayton 53, Tennessee 52; Virginia Tech 79, Indiana 70; Houston 66, Kansas 53; SMU 83, Louisville 81; Pacific 72, UTEP 63; UCLA 109, Wyoming 60. **Regional Third Place:** Princeton 78, St. John's (N.Y.) 58; Indiana 51, Tennessee 44; Kansas 70, Louisville 68; UTEP 69, Wyoming 67. **Regional Championships:** North Carolina 96, Boston College 80; Dayton 71, Virginia Tech 66 (ot); Houston 83, SMU 75; UCLA 80, Pacific 64. **Semifinals:** Dayton 76, North Carolina 62; UCLA 73, Houston 58. **Third Place:** Houston 84, North Carolina 62. **Championship:** UCLA 79, Dayton 64.

1968 First Round: St. Bonaventure 102, Boston College 93; Columbia 83, La Salle 69; Davidson 79, St. John's (N.Y.) 70; Marquette 72, Bowling Green 71; East Tenn. St. 79, Florida St. 69; Houston 94, Loyola (Ill.) 76; New Mexico St. 68, Weber St. 57. **Second Round:** North Carolina 91, St. Bonaventure 72; Davidson 61, Columbia 59 (ot); Kentucky 107, Marquette 89; Ohio St. 79, East Tenn. St. 72; Houston 91, Louisville 75; TCU 77, Kansas St. 72; UCLA 58, New Mexico St. 49; Santa Clara 86, New Mexico 73. **Regional Third Place:** Columbia 95, St. Bonaventure 75; Marquette 69, East Tenn. St. 57; Louisville 93, Kansas St. 63; New Mexico St. 62, New Mexico 58. **Regional Championships:** North Carolina 70, Davidson 66; Ohio St. 82, Kentucky 81; Houston 103, TCU 68; UCLA 87, Santa Clara 66. **Semifinals:** North Carolina 80, Ohio St. 66; UCLA 101, Houston 69. **Third Place:** Ohio St. 89, Houston 85. **Championship:** UCLA 78, North Carolina 55.

1969 First Round: Duquesne 74, St. Joseph's 52; Davidson 75, Villanova 61; St. John's (N.Y.) 72, Princeton 63; Marquette 82, Murray St. 62; Miami (Ohio) 63, Notre Dame 60; Texas A&M 81, Trinity (Tex.) 66; Colorado St. 52, Dayton 50; New Mexico St. 74, BYU 62; Weber St. 75, Seattle 73. **Second Round:** North Carolina 79, Duquesne 78; Davidson 79, St. John's (N.Y.) 69; Marquette 81, Kentucky 74; Purdue 91, Miami (Ohio) 71; Drake 81, Texas A&M 63; Colorado St. 64, Colorado 56; UCLA 53, New Mexico St. 38; Santa Clara 63, Weber St. 59. **Regional Third Place:** Duquesne 75, St. John's (N.Y.) 72; Kentucky 72, Miami (Ohio) 71; Colorado 97, Texas A&M 82; Weber St. 58, New Mexico St. 56. **Regional Championships:** North Carolina 87, Davidson 85; Purdue 75, Marquette 73 (ot); Drake 84, Colorado St. 77; UCLA 90, Santa Clara 52. **Semifinals:** Purdue 92, North Carolina 65; UCLA 85, Drake 82. **Third Place:** Drake 104, North Carolina 84. **Championship:** UCLA 92, Purdue 72.

1970 First Round: St. Bonaventure 85, Davidson 72; Niagara 79, Penn 69; Villanova 77, Temple 69; Notre Dame 112, Ohio 82; Jacksonville 109, Western Ky. 96; Houston 71, Dayton 64; New Mexico St. 101, Rice 77; Long Beach St. 92, Weber St. 73; Utah St. 91, UTEP 81. **Second Round:** St. Bonaventure 80, North Carolina St. 68; Villanova 98, Niagara 73; Kentucky 109, Notre Dame 99; Jacksonville 104, Iowa 103; Drake 92, Houston 87; New Mexico St. 70, Kansas St. 66; UCLA 88, Long Beach St. 65; Utah St. 69, Santa Clara 68. **Regional Third Place:** North Carolina St. 108, Niagara 88; Iowa 121, Notre Dame 106; Kansas St. 107, Houston 98; Santa Clara 89, Long Beach St. 86. **Regional Championships:** St. Bonaventure 97, Villanova 74; Jacksonville 106, Kentucky 100; New Mexico St. 87, Drake 78; UCLA 101, Utah St. 79. **Semifinals:** Jacksonville 91, St. Bonaventure 83; UCLA 93, New Mexico St. 77. **Third Place:** New Mexico St. 79, St. Bonaventure 73. **Championship:** UCLA 80, Jacksonville 69.

1971 First Round: Penn 70, Duquesne 65; *Villanova 93, St. Joseph's 75; Fordham 105, Furman 74; *Western Ky. 74, Jacksonville 72; Marquette 62, Miami (Ohio) 47; Notre Dame 102, TCU 94; Houston 72, New Mexico St. 69; BYU 91, Utah St. 82; *Long Beach St. 77, Weber St. 66. **Second Round:** Penn 79, South Carolina 64; *Villanova 85, Fordham 75; *Western Ky. 107, Kentucky 83; Ohio St. 60, Marquette 59; Drake 79, Notre Dame 72 (ot); Kansas 78, Houston 77; UCLA 91, BYU 73; *Long Beach St. 78, Pacific 65. **Regional Third Place:** Fordham 100, South Carolina 90; Marquette 91, Kentucky 74; Houston 119, Notre Dame 106; Pacific 84, BYU 81. **Regional Championships:** *Villanova 90, Penn 47; *Western Ky. 81, Ohio St. 78 (ot); Kansas 73, Drake 71; UCLA 57, *Long Beach St. 55. **Semifinals:** *Villanova 92, *Western Ky. 89 (2 ot); UCLA 68, Kansas 60. **Third Place:** *Western Ky. 77, Kansas 75. **Championship:** UCLA 68, *Villanova 62.

**Villanova's, Western Kentucky's and Long Beach State's participation in 1971 tournament vacated.*

1972 First Round: South Carolina 53, Temple 51; Villanova 85, East Caro. 70; Penn 76, Providence 60; Marquette 73, Ohio 49; Florida St. 83, Eastern Ky. 81; *La.-Lafayette 112, Marshall 101; Texas 85, Houston 74; Weber St. 91, Hawaii 64; *Long Beach St. 95, BYU 90 (ot). **Second Round:** North Carolina 92, South Carolina 69; Penn 78, Villanova 67; Kentucky 85, Marquette 69; Florida St. 70, *Minnesota 56; Louisville 88, *La.-Lafayette 84; Kansas St. 66, Texas 55; UCLA 90, Weber St. 58; *Long Beach St. 75, San Francisco 55. **Regional Third Place:** South Carolina 90, Villanova 78; *Minnesota 77, Marquette 72; *La.-Lafayette 100, Texas 70; San Francisco 74, Weber St. 64. **Regional Championships:** North Carolina 73, Penn 59; Florida St. 73, Kentucky 54; Louisville 72, Kansas St. 65; UCLA 73, *Long Beach St. 57. **Semifinals:** Florida St. 79, North Carolina 75; UCLA 96, Louisville 77. **Third Place:** North Carolina 105, Louisville 91. **Championship:** UCLA 81, Florida St. 76.

**Louisiana-Lafayette's, Long Beach State's and Minnesota's participation in 1972 tournament vacated.*

1973 First Round: Syracuse 83, Furman 82; Penn 62, St. John's (N.Y.) 61; Providence 89, St. Joseph's 76; South Carolina 78, Texas Tech 70; *La.-Lafayette 102, Houston 89; Marquette 77, Miami (Ohio) 62; *Austin Peay 77, Jacksonville 75; *Long Beach St. 88, Weber St. 75; Arizona St. 103, Oklahoma City 78. **Second Round:** Maryland 91, Syracuse 75; Providence 87, Penn 65; Memphis 90, South Carolina 76; Kansas St. 66, *La.-Lafayette 63; Indiana 75, Marquette 69; Kentucky 106, *Austin Peay 100 (ot); San Francisco 77, *Long Beach St. 67; UCLA 98, Arizona St. 81. **Regional Third Place:** Syracuse 69, Penn 68; South Carolina 90, *La.-Lafayette 85; Marquette 88, *Austin Peay 73; *Long Beach St. 84, Arizona St. 80. **Regional Championships:** Providence 103, Maryland 89; Memphis 92, Kansas St. 72; Indiana 72, Kentucky 65; UCLA 54, San Francisco 39. **Semifinals:** Memphis 98, Providence 85; UCLA 70, Indiana 59. **Third Place:** Indiana 97, Providence 79. **Championship:** UCLA 87, Memphis 66.

**Austin Peay's, Long Beach State's and Louisiana-Lafayette's participation in 1973 tournament vacated.*

1974 First Round: Providence 84, Penn 69; Pittsburgh 54, St. Joseph's 42; Furman 75, South Carolina 67; New Mexico 73, Idaho St. 65; Dayton 88, Cal St. L.A. 80; Notre Dame 108, Austin Peay 66; Marquette 85, Ohio 59; Oral Roberts 86, Syracuse 82 (ot); Creighton 77, Texas 61. **Second Round:** North Carolina St. 92, Providence 78; Pittsburgh 81, Furman 78; San Francisco 64, New Mexico 61; UCLA 111, Dayton 100 (3 ot); Michigan 77, Notre Dame 68; Marquette 69, Vanderbilt 61; Oral Roberts 96, Louisville 93; Kansas 55, Creighton 54. **Regional Third Place:** Providence 95, Furman 83; New Mexico 66, Dayton 61; Notre Dame 118, Vanderbilt 88; Creighton 80, Louisville 71. **Regional Championships:** North Carolina St. 100, Pittsburgh 72; UCLA 83, San Francisco 60; Marquette 72, Michigan 70; Kansas 93, Oral Roberts 90 (ot). **Semifinals:** North Carolina St. 80, UCLA 77 (2 ot); Marquette 64, Kansas 51. **Third Place:** UCLA 78, Kansas 61. **Championship:** North Carolina St. 76, Marquette 64.

1975 First Round: Syracuse 87, La Salle 83 (ot); North Carolina 93, New Mexico St. 69; Boston College 82, Furman 76; Kansas St. 69, Penn 62; Central Mich. 77, Georgetown 75; Kentucky 76, Marquette 54; Indiana 78, UTEP 53; Oregon St. 78, Middle Tenn. 67; Cincinnati 87, Texas A&M 79; Louisville 91, Rutgers 78; Maryland 83, Creighton 79; Notre Dame 77, Kansas 71; Arizona St. 97, Alabama 94; UNLV 90, San Diego St. 80; UCLA 103, Michigan 91 (ot); Montana 69, Utah St. 63. **Second Round:** Syracuse 78, North Carolina 76; Kansas St. 74, Boston College 65; Kentucky 90, Central Mich. 73; Indiana 81, Oregon St. 71; Louisville 78, Cincinnati 63; Maryland 83, Notre Dame 71; Arizona St. 84, UNLV 81; UCLA 67, Montana 64. **Regional Third Place:** North Carolina 110, Boston College 90; Central Mich. 88, Oregon St. 87; Cincinnati 95, Notre Dame 87 (ot); UNLV 75, Montana 67. **Regional Championships:** Syracuse 95, Kansas St. 87 (ot); Kentucky 92, Indiana 90; Louisville 96, Maryland 82; UCLA 89, Arizona St. 75. **Semifinals:** Kentucky 95, Syracuse 79; UCLA 75, Louisville 74 (ot). **Third Place:** Louisville 96, Syracuse 88 (ot). **Championship:** UCLA 92, Kentucky 85.

1976 First Round: DePaul 69, Virginia 60; VMI 81, Tennessee 75; Rutgers 54, Princeton 53; Connecticut 80, Hofstra 78 (ot); Michigan 74, Wichita St. 73; Notre Dame 79, Cincinnati 78; Missouri 69, Washington 67; Texas Tech 69, Syracuse 56; Alabama 79, North Carolina 64; Indiana 90, St. John's (N.Y.) 70; Marquette 79, Western Ky. 60; Western Mich. 77, Virginia Tech 67 (ot); Pepperdine 87, Memphis 77; UCLA 74, San Diego St. 64; Arizona 83, Georgetown 76; UNLV 103, Boise St. 78. **Second Round:** VMI 71, DePaul 66 (ot); Rutgers 93, Connecticut 79; Missouri 86, Texas Tech 75; Michigan 80, Notre Dame 76; Indiana 74, Alabama 69; Marquette 62, Western Mich. 57; UCLA 70, Pepperdine 61; Arizona 114, UNLV 109 (ot). **Regional Championships:** Rutgers 91, VMI 75; Michigan 95, Missouri 88; Indiana 65, Marquette 56; UCLA 82, Arizona 66. **Semifinals:** Michigan 86, Rutgers 70; Indiana 65, UCLA 51. **Third Place:** UCLA 106, Rutgers 92. **Championship:** Indiana 86, Michigan 68.

1977 First Round: VMI 73, Duquesne 66; Kentucky 72, Princeton 58; Notre Dame 90, Hofstra 83; North Carolina 69, Purdue 66; UCLA 87, Louisville 79; Idaho St. 83, Long Beach St. 72; Utah 72, St. John's (N.Y.) 68; UNLV 121, San Francisco 95; Michigan 92, Holy Cross 81; Detroit 93, Middle Tenn. 76; Charlotte 91, Central Mich. 86 (ot); Syracuse 93, Tennessee 88 (ot); Marquette 66, Cincinnati 51; Kansas St. 87, Providence 80; Wake Forest 86, Arkansas 80; Southern Ill. 81, Arizona 77. **Second Round:** Kentucky 93, VMI 78; North Carolina 79, Notre Dame 77; Idaho St. 76, UCLA 75; UNLV 88,

Utah 83; Michigan 86, Detroit 81; Charlotte 81, Syracuse 59; Marquette 67, Kansas St. 66; Wake Forest 86, Southern Ill. 81. **Regional Championships:** North Carolina 79, Kentucky 72; UNLV 107, Idaho St. 90; Charlotte 75, Michigan 68; Marquette 82, Wake Forest 68. **Semifinals:** Marquette 51, Charlotte 49; North Carolina 84, UNLV 83. **Third Place:** UNLV 106, Charlotte 94. **Championship:** Marquette 67, North Carolina 59.

1978 First Round: Michigan St. 77, Providence 63; Western Ky. 87, Syracuse 86 (ot); Miami (Ohio) 84, Marquette 81 (ot); Kentucky 85, Florida St. 76; UCLA 83, Kansas 76; Arkansas 73, Weber St. 52; San Francisco 68, North Carolina 64; Cal St. Fullerton 90, New Mexico 85; Duke 63, Rhode Island 62; Penn 92, St. Bonaventure 83; Indiana 63, Furman 62; Villanova 103, La Salle 97; Utah 86, Missouri 79 (2 ot); Notre Dame 100, Houston 77; DePaul 80, Creighton 78; Louisville 76, St. John's (N.Y.) 68. **Second Round:** Michigan St. 90, Western Ky. 69; Kentucky 91, Miami (Ohio) 69; Arkansas 74, UCLA 70; Cal St. Fullerton 75, San Francisco 72; Duke 84, Penn 80; Villanova 61, Indiana 60; Notre Dame 69, Utah 56; DePaul 90, Louisville 89 (2 ot). **Regional Championships:** Kentucky 52, Michigan St. 49; Arkansas 61, Cal St. Fullerton 58; Duke 90, Villanova 72; Notre Dame 84, DePaul 64. **Semifinals:** Kentucky 64, Arkansas 59; Duke 90, Notre Dame 86. **Third Place:** Arkansas 71, Notre Dame 69. **Championship:** Kentucky 94, Duke 88.

1979 First Round: St. John's (N.Y.) 75, Temple 70; Penn 73, Iona 69; Lamar 95, Detroit 87; Tennessee 97, Eastern Ky. 81; Southern California 86, Utah St. 67; Pepperdine 92, Utah 88 (ot); Weber St. 81, New Mexico St. 78 (ot); Virginia Tech 70, Jacksonville 53. **Second Round:** St. John's (N.Y.) 80, Duke 78; Rutgers 64, Georgetown 58; Penn 72, North Carolina 71; Syracuse 89, Connecticut 81; Michigan St. 95, Lamar 64; LSU 71, Appalachian St. 57; Notre Dame 73, Tennessee 67; Toledo 74, Iowa 72; DePaul 89, Southern California 78; Marquette 73, Pacific 48; UCLA 76, Pepperdine 71; San Francisco 86, BYU 63; Arkansas 74, Weber St. 63; Louisville 69, South Ala. 66; Indiana St. 86, Virginia Tech 69; Oklahoma 90, Texas 76. **Regional Semifinals:** St. John's (N.Y.) 67, Rutgers 65; Penn 84, Syracuse 76; Michigan St. 87, LSU 71; Notre Dame 79, Toledo 71; DePaul 62, Marquette 56; UCLA 99, San Francisco 81; Arkansas 73, Louisville 62; Indiana St. 93, Oklahoma 72. **Regional Championships:** Penn 64, St. John's (N.Y.) 62; Michigan St. 80, Notre Dame 68; DePaul 95, UCLA 91; Indiana St. 73, Arkansas 71. **Semifinals:** Michigan St. 101, Penn 67; Indiana St. 76, DePaul 74. **Third Place:** DePaul 96, Penn 93. **Championship:** Michigan St. 75, Indiana St. 64.

1980 First Round: Villanova 77, Marquette 59; Iowa 86, VCU 72; *Iona 84, Holy Cross 78; Tennessee 80, Furman 69; Alcorn St. 70, South Ala. 62; Missouri 61, San Jose St. 51; Texas A&M 55, Bradley 53; Kansas St. 71, Arkansas 53; Florida St. 94, Toledo 91; Penn 62, Washington St. 55; Purdue 90, La Salle 82; Virginia Tech 89, Western Ky. 85 (ot); *UCLA 87, Old Dominion 74; Arizona St. 99, *Loyola Marymount 71; Clemson 76, Utah St. 73; Lamar 87, Weber St. 86. **Second Round:** Syracuse 97, Villanova 83; Iowa 77, North Carolina St. 64; Georgetown 74, *Iona 71; Maryland 86, Tennessee 75; LSU 98, Alcorn St. 88; Missouri 87, Notre Dame 84 (ot); Texas A&M 78, North Carolina 61 (2 ot); Louisville 71, Kansas St. 69 (ot); Kentucky 97, Florida St. 78; Duke 52, Penn 42; Purdue 87, St. John's (N.Y.) 72; Indiana 68, Virginia Tech 59; *UCLA 77, DePaul 71; Ohio St. 89, Arizona St. 75; Clemson 71, BYU 66; Lamar 81, *Oregon St. 77. **Regional Semifinals:** Iowa 88, Syracuse 77; Georgetown 74, Maryland 68; LSU 68, Missouri 63; Louisville 66, Texas A&M 55 (ot); Duke 55, Kentucky 54; Purdue 76, Indiana 69; *UCLA 72, Ohio St. 68; Clemson 74, Lamar 66. **Regional Championships:** Iowa 81, Georgetown 80; Louisville 86, LSU 66; Purdue 68, Duke 60; *UCLA 85, Clemson 74. **Semifinals:** Louisville 80, Iowa 72; *UCLA 67, Purdue 62. **Third Place:** Purdue 75, Iowa 58. **Championship:** Louisville 59, *UCLA 54.

**Iona's, Loyola Marymount's, Oregon State's and UCLA's participation in 1980 tournament vacated.*

1981 First Round: Lamar 71, Missouri 67; Arkansas 73, Mercer 67; Wichita St. 95, Southern U. 70; Kansas 69, Mississippi 66; St. Joseph's 59, Creighton 57; Boston College 93, Ball St. 90; Maryland 81, Chattanooga 69; UAB 93, Western Ky. 68; Kansas St. 64, San Francisco 60; Wyoming 78, Howard 43; Northeastern 55, Fresno St. 53; Pittsburgh 70, Idaho 69 (ot); Villanova 90, Houston 72; VCU 85, Long Island 69; BYU 60, Princeton 51; James Madison 61, Georgetown 55. **Second Round:** LSU 100, Lamar 78; Arkansas 74, Louisville 73; Wichita St. 60, Iowa 56; Kansas 88, Arizona St. 71; St. Joseph's 49, DePaul 48; Boston College 67, Wake Forest 64; Indiana 99, Maryland 64; UAB 69, Kentucky 62; Kansas St. 50, *Oregon St. 48; Illinois 67, Wyoming 65; Utah 94, Northeastern 69; North Carolina 74, Pittsburgh 57; Virginia 54, Villanova 50; Tennessee 58, VCU 56 (ot); BYU 78, UCLA 55; Notre Dame 54, James Madison 45. **Regional Semifinals:** LSU 72, Arkansas 56; Wichita St. 66, Kansas 65; St. Joseph's 42, Boston College 41; Indiana 87, UAB 72; Kansas St. 57, Illinois 52; North Carolina 61, Utah 56; Virginia 62, Tennessee 48; BYU 51, Notre Dame 50. **Regional Championships:** LSU 96, Wichita St. 85; Indiana 78, St. Joseph's 46; North Carolina 82, Kansas St. 68; Virginia 74, BYU 60. **Semifinals:** Indiana 67, LSU 49; North Carolina 78, Virginia 65. **Third Place:** Virginia 78, LSU 74. **Championship:** Indiana 63, North Carolina 50.

**Oregon State's participation in 1981 tournament vacated.*

1982 First Round: James Madison 55, Ohio St. 48; St. John's (N.Y.) 66, Penn 56; Northeastern 63, St. Joseph's 62; Wake Forest 74, Old Dominion 57; Boston College 70, San Francisco 66; Kansas St. 77, Northern Ill. 68; Houston 94, Alcorn St. 84; Marquette 67, Evansville 62; Tennessee 61, La.-Lafayette 57; Indiana 94, Robert Morris 62; Middle Tenn. 50, Kentucky 44; Chattanooga 58, North Carolina St. 51; Wyoming 61, Southern California 58; West Virginia 102, N.C. A&T 72; Iowa 70, La.-Monroe 63; Pepperdine 99, Pittsburgh 88. **Second Round:** North Carolina 52, James Madison 50; Alabama 69, St. John's (N.Y.) 68; Villanova 76, Northeastern 72 (3 ot); *Memphis 56, Wake Forest 55; Boston College 82, DePaul 75; Kansas St. 65, Arkansas 64; Houston 78, Tulsa 74; Missouri 73, Marquette 69; Virginia 54, Tennessee 51; UAB 80, Indiana 70; Louisville 81, Middle Tenn. 56; Minnesota 62, Chattanooga 61; Georgetown 51, Wyoming 43; Fresno St. 50, West Virginia 46; Idaho 69, Iowa 67 (ot); *Oregon St. 70, Pepperdine 51. **Regional Semifinals:** North Carolina 74, Alabama 69; Villanova 70, *Memphis 66; Boston College 69, Kansas St. 65; Houston 79, Missouri 78; UAB 68, Virginia 66; Louisville 67, Minnesota 61; Georgetown 58, Fresno St. 40; *Oregon St. 60, Idaho 42. **Regional Championships:** North Carolina 70, Villanova 60; Houston 99, Boston College 92; Louisville 75, UAB 68; Georgetown 69, *Oregon St. 45. **Semifinals:** North Carolina 68, Houston 63; Georgetown 50, Louisville 46. **Championship:** North Carolina 63, Georgetown 62.

**Memphis' and Oregon State's participation in 1982 tournament vacated.*

1983 Opening Round: Robert Morris 64, Ga. Southern 54; Alcorn St. 81, Xavier 75; Princeton 53, N.C. A&T 41; La Salle 70, Boston U. 58. **First Round:** Maryland 52, Chattanooga 51; Lamar 73, Alabama 50; Georgetown 68, Alcorn St. 63; Iowa 64, Utah St. 59; Purdue 55, Robert Morris 53; Ohio 51, Illinois St. 49; Tennessee 57, Marquette 56; Oklahoma 71, UAB 63; Utah 52, Illinois 49; Washington St. 62, Weber St. 52; Princeton 56, Oklahoma St. 53; North Carolina St. 69, Pepperdine 67 (2 ot); James Madison 57, West Virginia 50; VCU 76, La Salle 67; Syracuse 74, Morehead St. 59; Rutgers 60, La.-Lafayette 53. **Second Round:** Villanova 60, Lamar 58; Houston 60, Maryland 50; Iowa 77, Missouri 63; *Memphis 66, Georgetown 57; Kentucky 57, Ohio 40; Arkansas 78, Purdue 68; Indiana 63, Oklahoma 49; Louisville 70, Tennessee 57; Virginia 54, Washington St. 49; Utah 67, UCLA 61; North Carolina St. 71, UNLV 70; Boston College 51, Princeton 42; North Carolina 68, James Madison 49; Georgia 56, VCU 54; Ohio St. 79, Syracuse 74; St. John's (N.Y.) 66, Rutgers 55. **Regional Semifinals:** Villanova 55, Iowa 54; Houston 70, *Memphis 63; Kentucky 64, Indiana 59; Louisville 65, Arkansas 63; North Carolina St. 75, Utah 56; Virginia 95, Boston College 92; North Carolina 64, Ohio St. 51; Georgia 70, St. John's (N.Y.) 67. **Regional Championships:** Houston 89, Villanova 71; Louisville 80, Kentucky 68 (ot); North Carolina St. 63, Virginia 62; Georgia 82, North Carolina 77. **Semifinals:** North Carolina St. 67, Georgia 60; Houston 94, Louisville 81. **Championship:** North Carolina St. 54, Houston 52.

**Memphis' participation in 1983 tournament vacated.*

1984 Opening Round: Morehead St. 70, N.C. A&T 69; Princeton 65, San Diego 56; Richmond 89, Rider 65; Northeastern 90, Long Island 87; Alcorn St. 79, Houston Baptist 60. **First Round:** BYU 84, UAB 68; Louisville 72, Morehead St. 59; West Virginia 64, Oregon St. 62; Villanova 84, Marshall 72; SMU 83, Miami (Ohio) 69; UNLV 68, Princeton 56; Washington 64, Nevada 54; Dayton 74, LSU 66; Temple 65, St. John's (N.Y.) 63; Richmond 72, Auburn 71; VCU 70, Northeastern 69; Virginia 58, Iona 57; Illinois St. 49, Alabama 48; Kansas 57, Alcorn St. 56; *Memphis 92, Oral Roberts 83; Louisiana Tech 66, Fresno St. 56. **Second Round:** Kentucky 93, BYU 68; Louisville 69, Tulsa 67; Maryland 102, West Virginia 77; Illinois 64, Villanova 56; Georgetown 37, SMU 36; UNLV 73, UTEP 60; Washington 80, Duke 78; Dayton 89, Oklahoma 85; North Carolina 77, Temple 66; Indiana 75, Richmond 67; Syracuse 78, VCU 63; Virginia 53, Arkansas 51 (ot); DePaul 75, Illinois St. 61; Wake Forest 69, Kansas 59; *Memphis 66, Purdue 48; Houston 77, Louisiana Tech 69. **Regional Semifinals:** Kentucky 72, Louisville 67; Illinois 72, Maryland 70; Georgetown 62, UNLV 48; Dayton 64, Washington 58; Indiana 72, North Carolina 68; Virginia 63, Syracuse 55; Wake Forest 73, DePaul 71 (ot); Houston 78, *Memphis 71. **Regional Championships:** Kentucky 54, Illinois 51; Georgetown 61, Dayton 49; Virginia 50, Indiana 48; Houston 68, Wake Forest 63. **Semifinals:** Georgetown 53, Kentucky 40; Houston 49, Virginia 47 (ot). **Championship:** Georgetown 84, Houston 75.

**Memphis' participation in 1984 tournament vacated.*

1985 First Round: Georgetown 68, Lehigh 43; Temple 60, Virginia Tech 57; SMU 85, Old Dominion 68; Loyola (Ill.) 59, Iona 58; Illinois 76, Northeastern 57; *Georgia 67, Wichita St. 59; Syracuse 70, DePaul 65; Georgia Tech 65, Mercer 58; Auburn 59, Purdue 58; Kansas 49, Ohio 38; Notre Dame 79, Oregon St. 70; North Carolina 76, Middle Tenn. 57; Michigan 59, Fairleigh Dickinson 55; Villanova 51, Dayton 49; Maryland 69, Miami (Ohio) 68 (ot); Navy 78, LSU 55; Oklahoma 96, N.C. A&T 83; Illinois St. 58, Southern California 55; Ohio St. 75, Iowa St. 64; Louisiana Tech 78, Pittsburgh 54; Boston College 55, Texas Tech 53; Duke 75, Pepperdine 62; UAB 70, Michigan St. 68; *Memphis 67, Penn 55; St. John's (N.Y.) 83, Southern U. 59; Arkansas 63, Iowa 54; Kentucky 66, Washington 58; UNLV 85, San Diego St. 80; UTEP 79, Tulsa 75; North Carolina St. 65, Nevada 56; Alabama 50, Arizona 41; VCU 81, Marshall 65. **Second Round:** Georgetown 63, Temple 46; Loyola (Ill.) 70, SMU 57; Illinois 74, *Georgia 58; Georgia Tech 70, Syracuse 53; Villanova 59, Michigan 55; Maryland 64, Navy 59; Auburn 66, Kansas 64; North Carolina 60, Notre Dame 58; Oklahoma 75, Illinois St. 69; Louisiana Tech 79, Ohio St. 67; Boston College 74, Duke 73; *Memphis 67, UAB 66 (ot); St. John's (N.Y.) 68, Arkansas 65; Kentucky 64, UNLV 61; Alabama 63, VCU 59; North Carolina St. 86, UTEP 73. **Regional Semifinals:** Georgetown 65, Loyola (Ill.) 53; Georgia Tech 61, Illinois 53; Villanova 46, Maryland 43; North Carolina 62, Auburn 56; Oklahoma 86, Louisiana Tech 84 (ot); *Memphis 59, Boston College 57; North Carolina St. 61, Alabama 55; St. John's (N.Y.) 86, Kentucky 70. **Regional Championships:** Georgetown 60, Georgia Tech 54; Villanova 56, North Carolina 44; *Memphis 63, Oklahoma 61; St. John's (N.Y.) 69, North Carolina St. 60. **Semifinals:** Villanova 52, *Memphis 45; Georgetown 77, St. John's (N.Y.) 59. **Championship:** Villanova 66, Georgetown 64.

**Georgia's and Memphis' participation in 1985 tournament vacated.*

1986 First Round: Duke 85, Mississippi Val. 78; Old Dominion 72, West Virginia 64; *DePaul 72, Virginia 68; Oklahoma 80, Northeastern 74; St. Joseph's 60, Richmond 59; Cleveland St. 83, Indiana 79; Navy 87, Tulsa 68; Syracuse 101, Brown 52; Kansas 71, N.C. A&T 46; Temple 61, Jacksonville 50 (ot); Michigan St. 72, Washington 70; Georgetown 70, Texas Tech 64; North Carolina St. 66, Iowa 64; Ark.-Little Rock 90, Notre Dame 83; Iowa St. 81, Miami (Ohio) 79 (ot); Michigan 70, Akron 64; Kentucky 75, Davidson 55; Western Ky. 67, Nebraska 59; Alabama 97, Xavier 80; Illinois 75, Fairfield 51; LSU 94, Purdue 87 (2 ot); *Memphis 95, Ball St. 63; Villanova 71, Virginia Tech 62; Georgia Tech 68, Marist 53; St. John's (N.Y.) 83, Montana St. 74; Auburn 73, Arizona 63; Maryland 69, Pepperdine 64; UNLV 74, La.-Monroe 51; UAB 66, Missouri 64; North Carolina 84, Utah 72; Bradley 83, UTEP 65; Louisville 93, Drexel 73. **Second Round:** Kentucky 71, Western Ky. 64; Alabama 58, Illinois 56; LSU 83, *Memphis 81; Georgia Tech 66, Villanova 61; Auburn 81, St. John's (N.Y.) 65; UNLV 70, Maryland 64; North Carolina 77, UAB 59; Louisville 82, Bradley 68; Duke 89, Old Dominion 61; *DePaul 74, Oklahoma 69; Cleveland St. 75, St. Joseph's 69; Navy 97, Syracuse 85; Kansas 65, Temple 43; Michigan St. 80, Georgetown 68; North Carolina St. 80, Ark.-Little Rock 66 (2 ot); Iowa St. 72, Michigan 69. **Regional Semifinals:** Duke 74, *DePaul 67; Navy 71, Cleveland St. 70; Kansas 96, Michigan St. 86 (ot); North Carolina St. 70, Iowa St. 66; Kentucky 68, Alabama 63; LSU 70, Georgia Tech 64; Auburn 70, UNLV 63; Louisville 94, North Carolina 79. **Regional Championships:** LSU 59, Kentucky 57; Louisville 84, Auburn 76; Duke 71, Navy 50; Kansas 75, North Carolina St. 67. **Semifinals:** Louisville 88, LSU 77; Duke 71, Kansas 67. **Championship:** Louisville 72, Duke 69.

**DePaul's and Memphis' participation in 1986 tournament vacated.*

1987 First Round: North Carolina 113, Penn 82; Michigan 97, Navy 82; Notre Dame 84, Middle Tenn. 71; TCU 76, *Marshall 60; *Florida 82, *North Carolina St. 70; Purdue 104, Northeastern 95; Western Ky. 64, West Virginia 62; Syracuse 79, Ga. Southern 73; Georgetown 75, Bucknell 53; Ohio St. 91, Kentucky 77; Kansas 66, Houston 55; Missouri St. 65, Clemson 60; Providence 90, UAB 68; Austin Peay 68, Illinois 67; New Orleans 83, BYU 79; *Alabama 88, N.C. A&T 71; Indiana 92, Fairfield 58; Auburn 62, San Diego 61; Duke 58, Texas A&M 51; Xavier 70, Missouri 69; St. John's (N.Y.) 57, Wichita St. 55; *DePaul 76, Louisiana Tech 62; LSU 85, Georgia Tech 79; Temple 75, Southern U. 56; Oklahoma 74, Tulsa 69; Pittsburgh 93, Marist 68; UTEP 98, Arizona 91 (ot); Iowa 99, Santa Clara 76; UNLV 95, Idaho St. 70; Kansas St. 82, Georgia 79 (ot); Wyoming 64, Virginia 60; UCLA 92, Central Mich. 73. **Second Round:** Notre Dame 58, TCU 57; North Carolina 109, Michigan 97; *Florida 85, Purdue 66; Syracuse 104, Western Ky. 86; Georgetown 82, Ohio St. 79; Kansas 67, Missouri St. 63; Providence 90, Austin Peay 87 (ot); *Alabama 101, New Orleans 76; Indiana 107, Auburn 90; Duke 65, Xavier 60; *DePaul 83, St. John's (N.Y.) 75 (ot); LSU 72, Temple 62; Oklahoma 96, Pittsburgh 93; Iowa 84, UTEP 82; UNLV 80, Kansas St. 61; Wyoming 78, UCLA 68. **Regional Semifinals:** North Carolina 74, Notre Dame 68; Syracuse 87, *Florida 81; Providence 103, *Alabama 82; Georgetown 70, Kansas 57; Indiana 88, Duke 82; LSU 63, *DePaul 58; UNLV 92, Wyoming 78; Iowa 93, Oklahoma 91 (ot). **Regional Championships:** Syracuse 79, North Carolina 75; Providence 88, Georgetown 73; Indiana 77, LSU 76; UNLV 84, Iowa 81. **Semifinals:** Syracuse 77, Providence 63; Indiana 97, UNLV 93. **Championship:** Indiana 74, Syracuse 73.

**Alabama's, DePaul's, Florida's, Marshall's and North Carolina State's participation in 1987 tournament vacated.*

1988 First Round: Purdue 94, Fairleigh Dickinson 79; Memphis 75, Baylor 60; *DePaul 83, Wichita St. 62; Kansas St. 66, La Salle 53; Kansas 85, Xavier 72; Murray St. 78, *North Carolina St. 75; Vanderbilt 80, Utah St. 77; Pittsburgh 108, Eastern Mich. 90; Temple 87, Lehigh 73; Georgetown 66, LSU 63; Georgia Tech 90, Iowa St. 78; Richmond 72, Indiana 69; Rhode Island 87, Missouri 80; Syracuse 69, N.C. A&T 55; SMU 83, Notre Dame 75; Duke 85, Boston U. 69; Arizona 90, Cornell 50; Seton Hall 80, UTEP 64; Iowa 102, Florida St. 98; UNLV 54, Missouri St. 50; *Florida 62, St. John's (N.Y.) 59; Michigan 63, Boise St. 58; Loyola Marymount 119, Wyoming 115; North Carolina 83, North Texas 65; Oklahoma 94, Chattanooga 66; Auburn 90, Bradley 86; Louisville 70, Oregon St. 61; BYU 98, Charlotte 92 (ot); Villanova 82, Arkansas 74; Illinois 81, UTSA 72; *Maryland 92, UC Santa Barbara 82; *Kentucky 99, Southern U. 84. **Second Round:** Purdue 100, Memphis 73; Kansas St. 66, *DePaul 58; Kansas 61, Murray St. 58; Vanderbilt 80, Pittsburgh 74 (ot); Temple 74, Georgetown 53; Richmond 59, Georgia Tech 55; Rhode Island 97, Syracuse 94; Duke 94, SMU 79; Arizona 84, Seton Hall 55; Iowa 104, UNLV 86; Michigan 108, *Florida 85; North Carolina 123, Loyola Marymount 97; Oklahoma 107, Auburn 87; Louisville 97, BYU 76; Villanova 66, Illinois 63; *Kentucky 90, *Maryland 81. **Regional Semifinals:** Kansas St. 73, Purdue 70; Kansas 77, Vanderbilt 64; Temple 69, Richmond 47; Duke 73, Rhode Island 72; Arizona 99, Iowa 79; North Carolina 78, Michigan 69; Oklahoma 108, Louisville 98; Villanova 80, *Kentucky 74. **Regional Championships:** Kansas 71, Kansas St. 58; Duke 63, Temple 53; Arizona 70, North Carolina 52; Oklahoma 78, Villanova 59. **Semifinals:** Kansas 66, Duke 59; Oklahoma 86, Arizona 78. **Championship:** Kansas 83, Oklahoma 79.

**DePaul's, Florida's, Kentucky's, Maryland's and North Carolina State's participation in 1988 tournament vacated.*

1989 First Round: Illinois 77, McNeese St. 71; Ball St. 68, Pittsburgh 64; Arkansas 120, Loyola Marymount 101; Louisville 76, Ark.-Little Rock 71; Texas 76, Georgia Tech 70; Missouri 85, Creighton 69; Colorado St. 68, Florida 46; Syracuse 104, Bucknell 81; Oklahoma 72, East Tenn. St. 71; Louisiana Tech 83, La Salle 74; Virginia 100, Providence 97; Middle Tenn. 97, Florida St. 83; South Ala. 86, Alabama 84; Michigan 92, Xavier 87; UCLA 84, Iowa St. 74; North Carolina 93, Southern U. 79; Georgetown 50, Princeton 49; Notre Dame 81, Vanderbilt 65; North Carolina St. 81, South Carolina 66; Iowa 87, Rutgers 73; Minnesota 86, Kansas St. 75; Siena 80, Stanford 78; West Virginia 84, Tennessee 68; Duke 90, South Carolina St. 69; Arizona 94, Robert Morris 60; Clemson 83, St. Mary's (Cal.) 70; *DePaul 66, Memphis 63; UNLV 68, Idaho 56; Evansville 94, Oregon St. 90 (ot); Seton Hall 60, Missouri St. 51; UTEP 85, LSU 74; Indiana 99, George Mason 85. **Second Round:** Illinois 72, Ball St. 60; Louisville 93, Arkansas 84; Missouri 108, Texas 89; Syracuse 65, Colorado St. 50; Oklahoma 124, Louisiana Tech 81; Virginia 104, Middle Tenn. 88; Michigan 91, South Ala. 82; North Carolina 88, UCLA 81; Georgetown 81, Notre Dame 74; North Carolina St. 102, Iowa 96 (2 ot); Minnesota 80, Siena 67; Duke 70, West Virginia 63; Arizona 94, Clemson 68; UNLV 85, *DePaul 70; Seton Hall 87, Evansville 73; Indiana 92, UTEP 69. **Regional Semifinals:** Illinois 83, Louisville 69; Syracuse 83, Missouri 80; Virginia 86, Oklahoma 80; Michigan 92, North Carolina 87; Georgetown 69, North Carolina St. 61; Duke 87, Minnesota 70; UNLV 68, Arizona 67; Seton Hall 78, Indiana 65. **Regional Championships:** Illinois 89, Syracuse 86; Michigan 102, Virginia 65; Duke 85, Georgetown 77; Seton Hall 84, UNLV 61. **Semifinals:** Seton Hall 95, Duke 78; Michigan 83, Illinois 81. **Championship:** Michigan 80, Seton Hall 79 (ot).

**DePaul's participation in 1989 tournament vacated.*

1990 First Round: Michigan St. 75, Murray St. 71 (ot); UC Santa Barbara 70, Houston 66; LSU 70, Villanova 63; Georgia Tech 99, East Tenn. St. 83; Minnesota 64, UTEP 61 (ot); UNI 74, Missouri 71; Virginia 75, Notre Dame 67; Syracuse 70, Coppin St. 48; UNLV 102, Ark.-Little Rock 72; Ohio St. 84, Providence 83 (ot); Ball St. 54, Oregon St. 53; Louisville 78, Idaho 59; Loyola Marymount 111, New Mexico St. 92; Michigan 76, Illinois St. 70; Alabama 71, Colorado St. 54; Arizona 79, South Fla. 67; Connecticut 76, Boston U. 52; California 65, Indiana 63; *Clemson 49, BYU 47; La Salle 79, Southern Miss. 63; St. John's (N.Y.) 81, Temple 65; Duke 81, Richmond 46; UCLA 68, UAB 56; Kansas 79, Robert Morris 71; Oklahoma 77, Towson 68; North Carolina 83, Missouri St. 70; Dayton 88, Illinois 86; Arkansas 68, Princeton 64; Xavier 87, Kansas St. 79; Georgetown 70, Texas Southern 52; Texas 100, Georgia 88; Purdue 75, La.-Monroe 63. **Second Round:** Michigan St. 62, UC Santa Barbara 58; Georgia Tech 94, LSU 91; Minnesota 81, UNI 78; Syracuse 63, Virginia 61; UNLV 76, Ohio St. 65; Ball St. 62, Louisville 60; Loyola Marymount 149, Michigan 115; Alabama 77, Arizona 55; Connecticut 74, California 54; *Clemson 79, La Salle 75; Duke 76, St. John's (N.Y.) 72; UCLA 71, Kansas 70; North Carolina 79, Oklahoma 77; Arkansas 86, Dayton 84; Xavier 74, Georgetown 71; Texas 73, Purdue 72. **Regional Semifinals:** Georgia Tech 81, Michigan St. 80 (ot); Minnesota 82, Syracuse 75; UNLV 69, Ball St. 67; Loyola Marymount 62, Alabama 60; Connecticut 71, *Clemson 70; Duke 90, UCLA 81; Arkansas 96, North Carolina 73; Texas 102, Xavier 89. **Regional Championships:** Georgia Tech 93, Minnesota 91; UNLV 131, Loyola Marymount 101; Duke 79, Connecticut 78 (ot); Arkansas 88, Texas 85. **Semifinals:** UNLV 90, Georgia Tech 81; Duke 97, Arkansas 83. **Championship:** UNLV 103, Duke 73.

**Clemson's participation in 1990 tournament vacated.*

1991 First Round: UNLV 99, Montana 65; Georgetown 70, Vanderbilt 60; Michigan St. 60, Green Bay 58; Utah 82, South Ala. 72; Creighton 64, New Mexico St. 56; Seton Hall 71, Pepperdine 51; BYU 61, Virginia 48; Arizona 93, St. Francis (Pa.) 80; Ohio St. 97, Towson 86; Georgia Tech 87, DePaul 70; Texas 73, St. Peter's 65; St. John's (N.Y.) 75, Northern Ill. 68; Connecticut 79, LSU 62; Xavier 89, Nebraska 84; Iowa 76, East Tenn. St. 73; Duke 102, La.-Monroe 73; North Carolina 101, Northeastern 66; Villanova 50, Princeton 48; Eastern Mich. 76, Mississippi St. 56; Penn St. 74, UCLA 69; North Carolina St. 114, Southern Miss. 85; Oklahoma St. 67, New Mexico 54; Temple 80, Purdue 63; Richmond 73, Syracuse 69; Arkansas 117, Georgia St. 76; Arizona St. 79, Rutgers 76; Wake Forest 71, Louisiana Tech 65; Alabama 89, Murray St. 79; Pittsburgh 76, Georgia 68 (ot); Kansas 55, New Orleans 49; Florida St. 75, Southern California 72; Indiana 79, Coastal Caro. 69. **Second Round:** UNLV 62, Georgetown 54; Utah 85, Michigan St. 84 (2 ot); Seton Hall 81, Creighton 69; Arizona 76, BYU 61; Ohio St. 65, Georgia Tech 61; St. John's (N.Y.) 84, Texas 76; Connecticut 66, Xavier 50; Duke 85, Iowa 70; North Carolina 84, Villanova 69; Eastern Mich. 71, Penn St. 68 (ot); Oklahoma St. 73, North Carolina St. 64; Temple 77, Richmond 64; Arkansas 97, Arizona St. 90; Alabama 96, Wake Forest 88; Kansas 77, Pittsburgh 66; Indiana 82, Florida St. 60. **Regional Semifinals:** UNLV 83, Utah 66; Seton Hall 81, Arizona 77; St. John's (N.Y.) 91, Ohio St. 74; Duke 81, Connecticut 67; North Carolina 93, Eastern Mich. 67; Temple 72, Oklahoma St. 63 (ot); Arkansas 93, Alabama 70; Kansas 83, Indiana 65. **Regional Championships:** UNLV 77, Seton Hall 65; Duke 78, St. John's (N.Y.) 61; North Carolina 75, Temple 72; Kansas 93, Arkansas 81. **Semifinals:** Duke 79, UNLV 77; Kansas 79, North Carolina 73. **Championship:** Duke 72, Kansas 65.

1992 First Round: Kansas 100, Howard 67; UTEP 55, Evansville 50; Michigan St. 61, Missouri St. 54; Cincinnati 85, Delaware 47; Memphis 80, Pepperdine 70; Arkansas 80, Murray St. 69; Georgia Tech 65, Houston 60; Southern California 84, La.-Monroe 54; Ohio St. 83, Mississippi Val. 56; Connecticut 86, Nebraska 65; Alabama 80, Stanford 75; North Carolina 68, Miami (Ohio) 63; *Michigan 73, Temple 66; East Tenn. St. 87, Arizona 80; Tulane 61, St. John's (N.Y.) 57; Oklahoma St. 100, Ga. Southern 73; Duke 82, Campbell 56; Iowa 98, Texas 92; Missouri 89, West Virginia 78; Seton Hall 78, La Salle 76; Syracuse 51, Princeton 43; Massachusetts 85, Fordham 58; Iowa St. 76, Charlotte 74; Kentucky 88, Old Dominion 69; UCLA 73, Robert Morris 53; Louisville 81, Wake Forest 58; *New Mexico St. 81, DePaul 73; La.-Lafayette 87, Oklahoma 83; Georgetown 75, South Fla. 60; Florida St. 78, Montana 68; LSU 94, BYU 83; Indiana 94, Eastern Ill. 55. **Second Round:** UTEP 66, Kansas 60; Cincinnati 77, Michigan St. 65; Memphis 82, Arkansas 80; Georgia Tech 79, Southern California 78; Ohio St. 78, Connecticut 55; North Carolina 64, Alabama 55; *Michigan 102, East Tenn. St. 90; Oklahoma St. 87, Tulane 71; Duke 75, Iowa 62; Seton Hall 88, Missouri 71; Massachusetts 77, Syracuse 71 (ot); Kentucky 106, Iowa St. 98; UCLA 85, Louisville 69; *New Mexico St. 81, La.-Lafayette 73; Florida St. 78, Georgetown 68; Indiana 89, LSU 79. **Regional Semifinals:** Cincinnati 69, UTEP 67; Memphis 83, Georgia Tech 79 (ot); Ohio St. 80, North Carolina 73; *Michigan 75, Oklahoma St. 72; Duke 81, Seton Hall 69; Kentucky 87, Massachusetts 77; UCLA 85, *New Mexico St. 78; Indiana 85, Florida St. 74. **Regional Championships:** Cincinnati 88, Memphis 57; *Michigan 75, Ohio St. 71 (ot); Duke 104, Kentucky 103 (ot); Indiana 106, UCLA 79. **Semifinals:** *Michigan 76, Cincinnati 72; Duke 81, Indiana 78. **Championship:** Duke 71, *Michigan 51.

**Michigan's and New Mexico State's participation in 1992 tournament vacated.*

1993 First Round: Kentucky 96, Rider 52; Utah 86, Pittsburgh 65; Wake Forest 81, Chattanooga 58; Iowa 82, La.-Monroe 69; Tulane 55, Kansas St. 53; Florida St. 82, Evansville 70; Western Ky. 55, Memphis 52; Seton Hall 81, Tennessee St. 59; *Michigan 84, Coastal Caro. 53; UCLA 81, Iowa St. 70; George Washington 82, New Mexico 68; Southern U. 93, Georgia Tech 78; Illinois 75, Long Beach St. 72; Vanderbilt 92, Boise St. 72; Temple 75, Missouri 61; Santa Clara 64, Arizona 61; North Carolina 85, East Caro. 65; Rhode Island 74, Purdue 68; St. John's (N.Y.) 85, Texas Tech 67; Arkansas 94, Holy Cross 64; Virginia 78, Manhattan 66; Massachusetts 54, Penn 50; *New Mexico St. 93, Nebraska 79; Cincinnati 93, Coppin St. 66; Indiana 97, Wright St. 54; Xavier 73, New Orleans 55; Oklahoma St. 74, Marquette 62; Louisville 76, Delaware 70; California 66, LSU 64; Duke 105, Southern Ill. 70; BYU 80, SMU 71; Kansas 94, Ball St. 72. **Second Round:** Kentucky 83, Utah 62; Wake Forest 84, Iowa 78; Florida St. 94, Tulane 63; Western Ky. 72, Seton Hall 68; *Michigan 86, UCLA 84 (ot); George Washington 90, Southern U. 80; Vanderbilt 85, Illinois 68; Temple 68, Santa Clara 57; North Carolina 112, Rhode Island 67; Arkansas 80, St. John's (N.Y.) 74; Virginia 71, Massachusetts 56; Cincinnati 92, *New Mexico St. 55; Indiana 73, Xavier 70; Louisville 78, Oklahoma St. 63; California 82, Duke 77; Kansas 90, BYU 76. **Regional Semifinals:** Kentucky 103, Wake Forest 69; Florida St. 81, Western Ky. 78 (ot); *Michigan 72, George Washington 64; Temple 67, Vanderbilt 59; North Carolina 80, Arkansas 74; Cincinnati 71, Virginia 54; Indiana 82, Louisville 69; Kansas 93, California 76. **Regional Championships:** Kentucky 106, Florida St. 81; *Michigan 77, Temple 72; North Carolina 75, Cincinnati 68 (ot); Kansas 83, Indiana 77. **Semifinals:** North Carolina 78, Kansas 68; *Michigan 81, Kentucky 78 (ot). **Championship:** North Carolina 77, *Michigan 71.

**Michigan's and New Mexico State's participation in 1993 tournament vacated.*

1994 First Round: *Missouri 76, Navy 53; Wisconsin 80, Cincinnati 72; Green Bay 61, California 57; Syracuse 92, Hawaii 78; *Minnesota 74, Southern Ill. 60; Louisville 67, Boise St. 58; Virginia 57, New Mexico 54; Arizona 81, Loyola (Md.) 55; Arkansas 94, N.C. A&T 79; Georgetown 84, Illinois 77; Tulsa 112, UCLA 102; Oklahoma St. 65, *New Mexico St. 55; Texas 91, Western Ky. 77; Michigan 78, Pepperdine 74 (ot); Maryland 74, St. Louis 66; Massachusetts 78, Texas St. 60; North Carolina 71, Liberty 51; Boston College 67, Washington St. 64; Indiana 84, Ohio 72; Temple 61, Drexel 39; Penn 90, Nebraska 80; Florida 64, James Madison 62; George Washington 51, UAB 46; Connecticut 64, Rider 46; Purdue 98, UCF 67; Alabama 76, Providence 70; Wake Forest 68, Col. of Charleston 58; Kansas 102, Chattanooga 73; Marquette 81, La.-Lafayette 59; Kentucky 83, Tennessee St. 70; Michigan St. 84, Seton Hall 73; Duke 82, Texas Southern 70. **Second Round:** *Missouri 109, Wisconsin 96; Syracuse 64, Green Bay 59; Louisville 60, *Minnesota 55; Arizona 71, Virginia 58; Arkansas 85, Georgetown 73; Tulsa 82, Oklahoma St. 80; Michigan 84, Texas 79; Maryland 95, Massachusetts

87; Boston College 75, North Carolina 72; Indiana 67, Temple 58; Florida 70, Penn 58; Connecticut 75, George Washington 63; Purdue 83, Alabama 73; Kansas 69, Wake Forest 58; Marquette 75, Kentucky 63; Duke 85, Michigan St. 74. **Regional Semifinals:** *Missouri 98, Syracuse 88 (ot); Arizona 82, Louisville 70; Arkansas 103, Tulsa 84; Michigan 78, Maryland 71; Boston College 77, Indiana 68; Florida 69, Connecticut 60 (ot); Purdue 83, Kansas 78; Duke 59, Marquette 49. **Regional Championships:** Arizona 92, *Missouri 72; Arkansas 76, Michigan 68; Florida 74, Boston College 66; Duke 69, Purdue 60. **Semifinals:** Arkansas 91, Arizona 82; Duke 70, Florida 65. **Championship:** Arkansas 76, Duke 72.

**Minnesota's, Missouri's and New Mexico State's participation in 1994 tournament vacated.*

1995 First Round: Kansas 82, Colgate 68; Western Ky. 82, Michigan 76 (ot); Miami (Ohio) 71, Arizona 62; Virginia 96, Nicholls St. 72; Memphis 77, Louisville 56; Purdue 49, Green Bay 48; Syracuse 96, Southern Ill. 92; Arkansas 79, Texas Southern 78; Kentucky 113, Mt. St. Mary's 67; Tulane 76, BYU 70; Arizona St. 81, Ball St. 66; Manhattan 77, Oklahoma 67; Georgetown 68, Xavier 63; Weber St. 79, Michigan St. 72; Iowa St. 64, Florida 61; North Carolina 80, Murray St. 70; Wake Forest 79, N.C. A&T 47; St. Louis 64, *Minnesota 61 (ot); Alabama 91, Penn 85 (ot); Oklahoma St. 73, Drexel 49; Tulsa 68, Illinois 62; Old Dominion 89, Villanova 81 (3 ot); Stanford 70, Charlotte 68; Massachusetts 68, St. Peter's 51; UCLA 92, Florida Int'l 56; Missouri 65, Indiana 60; Mississippi St. 75, Santa Clara 67; Utah 76, Long Beach St. 64; Texas 90, Oregon 73; Maryland 87, Gonzaga 63; Cincinnati 77, Temple 71; Connecticut 100, Chattanooga 71. **Second Round:** Kansas 75, Western Ky. 70; Virginia 60, Miami (Ohio) 54 (ot); Memphis 75, Purdue 73; Arkansas 96, Syracuse 94 (ot); Kentucky 82, Tulane 60; Arizona St. 64, Manhattan 54; Georgetown 53, Weber St. 51; North Carolina 73, Iowa St. 51; Wake Forest 64, St. Louis 59; Oklahoma St. 66, Alabama 52; Tulsa 64, Old Dominion 52; Massachusetts 75, Stanford 53; UCLA 75, Missouri 74; Mississippi St. 78, Utah 64; Maryland 82, Texas 68; Connecticut 96, Cincinnati 91. **Regional Semifinals:** Virginia 67, Kansas 58; Arkansas 96, Memphis 91 (ot); Kentucky 97, Arizona St. 73; North Carolina 74, Georgetown 64; Massachusetts 76, Tulsa 51; Oklahoma St. 71, Wake Forest 66; Connecticut 99, Maryland 89; UCLA 86, Mississippi St. 67. **Regional Championships:** Arkansas 68, Virginia 61; North Carolina 74, Kentucky 61; Oklahoma St. 68, Massachusetts 54; UCLA 102, Connecticut 96. **Semifinals:** Arkansas 75, North Carolina 68; UCLA 74, Oklahoma St. 61. **Championship:** UCLA 89, Arkansas 78.

**Minnesota's participation in 1995 tournament vacated.*

1996 First Round: *Connecticut 68, Colgate 59; Eastern Mich. 75, Duke 60; Mississippi St. 58, VCU 51; Princeton 43, UCLA 41; Boston College 64, Indiana 51; Georgia Tech 90, Austin Peay 79; Temple 61, Oklahoma 43; Cincinnati 66, UNC Greensboro 61; *Purdue 73, Western Caro. 71; Georgia 81, Clemson 74; Drexel 75, Memphis 63; Syracuse 88, Montana St. 55; Iowa 81, George Washington 79; Arizona 90, Valparaiso 51; Santa Clara 91, Maryland 79; Kansas 92, South Carolina St. 54; Massachusetts 92, UCF 70; Stanford 66, Bradley 58; Arkansas 86, Penn St. 80; Marquette 68, Monmouth 44; North Carolina 83, New Orleans 62; *Texas Tech 74, Northern Ill. 73; New Mexico 69, Kansas St. 48; Georgetown 93, Mississippi Val. 56; Kentucky 110, San Jose St. 72; Virginia Tech 61, Green Bay 48; Iowa St. 74, California 64; Utah 72, Canisius 43; Louisville 82, Tulsa 80 (ot); Villanova 92, Portland 58; Texas 80, *Michigan 76; Wake Forest 62, La.-Monroe 50. **Second Round:** *Connecticut 95, Eastern Mich. 81; Mississippi St. 63, Princeton 41; Georgia Tech 103, Boston College 89; Cincinnati 78, Temple 65; Georgia 76, *Purdue 69; Syracuse 69, Drexel 58; Arizona 87, Iowa 73; Kansas 76, Santa Clara 51; Massachusetts 79, Stanford 74; Arkansas 65, Marquette 56; *Texas Tech 92, North Carolina 73; Georgetown 73, New Mexico 62; Kentucky 84, Virginia Tech 60; Utah 73, Iowa St. 67; Louisville 68, Villanova 64; Wake Forest 65, Texas 62. **Regional Semifinals:** Mississippi St. 60, *Connecticut 55; Cincinnati 87, Georgia Tech 70; Syracuse 83, Georgia 81 (ot); Kansas 83, Arizona 80; Massachusetts 79, Arkansas 63; Georgetown 98, *Texas Tech 90; Kentucky 101, Utah 70; Wake Forest 60, Louisville 59. **Regional Championships:** Mississippi St. 73, Cincinnati 63; Syracuse 60, Kansas 57; Massachusetts 86, Georgetown 62; Kentucky 83, Wake Forest 63. **Semifinals:** Syracuse 77, Mississippi St. 69; Kentucky 81, Massachusetts 74. **Championship:** Kentucky 76, Syracuse 67.

**Connecticut's, Michigan's, Purdue's and Texas Tech's participation in 1996 tournament vacated.*

1997 First Round: Kentucky 92, Montana 54; Iowa 73, Virginia 60; Boston College 73, Valparaiso 66; St. Joseph's 75, Pacific 65; Stanford 80, Oklahoma 67; Wake Forest 68, St. Mary's (Cal.) 46; Charlotte 79, Georgetown 67; Utah 75, Navy 61; *Minnesota 78, Texas St. 46; Temple 62, Mississippi 40; Tulsa 81, Boston U. 52; Clemson 68, Miami (Ohio) 56; Iowa St. 69, Illinois St. 57; Cincinnati 86, Butler 69; Xavier 80, Vanderbilt 68; UCLA 109, Charleston So. 75; North Carolina 82, Fairfield 74; Colorado 80, Indiana 62; California 55, Princeton 52; Villanova 101, Long Island 91; Louisville 65, Massachusetts 57; New Mexico 59, Old Dominion 55; Texas 71, Wisconsin 58; Coppin St. 78, South Carolina 65; Kansas 78, Jackson St. 64; Purdue 83, Rhode Island 76 (ot); Col. of Charleston 75, Maryland 66; Arizona 65, South Ala. 57; Illinois 90, Southern California 77; Chattanooga 73, Georgia 70; Providence 81, Marquette 59; Duke 71, Murray St. 68. **Second Round:** Kentucky 75, Iowa 69; St. Joseph's 81, Boston College 77 (ot); Stanford 72, Wake Forest 66; Utah 77, Charlotte 58; *Minnesota 76, Temple 57; Clemson 65, Tulsa 59; Iowa St. 67, Cincinnati 66; UCLA 96, Xavier 83; North Carolina 73, Colorado 56; California 75, Villanova 68; Louisville 64, New Mexico 63; Texas 82, Coppin St. 81; Kansas 75, Purdue 61; Arizona 73, Col. of Charleston 69; Chattanooga 75, Illinois 63; Providence 98, Duke 87. **Regional Semifinals:** Kentucky 83, St. Joseph's 68; Utah 82, Stanford 77 (ot); *Minnesota 90, Clemson 84 (2 ot); UCLA 74, Iowa St. 73 (ot); North Carolina 63, California 57; Louisville 78, Texas 63; Arizona 85, Kansas 82; Providence 71, Chattanooga 65. **Regional Championships:** Kentucky 72, Utah 59; *Minnesota 80, UCLA 72; North Carolina 97, Louisville 74; Arizona 96, Providence 92 (ot). **Semifinals:** Kentucky 78, *Minnesota 69; Arizona 66, North Carolina 58. **Championship:** Arizona 84, Kentucky 79 (ot).

**Minnesota's participation in 1997 tournament vacated.*

1998 First Round: Kansas 110, Prairie View 52; Rhode Island 97, Murray St. 74; Florida St. 96, TCU 87; Valparaiso 70, Mississippi 69; Western Mich. 75, Clemson 72; Stanford 67, Col. of Charleston 57; Detroit 66, St. John's (N.Y.) 64; Purdue 95, Delaware 56; Duke 99, Radford 63; Oklahoma St. 74, George Washington 59; Syracuse 63, Iona 61; New Mexico 79, Butler 62; UCLA 65, Miami (Fla.) 62; *Michigan 80, Davidson 61; St. Louis 51, Massachusetts 46; Kentucky 82, South Carolina St. 67; North Carolina 88, Navy 52; Charlotte 77, Ill.-Chicago 62; Princeton 69, UNLV 57; Michigan St. 83, Eastern Mich. 71; Washington 69, Xavier 68; Richmond 62, South Carolina 61; Indiana 94, Oklahoma 87 (ot); Connecticut 93, Fairleigh Dickinson 85; Arizona 99, Nicholls St. 60; Illinois St. 82, Tennessee 81 (ot); Illinois 61, South Ala. 51; Maryland 82, Utah St. 68; Arkansas 74, Nebraska 65; Utah 85, San Francisco 68; West Virginia 82, Temple 52; Cincinnati 65, Northern Ariz. 62. **Second Round:** Rhode Island 80, Kansas 75; Valparaiso 83, Florida St. 77 (ot); Stanford 83, Western Mich. 65; Purdue 80, Detroit 65; Duke 79, Oklahoma St. 73; Syracuse 56, New Mexico 46; UCLA 85, *Michigan 82; Kentucky 88, St. Louis 61; North Carolina 93, Charlotte 83 (ot); Michigan St. 63, Princeton 56; Washington 81, Richmond 66; Connecticut 78, Indiana 68; Arizona 82, Illinois St. 49; Maryland 67, Illinois 61; Utah 75, Arkansas 69; West Virginia 75, Cincinnati 74. **Regional Semifinals:** Rhode Island 74, Valparaiso 68; Stanford 67, Purdue 59; Duke 80, Syracuse 67; Kentucky 94, UCLA 68; North Carolina 73, Michigan St. 58; Connecticut 75, Washington 74; Arizona 87, Maryland 79; Utah 65, West Virginia 62. **Regional Championships:** Stanford 79, Rhode Island 77; Kentucky 86, Duke 84; North Carolina 75, Connecticut 64; Utah 76, Arizona 51. **Semifinals:** Kentucky 86, Stanford 85 (ot); Utah 65, North Carolina 59. **Championship:** Kentucky 78, Utah 69.

**Michigan's participation in 1998 tournament vacated.*

1999 First Round: Auburn 80, Winthrop 41; Oklahoma St. 69, Syracuse 61; Detroit 56, *UCLA 53; *Ohio St. 72, Murray St. 58; Indiana 108, George Washington 88; St. John's (N.Y.) 69, Samford 43; Creighton 62, Louisville 58; Maryland 82, Valparaiso 60; Connecticut 91, UTSA 66; New Mexico 61, Missouri 59; Iowa 77, UAB 64; Arkansas 94, Siena 80; Florida 75, Penn 61; Weber St. 76, North Carolina 74; Gonzaga 75, Minnesota 63; Stanford 69, Alcorn St. 57; Duke 99, Florida A&M 58; Tulsa 62, Col. of Charleston 53; Missouri St. 43, Wisconsin 32; Tennessee 62, Delaware 52; Temple 61, Kent St. 54; Cincinnati 72, George Mason 48; Purdue 58, Texas 54; Miami (Fla.) 75, Lafayette 54; Michigan St. 76, Mt. St. Mary's 53; Mississippi 72, Villanova 70; Charlotte 81, Rhode Island 70 (ot); Oklahoma 61, *Arizona 60; Kansas 95, Evansville 74; Kentucky 82, New Mexico St. 60; Miami (Ohio) 59, Washington 58; Utah 80, Arkansas St. 58. **Second Round:** Auburn 81, Oklahoma St. 74; *Ohio St. 75, Detroit 44; St. John's (N.Y.) 86, Indiana 61; Maryland 75, Creighton 63; Connecticut 78, New Mexico 56; Iowa 82, Arkansas 72; Florida 82, Weber St. 74 (ot); Gonzaga 82, Stanford 74; Duke 97, Tulsa 56; Missouri St. 81, Tennessee 51; Temple 64, Cincinnati 54; Purdue 73, Miami (Fla.) 63; Michigan St. 74, Mississippi 66; Oklahoma 85, Charlotte 72; Kentucky 92, Kansas 88 (ot); Miami (Ohio) 66, Utah 58. **Regional Semifinals:** *Ohio St. 72, Auburn 64; St. John's (N.Y.) 76, Maryland 62; Connecticut 78, Iowa 68; Gonzaga 73, Florida 72; Duke 78, Missouri St. 61; Temple 77, Purdue 55; Michigan St. 54, Oklahoma 46; Kentucky 58, Miami (Ohio) 43. **Regional Finals:** *Ohio St. 77, St. John's (N.Y.) 74; Connecticut 67, Gonzaga 62; Duke 85, Temple 64; Michigan St. 73, Kentucky 66. **Semifinals:** Connecticut 64, *Ohio St. 58; Duke 68, Michigan St. 62. **Championship:** Connecticut 77, Duke 74.

**Arizona's, Ohio State's and UCLA's participation in 1999 tournament vacated.*

2000 First Round: Texas 77, Indiana St. 61; LSU 64, Southeast Mo. St. 61; Purdue 62, Dayton 61; Oklahoma 74, Winthrop 50; Gonzaga 77, Louisville 66; St. John's (N.Y.) 61, Northern Ariz. 56; Arizona 71, Jackson St. 47; Wisconsin 66, *Fresno St. 56; Michigan St. 65, Valparaiso 38; UCLA 65, Ball St. 57; Auburn 72, Creighton 69; Kentucky 85, St. Bonaventure 80 (2 ot); Iowa St. 88, Central Conn. St. 78; Syracuse 79, Samford 65; Maryland 74, Iona 59; Utah 48, St. Louis 45; Florida 69, Butler 68 (ot); Pepperdine 77, Indiana 57; Illinois 68, Penn 58; Seton Hall 72, Oregon 71 (ot); Temple 73, Lafayette 47; Oklahoma St. 86, Hofstra 66; Kansas 81, DePaul 77 (ot); Duke 82, Lamar 55; Tennessee 63, La.-Lafayette 58; Cincinnati 64, UNC Wilmington 47; Connecticut 75, Utah St. 67; Tulsa 89, UNLV 62; *Ohio St. 87, Appalachian St. 61; North Carolina 84, Missouri 70; Miami (Fla.) 75, Arkansas 71; Stanford 84, South Carolina St. 65. **Second Round:** LSU 72, Texas 67; Purdue 66, Oklahoma 62; Wisconsin 66, Arizona 59; Gonzaga 82, St. John's (N.Y.) 76; Syracuse 52, Kentucky 50; Michigan St. 73, Utah 61; Iowa St. 79, Auburn 60; UCLA 105, Maryland 70; Duke 69, Kansas 64; Florida 93, Illinois 76; Oklahoma St. 75, Pepperdine 67; Seton Hall 67, Temple 65 (ot); North Carolina 60, Stanford 53; Tennessee 65, Connecticut 51; Miami (Fla.) 75, *Ohio St. 62; Tulsa 69, Cincinnati 61. **Regional Semifinals:** Wisconsin 61, LSU 48; Purdue 75, Gonzaga 66; Michigan St. 75, Syracuse 58; Iowa St. 80, UCLA 56; Florida 87, Duke 78; Oklahoma St. 68, Seton Hall 66; North Carolina 74, Tennessee 69; Tulsa 80, Miami (Fla.) 71. **Regional Finals:** Wisconsin 64, Purdue 60; Michigan St. 75, Iowa St. 64; Florida 77, Oklahoma St. 65; North Carolina 59, Tulsa 55. **Semifinals:** Michigan St. 53, Wisconsin 41; Florida 71, North Carolina 59. **Championship:** Michigan St. 89, Florida 76.

**Fresno State's and Ohio State's participation in 2000 tournament vacated.*

2001 Opening Round: Northwestern St. 71, Winthrop 67. **First Round:** Illinois 96, Northwestern St. 54; Charlotte 70, Tennessee 63; Syracuse 79, Hawaii 69; Kansas 99, Cal St. Northridge 75; Notre Dame 83, Xavier 71; Mississippi 72, Iona 70; Butler 79, Wake Forest 63; Arizona 101, Eastern Ill. 76; Michigan St. 69, Alabama St. 35; Fresno St. 82, California 70; Gonzaga 86, Virginia 85; Indiana St. 70, Oklahoma 68 (ot); Temple 79, Texas 65; Florida 69, Western Ky. 56; Penn St. 69, Providence 59; North Carolina 70, Princeton 48; Duke 95, Monmouth 52; Missouri 70, Georgia 68; Utah St. 77, *Ohio St. 68 (ot); UCLA 61, Hofstra 48; Southern California 69, Oklahoma St. 54; Boston College 68, Southern Utah 65; Iowa 69, Creighton 56; Kentucky 72, Holy Cross 68; Stanford 89, UNC Greensboro 60; St. Joseph's 66, Georgia Tech 62; Cincinnati 84, BYU 59; Kent St. 77, Indiana 73; Georgia St. 50, Wisconsin 49; Maryland 83, George Mason 80; Georgetown 63, Arkansas 61; Hampton 58, Iowa St. 57. **Second Round:** Illinois 79, Charlotte 61; Kansas 87, Syracuse 58; Mississippi 59, Notre Dame 56; Arizona 73, Butler 52; Michigan St. 81, Fresno St. 65; Gonzaga 85, Indiana St. 68; Temple 75, Florida 54; Penn St. 82, North Carolina 74; Duke 94, Missouri 81; UCLA 75, Utah St. 50; Southern California 74, Boston College 71; Kentucky 92, Iowa 79; Stanford 90, St. Joseph's 83; Cincinnati 66, Kent St. 43; Maryland 79, Georgia St. 60; Georgetown 76, Hampton 57. **Regional Semifinals:** Illinois 80, Kansas 64; Arizona 66, Mississippi 56; Michigan St. 77, Gonzaga 62; Temple 84, Penn St. 72; Duke 76, UCLA 63; Southern California 80, Kentucky 76; Stanford 78, Cincinnati 65; Maryland 76, Georgetown 66. **Regional Finals:** Arizona 87, Illinois 81; Michigan St. 69, Temple 62; Duke 79, Southern California 69; Maryland 87, Stanford 73. **Semifinals:** Arizona 80, Michigan St. 61; Duke 95, Maryland 84. **Championship:** Duke 82, Arizona 72.

**Ohio State's participation in 2001 tournament vacated.*

2002 Opening Round: Siena 81, Alcorn St. 77. First Round: Maryland 85, Siena 70; Wisconsin 80, *St. John's (N.Y.) 70; Tulsa 71, Marquette 69; Kentucky 83, Valparaiso 68; Southern Ill. 76, Texas Tech 68; *Georgia 85, Murray St. 68; North Carolina St. 69, Michigan St. 58; Connecticut 78, Hampton 67; Kansas 70, Holy Cross 59; Stanford 84, Western Ky. 68; Creighton 83, Florida 82 (2 ot); Illinois 93, San Diego St. 64; Texas 70, Boston College 57; Mississippi St. 70, McNeese St. 58; Wake Forest 83, Pepperdine 74; Oregon 81, Montana 62; Duke 84, Winthrop 37; Notre Dame 82, Charlotte 63; Indiana 75, Utah 56; UNC Wilmington 93, Southern California 89 (ot); California 82, Penn 75; Pittsburgh 71, Central Conn. St. 54; Kent St. 69, Oklahoma St. 61; Alabama 86, Fla. Atlantic 78; Cincinnati 90, Boston U. 52; UCLA 80, Mississippi 58; Missouri 93, Miami (Fla.) 80; *Ohio St. 69, Davidson 64; Wyoming 73, Gonzaga 66; Arizona 86, UC Santa Barbara 81; Xavier 77, Hawaii 58; Oklahoma 71, Ill.-Chicago 63. **Second Round:** Maryland 87, Wisconsin 57; Kentucky 87, Tulsa 82; Southern Ill. 77, *Georgia 75; Connecticut 77, North Carolina St. 74; Kansas 86, Stanford 63; Illinois 72, Creighton 60; Texas 68, Mississippi St. 64; Oregon 92, Wake Forest 87; Duke 84, Notre Dame 77; Indiana 76, UNC Wilmington 67; Pittsburgh 63, California 50; Kent St. 71, Alabama 58; UCLA 105, Cincinnati 101 (2 ot); Missouri 83, *Ohio St. 67; Arizona 68, Wyoming 60; Oklahoma 78, Xavier 65. **Regional Semifinals:** Maryland 78, Kentucky 68; Connecticut 71, Southern Ill. 59; Kansas 73, Illinois 69; Oregon 72, Texas 70; Indiana 74, Kent St. 78, Pittsburgh 63 (ot); Missouri 82, UCLA 73; Oklahoma 88, Arizona 78. **Regional Finals:** Maryland 90, Connecticut 82; Kansas 104, Oregon 86; Indiana 81, Kent St. 69; Oklahoma 81, Missouri 75. **Semifinals:** Indiana 73, Oklahoma 64; Maryland 97, Kansas 88. **Championship:** Maryland 64, Indiana 52.

Georgia's, Ohio State's and St. John's (N.Y.) participation in 2002 tournament vacated.

2003 Opening Round: UNC Asheville 92, Texas Southern 84 (ot). **First Round:** Kentucky 95, IUPUI 64; Utah 60, Oregon 58; Wisconsin 81, Weber St. 74; Tulsa 84, Dayton 71; Missouri 72, Southern Ill. 71; Marquette 72, Holy Cross 68; Indiana 67, Alabama 62; Pittsburgh 87, Wagner 61; Arizona 80, Vermont 51; Gonzaga 74, Cincinnati 69; Notre Dame 70, Milwaukee 69; Illinois 65, Western Ky. 60; Central Mich. 79, Creighton 73; Duke 67, Colorado St. 57; Arizona St. 84, Memphis 71; Kansas 64, Utah St. 61; Texas 82, UNC Asheville 61; Purdue 80, LSU 56; Connecticut 58, BYU 53; Stanford 77, San Diego 69; Maryland 75, UNC Wilmington 73; Xavier 71, Troy 59; Michigan St. 79, Colorado 64; Florida 85, Sam Houston St. 55; Oklahoma 71, South Carolina 54; California 76, North Carolina St. 74 (ot); Butler 47, Mississippi St. 46; Louisville 86, Austin Peay 64; Oklahoma St. 77, Penn 63; Syracuse 76, Manhattan 65; Auburn 65, St. Joseph's 63 (ot); Wake Forest 76, East Tenn. St. 73. **Second Round:** Kentucky 74, Utah 54; Arizona 80, Tulsa 60; Marquette 101, Missouri 92; Pittsburgh 74, Indiana 52; Arizona 96, Gonzaga 95 (2 ot); Notre Dame 68, Illinois 60; Duke 86, Central Mich. 60; Kansas 108, Arizona St. 76; Texas 77, Purdue 67; Connecticut 85, Stanford 74; Maryland 77, Xavier 64; Michigan St. 68, Florida 46; Oklahoma 74, California 65; Butler 79, Louisville 71; Syracuse 68, Oklahoma St. 56; Auburn 68, Wake Forest 62. **Regional Semifinals:** Kentucky 63, Wisconsin 57; Marquette 77, Pittsburgh 74; Arizona 88, Notre Dame 71; Kansas 69, Duke 65; Texas 82, Connecticut 78; Michigan St. 60, Maryland 58; Oklahoma 65, Butler 54; Syracuse 79, Auburn 78. **Regional Finals:** Marquette 83, Kentucky 69; Kansas 78, Arizona 75; Texas 85, Michigan St. 76; Syracuse 63, Oklahoma 47. **Semifinals:** Kansas 94, Marquette 61; Syracuse 95, Texas 84. **Championship:** Syracuse 81, Kansas 78.

2004 Opening Round: Florida A&M 72, Lehigh 57. **First Round:** Kentucky 96, Florida A&M 76; UAB 102, Washington 100; Pacific 66, Providence 58; Kansas 78, Ill.-Chicago 53; Boston College 58, Utah 51; Georgia Tech 65, UNI 60; Nevada 72, Michigan St. 66; Gonzaga 76, Valparaiso 49; St. Joseph's 82, Liberty 63; Texas Tech 79, Charlotte 75; Manhattan 75, Florida 60; Wake Forest 79, VCU 78; Wisconsin 76, Richmond 64; Pittsburgh 53, UCF 44; Memphis 59, South Carolina 43; Oklahoma St. 75, Eastern Wash. 56; Duke 96, Alabama St. 61; Seton Hall 80, Arizona 76; Illinois 72, Murray St. 53; Cincinnati 80, East Tenn. St. 77; North Carolina 63, Air Force 52; Texas 66, Princeton 49; Xavier 80, Louisville 70; Mississippi St. 85, Monmouth 52; Stanford 71, UTSA 45; Alabama 65, Southern Ill. 64; Syracuse 80, BYU 75; Maryland 86, UTEP 83; Vanderbilt 71, Western Mich. 58; North Carolina St. 61, La.-Lafayette 52; DePaul 76, Dayton 69 (2 ot); Connecticut 70, Vermont 53. **Second Round:** UAB 76, Kentucky 75; Kansas 78, Pacific 63; Georgia Tech 57, Boston College 54; Nevada 91, Gonzaga 72; St. Joseph's 70, Texas Tech 65; Wake Forest 84, Manhattan 80; Pittsburgh 59, Wisconsin 55; Oklahoma St. 70, Memphis 53; Duke 90, Seton Hall 62; Illinois 92, Cincinnati 68; Texas 78, North Carolina 75; Xavier 89, Mississippi St. 74; Alabama 70, Stanford 67; Syracuse 72, Maryland 70; Vanderbilt 75, North Carolina St. 73; Connecticut 72, DePaul 55. **Regional Semifinals:** Kansas 100, UAB 74; Georgia Tech 72, Nevada 67; St. Joseph's 84, Wake Forest 80; Oklahoma St. 63, Pittsburgh 51; Duke 72, Illinois 62; Xavier 79, Texas 71; Alabama 80, Syracuse 71; Connecticut 73, Vanderbilt 53. **Regional Finals:** Georgia Tech 79, Kansas 71 (ot); Oklahoma St. 64, St. Joseph's 62; Duke 66, Xavier 63; Connecticut 87, Alabama 71. **Semifinals:** Georgia Tech 67, Oklahoma St. 65; Connecticut 79, Duke 78. **Championship:** Connecticut 82, Georgia Tech 73.

2005 Opening Round: Oakland 79, Alabama A&M 69. **First Round:** Illinois 67, Fairleigh Dickinson 55; Nevada 61, Texas 57; Milwaukee 83, Alabama 73; Boston College 85, Penn 65; UAB 82, LSU 68; Arizona 66, Utah St. 53; Southern Ill. 65, St. Mary's (Cal.) 56; Oklahoma St. 63, Southeastern La. 50; Washington 88, Montana 77; Pacific 79, Pittsburgh 71; Georgia Tech 80, George Washington 68; Louisville 68, La.-Lafayette 62; Texas Tech 78, UCLA 66; Gonzaga 74, Winthrop 64; West Virginia 63, Creighton 61; Wake Forest 70, Chattanooga 54; North Carolina 96, Oakland 68; Iowa St. 64, Minnesota 53; Villanova 55, New Mexico 47; Florida 67, Ohio 60; Wisconsin 57, UNI 52; Bucknell 64, Kansas 63; North Carolina St. 75, Charlotte 63; Connecticut 77, UCF 71; Duke 57, Delaware St. 46; Mississippi St. 93, Stanford 70; Michigan St. 89, Old Dominion 81; Vermont 60, Syracuse 57 (ot); Utah 60, UTEP 54; Oklahoma 84, Niagara 67; Cincinnati 76, Iowa 64; Kentucky 72, Eastern Ky. 64. **Second Round:** Illinois 71, Nevada 59; Milwaukee 83, Boston College 75; Arizona 85, UAB 63; Oklahoma St. 85, Southern Ill. 77; Washington 97, Pacific 79; Louisville 76, Georgia Tech 54; Texas Tech 71, Gonzaga 69; West Virginia 111, Wake Forest 105 (2 ot); North Carolina 92, Iowa St. 65; Villanova 76, Florida 65; Wisconsin 71, Bucknell 62; North Carolina St. 65, Connecticut 62; Duke 63, Mississippi St. 55; Michigan St. 72, Vermont 61; Utah 67, Oklahoma 58; Kentucky 69, Cincinnati 60. **Regional Semifinals:** Illinois 77, Milwaukee 63; Arizona 79, Oklahoma St. 78; Louisville 93, Washington 79; West Virginia 65, Texas Tech 60; North Carolina 67, Villanova 66; Wisconsin 65, North Carolina St. 56; Michigan St. 78, Duke 68; Kentucky 62, Utah 52. **Regional Finals:** Illinois 90, Arizona 89 (ot); Louisville 93, West Virginia 85 (ot); North Carolina 88, Wisconsin 82; Michigan St. 94, Kentucky 88 (2 ot). **Semifinals:** Illinois 72, Louisville 58; North Carolina 87, Michigan St. 71. **Championship:** North Carolina 75, Illinois 70.

2006 Opening Round: Monmouth 71, Hampton 49. **First Round:** Duke 70, Southern U. 54; George Washington 88, UNC Wilmington 85 (ot); Texas A&M 66, Syracuse 58; LSU 80, Iona 64; West Virginia 64, Southern Ill. 46; Northwestern St. 64, Iowa 63; North Carolina St. 58, California 52; Texas 60, Penn 52; Memphis 94, Oral Roberts 78; Bucknell 59, Arkansas 55; Pittsburgh 79, Kent St. 64; Bradley 77, Kansas 73; Indiana 87, San Diego St. 83; Gonzaga 79, Xavier 75; Alabama 90, Marquette 85; UCLA 78, Belmont 44; Connecticut 72, Albany (N.Y.) 59; Kentucky 69, UAB 64; Washington 75, Utah St. 61; Illinois 78, Air Force 69; George Mason 75, Michigan St. 65; North Carolina 69, Murray St. 65; Wichita St. 86, Seton Hall 66; Tennessee 63, Winthrop 61; Villanova 58, Monmouth 45; Arizona 94, Wisconsin 75; Montana 87, Nevada 79; Boston College 88, Pacific 76 (2 ot); Milwaukee 82, Oklahoma 74; Florida 76, South Ala. 50; Georgetown 54, UNI 49; Ohio St. 70, Davidson 62. **Second Round:** Duke 74, George Washington 61; LSU 58, Texas A&M 57; West Virginia 67, Northwestern St. 54; Texas 75, North Carolina St. 54; Memphis 80, Bucknell 59; Bradley 72, Pittsburgh 66; Gonzaga 90, Indiana 80; UCLA 62, Alabama 59; Connecticut 87, Kentucky 83; Washington 67, Illinois 64; George Mason 65, North Carolina 60; Wichita St. 80, Tennessee 73; Villanova 82, Arizona 78; Boston College 69, Montana 56; Florida 82, Milwaukee 60; Ohio St. 52. **Regional Semifinals:** LSU 62, Duke 54; Texas 74, West Virginia 71; Memphis 80, Bradley 64; UCLA 73, Gonzaga 71; Connecticut 98, Washington 92 (ot); George Mason 63, Wichita St. 55; Villanova 60, Boston College 59 (ot); Florida 57, Georgetown 53. **Regional Finals:** LSU 70, Texas 60 (ot); UCLA 50, Memphis 45; George Mason 86, Connecticut 84 (ot); Florida 75, Villanova 62. **Semifinals:** UCLA 59, LSU 45; Florida 73, George Mason 58. **Championship:** Florida 73, UCLA 57.

2007 Opening Round: Niagara 77, Florida A&M 69. **First Round:** Florida 112, Jackson St. 69; Purdue 72, Arizona 63; Butler 57, Old Dominion 46; Maryland 82, Davidson 70; Winthrop 84, Notre Dame 74; Oregon 58, Miami (Ohio) 56; UNLV 67, Ga. Tech 63; Wisconsin 76, A&M-Corpus Christi 63; Kansas 107, Niagara 67; Kentucky 67, Villanova 58; Va. Tech 54, Illinois 52; Southern Ill. 61, Holy Cross 51; VCU 79, Duke 77; Pittsburgh 79, Wright St. 58; Indiana 70, Gonzaga 57; UCLA 70, Weber St. 42; North Carolina 88, Eastern Ky. 65; Michigan St. 61, Marquette 49; Southern California 77, Arkansas 60; Texas 79, New Mexico St. 67; Vanderbilt 77, George Washington 44; Washington St. 70, Oral Roberts 54; Boston College 84, Texas Tech 75; Georgetown 80, Belmont 55; Ohio St. 78, Central Conn. St. 57; Xavier 79, BYU 77; Tennessee 121, Long Beach St. 86; Virginia 84, Albany (N.Y.) 57; Louisville 78, Stanford 58; Texas A&M 68, Penn 52; Nevada 77, Creighton 71 (ot); Memphis 73, North Texas 58. **Second Round:** Florida 74, Purdue 67; Butler 62, Maryland 59; Oregon 75, Winthrop 61; UNLV 74, Wisconsin 68; Kansas 88, Kentucky 76; Southern Ill. 63, Va. Tech 48; Pittsburgh 84, VCU 79, (ot); UCLA 54, Indiana 49; North Carolina 81, Michigan St. 67; Southern California 87, Texas 68; Vanderbilt 78, Washington St. 74, (2 ot); Georgetown 62, Boston College 55; Ohio St. 78, Xavier 71 (ot); Tennessee 77, Virginia 74; Texas A&M 72, Louisville 69; Memphis 78, Nevada 58. **Regional Semifinals:** Florida 65, Butler 57; Oregon 76, UNLV 72; Kansas 61, Southern Ill. 58; UCLA 64, Pittsburgh 55; North Carolina 74, Southern California 64; Georgetown 66, Vanderbilt 65; Ohio St. 85, Tennessee 84; Memphis 65, Texas A&M 64. **Regional Finals:** Florida 85, Oregon 77; UCLA 68, Kansas 55; Georgetown 96, North Carolina 84 (ot); Ohio St. 92, Memphis 76. **Semifinals:** Florida 76, UCLA 66; Ohio St. 67, Georgetown 60. **Championship:** Florida 84, Ohio St. 75

Division II Championship

2007 Results

FIRST ROUND
Findlay 70, Wis.-Parkside 60
Northern Ky. 73, Drury 68
Grand Valley St. 85, Quincy 75
Southern Ind. 84, Rockhurst 78
Barton 85, Queens (N.C.) 76
West Virginia St. 91, Alderson-Broaddus 75
Millersville 89, Mount Olive 85
California (Pa.) 82; West Liberty St. 79 (ot)
Augusta St. 79, Elizabeth City St. 63
Wingate 72, Armstrong Atlantic 68
Clayton St. 72, Catawba 69 (ot)
Virginia Union 74, Lander 68 (ot)
Humboldt St. 68, Alas. Anchorage 61
Grand Canyon 87, Seattle Pacific 65
Seattle 69, Cal Poly Pomona 55
Cal St. San B'dino 71, BYU-Hawaii 68
Montevallo 78, Albany St. (Ga.) 62
Henderson St. 58, Barry 44
Eckerd 66, Benedict 56
Rollins 61, Valdosta St. 60
Central Mo. 76, St. Edward's 39
Northwest Mo. St. 74, Pittsburg St. 53

Midwestern St. 86, West Tex. A&M 81
Southeastern Okla. St. 79, Emporia St. 66
Bentley 59, Caldwell 56
Bridgeport 67, Philadelphia U. 65
Bryant 77, Aldelphi 55
St. Rose 87, Pace 71
Winona St. 100, St. Cloud St. 73
Neb.-Kearney 95, South Dakota 88
Metro St. 71, Adams St. 48
Minn. St. Mankato 85, Fort Lewis 71

SECOND ROUND
Northern Ky. 60, Findlay 56
Grand Valley St. 90, Southern Ind. 83
Barton 88, West Virginia St. 85
Millersville 82, California (Pa.) 72
Wingate 79, Augusta St. 78
Virginia Union 71, Clayton St. 70 (ot)
Humboldt St. 95, Grand Canyon 81
Cal St. San B'dino 72, Seattle 66
Montevallo 68, Henderson St. 58 (ot)
Eckerd 85, Rollins 76
Central Mo. 72, Northwest Mo. St. 61
Southeastern Okla. St. 88, Midwestern St. 77 (ot)
Bentley 60, Bridgeport 45
Bryant 65, St. Rose 62
Winona St. 81, Neb.-Kearney 70

Minn. St. Mankato 70, Metro St. 68

REGIONAL FINALS
Grand Valley St. 66, Northern Ky. 42
Barton 76, Millersville 65
Wingate 73, Virginia Union 56
Cal St. San B'dino 68, Humboldt St. 66
Montevallo 64, Eckerd 61
Central Mo. 67, Southeastern Okla. St. 54
Bentley 63, Bryant 54
Winona St. 89, Minn. St. Mankato 76

QUARTERFINALS
Barton 83, Grand Valley St. 81 (ot)
Cal St. San B'dino 100, Wingate 73
Central Mo. 86, Montevallo 69
Winona St. 64, Bentley 51

SEMIFINALS
Barton 80, Cal St. San B'dino 79
Winona St. 90, Central Mo. 85 (ot)

CHAMPIONSHIP
Barton 77, Winona St. 75

Box Scores

SEMIFINALS
MARCH 22 AT SPRINGFIELD, MASSACHUSETTS

Barton 80, Cal St. San B'Dino 79

Cal St. San B'Dino

No.	Player	FG	FGA	FG	FGA	FT	FTA	OFF	DEF	TOT	PF	TP	A	TO	BLK	S	MIN
2	Marlon Pierce............ *	0	3	0	2	2	2	0	2	2	1	2	2	2	0	4	24
3	Yoseph Yaisrael............. *	5	7	2	4	0	1	0	0	0	5	12	3	0	0	1	25
5	Chet Johnson.................. *	3	5	1	2	0	0	2	2	4	5	7	2	1	0	0	18
23	Prentice Harris.............. *	5	7	4	4	3	3	0	0	0	3	17	1	1	0	2	28
32	Ivan Johnson.................. *	7	9	0	0	5	10	1	5	6	4	19	3	2	0	3	35
00	Greg Williams................	0	1	0	0	0	0	0	1	1	0	0	0	0	0	0	5
1	Jason Gilzene.................	0	1	0	0	0	0	0	0	0	0	0	0	0	0	0	3
12	Geoffrey Clayton	2	6	0	2	1	1	1	1	2	3	5	4	4	0	1	26
15	Lance Ortiz....................	1	4	1	2	2	2	1	0	1	2	5	1	1	0	2	18
30	David Reichel.................	4	6	2	4	0	0	0	0	0	4	10	0	0	0	0	15
50	Joseph Tillman..............	1	1	0	0	0	0	0	0	0	0	2	0	0	0	0	3
	TEAM......................	0	0	0	0	0	0	1	2	3	0	0	0	0	0	0	
	Totals	28	50	10	20	13	19	6	13	19	27	79	16	11	0	13	200

Deadball rebounds: 2

Barton

No.	Player	FG	FGA	FG	FGA	FT	FTA	OFF	DEF	TOT	PF	TP	A	TO	BLK	S	MIN
3	Bobby Buffaloe .... *	6	7	3	3	4	4	1	0	1	1	19	1	7	0	0	37
11	Anthony Atkinson .... *	6	11	0	1	7	9	0	3	3	1	19	2	3	0	2	40
20	Jeff Dalce .... *	0	0	0	0	0	0	1	2	3	2	0	0	1	0	0	8
33	Brian Leggett .... *	1	1	0	0	1	2	3	3	6	4	3	0	0	0	0	19
41	Mark Friscone .... *	2	5	1	3	3	3	1	1	2	2	8	0	0	0	0	15
10	Alejo Barovero	7	12	2	5	6	8	3	3	6	3	22	3	2	0	0	35
23	Bobby McNeil	0	0	0	0	0	0	0	1	1	0	0	3	0	0	0	2
30	L.J. Dunn	0	1	0	0	0	0	0	2	2	0	0	1	0	0	0	10
31	Errol Frails	1	4	1	4	2	4	0	0	0	2	5	0	1	0	0	14
44	David King.....................	2	2	0	0	0	0	1	1	2	4	4	1	1	0	0	20
	TEAM........................	0	0	0	0	0	0	0	4	4	0	0	0	0	0	0	0
	Totals	25	43	7	16	23	30	10	20	30	19	80	8	18	0	2	200

Deadball rebounds: 2

Officials: Mike McCloskey; Gary Tracy; Keith Winfrey
Technical Fouls: Cal St. San B'dino-Ivan Johnson. Barton-None

Score by Periods	1	2	Total
Cal St. San B'dino............	33	46	79
Barton	37	43	80

Winona St. 90, Central Mo 85 (ot)

Winona St.

No.	Player	TOT-FG FG	FGA	3-PT FG	FGA	FT	FTA	REBOUNDS OFF	DEF	TOT	PF	TP	A	TO	BLK	S	MIN
4	Quincy Henderson	* 0	2	0	2	0	0	0	5	5	5	0	0	4	0	2	26
11	Zach Malvik	* 7	12	0	2	5	8	0	4	4	1	19	5	7	0	2	45
21	Jonte Flowers	*13	17	1	1	5	5	0	4	4	2	32	3	5	1	2	45
32	Joe Ingvalson	* 2	2	0	0	0	0	0	1	1	2	4	0	0	0	1	12
42	John Smith	*10	12	0	0	5	8	2	10	12	3	25	3	4	2	2	45
3	Travis Whipple	0	0	0	0	2	2	0	0	0	4	2	1	0	0	1	31
24	David Johnson	3	5	2	2	0	0	0	2	2	5	8	3	0	0	0	18
33	Josh Korth	0	1	0	1	0	0	0	0	0	1	0	0	1	0	0	3
	TEAM	0	0	0	0	0	0	0	4	4	0	0	0	0	0	0	0
	Totals	35	51	3	8	17	23	2	30	32	23	90	15	21	3	8	225

Deadball rebounds: 5

Central Mo.

No.	Player	TOT-FG FG	FGA	3-PT FG	FGA	FT	FTA	REBOUNDS OFF	DEF	TOT	PF	TP	A	TO	BLK	S	MIN
00	Charles Stoker	* 1	4	0	0	4	4	5	3	8	1	6	1	0	0	1	40
1	Theo Jones	* 4	12	3	7	4	4	0	2	2	3	15	2	2	0	4	41
3	Zack Wright	*14	26	2	3	3	7	1	5	6	0	33	4	3	0	4	45
5	Wadale Williams	* 4	11	0	4	0	0	2	1	3	3	8	2	1	0	2	40
33	Darryl Sommerset	* 6	12	1	3	3	3	1	0	1	5	16	2	3	0	2	19
12	Kevin Wollbrinck	0	0	0	0	0	0	0	0	0	0	0	0	0	0	0	1
15	Fred Dudley	0	1	0	1	0	0	0	1	1	0	0	1	0	0	0	8
24	Michael Taylor	1	2	0	1	0	0	1	0	1	1	2	0	0	0	0	7
54	Alonzo Brooks	1	2	0	0	3	4	1	3	4	5	5	0	3	0	0	24
	TEAM	0	0	0	0	0	0	0	0	0	0	0	0	0	0	0	0
	Totals	31	70	6	19	17	22	11	15	26	18	85	12	12	0	10	225

Deadball rebounds: 3
Attendance: 2,679
Officials: Mike Greenstein; David White; Chris Beaver;
Technical fouls: Winona St.-None. Central Mo.-None

Score by Periods	1	2	OT	Total
Winona St.	37	41	12	90
Central Mo.	36	42	7	85

CHAMPIONSHIP
MARCH 24, AT SPRINGFIELD, MASSACHUSETTS

Barton 77, Winona St. 75

Barton

No.	Player	TOT-FG FG	FGA	3-PT FG	FGA	FT	FTA	REBOUNDS OFF	DEF	TOT	PF	TP	A	TO	BLK	S	MIN
3	Bobby Buffaloe	* 1	4	1	3	0	0	0	1	1	2	3	2	0	0	2	29
11	Anthony Atkinson	*13	24	2	7	1	2	0	0	0	3	29	4	2	0	2	40
20	Jeff Dalce	* 2	4	0	0	0	0	0	1	1	3	4	0	2	0	2	13
33	Brian Leggett	* 3	5	0	0	2	2	5	5	10	4	8	0	2	2	0	25
41	Mark Friscone	* 5	7	1	2	3	3	1	1	2	1	14	0	0	0	0	15
10	Alejo Barovero	3	12	0	2	3	5	2	2	4	1	9	1	3	0	3	30
30	L.J. Dunn	5	11	0	0	0	0	2	4	6	0	10	0	1	0	0	17
31	Errol Frails	0	0	0	0	0	2	0	1	1	1	0	0	1	0	1	10
44	David King	0	0	0	0	0	0	0	1	1	1	0	0	2	0	1	10
	TEAM	0	0	0	0	0	0	3	0	3	0	0	0	2	0	0	0
	Totals	32	67	4	14	9	14	13	16	29	15	77	8	15	2	14	200

Deadball rebounds: 2

Winona St.

No.	Player	TOT-FG FG	FGA	3-PT FG	FGA	FT	FTA	REBOUNDS OFF	DEF	TOT	PF	TP	A	TO	BLK	S	MIN
4	Quincy Henderson	* 7	9	5	7	0	0	1	4	5	3	19	1	4	1	2	40
11	Zach Malvik	*10	16	0	1	6	8	0	3	3	4	26	5	5	0	0	40
21	Jonte Flowers	* 6	11	0	0	1	2	2	10	12	4	13	4	6	0	1	33
32	Joe Ingvalson	* 1	2	0	1	0	0	0	0	0	2	2	0	0	0	0	5
42	John Smith	* 4	6	0	0	2	3	2	3	5	3	10	2	5	2	1	28
3	Travis Whipple	1	2	1	2	0	0	0	2	2	3	3	0	1	0	0	32
24	David Johnson	0	4	0	2	0	0	0	1	1	0	0	1	1	0	1	18
41	Ryan Gargaro	1	1	0	0	0	0	0	0	0	1	2	0	1	0	0	4
	TEAM	0	0	0	0	0	0	2	2	4	0	0	0	1	0	0	0
	Totals	30	51	6	13	9	13	7	25	32	20	75	13	24	3	5	200

Deadball rebounds: 2
Attendance: 4,974
Officials: Mike Greenstein; Gary Tracy; Mike McCloskey;
Technical fouls: Barton-None. Winona St.-None.

Score by Periods	1	2	Total
Barton	31	46	77
Winona St.	41	34	75

Year-by-Year Results

Season	Champion	Score	Runner-Up	Third Place	Fourth Place	Championship Game Attendance	Championship Total Attendance
1957	Wheaton (Ill.) (28-1)	89-65	Ky. Wesleyan	Mt. St. Mary's	Cal St. L.A.	5,000	13,000
1958	South Dakota (22-5)	75-53	St. Michael's	Evansville	Wheaton (Ill.)	4,709	16,007
1959	Evansville (21-6)	83-67	Missouri St.	N.C. A&T	Cal St. L.A.	8,651	22,287
1960	Evansville (25-4)	90-69	Chapman	Ky. Wesleyan	Cornell College	9,009	27,836
1961	Wittenberg (25-4)	42-38	Southeast Mo. St.	South Dakota St.	Mt. St. Mary's	5,138	13,002
1962	Mt. St. Mary's (24-6)	58-57 (ot)	Sacramento St.	Southern Ill.	Neb. Wesleyan	1,851	7,749
1963	South Dakota St. (22-5)	44-42	Wittenberg	Oglethorpe	Southern Ill.	5,261	18,526
1964	Evansville (26-3)	72-59	Akron	N.C. A&T	UNI	12,244	31,915
1965	Evansville (29-0)	85-82 (ot)	Southern Ill.	North Dakota	St. Michael's	12,797	36,084
1966	Ky. Wesleyan (24-6)	54-51	Southern Ill.	Akron	North Dakota	10,319	26,082
1967	Winston-Salem (30-2)	77-74	Missouri St.	Ky. Wesleyan	Illinois St.	6,041	20,608
1968	Ky. Wesleyan (28-3)	63-52	Indiana St.	Trinity (Tex.)	Ashland	13,062	33,899
1969	Ky. Wesleyan (25-5)	75-71	Missouri St.	** American Int'l	Ashland	12,132	30,003
1970	Philadelphia U. (29-2)	76-65	Tennessee St.	UC Riverside	Buffalo St.	5,748	16,075
1971	Evansville (22-8)	97-82	Old Dominion	** La.-Lafayette	Ky. Wesleyan	13,124	35,812
1972	Roanoke (28-4)	84-72	Akron	Tennessee St.	Eastern Mich.	5,233	17,450
1973	Ky. Wesleyan (24-6)	78-76 (ot)	Tennessee St.	Assumption	Brockport St.	6,768	18,318
1974	Morgan St. (28-5)	67-52	Missouri St.	Assumption	New Orleans	4,381	14,207
1975	Old Dominion (25-6)	76-74	New Orleans	Assumption	Chattanooga	4,046	12,909
1976	Puget Sound (27-7)	83-74	Chattanooga	Eastern Ill.	Old Dominion	4,195	70,149
1977	Chattanooga (27-5)	71-62	Randolph-Macon	North Ala.	Sacred Heart	5,718	70,766
1978	Cheyney (26-2)	47-40	Green Bay	Eastern Ill.	UCF	6,458	67,966
1979	North Ala. (22-9)	64-50	Green Bay	Cheyney	Bridgeport	3,768	47,907
1980	Virginia Union (26-4)	80-74	NYIT	Fla. Southern	North Ala.	3,555	44,815
1981	Fla. Southern (24-8)	73-68	Mt. St. Mary's	Cal Poly	Green Bay	5,928	64,659
1982	Dist. Columbia (25-5)	73-63	Fla. Southern	Ky. Wesleyan	Cal St. Bakersfield	4,725	65,884
1983	Wright St. (18-4)	92-73	Dist. Columbia	* Cal St. Bakersfield	* Morningside	4,747	57,893
1984	Central Mo. St. (29-3)	81-77	St. Augustine's	* Ky. Wesleyan	* North Ala.	4,886	67,392
1985	Jacksonville St. (31-1)	74-73	South Dakota St.	* Ky. Wesleyan	* Mt. St. Mary's	6,187	70,945
1986	Sacred Heart (30-4)	93-87	Southeast Mo. St.	* Cheyney	* Fla. Southern	5,863	59,370
1987	Ky. Wesleyan (28-5)	92-74	Gannon	* Delta St.	* Mont. St.-Billings	6,894	65,162
1988	Mass.-Lowell (27-7)	75-72	Alas. Anchorage	Fla. Southern	Troy	4,909	56,123
1989	N.C. Central (28-4)	73-46	Southeast Mo. St.	UC Riverside	Jacksonville St.	3,909	56,890
1990	Ky. Wesleyan (31-2)	93-79	Cal St. Bakersfield	North Dakota	Morehouse	3,904	60,966
1991	North Ala. (29-4)	79-72	Bridgeport	* Cal St. Bakersfield	* Virginia Union	4,582	45,580
1992	Virginia Union (30-3)	100-75	Bridgeport	* Cal St. Bakersfield	* California (Pa.)	5,431	41,219
1993	Cal St. Bakersfield (33-0)	85-72	Troy	* Wayne St. (Mich.)	* Southern N.H.	5,653	44,200
1994	Cal St. Bakersfield (27-6)	92-86	Southern Ind.	* Washburn	* Southern N.H.	6,683	35,599
1995	Southern Ind. (29-4)	71-63	UC Riverside	* Norfolk St.	* Indiana (Pa.)	4,806	130,780
1996	Fort Hays St. (34-0)	70-63	Northern Ky.	* Virginia Union	* California (Pa.)	3,707	55,826
1997	Cal St. Bakersfield (29-4)	57-56	Northern Ky.	* Salem Int'l	* Lynn	2,840	67,531
1998	UC Davis (31-2)	83-77	Ky. Wesleyan	* Virginia Union	* St. Rose	3,420	51,270
1999	Ky. Wesleyan (35-2)	75-60	Metro St.	* Truman	* Fla. Southern	4,013	45,348
2000	Metro St. (33-4)	97-99	Ky. Wesleyan	* Mo. Southern St.	* Seattle Pacific	4,648	40,048
2001	Ky. Wesleyan (31-3)	72-63	Washburn	Western Wash.	Tampa	3,025	46,711
2002	Metro St. (29-6)	80-72	Ky. Wesleyan	Shaw	Indiana (Pa.)	5,119	60,258
2003	Northeastern St. (32-3)	75-64	** Ky. Wesleyan	* Queens (N.C.)	* Bowie St.	2,378	50,912
2004	Kennesaw St. (35-4)	84-59	Southern Ind.	* Metro St.	* Humboldt St.	1,653	29,486
2005	Virginia Union (30-4)	63-58	Bryant	* Lynn	* Tarleton St.	1,717	32,938
2006	Winona St. (32-4)	73-61	Virginia Union	* Seattle Pacific	* Stonehill	4,093	63,176
2007	Barton (31-5)	77-75	Winona St.	* Cal St. San B'dino	* Central Mo.	4,974	76,073

*Indicates tied for third. **Student-athletes representing American International in 1969, La.-Lafayette in 1971 and Ky. Wesleyan in 2003 were declared ineligible after the tournament. Under NCAA rules, the teams' and ineligible student-athletes' records were deleted, and the teams' places in the final standings were vacated.

Season	Site of Finals	Coach of Champion	Outstanding Player Award
1957	Evansville, Ind.	Lee Pfund, Wheaton (Ill.)	Mel Peterson, Wheaton (Ill.)
1958	Evansville, Ind.	Duane Clodfelter, South Dakota	Ed Smallwood, Evansville
1959	Evansville, Ind.	Arad McCutchan, Evansville	Hugh Ahlering, Evansville
1960	Evansville, Ind.	Arad McCutchan, Evansville	Ed Smallwood, Evansville
1961	Evansville, Ind.	Ray Mears, Wittenberg	Don Jacobsen, South Dakota St.
1962	Evansville, Ind.	James Phelan, Mt. St. Mary's	Ron Rohrer, Sacramento St.
1963	Evansville, Ind.	Jim Iverson, South Dakota St.	Wayne Rasmussen, South Dakota St.
1964	Evansville, Ind.	Arad McCutchan, Evansville	Jerry Sloan, Evansville
1965	Evansville, Ind.	Arad McCutchan, Evansville	Jerry Sloan, Evansville
1966	Evansville, Ind.	Guy Strong, Ky. Wesleyan	Sam Smith, Ky. Wesleyan
1967	Evansville, Ind.	C.E. Gaines, Winston-Salem	Earl Monroe, Winston-Salem
1968	Evansville, Ind.	Bob Daniels, Ky. Wesleyan	Jerry Newsom, Indiana St.
1969	Evansville, Ind.	Bob Daniels, Ky. Wesleyan	George Tinsley, Ky. Wesleyan
1970	Evansville, Ind.	Herb Magee, Philadelphia U.	Ted McClain, Tennessee St.
1971	Evansville, Ind.	Arad McCutchan, Evansville	Don Buse, Evansville
1972	Evansville, Ind.	Charles Moir, Roanoke	Hal Johnston, Roanoke
1973	Evansville, Ind.	Bob Jones, Ky. Wesleyan	Mike Williams, Ky. Wesleyan
1974	Evansville, Ind.	Nathaniel Frazier, Morgan St.	Marvin Webster, Morgan St.
1975	Evansville, Ind.	Sonny Allen, Old Dominion	Wilson Washington, Old Dominion
1976	Evansville, Ind.	Don Zech, Puget Sound	Curt Peterson, Puget Sound
1977	Springfield, Mass.	Ron Shumate, Chattanooga	Wayne Golden, Chattanooga
1978	Springfield, Mo.	John Chaney, Cheyney	Andrew Fields, Cheyney
1979	Springfield, Mo.	Bill Jones, North Ala.	Perry Oden, North Ala.
1980	Springfield, Mass.	Dave Robbins, Virginia Union	Keith Valentine, Virginia Union
1981	Springfield, Mass.	Hal Wissel, Fla. Southern	John Ebeling, Fla. Southern

Season	Site of Finals	Coach of Champion	Outstanding Player Award
1982	Springfield, Mass.	Wil Jones, Dist. Columbia	Michael Britt, Dist. Columbia
1983	Springfield, Mass.	Ralph Underhill, Wright St.	Gary Monroe, Wright St.
1984	Springfield, Mass.	Lynn Nance, Central Mo. St.	Ron Nunnelly, Central Mo. St.
1985	Springfield, Mass.	Bill Jones, Jacksonville St.	Mark Tetzlaff, South Dakota St.
1986	Springfield, Mass.	Dave Bike, Sacred Heart	Roger Younger, Sacred Heart
1987	Springfield, Mass.	Wayne Chapman, Ky. Wesleyan	Sam Smith, Ky. Wesleyan
1988	Springfield, Mass.	Don Doucette, Mass.-Lowell	Leo Parent, Mass.-Lowell
1989	Springfield, Mass.	Michael Bernard, N.C. Central	Miles Clarke, N.C. Central
1990	Springfield, Mass.	Wayne Chapman, Ky. Wesleyan	Wade Green, Cal St. Bakersfield
1991	Springfield, Mass.	Gary Elliott, North Ala.	Lambert Shell, Bridgeport
1992	Springfield, Mass.	Dave Robbins, Virginia Union	Derrick Johnson, Virginia Union
1993	Springfield, Mass.	Pat Douglass, Cal St. Bakersfield	Tyrone Davis, Cal St. Bakersfield
1994	Springfield, Mass.	Pat Douglass, Cal St. Bakersfield	Stan Gouard, Southern Ind.
1995	Louisville, Ky.	Bruce Pearl, Southern Ind.	William Wilson, UC Riverside
1996	Louisville, Ky.	Gary Garner, Fort Hays St.	Sherick Simpson, Fort Hays St.
1997	Louisville, Ky.	Pat Douglass, Cal St. Bakersfield	Kebu Stewart, Cal St. Bakersfield
1998	Louisville, Ky.	Bob Williams, Ky. Wesleyan	Antonio Garcia, Ky. Wesleyan
1999	Louisville, Ky.	Bob Williams, Ky. Wesleyan	Antonio Garcia, Ky. Wesleyan
2000	Louisville, Ky.	Mike Dunlap, Metro St.	DeMarcos Anzures, Metro St.
2001	Bakersfield, Calif.	Ray Harper, Ky. Wesleyan	Lorico Duncan, Ky. Wesleyan
2002	Evansville, Ind.	Mike Dunlap, Metro St.	Patrick Mutombo, Metro St.
2003	Lakeland, Fla.	Larry Gipson, Northeastern St.	Darnell Hinson, Northeastern St.
2004	Bakersfield, Calif.	Tony Ingle, Kennesaw St.	Terrence Hill, Kennesaw St.
2005	Grand Forks, N.D.	Dave Robbins, Virginia Union	Antwan Walton, Virginia Union
2006	Springfield, Mass.	Mike Leaf, Winona St.	John Smith, Winona St.
2007	Springfield, Mass.	Ron Lievense, Barton	Anthony Atkinson, Barton

Individual Records

(Three-game minimum for series records and percentages)

POINTS, GAME
54—Willie Jones, American (91) vs. Evansville (101), 1960; Bill Fennelly, Central Mo. St. (112) vs. Jacksonville St. (91), 1980.

POINTS, TOURNAMENT
185—Jack Sullivan, Mt. St. Mary's, 1957 (36 vs. CCNY, 48 vs. N.C. Central, 39 vs. Rider, 19 vs. Ky. Wesleyan, 43 vs. Cal. St. L.A.).

FIELD GOALS, GAME
22—Phil Jackson, North Dakota (107) vs. Parsons (56), 1967.

FIELD GOALS, TOURNAMENT
71—Jack Sullivan, Mt. St. Mary's, 1957 (14 vs. CCNY, 19 vs. N.C. Central, 16 vs. Rider, 8 vs. Ky. Wesleyan, 14 vs. Cal. St. L.A.).

THREE-POINT FIELD GOALS, GAME
11—Kenny Warren, Cal St. Bakersfield (98) vs. Grand Canyon (68), 1993.

THREE-POINT FIELD GOALS, TOURNAMENT
23—John Williams, Bryant, 2005 (5 vs. Bloomfield, 4 vs. Adelphi, 1 vs. Bentley, 5 vs. Mount Olive, 6 vs. Tarleton St, 2 vs. Virginia Union.)

FREE THROWS MADE, GAME
24—Dave Twardzik, Old Dominion (102) vs. Norfolk St. (97), 1971.

FREE THROWS MADE, TOURNAMENT
55—Don Jacobsen, South Dakota St., 1961 (9 vs. Cornell College, 22 vs. Prairie View, 9 vs. UC Santa Barbara, 11 vs. Southeast Mo. St., 4 vs. Mt. St. Mary's).

HIGHEST FREE-THROW PERCENTAGE, GAME
(Minimum 18 Made)
100.0%—Ralph Talley, Norfolk St. (70) vs. Virginia Union (60), 1986 (18-18).

ASSISTS, GAME
20—Steve Ray, Bridgeport (132) vs. Stonehill (127) (ot), 1989.

ASSISTS, TOURNAMENT
49—Tyrone Tate, Southern Ind., 1994 (8 vs. Ky. Wesleyan, 3 vs. Wayne St. (Mich.), 16 vs. South Dakota, 16 vs. Southern N.H., 6 vs. Cal St. Bakersfield).

REBOUNDS, TOURNAMENT (SINCE 1968)
99—Marvin Webster, Morgan St., 1974 (5 games).

Team Records

(Three-game minimum for tournament records and percentages)

POINTS, GAME
132—Bridgeport vs. Stonehill (127) (ot), 1989; Central Okla. vs. Washburn (114), 1992.

POINTS, TOURNAMENT
567—Southern Ind., 1995 (95 vs. Hillsdale, 102 vs. Ky. Wesleyan, 102 vs. Northern Ky., 108 vs. Southern N.H., 89 vs. Norfolk St., 71 vs. UC Riverside).

FIELD GOALS, GAME
54—Bentley (129) vs. Stonehill (118), 1989.

FIELD GOALS, TOURNAMENT
198—Southern Ind., 1995 (37 vs. Hillsdale, 37 vs. Ky. Wesleyan, 34 vs. Northern Ky., 40 vs. Southern N.H., 26 vs. Norfolk St., 24 vs. UC Riverside).

THREE-POINT FIELD GOALS, GAME
23—Troy (126) vs. New Hamp. Col (123), 1993.

THREE-POINT FIELD GOALS, TOURNAMENT
57—Troy, 1993 (9 vs. Fla. Southern, 14 vs. Delta St., 6 vs. Washburn, 23 vs. Southern N.H., 5 vs. Cal St. Bakersfield).

FREE THROWS MADE, GAME
46—Evansville (110) vs. N.C. A&T (92), 1959.

FREE THROWS MADE, TOURNAMENT
142—Mt. St. Mary's, 157.

ASSISTS, GAME
36—Troy (126) vs. Southern N.H. (123), 1993.

ASSISTS, TOURNAMENT
120—North Dakota, 1990.

CHAMPIONSHIPS

All-Tournament Teams

*Most Outstanding Player.
#Participation voided by action of the NCAA Council.

1957
*Mel Peterson, Wheaton (Ill.)
Jack Sullivan, Mt. St. Mary's
Mason Cope, Ky. Wesleyan
Bob Whitehead, Wheaton (Ill.)
Jim Daniels, South Dakota

1958
*Ed Smallwood, Evansville
Jim Browne, St. Michael's
Jim Daniels, South Dakota
Mel Peterson, Wheaton (Ill.)
Dick Zeitler, St. Michael's

1959
*Hugh Ahlering, Evansville
Joe Cotton, N.C. A&T
Jack Israel, Missouri St.
Paul Benes, Hope
Leo Hill, Cal St. L.A.

1960
*Ed Smallwood, Evansville
Dale Wise, Evansville
Tom Cooke, Chapman
Gary Auten, Ky. Wesleyan
William Jones, American

1961
*Don Jacobsen, South Dakota St.
John O'Reilly, Mt. St. Mary's
George Fisher, Wittenberg
Vivan Reed, Southeast Mo. St.
Carl Ritter, Southeast Mo. St.

1962
*Ron Rohrer, Sacramento St.
Jim Mumford, Neb. Wesleyan
Ed Spila, Southern Ill.
John O'Reilly, Mt. St. Mary's
Ed Pfeiffer, Mt. St. Mary's

1963
*Wayne Rasmussen, South Dakota St.
Tom Black, South Dakota St.
Bob Cherry, Wittenberg
Bill Fisher, Wittenberg
Al Thrasher, Wittenberg

1964
*Jerry Sloan, Evansville
Maurice McHartley, N.C. A&T
Larry Humes, Evansville
Bill Stevens, Akron
Buster Briley, Evansville

1965
*Jerry Sloan, Evansville
Richard Tarrant, St. Michael's
Walt Frazier, Southern Ill.
George McNeil, Southern Ill.
Larry Humes, Evansville

1966
*Sam Smith, Ky. Wesleyan
Clarence Smith, Southern Ill.
George McNeil, Southern Ill.
David Lee, Southern Ill.
Phil Jackson, North Dakota

1967
*Earl Monroe, Winston-Salem
Lou Shepherd, Missouri St.
Sam Smith, Ky. Wesleyan
Danny Bolden, Missouri St.
Dallas Thornton, Ky. Wesleyan

1968
*Jerry Newsom, Indiana St.
Larry Jeffries, Trinity (Tex.)
George Tinsley, Ky. Wesleyan
Fred Hardman, Indiana St.
Dallas Thornton, Ky. Wesleyan

1969
*George Tinsley, Ky. Wesleyan
Curtis Perry, Missouri St.
Tommy Hobgood, Ky. Wesleyan
Mert Bancroft, Missouri St.
Bob Rutherford, American Int'l

1970
*Ted McClain, Tennessee St.
Randy Smith, Buffalo St.
Carl Poole, Philadelphia U.
Howard Lee, UC Riverside
John Pierantozzi, Philadelphia U.

1971
*Don Buse, Evansville
#Dwight Lamar, La.-Lafayette
Rick Coffey, Evansville
John Duncan, Ky. Wesleyan
Skip Noble, Old Dominion

1972
*Hal Johnston, Roanoke
Leonard Robinson, Tennessee St.
Lloyd Neal, Tennessee St.
Jay Piccola, Roanoke
Len Paul, Akron

1973
*Mike Williams, Ky. Wesleyan
Ron Gilliam, Brockport St.
Mike Boylan, Assumption
Leonard Robinson, Tennessee St.
Roger Zornes, Ky. Wesleyan

1974
*Marvin Webster, Morgan St.
John Grochowalski, Assumption
Randy Magers, Missouri St.
William Doolittle, Missouri St.
Alvin O'Neal, Morgan St.

1975
*Wilson Washington, Old Dominion
Wilbur Holland, New Orleans
John Grochowalski, Assumption
Joey Caruthers, Old Dominion
Paul Brennan, Assumption

1976
*Curt Peterson, Puget Sound
Wayne Golden, Chattanooga
Jeff Fuhrmann, Old Dominion
Jeff Furry, Eastern Ill.
Brant Gibler, Puget Sound

1977
*Wayne Golden, Chattanooga
Joe Allen, Randolph-Macon
Otis Boddie, North Ala.
William Gordon, Chattanooga
Hector Olivencia, Sacred Heart

1978
*Andrew Fields, Cheyney
Kenneth Hynson, Cheyney
Tom Anderson, Green Bay
Charlie Thomas, Eastern Ill.
Jerry Prather, UCF

1979
*Perry Oden, North Ala.
Carlton Hurdle, Bridgeport
Ron Ripley, Green Bay
Ron Darby, North Ala.
Rory Lindgren, Green Bay

1980
*Keith Valentine, Virginia Union
Larry Holmes, Virginia Union
Bobby Jones, NYIT
John Ebeling, Fla. Southern
Johnny Buckman, North Ala.

1981
*John Ebeling, Fla. Southern
Mike Hayes, Fla. Southern
Durelle Lewis, Mt. St. Mary's
Jim Rowe, Mt. St. Mary's
Jay Bruchak, Mt. St. Mary's

1982
*Michael Britt, Dist. Columbia
John Ebeling, Fla. Southern
Dwight Higgs, Ky. Wesleyan
Earl Jones, Dist. Columbia
Wayne McDaniel, Cal St. Bakersfield

1983
*Gary Monroe, Wright St.
Anthony Bias, Wright St.
Fred Moore, Wright St.
Earl Jones, Dist. Columbia
Michael Britt, Dist. Columbia

1984
*Ron Nunnelly, Central Mo. St.
Brian Pesko, Central Mo. St.
Kenneth Bannister, St. Augustine's
Rod Drake, Ky. Wesleyan
Robert Harris, North Ala.

1985
*Mark Tetzlaff, South Dakota St.
Dave Bennett, Ky. Wesleyan
Melvin Allen, Jacksonville St.
Robert Spurgeon, Jacksonville St.
Darryle Edwards, Mt. St. Mary's

1986
*Roger Younger, Sacred Heart
Kevin Stevens, Sacred Heart
Keith Johnson, Sacred Heart
Riley Ellis, Southeast Mo. St.
Ronny Rankin, Southeast Mo. St.

1987
*Sam Smith, Ky. Wesleyan
Andra Whitlow, Ky. Wesleyan
John Worth, Ky. Wesleyan
Mike Runski, Gannon
Jerome Johnson, Mont. St.-Billings

1988
*Leo Parent, Mass.-Lowell
Bobby Licare, Mass.-Lowell
Averian Parrish, Alas. Anchorage
Jerry Johnson, Fla. Southern
Darryl Thomas, Troy

1989
*Miles Clarke, N.C. Central
Dominique Stephens, N.C. Central
Antoine Sifford, N.C. Central
Earnest Taylor, Southeast Mo. St.
Maurice Pullum, UC Riverside

1990
*Wade Green, Cal St. Bakersfield
LeRoy Ellis, Ky. Wesleyan
Corey Crowder, Ky. Wesleyan
Dave Vonesh, North Dakota
Vincent Mitchell, Ky. Wesleyan

1991
*Lambert Shell, Bridgeport
Pat Morris, Bridgeport
Fred Stafford, North Ala.
Allen Williams, North Ala.
Carl Wilmer, North Ala.

1992
*Derrick Johnson, Virginia Union
Reggie Jones, Virginia Union
Winston Jones, Bridgeport
Steve Wills, Bridgeport
Kenney Toomer, California (Pa.)

1993
*Tyrone Davis, Cal St. Bakersfield
Roheen Oats, Cal St. Bakersfield
Terry McCord, Troy
Wayne Robertson, New Hamp. Col.
Danny Lewis, Wayne St. (Mich.)

1994
*Stan Gouard, Southern Ind.
Kenny Warren, Cal St. Bakersfield
Reggie Phillips, Cal St. Bakersfield
Roheen Oats, Cal St. Bakersfield
Tyrone Tate, Southern Ind.

1995
*William Wilson, UC Riverside
Brian Huebner, Southern Ind.
Chad Gilbert, Southern Ind.
Boo Purdom, UC Riverside
Corey Williams, Norfolk St.

1996
*Sherick Simpson, Fort Hays St.
Paul Cluxton, Northern Ky.
LaRon Moore, Northern Ky.
Alonzo Goldston, Fort Hays St.
Kebu Stewart, Cal St. Bakersfield

1997
*Kebu Stewart, Cal St. Bakersfield
Cliff Clinton, Northern Ky.
Paul Cluxton, Northern Ky.
Shannon Minor, Northern Ky.
Terrance Springer, Salem Int'l

1998
*Antonio Garcia, Ky. Wesleyan
Dana Williams, Ky. Wesleyan
Jason Cox, Ky. Wesleyan
Dante Ross, Ky. Wesleyan
William Davis, Virginia Union

1999
*Antonio Garcia, Ky. Wesleyan
Dana Williams, Ky. Wesleyan
Lee Barlow, Metro St.
DeMarcos Anzures, Metro St.
Innocent Kere, Fla. Southern

2000
*DeMarcos Anzures, Metro St.
Kane Oakley, Metro St.
John Bynum, Metro St.
Lee Barlow, Metro St.
Lorico Duncan, Ky. Wesleyan

2001
*Lorico Duncan, Ky. Wesleyan
Marshall Sanders, Ky. Wesleyan
Ewan Auguste, Washburn
Ryan Murphy, Washburn
Sylvere Bryan, Washburn

2002
*Patrick Mutombo, Metro St.
Clayton Smith, Metro St.
Chris Landry, Ky. Wesleyan
Ronald Evans, Ky. Wesleyan
Ronald Murray, Shaw

2003
*Darnell Hinson, Northeastern St.
Shon Robinson, Northeastern St.
Derek Cline, Northeastern St.
Marlon Parmer, Ky. Wesleyan
Eugene Dabney, Ky. Wesleyan

2004
*Terrence Hill, Kennesaw St.
Georgy Joseph, Kennesaw St.
Cris Brunson, Southern Ind.
Joe Gordon, Southern Ind.
Luke Kendall, Metro St.

2005
*Antwan Walton, Virginia Union
Luqman Jaaber, Virginia Union
Duan Crockett, Virginia Union
Chris Burns, Bryant
John Williams, Bryant

2006
*John Smith, Winona St.
David Zellman, Winona St.
Brad Byerson, Virginia Union
Darius Hargrove, Virginia Union
Tony Binetti, Seattle Pacific

2007
*Anthony Atkinson, Barton
Zack Wright, Central Mo.
Jonte Flowers, Winona St.
Zack Malvik, Winona St.
John Smith, Winona St.

#The participation of Dwight Lamar (Louisiana-Lafayette) in the 1971 tournament was voided by action of the NCAA Council.

Won-Lost Records in Tournament Play

Team (Years Participated)	Yrs.	Won	Lost	Pct.	1st	2nd	3rd	4th
Abilene Christian (1959-60-62-64-65-66-86-87-99-2003)	10	9	12	.429	0	0	0	0
Adams St. (2007)	1	0	1	.000	0	0	0	0
Adelphi (1958-59-64-78-95-96-97-98-99-2000-01-02-05-06-07)	15	12	16	.429	0	0	0	0
Akron (1958-64-65-66-67-71-72-73-75)	9	21	9	.700	0	2	1	0
Ala.-Huntsville (2000-03-06)	3	1	3	.250	0	0	0	0
Alabama A&M (1985-86-87-88-89-93-94-95-96-97)	10	11	13	.458	0	0	0	0
Alabama St. (1972-75)	2	0	3	.000	0	0	0	0
Alas. Anchorage (1982-86-87-88-90-91-93-94-96-97-2004-07)	12	10	13	.435	0	1	0	0
Alas. Fairbanks (1989-2003-04-05-06)	5	4	6	.400	0	0	0	0
Albany (N.Y.) (1969)	1	1	1	.500	0	0	0	0
Albany St. (Ga.) (1973-78-79-84-85-92-97-98-2007)	9	4	11	.267	0	0	0	0
Albright (1961-62-65-66-74)	5	4	6	.400	0	0	0	0
Alcorn St. (1969)	1	1	1	.500	0	0	0	0
Alderson-Broaddus (2002-03-04-05-06-07)	6	4	6	.400	0	0	0	0
American (1958-59-60)	3	6	3	.667	0	0	0	0
American Int'l (1966-67-68-83-84-85-94-2000)*	8	7	11	.389	0	0	0	0
Amherst (1957)	1	0	1	.000	0	0	0	0
Angelo St. (1988-89-2001)	3	1	4	.200	0	0	0	0
Ark.-Monticello (2006)	1	2	1	.667	0	0	0	0
Ark.-Pine Bluff (1967)	1	0	2	.000	0	0	0	0
Arkansas St. (1958-60-62-63-66-67)	6	5	7	.417	0	0	0	0
Armstrong Atlantic (1975-77-95-2001-04-06-07)	7	2	9	.182	0	0	0	0
Ashland (1968-69-70-71-88-90-91)	7	11	10	.524	0	0	0	2
Assumption (1960-63-64-65-66-67-68-69-70-71-72-73-74-75-76-77-79-83-88-91-92-98-2002-03)	24	32	27	.542	0	0	3	0
Augusta St. (1978-2001-02-07)	4	2	5	.286	0	0	0	0
Augustana (Ill.) (1959-60-63-71)	4	0	8	.000	0	0	0	0
Augustana (S.D.) (1975-77-78-86-88-89)	6	3	9	.250	0	0	0	0
Austin Peay (1958-60-61-63)	4	3	6	.333	0	0	0	0
Baldwin-Wallace (1967)	1	1	1	.500	0	0	0	0
Ball St. (1964)	1	0	2	.000	0	0	0	0
Baltimore (1975-76-77)	3	3	3	.500	0	0	0	0
Barry (2005-07)	2	0	2	.000	0	0	0	0
Barton (1997-2003-06-07)	4	10	3	.769	1	0	0	0
Bates (1961)	1	1	1	.500	0	0	0	0
Bellarmine (1963-65-69-70-77-82-84-89-91)	9	6	12	.333	0	0	0	0
Belmont Abbey (1959-60-61-2002-03)	5	4	5	.444	0	0	0	0
Beloit (1957)	1	1	1	.500	0	0	0	0
Bemidji St. (2004)	1	0	1	.000	0	0	0	0
Benedict (1980-2004-06-07)	4	0	5	.000	0	0	0	0
Bentley (1972-73-74-75-76-79-85-89-93-2002-05-06-07)	13	12	15	.444	0	0	0	0
Bethune-Cookman (1965-68-80)	3	0	6	.000	0	0	0	0
Bloomfield (2005-06)	2	1	2	.333	0	0	0	0
Bloomsburg (1963-74-81-82-83-89-95-96)	8	8	9	.471	0	0	0	0
Bluefield St. (1996)	1	0	1	.000	0	0	0	0
Boise St. (1970)	1	1	1	.500	0	0	0	0
Bowie St. (2003-04-05)	3	7	3	.700	0	0	1	0
Brandeis (1958)	1	1	1	.500	0	0	0	0
Bridgeport (1968-72-73-76-77-78-79-85-89-90-91-92-2003-04-06-07)	16	24	18	.571	0	2	0	1
BYU-Hawaii (2000-02-03-04-05-07)	6	1	6	.143	0	0	0	0
Brockport St. (1973)	1	4	2	.667	0	0	0	1
Bryant (1978-80-2004-05-06-07)	6	9	8	.529	0	1	0	0
Buffalo (1957-58-59-60-63-65)	6	6	7	.462	0	0	0	0
Buffalo St. (1967-68-70-71-72-76)	6	7	9	.438	0	0	0	1
C.W. Post (1962-71-73-75-83-84-85-87-90-91-94-2003-04)	13	12	15	.444	0	0	0	0
Caldwell (2007)	1	0	1	.000	0	0	0	0
UC Davis (1967-68-69-75-76-78-95-96-97-98-99-2000)	12	10	16	.385	1	0	0	0
UC Irvine (1968-69-72-75)	4	2	6	.250	0	0	0	0
UC Riverside (1970-72-73-74-75-79-80-84-86-88-89-90-91-92-94-95-97)	17	28	19	.596	0	1	2	0
UC Santa Barbara (1961-63)	2	3	2	.600	0	0	0	0
Cal Poly (1971-74-77-80-81-82-86)	7	10	8	.556	0	0	1	0
Cal Poly Pomona (1962-64-76-2003-04-05-07)	7	10	7	.588	0	0	0	0
Cal St. Bakersfield (1973-76-82-83-84-88-89-90-91-92-93-94-95-96-97-98-2001-02-03-04-06)	21	41	20	.672	3	1	3	1
Cal St. Chico (1958-74-81-91-92-93-2004-05)	8	1	13	.071	0	0	0	0
Cal St. Dom. Hills (1981-87-89)	3	2	4	.333	0	0	0	0
Cal St. East Bay (1977-85-86-87-88)	5	6	6	.500	0	0	0	0
Cal St. L.A. (1957-59-95-98-2000)	5	9	7	.563	0	0	0	2
Cal St. Northridge (1978-79-85)	3	2	4	.333	0	0	0	0
Cal St. San B'dino (1999-2000-01-02-03-04-05-07)	8	14	8	.636	0	0	0	0
California (Pa.) (1985-88-92-93-94-95-96-98-99-2003-04-07)	12	10	13	.435	0	0	2	0
Capital (1957-70-73)	3	2	3	.400	0	0	0	0
Carson-Newman (2002)	1	1	1	.500	0	0	0	0
Catawba (1998-99-2001-04-05-07)	6	1	6	.143	0	0	0	0
Catholic (1964)	1	0	2	.000	0	0	0	0
Centenary (La.) (1957-58-59)	3	1	4	.200	0	0	0	0
Central Ark. (2005)	1	1	1	.500	0	0	0	0
Central Conn. St. (1966-67-69-71-83-84)	6	6	8	.429	0	0	0	0
UCF (1976-77-78-80-81-82)	6	6	8	.429	0	0	0	1
Central Mich. (1965-70-71)	3	3	3	.500	0	0	0	0
Central Mo. (1965-70-80-81-82-83-84-85-89-90-91-94-95-96-97-2005-06-07)	18	24	18	.571	1	0	1	0
Central Okla. (1992-93-95-97-98-2003-05-06)	8	7	8	.467	0	0	0	0

CHAMPIONSHIPS

Team (Years Participated)	Yrs.	Won	Lost	Pct.	1st	2nd	3rd	4th
Central St. (Ohio) (1982)	1	1	1	.500	0	0	0	0
Central Wash. (1999-2000-01-06)	4	2	4	.333	0	0	0	0
Centre (1964)	1	0	2	.000	0	0	0	0
Chaminade (2006)	1	1	1	.500	0	0	0	0
Chapman (1957-58-59-60-61-63-78-83-84)	9	11	10	.524	0	1	0	0
Charleston (W.V.) (1999-2000-01-02)	4	2	4	.333	0	0	0	0
Chattanooga (1961-73-75-76-77)	5	11	5	.688	1	1	0	0
Cheyney (1965-66-67-68-69-70-71-72-73-76-77-78-79-80-81-82-83-86-2004)	19	33	20	.623	1	0	2	0
Chicago (1961-74)	2	2	2	.500	0	0	0	0
CCNY (1957)	1	0	1	.000	0	0	0	0
Clarion (1981-2001)	2	1	2	.333	0	0	0	0
Clark Atlanta (1996)	1	0	1	.000	0	0	0	0
Clayton St. (2007)	1	1	1	.500	0	0	0	0
Coe (1973-74)	2	2	2	.500	0	0	0	0
Colo. Christian (1993)	1	0	2	.000	0	0	0	0
Colorado Col. (1960-61)	2	0	4	.000	0	0	0	0
Colorado St.-Pueblo (1967-68-72-73-98)	5	2	8	.200	0	0	0	0
Columbus St. (1978-84-96-98-2000-03-04-05-06)	9	8	10	.444	0	0	0	0
Concord (1997)	1	2	1	.667	0	0	0	0
Concordia (Ill.) (1962-63-65-69)	4	2	6	.250	0	0	0	0
Cornell College (1960-61-63-70)	4	4	7	.364	0	0	0	1
Delta St. (1972-85-86-87-93-96-97-98-2000-02-03-06)	12	13	12	.520	0	0	1	0
Denison (1968)	1	1	1	.500	0	0	0	0
Denver (1992-96)	2	1	2	.333	0	0	0	0
DePauw (1957-68)	2	0	3	.000	0	0	0	0
Dist. Columbia (1982-83-87-2004)	4	9	4	.692	1	1	0	0
Doane (1965)	1	0	2	.000	0	0	0	0
Dowling (1995-98)	2	0	2	.000	0	0	0	0
Drexel (1957-60-66-67)	4	0	7	.000	0	0	0	0
Drury (2000-04-06-07)	4	2	4	.333	0	0	0	0
East Stroudsburg (1990)	1	1	1	.500	0	0	0	0
East Tenn. St. (1957)	1	1	1	.500	0	0	0	0
Eastern Ill. (1975-76-77-78-79-80)	6	12	6	.667	0	0	2	0
Eastern Mich. (1972)	1	3	2	.600	0	0	0	1
Eastern N.M. (1993-2004)	2	1	2	.333	0	0	0	0
Eckerd (1973-94-95-2001-03-04-05-07)	8	9	9	.500	0	0	0	0
Edinboro (1982-86-94-96-98-2005-06)	7	3	9	.250	0	0	0	0
Elizabeth City St. (1978-81-94-97-99-2007)	6	7	6	.538	0	0	0	0
Elizabethtown (1964)	1	1	1	.500	0	0	0	0
Elon (1997)	1	0	1	.000	0	0	0	0
Emporia St. (2004-07)	2	0	2	.000	0	0	0	0
Evansville (1957-58-59-60-61-62-63-64-65-66-68-71-72-74-76)	15	40	10	.800	5	0	1	0
Fairfield (1960-61-62)	3	2	4	.333	0	0	0	0
Fairleigh Dickinson (1963)	1	0	2	.000	0	0	0	0
Fairmont St. (1996-98-99-2000)	4	4	4	.500	0	0	0	0
Fayetteville St. (1973-93)	2	2	3	.400	0	0	0	0
Ferris St. (1983-87-88-89-90-98-2005-06)	8	7	9	.438	0	0	0	0
Findlay (2002-03-04-05-06-07)	6	7	6	.538	0	0	0	0
Fisk (1964-74)	2	3	2	.600	0	0	0	0
Florida A&M (1957-59-62-78)	4	3	4	.429	0	0	0	0
Fla. Gulf Coast (2005)	1	0	1	.000	0	0	0	0
Fla. Southern (1972-79-80-81-82-83-85-86-87-88-89-90-91-93-96-98-99-2000-01-03-04)	21	32	23	.582	1	1	4	0
Florida Tech (1989-90)	2	1	4	.200	0	0	0	0
Fort Hays St. (1995-96-97-98-2001-03-06)	7	8	6	.571	1	0	0	0
Fort Lewis (2002-03-05-07)	4	0	4	.000	0	0	0	0
Fort Valley St. (1998)	1	0	1	.000	0	0	0	0
Francis Marion (2004)	1	2	1	.667	0	0	0	0
Franklin Pierce (1991-93-96)	3	3	3	.500	0	0	0	0
Fresno St. (1958-60-62-63-64-65-66)	7	8	8	.500	0	0	0	0
Gannon (1962-72-75-77-80-84-85-86-87-88-90-93-94-95-2000-01-02-03-04-05)	20	14	25	.359	0	1	0	0
Gardner-Webb (2000)	1	0	1	.000	0	0	0	0
GC&SU (1997-99-2000-06)	4	5	4	.556	0	0	0	0
Ga. Southern (1970)	1	1	1	.500	0	0	0	0
Grambling (1958-76)	2	3	2	.600	0	0	0	0
Grand Canyon (1992-93-95-96-97-98-2007)	7	5	7	.417	0	0	0	0
Grand Valley St. (1985-91-92-97-2001-06-07)	7	5	8	.385	0	0	0	0
Green Bay (1974-76-77-78-79-81)	6	13	8	.619	0	2	0	1
Grinnell (1962)	1	0	2	.000	0	0	0	0
Gust. Adolphus (1958)	1	0	2	.000	0	0	0	0
Hamline (1962)	1	1	1	.500	0	0	0	0
Hampton (1983-91)	2	2	2	.500	0	0	0	0
Harding (2003)	1	0	1	.000	0	0	0	0
Hartford (1972-73-74-75)	4	2	4	.333	0	0	0	0
Hartwick (1965-70-71-73-74-75-76-77-78-79-80)	11	11	13	.458	0	0	0	0
Hawaii-Hilo (2003-05)	2	1	2	.333	0	0	0	0
Hawaii Pacific (1999)	1	0	1	.000	0	0	0	0
Henderson St. (1999-2000-01-02-03-04-07)	7	8	7	.533	0	0	0	0
High Point (1996-97)	2	2	2	.500	0	0	0	0
Hillsdale (1995-2001-02)	3	1	3	.250	0	0	0	0
Hiram (1973-74)	2	1	3	.250	0	0	0	0
Hofstra (1959-62-63-64)	4	5	4	.556	0	0	0	0
Hope (1958-59)	2	3	2	.600	0	0	0	0
Humboldt St. (1983-90-2001-02-03-04-06-07)	8	9	9	.500	0	0	1	0
Illinois St. (1957-62-67-68-69)	5	6	7	.462	0	0	0	1

Team (Years Participated)	Yrs.	Won	Lost	Pct.	1st	2nd	3rd	4th
Incarnate Word (2002)	1	1	1	.500	0	0	0	0
Indiana (Pa.) (1994-95-96-2000-02-04-05)	7	13	7	.650	0	0	2	0
IPFW (1993)	1	0	2	.000	0	0	0	0
Indiana St. (1966-67-68)	3	5	4	.556	0	1	0	0
Indianapolis (1996-97-2003-04-05)	5	1	5	.167	0	0	0	0
Ithaca (1964-72)	2	1	3	.250	0	0	0	0
Jackson St. (1957-64-65-66-68)	5	4	6	.400	0	0	0	0
Jacksonville St. (1980-81-83-84-85-89-90-92)	8	16	9	.640	1	0	0	1
James Madison (1974-76)	2	0	3	.000	0	0	0	0
Johns Hopkins (1974)	1	0	1	.000	0	0	0	0
Johnson C. Smith (1960-87-91-92-95-98-2001-02-03-06)	10	6	13	.316	0	0	0	0
Kennesaw St. (2003-04-05)	3	7	2	.778	1	0	0	0
Kentucky St. (1962-2001)	2	1	2	.333	0	0	0	0
Ky. Wesleyan (1957-60-61-64-66-67-68-69-70-71-72-73-74-82-83-84-85-86-87-88-89-90-91-92-94-95-98-99-2000-01-02-04)*	32	91	26	.777	8	4	5	1
King's (Pa.) (1974)	1	1	1	.500	0	0	0	0
Knox (1958-59)	2	2	2	.500	0	0	0	0
Kutztown (1988)	1	0	2	.000	0	0	0	0
Lake Superior St. (1996)	1	0	1	.000	0	0	0	0
Lamar (1960-62-63-64-66)	5	5	5	.500	0	0	0	0
Lander (1995-99-2007)	3	3	3	.500	0	0	0	0
Lane (2005)	1	0	1	.000	0	0	0	0
Lebanon Valley (1973)	1	0	1	.000	0	0	0	0
Le Moyne (1959-60-64-65-66-68-69-88-96-97)	10	4	13	.235	0	0	0	0
LeMoyne-Owen (1999-2000)	2	0	2	.000	0	0	0	0
Lenoir-Rhyne (1995-2003-04)	3	0	3	.000	0	0	0	0
Lewis (1982-83-84-85-86-88-98-99-2002-03-04)	11	6	13	.316	0	0	0	0
Lincoln (Mo.) (1959-60-61-67-68-69-72-75-76-77-78-81)	12	12	13	.480	0	0	0	0
Linfield (1957-58)	2	1	3	.250	0	0	0	0
Lock Haven (1987-89)	2	2	2	.500	0	0	0	0
Long Beach St. (1961)	1	1	1	.500	0	0	0	0
Long Island (1965-66-67)	3	6	3	.667	0	0	0	0
Longwood (1994-95-2001)	3	1	4	.200	0	0	0	0
Loras (1959)	1	0	2	.000	0	0	0	0
Louisiana Tech (1967-71)	2	2	2	.500	0	0	0	0
Loyola (Md.) (1973)	1	1	2	.333	0	0	0	0
Luther (1967)	1	1	1	.500	0	0	0	0
Lynn (1997-98-99-2005)	4	9	4	.692	0	0	2	0
MacMurray (1961)	1	0	2	.000	0	0	0	0
Mansfield (1984-97)	2	1	2	.333	0	0	0	0
UMBC (1979-80)	2	3	2	.600	0	0	0	0
Mass.-Lowell (1988-2001-02-03-04-06)	6	14	5	.737	1	0	0	0
McNeese St. (1968)	1	0	2	.000	0	0	0	0
Mercer (1972)	1	0	2	.000	0	0	0	0
Merrimack (1977-78-91-92-2000)	5	5	5	.500	0	0	0	0
Mesa St. (1994-95-99-2004)	4	0	5	.000	0	0	0	0
Metro St. (1990-91-98-99-2000-01-02-03-04-05-06-07)	12	29	10	.744	2	1	1	0
Michigan Tech (1963-98-2000-02-03-04)	6	5	6	.455	0	0	0	0
Midwestern St. (1999-2000-2007)	3	2	3	.400	0	0	0	0
Miles (1974)	1	0	1	.000	0	0	0	0
Millersville (1985-86-87-89-93-95-2003-05-07)	9	12	9	.571	0	0	0	0
Milwaukee (1960-89)	2	3	2	.600	0	0	0	0
Minn. Duluth (1957-65-97-2002-03)	5	1	5	.167	0	0	0	0
Minn. St. Mankato (1964-76-2005-06-07)	5	6	5	.545	0	0	0	0
Minn. St. Moorhead (1965)	1	1	1	.500	0	0	0	0
Mississippi Col. (1978-95)	2	3	2	.600	0	0	0	0
Mo.-Rolla (1975-76-96)	3	1	5	.167	0	0	0	0
Mo.-St. Louis (1972-88)	2	3	2	.600	0	0	0	0
Mo. Southern St. (1993-2000)	2	3	3	.500	0	0	1	0
Missouri St. (1958-59-66-67-68-69-70-73-74-78)	10	23	10	.697	0	4	0	0
Mo. Western St. (1990-91-92-95-97-98-99-2002-03)	9	1	12	.077	0	0	0	0
Monmouth (Ill.) (1957-74)	2	0	2	.000	0	0	0	0
Monmouth (1981-82)	2	1	3	.250	0	0	0	0
Mont. St.-Billings (1981-82-85-86-87-96-97-98-2002)	9	7	11	.389	0	0	1	0
Montclair St. (1969-70-71)	3	4	3	.571	0	0	0	0
Montevallo (2004-05-06-07)	4	10	4	.714	0	0	0	0
Morehouse (1981-90-91-95-2003-04)	6	3	9	.250	0	0	0	1
Morgan St. (1974-75-76)	3	6	3	.667	1	0	0	0
Morningside (1983-84-95)	3	8	3	.727	0	0	1	0
Mount Olive (2004-05-06-07)	4	4	4	.500	0	0	0	0
Mt. St. Mary's (1957-61-62-63-67-69-70-79-80-81-82-85-86-87)	14	25	17	.595	1	1	2	1
Muhlenberg (1968)	1	0	2	.000	0	0	0	0
Neb.-Kearney (1991-96-97-98-2002-03-04-05-06-07)	10	8	11	.421	0	0	0	0
Neb.-Omaha (1975-76-77-79-82-83-84-2002-04-05)	10	6	12	.333	0	0	0	1
Neb. Wesleyan (1962-63-64-99)	4	6	6	.500	0	0	0	0
Nevada (1957-61-64-66)	4	1	6	.143	0	0	0	0
UNLV (1965-67-68-69)	4	4	5	.444	0	0	0	0
New Haven (1987-88-90-2003-04)	5	2	7	.222	0	0	0	0
New Jersey City (1973-74)	2	0	2	.000	0	0	0	0
New Orleans (1971-72-74-75)	4	9	6	.600	0	1	0	1
NYIT (1978-80-2004)	3	5	4	.556	0	1	0	0
Nicholls St. (1976-79-80)	3	5	3	.625	0	0	0	0
Norfolk St. (1965-68-69-71-74-84-85-86-87-88-89-90-92-94-95)	15	19	18	.514	0	0	1	0

Team (Years Participated)	Yrs.	Won	Lost	Pct.	1st	2nd	3rd	4th
North Ala. (1977-79-80-81-84-88-91-94-95-96-2006)	11	27	10	.730	2	0	2	1
N.C. A&T (1958-59-62-64)	4	10	4	.714	0	0	2	0
N.C. Central (1957-88-89-90-93-96-97)	7	10	6	.625	1	0	0	0
North Dakota (1965-66-67-74-75-76-77-79-80-81-82-90-91-92-93-94-95-2000-03)	19	29	22	.569	0	0	2	0
North Dakota St. (1971-74-81-83-94-95-96-97)	8	8	8	.500	0	0	0	0
North Park (1969)	1	1	1	.500	0	0	0	0
Northeastern (1962-63-64-66-67-68)	6	8	6	.571	0	0	0	0
Northeastern St. (2000-01-02-03)	4	8	3	.727	1	0	0	0
Northern Colo. (1964-65-66-89)	4	1	6	.143	0	0	0	0
Northern Ill. (1958)	1	1	1	.500	0	0	0	0
UNI (1962-64-79)	3	5	4	.556	0	0	0	1
Northern Ky. (1978-95-96-97-98-2000-01-03-07)	9	15	10	.600	0	0	0	0
Northern Mich. (1979-80-81-84-85-93-99-2000)	8	7	10	.412	0	2	0	0
Northern St. (1996-97-98-99-2004-05-06)	7	5	7	.417	0	0	0	0
Northwest Mo. St. (1982-84-89-98-2000-01-02-03-04-06-07)	11	10	14	.417	0	0	0	0
Northwood (1999)	1	0	1	.000	0	0	0	0
Oakland (1994-95-96-97)	4	2	4	.333	0	0	0	0
Oglethorpe (1963-66-68-69)	4	8	4	.667	0	0	1	0
Ohio Northern (1974)	1	0	1	.000	0	0	0	0
Old Dominion (1969-70-71-73-74-75-76)	7	15	8	.652	1	1	0	1
Pace (1992-99-2002-07)	4	1	5	.167	0	0	0	0
Pacific (Ore.) (1957)	1	0	1	.000	0	0	0	0
Paine (1994-99-2002)	3	1	3	.250	0	0	0	0
Parsons (1967)	1	0	2	.000	0	0	0	0
Pfeiffer (1996-2000-04-05)	4	6	4	.600	0	0	0	0
Philadelphia U. (1958-63-64-65-66-67-68-69-70-71-72-73-75-76-77-78-79-83-85-89-91-92-93-94-95-2001-04-07)	28	31	32	.492	1	0	0	0
Philander Smith (1957-58)	2	0	3	.000	0	0	0	0
Pittsburg St. (1997-98-99-2005-07)	5	4	5	.444	0	0	0	0
Pitt.-Johnstown (1997-98)	2	1	2	.333	0	0	0	0
Portland St. (1967)	1	0	2	.000	0	0	0	0
Potsdam St. (1966-73-74)	3	2	6	.250	0	0	0	0
Prairie View (1960-61)	2	2	2	.500	0	0	0	0
Presbyterian (1996-97-2003-06)	4	3	4	.429	0	0	0	0
Puget Sound (1970-71-73-75-76-77-78-79-80-81-84)	11	17	11	.607	1	0	0	0
Queens (N.Y.) (2001-02-05)	3	0	3	.000	0	0	0	0
Queens (N.C.) (1996-98-99-2001-03-07)	6	8	6	.571	0	0	1	0
Quincy (1995-97-2005-06-07)	5	4	5	.444	0	0	0	0
Quinnipiac (1976-79-80-88)	4	2	6	.250	0	0	0	0
Randolph-Macon (1965-66-74-75-77-81-83-84-85)	9	6	14	.300	0	1	0	0
Regis (Colo.) (1957-58-95-96)	4	3	5	.375	0	0	0	0
Rensselaer (1958-73)	2	0	3	.000	0	0	0	0
Rider (1957)	1	2	1	.667	0	0	0	0
Roanoke (1968-71-72-73-74-79)	6	8	8	.500	1	0	0	0
Rochester (1961-62-67-68)	4	3	5	.375	0	0	0	0
Rockhurst (2002-07)	2	2	2	.500	0	0	0	0
Rollins (1974-76-79-92-96-2003-04-06-07)	9	9	11	.450	0	0	0	0
Sacramento St. (1959-62-70-88)	4	4	7	.364	0	1	0	0
Sacred Heart (1971-72-75-77-78-81-82-83-84-85-86-87-89)	13	22	15	.595	1	0	0	1
St. Andrews (2000)	1	0	1	.000	0	0	0	0
St. Anselm (1960-62-70-86-87-90-93-95-96-99-2000-01-05-06)	14	10	17	.370	0	0	0	0
St. Augustine's (1983-84-97)	3	7	3	.700	0	1	0	0
St. Cloud St. (1974-86-87-88-92-2000-01-03-06-07)	10	7	12	.368	0	0	0	0
St. Edward's (2006-07)	2	0	2	.000	0	0	0	0
St. Joseph's (Ind.) (1970-74-75-76-78-79-92-2006)	8	11	9	.550	0	0	0	0
St. Lawrence (1974)	1	0	1	.000	0	0	0	0
St. Mary's (Tex.) (2001-03-04-05)	4	0	4	.000	0	0	0	0
St. Michael's (1957-58-59-60-65-67-73-74-87-97-99-2001)	12	19	15	.559	0	1	0	1
St. Norbert (1958)	1	0	2	.000	0	0	0	0
St. Olaf (1969-71-72)	3	1	6	.143	0	0	0	0
St. Procopius (1966)	1	0	1	.000	0	0	0	0
St. Rose (1992-95-96-97-98-99-2000-03-05-07)	10	10	11	.476	0	0	1	0
St. Thomas (Fla.) (1972-73-82)	3	2	3	.400	0	0	0	0
Salem Int'l (1997-98-99-2000-01-02-03-05-06)	9	13	9	.591	0	0	1	0
Sam Houston St. (1986)	1	0	2	.000	0	0	0	0
San Diego (1966-73-74-78-79)	5	4	6	.400	0	0	0	0
San Diego St. (1957-67-68)	3	5	3	.625	0	0	0	0
San Fran. St. (1960-63-65-69-71-80-82-83-94)*	9	4	15	.211	0	0	0	0
Seattle (2007)	1	1	1	.500	0	0	0	0
Seattle Pacific (1962-64-65-66-71-72-77-95-96-98-99-2000-01-02-05-06-07)	17	22	17	.564	0	0	2	0
Shaw (1995-2002-03)	3	6	3	.667	0	0	1	0
Shippensburg (1991-2006)	2	0	3	.000	0	0	0	0
Siena (1974)	1	2	1	.667	0	0	0	0
Slippery Rock (1990-91)	2	1	3	.250	0	0	0	0
Sonoma St. (1973-74-89-99-2003-06)	6	2	7	.222	0	0	0	0
S.C.-Aiken (1998)	1	1	1	.500	0	0	0	0
S.C. Upstate (1991-92-96-98-2005-06)	6	5	6	.455	0	0	0	0
South Carolina St. (1958-61-63-66-67)	5	3	7	.300	0	0	0	0
South Dakota (1957-58-72-90-93-94-99-2000-03-04-05-06-07)	13	18	12	.600	1	0	0	0
South Dakota St. (1959-60-61-63-68-69-70-72-73-78-80-84-85-88-91-92-96-97-98-2000-01-02-04)	23	35	22	.614	1	1	1	1
Southampton (1972)	1	2	1	.667	0	0	0	0
Southeast Mo. St. (1961-62-63-64-79-82-83-85-86-87-88-89-90)	13	28	14	.667	0	3	0	0
Southeastern La. (1973)	1	1	1	.500	0	0	0	0
Southeastern Okla. (2007)	1	2	1	.667	0	0	0	0

Team (Years Participated)	Yrs.	Won	Lost	Pct.	1st	2nd	3rd	4th
Southern Conn. St. (1982-83-97-2000)	4	3	5	.375	0	0	0	0
Southern Ill. (1959-61-62-63-64-65-66)	7	17	9	.654	0	2	1	1
SIU Edwardsville (1986-87-89-2005-06)	5	6	5	.545	0	0	0	0
Southern Ind. (1978-80-81-85-87-90-93-94-95-96-97-98-99-2000-01-03-04-05-06-07)	20	30	22	.577	1	2	0	0
Southern N.H. (1980-81-86-87-90-92-93-94-95-96-97-98-99-2003-04-05)	16	23	16	.590	0	0	2	0
Southern U. (1974-75-77)	3	1	5	.167	0	0	0	0
Southwest Baptist (1990-91-2006)	3	3	4	.429	0	0	0	0
Southwest Minn. St. (2001)	1	3	1	.750	0	0	0	0
Southwestern Okla. (2005)	1	0	1	.000	0	0	0	0
Springfield (1961-63-64-66-68-69-70-80-81-82-86)	11	6	16	.273	0	0	0	0
Stephen F. Austin (1983)	1	1	1	.500	0	0	0	0
Stetson (1967-70-71)	3	3	4	.429	0	0	0	0
Steubenville (1965-66-73)	3	4	3	.571	0	0	0	0
Stillman (2006)	1	0	1	.000	0	0	0	0
Stonehill (1971-73-80-81-82-89-98-2006)	8	7	11	.389	0	0	1	0
Stony Brook (1970)	1	0	2	.000	0	0	0	0
Tampa (1984-85-86-87-88-89-90-93-94-95-97-2000-01-02)	14	15	15	.500	0	0	1	0
Tarleton St. (2002-03-04-05-06)	5	10	5	.667	0	0	1	0
Tenn.-Martin (1982-83)	2	1	3	.250	0	0	0	0
Tennessee St. (1963-67-70-71-72-73-74-75)	8	19	9	.679	0	2	1	1
Tex.-Pan American (1968)	1	1	1	.500	0	0	0	0
Tex. A&M-Commerce (1996-97-98-2005)	4	5	4	.556	0	0	0	0
Tex. A&M-Kingsville (1992-96-2004)	3	1	3	.250	0	0	0	0
Towson (1977-78)	2	3	2	.600	0	0	0	0
Transylvania (1969-70-72-73)	4	2	7	.222	0	0	0	0
Trinity (Tex.) (1960-61-68)	3	6	3	.667	0	0	1	0
Troy (1977-88-91-92-93)	5	10	6	.625	0	1	0	1
Truman (1960-71-79-81-99-2006)	6	8	7	.533	0	0	1	0
Tusculum (2005)	1	0	1	.000	0	0	0	0
Tuskegee (1959-79)	2	1	3	.250	0	0	0	0
Union (Tenn.) (1962-68)	2	1	3	.250	0	0	0	0
Upsala (1960)	1	1	1	.500	0	0	0	0
Valdosta St. (1976-77-79-2002-04-07)	6	5	6	.455	0	0	0	0
Valparaiso (1962-66-67-69-73)	5	7	5	.583	0	0	0	0
Virginia St. (1982-88)	2	1	3	.250	0	0	0	0
Virginia Union (1961-77-79-80-82-84-85-86-87-88-89-90-91-92-93-94-95-96-98-2000-03-04-05-06-07)	25	45	24	.652	3	1	3	0
Wabash (1958-59-60-61)	4	4	4	.500	0	0	0	0
Wagner (1958-67-68-69)	4	4	4	.500	0	0	0	0
Wartburg (1957-58-59-60)	4	2	5	.286	0	0	0	0
Washburn (1992-93-94-95-97-2000-01-03-04-05)	10	13	10	.565	0	1	1	0
Washington-St. Louis (1963-64-65)	3	4	3	.571	0	0	0	0
Wayne St. (Mich.) (1970-84-86-87-92-93-94-99-2004-05)	10	11	12	.478	0	0	1	0
Wayne St. (Neb.) (1999-2000)	2	2	2	.500	0	0	0	0
Wesleyan (Conn.) (1959)	1	0	2	.000	0	0	0	0
West Ala. (1978-82)	2	2	2	.500	0	0	0	0
West Chester (1983-95-99-2001-2003)	5	0	6	.000	0	0	0	0
West Ga. (1975-80-81-83-84-86-87-97-98-99-2001-02-05)	13	10	14	.417	0	0	0	0
West Liberty St. (2007)	1	0	1	.000	0	0	0	0
West Tex. A&M (1987-90-91-94-98-99-2001-03-06-07)	10	5	12	.294	0	0	0	0
West Virginia St. (2004-06-07)	3	3	3	.500	0	0	0	0
West Va. Wesleyan (2002)	1	0	1	.000	0	0	0	0
Western Ill. (1959-80-81)	3	2	4	.333	0	0	0	0
Western St. (1993)	1	1	1	.500	0	0	0	0
Western Wash. (2001-05-06)	3	6	3	.667	0	0	1	0
Wheaton (Ill.) (1957-58-59-60)	4	11	4	.733	1	0	0	1
Wheeling Jesuit (2005-06)	2	0	2	.000	0	0	0	0
Widener (1972)	1	0	1	.000	0	0	0	0
Willamette (1959)	1	1	1	.500	0	0	0	0
Williams (1959-61)	2	2	3	.400	0	0	0	0
Wingate (1999-2000-01-02-06-07)	6	4	6	.400	0	0	0	0
Winona St. (2001-05-06-07)	4	12	3	.800	1	1	0	0
Winston-Salem (1966-67-77-84-85-86-99-2000-01-02-05)	11	11	13	.458	1	0	0	0
Wis.-Parkside (2007)	1	0	1	.000	0	0	0	0
Wis.-Superior (1957-61)	2	0	3	.000	0	0	0	0
Wittenberg (1959-61-62-63-69-72-74)	7	14	8	.636	1	1	0	0
Wooster (1971-73)	2	0	4	.000	0	0	0	0
Wright St. (1976-79-80-81-82-83-85-86)	8	12	7	.632	1	0	0	0
Youngstown St. (1961-62-63-64-66-70-72-75-77)	9	8	11	.421	0	0	0	0

Participation in tournament vacated by the NCAA Committee on Infractions: American Int'l 1969-70; La.-Lafayette 1971 (only tournament berth); San Fran. St. 1984, Ky. Wesleyan 2003.

(Note: Losing semifinalists are credited with third place in years when there was no third-place game [1983-87, 1991-present].)

All-Time Results

1957 First Round: St. Michael's 80, Amherst 63; Rider 63, Drexel 61; Mt. St. Mary's 93, CCNY 84; N.C. Central 78, Florida A&M 61; Buffalo 75, Capital 64; Evansville 108, Illinois St. 96; Ky. Wesleyan 77, DePauw 62; East Tenn. St. 62, Centenary (La.) 61 (ot); South Dakota 62, Monmouth (Ill.) 52; Jackson St. 93, Philander Smith 65; Wheaton (Ill.) 84, Minn. Duluth 75; Beloit 103, Wis.-Superior 79; Regis (Colo.) 88, Wartburg 82; San Diego St. 75, Chapman 56; Cal St. L.A. 75, Nevada 69; Linfield 83, Pacific (Ore.) 79 (ot). **Second Round:** Rider 69,

St. Michael's 68; Mt. St. Mary's 106, N.C. Central 88; Buffalo 77, Evansville 75; Ky. Wesleyan 84, East Tenn. St. 73; South Dakota 2, Jackson St. 0 (forfeit); Wheaton (Ill.) 77, Beloit 75; San Diego St. 81, Regis (Colo.) 78; Cal St. L.A. 85, Linfield 74. **Quarterfinals:** Mt. St. Mary's 86, Rider 66; Ky. Wesleyan 72, Buffalo 68; Wheaton (Ill.) 90, South Dakota 80; Cal St. L.A. 57, San Diego St. 55. **Semifinals:** Ky. Wesleyan 99, Mt. St. Mary's 81; Wheaton (Ill.) 71, Cal St. L.A. 53. **Third Place:** Mt. St. Mary's 82, Cal St. L.A. 72. **Championship:** Wheaton (Ill.) 89, Ky. Wesleyan 65.
1958 First Round: Adelphi 90, Brandeis 72; St. Michael's 72, Rensselaer 56; Grambling 104, South Carolina St. 79;

N.C. A&T 68, Philander Smith 64; Wagner 94, Philadelphia U. 77; American 77, Buffalo 60; Evansville 70, Wabash 68 (ot); Akron 76, Austin Peay 61; Wheaton (Ill.) 68, St. Norbert 66; Hope 101, Northern Ill. 95; Fresno St. 69, Cal St. Chico 56; Chapman 78, Linfield 57; Missouri St. 74, Centenary (La.) 69; Regis (Colo.) 48, Arkansas St. 47; South Dakota 67, Wartburg 65; Knox 76, Gust. Adolphus 65. **Regional Third Place:** Brandeis 71, Rensselaer 69; South Carolina St. 80, Philander Smith 70; Buffalo 77, Philadelphia U. 73; Wabash 72, Austin Peay 69; Northern Ill. 76, St. Norbert 70; Cal St. Chico 76, Linfield 62; Arkansas St. 83, Centenary (La.) 70; Wartburg 83, Gust. Adolphus 73. **Regional Championships:** St. Michael's

97, Adelphi 58; Grambling 88, N.C. A&T 73; American 72, Wagner 65; Evansville 82, Akron 70; Wheaton (Ill.) 104, Hope 93; Chapman 52, Fresno St. 49; Missouri St. 73, Regis (Colo.) 65; South Dakota 102, Knox 51. **Quarterfinals:** Evansville 82, American 72; St. Michael's 84, Grambling 76; Wheaton (Ill.) 81, Chapman 64; South Dakota 63, Missouri St. 58. **Semifinals:** St. Michael's 78, Evansville 70; South Dakota 64, Wheaton (Ill.) 60. **Third Place:** Evansville 95, Wheaton (Ill.) 93. **Championship:** South Dakota 75, St. Michael's 53.

1959 First Round: N.C. A&T 101, Tuskegee 87; Florida A&M 90, Lincoln (Mo.) 73; American 80, Adelphi 73; Hofstra 67, Wesleyan (Conn.) 48; St. Michael's 53, Buffalo 51; Le Moyne 72, Williams 66; Evansville 66, Belmont Abbey 54; Wittenberg 80, Southern Ill. 70; Wheaton (Ill.) 102, Wabash 83; Hope 102, Loras 73; Missouri St. 87, Abilene Christian 67; Centenary (La.) 84, Western Ill. 76; South Dakota St. 73, Augustana (Ill.) 58; Knox 88, Wartburg 84; Cal St. L.A. 83, Sacramento St. 57; Chapman 73, Willamette 52. **Regional Third Place:** Belmont Abbey 79, Southern Ill. 70; Buffalo 78, Williams 53; Adelphi 69, Wesleyan (Conn.) 63; Lincoln (Mo.) 88, Tuskegee 64; Wartburg 69, Augustana (Ill.) 66 (ot); Abilene Christian 85, Western Ill. 81 (ot); Wabash 100, Loras 79; Willamette 76, Sacramento St. 57. **Regional Championships:** N.C. A&T 98, Florida A&M 75; American 66, Hofstra 65; St. Michael's 71, Le Moyne 70; Evansville 56, Wittenberg 50; Hope 81, Wheaton (Ill.) 76; Missouri St. 65, Centenary (La.) 62; South Dakota St. 106, Knox 80; Cal St. L.A. 86, Chapman 82. **Quarterfinals:** N.C. A&T 87, American 70; Evansville 82, St. Michael's 63; Missouri St. 76, Hope 74; Cal St. L.A. 92, South Dakota St. 67. **Semifinals:** Evansville 110, N.C. A&T 92; Missouri St. 72, Cal St. L.A. 59. **Third Place:** N.C. A&T 101, Cal St. L.A. 84. **Championship:** Evansville 83, Missouri St. 67.

1960 First Round: St. Michael's 73, Assumption 50; St. Anselm 108, Le Moyne 75; Ky. Wesleyan 108, Johnson C. Smith 80; Austin Peay 74, Belmont Abbey 63; Fairfield 56, Drexel 44; American 83, Upsala 74; Evansville 91, Arkansas St. 74; Wabash 76, Buffalo 65; Wheaton (Ill.) 82, Augustana (Ill.) 67; Lincoln (Mo.) 100, Milwaukee 92; Fresno St. 62, San Fran. St. 49; Chapman 73, Trinity (Tex.) 52; Cornell College 72, Wartburg 67; Prairie View 78, South Dakota St. 65; Truman 82, Lamar 81; Abilene Christian 109, Colorado Col. 65. **Regional Third Place:** Assumption 94, Le Moyne 68; Buffalo 53, Arkansas St. 52; Belmont Abbey 70, Johnson C. Smith 59; Upsala 74, Drexel 69; Lamar 88, Colorado Col. 67; Milwaukee 109, Augustana (Ill.) 82; Trinity (Tex.) 72, San Fran. St. 64; South Dakota St. 93, Wartburg 77. **Regional Championships:** St. Michael's 99, St. Anselm 95; Ky. Wesleyan 83, Austin Peay 69; American 75, Fairfield 74; Evansville 89, Wabash 68; Wheaton (Ill.) 78, Lincoln (Mo.) 59; Chapman 70, Fresno St. 62; Cornell College 93, Prairie View 79; Truman 79, Abilene Christian 76. **Quarterfinals:** Ky. Wesleyan 99, St. Michael's 55; Evansville 101, American 91; Chapman 73, Wheaton (Ill.) 67; Cornell College 83, Truman 81. **Semifinals:** Evansville 76, Ky. Wesleyan 69; Chapman 79, Cornell College 64. **Third Place:** Ky. Wesleyan 86, Cornell College 76. **Championship:** Evansville 90, Chapman 69.

1961 First Round: Belmont Abbey 74, Ky. Wesleyan 62; Austin Peay 77, Chattanooga 69; Mt. St. Mary's 83, Virginia Union 80; Albright 85, Fairfield 67; Williams 74, Rochester 72; Bates 75, Springfield 63; Wittenberg 43, Youngstown St. 28; Wabash 94, South Carolina St. 83; Lincoln (Mo.) 90, Evansville 77; Chicago 64, MacMurray 59; Southeast Mo. St. 99, Colorado Col. 68; Southern Ill. 96, Trinity (Tex.) 82; Prairie View 79, Wis.-Superior 68; South Dakota St. 90, Cornell College 71; Long Beach St. 70, Chapman 66; UC Santa Barbara 78, Nevada 57. **Regional Third Place:** Ky. Wesleyan 111, Chattanooga 80; Virginia Union 70, Fairfield 66; Youngstown St. 96, South Carolina St. 82; Rochester 82, Springfield 68; Evansville 98, MacMurray 97 (ot); Cornell College 83, Wis.-Superior 72; Trinity (Tex.) 75, Colorado Col. 58; Chapman 68, Nevada 63. **Regional Championships:** Austin Peay 70, Belmont Abbey 63; Mt. St. Mary's 82, Albright 76; Williams 75, Bates 68; Wittenberg 48, Wabash 42; Southeast Mo. St. 87, Southern Ill. 84; Chicago 55, Lincoln (Mo.) 42; South Dakota St. 88, Prairie View 84; UC Santa Barbara 58, Long Beach St. 54. **Quarterfinals:** Mt. St. Mary's 96, Austin Peay 78; Wittenberg 64, Williams 51; Southeast Mo. St. 67, Chicago 41; South Dakota St. 79, UC Santa Barbara 65. **Semifinals:** Wittenberg 65, Mt. St. Mary's 49; Southeast Mo. St. 81, South Dakota St. 69. **Third Place:** South Dakota St. 77, Mt. St. Mary's 76. **Championship:** Wittenberg 42, Southeast Mo. St. 38.

1962 First Round: Northeastern 88, St. Anselm 78; Fairfield 86, Rochester 75; Southern Ill. 78, Union (Tenn.) 56; Evansville 97, N.C. A&T 82; Mt. St. Mary's 67, Albright 64 (4 ot); Hofstra 56, C.W. Post 55; Florida A&M 74, Youngstown St. 60; Wittenberg 69, Gannon 43; Cal Poly Pomona 88, Fresno St. 81; Sacramento St. 68, Seattle Pacific 57; Concordia (Ill.) 79, Illinois St. 61; Valparaiso 75, Kentucky St. 61; Southeast Mo. St. 57, Abilene Christian 55; Arkansas St. 66, Lamar 65; UNI 81, Hamline 68; Neb. Wesleyan 71, Grinnell 65. **Regional Third Place:** St. Anselm 83, Rochester 64; Albright 65, C.W. Post 59; Youngstown St. 58, Gannon 52; N.C. A&T 84, Union (Tenn.) 80; Kentucky St. 77, Illinois St. 72; Lamar 83, Abilene Christian 74; Hamline 76, Grinnell 69; Seattle Pacific 73, Fresno St. 68. **Regional Championships:** Northeastern 80, Fairfield 69; Southern Ill. 88, Evansville 83; Mt. St. Mary's 66, Hofstra 51; Wittenberg 35, Florida A&M 33; Sacramento St. 73, Cal Poly Pomona 65; Valparaiso 75, Concordia (Ill.) 72; Southeast Mo. St. 76, Arkansas St. 64; Neb. Wesleyan 78, UNI 77. **Quarterfinals:** Southern Ill. 73, Northeastern 57; Mt. St. Mary's 43, Wittenberg 39; Sacramento St. 61, Valparaiso 54; Neb. Wesleyan 71, Southeast Mo. St. 61 (ot). **Semifinals:** Mt. St. Mary's 58, Southern Ill. 57; Sacramento St. 74, Neb. Wesleyan 73 (2 ot). **Third Place:** Southern Ill. 98, Neb. Wesleyan 81. **Championship:** Mt. St. Mary's 58, Sacramento St. 57 (ot).

1963 First Round: Tennessee St. 119, Austin Peay 94; Oglethorpe 57, Bellarmine 49; Bloomsburg 76, Mt. St. Mary's 61; Philadelphia U. 60, Hofstra 55; South Carolina St. 80, Buffalo 63; Wittenberg 38, Youngstown St. 31; Springfield 66, Fairleigh Dickinson 54; Northeastern 74, Assumption 60; Evansville 66, Concordia (Ill.) 56; Washington-St. Louis 71, Augustana (Ill.) 66; Lamar 89, Arkansas St. 88; Southern Ill. 87, Southeast Mo. St. 79; Neb. Wesleyan 86, Michigan Tech 69; South Dakota St. 71, Cornell College 64; Chapman 53, San Fran. St. 50; Fresno St. 68, UC Santa Barbara 60. **Regional Third Place:** Bellarmine 96, Austin Peay 86; Hofstra 78, Mt. St. Mary's 71; Youngstown St. 65, Buffalo 53; Assumption 65, Fairleigh Dickinson 51; Concordia (Ill.) 92, Augustana (Ill.) 84; Arkansas St. 77, Southeast Mo. St. 75; Michigan Tech 71, Cornell College 61; UC Santa Barbara 58, San Fran. St. 56. **Regional Championships:** Oglethorpe 55, Tennessee St. 51; Philadelphia U. 54, Bloomsburg 48; Wittenberg 70, South Carolina St. 63; Northeastern 47, Springfield 45; Evansville 85, Washington-St. Louis 76; Southern Ill. 93, Lamar 84; South Dakota St. 77, Neb. Wesleyan 75; Fresno St. 71, Chapman 59. **Quarterfinals:** Oglethorpe 36, Philadelphia U. 34; Wittenberg 48, Northeastern 47; Southern Ill. 86, Evansville 73; South Dakota St. 84, Fresno St. 71. **Semifinals:** Wittenberg 46, Oglethorpe 37; South Dakota St. 80, Southern Ill. 76. **Third Place:** Oglethorpe 68, Southern Ill. 64. **Championship:** South Dakota St. 44, Wittenberg 42.

1964 First Round: Elizabethtown 74, Philadelphia U. 73; Hofstra 92, Catholic 91 (2 ot); Le Moyne 64, Youngstown St. 53; Akron 94, Ithaca 77; Northeastern 79, Assumption 68; Adelphi 75, Springfield 71; Fisk 91, Ky. Wesleyan 86; N.C. A&T 86, Centre 68; Southeast Mo. St. 83, Northern Colo. 79; Abilene Christian 73, Lamar 71; Minn. St. Mankato 87, Neb. Wesleyan 72; UNI 71, Washington-St. Louis 56; Cal Poly Pomona 99, Nevada 71; Fresno St. 68, Seattle Pacific 53; Evansville 97, Jackson St. 69; Southern Ill. 88, Ball St. 81. **Regional Third Place:** Philadelphia U. 94, Catholic 64; Youngstown St. 91, Ithaca 79; Assumption 64, Springfield 60; Ky. Wesleyan 91, Centre 71; Lamar 116, Northern Colo. 85; Washington-St. Louis 77, Neb. Wesleyan 74; Seattle Pacific 76, Nevada 74; Jackson St. 92, Ball St. 71. **Regional Championships:** Hofstra 74, Elizabethtown 61; Akron 62, Le Moyne 38; Adelphi 68, Northeastern 66; N.C. A&T 112, Fisk 87; Southeast Mo. St. 90, Abilene Christian 87; UNI 71, Minn. St. Mankato 64 (ot); Cal Poly Pomona 79, Fresno St. 72; Evansville 64, Southern Ill. 59. **Quarterfinals:** Akron 77, Hofstra 58; N.C. A&T 83, Adelphi 80; UNI 93, Southeast Mo. St. 85; Evansville 95, Cal Poly Pomona 73. **Semifinals:** Akron 57, N.C. A&T 48; Evansville 82, UNI 67. **Third Place:** N.C. A&T 91, UNI 72. **Championship:** Evansville 72, Akron 59.

1965 First Round: Buffalo 81, Randolph-Macon 69; Akron 72, Steubenville 70; St. Michael's 77, Hartwick 72; Assumption 76, Le Moyne 58; Evansville 116, Bethune-Cookman 77; Bellarmine 91, Norfolk St. 74; Long Island 57, Cheyney 48; Philadelphia U. 50, Albright 49; Minn. St. Moorhead 74, Northern Colo. 73; North Dakota 67, Minn. Duluth 57; Fresno St. 74, UNLV 61; Seattle Pacific 107, San Fran. St. 78; Central Mich. 83, Jackson St. 79; Southern Ill. 71, Concordia (Ill.) 70; Abilene Christian 91, Doane 50; Washington-St. Louis 82, Central Mo. 67. **Regional Third Place:** Steubenville 94, Randolph-Macon 68; Hartwick 70, Le Moyne 68; Norfolk St. 91, Bethune-Cookman 74; Cheyney 52, Albright 51; Minn. Duluth 86, Northern Colo. 58; San Fran. St. 85, UNLV 78; Jackson St. 90, Concordia (Ill.) 80; Central Mo. 105, Doane 52. **Regional Championships:** Akron 69, Buffalo 58; St. Michael's 83, Assumption 76; Evansville 81, Bellarmine 74; Philadelphia U. 61, Long Island 58; North Dakota 82, Minn. St. Moorhead 57; Seattle Pacific 82, Fresno St. 68; Southern Ill. 90, Central Mich. 62; Washington-St. Louis 69, Abilene Christian 66. **Quarterfinals:** St. Michael's 101, Akron 87; Evansville 92, Philadelphia U. 76; North Dakota 97, Seattle Pacific 83; Southern Ill. 76, Washington-St. Louis 67. **Semifinals:** Evansville 93, St. Michael's 70; Southern Ill. 97, North Dakota 64. **Third Place:** North Dakota 94, St. Michael's 86. **Championship:** Evansville 85, Southern Ill. 82 (ot).

1966 First Round: Assumption 105, American Int'l 102; Northeastern 93, Springfield 80; Central Conn. St. 94, Potsdam St. 82; Philadelphia U. 83, Le Moyne 61. Consolations: American Int'l 96, Springfield 94 (ot); Le Moyne 86, Potsdam St. 63. **Second Round:** Assumption 96, Northeastern 69; Central Conn. St. 97, Philadelphia U. 75; Ky. Wesleyan 81, South Carolina St. 73 (ot); Oglethorpe 69, Winston-Salem 66; Cheyney 61, Albright 56; Long Island 62, Drexel 54; Steubenville 77, Randolph-Macon 56; Akron 70, Youngstown St. 63; Seattle Pacific 69, San Diego 63; Fresno St. 127, Nevada 78; Evansville 111, Lamar 103; Southern Ill. 83, Indiana St. 65; Abilene Christian 94, Jackson St. 79; Missouri St. 72, Arkansas St. 71; Valparaiso 107, St. Procopius 76; North Dakota 84, Northern Colo. 71. **Regional Third Place:** Winston-Salem 85, South Carolina St. 81; Albright 78, Drexel 61; Youngstown St. 94, Randolph-Macon 63; Nevada 74, San Diego 71; Lamar 93, Indiana St. 78; Arkansas St. 84, Jackson St. 77. **Regional Championships:** Central Conn. St. 96, Assumption 87; Ky. Wesleyan 48, Oglethorpe 41; Long Island 67, Cheyney 64; Akron 93, Steubenville 76; Fresno St. 64, Seattle Pacific 58; Southern Ill. 90, Evansville 77; Abilene Christian 63, Missouri St. 58; North Dakota 112, Valparaiso 82. **Quarterfinals:** Ky. Wesleyan 84, Central Conn. St. 76; Akron 74, Long Island 68; North Dakota 63, Abilene Christian 62; Southern Ill. 93, Fresno St. 70. **Semifinals:** Ky. Wesleyan 105, Akron 75; Southern Ill. 69, North Dakota 61. **Third Place:** Akron 76, North Dakota 71. **Championship:** Ky. Wesleyan 54, Southern Ill. 51.

1967 First Round: Assumption 87, American Int'l 85 (3 ot); St. Michael's 70, Northeastern 61; Central Conn. St. 90, Buffalo St. 73; Long Island 85, Rochester 76. **Consolations:** Northeastern 80, American Int'l 53; Rochester 76, Buffalo St. 70. **Second Round:** St. Michael's 77, Assumption 63; Long Island 114, Central Conn. St. 66; Akron 98, Mt. St. Mary's 72; Winston-Salem 91, Baldwin-Wallace 76; Philadelphia U. 90, Wagner 85 (ot); Cheyney 75, Drexel 53; Ky. Wesleyan 68, Stetson 55; South Carolina St. 66, Tennessee St. 59; Missouri St. 83, Ark.-Pine Bluff 80; Lincoln (Mo.) 93, Arkansas St. 80; Indiana St. 109, Luther 88; Valparaiso 89, Colorado St.-Pueblo 52; San Diego St. 101, Portland St. 73; UNLV 100, UC Davis 83; Louisiana Tech 86, North Dakota 77; Illinois St. 72, Parsons 68. **Regional Third Place:** Baldwin-Wallace 106, Mt. St. Mary's 82; Wagner 61, Drexel 53; Tennessee St. 65, Stetson 53; Arkansas St. 105, Ark.-Pine Bluff 93; Luther 99, Colorado St.-Pueblo 78; UC Davis 81, Portland St. 61; North Dakota 107, Parsons 56. **Regional Championships:** Long Island 72, St. Michael's 64; Winston-Salem 88, Akron 80; Cheyney 80, Philadelphia U. 64; Ky. Wesleyan 87, South Carolina St. 70; Missouri St. 87, Lincoln (Mo.) 77; Valparaiso 80, Indiana St. 77; San Diego St. 88, UNLV 71; Illinois St. 89, Louisiana Tech 66. **Quarterfinals:** Winston-Salem 62, Long Island 54; Ky. Wesleyan 66, Cheyney 53; Missouri St. 86, Valparaiso 72; Illinois St. 77, San Diego St. 76 (3 ot). **Semifinals:** Winston-Salem 82, Ky. Wesleyan 73; Missouri St. 93, Illinois St. 76. **Third Place:** Ky. Wesleyan 112, Illinois St. 73. **Championship:** Winston-Salem 77, Missouri St. 74.

1968 First Round: Bridgeport 86, Springfield 62; American Int'l 80, Assumption 78; Buffalo St. 83, Le Moyne 66; Rochester 73, Northeastern 70. **Consolations:** Assumption 94, Springfield 75; Northeastern 67, Le Moyne 54. **Second Round:** American Int'l 77, Bridgeport 67; Buffalo St. 79, Rochester 67; Ky. Wesleyan 86, Oglethorpe 59; Union (Tenn.) 81, Bethune-Cookman 67; Cheyney 94, Muhlenberg 67; Wagner 98, Philadelphia U. 84; Norfolk St. 108, Denison 86; Ashland 71, Roanoke 46; Evansville 95, Lincoln (Mo.) 80; Missouri St. 69, Colorado St.-Pueblo 68; Tex.-Pan American 96, Jackson St. 73; Trinity (Tex.) 95, McNeese St. 78; Indiana St. 101, South Dakota St. 96; Illinois St. 83, DePauw 81; UNLV 96, UC Davis 91; UC Irvine 78, San Diego St. 69. **Regional Third Place:** Oglethorpe 82, Bethune-Cookman 70; Philadelphia U. 105, Muhlenberg 94; Denison 90, Roanoke 77; Lincoln (Mo.) 92, Colorado St.-Pueblo 77; Jackson St. 75, McNeese St. 71; South Dakota St. 86, DePauw 84; San Diego St. 79, UC Davis 72. **Regional Championships:** American Int'l 79, Buffalo St. 64; Ky. Wesleyan 66, Union (Tenn.) 56; Cheyney 72, Wagner 57; Ashland 61, Norfolk St. 51; Evansville 79, Missouri

St. 73; Trinity (Tex.) 87, Tex.-Pan American 83 (ot); Indiana St. 98, Illinois St. 93; UNLV 79, UC Irvine 74. **Quarterfinals:** Ky. Wesleyan 90, American Int'l 78; Ashland 45, Cheyney 30; Trinity (Tex.) 93, Evansville 77; Indiana St. 94, UNLV 75. **Semifinals:** Ky. Wesleyan 45, Ashland 32; Indiana St. 77, Trinity (Tex.) 67. **Third Place:** Trinity (Tex.) 68, Ashland 52. **Championship:** Ky. Wesleyan 63, Indiana St. 52.

1969 First Round: Oglethorpe 68, Old Dominion 60; Mt. St. Mary's 95, Norfolk St. 80; Alcorn St. 76, Bellarmine 75; Ky. Wesleyan 77, Transylvania 61; San Fran. St. 81, UC Irvine 55; UNLV 84, UC Davis 81; Springfield 91, Central Conn. St. 80; *American Int'l 79, Assumption 77; Wagner 109, Albany (N.Y.) 64; Montclair St. 79, Le Moyne 75; South Dakota St. 79, Lincoln (Mo.) 77; Missouri St. 75, St. Olaf 47; Illinois St. 87, North Park 82; Valparaiso 91, Concordia (Ill.) 81; Cheyney 84, Wittenberg 70; Ashland 43, Philadelphia U. 40. **Regional Third Place:** Norfolk St. 113, Old Dominion 102; Transylvania 65, Bellarmine 64; UC Irvine 82, UC Davis 70; Assumption 98, Central Conn. St. 77; Albany (N.Y.) 71, Le Moyne 70; Lincoln (Mo.) 77, St. Olaf 72; North Park 90, Concordia (Ill.) 73; Philadelphia U. 76, Wittenberg 74. **Regional Championships:** Oglethorpe 74, Mt. St. Mary's 56; Ky. Wesleyan 83, Alcorn St. 79; San Fran. St. 77, UNLV 72; *American Int'l 91, Springfield 68; Montclair St. 101, Wagner 78; Missouri St. 87, South Dakota St. 74; Illinois St. 103, Valparaiso 87; Ashland 66, Cheyney 56. **Quarterfinals:** Ky. Wesleyan 82, Oglethorpe 68; *American Int'l 80, San Fran. St. 75; Missouri St. 92, Montclair St. 76; Ashland 41, Illinois St. 35. **Semifinals:** Ky. Wesleyan 83, *American Int'l 82 (ot); Missouri St. 58, Ashland 48. **Third Place:** *American Int'l 53, Ashland 51. **Championship:** Ky. Wesleyan 75, Missouri St. 71.

**American Int'l's participation in 1969 tournament vacated.*

1970 First Round: Philadelphia U. 79, Youngstown St. 52; Ashland 50, Cheyney 43; *American Int'l 89, St. Anselm 74; Assumption 106, Springfield 84; UC Riverside 83, Boise St. 71; Puget Sound 67, Sacramento St. 62; St. Joseph's (Ind.) 75, Capital 72; Central Mich. 73, Wayne St. (Mich.) 61; Montclair St. 63, Hartwick 54; Buffalo St. 93, Stony Brook 69; Stetson 78, Mt. St. Mary's 77; Ga. Southern 86, Old Dominion 79; Tennessee St. 82, Bellarmine 77; Ky. Wesleyan 74, Transylvania 67; Central Mo. 77, Cornell College 65; South Dakota St. 82, Missouri St. 71. **Regional Third Place:** Cheyney 94, Youngstown St. 91; Springfield 109, St. Anselm 103; Boise St. 63, Sacramento St. 61; Capital 83, Wayne St. (Mich.) 80; Hartwick 78, Stony Brook 70; Old Dominion 93, Mt. St. Mary's 90; Bellarmine 114, Transylvania 72; Missouri St. 76, Cornell College 65. **Regional Championships:** Philadelphia U. 45, Ashland 28; *American Int'l 83, Assumption 82; UC Riverside 83, Puget Sound 72; St. Joseph's (Ind.) 87, Central Mich. 68; Buffalo St. 81, Montclair St. 72; Stetson 93, Ga. Southern 86; Tennessee St. 75, Ky. Wesleyan 73; South Dakota St. 92, Central Mo. 73. **Quarterfinals:** Philadelphia U. 101, *American Int'l 53; UC Riverside 82, St. Joseph's (Ind.) 77; Tennessee St. 92, South Dakota St. 89; Buffalo St. 75, Stetson 74. **Semifinals:** Philadelphia U. 79, UC Riverside 63; Tennessee St. 101, Buffalo St. 80. **Third Place:** UC Riverside 94, Buffalo St. 83. **Championship:** Philadelphia U. 76, Tennessee St. 65.

**American Int'l's participation in 1970 tournament vacated.*

1971 First Round: Ky. Wesleyan 94, St. Olaf 79; Truman 75, North Dakota St. 66; Philadelphia U. 83, Wooster 81 (ot); Cheyney 100, Akron 89; Norfolk St. 97, Roanoke 77; Old Dominion 89, Stetson 65; Seattle Pacific 75, San Fran. St. 68; Puget Sound 81, Cal Poly 69; Assumption 106, Sacred Heart 83; Central Conn. St. 111, Stonehill 99; Tennessee St. 92, Louisiana Tech 91 (ot); *La.-Lafayette 113, New Orleans 107; Central Mich. 63, Augustana (Ill.) 59; Evansville 72, Ashland 64; Hartwick 77, C.W. Post 50; Buffalo St. 103, Montclair St. 93. **Regional Third Place:** North Dakota St. 96, St. Olaf 94; Akron 77, Wooster 68; Stetson 91, Roanoke 72; Cal Poly 70, San Fran. St. 68; Sacred Heart 86, Stonehill 81; Louisiana Tech 107, New Orleans 88; Ashland 88, Augustana (Ill.) 65; Montclair St. 80, C.W. Post 68. **Regional Championships:** Ky. Wesleyan 60, Truman 48; Cheyney 60, Philadelphia U. 58; Old Dominion 102, Norfolk St. 97; Puget Sound 85, Seattle Pacific 78; Assumption 105, Central Conn. St. 77; *La.-Lafayette 86, Tennessee St. 82; Evansville 78, Central Mich. 60; Hartwick 71, Buffalo St. 70. **Quarterfinals:** Ky. Wesleyan 89, Cheyney 83; Old Dominion 81, Puget Sound 80 (ot); *La.-Lafayette 110, Assumption 99; Evansville 105, Hartwick 69. **Semifinals:** Old Dominion 97, Ky. Wesleyan 83; Evansville 93, *La.-Lafayette 74. **Third Place:** *La.-Lafayette 105, Ky. Wesleyan 83. **Championship:** Evansville 97, Old Dominion 82.

**La.-Lafayette's participation in 1971 tournament vacated.*

1972 First Round: St. Olaf 87, South Dakota St. 72; New Orleans 80, Alabama St. 72; Philadelphia U. 67, Widener 62; Youngstown St. 81, Gannon 71. **Second Round:** Bentley 96, Sacred Heart 79; Assumption 112, Bridgeport 82; Eastern Mich. 61, Ky. Wesleyan 59; Evansville 81, Wittenberg 73; Lincoln (Mo.) 97, St. Olaf 81; Mo.-St. Louis 114, South Dakota 72; St. Thomas (Fla.) 68, Fla. Southern 62; Roanoke 78, Mercer 72; Tennessee St. 80, New Orleans 79; Delta St. 71, Transylvania 59; Hartford 81, Ithaca 66; Southampton 83, Buffalo St. 72; Youngstown St. 90, Cheyney 80; Akron 54, Philadelphia U. 52; Seattle Pacific 68, UC Riverside 63; Colorado St.-Pueblo 77, UC Irvine 58. **Regional Third Place:** Bridgeport 107, Sacred Heart 89; Ky. Wesleyan 68, Wittenberg 64; South Dakota 113, St. Olaf 91; Fla. Southern 85, Mercer 83; New Orleans 110, Transylvania 74; Ithaca 70, Buffalo St. 58; Philadelphia U. 86, Cheyney 82; UC Riverside 94, UC Irvine 75. **Regional Championships:** Assumption 109, Bentley 103; Eastern Mich. 93, Evansville 88; Mo.-St. Louis 84, Lincoln (Mo.) 75; Roanoke 67, St. Thomas (Fla.) 57; Tennessee St. 79, Delta St. 73; Southampton 86, Hartford 74; Akron 87, Youngstown St. 71; Colorado St.-Pueblo 86, Seattle Pacific 83. **Quarterfinals:** Eastern Mich. 93, Assumption 88; Roanoke 94, Mo.-St. Louis 69; Tennessee St. 95, Southampton 55; Akron 92, Colorado St.-Pueblo 77. **Semifinals:** Roanoke 99, Eastern Mich. 73; Akron 71, Tennessee St. 69 (ot). **Third Place:** Tennessee St. 107, Eastern Mich. 82. **Championship:** Roanoke 84, Akron 72.

1973 First Round: St. Michael's 108, Hartford 97; Bridgeport 77, Stonehill 74; Cheyney 74, Lebanon Valley 56; Steubenville 54, Hiram 51; Transylvania 72, Albany St. (Ga.) 71 (ot); Fayetteville St. 95, Eckerd 66; Loyola (Md.) 82, St. Thomas (Fla.) 79 (ot); Brockport St. 78, New Jersey City 68; Potsdam St. 54, Rensselaer 52; UC Riverside 70, Sonoma St. 68. **Second Round:** Coe 65, Colorado St.-Pueblo 63; South Dakota St. 85, Missouri St. 74; Assumption 81, St. Michael's 79; Bentley 109, Bridgeport 106 (3 ot); Akron 99, Cheyney 71; Steubenville 61, Philadelphia U. 51; Tennessee St. 53, Transylvania 45; Southeastern La. 67, Chattanooga 64; Ky. Wesleyan 93, Wooster 56; Valparaiso 69, Capital 64; Old Dominion 80, Fayetteville St. 74; Roanoke 84, Loyola (Md.) 63; Brockport St. 93, C.W. Post 77; Hartwick 75, Potsdam St. 58; UC Riverside 71, Puget Sound 51; Cal St. Bakersfield 50, San Diego 44. **Regional Third Place:** Missouri St. 76, Colorado St.-Pueblo 62; Bridgeport 93, St. Michael's 75; Cheyney 70, Philadelphia U. 63; Chattanooga 99, Transylvania 86; Capital 75, Wooster 47; Fayetteville St. 81, Loyola (Md.) 66; C.W. Post 79, Potsdam St. 75; San Diego 80, Puget Sound 73. **Regional Championships:** Coe 107, South Dakota St. 104; Assumption 87, Bentley 85; Akron 49, Steubenville 47; Tennessee St. 62, Southeastern La. 54 (ot); Ky. Wesleyan 74, Valparaiso 66; Roanoke 88, Old Dominion 87 (ot); Brockport St. 70, Hartwick 62; UC Riverside 61, Cal St. Bakersfield 54. **Quarterfinals:** Assumption 102, Coe 96; Tennessee St. 54, Akron 50; Ky. Wesleyan 87, Roanoke 63; Brockport St. 79, UC Riverside 70. **Semifinals:** Tennessee St. 106, Assumption 76; Ky. Wesleyan 96, Brockport St. 90. **Third Place:** Assumption 94, Brockport St. 90. **Championship:** Ky. Wesleyan 78, Tennessee St. 76 (ot).

1974 First Round: Norfolk St. 74, Randolph-Macon 72; Rollins 76, Miles 67; Potsdam St. 65, St. Lawrence 49; Siena 87, New Jersey City 64; Bloomsburg 78, Johns Hopkins 63; Hiram 56, Ohio Northern 50; St. Joseph's (Ind.) 91, Coe 76; Wittenberg 82, Chicago 58; St. Cloud St. 77, North Dakota St. 62; North Dakota 73, Monmouth (Ill.) 67; Fisk 59, James Madison 54; Sonoma St. 60, San Diego 54. **Second Round:** Norfolk St. 84, Roanoke 75; Old Dominion 80, Rollins 77; Hartford 102, St. Michael's 93; Assumption 85, Bentley 83; Morgan St. 54, Potsdam St. 43; Hartwick 81, Siena 72; Bloomsburg 66, King's (Pa.) 65; Albright 93, Hiram 79; St. Joseph's (Ind.) 70, Green Bay 54; Wittenberg 59, Evansville 55 (ot); Ky. Wesleyan 74, St. Cloud St. 72; Missouri St. 71, North Dakota 63; Fisk 65, Tennessee St. 54; New Orleans 85, Southern U. 80; Sonoma St. 73, Cal Poly 66; UC Riverside 62, Cal St. Chico 51. **Regional Third Place:** Roanoke 88, Rollins 77; St. Michael's 99, Bentley 91; Siena 82, Potsdam St. 74; King's (Pa.) 111, Hiram 81; Evansville 87, Green Bay 75; North Dakota 75, St. Cloud St. 71; Tennessee St. 98, Southern U. 88; Cal Poly 81, Cal St. Chico 63. **Regional Championships:** Norfolk St. 89, Old Dominion 76; Assumption 84, Hartford 68; Morgan St. 68, Hartwick 64; Bloomsburg 92, Albright 78; St. Joseph's (Ind.) 75, Wittenberg 60; Missouri St. 69, Ky. Wesleyan 66; New Orleans 78, Fisk 63; UC Riverside 71, Sonoma St. 56. **Quarterfinals:** Assumption 89, Norfolk St. 79; Morgan St. 71, Bloomsburg 57; Missouri St. 80, St. Joseph's (Ind.) 78; New Orleans 83, UC Riverside 78. **Semifinals:** Morgan St. 73, Assumption 70; Missouri St. 68, New Orleans 63. **Third Place:** Assumption 115, New Orleans 103. **Championship:** Morgan St. 67, Missouri St. 52.

1975 First Round: Assumption 111, Sacred Heart 95; Bentley 99, Hartford 82; C.W. Post 72, Philadelphia U. 68; Gannon 65, Hartwick 64 (ot); New Orleans 90, West Ga. 89; Lincoln (Mo.) 93, Southern U. 87; UC Riverside 78, UC Davis 77; Puget Sound 76, UC Irvine 74 (ot); North Dakota 72, Mo.-Rolla 61; Neb.-Omaha 69, Augustana (S.D.) 61; Old Dominion 95, Baltimore 72; Randolph-Macon 64, Morgan St. 60; Chattanooga 107, Alabama St. 83; Tennessee St. 63, Armstrong Atlantic 53; St. Joseph's (Ind.) 96, Youngstown St. 78; Akron 76, Eastern Ill. 62. **Regional Third Place:** Hartford 102, Sacred Heart 91; Philadelphia U. 80, Hartwick 75; Southern U. 103, West Ga. 98; UC Davis 84, UC Irvine 70; Augustana (S.D.) 71, Mo.-Rolla 64; Baltimore 77, Morgan St. 76; Armstrong Atlantic 110, Alabama St. 78; Eastern Ill. 86, Youngstown St. 80. **Regional Championships:** Assumption 87, Bentley 82; Gannon 67, C.W. Post 60; New Orleans 84, Lincoln (Mo.) 83; UC Riverside 59, Puget Sound 58; North Dakota 84, Neb.-Omaha 71; Old Dominion 83, Randolph-Macon 76; Tennessee St. 82, Chattanooga 81; Akron 58, St. Joseph's (Ind.) 52. **Quarterfinals:** Assumption 81, Gannon 69; New Orleans 73, UC Riverside 59; Old Dominion 78, North Dakota 62; Tennessee St. 72, Akron 69. **Semifinals:** New Orleans 84, Assumption 73 (ot); Old Dominion 77, Tennessee St. 60. **Third Place:** Assumption 88, Tennessee St. 80. **Championship:** Old Dominion 76, New Orleans 74.

1976 First Round: Evansville 85, Wright St. 75; Eastern Ill. 65, St. Joseph's (Ind.) 56; Valdosta St. 95, UCF 82; Chattanooga 86, Rollins 62; Puget Sound 80, Cal Poly Pomona 65; Cal St. Bakersfield 87, UC Davis 65; Baltimore 85, Morgan St. 65; Old Dominion 86, James Madison 77; Bridgeport 93, Bentley 86; Assumption 64, Quinnipiac 60; Nicholls St. 97, Lincoln (Mo.) 79; Grambling 67, Mo.-Rolla 61; North Dakota 86, Neb.-Omaha 74 (ot); Green Bay 72, Minn. St. Mankato 67 (2 ot); Philadelphia U. 89, Buffalo St. 69; Cheyney 73, Hartwick 72 (ot). **Regional Third Place:** Wright St. 72, St. Joseph's (Ind.) 68; Rollins 101, Florida Tech 91; Cal Poly Pomona 84, UC Davis 82 (ot); Morgan St. 86, James Madison 81; Bentley 83, Quinnipiac 77; Lincoln (Mo.) 86, Mo.-Rolla 84 (ot); Minn. St. Mankato 95, Neb.-Omaha 73; Buffalo St. 69, Hartwick 67. **Regional Championships:** Eastern Ill. 75, Evansville 73; Chattanooga 86, Valdosta St. 66; Puget Sound 75, Cal St. Bakersfield 65; Old Dominion 73, Baltimore 58; Bridgeport 86, Assumption 84; Nicholls St. 90, Grambling 89; North Dakota 65, Green Bay 61; Cheyney 60, Philadelphia U. 59. Quarterfinals: Eastern Ill. 81, Bridgeport 66; Chattanooga 107, Nicholls St. 78; Puget Sound 80, North Dakota 77; Old Dominion 90, Cheyney 85. **Semifinals:** Chattanooga 93, Eastern Ill. 84; Puget Sound 83, Old Dominion 78. **Third Place:** Eastern Ill. 78, Old Dominion 74. **Championship:** Puget Sound 83, Chattanooga 74.

1977 First Round: Baltimore 116, Virginia Union 96; Towson 102, Winston-Salem 83; Merrimack 107, Bridgeport 83; Sacred Heart 83, Assumption 78; UCF 91, Armstrong Atlantic 81; Chattanooga 92, Valdosta St. 76; North Dakota 71, Augustana (S.D.) 64; Green Bay 89, Neb.-Omaha 63; Eastern Ill. 87, Bellarmine 72; Randolph-Macon 71, Youngstown St. 69 (ot); Cheyney 62, Philadelphia U. 58; Hartwick 68, Gannon 66; Troy 81, Lincoln (Mo.) 75; North Ala. 105, Southern U. 88; Cal Poly 73, Seattle Pacific 58; Puget Sound 85, Cal St. East Bay 68. **Regional Third Place:** Virginia Union 107, Winston-Salem 93; Assumption 86, Bridgeport 84; Valdosta St. 83, Armstrong Atlantic 73; Neb.-Omaha 93, Augustana (S.D.) 91; Youngstown St. 81, Bellarmine 79; Gannon 85, Philadelphia U. 67; Lincoln (Mo.) 103, Southern U. 87; Seattle Pacific 94, Cal St. East Bay 74. **Regional Championships:** Towson 92, Baltimore 87 (ot); Sacred Heart 110, Merrimack 104; Chattanooga 88, UCF 79; North Dakota 45, Green Bay 43; Randolph-Macon 69, Eastern Ill. 66; Cheyney 88, Hartwick 61; North Ala. 77, Troy 70; Cal Poly 67, Puget Sound 54. **Quarterfinals:** Sacred Heart 85, Towson 82; Chattanooga 76, North Dakota 52; Randolph-Macon 65, Cheyney 63; North Ala. 67, Cal Poly 64 (ot). **Semifinals:** Chattanooga 95, Sacred Heart 81; Randolph-Macon 82, North Ala. 67. **Third Place:** North Ala. 93, Sacred Heart 77. **Championship:** Chattanooga 71, Randolph-Macon 62.

1978 First Round: Cheyney 78, Adelphi 64; Philadelphia U. 73, Hartwick 62; Merrimack 116, Bryant 91; Sacred Heart 73, Bridgeport 70; UCF 86, Augusta St. 66; Florida A&M 72, West Ala. 69; Cal St. Northridge 79, UC Davis 73; San Diego 91, Puget Sound 85; Eastern Ill. 100, St. Joseph's (Ind.) 93; Southern Ind. 86, Northern Ky. 78; Towson 106, Albany St. (Ga.) 89; Elizabeth City St. 64, NYIT 62; Missouri

CHAMPIONSHIPS

St. 69, Columbus St. 67; Lincoln (Mo.) 82, Mississippi Col. 73; Green Bay 80, South Dakota St. 57; Augustana (S.D.) 78, Chapman 66. **Regional Third Place:** Hartwick 77, Adelphi 74; Bridgeport 89, Bryant 85; West Ala. 91, Augusta St. 90; Puget Sound 96, UC Davis 73; St. Joseph's (Ind.) 93, Northern Ky. 87; Albany St. (Ga.) 81, NYIT 78; Mississippi Col. 96, Columbus St. 75; South Dakota St. 61, Chapman 59. **Regional Championships:** Cheyney 73, Philadelphia U. 60; Sacred Heart 84, Merrimack 83 (ot); UCF 85, Florida A&M 78; San Diego 70, Cal St. Northridge 67; Eastern Ill. 79, Southern Ind. 67; Elizabeth City St. 84, Towson 73; Lincoln (Mo.) 84, Missouri St. 83; Green Bay 72, Augustana (S.D.) 60. **Quarterfinals:** Cheyney 59, Sacred Heart 57; UCF 77, San Diego 71; Eastern Ill. 84, Elizabeth City St. 71; Green Bay 63, Lincoln (Mo.) 61. **Semifinals:** Cheyney 79, UCF 63; Green Bay 58, Eastern Ill. 43. **Third Place:** Eastern Ill. 77, UCF 67. **Championship:** Cheyney 47, Green Bay 40.

1979 First Round: Wright St. 75, Northern Mich. 66; St. Joseph's (Ind.) 76, Eastern Ill. 66; Bridgeport 92, Quinnipiac 75; Assumption 89, Bentley 78; Nicholls St. 89, Southeast Mo. St. 74; Rollins 97, Truman 88 (ot); Valdosta St. 102, Tuskegee 93; North Ala. 75, Fla. Southern 67; Puget Sound 81, Cal St. Northridge 67; UC Riverside 62, San Diego 48; UNI 84, Neb.-Omaha 72; Green Bay 63, North Dakota 48; Cheyney 82, Albany St. (Ga.) 61; Hartwick 49, Philadelphia U. 48; UMBC 79, Mt. St. Mary's 74; Virginia Union 68, Roanoke 67. **Regional Third Place:** Eastern Ill. 65, Northern Mich. 58; Bentley 104, Quinnipiac 93; Southeast Mo. St. 86, Truman 82; Tuskegee 107, Fla. Southern 102; San Diego 74, Cal St. Northridge 69 (ot); Neb.-Omaha 86, North Dakota 75; Albany St. (Ga.) 72, Philadelphia U. 61; Mt. St. Mary's 93, Roanoke 89. **Regional Championships:** St. Joseph's (Ind.) 73, Wright St. 68; Bridgeport 85, Assumption 75; Nicholls St. 100, Rollins 87; North Ala. 110, Valdosta St. 101; Puget Sound 77, UC Riverside 52; Green Bay 56, UNI 50; Cheyney 72, Hartwick 63; UMBC 58, Virginia Union 56. **Quarterfinals:** Bridgeport 92, St. Joseph's (Ind.) 82; North Ala. 103, Nicholls St. 97; Green Bay 65, Puget Sound 53; Cheyney 65, UMBC 62. **Semifinals:** North Ala. 85, Bridgeport 82; Green Bay 46, Cheyney 45. **Third Place:** Cheyney 81, Bridgeport 78. **Championship:** North Ala. 64, Green Bay 50.

1980 First Round: UMBC 86, Benedict 69; Virginia Union 72, Mt. St. Mary's 70; Springfield 91, Bryant 78; Southern N.H. 98, Quinnipiac 89; South Dakota St. 74, Stonehill 51; Western Ill. 102, North Dakota 79; Fla. Southern 81, Bethune-Cookman 72; UCF 81, West Ga. 78; UC Riverside 65, Puget Sound 61; Cal Poly 66, San Fran. St. 46; North Ala. 98, Central Mo. 86; Nicholls St. 78, Jacksonville St. 76; NYIT 81, Gannon 59; Hartwick 67, Cheyney 64; Eastern Ill. 74, Wright St. 63; Northern Mich. 93, Southern Ind. 83. **Regional Third Place:** Mt. St. Mary's 84, Benedict 82; Quinnipiac 102, Bryant 97; Stonehill 70, North Dakota 57; West Ga. 75, Bethune-Cookman 63; Puget Sound 93, San Fran. St. 86; Central Mo. 112, Jacksonville St. 91; Cheyney 87, Gannon 86; Wright St. 88, Southern Ind. 85. **Regional Championships:** Virginia Union 80, UMBC 65; Southern N.H. 89, Springfield 80; South Dakota St. 98, Western Ill. 86; Fla. Southern 71, UCF 64; UC Riverside 62, Cal Poly 53; North Ala. 77, Nicholls St. 68; NYIT 80, Hartwick 78; Northern Mich. 58, Eastern Ill. 56. **Quarterfinals:** Virginia Union 108, Southern N.H. 91; Fla. Southern 81, South Dakota St. 71; North Ala. 76, UC Riverside 69; NYIT 58, Northern Mich. 57. **Semifinals:** Virginia Union 78, Fla. Southern 71; NYIT 72, North Ala. 66. **Third Place:** Fla. Southern 68, North Ala. 67. **Championship:** Virginia Union 80, NYIT 74.

1981 First Round: Mt. St. Mary's 81, Cheyney 75; Elizabeth City St. 54, Randolph-Macon 53; Western Ill. 80, Southern Ind. 73; Northern Mich. 70, Wright St. 69; Green Bay 82, North Dakota St. 76; North Dakota 87, Central Mo. 80; North Ala. 67, Lincoln (Mo.) 53; Truman 82, Jacksonville St. 78; Puget Sound 62, Cal St. Chico 60; Cal St. Dom. Hills 61, Mont. St.-Billings 52; UCF 94, Morehouse 77; Fla. Southern 70, West Ga. 59; Clarion 80, Monmouth 78; Cal Poly 71, Bloomsburg 43; Southern N.H. 76, Springfield 75; Sacred Heart 89, Stonehill 86. **Regional Third Place:** Cheyney 76, Randolph-Macon 67; Wright St. 96, Southern Ind. 89; North Dakota St. 95, Central Mo. 87; Jacksonville St. 84, Lincoln (Mo.) 66; Mont. St.-Billings 54, Cal St. Chico 49; West Ga. 102, Morehouse 76; Monmouth 79, Bloomsburg 64; Stonehill 79, Springfield 78. **Regional Championships:** Mt. St. Mary's 78, Elizabeth City St. 76; Northern Mich. 93, Western Ill. 87; Green Bay 72, North Dakota 60; North Ala. 63, Truman 59; Puget Sound 72, Cal St. Dom. Hills 54; Fla. Southern 73, UCF 71; Cal Poly 84, Clarion 61; Southern N.H. 81, Sacred Heart 80. **Quarterfinals:** Mt. St. Mary's 88, Northern Mich. 74; Green Bay 65, North Ala. 39; Fla. Southern 56, Puget Sound 55; Cal Poly 77, Southern N.H. 73. **Semifinals:** Mt. St. Mary's 76, Green Bay 60; Fla. Southern 54, Cal Poly 51. **Third Place:** Cal Poly 62, Green Bay 61 (2 ot). **Championship:** Fla. Southern 73, Mt. St. Mary's 68.

1982 First Round: Dist. Columbia 68, Virginia Union 64 (ot); Mt. St. Mary's 90, Virginia St. 86; Cheyney 66, Monmouth 53; Bloomsburg 53, Edinboro 50; Neb.-Omaha 78, Lewis 69; North Dakota 59, Mont. St.-Billings 54; Cal Poly 66, Alas. Anchorage 60; Cal St. Bakersfield 58, San Fran. St. 50; Southeast Mo. St. 60, UCF 55; Tenn.-Martin 46, Central Mo. 42; West Ala. 75, St. Thomas (Fla.) 72; Fla. Southern 80, Northwest Mo. St. 74; Central St. (Ohio) 63, Bellarmine 61; Ky. Wesleyan 76, Wright St. 71 (ot); Sacred Heart 66, Springfield 61; Southern Conn. St. 76, Stonehill 61. **Regional Third Place:** Virginia St. 84, Virginia Union 82; Edinboro 56, Monmouth 53; Lewis 76, Mont. St.-Billings 70; Alas. Anchorage 89, San Fran. St. 84; Central Mo. 70, UCF 62; St. Thomas (Fla.) 89, Northwest Mo. St. 83; Wright St. 87, Bellarmine 86; Springfield 73, Stonehill 72. **Regional Championships:** Dist. Columbia 67, Mt. St. Mary's 66; Cheyney 70, Bloomsburg 48; North Dakota 83, Neb.-Omaha 75; Cal St. Bakersfield 58, Cal Poly 55; Southeast Mo. St. 56, Tenn.-Martin 53; Fla. Southern 86, West Ala. 79 (3 ot); Ky. Wesleyan 66, Central St. (Ohio) 65; Sacred Heart 78, Southern Conn. St. 67. **Quarterfinals:** Dist. Columbia 72, Cheyney 69; Cal St. Bakersfield 67, North Dakota 65; Fla. Southern 87, Southeast Mo. St. 73; Ky. Wesleyan 88, Sacred Heart 85. **Semifinals:** Dist. Columbia 76, Cal St. Bakersfield 71; Fla. Southern 90, Ky. Wesleyan 89 (2 ot). **Third Place:** Ky. Wesleyan 77, Cal St. Bakersfield 66. **Championship:** Dist. Columbia 73, Fla. Southern 63.

1983 First Round: St. Augustine's 78, Hampton 73; Dist. Columbia 34, Randolph-Macon 17; Sacred Heart 113, Assumption 108 (4 ot); American Int'l 65, Central Conn. St. 64; North Dakota St. 71, Ferris St. 68; Morningside 80, Neb.-Omaha 79; Jacksonville St. 67, Fla. Southern 61; West Ga. 74, West Chester 73; Central Mo. 66, Stephen F. Austin 57; Southeast Mo. St. 83, Tenn.-Martin 71; Chapman 80, San Fran. St. 70; Cal St. Bakersfield 72, Humboldt St. 48; Wright St. 71, Lewis 57; Ky. Wesleyan 90, Southern Conn. St. 68; Bloomsburg 76, Cheyney 75; Philadelphia U. 72, C.W. Post 68. **Regional Third Place:** Hampton 71, Randolph-Macon 51; Assumption 99, Central Conn. St. 89 (ot); Ferris St. 81, Neb.-Omaha 75; Fla. Southern 72, West Chester 71; Stephen F. Austin 83, Tenn.-Martin 70; San Fran. St. 78, Humboldt St. 71; Lewis 91, Southern Conn. St. 73; C.W. Post 83, Cheyney 69. **Regional Championships:** Dist. Columbia 93, St. Augustine's 88; Sacred Heart 72, American Int'l 68; Morningside 79, North Dakota St. 77; Jacksonville St. 92, West Ga. 76; Southeast Mo. St. 74, Central Mo. 69; Cal St. Bakersfield 78, Chapman 66; Wright St. 69, Ky. Wesleyan 67; Bloomsburg 73, Philadelphia U. 66. **Quarterfinals:** Dist. Columbia 45, Sacred Heart 38; Morningside 91, Jacksonville St. 90; Cal St. Bakersfield 75, Southeast Mo. St. 70; Wright St. 73, Bloomsburg 53. **Semifinals:** Wright St. 57, Cal St. Bakersfield 50; Dist. Columbia 92, Morningside 77. **Championship:** Wright St. 92, Dist. Columbia 73.

1984 First Round: St. Augustine's 66, Mansfield 65; C.W. Post 65, Gannon 62; Sacred Heart 72, American Int'l 69 (2 ot); South Dakota St. 74, Central Conn. St. 59; Lewis 93, Bellarmine 87; Ky. Wesleyan 96, Cal St. Bakersfield 85; Virginia Union 45, Randolph-Macon 30; Norfolk St. 70, Winston-Salem 61; Morningside 86, Northern Mich. 76; Wayne St. (Mich.) 82, Neb.-Omaha 70; Jacksonville St. 78, Northwest Mo. St. 75; Central Mo. 50, Columbus St. 47; *San Fran. St. 65, UC Riverside 57; Puget Sound 57, Chapman 52; West Ga. 64, Tampa 63; North Ala. 86, Albany St. (Ga.) 73. **Regional Third Place:** Mansfield 94, Gannon 78; Central Conn. St. 102, American Int'l 90; Bellarmine 81, Cal St. Bakersfield 71; Randolph-Macon 69, Winston-Salem 54; Neb.-Omaha 84, Northern Mich. 81; Columbus St. 65, Northwest Mo. St. 63; Chapman 74, UC Riverside 71; Tampa 87, Albany St. (Ga.) 77. **Regional Championships:** St. Augustine's 86, C.W. Post 80; Sacred Heart 88, South Dakota St. 81 (ot); Ky. Wesleyan 72, Lewis 70; Virginia Union 58, Norfolk St. 56; Morningside 75, Wayne St. (Mich.) 73; Central Mo. 79, Jacksonville St. 72; *San Fran. St. 59, Puget Sound 55; North Ala. 66, West Ga. 65. **Quarterfinals:** St. Augustine's 107, Sacred Heart 92; Ky. Wesleyan 72, Virginia Union 71; Central Mo. 74, Morningside 60; North Ala. 76, *San Fran. St. 68. **Semifinals:** St. Augustine's 89, Ky. Wesleyan 80; Central Mo. 89, North Ala. 85 (ot). **Championship:** Central Mo. 81, St. Augustine's 77.

**San Francisco St.'s participation in the 1984 tournament vacated.*

1985 First Round: Wright St. 61, Lewis 53; Ky. Wesleyan 77, Southern Ind. 64; Sacred Heart 47, Bridgeport 45; American Int'l 65, Bentley 49; Southeast Mo. St. 85, Alabama A&M 74; Delta St. 52, Central Mo. 47; Tampa 79, Fla. Southern 65; Jacksonville St. 120, Albany St. (Ga.) 84; Grand Valley St. 71, Northern Mich. 70; South Dakota St. 73, Gannon 64; Cal St. East Bay 64, Norfolk St. 61; Cal St. Northridge 70, Mont. St.-Billings 59; Mt. St. Mary's 62, Randolph-Macon 52 (3 ot); Winston-Salem 44, Virginia Union 42; Philadelphia U. 95, California (Pa.) 76; C.W. Post 57, Millersville 55. **Regional Third Place:** Southern Ind. 92, Lewis 78; Bridgeport 83, Bentley 67; Central Mo. 88, Alabama A&M 74; Fla. Southern 108, Albany St. (Ga.) 80; Northern Mich. 95, Gannon 65; Norfolk St. 90, Mont. St.-Billings 78; Virginia Union 78, Randolph-Macon 55; Millersville 96, California (Pa.) 86. **Regional Championships:** Ky. Wesleyan 84, Wright St. 72; American Int'l 80, Sacred Heart 74; Southeast Mo. St. 67, Delta St. 59; Jacksonville St. 76, Tampa 61; South Dakota St. 58, Grand Valley St. 57; Cal St. East Bay 51, Cal St. Northridge 48; Mt. St. Mary's 63, Winston-Salem 56; C.W. Post 71, Philadelphia U. 68. **Quarterfinals:** Ky. Wesleyan 76, American Int'l 73; Jacksonville St. 80, Southeast Mo. St. 79; South Dakota St. 62, Cal St. East Bay 58; Mt. St. Mary's 69, C.W. Post 67. **Semifinals:** Jacksonville St. 72, Ky. Wesleyan 61; South Dakota St. 78, Mt. St. Mary's 71. **Championship:** Jacksonville St. 74, South Dakota St. 73.

1986 First Round: SIU Edwardsville 70, Lewis 61; Wright St. 94, Ky. Wesleyan 84; Cheyney 106, Edinboro 85; Gannon 78, Millersville 66; Delta St. 61, Sam Houston St. 59; Southeast Mo. St. 94, Abilene Christian 72; Alas. Anchorage 86, UC Riverside 83; Cal St. East Bay 67, Cal Poly 65; Wayne St. (Mich.) 72, Augustana (S.D.) 57; St. Cloud St. 76, Mont. St.-Billings 67; Fla. Southern 83, West Ga. 82; Tampa 76, Alabama A&M 69; Norfolk St. 70, Virginia Union 60; Mt. St. Mary's 74, Winston-Salem 71; Sacred Heart 76, Springfield 74 (2 ot); Southern N.H. 67, St. Anselm 57. **Regional Third Place:** Ky. Wesleyan 91, Lewis 81; Millersville 107, Edinboro 86; Abilene Christian 73, Sam Houston St. 60; UC Riverside 55, Cal Poly 53; Mont. St.-Billings 86, Augustana (S.D.) 61; West Ga. 104, Alabama A&M 84; Virginia Union 95, Winston-Salem 77; Springfield 70, St. Anselm 65. **Regional Championships:** Wright St. 77, SIU Edwardsville 73; Cheyney 65, Gannon 62; Southeast Mo. St. 75, Delta St. 74; Cal St. East Bay 87, Alas. Anchorage 73; Wayne St. (Mich.) 75, St. Cloud St. 71; Fla. Southern 67, Tampa 57; Norfolk St. 78, Mt. St. Mary's 75; Sacred Heart 83, Southern N.H. 67. **Quarterfinals:** Cheyney 78, Wright St. 75; Southeast Mo. St. 85, Cal St. East Bay 69; Fla. Southern 77, Wayne St. (Mich.) 65; Sacred Heart 84, Norfolk St. 74. **Semifinals:** Southeast Mo. St. 90, Cheyney 81; Sacred Heart 86, Fla. Southern 80. **Championship:** Sacred Heart 93, Southeast Mo. St. 87.

1987 First Round: Sacred Heart 82, St. Anselm 80; Southern N.H. 71, New Haven 70; Millersville 83, St. Michael's 76; Gannon 80, C.W. Post 71; West Ga. 81, Tampa 73; Fla. Southern 92, Alabama A&M 83; Alas. Anchorage 68, Cal St. Dom. Hills 64; Mont. St.-Billings 78, Cal St. East Bay 54; Ferris St. 70, Wayne St. (Mich.) 67; St. Cloud St. 81, Lock Haven 64; Delta St. 88, Abilene Christian 71; Southeast Mo. St. 72, West Tex. A&M 71; Mt. St. Mary's 94, Virginia Union 84; Norfolk St. 68, Dist. Columbia 64; Ky. Wesleyan 112, Johnson C. Smith 77; SIU Edwardsville 88, Southern Ind. 82. **Regional Third Place:** St. Anselm 94, New Haven 88; C.W. Post 85, St. Michael's 72; Tampa 92, Alabama A&M 76; Cal St. East Bay 71, Cal St. Dom. Hills 55; Lock Haven 84, Wayne St. (Mich.) 83; West Tex. A&M 67, Abilene Christian 63; Virginia Union 99, Dist. Columbia 92; Southern Ind. 102, Johnson C. Smith 96. **Regional Championships:** Southern N.H. 73, Sacred Heart 67; Gannon 85, Millersville 82; Fla. Southern 84, West Ga. 69; Mont. St.-Billings 79, Alas. Anchorage 73; St. Cloud St. 77, Ferris St. 69; Delta St. 90, Southeast Mo. St. 84 (ot); Norfolk St. 70, Mt. St. Mary's 66; Ky. Wesleyan 89, SIU Edwardsville 86. **Quarterfinals:** Gannon 93, Southern N.H. 81; Mont. St.-Billings 75, Fla. Southern 62; Delta St. 78, St. Cloud St. 73 (ot); Ky. Wesleyan 80, Norfolk St. 74. **Semifinals:** Gannon 61, Mont. St.-Billings 55; Ky. Wesleyan 98, Delta St. 75. **Championship:** Ky. Wesleyan 92, Gannon 74.

1988 First Round: Mass.-Lowell 90, Assumption 65; New Haven 96, Quinnipiac 62; Ky. Wesleyan 82, Lewis 74; Alabama A&M 75, Ashland 73 (ot); Tampa 71, Norfolk St. 68; Fla. Southern 99, North Ala. 76; Mo.-St. Louis 68, South Dakota St. 63; Southeast Mo. St. 111, Angelo St. 75; Ferris St. 91, Augustana (S.D.) 75; UC Riverside 78, St. Cloud St. 71; Alas. Anchorage 89, Cal St. Bakersfield 82 (ot); Cal St. East Bay 96, Sacramento St. 85; N.C. Central 56, Virginia St. 49; Troy 75, Virginia Union 71; California (Pa.) 91, Le Moyne 88; Gannon 84, Kutztown 64. **Regional Third Place:** Quinnipiac 88, Assumption 73; Lewis 89, Ashland 73; North Ala. 87, Norfolk St. 76; South Dakota St. 87, Angelo St. 84; St.

Cloud St. 118, Augustana (S.D.) 114 (2 ot); Cal St. Bakersfield 90, Sacramento St. 89; Virginia Union 90, Virginia St. 89; Le Moyne 89, Kutztown 81. **Regional Championships:** Mass.-Lowell 84, New Haven 72; Alabama A&M 92, Ky. Wesleyan 88; Fla. Southern 76, Tampa 63; Southeast Mo. St. 73, Mo.-St. Louis 69; Ferris St. 80, UC Riverside 64; Alas. Anchorage 72, Cal St. East Bay 67; Troy 66, N.C. Central 65 (ot); Gannon 93, California (Pa.) 75. **Quarterfinals:** Mass.-Lowell 76, Alabama A&M 68; Fla. Southern 78, Southeast Mo. St. 75; Alas. Anchorage 97, Ferris St. 85; Troy 100, Gannon 79. **Semifinals:** Mass.-Lowell 88, Fla. Southern 81; Alas. Anchorage 77, Troy 72. **Third Place:** Fla. Southern 94, Troy 84. **Championship:** Mass.-Lowell 75, Alas. Anchorage 72.

1989 First Round: Bridgeport 132, Stonehill 127 (ot); Sacred Heart 103, Bentley 88; Virginia Union 116, Alabama A&M 80; N.C. Central 67, Norfolk St. 64; Ky. Wesleyan 100, SIU Edwardsville 87 (ot); Bellarmine 108, Ferris St. 92; Tampa 90, Fla. Southern 86; Jacksonville St. 94, Florida Tech 70; Milwaukee 99, Augustana (S.D.) 95; Northern Colo. 92, Alas. Fairbanks 70; Central Mo. 78, Northwest Mo. St. 74; Southeast Mo. St. 65, Angelo St. 60; Bloomsburg 74, Philadelphia U. 73 (ot); Millersville 97, Lock Haven 84; UC Riverside 79, Sonoma St. 65; Cal St. Bakersfield 64, Cal St. Dom. Hills 61. **Regional Third Place:** Bentley 129, Stonehill 118; Alabama A&M 93, Norfolk St. 80; SIU Edwardsville 102, Ferris St. 92; Fla. Southern 85, Florida Tech 75; Augustana (S.D.) 112, Alas. Fairbanks 107 (2 ot); Angelo St. 89, Northwest Mo. St. 80; Lock Haven 82, Philadelphia U. 78; Cal St. Dom. Hills 98, Sonoma St. 77. **Regional Championships:** Sacred Heart 69, Bridgeport 67; N.C. Central 60, Virginia Union 55; Ky. Wesleyan 84, Bellarmine 77; Jacksonville St. 89, Tampa 67; Milwaukee 89, Northern Colo. 88 (ot); Southeast Mo. St. 88, Central Mo. 73; Millersville 87, Bloomsburg 71; UC Riverside 63, Cal St. Bakersfield 60. **Quarterfinals:** N.C. Central 58, Sacred Heart 57; Jacksonville St. 107, Ky. Wesleyan 70; Southeast Mo. St. 93, Milwaukee 84; UC Riverside 92, Millersville 86. **Semifinals:** N.C. Central 90, Jacksonville St. 70; Southeast Mo. St. 84, UC Riverside 83 (ot). **Third Place:** UC Riverside 90, Jacksonville St. 81. **Championship:** N.C. Central 73, Southeast Mo. St. 46.

1990 First Round: Bridgeport 83, New Haven 78; St. Anselm 94, Southern N.H. 89; Central Mo. 69, UC Riverside 59; Cal St. Bakersfield 76, Humboldt St. 58; East Stroudsburg 99, Slippery Rock 98 (ot); Gannon 83, C.W. Post 78; Morehouse 82, Virginia Union 78; Florida Tech 73, Norfolk St. 63; Mo. Western St. 73, West Tex. A&M 71; Southeast Mo. St. 91, Southern Ind. 73; Ashland 68, Southwest Baptist 64; Ky. Wesleyan 97, Ferris St. 72; Metro St. 82, South Dakota 73; North Dakota 78, Alas. Anchorage 71; N.C. Central 66, Tampa 61; Jacksonville St. 97, Fla. Southern 96 (ot). **Regional Third Place:** Southern N.H. 91, New Haven 88; Humboldt St. 71, UC Riverside 70; C.W. Post 84, Slippery Rock 79; Norfolk St. 102, Virginia Union 93; West Tex. A&M 98, Southern Ind. 92 (ot); Ferris St. 88, Southwest Baptist 80 (ot); South Dakota 101, Alas. Anchorage 92; Fla. Southern 92, Tampa 82. **Regional Championships:** Bridgeport 91, St. Anselm 82; Cal St. Bakersfield 68, Central Mo. 64; Gannon 72, East Stroudsburg 63; Morehouse 81, Florida Tech 77; Southeast Mo. St. 88, Mo. Western St. 73; Ky. Wesleyan 79, Ashland 75; North Dakota 85, Metro St. 80; Jacksonville St. 95, N.C. Central 88 (ot). **Quarterfinals:** Cal St. Bakersfield 87, Bridgeport 72; Morehouse 75, Gannon 69; Ky. Wesleyan 91, Southeast Mo. St. 90 (ot); North Dakota 89, Jacksonville St. 67. **Semifinals:** Cal St. Bakersfield 85, Morehouse 60; Ky. Wesleyan 101, North Dakota 92. **Third Place:** North Dakota 98, Morehouse 77. **Championship:** Ky. Wesleyan 93, Cal St. Bakersfield 79.

1991 First Round: Franklin Pierce 82, Merrimack 79; Bridgeport 94, Assumption 87; Philadelphia U. 62, Shippensburg 50; C.W. Post 70, Slippery Rock 66; Southwest Baptist 98, Ky. Wesleyan 81; Central Mo. 72, West Tex. A&M 69; Alas. Anchorage 74, Cal St. Chico 69; Cal St. Bakersfield 75, UC Riverside 62; South Dakota St. 92, Metro St. 79; North Dakota 90, Neb.-Kearney 60; Virginia Union 89, Morehouse 79; S.C. Upstate 99, Johnson C. Smith 74; North Ala. 94, Hampton 80; Troy 78, Fla. Southern 73; Grand Valley St. 78, Bellarmine 72; Ashland 103, Mo. Western St. 72. **Regional Third Place:** Merrimack 89, Assumption 71; Slippery Rock 119, Shippensburg 101; Ky. Wesleyan 91, West Tex. A&M 78; UC Riverside 90, Cal St. Chico 82; Metro St. 99, Neb.-Kearney 92; Johnson C. Smith 102, Morehouse 89; Hampton 70, Fla. Southern 68; Bellarmine 94, Mo. Western St. 83. **Regional Championships:** Bridgeport 81, Franklin Pierce 77; Philadelphia U. 64, C.W. Post 63; Southwest Baptist 63, Central Mo. 61; Cal St. Bakersfield 78, Alas. Anchorage 68; North Dakota 54, South Dakota St. 51; Virginia Union 77, S.C. Upstate 73; North Ala. 93, Troy 86; Ashland 82, Grand Valley St. 75. **Quarterfinals:** Bridgeport 69, Philadelphia U. 62; Cal St. Bakersfield 55, Southwest Baptist 52; Virginia Union 64, North Dakota 63; North Ala. 92, Ashland 84. **Semifinals:** Bridgeport 73, Cal St. Bakersfield 66 (ot); North Ala. 97, Virginia Union 76. **Championship:** North Ala. 79, Bridgeport 72.

1992 First Round: Southern N.H. 89, Assumption 87; Bridgeport 91, Merrimack 84; Central Okla. 100, Mo. Western St. 96 (ot); Washburn 85, Tex. A&M-Kingsville 65; Denver 73, North Dakota 68; South Dakota St. 79, St. Cloud St. 74 (ot); Philadelphia U. 83, St. Rose 70; California (Pa.) 69, Pace 66 (ot); S.C. Upstate 87, Rollins 83; Jacksonville St. 96, Troy 91; UC Riverside 74, Grand Canyon 61; Cal St. Bakersfield 99, Cal St. Chico 78; Wayne St. (Mich.) 63, St. Joseph's (Ind.) 56; Ky. Wesleyan 84, Grand Valley St. 73; Johnson C. Smith 82, Norfolk St. 76; Virginia Union 79, Albany St. (Ga.) 67. **Regional Third Place:** Merrimack 105, Assumption 84; Tex. A&M-Kingsville 97, Mo. Western St. 83; North Dakota 80, St. Cloud St. 60; St. Rose 59, Pace 52; Troy 110, Rollins 92; Grand Canyon 88, Cal St. Chico 87; St. Joseph's (Ind.) 74, Grand Valley St. 64 (ot); Albany St. (Ga.) 73, Norfolk St. 70. **Regional Championships:** Bridgeport 100, Southern N.H. 87; Central Okla. 132, Washburn 114; South Dakota St. 87, Denver 57; California (Pa.) 90, Philadelphia U. 79; Jacksonville St. 105, S.C. Upstate 87; Cal St. Bakersfield 72, UC Riverside 70 (ot); Ky. Wesleyan 90, Wayne St. (Mich.) 72; Virginia Union 87, Johnson C. Smith 70. **Quarterfinals:** Bridgeport 127, Central Okla. 124 (ot); California (Pa.) 84, South Dakota St. 73; Cal St. Bakersfield 89, Jacksonville St. 59; Virginia Union 81, Ky. Wesleyan 69. **Semifinals:** Bridgeport 76, California (Pa.) 75; Virginia Union 69, Cal St. Bakersfield 66. **Championship:** Virginia Union 100, Bridgeport 75.

1993 First Round: N.C. Central 93, Alabama A&M 84; Virginia Union 67, Fayetteville St. 38; Alas. Anchorage 72, Cal St. Chico 70; Cal St. Bakersfield 98, Grand Canyon 68; Northern Mich. 86, Southern Ind. 85; Wayne St. (Mich.) 78, IPFW 72; Millersville 86, California (Pa.) 77; Philadelphia U. 70, Gannon 56; Delta St. 73, Tampa 61; Troy 75, Fla. Southern 72; Washburn 92, Central Okla. 88; Eastern N.M. 76, Mo. Southern St. 73; Franklin Pierce 95, Bentley 74; Southern N.H. 67, St. Anselm 63; North Dakota 80, Western St. 61; South Dakota 78, Colo. Christian 60. **Regional Third Place:** Alabama A&M 79, Fayetteville St. 62; Grand Canyon 103, Cal St. Chico 98; Southern Ind. 95, IPFW 93; East regional third-place game canceled due to inclement weather; Tampa 79, Fla. Southern 73; Central Okla. 116, Mo. Southern St. 109; Bentley 109, St. Anselm 90; Western St. 81, Colo. Christian 71. **Regional Championships:** N.C. Central 93, Virginia Union 81; Cal St. Bakersfield 78, Alas. Anchorage 59; Wayne St. (Mich.) 90, Northern Mich. 58; Philadelphia U. 70, Millersville 62; Troy 110, Delta St. 93; Washburn 79, Eastern N.M. 78; Southern N.H. 83, Franklin Pierce 73; South Dakota 66, North Dakota 64 (ot). **Quarterfinals:** Cal St. Bakersfield 86, N.C. Central 80; Wayne St. (Mich.) 78, Philadelphia U. 76; Troy 94, Washburn 82; Southern N.H. 100, South Dakota 96 (3 ot). **Semifinals:** Cal St. Bakersfield 61, Wayne St. (Mich.) 57; Troy 126, Southern N.H. 123. **Championship:** Cal St. Bakersfield 85, Troy 72.

1994 First Round: Virginia Union 88, Elizabeth City St. 71; Norfolk St. 61, Longwood 59; Washburn 83, Central Mo. 78; North Ala. 74, West Tex. A&M 67; UC Riverside 78, San Fran. St. 61; Cal St. Bakersfield 92, Alas. Anchorage 61; California (Pa.) 65, Gannon 64; Indiana (Pa.) 90, Edinboro 77; Wayne St. (Mich.) 99, Oakland 97; Southern Ind. 78, Ky. Wesleyan 67; South Dakota 94, North Dakota 76; North Dakota St. 75, Mesa St. 65 (ot); Philadelphia U. 56, C.W. Post 54; Southern N.H. 90, American Int'l 73; Alabama A&M 110, Paine 106 (2 ot); Tampa 83, Eckerd 61. **Regional Third Place:** Elizabeth City St. 88, Longwood 87; Central Mo. 79, West Tex. A&M 74; Alas. Anchorage 109, San Fran. St. 97; Gannon 75, Edinboro 66; Ky. Wesleyan 118, Oakland 91; North Dakota 97, Mesa St. 88; C.W. Post 84, American Int'l 81; Paine 57, Eckerd 52. **Regional Championships:** Norfolk St. 71, Virginia Union 69; Washburn 92, North Ala. 73; Cal St. Bakersfield 75, UC Riverside 62; Indiana (Pa.) 80, California (Pa.) 76; Southern Ind. 112, Wayne St. (Mich.) 84; South Dakota 61, North Dakota St. 58; Southern N.H. 79, Philadelphia U. 78 (2 ot); Alabama A&M 95, Tampa 90. **Quarterfinals:** Washburn 69, Norfolk St. 58; Cal St. Bakersfield 87, Indiana (Pa.) 69; Southern Ind. 98, South Dakota 77; Southern N.H. 100, Alabama A&M 90. **Semifinals:** Cal St. Bakersfield 67, Washburn 64; Southern Ind. 111, Southern N.H. 89. **Championship:** Cal St. Bakersfield 92, Southern Ind. 86.

1995 First Round: Gannon 82, Bloomsburg 81; Millersville 61, West Chester 60; Central Mo. 95, North Ala. 75; Mississippi Col. 87, Washburn 80 (2 ot); UC Davis 92, Grand Canyon 88 (ot); Cal St. L.A. 70, Cal St. Bakersfield 66 (ot); Morningside 92, North Dakota 86; North Dakota St. 85, Mesa St. 76; Shaw 83, Longwood 76; Johnson C. Smith 72, Lenoir-Rhyne 71; Eckerd 82, Lander 79; Armstrong Atlantic 78, Morehouse 70; Philadelphia U. 72, Adelphi 60; Southern N.H. 94, Dowling 79; Quincy 116, Oakland 94; Southern Ind. 95, Hillsdale 86. **Regional Semifinals:** Indiana (Pa.) 93, Gannon 71; California (Pa.) 93, Millersville 66; Central Mo. 80, Mo. Western St. 78; Central Okla. 94, Mississippi Col. 88; UC Riverside 84, UC Davis 66; Seattle Pacific 76, Cal St. L.A. 68; Morningside 93, Regis (Colo.) 70; Fort Hays St. 73, North Dakota St. 63; Virginia Union 94, Shaw 73; Norfolk St. 89, Johnson C. Smith 61; Alabama A&M 75, Eckerd 58; Tampa 65, Armstrong Atlantic 59; Philadelphia U. 84, St. Anselm 82; Southern N.H. 113, St. Rose 110 (ot); Northern Ky. 97, Quincy 91; Southern Ind. 102, Ky. Wesleyan 81. **Regional Third Place:** Millersville 89, Gannon 76 (ot); Mississippi Col. 90, Mo. Western St. 77; Cal St. L.A. 78, UC Davis 74; North Dakota St. 84, Regis (Colo.) 72; Shaw 96, Johnson C. Smith 90; Eckerd 72, Armstrong Atlantic 70; St. Anselm 109, St. Rose 92; Quincy 111, Ky. Wesleyan 104. **Regional Championships:** Indiana (Pa.) 80, California (Pa.) 69; Central Mo. 117, Central Okla. 112; UC Riverside 74, Seattle Pacific 68; Morningside 85, Fort Hays St. 82; Norfolk St. 84, Virginia Union 66; Alabama A&M 79, Tampa 78; Southern N.H. 84, Philadelphia U. 62; Southern Ind. 102, Northern Ky. 94. **Quarterfinals:** Indiana (Pa.) 90, Central Mo. 79; UC Riverside 71, Morningside 58; Norfolk St. 85, Alabama A&M 67; Southern Ind. 108, Southern N.H. 93. **Semifinals:** UC Riverside 73, Indiana (Pa.) 69; Southern Ind. 89, Norfolk St. 81. **Championship:** Southern Ind. 71, UC Riverside 63.

1996 First Round: Edinboro 90, Bloomsburg 82; Fairmont St. 78, Bluefield St. 66; S.C. Upstate 91, Clark Atlanta 71; Columbus St. 88, Rollins 80 (ot); Regis (Colo.) 73, Neb.-Kearney 70; North Dakota St. 71, Denver 70; Central Mo. 89, Tex. A&M-Commerce 86 (ot); North Ala. 78, Delta St. 69; Franklin Pierce 83, Le Moyne 53; Southern N.H. 68, Adelphi 52; Pfeiffer 71, N.C. Central 62; High Point 76, Presbyterian 67; Grand Canyon 105, Alas. Anchorage 96 (ot); UC Davis 89, Mont. St.-Billings 80; Indianapolis 105, Lake Superior St. 81; Northern St. 98, Oakland 92. **Regional Semifinals:** California (Pa.) 84, Edinboro 76; Indiana (Pa.) 84, Fairmont St. 83; Alabama A&M 106, S.C. Upstate 91; Columbus St. 83, Fla. Southern 77; Fort Hays St. 97, Regis (Colo.) 69; South Dakota St. 94, North Dakota St. 88; Mo.-Rolla 72, Central Mo. 67; North Ala. 85, Tex. A&M-Kingsville 80; St. Anselm 78, Franklin Pierce 70; St. Rose 83, Southern N.H. 82; Virginia Union 49, Pfeiffer 47; Queens (N.C.) 81, High Point 70; Cal St. Bakersfield 71, Grand Canyon 65; Seattle Pacific 79, UC Davis 65; Southern Ind. 75, Indianapolis 71; Northern Ky. 82, Northern St. 71. **Regional Championships:** California (Pa.) 78, Indiana (Pa.) 68; Alabama A&M 98, Columbus St. 82; Fort Hays St. 99, South Dakota St. 90; North Ala. 92, Mo.-Rolla 80; St. Rose 87, St. Anselm 76; Virginia Union 81, Queens (N.C.) 58; Cal St. Bakersfield 78, Seattle Pacific 65; Northern Ky. 99, Southern Ind. 87. **Quarterfinals:** California (Pa.) 95, Alabama A&M 85; Fort Hays St. 71, North Ala. 68; Virginia Union 99, St. Rose 72; Northern Ky. 56, Cal St. Bakersfield 55. **Semifinals:** Fort Hays St. 76, California (Pa.) 56; Northern Ky. 68, Virginia Union 66. **Championship:** Fort Hays St. 70, Northern Ky. 63.

1997 First Round: St. Michael's 86, Adelphi 85 (ot); St. Rose 92, Le Moyne 76; Grand Canyon 78, UC Davis 66; Mont. St.-Billings 97, UC Riverside 86; High Point 94, Pitt.-Johnstown 92 (ot); Concord 79, Barton 74; St. Augustine's 93, GC&SU 87; Elizabeth City St. 77, Elon 70; North Dakota St. 90, Northern St. 89 (ot); Neb.-Kearney 90, Minn. Duluth 76; Delta St. 88, Albany St. (Ga.) 64; Tampa 83, West Ga. 61; Pittsburg St. 72, Mo. Western St. 70; Tex. A&M-Commerce 80, Central Mo. 74; Oakland 79, Grand Valley St. 74; Quincy 125, Southern Ind. 118 (3 ot). **Regional Semifinals:** Southern N.H. 101, St. Michael's 90; Southern Conn. St. 83, St. Rose 80; Cal St. Bakersfield 80, Grand Canyon 70; Mont. St.-Billings 97, Alas. Anchorage 67; Salem Int'l 91, High Point 82; Concord 111, Mansfield 96; St. Augustine's 78, N.C. Central 66; Elizabeth City St. 76, Presbyterian 64; Fort Hays St. 82, North Dakota St. 78; South Dakota St. 102, Neb.-Kearney 83; Alabama A&M 81, Delta St. 80; Lynn 81, Tampa 76; Pittsburg St. 90, Central Okla. 84; Tex. A&M-Commerce 80, Washburn 75; Oakland 75, Indianapolis 72; Northern Ky. 82, Quincy 54. **Regional Championships:** Southern Conn. St. 80, Southern N.H. 61; Cal St. Bakersfield 90, Mont. St.-Billings 78; Salem Int'l 85, Concord 76; Elizabeth City St. 90, St. Augustine's 73; South Dakota St. 86, Fort Hays St. 74; Lynn 87, Alabama A&M 82; Tex. A&M-Commerce 89, Pittsburg St. 83; Northern

CHAMPIONSHIPS

Ky. 101, Oakland 87. **Quarterfinals:** Cal St. Bakersfield 65, Southern Conn. St. 62; Salem Int'l 91, Elizabeth City St. 74; Lynn 78, South Dakota St. 72; Northern Ky. 79, Tex. A&M-Commerce 67. **Semifinals:** Cal St. Bakersfield 81, Salem Int'l 68; Northern Ky. 79, Lynn 58. **Championship:** Cal St. Bakersfield 57, Northern Ky. 56.

1998 First Round: Pittsburg St. 85, Northwest Mo. St. 70; Central Okla. 107, Tex. A&M-Commerce 103; Cal St. L.A. 58, Grand Canyon 53; Seattle Pacific 82, Mont. St.-Billings 64; Assumption 87, Adelphi 63; Southern N.H. 89, Dowling 62; Edinboro 79, California (Pa.) 78; Pitt.-Johnstown 80, Queens (N.C.) 72; Metro St. 69, Fort Hays St. 61; Neb.-Kearney 77, Colorado St.-Pueblo 74; S.C. Upstate 95, Johnson C. Smith 67; S.C.-Aiken 74, Columbus St. 65; Albany St. (Ga.) 86, Fla. Southern 80; West Ga. 77, Fort Valley St. 74; Michigan Tech 76, Lewis 73; Northern Ky. 78, Ferris St. 63. **Regional Semifinals:** West Tex. A&M 90, Pittsburg St. 79; Central Okla. 109, Mo. Western St. 101; UC Davis 53, Cal St. L.A. 51; Seattle Pacific 62, Cal St. Bakersfield 60; St. Rose 87, Assumption 80; Stonehill 78, Southern N.H. 67 (ot); Salem Int'l 91, Edinboro 83; Fairmont St. 75, Pitt.-Johnstown 74; South Dakota St. 93, Metro St. 79; Northern St. 92, Neb.-Kearney 86; Virginia Union 91, S.C. Upstate 61; Catawba 82, S.C.-Aiken 76; Delta St. 84, Albany St. (Ga.) 62; Lynn 104, West Ga. 92; Ky. Wesleyan 78, Michigan Tech 68; Southern Ind. 81, Northern Ky. 66. **Regional Championships:** West Tex. A&M 105, Central Okla. 101; UC Davis 80, Seattle Pacific 52; St. Rose 97, Stonehill 87 (2 ot); Fairmont St. 79, Salem Int'l 78; Northern St. 88, South Dakota St. 82; Virginia Union 70, Catawba 58; Delta St. 63, Lynn 59 (ot); Ky. Wesleyan 98, Southern Ind. 79. **Quarterfinals:** UC Davis 63, West Tex. A&M 55; St. Rose 77, Fairmont St. 73 (ot); Virginia Union 67, Northern St. 63; Ky. Wesleyan 76, Delta St. 68. **Semifinals:** UC Davis 88, St. Rose 76; Ky. Wesleyan 80, Virginia Union 72. **Championship:** UC Davis 83, Ky. Wesleyan 77.

1999 First Round: Neb.-Kearney 85, Northern St. 80; South Dakota 79, Mesa St. 74; Charleston (W.V.) 79, West Chester 77; Queens (N.C.) 83, California (Pa.) 72; St. Michael's 87, Southern N.H. 76; Adelphi 57, Pace 56; Truman 82, Mo. Western St. 69; Abilene Christian 102, West Tex. A&M 96 (3 ot); Henderson St. 76, West Ga. 54; Lynn 83, Paine 71; Cal St. San B'dino 73, Sonoma St. 62; Seattle Pacific 83, Hawaii Pacific 61; Lander 68, Catawba 59; Winston-Salem 71, Elizabeth City St. 60; Northern Mich. 83, Lewis 77; Southern Ind. 89, Northwood 79. **Regional Semifinals:** Neb.-Kearney 94, Wayne St. (Neb.) 92 (ot); Metro St. 83, South Dakota 69; Salem Int'l 74, Charleston (W.V.) 60; Fairmont St. 61, Queens (N.C.) 54; St. Rose 78, St. Michael's 67; Adelphi 66, St. Anselm 50; Truman 81, Midwestern St. 68; Abilene Christian 79, Pittsburg St. 59; Henderson St. 76, LeMoyne-Owen 68; Fla. Southern 77, Lynn 69; Cal St. San B'dino 87, Central Wash. 71; Seattle Pacific 73, UC Davis 68; Lander 49, GC&SU 46; Winston-Salem 66, Wingate 63 (ot); Ky. Wesleyan 93, Northern Mich. 72; Southern Ind. 72, Wayne St. (Mich.) 69. **Regional Championships:** Metro St. 78, Neb.-Kearney 69; Salem Int'l 73, Fairmont St. 69; St. Rose 72, Adelphi 67 (2 ot); Truman 76, Abilene Christian 69; Fla. Southern 73, Henderson St. 63; Cal St. San B'dino 74, Seattle Pacific 67 (ot); Lander 47, Winston-Salem 46; Ky. Wesleyan 76, Southern Ind. 64. **Quarterfinals:** Metro St. 89, Salem Int'l 84; Truman 106, St. Rose 101 (3 ot); Fla. Southern 84, Cal St. San B'dino 69; Ky. Wesleyan 74, Lander 69. **Semifinals:** Metro St. 69, Truman 65; Ky. Wesleyan 87, Fla. Southern 67. **Championship:** Ky. Wesleyan 75, Metro St. 60.

2000 First Round: Delta St. 67, Henderson St. 64; Ala.-Huntsville 88, LeMoyne-Owen 71; Washburn 82, Drury 74; Northeastern St. 60, Northwest Mo. St. 56; St. Anselm 93, American Int'l 85; Merrimack 92, St. Rose 64; North Dakota 73, South Dakota St. 67; Wayne St. (Neb.) 90, St. Cloud St. 80; GC&SU 92, Gardner-Webb 81; Columbus St. 80, Virginia Union 60; UC Davis 60, BYU-Hawaii 53; Cal St. San B'dino 61, Cal St. L.A. 54; Indiana (Pa.) 79, Fairmont St. 73; Salem Int'l 74, St. Andrews 65; Northern Ky. 89, Northern Mich. 57; Michigan Tech 91, Gannon 86. **Regional Semifinals:** Fla. Southern 81, Delta St. 55; Tampa 64, Ala.-Huntsville 55; Mo. Southern St. 79, Washburn 73 (ot); Midwestern St. 91, Northeastern St. 88; St. Anselm 83, Southern Conn. St. 70; Adelphi 90, Merrimack 64; Metro St. 82, North Dakota 58; Wayne St. (Neb.) 86, South Dakota 83; GC&SU 72, Winston-Salem 68; Columbus St. 67, Wingate 57; Seattle Pacific 68, UC Davis 61; Central Wash. 101, Cal St. San B'dino 88; Indiana (Pa.) 108, Charleston (W.V.) 81; Pfeiffer 99, Salem Int'l 95; Ky. Wesleyan 66, Northern Ky. 62; Southern Ind. 85, Michigan Tech 68. **Regional Finals:** Fla. Southern 67, Tampa 53; Mo. Southern St. 92, Midwestern St. 83; St. Anselm 76, Adelphi 72; Metro St. 84, Wayne St. (Neb.) 72; GC&SU 68, Columbus St. 62; Seattle Pacific 85, Central Wash. 72; Indiana (Pa.) 104, Pfeiffer 71; Ky. Wesleyan 88, Southern Ind. 79. **Quarterfinals:** Mo. Southern St. 76, Fla. Southern 65; Metro St. 81, St. Anselm 61; Seattle Pacific 77, GC&SU 65; Ky. Wesleyan 84, Indiana (Pa.) 68. **Semifinals:** Metro St. 75, Mo. Southern St. 74; Ky. Wesleyan 87, Seattle Pacific 81 (ot). **Championship:** Metro St. 97, Ky. Wesleyan 79.

2001 First Round: Hillsdale 60, Gannon 58; Northern Ky. 106, Grand Valley St. 102; Metro St. 91, South Dakota St. 80; Southwest Minn. St. 88, Winona St. 77; Philadelphia U. 90, St. Anselm 77; Mass.-Lowell 85, Queens (N.Y.) 67; Henderson St. 68, West Ga. 57; Tampa 83, Kentucky St. 68; Wingate 88, Armstrong Atlantic 67; Augusta St. 96, Catawba 84; West Tex. A&M 67, St. Mary's (Tex.) 55; Northeastern St. 80, Angelo St. 75; Longwood 103, West Chester 95; Salem Int'l 77, Clarion 72; Cal St. Bakersfield 99, Humboldt St. 88; Central Wash. 101, Seattle Pacific 95. **Regional Semifinals:** Ky. Wesleyan 73, Hillsdale 71; Northern Ky. 93, Southern Ind. 92 (ot); St. Cloud St. 100, Metro St. 61; Southwest Minn. St. 82, Fort Hays St. 63; Adelphi 87, Philadelphia U. 66; St. Michael's 80, Mass.-Lowell 69; Henderson St. 69, Fla. Southern 64 (ot); Tampa 67, Eckerd 56; Johnson C. Smith 92, Wingate 60; Winston-Salem 65, Augusta St. 48; Washburn 86, West Tex. A&M 61; Northwest Mo. St. 62, Northeastern St. 60; Queens (N.C.) 77, Longwood 76; Salem Int'l 88, Charleston (W.V.) 70; Western Wash. 95, Cal St. Bakersfield 86 (ot); Cal St. San B'dino 79, Central Wash. 74. **Regional Finals:** Ky. Wesleyan 59, Northern Ky. 57; Southwest Minn. St. 67, St. Cloud St. 65; Adelphi 78, St. Michael's 66; Tampa 60, Henderson St. 51; Johnson C. Smith 64, Winston-Salem 52; Washburn 67, Northwest Mo. St. 61; Queens (N.C.) 81, Salem Int'l 67; Western Wash. 58, Cal St. San B'dino 55. **Quarterfinals:** Ky. Wesleyan 85, Southwest Minn. St. 66; Tampa 82, Adelphi 68; Washburn 70, Johnson C. Smith 64; Western Wash. 89, Queens (N.C) 85. **Semifinals:** Ky. Wesleyan 85, Tampa 84 (ot); Washburn 96, Western Wash. 90. **Championship:** Ky. Wesleyan 72, Washburn 63.

2002 First Round: Charleston (W.V.) 96, Alderson-Broaddus 93 (ot); Belmont Abbey 76, West Va. Wesleyan 59; Rockhurst 75, Mo. Western St. 68; Incarnate Word 72, Tarleton St. 59; Cal St. Bakersfield 84, Mont. St.-Billings 81; Seattle Pacific 82, BYU-Hawaii 57; Neb.-Omaha 88, Fort Lewis 58; Metro St. 66, Minn. Duluth 61; Johnson C. Smith 73, Augusta St. 70; Winston-Salem 90, Wingate 75; West Ga. 76, Delta St. 71; Valdosta St. 62, Paine 57; Mass.-Lowell 72, Bentley 70; Pace 92, Queens (N.Y.) 88; Findlay 70, Gannon 53; Lewis 67, Hillsdale 53. **Second Round:** Indiana (Pa.) 91, Charleston (W.V.) 81; Salem Int'l 75, Belmont Abbey 69; Rockhurst 75, Northeastern St. 70 (2 ot); Northwest Mo. St. 61, Incarnate Word 56; Cal St. San B'dino 66, Cal St. Bakersfield 62; Humboldt St. 89, Seattle Pacific 82; South Dakota St. 96, Neb.-Omaha 76; Metro St. 59, Neb.-Kearney 51; Carson-Newman 77, Johnson C. Smith 66; Shaw 62, Winston-Salem 61; West Ga. 77, Tampa 69; Valdosta St. 80, Henderson St. 54; Adelphi 72, Mass.-Lowell 57; Assumption 91, Pace 73; Ky. Wesleyan 94, Findlay 89; Lewis 62, Michigan Tech 51. **Regional Finals:** Indiana (Pa.) 85, Salem Int'l 81; Northwest Mo. St. 79, Rockhurst 73; Cal St. San B'dino 80, Humboldt St. 65; Metro St. 87, South Dakota St. 86; Shaw 69, Carson-Newman 68; West Ga. 81, Valdosta St. 69; Adelphi 77, Assumption 56; Ky. Wesleyan 80, Lewis 75. **Quarterfinals:** Indiana (Pa.) 78, Northwest Mo. St. 72; Metro St. 65, Cal St. San B'dino 48; Shaw 102, West Ga. 84; Ky. Wesleyan 71, Adelphi 46. **Semifinals:** Metro St. 82, Indiana (Pa.) 52; Ky. Wesleyan 101, Shaw 92. **Championship:** Metro St. 80, Ky. Wesleyan 72.

2003 First Round: Mass.-Lowell 91, St. Rose 68; Bridgeport 64, Adelphi 56; New Haven 76, Southern N.H. 71; C.W. Post 81, Assumption 75 (ot); Presbyterian 71, Columbus St. 59; Shaw 72, Johnson C. Smith 58; Kennesaw St. 74, Virginia Union 65; Bowie St. 88, Lenoir-Rhyne 82; Cal St. Bakersfield 50, BYU-Hawaii 41; Cal Poly Pomona 80, Alas. Fairbanks 76; Humboldt St. 102, Hawaii-Hilo 81; Cal St. San B'dino 86, Sonoma St. 58; Michigan Tech 90, Indianapolis 75; Southern Ind. 82, Lewis 63; Findlay 80, Northern Ky. 76; *Ky. Wesleyan 81, Gannon 74; Queens (N.C.) 72, West Chester 58; Salem Int'l 76, California (Pa.) 73; Millersville 62, Belmont Abbey 56; Barton 81, Alderson-Broaddus 76; Rollins 76, Ala.-Huntsville 61; Eckerd 83, Morehouse 66; Delta St. 72, Fla. Southern 70; Henderson St. 67, Harding 59; Tarleton St. 56, St. Mary's (Tex.) 43; Northwest Mo. St. 71, Mo. Western St. 61; Washburn 75, West Tex. A&M 73; Northeastern St. 78, Central Okla. 67; Neb.-Kearney 72, Minn. Duluth 67; South Dakota St. 84, Fort Hays St. 78; Metro St. 85, Fort Lewis 63; St. Cloud St. 74, North Dakota 69. **Second Round:** Mass.-Lowell 86, Bridgeport 73; C.W. Post 78, New Haven 61; Presbyterian 77, Shaw 58; Bowie St. 95, Kennesaw St. 70; Cal Poly Pomona 62, Cal St. Bakersfield 49; Cal St. San B'dino 80, Humboldt St. 68; Southern Ind. 74, Michigan Tech 71; *Ky. Wesleyan 83, Findlay 66; Queens (N.C.) 100, Salem Int'l 87; Millersville 80, Barton 63; Eckerd 74, Rollins 70; Henderson St. 67, Delta St. 60; Tarleton St. 73, Northwest Mo. St. 58; Northeastern St. 64, Washburn 59; Neb.-Kearney 86, South Dakota St. 85; Metro St. 75, St. Cloud St. 63. **Regional Finals:** Mass.-Lowell 69, C.W. Post 59; Bowie St. 67, Presbyterian 53; Cal Poly Pomona 91, Cal St. San B'dino 84 (2 ot); *Ky. Wesleyan 95, Southern Ind. 91; Queens (N.C.) 94, Millersville 77; Eckerd 85, Henderson St. 75; Northeastern St. 56, Tarleton St. 46; Neb.-Kearney 94, Metro St. 87 (2 ot). **Quarterfinals:** Bowie St. 72, Mass.-Lowell 62; *Ky. Wesleyan 85, Cal Poly Pomona 60; Queens (N.C.) 99, Eckerd 78; Northeastern St. 94, Neb.-Kearney 75. **Semifinals:** *Ky. Wesleyan 84, Bowie St. 64; Northeastern St. 84, Queens (N.C.) 69. **Championship:** Northeastern St. 75, *Ky. Wesleyan 64.

**Ky. Wesleyan's participation in the 2003 tournament vacated.*

2004 First Round: Tarleton St. 77, Tex. A&M-Kingsville 74; Drury 85, Emporia St. 81; Northwest Mo. St. 77, Eastern N.M. 57; Washburn 81, St. Mary's (Tex.) 70; Wayne St. (Mich.) 65, Lewis 62; Michigan Tech 81, Gannon 75; Southern Ind. 96, Ky. Wesleyan 83; Findlay 84, Indianapolis 83 (ot); Metro St. 102, Mesa St. 72; South Dakota St. 99, Northern St. 80; South Dakota 82, Neb.-Omaha 71; Neb.-Kearney 104, Bemidji St. 90; Montevallo 56, Valdosta St. 49; Henderson St. 71, Morehouse 51; Eckerd 70, Fla. Southern 62; Rollins 88, Benedict 79; Pfeiffer 104, Indiana (Pa.) 91; Cheyney 76, California (Pa.) 59; West Virginia St. 80, Dist. Columbia 69; Alderson-Broaddus 85, Mount Olive 80; Kennesaw St. 78, Catawba 63; Columbus St. 77, Virginia Union 75; Bowie St. 86, Lenoir-Rhyne 81; Francis Marion 86, Armstrong Atlantic 84; Mass.-Lowell 74, Bridgeport 64; Southern N.H. 74, New Haven 67; NYIT 81, Philadelphia U. 75; Bryant 65, C.W. Post 63; Cal St. San B'dino 92, Cal St. Chico 60; Alas. Fairbanks 91, Cal St. Bakersfield 82; Humboldt St. 86, Cal Poly Pomona 83; BYU-Hawaii 67, Alas. Anchorage 61. **Second Round:** Drury 78, Tarleton St. 73 (ot); Northwest Mo. St. 62, Washburn 61; Wayne St. (Mich.) 57, Michigan Tech 54; Southern Ind. 75, Findlay 67; Metro St. 109, South Dakota St. 69; Neb.-Kearney 96, South Dakota 80; Montevallo 78, Henderson St. 57; Rollins 77, Eckerd 54; Pfeiffer 121, Cheyney 101; Alderson-Broaddus 87, West Virginia St. 71; Kennesaw St. 70, Columbus St. 55; Francis Marion 95, Bowie St. 78; Mass.-Lowell 67, Southern N.H. 61 (ot); Bryant 64, NYIT 60; Alas. Fairbanks 82, Cal St. San B'dino 78 (ot); Humboldt St. 71, BYU-Hawaii 61. **Regional Finals:** Northwest Mo. St. 62, Drury 59; Southern Ind. 69, Wayne St. (Mich.) 68; Metro St. 79, Neb.-Kearney 68; Rollins 75, Montevallo 63; Pfeiffer 106, Alderson-Broaddus 77; Kennesaw St. 82, Francis Marion 73; Mass.-Lowell 63, Bryant 62; Humboldt St. 64, Alas. Fairbanks 60. **Quarterfinals:** Southern Ind. 88, Northwest Mo. St. 81; Metro St. 88, Rollins 54; Kennesaw St. 86, Pfeiffer 79; Humboldt St. 89, Mass.-Lowell 82. **Semifinals:** Southern Ind. 83, Metro St. 81; Kennesaw St. 81, Humboldt St. 67. **Championship:** Kennesaw St. 84, Southern Ind. 59.

2005 First Round: Bentley 85, Queens (N.Y.) 68; Southern N.H. 80, St. Rose 71; Bryant 69, Adelphi 48; Bloomfield 79, St. Anselm 77; Pfeiffer 110, Wheeling Jesuit 94; Salem Int'l 72, Alderson-Broaddus 61; Indiana (Pa.) 76, Edinboro 73; Mount Olive 86, Millersville 78; Tex. A&M-Commerce 62, Southwestern Okla. 57; Central Okla. 84, Washburn 66; Pittsburg St. 73, St. Mary's (Tex.) 59; Tarleton St. 75, Central Mo. 72; Western Wash. 80, BYU-Hawaii 69; Alas. Fairbanks 65, Cal St. San B'dino 59; Cal Poly Pomona 82, Seattle Pacific 77; Hawaii-Hilo 83, Cal St. Chico 81; Lynn 89, Lane 61; Central Ark. 74, West Ga. 71; Eckerd 81, Fla. Gulf Coast 79; Montevallo 74, Barry 48; Findlay 83, Quincy 73; Wayne St. (Mich.) 56, SIU Edwardsville 55; Ferris St. 99, Indianapolis 79; Southern Ind. 67, Gannon 61; Metro St. 83, Northern St. 60; Minn. St. Mankato 86, Fort Lewis 78; South Dakota 94, Neb.-Kearney 84; Winona St. 64, Neb.-Omaha 58; Bowie St. 91, Tusculum 88; Columbus St. 83, Kennesaw St. 78; S.C. Upstate 63, Winston-Salem 59; Virginia Union 85, Catawba 81. **Second Round:** Bentley 90, Southern N.H. 84; Bryant 76, Bloomfield 59; Salem Int'l 105, Pfeiffer 92; Mount Olive 72, Indiana (Pa.) 64; Tex. A&M-Commerce 81, Central Okla. 73; Tarleton St. 65, Pittsburg St. 59; Alas. Fairbanks 88, Western Wash. 66; Cal Poly Pomona 73, Hawaii-Hilo 62; Lynn 73, Central Ark. 69; Montevallo 65, Eckerd 62; Findlay 63, Wayne St. (Mich.) 49; Ferris St. 93, Southern Ind. 87; Metro St. 85, Minn. St. Mankato 64; South Dakota 73, Winona St. 68; Bowie St. 84, Columbus St. 72; Virginia Union 85, S.C. Upstate 67. **Regional Finals:** Bryant 74, Bentley 64; Mount Olive 80, Salem Int'l 73; Tarleton St. 75, Tex. A&M-Commerce 70; Cal Poly Pomona 65, Alas. Fairbanks 58; Lynn 67, Montevallo 54; Findlay 94,

Ferris St. 73; Metro St. 89, South Dakota 84; Virginia Union 70, Bowie St. 64. **Quarterfinals:** Bryant 84, Mount Olive 69; Tarleton St. 58, Cal Poly Pomona 56; Lynn 75, Findlay 66; Virginia Union 78, Metro St. 63. **Semifinals:** Bryant 60, Tarleton St. 55; Virginia Union 76, Lynn 61. **Championship:** Virginia Union 63, Bryant 58.

2006 First Round: Delta St. 76, Stillman 70; Ark.-Monticello 90, North Ala. 81; Rollins 63, Ala.-Huntsville 58; Montevallo 69, Benedict 59; Seattle Pacific 86, Central Wash. 76; Cal St. Bakersfield 71, Sonoma St. 65; Chaminade 84, Alas. Anchorage 67; Western Wash. 100, Humboldt St. 86; St. Joseph's (Ind.) 74, Ferris St. 69; Southern Ind. 78, Drury 58; Quincy 74, Findlay 67; SIU Edwardsville 65, Grand Valley St. 61; Virginia Union 82, Wingate 66; Columbus St. 90, S.C. Upstate 88 (ot); GC&SU 86, Johnson C. Smith 68; Presbyterian 73, Armstrong Atlantic 67; Winona St. 81, South Dakota 69 (ot); Minn. St. Mankato 82, Neb.-Kearney 70; Northern St. 72, Metro St. 67; Fort Hays St. 69, St. Cloud St. 54; Barton 93, Wheeling Jesuit 70; Mount Olive 86, Shippensburg 83; Alderson-Broaddus 64, Salem Int'l 58; West Virginia St. 103, Edinboro 89; Stonehill 96, Bloomfield 77; Adelphi 90, Bentley 86; Mass.-Lowell 77, Bryant 67; St. Anselm 83, Bridgeport 63; Southwest Baptist 75, St. Edward's 70; Northwest Mo. St. 66, West Tex. A&M 51; Central Mo. 67, Truman 63 (ot); Tarleton St. 75, Central Okla. 68. **Second Round:** Ark.-Monticello 83, Delta St. 68; Montevallo 81, Rollins 68; Seattle Pacific 81, Cal St. Bakersfield 75; Western Wash. 101, Chaminade

91; Southern Ind. 81, St. Joseph's (Ind.) 78; SIU Edwardsville 80, Quincy 69; Virginia Union 75, Columbus St. 69; GC&SU 77, Presbyterian 58; Winona St. 74, Minn. St. Mankato 71; Northern St. 60, Fort Hays St. 58; Barton 82, Mount Olive 79; Alderson-Broaddus 88, West Virginia St. 82; Stonehill 69, Adelphi 54; Mass.-Lowell 74, St. Anselm 70; Northwest Mo. St. 83, Southwest Baptist 80; Tarleton St. 62, Central Mo. 59. **Regional Finals:** Montevallo 89, Ark.-Monticello 86 (ot); Seattle Pacific 81, Western Wash. 77; SIU Edwardsville 64, Southern Ind. 60 (ot); Virginia Union 76, GC&SU 73; Winona St. 96, Northern St. 86; Barton 73, Alderson-Broaddus 70; Stonehill 89, Mass.-Lowell 80; Tarleton St. 72, Northwest Mo. St. 71. **Quarterfinals:** Seattle Pacific 79, Montevallo 65; Virginia Union 60, SIU Edwardsville 58; Winona St. 86, Barton 78 (ot); Stonehill 69, Tarleton St. 59. **Semifinals:** Virginia Union 68, Seattle Pacific 63; Winona St. 83, Stonehill 73. **Championship:** Winona St. 73, Virginia Union 61.

2007 First Round: Findlay 70, Wis.Parkside 60; Northern Ky. 73, Drury 68; Grand Valley St. 85, Quincy 75; Southern Ind. 84, Rockhurst 78; Barton 85, Queens (N.C.) 76; West Virginia St. 91, Alderson-Broaddus 75; Millersville 89, Mount Olive 85; California (Pa.) 82; West Liberty St. 79 (ot); Augusta St. 79, Elizabeth City St. 63; Wingate 72, Armstrong Atlantic 68; Clayton St. 72, Catawba 69 (ot); Virginia Union 74, Lander 68 (ot); Humboldt St. 68, Alas. Anchorage 61; Grand Canyon 87, Seattle Pacific 65; Seattle 69, Cal Poly Pomona 55; Cal St. San B'dino 71, BYU-Hawaii 68; Montevallo 78, Albany St.

(Ga.) 62; Henderson St. 58, Barry 44; Eckerd 66, Benedict 56; Rollins 61, Valdosta St. 60; Central Mo. 76, St. Edward's 39; Northwest Mo. St. 74, Pittsburg St. 53; Midwestern St. 86, West Tex. A&M 81; Southeastern Okla. St. 79, Emporia St. 66; Bentley 59, Caldwell 56; Bridgeport 67, Philadelphia U. 65; Bryant 77, Aldelphi 55; St. Rose 87, Pace 71; Winona St. 100, St. Cloud St. 73; Neb.-Kearney 95, South Dakota 88; Metro St. 71, Adams St. 48; Minn. St. Mankato 85, Fort Lewis 71. **Second Round:** Northern Ky. 60, Findlay 56; Grand Valley St. 90, Southern Ind. 83; Barton 88, West Virginia St. 85; Millersville 82, California (Pa.) 72; Wingate 79, Augusta St. 78; Virginia Union 71, Clayton St. 70 (ot); Humboldt St. 95, Grand Canyon 81; Cal St. San B'dino 72, Seattle 66; Montevallo 68, Henderson St. 58 (ot); Eckerd 85, Rollins 76; Central Mo. 72, Northwest Mo. St. 61; Southeastern Okla. St. 88, Midwestern St. 77 (ot); Bentley 60, Bridgeport 45; Bryant 65, St. Rose 62; Winona St. 81, Neb.-Kearney 70; Minn. St. Mankato 70, Metro St. 68. **Regional Finals:** Grand Valley St. 66, Northern Ky. 42; Barton 76, Millersville 65; Wingate 73, Virginia Union 56; Cal St. San B'dino 68, Humboldt St. 66; Montevallo 64, Eckerd 61; Central Mo. 67, Southeastern Okla. St. 54; Bentley 63, Bryant 54; Winona St. 89, Minn. St. Mankato 76. **Quarterfinals:** Barton 83, Grand Valley St. 81 (ot); Cal St. San B'dino 100, Wingate 73; Central Mo. 86, Montevallo 69;Winona St. 64, Bentley 51. **Semifinals:** Barton 80, Cal St. San B'dino 79; Winona St. 90, Central Mo. 85 (ot). **Championship:** Barton 77, Winona St. 75.

Division III Championship

2007 Results

FIRST ROUND

St. John's (Minn.) 85, Loras 82 (ot)
Washington-St. Louis 77, Fontbonne 58
Whitworth 62, DePauw 59
Calvin 69, Aurora 68
Hope 76, Chicago 54
Carroll (Wis.) 73, Augustana (Ill.) 69
Catholic 58, Messiah 37
Lincoln (Pa.) 91, Alvernia 76
Johns Hopkins 84, Villa Julie 72
Guilford 101, Manhattanville 81
Va. Wesleyan 63, Averett 60
Hampden-Sydney 68, Hood 65
Mississippi Col. 68, Occidental 51
Maryville (Tenn.) 73, Mary Hardin-Baylor 62
Widener 73, King's (Pa.) 63
Ramapo 77, York (N.Y.) 68
Stevens Inst. 68, WPI 57
Rhode Island Col. 64, Coast Guard 60
Brandeis 77, Trinity (Conn.) 70 (ot)
Keene St. 81, Rivier 47

St. John Fisher 98, Wentworth Inst. 72
Plattsburgh St. 61, Rochester 60
St. Lawrence 85, Elms 79
Brockport 74, Williams 66
Wooster 92, Transylvania 66
Centre 69, Capital 55
John Carroll 87, Westminster (Pa.) 83

SECOND ROUND

Wis.-Stevens Point 93, St. John's (Minn.) 76
Washington-St. Louis 63, Whitworth 61
Hope 80, Calvin 64
Carroll (Wis.) 86, St. Thomas (Minn.) 80
Lincoln (Pa.) 81, Catholic 70
Guilford 80, Johns Hopkins 73
Va. Wesleyan 61, Hampden-Sydney 51
Mississippi Col. 76, Maryville (Tenn.) 62
Amherst 87, Widener 70
Stevens Inst. 69, Ramapo 61
Rhode Island Col. 70, Brandeis 67
Keene St. 76, Salem St. 75
St. John Fisher 95, Plattsburgh St. 87
Brockport 74, St. Lawrence 49
Wooster 73, Centre 56
John Carroll 79, Lake Erie 77

SECTIONAL SEMIFINALS

Washington-St. Louis 78, Wis.-Stevens Point 66
Hope 89, Carroll 77
Guilford 129, Lincoln (Pa.) 128 (3 ot)
Va. Wesleyan 81, Mississippi Col. 55
Amherst 97, Stevens Inst. 74
Rhode Island Col. 75, Keene St. 73
Brockport St. 105, St. John Fisher 91
Wooster 83, John Carroll 73

SECTIONAL CHAMPIONSHIPS

Washington-St. Louis 58, Hope 55
Va. Wesleyan 81, Guilford 71
Amherst 81, Rhode Island Col. 69
Wooster 94, Brockport St. 87

SEMIFINALS

Va. Wesleyan 67, Washington-St. Louis 65
Amherst 67, Wooster 60

THIRD PLACE

Washington-St. Louis 92, Wooster 84

CHAMPIONSHIP

Amherst 80, Va. Wesleyan 67

Box Scores

SEMIFINALS
MARCH 16, AT SALEM, VIRGINIA

Va. Wesleyan 67, Washington-St. Louis 65

Va. Wesleyan

No.	Player	TOT-FG FG	FGA	3-PT FG	FGA	FT	FTA	REBOUNDS OFF	DEF	TOT	PF	TP	A	TO	BLK	S	MIN
00	TonTon Balenga	* 2	5	1	3	5	6	1	2	3	1	10	1	6	0	0	25
11	Thomas Sumpter	* 0	2	0	0	0	0	0	1	1	3	0	6	0	0	3	20
14	Terrell Dixon	* 4	7	1	3	0	0	0	1	1	3	9	1	0	0	1	34
30	Brandon Adair	*12	12	0	0	1	3	4	2	6	4	25	1	3	0	1	33
40	Tyler Fantin	* 3	8	2	5	2	2	0	5	5	4	10	2	1	1	1	33
10	D'Juan Tucker	1	5	1	4	1	2	0	3	3	1	4	4	1	0	1	22
33	T.J. Williams	0	0	0	0	0	0	0	0	0	0	0	0	0	0	0	5
34	Stephen Fields	3	5	1	2	2	3	0	2	2	2	9	0	2	0	0	14
44	Norman Hassell	0	2	0	2	0	0	0	0	0	1	0	1	0	0	0	14
	TEAM	0	0					0	0	0	0	0	0	0	0	0	0
	Totals	25	46	6	19	11	16	5	16	21	19	67	16	13	1	6	200

Deadball Rebounds: 5

Washington-St. Louis

No.	Player	TOT-FG FG	FGA	3-PT FG	FGA	FT	FTA	REBOUNDS OFF	DEF	TOT	PF	TP	A	TO	BLK	S	MIN
12	Sean Wallis	* 5	10	2	5	5	6	0	2	2	2	17	8	6	0	1	37
21	Tyler Nading	* 4	5	0	0	0	0	2	1	3	3	8	1	2	0	2	22
30	Nick Nikitas	* 3	7	0	2	2	2	0	0	0	1	8	2	3	0	0	34
33	Aaron Thompson	* 1	2	1	1	2	2	0	2	2	1	5	1	0	0	0	34
50	Troy Ruths	* 8	17	0	0	5	5	4	3	7	5	21	0	2	0	1	34
20	Ray Wagner	0	1	0	0	0	0	0	0	0	0	0	0	1	0	0	4
23	Phil Syvertsen	0	0	0	0	0	0	0	0	0	3	0	0	1	0	0	11
34	Cameron Smith	0	0	0	0	0	0	0	0	0	0	0	0	1	0	0	15
44	Zach Kelly	2	3	1	1	1	2	1	4	5	2	6	0	0	0	0	9
	Team	0	0	0	0	0	0	0	2	2	0	0	0	2	0	0	0
	Totals	23	45	4	9	15	17	7	14	21	17	65	12	18	0	4	200

Deadball Rebounds: 3

Officials: Curt Seter; Roland Simmons; Gary Wild
Technical fouls: Va. Wesleyan-None. Washington-St. Louis-None.

Score by Periods	1	2	Total
Va. Wesleyan	25	42	67
Washington-St. Louis	28	37	65

Amherst 67, Wooster 60

Wooster

No.	Player	TOT-FG		3-PT				REBOUNDS									
		FG	FGA	FG	FGA	FT	FTA	OFF	DEF	TOT	PF	TP	A	TO	BLK	S	MIN
10	Brandon Johnson *	1	5	0	2	3	5	1	6	7	2	5	2	2	0	0	31
22	James Cooper *	4	10	3	7	1	2	1	2	3	1	12	1	1	0	1	35
30	Andy Van Horn *	2	4	1	1	1	1	1	1	2	3	6	3	0	0	1	22
33	Tom Port *	3	9	1	6	6	7	0	4	4	0	13	2	5	1	1	37
40	Evan Will *	1	1	0	0	0	0	1	0	1	0	2	0	0	0	0	15
14	Marty Bidwell	0	2	0	1	0	0	0	3	3	1	0	1	4	0	0	16
24	Devin Fulk	1	4	0	2	0	0	1	2	3	2	2	1	1	0	1	15
34	Tim Vandervaart	9	10	0	0	2	2	0	4	4	4	20	2	2	1	2	28
	TEAM	0	0	0	0	0	0	0	3	3							0
	Totals	21	45	5	19	13	17	5	25	30	16	60	12	15	2	5	200

Deadball Rebounds: 1

Amherst

No.	Player	TOT-FG		3-PT				REBOUNDS									
		FG	FGA	FG	FGA	FT	FTA	OFF	DEF	TOT	PF	TP	A	TO	BLK	S	MIN
1	Andrew Olson *	4	11	1	6	6	6	1	5	6	1	15	9	5	0	3	40
20	Tim McLaughlin *	6	12	4	7	0	1	2	6	8	4	16	2	1	1	2	37
24	Brian Baskauskas *	2	4	2	3	3	4	0	4	4	3	9	1	0	0	0	29
34	Dan O'Shea *	1	2	0	0	2	2	1	3	4	1	4	0	0	0	0	12
41	Dan Wheeler *	5	13	1	6	0	4	2	1	3	1	11	0	2	0	1	30
4	Mike Salerno	0	0	0	0	0	0	2	1	3	1	0	1	0	0	1	13
32	Fletcher Walters	1	2	1	1	0	0	1	0	1	2	3	1	0	0	0	11
44	Kevin Hopkins	3	8	0	0	3	3	0	1	1	2	9	0	3	0	0	25
52	Brandon Jones	0	1	0	0	0	0	0	1	1	0	0	0	1	0	0	3
	TEAM	0	0	0	0	0	0	1	0	1							
	Totals	22	53	9	23	14	20	10	22	32	15	67	14	12	1	7	200

Deadball Rebounds: 2

Attendance: 2,252
Officials: David Dence; Todd Sweeney; Carl Gerlitos
Technical fouls: Wooster-None. Amherst-None.

Score by Periods	1	2	Total
Wooster	25	35	60
Amherst	39	28	67

THIRD PLACE
MARCH 17, AT SALEM, VIRGINIA

Washington-St. Louis 92, Wooster 84

Wooster

No.	Player	TOT-FG		3-PT				REBOUNDS									
		FG	FGA	FG	FGA	FT	FTA	OFF	DEF	TOT	PF	TP	A	TO	BLK	S	MIN
10	Brandon Johnson *	7	15	0	3	1	1	0	2	2	3	15	6	4	0	2	32
22	James Cooper *	2	4	1	4	0	0	0	0	0	2	5	2	3	0	0	23
30	Andy Van Horn *	3	3	1	1	4	5	2	0	2	3	11	2	1	0	0	27
33	Tom Port *	4	17	4	12	1	3	1	1	2	4	13	5	1	1	3	31
34	Tim Vandervaart *	8	13	0	0	0	1	6	5	11	4	16	1	1	1	0	14
14	Marty Bidwell	2	4	0	1	0	0	1	5	6	4	4	1	1	0	0	25
24	Devin Fulk	5	11	3	5	0	0	4	6	10	2	13	0	2	1	0	15
40	Evan Will	2	4	1	2	2	4	2	1	3	3	7	0	3	0	0	0
	TEAM	0	0	0	0	0	0	2	1	3							
	Totals	33	78	10	28	8	14	18	21	39	25	84	17	15	3	7	200

Deadball Rebounds: 8

Washington St.-Louis

No.	Player	TOT-FG		3-PT				REBOUNDS									
		FG	FGA	FG	FGA	FT	FTA	OFF	DEF	TOT	PF	TP	A	TO	BLK	S	MIN
12	Sean Wallis *	6	13	1	6	8	9	0	4	4	2	21	8	3	0	3	37
21	Tyler Nading *	8	11	1	2	5	6	4	5	9	4	22	4	4	3	0	29
30	Nick Nikitas *	1	3	0	2	2	2	0	2	2	1	4	0	1	0	0	21
33	Aaron Thompson *	4	7	4	7	4	4	0	4	4	2	16	2	0	2	2	36
50	Troy Ruths *	5	12	0	0	7	8	2	6	8	5	17	1	4	0	0	26
11	Moss Schermerhorn	0	1	0	0	0	0	0	1	1	0	0	1	0	0	0	3
20	Ray Wagner	0	1	0	1	0	0	0	0	0	1	0	0	1	0	0	4
23	Phil Syvertsen	0	1	0	1	0	0	0	0	0	0	0	0	1	0	0	27
34	Cameron Smith	4	7	1	3	1	1	1	2	3	1	10	0	1	0	0	1
40	Cameron Williams	0	0	0	0	0	0	0	0	0	0	0	0	0	0	0	11
44	Zach Kelly	1	3	0	1	0	2	2	2	4	1	2	0	1	0	1	3
52	Jonathan Breshears	0	0	0	0	0	0	1	1	2	0	0	0	0	0	0	0
	TEAM	0	0	0	0	0	0	1	0	1							
	Totals	29	59	7	23	27	32	10	27	37	18	92	17	15	5	6	200

Deadball Rebounds: 2

Officials: Ted Kessler; Johnny Pearson; Craign Murley
Technical fouls: Wooster-None. Washington-St. Louis-None.

Score by Periods	1	2	Total
Wooster	35	49	84
Washington-St. Louis	34	58	92

CHAMPIONSHIP
MARCH 18, AT SALEM, VIRGINIA
Amherst 80, Va. Wesleyan 67

Amherst

No.	Player	TOT-FG FG	FGA	3-PT FG	FGA	FT	FTA	REB OFF	DEF	TOT	PF	TP	A	TO	BLK	S	MIN
1	Andrew Olson *	3	8	2	4	7	8	0	1	1	1	15	5	4	0	0	39
20	Tim McLaughlin *	5	10	1	3	1	1	0	5	5	3	12	2	1	1	1	30
24	Brian Baskauskas *	6	9	0	2	2	2	1	5	6	5	14	3	1	0	0	28
34	Dan O'Shea *	0	1	0	0	0	0	1	0	1	5	0	0	0	1	2	10
41	Dan Wheeler *	4	7	1	2	4	4	3	4	7	0	13	0	0	0	0	32
4	Mike Salerno	0	0	0	0	0	0	0	1	1	1	0	2	1	0	2	24
32	Fletcher Walters	2	4	1	3	2	2	0	0	0	1	7	0	0	0	1	8
44	Kevin Hopkins	3	6	0	0	6	7	2	3	5	4	12	0	0	2	0	15
52	Brandon Jones	0	5	0	0	7	8	1	2	3	2	7	0	1	0	0	15
	TEAM	0	0	0	0	0	0	0	1	1	0	0	0	1	0	0	14
	Totals	23	50	5	14	29	32	8	22	30	22	80	12	8	4	6	200

Deadball Rebounds: 2

Va. Wesleyan

No.	Player	TOT-FG FG	FGA	3-PT FG	FGA	FT	FTA	REB OFF	DEF	TOT	PF	TP	A	TO	BLK	S	MIN
11	Thomas Sumpter *	2	6	0	0	2	2	3	2	5	2	6	3	0	0	1	27
14	Terrell Dixon *	2	6	2	4	2	2	0	2	2	0	8	0	2	0	0	25
24	TonTon Balenga *	5	12	2	7	7	7	0	2	2	4	19	0	4	0	0	30
30	Brandon Adair *	7	9	0	0	3	11	4	1	5	4	17	0	2	0	1	40
40	Tyler Fantin *	1	6	0	0	2	2	2	6	8	4	4	1	1	1	0	22
10	D'Juan Tucker	0	1	0	0	1	2	0	2	2	0	1	0	0	0	1	15
32	Rodney Young	0	1	0	0	2	2	1	1	2	5	2	0	0	0	1	11
34	Stephen Fields	2	5	1	1	3	5	0	2	2	1	8	3	2	1	1	22
44	Norman Hassell	0	0	0	0	0	0	0	0	0	4	0	0	0	0	1	7
54	Travis Klink	1	1	0	0	0	0	0	0	0	0	2	0	0	0	0	1
	TEAM	0	0	0	0	0	0	0	1	1	0	0	0	1	0	0	0
	Totals	20	48	5	12	22	33	10	19	29	24	67	7	12	2	5	200

Deadball Rebounds: 8
Attendance: 3,075
Officials: Carl Gerlitos; Gregg Durich; Jeff Benedict
Technical fouls: Amherst-None. Va. Wesleyan-None.

Score by Periods	1	2	Total
Amherst	39	41	80
Va. Wesleyan	28	39	67

Year-by-Year Results

Season	Champion	Score	Runner-Up	Third Place	Fourth Place	Championship Game Attendance	Championship Total Attendance
1975	LeMoyne-Owen (27-5)	57-54	Rowan	Augustana (Ill.)	Brockport St.	1,800	—
1976	Scranton (29-3)	60-57	Wittenberg	Augustana (Ill.)	Plattsburgh St.	4,000	24,345
1977	Wittenberg (23-5)	79-66	Oneonta St.	Scranton	Hamline	2,100	25,748
1978	North Park (29-2)	69-57	Widener	Albion	Stony Brook	2,800	24,458
1979	North Park (26-5)	66-62	Potsdam St.	Frank. & Marsh.	Centre	3,500	31,230
1980	North Park (28-3)	83-76	Upsala	Wittenberg	Longwood	3,500	30,624
1981	Potsdam St. (30-2)	67-65 (ot)	Augustana (Ill.)	Ursinus	Otterbein	4,237	38,199
1982	Wabash (24-4)	83-62	Potsdam St.	Brooklyn	Cal St. Stanislaus	3,500	33,661
1983	Scranton (27-5)	64-63	Wittenberg	Roanoke	Wis.-Whitewater	3,700	36,731
1984	Wis.-Whitewater (27-4)	103-86	Clark (Mass.)	DePauw	Upsala	3,200	30,311
1985	North Park (27-4)	72-71	Potsdam St.	Neb. Wesleyan	Widener	2,816	31,746
1986	Potsdam St. (32-0)	76-73	LeMoyne-Owen	Neb. Wesleyan	New Jersey City	—	34,366
1987	North Park (28-3)	106-100	Clark (Mass.)	Wittenberg	Richard Stockton	2,100	38,542
1988	Ohio Wesleyan (27-5)	92-70	Scranton	Neb. Wesleyan	Hartwick	2,500	34,373
1989	Wis.-Whitewater (29-2)	94-86	TCNJ	Southern Me.	Centre	2,882	37,396
1990	Rochester (27-5)	43-42	DePauw	Washington (Md.)	Calvin	3,000	46,365
1991	Wis.-Platteville (28-3)	81-74	Frank. & Marsh.	Otterbein	Ramapo	2,379	44,538
1992	Calvin (31-1)	62-49	Rochester	Wis.-Platteville	New Jersey City	2,941	45,611
1993	Ohio Northern (28-2)	71-68	Augustana (Ill.)	Rowan	Mass.-Dartmouth	2,120	32,360
1994	Lebanon Valley (28-4)	66-59 (ot)	New York U.	Wittenberg	St. Thomas (Minn.)	2,419	40,207
1995	Wis.-Platteville (31-0)	69-55	Manchester	Rowan	Trinity (Conn.)	3,000	68,731
1996	Rowan (28-4)	100-93	Hope	Ill. Wesleyan	Frank. & Marsh.	3,944	67,695
1997	Ill. Wesleyan (24-7)	89-86	Neb. Wesleyan	Williams	Alvernia	3,013	59,784
1998	Wis.-Platteville (30-0)	69-56	Hope	Williams	Wilkes	3,915	53,981
1999	Wis.-Platteville (30-2)	76-75 (ot)	Hampden-Sydney	Connecticut Col.	Wm. Paterson	4,461	45,348
2000	Calvin (30-2)	79-75	Wis-Eau Claire	Salem St.	Frank. & Marsh.	3,261	52,847
2001	Catholic (28-5)	76-62	Wm. Paterson	Ill. Wesleyan	Ohio Northern	3,317	57,784
2002	Otterbein (30-3)	102-83	Elizabethtown	Carthage	Rochester	2,852	74,437
2003	Williams (31-1)	67-65	Gust. Adolphus	Wooster	Hampden-Sydney	3,867	50,870
2004	Wis.-Stevens Point (29-5)	84-82	Williams	John Carroll	Amherst	2,374	52,066
2005	Wis.-Stevens Point (29-3)	73-49	Rochester	Calvin	York (Pa.)	2,877	47,640
2006	Va. Wesleyan (30-3)	59-56	Wittenberg	Ill. Wesleyan	Amherst	3,435	45,371
2007	Amherst (30-2)	80-67	Va. Wesleyan	Washington-St. Louis	Wooster	3,075	60,619

Season	Site of Finals	Coach of Champion	Outstanding Player Award
1975	Reading, Pa.	Jerry Johnson, LeMoyne-Owen	Bob Newman, LeMoyne-Owen
1976	Reading, Pa.	Bob Bessoir, Scranton	Jack Maher, Scranton
1977	Rock Island, Ill.	Larry Hunter, Wittenberg	Rick White, Wittenberg
1978	Rock Island, Ill.	Dan McCarrell, North Park	Michael Harper, North Park
1979	Rock Island, Ill.	Dan McCarrell, North Park	Michael Harper, North Park
1980	Rock Island, Ill.	Dan McCarrell, North Park	Michael Thomas, North Park
1981	Rock Island, Ill.	Jerry Welsh, Potsdam St.	Maxwell Artis, Augustana (Ill.)
1982	Grand Rapids, Mich.	Mac Petty, Wabash	Pete Metzelaars, Wabash
1983	Grand Rapids, Mich.	Bob Bessoir, Scranton	Bill Bessoir, Scranton
1984	Grand Rapids, Mich.	Dave Vander Meulen, Wis.-Whitewater	Andre McKoy, Wis.-Whitewater
1985	Grand Rapids, Mich.	Bosco Djurickovic, North Park	Earnest Hubbard, North Park
1986	Grand Rapids, Mich.	Jerry Welsh, Potsdam St.	Roosevelt Bullock, Potsdam St.
1987	Grand Rapids, Mich.	Bosco Djurickovic, North Park	Michael Starks, North Park
1988	Grand Rapids, Mich.	Gene Mehaffey, Ohio Wesleyan	Scott Tedder, Ohio Wesleyan
1989	Springfield, Ohio	Dave Vander Meulen, Wis.-Whitewater	Greg Grant, TCNJ
1990	Springfield, Ohio	Mike Neer, Rochester	Chris Fite, Rochester
1991	Springfield, Ohio	Bo Ryan, Wis.-Platteville	Shawn Frison, Wis.-Platteville
1992	Springfield, Ohio	Ed Douma, Calvin	Steve Honderd, Calvin
1993	Buffalo, N.Y.	Joe Campoli, Ohio Northern	Kirk Anderson, Augustana (Ill.)
1994	Buffalo, N.Y.	Pat Flannery, Lebanon Valley	Mike Rhoades, Lebanon Valley
			Adam Crawford, New York U.
1995	Buffalo, N.Y.	Bo Ryan, Wis.-Platteville	Ernie Peavy, Wis.-Platteville
1996	Salem, Va.	John Giannini, Rowan	Terrence Stewart, Rowan
1997	Salem, Va.	Dennie Bridges, Ill. Wesleyan	Bryan Crabtree, Ill. Wesleyan
1998	Salem, Va.	Bo Ryan, Wis.-Platteville	Ben Hoffmann, Wis.-Platteville
1999	Salem, Va.	Bo Ryan, Wis.-Platteville	Merrill Brunson, Wis.-Platteville
2000	Salem, Va.	Kevin Vande Streek, Calvin	Sherm Carstensen, Calvin
2001	Salem, Va.	Mike Lonergan, Catholic	Pat Maloney, Catholic
2002	Salem, Va.	Dick Reynolds, Otterbein	Jeff Gibbs, Otterbein
2003	Salem, Va.	David Paulsen, Williams	Benjamin Coffin, Williams
2004	Salem, Va.	Jack Bennett, Wis.-Stevens Point	Nick Bennett, Wis.-Stevens Point
2005	Salem, Va.	Jack Bennett, Wis.-Stevens Point	Jason Kalsow, Wis.-Stevens Point
2006	Salem, Va.	David Macedo, Va. Wesleyan	Ton Ton Balenga, Va. Wesleyan
2007	Salem, Va.	David Hixon, Amherst	Andrew Olson, Amherst

Individual Records

(Minimum three games for tournament records.)

POINTS, GAME
59—Ben Strong, Guilford (129) vs. Lincoln (Pa.) (128) (3 ot), 2007.

POINTS, TOURNAMENT
177—Michael Nogelo, Williams, 1998 (31 vs. Trinity [Conn.], 30 vs. Springfield, 25 vs. Hamilton, 35 vs. St. Lawrence, 18 vs. Wis.-Platteville, 38 vs. Wilkes).

SCORING AVERAGE, TOURNAMENT
37.3—Kyle Myrick, Lincoln (Pa.) (44 vs. Chris. Newport, 34 vs. Messiah, 34 vs. Va. Wesleyan), 2006.

FIELD GOALS, GAME
21—Gerald Reece, William Penn (85) vs. North Park (81), 1981.

FIELD GOALS, TOURNAMENT
68—Greg Grant, TCNJ, 1989 (11 vs. Shenandoah, 11 vs. New Jersey City, 16 vs. Potsdam St., 16 vs. Southern Me., 14 vs. Wis.-Whitewater).

THREE-POINT FIELD GOALS, GAME
12—Kirk Anderson, Augustana (Ill.) (100) vs. Wis.-Platteville (86), 1993.

THREE-POINT FIELD GOALS, TOURNAMENT
35—Kirk Anderson, Augustana (Ill.), 1993 (4 vs. DePauw, 5 vs. Beloit, 4 vs. La Verne, 12 vs. Wis.-Platteville, 6 vs. Rowan, 4 vs. Ohio Northern).

FREE THROWS MADE, GAME
21—Tom Montsma, Calvin (88) vs. Wabash (76), 1980.

FREE THROWS MADE, TOURNAMENT
52—Daimen Hunter, Alvernia, 1997 (6 vs. Lebanon Valley, 14 vs. Goucher, 5 vs. Rochester Inst., 11 vs. Salisbury, 0 vs. Ill. Wesleyan, 16 vs. Williams).

ASSISTS, GAME
20—Matt Nadelhoffer, Wheaton (Ill.) (131) vs. Grinnell (117), 1996.

ASSISTS, TOURNAMENT
62—Ricky Spicer, Wis.-Whitewater, 1989.

REBOUNDS, TOURNAMENT
83—Jeff Gibbs, Otterbein, 2002.

REBOUNDING AVERAGE, TOURNAMENT
16.6—Jeff Gibbs, Otterbein, 2002 (13 vs. Bethany [W.V.], 6 vs. Randolph-Macon, 24 vs. DePauw; 15 vs. Carthage; 25 vs. Elizabethtown).

Team Records

(Minimum three games for tournament records.)

POINTS, GAME
132—Ill. Wesleyan vs. Grinnell (91), 2001.

POINTS, TOURNAMENT
594—Rowan, 1996 [130 vs. York (N.Y.), 102 vs. New Jersey City, 85 vs. Williams, 98 vs. Richard Stockton, 79 vs. Ill. Wesleyan, 100 vs. Hope].

FIELD GOALS, GAME
52—Wheaton (Ill.) (131) vs. Grinnell (117), 1996.

FIELD GOALS, TOURNAMENT
206—Rowan, 1996 (45 vs. York [N.Y.], 31 vs. New Jersey City, 29 vs. Williams, 35 vs. Richard Stockton, 32 vs. Ill. Wesleyan, 34 vs. Hope).

THREE-POINT FIELD GOALS, GAME
22—Grinnell (117) vs. Wheaton (Ill.) (131), 1996.

THREE-POINT FIELD GOALS, TOURNAMENT
59—Augustana (Ill.), 1993 (6 vs. DePauw, 11 vs. Beloit, 11 vs. La Verne, 14 vs. Wis.-Platteville, 9 vs. Rowan, 8 vs. Ohio Northern).

FREE THROWS MADE, GAME
43—Capital (103) vs. Va. Wesleyan (93), 1982; Potsdam St. (91) vs. New Jersey City (89), 1986.

FREE THROWS MADE, TOURNAMENT
137—Catholic, 2001 [18 vs. CCNY; 11 vs. Widener; 18 vs. Brockport St.; 25 vs. Clark (Mass.); 33 vs. Ohio Northern; 32 vs. Wm. Paterson].

ASSISTS, GAME
34—Hampden-Sydney (105) vs. Greensboro (79), 1995.

ASSISTS, TOURNAMENT
136—Neb. Wesleyan, 1997 (25 vs. Buena Vista, 17 vs. Gust. Adolphus, 22 vs. Hope, 23 vs. Wis.-Stevens Point, 26 vs. Williams, 23 vs. Ill. Wesleyan).

All-Tournament Teams

Most Outstanding Player.

1975
*Robert Newman, LeMoyne-Owen
Clint Jackson, LeMoyne-Owen
Dan Panaggio, Brockport St.
Bruce Hamming, Augustana (Ill.)
Greg Ackles, Rowan

1976
*Jack Maher, Scranton
Tom Dunn, Wittenberg
Bob Heubner, Wittenberg
Ronnie Wright, Plattsburgh St.
Terry Lawrence, Augustana (Ill.)

1977
*Rick White, Wittenberg
Phil Smyczek, Hamline
Paul Miernicki, Scranton
Clyde Eberhardt, Wittenberg
Ralph Christian, Oneonta St.

1978
*Michael Harper, North Park
Dennis James, Widener
John Nibert, Albion
Earl Keith, Stony Brook
Tom Florentine, North Park

1979
*Michael Harper, North Park
Don Marsh, Frank. & Marsh.
Derrick Rowland, Potsdam St.
Michael Thomas, North Park
Modzel Greer, North Park

1980
*Michael Thomas, North Park
Ellonya Green, Upsala
Steve Keenan, Upsala
Tyronne Curtis, Wittenberg
Keith French, North Park

1981
*Max Artis, Augustana (Ill.)
Bill Rapier, Augustana (Ill.)
Ed Jachim, Potsdam St.
Derrick Rowland, Potsdam St.
Ron Stewart, Otterbein

1982
*Pete Metzelaars, Wabash
Doug Cornfoot, Cal St. Stanislaus
Rick Davis, Brooklyn
Merlin Nice, Wabash
Leroy Witherspoon, Potsdam St.
Maurice Woods, Potsdam St.

1983
*Bill Bessoir, Scranton
Mickey Banas, Scranton
Jay Ferguson, Wittenberg
Mark Linde, Wis.-Whitewater
Gerald Holmes, Roanoke

1984
*Andre McKoy, Wis.-Whitewater
Mark Linde, Wis.-Whitewater
James Gist, Upsala
Dan Trant, Clark (Mass.)
David Hathaway, DePauw

1985
*Earnest Hubbard, North Park
Justyne Monegain, North Park
Dana Janssen, Neb. Wesleyan
Brendan Mitchell, Potsdam St.
Lou Stevens, Widener

1986
*Roosevelt Bullock, Potsdam St.
Barry Stanton, Potsdam St.
Johnny Mayers, New Jersey City
Michael Neal, LeMoyne-Owen
Dana Janssen, Neb. Wesleyan

1987
*Michael Starks, North Park
Mike Barach, North Park
Steve Iannarino, Wittenberg
Kermit Sharp, Clark (Mass.)
Donald Ellison, Richard Stockton

1988
*Scott Tedder, Ohio Wesleyan
Lee Rowlinson, Ohio Wesleyan
J.P. Andrejko, Scranton
Charlie Burt, Neb. Wesleyan
Tim McGraw, Hartwick

1989
*Greg Grant, TCNJ
Danny Johnson, Centre
Jeff Bowers, Southern Me.
Ricky Spicer, Wis.-Whitewater
Elbert Gordon, Wis.-Whitewater
Jeff Seifriz, Wis.-Whitewater

1990
*Chris Fite, Rochester
Brett Crist, DePauw
Chris Brandt, Washington (Md.)
Brett Hecko, DePauw
Steve Honderd, Calvin

1991
*Shawn Frison, Wis.-Platteville
James Bradley, Otterbein
Robby Jeter, Wis.-Platteville
Will Lasky, Frank. & Marsh.
David Wilding, Frank. & Marsh.

1992
*Steve Honderd, Calvin
Matt Harrison, Calvin
Mike LeFebre, Calvin
Chris Fite, Rochester
Kyle Meeker, Rochester

1993
*Kirk Anderson, Augustana (Ill.)
Mark Gooden, Ohio Northern
Aaron Madry, Ohio Northern
Steven Haynes, Mass.-Dartmouth
Keith Wood, Rowan

1994
*Mike Rhoades, Lebanon Valley
*Adam Crawford, New York U.
Jonathan Gabriel, New York U.
John Harper, Lebanon Valley
Matt Croci, Wittenberg

1995
*Ernie Peavy, Wis.-Platteville
Brad Knoy, Manchester
Kyle Hupfer, Manchester
Aaron Lancaster, Wis.-Platteville
Charles Grasty, Rowan

1996
*Terrence Stewart, Rowan
Antwan Dasher, Rowan
Joel Holstege, Hope
Duane Bosma, Hope
Chris Simich, Ill. Wesleyan

1997
*Bryan Crabtree, Ill. Wesleyan
Korey Coon, Ill. Wesleyan
Mitch Mosser, Neb. Wesleyan
Damien Hunter, Alvernia
Michael Nogelo, Williams

1998
*Ben Hoffmann, Wis.-Platteville
Andre Dalton, Wis.-Platteville
Joel Holstege, Hope
Michael Nogelo, Williams
Dave Jannuzzi, Wilkes

1999
*Merrill Brunson, Wis.-Platteville
Mike Jones, Wis.-Platteville
T.J. Grimes, Hampden-Sydney
Jeremy Harris, Hampden-Sydney
Horace Jenkins, Wm. Paterson

2000
*Sherm Carstensen, Wis.-Eau Claire
Jeremy Veenstra, Calvin
Aaron Winkle, Calvin
Tishaun Jenkins, Salem St.
Alex Kraft, Frank. & Marsh.

2001
*Pat Maloney, Catholic
Matt Hilleary, Catholic
Horace Jenkins, Wm. Paterson
Chad Bostleman, Ohio Northern
Luke Kasten, Ill. Wesleyan

2002
*Jeff Gibbs, Otterbein
Kevin Shay, Otterbein
Bob Porambo, Elizabethtown
Seth Hauben Carthage
Jason Wiertel, Carthage

2003
*Benjamin Coffin, Williams
Michael Crotty, Williams
Doug Espenson, Gust. Adolphus
Jeff Monroe, Hampden-Sydney
Bryan Nelson, Wooster

2004
*Nick Bennett, Wis.-Stevens Point
Jason Kalsow, Wis.-Stevens Point
Tucker Kain, Williams
Michael Crotty, Williams
Jerry Angel, Wooster

2005
*Jason Kalsow, Wis.-Stevens Point
Nick Bennett, Wis.-Stevens Point
Jon Krull, Wis.-Stevens Point
Seth Hauben, Rochester
Joel Hoekstra, Calvin

2006
*Ton Ton Balenga, Va. Wesleyan
Brandon Adair, Va. Wesleyan
Dane Borchers, Wittenberg
Dan Russ, Wittenberg
Keelan Amelianovich, Ill. Wesleyan

2007
*Andrew Olson, Amherst
Tim McLaughlin, Amherst
Brandon Adair, Va. Wesleyan
Sean Wallis, Washington-St. Louis
Tim Vandervaart, Wooster

Won-Lost Records in Tournament Play

Team (Years Participated)	Yrs.	Won	Lost	Pct.	1st	2nd	3rd	4th
Albany (N.Y.) (1975-77-79-80-81-85-90-92-94-95)	10	10	12	.455	0	0	0	0
Albion (1978-79-98-2005)	4	7	4	.636	0	0	1	0
Albright (1977-79-80-2005)	4	4	5	.444	0	0	0	0
Alfred (1985-86-89-97)	4	1	5	.167	0	0	0	0
Allegheny (1975-79-80-81-87-88-89-98-99)	9	4	14	.222	0	0	0	0
Alvernia (1997-2000-02-03-06-07)	6	6	7	.462	0	0	0	1
Amherst (1994-97-2000-01-02-03-04-05-06-07)	10	20	12	.625	1	0	0	2
Anna Maria (1996)	1	2	1	.667	0	0	0	0
Ashland (1976-77-78)	3	2	3	.400	0	0	0	0
Augsburg (1985-98-99)	3	1	4	.200	0	0	0	0
Augustana (Ill.) (1975-76-77-80-81-82-83-93-2006-07)	10	22	11	.667	0	2	2	0
Aurora (1998-2001-03-05-07)	5	1	5	.167	0	0	0	0
Averett (1990-07)	2	1	3	.250	0	0	0	0
Babson (1992-95-96-2002-04)	5	2	5	.286	0	0	0	0
Baldwin-Wallace (1979-95-96-98-2005-06)	6	5	6	.455	0	0	0	0
Baruch (2000-06)	2	0	2	.000	0	0	0	0
Beloit (1977-79-80-81-82-83-89-93-95)	9	3	12	.200	0	0	0	0
Benedictine (Ill.) (1991-97-2000-01-04)	5	2	5	.286	0	0	0	0
Bethany (W.V.) (1978-82-2002-05-06)	5	2	6	.250	0	0	0	0
Bethel (Minn.) (1991)	1	0	1	.000	0	0	0	0
Bishop (1977-82-83)	3	2	3	.400	0	0	0	0
Bowdoin (1996-99)	2	2	2	.500	0	0	0	0
Blackburn (2003-05)	2	0	2	.000	0	0	0	0
Brandeis (1975-77-78-2007)	4	6	4	.600	0	0	0	0
Bridgewater (Va.) (1988-96-97)	3	2	4	.333	0	0	0	0
Bridgewater St. (1983-99-2006)	3	1	3	.250	0	0	0	0
Brockport St. (1975-94-97-98-2001-02-04-07)	8	13	9	.591	0	0	0	1
Brooklyn (1982)	1	4	1	.800	0	0	1	0
Buena Vista (1997-2000-02-03-04-05-06)	7	4	7	.364	0	0	0	0
Buffalo (1982)	1	0	2	.000	0	0	0	0
Buffalo St. (1984-85-88-89-90-91-92-93-95-96-97-2003)	12	9	12	.429	0	0	0	0
Cabrini (1988-94-95-96-97-2001-02)	7	4	8	.333	0	0	0	0
UC San Diego (1990-91-92-94)	4	2	4	.333	0	0	0	0
Cal Lutheran (1992-93-94-2001)	4	2	4	.333	0	0	0	0
Cal St. San B'dino (1989)	1	0	1	.000	0	0	0	0
Cal St. Stanislaus (1981-82-83-87-89)	5	8	7	.533	0	0	0	1
Calvin (1980-81-86-87-89-90-91-92-93-94-95-2000-01-04-05-06-07)	17	30	18	.625	2	0	1	1
Capital (1982-83-84-89-96-2007)	6	5	6	.455	0	0	0	0
Carleton (2006)	1	0	1	.000	0	0	0	0
Carnegie Mellon (1977-2006)	2	0	3	.000	0	0	0	0
Carroll (Wis.) (2006-07)	2	2	2	.500	0	0	0	0
Carthage (2000-01-02)	3	7	3	.700	0	0	1	0
Castleton (2004)	1	0	1	.000	0	0	0	0
Catholic (1993-96-98-99-2000-01-02-03-04-06-07)	11	14	10	.583	1	0	0	0
Cazenovia (2002)	1	0	1	.000	0	0	0	0
Central (Iowa) (1977-78-79-80-85-91-94-95)	8	5	9	.357	0	0	0	0
Centre (1979-83-84-85-86-87-88-89-92-2007)	10	11	15	.423	0	0	0	2
Chaminade (1979)	1	2	1	.667	0	0	0	0
Chicago (1997-98-2000-01-07)	5	6	5	.545	0	0	0	0
Chris. Newport (1986-88-89-90-91-93-94-95-96-97-98-99-2000-01-03-06)	16	10	17	.370	0	0	0	0
City Tech (2005)	1	1	1	.500	0	0	0	0
CCNY (1976-2001-03)	3	1	3	.250	0	0	0	0
Claremont-M-S (1984-87-88-90-91-96-2002-06)	8	3	9	.250	0	0	0	0
Clark (Mass.) (1978-79-80-81-82-83-84-85-86-87-88-99-2001-02-03)	15	26	15	.634	0	2	0	0
Clark Atlanta (1977)	1	0	2	.000	0	0	0	0
Coast Guard (1979-2007)	2	1	2	.333	0	0	0	0
Coe (1975-76)	2	2	2	.500	0	0	0	0
Colby (1994-95-97)	3	0	3	.000	0	0	0	0
Colby-Sawyer (2001-02-03)	3	0	3	.000	0	0	0	0
Colorado Col. (1992-2004)	2	1	2	.333	0	0	0	0
Connecticut Col. (1998-99)	2	5	2	.714	0	0	1	0
Concordia (Wis.) (2000)	1	0	1	.000	0	0	0	0
Concordia-M'head (1996)	1	0	1	.000	0	0	0	0
Cornell College (1976-94)	2	0	3	.000	0	0	0	0
Cortland St. (1997-99-2000-06)	4	4	4	.500	0	0	0	0
Dallas (2004)	1	0	1	.000	0	0	0	0
Defiance (1993-99-2001)	3	0	3	.000	0	0	0	0
DePauw (1978-84-85-86-87-90-91-92-93-2002-06-07)	12	12	14	.462	0	1	1	0
DeSales (1996)	1	0	1	.000	0	0	0	0
Denison (1997)	1	0	1	.000	0	0	0	0
Dickinson (1980-82-91-97)	4	1	5	.167	0	0	0	0
Doane (1975)	1	0	1	.000	0	0	0	0
Dubuque (1981-86-88-90)	4	4	4	.500	0	0	0	0
Eastern Conn. St. (1992-93-2000)	3	3	3	.500	0	0	0	0
Edgewood (2002-05)	2	0	2	.000	0	0	0	0
Elizabethtown (1979-93-2002-03-04)	5	5	5	.500	0	1	0	0
Elmhurst (1992-2001)	2	2	2	.500	0	0	0	0
Elmira (1995)	1	0	1	.000	0	0	0	0
Elms (2005-06-07)	3	0	3	.000	0	0	0	0
Emory (1990)	1	2	1	.667	0	0	0	0

Team (Years Participated)	Yrs.	Won	Lost	Pct.	1st	2nd	3rd	4th
Emory & Henry (1988-90-91-92-93)	5	4	5	.444	0	0	0	0
Endicott (2000-04-05-06)	4	0	4	.000	0	0	0	0
FDU-Florham (1990-98)	2	0	2	.000	0	0	0	0
Farmingdale St. (2006)	1	1	1	.500	0	0	0	0
Ferrum (1992)	1	1	1	.500	0	0	0	0
Fontbonne (1996-2007)	2	0	2	.000	0	0	0	0
Framingham St. (1979-80-84)	3	2	4	.333	0	0	0	0
Franklin (1998-99-2000-02)	4	3	4	.429	0	0	0	0
Frank. & Marsh. (1975-77-79-81-84-86-87-88-89-90-91-92-93-94-95-96-99-2000-04)	19	32	23	.582	0	1	1	2
Fredonia St. (1993)	1	0	1	.000	0	0	0	0
Geneseo St. (1991-93-94-95-96-98-99)	7	5	7	.417	0	0	0	0
Gettysburg (1996-2001-02)	3	0	3	.000	0	0	0	0
Gordon (2006)	1	0	1	.000	0	0	0	0
Goucher (1995-97-99)	3	2	3	.400	0	0	0	0
Greensboro (1985-94-95)	3	4	3	.571	0	0	0	0
Grinnell (1996-2001)	2	0	2	.000	0	0	0	0
Grove City (1976-79-83-89)	4	3	5	.375	0	0	0	0
Guilford (2007)	1	3	1	.750	0	0	0	0
Gust. Adolphus (1987-89-92-96-97-98-99-2001-02-03-04-05)	12	19	12	.613	0	1	0	0
Gwynedd-Mercy (2004-05)	2	1	2	.333	0	0	0	0
Hamilton (1995-96-97-98-99-2000-2003-04-06)	9	10	9	.526	0	0	0	0
Hamline (1975-77)	2	4	3	.571	0	0	0	1
Hampden-Sydney (1989-92-94-95-97-98-99-2000-01-02-03-04-07)	13	18	14	.563	0	1	0	1
Hanover (1995-96-2003-04-05)	5	5	5	.500	0	0	0	1
Hartwick (1983-85-88-96)	4	5	5	.500	0	0	0	1
Heidelberg (1984-95)	2	1	2	.333	0	0	0	0
Hendrix (1995-96)	2	1	2	.333	0	0	0	0
Hiram (1975-76-84)	3	2	4	.333	0	0	0	0
Hobart (2001)	1	0	1	.000	0	0	0	0
Hood (2007)	1	0	1	.000	0	0	0	0
Hope (1982-83-84-85-87-88-89-90-91-92-95-96-97-98-2002-03-06-07)	18	22	20	.524	0	2	0	0
Humboldt St. (1978-79-80)	3	3	3	.500	0	0	0	0
Hunter (1990-92-93-94-95-98)	6	4	6	.400	0	0	0	0
Illinois Col. (2003)	1	0	1	.000	0	0	0	0
Ill. Wesleyan (1984-86-87-88-90-91-92-94-95-96-97-98-99-2001-03-04-05-06)	18	39	18	.684	1	0	3	0
Ithaca (1977-82-83-87-93-2002)	6	2	9	.182	0	0	0	0
John Carroll (1983-86-96-97-98-99-2003-04-05-07)	10	17	12	.586	0	0	1	0
Johns Hopkins (1990-91-92-93-94-98-99-2007)	8	6	8	.429	0	0	0	0
Johnson & Wales (R.I.) (2004)	1	0	1	.000	0	0	0	0
Kalamazoo (1996)	1	0	1	.000	0	0	0	0
Kean (1978-91-92)	3	5	3	.625	0	0	0	0
Keene St. (2004-07)	2	4	2	.667	0	0	0	0
Kenyon (1994-95)	2	2	2	.500	0	0	0	0
King's (Pa.) (1990-91-92-2005-07)	5	3	5	.375	0	0	0	0
Knox (1975)	1	0	2	.000	0	0	0	0
Knoxville (1977-78)	2	3	2	.600	0	0	0	0
La Verne (1993)	1	1	1	.500	0	0	0	0
Lake Erie (2006-07)	2	0	2	.000	0	0	0	0
Lakeland (2004)	1	0	1	.000	0	0	0	0
Lane (1979-80)	2	2	3	.400	0	0	0	0
Lasell (2002-03-04)	3	0	3	.000	0	0	0	0
Lawrence (1997-2004-05-06)	4	5	4	.556	0	0	0	0
Lebanon Valley (1993-94-95-97-99-2005)	6	7	5	.583	1	0	0	0
Lehman (2004)	1	0	1	.000	0	0	0	0
LeMoyne-Owen (1975-76-83-84-85-86)	6	15	5	.750	1	1	0	0
Lewis & Clark (2000-01-02)	3	5	3	.625	0	0	0	0
Lincoln (Pa.) (2006-07)	2	4	2	.667	0	0	0	0
Linfield (2001)	1	1	1	.500	0	0	0	0
Longwood (1980)	1	3	2	.600	0	0	0	1
Loras (2007)	1	0	1	.000	0	0	0	0
Luther (1982-84)	2	1	3	.250	0	0	0	0
Lycoming (1985-96-2002-04)	4	4	4	.500	0	0	0	0
Lynchburg (1976-79)	2	0	2	.000	0	0	0	0
MacMurray (2001)	1	0	1	.000	0	0	0	0
Manchester (1993-94-95-99)	4	6	4	.600	0	1	0	0
Manhattanville (1978-79-2007)	3	0	5	.000	0	0	0	0
Mansfield (1975-76)	2	3	2	.600	0	0	0	0
Marian (Wis.) (2001)	1	0	1	.000	0	0	0	0
Marietta (1975)	1	1	1	.500	0	0	0	0
Mary Hardin-Baylor (2007)	1	0	1	.000	0	0	0	0
Mary Washington (2003)	1	0	1	.000	0	0	0	0
Marymount (Va.) (2000)	1	0	1	.000	0	0	0	0
Maryville (Mo.) (1997-2004-06)	3	0	3	.000	0	0	0	0
Maryville (Tenn.) (1991-92-93-95-97-99-2000-01-02-03-04-05-06-07)	14	13	14	.481	0	0	0	0
Mass.-Boston (1975-76-77-78-81-83-2006)	7	6	8	.429	0	0	0	0
Mass.-Dartmouth (1976-86-87-88-90-91-93-94-95-97-98-2001)	12	14	13	.519	0	0	0	1
Mass. Liberal Arts (1987-88-89-90)	4	3	6	.333	0	0	0	0
McMurry (2000-01)	2	3	2	.600	0	0	0	0
Merchant Marine (1989-97-98-99-2001-02-03)	7	4	7	.364	0	0	0	0
Messiah (2006-07)	2	1	2	.333	0	0	0	0
Methodist (1975-77-97-2004-05)	5	5	5	.500	0	0	0	0
Miles (1975-76)	2	3	2	.600	0	0	0	0
Millikin (1983-88-89)	3	2	4	.500	0	0	0	0
Millsaps (1984-95-96-2001)	4	4	4	.500	0	0	0	0

Team (Years Participated)	Yrs.	Won	Lost	Pct.	1st	2nd	3rd	4th
Milwaukee (1982)	1	1	1	.500	0	0	0	0
Milwaukee Engr. (2003)	1	0	1	.000	0	0	0	0
Minn.-Morris (1978-79)	2	1	3	.250	0	0	0	0
Mississippi Col. (1998-99-2000-01-02-03-05-06-07)	9	8	9	.471	0	0	0	0
Monmouth (Ill.) (1985-88-89-90)	4	3	5	.375	0	0	0	0
Monmouth (1976)	1	1	1	.500	0	0	0	0
Montclair St. (1981-82-84-94-95-2003)	6	6	6	.500	0	0	0	0
Moravian (1983)	1	0	2	.000	0	0	0	0
Mt. St. Mary (N.Y.) (2000-05)	2	0	2	.000	0	0	0	0
Mt. St. Vincent (1996-97)	2	0	2	.000	0	0	0	0
Mount Union (1997)	1	2	1	.667	0	0	0	0
Muhlenberg (1995-98)	2	0	2	.000	0	0	0	0
Muskingum (1977-81-83-88-90)	5	3	7	.300	0	0	0	0
Nazareth (1984-86-87-90-98)	5	5	5	.500	0	0	0	0
Neb. Wesleyan (1977-84-85-86-87-88-90-95-97-98-99-2000-01)	14	24	16	.600	0	1	3	0
TCNJ (1985-86-88-89-90-98)	6	8	6	.571	0	1	0	0
New Jersey City (1978-79-80-86-87-89-90-92-95-96-97-98-99-2004-05)	15	17	18	.486	0	0	0	2
NJIT (1991-93-94-95-96)	5	3	5	.375	0	0	0	0
New York U. (1986-92-93-94-95-96-97-98)	8	8	9	.471	0	1	0	0
UNC Greensboro (1980)	1	0	2	.000	0	0	0	0
N.C. Wesleyan (1983-84-87-2002)	4	3	5	.375	0	0	0	0
North Central (Ill.) (1984-85-89-90-2006)	5	2	6	.250	0	0	0	0
North Park (1978-79-80-81-82-85-86-87-90)	9	26	6	.813	5	0	0	0
Norwich (1984-87-2005-06)	4	2	5	.286	0	0	0	0
Oberlin (1976)	1	1	1	.500	0	0	0	0
Occidental (1980-2003-06-07)	4	3	5	.375	0	0	0	0
Oglethorpe (1994-95)	2	0	2	.000	0	0	0	0
Ohio Northern (1980-82-88-93-95-96-97-99-2000-01)	10	12	10	.545	1	0	0	1
Ohio Wesleyan (1988)	1	5	0	1.000	1	0	0	0
Old Westbury (2004)	1	0	1	.000	0	0	0	0
Oneonta St. (1977)	1	4	1	.800	0	1	0	0
Otterbein (1978-81-85-86-87-89-90-91-92-93-94-99-2002)	13	23	13	.639	1	0	1	1
Pacific (Ore.) (2000)	1	0	1	.000	0	0	0	0
Penn St.-Behrend (2000-04-05)	3	3	3	.500	0	0	0	0
Pitt.-Bradford (2002-03)	2	0	2	.000	0	0	0	0
Plattsburgh St. (1976-95-2006-07)	4	4	5	.444	0	0	0	1
Plymouth St. (1996-2004)	2	1	2	.333	0	0	0	0
Pomona-Pitzer (1986-89-94-95-97-98-99-2000-04-05)	10	4	11	.267	0	0	0	0
Potsdam St. (1978-79-80-81-82-83-84-85-86-87-88-89-90-2004-05)	15	36	13	.735	2	3	0	0
Puget Sound (2004-05-06)	3	4	3	.571	0	0	0	0
Ramapo (1991-2003-05-07)	4	7	5	.583	0	0	0	1
Randolph-Macon (1990-91-96-98-99-2002-03-04-06)	9	5	9	.357	0	0	0	0
Redlands (1985)	1	1	1	.500	0	0	0	0
Rensselaer (1975-76-91-96)	4	3	5	.375	0	0	0	0
Rhode Island Col. (1975-76-79-2007)	4	5	6	.455	0	0	0	0
Rhodes (1980-81-93)	3	3	3	.500	0	0	0	0
Richard Stockton (1987-88-89-90-92-93-94-96-97-99)	10	15	12	.556	0	0	0	1
Ripon (1978-80-86-87-91-92-95-96-98-99-2000-02)	12	5	14	.263	0	0	0	0
Rivier (2007)	1	0	1	.000	0	0	0	0
Roanoke (1981-82-83-84-85-86-87-94-95-96-97-2000-01)	13	13	15	.464	0	0	1	0
Rochester (1981-90-91-92-97-99-2002-03-04-05-07)	11	23	10	.697	1	2	0	1
Rochester Inst. (1976-95-96-97-99-2000)	6	3	6	.333	0	0	0	0
Rockford (2003)	1	0	1	.000	0	0	0	0
Rose-Hulman (1977-78-81-82-89-96-97-99)	8	5	10	.333	0	0	0	0
Rowan (1975-76-77-91-93-94-95-96-97-98-99-2000)	12	29	11	.725	1	1	2	0
Rust (1983-87-88-89-97)	5	3	5	.375	0	0	0	0
St. Andrews (1981-82-83)	3	3	3	.500	0	0	0	0
St. John Fisher (1992-94-95-96-97-98-99-2001-03-04-05-06-07)	13	8	13	.381	0	0	0	0
St. John's (Minn.) (1985-86-88-93-95-2000-01-07)	8	5	9	.357	0	0	0	0
St. Joseph's (Me.) (2003)	1	0	1	.000	0	0	0	0
St. Lawrence (1975-78-79-80-81-84-96-97-98-2007)	10	8	12	.400	0	0	0	0
St. Norbert (1984-2002)	2	1	2	.333	0	0	0	0
St. Thomas (Minn.) (1990-93-94-95-2000-02-06-07)	8	9	9	.500	0	0	0	1
Salem St. (1980-81-82-86-89-90-91-92-93-95-96-97-98-2000-01-02-03-04-05-07)	20	19	21	.475	0	0	1	0
Salisbury (1985-91-92-96-97)	5	6	5	.545	0	0	0	0
Salve Regina (1995)	1	0	1	.000	0	0	0	0
SCAD (2000-01-03)	3	1	3	.250	0	0	0	0
Savannah St. (1979-80-81)	3	4	3	.571	0	0	0	0
Scranton (1975-76-77-78-80-81-82-83-84-85-86-87-88-91-92-93-98-2000-03-06)	20	32	20	.615	2	1	1	0
Sewanee (1975-76-97-98)	4	1	6	.143	0	0	0	0
Shenandoah (1989-91-96)	3	1	4	.200	0	0	0	0
Shepherd (1976)	1	2	1	.667	0	0	0	0
Simpson (1976-92-95-96)	4	1	4	.200	0	0	0	0
Slippery Rock (1978)	1	1	1	.500	0	0	0	0
Sonoma St. (1983)	1	1	1	.500	0	0	0	0
Southern Me. (1988-89-90-91)	4	6	4	.600	0	0	1	0
Southern Vt. (2003)	1	1	1	.500	0	0	0	0
Springfield (1996-97-98-2000-05)	5	3	5	.375	0	0	0	0
Staten Island (1981-82-84-88-89-95-96-99-2002)	9	3	12	.200	0	0	0	0
Stevens Institute (2007)	1	2	1	.667	0	0	0	0
Stillman (1996)	1	0	1	.000	0	0	0	0
Stony Brook (1977-78-79-80-87-91)	6	7	7	.500	0	0	0	1
Suffolk (1975-76-77-78-2002)	5	2	7	.222	0	0	0	0

Team (Years Participated)	Yrs.	Won	Lost	Pct.	1st	2nd	3rd	4th
Sul Ross St. (2004)	1	2	1	.667	0	0	0	0
Susquehanna (1984-86-89-92-94)	5	4	6	.400	0	0	0	0
Texas-Dallas (2005)	1	0	1	.000	0	0	0	0
Transylvania (1975-76-77-78-2006-07)	6	7	6	.538	0	0	0	0
Trinity (Conn.) (1995-98-99-2002-03-07)	6	8	7	.533	0	0	0	1
Trinity (Tex.) (1998-2000-03-04-05-06)	6	4	6	.400	0	0	0	0
Tufts (1995-97-2006)	3	3	3	.500	0	0	0	0
Union (N.Y.) (1983-2002-05)	3	3	3	.500	0	0	0	0
Upper Iowa (1996-99)	2	0	2	.000	0	0	0	0
Upsala (1978-79-80-81-82-83-84-86)	8	13	10	.565	0	1	0	1
Ursinus (1980-81-82-2003-05-06)	6	6	7	.462	0	0	1	0
Utica (2006)	1	2	1	.667	0	0	0	0
Villa Julie (2006-07)	2	1	2	.333	0	0	0	0
Va. Wesleyan (1978-79-82-93-2005-06-07)	7	12	8	.600	1	1	0	0
Wabash (1980-81-82-97-98)	5	8	5	.615	0	0	0	0
Wartburg (1975-87-89-91-93-2001)	6	5	7	.417	0	0	0	0
Washington (Md.) (1984-86-89-90)	4	6	5	.545	0	0	1	0
Washington-St. Louis (1987-88-89-91-95-96-97-99-2001-02-07)	11	16	11	.593	0	0	1	0
Wash. & Jeff. (1985-94)	2	3	3	.500	0	0	0	0
Wash. & Lee (1975-77-78-80)	4	1	7	.125	0	0	0	0
Webster (2000-02)	2	0	2	.000	0	0	0	0
Wentworth Inst. (1997-2007)	2	0	2	.000	0	0	0	0
Westminster (Mo.) (1995)	1	0	1	.000	0	0	0	0
Westminster (Pa.) (2007)	1	0	1	.000	0	0	0	0
Western Conn. St. (1986-89-90-91-92-96-99-2002-03-05)	10	7	11	.389	0	0	0	0
Western New Eng. (1990-2000-01)	3	0	3	.000	0	0	0	0
Westfield St. (1985-93)	2	0	3	.000	0	0	0	0
Wheaton (Ill.) (1995-96-99-2005)	4	2	4	.333	0	0	0	0
Whittier (1979-81-82)	3	3	4	.429	0	0	0	0
Whitworth (2003-07)	2	1	2	.333	0	0	0	0
Widener (1975-76-77-78-82-83-85-87-95-97-2000-01-06-07)	14	17	16	.515	0	1	0	1
Wilkes (1995-96-97-98-99-2001)	6	10	7	.588	0	0	0	0
Wm. Paterson (1975-77-80-81-83-84-85-97-99-2000-01-02-06)	13	22	14	.611	0	1	0	1
William Penn (1979-81-83)	3	2	4	.333	0	0	0	0
Williams (1994-95-96-97-98-2000-02-03-04-07)	10	26	9	.743	1	1	2	0
Wis.-Eau Claire (2000-01)	2	6	2	.750	0	0	0	0
Wis.-La Crosse (2006)	1	0	1	.000	0	0	0	0
Wis. Lutheran (2006)	1	0	1	.000	0	0	0	0
Wis.-Oshkosh (1996-97-98-2002-03)	5	7	5	.583	0	0	0	0
Wis.-Platteville (1991-92-93-94-95-96-97-98-99)	9	30	5	.857	4	0	0	0
Wis.-Stevens Point (1997-2000-03-04-05-07)	6	17	4	.810	2	0	1	0
Wis.-Stout (2006)	1	1	1	.500	0	0	0	0
Wis.-Whitewater (1983-84-85-86-88-89-92-93-94-95-96-97-2006)	13	22	12	.647	2	0	0	1
Wittenberg (1975-76-77-79-80-81-82-83-85-86-87-89-90-91-92-94-95-96-97-2001-02-04-05-06)	24	47	24	.662	1	3	3	0
Wooster (1978-91-92-93-95-96-97-98-99-2000-01-03-04-05-06-07)	16	17	17	.500	0	0	1	1
Worcester St. (1977-94)	2	0	3	.000	0	0	0	0
WPI (1982-85-2005-06-07)	5	4	6	.400	0	0	0	0
York (N.Y.) (1995-96-97-2006-07)	5	0	5	.000	0	0	0	0
York (Pa.) (1995-2005-06)	3	4	4	.500	0	0	0	1

All-Time Results

1975 First Round: Suffolk 80, Mass.-Boston 75 (ot); Brandeis 94, Rhode Island Col. 84; St. Lawrence 82, Albany (N.Y.) 63; Brockport St. 83, Rensselaer 70; Mansfield 85, Frank. & Marsh. 70; Scranton 59, Widener 55; Wm. Paterson 53, Methodist 52; Rowan 66, Wash. & Lee 48; LeMoyne-Owen 92, Transylvania 84; Miles 80, Sewanee 60; Marietta 75, Allegheny 67; Wittenberg 71, Hiram 49; Wartburg 79, Coe 78; Augustana (Ill.) 67, Knox 64. **Regional Third Place:** Mass.-Boston 114, Rhode Island Col. 96; Rensselaer 72, Albany (N.Y.) 55; Widener 69, Frank. & Marsh. 50; Methodist 71, Wash. & Lee 58; Transylvania 68, Sewanee 66; Hiram 86, Allegheny 78; Coe 83, Knox 72. **Regional Championships:** Brandeis 89, Suffolk 77; Brockport St. 103, St. Lawrence 77; Mansfield 78, Scranton 65; Rowan 62, Wm. Paterson 59; LeMoyne-Owen 92, Miles 76; Wittenberg 85, Marietta 70; Augustana (Ill.) 62, Wartburg 61; Hamline 48, Doane 47. **Quarterfinals:** Brockport St. 96, Brandeis 76; Rowan 60, Mansfield 49; LeMoyne-Owen 68, Wittenberg 65; Augustana (Ill.) 48, Hamline 42. **Semifinals:** Rowan 76, Brockport St. 68; LeMoyne-Owen 84, Augustana (Ill.) 71. **Third Place:** Augustana (Ill.) 78, Brockport St. 71. **Championship:** LeMoyne-Owen 57, Rowan 54.

1976 First Round: Mass.-Dartmouth 79, Suffolk 76; Rhode Island Col. 87, Mass.-Boston 65; CCNY 94, Rochester Inst. 69; Plattsburgh St. 68, Rensselaer 65; Wittenberg 88, Oberlin 66; Ashland 75, Hiram 74; Miles 79, Sewanee 71; Transylvania 112, LeMoyne-Owen 92; Widener 65, Mansfield 54; Scranton 68, Grove City 45; Shepherd 77, Rowan 62; Monmouth 97, Lynchburg 73; Coe 70, Simpson 62; Augustana (Ill.) 83, Cornell College 77. **Regional Third Place:** Mass.-Boston 108, Suffolk 101; Rochester Inst. 81, Rensselaer 74; Oberlin 80, Hiram 77; LeMoyne-Owen 87, Sewanee 86; Mansfield 73, Grove City 59; Rowan 82, Lynchburg 62; Simpson 96, Cornell College 88. **Regional Championships:** Rhode Island Col. 89, Mass.-Dartmouth 87; Plattsburgh St. 83, CCNY 81; Wittenberg 61, Ashland 49; Miles 87, Transylvania 85; Scranton 70, Widener 65; Shepherd 79, Monmouth 71; Augustana (Ill.) 79, Coe 70. **Quarterfinals:** Plattsburgh St. 91, Rhode Island Col. 80; Wittenberg 101, Miles 75; Scranton 94, Shepherd 78. **Semifinals:** Wittenberg 71, Plattsburgh St. 58; Scranton 76, Augustana (Ill.) 65. **Third Place:** Augustana (Ill.) 93, Plattsburgh St. 69. **Championship:** Scranton 60, Wittenberg 57.

1977 First Round: Mass.-Boston 83, Suffolk 73; Brandeis 67, Worcester St. 65; Oneonta St. 71, Stony Brook 65; Albany (N.Y.) 75, Ithaca 58; Hamline 44, Beloit 42; Central (Iowa) 73, Augustana (Ill.) 69; Methodist 85, Rowan 82; Wm. Paterson 92, Wash. & Lee 68; Scranton 59, Widener 51; Albright 51, Frank. & Marsh. 49; Rose-Hulman 85, Knoxville 75; Transylvania 85, Clark Atlanta 84; Ashland 72, Muskingum 68; Wittenberg 82, Carnegie Mellon 68. **Regional Third Place:** Suffolk 81, Worcester St. 79; Stony Brook 74, Ithaca 63; Augustana (Ill.) 78, Beloit 68; Rowan 103, Wash. & Lee 87; Frank. & Marsh. 89, Widener 71; Knoxville 73, Clark Atlanta 67; Muskingum 74, Carnegie Mellon 71. **Regional Championships:** Mass.-Boston 95, Brandeis 69; Oneonta St. 47, Albany (N.Y.) 46; Hamline 53, Central (Iowa) 50; Wm. Paterson 62, Methodist 60; Scranton 75, Albright 60; Neb. Wesleyan 84, Bishop 83; Rose-Hulman 91, Transylvania 85 (ot); Wittenberg 69, Ashland 67. **Quarterfinals:** Oneonta St. 72, Mass.-Boston 61; Hamline 82, Neb. Wesleyan 60; Scranton 78, Wm. Paterson 69; Wittenberg 71, Rose-Hulman 57. **Semifinals:** Oneonta St. 61, Hamline 56; Wittenberg 53, Scranton 52 (ot). **Third Place:** Scranton 60, Hamline 59. **Championship:** Wittenberg 79, Oneonta St. 66.

1978 First Round: Mass.-Boston 93, Suffolk 90; Brandeis 79, Clark (Mass.) 77; Stony Brook 68, Potsdam St. 62; St. Lawrence 65, Manhattanville 62; Widener 47, Upsala 39; Slippery Rock 70, Scranton 65; Kean 84, Va. Wesleyan 75; Wash. & Lee 66, New Jersey City 65; Albion 72, Otterbein 61; Bethany (W.V.) 70, Rose-Hulman 68; Wooster 84, DePauw 74; Knoxville 86, Transylvania 67; North Park 78, Ripon 68; Minn.-Morris 62, Central (Iowa) 59. **Regional Third Place:** Clark (Mass.) 89, Suffolk 87; Potsdam St. 64, Manhattanville 60; Scranton 84, Upsala 77; New Jersey City 105, Va. Wesleyan 102; Otterbein 99, Rose-Hulman 82; Transylvania 96, DePauw 79; Central (Iowa) 81, Ripon 66. **Regional Championships:** Brandeis 69, Mass.-Boston 68; Stony Brook 40, St. Lawrence 34; Widener 63, Slippery Rock 60 (ot); Kean 80, Wash. & Lee 64; Albion 91, Bethany (W.V.) 74; Knoxville 84, Wooster 76; North Park 65, Minn.-Morris 62; Humboldt St. 69, Ashland 68. **Quarterfinals:** Stony Brook 98, Brandeis 84; Widener 55, Kean 49; Albion 78, Knoxville 77; North Park 79, Humboldt St. 76 (ot). **Semifinals:** Widener 48, Stony Brook 38; North Park 75, Albion 69. **Third Place:** Albion 87, Stony Brook 78. **Championship:** North Park 69, Widener 57.

1979 First Round: Framingham St. 89, Rhode Island Col. 80; Clark (Mass.) 68, Coast Guard 59 (2 ot); St. Lawrence 64, Manhattanville 59; Potsdam St. 70, Stony Brook 65; Baldwin-Wallace 70, Albion 66; Wittenberg 69, Allegheny 68; Savannah St. 82, Albany (N.Y.) 81 (ot); Centre 79, Lane 68; Elizabethtown 58, Grove City 53; Frank. & Marsh. 74, Albright 63 (ot); New Jersey City 85, Va. Wesleyan 64; Upsala 115, Lynchburg 85; Central (Iowa) 85, Minn.-Morris 57; North Park 63, Beloit 62; Chaminade 78, William Penn 69; Whittier 74, Humboldt St. 73 (2 ot). **Regional Third Place:** Coast Guard 76, Rhode Island Col. 71; Stony Brook 66, Manhattanville 61; Albion 91, Allegheny 78; Albany (N.Y.) 85, Lane 83 (ot); Grove City 79, Albright 73; Va. Wesleyan 108, Lynchburg 84;

Beloit 72, Minn.-Morris 64; Humboldt St. 95, William Penn 91. **Regional Championships:** Clark (Mass.) 85, Framingham St. 73; Potsdam St. 70, St. Lawrence 61; Baldwin-Wallace 68, Wittenberg 66; Centre 82, Savannah St. 54; Frank. & Marsh. 60, Elizabethtown 59; New Jersey City 91, Upsala 81; North Park 81, Central (Iowa) 66; Chaminade 78, Whittier 77. **Quarterfinals:** Potsdam St. 89, Clark (Mass.) 72; Centre 68, Baldwin-Wallace 65 (3 ot); Frank. & Marsh. 83, New Jersey City 72; North Park 95, Chaminade 74. **Semifinals:** Potsdam St. 67, Centre 63; North Park 83, Frank. & Marsh. 73. **Third Place:** Frank. & Marsh. 66, Centre 65. **Championship:** North Park 66, Potsdam St. 62.

1980 First Round: Longwood 73, Framingham St. 63; Clark (Mass.) 90, Salem St. 71; Potsdam St. 93, Stony Brook 75; Albany (N.Y.) 75, St. Lawrence 66; Humboldt St. 64, Occidental 54; New Jersey City 66, Beloit 55; North Park 91, Ripon 73; Augustana (Ill.) 76, Central (Iowa) 74; Albright 88, Ursinus 72; Scranton 51, Dickinson 48; Upsala 78, Wash. & Lee 70; Wm. Paterson 81, Allegheny 74; Ohio Northern 92, Calvin 90; Wittenberg 76, Wabash 68; Savannah St. 61, UNC Greensboro 58; Lane 57, Rhodes 54. **Regional Third Place:** Salem St. 84, Framingham St. 82; Stony Brook 85, St. Lawrence 70; Beloit 69, Occidental 57; Ripon 81, Central (Iowa) 71; Dickinson 77, Ursinus 64; Allegheny 103, Wash. & Lee 80; Calvin 88, Wabash 76; Rhodes 88, UNC Greensboro 80. **Regional Championships:** Longwood 70, Clark (Mass.) 60; Potsdam St. 87, Albany (N.Y.) 72; New Jersey City 74, Humboldt St. 73; North Park 72, Augustana (Ill.) 60; Albright 81, Scranton 73; Upsala 104, Wm. Paterson 79; Wittenberg 59, Ohio Northern 51; Lane 87, Savannah St. 70. **Quarterfinals:** Longwood 78, Potsdam St. 61; North Park 86, New Jersey City 63; Upsala 71, Albright 58; Wittenberg 69, Lane 59. **Semifinals:** North Park 57, Longwood 55; Upsala 67, Wittenberg 63. **Third Place:** Wittenberg 48, Longwood 47. **Championship:** North Park 83, Upsala 76.

1981 First Round: Clark (Mass.) 109, Mass.-Boston 69; Rochester 75, Salem St. 62; Potsdam St. 80, Staten Island 57; Albany (N.Y.) 45, St. Lawrence 44; Ursinus 69, Frank. & Marsh. 58; Wm. Paterson 87, Scranton 70; Upsala 73, Allegheny 66; Montclair St. 57, Roanoke 55; Beloit 68, William Penn 58; Augustana (Ill.) 81, North Park 68; Whittier 103, Cal St. Stanislaus 95; Muskingum 75, Dubuque 61; Wittenberg 72, Calvin 50; Otterbein 81, Wabash 69; Savannah St. 76, Rose-Hulman 62; Rhodes 72, St. Andrews 70. **Regional Third Place:** Salem St. 91, Mass.-Boston 90; St. Lawrence 62, Staten Island 60; Frank. & Marsh. 73, Scranton 68; Roanoke 84, Allegheny 75; William Penn 85, North Park 81; Dubuque 86, Cal St. Stanislaus 73; Wabash 93, Calvin 71; St. Andrews 84, Rose-Hulman 80. **Regional Championships:** Clark (Mass.) 78, Rochester 74; Potsdam St. 68, Albany (N.Y.) 63 (ot); Ursinus 66, Wm. Paterson 64; Upsala 86, Montclair St. 64; Augustana (Ill.) 56, Beloit 53; Whittier 66, Muskingum 61 (ot); Otterbein 72, Wittenberg 68; Savannah St. 76, Rhodes 75. **Quarterfinals:** Potsdam St. 87, Clark (Mass.) 81; Ursinus 71, Upsala 69; Augustana (Ill.) 69, Whittier 67; Otterbein 67, Savannah St. 64 (ot). **Semifinals:** Potsdam St. 63, Ursinus 61; Augustana (Ill.) 93, Otterbein 81. **Third Place:** Ursinus 82, Otterbein 79. **Championship:** Potsdam St. 67, Augustana (Ill.) 65 (ot).

1982 First Round: Salem St. 58, WPI 57 (ot); Potsdam St. 53, Clark (Mass.) 51; Ursinus 64, Scranton 62; Widener 61, Dickinson 53; Staten Island 64, Buffalo 53; Brooklyn 50, Ithaca 47; Roanoke 67, Montclair St. 66; Upsala 54, Bethany (W.V.) 39; Augustana (Ill.) 70, Milwaukee 63; Luther 66, Beloit 42; Hope 77, Wittenberg 60; Wabash 81, Ohio Northern 61; Cal St. Stanislaus 62, Whittier 60; Bishop 65, North Park 64; St. Andrews 91, Rose-Hulman 69; Capital 103, Va. Wesleyan 93 (ot). **Regional Third Place:** Clark (Mass.) 99, WPI 57; Scranton 91, Dickinson 77; Ithaca 74, Buffalo 73; Montclair St. 69, Bethany (W.V.) 68; Milwaukee 75, Beloit 73; Ohio Northern 80, Wittenberg 52; North Park 68, Whittier 66; Rose-Hulman 88, Va. Wesleyan 87. **Regional Championships:** Potsdam St. 59, Salem St. 58; Ursinus 63, Widener 53; Brooklyn 60, Staten Island 57; Augustana (Ill.) 76, Luther 57; Wabash 82, Hope 70; Roanoke 81, Upsala 72; Cal St. Stanislaus 84, Bishop 67; Capital 72, St. Andrews 68. **Quarterfinals:** Potsdam St. 62, Ursinus 44; Brooklyn 62, Roanoke 59; Wabash 54, Augustana (Ill.) 51; Cal St. Stanislaus 61, Capital 60. **Semifinals:** Potsdam St. 50, Brooklyn 49; Wabash 68, Cal St. Stanislaus 64. **Third Place:** Brooklyn 68, Cal St. Stanislaus 62. **Championship:** Wabash 83, Potsdam St. 62.

1983 First Round: Clark (Mass.) 82, Mass.-Boston 71; Bridgewater St. 56, Muskingum 54; Roanoke 66, N.C. Wesleyan 63; Wm. Paterson 70, Upsala 58; Potsdam St. 76, Ithaca 74 (3 ot); Hartwick 61, Union (N.Y.) 49; Scranton 73, Moravian 59; Widener 56, Grove City 52; Cal St. Stanislaus 80, Augustana (Ill.) 73; Sonoma St. 88, Bishop 65; Hope 81, John Carroll 72; Wittenberg 57, Capital 56; Millikin 66, Beloit 49; Wis.-Whitewater 62, William Penn 47; St. Andrews 69, Centre 57; LeMoyne-Owen 76, Rust 62. **Regional Third Place:** Mass.-Boston 75, Muskingum 68; Upsala 97, N.C. Wesleyan 88; Union (N.Y.) 89, Ithaca 69; Grove City 76, Moravian 54; Bishop 104, Augustana (Ill.) 100; Capital 75, John Carroll 64; William Penn 73, Beloit 68; Rust 59, Centre 58. **Regional Championships:** Clark (Mass.) 82, Bridgewater St. 80; Roanoke 58, Wm. Paterson 56; Potsdam St. 60, Hartwick 56; Scranton 74, Widener 69 (3 ot); Cal St. Stanislaus 71, Sonoma St. 61; Wittenberg 63, Hope 55; Wis.-Whitewater 63, Millikin 61; LeMoyne-Owen 90, St. Andrews 88 (ot). Quarterfinals: Roanoke 87, Clark (Mass.) 83; Scranton 65, Potsdam St. 64; Wittenberg 68, Cal St. Stanislaus 65; Wis.-Whitewater 94, LeMoyne-Owen 83. **Semifinals:** Scranton 82, Roanoke 67; Wittenberg 85, Wis.-Whitewater 80. **Third Place:** Roanoke 83, Wis.-Whitewater 77. **Championship:** Scranton 64, Wittenberg 63.

1984 First Round: Framingham St. 94, Hiram 76; Clark (Mass.) 88, Norwich 84; Staten Island 64, St. Lawrence 53; Nazareth 67, Buffalo St. 50; Roanoke 94, Washington (Md.) 74; Upsala 44, Wm. Paterson 43; Montclair St. 78, Scranton 60; Susquehanna 74, Frank. & Marsh. 58; Neb. Wesleyan 62, Claremont-M-S 47; Potsdam St. 68, Luther 57; St. Norbert 69, North Central (Ill.) 56; Wis.-Whitewater 75, Ill. Wesleyan 67; Heidelberg 73, Hope 69; DePauw 62, Capital 60; LeMoyne-Owen 88, Millsaps 69; N.C. Wesleyan 70, Centre 62. **Regional Third Place:** Hiram 105, Norwich 103; Buffalo St. 83, St. Lawrence 70; Wm. Paterson 83, Washington (Md.) 78; Scranton 86, Frank. & Marsh. 82; Claremont-M-S 84, Luther 83; North Central (Ill.) 82, Ill. Wesleyan 77; Capital 83, Hope 77; Millsaps 65, Centre 56. **Regional Championships:** Clark (Mass.) 84, Framingham St. 78; Nazareth 74, Staten Island 68; Upsala 63, Roanoke 62; Montclair St. 68, Susquehanna 62; Neb. Wesleyan 87, Potsdam St. 72; Wis.-Whitewater 87, St. Norbert 84 (3 ot); DePauw 54, Heidelberg 53 (ot); LeMoyne-Owen 71, N.C. Wesleyan 68. **Quarterfinals:** Clark (Mass.) 90, Nazareth 84; Upsala 57, Montclair St. 56; Wis.-Whitewater 65, Neb. Wesleyan 54; DePauw 98, LeMoyne-Owen 49. **Semifinals:** Clark (Mass.) 69, Upsala 68; Wis.-Whitewater 85, DePauw 69. **Third Place:** DePauw 73, Upsala 67. **Championship:** Wis.-Whitewater 103, Clark (Mass.) 86.

1985 First Round: Clark (Mass.) 88, Westfield St. 78; WPI 58, Albany (N.Y.) 57 (ot); Widener 54, Lycoming 52; Scranton 85, Wash. & Jeff. 74; Wm. Paterson 71, Roanoke 68 (ot); TCNJ 75, Salisbury 62; Buffalo St. 76, Alfred 68; Potsdam St. 63, Hartwick 62; Wittenberg 70, DePauw 62; Hope 78, Otterbein 71; North Park 95, Monmouth (Ill.) 55; Wis.-Whitewater 72, North Central (Ill.) 53; Neb. Wesleyan 74, St. John's (Minn.) 56; Central (Iowa) 72, Redlands 64; Centre 66, Greensboro 52; LeMoyne-Owen 74, Augsburg 55. **Regional Third Place:** Albany (N.Y.) 78, Westfield St. 70; Lycoming 102, Wash. & Jeff. 92 (2 ot); Salisbury 98, Roanoke 83; Hartwick 52, Alfred 47; Otterbein 79, DePauw 78; Monmouth (Ill.) 69, North Central (Ill.) 60; Redlands 80, St. John's (Minn.) 70; Greensboro 83, Augsburg 69. **Regional Championships:** WPI 67, Clark (Mass.) 62; Widener 55, Scranton 53 (ot); Wm. Paterson 59, TCNJ 48; Potsdam St. 69, Buffalo St. 56; Wittenberg 68, Hope 63; North Park 83, Wis.-Whitewater 81 (ot); Neb. Wesleyan 76, Central (Iowa) 54; Centre 91, LeMoyne-Owen 72. **Quarterfinals:** Widener 41, WPI 38; Potsdam St. 76, Wm. Paterson 59; North Park 73, Wittenberg 71; Neb. Wesleyan 69, Centre 62. **Semifinals:** Potsdam St. 54, Widener 38; North Park 85, Neb. Wesleyan 80. **Third Place:** Neb. Wesleyan 48, Widener 44. **Championship:** North Park 72, Potsdam St. 71.

1986 First Round: Salem St. 73, Clark (Mass.) 71; Mass.-Dartmouth 64, Western Conn. St. 62; New Jersey City 67, Roanoke 61; Upsala 66, TCNJ 64; Alfred 88, Nazareth 86; Potsdam St. 83, New York U. 67; DePauw 69, Wittenberg 55; Otterbein 100, Calvin 84; Ripon 68, North Park 65; Ill. Wesleyan 79, Wis.-Whitewater 75; LeMoyne-Owen 92, John Carroll 78; Centre 70, Chris. Newport 62; Neb. Wesleyan 89, Pomona-Pitzer 59; Dubuque 71, St. John's (Minn.) 47; Susquehanna 79, Washington (Md.) 75; Frank. & Marsh. 61, Scranton 57. **Regional Third Place:** Clark (Mass.) 78, Western Conn. St. 77; TCNJ 58, Roanoke 55; Nazareth 87, New York U. 73; Wittenberg 84, Calvin 77; Wis.-Whitewater 89, North Park 73; Chris. Newport 75, John Carroll 73; St. John's (Minn.) 71, Pomona-Pitzer 52; Washington (Md.) 94, Scranton 78. **Regional Championships:** Mass.-Dartmouth 81, Salem St. 66; New Jersey City 69, Upsala 64; Potsdam St. 80, Alfred 51; Otterbein 82, DePauw 76; Ill. Wesleyan 63, Ripon 57; LeMoyne-Owen 72, Centre 69; Neb. Wesleyan 61, Dubuque 50; Susquehanna 79, Frank. & Marsh. 72 (ot). **Quarterfinals:** LeMoyne-Owen 93, Ill. Wesleyan 85; Potsdam St. 80, Susquehanna 65; Neb. Wesleyan 87, Otterbein 82 (ot); New Jersey City 83, Mass.-Dartmouth 69. **Semifinals:** Potsdam St. 91, New Jersey City 89; LeMoyne-Owen 86, Neb. Wesleyan 80. **Third Place:** Neb. Wesleyan 97, New Jersey City 93. **Championship:** Potsdam St. 76, LeMoyne-Owen 73.

1987 First Round: Mass.-Dartmouth 110, Mass. Liberal Arts 82; Clark (Mass.) 108, Norwich 76; Potsdam St. 56, Ithaca 53; Nazareth 93, Stony Brook 81; Widener 67, Scranton 56; Frank. & Marsh. 77, Allegheny 59; Richard Stockton 67, Roanoke 64; Cal St. Stanislaus 101, New Jersey City 93; Washington-St. Louis 69, Rust 68; N.C. Wesleyan 64, Centre 62; Otterbein 95, Hope 80; Wittenberg 70, Calvin 69; Gust. Adolphus 70, Neb. Wesleyan 59; Wartburg 91, Claremont-M-S 81; North Park 91, Ripon 81; Ill. Wesleyan 69, DePauw 61. **Regional Third Place:** Norwich 89, Mass. Liberal Arts 70; Stony Brook 95, Ithaca 77; Scranton 97, Allegheny 90 (ot); Roanoke 96, New Jersey City 82; Rust 72, Centre 65; Calvin 92, Hope 90 (ot); Claremont-M-S 75, Neb. Wesleyan 60; DePauw 77, Ripon 66. **Regional Championships:** Clark (Mass.) 88, Mass.-Dartmouth 80; Potsdam St. 86, Nazareth 63; Widener 53, Frank. & Marsh. 50; Richard Stockton 88, Cal St. Stanislaus 80; N.C. Wesleyan 66, Washington-St. Louis 64; Wittenberg 78, Otterbein 71; Wartburg 74, Gust. Adolphus 72; North Park 82, Ill. Wesleyan 77. **Quarterfinals:** Clark (Mass.) 65, Potsdam St. 63; Richard Stockton 68, Widener 65 (ot); Wittenberg 77, N.C. Wesleyan 64; North Park 88, Wartburg 63. **Semifinals:** Clark (Mass.) 77, Richard Stockton 71; North Park 75, Wittenberg 70. **Third Place:** Wittenberg 82, Richard Stockton 80 (ot). **Championship:** North Park 106, Clark (Mass.) 100.

1988 First Round: Mass.-Dartmouth 91, Mass. Liberal Arts 75; Clark (Mass.) 82, Southern Me. 79; Scranton 59, Cabrini 51; Frank. & Marsh. 63, Allegheny 61; Buffalo St. 73, Potsdam St. 70; Hartwick 80, Staten Island 73; TCNJ 87, Bridgewater (Va.) 50; Emory & Henry 72, Richard Stockton 59; Ill. Wesleyan 99, Monmouth (Ill.) 74; Millikin 101, Wis.-Whitewater 86; Ohio Wesleyan 77, Ohio Northern 70; Hope 80, Muskingum 75; Neb. Wesleyan 72, St. John's (Minn.) 64; Dubuque 80, Claremont-M-S 78; Centre 73, Rust 67; Washington-St. Louis 64, Chris. Newport 62. **Regional Third Place:** Southern Me. 84, Mass. Liberal Arts 60; Allegheny 93, Cabrini 66; Potsdam St. 93, Staten Island 80; Richard Stockton 72, Bridgewater (Va.) 70; Wis.-Whitewater 103, Monmouth (Ill.) 93; Ohio Northern 69, Muskingum 43; St. John's (Minn.) 92, Claremont-M-S 75; Rust 74, Chris. Newport 63. **Regional Championships:** Clark (Mass.) 86, Mass.-Dartmouth 85; Scranton 61, Frank. & Marsh. 47; Hartwick 54, Buffalo St. 53; TCNJ 82, Emory & Henry 72; Ill. Wesleyan 91, Millikin 74; Ohio Wesleyan 110, Hope 107 (2 ot); Neb. Wesleyan 69, Dubuque 64; Washington-St. Louis 74, Centre 59. **Quarterfinals:** Scranton 73, Clark (Mass.) 55; Hartwick 84, TCNJ 69; Ohio Wesleyan 106, Ill. Wesleyan 103; Neb. Wesleyan 58, Washington-St. Louis 55. **Semifinals:** Scranton 84, Hartwick 61; Ohio Wesleyan 87, Neb. Wesleyan 71. **Third Place:** Neb. Wesleyan 73, Hartwick 70. **Championship:** Ohio Wesleyan 92, Scranton 70.

1989 First Round: Staten Island 96, Alfred 72; Shenandoah 74, Richard Stockton 64; Monmouth (Ill.) 82, Beloit 70; Allegheny 71, Hope 69; Calvin 69, Capital 64; Wartburg 78, Gust. Adolphus 62; Pomona-Pitzer 108, Cal St. San B'dino 104 (2 ot); Rose-Hulman 56, Chris. Newport 42. **Regional Semifinals:** Southern Me. 88, Mass. Liberal Arts 80; Western Conn. St. 89, Salem St. 84; Frank. & Marsh. 59, Susquehanna 54; Washington (Md.) 82, Grove City 69; Buffalo St. 76, Staten Island 51; Potsdam St. 80, Merchant Marine 68; TCNJ 96, Shenandoah 74; New Jersey City 94, Hampden-Sydney 84; Wis.-Whitewater 112, Monmouth (Ill.) 76; North Central (Ill.) 63, Millikin 59; Wittenberg 61, Allegheny 46; Otterbein 93, Calvin 90; Neb. Wesleyan 87, Wartburg 63; Cal St. Stanislaus 90, Pomona-Pitzer 78; Centre 88, Rose-Hulman 75; Washington-St. Louis 2, Rust 0 (forfeit). **Regional Third Place:** Mass. Liberal Arts 112, Salem St. 78; Grove City 74, Susquehanna 60; Merchant Marine 69, Staten Island 54; Hampden-Sydney 80, Shenandoah 78; Monmouth (Ill.) 87, Millikin 84; Calvin 89, Allegheny 87 (ot); Pomona-Pitzer 80, Wartburg 67. **Regional Championships:** Southern Me. 90, Western Conn. St. 88; Frank. & Marsh. 96, Washington (Md.) 76; Potsdam St. 74, Buffalo St. 60; TCNJ 78, New Jersey City 77; Wis.-Whitewater 95, North Central (Ill.) 83; Otterbein 76, Wittenberg 66; Cal St. Stanislaus 76, Neb. Wesleyan 66; Centre 69, Washington-St. Louis 68. **Quarterfinals:** Southern Me. 79, Frank. & Marsh. 71; TCNJ 78, Potsdam St. 62; Wis.-Whitewater 105, Otterbein 86; Centre 124, Cal St.

Stanislaus 123 (2 ot). **Semifinals:** TCNJ 84, Southern Me. 62; Wis.-Whitewater 88, Centre 81. **Third Place:** Southern Me. 81, Centre 70. **Championship:** Wis.-Whitewater 94, TCNJ 86.

1990 First Round: Southern Me. 74, Western New Eng. 52; Rochester 73, Nazareth 54; Johns Hopkins 90, FDU-Florham 72; Richard Stockton 100, Hunter 84; Muskingum 70, Otterbein 64; Emory & Henry 91, Chris. Newport 80; Ill. Wesleyan 83, North Park 68; Dubuque 84, Claremont-M-S 77. **Second Round:** Mass. Liberal Arts 88, Southern Me. 79; Albany (N.Y.) 85, Potsdam St. 75; Mass.-Dartmouth 122, Salem St. 112; Rochester 62, Buffalo St. 57; Johns Hopkins 85, Frank. & Marsh. 78; Western Conn. St. 69, TCNJ 68; Washington (Md.) 85, King's (Pa.) 83; Richard Stockton 73, New Jersey City 71; Wittenberg 69, Muskingum 50; Averett 91, Randolph-Macon 78 (ot); Calvin 95, Hope 68; Emory 91, Emory & Henry 81; Ill. Wesleyan 71, North Central (Ill.) 63; Neb. Wesleyan 77, UC San Diego 75; DePauw 71, Monmouth (Ill.) 69; St. Thomas (Minn.) 65, Dubuque 55. **Sectional Semifinals:** Mass. Liberal Arts 69, Albany (N.Y.) 66; Rochester 92, Mass.-Dartmouth 80; Western Conn. St. 79, Johns Hopkins 69; Washington (Md.) 89, Richard Stockton 88; Wittenberg 86, Averett 64; Calvin 80, Emory 73; Ill. Wesleyan 85, Neb. Wesleyan 63; DePauw 75, St. Thomas (Minn.) 69 (2 ot). **Sectional Third Place:** Mass.-Dartmouth 92, Albany (N.Y.) 91; Johns Hopkins 80, Richard Stockton 74; Emory 102, Averett 93; St. Thomas (Minn.) 77, Neb. Wesleyan 71. **Sectional Championships:** Rochester 50, Mass. Liberal Arts 47; Washington (Md.) 107, Western Conn. St. 104 (ot); Calvin 63, Wittenberg 59; DePauw 68, Ill. Wesleyan 65. **Semifinals:** Rochester 86, Washington (Md.) 70; DePauw 82, Calvin 79. **Third Place:** Washington (Md.) 87, Calvin 86. **Championship:** Rochester 43, DePauw 42.

1991 First Round: Rowan 88, NJIT 80; Johns Hopkins 65, Dickinson 60; Rochester 73, Rensselaer 69; Ripon 65, Ill. Wesleyan 63; Emory & Henry 88, Shenandoah 69; Washington-St. Louis 76, Maryville (Tenn.) 73; Calvin 85, Wooster 68; Central (Iowa) 88, Bethel (Minn.) 77. **Second Round:** Salem St. 83, Western Conn. St. 62; Ramapo 87, Salisbury 75; Mass.-Dartmouth 87, Southern Me. 76; Kean 85, Rowan 66; Frank. & Marsh. 65, Johns Hopkins 56; Geneseo St. 83, Buffalo St. 75; Scranton 85, King's (Pa.) 62; Rochester 71, Stony Brook 67; Wis.-Platteville 96, Ripon 77; Chris. Newport 81, Emory & Henry 71; Benedictine (Ill.) 76, DePauw 72; Randolph-Macon 77, Washington-St. Louis 53; Calvin 89, Hope 84 (ot); Wartburg 75, Central (Iowa) 73; Otterbein 88, Wittenberg 62; UC San Diego 76, Claremont-M-S 72. **Sectional Semifinals:** Ramapo 101, Salem St. 98; Kean 105, Mass.-Dartmouth 80; Frank. & Marsh. 94, Geneseo St. 63; Rochester 64, Scranton 62 (ot); Wis.-Platteville 110, Chris. Newport 50; Benedictine (Ill.) 74, Randolph-Macon 62; Calvin 76, Wartburg 71; Otterbein 108, UC San Diego 95. **Sectional Championships:** Ramapo 80, Kean 77; Frank. & Marsh. 76, Rochester 73 (ot); Wis.-Platteville 101, Benedictine (Ill.) 65; Otterbein 75, Calvin 73. **Semifinals:** Frank. & Marsh. 109, Ramapo 56; Wis.-Platteville 96, Otterbein 94. **Third Place:** Otterbein 113, Ramapo 84. **Championship:** Wis.-Platteville 81, Frank. & Marsh. 74.

1992 First Round: King's (Pa.) 74, Susquehanna 71; Albany (N.Y.) 72, New York U. 66; Wis.-Whitewater 86, Ripon 83; Elmhurst 56, DePauw 49; Ferrum 79, Emory & Henry 77; Kean 63, Richard Stockton 60; Hope 76, Wittenberg 60; Colorado Col. 87, Simpson 67. **Second Round:** Frank. & Marsh. 74, King's (Pa.) 62; Buffalo St. 73, St. John Fisher 56; Scranton 58, Johns Hopkins 49; Rochester 75, Albany (N.Y.) 49; Wis.-Platteville 90, Wis.-Whitewater 78; Hampden-Sydney 88, Centre 83 (2 ot); Ill. Wesleyan 95, Elmhurst 70; Maryville (Tenn.) 94, Ferrum 92; Eastern Conn. St. 69, Babson 67; New Jersey City 81, Hunter 68; Salem St. 89, Western Conn. St. 77; Salisbury 107, Kean 99 (ot); Calvin 91, Hope 88; Gust. Adolphus 77, Colorado Col. 73 (ot); Otterbein 80, Wooster 77; Cal Lutheran 88, UC San Diego 70. **Sectional Semifinals:** Frank. & Marsh 64, Buffalo St. 55; Rochester 69, Scranton 54; Wis.-Platteville 89, Hampden-Sydney 71; Maryville (Tenn.) 73, Ill. Wesleyan 71; New Jersey City 92, Eastern Conn. St. 86; Salisbury 95, Salem St. 85; Calvin 69, Gust. Adolphus 68; Otterbein 82, Cal Lutheran 78. **Sectional Championships:** Rochester 77, Frank. & Marsh. 68; Wis.-Platteville 87, Maryville (Tenn.) 83 (ot); New Jersey City 97, Salisbury 83; Calvin 88, Otterbein 67. **Semifinals:** Rochester 61, Wis.-Platteville 48; Calvin 81, New Jersey City 40. **Third Place:** Wis.-Platteville 72, New Jersey City 61. **Championship:** Calvin 62, Rochester 49.

1993 First Round: Ithaca 71, Fredonia St. 56; Otterbein 80, Defiance 66; Rhodes 71, Va. Wesleyan 62; Lebanon Valley 53, Johns Hopkins 49; Richard Stockton 106, Catholic 91; Augustana (Ill.) 79, DePauw 66; St. John's (Minn.) 80, Wartburg 75 (ot); Wis.-Whitewater 84, Manchester 68. **Second Round:** New York U. 75, Ithaca 61; Eastern Conn. St. 81, Salem St. 71; Geneseo St. 80, Buffalo St. 69; Mass.-Dartmouth 90, Westfield St. 81; Calvin 90, Otterbein 68; Emory & Henry 85, Maryville (Tenn.) 61; Ohio Northern 88, Wooster 62; Chris. Newport 84, Rhodes 74; Scranton 58, Lebanon Valley 56; Hunter 83, NJIT 70; Frank. & Marsh. 78, Elizabethtown 64; Rowan 84, Richard Stockton 61; La Verne 67, Cal Lutheran 56; Augustana (Ill.) 92, Beloit 66; St. Thomas (Minn.) 75, St. John's (Minn.) 61; Wis.-Platteville 88, Wis.-Whitewater 72. **Sectional Semifinals:** Eastern Conn. St. 78, New York U. 73 (2 ot); Mass.-Dartmouth 68, Geneseo St. 66; Calvin 101, Emory & Henry 67; Ohio Northern 83, Chris. Newport 67; Scranton 78, Hunter 62; Rowan 69, Frank. & Marsh. 68; Augustana (Ill.) 87, La Verne 84; Wis.-Platteville 70, St. Thomas (Minn.) 60. **Sectional Championships:** Mass.-Dartmouth 75, Eastern Conn. St. 64; Ohio Northern 67, Calvin 56; Rowan 80, Scranton 73; Augustana (Ill.) 100, Wis.-Platteville 86. **Semifinals:** Ohio Northern 74, Mass.-Dartmouth 73; Augustana (Ill.) 83, Rowan 81. **Third Place:** Rowan 95, Mass.-Dartmouth 74. **Championship:** Ohio Northern 71, Augustana (Ill.) 68.

1994 First Round: Hunter 79, Montclair St. 74; St. John Fisher 77, Brockport St. 72; UC San Diego 67, Pomona-Pitzer 66; Hampden-Sydney 91, Oglethorpe 79; Susquehanna 100, Cabrini 77; Williams 108, Worcester St. 88; Wis.-Platteville 78, Cornell College 54; Wash. & Jeff. 73, Otterbein 71. **Second Round:** Rowan 70, Hunter 55; New York U. 67, Geneseo St. 55; Richard Stockton 74, NJIT 69; Albany (N.Y.) 84, St. John Fisher 72; Cal Lutheran 95, UC San Diego 81; Greensboro 90, Chris. Newport 77; St. Thomas (Minn.) 73, Central (Iowa) 62; Hampden-Sydney 95, Roanoke 80; Frank. & Marsh. 87, Susquehanna 78; Amherst 80, Colby 77; Lebanon Valley 58, Johns Hopkins 48; Mass.-Dartmouth 82, Williams 78; Wis.-Platteville 76, Wis.-Whitewater 68; Wittenberg 86, Calvin 81; Ill. Wesleyan 79, Manchester 77; Wash. & Jeff. 75, Kenyon 58. **Sectional Semifinals:** New York U. 80, Rowan 75 (3 ot); Albany (N.Y.) 60, Richard Stockton 54; Greensboro 104, Cal Lutheran 99; St. Thomas (Minn.) 80, Hampden-Sydney 66; Amherst 80, Frank. & Marsh. 71; Lebanon Valley 83, Mass.-Dartmouth 62; Wittenberg 66, Wis.-Platteville 48; Wash. & Jeff. 97, Ill. Wesleyan 82. **Sectional Championships:** New York U. 67, Albany (N.Y.) 65; St. Thomas (Minn.) 84, Greensboro 74; Lebanon Valley 87, Amherst 79; Wittenberg 91, Wash. & Jeff. 65. Semifinals: New York U. 75, St. Thomas (Minn.) 68; Lebanon Valley 93, Wittenberg 83. **Third Place:** Wittenberg 73, St. Thomas (Minn.) 62. **Championships:** Lebanon Valley 66, New York U. 59 (ot).

1995 Play-in: Geneseo St. 74, Rochester Inst. 53; Albany (N.Y.) 92, St. John Fisher 84; Rowan 70, Montclair St. 45; New York U. 101, Hunter 71; Buffalo St. 58, Elmira 49; Hamilton 83, Plattsburgh St. 74; New Jersey City 109, Staten Island 91; NJIT 87, York (N.Y.) 70; Baldwin-Wallace 72, Hope 69; Wittenberg 62, Calvin 57; Ill. Wesleyan 115, Westminster (Mo.) 74; Washington-St. Louis 68, Beloit 60; Kenyon 74, Ohio Northern 72; Wooster 72, Heidelberg 64; Hanover 79, Wheaton (Ill.) 78; Manchester 93, Ripon 70; Hampden-Sydney 78, Chris. Newport 71; Greensboro 87, Oglethorpe 72; St. Thomas (Minn.) 62, Central (Iowa) 58; Neb. Wesleyan 120, Simpson 79; Maryville (Tenn.) 77, Roanoke 76; Millsaps 79, Hendrix 67; Wis.-Whitewater 82, Pomona-Pitzer 70; Wis.-Platteville 99, St. John's (Minn.) 67; Mass.-Dartmouth 117, Salve Regina 77; Williams 80, Colby 66; Goucher 102, Lebanon Valley 91; Wilkes 70, Widener 60; Salem St. 86, Tufts 80; Trinity (Conn.) 95, Babson 89; Cabrini 88, York (Pa.) 63; Frank. & Marsh. 69, Muhlenberg 54. **Second Round:** Geneseo St. 71, Albany (N.Y.) 70; Rowan 74, New York U. 58; Hamilton 79, Buffalo St. 64; NJIT 97, New Jersey City 86; Baldwin-Wallace 74, Wittenberg 70; Ill. Wesleyan 90, Washington-St. Louis 65; Kenyon 57, Wooster 55; Manchester 84, Hanover 79; Hampden-Sydney 105, Greensboro 79; Neb. Wesleyan 94, St. Thomas (Minn.) 74; Millsaps 88, Maryville (Tenn.) 86 (2 ot); Wis.-Platteville 100, Wis.-Whitewater 98; Williams 61, Mass.-Dartmouth 59; Wilkes 88, Goucher 70; Trinity (Conn.) 93, Salem St. 90 (ot); Frank. & Marsh. 87, Cabrini 83. **Sectional Semifinals:** Rowan 76, Geneseo St. 64; NJIT 96, Hamilton 86; Ill. Wesleyan 67, Baldwin-Wallace 51; Manchester 84, Kenyon 65; Hampden-Sydney 77, Neb. Wesleyan 65; Wis.-Platteville 82, Millsaps 68; Wilkes 91, Williams 89 (ot); Trinity (Conn.) 79, Frank. & Marsh. 58. **Sectional Championships:** Rowan 101, NJIT 87; Manchester 89, Ill. Wesleyan 82; Wis.-Platteville 99, Hampden-Sydney 85; Trinity (Conn.) 90, Wilkes 85. **Semifinals:** Manchester 79, Rowan 66; Wis.-Platteville 82, Trinity (Conn.) 59. **Third Place:** Rowan 105, Trinity (Conn.) 72. **Championship:** Wis.-Platteville 69, Manchester 55.

1996 First Round: Geneseo St. 73, Rochester Inst. 51; Buffalo St. 74, St. John Fisher 65; Wilkes 87, DeSales 72; Cabrini 85, Catholic 65; St. Lawrence 85, Hamilton 78; Rensselaer 68, Hartwick 55; Lycoming 103, Gettysburg 75; Frank. & Marsh. 118, Salisbury 69; Wis.-Whitewater 85, Wis.-Platteville 77; Claremont-M-S 70, Upper Iowa 58; Hope 65, Kalamazoo 62; John Carroll 86, Wooster 72; Wis.-Oshkosh 79, Simpson 74; Gust. Adolphus 72, Concordia-M'head 61; Capital 68, Ohio Northern 57; Wittenberg 70, Baldwin-Wallace 61; Williams 78, Plymouth St. 62; Bowdoin 62, Springfield 56; Rowan 130, York (N.Y.) 66; New Jersey City 73, Staten Island 63; Anna Maria 111, Babson 90; Salem St. 76, Western Conn. St. 60; New York. U. 105, NJIT 88; Richard Stockton 80, Mt. St. Vincent 54; Wheaton (Ill.) 131, Grinnell 117; Washington-St. Louis 76, Rose-Hulman 74; Chris. Newport 66, Randolph-Macon 57; Millsaps 83, Bridgewater (Va.) 72; Hanover 85, Fontbonne 43; Ill. Wesleyan 77, Ripon 66; Hendrix 97, Stillman 85; Roanoke 128, Shenandoah 110. **Second Round:** Buffalo St. 71, Geneseo St. 61; Wilkes 96, Cabrini 91 (ot); Rensselaer 78, St. Lawrence 70; Frank. & Marsh. 72, Lycoming 61; Wis.-Whitewater 63, Claremont-M-S 62; Hope 80, John Carroll 61; Gust. Adolphus 61, Wis.-Oshkosh 60 (2 ot); Wittenberg 65, Capital 60; Williams 91, Bowdoin 64; Rowan 102, New Jersey City 83; Anna Maria 74, Salem St. 67; Richard Stockton 81, New York U. 77 (ot); Washington-St. Louis 93, Wheaton (Ill.) 75; Chris. Newport 73, Millsaps 69; Ill. Wesleyan 73, Hanover 67; Roanoke 80, Hendrix 64. **Sectional Semifinals:** Wilkes 64, Buffalo St. 59; Frank. & Marsh. 74, Rensselaer 58; Hope 88, Wis.-Whitewater 66; Wittenberg 76, Gust. Adolphus 68; Rowan 85, Williams 77; Richard Stockton 95, Anna Maria 88; Washington-St. Louis 87, Chris. Newport 71; Ill. Wesleyan 116, Roanoke 88. **Sectional Championships:** Frank. & Marsh. 107, Wilkes 70; Hope 69, Wittenberg 60; Rowan 98, Richard Stockton 70; Ill. Wesleyan 73, Washington-St. Louis 61. **Semifinals:** Hope 76, Frank. & Marsh. 57; Rowan 79, Ill. Wesleyan 77. **Third Place:** Ill. Wesleyan 89, Frank. & Marsh. 57. **Championship:** Rowan 100, Hope 93.

1997 First Round: Widener 70, Dickinson 62; Salisbury 101, Wilkes 90; Brockport St. 64, St. Lawrence 63; St. John Fisher 77, Cortland St. 70; Alvernia 69, Lebanon Valley 55; Goucher 67, Cabrini 60; Buffalo St. 70, Hamilton 66; Rochester Inst. 65, Rochester 64; Chris. Newport 79, Hampden-Sydney 74; Methodist 67, Roanoke 63; Chicago 59, Benedictine (Ill.) 52; Wabash 69, Lawrence 63; Sewanee 68, Rust 61; Bridgewater (Va.) 64, Maryville (Tenn.) 62; Rose-Hulman 86, Washington-St. Louis 69; Ill. Wesleyan 105, Maryville (Mo.) 66; Rowan 72, Mt. St. Vincent 53; New York U. 94, New Jersey City 84; Tufts 65, Mass.-Dartmouth 63; Salem St. 69, Springfield 61; Wm. Paterson 51, Merchant Marine 43; Richard Stockton 78, York (N.Y.) 71; Amherst 83, Colby 60; Williams 76, Wentworth Inst. 51; Hope 69, Denison 66; Wooster 84, Ohio Northern 58; Gust. Adolphus 82, Wis.-Whitewater 67; Neb. Wesleyan 93, Buena Vista 54; Wittenberg 82, John Carroll 68; Mount Union 77, Alfred 69; Wis.-Stevens Point 68, Pomona-Pitzer 58; Wis.-Platteville 51, Wis.-Oshkosh 43. **Second Round:** Salisbury 77, Widener 65; Brockport St. 73, St. John Fisher 68; Alvernia 60, Goucher 55; Rochester Inst. 111, Buffalo St. 106 (2 ot); Methodist 72, Chris. Newport 67; Chicago 78, Wabash 70; Bridgewater (Va.) 65, Sewanee 62; Ill. Wesleyan 54, Rose-Hulman 53; Rowan 56, New York U. 53; Salem St. 83, Tufts 63; Richard Stockton 64, Wm. Paterson 60; Williams 86, Amherst 63; Hope 67, Wooster 56; Neb. Wesleyan 61, Gust. Adolphus 59; Mount Union 73, Wittenberg 65; Wis.-Stevens Point 46, Wis.-Platteville 43. **Sectional Semifinals:** Salisbury 79, Brockport St. 78; Alvernia 77, Rochester Inst. 71; Methodist 74, Chicago 70; Ill. Wesleyan 87, Bridgewater (Va.) 60; Rowan 82, Salem St. 72; Williams 85, Richard Stockton 61; Neb. Wesleyan 92, Hope 75; Wis.-Stevens Point 68, Mount Union 67 (ot). **Sectional Championships:** Alvernia 89, Salisbury 84; Ill. Wesleyan 95, Methodist 63; Williams 71, Rowan 62; Neb. Wesleyan 69, Wis.-Stevens Point 66. **Semifinals:** Ill. Wesleyan 85, Alvernia 82; Neb. Wesleyan 101, Williams 90. **Third Place:** Williams 78, Alvernia 77. **Championship:** Ill. Wesleyan 89, Neb. Wesleyan 86.

1998 First Round: Williams 89, Trinity (Conn.) 63; Hamilton 102, Geneseo St. 68; Salem St. 86, Mass.-Dartmouth 78 (ot); Nazareth 81, Brockport St. 78; Franklin 76, Ripon 73; Gust. Adolphus 78, Augsburg 70; Wabash 87, Aurora 80; Wis.-Oshkosh 93, Pomona-Pitzer 71; New Jersey City 71, New York U. 58; Johns Hopkins 87, FDU-Florham 47; Rowan 70, Merchant Marine 49; Scranton 77, Muhlenberg 61; Mississippi Col. 60, Sewanee 54; Allegheny 97, Baldwin-Wallace 88; Trinity (Tex.) 60, Randolph-Macon 55; John Carroll 72, Albion 50. **Second Round:** Williams 82, Springfield 75; Hamilton 87, St. John Fisher 72; Connecticut Col. 93, Salem St. 84; St. Lawrence 96, Nazareth 75; Ill. Wesleyan

95, Franklin 92 (ot); Gust. Adolphus 65, Neb. Wesleyan 51; Chicago 67, Wabash 62; Wis.-Platteville 69, Wis.-Oshkosh 59; Hunter 65, New Jersey City 60; Catholic 67, Johns Hopkins 62; Rowan 81, TCNJ 58; Wilkes 59, Scranton 57; Chris. Newport 78, Mississippi Col. 67; Hope 80, Allegheny 66; Hampden-Sydney 76, Trinity (Tex.) 62; John Carroll 78, Wooster 59. **Sectional Semifinals:** Williams 90, Hamilton 69; St. Lawrence 94, Connecticut Col. 77; Gust. Adolphus 67, Ill. Wesleyan 61; Wis.-Platteville 78, Chicago 63; Hunter 84, Catholic 82 (2 ot); Wilkes 83, Rowan 80 (2 ot); Hope 81, Chris. Newport 64; John Carroll 77, Hampden-Sydney 71. **Sectional Championships:** Williams 100, St. Lawrence 82; Wis.-Platteville 78, Gust. Adolphus 71; Wilkes 58, Hunter 55; Hope 84, John Carroll 66. **Semifinals:** Wis.-Platteville 82, Williams 68; Hope 81, Wilkes 61. **Third Place:** Williams 105, Wilkes 93. **Championship:** Wis.-Platteville 69, Hope 56.

1999 First Round: Hamilton 66, Rochester 58; Bowdoin 68, Bridgewater St. 48; Cortland St. 85, Rochester Inst. 49; Western Conn. St. 70, Clark (Mass.) 51; John Carroll 68, Allegheny 62; Maryville (Tenn.) 66, Rose-Hulman 59; Otterbein 104, Defiance 90; Randolph-Macon 68, Chris. Newport 66; Frank. & Marsh. 81, Johns Hopkins 66; New Jersey City 79, Merchant Marine 66; Catholic 77, Lebanon Valley 72; Wm. Paterson 76, Staten Island 59; Augsburg 102, Neb. Wesleyan 91; Wheaton (Ill.) 81, Washington-St. Louis 79; Gust. Adolphus 67, Pomona-Pitzer 37; Ripon 63, Ill. Wesleyan 58. **Second Round:** Hamilton 72, St. John Fisher 70; Trinity (Conn.) 71, Bowdoin 57; Cortland St. 71, Geneseo St. 61; Connecticut Col. 94, Western Conn. St. 76; John Carroll 88, Ohio Northern 83 (ot); Mississippi Col. 67, Maryville (Tenn.) 53; Wooster 89, Otterbein 80; Hampden-Sydney 74, Randolph-Macon 65; Wilkes 77, Frank. & Marsh. 58; Richard Stockton 62, New Jersey City 56; Catholic 73, Goucher 69; Wm. Paterson 58, Rowan 55; Wis.-Platteville 85, Augsburg 53; Manchester 62, Wheaton (Ill.) 60; Gust. Adolphus 58, Upper Iowa 55; Franklin 81, Ripon 73. **Sectional Semifinals:** Trinity (Conn.) 89, Hamilton 73; Connecticut Col. 80, Cortland St. 66; John Carroll 78, Mississippi Col. 57; Hampden-Sydney 74, Wooster 66; Richard Stockton 60, Wilkes 50; Wm. Paterson 79, Catholic 71; Wis.-Platteville 74, Manchester 65; Gust. Adolphus 66, Franklin 65. **Sectional Championships:** Connecticut Col. 73, Trinity (Conn.) 70; Hampden-Sydney 68, John Carroll 51; Wm. Paterson 50, Richard Stockton 49; Wis.-Platteville 61, Gust. Adolphus 47. **Semifinals:** Hampden-Sydney 74, Connecticut Col. 58; Wis.-Platteville 75, Wm. Paterson 51. **Third Place:** Connecticut Col. 92, Wm. Paterson 83 (ot). **Championship:** Wis.-Platteville 76, Hampden-Sydney 75 (2 ot).

2000 First Round: Springfield 80, Eastern Conn. St. 75; Amherst 79, Western New Eng. 77; Penn St.-Behrend 64, Alvernia 60; Hamilton 85, Endicott 68; St. Thomas (Minn.) 80, Neb. Wesleyan 58; Wis.-Eau Claire 72, Concordia (Wis.) 54; Lewis & Clark 77, Pacific (Ore.) 75; Ripon 58, St. John's (Minn.) 55; Pomona-Pitzer 65, Trinity (Tex.) 62; Maryville (Tenn.) 69, SCAD 54; Ohio Northern 74, Benedictine (Ill.) 66; Franklin 81, Webster 50; Scranton 78, Mt. St. Mary (N.Y.) 66; Chris. Newport 68, Mississippi Col. 61; Roanoke 83, Marymount (Va.) 72 (ot); Frank. & Marsh. 69, Baruch 46. **Second Round:** Springfield 75, Williams 74; Salem St. 81, Amherst 75; Penn St.-Behrend 80, Rochester Inst. 65; Cortland St. 60, Hamilton 55; Buena Vista 69, St. Thomas (Minn.) 66; Wis.-Eau Claire 74, Carthage 62; Wis.-Stevens Point 72, Lewis & Clark 68; Chicago 75, Ripon 68; McMurry 111, Pomona-Pitzer 76; Maryville (Tenn.) 76, Hampden-Sydney 75; Wooster 82, Ohio Northern 71; Calvin 92, Franklin 90 (ot); Wm. Paterson 60, Scranton 58; Catholic 65, Chris. Newport 64; Rowan 80, Roanoke 74; Frank. & Marsh. 65, Widener 62. **Sectional Semifinals:** Salem St. 70, Springfield 69; Penn St.-Behrend 58, Cortland St. 52; Wis.-Eau Claire 82, Buena Vista 75 (ot); Wis.-Stevens Point 63, Chicago 49; McMurry 112, Maryville (Tenn.) 95; Calvin 82, Wooster 53; Catholic 57, Wm. Paterson 52; Frank. & Marsh. 76, Rowan 72. **Sectional Championships:** Salem St. 75, Penn St.-Behrend 69; Wis.-Eau Claire 60, Wis.-Stevens Point 58; Calvin 115, McMurry 79; Frank. & Marsh. 85, Catholic 74. **Semifinals:** Wis.-Eau Claire 70, Salem St. 42; Calvin 79, Frank. & Marsh. 77. **Third Place:** Salem St. 79, Frank. & Marsh. 75. **Championship:** Calvin 79, Wis.-Eau Claire 74.

2001 First Round: Salem St. 96, Western New Eng. 71; Carthage 83, Marian (Wis.) 65; Maryville (Tenn.) 85, MacMurray 69; Calvin 89, Defiance 78; Merchant Marine 106, Cabrini 96; Amherst 89, St. John Fisher 76; Catholic 82, CCNY 65; Brockport St. 65, Colby-Sawyer 59; Wis.-Eau Claire 66, Benedictine (Ill.) 55; Linfield 85, Cal Lutheran 66; Washington-St. Louis 101, Aurora 84; Ill. Wesleyan 132, Grinnell 91; Roanoke 70, SCAD 62; Gust. Adolphus 69, Neb. Wesleyan 60; Mississippi Col. 61, Millsaps 45; Hampden-Sydney 60, Gettysburg 52. **Second Round:** Mass.-Dartmouth 86, Salem St. 64; Carthage 88, Wooster 80; Wittenberg 71, Maryville (Tenn.) 51; Ohio Northern 79, Calvin 68; Merchant Marine 100, Wilkes 98 (ot); Clark (Mass.) 89, Amherst 76; Catholic 69, Widener 67; Brockport St. 77, Hobart 75; Chicago 74, Wis.-Eau Claire 67; Lewis & Clark 101, Linfield 89; Elmhurst 78, Washington-St. Louis 77; Ill. Wesleyan 65, Wartburg 60; Chris. Newport 84, Roanoke 54; St. John's (Minn.) 84, Gust. Adolphus 75; McMurry 86, Mississippi Col. 82; Wm. Paterson 84, Hampden-Sydney 65. **Sectional Semifinals:** Carthage 90, Mass.-Dartmouth 41; Ohio Northern 82, Wittenberg 66; Clark (Mass.) 75, Merchant Marine 69; Catholic 69, Brockport St. 64; Chicago 62, Lewis & Clark 52; Ill. Wesleyan 63, Elmhurst 60; Chris. Newport 71, St. John's (Minn.) 65; Wm. Paterson 77, McMurry 59. **Sectional Championships:** Ohio Northern 66, Carthage 64; Catholic 82, Clark (Mass.) 78; Ill. Wesleyan 77, Chicago 68; Wm. Paterson 86, Chris. Newport 75. Semifinals: Catholic 82, Ohio Northern 77; Wm. Paterson 67, Ill. Wesleyan 52. **Third Place:** Ill. Wesleyan 76, Ohio Northern 73. **Championship:** Catholic 76, Wm. Paterson 62.

2002 First Round: Wis.-Oshkosh 71, Ripon 56; Lewis & Clark 81, Claremont-M-S 59; Hope 54, St. Norbert 53; Gust. Adolphus 74, Edgewood 65; Maryville (Tenn.) 70, Webster 45; Wittenberg 75, Franklin 44; Lycoming 78, Gettysburg 59; Bethany (W.V.) 110, Pitt.-Bradford 98; Williams 121, Cazenovia 49; Union (N.Y.) 75, Lasell 73; Western Conn. St. 92, Salem St. 89; Trinity (Conn.) 75, Colby-Sawyer 47; Alvernia 76, Ithaca 67; Cabrini 85, Merchant Marine 73; Clark (Mass.) 84, Suffolk 77; Hampden-Sydney 92, N.C. Wesleyan 79. **Second Round:** Wis.-Oshkosh 88, St. Thomas (Minn.) 85 (ot); Lewis & Clark 70, Mississippi Col. 57; Carthage 63, Hope 57; Gust. Adolphus 88, Buena Vista 60; Washington-St. Louis 71, Maryville (Tenn.) 57; DePauw 89, Wittenberg 76; Randolph-Macon 79, Lycoming 62; Otterbein 121, Bethany (W.V.) 98; Rochester 66, Williams 51; Babson 63, Union (N.Y.) 50; Amherst 82, Western Conn. St. 77; Brockport St. 80, Trinity (Conn.) 61; Elizabethtown 95, Alvernia 84; Cabrini 47, Wm. Paterson 43; Clark (Mass.) 101, Staten Island 72; Catholic 74, Hampden-Sydney 66. **Sectional Semifinals:** Lewis & Clark 79, Wis.-Oshkosh 71; Carthage 71, Gust. Adolphus 65; DePauw 90, Washington-St. Louis 87; Otterbein 85, Randolph-Macon 72; Rochester 71, Babson 60; Brockport St. 69, Amherst 64; Elizabethtown 87, Cabrini 85; Clark (Mass.) 75, Catholic 72. **Sectional Championships:** Carthage 85, Lewis & Clark 70; Otterbein 87, DePauw 79; Rochester 71, Brockport St. 62; Elizabethtown 94, Clark (Mass.) 90. **Semifinals:** Otterbein 70, Carthage 66; Elizabethtown 93, Rochester 83 (ot). **Third Place:** Carthage 72, Rochester 51. **Championship:** Otterbein 102, Elizabethtown 83.

2003 First Round: Alvernia 58, Mary Washington 53; Wis.-Oshkosh 78, Milwaukee Engr. 56; SCAD 66, Chris. Newport 61; Ill. Wesleyan 79, Blackburn 59; Buena Vista 96, Illinois Col. 66; Aurora 67, Trinity (Tex.) 66; Gust. Adolphus 65, Whitworth 55; Maryville (Tenn.) 70, Mississippi Col. 58; Salem St. 81, St. Joseph's (Me.) 76; Hamilton 93, Colby-Sawyer 68; Southern Vt. 63, Lasell 60; Western Conn. St. 84, Clark (Mass.) 82; Scranton 58, Buffalo St. 56; John Carroll 85, Pitt.-Bradford 65; Merchant Marine 63, CCNY 57; Montclair St. 74, Elizabethtown 69. Second Round: Randolph-Macon 72, Alvernia 69 (ot); Wis.-Oshkosh 84, Hope 77; Hampden-Sydney 56, SCAD 54; Ill. Wesleyan 85, Washington-St. Louis 73; Buena Vista 84, Rockford 72; Occidental 80, Aurora 61; Gust. Adolphus 75, Wis.-Stevens Point 62; Hanover 68, Maryville (Tenn.) 64; Williams 94, Salem St. 67; Hamilton 72, St. John Fisher 68; Amherst 84, Southern Vt. 60; Rochester 73, Western Conn. St. 62; Scranton 77, Ursinus 75; Wooster 77, John Carroll 75; Ramapo 92, Merchant Marine 76; Montclair St. 95, Catholic 78. **Sectional Semifinals:** Wis.-Oshkosh 53, Randolph-Macon 47; Hampden-Sydney 76, Ill. Wesleyan 68; Occidental 67, Buena Vista 62; Gust. Adolphus 79, Hanover 66; Williams 76, Hamilton 65; Amherst 74, Rochester 68; Wooster 75, Scranton 64; Ramapo 89, Montclair St. 80. **Sectional Finals:** Hampden-Sydney 68, Wis.-Oshkosh 63; Gust. Adolphus 74, Occidental 56; Williams 91, Amherst 74; Wooster 68, Ramapo 64. **Semifinals:** Williams 74, Wooster 72 (ot); Gust. Adolphus 79, Hampden-Sydney 68. **Third Place:** Wooster 78, Hampden-Sydney 74. **Championship:** Williams 67, Gust. Adolphus 65.

2004 First Round: Pomona-Pitzer 79, Colorado Col. 55; Wis.-Stevens Point 84, Benedictine (Ill.) 58; Sul Ross St. 71, Dallas 67; Lawrence 86, Lakeland 51; John Carroll 88, Calvin 77; Randolph-Macon 51, Methodist 50; Ill. Wesleyan 82, Maryville (Mo.) 73; Potsdam St. 60, Penn St.-Behrend 58; Trinity (Conn.) 72, Lasell 66; Salem St. 94, Johnson & Wales (R.I.) 80; St. John Fisher 90, Hamilton 83; Babson 66, Endicott 56; Lycoming 74, Lehman 68; Plymouth St. 75, Castleton 57; Hampden-Sydney 74, Elizabethtown 71; Catholic 75, Old Westbury 50. **Second Round:** Puget Sound 89, Pomona-Pitzer 75; Wis.-Stevens Point 66, Gust. Adolphus 55; Sul Ross St. 74, Trinity (Tex.) 72; Lawrence 72, Buena Vista 66; John Carroll 85, Wittenberg 64; Maryville (Tenn.) 75, Randolph-Macon 68; Ill. Wesleyan 77, Hanover 67; Wooster 70, Potsdam St. 56; Brockport St. 80, Trinity (Conn.) 76; Williams 91, Salem St. 77; Rochester 75, St. John Fisher 66; Keene St. 79, Babson 55; New Jersey City 74, Lycoming 67; Amherst 113, Plymouth St. 85; Frank. & Marsh. 78, Hampden-Sydney 76; Gwynedd-Mercy 74, Catholic 72 (ot). **Sectional Semifinals:** Wis.-Stevens Point 100, Puget Sound 79; Lawrence 86, Sul Ross St. 79 (ot); John Carroll 76, Maryville (Tenn.) 74; Wooster 58, Ill. Wesleyan 53; Williams 78, Brockport St. 50; Keene St. 82, Rochester 79; Amherst 92, New Jersey City 74; Frank. & Marsh. 92, Gwynedd-Mercy 74. **Sectional Finals:** Wis.-Stevens Point 82, Lawrence 81 (ot); John Carroll 70, Wooster 64; Williams 79, Keene St. 64; Amherst 82, Frank. & Marsh. 70. **Semifinals:** Wis.-Stevens Point 87, John Carroll 62; Williams 86, Amherst 81. **Third Place:** John Carroll 96, Amherst 85. **Championship:** Wis.-Stevens Point 84, Williams 82.

2005 First Round: Hanover 69, Blackburn 49; Trinity (Tex.) 72, Texas-Dallas 66; Buena Vista 91, Edgewood 74; Lawrence 70, Gust. Adolphus 56; City Tech 68, Ursinus 66; Albright 94, Mt. St. Mary (N.Y.) 84; Western Conn. St. 73, Endicott 62; Va. Wesleyan 76, New Jersey City 57; Springfield 71, Norwich 56; Union (N.Y.) 84, Gwynedd-Mercy 70; Salem St. 74, Elms 71; Lebanon Valley 71, Penn St.-Behrend 53; John Carroll 76, Bethany (W.V.) 48; Wooster 94, Baldwin-Wallace 78; Calvin 75, Wheaton (Ill.) 74; Maryville (Tenn.) 79, Methodist 64. **Second Round:** Hanover 81, Ill. Wesleyan 76; Trinity (Tex.) 65, Pomona-Pitzer 53; Puget Sound 85, Buena Vista 82; Wis.-Stevens Point 79, Lawrence 45; Ramapo 105, City Tech 60; King's (Pa.) 57, Albright 55; WPI 79, Western Conn. St. 77; York (Pa.) 90, Va. Wesleyan 80; Amherst 81, Springfield 68; Rochester 79, Union (N.Y.) 61; Potsdam St. 74, Salem St. 73 (ot); St. John Fisher 66, Lebanon Valley 58; John Carroll 75, Wittenberg 68 (2 ot); Albion 59, Wooster 58; Calvin 71, Aurora 59; Mississippi Col. 68, Maryville (Tenn.) 62. **Sectional Semifinals:** Trinity (Tex.) 73, Hanover 65; Wis.-Stevens Point 81, Puget Sound 63; King's (Pa.) 85, Ramapo 78; York (Pa.) 99, WPI 80; Rochester 69, Amherst 62; Potsdam St. 67, St. John Fisher 43; Albion 80, John Carroll 79; Calvin 79, Mississippi Col. 60. **Sectional Championships:** Wis.-Stevens Point 61, Trinity (Tex.) 55; York (Pa.) 70, King's (Pa.) 58; Rochester 67, Potsdam St. 51; Calvin 60, Albion 52. **Semifinals:** Wis.-Stevens Point 81, York (Pa.) 58; Rochester 65, Calvin 62. **Third Place:** Calvin 98, York (Pa.) 84. **Championship:** Wis.-Stevens Point 73, Rochester 49.

2006 First Round: St. Thomas (Minn.) 76, North Central (Ill.) 68; Wis.-Whitewater 76, DePauw 68; Ill. Wesleyan 81, Carroll (Wis.) 68; Occidental 48, Claremont M-S 41; Augustana (Ill.) 71, Buena Vista 66; Wis.-Stout 66, Carleton 64; Farmingdale St. 93, Ursinus 82; Lincoln (Pa.) 102, Chris. Newport 96; Messiah 83, Alvernia 77 (ot); Villa Julie 86, Baruch 71; Wm. Paterson 70, Scranton 45; York (Pa.) 87, York (N.Y.) 67; Widener 61, Catholic 59; Hamilton 66, Plattsburgh St. 65 (ot); Cortland St. 68, Mass.-Boston 54; Tufts 83, Endicott 60; WPI 79, Bridgewater St. 62; Utica 71, Gordon 66; Norwich 82, Elms 70; Mississippi Col. 88, Maryville (Mo.) 58; Maryville (Tenn.) 83, Trinity (Tex.) 64; Transylvania 75, Bethany (W.V.) 56; Wooster 84, Randolph-Macon 70; Hope 93, Wis. Lutheran 51; Calvin 79, Wis.-La Crosse 71; Wittenberg 76, Lake Erie 40; Baldwin-Wallace 79, Carnegie Mellon 71. **Second Round:** Lawrence 63, St. Thomas (Minn.) 59; Ill. Wesleyan 85, Wis.-Whitewater 71; Puget Sound 89, Occidental 81; Augustana (Ill.) 77, Wis.-Stout 70; Va. Wesleyan 71, Farmingdale St. 61; Lincoln (Pa.) 100, Messiah 80; Wm. Paterson 72, Villa Julie 48; Widener 71, York (Pa.) 69; Amherst 83, Hamilton 59; Tufts 68, Cortland St. 65; Utica 76, WPI 58; St. John Fisher 71, Norwich 50; Mississippi Col. 69, Maryville (Tenn.) 51; Transylvania 91, Wooster 88; Hope 70, Calvin 67; Wittenberg 78, Baldwin-Wallace 60. **Sectional Semifinals:** Ill. Wesleyan 71, Lawrence 68; Puget Sound 92, Augustana (Ill.) 86; Va. Wesleyan 72, Lincoln (Pa.) 71; Wm. Paterson 52, Widener 45; Amherst 90, Tufts 85; St. John Fisher 94, Utica 78; Transylvania 76, Mississippi Col. 64; Wittenberg 56, Hope 49. **Sectional Championships:** Ill. Wesleyan 113, Puget Sound 99; Va. Wesleyan 46, Wm. Paterson 35; Amherst 93, St. John Fisher 70; Wittenberg 74, Transylvania 61. **Semifinals:** Va. Wesleyan 81, Ill. Wesleyan 79; Wittenberg 64, Amherst 60. **Third Place:** Ill. Wesleyan 71, Amherst 68. **Championship:** Va. Wesleyan 59, Wittenberg 56.

2007 First Round: St. John's (Minn.) 85, Loras 82 (ot); Washington-St. Louis 77, Fontbonne 58; Whitworth 62, DePauw 59; Calvin 69, Aurora 68; Hope 76, Chicago 54;

Carroll (Wis.) 73, Augustana (Ill.) 69; Catholic 58, Messiah 37; Lincoln (Pa.) 91, Alvernia 76; Johns Hopkins 84, Villa Julie 72; Guilford 101, Manhattanville 81; Va. Wesleyan 63, Averett 60; Hampden-Sydney 68, Hood 65; Mississippi Col. 68, Occidental 51; Maryville (Tenn.) 73, Mary Hardin-Baylor 62; Widener 73, King's (Pa.) 63; Ramapo 77, York (N.Y.) 68; Stevens Inst. 68, WPI 57; Rhode Island Col. 64, Coast Guard 60; Brandeis 77, Trinity (Conn.) 70 (ot); Keene St. 81, River 47; St. John Fisher 98, Wentworth Inst. 72; Plattsburgh St. 61, Rochester 60; St. Lawrence 85, Elms 79; Brockport 74, Williams 66; Wooster 92, Transylvania 66; Centre 69, Capital 55; John Carroll 87, Westminster (Pa.) 83. **Second Round:** Wis.-Stevens Point 93, St. John's (Minn.) 76; Washington-St. Louis 63, Whitworth 61; Hope 80, Calvin 64; Carroll (Wis.) 86, St. Thomas (Minn.) 80; Lincoln (Pa.) 81, Catholic 70; Guilford 80, Johns Hopkins 73; Va. Wesleyan 61, Hampden-Sydney 51; Mississippi Col. 76, Maryville (Tenn.) 62; Amherst 87, Widener 70; Stevens Inst. 69, Ramapo 61; Rhode Island Col. 70, Brandeis 67; Keene St. 76, Salem St. 75; St. John Fisher 95, Plattsburgh St. 87; Brockport 74, St. Lawrence 49; Wooster 73, Centre 56; John Carroll 79, Lake Erie 77. **Sectional Semifinals:** Washington-St. Louis 78, Wis.-Stevens Point 66; Hope 89, Carroll 77; Guilford 129, Lincoln (Pa.) 128 (3 ot); Va. Wesleyan 81, Mississippi Col. 55; Amherst 97, Stevens Inst. 74; Rhode Island Col. 75, Keene St. 73; Brockport St. 105, St. John Fisher 91; Wooster 83, John Carroll 73. **Sectional Championships:** Washington-St. Louis 58, Hope 55; Va. Wesleyan 81, Guilford 71; Amherst 81, Rhode Island Col. 69; Wooster 94, Brockport St. 87. **Semifinals:** Va. Wesleyan 67, Washington-St. Louis 65; Amherst 67, Wooster 60. **Third Place:** Washington-St. Louis 92, Wooster 84. **Championship:** Amherst 80, Va. Wesleyan 67.

Statistical Leaders

2007 Division I Individual Leaders

Points Per Game

Rk. Name, School	Cl.	G	FGM	3FG	FT	Pts.	Avg.
1. #Reggie Williams, VMI	Jr.	33	338	76	176	928	28.1
2. Trey Johnson, Jackson St.	Sr.	35	311	79	246	947	27.1
3. Morris Almond, Rice	Sr.	32	263	77	241	844	26.4
4. #Kevin Durant, Texas	Fr.	35	306	82	209	903	25.8
5. Gary Neal, Towson	Sr.	32	267	93	183	810	25.3
6. Bo McCalebb, New Orleans	Jr.	31	287	26	176	776	25.0
7. #Rodney Stuckey, Eastern Wash.	So.	29	227	43	215	712	24.6
8. Gerald Brown, Loyola (Md.)	Jr.	29	205	58	175	643	22.2
9. Stephen Curry, Davidson	Fr.	34	242	122	124	730	21.5
10. Jaycee Carroll, Utah St.	Jr.	35	256	83	151	746	21.3
11. Alex Harris, UC Santa Barb.	Jr.	29	191	71	158	611	21.1
12. Adrian Banks, Arkansas St.	Jr.	33	232	97	134	695	21.1
13. Arizona Reid, High Point	Jr.	32	285	20	81	671	21.0
14. Kyle Hines, UNC Greensboro	Jr.	29	233	1	138	605	20.9
15. Chris Lofton, Tennessee	Jr.	31	205	106	129	645	20.8
16. Charron Fisher, Niagara	Jr.	27	188	37	142	555	20.6
17. Adam Haluska, Iowa	Sr.	31	190	90	167	637	20.5
18. Caleb Green, Oral Roberts	Sr.	34	207	6	278	698	20.5
19. Nick Fazekas, Nevada	Sr.	32	248	28	128	652	20.4
20. Larry Blair, Liberty	Sr.	31	237	52	105	631	20.4
21. Loren Stokes, Hofstra	Sr.	32	230	27	164	651	20.3
22. Bobby Brown, Cal St. Fullerton	Sr.	27	188	80	90	546	20.2
23. Antoine Agudio, Hofstra	Jr.	32	219	100	108	646	20.2
24. Jason Thompson, Rider	Jr.	31	221	6	176	624	20.1
25. Dionte Christmas, Temple	So.	30	192	88	128	600	20.0
26. Jarrius Jackson, Texas Tech	Sr.	34	224	79	150	677	19.9
27. Alando Tucker, Wisconsin	Sr.	36	256	40	164	716	19.9
28. Brandon Ewing, Wyoming	So.	31	186	50	194	616	19.9
29. Al Thornton, Florida St.	Sr.	35	244	36	166	690	19.7
30. DaShaun Wood, Wright St.	Sr.	33	223	59	143	648	19.6
31. Martin Samarco, Bowling Green	Sr.	31	200	80	124	604	19.5
32. Mark Tyndale, Temple	Jr.	24	164	24	113	465	19.4
33. Brandon Heath, San Diego St.	Sr.	33	225	87	100	637	19.3
34. James Florence, Mercer	Fr.	28	163	55	158	539	19.3
35. Chavis Holmes, VMI	So.	32	188	108	131	615	19.2
36. Robert McKiver, Houston	Jr.	33	201	116	116	634	19.2
37. Stefan Blaszczynski, Nicholls St.	Sr.	24	149	41	121	460	19.2
38. Jared Dudley, Boston College	Sr.	30	195	39	142	571	19.0
39. Sean Singletary, Virginia	Jr.	32	170	79	190	609	19.0
40. Mario Boggan, Oklahoma St.	Sr.	34	242	13	150	647	19.0
41. Demetris Nichols, Syracuse	Sr.	35	225	100	113	663	18.9
42. Carl Landry, Purdue	Sr.	34	219	4	201	643	18.9
43. Tre Kelley, South Carolina	Sr.	29	198	55	96	547	18.9
44. Quin Humphrey, Youngstown St.	Sr.	31	189	65	141	584	18.8
45. Jamar Wilson, Albany (N.Y.)	Sr.	33	209	46	156	620	18.8
46. Aaron Nixon, Long Beach St.	Sr.	32	198	81	124	601	18.8
47. Giordan Watson, Central Mich.	Jr.	31	186	64	146	582	18.8
48. Andre Harris, Fairleigh Dickinson	Sr.	30	227	10	99	563	18.8
Chris Oliver, Radford	Sr.	30	220	16	107	563	18.8
50. Stefon Jackson, UTEP	So.	31	194	31	159	578	18.6

#entered NBA draft

Field-Goal Percentage

Minimum 5 made per game

Rk. Name, School	Cl.	G	FGM	FGA	FG%
1. Mike Freeman, Hampton	Fr.	30	162	239	67.8
2. Roy Hibbert, Georgetown	Jr.	37	186	277	67.1
3. Florentino Valencia, Toledo	Sr.	32	164	246	66.7
4. Vladimir Kuljanin, UNC Wilmington	Jr.	29	165	249	66.3
5. Calvin Brown, Norfolk St.	Sr.	30	152	233	65.2
6. #Brandan Wright, North Carolina	Fr.	37	228	353	64.6
7. Herbert Hill, Providence	Sr.	31	240	375	64.0
8. Paul Butorac, Eastern Wash.	Sr.	28	158	247	64.0
9. Luke Nevill, Utah	So.	29	181	284	63.7
10. Ahmad Nivins, St. Joseph's	So.	31	176	279	63.1
11. Will Thomas, George Mason	Jr.	33	178	284	62.7
12. Jermaine Griffin, Texas-Arlington	Jr.	29	161	257	62.6
13. #Greg Oden, Ohio St.	Fr.	32	189	307	61.6
14. Stephane Lasme, Massachusetts	Sr.	33	165	270	61.1
15. Andrew Strait, Montana	Jr.	30	196	321	61.1
16. Rashaun Freeman, Massachusetts	Sr.	33	206	338	60.9
17. Amadi McKenzie, Tennessee Tech	Jr.	32	163	268	60.8
18. Richard Hendrix, Alabama	So.	32	186	309	60.2
19. Carlos Monroe, Fla. Atlantic	So.	27	200	335	59.7
20. Carl Landry, Purdue	Jr.	34	219	367	59.7

Rk. Name, School	Cl.	G	FGM	FGA	FG%
21. Tony Lee, Robert Morris	Jr.	28	169	285	59.3
22. Randolph Morris, Kentucky	Jr.	34	202	341	59.2
23. Chris Daniels, A&M-Corpus Christi	Sr.	33	194	329	59.0
24. Ben McCauley, North Carolina St.	So.	36	211	361	58.4
25. Kyle Visser, Wake Forest	Sr.	31	188	322	58.4
26. Leon Williams, Ohio	Jr.	32	162	278	58.3
27. #Jason Smith, Colorado St.	Jr.	30	175	302	57.9
28. Matt Nelson, Boise St.	Jr.	31	159	275	57.8
29. John Baumann, Columbia	Jr.	28	145	251	57.8
30. Kentrell Gransberry, South Fla.	Jr.	23	138	239	57.7

#entered NBA draft

Three-Point Field Goals Per Game

Rk. Name, School	Cl.	G	3FG	Avg.
1. Stephen Sir, Northern Ariz.	Sr.	30	124	4.13
2. Will Whittington, Marist	Sr.	34	137	4.03
3. Steven Rush, N.C. A&T	Jr.	30	115	3.83
4. Tristan Blackwood, Central Conn. St.	Jr.	34	122	3.59
Stephen Curry, Davidson	Fr.	34	122	3.59
6. Keddric Mays, Chattanooga	Sr.	33	118	3.58
7. Robert McKiver, Houston	Jr.	33	116	3.52
8. Daryl Cohen, Southeastern La.	Sr.	30	105	3.50
9. A.J. Abrams, Texas	So.	35	120	3.43
10. Chris Lofton, Tennessee	Jr.	31	106	3.42
11. Chavis Holmes, VMI	So.	32	108	3.38
12. Ryan Wittman, Cornell	Fr.	28	93	3.32
13. Erik Kangas, Oakland	So.	33	109	3.30
14. Colin Falls, Notre Dame	Sr.	30	99	3.30
15. Drew Neitzel, Michigan St.	Jr.	35	114	3.26
16. Frank Young, West Virginia	Sr.	36	117	3.25
17. David Holston, Chicago St.	Jr.	29	94	3.24
18. Adam Leonard, Eastern Ky.	Fr.	33	104	3.15
19. James Parlow, New Orleans	Jr.	27	85	3.15
20. Tajuan Porter, Oregon	Fr.	35	110	3.14
21. Antoine Agudio, Hofstra	Jr.	32	100	3.13
Andre' Ratliff, Grambling	Jr.	24	75	3.13
23. Jeremy Crouch, Bradley	Jr.	27	83	3.07
24. Ross DeRogatis, San Diego	Sr.	32	98	3.06
25. Leemire Goldwire, Charlotte	Jr.	30	91	3.03
26. Jimmy Baron, Rhode Island	So.	32	97	3.03
27. Jack Leasure, Coastal Caro.	Jr.	30	90	3.00
28. Joey Mundweiler, Wagner	So.	30	89	2.97
29. Bobby Brown, Cal St. Fullerton	Sr.	27	80	2.96
30. Leslie Robinson, Florida A&M	Jr.	35	103	2.94
31. Michael Jenkins, Winthrop	Jr.	34	100	2.94
32. Adrian Banks, Arkansas St.	Jr.	33	97	2.94
33. Jack McClinton, Miami (Fla.)	So.	31	91	2.94

Three-Point Field-Goal Percentage

Minimum 2.5 made per game

Rk. Name, School	Cl.	G	3FG	3FGA	3FG%
1. Josh Carter, Texas A&M	So.	34	86	172	50.0
Jeremy Crouch, Bradley	Jr.	27	83	166	50.0
3. Stephen Sir, Northern Ariz.	Sr.	30	124	253	49.0
4. Jimmy Baron, Rhode Island	So.	32	97	203	47.8
5. Josh Washington, A&M-Corpus Christi	Sr.	32	90	189	47.6
6. Adrian Banks, Arkansas St.	Jr.	33	97	204	47.5
7. James Parlow, New Orleans	Jr.	27	85	180	47.2
8. Blake Ahearn, Missouri St.	Sr.	33	94	202	46.5
9. Chad Toppert, New Mexico	So.	32	85	183	46.4
10. Lee Humphrey, Florida	Sr.	40	113	246	45.9
11. Brian Roberts, Dayton	Jr.	31	82	179	45.8
12. Samuel Haanpaa, Valparaiso	Fr.	29	75	164	45.7
13. Damon Huffman, Brown	Jr.	23	65	143	45.5
14. Matt Lawrence, Missouri	So.	30	81	183	44.3
15. DeWitt Scott, IPFW	Jr.	29	73	165	44.2
16. Andy Wicke, Belmont	So.	30	77	175	44.0
17. Jack McClinton, Miami (Fla.)	So.	31	91	207	44.0
18. Jason Holsinger, Evansville	So.	31	87	199	43.7
19. Tajuan Porter, Oregon	Fr.	35	110	252	43.7
20. Demetric Bennett, South Ala.	Jr.	31	81	186	43.5
21. Will Franklin, Bradley	Sr.	35	88	203	43.3
22. Frank Young, West Virginia	Sr.	36	117	270	43.3
23. Ryan Appleby, Washington	Jr.	32	84	194	43.3
24. Antoine Agudio, Hofstra	Jr.	32	100	231	43.3

Rk.	Name, School	Cl.	G	3FG	3FGA	3FG%
25.	Erik Kangas, Oakland	So.	33	109	253	43.1
26.	Ryan Wittman, Cornell	Fr.	28	93	216	43.1
27.	Donte Gennie, Ga. Southern	Sr.	31	82	191	42.9
28.	Levi Stukes, Georgia	Sr.	32	85	198	42.9
29.	Marquis Sullivan, Loyola (Md.)	So.	31	88	205	42.9
30.	Andre Ingram, American	Sr.	30	78	184	42.4

Free-Throw Percentage

Minimum 2.5 made per game

Rk.	Name, School	Cl.	G	FT	FTA	FT%
1.	Derek Raivio, Gonzaga	Sr.	34	148	154	96.1
2.	A.J. Graves, Butler	Jr.	35	145	153	94.8
3.	Blake Ahearn, Missouri St.	Sr.	33	111	120	92.5
4.	Tristan Blackwood, Central Conn. St.	Jr.	34	97	105	92.4
5.	David Kool, Western Mich.	Fr.	29	99	108	91.7
6.	Mike Schachtner, Green Bay	So.	33	104	114	91.2
7.	Arvydas Eitutavicius, American	Sr.	30	95	105	90.5
	Leemire Goldwire, Charlotte	Jr.	30	95	105	90.5
9.	Sharaud Curry, Providence	So.	27	82	91	90.1
10.	Brian Roberts, Dayton	Jr.	31	133	148	89.9
11.	Jack McClinton, Miami (Fla.)	So.	31	102	114	89.5
12.	Jaycee Carroll, Utah St.	Jr.	35	151	170	88.8
13.	Jim Goffredo, Harvard	Sr.	28	95	107	88.8
14.	Josh Mayo, Ill.-Chicago	So.	27	78	88	88.6
15.	Solomon Bozeman, South Fla.	Fr.	30	130	147	88.4
16.	DaShaun Wood, Wright St.	Sr.	33	143	162	88.3
17.	Derek Coleman, Robert Morris	Sr.	28	74	84	88.1
18.	Terry Bryant, Southeastern La.	Sr.	30	80	91	87.9
19.	Drew Neitzel, Michigan St.	Jr.	35	123	140	87.9
20.	Ivan Radenovic, Arizona	Sr.	31	150	172	87.2
21.	Sean Singletary, Virginia	Jr.	32	190	218	87.2
22.	Dionte Christmas, Temple	So.	30	128	147	87.1
23.	Adam Haluska, Iowa	Sr.	31	167	192	87.0
24.	Austin Ewing, N.C. A&T	Jr.	30	103	119	86.6
25.	Nate Carter, Oklahoma	Sr.	31	109	126	86.5
26.	Zarryon Fereti, St. Bonaventure	Jr.	24	64	74	86.5
27.	Austin Montgomery, IUPUI	Jr.	30	89	103	86.4
28.	Greg Sprink, Navy	Jr.	30	127	147	86.4
29.	Nate Funk, Creighton	Sr.	33	126	146	86.3
30.	Steven Rush, N.C. A&T	Jr.	30	91	106	85.8
31.	Dion Harris, Michigan	Sr.	35	103	120	85.8

Rebounds Per Game

Rk.	Name, School	Cl.	G	Reb.	Avg.
1.	Rashad Jones-Jennings, Ark.-Little Rock	Sr.	30	392	13.1
2.	Chris Holm, Vermont	Sr.	33	401	12.2
3.	Kentrell Gransberry, South Fla.	Jr.	23	263	11.4
4.	#Kevin Durant, Texas	Fr.	35	390	11.1
5.	Nick Fazekas, Nevada	Sr.	32	354	11.1
6.	Obie Nwadike, Central Conn. St.	Sr.	31	331	10.7
7.	Ryvon Covile, Detroit	Sr.	30	317	10.6
8.	#Glen Davis, LSU	Jr.	29	303	10.4
9.	#Jason Smith, Colorado St.	Jr.	30	304	10.1
10.	Jason Thompson, Rider	Jr.	31	312	10.1
11.	Christopher Moore, Texas Southern	Sr.	28	276	9.9
12.	Lamar Sanders, Lamar	Jr.	32	315	9.8
13.	#Dominic McGuire, Fresno St.	Jr.	32	314	9.8
14.	Clif Brown, Niagara	Sr.	33	321	9.7
15.	Jeff Adrien, Connecticut	So.	31	301	9.7
16.	Jon Brockman, Washington	So.	32	307	9.6
17.	#Greg Oden, Ohio St.	Fr.	32	306	9.6
18.	Stephane Lasme, Massachusetts	Sr.	33	315	9.5
19.	Arizona Reid, High Point	Jr.	32	304	9.5
	Scott Cutley, Cal St. Fullerton	Jr.	26	247	9.5
21.	#Al Horford, Florida	Jr.	38	360	9.5
22.	Aaron Gray, Pittsburgh	Sr.	36	341	9.5
23.	Carlos Monroe, Fla. Atlantic	So.	27	254	9.4
24.	Brandon Wallace, South Carolina	Sr.	30	282	9.4
25.	Joey Dorsey, Memphis	Jr.	37	347	9.4
26.	Chaz Crawford, Drexel	Sr.	31	289	9.3
27.	Yassin Idbihi, Buffalo	Sr.	28	261	9.3
28.	Caleb Green, Oral Roberts	Sr.	34	315	9.3
29.	Geoff McDermott, Providence	So.	31	283	9.1
30.	Jeff Pendergraph, Arizona St.	So.	30	272	9.1
31.	Eric Coleman, UNI	Jr.	31	281	9.1

#entered NBA draft

Assists Per Game

Rk.	Name, School	Cl.	G	Ast.	Avg.
1.	Jared Jordan, Marist	Sr.	33	286	8.67
2.	Jason Richards, Davidson	Jr.	34	249	7.32
3.	Mustafa Shakur, Arizona	Sr.	31	215	6.94
4.	D.J. Augustin, Texas	Fr.	35	233	6.66
5.	Eric Maynor, VCU	So.	35	224	6.40
6.	Keenan Jones, Northwestern St.	Sr.	32	200	6.25
7.	#Mike Conley Jr., Ohio St.	Fr.	39	238	6.10
8.	Dwayne Foreman, Ga. Southern	Sr.	29	176	6.07
9.	Josh Wilson, Northern Ariz.	So.	30	181	6.03
10.	Ishmael Smith, Wake Forest	Fr.	31	186	6.00
11.	Trant Simpson, Alabama A&M	Fr.	28	167	5.96
12.	Temi Soyebo, UNC Wilmington	Sr.	29	170	5.86
13.	Kevin Kanaskie, Middle Tenn.	So.	32	185	5.78
14.	Brooks McKowen, UNI	Sr.	31	179	5.77
	Charles Richardson Jr., Nebraska	Sr.	31	179	5.77
16.	#Javaris Crittenton, Georgia Tech	Fr.	32	184	5.75
17.	Steve Barnes, Southern Utah	Sr.	30	172	5.73
18.	Darren Collison, UCLA	So.	34	194	5.71
19.	Ty Lawson, North Carolina	Fr.	38	213	5.61
20.	Eugene Lawrence, St. John's (N.Y.)	Jr.	31	173	5.58
21.	Kevin Bell, Fresno St.	Jr.	32	178	5.56
22.	Jejuan Plair, Sam Houston St.	Sr.	31	172	5.55
23.	Darrell Jenkins, East Caro.	Jr.	30	166	5.53
24.	#Rodney Stuckey, Eastern Wash.	So.	29	160	5.52
25.	Todd Abernethy, Mississippi	Sr.	33	182	5.52
26.	Travis Walton, Michigan St.	So.	35	191	5.46
27.	Drew Gibson, Wofford	Jr.	25	136	5.44
28.	Al Stewart, Drake	Sr.	32	174	5.44
29.	Derek Coleman, Robert Morris	Sr.	28	152	5.43
30.	Tyrese Rice, Boston College	So.	33	178	5.39
31.	Frank Turner, Canisius	Fr.	31	167	5.39

#entered NBA draft

Blocked Shots Per Game

Rk.	Name, School	Cl.	G	Blk.	Avg.
1.	Mickell Gladness, Alabama A&M	Jr.	30	188	6.27
2.	Stephane Lasme, Massachusetts	Sr.	33	168	5.09
3.	Hasheem Thabeet, Connecticut	Fr.	31	118	3.81
4.	McHugh Mattis, South Fla.	Sr.	30	109	3.63
5.	#Dominic McGuire, Fresno St.	Jr.	32	114	3.56
6.	Scott VanderMeer, Ill.-Chicago	So.	32	111	3.47
7.	Darryl Watkins, Syracuse	Sr.	33	112	3.39
8.	#Greg Oden, Ohio St.	Fr.	32	105	3.28
9.	John Bunch, Monmouth	Sr.	29	95	3.28
10.	Chaz Crawford, Drexel	Sr.	31	94	3.03
11.	Joel Anthony, UNLV	Sr.	37	109	2.95
12.	Herbert Hill, Providence	Sr.	31	91	2.94
13.	Brandon Wallace, South Carolina	Sr.	30	86	2.87
14.	Steven Hill, Arkansas	Jr.	35	99	2.83
15.	Ekene Ibekwe, Maryland	Sr.	33	88	2.67
16.	Kieron Achara, Duquesne	Jr.	23	59	2.57
17.	Williams Byrd, Ark.-Pine Bluff	Sr.	31	78	2.52
18.	#Josh McRoberts, Duke	So.	33	82	2.48
19.	Bamba Fall, SMU	So.	25	62	2.48
20.	Diamon Simpson, St. Mary's (Cal.)	So.	32	79	2.47
21.	Roy Hibbert, Georgetown	Jr.	37	90	2.43
22.	Shawn King, Oral Roberts	Jr.	34	81	2.38
23.	Bryant Dunston, Fordham	Jr.	30	71	2.37
24.	Robin Lopez, Stanford	Fr.	31	73	2.35
25.	Jermareo Davidson, Alabama	Sr.	30	70	2.33
26.	Jemino Sobers, Central Conn. St.	Sr.	34	78	2.29
27.	D.J. White, Indiana	Jr.	32	73	2.28
28.	Kyle Hines, UNC Greensboro	Jr.	29	64	2.21
29.	Ahmet Gueye, Hawaii	Sr.	30	66	2.20
30.	Jarrad Henry, Pepperdine	Jr.	31	68	2.19
31.	Joey Dorsey, Memphis	Jr.	37	81	2.19
32.	Scott Morrison, Portland St.	Jr.	32	70	2.19

#entered NBA draft

Steals Per Game

Rk.	Name, School	Cl.	G	St.	Avg.
1.	Travis Holmes, VMI	So.	33	111	3.36
2.	Paul Gause, Seton Hall	So.	29	90	3.10

Rk. Name, School	Cl.	G	Stl.	Avg.
3. Ledell Eackles, Campbell	Sr.	31	94	3.03
4. Ibrahim Jaaber, Penn	Sr.	31	90	2.90
5. Chavis Holmes, VMI	So.	32	90	2.81
6. Torey Thomas, Holy Cross	Sr.	34	95	2.79
7. Jamon Gordon, Virginia Tech	Sr.	34	94	2.76
8. Tony Lee, Robert Morris	Jr.	28	77	2.75
9. Derek Johnson, Prairie View	So.	30	82	2.73
10. Jerel McNeal, Marquette	So.	29	76	2.62
11. Courtney Pigram, East Tenn. St.	So.	34	89	2.62
12. Carl Elliott, George Washington	Sr.	32	83	2.59
13. D.J. Thompson, Appalachian St.	Sr.	33	85	2.58
14. Sonny Troutman, Ohio	Sr.	32	82	2.56
15. Mario Chalmers, Kansas	So.	38	97	2.55
16. Alex Bausley, Sacramento St.	Sr.	29	72	2.48
17. Antonio Kellogg, San Francisco	So.	28	69	2.46
18. Mike Gordon, Binghamton	Jr.	29	71	2.45
#Rodney Stuckey, Eastern Wash.	So.	29	71	2.45
20. Stefhon Hannah, Missouri	Jr.	30	72	2.40
21. Oliver Lafayette, Houston	Sr.	33	78	2.36
22. Darren Collison, UCLA	So.	34	78	2.29
23. Bashir Mason, Drexel	Sr.	32	73	2.28
24. Drew Williamson, Old Dominion	Sr.	33	75	2.27
25. Damitrius Coleman, Bethune-Cookman	Sr.	26	59	2.27
26. Keith Simmons, Holy Cross	Sr.	34	77	2.26
27. Sundiata Gaines, Georgia	Jr.	32	72	2.25
28. Drew Gibson, Wofford	Jr.	25	56	2.24
29. #Mike Conley Jr., Ohio St.	Fr.	39	87	2.23
30. Royce Parran, Chicago St.	Sr.	29	64	2.21

#entered NBA draft

2007 Division I Individual Game Highs

Points

Rk. Name, School	Cl.	Opponent	Date	Pts.
1. Trey Johnson, Jackson St.	Sr.	UTEP	12/22/2006	49
2. Bobby Brown, Cal St. Fullerton	Sr.	Bethune-Cookman	12/16/2006	47
3. Al Thornton, Florida St.	Sr.	Miami (Fla.)	3/3/2007	45
Reggie Williams, VMI	Jr.	Virginia Intermont	11/15/2006	45
5. Jaycee Carroll, Utah St.	Jr.	New Mexico St.	2/5/2007	44
Morris Almond, Rice	Sr.	Vanderbilt	1/2/2007	44
7. Dwayne Jackson, Charleston So.	Sr.	VMI	1/13/2007	43
Martin Samarco, Bowling Green	Sr.	Buffalo	1/7/2007	43
Tony Murphy, Norfolk St.	Jr.	A&M-Corpus Christi	12/19/2006	43
David Holston, Chicago St.	Jr.	St. Bonaventure	11/9/2006	43
11. Morris Almond, Rice	Sr.	Utah	11/25/2006	42
12. Aleks Maric, Nebraska	Jr.	Kansas St.	2/13/2007	41
Reggie Williams, VMI	Jr.	Cornell	12/1/2006	41
Eugene Myatt, Howard	So.	VMI	11/25/2006	41
Gary Neal, Towson	Sr.	Samford	11/16/2006	41
16. JamesOn Curry, Oklahoma St.	Jr.	Baylor	3/3/2007	40
Scottie Reynolds, Villanova	Fr.	Connecticut	2/28/2007	40
Tristan Blackwood, Central Conn. St.	Jr.	Robert Morris	2/22/2007	40
Alex McLean, Liberty	Jr.	VMI	2/21/2007	40
Larry Blair, Liberty	Sr.	Coastal Caro.	2/12/2007	40
Reggie Williams, VMI	Jr.	Liberty	1/27/2007	40
J.R. Reynolds, Virginia	Sr.	Wake Forest	1/21/2007	40
Reggie Williams, VMI	Jr.	High Point	1/10/2007	40
Sammy Mejia, DePaul	Sr.	Northwestern St.	12/29/2006	40
Michael Jenkins, Winthrop	Jr.	North Greenville	11/10/2006	40

Field-Goal Percentage

Minimum 10 made

Rk. Name, School	Cl.	Opponent	Date	FGM	FGA	FG%
1. Andrew Strait, Montana	Jr.	Northern Ariz.	1/25/2007	11	11	100.0
Blagoj Janev, New Hampshire	Sr.	Vermont	1/9/2007	11	11	100.0
Anthony Tolliver, Creighton	Sr.	Illinois St.	1/1/2007	11	11	100.0
Vladimir Kuljanin, UNC Wilmington	Jr.	Toledo	12/16/2006	11	11	100.0
Tyler Troupe, Chattanooga	So.	King (Tenn.)	12/21/2006	10	10	100.0
Stephen DuCharme, Utah St.	Jr.	Drake	11/18/2006	10	10	100.0
Kyle Visser, Wake Forest	Sr.	James Madison	11/11/2006	10	10	100.0
8. Randall Gulina, Samford	Sr.	Tenn. Temple	11/14/2006	14	15	93.3
9. Longar Longar, Oklahoma	Jr.	Chaminade	11/22/2006	12	13	92.3
10. Antanas Kavaliauskas, Texas A&M	Sr.	Missouri	3/3/2007	11	12	91.7
Boomer Herndon, Belmont	Sr.	Kennesaw St.	1/4/2007	11	12	91.7
James Davis, Lamar	Jr.	Louisiana Col.	1/1/2007	11	12	91.7
Randolph Morris, Kentucky	Jr.	North Carolina	12/2/2006	11	12	91.7
Luke Nevill, Utah	So.	Weber St.	11/29/2006	11	12	91.7
James Hughes, Northern Ill.	Sr.	Duquesne	11/20/2006	11	12	91.7
16. John Cantrell, Chicago St.	Jr.	Centenary (La.)	2/17/2007	10	11	90.9
Antuane Miller, Stephen F. Austin	Sr.	Texas St.	1/25/2007	10	11	90.9
James Gist, Maryland	Jr.	Georgia Tech	1/24/2007	10	11	90.9
Will Thomas, George Mason	Jr.	Northeastern	1/20/2007	10	11	90.9
Jermaine Griffin, Texas-Arlington	Jr.	Northwestern St.	1/6/2007	10	11	90.9
Jimmy Tobias, Ga. Southern	Sr.	Flagler	12/12/2006	10	11	90.9
David Fisher, New Mexico St.	Sr.	New Mexico	12/5/2006	10	11	90.9
Kendall Chones, Colgate	Jr.	Harvard	12/2/2006	10	11	90.9
Sean Denison, Santa Clara	Sr.	Nevada	11/25/2006	10	11	90.9
Jerome Habel, San Diego St.	Jr.	California	11/18/2006	10	11	90.9
Herbert Hill, Providence	Sr.	Fairleigh Dickinson	11/14/2006	10	11	90.9
Russ Gibson, Campbell	Sr.	UNC Pembroke	11/11/2006	10	11	90.9

Three-Point Field Goals Made

Minimum 8 made

Rk. Name, School	Cl.	Opponent	Date	3FG
1. Michael Jenkins, Winthrop	Jr.	North Greenville	11/10/2006	12
2. Eric Moore, Buffalo	So.	Bowling Green	1/7/2007	11
Bobby Brown, Cal St. Fullerton	Sr.	Bethune-Cookman	12/16/2006	11
4. Tristan Blackwood, Central Conn. St.	Jr.	Robert Morris	2/22/2007	10
Andy Wicke, Belmont	So.	Gardner-Webb	1/20/2007	10
Nathan Cranford, Appalachian St.	Sr.	Chattanooga	1/6/2007	10
Leslie Robinson, Florida A&M	Jr.	Albany St. (Ga.)	12/9/2006	10
Tajuan Porter, Oregon	Fr.	Portland St.	11/12/2006	10
Daryl Cohen, Southeastern La.	Sr.	McNeese St.	2/1/2006	10
10. Isaiah Swann, Florida St.	Jr.	Mississippi St.	3/20/2007	9
Gary Patterson, IUPUI	So.	Oral Roberts	2/22/2007	9
Derek Stockalper, Cal Poly	Sr.	Portland St.	2/17/2007	9
Jamaal Womack, St. Francis (N.Y.)	Jr.	Robert Morris	2/17/2007	9
Derrick Low, Washington St.	Jr.	Oregon	1/27/2007	9
Fred Robinson, VMI	Sr.	Charleston So.	1/13/2007	9
Marico Stinson, Indiana St.	Fr.	Drake	12/30/2006	9
Ken Tutt, Oral Roberts	Sr.	Chattanooga	12/16/2006	9
Mike Jones, Maryland	Sr.	UMKC	12/13/2006	9
Robert McKiver, Houston	Jr.	Prairie View	11/29/2006	9
Stephen Curry, Davidson	Fr.	Colby	11/21/2006	9
Deonta Vaughn, Cincinnati	Fr.	Wofford	11/21/2006	9
Brandon Chappell, Lamar	Sr.	Nicholls St.	2/1/2006	9

Three-Point Field Goal Percentage

Minimum 7 made

Rk. Name, School	Cl.	Opponent	Date	3FG	3FGA	3FG%
1. Bryce Taylor, Oregon	Jr.	Southern Cal	3/10/2007	7	7	100.0
Matt Lojeski, Hawaii	Sr.	Boise St.	3/3/2007	7	7	100.0
Jawann McClellan, Arizona	Jr.	New Mexico St.	11/19/2006	7	7	100.0
4. Nathan Cranford, Appalachian St.	Sr.	Chattanooga	1/6/2007	10	11	90.9
5. Marico Stinson, Indiana St.	Fr.	Drake	12/30/2006	9	10	90.0
6. Levi Stukes, Georgia	Sr.	Fresno St.	3/14/2007	8	9	88.9
Quin Humphrey, Youngstown St.	Sr.	Ill.-Chicago	2/3/2007	8	9	88.9
Hector Hernandez, Fresno St.	Jr.	Cal Poly	12/23/2006	8	9	88.9
Jimmy Baron, Rhode Island	So.	Brown	12/5/2006	8	9	88.9
10. Andre Smith, George Mason	So.	James Madison	3/2/2007	7	8	87.5
Lee Humphrey, Florida	Sr.	South Carolina	1/13/2007	7	8	87.5
Donte Gennie, Ga. Southern	Sr.	Pikeville	1/2/2007	7	8	87.5
Mike Schachtner, Green Bay	Sr.	Chicago St.	12/12/2006	7	8	87.5
Adam Viet, UNI	Jr.	UMKC	12/9/2006	7	8	87.5
Corey Lewis, Colorado St.	Sr.	Kansas St.	12/2/2006	7	8	87.5
Marchello Vealy, Oral Roberts	So.	Kansas	11/15/2006	7	8	87.5
Billy Humphrey, Georgia	So.	Southern U.	11/10/2006	7	8	87.5
18. Bobby Brown, Cal St. Fullerton	Sr.	Beth.-Cookman	12/16/2006	11	13	84.6
19. Andy Wicke, Belmont	So.	Gardner-Webb	2/15/2007	10	12	83.3
Tajuan Porter, Oregon	Fr.	Portland St.	11/12/2006	10	12	83.3

Free-Throw Percentage

Minimum 12 made

Rk.	Name, School	Cl.	Opponent	Date	FT	FTA	FT%
1.	Jaycee Carroll, Utah St.	Jr.	New Mexico St.	2/5/2007	15	15	100.0
	Josh Mayo, Ill.-Chicago	So.	Loyola (Ill.)	3/2/2007	14	14	100.0
	Anthony Williams, Grambling	Sr.	Jackson St.	2/17/2007	14	14	100.0
	Blake Ahearn, Missouri St.	Sr.	Wichita St.	1/7/2007	14	14	100.0
	Jarrius Jackson, Texas Tech	Sr.	UTEP	11/25/2006	14	14	100.0
	Nate Carter, Oklahoma	Sr.	Texas A&M	1/27/2007	13	13	100.0
	Terrance Calvin, Ark.-Pine Bluff	Fr.	Philander Smith	1/8/2007	13	13	100.0
	Stephen Curry, Davidson	Fr.	Western Mich.	12/30/2006	13	13	100.0
	Chris Lofton, Tennessee	Jr.	East Tenn. St.	12/30/2006	13	13	100.0
	Eddie Ard, Lipscomb	Jr.	Liberty	12/21/2006	13	13	100.0
	Roderick Earls, Tulsa	Jr.	Cal St. Northridge	11/25/2006	13	13	100.0
	A.J. Graves, Butler	Jr.	Loyola (Ill.)	3/3/2007	12	12	100.0
	James Ulrich, Wagner	Jr.	Fairleigh Dickinson	2/24/2007	12	12	100.0
	Wesley Matthews, Marquette	So.	Villanova	2/19/2007	12	12	100.0
	Mike Trimboli, Vermont	So.	Binghamton	2/18/2007	12	12	100.0
	Derek Raivio, Gonzaga	Sr.	Santa Clara	2/12/2007	12	12	100.0
	Jermaine Anderson, New Hampshire	Sr.	Boston U.	2/11/2007	12	12	100.0
	Chuma Awaji, UC Irvine	Jr.	Cal St. Northridge	2/3/2007	12	12	100.0
	Rodney Stuckey, Eastern Wash.	So.	Montana St.	2/1/2007	12	12	100.0
	LeVonn Jordan, Elon	Sr.	Western Caro.	1/22/2007	12	12	100.0
	David Hoskins, Kansas St.	Jr.	Missouri	1/13/2007	12	12	100.0
	Tyrone Bazy, Northern Ariz.	Sr.	Eastern Wash.	1/6/2007	12	12	100.0
	Brandon Bush, Texas St.	So.	Central Ark.	1/6/2007	12	12	100.0
	DaShaun Wood, Wright St.	Sr.	IPFW	1/2/2007	12	12	100.0
	Devin Sweeney, St. Francis (Pa.)	Fr.	Liberty	12/16/2006	12	12	100.0
	Travis Jones, South Carolina St.	Sr.	Coastal Caro.	12/13/2006	12	12	100.0
	Ryan Werch, Green Bay	Jr.	Central Mich.	12/9/2006	12	12	100.0
	Calvin Chitwood, Cal St. Northridge	Jr.	Eastern Wash.	12/3/2006	12	12	100.0
	Rodney Stuckey, Eastern Wash.	So.	Eastern Ore.	11/29/2006	12	12	100.0
	Sean Singletary, Virginia	Jr.	UNC Asheville	11/22/2006	12	12	100.0
	Greg Sprink, Navy	Jr.	Stony Brook	11/19/2006	12	12	100.0
	Leemire Goldwire, Charlotte	Jr.	Hofstra	11/11/2006	12	12	100.0

Rebounds

Rk.	Name, School	Cl.	Opponent	Date	Reb.
1.	Arizona Reid, High Point	Jr.	VMI	2/24/2007	25
2.	Kentrell Gransberry, South Fla.	Jr.	DePaul	3/3/2007	23
	Kevin Durant, Texas	Fr.	Texas Tech	1/31/2007	23
4.	Jason Smith, Colorado St.	Jr.	Wyoming	2/24/2007	22
	Josh Heytvelt, Gonzaga	So.	Pepperdine	2/3/2007	22
	Moses Sonko, Coastal Caro.	Sr.	VMI	2/3/2007	22
	Calvin Henry, Mercer	So.	VMI	12/9/2006	22
	Paul Butorac, Eastern Wash.	Sr.	Lewis-Clark St.	11/18/2006	22
9.	Victor Akinyanju, Quinnipiac	Sr.	Mt. St. Mary's	2/3/2007	21
	Clif Brown, Niagara	Sr.	Binghamton	11/16/2006	21
11.	Terrence Roberts, Syracuse	Sr.	Notre Dame	3/8/2007	20
	Jason Thompson, Rider	Jr.	Manhattan	2/9/2007	20
	Calvin Brown, Norfolk St.	Sr.	Winston-Salem	1/18/2007	20
	Mario Boggan, Oklahoma St.	Sr.	Texas	1/16/2007	20
	Herbert Hill, Providence	Sr.	George Washington	11/26/2006	20

Assists

Rk.	Name, School	Cl.	Opponent	Date	Ast.
1.	Jason Richards, Davidson	Jr.	Mt. St. Mary (N.Y.)	12/15/2006	19
2.	Ryan Evanochko, Green Bay	Sr.	Chicago St.	12/12/2006	16
	Jason Richards, Davidson	Jr.	Colby	11/21/2006	16
4.	Ishmael Smith, Wake Forest	Fr.	Georgia Tech	3/8/2007	15
	Jared Jordan, Marist	Sr.	Siena	2/24/2007	15
	Darren Collison, UCLA	So.	Arizona	2/17/2007	15
	Acie Law IV, Texas A&M	Sr.	Texas	2/5/2007	15
	Eric Maynor, VCU	So.	Georgia St.	2/3/2007	15
	Charles Richardson Jr., Nebraska	Sr.	Rutgers	12/2/2006	15
	Keenan Jones, Northwestern St.	Sr.	Utah St.	11/10/2006	15
11.	C.C. Williams, Towson	Jr.	Georgia St.	2/10/2007	14
	Trant Simpson, Alabama A&M	Fr.	Ark.-Pine Bluff	2/5/2007	14
	Josh Wilson, Northern Ariz.	So.	Eastern Wash.	1/18/2007	14
	Acie Law IV, Texas A&M	Sr.	Grambling	12/28/2006	14
	Jerrel Green, Morgan St.	Jr.	Coppin St.	12/6/2006	14

Blocked Shots

Rk.	Name, School	Cl.	Opponent	Date	Blk.
1.	Mickell Gladness, Alabama A&M	Jr.	Texas Southern	2/24/2007	16
2.	Joel Anthony, UNLV	Sr.	TCU	2/7/2007	13
	Sean Williams, Boston College	Jr.	Duquesne	12/28/2006	13
4.	Brook Lopez, Stanford	Fr.	Southern California	1/25/2007	12
	Sean Williams, Boston College	Jr.	Providence	11/22/2006	12
6.	Jarrad Henry, Pepperdine	Jr.	Portland	2/5/2007	11
	Stephane Lasme, Massachusetts	Sr.	St. Francis (N.Y.)	11/22/2006	11
8.	Ronald Alexander, Mississippi Val.	Sr.	Jackson St.	2/24/2007	10
	John Bunch, Monmouth	Sr.	St. Francis (N.Y.)	2/3/2007	10
	Dominic McGuire, Fresno St.	Jr.	San Diego	12/30/2006	10
	Brad Kanis, Southern Utah	Jr.	Utah Valley St.	12/22/2006	10
	McHugh Mattis, South Fla.	Sr.	Winston-Salem	12/7/2006	10
	Hasheem Thabeet, Connecticut	Fr.	Texas Southern	12/3/2006	10
14.	Menelik Barbary, San Jose St.	Sr.	Idaho	3/6/2007	9
	Scott VanderMeer, Ill.-Chicago	So.	Cleveland St.	1/27/2007	9
	Mickell Gladness, Alabama A&M	Jr.	Southern U.	1/22/2007	9
	Mickell Gladness, Alabama A&M	Jr.	Alcorn St.	1/20/2007	9
	Mickell Gladness, Alabama A&M	Jr.	Mississippi	12/22/2006	9
	Jermareo Davidson, Alabama	Sr.	Southern Miss.	12/16/2006	9
	Mickell Gladness, Alabama A&M	Jr.	Paul Quinn	11/18/2006	9
	Hasheem Thabeet, Connecticut	Fr.	Fairfield	11/18/2006	9

Steals

Rk.	Name, School	Cl.	Opponent	Date	St.
1.	Travis Holmes, VMI	So.	Bridgewater (Va.)	1/18/2007	11
2.	Ledell Eackles, Campbell	Sr.	UNC Pembroke	11/11/2006	10
3.	D.J. Thompson, Appalachian St.	Jr.	UNC Greensboro	2/22/2007	9
	Kevin Bell, Fresno St.	Jr.	Hawaii	2/1/2007	9
	Chavis Holmes, VMI	So.	Bridgewater (Va.)	1/18/2007	9
	Damian Martin, Loyola Marymount	Jr.	Boise St.	12/19/2006	9
	Darren Collison, UCLA	So.	Long Beach St.	11/28/2006	9
8.	Eryk Thomas, East Tenn. St.	Sr.	Jacksonville	1/15/2007	8
	Travis Holmes, VMI	So.	Charleston So.	1/13/2007	8
	Brandon Johnson, Old Dominion	Jr.	George Mason	1/6/2007	8
	Paul Gause, Seton Hall	So.	St. Mary's (Cal.)	12/2/2006	8
	Tony Lee, Robert Morris	Jr.	Duquesne	12/2/2006	8
	Haron Hargrave, Sacramento St.	Sr.	Illinois St.	11/29/2006	8
	Temi Soyebo, UNC Wilmington	Sr.	Colorado	11/29/2006	8
	Ledell Eackles, Campbell	Sr.	Appalachian St.	11/27/2006	8
	Carlos Medlock, Eastern Mich.	So.	Davidson	11/10/2006	8
	Mike Robinson, Eastern Ill.	So.	La.-Monroe	11/10/2006	8

2007 Division I Team Leaders

Won-Lost Percentage

Rk.	Name	W	L	Pct.
1.	Ohio St.	35	4	89.7
2.	Memphis	33	4	89.2
3.	Florida	35	5	87.5
4.	Kansas	33	5	86.8
5.	UCLA	30	5	85.7
6.	Nevada	29	5	85.3
	Winthrop	29	5	85.3
	Davidson	29	5	85.3
9.	Wisconsin	30	6	83.3
10.	North Carolina	31	7	81.6
11.	UNLV	30	7	81.1
	Georgetown	30	7	81.1
13.	Butler	29	7	80.6
	Southern Ill.	29	7	80.6
15.	VCU	28	7	80.0
16.	Texas A&M	27	7	79.4
17.	Akron	26	7	78.8
	A&M-Corpus Christi	26	7	78.8
19.	Pittsburgh	29	8	78.4
	Oregon	29	8	78.4
21.	Washington St.	26	8	76.5
22.	Vermont	25	8	75.8
	Appalachian St.	25	8	75.8
24.	West Virginia	27	9	75.0
	Long Beach St.	24	8	75.0
	Notre Dame	24	8	75.0
27.	Air Force	26	9	74.3
28.	BYU	25	9	73.5
	Holy Cross	25	9	73.5
	Xavier	25	9	73.5
	Maryland	25	9	73.5
	New Mexico St.	25	9	73.5
	Marist	25	9	73.5

Scoring Offense

Rk.	School	G	W-L	Pts.	Avg.
1.	VMI	33	14-19	3,331	100.9
2.	North Carolina	38	31-7	3,258	85.7
3.	Eastern Wash.	29	15-14	2,443	84.2
4.	Northern Ariz.	30	18-12	2,490	83.0
5.	Cal St. Fullerton	30	20-10	2,462	82.1
6.	Texas	35	25-10	2,860	81.7
7.	Davidson	34	29-5	2,765	81.3
8.	Notre Dame	32	24-8	2,592	81.0
9.	Tennessee	35	24-11	2,831	80.9
10.	Long Beach St.	32	24-8	2,575	80.5
11.	Florida	40	35-5	3,193	79.8
12.	A&M-Corpus Christi	33	26-7	2,615	79.2
13.	Maryland	34	25-9	2,685	79.0
14.	Memphis	37	33-4	2,918	78.9
15.	Northwestern St.	32	17-15	2,523	78.8
16.	Georgia Tech	32	20-12	2,515	78.6
17.	Sacred Heart	32	18-14	2,513	78.5
18.	Campbell	31	14-17	2,433	78.5
19.	Gonzaga	34	23-11	2,668	78.5
20.	Kansas	38	33-5	2,978	78.4
21.	Duquesne	29	10-19	2,271	78.3
22.	Portland St.	32	19-13	2,503	78.2
23.	Western Ky.	33	22-11	2,580	78.2
24.	BYU	34	25-9	2,654	78.1
25.	New Mexico St.	34	25-9	2,652	78.0
26.	Arizona	31	20-11	2,417	78.0
27.	Missouri	30	18-12	2,328	77.6
28.	Texas St.	29	9-20	2,249	77.6
29.	Nevada	34	29-5	2,632	77.4
30.	Sam Houston St.	31	21-10	2,397	77.3
31.	Massachusetts	33	24-9	2,551	77.3

Scoring Defense

Rk.	School	G	W-L	Opp. Pts.	Opp. Avg.
1.	Princeton	28	11-17	1,493	53.3
2.	Air Force	35	26-9	1,960	56.0
3.	Southern Ill.	36	29-7	2,023	56.2
4.	Illinois	35	23-12	1,997	57.1
5.	Butler	36	29-7	2,056	57.1
6.	Michigan St.	35	23-12	2,001	57.2
7.	Miami (Ohio)	33	18-15	1,895	57.4
8.	Holy Cross	34	25-9	1,954	57.5
9.	Bucknell	31	22-9	1,791	57.8
10.	Wisconsin	36	30-6	2,083	57.9
11.	Georgetown	37	30-7	2,146	58.0
12.	Northwestern	31	13-18	1,821	58.7
13.	Delaware St.	34	21-13	1,998	58.8
14.	George Mason	33	18-15	1,951	59.1
15.	Texas A&M	34	27-7	2,021	59.4
16.	UCLA	35	30-5	2,081	59.5
17.	Washington St.	34	26-8	2,024	59.5
18.	Oklahoma	31	16-15	1,848	59.6
19.	Boston U.	30	12-18	1,801	60.0
20.	Samford	32	16-16	1,934	60.4
21.	Michigan	35	22-13	2,116	60.5
22.	Drexel	32	23-9	1,939	60.6
23.	Creighton	33	22-11	2,011	60.9
24.	Akron	33	26-7	2,014	61.0
25.	Army	31	15-16	1,892	61.0
26.	Colgate	29	10-19	1,771	61.1
27.	Winthrop	34	29-5	2,088	61.4
28.	Kansas	38	33-5	2,344	61.7
29.	Indiana	32	21-11	1,976	61.8
30.	Arizona St.	30	8-22	1,853	61.8

Scoring Margin

Rk.	School	W-L	Pts.	Avg.	Opp. Pts.	Opp. Avg.	Pt. Mar.
1.	Florida	35-5	3,193	79.8	2,504	62.6	17.2
2.	North Carolina	31-7	3,258	85.7	2,608	68.6	17.1
3.	Kansas	33-5	2,978	78.4	2,344	61.7	16.7
4.	Texas A&M	27-7	2,570	75.6	2,021	59.4	16.1
5.	Memphis	33-4	2,918	78.9	2,333	63.1	15.8
6.	Akron	26-7	2,485	75.3	2,014	61	14.3
7.	Winthrop	29-5	2,545	74.9	2,088	61.4	13.4
8.	Notre Dame	24-8	2,592	81	2,176	68	13.0
9.	Air Force	26-9	2,414	69	1,960	56	13.0
10.	Davidson	29-5	2,765	81.3	2,336	68.7	12.6
11.	Ohio St.	35-4	2,905	74.5	2,417	62	12.5
12.	Wisconsin	30-6	2,527	70.2	2,083	57.9	12.3
13.	UCLA	30-5	2,503	71.5	2,081	59.5	12.1
14.	Maryland	25-9	2,685	79	2,295	67.5	11.5
15.	Georgetown	30-7	2,555	69.1	2,146	58	11.1
16.	Xavier	25-9	2,595	76.3	2,228	65.5	10.8
17.	Butler	29-7	2,434	67.6	2,056	57.1	10.5
18.	West Virginia	27-9	2,610	72.5	2,245	62.4	10.1
19.	Nevada	29-5	2,632	77.4	2,296	67.5	9.9
20.	Oregon	29-8	2,807	75.9	2,450	66.2	9.6
21.	Texas	25-10	2,860	81.7	2,528	72.2	9.5
22.	A&M-Corpus Christi	26-7	2,615	79.2	2,302	69.8	9.5
23.	VCU	28-7	2,626	75	2,298	65.7	9.4
24.	Georgia Tech	20-12	2,515	78.6	2,222	69.4	9.2
25.	BYU	25-9	2,654	78.1	2,347	69	9.0
26.	Missouri St.	22-11	2,439	73.9	2,150	65.2	8.8
27.	Sam Houston St.	21-10	2,397	77.3	2,126	68.6	8.7
28.	Massachusetts	24-9	2,551	77.3	2,270	68.8	8.5
29.	Louisville	24-10	2,433	71.6	2,144	63.1	8.5
30.	Pittsburgh	29-8	2,637	71.3	2,324	62.8	8.5

Field-Goal Percentage

Rk.	School	G	W-L	FGM	FGA	FG%
1.	Florida	40	35-5	1,125	2,138	52.6
2.	A&M-Corpus Christi	33	26-7	912	1,747	52.2
3.	Georgetown	37	30-7	923	1,826	50.5
4.	North Carolina	38	31-7	1,187	2,379	49.9
5.	Texas A&M	34	27-7	908	1,823	49.8
6.	Eastern Wash.	29	15-14	846	1,708	49.5
7.	Northern Ariz.	30	18-12	873	1,766	49.4
8.	Kansas	38	33-5	1,106	2,241	49.4
9.	North Carolina St.	36	20-16	908	1,849	49.1
10.	BYU	34	25-9	972	1,981	49.1
11.	Air Force	35	26-9	815	1,662	49.0
12.	Georgia Tech	32	20-12	935	1,909	49.0
13.	Weber St.	32	20-12	772	1,579	48.9
14.	Fla. Atlantic	31	16-15	834	1,706	48.9
15.	Penn	31	22-9	836	1,712	48.8
16.	Colorado St.	30	17-13	768	1,573	48.8
17.	Utah	30	11-19	713	1,470	48.5
18.	Akron	33	26-7	900	1,857	48.5
19.	Providence	31	18-13	868	1,793	48.4
20.	Nevada	34	29-5	949	1,961	48.4
21.	Gonzaga	34	23-11	933	1,932	48.3
22.	Western Ky.	33	22-11	909	1,887	48.2
23.	Florida St.	35	22-13	936	1,947	48.1
24.	Liberty	31	14-17	895	1,862	48.1
25.	Sacred Heart	32	18-14	914	1,903	48.0
26.	UCLA	35	30-5	923	1,922	48.0
27.	New Mexico St.	34	25-9	906	1,890	47.9
28.	Appalachian St.	33	25-8	914	1,909	47.9
29.	Arizona	31	20-11	846	1,770	47.8
30.	Maryland	34	25-9	971	2,032	47.8
31.	Boston College	33	21-12	842	1,763	47.8

Field-Goal Percentage Defense

Rk.	School	G	W-L	Opp. FG	Opp. FGA	Opp. FG%
1.	Connecticut	31	17-14	677	1,824	37.1
2.	Texas A&M	34	27-7	672	1,793	37.5
3.	Syracuse	35	24-11	834	2,223	37.5
4.	Kansas	38	33-5	804	2,136	37.6
5.	Georgetown	37	30-7	742	1,935	38.3
6.	Michigan St.	35	23-12	671	1,746	38.4
7.	Fresno St.	32	22-10	792	2,058	38.5
8.	Maryland	34	25-9	823	2,117	38.9
9.	Tulsa	31	20-11	649	1,667	38.9
10.	Alabama A&M	30	39375	707	1,814	39.0
11.	Southern California	37	25-12	849	2,178	39.0
12.	Memphis	37	33-4	785	2,013	39.0
13.	Tulane	30	17-13	695	1,774	39.2
14.	Belmont	33	23-10	746	1,904	39.2
15.	Ark.-Pine Bluff	31	39435	695	1,765	39.4
16.	Hawaii	31	18-13	727	1,828	39.8
17.	Santa Clara	31	21-10	667	1,676	39.8
18.	Gonzaga	34	23-11	801	2,010	39.9
19.	East Tenn. St.	34	24-10	793	1,988	39.9
20.	Mississippi Val.	34	18-16	768	1,913	40.1
21.	Illinois	35	23-12	693	1,726	40.2
22.	Akron	33	26-7	717	1,785	40.2
23.	Drexel	32	23-9	674	1,677	40.2
24.	Southern Miss.	31	20-11	640	1,591	40.2
25.	Louisville	34	24-10	714	1,774	40.2
26.	Mississippi St.	35	21-14	856	2,125	40.3
27.	American	30	16-14	629	1,561	40.3
28.	Ohio St.	39	35-4	903	2,237	40.4
29.	Washington St.	34	26-8	709	1,754	40.4
30.	LSU	32	17-15	732	1,810	40.4

Three-Point Field Goals Made Per Game

Rk.	School	G	W-L	3FG	3PG
1.	VMI	33	14-19	442	13.4
2.	West Virginia	36	27-9	371	10.3
3.	Houston	33	18-15	330	10.0
4.	Bradley	35	22-13	349	10.0
5.	Wofford	30	10-20	297	9.9
6.	Pepperdine	31	8-23	303	9.8

Rk.	School	G	W-L	3FG	3PG
7.	Davidson	34	29-5	328	9.6
8.	Fresno St.	32	22-10	303	9.5
9.	Oregon	37	29-8	350	9.5
10.	New Mexico	32	15-17	299	9.3
11.	Tennessee	35	24-11	327	9.3
12.	Cal Poly	30	19-11	280	9.3
13.	Vanderbilt	34	22-12	317	9.3
14.	Troy	30	13-17	279	9.3
15.	Marist	34	25-9	312	9.2
16.	Air Force	35	26-9	316	9.0
17.	Notre Dame	32	24-8	287	9.0
	La.-Monroe	32	18-14	287	9.0
19.	Nicholls St.	30	8-22	269	9.0
20.	Butler	36	29-7	321	8.9
21.	Texas	35	25-10	308	8.8
22.	Belmont	33	23-10	288	8.7
23.	Charlotte	30	14-16	261	8.7
24.	Navy	30	14-16	260	8.7
25.	Lafayette	30	9-21	256	8.5
26.	Long Beach St.	32	24-8	273	8.5
27.	South Ala.	32	20-12	272	8.5
28.	Sam Houston St.	31	21-10	263	8.5
29.	Texas St.	29	9-20	244	8.4
30.	UMKC	32	12-20	267	8.3
31.	Lamar	32	15-17	266	8.3

Three-Point Field-Goal Percentage

Minimum 5 made per game

Rk.	School	G	W-L	3FG	3FGA	3FG%
1.	Northern Ariz.	30	18-12	229	537	42.6
2.	Texas A&M	34	27-7	215	510	42.2
3.	Bradley	35	22-13	349	831	42.0
4.	New Orleans	31	14-17	225	542	41.5
5.	BYU	34	25-9	256	617	41.5
6.	Utah	30	11-19	217	524	41.4
7.	Hofstra	32	22-10	256	621	41.2
8.	Texas Tech	34	21-13	208	505	41.2
9.	Florida	40	35-5	297	727	40.9
10.	Nevada	34	29-5	253	623	40.6
11.	Western Ky.	33	22-11	263	651	40.4
12.	Columbia	28	16-12	200	497	40.2
13.	A&M-Corpus Christi	33	26-7	192	478	40.2
14.	VCU	35	28-7	244	609	40.1
15.	Air Force	35	26-9	316	789	40.1
16.	Evansville	31	14-17	228	573	39.8
17.	Arkansas St.	33	18-15	241	608	39.6
18.	Cornell	28	16-12	198	500	39.6
19.	Southern California	37	25-12	207	523	39.6
20.	Kansas	38	33-5	231	584	39.6
21.	Army	31	15-16	187	473	39.5
22.	Weber St.	32	20-12	180	456	39.5
23.	Gonzaga	34	23-11	230	583	39.5
24.	UCF	31	22-9	239	606	39.4
25.	Cal Poly	30	19-11	280	713	39.3
26.	Akron	33	26-7	245	624	39.3
27.	Missouri St.	33	22-11	243	622	39.1
28.	Rhode Island	33	19-14	248	635	39.1
29.	Notre Dame	32	24-8	287	735	39.0
30.	Xavier	34	25-9	269	689	39.0
31.	Oregon	37	29-8	350	897	39.0

Free-Throw Percentage

Rk.	School	G	W-L	FT	FTA	FT%
1.	Villanova	33	22-11	594	761	78.1
2.	Utah St.	35	23-12	492	631	78.0
3.	California	33	16-17	400	520	76.9
4.	Oakland	33	19-14	546	711	76.8
5.	Oregon	37	29-8	531	698	76.1
6.	Green Bay	33	18-15	530	697	76.0
7.	Butler	36	29-7	553	728	76.0
8.	Harvard	28	12-16	497	655	75.9
9.	Florida St.	35	22-13	498	657	75.8
10.	Robert Morris	28	17-11	369	487	75.8
11.	Nevada	34	29-5	481	636	75.6
12.	Air Force	35	26-9	468	620	75.5
13.	IUPUI	30	15-15	464	615	75.4
14.	Seton Hall	29	13-16	450	597	75.4

STATISTICAL LEADERS

Rk.	School	G	W-L	FT	FTA	FT%
15.	Creighton	33	22-11	535	710	75.4
16.	Davidson	34	29-5	499	663	75.3
17.	Nicholls St.	30	8-22	391	520	75.2
18.	Gonzaga	34	23-11	572	762	75.1
19.	Cornell	28	16-12	376	501	75.0
20.	Arizona	31	20-11	553	737	75.0
21.	Navy	30	14-16	358	479	74.7
22.	Iowa	31	17-14	448	602	74.4
23.	Notre Dame	32	24-8	567	763	74.3
24.	Duquesne	29	10-19	422	568	74.3
25.	Virginia	32	21-11	582	784	74.2
26.	Northern Ariz.	30	18-12	515	694	74.2
27.	Brown	29	11-18	477	643	74.2
28.	Xavier	34	25-9	628	847	74.1
29.	UMKC	32	12-20	413	558	74.0
30.	Delaware St.	34	21-13	390	527	74.0
31.	Utah	30	11-19	432	584	74.0

Rebound Margin

Rk.	School	W-L	Reb.	Avg.	Opp Reb.	Opp Avg.	Reb Mar.
1.	Vermont	25-8	1,344	40.7	1,027	31.1	9.6
2.	Washington	19-13	1,225	38.3	938	29.3	9.0
3.	North Carolina	31-7	1,551	40.8	1,227	32.3	8.5
4.	Florida	35-5	1,504	37.6	1,164	29.1	8.5
5.	Massachusetts	24-9	1,334	40.4	1,081	32.8	7.7
6.	Southern Miss.	20-11	1,196	38.6	972	31.4	7.2
7.	Tulsa	20-11	1,230	39.7	1,007	32.5	7.2
8.	Michigan St.	23-12	1,217	34.8	972	27.8	7.0
9.	Cal St. Northridge	14-17	1,204	38.8	991	32.0	6.9
10.	Kansas	33-5	1,507	39.7	1,254	33.0	6.7
11.	Winthrop	29-5	1,279	37.6	1,053	31.0	6.6
12.	Connecticut	17-14	1,311	42.3	1,106	35.7	6.6
	Buffalo	12-19	1,186	38.3	981	31.6	6.6
14.	Davidson	29-5	1,378	40.5	1,156	34.0	6.5
15.	Nevada	29-5	1,300	38.2	1,080	31.8	6.5
16.	A&M-Corpus Christi	26-7	1,173	35.5	964	29.2	6.3
17.	Providence	18-13	1,158	37.4	964	31.1	6.3
18.	BYU	25-9	1,273	37.4	1,063	31.3	6.2
19.	Michigan	22-13	1,231	35.2	1,020	29.1	6.0
20.	Stanford	18-13	1,193	38.5	1,009	32.5	5.9
21.	Georgia Tech	20-12	1,166	36.4	982	30.7	5.8
22.	Georgia	19-14	1,250	37.9	1,063	32.2	5.7
23.	Arizona	20-11	1,158	37.4	984	31.7	5.6
24.	LSU	17-15	1,205	37.7	1,026	32.1	5.6
25.	North Texas	23-11	1,356	39.9	1,167	34.3	5.6
26.	Colorado St.	17-13	1,056	35.2	890	29.7	5.5
27.	Georgetown	30-7	1,250	33.8	1,050	28.4	5.4
28.	Memphis	33-4	1,468	39.7	1,272	34.4	5.3
29.	Illinois	23-12	1,231	35.2	1,049	30.0	5.2
30.	Santa Clara	21-10	1,121	36.2	961	31.0	5.2

Assists Per Game

Rk.	School	G	W-L	Ast.	Avg.
1.	VMI	33	14-19	681	20.6
2.	Sam Houston St.	31	21-10	596	19.2
3.	North Carolina	38	31-7	696	18.3
4.	Northern Ariz.	30	18-12	544	18.1
5.	A&M-Corpus Christi	33	26-7	595	18.0
6.	Eastern Wash.	29	15-14	514	17.7
7.	West Virginia	36	27-9	633	17.6
8.	Pittsburgh	37	29-8	647	17.5
9.	Hawaii	31	18-13	539	17.4
	Penn	31	22-9	539	17.4
11.	Texas A&M	34	27-7	591	17.4
12.	Lamar	32	15-17	554	17.3
13.	Cal St. Fullerton	30	20-10	519	17.3
14.	Maryland	34	25-9	587	17.3
15.	Notre Dame	32	24-8	552	17.3
16.	Kansas	38	33-5	651	17.1
17.	Vanderbilt	34	22-12	578	17.0
18.	Northwestern St.	32	17-15	539	16.8
19.	Nevada	34	29-5	569	16.7
20.	Winthrop	34	29-5	567	16.7
21.	Auburn	32	17-15	532	16.6
22.	Coastal Caro.	30	15-15	497	16.6
23.	High Point	32	22-10	530	16.6

Rk.	School	G	W-L	Ast.	Avg.
24.	Providence	31	18-13	513	16.5
25.	Arizona	31	20-11	511	16.5
26.	Davidson	34	29-5	559	16.4
27.	Missouri St.	33	22-11	542	16.4
28.	Campbell	31	14-17	509	16.4
29.	Robert Morris	28	17-11	452	16.1
30.	Duquesne	29	10-19	465	16.0
31.	Michigan St.	35	23-12	560	16.0

Blocked Shots Per Game

Rk.	School	G	W-L	Blk.	Avg.
1.	Connecticut	31	17-14	264	8.5
2.	Alabama A&M	30	10-20	236	7.9
3.	Massachusetts	33	24-9	246	7.5
4.	Syracuse	35	24-11	250	7.1
5.	Maryland	34	25-9	233	6.9
6.	Kansas	38	33-5	246	6.5
7.	Fresno St.	32	22-10	206	6.4
8.	Mississippi St.	35	21-14	222	6.3
9.	Arkansas	35	21-14	221	6.3
10.	Tulane	30	17-13	188	6.3
11.	Stanford	31	18-13	184	5.9
12.	Memphis	37	33-4	217	5.9
13.	Boston College	33	21-12	191	5.8
14.	Michigan	35	22-13	200	5.7
15.	Texas	35	25-10	197	5.6
16.	Ohio St.	39	35-4	218	5.6
17.	Tulsa	31	20-11	169	5.5
18.	St. Mary's (Cal.)	32	17-15	172	5.4
19.	UNLV	37	30-7	197	5.3
20.	Alabama	32	20-12	170	5.3
21.	Clemson	36	25-11	191	5.3
22.	Georgetown	37	30-7	189	5.1
23.	Monmouth	30	12-18	153	5.1
24.	Ill.-Chicago	32	14-18	162	5.1
25.	South Fla.	30	12-18	150	5.0
26.	Drexel	32	23-9	159	5.0
27.	Hawaii	31	18-13	154	5.0
28.	McNeese St.	32	15-17	158	4.9
29.	Minnesota	31	9-22	152	4.9
30.	Florida	40	35-5	194	4.9

Steals Per Game

Rk.	School	G	W-L	St.	Avg.
1.	VMI	33	14-19	490	14.8
2.	Sacramento St.	29	10-19	320	11.0
3.	Seton Hall	29	13-16	299	10.3
4.	Northwestern St.	32	17-15	326	10.2
5.	Missouri	30	18-12	302	10.1
6.	East Tenn. St.	34	24-10	338	9.9
7.	Georgia Tech	32	20-12	316	9.9
8.	Campbell	31	14-17	300	9.7
9.	Tennessee	35	24-11	336	9.6
10.	Prairie View	30	8-22	286	9.5
11.	Holy Cross	34	25-9	324	9.5
12.	Clemson	36	25-11	342	9.5
13.	Sacred Heart	32	18-14	302	9.4
14.	Memphis	37	33-4	344	9.3
15.	Toledo	32	19-13	297	9.3
16.	Coastal Caro.	30	15-15	277	9.2
17.	Kansas	38	33-5	350	9.2
18.	Hampton	31	15-16	285	9.2
19.	Pepperdine	31	8-23	283	9.1
20.	George Washington	32	23-9	292	9.1
21.	Radford	30	8-22	270	9.0
22.	Cal St. Northridge	31	14-17	278	9.0
23.	Georgia	33	19-14	293	8.9
24.	Texas St.	29	9-20	256	8.8
25.	Jacksonville	29	15-14	252	8.7
26.	Marquette	34	24-10	295	8.7
27.	Appalachian St.	33	25-8	285	8.6
28.	Penn	31	22-9	263	8.5
	Hartford	31	13-18	263	8.5
30.	Notre Dame	32	24-8	271	8.5

Turnovers Per Game

Rk.	School	G	W-L	TO	Avg.
1.	Butler	36	29-7	341	9.5
2.	Air Force	35	26-9	359	10.3
3.	Samford	32	16-16	334	10.4
4.	Washington St.	34	26-8	355	10.4
5.	Northwestern	31	13-18	338	10.9
6.	Virginia Tech	34	22-12	371	10.9
7.	UNLV	37	30-7	410	11.1
8.	South Carolina	30	14-16	337	11.2
9.	VCU	35	28-7	394	11.3
10.	West Virginia	36	27-9	406	11.3
11.	Wisconsin	36	30-6	407	11.3
12.	Ohio St.	39	35-4	443	11.4
13.	Bradley	35	22-13	399	11.4
14.	Hofstra	32	22-10	368	11.5
15.	UMKC	32	12-20	371	11.6
16.	Houston	33	18-15	383	11.6
17.	Texas Tech	34	21-13	396	11.6
18.	California	33	16-17	385	11.7
	Green Bay	33	18-15	385	11.7
20.	DePaul	34	20-14	397	11.7
21.	Lipscomb	31	18-13	369	11.9
22.	Pittsburgh	37	29-8	441	11.9
23.	New Orleans	31	14-17	370	11.9
24.	Mississippi	34	21-13	409	12
25.	Wichita St.	31	17-14	373	12
26.	Wright St.	33	23-10	400	12.1
27.	Delaware St.	34	21-13	413	12.1
28.	Wofford	30	10-20	365	12.2
29.	Seton Hall	29	13-16	353	12.2
30.	Texas A&M	34	27-7	415	12.2

Personal Fouls Per Game

Rk.	School	G	W-L	PF	Avg.	DQ
1.	Eastern Ky.	33	21-12	449	13.6	9
2.	Ohio St.	39	35-4	534	13.7	4
3.	Arizona	31	20-11	425	13.7	8
4.	Alabama	32	20-12	460	14.4	11
5.	Samford	32	16-16	467	14.6	14
6.	George Mason	33	18-15	491	14.9	1
7.	Northwestern	31	13-18	462	14.9	6
8.	South Carolina	30	14-16	448	14.9	11
9.	Air Force	35	26-9	526	15	7
10.	Northeastern	32	13-19	483	15.1	11
11.	West Virginia	36	27-9	544	15.1	6
12.	San Diego St.	33	22-11	501	15.2	8
13.	Boston College	33	21-12	505	15.3	10
14.	Wisconsin	36	30-6	551	15.3	2
15.	LSU	32	17-15	493	15.4	6
16.	Troy	30	13-17	466	15.5	10
17.	Col. of Charleston	33	22-11	516	15.6	12
18.	Florida	40	35-5	626	15.7	6
19.	Delaware St.	34	21-13	539	15.9	7
20.	North Carolina St.	36	20-16	572	15.9	11
21.	Youngstown St.	31	14-17	496	16	6
	Central Conn. St.	34	22-12	544	16	7
23.	Ohio	32	19-13	513	16	11
24.	Kentucky	34	22-12	547	16.1	4
25.	Washington St.	34	26-8	549	16.1	9
26.	Fresno St.	32	22-10	519	16.2	11
27.	UCLA	35	30-5	569	16.3	9
28.	Penn St.	30	11-19	488	16.3	6
29.	UC Santa Barb.	29	18-11	472	16.3	12
30.	DePaul	34	20-14	555	16.3	8

2007 Division I Team Game Highs

Points

Rk.	School	Opponent	Date	Pts.	Opp Pts.
1.	Cal St. Northridge	Redlands	11/15/06	159	97
2.	VMI	Virginia Intermont	11/15/06	156	95
3.	VMI	Southern Va.	11/20/06	144	127
4.	VMI	Lees-McRae	12/6/06	135	75
5.	Oklahoma St.	Southwestern Okla.	1/2/07	129	77
	Penn St.	VMI	12/30/06	129	111
7.	VMI	Bridgewater (Va.)	1/18/07	125	95
8.	Liberty	VMI	1/27/07	122	117
9.	Tennessee	Long Beach St.	3/16/07	121	86
10.	San Diego St.	Campbell	12/12/06	119	82
11.	Liberty	VMI	2/21/07	118	108
	Rice	Paul Quinn	11/11/06	118	66
13.	VMI	Liberty	1/27/07	117	122
	Western Caro.	Toccoa Falls	11/27/06	117	58
15.	VMI	Charleston So.	1/13/07	116	83
	Davidson	Mt. St. Mary (N.Y.)	12/15/06	116	55
	Howard	VMI	11/25/06	116	111
	Oregon	Portland St.	11/12/06	116	68
	Ga. Southern	UC Davis	11/12/06	116	73
20.	High Point	VMI	1/10/07	115	104
21.	Wake Forest	Georgia Tech	3/8/07	114	112
	Radford	VMI	2/14/07	114	107
23.	Citadel	Atlanta Christian	12/30/06	113	59
	Southern Miss.	Spring Hill	11/22/06	113	57
25.	Florida	Jackson St.	3/16/07	112	69
	Georgia Tech	Wake Forest	3/8/07	112	114
27.	VMI	Penn St.	12/30/06	111	126
	VMI	Howard	11/25/06	111	116
	Memphis	Jackson St.	11/16/06	111	69
30.	Eastern Wash.	Cal St. Fullerton	11/27/06	110	100
	Tennessee Tech	Bluefield Col.	11/13/06	110	69
	Texas-Arlington	Texas St.	2/3/06	110	103

Field-Goal Percentage

Rk.	School	Opponent	Date	FGM	FGA	FG%
1.	Ohio	Bellarmine	12/9/06	32	44	72.7
2.	Long Island	Old Westbury	11/25/06	42	58	72.4
3.	Richmond	Longwood	11/20/06	28	39	71.8
4.	Rice	Paul Quinn	11/11/06	43	60	71.7
5.	Cal St. Northridge	Redlands	11/15/06	62	87	71.3
6.	Utah	Air Force	1/16/07	29	41	70.7
7.	Howard	VMI	11/25/06	46	66	69.7
	Evansville	Samford	2/17/07	23	33	69.7
9.	San Diego St.	Campbell	12/12/06	48	69	69.6
10.	Boston College	Hartford	1/31/07	33	48	68.8
11.	Duke	Miami (Fla.)	1/14/07	28	41	68.3
12.	Oklahoma St.	Fla. Atlantic	11/10/06	36	53	67.9
13.	Alabama	Alabama St.	12/9/06	38	56	67.9
14.	Nebraska	Creighton	11/18/06	25	37	67.6
15.	Valparaiso	Chicago St.	2/5/07	33	49	67.3
	Weber St.	Eastern Wash.	1/27/07	33	49	67.3
17.	Long Beach St.	UC Davis	2/24/07	42	63	66.7
	New Mexico St.	New Mexico	12/5/06	38	57	66.7
	Wake Forest	Gardner-Webb	12/19/06	36	54	66.7
	DePaul	Rhode Island	12/16/06	34	51	66.7
	North Carolina St.	Virginia Tech	2/18/07	32	48	66.7
	Gonzaga	San Diego	1/29/07	32	48	66.7
	Northern Ariz.	Sacramento St.	1/13/07	32	48	66.7
	Louisiana Tech	Utah St.	2/24/07	30	45	66.7
	Weber St.	Sacramento St.	1/11/07	30	45	66.7

Three-Point Field Goals Made

Rk.	School	Opponent	Date	3FG
1.	VMI	Lees-McRae	12/6/06	22
2.	VMI	Charleston So.	1/13/07	21

STATISTICAL LEADERS

Rk.	School	Opponent	Date	3FG
	VMI	Virginia Intermont	11/15/06	21
	Pepperdine	Nicholls St.	11/14/06	21
	Nicholls St.	A&M-Corpus Christi	2/8/06	21
6.	Nicholls St.	Lamar	3/1/07	20
	Butler	Cleveland St.	2/8/07	20
	Bradley	Florida A&M	11/21/06	20
	VMI	Southern Va.	11/20/06	20
10.	VMI	Bridgewater (Va.)	1/18/07	19
	VMI	Penn St.	12/30/06	19
	VMI	Jacksonville St.	12/2/06	19
	VMI	Howard	11/25/06	19
	Davidson	Colby	11/21/06	19
15.	Fresno St.	Georgia	3/14/07	18
	Wofford	West Va. Wesleyan	1/3/07	18
	Virginia	Gonzaga	1/3/07	18
	Citadel	Atlanta Christian	12/30/06	18
	Houston	Rhode Island	11/13/06	18
20.	West Virginia	Providence	3/7/07	17
	New Mexico	Utah	2/24/07	17
	Marist	Siena	2/24/07	17
	Howard	Florida A&M	2/19/07	17
	Belmont	Gardner-Webb	2/15/07	17
	Appalachian St.	Citadel	1/27/07	17
	Long Beach St.	UC Santa Barb.	1/4/07	17
	Indiana St.	Drake	12/30/06	17
	Maryland	UMKC	12/13/06	17
	West Virginia	Duquesne	12/9/06	17
	Cincinnati	Wofford	11/21/06	17
	Washington	Nicholls St.	11/13/06	17
	Oregon	Portland St.	11/12/06	17
	Winthrop	North Greenville	11/10/06	17

Three-Point Field-Goal Percentage

Minimum 10 made

Rk.	School	Opponent	Date	3FG	3FGA	3FG%
1.	Youngstown St.	Ill.-Chicago	2/3/07	14	18	77.8
2.	New Mexico St.	Boise St.	3/9/07	10	13	76.9
3.	Valparaiso	Western Ill.	1/18/07	12	16	75.0
	Texas A&M	Idaho St.	11/25/06	12	16	75.0
	St. Louis	Louisiana Tech	11/17/06	12	16	75.0
6.	North Carolina St.	Virginia Tech	2/18/07	11	15	73.3
	UNI	Southern Ill.	1/23/07	11	15	73.3
	Northern Ariz.	Sacramento St.	1/13/07	11	15	73.3
	Southern Utah	Tex. A&M Int'l	12/16/06	11	15	73.3
10.	Oral Roberts	IUPUI	2/22/07	10	14	71.4
	Nevada	St. Mary's (Cal.)	12/12/06	10	14	71.4
12.	Youngstown St.	Slippery Rock	11/19/06	12	17	70.6
13.	Wake Forest	Georgia Tech	3/8/07	16	23	69.6
14.	Citadel	Atlanta Christian	12/30/06	18	26	69.2
15.	Citadel	Wofford	1/6/07	11	16	68.8
	Richmond	Longwood	11/20/06	11	16	68.8
17.	BYU	UNLV	2/3/07	15	22	68.2
18.	West Virginia	Rutgers	1/31/07	14	21	66.7
	Baylor	Oklahoma St.	3/3/07	12	18	66.7
	Rhode Island	Brown	12/5/06	12	18	66.7
	Texas Tech	Ark.-Little Rock	11/14/06	12	18	66.7
	Oakland	Western Ill.	3/3/07	10	15	66.7
	Virginia Tech	UNC Greensboro	1/10/07	10	15	66.7
	Wake Forest	Gardner-Webb	12/19/06	10	15	66.7
	BYU	UCLA	11/15/06	10	15	66.7

Free-Throw Percentage

Minimum 15 made

Rk.	School	Opponent	Date	FT	FTA	FT%
1.	A&M-Corpus Christi	Detroit	11/25/06	21	21	100.0
	Stephen F. Austin	Howard Payne	12/30/06	20	20	100.0
	Nevada	Idaho	2/22/07	16	16	100.0
	Air Force	Texas Tech	11/21/06	15	15	100.0
5.	Virginia	American	12/28/06	27	28	96.4
	Navy	Loyola (Md.)	11/10/06	27	28	96.4
7.	Montana St.	Northern Ariz.	1/27/07	26	27	96.3
8.	Texas	New Mexico St.	3/16/07	25	26	96.2
9.	Butler	Wright St.	2/10/07	24	25	96.0
10.	North Carolina	North Carolina St.	3/11/07	23	24	95.8
11.	William & Mary	UMBC	12/22/06	21	22	95.5
12.	Nevada	Hawaii	2/3/07	20	21	95.2
	Towson	VCU	1/13/07	20	21	95.2

Rk.	School	Opponent	Date	FT	FTA	FT%
	UNLV	Houston	12/30/06	20	21	95.2
15.	Mt. St. Mary's	St. Francis (Pa.)	1/18/07	19	20	95.0
	Tennessee Tech	Samford	1/14/07	19	20	95.0
	Evansville	Bradley	12/30/06	19	20	95.0
	California	Marshall	11/23/06	19	20	95.0
	Oklahoma	Memphis	11/20/06	19	20	95.0
20.	Portland	San Diego	2/24/07	18	19	94.7
	Virginia	Georgia Tech	2/24/07	18	19	94.7
	Valparaiso	UMKC	1/25/07	18	19	94.7
	Notre Dame	Winston-Salem	11/29/06	18	19	94.7
	Col. of Charleston	UNC Wilmington	11/26/06	18	19	94.7

Attendance

Rk.	School	Score	Opponent	Opp Score	Date	City, State	Att.
1.	Florida	76	UCLA	66	3/31/07	Atlanta	53,510
	Ohio St.	67	Georgetown	60	3/31/07	Atlanta	53,510
3.	Ohio St.	75	Florida	84	4/2/07	Atlanta	51,458
4.	Syracuse	73	Connecticut	63	2/17/07	Syracuse, NY	32,376
5.	Syracuse	75	Villanova	64	1/13/07	Syracuse, NY	26,874
6.	Ohio St.	85	Tennessee	84	3/22/07	San Antonio	26,776
7.	Syracuse	80	San Diego State	64	3/19/07	Syracuse, NY	26,752
8.	Florida	65	Butler	57	3/23/07	St. Louis	26,307
9.	Georgetown	58	Syracuse	72	2/26/07	Syracuse, NY	26,287
10.	Ohio St.	92	Memphis	76	3/24/07	San Antonio	26,260
11.	Memphis	65	Texas A&M	64	3/22/07	San Antonio	26,060
12.	Oregon	77	Florida	85	3/25/07	St. Louis	25,947
13.	Syracuse	75	DePaul	69	2/3/07	Syracuse, NY	24,638
14.	Florida	64	Kentucky	61	2/10/07	Lexington, KY	24,465
15.	Kentucky	76	Tennessee	57	1/28/07	Lexington, KY	24,311
16.	Kentucky	82	Massachusetts	68	12/22/06	Lexington, KY	24,307
17.	Vanderbilt	72	Kentucky	67	1/20/07	Lexington, KY	24,284
18.	Kentucky	59	Indiana	54	12/9/06	Lexington, KY	24,253
19.	Georgia	70	Kentucky	82	2/28/07	Lexington, KY	24,108
20.	Syracuse	76	St. John's (N.Y.)	74	2/11/07	Syracuse, NY	24,106

Winning Streak That Ended In 2006-07

Rk. When Lost	School	Lost To	Date Lost	Score	Streak
1.	Memphis	Ohio St.	3/24/07	76-92	25
1.	Ohio St.	Florida	4/2/07	75-84	22
1.	Clemson	Maryland	1/13/07	87-92	17
1.	Florida	Vanderbilt	2/17/07	70-83	17
1.	Wisconsin	Indiana	1/31/07	66-71	17
3.	Bucknell	Holy Cross	3/9/07	66-72	14
3.	Kansas	UCLA	3/24/07	55-68	14
2.	UCLA	Oregon	1/6/07	66-68	14
1.	Air Force	Utah	1/16/07	79-85	13
4.	Davidson	Maryland	3/15/07	70-82	13
1.	New Mexico St.	Louisiana Tech	1/17/07	71-73	13
2.	Oregon	Southern California	1/4/07	82-84	13
2.	South Ala.	Florida Int'l	2/18/07	67-69	13
5.	Southern Ill.	Creighton	3/4/07	61-67	13
4.	Vermont	Albany (N.Y.)	3/10/07	59-60	13
3.	Arizona	Washington St.	1/6/07	73-77	12
5.	Central Conn. St.	Fairleigh Dickinson	2/17/07	60-66	12
2.	Davidson	Appalachian St.	1/20/07	74-81	12
1.	Florida	Kansas	11/25/06	80-82	12
2.	Holy Cross	Bucknell	2/9/07	45-48	12
4.	Niagara	Kansas	3/16/07	67-107	12
2.	North Carolina	Virginia Tech	1/13/07	88-94	12
3.	Notre Dame	Georgetown	1/6/07	48-66	12
2.	Austin Peay	Murray St.	2/1/07	68-77	11
4.	Connecticut	West Virginia	12/30/06	71-81	11
5.	Georgetown	Syracuse	2/26/07	58-72	11
3.	Kentucky	Vanderbilt	1/20/07	67-72	11
1.	Oklahoma St.	Tennessee	12/18/06	77-79	11
2.	A&M-Corpus Christi	Sam Houston St.	2/3/07	79-84	10
1.	Butler	Indiana St.	12/9/06	64-72	10
6.	Drexel	Hofstra	1/11/07	53-55	10
4.	East Tenn. St.	Jacksonville	2/8/07	66-74	10
4.	Kansas	Texas Tech	1/20/07	64-69	10
4.	Nevada	New Mexico St.	1/20/07	73-80	10
7.	Penn	Texas A&M	3/15/07	52-68	10
2.	Pittsburgh	Wisconsin	12/16/06	75-89	10
5.	UNLV	Air Force	1/6/07	50-56	10
4.	VCU	Hofstra	1/31/07	68-79	10

Home Court Streaks That Ended In 2006-07

Rk. When Lost	School	Lost To	Date Lost	Score	Streak
1.	Gonzaga	Santa Clara	2/12/07	73-84	50
2.	Connecticut	Marquette	1/10/07	69-73	31
1.	Air Force	BYU	2/27/07	58-62	30
5.	George Washington	Xavier	2/10/07	58-87	24
5.	Butler	Southern Ill.	2/17/07	64-68	22

Rk. When Lost	School	Lost To	Date Lost	Score	Streak
6.	Texas	Kansas St.	2/3/07	72-73	22
4.	Akron	Nevada	12/22/06	71-73	21
5.	Texas A&M	Texas Tech	2/13/07	75-77	21
3.	Iowa	UNI	12/5/06	55-57	20
7.	New Mexico St.	Fresno St.	2/24/07	58-60	19
8.	UAB	Southern Miss.	1/20/07	55-57	19
9.	Lipscomb	East Tenn. St.	1/27/07	66-71	18
8.	Northwestern St.	A&M-Corpus Christi	1/11/07	57-69	18

2008 Division I Top Returnees

Career Totals

MOST POINTS

Seniors	Ht.	Yrs.	G	FG	3FG	FT	Pts.	Avg.
1. Bo McCalebb, New Orleans	6-0	4	96	716	68	437	1,937	20.18
2. Jaycee Carroll, Utah St.	6-2	3	99	613	255	256	1,737	17.55
3. Antoine Agudio, Hofstra	6-3	3	95	573	273	245	1,664	17.52
4. Kyle Hines, UNC Greensboro	6-6	3	89	647	3	294	1,591	17.88
5. Chris Lofton, Tennessee	6-2	3	92	520	313	219	1,572	17.09
6. Courtney Lee, Western Ky.	6-5	3	91	543	176	241	1,503	16.52
7. Richard Roby, Colorado	6-6	3	87	499	167	291	1,456	16.74
8. Sean Singletary, Virginia	6-0	3	90	439	164	384	1,426	15.84
9. Jack Leasure, Coastal Caro.	6-3	3	89	489	300	146	1,424	16.00
10. Martin Zeno, Texas Tech	6-5	3	99	487	26	416	1,416	14.30

Juniors	Ht.	Yrs.	G	FG	3FG	FT	Pts.	Avg.
1. Tyler Hansbrough, North Carolina.	6-9	2	69	427	3	429	1,286	18.64
2. Brandon Ewing, Wyoming	6-2	2	63	312	84	331	1,039	16.49
3. Dominic James, Marquette	5-11	2	65	345	91	198	979	15.06
4. Jamont Gordon, Mississippi St.	6-4	2	65	320	69	265	974	14.98
5. Brandon Rush, Kansas	6-6	2	71	356	125	133	970	13.66
6. Ben Woodside, North Dakota St.	5-11	2	56	283	99	285	950	16.96
7. Eric Devendorf, Syracuse	6-4	2	70	329	104	183	945	13.50
8. Mike Trimboli, Vermont	6-1	2	63	300	118	222	940	14.92
9. Courtney Pigram, East Tenn. St.	6-0	2	61	338	139	122	937	15.36
10. Jack McClinton, Siena & Miami (Fla.)	6-1	2	61	300	137	190	927	15.20

SCORING AVERAGE

Seniors (Min. 1,200 Pts.)	Ht.	Yrs.	G	FG	3FG	FT	Pts.	Avg.
1. Bo McCalebb, New Orleans	6-0	4	96	716	68	437	1,937	20.18
2. Kyle Hines, UNC Greensboro	6-6	3	89	647	3	294	1,591	17.88
3. Jaycee Carroll, Utah St.	6-2	3	99	613	255	256	1,737	17.55
4. Antoine Agudio, Hofstra	6-3	3	95	573	273	245	1,664	17.52
5. Chris Lofton, Tennessee	6-2	3	92	520	313	219	1,572	17.09
6. Richard Roby, Colorado	6-6	3	87	499	167	291	1,456	16.74
7. Courtney Lee, Western Ky.	6-5	3	91	543	176	241	1,503	16.52
8. Jack Leasure, Coastal Caro.	6-3	3	89	489	300	146	1,424	16.00
9. Sean Singletary, Virginia	6-0	3	90	439	164	384	1,426	15.84
10. Jason Thompson, Rider	6-10	3	88	484	19	359	1,346	15.30

Juniors (Min. 800 Pts.)	Ht.	Yrs.	G	FG	3FG	FT	Pts.	Avg.
1. Tyler Hansbrough, North Carolina.	6-9	2	69	427	3	429	1,286	18.64
2. Ben Woodside, North Dakota St.	5-11	2	56	283	99	285	950	16.96
3. Brandon Ewing, Wyoming	6-2	2	63	312	84	331	1,039	16.49
4. Courtney Pigram, East Tenn. St.	6-0	2	61	338	139	122	937	15.36
5. Jack McClinton, Siena & Miami (Fla.)	6-1	2	61	300	137	190	927	15.20
6. Dominic James, Marquette	5-11	2	65	345	91	198	979	15.06
7. Jamont Gordon, Mississippi St.	6-4	2	65	320	69	265	974	14.98
8. Mike Trimboli, Vermont	6-1	2	63	300	118	222	940	14.92
9. Toney Douglas, Auburn & Florida St.	6-1	2	61	322	93	168	905	14.84
10. Chavis Holmes, VMI	6-4	2	59	266	141	179	852	14.44

HIGHEST FIELD-GOAL PERCENTAGE

Seniors (Min. 300 FGM)	Ht.	Yrs.	G	FG	FGA	Pct.
1. Amadi McKenzie, Tennessee Tech	6-5	3	90	329	541	60.8
2. Andrew Strait, Montana	6-8	3	91	516	850	60.7
3. Leon Williams, Ohio	6-8	3	94	433	716	60.5
4. Will Thomas, George Mason	6-7	3	97	421	697	60.4
5. Jermaine Griffin, Texas-Arlington	6-8	3	87	337	559	60.3
6. Ra'Sean Dickey, Georgia Tech	6-9	3	89	301	501	60.1
7. Roy Hibbert, Georgetown	7-2	3	102	394	656	60.1
8. Kyle Hines, UNC Greensboro	6-6	3	89	647	1086	59.6
9. Tim Pollitz, Miami (Ohio)	6-5	3	79	398	686	58.0
10. David Padgett, Kansas & Louisville	6-11	3	88	305	534	57.1

Juniors (Min. 240 FGM)	Ht.	Yrs.	G	FG	FGA	Pct.
1. Ahmad Nivins, St. Joseph's	6-9	2	61	244	390	62.6
2. Luke Nevill, Utah	7-1	2	58	297	502	59.2
3. Richard Hendrix, Alabama	6-8	2	63	294	503	58.4
4. Carlos Monroe, Fla. Atlantic	6-8	2	44	278	478	58.2
5. Gyno Pomare, San Diego	6-7	3	63	315	548	57.5
6. Shawn James, Duquesne & Northeastern.	6-9	2	55	240	423	56.7
7. Tyler Hansbrough, North Carolina	6-9	2	69	427	783	54.5
8. Chris Douglas-Roberts, Memphis	6-6	2	69	296	549	53.9
9. Jon Brockman, Washington	6-7	2	65	291	542	53.7
10. Trent Plaisted, Brigham Young	6-11	3	68	311	585	53.2

MOST THREE-POINT FIELD GOALS MADE PER GAME

Seniors (Min. 120 3FGM)	Ht.	Yrs.	G	3FG	Avg.
1. Chris Lofton, Tennessee	6-2	3	92	313	3.40
2. Jack Leasure, Coastal Caro.	6-3	3	89	300	3.37
3. David Holston, Chicago St.	5-8	2	59	173	2.93
4. Antoine Agudio, Hofstra	6-3	3	95	273	2.87
5. Shane Nichols, St. Peter's & Wofford	6-0	3	87	246	2.83
6. Johnnie Bryant, Utah	6-0	2	59	156	2.64
7. Jaycee Carroll, Utah St.	6-2	3	99	255	2.58
8. Andre' Ratliff, Grambling	5-10	3	76	194	2.55
9. Darnell Harris, La Salle	6-1	3	87	219	2.52
10. Steven Rush, UNC Ashe. & N.C. A&T	5-11	3	85	213	2.51

Juniors (Min. 80 3FGM)	Ht.	Yrs.	G	3FG	Avg.
1. Adam Gore, Cornell	6-0	2	29	88	3.03
2. Jason Holsinger, Evansville	5-11	2	60	156	2.60
3. Josh Alexander, Stephen F. Austin	6-4	2	58	145	2.50
4. Ryan Bathie, Nicholls St.	6-6	2	50	124	2.48
5. Jimmy Baron, Rhode Island	6-2	2	59	144	2.44
6. Chavis Holmes, VMI	6-4	2	59	141	2.39
7. A.J. Abrams, Texas	5-10	2	72	166	2.31
8. Andy Wicke, Belmont	6-2	2	61	140	2.30
9. Courtney Pigram, East Tenn. St.	6-0	2	61	139	2.28
10. Loren Leath, Sacramento St.	6-2	2	56	127	2.27

HIGHEST THREE-POINT FIELD-GOAL PERCENTAGE

Seniors (Min. 120 3FGM)	Ht.	Yrs.	G	3FG	3FGA	Pct.
1. Jaycee Carroll, Utah St.	6-2	3	99	255	564	45.2
2. Pete Campbell, IPFW & Butler	6-7	2	63	146	327	44.6
3. Sean Taibi, Northern Colo.	6-3	3	85	210	472	44.5
4. Chris Lofton, Tennessee	6-2	3	92	313	714	43.8
5. Johnnie Bryant, Utah	6-0	2	59	156	356	43.8
6. Brian Roberts, Dayton	6-2	3	91	193	445	43.4
7. DeWitt Scott, Md.-East. Shore & IPFW	6-6	3	78	144	333	43.2
8. Jonathan Wallace, Georgetown	6-1	3	102	169	395	42.8
9. Ryan Appleby, Florida & Washington	6-2	3	78	159	373	42.6
10. Antoine Agudio, Hofstra	6-3	3	95	273	641	42.6

Juniors (Min. 80 3FGM)	Ht.	Yrs.	G	3FG	3FGA	Pct.
1. Harris Mansell, Rider	6-3	2	58	97	199	48.7
2. Josh Alexander, Stephen F. Austin	6-4	2	58	145	318	45.6
3. Josh Carter, Texas A&M	6-7	2	65	143	314	45.5
4. Shaun Green, Utah	6-8	2	59	107	238	45.0
5. Brandon Rush, Kansas	6-6	2	71	125	280	44.6
6. Mike Nelson, North Dakota St.	6-2	2	56	91	204	44.6
7. Chad Toppert, New Mexico	6-6	2	60	99	226	43.8
8. Matt Lawrence, Missouri	6-7	2	55	90	206	43.7
9. Jimmy Baron, Rhode Island	6-2	2	59	144	334	43.1
10. Stephan Gilling, Colorado St.	6-2	2	61	130	303	42.9

STATISTICAL LEADERS

HIGHEST FREE-THROW PERCENTAGE

Seniors (Min. 175 FTM)	Ht.	Yrs.	G	FT	FTA	FT%
1. A.J. Graves, Butler	6-1	3	96	290	321	90.3
2. Ronald Steele, Alabama	6-2	3	89	211	243	86.8
3. Drew Neitzel, Michigan St.	6-0	3	102	177	204	86.8
4. Sean Singletary, Virginia	6-0	3	90	384	455	84.4
5. Brian Roberts, Dayton	6-2	3	91	254	301	84.4
6. Chris Lofton, Tennessee	6-2	3	92	219	260	84.2
7. Jaycee Carroll, Utah St.	6-2	3	99	256	307	83.4
8. Greg Sprink, Navy	6-5	3	82	267	321	83.2
9. John Ford, McNeese St.	5-9	3	87	218	264	82.6
10. Mark McAndrew, Brown	6-3	3	81	179	218	82.1

Juniors (Min. 110 FTM)	Ht.	Yrs.	G	FT	FTA	FT%
1. A.J. Abrams, Texas	5-10	2	72	116	128	90.6
2. Sharaud Curry, Providence	5-10	2	54	131	146	89.7
3. Mike Schachtner, Green Bay	6-9	2	64	161	186	86.6
4. Jason Holsinger, Evansville	5-11	2	60	123	143	86.0
5. Josh Mayo, Ill.-Chicago	5-10	2	58	157	183	85.8
6. Jack McClinton, Siena & Miami (Fla.)	6-1	2	61	190	222	85.6
7. Mike Trimboli, Vermont	6-1	2	63	222	265	83.8
8. Terrel Harris, Oklahoma St.	6-5	2	66	112	135	83.0
9. Leon Young, Loyola (Ill.)	6-6	2	56	188	227	82.8
10. Vince Oliver, UC Davis	6-3	2	55	137	166	82.5

MOST REBOUNDS

Seniors	Ht.	Yrs.	G	Reb.	Avg.
1. Joey Dorsey, Memphis	6-9	3	111	847	7.63
2. Kyle Hines, UNC Greensboro	6-6	3	89	766	8.61
3. Leon Williams, Ohio	6-8	3	94	765	8.14
4. Jason Thompson, Rider	6-10	3	88	759	8.63
5. Eric Coleman, UNI	6-6	3	96	716	7.46
6. Bryant Dunston, Fordham	6-8	3	91	709	7.79
7. Louis Graham, Ga. Southern	6-8	3	92	692	7.52
8. Joe Reitz, Western Mich.	6-7	3	96	685	7.14
9. Aleks Maric, Nebraska	6-11	3	88	680	7.73
10. Arizona Reid, High Point	6-5	3	89	671	7.54

Juniors	Ht.	Yrs.	G	Reb.	Avg.
1. Luc Richard Mbah a Moute, UCLA	6-8	2	73	572	7.84
2. Tyler Hansbrough, North Carolina	6-9	2	69	544	7.88
3. Geoff McDermott, Providence	6-7	2	58	526	9.07
4. Richard Hendrix, Alabama	6-8	2	63	526	8.35
5. Jon Brockman, Washington	6-7	2	65	522	8.03
6. Jeff Adrien, Connecticut	6-7	2	64	466	7.28
7. Jamont Gordon, Mississippi St.	6-4	2	65	453	6.97
8. Diamon Simpson, St. Mary's (Cal.)	6-7	2	61	446	7.31
9. Jeff Pendergraph, Arizona St.	6-9	2	57	437	7.67
10. Robert Dozier, Memphis	6-9	2	74	434	5.86

MOST REBOUNDS PER GAME

Seniors (Min. 500 Rebs.)	Ht.	Yrs.	G	Reb.	Avg.
1. Jason Thompson, Rider	6-10	3	88	759	8.63
2. Kyle Hines, UNC Greensboro	6-6	3	89	766	8.61
3. Leon Williams, Ohio	6-8	3	94	765	8.14
4. Othyus Jeffers, Ill.-Chicago	6-5	2	63	511	8.11
5. Tyrone Nelson, Prairie View & New Mexico St.	6-9	3	81	637	7.86
6. Bryant Dunston, Fordham	6-8	3	91	709	7.79
7. Aleks Maric, Nebraska	6-11	3	88	680	7.73
8. Todd Sowell, St. Peter's	6-7	3	87	664	7.63
9. Joey Dorsey, Memphis	6-9	3	111	847	7.63
10. Haminn Quaintance, Jacksonville & Kent	6-7	3	84	640	7.62

Juniors (Min. 280 Rebs.)	Ht.	Yrs.	G	Reb.	Avg.
1. Geoff McDermott, Providence	6-7	2	58	526	9.07
2. Richard Hendrix, Alabama	6-8	2	63	526	8.35
3. Jon Brockman, Washington	6-7	2	65	522	8.03
4. Tyler Hansbrough, North Carolina	6-9	2	69	544	7.88
5. Luc Richard Mbah a Moute, UCLA	6-8	2	73	572	7.84
6. Shawn James, Duquesne & Northeastern	6-9	2	55	426	7.75
7. Jeff Pendergraph, Arizona St.	6-9	2	57	437	7.67
8. Carlos Monroe, Fla. Atlantic	6-8	2	44	332	7.55
9. Diamon Simpson, St. Mary's (Cal.)	6-7	2	61	446	7.31
10. Jeff Adrien, Connecticut	6-7	2	64	466	7.28

MOST ASSISTS PER GAME

Seniors (Min. 280 Asts.)	Ht.	Yrs.	G	Ast.	Avg.
1. Daniel Ruffin, Bradley	5-10	3	93	475	5.11
2. Kevin Bell, Fresno St.	5-10	3	84	412	4.90
3. Eugene Lawrence, St. John's (N.Y.)	6-1	3	85	410	4.82
4. Chris Gaynor, Winthrop	5-10	3	95	427	4.49
5. Ronald Steele, Alabama	6-2	3	89	397	4.46
6. Dwayne Foreman, Ga. Southern	5-10	3	90	395	4.39
7. Drew Neitzel, Michigan St.	6-0	3	102	437	4.28
8. Sean Singletary, Virginia	6-0	3	90	385	4.28
9. Roy Peake, Winston-Salem	5-11	3	87	369	4.24
10. Mike Green, Towson & Butler	6-0	3	94	396	4.21

Juniors (Min. 150 Asts.)	Ht.	Yrs.	G	Ast.	Avg.
1. Josh Wilson, Northern Ariz.	6-2	2	62	376	6.06
2. Mike Trimboli, Vermont	6-1	2	63	332	5.27
3. Dominic James, Marquette	5-11	2	65	334	5.14
4. Ben Woodside, North Dakota St.	5-11	2	56	287	5.13
5. Quantez Robertson, Auburn	6-3	2	60	293	4.88
6. Jamont Gordon, Mississippi St.	6-4	2	65	316	4.86
7. Jason Holsinger, Evansville	5-11	2	60	276	4.60
8. Chris Lowe, Massachusetts	6-0	2	60	271	4.52
9. Eric Maynor, VCU	6-2	2	64	289	4.52
10. Greg Paulus, Duke	6-1	2	69	311	4.51

MOST BLOCKED SHOTS PER GAME

Seniors (Min. 90 Blks.)	Ht.	Yrs.	G	Blk.	Avg.
1. Mickell Gladness, Alabama A&M	6-11	2	56	265	4.73
2. Durrell Nevels, Central Ark.	6-6	1	30	99	3.30
3. Kyle Hines, UNC Greensboro	6-6	3	89	254	2.85
4. Steven Hill, Arkansas	7-0	3	97	244	2.52
5. Haminn Quaintance, Jacksonville & Kent	6-7	3	84	198	2.36
6. Bryant Dunston, Fordham	6-8	3	91	214	2.35
7. D.J. White, Indiana	6-9	3	66	144	2.18
8. Randall Hanke, Providence	6-11	2	57	107	1.88
9. Roy Hibbert, Georgetown	7-2	3	102	184	1.80
10. Arturo Dubois, Manhattan	6-8	3	90	159	1.77

Juniors (Min. 70 Blks.)	Ht.	Yrs.	G	Blk.	Avg.
1. Shawn James, Duquesne & Northeastern	6-9	2	55	332	6.04
2. Bamba Fall, SMU	7-1	2	43	115	2.67
3. Scott VanderMeer, Bowling Green & Ill.-Chicago	6-11	2	61	142	2.33
4. Diamon Simpson, St. Mary's (Cal.)	6-7	2	61	124	2.03
5. Randall Hanke, Providence	6-11	2	57	107	1.88
6. Mamadou Diene, Baylor	7-0	2	43	79	1.84
7. Korvotney Barber, Auburn	6-7	2	60	98	1.63
8. John Bryant, Santa Clara	6-10	2	60	86	1.43
9. Richard Hendrix, Alabama	6-8	2	63	89	1.41
10. Robert Dozier, Memphis	6-9	2	74	99	1.34

MOST STEALS PER GAME

Seniors (Min. 120 St.)	Ht.	Yrs.	G	St.	Avg.
1. Sundiata Gaines, Georgia	6-1	3	89	198	2.22
2. Tony Lee, Robert Morris	6-0	3	85	180	2.12
3. Drew Gibson, Wofford	6-2	3	82	164	2.00
4. Courtney Lee, Western Ky.	6-5	3	91	177	1.95
5. Haminn Quaintance, Jacksonville & Kent	6-7	3	84	157	1.87
6. Bo McCalebb, New Orleans	6-0	4	96	174	1.81
7. Corey Johnson, Navy	6-2	3	77	139	1.81
8. Damian Martin, Loyola Marymount	6-2	3	88	158	1.80
9. Russell Robinson, Kansas	6-1	3	94	168	1.79
10. Roy Peake, Winston-Salem	5-11	3	87	154	1.77

Juniors (Min. 70 St.)	Ht.	Yrs.	G	St.	Avg.
1. Derek Johnson, Prairie View	6-1	1	30	82	2.73
2. Travis Holmes, VMI	6-4	2	60	159	2.65
3. Mario Chalmers, Kansas	6-1	2	71	186	2.62
4. Jerel McNeal, Marquette	6-3	2	60	140	2.33
5. Paul Gause, Seton Hall	5-11	2	57	126	2.21
6. Chavis Holmes, VMI	6-4	2	59	129	2.19
7. Courtney Pigram, East Tenn. St.	6-0	2	61	129	2.11
8. Bryan Mullins, Southern Ill.	6-1	2	69	143	2.07
9. Mike Robinson, Eastern Ill.	5-11	2	57	118	2.07
10. Zaire Taylor, Delaware	6-4	2	44	91	2.07

2007 Division II Individual Leaders

Points Per Game

Rk.	Name, School	Cl.	G	FGM	3FG	FT	Pts.	Avg.
1.	Ted Scott, West Virginia St.	Jr.	33	315	125	137	892	27.0
2.	Tyrone Anderson, Concord	Sr.	30	295	17	176	783	26.1
3.	Nate Newell, Ark.-Monticello	Sr.	26	186	104	192	668	25.7
4.	Gil Goodrich, Bowie St.	Sr.	28	210	115	177	712	25.4
5.	Andre Dabney, Bloomfield	Sr.	27	215	94	139	663	24.6
6.	DeMario Grier, Pfeiffer	Sr.	28	208	102	166	684	24.4
7.	Kris Krzyminski, Wayne St. (Mich.)	Sr.	26	210	83	117	620	23.8
8.	Jontae Vinson, Cal St. L.A.	Jr.	26	244	1	129	618	23.8
9.	Bradd Wierzbicki, Queens (N.Y.)	Sr.	25	195	55	140	585	23.4
10.	Damien Lolar, West Tex. A&M	Sr.	28	231	38	150	650	23.2
11.	Ricky Volcy, Northern Mich.	Sr.	29	222	67	142	653	22.5
12.	Barry Durosier, West Fla.	Sr.	27	201	65	128	595	22.0
13.	Matt Hall, Harding	Jr.	29	202	36	199	639	22.0
14.	Billy Arre, Lock Haven	So.	27	214	46	115	589	21.8
15.	Christian Burns, Philadelphia U.	Sr.	29	253	2	122	630	21.7
16.	Marcus Hubbard, Angelo St.	Jr.	26	201	56	106	564	21.7
17.	Antonio Fitzgerald, St. Augustine's	Sr.	28	187	57	176	607	21.7
18.	Milton Nance, North Ala.	Sr.	28	184	96	142	606	21.6
19.	Sean Barnette, Wingate	Jr.	34	263	75	134	735	21.6
20.	Patrick Hannaway, UC-Colo. Spgs.	Sr.	26	203	21	133	560	21.5
21.	Terrance Whiters, Arkansas Tech	Jr.	23	164	41	123	492	21.4
22.	Tyrone Beale, Bowie St.	Sr.	29	267	0	79	613	21.1
23.	Jason Thomas, East Central	Sr.	24	150	74	130	504	21.0
24.	Zack Whiting, Chaminade	Sr.	27	181	27	175	564	20.9
25.	Dusty Jura, Neb.-Kearney	Sr.	31	226	22	172	646	20.8
26.	Anthony Atkinson, Barton	Sr.	36	249	67	185	750	20.8
27.	Brian Stamer, Colo. Christian	Jr.	28	227	25	101	580	20.7
28.	Corey McDuffie, West Liberty St.	Sr.	29	189	83	139	600	20.7
29.	Michael Pierrot, Felician	Sr.	27	215	1	127	558	20.7
30.	Stephen Soriano, Mesa St.	Sr.	27	181	16	178	556	20.6
31.	Lance Den Boer, Central Wash.	Sr.	27	166	72	150	554	20.5
32.	Tyrekus Bowman, Augusta St.	Jr.	31	243	21	127	634	20.5
33.	Jason Smith, Ala.-Huntsville	Sr.	29	175	83	159	592	20.4
34.	Greg Brown, Montevallo	Sr.	34	244	68	138	694	20.4
35.	Anthony Brown, Central Okla.	Sr.	28	228	0	113	569	20.3
36.	Kevin Weybright, Christian Bros.	Jr.	28	211	67	79	568	20.3
37.	Matthew Reid, Cameron	Sr.	26	170	45	141	526	20.2
38.	Jake Linton, St. Martin's	So.	27	181	78	105	545	20.2
39.	Tim Bieri, Fort Lewis	Sr.	31	211	77	124	623	20.1
40.	Monyea Pratt, Stillman	Sr.	28	205	37	112	559	20.0
41.	Jushay Rockett, Alas. Fairbanks	Sr.	29	218	47	95	578	19.9
42.	John Davis, Tarleton St.	Sr.	28	194	26	142	556	19.9
43.	Eric Babers, Southeastern Okla.	Sr.	32	209	0	217	635	19.8
44.	Shane Maynard, West Liberty St.	Jr.	30	201	44	147	593	19.8
45.	Marcus Kennedy, Montevallo	Sr.	34	253	28	134	668	19.6
46.	Anthony Hilliard, Elizabeth City St.	So.	31	222	3	157	604	19.5
47.	Richard Fields, Concordia (N.Y.)	Jr.	26	146	66	146	504	19.4
48.	Kenny Jones, Kentucky St.	Jr.	30	223	3	131	580	19.3
49.	Brian Foster, Concord	Sr.	30	195	94	94	578	19.3
50.	Zack Wright, Central Mo.	Sr.	35	228	19	195	670	19.1
51.	Donta Watson, Emporia St.	Sr.	29	183	114	75	555	19.1
52.	Luke Anderson, Minn. St. Mankato	Sr.	33	210	91	119	630	19.1

Field-Goal Percentage

Min. 5 made per game

Rk.	Name, School	Cl.	G	FGM	FGA	FG%
1.	Garret Siler, Augusta St.	So.	31	166	241	68.9
2.	Dzaflo Larkai, Bellarmine	Jr.	27	146	220	66.4
3.	Chris Gilliam, Pitt.-Johnstown	Jr.	29	189	290	65.2
4.	Kenny Jones, Kentucky St.	Jr.	30	223	348	64.1
5.	Elijah Rouse, Mount Olive	Sr.	31	178	279	63.8
6.	Patrick Hannaway, UC-Colo. Spgs.	Sr.	26	203	319	63.6
7.	Brandon Butler, Regis (Colo.)	Sr.	26	184	291	63.2
8.	Ian Elseth, Colorado Mines	Sr.	21	114	181	63.0
9.	Willie Shaw, Dist. Columbia	Jr.	25	149	237	62.9
10.	Sam Carey, Southern N.H.	Jr.	26	140	223	62.8
11.	Devin Peal, Humboldt St.	Jr.	30	172	278	61.9
12.	Eric Dawson, Midwestern St.	Sr.	30	199	323	61.6
13.	Matt White, Southeastern Okla.	Sr.	32	168	273	61.5
14.	Chris Wooldridge, Catawba	Sr.	31	204	336	60.7
15.	Lucas Alves, BYU-Hawaii	Fr.	28	166	274	60.6
16.	Eric Babers, Southeastern Okla.	Sr.	32	209	346	60.4
17.	Mike Mosby, Adelphi	Sr.	31	155	259	59.8
18.	Anthony Brown, Central Okla.	Sr.	28	228	381	59.8

Rk.	Name, School	Cl.	G	FGM	FGA	FG%
19.	Nate Perry, Southwestern Okla.	Jr.	26	138	231	59.7
20.	Diego Aguiar, Nova Southeastern	Sr.	28	160	269	59.5
21.	Henrick Foster, West Ga.	Jr.	28	173	291	59.5
22.	Matt Cooper, Le Moyne	Sr.	29	151	255	59.2
23.	Esmir Guzonjic, North Ala.	Sr.	28	188	319	58.9
24.	Ryan Kuhl, Lake Superior St.	So.	27	165	280	58.9
25.	Jacob Mitchell, Western Ore.	Sr.	27	200	340	58.8
26.	Chris Jones, Queens (N.C.)	Sr.	29	174	296	58.8
27.	Dustin Kinney, Charleston (W.V.)	Sr.	29	148	252	58.7
28.	Tyronne Beale, Bowie St.	Sr.	29	267	455	58.7
29.	John Smith, Winona St.	Jr.	36	234	399	58.6
30.	Tyrone Anderson, Concord	Sr.	30	295	504	58.5

Three-Point Field Goals Per Game

Rk.	Name, School	Cl.	G	3FG	3PG
1.	Brett Rector, Davis & Elkins	Jr.	24	99	4.1
2.	Gil Goodrich, Bowie St.	Sr.	28	115	4.1
3.	Nate Newell, Ark.-Monticello	Sr.	26	104	4.0
4.	Donta Watson, Emporia St.	Sr.	29	114	3.9
5.	Taurean Moy, LeMoyne-Owen	Fr.	27	104	3.9
6.	Ted Scott, West Virginia St.	Jr.	33	125	3.8
7.	Chad Miller, Oakland City	Sr.	28	106	3.8
8.	Quinn Beckwith, North Ala.	Sr.	29	108	3.7
9.	Will Washington, Northern Mich.	Sr.	29	106	3.7
10.	DeMario Grier, Pfeiffer	Sr.	28	102	3.6
11.	Bryce Caldwell, Wayne St. (Neb.)	Jr.	28	99	3.5
12.	Chris Burns, Bryant	Sr.	32	113	3.5
13.	Ryan Williams, Pace	Jr.	33	115	3.5
14.	Andre Dabney, Bloomfield	Sr.	27	94	3.5
15.	Jason Stampley, Southeastern Okla.	Sr.	32	111	3.5
16.	Milton Nance, North Ala.	Sr.	28	96	3.4
	Zac Robinson, Neb.-Omaha	Sr.	28	96	3.4
18.	Brandon Wright, Erskine	Fr.	29	98	3.4
19.	Chris Vetrano, St. Anselm	Jr.	29	97	3.3
20.	Kevin Hill, Mansfield	Jr.	26	86	3.3
21.	Ricky Yahn, Wheeling Jesuit	Sr.	28	92	3.3
22.	Michael Bahl, Metro St.	Sr.	32	105	3.3
23.	Jon Baird, Cal St. Chico	Jr.	25	82	3.3
24.	Craig Nelson, Northern St.	Jr.	29	95	3.3
25.	David Lopez, Lincoln Memorial	Sr.	26	85	3.3
26.	Brett Bartlett, Ashland	Jr.	28	91	3.3
27.	Jason Fulwood, Coker	Sr.	29	94	3.2
28.	Memo Rodriguez, Ouachita Baptist	Jr.	28	90	3.2
29.	Kris Krzyminski, Wayne St. (Mich.)	Sr.	26	83	3.2
30.	Jordan Nuness, Minn. Duluth	Jr.	29	92	3.2

Three-Point Field-Goal Percentage

Minimum 2.5 made per game

Rk.	Name, School	Cl.	G	3FG	3FGA	3FG%
1.	Michael Bahl, Metro St.	Sr.	32	105	202	52.0
2.	Kris Krzyminski, Wayne St. (Mich.)	Sr.	26	83	164	50.6
3.	Andrew Kochevar, Sonoma St.	Jr.	26	65	134	48.5
4.	Chad Miller, Oakland City	Sr.	28	106	221	48.0
5.	Wes Jensen, Adams St.	Sr.	30	80	167	47.9
6.	Jordan Nuness, Minn. Duluth	Jr.	29	92	193	47.7
7.	Melvin Hall, Southern Ind.	Sr.	35	103	219	47.0
8.	Mark Morse, Lake Superior St.	So.	27	70	149	47.0
9.	Aaron Hill, Rockhurst	So.	29	84	179	46.9
10.	Jon Baird, Cal St. Chico	Jr.	25	82	176	46.6
11.	Sean-Claude Terrell, Tuskegee	Jr.	26	67	146	45.9
12.	Matt Fletcher, Southwest Minn. St.	Jr.	30	92	202	45.5
13.	Kevin Hill, Mansfield	Jr.	26	86	189	45.5
14.	Eric Boyce, BYU-Hawaii	Sr.	28	74	163	45.4
15.	Eric Hall, South Dakota	Jr.	30	93	205	45.4
16.	Drew Coffman, Midwestern St.	Sr.	31	78	173	45.1
17.	Tim Homan, Hillsdale	Jr.	26	65	145	44.8
18.	Pierce Caldwell, Incarnate Word	Fr.	29	78	175	44.6
19.	Corey McDuffie, West Liberty St.	Sr.	29	83	187	44.4
20.	Eric Draper, Alas. Anchorage	Sr.	28	78	176	44.3
21.	P.J. Schumacher, North Greenville	Sr.	24	64	145	44.1
22.	Steven Gum, Drury	Jr.	30	75	170	44.1
23.	Jake Linton, St. Martin's	So.	27	78	177	44.1
24.	David Lopez, Lincoln Memorial	Sr.	26	85	193	44.0

STATISTICAL LEADERS

Rk.	Name, School	Cl.	G	3FG	3FGA	3FG%
25.	Craig Nelson, Northern St.	Jr.	29	95	216	44.0
26.	Donta Watson, Emporia St.	Sr.	29	114	260	43.8
27.	Andre Coleman, Limestone	So.	23	65	149	43.6
28.	Ted Scott, West Virginia St.	Jr.	33	125	287	43.6
29.	Brett Bartlett, Ashland	Jr.	28	91	209	43.5
30.	Brian Foster, Concord	Sr.	30	94	218	43.1
31.	Lance Den Boer, Central Wash.	Sr.	27	72	167	43.1
	Turmaine Rice, Delta St.	Sr.	27	72	167	43.1

Free-Throw Percentage

Minimum 2.5 made per game

Rk.	Name, School	Cl.	G	FT	FTA	FT%
1.	Richard Stone, St. Andrews	Sr.	28	101	110	91.8
2.	Lance Den Boer, Central Wash.	Sr.	27	150	164	91.5
3.	Danley Shank, Shepherd	Sr.	25	76	84	90.5
4.	Radayl Richardson, Michigan Tech	Sr.	28	89	99	89.9
5.	Michael Jenkins, Neb.-Omaha	So.	27	133	148	89.9
6.	Lukas Henne, Western Wash.	Sr.	26	136	153	88.9
7.	Carl Arts, Alas. Anchorage	Jr.	28	86	97	88.7
8.	Dustin Bremerman, Seattle Pacific	Sr.	28	113	128	88.3
9.	Jake Linton, St. Martin's	So.	27	105	119	88.2
	Will Scheufelt, Humboldt St.	Jr.	30	90	102	88.2
11.	Vahn Knight, Ashland	Sr.	28	127	144	88.2
12.	Joey Deas, Rockhurst	Jr.	29	95	108	88.0
13.	Nic Fuller, UC-Colo. Spgs.	Jr.	28	89	102	87.3
14.	Dallas Hodges, Wayne St. (Neb.)	Sr.	25	130	149	87.2
15.	Herman Burge, Valdosta St.	Sr.	29	82	94	87.2
16.	Justin Parnell, Northwest Nazarene	Fr.	27	107	123	87.0
17.	Steve Dagostino, St. Rose	Jr.	31	140	161	87.0
	Darnell Evans, Queens (N.C.)	Jr.	30	120	138	87.0
	Murvin English, East Stroudsburg	Sr.	28	80	92	87.0
20.	Kevin Schappell, Northern Ky.	Sr.	33	86	99	86.9
21.	Rodney Edgerson, Ky. Wesleyan	Sr.	27	76	88	86.4
22.	Cody Loughry, Fairmont St.	Jr.	28	83	97	85.6
23.	Chris Burns, Bryant	Sr.	32	88	103	85.4
24.	Kenny Jones, Merrimack	Sr.	28	81	95	85.3
25.	Andrew Peschong, Southwest Minn. St.	Fr.	30	75	88	85.2
26.	Bryant Lassiter, NYIT	So.	29	137	161	85.1
27.	Troy Slaten, Mo.-St. Louis	Sr.	25	67	79	84.8
28.	Kris Krzyminski, Wayne St. (Mich.)	Sr.	26	117	138	84.8
	Kente Hart, Carson-Newman	Sr.	29	139	164	84.8
30.	Shawn Weinstein, St. Edward's	Jr.	30	111	131	84.7
31.	Drew Coffman, Midwestern St.	Sr.	31	122	144	84.7

Rebounds Per Game

Rk.	Name, School	Cl.	G	Reb.	Avg.
1.	Eric Dawson, Midwestern St.	Sr.	30	341	11.4
2.	Christian Burns, Philadelphia U.	Sr.	29	324	11.2
3.	Eric Babers, Southeastern Okla.	Sr.	32	345	10.8
4.	John Davis, Tarleton St.	Sr.	28	301	10.8
5.	Brandon Bingle, East Central	Sr.	26	276	10.6
6.	Anthony Hilliard, Elizabeth City St.	So.	31	328	10.6
7.	Jeff Fahnbulleh, Ky. Wesleyan	Jr.	26	273	10.5
8.	Brian Stamer, Colo. Christian	Sr.	28	293	10.5
9.	Tony Cornett, West Virginia St.	Sr.	32	334	10.4
10.	Michael Pierrot, Felician	Sr.	27	280	10.4
11.	Brian Monahan, St. Michael's	Jr.	29	295	10.2
12.	Dusty Jura, Neb.-Kearney	Sr.	31	314	10.1
13.	Aaron Williams, West Chester	Sr.	26	263	10.1
14.	Kevin Johnson, Humboldt St.	Sr.	29	291	10.0
15.	Stephan Bolt, Lewis	Jr.	25	250	10.0
16.	Magen McNeil, American Int'l	Sr.	29	287	9.9
17.	John Smith, Winona St.	Jr.	36	354	9.8
18.	Jason Gant, Incarnate Word	Sr.	29	285	9.8
19.	Marko Kolaric, Chaminade	Jr.	27	265	9.8
20.	Ricky Volcy, Northern Mich.	Sr.	29	279	9.6
21.	Andy Calmes, Truman	Sr.	28	269	9.6
22.	Amonzo Gantt, North Greenville	Sr.	29	278	9.6
23.	Devario Hudson, Valdosta St.	Jr.	29	273	9.4
24.	Chris LeBorious, Ohio Valley	Jr.	27	253	9.4
25.	Jeremy Benjamin, Bridgeport	Sr.	28	262	9.4
	Daren Tielsch, Edinboro	Sr.	28	262	9.4
27.	Jeremy Black, Tampa	Jr.	29	271	9.3
28.	Mike Mosby, Adelphi	Sr.	31	288	9.3
29.	Willie Shaw, Dist. Columbia	Jr.	25	232	9.3
30.	Ryan McLemore, Edinboro	Jr.	28	258	9.2

Assists Per Game

Rk.	Name, School	Cl.	G	Ast.	Avg.
1.	Zack Whiting, Chaminade	Sr.	27	289	10.7
2.	Luke Cooper, Alas. Anchorage	Jr.	28	230	8.2
3.	Jonny Reibel, Rollins	Jr.	32	245	7.7
4.	Gil Goodrich, Bowie St.	Sr.	28	207	7.4
5.	Shawn Poppie, Limestone	Sr.	26	176	6.8
6.	Ronnie Means, Fairmont St.	Jr.	28	189	6.8
7.	Shejdie Childs, GCSU	Sr.	29	191	6.6
8.	Brian Graves, Catawba	Sr.	31	203	6.5
9.	Darren Duncan, Merrimack	Fr.	28	183	6.5
	Ryan Webb, Seattle	Sr.	28	183	6.5
11.	Justin Argenal, Cal St. Chico	So.	27	175	6.5
12.	Herman Burge, Valdosta St.	Sr.	29	183	6.3
13.	Bruce Royal, St. Paul's	So.	28	170	6.1
14.	Anthony Atkinson, Barton	Sr.	36	216	6.0
15.	Kente Hart, Carson-Newman	Sr.	29	171	5.9
16.	Mark Covin, Le Moyne	Jr.	29	169	5.8
17.	J.B. Jones, SIU Edwardsville	Jr.	27	157	5.8
18.	Hassan Washington, Queens (N.Y.)	Jr.	28	158	5.6
19.	Dan Binggeli, West Liberty St.	Jr.	30	167	5.6
20.	Stephen Harrel, Southeastern Okla.	Sr.	32	178	5.6
21.	Tyrone Deacon, Wis.-Parkside	Jr.	32	175	5.5
22.	Edwin Torres, Virginia St.	Jr.	28	153	5.5
23.	Cory Knight, Gannon	So.	24	129	5.4
24.	Tyler Ryerson, Mo. Southern St.	Jr.	28	149	5.3
25.	Robert Quaintance, Fla. Gulf Coast	Sr.	31	163	5.3
26.	Tyrone Anderson, Concord	Sr.	30	156	5.2
27.	Aaron Nichols, Salem Int'l	Sr.	27	140	5.2
28.	Randall Stallworth, Stonehill	Fr.	28	145	5.2
29.	Brandon Kimbrough, Drury	Sr.	30	155	5.2
30.	Drew Coffman, Midwestern St.	Sr.	31	160	5.2

Blocked Shots Per Game

Rk.	Name, School	Cl.	G	Blk.	Avg.
1.	Sean McKeon, Kutztown	Jr.	28	117	4.2
2.	Jeremy Overstreet, Paine	Sr.	26	105	4.0
3.	Bryan Grier, Wingate	Jr.	34	119	3.5
4.	Avis Wyatt, Virginia St.	Sr.	28	92	3.3
5.	Ryan McLemore, Edinboro	Jr.	28	91	3.3
6.	Eric Dawson, Midwestern St.	Sr.	30	96	3.2
7.	DeMario Williams, Miles	Jr.	28	88	3.1
8.	Matthew Rogers, Southwest Baptist	Fr.	28	81	2.9
9.	John Smith, Winona St.	Jr.	36	100	2.8
10.	Ricky Volcy, Northern Mich.	Sr.	29	80	2.8
11.	Eric Babers, Southeastern Okla.	Sr.	32	79	2.5
12.	John Torson, Rockhurst	Jr.	29	71	2.4
13.	Mervyn Clarke, Oakland City	Jr.	28	68	2.4
14.	Garret Siler, Augusta St.	So.	31	74	2.4
15.	Michael Pierrot, Felician	Sr.	27	63	2.3
16.	Josh Kindred, Lenoir-Rhyne	Jr.	28	65	2.3
17.	Curtis Milner, Lander	Fr.	31	69	2.2
18.	Bryan Lee, Grand Canyon	Sr.	29	64	2.2
19.	Joel Box, Quincy	Sr.	29	63	2.2
20.	Tyler Cain, South Dakota	Fr.	30	64	2.1
21.	Channon Easley, East Stroudsburg	Jr.	27	57	2.1
22.	Monyea Pratt, Stillman	Sr.	28	59	2.1
23.	Christian Burns, Philadelphia U.	Sr.	29	61	2.1
24.	Will Graham, Fla. Southern	Jr.	28	58	2.1
25.	Devario Hudson, Valdosta St.	Jr.	29	60	2.1
26.	Craig Williams, Erskine	Sr.	22	45	2.0
27.	Ed Desir, Emporia St.	Sr.	28	56	2.0
	Robbie Will, Seattle Pacific	Jr.	28	56	2.0
	Tyrone Davidson, Mo.-Rolla	Sr.	26	52	2.0
30.	David White, Seattle	Sr.	29	57	2.0

Steals Per Game

Rk.	Name, School	Cl.	G	St.	Avg.
1.	Japhet McNeil, Bridgeport	Sr.	31	125	4.0
2.	Jeremy Byrd, S.C. Upstate	Jr.	26	90	3.5
3.	Charlie Parker, Millersville	Jr.	33	104	3.2
4.	Jonte Flowers, Winona St.	Jr.	36	107	3.0
5.	Monyea Pratt, Stillman	Sr.	28	82	2.9
6.	Shaun McKie, Salem Int'l	Sr.	25	73	2.9
7.	Terrance Whiters, Arkansas Tech	Jr.	23	64	2.8
8.	Paul Flowers, Mercy	Sr.	27	69	2.6
9.	Frank Pinson, Albany St. (Ga.)	Sr.	32	81	2.5

Rk.	Name, School	Cl.	G	Stl.	Avg.
10.	Robert Quaintance, Fla. Gulf Coast	Jr.	31	77	2.5
11.	Herman Burge, Valdosta St.	Sr.	29	71	2.4
12.	Zack Wright, Central Mo.	Sr.	35	85	2.4
	Leon Kennedy, Clarion	Sr.	28	68	2.4
14.	Elijah Rouse, Mount Olive	Sr.	31	75	2.4
15.	Jeff Dickson, St. Anselm	Jr.	25	60	2.4
16.	Gil Goodrich, Bowie St.	Sr.	28	67	2.4
17.	Ralph Mata, Lincoln (Mo.)	Jr.	26	62	2.4
18.	Sheanan Martinez, Nyack	Jr.	27	64	2.4
19.	Blake Strouth, Minn. St. Moorhead	Jr.	25	59	2.4
20.	Beau Brown, Lincoln Memorial	Fr.	28	66	2.4
	Kai Wells, Lincoln Memorial	Sr.	28	66	2.4

Rk.	Name, School	Cl.	G	Stl.	Avg.
22.	Chuck Davis, Shippensburg	Sr.	31	73	2.4
23.	Bryant Lassiter, NYIT	So.	29	68	2.3
24.	Terrell Eargle, Alderson-Broaddus	Fr.	30	70	2.3
	Zach Chandler, Newberry	Sr.	27	63	2.3
26.	Maurice Hooper, Johnson C. Smith	Jr.	25	58	2.3
27.	Marcus Grant, West Fla.	Sr.	27	62	2.3
	J.B. Jones, SIU Edwardsville	Jr.	27	62	2.3
29.	Jarrod Jackson, Tuskegee	Fr.	26	59	2.3
30.	Cornelius Gilleylen, St. Edward's	Sr.	30	68	2.3
31.	Winston Hines, Stillman	Jr.	28	63	2.3
	Damien Lolar, West Tex. A&M	Sr.	28	63	2.3
	Adrian Miles, Goldey-Beacom	Fr.	28	63	2.3

2007 Division II Individual Game Highs

Points

Rk.	Name, School	Cl.	Opponent	Date	Pts.
1.	Gil Goodrich, Bowie St.	Sr.	Mansfield	12/9/2006	52
2.	DeMario Grier, Pfeiffer	Sr.	Limestone	2/8/2007	48
3.	Damien Lolar, West Tex. A&M	Sr.	Ouachita Baptist	11/25/2006	47
4.	Ricky Yahn, Wheeling Jesuit	Sr.	Salem Int'l	1/6/2007	45
5.	Matt Otte, Bellarmine	Sr.	Lewis	2/10/2007	43
	Brian Foster, Concord	Sr.	West Liberty St.	2/1/2007	43
	Ted Scott, West Virginia St.	Jr.	West Liberty St.	1/20/2007	43
	Greg Brown, Montevallo	Sr.	West Ga.	1/13/2007	43
	Milton Nance, North Ala.	Sr.	Arkansas Tech	12/18/2006	43
	Dustin Bremerman, Seattle Pacific	Sr.	BYU-Hawaii	12/2/2006	43
11.	Torre Doty, Ark.-Monticello	Sr.	Arkansas Tech	1/20/2007	42
12.	Gil Goodrich, Bowie St.	Sr.	St. Augustine's	2/8/2007	41
	Luke Belt, Central Okla.	So.	Tex. A&M-Commerce	2/7/2007	41
	Troy Slaten, Mo.-St. Louis	Sr.	Mo.-Rolla	2/6/2007	41
	Nate Newell, Ark.-Monticello	Sr.	Harding	2/2/2007	41
	Andre Dabney, Bloomfield	Sr.	Post	1/16/2007	41
	Tyrone Anderson, Concord	Sr.	Pitt.-Johnstown	1/13/2007	41
	Japhet McNeil, Bridgeport	Sr.	Southern N.H.	1/8/2007	41
	Shane Maynard, West Liberty St.	Jr.	Pitt.-Johnstown	12/29/2006	41
	Kris Krzyminski, Wayne St. (Mich.)	Sr.	Gannon	11/30/2006	41
	Bryant Lassiter, NYIT	So.	Adelphi	11/29/2006	41
22.	Brian Stamer, Colo. Christian	Jr.	Chadron St.	2/17/2007	40
	Ryan Lancaster, Holy Family	Jr.	Bloomfield	1/13/2007	40
	Jason Thomas, East Central	Jr.	Southwestern Christ.	12/12/2006	40
	Brett Ledbetter, Mo.-St. Louis	Sr.	Rockhurst	12/9/2006	40
	Justin Wilson, Lock Haven	So.	East Stroudsburg	12/2/2006	40

Field-Goal Percentage

Minimum 10 made

Rk.	Name, School	Cl.	Opponent	Date	FGM	FGA	FG%
1.	Patrick Hannaway, UC-Colo. Spgs.	Sr.	Carroll (Wis.)	11/25/2006	15	15	100.0
	Esmir Guzonjic, North Ala.	Sr.	West Fla.	2/3/2007	13	13	100.0
	Dee Dee Drake, Henderson St.	Sr.	Rhema	12/4/2006	13	13	100.0
	Scott Mirich, West Liberty St.	Fr.	Davis & Elkins	1/13/2007	11	11	100.0
	Mikal Monette, Eastern N.M.	Sr.	S'western Christ.	11/30/2006	10	10	100.0
6.	Fernando Bonfim, Chadron St.	Sr.	Colo. Christian	2/17/2007	12	13	92.3
	Frank Phifer, Washburn	Sr.	Northwest Mo. St.	2/14/2007	12	13	92.3
8.	Anthony Brown, Central Okla.	Sr.	Tarleton St.	2/27/2007	11	12	91.7
	Artavius Mitchell, Lincoln Memorial	Sr.	Carson-Newman	2/17/2007	11	12	91.7
	Curt Ludtke, Northwood (Mich.)	Sr.	Ferris St.	2/3/2007	11	12	91.7
	Remi Yusuf, Tex. A&M-Kingsville	Sr.	Eastern N.M.	2/3/2007	11	12	91.7
12.	Aurimas Truskauskas, Gannon	Sr.	Wayne St. (Mich.)	2/10/2007	10	11	90.9
	Brad Ferstenou, Wis.-Parkside	Jr.	Bellarmine	2/8/2007	10	11	90.9
	Tyler Stoczynski, Gannon	So.	Penn St.-McKeesport	1/15/2007	10	11	90.9
	Channon Easley, East Stroudsburg	Jr.	Phila. Sciences	1/3/2007	10	11	90.9
	Joe Martinez, Northeastern St.	Jr.	Haskell	12/16/2006	10	11	90.9
	Emmanuel Little, North Dakota	Jr.	Dickinson St.	12/9/2006	10	11	90.9
	Raymond Shaw, West Ala.	Jr.	Clark Atlanta	12/6/2006	10	11	90.9
	Henrick Foster, West Ga.	Jr.	Columbus St.	11/24/2006	10	11	90.9

Three-Point Field Goals Made

Rk.	Name, School	Cl.	Opponent	Date	3FG
1.	Chad Miller, Oakland City	Sr.	Boyce	2/3/2007	11
	Kris Krzyminski, Wayne St. (Mich.)	Sr.	Gannon	11/30/2006	11
3.	Rodney Edgerson, Ky. Wesleyan	Sr.	Wis.-Parkside	1/25/2007	10
	Dominique Barron, Wilmington (Del.)	So.	Caldwell	12/16/2006	10
5.	E.J. Murray, Florida Tech	Jr.	Fla. Southern	2/28/2007	9
	Matt Otte, Bellarmine	Sr.	Lewis	2/10/2007	9
	Jason Stampley, Southeastern Okla.	Sr.	Cameron	2/7/2007	9
	Gil Goodrich, Bowie St.	Sr.	Virginia Union	1/23/2007	9
	Barry Jones, St. Augustine's	Sr.	Johnson C. Smith	1/23/2007	9
	Ted Scott, West Virginia St.	Jr.	West Liberty St.	1/20/2007	9
	Bryce Caldwell, Wayne St. (Neb.)	Jr.	Minn. St. Moorhead	1/19/2007	9
	Jeff Miner, Mont. St.-Billings	Fr.	Dallas Baptist	1/17/2007	9
	Milton Nance, North Ala.	Sr.	Arkansas Tech	12/18/2006	9
	Kevin Hill, Mansfield	Jr.	Bowie St.	12/9/2006	9
	Dustin Bremerman, Seattle Pacific	Sr.	BYU-Hawaii	12/2/2006	9
	Raul Mercedes, C.W. Post	Sr.	St. Anselm	11/17/2006	9

Three-Point Field-Goal Percentage

Minimum 8 made

Rk.	Name, School	Cl.	Opponent	Date	3FG	3FGA	3FG%
1.	Rodney Edgerson, Ky. Wesleyan	Sr.	Wis.-Parkside	1/25/2007	10	10	100.0
	Kyric Rambo, Southeastern Okla.	Jr.	Tex. A&M-Commerce	1/27/2007	8	8	100.0
	Justin Wilson, Lock Haven	So.	East Stroudsburg	12/2/2006	8	8	100.0
	Taurean Moy, LeMoyne-Owen	Fr.	Delta St.	11/25/2006	8	8	100.0
	Trey Mines, Virginia St.	Fr.	N.C. Central	1/23/2007	7	7	100.0
6.	Kevin Ratzsch, Northern St.	So.	Wayne St. (Neb.)	2/3/2007	8	9	88.9
7.	Jeff Martin, Neb.-Kearney	Fr.	Chadron St.	2/6/2007	7	8	87.5
	Theo Donley, Chadron St.	Sr.	Colo. Christian	2/2/2007	7	8	87.5
9.	Nick Certa, Truman	Jr.	Emporia St.	2/21/2007	7	9	77.8
	Lance Hazel, Queens (N.Y.)	Sr.	Concordia (N.Y.)	1/20/2007	7	9	77.8
	Charlie Smallwood, Dist. Columbia	Jr.	Kutztown	11/25/2006	7	9	77.8
12.	Matt Otte, Bellarmine	Sr.	Lewis	2/10/2007	9	12	75.0
	Dustin Bremerman, Seattle Pacific	Sr.	BYU-Hawaii	12/2/2006	9	12	75.0
14.	Chad Miller, Oakland City	Sr.	Boyce	2/3/2007	11	15	73.3
15.	Matt Fletcher, Southwest Minn. St.	Jr.	Bemidji St.	1/26/2007	8	11	72.7
16.	Matt Fletcher, Southwest Minn. St.	Jr.	Wayne St. (Neb.)	2/17/2007	7	10	70.0
	Champ Sylvester, Tex. A&M-Commerce	Jr.	Central Okla.	2/7/2007	7	10	70.0
	John Morris, C.W. Post	Sr.	Gannon	11/24/2006	7	10	70.0
19.	Sam Belt, Central Okla.	Jr.	Okla. Christian	11/28/2006	8	12	66.7
20.	Bryce Caldwell, Wayne St. (Neb.)	Jr.	Minn. St. Moorhead	1/19/2007	9	14	64.3
	Milton Nance, North Ala.	Sr.	Arkansas Tech	12/18/2006	9	14	64.3

STATISTICAL LEADERS

Free-Throw Percentage

Minimum 12 made

Rk. Name, School	Cl.	Opponent	Date	FT	FTA	FT%
1. Zack Wright, Central Mo.	Sr.	Pittsburg St.	12/9/2006	16	16	100.0
Bryant Lassiter, NYIT	So.	St. Thomas Aquinas	2/3/2007	15	15	100.0
Paul Flowers, Mercy	Jr.	Bloomfield	1/4/2007	15	15	100.0
Hunter Henry, Northwest Mo. St.	So.	Mo. Southern St.	3/1/2007	14	14	100.0
Lance Den Boer, Central Wash.	Sr.	Alas. Anchorage	2/22/2007	14	14	100.0
LaVontay Fenderson, Wis.-Parkside	So.	Mo.-St. Louis	1/20/2007	14	14	100.0
Shane Maynard, West Liberty St.	Jr.	Bluefield St.	2/3/2007	13	13	100.0
Antonio Fitzgerald, St. Augustine's	Sr.	Livingstone	1/11/2007	13	13	100.0
Ty McTyer, Colorado St.-Pueblo	Jr.	UC-Colo. Spgs.	12/30/2006	13	13	100.0
Jean Georges, Caldwell	Sr.	Nyack	2/20/2007	12	12	100.0
Greg Twomey, Assumption	Jr.	Stonehill	2/17/2007	12	12	100.0
Nate Newell, Ark.-Monticello	Sr.	Ouachita Baptist	2/8/2007	12	12	100.0
Troy Slaten, Mo.-St. Louis	Sr.	Mo.-Rolla	2/6/2007	12	12	100.0
Omari Knox, Bloomfield	So.	Goldey-Beacom	1/27/2007	12	12	100.0
Jonny Reibel, Rollins	Jr.	St. Leo	1/17/2007	12	12	100.0
Dustin Bremerman, Seattle Pacific	Sr.	Western Wash.	1/13/2007	12	12	100.0
Milton Nance, North Ala.	Sr.	Arkansas Tech	12/18/2006	12	12	100.0
David Walters, Wayne St. (Neb.)	So.	Mary	12/9/2006	12	12	100.0
Jake Linton, St. Martin's	So.	Ashland	11/17/2006	12	12	100.0
Radayl Richardson, Michigan Tech	Sr.	Wis.-Parkside	11/17/2006	12	12	100.0

Rebounds

Rk. Name, School	Cl.	Opponent	Date	Reb.
1. Brian Monahan, St. Michael's	Jr.	Assumption	1/11/2007	24
2. Barry Cornish, Shepherd	Jr.	Columbia Union	11/17/2006	23
3. Elijah Rouse, Mount Olive	Sr.	Barton	1/18/2007	22
4. Brandon Wash, Dallas Baptist	So.	Tex. Permian Basin	1/22/2007	21
Jason Gant, Incarnate Word	Sr.	Concordia (Tex.)	12/30/2006	21
Anthony Hilliard, Elizabeth City St.	So.	Livingstone	11/30/2006	21
7. Dusty Jura, Neb.-Kearney	Sr.	Metro St.	3/3/2007	20
Robert Strickland, Charleston (W.V.)	Jr.	Bluefield St.	1/6/2007	20
Eric Dawson, Midwestern St.	Sr.	Southeastern Okla.	12/2/2006	20
Aurimas Truskauskas, Gannon	Sr.	Edinboro	11/27/2006	20

Assists

Rk. Name, School	Cl.	Opponent	Date	Ast.
1. Edwin Torres, Virginia St.	Jr.	N.C. Central	1/23/2007	16
Luke Cooper, Alas. Anchorage	Jr.	UM-Kansas City	11/24/2006	16
3. Brian Graves, Catawba	Sr.	Carson-Newman	2/28/2007	15
Shon Caston, Montevallo	Jr.	Carver Bible	1/16/2007	15
Ronnie Means, Fairmont St.	Jr.	Pfeiffer	12/31/2006	15
Herman Burge, Valdosta St.	Sr.	Nova Southeastern	12/30/2006	15
7. Aaron Nichols, Salem Int'l	Sr.	Ohio Valley	1/20/2007	14
Mike Daniels, Tarleton St.	Jr.	Tex. A&M-Commerce	1/4/2007	14

Rk. Name, School	Cl.	Opponent	Date	Ast.
9. J.B. Jones, SIU Edwardsville	Jr.	Mo.-St. Louis	2/24/2007	13
Luke Cooper, Alas. Anchorage	Jr.	Western Ore.	2/1/2007	13
Sheanan Martinez, Nyack	Jr.	Bloomfield	1/30/2007	13
Raheem Scott, Holy Family	Sr.	Wilmington (Del.)	1/16/2007	13
Ryan Webb, Seattle	Sr.	Cheyney	12/30/2006	13
Edwin Torres, Virginia St.	Jr.	Alderson-Broaddus	12/29/2006	13
Hassan Washington, Queens (N.Y.)	Sr.	New Haven	12/6/2006	13
Marques Blank, Augustana (S.D.)	So.	Mo. Southern St.	12/2/2006	13
Ryan Webb, Seattle	Sr.	Ashland	11/18/2006	13

Blocked Shots

Rk. Name, School	Cl.	Opponent	Date	Blk.
1. Mervyn Clarke, Oakland City	Jr.	Ind.-East	11/15/2006	13
2. Sean McKeon, Kutztown	Jr.	Millersville	2/15/2007	11
3. Robert Espinosa, Shaw	Fr.	Livingstone	2/22/2007	10
4. John Smith, Winona St.	Jr.	Neb.-Kearney	3/11/2007	9
Avis Wyatt, Virginia St.	Sr.	Livingstone	1/25/2007	9
Ron Wyatt, Dominican (N.Y.)	Jr.	Bloomfield	12/21/2006	9
Ryan McLemore, Edinboro	Jr.	Mercyhurst	12/6/2006	9
Avis Wyatt, Virginia St.	Sr.	Johnson C. Smith	11/30/2006	9
Robbie Will, Seattle Pacific	Jr.	Cal St. L.A.	11/17/2006	9
10. Bryan Grier, Wingate	Jr.	Carson-Newman	2/24/2007	8
Ricky Volcy, Northern Mich.	Sr.	Northwood (Mich.)	2/17/2007	8
Michael Pierrot, Felician	Sr.	Goldey-Beacom	2/5/2007	8
John Smith, Winona St.	Jr.	Clarke	1/31/2007	8
Jeremy Black, Tampa	Jr.	Southeastern (Fla.)	12/18/2006	8
Tyrone Davidson, Mo.-Rolla	Sr.	Cent. Christian (Mo)	12/18/2006	8
Robert Strickland, Charleston (W.V.)	Jr.	Ohio-Eastern	12/16/2006	8
Sean McKeon, Kutztown	Jr.	Lock Haven	12/3/2006	8
Eric Dawson, Midwestern St.	Sr.	Southeastern Okla.	12/2/2006	8
Ryan McLemore, Edinboro	Jr.	Bloomsburg	1/14/2006	8
Sean McKeon, Kutztown	Jr.	West Chester	1/10/2006	8

Steals

Rk. Name, School	Cl.	Opponent	Date	St.
1. David Clark, Delta St.	So.	LeMoyne-Owen	11/25/2006	15
2. Frank Petersen, Dist. Columbia	Jr.	Ohio St.-Marion	1/1/2006	9
3. Hassan Robinson, St. Paul's	Sr.	Virginia St.	2/3/2007	8
Dan Binggeli, West Liberty St.	Jr.	Concord	2/1/2007	8
Kevin Widemond, Tex. A&M-Commerce	Jr.	Central Okla.	1/29/2007	8
Japhet McNeil, Bridgeport	Sr.	C.W. Post	1/27/2007	8
Terrance Whiters, Arkansas Tech	Jr.	Delta St.	1/25/2007	8
Shaun McKie, Salem Int'l	Sr.	Ohio Valley	1/20/2007	8
Gil Goodrich, Bowie St.	Sr.	Shaw	1/13/2007	8
Damon Harris, Ouachita Baptist	Sr.	Champion Bapt.	1/8/2007	8
Japhet McNeil, Bridgeport	Sr.	St. Thomas Aquinas	1/4/2007	8
Paul Flowers, Mercy	Jr.	NYIT	12/9/2006	8
Paul Flowers, Mercy	Jr.	Bloomfield	12/3/2006	8
Greg Brown, Montevallo	Sr.	Tuskegee	11/21/2006	8
Zach Chandler, Newberry	Sr.	Allen	11/21/2006	8
Chase Groves, Glenville St.	So.	Ohio St.-Newark	11/18/2006	8

2007 Division II Team Leaders

Won-Lost Percentage

Rk.	School	W	L	Pct.
1.	Winona St.	35	1	97.2
2.	Bentley	32	1	97.0
3.	Findlay	29	2	93.5
4.	Central Mo.	31	4	88.6
5.	Metro St.	28	4	87.5
6.	Humboldt St.	26	4	86.7
7.	Barton	31	5	86.1
8.	Grand Valley St.	29	5	85.3
9.	Minn. St. Mankato	28	5	84.8
	Millersville	28	5	84.8
11.	Southeastern Okla.	27	5	84.4
12.	Benedict	25	5	83.3
	West Liberty St.	25	5	83.3
14.	Southern Ind.	29	6	82.9
15.	Montevallo	28	6	82.4
16.	Eckerd	27	6	81.8
	Fla. Gulf Coast	27	6	81.8
18.	Cal St. San B'dino	26	6	81.3
19.	Alderson-Broaddus	24	6	80.0
	St. Edward's	24	6	80.0
21.	Virginia Union	23	6	79.3
22.	West Virginia St.	26	7	78.8
23.	Rollins	25	7	78.1
24.	Midwestern St.	24	7	77.4
	Augusta St.	24	7	77.4
	Neb.-Kearney	24	7	77.4
	California (Pa.)	24	7	77.4
	Northwest Mo. St.	24	7	77.4
29.	South Dakota	23	7	76.7
	Barry	23	7	76.7

Scoring Offense

Rk.	School	G	W-L	Pts.	Avg.
1.	West Liberty St.	30	25-5	2,962	98.7
2.	Pfeiffer	28	17-11	2,691	96.1
3.	West Virginia St.	33	26-7	2,979	90.3
4.	Southwestern Okla.	27	17-10	2,386	88.4
5.	Mount Olive	31	23-8	2,717	87.6
6.	Wheeling Jesuit	28	18-10	2,413	86.2
7.	Barton	36	31-5	3,090	85.8
8.	Winona St.	36	35-1	3,083	85.6
9.	Concord	30	17-13	2,567	85.6
10.	Cal St. Stanislaus	29	13-16	2,473	85.3
11.	North Ala.	29	15-14	2,471	85.1
12.	St. Paul's	28	11-17	2,383	85.1
13.	Bowie St.	29	19-10	2,468	85.1
14.	Southern Ind.	35	29-6	2,931	83.7
15.	Emporia St.	29	21-8	2,426	83.7
16.	Humboldt St.	30	26-4	2,496	83.2
17.	Midwestern St.	31	24-7	2,579	83.2
18.	Southeastern Okla.	32	27-5	2,654	82.9
19.	Central Okla.	28	20-8	2,322	82.9
20.	Alderson-Broaddus	30	24-6	2,487	82.9
21.	Montevallo	34	28-6	2,816	82.8
22.	Wingate	34	25-9	2,813	82.7
23.	Oakland City	28	16-12	2,312	82.6
24.	Valdosta St.	29	20-9	2,386	82.3
25.	UC-Colo. Spgs.	28	16-12	2,301	82.2
26.	Tex. A&M-Commerce	28	14-14	2,294	81.9
27.	Millersville	33	28-5	2,700	81.8
28.	Neb.-Kearney	31	24-7	2,530	81.6
29.	Catawba	31	20-11	2,509	80.9
30.	Carson-Newman	29	10-19	2,337	80.6

Scoring Defense

Rk.	School	G	W-L	Opp. Pts.	Opp. Avg.
1.	Bentley	33	32-1	1,898	57.5
2.	Grand Valley St.	34	29-5	1,956	57.5
3.	Henderson St.	32	23-9	1,873	58.5
4.	Northwest Mo. St.	31	24-7	1,855	59.8
5.	Findlay	31	29-2	1,867	60.2
6.	Clayton St.	32	24-8	1,947	60.8
7.	Southwest Minn. St.	30	20-10	1,841	61.4
8.	Christian Bros.	28	21-7	1,721	61.5
9.	Stillman	28	15-13	1,722	61.5
10.	Eckerd	33	27-6	2,035	61.7
11.	Holy Family	28	19-9	1,728	61.7
12.	SIU Edwardsville	27	15-12	1,667	61.7
13.	Michigan Tech	28	13-15	1,734	61.9
14.	Edinboro	29	19-10	1,796	61.9
15.	Presbyterian	29	20-9	1,810	62.4
16.	Barry	30	23-7	1,881	62.7
17.	Philadelphia U.	30	20-10	1,883	62.8
18.	Lander	31	20-11	1,949	62.9
19.	Shippensburg	31	17-14	1,951	62.9
20.	Benedict	30	25-5	1,890	63.0
21.	Caldwell	31	19-12	1,961	63.3
22.	Central Mo.	35	31-4	2,223	63.5
23.	St. Mary's (Tex.)	28	16-12	1,783	63.7
24.	Phila. Sciences	29	14-15	1,847	63.7
25.	California (Pa.)	31	24-7	1,978	63.8
26.	Fort Valley St.	30	18-12	1,926	64.2
27.	Truman	29	16-13	1,870	64.5
28.	Adelphi	31	18-13	2,000	64.5
29.	Southern Ark.	27	11-16	1,743	64.6
30.	Cal St. Bakersfield	29	15-14	1,875	64.7

Scoring Margin

Rk.	School	W-L	Pts.	Avg.	Opp. Pts.	Opp. Avg.	Pt. Mar.
1.	Winona St.	35-1	3,083	85.6	2,393	66.5	19.2
2.	Findlay	29-2	2,426	78.3	1,867	60.2	18.0
3.	Bentley	32-1	2,410	73.0	1,898	57.5	15.5
4.	Central Mo.	31-4	2,764	79.0	2,223	63.5	15.5
5.	Southern Ind.	29-6	2,931	83.7	2,406	68.7	15.0
6.	Grand Valley St.	29-5	2,453	72.1	1,956	57.5	14.6
7.	Montevallo	28-6	2,816	82.8	2,332	68.6	14.2
8.	Metro St.	28-4	2,544	79.5	2,105	65.8	13.7
9.	Northwest Mo. St.	24-7	2,261	72.9	1,855	59.8	13.1
10.	Millersville	28-5	2,700	81.8	2,283	69.2	12.6
11.	West Liberty St.	25-5	2,962	98.7	2,586	86.2	12.5
12.	Alas. Anchorage	19-9	2,182	77.9	1,838	65.6	12.3
13.	Alderson-Broaddus	24-6	2,487	82.9	2,128	70.9	12.0
14.	Oakland City	16-12	2,312	82.6	1,977	70.6	12.0
15.	California (Pa.)	24-7	2,339	75.5	1,978	63.8	11.6
16.	Wheeling Jesuit	18-10	2,413	86.2	2,089	74.6	11.6
17.	Humboldt St.	26-4	2,496	83.2	2,160	72.0	11.2
18.	Augusta St.	24-7	2,494	80.5	2,155	69.5	10.9
19.	Clayton St.	24-8	2,293	71.7	1,947	60.8	10.8
20.	Eckerd	27-6	2,387	72.3	2,035	61.7	10.7
21.	Cal St. San B'dino	26-6	2,520	78.8	2,181	68.2	10.6
22.	Mount Olive	23-8	2,717	87.6	2,390	77.1	10.5
23.	Fla. Gulf Coast	27-6	2,498	75.7	2,150	65.2	10.5
24.	Southeastern Okla.	27-5	2,654	82.9	2,319	72.5	10.5
25.	Pitt.-Johnstown	21-9	2,396	79.9	2,093	69.8	10.1
26.	Minn. St. Mankato	28-5	2,577	78.1	2,247	68.1	10.0
27.	Valdosta St.	20-9	2,386	82.3	2,097	72.3	10.0
28.	South Dakota	23-7	2,386	79.5	2,091	69.7	9.8
29.	St. Edward's	24-6	2,262	75.4	1,983	66.1	9.3
30.	Neb.-Kearney	24-7	2,530	81.6	2,251	72.6	9.0
	Virginia Union	23-6	2,174	75.0	1,913	66.0	9.0
32.	Christian Bros.	21-7	1,972	70.4	1,721	61.5	9.0

Field-Goal Percentage

Rk.	School	G	W-L	FGM	FGA	FG%
1.	Winona St.	36	35-1	1,128	2,162	52.2
2.	Pitt.-Johnstown	30	21-9	918	1,760	52.2
3.	Southern Ind.	35	29-6	1,070	2,060	51.9
4.	Humboldt St.	30	26-4	875	1,706	51.3
5.	North Greenville	29	16-13	798	1,559	51.2
6.	Alas. Anchorage	28	19-9	742	1,450	51.2
7.	Concord	30	17-13	957	1,874	51.1

Rk.	School	G	W-L	FGM	FGA	FG%
8.	Ky. Wesleyan	27	13-14	722	1,423	50.7
9.	BYU-Hawaii	28	20-8	778	1,536	50.7
10.	West Liberty St.	30	25-5	1,025	2,024	50.6
11.	Shepherd	29	16-13	857	1,696	50.5
12.	Montevallo	34	28-6	1,003	1,989	50.4
13.	UC-Colo. Spgs.	28	16-12	806	1,600	50.4
14.	Henderson St.	32	23-9	779	1,558	50.0
	West Tex. A&M	29	18-11	762	1,524	50.0
	Lenoir-Rhyne	28	18-10	728	1,456	50.0
17.	Augusta St.	31	24-7	887	1,781	49.8
18.	Seattle Pacific	28	18-10	790	1,588	49.7
19.	Alderson-Broaddus	30	24-6	909	1,828	49.7
20.	Cal St. San B'dino	32	26-6	895	1,800	49.7
21.	Quincy	30	20-10	798	1,606	49.7
22.	Bellarmine	27	12-15	723	1,456	49.7
23.	Fort Lewis	31	22-9	841	1,695	49.6
24.	Findlay	31	29-2	860	1,739	49.5
25.	Mesa St.	27	17-10	666	1,348	49.4
26.	Christian Bros.	28	21-7	723	1,465	49.4
27.	Drury	30	21-9	832	1,686	49.3
28.	Midwestern St.	31	24-7	889	1,805	49.3
29.	North Dakota	28	11-17	748	1,520	49.2
30.	Southeastern Okla.	32	27-5	926	1,888	49.0
31.	Oakland City	28	16-12	823	1,678	49.0

Field-Goal Percentage Defense

Rk.	School	G	W-L	Opp. FG	Opp. FGA	Opp. FG%
1.	Grand Valley St.	34	29-5	677	1,831	37.0
2.	Edinboro	29	19-10	670	1,773	37.8
3.	Paine	27	17-10	631	1,649	38.3
4.	Henderson St.	32	23-9	655	1,699	38.6
5.	Fla. Gulf Coast	33	27-6	741	1,900	39.0
6.	Virginia Union	29	23-6	695	1,768	39.3
7.	Shippensburg	31	17-14	672	1,707	39.4
8.	Bentley	33	32-1	717	1,807	39.7
9.	Michigan Tech	28	13-15	581	1,464	39.7
10.	NYIT	29	20-9	688	1,729	39.8
11.	Winona St.	36	35-1	906	2,275	39.8
12.	Northwest Mo. St.	31	24-7	627	1,563	40.1
13.	Eckerd	33	27-6	718	1,787	40.2
14.	Tarleton St.	28	18-10	664	1,641	40.5
15.	Holy Family	28	19-9	627	1,549	40.5
16.	Adelphi	31	18-13	639	1,577	40.5
17.	Clayton St.	32	24-8	684	1,682	40.7
18.	South Dakota	30	23-7	750	1,843	40.7
19.	Fort Valley St.	30	18-12	661	1,619	40.8
20.	Le Moyne	29	14-15	676	1,654	40.9
21.	Johnson C. Smith	25	16-9	619	1,514	40.9
22.	Kentucky St.	30	15-15	766	1,871	40.9
23.	C.W. Post	30	19-11	717	1,751	40.9
24.	Tusculum	28	13-15	647	1,577	41.0
25.	Barry	30	23-7	654	1,594	41.0
26.	Bridgeport	31	22-9	700	1,706	41.0
27.	Benedict	30	25-5	688	1,675	41.1
28.	Fla. Southern	28	8-20	706	1,718	41.1
29.	East Central	26	10-16	636	1,546	41.1
30.	Southwest Minn. St.	30	20-10	673	1,634	41.2
31.	Lynn	28	14-14	638	1,549	41.2
32.	Pitt.-Johnstown	30	21-9	741	1,798	41.2

Three-Point Field Goals Per Game

Rk.	School	G	W-L	3FG	3PG
1.	Fairmont St.	28	14-14	296	10.6
2.	Ashland	28	16-12	283	10.1
	Oakland City	28	16-12	283	10.1
4.	Rollins	32	25-7	321	10.0
5.	Northern Mich.	29	18-11	290	10.0
6.	Columbus St.	29	17-12	289	10.0
7.	Coker	29	8-21	286	9.9
8.	West Liberty St.	30	25-5	294	9.8
9.	Northwest Nazarene	27	10-17	261	9.7
10.	Southwestern Okla.	27	17-10	260	9.6
11.	St. Michael's	29	16-13	272	9.4
12.	Mont. St.-Billings	27	6-21	253	9.4
13.	West Virginia St.	33	26-7	309	9.4
14.	Southwest Baptist	28	16-12	261	9.3

Rk.	School	G	W-L	3FG	3PG
	Pfeiffer	28	17-11	261	9.3
16.	Metro St.	32	28-4	298	9.3
17.	Northern Ky.	33	24-9	298	9.0
18.	Valdosta St.	29	20-9	261	9.0
19.	Neb.-Kearney	31	24-7	277	8.9
20.	Davis & Elkins	28	6-22	250	8.9
	Wheeling Jesuit	28	18-10	250	8.9
22.	Chaminade	27	16-11	240	8.9
23.	Seattle Pacific	28	18-10	248	8.9
24.	Grand Canyon	29	21-8	255	8.8
25.	Emporia St.	29	21-8	252	8.7
26.	North Ala.	29	15-14	251	8.7
27.	Mansfield	26	9-17	225	8.7
28.	Limestone	29	20-9	250	8.6
29.	Western St.	27	12-15	231	8.6
30.	Ala.-Huntsville	29	18-11	248	8.6

Three-Point Field-Goal Percentage

Minimum 5 made per game

Rk.	School	G	W-L	3FG	3FGA	3FG%
1.	Metro St.	32	28-4	298	675	44.1
2.	Oakland City	28	16-12	283	661	42.8
3.	Northern St.	29	21-8	241	565	42.7
4.	West Virginia St.	33	26-7	309	726	42.6
5.	Alas. Anchorage	28	19-9	219	517	42.4
6.	LeMoyne-Owen	28	12-16	189	456	41.4
7.	Wayne St. (Mich.)	26	13-13	175	426	41.1
8.	Winona St.	36	35-1	263	646	40.7
9.	Augusta St.	31	24-7	222	546	40.7
10.	Montevallo	34	28-6	248	611	40.6
11.	Ky. Wesleyan	27	13-14	174	429	40.6
12.	Minn. Duluth	29	16-13	208	516	40.3
13.	West Liberty St.	30	25-5	294	735	40.0
14.	Neb.-Kearney	31	24-7	277	695	39.9
15.	Augustana (S.D.)	28	16-12	224	566	39.6
16.	Mo.-St. Louis	27	9-18	184	465	39.6
17.	BYU-Hawaii	28	20-8	207	524	39.5
18.	Sonoma St.	26	15-11	187	474	39.5
19.	Upper Iowa	28	3-25	180	457	39.4
20.	Pfeiffer	28	17-11	261	663	39.4
21.	Fairmont St.	28	14-14	296	752	39.4
22.	Rollins	32	25-7	321	816	39.3
23.	Midwestern St.	31	24-7	203	517	39.3
24.	Northern Ky.	33	24-9	298	759	39.3
25.	Emporia St.	29	21-8	252	642	39.3
26.	Southwest Minn. St.	30	20-10	250	637	39.2
27.	Fort Lewis	31	22-9	247	630	39.2
28.	S.C. Upstate	28	17-11	227	579	39.2
29.	Drury	30	21-9	207	528	39.2
30.	Mesa St.	27	17-10	176	449	39.2
31.	Limestone	29	20-9	250	638	39.2
32.	Seattle Pacific	28	18-10	248	633	39.2
33.	Adams St.	30	16-14	219	559	39.2
34.	Grand Canyon	29	21-8	255	651	39.2

Free-Throw Percentage

Rk.	School	G	W-L	FT	FTA	FT%
1.	Northwest Nazarene	27	10-17	384	473	81.2
2.	Augustana (S.D.)	28	16-12	363	455	79.8
3.	Ark.-Monticello	26	9-17	451	581	77.6
4.	Alas. Anchorage	28	19-9	479	620	77.3
5.	Ashland	28	16-12	429	556	77.2
6.	West Liberty St.	30	25-5	618	801	77.2
7.	Mesa St.	27	17-10	551	720	76.5
8.	Minn. Duluth	29	16-13	401	524	76.5
9.	Pfeiffer	28	17-11	608	797	76.3
10.	Neb.-Omaha	28	12-19	407	534	76.2
11.	St. Rose	32	22-10	416	546	76.2
12.	Carson-Newman	29	10-19	501	660	75.9
13.	Northern Ky.	33	24-9	488	643	75.9
14.	Northwest Mo. St.	31	24-7	515	679	75.8
15.	Minn. St. Mankato	33	28-5	561	741	75.7
16.	Mo.-Rolla	27	7-20	352	466	75.5
17.	Ferris St.	28	10-18	338	449	75.3
18.	Western Wash.	26	11-15	470	625	75.2
19.	Lake Superior St.	27	9-18	298	397	75.1
20.	Seattle Pacific	28	18-10	407	544	74.8

Rk.	School	G	W-L	FT	FTA	FT%
21.	Bentley	33	32-1	439	587	74.8
22.	St. Martin's	27	10-17	478	641	74.6
23.	St. Michael's	29	16-13	364	489	74.4
24.	Armstrong Atlantic	30	21-9	476	640	74.4
25.	Midwestern St.	31	24-7	598	805	74.3
26.	Hawaii-Hilo	27	9-18	456	614	74.3
27.	Kutztown	28	17-11	556	749	74.2
28.	Quincy	30	20-10	501	675	74.2
29.	Central Mo.	35	31-4	713	962	74.1
30.	Merrimack	28	8-20	362	489	74.0
31.	North Ala.	29	15-14	498	673	74.0

Rebound Margin

Rk.	School	W-L	Reb.	Avg.	Opp Reb.	Opp Avg.	Reb Mar.
1.	Fla. Gulf Coast	27-6	1,468	44.5	1,111	33.7	10.8
2.	Alderson-Broaddus	24-6	1,174	39.1	918	30.6	8.5
3.	Bentley	32-1	1,276	38.7	998	30.2	8.4
4.	Eckerd	27-6	1,241	37.6	988	29.9	7.7
5.	Fort Valley St.	18-12	1,199	40.0	974	32.5	7.5
6.	California (Pa.)	24-7	1,160	37.4	930	30.0	7.4
7.	East Central	10-16	1,127	43.3	935	36.0	7.4
8.	Grand Valley St.	29-5	1,271	37.4	1,025	30.1	7.2
9.	Henderson St.	23-9	1,142	35.7	913	28.5	7.2
10.	Southern Ind.	29-6	1,266	36.2	1,021	29.2	7.0
11.	Lynn	14-14	1,073	38.3	884	31.6	6.8
12.	St. Mary's (Tex.)	16-12	1,029	36.8	843	30.1	6.6
13.	Virginia Union	23-6	1,188	41.0	999	34.4	6.5
14.	Shepherd	16-13	1,080	37.2	893	30.8	6.4
15.	Elizabeth City St.	16-16	1,394	43.6	1,189	37.2	6.4
16.	Clayton St.	24-8	1,241	38.8	1,041	32.5	6.3
17.	Minn. Duluth	16-13	990	34.1	814	28.1	6.1
18.	Pittsburg St.	18-13	1,121	36.2	935	30.2	6.0
19.	Central Mo.	31-4	1,282	36.6	1,076	30.7	5.9
20.	Alas. Fairbanks	17-13	1,108	36.9	937	31.2	5.7
21.	Ky. Wesleyan	13-14	908	33.6	757	28.0	5.6
22.	Gannon	9-17	948	36.5	809	31.1	5.3
23.	Dist. Columbia	20-9	1,153	39.8	1,000	34.5	5.3
24.	Central Okla.	20-8	1,077	38.5	931	33.3	5.2
25.	Montevallo	28-6	1,280	37.6	1,103	32.4	5.2
26.	West Virginia St.	26-7	1,350	40.9	1,179	35.7	5.2
27.	Tampa	15-14	1,126	38.8	976	33.7	5.2
28.	Cheyney	15-15	1,120	37.3	969	32.3	5.0
29.	Tarleton St.	18-10	1,105	39.5	965	34.5	5.0
30.	Winona St.	35-1	1,390	38.6	1,211	33.6	5.0

Assists Per Game

Rk.	School	G	W-L	Ast.	Avg.
1.	Pitt.-Johnstown	30	21-9	586	19.5
2.	Oakland City	28	16-12	546	19.5
3.	Seattle Pacific	28	18-10	539	19.3
4.	Alas. Anchorage	28	19-9	536	19.1
5.	West Liberty St.	30	25-5	565	18.8
6.	Drury	30	21-9	561	18.7
7.	Central Okla.	28	20-8	518	18.5
8.	West Virginia St.	33	26-7	610	18.5
9.	North Greenville	29	16-13	536	18.5
10.	Chaminade	27	16-11	494	18.3
11.	Montevallo	34	28-6	616	18.1
12.	Rollins	32	25-7	578	18.1
13.	Mount Olive	31	23-8	557	18.0
14.	Augusta St.	31	24-7	556	17.9
15.	Southwestern Okla.	27	17-10	484	17.9
16.	Winona St.	36	35-1	641	17.8
17.	Ala.-Huntsville	29	18-11	515	17.8
18.	Alderson-Broaddus	30	24-6	532	17.7
19.	Southern Ind.	35	29-6	618	17.7
20.	Midwestern St.	31	24-7	544	17.5
21.	Wheeling Jesuit	28	18-10	491	17.5
22.	St. Paul's	28	11-17	485	17.3
23.	Humboldt St.	30	26-4	517	17.2
24.	Concord	30	17-13	513	17.1
25.	GCSU	29	19-10	494	17.0
26.	Christian Bros.	28	21-7	474	16.9
	Augustana (S.D.)	28	16-12	474	16.9
28.	Tex. A&M-Commerce	28	14-14	473	16.9
	BYU-Hawaii	28	20-8	473	16.9
30.	St. Cloud St.	30	19-11	504	16.8
31.	Fla. Gulf Coast	33	27-6	554	16.8

Blocked Shots Per Game

Rk.	School	G	W-L	Blk.	Avg.
1.	Paine	27	17-10	199	7.4
2.	Kutztown	28	17-11	186	6.6
3.	Wingate	34	25-9	224	6.6
4.	Edinboro	29	19-10	159	5.5
5.	Winona St.	36	35-1	195	5.4
6.	Midwestern St.	31	24-7	167	5.4
	Mount Olive	31	23-8	167	5.4
8.	BYU-Hawaii	28	20-8	148	5.3
9.	Tampa	29	15-14	151	5.2
10.	Charleston (W.V.)	29	15-14	146	5.0
11.	Valdosta St.	29	20-9	144	5.0
12.	Bridgeport	31	22-9	153	4.9
13.	Miles	29	14-15	142	4.9
14.	Catawba	31	20-11	146	4.7
15.	South Dakota	30	23-7	141	4.7
16.	Southwest Baptist	28	16-12	131	4.7
17.	Rockhurst	29	17-12	133	4.6
18.	Western Wash.	26	11-15	119	4.6
19.	Morehouse	25	9-16	113	4.5
20.	Augusta St.	31	24-7	136	4.4
21.	Concordia-St. Paul	29	21-8	127	4.4
22.	Post	29	17-12	126	4.3
23.	Lenoir-Rhyne	28	18-10	121	4.3
24.	Virginia St.	28	20-8	120	4.3
	Tarleton St.	28	18-10	120	4.3
26.	Northern Mich.	29	18-11	124	4.3
27.	Kentucky St.	30	15-15	126	4.2
	Pitt.-Johnstown	30	21-9	126	4.2
29.	Holy Family	28	19-9	117	4.2
30.	Lander	31	20-11	129	4.2

Steals Per Game

Rk.	School	G	W-L	St.	Avg.
1.	Cal St. San B'dino	32	26-6	393	12.3
2.	St. Edward's	30	24-6	334	11.1
3.	Southwestern Okla.	27	17-10	300	11.1
4.	Metro St.	32	28-4	349	10.9
5.	Albany St. (Ga.)	32	15-17	345	10.8
6.	Clayton St.	32	24-8	340	10.6
7.	Bridgeport	31	22-9	324	10.5
8.	Pfeiffer	28	17-11	288	10.3
9.	Oakland City	28	16-12	287	10.3
10.	Stillman	28	15-13	282	10.1
11.	Findlay	31	29-2	311	10.0
12.	Johnson C. Smith	25	16-9	250	10.0
13.	Millersville	33	28-5	329	10.0
14.	Delta St.	28	18-10	277	9.9
15.	Arkansas Tech	27	6-21	266	9.9
16.	Clarion	28	13-15	275	9.8
17.	Central Mo.	35	31-4	343	9.8
18.	Abilene Christian	26	10-16	254	9.8
19.	Wheeling Jesuit	28	18-10	272	9.7
20.	Salem Int'l	27	15-12	262	9.7
21.	Tuskegee	28	6-22	270	9.6
22.	Virginia Union	29	23-6	278	9.6
	Concordia-St. Paul	29	21-8	278	9.6
24.	West Liberty St.	30	25-5	287	9.6
25.	East Stroudsburg	28	18-10	267	9.5
26.	Miles	29	14-15	276	9.5
27.	Lincoln Memorial	28	13-15	264	9.4
28.	Virginia St.	28	20-8	259	9.3
29.	BYU-Hawaii	28	20-8	256	9.1
30.	Southern Ind.	35	29-6	319	9.1
31.	Tex. A&M-Kingsville	28	19-9	255	9.1
	S.C. Upstate	28	17-11	255	9.1
33.	Lincoln (Mo.)	26	7-19	236	9.1
34.	California (Pa.)	31	24-7	281	9.1
35.	St. Rose	32	22-10	290	9.1
36.	Fla. Gulf Coast	33	27-6	299	9.1

Turnovers Per Game

Rk.	School	G	W-L	TO	Avg.
1.	Wis.-Parkside	32	19-13	362	11.3
2.	Truman	29	16-13	330	11.4

STATISTICAL LEADERS

Rk.	School	G	W-L	TO	Avg.
3.	Northern Ky.	33	24-9	378	11.5
4.	Western St.	27	12-15	310	11.5
5.	Michigan Tech	28	13-15	325	11.6
6.	St. Cloud St.	30	19-11	350	11.7
7.	Fort Hays St.	28	13-15	327	11.7
8.	SIU Edwardsville	27	15-12	318	11.8
9.	Indianapolis	26	13-13	307	11.8
10.	Minn. Duluth	29	16-13	343	11.8
11.	Southwest Minn. St.	30	20-10	361	12.0
12.	Chaminade	27	16-11	325	12.0
13.	Northwest Mo. St.	31	24-7	374	12.1
14.	Winona St.	36	35-1	435	12.1
15.	Northwest Nazarene	27	10-17	328	12.1
16.	Findlay	31	29-2	387	12.5
17.	Ala.-Huntsville	29	18-11	363	12.5
18.	Minn. St. Mankato	33	28-5	414	12.5
19.	Ark.-Monticello	26	9-17	329	12.7
20.	Saginaw Valley	25	11-14	317	12.7
21.	Western N.M.	27	12-15	343	12.7
22.	Millersville	33	28-5	421	12.8
23.	Northern Mich.	29	18-11	371	12.8
24.	Bentley	33	32-1	424	12.8
25.	Valdosta St.	29	20-9	374	12.9
	St. Michael's	29	16-13	374	12.9
27.	Colorado St.-Pueblo	28	13-15	363	13.0
28.	Northern St.	29	21-8	380	13.1
29.	Mercyhurst	29	18-11	381	13.1
	GCSU	29	19-10	381	13.1

Personal Fouls Per Game

Rk.	School	G	W-L	PF	Avg.	DQ
1.	Bentley	33	32-1	457	13.8	1
2.	Ala.-Huntsville	29	18-11	405	14.0	7
3.	Winona St.	36	35-1	532	14.8	4
4.	Gannon	26	9-17	387	14.9	6
5.	Davis & Elkins	28	6-22	417	14.9	14
6.	Erskine	29	14-15	438	15.1	23
7.	Southwest Minn. St.	30	20-10	458	15.3	9
8.	Truman	29	16-13	445	15.3	7
9.	Humboldt St.	30	26-4	465	15.5	2
10.	Christian Bros.	28	21-7	437	15.6	7
11.	Philadelphia U.	30	20-10	469	15.6	19
12.	North Greenville	29	16-13	456	15.7	5
13.	Ashland	28	16-12	442	15.8	8
14.	Edinboro	29	19-10	459	15.8	10
15.	Hillsdale	26	15-11	413	15.9	11
16.	Stonehill	28	16-12	447	16.0	14
17.	Minn. St. Mankato	33	28-5	530	16.1	4
18.	St. Michael's	29	16-13	466	16.1	6
19.	American Int'l	29	16-13	468	16.1	6
20.	Grand Valley St.	34	29-5	551	16.2	8
21.	Montevallo	34	28-6	553	16.3	10
22.	Stillman	28	15-13	456	16.3	19
23.	Cal Poly Pomona	28	20-8	458	16.4	11
24.	Pace	33	20-13	541	16.4	11
25.	GCSU	29	19-10	476	16.4	7
26.	Northeastern St.	26	10-16	427	16.4	6
27.	Glenville St.	28	6-22	460	16.4	11
28.	New Haven	28	9-19	461	16.5	2
29.	Shepherd	29	16-13	479	16.5	15
30.	Franklin Pierce	27	13-14	446	16.5	5

2007 Division II Team Game Highs

Points

Rk.	School	Opponent	Date	Pts.	Opp Pts.
1.	Montevallo	Carver Bible	1/16/2007	150	72
2.	West Liberty St.	Ohio-Eastern	11/15/2006	141	76
3.	Charleston (W.V.)	Ohio-Eastern	12/16/2006	140	70
4.	Southwestern Okla.	Southwestern Christ.	12/20/2006	138	67
5.	Dist. Columbia	Ohio St.-Marion	12/1/2006	133	53
6.	California (Pa.)	Penn St.-Fayette	11/21/2006	132	47
	Oakland City	Ind.-East	11/15/2006	132	58
8.	Valdosta St.	Carver Bible	11/15/2006	130	62
9.	Southern Ind.	Judson (Ill.)	11/21/2006	125	68
	Alas. Fairbanks	Lancaster Bible	11/3/2006	125	61
11.	Northern Mich.	Finlandia	12/18/2006	123	68
12.	Wingate	Carson-Newman	2/24/2007	122	116
	Western Ore.	Cal St. Monterey Bay	12/15/2006	122	126
	Bowie St.	Mansfield	12/9/2006	122	117
15.	Lincoln Memorial	Carson-Newman	2/17/2007	120	118
16.	Winona St.	North Central (Minn.)	12/5/2006	119	38
17.	Carson-Newman	Lincoln Memorial	2/17/2007	118	120
	Ouachita Baptist	Ecclesia	11/18/2006	118	61
19.	East Stroudsburg	Penn St.-Schuylkill	2/3/2007	117	56
	Southern Ind.	Harris-Stowe	12/30/2006	117	78
	Mansfield	Bowie St.	12/9/2006	117	122
22.	Bowie St.	St. Augustine's	2/8/2007	116	104
	Abilene Christian	Concordia (Tex.)	11/18/2006	116	114
24.	Lynn	Wilmington (Del.)	12/21/2006	115	68
25.	Valdosta St.	Palm Beach Atl.	2/12/2007	114	70
	Southwestern Okla.	Midwestern St.	12/7/2006	114	99

Field-Goal Percentage

Rk.	School	Opponent	Date	FGM	FGA	FG%
1.	Dist. Columbia	Kutztown	11/25/2006	7	9	77.8
2.	Lenoir-Rhyne	Lincoln Memorial	2/28/2007	35	47	74.5
3.	Southwestern Okla.	Southwestern Christ.	12/20/2006	57	80	71.3
4.	Abilene Christian	Concordia (Tex.)	11/18/2006	39	55	70.9
5.	Seattle Pacific	Northwest Nazarene	1/18/2007	42	60	70.0
6.	Southern Ind.	Judson (Ill.)	11/21/2006	52	75	69.3

Rk.	School	Opponent	Date	FGM	FGA	FG%
7.	Cheyney	Bloomsburg	2/4/2007	36	52	69.2
	Seattle Pacific	Seattle	2/3/2007	36	52	69.2
9.	Northern Ky.	Rockhurst	2/3/2007	31	45	68.9
	West Tex. A&M	N.M. Highlands	1/22/2007	31	45	68.9
11.	Concordia-St. Paul	Minn.-Crookston	12/9/2006	42	61	68.9
12.	Wingate	Carson-Newman	2/24/2007	48	70	68.6
13.	North Dakota	Dickinson St.	12/8/2006	37	54	68.5
14.	Adams St.	Western N.M.	2/24/2007	28	41	68.3
15.	Christian Bros.	Ouachita Baptist	2/15/2007	30	44	68.2
16.	Christian Bros.	North Ala.	12/9/2006	37	55	67.3
17.	Alas. Anchorage	Lancaster Bible	11/4/2006	39	58	67.2
18.	Augustana (S.D.)	Peru St.	12/5/2006	41	61	67.2
19.	Drury	Indianapolis	1/11/2007	34	51	66.7
	Grand Valley St.	Marygrove	1/17/2007	32	48	66.7
	West Liberty St.	Dist. Columbia	11/17/2006	32	48	66.7
	Northwood (Mich.)	Ferris St.	2/3/2007	28	42	66.7
	Ala.-Huntsville	West Ga.	1/23/2007	28	42	66.7
	Philadelphia U.	Dominican (N.Y.)	1/13/2007	26	39	66.7

Three-Point Field Goals Made

Rk.	School	Opponent	Date	3FG
1.	Montevallo	Carver Bible	1/16/2007	32
2.	Oakland City	Boyce	2/3/2007	25
3.	Lincoln Memorial	North Greenville	2/20/2007	21
4.	Wis.-Parkside	Grace Bible (Mich.)	12/21/2006	20
	Fairmont St.	Ohio-Eastern	12/18/2006	20
	Mansfield	Bowie St.	12/9/2006	20
7.	Mo.-Rolla	Ky. Wesleyan	2/3/2007	19
8.	Concordia (N.Y.)	C.W. Post	2/8/2007	18
	Southwestern Okla.	Tex. A&M-Commerce	2/3/2007	18
	Valdosta St.	Nova Southeastern	12/30/2006	18
	Southwestern Okla.	Southwestern Christ.	12/20/2006	18
	Northern Mich.	Wis.-Stout	12/13/2006	18
	Northern Ky.	Tiffin	12/5/2006	18
	Ark.-Monticello	Central Baptist	11/22/2006	18
15.	Western St.	Fort Lewis	2/22/2007	17
	Northern Mich.	Northwood (Mich.)	2/17/2007	17
	Mars Hill	North Greenville	2/17/2007	17
	Northern Ky.	Rockhurst	2/3/2007	17
	Mont. St.-Billings	Okla. Panhandle	1/12/2007	17

Rk.	School	Opponent	Date	3FG
	Concordia-St. Paul	Wis.-River Falls	12/16/2006	17
	East Central	Southwestern Christ.	12/12/2006	17
	Northwest Nazarene	Mesa St.	11/18/2006	17
	Valdosta St.	Carver Bible	11/15/2006	17

Three-Point Field-Goal Percentage

Minimum 10 made

Rk.	School	Opponent	Date	3FG	3FGA	3FG%
1.	LeMoyne-Owen	Delta St.	11/25/2006	10	10	100.0
2.	Chadron St.	Colo. Christian	2/2/2007	16	20	80.0
3.	Florida Tech	Palm Beach Atl.	12/20/2006	12	16	75.0
	Fla. Southern	Armstrong Atlantic	11/25/2006	12	16	75.0
5.	Concordia-St. Paul	Wis.-River Falls	12/16/2006	17	23	73.9
6.	Christian Bros.	Ouachita Baptist	2/15/2007	13	18	72.2
	UC-Colo. Spgs.	Colorado St.-Pueblo	12/30/2006	13	18	72.2
	Shepherd	Valley Forge Chrst.	12/6/2006	13	18	72.2
9.	Mercyhurst	Hillsdale	2/10/2007	10	14	71.4
	Neb.-Kearney	Colorado Mines	2/8/2007	10	14	71.4
	Wayne St. (Mich.)	Indianapolis	12/20/2006	10	14	71.4
	Upper Iowa	Northern St.	12/2/2006	10	14	71.4
13.	Southwestern Okla.	Southwestern Christ.	12/20/2006	18	26	69.2
14.	Central Mo.	Mo. Western St.	1/10/2007	14	21	66.7
	Cheyney	Bloomsburg	2/4/2007	12	18	66.7
	Northwest Mo. St.	Emporia St.	1/24/2007	12	18	66.7
	Adams St.	Western N.M.	2/24/2007	10	15	66.7
	Rockhurst	Mo.-Rolla	2/15/2007	10	15	66.7
	Wayne St. (Mich.)	Ashland	2/3/2007	10	15	66.7
	Ky. Wesleyan	Wis.-Parkside	1/25/2007	10	15	66.7
	Western Wash.	Seattle	1/11/2007	10	15	66.7
	St. Joseph's (Ind.)	Ferris St.	1/3/2007	10	15	66.7

Rk.	School	Opponent	Date	3FG	3FGA	3FG%
	West Tex. A&M	N.M. Highlands	11/27/2006	10	15	66.7
	UC-Colo. Spgs.	Northern Colo.	11/17/2006	10	15	66.7

Free-Throw Percentage

Minimum 15 made

Rk.	School	Opponent	Date	FT	FTA	FT%
1.	Rockhurst	SIU Edwardsville	2/10/2007	19	19	100.0
	Southern Ind.	Mo.-St. Louis	2/1/2007	19	19	100.0
	Western Wash.	Alas. Anchorage	2/17/2007	16	16	100.0
4.	Minn. St. Mankato	Western St.	12/2/2006	25	26	96.2
5.	Central Mo.	Northwest Mo. St.	3/11/2007	22	23	95.7
	Western N.M.	Grand Canyon	11/15/2006	22	23	95.7
7.	Ark.-Monticello	West Ga.	11/30/2006	21	22	95.5
8.	Winona St.	St. Cloud St.	3/10/2007	20	21	95.2
9.	Lake Superior St.	Ferris St.	12/18/2006	19	20	95.0
	Arkansas Tech	Arkansas St.	12/9/2006	19	20	95.0
11.	Queens (N.Y.)	NYIT	2/15/2007	18	19	94.7
	Shaw	Virginia Union	2/13/2007	18	19	94.7
	Mo. Western St.	Emporia St.	2/3/2007	18	19	94.7
	Eastern N.M.	West Tex. A&M	1/29/2007	18	19	94.7
	Davis & Elkins	Goldey-Beacom	1/25/2007	18	19	94.7
	Michigan Tech	Wayne St. (Mich.)	1/18/2007	18	19	94.7
	Concordia (N.Y.)	Bridgeport	1/17/2007	18	19	94.7
18.	Quincy	Drury	1/27/2007	34	36	94.4
	Augustana (S.D.)	North Dakota	2/8/2007	17	18	94.4
	South Dakota	Minn. St. Mankato	2/8/2007	17	18	94.4
	Fort Hays St.	Mo. Western St.	1/13/2007	17	18	94.4
	Washburn	Emporia St.	1/3/2007	17	18	94.4
	Colorado Mines	Western N.M.	12/16/2006	17	18	94.4
	Mo.-Rolla	Rockhurst	12/7/2006	17	18	94.4

2007 Division III Individual Leaders

Points Per Game

Rk.	Name, School	Cl.	G	FGM	3FG	FT	Pts.	Avg.
1.	Mike Hoyt, Mt. St. Mary (N.Y.)	Sr.	26	274	121	229	898	34.5
2.	Amir Mazarei, Redlands	Sr.	23	220	143	75	658	28.6
3.	John Grotberg, Grinnell	So.	24	209	112	145	675	28.1
4.	Ben Strong, Guilford	Jr.	29	278	0	181	737	25.4
5.	Alex Kuchar, Centenary (N.J.)	So.	24	195	70	128	588	24.5
6.	Jake Baldwin, Piedmont	Jr.	26	239	22	126	626	24.1
7.	Thomas Baker, Rowan	Sr.	26	246	21	107	620	23.8
8.	Bryan Rouse, Emerson	Fr.	20	171	0	128	470	23.5
9.	Tony Barros, Mass.-Boston	Sr.	27	203	84	144	634	23.5
10.	John Murphy, Suffolk	Sr.	24	170	81	140	561	23.4
11.	Doug Williams, Mount Ida	Sr.	26	234	1	128	597	23.0
12.	Ryan Jaziri, New England Col.	Jr.	25	203	51	117	574	23.0
13.	Jephet Kerr, Johnson & Wales (RI)	Sr.	26	195	54	152	596	22.9
14.	Tori Davis, Baldwin-Wallace	Sr.	27	209	0	188	606	22.4
15.	Kent Raymond, Wheaton (Ill.)	So.	23	150	51	164	515	22.4
16.	Dallas Reinard, Hilbert	Jr.	28	219	83	105	626	22.4
17.	Rashawn Johnson, Wesley	So.	26	214	78	75	581	22.3
	Ray Williams, Salisbury	Sr.	26	205	69	102	581	22.3
19.	Chris Isom, East Tex. Baptist	Sr.	25	206	16	123	551	22.0
20.	Joel McDonald, Concordia (Tex.)	So.	26	184	82	118	568	21.8
21.	Chad McGowan, York (Pa.)	Jr.	26	207	8	143	565	21.7
22.	Zach Freeman, Ill. Wesleyan	Sr.	25	196	5	142	539	21.6
23.	Jimmy Bartolotta, MIT	So.	27	184	42	162	572	21.2
24.	Anthony Williams, Plattsburgh St.	Jr.	27	183	59	142	567	21.0
25.	Isaac Smith, Alma	Sr.	25	182	46	112	522	20.9
26.	Eric Downie, Salem St.	Sr.	27	194	30	145	563	20.9
27.	Dan Hodgkinson, Denison	Sr.	24	185	2	127	499	20.8
28.	Tyler Daugherty, Dubuque	Jr.	25	161	65	130	517	20.7
29.	Thomas Young, Polytechnic (N.Y.)	Sr.	21	165	5	98	433	20.6
30.	Brandon Mimes, John Carroll	Sr.	31	222	1	193	638	20.6
31.	Nick Shattuck, Ursinus	Jr.	26	202	31	99	534	20.5
32.	Kevin Guyden, Mary Hardin-Baylor	Sr.	28	182	47	164	575	20.5
	Ryan Junghans, Hood	So.	28	164	90	157	575	20.5
34.	Josh Flynn-Brown, Chapman	Sr.	26	174	80	105	533	20.5
35.	Josh Johnson, Louisiana Col.	So.	25	208	28	68	512	20.5
36.	Curtis Gadles, Westfield St.	Sr.	26	201	65	63	530	20.4
37.	Lenny Hall, N.C. Wesleyan	Jr.	27	171	33	175	550	20.4
38.	Chris Demarco, Edgewood	So.	24	158	1	164	481	20.0
39.	Larry Welton, Aurora	Jr.	28	192	60	115	559	20.0
40.	Nick Harrington, Southern Vt.	Jr.	21	159	9	92	419	20.0

Rk.	Name, School	Cl.	G	FGM	3FG	FT	Pts.	Avg.
41.	Bryan Schnettler, St. Thomas (Minn.)	Sr.	28	183	117	74	557	19.9
42.	William Maupins, St. Scholastica	Sr.	27	219	15	83	536	19.9
43.	Sherrad Prezzie-Blue, Wentworth Inst.	Jr.	29	219	65	72	575	19.8
44.	Luke Linz, Concordia-M'head	Jr.	25	181	0	132	494	19.8
45.	Nathan Drury, Carroll (Wis.)	Sr.	27	181	80	91	533	19.7
46.	Tyler Ousley, Otterbein	Sr.	27	166	6	194	532	19.7
47.	Virgil Gray II, Stevens Institute	So.	29	205	34	125	569	19.6
48.	Andrew Zimmer, Wabash	Jr.	25	179	12	120	490	19.6
49.	Joe Canori, Nazareth	Jr.	25	171	72	75	489	19.6
50.	Ryan Cain, WPI	Sr.	26	156	56	140	508	19.5
51.	Kyle Born, Whitman	Sr.	23	170	12	97	449	19.5
52.	Chris LaBoard, SUNYIT	Sr.	29	188	42	147	565	19.5
53.	Emanuel Maceira, Claremont-M-S	Sr.	25	184	39	80	487	19.5
54.	Jason Maclin, Knox	Sr.	23	137	54	120	448	19.5
55.	Tim Madson, Bethel (Minn.)	So.	26	162	46	136	506	19.5
56.	David Knowles, Pomona-Pitzer	Sr.	24	158	89	62	467	19.5

Field-Goal Percentage

Minimum 5 made per game

Rk.	Name, School	Cl.	G	FGM	FGA	FG%
1.	Brandon Adair, Va. Wesleyan	Sr.	32	246	356	69.1
2.	Michael Romes, Mt. St. Joseph	Fr.	22	145	212	68.4
3.	Mike Kilburg, Coe	Sr.	27	187	284	65.8
4.	Brian Schmidt, Heidelberg	Jr.	20	103	157	65.6
5.	Matt Griffin, Johns Hopkins	Sr.	29	170	262	64.9
6.	Tori Davis, Baldwin-Wallace	Sr.	27	209	323	64.7
7.	Brian Schmitting, Ripon	Sr.	23	172	266	64.7
8.	Robert Krauel, Puget Sound	So.	25	136	213	63.8
9.	David Goode, Chestnut Hill	Jr.	25	153	241	63.5
10.	Jack Lighthall, Utica	Sr.	26	146	232	62.9
11.	Craig Schafer, St. John's (Minn.)	Sr.	29	153	244	62.7
12.	Erich Bracht, MIT	Fr.	27	146	233	62.7
13.	Joshua Merlis, Yeshiva	Jr.	26	191	306	62.4
14.	Gari Blackett, Staten Island	Jr.	28	141	226	62.4
15.	Jesse Gutekunst, Hood	Jr.	29	211	341	61.9
16.	Brent Ruch, Elmhurst	So.	27	140	227	61.7
17.	Zach Freeman, Ill. Wesleyan	Sr.	25	196	319	61.4
18.	Ben Chojnacki, Ohio Wesleyan	Jr.	23	120	197	60.9
19.	Tyler Smith, Nazareth	Jr.	25	155	255	60.8
20.	Dan Hodgkinson, Denison	Sr.	24	185	306	60.5

STATISTICAL LEADERS

Rk.	Name, School	Cl.	G	FGM	FGA	FG%
21.	Amseshem Foluke-Henderson, New Paltz St.	Jr.	24	184	305	60.3
22.	Jerel Robertson, MacMurray	So.	24	145	241	60.2
23.	Steve Willson, Keuka	Sr.	26	140	233	60.1
24.	Mike Leonard, Aurora	Jr.	28	150	250	60.0
25.	Dennis Echols, York (N.Y.)	Sr.	25	160	267	59.9
26.	Kevin Reichlmayr, Fredonia St.	Sr.	24	146	244	59.8
27.	Brian Fogerty, Fontbonne	So.	28	194	325	59.7
28.	Lawrence Avitabile, Vassar	Jr.	28	185	310	59.7
29.	Clint Driftmier, Central (Iowa)	Sr.	25	192	322	59.6
30.	Derrick Thornton, Lake Erie	So.	28	169	285	59.3

Three-Point Field Goals Per Game

Rk.	Name, School	Cl.	G	3FG	Avg.
1.	Amir Mazarei, Redlands	Sr.	23	143	6.2
2.	John Grotberg, Grinnell	So.	24	112	4.7
3.	Mike Hoyt, Mt. St. Mary (N.Y.)	Sr.	26	121	4.7
4.	Bryan Schnettler, St. Thomas (Minn.)	Sr.	28	117	4.2
5.	Derek Johnson, St. Scholastica	Sr.	27	107	4.0
6.	Brad Liddell, Macalester	Jr.	25	98	3.9
7.	Connor Whitman, Occidental	Jr.	25	97	3.9
8.	Nick Farrell, Colby	Sr.	26	97	3.7
9.	David Knowles, Pomona-Pitzer	Sr.	24	89	3.7
10.	Stephen Harris, Cazenovia	So.	26	95	3.7
11.	Chris Faidley, Whitman	So.	25	91	3.6
	James Russo, Goucher	Sr.	25	91	3.6
13.	DeMonte Bynum, Clarke	Jr.	26	93	3.6
14.	Isaiah Creasap, Marietta	So.	25	89	3.6
15.	Dana John, New Jersey City	Sr.	28	98	3.5
16.	Martin Salinas, Texas-Dallas	Sr.	26	89	3.4
17.	John Murphy, Suffolk	Sr.	24	81	3.4
18.	Chris Matte, Southern Vt.	Sr.	21	70	3.3
19.	Kenneth Eusey, Old Westbury	Jr.	28	93	3.3
20.	Taylor Marsh, Puget Sound	Jr.	25	83	3.3
21.	Dave Maggiacomo, Cortland St.	Sr.	26	86	3.3
	Ian Ribald, Yeshiva	Sr.	26	86	3.3
23.	Sami Wylie, Lincoln (Pa.)	Sr.	28	92	3.3
24.	Pete Rortvedt, Wis.-Stevens Point	So.	29	95	3.3
25.	Daniel Markus, Redlands	Jr.	23	74	3.2
26.	Ryan Junghans, Hood	So.	28	90	3.2
	Glen Ufland, Hilbert	Sr.	28	90	3.2
28.	Pat Grace, Merchant Marine	So.	26	83	3.2
	Jake Phillips, Carleton	Sr.	26	83	3.2
30.	Tom Cuddihy, Bridgewater St.	Jr.	24	76	3.2
31.	Joel McDonald, Concordia (Tex.)	So.	26	82	3.2

Three-Point Field-Goal Percentage

Minimum 2.5 made per game

Rk.	Name, School	Cl.	G	3FG	3FGA	3FG%
1.	Nate Stahl, Capital	So.	28	74	146	50.7
2.	Steve Hicklin, Wis.-Stevens Point	Jr.	29	74	148	50.0
	Andrew Tulowitzky, Oglethorpe	Sr.	26	73	146	50.0
4.	Matt Henninger, Messiah	Sr.	25	64	129	49.6
5.	Matt Walsh, Cabrini	Fr.	24	65	134	48.5
6.	Dan Mueller, St. John Fisher	Sr.	30	93	194	47.9
7.	Ryan Junghans, Hood	So.	28	90	190	47.4
8.	Connor Whitman, Occidental	Jr.	25	97	206	47.1
9.	Sherod Harris, Brockport St.	Jr.	26	68	145	46.9
10.	Josh Flynn-Brown, Chapman	Sr.	26	80	171	46.8
11.	Trevor White, Fontbonne	Fr.	27	70	150	46.7
12.	Ian Ribald, Yeshiva	Sr.	26	86	185	46.5
13.	Bryan Schnettler, St. Thomas (Minn.)	Sr.	28	117	252	46.4
14.	Derek Griffin, Calvin	Jr.	29	80	173	46.2
15.	Andrew Harris, Middlebury	Jr.	24	67	147	45.6
16.	David Knowles, Pomona-Pitzer	Sr.	24	89	197	45.2
17.	Ryan Thompson, Wis.-River Falls	Jr.	26	70	155	45.2
18.	James Jones, Whitworth	Sr.	21	56	125	44.8
19.	Kase Gonzales, Louisiana Col.	Jr.	23	59	133	44.4
20.	Devin Ruocco, Plymouth St.	Sr.	26	74	169	43.8
21.	Jake Phillips, Carleton	Sr.	26	83	190	43.7
22.	Isaiah Creasap, Marietta	So.	25	89	204	43.6
23.	Dallas Reinard, Hilbert	Jr.	28	83	191	43.5
24.	Nick Adams, Westminster (Pa.)	Sr.	27	69	159	43.4
25.	Michael Decorso, New York U.	Sr.	28	81	187	43.3
26.	Jesse Meyer, Chicago	Sr.	26	71	164	43.3
27.	Anthony Passalacqua, Stevens Institute	So.	30	75	174	43.1
28.	Wes Gardner, Manchester	Sr.	25	73	170	42.9
29.	Dave Maggiacomo, Cortland St.	Sr.	26	86	201	42.8

Rk.	Name, School	Cl.	G	3FG	3FGA	3FG%
30.	Pat Grace, Merchant Marine	So.	26	83	194	42.8
31.	Curtis Gadles, Westfield St.	Sr.	26	65	152	42.8

Free-Throw Percentage

Minimum 2.5 made per game

Rk.	Name, School	Cl.	G	FT	FTA	FT%
1.	Joseph Chatman, Lesley	Jr.	27	126	133	94.7
2.	Bryan Schnettler, St. Thomas (Minn.)	Sr.	28	74	80	92.5
3.	Zachary Silas, Albion	Sr.	25	70	77	90.9
4.	Ryan Dupic, Buena Vista	Sr.	26	88	97	90.7
5.	Brendan Schuler, Baldwin-Wallace	Jr.	27	86	95	90.5
6.	Kevin Guyden, Mary Hardin-Baylor	Sr.	28	164	182	90.1
7.	Ryan Jaziri, New England Col.	Jr.	25	117	130	90.0
8.	Ryan Burks, Elmhurst	So.	27	130	145	89.7
9.	Sean Burton, Ithaca	So.	28	85	95	89.5
10.	Andrew Hippert, Bowdoin	Jr.	25	100	112	89.3
11.	Ryan Junghans, Hood	So.	28	157	176	89.2
12.	Jordan Beard, Oberlin	Jr.	25	64	72	88.9
13.	Mike Staley, Hiram	Fr.	24	68	77	88.3
14.	Randy Arnold, Scranton	Jr.	26	90	102	88.2
15.	Rob McCarter, Alfred	Sr.	23	133	151	88.1
16.	Zak Clark, Central (Iowa)	Jr.	25	88	100	88.0
17.	Michael Anthony, Bluffton	Sr.	26	129	147	87.8
18.	Kent Raymond, Wheaton (Ill.)	So.	23	164	187	87.7
19.	Brent Ruch, Elmhurst	So.	27	78	89	87.6
20.	Tonton Balenga, Va. Wesleyan	Jr.	33	125	143	87.4
21.	Todd Lincoln, Keuka	Sr.	26	69	79	87.3
22.	Luke Slater, Loras	Jr.	28	82	94	87.2
23.	Ryan Samuel, Merchant Marine	Fr.	21	54	62	87.1
24.	Andrew Tulowitzky, Oglethorpe	Sr.	26	91	105	86.7
25.	Jimmy Bartolotta, MIT	So.	27	162	187	86.6
26.	Dan Mueller, St. John Fisher	Sr.	30	76	88	86.4
27.	Stanley Chamblain, Lesley	Sr.	27	82	95	86.3
28.	Sean Wallis, Washington-St. Louis	So.	30	113	131	86.3
29.	Ross Banaszak, Otterbein	Jr.	27	100	116	86.2
30.	Tim Madson, Bethel (Minn.)	So.	26	136	158	86.1

Rebounds Per Game

Rk.	Name, School	Cl.	G	Reb.	Avg.
1.	Nick Harrington, Southern Vt.	Jr.	21	281	13.4
2.	Gari Blackett, Staten Island	Jr.	28	345	12.3
3.	Jeff Prebeck, Coast Guard	Jr.	28	344	12.3
4.	Mardochee Jean, Hardin-Simmons	Jr.	28	324	11.6
5.	Jesse Gutekunst, Hood	Jr.	29	332	11.4
6.	Jose Guitian, Lasell	So.	28	319	11.4
7.	Antoine Sylvia, New England Col.	Sr.	24	271	11.3
8.	Kyle Born, Whitman	Sr.	23	259	11.3
9.	Ben Strong, Guilford	Jr.	29	325	11.2
10.	Danny Nawrocki, Johns Hopkins	Sr.	29	319	11.0
11.	Ryan Murray, Colby-Sawyer	So.	25	270	10.8
12.	Tyler Ousley, Otterbein	Sr.	27	291	10.8
13.	Jeremy Jorgensen, Castleton	Sr.	27	290	10.7
14.	David Boettcher, Arcadia	Sr.	22	235	10.7
15.	Brandon Mimes, John Carroll	Sr.	31	327	10.5
16.	Travis Gorham, Plattsburgh St.	Jr.	28	295	10.5
17.	Tom Arthur, Phila. Biblical	So.	26	269	10.3
18.	Bruce MacLelland, Cabrini	Jr.	21	217	10.3
19.	Chris Isom, East Tex. Baptist	Sr.	25	258	10.3
20.	Charlie Averkamp, Edgewood	Jr.	26	268	10.3
21.	Mark Blasingame, Chris. Newport	So.	26	266	10.2
22.	Isaac Rosefelt, St. Thomas (Minn.)	Sr.	25	254	10.2
23.	Dane Borchers, Wittenberg	Sr.	27	272	10.1
24.	Ozi Menakaya, Salisbury	So.	21	211	10.0
25.	Chris Tarpley, Eureka	Sr.	26	260	10.0
	Issac Stickney, New England	Jr.	24	240	10.0
27.	Brian Schmitting, Ripon	Sr.	23	229	10.0
28.	Brandon McCombs, Salem St.	Sr.	27	267	9.9
29.	Jonathan Arthur, Montclair St.	Jr.	18	177	9.8
30.	Matt Fabian, Ursinus	Sr.	26	255	9.8
	Ahmad Kareem Shaheed, Oglethorpe	Jr.	26	255	9.8
32.	Edrick Montgomery, Millsaps	Jr.	27	264	9.8

Assists Per Game

Rk.	Name, School	Cl.	G	Ast.	Avg.
1.	David Arseneault, Grinnell	So.	24	203	8.5
2.	Davon Barton, Chris. Newport	So.	26	217	8.3
3.	Andrew Olson, Amherst	Jr.	32	243	7.6
4.	Eddie Ohlson, DeSales	Jr.	30	225	7.5
5.	Corey McAdam, Nazareth	Fr.	25	186	7.4
6.	Sean Wallis, Washington-St. Louis	So.	30	219	7.3
7.	Bryan Williams, Whitworth	Sr.	27	194	7.2
8.	Josh Winans, Cazenovia	Sr.	25	164	6.6
9.	Mike Staley, Hiram	Fr.	24	155	6.5
10.	Jake Green, Piedmont	Jr.	26	164	6.3
11.	Matt Kieselowsky, Albright	Sr.	24	150	6.3
12.	Michael Reyes, Hilbert	Jr.	28	167	6.0
13.	Travis Carruthers, Texas-Dallas	Sr.	26	155	6.0
14.	Richard Reilly, Castleton	Jr.	24	143	6.0
15.	Todd Lincoln, Keuka	Sr.	26	154	5.9
16.	Mike Parker, Eastern Conn. St.	Sr.	23	136	5.9
17.	Ryan Finger, Alvernia	Sr.	26	153	5.9
18.	Kyle Yocum, Staten Island	Fr.	28	164	5.9
19.	K.C. Grandfield, Bridgewater St.	Sr.	25	146	5.8
	Zak Ray, Bates	Sr.	25	146	5.8
21.	Michael Salamanca, York (N.Y.)	Jr.	29	169	5.8
22.	Donte Chisolm, Manhattanville	Jr.	29	168	5.8
23.	Abe Woldeslassie, Macalester	Jr.	25	143	5.7
24.	Darrick Leonard, Aurora	Sr.	28	160	5.7
25.	David Shepherd, Tufts	Sr.	24	135	5.6
26.	Steven Morris, Newbury	Sr.	26	146	5.6
27.	Greg Rosatelli, Westminster (Pa.)	Sr.	27	150	5.6
28.	Brandon Todd, Muskingum	Jr.	25	138	5.5
29.	David McMullen, Ripon	Sr.	23	126	5.5
30.	Jon Mowl, Gallaudet	So.	25	136	5.4
	Harel Vatavu, Yeshiva	Sr.	25	136	5.4
32.	Mike Moore, DePauw	So.	28	152	5.4
33.	Brendan Schuler, Baldwin-Wallace	Jr.	27	146	5.4
34.	Dwayne Powell, Lasell	Jr.	28	151	5.4
35.	Shawn Bolling, Chestnut Hill	Sr.	28	150	5.4

Blocked Shots Per Game

Rk.	Name, School	Cl.	G	Blk.	Avg.
1.	Kerry Gibson, Wis.-Oshkosh	Sr.	27	103	3.8
2.	Mark Blasingame, Chris. Newport	So.	26	95	3.7
3.	Drew Cohen, Colby	Sr.	24	84	3.5
4.	Timothy Broomfield, Mississippi Col.	Sr.	30	102	3.4
5.	Joe Spierenburg, Gettysburg	So.	26	86	3.3
6.	Jacob Nonemacher, Wis.-Stout	Sr.	25	82	3.3
7.	Mardochee Jean, Hardin-Simmons	Jr.	28	80	2.9
8.	Mike Johnson, Eastern	Jr.	27	74	2.7
9.	Heman Honore, Newbury	Fr.	27	73	2.7
10.	Ben Gunn, Capital	Jr.	28	75	2.7
11.	Tyler Ousley, Otterbein	Sr.	27	69	2.6
12.	Ben Strong, Guilford	Jr.	29	72	2.5
13.	Jim Stevens, Maranatha Baptist	Sr.	27	67	2.5
14.	David Ferezy, Simpson	So.	25	62	2.5
	Isaac Rosefelt, St. Thomas (Minn.)	Sr.	25	62	2.5
16.	Winfred Rembert, Worcester St.	Sr.	25	61	2.4

Rk.	Name, School	Cl.	G	Blk.	Avg.
17.	Matt Loretz, Redlands	Jr.	23	56	2.4
18.	Antoine Sylvia, New England Col.	Sr.	24	58	2.4
19.	Dylan Holmes, Salem St.	So.	27	64	2.4
20.	Jason Boone, New York U.	Sr.	28	66	2.4
21.	Jon Ciche, Edgewood	So.	21	48	2.3
22.	Michael Collins, Stevens Institute	Sr.	30	66	2.2
23.	Tori Davis, Baldwin-Wallace	Sr.	27	59	2.2
24.	Martin Cleveland, Husson	Fr.	28	60	2.1
25.	John Patterson, Centre	Sr.	29	62	2.1
26.	Ian McCormick, Swarthmore	Jr.	24	50	2.1
27.	Mike Haiduc, Dominican (Ill.)	Jr.	25	51	2.0
28.	Jonathan Marstaller, Gordon	Jr.	27	54	2.0
	Terry Smith, Widener	Sr.	25	50	2.0
30.	Jesse Gutekunst, Hood	Jr.	29	57	2.0
31.	Gene Rivera, Lewis & Clark	Jr.	26	51	2.0
32.	Zach Miller, Cal Lutheran	So.	25	49	2.0

Steals Per Game

Rk.	Name, School	Cl.	G	St.	Avg.
1.	Elbie Murphy, St. Joseph's (Me.)	So.	30	126	4.2
2.	Marquis Patton, Fisk	Sr.	22	87	4.0
3.	Amir Mazarei, Redlands	Sr.	23	87	3.8
4.	Doug Ticus, Grinnell	Sr.	24	87	3.6
5.	Corey McAdam, Nazareth	Fr.	25	81	3.2
	Josh Winans, Cazenovia	Sr.	25	81	3.2
7.	Corey McFarlane, Brooklyn	So.	22	71	3.2
8.	Tony Barros, Mass.-Boston	Sr.	27	86	3.2
9.	Kenneth Eusey, Old Westbury	Jr.	28	84	3.0
10.	Chris Reaves, SUNYIT	Sr.	29	85	2.9
11.	David Knowles, Pomona-Pitzer	Sr.	24	70	2.9
12.	Jephet Kerr, Johnson & Wales (RI)	Sr.	26	75	2.9
	Bryan Majors, Susquehanna	Fr.	26	75	2.9
14.	Beau Wilson, Waynesburg	Sr.	24	68	2.8
15.	Chris Goodridge, Salve Regina	Jr.	26	73	2.8
	Otis Saylee, City Tech	Sr.	26	73	2.8
17.	Bryson Taylor, Greenville	Sr.	25	70	2.8
18.	Demitrius Washington, Bard	Jr.	19	52	2.7
19.	Mike Moore, Concordia (Tex.)	Jr.	26	71	2.7
20.	Chris LaBoard, SUNYIT	Sr.	29	79	2.7
21.	Tony Cannon, New Paltz St.	Jr.	25	68	2.7
22.	David McMullen, Ripon	Sr.	23	62	2.7
23.	Terry Bailey, Oglethorpe	Sr.	26	70	2.7
24.	Travis Moulton, Concordia (Wis.)	So.	24	64	2.7
25.	Dan Selway, Redlands	So.	23	61	2.7
	Dave Thomas, Redlands	Jr.	23	61	2.7
27.	Joseph Chatman, Lesley	Jr.	27	71	2.6
28.	Kevin Tucker, New Jersey City	So.	28	73	2.6
29.	Jarrell Sweet, Colorado Col.	So.	25	65	2.6
30.	Michael Bennett, Hendrix	Sr.	25	64	2.6
	Godfrey Mascall, John Jay	So.	25	64	2.6
	Zak Ray, Bates	Sr.	25	64	2.6
	Antwan Williams, Puget Sound	So.	25	64	2.6
34.	John McMahon, Rivier	Sr.	29	74	2.6

2007 Division III Individual Game Highs

Points

Rk.	Name, School	Cl.	Opponent	Date	Pts.
1.	Sami Wylie, Lincoln (Pa.)	Sr.	Ohio St.-Marion	12/2/2006	69
2.	Ben Strong, Guilford	Jr.	Lincoln (Pa.)	3/9/2007	59
	Mike Hoyt, Mt. St. Mary (N.Y.)	Sr.	Farmingdale	1/27/2007	59
4.	Mike Hoyt, Mt. St. Mary (N.Y.)	Sr.	Stevens Institute	2/17/2007	57
5.	Bryan Rouse, Emerson	Fr.	Daniel Webster	12/9/2006	56
6.	Mike Hoyt, Mt. St. Mary (N.Y.)	Sr.	Manhattanville	2/1/2007	55
7.	Shawn Fuller, Becker	So.	Mitchell	2/10/2007	53
	Kyle Born, Whitman	Sr.	Redlands	1/3/2007	53
9.	John Grotberg, Grinnell	So.	MacMurray	11/25/2006	52
	Josh Robinson, Susquehanna	Jr.	King's (Pa.)	11/18/2006	52
11.	Mike Hoyt, Mt. St. Mary (N.Y.)	Sr.	Maritime (N.Y.)	1/18/2007	50
12.	Tony Barros, Mass.-Boston	Sr.	Western Conn. St.	2/20/2007	48
	Amir Mazarei, Redlands	Sr.	Pacific Union	1/6/2007	48
14.	Dave Bisesi, Mass. Liberal Arts	Jr.	Maritime (N.Y.)	11/28/2006	47
15.	Mike Hoyt, Mt. St. Mary (N.Y.)	Sr.	Centenary (N.J.)	1/16/2007	46
	John Grotberg, Grinnell	So.	Lawrence	1/12/2007	46
	Dallas Reinard, Hilbert	Jr.	Mt. Aloysius	1/6/2007	46
	Tony Barros, Mass.-Boston	Sr.	Colby-Sawyer	11/25/2006	46
19.	Cory Smith, Rhodes	So.	Oglethorpe	2/11/2007	44
	Kent Raymond, Wheaton (Ill.)	Sr.	Ill. Wesleyan	2/10/2007	44
	Nate Brodman, Colorado Col.	Jr.	Johnson & Wales (CO)	2/3/2007	44
22.	Tony Barros, Mass.-Boston	Sr.	Eastern Conn. St.	1/20/2007	43
	Mike Hoyt, Mt. St. Mary (N.Y.)	Sr.	Mt. St. Vincent	1/10/2007	43
	Amir Mazarei, Redlands	Sr.	Hope Int'l	12/9/2006	43
	Joel McDonald, Concordia (Tex.)	So.	Texas-Dallas	12/9/2006	43
26.	Josh Johnson, Louisiana Col.	So.	Mary Hardin-Baylor	2/23/2007	42
	Mike Hoyt, Mt. St. Mary (N.Y.)	Sr.	Centenary (N.J.)	2/5/2007	42
	Amir Mazarei, Redlands	Sr.	Pomona-Pitzer	2/3/2007	42
	Thomas Baker, Rowan	Sr.	Kean	1/17/2007	42
	Dave Maggiacomo, Cortland St.	Sr.	Fredonia St.	1/13/2007	42
	Jake Baldwin, Piedmont	Jr.	Wesley	12/1/2006	42

Field-Goal Percentage

Minimum 10 made

Rk.	Name, School	Cl.	Opponent	Date	FGM	FGA	FG%
1.	Danny Hagen, Cal Lutheran	So.	Redlands	1/13/2007	16	16	100.0
	David Goode, Chestnut Hill	Jr.	Delaware Valley	1/6/2007	13	13	100.0
	Brandon Adair, Va. Wesleyan	Sr.	Washington-St. Louis	3/16/2007	12	12	100.0
	Jason Sager, East. Mennonite	Sr.	Emory & Henry	1/20/2007	12	12	100.0
	Marc O'Leary, Hanover	Jr.	Westminster (Pa.)	12/21/2006	12	12	100.0
	Andrew Tulowitzky, Oglethorpe	Sr.	Piedmont	1/2/2007	11	11	100.0
	Zach Freeman, Ill. Wesleyan	Sr.	Judson (Ill.)	11/25/2006	11	11	100.0
	Trevor Tonkovich, New England Col.	Fr.	Me.-Presque Isle	11/17/2006	10	10	100.0

Three-Point Field Goals Made

Rk.	Name, School	Cl.	Opponent	Date	3FG
1.	Sami Wylie, Lincoln (Pa.)	Sr.	Ohio St.-Marion	12/2/2006	21
2.	Bill Carey, Framingham St.	Fr.	Salem St.	2/10/2007	11
	Nate Brodman, Colorado Col.	Jr.	Johnson & Wales (CO)	2/3/2007	11
	Amir Mazarei, Redlands	Sr.	Pacific Union	1/6/2007	11
	Clint Parker, Hanover	Jr.	Wabash	11/21/2006	11
6.	Stephen Harris, Cazenovia	So.	Morrisville St.	2/8/2007	10
	Mike Hoyt, Mt. St. Mary (N.Y.)	Sr.	Centenary (N.J.)	2/5/2007	10
	Stephen Harris, Cazenovia	So.	Bard	1/25/2007	10
	Dave Maggiacomo, Cortland St.	Sr.	Fredonia St.	1/13/2007	10
	James Russo, Goucher	Sr.	Ozarks (Mo.)	1/5/2007	10
	Amir Mazarei, Redlands	Sr.	Hope Int'l	12/9/2006	10
	Amir Mazarei, Redlands	Sr.	La Sierra	12/6/2006	10
	Isaiah Pinckney, Delaware Valley	Sr.	Richard Stockton	11/27/2006	10
	John Grotberg, Grinnell	So.	MacMurray	11/25/2006	10
15.	Chadd Barnes, Rutgers-Newark	So.	New York U.	3/2/2007	9
	Dusty Magee, Aurora	So.	Rockford	2/17/2007	9
	Chris Faidley, Whitman	So.	Puget Sound	2/10/2007	9
	James Russo, Goucher	Sr.	Gallaudet	2/6/2007	9
	Kevin Bradley, Bowdoin	Sr.	Me.-Presque Isle	2/5/2007	9
	Jordan Snipes, Guilford	Sr.	Lynchburg	2/3/2007	9
	Glen Ufland, Hilbert	Sr.	Mt. Aloysius	2/3/2007	9
	Kyle Enoch, Lebanon Valley	So.	Widener	1/31/2007	9
	Mike Hoyt, Mt. St. Mary (N.Y.)	Sr.	Farmingdale	1/27/2007	9
	Amir Mazarei, Redlands	Sr.	Occidental	1/24/2007	9

Rk.	Name, School	Cl.	Opponent	Date	3FG
	Bryan Schnettler, St. Thomas (Minn.)	Sr.	Hamline	1/24/2007	9
	Kase Gonzales, Louisiana Col.	Jr.	Texas-Tyler	1/11/2007	9
	Nick Farrell, Colby	Sr.	Maine Maritime	1/9/2007	9
	Glen Ufland, Hilbert	Sr.	Fredonia St.	1/8/2007	9
	Bo Mason, Maryville (Tenn.)	Jr.	Piedmont	1/7/2007	9
	Andy Root, Wabash	So.	Hiram	1/7/2007	9
	Jason Price, Wis.-Whitewater	Fr.	Carroll (Wis.)	12/28/2006	9
	Tony Barros, Mass.-Boston	Sr.	Colby-Sawyer	11/25/2006	9
	Daniel Markus, Redlands	Jr.	Biola	11/25/2006	9

Three-Point Field-Goal Percentage

Minimum 7 made

Rk.	Name, School	Cl.	Opponent	Date	3FG	3FGA	3FG%
1.	Andy Root, Wabash	So.	Hiram	1/7/2007	9	9	100.0
	Jake Phillips, Carleton	Sr.	Macalester	2/14/2007	7	7	100.0
	Andrew Tulowitzky, Oglethorpe	Sr.	Piedmont	1/2/2007	7	7	100.0
4.	Joe Canori, Nazareth	Jr.	Hartwick	2/10/2007	7	8	87.5
	Peter Lipka, Farmingdale St.	Jr.	Stevens Institute	1/30/2007	7	8	87.5
	Sherrad Prezzie-Blue, Wentworth Inst.	Jr.	Anna Maria	1/20/2007	7	8	87.5
	Cody Anderle, East Tex. Baptist	So.	Texas-Dallas	1/18/2007	7	8	87.5
	Timothy Broomfield, Mississippi Col.	Sr.	Westmont	12/30/2006	7	8	87.5
	Curtis Gadles, Westfield St.	Sr.	Western New Eng.	12/2/2006	7	8	87.5
	Thomas Bright, Pacific (Ore.)	Fr.	Multnomah Bible	11/28/2006	7	8	87.5
11.	Dave Maggiacomo, Cortland St.	Sr.	Fredonia St.	1/13/2007	10	12	83.3
12.	Bo Mason, Maryville (Tenn.)	Jr.	Piedmont	1/7/2007	9	11	81.8
13.	Ian Ribald, Yeshiva	Sr.	Centenary (N.J.)	2/7/2007	8	10	80.0
	Adam Garner, Mass. Liberal Arts	Sr.	Worcester St.	1/20/2007	8	10	80.0
	Brian Fenton, St. Joseph's (L.I.)	Sr.	Merchant Marine	1/6/2007	8	10	80.0
16.	Neal Wesson, Rensselaer	Fr.	Morrisville St.	12/5/2007	7	9	77.8
	Tyler Daugherty, Dubuque	Jr.	Loras	2/9/2007	7	9	77.8
	Justin Bestor, Marian (Wis.)	So.	Concordia (Ill.)	2/7/2007	7	9	77.8
	Nick Adams, Westminster (Pa.)	Sr.	Thomas More	2/3/2007	7	9	77.8
	James Cooper, Wooster	Jr.	Allegheny	1/31/2007	7	9	77.8
	Jephet Kerr, Johnson & Wales (RI)	Sr.	Albertus Magnus	1/29/2007	7	9	77.8
	Brody Jackson, Bethany (W.V.)	Jr.	St. Vincent	1/24/2007	7	9	77.8
	Damien Santana, Farmingdale St.	So.	Maritime (N.Y.)	1/10/2007	7	9	77.8
	Sean Wallis, Washington-St. Louis	So.	Chicago	1/6/2007	7	9	77.8
	Sean Burton, Ithaca	So.	Potsdam St.	12/9/2006	7	9	77.8
	Damien Santana, Farmingdale St.	So.	Yeshiva	12/6/2006	7	9	77.8
	Steve Austin, Daniel Webster	So.	Johnson St.	11/25/2006	7	9	77.8
	Mike Lee, Mary Washington	Sr.	Messiah	11/17/2006	7	9	77.8

Free-Throw Percentage

Minimum 12 made

Rk.	Name, School	Cl.	Opponent	Date	FT	FTA	FT%
1.	Kent Raymond, Wheaton (Ill.)	So.	Ill. Wesleyan	2/10/2007	20	20	100.0
	Dominic Trawick, Bridgewater (Va.)	Fr.	East. Mennonite	12/16/2006	19	19	100.0
	Mike Hoyt, Mt. St. Mary (N.Y.)	Sr.	Stevens Institute	2/17/2007	18	18	100.0
	Rob McCarter, Alfred	Sr.	Elmira	2/9/2007	16	16	100.0
	Raun Singleton, Monmouth (Ill.)	Sr.	William Penn	11/26/2006	15	15	100.0
	Josh Fox, Bridgewater (Va.)	Jr.	Emory & Henry	2/11/2007	14	14	100.0
	Ryan Jaziri, New England Col.	Jr.	Colby-Sawyer	1/25/2007	14	14	100.0
	Ryan Burks, Elmhurst	So.	Wheaton (Ill.)	1/20/2007	14	14	100.0
	Pete Moran, John Carroll	Sr.	Mount Union	1/17/2007	14	14	100.0
	David Knowles, Pomona-Pitzer	Sr.	La Sierra	1/6/2007	14	14	100.0
	Ryan Burks, Elmhurst	So.	Millikin	2/21/2007	13	13	100.0
	Zak Clark, Central (Iowa)	Jr.	Dubuque	2/10/2007	13	13	100.0
	Dave Jutton, Cortland St.	Sr.	St. John Fisher	12/29/2006	13	13	100.0
	Justin Short, Randolph-Macon	Sr.	Roanoke	12/3/2006	13	13	100.0
	Mike Hoyt, Mt. St. Mary (N.Y.)	Sr.	Westfield St.	11/18/2006	13	13	100.0
	Wahab Owolabi, Wash. & Jeff.	So.	Grove City	2/15/2007	12	12	100.0
	Marcus Minzel, Neb. Wesleyan	Jr.	Dana	2/10/2007	12	12	100.0
	Rob Andrus, Willamette	Sr.	George Fox	2/9/2007	12	12	100.0
	Chris Vallee, Nichols	Jr.	Anna Maria	2/6/2007	12	12	100.0

Rk.	Name, School	Cl.	Opponent	Date	FT	FTA	FT%
	Sean Wallis, Washington-St. Louis	So.	Brandeis	1/26/2007	12	12	100.0
	Alan Jaziri, Suffolk	Fr.	Johnson & Wales (RI)	1/17/2007	12	12	100.0
	Jesse Gutekunst, Hood	Jr.	Marymount (Va.)	1/10/2007	12	12	100.0
	Chris Demarco, Edgewood	So.	Marian (Wis.)	12/6/2006	12	12	100.0
	R.J. Smith, Greensboro	Fr.	Apprentice	11/25/2006	12	12	100.0
	Ray Williams, Salisbury	Sr.	Villa Julie	11/21/2006	12	12	100.0

Rebounds

Rk.	Name, School	Cl.	Opponent	Date	Reb.
1.	Pat Smithgall, Alfred	Fr.	Hilbert	11/21/2006	26
2.	Emmanuel Masumbuko, Becker	So.	Mitchell	2/10/2007	23
	Kyle Born, Whitman	Sr.	Pacific Lutheran	1/12/2007	23
4.	Jesse Gutekunst, Hood	Jr.	St. Mary's (Md.)	2/22/2007	22
	Tom Arthur, Phila. Biblical	So.	Purchase St.	1/30/2007	22
	Drew Cohen, Colby	Sr.	Lesley	1/6/2007	22
	Mardochee Jean, Hardin-Simmons	Jr.	Louisiana Col.	11/30/2006	22
8.	Femi Solaja, Augsburg	Jr.	Bethel (Minn.)	2/17/2007	21
	Chris Harrison, Mt. St. Mary (N.Y.)	So.	Old Westbury	1/13/2007	21
	Ozi Menakaya, Salisbury	So.	Mary Washington	1/10/2007	21
	Kyle Foster, Hamline	Sr.	St. Scholastica	12/16/2006	21
12.	Dane Borchers, Wittenberg	Sr.	Ohio Wesleyan	2/23/2007	20
	Emmanuel Masumbuko, Becker	So.	Elms	2/8/2007	20
	Adam Coleman, N.C. Wesleyan	So.	Chris. Newport	2/6/2007	20
	Jose Guitian, Lasell	So.	Mount Ida	1/18/2007	20
	Mardochee Jean, Hardin-Simmons	Jr.	Concordia (Tex.)	1/11/2007	20
	Ray Bryant, Utica	Sr.	Utica/Rome	12/9/2006	20

Assists

Rk.	Name, School	Cl.	Opponent	Date	Ast.
1.	K.C. Grandfield, Bridgewater St.	Sr.	Framingham St.	2/3/2007	17
2.	Sean Wallis, Washington-St. Louis	So.	Chicago	2/24/2007	16
	Jared McCoy, Maryville (Mo.)	Fr.	Lincoln Christian	12/9/2006	16
	Josh Winans, Cazenovia	Sr.	Bard	12/5/2006	16
5.	Davon Barton, Chris. Newport	So.	Methodist	2/16/2007	15
	Mike Staley, Hiram	Fr.	Denison	1/20/2007	15
	Andrew Olson, Amherst	Jr.	Elms	1/16/2007	15
8.	Jeremy Rivers, Becker	Jr.	Mitchell	2/10/2007	14
	Garth Brandal, Whitman	Jr.	Redlands	1/3/2007	14
	Mike Moore, Concordia (Tex.)	Jr.	Texas-Dallas	12/9/2006	14
	Nick Tokarski, Salem St.	Fr.	Newbury	12/5/2006	14
	David Arseneault, Grinnell	So.	Carthage	11/21/2006	14
13.	Brett De Hoogh, Central (Iowa)	Jr.	Martin Luther	12/16/2007	13
	Andrew Olson, Amherst	Jr.	Stevens Institute	3/9/2007	13
	Mike Parker, Eastern Conn. St.	Sr.	Old Westbury	2/8/2007	13
	Mike Parker, Eastern Conn. St.	Sr.	Mass.-Boston	1/20/2007	13
	Bo Mason, Maryville (Tenn.)	Jr.	Fisk	1/17/2007	13
	David Arseneault, Grinnell	So.	Beloit	1/13/2007	13
	David Shepherd, Tufts	Sr.	Trinity (Conn.)	1/13/2007	13
	David Arseneault, Grinnell	So.	Milwaukee Engr.	1/9/2007	13
	Corey McAdam, Nazareth	Fr.	Wheaton (Mass.)	12/29/2006	13
	Nathan Drury, Carroll (Wis.)	Sr.	Grinnell	12/2/2006	13
	Mike Moore, Concordia (Tex.)	Jr.	Texas-Tyler	12/2/2006	13
	Chris Stephens, Bethany (W.V.)	Sr.	Franciscan	11/30/2006	13
	Bryan Williams, Whitworth	Sr.	Whittier	11/25/2006	13
	Mike Moore, DePauw	So.	Earlham	11/18/2006	13

Blocked Shots

Rk.	Name, School	Cl.	Opponent	Date	Blk.
1.	Jesse Gutekunst, Hood	Jr.	Marymount (Va.)	1/10/2007	12
2.	Kerry Gibson, Wis.-Oshkosh	Sr.	Wis.-River Falls	1/27/2007	11
	Kerry Gibson, Wis.-Oshkosh	Sr.	Wis.-Superior	12/2/2006	11
4.	Jon Ciche, Edgewood	So.	Rockford	2/19/2007	9
	Jacob Nonemacher, Wis.-Stout	Sr.	Wis.-Whitewater	1/27/2007	9
	Mark Blasingame, Chris. Newport	So.	N.C. Wesleyan	1/16/2007	9
	Lance Bisson, Rivier	So.	Emerson	1/9/2007	9
	Drew Cohen, Colby	Sr.	Lesley	1/6/2007	9
	Mardochee Jean, Hardin-Simmons	Jr.	Va. Wesleyan	12/30/2006	9
	Isaac Rosefelt, St. Thomas (Minn.)	Sr.	Macalester	12/6/2006	9
	Jason Soppe, Simpson	Sr.	Augustana (Ill.)	12/2/2006	9
	Ben Chase, Emerson	Jr.	Mass.-Boston	11/28/2006	9
13.	Matt Loretz, Redlands	Jr.	Whittier	2/19/2007	8
	Drew Cohen, Colby	Sr.	Tufts	2/10/2007	8
	Jacob Nonemacher, Wis.-Stout	Sr.	Wis.-River Falls	1/31/2007	8
	Timothy Broomfield, Mississippi Col.	Sr.	East Tex. Baptist	1/27/2007	8
	Adam Blodgett, Thomas (Me.)	Sr.	Castleton St.	1/20/2007	8
	Mark Retallic, Worcester St.	Sr.	Mass. Liberal Arts	1/20/2007	8
	Jacob Nonemacher, Wis.-Stout	Sr.	Viterbo	12/29/2006	8
	Jacob Nonemacher, Wis.-Stout	Sr.	Buena Vista	12/21/2006	8

Steals

Rk.	Name, School	Cl.	Opponent	Date	St.
1.	James Parker, Lesley	Sr.	Johnson St.	12/8/2006	11
2.	Corey McAdam, Nazareth	Fr.	Elmira	2/16/2007	10
	Josh Winans, Cazenovia	Sr.	D'Youville	1/10/2007	10
4.	Amir Mazarei, Redlands	Sr.	Whitman	1/3/2007	9
	Mike Parker, Eastern Conn. St.	Sr.	Medaille	1/2/2007	9
	Darnell Edmonds, Hood	Sr.	Merchant Marine	12/30/2006	9
	Amir Mazarei, Redlands	Sr.	La Sierra	12/6/2006	9
	Doug Ticus, Grinnell	Sr.	MacMurray	11/25/2006	9
	Nathan Penley, Baptist Bible (Pa.)	Jr.	Marywood	11/17/2006	9
10.	Tyler Evans, New England Col.	Fr.	Nichols	2/17/2007	8
	Kevin Tucker, New Jersey City	So.	Rutgers-Camden	2/3/2007	8
	Anthony Hairston, Emory & Henry	So.	Roanoke	1/31/2007	8
	Bud Willis, McMurry	Fr.	Sul Ross St.	1/27/2007	8
	Michael Zasada, Eureka	Fr.	Fontbonne	1/27/2007	8
	Terry Bailey, Oglethorpe	Sr.	Southwestern (Tex.)	1/26/2007	8
	Travis Molton, Concordia (Wis.)	Sr.	Dominican (Ill.)	1/20/2007	8
	Zach Johnson, Carleton	So.	St. Mary's (Minn.)	1/10/2007	8
	Jered Gamble, Waynesburg	Jr.	La Roche	12/14/2006	8
	Terry Bailey, Oglethorpe	Sr.	Huntingdon	12/11/2006	8
	David McMullen, Ripon	Sr.	Knox	12/1/2006	8
	Jerry Beverly, Whitworth	Jr.	Caltech	11/26/2006	8
	Drew Gensler, Millikin	So.	Ind.-Northwest	11/21/2006	8
	Vincent Brock, Millikin	So.	MacMurray	11/18/2006	8
	Chris Goodridge, Salve Regina	Jr.	Bridgewater St.	11/18/2006	8
	Bart Hostetler, Ohio Northern	Sr.	Elizabethtown	11/18/2006	8
	Martin Salinas, Texas-Dallas	Sr.	Austin	11/18/2006	8

2007 Division III Team Leaders

Won-Lost Percentage

Rk.	Name	W	L	Pct.
1.	Amherst	30	2	93.8
2.	Mississippi Col.	27	3	90.0
3.	Wis.-Stevens Point	26	3	89.7
4.	Lake Erie	25	3	89.3
	Aurora	25	3	89.3
6.	Salem St.	24	3	88.9
7.	Rhode Island Col.	27	4	87.1
8.	St. Thomas (Minn.)	24	4	85.7
	Whitworth	24	4	85.7
10.	Wooster	29	5	85.3
11.	Va. Wesleyan	28	5	84.8
12.	WPI	22	4	84.6
13.	Hope	26	5	83.9
14.	Washington-St. Louis	25	5	83.3
15.	Centre	24	5	82.8
	Guilford	24	5	82.8
	Johns Hopkins	24	5	82.8
18.	Alvernia	23	5	82.1
19.	Wittenberg	22	5	81.5
20.	Brockport St.	26	6	81.3
21.	Chapman	21	5	80.8
	Trinity (Conn.)	21	5	80.8
23.	Keene St.	25	6	80.6
24.	St. John Fisher	24	6	80.0
25.	Catholic	23	6	79.3
	St. Lawrence	23	6	79.3
	Manhattanville	23	6	79.3
28.	Augustana (Ill.)	22	6	78.6
	DePauw	22	6	78.6
	Mary Hardin-Baylor	22	6	78.6
	Husson	22	6	78.6
	New York U.	22	6	78.6

Scoring Offense

Rk.	School	G	W-L	Pts.	Avg.
1.	Redlands	24	17-7	2,810	117.1
2.	Grinnell	24	17-7	2,662	110.9
3.	Emory & Henry	25	14-11	2,734	109.4
4.	Puget Sound	25	18-7	2,427	97.1
5.	Lincoln (Pa.)	29	20-9	2,626	90.6
6.	Brockport St.	32	26-6	2,814	87.9
7.	Wooster	34	29-5	2,989	87.9
8.	Concordia (Tex.)	26	10-16	2,280	87.7
9.	Westminster (Pa.)	27	18-9	2,346	86.9
10.	Aurora	28	25-3	2,417	86.3
11.	Guilford	29	24-5	2,457	84.7
12.	Bethel (Minn.)	26	18-8	2,202	84.7
13.	Piedmont	26	13-13	2,190	84.2
14.	Wis. Lutheran	26	15-11	2,180	83.8
15.	Keene St.	31	25-6	2,589	83.5
16.	Elms	29	20-9	2,416	83.3
17.	Lesley	27	14-13	2,248	83.3
18.	SUNYIT	29	17-12	2,410	83.1
19.	MacMurray	25	16-9	2,075	83.0
20.	Bethany (W.V.)	28	19-9	2,320	82.9
21.	Tufts	25	15-10	2,071	82.8
22.	Chris. Newport	26	15-11	2,151	82.7
23.	New England Col.	25	10-15	2,068	82.7
24.	Cazenovia	26	12-14	2,139	82.3
25.	Wis.-Stevens Point	29	26-3	2,372	81.8
26.	Carroll (Wis.)	27	18-9	2,205	81.7
27.	Amherst	32	30-2	2,604	81.4
28.	Salem St.	27	24-3	2,197	81.4
29.	Lake Erie	28	25-3	2,273	81.2
30.	Oglethorpe	26	14-12	2,104	80.9
31.	Manhattanville	29	23-6	2,346	80.9

Scoring Defense

Rk.	School	G	W-L	Opp. Pts.	Opp. Avg.
1.	Mississippi Col.	30	27-3	1,711	57.0
2.	Claremont-M-S	25	15-10	1,427	57.1
3.	Centre	29	24-5	1,680	57.9
4.	Penn St.-Behrend	29	21-8	1,690	58.3
5.	Wm. Paterson	25	15-10	1,464	58.6
6.	Wittenberg	27	22-5	1,587	58.8
7.	New York U.	28	22-6	1,650	58.9
8.	Western New Eng.	30	22-8	1,777	59.2
9.	Cal Lutheran	25	17-8	1,494	59.8
10.	Drew	24	9-15	1,445	60.2
11.	Alvernia	28	23-5	1,687	60.3
12.	Arcadia	25	11-14	1,511	60.4
13.	Messiah	26	19-7	1,577	60.7
14.	Amherst	32	30-2	1,944	60.8
15.	Scranton	26	19-7	1,590	61.2
16.	Bates	25	18-7	1,536	61.4
17.	Gettysburg	26	13-13	1,606	61.8
18.	Wis.-La Crosse	27	19-8	1,670	61.9
19.	Utica	26	19-7	1,610	61.9
20.	Catholic	29	23-6	1,800	62.1
21.	Southwestern (Tex.)	26	11-15	1,617	62.2
22.	Rose-Hulman	25	9-16	1,557	62.3
23.	Va. Wesleyan	33	28-5	2,056	62.3
24.	Wis.-Oshkosh	27	21-6	1,686	62.4
25.	Rochester (N.Y.)	26	18-8	1,624	62.5
26.	Connecticut Col.	24	11-13	1,500	62.5
27.	WPI	26	22-4	1,629	62.7
28.	St. Thomas (Minn.)	28	24-4	1,760	62.9
	Whitworth	28	24-4	1,760	62.9
30.	Haverford	26	14-12	1,636	62.9

Scoring Margin

Rk.	School	W-L	Pts.	Avg.	Opp. Pts.	Opp. Avg.	Pt. Mar.
1.	Amherst	30-2	2,604	81.4	1,944	60.8	20.6
2.	Aurora	25-3	2,417	86.3	1,944	69.4	16.9
3.	Wooster	29-5	2,989	87.9	2,416	71.1	16.9
4.	Hope	26-5	2,481	80.0	1,960	63.2	16.8
5.	Mississippi Col.	27-3	2,192	73.1	1,711	57.0	16.0
6.	Wis.-Stevens Point	26-3	2,372	81.8	1,913	66.0	15.8
7.	Husson	22-6	2,223	79.4	1,821	65.0	14.4
8.	Va. Wesleyan	28-5	2,528	76.6	2,056	62.3	14.3
9.	Brockport St.	26-6	2,814	87.9	2,374	74.2	13.8
10.	Whitworth	24-4	2,132	76.1	1,760	62.9	13.3
	New York U.	22-6	2,022	72.2	1,650	58.9	13.3
12.	St. Thomas (Minn.)	24-4	2,124	75.9	1,760	62.9	13.0
13.	Lake Erie	25-3	2,273	81.2	1,911	68.3	12.9
14.	Centre	24-5	2,051	70.7	1,680	57.9	12.8
15.	Chapman	21-5	1,994	76.7	1,668	64.2	12.5
16.	Wis.-Oshkosh	21-6	2,017	74.7	1,686	62.4	12.3
17.	St. Joseph's (Me.)	22-8	2,310	77.0	1,943	64.8	12.2
18.	Scranton	19-7	1,907	73.3	1,590	61.2	12.2
19.	Wittenberg	22-5	1,913	70.9	1,587	58.8	12.1
20.	Occidental	19-6	1,877	75.1	1,580	63.2	11.9
21.	Trinity (Conn.)	21-5	2,054	79.0	1,756	67.5	11.5
22.	WPI	22-4	1,925	74.0	1,629	62.7	11.4
23.	Ohio Wesleyan	18-10	2,116	75.6	1,798	64.2	11.4
24.	Cal Lutheran	17-8	1,777	71.1	1,494	59.8	11.3
25.	Salem St.	24-3	2,197	81.4	1,895	70.2	11.2
26.	Utica	19-7	1,899	73.0	1,610	61.9	11.1
27.	Bates	18-7	1,813	72.5	1,536	61.4	11.1
28.	Alvernia	23-5	1,992	71.1	1,687	60.3	10.9
29.	Manhattanville	23-6	2,346	80.9	2,036	70.2	10.7
30.	Wis.-Whitewater	18-9	2,122	78.6	1,839	68.1	10.5

Field-Goal Percentage

Rk.	School	G	W-L	FGM	FGA	FG%
1.	Mississippi Col.	30	27-3	789	1504	52.5
2.	Whitworth	28	24-4	779	1495	52.1
3.	Wooster	34	29-5	1112	2155	51.6
4.	Lawrence	23	13-10	611	1195	51.1
5.	Amherst	32	30-2	968	1895	51.1
6.	Randolph-Macon	26	14-12	702	1383	50.8
7.	Chris. Newport	26	15-11	821	1625	50.5
8.	North Central (Ill.)	26	16-10	690	1371	50.3
9.	St. Thomas (Minn.)	28	24-4	800	1591	50.3
10.	Wis.-Stevens Point	29	26-3	862	1729	49.9
11.	New York U.	28	22-6	717	1443	49.7
12.	Wis.-Oshkosh	27	21-6	711	1432	49.7
13.	Gust. Adolphus	27	14-13	671	1352	49.6
14.	Guilford	29	24-5	906	1828	49.6
15.	Occidental	25	19-6	714	1445	49.4
16.	Ripon	23	13-10	671	1360	49.3
17.	Ill. Wesleyan	25	11-14	666	1350	49.3
18.	DeSales	30	22-8	809	1643	49.2
19.	Bridgewater (Va.)	27	10-17	675	1376	49.1
20.	Piedmont	26	13-13	809	1651	49.0
21.	Elmhurst	27	21-6	730	1491	48.9
22.	Coe	27	19-8	710	1451	48.9
23.	Geneseo St.	26	15-11	651	1331	48.9
24.	Carroll (Wis.)	27	18-9	783	1604	48.8
25.	Va. Wesleyan	33	28-5	940	1928	48.8
26.	York (N.Y.)	29	18-11	762	1565	48.7
27.	Mt. St. Joseph	25	13-12	666	1369	48.6
28.	Baldwin-Wallace	27	18-9	726	1496	48.5
29.	Baptist Bible (Pa.)	26	18-8	780	1608	48.5
30.	Johns Hopkins	29	24-5	712	1468	48.5
31.	Brockport St.	32	26-6	983	2027	48.5
32.	King's (Pa.)	28	19-9	742	1531	48.5

Field-Goal Percentage Defense

Rk.	School	G	W-L	Opp. FG	Opp. FGA	Opp. FG%
1.	New York U.	28	22-6	552	1,560	35.4
2.	Mississippi Col.	30	27-3	602	1,671	36.0
3.	Rowan	26	20-6	631	1,682	37.5
4.	Claremont-M-S	25	15-10	462	1,231	37.5
5.	Western New Eng.	30	22-8	647	1,717	37.7
6.	Me.-Farmington	26	10-16	603	1,580	38.2
7.	Wm. Paterson	25	15-10	451	1,176	38.4
8.	St. Lawrence	29	23-6	717	1,863	38.5
9.	Wittenberg	27	22-5	565	1,468	38.5
10.	Amherst	32	30-2	686	1,772	38.7
11.	Farmingdale St.	28	18-10	648	1,672	38.8
12.	Gettysburg	26	13-13	569	1,465	38.8
13.	Centre	29	24-5	627	1,613	38.9
14.	Alvernia	28	23-5	633	1,617	39.1
15.	Southwestern (Tex.)	26	11-15	526	1,342	39.2
16.	Maine Maritime	24	12-12	546	1,391	39.3
17.	Salem St.	27	24-3	700	1,783	39.3
18.	Utica	26	19-7	575	1,460	39.4
19.	Bridgewater St.	25	17-8	649	1,643	39.5
20.	Catholic	29	23-6	680	1,721	39.5
21.	York (N.Y.)	29	18-11	705	1,783	39.5
22.	Hope	31	26-5	694	1,747	39.7
23.	Johns Hopkins	29	24-5	659	1,657	39.8
24.	Emmanuel (Mass.)	28	12-16	641	1,608	39.9
25.	Wis.-Stout	25	12-13	551	1,382	39.9
26.	Penn St.-Behrend	29	21-8	607	1,518	40.0
27.	Whitworth	28	24-4	601	1,498	40.1
28.	Yeshiva	26	15-11	589	1,467	40.1
29.	Ursinus	26	16-10	619	1,540	40.2
30.	Husson	28	22-6	662	1,646	40.2

Three-Point Field Goals Per Game

Rk.	School	G	W-L	3FG	3PG
1.	Redlands	24	17-7	440	18.3
2.	Grinnell	24	17-7	424	17.7
3.	Emory & Henry	25	14-11	436	17.4
4.	Mary Washington	26	16-10	325	12.5
5.	Westminster (Pa.)	27	18-9	330	12.2

Rk.	School	G	W-L	3FG	3PG
6.	Chicago	26	20-6	285	11.0
7.	Aurora	28	25-3	306	10.9
8.	Wis.-Stevens Point	29	26-3	309	10.7
9.	Pomona-Pitzer	24	16-8	251	10.5
10.	Macalester	25	11-14	260	10.4
11.	Merchant Marine	26	14-12	265	10.2
12.	Puget Sound	25	18-7	250	10.0
13.	Lewis & Clark	26	19-7	255	9.8
14.	Bethany (W.V.)	28	19-9	269	9.6
15.	Williams	28	16-12	268	9.6
16.	Wooster	34	29-5	324	9.5
17.	Suffolk	27	9-18	255	9.4
18.	Hanover	25	14-11	235	9.4
19.	Rhode Island Col.	31	27-4	287	9.3
20.	Transylvania	28	19-9	258	9.2
21.	Waynesburg	25	12-13	230	9.2
22.	Mass. Liberal Arts	25	6-19	229	9.2
23.	Lesley	27	14-13	246	9.1
24.	Louisiana Col.	25	8-17	227	9.1
25.	Mt. St. Mary (N.Y.)	26	9-17	234	9.0
	Union (N.Y.)	25	11-14	225	9.0
27.	Amherst	32	30-2	286	8.9
28.	Hope	31	26-5	274	8.8
29.	Cazenovia	26	12-14	228	8.8
30.	Clark (Mass.)	25	11-14	219	8.8
31.	Lasell	28	16-12	245	8.8

Three-Point Field-Goal Percentage

Minimum 5 made per game

Rk.	School	G	W-L	3FG	3FGA	3FG%
1.	Augustana (Ill.)	28	22-6	159	361	44.0
2.	Occidental	25	19-6	170	403	42.2
3.	Wis.-Stevens Point	29	26-3	309	744	41.5
4.	Endicott	28	16-12	147	356	41.3
5.	Wooster	34	29-5	324	792	40.9
6.	Aurora	28	25-3	306	749	40.9
7.	Amherst	32	30-2	286	701	40.8
8.	Hope	31	26-5	274	672	40.8
9.	Wis.-Platteville	25	13-12	169	415	40.7
10.	Union (N.Y.)	25	11-14	225	556	40.5
11.	Buena Vista	26	17-9	219	543	40.3
12.	St. Thomas (Minn.)	28	24-4	177	439	40.3
13.	Whitworth	28	24-4	183	456	40.1
14.	Rochester (N.Y.)	26	18-8	167	417	40.0
15.	Elmhurst	27	21-6	144	360	40.0
16.	St. John Fisher	30	24-6	224	562	39.9
17.	North Park	25	13-12	142	357	39.8
18.	Lasell	28	16-12	245	616	39.8
19.	Transylvania	28	19-9	258	649	39.8
20.	Scranton	26	19-7	219	552	39.7
21.	Bluffton	26	18-8	169	426	39.7
22.	New York U.	28	22-6	189	477	39.6
23.	Franklin	26	16-10	208	525	39.6
24.	Chicago	26	20-6	285	721	39.5
25.	Hampden-Sydney	30	19-11	210	532	39.5
26.	Wis.-Whitewater	27	18-9	171	434	39.4
27.	Brockport St.	32	26-6	275	700	39.3
28.	Capital	28	19-9	185	471	39.3
29.	Rensselaer	26	13-13	168	428	39.3
30.	Wheaton (Ill.)	26	17-9	165	421	39.2
31.	Alvernia	28	23-5	206	526	39.2

Free-Throw Percentage

Rk.	School	G	W-L	FT	FTA	FT%
1.	Wis.-Stevens Point	29	26-3	339	412	82.3
2.	MIT	27	14-13	380	481	79.0
3.	Hiram	26	7-19	404	512	78.9
4.	Bluffton	26	18-8	467	592	78.9
5.	Elmhurst	27	21-6	500	636	78.6
6.	Wheaton (Ill.)	26	17-9	476	607	78.4
7.	Wheaton (Mass.)	26	11-15	367	470	78.1
8.	Pomona-Pitzer	24	16-8	299	387	77.3
9.	Plymouth St.	26	10-16	458	593	77.2
10.	Moravian	25	11-14	442	577	76.6
11.	Wis.-Whitewater	27	18-9	501	655	76.5
12.	Oberlin	25	5-20	341	446	76.5
13.	Scranton	26	19-7	340	445	76.4
14.	Gust. Adolphus	27	14-13	394	516	76.4

Rk.	School	G	W-L	FT	FTA	FT%
15.	Baldwin-Wallace	27	18-9	497	651	76.3
16.	Carroll (Wis.)	27	18-9	405	531	76.3
17.	Wis.-Oshkosh	27	21-6	468	614	76.2
18.	Cornell College	25	8-17	337	443	76.1
19.	Susquehanna	26	16-10	389	512	76.0
20.	Willamette	25	10-15	423	557	75.9
21.	Bethel (Minn.)	26	18-8	437	577	75.7
22.	Knox	23	5-18	315	418	75.4
23.	Northland	25	9-16	425	565	75.2
24.	Wooster	34	29-5	441	588	75.0
25.	St. John's (Minn.)	29	21-8	381	509	74.9
26.	Westminster (Mo.)	24	15-9	322	431	74.7
27.	Otterbein	27	16-11	480	643	74.7
28.	Hope	31	26-5	429	575	74.6
29.	Westminster (Pa.)	27	18-9	436	585	74.5
30.	Manhattanville	29	23-6	451	606	74.4

Rebound Margin

Rk.	School	W-L	Reb.	Avg.	Opp Reb.	Opp Avg.	Reb Mar.
1.	New York U.	22-6	1,117	39.9	824	29.4	10.5
2.	Salem St.	24-3	1,255	46.5	1,003	37.1	9.3
3.	Guilford	24-5	1,243	42.9	981	33.8	9.0
4.	Occidental	19-6	939	37.6	726	29.0	8.5
5.	Wis.-Oshkosh	21-6	975	36.1	750	27.8	8.3
6.	Edgewood	18-8	1,006	38.7	798	30.7	8.0
7.	Ursinus	16-10	998	38.4	792	30.5	7.9
8.	Ill. Wesleyan	11-14	897	35.9	702	28.1	7.8
9.	Farmingdale St.	18-10	1,207	43.1	990	35.4	7.8
10.	Chapman	21-5	978	37.6	777	29.9	7.7
11.	Tufts	15-10	1,060	42.4	872	34.9	7.5
12.	Rowan	20-6	1,141	43.9	948	36.5	7.4
13.	Messiah	19-7	973	37.4	784	30.2	7.3
14.	Bates	18-7	942	37.7	762	30.5	7.2
15.	Mississippi Col.	27-3	1,107	36.9	893	29.8	7.1
16.	Vassar	18-10	1,112	39.7	919	32.8	6.9
17.	Wooster	29-5	1,281	37.7	1,054	31.0	6.7
18.	Worcester St.	11-16	1,166	43.2	987	36.6	6.6
19.	Ramapo	22-8	1,266	42.2	1,068	35.6	6.6
20.	Western New Eng.	22-8	1,222	40.7	1,027	34.2	6.5
21.	Elmhurst	21-6	944	35.0	773	28.6	6.3
22.	Endicott	16-12	1,036	37.0	860	30.7	6.3
23.	North Central (Ill.)	16-10	879	33.8	716	27.5	6.3
24.	FDU-Florham	17-10	1,088	40.3	921	34.1	6.2
25.	Pacific (Ore.)	12-13	965	38.6	812	32.5	6.1
26.	Otterbein	16-11	1,012	37.5	847	31.4	6.1
27.	Johns Hopkins	24-5	1,085	37.4	911	31.4	6.0
	Trinity (Conn.)	21-5	972	37.4	816	31.4	6.0
29.	Lakeland	16-11	1,060	39.3	902	33.4	5.9
30.	St. Thomas (Minn.)	24-4	1,014	36.2	851	30.4	5.8
31.	Bethel (Minn.)	18-8	1,033	39.7	883	34.0	5.8

Assists Per Game

Rk.	School	G	W-L	Ast.	Avg.
1.	Emory & Henry	25	14-11	523	20.9
2.	Redlands	24	17-7	489	20.4
3.	Piedmont	26	13-13	527	20.3
4.	Grinnell	24	17-7	480	20.0
5.	Amherst	32	30-2	617	19.3
6.	Chris. Newport	26	15-11	482	18.5
7.	Utica	26	19-7	470	18.1
8.	Washington-St. Louis	30	25-5	541	18.0
9.	Baptist Bible (Pa.)	26	18-8	468	18.0
10.	DeSales	30	22-8	536	17.9
11.	Brockport St.	32	26-6	570	17.8
12.	Coe	27	19-8	480	17.8
13.	Geneseo St.	26	15-11	462	17.8
14.	St. John Fisher	30	24-6	531	17.7
15.	Wooster	34	29-5	600	17.6
16.	Bethany (W.V.)	28	19-9	494	17.6
17.	Cazenovia	26	12-14	458	17.6
18.	St. John's (Minn.)	29	21-8	509	17.6
19.	Yeshiva	26	15-11	452	17.4
20.	Wis.-Stevens Point	29	26-3	499	17.2
21.	Greenville	25	13-12	430	17.2
22.	Merchant Marine	26	14-12	446	17.2
23.	Tufts	25	15-10	428	17.1

Rk.	School	G	W-L	Ast.	Avg.
24.	Maryville (Tenn.)	29	22-7	496	17.1
25.	Potsdam St.	25	9-16	426	17.0
26.	Keuka	26	13-13	442	17.0
	Ripon	23	13-10	391	17.0
28.	Guilford	29	24-5	492	17.0
	Manhattanville	29	23-6	492	17.0
30.	Webster	26	16-10	440	16.9

Blocked Shots Per Game

Rk.	School	G	W-L	Blk.	Avg.
1.	Chris. Newport	26	15-11	175	6.7
2.	Gettysburg	26	13-13	167	6.4
3.	Amherst	32	30-2	183	5.7
4.	Simpson	27	18-9	154	5.7
5.	Wis.-Stout	25	12-13	136	5.4
6.	New York U.	28	22-6	149	5.3
7.	Lincoln (Pa.)	29	20-9	152	5.2
8.	Wis.-Oshkosh	27	21-6	141	5.2
9.	Worcester St.	27	11-16	140	5.2
10.	Skidmore	24	2-22	121	5.0
11.	Redlands	24	17-7	118	4.9
12.	Mississippi Col.	30	27-3	147	4.9
13.	Salem St.	27	24-3	131	4.9
14.	Newbury	27	15-12	127	4.7
	Mass.-Boston	27	10-17	127	4.7
16.	Emmanuel (Mass.)	28	12-16	130	4.6
17.	St. Lawrence	29	23-6	134	4.6
18.	Colby	26	15-11	118	4.5
19.	Curry	30	16-14	136	4.5
20.	Salve Regina	26	13-13	116	4.5
21.	Hardin-Simmons	28	16-12	123	4.4
22.	Trinity (Conn.)	26	21-5	113	4.3
23.	Aurora	28	25-3	121	4.3
24.	Stevens Institute	30	23-7	129	4.3
25.	WPI	26	22-4	111	4.3
26.	Scranton	26	19-7	110	4.2
27.	York (N.Y.)	29	18-11	122	4.2
28.	Guilford	29	24-5	121	4.2
29.	Edgewood	26	18-8	108	4.2
30.	Gordon	27	19-8	112	4.1
31.	Western Conn. St.	26	14-12	107	4.1
32.	Johns Hopkins	29	24-5	119	4.1
	New Jersey City	29	19-10	119	4.1

Steals Per Game

Rk.	School	G	W-L	St.	Avg.
1.	Redlands	24	17-7	487	20.3
2.	Emory & Henry	25	14-11	444	17.8
3.	Grinnell	24	17-7	382	15.9
4.	Kean	25	13-12	343	13.7
5.	Lesley	27	14-13	347	12.9
6.	Brooklyn	24	10-14	306	12.8
7.	Lincoln (Pa.)	29	20-9	358	12.3
8.	Puget Sound	25	18-7	299	12.0
9.	Elizabethtown	24	9-15	287	12.0
10.	Fisk	22	5-17	262	11.9
11.	Lake Erie	28	25-3	332	11.8
12.	St. Joseph's (Me.)	30	22-8	354	11.8
13.	Concordia (Tex.)	26	10-16	301	11.6
14.	Neumann	26	13-13	300	11.5
15.	Concordia (Wis.)	25	8-17	287	11.5
16.	Wis. Lutheran	26	15-11	292	11.2
17.	LaGrange	27	18-9	301	11.1
18.	Buffalo St.	25	12-13	278	11.1
19.	Clark (Mass.)	25	11-14	276	11.0
20.	McMurry	27	20-7	297	11.0
	Greenville	25	13-12	275	11.0
22.	Western Conn. St.	26	14-12	284	10.9
23.	Piedmont	26	13-13	280	10.8
24.	Brockport St.	32	26-6	344	10.8
25.	New Paltz St.	25	11-14	268	10.8
26.	SUNYIT	29	17-12	306	10.6
27.	Baptist Bible (Pa.)	26	18-8	274	10.5
28.	Howard Payne	25	7-18	259	10.4
29.	Old Westbury	29	18-11	300	10.4
30.	Cazenovia	26	12-14	268	10.3
31.	Susquehanna	26	16-10	267	10.3
32.	Curry	30	16-14	308	10.3

Turnovers Per Game

Rk.	School	G	W-L	TO	Avg.
1.	Wis.-Stevens Point	29	26-3	247	8.5
2.	Lewis & Clark	26	19-7	249	9.6
3.	Muskingum	25	12-13	253	10.1
4.	Chicago	26	20-6	275	10.6
5.	Ohio Wesleyan	28	18-10	314	11.2
6.	Carleton	26	11-15	294	11.3
7.	Williams	28	16-12	324	11.6
8.	Westminster (Mo.)	24	15-9	281	11.7
9.	Earlham	26	8-18	306	11.8
10.	Wittenberg	27	22-5	318	11.8
11.	Blackburn	25	10-15	295	11.8
12.	Gordon	27	19-8	320	11.9
13.	Cortland St.	26	10-16	312	12.0
14.	Pacific (Ore.)	25	12-13	302	12.1
15.	Franklin	26	16-10	316	12.2
16.	Hanover	25	14-11	304	12.2
17.	Wis.-Oshkosh	27	21-6	331	12.3
18.	Pitt-Bradford	27	14-13	333	12.3
19.	Maryville (Tenn.)	29	22-7	359	12.4
20.	Trinity (Conn.)	26	21-5	324	12.5
21.	Va. Wesleyan	33	28-5	412	12.5
22.	St. John's (Minn.)	29	21-8	363	12.5
23.	Macalester	25	11-14	313	12.5
24.	Catholic	29	23-6	366	12.6
25.	Bowdoin	25	15-10	317	12.7
26.	Bluffton	26	18-8	330	12.7
27.	St. Thomas (Minn.)	28	24-4	357	12.8
28.	Wis.-Whitewater	27	18-9	345	12.8
29.	Carthage	25	16-9	321	12.8
30.	Phila. Biblical	26	9-17	334	12.8

Personal Fouls Per Game

Rk.	School	G	W-L	PF	Avg.	DQ
1.	Carleton	26	11-15	343	13.2	5
2.	Keuka	26	13-13	361	13.9	5
3.	Penn St.-Behrend	29	21-8	407	14.0	4
4.	Coast Guard	28	14-14	399	14.3	6
5.	St. Thomas (Minn.)	28	24-4	407	14.5	5
6.	Connecticut Col.	24	11-13	352	14.7	1
7.	Newbury	27	15-12	399	14.8	11
8.	Centre	29	24-5	429	14.8	3
9.	St. Olaf	27	13-14	402	14.9	5
10.	Yeshiva	26	15-11	388	14.9	5
11.	D'Youville	25	3-22	374	15.0	11
12.	Gust. Adolphus	27	14-13	409	15.1	5
13.	Earlham	26	8-18	394	15.2	7
14.	Wis.-Oshkosh	27	21-6	410	15.2	6
15.	Pomona-Pitzer	24	16-8	366	15.3	6
16.	Defiance	26	17-9	399	15.3	9
17.	Wis.-La Crosse	27	19-8	415	15.4	9
18.	DeSales	30	22-8	462	15.4	3
19.	Huntingdon	26	3-23	402	15.5	10
20.	Western New Eng.	30	22-8	469	15.6	10
21.	Centenary (N.J.)	24	3-21	378	15.8	16
22.	Lake Forest	25	15-10	394	15.8	5
23.	Southern Me.	26	6-20	410	15.8	8
24.	Gordon	27	19-8	426	15.8	7
25.	Chris. Newport	26	15-11	411	15.8	6
26.	SUNYIT	29	17-12	459	15.8	6
27.	Curry	30	16-14	476	15.9	15
28.	Cal Lutheran	25	17-8	397	15.9	5
	Northland	25	9-16	397	15.9	9
30.	Eastern	27	16-11	429	15.9	3
31.	Catholic	29	23-6	462	15.9	6

2007 Division III Team Game Highs

Points

Rk.	School	Opponent	Date	Pts.	Opp Pts.
1.	Lincoln (Pa.)	Ohio St.-Marion	12/2/2006	201	78
2.	Redlands	Whitman	1/3/2007	153	149
3.	Redlands	Pacific Union	1/6/2007	151	120
4.	Whitman	Redlands	1/3/2007	149	153
5.	Grinnell	Monmouth (Ill.)	12/6/2006	143	125
6.	Grinnell	Lawrence	1/12/2007	142	130
7.	Emory & Henry	Lynchburg	12/9/2006	141	98
8.	Puget Sound	Willamette	12/1/2006	140	137
9.	Grinnell	Simpson	12/9/2006	139	127
10.	Willamette	Puget Sound	12/1/2006	137	140
11.	Emory & Henry	Lynchburg	1/24/2007	136	107
12.	Redlands	Whittier	1/27/2007	132	122
13.	Redlands	UC Santa Cruz	11/30/2006	131	110
14.	Guilford	Emory & Henry	1/13/2007	130	114
	Redlands	La Sierra	12/6/2006	130	116
	Puget Sound	Menlo	11/18/2006	130	102
17.	Guilford	Lincoln (Pa.)	3/9/2007	129	128
	Emory & Henry	Cabrini	11/18/2006	129	112
19.	Va. Wesleyan	Emory & Henry	1/6/2007	128	84
20.	Simpson	Grinnell	12/9/2006	127	139
21.	Marymount (Va.)	Salisbury	2/14/2007	126	122
	Wis.-Whitewater	Grinnell	12/16/2006	126	90
	Maritime (N.Y.)	Mass. Liberal Arts	11/28/2006	126	124
24.	Emory & Henry	Va. Wesleyan	1/27/2007	124	101
	Mass. Liberal Arts	Maritime (N.Y.)	11/28/2006	124	126
	Puget Sound	UC Santa Cruz	11/17/2006	124	86
27.	Wis.-Oshkosh	Grinnell	1/4/2007	123	105
	Bethany (W.V.)	Mt. Aloysius	12/16/2006	123	105
	Redlands	Hope Int'l	12/9/2006	123	127
	Redlands	Cal St. East Bay	12/1/2006	123	115

Field-Goal Percentage

Rk.	School	Opponent	Date	FGM	FGA	FG%
1.	Carthage	Grinnell	11/21/2006	55	69	79.7
2.	Cal Lutheran	Redlands	1/13/2007	55	73	75.3
3.	Ramapo	Roanoke	12/27/2006	32	43	74.4
4.	Wash. & Lee	Emory & Henry	2/7/2007	43	59	72.9
5.	Bridgewater (Va.)	VMI	1/18/2007	40	55	72.7
	Thiel	Lancaster Bible	12/2/2006	32	44	72.7
7.	Dominican (Ill.)	Maranatha Baptist	12/5/2006	39	54	72.2
8.	Ill. Wesleyan	Albion	12/30/2006	36	50	72.0
9.	Carroll (Wis.)	Grinnell	12/2/2006	55	78	70.5
10.	Mt. St. Joseph	Franklin	1/3/2007	31	44	70.5
11.	Whitman	Redlands	1/2/2007	63	90	70.0
	Salve Regina	Mitchell	11/21/2006	35	50	70.0
13.	Willamette	Puget Sound	1/26/2007	37	53	69.8
14.	Va. Wesleyan	Emory & Henry	1/6/2007	46	66	69.7
15.	Randolph-Macon	Penn St.-Berks	11/17/2006	39	56	69.6
16.	Connecticut Col.	Bates	1/27/2007	25	36	69.4
17.	Central (Iowa)	Wartburg	1/3/2007	29	42	69.0
18.	Concordia (Ill.)	Greenville	11/17/2006	26	38	68.4
19.	Pomona-Pitzer	Redlands	1/10/2007	41	60	68.3
20.	Otterbein	Muskingum	1/27/2007	28	41	68.3
	Rochester (N.Y.)	Geneseo St.	1/13/2007	28	41	68.3

Three-Point Field Goals Made

Rk.	School	Opponent	Date	3FG
1.	Lincoln (Pa.)	Ohio St.-Marion	12/2/2006	28
2.	Grinnell	Kalamazoo	12/17/2006	27
	Grinnell	Monmouth (Ill.)	12/6/2006	27
4.	Emory & Henry	Virginia-Wise	11/30/2006	25

STATISTICAL LEADERS

Rk.	School	Opponent	Date	3FG
	Wooster	Cabrini	11/17/2006	25
6.	Redlands	Pacific Union	1/6/2007	24
	Redlands	Whitman	1/3/2007	24
8.	Emory & Henry	Guilford	2/17/2007	22
	Mary Washington	Goucher	2/10/2007	22
	Emory & Henry	Lynchburg	1/24/2007	22
11.	Redlands	Pomona-Pitzer	2/3/2007	21
	Emory & Henry	East. Mennonite	1/20/2007	21
	Emory & Henry	Guilford	1/13/2007	21
	Macalester	Concordia-M'head	1/3/2007	21
	Emory & Henry	Lynchburg	12/9/2006	21
	Redlands	Hope Int'l	12/9/2006	21
	Redlands	Chapman	12/2/2006	21
	Pacific (Ore.)	Multnomah Bible	11/28/2006	21
	Redlands	Biola	11/25/2006	21
	Puget Sound	Menlo	11/18/2006	21

Three-Point Field-Goal Percentage

Minimum 10 made

Rk.	School	Opponent	Date	3FG	3FGA	3FG%
1.	Phila. Biblical	Gordon	11/21/2006	12	15	80.0
2.	Union (N.Y.)	Hobart	1/20/2007	10	13	76.9
	Linfield	Evergreen St.	12/8/2006	10	13	76.9
4.	Skidmore	Hamilton	1/20/2007	11	15	73.3
5.	St. John Fisher	Elmira	2/10/2007	13	18	72.2
6.	Wheaton (Ill.)	Principia	12/6/2006	15	21	71.4
	Nazareth	Hartwick	2/10/2007	10	14	71.4
	Chris. Newport	Shenandoah	1/31/2007	10	14	71.4
9.	Brandeis	Rochester (N.Y.)	2/11/2007	11	16	68.8
	Grove City	Westminster (Pa.)	1/17/2007	11	16	68.8
	Rhodes	Dallas	1/8/2007	11	16	68.8
12.	Richard Stockton	Kean	2/10/2007	13	19	68.4
	Amherst	Southern Vt.	1/23/2007	13	19	68.4
14.	Mary Hardin-Baylor	Schreiner	1/27/2007	12	18	66.7
	Wentworth Inst.	Anna Maria	1/20/2007	12	18	66.7
	LeTourneau	Schreiner	1/6/2007	12	18	66.7
	New England Col.	Newbury	1/20/2007	10	15	66.7
	Earlham	Oberlin	1/20/2007	10	15	66.7
	Mississippi Col.	Westmont	12/30/2006	10	15	66.7
	Rivier	Johnson St.	11/17/2006	10	15	66.7

Free-Throw Percentage

Minimum 15 made

Rk.	School	Opponent	Date	FT	FTA	FT%
1.	Wash. & Jeff.	Thomas More	2/7/2007	21	21	100.0
	Lynchburg	Randolph-Macon	12/6/2006	21	21	100.0
	Oberlin	Kenyon	2/10/2007	20	20	100.0
	St. Mary's (Md.)	Hood	2/22/2007	17	17	100.0
	Richard Stockton	Rowan	2/17/2007	17	17	100.0
	St. John's (Minn.)	St. Mary's (Minn.)	1/22/2007	16	16	100.0
7.	Wheaton (Ill.)	Carthage	1/31/2007	21	22	95.5
	Lesley	Newbury	1/30/2007	21	22	95.5
	Hiram	Kenyon	1/10/2007	21	22	95.5
10.	DePauw	Southwestern (Tex.)	1/20/2007	20	21	95.2
	Wis.-Stevens Point	Northern Mich.	12/28/2006	20	21	95.2
	Potsdam St.	Clarkson	11/18/2006	20	21	95.2
13.	Buena Vista	Luther	2/10/2007	19	20	95.0
	Wis. Lutheran	Benedictine (Ill.)	2/10/2007	19	20	95.0
	Colby	Trinity (Conn.)	1/27/2007	19	20	95.0
	Westminster (Mo.)	Eureka	1/13/2007	19	20	95.0
	Willamette	Cal Lutheran	12/29/2006	19	20	95.0
18.	Hobart	Vassar	1/26/2007	18	19	94.7
	York (Pa.)	St. Mary's (Md.)	1/10/2007	18	19	94.7
20.	Wis.-Stevens Point	Wis.-Whitewater	2/22/2007	17	18	94.4
	Va. Wesleyan	Randolph-Macon	2/10/2007	17	18	94.4
	Cortland St.	Potsdam St.	2/2/2007	17	18	94.4
	Denison	Oberlin	1/10/2007	17	18	94.4
	St. Mary's (Md.)	Immaculata	1/6/2007	17	18	94.4

Attendance Records

Attendance

2007 Attendance Summary

(For All NCAA Varsity Teams)

	Total Teams	Games or Sessions	2007 Attendance	Avg.	Change in Total	Change in Avg.
Home Attendance, NCAA Division I	325	*4,735	*25,224,121	5,327	1,757,319	129
NCAA Championship Tournament		35	696,992	19,914	26,738	764
Other Division I Neutral-Site Attendance		224	*1,784,799	7,968	113,509	-145
NCAA DIVISION I TOTALS	**325**	***4,994**	***27,705,912**	**5,548**	**1,897,566**	**122**
Home Attendance, NCAA Division II	^262	3,551	2,892,820	815	-20,693	-10
Home Attendance, NCAA Division III	380	4,533	1,947,730	430	-7,990	0
Reclassifying Teams	*15	*178	*175,921	*988	--	--
Neutral-Site Attendance for Divisions II & III		131	85,315	651	--	--
NCAA Division II Tournament Neutral Sites		14	20,497	1,464	--	--
NCAA Division III Tournament Neutral Sites		5	7,668	1,534	--	--
NATIONAL TOTALS FOR 2007	**982**	***13,406**	***32,835,863**	**2,449**	**1,896,148**	**98**

*Record high. NOTES: The Neutral-Site Attendance for Divisions II and III does not include the NCAA tournaments. The total attendance for the Division II Tournament was 76,073 for a 2,113 average over 36 sessions and the Division III Tournament was 60,619 for a 1,443 average over 42 sessions.

^ Division II attendance figures do not include five NCAA Puerto Rican schools.

Division I Championship Tournament

Round	Site	Att.	Site	Att.	Site	Att.	Site	Att.
Opening Round	Dayton	8,257						
1st Round	Buffalo	18,843	Columbus	19,916	New Orleans	13,393	Spokane	11,551
	Buffalo	18,649	Columbus	19,916	New Orleans	13,585	Spokane	11,551
	Chicago	18,237	Lexington	20,752	Sacramento	15,880	Winston-Salem	14,148
	Chicago	19,274	Lexington	20,816	Sacramento	16,338	Winston-Salem	14,148
2nd Round	Buffalo	18,801	Columbus	19,916	New Orleans	13,594	Spokane	11,551
	Chicago	20,916	Lexington	20,882	Sacramento	16,407	Winston-Salem	14,148
Regional Semifinal	East Rutherford	19,557	San Antonio	26,776	San Jose	18,049	St. Louis	26,307
Regional Final	East Rutherford	19,557	San Antonio	26,260	San Jose	18,102	St. Louis	25,947

Final Four

National Semifinal	Atlanta	53,510
National Final	Atlanta	51,458
Final Four Total		104,968

Total Tournament Attendance	696,992
Average Per Session	19,914

All Division I Conferences

	Total Teams	Games or Sessions	Entire Season 2007 Attendance	Average	Change In Avg.	Conference Tournament Total Sessions	Conference Tournament Total Attendance	Average
1. Big Ten	11	201	*2,564,662	12,760	179	5	94,412	18,882
2. Southeastern	12	214	*2,562,073	11,972	890	6	94,134	15,689
3. Big East#	16	292	**3,259,992	11,164	103	6	117,564	19,594
4. Atlantic Coast	12	219	*2,434,902	11,118	-154	6	133,614	22,269
5. Big 12	12	211	*2,261,697	*10,719	598	6	113,274	18,879
6. Pacific 10	10	176	*1,500,188	*8,524	615	5	84,477	16,895
7. Mountain West	9	150	1,244,710	8,298	532	5	54,921	10,984
8. Missouri Valley	10	156	*1,251,050	*8,020	303	5	85,074	17,015
9. Western Athletic	9	137	908,282	6,630	790	5	49,650	9,930
10. Atlantic 10	14	213	*1,155,219	5,424	-306	6	32,498	5,416
11. Conference USA #	12	194	980,309	5,053	-602	6	62,538	10,423
12. Colonial	12	171	*632,914	3,701	70	6	42,259	7,043
13. Horizon	9	131	483,326	3,690	213	6	27,261	4,544
14. Mid-American	12	165	518,903	3,145	-364	5	39,995	7,999
15. West Coast	8	116	312,034	2,690	-243	4	17,994	4,499
16. Big Sky	8	111	282,057	2,541	-200	4	21,261	5,315
17. Mid-Continent #	8	107	270,743	2,530	76	4	14,726	3,682
18. Ohio Valley	11	154	374,554	2,432	-362	6	15,051	2,509
19. Sun Belt #	13	182	436,636	2,399	-570	9	13,767	1,530
20. Metro Atlantic	10	138	330,383	2,394	-13	5	15,976	3,195
21. Southern	11	151	357,848	2,370	96	5	27,711	5,542
22. America East	9	114	229,478	2,013	50	5	13,178	2,636
23. Atlantic Sun #	8	110	221,382	2,013	53	4	20,196	5,049
24. Ivy	8	101	194,907	1,930	-257	-	-	-
25. Big West	8	110	203,626	1,851	-124	4	12,211	3,053
26. Patriot	8	108	*199,338	1,846	41	7	18,796	2,685
27. Mid-Eastern	11	133	235,983	1,774	-93	5	26,918	5,384
28. Big South #	8	113	195,601	1,731	249	6	19,810	3,302
29. Southland #	11	147	237,734	1,617	75	4	5,372	1,343
30. Southwestern	10	121	176,918	1,462	-98	6	7,957	1,326
31. Northeast	11	151	182,149	1,206	45	7	13,595	1,942
Independents	4	46	54,235	1,179	-682	-	-	-

** All-Time record high. * Record high for that conference. # Different lineups in 2006.

NOTE: Entire season total attendance includes the conference tournaments.

Leading Division II Conferences

Rank	Division II	Total Teams	Games or Sessions	2007 Attendance	Average	Change In Avg.
1.	North Central	7	102	198,653	1,948	28
2.	Mid-America	10	142	268,946	1,894	36
3.	Northern Sun	9	134	201,880	1,507	88
4.	CIAA	11	134	186,342	1,391	-156
5.	SIAC	12	155	160,463	1,035	6
6.	Great Lakes Valley	14	199	205,095	1,031	83
7.	Lone Star	14	193	184,620	957	-62
8.	Great Northwest	9	115	107,029	931	-68
9.	Gulf South	15	202	168,932	836	-132
10.	California	11	144	119,679	831	-65

Leading Division III Conferences

Rank	Division III	Total Teams	Games or Sessions	2007 Attendance	Average	Change In Avg.
1.	Michigan	7	80	88,039	1,100	-134
2.	Illinois & Wisconsin	8	93	74,765	804	-62
3.	Wisconsin	9	114	89,897	789	-11
4.	Ohio	10	118	91,334	774	76
5.	North Coast	10	123	84,053	683	-22
6.	Northwest	9	98	62,050	633	-49
7.	Old Dominion	10	126	72,448	575	41
8.	UAA	8	110	62,444	568	122
9.	Iowa	9	101	56,926	564	-99
10.	American Southwest	14	166	92,775	559	10

Leading Teams

DIVISION I

Rank	School	G	Attendance	Average
1.	Kentucky	16	374,737	23,421
2.	Syracuse	22	473,353	21,516
3.	North Carolina	17	351,785	20,693
4.	Tennessee	16	314,571	19,661
5.	Louisville	20	369,763	18,488
6.	Ohio St.	18	315,539	17,530
7.	Wisconsin	19	326,610	17,190
8.	Maryland	19	319,616	16,822
9.	Arkansas	16	267,520	16,720
10.	Illinois	17	282,506	16,618
11.	Indiana	15	247,103	16,474
12.	Kansas	18	293,400	16,300
13.	Creighton	14	222,728	15,909
14.	Marquette	20	306,893	15,345
15.	Michigan St.	19	280,421	14,759
16.	Memphis	19	276,014	14,527
17.	Arizona	16	227,239	14,202
18.	North Carolina St.	20	279,035	13,952
19.	Virginia	17	229,858	13,521
20.	Connecticut	20	260,231	13,012
21.	Oklahoma St.	18	234,142	13,008
22.	Texas	16	207,504	12,969
23.	New Mexico	18	231,346	12,853
24.	South Carolina	17	218,240	12,838
25.	Iowa St.	17	212,310	12,489
26.	Kansas St.	17	209,123	12,301
27.	Alabama	16	196,552	12,285
28.	Dayton	17	208,522	12,266
29.	Iowa	16	195,139	12,196
30.	BYU	17	205,243	12,073

2007 DIVISION I TEAM-BY-TEAM ATTENDANCE

School	G	Attendance	Average
Air Force	17	86,080	5,064
Akron	14	50,308	3,593
Alabama	16	196,552	12,285
Alabama A&M	14	17,333	1,238
Alabama St.	12	31,183	2,599
UAB	13	61,779	4,752
Albany (N.Y.)	13	41,276	3,175
Alcorn St.	11	9,374	852
American	13	22,619	1,740
Appalachian St.	13	32,894	2,530
Arizona	16	227,239	14,202
Arizona St.	18	124,756	6,931
Arkansas	16	267,520	16,720
Arkansas St.	13	42,313	3,255
Ark.-Little Rock	13	42,713	3,286
Ark.-Pine Bluff	10	6,049	605
Army	14	13,562	969
Auburn	20	106,198	5,310
Austin Peay	15	41,481	2,765
Ball St.	14	60,116	4,294
Baylor	18	109,174	6,065
Belmont	11	14,860	1,351
Bethune-Cookman	12	25,106	2,092
Binghamton	13	41,684	3,206
Boise St.	15	65,889	4,393
Boston College	18	124,486	6,916
Boston U.	14	22,189	1,585
Bowling Green	15	21,049	1,403
Bradley	17	165,376	9,728

School	G	Attendance	Average
BYU	17	205,243	12,073
Brown	10	11,293	1,129
Bucknell	12	44,017	3,668
Buffalo	15	43,477	2,898
Butler	15	86,005	5,734
Cal Poly	14	28,647	2,046
California	15	126,650	8,443
UC Irvine	12	28,703	2,392
UC Riverside	12	8,837	736
UC Santa Barbara	14	29,666	2,119
Cal St. Fullerton	14	13,542	967
Cal St. Northridge	15	14,160	944
Campbell	15	13,246	883
Canisius	13	30,152	2,319
Centenary (La.)	12	7,791	649
Central Conn. St.	17	34,257	2,015
UCF	16	43,296	2,706
Central Mich.	13	27,259	2,097
Col. of Charleston	13	42,766	3,290
Charleston So.	13	15,428	1,187
Charlotte	14	84,360	6,026
Chattanooga	16	51,185	3,199
Chicago St.	6	3,703	617
Cincinnati	18	158,966	8,831
Citadel	14	23,637	1,688
Clemson	20	146,583	7,329
Cleveland St.	14	36,662	2,619
Coastal Caro.	17	17,032	1,002
Colgate	14	7,369	526
Colorado	15	49,862	3,324
Colorado St.	14	64,687	4,621
Columbia	14	18,458	1,318
Connecticut	20	260,231	13,012
Coppin St.	10	4,256	426
Cornell	13	17,424	1,340
Creighton	14	222,728	15,909
Dartmouth	13	10,398	800
Davidson	14	52,095	3,721
Dayton	17	208,522	12,266
Delaware	14	42,870	3,062
Delaware St.	10	13,513	1,351
Denver	14	20,177	1,441
DePaul	16	162,320	10,145
Detroit	12	27,749	2,312
Drake	15	81,870	5,458
Drexel	13	28,094	2,161
Duke	19	176,966	9,314
Duquesne	14	29,356	2,097
East Caro.	14	63,457	4,533
East Tenn. St.	17	78,625	4,625
Eastern Ill.	14	15,458	1,104
Eastern Ky.	14	35,375	2,527
Eastern Mich.	14	11,697	836
Eastern Wash.	13	31,152	2,396
Elon	13	13,116	1,009
Evansville	15	82,407	5,494
Fairfield	15	40,633	2,709
Fairleigh Dickinson	13	10,513	809
Florida	18	212,866	11,826
Florida A&M	13	16,688	1,284
Fla. Atlantic	13	12,062	928
Florida Int'l	13	6,796	523
Florida St.	19	142,416	7,496
Fordham	14	35,593	2,542
Fresno St.	18	210,828	11,713
Furman	14	29,897	2,136

School	G	Attendance	Average	School	G	Attendance	Average
Gardner-Webb	12	23,615	1,968	Morehead St.	16	37,098	2,319
George Mason	13	88,837	6,834	Morgan St.	13	20,239	1,557
George Washington	13	44,233	3,403	Mt. St. Mary's	12	11,809	984
Georgetown	17	177,501	10,441	Murray St.	13	41,726	3,210
Georgia	18	132,048	7,336	Navy	14	22,630	1,616
Ga. Southern	12	25,939	2,162	Nebraska	16	169,350	10,584
Georgia St.	15	17,678	1,179	Nevada	16	142,442	8,903
Georgia Tech	17	156,247	9,191	UNLV	20	227,074	11,354
Gonzaga	13	83,272	6,406	New Hampshire	11	10,643	968
Grambling	11	21,650	1,968	New Mexico	18	231,346	12,853
Green Bay	16	59,826	3,739	New Mexico St.	20	188,254	9,413
Hampton	12	25,668	2,139	New Orleans	14	7,286	520
Hartford	12	12,485	1,040	Niagara	15	25,058	1,671
Harvard	13	16,255	1,250	Nicholls St.	10	3,612	361
Hawaii	16	102,959	6,435	Norfolk St.	11	22,157	2,014
High Point	16	20,033	1,252	North Carolina	17	351,785	20,693
Hofstra	11	39,854	3,623	N.C. A&T	11	33,280	3,025
Holy Cross	14	42,611	3,044	UNC Asheville	13	13,119	1,009
Houston	14	59,902	4,279	UNC Greensboro	14	20,911	1,494
Howard	11	15,254	1,387	North Carolina St.	20	279,035	13,952
Idaho	14	19,371	1,384	UNC Wilmington	12	62,816	5,235
Idaho St.	12	34,170	2,848	North Texas	16	33,065	2,067
Ill.-Chicago	14	51,677	3,691	Northeastern	12	15,290	1,274
Illinois	17	282,506	16,618	Northern Ariz.	13	19,381	1,491
Illinois St.	15	76,380	5,092	Northern Ill.	13	20,760	1,597
Indiana	15	247,103	16,474	UNI	14	88,170	6,298
Indiana St.	16	69,243	4,328	Northwestern	18	82,282	4,571
IPFW	13	19,386	1,491	Northwestern St.	12	24,848	2,071
IUPUI	12	17,241	1,437	Notre Dame	18	162,485	9,027
Iona	11	21,160	1,924	Oakland	12	28,005	2,334
Iowa	16	195,139	12,196	Ohio	12	54,025	4,502
Iowa St.	17	212,310	12,489	Ohio St.	18	315,539	17,530
Jackson St.	10	24,969	2,497	Oklahoma	16	160,371	10,023
Jacksonville	13	24,807	1,908	Oklahoma St.	18	234,142	13,008
Jacksonville St.	13	30,306	2,331	Old Dominion	17	105,851	6,227
James Madison	14	46,230	3,302	Oral Roberts	14	90,775	6,484
Kansas	18	293,400	16,300	Oregon	18	151,576	8,421
Kansas St.	17	209,123	12,301	Oregon St.	19	98,128	5,165
Kent St.	13	43,614	3,355	Pacific	12	42,224	3,519
Kentucky	16	374,737	23,421	Penn	14	68,791	4,914
La Salle	18	43,615	2,423	Penn St.	19	151,785	7,989
Lafayette	13	27,465	2,113	Pepperdine	12	15,028	1,252
Lamar	14	50,107	3,579	Pittsburgh	18	208,997	11,611
Lehigh	14	19,065	1,362	Portland	16	31,059	1,941
Liberty	15	29,765	1,984	Portland St.	15	10,898	727
Lipscomb	14	20,581	1,470	Prairie View	11	13,348	1,213
Long Beach St.	13	25,636	1,972	Princeton	11	30,719	2,793
Long Island	13	7,991	615	Providence	19	159,798	8,410
LSU	18	180,038	10,002	Purdue	17	192,984	11,352
Louisiana Tech	11	25,164	2,288	Quinnipiac	14	23,621	1,687
La.-Lafayette	14	37,153	2,654	Radford	11	15,063	1,369
La.-Monroe	14	27,322	1,952	Rhode Island	15	67,293	4,486
Louisville	20	369,763	18,488	Rice	15	22,160	1,477
Loyola (Ill.)	16	45,603	2,850	Richmond	16	64,367	4,023
Loyola (Md.)	12	26,943	2,245	Rider	13	19,196	1,477
Loyola Marymount	13	31,114	2,393	Robert Morris	15	15,881	1,059
Maine	11	15,545	1,413	Rutgers	16	87,253	5,453
Manhattan	14	23,623	1,687	Sacramento St.	13	10,512	809
Marist	14	38,666	2,762	Sacred Heart	13	11,059	851
Marquette	20	306,893	15,345	St. Bonaventure	14	48,388	3,456
Marshall	14	49,617	3,544	St. Francis (N.Y.)	12	3,564	297
Maryland	19	319,616	16,822	St. Francis (Pa.)	15	21,572	1,438
UMBC	12	23,033	1,919	St. John's (N.Y.)	19	131,477	6,920
Md.-East. Shore	12	20,725	1,727	St. Joseph's	14	59,435	4,245
Massachusetts	14	83,542	5,967	St. Louis	15	145,002	9,667
McNeese St.	13	8,782	676	St. Mary's (Cal.)	17	42,065	2,474
Memphis	19	276,014	14,527	St. Peter's	13	11,478	883
Mercer	14	15,898	1,136	Sam Houston St.	13	25,569	1,967
Miami (Fla.)	15	51,974	3,465	Samford	13	21,161	1,628
Miami (Ohio)	13	42,253	3,250	San Diego	14	31,139	2,224
Michigan	21	209,327	9,968	San Diego St.	16	125,135	7,821
Michigan St.	19	280,421	14,759	San Francisco	12	29,104	2,425
Middle Tenn.	13	53,632	4,126	San Jose St.	11	20,627	1,875
Milwaukee	14	47,167	3,369	Santa Clara	16	35,602	2,225
Minnesota	17	186,554	10,974	Savannah St.	14	15,407	1,101
Mississippi	17	91,895	5,406	Seton Hall	16	106,169	6,636
Mississippi St.	19	168,763	8,882	Siena	14	81,670	5,834
Mississippi Val.	11	22,386	2,035	South Ala.	14	47,904	3,422
Missouri	19	156,612	8,243	South Carolina	17	218,240	12,838
Missouri St.	17	121,984	7,176	South Carolina St.	13	12,179	937
UMKC	13	19,568	1,505	South Fla.	15	57,781	3,852
Monmouth	13	23,219	1,786	Southeast Mo. St.	13	46,258	3,558
Montana	16	64,653	4,041	Southeastern La.	11	12,120	1,102
Montana St.	14	42,339	3,024				

School	G	Attendance	Average
Southern California	18	104,357	5,798
Southern Ill.	13	100,655	7,743
SMU	16	29,406	1,838
Southern Miss.	18	62,654	3,481
Southern U.	12	9,805	817
Southern Utah	14	36,453	2,604
Stanford	17	120,204	7,071
Stephen F. Austin	15	30,313	2,021
Stetson	13	26,292	2,022
Stony Brook	13	22,239	1,711
Syracuse	22	473,353	21,516
Temple	14	60,365	4,312
Tennessee	16	314,571	19,661
Tennessee St.	13	36,140	2,780
Tennessee Tech	14	36,680	2,620
Tenn.-Martin	14	26,152	1,868
Texas	16	207,504	12,969
Texas A&M	19	186,420	9,812
A&M-Corpus Christi	14	36,978	2,641
TCU	17	63,448	3,732
Texas Southern	13	12,864	990
Texas St.	15	17,997	1,200
Texas Tech	16	160,155	10,010
Texas-Arlington	12	6,046	504
UTEP	18	156,729	8,707
Tex.-Pan American	13	15,739	1,211
UTSA	14	15,990	1,142
Toledo	11	63,265	5,751
Towson	14	24,927	1,781
Troy	12	25,673	2,139
Tulane	16	32,065	2,004
Tulsa	18	97,656	5,425
UCLA	16	166,843	10,428
Utah	15	142,833	9,522
Utah St.	14	118,131	8,438
Valparaiso	12	42,240	3,520
Vanderbilt	17	204,511	12,030
Vermont	13	37,054	2,850
Villanova	14	149,884	10,706
Virginia	17	229,858	13,521
VCU	14	78,963	5,640
VMI	13	25,152	1,935
Virginia Tech	15	147,330	9,822
Wagner	14	18,663	1,333
Wake Forest	17	174,992	10,294
Washington	19	188,305	9,911
Washington St.	15	107,653	7,177
Weber St.	15	68,952	4,597
West Virginia	18	169,557	9,420
Western Caro.	11	22,097	2,009
Western Ill.	14	13,944	996
Western Ky.	15	78,435	5,229
Western Mich.	13	41,085	3,160
Wichita St.	15	157,170	10,478
William & Mary	16	39,245	2,453
Winthrop	15	60,009	4,001
Wisconsin	19	326,610	17,190
Wofford	12	15,600	1,300
Wright St.	15	87,962	5,864
Wyoming	14	84,963	6,069
Xavier	15	148,650	9,910
Yale	13	21,569	1,659
Youngstown St.	14	38,311	2,737

RECLASSIFYING TEAMS TO DIVISION I

School	G	Attendance	Average
UC Davis	11	20,113	1,828
Central Ark.	13	15,225	1,171
Kennesaw St.	13	12,515	963
Longwood	12	11,134	928
NJIT	12	5,790	483
North Dakota St.	14	36,745	2,625
North Fla.	14	10,618	758
Northern Colo.	12	8,957	746
South Dakota St.	12	22,199	1,850
Winston-Salem	6	15,689	2,615

LARGEST DIVISION I AVERAGE ATTENDANCE INCREASE FROM PREVIOUS YEAR

Rank	School	G	2007 Avg.	2006 Avg.	Change in Avg.
1.	Virginia	17	13,521	7,796	5,725
2.	Kansas St.	17	12,301	7,664	4,637

3.	South Carolina	17	12,838	9,090	3,748
4.	Washington St.	15	7,177	3,945	3,232
5.	New Mexico St.	20	9,413	6,525	2,888
6.	Texas Tech	16	10,010	7,279	2,731
7.	George Mason	13	6,834	4,533	2,301
8.	Ohio St.	18	17,530	15,389	2,141
9.	Creighton	14	15,909	13,900	2,009
10.	Butler	15	5,734	3,760	1,974
11.	Southern California	18	5,798	3,932	1,866
12.	Alabama	16	12,285	10,503	1,782
13.	Arkansas	16	16,720	14,958	1,762
14.	Tennessee	16	19,661	17,954	1,707
15.	Texas A&M	19	9,812	8,133	1,679
16.	Toledo	11	5,751	4,095	1,656
17.	Stanford	17	7,071	5,438	1,633
18.	Mississippi	17	5,406	3,835	1,571
19.	UCLA	16	10,428	8,894	1,534
20.	Oklahoma St.	18	13,008	11,591	1,417
21.	Marquette	20	15,345	13,998	1,347
22.	UNLV	20	11,354	10,040	1,314
23.	Fresno St.	18	11,713	10,407	1,306
24.	Canisius	13	2,319	1,107	1,212
25.	Drake	15	5,458	4,267	1,191
26.	Air Force	17	5,064	3,882	1,182
27.	Nebraska	16	10,584	9,417	1,167
28.	UCF	16	2,706	1,541	1,165
29.	La.-Monroe	14	1,952	792	1,160
30.	Penn St.	19	7,989	6,830	1,159

DIVISION I ALL GAMES ATTENDANCE (HOME, ROAD, NEUTRAL)

Rank	School	Attendance
1.	Ohio St.	747,457
2.	North Carolina	655,139
3.	Syracuse	650,811
4.	Florida	627,866
5.	Kentucky	623,163
6.	Kansas	582,761
7.	Louisville	570,799
8.	Wisconsin	569,555
9.	Tennessee	561,304
10.	Illinois	547,357
11.	Maryland	518,752
12.	Georgetown	508,597
13.	Michigan St.	502,755
14.	North Carolina St.	498,555
15.	Pittsburgh	489,703
16.	Indiana	487,674
17.	Marquette	479,873
18.	Arkansas	464,406
19.	Texas	461,917
20.	Memphis	457,350
21.	Connecticut	436,818
22.	UCLA	431,852
23.	Oklahoma St.	428,349
24.	Creighton	421,955

DIVISION II

Rank	School	G/S	Attendance	Average
1.	Central Mo. St.	18	65,520	3,640
2.	Winona St.	21	70,926	3,377
3.	Virginia St.	12	38,849	3,237
4.	Northern St.	18	56,886	3,160
5.	South Dakota	15	41,923	2,795
6.	Augustana (S.D.)	14	37,671	2,691
7.	Washburn	11	29,170	2,652
8.	St. Cloud St.	15	35,712	2,381
9.	Benedict	14	32,740	2,339
10.	Cal St. Bakersfield	11	25,006	2,273
11.	Neb.-Kearney	13	29,426	2,264
12.	Southern Ind.	18	40,284	2,238
13.	Emporia St.	17	37,306	2,194
14.	North Dakota	12	26,258	2,188
15.	Elizabeth City St.	14	28,889	2,064
16.	Midwestern St.	16	32,322	2,020
17.	Minn. St. Mankato	16	32,202	2,013
18.	Mo. Western St.	13	25,866	1,990
19.	Ky. Wesleyan	17	33,450	1,968
20.	Alas. Anchorage	17	33,248	1,956
21.	Southwest Minn. St.	15	29,325	1,955
22.	Harding	14	27,181	1,942
23.	Fort Hays St.	14	26,017	1,858
24.	Tarleton St.	17	31,102	1,830
25.	Johnson C. Smith	12	19,067	1,589
26.	Pittsburg St.	13	19,570	1,505

Rank	School	G/S	Attendance	Average
27.	Fla. Gulf Coast	23	32,856	1,429
28.	Central Wash.	8	10,784	1,348
29.	Findlay	21	27,929	1,330
30.	Fayetteville St.	13	17,145	1,319

DIVISION III

Rank	School	G/S	Attendance	Average
1.	Hope	18	52,719	2,928
2.	Ill. Wesleyan	10	24,700	2,470
3.	Calvin	14	29,252	2,089
4.	Wooster	16	26,658	1,666
5.	Lincoln (Pa.)	10	13,908	1,390
6.	Wis.-Stevens Point	11	15,154	1,377
7.	Otterbein	11	14,956	1,359
8.	Lawrence	13	16,869	1,297
9.	Maryville (Tenn.)	11	14,244	1,294
10.	Willamette	8	9,500	1,187
11.	Wittenberg	18	21,213	1,178
12.	Wis.-Stout	14	16,045	1,146
13.	Puget Sound	13	14,827	1,140
14.	New York U.	12	13,379	1,114
15.	Mississippi Col.	16	17,593	1,099
16.	Chris. Newport	19	20,705	1,089
17.	Wartburg	12	12,825	1,068
18.	Augustana (Ill.)	14	14,809	1,057
19.	Buena Vista	10	10,350	1,035
20.	Wis.-Whitewater	15	15,063	1,004
21.	Muskingum	12	11,963	996
22.	St. Thomas (Minn.)	13	12,250	942
23.	Capital	12	11,240	936
24.	Fredonia St.	11	10,092	917
25.	Wis.-Platteville	12	10,951	912
26.	Lebanon Valley	11	9,906	900
27.	Howard Payne	14	12,454	889
28.	Baldwin-Wallace	12	10,540	878
29.	Whitworth	10	8,750	875
30.	Louisiana Col.	11	9,106	827

All Time Attendance Leaders

DIVISION I

CONFERENCE LEADERS BY TOTAL ATTENDANCE

Conference	Season	Teams	Attendance	P/G Avg.
Big East	†2007	16	3,259,992	11,164
Big East	†2006	16	2,964,418	11,061
Big Ten	2007	11	2,564,662	12,760
Southeastern	2007	12	2,562,073	11,972
Atlantic Coast	2007	12	2,434,902	11,118
Big Ten	†2001	11	2,342,022	13,383
Big Ten	2006	11	2,277,085	12,581
Atlantic Coast	2006	12	2,277,076	11,273
Big 12	2007	12	2,261,697	10,719
Big Ten	†2002	11	2,258,255	13,362
Big Ten	†2000	11	2,255,913	13,428
Big Ten	†2005	11	2,255,332	12,530
Big Ten	†2003	11	2,254,658	12,526
Southeastern	†2004	12	2,230,546	11,439
Southeastern	2006	12	2,205,320	11,082
Big Ten	†1999	11	2,204,556	13,361
Big East	2004	14	2,184,497	9,296
Big Ten	†1998	11	2,166,264	12,450
Big Ten	†1993	11	2,163,693	12,728
Southeastern	2001	12	2,163,525	10,982

DIVISION I

CONFERENCE LEADERS BY AVERAGE ATTENDANCE

Conference	Season	Teams	Attendance	P/G Avg.
Big Ten	†1990	10	2,017,407	13,449
Big Ten	†2000	11	2,255,913	13,428
Big Ten	†2001	11	2,342,022	13,383
Big Ten	†2002	11	2,258,255	13,362
Big Ten	†1999	11	2,204,556	13,361
Big Ten	†1991	10	2,042,836	13,095
Big Ten	†1992	10	1,994,144	12,865
Big Ten	†2004	11	2,122,586	12,787
Big Ten	†1996	11	2,106,810	12,769
Big Ten	†2007	11	2,564,662	12,760
Big Ten	†1993	11	2,163,693	12,728
Big Ten	†1995	11	2,058,763	12,708
Big Ten	†1994	11	2,107,600	12,696

Conference	Season	Teams	Attendance	P/G Avg.
Big Ten	†1989	10	1,971,110	12,635
Big Ten	†2006	11	2,277,085	12,581
Big East	1991	9	1,771,386	12,563
Big Ten	†2005	11	2,255,332	12,530
Big Ten	†2003	11	2,254,658	12,526
Big Ten	†1998	11	2,166,264	12,450
Big Ten	†1988	10	1,925,617	12,423

DIVISION II

CONFERENCE LEADERS BY TOTAL ATTENDANCE

Conference	Season	Teams	Attendance	P/G Avg.
North Central Intercollegiate	†1992	10	482,213	3,014
North Central Intercollegiate	†1991	10	438,746	2,868
North Central Intercollegiate	†1989	10	438,403	2,923
North Central Intercollegiate	†1990	10	436,292	2,889
North Central Intercollegiate	†1988	10	413,956	2,797
North Central Intercollegiate	†1993	10	408,624	2,919
Central Intercollegiate	1990	14	395,884	2,262
North Central Intercollegiate	†1987	10	393,940	2,626
North Central Intercollegiate	†1984	10	392,154	2,801
Central Intercollegiate	1991	14	384,978	2,139
North Central Intercollegiate	†1995	10	382,042	2,497
Central Intercollegiate	†1980	13	380,798	2,457
North Central Intercollegiate	†1985	10	380,087	2,639
North Central Intercollegiate	†1986	10	379,701	2,601
Central Intercollegiate	1989	14	378,046	2,211
Central Intercollegiate	†1981	14	377,322	2,233
Central Intercollegiate	†1979	12	375,370	2,760
Central Intercollegiate	1988	14	374,803	2,142
Central Intercollegiate	†1982	14	373,236	2,290
Central Intercollegiate	1987	14	370,957	2,169

DIVISION II

CONFERENCE LEADERS BY AVERAGE ATTENDANCE

Conference	Season	Teams	Attendance	P/G Avg.
North Central Intercollegiate	†1992	10	482,213	3,014
North Central Intercollegiate	†1989	10	438,403	2,923
North Central Intercollegiate	†1993	10	408,624	2,919
North Central Intercollegiate	†1990	10	436,292	2,889
North Central Intercollegiate	†1991	10	438,746	2,868
North Central Intercollegiate	†1981	8	312,410	2,840
North Central Intercollegiate	†1984	10	392,154	2,801
North Central Intercollegiate	†1988	10	413,956	2,797
Mid-Continent	†1980	5	189,193	2,782
North Central Intercollegiate	1980	8	302,752	2,778
Central Intercollegiate	†1979	12	375,370	2,760
North Central Intercollegiate	1979	7	257,030	2,677
North Central Intercollegiate	†1985	10	380,087	2,639
North Central Intercollegiate	†1994	10	362,572	2,627
North Central Intercollegiate	†1987	10	393,940	2,626
North Central Intercollegiate	†1982	8	290,995	2,622
North Central Intercollegiate	†1986	10	379,701	2,601
North Central Intercollegiate	†2004	8	301,111	2,574
North Central Intercollegiate	†1983	8	356,777	2,567
North Central Intercollegiate	†2002	10	369,858	2,551

DIVISION III

CONFERENCE LEADERS BY TOTAL ATTENDANCE

Conference	Season	Teams	Attendance	P/G Avg.
Wisconsin State University	†1979	9	183,122	1,621
Wisconsin State University	†1990	9	170,276	1,362
Wisconsin State University	†1986	9	164,207	1,368
Wisconsin State University	†1982	9	160,860	1,411
Wisconsin State University	†1980	9	154,665	1,333
Wisconsin State University	†1985	9	153,102	1,255
Minnesota Intercollegiate	†1987	11	153,090	1,169
Wisconsin State University	†1991	9	152,289	1,238
Minnesota Intercollegiate	†1984	11	148,041	1,130
Wisconsin State University	1984	9	142,859	1,181
Illinois & Wisconsin	1980	9	138,820	1,251
Wisconsin State University	†1992	9	135,735	1,122
Wisconsin State University	†1993	9	130,870	1,091
Minnesota Intercollegiate	1990	9	120,849	1,079
Minnesota Intercollegiate	1992	11	118,504	898
Middle Atlantic	†1998	16	115,253	597
Middle Atlantic	†2003	16	111,519	575
Michigan Intercollegiate	†2000	8	111,310	1,091
Illinois & Wisconsin	†2001	8	110,868	1,131
Middle Atlantic	2000	16	110,833	568

DIVISION III

CONFERENCE LEADERS BY AVERAGE ATTENDANCE

Conference	Season	Teams	Attendance	P/G Avg.
Wisconsin State University	†1979	9	183,122	1,621
Wisconsin State University	†1982	9	160,860	1,411
Wisconsin State University	†1986	9	164,207	1,368
Wisconsin State University	†1990	9	170,276	1,362
Wisconsin State University	†1980	9	154,665	1,333
Wisconsin State University	†1985	9	153,102	1,255
Illinois & Wisconsin	1980	9	138,820	1,251
Michigan Intercollegiate	†2002	7	98,263	1,244
Wisconsin State University	†1991	9	152,289	1,238
Michigan Intercollegiate	†1993	7	97,624	1,236
Michigan Intercollegiate	†2006	7	107,400	1,234
Michigan Intercollegiate	†1994	7	97,418	1,203
Michigan Intercollegiate	1990	7	84,548	1,191
Michigan Intercollegiate	†1995	7	86,353	1,183
Wisconsin State University	†1984	9	142,859	1,181
Minnesota Intercollegiate	†1987	11	153,090	1,169
Michigan Intercollegiate	†1992	7	89,549	1,163
Michigan Intercollegiate	†2001	7	95,378	1,163
Illinois & Wisconsin	2001	8	110,868	1,131
Minnesota Intercollegiate	1984	11	148,041	1,130

DIVISION I

TEAM LEADERS BY TOTAL ATTENDANCE

Conference	Season	Teams	Attendance	P/G Avg.
Syracuse	†1989	19	537,949	28,313
Syracuse	†1986	19	498,850	26,255
Syracuse	†1991	17	497,179	29,246
Syracuse	†1990	16	478,686	29,918
Syracuse	†1987	19	474,214	24,959
Syracuse	†2007	22	473,353	21,516
Syracuse	†1988	16	461,223	28,826
Syracuse	†1992	17	460,752	27,103
Kentucky	1986	19	426,740	22,460
Kentucky	†1994	17	419,039	24,649
Syracuse	†2005	18	413,605	22,978
Syracuse	†2006	19	410,153	21,587
Syracuse	†1993	16	405,620	25,351
Louisville	2006	22	402,963	18,316
Kentucky	1992	17	396,688	23,335
Kentucky	†1988	17	393,725	23,160
Syracuse	†1985	15	388,049	25,870
Syracuse	†1995	16	387,925	24,245
Kentucky	1993	16	382,869	23,929
Syracuse	†1984	17	380,465	22,380

DIVISION I

TEAM LEADERS BY AVERAGE ATTENDANCE

Conference	Season	Teams	Attendance	P/G Avg.
Syracuse	†1990	16	478,686	29,918
Syracuse	†1991	17	497,179	29,246
Syracuse	†1988	16	461,223	28,826
Syracuse	†1989	19	537,949	28,313
Syracuse	†1992	17	460,752	27,103
Syracuse	†1986	19	498,850	26,255
Syracuse	†1985	15	388,049	25,870
Syracuse	†1993	16	405,620	25,351
Syracuse	†1987	19	474,214	24,959
Syracuse	†1994	17	419,039	24,649
Syracuse	†1995	16	387,925	24,245
Kentucky	†1998	12	287,354	23,946
Kentucky	1993	16	382,869	23,929
Kentucky	†1996	13	310,633	23,895
Kentucky	1995	13	309,477	23,806
Kentucky	†1997	13	309,457	23,804
Kentucky	†1983	15	356,776	23,785
Kentucky	†1984	16	380,453	23,778
Kentucky	1991	14	331,404	23,672
Kentucky	†1981	15	354,996	23,666

DIVISION II

TEAM LEADERS BY TOTAL ATTENDANCE

Conference	Season	Teams	Attendance	P/G Avg.
Norfolk St.	†1984	18	119,925	6,663
Southeast Mo. St.	†1989	21	106,102	5,052
Southeast Mo. St.	†1988	20	104,538	5,227
Norfolk St.	†1983	17	101,854	5,991
Southeast Mo. St.	†1990	19	100,448	5,287
Norfolk St.	†1985	16	97,854	6,116
Norfolk St.	†1979	19	97,700	4,984
Ky. Wesleyan	1984	19	96,344	5,071

Conference	Season	Teams	Attendance	P/G Avg.
North Dakota St.	1983	15	90,850	6,057
Ky. Wesleyan	1985	19	88,612	4,664
Ky. Wesleyan	1990	20	87,371	4,369
Southeast Mo. St.	†1991	16	85,927	5,370
South Dakota St.	†1998	16	85,599	5,350
Ky. Wesleyan	1988	19	84,009	4,422
Ky. Wesleyan	†1982	20	84,008	4,200
Ky. Wesleyan	1987	19	82,459	4,340
Alabama A&M	†1995	16	82,249	5,141
Alabama A&M	†1994	17	80,877	4,757
North Dakota St.	1984	15	79,000	5,267
Ky. Wesleyan	1983	17	78,895	4,461

DIVISION II

TEAM LEADERS BY AVERAGE ATTENDANCE

Conference	Season	Teams	Attendance	P/G Avg.
Norfolk St.	†1984	18	119,925	6,663
Norfolk St.	†1985	16	97,854	6,116
North Dakota St.	†1983	15	90,850	6,057
Norfolk St.	1983	17	101,854	5,991
Southeast Mo. St.	†1991	16	85,927	5,370
South Dakota St.	†1998	16	85,599	5,350
North Dakota St.	†1981	13	69,000	5,308
Southeast Mo. St.	†1990	19	100,448	5,287
North Dakota St.	1984	15	79,000	5,267
Southeast Mo. St.	†1988	20	104,538	5,227
Alabama A&M	†1995	16	82,249	5,141
Ky. Wesleyan	1984	19	96,344	5,071
Southeast Mo. St.	†1989	21	106,102	5,052
Norfolk St.	†1979	19	94,700	4,984
Norfolk St.	1990	14	69,536	4,967
South Dakota St.	†1996	14	69,229	4,945
North Dakota	†1992	13	64,261	4,943
Norfolk St.	†1980	15	73,750	4,917
Alabama A&M	1992	15	73,633	4,909
North Dakota St.	1985	15	73,100	4,873

DIVISION III

TEAM LEADERS BY TOTAL ATTENDANCE

Conference	Season	Teams	Attendance	P/G Avg.
Hope	†2006	18	52,719	2,928
Calvin	†2000	14	48,941	3,496
Calvin	†1993	12	48,215	4,018
St. John's (Minn.)	†1978	15	45,000	3,000
Hope	†2007	15	43,848	2,923
Calvin	†2001	13	43,796	3,369
Wis.-Stevens Point	†1982	14	41,000	2,929
Wis.-Eau Claire	†1989	17	40,900	2,406
Otterbein	†1983	17	40,900	2,406
Otterbein	†1991	18	40,101	2,228
Wis.-Whitewater	†1986	16	40,000	2,500
Wis.-Eau Claire	†1987	17	39,800	2,341
Concordia (Minn.)	1982	14	39,700	2,836
Augustana (Ill.)	1982	14	38,700	2,764
Calvin	†1992	14	38,600	2,757
Calvin	†1994	14	38,271	2,734
Scranton	†1977	14	37,900	2,707
Wis.-Eau Claire	1991	18	37,750	2,097
Ill. Wesleyan	†1995	15	37,700	2,513
Calvin	†2002	13	37,613	2,893

DIVISION III

TEAM LEADERS BY AVERAGE ATTENDANCE

Conference	Season	Teams	Attendance	P/G Avg.
Calvin	†1993	12	48,215	4,018
Calvin	†1978	10	36,300	3,630
Calvin	†2000	14	48,941	3,496
Calvin	†2001	13	43,796	3,369
Augustana (Ill.)	†1983	12	36,400	3,033
St. John's (Minn.)	1978	15	45,000	3,000
Wis.-Stevens Point	†1982	14	41,000	2,929
Hope	†2006	18	52,719	2,928
Hope	†2007	15	43,848	2,923
Savannah St.	†1980	6	17,502	2,917
Calvin	†2002	13	37,613	2,893
Potsdam St.	†1981	11	31,600	2,873
Savannah St.	†1979	10	28,700	2,870
Concordia-M'head	†1987	13	37,300	2,869
Concordia (Minn.)	1982	14	39,700	2,836
Calvin	†1997	10	28,206	2,821
Calvin	†1995	11	30,717	2,792
Augustana (Ill.)	1982	14	38,700	2,764

Conference	Season	Teams	Attendance	P/G Avg.
Calvin	†1992	14	38,600	2,757
Calvin	†1994	14	37,271	2,734

†national leader

Annual NCAA Attendance

ALL DIVISIONS

Season	Teams	Attendance	Per Game Average	Change in Avg.	
1977	717	23,324,040	2,710	—	—
1978	726	23,590,952	2,678	Down	32
1979	718	24,482,516	2,757	Up	79
1980	715	24,861,722	2,765	Up	8
1981	730	25,159,358	2,737	Down	28
1982	741	25,416,017	2,727	Down	10
1983	755	26,122,785	2,706	Down	21
1984	750	26,271,613	2,728	Up	22
1985	753	26,584,426	2,712	Down	16
1986	760	26,368,815	2,654	Down	58
1987	760	26,797,644	2,698	Up	44
1988	761	27,452,948	2,777	Up	79
1989	772	28,270,260	2,814	Up	37
1990	767	28,740,819	*2,860	Up	46
1991	796	29,249,583	2,796	Down	64
1992	813	29,378,161	2,747	Down	49
1993	831	28,527,348	2,703	Down	44
1994	858	28,390,491	2,604	Down	99
1995	868	28,548,158	2,581	Down	23
1996	866	28,225,352	2,563	Down	18
1997	865	27,738,284	2,508	Down	55
1998	895	28,031,879	2,445	Down	63
1999	926	28,505,428	2,401	Down	44
2000	932	29,024,876	2,410	Up	9
2001	937	28,949,093	2,392	Down	18
2002	936	29,395,240	2,373	Down	19
2003	967	30,124,304	2,339	Down	34
2004	981	30,760,510	2,355	Up	16
2005	983	30,568,645	2,327	Down	28
2006	*984	30,939,715	2,351	Up	24
2007	982	*32,835,863	2,449	Up	98

DIVISION I

Season	Teams	Attendance	Per Game Average	Change in Avg.	
1976	235	15,059,892	4,759	—	—
1977	245	16,469,250	5,021	Up	262
1978	254	17,669,080	5,124	Up	103
1979	257	18,649,383	5,271	Up	147
1980	261	19,052,743	5,217	Down	54
1981	264	19,355,690	5,131	Down	86
1982	273	19,789,706	5,191	Up	60
1983	274	20,488,437	5,212	Up	21
1984	276	20,715,426	5,243	Up	31
1985	282	21,394,261	5,258	Up	15
1986	283	21,244,519	5,175	Down	83
1987	290	21,756,709	5,205	Up	30
1988	290	22,463,476	5,443	Up	238
1989	293	23,059,429	5,565	Up	122
1990	292	23,581,823	5,721	Up	156
1991	295	23,777,437	*5,735	Up	14
1992	298	23,893,993	5,643	Down	92
1993	298	23,321,655	5,635	Down	8
1994	301	23,275,158	5,571	Down	64
1995	302	23,560,495	5,641	Up	70
1996	305	23,542,652	5,588	Down	53
1997	305	23,190,856	5,485	Down	103
1998	306	23,282,774	5,459	Down	26
1999	310	23,587,824	5,451	Down	8
2000	318	24,281,774	5,386	Down	65
2001	318	24,100,555	5,311	Down	75
2002	321	24,499,611	5,287	Down	24
2003	325	25,001,678	5,372	Up	85
2004	*326	25,548,468	5,443	Up	71
2005	*326	25,366,317	5,334	Down	109
2006	*326	25,808,346	5,426	Up	92
2007	325	*27,705,912	5,548	Up	122

DIVISION II

Season	Teams	Attendance	Per Game Average	Change in Avg.	
1977	177	*3,846,907	*1,811	—	—
1978	173	3,168,419	1,515	Down	296
1979	172	3,295,149	1,535	Up	20
1980	177	3,324,670	1,479	Down	56
1981	190	3,543,766	1,486	Up	7
1982	190	3,329,518	1,391	Down	95
1983	195	3,364,184	1,324	Down	67
1984	189	3,199,307	1,306	Down	18
1985	181	2,988,083	1,255	Down	51
1986	184	2,946,020	1,204	Down	51
1987	179	2,893,392	1,220	Up	16
1988	175	2,902,400	1,242	Up	22
1989	189	3,157,464	1,273	Up	31
1990	189	3,104,462	1,223	Down	50
1991	204	3,388,278	1,221	Down	2
1992	214	3,395,684	1,188	Down	33
1993	220	3,201,765	1,145	Down	43
1994	243	3,219,979	1,036	Down	109
1995	244	3,125,974	992	Down	44
1996	242	2,918,802	938	Down	54
1997	242	2,873,311	915	Down	23
1998	252	2,976,420	904	Down	8
1999	266	3,063,436	892	Down	15
2000	258	2,942,477	882	Down	10
2001	261	2,951,969	877	Down	5
2002	258	2,990,641	888	Up	11
2003	269	3,076,804	855	Down	33
2004	*271	3,107,628	864	Up	9
2005	268	3,054,549	854	Down	10
2006	264	2,913,513	825	Down	29
2007	262	2,892,820	815	Down	10

DIVISION III

Season	Teams	Attendance	Per Game Average	Change in Avg.	
1977	295	*2,881,400	*912	—	—
1978	299	2,632,678	816	Down	96
1979	289	2,427,688	770	Down	46
1980	277	2,387,142	783	Up	13
1981	276	2,132,000	693	Down	90
1982	278	2,183,895	711	Up	18
1983	286	2,148,736	685	Down	26
1984	286	2,233,340	701	Up	16
1985	290	2,081,452	629	Down	72
1986	293	2,053,693	615	Down	14
1987	291	2,021,459	606	Down	9
1988	296	1,970,823	583	Down	23
1989	290	1,935,058	573	Down	10
1990	286	1,939,795	581	Up	8
1991	297	1,967,087	564	Down	1
1992	301	1,962,598	553	Down	11
1993	313	1,883,283	531	Down	22
1994	314	1,741,867	493	Down	38
1995	322	1,802,301	487	Down	6
1996	319	1,730,357	472	Down	15
1997	318	1,626,240	444	Down	28
1998	337	1,736,409	447	Up	3
1999	350	1,824,391	446	Down	1
2000	356	1,750,621	426	Down	20
2001	358	1,846,043	444	Up	18
2002	357	1,804,209	424	Down	20
2003	373	1,869,592	426	Up	2
2004	*384	1,944,957	427	Up	1
2005	383	1,960,141	431	Up	4
2006	382	1,955,720	430	Down	1
2007	380	1,947,730	430	None	0

*record

Annual Conference Attendance Champions

DIVISION I

Season	Conference	Teams	Attendance	P/G Avg.
1976	Atlantic Coast	7	863,082	9,590
1977	Big Ten	10	1,346,889	9,977
1978	Big Ten	10	1,539,589	11,238
1979	Big Ten	10	1,713,380	12,238
1980	Big Ten	10	1,877,048	12,189
1981	Big Ten	10	1,779,892	12,026
1982	Big Ten	10	1,688,834	11,810
1983	Big Ten	10	1,747,910	11,499

Season	Conference	Teams	Attendance	P/G Avg.
1984	Big Ten	10	1,774,140	12,069
1985	Big Ten	10	1,911,325	12,097
1986	Big Ten	10	1,908,629	11,929
1987	Big Ten	10	1,805,263	11,877
1988	Big Ten	10	1,925,617	12,423
1989	Big Ten	10	1,971,110	12,635
1990	Big Ten	10	2,017,407	*13,449
1991	Big Ten	10	2,042,836	13,095
1992	Big Ten	10	1,994,144	12,865
1993	Big Ten	11	2,163,693	12,728
1994	Big Ten	11	2,107,600	12,696
1995	Big Ten	11	2,058,763	12,708
1996	Big Ten	11	2,106,810	12,769
1997	Big Ten	11	2,004,893	12,376
1998	Big Ten	11	2,166,264	12,450
1999	Big Ten	11	2,204,556	13,361
2000	Big Ten	11	2,255,913	13,428
2001	Big Ten	11	2,342,022	13,383
2002	Big Ten	11	2,258,255	13,362
2003	Big Ten	11	2,254,658	12,526
2004	Big Ten	11	2,122,586	12,787
2005	Big Ten	11	2,255,332	12,530
2006	Big Ten	11	2,277,085	12,581
2007	Big Ten	11	2,564,662	12,760

DIVISION II

Season	Conference	Teams	Attendance	P/G Avg.
1979	Central Intercollegiate	12	375,370	2,760
1980	Mid-Continent	5	189,193	2,782
1981	North Central Intercollegiate	8	312,410	2,840
1982	North Central Intercollegiate	8	290,995	2,622
1983	North Central Intercollegiate	8	356,777	2,567
1984	North Central Intercollegiate	10	392,154	2,801
1985	North Central Intercollegiate	10	380,087	2,639
1986	North Central Intercollegiate	10	379,701	2,601
1987	North Central Intercollegiate	10	393,940	2,626
1988	North Central Intercollegiate	10	413,956	2,797
1989	North Central Intercollegiate	10	438,403	2,923
1990	North Central Intercollegiate	10	436,292	2,889
1991	North Central Intercollegiate	10	438,746	2,868
1992	North Central Intercollegiate	10	*482,213	*3,014
1993	North Central Intercollegiate	10	408,624	2,919
1994	North Central Intercollegiate	10	362,572	2,627
1995	North Central Intercollegiate	10	382,042	2,497
1996	North Central Intercollegiate	10	341,119	2,336
1997	North Central Intercollegiate	10	319,703	2,160
1998	North Central Intercollegiate	10	315,918	2,225
1999	North Central Intercollegiate	10	299,228	2,050
2000	North Central Intercollegiate	10	300,257	2,114
2001	North Central Intercollegiate	10	300,822	2,118
2002	North Central Intercollegiate	10	369,858	2,551
2003	North Central Intercollegiate	9	328,903	2,473
2004	North Central Intercollegiate	8	301,111	2,574
2005	North Central Intercollegiate	7	229,745	2,252
2006	North Central Intercollegiate	7	197,739	1,920
2007	North Central Intercollegiate	7	198,653	1,948

DIVISION III

Season	Conference	Teams	Attendance	P/G Avg.
1990	Wisconsin State University	9	*170,276	*1,362
1991	Wisconsin State University	9	152,289	1,238
1992	Michigan Intercollegiate	7	89,549	1,163
1993	Michigan Intercollegiate	7	97,624	1,236
1994	Michigan Intercollegiate	7	97,418	1,203
1995	Michigan Intercollegiate	7	86,353	1,183
1996	Michigan Intercollegiate	7	80,376	1,058
1997	Michigan Intercollegiate	7	81,370	1,085
1998	Michigan Intercollegiate	8	91,267	941
1999	Michigan Intercollegiate	8	87,055	957
2000	Michigan Intercollegiate	8	111,310	1,091
2001	Michigan Intercollegiate	7	95,378	1,163
2002	Michigan Intercollegiate	7	98,263	1,244
2003	Michigan Intercollegiate	8	79,798	1,050
2004	Michigan Intercollegiate	8	88,153	1,049
2005	Michigan Intercollegiate	7	89,165	1,115
2006	Michigan Intercollegiate	7	107,400	1,234
2007	Michigan Intercollegiate	7	88,039	1,100

*record

Annual Team Attendance Champions

DIVISION I

Season	Champion	Games	Attendance	Avg.
1970	Illinois	11	157,206	14,291
1971	Illinois	11	177,408	16,128
1972	BYU	12	261,815	21,818
1973	BYU	14	260,102	18,579
1974	BYU	10	162,510	16,251
1975	Minnesota	13	219,047	16,850
1976	Indiana	12	202,700	16,892
1977	Kentucky	14	312,527	22,323
1978	Kentucky	16	373,367	23,335
1979	Kentucky	15	351,042	23,403
1980	Kentucky	15	352,511	23,501
1981	Kentucky	15	354,996	23,666
1982	Kentucky	16	371,093	23,193
1983	Kentucky	15	356,776	23,785
1984	Kentucky	16	380,453	23,778
1985	Syracuse	15	388,049	25,870
1986	Syracuse	19	498,850	26,255
1987	Syracuse	19	474,214	24,959
1988	Syracuse	16	461,223	28,826
1989	Syracuse	19	*537,949	28,313
1990	Syracuse	16	478,686	*29,918
1991	Syracuse	17	497,179	29,246
1992	Syracuse	17	460,752	27,103
1993	Syracuse	16	405,620	25,351
1994	Syracuse	17	419,039	24,649
1995	Syracuse	16	387,925	24,245
1996	Kentucky	13	310,633	23,895
1997	Kentucky	13	309,457	23,804
1998	Kentucky	12	287,354	23,946
1999	Kentucky	13	303,771	23,367
2000	Kentucky	14	314,267	22,448
2001	Kentucky	12	261,435	21,786
2002	Kentucky	15	315,203	21,014
2003	Kentucky	13	289,526	22,271
2004	Kentucky	13	295,227	22,710
2005	Syracuse	18	413,605	22,978
2006	Kentucky	15	341,445	22,763
2007	Kentucky	16	374,737	23,421

DIVISION I LARGEST INCREASE FROM PREVIOUS YEAR

Season	Champion	Games	Att. Avg.	Previous Yr. Avg.	Increase
1977	Kentucky	14	22,323	11,511	10,812
1978	Texas	15	12,583	5,846	6,737
1979	Illinois	13	14,209	8,719	5,490
1980	Missouri	16	9,460	6,624	2,836
1981	DePaul	14	15,410	5,308	10,102
1982	Georgetown	17	8,591	4,197	4,394
1983	Chattanooga	16	7,547	3,931	3,616
1984	UNLV	16	15,779	6,380	9,399
1985	Villanova	9	10,218	5,744	4,474
1986	North Carolina	15	15,838	9,954	5,884
1987	North Carolina	13	20,149	15,838	4,311
1988	Tennessee	16	20,823	12,191	8,632
1989	Texas	14	10,011	4,028	5,983
1990	Cincinnati	15	9,273	3,572	5,701
1991	Wright St.	15	8,503	2,716	5,787
1992	Memphis	16	16,142	10,935	5,207
1993	Boise St.	15	12,113	7,536	4,577
1994	Arkansas	16	20,134	8,975	*11,159
1995	St. Louis	16	17,714	13,008	4,706
1996	Memphis	17	14,235	9,765	4,470
1997	Wichita St.	15	9,449	5,528	3,921
1998	Temple	13	7,964	3,891	4,073
1999	Ohio St.	15	17,223	9,970	7,253
2000	North Carolina St.	20	16,535	10,800	5,735
2001	Oklahoma St.	12	12,044	5,907	6,137
2002	Texas Tech	17	13,743	9,557	4,186
2003	BYU	16	14,468	8,630	5,838
2004	UTEP	17	10,282	6,038	4,244
2005	Virginia Tech	16	9,405	6,342	3,063
2006	Tennessee	15	17,954	12,225	5,729
2007	Virginia	17	13,521	7,796	5,725

DIVISION I ALL GAMES (HOME, ROAD & NEUTRAL)

Season	Champion	Games	Attendance	Avg.
1978	Kentucky	30	586,250	19,542
1979	Kentucky	31	546,288	17,622
1980	Kentucky	35	563,160	16,090
1981	Kentucky	28	499,461	17,838
1982	Kentucky	30	541,786	18,060
1983	Kentucky	31	562,947	18,160
1984	Kentucky	34	633,618	18,636
1985	Syracuse	31	581,347	18,753
1986	Syracuse	32	641,146	20,036
1987	Syracuse	38	826,182	21,742
1988	Syracuse	35	719,910	20,569
1989	Syracuse	38	*855,053	*22,501
1990	Syracuse	33	716,945	21,726
1991	Syracuse	32	680,261	21,258
1992	Kentucky	36	709,078	19,697
1993	North Carolina	38	721,760	18,994
1994	Kentucky	34	647,722	19,051
1995	Arkansas	39	695,026	17,821
1996	Kentucky	36	725,884	20,163
1997	Kentucky	40	822,863	20,572
1998	Kentucky	39	784,614	20,118
1999	Kentucky	37	737,738	19,939
2000	Michigan St.	39	621,108	15,926
2001	Duke	39	650,550	16,681
2002	Indiana	37	644,641	17,423
2003	Syracuse	35	686,997	19,628
2004	Kentucky	32	663,298	20,728
2005	Illinois	39	711,798	18,251
2006	Syracuse	35	640,949	18,313
2007	Ohio St.	39	747,457	19,166

DIVISION II

Season	Champion	Avg.
1977	Evansville	4,576
1978	Norfolk St.	4,226
1979	Norfolk St.	4,984
1980	Norfolk St.	4,917
1981	North Dakota St.	5,300
1982	North Dakota St.	4,385
1983	North Dakota St.	6,057
1984	Norfolk St.	*6,663
1985	Norfolk St.	6,116
1986	St. Cloud St.	4,539
1987	North Dakota St.	4,820
1988	Southeast Mo. St.	5,227
1989	Southeast Mo. St.	5,052
1990	Southeast Mo. St.	5,287
1991	Southeast Mo. St.	5,370
1992	North Dakota	4,943
1993	Alabama A&M	4,748
1994	South Dakota	4,852
1995	Alabama A&M	5,141
1996	South Dakota St.	4,945
1997	South Dakota St.	4,423
1998	South Dakota St.	5,350
1999	Ky. Wesleyan	4,247
2000	South Dakota St.	4,077
2001	Morehouse	4,404
2002	South Dakota St.	4,449
2003	Neb.-Kearney	3,839
2004	South Dakota St.	3,375
2005	Virginia St.	3,471
2006	Northern St.	3,916
2007	Central Mo. St.	3,640

*record

DIVISION III

Season	Champion	Avg.
1977	Scranton	2,707
1978	Calvin	3,630
1979	Savannah St.	2,870
1980	Savannah St.	2,917
1981	Potsdam St.	2,873
1982	Wis.-Stevens Point	2,929
1983	Augustana (Ill.)	3,033
1984	Hope	2,144
1985	Wis.-Stevens Point	2,313
1986	Calvin	2,570
1987	Concordia-M'head	2,869
1988	Calvin	2,627
1989	Calvin	2,544
1990	Calvin	2,622
1991	Hope	2,480
1992	Calvin	2,757
1993	Calvin	*4,018
1994	Calvin	2,734
1995	Calvin	2,792
1996	Hope	2,409
1997	Calvin	2,821
1998	Ill. Wesleyan	2,615
1999	Hope	2,440
2000	Calvin	3,496
2001	Calvin	3,369
2002	Calvin	2,893
2003	Hope	2,383
2004	Hope	2,491
2005	Hope	2,462
2006	Hope	2,928
2007	Hope	2,923

*record

Annual NCAA Tournament Attendance

DIVISION I

Season	Sess.	Attend.	P/G Avg.
1939	5	15,025	3,005
1940	5	36,880	7,376
1941	5	48,055	9,611
1942	5	24,372	4,874
1943	5	56,876	11,375
1944	5	59,369	11,874
1945	5	67,780	13,556
1946	5	73,116	14,623
1947	5	72,959	14,592
1948	5	72,523	14,505
1949	5	66,077	13,215
1950	5	75,464	15,093
1951	9	110,645	12,294
1952	10	115,712	11,571
1953	14	127,149	9,082
1954	15	115,391	7,693
1955	15	116,983	7,799
1956	15	132,513	8,834
1957	14	108,891	7,778
1958	14	176,878	12,634
1959	14	161,809	11,558
1960	16	155,491	9,718
1961	14	169,520	12,109
1962	14	177,469	12,676
1963	14	153,065	10,933
1964	14	140,790	10,056
1965	13	140,673	10,821
1966	13	140,925	10,840
1967	14	159,570	11,398
1968	14	160,888	11,492
1969	15	165,712	11,047
1970	16	146,794	9,175
1971	16	207,200	12,950
1972	16	147,304	9,207
1973	16	163,160	10,198
1974	16	154,112	9,632
1975	18	183,857	10,214
1976	18	202,502	11,250
1977	18	241,610	13,423
1978	18	227,149	12,619
1979	22	262,101	11,914
1980	26	321,260	12,356
1981	26	347,414	13,362
1982	26	427,251	16,433
1983	28	364,356	13,013
1984	28	397,481	14,196
1985	34	422,519	12,427
1986	34	499,704	14,697
1987	34	654,744	19,257
1988	34	558,998	16,441
1989	34	613,242	18,037
1990	34	537,138	15,798
1991	34	665,707	19,580
1992	34	580,462	17,072
1993	34	707,719	20,815
1994	34	578,007	17,000
1995	34	539,440	15,866
1996	34	643,290	18,920
1997	34	634,584	18,664
1998	34	682,530	20,074
1999	34	*720,685	*21,197
2000	34	638,577	18,782
2001	35	596,075	17,031
2002	35	720,433	20,584
2003	35	715,080	20,431
2004	35	716,899	20,483
2005	35	689,317	19,695
2006	35	670,254	19,150
2007	35	696,992	19,914

*record

DIVISION II

Season	Sess.	Attend.	P/G Avg.
1977	22	*87,602	*3,982
1978	22	83,058	3,775
1979	22	66,446	3,020
1980	22	50,649	2,302
1981	22	69,470	3,158
1982	22	67,925	3,088
1983	22	70,335	3,197
1984	22	81,388	3,699
1985	22	81,476	3,703
1986	22	71,083	3,231
1987	22	77,934	3,542
1988	22	72,462	3,294
1989	20	69,008	3,450
1990	20	64,212	3,211
1991	20	59,839	2,992
1992	20	60,629	3,031
1993	20	56,125	2,806
1994	20	60,511	3,026
1995	36	86,767	2,410
1996	28	65,882	2,353
1997	28	66,626	2,380
1998	28	59,946	2,141
1999	28	49,144	1,755
2000	28	50,130	1,790
2001	28	60,418	2,158
2002	28	60,258	2,152
2003	36	51,054	1,418
2004	36	41,126	1,142
2005	36	51,896	1,442
2006	36	60,640	1,684
2007	36	76,073	2,113

*record

DIVISION III

Season	Sess.	Attend.	P/G Avg.
1977	21	38,881	1,851
1978	21	37,717	1,796
1979	22	43,850	1,993
1980	22	46,518	2,114
1981	22	58,432	*2,656
1982	22	44,973	2,044
1983	22	51,093	2,322
1984	22	42,152	1,916
1985	22	39,154	1,780
1986	22	53,500	2,432
1987	22	48,150	2,189
1988	22	43,787	1,990
1989	28	49,301	1,761
1990	26	50,527	1,943
1991	34	56,942	1,675
1992	34	65,257	1,919
1993	34	49,675	1,461
1994	34	54,848	1,613
1995	59	*88,684	1,503
1996	58	87,437	1,508
1997	58	70,647	1,218
1998	42	63,330	1,508
1999	42	53,928	1,284
2000	42	62,527	1,489
2001	42	77,110	1,836
2002	46	74,437	1,618
2003	42	66,379	1,580
2004	42	66,693	1,588
2005	42	64,289	1,531
2006	42	99,394	2,367
2007	42	60,619	1,443

*record

Division I Attendance Records

SINGLE GAME (PAID)
78,129—Kentucky (79) vs. Michigan St. (74), Dec. 13, 2003, at Ford Field, Detroit (regular-season game)

SINGLE GAME (TURNSTILE)
58,903—North Carolina (78) vs. Kansas (68) and Michigan (81) vs. Kentucky (78) (ot), Apr. 3, 1993 (NCAA semifinals), at Louisiana Superdome, New Orleans

HOME COURT, SINGLE GAME
33,633—Villanova (92) at Syracuse (82), Mar. 5, 2006, Carrier Dome, Syracuse, NY

HOME-COURT AVERAGE, SEASON
29,918—Syracuse, 1990 (478,686 in 16 games at Carrier Dome)

HOME-COURT TOTAL, SEASON
537,949—Syracuse, 1989 (19 games)

FULL-SEASON AVERAGE, ALL GAMES (home, road, neutral, tournaments)
22,501—Syracuse, 1989 (855,053 in 38 games)

FULL-SEASON TOTAL, ALL GAMES (home, road, neutral, tournaments)
855,053—Syracuse, 1989 (38 games)

TOP 10 ATTENDANCE GAMES (PAID)*
78,129—Kentucky (79) vs. Michigan St. (74), Dec. 13, 2003, at Ford Field, Detroit

68,112—LSU (87) vs. Notre Dame (64), Jan. 20, 1990, at Louisiana Superdome, New Orleans

66,144—LSU (82) vs. Georgetown (80), Jan. 28, 1989, at Louisiana Superdome, New Orleans

64,959—Indiana (74) vs. Syracuse (73), Mar. 30, 1987 (NCAA final); Indiana (97) vs. UNLV (93) and Syracuse (77) vs. Providence (63), Mar. 28, 1987 (NCAA semifinals), at Louisiana Superdome, New Orleans

64,151—North Carolina (77) vs. Michigan (71), Apr. 5, 1993 (NCAA final); North Carolina (78) vs. Kansas (68) and Michigan (81) vs. Kentucky (78) (ot), Apr. 3, 1993 (NCAA semifinals), at Louisiana Superdome, New Orleans

61,612—North Carolina (63) vs. Georgetown (62), Mar. 29, 1982 (NCAA final); North Carolina (68) vs. Houston (63) and Georgetown (50) vs. Louisville (46), Mar. 27, 1982 (NCAA semifinals), at Louisiana Superdome, New Orleans

61,304—LSU (84) vs. Texas (83), Jan. 3, 1992, at Louisiana Superdome, New Orleans

54,524—Syracuse (81) vs. Kansas (78), Apr. 7, 2003 (NCAA final); Kansas (94) vs. Marquette (61) and Syracuse (95) vs. Texas (84), Apr. 5, 2003 (NCAA semifinals), at Louisiana Superdome, New Orleans (attendance for the semifinals was 54,432)

53,510—Florida (76) vs. UCLA (66) and Ohio St. (67) vs. Georgetown (60), Mar. 31, 2007 (NCAA semifinals), at Georgia Dome, Atlanta (attendance for the finals was 51,458)

52,693—Houston (71) vs. UCLA (69), Jan. 20, 1968, at Astrodome, Houston

* Figures for games at the Final Four include the media.

TOP FIVE ATTENDANCE GAMES (TURNSTILE)
58,903—North Carolina (78) vs. Kansas (68) and Michigan (81) vs. Kentucky (78) (ot), Apr. 3, 1993 (NCAA semifinals), at Louisiana Superdome, New Orleans

56,707—Indiana (74) vs. Syracuse (73), Mar. 30, 1987 (NCAA final), at Louisiana Superdome, New Orleans

56,264—North Carolina (77) vs. Michigan (71), Apr. 5, 1993 (NCAA final), at Louisiana Superdome, New Orleans

55,841—Indiana (97) vs. UNLV (93) and Syracuse (77) vs. Providence (63), Mar. 28, 1987 (NCAA semifinals), at Louisiana Superdome, New Orleans

54,321—LSU (82) vs. Georgetown (80), Jan. 28, 1989, at Louisiana Superdome, New Orleans

TOP 10 REGULAR-SEASON GAMES (PAID)
78,129—Kentucky (79) vs. Michigan St. (74), Dec. 13, 2003, at Ford Field, Detroit

68,112—LSU (87) vs. Notre Dame (64), Jan. 20, 1990, at Louisiana Superdome, New Orleans

66,144—LSU (82) vs. Georgetown (80), Jan. 28, 1989, at Louisiana Superdome, New Orleans

61,304—LSU (84) vs. Texas (83), Jan. 3, 1992, at Louisiana Superdome, New Orleans

52,693—Houston (71) vs. UCLA (69), Jan. 20, 1968, at Astrodome, Houston

45,214—Louisville (101) vs. Indiana (79) and Notre Dame (81) vs. Kentucky (65), Dec. 3, 1988, at RCA Dome, Indianapolis

43,601—Notre Dame (69) vs. Louisville (54) and Kentucky (82) vs. Indiana (76), Dec. 5, 1987, at RCA Dome, Indianapolis

41,071—Kentucky (89) vs. Indiana (82), Dec. 2, 1995, at RCA Dome, Indianapolis

40,128—Louisville (84) vs. Notre Dame (73) and Indiana (71) vs. Kentucky (69), Dec. 2, 1989, at RCA Dome, Indianapolis

38,504—Kentucky (75) vs. Indiana (72), Dec. 6, 1997, at RCA Dome, Indianapolis

ON-CAMPUS REGULAR-SEASON, SINGLE GAME
33,633—Villanova (92) at Syracuse (82), Mar. 5, 2006, Carrier Dome, Syracuse, NY

33,199—Notre Dame (57) at Syracuse (60), Feb. 5, 2005, Carrier Dome, Syracuse, NY

33,071—Rutgers (74) at Syracuse (82), Mar. 9, 2003, Carrier Dome, Syracuse, NY

33,048—Georgetown (58) at Syracuse (62), Mar. 3, 1991, Carrier Dome, Syracuse, NY

33,015—Georgetown (87) at Syracuse (89), Mar. 4, 1990 (ot), Carrier Dome, Syracuse, NY

32,996—Georgetown (72) at Syracuse (68), Feb. 23, 1992, Carrier Dome, Syracuse, NY

32,944—Connecticut (56) at Syracuse (67), Mar. 7, 2004, Carrier Dome, Syracuse, NY

32,820—Connecticut (86) at Syracuse (90), Feb. 10, 1990, Carrier Dome, Syracuse, NY

32,804—Providence (66) at Syracuse (91), Feb. 26, 2005, Carrier Dome, Syracuse, NY

32,763—Pittsburgh (68) at Syracuse (89), Feb. 24, 1991, Carrier Dome, Syracuse, NY

2007 Division I Attendance Single-Game Highs

REGULAR-SEASON

32,376—Connecticut (63) at Syracuse (73), Feb. 17, 2007, at Carrier Dome, Syracuse, N.Y.

26,874—Villanova (64) at Syracuse (75), Jan. 13, 2007, at Carrier Dome in Syracuse, NY

26,287—Georgetown (58) at Syracuse (72), Feb. 26, 2007, at Carrier Dome in Syracuse, NY

24,638—DePaul (69) at Syracuse (75), Feb. 3, 2007, at Carrier Dome in Syracuse, NY

24,465—Florida (64) at Kentucky (61), Feb. 10, 2007, at Rupp Arena in Lexington, KY

POSTSEASON

53,510—Florida (76) vs. UCLA (66) and Ohio St. (67) vs. Georgetown (60), Mar. 31, 2007 (NCAA semifinal), at Georgia Dome in Atlanta

51,458—Florida (84) vs. Ohio St. (75), Apr. 2, 2007 (NCAA final), at Georgia Dome in Atlanta

26,776—Ohio St. (85) vs. Tennessee (84) and Memphis (65) vs. Texas A&M (69), Mar. 22, 2007 (South Regional semifinals), at Alamodome in San Antonio

26,752—Syracuse (80) vs. San Diego St. (64), Mar. 19, 2007 (NIT second round), at Carrier Dome in Syracuse, NY

26,307—Florida (65) vs. Butl;er (57) and Oregon (76) vs. UNLV (72), Mar. 23, 2007 (Midwest Regional semifinals), at Edward Jones Dome in St. Louis

Division II Attendance Records

HOME-COURT AVERAGE, SEASON

6,663—Norfolk St., 1984

PAID ATTENDANCE, SINGLE GAME

21,786—Bowie St. (72) vs. Virginia Union (71), Mar. 1, 2003, at RBC Center, Raleigh, NC (Central Intercollegiate Athletic Association final; early rounds had crowds of 16,536, 15,786 and 11,761)

20,432—Shaw (82) vs. Johnson Smith (68), Mar. 2, 2002, at RBC Center, Raleigh, NC (Central Intercollegiate Athletic Association final; early rounds had crowds of 18,054, 17,827 and 14,386)

15,731—Virginia Union (80) vs. N.C. Central (72), Feb. 28, 2004, at RBC Center, Raleigh, NC (CIAA final; early rounds had crowds of 9,718, 8,493 & 7,115)

13,913—Evansville (93) vs. Ky. Wesleyan (87), Feb. 13, 1960, at Roberts Stadium, Evansville, IN

13,240—La.-Lafayette (105) vs. Ky. Wesleyan (83), Mar. 19, 1971, at Roberts Stadium, Evansville, IN (NCAA third place)

2007 ATTENDANCE SINGLE-GAME HIGHS

6,213—Winona St. (76) at Northern St. (66), Jan. 27, 2007

6,147—Emporia St. (79) at Central Mo. (88), Feb. 10, 2007

5,675—Northwest Mo. St. (55) at Central Mo. (69), Jan. 20, 2007

5,528—Truman (47) at Central Mo. (66), Jan. 31, 2007

5,281—Minn. St. (69) at Northern St. (75), Feb. 20, 2007

Division III Attendance Records

HOME-COURT AVERAGE, SEASON

4,018—Calvin, 1993

PAID ATTENDANCE, SINGLE GAME

11,442—Hope (70) vs. Calvin (56), Jan. 29, 1997, at Van Andel Arena, Grand Rapids, Michigan

2007 ATTENDANCE SINGLE-GAME HIGHS

4,700—Redlands (102) at Pomona-Pitzer (113), Feb. 3, 2007

4,500—Hope (65) at Calvin (62), Jan. 13, 2007

3,776—Wittenberg (74) at Wooster (71), Feb. 3, 2007

3,435—Calvin (77) at Hope (71), Feb. 7, 2007

3,302—Olivet (43) at Calvin (90), Feb. 10, 2007

Playing-Rules History

Dr. James Naismith's 13 Original Rules of Basketball

Photo from NCAA archives

1. The ball could be thrown in any direction with one or both hands.
2. The ball could be batted in any direction with one or both hands (never with the fist).
3. A player cannot run with the ball. The player must throw it from the spot on which he catches it, allowance to be made for a man who catches the ball when running at a good speed if he tries to stop.
4. The ball had to be held in or between the hands; the arms or body must not be used for holding it.
5. No shouldering, holding, pushing, tripping, or striking in any way the person of an opponent should be allowed; the first infringement of this rule by any player should count as a foul, the second should disqualify him until the next goal was made, or, if there was evident intent to injure the person, for the whole of the game, no substitute allowed.
6. A foul was striking at the ball with the fist, violation of Rules 3, 4, and such as described in Rule 5.
7. If either side makes three consecutive fouls, it should count a goal for the opponents (consecutive means without the opponents in the meantime making a foul).
8. A goal should be made when the ball was thrown or batted from the grounds into the basket and stays there, providing those defending the goal do not touch or disturb the goal. If the ball rests on the edges, and the opponent moves the basket, it should count as a goal.
9. When the ball goes out of bounds, it should be thrown into the field of play by the person first touching it. In case of a dispute, the umpire should throw it straight into the field. The thrower-in was allowed five seconds; if he holds it longer, it should go to the opponent. If any side persists in delaying the game, the umpire should call a foul on that side.
10. The umpire should be judge of the men and should note the fouls and notify the referee when three consecutive fouls have been made. He should have power to disqualify men according to Rule 5.
11. The referee should be judge of the ball and should decide when the ball was in play, in bounds, to which side it belongs, and should keep the time. He should decide when a goal had been made, and keep account of the goals with any other duties that were usually performed by a referee.
12. The time should be two 15-minute halves, with five minutes' rest between.
13. The side making the most goals in that time should be declared the winner. In case of a draw, the game may, by agreement of the captains, be continued until another goal was made.

Note: These original rules were published in January 1892 in the Springfield College school newspaper, The Triangle.

Important Rules Changes by Year

The earliest rules book available for this research was from the 1905-06 season. Some of the rules listed in 1905-06 could have actually been instituted before that season.

1891-92
- The 13 original rules of basketball were written by Dr. James Naismith in December 1891 in Springfield, Massachusetts.

1894-95
- The free-throw line was set at 20 feet.

1895-96
- Points awarded for field goal change from three to two, and points awarded for each successful free throw from three points to one point.

1896-97
- Backboards were installed.

1900-01
- A dribbler could not shoot for a field goal and could dribble only once, and then with two hands.

1905-06
- Personal fouls were separated into two classes: "A" for general fouls and "B" for more flagrant fouls. Class A fouls were called for delay of game, tackling the ball (touching the ball when a teammate was already touching it), kicking the ball, striking the ball, advancing the ball, hugging the ball, shooting after dribbling, tackling the opponent, holding the opponent, pushing the opponent, or addressing the game officials. Class B fouls could lead to possible game disqualification and were called for striking the opponent, kicking the opponent, shouldering the opponent, tripping the opponent, hacking the opponent, unnecessary roughness, or using profane or abusive language. If two class B fouls were committed by one player, he was disqualified for the rest of the game.
- If a player was fouled during the act of shooting, his team was automatically awarded one point and one free-throw attempt. If the original shot from the field for goal was good, it counted along with the awarded extra point and free-throw attempt.
- Each game had one referee, one umpire and two inspectors. The referee was the superior officer of the game and had supreme authority once the game began until it concluded. The referee's main duties were calling fouls and stopping play. The umpire could call fouls and reported to the referee. Inspectors were the referee's assistants and were stationed one at each end of the court. Inspectors had no power to make decisions but noted whether goals were made in accordance with the rules and reported such to the referee. The official scorer kept a book containing the scoring and fouls made for each player and each team. The duties of the official scorer have basically remained the same through all the years.
- One timekeeper was appointed by the home team. The visiting team could appoint an assistant timekeeper if it chose to.
- A timeout called while the ball was in play resulted in a jump ball when play was resumed. If the ball was out-of-bounds when a timeout was called, the team in possession of the ball kept possession.
- Time stopped only when ordered by the referee. It did not stop for dead-ball situations such as free throws or when the ball was out-of-bounds.
- Halftime increased to 10 minutes.
- Although not yet known as defensive goaltending, if a player touched the ball or basket when the ball was on the edge of the rim, the referee awarded one point to the shooting team.

1906-07
- The free-throw line was moved from 20 to 15 feet.

1907-08
- Inspector was no longer a game official position.

1908-09
- A dribbler became permitted to shoot. The dribble was defined as the "continuous passage of the ball," making the double dribble illegal.

- A second official was added for games in an effort to curb the rough play.

1910-11
- Within Class B fouls, personal fouls were distinguished from the other.
- Players were disqualified upon committing their fourth personal foul.
- No coaching was allowed during the progress of the game by anybody connected with either team. A warning was given for the first violation and a free throw was awarded after that.

1913-14
- The bottom of the net was left open.

1914-15
- College, YMCA and AAU rules were made the same.

1915-16
- Class A fouls were changed to violations, and Class B fouls became technical and personal fouls.
- If a player was fouled in the act of shooting, his team was awarded two free throws regardless of whether the original field goal was made or missed. If it was made, those two points counted.
- Defensive interference with the ball or basket while the ball was on the basket's rim resulted in one free throw attempt for the shooting team.

1920-21
- A player could re-enter the game once. Before this rule, if a player left the game, he could not re-enter for the rest of the game.
- The backboards were moved two feet from the wall of the court. Before this rule, players would "climb" the padded wall to sink baskets.

1921-22
- Running with the ball changed from a foul to a violation.

1922-23
- Defensive interference with the ball or basket while the ball was on the basket's rim was declared a goal for the shooting team.

1923-24
- The player fouled must shoot his own free throws. Before this rule, one person usually shot all his team's free throws.

1924-25
- Time stopped when ordered by the referee for injuries, substitutions, two-shot fouls and timeouts requested by the team captain. The clock kept running at all other times including dead-ball situations, such as out-of-bounds.
- Two timekeepers were used, one from each team, and shared a watch placed on a table so both could see it. The timekeepers kept track of all the incidents that time was out and added that to the game time. The timekeepers indicated when time expired by using a gong, pistol or whistle.
- Only team captains could call for a timeout. Each team had three timeouts per game.

1928-29
- The charging foul by the dribbler was introduced.

1930-31
- A held ball could be called when a closely guarded player was withholding the ball from play for five seconds. The result was a jump ball.
- The maximum circumference of the ball was reduced from 32 to 31 inches, and the maximum weight from 23 to 22 ounces.
- If a player was fouled in the act of shooting, his team was awarded two free throws if the original field goal was missed. If it was made, those two points counted and only one free throw was attempted.

1932-33
- The 10-second center (division) line was introduced to reduce stalling.
- No player could stand in the free-throw lane with the ball for more than three seconds.

1933-34
- A player could re-enter the game twice.

1934-35
- The circumference of the ball again was reduced to between 29½ and 30¼ inches.

1935-36
- No offensive player could remain in the free-throw lane, with or without the ball, for more than three seconds.
- After a made free throw, the team scored upon put the ball in play at the end of the court where the goal had been scored.

1937-38
- The center jump after every goal scored was eliminated.

1938-39
- The ball was thrown in from out of bounds at mid-court by the team shooting a free throw after a technical foul. Before this rule, the ball was put into play with a center jump after a technical-foul free throw.
- The circumference of the ball was established as 30 inches.

1939-40
- Teams had the choice of whether to take a free throw or take the ball out of bounds at mid-court. If two or more free throws were awarded, this option applied to the last throw.
- The backboards were moved from 2 to 4 feet from the end line to permit freer movement under the basket.

1940-41
- Fan-shaped backboards were made legal.

1942-43
- Any player who was eligible to start an overtime period was allowed an extra personal foul, increasing the total so disqualification was on the fifth foul.

1944-45
- Along with the ball on the rim, defensive interference by touching the ball after it had started its downward flight during an opponent's field goal attempt was declared a goal for the shooting team.
- Five personal fouls disqualify a player. An extra foul was not permitted in overtime games.
- Unlimited substitution was introduced.
- It became a violation for an offensive player to remain in the free-throw lane for more than three seconds.

1946-47
- Transparent backboards were authorized.

1947-48
- The clock was stopped on every dead ball the last three minutes of the second half and of every overtime period. This included every time a goal was scored because the ball was considered dead until put into play again. (This rule was abolished in 1951.)

1948-49
- Coaches were allowed to speak to players during a timeout.

1951-52
- Games were played in four 10-minute quarters.

1952-53
- Teams could no longer waive free throws in favor of taking the ball out of bounds.
- The one-and-one free-throw rule was introduced, although the bonus was used only if the first shot was missed. The rule was in effect the entire game except the last three minutes, when every foul resulted in two free throws.

1954-55
- The one-and-one free throw was changed so that the bonus shot was given only if the first shot was made.
- Games were changed back to being played in two 20-minute halves.

1955-56
- The free-throw lane was increased from 6 feet to 12 feet.
- The two-shot penalty in the last three minutes of the game was eliminated. The one-and-one became in effect the entire game.

1956-57
- On the lineup for a free throw, the two spaces adjacent to the end line were occupied by opponents of the free-thrower. In the past, one space was marked "H" for a home team player to occupy, and across the lane the first space was marked "V" for a visiting team player to stand in.
- Grasping the basket became classified as a technical foul under unsportsmanlike tactics.

1957-58
- Offensive goaltending was banned so that no player from either team could touch the ball or basket when the ball was on the basket's rim or above the cylinder. The only exception was the shooter in the original act of shooting.
- One free throw for each common foul was taken for the first six personal fouls by one team in each half, and the one-and-one was used thereafter.
- On uniforms, the use of the single digit numbers one and two and any digit greater than five was prohibited.
- A ball that passed over the backboard—either front to back or back to front—was considered out of bounds.

1964-65

- Coaches had to remain seated on the bench except while the clock was stopped or to direct or encourage players on the court. This rule was to help keep coaches from inciting undesirable crowd reactions toward the officials.

1967-68

- The dunk was made illegal during the game and pregame warm-up.

1970-71

- During a jump ball, a nonjumper could not change his position from the time the official was ready to make the toss until after the ball had been touched.

1972-73

- The free throw on the first six common fouls each half by a team was eliminated.
- Players could not attempt to create the false impression that they had been fouled in charging/guarding situations or while screening when the contact was only incidental. An official could charge the "actor" with a technical foul for unsportsmanlike conduct if, in the official's opinion, the actor was making a travesty of the game.
- Freshmen became eligible to play varsity basketball. This was the result of a change in the NCAA bylaws, not the basketball playing rules.

1973-74

- Officials could now penalize players for fouls occurring away from the ball, such as grabbing, holding and setting illegal screens.

1974-75

- During a jump ball, a non-jumper on the restraining circle could move around the circle after the ball had left the official's hands.
- A player charged with a foul was no longer required to raise his hand. (In 1978, however, it was strongly recommended that a player start raising his hand again.)

1976-77

- The dunk was made legal again.

1980-81

- Conferences began experimenting with the three-point field-goal at different distances.

1981-82

- The jump ball was used only at the beginning of the game and the start of each overtime. An alternating arrow was used to indicate possession in jump-ball situations during the game.
- All fouls charged to bench personnel were assessed to the head coach.

1982-83

- When the closely guarded five-second count was reached, it was no longer a jump-ball situation. It was a violation, and the ball was awarded to the defensive team out of bounds.

1983-84

- Two free throws were taken for each common foul committed within the last two minutes of the second half and the entire overtime period, if the bonus rule was in effect. (This rule was rescinded one month into the season.)

1984-85

- The coaching box was introduced, whereby a coach and all bench personnel had to remain in the 28-foot-long coaching box unless seeking information from the scorers' table.

1985-86

- The 45-second clock was introduced. The team in control of the ball had to shoot for a goal within 45 seconds after it attained team control.
- If a shooter was fouled intentionally and the shot was missed, the penalty was two shots and possession of the ball out of bounds to the team that was fouled.
- The head coach could stand throughout the game, while all other bench personnel had to remain seated.

1986-87

- The three-point field goal was introduced and set at 19 feet 9 inches from the center of the basket.
- A coach could leave the confines of the bench at any time without penalty to correct a scorer's or timer's mistake. A technical foul was assessed if there was no mistake. (This was changed the next year to a timeout.) Also, a television replay could be used to prevent or rectify a scorer's or timer's mistake or a malfunction of the clock.

1987-88

- Each intentional personal foul carried a two-shot penalty plus possession of the ball.

1988-89

- Any squad member who participated in a fight was ejected from the game and was placed on probation. If that player participated in a second fight during the season, he was suspended for one game. A third fight involving the same person resulted in suspension for the rest of the season including championship competition.

1990-91

- Beginning with the team's 10th personal foul in a half, two free throws were awarded for each common foul, except player-control fouls.
- Three free throws were awarded when a shooter was fouled during an unsuccessful three-point try.
- The fighting rule was amended. The first time any squad member or bench personnel participated in a fight, he was suspended for the team's next game. If that same person participated in a second fight, he was suspended for the rest of the season, including championship competition.

1991-92

- Contact technical fouls counted toward the five fouls for player disqualification and toward the team fouls in reaching bonus free-throw situations.
- The shot clock was reset when the ball struck the basket ring, not when a shot left the shooter's hands as it had been since the rule was introduced in 1986.

1992-93

- Unsporting technical fouls, in addition to contact technical fouls, counted toward the five fouls for player disqualification and toward the team fouls in reaching bonus free-throw situations.

1993-94

- The shot clock was reduced from 45 seconds to 35. The team in control of the ball must shoot for a goal within 35 seconds after it attained team control.
- A foul was ruled intentional if, while playing the ball, a player caused excessive contact with an opponent.
- The game clock was stopped after successful field goals in the last minute of the game and the last minute of any overtime period with no substitution allowed.
- The five-second dribbling violation when closely guarded was eliminated.
- The rule concerning the use of profanity was expanded to include abusive and obscene language in an effort to curtail verbal misconduct by players and coaches.

1994-95

- The inner circle at mid-court was eliminated.
- Scoring was restricted to a tap-in when (3/10) (.3) of a second or less remained on the game clock or shot clock.
- The fighting and suspension rules were expanded to include coaches and team personnel.

1995-96

- All unsporting technical fouls charged to anyone on the bench counted toward the team foul total.
- Teams were allowed one 20-second timeout per half. This was an experimental rule in the 1994-95 season.

1996-97

- Teams had to warm up and shoot at the end of the court farthest from their own bench for the first half. Previously, teams had the choice of baskets in the first half.
- In games not involving commercial electronic media, teams were entitled to four full-length timeouts and two 20-second timeouts per game. In games involving commercial electronic media, teams were entitled to two full-length timeouts and three 20-second timeouts per game.

1997-98

- The five-second dribbling violation when closely guarded was reinstated.
- Timeout requests could be made by a player on the court or by the head coach.

1998-99

- In a held-ball situation initiated by the defense, the ball would be awarded to the defensive team. Previously, possession was awarded by the direction of the possession arrow.

1999-00
- Held-ball change from previous season rescinded.
- Twenty-second timeouts increased to 30 seconds in length. New electronic- media timeout format adopted.
- Uniform numbers one and two were permitted.
- Officials must consult courtside television monitors, when available, to judge whether a game-deciding last-second shot in the second half or any extra period counts. (This was passed during the season.)

2000-01
- Technical fouls divided into direct (two-shot penalty) and indirect (one-shot penalty) with ball returned to point of interruption.

2001-02
- Both direct and indirect technical fouls penalized by two shots and returned to point of interruption.
- Officials could check an official courtside monitor to determine if a try was a three- or two-point attempt, regardless of whether the try was successful.

2002-03
- Composite ball could be used without mutual consent of coaches.
- Two free-throw lane spaces closest to the free-thrower would remain unoccupied.
- No free throws were awarded to the offended team in bonus for personal fouls committed by a team while in team control or in possession of the ball during a throw-in (team-control foul).

2003-04
- Officials could consult courtside monitor at the end of either half or any extra period to determine: (1) if a field-goal try beat the horn; (2) whether a shot-clock violation at the end of the first half beat the horn; or, (3) whether a shot-clock violation that would determine the outcome of a game beat the horn. The officials also could use a courtside monitor to correct a timer's mistake or to determine if the game clock or shot clock expired at or near the end of a period.
- A team would have control when a player of that team had disposal of the ball for a throw-in.

2005-06
- Expanding on the rule from two seasons before, officials who consult a courtside monitor at the end of either half or any extra period could correct the official game time if needed and/or determine whether a foul was committed before time expired. Officials could also consult a courtside monitor any time during the game to correct a timer's mistake.
- The time allowed to replace a disqualified player was reduced from 30 to 20 seconds and the warning signal was sounded five seconds before the expiration of the time limit.
- Violations when the ball had been intentionally kicked no longer resulted in the reset of the shot clock to 35 seconds. When the violation occured with 15 or fewer seconds remaining, the shot clock was reset to 15 seconds. Otherwise, when the violation occured with more than 15 seconds remaining, there was no reset of the shot clock.

2006-07
- A timeout would not be recognized when an airborne player's momentum carried him either out-of-bounds or into the backcourt.

2007-08
- During free throws, eliminated the first lane space nearest the basket on each side of the lane and used the second, third and fourth lane space on each side as an alignment for free throws.
- Use of courtside monitor allowed for determining whether a flagrant foul occurred or to assess the situation during a fight.

2008-09
- The three-point line will be extended to 20 feet, 9 inches.

2009-10
- Division II and III institutions will be required to have a game clock with a 10th-of-a-second display, a red light or LED lights, and shot clocks mounted on the backboard.

Important Rules Changes by Subject

Ball: 1930-31, The maximum circumference of the ball was reduced from 32 to 31 inches, and the maximum weight from 23 to 22 ounces. 1934-35, The circumference of the ball again was reduced to between 29½ and 30¼ inches. 1938-39, The circumference of the ball was established as 30 inches. 2002-03, Mutual consent no longer needed for composite ball to be legal.

Basket Equipment: 1896-97, Backboards were installed. 1913-14, The bottom of the net was left open. 1920-21, The backboards were moved two feet from the wall of the court. Before this rule, players would "climb" the padded wall to sink baskets. 1939-40, The backboards were moved from 2 to 4 feet from the end line to permit freer movement under the basket. 1940-41, Fan-shaped backboards were made legal. 1946-47, Transparent backboards were authorized. 1957-58, A ball that passed over the backboard—either front to back or back to front—was considered out of bounds. 1996-97, Teams had to warm up and shoot at the end of the court farthest from their own bench for the first half. Previously, teams had the choice of baskets in the first half. 2002-03, For Division I, shot clocks had to be mounted and recessed on backboard, red warning light had to be added and game clock had to show 10th-of-a-second display. 2003-04, for Division II, shot clocks were recessed and mounted. 2009-10, Division II and III institutions were required to have a game clock with a 10th-of-a-second display, a red light or LED lights, and shot clocks mounted on the backboard. 2009-10, Division II and III institutions will be required to have a game clock with a 10th-of-a-second display, a red light or LED lights, and shot clocks mounted on the backboard.

Block/Charge: 1928-29, The charging foul by the dribbler was introduced. 1972-73, Players could not attempt to create the false impression that they had been fouled in charging/guarding situations or while screening when the contact was only incidental. An official could charge the "actor" with a technical foul for unsportsmanlike conduct if, in the official's opinion, the actor was making a travesty of the game. 2002, Prior rule was deleted because of lack of use.

Clock Stoppage: 1947-48, The clock was stopped on every dead ball the last three minutes of the second half and of every extra period. This includes every time a goal was scored because the ball was considered dead until put into play again. (This rule was abolished in 1951.)

Closely Guarded: 1982-83, When the closely guarded five-second count was reached, it was no longer a jump-ball situation. It was a violation, and the ball was awarded to the defensive team out of bounds. 1993-94, The five-second dribbling violation when closely guarded was eliminated. 1997-98, The five-second dribbling violation when closely guarded was reinstated.

Coaching: 1910-11, No coaching was allowed during the progress of the game by anybody connected with either team. A warning was given for the first violation and a free throw was awarded after that. 1948-49, Coaches were allowed to speak to players during a timeout. 1964-65, Coaches had to remain seated on the bench except while the clock was stopped or to direct or encourage players on the court. This rule was to help keep coaches from inciting undesirable crowd reactions toward the officials. 1984-85, The coaching box was introduced, whereby a coach and all bench personnel had to remain in the 28-foot-long coaching box unless seeking information from the scorers' table. 1985-86, The head coach could stand throughout the game, while all other bench personnel had to remain seated. 1986-87, A coach could leave the confines of the bench at any time without penalty to correct a scorer's or timer's mistake. A technical foul was assessed if there was no mistake. (This penalty was changed the next year to a timeout.) Also, a television replay could be used to prevent or rectify a scorer's or timer's mistake or a malfunction of the clock. 1994-95, The fighting and suspension rules were expanded to include coaches and team personnel. 1995-96, All unsporting technical fouls charged to anyone on the bench counted toward the team foul total.

Dunk: 1967-68, The dunk was made illegal during the game and pregame warm-up. 1976-77, The dunk was made legal again but remains illegal during warm-up.

Field Goals: 1895-96, A field goal changes from three to two points, and free throws from three points to one point. 1905-06, If a player was fouled during the act of shooting, his team was automatically awarded one point and one free-throw attempt. If the original shot from the field for goal was good, it counted along with the awarded extra point and free-throw attempt. 1915-16, If a player was fouled in the act of shooting, his team was awarded two free throws regardless of whether the original field goal was made or missed. If it was made, those two points counted. 1930-31, If a player was fouled in the act of shooting, his team was awarded two free throws if the original field goal was missed. If it was made, those two points counted and only one free throw was attempted.

Fighting: 1988-89, Any squad member who participated in a fight was ejected from the game and placed on probation. If that individual participated in a second fight during the season, he was suspended for one game. A third fight involving the same person resulted in suspension for the rest of the season including championship competition. 1990-91, The fighting rule was amended. The first time any squad member or bench personnel participated in a fight, he was suspended for the team's next game. If that same person participated in a second fight, he was suspended for the rest of the season, including championship competition. 1994-95, The fighting and suspension rules were expanded to include coaches and team personnel.

Fouls: 1905-06, Personal fouls were separated into two classes: "A" for general fouls and "B" for more flagrant fouls. Class A fouls were called for delay of game, tackling the ball (touching the ball when a teammate was already touching it), kicking the ball, striking the ball, advancing the ball, hugging the ball, shooting after dribbling, tackling the opponent,

holding the opponent, pushing the opponent, or addressing the game officials. Class B fouls could lead to possible game disqualification and were called for striking the opponent, kicking the opponent, shouldering the opponent, tripping the opponent, hacking the opponent unnecessary roughness, or using profane or abusive language. If two Class B fouls were committed by one player, he was disqualified for the rest of the game. 1910-11, Within Class B fouls, personal fouls were distinguished from the other. 1915-16, Class A fouls were changed to violations, and Class B fouls became technical and personal fouls.

Fouling Out: 1905-06, Players were disqualified upon committing their second Class "B" foul (as described in the preceding "Fouls" section). 1910-11, Players were disqualified upon committing their fourth personal foul. 1942-43, Any player who was eligible to start an extra period was allowed an extra personal foul, increasing the total so disqualification was on the fifth foul. 1944-45, Five personal fouls disqualify a player. An extra foul was not permitted in overtime games. 1991-92, Contact technical fouls counted toward the five fouls for player disqualification and toward the team fouls in reaching bonus free-throw situations.

Free Throws: 1894-95, The free-throw line was set at 20 feet. 1906-07, The free-throw line was moved from 20 to 15 feet. 1923-24, The player fouled must shoot his own free throws. Before this rule, one person usually shot all his team's free throws. 1935-36, After a made free throw, the team scored upon would put the ball in play at the end of the court where the goal had been scored. 1939-40, Teams had the choice of whether to take a free throw or take the ball out of bounds at mid-court. If two or more free throws were awarded, this option applied to the last throw. 1952-53, Teams could no longer waive free throws in favor of taking the ball out of bounds. 1952-53, The one-and-one free-throw rule was introduced, although the bonus was used only if the first shot was missed. The rule was in effect the entire game except the last three minutes, when every foul was two shots. 1954-55, The one-and-one free throw was changed so that the bonus shot was given only if the first shot was made. 1955-56, The two-shot penalty in the last three minutes of the game was eliminated. The one-and-one became in effect the entire game. 1956-57, The free-throw lane was increased from 6 feet to 12 feet. On the lineup for a free throw, the two spaces adjacent to the end line were occupied by opponents of the free thrower. In the past, one space was marked "H" for a home team player to occupy, and across the lane the first space was marked "V" for a visiting team player to stand in. 1957-58, One free throw for each common foul was taken for the first six personal fouls by one team in each half, and the one-and-one was used thereafter. 1972-73, The free throw on the first six common fouls each half by a team was eliminated. 1974-75, A player charged with a foul was no longer required to raise his hand. (In 1978, however, it was strongly recommended that a player start raising his hand again.) 1983-84, Two free throws were taken for each common foul committed within the last two minutes of the second half and the entire overtime period, if the bonus rule was in effect. (This rule was rescinded one month into the season.) 1985-86, If a shooter was fouled intentionally and the shot was missed, the penalty was two shots and possession of the ball out of bounds to the team that was fouled. 1987-88, Each intentional personal foul carried a two-shot penalty plus possession of the ball. 1990-91, Beginning with the team's 10th personal foul in a half, two free throws were awarded for each common foul, except player-control fouls. 1990-91, Three free throws were awarded when a shooter was fouled during an unsuccessful three-point try. 1991-92, Contact technical fouls counted toward the five fouls for player disqualification and toward the team fouls in reaching bonus free-throw situations. 1992-93, Unsporting technical fouls, in addition to contact technical fouls, counted toward the five fouls for player disqualification and toward the team fouls in reaching bonus free-throw situations. 1995-96, All unsporting technical fouls charged to anyone on the bench counted toward the team foul total. 2000-01, Number of players permitted on free-throw lane reduced from eight to six. 2002-03, Lane spaces closest to the free-thrower would remain unoccupied. 2007-08, During free throws, eliminated the first lane space nearest the basket on each side of the lane and used the second, third and fourth lane space on each side as an alignment for free throws.

Freshmen: 1972-73, Freshmen became eligible to play varsity basketball. This was the result of a change in the NCAA bylaws, not the basketball playing rules.

Game Officials: 1905-06, Each game had one referee, one umpire and two inspectors. The referee was the superior officer of the game and had supreme authority once the game began until it concluded. The referee's main duties were calling fouls and stopping play. The umpire could call fouls and reported to the referee. Inspectors were the referee's assistants and were stationed one at each end of the court. Inspectors had no power to make decisions but noted whether goals were made in accordance with the rules and reported such to the referee. The official scorer kept a book containing the scoring and fouls made for each player and each team. The duties of the official scorer have basically remained the same through all the years. For timekeepers, see the section on timekeepers. 1907-08, Inspector was no longer a game official position.

Goaltending/Basket Interference: 1905-06, Although not yet known as defensive goaltending, if a player touched the ball or basket when the ball was on the edge of the rim, the referee awarded one point to the shooting team. 1915-16, Defensive interference with the ball or basket while the ball was on the basket's rim resulted in one free throw attempt for the shooting team. 1922-23, Defensive interference with the ball or basket while the ball was on the basket's rim was declared a goal for the shooting team. 1944-45, Along with the ball on the rim, defensive interference by touching the ball after it had started its downward flight during an opponent's field goal attempt was declared a goal for the shooting team. 1957-58, Offensive goaltending was banned so that no player from either team could touch the ball or basket when the ball was on the basket's rim or above the cylinder. The only exception was the shooter in the original act of shooting.

Held Ball: 1930-31, A held ball could be called when a closely guarded player was withholding the ball from play for five seconds. The result was a jump ball. 1998-99, In a held-ball situation initiated by the defense, the ball would be awarded to the defensive team. Previously, possession was awarded by the direction of the possession arrow. This was rescinded the next season.

Intentional Foul: 1985-86, If a shooter was fouled intentionally and the shot was missed, the penalty was two shots and possession of the ball out of bounds to the team that was fouled. 1987-88, Each intentional personal foul carried a two-shot penalty plus possession of the ball. 1993-94, A foul would be ruled intentional if, while playing the ball, a player caused excessive contact with an opponent.

Jump Ball/Alternate Possession: 1905-06, A timeout called while the ball was in play resulted in a jump ball when play was resumed. If the ball was out-of-bounds when a timeout was called, the team in possession of the ball kept possession. 1930-31, A held ball could be called when a closely guarded player was withholding the ball from play for five seconds. The result was a jump ball. 1937-38, The center jump after every goal scored was eliminated. 1970-71, During a jump ball, a non-jumper could not change his position from the time the official was ready to make the toss until after the ball had been touched. 1974-75, During a jump ball, a non-jumper on the restraining circle could move around it after the ball had left the official's hands. 1981-82, The jump ball was used only at the beginning of the game and the start of each extra period. An alternating arrow would indicate possession in held-ball situations during the game. 1994-95, The inner circle at mid-court was eliminated.

Lines: 1894-95, The free-throw line was moved from 20 to 15 feet. 1932-33, The 10-second center (division) line was introduced to reduce stalling. 1956-57, The free-throw lane was increased from 6 feet to 12 feet. On the lineup for a free throw, the two spaces adjacent to the end line were occupied by opponents of the free-thrower. In the past, one space was marked "H" for a home team player to occupy, and across the lane the first space was marked "V" for a visiting team player to stand in. 1984-85, The coaching box was introduced, whereby a coach and all bench personnel had to remain in the 28-foot-long coaching box unless seeking information from the scorers' table. 1986-87, The three-point field goal was introduced and set at 19 feet 9 inches from the center of the basket. 1994-95, The inner circle at mid-court was eliminated.

Officials: 1908-09, A second official was added for games in an effort to curb the rough play. 1977-78, The option of a third official was allowed.

Out of Bounds: 1957-58, A ball that passed over the backboard—either front to back or back to front—was considered out of bounds.

Overtime: 1942-43, Any player who was eligible to start an extra period was allowed an extra personal foul, increasing the total so disqualification was on the fifth foul. 1944-45, An extra foul was not permitted in overtime games. 1993-94, The game clock was stopped after successful field goals in the last minute of the game and the last minute of any extra period with no substitution allowed.

Periods: 1905-06, Games were played in two 20-minute halves with a 10-minute rest time between the halves. 1951-52, Games were played in four 10-minute quarters. 1954-55, Games were changed back to being played in two 20-minute halves. 1996-97, Teams had to warm up and shoot at the end of the court farthest from their own bench for the first half. Previously, teams had the choice of baskets in the first half.

Rough Play: 1908-09, A second official was added for games in an effort to curb the rough play. 1939-40, Teams had the choice of whether to take a free throw or take the ball out of bounds at mid-court. If two or more free throws were awarded, this option applied to the last throw. 1952-53, Teams could no longer waive free throws in favor of taking the ball out of bounds. 1957-58, One free throw for each common foul was taken for the first six personal fouls by one team in each half, and the one-and-one was used thereafter. 1972-73, The free throw on the first six common fouls each half by a team was eliminated. 1973-74, Officials could now penalize players for fouls occurring away from the ball, such as grabbing, holding and setting illegal screens. 1974-75, A player charged with a foul was no longer required to raise his hand. (In 1978, however, it was strongly recommended that a player start raising his hand again.) 1983-84, Two free throws were taken for each common foul committed within the last two minutes of the second half and the entire overtime period, if the bonus rule was in effect. (This rule was rescinded one month into the season.) 1987-88, Each intentional personal foul carried a two-shot penalty plus possession of the ball. 1990-91, Beginning with the team's 10th personal foul in a half, two free throws were awarded for each common foul, except player-control fouls. 1991-92, Contact technical fouls counted toward the five fouls for player disqualification and toward the team fouls in reaching bonus free-throw situations. 1992-93, Unsporting technical fouls, in addition to contact technical fouls, counted toward the five fouls for player disqualification and toward the team fouls in reaching bonus free-throw situations. 1993-94, A foul would be ruled intentional if, while playing the ball, a player caused excessive contact with an opponent. 2000-01, Number of players permitted on free-throw lane reduced from eight to six. 2007-08, Use of courtside monitor allowed for determining whether a flagrant foul occurred or to assess the situation during a fight.

Shot Clock/Stalling: 1932-33, The 10-second center (division) line was introduced to reduce stalling. 1985-86, The 45-second clock was introduced. The team in control of the ball must now shoot for a goal within 45 seconds after it attains team control. 1991-92, The shot clock was reset when the ball struck the basket ring, not when a shot left the shooter's hands as it had been since the rule was introduced in 1986. 1993-94, The shot clock was reduced to 35 seconds from 45. The team in control of the ball must shoot for a goal within 35 seconds after it attained team control. 1993-94, The game clock was stopped after successful field goals in the last minute of the game and the last minute of any overtime period with no substitution allowed. Officials could consult courtside monitor at the end of either half or any extra period to determine: (1) if a field-goal try beat the horn; (2) whether a shot-clock violation at the end of the first half beat the horn; or, (3) whether a shot-clock violation that would determine the outcome of a game beat the horn. The officials also could use a courtside monitor to correct a timer's mistake or to determine if the game clock or shot clock expired at or near the end of a period. 2005-06, Violations when the ball had been intentionally kicked would no longer result in the reset of the shot clock to 35 seconds. When the violation occured with 15 or fewer seconds remaining, the shot clock was reset to

15 seconds. Otherwise, when the violation occured with more than 15 seconds remaining, there was no reset of the shot clock.

Shot in Closing Seconds: 1994-95, Scoring was restricted to a tap-in when 3/10 (.3) of a second or less remained on the game clock or shot clock. 1999-2000, During the season, the rules committee made a rule that required the official to look at the courtside monitor to determine if a potential game-winning shot in the last second of the game or overtime would count. 2003-04, Officials could consult courtside monitor at the end of either half or any extra period to determine: (1) if a field-goal try beat the horn; (2) whether a shot-clock violation at the end of the first half beat the horn; or, (3) whether a shot-clock violation that would determine the outcome of a game beat the horn. The officials also could use a courtside monitor to correct a timer's mistake or to determine if the game clock or shot clock expired at or near the end of a period.

Substitution: 1920-21, A player could re-enter the game once. Before this rule, if a player left the game, he could not re-enter for the rest of the game. 1933-34, A player could re-enter the game twice. 1944-45, Unlimited substitution was introduced. 1993-94, The game clock was stopped after successful field goals in the last minute of the game and the last minute of any extra period with no substitution allowed. 2005-06, The time allowed to replace a disqualified player was reduced from 30 to 20 seconds and the warning signal was sounded five seconds before the expiration of the time limit.

Technical Fouls: 1938-39, The ball was thrown in from out of bounds at mid-court by the team shooting a free throw after a technical foul. Before, the ball was put into play with a center jump after a technical-foul free throw. 1956-57, Grasping the basket became classified as a technical foul under unsportsmanlike tactics. 1981-82, All fouls charged to bench personnel were assessed to the head coach. 1988-89, Any squad member who participated in a fight was ejected from the game and was placed on probation. If that player participated in a second fight during the season, he was suspended for one game. A third fight involving the same person resulted in suspension for the rest of the season including championship competition. 1990-91, The fighting rule was amended. The first time any squad member or bench personnel participated in a fight, he was suspended for the team's next game. If that same person participated in a second fight, he was suspended for the rest of the season, including championship competition. 1991-92, Contact technical fouls counted toward the five fouls for player disqualification and toward the team fouls in reaching bonus free-throw situations. 1992-93, Unsporting technical fouls, in addition to contact technical fouls, counted toward the five fouls for player disqualification and toward the team fouls in reaching bonus free-throw situations. 1993-94, The rule concerning the use of profanity was expanded to include abusive and obscene language in an effort to curtail verbal misconduct by players and coaches. 1994-95, The fighting and suspension rules were expanded to include coaches and team personnel. 2000-01, technical fouls divided into direct (two-shot penalty) and indirect (one-shot penalty) with ball returned to point of interruption. 2001-02, Both direct and indirect technical fouls penalized by two shots and return to point of interruption.

Television Replay: 1986-87, A coach could leave the confines of the bench at any time without penalty to correct a scorer's or timer's mistake. A technical foul was assessed if there was no mistake. (This was changed the next year to a timeout.) Also, a television replay could be used to prevent or rectify a scorer's or timer's mistake or a malfunction of the clock. 1999-00, Officials must consult courtside television monitors, when available, to judge whether a game-deciding last-second shot in the second half or any extra period counts. (This was passed during season.) 2001-02, Officials could check an official courtside monitor to determine if a try was a three- or two-point attempt, regardless of whether the try was successful. 2003-04, Officials could consult courtside monitor at the end of either half or any extra period to determine: (1) if a field-goal try beat the horn; (2) whether a shot-clock violation at the end of the first half beat the horn; or, (3) whether a shot-clock violation that would determine the outcome of a game beat the horn. The officials also could use a courtside monitor to correct a timer's mistake or to determine if the game clock or shot clock expired at or near the end of a period. 2005-06, Expanding on the rule from two seasons before, officials who consult a courtside monitor at the end of either half or any extra period could correct the official game time if needed and/or determine whether a foul was committed before time expired. Officials could also consult a courtside monitor any time during the game to correct a timer's mistake. 2007-08, Use of courtside monitor allowed for determining whether a flagrant foul occurred or to assess the situation during a fight.

Three Seconds: 1932-33, No player could stand in the free-throw lane with the ball more than three seconds. 1935-36, No offensive player could remain in the free-throw lane, with or without the ball, for more than three seconds. 1944-45, It became a violation for an offensive player to remain in the free-throw lane more than three seconds.

Three-Point Shot: 1980-81, Conferences began experimenting with the three-point field-goal at different distances. 1986-87, The three-point field goal was introduced nationally and set at 19 feet 9 inches from the center of the basket. 1990-91, Three free throws were awarded when a shooter was fouled during an unsuccessful three-point try. 2008-09, The three-point line will be extended to 20 feet, 9 inches.

Time Stoppage: 1905-06, Time stopped only when ordered by the referee. It did not stop for dead-ball situations such as free throws or when the ball was out-of-bounds. 1924-25, Time stopped when ordered by the referee for injuries, substitutions, two-shot fouls and timeouts requested by the team captain. The clock kept running at all other times including dead-ball situations, such as out-of-bounds.

Timekeepers: 1905-06, One timekeeper was appointed by the home team. The visiting team could appoint an assistant timekeeper if it chose to. 1924-25, Two timekeepers were used, one from each team, and shared a watch placed on a table so both could see it. The timekeepers kept track of all the incidents that time was out and added that to the game time. The timekeepers indicated when time expired by using a gong, pistol or whistle.

Timeouts: 1924-25, Only team captains could call for a timeout. Each team had three timeouts per game. 1948-49, Coaches were allowed to speak to players during a timeout. 1995-96, Teams were allowed one 20-second timeout per half. This was an experimental rule in the 1994-95 season. 1996-97, In games not involving commercial electronic media, teams were entitled to four full-length timeouts and two 20-second timeouts per game. In games involving commercial electronic media, teams were entitled to two full-length timeouts and three 20-second timeouts per game. 1997-98, Timeout requests could be made by a player on the court or by the head coach. 1999-00, Twenty-second timeouts increased to 30 seconds in length. New electronic-media timeout format adopted. 2006-07, A timeout would not be recognized when an airborne player's momentum carried him either out-of-bounds or into the backcourt.

Traveling: 1900-01, A dribbler could not shoot for a field goal and could dribble only once, and then with two hands. 1908-09, A dribbler was permitted to shoot. The dribble was defined as the "continuous passage of the ball," making the double dribble illegal. 1921-22, Running with the ball changes from a foul to a violation.

Uniforms: 1957-58, On uniforms, the use of the single digit numbers one and two and any digit greater than five was prohibited. 1999-00, Uniform numbers one and two were permitted.

Basketball Rules Committee Secretary-Rules Editor Roster

Name	Affiliation	Years
Oswald Tower	non-NCAA	1939-59
John Bunn	Colorado St.	1960-67
Ed Steitz	Springfield	1967-91
Henry Nichols	Villanova	1992-96
Ed Bilik	Springfield	1997-present

Division I Basketball Rules Committee Chair Roster

Name	Affiliation	Years
H.H. Salmon Jr.	Princeton	1939-40
Floyd Rowe	non-NCAA	1941
James W. St. Clair	SMU	1942-44
E.J. Hickox	non-NCAA	1945, 1947
H.G. Olsen	Ohio St.	1946
George Edwards	Missouri	1948-51
Bruce Drake	Oklahoma	1952-55
Paul Hinkle	Butler	1956-59
H.E. Foster	Wisconsin	1960-65
Polk Robison	Texas Tech	1966
Norvall Neve	Atlantic Coast, Missouri Valley Conferences	1967-75
Richard Wilson	Amherst	1976
John Carpenter	Rider	1977-78
Jack Thurnblad	Carleton	1979-80
C.M. Newton	Alabama, Southeastern Conference	1981-85
James Dutcher	Minnesota	1986
Jerry Krause	Eastern Wash.	1987
Richard Sauers	Albany (N.Y.)	1988
Gene Bartow	UAB	1989-93
George Raveling	Southern California	1994-96
Larry Keating Jr.	Seton Hall	1997
Herb Kenny	Wesleyan (Conn.)	1998
Reggie Minton	Air Force	1999-2000
Roy Williams	Kansas	2001
Art Hyland	Big East Conference	2002-03
Willis Wilson	Rice	2004
Perry Watson	Detroit	2005
Larry Keating Jr.	Kansas	2006-07

Basketball Rules Committee Roster

Name	Affiliation	Years
Phog Allen	Kansas	1939-41
William Anderson	Lafayette	1951-54
Lewis Andreas	Syracuse	1946-49
Tom Apke	Creighton, Colorado	1979-84
Tim Autry	South Carolina St.	1998-2002
Joe Baker	Wis.-La Crosse	2003-05
Ralph Barkey	Sonoma St.	1996
Sam Barry	Southern California	1946-48
Justin Barry	Southern California	1949-51

Name	Affiliation	Years
Gene Bartow	Memphis, Illinois, UCLA, UAB	1974-78, 88-93
Mike Brey	Notre Dame	2008-present
Steve Belko	Oregon	1966-69
John Bennington	St. Louis, Michigan St.	1960-65
Bill Berry	San Jose St.	1988-90
Ed Bilik	Springfield	1968-69, 72-78, 96-2002
Hoyt Brawner	Denver	1960-66
Charlie Brock	Springfield	2003-07
Clint Bryant	Augusta St.	1996-99
Tom Bryant	Centre	1996-98
John Bunn	Stanford, Springfield, Colorado St.	1939-40, 54-67
Clarence Burch	Lycoming	1979-82
Jim Burson	Muskingum	1987-92
L.C. Butler	Colorado St.	1951-53
E.M. Cameron	Duke	1956-61
John Carpenter	Rider	1973-78
Don Casey	Temple	1979-82
Dale Clayton	Carson-Newman	2003-07
Gary Colson	New Mexico, California	1986-92
Robert Corn	Mo. Southern St.	2008-present
Forrest Cox	Colorado	1940-44
Joe Dean Jr.	Birmingham So.	2003-07
Sumner A. Dole	Connecticut	1939-41
Ed Douma	Hillsdale	2001-04
Bruce Drake	Oklahoma	1947-55
Fran Dunphy	Penn	2004-06
James Dutcher	Minnesota	1983-86
W.H.H. Dye	Washington	1955-59
C.S. Edmundson	Washington	1941-45
George Edwards	Missouri	1942-51
Fred Enke	Arizona	1957-61
Wesley E. Fesler	Wesleyan (Conn.)	1944
Dan Fitzgerald	Gonzaga	1996-97
H.E. Foster	Wisconsin	1958-66
Clarence Gaines	Winston-Salem	1992-93
Jayson Gee	Charleston (W.V.)	2001-03
Pete Gillen	Xavier	1993-97
Jack Gray	Texas	1951-52
Hugh Greer	Connecticut	1963
Jim Gudger	Tex. A&M-Commerce	1976, 78
Dick Hack	Medaille	2006-present
Richard Harter	Penn	1972
Rick Hartzell	UNI	2008-present
Clem Haskins	Minnesota	1992-96
E.O. "Doc" Hayes	SMU	1967-69
R.E. Henderson	Baylor	1953-56
Paul Hinkle	Butler	1954-59
Howard Hobson	Yale	1952-55
Ron Holmes	McMurry	1999-2002
Art Hyland	Big East Conference	1998-2003
Henry Iba	Oklahoma St.	1952-54, 67-69
Clarence Iba	Tulsa	1956-59
George Ireland	Loyola (Ill.)	1963-66
Calvin Irvin	N.C. A&T	1979
Brad Jackson	Western Wash.	2004-present
Bill Jones	North Ala.	1985-91
Larry Keating, Jr.	Seton Hall, Kansas	1994-97; 2003-07
Herb Kenny	Wesleyan (Conn.)	1993-98
William Knapton	Beloit	1981-86
Jack Kraft	Villanova	1968-69
Jerry Krause	Eastern Wash. St.	1976-78, 83-87
Mike Kryzewski	Duke	1991
John Kundla	Minnesota	1968-69, 72-74
Eugene Lambert	Arkansas	1945-49
Dale Lash	Springfield	1942-43
Debora Lazorik	Marietta	1999-2002
Harry Litwack	Temple	1960-65
Bobby Lutz	Charlotte	2007-present
Edward P. Markey	St. Michael's	1992-95
Jack Martin	Lamar	1974-79
Rollie Massimino	UNLV	1993-95
Arthur McAfee	Morehouse	1975-80
Walter "Doc" Meanwell	Wisconsin	1939
Gene Mehaffey	Ohio Wesleyan	1993-98
Bill Menefee	Baylor	1972-73

Name	Affiliation	Years
Ray Meyer	DePaul	1979-82
Joey Meyer	DePaul	1993-95
Douglas Mills	Illinois	1947-53
Reggie Minton	Air Force	1997-2000
Mike Montgomery	Stanford	1997-2000
Steve Moore	Wooster	2007-present
Gerald Myers	Texas Tech	1986-92
Norvall Neve	Atlantic Coast, Missouri Valley Conferences	1967-75
C.M. Newton	Alabama, Southeastern Conference	1981-85
Henry Nichols	Villanova	1992-96
Thomas Niland Jr.	Le Moyne	1985-91
Kenneth Norton	Manhattan	1955-59
Tom O'Connor	George Mason	1998-2003
Dave Odom	Wake Forest	2001-04
H.G. Olsen	Ohio St.	1940-46
Ray Oosting	Trinity (Conn.)	1946-49, 51, 58-62
James Padgett	California, Nevada	1972-74
Curtis Parker	Centenary (La.)	1939-41
Ted Paulauskas	St. Anselm	1997-99
Richard H. Perry	UC Riverside	1992
Vadal Peterson	Utah	1945-48
Mac Petty	Wabash	1987-92
Digger Phelps	Notre Dame	1988-91
Jerry Pimm	Utah	1979-84
Lonnie Porter	Regis (Colo.)	2004-present
Clarence Price	California	1952-54
Skip Prosser	Wake Forest	2004-07
Jack Ramsay	St. Joseph's	1966-67
George Raveling	Southern California	1993-96
Lonn Reisman	Tarleton St.	2000-03
Polk Robison	Texas Tech	1962-66
Paul Rundell	San Fran. St.	1980-81
Adolph Rupp	Kentucky	1962-66
Andy Russo	Florida Tech, Lynn	1997-2000
H.H. Salmon Jr.	Princeton	1939-40
Richard Sauers	Albany (N.Y)	1983-87
William Scanlon	Union (N.Y.)	1989-94
Norman Shepard	Davidson	1942-47
J. Dallas Shirley	Southern Conference	1984-87
Dean Smith	North Carolina	1967-69, 72-73
James W. St. Clair	SMU	1939-44
Floyd Stahl	Ohio St.	1956-57, 60-61
Ed Steitz	Springfield	1959-91
Norm Stewart	Missouri	1985-91
Kenneth Stibler	Biscayne	1978-84
Eddie Sutton	Arkansas	1980-85
H. Jamison Swarts	Penn	1941-45
A.K. Tebell	Virginia	1948-52
Bob Thomason	Pacific	2004-present
John M. Thompson	N.C. Wesleyan	2008-present
John Thompson III	Princeton	2003-04
Jack Thurnblad	Carleton	1975-80
Alvin J. Van Wie	Wooster	1981-86
Bob Vanatta	Sunshine State Conference	1994-95
Kevin Vande Streek	Calvin	2003-06
M. Edward Wagner	California Collegiate Athletic Association	1976-79
Russell Walseth	Colorado	1972-75, 77-78
Perry Watson	Detroit	2002-05
Stanley Watts	BYU	1954-57
Clifford Wells	Tulane	1953-56
Don White	Connecticut	1945
Phillip Witherspoon	Buffalo	2006-present
Vining William	Ouachita Baptist	1977
James Williams	Colorado St.	1972-78
Roy Williams	Kansas	1997-2000
Floyd Wilson	Harvard	1964-69
Richard Wilson	Amherst	1972-75
Willis Wilson	Rice	2001-04
Willard A. Witte	Wyoming	1939
John Wooden	UCLA	1961-64
Ned Wulk	Arizona St.	1968-69
Jim Zalacca	New Paltz St., Potsdam St.	1999-2002

Division I Basketball Firsts

The First Time...

Playing rules were published:
January 1892 in the Springfield College school newspaper, The Triangle.

A game was played:
January 20, 1892, at the Training School of the International YMCA College, now known as Springfield College in Massachusetts.

A game was played in public:
March 11, 1892, at Springfield College. A crowd of 200 saw the students defeat the teachers, 5-1.

A full schedule of games was played by a college:
1894, when the University of Chicago compiled a 6-1 season record.

A game between two colleges was played:
February 9, 1895, when the Minnesota School of Agriculture defeated Hamline, 9-3. Nine players were allowed on the court at the same time for both teams.

A game between two colleges was played with five players on each team:
January 16, 1896, when Chicago defeated Iowa, 15-12, in Iowa City. Iowa's starting lineup was composed of a YMCA team that just happened to be university students.

A game between two true college teams with five players on a team was played:
1897, when Yale defeated Penn, 32-10.

A conference season was played:
1901-02 by the East League, known today as the Ivy Group.

A conference tournament was played:
1921 by the Southern Conference. Kentucky was the winner.

A consensus all-America team was selected:
1929. Members were Charley Hyatt, Pittsburgh; Joe Schaaf, Penn; Charles Murphy, Purdue; Vern Corbin, California; Thomas Churchill, Oklahoma; and John Thompson, Montana State.

A game was filmed for a newsreel:
February 20, 1931, St. John's (N.Y.) against Carnegie Mellon.

The National Invitation Tournament was played:
1938, when Temple was the winner.

A college game was televised:
February 28, 1940, when Pittsburgh defeated Fordham, 50-37, at Madison Square Garden in New York City. In the second game, New York University defeated Georgetown, 50-27. The games were broadcast on New York station W2XBS.

The three-point shot was used experimentally in a game:
February 7, 1945, Columbia defeated Fordham, 73-58. The three-point line was set at 21 feet from the basket and Columbia scored 11 "long goals" to Fordham's nine. Also, free-throwers had an option to take their shots from the regular 15-foot distance for one point or from 21 feet for two points. Eight "long fouls" were made during the game.

The 12-foot free-throw lane was used experimentally in a game:
February 7, 1945, Columbia defeated Fordham, 73-58 in the same game as mentioned above. The free-throw lane was widened from 6 feet to 12 for this game and the rule was adopted 11 years later.

An Associated Press poll was published:
1949, when St. Louis was ranked No. 1. By the end of the season, Kentucky had taken over the top spot.

All the games of a conference tournament were televised:
1979, the Sun Belt on ESPN.

The RPI was released to the public:
Febuary 1, 2006, when the Rating Percentage Index (RPI) appeared on the NCAA Web site.

NCAA Tournament Firsts

The first game:
March 17, 1939, when Villanova defeated Brown, 42-30, in Philadelphia.

The first championship game:
March 27, 1939, when Oregon defeated Ohio State, 46-33, in Evanston, Illinois.

The first NCAA tournament MOP:
1939, Jimmy Hull of Ohio State was named the tournament's Most Outstanding Player.

The first player to score 30 points or more in a tournament game:
1941, George Glamack of North Carolina scored 31 points against Dartmouth in a regional third-place game.

The first time two teams from the same conference played in the NCAA tournament:
1944, when Iowa State and Missouri, both of the Big Six, played in the Western regional.

The first freshman named NCAA tournament MOP:
1944, Arnie Ferrin of Utah.

The first two-time NCAA tournament MOP:
1946, Bob Kurland of Oklahoma State was MOP in 1945 and 1946.

The first time four teams advanced to the final site:
1946 (North Carolina, Ohio State, Oklahoma State and California).

The first championship game televised:
1946, locally in New York City by WCBS-TV. Oklahoma State defeated North Carolina, 43-40. An estimated 500,000 watched the game on television.

The first player to dunk:
March 26 1946, when Bob Kurland, the 7-foot center for Oklahoma State, threw down two dunks late in the game to help preserve a 43-40 victory over North Carolina in the championship game.

The first repeat champion:
1946, Oklahoma State followed its 1945 championship with a title in 1946.

The first player to score 30 points or more in a Final Four game:
1947, George Kaftan of Holy Cross scored 30 points against CCNY in the national semifinal game.

The first school to win the NCAA championship in its home town:
1950, CCNY won the title in New York.

The first NCAA championship team to have an integrated roster of white and black players:
1950, CCNY's squad was the first integrated championship team, starting three black players

The first time conference champions qualified automatically:
1951.

The first time a team entered the tournament undefeated:
1951, Columbia at 21-0. The Lions lost to Illinois in the first round, 79-71.

The first time a conference tournament champion qualified automatically for the NCAA tournament instead of the regular-season champion:
1952, North Carolina State finished second in the Southern Conference but won the conference postseason tournament.

The first time there were four regional sites:
1952.

The first time games were televised regionally:
1952.

The first NCAA tournament MOP not to play on the national championship team:
1953, B.H. Born of Kansas.

The first player to score 40 points or more in a tournament game:
1952, Clyde Lovellette of Kansas scored 44 points against St. Louis in the regional final game.

The first player to score 40 points or more in a Final Four game:
1953, Bob Houbregs of Washington scored 42 points against LSU in the national third-place game.

The first time a Final Four was played on Friday and Saturday:
1954.

The first tournament championship game televised nationally:
1954, for a broadcast rights fee of $7,500.

The first time an undefeated team won the NCAA championship:
1956, when San Francisco went 29-0.

The first player to score 50 points or more in a tournament game:
1958, Oscar Robertson of Cincinnati scored 56 points against Arkansas in the regional third-place game.

The first time two teams from the same state played in the NCAA title game:
1961, when Cincinnati defeated Ohio State, 70-65, in overtime.

The first football Heisman Trophy winner to play in the Final Four:
1963, Terry Baker of Oregon State.

The first player to score 50 points or more in a Final Four game:
1965, Bill Bradley of Princeton scored 58 points against Wichita State in the national third-place game.

The first championship team to start five African-Americans:
1966, UTEP with Harry Flournoy, David Lattin, Bobby Joe Hill, Orsten Artis and Willie Worsley.

The first three-time NCAA tournament MOP:
1969, Lew Alcindor of UCLA was MOP in 1967, 1968 and 1969.

The first time the Final Four was played on Thursday and Saturday:
1969.

The first time the Final Four was played on Saturday and Monday:
1973.

The first NCAA title game televised during prime time:
1973, UCLA's win over Memphis was televised by NBC.

The first time television rights totaled more than $1 million:
1973.

The first public draw for Final Four tickets:
1973 for the 1974 championship.

The first time teams other than the conference champion could be chosen at large from the same conference:
1975.

The first reference to the term "Final Four":
1975 Official Collegiate Basketball Guide, page 5 in national preview-review section written by Ed Chay of the Cleveland Plain Dealer. Chay wrote, "Outspoken Al McGuire of Marquette, whose team was one of the final four in Greensboro, was among several coaches who said it was good for college basketball that UCLA was finally beaten."

The first time two African-American coaches played each other in a tournament game:
March 13, 1976, when Fred Snowden's Arizona Wildcats defeated John Thompson's Georgetown Hoyas, 83-76, in a first round game.

The first time two teams from the same conference played in the Final Four title game:
March 29, 1976, when Indiana defeated Michigan, 86-68. Both teams were Big Ten members.

The first player to play for two teams in the Final Four championship game:
1978, Bob Bender with Indiana in 1976 and Duke in 1978.

The first time the seeding process was used to align teams in the bracket:
1978.

The first reference to term "Final Four" was capitalized:
1978 Official Collegiate Basketball Guide (page 7, first line).

The first time all teams were seeded in the bracket:
1979.

The first public lottery for Final Four tickets:
1979.

The first time more than two teams from the same conference were allowed in the NCAA tournament:
1980.

The first time none of the No. 1 seeds in the NCAA tournament advanced to the Final Four:
1980.

The first time the Rating Percentage Index (RPI), a computer ranking system, was used as an aid in evaluating teams for at-large selections and seeding:
1981.

The first time two No. 1 seeds in the NCAA tournament advanced to the Final Four:
1981.

The first time a Final Four logo was produced that was specific to the site of the championship game:
1981, when the final game was played in Philadelphia and the logo included the Liberty Bell.

The first live television broadcast of the selection show announcing the NCAA tournament bracket:
1982.

The first time CBS was awarded the television rights for the NCAA tournament:
1982.

The first TV announcer to use "March Madness" in referring the tournament:
1982, Brent Musburger of CBS Sports.

The first African-American to coach a team into the Final Four:
1982, John Thompson of Georgetown.

The first time a men's and women's team from the same school advanced to the Final Four in the same year:
1983, when both Georgia teams lost in the national semifinals.

The first time awards were presented to all participating teams in the NCAA championship tournament:
1984.

The first African-American to coach a team to the NCAA basketball championship:
1984, John Thompson of Georgetown.

The first time 64 teams participated in the NCAA tournament:
1985.

The first unranked team to win the championship:
1985, Villanova.

The first double-digit seed to reach the Final Four:
1986, LSU as an 11-seed.

The first coach to win the NCAA title in his first year as a head coach:
Steve Fisher of Michigan in 1989.

The first time 65 teams participated in the NCAA tournament:
2001.

The first time two persons of color faced each other as coaches in a Final Four game:
March 30, 2002, when Mike Davis' Indiana Hoosiers defeated Kelvin Sampson's Oklahoma Sooners, 73-64, in a national semifinal game.

The first time three teams from the same conference advanced to the Final Four:
1985, when Georgetown, St. John's (New York) and Villanova represented the Big East.

The first time all 64 NCAA tournament teams were subject to drug testing:
1987.

The first time neutral courts were used in all rounds of the NCAA tournament:
1989.

The first time all the Nos. 1 and 2 seeds in the NCAA tournament advanced to the Sweet Sixteen:
1989.

The first time a bearded coach advanced to the Final Four:
1989, P.J. Carlesimo of Seton Hall.

The first No. 15-seed to defeat a No. 2-seed:
1991, Richmond over Syracuse, 73-69.

The first time a minimum facility seating capacity of 12,000 for first and second rounds and regionals was established:
1993.

The first time three No. 1 seeds in the NCAA tournament advanced to the Final Four:
1993.

The first time two former Final Four most outstanding players returned to the Final Four:
1995, when North Carolina's Donald Williams (1993) and Arkansas' Corliss Williamson (1994) returned to the Final Four.

The First School...

To play in both the NIT and the NCAA tournaments in the same year:
Duquesne in 1940

To win 30 games in a season:
Wyoming went 31-2 in 1943.

To win a football bowl game and the NCAA tournament title in the same academic year:
Oklahoma State won the Cotton Bowl and the NCAA championship in 1944-45.

To be ranked No. 1 in the final regular-season poll and go on to win the NCAA championship:
Kentucky ended the 1949 regular season ranked No. 1 and proceeded to win its second NCAA title.

To win the NCAA tournament and the NIT in the same year:
CCNY won both tournaments in 1950.

To play for the national championship in both football and basketball in the same academic year:
Oklahoma lost in both the Orange Bowl and the Final Four title game in 1987-88.

To be ranked No. 1 in the men's and women's polls:
Connecticut's men's and women's basketball programs were ranked No. 1 in their respective top-25 polls February 13, 1995.

To be voted the national champion in football and win the NCAA basketball tournament in the same academic year:
Florida in 2006-07

The First Coach...

Who also happened to be the inventor of the game:
Dr. James Naismith invented the game in December 1891 at Springfield College in Massachusetts.

To have won the NCAA tournament at his alma mater:
Howard Hobson of Oregon in 1939.

To lead his team to a finish among the final four teams in the nation in his first season as a head coach:
Bruce Drake of Oklahoma in 1939.

To take two different teams to the NCAA tournament:
Ben Carnevale—North Carolina in 1946 and Navy in 1947.

To lead his alma mater into the NCAA tournament after having played in the tournament:
Elmer Gross played for Penn State in the 1942 NCAA tournament and later coached them in the 1952 tournament.

To lead a school other than his alma mater into the NCAA tournament after having played in the tournament:
Doyle Parrack played for Oklahoma State in the 1945 NCAA tournament and later coached Oklahoma City in the 1952 tournament.

To be recognized as national coach of the year:
Phil Woolpert of San Francisco was named the 1955 coach of the year by United Press International.

To take two different teams to the Final Four:
Forddy Anderson and Frank McGuire. Anderson—Bradley in 1950 and Michigan State in 1957; McGuire—St. John's (New York) in 1952 and North Carolina in 1957.

To take two different schools to the NCAA championship game:
Frank McGuire in 1957 with North Carolina after St. John's (New York) in 1952.

To take three different teams to the NCAA tournament:
Eddie Hickey—Creighton in 1941 (first year), Saint Louis in 1952 and Marquette in 1959.

To have won the NCAA championship his first year at a school:
Ed Jucker at Cincinnati in 1961.

Who was African-American to coach at a Division I school:
Will Robinson at Illinois State in the 1971-72 season.

To win the NCAA championship after playing for an NCAA championship team:
Bob Knight coached Indiana to the championship in 1976 after playing for the 1960 Ohio State champions.

To take four different teams to the NCAA tournament:
Eddie Sutton—Creighton in 1974 (first year), Arkansas in 1977, Kentucky in 1986 and Oklahoma State in 1991.

To take a school to the Final Four in four different decades:
Dean Smith took North Carolina to the Final Four 11 times from 1967 to 1997.

To take three different teams to the Final Four:
Rick Pitino—Providence in 1987, Kentucky in 1993 and Louisville in 2005.

The First Player...

To score 1,000 points in his career:
Christian Steinmetz of Wisconsin from 1903-05.

To be named consensus all-American three times:
John Wooden of Purdue from 1930-32.

To popularize the jump shot:
John Cooper of Missouri in 1932-34, Hank Luisetti of Stanford in 1936-38 and Kenny Sailors of Wyoming in 1941-43 and 1946.

To score 50 points in one game:
Hank Luisetti of Stanford, who scored 50 in a win over Duquesne, January 1, 1938.

To dribble behind his back:
Bob Davies, an all-American from Seton Hall, is believed to be one of the first innovators of the behind-the-back dribble around 1941 and was photographed doing so.

To dunk in a game:
Bob Kurland, the 7-foot center for Oklahoma State, in 1946. His first dunk was disallowed, although his subsequent dunks were allowed.

Who was African-American to be named to the consensus all-America team:
Don Barksdale of UCLA in 1947.

Who was African-American to play on the U.S. Olympic team:
Don Barksdale of UCLA in 1948.

To score 2,000 points in his career:
Jim Lacy of Loyola (Md.) scored 2,154 points from 1946-49.

To lead the nation in scoring during the regular season and play for the NCAA championship team in the same year:
Clyde Lovellette of Kansas in 1952.

To grab 50 rebounds in one game:
Bill Chambers of William and Mary brought down 51 boards against Virginia on February 14, 1953.

To grab 700 rebounds in a season:
Walt Dukes of Seton Hall brought down 734 boards during the 1953 season.

To score 100 points in a game:
Frank Selvy of Furman scored 100 points in a 149-95 victory over Newberry on February 13, 1954, in Greenville, South Carolina.

To score 1,000 points in a single season:
Frank Selvy of Furman scored 1,209 during the 1954 season.

To average 40 points a game for a season:
Frank Selvy of Furman averaged 41.7 points a game during the 1954 season.

To average 30 points a game for a career:
Frank Selvy of Furman averaged 32.5 points a game from 1952-54.

To achieve 2,000 points and 2,000 rebounds in his career:
Tom Gola of La Salle scored 2,462 points and pulled down 2,201 rebounds from 1952-55.

Recognized as the national player of the year:
Tom Gola of La Salle was named the 1955 player of the year by United Press International.

To average more than 20 points and 20 rebounds per game during his career:
Bill Russell of San Francisco from 1954-56. He averaged 20.7 points and 20.3 rebounds.

To score 3,000 points in his career:
Pete Maravich of LSU scored 3,667 points from 1968-70.

To average 40 points a game for a career:
Pete Maravich of LSU averaged 44.2 points a game from 1968-70.

To score a three-point field goal (not counting the Columbia-Fordham game in 1945):
Ronnie Carr of Western Carolina drilled a 23-footer against Middle Tennessee State at 7:06 p.m. on November 29, 1980. The three-pointer was used as an experiment by several conferences until the rule was adopted nationally for the 1986-87 season.

To be named consensus all-American his freshman season:
Wayman Tisdale of Oklahoma in 1983.

To lead the nation in scoring and rebounding in the same season:
Xavier McDaniel of Wichita State in 1985.

To make 400 three-point field goals in his career:
Doug Day of Radford hit 401 three-pointers from 1990-93.

To be named national player-of-the-year his freshman season:
Kevin Durant of Texas in 2007.

Conferences

2007 Division I Conference Standings

AMERICA EAST CONFERENCE

	Conference			Full Season		
	W	L	Pct.	W	L	Pct.
Vermont	15	1	.938	25	8	.758
Albany (N.Y.) #	13	3	.813	23	10	.697
Boston U.	8	8	.500	12	18	.400
Maine	7	9	.438	12	18	.400
UMBC	7	9	.438	12	19	.387
Binghamton	6	10	.375	13	16	.448
Hartford	6	10	.375	13	18	.419
New Hampshire	6	10	.375	10	20	.333
Stony Brook	4	12	.250	9	20	.310

ATLANTIC COAST CONFERENCE

	Conference			Full Season		
	W	L	Pct.	W	L	Pct.
North Carolina #	11	5	.688	31	7	.816
Virginia	11	5	.688	21	11	.656
Virginia Tech	10	6	.625	22	12	.647
Boston College	10	6	.625	21	12	.636
Maryland	10	6	.625	25	9	.735
Georgia Tech	8	8	.500	20	12	.625
Duke	8	8	.500	22	11	.667
Clemson	7	9	.438	25	11	.694
Florida St.	7	9	.438	22	13	.629
North Carolina St.	5	11	.313	20	16	.556
Wake Forest	5	11	.313	15	16	.484
Miami (Fla.)	4	12	.250	12	20	.375

ATLANTIC SUN CONFERENCE

	Conference			Full Season		
	W	L	Pct.	W	L	Pct.
East Tenn. St.	16	2	.889	24	10	.706
Belmont #	14	4	.778	23	10	.697
Jacksonville	11	7	.611	15	14	.517
Lipscomb	11	7	.611	18	13	.581
Kennesaw St.^	9	9	.500	14	18	.438
Mercer	8	10	.444	13	17	.433
Campbell	7	11	.389	14	17	.452
Gardner-Webb	7	11	.389	9	21	.300
Stetson	6	12	.333	11	20	.355
North Fla.^	1	17	.056	3	26	.103

ATLANTIC 10 CONFERENCE

	Conference			Full Season		
	W	L	Pct.	W	L	Pct.
Massachusetts	13	3	.813	24	9	.727
Xavier	13	3	.813	25	9	.735
George Washington #	11	5	.688	23	9	.719
Fordham	10	6	.625	18	12	.600
Rhode Island	10	6	.625	19	14	.576
St. Joseph's	9	7	.563	18	14	.563
Dayton	8	8	.500	19	12	.613
St. Louis	8	8	.500	20	13	.606
Charlotte	7	9	.438	14	16	.467
Duquesne	6	10	.375	10	19	.345
Temple	6	10	.375	12	18	.400
Richmond	4	12	.250	8	22	.267
St. Bonaventure	4	12	.250	7	22	.241
La Salle	3	13	.188	10	20	.333

BIG EAST CONFERENCE

	Conference			Full Season		
	W	L	Pct.	W	L	Pct.
Georgetown #	13	3	.813	30	7	.811
Louisville	12	4	.750	24	10	.706
Pittsburgh	12	4	.750	28	9	.757
Notre Dame	11	5	.688	24	8	.750
Syracuse	10	6	.625	24	11	.686
Marquette	10	6	.625	24	10	.706
West Virginia	9	7	.563	27	9	.750
DePaul	9	7	.563	20	14	.588
Villanova	9	7	.563	22	11	.667
Providence	8	8	.500	18	13	.581
St. John's (N.Y.)	7	9	.438	16	15	.516
Connecticut	6	10	.375	17	14	.548
Seton Hall	4	12	.250	13	16	.448
South Fla.	3	13	.188	12	18	.400
Rutgers	3	13	.188	10	19	.345
Cincinnati	2	14	.125	11	19	.367

BIG SKY CONFERENCE

	Conference			Full Season		
	W	L	Pct.	W	L	Pct.
Weber St. #	11	5	.688	20	12	.625
Northern Ariz.	11	5	.688	18	12	.600
Montana	10	6	.625	17	15	.531
Portland St.	9	7	.563	19	13	.594
Montana St.	8	8	.500	11	19	.367
Idaho St.	8	8	.500	13	17	.433
Eastern Wash.	8	8	.500	15	14	.517
Sacramento St.	5	11	.313	10	19	.345
Northern Colo.^	2	14	.125	4	24	.143

BIG SOUTH CONFERENCE

	Conference			Full Season		
	W	L	Pct.	W	L	Pct.
Winthrop #	14	0	1.000	29	5	.853
High Point	11	3	.786	22	10	.688
Liberty	8	6	.571	14	17	.452
Coastal Caro.	7	7	.500	15	15	.500
UNC Asheville	6	8	.429	12	19	.387
VMI	5	9	.357	14	19	.424
Radford	3	11	.214	8	22	.267
Charleston So.	2	12	.143	8	22	.267

BIG TEN CONFERENCE

	Conference			Full Season		
	W	L	Pct.	W	L	Pct.
Ohio St. #	15	1	.938	35	4	.897
Wisconsin	13	3	.813	30	6	.833
Indiana	10	6	.625	21	11	.656
Illinois	9	7	.563	23	12	.657
Purdue	9	7	.563	22	12	.647
Iowa	9	7	.563	17	14	.548
Michigan St.	8	8	.500	23	12	.657
Michigan	8	8	.500	22	13	.629
Minnesota	3	13	.188	9	22	.290
Northwestern	2	14	.125	13	18	.419
Penn St.	2	14	.125	11	19	.367

BIG 12 CONFERENCE

	Conference			Full Season		
	W	L	Pct.	W	L	Pct.
Kansas #	14	2	.875	33	5	.868
Texas A&M	13	3	.813	27	7	.794
Texas	12	4	.750	25	10	.714
Kansas St.	10	6	.625	23	12	.657
Texas Tech	9	7	.563	21	13	.618
Missouri	7	9	.438	18	12	.600
Oklahoma St.	6	10	.375	22	13	.629
Iowa St.	6	10	.375	15	16	.484
Oklahoma	6	10	.375	16	15	.516
Nebraska	6	10	.375	17	14	.548
Baylor	4	12	.250	15	16	.484
Colorado	3	13	.188	7	20	.259

BIG WEST CONFERENCE

	Conference			Full Season		
	W	L	Pct.	W	L	Pct.
Long Beach St. #	12	2	.857	24	8	.750
Cal St. Fullerton	9	5	.643	20	10	.667
Cal Poly	9	5	.643	19	11	.633
UC Santa Barbara	9	5	.643	18	11	.621
UC Irvine	6	8	.429	15	18	.455
Cal St. Northridge	5	9	.357	14	17	.452
Pacific	5	9	.357	12	19	.387
UC Riverside	1	13	.071	7	24	.226

COLONIAL ATHLETIC ASSOCIATION

	Conference			Full Season		
	W	L	Pct.	W	L	Pct.
VCU #	16	2	.889	28	7	.800
Old Dominion	15	3	.833	24	9	.727
Hofstra	14	4	.778	22	10	.688
Drexel	13	5	.722	23	9	.719
George Mason	9	9	.500	18	15	.545
Northeastern	9	9	.500	13	19	.406
William & Mary	8	10	.444	15	15	.500
Towson	8	10	.444	15	17	.469
Georgia St.	5	13	.278	11	20	.355
UNC Wilmington	4	14	.222	7	22	.241
James Madison	4	14	.222	7	23	.233
Delaware	3	15	.167	5	26	.161

CONFERENCE USA

	Conference			Full Season		
	W	L	Pct.	W	L	Pct.
Memphis #	16	0	1.000	32	5	.865
UCF	11	5	.688	22	9	.710
Houston	10	6	.625	18	15	.545
Tulane	9	7	.563	17	13	.567
Tulsa	9	7	.563	20	11	.645
Southern Miss.	9	7	.563	20	11	.645
Rice	8	8	.500	16	16	.500
Marshall	7	9	.438	13	19	.406
UAB	7	9	.438	15	16	.484
UTEP	6	10	.375	14	17	.452
SMU	3	13	.188	14	17	.452
East Caro.	1	15	.063	6	24	.200

HORIZON LEAGUE

	Conference			Full Season		
	W	L	Pct.	W	L	Pct.
Wright St. #	13	3	.813	23	10	.697
Butler	13	3	.813	29	7	.806
Loyola (Ill.)	10	6	.625	21	11	.656
Green Bay	7	9	.438	18	15	.545
Youngstown St.	7	9	.438	14	17	.452
Ill.-Chicago	7	9	.438	14	18	.438
Milwaukee	6	10	.375	9	22	.290
Detroit	6	10	.375	11	19	.367
Cleveland St.	3	13	.188	10	21	.323

IVY GROUP

	Conference			Full Season		
	W	L	Pct.	W	L	Pct.
Penn	13	1	.929	22	9	.710
Yale	10	4	.714	14	13	.519
Cornell	9	5	.643	16	12	.571
Columbia	7	7	.500	16	12	.571
Brown	6	8	.429	11	18	.379
Harvard	5	9	.357	12	16	.429
Dartmouth	4	10	.286	9	18	.333
Princeton	2	12	.143	11	17	.393

METRO ATLANTIC ATHLETIC CONFERENCE

	Conference			Full Season		
	W	L	Pct.	W	L	Pct.
Marist	14	4	.778	25	9	.735
Niagara #	13	5	.722	23	12	.657
Loyola (Md.)	12	6	.667	18	13	.581
Siena	12	6	.667	20	12	.625
Manhattan	10	8	.556	13	17	.433
Fairfield	10	8	.556	13	19	.406
Rider	9	9	.500	16	15	.516
Canisius	6	12	.333	12	19	.387
St. Peter's	3	15	.167	5	25	.167
Iona	1	17	.056	2	28	.067

MID-AMERICAN CONFERENCE

	Conference			Full Season		
East Division	W	L	Pct.	W	L	Pct.
Akron	13	3	.813	26	7	.788
Kent St.	12	4	.750	21	11	.656
Miami (Ohio) #	10	6	.625	18	15	.545
Ohio	9	7	.563	19	13	.594
Buffalo	4	12	.250	12	19	.387
Bowling Green	3	13	.188	13	18	.419
West Division						
Toledo	14	2	.875	19	13	.594
Western Mich.	9	7	.563	16	16	.500
Central Mich.	7	9	.438	13	18	.419
Eastern Mich.	6	10	.375	13	19	.406
Ball St.	5	11	.313	9	22	.290
Northern Ill.	4	12	.250	7	23	.233

MID-CONTINENT CONFERENCE

	Conference			Full Season		
	W	L	Pct.	W	L	Pct.
Oral Roberts #	12	2	.857	23	11	.676
Oakland	10	4	.714	19	14	.576
Valparaiso	9	5	.643	16	15	.516
IUPUI	7	7	.500	15	15	.500
Southern Utah	6	8	.429	16	14	.533
UMKC	6	8	.429	12	20	.375
Centenary (La.)	3	11	.214	10	21	.323
Western Ill.	3	11	.214	7	23	.233

MID-EASTERN ATHLETIC CONFERENCE

	Conference			Full Season		
	W	L	Pct.	W	L	Pct.
Delaware St.	16	2	.889	21	12	.636
Florida A&M #	12	6	.667	21	14	.600
Hampton	10	8	.556	15	16	.484
N.C. A&T	10	8	.556	15	17	.469
South Carolina St.	10	8	.556	13	17	.433
Morgan St.	10	8	.556	13	18	.419
Norfolk St.	10	8	.556	11	19	.367
Coppin St.	9	9	.500	12	20	.375
Bethune-Cookman	6	12	.333	9	21	.300
Howard	5	13	.278	9	22	.290
Md.-East. Shore	1	17	.056	4	27	.129

MISSOURI VALLEY CONFERENCE

	Conference			Full Season		
	W	L	Pct.	W	L	Pct.
Southern Ill.	15	3	.833	29	7	.806
Creighton #	13	5	.722	22	11	.667
Missouri St.	12	6	.667	22	11	.667
Bradley	10	8	.556	22	13	.629
UNI	9	9	.500	18	13	.581
Wichita St.	8	10	.444	17	14	.548
Drake	6	12	.333	17	15	.531
Illinois St.	6	12	.333	15	16	.484
Evansville	6	12	.333	14	17	.452
Indiana St.	5	13	.278	13	18	.419

MOUNTAIN WEST CONFERENCE

	Conference			Full Season		
	W	L	Pct.	W	L	Pct.
BYU	13	3	.813	25	9	.735
UNLV #	12	4	.750	30	7	.811
Air Force	10	6	.625	26	9	.743
San Diego St.	10	6	.625	22	11	.667
Wyoming	7	9	.438	17	15	.531
Colorado St.	6	10	.375	17	13	.567
Utah	6	10	.375	11	19	.367
New Mexico	4	12	.250	15	17	.469
TCU	4	12	.250	13	17	.433

NORTHEAST CONFERENCE

	Conference			Full Season		
	W	L	Pct.	W	L	Pct.
Central Conn. St. #	16	2	.889	22	12	.647
Sacred Heart	12	6	.667	18	14	.563
Quinnipiac	11	7	.611	14	15	.483
Robert Morris	9	9	.500	17	11	.607
Fairleigh Dickinson	9	9	.500	14	16	.467
Mt. St. Mary's	9	9	.500	11	20	.355
Wagner	8	10	.444	11	19	.367
Monmouth	7	11	.389	12	18	.400
St. Francis (N.Y.)	7	11	.389	9	22	.290
Long Island	6	12	.333	10	19	.345
St. Francis (Pa.)	5	13	.278	8	21	.276

OHIO VALLEY CONFERENCE

	Conference			Full Season		
	W	L	Pct.	W	L	Pct.
Austin Peay	16	4	.800	21	12	.636
Eastern Ky. #	13	7	.650	21	12	.636
Tennessee Tech	13	7	.650	19	13	.594
Murray St.	13	7	.650	16	14	.533
Samford	12	8	.600	16	16	.500
Southeast Mo. St.	9	11	.450	11	20	.355
Morehead St.	8	12	.400	12	18	.400
Tennessee St.	8	12	.400	12	20	.375
Jacksonville St.	7	13	.350	9	21	.300
Eastern Ill.	6	14	.300	10	20	.333
Tenn.-Martin	5	15	.250	8	23	.258

PACIFIC-10 CONFERENCE

	Conference			Full Season		
	W	L	Pct.	W	L	Pct.
UCLA	15	3	.833	30	6	.833
Washington St.	13	5	.722	26	8	.765
Oregon #	11	7	.611	29	8	.784
Arizona	11	7	.611	20	11	.645
Southern California	11	7	.611	25	12	.676
Stanford	10	8	.556	18	13	.581
Washington	8	10	.444	19	13	.594
California	6	12	.333	16	17	.485
Oregon St.	3	15	.167	11	21	.344
Arizona St.	2	16	.111	8	22	.267

PATRIOT LEAGUE

	Conference			Full Season		
	W	L	Pct.	W	L	Pct.
Holy Cross #	13	1	.929	25	9	.735
Bucknell	13	1	.929	22	9	.710
Lehigh	7	7	.500	12	19	.387
American	7	7	.500	16	14	.533
Colgate	5	9	.357	10	19	.345
Army	4	10	.286	15	16	.484
Navy	4	10	.286	14	16	.467
Lafayette	3	11	.214	9	21	.300

SOUTHEASTERN CONFERENCE

Eastern Division	Conference			Full Season		
	W	L	Pct.	W	L	Pct.
Florida #	13	3	.813	35	5	.875
Vanderbilt	10	6	.625	22	12	.647
Tennessee	10	6	.625	24	11	.686
Kentucky	9	7	.563	22	12	.647
Georgia	8	8	.500	19	14	.576
South Carolina	4	12	.250	14	16	.467
Western Division						
Mississippi St.	8	8	.500	21	14	.600
Mississippi	8	8	.500	21	13	.618
Arkansas	7	9	.438	21	14	.600
Auburn	7	9	.438	17	15	.531
Alabama	7	9	.438	20	12	.625
LSU	5	11	.313	17	15	.531

SOUTHERN CONFERENCE

North Division	Conference			Full Season		
	W	L	Pct.	W	L	Pct.
Appalachian St.	15	3	.833	25	8	.758
UNC Greensboro	12	6	.667	16	14	.533
Western Caro.	7	11	.389	11	20	.355
Chattanooga	6	12	.333	15	18	.455
Elon	5	13	.278	7	23	.233
South Division						
Davidson #	17	1	.944	29	5	.853
Col. of Charleston	13	5	.722	22	11	.667
Furman	8	10	.444	15	16	.484
Ga. Southern	7	11	.389	15	16	.484
Wofford	5	13	.278	10	20	.333
Citadel	4	14	.222	7	23	.233

SOUTHLAND CONFERENCE

East Division	Conference			Full Season		
	W	L	Pct.	W	L	Pct.
Northwestern St.	10	6	.625	17	15	.531
McNeese St.	9	7	.563	15	17	.469
Southeastern La.	8	8	.500	16	14	.533
Lamar	8	8	.500	15	17	.469
Nicholls St.	7	9	.438	8	22	.267
Central Ark.^	4	12	.250	10	20	.333
West Division						
A&M Corpus Christi #	14	2	.875	26	7	.788
Sam Houston St.	13	3	.813	21	10	.677
Stephen F. Austin	8	8	.500	15	14	.517
Texas-Arlington	8	8	.500	13	17	.433
Texas St.	4	12	.250	9	20	.310
UTSA	3	13	.188	7	22	.241

SOUTHWESTERN ATHLETIC CONFERENCE

	Conference			Full Season		
	W	L	Pct.	W	L	Pct.
Mississippi Val.	13	5	.722	18	16	.529
Jackson St. #	12	6	.667	21	14	.600
Grambling	10	8	.556	12	14	.462
Alcorn St.	10	8	.556	11	19	.367
Texas Southern	9	9	.500	14	17	.452
Ark.-Pine Bluff	9	9	.500	12	19	.387
Southern U.	9	9	.500	10	21	.323
Alabama St.	8	10	.444	10	20	.333
Prairie View	6	12	.333	8	22	.267
Alabama A&M	4	14	.222	10	20	.333

SUN BELT CONFERENCE

Eastern Division	Conference			Full Season		
	W	L	Pct.	W	L	Pct.
South Ala.	13	5	.722	20	12	.625
Western Ky.	12	6	.667	22	11	.667
Fla. Atlantic	10	8	.556	16	15	.516
Middle Tenn.	8	10	.444	15	17	.469
Troy	8	10	.444	13	17	.433
Florida Int'l	7	11	.389	12	17	.414
Western Division						
Arkansas St.	11	7	.611	18	15	.545
La.-Monroe	11	7	.611	18	14	.563
North Texas #	10	8	.556	23	11	.676
New Orleans	9	9	.500	14	17	.452
Ark.-Little Rock	8	10	.444	13	17	.433
La.-Lafayette	7	11	.389	9	21	.300
Denver	3	15	.167	4	25	.138

WEST COAST CONFERENCE

	Conference			Full Season		
	W	L	Pct.	W	L	Pct.
Gonzaga #	11	3	.786	23	11	.676
Santa Clara	10	4	.714	21	10	.677
St. Mary's (Cal.)	8	6	.571	17	15	.531
San Francisco	8	6	.571	13	18	.419
San Diego	6	8	.429	18	14	.563
Loyola Marymount	5	9	.357	13	18	.419
Portland	4	10	.286	9	23	.281
Pepperdine	4	10	.286	8	23	.258

WESTERN ATHLETIC CONFERENCE

	Conference			Full Season		
	W	L	Pct.	W	L	Pct.
Nevada	14	2	.875	29	5	.853
New Mexico St. #	11	5	.688	25	9	.735
Fresno St.	10	6	.625	22	10	.688
Utah St.	9	7	.563	23	12	.657
Hawaii	8	8	.500	18	13	.581
Boise St.	8	8	.500	17	14	.548
Louisiana Tech	7	9	.438	10	20	.333
San Jose St.	4	12	.250	5	25	.167
Idaho	1	15	.063	4	27	.129

INDEPENDENTS

	W	L	Pct.
Tex.-Pan American	14	15	.483
IPFW	12	17	.414
Savannah St.	12	18	.400
Chicago St.	9	20	.310

RECLASSIFYING AND PROVISIONAL TEAMS

	W	L	Pct.
Utah Valley St.	22	7	.759
North Dakota St.	20	8	.714
Cal St. Bakersfield	15	14	.517
Kennesaw St.	13	18	.419
Central Ark.	10	20	.333
Longwood	9	22	.290
South Dakota St.	6	24	.200
UC Davis	5	23	.179
NJIT	5	24	.172
Winston-Salem	5	24	.172
Northern Colo.	4	24	.143
North Fla.	3	26	.103

#won conference tournament
^not full-fledged Division I

CONFERENCES

Division I Conference Champions Season-By-Season

Regular-season and conference tournament champions; No. refers to the number of teams in the conference or tournament.

AMERICA EAST CONFERENCE

Season	No.	Regular Season
1980	10	Boston U./Northeastern
1981	9	Northeastern
1982	9	Northeastern
1983	9	Boston U./New Hampshire
1984	8	Northeastern
1985	9	Northeastern/Canisius
1986	10	Northeastern
1987	10	Northeastern
1988	10	Siena
1989	10	Siena
1990	7	Northeastern
1991	6	Northeastern
1992	8	Delaware
1993	8	Drexel/Northeastern
1994	8	Drexel
1995	9	Drexel
1996	10	Drexel
1997	10	Boston U.
1998	10	Delaware/Boston U.
1999	10	Delaware/Drexel
2000	10	Hofstra
2001	10	Hofstra
2002	9	Boston U./Vermont
2003	9	Boston U.
2004	10	Boston U.
2005	10	Vermont
2006	9	Albany (N.Y.)
2007	9	Vermont

Season	No.	Conference Tournament
1980	8	Holy Cross
1981	6	Northeastern
1982	6	Northeastern
1983	9	Boston U.
1984	8	Northeastern
1985	9	Northeastern
1986	10	Northeastern
1987	10	Northeastern
1988	10	Boston U.
1989	10	Siena
1990	7	Boston U.
1991	6	Northeastern
1992	8	Delaware
1993	8	Delaware
1994	8	Drexel
1995	9	Drexel
1996	10	Drexel
1997	10	Boston U.
1998	10	Delaware
1999	10	Delaware
2000	10	Hofstra
2001	10	Hofstra
2002	8	Boston U.
2003	8	Vermont
2004	10	Vermont
2005	10	Vermont
2006	9	Albany (N.Y.)
2007	9	Albany (N.Y.)

AMERICAN SOUTH CONFERENCE

Season	No.	Regular Season
1988	6	Louisiana Tech/New Orleans
1989	6	New Orleans
1990	6	Louisiana Tech/New Orleans
1991	7	New Orleans/Arkansas St.

Season	No.	Conference Tournament
1988	6	Louisiana Tech
1989	6	Louisiana Tech
1990	6	New Orleans
1991	7	Louisiana Tech

AMERICAN WEST CONFERENCE

Season	No.	Regular Season
1995	4	Southern Utah
1996	4	Cal Poly

Season	No.	Conference Tournament
1995	4	Southern Utah
1996	4	Southern Utah

ATLANTIC COAST CONFERENCE

Season	No.	Regular Season
1954	8	Duke
1955	8	North Carolina St.
1956	8	North Carolina St./North Carolina
1957	8	North Carolina
1958	8	Duke
1959	8	North Carolina St./North Carolina
1960	8	North Carolina
1961	8	North Carolina
1962	8	Wake Forest
1963	8	Duke
1964	8	Duke
1965	8	Duke
1966	8	Duke
1967	8	North Carolina
1968	8	North Carolina
1969	8	North Carolina
1970	8	South Carolina
1971	8	North Carolina
1972	7	North Carolina
1973	7	North Carolina St.
1974	7	North Carolina St.
1975	7	Maryland
1976	7	North Carolina
1977	7	North Carolina
1978	7	North Carolina
1979	7	Duke/North Carolina
1980	8	Maryland
1981	8	Virginia
1982	8	North Carolina/Virginia
1983	8	North Carolina/Virginia
1984	8	North Carolina
1985	8	Georgia Tech/North Carolina/North Carolina St.
1986	8	Duke
1987	8	North Carolina
1988	8	North Carolina
1989	8	North Carolina St.
1990	8	Clemson
1991	8	Duke
1992	9	Duke
1993	9	North Carolina
1994	9	Duke
1995	9	Maryland/North Carolina/Virginia/Wake Forest
1996	9	Georgia Tech
1997	9	Duke
1998	9	Duke
1999	9	Duke
2000	9	Duke
2001	9	Duke/North Carolina
2002	9	Maryland
2003	9	Wake Forest
2004	9	Duke
2005	11	North Carolina
2006	12	Duke
2007	12	North Carolina/Virginia

Season	No.	Conference Tournament
1954	8	North Carolina St.
1955	8	North Carolina St.
1956	8	North Carolina St.
1957	8	North Carolina
1958	8	Maryland
1959	8	North Carolina St.
1960	8	Duke
1961	7	Wake Forest
1962	8	Wake Forest
1963	8	Duke
1964	8	Duke
1965	8	North Carolina St.
1966	8	Duke
1967	8	North Carolina
1968	8	North Carolina
1969	8	North Carolina
1970	8	North Carolina St.
1971	8	South Carolina
1972	7	North Carolina
1973	7	North Carolina St.
1974	7	North Carolina St.
1975	7	North Carolina
1976	7	Virginia
1977	7	North Carolina
1978	7	Duke
1979	7	North Carolina
1980	8	Duke
1981	8	North Carolina

Season	No.	Conference Tournament
1982	8	North Carolina
1983	8	North Carolina St.
1984	8	Maryland
1985	8	Georgia Tech
1986	8	Duke
1987	8	North Carolina St.
1988	8	Duke
1989	8	North Carolina
1990	8	Georgia Tech
1991	7	North Carolina
1992	9	Duke
1993	9	Georgia Tech
1994	9	North Carolina
1995	9	Wake Forest
1996	9	Wake Forest
1997	9	North Carolina
1998	9	North Carolina
1999	9	Duke
2000	9	Duke
2001	9	Duke
2002	9	Duke
2003	9	Duke
2004	9	Maryland
2005	11	Duke
2006	12	Duke
2007	12	North Carolina

ATLANTIC SUN CONFERENCE

Season	No.	Regular Season
1979	8	La.-Monroe
1980	7	La.-Monroe
1981	9	Houston Baptist
1982	9	Ark.-Little Rock
1983	8	Ark.-Little Rock
1984	8	Houston Baptist
1985	8	Ga. Southern
1986	8	Ark.-Little Rock
1987	10	Ark.-Little Rock
1988	10	Ark.-Little Rock/Ga. Southern
1989	10	Ga. Southern
1990	9	Centenary (La.)
1991	8	UTSA
1992	8	Ga. Southern
1993	7	Florida Int'l
1994	10	Col. of Charleston
1995	11	Col. of Charleston
1996	12	Col. of Charleston (East)/Samford (West)/Southeastern La. (West)
1997	12	Col. of Charleston (East)/Samford (West)
1998	12	Col. of Charleston (East)/Georgia St. (West)
1999	11	Samford
2000	10	Georgia St./Troy
2001	10	Georgia
2002	11	Georgia St./Troy
2003	12	Belmont (North)/Mercer (South)/Troy (South)
2004	11	Troy
2005	11	UCF/Gardner-Webb
2006	11	Lipscomb/Belmont
2007	8	East Tenn. St.

Season	No.	Conference Tournament
1979	6	La.-Monroe
1980	7	Centenary (La.)
1981	9	Mercer
1982	7	La.-Monroe
1983	8	Ga. Southern
1984	8	Houston Baptist
1985	8	Mercer
1986	8	Ark.-Little Rock
1987	8	Ga. Southern
1988	8	UTSA
1989	8	Ark.-Little Rock
1990	8	Ark.-Little Rock
1991	8	Georgia St.
1992	8	Ga. Southern
1993		DNP
1994	8	UCF
1995		Florida Int'l
1996	8	UCF
1997	8	Col. of Charleston
1998	8	Col. of Charleston
1999	8	Samford

Season	No.	Conference Tournament
2000	10	Samford
2001	10	Georgia St.
2002	8	Fla. Atlantic
2003	8	Troy
2004	8	UCF
2005	8	UCF
2006	8	Belmont
2007	8	Belmont

ATLANTIC 10 CONFERENCE

Season	No.	Regular Season
1977	8	Rutgers (Eastern)/West Virginia (Western)/Penn St. (Western)
1978	8	Rutgers/Villanova
1979	8	Villanova
1980	8	Villanova/Duquesne/Rutgers
1981	8	Rhode Island/Duquesne
1982	8	West Virginia
1983	10	Rutgers (Eastern)/St. Bonaventure (Western)/West Virginia (Western)
1984	10	Temple
1985	10	West Virginia
1986	10	St. Joseph's
1987	10	Temple
1988	10	West Virginia
1989	10	West Virginia
1990	10	Temple
1991	10	Rutgers
1992	9	Massachusetts
1993	8	Massachusetts
1994	9	Massachusetts
1995	9	Massachusetts
1996	12	Massachusetts (East)/George Washington (West)/Virginia Tech (West)
1997	12	St. Joseph's (East)/Xavier (West)
1998	12	Temple (East)/Xavier (West)/George Washington (West)/Dayton (West)
1999	12	Temple (East)/George Washington (West)
2000	12	Temple (East)/Dayton (West)
2001	11	St. Joseph's
2002	12	Temple (East)/St. Joseph's (East)/Xavier (West)
2003	12	St. Joseph's (East)/Xavier (West)
2004	12	St. Joseph's (East)/Dayton (West)
2005	12	St. Joseph's (East)/George Washington (West)
2006	14	George Washington
2007	14	Massachusetts/Xavier

Season	No.	Conference Tournament
1977	8	Duquesne
1978	8	Villanova
1979	8	Rutgers
1980	8	Villanova
1981	8	Pittsburgh
1982	8	Pittsburgh
1983	10	West Virginia
1984	10	West Virginia
1985	10	Temple
1986	10	St. Joseph's
1987	10	Temple
1988	10	Temple
1989	10	Rutgers
1990	10	Temple
1991	10	Penn St.
1992	9	Massachusetts
1993	8	Massachusetts
1994	9	Massachusetts
1995	9	Massachusetts
1996	12	Massachusetts
1997	12	St. Joseph's
1998	12	Xavier
1999	12	Rhode Island
2000	12	Temple
2001	11	Temple
2002	12	Xavier
2003	11	Dayton
2004	12	Xavier
2005	12	George Washington
2006	12	Xavier
2007	12	George Washington

BIG EAST CONFERENCE

Season	No.	Regular Season
1980	7	Syracuse/Georgetown/St. John's (N.Y.)
1981	8	Boston College
1982	8	Villanova
1983	9	Boston College/Villanova/St. John's (N.Y.)
1984	9	Georgetown
1985	9	St. John's (N.Y.)
1986	9	St. John's (N.Y.)/Syracuse
1987	9	Syracuse/Georgetown/Pittsburgh
1988	9	Pittsburgh
1989	9	Georgetown
1990	9	Connecticut/Syracuse
1991	9	Syracuse
1992	10	Seton Hall/Georgetown/St. John's (N.Y.)
1993	10	Seton Hall
1994	10	Connecticut
1995	10	Connecticut
1996	13	Georgetown (Big East 7)/Connecticut (Big East 6)
1997	13	Georgetown (Big East 7)/Villanova (Big East 6)/Boston College (Big East 6)
1998	13	Syracuse (Big East 7)/Connecticut (Big East 6)
1999	13	Connecticut
2000	13	Syracuse/Miami (Fla.)
2001	14	Boston College (East)/Notre Dame (West)
2002	14	Connecticut (East)/Pittsburgh (West)
2003	14	Boston College (East)/Connecticut (East)/Pittsburgh (West)/Syracuse (West)
2004	14	Pittsburgh
2005	12	Boston College/Connecticut
2006	16	Connecticut/Villanova
2007	16	Georgetown

Season	No.	Conference Tournament
1980	7	Georgetown
1981	8	Syracuse
1982	8	Georgetown
1983	9	St. John's (N.Y.)
1984	9	Georgetown
1985	9	Georgetown
1986	9	St. John's (N.Y.)
1987	9	Georgetown
1988	9	Syracuse
1989	9	Georgetown
1990	9	Connecticut
1991	9	Seton Hall
1992	10	Syracuse
1993	10	Seton Hall
1994	10	Providence
1995	10	Villanova
1996	13	Connecticut
1997	13	Boston College
1998	13	Connecticut
1999	13	Connecticut
2000	13	St. John's (N.Y.)
2001	12	Boston College
2002	12	Connecticut
2003	12	Pittsburgh
2004	12	Connecticut
2005	11	Syracuse
2006	12	Syracuse
2007	12	Georgetown

BIG EIGHT CONFERENCE

(Note: The Big Eight and Missouri Valley conferences share the same history from 1908-28.)

Season	No.	Regular Season
1908	6	Kansas
1909	6	Kansas
1910	6	Kansas
1911	5	Kansas
1912	6	Nebraska/Kansas
1913	6	Nebraska
1914	7	Kansas/Nebraska
1915	7	Kansas
1916	7	Nebraska
1917	7	Kansas St.
1918	7	Missouri
1919	8	Kansas St.
1920	8	Missouri

Season	No.	Regular Season
1921	9	Missouri
1922	9	Missouri/Kansas
1923	9	Kansas
1924	9	Kansas
1925	9	Kansas
1926	10	Kansas
1927	10	Kansas
1928	10	Oklahoma
1929	6	Oklahoma
1930	6	Missouri
1931	6	Kansas
1932	6	Kansas
1933	6	Kansas
1934	6	Kansas
1935	6	Iowa St.
1936	6	Kansas
1937	6	Kansas/Nebraska
1938	6	Kansas
1939	6	Missouri/Oklahoma
1940	6	Kansas/Missouri/Oklahoma
1941	6	Iowa St./Kansas
1942	6	Kansas/Oklahoma
1943	6	Kansas
1944	6	Iowa St./Oklahoma
1945	6	Iowa St.
1946	6	Kansas
1947	6	Oklahoma
1948	7	Kansas St.
1949	7	Nebraska/Oklahoma
1950	7	Kansas/Kansas St./Nebraska
1951	7	Kansas St.
1952	7	Kansas
1953	7	Kansas
1954	7	Kansas/Colorado
1955	7	Colorado
1956	7	Kansas St.
1957	7	Kansas
1958	7	Kansas St.
1959	8	Kansas St.
1960	8	Kansas/Kansas St.
1961	8	Kansas St.
1962	8	Colorado
1963	8	Colorado/Kansas St.
1964	8	Kansas St.
1965	8	Oklahoma St.
1966	8	Kansas
1967	8	Kansas
1968	8	Kansas St.
1969	8	Colorado
1970	8	Kansas St.
1971	8	Kansas
1972	8	Kansas St.
1973	8	Kansas St.
1974	8	Kansas
1975	8	Kansas
1976	8	Missouri
1977	8	Kansas St.
1978	8	Kansas
1979	8	Oklahoma
1980	8	Missouri
1981	8	Missouri
1982	8	Missouri
1983	8	Missouri
1984	8	Oklahoma
1985	8	Oklahoma
1986	8	Kansas
1987	8	Missouri
1988	8	Oklahoma
1989	8	Oklahoma
1990	8	Missouri
1991	8	Oklahoma St./Kansas
1992	8	Kansas
1993	8	Kansas
1994	8	Missouri
1995	8	Kansas
1996	8	Kansas

Season	No.	Conference Tournament
1977	8	Kansas St.
1978	8	Missouri
1979	8	Oklahoma
1980	8	Kansas St.
1981	8	Kansas
1982	8	Missouri
1983	8	Oklahoma St.
1984	8	Kansas
1985	8	Oklahoma
1986	8	Kansas
1987	8	Missouri
1988	8	Oklahoma

CONFERENCES

Season	No.	Conference Tournament
1989	8	Missouri
1990	8	Oklahoma
1991	8	Missouri
1992	8	Kansas
1993	8	Missouri
1994	8	Nebraska
1995	8	Oklahoma St.
1996	8	Iowa St.

BIG SKY CONFERENCE

Season	No.	Regular Season
1964	6	Montana St.
1965	6	Weber St.
1966	6	Weber St./Gonzaga
1967	6	Gonzaga/Montana St.
1968	6	Weber St.
1969	6	Weber St.
1970	6	Weber St.
1971	6	Weber St.
1972	8	Weber St.
1973	8	Weber St.
1974	8	Idaho St./Montana
1975	8	Montana
1976	8	Boise St./Weber St./Idaho St.
1977	8	Idaho St.
1978	8	Montana
1979	8	Weber St.
1980	8	Weber St.
1981	8	Idaho
1982	8	Idaho
1983	8	Weber St./Nevada
1984	8	Weber St.
1985	8	Nevada
1986	8	Northern Ariz./Montana
1987	8	Montana St.
1988	9	Boise St.
1989	9	Boise St./Idaho
1990	9	Idaho
1991	9	Montana
1992	9	Montana
1993	8	Idaho
1994	8	Weber St./Idaho St.
1995	8	Montana/Weber St.
1996	8	Montana St.
1997	9	Northern Ariz.
1998	9	Northern Ariz.
1999	9	Weber St.
2000	9	Montana/Eastern Wash.
2001	9	Cal St. Northridge
2002	8	Montana St.
2003	8	Weber St.
2004	8	Eastern Wash.
2005	8	Portland St.
2006	8	Northern Ariz.
2007	8	Northern Ariz./Weber St.

Season	No.	Conference Tournament
1976	8	Boise St.
1977	8	Idaho St.
1978	8	Weber St.
1979	8	Weber St.
1980	8	Weber St.
1981	8	Idaho
1982	8	Idaho
1983	8	Weber St.
1984	8	Nevada
1985	8	Nevada
1986	7	Montana St.
1987	8	Idaho St.
1988	9	Boise St.
1989	9	Idaho
1990	9	Idaho
1991	9	Montana
1992	6	Montana
1993	6	Boise St.
1994	6	Boise St.
1995	6	Weber St.
1996	6	Montana St.
1997	6	Montana
1998	6	Northern Ariz.
1999	6	Weber St.
2000	6	Northern Ariz.
2001	6	Cal St. Northridge
2002	6	Montana
2003	6	Weber St.
2004	6	Eastern Wash.
2005	6	Montana
2006	6	Montana
2007	6	Weber St.

BIG SOUTH CONFERENCE

Season	No.	Regular Season
1986	8	Charleston So.
1987	8	Charleston So.
1988	7	Coastal Caro.
1989	7	Coastal Caro.
1990	7	Coastal Caro.
1991	8	Coastal Caro.
1992	8	Radford
1993	9	Towson
1994	10	Towson
1995	9	UNC Greensboro
1996	9	UNC Greensboro
1997	8	Liberty/UNC Asheville
1998	7	UNC Asheville
1999	6	Winthrop
2000	8	Radford
2001	8	Radford
2002	8	Winthrop/UNC Asheville
2003	8	Winthrop
2004	9	Birmingham So./Liberty
2005	9	Winthrop
2006	9	Winthrop
2007	8	Winthrop

Season	No.	Conference Tournament
1986	8	Charleston So.
1987	8	Charleston So.
1988	7	Winthrop
1989	7	UNC Asheville
1990	7	Coastal Caro.
1991	8	Coastal Caro.
1992	8	Campbell
1993	9	Coastal Caro.
1994	8	Liberty
1995	8	Charleston So.
1996	8	UNC Greensboro
1997	8	Charleston So.
1998	7	Radford
1999	6	Winthrop
2000	6	Winthrop
2001	6	Winthrop
2002	8	Winthrop
2003	8	UNC Asheville
2004	8	Liberty
2005	8	Winthrop
2006	8	Winthrop
2007	8	Winthrop

BIG TEN CONFERENCE

Season	No.	Regular Season
1906	6	Minnesota
1907	5	Chicago/Minnesota/Wisconsin
1908	5	Chicago/Wisconsin
1909	8	Chicago
1910	8	Chicago
1911	8	Purdue/Minnesota
1912	8	Purdue/Wisconsin
1913	9	Wisconsin
1914	9	Wisconsin
1915	9	Illinois
1916	9	Wisconsin
1917	9	Minnesota/Illinois
1918	10	Wisconsin
1919	10	Minnesota
1920	10	Chicago
1921	10	Michigan/Wisconsin/Purdue
1922	10	Purdue
1923	10	Iowa/Wisconsin
1924	10	Wisconsin/Illinois/Chicago
1925	10	Ohio St.
1926	10	Purdue/Indiana/Michigan/Iowa
1927	10	Michigan
1928	10	Indiana/Purdue
1929	10	Wisconsin/Michigan
1930	10	Purdue
1931	10	Northwestern
1932	10	Purdue
1933	10	Northwestern/Ohio St.
1934	10	Purdue
1935	10	Purdue/Illinois/Wisconsin
1936	10	Indiana/Purdue
1937	10	Minnesota/Illinois
1938	10	Purdue
1939	10	Ohio St.
1940	10	Purdue
1941	10	Wisconsin
1942	10	Illinois
1943	10	Illinois
1944	10	Ohio St.

Season	No.	Regular Season
1945	10	Iowa
1946	10	Ohio St.
1947	9	Wisconsin
1948	9	Michigan
1949	9	Illinois
1950	9	Ohio St.
1951	10	Illinois
1952	10	Illinois
1953	10	Indiana
1954	10	Indiana
1955	10	Iowa
1956	10	Iowa
1957	10	Indiana/Michigan St.
1958	10	Indiana
1959	10	Michigan St.
1960	10	Ohio St.
1961	10	Ohio St.
1962	10	Ohio St.
1963	10	Ohio St./Illinois
1964	10	Michigan/Ohio St.
1965	10	Michigan
1966	10	Michigan
1967	10	Indiana/Michigan St.
1968	10	Ohio St./Iowa
1969	10	Purdue
1970	10	Iowa
1971	10	Ohio St.
1972	10	Minnesota
1973	10	Indiana
1974	10	Indiana/Michigan
1975	10	Indiana
1976	10	Indiana
1977	10	Michigan
1978	10	Michigan St.
1979	10	Michigan St./Purdue/Iowa
1980	10	Indiana
1981	10	Indiana
1982	10	Minnesota
1983	10	Indiana
1984	10	Illinois/Purdue
1985	10	Michigan
1986	10	Michigan
1987	10	Indiana/Purdue
1988	10	Purdue
1989	10	Indiana
1990	10	Michigan St.
1991	10	Ohio St./Indiana
1992	10	Ohio St.
1993	11	Indiana
1994	11	Purdue
1995	11	Purdue
1996	11	Purdue
1997	11	Minnesota
1998	11	Michigan St./Illinois
1999	11	Michigan St.
2000	11	Michigan St./Ohio St.
2001	11	Michigan St./Illinois
2002	11	Illinois/Ohio St./Indiana/Wisconsin
2003	11	Wisconsin
2004	11	Illinois
2005	11	Illinois
2006	11	Ohio St.
2007	11	Ohio St.

Season	No.	Conference Tournament
1998	11	Michigan
1999	11	Michigan St.
2000	11	Michigan St.
2001	11	Iowa
2002	11	Ohio St.
2003	11	Illinois
2004	11	Wisconsin
2005	11	Illinois
2006	11	Iowa
2007	11	Ohio St.

BIG 12 CONFERENCE

Season	No.	Regular Season
1997	12	Kansas
1998	12	Kansas
1999	12	Texas
2000	12	Iowa St.
2001	12	Iowa St.
2002	12	Kansas
2003	12	Kansas
2004	12	Oklahoma St.
2005	12	Oklahoma/Kansas
2006	12	Texas/Kansas
2007	12	Kansas

Season	No.	Conference Tournament
1997	12	Kansas
1998	12	Kansas
1999	12	Kansas
2000	12	Iowa St.
2001	12	Oklahoma
2002	12	Oklahoma
2003	12	Oklahoma
2004	11	Oklahoma St.
2005	12	Oklahoma St.
2006	12	Kansas
2007	12	Kansas

BIG WEST CONFERENCE

Season	No.	Regular Season
1970	6	Long Beach St.
1971	6	Long Beach St.
1972	7	Long Beach St.
1973	7	Long Beach St.
1974	7	Long Beach St.
1975	6	Long Beach St.
1976	6	Long Beach St./Cal St. Fullerton
1977	7	Long Beach St./San Diego St.
1978	8	Fresno St./San Diego St.
1979	8	Pacific
1980	8	Utah St.
1981	8	Fresno St.
1982	8	Fresno St.
1983	9	UNLV
1984	10	UNLV
1985	10	UNLV
1986	10	UNLV
1987	10	UNLV
1988	10	UNLV
1989	10	UNLV
1990	10	UNLV
1991	10	UNLV
1992	10	UNLV
1993	10	New Mexico St.
1994	10	New Mexico St.
1995	10	Utah St.
1996	10	Long Beach St.
1997	12	Nevada (Eastern)/New Mexico St. (Eastern)/Utah St. (Eastern)/ Pacific (Western)
1998	12	Utah St. (Eastern)/ Pacific (Western)
1999	12	Boise St. (Eastern)/New Mexico St. (Eastern)/UC Santa Barb. (Western)
2000	12	Utah St. (Eastern)/Long Beach St. (Western)
2001	9	UC Irvine
2002	10	Utah St./UC Irvine
2003	10	UC Santa Barb.
2004	10	Utah St./Pacific
2005	10	Pacific
2006	8	Pacific
2007	8	Long Beach St.

Season	No.	Conference Tournament
1976	4	San Diego St.
1977	7	Long Beach St.
1978	7	Cal St. Fullerton
1979	8	Pacific
1980	7	San Jose St.
1981	7	Fresno St.
1982	7	Fresno St.
1983	8	UNLV
1984	8	Fresno St.
1985	8	UNLV
1986	8	UNLV
1987	8	UNLV
1988	10	Utah St.
1989	10	UNLV
1990	10	UNLV
1991	8	UNLV
1992	8	New Mexico St.
1993	8	Long Beach St.
1994	10	New Mexico St.
1995	10	Long Beach St.
1996	6	San Jose St.
1997	8	Pacific
1998	8	Utah St.
1999	8	New Mexico St.
2000	8	Utah St.
2001	8	Utah St.
2002	8	UC Santa Barb.
2003	8	Utah St.
2004	8	Pacific
2005	8	Utah St.
2006	8	Pacific
2007	8	Long Beach St.

BORDER CONFERENCE

Season	No.	Regular Season
1932	5	Arizona
1933	6	Texas Tech
1934	6	Texas Tech
1935	6	Texas Tech
1936	7	Arizona
1937	7	New Mexico St.
1938	7	New Mexico St.
1939	7	New Mexico St.
1940	7	New Mexico St.
1941		DNP
1942	9	West Tex. A&M
1943	8	West Tex. A&M
1944	4	Northern Ariz.
1945	9	New Mexico
1946	9	Arizona
1947	9	Arizona
1948	9	Arizona
1949	9	Arizona
1950	9	Arizona
1951	9	Arizona
1952	8	New Mexico St./West Tex. A&M
1953	8	Arizona/Hardin-Simmons
1954	7	Texas Tech
1955	7	Texas Tech/West Tex. A&M
1956	7	Texas Tech
1957	6	UTEP
1958	6	Arizona St.
1959	6	Arizona St./New Mexico St./UTEP
1960	6	New Mexico St.
1961	6	Arizona St./New Mexico St.
1962	5	Arizona St.

COLONIAL ATHLETIC ASSOCIATION

Season	No.	Regular Season
1983	6	William & Mary
1984	6	Richmond
1985	8	Navy/Richmond
1986	8	Navy
1987	8	Navy
1988	8	Richmond
1989	8	Richmond
1990	8	James Madison
1991	8	James Madison
1992	8	Richmond/James Madison
1993	8	James Madison/Old Dominion
1994	8	James Madison/Old Dominion
1995	8	Old Dominion
1996	9	VCU
1997	9	Old Dominion/UNC Wilmington
1998	9	William & Mary/UNC Wilmington
1999	9	George Mason
2000	9	James Madison/George Mason
2001	9	Richmond
2002	10	UNC Wilmington
2003	10	UNC Wilmington
2004	10	VCU
2005	10	Old Dominion
2006	12	George Mason/UNC Wilmington
2007	12	VCU

Season	No.	Conference Tournament
1983	6	James Madison
1984	6	Richmond
1985	8	Navy
1986	8	Navy
1987	8	Navy
1988	8	Richmond
1989	8	George Mason
1990	8	Richmond
1991	8	Richmond
1992	8	Old Dominion
1993	8	East Caro.
1994	8	James Madison
1995	8	Old Dominion
1996	9	VCU
1997	9	Old Dominion
1998	9	Richmond
1999	9	George Mason
2000	9	UNC Wilmington
2001	6	George Mason
2002	10	UNC Wilmington
2003	10	UNC Wilmington
2004	10	VCU
2005	10	Old Dominion
2006	12	UNC Wilmington
2007	12	VCU

CONFERENCE USA

Season	No.	Regular Season
1996	11	Tulane (Red)/Memphis (White)/Cincinnati (Blue)
1997	12	Tulane (Red)/Memphis (White)/Charlotte (White)/Cincinnati (Blue)
1998	12	Cincinnati (American)/Memphis (National)
1999	12	Cincinnati (American)/UAB (National)
2000	12	Cincinnati (American)/Tulane (National)/South Fla. (National)
2001	12	Cincinnati (American)/Southern Miss. (National)
2002	14	Cincinnati (American)/Memphis (National)
2003	14	Marquette (American)/Memphis (National)
2004	14	DePaul/Memphis/Cincinnati/UAB/Charlotte
2005	14	Louisville
2006	12	Memphis
2007	12	Memphis

Season	No.	Conference Tournament
1996	11	Cincinnati
1997	12	Marquette
1998	12	Cincinnati
1999	12	Charlotte
2000	12	St. Louis
2001	12	Charlotte
2002	12	Cincinnati
2003	12	Louisville
2004	12	Cincinnati
2005	12	Louisville
2006	12	Memphis
2007	12	Memphis

EAST COAST CONFERENCE

Season	No.	Regular Season
1959	10	St. Joseph's
1960	10	St. Joseph's
1961	10	St. Joseph's
1962	10	St. Joseph's
1963	9	St. Joseph's
1964	8	Temple
1965	8	St. Joseph's
1966	10	St. Joseph's
1967	12	Temple
1968	11	La Salle
1969	12	Temple
1970	12	St. Joseph's (East)/Rider (West)/Lehigh (West)/Lafayette (West)
1971	13	St. Joseph's (East)/Lafayette (West)
1972	13	Temple (East)/Rider (West)
1973	13	St. Joseph's (East)/Lafayette (West)
1974	13	St. Joseph's (East)/La Salle (East)/Rider (West)
1975	12	American (East)/La Salle (East)/Lafayette (West)
1976	12	St. Joseph's (East)/Lafayette (West)
1977	12	Temple (East)/Hofstra (East)/Lafayette (West)
1978	12	La Salle (East)/Lafayette (West)
1979	12	Temple (East)/Bucknell (West)
1980	12	St. Joseph's (East)/Lafayette (West)
1981	12	American (East)/Lafayette (West)/Rider (West)
1982	12	Temple (East)/West Chester (West)
1983	10	American (East)/La Salle (East)/Hofstra (East)/Rider (West)
1984	9	Bucknell
1985	8	Bucknell
1986	8	Drexel
1987	8	Bucknell
1988	8	Lafayette
1989	8	Bucknell
1990	8	Towson/Hofstra/Lehigh
1991	7	Towson
1992	7	Hofstra
1993		DNP
1994	6	Troy

Season	No.	Conference Tournament
1975	12	La Salle
1976	12	Hofstra
1977	12	Hofstra
1978	12	La Salle
1979	12	Temple
1980	12	La Salle
1981	12	St. Joseph's
1982	12	St. Joseph's
1983	10	La Salle
1984	9	Rider
1985	8	Lehigh
1986	8	Drexel
1987	8	Bucknell
1988	8	Lehigh
1989	8	Bucknell
1990	8	Towson
1991	7	Towson
1992	7	Towson
1993		DNP
1994	6	Hofstra

EASTERN INTERCOLLEGIATE CONFERENCE

Season	No.	Regular Season
1933	5	Pittsburgh
1934	6	Pittsburgh
1935	5	Pittsburgh/West Virginia
1936	6	Carnegie Mellon/Pittsburgh
1937	6	Pittsburgh/Temple
1938	6	Temple
1939	6	Carnegie Mellon/Georgetown

GREAT MIDWEST CONFERENCE

Season	No.	Regular Season
1992	6	DePaul/Cincinnati
1993	6	Cincinnati
1994	7	Marquette
1995	7	Memphis

Season	No.	Conference Tournament
1992	6	Cincinnati
1993	6	Cincinnati
1994	7	Cincinnati
1995	7	Cincinnati

GULF STAR CONFERENCE

Season	No.	Regular Season
1985	6	Southeastern La.
1986	6	Sam Houston St.
1987	6	Stephen F. Austin

HORIZON LEAGUE

Season	No.	Regular Season
1980	6	Loyola (Ill.)
1981	7	Xavier
1982	7	Evansville
1983	8	Loyola (Ill.)
1984	8	Oral Roberts
1985	8	Loyola (Ill.)
1986	7	Xavier
1987	7	Evansville/Loyola (Ill.)
1988	6	Xavier
1989	7	Evansville
1990	8	Xavier
1991	8	Xavier
1992	6	Evansville
1993	8	Evansville/Xavier
1994	6	Xavier
1995	11	Xavier
1996	9	Green Bay
1997	9	Butler
1998	8	Detroit/Ill.-Chicago
1999	8	Detroit
2000	8	Butler
2001	8	Butler
2002	9	Butler
2003	9	Butler
2004	9	Milwaukee
2005	9	Milwaukee
2006	9	Milwaukee
2007	9	Butler/Wright St.

Season	No.	Conference Tournament
1980	6	Oral Roberts
1981	7	Oklahoma City
1982	7	Evansville
1983	8	Xavier
1984	8	Oral Roberts
1985	8	Loyola (Ill.)
1986	7	Xavier
1987	7	Xavier
1988	6	Xavier
1989	7	Evansville
1990	8	Dayton
1991	8	Xavier
1992	6	Evansville
1993	8	Evansville
1994	6	Detroit
1995	10	Green Bay
1996	8	Northern Ill.
1997	9	Butler
1998	8	Butler
1999	8	Detroit
2000	8	Butler
2001	8	Butler
2002	9	Ill.-Chicago
2003	9	Milwaukee
2004	9	Ill.-Chicago
2005	9	Milwaukee
2006	9	Milwaukee
2007	9	Wright St.

IVY GROUP

Season	No.	Regular Season
1902	5	Yale
1903	5	Yale
1904	6	Columbia
1905	5	Columbia
1906	6	Penn
1907	6	Yale
1908	5	Penn
1909-10		DNP
1911	5	Columbia
1912	6	Columbia
1913	5	Cornell
1914	6	Cornell/Columbia
1915	6	Yale
1916	6	Penn
1917	6	Yale
1918	6	Penn
1919	5	Penn
1920	6	Penn
1921	6	Penn
1922	6	Princeton
1923	6	Yale
1924	6	Cornell
1925	6	Princeton
1926	6	Columbia
1927	6	Dartmouth
1928	6	Penn
1929	6	Penn
1930	6	Columbia
1931	6	Columbia
1932	6	Princeton
1933	6	Yale
1934	7	Penn
1935	7	Penn
1936	7	Columbia
1937	7	Penn
1938	7	Dartmouth
1939	7	Dartmouth
1940	7	Dartmouth
1941	7	Dartmouth
1942	7	Dartmouth
1943	7	Dartmouth
1944	5	Dartmouth
1945	4	Penn
1946	5	Dartmouth
1947	7	Columbia
1948	7	Columbia
1949	7	Yale
1950	7	Princeton
1951	7	Columbia
1952	7	Princeton
1953	7	Penn
1954	8	Cornell
1955	8	Princeton
1956	8	Dartmouth
1957	8	Yale
1958	8	Dartmouth
1959	8	Dartmouth
1960	8	Princeton
1961	8	Princeton
1962	8	Yale
1963	8	Princeton
1964	8	Princeton
1965	8	Princeton
1966	8	Penn
1967	8	Princeton
1968	8	Columbia
1969	8	Princeton
1970	8	Penn
1971	8	Penn
1972	8	Penn
1973	8	Penn
1974	8	Penn
1975	8	Penn
1976	8	Princeton
1977	8	Princeton
1978	8	Penn
1979	8	Penn
1980	8	Penn
1981	8	Princeton
1982	8	Penn
1983	8	Princeton
1984	8	Princeton
1985	8	Penn
1986	8	Brown
1987	8	Penn
1988	8	Cornell
1989	8	Princeton
1990	8	Princeton
1991	8	Princeton
1992	8	Princeton
1993	8	Penn
1994	8	Penn
1995	8	Penn
1996	8	Princeton
1997	8	Princeton
1998	8	Princeton
1999	8	Penn
2000	8	Penn
2001	8	Princeton
2002	8	Penn/Yale/Princeton
2003	8	Penn
2004	8	Princeton
2005	8	Penn
2006	8	Penn
2007	8	Penn

METRO ATLANTIC ATHLETIC CONFERENCE

Season	No.	Regular Season
1982	6	St. Peter's
1983	6	Iona
1984	8	La Salle/St. Peter's/Iona
1985	8	Iona
1986	8	Fairfield
1987	8	St. Peter's
1988	8	La Salle
1989	8	La Salle
1990	12	Holy Cross (North)/La Salle (South)
1991	9	Siena
1992	9	Manhattan
1993	8	Manhattan
1994	8	Canisius
1995	8	Manhattan
1996	8	Fairfield/Iona
1997	8	Iona
1998	10	Iona
1999	10	Niagara/Siena
2000	10	Siena
2001	10	Iona/Siena/Niagara
2002	10	Marist/Rider
2003	10	Manhattan
2004	10	Manhattan
2005	10	Niagara/Rider
2006	10	Manhattan
2007	10	Marist

Season	No.	Conference Tournament
1982	6	Fordham
1983	6	Fordham
1984	8	Iona
1985	8	Iona
1986	8	Fairfield
1987	8	Fairfield
1988	8	La Salle
1989	8	La Salle
1990	12	La Salle
1991	9	St. Peter's
1992	9	La Salle
1993	8	Manhattan
1994	8	Loyola (Md.)

Season	No.	Conference Tournament
1995	8	St. Peter's
1996	8	Canisius
1997	8	Fairfield
1998	10	Iona
1999	10	Siena
2000	10	Iona
2001	10	Iona
2002	10	Siena
2003	10	Manhattan
2004	10	Manhattan
2005	10	Niagara
2006	10	Iona
2007	10	Niagara

METROPOLITAN COLLEGIATE ATHLETIC CONFERENCE

Season	No.	Regular Season
1976	6	Tulane
1977	7	Louisville
1978	7	Florida St.
1979	7	Louisville
1980	7	Louisville
1981	7	Louisville
1982	7	Memphis
1983	7	Louisville
1984	8	Memphis/Louisville
1985	8	Memphis
1986	7	Louisville
1987	7	Louisville
1988	7	Louisville
1989	7	Florida St.
1990	8	Louisville
1991	8	Southern Miss.
1992	7	Tulane
1993	7	Louisville
1994	7	Louisville
1995	7	Charlotte

Season	No.	Conference Tournament
1976	6	Cincinnati
1977	7	Cincinnati
1978	7	Louisville
1979	7	Virginia Tech
1980	7	Louisville
1981	7	Louisville
1982	7	Memphis
1983	7	Louisville
1984	8	Memphis
1985	8	Memphis
1986	7	Louisville
1987	7	Memphis
1988	7	Louisville
1989	5	Louisville
1990	8	Louisville
1991	8	Florida St.
1992	7	Charlotte
1993	7	Louisville
1994	7	Louisville
1995	7	Louisville

METROPOLITAN NEW YORK CONFERENCE

Season	No.	Regular Season
1943	8	St. John's (N.Y.)
1944-45		DNP
1946	7	New York U./St. John's (N.Y.)
1947	7	St. John's (N.Y.)
1948	7	New York U.
1949	7	Manhattan/St. John's (N.Y.)
1950	7	CCNY
1951	7	St. John's (N.Y.)
1952	7	St. John's (N.Y.)
1953	7	Manhattan
1954	7	St. Francis (N.Y.)
1955	7	Manhattan
1956	7	St. Francis (N.Y.)
1957	7	New York U.
1958	7	St. John's (N.Y.)
1959	7	Manhattan
1960	7	New York U.
1961	7	St. John's (N.Y.)
1962	7	St. John's (N.Y.)
1963	7	Fordham

MID-AMERICAN CONFERENCE

Season	No.	Regular Season
1947	5	Butler/Cincinnati
1948	6	Cincinnati
1949	6	Cincinnati
1950	6	Cincinnati
1951	5	Cincinnati
1952	7	Miami (Ohio)/Western Mich.
1953	7	Miami (Ohio)
1954	8	Toledo
1955	8	Miami (Ohio)
1956	7	Marshall
1957	7	Miami (Ohio)
1958	7	Miami (Ohio)
1959	7	Bowling Green
1960	7	Ohio
1961	7	Ohio
1962	7	Bowling Green
1963	7	Bowling Green
1964	7	Ohio
1965	7	Ohio
1966	7	Miami (Ohio)
1967	7	Toledo
1968	7	Bowling Green
1969	7	Miami (Ohio)
1970	6	Ohio
1971	6	Miami (Ohio)
1972	6	Ohio
1973	7	Miami (Ohio)
1974	7	Ohio
1975	8	Central Mich.
1976	10	Western Mich.
1977	10	Central Mich.
1978	10	Miami (Ohio)
1979	10	Toledo
1980	10	Toledo
1981	10	Ball St./Northern Ill./Toledo/ Western Mich./Bowling Green
1982	10	Ball St.
1983	10	Bowling Green
1984	10	Miami (Ohio)
1985	10	Ohio
1986	10	Miami (Ohio)
1987	9	Central Mich.
1988	9	Eastern Mich.
1989	9	Ball St.
1990	9	Ball St.
1991	9	Eastern Mich.
1992	8	Miami (Ohio)
1993	10	Ball St./Miami (Ohio)
1994	10	Ohio
1995	10	Miami (Ohio)
1996	10	Eastern Mich.
1997	10	Bowling Green/Miami (Ohio)
1998	12	Akron (East)/Ball St. (West)/
1999	13	Miami (Ohio)(East)/Toledo (West)
2000	13	Bowling Green (East)/ Ball St. (West)/Toledo (West)
2001	13	Kent St. (East)/ Central Mich. (West)
2002	13	Kent St. (East)/Ball St. (West)
2003	13	Kent St. (East)/ Central Mich. (West)
2004	13	Kent St.(East)/Western Mich. (West)
2005	13	Miami (Ohio) (East)/Toledo (West)/Western Mich. (West)
2006	12	Kent St. (East)/ Northern Ill. (West)
2007	12	Akron (East)/Toledo (West)

Season	No.	Conference Tournament
1980	7	Toledo
1981	7	Ball St.
1982	7	Northern Ill.
1983	7	Ohio
1984	7	Miami (Ohio)
1985	7	Ohio
1986	7	Ball St.
1987	7	Central Mich.
1988	7	Eastern Mich.
1989	8	Ball St.
1990	8	Ball St.
1991	8	Eastern Mich.
1992	8	Miami (Ohio)
1993	10	Ball St.
1994	8	Ohio
1995	8	Ball St.
1996	8	Eastern Mich.
1997	8	Miami (Ohio)
1998	8	Eastern Mich.

Season	No.	Conference Tournament
1999	8	Kent St.
2000	13	Ball St.
2001	13	Kent St.
2002	13	Kent St.
2003	13	Central Mich.
2004	13	Western Mich.
2005	13	Ohio
2006	12	Kent St.
2007	12	Miami (Ohio)

MID-EASTERN ATHLETIC CONFERENCE

Season	No.	Regular Season
1972	7	N.C. A&T
1973	7	Md.-East. Shore
1974	7	Md.-East. Shore/Morgan St.
1975	7	N.C. A&T
1976	7	N.C. A&T/Morgan St.
1977	7	South Carolina St.
1978	7	N.C. A&T
1979	7	N.C. A&T
1980	7	Howard
1981	6	N.C. A&T
1982	7	N.C. A&T
1983	7	Howard
1984	6	N.C. A&T
1985	7	N.C. A&T
1986	8	N.C. A&T
1987	8	Howard
1988	9	N.C. A&T
1989	9	South Carolina St.
1990	9	Coppin St.
1991	9	Coppin St.
1992	9	N.C. A&T/Howard
1993	9	Coppin St.
1994	9	Coppin St.
1995	9	Coppin St.
1996	10	Coppin St./South Carolina St.
1997	10	Coppin St.
1998	11	Coppin St.
1999	11	Coppin St./South Carolina St.
2000	11	South Carolina St.
2001	11	Hampton/South Carolina St.
2002	11	Hampton
2003	11	South Carolina St.
2004	11	South Carolina St./Coppin St.
2005	11	Delaware St.
2006	11	Delaware St.
2007	11	Delaware St.

Season	No.	Conference Tournament
1972	7	N.C. A&T
1973	7	N.C. A&T
1974	7	Md.-East. Shore
1975	7	N.C. A&T
1976	7	N.C. A&T
1977	7	Morgan St.
1978	7	N.C. A&T
1979	7	N.C. A&T
1980	7	Howard
1981	6	Howard
1982	7	N.C. A&T
1983	7	N.C. A&T
1984	6	N.C. A&T
1985	6	N.C. A&T
1986	6	N.C. A&T
1987	7	N.C. A&T
1988	7	N.C. A&T
1989	8	South Carolina St.
1990	8	Coppin St.
1991	9	Florida A&M
1992	9	Howard
1993	9	Coppin St.
1994	9	N.C. A&T
1995	9	N.C. A&T
1996	8	South Carolina St.
1997	9	Coppin St.
1998	9	South Carolina St.
1999	10	Florida A&M
2000	11	South Carolina St.
2001	11	Hampton
2002	11	Hampton
2003	11	South Carolina St.
2004	11	Florida A&M
2005	11	Delaware St.
2006	11	Hampton
2007	11	Florida A&M

MISSOURI VALLEY CONFERENCE

(Note: The Big Eight and Missouri Valley conferences share the same history from 1908-28.)

Season	No.	Regular Season
1908	6	Kansas
1909	6	Kansas
1910	6	Kansas
1911	5	Kansas
1912	6	Nebraska/Kansas
1913	6	Nebraska
1914	7	Kansas/Nebraska
1915	7	Kansas
1916	7	Nebraska
1917	7	Kansas St.
1918	7	Missouri
1919	8	Kansas St.
1920	8	Missouri
1921	9	Missouri
1922	9	Missouri/Kansas
1923	9	Kansas
1924	9	Kansas
1925	9	Kansas
1926	10	Kansas
1927	10	Kansas
1928	10	Oklahoma
1929	5	Washington-St. Louis
1930	5	Creighton/Washington-St. Louis
1931	5	Creighton/Oklahoma St.
1932	5	Creighton
1933	6	Butler
1934	6	Butler
1935	7	Creighton/Drake
1936	7	Creighton/Oklahoma St./Drake
1937	7	Oklahoma St.
1938	7	Oklahoma St.
1939	8	Oklahoma St./Drake
1940	7	Oklahoma St.
1941	7	Creighton
1942	6	Oklahoma St./Creighton
1943	6	Creighton
1944	4	Oklahoma St.
1945	5	Oklahoma St.
1946	7	Oklahoma St.
1947	7	St. Louis
1948	6	Oklahoma St.
1949	6	Oklahoma St.
1950	7	Bradley
1951	8	Oklahoma St.
1952	6	St. Louis
1953	6	Oklahoma St.
1954	6	Oklahoma St.
1955	6	Tulsa/St. Louis
1956	7	Houston
1957	8	St. Louis
1958	8	Cincinnati
1959	8	Cincinnati
1960	8	Cincinnati
1961	8	Cincinnati
1962	7	Bradley/Cincinnati
1963	7	Cincinnati
1964	7	Drake/Wichita St.
1965	8	Wichita St.
1966	8	Cincinnati
1967	8	Louisville
1968	9	Louisville
1969	9	Drake/Louisville
1970	9	Drake
1971	8	Drake/Louisville/St. Louis
1972	8	Memphis/Louisville
1973	10	Memphis
1974	9	Louisville
1975	8	Louisville
1976	7	Wichita St.
1977	7	Southern Ill./New Mexico St.
1978	9	Creighton
1979	9	Indiana St.
1980	9	Bradley
1981	9	Wichita St.
1982	10	Bradley
1983	10	Wichita St.
1984	9	Tulsa/Illinois St.
1985	9	Tulsa
1986	9	Bradley
1987	8	Tulsa
1988	9	Bradley
1989	8	Creighton
1990	8	Southern Ill.
1991	9	Creighton
1992	10	Southern Ill./Illinois St.
1993	10	Illinois St.
1994	10	Southern Ill./Tulsa
1995	11	Tulsa
1996	11	Bradley
1997	10	Illinois St.
1998	10	Illinois St.
1999	10	Evansville
2000	10	Indiana St.
2001	10	Creighton
2002	10	Southern Ill./Creighton
2003	10	Southern Ill.
2004	10	Southern Ill.
2005	10	Southern Ill.
2006	10	Wichita St.
2007	10	Southern Ill.

Season	No.	Conference Tournament
1977	8	Southern Ill.
1978	9	Creighton
1979	8	Indiana St.
1980	8	Bradley
1981	8	Creighton
1982	8	Tulsa
1983	8	Illinois St.
1984	8	Tulsa
1985	8	Wichita St.
1986	8	Tulsa
1987	7	Wichita St.
1988	8	Bradley
1989	8	Creighton
1990	8	Illinois St.
1991	9	Creighton
1992	8	Missouri St.
1993	8	Southern Ill.
1994	8	Southern Ill.
1995	8	Southern Ill.
1996	8	Tulsa
1997	10	Illinois St.
1998	10	Illinois St.
1999	10	Creighton
2000	10	Creighton
2001	10	Indiana St.
2002	10	Creighton
2003	10	Creighton
2004	10	UNI
2005	10	Creighton
2006	10	Southern Ill.
2007	10	Creighton

MOUNTAIN STATES CONFERENCE

Season	No.	Regular Season
1938	7	Colorado/Utah
1939	7	Colorado
1940	7	Colorado
1941	7	Wyoming
1942	7	Colorado
1943	5	Wyoming
1944	7	Utah
1945	7	Utah
1946	7	Wyoming
1947	7	Wyoming
1948	6	BYU
1949	6	Wyoming
1950	6	BYU
1951	6	BYU
1952	8	Wyoming
1953	8	Wyoming
1954	8	Colorado
1955	8	Utah
1956	8	Utah
1957	8	BYU
1958	8	Wyoming
1959	8	Utah
1960	8	Utah
1961	8	Colorado St./Utah
1962	8	Utah

MOUNTAIN WEST CONFERENCE

Season	No.	Regular Season
2000	8	UNLV/Utah
2001	8	BYU/Wyoming/Utah
2002	8	Wyoming
2003	8	BYU/Utah
2004	8	Air Force
2005	8	Utah
2006	9	San Diego St.
2007	9	Brigham Young

Season	No.	Conference Tournament
2000	8	UNLV
2001	7	BYU
2002	8	San Diego St.
2003	8	Colorado St.
2004	8	Utah
2005	8	New Mexico
2006	8	San Diego St.
2007	9	UNLV

NEW ENGLAND CONFERENCE

Season	No.	Regular Season
1938	5	Rhode Island
1939	5	Rhode Island
1940	5	Rhode Island
1941	5	Rhode Island
1942	5	Rhode Island
1943	5	Rhode Island
1944	4	Rhode Island
1945		DNP
1946	5	Rhode Island

NEW JERSEY-NEW YORK 7 CONFERENCE

Season	No.	Regular Season
1977	7	Columbia/Seton Hall
1978	7	Rutgers/St. John's (N.Y.)
1979	7	Rutgers

NORTHEAST CONFERENCE

Season	No.	Regular Season
1982	11	Fairleigh Dickinson (North)/Robert Morris (South)
1983	10	Long Island (North)/Robert Morris (South)
1984	9	Long Island/Robert Morris
1985	8	Marist
1986	9	Fairleigh Dickinson
1987	9	Marist
1988	9	Fairleigh Dickinson/Marist
1989	9	Robert Morris
1990	9	Robert Morris
1991	9	St. Francis (Pa.)/Fairleigh Dickinson
1992	9	Robert Morris
1993	10	Rider
1994	10	Rider
1995	10	Rider
1996	10	Mt. St. Mary's
1997	10	Long Island
1998	9	Long Island
1999	11	UMBC
2000	12	Central Conn. St.
2001	12	St. Francis (N.Y.)
2002	12	Central Conn. St.
2003	12	Wagner
2004	11	Monmouth/St. Francis (N.Y.)
2005	11	Monmouth
2006	11	Fairleigh Dickinson
2007	11	Central Conn. St.

Season	No.	Conference Tournament
1982	8	Robert Morris
1983	8	Robert Morris
1984	8	Long Island
1985	8	Fairleigh Dickinson
1986	8	Marist
1987	6	Marist
1988	6	Fairleigh Dickinson
1989	6	Robert Morris
1990	6	Robert Morris
1991	7	St. Francis (Pa.)
1992	9	Robert Morris
1993	10	Rider
1994	10	Rider
1995	10	Mt. St. Mary's
1996	10	Monmouth
1997	8	Long Island
1998	8	Fairleigh Dickinson
1999	8	Mt. St. Mary's
2000	8	Central Conn. St.
2001	7	Monmouth
2002	8	Central Conn. St.
2003	8	Wagner
2004	8	Monmouth
2005	8	Fairleigh Dickinson
2006	8	Monmouth
2007	8	Central Conn. St.

OHIO VALLEY CONFERENCE

Season	No.	Regular Season
1949	8	Western Ky.
1950	7	Western Ky.
1951	7	Murray St.
1952	7	Western Ky.
1953	6	Eastern Ky.
1954	6	Western Ky.
1955	6	Western Ky.
1956	6	Morehead St./Tennessee Tech/ Western Ky.
1957	6	Morehead St./Western Ky.
1958	7	Tennessee Tech
1959	7	Eastern Ky.
1960	7	Western Ky.
1961	7	Morehead St./Western Ky./ Eastern Ky.
1962	6	Western Ky.
1963	7	Tennessee Tech/Morehead St.
1964	8	Murray St.
1965	8	Eastern Ky.
1966	8	Western Ky.
1967	8	Western Ky.
1968	8	East Tenn. St./Murray St.
1969	8	Murray St./Morehead St.
1970	8	Western Ky.
1971	8	Western Ky.
1972	8	Eastern Ky./Morehead St./ Western Ky.
1973	8	Austin Peay
1974	8	Austin Peay/Morehead St.
1975	8	Middle Tenn.
1976	8	Western Ky.
1977	8	Austin Peay
1978	8	Middle Tenn./Eastern Ky.
1979	7	Eastern Ky.
1980	7	Western Ky./Murray St.
1981	8	Western Ky.
1982	8	Murray St./Western Ky.
1983	8	Murray St.
1984	8	Morehead St.
1985	8	Tennessee Tech
1986	8	Akron/Middle Tenn.
1987	8	Middle Tenn.
1988	8	Murray St.
1989	7	Middle Tenn./Murray St.
1990	7	Murray St.
1991	7	Murray St.
1992	8	Murray St.
1993	9	Tennessee St.
1994	9	Murray St.
1995	9	Murray St./Tennessee St.
1996	9	Murray St.
1997	10	Austin Peay/Murray St.
1998	10	Murray St.
1999	10	Murray St.
2000	10	Southeast Mo. St./ Murray St.
2001	9	Tennessee Tech
2002	9	Tennessee Tech
2003	9	Austin Peay/ Morehead St.
2004	11	Austin Peay
2005	11	Tennessee Tech
2006	11	Murray St.
2007	11	Austin Peay

Season	No.	Conference Tournament
1949	8	Western Ky.
1950	7	Eastern Ky.
1951	7	Murray St.
1952	7	Western Ky.
1953	6	Western Ky.
1954	6	Western Ky.
1955	6	Eastern Ky.
1956-63		DNP
1964	8	Murray St.
1965	8	Western Ky.
1966	8	Western Ky.
1967	8	Tennessee Tech
1968-74		DNP
1975	4	Middle Tenn.
1976	8	Western Ky.
1977	4	Middle Tenn.
1978	4	Western Ky.
1979	4	Eastern Ky.
1980	4	Western Ky.
1981	4	Western Ky.
1982	4	Middle Tenn.
1983	4	Morehead St.
1984	4	Morehead St.
1985	7	Middle Tenn.
1986	7	Akron
1987	7	Austin Peay
1988	7	Murray St.
1989	7	Middle Tenn.
1990	7	Murray St.
1991	7	Murray St.
1992	7	Murray St.
1993	6	Tennessee St.
1994	7	Tennessee St.
1995	7	Murray St.
1996	7	Austin Peay
1997	8	Murray St.
1998	8	Murray St.
1999	8	Murray St.
2000	8	Southeast Mo. St.
2001	8	Eastern Ill.
2002	8	Murray St.
2003	8	Austin Peay
2004	8	Murray St.
2005	8	Eastern Ky.
2006	8	Murray St.
2007	8	Eastern Ky.

PACIFIC-10 CONFERENCE

Season	No.	Regular Season
1916	3	California/Oregon St.
1917	6	Washington St.
1918		DNP
1919	6	Oregon
1920	6	Stanford
1921	6	Stanford
1922	8	Idaho
1923	8	Idaho
1924	9	California
1925	8	California
1926	9	California
1927	9	California
1928	10	Southern California
1929	10	California
1930	9	Southern California
1931	9	Washington
1932	9	California
1933	9	Oregon St.
1934	9	Washington
1935	9	Southern California
1936	9	Stanford
1937	9	Stanford
1938	10	Stanford
1939	9	Oregon
1940	9	Southern California
1941	9	Washington St.
1942	9	Stanford
1943	9	Washington
1944	8	Washington (North)/ California (South)
1945	8	Oregon (North)/UCLA (South)
1946	9	California
1947	9	Oregon St.
1948	9	Washington
1949	9	Oregon St.
1950	9	UCLA
1951	9	Washington
1952	9	UCLA
1953	9	Washington
1954	9	Southern California
1955	9	Oregon St.
1956	9	UCLA
1957	9	California
1958	9	Oregon St./California
1959	9	California
1960	5	California
1961	5	Southern California
1962	5	UCLA
1963	5	UCLA/Stanford
1964	6	UCLA
1965	8	UCLA
1966	8	Oregon St.
1967	8	UCLA
1968	8	UCLA
1969	8	UCLA
1970	8	UCLA
1971	8	UCLA
1972	8	UCLA
1973	8	UCLA
1974	8	UCLA
1975	8	UCLA
1976	8	UCLA
1977	8	UCLA
1978	8	UCLA
1979	10	UCLA
1980	10	Oregon St.
1981	10	Oregon St.
1982	10	Oregon St.
1983	10	UCLA
1984	10	Washington/Oregon St.
1985	10	Washington/Southern California
1986	10	Arizona
1987	10	UCLA
1988	10	Arizona
1989	10	Arizona
1990	10	Oregon St./Arizona
1991	10	Arizona
1992	10	UCLA
1993	10	Arizona
1994	10	Arizona
1995	10	UCLA
1996	10	UCLA
1997	10	UCLA
1998	10	Arizona
1999	10	Stanford
2000	10	Arizona/Stanford
2001	10	Stanford
2002	10	Oregon
2003	10	Arizona
2004	10	Stanford
2005	10	Arizona
2006	10	UCLA
2007	10	UCLA

Season	No.	Conference Tournament
1987	10	UCLA
1988	10	Arizona
1989	10	Arizona
1990	10	Arizona
1991-2001		DNP
2002	8	Arizona
2003	8	Oregon
2004	8	Stanford
2005	8	Washington
2006	10	UCLA
2007	10	Oregon

PATRIOT LEAGUE

Season	No.	Regular Season
1991	7	Fordham
1992	8	Bucknell/Fordham
1993	8	Bucknell
1994	8	Navy/Fordham/ Colgate/Holy Cross
1995	8	Bucknell/Colgate
1996	7	Colgate/Navy
1997	7	Navy
1998	7	Lafayette/Navy
1999	7	Lafayette
2000	7	Lafayette/Navy
2001	7	Holy Cross
2002	8	American
2003	8	Holy Cross
2004	8	Lehigh/American
2005	8	Holy Cross
2006	8	Bucknell
2007	8	Holy Cross

Season	No.	Conference Tournament
1991	7	Fordham
1992	8	Fordham
1993	8	Holy Cross
1994	8	Navy
1995	8	Colgate
1996	7	Colgate
1997	7	Navy
1998	7	Navy
1999	7	Lafayette
2000	7	Lafayette
2001	7	Holy Cross
2002	8	Holy Cross
2003	8	Holy Cross
2004	8	Lehigh
2005	8	Bucknell
2006	8	Bucknell
2007	8	Holy Cross

ROCKY MOUNTAIN CONFERENCE

Season	No.	Regular Season
1922	6	Colorado Col.
1923	5	Colorado Col.
1924	6	Colorado Col.
1925	12	Colorado Col. (East)/BYU (West)
1926	12	Colorado St. (East)/Utah (West)

Season	No.	Regular Season
1927	12	Colorado Col. (East)/Montana St. (West)
1928	12	Wyoming (East)/Montana St. (West)
1929	12	Colorado (East)/Montana St. (West)
1929	12	Colorado (East)/Montana St. (West)
1930	12	Colorado (East)/Montana St. (West)/Utah St. (West)
1931	12	Wyoming (East)/Utah (West)
1932	12	Wyoming (East)/BYU (West)/Utah (West)
1933	12	Wyoming (East)/Colorado St. (East)/BYU (West)/Utah (West)
1934	12	Wyoming (East)/ BYU (West)
1935	12	Northern Colo. (East)/Utah St. (West)
1936	12	Wyoming (East)/Utah (West)
1937	12	Denver (East)/Colorado (East)/Montana St. (West)/Utah (West)
1938	5	Montana St.
1939	5	Northern Colo.
1940	5	Northern Colo.
1941	5	Northern Colo.
1942	5	Northern Colo.
1943	3	Northern Colo.
1944	3	Colorado Col.
1945	3	Colorado Col.
1946	5	Colorado St.
1947	5	Montana St.
1948	4	Colorado St.
1949	5	Colorado St.
1950	6	Montana St.
1951	6	Montana St.
1952	6	Colorado St./Montana St.
1953	6	Idaho St.
1954	6	Idaho St.
1955	6	Idaho St.
1956	6	Idaho St.
1957	6	Idaho St.
1958	6	Idaho St.
1959	6	Idaho St.
1960	6	Idaho St.

SOUTHEASTERN CONFERENCE

Season	No.	Regular Season
1933	13	Kentucky
1934	13	Alabama
1935	13	LSU/Kentucky
1936	13	Tennessee
1937	13	Kentucky
1938	13	Georgia Tech
1939	13	Kentucky
1940	13	Kentucky
1941	12	Tennessee
1942	12	Kentucky
1943	12	Tennessee
1944	6	Kentucky
1945	12	Kentucky
1946	12	Kentucky
1947	12	Kentucky
1948	12	Kentucky
1949	12	Kentucky
1950	12	Kentucky
1951	12	Kentucky
1952	12	Kentucky
1953	11	LSU
1954	12	Kentucky/LSU
1955	12	Kentucky
1956	12	Alabama
1957	12	Kentucky
1958	12	Kentucky
1959	12	Mississippi St.
1960	12	Auburn
1961	12	Mississippi St.
1962	12	Mississippi St./Kentucky
1963	12	Mississippi St.
1964	12	Kentucky
1965	11	Vanderbilt
1966	11	Kentucky
1967	10	Tennessee
1968	10	Kentucky
1969	10	Kentucky
1970	10	Kentucky
1971	10	Kentucky
1972	10	Tennessee/Kentucky
1973	10	Kentucky
1974	10	Vanderbilt/Alabama

Season	No.	Regular Season
1975	10	Kentucky/Alabama
1976	10	Alabama
1977	10	Kentucky/Tennessee
1978	10	Kentucky
1979	10	LSU
1980	10	Kentucky
1981	10	LSU
1982	10	Kentucky/Tennessee
1983	10	Kentucky
1984	10	Kentucky
1985	10	LSU
1986	10	Kentucky
1987	10	Alabama
1988	10	Kentucky*
1989	10	Florida
1990	10	Georgia
1991	10	Mississippi St./LSU
1992	12	Kentucky (Eastern)/Arkansas (Western)
1993	12	Vanderbilt (Eastern)/Arkansas (Western)
1994	12	Florida (Eastern)/Kentucky (Eastern)/Arkansas (Western)
1995	12	Kentucky (Eastern)/Arkansas (Western)/Mississippi St. (Western)
1996	12	Kentucky (Eastern)/Mississippi St. (Western)
1997	12	South Carolina (Eastern)/Mississippi (Western)
1998	12	Kentucky (Eastern)/Mississippi (Western)
1999	12	Tennessee (Eastern)/Auburn (Western)
2000	12	Tennessee (Eastern)/ Florida (Eastern)/Kentucky (Eastern)/LSU (Western)
2001	12	Florida (Eastern)/Kentucky (Eastern)/Mississippi (Western)
2002	12	Georgia (Eastern)/Kentucky (Eastern)/Florida (Eastern)/Alabama (Western)
2003	12	Kentucky (Eastern)/Mississippi St. (Western)
2004	12	Kentucky (Eastern)/Mississippi St. (Western)
2005	12	Kentucky (Eastern)/Alabama (Western)/LSU (Western)
2006	12	Tennessee (Eastern)/LSU (Western)
2007	12	Florida (Eastern)/Mississippi (Western)/Mississippi St. (Western)

Season	No.	Conference Tournament
1933	13	Kentucky
1934	10	Alabama
1935		DNP
1936	9	Tennessee
1937	8	Kentucky
1938	11	Georgia Tech
1939	12	Kentucky
1940	12	Kentucky
1941	12	Tennessee
1942	12	Kentucky
1943	11	Tennessee
1944	6	Kentucky
1945	11	Kentucky
1946	12	Kentucky
1947	12	Kentucky
1948	12	Kentucky
1949	12	Kentucky
1950	12	Kentucky
1951	12	Vanderbilt
1952	12	Kentucky
1953-78		DNP
1979	10	Tennessee
1980	10	LSU
1981	10	Mississippi
1982	10	Alabama
1983	10	Georgia
1984	10	Kentucky
1985	10	Auburn
1986	10	Kentucky
1987	10	Alabama
1988	10	Kentucky*
1989	10	Alabama
1990	9	Alabama
1991	9	Alabama
1992	11	Kentucky

Season	No.	Conference Tournament
1993	12	Kentucky
1994	12	Kentucky
1995	12	Kentucky
1996	12	Mississippi St.
1997	12	Kentucky
1998	12	Kentucky
1999	12	Kentucky
2000	12	Arkansas
2001	12	Kentucky
2002	12	Mississippi St.
2003	11	Kentucky
2004	12	Kentucky
2005	12	Florida
2006	12	Florida
2007	12	Florida

*later vacated

SOUTHERN CONFERENCE

Season	No.	Regular Season
1922	13	Virginia
1923	19	North Carolina
1924	21	Tulane
1925	21	North Carolina
1926	22	Kentucky
1927	22	South Carolina
1928	22	Auburn
1929	23	Wash. & Lee
1930	23	Alabama
1931	22	Georgia
1932	23	Kentucky/Maryland
1933	10	South Carolina
1934	10	South Carolina
1935	10	North Carolina
1936	10	Wash. & Lee
1937	16	Wash. & Lee
1938	15	North Carolina
1939	15	Wake Forest
1940	15	Duke
1941	15	North Carolina
1942	16	Duke
1943	15	Duke
1944	12	North Carolina
1945	14	South Carolina
1946	16	North Carolina
1947	16	North Carolina St.
1948	16	North Carolina St.
1949	16	North Carolina St.
1950	16	North Carolina St.
1951	17	North Carolina St.
1952	17	West Virginia
1953	17	North Carolina St.
1954	10	George Washington
1955	10	West Virginia
1956	10	George Washington/West Virginia
1957	10	West Virginia
1958	10	West Virginia
1959	9	West Virginia
1960	9	Virginia Tech
1961	9	West Virginia
1962	9	West Virginia
1963	9	West Virginia
1964	9	Davidson
1965	10	Davidson
1966	9	Davidson
1967	9	West Virginia
1968	9	Davidson
1969	8	Davidson
1970	8	Davidson
1971	7	Davidson
1972	8	Davidson
1973	8	Davidson
1974	8	Furman
1975	8	Furman
1976	8	VMI
1977	10	Furman/VMI
1978	8	Appalachian St.
1979	9	Appalachian St.
1980	9	Furman
1981	9	Appalachian St./Davidson/Chattanooga
1982	9	Chattanooga
1983	9	Chattanooga
1984	9	Marshall
1985	9	Chattanooga
1986	9	Chattanooga
1987	9	Marshall
1988	9	Marshall
1989	8	Chattanooga

Season	No.	Regular Season
1990	8	East Tenn. St.
1991	8	East Tenn. St./Furman/ Chattanooga
1992	8	East Tenn. St./Chattanooga
1993	10	Chattanooga
1994	10	Chattanooga
1995	10	Marshall (Northern)/ Chattanooga (Southern)
1996	10	Davidson (Northern)/ Western Caro. (Southern)
1997	10	Davidson (Northern)/ Marshall (Northern)/ Chattanooga (Southern)
1998	11	Appalachian St. (North)/Davidson (North)/Chattanooga (South)
1999	12	Appalachian St.(North)/ Col. of Charleston (South)
2000	12	Appalachian St. (North)/ Col. of Charleston (South)
2001	12	East Tenn. St. (North)/ Col. of Charleston (South)
2002	12	Davidson (North)/ UNC Greensboro (North)/East Tenn. St. (North)/ Col. of Charleston (South)/ Ga. Southern (South)/Chattanooga (South)
2003	12	Appalachian St. (North)/Davidson (North)/East Tenn. St. (North)/ Col. of Charleston (South)
2004	12	East Tenn. St. (North)/ Ga. Southern (South)/Davidson (South)/ Col. of Charleston (South)
2005	12	Chattanooga (North)/Davidson (South)
2006	11	Elon (North)/Ga. Southern (South)
2007	11	Appalachian St. (North)/ Davidson (South)

Season	No.	Conference Tournament
1921		Kentucky
1922	23	North Carolina
1923	22	Mississippi St.
1924	16	North Carolina
1925	17	North Carolina
1926	16	North Carolina
1927	14	Vanderbilt
1928	16	Mississippi
1929	16	North Carolina St.
1930	16	Alabama
1931	16	Maryland
1932	16	Georgia
1933	8	South Carolina
1934	8	Wash. & Lee
1935	8	North Carolina
1936	8	North Carolina
1937	8	Wash. & Lee
1938	8	Duke
1939	11	Clemson
1940	8	North Carolina
1941	8	Duke
1942	8	Duke
1943	8	George Washington
1944	8	Duke
1945	8	North Carolina
1946	8	Duke
1947	8	North Carolina St.
1948	10	North Carolina St.
1949	8	North Carolina St.
1950	8	North Carolina St.
1951	8	North Carolina St.
1952	8	North Carolina St.
1953	8	Wake Forest
1954	8	George Washington
1955	8	West Virginia
1956	8	West Virginia
1957	8	West Virginia
1958	8	West Virginia
1959	8	West Virginia
1960	8	West Virginia
1961	8	George Washington
1962	8	West Virginia
1963	8	West Virginia
1964	8	VMI
1965	8	West Virginia
1966	8	Davidson
1967	8	West Virginia
1968	8	Davidson
1969	8	Davidson
1970	8	Davidson
1971	7	Furman
1972	8	East Caro.

Season	No.	Conference Tournament
1973	8	Furman
1974	8	Furman
1975	8	Furman
1976	8	VMI
1977	7	VMI
1978	8	Appalachian St.
1979	8	Appalachian St.
1980	8	Furman
1981	8	Chattanooga
1982	8	Chattanooga
1983	8	Chattanooga
1984	8	Marshall
1985	8	Marshall
1986	8	Davidson
1987	8	Marshall
1988	8	Chattanooga
1989	8	East Tenn. St.
1990	8	East Tenn. St.
1991	8	East Tenn. St.
1992	8	East Tenn. St.
1993	10	Chattanooga
1994	10	Chattanooga
1995	10	Chattanooga
1996	9	Western Caro.
1997	10	Chattanooga
1998	10	Davidson
1999	12	Col. of Charleston
2000	12	Appalachian St.
2001	12	UNC Greensboro
2002	12	Davidson
2003	12	East Tenn. St.
2004	12	East Tenn. St.
2005	12	UNC Greensboro
2006	11	Davidson
2007	11	Davidson

SOUTHLAND CONFERENCE

Season	No.	Regular Season
1964	5	Lamar
1965	5	Abilene Christian/Arkansas St.
1966	5	Abilene Christian
1967	5	Arkansas St.
1968	5	Abilene Christian
1969	5	Trinity (Tex.)
1970	5	Lamar
1971	5	Arkansas St.
1972	7	Louisiana Tech
1973	7	Louisiana Tech
1974	3	Arkansas St.
1975	5	McNeese St.
1976	6	Louisiana Tech
1977	6	La.-Lafayette
1978	6	McNeese St./Lamar
1979	6	Lamar
1980	6	Lamar
1981	6	Lamar
1982	6	La.-Lafayette
1983	7	Lamar
1984	7	Lamar
1985	7	Louisiana Tech
1986	7	La.-Monroe
1987	6	Louisiana Tech
1988	8	North Texas
1989	8	North Texas
1990	8	La.-Monroe
1991	8	La.-Monroe
1992	10	UTSA
1993	10	La.-Monroe
1994	10	La.-Monroe
1995	10	Nicholls St.
1996	10	La.-Monroe
1997	10	McNeese St./La.-Monroe/ Texas St.
1998	10	Nicholls St.
1999	10	Texas St.
2000	11	Sam Houston St.
2001	11	McNeese St.
2002	11	McNeese St.
2003	11	Sam Houston St.
2004	11	Southeastern La./ Texas-Arlington/UTSA
2005	11	Northwestern St./Southeastern La.
2006	11	Northwestern St.
2007	11	Northwestern St. (East)/ A&M Corpus Christi (West)

Season	No.	Conference Tournament
1981	6	Lamar
1982	5	La.-Lafayette

Season	No.	Conference Tournament
1983	7	Lamar
1984	7	Louisiana Tech
1985	7	Louisiana Tech
1986	7	La.-Monroe
1987	6	Louisiana Tech
1988	6	North Texas
1989	6	McNeese St.
1990	7	La.-Monroe
1991	4	La.-Monroe
1992	6	La.-Monroe
1993	6	La.-Monroe
1994	8	Texas St.
1995	8	Nicholls St.
1996	6	La.-Monroe
1997	6	Texas St.
1998	6	Nicholls St.
1999	6	UTSA
2000	8	Lamar
2001	8	Northwestern St.
2002	6	McNeese St.
2003	6	Sam Houston St.
2004	8	UTSA
2005	8	Southeastern La.
2006	8	Northwestern St.
2007	8	A&M Corpus Christi

SOUTHWEST CONFERENCE

Season	No.	Regular Season
1915	5	Texas
1916	5	Texas
1917	3	Texas
1918	5	Rice
1919	5	Texas
1920	6	Texas A&M
1921	5	Texas A&M
1922	6	Texas A&M
1923	6	Texas A&M
1924	8	Texas
1925	8	Oklahoma St.
1926	7	Arkansas
1927	7	Arkansas
1928	7	Arkansas
1929	7	Arkansas
1930	7	Arkansas
1931	7	TCU
1932	7	Baylor
1933	7	Texas
1934	7	TCU
1935	7	Arkansas/Rice/SMU
1936	7	Arkansas
1937	7	SMU
1938	7	Arkansas
1939	7	Texas
1940	7	Rice
1941	7	Arkansas
1942	7	Rice/Arkansas
1943	7	Texas/Rice
1944	7	Arkansas/Rice
1945	7	Rice
1946	7	Baylor
1947	7	Texas
1948	7	Baylor
1949	7	Arkansas/Baylor/Rice
1950	7	Baylor/Arkansas
1951	7	Texas A&M/TCU/Texas
1952	7	TCU
1953	7	TCU
1954	7	Rice/Texas
1955	7	SMU
1956	7	SMU
1957	7	SMU
1958	8	Arkansas/SMU
1959	8	TCU
1960	8	Texas
1961	8	Texas Tech
1962	8	SMU/Texas Tech
1963	8	Texas
1964	8	Texas A&M
1965	8	SMU/Texas
1966	8	SMU
1967	8	SMU
1968	8	TCU
1969	8	Texas A&M
1970	8	Rice
1971	8	TCU
1972	8	Texas/SMU
1973	8	Texas Tech
1974	8	Texas
1975	8	Texas A&M

Season	No.	Regular Season
1976	9	Texas A&M
1977	9	Arkansas
1978	9	Texas/Arkansas
1979	9	Texas/Arkansas
1980	9	Texas A&M
1981	9	Arkansas
1982	9	Arkansas
1983	9	Houston
1984	9	Houston
1985	9	Texas Tech
1986	9	TCU/Texas/Texas A&M
1987	9	TCU
1988	9	SMU
1989	9	Arkansas
1990	9	Arkansas
1991	9	Arkansas
1992	8	Houston/Texas
1993	8	SMU
1994	8	Texas
1995	8	Texas/Texas Tech
1996	8	Texas Tech

Season	No.	Conference Tournament
1976	9	Texas Tech
1977	9	Arkansas
1978	9	Houston
1979	9	Arkansas
1980	9	Texas A&M
1981	9	Houston
1982	9	Arkansas
1983	9	Houston
1984	9	Houston
1985	8	Texas Tech
1986	8	Texas Tech
1987	8	Texas A&M
1988	8	SMU
1989	8	Arkansas
1990	8	Arkansas
1991	9	Arkansas
1992	8	Houston
1993	8	Texas Tech
1994	8	Texas
1995	7	Texas
1996	8	Texas Tech

SOUTHWESTERN ATHLETIC CONFERENCE

Season	No.	Regular Season
1957	6	Texas Southern
1958	6	Texas Southern
1959	8	Grambling
1960	8	Grambling
1961	8	Prairie View
1962	7	Prairie View
1963	8	Grambling
1964	8	Grambling/Jackson St.
1965	8	Southern U.
1966	8	Alcorn St./Grambling
1967	8	Alcorn St./Ark.-Pine Bluff/Grambling
1968	8	Alcorn St./Jackson St.
1969	8	Alcorn St.
1970	8	Jackson St.
1971	7	Grambling
1972	7	Grambling
1973	7	Alcorn St.
1974	7	Jackson St.
1975	7	Jackson St.
1976	7	Alcorn St.
1977	7	Texas Southern
1978	7	Jackson St./Southern U.
1979	7	Alcorn St.
1980	7	Alcorn St.
1981	7	Alcorn St./Southern U.
1982	7	Alcorn St./Jackson St.
1983	8	Texas Southern
1984	8	Alcorn St.
1985	8	Alcorn St.
1986	8	Alcorn St./Southern U.
1987	8	Grambling
1988	8	Southern U.
1989	8	Grambling/Southern U./Texas Southern
1990	8	Southern U.
1991	8	Jackson St.
1992	8	Mississippi Val./Texas Southern
1993	8	Jackson St.
1994	8	Texas Southern
1995	8	Texas Southern
1996	8	Jackson St./Mississippi Val.
1997	8	Mississippi Val.
1998	9	Texas Southern
1999	9	Alcorn St.
2000	10	Alcorn St.
2001	10	Alabama St.
2002	10	Alcorn St.
2003	10	Prairie View
2004	10	Mississippi Val.
2005	10	Alabama A&M
2006	10	Southern U.
2007	10	Mississippi Val.

Season	No.	Conference Tournament
1980	7	Alcorn St.
1981	7	Southern U.
1982	7	Alcorn St.
1983	7	Alcorn St.
1984	8	Alcorn St.
1985	4	Southern U.
1986	8	Mississippi Val.
1987	8	Southern U.
1988	8	Southern U.
1989	8	Southern U.
1990	8	Texas Southern
1991	8	Jackson St.
1992	8	Mississippi Val.
1993	8	Southern U.
1994	8	Texas Southern
1995	6	Texas Southern
1996	6	Mississippi Val.
1997	8	Jackson St.
1998	8	Prairie View
1999	8	Alcorn St.
2000	8	Jackson St.
2001	8	Alabama St.
2002	8	Alcorn St.
2003	8	Texas Southern
2004	8	Alabama St.
2005	8	Alabama A&M
2006	8	Southern U.
2007	8	Jackson St.

SUMMIT LEAGUE

Season	No.	Regular Season
1983	8	Western Ill.
1984	8	Ill.-Chicago
1985	8	Cleveland St.
1986	8	Cleveland St.
1987	8	Missouri St.
1988	8	Missouri St.
1989	8	Missouri St.
1990	7	Missouri St.
1991	9	Northern Ill.
1992	9	Green Bay
1993	9	Cleveland St.
1994	10	Green Bay
1995	10	Valparaiso
1996	10	Valparaiso
1997	8	Valparaiso
1998	9	Valparaiso
1999	8	Valparaiso
2000	9	Oakland
2001	9	Southern Utah/Valparaiso
2002	8	Valparaiso
2003	8	Valparaiso
2004	9	Valparaiso
2005	9	Oral Roberts
2006	9	IUPUI/Oral Roberts
2007	8	Oral Roberts

Season	No.	Conference Tournament
1984	8	Western Ill.
1985	8	Eastern Ill.
1986	8	Cleveland St.
1987	8	Missouri St.
1988		DNP
1989	7	Missouri St.
1990	7	UNI
1991	8	Green Bay
1992	8	Eastern Ill.
1993	8	Wright St.
1994	8	Green Bay
1995	6	Valparaiso
1996	8	Valparaiso
1997	8	Valparaiso
1998	7	Valparaiso
1999	7	Valpairaso
2000	7	Valparaiso
2001	8	Southern Utah
2002	8	Valparaiso
2003	8	IUPUI
2004	8	Valparaiso
2005	8	Oakland
2006	8	Oral Roberts
2007	8	Oral Roberts

SUN BELT CONFERENCE

Season	No.	Regular Season
1977	6	Charlotte
1978	6	Charlotte
1979	6	South Ala.
1980	8	South Ala.
1981	7	VCU/South Ala./UAB
1982	6	UAB
1983	8	VCU/Old Dominion
1984	8	VCU
1985	8	VCU
1986	8	Old Dominion
1987	8	Western Ky.
1988	8	Charlotte
1989	8	South Ala.
1990	8	UAB
1991	8	South Ala.
1992	11	Louisiana Tech/La.-Lafayette
1993	10	New Orleans
1994	10	Western Ky.
1995	10	Western Ky.
1996	10	Ark.-Little Rock/New Orleans
1997	10	New Orleans/South Ala.
1998	10	South Ala./Arkansas St.
1999	8	Louisiana Tech
2000	9	La.-Lafayette/South Ala.
2001	12	Western Ky. (East)/South Ala. (West)
2002	11	Western Ky. (East)/La.-Lafayette (West)/New Mexico St. (West)
2003	12	Western Ky. (East)/La.-Lafayette (West)
2004	11	Ark.-Little Rock (East)/La.-Lafayette (West)
2005	11	Ark.-Little Rock (East)/Denver (West)
2006	11	Western Ky. (East)/South Ala. (West)
2007	13	South Ala. (Eastern)/Arkansas St. (Western)/La.-Monroe (Western)

Season	No.	Conference Tournament
1977	6	Charlotte
1978	6	New Orleans
1979	6	Jacksonville
1980	8	VCU
1981	7	VCU
1982	6	UAB
1983	8	UAB
1984	8	UAB
1985	8	VCU
1986	8	Jacksonville
1987	8	UAB
1988	8	Charlotte
1989	8	South Ala.
1990	8	South Fla.
1991	8	South Ala.
1992	11	La.-Lafayette
1993	9	Western Ky.
1994	10	La.-Lafayette
1995	10	Western Ky.
1996	10	New Orleans
1997	10	South Ala.
1998	10	South Ala.
1999	8	Arkansas St.
2000	9	La.-Lafayette
2001	11	Western Ky.
2002	11	Western Ky.
2003	11	Western Ky.
2004	8	La.-Lafayette
2005	11	La.-Lafayette
2006	11	South Ala.
2007	13	North Texas

WEST COAST CONFERENCE

Season	No.	Regular Season
1953	5	Santa Clara
1954	5	Santa Clara
1955	5	San Francisco
1956	8	San Francisco
1957	8	San Francisco

Season	No.	Regular Season
1958	7	San Francisco
1959	7	St. Mary's (Cal.)
1960	7	Santa Clara
1961	7	Loyola Marymount
1962	7	Pepperdine
1963	7	San Francisco
1964	7	San Francisco
1965	8	San Francisco
1966	8	Pacific
1967	8	Pacific
1968	8	Santa Clara
1969	8	Santa Clara
1970	8	Santa Clara
1971	8	Pacific
1972	8	San Francisco
1973	8	San Francisco
1974	8	San Francisco
1975	8	UNLV
1976	7	Pepperdine
1977	8	San Francisco
1978	8	San Francisco
1979	8	San Francisco
1980	9	San Francisco/St. Mary's (Cal.)
1981	8	San Francisco/Pepperdine
1982	8	Pepperdine
1983	7	Pepperdine
1984	7	San Diego
1985	7	Pepperdine
1986	8	Pepperdine
1987	8	San Diego
1988	8	Loyola Marymount
1989	8	St. Mary's (Cal.)
1990	8	Loyola Marymount
1991	8	Pepperdine
1992	8	Pepperdine
1993	8	Pepperdine
1994	8	Gonzaga
1995	8	Santa Clara
1996	8	Gonzaga/Santa Clara
1997	8	St. Mary's (Cal.)/Santa Clara
1998	8	Gonzaga
1999	8	Gonzaga
2000	8	Pepperdine
2001	8	Gonzaga
2002	8	Gonzaga/Pepperdine
2003	8	Gonzaga
2004	8	Gonzaga
2005	8	Gonzaga
2006	8	Gonzaga
2007	8	Gonzaga

Season	No.	Conference Tournament
1987	8	Santa Clara
1988	8	Loyola Marymount
1989	8	Loyola Marymount
1990		DNP
1991	8	Pepperdine
1992	8	Pepperdine
1993	8	Santa Clara
1994	8	Pepperdine
1995	8	Gonzaga
1996	8	Portland
1997	8	St. Mary's (Cal.)
1998	8	San Francisco
1999	8	Gonzaga
2000	8	Gonzaga
2001	8	Gonzaga
2002	8	Gonzaga
2003	6	San Diego
2004	8	Gonzaga
2005	8	Gonzaga
2006	8	Gonzaga
2007	8	Gonzaga

WESTERN ATHLETIC CONFERENCE

Season	No.	Regular Season
1963	6	Arizona St.
1964	6	New Mexico/Arizona St.
1965	6	BYU
1966	6	Utah
1967	6	Wyoming/BYU
1968	6	New Mexico
1969	6	BYU/Wyoming
1970	8	UTEP
1971	8	BYU
1972	8	BYU
1973	8	Arizona St.
1974	8	New Mexico
1975	8	Arizona St.

Season	No.	Regular Season
1976	8	Arizona
1977	8	Utah
1978	8	New Mexico
1979	7	BYU
1980	8	BYU
1981	9	Utah/Wyoming
1982	9	Wyoming
1983	9	UTEP/Utah
1984	9	UTEP
1985	9	UTEP
1986	9	Wyoming/UTEP/Utah
1987	9	UTEP
1988	9	BYU
1989	9	Colorado St.
1990	9	Colorado St./BYU
1991	9	Utah
1992	9	UTEP/BYU
1993	10	BYU/Utah
1994	10	New Mexico
1995	10	Utah
1996	10	Utah
1997	16	Fresno St. (Pacific)/Hawaii (Pacific)/Utah (Mountain)
1998	16	TCU (Pacific)/Utah (Mountain)
1999	16	UNLV (Mountain)/Tulsa (Mountain)/Utah (Pacific)
2000	8	Tulsa
2001	9	Fresno St.
2002	10	Hawaii/Tulsa
2003	10	Fresno St.
2004	10	UTEP/Nevada
2005	10	Nevada
2006	9	Nevada
2007	9	Nevada

Season	No.	Conference Tournament
1984	9	UTEP
1985	9	San Diego St.
1986	9	UTEP
1987	9	Wyoming
1988	9	Wyoming
1989	9	UTEP
1990	9	UTEP
1991	9	BYU
1992	8	BYU
1993	10	New Mexico
1994	10	Hawaii
1995	10	Utah
1996	10	New Mexico
1997	12	Utah
1998	12	UNLV
1999	12	Utah
2000	8	Fresno St.
2001	9	Hawaii
2002	10	Hawaii
2003	9	Tulsa
2004	10	Nevada
2005	10	UTEP
2006	8	Nevada
2007	9	New Mexico St.

WESTERN NEW YORK LITTLE THREE CONFERENCE

Season	No.	Regular Season
1947	3	Canisius
1948	3	Niagara
1949	3	Niagara
1950	3	Canisius/Niagara/St. Bonaventure
1951	3	St. Bonaventure
1952		DNP
1953	3	Niagara
1954	3	Niagara
1955	3	Niagara
1956	3	Canisius
1957	3	Canisius/St. Bonaventure
1958	3	St. Bonaventure

YANKEE CONFERENCE

Season	No.	Regular Season
1947	6	Vermont
1948	6	Connecticut
1949	6	Connecticut
1950	6	Rhode Island
1951	6	Connecticut
1952	6	Connecticut
1953	6	Connecticut
1954	6	Connecticut

Season	No.	Regular Season
1955	6	Connecticut
1956	6	Connecticut
1957	6	Connecticut
1958	6	Connecticut
1959	6	Connecticut
1960	6	Connecticut
1961	6	Rhode Island
1962	6	Massachusetts
1963	6	Connecticut
1964	6	Connecticut/Rhode Island
1965	6	Connecticut
1966	6	Connecticut/Rhode Island
1967	6	Connecticut
1968	6	Massachusetts/Rhode Island
1969	6	Massachusetts
1970	6	Connecticut/Massachusetts
1971	6	Massachusetts
1972	6	Rhode Island
1973	7	Massachusetts
1974	7	Massachusetts
1975	7	Massachusetts

INDEPENDENTS
(Best Record)

Season	No.	Regular Season
1946	30	Yale
1947	32	Duquesne
1948	40	Bradley
1949	34	Villanova
1950	36	Toledo
1951	37	Dayton
1952	42	Seton Hall
1953	42	Seattle
1954	39	Holy Cross/Seattle
1955	41	Marquette
1956	35	Temple
1957	32	Seattle
1958	29	Temple
1959	32	St. Bonaventure
1960	34	Providence
1961	35	Memphis
1962	34	Loyola (Ill.)
1963	47	Loyola (Ill.)
1964	51	UTEP
1965	45	Providence
1966	44	UTEP
1967	47	Boston College
1968	47	Houston
1969	47	Boston College
1970	52	Jacksonville
1971	55	Marquette
1972	59	Oral Roberts
1973	68	Providence
1974	73	Notre Dame
1975	79	Tex.-Pan American
1976	79	Rutgers
1977	73	UNLV
1978	70	DePaul
1979	68	Syracuse
1980	55	DePaul
1981	54	DePaul
1982	52	DePaul
1983	19	New Orleans
1984	19	DePaul
1985	22	Notre Dame
1986	17	Notre Dame
1987	18	DePaul
1988	18	Akron
1989	22	Akron
1990	19	Wright St.
1991	17	DePaul
1992	12	Penn St.
1993	14	Milwaukee
1994	6	Southern Utah
1995	2	Notre Dame
1996	2	Oral Roberts
1997	3	Oral Roberts
1998	0	
1999	2	Denver
2000	5	Tex.-Pan American
2001	5	Stony Brook
2002	3	Tex.-Pan American
2003	6	Centenary (La.)
2004	4	A&M-Corpus Christi
2005	4	A&M-Corpus Christi
2006	4	A&M-Corpus Christi
2007	4	Tex.-Pan American

CONFERENCES

CONSECUTIVE REGULAR-SEASON WINNER

No.	Team	Conference	Seasons
13	UCLA	Pacific-10	1967-79
10	Connecticut	Yankee	1951-60
10	UNLV	Big West	1983-92
9	Kentucky	Southeastern	1944-52
8	Idaho St.	Rocky Mountain	1953-60
8	Long Beach St.	Big West	1970-77
7	Cincinnati	Conference USA	1996-2002
7	Coppin St.	Mid-Eastern	1993-99
7	Dartmouth	Ivy	1938-44
7	Gonzaga	West Coast	2001-07
7	Murray St.	Ohio Valley	1994-2000
7	Rhode Island	New England	1938-44
6	Arizona	Border	1946-51
6	Col. of Charleston	Southern	1999-2004
6	Cincinnati	Missouri Valley	1958-63
6	Davidson	Southern	1968-73
6	Kansas	Missouri Valley	1922-27
6	Kentucky	Southeastern	1968-73
6	Kentucky	Southeastern	2000-05
6	Penn	Ivy	1970-75
6	Weber St.	Big Sky	1968-73

CONSECUTIVE CONFERENCE TOURNAMENT WINNER

No.	Team	Conference	Seasons
7	Kentucky	Southeastern	1944-50
7	N.C. A&T	Mid-Eastern	1982-88
6	North Carolina St.	Southern	1947-52
6	Valparaiso	Mid-Continent	1995-2000
6	West Virginia	Southern	1955-60
5	Duke	Atlantic Coast	1999-2003
5	Massachusetts	Atlantic 10	1992-96
4	Arizona	Pacific-10	1988-90, 2002
4	Cincinnati	Great Midwest	1992-95
4	East Tenn. St.	Southern	1989-92
4	Gonzaga	West Coast	1999-2002
4	Gonzaga	West Coast	2004-07
4	Kentucky	Southeastern	1992-95
4	La.-Monroe	Southland	1990-93
4	Northeastern	America East	1984-87
4	Winthrop	Big South	1999-2002
3	28 tied		

REGULAR SEASON CONFERENCE TITLES WON OR SHARED
(Includes divisional crowns)

No.	School	Conferences
50	Kansas	MVC, Big 8, Big 12
49	Kentucky	Southern, SEC
37	Penn	Ivy
32	North Carolina	Southern, ACC
31	Utah	Rocky Mountain, Mountain States, WAC, MWC
29	UCLA	Pac-10
28	Connecticut	Yankee, Big East
28	Princeton	Ivy
26	Arkansas	Southwest, SEC
26	Western Ky.	OVC, Sun Belt
24	Texas	Southwest, Big 12
22	BYU	Rocky Mountain Mountain States WAC, MWC
22	Cincinnati	MAC, MVC, Great Midwest, C-USA
21	Arizona	Border, WAC, Pac-10
21	Duke	Southern
21	Purdue	Big Ten
21	Wyoming	Rocky Mountain Mountain States WAC, MWC
20	Indiana	Big Ten
20	Louisville	MVC, Metropolitan, C-USA
20	Murray St.	OVC
20	St. Joseph's	East Coast, A-10

DIVISION I UNDEFEATED IN CONFERENCE PLAY
Minimum 6 conference games.

Year	Conference	Team	Conference W-L	Overall W-L
1904	Ivy	Columbia	10-0	14-0
1905	Ivy	Columbia	8-0	13-0
1908	Ivy	Penn	8-0	23-4
1908	Missouri Valley	Kansas	6-0	18-6
1909	Big Ten	Chicago	12-0	12-0
1912	Big Ten	Purdue	12-0	12-0
1912	Big Ten	Wisconsin	12-0	15-0
1912	Missouri Valley	Nebraska	8-0	14-1
1913	Big Ten	Wisconsin	12-0	14-1
1913	Missouri Valley	Nebraska	10-0	17-2
1914	Big Ten	Wisconsin	12-0	15-0
1914	Missouri Valley	Nebraska	7-0	15-3
1915	Big Ten	Illinois	12-0	16-0
1916	Big Ten	Wisconsin	12-0	20-1
1916	Missouri Valley	Nebraska	12-0	13-1
1916	Southwest	Texas	6-0	12-0
1920	Ivy	Penn	10-0	22-1
1920	Southwest	Texas A&M	16-0	19-0
1922	Pacific Coast	Idaho	7-0	19-1
1923	Missouri Valley	Kansas	16-0	17-1
1924	Southwest	Texas	20-0	23-0
1926	Pacific Coast	California	7-0	14-0
1927	Pacific Coast	California	7-0	13-0
1928	Missouri Valley	Oklahoma	18-0	18-0
1928	Southwest	Arkansas	12-0	19-1
1929	Big Six	Oklahoma	10-0	13-2
1929	Missouri Valley	Washington-St. Louis	7-0	11-7
1929	Pacific Coast	California	11-0	17-3
1930	Big Ten	Purdue	10-0	13-2
1931	Ivy	Columbia	10-0	20-2
1932	Missouri Valley	Creighton	8-0	17-4
1934	Eastern Intercollegiate	Pittsburgh	8-0	18-4
1936	Big Six	Kansas	10-0	21-2
1936	Ivy	Columbia	12-0	19-3
1937	Ivy	Penn	12-0	17-3
1938	Border	New Mex. St.	18-0	22-3
1940	Missouri Valley	Oklahoma St.	12-0	26-3
1941	Southwest	Arkansas	12-0	20-3
1942	Border	West Tex. A&M	16-0	28-3
1943	Big Six	Kansas	10-0	22-6
1943	Big Ten	Illinois	12-0	17-1
1943	Border	West Tex. A&M	10-0	15-7
1943	Missouri Valley	Creighton	10-0	16-1
1944	Ivy	Dartmouth	8-0	19-2
1945	Border	New Mexico	12-0	14-2
1945	Southwest	Rice	12-0	20-1
1946	Big Six	Kansas	10-0	19-2
1946	Missouri Valley	Oklahoma St.	12-0	31-2
1947	Southwest	Texas	12-0	26-2
1948	Missouri Valley	Oklahoma St.	10-0	27-4
1948	Southeastern	Kentucky	9-0	36-3
1949	Southeastern	Kentucky	13-0	32-2
1951	Ivy	Columbia	12-0	22-1
1951	Southeastern	Kentucky	14-0	32-2
1952	Southeastern	Kentucky	14-0	29-3
1953	Rocky Mountain	Idaho St.	10-0	18-7
1953	Southeastern	LSU	13-0	22-3
1954	Southeastern	Kentucky	14-0	25-0
1954	Southeastern	LSU	14-0	20-5
1954	Southern	George Washington	10-0	23-3
1954	Yankee	Connecticut	7-0	23-3
1955	West Coast	San Francisco	12-0	28-1
1955	Yankee	Connecticut	7-0	20-5
1956	Pacific Coast	UCLA	16-0	22-6
1956	Southeastern	Alabama	14-0	21-3
1956	Southwest	Southern Methodist	12-0	25-4
1956	West Coast	San Francisco	14-0	29-0
1957	Atlantic Coast	North Carolina	14-0	32-0
1957	Rocky Mountain	Idaho St.	12-0	25-4
1957	Southern	West Virginia	12-0	25-5
1957	Yankee	Connecticut	8-0	17-8
1958	Mid-American	Miami (Ohio)	12-0	18-9
1958	Rocky Mountain	Idaho St.	10-0	22-6
1958	Southern	West Virginia	12-0	26-2
1958	West Coast	San Francisco	12-0	25-2

Year	Conference	Team	Conference W-L	Overall W-L
1958	Yankee	Connecticut	10-0	17-10
1959	Big Eight	Kansas St.	14-0	25-2
1959	Middle Atlantic	St. Joseph's	7-0	22-5
1959	Southern	West Virginia	11-0	29-5
1960	Rocky Mountain	Idaho St.	8-0	21-5
1961	Big Ten	Ohio St.	14-0	27-1
1961	Middle Atlantic	St. Joseph's	8-0	25-5
1962	Border	Arizona St.	8-0	23-4
1963	Atlantic Coast	Duke	14-0	27-3
1963	Middle Atlantic	St. Joseph's	8-0	23-5
1964	AAWU	UCLA	15-0	30-0
1964	West Coast	San Francisco	12-0	23-5
1965	AAWU	UCLA	14-0	28-2
1965	Southern	Davidson	12-0	24-2
1965	Yankee	Connecticut	10-0	23-3
1966	Ohio Valley	Western Ky.	14-0	25-3
1967	AAWU	UCLA	14-0	30-0
1967	West Coast	Pacific	14-0	24-4
1968	AAWU	UCLA	14-0	29-1
1969	Big Sky	Weber St.	15-0	27-3
1969	Ivy	Princeton	14-0	19-7
1969	Southern	Davidson	9-0	27-3
1970	Atlantic Coast	South Carolina	14-0	25-3
1970	Big Ten	Iowa	14-0	20-5
1970	Ivy	Penn	14-0	25-2
1970	Ohio Valley	Western Ky.	14-0	22-3
1970	Pacific Coast	Long Beach St.	10-0	24-5
1970	Southern	Davidson	10-0	22-5
1971	Big Eight	Kansas	14-0	27-3
1971	Ivy	Penn	14-0	28-1
1971	Middle Atlantic (E)	St. Joseph's	6-0	19-9
1971	Pacific Coast	Long Beach St.	10-0	24-5
1971	Pacific-8	UCLA	14-0	29-1
1971	Yankee	Massachusetts	10-0	23-4
1972	Middle Atlantic (E)	Temple	6-0	23-8
1972	Pacific-8	UCLA	14-0	30-0
1972	Southland	La.-Lafayette	8-0	25-4
1973	Atlantic Coast	North Caro. St.	12-0	27-0
1973	Middle Atlantic (E)	St. Joseph's	6-0	22-6
1973	Pacific-8	UCLA	14-0	30-0
1973	Southland	La.-Lafayette	12-0	24-5
1974	Atlantic Coast	North Caro. St.	12-0	30-1
1974	Pacific Coast	Long Beach St.	12-0	24-2
1975	Big Ten	Indiana	18-0	31-1
1975	Southern	Furman	13-0	22-7
1976	Big Ten	Indiana	18-0	32-0
1976	Ivy	Princeton	14-0	22-5
1977	Southwest	Arkansas	16-0	26-2
1977	West Coast	San Francisco	14-0	29-2
1978	East Coast (W)	Lafayette	10-0	23-8
1978	Pacific-8	UCLA	14-0	25-3
1979	East Coast	Temple	13-0	25-4
1979	Missouri Valley	Indiana St.	16-0	33-1
1979	New Jersey-New York 7	Rutgers	6-0	22-9
1979	Southwestern	Alcorn St.	12-0	28-1
1979	Sun Belt	South Ala.	10-0	20-7
1980	Metro	Louisville	12-0	33-3
1980	Southwestern	Alcorn St.	12-0	28-2
1980	Trans America	La.-Monroe	6-0	17-11
1981	East Coast (E)	American	11-0	24-6
1982	East Coast	Temple	11-0	19-8
1982	West Coast	Pepperdine	14-0	22-7
1983	ECAC South	William & Mary	9-0	20-9
1983	Metro	Louisville	12-0	32-4
1983	Southwest	Houston	16-0	31-3
1984	Atlantic 10	Temple	18-0	26-5
1984	Atlantic Coast	North Carolina	14-0	28-3
1984	ECAC North Atlantic	Northeastern	14-0	27-5
1986	Missouri Valley	Bradley	16-0	32-3
1987	Atlantic Coast	North Carolina	14-0	32-4
1987	Gulf Star	Stephen F. Austin	10-0	22-6
1987	Pacific Coast	UNLV	18-0	37-2
1988	Atlantic 10	Temple	18-0	32-2
1988	Metro Atlantic	La Salle	14-0	24-10
1988	Mid-Eastern	N.C. A&T	16-0	26-3

Year	Conference	Team	Conference W-L	Overall W-L
1988	West Coast	Loyola Marymount	14-0	28-4
1990	Metro Atlantic	La Salle	16-0	30-2
1991	Big West	UNLV	18-0	34-1
1991	Ivy	Princeton	14-0	24-3
1992	Big West	UNLV	18-0	26-2
1992	North Atlantic	Delaware	14-0	27-4
1992	West Coast	Pepperdine	14-0	24-7
1993	Ivy	Penn	14-0	22-5
1993	Mid-Eastern	Coppin St.	16-0	22-8
1993	Sun Belt	New Orleans	18-0	26-4
1994	Big Eight	Missouri	14-0	28-4
1994	Ivy	Penn	14-0	25-3
1994	Mid-Eastern	Coppin St.	16-0	22-8
1995	American West	Southern Utah	6-0	17-11
1995	Ivy	Penn	14-0	22-6
1995	Midwestern	Xavier	14-0	23-5

Year	Conference	Team	Conference W-L	Overall W-L
1996	Midwestern	Wis.-G.B.	16-0	25-4
1996	Southeastern (E)	Kentucky	16-0	34-2
1996	Southern	Davidson	14-0	25-5
1996	Southwest	Texas Tech	14-0	30-2
1997	Ivy	Princeton	14-0	24-4
1997	Trans America (E)	Col. of Charleston	16-0	29-3
1998	Ivy	Princeton	14-0	27-2
1998	Western Athletic (P)	TCU	14-0	27-6
1999	Atlantic Coast	Duke	16-0	37-2
1999	Southern (S)	Col. of Charleston	16-0	28-3
1999	Western Athletic (P)	Utah	14-0	28-5
2000	Big West (E)	Utah St.	16-0	28-6
2000	Conference USA (A)	Cincinnati	16-0	29-4

Year	Conference	Team	Conference W-L	Overall W-L
2000	Ivy	Penn	14-0	21-8
2002	Big 12	Kansas	16-0	33-4
2003	Big Sky	Weber St.	14-0	26-6
2003	Ivy	Penn	14-0	22-6
2003	Southeastern	Kentucky	16-0	32-4
2004	Atlantic 10 (E)	St. Joseph's	16-0	30-2
2004	Ohio Valley	Austin Peay	16-0	22-10
2004	West Coast	Gonzaga	14-0	28-3
2005	Big West	Pacific	18-0	27-4
2005	Southern (S)	Davidson	16-0	23-9
2006	Atlantic 10	George Washington	16-0	27-3
2006	Patriot	Bucknell	14-0	27-5
2006	West Coast	Gonzaga	14-0	29-4
2007	Big South	Winthrop	14-0	29-5
2007	Conference USA	Memphis	16-0	32-5

Division I Conference Alignment History

CHANGES FOR 2007-08

Team	Old Conference	New Conference
UC Davis	Division II	Big West
IPFW	Independent	Summit
Longwood	Division II	Independent
Northern Colo.	Division II	Big Sky
Valparaiso	Mid-Continent	Horizon

CHANGES FOR TEAMS NOT YET FULL-FLEDGE DIVISION I

Team	Status	New Conference
Central Ark.	Reclassifying	Southland
Fla. Gulf Coast	Reclassifying	Atlantic Sun
Kennesaw St.	Reclassifying	Atlantic Sun
North Dakota St.	Reclassifying	Summit
North Fla.	Reclassifying	Atlantic Sun
Presbyterian	Reclassifying	Big South
S.C. Upstate	Reclassifying	Atlantic Sun
South Dakota St.	Reclassifying	Summit
Utah Valley St.	Provisional	Western Athletic

AMERICA EAST CONFERENCE
(1980-present)
ECAC North (1980-82)
ECAC North Atlantic (1983-89)
North Atlantic (1990-96)
America East (1997-present)

Albany (N.Y.)	2002-present
Binghamton	2002-present
Boston U.	1980-present
Canisius	1980-89
Colgate	1980-90
Delaware	1992-2001
Drexel	1992-2001
Hartford	1986-present
Hofstra	1995-2001
Holy Cross	1980-83
Maine	1980-present
UMBC	2004-present
New Hampshire	1980-present
Niagara	1980-89
Northeastern	1980-2005
Rhode Island	1980
Siena	1985-89
Stony Brook	2002-present
Towson	1996-2001
Vermont	1980-present

AMERICAN SOUTH CONFERENCE
(1988-91)

Arkansas St.	1988-91
UCF	1991
Lamar	1988-91
Louisiana Tech	1988-91
New Orleans	1988-91
La.-Lafayette	1988-91
Tex.-Pan American	1988-91

AMERICAN WEST CONFERENCE
(1995-96)

Cal Poly	1995-96
Cal St. Northridge	1995-96
Sacramento St.	1995-96
Southern Utah	1995-96

ATLANTIC COAST CONFERENCE
(1954-present)

Boston College	2006-present
Clemson	1954-present
Duke	1954-present
Florida St.	1992-present
Georgia Tech	1980-present
Maryland	1954-present
Miami (Fla.)	2005-present
North Carolina	1954-present
North Carolina St.	1954-present
South Carolina	1954-71
Virginia	1954-present
Virginia Tech	2005-present
Wake Forest	1954-present

ATLANTIC SUN CONFERENCE
(1979-present)
Trans America Athletic (1979-2001)

Ark.-Little Rock	1981-91
Belmont	2002-present
Campbell	1995-present
Centenary (La.)	1979-99
UCF	1993-2005
Col. of Charleston	1993-98
East Tenn. St.	2006-present
Fla. Atlantic	1994-present
Florida Int'l	1992-98
Gardner-Webb	2003-present
Ga. Southern	1981-92
Georgia St.	1985-2005
Hardin-Simmons	1979-89
Houston Baptist	1979-89
Jacksonville	1999-present
Jacksonville St.	1996-2003
Lipscomb	2004-present
Mercer	1979-present
Nicholls St.	1983-84
La.-Monroe	1979-82
Northwestern St.	1981-84
Oklahoma City	1979
Samford	1979-2003
Southeastern La.	1992-97
Stetson	1987-present
Tex.-Pan American	1979-80
Troy	1998-2005

ATLANTIC 10 CONFERENCE
(1977-present)
Eastern Collegiate Basketball League (1977-78)
Eastern AA (1979-82)
Eastern 8
Atlantic 10 (1983-present)

Charlotte	2006-present
Dayton	1996-present
Duquesne	1977-92, 94-present
Fordham	1996-present
George Washington	1977-present
La Salle	1996-present
Massachusetts	1977-present
Penn St.	1977-79, 83-91
Pittsburgh	1977-82
Rhode Island	1981-present
Richmond	2002-present
Rutgers	1977-95
St. Bonaventure	1980-present
St. Joseph's	1983-present
St. Louis	2006-present
Temple	1983-present
Villanova	1977-80
Virginia Tech	1996-2000
West Virginia	1977-95
Xavier	1996-present

BIG EAST CONFERENCE
(1980-present)

Boston College	1980-2005
Cincinnati	2006-present
Connecticut	1980-present
DePaul	2006-present
Georgetown	1980-present
Louisville	2006-present
Marquette	2006-present
Miami (Fla.)	1992-2004
Notre Dame	1996-present
Pittsburgh	1983-present
Providence	1980-present
Rutgers	1996-present
St. John's (N.Y.)	1980-present
Seton Hall	1980-present
South Fla.	2006-present
Syracuse	1980-present
Villanova	1981-present
Virginia Tech	2001-2004
West Virginia	1996-present

BIG EIGHT CONFERENCE

(1908-96)
Missouri Valley (1908-28)
Big Six (1929-47)
Big Seven (1948-58)
Big Eight (1959-96)

Colorado	1948-96
Drake	1908-28
Grinnell	1919-28
Iowa St.	1908-96
Kansas	1908-96
Kansas St.	1914-96
Missouri	1908-96
Nebraska	1908-19, 21-96
Oklahoma	1920-96
Oklahoma St.	1926-28, 59-96
Washington-St. Louis	1908-10, 12-28

BIG SKY CONFERENCE

(1964-present)

Boise St.	1971-96
Cal St. Northridge	1997-2001
Eastern Wash.	1988-present
Gonzaga	1964-79
Idaho	1964-96
Idaho St.	1964-present
Montana	1964-present
Montana St.	1964-present
Nevada	1980-92
Northern Ariz.	1971-present
Northern Colo.	2008-present
Portland St.	1999-present
Sacramento St.	1997-present
Weber St.	1964-present

BIG SOUTH CONFERENCE

(1986-present)

Armstrong Atlantic	1986-87
Augusta St.	1986-91
Birmingham-So.	2004-06
Campbell	1986-94
Charleston So.	1986-present
Coastal Caro.	1986-present
Davidson	1991-92
Elon	2000-2003
High Point	2000-present
Liberty	1992-present
UMBC	1993-98
UNC Asheville	1986-present
UNC Greensboro	1993-97
Radford	1986-present
Towson	1993-95
VMI	2004-present
Winthrop	1986-present

BIG TEN CONFERENCE

(1895-present)
Intercollegiate Conference of Faculty
   Representatives
Western Intercollegiate
Big Nine (1947-48)
Big Ten (1912-46, 49-present)

Chicago	1895-46
Illinois	1895-present
Indiana	1899-present
Iowa	1899-present
Michigan	1895-present
Michigan St.	1949-present
Minnesota	1895-present
Northwestern	1895-present
Ohio St.	1912-present
Penn St.	1993-present
Purdue	1895-present
Wisconsin	1895-present

BIG 12 CONFERENCE

(1997-present)

Baylor	1997-present
Colorado	1997-present
Iowa St.	1997-present
Kansas	1997-present
Kansas St.	1997-present
Missouri	1997-present
Nebraska	1997-present
Oklahoma	1997-present
Oklahoma St.	1997-present
Texas	1997-present
Texas A&M	1997-present
Texas Tech	1997-present

BIG WEST CONFERENCE

(1970-present)
Pacific Coast (1970-88)
Big West (1989-present)

Boise St.	1997-2001
UC Davis	2008-present
UC Irvine	1978-present
UC Riverside	2002-present
UC Santa Barb.	1970-74, 77-present
Cal Poly	1997-present
Cal St. Fullerton	1975-present
Cal St. L.A.	1970-74
Cal St. Northridge	2002-present
Fresno St.	1970-92
Idaho	1997-2005
Long Beach St.	1970-present
Nevada	1993-2000
UNLV	1983-96
New Mexico St.	1984-2000
North Texas	1997-2000
Pacific	1972-present
San Diego St.	1970-78
San Jose St.	1970-96
Utah St.	1979-2005

BORDER CONFERENCE

(1932-40, 42-62)

Arizona	1932-40, 42-61
Arizona St.	1932-40, 42-43, 44-62
Hardin-Simmons	1942-43, 45-62
New Mexico	1932-40, 42, 45-51
New Mexico St.	1932-40, 42-62
Northern Ariz.	1932-40, 42-53
UTEP	1936-40, 42-43, 44-62
Texas Tech	1933-40, 42-56
West Tex. A&M	1942-43, 45-62

COLONIAL ATHLETIC ASSOCIATION

(1983-present)

American	1985-2001
Delaware	2002-present
Drexel	2002-present
East Caro.	1983-2001
George Mason	1983-present
Georgia St.	2006-present
Hofstra	2002-present
James Madison	1983-present
Navy	1983-91
UNC Wilmington	1985-present
Northeastern	2006-present
Old Dominion	1992-present
Richmond	1983-2001
Towson	2002-present
VCU	1996-present
William & Mary	1983-present

CONFERENCE USA

(1996-present)

UAB	1996-present
UCF	2006-present
Charlotte	1996-2005
Cincinnati	1996-2005
DePaul	1996-2005
East Caro.	2002-present
Houston	1997-present
Louisville	1996-2005
Marquette	1996-2005
Marshall	2006-present
Memphis	1996-present
Rice	2006-present
St. Louis	1996-2005
South Fla.	1996-2005
SMU	2006-present
Southern Miss.	1996-present
UTEP	2006-present
TCU	2002-05
Tulane	1996-present
Tulsa	2006-present

EAST COAST CONFERENCE

(1959-92, 94)
Middle Atlantic (1959-74)
East Coast (1975-92, 94)

American	1967-84
Brooklyn	1992
Bucknell	1959-90
Buffalo	1992, 94
Central Conn. St.	1991-92, 94
Chicago St.	1994
Delaware	1959-91
Drexel	1959-91
Gettysburg	1959-74
Hofstra	1966-92, 94
Lafayette	1959-90
La Salle	1959-83
Lehigh	1959-90
UMBC	1991-92
Muhlenberg	1959-64
Northeastern Ill.	1994
Rider	1967-92
Rutgers	1959-62
St. Joseph's	1959-82
Temple	1959-82
Towson	1983-92
Troy	1994
West Chester	1966-67, 69-74

EASTERN INTERCOLLEGIATE CONFERENCE

(1933-39)

Bucknell	1934
Carnegie Mellon	1933-39
Georgetown	1933-39
Penn St.	1936-39
Pittsburgh	1933-39
Temple	1933-39
West Virginia	1933-39

GREAT MIDWEST CONFERENCE

(1992-95)

UAB	1992-95
Cincinnati	1992-95
Dayton	1994-95
DePaul	1992-95
Marquette	1992-95
Memphis	1992-95
St. Louis	1992-95

GULF STAR CONFERENCE

(1985-87)

Nicholls St.	1985-87
Northwestern St.	1985-87
Sam Houston St.	1985-87
Southeastern La.	1985-87
Stephen F. Austin	1985-87
Texas St.	1985-87

HORIZON LEAGUE

(1980-present)
Midwestern Collegiate (1980-2001)

Butler	1980-present
Cleveland St.	1995-present
Dayton	1989-93
Detroit	1981-present
Duquesne	1993
Evansville	1980-94
Green Bay	1995-present
Ill.-Chicago	1995-present
La Salle	1993-95
Loyola (Ill.)	1980-present
Marquette	1990-91
Milwaukee	1995-present
Northern Ill.	1995-97
Oklahoma City	1980-85
Oral Roberts	1980-87
St. Louis	1983-91
Valparaiso	2008-present
Wright St.	1995-present
Xavier	1980-95
Youngstown St.	2002-present

IVY GROUP

(1902-08, 11-18, 20-present)
Eastern Intercollegiate League

Brown	1954-present
Columbia	1902-08, 11-18, 20-present
Cornell	1902-08, 11-18, 20-present
Dartmouth	1912-18, 20-present
Harvard	1902-04, 06-07, 34-43, 47-present
Penn	1904-08, 11-18, 20-present

Princeton	1902-08, 11-18, 20-44, 46-present
Yale	1902-08, 11-18, 20-43, 47-present

METRO ATLANTIC ATHLETIC CONFERENCE
(1982-present)

Army	1982-90
Canisius	1990-present
Fairfield	1982-present
Fordham	1982-90
Holy Cross	1984-90
Iona	1982-present
La Salle	1984-92
Loyola (Md.)	1990-present
Manhattan	1982-present
Marist	1998-present
Niagara	1990-present
Rider	1998-present
St. Peter's	1982-present
Siena	1990-present

METROPOLITAN COLLEGIATE ATHLETIC CONFERENCE
(1976-95)

Charlotte	1992-95
Cincinnati	1976-91
Florida St.	1977-91
Georgia Tech	1976-78
Louisville	1976-95
Memphis	1976-91
St. Louis	1976-82
South Carolina	1984-91
South Fla.	1992-95
Southern Miss.	1983-95
Tulane	1976-85, 90-95
VCU	1992-95
Virginia Tech	1979-95

METROPOLITAN COLLEGIATE CONFERENCE (1966-69)

Fairleigh Dickinson	1966-69
Hofstra	1966-69
Iona	1966-69
Long Island	1966-69
Manhattan	1966-69
New York U.	1966-67
St. Francis (N.Y.)	1966-68
St. Peter's	1966-69
Seton Hall	1966-69
Wagner	1966-69

METROPOLITAN NEW YORK CONFERENCE (1943, 46-63)

Brooklyn	1943, 46-63
CCNY	1943, 46-63
Fordham	1943, 46-63
Hofstra	1943
Manhattan	1943, 46-63
New York U.	1943, 46-63
St. Francis (N.Y.)	1943, 46-63
St. John's (N.Y.)	1943, 46-63

MID-AMERICAN CONFERENCE
(1947-present)

Akron	1993-present
Ball St.	1976-present
Bowling Green	1954-present
Buffalo	1999-present
Butler	1947-50
Case Reserve	1947-55
Central Mich.	1973-present
Cincinnati	1947-53
Eastern Mich.	1975-present
Kent St.	1952-present
Marshall	1954-69, 98-2005
Miami (Ohio)	1948-present
Northern Ill.	1976-86, 98-present
Ohio	1947-present
Toledo	1952-present
Wayne St. (Mich.)	1947
Western Mich.	1948-present

MID-EASTERN ATHLETIC CONFERENCE
(1972-present)

Bethune-Cookman	1981-present
Coppin St.	1986-present

Delaware St.	1972-87, 89-present
Florida A&M	1981-83, 88-present
Hampton	1996-present
Howard	1972-present
Md.-East. Shore	1972-79, 83-present
Morgan St.	1972-80, 85-present
Norfolk St.	1998-present
N.C. A&T	1972-present
N.C. Central	1972-80
South Carolina St.	1972-present

MISSOURI VALLEY CONFERENCE
(1908-present)

Bradley	1949-51, 56-present
Butler	1933-34
Cincinnati	1958-70
Creighton	1928-43, 46-48, 78-present
Detroit	1950-57
Drake	1908-51, 57-present
Evansville	1995-present
Grinnell	1919-39
Houston	1951-60
Illinois St.	1982-present
Indiana St.	1978-present
Iowa St.	1908-28
Kansas	1908-28
Kansas St.	1914-28
Louisville	1965-75
Memphis	1968-73
Missouri	1908-28
Missouri St.	1991-present
Nebraska	1908-19, 21-28
New Mexico St.	1973-83
North Texas	1958-75
UNI	1992-present
Oklahoma	1920-28
Oklahoma St.	1926-57
St. Louis	1938-43, 45-74
Southern Ill.	1976-present
Tulsa	1935-96
Washburn	1935-41
Washington-St. Louis	1908-10, 12-47
West Tex. A&M	1973-86
Wichita St.	1946-present

MOUNTAIN STATES CONFERENCE
(1911-43, 46-62)
Also known as:
Rocky Mountain (1911-37)
Big Seven (1938-43, 46-47)
Skyline Six (1948-51)
Skyline Eight (1952-62)
Mountain States (1938-43, 46-62)

BYU	1924-42, 46-62
Colorado	1911-42, 46-47
Colorado Col.	1911-37
Colorado Mines	1911-37
Colorado St.	1911-22, 24-42, 46-62
Denver	1911-42, 46-62
Montana	1952-62
Montana St.	1925-37
New Mexico	1952-62
Northern Colo.	1925-37
Utah	1924-42, 46-62
Utah St.	1924-42, 46-62
Western St.	1925-37
Wyoming	1923-43, 46-62

MOUNTAIN WEST CONFERENCE
(2000-present)

Air Force	2000-present
BYU	2000-present
Colorado St.	2000-present
UNLV	2000-present
New Mexico	2000-present
San Diego St.	2000-present
TCU	2006-present
Utah	2000-present
Wyoming	2000-present

NEW JERSEY-NEW YORK 7 CONFERENCE (1977-79)

Columbia	1977-79
Fordham	1977-79
Manhattan	1977-79
Princeton	1977-79
Rutgers	1977-79
St. John's (N.Y.)	1977-79
Seton Hall	1977-79

NORTHEAST CONFERENCE
(1982-present)
ECAC Metro (1982-88)
Northeast (1989-present)

Baltimore	1982-83
Central Conn. St.	1998-present
Fairleigh Dickinson	1982-present
Long Island	1982-present
Loyola (Md.)	1982-89
Marist	1982-97
UMBC	1999-2003
Monmouth	1986-present
Mt. St. Mary's	1990-present
Quinnipiac	1999-present
Rider	1993-97
Robert Morris	1982-present
Sacred Heart	2000-present
St. Francis (N.Y.)	1982-present
St. Francis (Pa.)	1982-present
Siena	1982-84
Towson	1982
Wagner	1982-present

OHIO VALLEY CONFERENCE
(1949-present)

Akron	1981-87
Austin Peay	1964-present
East Tenn. St.	1958-78
Eastern Ill.	1997-present
Eastern Ky.	1949-present
Evansville	1949-52
Jacksonville St.	2004-present
Louisville	1949
Marshall	1949-52
Middle Tenn.	1953-2000
Morehead St.	1949-present
Murray St.	1949-present
Samford	2004-present
Southeast Mo. St.	1992-present
Tenn.-Martin	1993-present
Tennessee St.	1988-present
Tennessee Tech	1949-present
Western Ky.	1949-82
Youngstown St.	1982-88

PACIFIC-10 CONFERENCE
(1916-17, 19-present)
Pacific Coast (1916-59)
Big Five (1960-62)
Big Six (1963)
Athletic Association of Western Universities—AAWU (1963-68)
Pacific 8 (1969-78)
Pacific-10 (1979-present)

Arizona	1979-present
Arizona St.	1979-present
California	1916-17, 19-present
Idaho	1922-59
Montana	1924-29
Oregon	1917, 19-59, 65-present
Oregon St.	1916-17, 19-59, 65-present
Southern California	1922-24, 26-present
Stanford	1917, 19-43, 46-present
UCLA	1928-present
Washington	1916-17, 19-present
Washington St.	1917, 19-59, 64-present

PATRIOT LEAGUE
(1991-present)

American	2002-present
Army	1991-present
Bucknell	1991-present
Colgate	1991-present
Fordham	1991-95
Holy Cross	1991-present
Lafayette	1991-present
Lehigh	1991-present
Navy	1992-present

SOUTHEASTERN CONFERENCE
(1933-present)

Alabama	1933-43, 45-present
Arkansas	1992-present
Auburn	1933-43, 45-present
Florida	1933-43, 45-present
Georgia	1933-present
Georgia Tech	1933-64
Kentucky	1933-52, 54-present

CONFERENCES

LSU	1933-present
Mississippi	1933-43, 45-present
Mississippi St.	1933-43, 45-present
Sewanee	1933-40
South Carolina	1992-present
Tennessee	1933-43, 45-present
Tulane	1933-66
Vanderbilt	1933-present

SOUTHERN CONFERENCE
(1922-present)
Southern Intercollegiate Athletic Association—
   SIAA (1895-1921)

Alabama	1922-32
Appalachian St.	1973-present
Auburn	1922-32
Col. of Charleston	1999-present
Chattanooga	1977-present
Citadel	1937-present
Clemson	1922-53
Davidson	1937-88, 93-present
Duke	1929-53
East Caro.	1966-77
East Tenn. St.	1979-2005
Elon	2004-present
Florida	1923-32
Furman	1937-42, 45-present
George Washington	1942-43, 46-70
Georgia	1922-32
Ga. Southern	1993-present
Georgia Tech	1922-32
Kentucky	1922-32
LSU	1923-32
Marshall	1977-97
Maryland	1924-53
Mississippi	1923-32
Mississippi St.	1922-30, 32
North Carolina	1922-53
UNC Greensboro	1998-present
North Carolina St.	1922-53
Richmond	1937-76
Sewanee	1924-32
South Carolina	1923-53
Tennessee	1922-32
Tulane	1923-32
Vanderbilt	1923-32
Virginia	1922-37
VMI	1926-2003
Virginia Tech	1922-65
Wake Forest	1937-43, 45-53
Wash. & Lee	1922-43, 46-58
West Virginia	1951-68
Western Caro.	1977-present
William & Mary	1937-77
Wofford	1998-present

SOUTHLAND CONFERENCE
(1964-present)

Abilene Christian	1964-73
Arkansas St.	1964-87
Lamar	1964-87, 99-present
La.-Lafayette	1972-82
La.-Monroe	1983-2006
Louisiana Tech	1972-87
McNeese St.	1973-present
Nicholls St.	1992-present
North Texas	1983-96
Northwestern St.	1988-present
Sam Houston St.	1988-present
Southeastern La.	1998-present
Stephen F. Austin	1988-present
Texas-Arlington	1964-86, 88-present
UTSA	1992-present
A&M-Corpus Christi	2007-present
Texas St.	1988-present
Trinity (Tex.)	1964-72

SOUTHWEST CONFERENCE
(1915-96)

Arkansas	1924-91
Baylor	1915-96
Houston	1976-96
Oklahoma St.	1918, 22-25
Phillips	1920
Rice	1915-16, 18-96
SMU	1919-96
Southwestern (Tex.)	1915-16
Texas	1915-96
Texas A&M	1915-96
TCU	1924-96
Texas Tech	1958-96

SOUTHWESTERN ATHLETIC CONFERENCE
(1978-present)

Alabama A&M	2000-present
Alabama St.	1983-present
Alcorn St.	1978-present
Ark.-Pine Bluff	1999-present
Grambling	1978-present
Jackson St.	1978-present
Mississippi Val.	1978-present
Prairie View	1978-present
Southern U.	1978-present
Texas Southern	1978-present

SUMMIT LEAGUE
(1983-present)
Mid-Continent (1983-2007)

Akron	1991-92
Buffalo	1995-98
Centenary (La.)	2004-present
Central Conn. St.	1995-97
Chicago St.	1995-2006
Cleveland St.	1983-94
Eastern Ill.	1983-96
Green Bay	1983-94
Ill.-Chicago	1983-94
IPFW	2008-present
IUPUI	1999-present
Milwaukee	1994
UMKC	1995-present
Missouri St.	1983-90
Northeastern Ill.	1995-98
Northern Ill.	1991-94
UNI	1983-91
Oakland	2000-present
Oral Roberts	1998-present
Southern Utah	1998-present
Troy	1995-97
Valparaiso	1983-2007
Western Ill.	1983-present
Wright St.	1992-94
Youngstown St.	1993-2001

SUN BELT CONFERENCE
(1977-present)

UAB	1980-91
Ark.-Little Rock	1992-present
Arkansas St.	1992-present
UCF	1992
Charlotte	1977-91
Denver	2000-present
Florida Int'l	1999-present
Georgia St.	1977-81
Jacksonville	1977-98
Lamar	1992-98
La.-Lafayette	1992-present
La.-Monroe	2007-present
Louisiana Tech	1992-2001
Middle Tenn.	2001-present
New Mexico St.	2001-05
New Orleans	1977-80, 92-present

North Texas	2001-present
Old Dominion	1983-91
South Ala.	1977-present
South Fla.	1977-91
Tex.-Pan American	1992-98
Troy	2006-present
VCU	1980-91
Western Ky.	1983-present

WEST COAST CONFERENCE
(1953-present)

UC Santa Barb.	1965-69
Fresno St.	1956-57
Gonzaga	1980-present
Loyola Marymount	1956-present
Nevada	1970-79
UNLV	1970-75
Pacific	1953-71
Pepperdine	1956-present
Portland	1977-present
St. Mary's (Cal.)	1953-present
San Diego	1980-present
San Francisco	1953-82, 86-present
San Jose St.	1953-69
Santa Clara	1953-present
Seattle	1972-80

WESTERN ATHLETIC CONFERENCE
(1963-present)

Air Force	1981-99
Arizona	1963-78
Arizona St.	1963-78
Boise St.	2002-present
BYU	1963-99
Colorado St.	1970-99
Fresno St.	1993-present
Hawaii	1980-present
Idaho	2006-present
Louisiana Tech	2002-present
Nevada	2001-present
UNLV	1997-99
New Mexico	1963-99
New Mexico St.	2006-present
Rice	1997-99
San Diego St.	1979-present
San Jose St.	1997-present
SMU	1997-2005
UTEP	1970-2005
TCU	1997-2001
Tulsa	1997-2005
Utah	1963-99
Utah St.	2006-present
Wyoming	1963-99

WESTERN NEW YORK LITTLE THREE CONFERENCE
(1947-51, 53-58)

Canisius	1947-51, 53-58
Niagara	1947-51, 53-58
St. Bonaventure	1947-51, 53-58

YANKEE CONFERENCE
(1938-43, 46-76)

Boston U.	1973-76
Connecticut	1938-43, 46-76
Maine	1938-43, 46-76
Massachusetts	1947-76
New Hampshire	1938-43, 46-76
Northeastern	1938-43, 46
Rhode Island	1938-43, 46-76
Vermont	1947-76

Division I Alignment History

Abilene Christian	1971-73
Air Force	1958-present
Akron	1948-50, 1981-present
Alabama	1948-present
UAB	1980-present
Alabama A&M	2000-present
Alabama St.	1983-present
Albany (N.Y.)	2000-present
Alcorn St.	1978-present
Alliant Int'l	1982-91
American	1967-present
Appalachian St.	1974-present
Arizona	1948, 1951-present
Arizona St.	1951-present
Arkansas	1948-present
Ark.-Little Rock	1979-present
Ark.-Pine Bluff	1999-present
Arkansas St.	1971-present
Armstrong Atlantic	1987
Army	1948-present
Auburn	1948-present
Augusta	1985-91
Austin Peay	1964-present
Baldwin-Wallace	1948-53
Ball St.	1972-present
Baltimore	1979-83
Baylor	1948-present
Belmont	2000-present
Bethune-Cookman	1981-present
Binghamton	2002-present
Birmingham-So.	2004-06
Boise St.	1972-present
Boston College	1948-present
Boston U.	1948-49, 1958-present
Bowling Green	1948-present
Bradley	1948-present
BYU	1948-present
Brooklyn	1948-49, 1983-92
Brown	1948-present
Bucknell	1948-present
Buffalo	1974-77, 1992-present
Butler	1948-present
California	1948-present
UC Davis	2008-present
UC Irvine	1978-present
UC Riverside	2002-present
UC Santa Barb.	1964-present
Cal Poly	1995-present
Cal St. Fullerton	1975-present
Cal St. L.A.	1971-75
Cal St. Northridge	1991-present
Campbell	1978-present
Canisius	1948-present
Case Reserve	1948-55
Catholic	1977-81
Centenary (La.)	1960-present
Central Conn. St.	1987-present
UCF	1985-present
Central Mich.	1974-present
Col. of Charleston	1992-present
Charleston So.	1975-present
Charlotte	1973-present
Chattanooga	1978-present
Chicago St.	1985-present
Cincinnati	1948-present
Citadel	1948-present
CCNY	1948-53
Clemson	1948-present
Cleveland St.	1973-present
Coastal Caro.	1987-present
Colgate	1948-present
Colorado	1948-present
Colorado St.	1948-present
Columbia	1948-present
Connecticut	1948, 1952-present
Coppin St.	1986-present
Cornell	1948-present
Creighton	1948-56, 1960-present
Dartmouth	1948-present
Davidson	1948-present
Dayton	1948-present
Delaware	1958-present
Delaware St.	1974-present
Denver	1948-80, 1999-present
DePaul	1948-present
Detroit	1948-present
Drake	1948-present
Drexel	1974-present
Duke	1948-present
Duquesne	1948-present
East Caro.	1965-present
East Tenn. St.	1959-present
Eastern Ill.	1982-present
Eastern Ky.	1948, 1952-present
Eastern Mich.	1974-present
Eastern Wash.	1984-present
Elon	2000-present
Evansville	1978-present
Fairfield	1965-present
Fairleigh Dickinson	1968-present
Florida	1948-present
Florida A&M	1979-present
Fla. Atlantic	1994-present
Florida Int'l	1988-present
Florida St.	1957-present
Fordham	1948-present
Fresno St.	1956-58, 1971-present
Furman	1948-present
Gardner-Webb	2003-present
George Mason	1979-present
George Washington	1948-present
Georgetown	1948-present
Georgia	1948-present
Ga. Southern	1974-present
Georgia St.	1974-present
Georgia Tech	1948-present
Gettysburg	1948-51, 1959-73
Gonzaga	1953-present
Grambling	1978-present
Green Bay	1982-present
Hamline	1948
Hampton	1996-present
Hardin-Simmons	1951-63, 1965-90
Hartford	1985-present
Harvard	1948-present
Hawaii	1971-present
High Point	2000-present
Hofstra	1967-present
Holy Cross	1948-present
Houston	1951-present
Houston Baptist	1974-89
Howard	1974-present
Idaho	1948-present
Idaho St.	1959-present
Illinois	1948-present
Ill.-Chicago	1982-present
Illinois St.	1972-present
Indiana	1948-present
IPFW	2003-present
IUPUI	1999-present
Indiana St.	1948, 1972-present
Iona	1954-present
Iowa	1948-present
Iowa St.	1948-present
Jackson St.	1978-present
Jacksonville	1967-present
Jacksonville St.	1996-present
James Madison	1977-present
John Carroll	1948-55
Kansas	1948-present
Kansas St.	1948-present
Kent St.	1948, 1952-present
Kentucky	1948-52, 1954-present
Ky. Wesleyan	1957-58
La Salle	1948-present
Lafayette	1948-present
Lamar	1970-present
Lawrence Tech	1948
Lehigh	1948-present
Liberty	1989-present
Lipscomb	2004-present
Long Beach St.	1970-present
Long Island	1948-51, 1969-present
Longwood	2008-present
La.-Lafayette	1972-73, 1976-present
La.-Monroe	1974-present
LSU	1948-present
Louisiana Tech	1974-present
Louisville	1948-present
Loyola Marymount	1950-present
Loyola (Ill.)	1948-present
Loyola (La.)	1952-53, 1955-72
Loyola (Md.)	1948-50, 1982-present
Maine	1962-present
Manhattan	1948-present
Marist	1982-present
Marquette	1948-present
Marshall	1948, 1954-present
Maryland	1948-present
UMBC	1987-present
Md.-East. Shore	1974-75, 1982-present
Massachusetts	1962-present
McNeese St.	1974-present
Memphis	1956-present
Mercer	1974-present
Miami (Fla.)	1949-53, 1955-71, 1986-present
Miami (Ohio)	1948-present
Michigan	1948-present
Michigan St.	1948-present
Middle Tenn.	1959-present
Milwaukee	1974-80, 1991-present
Minnesota	1948-present
Mississippi	1948-present
Mississippi St.	1948-present
Mississippi Val.	1980-present
Missouri	1948-present
UMKC	1990-present
Missouri St.	1983-present
Monmouth	1984-present
Montana	1948, 1952-present
Montana St.	1948, 1958-present
Morehead St.	1956-present
Morgan St.	1985-present
Morris Brown	2002-03
Mt. St. Mary's	1989-present
Muhlenberg	1948-63
Murray St.	1954-present
Navy	1948-present
Nebraska	1948-present
UNLV	1970-present
Nevada	1948, 1970-present
New Hampshire	1962-present
New Mexico	1951-present
New Mexico St.	1951-present
New Orleans	1976-present
New York U.	1948-71; 84
Niagara	1948-present
Nicholls St.	1981-present
Norfolk St.	1998-present
North Carolina	1948-present
UNC Asheville	1987-present
UNC Greensboro	1992-present
UNC Wilmington	1977-present
N.C. A&T	1974-present
North Carolina St.	1948-present
North Texas	1958-present
Northeastern	1973-present
Northeastern Ill.	1991-98
Northern Ariz.	1951-53, 1972-present
Northern Colo.	1974-78, 2008-present
Northern Ill.	1968-present
UNI	1981-present
Northwestern	1948-present
Northwestern St.	1977-present
Notre Dame	1948-present
Oakland	2000-present
Ohio	1948-present
Ohio St.	1948-present
Oklahoma	1948-present
Oklahoma City	1951-85
Oklahoma St.	1948-present
Old Dominion	1977-present
Oral Roberts	1972-89, 1994-present
Oregon	1948-present
Oregon St.	1948-present
Pacific	1954-present
Penn	1948-present

Penn St.	1948-present
Pepperdine	1956-present
Pittsburgh	1948-present
Portland	1954-present
Portland St.	1973-81, 1999-present
Prairie View	1981-present
Princeton	1948-present
Providence	1949, 1958-present
Purdue	1948-present
Quinnipiac	1999-present
Radford	1985-present
Regis (Colo.)	1962-64
Rhode Island	1948-present
Rice	1948-present
Richmond	1948-present
Rider	1968-present
Robert Morris	1977-present
Rutgers	1948-present
Sacramento St.	1992-present
Sacred Heart	2000-present
St. Bonaventure	1948-present
St. Francis (N.Y.)	1948-present
St. Francis (Pa.)	1956-present
St. John's (N.Y.)	1948-present
St. Joseph's	1948-present
St. Louis	1948-present
St. Mary's (Cal.)	1948-present
St. Peter's	1965-present
Sam Houston St.	1987-present
Samford	1973-present
San Diego	1980-present
San Diego St.	1971-present
San Francisco	1948-82, 1986-present
San Jose St.	1953-present
Santa Clara	1948-present
Savannah St.	2003-present
Scranton	1948
Seattle	1953-80
Seton Hall	1948-present
Siena	1948-49, 1951-60, 1977-present
South Ala.	1972-present
South Carolina	1948-present
South Carolina St.	1974-present
South Fla.	1974-present
Southeast Mo. St.	1992-present
Southeastern La.	1981-89, 1991-present
Southern U.	1978-present
Southern California	1948-present
Southern Ill.	1968-present
SMU	1948-present
Southern Miss.	1969, 1973-present
Southern Utah	1989-present
Stanford	1948-present
Stephen F. Austin	1987-present
Stetson	1972-present
Stony Brook	2000-present
Syracuse	1948-present
Temple	1948-present
Tennessee	1948-present
Tenn.-Martin	1993-present
Tennessee St.	1978-present
Tennessee Tech	1956-present
Texas	1948-present
Texas-Arlington	1969-present
UTEP	1951-present
Tex.-Pan American	1969-present
UTSA	1982-present
Texas A&M	1948-present
A&M-Corpus Christi	1973, 2003-present
TCU	1948-present
Texas Southern	1978-present
Texas St.	1985-present
Texas Tech	1951-present
Texas Wesleyan	1948
Toledo	1948-present
Towson	1980-present
Trinity (Tex.)	1971-73
Troy	1994-present
Tulane	1948-85, 1990-present
Tulsa	1948-present
UCLA	1948-present
Utah	1948-present
Utah St.	1948-present
Utica	1982-87
Valparaiso	1948-58, 1977-present
Vanderbilt	1948-present
Vermont	1962-present
Villanova	1948-present
Virginia	1948-present
VCU	1974-present
VMI	1948-present
Virginia Tech	1948-present
Wagner	1977-present
Wake Forest	1948-present
Washington	1948-present
Washington-St. Louis	1948-50, 1954-60
Wash. & Lee	1948-59
Washington St.	1948-present
Wayne St. (Neb.)	1948-50
Weber St.	1964-present
West Chester	1974-82
West Texas	1951-86
West Virginia	1948-present
Western Caro.	1977-present
Western Ill.	1982-present
Western Ky.	1948-present
Western Mich.	1948-present
Wichita St.	1948-present
William & Mary	1948-present
Winthrop	1987-present
Wisconsin	1948-present
Wofford	1996-present
Wright St.	1988-present
Wyoming	1948-present
Xavier	1948-present
Yale	1948-present
Youngstown St.	1948, 1982-present

2007 Division II Conference Standings

CALIFORNIA COLLEGIATE ATHLETIC ASSOCIATION

	Conference			Full Season		
	W	L	Pct.	W	L	Pct.
Humbolt St. #	19	3	.864	26	4	.867
Cal St. San B'dino	18	4	.818	26	6	.813
Cal Poly Pomona	16	6	.727	20	8	.714
Sonoma St.	14	8	.636	15	11	.577
Cal St. Bakersfield	14	8	.636	15	14	.517
UC San Diego	10	12	.455	12	15	.444
Cal St. Stanislaus	9	13	.409	13	16	.448
Cal St. Dom. Hills	9	13	.409	12	15	.444
Cal St. Monterey Bay	9	13	.409	12	15	.444
Cal St. LA	7	15	.318	10	17	.370
Cal St. Chico	5	17	.227	7	20	.259
San Fran. St.	2	20	.091	6	21	.222

CENTRAL ATLANTIC COLLEGIATE CONFERENCE

	Conference			Full Season		
	W	L	Pct.	W	L	Pct.
Philadelphia U.	14	6	.700	20	10	.667
Holy Family	14	6	.700	19	9	.679
Post	14	6	.700	17	12	.586
Caldwell #	11	9	.550	19	12	.613
Goldey Beacom	11	9	.550	15	13	.536
Phila. Sciences	10	10	.500	14	15	.483
Dominican (N.Y.)	10	10	.500	13	15	.464
Felician	10	10	.500	12	16	.429
Bloomfield	8	12	.400	10	17	.370
Nyack	7	13	.350	9	18	.333
Wilmington (Del.)	1	19	.050	1	26	.037

CENTRAL INTERCOLLEGIATE ATHLETIC ASSOCIATION

	Conference			Full Season		
Eastern Division	W	L	Pct.	W	L	Pct.
Virginia Union	16	4	.800	23	6	.793
Virginia St.	15	5	.750	20	8	.714
Bowie St.	11	9	.550	19	10	.655
Elizabeth City St. #	8	12	.400	16	16	.500
St. Paul's	7	13	.350	11	17	.393
Shaw	1	19	.050	3	25	.107
Western Division						
St. Augustine's	14	6	.700	19	9	.679
Johnson C. Smith	14	6	.700	16	9	.640
Fayetteville St.	11	9	.550	16	13	.552
N.C. Central	8	12	.400	13	15	.464
Livingstone	5	15	.250	8	20	.286

CONFERENCE CAROLINAS

	Conference			Full Season		
	W	L	Pct.	W	L	Pct.
Barton #	19	1	.950	31	5	.861
Mount Olive	15	5	.750	23	8	.742
Queens (N.C.)	15	5	.750	20	10	.667
Limestone	14	6	.700	20	9	.690
Pfeiffer	11	9	.550	17	11	.607
Erskine	9	11	.450	14	15	.483
St. Andrews	8	12	.400	11	17	.393
Belmont Abbey	6	14	.300	8	20	.286
Lees-McRae	5	15	.250	6	22	.214
Coker	4	16	.200	8	21	.276
Anderson (S.C.)	4	16	.200	4	24	.143

EAST COAST CONFERENCE

	Conference			Full Season		
	W	L	Pct.	W	L	Pct.
NYIT	15	5	.750	19	9	.679
Bridgeport	14	6	.700	22	9	.710
Post	13	7	.650	19	11	.633
Adelphi #	12	8	.600	18	13	.581
Queens (N.Y.)	11	9	.550	14	14	.500
St. Thomas Aquinas	11	9	.550	11	17	.393
Molloy	10	10	.500	14	15	.483
New Haven	8	12	.400	9	19	.321
Concordia (N.Y.)	8	12	.400	8	18	.308
Dowling	5	15	.250	6	21	.222
Mercy	4	16	.200	5	22	.185

GREAT LAKES INTERCOLLEGIATE ATHLETIC CONFERENCE

	Conference			Full Season		
North Division	W	L	Pct.	W	L	Pct.
Grand Valley St.	15	3	.833	29	5	.853
Northern Mich.	11	7	.611	18	11	.621
Ferris St.	9	9	.500	11	17	.393
Michigan Tech	8	10	.444	13	15	.464
Saginaw Valley	8	10	.444	11	14	.440
Lake Superior St.	6	12	.333	9	18	.333
Northwood	3	15	.167	8	19	.296
South Division						
Findlay #	17	0	1.000	29	2	.935
Mercyhurst	9	8	.529	18	11	.621
Wayne St. (Mich.)	9	8	.529	13	13	.500
Ashland	8	9	.471	16	12	.571
Hillsdale	7	10	.412	15	11	.577
Gannon	4	13	.235	9	17	.346

GREAT LAKES VALLEY CONFERENCE

East Division	Conference			Full Season		
	W	L	Pct.	W	L	Pct.
Northern Ky.	13	6	.684	24	9	.727
St. Joseph's (Ind.)	11	8	.579	16	12	.571
Wis.-Parkside	10	9	.526	19	13	.594
Lewis	10	9	.526	15	13	.536
Indianapolis	9	10	.474	13	13	.500
Bellarmine	8	11	.421	12	15	.444
Ky. Wesleyan	6	13	.316	13	14	.481
West Division						
Southern Ind. #	14	5	.737	29	6	.829
Drury	13	6	.684	21	9	.700
Quincy	12	7	.632	20	10	.667
Rockhurst	11	8	.579	17	12	.586
SIU Edwardsville	10	9	.526	15	12	.556
Mo.-St. Louis	4	15	.211	9	18	.333
Mo. Rolla	2	17	.105	7	20	.259

GREAT NORTHWEST ATHLETIC CONFERENCE

	Conference			Full Season		
	W	L	Pct.	W	L	Pct.
Seattle #	11	5	.688	20	9	.690
Seattle Pacific	11	5	.688	18	10	.643
Alas. Anchorage	10	6	.625	19	9	.679
Central Wash.	10	6	.625	15	12	.556
Alas. Fairbanks	8	8	.500	17	13	.567
St. Martin's	7	9	.438	10	17	.370
Western Wash.	5	11	.313	11	15	.423
Northwest Nazarene	5	11	.313	10	17	.370
Western Ore.	5	11	.313	10	17	.370

GULF SOUTH CONFERENCE

East Division	Conference			Full Season		
	W	L	Pct.	W	L	Pct.
Montevallo #	11	1	.917	28	6	.824
Valdosta St.	8	4	.667	20	9	.690
North Ala.	7	5	.583	15	14	.517
Ala.-Huntsville	6	6	.500	18	11	.621
West Ga.	5	7	.417	13	15	.464
West Ala.	3	9	.250	10	17	.370
West Fla.	2	10	.167	10	17	.370
West Division						
Henderson St.	11	3	.786	23	9	.719
Christian Bros.	10	4	.714	21	7	.750
Harding	9	5	.643	17	12	.586
Delta St.	8	6	.571	18	10	.643
Ouachita Baptist	8	6	.571	14	14	.500
Southern Ark.	5	9	.357	11	16	.407
Ark.-Monticello	4	10	.286	9	17	.346
Arkansas Tech	1	13	.071	6	21	.222

HEARTLAND CONFERENCE

	Conference			Full Season		
	W	L	Pct.	W	L	Pct.
St. Edward's #	10	2	.833	24	6	.800
Incarnate Word	9	3	.750	18	11	.621
St. Mary's (Tex.)	8	4	.667	16	12	.571
Dallas Baptist	5	7	.417	11	20	.355
Mont. St.-Billings	4	8	.333	6	21	.222
Lincoln (Mo.)	3	9	.250	7	19	.269
Okla. Panhandle St.	3	9	.250	7	20	.259
Texas A&M Int'l *	-	-	-	12	15	.444
Newman *	-	-	-	11	17	.393
Tex.-Permian Basin *	-	-	-	10	17	.370

LONE STAR CONFERENCE

North Division	Conference			Full Season		
	W	L	Pct.	W	L	Pct.
Southeastern Okla.	11	1	.917	27	5	.844
Central Okla.	9	3	.750	20	8	.714
Tex. A&M-Commerce	7	5	.583	14	14	.500
Southwestern Okla.	5	7	.417	17	10	.630
Northeastern St.	5	7	.417	9	16	.360
Cameron	3	9	.250	12	14	.462
East Central	2	10	.167	10	16	.385
South Division						
Midwestern St. #	9	3	.750	24	7	.774
West Tex. A&M	9	3	.750	18	11	.621
Tarleton St.	7	5	.583	18	10	.643
Tex. A&M-Kingsville	6	6	.500	19	9	.679
Eastern N.M.	6	6	.500	12	14	.462
Angelo St.	4	8	.333	9	17	.346
Abilene Christian	1	11	.083	10	16	.385

MID-AMERICA INTERCOLLEGIATE ATHLETICS ASSOCIATION

	Conference			Full Season		
	W	L	Pct.	W	L	Pct.
Central Mo. St. #	15	3	.833	31	4	.886
Northwest Mo. St.	15	3	.833	24	7	.774
Emporia St.	12	6	.667	21	8	.724
Southwest Baptist	10	8	.556	16	12	.571
Pittsburg St.	9	9	.500	18	13	.581
Truman St.	9	9	.500	16	13	.552
Fort Hays St.	6	12	.333	13	15	.464
Mo. Western St.	5	13	.278	12	15	.444
Mo. Southern St.	5	13	.278	10	18	.357
Washburn	4	14	.222	8	19	.296

NORTH CENTRAL CONFERENCE

	Conference			Full Season		
	W	L	Pct.	W	L	Pct.
Minn. St. Mankato	10	2	.833	28	5	.848
South Dakota #	10	2	.833	23	7	.767
St. Cloud St.	7	5	.583	19	11	.633
Minn.-Duluth	6	6	.500	16	13	.552
Augustana (S.D.)	3	9	.250	16	12	.571
Neb.-Omaha	3	9	.250	12	16	.429
North Dakota	3	9	.250	11	17	.393

NORTHEAST-10 CONFERENCE

	Conference			Full Season		
	W	L	Pct.	W	L	Pct.
Bentley #	22	0	1.000	32	1	.970
St. Rose	15	7	.682	22	10	.688
Pace	15	7	.682	20	13	.606
Bryant	14	8	.636	21	11	.656
American Int'l	13	9	.591	16	13	.552
St. Michael's	12	10	.545	16	13	.552
Stonehill	11	11	.500	16	12	.571
Franklin Pierce	11	11	.500	13	14	.481
St. Anselm	10	12	.455	15	14	.517
Le Moyne	10	12	.455	14	15	.483
Assumption	9	13	.409	11	17	.393
Merrimack	7	15	.318	8	20	.286
Mass.-Lowell	6	16	.273	9	18	.333
Southern Conn. St.	5	17	.227	7	20	.259
Southern N.H.	5	17	.227	6	21	.222

NORTHERN SUN INTERCOLLEGIATE CONFERENCE

	Conference			Full Season		
	W	L	Pct.	W	L	Pct.
Winona St. #	18	0	1.000	35	1	.972
Southwest Minn. St.	14	4	.778	20	10	.667
Concordia-St. Paul	13	5	.722	21	8	.724
Northern St.	13	5	.722	21	8	.724
Wayne St. (Neb.)	10	8	.556	15	13	.536
Minn. St. Moorhead	8	10	.444	13	15	.464
Mary	5	13	.278	9	18	.333
Bemidji St.	5	13	.278	5	23	.179
Minn.-Crookston	2	16	.111	3	24	.111
Upper Iowa	2	16	.111	3	25	.107

PACIFIC WEST CONFERENCE

	Conference			Full Season		
	W	L	Pct.	W	L	Pct.
Grand Canyon #	13	2	.867	21	8	.724
BYU-Hawaii	12	3	.800	20	8	.714
Chaminade	8	7	.533	16	11	.593
Hawaii-Hilo	6	9	.400	9	19	.321
Hawaii-Pacific	4	11	.267	10	17	.370
Nortre Dame de Namur	2	13	.133	9	18	.333

PEACH BELT CONFERENCE

North Division	Conference			Full Season		
	W	L	Pct.	W	L	Pct.
Lander #	11	5	.688	20	11	.645
S.C. Upstate	9	7	.563	16	12	.571
Francis Marion	5	11	.313	9	19	.321
UNC Pembroke	5	11	.313	6	22	.214
North Ga.	4	12	.250	9	21	.300
S.C.-Aiken	3	13	.188	9	22	.290
South Division						
Augusta St.	14	2	.875	24	7	.774
Armstrong Atlantic	11	5	.688	21	9	.700
Clayton St.	10	6	.625	24	8	.750
Columbus St.	9	7	.563	17	12	.586
GCSU	8	8	.500	19	10	.655
Ga. Southwestern	7	9	.438	16	13	.552

PENNSYLVANIA STATE ATHLETIC CONFERENCE

Eastern Division	Conference			Full Season		
	W	L	Pct.	W	L	Pct.
Millersville #	9	3	.750	28	5	.848
East Stroudsburg	6	6	.500	18	10	.643
Kutztown	6	6	.500	17	11	.607
Cheyney	6	6	.500	15	15	.500
Bloomsburg	5	7	.417	13	14	.481
West Chester	5	7	.417	13	14	.481
Mansfield	5	7	.417	10	17	.370
Western Division						
California (Pa.)	10	2	.833	24	7	.774
Edinboro	8	4	.667	19	10	.655
Shippensburg	7	5	.583	16	15	.516
Clarion	6	6	.500	12	16	.429
Lock Haven	5	7	.417	12	15	.444
Indiana (Pa.)	3	9	.250	6	21	.222
Slippery Rock	3	9	.250	6	21	.222

ROCKY MOUNTAIN ATHLETIC CONFERENCE

East Division	Conference			Full Season		
	W	L	Pct.	W	L	Pct.
Metro St. #	17	2	.895	28	4	.875
Neb.-Kearney	16	3	.842	24	7	.774
UC-Colo. Springs	9	10	.474	16	12	.571
Colorado Mines	8	11	.421	14	14	.500
Colo. Christian	8	11	.421	13	15	.464
Regis (Colo.)	4	15	.211	9	17	.346
Chadron St.	4	15	.211	6	21	.222
West Division						
Fort Lewis	13	6	.684	21	9	.700
Mesa St.	13	6	.684	17	10	.630
Adams St.	13	6	.684	16	14	.533
Colorado St.-Pueblo	9	10	.474	13	15	.464
Western N.M.	8	11	.421	12	14	.462
Western St.	7	12	.368	12	15	.444
N.M. Highlands	4	15	.211	4	23	.148

SOUTH ATLANTIC CONFERENCE

	Conference			Full Season		
	W	L	Pct.	W	L	Pct.
Catawba	13	3	.813	20	11	.645
Presbyterian	12	4	.750	20	9	.690
Wingate #	11	5	.688	25	9	.735
Lenoir-Rhyne	11	5	.688	18	10	.643
Lincoln-Memorial	7	9	.438	13	15	.464
Tusculum	6	10	.375	13	15	.464
Newberry	6	10	.375	12	15	.444
Mars Hill	4	12	.250	8	20	.286
Carson-Newman	2	14	.125	10	19	.345

SOUTHERN INTERCOLLEGIATE ATHLETIC CONFERENCE

	Conference			Full Season		
	W	L	Pct.	W	L	Pct.
Benedict	20	2	.909	25	5	.833
Paine	15	7	.682	17	10	.630
Fort Valley St.	15	7	.682	18	12	.600
Stillman	13	9	.591	15	13	.536
Kentucky St.	11	11	.500	15	15	.500
Albany St. (Ga.) #	11	11	.500	15	17	.469
Miles	10	12	.455	14	15	.483
Lane	10	12	.455	13	16	.448
LeMoyne-Owen	10	12	.455	12	16	.429
Morehouse	9	13	.409	9	16	.360
Tuskegee	6	16	.273	6	22	.214
Clark Atlanta	2	20	.091	2	26	.071
Claflin	-	-	-	9	17	.346

SUNSHINE STATE CONFERENCE

	Conference			Full Season		
	W	L	Pct.	W	L	Pct.
Rollins	13	3	.813	25	7	.781
Barry	13	3	.813	23	7	.767
Eckerd	12	4	.750	26	7	.788
Nova Southeastern	8	8	.500	14	15	.483
Tampa	7	9	.438	15	14	.517
Lynn	6	10	.375	14	14	.500
St. Leo	6	10	.375	13	15	.464
Florida Tech	4	12	.250	10	21	.323
Fla. Southern	3	13	.188	8	20	.286

CONFERENCES

WEST VIRGINIA INTERCOLLEGIATE ATHLETIC CONFERENCE

	Conference			Full Season		
	W	L	Pct.	W	L	Pct.
Alderson-Broaddus ...	18	0	1.000	24	6	.800
West Liberty St.	17	1	.944	25	5	.833
West Va. St. #	13	5	.722	26	7	.788
Concord........................	12	6	.667	17	13	.567
Wheeling Jesuit	11	7	.611	18	10	.643
Salem Int'l...................	11	7	.611	15	12	.556
Shepherd.....................	9	9	.500	16	13	.552
Charleston (W.Va.).......	9	9	.500	15	14	.517
Fairmont St.	8	10	.444	14	14	.500
Bluefield St.	5	13	.278	10	19	.345
Ohio Valley	5	13	.278	8	20	.286
Davis & Elkins	3	15	.167	6	21	.222
Glenville St.	3	15	.167	6	22	.214
W.V. Wesleyan	2	16	.111	3	25	.107
Pitt.-Johnstown *.........	-	-	-	21	9	.700
Seton Hill *	-	-	-	15	11	.577

DIVISION II INDEPENDENTS

	W	L	Pct.
Fla. Gulf Coast.............	27	6	.818
Central St. (Ohio)	22	5	.815
Dist. Columbia.............	20	9	.690
Oakland City................	17	12	.586
North Greenville	16	13	.552
Flagler	14	13	.519
Dixie St.	11	14	.440
Chowan	11	15	.423
Columbia Union	4	21	.160
Palm Beach Atl.	3	27	.100

#won conference tournament
*not eligible for conference championship

2007 Division III Conference Standings

ALLEGHENY MOUNTAIN COLLEGIATE CONFERENCE

	Conference			Full Season		
	W	L	Pct.	W	L	Pct.
Lake Erie #	17	1	.944	25	3	.893
Penn St.-Behrend........	16	2	.889	19	8	.704
Pitt.-Bradford..............	10	8	.556	14	13	.519
Hilbert.........................	9	9	.500	14	16	.467
Frostburg St.	9	9	.500	10	16	.385
Penn St.-Altoona.........	8	10	.444	10	16	.385
Medaille......................	7	11	.389	11	14	.440
La Roche	6	12	.333	8	16	.333
Mt. Aloysius	3	15	.167	9	16	.360
Pitt.-Greensburg	3	15	.167	3	22	.120

AMERICAN SOUTHWEST CONFERENCE

	Conference			Full Season		
East Division	W	L	Pct.	W	L	Pct.
Mississippi Col. #.........	19	1	.950	27	3	.900
Texas-Dallas	13	7	.650	18	8	.692
LeTourneau	13	7	.650	15	10	.600
Louisiana Col.	8	12	.400	8	17	.320
East Tex. Baptist	7	13	.350	8	17	.320
Ozarks (Ark.)	7	13	.350	8	17	.320
Texas-Tyler	5	15	.250	7	17	.292
West Division						
Mary Hardin-Baylor....	17	4	.810	22	6	.786
McMurry......................	17	4	.810	20	7	.741
Hardin-Simmons	14	7	.667	16	12	.571
Concordia (Tex.)..........	9	12	.429	10	16	.385
Sul Ross St.	8	13	.381	8	16	.333
Howard Payne	7	14	.333	7	18	.280
Schreiner	6	15	.286	6	19	.240
Texas Lutheran	4	17	.190	4	20	.167

CAPITAL ATHLETIC CONFERENCE

	Conference			Full Season		
	W	L	Pct.	W	L	Pct.
Hood	12	4	.750	21	8	.724
Catholic #....................	11	5	.688	23	6	.793
York (Pa.)....................	10	6	.625	16	10	.615
Mary Washington........	9	7	.563	16	10	.615
St. Mary's (Md.)	9	7	.563	16	11	.593
Marymount (Va.)	9	7	.563	14	11	.560
Salisbury......................	7	9	.438	12	14	.462
Goucher	4	12	.250	7	18	.280
Gallaudet	1	15	.063	4	21	.160

CENTENNIAL CONFERENCE

	Conference			Full Season		
	W	L	Pct.	W	L	Pct.
Johns Hopkins #..........	15	3	.833	24	5	.828
Ursinus........................	13	5	.722	16	10	.615
Haverford....................	12	6	.667	14	12	.538
Gettysburg..................	10	8	.556	13	13	.500
Muhlenberg.................	9	9	.500	10	15	.400
McDaniel.....................	8	10	.444	11	14	.440
Swarthmore.................	8	10	.444	11	14	.440
Frank. & Marsh.	7	11	.389	8	17	.320
Dickinson....................	5	13	.278	7	17	.292
Washington (Md.)	3	15	.167	4	20	.167

CITY UNIVERSITY OF NEW YORK ATHLETIC CONFERENCE

	Conference			Full Season		
	W	L	Pct.	W	L	Pct.
York (N.Y.) #	10	3	.769	18	11	.621
Staten Island...............	9	4	.692	15	13	.536
Baruch.........................	8	5	.615	11	16	.407
CCNY	7	6	.538	12	14	.462
Hunter..........................	6	7	.462	12	14	.462
Lehman	6	7	.462	10	16	.385
John Jay.......................	6	7	.462	7	19	.269
City Tech......................	6	7	.462	7	19	.269
Medgar Evers	5	8	.385	8	16	.333
Brooklyn	2	11	.154	10	14	.417

COMMONWEALTH COAST CONFERENCE

	Conference			Full Season		
North Division	W	L	Pct.	W	L	Pct.
Gordon........................	13	3	.813	19	8	.704
Endicott.......................	12	4	.750	16	12	.571
Wentworth Inst. #	9	7	.563	17	12	.586
Colby-Sawyer...............	8	8	.500	10	15	.400
New England Col.	5	11	.313	10	15	.400
New England	5	11	.313	5	20	.200
South Division						
Curry............................	11	5	.688	16	14	.533
Roger Williams.............	10	6	.625	15	11	.577
Nichols.........................	9	7	.563	14	11	.560
Salve Regina	8	8	.500	13	13	.500
Anna Maria	4	12	.250	7	18	.280
Eastern Nazarene	2	14	.125	2	23	.080

EMPIRE 8

	Conference			Full Season		
	W	L	Pct.	W	L	Pct.
St. John Fisher #..........	11	3	.786	24	6	.800
Utica...........................	10	4	.714	19	7	.731
Ithaca	9	5	.643	15	13	.536
Rochester Inst.	8	6	.571	14	13	.519
Alfred..........................	8	6	.571	10	14	.417
Nazareth......................	6	8	.429	11	14	.440
Hartwick......................	3	11	.214	10	15	.400
Elmira..........................	1	13	.071	2	23	.080

GREAT NORTHEAST ATHLETIC CONFERENCE

	Conference			Full Season		
	W	L	Pct.	W	L	Pct.
Western New Eng.	14	2	.875	22	8	.733
Emerson.......................	12	4	.750	16	10	.615
Rivier #	10	6	.625	20	9	.690
Norwich.......................	9	7	.563	13	12	.520
Emmanuel....................	8	8	.500	12	16	.429
Johnson & Wales	8	8	.500	10	16	.385
Suffolk.........................	7	9	.438	9	18	.333
Daniel Webster............	2	14	.125	6	18	.250
Albertus Magnus..........	2	14	.125	2	23	.080

GREAT SOUTH ATHLETIC CONFERENCE

	Conference			Full Season		
	W	L	Pct.	W	L	Pct.
Maryville (Tenn.) #	6	0	1.000	22	7	.759
LaGrange.....................	4	2	.667	18	9	.667
Piedmont.....................	2	4	.333	13	13	.500
Huntington..................	0	6	.000	3	23	.115

HEARTLAND COLLEGIATE ATHLETIC CONFERENCE

	Conference			Full Season		
	W	L	Pct.	W	L	Pct.
Franklin	11	5	.688	16	10	.615
Bluffton.......................	10	6	.625	18	8	.692
Transylvania #	10	6	.625	19	9	.679
Defiance	9	7	.563	17	9	.654
Hanover.......................	9	7	.563	14	11	.560
Mt. St. Joseph..............	9	7	.563	13	12	.520
Manchester..................	7	9	.438	15	10	.600
Rose-Hulman................	5	11	.313	9	16	.360
Anderson (Ind.)	2	14	.125	9	16	.360

COLLEGE CONFERNCE OF ILLINOIS & WISCONSIN

	Conference			Full Season		
	W	L	Pct.	W	L	Pct.
Augustana (Ill.) #	11	3	.786	22	6	.786
Elmhurst	10	4	.714	21	6	.778
Wheaton (Ill.)	9	5	.643	17	9	.654
North Central (Ill.)	8	6	.571	16	10	.615
Carthage	7	7	.500	16	9	.640
North Park	5	9	.357	13	12	.520
Ill. Wesleyan	4	10	.286	11	14	.440
Millikin	2	12	.143	9	16	.360

IOWA INTERCOLLEGIATE ATHLETIC CONFERENCE

	Conference			Full Season		
	W	L	Pct.	W	L	Pct.
Loras #	15	1	.938	21	7	.750
Coe	11	5	.688	19	8	.704
Buena Vista	11	5	.688	17	9	.654
Simpson	10	6	.625	18	9	.667
Central (Iowa)	8	8	.500	11	14	.440
Dubuque	5	11	.313	11	14	.440
Wartburg	5	11	.313	11	15	.423
Cornell College	4	12	.250	8	17	.320
Luther	3	13	.188	5	20	.200

LIBERTY LEAGUE

	Conference			Full Season		
	W	L	Pct.	W	L	Pct.
Hamilton	11	3	.786	19	7	.731
St. Lawrence #	10	4	.714	23	6	.793
Vassar	8	6	.571	18	10	.643
Union (N.Y.)	8	6	.571	11	14	.440
Hobart	7	7	.500	11	14	.440
RPI	6	8	.429	13	13	.500
Clarkson	5	9	.357	14	11	.560
Skidmore	1	13	.071	2	22	.083

LITTLE EAST CONFERENCE

	Conference			Full Season		
	W	L	Pct.	W	L	Pct.
Rhode Island Col. #	12	2	.857	27	4	.871
Keene St.	11	3	.786	25	6	.806
Western Conn. St.	8	6	.571	14	12	.538
Mass.-Dartmouth	8	6	.571	14	13	.519
Eastern Conn. St.	7	7	.500	15	11	.577
Mass.-Boston	5	9	.357	10	16	.385
Plymouth St.	3	11	.214	10	16	.385
Southern Me.	2	12	.143	6	20	.231

MASSACHUSETTS STATE COLLEGE ATHLETIC CONFERENCE

	Conference			Full Season		
	W	L	Pct.	W	L	Pct.
Salem St. #	12	0	1.000	24	3	.889
Bridgewater St.	9	3	.750	17	8	.680
Westfield St.	6	6	.500	17	11	.607
Worcester St.	5	7	.417	11	16	.407
Fitchburg St.	5	7	.417	7	18	.280
Framingham St.	4	8	.333	10	15	.400
Mass. College	1	11	.083	6	19	.240

MICHIGAN INTERCOLLEGIATE ATHLETIC ASSOCIATION

	Conference			Full Season		
	W	L	Pct.	W	L	Pct.
Hope	13	1	.929	26	5	.839
Clavin #	10	4	.714	19	10	.655
Tri-State	9	5	.643	16	9	.640
Adrian	8	6	.571	10	15	.400
Albion	8	6	.571	10	15	.400
Kalamazoo	3	11	.214	5	19	.208
Olivet	3	11	.214	5	20	.200
Alma	2	12	.143	3	22	.120

MIDDLE ATLANTIC CORPORATION

	Conference			Full Season		
	W	L	Pct.	W	L	Pct.
Commonwealth League						
Messiah	13	1	.929	19	7	.731
Juniata	9	5	.643	17	11	.607
Susquehanna	8	6	.571	16	10	.615
Widener #	7	7	.500	15	13	.536
Lebanon Valley	6	8	.429	15	12	.556
Albright	5	9	.357	10	14	.417
Moravian	4	10	.286	11	14	.440
Elizabethtown	4	10	.286	9	15	.375
Freedom League						
King's (Pa.) #	11	3	.786	19	9	.679
Scranton	10	4	.714	19	7	.731
DeSales	9	5	.643	22	8	.733
FDU-Florham	9	5	.643	17	10	.630
Lycoming	6	8	.429	13	12	.520
Wilkes	4	10	.286	12	11	.522
Drew	4	10	.286	9	15	.375
Delaware Valley	3	11	.214	5	20	.200

MIDWEST CONFERENCE

	Conference			Full Season		
	W	L	Pct.	W	L	Pct.
Grinnell	13	3	.813	17	7	.708
Carroll (Wis.) #	12	4	.750	18	9	.667
Ripon	11	5	.688	13	10	.565
Lake Forest	10	6	.625	15	10	.600
Lawrence	9	7	.563	13	10	.565
St. Norbert	8	8	.500	9	13	.409
Monmouth (Ill.)	7	9	.438	11	11	.500
Beloit	4	12	.250	4	19	.174
Illinois Col.	3	13	.188	8	15	.348
Knox	3	13	.188	5	18	.217

MINNESOTA INTERCOLLEGIATE ATHLETIC CONFERENCE

	Conference			Full Season		
	W	L	Pct.	W	L	Pct.
St. Thomas (Minn.) #	18	2	.900	24	4	.857
St. John's (Minn.)	17	3	.850	21	8	.724
Bethel (Minn.)	13	7	.650	18	8	.692
Gust. Adolphus	11	9	.550	14	13	.519
Carleton	10	10	.500	11	15	.423
St. Olaf	9	11	.450	13	14	.481
Macalester	8	12	.400	11	14	.440
Augsburg	7	13	.350	10	15	.400
Hamline	7	13	.350	9	16	.360
St. Mary's (Minn.)	6	14	.300	7	17	.292
Concordia-M'head	4	16	.200	4	21	.160

NEW ENGLAND SMALL COLLEGE ATHLETIC CONFERENCE

	Conference			Full Season		
	W	L	Pct.	W	L	Pct.
Amherst	8	1	.889	30	2	.938
Trinity (Conn.)	7	2	.778	21	5	.808
Williams #	6	3	.667	16	12	.571
Colby	5	4	.556	15	11	.577
Middlebury	5	4	.556	15	10	.600
Tufts	5	4	.556	15	10	.600
Bates	3	6	.333	18	7	.720
Bowdoin	3	6	.333	15	10	.600
Wesleyan (Conn.)	2	7	.222	7	16	.304
Connecticut Col.	1	8	.111	11	13	.458

NEW ENGLAND WOMEN'S AND MEN'S ATHLETICS CONFERENCE

	Conference			Full Season		
	W	L	Pct.	W	L	Pct.
WPI	11	1	.917	22	4	.846
Babson	9	3	.750	16	10	.615
Springfield	7	5	.583	12	14	.462
MIT	5	7	.417	14	13	.519
Clark (Mass.)	5	7	.417	11	14	.440
Wheaton (Mass.)	3	9	.250	11	15	.423
Coast Guard #	2	10	.167	14	14	.500

NEW JERSEY ATHLETIC CONFERENCE

	Conference			Full Season		
	W	L	Pct.	W	L	Pct.
North Division						
New Jersey City	11	2	.846	19	10	.655
Ramapo #	9	4	.692	22	8	.733
Rutgers-Newark	6	7	.462	18	11	.621
Wm. Paterson	6	7	.462	15	10	.600
Montclair St.	5	8	.385	12	12	.500
South Division						
Rowan	9	4	.692	20	6	.769
Richard Stockton	8	5	.615	18	10	.643
New Jersey	5	8	.385	12	14	.462
Kean	4	9	.308	13	12	.520
Rutgers-Camden	2	11	.154	6	19	.240

NORTH ATLANTIC CONFERENCE

	Conference			Full Season		
East Division	W	L	Pct.	W	L	Pct.
Husson	14	0	1.000	22	6	.786
Maine Maritime	8	6	.571	12	12	.500
Me.-Farmington	7	7	.500	10	16	.385
Mount Ida	3	11	.214	7	19	.269
Thomas	3	11	.214	5	20	.200
West Division						
Elms #	12	3	.800	20	9	.690
Lasell	12	3	.800	16	12	.571
Castleton	9	6	.600	15	12	.556
Lesley	9	6	.600	14	13	.519
Johnson St.	2	13	.133	5	20	.200
Becker	1	14	.067	3	22	.120

NORTH COAST ATHLETIC CONFERENCE

	Conference			Full Season		
	W	L	Pct.	W	L	Pct.
Wooster #	15	1	.938	29	5	.853
Wittenberg	13	3	.813	22	5	.815
Ohio Wesleyan	10	6	.625	18	10	.643
Allegheny	8	8	.500	12	13	.480
Wabash	7	9	.438	11	16	.407
Kenyon	6	10	.375	10	16	.385
Earlham	6	10	.375	8	18	.308
Hiram	6	10	.375	7	19	.269
Denison	5	11	.313	6	18	.250
Oberlin	4	12	.250	5	20	.200

NORTH EASTERN ATHLETIC CONFERENCE

	Conference			Full Season		
North Division	W	L	Pct.	W	L	Pct.
Baptist Bible (Pa.)	13	3	.813	18	8	.692
Keuka	10	6	.625	13	13	.500
Keystone	10	6	.625	13	13	.500
Cazenovia	9	7	.563	12	14	.462
D'Youville	3	13	.188	3	22	.120
Bard	2	14	.125	3	22	.120
South Division						
Villa Julie #	14	2	.875	20	8	.714
Chestnut Hill	14	2	.875	19	9	.679
Penn St.-Berks	8	8	.500	8	18	.308
Phila. Biblical	6	10	.375	9	17	.346
Purchase	4	12	.250	2	20	.091
Polytechnic (N.Y.)	3	13	.188	4	20	.167

NORTHERN ATHLETICS CONFERENCE

	Conference			Full Season		
	W	L	Pct.	W	L	Pct.
Aurora #	16	2	.889	25	3	.893
Edgewood	15	3	.833	18	8	.692
Dominican (Ill.)	12	6	.667	17	10	.630
Lakeland	12	6	.667	16	11	.593
Wisc. Lutheran	12	6	.667	15	11	.577
Marian (Wis.)	10	8	.556	13	12	.520
Benedictine (Ill.)	10	8	.556	12	14	.462
Concordia (Wis.)	7	11	.389	8	17	.320
Concordia (Chicago)	3	15	.167	4	21	.160
Rockford	2	16	.111	3	22	.120
Maranatha Baptist	0	18	.000	3	22	.120

NORTHWEST CONFERENCE

	Conference			Full Season		
	W	L	Pct.	W	L	Pct.
Whitworth #	13	3	.813	24	4	.857
Lewis & Clark	13	3	.813	19	7	.731
Puget Sound	11	5	.688	18	7	.720
Pacific (Ore.)	8	8	.500	12	13	.480
George Fox	7	9	.438	12	13	.480
Willamette	6	10	.375	10	15	.400
Pacific Lutheran	6	10	.375	9	14	.391
Whitman	5	11	.313	9	16	.360
Linfield	3	13	.188	8	17	.320

OHIO ATHLETIC CONFERENCE

	Conference			Full Season		
	W	L	Pct.	W	L	Pct.
Capital#	13	5	.722	19	9	.679
John Carroll	13	5	.722	21	10	.677
Ohio Northern	12	6	.667	19	7	.731
Baldwin-Wallace	12	6	.667	18	9	.667
Otterbein	11	7	.611	16	11	.593
Heidelberg	9	9	.500	13	13	.500
Wilmington	8	10	.444	13	13	.500
Muskingum	6	12	.333	12	13	.480
Mt. Union	5	13	.278	10	15	.400
Marietta	1	17	.056	5	20	.200

OLD DOMINION ATHLETIC CONFERENCE

	Conference			Full Season		
	W	L	Pct.	W	L	Pct.
Va. Wesleyan	17	1	.944	28	5	.848
Guilford	15	3	.833	24	5	.828
Roanoke	11	7	.611	17	11	.607
Hampden-Sydney #	10	8	.556	19	11	.633
Emory & Henry	10	8	.556	14	11	.560
Randolph-Macon	9	9	.500	14	12	.538
Wash. & Lee	6	12	.333	11	14	.440
Bridgewater (Va.)	6	12	.333	10	17	.370
Eastern Mennonite	3	15	.167	7	17	.292
Lynchburg	3	15	.167	6	19	.240

PENNSYLVANIA ATHLETIC CONFERENCE

	Conference			Full Season		
	W	L	Pct.	W	L	Pct.
Alvernia #	16	2	.889	23	5	.821
Gwynedd-Mercy	12	6	.667	14	13	.519
Eastern	10	8	.556	16	11	.593
Neumann	10	8	.556	13	13	.500
Immaculata	10	8	.556	12	16	.429
Arcadia	9	9	.500	11	14	.440
Wesley	9	9	.500	11	15	.423
Misericordia	8	10	.444	10	15	.400
Cabrini	4	14	.222	5	20	.200
Marywood	2	16	.111	5	20	.200

PRESIDENTS' ATHLETIC CONFERENCE

	Conference			Full Season		
	W	L	Pct.	W	L	Pct.
Westminster (Pa.)	10	2	.833	18	9	.667
Bethany (W.V.)	9	3	.750	19	9	.679
Wash. and Jeff.	8	4	.667	14	14	.500
Grove City #	6	6	.500	16	12	.571
Waynesburg	4	8	.333	12	13	.480
Thomas More	3	9	.250	3	23	.115
Thiel	2	10	.167	5	20	.200

ST. LOUIS INTERCOLLEGIATE ATHLETIC CONFERENCE

	Conference			Full Season		
	W	L	Pct.	W	L	Pct.
MacMurray	14	4	.778	16	9	.640
Webster	14	4	.778	16	10	.615
Eureka	12	6	.667	16	10	.615
Fontbonne #	12	6	.667	16	12	.571
Westminster (Mo.)	11	7	.611	15	9	.625
Greenville	11	7	.611	13	12	.520
Blackburn	8	10	.444	10	15	.400
Maryville (Mo.)	5	13	.278	6	19	.240
Lincoln Christian	2	16	.111	4	18	.182
Principia	1	17	.056	1	22	.043

SKYLINE CONFERENCE

	Conference			Full Season		
	W	L	Pct.	W	L	Pct.
Manhattanville #	13	3	.813	23	6	.793
Stevens Tech.	13	3	.813	23	7	.767
Old Westbury	12	4	.750	18	10	.643
Farmingdale St.	11	5	.688	18	10	.643
St. Joseph's (L.I.)	11	5	.688	17	10	.630
Merchant Marine	9	7	.563	14	12	.538
Yeshiva	8	8	.500	15	11	.577
Mt. St. Mary	6	10	.375	9	16	.360
Maritime (N.Y.)	3	13	.188	4	21	.160
Centenary (N.J.)	1	15	.063	3	21	.125
Mt. St. Vincent	1	15	.063	3	22	.120

SOUTHERN CALIFORNIA INTERCOLLEGIATE ATHLETIC CONFERENCE

	Conference			Full Season		
	W	L	Pct.	W	L	Pct.
Occidental #	12	2	.857	19	6	.760
Redlands	10	4	.714	17	7	.708
Cal Lutheran	10	4	.714	17	8	.680
Pomona-Pitzer	10	4	.714	16	8	.667
Claremont-M-S	7	7	.500	15	10	.600
LaVerne	4	10	.286	6	20	.231
Whittier	3	11	.214	9	16	.360
Caltech	0	14	.000	1	24	.040

SOUTHERN COLLEGIATE ATHLETIC CONFERENCE

	Conference			Full Season		
	W	L	Pct.	W	L	Pct.
Centre #	12	2	.857	24	5	.828
DePauw	12	2	.857	22	6	.786
Millsaps	11	3	.786	18	9	.667
Trinity (Tex.)	8	6	.571	16	12	.571
Hendrix	7	7	.500	15	10	.600
Ogelthorpe	7	7	.500	14	12	.538
Southwestern (Tex.)	5	9	.357	11	15	.423
Sewanee	5	9	.357	6	19	.240
Rhodes	3	11	.214	8	15	.348
Austin	0	14	.000	5	19	.208

STATE UNIVERSITY OF NEW YORK ATHLETIC CONFERENCE

	Conference			Full Season		
	W	L	Pct.	W	L	Pct.
Brockport St.	14	2	.875	26	6	.813
Plattsburgh St. #	11	5	.688	21	9	.700
Oswego St.	10	6	.625	17	13	.567
Geneseo St.	9	7	.563	15	11	.577
SUNYIT	9	7	.563	16	12	.571
Oneonta St.	9	7	.563	11	15	.423
Buffalo St.	7	9	.438	12	13	.480
Cortland St.	6	10	.375	10	16	.385
Potsdam St.	6	10	.375	9	16	.360
New Paltz St.	4	12	.250	11	14	.440
Fredonia St.	3	13	.188	6	18	.250

USA SOUTH ATHLETIC CONFERENCE

	Conference			Full Season		
	W	L	Pct.	W	L	Pct.
Averett #	9	3	.750	20	7	.741
Greensboro	9	3	.750	20	7	.741
Chris. Newport	7	5	.583	15	11	.577
Methodist	6	6	.500	11	14	.440
Ferrum	5	7	.417	12	15	.444
N.C. Wesleyan	5	7	.417	12	15	.444
Shenandoah	1	11	.083	7	18	.280

UNIVERSITY ATHLETIC ASSOCIATION

	Conference			Full Season		
	W	L	Pct.	W	L	Pct.
Washington-St. Louis #.	11	3	.786	25	5	.833
Chicago	11	3	.786	20	6	.769
Brandeis	9	5	.643	20	7	.741
Rochester	9	5	.643	18	8	.692
New York U.	8	6	.571	22	6	.786
Carnegie Mellon	5	9	.357	12	13	.480
Emory	2	12	.143	8	17	.320
Case Reserve	1	13	.071	5	20	.200

UPPER MIDWEST ATHLETIC CONFERENCE

	Conference			Full Season		
	W	L	Pct.	W	L	Pct.
Northwestern (Minn.).	12	2	.857	21	6	.778
Bethany Lutheran	10	4	.714	13	12	.520
St. Scholastica #	9	5	.643	14	13	.519
Martin Luther	9	5	.643	12	14	.462
Presentation	6	8	.429	9	15	.375
Minn.-Morris	6	8	.429	9	16	.360
Northland	4	10	.286	9	16	.360
Crown (Minn.)	0	14	.000	1	22	.043

WISCONSIN INTERCOLLEGIATE ATHLETIC CONFERENCE

	Conference			Full Season		
	W	L	Pct.	W	L	Pct.
Wis.-Stevens Point #.	15	1	.938	26	3	.897
Wis.-Oshkosh	12	4	.750	21	6	.778
Wis.-La Crosse	12	4	.750	19	8	.704
Wis.-Whitewater	10	6	.625	18	9	.667
Wis.-Platteville	8	8	.500	13	12	.520
Wis.-Stout	5	11	.313	12	13	.480
Wis.-River Falls	5	11	.313	10	16	.385
Wis.-Eau Claire	3	13	.188	10	16	.385
Wis.-Superior	2	14	.125	7	18	.280

DIVISION III INDEPENDENTS

	W	L	Pct.
Chapman	21	5	.808
Menlo	11	3	.786
St. Joseph's (Me.)	22	8	.733
Lincoln (Pa.)	20	9	.690
Milwaukee Engr.	16	11	.593
Newbury	15	12	.556
Lyndon St.	10	11	.476
Dallas	12	14	.462
La Sierra	11	14	.440
Rust	11	14	.440
Mitchell	11	16	.407
Southern Vt.	9	14	.391
Morrisville St.	8	18	.308
North Central (Minn.)	7	16	.304
Neb. Wesleyan	7	19	.269
Fisk	6	18	.250
Finlandia	5	18	.217
Colorado Col.	4	21	.160
Me.-Presque Isle	3	19	.136
Clarke	2	18	.100
UC Santa Cruz	2	21	.087
Green Mountain	2	22	.083

#won conference tournament

2007 Results, All Divisions

2006-07 Results—All Divisions

Following is an alphabetical listing of the 2006-07 season's game-by-game scores for the men's teams of the member colleges and universities of the National Collegiate Athletic Association.

Below each team's name and location appear the name of its 2006-07 head coach and his alma mater, where available. All other information is from the current season. Divisional designation for each team is indicated in the upper right-hand corner of each listing.

Squares (⊠) indicate home games and daggers (†) indicate neutral-site games.

All records are restricted to varsity games between four-year college institutions.

The 2007-08 schedules and updated information can be found on the World Wide Web at www.ncaasports.com.

ABILENE CHRISTIAN
Abilene, TX 79699 II

Coach: Jason Copeland, Lubbock Chrst. 1997

2006-07 RESULTS (10-16)
71	Hillsdale Baptist ⊠	46
116	Concordia (Tex.) ⊠	114
87	Howard Payne ⊠	81
60	St. Edward's	65
88	Tex. A&M-Commerce ⊠	84
76	Dallas Baptist	61
65	Northeastern St.	66
66	Central Okla.	92
95	Rhema	50
70	St. Mary's (Tex.) ⊠	68
72	St. Edward's ⊠	61
62	East Central	57
66	Southeastern Okla. ⊠	77
84	Southwestern Okla.	91
82	Eastern N.M.	86
69	West Tex. A&M	78
92	Angelo St. ⊠	76
74	Tex. A&M-Kingsville ⊠	85
75	Midwestern St. ⊠	93
67	Tarleton St.	87
67	Midwestern St.	93
80	Tarleton St. ⊠	81
76	Eastern N.M. ⊠	89
68	West Tex. A&M ⊠	80
62	Angelo St.	67
87	Tex. A&M-Kingsville	92

Nickname: Wildcats
Colors: Purple & White
Arena: Moody Coliseum
  Capacity: 4,600; Year Built: 1968
AD: Jared Mosley
SID: Lance Fleming

ADAMS ST.
Alamosa, CO 81102 II

Coach: Larry Mortensen, Adams St. 1988

2006-07 RESULTS (16-14)
75	Tex. Permian Basin ⊠	78
55	Dixie St.	66
69	West Tex. A&M	62
69	Southwestern Okla. †	84
52	Dixie St.	68
45	Carroll (Mont.) †	65
62	Westminster (Utah) †	63
59	Regis (Colo.)	60
89	UC-Colo. Springs ⊠	76
68	Colo. Christian	64
49	Metro St.	81
77	Neb.-Kearney ⊠	84
82	Chadron St. ⊠	69
58	Colorado Mines	59
79	Western N.M. ⊠	65
95	N.M. Highlands ⊠	70
80	Colorado St.-Pueblo	76
64	Western St.	51
77	Fort Lewis	85
79	Mesa St.	75
85	Colorado St.-Pueblo ⊠	74
70	Western St. ⊠	77
91	Mesa St. ⊠	78
85	Fort Lewis ⊠	77
87	N.M. Highlands	79
82	Western N.M.	73
98	UC-Colo. Springs ⊠	83
97	Neb.-Kearney †	90
60	Metro St. †	70
48	Metro St. †	71

Nickname: Grizzlies
Colors: Green & White
Arena: Plachy Hall
  Capacity: 2,300; Year Built: 1960
AD: Larry Mortensen
SID: Chris Day

ADELPHI
Garden City, NY 11530-0701 II

Coach: James Cosgrove, St. Anselm 1987

2006-07 RESULTS (18-13)
43	Bentley ⊠	69
75	Bloomfield ⊠	60
85	NYIT	92
72	Concordia (N.Y.)	64
54	St. Thomas Aquinas	64
74	Mercy ⊠	37
63	Assumption	76
78	St. Michael's †	79
70	Pace	67
66	Philadelphia U. ⊠	62
59	New Haven ⊠	61
64	Queens (N.Y.)	50
72	Dowling	55
71	Bridgeport ⊠	76
77	C.W. Post ⊠	67
60	Molloy ⊠	64
75	NYIT	72
56	Caldwell	69
71	Concordia (N.Y.) ⊠	59
54	St. Thomas Aquinas ⊠	61
73	Mercy	54
74	New Haven	60
96	Queens (N.Y.) ⊠	84
65	Dowling ⊠	44
60	Bridgeport	63
53	C.W. Post	66
76	Molloy ⊠	52
85	Queens (N.Y.) ⊠	79
65	NYIT †	59
61	C.W. Post †	58
55	Bryant †	77

Nickname: Panthers
Colors: Brown & Gold
Arena: Woodruff Hall
  Capacity: 800; Year Built: 1929
AD: Robert E. Hartwell
SID: Adam Siepiola

ADRIAN
Adrian, MI 49221 III

Coach: Buck Riley, Southwestern Okla. 1967

2006-07 RESULTS (10-15)
51	Albright †	74
62	Neumann †	68
55	Rochester College	66
54	Siena Heights	58
74	Rochester College ⊠	85
66	Azusa Pacific †	82
63	Mont. St.-Northern †	71
79	Manchester ⊠	80
77	Oberlin ⊠	40
81	Albion	76
77	Kalamazoo ⊠	65
79	Calvin ⊠	75
69	Olivet	66
42	Hope ⊠	81
59	Tri-State ⊠	75
79	Alma	73
71	Albion ⊠	64
67	Kalamazoo	80
65	Calvin	84
63	Olivet ⊠	44
71	Hope	84
62	Tri-State	70
86	Alma ⊠	81
66	Albion	64
61	Hope	77

Nickname: Bulldogs
Colors: Gold & Black
Arena: Merillat Center
  Capacity: 1,350; Year Built: 1990
AD: Michael Duffy
SID: Nate Jorgensen

AIR FORCE
USAF Academy, CO 80840-5001 ..I

Coach: Jeff Bzdelik, Ill.-Chicago 1976

2006-07 RESULTS (26-9)
81	Ark.-Pine Bluff ⊠	45
69	Long Beach St. †	68
79	Stanford	45
84	Colorado	46
56	Duke †	71
67	Texas Tech †	53
83	Radford †	59
94	Wake Forest †	58
78	IPFW ⊠	66
70	Tex.-Pan American ⊠	58
82	Colorado Col. ⊠	31
70	Norfolk St.	47
66	George Washington †	52
78	Santa Clara	48
81	Colorado St.	75
56	UNLV ⊠	50
65	New Mexico ⊠	57
58	Wyoming	56
79	Utah	85
56	San Diego St. ⊠	51
72	TCU	39
52	BYU	61
88	Wyoming ⊠	43
41	San Diego St.	62
60	New Mexico	51
69	Utah ⊠	43
67	Colorado St. ⊠	58
50	UNLV	71
66	TCU	71
58	BYU ⊠	62
62	Wyoming †	67
75	Austin Peay †	51
83	Georgia	52
52	DePaul ⊠	51
67	Clemson †	68

Nickname: Falcons
Colors: Blue & Silver

Arena: Clune Arena
  Capacity: 5,939; Year Built: 1968
AD: Hans J. Mueh
SID: Jerry Cross

AKRON
Akron, OH 44325 I

Coach: Keith Dambrot, Akron 1982

2006-07 RESULTS (26-7)
79	Ark.-Little Rock †	81
89	Gardner-Webb †	61
97	Tiffin ⊠	35
63	Niagara	48
61	Oral Roberts	59
90	Binghamton	55
79	Winston-Salem ⊠	67
80	Ill.-Chicago	86
79	St. Francis (Pa.) ⊠	44
71	Nevada ⊠	73
92	Loyola Marymount ⊠	52
70	Youngstown St.	61
72	Ohio	77
54	Miami (Ohio) ⊠	52
83	Bowling Green	62
78	Kent St. ⊠	68
66	Buffalo ⊠	59
87	Northern Ill.	64
69	Western Mich.	36
70	Eastern Mich.	60
70	Ball St. ⊠	52
78	Central Mich. ⊠	64
65	Toledo	68
79	Ohio ⊠	48
74	Austin Peay ⊠	57
62	Miami (Ohio)	64
93	Bowling Green ⊠	87
87	Duquesne	74
87	Buffalo	69
66	Kent St.	64
62	Central Mich. †	53
61	Kent St. †	54
52	Miami (Ohio) †	53

Nickname: Zips
Colors: Blue & Gold
Arena: James A. Rhodes Arena
  Capacity: 5,500; Year Built: 1983
AD: Mack Rhoades
SID: Gregg Bach

ALABAMA
Tuscaloosa, AL 35487 I

Coach: Mark Gottfried, Alabama 1987

2006-07 RESULTS (20-12)
96	Jackson St. ⊠	65
71	Middle Tenn. †	62
72	Iowa †	60
63	Xavier †	56
74	Texas Southern ⊠	44
75	La.-Monroe ⊠	61
78	Tennessee St. ⊠	60
85	Notre Dame	99
92	Alabama St. ⊠	58
77	Southern Miss. †	64
82	North Carolina St.	75
99	Coppin St. ⊠	49
80	Lipscomb ⊠	58
70	Oklahoma ⊠	55
61	Arkansas	88
71	LSU ⊠	61
73	Vanderbilt	94
78	Georgia ⊠	76
57	Auburn	81
57	Arkansas ⊠	63
73	LSU	70
64	South Carolina	61
80	Mississippi St. ⊠	79
69	Mississippi	75
67	Florida	76

72	Kentucky ⊠	61
66	Tennessee	69
77	Auburn ⊠	86
69	Mississippi	58
67	Mississippi St.	91
67	Kentucky †	79
87	Massachusetts	89

Nickname: Crimson Tide
Colors: Crimson & White
Arena: Coleman Coliseum
　　Capacity: 15,316; Year Built: 1968
AD: Mal Moore
SID: Becky Hopf

ALABAMA A&M
Normal, AL 35762 I

Coach: L. Vann Pettaway, Alabama
A&M 1980

2006-07 RESULTS (10-20)

47	IUPUI †	86
70	South Dakota St. †	66
39	Princeton †	56
87	Paul Quinn ⊠	59
65	Stillman ⊠	64
36	Georgia	80
84	Oakwood ⊠	63
59	Tuskegee ⊠	57
55	Nebraska	82
57	Mississippi	81
47	Vanderbilt	86
52	Grambling ⊠	63
52	Jackson St. ⊠	68
41	Mississippi Val.	55
45	Ark.-Pine Bluff	52
61	Alabama St. ⊠	55
58	Alcorn St.	59
68	Southern U. ⊠	63
66	Texas Southern	68
58	Prairie View	60
54	Mississippi Val. ⊠	65
65	Ark.-Pine Bluff ⊠	66
70	Alabama St.	74
79	Winston-Salem ⊠	63
77	Alcorn St.	86
60	Southern U.	62
79	Texas Southern ⊠	73
86	Prairie View ⊠	66
69	Grambling	93
70	Jackson St.	81

Nickname: Bulldogs
Colors: Maroon & White
Arena: Elmore Health Science Building
　　Capacity: 6,000; Year Built: 1973
AD: Betty Kelly Austin
SID: Thomas Galbraith

ALABAMA ST.
Montgomery, AL 36101-0271 I

Coach: Lewis Jackson, Alabama St.
1984

2006-07 RESULTS (10-20)

43	Southern Miss.	80
59	Georgia St.	70
80	Tuskegee ⊠	77
63	Troy ⊠	56
49	Missouri St.	89
45	Santa Clara †	71
58	Alabama	92
56	Georgia St. ⊠	64
59	Mississippi St.	74
55	Colorado St. †	61
72	Kennesaw St. †	78
68	Jackson St. ⊠	81
76	Grambling ⊠	66
46	Ark.-Pine Bluff	43
57	Mississippi Val.	59
45	Alabama A&M	61
49	Southern U. ⊠	44
77	Alcorn St. ⊠	80
47	Prairie View	50
78	Texas Southern	61

60	Ark.-Pine Bluff ⊠	56
44	Mississippi Val. ⊠	52
74	Alabama A&M ⊠	70
71	Southern U.	58
65	Alcorn St.	66
60	Prairie View ⊠	74
72	Texas Southern ⊠	67
65	Jackson St.	69
70	Grambling	76
52	Mississippi Val. †	62

Nickname: Hornets
Colors: Black & Old Gold
Arena: Joe L. Reed Acadome
　　Capacity: 7,400; Year Built: 1992
AD: Ron Dickerson Sr.
SID: Kelvin Datcher

UAB
Birmingham, AL 35294-0110.........I

Coach: Mike Davis, Alabama 1985

2006-07 RESULTS (15-16)

60	Washington St. †	71
76	Radford †	63
75	Milwaukee	60
87	Wyoming	93
92	Wyoming ⊠	71
54	Western Ky.	69
59	Cincinnati	57
88	Minnesota ⊠	81
58	DePaul ⊠	57
44	VCU	53
42	Old Dominion	56
84	Winston-Salem ⊠	53
78	South Fla. ⊠	62
70	Florida †	75
63	UTEP	76
74	UCF ⊠	64
67	Tulane	60
54	Memphis	79
55	Southern Miss. ⊠	57
58	East Caro.	42
56	SMU ⊠	60
54	Marshall	61
56	Memphis ⊠	70
73	UTEP ⊠	64
84	Rice ⊠	73
64	Houston	70
62	Tulsa	57
70	Marshall ⊠	57
68	Southern Miss.	76
74	Tulane ⊠	76
52	Marshall †	53

Nickname: Blazers
Colors: Forest Green & Old Gold
Arena: Bartow Arena
　　Capacity: 8,500; Year Built: 1987
AD: Brian Mackin
SID: Aaron Jordan

ALA.-HUNTSVILLE
Huntsville, AL 35899 II

Coach: Lennie Acuff, Shorter 1988

2006-07 RESULTS (18-11)

79	Nova Southeastern ⊠	60
82	Incarnate Word †	78
61	St. Edward's	71
84	Paul Quinn ⊠	60
72	Carson-Newman ⊠	71
55	Harding	68
67	Carson-Newman	66
71	Harding ⊠	57
93	Berry ⊠	74
58	Barry	62
83	Nova Southeastern	73
89	St. Thomas Aquinas †	59
85	Loyola (La.) †	79
80	West Ala.	58
73	Montevallo	86
80	West Fla. ⊠	74
59	Valdosta St. ⊠	73
82	Oakland City ⊠	66

85	West Ga.	78
88	North Ala. ⊠	92
51	Valdosta St.	70
80	West Fla.	61
67	Montevallo ⊠	74
93	West Ala. ⊠	78
72	West Ga. ⊠	59
77	Oakland City	78
73	North Ala.	89
74	Delta St. ⊠	69
59	Henderson St. †	70

Nickname: Chargers
Colors: Royal Blue & White
Arena: Spragins Hall
　　Capacity: 2,000; Year Built: 1977
AD: James E. Harris
SID: Antoine Bell

ALAS. ANCHORAGE
Anchorage, AK 99508 II

Coach: Rusty Osborne, Texas 1988

2006-07 RESULTS (19-9)

105	Lancaster Bible ⊠	58
102	Lancaster Bible ⊠	30
79	Bemidji St. ⊠	58
88	Bemidji St. ⊠	42
58	Loyola Marymount ⊠	69
77	UMKC ⊠	70
65	Hofstra ⊠	75
78	Florida Tech †	60
83	Augustana (S.D.) †	65
79	BYU-Hawaii ⊠	68
85	Hawaii-Hilo ⊠	72
65	Seattle Pacific ⊠	68
80	Central Wash. ⊠	60
60	Northwest Nazarene ⊠	57
74	St. Martin's	76
70	Western Ore.	49
92	Western Wash.	72
64	Seattle	65
73	Western Ore. ⊠	81
93	St. Martin's ⊠	76
78	Alas. Fairbanks ⊠	69
89	Northwest Nazarene	75
66	Seattle ⊠	69
77	Western Wash. ⊠	61
76	Central Wash.	61
80	Seattle Pacific	89
85	Alas. Fairbanks	75
61	Humboldt St. †	68

Nickname: Seawolves
Colors: Green & Gold
Arena: Wells Fargo Sports Complex
　　Capacity: 1,250; Year Built: 1977
AD: Steve Cobb
SID: Nate Sagan

ALAS. FAIRBANKS
Fairbanks, AK 99775-7500..............II

Coach: Frank Ostanik, Alas. Fairbanks
1993

2006-07 RESULTS (17-13)

91	Lancaster Bible ⊠	58
125	Lancaster Bible ⊠	61
96	Pace †	91
79	North Georgia †	76
73	Southern Ind. †	94
66	Weber St. ⊠	71
73	Rhode Island	77
66	Southeast Mo. St. ⊠	69
80	Golden St. Baptist ⊠	45
86	Golden St. Baptist ⊠	36
58	Augustana (S.D.) ⊠	82
78	Florida Tech †	68
85	Hawaii-Hilo †	74
76	BYU-Hawaii †	71
72	Central Wash. ⊠	79
90	Seattle Pacific ⊠	78
79	Northwest Nazarene ⊠	60
64	Western Ore.	79
84	St. Martin's	89

57	Seattle	56
73	Western Wash.	64
75	St. Martin's ⊠	67
79	Western Ore. ⊠	76
69	Alas. Anchorage	78
84	Western Wash. ⊠	62
48	Seattle ⊠	50
75	Seattle Pacific	70
67	Central Wash.	74
67	Northwest Nazarene	77
75	Alas. Anchorage ⊠	85

Nickname: Nanooks
Colors: Blue & Gold
Arena: Patty Center
　　Capacity: 2,000; Year Built: 1962
AD: Forrest Karr
SID: Jamie Schanback

ALBANY ST. (GA.)
Albany, GA 31705 II

Coach: Christopher Cameron, Tulane
1997

2006-07 RESULTS (15-17)

73	Montevallo	89
81	Valdosta St.	111
68	Ga. Southwestern ⊠	69
80	LeMoyne-Owen ⊠	72
87	Florida A&M	96
67	Fla. Gulf Coast	76
64	Miles ⊠	57
56	Stillman ⊠	64
96	Tuskegee ⊠	71
64	Lane	66
84	Kentucky St.	100
50	Fort Valley St.	66
68	Benedict ⊠	70
62	Paine ⊠	64
77	Lane ⊠	65
67	Kentucky St. ⊠	66
69	LeMoyne-Owen	77
75	Miles	68
59	Morehouse	56
58	Clark Atlanta	63
45	Stillman	50
85	Tuskegee	64
99	Clark Atlanta	69
61	Morehouse ⊠	64
77	Fort Valley St. ⊠	71
70	Benedict	77
71	Paine	67
67	Clark Atlanta †	43
64	Stillman †	58
73	Benedict †	64
54	Fort Valley St. †	50
62	Montevallo	78

Nickname: Golden Rams
Colors: Blue & Gold
Arena: HPER Gym Complex
　　Capacity: 4,000; Year Built: 1998
AD: Joshua Murfree, Jr.
SID: Edythe Bradley

ALBANY (N.Y.)
Albany, NY 12222................................I

Coach: Will Brown, Dowling 1995

2006-07 RESULTS (23-10)

55	Bucknell ⊠	49
87	Delaware ⊠	67
71	Sacred Heart	90
55	Connecticut	86
75	Siena	76
57	VCU ⊠	75
62	Brown ⊠	52
79	Harvard	76
71	St. Bonaventure ⊠	56
78	Cornell	75
59	Utah	58
66	Utah Valley St.	73
69	New Hampshire ⊠	52
72	Binghamton	83
65	UMBC	61

82	Maine ⊠	73
66	Vermont	75
66	Stony Brook ⊠	61
80	Hartford ⊠	67
52	Boston U.	50
71	New Hampshire	64
82	UMBC ⊠	58
65	Binghamton ⊠	62
61	Hartford	55
71	Maine	55
63	Vermont ⊠	67
82	Boise St.	83
66	Stony Brook	46
73	Boston U. ⊠	63
64	New Hampshire †	47
59	Boston U.	49
60	Vermont	59
57	Virginia †	84

Nickname: Great Danes
Colors: Purple & Gold
Arena: Recreation & Convocation Center
  Capacity: 5,000; Year Built: 1992
AD: Lee McElroy
SID: Brian DePasquale

ALBERTUS MAGNUS
New Haven, CT 06511-1189........ III

Coach: Bob McMahon, Boston U. 1976

2006-07 RESULTS (2-23)

73	Merchant Marine	76
54	Western Conn. St.	93
49	Coast Guard	88
71	Newbury	77
88	Daniel Webster	99
58	Connecticut Col. ⊠	75
63	Norwich ⊠	78
71	Wesleyan (Conn.)	98
70	Emerson ⊠	75
90	Daniel Webster ⊠	81
63	Suffolk	87
83	Southern Vt. ⊠	92
59	Emmanuel (Mass.)	82
55	Western New Eng. ⊠	72
67	Norwich	70
82	Rivier	87
68	Johnson & Wales (RI)	108
67	Emerson	92
97	Suffolk ⊠	88
74	Southern Vt.	78
81	Mitchell ⊠	86
59	Emmanuel (Mass.) ⊠	80
54	Western New Eng.	69
66	Johnson & Wales (RI) ⊠	107
75	Rivier ⊠	78

Nickname: Falcons
Colors: Royal Blue & White
Arena: Cosgrove Marcus Messer Center
  Capacity: 700; Year Built: 1989
AD: Jennifer Pacelli
SID: Brian Leighton

ALBION
Albion, MI 49224 III

Coach: Mike Turner, Albion 1969

2006-07 RESULTS (10-15)

49	Rochester College ⊠	62
68	John Carroll ⊠	82
71	Centre †	69
69	Hanover	83
98	Finlandia †	55
58	Spring Arbor ⊠	79
59	Buffalo St. †	65
46	Elmhurst †	76
58	North Central (Ill.)	69
80	Ill. Wesleyan	94
76	Adrian ⊠	81
66	Tri-State	74
58	Hope	94
81	Alma ⊠	69
77	Kalamazoo	59
71	Calvin	78

73	Olivet ⊠	43
64	Adrian	71
69	Tri-State ⊠	59
71	Hope ⊠	78
73	Alma	64
83	Kalamazoo ⊠	62
82	Calvin	77
68	Olivet	54
64	Adrian	66

Nickname: Britons
Colors: Purple & Gold
Arena: Kresge Gymnasium
  Capacity: 1,400; Year Built: 1925
AD: Lisa Roschek
SID: Bobby Lee

ALBRIGHT
Reading, PA 19612-5234 III

Coach: Rick Ferry, Susquehanna 1985

2006-07 RESULTS (10-14)

74	Adrian ⊠	51
62	Catholic ⊠	67
85	King's (Pa.)	84
70	York (Pa.)	72
74	Lebanon Valley ⊠	79
65	Messiah ⊠	66
67	DeSales ⊠	77
85	Alvernia ⊠	93
76	New Jersey City †	62
92	Shenandoah †	94
73	Pa. Col. of Bible †	48
94	New Jersey City ⊠	71
55	Widener	57
81	Elizabethtown	78
78	Moravian ⊠	81
75	Juniata	76
77	Susquehanna ⊠	90
81	Elizabethtown ⊠	73
87	Moravian	73
63	Messiah	69
70	Widener ⊠	66
62	Susquehanna	69
72	Lebanon Valley	65
70	Juniata	82

Nickname: Lions
Colors: Red & White
Arena: Bollman Center
  Capacity: 2,500; Year Built: 1950
AD: Stephen George
SID: Jeff Feiler

ALCORN ST.
Alcorn State, MS 39096-7500 I

Coach: Samuel West, Texas Southern 1977

2006-07 RESULTS (11-19)

44	Texas	103
59	St. Bonaventure †	68
57	Miami (Fla.)	96
61	Florida Int'l	74
49	Radford †	77
59	Baylor	90
71	Texas St.	77
78	Sam Houston St. ⊠	81
98	Paul Quinn ⊠	83
59	New Mexico	91
65	Binghamton †	78
71	Prairie View ⊠	64
69	Texas Southern ⊠	72
70	Jackson St.	86
58	Grambling	61
61	Mississippi Val. ⊠	60
61	Ark.-Pine Bluff ⊠	57
59	Alabama A&M	58
80	Alabama St.	77
85	Southern U. ⊠	73
88	Jackson St. ⊠	80
76	Grambling ⊠	83
63	Mississippi Val.	76
56	Ark.-Pine Bluff	78
86	Alabama A&M ⊠	77

66	Alabama St. ⊠	65
56	Southern U.	61
73	Prairie View	78
70	Texas Southern	67
64	Texas Southern †	74

Nickname: Braves
Colors: Purple & Gold
Arena: Davey L. Whitney Complex
  Capacity: 7,000; Year Built: 1974
AD: Wiley Jones
SID: LaToya Shields

ALDERSON-BROADDUS
Philippi, WV 26416 II

Coach: Greg Zimmerman, Alderson-Broaddus 1978

2006-07 RESULTS (24-6)

61	Shippensburg †	62
73	West Chester	68
63	Indiana (Pa.) ⊠	74
91	Northwest Nazarene	79
97	Central Wash. †	74
116	Penn St.-New Kens. ⊠	34
77	Virginia St.	85
67	Edinboro	84
97	Glenville St. ⊠	77
66	Bluefield St.	62
84	West Va. Wesleyan ⊠	60
72	Charleston (W.V.) ⊠	66
69	Davis & Elkins	41
72	Wheeling Jesuit	65
92	Salem Int'l	72
105	West Virginia St. ⊠	82
98	Glenville St.	72
98	Ohio Valley	71
80	Charleston (W.V.)	57
92	Shepherd ⊠	74
91	Concord	83
80	West Virginia St.	77
65	Davis & Elkins ⊠	60
88	West Liberty St.	83
80	Fairmont St. ⊠	73
82	West Va. Wesleyan	65
86	Charleston (W.V.) †	70
91	Concord †	87
79	West Virginia St. †	80
75	West Virginia St. †	91

Nickname: Battlers
Colors: Blue, Gray & Gold
Arena: Rex Pyles Arena
  Capacity: 2,500; Year Built: 1968
AD: Jerrell D. Long
SID: Carrie Bodkins

ALFRED
Alfred, NY 14802 III

Coach: Jay Murphy, Brockport St. 1981

2006-07 RESULTS (10-14)

44	New York U.	73
83	Moravian †	94
79	Hilbert ⊠	77
73	Allegheny ⊠	57
58	Cortland St.	72
50	Geneseo St.	67
62	Potsdam St.	68
65	St. Lawrence	74
59	Randolph-Macon	70
51	Richard Stockton †	59
72	Nazareth	75
69	Rochester Inst.	60
51	Utica	60
74	Hartwick	58
51	St. John Fisher ⊠	50
57	Ithaca ⊠	68
73	Elmira ⊠	58
64	Rochester Inst. ⊠	77
82	Nazareth ⊠	77
41	St. John Fisher	81
62	Elmira	55
73	Ithaca	88
76	Hartwick ⊠	55

62	Utica ⊠	61

Nickname: Saxons
Colors: Purple & Gold
Arena: James A. McLane Physical
  Capacity: 3,200; Year Built: 1971
AD: James M. Moretti
SID: Mark Whitehouse

ALLEGHENY
Meadville, PA 16335 III

Coach: Rob Clune, Albany (N.Y.) 1981

2006-07 RESULTS (12-13)

78	Grove City †	75
81	Wash. & Jeff. ⊠	75
56	Penn St.-Behrend ⊠	55
57	Alfred	73
59	Kenyon	61
97	Westminster (Pa.)	102
73	Ohio Wesleyan ⊠	70
49	Thiel ⊠	42
57	Lawrence †	69
61	Mary Washington †	68
55	Earlham ⊠	56
72	Wabash ⊠	69
87	Wooster ⊠	97
67	Denison	87
93	Oberlin ⊠	68
51	Wittenberg ⊠	83
81	Hiram ⊠	82
70	Kenyon ⊠	65
71	Wooster	109
58	Ohio Wesleyan	87
74	Oberlin	69
94	Denison ⊠	67
79	Hiram	66
62	Wittenberg ⊠	57
84	Wabash	87

Nickname: Gators
Colors: Blue & Gold
Arena: Wise Center
  Capacity: 960; Year Built: 1997
AD: Betsy Mitchell
SID: Bill Salyer

ALMA
Alma, MI 48801 III

Coach: Ed Kohtala, Maine 1981

2006-07 RESULTS (3-22)

61	Wis.-Eau Claire †	69
62	Eureka †	73
62	Grace Bible (Mich.)	60
53	Ferris St.	81
66	Madonna ⊠	79
66	Elmhurst ⊠	74
52	Aquinas	86
67	Northwood (Mich.)	79
63	Franklin	85
68	Lakeland †	81
70	Olivet	86
61	Calvin ⊠	86
64	Kalamazoo ⊠	56
69	Albion	81
81	Tri-State	89
53	Hope	86
73	Adrian ⊠	79
50	Olivet ⊠	55
49	Calvin	105
66	Kalamazoo	73
64	Albion ⊠	73
76	Tri-State ⊠	62
62	Hope ⊠	88
81	Adrian	86
49	Hope	89

Nickname: Scots
Colors: Maroon & Cream
Arena: Cappaert Gymnasium
  Capacity: 3,000; Year Built: 1967
AD: Ellen Curtis
SID: Lindsay Carpenter

ALVERNIA
Reading, PA 19607.................III

Coach: Mike Miller, Delaware Valley 1980

2006-07 RESULTS (23-5)

74	Rutgers-Camden ⊠	55
71	Baldwin-Wallace ⊠	62
67	Cal Lutheran †	71
56	George Fox †	63
59	Immaculata ⊠	58
80	Wesley ⊠	65
93	Albright	85
72	Frank. & Marsh. ⊠	58
94	Penn St.-Berks ⊠	60
66	Arcadia	56
93	Marywood	76
69	Cabrini ⊠	34
60	Neumann ⊠	61
66	Arcadia	60
65	Misericordia ⊠	49
79	Wesley	69
70	Eastern ⊠	49
54	Gwynedd-Mercy	57
73	Cabrini	66
71	Neumann ⊠	59
64	Gwynedd-Mercy ⊠	61
48	Immaculata	45
81	Marywood ⊠	51
66	Misericordia	49
84	Eastern	74
71	Eastern ⊠	48
70	Immaculata ⊠	55
76	Lincoln (Pa.) †	91

Nickname: Crusaders
Colors: Maroon & Gold
Arena: Physical Education Center
  Capacity: 1,500; Year Built: 1987
AD: John McCloskey
SID: Jon King

AMERICAN
Washington, DC 20016...................I

Coach: Jeff Jones, Virginia 1982

2006-07 RESULTS (16-14)

59	Fairfield	54
97	Morgan St. ⊠	84
50	Richmond	61
81	Loyola (Md.) ⊠	74
68	Xavier	86
59	Mt. St. Mary's	46
75	NJIT ⊠	50
60	Longwood ⊠	49
85	Howard	75
53	Yale	70
54	Maryland	66
70	Virginia	91
79	Longwood	81
73	St. Francis (Pa.) ⊠	63
49	Lehigh	51
60	Bucknell	66
70	Colgate ⊠	48
55	Army	60
64	Holy Cross ⊠	69
55	Navy ⊠	46
73	Lafayette	59
47	Holy Cross	58
54	Lehigh ⊠	56
66	Bucknell ⊠	69
64	Colgate	58
64	Army ⊠	49
71	Navy	60
78	Lafayette ⊠	67
59	Colgate ⊠	44
53	Holy Cross	55

Nickname: Eagles
Colors: AU Red, White & Blue
Arena: Bender Arena
  Capacity: 4,500; Year Built: 1988
AD: Athena Argyropoulos/Rob Acunto
SID: Anthony Wilson

AMERICAN INT'L
Springfield, MA 01109-3189.........II

Coach: Arthur Luptowski, Bloomsburg 1973

2006-07 RESULTS (16-13)

68	Dowling	65
68	Bryant	72
75	Pace ⊠	87
59	St. Rose	74
53	Bentley ⊠	79
69	Merrimack ⊠	61
66	St. Michael's ⊠	60
75	Southern N.H.	89
89	Southern Conn. St.	81
75	Mass.-Lowell ⊠	72
57	Philadelphia U. ⊠	63
63	Franklin Pierce	78
60	Holy Family ⊠	62
82	Le Moyne	75
75	Southern Conn. St. ⊠	69
68	New Haven	53
63	Stonehill ⊠	58
63	St. Anselm	75
70	Mass.-Lowell	57
76	St. Michael's	75
61	Assumption ⊠	76
74	Merrimack	65
58	Bryant ⊠	47
71	Le Moyne ⊠	68
56	Bentley	87
69	St. Rose ⊠	62
64	Pace	74
68	Merrimack ⊠	60
63	Bryant	79

Nickname: Yellow Jackets
Colors: Gold, White & Black
Arena: Henry A. Butova Gym
  Capacity: 2,500; Year Built: 1965
AD: Richard F. Bedard
SID: Greg Royce

AMHERST
Amherst, MA 01002-5000.............III

Coach: David Hixon, Amherst 1975

2006-07 RESULTS (30-2)

101	City Tech ⊠	66
98	Thomas (Me.) ⊠	64
84	Emmanuel (Mass.)	45
92	Western New Eng. ⊠	56
91	Springfield ⊠	52
79	MIT	47
84	Brandeis ⊠	74
70	Worcester St.	42
66	Trinity (Tex.)	54
89	Babson ⊠	70
64	Williams	45
76	Wesleyan (Conn.)	52
96	Tufts	92
79	Bates	64
103	Elms ⊠	69
79	Middlebury ⊠	73
72	Williams ⊠	51
111	Southern Vt. ⊠	67
69	Colby	58
73	Bowdoin	55
62	Rhode Island Col.	48
91	Connecticut Col. ⊠	49
81	Wesleyan (Conn.) ⊠	56
59	Trinity (Conn.)	62
72	Bates ⊠	68
82	Colby ⊠	55
69	Williams ⊠	70
87	Widener ⊠	70
97	Stevens Institute ⊠	74
81	Rhode Island Col. ⊠	69
67	Wooster †	60
80	Va. Wesleyan †	67

Nickname: Lord Jeffs
Colors: Purple & White
Arena: LeFrak Gymnasium
  Capacity: 2,450; Year Built: 1986
AD: Suzanne R. Coffey
SID: Tanner Lipsett

ANDERSON (IND.)
Anderson, IN 46012-3495.............III

Coach: Tom Slyder, Anderson (Ind.) 1988

2006-07 RESULTS (9-16)

69	Wilmington (Ohio) †	67
76	Thomas More †	59
69	Taylor (Ind.) ⊠	59
50	Rose-Hulman ⊠	63
60	Defiance ⊠	62
33	Murray St.	78
86	Transylvania ⊠	91
69	Mt. St. Joseph ⊠	72
84	Earlham ⊠	74
74	La Verne ⊠	54
75	Whittier ⊠	61
59	IPFW	107
77	Bluffton ⊠	73
73	Oberlin	72
69	Hanover	72
74	Franklin ⊠	79
59	Manchester ⊠	64
64	Defiance	78
59	Rose-Hulman	71
71	Mt. St. Joseph ⊠	80
64	Transylvania	61
68	Bluffton	77
74	Hanover ⊠	77
66	Manchester ⊠	69
74	Franklin	84

Nickname: Ravens
Colors: Orange & Black
Arena: O.C. Lewis Gym
  Capacity: 3,000; Year Built: 1962
AD: Michael Zapolski
SID: Justin Bates

ANDERSON (S.C.)
Anderson, SC 29621.........................II

Coach: Jason Taylor, Jacksonville St. 2000

2006-07 RESULTS (4-24)

60	Lenoir-Rhyne †	83
63	S.C.-Aiken	73
42	Lees-McRae	63
61	Wingate	83
43	Limestone	62
70	Belmont Abbey ⊠	66
71	Wingate ⊠	92
56	Newberry ⊠	68
59	North Greenville ⊠	69
69	St. Andrews ⊠	48
37	Queens (N.C.) ⊠	75
64	Barton	98
80	Erskine ⊠	82
80	Pfeiffer ⊠	87
57	Mount Olive ⊠	97
51	Coker ⊠	58
49	St. Andrews	79
66	Lees-McRae ⊠	74
54	North Greenville	62
56	Erskine	53
49	Queens (N.C.)	59
73	Barton ⊠	83
48	Coker	69
66	Pfeiffer	77
52	Belmont Abbey	49
68	Limestone ⊠	72
60	Mount Olive	68
75	Erskine	95

Nickname: Trojans
Colors: Gold & Black
Arena: Abney Athletic Center
  Capacity: 1,000; Year Built: 1979
AD: Robert G. Beville
SID: Cobb Oxford

ANGELO ST.
San Angelo, TX 76909.....................II

Coach: Fred Rike, West Tex. A&M 1989

2006-07 RESULTS (9-17)

70	Metro St.	82
87	Colo. Christian †	69
66	Regis (Colo.)	72
70	Okla. Panhandle ⊠	67
75	Tex. A&M-Commerce ⊠	81
70	Incarnate Word	69
64	Central Okla.	91
67	Northeastern St.	62
60	Incarnate Word ⊠	63
69	St. Augustine's ⊠	72
57	Texas Southern	76
63	Southeastern Okla. ⊠	72
59	East Central ⊠	69
72	Cameron	71
94	West Tex. A&M ⊠	84
78	Eastern N.M.	94
76	Abilene Christian	92
81	Tex. A&M-Kingsville ⊠	57
78	Tarleton St. ⊠	81
96	Midwestern St.	107
73	Tarleton St.	76
89	Midwestern St. ⊠	88
56	West Tex. A&M	86
65	Eastern N.M. ⊠	68
67	Abilene Christian ⊠	62
61	Tex. A&M-Kingsville	85

Nickname: Rams
Colors: Blue & Gold
Arena: Junell Center/Stephens Arena
  Capacity: 5,500; Year Built: 2001
AD: Kathleen Brasfield
SID: Dave Wester

ANNA MARIA
Paxton, MA 01612-1198.................III

Coach: Shawn Conrad, Assumption 1984

2006-07 RESULTS (7-18)

72	Bard †	56
49	Rivier	51
70	Newbury ⊠	68
74	Daniel Webster ⊠	81
73	Becker	76
64	Salve Regina	81
52	Nichols	68
62	Bard	66
59	Mass. Liberal Arts †	64
55	Endicott ⊠	70
59	Eastern Nazarene ⊠	55
60	Worcester St.	65
49	Roger Williams ⊠	89
43	Colby-Sawyer	75
66	Eastern Nazarene	62
84	Wentworth Inst.	91
75	New England Col. ⊠	74
69	New England ⊠	50
54	Curry ⊠	66
81	Mitchell	79
83	Nichols ⊠	95
57	Roger Williams	74
60	Salve Regina ⊠	71
52	Gordon	74
48	Curry	73

Nickname: AMCATS
Colors: Royal Blue & White
Arena: Fuller Activities Center
  Capacity: 500; Year Built: 1986
AD: David Shea
SID: David Gentleman

RESULTS

APPALACHIAN ST.
Boone, NC 28608 I

Coach: Houston Fancher, Middle Tenn. 1988

2006-07 RESULTS (25-8)

109	North Greenville ⊠	71
49	Clemson	79
78	Montreat ⊠	63
78	Wake Forest	88
84	Campbell ⊠	71
68	Col. of Charleston	57
56	Citadel	52
37	Virginia Tech	69
93	Brevard ⊠	53
87	Ga. Southern ⊠	84
80	Virginia †	69
75	UCF †	64
87	Vanderbilt †	79
73	VCU	70
77	Chattanooga	63
63	Elon ⊠	64
100	Western Caro. ⊠	91
76	UNC Greensboro	80
81	Davidson	74
77	Furman ⊠	63
95	Citadel ⊠	54
67	Col. of Charleston ⊠	56
72	Furman	76
77	Ga. Southern	55
72	Wofford ⊠	52
85	Chattanooga ⊠	69
60	Wichita St.	58
76	Western Caro.	65
80	UNC Greensboro ⊠	66
72	Elon	63
78	Western Caro. †	59
87	Col. of Charleston †	89
59	Mississippi	73

Nickname: Mountaineers
Colors: Black & Gold
Arena: Holmes Convocation Center
  Capacity: 8,325; Year Built: 2000
AD: Charles Cobb
SID: Ty Patton

ARCADIA
Glenside, PA 19038-3295 III

Coach: Patrick Dorney, Lebanon Valley

2006-07 RESULTS (11-14)

54	Stevens Institute †	59
55	Rensselaer †	57
66	Swarthmore	75
49	Penn St.-Delco ⊠	45
62	Immaculata	64
47	Eastern	68
62	Neumann ⊠	67
49	Lebanon Valley	56
55	Delaware Valley ⊠	59
86	Chestnut Hill	75
64	Misericordia	61
54	Cabrini	48
56	Alvernia	66
64	Eastern ⊠	59
65	Marywood ⊠	54
60	Alvernia ⊠	66
49	Neumann	60
71	Gwynedd-Mercy	48
76	Misericordia ⊠	56
70	Immaculata ⊠	56
69	Wesley	73
77	Cabrini ⊠	61
56	Wesley ⊠	62
61	Gwynedd-Mercy ⊠	69
63	Marywood	47

Nickname: Knights
Colors: Scarlet & Gray
Arena: Kuch Center
  Capacity: 1,500; Year Built: 1993
AD: Shirley M. Liddle
SID: Joy Zazzera

ARIZONA
Tucson, AZ 85721-0096 I

Coach: Lute Olson, Augsburg 1956

2006-07 RESULTS (20-11)

90	Virginia	93
101	Northern Ariz. ⊠	79
102	New Mexico St. ⊠	87
86	Samford ⊠	57
89	UNLV ⊠	75
84	Illinois †	72
72	Louisville †	65
69	San Diego St.	48
87	Houston	62
79	Memphis	71
94	California ⊠	85
89	Stanford ⊠	75
96	Washington	87
73	Washington St.	77
83	Oregon St. ⊠	72
77	Oregon ⊠	79
73	Southern California	80
69	UCLA	73
71	Arizona St. ⊠	47
64	North Carolina	92
66	Washington St. ⊠	72
84	Washington ⊠	54
72	Oregon St.	66
77	Oregon	74
75	Southern California ⊠	80
66	UCLA ⊠	81
61	Arizona St.	58
70	California	65
85	Stanford †	80
50	Oregon †	69
63	Purdue †	72

Nickname: Wildcats
Colors: Cardinal & Navy
Arena: McKale Center
  Capacity: 14,545; Year Built: 1973
AD: Jim Livengood
SID: Richard Paige

ARIZONA ST.
Tempe, AZ 85287-2505 I

Coach: Herb Sendek, Carnegie Mellon 1985

2006-07 RESULTS (8-22)

71	Northern Ariz. ⊠	75
69	Cal St. San B'dino ⊠	52
67	Portland St. ⊠	71
64	San Jose St. ⊠	52
67	Iowa ⊠	64
66	Northern Colo. ⊠	51
63	Minnesota	66
58	Xavier	76
52	Colgate ⊠	36
71	N.C. A&T ⊠	66
70	Davidson ⊠	75
60	Stanford ⊠	71
62	California ⊠	66
55	Washington St.	75
53	Washington	64
55	Oregon ⊠	60
59	Oregon St. ⊠	67
50	UCLA	60
49	Southern California	58
47	Arizona	71
61	Washington ⊠	66
47	Washington St. ⊠	48
51	Oregon	55
55	Oregon St.	59
61	UCLA ⊠	67
68	Southern California ⊠	58
58	Arizona ⊠	61
53	Stanford	63
42	California	41
51	Washington †	59

Nickname: Sun Devils
Colors: Maroon & Gold
Arena: Wells Fargo Arena
  Capacity: 14,198; Year Built: 1974
AD: Lisa Love
SID: Doug Tammaro

ARKANSAS
Fayetteville, AR 72701 I

Coach: Stan Heath, Eastern Mich. 1988

2006-07 RESULTS (21-14)

92	Southeast Mo. St. ⊠	52
70	Stephen F. Austin ⊠	59
61	Southern Ill. †	53
73	Marist †	64
71	West Virginia †	64
64	Missouri	86
71	UMKC ⊠	61
75	Central Mich. ⊠	59
91	Oakland ⊠	57
56	Texas Tech †	71
76	Texas	80
68	Oral Roberts ⊠	56
80	Louisiana Tech ⊠	50
68	Tulsa ⊠	59
88	Alabama ⊠	61
72	Florida	79
72	Mississippi	74
64	Georgia ⊠	67
72	LSU ⊠	52
60	South Carolina	66
63	Alabama	57
74	Kentucky ⊠	82
65	Auburn ⊠	57
67	LSU	71
60	Mississippi St.	84
83	Mississippi ⊠	66
59	Auburn	67
72	Tennessee ⊠	83
67	Mississippi St. ⊠	58
82	Vanderbilt	67
82	South Carolina †	52
72	Vanderbilt †	71
81	Mississippi St. †	72
56	Florida †	77
60	Southern California †	77

Nickname: Razorbacks
Colors: Cardinal & White
Arena: Bud Walton Arena
  Capacity: 19,200; Year Built: 1993
AD: J. Frank Broyles
SID: Robby Edwards

ARKANSAS ST.
State University, AR 72467 I

Coach: Dickey Nutt, Oklahoma St. 1982

2006-07 RESULTS (18-15)

44	Clemson †	83
61	Old Dominion	69
67	Monmouth †	69
64	Bowling Green ⊠	54
87	Lyon ⊠	51
68	Tenn.-Martin	63
77	Austin Peay ⊠	70
78	South Dakota St.	84
60	Memphis	86
70	Eastern Ill.	73
72	Bowling Green	81
86	Arkansas Tech ⊠	74
81	Denver ⊠	66
73	La.-Lafayette	63
78	South Ala. ⊠	91
69	La.-Monroe	77
84	North Texas ⊠	60
77	Ark.-Little Rock ⊠	51
79	Troy	87
54	Middle Tenn.	51
76	Western Ky. ⊠	75
61	Florida Int'l	80
84	Fla. Atlantic ⊠	77
68	Denver	76
70	La.-Lafayette ⊠	76
67	South Ala.	85
90	New Orleans ⊠	79
76	La.-Monroe ⊠	68
74	North Texas	71
61	Ark.-Little Rock.	55
81	New Orleans †	74
80	Western Ky. †	73
75	North Texas †	83

Nickname: Indians
Colors: Scarlet & Black
Arena: Convocation Center
  Capacity: 10,038; Year Built: 1987
AD: Dean Lee
SID: Bill Bowen

ARKANSAS TECH
Russellville, AR 72801-2222 II

Coach: Mark Downey, Charleston (W.V.) 1995

2006-07 RESULTS (6-21)

72	Southwestern Okla.	85
58	P.R.-Bayamon †	69
81	Palm Beach Atl. †	71
80	Fla. Gulf Coast	86
79	Northeastern St.	83
78	North Ala. ⊠	79
91	Central Baptist ⊠	86
74	Arkansas St.	86
91	North Ala.	94
82	Crichton ⊠	70
101	Lincoln (Mo.) ⊠	84
86	Mid-America Naz. ⊠	87
67	Henderson St.	80
61	Christian Bros.	74
63	Southern Ark. ⊠	68
69	Harding ⊠	77
78	Ark.-Monticello	87
77	Delta St.	90
74	Ouachita Baptist	81
85	Rhema ⊠	66
42	Henderson St. ⊠	66
60	Christian Bros. ⊠	63
62	Southern Ark.	71
74	Harding	86
79	Ark.-Monticello ⊠	73
69	Delta St.	74
70	Ouachita Baptist ⊠	77

Nickname: Wonder Boys
Colors: Green & Gold
Arena: Tucker Coliseum
  Capacity: 3,500; Year Built: 1976
AD: Steve Mullins
SID: Ben Greenberg

ARK.-LITTLE ROCK
Little Rock, AR 72204 I

Coach: Steve Shields, Baylor 1988

2006-07 RESULTS (13-17)

83	Central Methodist ⊠	54
81	Akron †	79
59	Texas Tech	93
60	Tulsa	66
83	Texas St.	77
58	Tenn.-Martin ⊠	56
35	Texas A&M	75
59	Centenary (La.)	69
46	McNeese St. ⊠	60
67	Minnesota	66
57	Belmont ⊠	72
73	Denver †	47
68	La.-Monroe	76
59	La.-Lafayette	55
70	Troy	82
86	North Texas ⊠	75
73	New Orleans ⊠	82
51	Arkansas St.	77
54	South Ala.	68
71	Western Ky. ⊠	69
60	Middle Tenn. ⊠	61
71	Fla. Atlantic	75
86	Florida Int'l ⊠	68
57	La.-Monroe ⊠	58
74	Denver	68
69	Troy ⊠	71
69	North Texas	75
65	New Orleans	64
55	Arkansas St. ⊠	61
70	New Orleans	77

Nickname: Trojans
Colors: Maroon, Silver & Black
Arena: Jack Stephens Center
   Capacity: 5,600; Year Built: 2005
AD: Chris Peterson
SID: Joe Angolia

ARK.-MONTICELLO
Monticello, AR 71656 II

Coach: Mike Newell, Sam Houston St. 1973

2006-07 RESULTS (9-17)

87	LeMoyne-Owen ⊠	83
99	Central Baptist ⊠	71
73	Southwest Baptist ⊠	98
72	West Ga. ⊠	82
85	Ecclesia ⊠	70
85	Loyola (La.) ⊠	82
72	Hawaii-Hilo	83
75	Hawaii Pacific	84
68	BYU-Hawaii †	101
89	Lincoln (Mo.) ⊠	81
70	West Ga.	77
54	Clayton St.	88
76	Harding ⊠	87
78	Ouachita Baptist ⊠	77
69	Delta St.	79
66	Henderson St.	68
87	Arkansas Tech ⊠	78
65	Christian Bros.	49
48	Southern Ark.	65
70	Harding	79
55	Ouachita Baptist	73
79	Delta St. ⊠	82
60	Henderson St. ⊠	82
73	Arkansas Tech	79
60	Christian Bros.	90
76	Southern Ark. ⊠	65

Nickname: Boll Weevils
Colors: Kelly Green & White
Arena: Steelman Fieldhouse
   Capacity: 2,600; Year Built: 1959
AD: Alvy Early
SID: Paul Smith

ARK.-PINE BLUFF
Pine Bluff, AR 71601 I

Coach: Van Holt, Ark.-Pine Bluff 1965

2006-07 RESULTS (12-19)

45	Air Force	81
63	Nevada	82
55	Fresno St.	82
42	Nebraska	71
39	Creighton	74
84	Philander Smith ⊠	68
77	Philander Smith	69
62	New Mexico St.	78
51	UTEP	79
57	TCU	73
68	Tulane	70
55	Mississippi Val. ⊠	63
43	Alabama St.	46
52	Alabama A&M ⊠	45
54	Southern U.	47
57	Alcorn St.	61
56	Texas Southern ⊠	58
61	Prairie View ⊠	56
68	Grambling	74
56	Jackson St.	59
56	Alabama St.	60
66	Alabama A&M	65
73	Southern U. ⊠	58
78	Alcorn St. ⊠	56
80	Texas Southern	83
70	Prairie View	67
72	Grambling ⊠	68
59	Jackson St. ⊠	54
50	Mississippi Val.	63
51	Grambling †	48
62	Jackson St. †	64

Nickname: Golden Lions
Colors: Black & Gold
Arena: K.L. Johnson HPER Complex
   Capacity: 4,500; Year Built: 1982
AD: Craig Curry
SID: Carl Whimper

ARMSTRONG ATLANTIC
Savannah, GA 31419-1997 II

Coach: Jeff Burkhamer, Alderson-Broaddus 1984

2006-07 RESULTS (21-9)

70	Truman †	67
65	Mo. Western St.	61
61	Fla. Southern ⊠	58
70	Brewton Parker ⊠	47
94	Catawba	86
53	Lenoir-Rhyne †	64
60	Eckerd ⊠	59
71	Lenoir-Rhyne ⊠	68
81	Fla. Southern	93
74	Southern Ark. ⊠	64
76	Ferris St. ⊠	68
66	GCSU	64
78	North Georgia ⊠	70
64	Clayton St.	69
75	Francis Marion	60
74	Augusta St. ⊠	83
55	Lander	54
63	Clayton St. ⊠	58
60	UNC Pembroke ⊠	62
53	Augusta St.	77
85	S.C.-Aiken	56
59	Ga. Southwestern	56
80	Columbus St. ⊠	64
62	GCSU	53
68	S.C. Upstate ⊠	61
64	Ga. Southwestern	76
72	Columbus St.	60
78	Francis Marion †	68
56	Lander	60
68	Wingate †	72

Nickname: Pirates
Colors: Maroon & Gold
Arena: Alumni Arena
   Capacity: 5,000; Year Built: 1995
AD: Eddie Aenchbacher
SID: Chad Jackson

ARMY
West Point, NY 10996-2101 I

Coach: Jim Crews, Indiana 1976

2006-07 RESULTS (15-16)

80	Stetson †	68
58	Missouri	67
63	N.C. A&T †	49
62	Hartford ⊠	53
56	Cornell ⊠	65
62	Brown	54
79	VMI ⊠	72
63	Citadel	55
60	NJIT ⊠	40
101	Purchase St. ⊠	40
92	Maritime (N.Y.) ⊠	42
47	Notre Dame	88
50	Michigan	62
59	Sacred Heart ⊠	58
58	Dartmouth	66
71	Colgate	73
42	Holy Cross	66
64	Lehigh ⊠	59
60	American ⊠	55
53	Navy ⊠	50
68	Lafayette	76
49	Bucknell	74
38	Colgate ⊠	42
54	Holy Cross ⊠	70
64	Lehigh	75
49	American	64
68	Navy	76
83	Lafayette ⊠	65
49	Bucknell ⊠	54

47	Lehigh	46
47	Bucknell	68

Nickname: Black Knights/Cadets
Colors: Black, Gold & Gray
Arena: Christl Arena
   Capacity: 5,043; Year Built: 1985
AD: Kevin Anderson
SID: Christian Anderson

ASHLAND
Ashland, OH 44805 II

Coach: Roger Lyons, Ashland 1974

2006-07 RESULTS (16-12)

99	Ohio Dominican ⊠	83
92	St. Martin's †	79
81	Seattle	91
73	St. Joseph's (Ind.)	89
87	West Va. Wesleyan ⊠	78
97	Slippery Rock ⊠	71
83	Lake Superior St. ⊠	68
78	Michigan Tech ⊠	57
86	Mt. Vernon Naz. ⊠	74
67	Findlay	92
80	Northern Mich. ⊠	82
76	Tiffin ⊠	60
76	Notre Dame (Ohio) ⊠	68
80	Aquinas ⊠	64
95	Gannon	96
71	Mercyhurst	79
92	Wayne St. (Mich.) ⊠	71
71	Hillsdale ⊠	67
85	Northwood (Mich.) ⊠	77
79	Saginaw Valley ⊠	68
78	Ferris St.	81
38	Grand Valley St.	79
75	Hillsdale	71
65	Wayne St. (Mich.)	84
83	Gannon ⊠	86
86	Mercyhurst ⊠	56
67	Findlay ⊠	76
54	Findlay	70

Nickname: Eagles
Colors: Purple & Gold
Arena: Charles Kates Gym
   Capacity: 3,000; Year Built: 1967
AD: Bill Goldring
SID: Al King

ASSUMPTION
Worcester, MA 01609 II

Coach: Serge DeBari, Assumption 1971

2006-07 RESULTS (11-17)

64	Nyack	81
67	Mercyhurst †	81
61	Franklin Pierce ⊠	51
65	St. Anselm	62
48	Bryant	62
65	Bentley	72
56	Stonehill ⊠	69
97	Merrimack ⊠	88
84	Southern N.H. ⊠	69
76	Adelphi ⊠	63
86	P.R.-Rio Piedras †	55
73	P.R.-Bayamon	75
63	Pace ⊠	70
76	Le Moyne ⊠	62
67	Bryant ⊠	77
76	St. Michael's	87
68	Mass.-Lowell ⊠	69
78	Southern Conn. St.	75
52	Franklin Pierce	62
68	Mass.-Lowell	62
66	St. Anselm ⊠	69
76	American Int'l	61
68	Southern N.H.	79
83	St. Rose	79
57	Merrimack	66
81	Stonehill	83
71	Bentley ⊠	82
60	St. Michael's	68

Nickname: Greyhounds
Colors: Blue, White, & Grey
Arena: Andrew Laska Gym
   Capacity: 3,000; Year Built: 1962
AD: Ted Paulauskas
SID: Steve Morris

AUBURN
Auburn , AL 36849 I

Coach: Jeff Lebo, North Carolina 1989

2006-07 RESULTS (17-15)

71	Troy ⊠	68
95	Winston-Salem ⊠	62
64	East Tenn. St. ⊠	58
79	Miles ⊠	58
65	Oklahoma St. †	66
63	Wisconsin †	77
92	Nicholls St. ⊠	87
81	La.-Monroe ⊠	60
66	Pittsburgh ⊠	74
82	South Ala. ⊠	71
86	Wofford ⊠	76
86	Tennessee St. ⊠	59
58	Texas A&M	87
69	Charleston So. ⊠	53
54	Southern Miss.	56
68	Vanderbilt ⊠	65
57	Kentucky ⊠	84
63	LSU	65
83	Tennessee ⊠	80
76	Mississippi St.	87
81	Alabama ⊠	57
66	Florida ⊠	91
80	South Carolina	75
59	Mississippi ⊠	82
57	Arkansas	65
83	Mississippi St. ⊠	91
79	Georgia	86
67	Arkansas ⊠	59
86	Alabama	77
80	LSU ⊠	68
79	Mississippi	83
65	Georgia †	80

Nickname: Tigers
Colors: Burnt Orange & Navy Blue
Arena: Beard-Eaves-Memorial
   Capacity: 10,500; Year Built: 1969
AD: Jay Jacobs
SID: Chuck Gallina

AUGSBURG
Minneapolis, MN 55454 III

Coach: Aaron Griess, Colorado Col. 1993

2006-07 RESULTS (10-15)

100	Crown (Minn.) ⊠	71
93	Presentation ⊠	72
93	Bethany Lutheran ⊠	84
67	Gust. Adolphus	84
79	St. Scholastica ⊠	95
69	St. Olaf	59
80	Carleton ⊠	69
77	Northwestern (Minn.) ⊠	91
65	Hamline ⊠	45
76	Macalester	90
63	St. Thomas (Minn.)	80
65	St. John's (Minn.) ⊠	75
83	St. Mary's (Minn.)	73
77	Concordia-M'head ⊠	66
83	Bethel (Minn.)	93
59	Carleton	76
56	Gust. Adolphus ⊠	69
74	St. Olaf ⊠	90
84	Hamline	85
81	Macalester ⊠	94
75	St. Thomas (Minn.) ⊠	80
54	St. John's (Minn.)	67
68	St. Mary's (Minn.) ⊠	80
65	Concordia-M'head	59
87	Bethel (Minn.) ⊠	82

RESULTS

Nickname: Auggies
Colors: Maroon & Gray
Arena: Si Melby Hall
   Capacity: 2,200; Year Built: 1961
AD: Paul Grauer
SID: Don Stoner

AUGUSTA ST.
Augusta, GA 30904 II

Coach: Darren Metress, Belmont Abbey 1988

2006-07 RESULTS (24-7)
73	Carson-Newman	58
70	Benedict	64
78	Paine	60
78	Queens (N.C.) ⊠	66
76	N.C. Central	77
77	Cheyney †	81
87	Paine ⊠	59
87	Carson-Newman ⊠	67
97	Queens (N.C.)	82
88	Lenoir-Rhyne	74
70	Catawba †	92
81	Columbus St. ⊠	75
89	S.C.-Aiken	70
83	GCSU	70
86	S.C. Upstate ⊠	69
83	Armstrong Atlantic	74
75	North Georgia	58
76	GCSU	45
79	Francis Marion	63
77	Armstrong Atlantic ⊠	53
84	Lander ⊠	70
76	Clayton St. ⊠	67
85	Ga. Southwestern	76
102	Columbus St.	91
80	UNC Pembroke ⊠	57
68	Clayton St.	70
72	Ga. Southwestern ⊠	81
91	GCSU †	82
69	Clayton St. †	72
79	Elizabeth City St. ⊠	53
78	Wingate ⊠	79

Nickname: Jaguars
Colors: Royal Blue & White
Arena: George A. Christenberry Fieldhouse
   Capacity: 2,216; Year Built: 1991
AD: Clint Bryant
SID: Joey Warren

AUGUSTANA (ILL.)
Rock Island, IL 61201-2296 III

Coach: Grey Giovanine, Central Mo. St. 1981

2006-07 RESULTS (22-6)
78	St. Norbert ⊠	57
69	Beloit ⊠	52
75	Washington-St. Louis ⊠	73
54	St. Ambrose	77
55	Simpson	53
74	Clarke ⊠	56
70	Coe ⊠	47
64	Cornell College	60
92	Wartburg ⊠	77
78	Rockford	44
68	Wis.-Stevens Point	71
62	North Park ⊠	48
71	Elmhurst	82
75	Wheaton (Ill.)	69
70	Carthage ⊠	54
80	Millikin	65
60	North Central (Ill.)	59
64	Ill. Wesleyan ⊠	62
86	Elmhurst ⊠	74
71	North Park	56
56	Carthage	66
63	Wheaton (Ill.) ⊠	60
71	Millikin ⊠	59
80	Ill. Wesleyan	77
81	North Central (Ill.) ⊠	85
74	North Central (Ill.) ⊠	67

78	Elmhurst ⊠	70
69	Carroll (Wis.) ⊠	73

Nickname: Vikings
Colors: Gold & Blue
Arena: Carver PE Center
   Capacity: 3,200; Year Built: 1971
AD: Charles J. Gordon
SID: Dave Wrath

AUGUSTANA (S.D.)
Sioux Falls, SD 57197 II

Coach: Tom Billeter, Illinois 1983

2006-07 RESULTS (16-12)
70	Dakota St. ⊠	50
70	Northern St.	72
64	Mary	59
68	Bemidji St.	48
73	Minn.-Crookston	70
81	Neb.-Kearney ⊠	69
85	Mo. Southern St. ⊠	76
108	Peru St. ⊠	67
82	Alas. Fairbanks	58
65	Alas. Anchorage †	83
70	Dakota Wesleyan ⊠	57
64	Wayne St. (Neb.)	55
94	Illinois Tech ⊠	41
81	Upper Iowa ⊠	59
66	Southwest Minn. St. ⊠	61
83	Neb.-Omaha ⊠	60
57	South Dakota	69
86	Minn. Duluth ⊠	65
76	St. Cloud St. ⊠	81
76	Minn. St. Mankato	81
62	Neb.-Omaha	64
67	North Dakota ⊠	59
59	Minn. Duluth	63
66	North Dakota	68
64	Minn. St. Mankato ⊠	68
80	St. Cloud St.	85
71	South Dakota ⊠	86
63	Minn. St. Mankato	80

Nickname: Vikings
Colors: Navy & Yellow
Arena: Elmen Center
   Capacity: 4,000; Year Built: 1988
AD: Bill Gross
SID: Kevin Ludwig

AURORA
Aurora, IL 60506 III

Coach: James Lancaster, Aurora 1986

2006-07 RESULTS (25-3)
71	Ind.-South Bend †	63
66	Rose-Hulman ⊠	61
85	North Central (Ill.)	69
101	Lakeland	94
100	Wis. Lutheran ⊠	91
110	Maranatha Baptist	44
65	Edgewood ⊠	68
99	Loras ⊠	71
90	Millikin ⊠	75
72	Beloit ⊠	61
76	Marian (Wis.)	70
90	Dominican (Ill.) ⊠	66
72	Clarke	63
77	Concordia (Ill.)	71
95	Concordia (Wis.)	71
90	Rockford ⊠	47
94	Lakeland ⊠	76
83	Benedictine (Ill.) ⊠	79
82	Wis. Lutheran	87
100	Maranatha Baptist ⊠	49
81	Marian (Wis.) ⊠	53
90	Edgewood ⊠	62
83	Dominican (Ill.) ⊠	80
109	Concordia (Ill.) ⊠	86
97	Rockford	77
86	Lakeland ⊠	72
85	Edgewood ⊠	69
68	Calvin	69

Nickname: Spartans
Colors: Royal Blue & White
Arena: Thornton Gymnasium
   Capacity: 2,200; Year Built: 1970
AD: Mark Walsh
SID: Brian Kipley

AUSTIN
Sherman, TX 75090-4440 III

Coach: Chris Oestreich, St. Mary (Kan.) 1988

2006-07 RESULTS (5-19)
74	Ozarks (Ark.) ⊠	69
64	Texas-Dallas ⊠	83
64	LeTourneau	78
78	Rhema †	80
89	Principia †	50
55	Hendrix	72
52	Texas-Dallas	61
70	Dallas	68
65	LeTourneau ⊠	56
33	Southwestern (Tex.) ⊠	52
45	Trinity (Tex.) ⊠	64
60	Centre	84
51	DePauw	70
63	Millsaps ⊠	72
67	Rhodes ⊠	71
70	Dallas ⊠	68
72	Hendrix ⊠	91
63	Texas-Arlington	105
80	Oglethorpe	92
58	Sewanee	70
37	Centre ⊠	56
58	DePauw ⊠	63
64	Southwestern (Tex.)	68
48	Trinity (Tex.)	64

Nickname: Kangaroos
Colors: Crimson & Gold
Arena: Hughey Gym
   Capacity: 2,000; Year Built: 1949
AD: Timothy P. Millerick
SID: Jeff Kelly

AUSTIN PEAY
Clarksville, TN 37044-4576 I

Coach: Dave Loos, Memphis 1970

2006-07 RESULTS (21-12)
62	Dayton	78
35	Illinois	80
70	Arkansas St.	77
79	Tenn. Wesleyan ⊠	64
77	Tennessee Tech ⊠	70
66	Morehead St.	70
59	Eastern Ky.	57
63	Memphis	88
75	Evansville ⊠	80
64	Middle Tenn. ⊠	63
83	Marian (Ind.) ⊠	50
74	Tenn.-Martin ⊠	61
78	Jacksonville St.	63
81	Eastern Ill.	76
68	Southeast Mo. St. ⊠	67
68	Murray St. ⊠	59
75	Tenn.-Martin	60
73	Jacksonville St. ⊠	58
66	Samford ⊠	48
75	Southeast Mo. St.	73
68	Murray St.	77
62	Tennessee St.	53
98	Eastern Ill. ⊠	71
52	Samford	50
89	Tennessee St. ⊠	44
57	Akron	74
72	Tennessee Tech	73
77	Eastern Ky. ⊠	68
77	Morehead St. ⊠	82
89	Tennessee St. ⊠	84
65	Samford †	55
62	Eastern Ky. †	63
51	Air Force	75

Nickname: Governors
Colors: Red & White
Arena: Winfield Dunn Center
   Capacity: 7,875; Year Built: 1975
AD: Dave Loos
SID: Brad Kirtley

AVERETT
Danville, VA 24541 III

Coach: Jimmy Allen, Emory & Henry 1993

2006-07 RESULTS (20-7)
71	Oneonta St. †	55
79	Wash. & Lee	56
66	Hampden-Sydney	59
81	Va. Wesleyan ⊠	73
84	Lynchburg ⊠	77
79	Rust †	61
73	Piedmont †	67
85	Apprentice ⊠	68
88	Marymount (Va.) ⊠	72
69	Guilford ⊠	74
51	Richard Stockton †	57
66	Hobart †	73
77	Ferrum	69
55	Greensboro	79
61	Methodist	58
82	Shenandoah	86
75	Chris. Newport	79
81	N.C. Wesleyan ⊠	72
68	Ferrum	62
83	Greensboro ⊠	79
71	Methodist	52
74	Chris. Newport ⊠	73
60	Shenandoah ⊠	57
70	N.C. Wesleyan	53
76	Ferrum †	73
108	N.C. Wesleyan †	105
60	Va. Wesleyan	63

Nickname: Cougars
Colors: Navy & Gold
Arena: Grant Center
   Capacity: 2,500; Year Built: 1998
AD: Charles S. Harris
SID: Sam Ferguson

BABSON
Babson Park, MA 02457-0310 III

Coach: Steve Brennan, Bates 1987

2006-07 RESULTS (16-10)
75	Colby ⊠	78
84	Vassar ⊠	72
83	Emerson ⊠	70
68	Trinity (Conn.) ⊠	71
66	Brandeis ⊠	76
69	Newbury †	52
71	Norwich	64
75	Lasell ⊠	73
62	Bridgewater St. †	79
73	Sewanee †	61
70	Amherst	89
75	Wheaton (Mass.) ⊠	67
56	MIT	47
53	WPI	59
74	Clark (Mass.)	65
72	MIT ⊠	59
58	Springfield ⊠	64
74	Coast Guard	62
84	Tufts ⊠	76
60	Bowdoin	69
79	WPI ⊠	69
82	Wheaton (Mass.)	72
73	Clark (Mass.) ⊠	63
62	Coast Guard ⊠	61
67	Springfield	59
66	Coast Guard ⊠	70

Nickname: Beavers
Colors: Green & White
Arena: Staake Gymnasium
   Capacity: 1,000; Year Built: 1989
AD: Josh MacArthur
SID: Chris Buck

BALDWIN-WALLACE
Berea, OH 44017 III

Coach: Steve Bankson, Graceland (Iowa) 1963

2006-07 RESULTS (18-9)
110	Curry †	70
62	Alvernia	71
81	Oberlin ⊠	66
74	Olivet ⊠	71
85	Capital	93
94	Ohio Northern	77
65	Marietta	57
81	Mount Union ⊠	75
69	Linfield †	61
64	Edgewood †	72
72	Ramapo †	60
80	John Carroll	73
74	Muskingum	61
74	Otterbein	83
88	Wilmington (Ohio) ⊠	95
72	Heidelberg ⊠	75
81	Capital ⊠	78
84	Mount Union	66
74	Ohio Northern ⊠	83
93	Heidelberg ⊠	80
68	Wilmington (Ohio)	75
84	Otterbein	76
76	Muskingum ⊠	66
81	John Carroll ⊠	77
74	Marietta	68
95	Heidelberg ⊠	82
69	John Carroll †	76

Nickname: Yellow Jackets
Colors: Brown & Gold
Arena: Ursprung Gymnasium
Capacity: 2,800; Year Built: 1949
AD: Stephen Bankson
SID: Kevin Ruple

BALL ST.
Muncie, IN 47306 I

Coach: Ronny Thompson, Georgetown 1992

2006-07 RESULTS (9-22)
81	Northern Colo. ⊠	42
65	Prairie View ⊠	48
55	Chattanooga ⊠	70
46	Kansas ⊠	64
66	Western Ky. †	76
54	Georgetown	69
73	Indiana St. ⊠	70
41	Butler	65
56	Oklahoma St. †	75
61	Valparaiso ⊠	40
70	Temple ⊠	75
60	Tennessee St.	67
57	Indiana	71
60	Toledo ⊠	62
61	Western Mich.	74
52	Eastern Mich. ⊠	56
71	Northern Ill. ⊠	60
64	Central Mich.	57
54	Kent St. ⊠	60
69	Ohio ⊠	57
57	Bowling Green	67
52	Akron	70
79	Buffalo ⊠	73
44	Miami (Ohio)	66
57	Northern Ill.	55
57	Illinois St.	70
59	Central Mich. ⊠	61
51	Eastern Mich.	61
61	Toledo	71
67	Western Mich. ⊠	71
48	Eastern Mich. †	51

Nickname: Cardinals
Colors: Cardinal & White
Arena: Worthen Arena
Capacity: 11,500; Year Built: 1992
AD: Thomas J. Collins
SID: Chris Taylor

BAPTIST BIBLE (PA.)
Clarks Summit, PA 18411 III

Coach: Mike Show, Baptist Bible (Pa.) 1992

2006-07 RESULTS (18-8)
60	Marywood	53
55	Misericordia †	52
63	Chestnut Hill	80
55	Keystone	56
75	King's (Pa.)	80
81	Villa Julie ⊠	69
71	Rutgers-Camden	64
81	Lancaster Bible	83
67	Wilkes	83
70	Lincoln (Pa.)	84
82	Purchase St.	57
91	Cazenovia ⊠	86
95	Bard ⊠	68
56	Keuka ⊠	54
75	D'Youville	64
81	Keystone	57
80	Polytechnic (N.Y.) ⊠	65
89	Bard	57
86	Phila. Biblical	63
105	Cazenovia	88
86	Penn St.-Berks ⊠	57
69	D'Youville ⊠	55
89	Valley Forge Chrst. ⊠	68
93	Keuka	100
120	Cazenovia ⊠	101
71	Chestnut Hill †	79

Nickname: Defenders
Colors: Royal Blue & White
AD: James M. Huckaby
SID: Eryl Christiansen

BARD
Annandale-On-Hudson, NY 12504-5000 III

Coach: Chris Wood, Plymouth St. 1989

2006-07 RESULTS (3-22)
56	Anna Maria †	72
75	Johnson St. †	84
53	Mt. St. Mary (N.Y.) †	91
86	New Paltz St. †	108
60	Villa Julie	95
87	Cazenovia	99
54	Hartwick	81
66	Anna Maria ⊠	62
72	Newbury ⊠	75
47	LIFE Pacific	75
52	Caltech	81
74	Purchase St.	75
73	Polytechnic (N.Y.)	57
67	Keuka ⊠	71
68	Baptist Bible (Pa.)	95
64	D'Youville ⊠	53
70	Keystone	78
94	Cazenovia ⊠	109
86	Phila. Biblical ⊠	94
57	Baptist Bible (Pa.) ⊠	89
70	Penn St.-Berks	84
71	Chestnut Hill ⊠	100
80	Keystone ⊠	101
77	D'Youville	78
73	Keuka	89

Nickname: Raptors
Colors: White & Black
Arena: Stevenson Gym
Capacity: 850; Year Built: 1988
AD: Kristen E. Hall
SID: Scott Swere

BARRY
Miami Shores, FL 33161 II

Coach: Cesar Odio, Fla. Southern 1981

2006-07 RESULTS (23-7)
67	P.R.-Cayey ⊠	58
76	Valdosta St. †	82
71	North Ala. †	69
79	Palm Beach Atl.	75
78	Fla. Memorial	63
70	P.R.-Rio Piedras ⊠	57
62	Ala.-Huntsville	58
102	Wilmington (Del.) †	76
47	Washburn †	63
67	Fla. Memorial ⊠	61
55	Eckerd	52
60	Tampa ⊠	55
63	Nova Southeastern	69
86	Fla. Southern ⊠	63
71	Florida Tech	59
74	St. Leo ⊠	68
68	Lynn	62
38	Rollins	63
61	Nova Southeastern ⊠	50
62	Eckerd ⊠	47
65	Tampa	55
69	Palm Beach Atl. ⊠	58
68	Fla. Southern	58
80	Florida Tech ⊠	63
73	St. Leo	71
71	Lynn ⊠	68
47	Rollins ⊠	76
64	Lynn	61
59	Eckerd †	63
44	Henderson St. †	58

Nickname: Buccaneers
Colors: Red, Black & Silver
Arena: Health & Sports Center
Capacity: 1,500; Year Built: 1990
AD: Michael L. Covone
SID: Dennis Jezek, Jr.

BARTON
Wilson, NC 27893-7000 II

Coach: Ron Lievense, St. Thomas (Minn.) 1981

2006-07 RESULTS (31-5)
83	Elizabeth City St. ⊠	82
106	St. Augustine's †	102
65	N.C. Central	67
68	St. Andrews	55
77	Coker ⊠	70
94	Lees-McRae ⊠	66
74	Chowan ⊠	78
76	Catawba †	79
61	Lenoir-Rhyne	95
75	Erskine	68
122	Pfeiffer ⊠	97
98	Anderson (S.C.) ⊠	64
101	Queens (N.C.) ⊠	94
80	Mount Olive	73
80	Limestone	83
85	Belmont Abbey	72
68	Erskine ⊠	50
84	Coker	52
99	St. Andrews ⊠	88
82	Lees-McRae	58
94	Chowan	90
83	Anderson (S.C.)	73
86	Mount Olive ⊠	82
95	Queens (N.C.)	87
94	Belmont Abbey ⊠	67
114	Pfeiffer	99
88	Limestone	80
93	Belmont Abbey ⊠	82
86	Limestone †	81
92	Mount Olive †	80
85	Queens (N.C.) †	76
86	West Virginia St. ⊠	85
76	Millersville ⊠	65
83	Grand Valley St. †	81
80	Cal St. San B'dino †	79
77	Winona St. †	75

Nickname: Bulldogs
Colors: Royal Blue & White
Arena: Wilson Gym
Capacity: 2,500; Year Built: 1966
AD: Gary W. Hall
SID: John Hackney

BARUCH
New York, NY 10010-5585 III

Coach: Ray Rankis, Lehman 1976

2006-07 RESULTS (11-16)
74	Yeshiva ⊠	64
79	Polytechnic (N.Y.)	61
55	Methodist †	71
73	Brevard †	79
55	John Jay ⊠	48
65	Lehman	77
72	St. Mary's (Md.) ⊠	79
59	Ramapo ⊠	90
80	Clark (Mass.) †	81
60	Old Westbury †	71
66	Wheaton (Ill.) ⊠	75
59	CCNY	52
64	York (N.Y.) ⊠	78
63	City Tech	54
59	Brooklyn ⊠	52
51	Wm. Paterson	70
77	Staten Island ⊠	64
68	Medgar Evers	66
51	John Jay	68
96	Hunter ⊠	82
64	New Paltz St. ⊠	65
59	CCNY ⊠	62
58	Lehman ⊠	60
70	Hunter	67
69	Farmingdale St. ⊠	79
66	John Jay †	58
59	Staten Island †	68

Nickname: Bearcats
Colors: Navy Blue, Columbia Blue, White
Arena: Baruch College ARC Arena
Capacity: 1,200; Year Built: 2002
AD: William Eng
SID: John Neves

BATES
Lewiston, ME 04240 III

Coach: Joe Reilly, Trinity (Conn.) 1991

2006-07 RESULTS (18-7)
66	Western New Eng. †	59
77	Southern Vt. †	51
78	Southern Me. ⊠	55
91	Endicott ⊠	53
82	Colby	69
61	Bowdoin	60
76	Thomas (Me.)	54
76	Me.-Farmington ⊠	56
73	Elms †	56
81	Union (N.Y.)	66
90	New England ⊠	46
63	Trinity (Conn.) ⊠	68
64	Amherst ⊠	79
89	St. Joseph's (Me.)	80
70	Husson ⊠	55
72	Tufts ⊠	44
75	Emmanuel (Mass.) ⊠	57
59	Wesleyan (Conn.)	56
65	Connecticut Col.	82
54	Williams	67
81	Middlebury	48
82	Gordon	74
62	Colby ⊠	63
58	Bowdoin ⊠	66
68	Amherst	72

Nickname: Bobcats
Colors: Garnet
Arena: Alumni Gymnasium
Capacity: 750; Year Built: 1925
AD: Dana Mulholland
SID: Andy Walter

BAYLOR
Waco, TX 76798-7096 I

Coach: Scott Drew, Butler 1993

2006-07 RESULTS (15-16)

90	Angelo St. ⊠	65
87	Colorado St. †	82
69	Gonzaga †	78
74	Texas Southern ⊠	50
90	Alcorn St. ⊠	59
95	Grambling ⊠	69
89	Texas St. ⊠	64
59	South Carolina ⊠	64
71	Syracuse	94
103	Prairie View ⊠	61
91	N.C. A&T ⊠	71
59	Delaware St. ⊠	56
76	Centenary (La.) ⊠	63
77	Oklahoma St.	81
51	Texas A&M ⊠	61
73	Texas Tech	70
60	Kansas St.	69
51	Oklahoma	91
56	Kansas ⊠	82
79	Texas	84
97	Colorado ⊠	83
58	Iowa St.	71
64	Oklahoma ⊠	68
71	Missouri	78
67	Texas ⊠	68
63	Nebraska ⊠	59
87	Texas A&M	97
74	Texas Tech	85
86	Oklahoma St. ⊠	82
97	Missouri †	83
69	Texas †	74

Nickname: Bears
Colors: Green & Gold
Arena: Ferrell Center
    Capacity: 10,284; Year Built: 1988
AD: Ian McCaw
SID: Heath Nielsen

BECKER
Leicester, MA 01524 III

Coach: Ron Abegglen, BYU 1962

2006-07 RESULTS (3-22)

53	WPI ⊠	86
55	Worcester St. ⊠	79
62	Clark (Mass.) ⊠	82
75	Wentworth Inst.	90
76	Anna Maria ⊠	73
60	Lasell ⊠	70
48	Coast Guard	83
53	Maine Maritime	56
48	Husson	87
63	Fitchburg St.	72
40	Worcester St.	77
60	Thomas (Me.) ⊠	73
61	Me.-Farmington ⊠	96
65	Lesley	92
75	Elms	94
71	Nichols ⊠	95
69	Lesley ⊠	78
84	Johnson St. ⊠	73
76	Castleton ⊠	82
58	Lasell	84
69	Elms ⊠	88
102	Mitchell ⊠	98
73	Mount Ida	80
84	Castleton	95
72	Johnson St.	92

Nickname: Hawks
Colors: Royal Blue, White & Black
Arena: Leicester Gymnasium
    Capacity: 500; Year Built: 1972
AD: Frank Millerick/Craig Barnett
SID: Bettiann Michalik

BELLARMINE
Louisville, KY 40205-0671 II

Coach: Scott Davenport, Louisville 1978

2006-07 RESULTS (12-15)

82	S.C. Upstate	73
74	Limestone †	84
78	Northern Ky. ⊠	66
44	SIU Edwardsville ⊠	54
81	Quincy ⊠	67
63	St. Joseph's †	75
74	Ohio †	91
64	Louisville	76
88	Lindsay Wilson ⊠	67
82	California (Pa.) †	75
81	Gannon	65
66	Lewis	71
76	Wis.-Parkside ⊠	93
73	Mo.-St. Louis ⊠	53
85	Mo.-Rolla ⊠	72
80	Southern Ind.	88
75	Ky. Wesleyan ⊠	61
73	St. Joseph's (Ind.) ⊠	64
64	Indianapolis ⊠	66
72	Rockhurst	75
67	Drury ⊠	81
71	Wis.-Parkside ⊠	63
99	Lewis ⊠	103
72	Ky. Wesleyan ⊠	69
82	Northern Ky.	91
68	Indianapolis	71
74	St. Joseph's (Ind.)	81

Nickname: Knights
Colors: Scarlet & Silver
Arena: Knights Hall
    Capacity: 3,000; Year Built: 1960
AD: Scott Wiegandt
SID: Nels Popp

BELMONT
Nashville, TN 37212-3757 I

Coach: Rick Byrd, Tennessee 1976

2006-07 RESULTS (23-10)

83	UNC Wilmington †	88
56	Fordham †	49
67	IUPUI	61
83	Fisk ⊠	54
57	Middle Tenn.	64
87	North Fla. ⊠	32
76	Jacksonville ⊠	62
76	IUPUI ⊠	66
72	Ark.-Little Rock	57
51	Illinois	77
58	Michigan St.	67
87	Rice †	85
60	St. Mary's (Cal.)	71
75	East Tenn. St.	74
63	Kennesaw St.	45
72	Mercer ⊠	47
73	Stetson ⊠	71
50	Lipscomb ⊠	55
67	Campbell	79
70	Gardner-Webb	54
70	East Tenn. St. ⊠	80
85	Kennesaw St. ⊠	66
62	Stetson	58
84	Mercer	77
60	Lipscomb	70
87	Gardner-Webb ⊠	55
92	Campbell ⊠	68
86	Jacksonville	71
74	North Fla.	54
79	Gardner-Webb †	61
79	Campbell †	63
94	East Tenn. St. †	67
55	Georgetown †	80

Nickname: Bruins
Colors: Red, White & Navy Blue
Arena: Curb Event Center
    Capacity: 5,000; Year Built: 2003
AD: Michael D. Strickland
SID: Greg Sage

BELMONT ABBEY
Belmont, NC 28012-1802 II

Coach: Dale Kuhl, Tiffin 1992

2006-07 RESULTS (8-20)

76	Shaw ⊠	79
84	Concord ⊠	81
75	Erskine ⊠	72
72	Lenoir-Rhyne ⊠	84
70	Carson-Newman	82
71	Pfeiffer	96
66	Anderson (S.C.)	70
64	Chowan	81
57	Limestone ⊠	67
76	Lees-McRae ⊠	64
63	St. Andrews	66
64	Coker ⊠	55
62	Mount Olive	81
80	North Greenville	87
68	Queens (N.C.)	70
72	Barton	85
110	Pfeiffer ⊠	107
59	Erskine	77
51	Coker	54
84	Lees-McRae	91
96	Limestone	91
82	St. Andrews ⊠	78
67	Barton	94
49	Anderson (S.C.) ⊠	52
69	Mount Olive ⊠	88
69	Queens (N.C.) ⊠	84
73	Lees-McRae ⊠	72
82	Barton	93

Nickname: Crusaders
Colors: Red & White
Arena: The Wheeler Center
    Capacity: 2,500; Year Built: 1971
AD: Eliane Kebbe
SID: Chris Poore

BELOIT
Beloit, WI 53511-5595 III

Coach: Cecil Youngblood, Augustana (Ill.) 1976

2006-07 RESULTS (4-19)

55	Milwaukee Engr.	62
52	Augustana (Ill.)	69
51	Wis.-Whitewater	76
58	Lake Forest ⊠	66
72	Illinois Col. ⊠	71
59	Carroll (Wis.)	103
48	Carthage ⊠	60
89	Judson (Ill.) ⊠	90
55	Elmhurst	70
61	Aurora	72
61	St. Norbert ⊠	54
57	Lawrence	69
73	Monmouth (Ill.)	80
79	Grinnell	98
79	Knox ⊠	63
74	Monmouth (Ill.) ⊠	67
77	Ripon ⊠	81
63	Carroll (Wis.) ⊠	70
52	Lake Forest	71
47	Illinois Col.	60
47	St. Norbert	76
62	Lawrence ⊠	74
60	Ripon	82

Nickname: Buccaneers
Colors: Navy Blue & Gold
Arena: Flood Arena
    Capacity: 2,250; Year Built: 1986
AD: Kim Chandler
SID: Keith Domke

BEMIDJI ST.
Bemidji, MN 56601-2699 II

Coach: Matt Bowen, Indiana 1995

2006-07 RESULTS (5-23)

59	Minn. Duluth	90
58	Alas. Anchorage	79
42	Alas. Anchorage	88
49	Wis.-Stout ⊠	67
48	Augustana (S.D.) ⊠	68
50	St. Cloud St. ⊠	80
68	Wayne St. (Neb.) ⊠	81
45	Southwest Minn. St.	87
49	North Dakota	94
55	Concordia-St. Paul ⊠	72
61	Minn. St. Moorhead ⊠	72
56	North Dakota ⊠	79
69	Wis.-Superior ⊠	75
64	Minn.-Crookston ⊠	62
48	Mary	76
51	Northern St.	87
37	Winona St. ⊠	82
53	Upper Iowa ⊠	51
54	Southwest Minn. St. ⊠	63
66	Wayne St. (Neb.) ⊠	59
56	Minn. St. Moorhead	70
68	Concordia-St. Paul	75
67	Minn.-Crookston ⊠	63
57	Northern St. ⊠	61
50	Mary ⊠	70
60	Upper Iowa	59
60	Winona St.	76
43	Southwest Minn. St.	86

Nickname: Beavers
Colors: Kelly Green & White
Arena: BSU Gymnasium
    Capacity: 2,000; Year Built: 1959
AD: Rick Goeb
SID: Brad Folestad

BENEDICT
Columbia, SC 29204 II

Coach: Freddrell Watson, Benedict 1998

2006-07 RESULTS (25-5)

63	Livingstone	59
64	Augusta St. ⊠	70
84	Lane	80
78	Kentucky St.	65
81	Lincoln Memorial ⊠	68
76	Miles	64
89	LeMoyne-Owen ⊠	74
81	Morehouse ⊠	69
62	Clark Atlanta ⊠	53
50	Claflin	44
56	Lane ⊠	54
84	Kentucky St. ⊠	63
70	Albany St. (Ga.)	68
73	Fort Valley St.	70
73	Miles ⊠	62
78	LeMoyne-Owen ⊠	76
53	Paine ⊠	72
51	Claflin ⊠	40
72	Tuskegee ⊠	70
59	Stillman ⊠	50
68	Morehouse	66
78	Clark Atlanta	46
71	Paine	59
76	Tuskegee	72
64	Stillman	61
77	Albany St. (Ga.) ⊠	70
56	Fort Valley St. ⊠	60
84	Lane †	58
64	Albany St. (Ga.) †	73
56	Eckerd †	66

Nickname: Tigers
Colors: Purple & Gold
Arena: Benjamin E. Mays Arena
Capacity: 3,500
AD: Willie Washington
SID: Derrick Johnson

BENEDICTINE (ILL.)
Lisle, IL 60532-0900............................III

Coach: Keith Bunkenburg, Benedictine (Ill.) 1989

2006-07 RESULTS (12-14)

84	Grace Bible (Mich.) †	63
60	Calvin	79
58	Wheaton (Ill.) ⊠	70
65	Kalamazoo	78
78	Concordia (Ill.)	67
74	Rockford ⊠	54
89	Concordia (Wis.)	69
66	Lakeland	74
54	North Central (Ill.) ⊠	74
82	Cornell College ⊠	88
78	Coe	77
72	Wis. Lutheran	71
59	Maranatha Baptist ⊠	42
66	Marian (Wis.)	57
63	Dominican (Ill.) ⊠	46
49	Edgewood	65
64	Concordia (Ill.) ⊠	72
79	Aurora	83
64	Rockford	57
62	Concordia (Wis.) ⊠	60
65	Lakeland	66
62	Wis. Lutheran ⊠	84
74	Maranatha Baptist	64
60	Marian (Wis.) ⊠	68
58	Edgewood	64
43	Dominican (Ill.)	60

Nickname: Eagles
Colors: Red & White
Arena: Dan & Ada Rice Center
 Capacity: 2,000; Year Built: 1976
AD:
SID: Dave Beyer

BENTLEY
Waltham, MA 02154-4705 II

Coach: Jay Lawson, New Hampshire 1979

2006-07 RESULTS (32-1)

69	Adelphi	43
71	NYIT †	42
70	C.W. Post	60
78	Southern Conn. St. ⊠	61
69	Mass.-Lowell	47
79	American Int'l	53
72	Assumption	65
61	Bryant ⊠	49
80	Stonehill	72
72	Merrimack	37
78	St. Michael's ⊠	74
81	New Haven ⊠	62
81	Southern Conn. St.	58
84	Southern N.H. ⊠	64
77	Franklin Pierce ⊠	65
67	Le Moyne	57
74	St. Anselm ⊠	45
65	St. Rose	54
65	Pace	62
88	Merrimack ⊠	71
78	Bryant	76
83	St. Michael's	59
68	Stonehill ⊠	51
87	American Int'l ⊠	56
65	Mass.-Lowell ⊠	47
82	Assumption	71
77	St. Anselm	43
85	Bryant ⊠	74
71	St. Rose ⊠	61
59	Caldwell ⊠	56
60	Bridgeport ⊠	45
63	Bryant ⊠	54
51	Winona St. †	64

Nickname: Falcons
Colors: Blue & Gold
Arena: Charles Dana PE Center
 Capacity: 2,600; Year Built: 1973
AD: Robert DeFelice
SID: Dick Lipe

BETHANY (W.V.)
Bethany, WV 26032-0417 III

Coach: Aaron Huffman, West Virginia 1997

2006-07 RESULTS (19-9)

91	Penn St.-Altoona †	87
64	Juniata	76
90	Pitt.-Greensburg	70
87	West Liberty St.	110
109	Ohio-Eastern †	80
98	Franciscan	62
77	Carnegie Mellon ⊠	78
78	Thiel ⊠	76
86	Penn St.-Altoona	64
62	Marietta	55
123	Mt. Aloysius ⊠	105
74	Lake Erie	79
75	Grove City	63
70	Thomas More	64
82	Wash. & Jeff. ⊠	73
102	Waynesburg	80
82	Westminster (Pa.) ⊠	96
107	St. Vincent	105
75	Thiel	72
74	Thomas More ⊠	65
58	Grove City	72
80	Waynesburg ⊠	68
79	Wash. & Jeff.	76
76	St. Vincent ⊠	73
90	Westminster (Pa.)	102
94	Thiel	80
75	Wash. & Jeff. ⊠	78
62	Juniata	72

Nickname: Bison
Colors: Kelly Green & White
Arena: Hummel Field House
 Capacity: 800; Year Built: 1948
AD: Kosmas Mouratidis
SID: Brian Rose

BETHANY LUTHERAN
Mankato, MN 56001 III

Coach: Rick Jeddeloh

2006-07 RESULTS (14-12)

96	Central (Iowa) ⊠	92
56	Whitworth †	68
73	Lewis & Clark †	96
83	Concordia (Cal.) †	109
84	Augsburg	93
77	Minn. St. Mankato	93
78	Martin Luther	62
74	Wis.-River Falls	96
79	Clarke ⊠	67
72	Luther	86
87	Gust. Adolphus ⊠	85
100	Crown (Minn.) ⊠	61
80	Minn.-Morris ⊠	69
65	Presentation	68
99	Crown (Minn.)	55
72	Northwestern (Minn.)	92
86	Northland ⊠	65
68	St. Scholastica ⊠	60
82	St. Scholastica	76
81	Northland	53
67	Presentation	56
78	Minn.-Morris	60
59	Northwestern (Minn.) ⊠	69
74	Martin Luther ⊠	68
70	St. Scholastica †	72
78	Bethel (Ind.) †	91

Nickname: Vikings
Colors: Red, white & black
Arena: Sports & Fitness Center
 Capacity: 1,000
AD: Karl Fager
SID: To be named

BETHEL (MINN.)
St. Paul, MN 55112-6999................III

Coach: Jeff Westlund, Bethel 1983

2006-07 RESULTS (18-8)

113	Dakota St. ⊠	83
107	Wis.-River Falls ⊠	77
111	Minn.-Morris ⊠	84
68	Crown (Minn.) ⊠	62
93	Hamline	89
77	Gust. Adolphus ⊠	78
62	Carleton ⊠	66
85	Martin Luther	73
77	St. John's (Minn.)	81
86	St. Thomas (Minn.) ⊠	91
65	St. Olaf	75
95	Concordia-M'head ⊠	83
87	Macalester	73
71	St. Mary's (Minn.)	58
93	Augsburg ⊠	83
83	Hamline ⊠	68
72	Gust. Adolphus	66
67	Carleton	63
83	St. John's (Minn.) ⊠	71
67	St. Thomas (Minn.)	89
85	St. Olaf ⊠	76
86	Concordia-M'head	71
105	Macalester ⊠	96
103	St. Mary's (Minn.) ⊠	57
82	Augsburg	87
79	St. Olaf ⊠	81

Nickname: Royals
Colors: Blue & Gold
Arena: Robertson PE Center
 Capacity: 2,000; Year Built: 1971
AD: Robert Bjorklund
SID: Dan Berglund

BETHUNE-COOKMAN
Daytona Beach, FL 32114-3099.....I

Coach: Clifford Reed, Bethune-Cookman 1991

2006-07 RESULTS (9-21)

67	Florida Tech ⊠	59
46	UCF	81
80	Warner Southern ⊠	72
73	Florida A&M	83
49	Oregon St.	72
64	Oregon	92
36	Southern California	88
65	Cal St. Fullerton	94
49	Savannah St.	52
49	South Fla.	82
58	Coppin St.	66
55	Hampton	59
65	Norfolk St. ⊠	68
57	N.C. A&T	52
56	South Carolina St. ⊠	68
60	Howard	63
59	Md.-East. Shore	57
48	Winston-Salem	56
46	Delaware St. ⊠	62
45	Hampton	67
52	Norfolk St.	66
58	N.C. A&T	55
46	South Carolina St.	44
54	Howard ⊠	56
49	Md.-East. Shore †	48
47	Savannah St. ⊠	42
40	Delaware St.	47
52	Morgan St. ⊠	50
62	Florida A&M ⊠	68
44	Coppin St.	56

Nickname: Wildcats
Colors: Maroon & Gold
Arena: Moore Gymnasium
 Capacity: 3,000; Year Built: 1953
AD: Lynn W. Thompson
SID: Bryan J. Harvey

BINGHAMTON
Binghamton, NY 13902-6000........I

Coach: Al Walker, Brockport St. 1981

2006-07 RESULTS (13-16)

59	Long Island	73
74	Niagara	66
66	Mt. St. Mary's ⊠	59
57	Cornell ⊠	56
70	Colgate	78
65	Rider ⊠	79
55	Akron ⊠	90
91	Long Island ⊠	80
79	North Fla.	61
79	Miami (Fla.)	74
83	Pepperdine †	90
78	Alcorn St. †	65
71	UMBC ⊠	73
83	Albany (N.Y.) ⊠	72
55	Stony Brook	67
49	Boston U. ⊠	61
64	Maine	69
57	Hartford	55
72	New Hampshire ⊠	75
61	Vermont ⊠	65
48	UMBC	51
66	Stony Brook ⊠	65
62	Albany (N.Y.)	65
54	Boston U.	66
67	Maine ⊠	40
61	Vermont	71
66	New Hampshire	37
55	Hartford ⊠	53
58	Boston U.	62

Nickname: Bearcats
Colors: Green & Black
Arena: Events Center
 Capacity: 5,142; Year Built: 2004
AD: Joel Thirer
SID: John Hartrick

BLACKBURN
Carlinville, IL 62626 III

Coach: Kirk Chandler, Elon 1981

2006-07 RESULTS (10-15)

57	Dominican (Ill.) ⊠	52
66	Concordia (Ill.) ⊠	60
43	Washington-St. Louis	78
57	Rose-Hulman ⊠	74
70	Robert Morris-S'fiel ⊠	73
75	Greenville ⊠	88
72	Eureka ⊠	81
74	Millikin	81
68	Mo.-St. Louis	80
78	Fontbonne ⊠	97
65	Maryville (Mo.)	59
71	Webster	70
75	Principia ⊠	64
74	MacMurray	89
62	Westminster (Mo.) ⊠	48
78	Lincoln Christian	89
74	Greenville	70
76	Eureka	81
75	Fontbonne	93
77	Principia	53
55	Maryville (Mo.) ⊠	54
75	Webster	84
75	MacMurray ⊠	76
62	Westminster (Mo.)	65
77	Lincoln Christian ⊠	50

Nickname: Battlin' Beavers
Colors: Scarlet & Black
Arena: Dawes Gymnasium
 Capacity: 500; Year Built: 1938
AD: Curtis Campbell
SID: Tom Emery

BLOOMFIELD

Bloomfield, NJ 07003 II

Coach: Gerald Holmes, NJIT 1987

2006-07 RESULTS (10-17)

68	West Chester	84
68	Shippensburg †	86
60	Adelphi	75
71	Caldwell †	74
68	Dowling †	65
78	Mercy †	75
69	Philadelphia U. ⊠	102
64	Goldey-Beacom	81
69	Phila. Sciences	73
81	Dominican (N.Y.) ⊠	78
69	Queens (N.Y.) †	87
80	Mercy †	87
86	Felician	93
91	Holy Family	94
95	Post	96
96	Wilmington (Del.) ⊠	85
74	Caldwell ⊠	83
78	Goldey-Beacom ⊠	74
67	Nyack	78
83	Dominican (N.Y.)	93
64	Philadelphia U.	90
76	Phila. Sciences	67
80	Wilmington (Del.)	79
99	Felician	93
85	Post ⊠	79
78	Nyack ⊠	69
88	Holy Family ⊠	91

Nickname: Deacons
Colors: Maroon & Gold
Arena: Bloomfield College Gymnasium
Capacity: 450; Year Built: 1958
AD: Sheila Wooten
SID: Gladstone Harris

BLOOMSBURG

Bloomsburg, PA 17815 II

Coach: John Sanow, Indiana (Pa.) 1987

2006-07 RESULTS (13-14)

70	Penn St.-Hazleton ⊠	56
64	Seton Hill †	54
84	Wilmington (Del.) †	61
60	Davis & Elkins ⊠	53
70	Indiana (Pa.) ⊠	67
67	Clarion ⊠	65
50	Dist. Columbia ⊠	56
54	Shippensburg	70
69	Lock Haven	80
61	California (Pa.)	71
72	Cheyney ⊠	80
62	Slippery Rock ⊠	60
63	Edinboro ⊠	73
47	Millersville	73
70	Kutztown	73
70	Penn St.-Hazleton	62
77	East Stroudsburg ⊠	75
73	Dist. Columbia	76
82	West Chester ⊠	85
82	Mansfield	85
61	Cheyney	100
76	Millersville ⊠	84
82	Kutztown ⊠	80
71	East Stroudsburg	69
82	Pitt.-Johnstown	88
75	West Chester	69
89	Mansfield ⊠	85

Nickname: Huskies
Colors: Maroon & Gold
Arena: E.H. Nelson Fieldhouse
Capacity: 2,000; Year Built: 1972
AD: Mary Gardner
SID: Tom McGuire

BLUEFIELD ST.

Bluefield, WV 24701-2198 II

Coach: Donald Jones, Bluefield St.

2006-07 RESULTS (10-19)

84	Fayetteville St. ⊠	78
59	Johnson C. Smith	89
56	St. Paul's †	78
77	Livingstone ⊠	73
79	Concord	70
77	Johnson C. Smith ⊠	68
89	Bluefield Col.	94
64	Fayetteville St.	76
63	Charleston (W.V.) ⊠	75
62	Alderson-Broaddus ⊠	66
75	West Virginia St.	98
92	Glenville St. ⊠	80
79	Concord	103
57	West Va. Wesleyan ⊠	53
73	Charleston (W.V.)	81
67	Fairmont St. ⊠	78
60	Shepherd	80
65	Wheeling Jesuit ⊠	74
81	West Liberty St.	115
70	Davis & Elkins ⊠	68
79	West Va. Wesleyan	77
73	Ohio Valley	62
78	West Virginia St. ⊠	103
67	Salem Int'l	77
71	Livingstone	84
75	Glenville St.	76
73	Concord ⊠	108
71	Wheeling Jesuit	69
61	West Virginia St. †	87

Nickname: Big Blues
Colors: Blue & Gold
Arena: Ned Shott Gymnasium
Capacity: 1,500; Year Built: 1969
AD: Terry W. Brown
SID: TBA

BLUFFTON

Bluffton, OH 45817-2104 III

Coach: Guy Neal, Bowling Green 1982

2006-07 RESULTS (18-8)

81	Cardinal Stritch †	65
49	North Central (Ill.) †	63
81	Earlham	68
79	Goshen ⊠	73
75	Heidelberg ⊠	73
94	Hiram	74
82	Franklin ⊠	74
103	Defiance ⊠	93
54	Rose-Hulman	49
69	Carnegie Mellon	65
94	Wright St.-Lake	59
76	Cincinnati-Clermont ⊠	74
95	Transylvania ⊠	92
73	Anderson (Ind.)	77
62	Manchester	72
94	Hanover ⊠	83
85	Mt. St. Joseph	88
76	Franklin	93
62	Rose-Hulman ⊠	53
72	Defiance	70
77	Anderson (Ind.) ⊠	68
82	Manchester ⊠	79
65	Transylvania	75
66	Mt. St. Joseph ⊠	65
68	Hanover	82
66	Transylvania †	78

Nickname: Beavers
Colors: Royal Purple and White
Arena: Founders Hall
Capacity: 1,500; Year Built: 1952
AD: Phill Talavinia
SID: Bill Hanefeld Jr.

BOISE ST.

Boise, ID 83725-1020 I

Coach: Greg Graham, Oregon 1978

2006-07 RESULTS (17-14)

79	Wyoming	94
77	Southern Utah ⊠	68
50	Colorado St.	67
63	Washington St.	65
72	BYU ⊠	68
58	Montana	62
94	Montana St. ⊠	69
84	Cal St. Northridge ⊠	75
99	Sacramento St. ⊠	66
82	Loyola Marymount	84
54	Idaho St. ⊠	45
77	Utah St. ⊠	66
86	Nevada	90
82	Louisiana Tech ⊠	56
69	New Mexico St. ⊠	73
79	Utah St	80
73	Hawaii ⊠	62
65	Fresno St. ⊠	61
75	Idaho	57
68	New Mexico St.	78
76	Louisiana Tech	84
86	Idaho ⊠	63
65	San Jose St.	64
101	Montana Western ⊠	65
83	Albany (N.Y.) ⊠	82
83	San Jose St. ⊠	64
81	Nevada ⊠	95
77	Fresno St.	78
75	Hawaii	92
78	Fresno St. †	73
69	New Mexico St.	88

Nickname: Broncos
Colors: Blue & Orange
Arena: Taco Bell Arena
Capacity: 12,380; Year Built: 1982
AD: Gene Bleymaier
SID: Todd Miles

BOSTON COLLEGE

Chestnut Hill, MA 02467-3861 I

Coach: Al Skinner, Massachusetts 1974

2006-07 RESULTS (21-12)

86	New Hampshire ⊠	47
63	Vermont ⊠	77
64	Providence	73
86	Rhode Island ⊠	68
65	Michigan St. ⊠	58
84	Massachusetts	73
75	Fairfield ⊠	52
73	Maryland ⊠	62
101	Sacred Heart ⊠	68
66	Kansas	84
93	Duquesne ⊠	98
87	Northeastern ⊠	82
72	Yale ⊠	56
74	North Carolina St.	58
95	Wake Forest	85
78	Virginia ⊠	73
82	Miami (Fla.) ⊠	63
54	Clemson	74
85	Florida St. ⊠	82
61	Duke	79
94	Hartford ⊠	60
80	Virginia Tech ⊠	59
75	Miami (Fla.)	80
68	Florida St.	67
70	Duke ⊠	78
72	North Carolina ⊠	77
62	Virginia Tech.	79
59	Clemson ⊠	54
60	Georgia Tech	74
74	Miami (Fla.) †	71
56	North Carolina †	71
84	Texas Tech †	75
55	Georgetown †	62

Nickname: Eagles
Colors: Maroon & Gold
Arena: Silvio O. Conte Forum

Capacity: 8,606; Year Built: 1988
AD: Gene DeFilippo
SID: Chris Cameron

BOSTON U.

Boston, MA 02215 I

Coach: Dennis Wolff, Connecticut 1978

2006-07 RESULTS (12-18)

57	George Washington ⊠	70
78	Harvard	74
60	Rider ⊠	66
54	Northeastern	73
74	Manhattan	65
39	St. Joseph's	55
74	St. Bonaventure	46
54	Massachusetts ⊠	56
51	Rhode Island	65
44	St. John's (N.Y.)	45
53	St. Joseph's †	58
70	Holy Cross ⊠	73
75	Hartford	80
65	Maine ⊠	63
61	Binghamton	49
53	New Hampshire ⊠	29
62	Stony Brook	68
59	UMBC ⊠	53
50	Albany (N.Y.) ⊠	52
66	Maine	55
59	Hartford ⊠	51
63	Vermont	72
66	Binghamton ⊠	54
55	New Hampshire	60
68	Stony Brook ⊠	55
63	UMBC	67
55	Vermont ⊠	57
63	Albany (N.Y.)	73
62	Binghamton ⊠	58
49	Albany (N.Y.) ⊠	59

Nickname: Terriers
Colors: Scarlet & White
Arena: Case Gym
Capacity: 1,800; Year Built: 1971
AD: Michael P. Lynch
SID: Megan Bradshaw

BOWDOIN

Brunswick, ME 04011 III

Coach: Tim Gilbride, Providence 1974

2006-07 RESULTS (15-10)

64	Salem St. ⊠	74
104	Me.-Fort Kent †	54
81	New England	75
84	Thomas (Me.)	63
68	Southern Me. ⊠	36
60	Bates ⊠	61
82	Colby-Sawyer	78
67	Colby	68
65	Plymouth St.	64
61	Me.-Farmington	57
64	Williams	69
58	Middlebury	81
71	Clark (Mass.) ⊠	66
74	Connecticut Col. ⊠	46
61	Wesleyan (Conn.) ⊠	63
72	Maine Maritime	47
75	Trinity (Conn.) ⊠	69
55	Amherst ⊠	73
69	Babson	60
67	Colby	81
98	Me.-Presque Isle ⊠	45
84	Tufts	94
66	Bates	58
87	St. Joseph's (Me.)	83
67	Trinity (Conn.)	77

Nickname: Polar Bears
Colors: White
Arena: Morrell Gymnasium
Capacity: 2,000; Year Built: 1965
AD: Jeffrey H. Ward
SID: Jim Caton

BOWIE ST.
Bowie, MD 20715-9465 II

Coach: Luke D'Alessio, Catholic 1983

2006-07 RESULTS (19-10)

90	Salem Int'l ⊠	73
89	Dowling ⊠	77
90	Livingstone ⊠	78
42	Virginia Union †	87
111	St. Paul's	75
122	Mansfield ⊠	117
80	St. Augustine's ⊠	87
84	St. Cloud St. ⊠	77
76	Virginia St.	84
85	N.C. Central ⊠	64
79	Fayetteville St.	70
92	Shaw ⊠	64
53	Johnson C. Smith	81
79	Livingstone	83
92	Virginia Union ⊠	70
99	Johnson C. Smith ⊠	88
109	Elizabeth City St. ⊠	101
72	Fayetteville St. ⊠	64
116	St. Augustine's	104
86	Shaw	68
75	N.C. Central	80
95	St. Paul's ⊠	106
74	Elizabeth City St.	77
113	Columbia Union	82
69	Virginia St. ⊠	75
92	Columbia Union ⊠	48
82	Shaw †	65
68	Johnson C. Smith †	62
54	Elizabeth City St. †	59

Nickname: Bulldogs
Colors: Black & Gold
Arena: A.C. Jordan Arena
   Capacity: 2,200; Year Built: 1973
AD: Derek Carter
SID: Gregory C. Goings

BOWLING GREEN
Bowling Green, OH 43403 I

Coach: Dan Dakich, Indiana 1985

2006-07 RESULTS (13-18)

89	Denison ⊠	52
54	Arkansas St.	64
59	Furman ⊠	63
65	South Ala. ⊠	64
71	Troy ⊠	69
81	Arkansas St. ⊠	72
58	Central Ark. ⊠	72
59	Wright St.	56
63	Northern Colo. ⊠	53
79	Marshall	78
58	Michigan Tech †	46
77	Jacksonville St. †	69
62	Green Bay	65
74	Buffalo ⊠	73
49	Ohio	67
62	Akron ⊠	83
60	Miami (Ohio)	66
61	Kent St.	62
63	Western Mich. ⊠	72
68	Central Mich.	71
67	Ball St. ⊠	57
48	Toledo	64
51	Northern Ill.	73
63	Eastern Mich. ⊠	65
90	Buffalo	98
90	Morehead St.	72
63	Ohio ⊠	88
87	Akron	93
64	Kent St. ⊠	77
68	Miami (Ohio) ⊠	64
59	Ohio †	69

Nickname: Falcons
Colors: Orange & Brown
Arena: Anderson Arena
   Capacity: 4,700; Year Built: 1960
AD: Greg Christopher
SID: J.D. Campbell

BRADLEY
Peoria, IL 61625 I

Coach: Jim Les, Bradley 1986

2006-07 RESULTS (22-13)

78	DePaul ⊠	58
74	SIU Edwardsville ⊠	58
81	Ill.-Chicago ⊠	72
107	Florida A&M ⊠	75
101	Rutgers †	72
71	Illinois †	75
84	Tennessee Tech	86
53	Michigan St.	82
88	Wright St. ⊠	49
76	Iowa St. †	66
82	Loyola (Ill.)	73
83	Southern Miss. ⊠	73
65	UNI	76
85	Evansville	78
78	Missouri St. ⊠	86
63	Wichita St.	84
89	Drake	86
48	Southern Ill. ⊠	46
76	Indiana St.	59
54	Creighton	65
78	Wichita St. ⊠	63
88	Illinois St. ⊠	67
70	Missouri St.	85
71	Creighton ⊠	82
70	Illinois St.	62
50	Southern Ill.	60
100	Drake ⊠	85
72	Evansville	71
73	VCU	64
70	UNI ⊠	79
74	Indiana St. ⊠	58
51	UNI †	48
51	Southern Ill. †	53
90	Providence	78
72	Mississippi St.	101

Nickname: Braves
Colors: Red & White
Arena: Carver Arena
   Capacity: 11,164; Year Built: 1982
AD: Kenneth E. Kavanagh
SID: Bobby Parker

BRANDEIS
Waltham, MA 02454-9110 III

Coach: Brian Meehan, Clark (Mass.)
1986

2006-07 RESULTS (20-7)

73	Newbury ⊠	60
90	Springfield ⊠	63
87	Suffolk ⊠	60
99	Tufts ⊠	89
76	Babson	66
62	Mass.-Dartmouth ⊠	47
87	Framingham St. ⊠	57
74	Elms ⊠	59
66	Clark (Mass.) ⊠	51
74	Amherst	84
81	Curry	73
65	Rochester (N.Y.)	83
68	Carnegie Mellon	75
52	New York U. ⊠	48
85	Case Reserve ⊠	68
74	Emory ⊠	50
64	Washington-St. Louis	68
76	Chicago	88
69	Chicago ⊠	74
81	Washington-St. Louis ⊠	75
75	Carnegie Mellon ⊠	52
73	Rochester (N.Y.) ⊠	66
76	Emory	67
56	Case Reserve	51
76	New York U.	67
77	Trinity (Conn.) †	70
67	Rhode Island Col.	70

Nickname: Judges
Colors: Blue & White
Arena: Auerbach Arena
   Capacity: 2,500; Year Built: 1992

AD: Sheryl Sousa
SID: Adam Levin

BRIDGEPORT
Bridgeport, CT 06601 II

Coach: Mike Ruane, Alvernia 1992

2006-07 RESULTS (22-9)

70	Post ⊠	67
56	Holy Family ⊠	53
74	C.W. Post ⊠	82
81	New Haven ⊠	69
68	St. Rose ⊠	64
85	Molloy ⊠	73
77	Merrimack †	70
57	Bryant	64
69	St. Thomas Aquinas	60
74	Southern N.H.	68
83	Queens (N.Y.) ⊠	67
58	NYIT	66
88	Concordia (N.Y.) ⊠	79
76	Adelphi	71
58	Mercy	63
69	Dowling	42
80	C.W. Post ⊠	75
60	New Haven ⊠	49
92	Molloy	95
53	St. Thomas Aquinas ⊠	57
72	Queens (N.Y.)	86
68	NYIT ⊠	62
62	Concordia (N.Y.)	46
63	Adelphi ⊠	60
82	Phila. Sciences	71
69	Mercy ⊠	66
76	Dowling ⊠	55
74	Molloy ⊠	64
60	C.W. Post ⊠	63
67	Philadelphia U. †	65
45	Bentley	60

Nickname: Purple Knights
Colors: Purple & White
Arena: Harvey Hubbell Gym
   Capacity: 2,000; Year Built: 1963
AD: Jay Moran
SID: Courtney Nogas

BRIDGEWATER (VA.)
Bridgewater, VA 22812-1599........ III

Coach: Bill Leatherman, Milligan 1966

2006-07 RESULTS (10-17)

78	Southern Va. †	62
93	Lancaster Bible †	63
93	Valley Forge Chrst. ⊠	52
52	Greensboro ⊠	68
57	Va. Wesleyan ⊠	82
90	East. Mennonite ⊠	77
69	Marietta †	72
67	Olivet †	72
88	Hampden-Sydney	91
60	Lynchburg	66
74	Wash. & Lee ⊠	81
63	Randolph-Macon ⊠	64
95	VMI	125
66	Guilford	70
93	Emory & Henry	115
59	Roanoke	64
61	Hampden-Sydney ⊠	58
83	Lynchburg ⊠	62
46	Va. Wesleyan	85
60	East. Mennonite	69
65	Randolph-Macon	63
52	Guilford ⊠	74
106	Emory & Henry ⊠	96
43	Roanoke ⊠	60
48	Wash. & Lee	46
88	Guilford †	78
62	Roanoke	87

Nickname: Eagles
Colors: Cardinal & Vegas Gold
Arena: Nininger Hall
   Capacity: 1,200; Year Built: 1957
AD: Curtis L. Kendall
SID: Steve Cox

BRIDGEWATER ST.
Bridgewater, MA 02325-9998......III

Coach: Joe Farroba, Boston St. 1976

2006-07 RESULTS (17-8)

66	St. Joseph's (Me.) ⊠	49
75	Salve Regina ⊠	62
61	WPI ⊠	75
69	Mass.-Dartmouth ⊠	66
88	Wheaton (Mass.)	77
82	Plymouth St. ⊠	73
79	Babson †	62
71	Keene St. †	80
80	Rhode Island Col.	88
73	Westfield St. ⊠	58
72	Endicott	74
82	Framingham St.	63
82	Mass. Liberal Arts ⊠	73
74	Mass.-Boston	71
62	Worcester St. ⊠	53
72	Salem St.	87
62	Fitchburg St.	54
75	Westfield St.	74
82	Western Conn. St. ⊠	76
95	Framingham St. ⊠	97
78	Mass. Liberal Arts	73
79	Worcester St.	71
72	Salem St. ⊠	81
75	Fitchburg St. ⊠	59
49	Westfield St. †	59

Nickname: Bears
Colors: Crimson & White
Arena: Adrian Tinsley Center
   Capacity: 1,000; Year Built: 2002
AD: John C. Harper
SID: Mike Holbrook

BYU
Provo, UT 84602................................ I

Coach: Dave Rose, Houston 1984

2006-07 RESULTS (25-9)

69	UCLA	82
84	Idaho St. ⊠	78
79	Portland ⊠	50
80	Southern Utah ⊠	61
68	Boise St.	72
73	Weber St.	69
81	San Jose St. ⊠	69
61	Michigan St. †	76
77	Lamar	86
75	Utah St. ⊠	62
102	Western Ore. ⊠	40
73	Liberty ⊠	59
72	Oral Roberts ⊠	62
77	Seton Hall ⊠	68
80	San Diego St. ⊠	58
89	TCU ⊠	65
75	UNLV	83
89	Wyoming ⊠	81
78	Colorado St.	90
70	New Mexico	49
61	Air Force ⊠	52
76	Utah	66
90	UNLV ⊠	63
77	Wyoming	73
85	TCU	72
96	New Mexico ⊠	83
76	Colorado St. ⊠	67
74	San Diego St.	86
62	Air Force	58
85	Utah ⊠	62
77	TCU †	64
96	Wyoming †	84
70	UNLV	78
77	Xavier †	79

Nickname: Cougars
Colors: Dark Blue and White
Arena: Marriott Center
   Capacity: 22,700; Year Built: 1971
AD: Tom Holmoe
SID: Brett Pyne

RESULTS

BYU-HAWAII
Laie, HI 96762-1294................II

Coach: Ken Wagner, BYU 1979

2006-07 RESULTS (20-8)
116	Cal St. Stanislaus ⊠	101
83	Central Wash. ⊠	75
93	Oakland City ⊠	69
97	Oakland City ⊠	56
72	Fort Lewis †	66
78	Dixie St.	72
93	Seattle Pacific	98
65	Seattle ⊠	76
75	Harding †	72
101	Ark.-Monticello †	68
68	Alas. Anchorage	79
71	Alas. Fairbanks †	76
71	Notre Dame de Namur ⊠	62
85	Notre Dame de Namur ⊠	65
79	Grand Canyon ⊠	73
69	Chaminade	83
76	Chaminade ⊠	68
74	Hawaii Pacific	63
74	Hawaii Pacific	70
86	Hawaii-Hilo ⊠	56
93	Hawaii-Hilo ⊠	83
93	Chaminade ⊠	89
79	Grand Canyon	89
67	Grand Canyon	78
81	Notre Dame de Namur	62
76	Hawaii-Hilo	62
72	Hawaii Pacific ⊠	51
68	Cal St. San B'dino †	71

Nickname: Seasiders
Colors: Crimson, Gold & Gray
Arena: Cannon Activities Center
  Capacity: 4,338; Year Built: 1981
AD: A. Kenyon Wagner
SID: Scott Lowe

BROCKPORT ST.
Brockport, NY 14420-2989............III

Coach: Nelson Whitmore, St. John Fisher 1992

2006-07 RESULTS (26-6)
78	Oberlin ⊠	66
105	Pitt.-Bradford ⊠	80
97	St. John Fisher	86
70	Fredonia St. ⊠	62
74	Plattsburgh St.	72
95	Potsdam St.	98
112	D'Youville ⊠	63
94	Hamilton ⊠	75
102	St. Lawrence ⊠	72
98	Keuka	58
73	Geneseo St. †	84
81	St. John Fisher †	85
89	Oswego St.	102
60	Oneonta St.	58
72	Cortland St.	63
103	Oneonta St. ⊠	71
109	New Paltz St. ⊠	81
82	Geneseo St.	70
74	Fredonia St.	51
91	Oswego St. ⊠	76
94	Buffalo St. ⊠	67
92	Potsdam St. ⊠	75
114	SUNYIT	108
83	Cortland St. ⊠	63
79	Geneseo St. ⊠	63
74	Cortland St. ⊠	56
104	SUNYIT	89
75	Plattsburgh St. ⊠	80
74	Williams †	66
74	St. Lawrence	49
105	St. John Fisher	91
87	Wooster †	94

Nickname: Golden Eagles
Colors: Green & Gold
Arena: Tuttle North Gym
  Capacity: 3,000; Year Built: 1973
AD: Linda J. Case
SID: Kelly Vergin

BROOKLYN
Brooklyn, NY 11210........................III

Coach: Steve Podias, Fordham 1978

2006-07 RESULTS (10-14)
63	New Paltz St.	94
75	Briarcliffe (N.Y.)	73
77	Pratt	42
87	Centenary (N.J.) ⊠	75
67	York (N.Y.)	89
72	Staten Island ⊠	85
71	Purchase St.	70
70	Maritime (N.Y.)	57
88	City Tech ⊠	93
78	Hunter	96
76	Berkeley ⊠	63
69	John Jay	70
52	Baruch	59
51	TCNJ	73
76	Lehman ⊠	80
61	City Tech	58
54	Yeshiva ⊠	59
77	Medgar Evers	80
56	York (N.Y.) ⊠	74
75	Briarcliffe (N.Y.) ⊠	68
83	St. Joseph's (Brkln) ⊠	74
84	Staten Island	99
43	CCNY	76
88	Medgar Evers ⊠	81

Nickname: Bridges
Colors: Maroon & Gold
Arena: Roosevelt Gymnasium
  Capacity: 800; Year Built: 1935
AD: Bruce Filosa
SID: Alex Lang

BROWN
Providence, RI 02912........................I

Coach: Craig Robinson, Princeton 1983

2006-07 RESULTS (11-18)
34	Michigan St.	45
58	Central Mich. †	71
47	Navy †	70
51	Providence	41
40	Northwestern	64
54	Army ⊠	62
66	Wagner	61
80	Quinnipiac ⊠	74
68	Rhode Island	72
52	Albany (N.Y.)	62
95	Hartford ⊠	82
63	Western Ill. †	59
57	A&M-Corpus Christi	71
47	UC Davis	49
56	SMU	60
42	Yale ⊠	56
76	Yale	71
52	Dartmouth	56
88	Harvard	92
61	Penn ⊠	77
63	Princeton ⊠	48
59	Cornell	61
68	Columbia	77
70	Harvard ⊠	66
53	Dartmouth ⊠	33
64	Columbia ⊠	59
67	Cornell ⊠	79
64	Princeton	55
64	Penn	67

Nickname: Bears
Colors: Brown, Red & White
Arena: Pizzitola Sports Center
  Capacity: 3,100; Year Built: 1989
AD: Michael Goldberger
SID: Chris Humm

BRYANT
Smithfield, RI 02917-1284.............II

Coach: Max Good, Eastern Ky. 1969

2006-07 RESULTS (21-11)
63	Philadelphia U.	85
72	American Int'l ⊠	68
84	St. Anselm ⊠	80
69	Franklin Pierce	71
62	Assumption	48
69	Mass.-Lowell	66
49	Bentley	61
76	Southern N.H. ⊠	46
59	Stonehill	77
70	Le Moyne ⊠	68
64	Bridgeport ⊠	57
52	Merrimack ⊠	73
72	St. Rose ⊠	71
77	Assumption	67
80	Pace ⊠	72
70	Stonehill ⊠	55
67	Southern N.H.	60
67	Le Moyne	61
66	Mass.-Lowell ⊠	55
70	St. Anselm	71
76	Bentley ⊠	78
65	Franklin Pierce ⊠	61
47	American Int'l	58
75	C.W. Post	60
68	St. Michael's	74
78	Southern Conn. St.	72
74	Merrimack ⊠	69
79	American Int'l ⊠	63
74	Bentley	85
77	Adelphi †	55
65	St. Rose †	62
54	Bentley †	63

Nickname: Bulldogs
Colors: Black, Gold & White
Arena: Chace Athletic Center
  Capacity: 2,700; Year Built: 1971
AD: Bill Smith
SID: Jason Sullivan

BUCKNELL
Lewisburg, PA 17837........................I

Coach: Pat Flannery, Bucknell 1980

2006-07 RESULTS (22-9)
49	Albany (N.Y.)	55
83	Wake Forest ⊠	86
53	St. Joseph's ⊠	63
60	Penn St.	63
72	Yale	57
60	St. Francis (Pa.)	56
48	UNI ⊠	57
60	George Mason †	57
70	Cornell	66
68	Xavier	67
60	Texas Tech	72
48	Central Ark. †	50
77	Northern Ill. †	59
59	Navy ⊠	51
66	American ⊠	60
60	Holy Cross	65
67	Lafayette	61
50	Colgate ⊠	36
62	Lehigh ⊠	44
74	Army ⊠	49
56	Colgate	53
78	Navy	63
69	American	66
48	Holy Cross ⊠	45
76	Lafayette ⊠	58
73	Towson ⊠	63
69	Lehigh	56
54	Army	49
62	Navy †	43
68	Army ⊠ †	47
66	Holy Cross	74

Nickname: Bison
Colors: Orange & Blue
Arena: Sojka Pavilion
  Capacity: 4,000; Year Built: 2003

AD: John P. Hardt
SID: Jon Terry

BUENA VISTA
Storm Lake, IA 50588-9990...........III

Coach: Brian VanHaaften, Northwestern (Iowa)

2006-07 RESULTS (17-9)
85	Ripon †	80
65	Wis.-Platteville	78
78	Gust. Adolphus	70
99	Northwestern (Iowa) ⊠	86
68	Luther	63
66	Dordt	61
103	St. Ambrose ⊠	98
56	Wis.-Stout †	57
77	St. Joseph's (L.I.) †	88
81	Simpson ⊠	66
84	Coe ⊠	79
70	Central (Iowa)	72
69	Loras ⊠	75
84	Wartburg	70
91	Dubuque ⊠	82
73	Cornell College	58
90	Wartburg ⊠	77
87	Central (Iowa) ⊠	66
56	Coe	59
59	Simpson	68
94	Cornell College ⊠	86
81	Luther ⊠	69
98	Dubuque	90
56	Loras	68
88	Coe ⊠	81
62	Loras	77

Nickname: Beavers
Colors: Navy Blue & Gold
Arena: Siebens Fieldhouse
  Capacity: 3,500; Year Built: 1969
AD: Jan Travis
SID: Nick Huber

BUFFALO
Buffalo, NY 14260........................I

Coach: Reggie Witherspoon, Empire St. 1995

2006-07 RESULTS (12-19)
72	Canisius	69
61	South Fla.	77
77	Cleveland St. †	73
60	Miami (Fla.) †	57
44	Evansville	74
65	Iona ⊠	54
64	Temple	62
74	Niagara ⊠	62
63	Tulane	80
67	Pittsburgh ⊠	77
72	Liberty ⊠	66
62	Delaware St. ⊠	65
69	Siena	64
73	Bowling Green	74
56	Kent St. ⊠	69
68	Miami (Ohio) ⊠	51
51	Ohio	67
59	Akron	66
62	Toledo	78
76	Eastern Mich.	89
64	Western Mich.	85
80	Northern Ill. ⊠	74
73	Ball St.	79
56	Central Mich. ⊠	59
98	Bowling Green ⊠	90
84	Detroit ⊠	92
64	Kent St.	68
68	Miami (Ohio)	80
69	Akron ⊠	87
84	Ohio ⊠	65
74	Central Mich. †	80

Nickname: Bulls
Colors: Royal Blue & White
Arena: Alumni Arena
  Capacity: 8,500; Year Built: 1982

AD: Warde Manuel
SID: Jon Fuller

BUFFALO ST.
Buffalo, NY 14222-1095 III

Coach: Fajri Ansari, Buffalo 1981

2006-07 RESULTS (12-13)

88	Clark (Mass.) ⊠	.74
82	Point Park ⊠	108
83	Wash. & Jeff. †	.71
57	Rochester (N.Y.)	.88
72	Oneonta St.	.79
76	New Paltz St.	.71
78	Medaille ⊠	.44
85	Hilbert ⊠	.75
65	Albion †	.59
103	Lincoln (Pa.) †	110
68	Cortland St.	.53
99	SUNYIT ⊠	.85
81	Oswego St. ⊠	.76
76	Potsdam St. ⊠	.94
84	Plattsburgh St. ⊠	.90
66	Geneseo St. ⊠	.75
66	Plattsburgh St.	.78
80	SUNYIT	.84
75	Fredonia St.	.78
67	Brockport St.	.94
72	Cortland St. ⊠	.69
96	New Paltz St. ⊠	.83
74	Fredonia St. ⊠	.59
69	Oswego St.	.77
72	Plattsburgh St.	.82

Nickname: Bengals
Colors: Orange & Black
Arena: Sports Arena
   Capacity: 3,500; Year Built: 1991
AD: Jerry S. Boyes
SID: Jeff Ventura

BUTLER
Indianapolis, IN 46208-3485 I

Coach: Todd Lickliter, Butler 1979

2006-07 RESULTS (29-7)

77	Tulane	.37
71	Notre Dame †	.69
60	Indiana †	.55
62	Ill.-Springfield ⊠	.56
56	Tennessee †	.44
79	Gonzaga †	.71
83	Kent St. ⊠	.80
60	Valparaiso	.47
70	Cleveland St. ⊠	.45
65	Ball St. ⊠	.41
64	Indiana St.	.72
68	Purdue †	.65
76	Evansville ⊠	.65
55	Milwaukee	.50
73	Wright St. ⊠	.42
67	Ill.-Chicago	.73
62	South Dakota St. ⊠	.47
67	Youngstown St. ⊠	.39
80	Green Bay †	.59
70	Loyola (Ill.)	.66
68	Detroit	.58
71	Ill.-Chicago ⊠	.45
71	Youngstown St.	.58
66	Milwaukee ⊠	.47
92	Cleveland St.	.50
65	Wright St.	.77
79	Fla. Gulf Coast ⊠	.65
64	Southern Ill. ⊠	.68
68	Green Bay	.58
71	Loyola (Ill.) ⊠	.75
56	Detroit ⊠	.36
67	Loyola (Ill.) †	.66
55	Wright St.	.60
57	Old Dominion †	.46
62	Maryland †	.59
57	Florida †	.65

Nickname: Bulldogs
Colors: Blue & White

Arena: Hinkle Fieldhouse
   Capacity: 11,043; Year Built: 1928
AD: Barry Collier
SID: Jim McGrath

C.W. POST
Brookville, NY 11548 II

Coach: Tim Cluess, Hofstra 1983

2006-07 RESULTS (19-11)

79	St. Anselm ⊠	.62
60	Bentley ⊠	.70
69	Gannon	.76
101	Lock Haven †	.71
82	Bridgeport	.74
85	Molloy	.82
86	Dowling ⊠	.51
74	Concordia (N.Y.) ⊠	.58
72	Queens (N.Y.)	.82
85	Post ⊠	.73
56	Southern Conn. St.	.48
60	St. Thomas Aquinas	.65
81	New Haven ⊠	.65
88	Mercy ⊠	.60
67	Adelphi	.77
85	NYIT	.87
75	Bridgeport ⊠	.80
85	Molloy ⊠	.79
82	Dowling	.64
83	Queens (N.Y.) ⊠	.74
81	Concordia (N.Y.)	.84
60	Bryant ⊠	.75
65	St. Thomas Aquinas ⊠	.56
68	New Haven	.77
67	Mercy	.52
66	Adelphi ⊠	.53
70	NYIT ⊠	.60
58	St. Thomas Aquinas ⊠	.55
63	Bridgeport	.60
58	Adelphi †	.61

Nickname: Pioneers
Colors: Green & Gold
Arena: Pratt Recreation Center
   Capacity: 3,000; Year Built: 2002
AD: Bryan Collins
SID: Tom Emberley

CABRINI
Radnor, PA 19087-3698 III

Coach: Matthew Macciocca, DeSales 1996

2006-07 RESULTS (5-20)

71	Wooster	128
112	Emory & Henry †	129
79	Penn St.-Berks	.63
81	Misericordia ⊠	.88
66	Marywood	.74
70	Wesley	.72
63	DeSales ⊠	.69
46	Widener	.61
50	Rowan	.72
60	Scranton ⊠	.89
48	Arcadia ⊠	.54
48	Eastern	.60
34	Alvernia	.69
71	Gwynedd-Mercy ⊠	.84
73	Neumann ⊠	.74
67	Immaculata ⊠	.65
61	Misericordia	.82
57	Wesley ⊠	.80
66	Alvernia ⊠	.73
77	Marywood ⊠	.65
61	Arcadia	.77
54	Eastern ⊠	.66
54	Immaculata	.50
63	Neumann ⊠	.61
73	Gwynedd-Mercy	.74

Nickname: Cavaliers
Colors: Royal Blue & White
Arena: Sacred Heart Gymnasium
   Capacity: 750; Year Built: 1958
AD: Leslie Danehy
SID: Rich Schepis

CALDWELL
Caldwell, NJ 07006-6195 II

Coach: Mark Corino, Kean 1977

2006-07 RESULTS (19-12)

66	Mesa St. †	.65
51	Colorado Mines	.59
74	Bloomfield ⊠	.71
69	Mercy ⊠	.58
65	Dowling ⊠	.54
82	Felician ⊠	.58
59	Dominican (N.Y.)	.63
52	Phila. Sciences	.65
83	Wilmington (Del.) ⊠	.76
56	St. Anselm	.70
66	Franklin Pierce	.63
63	Holy Family	.77
67	Philadelphia U. ⊠	.68
51	Goldey-Beacom	.56
67	Nyack	.56
53	Post	.61
68	Wilmington (Del.)	.60
83	Bloomfield	.74
75	Phila. Sciences ⊠	.65
69	Adelphi ⊠	.56
76	Felician	.80
63	Dominican (N.Y.) ⊠	.56
67	Holy Family ⊠	.66
56	Post	.73
53	Philadelphia U.	.57
73	Nyack ⊠	.54
53	Goldey-Beacom ⊠	.52
74	Goldey-Beacom	.65
73	Philadelphia U. †	.64
61	Phila. Sciences †	.60
56	Bentley	.59

Nickname: Cougars
Colors: Scarlet & Gold
Arena: George R. Newman
   Capacity: 1,800; Year Built: 2002
AD: Mark A. Corino
SID: Matt McLagan

CALIFORNIA
Berkeley, CA 94720 I

Coach: Ben Braun, Wisconsin 1975

2006-07 RESULTS (16-17)

60	Utah Valley St. ⊠	.47
79	San Diego St.	.86
73	Santa Clara ⊠	.48
72	Marshall †	.70
72	Hawaii †	.56
78	Loyola Marymount †	.70
78	Kansas St. ⊠	.48
71	Nevada †	.77
75	Chicago St. ⊠	.51
67	San Diego ⊠	.72
84	Furman ⊠	.50
62	DePaul	.90
85	Arizona	.94
66	Arizona St.	.62
67	Stanford	.63
56	Washington St. ⊠	.73
77	Washington ⊠	.69
77	Oregon St.	.74
84	Oregon	.92
46	UCLA ⊠	.62
73	Southern California ⊠	.76
71	Stanford ⊠	.90
71	Washington	.79
46	Washington St.	.59
63	Oregon ⊠	.61
84	Oregon St. ⊠	.80
75	UCLA	.85
66	Southern California	.84
65	Arizona ⊠	.70
41	Arizona St. ⊠	.42
70	Oregon St. †	.51
76	UCLA †	.69
63	Oregon †	.81

Nickname: Golden Bears
Colors: Blue & Gold
Arena: Haas Pavilion

Capacity: 11,877; Year Built: 1999
AD: Sandy Barbour
SID: Herb Benenson

UC DAVIS
Davis, CA 95616-8674 II

Coach: Gary Stewart, La Verne 1984

2006-07 RESULTS (5-23)

73	Ga. Southern †	116
90	Columbia †	.95
76	UTEP	.80
72	Portland	.76
77	Sacramento St.	100
72	Stanford	.84
66	Jackson St. ⊠	.58
49	Idaho St.	.76
61	Portland St.	.93
75	Long Beach St. ⊠	.89
48	UC Irvine ⊠	.68
49	Brown ⊠	.47
38	Utah Valley St. ⊠	.57
68	Cal Poly	.72
70	UC Santa Barbara ⊠	.66
93	Cal St. Northridge ⊠	.88
71	Pacific ⊠	.79
77	Cal St. Fullerton	.84
50	UC Riverside	.70
48	UC Santa Barbara ⊠	.66
64	Cal Poly ⊠	.88
59	Utah Valley St.	.88
74	Cal St. Northridge	.91
58	Pacific	.65
59	UC Irvine	.73
77	Long Beach St.	102
76	UC Riverside ⊠	.80
77	Cal St. Fullerton ⊠	.68

Nickname: Aggies
Colors: Yale Blue & Gold
Arena: The Pavilion
   Capacity: 7,000; Year Built: 1977
AD: Greg Warzecka
SID: Mike Robles

UC IRVINE
Irvine, CA 92697-4125 I

Coach: Pat Douglass, Pacific 1972

2006-07 RESULTS (15-18)

63	South Ala. †	.67
53	Winston-Salem †	.41
51	Fresno St.	.82
67	South Carolina ⊠	.52
42	Oregon	.85
64	Nevada	.83
68	Pepperdine ⊠	.66
65	Loyola Marymount	.73
73	Drake	.76
70	Sam Houston St. ⊠	.62
53	DePaul	.65
69	Loyola (Ill.)	.72
81	Harvard ⊠	.48
68	UC Davis	.48
66	Cal Poly ⊠	.62
59	UC Santa Barbara ⊠	.64
61	Cal St. Northridge	.67
67	Pacific	.42
64	UC Riverside ⊠	.48
68	Cal St. Fullerton ⊠	.71
88	Long Beach St. ⊠	.84
60	Cal St. Fullerton	.75
82	Pacific ⊠	.89
75	Cal St. Northridge ⊠	.66
62	UC Santa Barbara	.71
80	Cal Poly	.89
66	UC Riverside	.61
62	San Francisco	.76
73	UC Davis ⊠	.59
80	Long Beach St.	.85
53	UC Riverside †	.52
70	UC Santa Barbara †	.52
63	Long Beach St. †	.77

Nickname: Anteaters
Colors: Blue & Gold
Arena: Bren Events Center
    Capacity: 5,000; Year Built: 1987
AD: Paula Smith
SID: Bob Olson

UC RIVERSIDE

Riverside, CA 92521 I

Coach: Vonn Webb, Western N.M. 1989

2006-07 RESULTS (7-24)

61	Iowa St.	69
64	Eastern Ill. †	55
64	La.-Monroe †	76
88	Vanguard ⊠	63
75	Hope Int'l ⊠	55
45	San Diego St.	79
75	Southeast Mo. St.	78
38	UCLA	61
65	Montana	72
77	Texas-Arlington ⊠	78
56	Colgate ⊠	59
65	UC Santa Barbara	73
64	Cal Poly	67
55	UTEP	95
49	Pacific ⊠	62
60	Cal St. Northridge ⊠	67
62	San Diego	78
58	Cal St. Fullerton	98
48	UC Irvine	64
65	Long Beach St.	99
70	UC Davis ⊠	50
82	Cal St. Fullerton ⊠	76
69	Cal St. Northridge	89
66	Pacific	86
61	UC Irvine ⊠	66
81	Idaho	76
54	Cal Poly ⊠	70
67	UC Santa Barbara ⊠	68
80	UC Davis	76
75	Long Beach St. ⊠	91
52	UC Irvine †	53

Nickname: Highlanders
Colors: Blue & Gold
Arena: UCR Student Rec Center
    Capacity: 3,168; Year Built: 1994
AD: Stanley M. Morrison
SID: Ross French

UC SAN DIEGO

La Jolla, CA 92093-0531 II

Coach: Bill Carr, San Francisco 1992

2006-07 RESULTS (12-15)

48	San Diego St.	84
62	Grand Canyon	64
62	Seattle Pacific †	52
61	Montevallo †	60
67	Cal St. Chico ⊠	74
76	Cal St. Stanislaus ⊠	72
50	Hawaii Pacific ⊠	53
51	Cal St. Dom. Hills	60
76	Humboldt St.	90
70	Sonoma St.	75
59	Cal St. L.A.	54
36	Cal St. Bakersfield	67
69	Cal St. San B'dino ⊠	63
54	Cal Poly Pomona	60
63	San Fran. St.	58
55	Cal St. Monterey Bay	71
116	Cal St. Stanislaus	103
69	Cal St. Chico	54
45	Cal St. Dom. Hills ⊠	44
90	Sonoma St. ⊠	76
59	Humboldt St. ⊠	61
56	Cal St. Bakersfield ⊠	67
77	Cal St. L.A. ⊠	86
65	Cal Poly Pomona	68
59	Cal St. San B'dino	77
100	Cal St. Monterey Bay ⊠	82
73	San Fran. St. ⊠	47

Nickname: Tritons
Colors: Blue & Gold
Arena: RIMAC Arena
    Capacity: 5,000; Year Built: 1995
AD: Earl W. Edwards
SID: David Wahlstrom

UC SANTA BARBARA

Santa Barbara, CA 93106-5200 I

Coach: Bob Williams, San Jose St. 1975

2006-07 RESULTS (18-11)

75	San Jose St. ⊠	67
88	Montana St.	56
79	UNLV	76
89	Pepperdine	80
72	San Diego St. ⊠	76
55	Loyola Marymount ⊠	58
75	Portland	67
70	Fresno St. ⊠	42
74	San Francisco	69
90	Vanguard ⊠	63
63	San Diego	81
73	UC Riverside ⊠	65
84	Cal St. Fullerton ⊠	76
65	Long Beach St.	101
64	UC Irvine	59
66	UC Davis ⊠	70
61	Cal Poly ⊠	71
67	Cal St. Northridge	57
70	Pacific	62
66	UC Davis	48
71	UC Irvine ⊠	62
67	Long Beach St. ⊠	68
79	Cal Poly	86
70	Eastern Wash. ⊠	71
73	Cal St. Fullerton	79
68	UC Riverside	67
64	Pacific ⊠	49
75	Cal St. Northridge ⊠	59
52	UC Irvine †	70

Nickname: Gauchos
Colors: Blue & Gold
Arena: The Thunderdome
    Capacity: 6,000; Year Built: 1979
AD: Gary A. Cunningham
SID: Bill Mahoney

UC SANTA CRUZ

Santa Cruz, CA 95064 III

Coach: Gordie Johnson, UNI

2006-07 RESULTS (3-23)

86	Puget Sound	124
79	Pacific Lutheran †	84
56	Cal St. Stanislaus	112
58	Notre Dame de Namur †	69
52	San Diego Christian ⊠	84
110	Redlands	131
59	Colorado Col. †	54
57	Golden St. Baptist	52
52	Whitworth †	76
61	Caltech	49
47	Cal Lutheran	82
57	Cal St. East Bay	73
65	Cal Maritime †	98
44	Whitworth ⊠	89
62	Holy Names ⊠	97
56	Chapman †	77
68	Colorado Col. †	90
55	Dallas	71
57	Chapman	78
71	La Sierra	87
45	Dominican (Cal.) ⊠	73
41	Menlo	77
68	Cal St. East Bay	83
64	Chapman ⊠	76
52	Neb. Wesleyan	79
63	Colorado Col. †	79

Nickname: Banana Slugs
Colors: Navy Blue & Gold
Arena: West Field House
    Capacity: 300

AD: Linda Spradley
SID: Nikki Turner

CALIFORNIA (PA.)

California, PA 15419 II

Coach: Bill Brown, Ohio 1974

2006-07 RESULTS (24-7)

87	Penn St.-McKeesport ⊠	40
80	East Stroudsburg †	74
60	Shepherd	64
132	Penn St.-Fayette ⊠	47
69	Cheyney	61
88	Wheeling Jesuit ⊠	65
67	Millersville ⊠	74
66	West Chester ⊠	65
75	Bellarmine †	82
97	Roberts Wesleyan †	76
82	Mansfield ⊠	76
71	Bloomsburg ⊠	61
66	Clarion	63
94	East Stroudsburg ⊠	83
83	Kutztown	75
78	Lock Haven ⊠	50
75	Shippensburg ⊠	63
74	Indiana (Pa.)	63
79	Slippery Rock ⊠	56
48	Edinboro	49
80	Clarion ⊠	60
67	Pitt.-Johnstown ⊠	61
59	Lock Haven	61
67	Indiana (Pa.) ⊠	46
71	Shippensburg	51
65	Slippery Rock	63
73	Edinboro ⊠	59
67	Clarion	62
65	Cheyney ⊠	67
82	West Liberty St. †	79
72	Millersville †	82

Nickname: Vulcans
Colors: Red & Black
Arena: Hamer Hall
    Capacity: 2,500; Year Built: 1962
AD: Thomas G. Pucci
SID: Tom Byrnes

CAL LUTHERAN

Thousand Oaks, CA 91360-2787 III

Coach: Rich Rider, Truman 1970

2006-07 RESULTS (17-8)

79	La Sierra ⊠	57
71	Alvernia †	67
55	Whitworth †	68
65	Lewis & Clark †	61
48	Chapman	59
96	West Coast Baptist ⊠	45
57	Pacific (Ore.) ⊠	66
82	UC Santa Cruz ⊠	47
72	Willamette ⊠	85
64	Milwaukee Engr. ⊠	57
71	Messiah	66
64	Whittier ⊠	49
129	Redlands	85
64	La Verne	44
56	Occidental ⊠	68
68	Pomona-Pitzer ⊠	66
110	Caltech	47
51	Claremont-M-S ⊠	49
76	Whittier	67
97	Redlands ⊠	90
56	La Verne ⊠	53
40	Occidental	41
64	Pomona-Pitzer	69
93	Caltech ⊠	26
49	Claremont-M-S	62

Nickname: Kingsmen
Colors: Violet & Gold
Arena: Gilbert Arena
    Capacity: 1,500; Year Built: 2006
AD: Daniel E. Kuntz
SID: Tracy Maple

CAL POLY

San Luis Obispo, CA 93407 I

Coach: Kevin Bromley, Colorado St. 1983

2006-07 RESULTS (19-11)

69	Southeastern La. †	76
56	Portland †	53
65	Oregon St.	78
91	Cal St. Stanislaus ⊠	72
72	St. Mary's (Cal.) ⊠	59
81	Occidental ⊠	62
63	San Jose St.	80
58	Utah	77
82	Northern Ariz. ⊠	60
75	Fresno St.	95
91	Cal St. Fullerton ⊠	99
67	UC Riverside ⊠	64
62	UC Irvine ⊠	66
70	Long Beach St.	77
72	UC Davis ⊠	68
74	Sacramento St. ⊠	65
71	UC Santa Barbara	61
43	Pacific	66
79	Cal St. Northridge ⊠	68
88	UC Davis	64
77	Long Beach St. ⊠	80
89	UC Irvine ⊠	80
86	UC Santa Barbara ⊠	79
92	Portland St. ⊠	87
70	UC Riverside	54
90	Cal St. Fullerton	80
86	Cal St. Northridge ⊠	70
82	Pacific ⊠	70
81	Cal St. Fullerton †	56
83	Long Beach St. †	94

Nickname: Mustangs
Colors: Green & Gold
Arena: Robert A. Mott Gymnasium
    Capacity: 3,032; Year Built: 1960
AD: Alison Cone
SID: Brian Thurmond

CAL POLY POMONA

Pomona, CA 91768 II

Coach: Greg Kamansky, UC San Diego 1988

2006-07 RESULTS (20-8)

75	Western Wash. †	66
71	Seattle Pacific	84
68	Cal St. San B'dino ⊠	64
77	Sonoma St. ⊠	71
58	Humboldt St. ⊠	55
77	Vanguard ⊠	69
67	Western Wash. †	64
83	Central Wash. †	66
66	San Fran. St.	60
60	Cal St. Monterey Bay	68
76	Cal St. Chico ⊠	44
82	Cal St. Stanislaus ⊠	85
79	Cal St. Dom. Hills	76
60	UC San Diego	54
59	Cal St. Bakersfield ⊠	65
77	Cal St. L.A. ⊠	75
62	Humboldt St.	84
43	Sonoma St.	65
75	Cal St. San B'dino	69
78	Cal St. Monterey Bay ⊠	67
79	San Fran. St. ⊠	63
89	Cal St. Stanislaus	83
73	Cal St. Chico	60
68	UC San Diego ⊠	65
70	Cal St. Dom. Hills ⊠	69
65	Cal St. L.A.	61
49	Cal St. Bakersfield	58
55	Seattle †	69

Nickname: Broncos
Colors: Green & Gold
Arena: Kellogg Gym
    Capacity: 5,000; Year Built: 1966
AD: Brian Swanson
SID: Paul Helms

CAL ST. BAKERSFIELD
Bakersfield, CA 93311-1099........... II

Coach: Keith Brown, Pacific 1979

2006-07 RESULTS (15-14)

67	Pacific	75
70	Long Beach St.	73
75	Loyola Marymount	83
80	San Fran. St.	64
90	Cal St. Monterey Bay	53
72	San Diego	92
57	St. Mary's (Cal.)	65
82	Pepperdine	76
64	Cal St. L.A.	50
49	Utah St.	65
59	Cal St. Stanislaus	57
55	Cal St. Chico	61
66	Cal St. Dom. Hills ⊠	50
67	UC San Diego ⊠	36
58	Sonoma St. ⊠	65
57	Humboldt St. ⊠	61
65	Cal Poly Pomona	59
71	Cal St. San B'dino	77
76	Cal St. Monterey Bay ⊠	74
68	San Fran. St. ⊠	42
63	Cal St. L.A. ⊠	70
74	Cal St. Chico ⊠	54
90	Cal St. Stanislaus ⊠	78
67	UC San Diego	56
81	Cal St. Dom. Hills	72
77	Humboldt St.	86
53	Sonoma St.	58
66	Cal St. San B'dino ⊠	74
58	Cal Poly Pomona ⊠	49

Nickname: Roadrunners
Colors: Blue & Gold
Arena: Rabobank Arena
   Capacity: 10,000; Year Built: 1998
AD: Rudy Carvajal
SID: Kevin Gilmore

CAL ST. CHICO
Chico, CA 95929 II

Coach: Prescott Smith, Southwestern
Okla. 1965

2006-07 RESULTS (7-20)

63	Tarleton St.	86
66	Tex. A&M-Commerce †	89
83	Western Ore. ⊠	54
78	Central Wash. ⊠	92
74	UC San Diego	67
60	Cal St. Dom. Hills	68
85	Cal St. Stanislaus ⊠	87
77	Cal St. Stanislaus	85
75	Seattle ⊠	47
72	Cal St. L.A. ⊠	58
61	Cal St. Bakersfield ⊠	55
44	Cal Poly Pomona	76
56	Cal St. San B'dino	62
66	San Fran. St. ⊠	56
104	Cal St. Monterey Bay ⊠	106
67	Sonoma St.	76
56	Humboldt St.	74
56	Cal St. Dom. Hills ⊠	66
54	UC San Diego ⊠	69
54	Cal St. Bakersfield ⊠	74
85	Cal St. L.A.	99
82	Cal St. San B'dino ⊠	83
60	Cal Poly Pomona ⊠	73
86	Cal St. Monterey Bay	99
82	San Fran. St.	66
75	Humboldt St. ⊠	90
55	Sonoma St. ⊠	71

Nickname: Wildcats
Colors: Cardinal & White
Arena: Art Acker Gym
   Capacity: 1,997; Year Built: 1962
AD: Anita S. Barker
SID: Teresa Clements

CAL ST. DOM. HILLS
Carson, CA 90747 II

Coach: Damaine Powell, Southern
California 1994

2006-07 RESULTS (12-15)

67	Montevallo †	70
65	Seattle Pacific †	84
75	Cal St. Stanislaus ⊠	82
68	Cal St. Chico ⊠	60
83	Hawaii-Hilo ⊠	51
84	Master's ⊠	76
60	UC San Diego ⊠	51
70	Grand Canyon	69
62	Sonoma St.	68
64	Humboldt St.	65
50	Cal St. Bakersfield	66
80	Cal St. L.A.	66
76	Cal Poly Pomona ⊠	79
60	Cal St. San B'dino ⊠	77
67	Cal St. Monterey Bay ⊠	69
79	San Fran. St. ⊠	51
66	Cal St. Chico	56
81	Cal St. Stanislaus	83
44	UC San Diego	45
62	Humboldt St. ⊠	70
79	Sonoma St. ⊠	57
76	Cal St. L.A. ⊠	74
72	Cal St. Bakersfield ⊠	81
75	Cal St. San B'dino ⊠	84
69	Cal Poly Pomona	70
91	San Fran. St. ⊠	51
70	Cal St. Monterey Bay ⊠	65

Nickname: Toros
Colors: Cardinal & Gold
Arena: Torodome
   Capacity: 4,200; Year Built: 1978
AD: Patrick Guillen
SID: Mel Miranda

CAL ST. EAST BAY
Hayward, CA 94542 III

Coach: Will Biggs, Cal St. East Bay 1988

2006-07 RESULTS (8-18)

66	Pacific Union	64
66	Concordia (Cal.)	81
50	Lewis & Clark	68
74	San Fran. St.	97
115	Redlands	123
71	Whittier †	88
73	William Jessup	80
62	Simpson (Cal.)	67
73	UC Santa Cruz ⊠	57
75	Malone ⊠	88
66	Menlo ⊠	81
81	Holy Names ⊠	87
54	Dominican (Cal.)	70
87	Bethany (Cal.) ⊠	78
86	Cal St. Maritime ⊠	82
70	William Jessup ⊠	64
86	Pacific Union	96
70	Bethany (Cal.)	76
52	Menlo	62
78	Simpson (Cal.) ⊠	77
82	Holy Names	98
68	Dominican (Cal.) ⊠	86
83	UC Santa Cruz	68
70	Cal St. Maritime	92
88	Dominican (Cal.)	71
52	Menlo	69

Nickname: Pioneers
Colors: Red & White
Arena: Pioneer Gym
   Capacity: 5,000; Year Built: 1967
AD: Debby De Angelis
SID: Marty Valdez

CAL ST. FULLERTON
Fullerton, CA 92834-6810 I

Coach: Bob Burton, Fresno St. 1968

2006-07 RESULTS (20-10)

108	Cal Maritime ⊠	56
98	Hope Int'l ⊠	65
67	UTSA	63
91	La.-Lafayette	89
100	Eastern Wash.	110
76	UTSA	67
54	UCLA	78
83	Pepperdine	81
94	Bethune-Cookman ⊠	65
85	La.-Lafayette ⊠	49
104	San Jose St. ⊠	77
99	Cal Poly	91
76	UC Santa Barbara	84
76	Cal St. Northridge ⊠	72
76	Pacific ⊠	70
98	UC Riverside ⊠	58
85	Long Beach St.	95
71	UC Irvine	68
84	UC Davis ⊠	77
75	UC Irvine ⊠	60
76	UC Riverside	82
82	Pacific	77
75	Cal St. Northridge	73
84	Long Beach St. ⊠	94
62	Wright St.	77
79	UC Santa Barbara ⊠	73
80	Cal Poly ⊠	90
68	UC Davis	77
100	Pacific †	92
56	Cal Poly †	81

Nickname: Titans
Colors: Navy, Orange & White
Arena: Titan Gym
   Capacity: 4,000; Year Built: 1964
AD: Brian Quinn
SID: Mel Franks

CAL ST. L.A.
Los Angeles, CA 90032-8240 II

Coach: Stephen Thompson, Syracuse
1990

2006-07 RESULTS (10-17)

67	Seattle Pacific	85
66	Western Wash. †	67
95	West Coast Chrst. ⊠	42
85	Master's ⊠	68
74	Cal St. Monterey Bay	75
82	San Fran. St.	72
129	Redlands	105
50	Cal St. Bakersfield ⊠	64
58	Cal St. Chico	72
88	Cal St. Stanislaus	85
54	UC San Diego	59
66	Cal St. Dom. Hills ⊠	80
94	Humboldt St. ⊠	85
69	Sonoma St. ⊠	74
57	Cal St. San B'dino	69
75	Cal Poly Pomona	77
76	San Fran. St. ⊠	79
106	Cal St. Monterey Bay ⊠	109
70	Cal St. Bakersfield	63
86	Cal St. Stanislaus ⊠	83
99	Cal St. Chico ⊠	85
74	Cal St. Dom. Hills	76
86	UC San Diego	77
53	Sonoma St.	75
75	Humboldt St.	77
61	Cal Poly Pomona ⊠	65
63	Cal St. San B'dino ⊠	83

Nickname: Golden Eagles
Colors: Black & Gold
Arena: Eagles Nest
   Capacity: 5,000; Year Built: 1947
AD: Daniel Bridges
SID: Tommy Mahoney

CAL ST. MONTEREY BAY
Seaside, CA 93955 II

Coach: Pat Kosta, Cal St. Monterey Bay

2006-07 RESULTS (12-15)

41	St. Mary's (Cal.)	89
75	Cal St. L.A. ⊠	74
53	Cal St. Bakersfield ⊠	90
80	Chaminade †	77
87	St. Martin's †	83
126	Western Ore. †	122
86	Humboldt St.	111
82	San Fran. St.	86
70	Cal St. San B'dino ⊠	74
68	Cal Poly Pomona ⊠	60
93	Sonoma St.	105
85	Humboldt St.	92
107	Cal St. Stanislaus	96
106	Cal St. Chico	104
69	Cal St. Dom. Hills ⊠	67
71	UC San Diego ⊠	55
74	Cal St. Bakersfield	76
109	Cal St. L.A.	106
75	San Fran. St.	74
67	Cal Poly Pomona	78
81	Cal St. San B'dino	105
91	Humboldt St. ⊠	106
74	Sonoma St. ⊠	77
99	Cal St. Chico ⊠	86
89	Cal St. Stanislaus ⊠	96
82	UC San Diego	100
65	Cal St. Dom. Hills	70

Nickname: Otters
Colors: Forest green, teal & gold
Arena: Kelp Bed Gym
Capacity: 1,200
AD: Howard L. Gauthier
SID: Embele Awipi

CAL ST. NORTHRIDGE
Northridge, CA 91330-8276 I

Coach: Bobby Braswell, Cal St.
Northridge 1985

2006-07 RESULTS (14-17)

90	Portland St. †	65
73	Oregon	84
74	Lehigh †	68
159	Redlands ⊠	97
95	Pepperdine ⊠	92
44	Illinois St.	66
70	Tulsa	91
102	Eastern Wash. ⊠	98
75	Boise St. ⊠	84
73	Master's ⊠	66
50	Washington St.	69
64	Pacific	68
72	Cal St. Fullerton	76
67	UC Riverside	60
67	UC Irvine	61
90	Long Beach St. ⊠	83
88	UC Davis	93
72	South Dakota St. ⊠	61
57	UC Santa Barbara ⊠	67
68	Cal Poly ⊠	79
72	Long Beach St.	79
66	UC Irvine	75
89	UC Riverside ⊠	69
73	Cal St. Fullerton ⊠	75
91	UC Davis ⊠	74
76	Cleveland St.	85
64	South Dakota St.	63
76	Pacific ⊠	73
70	Cal Poly	86
59	UC Santa Barbara	75
54	Pacific †	71

Nickname: Matadors
Colors: Red, White & Black
Arena: The Matadome
   Capacity: 1,600; Year Built: 1962
AD: Rick Mazzuto
SID: TBA

RESULTS

CAL ST. SAN B'DINO
San Bernardino, CA 92407-2397 . II

Coach: Jeff Oliver, Cal Poly 1995
2006-07 RESULTS (26-6)

52	Arizona St.	69
64	Cal Poly Pomona	68
76	Humboldt St. ⊠	68
75	Sonoma St. ⊠	55
86	Seattle Pacific ⊠	66
104	Grand Canyon ⊠	60
94	Central Wash. †	84
86	Western Wash. †	67
74	Cal St. Monterey Bay	70
73	San Fran. St.	60
103	Cal St. Stanislaus ⊠	75
62	Cal St. Chico ⊠	56
63	UC San Diego	69
77	Cal St. Dom. Hills ⊠	60
69	Cal St. L.A. ⊠	57
77	Cal St. Bakersfield ⊠	71
74	Sonoma St.	52
78	Humboldt St.	89
69	Cal Poly Pomona ⊠	75
86	San Fran. St. ⊠	55
105	Cal St. Monterey Bay ⊠	81
83	Cal St. Chico	82
82	Cal St. Stanislaus	76
84	Cal St. Dom. Hills ⊠	75
77	UC San Diego ⊠	59
74	Cal St. Bakersfield	66
83	Cal St. L.A.	63
71	BYU-Hawaii †	68
72	Seattle †	66
68	Humboldt St. †	66
100	Wingate †	73
79	Barton †	80

Nickname: Coyotes
Colors: Columbia Blue & Black
Arena: Coussoulis Arena
   Capacity: 4,140; Year Built: 1995
AD: Nancy Simpson
SID: Mike Murphy

CAL ST. STANISLAUS
Turlock, CA 95382-0299 II

Coach: Keith Larsen, San Fran. St. 1985
2006-07 RESULTS (13-16)

101	BYU-Hawaii	116
75	Hawaii Pacific †	79
112	Central Wash. †	96
72	Cal Poly	91
112	UC Santa Cruz ⊠	56
75	Occidental ⊠	71
82	Cal St. Dom. Hills	75
72	UC San Diego	76
94	Cal Baptist ⊠	91
87	Cal St. Chico	85
85	Cal St. Chico ⊠	77
57	Cal St. Bakersfield ⊠	59
85	Cal St. L.A. ⊠	88
75	Cal St. San B'dino	103
85	Cal Poly Pomona	82
96	Cal St. Monterey Bay ⊠	107
95	San Fran. St.	72
88	Humboldt St.	94
87	Sonoma St.	85
103	UC San Diego ⊠	116
83	Cal St. Dom. Hills ⊠	81
83	Cal St. L.A.	86
78	Cal St. Bakersfield	90
83	Cal Poly Pomona ⊠	89
76	Cal St. San B'dino ⊠	82
97	San Fran. St.	92
96	Cal St. Monterey Bay	89
62	Sonoma St. ⊠	77
77	Humboldt St. ⊠	91

Nickname: Warriors
Colors: Red & Gold
Arena: Warrior Gym
   Capacity: 2,000; Year Built: 1978
AD: Milton E. Richards
SID: Brian F. Blank

CALTECH
Pasadena, CA 91125 III

Coach: Roy Dow, Colby 1984
2006-07 RESULTS (1-24)

40	Dubuque ⊠	81
68	West Coast Baptist ⊠	81
49	Chapman ⊠	81
32	La Sierra ⊠	78
30	Whitworth †	83
49	UC Santa Cruz ⊠	61
57	Pacific (Ore.) †	98
54	Williams ⊠	74
57	Wis. Lutheran ⊠	117
39	Robert Morris-S'fiel ⊠	73
81	Bard ⊠	52
40	Occidental	103
55	Pomona-Pitzer ⊠	98
41	Whittier	96
35	Claremont-M-S	78
55	La Verne ⊠	58
47	Cal Lutheran ⊠	110
59	Redlands	121
31	Occidental ⊠	108
50	Pomona-Pitzer	97
38	Whittier ⊠	71
45	Claremont-M-S ⊠	70
52	La Verne	85
26	Cal Lutheran	93
43	Redlands ⊠	125

Nickname: Beavers
Colors: Orange, Black, & White
Arena: Braun Athletic Center
   Capacity: 300; Year Built: 1992
AD: Wendell P. Jack
SID: Wendell P. Jack

CALVIN
Grand Rapids, MI 49546-4388 III

Coach: Kevin Van de Streek, Dordt 1981
2006-07 RESULTS (19-10)

98	Concordia (Wis.) ⊠	76
79	Benedictine (Ill.) ⊠	60
81	Aquinas ⊠	65
54	Hope ⊠	76
62	Wheaton (Ill.) †	73
54	Carthage	74
77	Aquinas ⊠	68
72	Trinity Christian †	63
77	Wis.-La Crosse †	87
82	Wooster	98
80	Tri-State ⊠	64
79	Alma	61
75	Adrian	79
62	Hope ⊠	65
74	Olivet	58
78	Albion ⊠	71
74	Kalamazoo ⊠	63
58	Tri-State	68
105	Alma ⊠	49
84	Adrian ⊠	65
77	Hope	71
90	Olivet ⊠	43
77	Albion	82
72	Kalamazoo	67
69	Olivet ⊠	39
82	Tri-State †	66
78	Hope	76
69	Aurora ⊠	68
64	Hope †	80

Nickname: Knights
Colors: Maroon & Gold
Arena: Calvin Fieldhouse
   Capacity: 4,500; Year Built: 1965
AD: James Timmer Jr.
SID: Jeff Febus

CAMERON
Lawton, OK 73505-6377 II

Coach: Maurice Leitzke, Evangel 1996
2006-07 RESULTS (12-14)

84	Dallas Baptist ⊠	82
67	Okla. Panhandle ⊠	58
60	Washburn ⊠	64
87	Pittsburg St. ⊠	72
90	West Tex. A&M ⊠	84
81	Eastern N.M. ⊠	90
71	Tarleton St. ⊠	69
79	Midwestern St. ⊠	77
73	Washburn ⊠	65
98	Dallas Baptist	87
79	Rhema †	60
84	Midwestern St.	94
70	Tex. A&M-Kingsville	87
71	Angelo St. ⊠	72
82	Southeastern Okla. ⊠	91
71	East Central	66
72	Northeastern St.	84
78	Central Okla. ⊠	82
101	Southwestern Okla. ⊠	100
83	Tex. A&M-Commerce	102
93	Southeastern Okla.	108
79	East Central ⊠	77
63	Northeastern St. ⊠	73
75	Central Okla.	95
73	Southwestern Okla.	95
81	Tex. A&M-Commerce ⊠	92

Nickname: Aggies
Colors: Black & Gold
Arena: Aggie Gymnasium
   Capacity: 1,800; Year Built: 1958
AD: Jim Jackson
SID: Craig Martin

CAMPBELL
Buies Creek, NC 27506 I

Coach: Robbie Laing, Troy 1982
2006-07 RESULTS (14-17)

106	UNC Pembroke ⊠	66
83	Coastal Caro. ⊠	63
100	UNC Wilmington ⊠	94
80	Radford	87
71	Appalachian St.	84
82	San Diego St.	119
69	San Diego	81
101	Radford ⊠	88
70	Virginia Tech	94
107	Ohio Valley ⊠	65
78	North Fla.	48
71	Jacksonville	90
88	Kennesaw St. ⊠	85
76	East Tenn. St. ⊠	100
93	Mercer	94
73	Stetson	82
79	Belmont ⊠	67
64	Lipscomb ⊠	65
54	North Fla. ⊠	49
84	Jacksonville ⊠	74
55	Gardner-Webb ⊠	64
64	Kennesaw St.	74
57	East Tenn. St.	87
104	Stetson ⊠	82
80	Mercer ⊠	81
64	Lipscomb	67
68	Belmont	92
88	Longwood ⊠	80
71	Gardner-Webb ⊠	60
90	Jacksonville †	85
63	Belmont †	79

Nickname: Fighting Camels
Colors: Orange & Black
Arena: Carter Gymnasium
   Capacity: 947; Year Built: 1953
AD: Stan Williamson
SID: Stan Cole

CANISIUS
Buffalo, NY 14208-1098 I

Coach: Tom Parrotta, Fordham 1988
2006-07 RESULTS (12-19)

69	Buffalo ⊠	72
43	West Virginia	66
78	Colgate	73
71	Syracuse ⊠	81
71	Youngstown St.	59
83	Fairleigh Dickinson	85
69	Marist	80
64	Fairfield	75
75	Detroit	72
77	Robert Morris ⊠	81
80	St. Bonaventure ⊠	71
81	Hartford	71
60	Siena	78
64	St. Peter's ⊠	61
51	Manhattan ⊠	60
48	Siena	70
68	St. Peter's	47
72	Iona ⊠	65
84	Marist ⊠	74
67	Manhattan	64
71	Iona	61
63	Fairfield ⊠	67
61	Niagara	79
74	Loyola (Md.)	77
88	Rider	98
88	Niagara ⊠	89
66	Coastal Caro.	83
72	Rider	81
71	Loyola (Md.) ⊠	74
62	St. Peter's †	48
63	Marist †	87

Nickname: Golden Griffins
Colors: Blue & Gold
Arena: Koessler Athletic Center
   Capacity: 2,176; Year Built: 1968
AD: William J. Maher
SID: Marc Gignac

CAPITAL
Columbus, OH 43209 III

Coach: Damon Goodwin, Dayton 1986
2006-07 RESULTS (19-9)

68	Wittenberg ⊠	73
62	Kenyon †	52
81	Denison †	68
71	Ohio Wesleyan	81
93	Baldwin-Wallace ⊠	85
83	Wilmington (Ohio) ⊠	76
72	John Carroll	80
77	Otterbein	59
77	Mt. St. Joseph ⊠	67
63	Carnegie Mellon	64
65	Heidelberg	63
68	Ohio Northern	57
74	Mount Union ⊠	84
54	Muskingum	66
67	Marietta ⊠	41
78	Baldwin-Wallace	81
73	Wilmington (Ohio)	65
89	John Carroll ⊠	82
65	Marietta	52
64	Muskingum ⊠	62
56	Mount Union	44
74	Ohio Northern ⊠	70
79	Heidelberg ⊠	67
69	Otterbein	73
82	Muskingum ⊠	60
69	Otterbein ⊠	49
78	John Carroll ⊠	73
55	Centre †	69

Nickname: Crusaders
Colors: Purple & White
Arena: The Capital Center
   Capacity: 2,100; Year Built: 2001
AD: Roger Welsh
SID: Leonard Reich

CARLETON
Northfield, MN 55057 III

Coach: Guy Kalland, Concordia-M'head 1974

2006-07 RESULTS (11-15)
66	Hawaii-Hilo	73
76	Hawaii Pacific	79
67	Chaminade	90
71	St. John's (Minn.) ⊠	73
66	Bethel (Minn.)	62
69	Augsburg	80
69	Concordia-M'head	52
75	Wis.-La Crosse ⊠	64
69	Minn. St. Mankato	72
62	St. Thomas (Minn.) ⊠	64
70	Hamline	75
77	St. Mary's (Minn.) ⊠	49
51	St. Olaf	67
64	Macalester	56
66	Gust. Adolphus	53
76	Augsburg ⊠	59
57	Concordia-M'head ⊠	62
60	St. John's (Minn.)	65
63	Bethel (Minn.) ⊠	67
41	St. Thomas (Minn.)	51
98	Hamline ⊠	61
66	St. Mary's (Minn.)	43
75	St. Olaf ⊠	59
77	Macalester ⊠	81
71	Gust. Adolphus ⊠	65
59	Gust. Adolphus	70

Nickname: Knights
Colors: Maize & Blue
Arena: West Gymnasium
 Capacity: 1,850; Year Built: 1964
AD: Leon Lunder
SID: Eric Sieger

CARNEGIE MELLON
Pittsburgh, PA 15213-3890 III

Coach: Tony Wingen, Springfield 1982

2006-07 RESULTS (12-13)
77	Wash. & Jeff.	66
70	Grove City †	52
121	Penn St.-Fayette ⊠	51
95	Point Park ⊠	101
51	Rochester (N.Y.) ⊠	60
77	La Roche	58
78	Bethany (W.V.)	77
65	Bluffton ⊠	69
64	Capital ⊠	63
91	Oberlin	65
68	New York U. ⊠	64
75	Brandeis ⊠	68
65	Lycoming	66
69	Chicago	100
49	Washington-St. Louis	73
71	Emory ⊠	70
58	Case Reserve ⊠	53
70	Case Reserve	68
83	Emory	94
52	Brandeis	75
57	New York U.	78
73	Washington-St. Louis ⊠	94
75	Chicago ⊠	82
60	Rochester (N.Y.)	72
75	Lebanon Valley	84

Nickname: Tartans
Colors: Cardinal, White & Grey
Arena: Skibo Gymnasium
 Capacity: 1,500; Year Built: 1924
AD: Susan Bassett
SID: Mark Fisher

CARROLL (WIS.)
Waukesha, WI 53186-5593 III

Coach: David Schultz, Wis.-Oshkosh 1986

2006-07 RESULTS (18-9)
75	Wis.-Stevens Point ⊠	93
86	UC-Colo. Springs †	105
91	Colorado Col.	79
75	Carthage ⊠	67
136	Grinnell ⊠	134
81	Monmouth (Ill.) ⊠	83
103	Beloit ⊠	59
59	Wis.-Oshkosh	78
81	Wis.-Whitewater	93
69	St. Norbert	55
72	Knox	52
84	Illinois Col.	71
70	Lake Forest ⊠	72
70	Knox	64
76	Ripon	80
72	Lawrence ⊠	45
70	Beloit	63
104	Grinnell	113
81	Monmouth (Ill.)	59
77	St. Norbert †	70
89	Ripon ⊠	75
76	Lawrence	63
92	Ripon †	79
80	Lake Forest †	71
73	Augustana (Ill.)	69
86	St. Thomas (Minn.)	80
77	Hope †	89

Nickname: Pioneers
Colors: Orange & White
Arena: Van Male Fieldhouse
 Capacity: 2,000; Year Built: 1965
AD: Kris Jacobsen
SID: Rick Mobley

CARSON-NEWMAN
Jefferson City, TN 37760 II

Coach: Dale Clayton, Milligan 1973

2006-07 RESULTS (10-19)
83	Brevard ⊠	72
58	Augusta St. ⊠	73
71	Ala.-Huntsville	72
82	Belmont Abbey ⊠	70
71	King (Tenn.) ⊠	64
66	Ala.-Huntsville ⊠	67
74	Maryville (Tenn.) ⊠	65
79	North Greenville ⊠	67
90	Brevard	61
67	Augusta St.	87
73	Lincoln Memorial ⊠	78
60	Newberry	63
67	Mars Hill ⊠	71
74	Wingate	87
98	North Greenville	65
73	Tusculum ⊠	81
51	Presbyterian ⊠	59
70	Lenoir-Rhyne	74
81	Catawba	97
67	Newberry ⊠	78
101	Mars Hill	93
82	Lenoir-Rhyne ⊠	80
74	Tusculum	86
72	Presbyterian	77
118	Lincoln Memorial	120
107	Catawba ⊠	112
116	Wingate ⊠	122
99	Mars Hill	88
113	Catawba	115

Nickname: Eagles
Colors: Orange & Blue
Arena: Holt Fieldhouse
 Capacity: 2,000; Year Built: 1961
AD: David W. Barger
SID: Mike Baur

CARTHAGE
Kenosha, WI 53140-1994 III

Coach: Bosko Djurickovic, North Park 1973

2006-07 RESULTS (16-9)
118	Grinnell	106
63	Gust. Adolphus	58
67	Carroll (Wis.)	75
71	Hope ⊠	65
74	Calvin ⊠	54
60	Beloit	48
93	Lawrence	86
82	Olivet †	63
82	Marietta †	51
60	Lewis	78
84	Northland ⊠	74
76	Ill. Wesleyan ⊠	79
62	Elmhurst ⊠	72
54	Augustana (Ill.)	70
80	North Central (Ill.)	69
64	Millikin ⊠	60
64	North Park	62
94	Ill. Wesleyan	83
67	Wheaton (Ill.)	71
66	Augustana (Ill.) ⊠	56
59	Elmhurst	81
60	North Central (Ill.) ⊠	62
85	North Park ⊠	79
70	Millikin	65
59	Wheaton (Ill.) ⊠	61

Nickname: Red Men
Colors: Red, White & Black
Arena: PE Center
 Capacity: 2,440; Year Built: 1964
AD: Robert R. Bonn
SID: Steve Marovich

CASE RESERVE
Cleveland, OH 44106-7223 III

Coach: Sean McDonnell, Boston College 1996

2006-07 RESULTS (5-20)
65	Medaille ⊠	73
62	Thiel ⊠	66
76	Hiram	74
64	Oberlin	78
76	Wash. & Jeff. ⊠	66
76	Kenyon ⊠	85
72	WPI †	83
71	Illinois Tech †	69
57	Illinois Col. †	60
77	Juniata ⊠	64
57	Grove City	65
67	Emory ⊠	76
56	Washington-St. Louis ⊠	73
67	Chicago ⊠	69
68	Brandeis	85
52	New York U.	69
43	Rochester (N.Y.)	84
53	Carnegie Mellon	58
68	Carnegie Mellon ⊠	70
56	Rochester (N.Y.) ⊠	67
73	Chicago	77
65	Washington-St. Louis	86
47	New York U. ⊠	65
51	Brandeis ⊠	56
84	Emory	83

Nickname: Spartans
Colors: Blue, Gray & White
Arena: Emerson PE Center
 Capacity: 1,220; Year Built: 1958
AD: David L. Diles
SID: Creg Jantz

CASTLETON
Castleton, VT 05735 III

Coach: Ted Shipley, Lyndon St. 1987

2006-07 RESULTS (15-12)
46	Clarkson †	65
86	Green Mountain †	55
87	Plymouth St. ⊠	88
90	Middlebury ⊠	99
68	Chris. Newport	90
67	Lasell	86
66	Lesley	110
81	New England Col.	78
85	Lyndon St.	66
67	Husson ⊠	92
76	Maine Maritime ⊠	57
88	Johnson St. ⊠	62
53	Me.-Farmington	68
70	Thomas (Me.) ⊠	54
75	Skidmore	68
80	Mount Ida ⊠	64
76	Lasell ⊠	83
79	Elms	92
82	Becker	76
80	Johnson St.	65
90	Lyndon St. ⊠	83
90	Lesley ⊠	79
71	Green Mountain	49
95	Becker ⊠	84
102	Elms ⊠	94
71	Husson	93
58	Western New Eng.	74

Nickname: Spartans
Colors: Green & White
Arena: Glenbrook
 Capacity: 1,000; Year Built: 1959
AD: Deanna Tyson
SID: Jeff Weld

CATAWBA
Salisbury, NC 28144-2488 II

Coach: Jim Baker, Catawba 1978

2006-07 RESULTS (20-11)
104	Allen ⊠	69
74	GCSU ⊠	82
69	S.C. Upstate ⊠	78
86	Armstrong Atlantic ⊠	94
75	Clayton St. ⊠	76
93	Montreat ⊠	87
61	Lander	78
75	S.C. Upstate	87
66	Lander ⊠	54
79	Barton †	76
92	Augusta St. †	70
93	Lenoir-Rhyne ⊠	82
81	Wingate	90
53	Tusculum ⊠	50
56	Presbyterian	69
83	Mars Hill ⊠	61
70	Lincoln Memorial	65
77	Newberry	83
97	Carson-Newman ⊠	81
108	Wingate ⊠	105
60	Tusculum	46
89	Newberry ⊠	80
83	Mars Hill	64
89	Lincoln Memorial ⊠	67
81	Lenoir-Rhyne	73
112	Carson-Newman	107
63	Presbyterian ⊠	57
115	Carson-Newman ⊠	113
74	Lenoir-Rhyne	70
82	Wingate †	97
69	Clayton St. †	72

Nickname: Catawba Indians
Colors: Blue & White
Arena: Goodman Gym
 Capacity: 3,500; Year Built: 1970
AD: Dennis Davidson
SID: Jim Lewis

CATHOLIC
Washington, DC 20064.................III

Coach: Steve Howes, Catholic 1996

2006-07 RESULTS (23-6)
85	Neumann †	73
67	Albright	62
61	Haverford	55
71	Scranton	61
67	St. Mary's (Md.) ⊠	62
62	Goucher ⊠	68
68	Marymount (Va.)	55
73	Hood ⊠	79
77	Villa Julie ⊠	67
78	Susquehanna ⊠	76
72	Methodist ⊠	43
61	Elizabethtown ⊠	42
78	York (Pa.) ⊠	61
62	Salisbury	58
51	Gallaudet ⊠	55
56	Mary Washington	64
75	St. Mary's (Md.) ⊠	73
80	Goucher	49
67	Marymount (Va.) ⊠	64
69	Hood	62
63	York (Pa.)	67
74	Salisbury ⊠	72
70	Gallaudet	52
74	Mary Washington ⊠	61
79	Salisbury ⊠	59
69	Mary Washington ⊠	67
85	Hood	75
58	Messiah †	37
70	Lincoln (Pa.) †	81

Nickname: Cardinals
Colors: Cardinal Red & Black
Arena: DuFour Center
    Capacity: 2,000; Year Built: 1985
AD: Mike Allen
SID: Barbara Jonas

CAZENOVIA
Cazenovia, NY 13035.................III

Coach: Michael Bowser, Holy Cross 1966

2006-07 RESULTS (12-14)
60	Oswego St.	114
87	Purchase St. †	80
54	Utica	79
69	Hobart	76
106	Purchase St.	103
99	Bard ⊠	87
75	Oneonta St. ⊠	72
80	Polytechnic (N.Y.) ⊠	84
81	SUNYIT ⊠	88
63	Clarkson	74
93	D'Youville ⊠	60
93	Morrisville St. ⊠	88
78	Phila. Biblical	63
86	Baptist Bible (Pa.)	91
89	Keystone ⊠	77
57	Keuka	100
109	Bard	94
96	Penn St.-Berks ⊠	89
75	Villa Julie ⊠	93
77	D'Youville	72
76	Chestnut Hill	93
88	Baptist Bible (Pa.) ⊠	105
89	Morrisville St. ⊠	94
93	Keuka ⊠	91
65	Keystone	94
101	Baptist Bible (Pa.)	120

Nickname: Wildcats
Colors: Navy Blue & Gold
Arena: Schneweiss Athletic Center
    Capacity: 800; Year Built: 1988
AD: Robert Kenna
SID: Brian Small

CENTENARY (LA.)
Shreveport, LA 71134-1188.............I

Coach: Rob Flaska, Michigan Tech 1982

2006-07 RESULTS (10-21)
66	TCU	72
91	Texas St. ⊠	85
71	Utah St. †	77
83	Southeast Mo. St. †	51
82	Rhode Island †	92
86	Northwestern St.	89
69	Ark.-Little Rock ⊠	59
84	Nicholls St. ⊠	71
64	Texas Tech	98
40	SMU	68
52	Georgia Tech	92
82	Louisiana Tech †	73
66	Texas	76
82	Texas St.	81
63	Baylor	76
62	Valparaiso ⊠	66
64	Western Ill. ⊠	58
75	UMKC	80
57	Southern Utah	78
66	Oral Roberts ⊠	89
68	IUPUI ⊠	70
74	Oakland ⊠	82
42	Western Ill.	45
50	Valparaiso	68
70	Southern Utah ⊠	63
69	UMKC ⊠	68
80	Oral Roberts	85
83	Chicago St. ⊠	80
63	Oakland	70
62	IUPUI	87
59	Oral Roberts †	79

Nickname: Gentlemen
Colors: Maroon & White
Arena: Gold Dome
    Capacity: 3,000; Year Built: 1971
AD: Glenn S. Evans
SID: David Pratt

CENTENARY (N.J.)
Hackettstown, NJ 07840.................III

Coach: Andy DeStephano, St. John's (N.Y.) 1998

2006-07 RESULTS (3-21)
67	Plymouth St.	82
54	Husson †	85
84	Berkeley ⊠	61
75	Brooklyn	87
57	Farmingdale St.	98
76	Mt. St. Vincent	74
63	Old Westbury	71
74	CCNY	83
75	Briarcliffe (N.Y.)	77
73	Green Mountain	62
74	Hunter	92
61	St. Joseph's (L.I.)	91
69	Mt. St. Mary (N.Y.) ⊠	97
72	Maritime (N.Y.) ⊠	85
70	Stevens Institute	108
62	Manhattanville ⊠	93
65	Merchant Marine	66
58	Mt. St. Vincent	96
66	Farmingdale St. ⊠	86
67	Mt. St. Mary (N.Y.)	94
66	Yeshiva ⊠	87
68	Maritime (N.Y.)	75
79	Manhattanville	112
71	Old Westbury ⊠	105

Nickname: Cyclones
Colors: Blue & White
Arena: Reeves Center
    Capacity: 250; Year Built: 1954
AD: Billie Jo Blackwell
SID: Josh Huber

CENTRAL (IOWA)
Pella, IA 50219.................III

Coach: Mike Boschee, North Dakota 1990

2006-07 RESULTS (11-14)
92	Bethany Lutheran	96
81	Cornell College ⊠	67
64	Westminster (Mo.)	66
106	Faith Bapt. Bible	44
74	Ashford	86
82	Monmouth (Ill.) ⊠	88
80	Martin Luther ⊠	68
68	Presentation †	63
63	Chaminade	91
83	Wartburg	69
60	Loras	82
72	Buena Vista ⊠	70
58	Dubuque	81
65	Simpson ⊠	83
59	Luther ⊠	47
65	Coe ⊠	61
57	Simpson	74
71	Cornell College	79
66	Buena Vista	87
65	Loras ⊠	76
88	Wartburg ⊠	73
68	Dubuque ⊠	62
60	Luther	57
68	Coe	71
87	Simpson	95

Nickname: Dutch
Colors: Red & White
Arena: Kuyper Gymnasium
    Capacity: 3,000; Year Built: 1970
AD: Al Dorenkamp
SID: Larry Happel

CENTRAL ARK.
Conway, AR 72035-0001.................II

Coach: Rand Chappell, Missouri St. 1985

2006-07 RESULTS (10-20)
71	Central Methodist ⊠	53
64	St. Bonaventure	69
59	Connecticut	88
61	Mississippi †	75
43	Fairfield †	46
64	Mississippi Val. ⊠	66
85	Rhema ⊠	52
81	Texas Col. ⊠	64
72	Bowling Green	58
68	UMKC	80
51	Mississippi Val.	66
50	Bucknell †	48
56	Marist	71
60	Texas-Arlington ⊠	66
80	Texas St.	93
59	UTSA ⊠	49
73	A&M-Corpus Christi ⊠	85
50	Lamar	62
56	McNeese St.	61
66	Southeastern La. ⊠	74
64	Nicholls St. ⊠	53
75	Ozarks (Ark.) ⊠	58
66	Northwestern St.	78
54	Stephen F. Austin ⊠	60
68	Sam Houston St.	81
82	Lamar ⊠	86
55	McNeese St. ⊠	58
63	Southeastern La.	66
70	Nicholls St.	66
92	Northwestern St. ⊠	86

Nickname: Bears
Colors: Purple & Gray
Arena: Jeff Farris Center
    Capacity: 5,500; Year Built: 1973
AD: Bradley Teague
SID: Steve East

CENTRAL CONN. ST.
New Britain, CT 06050-4010.........I

Coach: Howie Dickenman, Central Conn. St. 1970

2006-07 RESULTS (22-12)
40	Michigan	60
69	Eastern Mich. †	76
64	Davidson †	91
73	New Hampshire	66
57	St. Bonaventure ⊠	60
77	St. Francis (N.Y.) ⊠	64
52	Lehigh	55
63	Delaware ⊠	60
66	Massachusetts †	79
65	Harvard ⊠	72
73	La Salle ⊠	86
48	Vermont ⊠	55
66	UMBC	52
80	St. Francis (Pa.) ⊠	61
48	Robert Morris	64
71	Mt. St. Mary's	63
61	Long Island ⊠	48
60	Fairleigh Dickinson ⊠	56
49	Monmouth ⊠	46
69	St. Francis (N.Y.)	61
103	Sacred Heart ⊠	96
65	Quinnipiac	54
74	Mt. St. Mary's ⊠	62
96	Long Island	75
94	Quinnipiac ⊠	71
80	Sacred Heart	66
70	Monmouth	65
60	Fairleigh Dickinson	66
88	Robert Morris ⊠	86
79	Wagner ⊠	54
79	St. Francis (N.Y.) ⊠	61
74	Mt. St. Mary's ⊠	68
74	Sacred Heart ⊠	70
57	Ohio St. †	78

Nickname: Blue Devils
Colors: Blue & White
Arena: Detrick Gymnasium
    Capacity: 4,500; Year Built: 1965
AD: Charles Jones Jr.
SID: Thomas Pincince

UCF
Orlando, FL 32816-3555.................I

Coach: Kirk Speraw, Iowa 1980

2006-07 RESULTS (22-9)
83	Rollins ⊠	80
73	Stetson ⊠	60
81	Bethune-Cookman ⊠	46
81	Florida Tech ⊠	37
99	Jacksonville ⊠	62
87	Fla. Atlantic ⊠	65
63	Minnesota	74
67	Utah †	61
64	Appalachian St. †	75
73	Tennessee Tech †	66
75	NJIT ⊠	63
88	Tex.-Pan American ⊠	62
87	Colorado	96
72	South Dakota St.	61
64	UAB	74
78	Marshall	71
64	SMU ⊠	56
72	Rice ⊠	67
70	Houston	73
67	UTEP	64
65	Memphis ⊠	87
63	Tulsa ⊠	53
67	East Caro.	49
75	Marshall ⊠	58
80	Tulane	86
74	Rice	63
59	Southern Miss. ⊠	56
64	Tulsa	66
75	Houston ⊠	72
77	East Caro. ⊠	64
51	Rice †	53

Nickname: Golden Knights
Colors: Black & Gold
Arena: UCF Arena
  Capacity: 5,100; Year Built: 1991
AD: Keith R. Tribble
SID: Doug Richards

CENTRAL MICH.
Mount Pleasant, MI 48859-0001 .. I

Coach: Ernie Zeigler, Cleary 1984

2006-07 RESULTS (13-18)

50	Youngstown St. †	74
71	Brown †	58
85	UMKC	68
50	Cincinnati	60
76	Milwaukee	61
66	San Diego	67
59	Arkansas	75
71	Green Bay	89
78	Cleveland St.	76
61	Southern Ill.	74
73	Niagara	80
52	Morehead St.	51
74	Eastern Mich.	68
60	Toledo	65
67	Northern Ill.	64
76	Western Mich.	86
57	Ball St.	64
52	Miami (Ohio)	72
71	Bowling Green	68
45	Kent St.	61
73	Ohio	74
71	Akron	78
59	Buffalo	56
71	Western Mich.	66
62	Ill.-Chicago	84
61	Ball St.	59
71	Northern Ill.	64
83	Eastern Mich.	87
57	Toledo	77
80	Buffalo †	74
53	Akron †	82

Nickname: Chippewas
Colors: Maroon & Gold
Arena: Rose Arena
  Capacity: 5,200; Year Built: 1973
AD: David W. Heeke Jr.
SID: Don Helinski

CENTRAL MO.
Warrensburg, MO 64093 ... II

Coach: Kim Anderson, Missouri 1979

2006-07 RESULTS (31-4)

81	Monmouth (Ill.)	53
89	Central Methodist	58
82	Bacone	48
92	Eastern N.M.	65
88	Lincoln (Mo.)	60
77	Westminster (Mo.)	40
87	Pittsburg St.	67
71	Seattle Pacific †	60
81	Rollins †	74
103	Sterling (Kan.)	67
67	Washburn	50
77	Southwest Baptist	66
86	Mo. Southern St.	70
90	Mo. Western St.	70
80	Fort Hays St.	63
69	Northwest Mo. St.	55
77	Truman	64
81	Pittsburg St.	59
66	Truman	47
64	Northwest Mo. St.	82
77	Fort Hays St.	87
88	Emporia St.	79
94	Mo. Southern St.	66
84	Mo. Western St.	73
72	Emporia St.	78
69	Southwest Baptist	59
78	Washburn	62
78	Fort Hays St. †	64
72	Truman †	68

59	Pittsburg St. †	56
76	St. Edward's	39
72	Northwest Mo. St.	61
67	Southeastern Okla.	54
86	Montevallo †	69
85	Winona St. †	90

Nickname: Mules
Colors: Cardinal & Black
Arena: CMSU Multipurpose Building
  Capacity: 8,500; Year Built: 1976
AD: Jerry M. Hughes
SID: Rob McCutcheon

CENTRAL OKLA.
Edmond, OK 73034 ... II

Coach: Terry Evans, Oklahoma 1992

2006-07 RESULTS (20-8)

79	Okla. Baptist †	65
63	Okla. Christian	62
99	St. Gregory's	70
64	Mo. Western St. †	81
89	Emporia St.	98
104	Okla. Christian	87
62	Tex. A&M-Kingsville	72
82	Washburn	72
91	Angelo St.	64
92	Abilene Christian	66
68	West Tex. A&M	78
87	Eastern N.M.	78
108	Mid-America Bible	77
71	Tarleton St.	54
75	Northeastern St.	59
83	Southwestern Okla.	77
82	Cameron	78
63	Tex. A&M-Commerce	64
69	Southeastern Okla.	87
73	East Central	64
84	Northeastern St.	78
111	Tex. A&M-Commerce	106
79	Southwestern Okla.	80
95	Cameron	75
94	Southeastern Okla.	88
89	East Central	68
92	Tarleton St.	67
74	Midwestern St.	78

Nickname: Bronchos
Colors: Bronze & Blue
Arena: Hamilton Field House
  Capacity: 3,000; Year Built: 1965
AD: Bill Farley
SID: Mike Kirk

CENTRAL WASH.
Ellensburg, WA 98926 ... II

Coach: Greg Sparling, Central Wash. 1993

2006-07 RESULTS (15-12)

75	BYU-Hawaii	83
96	Cal St. Stanislaus †	112
93	Hawaii Pacific †	57
79	Humboldt St. †	90
92	Cal St. Chico	78
92	Mont. St.-Billings †	63
74	Alderson-Broaddus †	97
84	Cal St. San B'dino †	94
66	Cal Poly Pomona †	83
84	Shepherd †	64
67	North Dakota †	62
79	Alas. Fairbanks	72
60	Alas. Anchorage	80
73	St. Martin's	84
70	Western Ore.	65
71	Seattle	75
77	Western Wash.	79
98	Seattle Pacific	91
82	Western Wash.	68
83	Northwest Nazarene	53
80	Seattle Pacific	73
103	St. Martin's	85
69	Western Ore.	68
61	Alas. Anchorage	76

74	Alas. Fairbanks	67
73	Seattle	88
105	Northwest Nazarene	91

Nickname: Wildcats
Colors: Crimson & Black
Arena: Nicholson Pavilion
  Capacity: 3,600; Year Built: 1959
AD: Jack Bishop
SID: Jonathan Gordon

CENTRE
Danville, KY 40422-1394 ... III

Coach: Greg Mason, Centre 1994

2006-07 RESULTS (24-5)

84	Virginia-Wise †	60
82	Berea	66
63	Maryville (Tenn.)	71
69	Albion †	71
83	Cincinnati-Clermont †	69
72	Berea	55
67	DePauw	73
76	Thomas More	56
56	Transylvania	54
59	St. Norbert	47
60	Messiah	56
76	Oglethorpe	57
80	Sewanee	68
84	Austin	60
75	Hendrix	38
55	Southwestern (Tex.)	38
61	Trinity (Tex.)	52
67	Millsaps	79
77	Rhodes	52
73	DePauw	41
56	Austin	37
72	Hendrix	71
96	Oglethorpe	68
73	Sewanee	54
63	Southwestern (Tex.) †	43
75	Millsaps †	59
72	Trinity (Tex.) †	57
69	Capital †	55
56	Wooster	73

Nickname: Colonels
Colors: Gold & White
Arena: Alumni Memorial Gym
  Capacity: 1,800; Year Built: 1950
AD: Brian E. Chafin
SID: Mike Pritchard

CHADRON ST.
Chadron, NE 69337-2690 ... II

Coach: Brent Bargen, Doane 1993

2006-07 RESULTS (6-21)

75	Minn. St. Moorhead	99
79	Concordia-St. Paul †	102
65	Black Hills St.	75
67	Neb.-Omaha	93
75	South Dakota †	84
73	South Dakota	68
96	N.M. Highlands	104
84	Western N.M.	97
81	Mesa St.	87
76	Fort Lewis	86
63	Colorado St.-Pueblo	72
69	Adams St.	82
70	Western St.	69
85	UC-Colo. Springs	90
77	Regis (Colo.)	67
69	Neb.-Kearney	82
58	Colorado Mines	59
97	Johnson & Wales (CO)	96
83	Colo. Christian	78
58	Metro St.	96
65	Neb.-Kearney	98
76	Colorado Mines	71
84	Johnson & Wales (CO)	92
65	Metro St.	69
74	Colo. Christian	87
72	Regis (Colo.)	81
66	UC-Colo. Springs	70

Nickname: Eagles
Colors: Cardinal & White
Arena: Armstrong
  Capacity: 2,500; Year Built: 1965
AD: Bradley Roy Smith
SID: Con Marshall

CHAMINADE
Honolulu, HI 96816-1578 ... II

Coach: Matt Mahar, Johnson St. 1996

2006-07 RESULTS (16-11)

63	UCLA †	88
74	DePaul †	93
57	Oklahoma †	72
90	Carleton	67
92	St. Martin's	73
91	Holy Names	76
77	Cal St. Monterey Bay †	80
71	Sonoma St.	64
92	Presentation	50
91	Central (Iowa)	63
87	Indianapolis	71
101	New Paltz St.	86
79	Hawaii-Hilo	81
88	Hawaii-Hilo	85
83	BYU-Hawaii	69
68	BYU-Hawaii	76
64	Notre Dame de Namur	62
75	Notre Dame de Namur	70
72	Grand Canyon	86
86	Hawaii Pacific	56
89	BYU-Hawaii	93
54	Grand Canyon	50
68	Grand Canyon	71
78	Notre Dame de Namur	48
85	Hawaii Pacific	90
93	Hawaii Pacific	68
76	Hawaii-Hilo	60

Nickname: Silverswords
Colors: Royal Blue & White
Arena: McCabe Gym
Capacity: 2,500
AD: Kaia Hedlund
SID: Maurice Maggiolino

CHAPMAN
Orange, CA 92866 ... III

Coach: Mike Bokosky, Fort Lewis 1978

2006-07 RESULTS (21-5)

57	Whittier	60
72	La Verne	63
81	Caltech	49
73	Colorado Col. †	47
94	Whittier †	62
107	Redlands	110
59	Cal Lutheran	48
70	La Verne	62
62	Occidental	67
81	Hope Int'l	52
111	Puget Sound	117
66	Whittier	65
43	Claremont-M-S	54
83	La Sierra	56
77	UC Santa Cruz †	56
71	Dallas	64
89	Colorado Col. †	56
88	La Sierra	81
78	UC Santa Cruz	57
92	West Coast Chrst.	54
89	La Sierra	78
69	Hawaii Pacific	67
81	West Coast Chrst.	63
76	UC Santa Cruz	64
84	Colorado Col. †	67
64	Neb. Wesleyan	49

Nickname: Panthers
Colors: Cardinal & Gray
Arena: Hutton Sports Center
  Capacity: 2,400; Year Built: 1978
AD: David Currey
SID: Doug Aiken

COL. OF CHARLESTON
Charleston, SC 29424 I

Coach: Bobby Cremins, South Carolina 1970

2006-07 RESULTS (22-11)
72	Georgia St.	66
68	Villanova †	81
59	VCU †	71
64	Middle Tenn. †	56
91	UNC Wilmington ⊠	70
61	Kentucky	77
80	Charleston So.	84
57	Appalachian St. ⊠	68
55	South Carolina	67
62	Chattanooga ⊠	60
70	Coastal Caro.	49
82	Western Caro.	75
65	Fordham ⊠	56
68	Radford ⊠	46
71	Fairleigh Dickinson ⊠	67
73	Davidson	81
74	Citadel	62
67	Furman ⊠	55
67	Ga. Southern ⊠	64
67	Elon ⊠	45
77	Wofford ⊠	75
67	Chattanooga	54
56	Appalachian St.	67
76	Western Caro. ⊠	64
81	UNC Greensboro	59
63	Davidson ⊠	73
71	Wofford	58
80	Furman	77
50	Citadel ⊠	40
65	Ga. Southern	74
77	Ga. Southern †	66
89	Appalachian St. †	87
65	Davidson †	72

Nickname: Cougars
Colors: Maroon & White
Arena: F. Mitchell Johnson Center
Capacity: 3,500; Year Built: 1983
AD: Jerry I. Baker
SID: Tony Ciuffo

CHARLESTON (W.V.)
Charleston, WV 25304 II

Coach: Greg White, Marshall 1982

2006-07 RESULTS (15-14)
84	Lock Haven ⊠	80
49	Findlay	81
50	Central St. (Ohio) ⊠	68
75	Edinboro ⊠	77
140	Ohio-Eastern ⊠	70
72	Chowan ⊠	68
80	West Va. Tech †	67
77	Mount Olive †	81
75	Bluefield St.	63
89	Concord ⊠	72
72	Salem Int'l ⊠	77
66	Alderson-Broaddus	72
80	West Virginia St. ⊠	92
73	Shepherd	70
81	Bluefield St. ⊠	73
72	West Liberty St. ⊠	77
87	Davis & Elkins	71
57	Alderson-Broaddus ⊠	80
68	Chowan	65
66	Concord	73
83	Ohio Valley ⊠	71
85	West Va. Wesleyan	78
69	Wheeling Jesuit ⊠	75
82	Glenville St.	60
60	Fairmont St.	68
87	Davis & Elkins ⊠	60
68	West Virginia St.	82
70	Fairmont St.	62
70	Alderson-Broaddus †	86

Nickname: Golden Eagles
Colors: Maroon & Gold
Arena: Eddie King Gym
Capacity: 2,080; Year Built: 1988

AD: Tom Nozica
SID: Jim Workman

CHARLESTON SO.
Charleston, SC 29423-8087 I

Coach: Barclay Radebaugh, East Tenn. St. 1987

2006-07 RESULTS (8-22)
69	Furman	88
101	Fla. Christian	43
72	Citadel ⊠	63
69	Tulane	75
93	Asbury ⊠	68
50	Clemson	74
87	Coker ⊠	46
84	Col. of Charleston ⊠	80
59	Mercer	78
58	Southern California	70
69	New Mexico	76
67	Longwood ⊠	73
49	Md.-East. Shore †	74
53	Auburn	69
54	Coastal Caro.	66
52	Winthrop ⊠	75
83	VMI	116
53	Radford	61
87	High Point ⊠	95
63	Liberty ⊠	66
40	UNC Asheville	53
86	Coastal Caro. ⊠	77
89	Covenant ⊠	61
84	Radford ⊠	70
97	VMI	105
73	Liberty	83
54	Winthrop	78
50	High Point	70
56	UNC Asheville ⊠	73
42	Winthrop	72

Nickname: Buccaneers
Colors: Navy & Old Gold
Arena: CSU Fieldhouse
Capacity: 798; Year Built: 1965
AD: Hank Small
SID: Blake Freeland

CHARLOTTE
Charlotte, NC 28223 I

Coach: Bobby Lutz, Charlotte 1980

2006-07 RESULTS (14-16)
88	Hofstra ⊠	82
72	North Texas ⊠	90
67	Syracuse	79
72	Georgia St. ⊠	63
69	Mississippi St.	78
57	Indiana	74
81	UNC Asheville ⊠	73
51	Davidson	79
46	Houston †	68
74	Valparaiso †	62
79	Wyoming †	78
83	Wofford ⊠	62
63	Dayton	66
70	St. Joseph's ⊠	75
66	Richmond	51
80	Dayton ⊠	59
68	George Washington ⊠	76
63	St. Louis	76
61	Massachusetts ⊠	66
87	La Salle ⊠	80
57	Xavier	91
61	Richmond ⊠	46
72	Fordham ⊠	68
80	La.-Lafayette ⊠	56
69	Rhode Island	86
99	Duquesne	90
69	Temple	81
60	George Washington ⊠	62
74	St. Bonaventure †	53
63	Dayton †	81

Nickname: 49ers
Colors: Green & White

Arena: Dale F. Halton Arena
Capacity: 9,105; Year Built: 1996
AD: Judith W. Rose
SID: Thomas E. Whitestone

CHATTANOOGA
Chattanooga, TN 37403-2598 I

Coach: John Shulman, East Tenn. St. 1989

2006-07 RESULTS (15-18)
108	Ohio Valley ⊠	85
70	East Tenn. St.	71
44	Florida	93
70	Ball St.	55
55	Towson †	56
79	Prairie View †	66
97	Berea ⊠	63
63	Kentucky †	79
60	Col. of Charleston	62
76	Oral Roberts ⊠	72
80	Davidson ⊠	92
91	King (Tenn.) ⊠	50
83	Kennesaw St. ⊠	67
65	Colorado St. ⊠	76
56	Furman	69
63	Appalachian St. ⊠	77
67	Western Caro. ⊠	73
67	Ga. Southern ⊠	58
57	UNC Greensboro	67
66	Elon	56
63	Wofford	66
54	Col. of Charleston ⊠	67
61	Furman ⊠	68
62	Ga. Southern	57
57	Davidson	87
73	Citadel ⊠	43
75	Western Caro.	72
69	Appalachian St.	85
75	Jacksonville St. ⊠	64
62	Elon ⊠	59
61	UNC Greensboro ⊠	68
64	Wofford †	55
68	Davidson †	78

Nickname: Mocs
Colors: Navy Blue & Old Gold
Arena: The McKenzie Arena
Capacity: 11,218; Year Built: 1982
AD: Rick Hart
SID: Jeff Romero

CHESTNUT HILL
Philadelphia, PA 19118-2693 III

Coach: Jesse Balcer, Philadelphia U.

2006-07 RESULTS (19-9)
63	Philadelphia U.	75
58	Widener	81
83	Valley Forge Chrst.	79
80	Baptist Bible (Pa.) ⊠	63
69	Villa Julie	79
75	Keystone	74
63	Keuka	61
75	Arcadia ⊠	86
61	Rowan ⊠	79
53	Phila. Sciences	64
65	Roanoke	89
81	Ferrum †	74
76	Delaware Valley	59
88	Penn St.-Berks	59
76	Villa Julie ⊠	70
75	Phila. Biblical	72
74	Polytechnic (N.Y.) †	60
72	Purchase St. †	44
70	D'Youville	54
76	Penn St.-Berks	79
93	Cazenovia ⊠	76
63	Phila. Biblical ⊠	60
100	Bard	71
89	Purchase St.	72
86	Polytechnic (N.Y.)	65
89	Penn St.-Berks ⊠	64
79	Baptist Bible (Pa.) †	71
92	Villa Julie	94

Nickname: Griffins
Colors: Scarlet & White
Arena: Sorgenti Arena
Capacity: 1,400; Year Built: 2000
AD: Bill Stiles
SID: Greg Gornick

CHEYNEY
Cheyney, PA 19319-0200 II

Coach: Cleo Hill Jr., N.C. Central 1994

2006-07 RESULTS (15-15)
55	Dowling †	60
72	Salem Int'l †	76
95	Lincoln (Pa.) †	103
61	California (Pa.) ⊠	69
72	Shaw †	45
81	Augusta St. †	77
67	Virginia St. ⊠	73
64	Clarion	61
67	Indiana (Pa.)	41
71	Seattle Pacific	75
79	Seattle †	61
57	Edinboro ⊠	41
70	Slippery Rock ⊠	50
80	Bloomsburg	72
61	Lock Haven	62
57	Shippensburg	71
81	East Stroudsburg ⊠	66
71	Mansfield	81
65	West Chester	59
76	Kutztown ⊠	71
85	Millersville	92
100	Bloomsburg ⊠	61
56	East Stroudsburg	60
79	Mansfield	71
58	West Chester ⊠	59
70	Kutztown	73
81	Millersville ⊠	83
79	Kutztown	63
67	California (Pa.)	65
68	Millersville †	79

Nickname: Wolves
Colors: Blue & White
Arena: Cope Hall
Capacity: 1,500; Year Built: 1961
AD: Patric Simon
SID: Lenn Margolis

CHICAGO
Chicago, IL 60637 III

Coach: Mike McGrath, DePauw 1992

2006-07 RESULTS (20-6)
78	Coast Guard ⊠	61
79	DePauw ⊠	71
66	Lake Forest	39
60	Trinity (Tex.)	57
62	Southwestern (Tex.) †	74
81	Wheaton (Ill.) ⊠	77
93	Kalamazoo	59
64	Ill. Wesleyan	60
67	Coe ⊠	70
76	Cornell College ⊠	51
70	Milwaukee Engr.	53
59	Washington-St. Louis ⊠	70
99	Emory	75
69	Case Reserve	67
100	Carnegie Mellon ⊠	69
81	Rochester (N.Y.) ⊠	74
62	New York U. ⊠	60
88	Brandeis ⊠	76
74	Brandeis	69
76	New York U.	79
77	Case Reserve ⊠	73
89	Emory ⊠	71
76	Rochester (N.Y.)	73
82	Carnegie Mellon	75
74	Washington-St. Louis	70
54	Hope †	76

Nickname: Maroons
Colors: Maroon & White
Arena: Gerald Ratner Athletics Center

Capacity: 1,558; Year Built: 2003
AD: Thomas Weingartner
SID: Dave Hilbert

CHICAGO ST.
Chicago, IL 60628-1598 I

Coach: Kevin Jones, Eastern Ill. 1987

2006-07 RESULTS (9-20)

98	St. Bonaventure †	95
66	Texas	92
64	Wichita St.	76
69	Indiana	90
86	Wright St. ⊠	70
86	UTEP	82
74	New Mexico St.	80
44	Southeastern La. †	59
56	DePaul	83
51	California	75
72	Eastern Mich. †	61
81	Green Bay	92
61	Michigan St.	69
82	Cleveland St.	77
62	Wright St.	63
66	Southern Utah	84
64	Valparaiso	67
78	New Mexico St. ⊠	88
78	UMKC	86
79	Oakland	78
109	Ind.-South Bend ⊠	73
53	Oral Roberts	59
82	Western Ill.	72
36	Kansas St.	73
68	Detroit	78
77	IUPUI	79
76	Valparaiso	91
112	East-West U. ⊠	77
80	Centenary (La.)	83

Nickname: Cougars
Colors: Green & White
Arena: Jacoby Dickens Center
  Capacity: 2,500; Year Built: 1971
AD: Wayne L. Baskerville
SID: Quenjana Adams

CHOWAN
Murfreesboro, NC 27855 III

Coach: Jim Tribbett, Florida St. 1977

2006-07 RESULTS (11-15)

83	Coker †	64
70	Mount Olive	79
59	High Point	75
65	Millersville ⊠	76
79	Virginia St. ⊠	81
92	Concord ⊠	81
78	Barton	74
61	UNC Pembroke ⊠	64
81	Belmont Abbey ⊠	64
68	Charleston (W.V.)	72
74	Mount Olive †	93
76	UNC Pembroke	64
57	Millersville	94
50	East Caro.	68
77	Allen ⊠	60
66	Francis Marion ⊠	47
56	Elizabeth City St.	66
66	Concord	70
81	Apprentice	72
65	Charleston (W.V.) ⊠	68
90	Barton ⊠	94
92	Southern Va. ⊠	85
72	Francis Marion	78
85	Apprentice ⊠	70
107	Carver Bible †	51
60	Tenn. Temple †	67

Nickname: Hawks
Colors: Columbia Blue & White
Arena: Helms Center
  Capacity: 3,000; Year Built: 1979
AD: Dennis E. Helsel
SID: Meredith Davies Long

CHRISTIAN BROS.
Memphis, TN 38104-5519 II

Coach: Mike Nienaber, Mississippi Col.
1977

2006-07 RESULTS (21-7)

70	Lynn ⊠	52
66	Wayne St. (Mich.) †	51
67	Ferris St. †	62
78	LeMoyne-Owen	64
47	Grand Valley St. †	56
95	Central Baptist †	45
55	Lane	53
63	Williams Baptist ⊠	53
56	Montevallo	67
107	North Ala.	94
94	LeMoyne-Owen	56
73	Mo.-St. Louis ⊠	54
96	Lane	79
71	Southern Ark.	51
74	Arkansas Tech ⊠	61
48	Henderson St.	57
72	Ouachita Baptist	68
68	Delta St. ⊠	65
49	Ark.-Monticello ⊠	65
52	Harding ⊠	64
69	Southern Ark.	49
63	Arkansas Tech	60
53	Henderson St. ⊠	56
84	Ouachita Baptist ⊠	69
65	Delta St.	61
90	Ark.-Monticello ⊠	60
76	Harding	71
71	North Ala. †	78

Nickname: Buccaneers
Colors: Scarlet & Gray
Arena: Canale Arena
  Capacity: 1,000; Year Built: 1951
AD: Joseph Nadicksbernd
SID: Eric Opperman

CHRIS. NEWPORT
Newport News, VA 23606-2998 .. III

Coach: C.J. Woollum, Ky. Wesleyan 1971

2006-07 RESULTS (15-11)

92	York (N.Y.) ⊠	98
71	Va. Wesleyan	72
91	Southern Va. ⊠	87
87	Maryland Bible ⊠	67
84	Randolph-Macon ⊠	77
90	Castleton	68
92	Frostburg St. ⊠	84
71	John Carroll †	92
71	Fisk	72
86	Fisk ⊠	74
87	Oswego St. ⊠	85
78	Wesley ⊠	74
84	Shenandoah	81
72	Piedmont ⊠	74
85	N.C. Wesleyan ⊠	92
80	Ferrum ⊠	79
79	Averett ⊠	75
85	Methodist	86
67	Greensboro	65
85	Shenandoah ⊠	75
96	N.C. Wesleyan	102
73	Averett	74
97	Ferrum	89
93	Methodist ⊠	91
86	Greensboro ⊠	96
69	N.C. Wesleyan ⊠	71

Nickname: Captains
Colors: Blue & Silver
Arena: Freeman Center
  Capacity: 2,300; Year Built: 2000
AD: C.J. Woollum
SID: Francis Tommasino

CINCINNATI
Cincinnati, OH 45221-0021 I

Coach: Mick Cronin, Cincinnati 1997

2006-07 RESULTS (11-19)

70	Howard ⊠	39
67	Tenn.-Martin ⊠	49
63	High Point ⊠	51
90	Wofford ⊠	91
60	Central Mich. ⊠	50
68	Oakland ⊠	61
57	UAB ⊠	59
80	Temple †	71
67	Xavier ⊠	57
50	Ohio St. †	72
80	North Carolina St. ⊠	71
60	Miami (Ohio) ⊠	52
66	Ohio †	79
55	Memphis	88
42	Rutgers ⊠	54
59	South Fla.	74
76	Syracuse	77
96	West Virginia ⊠	83
51	Pittsburgh ⊠	67
67	Georgetown	82
53	Louisville ⊠	69
64	St. John's (N.Y.) ⊠	73
70	Providence	71
69	Rutgers	73
48	Villanova ⊠	64
64	Notre Dame ⊠	76
65	Georgetown ⊠	75
45	DePaul	58
70	Seton Hall ⊠	67
65	West Virginia	79

Nickname: Bearcats
Colors: Red & Black
Arena: Fifth Third Arena
  Capacity: 13,176; Year Built: 1989
AD: Michael J. Thomas
SID: Tom Hathaway

CITADEL
Charleston, SC 29409-6150 I

Coach: Ed Conroy, Citadel 1989

2006-07 RESULTS (7-23)

79	Ohio Valley ⊠	58
41	Michigan St.	73
53	Iowa	75
63	Charleston So.	72
50	Notre Dame	74
58	Southern California	74
81	Asbury ⊠	60
59	South Carolina ⊠	74
55	Army ⊠	63
52	Appalachian St. ⊠	56
63	Western Caro.	82
36	West Virginia	63
113	Atlanta Christian ⊠	59
53	Elon	50
74	Wofford	71
62	Col. of Charleston ⊠	74
74	Ga. Southern ⊠	69
54	Davidson	79
44	UNC Greensboro ⊠	47
59	Furman	63
54	Appalachian St.	95
68	Western Caro. ⊠	78
52	Elon ⊠	49
43	Chattanooga	73
49	Wofford ⊠	61
51	Furman ⊠	69
62	Ga. Southern	81
40	Col. of Charleston	50
70	Davidson ⊠	87
46	Ga. Southern †	62

Nickname: Bulldogs
Colors: Blue & White
Arena: McAlister Field House
  Capacity: 6,000; Year Built: 1939
AD: Les Robinson
SID: Noelle Orr

CCNY
New York, NY 10031 III

Coach: Andre Stampfel, Baruch 1996

2006-07 RESULTS (12-14)

56	Cortland St. ⊠	58
66	Rutgers-Newark ⊠	75
74	St. Joseph's (L.I.)	65
65	Stevens Institute	79
86	Wesleyan (Conn.)	83
62	Hunter	77
79	City Tech	71
83	Centenary (N.J.) ⊠	74
98	Yeshiva	101
51	Wm. Paterson ⊠	63
78	John Jay	59
52	Baruch	59
48	Mt. St. Mary (N.Y.) ⊠	75
58	Medgar Evers ⊠	60
59	Lehman ⊠	50
50	York (N.Y.)	65
58	Staten Island ⊠	64
58	Merchant Marine	91
62	Hunter ⊠	60
59	John Jay ⊠	54
85	Mitchell ⊠	70
62	Baruch	59
76	Brooklyn ⊠	43
55	Lehman	61
70	City Tech ⊠	61
62	York (N.Y.) ⊠	65

Nickname: Beavers
Colors: Lavender & Black
Arena: Nat Holman Gymnasium
  Capacity: 2,700; Year Built: 1975
AD: Jackee Meadow
SID: Karina Jorge

CLAREMONT-M-S
Claremont, CA 91711-6400 III

Coach: Ken Scalmanini, Cal Poly
Pomona 1993

2006-07 RESULTS (15-10)

63	West Coast Baptist †	40
61	Dubuque ⊠	59
60	Willamette ⊠	50
51	Hope Int'l †	48
62	Dominican (Cal.)	44
51	Menlo	50
74	Westmont ⊠	82
66	La Sierra	51
56	Concordia (Cal.)	77
47	Pt. Loma Nazarene ⊠	56
54	Chapman ⊠	43
59	La Verne	43
56	Occidental	71
94	Redlands ⊠	98
78	Caltech	35
65	Whittier	75
62	Pomona-Pitzer ⊠	66
49	Cal Lutheran ⊠	51
59	La Verne ⊠	50
68	Occidental ⊠	51
86	Redlands	94
70	Caltech	45
64	Whittier ⊠	38
47	Pomona-Pitzer	61
62	Cal Lutheran ⊠	49

Nickname: Stags
Colors: Maroon, Gold & White
Arena: Ducey Gymnasium
  Capacity: 1,200; Year Built: 1959
AD: Michael L. Sutton
SID: Kelly Beck

RESULTS

CLARION

Clarion, PA 16214 II

Coach: Ron Righter, St. Joseph's 1975

2006-07 RESULTS (13-15)

78	Briar Cliff (Iowa)	47
59	Wayne St. (Mich.)	72
82	Mansfield	77
65	Bloomsburg	67
91	Penn St.-Beaver ⊠	49
91	Briar Cliff (Iowa) ⊠	44
93	Penn St.-McKeesport ⊠	37
61	Cheyney	64
44	Wayne St. (Mich.) ⊠	52
78	East Stroudsburg ⊠	83
69	Kutztown ⊠	79
63	California (Pa.) ⊠	66
68	Millersville	77
61	West Chester	73
72	Indiana (Pa.) ⊠	77
49	Shippensburg	64
76	Lock Haven	87
75	Edinboro ⊠	67
70	Slippery Rock	57
60	California (Pa.)	80
62	Indiana (Pa.)	60
64	Shippensburg ⊠	63
107	Penn St.-DuBois ⊠	68
60	Lock Haven ⊠	54
94	Columbia Union ⊠	88
58	Edinboro	81
76	Slippery Rock ⊠	59
62	California (Pa.)	67

Nickname: Golden Eagles
Colors: Blue & Gold
Arena: W.S. Tippin Gymnasium
  Capacity: 4,000; Year Built: 1968
AD: David Katis
SID: Rich Herman

CLARK ATLANTA

Atlanta, GA 30314 II

Coach: Larry Nolley, Clark Atlanta 1981

2006-07 RESULTS (2-26)

49	Delta St.	66
62	Southern Ark. †	75
58	Stillman	74
56	Tuskegee	65
36	Claflin	56
58	West Ala.	81
54	Ga. Southwestern ⊠	56
90	Lane ⊠	95
54	Kentucky St. ⊠	86
41	Paine	53
53	Benedict	62
51	Miles ⊠	61
32	Lane	66
50	Kentucky St.	65
53	Tuskegee ⊠	66
41	Stillman ⊠	48
57	Morehouse	69
66	Fort Valley St. ⊠	87
63	Albany St. (Ga.) ⊠	58
53	Paine ⊠	59
46	Benedict ⊠	78
69	Albany St. (Ga.)	99
44	Morehouse	63
53	LeMoyne-Owen ⊠	76
62	LeMoyne-Owen	84
46	Fort Valley St.	49
64	Miles	62
43	Albany St. (Ga.) †	67

Nickname: Panthers
Colors: Red, Black & Grey
Arena: L.S. Epps Gym
Capacity: 1,800
AD: Brenda Edmond
SID: Charles Ward

CLARK (MASS.)

Worcester, MA 01610-1477 III

Coach: Paul Phillips, Assumption 1976

2006-07 RESULTS (11-14)

74	Buffalo St.	88
96	Fisher †	61
82	Becker	62
85	Worcester St. ⊠	68
51	Brandeis	66
83	Fitchburg St.	63
79	Tufts	87
81	Baruch †	80
64	New York U.	74
102	Coast Guard ⊠	91
81	Newbury	77
89	Wheaton (Mass.)	96
61	WPI ⊠	77
66	Bowdoin	71
65	Babson ⊠	74
67	MIT ⊠	68
83	Springfield	89
53	WPI	77
75	Wheaton (Mass.) ⊠	71
70	Trinity (Conn.) ⊠	72
55	Coast Guard	53
63	Babson	73
73	Springfield ⊠	72
81	MIT	73
53	MIT †	64

Nickname: Cougars
Colors: Scarlet & White
Arena: Kneller Athletic Center
  Capacity: 2,000; Year Built: 1977
AD: Linda S. Moulton
SID: Dalya Qualls

CLARKE

Dubuque, IA 52001 III

Coach: Jon Davison, Dubuque 1961

2006-07 RESULTS (9-18)

59	Ill. Wesleyan †	86
69	Martin Luther †	79
70	Loras ⊠	84
59	Dubuque ⊠	88
59	Cornell College	67
56	Augustana (Ill.)	74
70	Wartburg ⊠	82
80	Knox	70
67	Bethany Lutheran	79
61	Manhattanville †	68
69	Denison †	52
60	Graceland (Iowa) ⊠	72
63	Bethel (Kan.) ⊠	66
60	Tri-State ⊠	70
77	Cornell College ⊠	55
66	Dubuque	73
63	Aurora ⊠	72
73	Milwaukee Engr. ⊠	68
77	St. Ambrose ⊠	95
74	Wis.-Platteville ⊠	71
53	Franklin	72
52	Winona St.	79
88	Mt. Mercy ⊠	83
100	Emmaus ⊠	48
70	Milwaukee Engr.	62
88	Dallas †	76
53	Milwaukee Engr.	56

Nickname: Crusaders
Colors: Navy & Gold
Arena: Kehl Center
  Capacity: 900; Year Built: 1994
AD: Curt Long
SID: Jerry Hanson

CLARKSON

Potsdam, NY 13699-5830 III

Coach: Adam Stockwell, Le Moyne 1996

2006-07 RESULTS (14-12)

65	Castleton †	46
58	Potsdam St.	55
74	Potsdam St. ⊠	63
62	Rochester Inst. ⊠	51
60	Elmira ⊠	53
63	Plattsburgh St.	73
38	Scranton	62
75	Wilkes	65
59	Utica ⊠	48
64	Oswego St.	62
74	Cazenovia ⊠	63
65	Hamilton	59
56	Hobart	65
59	St. Lawrence ⊠	73
49	Rensselaer ⊠	67
62	Vassar ⊠	70
71	Union (N.Y.) ⊠	75
65	Skidmore ⊠	60
48	St. Lawrence	74
57	Vassar	53
57	Rensselaer	77
68	Hobart ⊠	47
60	Hamilton ⊠	71
79	Skidmore	67
69	Union (N.Y.)	74
84	SUNYIT	96

Nickname: Golden Knights
Colors: Green & Gold
Arena: Alumni Gymnasium
  Capacity: 2,000; Year Built: 1952
AD: Steve Yianoukos
SID: Tommy Szarka

CLAYTON ST.

Morrow, GA 30260 II

Coach: Gordon Gibbons, Springfield 1968

2006-07 RESULTS (24-8)

83	Southeastern (Fla.) ⊠	53
80	North Ala.	74
68	Lenoir-Rhyne †	49
76	Catawba	75
70	West Ga. ⊠	69
103	Carver Bible ⊠	58
62	West Ga.	54
67	Lee ⊠	58
80	Tex. Permian Basin ⊠	56
84	Edward Waters ⊠	35
88	Ark.-Monticello ⊠	54
67	Ga. Southwestern	64
78	Francis Marion ⊠	50
69	Armstrong Atlantic ⊠	64
70	Lander ⊠	63
76	Columbus St.	57
64	UNC Pembroke	54
58	Armstrong Atlantic	63
89	S.C.-Aiken ⊠	73
76	Columbus St. ⊠	77
74	S.C. Upstate	49
67	Augusta St.	76
60	GCSU	44
55	Ga. Southwestern ⊠	58
59	North Georgia	61
70	Augusta St. ⊠	68
62	GCSU ⊠	64
63	S.C. Upstate †	43
72	Augusta St. †	69
61	Lander	75
72	Catawba †	69
70	Virginia Union †	71

Nickname: Lakers
Colors: Blue & Orange
Arena: Athletics Center
  Capacity: 2,000; Year Built: 1983
AD: Mason Barfield
SID: Lee Wright

CLEMSON

Clemson, SC 29634 I

Coach: Oliver Purnell, Old Dominion 1975

2006-07 RESULTS (25-11)

83	Arkansas St. †	44
77	Monmouth †	65
74	Old Dominion	70
67	Furman	58
79	Appalachian St. ⊠	49
69	Mississippi St. ⊠	66
74	Charleston So. ⊠	50
90	Minnesota	68
74	South Carolina	53
90	Wofford ⊠	66
72	Ga. Southern ⊠	60
103	Western Caro. ⊠	60
75	Georgia ⊠	60
67	Georgia St. ⊠	57
68	Florida St.	66
75	Georgia Tech ⊠	74
87	North Carolina St.	76
87	Maryland	92
55	North Carolina	77
74	Boston College ⊠	54
66	Duke	68
63	Virginia ⊠	64
62	Georgia Tech	80
71	Florida St. ⊠	58
65	Wake Forest	67
66	Maryland ⊠	82
66	Duke ⊠	71
54	Boston College	59
74	Miami (Fla.) ⊠	70
75	Virginia Tech	74
66	Florida St. †	67
64	East Tenn. St. ⊠	57
89	Mississippi ⊠	68
74	Syracuse ⊠	70
68	Air Force †	67
73	West Virginia †	78

Nickname: Tigers
Colors: Burnt Orange & Northwest Purple
Arena: Littlejohn Coliseum
  Capacity: 10,000; Year Built: 1968
AD: Terry Don Phillips
SID: Tim Bourret

CLEVELAND ST.

Cleveland, OH 44115-2440 I

Coach: Gary Waters, Ferris St. 1975

2006-07 RESULTS (10-21)

74	George Mason ⊠	79
88	Notre Dame (Ohio) ⊠	62
73	Buffalo †	77
49	Evansville	63
78	Miami (Fla.) †	67
84	John Carroll ⊠	65
59	Delaware	53
66	Kent St. ⊠	59
45	Butler	70
60	Kansas St.	93
57	Ohio St.	78
76	Central Mich.	78
77	Chicago St. ⊠	82
62	Ill.-Chicago ⊠	72
73	West Va. Tech ⊠	52
55	Loyola (Ill.)	66
53	Green Bay	65
48	Milwaukee ⊠	60
63	Detroit ⊠	61
67	Wright St. ⊠	68
63	Youngstown St.	68
60	Ill.-Chicago	55
56	Milwaukee	57
57	Loyola (Ill.) ⊠	61
66	Green Bay ⊠	79
50	Butler ⊠	92
55	Wright St.	68
85	Cal St. Northridge	76
48	Detroit	60
68	Youngstown St. ⊠	55

59	Green Bay	78

Nickname: Vikings
Colors: Forest Green & White
Arena: Henry J. Goodman Arena
Capacity: 13,610; Year Built: 1991
AD: Lee Reed
SID: Brian McCann

COAST GUARD

New London, CT 06320-4195 III

Coach: Peter Barry, San Francisco 1970

2006-07 RESULTS (14-14)

61	Chicago	78
70	Earlham †	57
88	Albertus Magnus ⊠	49
68	Roger Williams ⊠	57
77	Johnson & Wales (RI)	68
83	Becker ⊠	48
56	Wentworth Inst. †	58
78	Merchant Marine	57
71	Rhode Island Col. ⊠	76
99	Lesley ⊠	76
91	Clark (Mass.)	102
69	Wheaton (Mass.) ⊠	56
59	MIT ⊠	62
60	Springfield ⊠	67
65	Connecticut Col. ⊠	60
84	Mitchell	63
59	Wheaton (Mass.)	60
68	WPI	76
62	Babson ⊠	74
77	Springfield	67
47	MIT	51
53	Clark (Mass.) ⊠	55
61	Babson	62
57	WPI ⊠	67
70	Babson	66
62	Wheaton (Mass.) †	60
71	WPI	66
60	Rhode Island Col.	64

Nickname: Bears
Colors: Blue & White
Arena: John Merriman Gymnasium
Capacity: 2,400; Year Built: 1964
AD: Raymond Cieplik
SID: Jason Southard

COASTAL CARO.

Conway, SC 29528-6054 I

Coach: Buzz Peterson, North Carolina 1986

2006-07 RESULTS (15-15)

46	Xavier	79
63	Campbell	83
70	Wright St. ⊠	63
93	Asbury ⊠	64
104	Southern Va. ⊠	62
72	Jacksonville	85
80	South Carolina St.	81
85	Brevard ⊠	46
49	Col. of Charleston ⊠	70
65	Florida St.	78
74	St. Andrews ⊠	54
81	McNeese St. ⊠	67
66	Charleston So. ⊠	54
68	UNC Asheville	60
83	Savannah St. ⊠	56
76	Radford	80
99	VMI	97
70	Liberty ⊠	65
56	High Point ⊠	59
63	Winthrop	65
77	Charleston So.	86
65	Savannah St.	66
108	VMI ⊠	99
85	Radford ⊠	67
63	High Point	71
77	Liberty	76
83	Canisius ⊠	66
77	UNC Asheville ⊠	82
69	Winthrop ⊠	83
64	UNC Asheville ⊠	77

Nickname: Chanticleers
Colors: Coastal Green, Bronze & Black
Arena: Kimbel Arena
Capacity: 1,039; Year Built: 1974
AD: Warren Koegel
SID: John Martin

COE

Cedar Rapids, IA 52402-5092 III

Coach: Pat Juckem, Lawrence 1995

2006-07 RESULTS (19-8)

93	Wis. Lutheran ⊠	62
67	Marian (Wis.) ⊠	53
82	Mt. Mercy	62
92	Wartburg ⊠	88
79	Grand View	66
47	Augustana (Ill.)	70
72	Dominican (Ill.) †	61
70	North Park †	56
70	Chicago	67
77	Benedictine (Ill.)	78
80	Dubuque	61
79	Buena Vista	84
60	Loras ⊠	61
76	Simpson	68
61	Central (Iowa)	65
69	Cornell College ⊠	54
64	Luther ⊠	40
71	Dubuque ⊠	56
82	Wartburg	60
59	Buena Vista ⊠	56
83	Cornell College	50
61	Luther	44
68	Loras	79
73	Simpson ⊠	78
71	Central (Iowa) ⊠	68
83	Wartburg ⊠	69
81	Buena Vista	88

Nickname: Kohawks
Colors: Crimson & Gold
Arena: Moray L. Eby Fieldhous
Capacity: 2,600; Year Built: 1931
AD: John Chandler
SID: Ryan Workman

COKER

Hartsville, SC 29550 II

Coach: Dan Schmotzer, St. Edward's 1974

2006-07 RESULTS (8-21)

62	Francis Marion ⊠	47
64	Chowan †	83
83	Ohio Valley †	91
46	Charleston So.	87
70	Barton	77
86	Pfeiffer ⊠	88
72	Morris	57
73	North Greenville ⊠	47
58	Queens (N.C.) ⊠	72
70	Erskine	79
68	Mount Olive ⊠	95
55	Belmont Abbey	64
65	Limestone ⊠	82
67	St. Andrews	77
70	Lees-McRae ⊠	64
58	Anderson (S.C.)	51
53	Queens (N.C.)	61
52	Barton ⊠	84
65	Mount Olive	99
54	Belmont Abbey ⊠	51
57	Erskine ⊠	65
71	Pfeiffer	82
69	Anderson (S.C.) ⊠	48
61	Morris ⊠	71
50	Limestone	77
61	St. Andrews ⊠	74
58	Lees-McRae	73
66	St. Andrews	59
62	Mount Olive	88

Nickname: Cobras
Colors: Navy Blue & Gold
Arena: Timberlake-Lawton Gym
Capacity: 750; Year Built: 1963
AD: C. Timothy Griggs
SID: Christian Stryker

COLBY

Waterville, ME 04901-8849 III

Coach: Dick Whitmore, Bowdoin 1965

2006-07 RESULTS (15-11)

78	Babson	75
71	Washington-St. Louis †	79
69	Davidson	99
79	New England	55
69	Bates ⊠	82
89	Fisher ⊠	73
83	Southern Me. ⊠	57
68	Bowdoin	67
78	Southern Me. †	59
73	St. Joseph's (Me.)	61
48	Springfield	64
70	Plattsburgh St. †	86
76	Lesley	85
73	Maine Maritime ⊠	56
93	Middlebury	100
55	Williams	62
75	Wesleyan (Conn.) ⊠	55
60	Connecticut Col. ⊠	57
58	Amherst ⊠	69
68	Trinity (Conn.) ⊠	77
70	Me.-Farmington	53
81	Bowdoin ⊠	67
63	Bates	62
89	Tufts	84
91	Middlebury	79
55	Amherst	82

Nickname: Mules
Colors: Blue & Gray
Arena: Wadsworth Gymnasium
Capacity: 2,500; Year Built: 1966
AD: Marcella K. Zalot
SID: Bill Sodoma

COLBY-SAWYER

New London, NH 03257 III

Coach: Bill Foti, New Hampshire 1986

2006-07 RESULTS (10-15)

53	Springfield †	77
74	Newbury †	70
85	Curry †	89
100	Mass.-Boston	102
77	Plymouth St. †	86
51	Roger Williams	72
81	Wentworth Inst. ⊠	69
78	Bowdoin ⊠	82
69	Salve Regina ⊠	53
85	Middlebury ⊠	96
63	Gordon	83
80	Nichols	77
75	Anna Maria ⊠	43
71	Endicott ⊠	61
62	New England ⊠	64
96	New England Col.	120
68	Wentworth Inst.	63
91	New England Col. ⊠	79
72	Eastern Nazarene	66
75	Curry ⊠	81
61	Endicott	70
56	Gordon ⊠	59
67	New England	73
89	Lesley ⊠	64
76	Curry	95

Nickname: Chargers
Colors: Royal Blue and White
Arena: David L. Coffin Fieldhouse
Capacity: 650; Year Built: 1991
AD: Deborah McGrath
SID: Mitch Capelle

COLGATE

Hamilton, NY 13346-1304 I

Coach: Emmett Davis, St. Lawrence 1981

2006-07 RESULTS (10-19)

59	Stony Brook ⊠	65
55	Dartmouth	43
73	Canisius ⊠	78
78	Binghamton ⊠	70
80	Quinnipiac ⊠	71
64	Harvard ⊠	76
82	Elmira ⊠	34
52	Syracuse	79
36	Arizona St.	52
59	UC Riverside	56
39	Santa Clara	53
42	George Washington †	75
53	Cornell ⊠	64
73	Army ⊠	71
65	Lafayette ⊠	71
48	American	70
59	Lehigh	60
36	Bucknell	50
55	Holy Cross ⊠	58
66	Navy	58
53	Bucknell ⊠	56
42	Army	38
54	Lafayette	51
58	American ⊠	64
53	Lehigh ⊠	56
47	Marist	63
57	Holy Cross	68
70	Navy ⊠	62
44	American	59

Nickname: Raiders
Colors: Maroon, Gray & White
Arena: Cotterell Court
Capacity: 3,091; Year Built: 1966
AD: David T. Roach
SID: Bob Cornell

COLORADO

Boulder, CO 80309 I

Coach: Ricardo Patton, Belmont 1980

2006-07 RESULTS (7-20)

78	Denver ⊠	64
65	New Mexico	106
46	Air Force ⊠	84
60	Utah	59
73	Wyoming ⊠	76
55	UNC Wilmington	67
88	Northern Colo. ⊠	86
72	Pepperdine ⊠	78
69	Colorado St. ⊠	72
96	UCF ⊠	87
78	Texas ⊠	102
54	Oklahoma	78
69	Texas A&M ⊠	87
74	Iowa St. ⊠	65
50	Nebraska	71
65	Missouri ⊠	79
74	Kansas	97
83	Baylor	97
89	Oklahoma St. ⊠	77
59	Kansas St.	78
46	Kansas ⊠	75
74	Texas Tech	95
53	Iowa St.	55
71	Kansas St. ⊠	87
82	Missouri	91
73	Nebraska ⊠	69
71	Texas Tech †	81

Nickname: Buffaloes
Colors: Silver, Black & Gold
Arena: Coors Events/Conference Center
Capacity: 11,064; Year Built: 1979
AD: Mike R. Bohn
SID: David Plati

COLO. CHRISTIAN
Lakewood, CO 80226 II

Coach: David Daniels, Colo. Christian 1995

2006-07 RESULTS (13-15)
93	St. Leo †	65
69	Angelo St. †	87
68	Northern Colo.	89
79	Seattle ⊠	83
85	Colorado Col. ⊠	41
61	Fort Lewis	72
47	Mesa St.	61
64	Adams St. ⊠	68
64	Colorado St.-Pueblo ⊠	66
77	Johnson & Wales (CO) ⊠	61
55	Western St.	62
71	Western N.M. ⊠	68
87	N.M. Highlands ⊠	75
53	Metro St.	77
67	Colorado Mines ⊠	51
80	UC-Colo. Springs	93
61	Regis (Colo.)	48
73	Colorado Col.	71
78	Chadron St.	83
67	Neb.-Kearney ⊠	84
99	Johnson & Wales (CO) ⊠	87
59	Regis (Colo.) ⊠	37
81	UC-Colo. Springs ⊠	69
72	Neb.-Kearney	79
87	Chadron St.	74
51	Metro St. ⊠	62
66	Colorado Mines	53
68	Metro St.	81

Nickname: Cougars
Colors: Navy & Gold
Arena: Cougar Fieldhouse
   Capacity: 1,800; Year Built: 1990
AD: Douglas Yager
SID: Dustin Main

COLORADO COL.
Colorado Springs, CO 80903 III

Coach: Andy Partee, Monmouth 1992

2006-07 RESULTS (4-22)
84	Hamline †	91
58	Wartburg †	78
71	Menlo ⊠	79
79	Carroll (Wis.) ⊠	91
41	Colo. Christian	85
47	Chapman †	73
69	LIFE Pacific †	59
54	UC Santa Cruz †	59
66	Regis (Colo.)	83
31	Air Force	82
77	UC-Colo. Springs	85
57	Edgewood †	72
57	Linfield †	73
40	Roanoke †	69
54	Fort Lewis ⊠	78
38	Western St.	60
50	Dallas	55
90	UC Santa Cruz †	68
56	Chapman †	89
69	UC-Colo. Springs ⊠	94
71	Colo. Christian ⊠	73
104	Johnson & Wales (CO) ⊠	93
53	Johnson & Wales (CO)	79
72	Dallas ⊠	77
67	Chapman †	84
79	UC Santa Cruz †	63

Nickname: Tigers
Colors: Black & Gold
Arena: J. Juan Reid Gymnasium
   Capacity: 1,000; Year Built: 1970
AD: Ken Ralph
SID: Dave Reed

COLORADO MINES
Golden, CO 80401 II

Coach: Pryor Orser, Mont. St.-Billings 1990

2006-07 RESULTS (14-14)
75	Northwest Nazarene ⊠	63
59	Caldwell ⊠	51
64	Mo. Southern St. †	69
39	Pittsburg St.	53
67	Wyoming	78
73	South Dak. Tech ⊠	64
46	Western St.	61
70	N.M. Highlands ⊠	60
79	Western N.M. ⊠	50
84	Tex. A&M-Commerce ⊠	80
74	St. Francis (Ill.) ⊠	56
67	Fort Lewis	73
54	Mesa St.	69
46	Colorado St.-Pueblo ⊠	55
59	Adams St. ⊠	58
48	Metro St.	64
51	Colo. Christian	67
72	Johnson & Wales (CO) ⊠	58
59	Chadron St.	58
63	Neb.-Kearney ⊠	80
88	UC-Colo. Springs ⊠	75
71	Regis (Colo.) ⊠	49
67	Neb.-Kearney	88
71	Chadron St.	76
81	Regis (Colo.)	55
76	UC-Colo. Springs	74
53	Colo. Christian ⊠	66
71	Metro St. ⊠	81

Nickname: Orediggers
Colors: Silver & Blue
Arena: Volk Gymnasium
   Capacity: 1,000; Year Built: 1959
AD: Thomas E. Spicer
SID: Greg Murphy

COLORADO ST.
Fort Collins, CO 80523-6011 I

Coach: Dale Layer, Eckerd 1980

2006-07 RESULTS (17-13)
76	Colorado St.-Pueblo ⊠	67
82	Baylor †	87
61	Rice †	70
74	Mont. St.-Northern †	56
67	Boise St. ⊠	50
81	Denver	73
84	Kansas St. ⊠	83
75	Northern Colo. ⊠	66
72	Colorado	69
82	North Dakota St. ⊠	80
61	Alabama St. †	56
76	Chattanooga	65
75	Air Force ⊠	81
88	New Mexico	79
73	Utah ⊠	57
76	San Diego St.	81
66	TCU	54
90	BYU ⊠	78
70	Wyoming	75
59	UNLV ⊠	76
66	New Mexico ⊠	70
77	Utah	82
66	San Diego St. ⊠	81
82	TCU ⊠	66
58	Air Force	67
67	BYU	76
86	Wyoming ⊠	68
47	UNLV	65
69	San Diego St. †	64
72	UNLV	88

Nickname: Rams
Colors: Green & Gold
Arena: Moby Arena
   Capacity: 8,745; Year Built: 1966
AD: Paul Kowalczyk
SID: Gary Ozzello

COLORADO ST.-PUEBLO
Pueblo, CO 81001-4901 II

Coach: Pat Eberhart, Adams St. 1991

2006-07 RESULTS (13-15)
84	Wartburg ⊠	77
86	Hamline ⊠	71
56	Wayland Baptist †	69
59	Dixie St. †	68
80	Minn. Duluth ⊠	78
60	Neb.-Omaha ⊠	66
76	UC-Colo. Springs ⊠	87
75	Regis (Colo.) ⊠	64
65	Metro St.	73
66	Colo. Christian	64
100	UC-Colo. Springs	107
72	Chadron St. ⊠	63
79	Neb.-Kearney ⊠	88
90	Johnson & Wales (CO) ⊠	69
55	Colorado Mines	46
67	N.M. Highlands ⊠	58
73	Western N.M. ⊠	63
76	Adams St. ⊠	80
71	Western St.	42
63	Mesa St.	74
79	Fort Lewis	89
74	Adams St.	85
64	Western St. ⊠	62
63	Fort Lewis ⊠	79
72	Mesa St. ⊠	74
62	Western N.M.	75
80	N.M. Highlands	79
74	Neb.-Kearney	91

Nickname: ThunderWolves
Colors: Red & Blue
Arena: State Fair Events Center
   Capacity: 5,500; Year Built: 1978
AD: Joe Folda
SID: Mike McNeely

UC-COLO. SPRINGS
Colorado Springs, CO 80933-7150 .. II

Coach: Russ Caton, Adams St. 1997

2006-07 RESULTS (16-12)
96	Northern Colo.	91
105	Carroll (Wis.) †	86
85	Menlo	68
71	Minn. St. Mankato †	74
95	Okla. Panhandle †	71
87	Colorado St.-Pueblo	76
76	Adams St.	89
85	Colorado Col. ⊠	77
84	Western St. ⊠	71
107	Colorado St.-Pueblo ⊠	100
65	Western N.M.	89
78	N.M. Highlands	77
89	Fort Lewis ⊠	87
98	Mesa St. ⊠	87
90	Chadron St.	85
54	Neb.-Kearney	85
94	Colorado Col.	69
93	Colo. Christian ⊠	80
82	Metro St. ⊠	87
65	Regis (Colo.) ⊠	71
75	Colorado Mines	88
67	Metro St.	83
69	Colo. Christian	81
75	Regis (Colo.)	78
74	Colorado Mines ⊠	76
89	Neb.-Kearney ⊠	81
70	Chadron St. ⊠	66
83	Adams St.	98

Nickname: Mountain Lions
Colors: Black & Gold
Arena: Lions Den
   Capacity: 500; Year Built: 1988
AD: Steve Kirkham
SID: Doug Fitzgerald

COLUMBIA
New York, NY 10027 I

Coach: Joe Jones, Oswego St. 1987

2006-07 RESULTS (16-12)
43	Duke	86
95	UC Davis †	90
73	NJIT	60
63	Kennesaw St. ⊠	51
90	Long Island ⊠	63
41	Stony Brook ⊠	54
55	Providence	81
76	Sacred Heart ⊠	71
70	Wagner ⊠	44
75	Lafayette	58
70	St. John's (N.Y.)	76
58	St. Francis (N.Y.)	67
55	Lehigh	54
87	Marywood ⊠	38
64	Princeton ⊠	56
43	Penn	69
45	Cornell ⊠	49
51	Cornell	56
90	Harvard	70
61	Dartmouth	55
71	Yale ⊠	85
77	Brown ⊠	68
54	Penn	73
49	Princeton	54
59	Brown	64
82	Yale	64
69	Dartmouth ⊠	67
76	Harvard ⊠	66

Nickname: Lions
Colors: Columbia Blue & White
Arena: Levien Gym
   Capacity: 3,408; Year Built: 1974
AD: M. Dianne Murphy
SID: Casey Taylor

COLUMBIA UNION
Takoma Park, MD 20912 II

Coach: Calvin Dunbar, Bishop 1981

2006-07 RESULTS (4-22)
65	Pitt.-Johnstown ⊠	82
78	Shepherd	98
65	East Stroudsburg †	81
85	St. Paul's ⊠	
78	Kutztown †	84
82	Davis & Elkins †	88
64	Fairmont St.	93
88	Kutztown ⊠	100
60	Mercyhurst	89
65	Slippery Rock †	76
73	St. Cloud St. ⊠	99
111	Pfeiffer ⊠	119
77	St. Paul's	112
71	Nyack	85
78	Apprentice	75
58	Davis & Elkins ⊠	64
95	Maryland Bible ⊠	80
61	Pitt.-Johnstown	101
89	Southern Va.	82
77	Dist. Columbia ⊠	86
106	Southern Va. ⊠	104
61	Winston-Salem	77
88	Clarion	94
82	Bowie St. ⊠	113
48	Bowie St.	92
83	Dist. Columbia	93

Nickname: Pioneers
Colors: Blue, Gold and White
Arena: The Pit
   Capacity: 350; Year Built: 1954
AD: Bruce Peifer
SID: Wayne Stewart

COLUMBUS ST.
Columbus, GA 31907-5645 II

Coach: Doug Branson, Troy 1997

2006-07 RESULTS (17-12)
82	N.C. Central	95
50	St. Augustine's †	71
83	Virginia St.	73
84	West Ga. ⊠	79
76	Morehouse	73
121	Carver Bible ⊠	74
96	Virginia St. ⊠	80
61	Valdosta St. †	63
87	Dist. Columbia	67
73	St. Augustine's ⊠	80
74	N.C. Central ⊠	63
75	Augusta St.	81
69	UNC Pembroke	54
81	Ga. Southwestern	72
83	S.C.-Aiken ⊠	71
57	Clayton St. ⊠	76
63	S.C. Upstate	68
74	Ga. Southwestern ⊠	81
84	North Georgia ⊠	77
77	Clayton St. ⊠	76
86	Francis Marion ⊠	77
104	GCSU ⊠	103
64	Armstrong Atlantic	80
91	Augusta St. ⊠	102
103	Lander	96
87	GCSU	81
60	Armstrong Atlantic ⊠	72
66	S.C.-Aiken †	58
81	Lander	83

Nickname: Cougars
Colors: Red, White & Blue
Arena: Lumpkin Center
　Capacity: 4,500; Year Built: 2000
AD: Herbert Greene
SID: Brian Padgett

CONCORD
Athens, WV 24712 II

Coach: Steve Cox, Salem Int'l 1975

2006-07 RESULTS (17-13)
95	Queens (N.C.) †	97
81	Belmont Abbey	84
70	Bluefield St.	79
95	West Va. Tech †	77
67	Tusculum	80
81	Chowan	92
84	Davis & Elkins ⊠	72
68	Tusculum ⊠	61
72	Charleston (W.V.)	89
87	Fairmont St. ⊠	69
88	Pitt.-Johnstown	100
96	West Virginia St.	102
103	Bluefield St. ⊠	79
98	Glenville St.	90
77	Ohio Valley	79
70	Chowan ⊠	66
81	Shepherd ⊠	78
97	West Va. Wesleyan ⊠	79
90	West Liberty St.	100
83	Wheeling Jesuit	80
73	Charleston (W.V.) ⊠	66
83	Alderson-Broaddus ⊠	91
82	Salem Int'l	97
116	Glenville St. ⊠	93
85	West Virginia St. ⊠	84
101	West Va. Wesleyan	81
108	Bluefield St.	73
78	Glenville St. ⊠	73
71	Salem Int'l †	69
87	Alderson-Broaddus †	91

Nickname: Mountain Lions
Colors: Maroon & Gray
Arena: Carter Center
　Capacity: 2,000; Year Built: 1972
AD: Greg Quick
SID: Stephen Ziegler

CONCORDIA (ILL.)
River Forest, IL 60305-1499 III

Coach: Brian Sommerhauser, Denison 1998

2006-07 RESULTS (4-21)
82	Greenville †	74
60	Blackburn	66
31	North Park ⊠	68
66	Concordia (Wis.) ⊠	69
67	Benedictine (Ill.) ⊠	78
72	Lakeland	86
83	Wis. Lutheran ⊠	90
63	Maranatha Baptist	43
56	Marian (Wis.)	68
59	Milwaukee Engr. ⊠	67
66	Knox	75
54	Edgewood	70
70	Dominican (Ill.)	85
71	Aurora ⊠	77
68	Rockford	69
72	Benedictine (Ill.)	64
47	Concordia (Neb.) †	66
62	Concordia (Wis.) †	76
69	Lakeland	84
74	Wis. Lutheran	98
73	Maranatha Baptist ⊠	61
64	Marian (Wis.) ⊠	74
68	Edgewood ⊠	81
70	Dominican (Ill.) ⊠	83
86	Aurora	109

Nickname: Cougars
Colors: Maroon & Gold
Arena: Geiseman Gymnasium
　Capacity: 2,200; Year Built: 1964
AD: Pete Gnan
SID: Jim Egan

CONCORDIA (N.Y.)
Bronxville, NY 10708 II

Coach: John Dwinell, Springfield 1981

2006-07 RESULTS (8-18)
77	Quinnipiac	92
57	Edward Waters	73
72	North Fla.	77
63	St. Thomas Aquinas	59
64	Adelphi ⊠	72
109	Pace ⊠	96
58	C.W. Post	74
58	Dowling ⊠	44
64	Mercyhurst	82
84	Mercy	77
76	NYIT	91
71	Molloy	68
56	Southern Conn. St.	74
79	Bridgeport	88
67	Queens (N.Y.) ⊠	65
62	New Haven	72
52	St. Thomas Aquinas ⊠	62
59	Adelphi	71
58	Mercy ⊠	54
51	Dowling	63
84	C.W. Post ⊠	81
63	NYIT ⊠	68
75	Molloy ⊠	95
46	Bridgeport ⊠	62
74	Queens (N.Y.)	88
66	New Haven ⊠	73

Nickname: Clippers
Colors: Blue & Gold
Arena: Meyer Athletic Center
　Capacity: 1,000; Year Built: 1963
AD: Ivan Marquez
SID: Craig Boston

CONCORDIA (WIS.)
Mequon, WI 53097-2402 III

Coach: Wayne Rasmussen, Concordia (Ind.) 1960

2006-07 RESULTS (8-17)
76	Calvin	98
88	Grace Bible (Mich.) †	92
73	Voorhees ⊠	105
62	Lawrence	72
69	Concordia (Ill.)	66
69	Benedictine (Ill.) ⊠	89
90	Wis. Lutheran	94
73	Lakeland	74
68	Rockford ⊠	57
91	Maranatha Baptist ⊠	76
77	Marian (Wis.) ⊠	75
65	Edgewood ⊠	78
71	Aurora ⊠	95
71	Dominican (Ill.)	83
71	Rockford	64
59	Concordia (Mich.)	96
76	Concordia (Ill.) †	62
77	Milwaukee Engr.	81
60	Benedictine (Ill.)	62
92	Lakeland ⊠	95
76	Wis. Lutheran ⊠	100
83	Maranatha Baptist	70
67	Marian (Wis.)	59
55	Edgewood	83
90	Dominican (Ill.) ⊠	94

Nickname: Falcons
Colors: Royal Blue & White
Arena: Buuck Fieldhouse
　Capacity: 2,000; Year Built: 1989
AD: Robert M. Barnhill
SID: Rick Riehl

CONCORDIA (TEX.)
Austin, TX 78705-2799 III

Coach: Stan Bonewitz, Texas Tech 2001

2006-07 RESULTS (10-16)
84	Lubbock Chrst. †	97
114	Abilene Christian	116
89	St. Edward's	105
81	Louisiana Col.	79
70	Mississippi Col.	91
122	Texas-Tyler ⊠	112
112	Texas-Dallas ⊠	118
92	East Tex. Baptist	100
79	LeTourneau	88
89	Incarnate Word	85
85	Ozarks (Ark.) ⊠	98
97	Hardin-Simmons ⊠	85
87	McMurry ⊠	94
85	Sul Ross St.	62
87	Howard Payne	91
91	Schreiner	85
82	Texas Lutheran	70
80	Mary Hardin-Baylor ⊠	87
77	Schreiner ⊠	82
93	Texas Lutheran ⊠	79
77	Mary Hardin-Baylor	96
118	Howard Payne ⊠	109
99	Sul Ross St. ⊠	67
71	Hardin-Simmons	99
57	McMurry	99
62	Mississippi Col.	86

Nickname: Tornados
Colors: Purple & White
Arena: Woltman Center
　Capacity: 1,600; Year Built: 1982
AD: Linda Lowery
SID: Jim Jost

CONCORDIA-M'HEAD
Moorhead, MN 56562-3597 III

Coach: Duane Siverson, Yankton 1978

2006-07 RESULTS (4-21)
84	Minn. St. Moorhead ⊠	85
72	Maryland Bible †	78
80	Southern Va. †	87
79	St. John's (Minn.) ⊠	85
68	St. Olaf	76
58	Mayville St.	62
52	Carleton	69
54	Minn. St. Mankato	82
70	Macalester	92
84	Hamline ⊠	65
63	Gust. Adolphus ⊠	58
83	Bethel (Minn.)	95
65	St. Thomas (Minn.) ⊠	68
66	Augsburg	77
67	St. Mary's (Minn.) ⊠	79
72	St. John's (Minn.) ⊠	78
62	Carleton	57
56	St. Olaf ⊠	63
74	Macalester ⊠	84
66	Hamline	74
57	Gust. Adolphus	80
71	Bethel (Minn.) ⊠	86
57	St. Thomas (Minn.)	77
59	Augsburg ⊠	65
70	St. Mary's (Minn.)	61

Nickname: Cobbers
Colors: Maroon & Gold
Arena: Memorial Auditorium
　Capacity: 3,500; Year Built: 1951
AD: Larry Papenfuss
SID: Jim Cella

CONCORDIA-ST. PAUL
St. Paul, MN 55104 II

Coach: Kelly Boe, St. John's (Minn.) 1997

2006-07 RESULTS (21-8)
76	North Dakota †	72
102	Chadron St. †	79
71	Minn. St. Mankato ⊠	65
50	St. Cloud St.	76
83	Minn. St. Moorhead	74
72	Bemidji St.	55
108	Minn.-Crookston	82
73	Macalester ⊠	64
105	Wis.-River Falls ⊠	72
55	Minn. Duluth ⊠	72
79	Neb.-Omaha	76
82	Mary	50
76	Northern St. ⊠	58
83	Winona St.	86
77	Upper Iowa	44
64	Southwest Minn. St. ⊠	70
77	Wayne St. (Neb.) ⊠	66
81	Minn. St. Moorhead ⊠	79
60	Minn.-Crookston ⊠	54
75	Bemidji St. ⊠	68
110	North Central (Minn. ⊠	73
65	Northern St.	72
72	Mary	70
77	Upper Iowa ⊠	63
68	Winona St. ⊠	87
80	Wayne St. (Neb.)	72
45	Southwest Minn. St.	59
77	Wayne St. (Neb.) ⊠	61
71	Winona St.	87

Nickname: Golden Bears
Colors: Navy Blue & Vegas Gold
Arena: Gangelhoff Center
　Capacity: 1,000; Year Built: 1993
AD: Thomas Rubbelke
SID: Jen Foley

CONNECTICUT
Storrs, CT 06269.....................I

Coach: Jim Calhoun, American Int'l 1968

2006-07 RESULTS (17-14)
53	Quinnipiac ⊠	46
88	Central Ark. ⊠	59
74	Fairfield	49
77	Mississippi ⊠	59
86	Albany (N.Y.) ⊠	55
89	Sacred Heart ⊠	46
106	Texas Southern ⊠	55
81	Northeastern ⊠	53
89	St. Mary's (Cal.) ⊠	73
88	Pepperdine ⊠	66
84	Coppin St. ⊠	41
71	West Virginia	81
69	South Fla. ⊠	50
49	LSU	66
69	Marquette ⊠	73
68	St. John's (N.Y.) ⊠	59
54	Pittsburgh	63
73	Indiana ⊠	77
54	Louisville	68
72	Providence ⊠	84
58	DePaul	66
61	Rutgers ⊠	50
67	Syracuse ⊠	60
52	Georgia Tech †	65
67	Seton Hall ⊠	55
63	Syracuse	73
65	Rutgers	55
69	Louisville ⊠	76
74	Villanova ⊠	78
46	Georgetown	59
65	Syracuse †	78

Nickname: Huskies, UConn
Colors: National Flag Blue & White
Arena: Harry A. Gampel Pavilion
Capacity: 10,167; Year Built: 1990
AD: Jeffrey A. Hathaway
SID: Kyle Muncy

CONNECTICUT COL.
New London, CT 06320-4196......III

Coach: Tom Satran, Connecticut Col. 1994

2006-07 RESULTS (11-13)
55	Plattsburgh St. †	52
63	Rutgers-Newark	64
66	MIT ⊠	48
60	Eastern Conn. St.	63
76	Mitchell	60
59	Rensselaer	55
77	Wheaton (Mass.) ⊠	74
75	Albertus Magnus	58
70	Salve Regina ⊠	76
69	Springfield ⊠	56
71	John Jay ⊠	49
65	Roger Williams ⊠	60
57	Eastern Nazarene	46
63	Johnson & Wales (RI) ⊠	67
61	Wesleyan (Conn.)	62
60	Coast Guard	65
46	Bowdoin	74
57	Colby	60
56	Tufts ⊠	63
82	Bates ⊠	65
49	Amherst	91
47	Trinity (Conn.)	62
55	Williams ⊠	61
59	Middlebury ⊠	69

Nickname: Camels
Colors: Royal Blue & White
Arena: Luce Fieldhouse/Gymnasium
Capacity: 800; Year Built: 1984
AD: Fran Shields
SID: Will Tomasian

COPPIN ST.
Baltimore, MD 21216-3698.............I

Coach: Fang Mitchell, Edison St. 1984

2006-07 RESULTS (12-20)
43	Virginia Tech	94
67	Hawaii	79
65	Tennessee	99
81	Winston-Salem ⊠	56
57	Kansas St.	68
77	Missouri	98
69	La Salle †	68
67	Iowa	83
82	Morgan St.	86
47	Oklahoma	64
49	Alabama	99
41	Connecticut	84
54	Ohio St.	91
66	Bethune-Cookman ⊠	58
49	Delaware St. ⊠	54
61	Norfolk St.	62
69	Hampton	77
60	N.C. A&T ⊠	69
70	South Carolina St. ⊠	67
62	Howard	59
64	Md.-East. Shore	57
45	Delaware St.	53
77	Norfolk St. ⊠	70
56	Hampton ⊠	71
64	N.C. A&T	58
65	South Carolina St.	76
50	Howard ⊠	46
80	Md.-East. Shore ⊠	65
59	Florida A&M	73
71	Morgan St. ⊠	62
56	Bethune-Cookman †	44
49	Delaware St. †	68

Nickname: Eagles
Colors: Royal Blue & Gold
Arena: Coppin Center
Capacity: 1,720; Year Built: 1987
AD: Ronald Mitchell
SID: Roger McAfee

CORNELL
Ithaca, NY 14853 I

Coach: Steve Donahue, Ursinus 1984

2006-07 RESULTS (16-12)
64	Northwestern	61
76	Stony Brook ⊠	72
71	Lehigh	90
65	Army	56
56	Binghamton	57
61	Hartford ⊠	63
99	VMI †	94
68	William & Mary	73
66	Bucknell ⊠	70
75	Albany (N.Y.) ⊠	78
50	Iowa	65
64	Colgate	53
80	Ithaca ⊠	47
69	NJIT ⊠	58
56	Penn ⊠	74
55	Princeton ⊠	35
49	Columbia	45
56	Columbia ⊠	51
74	Dartmouth	61
64	Harvard	65
61	Brown ⊠	59
60	Yale ⊠	59
57	Princeton	50
71	Penn	83
55	Yale	68
79	Brown	67
79	Harvard ⊠	85
76	Dartmouth ⊠	53

Nickname: Big Red
Colors: Carnelian Red & White
Arena: Newman Arena
Capacity: 4,473; Year Built: 1989
AD: J. Andrew Noel
SID: Jeremy Hartigan

CORNELL COLLEGE
Mt. Vernon, IA 52314-1098 III

Coach: Mike DeGeorge, Monmouth (Ill.) 1992

2006-07 RESULTS (8-17)
63	Marian (Wis.) ⊠	67
87	Wis. Lutheran ⊠	94
67	Central (Iowa)	81
67	Clarke ⊠	59
77	Faith Bapt. Bible ⊠	46
60	Augustana (Ill.) ⊠	64
73	Mt. Mercy	67
88	Benedictine (Ill.)	82
51	Chicago	76
55	Clarke	77
45	Luther	68
89	Wartburg ⊠	80
58	Loras ⊠	73
84	Dubuque ⊠	73
60	Simpson	80
54	Coe	69
58	Buena Vista ⊠	73
79	Central (Iowa) ⊠	71
63	Dubuque	74
78	Simpson ⊠	92
50	Coe ⊠	83
86	Buena Vista	94
68	Wartburg	89
44	Loras	63
68	Luther ⊠	60

Nickname: Rams
Colors: Purple & White
Arena: Small Multi-Sport Center
Capacity: 2,500; Year Built: 1953
AD: Tina Hill
SID: Darren Miller

CORTLAND ST.
Cortland, NY 13045 III

Coach: Tom Spanbauer, Cortland St. 1983

2006-07 RESULTS (10-16)
58	CCNY	56
99	Elmira	56
67	Oneonta St.	74
88	SUNYIT ⊠	93
72	Alfred ⊠	58
61	Ithaca ⊠	67
58	Utica	72
62	Rochester Inst. ⊠	63
76	St. John Fisher †	82
60	Susquehanna †	77
65	Rensselaer ⊠	48
53	Buffalo St. ⊠	68
74	Fredonia St.	66
61	Geneseo St.	64
51	Oswego St. ⊠	56
63	Brockport St. ⊠	72
64	Oswego St.	82
73	New Paltz St.	70
89	Potsdam St. ⊠	74
55	Plattsburgh St. ⊠	62
59	Oneonta St. ⊠	55
69	Buffalo St.	72
67	Potsdam St.	65
63	Brockport St.	83
80	Fredonia St. ⊠	73
56	Brockport St.	74

Nickname: Red Dragons
Colors: Red & White
Arena: Corey Gymnasium
Capacity: 3,500; Year Built: 1973
AD: Joan Sitterly
SID: Fran Elia

CREIGHTON
Omaha, NE 68178-0001 I

Coach: Dana Altman, Eastern N.M. 1980

2006-07 RESULTS (22-11)
78	Mississippi Val. ⊠	42
61	Nebraska	73
58	George Mason ⊠	56
74	Ark.-Pine Bluff ⊠	39
54	Dayton	60
73	Xavier	67
54	Fresno St.	69
68	Valparaiso †	43
80	Houston †	72
60	Hawaii	76
77	Missouri St. ⊠	74
79	Illinois St. ⊠	71
52	Indiana St.	55
75	Evansville	62
79	Drake ⊠	56
62	UNI	54
59	Wichita St.	62
65	Bradley ⊠	54
57	Southern Ill. ⊠	58
66	Missouri St.	62
71	Indiana St. ⊠	55
82	Bradley	71
67	Drake	62
79	Evansville ⊠	74
68	Southern Ill.	72
66	UNI ⊠	55
58	Drexel ⊠	64
55	Illinois St.	65
71	Wichita St. ⊠	54
59	Indiana St. †	38
75	Missouri St. †	58
67	Southern Ill. †	61
71	Nevada †	77

Nickname: Bluejays
Colors: Blue & White
Arena: Qwest Center OMAHA
Capacity: 17,272; Year Built: 2003
AD: Bruce D. Rassmussen
SID: Rob Anderson

CROWN (MINN.)
St. Bonifacius, MN 55387 III

Coach: Jon High, Pillsbury 1990

2006-07 RESULTS (3-23)
71	Augsburg	100
48	St. Olaf	100
62	Bethel (Minn.) ⊠	68
64	Trinity Bible (N.D.) ⊠	50
98	Providence-Manitoba †	54
56	Northwestern (Minn.)	76
64	Wis.-Superior ⊠	72
57	Wis.-River Falls ⊠	97
61	Bethany Lutheran	100
64	Pillsbury ⊠	77
59	Northland	74
53	St. Scholastica	103
56	Faith Bapt. Bible	55
55	Bethany Lutheran ⊠	99
37	Martin Luther ⊠	70
69	North Central (Minn. ⊠	77
58	Minn.-Morris ⊠	72
43	Presentation ⊠	61
56	Martin Luther	73
52	Presentation	79
64	Minn.-Morris	79
75	St. Scholastica ⊠	85
58	Northland ⊠	83
82	Trinity Bible (N.D.)	68
58	North Central (Minn.)	99
57	Northwestern (Minn.) ⊠	81

Nickname: Storm
Colors: Purple & gold
Arena: Storm Field
Capacity: 400
AD: Jim Hunter
SID: To be named

CURRY

Milton, MA 02186 III

Coach: Malcolm Wynn, Illinois St. 1978

2006-07 RESULTS (16-14)

70	Baldwin-Wallace †	110
51	Rutgers-Camden †	53
67	Springfield	76
89	Colby-Sawyer †	85
82	Framingham St. †	85
87	Trinity (Conn.) ⊠	104
73	Nichols ⊠	68
50	Roger Williams ⊠	65
53	Western New Eng.	70
73	Brandeis ⊠	81
73	New England	74
69	Salve Regina ⊠	72
74	Nichols	71
69	Roger Williams	67
84	Salve Regina	77
79	Eastern Nazarene	71
62	Endicott ⊠	64
66	Anna Maria	54
76	Newbury ⊠	55
53	Gordon ⊠	77
81	Colby-Sawyer	75
93	New England Col.	85
84	Eastern Nazarene	75
79	Wentworth Inst. ⊠	74
73	Anna Maria ⊠	48
95	Colby-Sawyer ⊠	76
71	Endicott ⊠	65
90	Wentworth Inst. ⊠	98
108	Emerson ⊠	88
67	St. Joseph's (Me.)	76

Nickname: Colonels
Colors: Purple & White
Arena: Miller Gymnasium
　Capacity: 300; Year Built: 1952
AD: Vincent Eruzione
SID: Ken Golner

D'YOUVILLE

Buffalo, NY 14201 III

Coach: Brian Miller, St. Bonaventure

2006-07 RESULTS (3-22)

31	Ohio Wesleyan †	96
37	Elmira	76
70	Medaille ⊠	76
41	St. John Fisher ⊠	74
46	Rochester Inst. ⊠	86
69	Polytechnic (N.Y.)	64
46	Keuka ⊠	76
54	Hilbert †	69
66	Medaille †	77
63	Brockport St.	112
48	Hilbert	82
58	Phila. Biblical ⊠	73
60	Cazenovia	93
66	Penn St.-Berks	69
53	Bard	64
45	Keystone	68
64	Baptist Bible (Pa.) ⊠	75
49	Keuka	73
54	Chestnut Hill ⊠	70
72	Cazenovia ⊠	77
50	Villa Julie	81
79	Keystone ⊠	77
66	Purchase St. ⊠	68
55	Baptist Bible (Pa.)	69
78	Bard ⊠	77

Nickname: Spartans
Colors: Red/White/Black
Arena: College Center
Capacity: 500
AD: Brian M. Cavanaugh
SID: To be named

DALLAS

Irving, TX 75062 III

Coach: Brian Stanfield, Drury 1990

2006-07 RESULTS (12-15)

56	Texas-Dallas †	90
86	Ozarks (Ark.) †	85
69	Rhodes	57
73	Millsaps †	64
58	Southwestern (Tex.) ⊠	46
77	Dallas Christian ⊠	67
68	Hendrix ⊠	71
79	LaGrange ⊠	71
68	Austin ⊠	70
78	DePauw †	104
49	Haverford †	62
60	Huntingdon	51
59	Rust †	55
53	Rhodes ⊠	81
46	Yeshiva ⊠	54
62	Dallas Christian ⊠	69
55	Colorado Col. ⊠	50
64	Chapman ⊠	71
71	UC Santa Cruz ⊠	55
68	Austin	70
78	Texas-Tyler	87
65	Trinity (Tex.) ⊠	68
75	Southwestern (Tex.)	77
84	Johnson & Wales (CO)	77
77	Colorado Col.	72
76	Clarke †	88
76	Finlandia †	86

Nickname: Crusaders
Colors: Navy & White
Arena: Maher Athletic Center
　Capacity: 1,000; Year Built: 1965
AD: Richard L. Strockbine
SID: Ryan Frey

DALLAS BAPTIST

Dallas , TX 75211-9299 II

Coach: Blake Flickner, Kansas 1998

2006-07 RESULTS (13-20)

82	Cameron	84
83	Howard Payne ⊠	64
60	East Central ⊠	69
72	Southern Ark.	67
61	Abilene Christian	76
65	Southern Ark. ⊠	58
64	Grand Canyon ⊠	78
87	Cameron ⊠	98
47	East Central	82
83	St. Edward's	88
64	Tex. A&M Int'l	88
72	Incarnate Word ⊠	71
61	Incarnate Word	72
80	St. Mary's (Tex.)	85
78	Mont. St.-Billings ⊠	69
73	Okla. Panhandle ⊠	52
63	Tex. Permian Basin ⊠	76
69	Lincoln (Mo.)	79
76	Tex. A&M Int'l ⊠	69
68	Okla. Panhandle	67
93	Lincoln (Mo.) ⊠	79
67	St. Edward's ⊠	78
74	St. Mary's (Tex.) ⊠	79
74	Mont. St.-Billings	77
79	Mont. St.-Billings	71
61	Grand Canyon	98
63	Tex. Permian Basin	78
64	St. Edward's †	73
60	Okla. Wesleyan ⊠	55
86	Central Baptist ⊠	74
68	Northwestern (Minn.) †	73
73	Manhattan Chrst. †	89
93	Oakland City	82

Nickname: Patriots
Colors: 1332
AD: Ryan Erwin
SID: To be named

DANIEL WEBSTER

Nashua, NH 03063-1300 III

Coach: Eddie Quick, Western Conn. St. 1991

2006-07 RESULTS (6-18)

83	Framingham St. ⊠	96
86	Johnson St.	85
81	Anna Maria	74
99	Albertus Magnus ⊠	88
80	New England Col. ⊠	95
74	Emerson	107
60	Emmanuel (Mass.) ⊠	82
68	Western New Eng. ⊠	86
81	Albertus Magnus	90
52	Norwich	86
89	Suffolk ⊠	88
74	Rivier	100
61	Emerson ⊠	93
62	Johnson & Wales (RI) ⊠	84
61	Emmanuel (Mass.)	83
46	Western New Eng.	80
93	Southern Vt. ⊠	92
57	Norwich ⊠	74
86	Hampshire ⊠	30
58	Suffolk	95
71	Rivier ⊠	80
71	Newbury	80
65	Johnson & Wales (RI)	78
50	Western New Eng.	81

Nickname: Eagles
Colors: Navy & White, Red
Arena: Vagge Gymnasium
　Capacity: 600; Year Built: 1977
AD: John Griffith
SID: Greg Andruskevich

DARTMOUTH

Hanover, NH 03755 I

Coach: Terry Dunn, Northern Colo. 1977

2006-07 RESULTS (9-18)

61	Massachusetts	98
49	George Washington	94
43	Colgate	55
69	Siena ⊠	83
50	Hartford	60
32	Kansas	83
74	James Madison	70
71	Stony Brook ⊠	50
56	Quinnipiac ⊠	53
62	Vermont	73
64	Md.-East. Shore	59
66	Army ⊠	58
80	Harvard ⊠	73
71	Harvard	77
61	New Hampshire ⊠	65
56	Brown ⊠	52
64	Yale ⊠	71
61	Cornell ⊠	74
55	Columbia ⊠	61
53	Penn	73
45	Princeton	44
64	Yale	69
33	Brown	53
53	Princeton ⊠	43
78	Penn ⊠	80
67	Columbia	69
53	Cornell	76

Nickname: Big Green
Colors: Dartmouth Green and White
Arena: Leede Arena
　Capacity: 2,100; Year Built: 1986
AD: Jo Ann Harper
SID: Kathy Slattery Phillips

DAVIDSON

Davidson, NC 28035 I

Coach: Bob McKillop, Hofstra 1972

2006-07 RESULTS (29-5)

81	Eastern Mich. †	77
68	Michigan	78
91	Central Conn. St. †	64
100	Ill.-Chicago ⊠	89
75	Missouri	81
99	Colby ⊠	69
47	Duke	75
86	Elon ⊠	61
66	UNC Greensboro	63
79	Charlotte ⊠	51
116	Mt. St. Mary (N.Y.) ⊠	55
92	Chattanooga ⊠	80
83	Ohio †	74
75	Arizona St.	70
71	Western Mich. ⊠	64
81	Col. of Charleston ⊠	73
71	Furman	63
83	Wofford	78
79	Citadel ⊠	54
74	Appalachian St. ⊠	81
101	Ga. Southern ⊠	92
79	Western Caro. ⊠	59
88	Elon	58
75	UNC Greensboro ⊠	65
87	Chattanooga ⊠	57
73	Col. of Charleston	63
92	Western Caro.	59
80	Wofford ⊠	73
75	Furman ⊠	57
87	Citadel	70
78	Chattanooga †	68
91	Furman †	68
72	Col. of Charleston †	65
70	Maryland †	82

Nickname: Wildcats
Colors: Red & Black
Arena: Belk Arena
　Capacity: 5,700; Year Built: 1989
AD: James E. Murphy III
SID: Rick Bender

DAVIS & ELKINS

Elkins, WV 26241-3996 II

Coach: Amrit Rayfield, Davis & Elkins 1997

2006-07 RESULTS (6-22)

53	Bloomsburg	60
49	Dist. Columbia	64
88	Columbia Union †	82
78	Fairmont St. ⊠	70
64	Shepherd ⊠	74
72	Concord	84
102	Pfeiffer ⊠	112
72	Goldey-Beacom ⊠	57
65	Shenandoah	68
61	Dist. Columbia ⊠	72
47	West Virginia St. ⊠	60
77	Glenville St.	70
80	West Liberty St.	113
41	Alderson-Broaddus ⊠	69
64	Columbia Union	58
59	West Va. Wesleyan	73
66	Goldey-Beacom	73
79	Ohio Valley ⊠	85
71	Charleston (W.V.) ⊠	87
65	Salem Int'l ⊠	68
68	Bluefield St.	70
68	Wheeling Jesuit	76
60	Alderson-Broaddus	65
62	West Va. Wesleyan ⊠	58
68	West Virginia St.	86
60	Charleston (W.V.)	87
69	Glenville St. ⊠	71
44	Salem Int'l	73

Nickname: Senators
Colors: Scarlet & White
Arena: Memorial Gymnasium
　Capacity: 1,875; Year Built: 1950

AD: Ralph Hill
SID: Kristi Kirkpatrick

DAYTON
Dayton, OH 45469 I

Coach: Brian Gregory, Oakland 1990

2006-07 RESULTS (19-12)
78	Austin Peay ⊠	62
79	N.C. A&T ⊠	66
48	SMU	53
73	Yale ⊠	62
68	Louisville †	64
67	South Carolina St. ⊠	55
69	Holy Cross ⊠	53
60	Creighton ⊠	54
58	Grambling	49
66	Western Caro. ⊠	55
56	Miami (Ohio) ⊠	54
54	Pittsburgh	84
51	North Carolina	81
66	Charlotte ⊠	63
74	Rhode Island	75
84	La Salle ⊠	82
59	Charlotte	80
72	Richmond ⊠	54
89	Duquesne	93
67	Xavier	83
84	George Washington ⊠	69
65	St. Joseph's	71
57	Fordham ⊠	45
69	St. Bonaventure	62
69	Massachusetts ⊠	77
56	St. Louis	66
67	Xavier ⊠	75
73	Temple	65
65	St. Louis †	64
81	Charlotte †	63
51	Xavier †	72

Nickname: Flyers
Colors: Red & Blue
Arena: University of Dayton Arena
   Capacity: 13,266; Year Built: 1969
AD: Ted Kissell
SID: Doug Hauschild

DEPAUL
Chicago, IL 60614 I

Coach: Jerry Wainwright, Colorado Col. 1968

2006-07 RESULTS (20-14)
58	Bradley	78
39	Northwestern	49
71	Eastern Ill. ⊠	41
81	Kentucky †	87
93	Chaminade †	74
73	Purdue †	81
64	Kansas	57
83	Chicago St. ⊠	56
57	UAB	58
78	Wake Forest ⊠	63
89	Rhode Island	81
65	UC Irvine ⊠	53
90	California	62
97	Northwestern St. ⊠	67
53	St. John's (N.Y.)	64
73	Villanova	65
49	Pittsburgh ⊠	59
60	Rutgers	37
71	St. John's (N.Y.) ⊠	63
50	Louisville ⊠	59
52	Georgetown	66
52	West Virginia	64
66	Connecticut ⊠	58
69	Syracuse	75
67	Notre Dame ⊠	66
72	Marquette ⊠	67
75	South Fla.	62
54	Notre Dame	78
58	Cincinnati ⊠	45
70	South Fla. ⊠	54
67	Villanova †	75
83	Hofstra ⊠	71

| 70 | Kansas St. | 65 |
| 51 | Air Force | 52 |

Nickname: Blue Demons
Colors: Royal Blue & Scarlet
Arena: Allstate Arena
   Capacity: 18,500; Year Built: 1980
AD: Jean Lenti Ponsetto
SID: Scott Reed

DEPAUW
Greencastle, IN 46135 III

Coach: Bill Fenlon, Northwestern 1979

2006-07 RESULTS (22-6)
85	Earlham †	80
71	Chicago	79
88	Judson (Ill.) ⊠	84
85	Ohio Wesleyan ⊠	79
92	Wabash ⊠	82
73	Centre ⊠	67
68	Maryville (Mo.)	50
84	Illinois Tech ⊠	63
53	Kenyon	52
104	Dallas †	78
77	Hamilton †	85
70	Sewanee	77
76	Oglethorpe	70
75	Hendrix ⊠	62
70	Austin	51
58	Rose-Hulman ⊠	43
66	Trinity (Tex.) ⊠	51
59	Southwestern (Tex.) ⊠	51
78	Rhodes	65
76	Millsaps	74
41	Centre	73
77	Hendrix	72
63	Austin	58
94	Sewanee ⊠	82
90	Oglethorpe ⊠	71
84	Sewanee †	72
72	Trinity (Tex.) †	77
59	Whitworth †	62

Nickname: Tigers
Colors: Old Gold & Black
Arena: Neal Fieldhouse
   Capacity: 2,800; Year Built: 1982
AD: Page Cotton Jr.
SID: Bill Wagner

DEFIANCE
Defiance, OH 43512 III

Coach: Jonathan Miller, Hanover

2006-07 RESULTS (17-9)
76	Thomas More ⊠	48
65	Wilmington (Ohio) ⊠	75
87	Heidelberg	82
64	Manchester ⊠	48
62	Anderson (Ind.)	60
93	Bluffton	103
81	Hanover ⊠	72
61	Olivet ⊠	55
72	Wash. & Jeff. ⊠	67
79	Juniata †	56
76	Illinois Col. †	71
60	Rose-Hulman ⊠	39
62	Mt. St. Joseph	80
50	Transylvania	74
66	Franklin ⊠	49
78	Anderson (Ind.) ⊠	64
73	Manchester	80
83	Hanover	80
70	Bluffton ⊠	72
74	Mt. St. Joseph ⊠	67
65	Marygrove ⊠	50
61	Rose-Hulman	52
77	Franklin	88
58	Transylvania ⊠	61
80	Franklin	73
64	Transylvania †	77

Nickname: Yellow Jackets
Colors: Purple & Gold
Arena: Weaner Community Center

Capacity: 2,200; Year Built: 1964
AD: Dick Kaiser
SID: Seth Mikel

DELAWARE
Newark, DE 19716 I

Coach: Monte Ross, Winston-Salem 1992

2006-07 RESULTS (5-26)
62	Marist	78
67	Albany (N.Y.)	87
67	Rider ⊠	77
53	Cleveland St. ⊠	59
63	Loyola (Md.)	75
55	Vermont ⊠	57
60	Central Conn. St.	63
60	VCU	79
64	UNC Greensboro	74
71	Niagara †	53
58	La Salle	56
47	Holy Cross †	49
47	James Madison	62
50	Hofstra	75
68	Towson ⊠	75
48	Old Dominion	83
77	William & Mary ⊠	62
44	Georgia St. ⊠	61
61	Drexel ⊠	69
63	Towson	85
64	Northeastern	73
72	Hofstra ⊠	68
59	George Mason	89
64	James Madison ⊠	69
78	UNC Wilmington ⊠	69
62	Drexel	77
46	George Mason ⊠	66
50	Iona ⊠	52
61	Northeastern ⊠	70
66	UNC Wilmington	75
67	Northeastern †	77

Nickname: Fightin' Blue Hens
Colors: Blue & Gold
Arena: Bob Carpenter Center
   Capacity: 5,000; Year Built: 1992
AD: Edgar N. Johnson
SID: Kevin Tritt

DELAWARE ST.
Dover, DE 19901 I

Coach: Greg Jackson, St. Paul's 1982

2006-07 RESULTS (21-13)
90	St. Paul's ⊠	53
50	Pittsburgh	67
43	North Carolina St.	63
54	Missouri St.	77
52	Wisconsin	64
65	Southern U. †	63
55	Sam Houston St. †	62
40	Purdue	62
48	Marquette	65
43	Michigan	70
65	Buffalo	62
56	Baylor	59
59	South Carolina St.	53
54	Coppin St.	49
68	Morgan St.	61
66	Howard	57
61	Md.-East. Shore	47
75	Hampton ⊠	64
66	Norfolk St. ⊠	56
69	Florida A&M	73
62	Bethune-Cookman	46
53	Coppin St. ⊠	45
40	Morgan St. ⊠	54
59	Howard	40
69	Md.-East. Shore ⊠	59
81	Hampton	74
72	Norfolk St.	61
77	Florida A&M ⊠	65
47	Bethune-Cookman ⊠	40
62	N.C. A&T ⊠	53
68	Coppin St. †	49

56	Morgan St. †	53
56	Florida A&M †	58
50	West Virginia	74

Nickname: Hornets
Colors: Red & Columbia Blue
Arena: Memorial Hall
   Capacity: 3,000; Year Built: 1982
AD: Chuck Bell
SID: Dennis Jones

DELAWARE VALLEY
Doylestown, PA 18901-2699 III

Coach: Denny Surovec, Penn St. 1997

2006-07 RESULTS (5-20)
74	Frank. & Marsh.	67
90	Lincoln (Pa.) †	119
58	Vassar	82
70	Richard Stockton	84
62	DeSales ⊠	85
77	Wilkes ⊠	66
65	Lebanon Valley ⊠	92
62	Moravian ⊠	66
59	Arcadia	55
40	Navy	65
70	Eastern	77
59	Chestnut Hill ⊠	76
84	Gwynedd-Mercy ⊠	93
47	Drew	71
61	King's (Pa.)	80
69	FDU-Florham ⊠	71
56	Lycoming	72
68	Scranton ⊠	84
66	King's (Pa.) ⊠	63
54	FDU-Florham	81
53	Wilkes	62
59	Drew ⊠	54
59	Scranton	90
51	DeSales	76
75	Lycoming ⊠	80

Nickname: Aggies
Colors: Green & Gold
Arena: James Work Gymnasium
   Capacity: 1,800; Year Built: 1969
AD: Frank Wolfgang
SID: Matthew Levy

DELTA ST.
Cleveland, MS 38733 II

Coach: Jason Conner, Belhaven 1987

2006-07 RESULTS (18-10)
66	Clark Atlanta ⊠	49
60	Miles ⊠	61
92	Southern-N.O.	57
71	LeMoyne-Owen	82
90	North Ala. ⊠	84
106	Ecclesia ⊠	48
75	West Ala.	68
102	Dillard	97
80	West Ga.	65
66	Tougaloo ⊠	61
72	Tougaloo †	65
67	West Ala. ⊠	56
80	Ouachita Baptist ⊠	60
78	Harding	65
79	Ark.-Monticello ⊠	69
66	Southern Ark. ⊠	61
65	Christian Bros.	68
90	Arkansas Tech	77
55	Henderson St. ⊠	62
80	Central St. (Ohio) ⊠	85
81	Ouachita Baptist	92
87	Harding ⊠	83
82	Ark.-Monticello	79
63	Southern Ark.	65
61	Christian Bros. ⊠	65
74	Arkansas Tech ⊠	69
54	Henderson St.	66
69	Ala.-Huntsville †	74

Nickname: Statesmen
Colors: Forest Green & White
Arena: Walter Sillers Coliseum

Capacity: 4,000; Year Built: 1961
AD: Ron Mayers
SID: Matt Jones

DENISON
Granville, OH 43023 III

Coach: Bob Ghiloni, Ohio St.-Newark
1981

2006-07 RESULTS (6-18)
71	Wash. & Lee	82
77	Oneonta St. †	62
70	Lake Erie	82
71	Muskingum ⊠	79
68	Capital †	81
85	Wittenberg ⊠	100
49	Wash. & Jeff.	71
56	Wabash ⊠	62
53	Scranton †	70
52	Clarke †	69
50	Ohio Wesleyan ⊠	72
67	Wooster	96
75	Oberlin ⊠	48
87	Allegheny ⊠	67
70	Kenyon	73
117	Hiram	120
60	Earlham ⊠	80
65	Wittenberg	87
76	Oberlin	82
52	Wabash	63
68	Kenyon ⊠	65
67	Allegheny	94
74	Earlham	73
79	Hiram ⊠	74

Nickname: Big Red
Colors: Red & White
Arena: Livingston Gymnasium
   Capacity: 2,500; Year Built: 1949
AD: Larry Scheiderer
SID: Craig Hicks

DENVER
Denver, CO 80208 I

Coach: Terry Carroll, UNI 1978

2006-07 RESULTS (4-25)
64	Colorado	78
68	Southern Utah ⊠	74
53	Sacramento St. ⊠	74
74	Northern Colo. ⊠	68
39	Stanford	82
63	Southern Utah	73
73	Colorado St. ⊠	81
56	South Dakota St. ⊠	67
59	Wyoming	91
59	Northern Colo.	74
66	Arkansas St.	81
47	Ark.-Little Rock	73
66	New Orleans ⊠	76
79	North Texas	91
64	La.-Lafayette	66
75	La.-Monroe ⊠	65
59	Florida Int'l	61
90	Fla. Atlantic ⊠	85
64	South Ala. ⊠	70
63	Troy	66
67	Western Ky. ⊠	77
49	Middle Tenn.	75
76	Arkansas St. ⊠	68
68	Ark.-Little Rock ⊠	74
66	New Orleans	89
65	North Texas ⊠	78
65	La.-Lafayette ⊠	67
51	La.-Monroe	87
67	La.-Monroe	83

Nickname: Pioneers
Colors: Crimson & Gold
Arena: Magness Arena
   Capacity: 7,200; Year Built: 1999
AD: Peggy Bradley-Doppes
SID: Derek Nagy

DESALES
Center Valley, PA 18034-9568 III

Coach: Scott Coval, William & Mary
1986

2006-07 RESULTS (22-8)
57	Ohio Northern †	74
119	Penn St.-Harrisburg †	49
72	Moravian	68
80	Misericordia ⊠	85
85	Delaware Valley	62
82	King's (Pa.) ⊠	55
69	Cabrini	63
77	Albright	67
76	Briarcliffe (N.Y.) ⊠	58
71	Muhlenberg ⊠	63
73	Immaculata ⊠	68
76	TCNJ ⊠	64
38	FDU-Florham	72
68	Wilkes	58
67	Drew ⊠	62
70	Scranton	78
64	Lycoming ⊠	63
75	Wilkes ⊠	51
99	Penn St.-Berks	70
53	Drew	56
70	King's (Pa.)	73
81	FDU-Florham ⊠	68
65	Lycoming	74
76	Delaware Valley ⊠	51
75	Scranton ⊠	70
62	Scranton	60
64	King's (Pa.) ⊠	67
88	Gwynedd-Mercy ⊠	77
83	Lebanon Valley ⊠	73
72	Penn St.-Behrend ⊠	63

Nickname: Bulldogs
Colors: Navy Blue & Scarlet
Arena: Billera Hall
   Capacity: 1,000; Year Built: 1964
AD: Scott Coval
SID: B.J. Spigelmyer

DETROIT
Detroit, MI 48219-0900 I

Coach: Perry Watson, Eastern Mich.
1972

2006-07 RESULTS (11-19)
57	Maine †	50
45	Marquette	87
48	Kent St.	61
67	Western Mich.	69
73	A&M-Corpus Christi ⊠	82
72	Eastern Mich. ⊠	52
49	Wright St.	50
55	Xavier	88
72	Canisius ⊠	75
63	Toledo	73
60	Northeastern ⊠	51
43	Kansas	63
60	Green Bay	42
64	Milwaukee	65
66	Youngstown St. ⊠	51
61	Cleveland St.	63
64	Loyola (Ill.) ⊠	70
66	Ill.-Chicago	54
91	Milwaukee ⊠	84
58	Butler ⊠	68
78	Chicago St.	68
76	Green Bay ⊠	72
59	Wright St. ⊠	66
61	Loyola (Ill.)	71
67	Ill.-Chicago ⊠	75
70	Youngstown St.	82
92	Buffalo	84
60	Cleveland St. ⊠	48
36	Butler	56
80	Youngstown St.	82

Nickname: Titans
Colors: Red, White & Blue
Arena: Calihan Hall
   Capacity: 8,295; Year Built: 1952
AD: Keri Gaither
SID: Mark Engel

DICKINSON
Carlisle, PA 17013 III

Coach: Dennis Csensits, DeSales 1990

2006-07 RESULTS (7-17)
100	Pitt.-Greensburg ⊠	88
60	Mary Washington ⊠	61
65	Wash. & Lee ⊠	78
72	Moravian ⊠	75
58	McDaniel	75
71	Washington (Md.)	73
56	Frank. & Marsh. ⊠	66
60	Johns Hopkins	76
77	Lancaster Bible ⊠	64
59	Wesley	84
67	Swarthmore ⊠	61
71	Ursinus ⊠	80
48	Haverford ⊠	50
59	Washington (Md.) ⊠	56
42	Gettysburg	68
40	Johns Hopkins ⊠	77
69	Muhlenberg ⊠	50
60	Swarthmore	66
77	McDaniel ⊠	75
80	Ursinus	100
73	Frank. & Marsh.	68
50	Haverford	51
84	Muhlenberg	91
65	Gettysburg ⊠	71

Nickname: Red Devils
Colors: Red & White
Arena: Kline Center
   Capacity: 2,000; Year Built: 1980
AD: Leslie J. Poolman
SID: Charlie McGuire

DIST. COLUMBIA
Washington, DC 20008 II

Coach: Julius Smith, Morehouse 1979

2006-07 RESULTS (20-9)
95	West Liberty St. †	99
66	Wheeling Jesuit †	63
64	Davis & Elkins ⊠	49
78	Kutztown ⊠	66
133	Ohio St.-Marion †	53
67	Salem Int'l	50
87	Salem Int'l ⊠	74
56	Bloomsburg	50
51	Ga. Southwestern	74
67	Columbus St.	87
72	Davis & Elkins	61
72	Virginia Union	86
57	Claflin	54
89	Felician	75
69	Virginia Union ⊠	74
70	Pitt.-Johnstown ⊠	71
76	Bloomsburg ⊠	73
75	Lincoln (Pa.) ⊠	70
86	Columbia Union	77
71	West Chester	61
73	Pitt.-Johnstown	82
74	Claflin ⊠	50
87	West Chester ⊠	79
84	Kutztown	81
76	Palm Beach Atl. †	62
71	North Georgia †	79
72	Flagler †	64
65	Pitt.-Johnstown †	82
93	Columbia Union ⊠	83

Nickname: Firebirds
Colors: Red & Yellow
Arena: Physical Activities Center
   Capacity: 3,000; Year Built: 1976
AD: Harold Merritt
SID: Bernard S. Payton

DIXIE ST.
St. George, UT 84770 II

Coach: Jon Judkins, Utah St. 1988

2006-07 RESULTS (11-13)
57	Fort Lewis †	79
66	Adams St.	55
75	Bethany (Cal.) †	70
60	Mesa St.	63
68	Colorado St.-Pueblo †	59
72	BYU-Hawaii ⊠	78
68	Adams St. ⊠	52
71	Carroll (Mont.) ⊠	81
67	Westminster (Utah)	64
68	Northwest Nazarene †	67
81	Montana Western	78
65	Carroll (Mont.)	60
55	Mont. St.-Northern	77
67	Tex. A&M Int'l ⊠	51
76	Seattle Pacific ⊠	82
72	Western Wash.	90
70	Seattle †	87
67	Seattle Pacific	71
76	Fort Lewis	86
72	Tex. A&M-Kingsville	93
66	Tex. A&M Int'l	54
90	Grand Canyon	81
63	Notre Dame de Namur ⊠	64
51	Notre Dame de Namur	65

Nickname: Rebels
Colors: Red, navy blue & white
Arena: Burns
   Capacity: 5,200; Year Built: 1992
AD: Dexter Irvin
SID: Jeff Cluff

DOMINICAN (ILL.)
River Forest, IL 60305 III

Coach: Mark White, Macalester 1984

2006-07 RESULTS (17-10)
52	Blackburn	57
80	Greenville †	74
57	Milwaukee Engr. ⊠	70
61	Edgewood ⊠	59
85	Wis. Lutheran ⊠	91
101	Maranatha Baptist ⊠	37
61	Marian (Wis.)	63
61	Coe †	72
57	Lake Forest †	55
74	Eureka ⊠	65
66	Aurora	90
85	Concordia (Ill.) ⊠	70
89	Rockford	67
46	Benedictine (Ill.)	63
83	Concordia (Wis.) ⊠	71
66	Wis. Lutheran	62
73	Lakeland ⊠	72
89	Maranatha Baptist	52
85	Marian (Wis.) ⊠	78
76	Edgewood	77
68	Milwaukee Engr.	61
80	Aurora ⊠	83
83	Concordia (Ill.)	70
92	Rockford ⊠	65
94	Concordia (Wis.)	90
60	Benedictine (Ill.) ⊠	43
62	Edgewood	73

Nickname: Stars
Colors: Royal Blue, Black & White
Arena: IGINI Sports Forum
   Capacity: 1,000; Year Built: 1985
AD: Erick Baumann
SID: Ken Trendel

DOMINICAN (N.Y.)
Orangeburg , NY 10962-1299 II

Coach: Joe Clinton, Union (N.Y.) 1983

2006-07 RESULTS (13-15)

53	Minn. Duluth †	67
44	Minn. St. Mankato	81
68	Felician	73
79	Nyack ⊠	67
59	Goldey-Beacom	56
63	Caldwell	59
85	Wilmington (Del.)	77
42	Stonehill	60
78	Bloomfield	81
65	Mercy ⊠	55
54	Queens (N.Y.) ⊠	59
60	Phila. Sciences	49
65	Holy Family ⊠	51
57	Philadelphia U.	77
66	Queens (N.Y.)	57
58	Goldey-Beacom ⊠	60
54	Post	89
68	Felician ⊠	73
87	Wilmington (Del.) ⊠	69
93	Bloomfield ⊠	83
56	Caldwell	63
56	Nyack	68
75	Phila. Sciences ⊠	68
84	Southern Conn. St. ⊠	69
57	Holy Family	71
73	Post	74
51	Philadelphia U. ⊠	36
67	Philadelphia U.	71

Nickname: Chargers
Colors: Black & Red
Arena: Hennessy Center
  Capacity: 1,000; Year Built: 1990
AD: Joseph S. Clinton
SID: Kelly-Ann Di Giulio

DOWLING
Oakdale, NY 11769 II

Coach: Stephen Hayn, Stony Brook 1991

2006-07 RESULTS (6-21)

65	American Int'l ⊠	68
60	Cheyney †	55
77	Bowie St.	89
49	Merrimack ⊠	71
66	Molloy ⊠	61
65	Bloomfield †	68
54	Caldwell	65
51	C.W. Post	86
44	Concordia (N.Y.)	58
79	Stonehill ⊠	91
64	Mercy ⊠	65
67	St. Thomas Aquinas ⊠	54
72	New Haven ⊠	64
55	Adelphi ⊠	72
52	NYIT ⊠	64
62	Queens (N.Y.)	85
42	Bridgeport ⊠	69
66	Molloy	71
57	Mercy	44
64	C.W. Post ⊠	82
63	Concordia (N.Y.) ⊠	51
61	St. Thomas Aquinas	68
64	New Haven	78
44	Adelphi	65
60	NYIT	68
77	Queens (N.Y.) ⊠	97
55	Bridgeport	76

Nickname: Golden Lions
Colors: Navy & Vegas Gold
Arena: Lasalle Center
Capacity: 1,500
AD: Rick Cole Jr.
SID: Melissa Perry

DRAKE
Des Moines, IA 50311-4505 I

Coach: Tom Davis, Wis.-Platteville 1960

2006-07 RESULTS (17-15)

78	Southeast Mo. St. †	51
74	Utah St. †	92
75	Troy †	80
104	Waldorf ⊠	51
80	Iowa St.	78
102	Troy ⊠	90
87	Ga. Southern ⊠	75
76	UC Irvine ⊠	73
75	Iowa ⊠	59
70	Toledo †	52
71	Jackson St. †	70
57	Evansville	78
73	Indiana St.	84
54	Southern Ill. ⊠	59
86	Bradley ⊠	89
56	Creighton	79
70	Illinois St. ⊠	66
62	Southern Ill.	72
74	Indiana St. ⊠	68
65	Illinois St.	80
77	Wichita St.	82
74	UNI ⊠	61
82	Missouri St. ⊠	87
62	Creighton ⊠	67
67	UNI	59
85	Bradley	100
62	Wichita St. ⊠	58
84	Milwaukee ⊠	76
82	Evansville ⊠	79
74	Missouri St.	92
101	Evansville †	96
59	Southern Ill. †	71

Nickname: Bulldogs
Colors: Blue & White
Arena: Drake Knapp Center
  Capacity: 7,002; Year Built: 1992
AD: Sandy Hatfield Clubb
SID: Mike Mahon

DREW
Madison, NJ 07940 III

Coach: Walter Townes, Clark (Mass.) 1984

2006-07 RESULTS (9-15)

72	Hunter ⊠	67
37	Wm. Paterson ⊠	55
55	Muhlenberg	54
62	FDU-Florham	69
53	Lycoming	65
58	Vassar	63
50	Ursinus ⊠	53
70	Ferrum †	65
48	Roanoke	60
50	Moravian	87
67	Salisbury †	54
71	Delaware Valley ⊠	47
34	Scranton ⊠	55
62	DeSales	67
58	Wilkes ⊠	49
57	Staten Island ⊠	52
55	King's (Pa.)	62
51	Scranton	65
56	DeSales ⊠	53
69	Lycoming ⊠	49
54	Delaware Valley	59
40	King's (Pa.) ⊠	80
39	FDU-Florham ⊠	53
50	Wilkes	62

Nickname: Rangers
Colors: Green & Blue
Arena: Baldwin Gym
  Capacity: 800; Year Built: 1958
AD: Connee Zotos
SID: Jennifer Brauner

DREXEL
Philadelphia, PA 19104 I

Coach: Bruiser Flint, St. Joseph's 1987

2006-07 RESULTS (23-9)

73	Fla. Gulf Coast ⊠	37
59	Vermont	46
49	Penn	68
81	Rider	89
57	Toledo ⊠	52
72	St. Joseph's	56
80	Fairleigh Dickinson ⊠	58
81	Villanova	76
84	Syracuse	79
69	Temple	54
61	George Mason ⊠	49
61	Georgia St.	55
69	UNC Wilmington ⊠	55
65	James Madison ⊠	54
53	Hofstra ⊠	55
57	Old Dominion	84
67	Northeastern ⊠	41
69	Delaware	61
66	UNC Wilmington	50
68	VCU ⊠	75
68	Northeastern	59
52	Old Dominion ⊠	62
66	Towson ⊠	56
95	Hofstra	87
77	Delaware ⊠	62
47	William & Mary	60
64	Creighton	58
64	William & Mary ⊠	57
77	Towson	68
64	Northeastern †	50
56	VCU †	63
56	North Carolina St. ⊠	63

Nickname: Dragons
Colors: Navy Blue & Gold
Arena: Daskalakis Athletic Center
  Capacity: 2,500; Year Built: 1975
AD: Eric A. Zillmer
SID: Mike Tuberosa

DRURY
Springfield, MO 65802 II

Coach: Steve Hesser, Oklahoma St. 1980

2006-07 RESULTS (21-9)

96	St. Mary (Kan.) ⊠	58
80	Southwest Baptist	79
66	Hannibal-La Grange ⊠	32
81	St. Gregory's ⊠	73
80	Lewis	83
84	Wis.-Parkside ⊠	75
86	Mo.-St. Louis ⊠	51
80	Mo.-Rolla ⊠	66
85	Harding	82
61	Hillsdale †	71
81	Wingate †	67
83	Missouri Valley ⊠	63
53	Ky. Wesleyan	62
70	Southern Ind.	89
81	St. Joseph's (Ind.) ⊠	69
66	Indianapolis ⊠	77
70	Rockhurst ⊠	78
60	SIU Edwardsville	78
74	Quincy	78
78	Northern Ky. ⊠	69
81	Bellarmine ⊠	67
79	SIU Edwardsville ⊠	71
76	Quincy ⊠	69
91	Mo.-St. Louis	87
86	Mo.-Rolla	82
69	Rockhurst	60
77	Southern Ind. ⊠	72
88	Wis.-Parkside †	75
62	Northern Ky. †	69
68	Northern Ky. †	73

Nickname: Panthers
Colors: Scarlet & Gray
Arena: Weiser Gymnasium
  Capacity: 2,250; Year Built: 1948

AD: Edsel Matthews
SID: Scott Puryear

DUBUQUE
Dubuque, IA 52001 III

Coach: Marty McDermott, North Dakota 1993

2006-07 RESULTS (11-14)

81	Caltech	40
59	Claremont-M-S	61
89	West Coast Baptist	72
61	Wis.-Platteville †	66
88	Clarke	59
84	Martin Luther ⊠	72
70	Mt. Mercy	76
61	Coe ⊠	80
101	Faith Bapt. Bible ⊠	74
81	Simpson ⊠	68
73	Clarke ⊠	66
81	Central (Iowa) ⊠	58
58	Luther	62
73	Cornell College	84
73	Loras ⊠	88
82	Buena Vista	91
74	Wartburg ⊠	65
56	Coe	71
74	Cornell College ⊠	63
63	Wartburg	69
67	Luther ⊠	52
64	Loras	71
62	Central (Iowa) ⊠	68
90	Buena Vista ⊠	98
58	Simpson	84

Nickname: Spartans
Colors: Blue & White
Arena: McCormick Gym
  Capacity: 1,500; Year Built: 1916
AD: Dan Runkle
SID: Paul Misner

DUKE
Durham, NC 27708-0555 I

Coach: Mike Krzyzewski, Army 1969

2006-07 RESULTS (22-11)

86	Columbia ⊠	43
72	Ga. Southern ⊠	48
75	UNC Greensboro ⊠	48
71	Air Force †	56
62	Marquette †	73
75	Davidson ⊠	47
54	Indiana ⊠	51
61	Georgetown ⊠	52
57	Holy Cross ⊠	45
69	George Mason ⊠	53
79	Kent St. ⊠	72
61	Gonzaga †	54
70	San Jose St. ⊠	51
73	Temple ⊠	55
67	Virginia Tech ⊠	69
63	Georgia Tech	74
85	Miami (Fla.) ⊠	63
62	Wake Forest ⊠	40
79	North Carolina St.	56
68	Clemson ⊠	66
75	Boston College ⊠	61
66	Virginia	68
67	Florida St. ⊠	68
73	North Carolina	79
60	Maryland	72
78	Boston College	70
71	Georgia Tech ⊠	62
71	Clemson	66
67	St. John's (N.Y.)	50
77	Maryland ⊠	85
72	North Carolina	86
80	North Carolina St. †	85
77	VCU †	79

Nickname: Blue Devils
Colors: Royal Blue & White
Arena: Cameron Indoor Stadium
  Capacity: 9,314; Year Built: 1939

AD: Joe Alleva
SID: Jon Jackson

DUQUESNE
Pittsburgh, PA 15282 I

Coach: Ron Everhart, Virginia Tech 1985

2006-07 RESULTS (10-19)
81 Youngstown St. ⊠ 75
77 UNC Asheville ⊠ 76
82 Northern Ill. ⊠ 87
53 Oakland ⊠ 67
74 Northern Ill. 85
72 Robert Morris 73
56 Pittsburgh 73
54 West Virginia ⊠ 85
74 Niagara 78
72 St. Francis (Pa.) 71
98 Boston College 93
41 St. Joseph's 89
73 St. Louis 63
63 La Salle ⊠ 79
59 Fordham 71
87 Massachusetts 101
93 Dayton ⊠ 89
96 Temple ⊠ 92
93 Xavier ⊠ 91
111 St. Bonaventure 92
111 La Salle 105
87 Rhode Island ⊠ 111
66 Richmond 69
83 Fordham 86
90 Charlotte ⊠ 99
94 St. Bonaventure ⊠ 97
74 Akron ⊠ 87
80 George Washington 88
77 St. Louis † 78

Nickname: Dukes
Colors: Red & Blue
Arena: A.J. Palumbo Center
   Capacity: 5,358; Year Built: 1988
AD: Greg Amodio
SID: Dave Saba

EARLHAM
Richmond, IN 47374 III

Coach: Jeff Justus, Rose-Hulman 1978

2006-07 RESULTS (8-18)
80 DePauw † 85
57 Coast Guard † 70
68 Bluffton 81
56 Manchester ⊠ 72
62 Wooster 84
69 Kenyon ⊠ 60
70 Rose-Hulman ⊠ 62
71 Franklin 66
74 Anderson (Ind.) 84
59 Muskingum † 61
60 Wash. & Jeff. 62
56 Allegheny 55
65 Hiram 67
60 Wittenberg ⊠ 71
68 Ohio Wesleyan ⊠ 65
57 Wabash 73
76 Oberlin ⊠ 59
80 Denison 60
51 Wooster ⊠ 64
40 Wittenberg 87
47 Kenyon 53
72 Wabash ⊠ 70
70 Ohio Wesleyan 82
73 Denison ⊠ 74
76 Oberlin 79
76 Wooster 94

Nickname: Quakers
Colors: Maroon & White
Arena: Schuckman Court
   Capacity: 1,800; Year Built: 1999
AD: Frank Carr
SID: Donald Tincher

EAST CARO.
Greenville, NC 27858-4353 I

Coach: Ricky Stokes, Virginia 1984

2006-07 RESULTS (6-24)
86 Morgan St. ⊠ 67
67 Richmond 71
72 UNC Greensboro 64
80 Limestone ⊠ 54
68 N.C. Central 47
56 Liberty 64
44 UNC Wilmington 59
52 South Fla. ⊠ 65
70 Morgan St. 76
50 Winthrop ⊠ 69
57 North Carolina St. 64
65 Wake Forest 81
68 Chowan ⊠ 50
49 Tulsa 67
47 Rice ⊠ 64
56 Tulane ⊠ 65
44 Memphis ⊠ 61
72 Southern Miss. 83
42 UAB ⊠ 58
52 Marshall 56
74 Rice 83
49 UCF ⊠ 67
59 Houston 83
42 Southern Miss. ⊠ 80
42 SMU 65
51 Marshall ⊠ 54
79 UTEP ⊠ 78
72 Tulane 88
64 UCF 77
50 Tulsa † 65

Nickname: Pirates
Colors: Purple & Gold
Arena: Williams Arena at Minges
   Capacity: 8,000; Year Built: 1967
AD: Terry Holland
SID: Jody Jones

EAST CENTRAL
Ada, OK 74820 II

Coach: Terry Shannon, Southeastern Okla. 1989

2006-07 RESULTS (10-16)
69 Dallas Baptist 60
81 Southwestern Christ. 82
55 Tarleton St. 63
73 Tex. A&M-Kingsville ⊠ 76
61 Midwestern St. 64
89 Southwestern Christ. 71
71 St. Edward's ⊠ 67
79 Rhema 61
82 Dallas Baptist ⊠ 47
84 Paul Quinn 69
90 Huston-Tillotson † 55
57 Abilene Christian 62
69 Angelo St. 59
62 Eastern N.M. 72
72 Southwestern Okla. 88
66 Cameron ⊠ 71
60 Southeastern Okla. 74
74 Tex. A&M-Commerce ⊠ 71
64 Northeastern St. 75
64 Central Okla. ⊠ 73
102 Southwestern Okla. ⊠ 101
77 Cameron 79
78 Southeastern Okla. ⊠ 83
64 Tex. A&M-Commerce 78
56 Northeastern St. ⊠ 70
68 Central Okla. 89

Nickname: Tigers
Colors: Orange & Black
Arena: Kerr Activities Center
   Capacity: 4,000; Year Built: 1973
AD: Brian DeAngelis
SID: Brian Johnson

EAST STROUDSBURG
East Stroudsburg, PA 18301 II

Coach: Jeff Wilson, East Stroudsburg 1986

2006-07 RESULTS (18-10)
74 California (Pa.) † 80
81 Columbia Union † 65
83 Lock Haven ⊠ 77
54 Shippensburg ⊠ 46
90 Penn St.-Harrisburg ⊠ 38
62 Pitt.-Johnstown ⊠ 69
86 Penn St.-Hazleton 46
82 Edinboro 72
68 Slippery Rock 54
98 Phila. Sciences 94
83 Clarion 78
71 Indiana (Pa.) 59
83 California (Pa.) ⊠ 94
66 Cheyney 81
78 West Chester ⊠ 77
75 Bloomsburg 77
65 Millersville ⊠ 83
76 Mansfield ⊠ 58
69 Kutztown 74
117 Penn St.-Schuylkill ⊠ 56
106 Briar Cliff (Iowa) ⊠ 61
60 Cheyney ⊠ 56
79 West Chester 67
69 Bloomsburg ⊠ 71
79 Millersville 80
87 Mansfield 79
74 Kutztown ⊠ 72
59 Millersville 63

Nickname: Warriors
Colors: Red & Black
Arena: Koehler Fieldhouse
   Capacity: 2,650; Year Built: 1967
AD: Thomas Gioglio
SID: Ryan Yanoshak

EAST TENN. ST.
Johnson City, TN 37614 I

Coach: Murry Bartow, UAB 1985

2006-07 RESULTS (24-10)
90 Virginia-Wise ⊠ 43
53 Eastern Ky. 70
71 Chattanooga ⊠ 70
58 Auburn 64
56 Morehead St. 77
61 Sam Houston St. † 72
66 Southern U. † 52
76 Mercer 70
75 Stetson 61
62 Vanderbilt 104
73 Milligan ⊠ 47
73 UNC Asheville ⊠ 65
71 Radford 51
88 Tennessee 93
74 Belmont ⊠ 75
75 Lipscomb ⊠ 72
66 Gardner-Webb 63
100 Campbell ⊠ 76
77 North Fla. ⊠ 58
71 Jacksonville ⊠ 59
78 Kennesaw St. ⊠ 66
80 Belmont 70
71 Lipscomb 66
63 Gardner-Webb ⊠ 61
87 Campbell ⊠ 57
66 Jacksonville 74
56 North Fla. 51
75 Kennesaw St. 71
84 Stetson ⊠ 49
112 Mercer ⊠ 89
77 Stetson 61
77 Lipscomb 72
67 Belmont ⊠ 94
57 Clemson 64

Nickname: Buccaneers
Colors: Navy Blue & Old Gold
Arena: Memorial Center
   Capacity: 5,780; Year Built: 1977

AD: Dave Mullins
SID: Michael White

EAST TEX. BAPTIST
Marshall, TX 75670-1498 III

Coach: Bert West, East Tex. Baptist 1973

2006-07 RESULTS (7-18)
58 Wiley 73
78 Jarvis Christian ⊠ 83
85 LSU-Shreveport 89
63 Hardin-Simmons ⊠ 86
50 Jarvis Christian 78
79 Howard Payne 70
62 Sul Ross St. 70
62 LeTourneau ⊠ 72
78 Belhaven 82
100 Concordia (Tex.) ⊠ 92
50 Mary Hardin-Baylor ⊠ 73
70 McMurry ⊠ 69
78 Schreiner 83
50 Texas Lutheran 66
73 LeTourneau 84
79 Ozarks (Ark.) ⊠ 64
81 Texas-Dallas 77
62 Texas-Tyler 66
63 Louisiana Col. 71
46 Mississippi Col. 66
80 Louisiana Col. ⊠ 77
32 Mississippi Col. ⊠ 61
76 Texas-Dallas ⊠ 85
85 Texas-Tyler ⊠ 83
60 Ozarks (Ark.) 84

Nickname: Tigers
Colors: Navy & Gold
Arena: Ornelas Gymnasium
   Capacity: 1,700; Year Built: 1995
AD: Kent Reeves
SID: David Weaver

EASTERN
St. Davids, PA 19087-3696 III

Coach: Matt Nadelhoffer, Wheaton (Ill.) 1998

2006-07 RESULTS (16-11)
67 Whitworth † 95
71 Franklin † 94
87 Lancaster Bible 78
61 Gwynedd-Mercy ⊠ 77
68 Arcadia ⊠ 47
55 Misericordia 51
79 Neumann ⊠ 73
76 Widener 70
77 Delaware Valley ⊠ 70
76 Wesley ⊠ 81
60 Cabrini ⊠ 48
59 Arcadia 64
74 Marywood 72
60 Immaculata ⊠ 73
75 Wesley 78
65 Gwynedd-Mercy 59
60 Misericordia ⊠ 43
49 Alvernia 70
71 Marywood ⊠ 51
82 Neumann 68
79 Valley Forge Chrst. ⊠ 66
66 Rutgers-Camden ⊠ 53
66 Cabrini ⊠ 54
57 Immaculata 76
74 Alvernia ⊠ 84
77 Neumann ⊠ 67
48 Alvernia 71

Nickname: Eagles
Colors: Maroon & White
Arena: Eastern University Gymnasium
   Capacity: 800; Year Built: 1958
AD: Harry Gutelius
SID: Mark Birtwistle

EASTERN CONN. ST.
Willimantic, CT 06226 III

Coach: Bill Geitner, Hamilton 1987
2006-07 RESULTS (15-11)
75	Mt. St. Vincent ⊠	69
74	Elms ⊠	92
55	Trinity (Conn.)	72
63	Connecticut Col.	60
85	Wesleyan (Conn.) ⊠	75
60	Mass.-Boston	57
74	Southern Me.	70
93	Purchase St. ⊠	66
72	Medaille †	44
54	Embry-Riddle	66
79	Rhode Island Col. ⊠	87
72	Mass.-Dartmouth ⊠	61
51	Plymouth St.	52
73	Keene St.	71
114	Mass.-Boston ⊠	115
52	Western Conn. St.	63
73	Southern Me. ⊠	72
85	Green Mountain ⊠	59
62	Rhode Island Col.	84
71	Keene St. ⊠	79
78	Old Westbury ⊠	64
60	Mass.-Dartmouth	70
79	Western Conn. St. ⊠	63
85	Mitchell	69
87	Plymouth St. ⊠	80
64	Mass.-Dartmouth	73

Nickname: Warriors
Colors: Navy & Burgundy
Arena: Geissler Gymnasium
Capacity: 3,000; Year Built: 1974
AD: Joyce S. Wong
SID: Bob Molta

EASTERN ILL.
Charleston, IL 61920-3099 I

Coach: Mike Miller, Tex. A&M-Commerce 1987
2006-07 RESULTS (10-20)
60	La.-Monroe †	70
55	UC Riverside †	64
54	Iowa St.	56
64	Ind.-South Bend ⊠	49
41	DePaul	71
63	Green Bay ⊠	61
50	Murray St.	53
73	Arkansas St.	70
74	Tennessee Tech	69
56	Tennessee St.	59
57	Eastern Ky. ⊠	73
63	Morehead St. ⊠	71
76	Western Ill. ⊠	56
51	Eastern Mich.	63
62	Murray St. ⊠	73
65	Southeast Mo. St.	80
76	Austin Peay ⊠	81
43	Tenn.-Martin	67
62	Eastern Ky.	63
64	Tennessee Tech ⊠	76
58	Tennessee St. ⊠	61
65	Morehead St.	62
73	Jacksonville St. ⊠	59
48	Samford ⊠	53
71	Austin Peay	98
74	Tenn.-Martin ⊠	59
77	Southeast Mo. St. ⊠	69
43	Loyola (Ill.)	66
69	Jacksonville St.	65
45	Samford	71

Nickname: Panthers
Colors: Blue & Gray
Arena: Lantz Arena
Capacity: 5,300; Year Built: 1966
AD: Richard A. McDuffie
SID: Rich Moser

EASTERN KY.
Richmond, KY 40475-3101 I

Coach: Jeff Neubauer, La Salle 1993
2006-07 RESULTS (21-12)
63	Asbury ⊠	46
70	East Tenn. St. ⊠	53
45	Ohio St.	74
63	Kenyon ⊠	52
73	UNC Asheville ⊠	54
70	James Madison	66
55	Western Ky.	78
72	Murray St. ⊠	66
57	Austin Peay ⊠	59
73	Eastern Ill.	57
82	Tenn.-Martin	69
65	Kentucky	78
74	Southeast Mo. St. ⊠	88
53	Tennessee Tech	75
73	Morehead St. ⊠	65
63	Eastern Ill. ⊠	62
56	Jacksonville St. ⊠	66
46	Samford ⊠	55
62	Tennessee St. ⊠	63
94	Tenn.-Martin ⊠	57
69	Morehead St. ⊠	61
92	Tennessee Tech ⊠	90
64	Murray St.	62
66	Southeast Mo. St.	61
46	Samford ⊠	38
63	Jacksonville St. ⊠	51
61	Youngstown St. ⊠	66
68	Austin Peay	77
65	Tennessee St.	53
63	Morehead St. ⊠	45
57	Tennessee Tech †	54
63	Austin Peay †	62
65	North Carolina †	86

Nickname: Colonels
Colors: Maroon & White
Arena: McBrayer Arena
Capacity: 6,500; Year Built: 1963
AD: Mark S. Sandy
SID: Michael Clark

EAST. MENNONITE
Harrisonburg, VA 22802 III

Coach: Kirby Dean, East. Mennonite 1992
2006-07 RESULTS (7-17)
88	Lancaster Bible ⊠	71
77	Southern Va. ⊠	73
81	Shenandoah	83
73	Ferrum	67
68	Greensboro †	76
95	Valley Forge Chrst. †	83
77	Wash. & Lee	81
80	Randolph-Macon ⊠	77
77	Bridgewater (Va.)	90
76	Lynchburg	87
55	Hampden-Sydney ⊠	78
58	Roanoke ⊠	78
56	Va. Wesleyan ⊠	85
109	Emory & Henry	121
69	Guilford	79
62	Wash. & Lee ⊠	86
87	Lynchburg ⊠	83
67	Hampden-Sydney	74
69	Bridgewater (Va.) ⊠	60
60	Va. Wesleyan	87
95	Emory & Henry ⊠	108
75	Guilford ⊠	84
48	Randolph-Macon	73
65	Roanoke	79

Nickname: Royals
Colors: Royal Blue & White
Arena: University Gym
Capacity: 1,800; Year Built: 1999
AD: David King
SID: Mike Zucconi

EASTERN MICH.
Ypsilanti, MI 48197 I

Coach: Charles Ramsey, Eastern Mich. 1992
2006-07 RESULTS (13-19)
77	Davidson †	81
76	Central Conn. St. †	69
51	Michigan	80
62	Marquette	95
52	Detroit	72
54	Oakland ⊠	66
76	San Diego †	78
61	Chicago St. ⊠	72
71	Northern Colo. ⊠	61
48	Tulsa	66
63	Eastern Ill. ⊠	51
62	IPFW ⊠	61
74	North Dakota St. ⊠	66
68	Central Mich. ⊠	74
63	Northern Ill. ⊠	62
56	Ball St.	52
56	Toledo ⊠	66
80	Western Mich.	84
61	Ohio	67
89	Buffalo ⊠	76
60	Akron ⊠	70
46	Kent St.	82
64	Miami (Ohio) ⊠	74
65	Bowling Green	63
56	Toledo	68
65	Manhattan ⊠	51
61	Western Mich. ⊠	80
61	Ball St. ⊠	51
87	Central Mich.	83
69	Northern Ill.	76
51	Ball St. †	48
54	Toledo †	62

Nickname: Eagles
Colors: Green & White
Arena: Convocation Center
Capacity: 8,824; Year Built: 1998
AD: Derrick L. Gragg
SID: Jim Streeter

EASTERN NAZARENE
Quincy, MA 02170-2999 III

Coach: Jon Yeh, Taylor-Ft. Wayne 1996
2006-07 RESULTS (2-23)
65	Keene St.	103
55	Marymount (Va.) †	66
79	Lesley ⊠	84
70	Mount Ida ⊠	74
73	Framingham St. ⊠	80
41	New England ⊠	46
70	Mitchell ⊠	72
61	Emerson	83
46	Connecticut Col. ⊠	57
55	Anna Maria	59
47	Roger Williams ⊠	84
82	New England Col.	91
53	Newbury	58
62	Anna Maria ⊠	66
58	Gordon	72
52	Nichols ⊠	70
71	Curry	79
58	Nichols	71
63	Salve Regina ⊠	81
66	Colby-Sawyer ⊠	72
78	Endicott	102
71	Roger Williams	63
75	Curry ⊠	84
57	Salve Regina	76
87	Wentworth Inst. ⊠	76

Nickname: Crusaders
Colors: Red & White
Arena: Lahue Center
Capacity: 1,600; Year Built: 1973
AD: Nancy Detwiler
SID: Thomas Newell

EASTERN N.M.
Portales, NM 88130 II

Coach: Shawn Scanlan, Kansas 1978
2006-07 RESULTS (12-14)
64	Western St. ⊠	66
55	Washburn ⊠	63
81	N.M. Highlands ⊠	71
78	Tabor †	56
65	Central Mo.	92
65	Southwestern Okla. ⊠	80
90	Cameron ⊠	81
81	Okla. Panhandle ⊠	53
68	Tex. A&M-Commerce	77
90	N.M. Highlands	63
64	Lubbock Chrst. ⊠	73
58	Northeastern St. ⊠	63
78	Central Okla. ⊠	87
72	East Central	62
86	Abilene Christian	82
94	Angelo St. ⊠	78
86	Midwestern St. ⊠	81
72	Tarleton St.	77
72	West Tex. A&M	87
84	Tex. A&M-Kingsville	85
79	West Tex. A&M	91
76	Tex. A&M-Kingsville ⊠	78
89	Abilene Christian ⊠	76
68	Angelo St.	65
62	Midwestern St. ⊠	77
77	Tarleton St. ⊠	74

Nickname: Greyhounds
Colors: Green & Silver
Arena: Greyhound Arena
Capacity: 4,800; Year Built: 1967
AD: Michael Maguire
SID: Adam Pitterman

EASTERN WASH.
Cheney, WA 99004 I

Coach: Mike Burns, Central Wash. 1997
2006-07 RESULTS (15-14)
75	Gonzaga	90
79	UNLV	82
85	Lewis-Clark St. ⊠	70
106	Evergreen St. ⊠	65
83	Washington	90
110	Cal St. Fullerton ⊠	100
90	Eastern Ore. ⊠	81
98	Cal St. Northridge ⊠	102
87	Portland	66
68	Santa Clara	91
74	Oregon	100
85	Idaho ⊠	56
79	Montana St. ⊠	82
74	Montana ⊠	71
88	Northern Colo.	87
101	Northern Ariz.	109
65	Idaho St.	70
88	Portland St. ⊠	70
80	Northern Ariz. ⊠	91
91	Northern Colo. ⊠	79
100	Sacramento St. ⊠	85
84	Weber St. ⊠	93
67	Montana St.	84
78	Montana	85
89	Weber St. ⊠	74
86	Portland St. ⊠	92
71	UC Santa Barbara	70
82	Idaho St. ⊠	79
80	Sacramento St. ⊠	72

Nickname: Eagles
Colors: Red & White
Arena: Reese Court
Capacity: 6,000; Year Built: 1975
AD: Michael Westfall
SID: Dave Cook

ECKERD
St. Petersburg, FL 33711 II

Coach: Tom Ryan, Eckerd 1987

2006-07 RESULTS (27-6)

90	West Ga. †	87
76	Goldey-Beacom †	64
62	Fla. Memorial	56
83	P.R.-Mayaguez ⊠	60
75	P.R.-Bayamon ⊠	67
58	Florida Tech	56
62	Palm Beach Atl.	59
101	Fla. Christian	59
59	Armstrong Atlantic	60
80	Francis Marion †	66
75	Fayetteville St. ⊠	63
52	Barry ⊠	55
59	Lynn ⊠	67
80	St. Leo ⊠	75
76	Nova Southeastern ⊠	61
88	Palm Beach Atl. ⊠	60
66	Rollins	73
74	Tampa ⊠	53
73	Fla. Southern	65
66	St. Leo ⊠	52
47	Barry	62
70	Lynn	62
73	Florida Tech ⊠	61
81	Nova Southeastern	57
62	Rollins ⊠	57
96	Tampa	54
85	Fla. Southern ⊠	72
76	St. Leo †	45
63	Barry †	59
67	Rollins †	52
66	Benedict †	56
85	Rollins †	76
61	Montevallo	64

Nickname: Tritons
Colors: Navy, Teal, White & Black
Arena: McArthur Center
  Capacity: 1,300; Year Built: 1970
AD: Bob Fortosis
SID: Evan Ortiz

EDGEWOOD
Madison, WI 53711-1998 III

Coach: Todd Adrian, Kansas 1995

2006-07 RESULTS (18-8)

80	Maranatha Baptist ⊠	55
56	Wis.-Oshkosh ⊠	82
61	Lake Forest ⊠	62
59	Dominican (Ill.)	61
77	Marian (Wis.) ⊠	67
47	Wis.-Stevens Point	69
68	Aurora	65
72	Colorado Col. †	57
72	Baldwin-Wallace †	64
50	Simpson †	69
68	Lakeland	64
70	Concordia (Ill.) ⊠	54
69	Rockford	50
78	Concordia (Wis.)	65
65	Benedictine (Ill.)	49
62	Maranatha Baptist	37
96	Wis. Lutheran ⊠	90
57	Marian (Wis.)	60
77	Dominican (Ill.) ⊠	76
62	Aurora	90
81	Concordia (Ill.)	68
83	Concordia (Wis.) ⊠	55
64	Benedictine (Ill.) ⊠	58
71	Rockford	59
73	Dominican (Ill.) ⊠	62
69	Aurora	85

Nickname: Eagles
Colors: Black, Red & White
Arena: Todd Wehr Edgedome
  Capacity: 1,000; Year Built: 1961
AD: Al Brisack
SID: Luke LeNoble

EDINBORO
Edinboro, PA 16444-0001 II

Coach: Greg Walcavich, Rutgers 1973

2006-07 RESULTS (19-10)

57	West Va. Wesleyan	61
79	Penn St.-McKeesport ⊠	51
67	Gannon ⊠	60
70	Penn St.-New Kens. ⊠	26
78	Millersville ⊠	82
75	West Chester ⊠	67
63	Mercyhurst ⊠	57
77	Charleston (W.V.)	75
72	East Stroudsburg ⊠	82
75	Kutztown ⊠	62
84	Alderson-Broaddus ⊠	67
41	Cheyney	57
76	Shippensburg ⊠	51
66	Mansfield	80
73	Bloomsburg	63
87	Slippery Rock ⊠	59
63	Indiana (Pa.)	51
85	Franciscan ⊠	53
58	Lock Haven	61
67	Clarion	75
49	California (Pa.) ⊠	48
54	Shippensburg	69
76	Slippery Rock	64
76	Indiana (Pa.) ⊠	46
92	Lock Haven ⊠	73
81	Clarion ⊠	58
59	California (Pa.)	73
67	Shippensburg ⊠	60
55	Millersville †	65

Nickname: Fighting Scots
Colors: Red & White
Arena: McComb Fieldhouse
  Capacity: 4,000; Year Built: 1970
AD: Bruce R. Baumgartner
SID: Bob Shreve

ELIZABETH CITY ST.
Elizabeth City, NC 27909 II

Coach: Shawn Walker, Elizabeth City St. 1994

2006-07 RESULTS (16-16)

82	Barton	83
81	Kentucky St. ⊠	87
55	Claflin ⊠	59
78	Johnson C. Smith	70
73	Livingstone	61
87	Glenville St. ⊠	79
93	N.C. Central ⊠	66
67	Johnson C. Smith ⊠	76
89	Fairmont St. †	87
93	Glenville St.	87
99	Shaw	78
53	Livingstone ⊠	55
74	St. Augustine's ⊠	84
87	Virginia St. ⊠	94
73	Fayetteville St.	82
66	Chowan ⊠	56
91	St. Paul's ⊠	82
70	Virginia Union	73
101	Bowie St.	109
70	Fayetteville St. ⊠	71
73	Shaw ⊠	66
111	St. Paul's	103
71	N.C. Central	77
72	St. Augustine's	78
76	Virginia St.	83
77	Bowie St. ⊠	74
94	Virginia Union ⊠	95
71	Livingstone †	54
57	Virginia St. †	55
59	Bowie St. †	54
63	Virginia Union †	60
53	Augusta St.	79

Nickname: Vikings
Colors: Royal Blue & White
Arena: R.L. Vaughan Center
  Capacity: 5,000; Year Built: 1976
AD: Thurlis J. Little Jr.
SID: April Emory

ELIZABETHTOWN
Elizabethtown, PA 17022-2298 ... III

Coach: Robert Schlosser, East Stroudsburg 1977

2006-07 RESULTS (9-15)

84	Penn St.-Harrisburg ⊠	23
60	Ohio Northern ⊠	76
74	Lycoming	77
69	Neumann ⊠	72
84	Susquehanna ⊠	79
73	Lebanon Valley	79
59	Millersville	96
84	King's (Pa.) ⊠	71
75	Rutgers-Camden	70
70	Gettysburg ⊠	64
87	Rutgers-Newark †	73
42	Catholic	61
44	Messiah ⊠	53
78	Albright ⊠	81
68	Juniata	74
74	Moravian	82
65	Widener ⊠	70
73	Albright	81
84	Susquehanna	74
67	Lebanon Valley ⊠	62
51	Juniata ⊠	63
53	Widener	69
59	Messiah	70
88	Moravian ⊠	69

Nickname: Blue Jays
Colors: Blue & Grey
Arena: Thompson Gymnasium
  Capacity: 2,200; Year Built: 1969
AD: Nancy J. Latimore
SID: Ian Showalter

ELMHURST
Elmhurst, IL 60126-3296 III

Coach: Mark Scherer, Eureka 1983

2006-07 RESULTS (21-6)

71	Simpson	82
56	St. Norbert	54
78	Rockford	59
87	Illinois Tech ⊠	77
55	Wis.-Oshkosh ⊠	52
74	Alma	66
84	Kalamazoo ⊠	57
98	Wis.-Whitewater ⊠	91
79	Gwynedd-Mercy †	62
76	Albion †	46
70	Beloit ⊠	55
82	Augustana (Ill.) ⊠	71
72	Carthage	62
76	Ill. Wesleyan ⊠	57
79	North Park	76
74	Wheaton (Ill.)	77
98	North Central (Ill.) ⊠	84
74	Augustana (Ill.)	86
85	Millikin ⊠	89
84	Ill. Wesleyan	69
81	Carthage ⊠	59
83	North Park ⊠	80
74	North Central (Ill.)	89
80	Wheaton (Ill.) ⊠	74
79	Millikin	63
85	Wheaton (Ill.) †	82
70	Augustana (Ill.)	78

Nickname: Bluejays
Colors: Blue & White
Arena: R.A. Faganel Hall
  Capacity: 1,800; Year Built: 1983
AD: Paul Krohn
SID: Kevin Juday

ELMIRA
Elmira, NY 14901 III

Coach: Chris Connolly, Hartwick 1996

2006-07 RESULTS (2-23)

50	Penn St.-Behrend	65
76	D'Youville ⊠	37
56	Cortland St. ⊠	99
70	Pitt.-Bradford	80
67	St. Lawrence	91
53	Clarkson	60
34	Colgate	82
55	Lycoming ⊠	60
57	Ferrum ⊠	72
55	Geneseo St. ⊠	76
61	Ithaca	85
64	Utica ⊠	83
74	Hartwick ⊠	62
66	Hobart ⊠	68
70	Rochester Inst. ⊠	82
60	Nazareth ⊠	68
61	St. John Fisher	91
58	Alfred	73
53	Hartwick	73
49	Utica	72
55	Alfred ⊠	62
60	St. John Fisher ⊠	86
68	Ithaca ⊠	86
56	Nazareth	71
63	Rochester Inst.	73

Nickname: Soaring Eagles
Colors: Purple & Gold
Arena: Speidel Gymnasium
  Capacity: 1,000; Year Built: 1995
AD: Patricia A. Thompson
SID: Matt Donohue

ELMS
Chicopee, MA 01013-2839 III

Coach: Ed Silva, Eastern Conn. St.

2006-07 RESULTS (20-9)

99	Mitchell †	81
92	Eastern Conn. St. ⊠	74
75	Westfield St. ⊠	84
65	WPI	83
73	Hartwick ⊠	68
59	Brandeis	74
76	Husson	85
77	Maine Maritime	59
56	Bates †	73
91	Mt. St. Vincent †	78
109	Lesley ⊠	73
78	Me.-Farmington ⊠	57
78	Thomas (Me.) ⊠	60
69	Amherst	103
94	Becker ⊠	75
75	Worcester St. ⊠	53
87	Lasell	83
92	Castleton ⊠	79
109	Johnson St. ⊠	81
79	Mount Ida	78
88	Becker	69
115	Lasell ⊠	107
82	Lesley	94
88	Johnson St.	75
94	Castleton	102
88	Mount Ida ⊠	76
68	Lasell ⊠	64
81	Husson	69
79	St. Lawrence	85

Nickname: Blazers
Colors: Green & Gold
Arena: Picknelly Arena
  Capacity: 481; Year Built: 1994
AD: Louise McCleary
SID: Justin Mokerzecki

ELON

Elon, NC 27244-2010 I

Coach: Ernie Nestor, Alderson-
Broaddus 1968

2006-07 RESULTS (7-23)

49	Georgia Tech	83
85	Montreat ⊠	72
48	Wake Forest	73
70	Vanderbilt ⊠	81
49	VCU ⊠	91
61	Davidson	86
48	High Point ⊠	62
63	Notre Dame	94
79	Wofford ⊠	69
64	New Hampshire †	65
75	Shawnee St. ⊠	53
50	Citadel ⊠	53
64	Penn ⊠	66
68	UNC Greensboro ⊠	72
64	Appalachian St.	63
56	Chattanooga ⊠	66
45	Col. of Charleston	67
77	Western Caro.	64
67	Ga. Southern ⊠	68
58	Davidson ⊠	88
64	Wofford	71
49	Citadel	52
64	Furman ⊠	69
73	UNC Greensboro	86
70	Ga. Southern	67
53	Georgia St.	63
59	Chattanooga	62
74	Western Caro. ⊠	65
63	Appalachian St. ⊠	72
65	Western Caro. †	69

Nickname: Phoenix
Colors: Maroon & Gold
Arena: Alumni Gym
    Capacity: 1,558; Year Built: 1949
AD: Dave Blank
SID: Megan Donald

EMERSON

Boston, MA 02116 III

Coach: Hank Smith, Franklin Pierce

2006-07 RESULTS (16-10)

85	Moravian †	81
49	New York U.	63
70	Babson	83
85	Mass.-Boston ⊠	62
76	Wheaton (Mass.)	81
91	Southern Vt. ⊠	69
83	Eastern Nazarene ⊠	61
107	Daniel Webster ⊠	74
72	MIT	79
66	Rivier ⊠	69
75	Albertus Magnus	70
87	Johnson & Wales (RI)	69
53	Western New Eng.	51
76	Norwich ⊠	77
77	Suffolk	72
93	Daniel Webster	61
84	Emmanuel (Mass.)	76
78	Rivier	81
92	Albertus Magnus ⊠	67
75	Johnson & Wales (RI) ⊠	72
46	Western New Eng.	68
76	Norwich	65
86	Suffolk ⊠	67
73	Emmanuel (Mass.) ⊠	68
75	Suffolk ⊠	80
88	Curry ⊠	108

Nickname: Lions
Colors: Royal Purple & Gold
Arena: Piano Row Gymnasium
    Capacity: 263; Year Built: 2006
AD: Kristin Parnell
SID: Roger Crosley

EMMANUEL (MASS.)

Boston, MA 02115 III

Coach: Jamahl Jackson, New
Hampshire

2006-07 RESULTS (12-16)

77	Gwynedd-Mercy ⊠	80
77	Staten Island ⊠	83
45	Amherst ⊠	84
78	Suffolk	85
63	Wesleyan (Conn.) ⊠	69
57	Western New Eng.	61
56	Northwood (Fla.)	54
44	Olivet Nazarene †	63
82	Daniel Webster	60
77	Johnson & Wales (RI) ⊠	71
96	Suffolk ⊠	70
69	Rivier	67
62	Salem St. ⊠	68
82	Albertus Magnus ⊠	59
57	Bates	75
67	Western New Eng. ⊠	71
76	Emerson ⊠	84
83	Daniel Webster ⊠	61
70	Johnson & Wales (RI)	78
66	Norwich	67
75	Rivier ⊠	74
67	Norwich ⊠	68
80	Albertus Magnus	59
76	Southern Vt. ⊠	68
68	Emerson	73
60	Norwich	55
71	Western New Eng.	62
57	Rivier	59

Nickname: Saints
Colors: Royal Blue & Gold
Arena: Jean Yawkey Center
    Capacity: 1,440; Year Built: 2004
AD: Pamela Roecker
SID: Alexis Mastronardi

EMORY

Atlanta, GA 30322 III

Coach: Brett Zuver, Lake Superior St.
1991

2006-07 RESULTS (8-17)

71	Mercer	89
96	LaGrange ⊠	93
93	Maryville (Tenn.) ⊠	82
77	Oglethorpe ⊠	73
78	Sewanee	61
77	LaGrange	91
91	Sewanee ⊠	62
52	Maryville (Tenn.)	92
62	Hood †	59
57	Wash. & Lee	69
76	Case Reserve	67
75	Chicago ⊠	99
73	Washington-St. Louis ⊠	78
50	New York U.	69
50	Brandeis	74
70	Carnegie Mellon	71
75	Rochester (N.Y.)	84
65	Rochester (N.Y.) ⊠	81
94	Carnegie Mellon ⊠	83
73	Oglethorpe	90
62	Washington-St. Louis	74
71	Chicago	89
67	Brandeis ⊠	76
66	New York U. ⊠	69
83	Case Reserve ⊠	84

Nickname: Eagles
Colors: Blue & Gold
Arena: Woodruff PE Center
    Capacity: 2,000; Year Built: 1983
AD: Tim Downes
SID: John Arenberg

EMORY & HENRY

Emory, VA 24327-0947 III

Coach: Bob Johnson, Dickinson 1968

2006-07 RESULTS (14-11)

83	Mount Union †	103
129	Cabrini ⊠	112
120	Virginia-Wise	101
110	Huntingdon ⊠	65
112	John Carroll ⊠	119
105	Virginia-Wise ⊠	84
102	Hampden-Sydney ⊠	113
101	Roanoke	92
141	Lynchburg ⊠	98
84	Va. Wesleyan	128
113	Randolph-Macon	105
114	Guilford	130
96	Wash. & Lee	98
121	East. Mennonite ⊠	109
115	Bridgewater (Va.) ⊠	93
136	Lynchburg	107
124	Va. Wesleyan ⊠	101
102	Randolph-Macon ⊠	106
107	Roanoke ⊠	112
108	Hampden-Sydney	100
100	Wash. & Lee ⊠	95
108	East. Mennonite	95
96	Bridgewater (Va.)	106
107	Guilford ⊠	108
100	Hampden-Sydney †	102

Nickname: Wasps
Colors: Blue & Gold
Arena: King Health & Physical Ed
    Capacity: 1,300; Year Built: 1970
AD: Robert J. Johnson
SID: Nathan Graybeal

EMPORIA ST.

Emporia, KS 66801-5087 II

Coach: David Moe, Texas Lutheran
1986

2006-07 RESULTS (21-8)

105	Ottawa ⊠	69
75	Northeastern St.	70
113	Baker ⊠	87
70	Northeastern St. ⊠	58
98	Central Okla. ⊠	89
85	Avila ⊠	79
78	Neb.-Omaha ⊠	55
86	Fort Hays St. ⊠	71
109	Bethany (Kan.) ⊠	76
83	Friends ⊠	71
93	Southwest Baptist ⊠	84
80	Washburn ⊠	77
86	Pittsburg St.	77
63	Truman	60
105	Mo. Southern St. ⊠	67
88	Mo. Western St.	76
72	Northwest Mo. St. ⊠	89
76	Fort Hays St.	73
58	Northwest Mo. St.	63
89	Mo. Western St. ⊠	79
73	Mo. Southern St.	72
79	Central Mo.	88
88	Pittsburg St. ⊠	91
88	Washburn	74
78	Central Mo. ⊠	71
78	Truman ⊠	88
89	Southwest Baptist	108
75	Truman †	88
66	Southeastern Okla. †	79

Nickname: Hornets
Colors: Old Gold & Black
Arena: White Auditorium
    Capacity: 5,000; Year Built: 1940
AD: Kent Weiser
SID: Don Weast

ENDICOTT

Beverly, MA 01915 III

Coach: Chris Millette, Boston College
1999

2006-07 RESULTS (16-12)

59	Rhode Island Col. †	73
73	Lasell †	63
61	Keene St. ⊠	79
53	Bates	91
66	MIT ⊠	74
68	New England ⊠	55
70	WPI	81
64	Wheaton (Mass.) ⊠	67
70	Anna Maria	55
74	Bridgewater St. ⊠	72
58	New England	51
61	Colby-Sawyer	71
69	Gordon	73
83	Wentworth Inst. ⊠	68
64	Curry	62
71	Wentworth Inst.	73
83	New England Col. ⊠	64
62	Roger Williams	58
102	Eastern Nazarene ⊠	78
70	Colby-Sawyer ⊠	61
101	Nichols ⊠	72
62	Gordon ⊠	61
70	New England Col.	82
68	Salve Regina ⊠	67
67	Nichols ⊠	57
65	Curry	71
68	Lasell †	67
57	Western New Eng.	74

Nickname: Gulls
Colors: Blue, Kelly Green & White
Arena: Post Center (MacDonald
Gymnasium)
    Capacity: 1,400; Year Built: 1999
AD: Larry R. Hiser
SID: Mike Deplacido

ERSKINE

Due West, SC 29639 II

Coach: Mark Peeler, Sewanee 1984

2006-07 RESULTS (14-15)

83	Montreat ⊠	76
72	Belmont Abbey	75
85	Queens (N.C.) ⊠	86
66	Francis Marion ⊠	51
67	St. Andrews	52
65	Lander	63
51	Newberry	52
59	Presbyterian	64
68	Barton ⊠	75
79	Coker ⊠	70
80	Pfeiffer	83
60	Mount Olive	93
82	Anderson (S.C.)	80
58	Limestone ⊠	67
29	Lander ⊠	62
83	Lees-McRae	68
50	Barton	68
77	Belmont Abbey ⊠	59
76	Mount Olive ⊠	90
53	Anderson (S.C.) ⊠	56
65	Coker	57
64	St. Andrews ⊠	53
75	S.C.-Aiken	57
56	Limestone	58
55	Queens (N.C.)	64
66	Lees-McRae ⊠	57
88	Pfeiffer ⊠	77
95	Anderson (S.C.) ⊠	75
76	Queens (N.C.)	85

Nickname: The Flying Fleet
Colors: Maroon & Gold
Arena: Galloway PE Center
    Capacity: 2,000; Year Built: 1980
AD: Mark Peeler
SID: Tiffany Mast

EUREKA

Eureka, IL 61530-1500 III

Coach: Jay Bruer, UNC Pembroke 2001

2006-07 RESULTS (16-10)

55	Manchester	62
73	Alma †	62
83	Knox ⊠	78
66	North Park ⊠	75
68	Millikin	62
81	Blackburn ⊠	72
75	Fontbonne	74
65	Dominican (Ill.)	74
75	Maryville (Mo.) ⊠	63
73	Lincoln Christian	69
57	Webster	62
67	Westminster (Mo.)	76
62	MacMurray ⊠	69
90	Greenville ⊠	78
72	Principia	56
75	Fontbonne ⊠	59
81	Blackburn	76
71	Lincoln Christian ⊠	49
74	Maryville (Mo.)	66
89	MacMurray ⊠	106
68	Webster ⊠	76
64	Westminster (Mo.) ⊠	81
92	Greenville	88
84	Principia ⊠	78
95	MacMurray †	81
79	Fontbonne †	88

Nickname: Red Devils
Colors: Maroon & Gold
Arena: Reagan Gym
Capacity: 2,200; Year Built: 1970
AD: Sandy Schuster
SID: Brian Sullivan

EVANSVILLE

Evansville, IN 47722 I

Coach: Steve Merfeld, Wis.-La Crosse 1984

2006-07 RESULTS (14-17)

64	Lipscomb	67
69	Miami (Fla.) ⊠	74
63	Cleveland St. ⊠	49
74	Buffalo ⊠	44
65	Southeast Mo. St. ⊠	45
75	Tenn.-Martin	57
54	Missouri	73
69	Valparaiso ⊠	64
69	Illinois St. ⊠	41
80	Lipscomb ⊠	73
80	Austin Peay	75
65	Butler	76
78	Drake ⊠	57
78	Bradley	85
61	UNI	64
62	Creighton ⊠	75
54	Missouri St.	106
56	Wichita St.	69
75	Southern Ill. ⊠	68
63	Missouri St. ⊠	56
50	Indiana St.	49
61	Wichita St. ⊠	66
61	Illinois St.	65
71	UNI ⊠	79
74	Creighton	79
76	Indiana St. ⊠	61
71	Bradley ⊠	72
69	Samford	65
79	Drake	82
69	Southern Ill.	76
96	Drake †	101

Nickname: Purple Aces
Colors: Purple, White & Orange
Arena: Roberts Stadium
Capacity: 12,144; Year Built: 1956
AD: Bill McGillis
SID: Bob Boxell

FAIRFIELD

Fairfield, CT 06824 I

Coach: Ed Cooley, Stonehill 1994

2006-07 RESULTS (13-19)

54	American ⊠	59
65	Holy Cross	67
47	St. Joseph's	63
67	Mississippi †	70
49	Connecticut	74
46	Central Ark. †	43
60	Georgetown ⊠	73
72	Loyola (Ill.) ⊠	83
68	St. Francis (N.Y.) ⊠	64
50	Providence	67
52	Boston College	75
54	Manhattan ⊠	57
75	Canisius ⊠	64
47	Fordham	56
55	Rider	58
54	Manhattan	58
76	Niagara	85
63	Rider ⊠	64
83	Iona	76
72	Siena	67
70	Iona ⊠	67
66	St. Peter's ⊠	58
68	Niagara ⊠	56
67	Canisius	63
65	Loyola (Md.) ⊠	62
64	Marist	65
67	Loyola (Md.)	59
64	Siena ⊠	69
61	William & Mary ⊠	45
60	Marist ⊠	67
63	St. Peter's	60
72	Loyola (Md.) ⊠	76

Nickname: Stags
Colors: Cardinal Red
Arena: Arena at Harbor Yard
Capacity: 9,500; Year Built: 2001
AD: Eugene Doris
SID: Jack Jones

FAIRLEIGH DICKINSON

Teaneck, NJ 07666 I

Coach: Tom Green, Syracuse 1971

2006-07 RESULTS (14-16)

71	Providence	96
76	Seton Hall	71
72	St. Peter's	65
67	Green Bay ⊠	76
85	Canisius ⊠	83
58	Drexel	80
80	Quinnipiac	75
86	Mercy ⊠	59
58	Stony Brook	82
72	Rider ⊠	74
61	IUPUI †	58
67	Col. of Charleston	71
96	Wagner ⊠	95
91	St. Francis (Pa.) ⊠	84
66	Robert Morris ⊠	70
56	Central Conn. St.	60
74	Long Island	73
63	Quinnipiac ⊠	64
65	Mt. St. Mary's	74
91	Sacred Heart	88
84	Robert Morris	79
64	Monmouth ⊠	63
69	St. Francis (N.Y.) ⊠	71
84	Monmouth	71
80	Long Island ⊠	85
66	Central Conn. St. ⊠	60
82	Sacred Heart ⊠	86
63	Wagner	91
69	St. Francis (N.Y.)	72
77	Quinnipiac	78

Nickname: Knights
Colors: Blue & Maroon
Arena: Rothman Center
Capacity: 5,000; Year Built: 1987
AD: David Langford
SID: Drew Brown

FDU-FLORHAM

Madison, NJ 07940 III

Coach: Peter Marion, Seton Hall 1995

2006-07 RESULTS (17-10)

77	Stevens Institute ⊠	65
84	Southwestern (Tex.) †	75
71	Trinity (Tex.)	66
85	Staten Island	68
69	Drew ⊠	62
70	Scranton	78
67	Moravian	85
85	City Tech	46
70	Hunter ⊠	74
57	Wm. Paterson	70
92	Briarcliffe (N.Y.) ⊠	61
84	Wentworth Inst. †	55
63	Marymount (Va.)	60
72	DeSales	38
66	Lycoming ⊠	51
71	Delaware Valley	69
75	King's (Pa.) ⊠	78
70	Wilkes	63
75	Lycoming	82
81	Delaware Valley ⊠	54
79	Scranton ⊠	71
68	DeSales	81
89	Wilkes ⊠	78
53	Drew	39
66	King's (Pa.)	91
74	King's (Pa.)	83
71	New Jersey City	88

Nickname: Devils
Colors: Cardinal and Navy
Arena: Ferguson Recreation Center
Capacity: 3,000; Year Built: 1995
AD: William T. Klika
SID: Jim Henry

FAIRMONT ST.

Fairmont, WV 26554 II

Coach: Tim Murphy, Fairmont St. 1985

2006-07 RESULTS (14-14)

92	Ohio St.-Newark ⊠	44
81	West Va. Wesleyan ⊠	64
85	Central St. (Ohio)	94
70	Davis & Elkins	78
93	Columbia Union ⊠	64
107	Ohio-Eastern	65
71	Central St. (Ohio) ⊠	66
87	Elizabeth City St. †	89
104	Pfeiffer †	94
71	Lock Haven ⊠	76
73	West Virginia St. ⊠	70
68	Wheeling Jesuit	95
69	Concord	87
66	Salem Int'l ⊠	68
58	Shepherd	66
86	Glenville St. ⊠	49
78	Bluefield St.	67
73	West Liberty St.	91
83	Ohio Valley ⊠	89
91	Salem Int'l	101
81	Wheeling Jesuit ⊠	76
83	Shepherd	79
77	West Va. Wesleyan ⊠	64
81	Ohio Valley	63
68	Charleston (W.V.) ⊠	60
73	Alderson-Broaddus	80
102	West Liberty St. ⊠	118
62	Charleston (W.V.) ⊠	70

Nickname: Falcons
Colors: Maroon, White & Fairmont Gold
Arena: Joe Retton Arena
Capacity: 4,000; Year Built: 1978
AD: David Scott Gines
SID: Adam Zundell

FARMINGDALE ST.

Farmingdale St., NY 11735-1021 III

Coach: Erik Smiles, Bridgeport 2001

2006-07 RESULTS (18-10)

90	Berkeley †	29
65	Ramapo	70
98	Centenary (N.J.) ⊠	57
57	Yeshiva	55
83	Mt. St. Vincent	70
81	Staten Island	77
87	Rutgers-Newark	93
83	New Jersey City ⊠	78
63	Alice Lloyd †	73
60	Husson †	57
77	Maritime (N.Y.)	62
78	Merchant Marine ⊠	66
81	St. Joseph's (L.I.)	64
69	Manhattanville	70
69	Old Westbury ⊠	92
81	Mt. St. Mary (N.Y.) ⊠	84
81	Stevens Institute	85
64	Yeshiva ⊠	60
86	Centenary (N.J.)	66
83	City Tech	61
100	Maritime (N.Y.) ⊠	68
61	Manhattanville ⊠	71
79	Baruch	69
75	Mt. St. Mary (N.Y.)	69
112	Mt. St. Vincent ⊠	58
74	St. Joseph's (L.I.) ⊠	72
76	Manhattanville	93
73	Rutgers-Newark	82

Nickname: Rams
Colors: Green & White
Arena: Walter A. Lynch Sports Center-Nold Hall
Capacity: 4,000; Year Built: 1972
AD: Michael Harrington
SID: Deana Ward

FAYETTEVILLE ST.

Fayetteville, NC 28301-4298 II

Coach: Samuel Hanger, Binghamton 1974

2006-07 RESULTS (15-13)

78	Bluefield St.	84
76	Shaw ⊠	55
64	S.C. Upstate ⊠	82
74	UNC Pembroke	64
76	Bluefield St. ⊠	64
68	Virginia Union ⊠	77
78	UNC Pembroke ⊠	60
63	Eckerd	75
75	Tampa	67
57	Virginia St. ⊠	71
71	N.C. Central ⊠	68
54	Virginia Union	85
70	Bowie St. ⊠	79
61	Johnson C. Smith	54
98	St. Paul's	90
82	Elizabeth City St. ⊠	73
78	Livingstone ⊠	68
68	Shaw	56
77	St. Paul's	89
71	Elizabeth City St.	70
64	Bowie St.	72
67	N.C. Central	60
61	St. Augustine's ⊠	60
62	Virginia St.	84
72	Johnson C. Smith ⊠	75
66	St. Augustine's	81
59	Livingstone	47
60	St. Augustine's †	61

Nickname: Broncos
Colors: Royal Blue & Lily White
Arena: Capel Arena
Capacity: 5,024; Year Built: 1995
AD: Edward McLean/Major Boyd
SID: Marion Crowe

FELICIAN

Lodi, NJ 07644 II

Coach: Del Harrison, New Jersey City 1991

2006-07 RESULTS (12-16)

63	Minn. St. Mankato	96
62	Minn. Duluth †	74
90	Queens (N.Y.)	102
73	Dominican (N.Y.) ⊠	68
78	Post	83
69	Philadelphia U. ⊠	66
58	Caldwell	82
62	Goldey-Beacom	67
89	Molloy ⊠	76
58	Pace	88
90	St. Michael's †	83
69	Holy Family ⊠	79
92	Wilmington (Del.) ⊠	67
93	Bloomfield	86
53	Phila. Sciences	83
75	Dist. Columbia	89
79	Nyack ⊠	67
67	Philadelphia U.	79
73	Dominican (N.Y.)	68
92	Post ⊠	89
80	Caldwell ⊠	76
92	Goldey-Beacom ⊠	88
68	Holy Family	84
92	Wilmington (Del.)	80
73	Nyack	82
93	Bloomfield ⊠	99
73	Phila. Sciences ⊠	83
71	Post	78

Nickname: Golden Falcons
Colors: Hunter Green & Gold
Arena: Joal & Joseph Job
　　Capacity: 900; Year Built: 1949
AD: Ben Di Nallo
SID: Mark Mentone

FERRIS ST.

Big Rapids, MI 49307-2295 II

Coach: Bill Sall, Calvin 1994

2006-07 RESULTS (10-18)

59	Northern Ky.	73
62	Christian Bros. †	67
57	SIU Edwardsville ⊠	52
81	Alma ⊠	53
69	Northwood (Mich.)	63
62	Saginaw Valley ⊠	64
63	Grand Valley St.	70
77	Lake Superior St. ⊠	84
60	Indianapolis †	71
76	Southern Ind. †	91
61	GCSU †	68
68	Armstrong Atlantic	76
69	St. Joseph's (Ind.) ⊠	86
65	Hillsdale	51
65	Northern Mich.	64
49	Michigan Tech	61
65	Mercyhurst	70
83	Gannon	85
81	Ashland ⊠	78
70	Findlay ⊠	75
84	Saginaw Valley	73
71	Northwood (Mich.) ⊠	79
61	Michigan Tech ⊠	59
89	Northern Mich. ⊠	81
78	Wayne St. (Mich.)	89
68	Lake Superior St.	62
68	Grand Valley St. ⊠	75
59	Grand Valley St	72

Nickname: Bulldogs
Colors: Crimson & Gold
Arena: Jim Wink Arena
　　Capacity: 2,400; Year Built: 1999
AD: Tom Kirinovic
SID: Rob Bentley

FERRUM

Ferrum, VA 24088 III

Coach: Bill Tharp, Army 1996

2006-07 RESULTS (12-15)

73	Huntingdon ⊠	52
70	Piedmont ⊠	64
66	Lynchburg	57
64	Hampden-Sydney	77
67	East. Mennonite ⊠	73
53	Gardner-Webb	70
70	Southern Va.	91
83	Lancaster Bible ⊠	73
72	Elmira	57
90	Maritime (N.Y.) ⊠	73
65	Drew †	70
74	Chestnut Hill †	81
56	Winston-Salem	77
69	Averett	77
73	Methodist ⊠	78
79	Greensboro ⊠	68
79	Chris. Newport	80
75	Shenandoah	71
83	N.C. Wesleyan ⊠	79
62	Averett ⊠	68
59	Methodist	63
84	Greensboro	94
68	Shenandoah ⊠	52
89	Chris. Newport ⊠	97
86	N.C. Wesleyan	73
77	Methodist	71
73	Averett †	76

Nickname: Panthers
Colors: Black & Gold
Arena: Swartz Gymnasium
　　Capacity: 1,200; Year Built: 1960
AD: Abe Naff
SID: Gary Holden

FINDLAY

Findlay, OH 45840 II

Coach: Ron Niekamp, Miami (Ohio) 1972

2006-07 RESULTS (29-2)

89	Tex. A&M-Commerce †	72
82	Tarleton St.	85
81	Charleston (W.V.) ⊠	49
89	Rio Grande ⊠	65
99	Lake Erie ⊠	67
70	Northern Mich. ⊠	56
77	Lake Superior St.	55
92	Ashland	67
71	Michigan Tech	63
59	Northern Ky. ⊠	53
100	Tiffin ⊠	61
59	Mercyhurst	47
91	Gannon	63
82	Hillsdale ⊠	55
68	Wayne St. (Mich.) ⊠	52
77	Saginaw Valley ⊠	60
74	Northwood (Mich.) ⊠	59
86	Marygrove ⊠	58
75	Ferris St.	70
72	Wayne St. (Mich.)	56
79	Hillsdale	66
83	Notre Dame (Ohio) ⊠	65
76	Grand Valley St. ⊠	62
86	Mercyhurst ⊠	60
85	Gannon ⊠	59
76	Ashland	67
70	Ashland ⊠	54
77	Mercyhurst ⊠	40
71	Grand Valley St. ⊠	61
74	Wis.-Parkside †	60
56	Northern Ky. ⊠	60

Nickname: Oilers
Colors: Orange & Black
Arena: Croy Gymnasium
　　Capacity: 2,200; Year Built: 1969
AD: Steven Rackley
SID: David Buck

FISK

Nashville, TN 37208-3051 III

Coach: Robert Moore, Fisk 1972

2006-07 RESULTS (5-18)

84	Crichton ⊠	102
54	Belmont	83
68	Lipscomb	80
83	Fontbonne	80
60	Webster	84
73	Otterbein ⊠	78
55	Crichton	110
62	Mississippi Col.	83
65	Greensboro	69
72	Chris. Newport ⊠	71
74	Chris. Newport	86
75	Greensboro †	83
52	Tennessee St.	85
82	Maryville (Tenn.)	91
64	Huntingdon ⊠	66
96	Philander Smith ⊠	86
81	Rust	86
54	Huntingdon	65
85	Oakwood ⊠	79
66	Maryville (Tenn.) ⊠	73
70	LaGrange	76
66	Rust ⊠	92
70	Oakwood ⊠	69

Nickname: Bulldogs
Colors: Blue & Gold
Arena: Johnson, Henderson Gym
　　Capacity: 2,500; Year Built: 1950
AD: William K Head
SID: Andrea Campbell

FITCHBURG ST.

Fitchburg, MA 01420-2697 III

Coach: Derek Shell, St. Thomas (Fla.) 1997

2006-07 RESULTS (7-18)

50	Mass.-Dartmouth	84
89	Suffolk †	91
80	Mass.-Boston ⊠	86
63	Rhode Island Col.	74
67	Nichols	79
54	WPI	74
63	Clark (Mass.) ⊠	83
72	Becker ⊠	63
67	Wheaton (Mass.) †	71
83	Wesleyan (Conn.) †	82
72	Worcester St.	67
73	Salem St.	81
63	Wheaton (Mass.)	74
68	Westfield St.	82
76	Framingham St. ⊠	83
73	Mass. Liberal Arts	68
54	Bridgewater St. ⊠	62
67	Worcester St. ⊠	52
62	Salem St.	83
54	Newbury	62
58	Westfield St. ⊠	53
85	Framingham St.	93
79	Mass. Liberal Arts ⊠	77
59	Bridgewater St.	75
72	Worcester St. ⊠	81

Nickname: Falcons
Colors: Green, Gold & White
Arena: Recreation Center
　　Capacity: 1,000; Year Built: 2000
AD: Sue E. Lauder
SID: To be named

FLORIDA

Gainesville, FL 32611 I

Coach: Billy Donovan, Providence 1987

2006-07 RESULTS (35-5)

79	Samford	54
86	North Fla. ⊠	40
90	Jacksonville ⊠	61
93	Chattanooga ⊠	44
94	Prairie View ⊠	33
101	Western Ky. †	68
80	Kansas †	82
83	Southern U. ⊠	27
66	Florida St.	70
85	Providence ⊠	67
72	Florida A&M †	57
88	Stetson ⊠	67
86	Ohio St. ⊠	60
75	UAB †	70
89	Liberty ⊠	58
67	Georgia ⊠	51
79	Arkansas ⊠	72
84	South Carolina	50
79	Mississippi	70
70	Mississippi St.	67
91	Auburn	66
74	Vanderbilt ⊠	64
94	Tennessee ⊠	78
71	Georgia	61
64	Kentucky	61
76	Alabama ⊠	67
70	Vanderbilt	83
63	South Carolina ⊠	49
56	LSU	66
76	Tennessee	86
85	Kentucky ⊠	72
74	Georgia †	57
80	Mississippi †	59
77	Arkansas †	56
112	Jackson St. †	69
74	Purdue †	67
65	Butler †	57
85	Oregon †	77
76	UCLA †	66
84	Ohio St. †	75

Nickname: Gators
Colors: Orange & Blue
Arena: Stephen C. O'Connell Center
　　Capacity: 12,000; Year Built: 1980
AD: Jeremy N. Foley
SID: Steve McClain

FLORIDA A&M

Tallahassee, FL 32307 I

Coach: Mike Gillespie, DePaul 1974

2006-07 RESULTS (21-14)

54	Maryland	93
88	Warner Southern ⊠	61
33	Miami (Ohio)	52
63	Illinois	84
75	Bradley	107
57	Ill.-Chicago †	75
74	Savannah St. †	75
83	Bethune-Cookman ⊠	73
76	Edward Waters ⊠	61
96	Albany St. (Ga.) ⊠	87
57	Florida †	72
66	North Fla.	65
51	Pittsburgh	77
62	Morgan St.	59
81	Norfolk St. ⊠	71
74	Hampton ⊠	76
73	South Carolina St. ⊠	58
78	N.C. A&T ⊠	82
65	Md.-East. Shore	55
65	Howard	73
73	Delaware St. ⊠	69
83	Winston-Salem ⊠	68
68	Norfolk St.	81
72	Hampton	74
72	South Carolina St.	69
82	N.C. A&T	90
93	Md.-East. Shore ⊠	60
85	Howard ⊠	75
65	Delaware St.	77
73	Coppin St. ⊠	59
68	Bethune-Cookman	62
61	Hampton †	58
74	N.C. A&T †	66
58	Delaware St. †	56
69	Niagara †	77

Nickname: Rattlers
Colors: Orange & Green
Arena: Gaither Athletic Center

Capacity: 3,365; Year Built: 1963
AD: Nelson E. Townsend
SID: Alvin Hollins

FLA. ATLANTIC
Boca Raton, FL 33431-0991 I

Coach: Rex Walters, Kansas 1993

2006-07 RESULTS (16-15)
50	Oklahoma St.	95
70	UMKC	85
55	Old Dominion	70
67	Marist	83
59	North Fla.	44
94	Fla. Memorial ■	60
77	Norfolk St. ■	64
65	UCF	87
91	Troy	87
52	North Carolina	105
70	UMKC ■	61
68	Florida Int'l	66
83	Western Ky. ■	93
93	New Orleans	86
76	South Ala.	101
68	Middle Tenn.	72
73	La.-Monroe ■	62
85	Denver	90
59	North Texas	76
75	La.-Lafayette ■	72
75	Ark.-Little Rock ■	71
77	Arkansas St.	84
87	Troy	92
81	Longwood	63
85	Florida Int'l ■	78
78	Western Ky.	73
98	New Orleans ■	77
79	South Ala. ■	69
59	Middle Tenn.	79
91	Florida Int'l ■	88
81	Western Ky. †	86

Nickname: Owls
Colors: Blue & Red
Arena: FAU Arena
    Capacity: 5,000; Year Built: 1984
AD: Craig W. Angelos
SID: Mike Boseak

FLA. GULF COAST
Fort Myers, FL 33965-6565 II

Coach: Dave Balza, Michigan 1991

2006-07 RESULTS (27-6)
37	Drexel	73
74	Penn	97
79	P.R.-Cayey ■	63
77	West Ala. ■	66
48	Henderson St. ■	45
86	Arkansas Tech ■	80
93	P.R.-Bayamon ■	70
77	Lynn ■	83
91	Tuskegee ■	72
65	Lynn	64
76	Albany St. (Ga.) ■	67
65	Montevallo	74
67	Valdosta St. ■	77
70	P.R.-Rio Piedras ■	61
73	Fort Valley St. ■	58
60	Florida Tech ■	47
75	P.R.-Cayey †	46
74	P.R.-Rio Piedras †	46
80	P.R.-Bayamon	73
78	Palm Beach Atl. ■	67
88	Stillman ■	63
69	Fla. Southern ■	56
70	Nova Southeastern ■	59
78	West Ga. ■	62
90	Palm Beach Atl.	63
81	Apprentice ■	52
77	Johnson & Wales (CO) ■	52
65	Butler	79
90	Marygrove †	61
85	Nova Southeastern	75
79	Flagler	59
99	North Georgia ■	62

82	Central St. (Ohio) ■	78

Nickname: Eagles
Colors: Green & Blue
Arena: Alico Arena
    Capacity: 4,500; Year Built: 2002
AD: Carl McAloose
SID: Matt Fairchild

FLORIDA INT'L
Miami, FL 33199 I

Coach: Sergio Rouco, Nova
Southeastern 1987

2006-07 RESULTS (12-17)
50	Miami (Fla.)	73
72	Robert Morris	96
74	Alcorn St. ■	61
62	Western Ill. ■	60
50	South Fla.	79
70	Kennesaw St.	68
39	George Mason	65
63	Wisconsin	79
72	Florida Tech ■	59
67	Troy	64
90	Palm Beach Atl. ■	74
66	Fla. Atlantic ■	68
46	Middle Tenn. ■	60
52	South Ala.	69
71	La.-Lafayette	74
74	Western Ky. ■	86
61	Denver ■	59
67	North Texas	66
69	La.-Monroe	77
67	New Orleans	77
80	Arkansas St. ■	61
68	Ark.-Little Rock	86
51	Troy	56
78	Fla. Atlantic	85
69	Middle Tenn.	67
69	South Ala. ■	67
71	La.-Lafayette ■	68
64	Western Ky.	82
88	Fla. Atlantic	91

Nickname: Golden Panthers
Colors: Blue & Gold
Arena: Pharmed Arena
    Capacity: 5,000; Year Built: 1986
AD: Peter Garcia
SID: Rich Kelch

FLA. SOUTHERN
Lakeland, FL 33801-5698 II

Coach: Linc Darner, Purdue 1995

2006-07 RESULTS (8-20)
101	P.R.-Mayaguez ■	64
58	Armstrong Atlantic	61
80	Northwood (Fla.)	84
70	Lynn	77
95	Palm Beach Atl.	100
82	Fla. Memorial ■	74
71	West Virginia St. ■	81
93	Armstrong Atlantic ■	81
67	Presbyterian	66
42	Grand Valley St. ■	62
72	Nova Southeastern	76
69	Florida Tech ■	66
59	Rollins ■	70
63	Barry	86
81	Tampa ■	73
56	Fla. Gulf Coast	69
95	St. Leo	102
65	Eckerd ■	73
69	Rollins	71
68	Nova Southeastern ■	73
52	Florida Tech	56
70	Lynn ■	80
58	Barry ■	68
63	Tampa	68
90	Palm Beach Atl. ■	70
92	St. Leo ■	69
72	Eckerd	85
62	Florida Tech †	64

Nickname: Moccasins
Colors: Scarlet & White
Arena: Jenkins Field House
    Capacity: 2,500; Year Built: 1966
AD: Lois Webb
SID: Bill Turnage

FLORIDA ST.
Tallahassee, FL 32306 I

Coach: Leonard Hamilton, Tenn.-Martin
1971

2006-07 RESULTS (22-13)
85	McNeese St. ■	65
73	Illinois St. ■	59
59	SMU ■	52
69	New Orleans ■	50
66	Pittsburgh	88
66	Wisconsin	81
70	Florida ■	66
82	Stetson	63
87	Georgia St.	55
88	Southeastern La. ■	62
81	High Point ■	64
78	Coastal Caro. ■	65
76	St. Peter's ■	63
92	Providence †	62
66	Clemson ■	68
58	North Carolina	84
80	Georgia Tech	88
82	Virginia Tech ■	73
86	Miami (Fla.) ■	67
82	Boston College	85
74	Wake Forest ■	66
96	Maryland ■	79
68	Duke	67
58	Clemson	71
67	Boston College ■	68
57	Georgia Tech ■	63
70	Virginia	73
55	Maryland	73
78	North Carolina St. ■	52
98	Miami (Fla.)	90
67	Clemson †	66
58	North Carolina †	73
77	Toledo	61
87	Michigan ■	66
71	Mississippi St.	86

Nickname: Seminoles
Colors: Garnet & Gold
Arena: Donald L. Tucker Center
    Capacity: 12,100; Year Built: 1981
AD: David R. Hart Jr.
SID: Chuck Walsh

FLORIDA TECH
Melbourne, FL 32901 II

Coach: Billy Mims, Charleston So. 1981

2006-07 RESULTS (10-21)
59	Bethune-Cookman	67
88	P.R.-Mayaguez ■	77
60	Jacksonville	89
37	UCF	81
77	Palm Beach Atl. ■	67
56	Eckerd	58
59	Florida Int'l	72
60	Alas. Anchorage †	78
68	Alas. Fairbanks	78
77	Waldorf ■	60
87	Palm Beach Atl.	78
66	Valdosta St.	89
47	Fla. Gulf Coast	60
57	Lynn	71
66	Fla. Southern	69
63	Tampa ■	52
70	St. Leo ■	73
59	Barry ■	71
59	Nova Southeastern	65
74	Rollins ■	87
47	Tampa	63
56	Lynn	52
56	Fla. Southern ■	52
61	Eckerd	73

71	St. Leo ■	77
63	Barry	80
63	Nova Southeastern ■	59
68	Rollins	70
78	Johnson & Wales (FL) ■	73
64	Fla. Southern †	62
65	Rollins †	80

Nickname: Panthers
Colors: Crimson & Gray
Arena: Charles & Ruth Clemente Center
    Capacity: 1,500; Year Built: 2001
AD: William K. Jurgens
SID: Christa Parulis-Kaye

FONTBONNE
St Louis, MO 63105-3098 III

Coach: Lee McKinney, Southeast Mo.
St. 1960

2006-07 RESULTS (16-12)
78	Hannibal-La Grange †	81
95	Moody Bible	83
80	Fisk ■	83
89	Concordia (Mich.)	66
77	Greenville	79
74	Eureka	75
78	Rose-Hulman	80
68	Washington-St. Louis	83
71	Tampa	84
97	Blackburn	78
69	Principia	52
95	MacMurray ■	86
76	Westminster (Mo.) ■	58
78	Webster ■	89
83	Lincoln Christian	78
78	Maryville (Mo.) ■	69
59	Eureka	75
90	Greenville ■	75
93	Blackburn ■	75
79	Westminster (Mo.)	53
94	Principia ■	53
79	MacMurray	92
79	Webster	86
90	Lincoln Christian ■	59
80	Maryville (Mo.)	65
67	Webster	62
88	Eureka †	79
58	Washington-St. Louis	77

Nickname: Griffins
Colors: Purple & Gold
Arena: Dunham Student Activities
    Capacity: 1,800; Year Built: 1993
AD: Lee McKinney
SID: Brian Hoener

FORDHAM
Bronx, NY 10458-5155 I

Coach: Dereck Whittenburg, North
Carolina St. 1984

2006-07 RESULTS (18-12)
70	Sacred Heart ■	68
71	Tennessee †	78
49	Belmont †	56
76	St. Francis (N.Y.) ■	49
70	Manhattan ■	66
70	Iona ■	54
59	Maryland	79
77	Penn	60
61	Texas A&M	84
56	Col. of Charleston	65
56	Fairfield ■	47
67	Quinnipiac ■	66
59	George Washington	70
58	Richmond	55
56	Xavier ■	71
71	Duquesne	59
56	St. Joseph's ■	55
77	St. Louis ■	68
62	La Salle	54
67	St. Bonaventure ■	61
44	Rhode Island ■	45
45	Dayton	57

68	Charlotte	72
59	Massachusetts ⊠	74
86	Duquesne ⊠	83
71	Rhode Island	62
91	St. Bonaventure ⊠	60
80	Temple ⊠	73
63	Richmond †	61
69	Rhode Island †	73

Nickname: Rams
Colors: Maroon & White
Arena: Rose Hill Gym
    Capacity: 3,200; Year Built: 1926
AD: Francis X. McLaughlin
SID: Joe DiBari

FORT HAYS ST.
Hays, KS 67601 II

Coach: Mark Johnson, Pittsburg St. 1993

2006-07 RESULTS (13-15)

96	Bethany (Kan.) ⊠	45
70	Washburn †	69
62	Western St. †	57
90	Baker ⊠	66
63	Cent. Christian (Mo) ⊠	45
65	Neb.-Kearney ⊠	70
71	Emporia St.	86
75	Kan. Wesleyan ⊠	52
68	Southeastern Okla. †	84
49	St. Mary's (Tex.)	47
54	Northwest Mo. St. ⊠	72
59	Truman	70
59	Southwest Baptist ⊠	69
57	Washburn	69
97	Mo. Western St. ⊠	80
63	Central Mo.	80
80	Mo. Southern St. ⊠	86
77	Pittsburg St.	75
73	Emporia St. ⊠	76
55	Pittsburg St. ⊠	56
89	Mo. Southern St. ⊠	61
87	Central Mo. ⊠	77
60	Mo. Western St.	61
74	Southwest Baptist	64
59	Truman ⊠	64
58	Washburn ⊠	57
40	Northwest Mo. St.	66
64	Central Mo. †	78

Nickname: Tigers
Colors: Black & Gold
Arena: Gross Memorial Coliseum
    Capacity: 6,814; Year Built: 1973
AD: Curtis Hammeke
SID: Ryan Prickett

FORT LEWIS
Durango, CO 81301-3999.............. II

Coach: Bob Hofman, Colorado 1974

2006-07 RESULTS (22-9)

79	Dixie St. †	57
77	Tex. Permian Basin †	64
79	Western N.M. †	77
66	BYU-Hawaii †	72
80	Hawaii-Hilo	59
103	Haskell †	79
89	Johnson & Wales (CO) ⊠	61
72	Colo. Christian ⊠	61
65	Metro St. ⊠	82
86	Chadron St.	76
58	Neb.-Kearney	75
78	Colorado Col.	54
73	Colorado Mines ⊠	67
86	Dixie St. ⊠	76
87	UC-Colo. Springs	89
79	Regis (Colo.)	71
79	Mesa St.	75
79	Western St. ⊠	67
63	Western N.M.	69
98	N.M. Highlands	61
85	Adams St. ⊠	77
89	Colorado St.-Pueblo ⊠	79

78	N.M. Highlands ⊠	68
77	Western N.M. ⊠	65
79	Colorado St.-Pueblo	63
77	Adams St.	85
80	Mesa St. ⊠	69
95	Western St.	103
81	Mesa St. ⊠	74
58	Metro St. †	73
71	Minn. St. Mankato †	85

Nickname: Skyhawks
Colors: Navy Blue, Light Blue & Gold
Arena: Whalen Gymnasium
Capacity: 2,750
AD: Kent Stanley
SID: Andrew Beardsley

FORT VALLEY ST.
Fort Valley, GA 31030 II

Coach: Travis Williams, Georgia St. 1995

2006-07 RESULTS (18-12)

56	Miles ⊠	58
80	LeMoyne-Owen ⊠	85
74	Mercer	79
60	Claflin ⊠	63
65	Ga. Southwestern	80
58	Fla. Gulf Coast	73
59	Tuskegee ⊠	57
52	Stillman	54
71	Kentucky St.	86
73	Lane	69
66	Albany St. (Ga.) ⊠	50
61	Claflin	48
65	Paine ⊠	49
70	Benedict ⊠	73
77	Kentucky St. ⊠	63
74	Lane ⊠	55
97	Miles	82
84	LeMoyne-Owen	77
87	Clark Atlanta ⊠	66
84	Morehouse	69
60	Tuskegee	61
62	Stillman	47
58	Morehouse ⊠	46
71	Albany St. (Ga.)	77
78	Paine	74
60	Benedict	56
49	Clark Atlanta ⊠	46
72	Miles	59
86	Kentucky St. †	70
50	Albany St. (Ga.) †	54

Nickname: Wildcats
Colors: Royal Blue & Old Gold
Arena: Health and Physical Education Complex
    Capacity: 5,100; Year Built: 2004
AD: Gwendolyn Reeves
SID: Russell Boone

FRAMINGHAM ST.
Framingham, MA 01701-9101 III

Coach: Don Spellman, Suffolk 1985

2006-07 RESULTS (10-15)

75	Medgar Evers †	69
79	New England Col.	92
96	Daniel Webster	83
87	Mass.-Boston	85
85	Curry †	82
61	Williams	56
80	Eastern Nazarene ⊠	73
57	Brandeis	87
69	St. Joseph's (Me.)	82
61	Trinity (Conn.)	100
66	Potsdam St. †	85
62	Mass. Liberal Arts	79
60	Rhode Island Col. ⊠	85
63	Bridgewater St. ⊠	82
73	Worcester St.	91
96	Salem St. ⊠	115
83	Fitchburg St.	76
79	Westfield St.	82
110	Mass. Liberal Arts ⊠	89

97	Bridgewater St.	95
84	Worcester St. ⊠	89
98	Salem St.	115
93	Fitchburg St. ⊠	85
75	Westfield St. ⊠	93
83	Westfield St.	98

Nickname: Rams
Colors: Black & Gold
Arena: Athletic & Recreation Center
    Capacity: 1,000; Year Built: 2002
AD: Thomas M. Kelley
SID: Kathy Lynch

FRANCIS MARION
Florence, SC 29501-0547 II

Coach: Gary Edwards, Va. Wesleyan 1979

2006-07 RESULTS (9-19)

47	Coker	62
68	SCAD ⊠	65
66	Apprentice	57
78	Morris ⊠	65
51	Erskine	66
68	Newberry	84
74	Mount Olive ⊠	89
47	Lenoir-Rhyne †	55
66	Eckerd †	80
56	Lander ⊠	78
50	Clayton St.	78
48	S.C. Upstate	65
60	Armstrong Atlantic ⊠	75
47	Chowan	66
85	S.C.-Aiken ⊠	78
56	Ga. Southwestern	68
66	S.C. Upstate ⊠	62
63	Augusta St. ⊠	79
72	S.C.-Aiken	68
77	Columbus St.	86
52	UNC Pembroke	48
61	North Georgia ⊠	64
78	Chowan ⊠	72
68	Lander	86
64	GCSU ⊠	95
75	UNC Pembroke ⊠	70
75	North Georgia	78
68	Armstrong Atlantic †	78

Nickname: Patriots
Colors: Red, White & Blue
Arena: Smith University Center
    Capacity: 3,027; Year Built: 1974
AD: Murray Hartzler
SID: Michael G. Hawkins

FRANKLIN
Franklin, IN 46131 III

Coach: Kerry Prather, Indiana 1977

2006-07 RESULTS (16-10)

78	Wheaton (Ill.)	81
94	Eastern †	71
61	North Central (Ill.)	85
90	Hanover ⊠	84
74	Bluffton	82
58	Rose-Hulman	50
68	Millikin	76
66	Earlham ⊠	71
82	Wabash ⊠	58
85	Alma ⊠	63
80	Wabash ⊠	68
72	Mt. St. Joseph ⊠	82
62	Manchester	59
84	Transylvania ⊠	85
79	Anderson (Ind.)	74
49	Defiance	66
93	Bluffton ⊠	76
73	Hanover	58
72	Clarke ⊠	53
68	Rose-Hulman ⊠	51
69	Manchester ⊠	73
76	Transylvania	66
83	Mt. St. Joseph	76
88	Defiance ⊠	77

84	Anderson (Ind.) ⊠	74
73	Defiance ⊠	80

Nickname: Grizzlies
Colors: Navy & Old Gold
Arena: Spurlock Center
    Capacity: 1,500; Year Built: 1975
AD: Kerry N. Prather
SID: Kevin Elixman

FRANK. & MARSH.
Lancaster, PA 17604-3003 III

Coach: Glenn Robinson, West Chester 1967

2006-07 RESULTS (8-17)

67	Delaware Valley ⊠	74
71	Widener ⊠	44
52	Lebanon Valley ⊠	57
67	Juniata	78
67	Gettysburg ⊠	48
64	Swarthmore	73
66	Dickinson	56
69	Haverford ⊠	43
58	Alvernia	72
68	Western Conn. St. ⊠	69
43	Lincoln (Pa.) ⊠	64
52	Ursinus	64
69	Muhlenberg ⊠	49
80	Washington (Md.)	54
71	Swarthmore ⊠	73
66	Johns Hopkins ⊠	69
55	Haverford	60
82	McDaniel ⊠	70
69	Ursinus ⊠	75
66	Gettysburg	67
69	Muhlenberg	71
68	Dickinson ⊠	73
90	Washington (Md.) ⊠	64
75	McDaniel	78
68	Johns Hopkins	84

Nickname: Diplomats
Colors: Blue & White
Arena: Mayser Center
    Capacity: 3,000; Year Built: 1960
AD: Patricia Epps
SID: Edward Haas

FRANKLIN PIERCE
Rindge, NH 03461 II

Coach: David Chadbourne, St. Joseph's (Me.) 1987

2006-07 RESULTS (13-14)

74	St. Michael's	63
59	New Haven †	73
51	Assumption	61
71	Bryant †	69
87	St. Joseph (Vt.) ⊠	61
87	Pace	84
78	Stonehill †	70
60	Le Moyne	69
61	St. Rose	70
73	Southern N.H. ⊠	72
63	Caldwell ⊠	66
73	St. Anselm	62
78	American Int'l ⊠	63
87	Southern Conn. St. ⊠	79
65	Bentley	77
57	Southern N.H.	46
40	Le Moyne ⊠	46
71	Stonehill	72
62	Assumption ⊠	52
61	St. Rose ⊠	66
53	Pace ⊠	72
74	Mass.-Lowell	51
61	Bryant	65
62	St. Anselm ⊠	61
60	Merrimack	83
86	St. Michael's ⊠	83
65	St. Anselm ⊠	66

Nickname: Ravens
Colors: Crimson, Gray & Black
Arena: FPC Fieldhouse

Capacity: 2,000; Year Built: 1967
AD: Bruce Kirsh
SID: Doug Monson

FREDONIA ST.
Fredonia, NY 14063 III

Coach: Kevin Moore, Brockport St. 1983

2006-07 RESULTS (6-18)

56	Keystone †	54
61	Nazareth	66
62	Brockport St.	70
58	New Paltz St.	61
51	Oneonta St.	56
57	Pitt.-Bradford ⊠	66
63	Houghton †	70
54	Hobart †	58
76	Houghton ⊠	83
86	Hilbert ⊠	82
62	Oswego St. ⊠	64
66	Cortland St.	74
51	Geneseo St.	67
64	Plattsburgh St. ⊠	73
63	Potsdam St. ⊠	53
61	Morrisville St. ⊠	44
56	SUNYIT	72
55	Plattsburgh St.	69
78	Buffalo St. ⊠	75
51	Brockport St. ⊠	74
78	SUNYIT ⊠	74
59	Buffalo St.	74
44	Geneseo St. ⊠	66
73	Cortland St.	80

Nickname: Blue Devils
Colors: Blue & White
Arena: Steele Hall
    Capacity: 3,500; Year Built: 1983
AD: Gregory Prechtl
SID: Jerry Reilly

FRESNO ST.
Fresno, CA 93740-0048 I

Coach: Steve Cleveland, UC Irvine 1976

2006-07 RESULTS (22-10)

85	Winston-Salem ⊠	63
73	South Ala. ⊠	63
82	UC Irvine ⊠	51
86	San Francisco	66
82	Ark.-Pine Bluff ⊠	55
80	Montana ⊠	41
74	Oregon St.	69
42	UC Santa Barbara	70
82	Montana St.	77
69	Creighton ⊠	54
67	Stanford ⊠	69
95	Cal Poly ⊠	75
68	San Diego ⊠	65
60	Idaho ⊠	41
79	Utah St. ⊠	70
66	Hawaii	83
61	San Jose St.	64
75	Nevada	85
67	San Jose St. ⊠	64
61	Boise St.	65
70	Louisiana Tech ⊠	64
42	Hawaii ⊠	54
72	Idaho	70
68	Nevada ⊠	81
75	New Mexico St. ⊠	69
78	Sam Houston St. ⊠	60
64	Louisiana Tech	63
60	New Mexico St.	58
78	Boise St. ⊠	77
71	Utah St.	66
73	Boise St. †	78
78	Georgia	88

Nickname: Bulldogs
Colors: Red & Blue
Arena: Save Mart Center
    Capacity: 15,596; Year Built: 2003
AD: Thomas C. Boeh
SID: Steve Weakland

FROSTBURG ST.
Frostburg, MD 21532-1099 III

Coach: Webb Hatch, VMI 1969

2006-07 RESULTS (10-16)

72	Goucher ⊠	77
68	St. Mary's (Md.) †	84
58	Villa Julie †	64
89	Pitt.-Greensburg ⊠	79
56	Penn St.-Behrend ⊠	69
74	Shenandoah ⊠	65
72	La Roche ⊠	71
78	Medaille	69
84	Chris. Newport	92
72	Waynesburg	97
66	Mary Washington ⊠	100
54	Pitt.-Bradford ⊠	52
73	Penn St.-Altoona ⊠	65
59	Hilbert	83
70	Lake Erie ⊠	80
98	Mt. Aloysius ⊠	83
43	Penn St.-Behrend	67
75	Pitt.-Greensburg	73
85	Medaille ⊠	70
59	La Roche	67
63	Pitt.-Bradford	56
73	Penn St.-Altoona	76
69	Hilbert ⊠	86
91	Mt. Aloysius ⊠	98
51	Lake Erie	71
73	Hilbert	87

Nickname: Bobcats
Colors: Red, White & Black
Arena: Bobcat Arena
    Capacity: 3,600; Year Built: 1977
AD: Ralph L. Brewer
SID: To be named

FURMAN
Greenville, SC 29613 I

Coach: Jeff Jackson, Cornell 1984

2006-07 RESULTS (15-16)

88	Charleston So. ⊠	69
67	Erskine ⊠	55
58	Clemson	67
63	Bowling Green	59
58	North Dakota St.	60
70	Vanderbilt	62
67	UNC Asheville ⊠	75
79	S.C.-Aiken ⊠	54
86	UNC Greensboro ⊠	91
70	San Diego	81
50	California	84
83	Mercer ⊠	69
69	Chattanooga ⊠	56
70	Ga. Southern	72
63	Davidson ⊠	71
55	Col. of Charleston	67
68	Wofford ⊠	65
79	Western Caro. ⊠	67
63	Citadel ⊠	59
63	Appalachian St.	77
54	UNC Greensboro	69
68	Chattanooga	61
76	Appalachian St. ⊠	72
69	Elon	64
55	Ga. Southern ⊠	57
69	Citadel	51
77	Col. of Charleston ⊠	80
57	Davidson	75
67	Wofford	76
73	UNC Greensboro †	71
68	Davidson †	91

Nickname: Paladins
Colors: Purple & White
Arena: Timmons Arena
    Capacity: 5,500; Year Built: 1997
AD: Gary Clark
SID: Hunter Reid

GALLAUDET
Washington, DC 20002-3695 III

Coach: James DeStefano, Gallaudet 1985

2006-07 RESULTS (4-21)

83	Mt. Aloysius ⊠	86
89	Waynesburg †	91
74	Maryland Bible ⊠	78
73	Southern Vt. ⊠	75
77	John Jay ⊠	52
64	Hood	77
79	York (Pa.) ⊠	96
60	Salisbury ⊠	74
61	Wesley	73
78	Penn St.-Berks	66
31	Juniata	77
68	Goucher	75
53	Mary Washington	97
61	St. Mary's (Md.) ⊠	68
55	Catholic	51
50	Marymount (Va.) ⊠	70
63	Hood ⊠	77
53	Christendom ⊠	37
73	York (Pa.) ⊠	78
59	Salisbury	71
67	Goucher ⊠	85
62	Mary Washington ⊠	73
64	St. Mary's (Md.)	85
52	Catholic ⊠	70
78	Marymount (Va.)	81

Nickname: Bison
Colors: Buff & Blue
Arena: Field House
    Capacity: 1,892; Year Built: 1984
AD: James De Stefano
SID: Jeremy Bunblasky

GANNON
Erie, PA 16541-0001 II

Coach: John T. Reilly, Bowie St. 1986

2006-07 RESULTS (9-17)

76	C.W. Post ⊠	69
73	Pitt.-Johnstown ⊠	68
60	Edinboro	67
67	Wayne St. (Mich.)	70
51	Hillsdale	73
61	Quincy	90
80	Southwest Baptist †	92
84	Roberts Wesleyan ⊠	65
65	Bellarmine ⊠	81
96	Ashland	95
63	Findlay ⊠	91
63	Saginaw Valley	71
52	Northwood (Mich.)	60
100	Penn St.-McKeesport ⊠	50
61	Lake Superior St. ⊠	71
85	Ferris St. ⊠	83
49	Grand Valley St. ⊠	61
53	Mercyhurst	64
44	Michigan Tech	58
72	Northern Mich.	80
69	Hillsdale ⊠	59
66	Wayne St. (Mich.) ⊠	71
86	Ashland	83
59	Findlay	85
85	Indiana (Pa.) ⊠	66
74	Mercyhurst ⊠	79

Nickname: Golden Knights
Colors: Maroon & Gold
Arena: Hammermill Center
    Capacity: 2,800; Year Built: 1949
AD: Bill Elias
SID: Dan Teliski

GARDNER-WEBB
Boiling Springs, NC 28017 I

Coach: Rick Scruggs, Georgia 1979

2006-07 RESULTS (9-21)

74	Texas Tech	86
61	Akron †	89
50	North Carolina	103
67	UNC Greensboro ⊠	79
76	North Carolina St.	88
70	Ferrum ⊠	53
67	Georgia	96
74	Western Caro. ⊠	73
51	High Point	65
60	Wake Forest	92
40	Wisconsin	98
64	Jacksonville	73
72	North Fla.	52
63	East Tenn. St. ⊠	66
60	Kennesaw St. ⊠	77
77	Stetson	64
74	Mercer	85
61	Lipscomb ⊠	55
54	Belmont ⊠	70
59	Jacksonville ⊠	64
72	North Fla. ⊠	46
64	Campbell ⊠	55
61	East Tenn. St.	63
56	Kennesaw St.	59
69	Mercer ⊠	68
73	Stetson ⊠	48
55	Belmont	87
57	Lipscomb	59
60	Campbell	71
61	Belmont †	79

Nickname: Runnin' Bulldogs
Colors: Scarlet, White & Black
Arena: Paul Porter Arena
    Capacity: 5,500; Year Built: 1982
AD: Chuck Burch
SID: Marc Rabb

GENESEO ST.
Geneseo, NY 14454 III

Coach: Steve Minton, Heidelberg 1986

2006-07 RESULTS (15-11)

76	Lake Erie †	85
78	Ithaca †	67
82	Oswego St. ⊠	70
67	Potsdam St.	64
59	Plattsburgh St.	65
67	Alfred ⊠	50
62	St. John Fisher	63
77	Pitt.-Bradford	57
76	Elmira	55
75	Roberts Wesleyan †	72
84	Brockport St. †	73
53	Rochester (N.Y.) †	80
67	Fredonia St.	51
64	Cortland St. ⊠	61
71	New Paltz St.	54
75	Buffalo St.	66
71	New Paltz St. ⊠	75
49	Oneonta St. ⊠	72
70	Brockport St. ⊠	82
63	SUNYIT	70
60	Oswego St.	67
80	Plattsburgh St. ⊠	74
85	Potsdam St. ⊠	59
66	Fredonia St.	44
63	Brockport St.	79
51	Oswego St.	61

Nickname: Blue Knights
Colors: Navy Blue & White
Arena: Alumni Fieldhouse
    Capacity: 3,000; Year Built: 1973
AD: Marilyn Moore
SID: George Gagnier

RESULTS

GEORGE FOX
Newberg, OR 97132-2697 III

Coach: Mark Sundquist, Seattle Pacific 1989

2006-07 RESULTS (12-13)

74	Corban ⊠	61
85	Holy Names ⊠	65
61	Concordia (Cal.) †	84
63	Alvernia †	56
91	Linfield ⊠	85
79	Puget Sound	92
68	Northwest (Wash.)	72
73	Oregon Tech †	84
80	Corban	63
67	St. Martin's	78
77	Whitman	63
53	Whitworth ⊠	83
72	Willamette ⊠	52
57	Pacific (Ore.)	64
77	Pacific Lutheran	68
61	Lewis & Clark	74
65	Linfield	64
75	Puget Sound ⊠	63
73	Northwest Chrst.	68
59	Whitman	69
64	Whitworth	90
79	Willamette	84
68	Pacific (Ore.) ⊠	59
66	Pacific Lutheran ⊠	78
63	Lewis & Clark ⊠	75

Nickname: Bruins
Colors: Navy & Gold
Arena: Wheeler Sports Center/Miller Gym
Capacity: 2,750; Year Built: 1977
AD: Craig Taylor
SID: Blair Cash

GEORGE MASON
Fairfax, VA 22030 I

Coach: Jim Larranaga, Providence 1971

2006-07 RESULTS (18-15)

79	Cleveland St.	74
66	Wichita St. ⊠	72
55	Hampton	46
56	Creighton	58
65	Florida Int'l ⊠	39
57	Bucknell †	60
62	Radford	60
53	Duke	69
58	Holy Cross †	46
49	Drexel	61
63	Mississippi St. ⊠	59
63	William & Mary ⊠	67
63	Old Dominion	65
55	UNC Wilmington ⊠	34
73	Towson	44
73	James Madison ⊠	52
76	William & Mary	63
78	Northeastern ⊠	53
62	VCU	75
59	James Madison	41
58	UNC Wilmington	65
89	Delaware ⊠	59
56	Old Dominion ⊠	66
49	VCU	63
60	Hofstra ⊠	68
66	Delaware	46
62	Kent St. ⊠	68
60	Georgia St. ⊠	54
50	Northeastern	73
73	James Madison †	62
64	Hofstra †	61
79	Old Dominion †	63
59	VCU †	65

Nickname: Patriots
Colors: Green & Gold
Arena: Patriot Center
Capacity: 10,000; Year Built: 1985
AD: Thomas J. O'Connor
SID: Richard Coco

GEORGE WASHINGTON
Washington, DC 20052 I

Coach: Karl Hobbs, Connecticut 1985

2006-07 RESULTS (23-9)

70	Boston U.	57
94	Dartmouth ⊠	49
74	Longwood ⊠	60
69	Kennesaw St.	52
67	Providence	86
63	Virginia Tech †	62
79	Md.-East. Shore ⊠	56
65	Southern California †	74
72	UMBC ⊠	51
52	Air Force †	66
75	Colgate †	42
70	Fordham ⊠	59
74	Marshall ⊠	65
84	Massachusetts	91
80	St. Bonaventure ⊠	63
63	Richmond	58
76	Charlotte ⊠	62
74	St. Joseph's ⊠	65
82	Rhode Island	78
69	Dayton	84
53	St. Louis	63
58	Xavier ⊠	87
56	St. Joseph's	62
84	Temple ⊠	72
68	Richmond ⊠	49
86	La Salle	74
62	Charlotte	60
88	Duquesne ⊠	80
58	St. Joseph's †	48
60	St. Louis †	40
78	Rhode Island †	69
44	Vanderbilt †	77

Nickname: Colonials
Colors: Buff & Blue
Arena: Charles E. Smith Athletic Center
Capacity: 5,000; Year Built: 1975
AD: Jack E. Kvancz
SID: Brad Bower

GEORGETOWN
Washington, DC 20057-1121 I

Coach: John Thompson III, Princeton 1988

2006-07 RESULTS (30-7)

69	Hartford ⊠	59
86	Vanderbilt	70
62	Old Dominion ⊠	75
73	Fairfield	60
69	Ball St. ⊠	54
50	Oregon ⊠	57
52	Duke	61
89	James Madison ⊠	53
73	Oral Roberts ⊠	58
76	Winston-Salem ⊠	32
69	Towson ⊠	41
65	Navy ⊠	44
67	Michigan	51
66	Notre Dame ⊠	48
52	Villanova ⊠	56
69	Pittsburgh	74
68	Rutgers	58
74	Seton Hall ⊠	58
66	DePaul ⊠	52
82	Cincinnati ⊠	67
72	St. John's (N.Y.)	48
73	Louisville	65
76	Marquette ⊠	58
71	West Virginia	53
58	Villanova	55
75	Cincinnati	65
61	Pittsburgh ⊠	53
58	Syracuse	72
59	Connecticut ⊠	46
62	Villanova †	57
84	Notre Dame †	82
65	Pittsburgh †	42
80	Belmont †	55
62	Boston College †	55
66	Vanderbilt †	65

Nickname: Hoyas
Colors: Blue & Gray
Arena: Verizon Center
Capacity: 20,600; Year Built: 1997
AD: Bernard Muir
SID: Bill Shapland

| 96 | North Carolina † | 84 |
| 60 | Ohio St. † | 67 |

GEORGIA
Athens, GA 30602-1661 I

Coach: Dennis Felton, Howard 1985

2006-07 RESULTS (19-14)

97	Southern U. ⊠	37
67	Western Ky. ⊠	70
105	Valdosta St. ⊠	74
105	South Carolina St. ⊠	60
80	Alabama A&M ⊠	36
87	Wake Forest	86
96	Gardner-Webb ⊠	67
96	Gonzaga †	83
93	Jacksonville ⊠	77
69	Georgia Tech	78
60	Clemson	75
54	Wisconsin	64
51	Florida	67
80	South Carolina ⊠	56
85	Vanderbilt ⊠	73
67	Arkansas	64
76	Alabama	78
78	Kentucky ⊠	69
57	LSU	54
71	Tennessee	82
61	Vanderbilt	66
61	Florida ⊠	71
73	South Carolina	54
75	Kennesaw St. ⊠	66
86	Auburn ⊠	79
49	Mississippi	67
86	Mississippi St. ⊠	73
70	Kentucky	82
65	Tennessee ⊠	71
80	Auburn †	65
57	Florida †	74
88	Fresno St. ⊠	78
52	Air Force	83

Nickname: Bulldogs
Colors: Red & Black
Arena: Stegeman Coliseum
Capacity: 10,523; Year Built: 1963
AD: Damon Evans
SID: Tim Hix

GCSU
Milledgeville, GA 31061 II

Coach: Terry Sellers, Aub.-Montgomery 1976

2006-07 RESULTS (19-10)

61	Livingstone †	51
82	Catawba	74
96	S.C.-Aiken ⊠	82
80	Morehouse †	76
84	West Ga. †	71
73	Lander ⊠	56
127	Carver Bible ⊠	74
58	Presbyterian	71
88	Presbyterian ⊠	77
68	Ferris St. †	61
50	Southern Ark. †	40
64	Armstrong Atlantic	66
53	Lander	67
70	Augusta St. ⊠	83
66	UNC Pembroke	37
68	Ga. Southwestern ⊠	53
93	S.C.-Aiken	81
45	Augusta St.	76
66	S.C. Upstate ⊠	62
71	Ga. Southwestern	58
86	North Georgia ⊠	63
103	Columbus St.	104
44	Clayton St. ⊠	60

GA. SOUTHERN
Statesboro, GA 30460-8086 I

53	Armstrong Atlantic ⊠	62
95	Francis Marion	64
81	Columbus St. ⊠	87
64	Clayton St.	62
68	UNC Pembroke †	53
82	Augusta St. †	91

Nickname: Bobcats
Colors: Navy Blue & Hunter Green
Arena: Centennial Center
Capacity: 4,071; Year Built: 1989
AD: Stan Aldridge
SID: Brad Muller

Coach: Jeff Price, Pikeville 1981

2006-07 RESULTS (15-16)

116	UC Davis †	73
48	Duke	72
50	Illinois	85
70	Winston-Salem ⊠	41
61	Mercer	59
59	Winston-Salem	49
72	Northern Ill. †	70
75	Drake	87
101	Flagler ⊠	67
84	Appalachian St.	87
60	Clemson	72
47	UNC Greensboro ⊠	68
89	Pikeville ⊠	68
72	Furman ⊠	70
83	Wofford ⊠	78
58	Chattanooga	67
69	Citadel	74
64	Col. of Charleston	67
92	Davidson	101
68	Elon	67
62	UNC Greensboro	65
57	Chattanooga ⊠	62
55	Appalachian St. ⊠	77
57	Western Caro.	69
57	Furman	55
67	Elon ⊠	70
81	Citadel ⊠	62
68	Wofford	46
74	Col. of Charleston ⊠	65
62	Citadel †	46
66	Col. of Charleston †	77

Nickname: Eagles
Colors: Blue & White
Arena: Hanner Fieldhouse
Capacity: 4,378; Year Built: 1969
AD: Samuel Q. Baker
SID: Matt Horne

GA. SOUTHWESTERN
Americus, GA 31709-4693 II

Coach: Michael Leeder, Florida St. 1992

2006-07 RESULTS (16-13)

69	Albany St. (Ga.)	68
100	Carver Bible ⊠	72
73	West Ala. †	64
59	Valdosta St.	66
42	Virginia St. ⊠	66
74	Dist. Columbia ⊠	51
80	Fort Valley St. ⊠	65
56	Clark Atlanta	54
74	Southern Conn. St. †	72
72	Rollins	82
64	Clayton St. ⊠	67
43	S.C. Upstate	57
72	Columbus St. ⊠	81
78	North Georgia	64
53	GCSU	68
68	Francis Marion ⊠	56
81	Columbus St.	64
66	Lander ⊠	74
58	GCSU ⊠	71
48	UNC Pembroke	51
56	Armstrong Atlantic	59
76	Augusta St. ⊠	85

58	Clayton St.	55
70	S.C.-Aiken ⊠	49
76	Armstrong Atlantic ⊠	64
81	Augusta St.	72
70	Pitt.-Johnstown †	61
60	Central St. (Ohio) †	72
76	North Georgia †	66

Nickname: Hurricanes
Colors: Navy & Gold
Arena: Storm Dome
Capacity: 1,500
AD: A. Randolph Barksdale
SID: To be named

GEORGIA ST.

Atlanta, GA 30302-3975 I

Coach: Michael Perry, Richmond 1981

2006-07 RESULTS (11-20)

66	Col. of Charleston ⊠	72
74	Georgia Tech	103
94	Winston-Salem ⊠	87
70	Alabama St. ⊠	59
63	Charlotte	72
70	Savannah St. ⊠	60
59	Hofstra	62
55	Florida St. ⊠	87
64	Alabama St.	56
59	Iowa	101
57	Clemson	67
55	Drexel ⊠	61
87	Towson ⊠	81
43	William & Mary ⊠	57
69	Northeastern	84
59	UNC Wilmington	54
61	Delaware	44
52	James Madison ⊠	59
63	Hofstra ⊠	76
65	William & Mary	81
57	Old Dominion	92
72	UNC Wilmington ⊠	60
71	VCU	100
55	Old Dominion ⊠	68
65	Towson	92
71	Northeastern ⊠	65
63	Elon ⊠	53
54	George Mason	60
70	VCU ⊠	72
70	William & Mary †	68
60	VCU †	73

Nickname: Panthers
Colors: Blue & White
Arena: GSU Sports Arena
Capacity: 4,500; Year Built: 1972
AD: Mary A. McElroy
SID: Charlie Taylor

GEORGIA TECH

Atlanta, GA 30332-0455 I

Coach: Paul Hewitt, St. John Fisher 1985

2006-07 RESULTS (20-12)

83	Elon ⊠	49
100	Jackson St. ⊠	70
103	Georgia St. ⊠	74
79	Purdue †	61
92	Memphis †	85
73	UCLA †	88
77	Penn St. ⊠	73
82	Miami (Fla.)	90
64	Vanderbilt	73
92	Centenary (La.) ⊠	52
78	Georgia ⊠	69
85	Troy ⊠	55
87	St. Francis (Pa.) ⊠	43
97	Winston-Salem ⊠	46
74	Clemson	75
74	Duke ⊠	63
88	Florida St. ⊠	80
61	North Carolina	77
65	Maryland	80
65	Virginia Tech ⊠	73
75	Wake Forest	85
80	Clemson ⊠	62
74	North Carolina St. ⊠	65
65	Connecticut †	52
63	Florida St.	57
62	Duke	71
75	Wake Forest ⊠	61
69	Virginia	75
84	North Carolina ⊠	77
74	Boston College ⊠	60
112	Wake Forest †	114
63	UNLV †	67

Nickname: Yellow Jackets
Colors: Old Gold & White
Arena: Alexander Memorial Coliseum
Capacity: 9,191; Year Built: 1956
AD: Dan Radakovich
SID: Mike Stamus

GETTYSBURG

Gettysburg, PA 17325-1668 III

Coach: George Petrie, Lebanon Valley 1972

2006-07 RESULTS (13-13)

55	Otterbein ⊠	56
77	Wesley ⊠	67
42	York (Pa.) ⊠	58
48	Frank. & Marsh.	67
52	Haverford	53
60	Ursinus ⊠	65
51	McDaniel ⊠	54
64	Union (N.Y.) †	49
61	Methodist †	71
64	Elizabethtown	70
64	Muhlenberg ⊠	67
70	Washington (Md.)	55
52	Swarthmore	49
65	Haverford ⊠	60
68	Dickinson ⊠	42
65	McDaniel	71
67	Johns Hopkins	83
71	Muhlenberg	64
67	Frank. & Marsh. ⊠	66
88	Washington (Md.) ⊠	51
73	Ursinus	85
60	Swarthmore ⊠	49
65	Johns Hopkins ⊠	58
71	Dickinson	65
60	Muhlenberg ⊠	51
73	Johns Hopkins	80

Nickname: Bullets
Colors: Orange & Blue
Arena: Bream Gymnasium
Capacity: 3,000; Year Built: 1962
AD: David Wright
SID: Eric Lawrence

GLENVILLE ST.

Glenville, WV 26351 II

Coach: Dwaine Osborne

2006-07 RESULTS (6-22)

74	West Va. Wesleyan †	70
95	Ohio St.-Newark †	85
84	Slippery Rock ⊠	82
79	Elizabeth City St.	87
68	Tusculum	81
89	West Liberty St. ⊠	107
80	Southern Ind.	108
75	Ky. Wesleyan	86
105	Pfeiffer ⊠	112
87	Elizabeth City St. ⊠	93
77	Alderson-Broaddus	97
89	West Va. Wesleyan	92
70	Davis & Elkins ⊠	77
80	Bluefield St.	92
87	Ohio Valley	98
90	Concord ⊠	98
49	Fairmont St.	86
78	Wheeling Jesuit ⊠	93
72	Alderson-Broaddus ⊠	98
62	Shepherd	94
66	Salem Int'l	77
70	West Va. Wesleyan ⊠	63
92	West Virginia St. ⊠	107
93	Concord	116
60	Charleston (W.V.) ⊠	82
76	Bluefield St. ⊠	75
71	Davis & Elkins	69
73	Concord	78

Nickname: Pioneers
Colors: Royal Blue & White
Arena: Jesse Lilly Gym
Capacity: 1,600; Year Built: 1950
AD: Steven Harold
SID: Dwaine Osborne

GOLDEY-BEACOM

Wilmington, DE 19808 II

Coach: Chuck Hammond, Philadelphia U. 1999

2006-07 RESULTS (15-13)

70	Tampa	76
64	Eckerd †	76
73	Molloy	72
82	NYIT ⊠	76
56	Dominican (N.Y.) ⊠	59
67	Phila. Sciences	76
67	Felician ⊠	62
81	Bloomfield ⊠	64
57	Davis & Elkins	72
67	Philadelphia U.	90
64	Nyack	52
58	Post	59
56	Caldwell ⊠	51
55	Holy Family ⊠	53
60	Dominican (N.Y.)	58
85	Wilmington (Del.)	79
73	Davis & Elkins ⊠	66
74	Bloomfield	78
68	Phila. Sciences ⊠	55
66	Nyack ⊠	82
88	Felician	92
72	Philadelphia U. ⊠	55
68	Post ⊠	59
58	Holy Family	70
54	Wilmington (Del.) ⊠	49
52	Caldwell	53
65	Caldwell ⊠	74
86	Molloy ⊠	70

Nickname: Lightning
Colors: Navy, Gold & White
Arena: MBNA America Hall Gymnasium
Capacity: 1,000; Year Built: 1998
AD: Chris Morgan
SID: Jennifer Smith

GONZAGA

Spokane, WA 99258-0066 I

Coach: Mark Few, Oregon 1987

2006-07 RESULTS (23-11)

90	Eastern Wash. ⊠	75
88	Rice †	50
78	Baylor †	69
92	UTSA ⊠	48
82	North Carolina †	74
71	Butler †	79
76	Idaho ⊠	51
69	Portland St. ⊠	51
87	Texas †	77
67	Washington St.	77
97	Washington ⊠	77
83	Georgia †	96
54	Duke †	61
74	Nevada †	82
87	Virginia	108
97	Loyola Marymount ⊠	62
69	Pepperdine ⊠	52
77	Santa Clara	69
75	St. Mary's (Cal.)	80
80	Portland	68
72	San Francisco ⊠	56
91	San Diego ⊠	82
90	Stanford	86
82	Pepperdine	57
61	Loyola Marymount	67
60	St. Mary's (Cal.) ⊠	49
73	Santa Clara ⊠	84
77	Memphis ⊠	78
87	Portland ⊠	67
86	San Francisco	79
74	San Diego	64
88	San Diego †	70
77	Santa Clara †	68
57	Indiana †	70

Nickname: Bulldogs, Zags
Colors: Blue, White & Red
Arena: McCarthey Athletic Center
Capacity: 6,000; Year Built: 2004
AD: Michael L. Roth
SID: Oliver Pierce

GORDON

Wenham, MA 01984-1899 III

Coach: Mike Schauer, Wheaton (Ill.) 1993

2006-07 RESULTS (19-8)

89	Mount Ida ⊠	72
78	MIT ⊠	71
79	Phila. Biblical	76
92	Mitchell ⊠	54
79	Wentworth Inst. ⊠	62
89	New England Col.	76
70	Salem St. ⊠	76
53	Husson	70
87	Northwestern (Minn.) ⊠	82
67	Roger Williams	77
83	Colby-Sawyer ⊠	63
86	New England Col. ⊠	60
68	Salve Regina	51
63	Wentworth Inst.	76
72	Eastern Nazarene ⊠	58
73	Endicott ⊠	69
69	Newbury	70
74	Nichols ⊠	66
66	New England	33
77	Curry	53
74	Bates ⊠	82
59	Colby-Sawyer	56
61	Endicott	62
74	Anna Maria ⊠	52
76	New England ⊠	38
63	Salve Regina ⊠	56
68	Wentworth Inst. ⊠	69

Nickname: Fighting Scots
Colors: Cyan & White
Arena: Bennett Center
Capacity: 2,300; Year Built: 1996
AD: Joe Hakes
SID: Patrick Byrne

GOUCHER

Baltimore, MD 21204-2794 III

Coach: Leonard Trevino, Texas Tech 1987

2006-07 RESULTS (7-18)

77	Maryland Bible ⊠	59
77	Frostburg St.	72
69	Johns Hopkins ⊠	85
68	McDaniel ⊠	76
55	York (Pa.) ⊠	69
68	Catholic	62
67	Salisbury ⊠	73
83	Marymount (Va.)	76
62	Lebanon Valley	74
38	Robert Morris	83
79	Mt. St. Mary (N.Y.) †	60
62	Ozarks (Mo.) †	67
75	Gallaudet ⊠	68
65	Hood	73
59	Mary Washington ⊠	87
80	St. Mary's (Md.) ⊠	86
78	York (Pa.)	91
49	Catholic ⊠	80

65	Salisbury	80
67	Marymount (Va.) ⊠	70
85	Gallaudet	67
74	Hood ⊠	78
59	Mary Washington	100
73	St. Mary's (Md.)	87
72	Hood	82

Nickname: Gophers
Colors: Blue & Gold
Arena: Sports/Recreation Center
Capacity: 1,200; Year Built: 1991
AD: Geoffrey Miller
SID: Mike Sanders

GRAMBLING
Grambling, LA 71245 I

Coach: Larry Wright, Grambling 1982

2006-07 RESULTS (12-14)

69	Texas Col. ⊠	67
61	Houston	96
46	TCU	64
69	Baylor	95
49	Dayton	58
68	Jarvis Christian ⊠	64
27	Texas A&M	101
63	Alabama A&M	52
66	Alabama St.	76
70	Southern U. ⊠	67
61	Alcorn St. ⊠	58
66	Prairie View	52
47	Texas Southern	55
77	Jackson St. ⊠	74
74	Ark.-Pine Bluff	68
78	Mississippi Val. ⊠	84
43	Southern U.	76
83	Alcorn St.	76
87	Prairie View ⊠	73
68	Texas Southern ⊠	76
57	Jackson St.	66
68	Ark.-Pine Bluff	72
55	Mississippi Val.	64
93	Alabama A&M ⊠	69
76	Alabama St. ⊠	70
48	Ark.-Pine Bluff †	51

Nickname: Tigers
Colors: Black & Gold
Arena: Tiger Memorial Gym
Capacity: 4,500; Year Built: 1954
AD: Troy A. Mathieu
SID: Ryan McGinty

GRAND CANYON
Phoenix, AZ 85017 II

Coach: Scott Mossman, Mid-America Naz. 1982

2006-07 RESULTS (21-8)

75	Western N.M.	82
64	UC San Diego ⊠	62
80	St. Martin's †	60
67	Western Wash.	77
79	Western N.M. ⊠	63
78	Dallas Baptist	64
60	Cal St. San B'dino	104
69	Cal St. Dom. Hills ⊠	70
54	Hawaii Pacific	49
58	Hawaii Pacific	50
73	BYU-Hawaii	79
123	S'western (Ariz.)	60
73	Hawaii-Hilo	60
89	Hawaii-Hilo ⊠	91
86	Chaminade ⊠	72
83	Notre Dame de Namur	77
51	Notre Dame de Namur	49
81	Dixie St. ⊠	90
89	BYU-Hawaii	79
78	BYU-Hawaii ⊠	67
61	Hawaii Pacific ⊠	47
56	Chaminade	54
71	Chaminade	68
72	Hawaii-Hilo	64
98	Dallas Baptist ⊠	61

82	Notre Dame de Namur ⊠	62
80	Notre Dame de Namur ⊠	68
87	Seattle Pacific †	65
81	Humboldt St. †	95

Nickname: Antelopes
Colors: Purple, Black & White
Arena: Antelope Gym
Capacity: 2,000; Year Built: 1994
AD: Keith Baker
SID: Cory Hitchcock

GRAND VALLEY ST.
Allendale, MI 49401 II

Coach: Ric Wesley, Central Mich. 1980

2006-07 RESULTS (29-5)

81	Davenport ⊠	52
74	Upper Iowa ⊠	40
56	Christian Bros. †	47
86	Mo.-St. Louis	57
71	Saginaw Valley ⊠	72
72	Northwood (Mich.)	53
70	Ferris St. ⊠	63
74	Mercyhurst	79
57	Lewis	38
89	Rochester College ⊠	67
59	Montevallo †	58
62	Fla. Southern	42
48	Michigan Tech ⊠	43
87	Northern Mich. ⊠	49
63	Lake Superior St.	33
63	Northern Mich.	52
79	Marygrove ⊠	40
61	Gannon	49
54	Wayne St. (Mich.) ⊠	44
79	Ashland	38
82	Lake Superior St. ⊠	48
74	Northwood (Mich.) ⊠	49
62	Findlay	76
69	Michigan Tech	64
87	Hillsdale	64
76	Saginaw Valley	71
75	Ferris St.	68
72	Ferris St. ⊠	59
88	Northern Mich. †	87
61	Findlay	71
85	Quincy †	75
90	Southern Ind. †	83
66	Northern Ky. †	42
81	Barton †	83

Nickname: Lakers
Colors: Blue, Black & White
Arena: Grand Valley Field House
Capacity: 4,010; Year Built: 1982
AD: Tim W. Selgo
SID: Tim Nott

GREEN MOUNTAIN
Poultney, VT 05764 II

Coach: Todd Montana, Ithaca 2001

2006-07 RESULTS (2-22)

57	Potsdam St.	82
55	Castleton †	86
57	Southern Vt. ⊠	73
57	Johnson St.	70
56	Morrisville St.	89
48	Hartwick	72
61	Fisher	76
59	Paul Smith	58
62	Centenary (N.J.) ⊠	73
47	Middlebury	102
41	Newbury ⊠	62
63	Mitchell	91
62	Lyndon St. ⊠	71
49	Mount Ida	57
59	Eastern Conn. St.	85
66	Vermont Tech	78
67	Mass. Liberal Arts	91
46	Albany Pharmacy	70
85	Life (Ga.) †	63
49	Mt. St. Vincent	70
75	Me.-Presque Isle ⊠	77

49	Castleton ⊠	71
42	Morrisville St. ⊠	71
60	Mitchell ⊠	64

Nickname: Eagles
Colors: Green & Gold
AD: Jamey Ventura
SID: To be named

GREENSBORO
Greensboro, NC 27401-1875....... III

Coach: Bryan Galuski, Eckerd 1998

2006-07 RESULTS (20-7)

81	Piedmont †	71
65	Huntingdon †	56
85	Apprentice	72
74	Guilford †	78
76	East. Mennonite †	68
68	Bridgewater (Va.)	52
69	Fisk ⊠	65
66	John Carroll ⊠	63
85	Oswego St. †	82
83	Fisk †	75
49	Maryville (Tenn.) ⊠	62
86	Southern Va.	88
62	Methodist	47
79	Averett ⊠	55
68	Ferrum	79
91	N.C. Wesleyan ⊠	80
83	Southern Va. ⊠	60
65	Shenandoah ⊠	52
65	Chris. Newport ⊠	67
68	Methodist ⊠	60
79	Averett	83
94	Ferrum †	84
78	N.C. Wesleyan ⊠	62
77	Shenandoah	67
96	Chris. Newport	86
86	Shenandoah †	75
76	N.C. Wesleyan †	84

Nickname: The Pride
Colors: Green, White & Silver
Arena: Hanes Gymnasium
Capacity: 850; Year Built: 1964
AD: Kim A. Strable
SID: Bob Lowe

GREENVILLE
Greenville, IL 62246.......................... III

Coach: George Barber, Asbury 1986

2006-07 RESULTS (13-12)

74	Concordia (Ill.) †	82
74	Dominican (Ill.) †	80
59	McKendree	82
96	Logan Chiropractic ⊠	57
88	Blackburn	75
79	Fontbonne ⊠	77
80	Robert Morris-S'fiel ⊠	90
78	Harris-Stowe ⊠	80
91	Principia ⊠	58
61	Maryville (Mo.)	58
88	MacMurray ⊠	86
93	Lincoln Christian ⊠	62
76	Webster	93
78	Eureka	90
67	Westminster (Mo.)	75
70	Blackburn ⊠	74
75	Fontbonne	90
72	Maryville (Mo.) ⊠	70
96	Principia	89
85	Webster ⊠	80
78	MacMurray	86
74	Lincoln Christian	71
90	St. Louis Pharmacy	80
88	Eureka ⊠	92
85	Westminster (Mo.) ⊠	77

Nickname: Panthers
Colors: Orange & Black
Arena: H.J. Long Gymnasium
Capacity: 2,000; Year Built: 1960
AD: Doug Faulkner
SID: B.J. Schneck

GRINNELL
Grinnell, IA 50112.......................... III

Coach: David Arseneault, Colby 1976

2006-07 RESULTS (17-7)

106	Carthage ⊠	118
136	MacMurray ⊠	116
134	Carroll (Wis.)	136
97	St. Norbert	122
143	Monmouth (Ill.) ⊠	125
139	Simpson ⊠	127
90	Wis.-Whitewater †	126
124	Kalamazoo †	104
105	Wis.-Oshkosh	123
79	Lake Forest	80
125	Milwaukee Engr. ⊠	106
142	Lawrence ⊠	130
98	Beloit ⊠	79
120	Ripon	118
106	Lawrence	103
90	Knox ⊠	70
116	Illinois Col.	105
127	Monmouth (Ill.)	111
113	Carroll (Wis.) ⊠	104
93	St. Norbert ⊠	66
100	Lake Forest ⊠	65
91	Knox	74
109	Illinois Col. ⊠	86
79	Lake Forest ⊠	94

Nickname: Pioneers
Colors: Scarlet & Black
Arena: Darby Gym
Capacity: 1,250; Year Built: 2005
AD: Dee Fairchild
SID: Steven Phelps

GROVE CITY
Grove City, PA 16127-2104 III

Coach: Steve Lamie, Grove City 1985

2006-07 RESULTS (16-13)

75	Allegheny †	78
52	Carnegie Mellon †	70
69	Penn St.-Altoona ⊠	59
74	Geneva	64
51	Juniata	61
82	Waynesburg ⊠	89
76	Kenyon	70
93	Hiram ⊠	97
82	Cincinnati-Clermont †	87
87	Wright St.-Lake †	77
65	Case Reserve ⊠	57
63	Bethany (W.V.)	75
57	Thiel	71
63	St. Vincent	62
68	Penn St.-Beaver ⊠	58
101	Westminster (Pa.)	91
49	Thomas More	48
74	Wash. & Jeff. ⊠	59
86	Waynesburg	75
65	Thiel ⊠	56
72	Bethany (W.V.) ⊠	58
59	Westminster (Pa.) ⊠	71
74	St. Vincent	84
84	Wash. & Jeff.	87
101	Thomas More ⊠	65
89	Waynesburg ⊠	60
86	Westminster (Pa.)	67
60	Wash. & Jeff.	58
46	Penn St.-Behrend	76

Nickname: Wolverines
Colors: Crimson and White
Arena: College Arena
Capacity: 1,800; Year Built: 1953
AD: Donald L. Lyle
SID: Ryan Briggs

GUILFORD
Greensboro, NC 27410-4173.........III

Coach: Tom Palombo, Va. Wesleyan 1989

2006-07 RESULTS (24-5)

101	Robert Morris-Chi. †	77
91	Sewanee †	78
78	Greensboro †	74
102	Lynchburg ⊠	80
66	Hampden-Sydney	63
77	Roanoke	67
70	Shenandoah ⊠	58
108	Methodist ⊠	102
74	Averett	69
80	Randolph-Macon	73
55	Va. Wesleyan	75
130	Emory & Henry ⊠	114
68	Roanoke	72
70	Bridgewater (Va.) ⊠	66
79	East. Mennonite ⊠	69
76	Randolph-Macon ⊠	65
69	Va. Wesleyan ⊠	72
62	Wash. & Lee	61
95	Lynchburg	70
86	Hampden-Sydney ⊠	72
74	Bridgewater (Va.)	52
84	East. Mennonite	75
95	Wash. & Lee ⊠	77
108	Emory & Henry	107
78	Bridgewater (Va.) †	88
101	Manhattanville †	81
80	Johns Hopkins	73
129	Lincoln (Pa.) †	128
71	Va. Wesleyan	81

Nickname: Quakers
Colors: Crimson & Gray
Arena: Ragan-Brown Field House
   Capacity: 2,500; Year Built: 1980
AD: Marion Kirby
SID: Dave Walters

GUST. ADOLPHUS
Saint Peter, MN 56082-1498.........III

Coach: Mark Hanson, Gust. Adolphus 1983

2006-07 RESULTS (14-13)

76	Luther	68
70	Buena Vista ⊠	78
58	Carthage ⊠	63
77	Macalester ⊠	72
84	Augsburg ⊠	67
78	Bethel (Minn.)	77
54	St. John's (Minn.) ⊠	63
91	Minn.-Morris ⊠	58
85	Bethany Lutheran	87
77	St. Mary's (Minn.)	70
58	Concordia-M'head	63
57	St. Thomas (Minn.)	74
73	Hamline ⊠	50
60	St. Olaf	57
53	Carleton ⊠	66
79	Macalester	70
69	Augsburg	56
66	Bethel (Minn.) ⊠	72
66	St. John's (Minn.)	100
72	St. Mary's (Minn.) ⊠	61
80	Concordia-M'head ⊠	57
80	St. Thomas (Minn.) ⊠	74
78	Hamline	79
52	St. Olaf ⊠	58
65	Carleton	71
70	Carleton ⊠	59
65	St. John's (Minn.)	87

Nickname: Golden Gusties
Colors: Black & Gold
Arena: Gus Young Court
   Capacity: 3,000; Year Built: 1984
AD: Alan Molde
SID: Tim Kennedy

GWYNEDD-MERCY
Gwynedd Valley, PA 19437-0901 III

Coach: John Baron, York (Pa.) 1995

2006-07 RESULTS (14-13)

80	Emmanuel (Mass.)	77
76	New Jersey City †	91
77	Eastern	61
70	Misericordia ⊠	66
77	Marywood	80
61	Immaculata	56
76	Rowan	92
62	Elmhurst †	79
44	North Central (Ill.) †	66
57	Richard Stockton ⊠	68
93	Delaware Valley	84
76	Immaculata ⊠	64
71	Neumann	67
88	Wesley ⊠	87
84	Cabrini	71
59	Eastern ⊠	65
101	Marywood ⊠	54
48	Arcadia	71
57	Alvernia ⊠	54
70	Misericordia	78
61	Alvernia	64
75	Neumann ⊠	90
69	Arcadia	61
72	Wesley	65
74	Cabrini ⊠	73
59	Immaculata ⊠	65
77	DeSales	88

Nickname: Griffins
Colors: Cardinal & Gold
Arena: Griffin Complex
   Capacity: 1,200; Year Built: 1991
AD: Keith Mondillo
SID: Chris Panter

HAMILTON
Clinton, NY 13323.............III

Coach: Tobin Anderson, Wesleyan (Conn.) 1995

2006-07 RESULTS (19-7)

78	Hartwick ⊠	67
75	Norwich ⊠	67
97	Medgar Evers ⊠	70
68	Utica ⊠	64
79	Wesleyan (Conn.) ⊠	76
84	Middlebury ⊠	86
60	Haverford †	51
85	DePauw †	77
75	Brockport St.	94
91	Hobart	67
59	Clarkson ⊠	65
81	St. Lawrence ⊠	74
79	Union (N.Y.)	59
84	Skidmore ⊠	88
61	Williams	63
64	Rensselaer ⊠	58
82	Vassar	76
78	Skidmore ⊠	47
63	Union (N.Y.) ⊠	58
76	St. Lawrence	68
71	Clarkson	60
86	Hobart ⊠	87
85	Vassar ⊠	70
86	Rensselaer	64
74	Union (N.Y.) ⊠	62
64	St. Lawrence	65

Nickname: Continentals
Colors: Buff & Blue
Arena: Margaret Bundy Scott Field House
   Capacity: 2,500; Year Built: 1978
AD: Susan Viscomi
SID: Jim Taylor

HAMLINE
St. Paul, MN 55104.............III

Coach: Barry Wohler, Minnesota 1982

2006-07 RESULTS (8-17)

91	Colorado Col. †	84
71	Colorado St.-Pueblo	86
78	Northwestern (Minn.)	79
89	Bethel (Minn.) ⊠	93
66	St. Thomas (Minn.) ⊠	81
87	St. Mary's (Minn.) ⊠	89
47	Minn. St. Mankato	76
73	St. Olaf	67
85	St. Scholastica ⊠	81
45	Augsburg	65
65	Concordia-M'head	84
75	Carleton ⊠	70
50	Gust. Adolphus	73
83	St. John's (Minn.)	92
77	Macalester	79
70	St. Olaf ⊠	66
68	Bethel (Minn.)	83
71	St. Thomas (Minn.)	90
70	St. Mary's (Minn.)	84
85	Augsburg ⊠	84
74	Concordia-M'head ⊠	66
61	Carleton	98
79	Gust. Adolphus ⊠	78
61	St. John's (Minn.)	97
72	Macalester ⊠	84

Nickname: Pipers
Colors: Burgundy & Gray
Arena: Hutton Arena
   Capacity: 2,000; Year Built: 1937
AD: Dan O'Brien
SID: Troy Mallat

HAMPDEN-SYDNEY
Hampden-Sydney, VA 23943.......III

Coach: Ryan "Bubba" Smith, Furman 2000

2006-07 RESULTS (19-11)

87	Roberts Wesleyan †	85
93	Westminster (Pa.)	84
59	Averett ⊠	66
77	Ferrum ⊠	64
113	Emory & Henry	102
63	Guilford ⊠	66
60	Va. Wesleyan ⊠	78
81	N.C. Wesleyan	69
69	Shenandoah ⊠	70
120	New Jersey City ⊠	113
91	Bridgewater (Va.) ⊠	88
78	East. Mennonite	55
59	Randolph-Macon	60
90	Lynchburg ⊠	63
66	Wash. & Lee ⊠	58
65	Roanoke	62
49	Va. Wesleyan	75
58	Bridgewater (Va.)	61
74	East. Mennonite ⊠	67
100	Emory & Henry ⊠	108
72	Guilford	86
71	Wash. & Lee	60
79	Roanoke ⊠	80
80	Lynchburg	68
82	Randolph-Macon ⊠	53
102	Emory & Henry †	100
70	Va. Wesleyan †	67
77	Roanoke	62
68	Hood †	65
51	Va. Wesleyan	61

Nickname: Tigers
Colors: Garnet & Gray
Arena: S. Douglas Fleet Gym
   Capacity: 2,500; Year Built: 1979
AD: Joseph E. Bush
SID: Donnie Turlington

HAMPTON
Hampton, VA 23668.............I

Coach: Kevin Nickelberry, Va. Wesleyan 1986

2006-07 RESULTS (15-16)

75	Maryland	102
74	New Orleans †	73
47	Holy Cross	62
49	UMBC ⊠	56
46	George Mason ⊠	55
51	VCU	74
72	Norfolk St.	74
71	UNC Greensboro ⊠	64
84	Howard †	95
69	Virginia	91
89	St. Bonaventure	74
67	William & Mary	72
59	Bethune-Cookman	55
76	Florida A&M	74
70	Morgan St.	75
77	Coppin St. ⊠	69
64	Delaware St.	75
80	Longwood	59
63	South Carolina St.	74
70	N.C. A&T	64
67	Bethune-Cookman ⊠	45
74	Florida A&M ⊠	72
67	Morgan St.	65
71	Coppin St.	56
74	Delaware St. ⊠	81
66	Norfolk St. ⊠	52
60	South Carolina St. ⊠	61
76	N.C. A&T ⊠	79
71	Md.-East. Shore ⊠	58
76	Howard †	61
58	Florida A&M †	61

Nickname: Pirates
Colors: Royal Blue & White
Arena: Convocation Center
   Capacity: 7,200; Year Built: 1993
AD: Joseph Taylor
SID: Jamar Ross

HANOVER
Hanover, IN 47243-0108.............III

Coach: Mike Beitzel, Wooster 1968

2006-07 RESULTS (14-11)

78	Maryville (Mo.) †	64
82	Webster †	84
90	Wabash	85
100	Cincinnati-Clermont ⊠	70
83	Albion	69
84	Franklin	90
72	Rose-Hulman ⊠	71
101	Mt. St. Joseph ⊠	68
72	Defiance	81
65	Ill. Wesleyan ⊠	84
116	Westminster (Pa.) ⊠	90
83	Mt. Vernon Naz. †	121
85	Loras †	91
74	Manchester ⊠	66
72	Anderson (Ind.) ⊠	69
83	Bluffton	94
71	Transylvania	70
56	Rose-Hulman	61
58	Franklin ⊠	73
80	Defiance ⊠	83
59	Mt. St. Joseph	58
77	Anderson (Ind.)	74
83	Manchester	73
47	Transylvania ⊠	64
82	Bluffton ⊠	68

Nickname: Panthers
Colors: Red & Blue
Arena: John Collier Arena
   Capacity: 2,000; Year Built: 1995
AD: Lynn Hall
SID: Carter Cloyd

HARDIN-SIMMONS
Abilene, TX 79698 III

Coach: Dylan Howard, UAB 1989

2006-07 RESULTS (16-12)

56	Southwestern (Tex.)	58
86	East Tex. Baptist	63
60	LeTourneau	61
90	Louisiana Col.	74
67	Mississippi Col. ⊠	70
64	McMurry ⊠	63
86	Ozarks (Ark.)	79
60	Trinity (Tex.) ⊠	67
69	Ripon †	80
61	Va. Wesleyan †	67
75	Texas-Dallas ⊠	56
77	Texas-Tyler ⊠	70
85	Concordia (Tex.)	97
61	Mary Hardin-Baylor	72
89	Schreiner	74
66	Texas Lutheran ⊠	60
53	McMurry	67
95	Howard Payne ⊠	70
84	Sul Ross St. ⊠	58
77	Howard Payne	69
49	Sul Ross St.	53
86	Schreiner	64
70	Texas Lutheran	66
99	Concordia (Tex.) ⊠	71
72	Mary Hardin-Baylor ⊠	75
74	LeTourneau †	65
71	Mary Hardin-Baylor †	67
64	Mississippi Col.	77

Nickname: Cowboys
Colors: Purple & Gold
Arena: Mabee Complex
Capacity: 3,003; Year Built: 1979
AD: John Neese
SID: Chad Grubbs

HARDING
Searcy, AR 72149-2281 II

Coach: Jeff Morgan, West Tex. A&M 1989

2006-07 RESULTS (17-12)

91	St. Edward's	89
70	Incarnate Word †	79
68	Ala.-Huntsville ⊠	55
109	Ecclesia ⊠	50
94	Texas Col. ⊠	71
103	North Ala. ⊠	96
97	Champion Bapt. ⊠	44
68	North Ala.	79
57	Ala.-Huntsville	71
82	Drury ⊠	85
72	BYU-Hawaii †	75
65	Hawaii Pacific	67
99	Central Baptist ⊠	78
87	Ark.-Monticello ⊠	76
65	Delta St. ⊠	78
76	Ouachita Baptist	77
77	Arkansas Tech	69
58	Henderson St. ⊠	60
65	Southern Ark. ⊠	55
64	Christian Bros.	52
79	Ark.-Monticello ⊠	70
83	Delta St.	87
77	Ouachita Baptist ⊠	68
86	Arkansas Tech ⊠	74
58	Henderson St.	55
64	Southern Ark.	61
71	Christian Bros. ⊠	76
73	Valdosta St. †	72
71	Henderson St. †	76

Nickname: Bisons
Colors: Black & Gold
Arena: Rhodes Fieldhouse
Capacity: 3,000; Year Built: 1949
AD: Greg Harnden
SID: Scott Goode

HARTFORD
West Hartford, CT 06117-1599 I

Coach: Dan Leibovitz, Penn 1996

2006-07 RESULTS (13-18)

59	Georgetown	69
64	Towson	78
53	Army	62
60	Dartmouth ⊠	50
63	Cornell	61
64	Long Island ⊠	49
55	Penn St.	56
76	Monmouth	75
66	Yale	65
58	St. Francis (N.Y.) ⊠	52
82	Brown	95
71	Canisius ⊠	81
62	Maine	60
80	Boston U. ⊠	75
59	New Hampshire	72
50	Stony Brook ⊠	47
55	Binghamton ⊠	57
68	UMBC	73
67	Albany (N.Y.)	80
63	Vermont ⊠	76
64	Maine ⊠	65
60	Boston College	94
51	Boston U.	59
55	Albany (N.Y.) ⊠	61
62	New Hampshire ⊠	46
59	Stony Brook	44
62	UMBC ⊠	54
53	Binghamton	55
73	Vermont	90
49	Stony Brook †	47
62	Vermont †	81

Nickname: Hawks
Colors: Scarlet & White
Arena: Chase Arena at Reich Family Pavilion
Capacity: 3,977; Year Built: 1990
AD: Patricia H. Meiser
SID: David Longolucco

HARTWICK
Oneonta, NY 13820-4020 III

Coach: Paul Culpo, St. Michael's 1993

2006-07 RESULTS (10-15)

67	Hamilton	78
63	New England †	40
87	Mass. Liberal Arts	78
84	Maritime (N.Y.) ⊠	63
62	Skidmore	56
68	Elms	73
72	Green Mountain ⊠	48
81	Bard ⊠	54
57	Oneonta St.	49
61	Scranton ⊠	85
54	Utica	72
59	Vassar	65
57	Ithaca	74
62	Elmira	74
48	St. John Fisher ⊠	65
58	Alfred ⊠	74
87	Nazareth	92
86	Rochester Inst.	82
59	Utica ⊠	71
73	Elmira ⊠	53
53	Ithaca ⊠	62
73	Rochester Inst. ⊠	69
73	Nazareth ⊠	81
55	Alfred	76
49	St. John Fisher	73

Nickname: Hawks
Colors: Royal Blue & White
Arena: Binder Gymnasium
Capacity: 1,800; Year Built: 1968
AD: Debra P. Warren
SID: April Raynovich

HARVARD
Boston, MA 02163 I

Coach: Frank Sullivan, Westfield St. 1973

2006-07 RESULTS (12-16)

75	Maine ⊠	71
74	Boston U. ⊠	78
50	Michigan	82
69	Holy Cross ⊠	82
83	Lehigh ⊠	75
83	New Hampshire	81
76	Colgate	64
87	Long Island	79
76	Albany (N.Y.)	79
72	Central Conn. St.	65
84	Vermont	76
75	Sacred Heart ⊠	95
92	Providence	101
48	UC Irvine	81
73	Dartmouth	80
77	Dartmouth ⊠	71
78	Yale ⊠	88
92	Brown ⊠	88
70	Columbia ⊠	90
65	Cornell ⊠	64
68	Princeton	74
53	Penn	67
66	Brown	70
71	Yale	86
67	Penn ⊠	83
50	Princeton ⊠	43
85	Cornell	79
66	Columbia	76

Nickname: Crimson
Colors: Crimson, Black & White
Arena: Lavietes Pavilion
Capacity: 2,195; Year Built: 1926
AD: Robert L. Scalise
SID: Kurt Svoboda

HAVERFORD
Haverford, PA 19041-1392 III

Coach: Michael Mucci, Villanova 1977

2006-07 RESULTS (14-12)

50	Trinity (Conn.) ⊠	78
53	Wittenberg †	68
55	Catholic ⊠	61
71	Muhlenberg	77
53	Gettysburg ⊠	52
72	Washington (Md.) ⊠	61
43	Frank. & Marsh.	69
39	Lehigh	83
51	Hamilton †	60
62	Dallas †	49
60	McDaniel ⊠	56
64	Johns Hopkins	59
50	Dickinson ⊠	48
60	Gettysburg	65
50	Swarthmore	51
60	Frank. & Marsh. ⊠	55
53	Ursinus	70
67	McDaniel	63
56	Muhlenberg ⊠	39
68	Johns Hopkins ⊠	72
65	Washington (Md.)	61
51	Dickinson	50
75	Ursinus ⊠	74
84	Swarthmore ⊠	78
70	Ursinus †	69
61	Johns Hopkins	68

Nickname: Fords
Colors: Scarlet & Black
Arena: Calvin J. Gooding '84
Capacity: 1,200; Year Built: 2005
AD: John E. Douglas/Wendy Smith
SID: Ryan Griswold

HAWAII
Honolulu, HI 96822-2370 I

Coach: Riley Wallace, Centenary (La.) 1964

2006-07 RESULTS (18-13)

59	UNLV	73
79	Coppin St. ⊠	67
85	Oregon St. ⊠	41
80	Hofstra †	79
56	California †	72
71	Pacific †	60
59	Santa Clara	68
58	UNLV ⊠	61
89	Northwestern St. ⊠	78
89	San Francisco ⊠	85
81	Nebraska ⊠	72
76	Creighton ⊠	60
66	Tenn.-Martin ⊠	53
86	New Mexico St.	92
67	Louisiana Tech ⊠	70
83	Fresno St. ⊠	66
66	Nevada ⊠	68
75	Idaho	76
62	Boise St.	73
72	San Jose St. ⊠	52
69	Utah St. ⊠	61
54	Fresno St.	42
68	Nevada	69
74	Louisiana Tech ⊠	50
68	New Mexico St. ⊠	71
50	Utah St.	58
93	Long Beach St. ⊠	78
67	San Jose St.	55
81	Idaho ⊠	64
92	Boise St. ⊠	75
70	Utah St. †	73

Nickname: Rainbow Warriors
Colors: Green, Black, Silver & White
Arena: Stan Sheriff Center
Capacity: 10,300; Year Built: 1994
AD: Herman R. Frazier
SID: Derek Inouchi

HAWAII PACIFIC
Honolulu, HI 96813 II

Coach: Darren Vorderbruegge, Bethany (Kan.)

2006-07 RESULTS (10-17)

79	Cal St. Stanislaus †	75
57	Central Wash. †	93
79	Carleton	85
65	St. Martin's ⊠	60
63	Holy Names ⊠	76
51	Menlo	53
53	UC San Diego	50
50	Seattle ⊠	53
84	Ark.-Monticello ⊠	75
67	Harding	65
66	Indianapolis ⊠	70
49	Grand Canyon ⊠	54
50	Grand Canyon ⊠	58
71	Notre Dame de Namur ⊠	60
66	Hawaii-Hilo	84
74	Hawaii-Hilo	64
63	BYU-Hawaii ⊠	74
70	BYU-Hawaii ⊠	74
56	Chaminade	86
65	Hawaii-Hilo ⊠	64
55	Notre Dame de Namur	71
59	Notre Dame de Namur	55
47	Grand Canyon	61
67	Chapman	69
90	Chaminade ⊠	85
68	Chaminade ⊠	93
51	BYU-Hawaii	72

Nickname: Sea Warriors
Colors: Columbia Blue, Kelly Green & White
Arena: Neal Blaisdell Center
Capacity: 7,500
AD: Darren Vorderbruegge
SID: Jeff Harada

HAWAII-HILO
Hilo, HI 96720-4091 II

Coach: Jeff Law, Plattsburgh St. 1985

2006-07 RESULTS (9-18)

93	Lewis & Clark ⊠	98
73	Carleton ⊠	66
70	Western N.M. ⊠	83
78	Western N.M. ⊠	62
59	Fort Lewis ⊠	80
67	Western Wash.	75
63	Seattle	80
57	Master's	63
51	Cal St. Dom. Hills	83
83	Ark.-Monticello ⊠	72
74	Alas. Fairbanks †	85
72	Alas. Anchorage	85
81	Chaminade	79
85	Chaminade	88
84	Hawaii Pacific ⊠	66
80	Hawaii Pacific ⊠	74
60	Grand Canyon	73
91	Grand Canyon	89
78	Notre Dame de Namur	70
56	BYU-Hawaii	86
83	BYU-Hawaii	93
64	Hawaii Pacific	65
69	Notre Dame de Namur ⊠	73
71	Notre Dame de Namur ⊠	60
64	Grand Canyon ⊠	72
62	BYU-Hawaii ⊠	76
60	Chaminade ⊠	76

Nickname: Vulcans
Colors: Red, White & Blue
Arena: Afook-Chinen Civic Center
 Capacity: 3,000; Year Built: 1955
AD: Kathleen McNally
SID: Kelly Leong

HEIDELBERG
Tiffin, OH 44883-2462 III

Coach: Duane Sheldon, Baldwin-Wallace 1993

2006-07 RESULTS (13-13)

69	Kalamazoo †	44
79	Mt. St. Joseph	76
82	Defiance ⊠	87
73	Bluffton	75
62	Myers ⊠	63
90	Wilmington (Ohio)	78
70	Ohio Northern ⊠	75
68	Mount Union	61
76	Muskingum ⊠	66
88	Hiram ⊠	50
68	Penn St.-Altoona ⊠	46
63	Capital ⊠	65
95	Otterbein	77
84	John Carroll ⊠	80
74	Marietta	70
75	Baldwin-Wallace ⊠	72
71	Wilmington (Ohio) ⊠	89
80	Ohio Northern	83
75	Mount Union ⊠	62
80	Baldwin-Wallace	93
87	Marietta ⊠	70
86	John Carroll	91
74	Otterbein ⊠	77
67	Capital	79
66	Muskingum	78
82	Baldwin-Wallace	95

Nickname: Berg
Colors: Red, Orange & Black
Arena: Seiberling Gymnasium
 Capacity: 1,900; Year Built: 1952
AD: Jerry McDonald
SID: Aaron Chimenti

HENDERSON ST.
Arkadelphia, AR 71999-0001 II

Coach: Sam Weaver, Henderson St. 1981

2006-07 RESULTS (23-9)

104	Central Baptist ⊠	60
57	West Ala. ⊠	49
64	Northwestern St.	84
58	Palm Beach Atl. †	48
45	Fla. Gulf Coast	48
70	P.R.-Bayamon †	60
36	UTSA	55
59	Nova Southeastern †	66
75	St. Leo †	63
76	Rhema ⊠	53
74	Southwest Baptist †	59
67	Quincy	64
85	Crichton ⊠	53
80	Arkansas Tech ⊠	67
56	Southern Ark.	48
57	Christian Bros. ⊠	48
68	Ark.-Monticello ⊠	66
60	Harding	58
62	Ouachita Baptist ⊠	65
62	Delta St.	55
66	Arkansas Tech	42
72	Southern Ark. ⊠	41
56	Christian Bros.	53
82	Ark.-Monticello	60
55	Harding ⊠	58
80	Ouachita Baptist	90
66	Delta St. ⊠	54
70	Ala.-Huntsville †	59
76	Harding †	71
52	Montevallo †	66
58	Barry †	44
58	Montevallo	66

Nickname: Reddies
Colors: Red & Gray
Arena: Duke Wells Center
 Capacity: 3,000; Year Built: 1971
AD: Sam Goodwin
SID: Troy Mitchell

HENDRIX
Conway, AR 72032-3080 III

Coach: Dan Priest, Ohio Northern

2006-07 RESULTS (15-10)

84	Rhema †	77
59	Westminster (Mo.) †	60
61	Rust	64
97	Principia ⊠	50
88	Rhema ⊠	71
76	Rust ⊠	71
72	Austin ⊠	55
80	Central Baptist ⊠	67
79	Dallas Christian †	48
71	Dallas	68
73	Ozarks (Ark.)	67
63	Trinity (Tex.) ⊠	45
43	Southwestern (Tex.) ⊠	57
62	DePauw	75
38	Centre	75
70	Rhodes ⊠	68
73	Millsaps ⊠	78
91	Austin	72
81	Sewanee	66
67	Oglethorpe	81
72	DePauw ⊠	77
71	Centre ⊠	72
70	Trinity (Tex.)	54
68	Southwestern (Tex.)	64
64	Millsaps †	77

Nickname: Warriors
Colors: Orange & Black
Arena: Ivan H. Grove
 Capacity: 1,200; Year Built: 1961
AD: Danny Powell
SID: Parker Griffith

HIGH POINT
High Point, NC 27262-3598 I

Coach: Bart Lundy, Winthrop 1993

2006-07 RESULTS (22-10)

61	Tenn.-Martin †	64
81	Howard †	62
51	Cincinnati	63
94	Covenant ⊠	67
75	Chowan ⊠	59
63	Maryland	81
93	Ohio Valley ⊠	48
62	Elon ⊠	48
59	Longwood ⊠	57
69	North Carolina	94
65	Gardner-Webb ⊠	51
64	Florida St.	81
63	Loyola (Md.) ⊠	57
88	Lees-McRae ⊠	62
81	Radford ⊠	74
115	VMI	104
90	UNC Asheville ⊠	64
77	Liberty ⊠	71
95	Charleston So.	87
59	Coastal Caro.	56
63	Winthrop ⊠	64
64	Longwood	69
75	Radford	65
79	Liberty	96
70	Savannah St.	49
71	Coastal Caro. ⊠	63
69	UNC Asheville	67
70	Charleston So. ⊠	50
60	Winthrop	72
109	VMI ⊠	92
90	Radford	73
81	VMI †	91

Nickname: Panthers
Colors: Purple & White
Arena: Millis Center
 Capacity: 2,565; Year Built: 1992
AD: Woody Gibson
SID: Brian Morgan

HILBERT
Hamburg, NY 14075-1597 III

Coach: Rob deGrandpre, Brockport St. 1995

2006-07 RESULTS (14-14)

73	Hobart ⊠	70
77	Alfred	79
89	Keuka ⊠	74
65	Lake Erie	68
53	Penn St.-Altoona	73
39	Penn St.-Behrend ⊠	59
79	La Roche ⊠	73
69	D'Youville †	54
75	Buffalo St.	85
82	D'Youville ⊠	48
117	Mt. Aloysius	110
82	Fredonia St.	86
84	Pitt.-Greensburg	77
83	Frostburg St. ⊠	59
72	Medaille	68
73	Pitt.-Bradford ⊠	75
73	Penn St.-Altoona ⊠	75
66	Lake Erie ⊠	96
63	La Roche	68
50	Penn St.-Behrend	65
103	Mt. Aloysius ⊠	96
94	Pitt.-Greensburg ⊠	91
86	Frostburg St.	69
59	Pitt.-Bradford	67
71	Medaille ⊠	55
87	Frostburg St. ⊠	73
67	Lake Erie	80
63	Vassar	80

Nickname: Hawks
Colors: Royal Blue & White
Arena: Brad Hafner Recreation Center
 Capacity: 1,200; Year Built: 1973
AD: Richard L. Walsh
SID: Rob deGrandpre

HILLSDALE
Hillsdale, MI 49242-1298 II

Coach: Ed Douma, Calvin 1973

2006-07 RESULTS (15-11)

73	Siena Heights	56
83	Indianapolis ⊠	70
81	Saginaw Valley ⊠	72
72	Mercyhurst ⊠	69
73	Gannon ⊠	51
69	Wayne St. (Mich.) ⊠	73
97	St. Francis (Ill.) ⊠	70
92	Siena Heights ⊠	62
71	Drury †	61
67	Winona St. †	81
76	Tiffin	58
66	Northwood (Mich.)	57
68	Saginaw Valley	60
51	Ferris St.	65
55	Findlay	82
67	Ashland	71
57	Northern Mich. ⊠	65
77	Michigan Tech ⊠	61
47	Lake Superior St.	59
71	Ashland ⊠	75
66	Findlay ⊠	79
59	Gannon	69
81	Mercyhurst	65
75	Northwood (Mich.) ⊠	57
64	Grand Valley St.	87
88	Wayne St. (Mich.) ⊠	83

Nickname: Chargers
Colors: Royal Blue & White
Arena: Jesse Philips Arena
 Capacity: 2,500; Year Built: 1989
AD: Michael J. Kovalchik
SID: Brad Monastiere

HIRAM
Hiram, OH 44234-0067 III

Coach: Steve Fleming, Hiram 1994

2006-07 RESULTS (7-19)

74	Case Reserve ⊠	76
74	Bluffton ⊠	94
49	Ohio Wesleyan	90
54	Mount Union ⊠	81
74	Oberlin	71
97	Grove City	93
62	Thiel	63
50	Heidelberg	88
62	Maryville (Tenn.) †	98
81	Kalamazoo †	89
85	La Roche ⊠	89
67	Earlham ⊠	65
83	Wabash ⊠	80
84	Kenyon	86
50	Wittenberg ⊠	72
57	Wooster ⊠	111
120	Denison ⊠	117
82	Allegheny	81
86	Ohio Wesleyan ⊠	92
54	Kenyon ⊠	73
82	Oberlin ⊠	74
73	Wooster	90
41	Wittenberg	78
66	Allegheny ⊠	79
74	Denison	79
49	Wittenberg	72

Nickname: Terriers
Colors: Blue and Red
Arena: Price Gymnasium
 Capacity: 2,000; Year Built: 1959
AD: Thomas E. Mulligan
SID: Jeff Hoedt

HOBART

Geneva, NY 14456 III

Coach: Izzi Metz, Hobart 1998

2006-07 RESULTS (11-14)

70	Hilbert	73
78	Keuka	82
76	Cazenovia ⊠	69
58	Ithaca	69
63	Rochester (N.Y.)	80
48	Rochester Inst.	67
58	Fredonia St. †	54
43	St. John Fisher ⊠	64
70	York (Pa.)	75
73	Averett †	66
67	Hamilton ⊠	91
57	St. Lawrence	66
65	Clarkson ⊠	56
68	Elmira	66
69	Skidmore	54
72	Union (N.Y.)	85
49	Vassar	66
58	Rensselaer	64
68	Union (N.Y.) ⊠	86
65	Skidmore ⊠	53
47	Clarkson	68
70	St. Lawrence	68
87	Hamilton	86
69	Rensselaer ⊠	62
85	Vassar ⊠	78

Nickname: Statesmen
Colors: Royal Purple and Orange
Arena: Bristol Gym
Capacity: 1,500; Year Built: 1965
AD: Michael J. Hanna
SID: Ken DeBolt

HOFSTRA

Hempstead, NY 11549 I

Coach: Tom Pecora, Adelphi 1983

2006-07 RESULTS (22-10)

82	Charlotte	88
77	Manhattan	79
79	Hawaii †	80
73	Marshall †	70
75	Alas. Anchorage	65
84	Siena	80
62	Georgia St. ⊠	59
73	Stony Brook	57
67	St. Francis (N.Y.) ⊠	64
60	Syracuse	85
65	St. Joseph's †	63
63	St. John's (N.Y.)	51
80	UNC Wilmington	69
75	Delaware ⊠	50
70	Old Dominion ⊠	58
55	Drexel	53
74	Northeastern	84
79	Towson ⊠	74
77	William & Mary ⊠	69
76	Georgia St.	63
64	Towson	60
68	Delaware	72
79	VCU ⊠	68
82	Northeastern ⊠	66
87	Drexel ⊠	95
68	George Mason	60
82	Old Dominion	96
65	Holy Cross ⊠	64
68	UNC Wilmington ⊠	65
98	James Madison	78
61	George Mason †	64
71	DePaul	83

Nickname: Pride
Colors: Gold, White and Blue
Arena: Hofstra Arena
Capacity: 5,124; Year Built: 1999
AD: Jack W. Hayes
SID: Jeremy Kniffin

HOLY CROSS

Worcester, MA 01610-2395 I

Coach: Ralph Willard, Holy Cross 1967

2006-07 RESULTS (25-9)

67	Fairfield ⊠	65
62	Hampton ⊠	47
65	Siena ⊠	57
82	Harvard	69
66	William & Mary ⊠	57
64	Syracuse	72
63	Yale	58
53	Dayton	69
45	Duke	57
68	Providence	77
46	George Mason †	58
68	La Salle	48
61	Niagara †	67
49	Delaware †	47
73	Boston U.	70
84	Lafayette	74
66	Army ⊠	42
65	Bucknell ⊠	60
61	Navy ⊠	42
69	American	64
58	Colgate	55
64	Lehigh ⊠	53
58	American ⊠	47
74	Lafayette ⊠	52
70	Army ⊠	54
45	Bucknell	48
68	Navy	40
64	Hofstra	65
68	Colgate ⊠	57
62	Lehigh	50
83	Lafayette ⊠	53
55	American ⊠	53
74	Bucknell ⊠	66
51	Southern Ill. †	61

Nickname: Crusaders
Colors: Royal Purple
Arena: Hart Recreation Center
Capacity: 3,600; Year Built: 1975
AD: Richard M. Regan Jr.
SID: Charles Bare

HOLY FAMILY

Philadelphia, PA 19114-2009 II

Coach: Alfred Johnson, Elizabeth City St. 1994

2006-07 RESULTS (19-9)

69	Mass.-Lowell †	58
53	Bridgeport	56
57	Claflin †	47
56	Kentucky St. †	43
61	Philadelphia U.	65
75	Post ⊠	63
49	Phila. Sciences	39
61	Nyack ⊠	48
73	St. Rose	88
62	Southern N.H. †	50
79	Felician	69
62	American Int'l	60
77	Caldwell ⊠	63
51	Dominican (N.Y.)	65
94	Bloomfield ⊠	91
89	Wilmington (Del.) ⊠	80
53	Goldey-Beacom	55
65	Post	67
56	Philadelphia U. ⊠	63
68	Nyack	62
61	Phila. Sciences ⊠	58
84	Felician ⊠	68
66	Caldwell	67
70	Goldey-Beacom ⊠	58
71	Dominican (N.Y.) ⊠	57
73	Wilmington (Del.)	45
91	Bloomfield	88
50	Phila. Sciences ⊠	55

Nickname: Tigers
Colors: Copenhagen Blue & White
Arena: Campus Center
Capacity: 1,000; Year Built: 1987

AD: Sandra Michael
SID: James Wagner

HOOD

Frederick, MD 21701-8575 III

Coach: Tom Dickman, Shepherd 1973

2006-07 RESULTS (21-8)

55	Montclair St. †	53
88	McDaniel †	72
64	McDaniel	66
83	Villa Julie †	72
70	St. Mary's (Md.) †	61
77	Gallaudet ⊠	64
60	Mary Washington	76
99	St. Mary's (Md.) ⊠	70
79	Catholic	73
59	Emory †	62
92	Merchant Marine †	82
73	Messiah	66
83	Marymount (Va.) ⊠	74
73	Goucher	65
77	Waynesburg ⊠	54
80	York (Pa.) ⊠	78
80	Salisbury	74
77	Gallaudet	63
91	Mary Washington ⊠	90
81	St. Mary's (Md.)	87
62	Catholic ⊠	69
58	Marymount (Va.)	71
78	Goucher	74
78	York (Pa.)	71
100	Salisbury ⊠	83
82	Goucher ⊠	72
92	St. Mary's (Md.) ⊠	76
75	Catholic	85
65	Hampden-Sydney †	68

Nickname: Blazers
Colors: Blue and Grey
Arena: Gov. Thomas Johnson High School
Capacity: 2,500; Year Built: 1969
AD: Gilbert Romaine
SID: Adrienne Gonzales

HOPE

Holland, MI 49422-9000 III

Coach: Glenn Van Wieren, Hope 1964

2006-07 RESULTS (26-5)

80	Cornerstone †	76
76	Calvin	54
65	Carthage	71
70	Wheaton (Ill.) †	73
88	Grace Bible (Mich.) ⊠	63
85	Goshen ⊠	72
65	Aquinas	62
88	Purdue-North Cent. ⊠	79
69	Trinity Christian ⊠	53
76	Rochester College ⊠	74
87	Kalamazoo	55
99	Olivet ⊠	70
94	Albion ⊠	58
65	Calvin	62
81	Adrian	42
86	Alma ⊠	53
101	Tri-State ⊠	57
86	Kalamazoo ⊠	48
79	Olivet	57
78	Albion	71
71	Calvin ⊠	77
84	Adrian ⊠	71
88	Alma	62
78	Tri-State	59
89	Alma ⊠	49
77	Adrian ⊠	61
76	Calvin ⊠	78
76	Chicago †	54
80	Calvin †	64
89	Carroll (Wis.) †	77
55	Washington-St. Louis †	58

Nickname: Flying Dutchmen
Colors: Orange & Blue

Arena: De Vos Fieldhouse
Capacity: 3,500; Year Built: 2005
AD: Raymond E. Smith
SID: Tom Renner

HOUSTON

Houston, TX 77204 I

Coach: Tom Penders, Connecticut 1967

2006-07 RESULTS (18-15)

102	Rhode Island	99
89	Monmouth ⊠	80
96	Grambling	61
78	St. Louis	81
101	Prairie View ⊠	54
84	VCU	102
62	Arizona	87
68	Charlotte †	46
72	Creighton †	80
57	Nebraska †	70
62	UNLV ⊠	78
70	Kentucky	77
69	Memphis ⊠	79
82	SMU ⊠	67
71	Rice	76
69	Tulsa	67
73	UCF	70
77	Marshall	61
59	St. Louis ⊠	58
70	Rice ⊠	63
71	UTEP	79
64	SMU	49
83	East Caro. ⊠	59
61	South Ala. ⊠	66
70	UAB ⊠	64
69	Southern Miss.	74
78	Tulane ⊠	70
64	Memphis	77
72	UCF	75
74	UTEP ⊠	67
62	Southern Miss. †	59
77	Rice †	62
59	Memphis	71

Nickname: Cougars
Colors: Scarlet & White with Navy Trim
Arena: Hofheinz Pavilion
Capacity: 8,479; Year Built: 1969
AD: Dave Maggard
SID: Chris Burkhalter

HOWARD

Washington, DC 20059 I

Coach: Gil Jackson, Elizabethtown 1969

2006-07 RESULTS (9-22)

39	Cincinnati	70
62	High Point †	81
86	Tenn.-Martin †	81
78	La Salle	84
116	VMI	111
75	St. Francis (Pa.) ⊠	69
95	Hampton †	84
75	Navy	79
75	American ⊠	85
65	Md.-East. Shore	63
67	Oregon St.	84
49	Portland St.	78
57	A&M-Corpus Christi	75
68	Western Ill. †	67
45	South Carolina St.	51
66	N.C. A&T	70
57	Delaware St.	66
63	Bethune-Cookman ⊠	60
53	Florida A&M ⊠	65
59	Coppin St. ⊠	62
53	Morgan St.	66
58	South Carolina St. ⊠	65
80	N.C. A&T ⊠	75
40	Delaware St. ⊠	59
56	Bethune-Cookman	54
75	Florida A&M	85
46	Coppin St.	50
62	Morgan St.	85
68	Norfolk St.	69

60	Md.-East. Shore ⊠	63
61	Hampton †	76

Nickname: Bison
Colors: Blue, White & Red
Arena: Burr Gymnasium
   Capacity: 2,700; Year Built: 1963
AD: Dwight F. Datcher
SID: Edward Hill Jr.

HOWARD PAYNE
Brownwood, TX 76801 III

Coach: Charles Pattillo, Howard Payne 1965

2006-07 RESULTS (7-18)

64	Dallas Baptist	83
81	Abilene Christian	87
74	Ozarks (Ark.)	86
70	East Tex. Baptist ⊠	79
95	LeTourneau ⊠	62
58	Sul Ross St.	62
80	Wayland Baptist ⊠	87
78	Texas-Tyler	67
71	Texas-Dallas	85
63	Stephen F. Austin	89
63	Louisiana Col. ⊠	68
64	Mississippi Col. ⊠	76
82	Schreiner	88
100	Texas Lutheran	85
91	Sul Ross St. ⊠	59
67	Mary Hardin-Baylor ⊠	71
91	Concordia (Tex.) ⊠	87
70	Hardin-Simmons	95
92	McMurry	97
69	Hardin-Simmons ⊠	77
60	McMurry ⊠	90
109	Concordia (Tex.)	118
76	Mary Hardin-Baylor	84
99	Schreiner	97
87	Texas Lutheran ⊠	72

Nickname: Yellow Jackets
Colors: Navy Blue and Old Gold
Arena: Brownwood Coliseum
   Capacity: 5,000; Year Built: 1968
AD: Mike Jones
SID: Abram Choate

HUMBOLDT ST.
Arcata, CA 95521-8299 II

Coach: Tom Wood, UC Davis 1971

2006-07 RESULTS (26-4)

106	Dominican (Cal.) ⊠	52
90	Central Wash. †	79
89	Western Ore. †	82
68	Cal St. San B'dino	76
55	Cal Poly Pomona	58
76	Notre Dame de Namur ⊠	62
111	Cal St. Monterey Bay ⊠	86
72	Sonoma St.	57
90	Sonoma St. ⊠	78
90	UC San Diego ⊠	76
65	Cal St. Dom. Hills ⊠	64
101	San Fran. St. ⊠	82
92	Cal St. Monterey Bay ⊠	85
85	Cal St. L.A.	94
61	Cal St. Bakersfield	57
94	Cal St. Stanislaus ⊠	88
74	Cal St. Chico ⊠	56
84	Cal Poly Pomona ⊠	62
89	Cal St. San B'dino ⊠	78
70	Cal St. Dom. Hills	62
61	UC San Diego	59
106	Cal St. Monterey Bay	91
94	San Fran. St.	62
86	Cal St. Bakersfield ⊠	77
77	Cal St. L.A. ⊠	75
90	Cal St. Chico	75
91	Cal St. Stanislaus	77
68	Alas. Anchorage †	61
95	Grand Canyon †	81
66	Cal St. San B'dino ⊠	68

Nickname: Lumberjacks
Colors: Green & Gold
Arena: HSU East Gym
   Capacity: 1,400; Year Built: 1956
AD: Dan Collen
SID: Dan Pambianco

HUNTER
New York, NY 10021 III

Coach: Nick Plevritis, Hunter 2000

2006-07 RESULTS (12-14)

67	Drew	72
70	Wentworth Inst. †	61
74	Manhattanville ⊠	77
99	Mt. St. Vincent ⊠	80
70	St. Joseph's (Brkln) ⊠	66
77	CCNY ⊠	62
72	John Jay ⊠	64
74	FDU-Florham	70
75	Maritime (N.Y.)	58
65	Rutgers-Newark	67
79	Lehman ⊠	69
96	Brooklyn ⊠	78
92	Centenary (N.J.) ⊠	74
69	Staten Island	68
59	New York U.	94
79	Medgar Evers	77
58	Lehman	62
80	Stevens Institute ⊠	95
60	CCNY	62
82	Baruch	96
73	York (N.Y.)	92
67	City Tech ⊠	71
59	John Jay	61
67	Baruch ⊠	70
43	St. Joseph's (L.I.)	71
62	York (N.Y.) †	81

Nickname: Hawks
Colors: Purple, White & Gold
Arena: Hunter College Sportsplex
   Capacity: 1,500; Year Built: 1985
AD: Terry Ann Wansart
SID: Camille Currie

HUNTINGDON
Montgomery, AL 36106 III

Coach: Tony Duckworth, Bob Jones 1990

2006-07 RESULTS (3-23)

52	Ferrum	73
56	Greensboro †	65
65	Emory & Henry	110
36	TCNJ †	62
64	Atlanta Christian ⊠	61
64	Pensacola Christian	81
59	Oglethorpe ⊠	63
49	Rhodes ⊠	50
57	MacMurray †	67
60	Millsaps †	68
50	Rhodes	59
51	Dallas	60
51	Rust ⊠	67
63	Piedmont ⊠	74
64	Maryville (Tenn.)	69
61	Sewanee	74
66	Fisk	64
58	LaGrange ⊠	66
29	Maryville (Tenn.) ⊠	60
53	Atlanta Christian	56
65	Fisk ⊠	54
77	Piedmont	96
58	Pensacola Christian ⊠	65
41	LaGrange	62
58	Wesley (Miss.)	73
57	Maryville (Tenn.) †	80

Nickname: Hawks
Colors: Scarlet Red, White and Pearl Gray
Arena: Delchamps Student Center
AD: Hugh Phillips
SID: To be named

HUSSON
Bangor, ME 04401 III

Coach: Warren Caruso, Husson 1989

2006-07 RESULTS (22-6)

82	Wheaton (Mass.) †	88
85	Centenary (N.J.) †	54
80	St. Joseph's (Me.) ⊠	67
94	Mount Ida	50
93	Lesley	90
85	Elms	76
87	Becker ⊠	48
70	Gordon ⊠	53
53	St. Joseph's (Me.)	73
77	Southern Me. †	73
58	Embry-Riddle	75
57	Farmingdale St. †	60
92	Castleton	67
85	Johnson St.	46
79	Thomas (Me.)	35
55	Bates	70
109	Me.-Presque Isle ⊠	49
64	Maine Maritime ⊠	61
93	Me.-Farmington ⊠	83
87	Mount Ida ⊠	68
81	Lasell ⊠	75
88	Thomas (Me.) ⊠	53
67	Me.-Farmington	63
72	Southern Me.	62
73	Maine Maritime	51
93	Castleton ⊠	71
95	Lesley ⊠	79
69	Elms ⊠	81

Nickname: Eagles
Colors: Green , White & Gold
AD: Jonathan Price
SID: Warren Caruso

IDAHO
Moscow, ID 83844-2302 I

Coach: George Pfeifer, Lewis-Clark St. 1979

2006-07 RESULTS (4-27)

76	North Dakota St. ⊠	91
74	South Dakota St.	66
65	Montana St. ⊠	72
50	Southern Utah	67
51	Gonzaga	76
66	Washington	87
50	Southern Utah ⊠	72
61	Idaho St.	82
54	Washington St. ⊠	66
59	North Dakota St.	79
56	Eastern Wash.	85
72	South Dakota St. ⊠	67
41	Fresno St.	60
55	Nevada	81
56	New Mexico St. ⊠	61
56	Utah St.	74
76	Hawaii ⊠	75
72	Louisiana Tech ⊠	73
66	New Mexico St.	84
57	Boise St. ⊠	75
65	San Jose St. ⊠	68
70	Fresno St. ⊠	72
63	Boise St.	86
66	Utah St. ⊠	75
59	Louisiana Tech	68
76	UC Riverside ⊠	81
68	Nevada ⊠	84
64	Hawaii	81
57	San Jose St.	62
50	San Jose St. †	49
56	Nevada †	88

Nickname: Vandals
Colors: Silver & Gold
Arena: Cowan Spectrum
   Capacity: 7,000; Year Built: 1975
AD: Robert Spear
SID: Amy Rysdam

IDAHO ST.
Pocatello, ID 83209-8173 I

Coach: Joe O'Brien, Monmouth (Ill.) 1977

2006-07 RESULTS (13-17)

56	Marquette	59
66	Maine †	57
78	BYU	84
60	Washington St.	66
44	Texas A&M	74
75	Carroll (Mont.) ⊠	74
46	Utah St.	83
82	Idaho ⊠	61
76	UC Davis ⊠	49
55	Oregon	84
76	Utah Valley St. ⊠	62
60	Illinois	71
45	Boise St.	54
58	Weber St.	55
73	Sacramento St.	58
78	Eastern Wash. ⊠	65
70	Northern Colo. ⊠	60
79	Montana	69
57	Montana St.	58
58	Weber St. ⊠	71
65	Portland St. ⊠	67
98	Northern Ariz. ⊠	102
85	Sacramento St. ⊠	62
66	Northern Colo.	55
63	Northern Ariz.	73
79	Eastern Wash.	82
63	Portland St.	70
71	Montana	72
67	Montana St. †	58
63	Montana	70

Nickname: Bengals
Colors: Orange & Black
Arena: Reed Gymnasium
   Capacity: 3,241; Year Built: 1951
AD: Paul A. Bubb
SID: Frank Mercogliano

ILLINOIS
Champaign, IL 61820 I

Coach: Bruce Weber, Milwaukee 1978

2006-07 RESULTS (23-12)

80	Austin Peay ⊠	35
76	Jackson St. ⊠	55
85	Ga. Southern ⊠	50
84	Florida A&M ⊠	63
81	Savannah St. ⊠	34
51	Miami (Ohio) †	49
75	Bradley †	71
66	Maryland ⊠	72
72	Arizona †	84
87	IUPUI ⊠	59
71	Ill.-Chicago †	66
77	Belmont	51
73	Missouri †	70
71	Idaho St. ⊠	60
59	Xavier †	65
61	Michigan	71
44	Ohio St. ⊠	62
74	Iowa ⊠	70
57	Michigan St.	63
64	Minnesota	52
64	Wisconsin ⊠	71
51	Indiana ⊠	43
47	Purdue	64
57	Michigan St. ⊠	50
59	Minnesota ⊠	49
58	Northwestern	43
61	Indiana	65
48	Northwestern ⊠	37
54	Michigan ⊠	42
68	Penn St.	50
53	Iowa	60
66	Penn St. †	60
58	Indiana †	54
41	Wisconsin †	53
52	Virginia Tech †	54

Nickname: Fighting Illini
Colors: Orange & Blue
Arena: Assembly Hall
Capacity: 16,618; Year Built: 1963
AD: Ronald E. Guenther
SID: Kent Brown

ILLINOIS COL.
Jacksonville, IL 62650-2299 III

Coach: Mike Worrell, Urbana 1986

2006-07 RESULTS (8-15)

70	Ill. Wesleyan	75
66	North Park ⊠	62
107	Concordia (Mo.)	57
71	Beloit	72
83	Knox ⊠	86
81	Millikin	72
59	Westminster (Mo.) ⊠	56
60	Case Reserve	57
71	Defiance †	76
70	Ripon	72
84	Monmouth (Ill.)	71
53	Lake Forest ⊠	51
51	St. Norbert ⊠	54
71	Carroll (Wis.) ⊠	84
67	Lawrence	79
69	St. Norbert	75
105	Grinnell ⊠	116
63	Knox	70
77	Ripon ⊠	91
60	Beloit	47
61	Lake Forest	65
70	Monmouth (Ill.) ⊠	82
86	Grinnell	109

Nickname: Blueboys
Colors: Blue & White
Arena: Sherman Gymnasium
Capacity: 1,600; Year Built: 2003
AD: Gale F. Vaughn
SID: Jim Murphy

ILLINOIS ST.
Normal, IL 61790-2660 I

Coach: Porter Moser, Creighton 1990

2006-07 RESULTS (15-16)

55	SMU †	57
59	Florida St.	73
67	McNeese St. †	50
66	Cal St. Northridge ⊠	44
78	St. John's (N.Y.)	65
86	Sacramento St. ⊠	69
86	Texas-Arlington ⊠	61
64	Miami (Ohio) ⊠	40
41	Evansville	69
57	Western Mich.	65
85	Lewis ⊠	66
77	Ill.-Chicago	69
49	Southern Ill. ⊠	68
71	Creighton	79
50	Indiana St. ⊠	54
67	UNI	64
66	Drake	70
66	Missouri St. ⊠	75
83	Wichita St. ⊠	75
80	Drake ⊠	65
67	Bradley	88
62	Southern Ill.	73
65	Evansville ⊠	61
62	Bradley ⊠	70
61	Missouri St.	73
64	Wichita St.	69
68	Indiana St.	53
70	Ball St. ⊠	57
65	Creighton ⊠	55
66	UNI	71
65	Indiana St. †	68

Nickname: Redbirds
Colors: Red & White
Arena: Redbird Arena
Capacity: 10,200; Year Built: 1989
AD: Sheahon Zenger
SID: Todd Kober

ILL. WESLEYAN
Bloomington, IL 61702-2900 III

Coach: Ron Rose, Ill. Wesleyan 1988

2006-07 RESULTS (11-14)

86	Clarke †	59
69	Wis.-Whitewater	68
75	Illinois Col. ⊠	70
74	Ohio Wesleyan †	87
92	Judson (Ill.) †	50
73	St. Xavier	75
64	Olivet Nazarene	63
63	Washington-St. Louis ⊠	75
60	Chicago ⊠	64
84	Hanover	65
94	Albion ⊠	80
79	Carthage ⊠	76
82	Millikin ⊠	84
57	Elmhurst	76
65	Wheaton (Ill.)	79
81	North Park ⊠	90
62	Augustana (Ill.)	64
83	Carthage	94
65	North Central (Ill.) ⊠	51
69	Elmhurst ⊠	84
66	Millikin	60
84	Wheaton (Ill.) ⊠	93
77	Augustana (Ill.) ⊠	80
81	North Park	80
70	North Central (Ill.)	77

Nickname: Titans
Colors: Green & White
Arena: Shirk Center
Capacity: 2,680; Year Built: 1994
AD: Dennis Bridges
SID: Stew Salowitz

ILL.-CHICAGO
Chicago, IL 60608............................... I

Coach: Jimmy Collins, New Mexico St. 1970

2006-07 RESULTS (14-18)

75	St. Edward's ⊠	60
89	Davidson	100
72	Bradley	81
61	Miami (Ohio)	72
75	Florida A&M †	57
68	Jackson St. †	71
74	Murray St. ⊠	68
80	Youngstown St. ⊠	64
71	Northern Ill.	48
66	Illinois †	71
86	Akron ⊠	80
64	Mississippi	77
78	Penn	90
69	Illinois St. ⊠	77
72	Cleveland St.	62
62	Wright St.	76
73	Butler ⊠	67
79	Loyola (Ill.) ⊠	73
65	Milwaukee	76
54	Detroit ⊠	66
57	Green Bay	77
55	Cleveland St. ⊠	60
45	Butler	71
87	Youngstown St.	92
64	Wright St. ⊠	74
75	Detroit	67
55	Green Bay ⊠	65
84	Central Mich. ⊠	62
72	Milwaukee ⊠	59
52	Loyola (Ill.)	51
83	Milwaukee	77
62	Loyola (Ill.) †	66

Nickname: Flames
Colors: Navy Blue & Fire Engine Red
Arena: UIC Pavilion
Capacity: 8,000; Year Built: 1982
AD: James W. Schmidt
SID: Mike Cassidy

IMMACULATA
Immaculata, PA 19345-0654 III

Coach: Jaime Chadwin, Delaware 2002

2006-07 RESULTS (12-16)

58	Johns Hopkins	71
61	McMurry †	75
61	Marymount (Va.) ⊠	69
72	Wilkes	78
64	Arcadia ⊠	62
58	Alvernia	59
78	Widener ⊠	87
56	Gwynedd-Mercy ⊠	61
68	DeSales	73
67	St. Mary's (Md.) †	86
64	Gwynedd-Mercy	76
69	Misericordia ⊠	65
73	Eastern	60
89	Marywood ⊠	74
75	Wesley	66
65	Cabrini	67
69	Marywood	58
74	Neumann ⊠	70
56	Arcadia	70
76	Misericordia	62
74	Wesley ⊠	65
45	Alvernia ⊠	48
50	Cabrini ⊠	54
76	Eastern ⊠	57
65	Neumann	67
77	Wesley	62
65	Gwynedd-Mercy	59
55	Alvernia	70

Nickname: Mighty Macs
Colors: Blue & White
Arena: Alumni Hall
Capacity: 500; Year Built: 1970
AD: Patricia Canterino
SID: Tom Machamer

INCARNATE WORD
San Antonio, TX 78209 II

Coach: Ken Burmeister, St. Mary's (Tex.) 1971

2006-07 RESULTS (18-11)

78	Ala.-Huntsville †	82
79	Harding †	70
73	Midwestern St. ⊠	75
63	Tex. A&M-Kingsville ⊠	67
69	Angelo St. ⊠	70
63	Angelo St.	60
91	S'western Aly God ⊠	80
73	Tex. A&M-Kingsville	83
85	Concordia (Tex.) ⊠	89
67	Houston Baptist ⊠	80
71	Tex. Permian Basin ⊠	65
76	Okla. Panhandle ⊠	69
71	Dallas Baptist	72
72	Dallas Baptist ⊠	61
96	St. Mary's (Tex.)	94
60	St. Edward's	64
58	Tex. A&M Int'l	54
70	Lincoln (Mo.)	65
82	Mont. St.-Billings	62
72	Mont. St.-Billings	66
70	St. Mary's (Tex.) ⊠	68
87	Lincoln (Mo.) ⊠	77
79	Mont. St.-Billings ⊠	65
61	St. Edward's ⊠	66
64	Texas A&M Int'l ⊠	54
93	Tex. Permian Basin	90
76	Okla. Panhandle	57
68	St. Mary's (Tex.) †	65
73	St. Edward's	85

Nickname: Cardinals
Colors: Red, Black & White
Arena: McDermott Center
Capacity: 2,000; Year Built: 1990
AD: Mark Papich
SID: Wayne Witt

INDIANA
Bloomington, IN 47408-1590 I

Coach: Kelvin Sampson, UNC Pembroke 1978

2006-07 RESULTS (21-11)

91	Lafayette †	66
55	Butler †	60
73	Indiana St. ⊠	66
90	Chicago St. ⊠	69
51	Duke	54
74	Charlotte ⊠	57
92	Western Ill. ⊠	40
54	Kentucky	59
57	Southern Ill. ⊠	47
77	Western Mich. ⊠	69
86	IUPUI †	57
71	Ball St. ⊠	57
67	Ohio St.	74
73	Michigan St. ⊠	51
85	Purdue ⊠	58
84	Penn St.	74
71	Iowa	64
77	Connecticut	73
43	Illinois	51
76	Michigan ⊠	61
71	Wisconsin ⊠	66
75	Iowa	81
65	Illinois ⊠	61
68	Purdue	81
55	Michigan	58
71	Minnesota ⊠	59
58	Michigan St.	66
69	Northwestern	65
94	Penn St. ⊠	63
54	Illinois †	58
70	Gonzaga †	57
49	UCLA †	54

Nickname: Hoosiers
Colors: Cream & Crimson
Arena: Assembly Hall
Capacity: 17,357; Year Built: 1971
AD: Richard I. Greenspan
SID: Pete Rhoda

INDIANA (PA.)
Indiana, PA 15705-1077 II

Coach: Joe Lombardi, Youngstown St. 1981

2006-07 RESULTS (6-21)

74	Alderson-Broaddus	63
85	Pitt.-Greensburg ⊠	52
67	Bloomsburg	70
54	Mansfield	68
53	Wheeling Jesuit	73
41	Cheyney ⊠	67
51	Mercyhurst	67
64	Kutztown ⊠	69
59	East Stroudsburg ⊠	71
61	Pitt.-Johnstown	89
64	West Chester	70
57	Millersville	75
77	Clarion	72
51	Edinboro ⊠	63
76	Slippery Rock	69
63	California (Pa.) ⊠	74
50	Shippensburg	70
61	Lock Haven ⊠	66
63	Pitt.-Johnstown ⊠	72
60	Clarion ⊠	62
46	Edinboro	76
79	Penn St.-McKeesport ⊠	57
47	Slippery Rock ⊠	44
46	California (Pa.)	67
66	Gannon	85
51	Shippensburg ⊠	72
59	Lock Haven	66

Nickname: Crimson Hawks
Colors: Crimson & Gray
Arena: Memorial Field House
Capacity: 2,365; Year Built: 1966
AD: Frank J. Condino
SID: Michael Hoffman

IPFW
Fort Wayne, IN 46805-1499 I

Coach: Dane Fife, Indiana 2002

2006-07 RESULTS (12-17)

49	Notre Dame	92
67	Valparaiso ⊠	75
77	Rochester (N.Y.) ⊠	44
61	Indiana St. ⊠	67
97	Western Ill.	95
60	IUPUI ⊠	70
84	Southeast Mo. St.	65
66	Air Force	78
43	Michigan St.	80
69	Kent St. ⊠	79
57	IUPUI	74
100	Marygrove ⊠	48
63	Utah St.	77
61	Eastern Mich.	62
58	Wright St.	72
107	Anderson (Ind.) ⊠	59
79	Western Ill. ⊠	77
82	NJIT ⊠	65
53	Loyola (Ill.)	69
45	Valparaiso	59
61	Tex.-Pan American	77
66	Utah Valley St.	96
72	North Dakota St. ⊠	69
68	South Dakota St. ⊠	52
52	NJIT	47
63	Utah Valley St. ⊠	72
82	Tex.-Pan American ⊠	64
83	South Dakota St.	72
57	North Dakota St.	73

Nickname: Mastodons
Colors: Blue & White
Arena: Allen County War Memorial Coliseum
   Capacity: 11,500; Year Built: 1964
AD: Mark A. Pope
SID: Rudy Yovich

IUPUI
Indianapolis, IN 46202 I

Coach: Ron Hunter, Miami (Ohio) 1986

2006-07 RESULTS (15-15)

86	Alabama A&M †	47
74	Kent St. †	81
73	Loyola (Ill.) †	77
74	Ind.-Southeast ⊠	59
61	Belmont ⊠	67
70	IPFW	60
66	Belmont	76
59	Illinois	87
66	Ind. Wesleyan ⊠	59
74	IPFW ⊠	57
57	Indiana †	86
58	Fairleigh Dickinson †	61
67	Radford †	64
57	Oakland	62
68	Western Ill.	55
55	Valparaiso	69
77	UMKC ⊠	72
53	Southern Utah ⊠	56
70	Centenary (La.)	68
66	Oral Roberts	77
79	Chicago St. ⊠	77
60	Oakland ⊠	70
68	Valparaiso ⊠	54
69	Western Ill. ⊠	47
57	Southern Utah	74
72	UMKC	85
73	Oral Roberts ⊠	83
87	Centenary (La.) ⊠	62
71	Southern Utah †	59
54	Oral Roberts †	75

Nickname: Jaguars
Colors: Red & Gold
Arena: IUPUI Gymnasium
   Capacity: 2,000; Year Built: 1982
AD: Michael R. Moore
SID: Ed Holdaway

INDIANA ST.
Terre Haute, IN 47809 I

Coach: Royce Waltman, Slippery Rock 1964

2006-07 RESULTS (13-18)

73	Western Mich. ⊠	71
66	Indiana	73
67	IPFW	61
59	Tulane ⊠	47
66	Oakland City ⊠	52
58	Middle Tenn.	65
70	Ball St.	73
72	Butler ⊠	64
60	Missouri St.	80
92	Wagner ⊠	86
89	Purdue ⊠	70
84	Drake ⊠	73
55	Creighton ⊠	52
54	Illinois St.	50
68	Wichita St. ⊠	63
59	Bradley ⊠	76
68	Drake	74
64	UNI	74
49	Evansville ⊠	50
55	Creighton	71
48	Southern Ill.	61
42	Missouri St. ⊠	71
59	UNI ⊠	46
45	Wichita St.	61
61	Evansville	76
53	Illinois St. ⊠	68
58	Miami (Ohio) ⊠	70
50	Southern Ill. ⊠	58
58	Bradley	74
68	Illinois St. †	65
38	Creighton †	59

Nickname: Sycamores
Colors: Royal Blue & White
Arena: Hulman Center
   Capacity: 10,200; Year Built: 1972
AD: Ron Prettyman
SID: Ace Hunt

INDIANAPOLIS
Indianapolis, IN 46227-3697 II

Coach: Todd Sturgeon, DePauw 1988

2006-07 RESULTS (13-13)

56	Brescia ⊠	54
70	Hillsdale ⊠	83
71	Mo.-Rolla	85
77	Ky. Wesleyan ⊠	70
56	Southern Ind. ⊠	55
73	Saginaw Valley ⊠	62
71	Ferris St. †	60
65	Wayne St. (Mich.)	73
70	Hawaii Pacific	66
71	Chaminade	87
61	St. Joseph's (Ind.)	64
64	Mo.-St. Louis	59
46	Rockhurst	63
77	Drury	66
68	Quincy ⊠	63
69	SIU Edwardsville ⊠	67
62	Northern Ky.	67
66	Bellarmine	64
62	Lewis ⊠	68
67	Wis.-Parkside ⊠	72
72	Ky. Wesleyan	67
80	Wis.-Parkside	89
60	Lewis	65
56	St. Joseph's (Ind.) ⊠	82
71	Bellarmine ⊠	68
60	Northern Ky. ⊠	68

Nickname: Greyhounds
Colors: Crimson & Grey
Arena: Nicoson Hall
   Capacity: 4,000; Year Built: 1960
AD: Sue Willey
SID: Mitch Wigness

IONA
New Rochelle, NY 10801 I

Coach: Jeff Ruland, Iona 1991

2006-07 RESULTS (2-28)

38	Winthrop †	57
61	Sacred Heart †	68
54	Buffalo	65
60	Rhode Island	85
54	Fordham	70
55	Rider	69
50	Vermont	63
51	Rutgers	66
58	Niagara ⊠	79
52	New Hampshire ⊠	67
46	Princeton ⊠	57
57	Maryland	88
66	Loyola (Md.)	75
65	Marist	87
63	Manhattan ⊠	73
76	Fairfield ⊠	83
65	Canisius	72
80	Niagara	81
67	Fairfield	70
61	Loyola (Md.) ⊠	71
61	Canisius ⊠	71
60	Siena	61
69	Rider ⊠	57
53	Siena ⊠	71
53	Marist ⊠	79
52	St. Peter's	59
52	Delaware	50
52	St. Peter's ⊠	54
65	Manhattan	71
62	Rider †	77

Nickname: Gaels
Colors: Maroon & Gold
Arena: Hynes Athletics Center
   Capacity: 2,611; Year Built: 1974
AD: Patrick Lyons
SID: Brian Beyrer

IOWA
Iowa City, IA 52242 I

Coach: Steve Alford, Indiana 1987

2006-07 RESULTS (17-14)

75	Citadel ⊠	53
78	Toledo †	65
60	Alabama †	72
60	Villanova †	89
64	Arizona St.	67
65	Virginia Tech	69
62	Tex.-Pan American ⊠	46
83	Coppin St. ⊠	67
55	UNI ⊠	57
77	Iowa St. ⊠	59
59	Drake	75
101	Georgia St. ⊠	59
90	Texas Southern ⊠	63
65	Cornell ⊠	50
62	Michigan St. ⊠	60
70	Illinois	74
60	Minnesota ⊠	49
64	Indiana	71
63	Ohio St.	82
79	Penn St. ⊠	63
46	Wisconsin	57
69	Michigan	62
81	Indiana ⊠	75
91	Minnesota	78
62	Wisconsin	74
66	Northwestern ⊠	58
49	Michigan St.	81
78	Purdue ⊠	59
72	Penn St.	74
60	Illinois ⊠	53
55	Purdue †	74

Nickname: Hawkeyes
Colors: Black and Gold
Arena: Carver-Hawkeye Arena
   Capacity: 15,500; Year Built: 1983
AD: Gary Barta
SID: Steve Roe

IOWA ST.
Ames, IA 50011 I

Coach: Greg McDermott, UNI 1988

2006-07 RESULTS (15-16)

69	UC Riverside ⊠	61
68	La.-Monroe ⊠	40
56	Eastern Ill. ⊠	54
57	Norfolk St. ⊠	49
68	Minnesota	63
90	Lake Superior St. ⊠	61
57	UNI	70
78	Drake ⊠	80
59	Iowa	77
70	Savannah St. ⊠	59
66	Bradley †	76
56	Ohio St.	75
87	Southeast Mo. St. ⊠	71
67	North Dakota St. ⊠	54
66	Missouri	65
71	Nebraska ⊠	62
64	Kansas ⊠	68
65	Colorado	74
60	Kansas St. ⊠	69
50	Oklahoma St.	62
49	Texas A&M	73
71	Baylor ⊠	58
55	Missouri ⊠	77
68	Texas	77
58	Oklahoma ⊠	51
47	Kansas St.	65
55	Colorado ⊠	53
52	Kansas	89
69	Nebraska	63
61	Texas Tech ⊠	63
63	Oklahoma †	68

Nickname: Cyclones
Colors: Cardinal & Gold
Arena: James H. Hilton Coliseum
   Capacity: 14,092; Year Built: 1971
AD: Jamie Pollard
SID: Mike Green

ITHACA
Ithaca, NY 14850 III

Coach: Jim Mullins, Connecticut 1980

2006-07 RESULTS (15-13)

72	Rochester (N.Y.)	81
67	Geneseo St. †	78
82	Morrisville St. ⊠	60
69	Hobart ⊠	58
67	Cortland St.	61
63	St. Lawrence	76
91	Potsdam St.	78
73	Kean ⊠	74
47	Cornell	80
85	Elmira ⊠	61
74	Hartwick ⊠	57
63	Utica ⊠	85
80	Morrisville St.	67
75	Nazareth ⊠	68
84	Rochester Inst. ⊠	90
68	Alfred	57
59	St. John Fisher	88
62	Oneonta St.	68
70	Utica	68
62	Hartwick	53
99	St. John Fisher ⊠	111
88	Alfred ⊠	73
86	Elmira	68
83	Rochester Inst.	74
80	Nazareth	84
56	Utica †	72
80	Rensselaer ⊠	69
76	Vassar	84

Nickname: Bombers
Colors: Blue & Gold
Arena: Ben Light Gymnasium
   Capacity: 2,500; Year Built: 1964
AD: Ken Kutler
SID: Mike Warwick

JACKSON ST.
Jackson, MS 39217 I

Coach: Tevester Anderson, Ark.-Pine Bluff 1962

2006-07 RESULTS (21-14)
65	Alabama	96
70	Georgia Tech	100
55	Illinois	76
69	Memphis	111
71	Rutgers	70
72	Savannah St. †	71
71	Ill.-Chicago †	68
81	Southeastern La.	73
58	UC Davis	66
54	Tulsa	79
77	Tougaloo ⊠	74
100	UTEP	97
70	Drake †	71
81	Alabama St.	68
68	Alabama A&M	52
86	Alcorn St. ⊠	70
62	Southern U.	73
73	Texas Southern	62
74	Prairie View	62
74	Grambling	77
66	Mississippi Val. ⊠	60
59	Ark.-Pine Bluff ⊠	56
80	Alcorn St.	88
64	Southern U.	57
83	Texas Southern ⊠	90
79	Prairie View ⊠	67
66	Grambling ⊠	57
70	Mississippi Val.	77
54	Ark.-Pine Bluff	59
69	Alabama St. ⊠	65
81	Alabama A&M ⊠	70
74	Southern U. †	65
64	Ark.-Pine Bluff †	62
81	Mississippi Val. †	71
69	Florida †	112

Nickname: Tigers
Colors: Royal Blue & White
Arena: Lee E. Williams Athletics and Assembly Center
   Capacity: 8,000; Year Built: 1981
AD: Robert L Braddy Sr.
SID: Henry Goolsby

JACKSONVILLE
Jacksonville, FL 32211-3394 I

Coach: Cliff Warren, Mt. St. Mary's 1990

2006-07 RESULTS (15-14)
64	Savannah St.	67
77	St. Leo ⊠	73
61	Florida	90
89	Florida Tech ⊠	60
87	South Carolina St. ⊠	74
62	UCF	99
61	Lipscomb	73
62	Belmont	76
85	Coastal Caro. ⊠	72
58	Texas A&M	97
77	Georgia	93
73	South Carolina	80
73	Gardner-Webb ⊠	64
90	Campbell ⊠	71
64	North Fla.	60
76	Kennesaw St.	83
59	East Tenn. St.	71
87	Mercer ⊠	77
69	Stetson ⊠	65
64	Gardner-Webb	59
74	Campbell	84
75	North Fla. ⊠	61
74	East Tenn. St.	66
76	Kennesaw St. ⊠	72
101	Mercer	97
57	Stetson	62
71	Belmont ⊠	86
74	Lipscomb ⊠	67
85	Campbell †	90

JACKSONVILLE ST.
Jacksonville, AL 36265-1602 I

Coach: Mike LaPlante, Maine 1989

2006-07 RESULTS (9-21)
54	New Orleans	66
80	Wofford ⊠	82
95	Reinhardt ⊠	72
69	Massachusetts ⊠	100
56	William & Mary	59
87	VMI †	85
53	Samford ⊠	54
69	Tenn.-Martin ⊠	70
70	Southeast Mo. St.	67
71	Murray St.	72
67	Green Bay	90
69	Bowling Green †	77
58	Michigan Tech †	76
63	Austin Peay ⊠	78
63	Samford	64
71	Tennessee Tech	75
74	Tennessee St.	83
66	Eastern Ky. ⊠	56
67	Morehead St. ⊠	62
58	Austin Peay	73
60	Tenn.-Martin	83
72	Tennessee St. ⊠	64
59	Eastern Ill.	73
61	Murray St. ⊠	63
72	Tennessee Tech ⊠	71
57	Morehead St.	52
51	Eastern Ky.	63
64	Chattanooga	75
65	Eastern Ill. ⊠	69
78	Southeast Mo. St. ⊠	72

Nickname: Gamecocks
Colors: Red & White
Arena: Pete Mathews Coliseum
   Capacity: 5,500; Year Built: 1974
AD: Jim Fuller
SID: Josh Underwood

JAMES MADISON
Harrisonburg, VA 22807 I

Coach: Dean Keener, Davidson 1988

2006-07 RESULTS (7-23)
82	Wake Forest	91
70	Mt. St. Mary's	81
89	VMI ⊠	87
78	Wofford ⊠	74
66	Eastern Ky. ⊠	70
57	Old Dominion	70
53	Georgetown	89
70	Dartmouth ⊠	74
58	Youngstown St. ⊠	78
57	Tex.-Pan American †	70
70	NJIT †	66
62	Delaware ⊠	47
61	VCU ⊠	77
54	Drexel ⊠	65
66	UNC Wilmington	80
52	George Mason	73
72	Old Dominion ⊠	65
59	Georgia St.	52
51	Northeastern	67
41	George Mason ⊠	59
60	Towson ⊠	69
62	William & Mary	65
69	Delaware	64
56	William & Mary ⊠	71
64	Northeastern ⊠	67
62	Towson	76
66	Siena	77
72	VCU	83
78	Hofstra ⊠	98
62	George Mason †	73

Nickname: Dolphins
Colors: Green & White
Arena: Swisher Gymnasium
   Capacity: 1,500; Year Built: 1953
AD: C. Alan Verlander
SID: Joel Lamp

JOHN CARROLL
University Heights, OH 44118-4581 III

Coach: Mike Moran, Xavier 1973

2006-07 RESULTS (21-10)
74	Loyola (Ill.)	96
82	Albion	68
65	Cleveland St.	84
80	TCNJ †	48
119	Emory & Henry	112
86	Otterbein ⊠	77
81	Muskingum	74
80	Capital ⊠	72
72	Wilmington (Ohio)	85
92	Chris. Newport †	71
63	Greensboro	66
73	Baldwin-Wallace ⊠	80
87	Marietta ⊠	71
80	Heidelberg	84
63	Ohio Northern ⊠	61
83	Mount Union	72
70	Otterbein	68
65	Muskingum ⊠	63
82	Capital	89
85	Mount Union ⊠	66
79	Ohio Northern	67
91	Heidelberg ⊠	86
85	Marietta	58
77	Baldwin-Wallace	81
94	Wilmington (Ohio) ⊠	78
102	Wilmington (Ohio) ⊠	88
76	Baldwin-Wallace †	69
73	Capital	78
87	Westminster (Pa.) ⊠	83
79	Lake Erie	77
73	Wooster †	83

Nickname: Blue Streaks
Colors: Blue & Gold
Arena: Tony DeCarlo Varsity Center
   Capacity: 1,350; Year Built: 1957
AD: Laurie Massa
SID: Chris Wenzler

JOHN JAY
New York, NY 10019 III

Coach: Charles Jackson, Pittsburgh

2006-07 RESULTS (7-19)
49	Lycoming	69
71	Penn St.-Berks †	53
59	Ramapo ⊠	74
73	N.C. Wesleyan †	92
52	Gallaudet	77
70	New Jersey City ⊠	81
45	Wm. Paterson ⊠	77
48	Baruch	55
64	Hunter	72
68	New Paltz St. ⊠	76
49	Connecticut Col.	71
59	CCNY ⊠	78
86	Lehman	79
76	Kean ⊠	80
70	Brooklyn ⊠	69
54	Medgar Evers ⊠	78
61	Lincoln (Pa.)	75
75	City Tech ⊠	72
75	York (N.Y.) ⊠	72
47	Rutgers-Newark ⊠	61
68	Baruch ⊠	51
54	CCNY	59
53	Lehman ⊠	67
61	Hunter ⊠	59
76	Staten Island ⊠	79
58	Baruch †	66

Nickname: Dukes
Colors: Purple & Gold
Arena: JMU Convocation Center
   Capacity: 7,156; Year Built: 1982
AD: Jeffrey T. Bourne
SID: Gary Michael

JOHNS HOPKINS
Baltimore, MD 21218-2684 III

Coach: Bill Nelson, Brockport St. 1965

2006-07 RESULTS (24-5)
71	Immaculata ⊠	58
70	Rowan ⊠	68
78	St. Mary's (Md.)	60
85	Goucher	69
71	Salisbury †	60
73	Swarthmore ⊠	57
62	Muhlenberg	56
91	McDaniel	66
76	Dickinson ⊠	60
51	Mississippi Col. †	75
72	Thomas More †	50
77	Washington (Md.) ⊠	72
59	Haverford ⊠	64
66	Ursinus	50
78	Muhlenberg ⊠	58
69	Frank. & Marsh. ⊠	66
77	Dickinson	40
83	Gettysburg ⊠	67
72	Washington (Md.)	54
63	Swarthmore	59
72	Haverford	68
68	McDaniel ⊠	70
74	Ursinus ⊠	68
58	Gettysburg	65
84	Frank. & Marsh. ⊠	68
80	Gettysburg ⊠	73
68	Haverford ⊠	61
84	Villa Julie ⊠	72
73	Guilford ⊠	80

Nickname: Blue Jays
Colors: Columbia Blue & Black
Arena: Goldfarb Gymnasium
   Capacity: 1,200; Year Built: 1965
AD: Thomas P. Calder
SID: Ernie Larossa

JOHNSON & WALES (RI)
Providence, RI 02903 III

Coach: Jamie Benton, Boston College 1988

2006-07 RESULTS (10-16)
78	Roger Williams	92
68	Coast Guard ⊠	77
49	Salve Regina ⊠	67
68	Rivier	55
53	Rhode Island Col. ⊠	82
67	Southern Vt.	75
59	Mass.-Dartmouth ⊠	73
86	Plymouth St.	92
64	Norwich	62
67	Connecticut Col.	63
71	Emmanuel (Mass.)	77
63	Rivier ⊠	74
69	Emerson ⊠	87
91	Suffolk ⊠	97
55	Western New Eng.	60
70	Southern Vt. ⊠	63
84	Daniel Webster	62
108	Albertus Magnus ⊠	68
78	Emmanuel (Mass.) ⊠	70
72	Emerson	75
94	Suffolk	99
64	Western New Eng. ⊠	69
62	Norwich	59
107	Albertus Magnus	66
78	Daniel Webster	65
76	Rivier	88

Nickname: Wildcats
Colors: Red & Gold
Arena: Harborside Student Center

Capacity: 1,500; Year Built: 1998
AD: John Parente
SID: Dan Booth

JOHNSON C. SMITH
Charlotte, NC 28216.........................II

Coach: Steve Joyner, Johnson C. Smith 1973

2006-07 RESULTS (16-9)
89	Bluefield St. ⊠	59
86	West Virginia St. ⊠	95
84	West Va. Tech †	71
68	Bluefield St.	77
70	Elizabeth City St. ⊠	78
59	Virginia St. ⊠	68
80	Shaw ⊠	65
76	Elizabeth City St.	67
79	Virginia Union ⊠	70
54	Fayetteville St. ⊠	61
81	Bowie St. ⊠	53
77	St. Paul's	75
80	St. Augustine's ⊠	76
82	Virginia Union	79
88	Bowie St.	99
60	N.C. Central ⊠	55
76	Livingstone	79
66	Virginia ⊠	74
91	St. Paul's ⊠	81
82	St. Augustine's	73
73	Livingstone ⊠	62
94	Shaw	78
75	Fayetteville St.	72
61	N.C. Central ⊠	54
62	Bowie St. †	68

Nickname: Golden Bulls
Colors: Gold & Blue
Arena: Brayboy Gymnasium
   Capacity: 2,316; Year Built: 1961
AD: Stephen W. Joyner
SID: Kristene Kelly

JOHNSON ST.
Johnson, VT 05656-9464 III

Coach: Michael Osborne, Johnson St. 1998

2006-07 RESULTS (5-20)
74	Rivier	94
84	Bard †	75
85	Daniel Webster ⊠	86
70	Green Mountain ⊠	57
77	Vermont Tech	80
99	St. Joseph (Vt.) ⊠	93
96	Lesley	101
82	Lasell	106
87	Mass. Liberal Arts	89
58	New England Col. ⊠	83
60	Maine Maritime ⊠	73
46	Husson ⊠	85
62	Castleton	88
63	Thomas (Me.)	73
46	Me.-Farmington	79
59	Middlebury	92
73	Lasell ⊠	89
86	Mount Ida ⊠	74
73	Becker	84
81	Elms	109
65	Castleton ⊠	80
59	Lesley ⊠	77
84	Lyndon St. ⊠	93
75	Elms ⊠	88
92	Becker ⊠	72

Nickname: Badgers
Colors: Green, Blue & White
Arena: Carter Gymnasium
   Capacity: 850; Year Built: 1965
AD: Barbara Lougee
SID: Michael Osborne

JUNIATA
Huntingdon, PA 16652 III

Coach: Greg Curley, Allegheny 1995

2006-07 RESULTS (17-12)
88	Franciscan ⊠	54
76	Bethany (W.V.) ⊠	64
78	Frank. & Marsh. ⊠	67
61	Messiah	81
59	Widener ⊠	69
61	Grove City ⊠	51
66	Waynesburg	69
57	York (Pa.)	70
56	Defiance †	79
64	Case Reserve	77
94	Rutgers-Camden ⊠	51
61	Penn St.-DuBois ⊠	62
77	Gallaudet	31
61	Susquehanna	63
80	Moravian	76
74	Elizabethtown ⊠	68
76	Albright ⊠	75
54	Lebanon Valley	58
70	Moravian ⊠	50
76	Messiah ⊠	67
71	Widener	62
63	Elizabethtown	51
65	Lebanon Valley ⊠	74
82	Susquehanna ⊠	67
82	Albright	70
76	Susquehanna ⊠	64
60	Widener ⊠	63
72	Bethany (W.V.) ⊠	62
69	Penn St.-Behrend †	77

Nickname: Eagles
Colors: Yale Blue & Old Gold
Arena: Kennedy Sports & Recreation Center
   Capacity: 1,500; Year Built: 1982
AD: Lawrence R. Bock
SID: Joel Cookson

KALAMAZOO
Kalamazoo, MI 49006 III

Coach: Rob Passage, Kalamazoo 1993

2006-07 RESULTS (5-19)
44	Heidelberg †	69
64	North Park †	69
78	Benedictine (Ill.) ⊠	65
63	Manchester ⊠	70
59	Chicago ⊠	93
57	Elmhurst	84
104	Grinnell †	124
63	Otterbein	83
89	Hiram †	81
55	Hope ⊠	87
65	Adrian	77
56	Alma	64
68	Tri-State ⊠	69
59	Albion ⊠	77
60	Olivet	63
63	Calvin	74
48	Hope	86
80	Adrian ⊠	67
73	Alma ⊠	66
53	Tri-State	75
62	Albion	83
77	Olivet ⊠	69
67	Calvin ⊠	72
47	Tri-State	60

Nickname: Hornets
Colors: Orange & Black
Arena: Anderson Athletic Center
   Capacity: 2,000; Year Built: 1980
AD: Timon Corwin
SID: Steve Wideen

KANSAS
Lawrence, KS 66045-8881 I

Coach: Bill Self, Oklahoma St. 1985

2006-07 RESULTS (33-5)
91	Northern Ariz. ⊠	57
71	Oral Roberts ⊠	78
87	Towson ⊠	61
89	Tennessee St. ⊠	54
64	Ball St. †	46
82	Florida †	80
83	Dartmouth ⊠	32
57	DePaul	64
72	Southern California ⊠	62
68	Toledo ⊠	58
94	Winston-Salem ⊠	43
84	Boston College ⊠	66
63	Detroit ⊠	43
80	Rhode Island ⊠	69
70	South Carolina ⊠	54
87	Oklahoma St. ⊠	57
68	Iowa St.	64
80	Missouri ⊠	77
64	Texas Tech	69
82	Baylor	56
97	Colorado ⊠	74
76	Nebraska	56
66	Texas A&M ⊠	69
97	Kansas St. ⊠	70
92	Missouri	74
75	Colorado	46
92	Nebraska ⊠	39
71	Kansas St.	62
89	Iowa St. ⊠	52
67	Oklahoma	65
90	Texas ⊠	86
64	Oklahoma †	47
67	Kansas St. †	61
88	Texas †	84
107	Niagara †	67
88	Kentucky †	76
61	Southern Ill. †	58
55	UCLA †	68

Nickname: Jayhawks
Colors: Crimson & Blue
Arena: Allen Fieldhouse
   Capacity: 16,300; Year Built: 1955
AD: Lew Perkins
SID: Chris Theisen

KANSAS ST.
Manhattan, KS 66502-3355 I

Coach: Bob Huggins, West Virginia 1977

2006-07 RESULTS (23-12)
70	William & Mary ⊠	60
55	Rutgers	41
101	Tennessee Tech ⊠	79
54	New Mexico	78
68	Coppin St. ⊠	57
48	California	78
83	Colorado St.	84
93	Cleveland St. ⊠	60
83	North Dakota St.	81
82	Kennesaw St. ⊠	54
79	Md.-East. Shore ⊠	58
68	Southern California †	55
72	New Mexico †	56
66	Xavier †	76
65	Texas A&M	69
52	Texas Tech ⊠	62
85	Missouri	81
69	Baylor ⊠	60
69	Iowa St.	60
73	Chicago St. ⊠	36
61	Nebraska ⊠	45
80	Missouri ⊠	73
73	Texas	72
70	Kansas	97
78	Colorado ⊠	59
63	Nebraska	74
65	Iowa St. ⊠	47
62	Kansas ⊠	71
87	Colorado	71

(continued)
70	Oklahoma St.	84
72	Oklahoma ⊠	61
66	Texas Tech †	45
61	Kansas †	67
59	Vermont ⊠	57
65	DePaul ⊠	70

Nickname: Wildcats
Colors: Purple & White
Arena: Bramlage Coliseum
   Capacity: 13,344; Year Built: 1988
AD: Tim Weiser
SID: Tom Gilbert

KEAN
Union, NJ 07083 III

Coach: Sean Drennan, Montclair St. 1997

2006-07 RESULTS (13-12)
73	Manhattanville	72
82	St. Vincent †	66
107	Merchant Marine ⊠	85
97	Ramapo	87
72	TCNJ	69
59	New Jersey City	67
96	Moravian	91
85	City Tech ⊠	79
74	Ithaca	73
73	Wilkes	83
67	Plattsburgh St. †	62
73	Springfield	76
60	King's (Pa.)	74
80	John Jay	76
82	Richard Stockton ⊠	91
89	Staten Island ⊠	67
87	Rowan	93
67	Montclair St. ⊠	80
80	Rutgers-Camden ⊠	49
73	Wm. Paterson	77
75	TCNJ ⊠	57
93	Rutgers-Newark	95
89	Richard Stockton	96
68	Rowan ⊠	88
77	Rutgers-Camden	86

Nickname: Cougars
Colors: Blue & White
Arena: Harwood Arena
   Capacity: 2,500; Year Built: 2005
AD: Glenn Hedden
SID: Karyn Pinter

KEENE ST.
Keene, NH 03435-0000 III

Coach: Rob Colbert, Marist 1992

2006-07 RESULTS (25-6)
103	Eastern Nazarene ⊠	65
109	Lesley ⊠	75
79	Endicott	61
92	New England Col. †	77
82	Rhode Island Col.	78
109	Tufts	118
89	Mass.-Dartmouth ⊠	81
67	Sewanee †	54
80	Bridgewater St. †	71
82	Northwestern (Minn.) ⊠	73
67	Mass.-Boston	61
101	Western Conn. St. ⊠	88
84	Springfield ⊠	79
81	Southern Me.	56
71	Eastern Conn. St. ⊠	73
92	Rhode Island Col. ⊠	81
58	Plymouth St. ⊠	57
79	Mitchell	69
74	Mass.-Dartmouth	97
92	Williams ⊠	85
86	Mass.-Boston ⊠	90
79	Eastern Conn. St.	71
84	Western Conn. St.	77
88	Plymouth St. ⊠	73
79	Southern Me. ⊠	65
98	Plymouth St. ⊠	86
79	Mass.-Boston †	67

75	Rhode Island Col.	87
81	Rivier	47
76	Salem St.	75
73	Rhode Island Col. †	75

Nickname: Owls
Colors: Red & White
Arena: Spaulding Gym
  Capacity: 2,100; Year Built: 1968
AD: John C. Ratliff
SID: Stuart Kaufman

KENNESAW ST.
Kennesaw, GA 30144-5591............ II

Coach: Tony Ingle, Huntington 1976

2006-07 RESULTS (13-18)

55	Western Ky. ⊠	96
67	St. Peter's †	60
51	Columbia	63
52	George Washington ⊠	69
68	Florida Int'l ⊠	70
68	Newberry ⊠	55
56	Stetson	61
77	Mercer	84
54	Kansas St.	82
65	Wichita St.	74
67	Md.-East. Shore †	49
85	Longwood †	87
67	Chattanooga	83
78	Alabama St. †	72
66	Lipscomb ⊠	55
45	Belmont ⊠	63
85	Campbell	88
77	Gardner-Webb	60
83	Jacksonville ⊠	76
77	North Fla. ⊠	57
66	East Tenn. St.	78
62	Lipscomb	73
66	Belmont	85
74	Campbell ⊠	64
59	Gardner-Webb ⊠	56
68	North Fla.	66
72	Jacksonville	76
66	Georgia	75
71	East Tenn. St. ⊠	75
87	Mercer ⊠	51
72	Stetson ⊠	67

Nickname: Owls
Colors: Black & Gold
Arena: KSU Convocation Center
  Capacity: 4,500; Year Built: 2005
AD: Dave Waples
SID: Mark Toma

KENT ST.
Kent, OH 44242-0001 I

Coach: Jim Christian, Rhode Island 1988

2006-07 RESULTS (21-11)

105	South Dakota St. †	50
81	IUPUI †	74
59	Ohio St.	81
61	Detroit ⊠	48
63	Temple ⊠	54
80	Butler	83
59	Cleveland St.	66
79	IPFW	69
72	Duke	79
58	Youngstown St. ⊠	62
70	Shawnee St. ⊠	47
74	New Hampshire ⊠	47
73	A&M-Corpus Christi	81
63	Miami (Ohio)	65
69	Buffalo	56
67	Ohio ⊠	65
68	Akron	78
62	Bowling Green ⊠	61
60	Ball St.	54
68	Northern Ill.	49
61	Central Mich. ⊠	45
82	Eastern Mich. ⊠	46
64	Toledo ⊠	60

57	Western Mich.	79
61	Miami (Ohio) ⊠	45
68	George Mason	62
68	Buffalo ⊠	64
73	Ohio	71
77	Bowling Green	64
64	Akron ⊠	66
75	Western Mich. †	66
54	Akron †	61

Nickname: Golden Flashes
Colors: Navy Blue & Gold
Arena: Memorial Athletic & Convocation Center
  Capacity: 6,327; Year Built: 1950
AD: Laing E. Kennedy
SID: Jason Tirotta

KENTUCKY
Lexington, KY 40506-0032.............. I

Coach: Tubby Smith, High Point 1973

2006-07 RESULTS (22-12)

57	Miami (Ohio) ⊠	46
79	Mississippi Val. ⊠	56
87	DePaul †	81
68	UCLA †	73
63	Memphis †	80
77	Col. of Charleston ⊠	61
63	North Carolina	75
79	Chattanooga †	63
59	Indiana ⊠	54
61	Louisville	49
74	Santa Clara ⊠	60
82	Massachusetts ⊠	68
78	Eastern Ky. ⊠	65
77	Houston ⊠	70
68	Mississippi	58
84	Auburn ⊠	57
64	Mississippi St. ⊠	60
87	South Carolina	49
67	Vanderbilt †	72
69	Georgia	78
76	Tennessee ⊠	57
82	Arkansas	74
95	South Carolina ⊠	89
61	Florida	64
85	Tennessee	89
61	Alabama	72
70	LSU ⊠	63
65	Vanderbilt	67
82	Georgia ⊠	70
72	Florida	85
79	Alabama †	67
82	Mississippi St. †	84
67	Villanova †	58
76	Kansas †	88

Nickname: Wildcats
Colors: Blue & White
Arena: Rupp Arena
  Capacity: 23,000; Year Built: 1976
AD: Mitch S. Barnhart
SID: Scott Stricklin

KENTUCKY ST.
Frankfort, KY 40601.......................... II

Coach: Thomas Patterson, Grace Bible (Mich.) 1995

2006-07 RESULTS (15-15)

64	Claflin	53
87	Elizabeth City St.	81
43	Holy Family †	56
59	Paine ⊠	69
65	Benedict ⊠	78
71	Morehouse	54
86	Clark Atlanta	54
84	Lane ⊠	73
86	Fort Valley St. ⊠	71
100	Albany St. (Ga.) ⊠	84
80	Paine	93
63	Benedict	84
67	Morehouse ⊠	78
65	Clark Atlanta ⊠	50

63	Fort Valley St.	77
66	Albany St. (Ga.)	67
51	Central St. (Ohio) ⊠	63
70	Tuskegee	51
67	Stillman	69
79	Central St. (Ohio)	85
75	LeMoyne-Owen	71
98	Miles	85
54	Lane	76
88	LeMoyne-Owen ⊠	80
84	Miles ⊠	80
57	Stillman ⊠	60
72	Tuskegee ⊠	79
101	Tuskegee †	85
88	Paine †	82
70	Fort Valley St. †	86

Nickname: Thorobreds
Colors: Green & Gold
Arena: William Exum HPER Center
  Capacity: 2,750; Year Built: 1994
AD: Derita Ratcliffe
SID: Ron Braden

KY. WESLEYAN
Owensboro, KY 42302-1039 II

Coach: Todd Lee, South Dakota 1983

2006-07 RESULTS (13-14)

100	Goshen ⊠	72
99	Illinois Tech ⊠	50
104	Mid-Continent ⊠	59
78	Cumberland (Ky.) ⊠	74
69	Southern Ind.	84
70	Indianapolis	77
64	St. Joseph's (Ind.)	69
81	SIU Edwardsville ⊠	80
86	Glenville St. ⊠	75
86	Saginaw Valley ⊠	80
62	Drury ⊠	53
61	Rockhurst ⊠	67
72	Quincy	81
47	SIU Edwardsville	64
65	Northern Ky. ⊠	76
61	Bellarmine ⊠	75
72	Wis.-Parkside	73
74	Lewis	84
106	Mo.-Rolla ⊠	97
97	Mo.-St. Louis ⊠	90
88	St. Joseph's (Ind.) ⊠	80
67	Indianapolis ⊠	72
49	Northern Ky.	67
69	Bellarmine	72
67	Western Ky.	74
86	Lewis ⊠	73
75	Wis.-Parkside ⊠	73

Nickname: Panthers
Colors: Purple & White
Arena: Owensboro Sportscenter
  Capacity: 5,002; Year Built: 1949
AD: Gary Gallup
SID: Roy Pickerill

KENYON
Gambier, OH 43022-9223.............. III

Coach: Matt Croci, Wittenberg 1994

2006-07 RESULTS (10-16)

67	La Roche †	48
83	Myers ⊠	67
52	Eastern Ky.	63
52	Capital ⊠	62
61	Muskingum	86
69	Wash. & Jeff.	58
61	Allegheny ⊠	59
85	Case Reserve	76
60	Earlham	69
70	Grove City ⊠	76
52	DePauw ⊠	53
67	Wittenberg ⊠	72
47	Ohio Wesleyan	53
86	Hiram ⊠	76
62	Oberlin	63
73	Denison ⊠	70

81	Wabash ⊠	87
54	Wooster	89
65	Allegheny	70
73	Hiram	54
53	Earlham	47
65	Denison	68
73	Oberlin ⊠	66
62	Wooster ⊠	87
74	Wabash	77
54	Ohio Wesleyan ⊠	60

Nickname: Lords
Colors: Purple & White
Arena: Tomsich Arena
  Capacity: 2,000; Year Built: 2006
AD: Peter Smith
SID: Marty Fuller

KEUKA
Keuka Park, NY 14478-0098 III

Coach: George Wunder, Rochester 1986

2006-07 RESULTS (13-13)

60	SUNYIT †	110
90	Paul Smith †	71
82	Hobart ⊠	78
74	Hilbert ⊠	89
78	Phila. Biblical	69
76	D'Youville	46
80	Penn St.-Berks ⊠	62
61	Chestnut Hill	63
58	Brockport St. ⊠	98
59	Roberts Wesleyan	95
66	Nazareth	90
71	Bard	67
61	Keystone ⊠	68
54	Baptist Bible (Pa.)	56
100	Cazenovia ⊠	57
73	D'Youville ⊠	49
71	Villa Julie ⊠	84
78	Albany Pharmacy ⊠	79
66	Keystone	68
70	Purchase St.	59
82	Polytechnic (N.Y.) ⊠	54
91	Cazenovia	93
100	Baptist Bible (Pa.) ⊠	93
89	Bard ⊠	73
76	Keystone	69
73	Villa Julie	95

Nickname: Storm
Colors: Green & Gold
Arena: Weed Physical Arts Center
  Capacity: 1,800; Year Built: 1973
AD: David M. Sweet
SID: Seth Fikes

KEYSTONE
La Plume, PA 18440.......................... III

Coach: Marc L. Smith, Lincoln Memorial 1993

2006-07 RESULTS (12-13)

54	Fredonia St. †	56
66	Morrisville St. †	63
58	TCNJ	61
55	Mansfield	79
47	Rutgers-Camden ⊠	55
56	Baptist Bible (Pa.) ⊠	55
79	Penn St.-Berks	76
74	Chestnut Hill ⊠	75
55	Washington (Md.)	61
57	Lincoln (Pa.)	74
50	Rutgers-Camden †	46
64	Villa Julie	81
68	Keuka	61
77	Cazenovia	89
68	D'Youville ⊠	45
78	Bard ⊠	70
57	Baptist Bible (Pa.)	81
65	Purchase St. ⊠	46
68	Keuka ⊠	66
85	Polytechnic (N.Y.)	67
77	D'Youville	79

54	Phila. Biblical ⊠	57
101	Bard	80
94	Cazenovia ⊠	65
69	Keuka	76

Nickname: Giants
Colors: Navy Blue, Oreange & White
Arena: Ace Spalding Arena
    Capacity: 1,000; Year Built: 1989
AD: Matthew T. Grimaldi
SID: J.R. Rupp

KING'S (PA.)
Wilkes-Barre, PA 18711-0801 III

Coach: J.P. Andrejko, Scranton 1988
2006-07 RESULTS (19-9)

67	TCNJ †	44
97	Susquehanna	98
84	Albright ⊠	85
94	Widener ⊠	81
75	Scranton ⊠	69
55	DeSales	82
80	Baptist Bible (Pa.) ⊠	75
71	Elizabethtown	84
80	Lafayette	89
81	Misericordia ⊠	73
76	Ursinus	50
87	York (Pa.)	91
74	Kean ⊠	60
76	Wilkes ⊠	55
80	Delaware Valley ⊠	61
58	Lycoming	52
78	FDU-Florham	75
62	Drew ⊠	55
63	Delaware Valley	66
75	Scranton	72
73	DeSales ⊠	70
79	Lycoming ⊠	61
80	Drew	40
58	Wilkes	66
91	FDU-Florham ⊠	66
83	FDU-Florham ⊠	74
67	DeSales ⊠	64
63	Widener ⊠	76

Nickname: Monarchs
Colors: Red & Gold
Arena: Scandlon Gym
    Capacity: 3,200; Year Built: 1968
AD: Cheryl J. Ish
SID: Bob Ziadie

KNOX
Galesburg, IL 61401-4999 III

Coach: Tim Heimann, Knox 1970
2006-07 RESULTS (5-18)

78	Eureka	83
79	William Penn ⊠	75
47	Hannibal-La Grange ⊠	64
75	Ripon	89
61	St. Norbert	74
86	Illinois Col.	83
70	Clarke ⊠	80
49	Southeastern (Fla.)	61
55	Warner Southern	78
75	Concordia (Ill.)	66
70	Monmouth (Ill.) ⊠	63
52	Carroll (Wis.) ⊠	72
63	Lawrence	74
63	Beloit	79
64	Carroll (Wis.)	70
70	Grinnell	90
53	Lake Forest ⊠	65
70	Illinois Col. ⊠	63
49	St. Norbert ⊠	58
66	Ripon ⊠	76
70	Monmouth (Ill.)	73
74	Grinnell ⊠	91
56	Lake Forest	76

Nickname: Prairie Fire
Colors: Purple & Gold
Arena: Memorial Gym
    Capacity: 3,000; Year Built: 1951

AD: Chad Eisele
SID: Brian Thiessen

KUTZTOWN
Kutztown, PA 19530-0721 II

Coach: Bernie Driscoll, Dickinson 1977
2006-07 RESULTS (17-11)

103	Penn St.-Hazleton ⊠	55
90	Wilmington (Del.)	84
84	Columbia Union †	78
66	Dist. Columbia	78
55	Phila. Sciences	53
69	Shippensburg ⊠	64
81	Lock Haven ⊠	68
100	Columbia Union	88
95	Slippery Rock ⊠	88
62	Edinboro	75
96	Penn St.-Berks	59
69	Indiana (Pa.) ⊠	64
79	Clarion	69
93	West Chester ⊠	97
75	California (Pa.) ⊠	83
74	Mansfield	85
73	Bloomsburg ⊠	70
67	Millersville ⊠	64
71	Cheyney	76
74	East Stroudsburg ⊠	69
88	West Chester	86
71	Mansfield ⊠	73
80	Bloomsburg	82
82	Millersville ⊠	79
73	Cheyney ⊠	70
81	Dist. Columbia ⊠	84
72	East Stroudsburg ⊠	74
63	Cheyney ⊠	79

Nickname: Golden Bears
Colors: Maroon & Gold
Arena: Keystone Hall
    Capacity: 3,400; Year Built: 1971
AD: Greg Bamberger
SID: Josh Leiboff

LA ROCHE
Pittsburgh, PA 15237 III

Coach: Scott Lang, Clarion 1993
2006-07 RESULTS (8-17)

48	Kenyon †	67
53	Mt. Vernon Naz. †	85
75	Thiel ⊠	70
89	Westminster (Pa.) ⊠	92
48	Penn St.-Altoona	46
62	Pitt.-Bradford ⊠	66
58	Carnegie Mellon	77
71	Frostburg St. ⊠	72
73	Hilbert	79
69	Waynesburg ⊠	83
89	Hiram	85
73	Lake Erie ⊠	82
92	Mt. Aloysius	77
56	Penn St.-Behrend	74
87	Pitt.-Greensburg ⊠	86
59	Medaille ⊠	60
73	Pitt.-Bradford	85
50	Penn St.-Altoona ⊠	59
68	Hilbert ⊠	63
67	Frostburg St.	59
45	Lake Erie	71
77	Mt. Aloysius ⊠	79
71	Penn St.-Behrend ⊠	61
62	Medaille	69
67	Pitt.-Greensburg	82

Nickname: Redhawks
Colors: Red & White
Arena: Kerr Fitness & Sports Center
    Capacity: 1,200; Year Built: 1993
AD: Jim Tinkey
SID: Chase Rowe

LA SALLE
Philadelphia, PA 19141-1199 I

Coach: John Giannini, North Central 1984
2006-07 RESULTS (10-20)

66	Mt. St. Mary's ⊠	60
84	Howard ⊠	78
69	St. Francis (Pa.)	60
68	Coppin St. †	69
64	Tex.-Pan American †	63
67	UMBC ⊠	78
86	Central Conn. St.	73
102	Morgan St. ⊠	76
51	Villanova ⊠	64
48	Holy Cross ⊠	68
56	Delaware ⊠	58
82	Niagara ⊠	88
66	Rhode Island	69
71	Massachusetts ⊠	79
79	Duquesne	63
82	Dayton	84
78	NJIT	59
92	Penn	93
73	St. Bonaventure	87
79	Richmond ⊠	56
54	Fordham	62
80	Charlotte	87
64	Temple	89
105	Duquesne ⊠	111
50	St. Joseph's ⊠	72
77	Temple ⊠	72
55	St. Louis	59
74	George Washington ⊠	86
63	Massachusetts	102
65	Xavier ⊠	76

Nickname: Explorers
Colors: Blue & Gold
Arena: Tom Gola Arena
    Capacity: 4,000; Year Built: 1972
AD: Thomas M. Brennan
SID: Kale Beers

LA VERNE
La Verne, CA 91750-4443 III

Coach: Gabe Duran, La Verne 1998
2006-07 RESULTS (5-20)

46	St. Thomas (Minn.) ⊠	60
63	Chapman	72
76	LIFE Pacific ⊠	46
60	La Sierra ⊠	66
79	West Coast Baptist	81
54	Pt. Loma Nazarene	101
62	Chapman ⊠	70
104	Puget Sound ⊠	114
54	Anderson (Ind.) ⊠	74
61	Millikin ⊠	74
70	La Sierra ⊠	74
43	Claremont-M-S ⊠	59
67	Whittier ⊠	63
44	Cal Lutheran ⊠	64
104	Redlands	116
58	Caltech	55
49	Occidental ⊠	70
61	Pomona-Pitzer	77
50	Claremont-M-S	59
67	Whittier	63
53	Cal Lutheran	56
93	Redlands ⊠	97
85	Caltech ⊠	52
54	Occidental	85
72	Pomona-Pitzer ⊠	77

Nickname: Leopards, Leos
Colors: Orange & Green
Arena: Sports Sci. Athletic Pavillion
    Capacity: 1,250; Year Built: 1973
AD: Christopher M. Ragsdale
SID: Will Darity

LAFAYETTE
Easton, PA 18042 I

Coach: Fran O'Hanlon, Villanova 1970
2006-07 RESULTS (9-21)

76	Wagner	70
66	Indiana †	91
60	Notre Dame †	92
73	St. Joseph's ⊠	81
51	UMBC	86
66	Miami (Fla.)	98
42	Princeton ⊠	44
72	St. Peter's	69
76	NJIT	57
72	Lycoming	54
58	Columbia ⊠	75
89	King's (Pa.) ⊠	80
58	Mt. St. Mary's ⊠	56
73	Temple	96
68	San Diego St.	78
74	Holy Cross	84
71	Colgate	65
44	Navy	60
61	Bucknell	67
69	Lehigh	77
76	Army ⊠	68
59	American ⊠	73
52	Holy Cross	74
51	Colgate ⊠	54
63	Navy ⊠	70
58	Bucknell	76
75	Lehigh ⊠	71
65	Army	83
67	American	78
53	Holy Cross	83

Nickname: Leopards
Colors: Maroon & White
Arena: Kirby Sports Center
    Capacity: 3,500; Year Built: 1973
AD: Bruce McCutcheon
SID: Phil LaBella

LAGRANGE
La Grange, GA 30240 III

Coach: Warren Haynes, LaGrange 1998
2006-07 RESULTS (18-9)

110	N.C. Wesleyan †	88
101	Carver Bible †	79
73	Sewanee ⊠	69
93	Emory	96
83	Oglethorpe †	87
83	Atlanta Christian	64
91	Emory ⊠	77
75	Berry	73
77	Valdosta St.	104
84	Dallas Christian †	67
71	Dallas	79
75	Millsaps ⊠	81
84	MacMurray	72
70	Emmanuel (Ga.) ⊠	97
60	Maryville (Tenn.) ⊠	73
75	Rust ⊠	69
95	Oglethorpe ⊠	90
71	Piedmont ⊠	66
66	Huntingdon	58
84	Pensacola Christian ⊠	70
87	Piedmont	80
57	Maryville (Tenn.)	87
76	Fisk	70
62	Huntingdon ⊠	41
97	Carver Bible ⊠	93
102	Piedmont ⊠	97
58	Maryville (Tenn.) ⊠	80

Nickname: Panthers
Colors: Red & Black
Arena: Mariotti Gymnasium
    Capacity: 500; Year Built: 1958
AD: Philip R. Williamson
SID: John Hughes

LAKE ERIE
Painesville, OH 44077 III

Coach: Cliff Hunt, Hiram 1971

2006-07 RESULTS (25-3)

85	Geneseo St. †	76
73	Rochester (N.Y.)	62
82	Denison	70
67	Findlay	99
68	Hilbert	65
97	Pitt.-Greensburg	58
67	Medaille	50
86	Penn St.-Altoona ⊠	68
88	St. Vincent	80
79	Bethany (W.V.) ⊠	74
82	La Roche	73
69	Pitt.-Bradford ⊠	52
104	Mt. Aloysius ⊠	90
80	Frostburg St.	70
63	Penn St.-Behrend	51
98	Pitt.-Greensburg ⊠	86
96	Hilbert	66
94	Penn St.-Altoona	66
97	Franciscan ⊠	72
78	Medaille ⊠	60
71	La Roche ⊠	45
93	Pitt.-Bradford	64
109	Mt. Aloysius	93
60	Penn St.-Behrend ⊠	66
71	Frostburg St. ⊠	51
80	Hilbert ⊠	67
59	Penn St.-Behrend ⊠	58
77	John Carroll ⊠	79

Nickname: Storm
Colors: Green & White
Arena: Athletics and Wellness Center
 Capacity: 800; Year Built: 2004
AD: Ken Krsolovic
SID: Kristy Booher

LAKE FOREST
Lake Forest, IL 60045 III

Coach: Chris Conger, Wisconsin 1995

2006-07 RESULTS (15-10)

65	Lakeland	58
39	Chicago ⊠	66
62	Edgewood	61
76	Illinois Tech ⊠	69
66	Beloit	58
59	Lawrence	69
68	Milwaukee Engr. ⊠	61
56	North Park †	57
55	Dominican (Ill.) †	57
80	Grinnell ⊠	79
51	Illinois Col.	53
72	Ripon ⊠	73
51	St. Norbert ⊠	52
72	Carroll (Wis.)	70
62	Ripon	49
53	Monmouth (Ill.) ⊠	55
65	Knox	53
71	Beloit ⊠	52
72	Lawrence ⊠	69
65	Illinois Col. ⊠	61
65	Grinnell	100
69	Monmouth (Ill.)	59
76	Knox ⊠	56
94	Grinnell	79
71	Carroll (Wis.) †	80

Nickname: Foresters
Colors: Red & Black
Arena: Sports Center
 Capacity: 1,200; Year Built: 1968
AD: Jackie A. Slaats
SID: Mike Wajerski

LAKE SUPERIOR ST.
Sault Ste. Marie, MI 49783 II

Coach: Mike Fitzner, Wayne St. (Neb.)
1997

2006-07 RESULTS (9-18)

72	Lewis †	75
65	Wis.-Parkside †	82
82	Finlandia ⊠	47
61	Iowa St.	90
68	Ashland	83
73	Concordia (Mich.)	64
55	Findlay ⊠	77
50	Northwood (Mich.) ⊠	52
74	Central St. (Ohio)	85
84	Ferris St.	77
72	St. Joseph's (Ind.) ⊠	75
77	Northern Mich.	75
71	Michigan Tech ⊠	63
33	Grand Valley St. ⊠	63
58	Central St. (Ohio) ⊠	76
55	Northland Bapt. ⊠	28
71	Gannon	61
62	Mercyhurst	66
59	Hillsdale ⊠	47
54	Wayne St. (Mich.) ⊠	77
48	Grand Valley St	82
78	Saginaw Valley	90
64	Northern Mich. ⊠	73
53	Michigan Tech ⊠	63
60	Saginaw Valley ⊠	63
62	Ferris St. ⊠	68
64	Northwood (Mich.)	60

Nickname: Lakers
Colors: Royal Blue & Gold
Arena: James Norris Center
 Capacity: 2,500; Year Built: 1976
AD: Kris Dunbar
SID: Linda Bouvet

LAKELAND
Sheboygan, WI 53082-0359 III

Coach: Kyle Brumett, Hanover 1998

2006-07 RESULTS (16-11)

58	Lake Forest ⊠	65
81	Wis.-La Crosse	91
94	Aurora ⊠	101
86	Concordia (Ill.)	72
108	Rockford	64
74	Benedictine (Ill.)	66
71	Wabash †	89
81	Alma †	68
74	Concordia (Wis.) ⊠	73
64	Edgewood ⊠	68
59	Wis.-Stevens Point	97
104	Northland Bapt. ⊠	65
80	Wis. Lutheran ⊠	63
86	Maranatha Baptist	50
66	Marian (Wis.)	71
76	Aurora	94
72	Dominican (Ill.)	73
84	Concordia (Ill.) ⊠	69
90	Rockford ⊠	57
95	Concordia (Wis.)	92
66	Benedictine (Ill.) ⊠	65
90	Milwaukee Engr. ⊠	75
81	Wis. Lutheran	87
85	Maranatha Baptist ⊠	56
80	Marian (Wis.) ⊠	64
51	Wis. Lutheran ⊠	50
72	Aurora	86

Nickname: Muskies
Colors: Navy & Gold
Arena: Todd Wehr Center
 Capacity: 1,500; Year Built: 1985
AD: Jane Bouche
SID: David Gallianetti

LAMAR
Beaumont, TX 77710 I

Coach: Steve Roccaforte, Lamar 1989

2006-07 RESULTS (15-17)

72	Texas Southern ⊠	64
60	Texas A&M	94
69	St. Louis †	82
71	Louisiana Tech †	68
62	New Orleans ⊠	64
92	St. Gregory's ⊠	72
64	Tulsa	78
63	Oral Roberts	88
71	Rice	83
86	BYU ⊠	77
64	Wyoming	69
74	Northern Ill. ⊠	53
62	Memphis	87
91	Louisiana Col. ⊠	76
71	UTSA	59
72	Stephen F. Austin ⊠	73
52	Sam Houston St.	88
62	Central Ark. ⊠	50
68	Northwestern St. ⊠	81
60	McNeese St.	68
89	Nicholls St. ⊠	82
64	Southeastern La.	73
74	Texas-Arlington	76
96	Texas St. ⊠	69
86	Central Ark.	82
78	A&M-Corpus Christi ⊠	77
75	McNeese St. ⊠	71
82	Northwestern St.	89
90	Nicholls St.	105
83	Southeastern La. ⊠	64
99	Sam Houston St. †	98
65	Northwestern St. †	78

Nickname: Cardinals
Colors: Red & White
Arena: Montagne Center
 Capacity: 10,080; Year Built: 1984
AD: Billy Tubbs
SID: Daucy Crizer

LANDER
Greenwood, SC 29649-2099 II

Coach: Bruce Evans, Furman 1991

2006-07 RESULTS (20-11)

63	Presbyterian	69
74	Southern Wesleyan ⊠	57
74	Wingate	61
78	Newberry ⊠	57
59	Presbyterian ⊠	60
56	GCSU	73
63	Erskine ⊠	65
78	Catawba ⊠	61
60	Claflin ⊠	52
54	Catawba	66
78	Francis Marion	56
67	GCSU ⊠	53
92	North Georgia	63
63	Clayton St.	70
56	UNC Pembroke	39
54	Armstrong Atlantic ⊠	55
62	Erskine	29
73	North Georgia ⊠	64
74	Ga. Southwestern	66
62	UNC Pembroke ⊠	54
70	Augusta St.	84
59	S.C. Upstate ⊠	65
80	S.C.-Aiken	62
86	Francis Marion ⊠	68
96	Columbus St. ⊠	103
67	S.C. Upstate	66
70	S.C.-Aiken ⊠	59
83	Columbus St. ⊠	81
60	Armstrong Atlantic	56
75	Clayton St. ⊠	61
68	Virginia Union †	74

Nickname: Bearcats
Colors: Blue & Gold
Arena: Finis Horne Arena
 Capacity: 2,500; Year Built: 1993

AD: Jefferson J. May
SID: Bob Stoner

LANE
Jackson, TN 38301-4598 I

Coach: J.L. Perry, Lane 1971

2006-07 RESULTS (13-16)

53	Christian Bros. ⊠	55
80	Benedict ⊠	84
66	Paine ⊠	70
79	Christian Bros.	96
95	Clark Atlanta	90
88	Morehouse	93
73	Kentucky St.	84
66	Albany St. (Ga.) ⊠	64
69	Fort Valley St. ⊠	73
54	Benedict	56
77	Paine	57
66	Clark Atlanta ⊠	32
73	Morehouse ⊠	59
65	Albany St. (Ga.)	77
55	Fort Valley St.	74
45	Claflin	58
59	Stillman	65
76	Tuskegee	79
103	Knoxville	54
63	Claflin ⊠	55
95	Miles	90
90	LeMoyne-Owen ⊠	93
76	Kentucky St. ⊠	54
69	Miles ⊠	72
83	LeMoyne-Owen ⊠	77
80	Tuskegee ⊠	67
69	Stillman ⊠	55
80	LeMoyne-Owen †	67
58	Benedict †	84

Nickname: Dragons
Colors: Cardinal Red & Royal Blue
Arena: J.F. Lane Center
 Capacity: 2,500; Year Built: 1974
AD: Ronald Abernathy
SID: Gregory Borman

LASELL
Newton, MA 02466 III

Coach: Aaron Galletta, Union (N.Y.)
2001

2006-07 RESULTS (16-12)

80	Tufts	85
63	Endicott †	73
77	Union (N.Y.) ⊠	56
70	Becker	60
63	Trinity (Conn.)	82
73	Babson	75
86	Castleton ⊠	67
106	Johnson St. ⊠	82
90	Western Conn. St.	79
64	WPI	75
71	Salem St. ⊠	78
79	Lesley	72
86	Williams ⊠	60
74	Mount Ida	58
89	Lesley ⊠	78
89	Johnson St.	58
83	Castleton	76
83	Elms	87
58	Maine Maritime	56
75	Husson	81
84	Becker ⊠	58
107	Elms	115
68	MIT	76
70	Me.-Farmington ⊠	54
89	Thomas (Me.) ⊠	46
81	Me.-Farmington ⊠	77
64	Elms	68
67	Endicott †	68

Nickname: Lasers
Colors: Columbia & Navy
Arena: Lasell Gymnasium
 Capacity: 300; Year Built: 1997
AD: Kristy Walter
SID: Jessica King

LAWRENCE
Appleton, WI 54912-0599 III

Coach: John Tharp, Beloit 1991

2006-07 RESULTS (13-10)

67	Wis.-Stevens Point ⊠	70
89	Wis. Lutheran †	75
72	Concordia (Wis.) ⊠	62
91	Monmouth (Ill.) ⊠	63
69	Lake Forest ⊠	59
86	Carthage ⊠	93
75	Wis.-Oshkosh	88
69	Allegheny †	57
70	Ursinus †	65
56	Ripon	60
69	Beloit ⊠	57
130	Grinnell	142
74	Knox	63
79	Illinois Col. ⊠	67
103	Grinnell ⊠	106
55	St. Norbert ⊠	49
45	Carroll (Wis.)	72
63	Monmouth (Ill.)	71
69	Lake Forest	72
72	Ripon ⊠	57
74	Beloit	62
71	St. Norbert	57
63	Carroll (Wis.) ⊠	76

Nickname: Vikings
Colors: Blue & White
Arena: Alexander Gym
    Capacity: 1,100; Year Built: 1929
AD: Robert Beeman
SID: Joe Vanden Acker

LE MOYNE
Syracuse, NY 13214-1399 II

Coach: Steve Evans, Union (N.Y.) 1994

2006-07 RESULTS (14-15)

48	Molloy	60
86	Mansfield ⊠	70
77	St. Rose ⊠	84
84	Southern N.H. ⊠	69
60	Southern Conn. St.	64
81	St. Anselm ⊠	84
69	Franklin Pierce ⊠	60
73	St. Michael's	75
80	Pace ⊠	63
68	Bryant	70
70	Merrimack †	57
69	Nyack	50
62	Assumption	76
75	American Int'l ⊠	82
89	Southern Conn. St. ⊠	60
57	Bentley ⊠	67
46	Franklin Pierce	40
61	Bryant ⊠	67
57	St. Rose	69
80	Merrimack ⊠	62
86	St. Michael's ⊠	75
74	Stonehill	69
63	Pace	64
65	Mass.-Lowell ⊠	59
68	American Int'l	71
49	St. Anselm	66
59	Southern N.H.	53
61	Stonehill	54
70	Pace	79

Nickname: Dolphins
Colors: Green & Gold
Arena: Ted Grant Court
    Capacity: 2,000; Year Built: 1954
AD: Richard W. Rockwell
SID: Mike Donlin

LEBANON VALLEY
Annville, PA 17003-1400 III

Coach: Brad McAlester, Southampton 1975

2006-07 RESULTS (15-12)

56	McDaniel ⊠	59
66	Montclair St. ⊠	60
57	Frank. & Marsh.	52
51	Ursinus ⊠	60
79	Albright	74
79	Elizabethtown ⊠	73
92	Delaware Valley	65
56	Arcadia ⊠	49
74	Goucher ⊠	62
56	Penn St.-Behrend †	48
63	Embry-Riddle	59
62	Villa Julie	63
93	Maryland Bible †	80
87	Moravian	94
65	Messiah	69
58	Widener ⊠	71
66	Susquehanna ⊠	78
58	Juniata ⊠	54
61	Messiah ⊠	67
87	Widener	78
62	Elizabethtown	67
71	Moravian ⊠	64
74	Juniata	65
65	Albright ⊠	72
69	Susquehanna ⊠	74
84	Carnegie Mellon ⊠	75
73	DeSales	83

Nickname: Flying Dutchmen
Colors: Blue, White
Arena: LVC Gymnasium
    Capacity: 1,650; Year Built: 2003
AD: Kathleen Tierney
SID: Braden Snyder

LEES-MCRAE
Banner Elk, NC 28604-0128 II

Coach: Scott Polsgrove, Taylor (Ind.) 1987

2006-07 RESULTS (6-22)

60	Lincoln Memorial	77
63	Anderson (S.C.) ⊠	42
76	UNC Pembroke †	72
75	Pfeiffer	88
86	Mount Olive ⊠	77
66	Barton	94
75	VMI	135
62	High Point	88
64	Belmont Abbey ⊠	76
82	Limestone	91
71	St. Andrews ⊠	75
98	Pfeiffer ⊠	110
77	Queens (N.C.) ⊠	88
64	Coker	70
80	Erskine ⊠	83
66	Brevard ⊠	70
74	Anderson (S.C.)	66
58	Barton ⊠	82
71	North Greenville	82
91	Belmont Abbey ⊠	84
85	Mount Olive	95
58	Queens (N.C.)	72
77	Pfeiffer	105
53	St. Andrews	75
71	Limestone ⊠	81
57	Erskine	66
73	Coker ⊠	58
72	Belmont Abbey	73

Nickname: Bobcats
Colors: Forest Green & Gold
Arena: Williams Gym
    Capacity: 1,200; Year Built: 1975
AD: Ried Estus
SID: Jason Levesque

LEHIGH
Bethlehem, PA 18015-3089 I

Coach: Billy Taylor, Notre Dame 1995

2006-07 RESULTS (12-19)

65	Oregon	77
90	Portland St. †	94
68	Cal St. Northridge †	74
90	Cornell ⊠	71
72	Sacred Heart ⊠	63
55	Quinnipiac	71
75	Harvard	83
87	Notre Dame	93
96	Swarthmore ⊠	33
55	Central Conn. St. ⊠	52
43	Princeton	44
58	Miami (Fla.)	79
83	Haverford ⊠	39
61	Rutgers	67
39	Monmouth	67
54	Columbia ⊠	55
51	American ⊠	49
71	Navy	61
59	Army	64
60	Colgate ⊠	59
77	Lafayette ⊠	69
44	Bucknell ⊠	62
53	Holy Cross	64
56	American	54
65	Navy ⊠	70
75	Army ⊠	64
56	Colgate	53
71	Lafayette	75
56	Bucknell ⊠	69
50	Holy Cross ⊠	62
46	Army ⊠	47

Nickname: Mountain Hawks
Colors: Brown & White
Arena: Stabler Arena
    Capacity: 5,600; Year Built: 1979
AD: Joseph D. Sterrett
SID: Mike Stagnitta

LEHMAN
Bronx, NY 10468-1589 III

Coach: Steve Schluman, Syracuse 1989

2006-07 RESULTS (10-16)

70	Purchase St. †	58
54	Oswego St.	76
43	Wm. Paterson ⊠	63
60	Mt. St. Vincent ⊠	57
27	Medgar Evers	37
77	Baruch	65
62	Union (N.Y.)	76
54	Merchant Marine ⊠	61
44	Yeshiva	68
52	St. Joseph's (L.I.)	88
57	City Tech	62
63	Briarcliffe (N.Y.) ⊠	41
58	Medgar Evers ⊠	66
69	Hunter	79
79	John Jay ⊠	86
63	York (N.Y.) ⊠	76
50	CCNY	59
80	Brooklyn	76
62	Hunter ⊠	58
62	Mitchell	89
64	Staten Island	70
67	John Jay	53
56	Morrisville St. ⊠	46
60	Baruch	58
61	CCNY ⊠	55
55	Staten Island †	62

Nickname: Lightning
Colors: Royal Blue, Vegas Gold & White
Arena: Lehman College APEX
    Capacity: 1,200; Year Built: 1994
AD: Martin L. Zwiren
SID: Eric Harrison

LEMOYNE-OWEN
Memphis, TN 38126 II

Coach: Smokey Gaines, LeMoyne-Owen 1967

2006-07 RESULTS (12-16)

83	Ark.-Monticello	87
64	Christian Bros. ⊠	78
82	Delta St. ⊠	71
72	Albany St. (Ga.)	80
85	Fort Valley St.	80
56	Christian Bros.	94
79	Paine	93
74	Benedict ⊠	89
66	Stillman	80
78	Tuskegee	65
62	Morehouse	85
69	Miles ⊠	71
76	Stillman ⊠	64
71	Tuskegee ⊠	64
65	Paine	63
76	Benedict	78
77	Albany St. (Ga.) ⊠	69
77	Fort Valley St. ⊠	84
89	Rust	73
71	Kentucky St. ⊠	75
93	Lane ⊠	90
80	Kentucky St.	88
77	Lane	83
76	Clark Atlanta	53
84	Clark Atlanta ⊠	62
71	Morehouse ⊠	51
94	Miles	106
67	Lane †	80

Nickname: Magicians
Colors: Purple & Old Gold
Arena: Bruce Hall
    Capacity: 1,000; Year Built: 1954
AD: David "Smokey" Gaines
SID: LaKeisha Henderson

LENOIR-RHYNE
Hickory, NC 28603 II

Coach: John Lentz, Lenoir-Rhyne 1974

2006-07 RESULTS (18-10)

83	Anderson (S.C.) †	60
82	Morris †	56
84	Belmont Abbey	72
59	UNC Asheville	69
49	Clayton St. †	68
64	Armstrong Atlantic †	53
55	Francis Marion †	47
68	Armstrong Atlantic	71
74	Augusta St. ⊠	88
95	Barton ⊠	61
82	Catawba	93
72	Tusculum	62
75	Presbyterian	61
61	Newberry ⊠	54
69	Mars Hill	55
63	Lincoln Memorial	55
74	Carson-Newman ⊠	70
79	Wingate ⊠	67
78	Tusculum ⊠	66
72	Presbyterian	75
63	Newberry	54
80	Carson-Newman	82
59	Lincoln Memorial	44
73	Catawba	81
67	Wingate	81
85	Mars Hill	50
101	Lincoln Memorial ⊠	90
70	Catawba ⊠	74

Nickname: Bears
Colors: Red & Black
Arena: Shuford Memorial Gym
    Capacity: 3,200; Year Built: 1957
AD: Neill McGeachy
SID: John Karrs

LESLEY
Cambridge, MA 02138-2790 III

Coach: Scott Willard,

2006-07 RESULTS (14-13)

100	Marymount (Va.) †	89
75	Keene St.	109
84	Eastern Nazarene	79
79	MIT ⊠	80
105	Maine Maritime ⊠	87
90	Husson ⊠	93
87	Mount Ida	98
101	Johnson St. ⊠	96
110	Castleton ⊠	66
84	Westfield St.	92
76	Coast Guard	99
85	Colby ⊠	76
73	Elms	109
72	Lasell ⊠	79
92	Becker ⊠	65
78	Lasell	89
78	Becker	69
67	Newbury	74
93	Suffolk	90
72	Thomas (Me.)	70
79	Me.-Farmington	75
77	Johnson St.	59
79	Castleton	90
94	Elms ⊠	82
64	Colby-Sawyer	89
75	Maine Maritime	71
79	Husson	95

Nickname: Lynx
Colors: Forest Green & Gold
AD: Stanley C. Vieira
SID: Josh Streit

LETOURNEAU
Longview, TX 75607-7001 III

Coach: Robert Davis, Midland Lutheran 1970

2006-07 RESULTS (15-10)

84	Jarvis Christian ⊠	81
78	Austin ⊠	64
61	McMurry ⊠	73
61	Hardin-Simmons ⊠	60
63	Sul Ross St.	77
62	Howard Payne	95
72	East Tex. Baptist	62
88	Concordia (Tex.) ⊠	79
71	Mary Hardin-Baylor ⊠	68
56	Austin	65
69	Texas Lutheran	63
89	Schreiner	75
84	East Tex. Baptist ⊠	73
86	Ozarks (Ark.) ⊠	84
67	Texas-Tyler	70
40	Texas-Dallas	54
51	Mississippi Col.	72
76	Louisiana Col.	62
64	Mississippi Col. ⊠	62
67	Louisiana Col. ⊠	76
57	Texas-Tyler ⊠	54
58	Texas-Dallas ⊠	54
81	Jarvis Christian	95
77	Ozarks (Ark.)	53
65	Hardin-Simmons †	74

Nickname: YellowJackets
Colors: Blue & Gold
Arena: Solheim Arena
   Capacity: 1,200; Year Built: 1996
AD: Duane Trogdon
SID: Shane Meling

LEWIS
Romeoville, IL 60446 II

Coach: Scott Trost, Minn.-Morris 1985

2006-07 RESULTS (15-13)

75	Lake Superior St. †	72
59	Michigan Tech	61

75	Trinity Christian ⊠	73
72	Northwood (Mich.) ⊠	53
83	Drury ⊠	80
71	Rockhurst ⊠	61
64	Quincy	79
46	SIU Edwardsville	65
38	Grand Valley St.	57
66	Illinois St.	85
78	Olivet Nazarene ⊠	59
78	Carthage	60
71	Bellarmine ⊠	66
66	Northern Ky. ⊠	72
62	Wis.-Parkside ⊠	84
74	Mo.-St. Louis	63
79	Mo.-Rolla	59
68	Southern Ind. ⊠	82
84	Ky. Wesleyan ⊠	74
68	Indianapolis	62
74	St. Joseph's (Ind.) ⊠	82
66	Northern Ky.	82
103	Bellarmine	99
87	St. Joseph's (Ind.) ⊠	70
65	Indianapolis ⊠	60
69	Wis.-Parkside ⊠	70
73	Ky. Wesleyan	86
45	Southern Ind.	57

Nickname: Flyers
Colors: Red & White
Arena: Neil Carey Arena
   Capacity: 855; Year Built: 1961
AD: Dan Schumacher
SID: Mickey Smith

LEWIS & CLARK
Portland, OR 97219-7899 III

Coach: Bob Gaillard, San Francisco 1962

2006-07 RESULTS (19-7)

68	Cal St. East Bay ⊠	50
98	Hawaii-Hilo	93
74	Concordia (Cal.) †	75
96	Bethany Lutheran †	73
61	Cal Lutheran †	65
77	Evergreen St. ⊠	57
72	Whitman	69
73	Whitworth	82
80	Evergreen St.	64
64	Portland	74
102	Pacific Lutheran	76
76	Willamette	66
75	Pacific (Ore.)	80
85	Linfield	66
88	Puget Sound	94
74	George Fox ⊠	61
103	Whitman ⊠	84
66	Whitworth ⊠	60
59	Pacific Lutheran	55
60	Willamette	55
80	Pacific (Ore.) ⊠	54
77	Linfield	71
98	Puget Sound ⊠	86
75	George Fox	63
66	Puget Sound ⊠	60
62	Whitworth	69

Nickname: Pioneers
Colors: Orange & Black
Arena: Pamplin Sports Center
   Capacity: 2,300; Year Built: 1969
AD: Clark Yeager
SID: Melissa Dudek

LIBERTY
Lynchburg, VA 24502-2269 I

Coach: Randy Dunton, Baptist Bible (Mo.) 1984

2006-07 RESULTS (14-17)

48	Oklahoma	74
101	Cincinnati Christian ⊠	65
92	Houghton ⊠	46
109	Southern Va. ⊠	64
64	East Caro. ⊠	56

84	St. Francis (Pa.) ⊠	67
89	Longwood ⊠	61
56	St. Francis (Pa.) ⊠	70
66	Buffalo	72
61	Lipscomb ⊠	66
59	BYU	73
81	Seton Hall ⊠	85
58	Oral Roberts †	90
58	Florida	89
77	UNC Asheville	84
80	Radford ⊠	66
40	Winthrop ⊠	68
71	High Point	77
65	Coastal Caro.	70
66	Charleston So.	63
122	VMI	117
80	UNC Asheville ⊠	65
96	High Point ⊠	79
76	Winthrop	80
83	Charleston So. ⊠	73
76	Coastal Caro. ⊠	77
70	Longwood	76
81	Niagara	90
118	VMI	108
64	Radford	48
78	VMI ⊠	79

Nickname: Flames
Colors: Red, White & Blue
Arena: Vines Center
   Capacity: 9,000; Year Built: 1990
AD: Jeff Barber
SID: Vincent Briedis

LIMESTONE
Gaffney, SC 29340-3799 II

Coach: Larry Epperly, Emory & Henry 1975

2006-07 RESULTS (20-9)

79	Newberry †	78
84	Bellarmine †	74
54	East Caro.	80
62	Anderson (S.C.) ⊠	43
63	Mount Olive	78
46	Winthrop	80
86	North Greenville ⊠	81
78	S.C.-Aiken ⊠	52
67	Queens (N.C.) ⊠	69
67	Belmont Abbey	57
60	St. Andrews	58
91	Lees-McRae ⊠	82
90	North Greenville	79
82	Coker	65
67	Erskine	58
83	Barton ⊠	80
80	Pfeiffer ⊠	78
73	Mount Olive	78
89	St. Andrews ⊠	64
97	Pfeiffer	91
63	Queens (N.C.)	66
91	Belmont Abbey ⊠	96
77	Coker ⊠	50
58	Erskine ⊠	56
81	Lees-McRae	71
72	Anderson (S.C.) ⊠	68
80	Barton	88
98	Pfeiffer ⊠	77
81	Barton †	86

Nickname: Saints
Colors: Blue, White & Gold
Arena: Timken Center
   Capacity: 1,500; Year Built: 1976
AD: Larry Epperly
SID: Leah Melichar

LINCOLN (MO.)
Jefferson City, MO 65102-0029 II

Coach: Charles Terry, Arkansas 1976

2006-07 RESULTS (7-19)

73	Harris-Stowe ⊠	69
88	Cent. Christian (Mo) ⊠	14
68	Upper Iowa †	67

46	Northwest Mo. St.	75
56	Missouri St.	88
60	Mo.-Rolla ⊠	64
60	Central Mo. ⊠	88
81	Ark.-Monticello	89
84	Arkansas Tech	101
60	St. Edward's ⊠	91
71	Tex. A&M Int'l ⊠	78
87	Tex. Permian Basin	93
57	Okla. Panhandle	75
84	Mont. St.-Billings	95
65	Incarnate Word ⊠	70
67	St. Mary's (Tex.) ⊠	69
79	Dallas Baptist ⊠	69
80	Mont. St.-Billings ⊠	71
67	Mont. St.-Billings ⊠	68
79	Dallas Baptist	93
77	Incarnate Word	87
52	St. Mary's (Tex.)	87
74	Tex. Permian Basin	88
87	Okla. Panhandle ⊠	72
64	St. Edward's	83
64	Tex. A&M Int'l.	61

Nickname: Blue Tigers
Colors: Navy Blue & White
Arena: Jason Gym
   Capacity: 2,500; Year Built: 1958
AD: Tim Abney
SID: Jeremy Copeland

LINCOLN (PA.)
Lincoln Univ., PA 19352 III

Coach: Garfield Yuille, Lincoln (Pa.) 1991

2006-07 RESULTS (20-9)

98	Widener †	91
119	Delaware Valley †	90
103	Cheyney †	95
92	New Jersey City ⊠	84
79	Salem Int'l	90
201	Ohio St.-Marion †	78
75	Ramapo	91
86	Penn St.-Altoona	95
75	North Central (Ill.) †	53
110	Buffalo St. ⊠	103
99	Seton Hill †	109
64	Frank. & Marsh.	43
74	Keystone ⊠	57
96	Rutgers-Camden ⊠	62
84	Baptist Bible (Pa.) ⊠	70
88	Point Park	110
75	John Jay ⊠	61
69	Richard Stockton	83
70	Dist. Columbia	75
73	Ramapo ⊠	72
79	Penn St.-Abington	75
83	Apprentice	78
79	New Jersey City	76
91	Penn St.-Delco	75
84	Newbury †	72
80	St. Joseph's (Me.)	89
91	Alvernia †	76
81	Catholic †	70
128	Guilford †	129

Nickname: Lions
Colors: Orange & Blue
Arena: Manuel Rivero Hall
   Capacity: 3,000; Year Built: 1973
AD: Alfonso Scandrett Jr.
SID: Rob Knox

LINCOLN CHRISTIAN
Lincoln, IL 62656 III

Coach: Garfield Yuille, Lincoln (Pa.) 1991

2006-07 RESULTS (5-19)

61	St. Louis Christian	84
90	Great Lake Christian ⊠	55
63	Maranatha Baptist ⊠	70
90	Northland Bapt. ⊠	69
61	Grace Bible (Mich.) ⊠	81

70	MacMurray ⊠	71
65	Maryville (Mo.)	91
63	Webster ⊠	65
69	Eureka ⊠	73
64	Westminster (Mo.)	85
62	Greenville	93
53	Principia	87
78	Fontbonne ⊠	83
89	Blackburn ⊠	78
56	Maryville (Mo.) ⊠	69
70	MacMurray	90
49	Eureka	71
72	Webster	83
63	Westminster (Mo.)	75
71	Greenville ⊠	74
93	Principia ⊠	68
78	Emmaus ⊠	42
59	Fontbonne	90
50	Blackburn	77

Nickname: Preachers
Colors: Red, white & black
Arena: Laughlin Center
Capacity: 1,500
AD: Kevin Crawford
SID: To be named

LINCOLN MEMORIAL
Harrogate, TN 37752-1901 II

Coach: Hugh Watson, Lee 1968
2006-07 RESULTS (13-15)
77	Lees-McRae ⊠	60
74	King (Tenn.) ⊠	71
87	Brevard ⊠	52
69	Simmons ⊠	56
66	Brevard	73
68	Benedict	81
84	King (Tenn.)	91
64	UNC Pembroke	52
63	Mount Olive †	78
78	Carson-Newman	73
71	Wingate ⊠	77
67	Tusculum ⊠	63
74	Presbyterian	57
79	Newberry	77
55	Lenoir-Rhyne	63
65	Catawba	70
82	Mars Hill	62
66	North Greenville ⊠	65
86	Wingate	89
58	Tusculum	61
57	Presbyterian ⊠	73
67	Mars Hill ⊠	81
44	Lenoir-Rhyne	59
67	Catawba	89
120	Carson-Newman ⊠	118
90	North Greenville	93
75	Newberry ⊠	68
90	Lenoir-Rhyne	101

Nickname: Railsplitters
Colors: Blue & Gray
Arena: B. Frank Turner Arena
Capacity: 5,009; Year Built: 1990
AD: Jay Nidiffer
SID: Michael Peace

LINFIELD
Mc Minnville, OR 97128-6894 III

Coach: Larry Doty, Linfield 1978
2006-07 RESULTS (8-17)
86	Holy Names ⊠	88
93	Corban ⊠	80
83	Cascade ⊠	73
85	George Fox	91
79	Pacific Lutheran	85
85	Warner Pacific ⊠	89
87	Evergreen St.	83
75	Walla Walla †	71
61	Baldwin-Wallace †	69
73	Colorado Col. †	57
67	Mount Union †	73
64	Whitworth ⊠	77

88	Whitman ⊠	90
66	Lewis & Clark ⊠	85
68	Willamette	80
61	Pacific (Ore.) ⊠	53
64	Puget Sound	70
64	George Fox ⊠	65
80	Pacific Lutheran ⊠	73
58	Whitworth	71
57	Whitman	60
71	Lewis & Clark ⊠	77
83	Willamette ⊠	80
50	Pacific (Ore.)	54
76	Puget Sound ⊠	83

Nickname: Wildcats
Colors: Purple & Red
Arena: Ted Wilson Gymnasium
Capacity: 1,924; Year Built: 1989
AD: Scott Carnahan
SID: Kelly Bird

LIPSCOMB
Nashville, TN 37204-3951 I

Coach: Scott Sanderson, South Carolina 1984
2006-07 RESULTS (18-13)
70	Tusculum ⊠	67
67	Evansville ⊠	64
69	Missouri	89
68	South Carolina	75
80	Fisk ⊠	68
62	Winston-Salem ⊠	46
73	Jacksonville ⊠	61
68	North Fla. ⊠	54
50	Vanderbilt	59
75	Nicholls St. ⊠	55
73	Evansville	80
66	Liberty	61
58	Alabama	80
55	Kennesaw St.	66
72	East Tenn. St.	75
79	Stetson ⊠	68
89	Mercer ⊠	68
55	Belmont	50
55	Gardner-Webb	61
65	Campbell	64
73	Kennesaw St. ⊠	62
66	East Tenn. St. ⊠	71
62	Mercer	50
67	Stetson	69
70	Belmont ⊠	60
67	Campbell ⊠	64
59	Gardner-Webb ⊠	57
64	North Fla.	73
67	Jacksonville	74
85	Mercer †	49
72	East Tenn. St.	77

Nickname: Bisons
Colors: Purple & Gold
Arena: Allen Arena
Capacity: 5,000; Year Built: 2001
AD: Steve Potts
SID: Mark McGee

LIVINGSTONE
Salisbury, NC 28144 II

Coach: James Stinson, Barber-Scotia 1987
2006-07 RESULTS (8-20)
59	Benedict ⊠	63
51	GCSU †	61
80	Allen †	66
73	Bluefield St.	77
78	Bowie St.	90
61	Elizabeth City St. ⊠	73
62	Morris ⊠	54
48	Virginia Union	55
55	Virginia St.	79
73	St. Augustine's ⊠	76
55	Elizabeth City St.	53
64	N.C. Central	75
83	Bowie St.	79

68	Fayetteville St.	78
57	Virginia St. ⊠	66
72	Shaw ⊠	67
80	St. Paul's ⊠	95
79	Johnson C. Smith ⊠	76
52	Virginia Union ⊠	67
60	Morris	67
51	N.C. Central	59
90	St. Paul's	99
62	Johnson C. Smith	73
84	Bluefield St. ⊠	71
47	St. Augustine's	74
72	Shaw	69
47	Fayetteville St. ⊠	59
54	Elizabeth City St. †	71

Nickname: Blue Bears
Colors: Columbia Blue & Black
Arena: William Trent Gymnasium
Capacity: 1,500; Year Built: 1970
AD: Clifton Huff
SID: Adrian Ferguson

LOCK HAVEN
Lock Haven, PA 17745 II

Coach: John Wilson, Washburn 1980
2006-07 RESULTS (12-15)
80	Charleston (W.V.)	84
60	St. Francis (Pa.)	94
71	Pitt.-Johnstown †	86
71	C.W. Post †	101
81	Shepherd ⊠	79
77	East Stroudsburg	83
68	Kutztown	81
36	Youngstown St.	70
68	Mansfield ⊠	65
80	Bloomsburg ⊠	69
76	Fairmont St.	71
63	Millersville	88
86	West Chester	80
60	Slippery Rock	79
62	Cheyney	61
52	Shippensburg ⊠	75
50	California (Pa.)	78
87	Clarion	76
61	Edinboro	58
66	Indiana (Pa.)	61
62	Slippery Rock ⊠	76
61	Shippensburg	76
61	California (Pa.) ⊠	59
54	Clarion	60
73	Edinboro	92
71	Pitt.-Johnstown ⊠	70
66	Indiana (Pa.) ⊠	59

Nickname: Bald Eagles
Colors: Crimson & White
Arena: Thomas Fieldhouse
Capacity: 2,500; Year Built: 1928
AD: Sharon E. Taylor
SID: Al Weston

LONG BEACH ST.
Long Beach, CA 90840-0118 I

Coach: Larry Reynolds, UC Riverside 1976
2006-07 RESULTS (24-8)
68	Air Force †	69
86	San Jose St. †	67
73	Cal St. Bakersfield ⊠	70
61	Southern California	79
58	UCLA	88
49	Temple	74
57	UMBC	53
95	Pepperdine ⊠	90
76	Sacramento St. ⊠	55
76	San Jose St.	67
66	Loyola Marymount	65
89	UC Davis	75
74	Manhattan ⊠	61
101	UC Santa Barbara ⊠	65
77	Cal Poly ⊠	70
83	Cal St. Northridge	90

95	Cal St. Fullerton ⊠	85
99	UC Riverside ⊠	65
84	UC Irvine	88
79	Cal St. Northridge ⊠	72
92	Pacific ⊠	64
80	Cal Poly	77
68	UC Santa Barbara	67
94	Cal St. Fullerton	84
78	Hawaii ⊠	93
102	UC Davis ⊠	77
82	Pacific	76
85	UC Irvine ⊠	80
91	UC Riverside	75
77	UC Irvine †	63
94	Cal Poly †	83
86	Tennessee †	121

Nickname: Forty Niners
Colors: Black & Gold
Arena: The Walter Pyramid
Capacity: 5,000; Year Built: 1994
AD: Vic Cegles
SID: Steve Janisch

LONG ISLAND
Brooklyn, NY 11201 I

Coach: Jim Ferry, Keene St. 1990
2006-07 RESULTS (10-19)
73	Binghamton ⊠	59
54	Minnesota	70
63	Columbia	90
105	Old Westbury ⊠	50
46	St. John's (N.Y.)	64
49	Hartford	64
70	New Hampshire ⊠	62
74	Monmouth	71
79	Harvard ⊠	87
45	Penn St.	66
80	Binghamton	91
72	St. Peter's	61
76	Mt. St. Mary's ⊠	78
52	St. Francis (N.Y.) ⊠	68
59	Robert Morris ⊠	56
72	St. Francis (Pa.) ⊠	60
48	Central Conn. St.	61
73	Fairleigh Dickinson ⊠	74
74	Wagner	88
71	Quinnipiac	73
77	Wagner ⊠	80
72	Sacred Heart	80
75	Central Conn. St. ⊠	96
82	St. Francis (N.Y.)	79
85	Fairleigh Dickinson	80
68	Quinnipiac ⊠	70
82	Monmouth ⊠	78
56	St. Francis (Pa.)	72
74	Robert Morris	90

Nickname: Blackbirds
Colors: Black, Silver & Royal Blue
Arena: Wellness Center
Capacity: 2,500; Year Built: 2006
AD: John Suarez
SID: Stacey Brann

LONGWOOD
Farmville, VA 23909-1899 II

Coach: Mike Gillian, Mass. Liberal Arts 1986
2006-07 RESULTS (9-22)
71	Virginia-Wise ⊠	49
63	VCU ⊠	75
65	Norfolk St.	54
60	George Washington	74
72	Richmond	83
88	Shenandoah ⊠	60
59	N.C. A&T	71
59	Navy ⊠	61
49	American	60
57	High Point	59
61	Liberty	89
60	New Mexico	79
53	Southern California	83

RESULTS

73 Charleston So. † 67
87 Kennesaw St. † 85
81 American 79
69 Providence 107
62 Yale 74
55 NJIT 59
52 Utah Valley St. 80
59 Savannah St. 65
59 Hampton 80
69 High Point 64
40 Oklahoma 81
75 Morgan St. 73
63 Fla. Atlantic 81
49 Virginia 90
76 Liberty 70
74 NJIT 78
80 Campbell 88
72 Savannah St. 74

Nickname: Lancers
Colors: Blue & White
Arena: Willett Hall
  Capacity: 2,522; Year Built: 1980
AD: Troy Austin
SID: Greg Prouty

LORAS
Dubuque, IA 52004-0178 III

Coach: Chad Walthall, Concordia-M'head 1991

2006-07 RESULTS (21-7)
82 Wis.-La Crosse 74
84 Clarke 70
73 Wis.-Platteville † 81
84 Simpson 68
69 North Park 87
73 Ashford 67
61 Mt. Mercy 70
71 Aurora 99
62 Bellevue † 72
91 Hanover † 85
59 Luther 49
82 Central (Iowa) 60
61 Coe 60
75 Buena Vista 69
73 Cornell College 58
62 Wartburg 61
88 Dubuque 73
56 Luther 54
70 Simpson 58
76 Central (Iowa) 65
59 Wartburg 71
71 Dubuque 64
79 Coe 68
63 Cornell College 44
68 Buena Vista 56
69 Simpson 52
77 Buena Vista 62
82 St. John's (Minn.) 85

Nickname: Duhawks
Colors: Purple & Gold
Arena: Loras Fieldhouse
  Capacity: 1,200; Year Built: 1923
AD: Chad Walthall
SID: Tim Calderwood

LOUISIANA COL.
Pineville, LA 71360-0001 III

Coach: Gene Rushing, Louisiana Col. 1970

2006-07 RESULTS (8-17)
60 McNeese St. 89
31 Sam Houston St. 95
79 Concordia (Tex.) 81
57 Mary Hardin-Baylor 71
74 Hardin-Simmons 90
71 McMurry 85
62 Jarvis Christian 74
62 Schreiner 79
80 Texas Lutheran 68
76 Lamar 91
68 Howard Payne 63

57 Sul Ross St. 63
79 Texas-Tyler 62
64 Texas-Dallas 42
43 Mississippi Col. 63
71 Ozarks (Ark.) 68
71 East Tex. Baptist 63
62 LeTourneau 76
77 East Tex. Baptist 80
76 LeTourneau 67
52 Mississippi Col 88
80 Ozarks (Ark.) 70
47 Texas-Tyler 68
57 Texas-Dallas 72
86 Mary Hardin-Baylor † 96

Nickname: Wildcats
Colors: Orange & Blue
Arena: H.O. West
  Capacity: 4,000; Year Built: 1968
AD: Tim Whitman
SID: Alex Goodling

LA.-LAFAYETTE
Lafayette, LA 70506 I

Coach: Robert Lee, Nicholls St. 1991

2006-07 RESULTS (9-21)
76 Ouachita Baptist 68
54 Mississippi 69
51 Oral Roberts 54
89 Cal St. Fullerton 91
67 Tennessee 77
74 Nevada 86
65 Louisiana Tech 60
42 Stephen F. Austin 80
76 New Orleans 80
63 Arkansas St. 73
49 Cal St. Fullerton 85
63 McNeese St. 68
55 Ark.-Little Rock 59
69 La.-Monroe 88
66 Denver 64
74 Florida Int'l 71
72 North Texas 73
72 Western Ky. 82
69 South Ala. 73
69 Troy 62
72 Fla. Atlantic 75
59 Middle Tenn. 71
67 New Orleans 64
76 Arkansas St. 70
56 Charlotte 80
85 La.-Monroe 56
67 Denver 65
68 Florida Int'l. 71
70 North Texas 72
78 North Texas 93

Nickname: Ragin' Cajuns
Colors: Vermilion & White
Arena: Cajundome
  Capacity: 11,550; Year Built: 1985
AD: David Walker
SID: Matt Hebert

LA.-MONROE
Monroe, LA 71209-3000 I

Coach: Orlando Early, Gardner-Webb 1990

2006-07 RESULTS (18-14)
70 Eastern Ill. † 60
40 Iowa St. 68
76 UC Riverside † 64
57 LSU 88
66 SMU 99
88 Loyola (La.) 53
61 Alabama 75
60 Auburn 81
76 William Carey 57
53 Mississippi 87
67 Middle Tenn. 65
101 Wesley (Miss.) 64
76 Ark.-Little Rock 68
87 Nicholls St. 83

88 La.-Lafayette 69
77 Arkansas St. 69
65 Denver 75
68 New Orleans 66
62 Fla. Atlantic 73
77 Florida Int'l 69
57 South Ala. 64
91 Troy 78
96 Western Ky. 103
58 Ark.-Little Rock 57
82 Middle Tenn. 76
66 North Texas 62
56 La.-Lafayette 85
68 Arkansas St. 76
87 Denver 51
75 New Orleans 88
83 Denver 67
71 North Texas † 77

Nickname: Warhawks
Colors: Maroon & Gold
Arena: Fant-Ewing Coliseum
  Capacity: 8,000; Year Built: 1971
AD: Bobby Staub
SID: John Holinka

LSU
Baton Rouge, LA 70893 I

Coach: John Brady, Belhaven 1976

2006-07 RESULTS (17-15)
96 Nicholls St. 42
88 La.-Monroe 57
53 Wichita St. 57
91 McNeese St. 57
74 Tulane 67
64 Texas A&M 52
75 Texas † 76
60 Oregon St. 53
72 Washington 88
68 Louisiana Tech 52
71 Wright St. 45
92 Mississippi Val. 58
60 Samford 45
66 Connecticut 49
61 Alabama 71
65 Auburn 63
62 Mississippi 55
52 Arkansas 72
53 Vanderbilt 64
54 Georgia 57
70 Alabama 73
78 Mississippi St. 85
67 Tennessee 70
71 Arkansas 67
70 Mississippi 71
50 Mississippi St. 56
63 Kentucky 70
66 Florida 56
68 Auburn 80
61 South Carolina 52
76 Tennessee † 67
60 Mississippi † 80

Nickname: Fighting Tigers
Colors: Purple & Gold
Arena: Maravich Assembly Center
  Capacity: 13,215; Year Built: 1972
AD: Skip Bertman
SID: Michael Bonnette

LOUISIANA TECH
Ruston, LA 71272 I

Coach: Keith Richard, La.-Monroe 1982

2006-07 RESULTS (10-20)
65 St. Louis 87
59 Texas A&M 75
68 Lamar † 71
59 McNeese St. 50
36 Southern Ill. 50
60 La.-Lafayette 65
59 Texas Tech 66
74 Southern U. 66
47 Southern U. 62

73 Centenary (La.) † 82
52 LSU 68
50 Arkansas 80
92 San Jose St. 56
70 Hawaii 67
56 Boise St. 82
49 Utah St. 69
73 New Mexico St. 71
73 Idaho 72
67 Nevada 84
64 Fresno St. 70
71 Nevada 79
84 Boise St. 76
50 San Jose St. 53
50 Hawaii 74
68 Idaho 59
72 Southeast Mo. St. 56
63 Fresno St. 64
84 Utah St. 71
64 New Mexico St. 79
70 New Mexico St. 77

Nickname: Bulldogs
Colors: Red & Blue
Arena: Thomas Assembly Center
  Capacity: 8,000; Year Built: 1982
AD: Jim M. Oakes
SID: Josh Milton

LOUISVILLE
Louisville, KY 40292 I

Coach: Rick Pitino, Massachusetts 1974

2006-07 RESULTS (24-10)
100 Northwestern St. 87
64 Dayton † 68
99 Sacramento St. 69
65 Arizona † 72
74 Ohio 71
74 St. Joseph's 64
76 Bellarmine 64
68 Massachusetts 72
49 Kentucky 61
71 Savannah St. 45
82 Miami (Fla.) 59
61 Northeastern 41
76 San Francisco 63
66 UNC Asheville 51
62 Notre Dame 78
81 South Fla. 55
78 Providence 63
65 Marquette 74
59 DePaul 50
68 Connecticut 54
76 Syracuse 71
69 Cincinnati 53
53 Villanova 57
65 Georgetown 73
83 South Fla. 63
66 Pittsburgh 53
61 Marquette 59
72 St. John's (N.Y.) 48
76 Connecticut 69
86 Seton Hall 71
82 West Virginia † 71
59 Pittsburgh † 65
78 Stanford † 58
69 Texas A&M † 72

Nickname: Cardinals
Colors: Red, Black & White
Arena: Freedom Hall
  Capacity: 18,865; Year Built: 1956
AD: Thomas M. Jurich
SID: Kenny Klein

LOYOLA (ILL.)
Chicago, IL 60611 I

Coach: Jim Whitesell, Luther 1982

2006-07 RESULTS (21-11)
68 Princeton † 57
75 Ohio St. 87
77 IUPUI † 73
96 John Carroll 74

69	San Diego ⊠	55
83	Fairfield	72
64	St. Louis ⊠	67
71	Green Bay ⊠	52
62	Purdue	78
76	Loyola (La.) ⊠	42
76	UNI ⊠	67
73	Bradley	82
72	UC Irvine ⊠	69
71	Youngstown St.	76
66	Cleveland St.	55
87	Milwaukee ⊠	74
55	Wright St.	81
73	Ill.-Chicago	79
70	Detroit	64
69	IPFW	53
66	Butler ⊠	70
47	Wright St. ⊠	59
80	Youngstown St. ⊠	68
61	Cleveland St.	57
71	Detroit ⊠	61
69	Green Bay	52
66	Milwaukee	56
66	Eastern Ill. ⊠	43
75	Butler	71
51	Ill.-Chicago ⊠	52
66	Ill.-Chicago †	62
66	Butler †	67

Nickname: Ramblers
Colors: Maroon & Gold
Arena: Joseph J. Gentile Center
   Capacity: 5,200; Year Built: 1996
AD: John Planek
SID: Bill Behrns

LOYOLA (MD.)
Baltimore, MD 21210........................I

Coach: Jimmy Patsos, Catholic 1989

2006-07 RESULTS (18-13)

61	Navy †	73
65	North Fla. †	50
69	UMBC	56
74	American	81
75	Delaware ⊠	63
83	Mt. St. Mary's ⊠	66
55	St. Peter's ⊠	66
77	Manhattan	58
57	High Point	63
60	Northwestern	66
61	Michigan St.	74
77	Marist ⊠	69
75	Iona ⊠	66
94	Siena	87
96	Niagara ⊠	95
62	Towson ⊠	70
62	St. Peter's	55
78	Rider	73
68	Manhattan ⊠	70
71	Iona	61
72	Siena ⊠	71
66	Marist	71
62	Fairfield	65
77	Canisius ⊠	74
59	Fairfield ⊠	67
95	Rider ⊠	73
62	Tennessee St.	60
71	Niagara	73
74	Canisius	71
76	Fairfield	72
79	Niagara †	89

Nickname: Greyhounds
Colors: Green & Grey
Arena: Reitz Arena
   Capacity: 3,000; Year Built: 1984
AD: Joseph Boylan
SID: Thomas Milajecki

LOYOLA MARYMOUNT
Los Angeles, CA 90045-8235 I

Coach: Rodney Tention, San Francisco
1988

2006-07 RESULTS (13-18)

68	Oral Roberts ⊠	65
37	Mississippi St.	61
71	New Mexico St. ⊠	69
83	Cal St. Bakersfield ⊠	75
69	Alas. Anchorage	58
88	Pacific †	85
70	California †	78
58	UC Santa Barbara	55
50	Southern California	67
77	Sam Houston St.	92
73	UC Irvine ⊠	65
63	San Diego St.	74
84	Boise St.	82
65	Long Beach St. ⊠	66
52	Akron	92
53	Monmouth	81
62	Gonzaga	97
65	Portland	81
61	San Francisco ⊠	68
74	San Diego ⊠	79
55	Pepperdine ⊠	57
74	Santa Clara	71
54	St. Mary's (Cal.)	69
74	Portland ⊠	59
67	Gonzaga ⊠	61
71	San Diego	66
69	San Francisco	76
88	Pepperdine	95
67	Santa Clara ⊠	66
47	St. Mary's (Cal.) ⊠	63
41	Portland	55

Nickname: Lions
Colors: Crimson & Navy Blue
Arena: Albert Gersten Pavilion
   Capacity: 4,156; Year Built: 1982
AD: William S. Husak
SID: John Shaffer

LUTHER
Decorah, IA 52101-1045 III

Coach: Mark Franzen, Wartburg 1994

2006-07 RESULTS (5-20)

68	Gust. Adolphus ⊠	76
60	St. Olaf	57
53	Mt. Mercy ⊠	55
63	Buena Vista ⊠	68
71	Washington-St. Louis	87
56	Worcester St. †	59
62	Northwestern (Minn.)	74
59	Waldorf	69
86	Bethany Lutheran ⊠	72
49	Iowa Wesleyan ⊠	59
49	Loras	59
70	Wartburg	56
68	Cornell College ⊠	45
50	Simpson ⊠	51
62	Dubuque ⊠	58
47	Central (Iowa)	59
55	Wartburg ⊠	56
54	Loras ⊠	56
40	Coe	64
53	Simpson	66
52	Dubuque	67
44	Coe ⊠	61
69	Buena Vista	81
57	Central (Iowa) ⊠	60
60	Cornell College	68

Nickname: Norse
Colors: Blue & White
Arena: Luther Field House
   Capacity: 3,500; Year Built: 1964
AD: Joe Thompson
SID: Dave Blanchard

LYCOMING
Williamsport, PA 17701-5192 III

Coach: Don Friday, Lebanon Valley
1990

2006-07 RESULTS (13-12)

69	John Jay ⊠	49
66	Randolph-Macon ⊠	81
77	Elizabethtown ⊠	74
48	Wilkes	65
65	Drew ⊠	53
54	Lafayette	72
54	Susquehanna	78
60	Elmira	55
95	Penn St. Tech ⊠	55
67	Shenandoah ⊠	58
56	New Jersey City †	59
64	Penn St. Tech †	49
72	Scranton	83
51	FDU-Florham	66
66	Carnegie Mellon ⊠	65
52	King's (Pa.)	58
72	Delaware Valley ⊠	56
63	DeSales	64
82	FDU-Florham ⊠	75
78	Wilkes ⊠	52
49	Drew	69
61	King's (Pa.) ⊠	79
74	DeSales ⊠	65
58	Scranton ⊠	65
80	Delaware Valley	75

Nickname: Warriors
Colors: Blue & Gold
Arena: Lamade Gymnasium
   Capacity: 2,300; Year Built: 1979
AD: Frank L. Girardi
SID: James Nekoloff

LYNCHBURG
Lynchburg, VA 24501-3199 III

Coach: John Swickrath, Denison 2001

2006-07 RESULTS (6-19)

101	Westminster (Pa.)	83
86	Roberts Wesleyan †	91
57	Ferrum ⊠	66
77	Averett	84
80	Guilford	102
78	Randolph-Macon ⊠	70
98	Emory & Henry	141
68	Marietta	84
80	Olivet †	76
95	Southern Va. ⊠	91
87	East. Mennonite ⊠	76
66	Bridgewater (Va.) ⊠	60
57	Va. Wesleyan ⊠	79
63	Hampden-Sydney	90
34	Roanoke	91
67	Wash. & Lee ⊠	84
107	Emory & Henry ⊠	136
83	East. Mennonite	87
62	Bridgewater (Va.)	83
66	Randolph-Macon	70
70	Guilford ⊠	95
56	Roanoke ⊠	69
56	Wash. & Lee	74
68	Hampden-Sydney ⊠	80
73	Va. Wesleyan	90

Nickname: Hornets
Colors: Grey & Crimson
Arena: Turner Gym
   Capacity: 2,400; Year Built: 1970
AD: Jack M. Toms
SID: Mike Carpenter

LYNN
Boca Raton, FL 33431 II

Coach: Scott McMillin, Buffalo 1998

2006-07 RESULTS (14-14)

52	Christian Bros.	70
84	North Ala.	94

85	P.R.-Cayey ⊠	51
94	P.R.-Mayaguez ⊠	79
83	Fla. Gulf Coast	77
77	Fla. Southern ⊠	70
64	Fla. Gulf Coast ⊠	65
79	Palm Beach Atl. ⊠	70
68	Washburn ⊠	61
115	Wilmington (Del.) ⊠	68
72	Shaw ⊠	44
71	Florida Tech	57
67	Eckerd ⊠	59
69	Palm Beach Atl.	61
52	Rollins ⊠	68
61	Nova Southeastern	56
62	Tampa	61
62	Barry ⊠	68
62	St. Leo ⊠	64
52	Florida Tech ⊠	56
62	Eckerd ⊠	70
80	Fla. Southern	70
71	Rollins	93
62	Nova Southeastern ⊠	66
59	Tampa ⊠	60
68	Barry	71
68	St. Leo ⊠	73
61	Barry ⊠	64

Nickname: Fighting Knights
Colors: Royal Blue & White
Arena: De Hoernle Center
   Capacity: 1,000; Year Built: 1993
AD: Kristen Moraz
SID: Jeff Messman

MACALESTER
St. Paul, MN 55105...........................III

Coach: Curt Kietzer, St. Thomas (Minn.)
1988

2006-07 RESULTS (11-14)

87	Embry-Riddle	85
70	Northwestern (Minn.)	85
87	Wis.-River Falls	73
72	Gust. Adolphus	77
73	St. Mary's (Minn.)	81
72	St. Thomas (Minn.)	77
64	Concordia-St. Paul	73
78	Viterbo ⊠	75
92	Concordia-M'head ⊠	70
90	Augsburg ⊠	76
68	St. John's (Minn.) ⊠	74
68	St. Olaf ⊠	65
73	Bethel (Minn.) ⊠	87
56	Carleton ⊠	64
79	Hamline ⊠	77
70	Gust. Adolphus ⊠	79
49	St. Mary's (Minn.) ⊠	60
55	St. Thomas (Minn.) ⊠	87
84	Concordia-M'head	74
94	Augsburg	81
76	St. John's (Minn.)	96
58	St. Olaf	61
96	Bethel (Minn.)	105
81	Carleton	77
84	Hamline	72

Nickname: Scots
Colors: Orange & Blue
Arena: Macalester Gymnasium
   Capacity: 600; Year Built: 1933
AD: Travis Feezell
SID: Andy Johnson

MACMURRAY
Jacksonville, IL 62650-2590 III

Coach: Steve Hettinga, Olivet 1993

2006-07 RESULTS (16-9)

76	Millikin ⊠	88
86	Monmouth (Ill.) ⊠	92
116	Grinnell ⊠	136
71	Lincoln Christian	70
71	Webster	66
67	Huntingdon †	57
72	LaGrange	84

RESULTS

94	Rockford ⊠	66
73	Westminster (Mo.)	70
83	Principia	72
86	Greenville	88
86	Fontbonne	95
69	Eureka	62
89	Blackburn ⊠	74
68	Maryville (Mo.)	62
75	Webster	87
90	Lincoln Christian ⊠	70
95	Principia	67
85	Westminster (Mo.)	95
106	Eureka	89
86	Greenville ⊠	78
92	Fontbonne ⊠	79
76	Blackburn	75
82	Maryville (Mo.) ⊠	79
81	Eureka †	95

Nickname: Highlanders
Colors: Scarlet & Navy
Arena: Bill Wall Gymnasium
Capacity: 1,500; Year Built: 1975
AD: Kevin Haslam
SID: Shelley Whitaker

MAINE
Orono, ME 04469-5747 ... I

Coach: Ted Woodward, Bucknell 1986

2006-07 RESULTS (12-18)

71	Harvard	75
50	Detroit †	57
57	Idaho St. †	66
79	St. Francis (N.Y.)	60
97	St. Joseph (Vt.) ⊠	69
43	Robert Morris ⊠	55
68	Mt. St. Mary's	65
68	NJIT	58
79	Providence	94
75	Me.-Farmington ⊠	34
42	Penn St.	75
69	Nevada	89
60	Hartford ⊠	62
68	New Hampshire ⊠	73
63	Boston U.	65
73	Albany (N.Y.)	82
69	Binghamton ⊠	64
70	UMBC ⊠	56
69	Vermont	64
74	Stony Brook	66
65	Hartford	64
55	Boston U. ⊠	66
65	New Hampshire	56
55	Albany (N.Y.) ⊠	71
40	Binghamton	67
75	Vermont ⊠	90
61	Northeastern	71
77	UMBC	80
63	Stony Brook ⊠	61
61	UMBC †	70

Nickname: Black Bears
Colors: Blue & White
Arena: Alfond Arena
Capacity: 5,712; Year Built: 1977
AD: Blake James
SID: Laura Reed

ME.-FARMINGTON
Farmington, ME 04938 ... III

Coach: Dick Meader, Me.-Farmington 1968

2006-07 RESULTS (10-16)

70	Mass. Liberal Arts ⊠	53
65	Southern Me. ⊠	70
41	St. Joseph's (Me.)	64
76	Thomas (Me.) ⊠	58
56	Bates	76
88	New England ⊠	79
61	St. Joseph's (Me.) ⊠	55
34	Maine	75
53	Southern Me.	66
57	Bowdoin ⊠	61

64	Plymouth St.	87
57	Elms	78
96	Becker	61
68	Castleton ⊠	53
79	Johnson St. ⊠	46
36	Maine Maritime ⊠	41
80	Thomas (Me.)	48
83	Husson	93
53	Colby ⊠	70
75	Lesley	79
61	Maine Maritime	77
62	Mount Ida ⊠	41
63	Husson ⊠	67
54	Lasell	70
65	Mount Ida	62
56	Lasell	81

Nickname: Beavers
Colors: Maroon and White
Arena: Dearborn Gymnasium
Capacity: 600; Year Built: 1963
AD: Julie Davis
SID: Pat McBride

MAINE MARITIME
Castine, ME 04420 ... III

Coach: Chris Murphy, Maine 1973

2006-07 RESULTS (12-12)

55	Maritime (N.Y.) ⊠	52
35	Cal Maritime ⊠	54
84	Unity ⊠	63
87	Lesley	105
68	Mount Ida	63
56	Becker ⊠	53
59	Elms ⊠	77
66	Me.-Presque Isle	45
97	Fisher †	94
50	Me.-Presque Isle ⊠	53
56	Colby	73
73	Johnson St.	60
57	Castleton	76
60	St. Joseph's (Me.) ⊠	84
47	Bowdoin	72
41	Me.-Farmington	36
61	Husson	64
57	Thomas (Me.) ⊠	49
56	Lasell ⊠	58
73	Mount Ida ⊠	62
77	Me.-Farmington ⊠	61
78	Thomas (Me.) ⊠	51
51	Husson ⊠	73
71	Lesley ⊠	75

Nickname: Mariners
Colors: Royal Blue & Gold
Arena: Margaret Chase Smith Gym
Capacity: 1,000; Year Built: 1965
AD: James Dyer
SID: Katrina Dagan

MANCHESTER
North Manchester, IN 46962 ... III

Coach: Brad Nadborne, DePauw 1981

2006-07 RESULTS (15-10)

62	Eureka ⊠	55
68	Wis.-Eau Claire ⊠	59
67	Tri-State ⊠	62
72	Earlham ⊠	56
48	Defiance	64
69	Mt. St. Joseph ⊠	65
70	Kalamazoo	63
74	Transylvania ⊠	86
62	Taylor-Ft. Wayne ⊠	51
59	Wash. & Jeff.	57
53	Muskingum †	56
80	Adrian	79
66	Hanover	74
59	Franklin ⊠	62
72	Bluffton ⊠	62
47	Rose-Hulman	50
64	Anderson (Ind.) ⊠	59
80	Defiance ⊠	73
91	Transylvania	75

73	Franklin	69
79	Bluffton	82
73	Hanover ⊠	83
69	Anderson (Ind.)	66
56	Rose-Hulman ⊠	68
63	Mt. St. Joseph	81

Nickname: Spartans
Colors: Black & Gold
Arena: Stauffer Wolfe Arena
Capacity: 1,700; Year Built: 1983
AD: Tom Jarman
SID: Doug Shoemaker

MANHATTAN
Riverdale, NY 10471 ... I

Coach: Barry Rohrssen, St. Francis (N.Y.) 1983

2006-07 RESULTS (13-17)

55	NJIT ⊠	56
63	Wagner ⊠	60
79	Hofstra ⊠	77
45	Princeton	57
65	Boston U. ⊠	74
66	Fordham	70
59	Memphis	77
57	Fairfield	54
58	Loyola (Md.) ⊠	77
73	St. Francis (N.Y.)	76
61	Long Beach St.	74
89	Pepperdine	87
58	Fairfield ⊠	54
60	Canisius	51
73	Iona	63
71	St. Peter's	66
86	Rider	75
69	Siena ⊠	80
70	Loyola (Md.)	68
64	Canisius ⊠	67
75	Marist ⊠	74
70	Niagara	81
58	St. Peter's ⊠	51
68	Rider	75
74	Niagara ⊠	76
57	Marist	73
51	Eastern Mich.	65
61	Siena	78
71	Iona ⊠	65
72	Siena †	75

Nickname: Jaspers
Colors: Kelly Green & White
Arena: Draddy Gymnasium
Capacity: 2,345; Year Built: 1979
AD: Robert J. Byrnes
SID: Michael Antonaccio

MANHATTANVILLE
Purchase, NY 10577 ... III

Coach: Pat Scanlon, Manhattanville 2003

2006-07 RESULTS (23-6)

72	Kean ⊠	73
94	Washington (Md.) ⊠	79
77	Hunter	74
78	Vassar ⊠	69
72	Yeshiva ⊠	64
73	Maritime (N.Y.)	56
94	Western Conn. St.	73
86	Mt. St. Mary (N.Y.) ⊠	67
68	Clarke †	61
66	Scranton †	79
84	Rutgers-Newark	79
67	Wm. Paterson ⊠	66
68	Merchant Marine	70
85	Stevens Institute ⊠	79
73	Old Westbury	75
70	Farmingdale St. ⊠	69
97	Mt. St. Vincent	54
93	Centenary (N.J.)	62
81	St. Joseph's (L.I.) ⊠	84
92	Mt. St. Mary (N.Y.)	74
80	Maritime (N.Y.) ⊠	55

62	Yeshiva	56
88	Merchant Marine ⊠	69
71	Farmingdale St.	61
112	Centenary (N.J.)	79
82	Mt. St. Mary (N.Y.) ⊠	64
93	Farmingdale St. ⊠	76
87	Old Westbury ⊠	68
81	Guilford †	101

Nickname: Valiants
Colors: Red & White
Arena: Kennedy Gymnasium
Capacity: 700; Year Built: 1947
AD: Keith Levinthal
SID: Michael LaPlaca

MANSFIELD
Mansfield, PA 16933 ... II

Coach: Rich Miller, Bucknell 1996

2006-07 RESULTS (9-18)

70	Le Moyne	86
66	Messiah	74
79	Keystone ⊠	55
77	Clarion	82
68	Indiana (Pa.) ⊠	54
117	Bowie St.	122
65	Lock Haven	68
64	Shippensburg	95
81	Wheeling Jesuit	104
90	West Liberty St. †	101
76	California (Pa.)	82
70	Millersville ⊠	85
80	Edinboro ⊠	66
96	Slippery Rock ⊠	92
85	Kutztown ⊠	74
81	Cheyney	71
82	Pitt.-Johnstown ⊠	86
65	West Chester	74
58	East Stroudsburg	76
85	Bloomsburg ⊠	82
75	Millersville	86
73	Kutztown	71
71	Cheyney ⊠	79
85	West Chester ⊠	71
58	Pitt.-Johnstown	69
79	East Stroudsburg ⊠	87
85	Bloomsburg	89

Nickname: Mountaineers
Colors: Red & Black
Arena: Decker Gymnasium
Capacity: 2,500; Year Built: 1970
AD: Roger N. Maisner
SID: Steve McCloskey

MARANATHA BAPTIST
Watertown, WI 53094-0000 ... III

Coach: Rob Cronin, Maranatha Baptist 1985

2006-07 RESULTS (4-23)

55	Edgewood	80
76	Emmaus †	53
70	Lincoln Christian	63
65	Grace Bible (Mich.) †	85
75	Moody Bible †	69
37	Dominican (Ill.)	101
44	Aurora ⊠	110
43	Concordia (Ill.) ⊠	63
56	Rockford ⊠	67
27	Wis.-Whitewater	92
76	Concordia (Wis.)	91
42	Benedictine (Ill.)	59
50	Lakeland ⊠	86
42	Milwaukee Engr. ⊠	74
48	Wis. Lutheran ⊠	105
37	Edgewood ⊠	62
53	Marian (Wis.)	87
52	Dominican (Ill.) ⊠	89
49	Aurora	100
61	Concordia (Ill.)	73
76	Northland Bapt. ⊠	88
70	Concordia (Wis.) ⊠	83
64	Benedictine (Ill.) ⊠	74

56	Lakeland	85
60	Wis. Lutheran	89
70	Emmaus ⊠	50
90	Northland Bapt. †	98

Nickname: Crusaders
Colors: Navy Blue & Gold
Arena: Maranatha Gymnasium
  Capacity: 800; Year Built: 1977
AD: Rob Thompson
SID: Robert Thompson

MARIAN (WIS.)
Fond Du Lac, WI 54935-4699 III

Coach: Mark Boyle, Wis.-Eau Claire 1978
2006-07 RESULTS (13-12)

68	Northland Bapt.	57
67	Cornell College	63
53	Coe	67
70	Wis.-Whitewater ⊠	74
63	Milwaukee Engr.	64
67	Edgewood	77
63	Dominican (Ill.) ⊠	61
68	Concordia (Ill.) ⊠	56
54	Wis.-Eau Claire	73
72	Finlandia †	52
70	Aurora	76
74	Rockford	55
75	Concordia (Wis.)	77
57	Benedictine (Ill.) ⊠	66
81	Wis. Lutheran	63
71	Lakeland ⊠	66
87	Maranatha Baptist ⊠	53
60	Edgewood ⊠	57
78	Dominican (Ill.)	85
53	Aurora	81
74	Concordia (Ill.)	64
86	Rockford	61
59	Concordia (Wis.) ⊠	67
68	Benedictine (Ill.)	60
64	Lakeland	80

Nickname: Sabres
Colors: Blue, White & Scarlet
Arena: Sadoff Gym
  Capacity: 1,000; Year Built: 1982
AD: Doug Hammonds
SID: Michael Schoenborn

MARIETTA
Marietta, OH 45750 III

Coach: Doug Foote, Morehead St. 1983
2006-07 RESULTS (5-20)

75	Thiel †	59
81	Medaille †	59
50	Ohio Northern	80
55	Otterbein ⊠	61
64	Wilmington (Ohio) ⊠	75
55	Bethany (W.V.) ⊠	62
57	Baldwin-Wallace	65
72	Bridgewater (Va.) †	69
51	Carthage †	82
84	Lynchburg	68
73	Westminster (Pa.) ⊠	98
59	Mount Union ⊠	64
71	John Carroll	87
51	Muskingum ⊠	63
70	Heidelberg ⊠	74
41	Capital	67
72	Ohio Northern ⊠	68
69	Otterbein	78
64	Wilmington (Ohio)	67
52	Capital ⊠	65
70	Heidelberg	87
58	Muskingum	64
58	John Carroll	85
56	Mount Union	69
68	Baldwin-Wallace ⊠	74

Nickname: Pioneers
Colors: Navy Blue & White
Arena: Ban Johnson Gymnasium
  Capacity: 1,457; Year Built: 1929
AD: To be named
SID: Dan May

MARIST
Poughkeepsie, NY 12601-1387 I

Coach: Matt Brady, Siena 1987
2006-07 RESULTS (25-9)

66	Ohio	83
78	Delaware	62
83	Fla. Atlantic ⊠	67
63	Minnesota †	56
64	Arkansas †	73
89	Western Mich. †	78
84	Old Dominion ⊠	71
80	Richmond	73
80	Canisius ⊠	69
89	St. Peter's	70
53	Wright St.	63
67	Northern Ill.	63
71	Central Ark. ⊠	56
69	Loyola (Md.)	77
71	Rider ⊠	55
87	Iona ⊠	65
84	Siena	75
91	Niagara ⊠	86
74	Canisius	84
67	St. Peter's ⊠	58
75	Niagara ⊠	83
74	Manhattan	75
71	Loyola (Md.) ⊠	66
79	Rider	78
65	Fairfield ⊠	64
79	Iona	53
73	Manhattan ⊠	57
63	Colgate ⊠	47
67	Fairfield	60
98	Siena ⊠	88
87	Canisius †	63
78	Siena †	86
67	Oklahoma St.	64
62	North Carolina St.	69

Nickname: Red Foxes
Colors: Red & White
Arena: McCann Recreation Center
  Capacity: 3,750; Year Built: 1977
AD: Timothy S. Murray
SID: Chris O'Connor

MARITIME (N.Y.)
Throggs Neck, NY 10465 III

Coach: Thomas Spina, Maritime (N.Y.) 1994
2006-07 RESULTS (4-21)

52	Maine Maritime	55
56	Cal Maritime †	75
63	Hartwick	84
126	Mass. Liberal Arts	124
56	Manhattanville ⊠	73
61	Stevens Institute ⊠	89
49	Yeshiva	61
42	Army	92
73	Ferrum ⊠	90
58	Hunter ⊠	75
57	Brooklyn ⊠	70
52	Marymount (Va.) ⊠	74
62	Farmingdale St. ⊠	77
83	Mt. St. Vincent ⊠	72
66	Merchant Marine ⊠	90
69	Mt. St. Mary (N.Y.) ⊠	98
85	Centenary (N.J.)	72
94	St. Joseph's (L.I.) ⊠	106
57	Old Westbury	83
55	Stevens Institute	68
55	Manhattanville	80
61	Merchant Marine	81
68	Farmingdale St.	100
75	Centenary (N.J.) ⊠	68
69	Yeshiva ⊠	84

Nickname: Privateers
Colors: Cardinal, Navy & White
Arena: Riesenberg Hall
  Capacity: 800; Year Built: 1964
AD: William E. Martinov, Jr.
SID: Joseph DeBenedictis

MARQUETTE
Milwaukee, WI 53233 I

Coach: Tom Crean, Central Mich. 1989
2006-07 RESULTS (24-10)

76	Hillsdale ⊠	66
59	Idaho St. ⊠	56
87	Detroit ⊠	45
95	Eastern Mich. ⊠	62
87	Texas Tech †	72
73	Duke †	62
65	Valparaiso	62
83	Northwestern St. ⊠	67
60	North Dakota St. ⊠	64
65	Delaware St. ⊠	48
66	Wisconsin	70
68	UMBC ⊠	46
80	Oakland ⊠	62
77	Morgan St. ⊠	57
69	Savannah St. ⊠	51
59	Providence	74
58	Syracuse ⊠	70
73	Connecticut	69
81	West Virginia ⊠	63
74	Louisville	65
77	Pittsburgh	74
89	Seton Hall ⊠	76
70	South Fla.	68
69	Providence ⊠	62
67	Rutgers ⊠	47
58	Georgetown	76
67	DePaul	72
59	Louisville ⊠	61
80	Villanova ⊠	67
73	Notre Dame	85
75	Pittsburgh ⊠	71
76	St. John's (N.Y.) †	67
79	Pittsburgh †	89
49	Michigan St. †	61

Nickname: Golden Eagles
Colors: Blue & Gold
Arena: Bradley Center
  Capacity: 18,850; Year Built: 1988
AD: Steven Cottingham
SID: Mike Broeker

MARS HILL
Mars Hill, NC 28754 II

Coach: Terry Rogers, Gardner-Webb
2006-07 RESULTS (8-20)

55	St. Andrews	70
66	N.C. A&T	98
73	Brevard	65
77	S.C.-Aiken	88
66	S.C. Upstate	82
74	S.C.-Aiken ⊠	72
79	North Greenville	67
70	S.C. Upstate ⊠	73
73	St. Andrews ⊠	46
42	Presbyterian	65
80	Newberry ⊠	75
71	Carson-Newman ⊠	67
55	Lenoir-Rhyne ⊠	69
61	Catawba ⊠	83
70	Wingate	75
62	Lincoln Memorial ⊠	82
67	Tusculum ⊠	64
75	Brevard	81
63	Presbyterian ⊠	66
53	Newberry	64
93	Carson-Newman ⊠	101
81	Lincoln Memorial	67
64	Catawba	83
79	Wingate ⊠	96
73	North Greenville ⊠	74
48	Tusculum	79
50	Lenoir-Rhyne	85
88	Carson-Newman ⊠	99

Nickname: Lions
Colors: Royal Blue & Gold
Arena: Stanford Arena
  Capacity: 2,300; Year Built: 1969
AD: David Riggins
SID: Rick Baker

MARSHALL
Huntington, WV 25755 I

Coach: Ron Jirsa, Gettysburg 1981
2006-07 RESULTS (13-19)

82	UNC Greensboro ⊠	80
69	Robert Morris ⊠	73
70	California †	72
70	Hofstra †	73
75	UMKC †	79
81	Morehead St.	80
78	Ohio	84
59	Memphis	78
79	Wright St. ⊠	72
45	Princeton	61
78	Bowling Green ⊠	79
59	Virginia Tech ⊠	58
70	Ohio ⊠	60
65	George Washington	74
64	UTEP	88
71	UCF ⊠	78
65	Tulsa ⊠	53
79	Tulane	73
63	West Virginia †	77
61	Houston ⊠	77
56	East Caro. ⊠	52
61	UAB ⊠	54
60	Tulsa	63
58	UCF	75
52	SMU ⊠	49
65	Tulane ⊠	73
54	East Caro.	51
57	UAB	70
69	Rice ⊠	64
73	Southern Miss.	83
53	UAB †	52
71	Memphis	92

Nickname: Thundering Herd
Colors: Green & White
Arena: Henderson Center
  Capacity: 9,043; Year Built: 1981
AD: Robert K. (Bob) Marcum
SID: Andy Boggs

MARTIN LUTHER
New Ulm, MN 56073-3965 III

Coach: James Unke, Martin Luther 1983
2006-07 RESULTS (11-15)

61	Wis.-Whitewater	85
79	Clarke †	69
59	St. Olaf ⊠	69
76	Waldorf	82
72	Dubuque	84
61	Viterbo	77
62	Bethany Lutheran ⊠	78
56	Mayville St. ⊠	93
73	Bethel (Minn.) ⊠	85
68	Central (Iowa)	80
69	Presentation ⊠	62
78	Minn.-Morris ⊠	61
87	North Central (Minn.	68
69	Northwestern (Minn.) †	72
70	Crown (Minn.)	37
70	St. Scholastica ⊠	68
73	Northland ⊠	66
73	Crown (Minn.) ⊠	56
76	Northland	45
71	St. Scholastica	82
58	Minn.-Morris	74
86	Presentation	66
82	North Central (Minn. ⊠	48
70	Northwestern (Minn.) ⊠	75
68	Bethany Lutheran	74
65	Northwestern (Minn.)	75

Nickname: Knights
Colors: Black, Red & White
Arena: Luther Student Center
  Capacity: 1,500; Year Built: 1967
AD: James M. Unke
SID: Dan Lewig & Tom Rosenow

MARY
Bismarck, ND 58504...................... II

Coach: Juno Pintar, North Dakota St. 1989

2006-07 RESULTS (9-18)
61	Neb.-Omaha †	64
86	St. Cloud St.	77
59	Augustana (S.D.) ⊠	64
70	Neb.-Kearney †	71
65	Northwest Mo. St. †	57
57	North Dakota	68
59	Upper Iowa	67
57	Winona St.	77
56	Southwest Minn. St. ⊠	64
71	Wayne St. (Neb.) ⊠	84
78	Mayville St. ⊠	75
69	North Dakota ⊠	67
50	Concordia-St. Paul	82
75	Minn. St. Moorhead	72
76	Bemidji St. ⊠	48
68	Minn.-Crookston ⊠	63
47	North Dakota St.	88
57	Northern St.	60
82	Upper Iowa ⊠	76
63	Winona St. ⊠	80
65	Wayne St. (Neb.)	75
41	Southwest Minn. St.	58
69	Minn. St. Moorhead ⊠	80
70	Concordia-St. Paul ⊠	72
60	Minn.-Crookston	73
70	Bemidji St.	50
59	Northern St. ⊠	77

Nickname: Marauders
Colors: Blue, white and orange
Arena: Activity Center
Capacity: 2,000
AD: Al Bortke
SID: Brian Larson

MARY HARDIN-BAYLOR
Belton, TX 76513 III

Coach: Ken DeWeese, Louisiana Col. 1969

2006-07 RESULTS (22-6)
63	Trinity (Tex.) ⊠	49
47	Mississippi Col.	75
71	Louisiana Col.	57
84	Texas-Tyler ⊠	81
70	Texas-Dallas ⊠	78
73	East Tex. Baptist	50
68	LeTourneau	71
63	Va. Wesleyan ⊠	62
86	Ripon ⊠	72
72	Southwestern (Tex.) ⊠	66
90	Ozarks (Ark.) ⊠	56
91	McMurry ⊠	80
72	Hardin-Simmons ⊠	61
71	Howard Payne	67
64	Sul Ross St.	52
75	Texas Lutheran	68
101	Schreiner ⊠	90
87	Concordia (Tex.)	80
71	Texas Lutheran ⊠	51
91	Schreiner	83
96	Concordia (Tex.) ⊠	77
77	Sul Ross St. ⊠	55
84	Howard Payne ⊠	76
76	McMurry	80
75	Hardin-Simmons	72
96	Louisiana Col. †	86
67	Hardin-Simmons †	71
62	Maryville (Tenn.) †	73

Nickname: Crusaders
Colors: Purple, Gold & White
Arena: Mayborn Campus Center
Capacity: 2,500; Year Built: 2005
AD: Ben Shipp
SID: Jon Wallin

MARY WASHINGTON
Fredericksburg, VA 22401-5358..III

Coach: Rod Wood, Randolph-Macon 1985

2006-07 RESULTS (16-10)
83	Messiah †	76
61	Dickinson	60
85	N.C. Wesleyan	79
73	Marymount (Va.)	64
76	Hood ⊠	60
55	York (Pa.)	52
72	Shenandoah	78
76	McDaniel	64
36	Embry-Riddle	67
68	Allegheny †	61
100	Frostburg St.	66
68	Salisbury	73
97	Gallaudet ⊠	53
87	Goucher ⊠	59
75	St. Mary's (Md.)	78
64	Catholic ⊠	56
73	Marymount (Va.) ⊠	77
90	Hood	91
75	York (Pa.) ⊠	90
57	Salisbury ⊠	56
73	Gallaudet	62
100	Goucher	59
64	St. Mary's (Md.) ⊠	76
61	Catholic	74
78	York (Pa.) ⊠	76
67	Catholic	69

Nickname: Eagles
Colors: Navy, Gray & White
Arena: Goolrick Gymnasium
Capacity: 600; Year Built: 1967
AD: Edward H. Hegmann
SID: Clint Often

MARYLAND
College Park, MD 20742................... I

Coach: Gary Williams, Maryland 1968

2006-07 RESULTS (25-9)
102	Hampton ⊠	75
81	Vermont ⊠	63
93	Florida A&M ⊠ †	54
92	St. John's (N.Y.) †	60
62	Michigan St. †	60
71	Winthrop ⊠	60
81	High Point ⊠	63
72	Illinois	66
74	Notre Dame †	81
79	Fordham ⊠	59
62	Boston College	73
101	UMKC ⊠	50
66	American ⊠	54
91	Mt. St. Mary's ⊠	50
94	Siena ⊠	75
88	Iona ⊠	57
58	Miami (Fla.) ⊠	63
92	Clemson ⊠	87
91	Virginia	103
64	Virginia Tech	67
80	Georgia Tech ⊠	65
79	Florida St.	96
79	Wake Forest	72
65	Virginia ⊠	69
72	Duke ⊠	60
85	North Carolina St.	70
82	Clemson	66
73	Florida St. ⊠	55
89	North Carolina ⊠	87
85	Duke	77
79	North Carolina St. ⊠	59
62	Miami (Fla.) †	67
82	Davidson †	70
59	Butler †	62

Nickname: Terrapins, Terps
Colors: Red, White, Black & Gold
Arena: Comcast Center
Capacity: 17,950; Year Built: 2002
AD: Deborah A. Yow
SID: Jason Yaman

UMBC
Baltimore, MD 21250-0000............. I

Coach: Randy Monroe, Cheyney 1987

2006-07 RESULTS (12-19)
56	St. Peter's	67
56	Loyola (Md.) ⊠	69
56	Hampton	49
86	Lafayette ⊠	51
54	Michigan	66
86	Morgan St.	72
57	St. John's (N.Y.)	78
53	Long Beach St. ⊠	57
78	La Salle	67
51	George Washington	72
46	Marquette	68
58	William & Mary	70
52	Central Conn. St. ⊠	66
73	Binghamton	71
72	Stony Brook	53
61	Albany (N.Y.) ⊠	65
63	Vermont ⊠	83
56	Maine	70
73	Hartford ⊠	68
53	Boston U.	59
45	New Hampshire ⊠	44
51	Binghamton ⊠	48
58	Albany (N.Y.)	82
39	Stony Brook ⊠	56
57	Vermont	66
54	Hartford	62
67	Boston U. ⊠	63
80	Maine ⊠	77
51	New Hampshire	64
70	Maine †	61
63	Vermont †	72

Nickname: Retrievers
Colors: Black, Gold & Red
Arena: RAC Arena
Capacity: 4,024; Year Built: 1974
AD: Charles R. Brown
SID: Steve Levy

MD.-EAST. SHORE
Princess Anne, MD 21853-1299.... I

Coach: Lawrence Lesett Jr., Cal St. Northridge 1983

2006-07 RESULTS (4-27)
76	Wagner ⊠	82
59	Navy	82
63	Virginia	104
64	Stony Brook	58
56	George Washington	79
63	Howard ⊠	65
46	Wichita St.	102
58	Kansas St.	79
49	Kennesaw St. †	67
74	Charleston So. †	49
49	West Virginia	95
59	Dartmouth ⊠	64
62	Norfolk St. ⊠	74
66	N.C. A&T	80
49	South Carolina St.	61
47	Delaware St. ⊠	61
88	Shenandoah ⊠	64
55	Florida A&M ⊠	65
57	Bethune-Cookman ⊠	59
59	Morgan St.	93
57	Coppin St. ⊠	64
57	N.C. A&T ⊠	70
74	South Carolina St. ⊠	77
59	Delaware St.	69
60	Florida A&M	93
48	Bethune-Cookman †	49
70	Morgan St. ⊠	81
65	Coppin St.	80
58	Hampton	71
63	Howard	60
70	Norfolk St. †	81

Nickname: Fighting Hawks
Colors: Maroon & Gray
Arena: Hytche Athletic Center
Capacity: 5,500; Year Built: 1998

AD: Keith Davidson
SID: G. Stan Bradley

MARYMOUNT (VA.)
Arlington, VA 22207-4299 III

Coach: Scott McClary, Muhlenberg

2006-07 RESULTS (14-11)
89	Lesley †	100
66	Eastern Nazarene †	55
69	Immaculata	61
64	Mary Washington ⊠	73
64	St. Mary's (Md.)	52
55	Catholic ⊠	68
76	Goucher ⊠	83
72	Averett	88
74	Maritime (N.Y.)	52
80	Mass. Liberal Arts ⊠	55
60	FDU-Florham ⊠	63
74	Hood	83
87	Lancaster Bible ⊠	58
75	York (Pa.)	96
76	Salisbury ⊠	65
70	Gallaudet	50
77	Mary Washington	73
89	St. Mary's (Md.) ⊠	80
64	Catholic	67
70	Goucher	67
71	Hood ⊠	58
82	York (Pa.) ⊠	94
126	Salisbury	122
81	Gallaudet ⊠	78
76	St. Mary's (Md.) ⊠	89

Nickname: Saints
Colors: Royal Blue & White
Arena: Verizon Sports Arena
Capacity: 1,000; Year Built: 1999
AD: William Finney
SID: Judy Finney

MARYVILLE (MO.)
St. Louis, MO 63141-7299............. III

Coach: Matt Rogers, Coe 1997

2006-07 RESULTS (6-19)
64	Hanover †	78
70	Transylvania	85
65	Reinhardt ⊠	54
52	Milwaukee Engr. ⊠	70
67	Webster	83
50	DePauw ⊠	68
91	Lincoln Christian ⊠	65
67	Washington-St. Louis	101
62	Mo.-St. Louis	99
63	Eureka	75
58	Greenville ⊠	61
59	Blackburn ⊠	65
58	Westminster (Mo.)	55
62	MacMurray ⊠	68
69	Fontbonne	78
78	Principia ⊠	61
69	Lincoln Christian	56
66	Webster ⊠	69
70	Greenville	72
66	Eureka ⊠	74
54	Blackburn	55
75	Principia	55
75	Westminster (Mo.) ⊠	91
79	MacMurray	82
65	Fontbonne	80

Nickname: Saints
Colors: Red & White
Arena: Moloney Arena
Capacity: 3,000; Year Built: 1980
AD: Linda Anderson
SID: Nicole Heasley

MARYVILLE (TENN.)

Maryville, TN 37804-5907.............III

Coach: Randy Lambert, Maryville (Tenn.) 1976

2006-07 RESULTS (22-7)

71	Centre ⊠	63
92	Oglethorpe †	88
82	Emory	93
55	Otterbein ⊠	58
92	Rust	78
65	Carson-Newman	74
92	Emory	52
64	Sewanee ⊠	47
70	Transylvania	81
98	Hiram †	62
84	Otterbein	81
62	Greensboro	49
73	LaGrange	60
87	Piedmont	84
69	Huntingdon ⊠	64
91	Fisk ⊠	82
78	Methodist	65
84	Oglethorpe	80
60	Huntingdon	29
64	King (Tenn.)	71
73	Fisk	66
87	LaGrange ⊠	57
101	Piedmont ⊠	78
64	Tenn. Wesleyan ⊠	65
88	Rust ⊠	69
80	Huntingdon †	57
80	LaGrange	58
73	Mary Hardin-Baylor †	62
56	Mississippi Col.	76

Nickname: Scots
Colors: Orange & Garnet
Arena: Boydson Baird Gymnasium
 Capacity: 2,000; Year Built: 1971
AD: Randall D. Lambert
SID: Eric S. Etchison

MARYWOOD

Scranton, PA 18509-1598 III

Coach: Eric Grundman, Empire St. 1990

2006-07 RESULTS (5-20)

53	Baptist Bible (Pa.) ⊠	60
93	Penn St.-Hazleton ⊠	60
57	Susquehanna ⊠	95
98	Davis ⊠	56
62	Neumann	77
74	Cabrini ⊠	66
80	Gwynedd-Mercy ⊠	77
63	Wilkes	100
38	Columbia	87
59	Misericordia	88
77	Wesley	80
76	Alvernia ⊠	93
72	Eastern ⊠	74
83	Lancaster Bible ⊠	76
54	Arcadia	65
74	Immaculata	89
69	Neumann	99
54	Gwynedd-Mercy	101
58	Immaculata ⊠	69
51	Eastern	71
74	Wesley ⊠	79
65	Cabrini	77
47	Misericordia ⊠	74
51	Alvernia	81
47	Arcadia ⊠	63

Nickname: Pacers
Colors: Forest Green & White
Arena: Insalaco Arena
 Capacity: 1,500; Year Built: 2006
AD: Mary Jo Gunning
SID: Andrew Smith

MASSACHUSETTS

Amherst, MA 01003 I

Coach: Travis Ford, Kentucky 1994

2006-07 RESULTS (24-9)

98	Dartmouth ⊠	61
65	Oakland †	56
68	Pittsburgh	85
79	Northeastern †	56
63	St. Francis (N.Y.) ⊠	49
100	Jacksonville St.	69
72	Savannah St.	49
73	Boston College ⊠	84
56	Boston U.	54
79	Central Conn. St. †	66
72	Louisville	68
68	Kentucky	82
78	Yale ⊠	69
71	Miami (Fla.) ⊠	72
79	La Salle	71
91	George Washington ⊠	84
88	Temple ⊠	77
77	Xavier	83
101	Duquesne ⊠	87
72	Rhode Island	75
66	Charlotte	61
72	Richmond ⊠	56
77	Rhode Island ⊠	55
89	Temple	98
74	Fordham	59
77	Dayton	69
83	St. Bonaventure ⊠	44
53	St. Louis	50
102	La Salle ⊠	63
71	St. Joseph's	67
71	St. Louis †	74
89	Alabama ⊠	87
77	West Virginia	90

Nickname: Minutemen
Colors: Maroon & White
Arena: Mullins Center
 Capacity: 9,493; Year Built: 1993
AD: John F. McCutcheon
SID: Matt Bourque

MASS.-DARTMOUTH

North Dartmouth, MA 02747-
2300 III

Coach: Brian Baptiste, American Int'l 1976

2006-07 RESULTS (14-13)

84	Fitchburg St. ⊠	50
84	Wesleyan (Conn.) ⊠	77
90	Worcester St. ⊠	64
66	Bridgewater St.	69
47	Brandeis	62
75	Southern Me.	70
72	Roger Williams ⊠	61
81	Keene St.	89
73	Johnson & Wales (RI)	59
63	Olivet Nazarene †	72
62	Northwood (Fla.)	79
64	Plymouth St. ⊠	51
61	Eastern Conn. St.	72
64	Western Conn. St. ⊠	67
79	Mass.-Boston	66
79	Tufts ⊠	82
64	Southern Me. ⊠	62
71	Rhode Island Col. ⊠	78
97	Keene St. ⊠	74
68	Salem St. ⊠	70
71	Plymouth St.	69
89	Mass.-Boston ⊠	81
70	Eastern Conn. St. ⊠	60
77	Rhode Island Col.	87
64	Western Conn. St.	74
73	Eastern Conn. St. ⊠	64
68	Rhode Island Col.	76

Nickname: Corsairs
Colors: Blue, White & Gold
Arena: Tripp Athletic Center
 Capacity: 2,500; Year Built: 1972
AD: Louise Goodrum
SID: Dave Geringer

MIT

Cambridge, MA 02139.................III

Coach: Larry Anderson, Rust 1987

2006-07 RESULTS (14-13)

83	Middlebury †	73
71	Gordon	78
48	Connecticut Col.	66
94	Suffolk	81
80	Lesley	79
74	Endicott	66
81	Tufts	88
52	Western New Eng.	61
47	Amherst	79
79	Emerson ⊠	72
80	Fisher ⊠	63
56	Springfield ⊠	57
47	Babson	56
62	Coast Guard	59
65	Wheaton (Mass.) ⊠	53
43	WPI ⊠	64
59	Babson	72
68	Clark (Mass.)	67
71	Newbury ⊠	62
52	Wheaton (Mass.)	71
51	Coast Guard ⊠	47
71	Springfield	68
47	WPI	68
76	Lasell ⊠	68
73	Clark (Mass.) ⊠	81
64	Clark (Mass.)	53
49	WPI	66

Nickname: Engineers
Colors: Cardinal Red & Silver Gray
Arena: Rockwell Cage
 Capacity: 600; Year Built: 1959
AD: John A. Benedick
SID: James Kramer

MASS. LIBERAL ARTS

North Adams, MA 01247-4100 ...III

Coach: Devin Gotham, Nazareth 1996

2006-07 RESULTS (6-19)

53	Me.-Farmington	70
78	Lyndon St. †	82
78	Hartwick	87
124	Maritime (N.Y.) ⊠	126
76	Lyndon St. ⊠	68
71	Mitchell ⊠	74
61	Newbury †	75
64	Anna Maria †	59
89	Johnson St. ⊠	87
55	Marymount (Va.)	80
74	Wentworth Inst. †	86
79	Framingham St. ⊠	62
93	Mount Ida ⊠	84
73	Bridgewater St.	82
67	Worcester St.	77
62	Salem St. ⊠	81
68	Fitchburg St. ⊠	73
67	Westfield St.	95
89	Framingham St.	110
91	Green Mountain ⊠	67
73	Bridgewater St. ⊠	78
69	Worcester St. ⊠	87
62	Salem St.	95
77	Fitchburg St.	79
91	Westfield St.	101

Nickname: Trailblazers
Colors: Navy & Gold
Arena: Amsler Campus Center Gym
 Capacity: 2,500; Year Built: 1975
AD: Scott F. Nichols
SID: Deb Raber

MASS.-BOSTON

Boston, MA 02125 III

Coach: Charlie Titus, St. Michael's 1972

2006-07 RESULTS (10-17)

86	Fitchburg St.	80
85	Framingham St. ⊠	87
102	Colby-Sawyer ⊠	100
62	Emerson	85
77	Suffolk ⊠	63
57	Eastern Conn. St. ⊠	60
74	Salem St. ⊠	97
80	Western Conn. St.	82
54	Ozarks (Mo.) †	67
75	Mt. St. Mary (N.Y.) †	59
61	Keene St. ⊠	67
97	Plymouth St. ⊠	90
77	Rhode Island Col.	86
66	Mass.-Dartmouth ⊠	79
71	Bridgewater St. ⊠	74
115	Eastern Conn. St.	114
60	Southern Me.	73
99	Western Conn. St. ⊠	90
90	Keene St.	86
81	Mass.-Dartmouth	89
67	WPI	89
67	Plymouth St.	96
96	Southern Me. ⊠	61
76	Tufts	93
72	Rhode Island Col. ⊠	90
88	Western Conn. St.	82
67	Keene St. †	79

Nickname: Beacons
Colors: Beacon Blue, Black & White
Arena: Clark Athletic Center
 Capacity: 3,500; Year Built: 1981
AD: Charlie Titus
SID: Alan Wickstrom

MASS.-LOWELL

Lowell, MA 01854.............................II

Coach: Ken Barer, George Washington 1988

2006-07 RESULTS (9-18)

70	New Haven	54
58	Holy Family †	69
75	Post †	70
75	St. Michael's	78
47	Bentley ⊠	69
75	Stonehill	74
66	Bryant ⊠	69
89	Merrimack ⊠	83
69	Southern Conn. St.	72
96	Queens (N.Y.) ⊠	75
72	American Int'l	75
71	NYIT	73
55	St. Rose	69
61	St. Anselm ⊠	67
56	Merrimack	72
65	Pace	75
69	Assumption	68
65	St. Michael's ⊠	69
57	American Int'l ⊠	70
62	Assumption ⊠	68
55	Bryant	66
68	Southern N.H. ⊠	63
51	Franklin Pierce ⊠	74
72	Stonehill ⊠	68
59	Le Moyne	65
47	Bentley	65
92	Southern Conn. St. ⊠	76

Nickname: River Hawks
Colors: Red, White & Royal Blue
Arena: Costello Gymnasium
 Capacity: 2,100; Year Built: 1960
AD: Dana K. Skinner
SID: Chris O'Donnell

MCMURRY
Abilene, TX 79697 III

Coach: Ron Holmes, McMurry 1977

2006-07 RESULTS (20-7)
63	Rowan †	68
75	Immaculata †	61
73	LeTourneau	61
57	Mississippi Col. ⊠	73
85	Louisiana Col. ⊠	71
63	Hardin-Simmons	64
75	Trinity (Tex.) ⊠	62
69	East Tex. Baptist	70
55	Sam Houston St.	86
89	Texas-Tyler ⊠	74
81	Texas-Dallas ⊠	57
75	Ozarks (Ark.) †	69
80	Mary Hardin-Baylor	91
94	Concordia (Tex.)	87
69	Texas Lutheran ⊠	64
90	Schreiner ⊠	71
67	Hardin-Simmons ⊠	53
90	Sul Ross St. ⊠	59
97	Howard Payne ⊠	92
69	Sul Ross St.	55
90	Howard Payne	60
77	Texas Lutheran	58
96	Schreiner	83
80	Mary Hardin-Baylor ⊠	76
99	Concordia (Tex.) ⊠	57
71	Texas-Dallas †	70
56	Mississippi Col.	66

Nickname: Indians
Colors: Maroon & White
Arena: Kimbrell Arena
   Capacity: 2,250; Year Built: 1973
AD: Bill Libby
SID: Kyle Robarts

MCNEESE ST.
Lake Charles, LA 70609 I

Coach: Dave Simmons, Louisiana Tech 1981

2006-07 RESULTS (15-17)
65	Florida St.	85
54	SMU †	70
50	Illinois St. †	67
89	Louisiana Col. ⊠	60
50	Louisiana Tech ⊠	59
77	Texas Col. ⊠	53
57	LSU	91
61	Mississippi Val. ⊠	44
60	Ark.-Little Rock	46
63	Mississippi St.	89
45	Mississippi Val.	76
68	La.-Lafayette ⊠	63
41	Southern Miss.	58
67	Coastal Caro.	81
62	A&M-Corpus Christi	74
59	Sam Houston St.	58
53	Stephen F. Austin ⊠	67
90	Northwestern St.	98
61	Central Ark. ⊠	56
68	Lamar ⊠	60
64	Southeastern La.	69
53	Nicholls St.	61
67	Texas St.	65
46	Texas-Arlington ⊠	52
83	Northwestern St. ⊠	81
58	Central Ark.	55
63	UTSA ⊠	57
71	Lamar	75
63	Southeastern La. ⊠	45
77	Nicholls St. ⊠	76
77	Texas-Arlington †	76
66	A&M-Corpus Christi †	87

Nickname: Cowboys
Colors: Blue & Gold
Arena: Burton Coliseum
   Capacity: 8,000; Year Built: 1986
AD: Sonny Watkins
SID: Louis Bonnette

MEDAILLE
Buffalo, NY 14214-2695 III

Coach: Mike MacDonald,
St. Bonaventure 1988

2006-07 RESULTS (11-14)
73	Case Reserve	65
59	Marietta †	81
76	D'Youville †	70
57	Pitt.-Bradford	66
85	Mt. Aloysius	89
50	Lake Erie ⊠	67
69	Frostburg St. ⊠	78
44	Buffalo St.	78
77	D'Youville †	66
44	Eastern Conn. St. †	72
52	Albany Pharmacy †	40
71	Pitt.-Greensburg	74
54	Penn St.-Behrend	65
57	Penn St.-Altoona ⊠	55
68	Hilbert ⊠	72
60	La Roche	59
74	Mt. Aloysius ⊠	57
69	Pitt.-Bradford ⊠	66
70	Frostburg St.	85
60	Lake Erie	78
80	Pitt.-Greensburg ⊠	77
46	Penn St.-Behrend ⊠	66
77	Penn St.-Altoona	76
69	La Roche ⊠	62
55	Hilbert	71

Nickname: Mavericks
Colors: Navy, Yellow & White
Arena: Kevin I. Sullivan Campus Center
   Capacity: 300; Year Built: 1995
AD: Pete Lonergan
SID: Michael P. Carbery

MEDGAR EVERS
Brooklyn, NY 11225-2298 III

Coach: Merrill Davis,

2006-07 RESULTS (9-16)
69	Framingham St. †	75
83	Me.-Presque Isle †	73
73	Rowan ⊠	93
70	Hamilton ⊠	97
71	St. Joseph's (L.I.)	82
96	Pratt ⊠	33
53	New York U.	92
37	Lehman ⊠	27
58	York (N.Y.)	69
56	Rutgers-Newark ⊠	70
70	Yeshiva	84
93	St. Joseph (Vt.) †	83
66	Lehman	58
78	Staten Island ⊠	80
62	City Tech	76
60	CCNY	58
78	John Jay ⊠	54
77	Hunter ⊠	79
66	Baruch ⊠	68
62	Ramapo	95
80	Brooklyn ⊠	77
70	Staten Island	76
80	York (N.Y.) ⊠	90
64	City Tech ⊠	61
81	Brooklyn	88

Nickname: Cougars
Colors: Gold & Black
Arena: Medgar Evers College Gym
   Capacity: 300; Year Built: 1971
AD: Roy Anderson
SID: Brent Davis

MEMPHIS
Memphis, TN 38152-3370 I

Coach: John Calipari, Clarion 1982

2006-07 RESULTS (33-4)
111	Jackson St. ⊠	69
77	Oklahoma †	65
85	Georgia Tech †	92
80	Kentucky †	63
86	Arkansas St. ⊠	60
77	Manhattan ⊠	59
78	Marshall ⊠	59
58	Tennessee	76
82	Mississippi ⊠	70
88	Austin Peay ⊠	63
71	Arizona	79
86	Middle Tenn. ⊠	46
87	Lamar ⊠	62
88	Cincinnati ⊠	55
79	Houston	69
75	Southern Miss.	62
79	UAB ⊠	54
61	East Caro.	44
72	Tulsa ⊠	59
67	Southern Miss. ⊠	64
87	UCF	65
88	SMU ⊠	52
70	UAB	56
95	Tulane ⊠	51
69	Tulsa	52
78	Gonzaga	77
99	Rice ⊠	63
77	Houston ⊠	64
78	UTEP	67
64	SMU	61
92	Marshall ⊠	71
71	Tulane ⊠	49
71	Houston ⊠	59
73	North Texas †	58
78	Nevada †	62
65	Texas A&M †	64
76	Ohio St. †	92

Nickname: Tigers
Colors: Blue & Gray
Arena: FedExForum
   Capacity: 18,400; Year Built: 2004
AD: R.C. Johnson
SID: Lamar Chance

MERCER
Macon, GA 31207 I

Coach: Mark Slonaker, Georgia 1980

2006-07 RESULTS (13-17)
48	Wisconsin	72
61	Savannah St.	71
89	Emory ⊠	71
59	Ga. Southern ⊠	61
70	East Tenn. St. ⊠	76
84	Kennesaw St. ⊠	77
78	Charleston So.	59
79	Fort Valley St. ⊠	74
62	Oregon St.	93
64	Oregon	84
69	Furman	83
84	Stetson ⊠	63
47	Belmont	72
68	Lipscomb	89
94	Campbell ⊠	93
85	Gardner-Webb ⊠	74
77	Jacksonville	87
77	North Fla.	58
68	Savannah St. ⊠	64
78	Stetson	66
50	Lipscomb ⊠	62
77	Belmont ⊠	84
68	Gardner-Webb	69
81	Campbell	80
97	Jacksonville ⊠	101
69	North Fla. ⊠	59
51	Kennesaw St.	87
89	East Tenn. St.	112
49	Lipscomb †	85

Nickname: Bears
Colors: Orange & Black
Arena: University Center
   Capacity: 3,200; Year Built: 2003
AD: Bobby A. Pope
SID: Randy Jones

MERCHANT MARINE
Kings Point, NY 11024-1699 III

Coach: Chris Carideo, Widener 1996

2006-07 RESULTS (14-12)
76	Albertus Magnus ⊠	73
85	Kean	107
86	St. Joseph's (Brkln) ⊠	72
96	Old Westbury ⊠	91
57	Coast Guard ⊠	78
61	Lehman	54
70	Staten Island ⊠	67
53	Wash. & Lee	75
82	Hood †	92
72	St. Joseph's (L.I.)	89
70	Manhattanville ⊠	68
66	Farmingdale St.	78
90	Maritime (N.Y.)	66
87	Mt. St. Vincent ⊠	66
92	Mt. St. Mary (N.Y.)	83
91	CCNY ⊠	58
60	Yeshiva	70
74	Stevens Institute ⊠	85
66	Centenary (N.J.) ⊠	65
71	Old Westbury	67
81	Maritime (N.Y.) ⊠	61
69	Manhattanville	88
82	Mt. St. Mary (N.Y.) ⊠	52
86	Stevens Institute	92
81	St. Joseph's (L.I.) ⊠	91
70	Old Westbury	78

Nickname: Mariners
Colors: Blue & Gray
Arena: Liebertz Gymnasium
   Capacity: 1,211; Year Built: 1943
AD: Susan Petersen-Lubow
SID: Tyrone C. Broxton

MERCY
Dobbs Ferry, NY 10522 II

Coach: Steve Kelly, Fordham 1969

2006-07 RESULTS (5-22)
61	Pace ⊠	81
55	Stonehill †	72
76	New Haven ⊠	69
58	Caldwell	69
75	Bloomfield †	69
51	NYIT ⊠	59
59	Fairleigh Dickinson	86
37	Adelphi	74
55	Dominican (N.Y.)	65
87	Bloomfield †	80
65	Dowling	64
77	Concordia (N.Y.) ⊠	84
68	Molloy ⊠	67
51	St. Thomas Aquinas ⊠	65
60	C.W. Post	88
63	Bridgeport ⊠	58
60	Queens (N.Y.) ⊠	76
60	New Haven	70
44	Dowling ⊠	57
54	Concordia (N.Y.)	58
68	NYIT	86
54	Adelphi ⊠	73
80	Molloy	85
53	St. Thomas Aquinas	63
52	C.W. Post ⊠	67
66	Bridgeport	69
61	Queens (N.Y.)	72

Nickname: Flyers
Colors: Blue & White
Arena: Westchester County Center
   Capacity: 3,500; Year Built: 1930
AD: Kevin T. McGinniss
SID: Drew Brown

MERCYHURST

Erie, PA 16546 II

Coach: Gary Manchel, Vermont 1985

2006-07 RESULTS (18-11)

73	Molloy †	75
81	Assumption †	67
89	Roberts Wesleyan ⊠	63
87	Ohio Valley	82
69	Hillsdale	72
65	Wayne St. (Mich.)	57
57	Edinboro	63
79	Grand Valley St. ⊠	74
89	Columbia Union ⊠	60
72	Northwood (Mich.) ⊠	43
67	Indiana (Pa.) ⊠	51
82	Concordia (N.Y.) ⊠	64
86	Slippery Rock ⊠	61
47	Findlay	59
79	Ashland ⊠	71
66	Northwood (Mich.) ⊠	74
68	Saginaw Valley	71
70	Ferris St.	65
66	Lake Superior St. ⊠	62
64	Gannon ⊠	53
69	Northern Mich.	82
66	Michigan Tech	59
67	Wayne St. (Mich.) ⊠	57
65	Hillsdale ⊠	81
60	Findlay	86
56	Ashland	86
79	Gannon	74
59	Wayne St. (Mich.) ⊠	54
40	Findlay	77

Nickname: Lakers
Colors: Blue & Green
Arena: Mercyhurst Athletic Center
  Capacity: 1,800; Year Built: 1978
AD: Peter J. Russo
SID: Jason Knavel

MERRIMACK

North Andover, MA 01845 II

Coach: Bert Hammel, Bentley 1973

2006-07 RESULTS (8-20)

52	Post	61
71	Dowling	49
84	Southern Conn. St. ⊠	77
79	St. Michael's ⊠	88
70	St. Rose ⊠	87
61	American Int'l	69
83	Mass.-Lowell	89
88	Assumption	97
37	Bentley ⊠	72
71	Stonehill	72
70	Bridgeport †	77
57	Le Moyne †	70
73	Bryant ⊠	52
94	Pace	99
72	Mass.-Lowell ⊠	56
56	Stonehill	68
66	St. Rose	88
62	St. Michael's	67
78	Southern N.H. ⊠	65
83	St. Anselm ⊠	71
62	Le Moyne	80
71	Bentley	88
65	American Int'l ⊠	74
57	Southern Conn. St.	73
66	Assumption ⊠	57
75	Franklin Pierce ⊠	60
69	Bryant	74
60	American Int'l	68

Nickname: Warriors
Colors: Navy Blue & Gold
Arena: Volpe Complex
  Capacity: 1,200; Year Built: 1972
AD: Sean T. Frazier
SID: Lisa Cascio

MESA ST.

Grand Junction, CO 81501 II

Coach: Jim Heaps, Mesa St. 1982

2006-07 RESULTS (17-10)

65	Caldwell †	66
91	Northwest Nazarene †	85
63	Dixie St. ⊠	60
70	Wayland Baptist ⊠	76
73	Bethany (Cal.) ⊠	54
80	Metro St. ⊠	71
61	Colo. Christian ⊠	47
87	Chadron St.	81
84	Neb.-Kearney	72
86	Johnson & Wales (CO)	88
86	Johnson & Wales (CO) ⊠	70
69	Colorado Mines ⊠	54
63	Regis (Colo.)	55
87	UC-Colo. Springs	98
75	Fort Lewis	79
85	Western St. ⊠	66
72	N.M. Highlands ⊠	74
71	Western N.M. ⊠	67
74	Colorado St.-Pueblo ⊠	63
75	Adams St. ⊠	79
80	Western N.M. ⊠	63
89	N.M. Highlands ⊠	59
78	Adams St.	91
74	Colorado St.-Pueblo	72
69	Fort Lewis	80
78	Western St.	71
74	Fort Lewis	81

Nickname: Mavericks
Colors: Maroon, Gold & White
Arena: Brownson Arena
  Capacity: 2,500; Year Built: 1969
AD: Jamie Hamilton
SID: Tish Elliott

MESSIAH

Grantham, PA 17027 III

Coach: Rick Van Pelt, Messiah 1991

2006-07 RESULTS (19-7)

76	Mary Washington †	83
92	Pitt.-Greensburg †	72
74	Mansfield ⊠	66
81	Juniata ⊠	61
66	Albright	65
104	Pa. Col. of Bible ⊠	35
55	Richard Stockton ⊠	49
78	Phila. Biblical ⊠	43
73	Geneva †	60
56	Centre	60
66	Cal Lutheran	71
66	Hood	73
53	Elizabethtown	44
69	Lebanon Valley ⊠	65
55	Susquehanna	52
74	Widener	61
70	Moravian ⊠	50
67	Lebanon Valley	61
67	Juniata	76
69	Albright ⊠	63
68	Susquehanna ⊠	53
79	Moravian	47
70	Elizabethtown ⊠	59
75	Widener ⊠	59
84	Widener	91
37	Catholic †	58

Nickname: Falcons
Colors: Navy & White
Arena: Brubaker Auditorium
  Capacity: 1,800; Year Built: 1972
AD: Jerry Chaplin
SID: Scott Frey

METHODIST

Fayetteville, NC 28311-1420 III

Coach: David Smith, Methodist 1981

2006-07 RESULTS (11-14)

85	Newport News ⊠	59
73	Piedmont	87
71	Baruch †	55
68	Embry-Riddle	77
76	Randolph-Macon	69
71	Gettysburg †	61
102	Guilford	108
49	Va. Wesleyan ⊠	84
43	Catholic	72
72	Rutgers-Newark †	76
47	Greensboro ⊠	62
78	Ferrum ⊠	73
71	Piedmont ⊠	55
58	Averett	61
65	Maryville (Tenn.) ⊠	78
86	N.C. Wesleyan	88
86	Chris. Newport ⊠	85
89	Shenandoah ⊠	78
60	Greensboro	68
63	Ferrum	59
52	Averett ⊠	71
79	N.C. Wesleyan ⊠	73
91	Chris. Newport	93
74	Shenandoah	73
71	Ferrum	77

Nickname: Monarchs
Colors: Green & Gold
Arena: March F. Riddle Center
  Capacity: 1,200; Year Built: 1990
AD: Bob McEvoy
SID: Kirbie Britt

METRO ST.

Denver, CO 80217-3362 II

Coach: Brannon Hays, Cal Lutheran 1993

2006-07 RESULTS (28-4)

82	Angelo St. ⊠	70
85	St. Leo ⊠	60
84	Seattle ⊠	76
75	Johnson & Wales (CO) ⊠	55
71	Mesa St.	80
82	Fort Lewis	65
73	Colorado St.-Pueblo ⊠	65
81	Adams St. ⊠	49
53	Northwest Mo. St. †	59
70	Mo. Western St. †	67
92	St. Francis (Ill.) ⊠	73
92	Tex. A&M-Commerce ⊠	76
81	Western St.	71
108	N.M. Highlands ⊠	77
78	Western N.M. ⊠	67
77	Colo. Christian ⊠	53
64	Colorado Mines ⊠	48
90	Regis (Colo.)	70
87	UC-Colo. Springs	82
92	Neb.-Kearney ⊠	75
96	Chadron St. ⊠	58
83	UC-Colo. Springs ⊠	67
86	Regis (Colo.) ⊠	61
69	Chadron St.	65
87	Neb.-Kearney	90
62	Colo. Christian	51
81	Colorado Mines	71
81	Colo. Christian ⊠	68
73	Fort Lewis †	58
70	Adams St. †	60
71	Adams St. †	48
68	Minn. St. Mankato †	70

Nickname: Roadrunners
Colors: Navy Blue & Burgundy
Arena: Auraria Events Center
  Capacity: 2,300; Year Built: 1965
AD: Joan M. McDermott
SID: Michelle Zents

MIAMI (FLA.)

Coral Gables, FL 33146 I

Coach: Frank Haith, Elon 1988

2006-07 RESULTS (12-20)

73	Florida Int'l ⊠	50
96	Alcorn St. ⊠	57
74	Evansville ⊠	69
57	Buffalo †	60
67	Cleveland St. †	78
98	Lafayette ⊠	66
59	Northwestern	61
90	Georgia Tech ⊠	82
79	Lehigh ⊠	58
52	Mississippi St. ⊠	70
89	Stetson ⊠	64
74	Binghamton ⊠	79
59	Louisville	82
67	Nebraska †	82
72	Massachusetts ⊠	71
58	Wake Forest ⊠	59
63	Maryland	58
63	Duke ⊠	85
63	Boston College	82
67	Florida St.	86
85	Virginia Tech ⊠	92
64	North Carolina	105
70	Virginia	81
68	Boston College ⊠	75
80	North Carolina St. ⊠	65
69	Wake Forest	74
68	Virginia ⊠	60
57	Virginia Tech	73
70	Clemson	74
90	Florida St. ⊠	98
67	Maryland †	62
71	Boston College †	74

Nickname: Hurricanes
Colors: Orange, Green & White
Arena: BankUnited Center
  Capacity: 7,000; Year Built: 2003
AD: Paul T. Dee
SID: Sam Henderson

MIAMI (OHIO)

Oxford, OH 45056 I

Coach: Charlie Coles, Miami (Ohio) 1965

2006-07 RESULTS (18-15)

56	Wright St. ⊠	57
46	Kentucky	57
52	Florida A&M ⊠	33
72	Ill.-Chicago ⊠	61
49	Illinois †	51
57	Rutgers †	44
53	Xavier	68
40	Illinois St.	64
56	Michigan ⊠	62
72	Oakland ⊠	46
54	Dayton	56
52	Cincinnati	60
65	Kent St. ⊠	63
52	Akron	54
51	Buffalo	68
66	Bowling Green ⊠	60
72	Ohio ⊠	69
72	Central Mich.	52
56	Toledo	61
62	Northern Ill. ⊠	59
62	Western Mich. ⊠	59
74	Eastern Mich.	64
66	Ball St. ⊠	44
45	Kent St.	61
70	Indiana St.	58
64	Akron	62
80	Buffalo ⊠	68
45	Ohio	52
64	Bowling Green	68
70	Ohio †	51
58	Toledo †	53
53	Akron †	52
56	Oregon †	58

Nickname: RedHawks
Colors: Red & White
Arena: Millett Hall
　　Capacity: 6,400; Year Built: 1968
AD: Brad Bates
SID: Angie Renninger

MICHIGAN
Ann Arbor, MI 48109-2201 I

Coach: Tommy Amaker, Duke 1987

2006-07 RESULTS (22-13)

60	Central Conn. St. ⊠	40
78	Davidson	68
80	Eastern Mich. ⊠	51
66	Milwaukee ⊠	59
82	Harvard ⊠	50
65	Youngstown St. ⊠	56
66	UMBC ⊠	54
67	North Carolina St.	74
83	Wofford ⊠	49
62	Miami (Ohio)	56
70	Delaware St. ⊠	43
67	Northern Ill. ⊠	52
55	UCLA	92
62	Army ⊠	50
51	Georgetown ⊠	67
71	Illinois ⊠	61
58	Northwestern	46
53	Purdue	67
77	Penn St. ⊠	57
71	Purdue ⊠	55
58	Wisconsin	71
61	Indiana	76
62	Iowa ⊠	69
63	Ohio St.	76
82	Minnesota ⊠	80
44	Michigan St.	59
58	Indiana ⊠	55
42	Illinois	54
62	Minnesota	51
67	Michigan St. ⊠	56
61	Ohio St. ⊠	65
49	Minnesota †	40
62	Ohio St. †	72
68	Utah St. ⊠	58
66	Florida St.	87

Nickname: Wolverines
Colors: Maize & Blue
Arena: Crisler Arena
　　Capacity: 13,751; Year Built: 1967
AD: William C. Martin
SID: Tom Wywrot

MICHIGAN ST.
East Lansing, MI 48824-1025 I

Coach: Tom Izzo, Northern Mich. 1977

2006-07 RESULTS (23-12)

45	Brown ⊠	34
86	Youngstown St. ⊠	61
73	Citadel ⊠	41
63	Texas †	61
60	Maryland †	62
66	Vermont ⊠	46
71	Oakland ⊠	53
58	Boston College	65
82	Bradley ⊠	53
80	IPFW ⊠	43
76	BYU †	61
69	Chicago St. ⊠	61
67	Belmont ⊠	58
76	Green Bay ⊠	64
74	Loyola (Md.) ⊠	61
60	Iowa	62
51	Indiana	73
66	Northwestern ⊠	45
63	Illinois	57
91	Penn St.	64
70	Minnesota ⊠	46
64	Ohio St.	66
50	Illinois	57
54	Ohio St. ⊠	63
38	Purdue	62

MICHIGAN TECH
Houghton, MI 49931-1295 II

Coach: Kevin Luke, Northern Mich. 1982

2006-07 RESULTS (13-15)

80	Wis.-Parkside ⊠	69
61	Lewis ⊠	59
48	Minn. St. Mankato †	67
76	Minn. Duluth	80
78	Northern Mich.	69
57	Ashland	78
70	Northwood (Mich.) ⊠	52
64	Saginaw Valley ⊠	56
63	Findlay	71
62	St. Joseph's (Ind.) ⊠	48
62	Minn. Duluth ⊠	55
46	Bowling Green †	58
50	Green Bay	62
76	Jacksonville St. †	58
43	Grand Valley St.	48
63	Lake Superior St. ⊠	71
61	Ferris St. ⊠	49
74	Wayne St. (Mich.)	80
61	Hillsdale	77
50	Saginaw Valley	44
66	Northwood (Mich.)	57
58	Gannon	44
59	Mercyhurst ⊠	66
59	Ferris St.	61
63	Lake Superior St.	53
64	Grand Valley St. ⊠	69
34	Northern Mich. ⊠	56
54	Northern Mich.	77

Nickname: Huskies
Colors: Silver, Gold & Black
Arena: SDC Gymnasium
　　Capacity: 3,200; Year Built: 1981
AD: Suzanne R. Sanregret
SID: Wes Frahm

MIDDLE TENN.
Murfreesboro, TN 37132 I

Coach: Kermit Davis Jr., Mississippi St. 1982

2006-07 RESULTS (15-17)

52	Tennessee	83
60	Cumberland (Ky.) ⊠	47
62	Alabama †	71
69	Toledo ⊠	75
56	Col. of Charleston †	64
64	Belmont ⊠	57
65	Indiana St. ⊠	58
67	Tennessee St. ⊠	56
65	La.-Monroe ⊠	67
63	Austin Peay	64
46	Memphis	86
64	Western Ky. ⊠	73
60	Florida Int'l	46
59	South Ala.	51
57	Troy ⊠	71
72	Fla. Atlantic ⊠	68
76	New Orleans	67
51	Arkansas St. ⊠	54
61	Ark.-Little Rock	60

53	North Texas	66
71	La.-Lafayette ⊠	59
57	South Dakota St.	56
75	Denver †	49
38	South Ala. ⊠	61
76	La.-Monroe	82
53	Western Ky.	65
67	Florida Int'l ⊠	69
70	Troy	73
79	Fla. Atlantic ⊠	59
72	Troy	64
63	South Ala. †	60
52	North Texas †	59

Nickname: Blue Raiders
Colors: Royal Blue & White
Arena: Murphy Athletic Center
　　Capacity: 11,520; Year Built: 1972
AD: Chris Massaro
SID: Tony Stinnett

MIDDLEBURY
Middlebury, VT 05753 III

Coach: Jeff Brown, Vermont 1982

2006-07 RESULTS (15-10)

73	MIT †	83
120	Mount Ida †	61
64	St. Lawrence	80
99	Castleton	90
64	Rensselaer ⊠	69
76	Union (N.Y.)	70
100	Southern Vt. ⊠	76
86	Hamilton	84
79	New England	53
81	Skidmore ⊠	65
96	Colby-Sawyer	85
102	Green Mountain ⊠	47
100	Colby	93
81	Bowdoin ⊠	58
73	Amherst	79
67	Trinity (Conn.)	82
92	Johnson St. ⊠	59
79	Williams	86
57	Norwich	61
102	Tufts ⊠	91
48	Bates ⊠	81
69	Plattsburgh St.	86
64	Wesleyan (Conn.)	58
69	Connecticut Col.	59
79	Colby	91

Nickname: Panthers
Colors: Blue & White
Arena: Pepin Gymnasium
　　Capacity: 1,200; Year Built: 1949
AD: Erin Quinn
SID: Brad Nadeau

MIDWESTERN ST.
Wichita Falls, TX 76308-2099 II

Coach: Jeff Ray, Midwestern St. 1984

2006-07 RESULTS (24-7)

82	Okla. Panhandle	63
113	Dallas Christian ⊠	42
75	Incarnate Word	73
70	Southeastern Okla. ⊠	92
99	Southwestern Okla.	114
77	Cameron	79
64	East Central	61
74	Pittsburg St. †	71
72	Northwest Mo. St. †	70
92	Southern Nazarene	90
94	Cameron	84
101	Tex. A&M-Commerce ⊠	84
89	Okla. Panhandle ⊠	73
64	Northeastern St.	55
76	Tex. A&M-Kingsville	73
81	Eastern N.M. ⊠	86
90	West Tex. A&M ⊠	81
72	Tarleton St.	59
93	Abilene Christian	75
107	Angelo St. ⊠	96
93	Abilene Christian ⊠	67

88	Angelo St.	89
76	Tarleton St. ⊠	70
79	Tex. A&M-Kingsville ⊠	82
77	Eastern N.M.	62
61	West Tex. A&M	55
90	Southwestern Okla. ⊠	67
78	Central Okla. ⊠	74
89	Southeastern Okla. ⊠	80
86	West Tex. A&M †	81
77	Southeastern Okla. †	88

Nickname: Mustangs
Colors: Maroon and Gold
Arena: D.L. Ligon Coliseum/Gerald Stockton Court
　　Capacity: 5,200; Year Built: 1969
AD: Ed Harris
SID: Bill Powers

MILES
Fairfield, AL 35064 II

Coach: Christopher Giles, UAB

2006-07 RESULTS (14-15)

63	Montevallo ⊠	60
72	Southern Ark. †	64
61	Delta St.	60
58	Auburn	79
51	Montevallo	84
58	Fort Valley St.	56
78	Stillman	61
67	Morehouse	81
57	Albany St. (Ga.)	64
64	Benedict ⊠	76
84	Paine ⊠	74
78	Tuskegee	64
70	Morehouse	63
61	Clark Atlanta	51
71	LeMoyne-Owen	69
71	Tuskegee ⊠	72
65	Stillman ⊠	62
62	Benedict	73
48	Paine	79
82	Fort Valley St. ⊠	97
68	Albany St. (Ga.) ⊠	75
90	Lane ⊠	95
85	Kentucky St. ⊠	98
72	Lane	69
80	Kentucky St.	84
106	LeMoyne-Owen ⊠	94
62	Clark Atlanta ⊠	64
75	Morehouse ⊠	73
59	Fort Valley St. ⊠	72

Nickname: Golden Bears
Colors: Purple & Gold
Arena: Knox-Windham Gym/Fair Park Arena
　　Capacity: 5,000; Year Built: 1949
AD: Augustus James
SID: Willie Patterson

MILLERSVILLE
Millersville, PA 17551-0302 II

Coach: Fred Thompson, La.-Monroe 1990

2006-07 RESULTS (28-5)

67	Shippensburg	69
113	Wilmington (Del.) ⊠	74
89	Seton Hill ⊠	79
76	Chowan	65
116	Penn St.-Harrisburg ⊠	48
82	Edinboro	78
81	Slippery Rock	65
96	Elizabethtown ⊠	59
101	Morris	80
74	California (Pa.)	67
94	Chowan ⊠	57
88	Lock Haven ⊠	63
65	Shippensburg ⊠	59
85	Mansfield	70
77	Clarion ⊠	68
75	Indiana (Pa.) ⊠	57
73	Bloomsburg ⊠	47

(Michigan mid-column results:)

59	Michigan ⊠	44
81	Iowa ⊠	49
64	Wisconsin ⊠	55
66	Indiana ⊠	58
56	Michigan	67
50	Wisconsin	52
62	Northwestern †	57
57	Wisconsin †	70
61	Marquette †	49
67	North Carolina †	81

Nickname: Spartans
Colors: Green & White
Arena: Breslin Events Center
　　Capacity: 14,759; Year Built: 1989
AD: Ronald H. Mason
SID: Matt Larson

64	Kutztown ⊠	67
83	East Stroudsburg	65
92	Cheyney ⊠	85
64	West Chester	72
86	Mansfield ⊠	75
84	Bloomsburg	76
79	Kutztown	82
80	East Stroudsburg ⊠	79
83	Cheyney	81
90	West Chester ⊠	81
63	East Stroudsburg ⊠	59
65	Edinboro †	55
79	Cheyney †	68
89	Mount Olive †	85
82	California (Pa.) †	72
65	Barton	76

Nickname: Marauders
Colors: Black & Gold
Arena: Pucillo Gymnasium
　Capacity: 2,850; Year Built: 1970
AD: Daniel N. Audette
SID: Greg Wright

MILLIKIN
Decatur, IL 62522-2084 III

Coach: Tim Littrell, Millikin 1977

2006-07 RESULTS (9-16)

88	MacMurray	76
88	Ind.-Northwest	73
62	Eureka ⊠	68
83	Webster ⊠	68
91	Robert Morris-S'fiel	94
76	Franklin ⊠	68
72	Illinois Col. ⊠	81
81	Blackburn ⊠	74
75	Aurora	90
75	West Coast Baptist	57
74	La Verne	61
65	North Park	73
84	Ill. Wesleyan ⊠	82
72	North Central (Ill.) ⊠	79
65	Augustana (Ill.) ⊠	80
60	Carthage	64
57	Wheaton (Ill.) ⊠	71
72	North Park ⊠	76
89	Elmhurst	85
76	North Central (Ill.)	82
60	Ill. Wesleyan ⊠	66
59	Augustana (Ill.)	71
72	Wheaton (Ill.)	83
65	Carthage ⊠	70
63	Elmhurst ⊠	79

Nickname: Big Blue
Colors: Royal Blue & White
Arena: Griswold Gymnasium
　Capacity: 3,052; Year Built: 1970
AD: Lori Kerans
SID: Julie Farr

MILLSAPS
Jackson, MS 39210 III

Coach: Tim Wise, Millsaps 1989

2006-07 RESULTS (18-9)

93	Pensacola Christian ⊠	62
79	Rust ⊠	69
60	Belhaven	69
70	Wesley (Miss.) †	57
64	Dallas †	73
70	Southwestern (Tex.)	68
53	Trinity (Tex.)	57
63	Pensacola Christian	72
67	Southeastern La.	90
81	LaGrange	75
68	Huntingdon †	60
84	Rhodes	67
70	Rust	92
78	Oglethorpe ⊠	76
77	Sewanee ⊠	69
72	Austin	63
78	Hendrix	73
79	Centre ⊠	67

74	DePauw ⊠	76
71	Southwestern (Tex.) ⊠	65
53	Trinity (Tex.) ⊠	54
78	Oglethorpe	74
93	Sewanee	80
86	Wesley (Miss.)	71
88	Rhodes ⊠	82
77	Hendrix †	64
59	Centre †	75

Nickname: Majors
Colors: Purple & White
Arena: The Hangar Dome
　Capacity: 3,500; Year Built: 1974
AD: Tim Wise
SID: Kevin Maloney

MILWAUKEE ENGR.
Milwaukee, WI 53202-3109 III

Coach: Brian Miller, Milwaukee 1987

2006-07 RESULTS (16-11)

62	Beloit ⊠	55
70	Dominican (Ill.)	57
82	Webster	79
70	Maryville (Mo.)	52
70	Rockford	66
64	Marian (Wis.) ⊠	63
61	Lake Forest	68
69	Illinois Tech ⊠	61
71	WPI ⊠	74
67	Concordia (Ill.)	59
69	Bethany (Kan.) †	75
57	Cal Lutheran	64
53	Chicago ⊠	70
71	Northland ⊠	63
73	Finlandia	51
106	Grinnell	125
68	Clarke	73
74	Maranatha Baptist	42
62	Wis.-Whitewater ⊠	95
71	Finlandia ⊠	63
81	Concordia (Wis.) ⊠	77
69	Northland Bapt.	55
61	Dominican (Ill.) ⊠	68
75	Lakeland	90
62	Clarke ⊠	70
75	Finlandia ⊠	68
56	Clarke ⊠	53

Nickname: Raiders
Colors: Red & White
Arena: Kern Center Arena
　Capacity: 600; Year Built: 2004
AD: Daniel I. Harris
SID: Brian Gibboney

MINNESOTA
Minneapolis, MN 55455 I

Coach: Jim Molinari, Ill. Wesleyan 1977

2006-07 RESULTS (9-22)

63	North Dakota St. ⊠	49
70	Long Island ⊠	54
63	Iowa St. ⊠	68
56	Marist †	63
53	Southern Ill. †	69
65	Montana ⊠	72
68	Clemson ⊠	90
66	Arizona St. ⊠	63
81	UAB	88
77	South Dakota St. ⊠	53
66	Ark.-Little Rock ⊠	67
74	UCF ⊠	63
58	UNLV	62
63	Southeastern La. ⊠	61
65	Purdue ⊠	59
45	Wisconsin	68
49	Iowa	60
52	Illinois	64
40	Northwestern ⊠	55
46	Michigan St.	70
65	Penn St. ⊠	60
62	Northwestern	55
49	Illinois	59

78	Iowa ⊠	91
80	Michigan	82
62	Wisconsin ⊠	75
67	Ohio St. ⊠	85
59	Indiana	71
51	Michigan ⊠	62
47	Purdue	66
40	Michigan †	49

Nickname: Golden Gophers
Colors: Maroon & Gold
Arena: Williams Arena
　Capacity: 14,625; Year Built: 1928
AD: Joel Maturi
SID: Kyle Coughlin

MINN. DULUTH
Duluth, MN 55812-2496 II

Coach: Gary Holquist, Milton 1979

2006-07 RESULTS (16-13)

90	Bemidji St. ⊠	59
67	Dominican (N.Y.) †	53
74	Felician †	62
78	St. Scholastica ⊠	68
77	Northern Mich. ⊠	80
80	Michigan Tech ⊠	76
78	Colorado St.-Pueblo	80
61	Regis (Colo.) †	67
88	Northland	46
77	Minn. St. Moorhead ⊠	70
74	Winona St. ⊠	84
95	Minn.-Crookston ⊠	71
55	Michigan Tech	62
72	Concordia-St. Paul	55
56	Southwest Minn. St.	69
81	Minn. St. Mankato	86
79	St. Cloud St. ⊠	86
65	Augustana (S.D.)	86
68	Neb.-Omaha	79
69	St. Cloud St.	88
62	South Dakota ⊠	68
75	Minn. St. Mankato ⊠	63
63	Augustana (S.D.)	59
73	North Dakota	68
83	South Dakota	75
69	Neb.-Omaha ⊠	64
91	North Dakota ⊠	67
85	North Dakota	63
56	South Dakota	60

Nickname: Bulldogs
Colors: Maroon & Gold
Arena: Romano Gymnasium
　Capacity: 2,759; Year Built: 1953
AD: Robert Nielson
SID: Kelly Grgas-Wheeler

MINN. ST. MANKATO
Mankato, MN 56001 II

Coach: Matt Margenthaler, Western Ill. 1991

2006-07 RESULTS (28-5)

96	Felician ⊠	63
81	Dominican (N.Y.) ⊠	44
65	Concordia-St. Paul	71
67	Michigan Tech †	48
88	Northern Mich. †	86
65	Upper Iowa ⊠	47
74	UC-Colo. Springs †	71
74	Western St.	57
93	Bethany Lutheran ⊠	77
76	Hamline	47
79	St. Mary's (Minn.) ⊠	57
87	Minn.-Crookston	63
55	Southwest Minn. St.	50
82	Concordia-M'head ⊠	54
72	Carleton ⊠	69
86	Minn. Duluth ⊠	81
92	North Dakota	91
83	St. Cloud St.	73
81	Augustana (S.D.) ⊠	76
71	North Dakota ⊠	65
91	South Dakota ⊠	87

63	Minn. Duluth	75
96	St. Cloud St. ⊠	68
75	South Dakota ⊠	85
62	Neb.-Omaha	59
68	Augustana (S.D.)	64
80	Neb.-Omaha ⊠	58
80	Augustana (S.D.) ⊠	63
78	St. Cloud St. ⊠	73
86	South Dakota	97
85	Fort Lewis †	71
70	Metro St. †	68
76	Winona St.	89

Nickname: Mavericks
Colors: Purple & Gold
Arena: Bresnan Arena In Taylor Center
　Capacity: 4,521; Year Built: 2000
AD: Kevin Buisman
SID: Paul Allan

MINN. ST. MOORHEAD
Moorhead, MN 56563-2996 II

Coach: Stu Engen, Augsburg 1986

2006-07 RESULTS (13-15)

99	Chadron St. ⊠	75
70	North Dakota ⊠	63
85	Concordia-M'head	84
66	St. Cloud St.	68
72	Valley City St.	71
74	Concordia-St. Paul ⊠	83
81	Minn.-Crookston	68
72	Bemidji St.	61
70	Minn. Duluth	77
63	South Dakota	75
68	Mayville St.	81
60	Northern St. ⊠	81
72	Mary ⊠	75
89	Trinity Bible (N.D.) ⊠	65
74	Upper Iowa ⊠	52
66	Winona St.	69
88	Wayne St. (Neb.)	91
58	Southwest Minn. St. ⊠	56
79	Concordia-St. Paul	81
70	Bemidji St. ⊠	56
79	Minn.-Crookston ⊠	59
80	Mary	69
69	Northern St.	75
56	Winona St. ⊠	89
72	Upper Iowa ⊠	59
64	Southwest Minn. St.	75
62	Wayne St. (Neb.)	65
62	Northern St.	68

Nickname: Dragons
Colors: Scarlet & White
Arena: Alex Nemzek Hall
　Capacity: 3,400; Year Built: 1960
AD: Sylvia M. Barnier
SID: Larry Scott

MINN.-CROOKSTON
Crookston, MN 56716-5001 II

Coach: Jeff Oseth, Minn. St. Moorhead 1994

2006-07 RESULTS (3-24)

62	North Dakota ⊠	75
58	Valley City St.	60
73	Mayville St.	87
70	Augustana (S.D.) ⊠	73
77	Minn.-Morris	83
50	Southwest Minn. St.	66
89	Wayne St. (Neb.)	96
68	Minn. St. Moorhead ⊠	81
82	Concordia-St. Paul ⊠	108
63	Minn. St. Mankato	87
71	Minn. Duluth	95
57	St. Cloud St. ⊠	83
85	Dakota St.	81
62	Bemidji St. ⊠	64
60	Northern St.	84
63	Mary	68
61	Upper Iowa ⊠	75
79	Winona St. ⊠	93

80	Wayne St. (Neb.) ⊠	82
60	Southwest Minn. St. ⊠	81
54	Concordia-St. Paul	60
59	Minn. St. Moorhead	79
63	Bemidji St.	67
73	Mary ⊠	60
72	Northern St. ⊠	90
66	Winona St.	104
73	Upper Iowa	62

Nickname: Golden Eagle
Colors: Maroon & Gold
Arena: Lysaker Gym
   Capacity: 3,500; Year Built: 1970
AD: Stephanie Helgeson
SID: Mitch Bakken

MINN.-MORRIS
Morris, MN 56267 II

Coach: Paul Grove, Gust. Adolphus 1989

2006-07 RESULTS (9-16)
79	Jamestown ⊠	89
77	St. John's (Minn.)	100
84	Bethel (Minn.)	111
83	Minn.-Crookston ⊠	77
80	Mayville St.	119
65	Valley City St. ⊠	73
65	Jamestown	87
69	Presentation	83
58	Gust. Adolphus	91
56	St. John's (Minn.) ⊠	74
94	North Central (Minn. ⊠	76
69	Bethany Lutheran	80
61	Martin Luther	78
99	Northland ⊠	53
69	St. Scholastica ⊠	74
72	Crown (Minn.)	58
62	Northwestern (Minn.)	72
54	Northwestern (Minn.) ⊠	78
79	Crown (Minn.) ⊠	64
90	North Central (Minn.	67
74	Martin Luther ⊠	58
60	Bethany Lutheran ⊠	78
81	St. Scholastica	91
65	Northland	57
73	Presentation ⊠	59

Nickname: Cougars
Colors: Maroon & Gold
Arena: Physical Education Center
   Capacity: 4,000; Year Built: 1971
AD: Mark Fohl
SID: Brian Curtis

MISERICORDIA
Dallas, PA 18612 III

Coach: Trevor Woodruff, Misericordia

2006-07 RESULTS (10-15)
69	Penn St.-Hazleton †	59
52	Baptist Bible (Pa.) †	55
48	Scranton ⊠	57
85	DeSales	80
88	Cabrini	81
66	Gwynedd-Mercy	70
51	Eastern ⊠	55
68	Susquehanna ⊠	70
73	King's (Pa.)	81
73	Wilkes †	75
61	Arcadia ⊠	64
88	Marywood ⊠	59
79	Neumann	75
65	Immaculata	69
83	Wesley ⊠	64
49	Alvernia	65
43	Eastern	60
82	Cabrini ⊠	61
56	Arcadia	76
78	Gwynedd-Mercy ⊠	70
62	Immaculata ⊠	76
74	Marywood	47
68	Neumann ⊠	62
49	Alvernia ⊠	66

| 65 | Wesley | 75 |

Nickname: Cougars
Colors: Royal Blue & Gold
Arena: Anderson Sports-Health Center
   Capacity: 1,500; Year Built: 1992
AD: David L. Martin
SID: Scott Crispell

MISSISSIPPI
University, MS 38677-1848 I

Coach: Andy Kennedy, UAB 1991

2006-07 RESULTS (21-13)
72	Mississippi Val. ⊠	49
69	La.-Lafayette ⊠	54
70	Fairfield †	67
75	Central Ark. †	61
59	Connecticut	77
86	Tennessee Tech ⊠	77
100	Nicholls St. ⊠	80
85	New Orleans ⊠	77
70	Memphis	82
87	La.-Monroe ⊠	53
82	South Ala.	72
77	Ill.-Chicago ⊠	64
81	Alabama A&M ⊠	57
56	St. Louis	59
58	Kentucky ⊠	68
67	Mississippi St.	77
74	Arkansas ⊠	72
55	LSU	62
70	Florida	79
83	Tennessee ⊠	69
80	Vanderbilt	85
85	Mississippi St. ⊠	73
82	Auburn	59
75	Alabama ⊠	69
71	LSU ⊠	70
66	Arkansas	83
67	Georgia ⊠	49
63	South Carolina	76
58	Alabama	69
83	Auburn ⊠	79
80	LSU †	60
59	Florida †	80
73	Appalachian St. ⊠	59
68	Clemson	89

Nickname: Rebels
Colors: Cardinal Red & Navy Blue
Arena: C.M. "Tad" Smith Coliseum
   Capacity: 8,700; Year Built: 1966
AD: Pete Boone
SID: Kyle Campbell

MISSISSIPPI COL.
Clinton, MS 39058 III

Coach: Mike Jones, Mississippi Col. 1975

2006-07 RESULTS (27-3)
82	Wesley (Miss.) ⊠	84
75	Mary Hardin-Baylor ⊠	47
91	Concordia (Tex.) ⊠	70
73	McMurry	57
70	Hardin-Simmons	67
83	Fisk ⊠	62
83	Schreiner	69
77	Texas Lutheran ⊠	53
75	Johns Hopkins †	51
81	Westmont	77
69	Sul Ross St.	39
76	Howard Payne	64
66	Texas-Dallas ⊠	54
66	Texas-Tyler ⊠	45
63	Louisiana Col.	43
65	Ozarks (Ark.)	47
72	LeTourneau ⊠	51
66	East Tex. Baptist ⊠	46
62	LeTourneau	64
61	East Tex. Baptist	32
88	Louisiana Col. ⊠	52
89	Ozarks (Ark.) ⊠	63
70	Texas-Dallas	67

61	Texas-Tyler	37
86	Concordia (Tex.) ⊠	62
66	McMurry	56
77	Hardin-Simmons ⊠	64
68	Occidental ⊠	51
76	Maryville (Tenn.) ⊠	56
55	Va. Wesleyan	81

Nickname: Choctaws
Colors: Blue & Gold
Arena: A.E. Wood Coliseum
   Capacity: 3,500; Year Built: 1979
AD: Mike Jones
SID: Chris Brooks

MISSISSIPPI ST.
Mississippi State, MS 39762-5509.. I

Coach: Rick Stansbury, Campbellsville 1982

2006-07 RESULTS (21-14)
90	Nicholls St. ⊠	55
61	Loyola Marymount ⊠	37
63	Winthrop ⊠	74
66	Clemson ⊠	69
78	Charlotte ⊠	69
96	A&M-Corpus Christi ⊠	72
84	South Ala. ⊠	46
70	Miami (Fla.)	52
89	McNeese St. ⊠	63
74	Alabama St. ⊠	59
89	New Orleans †	63
59	George Mason ⊠	63
75	Missouri	83
84	Tennessee	92
77	Mississippi ⊠	67
60	Kentucky	64
87	Auburn ⊠	76
67	Florida ⊠	70
63	South Carolina ⊠	66
73	Mississippi	85
85	LSU ⊠	78
79	Alabama	80
91	Auburn	83
84	Arkansas ⊠	60
56	LSU	50
83	Vanderbilt ⊠	70
73	Georgia	86
58	Arkansas	67
91	Alabama ⊠	67
84	Kentucky †	82
72	Arkansas †	81
82	Mississippi Val. ⊠	63
101	Bradley ⊠	72
86	Florida St. ⊠	71
62	West Virginia †	63

Nickname: Bulldogs
Colors: Maroon & White
Arena: Humphrey Coliseum
   Capacity: 10,500; Year Built: 1975
AD: Larry Templeton
SID: David Rosinski

MISSISSIPPI VAL.
Itta Bena, MS 38941-1400 I

Coach: James Green, Mississippi 1983

2006-07 RESULTS (18-16)
49	Mississippi	72
42	Creighton	78
56	Kentucky	79
66	Central Ark.	64
77	Northern Ariz.	104
39	Southern California	63
44	McNeese St.	61
76	McNeese St. ⊠	45
66	Central Ark. ⊠	51
59	Samford †	64
58	LSU	92
54	Wright St. †	55
63	Ark.-Pine Bluff	55
55	Alabama A&M ⊠	41
59	Alabama St. ⊠	57
60	Alcorn St.	61

64	Southern U.	72
64	Prairie View ⊠	61
64	Texas Southern ⊠	54
60	Jackson St.	66
84	Grambling	78
65	Alabama A&M	54
52	Alabama St.	44
76	Alcorn St. ⊠	63
62	Southern U. ⊠	63
45	Prairie View	47
63	Texas Southern	47
77	Jackson St. ⊠	70
64	Grambling ⊠	55
63	Ark.-Pine Bluff ⊠	50
62	Alabama St. †	52
54	Texas Southern †	50
71	Jackson St. †	81
63	Mississippi St.	82

Nickname: Delta Devils
Colors: Forest Green & White
Arena: Harrison HPER Complex
   Capacity: 6,000; Year Built: 1970
AD: Lonza Hardy Jr.
SID: Roderick Mosley

MISSOURI
Columbia, MO 65211-1050 I

Coach: Mike Anderson, Tulsa 1982

2006-07 RESULTS (18-12)
101	N.C. A&T ⊠	80
67	Army ⊠	58
66	Stetson ⊠	45
89	Lipscomb ⊠	69
81	Davidson ⊠	75
85	Stephen F. Austin ⊠	56
98	Coppin St. ⊠	77
86	Arkansas ⊠	64
73	Evansville ⊠	54
62	Purdue	79
70	Illinois †	73
87	Southern U. ⊠	58
83	Mississippi St. ⊠	75
65	Iowa St. ⊠	66
68	Texas	88
81	Kansas St. ⊠	80
77	Kansas	92
79	Colorado	65
71	Texas Tech ⊠	58
73	Kansas St.	80
61	Nebraska ⊠	66
77	Iowa St.	55
74	Kansas ⊠	92
78	Baylor ⊠	71
75	Oklahoma St.	64
72	Oklahoma ⊠	68
77	Nebraska	82
91	Colorado ⊠	82
78	Texas A&M	94
83	Baylor †	97

Nickname: Tigers
Colors: Old Gold & Black
Arena: Mizzou Arena
   Capacity: 15,061; Year Built: 2004
AD: Michael F. Alden
SID: David Reiter

UMKC
Kansas City, MO 64110 I

Coach: Rich Zvosec, Defiance 1983

2006-07 RESULTS (12-20)
85	Fla. Atlantic ⊠	70
97	Baker ⊠	58
68	Central Mich.	85
70	Pacific †	71
70	Alas. Anchorage	77
79	Marshall †	75
55	Wichita St.	85
61	Arkansas	71
79	Utah Valley St. ⊠	91
53	UNI	85
50	Maryland	101

80	Central Ark. ⊠	68
71	South Dakota St. ⊠	79
61	Fla. Atlantic	70
59	Utah Valley St.	74
86	Chicago St. ⊠	78
66	Southern Utah ⊠	62
80	Centenary (La.) ⊠	75
68	Oral Roberts ⊠	75
72	IUPUI	77
60	Oakland	78
52	Valparaiso	56
95	Western Ill. ⊠	89
59	Southern Utah	66
68	Oral Roberts	74
68	Centenary (La.)	69
80	Oakland ⊠	76
85	IUPUI ⊠	72
89	Western Ill.	54
61	Valparaiso	77
84	Valparaiso †	76
79	Oakland †	83

Nickname: Kangaroos
Colors: Blue & Gold
Arena: Municipal Auditorium
  Capacity: 9,827; Year Built: 1936
AD: Timothy W. Hall
SID: James Allan

MO.-ROLLA
Rolla, MO 65409-0740 ... II

Coach: Dale Martin, Central Mo. St. 1976

2006-07 RESULTS (7-20)

71	Rhema ⊠	55
49	Mo. Western St.	98
62	Truman †	76
64	Lincoln (Mo.)	60
76	St. Louis Pharmacy ⊠	60
73	St. Joseph's (Ind.) ⊠	80
85	Indianapolis ⊠	71
76	Rockhurst	82
66	Drury	80
104	Cent. Christian (Mo) ⊠	30
78	Oakland City ⊠	62
43	SIU Edwardsville ⊠	60
79	Quincy ⊠	86
73	Northern Ky.	81
72	Bellarmine	85
97	Wis.-Parkside ⊠	92
59	Lewis ⊠	79
59	Oakland City	63
76	Mo.-St. Louis ⊠	78
97	Ky. Wesleyan	106
80	Southern Ind.	98
81	Mo.-St. Louis	87
64	Southern Ind. ⊠	80
58	Rockhurst ⊠	80
82	Drury ⊠	86
58	SIU Edwardsville	72
83	Quincy	92

Nickname: Miners
Colors: Silver & Gold
Arena: Bullman Multi-Purpose
  Capacity: 4,000; Year Built: 1969
AD: Mark Mullin
SID: John Kean

MO.-ST. LOUIS
St. Louis, MO 63121-4499 ... II

Coach: Chris Pilz, Mo.-St. Louis 1991

2006-07 RESULTS (9-18)

64	Mo. Southern St.	74
92	Harris-Stowe ⊠	68
85	Central Bible (Mo.) ⊠	61
57	Grand Valley St. ⊠	86
51	Drury	86
83	Rockhurst	82
99	Maryville (Mo.) ⊠	62
54	Christian Bros.	73
80	Blackburn ⊠	68
69	Quincy ⊠	76

68	SIU Edwardsville ⊠	70
59	Indianapolis ⊠	64
53	Bellarmine	73
53	Northern Ky.	68
63	Lewis ⊠	74
77	Wis.-Parkside ⊠	74
90	St. Louis Pharmacy ⊠	58
78	Mo.-Rolla	76
61	Southern Ind.	83
90	Ky. Wesleyan	97
87	Mo.-Rolla	81
59	Southern Ind.	72
67	St. Joseph's (Ind.) ⊠	80
87	Drury	91
67	Rockhurst ⊠	76
70	Quincy	80
63	SIU Edwardsville	92

Nickname: Rivermen
Colors: Red & Gold
Arena: Mark Twain Building
  Capacity: 4,736; Year Built: 1971
AD: Patricia A. Dolan
SID: Todd Addington

MO. SOUTHERN ST.
Joplin, MO 64801-1595 ... II

Coach: Robert Corn, Mo. Southern St. 1978

2006-07 RESULTS (10-18)

74	Mo.-St. Louis ⊠	64
96	Central Bible (Mo.) ⊠	44
75	West Tex. A&M ⊠	70
69	Colorado Mines †	64
67	Evangel †	72
49	Rockhurst ⊠	64
76	Augustana (S.D.)	85
77	Northeastern St. ⊠	69
53	Truman ⊠	70
67	Southwestern Okla.	83
71	Mo. Western St.	84
71	Pittsburg St.	84
70	Central Mo. ⊠	86
59	Northwest Mo. St. ⊠	57
67	Emporia St.	105
86	Fort Hays St. ⊠	80
77	Southwest Baptist	84
68	Washburn ⊠	57
68	Truman	76
79	Washburn	70
61	Fort Hays St.	89
72	Emporia St. ⊠	73
77	Southwest Baptist ⊠	87
66	Central Mo.	94
60	Northwest Mo. St.	75
67	Pittsburg St. ⊠	72
82	Mo. Western St. ⊠	70
56	Northwest Mo. St. †	89

Nickname: Lions
Colors: Green & Gold
Arena: Leggett & Platt A.C.
  Capacity: 3,240; Year Built: 1999
AD: Sallie Beard
SID: Justin Maskus

MISSOURI ST.
Springfield, MO 65897 ... I

Coach: Barry Hinson, Oklahoma St. 1983

2006-07 RESULTS (22-11)

79	Toledo ⊠	66
77	Delaware St. ⊠	54
88	Lincoln (Mo.) ⊠	56
66	Wisconsin †	64
70	Oklahoma St. †	73
89	Alabama St. ⊠	49
78	Santa Clara	51
79	Milwaukee ⊠	60
78	UNC Wilmington	62
80	Indiana St. ⊠	60
50	St. Louis	51
81	South Fla.	69

74	Creighton	77
86	Bradley	78
95	Wichita St. ⊠	87
106	Evansville ⊠	54
56	Southern Ill.	76
75	Illinois St.	66
65	UNI	75
56	Evansville	63
62	Creighton	66
85	Bradley ⊠	70
87	Drake	82
71	Indiana St.	42
73	Illinois St. ⊠	61
62	UNI	58
47	Southern Ill.	51
66	Winthrop ⊠	77
71	Wichita St.	65
92	Drake ⊠	74
67	Wichita St. †	64
58	Creighton †	75
70	San Diego St. ⊠	74

Nickname: Bears
Colors: Maroon & White
Arena: Hammons Student Center
  Capacity: 8,846; Year Built: 1976
AD: William L. Rowe Jr.
SID: Mark Stillwell

MO. WESTERN ST.
St. Joseph, MO 64507 ... II

Coach: Tom Smith, Valparaiso 1967

2006-07 RESULTS (12-15)

98	Mo.-Rolla ⊠	49
61	Armstrong Atlantic ⊠	65
95	Neb.-Omaha	88
81	Central Okla. †	64
74	Northeastern St. †	73
95	Ottawa	78
80	York (Neb.) ⊠	55
76	Washburn	77
75	St. Mary's (Tex.)	66
67	Metro St. †	70
84	Mo. Southern St. ⊠	71
72	Northwest Mo. St.	78
60	Truman ⊠	74
70	Central Mo.	90
80	Fort Hays St.	97
71	Pittsburg St.	69
76	Emporia St. ⊠	88
66	Southwest Baptist ⊠	81
62	Washburn ⊠	77
75	Southwest Baptist	95
79	Emporia St.	89
73	Pittsburg St.	64
61	Fort Hays St. ⊠	60
68	Truman	64
73	Central Mo. ⊠	84
61	Northwest Mo. St. ⊠	69
70	Mo. Southern St.	82

Nickname: Griffons
Colors: Black & Gold
Arena: MWSU Fieldhouse
  Capacity: 3,750; Year Built: 1981
AD: Mark Linder
SID: Brett King

MOLLOY
Rockville Centre, NY 11571-5002 II

Coach: Charles Marquardt, St. Joseph's (Me.) 1986

2006-07 RESULTS (14-15)

60	Le Moyne ⊠	48
75	Mercyhurst †	73
78	Nyack	62
74	Post ⊠	71
72	Goldey-Beacom	73
61	Dowling	66
82	C.W. Post ⊠	85
73	Bridgeport	85
76	Felician	89
64	Queens (N.Y.) ⊠	76

78	Stonehill	90
67	Mercy	68
68	Concordia (N.Y.) ⊠	71
75	New Haven	62
89	NYIT	88
64	Adelphi ⊠	60
71	Dowling ⊠	66
72	St. Thomas Aquinas ⊠	64
79	C.W. Post	85
95	Bridgeport ⊠	92
73	New Haven ⊠	55
103	Queens (N.Y.) ⊠	94
85	Mercy ⊠	80
95	Concordia (N.Y.)	75
60	St. Thomas Aquinas	71
68	NYIT ⊠	76
52	Adelphi	76
64	Bridgeport	74
70	Goldey-Beacom	86

Nickname: Lions
Colors: Maroon & White
Arena: Quealy Gymnasium
  Capacity: 400; Year Built: 1955
AD: Susan Cassidy-Lyke
SID: Jen Mischke

MONMOUTH
West Long Branch, NJ 07764 ... I

Coach: Dave Calloway, Monmouth 1991

2006-07 RESULTS (12-18)

40	Old Dominion	54
65	Clemson †	77
69	Arkansas St. †	67
80	Houston	89
54	A&M-Corpus Christi	71
51	St. Peter's ⊠	50
66	Penn	80
67	Rider	66
49	Seton Hall	83
71	Long Island ⊠	74
75	Hartford	76
67	Lehigh ⊠	39
81	Loyola Marymount ⊠	53
69	Wagner	58
62	Mt. St. Mary's ⊠	56
57	Sacred Heart	74
51	Quinnipiac	71
46	Central Conn. St.	49
57	St. Francis (N.Y.)	69
71	St. Francis (Pa.) ⊠	66
76	Robert Morris ⊠	68
69	St. Francis (N.Y.) ⊠	60
63	Fairleigh Dickinson	64
70	Wagner	63
71	Fairleigh Dickinson ⊠	84
65	Central Conn. St. ⊠	70
61	Mt. St. Mary's	60
78	Long Island	82
75	Sacred Heart ⊠	82
62	St. Francis (Pa.)	73

Nickname: Hawks
Colors: Midnight Blue & White
Arena: Boylan Gymnasium
  Capacity: 2,500; Year Built: 1965
AD: Marilyn A. McNeil
SID: Thomas Dick

MONMOUTH (ILL.)
Monmouth, IL 61462-1998 ... III

Coach: Terry Glasgow, Parsons 1966

2006-07 RESULTS (11-11)

53	Central Mo.	81
92	MacMurray	86
61	Hannibal-La Grange ⊠	58
86	William Penn ⊠	73
63	Lawrence	91
83	Carroll (Wis.)	81
125	Grinnell	143
88	Central (Iowa)	82
52	Robert Morris-Chi.	92

RESULTS

71	Illinois Col. ⊠	84
63	Knox	70
80	Beloit ⊠	73
80	Ripon ⊠	79
56	St. Norbert	68
67	Beloit	74
55	Lake Forest	53
111	Grinnell ⊠	127
71	Lawrence ⊠	63
59	Carroll (Wis.) ⊠	81
73	Knox ⊠	70
82	Illinois Col. ⊠	70
59	Lake Forest ⊠	69

Nickname: Fighting Scots
Colors: Red & White
Arena: Glennie Gymnasium
　　　Capacity: 1,600; Year Built: 1982
AD: Terry L. Glasgow
SID: Barry McNamara, Dan Nolan

MONTANA
Missoula, MT 59812-1291 I

Coach: Wayne Tinkle, Montana 1989

2006-07 RESULTS (17-15)

83	Mont. St.-Northern ⊠	42
57	Utah Valley St.	74
71	Wyoming	76
56	West Virginia †	73
56	Virginia Tech †	77
72	Minnesota †	65
62	Boise St. ⊠	58
65	Western Ky. ⊠	81
72	UC Riverside ⊠	65
87	South Dakota St. ⊠	47
92	Montana Tech ⊠	63
58	Oral Roberts	69
58	Portland	61
80	Portland ⊠	74
71	Eastern Wash.	74
72	Sacramento St.	80
73	Montana St. ⊠	65
69	Idaho St. ⊠	79
90	Weber St. ⊠	86
74	Northern Ariz.	71
68	Northern Colo.	51
68	Portland St. ⊠	70
85	Eastern Wash. ⊠	78
76	Sacramento St. ⊠	69
72	Montana St.	63
67	Weber St.	73
77	Pacific ⊠	78
81	Northern Ariz. ⊠	88
85	Northern Colo. ⊠	64
72	Idaho St.	71
70	Idaho St. ⊠	63
71	Northern Ariz. †	78

Nickname: Grizzlies
Colors: Maroon and Silver
Arena: Adams Center/Dahlberg Arena
　　　Capacity: 7,500; Year Built: 1953
AD: Jim O'Day
SID: Dave Guffey

MONTANA ST.
Bozeman, MT 59717-3380 I

Coach: Brad Huse, Montana Tech 1989

2006-07 RESULTS (11-19)

37	Utah Valley St.	69
56	UC Santa Barbara ⊠	88
53	Portland	59
72	Idaho	65
84	Montana Western ⊠	59
63	Oregon St. ⊠	72
41	Fresno St.	80
62	Wyoming †	73
69	Boise St.	94
77	Fresno St. ⊠	82
53	Utah Valley St. ⊠	60
97	Great Falls ⊠	52
62	South Dakota St.	65
82	Eastern Wash.	79

65	Portland St.	79
63	Weber St.	84
65	Montana	73
63	Weber St. ⊠	48
58	Idaho St. ⊠	57
58	Northern Colo.	57
76	Northern Ariz.	86
84	Eastern Wash. ⊠	67
79	Portland St. ⊠	71
74	Sacramento St. ⊠	59
63	Montana ⊠	72
82	Sacramento St.	90
89	Northern Colo. ⊠	66
84	Northern Ariz. ⊠	92
58	Idaho St.	67
71	Portland St.	96

Nickname: Bobcats
Colors: Blue & Gold
Arena: Worthington Arena
　　　Capacity: 7,250; Year Built: 1956
AD: Peter Fields
SID: Bill Lamberty

MONT. ST.-BILLINGS
Billings, MT 59101-0298 II

Coach: Craig Carse, Bethany (W.V.) 1978

2006-07 RESULTS (6-21)

63	Central Wash. †	92
74	Northwest Nazarene	88
58	Tex. A&M Int'l	59
52	St. Mary's (Tex.)	64
85	West Liberty St. ⊠	103
50	Northwest Nazarene ⊠	70
89	Northwest Nazarene ⊠	90
65	Okla. Panhandle ⊠	54
73	Tex. A&M Int'l ⊠	80
60	St. Edward's ⊠	56
60	St. Edward's ⊠	91
64	Okla. Panhandle ⊠	69
48	Okla. Panhandle	62
87	Tex. Permian Basin	93
69	Dallas Baptist	78
95	Lincoln (Mo.) ⊠	84
51	St. Mary's (Tex.)	67
62	Incarnate Word ⊠	82
66	Incarnate Word ⊠	72
71	Lincoln (Mo.)	80
68	Lincoln (Mo.)	67
62	St. Mary's (Tex.)	70
65	Incarnate Word	79
111	Tex. Permian Basin ⊠	61
77	Dallas Baptist ⊠	74
71	Dallas Baptist ⊠	79
67	St. Edward's	84

Nickname: Yellowjackets
Colors: Cobalt Blue & Yellow
Arena: Alterowitz Gymnasium
　　　Capacity: 3,500; Year Built: 1961
AD: Gary R. Gray
SID: Travis Elam

MONTCLAIR ST.
Montclair, NJ 07043 III

Coach: Ted Fiore, Seton Hall 1962

2006-07 RESULTS (12-12)

53	Hood †	55
60	Lebanon Valley	66
91	Berkeley ⊠	43
64	Staten Island	66
79	Williams †	69
73	St. Joseph (Vt.) †	56
50	Wm. Paterson	66
54	TCNJ	65
81	Rutgers-Camden ⊠	62
93	Briarcliffe (N.Y.) ⊠	61
78	Salisbury †	71
65	Moravian	73
97	Berkeley ⊠	55
63	New Jersey City ⊠	76
74	Ramapo ⊠	77
80	Kean	67

76	Rutgers-Newark ⊠	77
84	Richard Stockton ⊠	78
45	Wm. Paterson ⊠	48
68	Rowan	78
87	Phila. Biblical	57
66	New Jersey City	90
71	Ramapo	68
78	Rutgers-Newark ⊠	71

Nickname: Red Hawks
Colors: Scarlet & White
Arena: Panzer Gymnasium
　　　Capacity: 1,200; Year Built: 1954
AD: Holly P. Gera
SID: Mike Scala

MONTEVALLO
Montevallo, AL 35115-6001 II

Coach: Danny Young, Grand Canyon 1990

2006-07 RESULTS (28-6)

60	Miles	63
71	Stillman	60
96	Concordia-Selma ⊠	64
89	Albany St. (Ga.) ⊠	73
103	Tuskegee	69
70	Cal St. Dom. Hills †	67
60	UC San Diego †	61
84	Miles ⊠	51
67	Christian Bros. ⊠	56
74	Fla. Gulf Coast	65
80	P.R.-Rio Piedras †	68
58	Grand Valley St. †	59
72	Presbyterian †	82
94	North Ala. ⊠	101
86	Ala.-Huntsville ⊠	73
98	West Ga.	84
150	Carver Bible ⊠	72
90	West Fla. ⊠	70
81	Valdosta St. ⊠	68
83	West Ala.	75
99	Oakwood ⊠	74
77	West Ga. ⊠	61
74	Ala.-Huntsville	67
98	North Ala.	95
101	West Fla.	63
89	Valdosta St. ⊠	77
93	West Ala.	62
78	West Ga. †	62
98	North Ala. †	71
66	Henderson St. †	52
78	Albany St. (Ga.) ⊠	62
66	Henderson St. ⊠	58
64	Eckerd ⊠	61
69	Central Mo. †	86

Nickname: Falcons
Colors: Purple & Gold
Arena: Student Activity Center
　　　Capacity: 2,000; Year Built: 2004
AD: Dennis S. Toney
SID: Alfred Kojima

MORAVIAN
Bethlehem, PA 18018-6650 III

Coach: Jim Walker, Gettysburg 1965

2006-07 RESULTS (11-14)

81	Emerson †	85
94	Alfred †	83
68	DeSales ⊠	72
75	Dickinson	72
65	Widener ⊠	78
73	Susquehanna	82
85	FDU-Florham ⊠	67
66	Delaware Valley	62
59	Scranton	72
91	Kean ⊠	96
80	Muhlenberg	61
87	Drew ⊠	50
73	Montclair St. ⊠	65
94	Lebanon Valley ⊠	87
76	Juniata ⊠	80
81	Albright	78

82	Elizabethtown ⊠	74
50	Messiah	70
50	Juniata	70
73	Albright ⊠	87
70	Susquehanna ⊠	76
64	Lebanon Valley	71
47	Messiah ⊠	79
108	Widener ⊠	102
69	Elizabethtown ⊠	88

Nickname: Greyhounds
Colors: Blue & Grey
Arena: Johnston Hall
　　　Capacity: 1,200; Year Built: 1952
AD: Paul R. Moyer
SID: Mark Fleming

MOREHEAD ST.
Morehead, KY 40351-1689 ....

Coach: Donnie Tyndall, Morehead St. 1993

2006-07 RESULTS (12-18)

46	Penn St.	63
80	Asbury ⊠	57
55	South Ala.	70
77	East Tenn. St. ⊠	56
80	Marshall ⊠	81
57	Western Ill.	56
70	Austin Peay ⊠	66
67	Murray St. ⊠	70
56	Tenn.-Martin	55
71	Eastern Ill.	63
90	Ind.-South Bend ⊠	52
51	Central Mich. ⊠	52
62	Tennessee St. ⊠	60
82	Tennessee Tech ⊠	71
65	Eastern Ky.	73
70	Tenn.-Martin ⊠	48
53	Samford	66
62	Jacksonville St.	67
59	Southeast Mo. St. ⊠	61
62	Eastern Ill. ⊠	58
52	Tennessee Tech	65
61	Eastern Ky. ⊠	69
78	Southeast Mo. St.	81
56	Murray St.	74
52	Jacksonville St. ⊠	57
71	Samford ⊠	58
72	Bowling Green ⊠	90
46	Tennessee St.	62
82	Austin Peay	77
45	Eastern Ky. ⊠	63

Nickname: Eagles
Colors: Blue & Gold
Arena: Ellis T. Johnson Arena
　　　Capacity: 6,500; Year Built: 1981
AD: Brian Hutchinson
SID: Randy Stacy

MOREHOUSE
Atlanta, GA 30314.............................

Coach: Grady L. Brewer, Morehouse 1980

2006-07 RESULTS (9-16)

76	GCSU †	80
73	Columbus St.	70
52	Stillman	64
81	Miles	62
54	Kentucky St. ⊠	71
93	Lane ⊠	88
69	Benedict	81
60	Paine	72
63	Miles ⊠	70
85	LeMoyne-Owen ⊠	70
78	Kentucky St.	62
59	Lane	72
71	Paine ⊠	76
71	Stillman ⊠	72
78	Tuskegee ⊠	67
69	Clark Atlanta	75
56	Albany St. (Ga.) ⊠	59
69	Fort Valley St. ⊠	84

66	Benedict ⊠	68
46	Fort Valley St.	58
64	Albany St. (Ga.)	61
63	Clark Atlanta ⊠	44
70	Tuskegee	66
51	LeMoyne-Owen	71
73	Miles	75

Nickname: Maroon Tigers
Colors: Maroon & White
Arena: Frank L. Forbes Arena
   Capacity: 6,000; Year Built: 1996
AD: Andre' Pattillo
SID: Yusuf Davis

MORGAN ST.
Baltimore, MD 21251..........................I

Coach: Todd Bozeman, Rhode Island 1986

2006-07 RESULTS (13-18)

67	East Caro.	86
84	American	97
66	Virginia	85
63	Seton Hall ⊠	83
72	UMBC ⊠	86
71	Penn St.	80
86	Coppin St. ⊠	82
76	East Caro. ⊠	70
76	La Salle	102
57	Marquette	77
59	Florida A&M ⊠	62
53	Winston-Salem ⊠	50
61	Delaware St. ⊠	68
75	Hampton	70
54	Norfolk St.	68
65	South Carolina St. ⊠	62
69	N.C. A&T ⊠	60
93	Md.-East. Shore ⊠	59
66	Howard	53
73	Longwood	75
54	Delaware St.	40
65	Hampton ⊠	67
71	Norfolk St. ⊠	61
56	South Carolina St.	70
79	N.C. A&T	91
81	Md.-East. Shore	70
85	Howard ⊠	62
50	Bethune-Cookman	52
62	Coppin St.	71
66	South Carolina St. †	64
53	Delaware St. †	56

Nickname: Bears
Colors: Blue & Orange
Arena: Hill Field House
   Capacity: 6,500; Year Built: 1975
AD: Floyd Kerr
SID: Leonard L. Haynes IV

MT. ALOYSIUS
Cresson, PA 16630 III

Coach: Lance Loya, S.C. Upstate

2006-07 RESULTS (9-16)

86	Gallaudet ⊠	83
76	Salisbury ⊠	97
59	Penn St.-Behrend	73
116	Lancaster Bible ⊠	107
89	Medaille ⊠	85
84	Pitt.-Greensburg	96
91	Pitt.-Bradford	99
105	Bethany (W.V.)	123
110	Hilbert ⊠	117
77	La Roche ⊠	92
90	Lake Erie	104
81	Penn St.-Altoona	90
83	Frostburg St. ⊠	98
57	Medaille	74
75	Penn St.-Behrend ⊠	104
90	Pitt.-Bradford ⊠	108
106	Pitt.-Greensburg ⊠	86
96	Lancaster Bible	84
96	Hilbert	103
88	Valley Forge Chrst.	102
79	La Roche	77

93	Lake Erie ⊠	109
91	Franciscan ⊠	78
98	Frostburg St.	91
77	Penn St.-Altoona ⊠	68

Nickname: Mounties
Colors: Blue & silver
Arena: Health & Physical Fitness Center
Capacity: 1,800
AD: Timothy Kelly
SID: To be named

MOUNT IDA
Newton, MA 02459-3323 III

Coach: Rico Cabral, Boston St. 1976

2006-07 RESULTS (7-19)

72	Gordon	89
61	Middlebury †	120
61	Wentworth Inst. ⊠	77
79	Mitchell †	62
70	Western Conn. St.	95
74	Eastern Nazarene	70
50	Husson ⊠	94
63	Maine Maritime ⊠	68
98	Lesley ⊠	87
64	Rivier	65
89	Fisher ⊠	83
84	Mass. Liberal Arts.	93
92	Mitchell ⊠	100
58	Lasell ⊠	74
57	Green Mountain ⊠	49
64	Castleton	80
74	Johnson St.	86
68	Husson	87
62	Maine Maritime	73
78	Elms ⊠	79
74	Thomas (Me.)	80
41	Me.-Farmington	62
80	Becker ⊠	73
90	Thomas (Me.) ⊠	71
62	Me.-Farmington ⊠	65
76	Elms	88

Nickname: Mustangs
Colors: Green & White
Arena: Mount Ida College Athletic Center
   Capacity: 500; Year Built: 1999
AD: Jacqueline Palmer
SID: Mike Raposo

MOUNT OLIVE
Mount Olive, NC 28365 II

Coach: Bill Clingan, Northeastern St.

2006-07 RESULTS (23-8)

101	Ohio Valley ⊠	94
79	Chowan ⊠	70
97	Pfeiffer	103
77	Lees-McRae	86
87	St. Andrews ⊠	71
78	Limestone ⊠	63
89	Francis Marion	74
93	Chowan †	74
78	Lincoln Memorial †	63
93	West Virginia St.	94
81	Charleston (W.V.) †	77
91	Queens (N.C.)	96
95	Coker	68
93	Erskine ⊠	60
81	Belmont Abbey ⊠	62
73	Barton ⊠	80
97	Anderson (S.C.)	57
78	Limestone	73
110	Pfeiffer ⊠	104
99	Coker ⊠	65
90	Erskine	76
83	St. Andrews	80
95	Lees-McRae ⊠	85
82	Barton	86
95	Queens (N.C.) ⊠	71
88	Belmont Abbey	69
68	Anderson (S.C.) ⊠	60
88	Coker ⊠	62
93	Queens (N.C.) †	86

80	Barton †	92
85	Millersville †	89

Nickname: Trojans
Colors: Green & White
Arena: Kornegay Arena
   Capacity: 1,500; Year Built: 1984
AD: Jeffrey M. Eisen
SID: David Shulimson

MT. ST. JOSEPH
Cincinnati, OH 45233-1670 III

Coach: Larry Cox, Hanover 1981

2006-07 RESULTS (13-12)

82	North Park ⊠	80
76	Heidelberg ⊠	79
74	Thomas More	68
73	Notre Dame (Ohio)	75
75	Transylvania ⊠	73
65	Manchester	69
68	Hanover	101
72	Anderson (Ind.) ⊠	69
68	Cincinnati Christian	71
67	Capital	77
73	Wilmington (Ohio) ⊠	60
82	Franklin	72
80	Defiance ⊠	62
77	Rose-Hulman	61
77	Cincinnati-Clermont	83
88	Bluffton ⊠	85
69	Transylvania	84
80	Anderson (Ind.)	71
58	Hanover ⊠	59
67	Defiance	74
67	Rose-Hulman ⊠	46
76	Franklin ⊠	83
65	Bluffton	66
88	Robert Morris-S'fiel ⊠	74
81	Manchester ⊠	63

Nickname: Lions
Colors: Blue & Gold
Arena: Harrington Center
   Capacity: 2,000; Year Built: 1998
AD: Steven F. Radcliffe
SID: Dane Neumeister

MT. ST. MARY (N.Y.)
Newburgh, NY 12550.....................III

Coach: Duane Davis, Empire St. 1969

2006-07 RESULTS (9-17)

102	Albany Pharmacy ⊠	58
69	Westfield St. ⊠	82
71	Rensselaer	83
91	Bard †	53
60	Vassar	72
72	St. Joseph's (L.I.)	86
67	Manhattanville	86
55	Stevens Institute	86
55	Davidson	116
60	Goucher †	79
59	Mass.-Boston †	75
75	CCNY ⊠	48
88	Mt. St. Vincent	59
75	Old Westbury ⊠	85
97	Centenary (N.J.)	69
98	Maritime (N.Y.) ⊠	69
83	Merchant Marine ⊠	92
84	Farmingdale St.	81
57	Yeshiva	68
74	Manhattanville ⊠	92
77	St. Joseph's (L.I.) ⊠	92
94	Centenary (N.J.)	67
52	Merchant Marine	82
69	Farmingdale St. ⊠	75
95	Stevens Institute ⊠	77
64	Manhattanville	82

Nickname: Blue Knights
Colors: Royal Blue, Black & White
Arena: Elaine & William Kaplan Recreation Center
   Capacity: 1,500; Year Built: 1992
AD: John J. Wright

SID: Justin Satkowski

MT. ST. MARY'S
Emmitsburg, MD 21727-7799 I

Coach: Milan Brown, Howard 1993

2006-07 RESULTS (11-20)

42	West Virginia	50
81	James Madison ⊠	70
60	La Salle	66
59	Binghamton	66
46	American ⊠	59
65	Maine ⊠	68
66	Loyola (Md.)	83
78	Quinnipiac ⊠	73
65	North Carolina St.	80
59	Winthrop	74
56	Lafayette	58
50	Maryland	91
78	Long Island	76
56	Monmouth	62
91	Sacred Heart ⊠	80
72	St. Francis (N.Y.) ⊠	54
63	Central Conn. St. ⊠	71
67	St. Francis (Pa.)	63
78	Robert Morris	81
80	Wagner ⊠	70
74	Fairleigh Dickinson ⊠	65
62	Central Conn. St.	74
62	Quinnipiac	70
58	St. Francis (Pa.) ⊠	43
60	Robert Morris ⊠	65
51	Sacred Heart	79
60	Monmouth ⊠	61
82	Wagner	77
55	St. Francis (N.Y.)	56
78	Robert Morris	61
68	Central Conn. St.	74

Nickname: Mountaineers
Colors: Blue & White
Arena: Knott Arena
   Capacity: 3,121; Year Built: 1987
AD: Harold P. Menninger
SID: Mark Vandergrift

MT. ST. VINCENT
Riverdale, NY 10471-1093 III

Coach: Michael Murphy, Hamilton 1997

2006-07 RESULTS (3-22)

69	Eastern Conn. St.	75
101	Mitchell †	76
76	SUNYIT ⊠	101
80	Hunter ⊠	99
57	Lehman	60
78	Yeshiva ⊠	88
74	Centenary (N.J.) ⊠	76
70	Farmingdale St. ⊠	83
47	New York U.	86
74	Union (N.Y.)	82
78	Elms †	91
59	Mt. St. Mary (N.Y.) ⊠	88
72	Maritime (N.Y.)	83
59	Stevens Institute	83
66	Merchant Marine	87
82	St. Joseph's (L.I.) ⊠	100
54	Manhattanville ⊠	97
72	Old Westbury	87
96	Centenary (N.J.) ⊠	58
51	Yeshiva	65
76	Stevens Institute ⊠	91
70	Green Mountain ⊠	49
61	St. Joseph's (L.I.)	76
93	Old Westbury ⊠	108
58	Farmingdale St.	112

Nickname: Dolphins
Colors: Blue, White & Gold
Arena: Mount Saint Vincent Athletics Center
   Capacity: 450; Year Built: 1910
AD: Cathy Ingram
SID: Michael Spinner

RESULTS

MOUNT UNION
Alliance, OH 44601 III

Coach: Lee Hood, Ohio Northern 1982

2006-07 RESULTS (10-15)

103	Emory & Henry †	83
60	Wooster	85
86	Franciscan	43
71	Muskingum ⬚	64
81	Hiram	54
61	Heidelberg	68
51	Ohio Northern ⬚	64
75	Baldwin-Wallace	81
76	Simpson †	80
50	Roanoke †	48
73	Linfield †	67
64	Marietta	59
60	Wilmington (Ohio) ⬚	80
84	Capital	74
61	Otterbein	77
72	John Carroll ⬚	83
61	Muskingum	65
66	Baldwin-Wallace ⬚	84
62	Heidelberg	75
66	John Carroll	85
68	Otterbein ⬚	78
44	Capital ⬚	56
96	Wilmington (Ohio)	73
69	Marietta ⬚	56
59	Ohio Northern	74

Nickname: Purple Raiders
Colors: Purple & White
Arena: Timken PE Building
    Capacity: 2,200; Year Built: 1970
AD: Larry Kehres
SID: Michael De Matteis

MUHLENBERG
Allentown, PA 18104-5586 III

Coach: Dave Madeira, Concord 1969

2006-07 RESULTS (10-15)

62	Rensselaer ⬚	60
66	Stevens Institute ⬚	73
54	Drew ⬚	55
77	Haverford ⬚	71
56	Johns Hopkins ⬚	62
73	Swarthmore	69
87	Washington (Md.) ⬚	61
105	TCNJ ⬚	109
63	DeSales	71
61	Moravian ⬚	80
67	Gettysburg	64
49	Frank. & Marsh.	69
50	McDaniel	72
58	Johns Hopkins	78
49	Ursinus ⬚	89
65	Washington (Md.)	71
50	Dickinson	69
64	Gettysburg ⬚	71
39	Haverford	56
71	Frank. & Marsh. ⬚	69
78	Swarthmore ⬚	65
69	McDaniel	68
91	Dickinson ⬚	84
76	Ursinus	68
51	Gettysburg	60

Nickname: Mules
Colors: Cardinal & Grey
Arena: Memorial Hall
    Capacity: 3,529; Year Built: 1954
AD: Samuel T. Beidleman
SID: Mike Falk

MURRAY ST.
Murray, KY 42071-3318 I

Coach: Billy Kennedy, Southeastern
La. 1986

2006-07 RESULTS (16-14)

84	San Diego St. †	87
68	Seattle Pacific †	76

44	St. Mary's (Cal.)	62
73	Belhaven ⬚	72
46	Southern Ill.	62
53	Eastern Ill. ⬚	50
68	Ill.-Chicago	74
64	Tennessee	89
78	Anderson (Ind.) ⬚	33
66	Eastern Ky.	72
70	Morehead St.	67
72	Jacksonville St. ⬚	71
44	Samford ⬚	55
73	Eastern Ill.	62
86	Tennessee St.	83
85	Southeast Mo. St. ⬚	96
59	Austin Peay	68
78	Tenn.-Martin ⬚	65
52	Tennessee Tech	63
85	Southeast Mo. St.	67
57	Samford	51
77	Austin Peay ⬚	68
63	Jacksonville St.	61
62	Eastern Ky. ⬚	64
74	Morehead St. ⬚	62
60	Tennessee St. ⬚	64
58	Rider	51
60	Tennessee Tech ⬚	56
74	Tenn.-Martin ⬚	52
60	Samford ⬚	70

Nickname: Racers
Colors: Navy & Gold
Arena: Regional Special Events Center
    Capacity: 8,600; Year Built: 1998
AD: Allen Ward
SID: Dave Winder

MUSKINGUM
New Concord, OH 43762 III

Coach: Geno Ford, Ohio 1997

2006-07 RESULTS (12-13)

69	Franciscan	43
79	Denison	71
86	Kenyon ⬚	61
67	Thiel ⬚	43
64	Mount Union	71
74	John Carroll ⬚	81
84	Otterbein	95
66	Heidelberg	76
61	Earlham †	59
56	Manchester †	53
57	Ohio Northern ⬚	69
61	Baldwin-Wallace ⬚	74
63	Marietta	51
66	Capital ⬚	54
55	Wilmington (Ohio)	65
65	Mount Union ⬚	61
63	John Carroll	65
79	Otterbein ⬚	80
71	Wilmington (Ohio) ⬚	67
62	Capital	64
64	Marietta ⬚	58
66	Baldwin-Wallace	76
57	Ohio Northern	63
78	Heidelberg ⬚	66
60	Capital	82

Nickname: Fighting Muskies
Colors: Black & Magenta
Arena: Muskingum Recreation Center
    Capacity: 3,000; Year Built: 1986
AD: Larry Shank
SID: Tom Caudill

MCDANIEL
Westminster, MD 21157-4390 III

Coach: Bob Flynn, Mt. St. Mary's 1979

2006-07 RESULTS (11-14)

59	Lebanon Valley	56
72	Hood †	88
66	Hood ⬚	64
53	Salisbury †	57
76	Goucher	68
75	Dickinson ⬚	58

76	Ursinus	75
66	Johns Hopkins ⬚	91
54	Gettysburg	51
64	Mary Washington ⬚	76
56	Haverford	60
63	Swarthmore ⬚	66
72	Muhlenberg	50
71	Gettysburg ⬚	65
70	Frank. & Marsh.	82
63	Haverford ⬚	67
68	Ursinus ⬚	82
75	Dickinson	77
75	Swarthmore	85
79	Washington (Md.) ⬚	69
70	Johns Hopkins	68
68	Muhlenberg ⬚	69
66	St. Mary's (Md.) ⬚	74
78	Frank. & Marsh. ⬚	75
84	Washington (Md.)	88

Nickname: Green Terror
Colors: Green & Gold
Arena: Gill P.E. Learning Center
    Capacity: 4,000; Year Built: 1984
AD: James M. Smith
SID: Luke Stillson

NAVY
Annapolis, MD 21402-5000 I

Coach: Billy Lange, Rowan 1994

2006-07 RESULTS (14-16)

73	Loyola (Md.) †	61
49	St. John's (N.Y.)	72
70	Brown †	47
87	Stony Brook	76
82	Md.-East. Shore ⬚	59
61	Villanova	70
79	William & Mary ⬚	63
61	Longwood	59
79	Howard ⬚	75
58	Penn ⬚	79
65	Delaware Valley ⬚	40
83	Washington (Md.) ⬚	37
44	Georgetown	65
59	Yale ⬚	74
52	NJIT	50
51	Bucknell	59
61	Lehigh ⬚	71
60	Lafayette	44
42	Holy Cross	61
50	Army	53
46	American	55
58	Colgate	66
63	Bucknell ⬚	78
70	Lehigh	65
70	Lafayette	63
40	Holy Cross ⬚	68
76	Army ⬚	68
60	American ⬚	71
62	Colgate	70
43	Bucknell	62

Nickname: Midshipmen
Colors: Navy Blue & Gold
Arena: Alumni Hall
    Capacity: 5,710; Year Built: 1991
AD: Chester S. Gladchuk
SID: Chris Forman

NAZARETH
Rochester, NY 14618-3790 III

Coach: Mike Daley, St. Bonaventure
1966

2006-07 RESULTS (11-14)

91	Morrisville St. ⬚	69
66	Fredonia St. ⬚	61
71	Rochester (N.Y.)	74
73	Oswego St. ⬚	81
81	Pitt.-Bradford ⬚	61
91	Old Westbury ⬚	82
89	Wheaton (Ill.) †	93
75	Staten Island	84
75	Alfred ⬚	72

63	St. John Fisher ⬚	73
57	Rochester (N.Y.) †	70
76	Rochester Inst. †	82
90	Keuka ⬚	66
68	Ithaca	75
68	Elmira	60
79	Rochester Inst. ⬚	86
92	Hartwick ⬚	87
72	Utica ⬚	73
61	St. John Fisher	69
77	Alfred	82
60	Rochester Inst.	69
45	Utica	65
81	Hartwick	73
71	Elmira ⬚	56
84	Ithaca ⬚	80

Nickname: Golden Flyers
Colors: Purple & Gold
Arena: Robert A. Kidera Gym
    Capacity: 1,200; Year Built: 1976
AD: Peter Bothner
SID: Joe Seil

NEBRASKA
Lincoln, NE 68508-0219 I

Coach: Doc Sadler, Arkansas 1982

2006-07 RESULTS (17-14)

76	Neb.-Omaha ⬚	62
73	Creighton	61
65	Lubbock Chrst. ⬚	42
71	Ark.-Pine Bluff ⬚	42
76	North Texas ⬚	57
73	Rutgers	75
56	Oregon †	68
82	Alabama A&M ⬚	55
73	Wyoming †	58
72	Hawaii	81
70	Houston †	57
82	Miami (Fla.) †	67
81	Savannah St. ⬚	53
82	Western Ky. ⬚	71
62	Iowa St.	71
53	Oklahoma	70
71	Colorado ⬚	50
61	Texas	62
45	Kansas St.	61
56	Kansas ⬚	76
61	Missouri	61
61	Texas Tech	59
55	Texas A&M ⬚	66
74	Kansas St. ⬚	63
39	Kansas	92
59	Baylor	63
82	Missouri ⬚	77
63	Iowa St. ⬚	69
69	Colorado	63
85	Oklahoma St. ⬚	73
39	Oklahoma St. †	54

Nickname: Cornhuskers, Huskers
Colors: Scarlet & Cream
Arena: Bob Devaney Sports Center
    Capacity: 13,595; Year Built: 1976
AD: Steven C. Pederson
SID: Jerry Trickie, Asst. SID

NEB.-KEARNEY
Kearney, NE 68849 II

Coach: Tom Kropp, Neb.-Kearney 1976

2006-07 RESULTS (24-7)

68	Doane ⬚	71
71	Mary †	70
84	Northern St.	73
80	Wayne St. (Neb.)	77
69	Augustana (S.D.)	81
70	Fort Hays St.	65
76	Western N.M.	62
97	N.M. Highlands	60
72	Mesa St. ⬚	84
75	Fort Lewis ⬚	58
84	Adams St.	77
88	Colorado St.-Pueblo	79

79	Dana ⊠	63
84	Western St. ⊠	67
73	Regis (Colo.) ⊠	56
85	UC-Colo. Springs ⊠	54
82	Chadron St.	69
80	Colorado Mines	63
75	Metro St.	92
84	Colo. Christian	67
98	Chadron St. ⊠	65
88	Colorado Mines ⊠	67
87	Neb.-Omaha ⊠	71
79	Colo. Christian ⊠	72
90	Metro St. ⊠	87
81	UC-Colo. Springs	89
85	Regis (Colo.)	72
91	Colorado St.-Pueblo ⊠	74
90	Adams St. †	97
95	South Dakota †	88
70	Winona St.	81

Nickname: Antelopes, Lopers
Colors: Royal Blue & Light Old Gold
Arena: Health & Sports Center
Capacity: 6,000; Year Built: 1990
AD: Jon McBride
SID: Peter Yazvac

NEB.-OMAHA
Omaha, NE 68182 II

Coach: Derrin Hansen, Neb. Wesleyan 1991

2006-07 RESULTS (12-16)

64	Mary †	61
63	Rockhurst †	76
88	Mo. Western St. ⊠	95
93	Chadron St. ⊠	67
58	Quincy ⊠	62
95	Peru St.	85
69	Regis (Colo.) †	67
66	Colorado St.-Pueblo	60
80	York (Neb.)	68
55	Emporia St.	78
91	Midland Lutheran ⊠	69
80	Doane	61
94	Dana ⊠	60
76	Concordia-St. Paul ⊠	79
60	Augustana (S.D.)	83
79	Minn. Duluth ⊠	68
78	South Dakota ⊠	93
73	North Dakota	75
64	Augustana (S.D.) ⊠	62
67	St. Cloud St.	76
67	South Dakota	86
62	St. Cloud St. ⊠	75
59	Minn. St. Mankato ⊠	62
71	Neb.-Kearney	87
52	North Dakota ⊠	50
64	Minn. Duluth	69
58	Minn. St. Mankato	80
52	St. Cloud St.	63

Nickname: Mavericks
Colors: Black & Crimson
Arena: UNO Fieldhouse
Capacity: 3,500; Year Built: 1950
AD: Thomas A Frette
SID: Gary Anderson

NEB. WESLEYAN
Lincoln, NE 68504-2796 III

Coach: Cam Schuknecht, Wartburg 1998

2006-07 RESULTS (8-19)

73	St. Scholastica †	72
101	Finlandia †	57
70	Concordia (Neb.) ⊠	65
89	St. Scholastica ⊠	79
58	Wartburg ⊠	81
73	Hastings	80
62	Morningside	78
54	Dana	61
66	Sioux Falls ⊠	81
66	Simpson ⊠	68

61	St. Mary's (Minn.)	76
63	St. Olaf	82
61	Doane ⊠	70
78	Northwestern (Iowa) ⊠	92
76	Midland Lutheran	66
73	Briar Cliff (Iowa)	77
58	Concordia (Neb.) ⊠	73
71	Dordt ⊠	83
55	Hastings	65
65	Mt. Marty	68
62	Doane	72
53	Dakota Wesleyan	74
69	Midland Lutheran ⊠	82
87	Dana	71
78	Briar Cliff (Iowa) ⊠	66
79	UC Santa Cruz ⊠	52
49	Chapman ⊠	64

Nickname: Prairie Wolves
Colors: Gold, Brown & Black
Arena: Snyder Arena
Capacity: 2,350; Year Built: 1995
AD: Ira Zeff
SID: Karl Skinner

NEUMANN
Aston, PA 19014-1298 III

Coach: Corey Stitzel, Elizabethtown 2002

2006-07 RESULTS (13-13)

73	Catholic †	85
68	Adrian †	62
80	Wesley	69
72	Elizabethtown	69
77	Marywood ⊠	62
67	Arcadia	62
73	Eastern	79
65	Richard Stockton †	68
113	Pa. Col. of Bible †	61
50	Shippensburg ⊠	72
68	Rowan	79
75	Misericordia ⊠	79
67	Gwynedd-Mercy ⊠	71
61	Alvernia ⊠	60
74	Cabrini	73
99	Marywood	69
60	Arcadia ⊠	49
82	Wesley ⊠	62
70	Immaculata	74
68	Eastern ⊠	82
59	Alvernia	71
90	Gwynedd-Mercy	75
62	Misericordia	68
61	Cabrini ⊠	63
67	Immaculata ⊠	65
67	Eastern	77

Nickname: Knights
Colors: Blue, Gold & White
Arena: Bruder Gym
Capacity: 350; Year Built: 1985
AD: Chuck Sack
SID: Leigh Matejkovic

NEVADA
Reno, NV 89557 I

Coach: Mark Fox, Eastern N.M. 1991

2006-07 RESULTS (29-5)

85	Alas. Anchorage ⊠	62
75	Oregon St. ⊠	47
82	Ark.-Pine Bluff ⊠	63
83	UC Irvine ⊠	64
78	Santa Clara	70
86	La.-Lafayette	74
77	California †	71
49	UNLV	58
76	St. Mary's (Cal.) ⊠	58
60	Pacific ⊠	53
73	Akron	71
89	Maine ⊠	69
82	Gonzaga †	74
81	Idaho ⊠	55
90	Boise St. ⊠	86

72	San Jose St.	63
68	Hawaii	66
85	Fresno St. ⊠	75
73	New Mexico St.	80
84	Louisiana Tech ⊠	67
79	Utah St. ⊠	62
79	Louisiana Tech	71
69	Hawaii	68
81	Fresno St.	68
68	San Jose St. ⊠	60
79	UNI	64
84	Idaho	68
95	Boise St.	81
77	Utah St.	79
69	New Mexico St. ⊠	65
88	Idaho †	56
77	Utah St. †	79
77	Creighton †	71
62	Memphis †	78

Nickname: Wolf Pack
Colors: Silver & Blue
Arena: Lawlor Events Center
Capacity: 11,200; Year Built: 1983
AD: Cary Groth
SID: Rhonda Lundin

UNLV
Las Vegas, NV 89154 I

Coach: Lon Kruger, Kansas St. 1975

2006-07 RESULTS (30-7)

73	Hawaii ⊠	59
82	Eastern Wash. ⊠	79
76	UC Santa Barbara ⊠	79
83	Washburn ⊠	55
96	San Francisco ⊠	88
75	Arizona	89
93	Northern Ariz. †	53
61	Hawaii	58
58	Nevada	49
67	A&M-Corpus Christi ⊠	57
103	Norfolk St. ⊠	56
74	South Fla.	59
62	Minnesota ⊠	58
74	Texas Tech	66
78	Houston	62
97	Utah ⊠	94
50	Air Force	56
76	Wyoming	86
83	BYU ⊠	75
75	TCU	66
68	San Diego St. ⊠	61
76	New Mexico ⊠	72
76	Colorado St.	59
63	BYU	90
82	TCU ⊠	67
80	Wyoming ⊠	70
52	San Diego St.	67
70	Utah	57
60	Air Force ⊠	50
85	New Mexico	83
65	Colorado St. ⊠	47
80	Utah ⊠	54
88	Colorado St. ⊠	72
78	BYU ⊠	70
67	Georgia Tech †	63
74	Wisconsin †	68
72	Oregon †	76

Nickname: Rebels
Colors: Scarlet & Gray
Arena: Thomas & Mack Center
Capacity: 18,500; Year Built: 1983
AD: Mike Hamrick
SID: Andy Grossman

NEW ENGLAND
Biddeford, ME 04005 III

Coach: Jon Hayes, Me.-Farmington 1997

2006-07 RESULTS (5-20)

59	Norwich †	76
40	Hartwick †	63

75	Bowdoin ⊠	81
55	Colby ⊠	79
46	Eastern Nazarene	41
55	Endicott	68
79	Me.-Farmington	88
51	Southern Me.	83
53	Middlebury	79
74	Curry ⊠	73
46	Bates	90
66	Wentworth Inst.	72
51	Endicott ⊠	58
65	New England Col.	80
57	Roger Williams ⊠	61
64	Colby-Sawyer	62
50	Anna Maria	69
58	Salve Regina ⊠	55
33	Gordon	66
62	Wentworth Inst. ⊠	75
65	Nichols	74
77	New England Col. ⊠	79
64	St. Joseph's (Me.) ⊠	81
73	Colby-Sawyer ⊠	67
38	Gordon	76

Nickname: Nor'easters
Colors: Royal & Grey
Arena: Campus Center
Capacity: 1,500; Year Built: 1989
AD: Kimberly J. Allen
SID: Curt Smyth

NEW ENGLAND COL.
Henniker, NH 03242-3293 III

Coach: Charles Mason, Concordia-M'head 1991

2006-07 RESULTS (10-15)

117	Me.-Presque Isle ⊠	95
92	Framingham St. ⊠	79
69	Rivier ⊠	84
77	Keene St. †	92
96	Thomas (Me.) ⊠	80
76	Gordon ⊠	89
95	Daniel Webster ⊠	80
78	Castleton ⊠	81
83	Johnson St.	58
66	Wentworth Inst. ⊠	67
60	Gordon	86
91	Eastern Nazarene ⊠	82
80	New England ⊠	65
87	Newbury ⊠	90
74	Anna Maria	75
120	Colby-Sawyer ⊠	96
85	Roger Williams ⊠	95
79	Colby-Sawyer	91
64	Endicott	83
61	Salve Regina	89
79	New England	77
85	Curry ⊠	93
75	Wentworth Inst. ⊠	87
82	Endicott ⊠	70
97	Nichols	108

Nickname: Pilgrims
Colors: Scarlet & Royal Blue
Arena: Bridges Gym
Capacity: 400; Year Built: 1965
AD: Lori Runksmeier
SID: Renee Hellert

NEW HAMPSHIRE
Durham, NH 03824 I

Coach: Bill Herrion, Merrimack 1981

2006-07 RESULTS (10-20)

47	Boston College	86
69	Franklin Pierce ⊠	70
66	Central Conn. St. ⊠	73
64	Robert Morris	77
64	Quinnipiac	59
81	Harvard	83
62	Long Island	70
48	Rutgers	55
41	Northeastern	51
67	Iona	52

RESULTS

65	Elon †	64
47	Kent St.	74
52	Albany (N.Y.)	69
73	Maine	68
60	Vermont ⊠	62
72	Hartford	59
29	Boston U.	53
65	Dartmouth	61
75	Binghamton	72
69	Stony Brook ⊠	56
44	UMBC ⊠	45
64	Albany (N.Y.) ⊠	71
79	Vermont	82
56	Maine ⊠	65
46	Hartford	62
60	Boston U. ⊠	55
49	Stony Brook	67
37	Binghamton ⊠	66
64	UMBC ⊠	51
47	Albany (N.Y.) †	64

Nickname: Wildcats
Colors: Blue & White
Arena: Lundholm Gymnasium
Capacity: 3,500; Year Built: 1961
AD: Marty Scarano
SID: Scott Stapin

NEW HAVEN
West Haven, CT 06516-1999 II

Coach: Al Seibert, Fredonia St. 1985

2006-07 RESULTS (9-19)

54	Mass.-Lowell ⊠	70
73	Franklin Pierce †	59
79	St. Michael's	91
69	Mercy	76
69	Bridgeport ⊠	81
67	Queens (N.Y.)	84
54	NYIT	74
62	Bentley	81
61	Post	83
61	Adelphi	59
64	Dowling	72
53	American Int'l ⊠	68
65	C.W. Post ⊠	81
62	Molloy ⊠	75
54	St. Thomas Aquinas	65
72	Concordia (N.Y.) ⊠	62
70	Mercy ⊠	60
49	Bridgeport	60
73	Queens (N.Y.) ⊠	65
55	Molloy	73
61	NYIT ⊠	80
60	Adelphi ⊠	74
78	Dowling ⊠	64
77	C.W. Post ⊠	68
71	Southern N.H. ⊠	86
61	St. Thomas Aquinas ⊠	53
73	Concordia (N.Y.)	66
59	NYIT	66

Nickname: Chargers
Colors: Blue & Gold
Arena: Charger Gymnasium
Capacity: 2,500; Year Built: 1971
AD: Deborah Chin
SID: Matt McCullough

NEW JERSEY CITY
Jersey City, NJ 07305-1597 III

Coach: Charles Brown, New Jersey City 1965

2006-07 RESULTS (19-10)

90	Staten Island †	77
91	Gwynedd-Mercy †	76
98	Briarcliffe (N.Y.) ⊠	65
81	John Jay	70
84	Lincoln (Pa.)	92
70	TCNJ	72
72	Rutgers-Newark	77
67	Kean ⊠	59
78	Farmingdale St.	83
62	Albright †	76

113	Hampden-Sydney	120
59	Lycoming †	56
71	Albright	94
56	Wm. Paterson ⊠	42
76	Montclair St.	63
64	Richard Stockton ⊠	53
73	Ramapo ⊠	66
95	Rowan	82
76	City Tech ⊠	58
77	Rutgers-Newark ⊠	56
69	Rutgers-Camden ⊠	46
71	Wm. Paterson	60
90	Montclair St. ⊠	66
76	Lincoln (Pa.) ⊠	79
79	Ramapo	64
79	Rutgers-Newark ⊠	69
81	Ramapo ⊠	83
88	FDU-Florham ⊠	71
69	Richard Stockton ⊠	80

Nickname: Gothic Knights
Colors: Green & Gold
Arena: John J. Moore Athletics & Fitness Center
Capacity: 2,000; Year Built: 1994
AD: Alice De Fazio
SID: Ira Thor

NJIT
Newark, NJ 07102 II

Coach: James Paul Casciano, Drexel 1974

2006-07 RESULTS (5-24)

56	Manhattan	55
63	Rider ⊠	52
60	Columbia	73
57	St. Peter's †	75
40	Siena ⊠	64
50	American	75
58	Maine ⊠	68
57	Lafayette ⊠	76
40	Army	60
61	Stony Brook ⊠	65
50	St. John's (N.Y.)	68
63	UCF	75
66	James Madison †	70
50	Navy ⊠	52
58	Cornell	69
59	Longwood ⊠	55
65	IPFW	82
59	La Salle	78
63	Siena	87
55	Utah Valley St.	86
60	Tex.-Pan American	72
67	South Dakota St. ⊠	62
57	North Dakota St. ⊠	80
47	IPFW ⊠	52
78	Longwood	74
47	Utah Valley St. ⊠	77
58	Tex.-Pan American ⊠	70
52	North Dakota St.	104
61	South Dakota St.	71

Nickname: Highlanders
Colors: Red & White
Arena: Fleisher Athletic Center
Capacity: 1,500; Year Built: 1960
AD: Leonard Kaplan
SID: Tim Camp

TCNJ
Ewing, NJ 08628-0718 III

Coach: John Castaldo, TCNJ 1982

2006-07 RESULTS (12-14)

44	King's (Pa.) †	67
79	Pa. Col. of Bible †	56
61	Keystone ⊠	58
48	John Carroll †	80
62	Huntingdon †	36
72	New Jersey City ⊠	70
49	Scranton	71
69	Kean ⊠	72
65	Montclair St.	54

109	Muhlenberg	105
63	St. Mary's (Md.) ⊠	64
70	Valley Forge Chrst. ⊠	53
93	St. Mary's (Md.) †	73
64	DeSales	76
57	Richard Stockton	66
59	Rowan ⊠	68
73	Brooklyn ⊠	51
65	Rutgers-Camden ⊠	62
56	Wm. Paterson ⊠	53
52	Rutgers-Newark	76
57	Kean	75
55	Ramapo ⊠	74
58	Richard Stockton ⊠	66
61	Rowan	81
70	Rutgers-Camden ⊠	56
61	Ramapo	77

Nickname: Lions
Colors: Blue & Gold
Arena: Packer Hall
Capacity: 1,200; Year Built: 1962
AD: Kevin A. McHugh
SID: Ann King

NEW MEXICO
Albuquerque, NM 87131 I

Coach: Ritchie McKay, Seattle Pacific 1987

2006-07 RESULTS (15-17)

91	Abilene Christian ⊠	54
92	Sacramento St. ⊠	56
106	Colorado ⊠	65
78	Kansas St. ⊠	54
79	New Mexico St. ⊠	76
63	UTEP	87
72	New Mexico St.	103
86	N.C. A&T ⊠	78
79	Longwood ⊠	60
76	Charleston So. ⊠	69
71	Wichita St. †	68
56	Kansas St. †	72
91	Alcorn St. ⊠	59
101	Pepperdine ⊠	96
68	Texas Tech	70
52	TCU	64
79	Colorado St. ⊠	88
57	Air Force ⊠	65
86	Utah ⊠	82
68	San Diego St. ⊠	73
49	BYU ⊠	70
72	UNLV	76
91	Wyoming ⊠	83
70	Colorado St.	66
51	Air Force ⊠	60
83	BYU	96
74	TCU ⊠	58
74	San Diego St. ⊠	81
91	Utah	93
83	UNLV ⊠	85
67	Wyoming	76
54	TCU †	62

Nickname: Lobos
Colors: Cherry & Silver
Arena: The Pit/Bob King Court
Capacity: 18,018; Year Built: 1966
AD: Paul Krebs
SID: Greg Remington

N.M. HIGHLANDS
Las Vegas, NM 87701 II

Coach: Greg Berry, Bradley 1968

2006-07 RESULTS (4-23)

59	Okla. Panhandle	77
71	Wayland Baptist ⊠	88
71	Eastern N.M.	81
64	West Tex. A&M ⊠	83
75	Lubbock Chrst. †	95
61	Wayland Baptist †	78
104	Chadron St. ⊠	96
60	Neb.-Kearney ⊠	97
60	Colorado Mines	70

63	Eastern N.M. ⊠	90
67	Regis (Colo.) ⊠	64
77	UC-Colo. Springs ⊠	78
77	Metro St.	108
75	Colo. Christian.	87
58	Colorado St.-Pueblo	67
70	Adams St.	95
63	West Tex. A&M ⊠	92
74	Mesa St. ⊠	72
61	Fort Lewis	98
52	Western N.M.	57
71	Western St. ⊠	63
68	Fort Lewis	78
59	Mesa St.	89
83	Western N.M. ⊠	90
51	Western St. ⊠	67
79	Adams St. ⊠	87
79	Colorado St.-Pueblo ⊠	80

Nickname: Cowboys
Colors: Purple & White
Arena: John A. Wilson Complex
Capacity: 5,000; Year Built: 1986
AD: Ben Santistevan
SID: Dan Corbett

NEW MEXICO ST.
Las Cruces, NM 88003 I

Coach: Reggie Theus, UNLV 2002

2006-07 RESULTS (25-9)

76	Pacific ⊠	74
69	Loyola Marymount	71
87	Arizona	102
76	New Mexico	79
80	Chicago St. ⊠	74
89	San Francisco ⊠	78
103	New Mexico ⊠	72
71	UTEP ⊠	69
78	Ark.-Pine Bluff ⊠	62
68	UTEP	62
100	Western N.M. ⊠	76
107	Norfolk St. ⊠	84
88	Chicago St.	78
92	Hawaii ⊠	86
74	San Jose St. ⊠	68
61	Idaho	56
73	Boise St.	69
71	Louisiana Tech ⊠	73
80	Nevada ⊠	73
84	Idaho ⊠	66
85	San Jose St.	78
78	Boise St. ⊠	68
63	Utah St.	75
69	Fresno St.	71
71	Hawaii	68
77	Ohio ⊠	72
76	Utah St. ⊠	73
58	Fresno St. ⊠	60
79	Louisiana Tech ⊠	64
65	Nevada	69
77	Louisiana Tech ⊠	70
88	Boise St. ⊠	69
72	Utah St. ⊠	70
67	Texas †	79

Nickname: Aggies
Colors: Crimson & White
Arena: Pan American Center
Capacity: 13,071; Year Built: 1968
AD: McKinley Boston Jr.
SID: Garret Ward

NEW ORLEANS
New Orleans, LA 70148 I

Coach: Buzz Williams, Oklahoma City 1994

2006-07 RESULTS (14-17)

65	Vermont †	82
73	Hampton †	74
66	Jacksonville St. ⊠	54
64	Tulane	78
50	Florida St.	69
64	Lamar	62

67	Northwestern St. ⊠	71
77	Mississippi	85
76	Texas-Tyler ⊠	52
80	La.-Lafayette ⊠	76
97	North Texas ⊠	93
63	Mississippi St. †	89
76	Denver	66
84	Tulane	77
86	Fla. Atlantic ⊠	93
82	Ark.-Little Rock	73
66	La.-Monroe	68
67	Middle Tenn. ⊠	76
86	Troy	85
70	Western Ky.	73
77	Florida Int'l ⊠	67
58	South Ala. ⊠	76
64	La.-Lafayette	67
64	North Texas	62
89	Denver ⊠	66
79	Arkansas St.	90
77	Fla. Atlantic	98
64	Ark.-Little Rock ⊠	65
88	La.-Monroe ⊠	75
77	Ark.-Little Rock ⊠	70
74	Arkansas St. †	81

Nickname: Privateers
Colors: Royal Blue & Silver
Arena: Kiefer Lakefront Arena
    Capacity: 8,933; Year Built: 1983
AD: James W. Miller
SID: Rob Broussard

NEW PALTZ ST.
New Paltz, NY 12561-2499 III

Coach: Doug Pasquerella, Cortland St. 1996

2006-07 RESULTS (11-14)

94	Brooklyn ⊠	63
72	Vassar	77
108	Bard †	86
61	Fredonia St. ⊠	58
71	Buffalo St. ⊠	76
85	SUNYIT	87
76	John Jay	68
81	Bethany (Cal.)	71
86	Chaminade	101
83	Old Westbury ⊠	80
73	Potsdam St.	61
66	Plattsburgh St.	86
83	SUNYIT ⊠	94
54	Geneseo St. ⊠	71
75	Geneseo St.	71
81	Brockport St.	109
70	Cortland St. ⊠	73
65	Baruch	64
57	Oneonta St. ⊠	75
91	Morrisville St. ⊠	61
87	Oswego St.	92
83	Buffalo St.	96
69	Oneonta St.	79
75	Potsdam St. ⊠	66
66	Plattsburgh St. ⊠	71

Nickname: Hawks
Colors: Orange & Blue
Arena: Elting Gymnasium
    Capacity: 2,200; Year Built: 1964
AD: Stuart Robinson
SID: Janelle Feuz

CITY TECH
Brooklyn, NY 11201 III

Coach: Otis Fenn, City Tech 1975

2006-07 RESULTS (7-19)

66	Amherst	101
66	Polytechnic (N.Y.) †	63
52	Wm. Paterson	78
65	Union (N.Y.)	90
73	Ramapo	91
49	Staten Island	73
71	CCNY ⊠	79
46	FDU-Florham ⊠	85

65	St. Joseph's (L.I.) ⊠	78
79	Kean	85
62	Lehman	57
93	Brooklyn	88
76	Medgar Evers ⊠	62
54	Baruch ⊠	63
67	York (N.Y.)	86
66	Rutgers-Newark ⊠	73
72	John Jay	75
58	Brooklyn ⊠	61
77	Vassar	85
70	Staten Island ⊠	58
58	New Jersey City	76
71	Hunter	67
61	Farmingdale St.	83
61	Medgar Evers	64
82	York (N.Y.) ⊠	79
61	CCNY	70

Nickname: Yellow Jackets
Colors: Royal Blue & Gold
AD: Jerry Albig
SID: Gregg Cohen

SUNYIT
Utica, NY 13504-3050 III

Coach: Tom Murphy, Springfield 1960

2006-07 RESULTS (17-12)

110	Keuka †	60
82	Utica	99
101	Mt. St. Vincent ⊠	76
90	Paul Smith ⊠	66
93	Cortland St.	88
57	Oswego St.	85
87	New Paltz St. ⊠	85
76	Utica ⊠	99
75	St. Joseph's (L.I.) †	74
62	Wis.-Stout †	79
88	Cazenovia	81
76	Potsdam St. ⊠	88
85	Buffalo St.	99
71	Oneonta St. ⊠	74
94	New Paltz St.	83
62	Morrisville St. ⊠	54
72	Fredonia St. ⊠	56
84	Buffalo St. ⊠	80
76	Plattsburgh St.	91
70	Geneseo St. ⊠	63
90	Potsdam St.	79
79	Oneonta St.	74
74	Fredonia St.	78
108	Brockport St. ⊠	114
89	Plattsburgh St. ⊠	84
90	Oneonta St. ⊠	73
89	Brockport St.	104
96	Clarkson ⊠	84
84	Oswego St. †	91

Nickname: Wildcats
Colors: Royal Blue & Grey
Arena: Campus Center Gym
    Capacity: 1,400; Year Built: 1987
AD: Kevin Grimmer
SID: Jim Lipocky

NYIT
Old Westbury, NY 11568-8000 II

Coach: Sal Lagano, Hofstra 1988

2006-07 RESULTS (20-9)

42	Bentley †	71
75	St. Anselm †	85
81	Wilmington (Del.)	63
76	Goldey-Beacom	82
92	Adelphi	85
59	St. Thomas Aquinas ⊠	51
59	Mercy	51
74	New Haven ⊠	54
77	Northwood (Fla.) †	62
73	Mass.-Lowell	71
91	Concordia (N.Y.) ⊠	76
66	Bridgeport ⊠	58
71	Queens (N.Y.)	73
64	Dowling	52

88	Molloy ⊠	89
87	C.W. Post ⊠	85
72	Adelphi ⊠	75
65	Southern N.H. ⊠	62
61	St. Thomas Aquinas	47
86	Mercy ⊠	68
80	New Haven	61
68	Concordia (N.Y.)	63
62	Bridgeport	68
96	Queens (N.Y.) ⊠	87
68	Dowling ⊠	60
76	Molloy	68
60	C.W. Post	70
66	New Haven ⊠	59
59	Adelphi †	65

Nickname: Bears
Colors: Navy Blue
Arena: Recreation Hall
    Capacity: 500; Year Built: 1955
AD: Clyde Doughty Jr.
SID: Ben Arcuri

NEW YORK U.
New York, NY 10012 III

Coach: Joe Nesci, Brooklyn 1979

2006-07 RESULTS (22-6)

73	Alfred ⊠	44
63	Emerson ⊠	49
77	Potsdam St. ⊠	67
56	York (N.Y.)	36
92	Medgar Evers ⊠	53
76	Stevens Institute ⊠	67
77	Polytechnic (N.Y.)	53
85	Old Westbury ⊠	55
74	Clark (Mass.)	64
86	Mt. St. Vincent ⊠	47
64	Carnegie Mellon	68
70	Rochester (N.Y.)	61
48	Brandeis	52
94	Hunter	59
69	Emory ⊠	50
69	Case Reserve ⊠	52
60	Chicago	62
78	Washington-St. Louis	79
73	Washington-St. Louis ⊠	57
79	Chicago ⊠	76
53	Rochester (N.Y.) ⊠	58
78	Carnegie Mellon ⊠	57
65	Case Reserve	47
69	Emory	66
67	Brandeis ⊠	76
87	St. Joseph's (L.I.) ⊠	68
82	Rutgers-Newark ⊠	72
58	Richard Stockton ⊠	55

Nickname: Violets
Colors: Purple & White
Arena: Coles Sports Center
    Capacity: 1,900; Year Built: 1981
AD: Christopher Bledsoe
SID: Jeffrey Bernstein

NEWBERRY
Newberry, SC 29108 II

Coach: Shaun Golden, Georgia 1993

2006-07 RESULTS (12-15)

78	Limestone †	79
61	S.C. Upstate	64
93	Allen ⊠	59
57	Lander	78
55	Kennesaw St.	68
84	Francis Marion ⊠	68
52	Erskine ⊠	51
68	Anderson (S.C.)	56
89	Wingate ⊠	79
63	Carson-Newman	60
75	Mars Hill	80
54	Lenoir-Rhyne	61
77	Lincoln Memorial ⊠	79
57	Claflin	54
64	Tusculum	76
83	Catawba ⊠	77

43	Presbyterian	70
78	Carson-Newman ⊠	67
64	Mars Hill ⊠	53
71	Brevard ⊠	63
54	Lenoir-Rhyne ⊠	63
80	Catawba	89
42	Tusculum ⊠	64
87	Wingate	84
29	Presbyterian ⊠	60
68	Lincoln Memorial	75
48	Presbyterian	56

Nickname: Indians
Colors: Scarlet & Gray
Arena: Eleazer Arena
    Capacity: 1,600; Year Built: 1981
AD: Andy Carter
SID: Ross Vaughn

NEWBURY
Brookline, MA 02445 III

Coach: L.J. Harrington, Whittier 1985

2006-07 RESULTS (15-12)

60	Brandeis	73
70	Colby-Sawyer †	74
68	Anna Maria	70
77	Albertus Magnus ⊠	71
52	Babson †	69
79	Lyndon St. †	64
61	Salem St.	73
75	Mass. Liberal Arts †	61
75	Bard	72
77	Clark (Mass.)	81
62	Green Mountain	41
58	Eastern Nazarene ⊠	53
77	Worcester St.	70
90	New England Col.	87
55	Wentworth Inst.	66
70	Gordon ⊠	69
62	MIT	71
74	Lesley ⊠	67
55	Curry	76
86	Mitchell ⊠	72
62	Fitchburg St. ⊠	54
65	St. Joseph's (Me.) ⊠	82
80	Daniel Webster ⊠	71
75	Mitchell	80
74	St. Joseph's (Me.) ⊠	68
72	Lincoln (Pa.) †	84
92	Mitchell †	52

Nickname: Nighthawks
Colors: Green & Gold
Arena: Papas Gymasium
    Capacity: 300; Year Built: 1950
AD: Peter Centola
SID: Peter Centola

NIAGARA
Niagara University, NY 14109 I

Coach: Joe Mihalich, La Salle 1978

2006-07 RESULTS (23-12)

66	Binghamton ⊠	74
58	Valparaiso ⊠	70
48	Akron ⊠	63
74	St. Bonaventure ⊠	63
62	Buffalo	74
69	Siena	81
64	St. John's (N.Y.) ⊠	86
78	Duquesne ⊠	74
79	Iona	58
80	Central Mich.	73
53	Delaware †	71
67	Holy Cross †	61
88	La Salle	82
88	St. Peter's ⊠	55
81	Siena ⊠	92
85	Fairfield ⊠	76
95	Loyola (Md.) ⊠	96
80	Rider	79
86	Marist ⊠	91
81	Iona ⊠	80
83	Marist	75

56	Fairfield	68
81	Manhattan ⊠	70
79	Canisius ⊠	61
63	St. Peter's	59
76	Manhattan	74
89	Canisius	88
90	Liberty ⊠	81
73	Loyola (Md.) ⊠	71
89	Rider ⊠	77
77	Rider †	52
89	Loyola (Md.) †	79
83	Siena †	79
77	Florida A&M †	69
67	Kansas †	107

Nickname: Purple Eagles
Colors: Purple and White
Arena: Gallagher Center
Capacity: 2,400; Year Built: 1949
AD: Ed McLaughlin
SID: Michele Schmidt

NICHOLLS ST.
Thibodaux, LA 70310 I

Coach: J.P. Piper, Southeastern La. 1991

2006-07 RESULTS (8-22)

55	Mississippi St.	90
63	UNI †	68
74	Washington	102
83	Pepperdine †	98
42	LSU	96
60	Texas	91
80	Mississippi	100
87	Auburn	92
71	Centenary (La.)	84
71	North Texas ⊠	74
76	Xavier (La.) ⊠	63
55	Lipscomb	75
40	Vanderbilt	76
83	La.-Monroe	87
55	Stephen F. Austin	61
61	Sam Houston St. ⊠	81
83	Texas-Arlington ⊠	81
82	Texas St. ⊠	67
69	Southeastern La.	75
88	Northwestern St. ⊠	98
53	Central Ark.	64
82	Lamar	89
61	McNeese St. ⊠	53
91	A&M-Corpus Christi	107
65	UTSA	54
74	Southeastern La. ⊠	72
93	Northwestern St.	92
66	Central Ark. ⊠	70
105	Lamar ⊠	90
76	McNeese St.	77

Nickname: Colonels
Colors: Red & Grey
Arena: David Stopher Gymnasium
Capacity: 3,800; Year Built: 1967
AD: Robert J. Bernardi
SID: Brandon Rizzuto

NICHOLS
Dudley, MA 01571-5000 III

Coach: Dave Sokolnicki, Nichols 1997

2006-07 RESULTS (14-11)

91	Worcester St. †	65
64	WPI †	83
77	Westfield St. ⊠	84
79	Fitchburg St. ⊠	67
68	Curry	73
68	Anna Maria ⊠	52
76	Worcester St.	81
90	Wesleyan (Conn.)	87
66	Western New Eng. ⊠	61
49	Roger Williams	82
71	Curry ⊠	74
77	Colby-Sawyer ⊠	80
64	Wentworth Inst.	79
77	Salve Regina	65
70	Eastern Nazarene	52

95	Becker ⊠	71
66	Gordon	74
71	Eastern Nazarene ⊠	58
74	New England ⊠	65
95	Anna Maria	83
76	Salve Regina ⊠	74
72	Endicott	101
65	Roger Williams ⊠	60
108	New England Col. ⊠	97
57	Endicott	67

Nickname: Bison
Colors: Black, White and Green
Arena: Chalmers Field House
Capacity: 800; Year Built: 2000
AD: Charlyn Robert
SID: Kristin DiChiaro

NORFOLK ST.
Norfolk, VA 23504 I

Coach: Dwight Freeman, Western St. 1982

2006-07 RESULTS (11-19)

36	Oklahoma	99
54	Longwood ⊠	65
49	Iowa St.	57
74	Hampton ⊠	72
64	Fla. Atlantic	77
47	Air Force	70
56	South Fla. †	87
56	UNLV	103
82	A&M-Corpus Christi †	98
84	New Mexico St.	107
74	Md.-East. Shore	62
71	Florida A&M	81
68	Bethune-Cookman	65
62	Coppin St. ⊠	61
68	Morgan St. ⊠	54
71	Winston-Salem ⊠	81
56	Delaware St.	66
60	N.C. A&T	80
62	South Carolina St.	56
81	Florida A&M ⊠	68
66	Bethune-Cookman ⊠	52
70	Coppin St.	77
61	Morgan St.	71
61	Delaware St. ⊠	72
52	Hampton	66
99	N.C. A&T ⊠	104
70	South Carolina St. ⊠	65
69	Howard ⊠	68
81	Md.-East. Shore †	70
66	N.C. A&T †	81

Nickname: Spartans
Colors: Green & Gold
Arena: Echols Memorial Hall
Capacity: 7,000; Year Built: 1982
AD: Marty L. Miller
SID: Matt Michalec

NORTH ALA.
Florence, AL 35632-0001 II

Coach: Bobby Champagne, South Ala. 1990

2006-07 RESULTS (15-14)

94	Lynn ⊠	84
94	Southern Ark. ⊠	70
107	Nova Southeastern	108
69	Barry †	71
74	Clayton St. ⊠	80
84	Delta St.	90
96	Harding	103
79	Arkansas Tech	78
79	Harding	68
94	Christian Bros.	107
98	Ouachita Baptist	94
94	Arkansas Tech	91
64	Southern Ark.	79
94	Northern Ky. ⊠	100
78	Ouachita Baptist ⊠	64
101	Montevallo	94
69	West Ala.	79

77	Valdosta St. ⊠	63
89	West Fla. ⊠	60
73	West Ga.	81
92	Ala.-Huntsville	88
85	West Fla.	78
65	Valdosta St.	73
109	West Ala.	85
95	Montevallo ⊠	98
80	West Ga. ⊠	84
89	Ala.-Huntsville	73
78	Christian Bros. †	71
71	Montevallo †	98

Nickname: Lions
Colors: Purple & Gold
Arena: Flowers Hall
Capacity: 3,500; Year Built: 1972
AD: Joel W. Erdmann
SID: Jeff Hodges

NORTH CAROLINA
Chapel Hill, NC 27515 I

Coach: Roy Williams, North Carolina 1972

2006-07 RESULTS (31-7)

103	Sacred Heart †	81
73	Winthrop †	66
103	Gardner-Webb ⊠	50
74	Gonzaga ⊠	82
101	Tennessee †	87
98	Ohio St. ⊠	89
75	Kentucky ⊠	63
94	High Point ⊠	69
93	UNC Asheville ⊠	62
105	Fla. Atlantic ⊠	52
69	St. Louis	48
87	Rutgers	48
81	Dayton ⊠	51
102	Penn ⊠	64
84	Florida St. ⊠	58
79	Virginia	69
88	Virginia Tech	94
77	Clemson	55
77	Georgia Tech ⊠	61
88	Wake Forest	60
92	Arizona	64
105	Miami (Fla.) ⊠	64
79	North Carolina St.	83
79	Duke	73
104	Wake Forest ⊠	67
80	Virginia Tech ⊠	81
77	Boston College	72
83	North Carolina St. ⊠	64
87	Maryland	89
77	Georgia Tech	84
86	Duke ⊠	72
73	Florida St. †	58
71	Boston College †	56
89	North Carolina St. †	80
86	Eastern Ky. †	65
81	Michigan St. †	67
74	Southern California †	64
84	Georgetown †	96

Nickname: Tar Heels
Colors: Carolina Blue & White
Arena: Smith Center
Capacity: 21,800; Year Built: 1986
AD: Richard Baddour
SID: Steve Kirschner

N.C. A&T
Greensboro, NC 27411 I

Coach: Jerry Eaves, Louisville 1986

2006-07 RESULTS (15-17)

80	Missouri	101
69	Stetson †	72
49	Army †	63
66	Dayton	79
98	Mars Hill ⊠	66
71	Longwood ⊠	59
67	South Carolina St.	77
92	St. Andrews	58

78	New Mexico	86
66	Arizona St.	71
83	Ohio †	95
71	Baylor	91
80	SMU	76
80	Md.-East. Shore ⊠	66
70	Howard	66
52	Bethune-Cookman	57
82	Florida A&M	78
69	Coppin St.	60
60	Morgan St.	69
80	Norfolk St. ⊠	60
64	Hampton ⊠	70
70	Md.-East. Shore	57
75	Howard	80
55	Bethune-Cookman ⊠	58
90	Florida A&M ⊠	82
58	Coppin St. ⊠	64
91	Morgan St. ⊠	79
104	Norfolk St.	99
79	Hampton	76
53	Delaware St.	62
81	Norfolk St. †	66
66	Florida A&M †	74

Nickname: Aggies
Colors: Blue & Gold
Arena: Ellis Corbett Sports Center
Capacity: 5,700; Year Built: 1978
AD: Dee Todd
SID: Brian Holloway

UNC ASHEVILLE
Asheville, NC 28804-3299 I

Coach: Eddie Biedenbach, North Carolina St. 1968

2006-07 RESULTS (12-19)

87	Montreat ⊠	72
46	Western Caro. ⊠	61
76	Duquesne	77
64	Virginia	81
54	Eastern Ky. ⊠	73
69	Lenoir-Rhyne ⊠	59
75	Furman	67
73	Charlotte	81
84	Tusculum ⊠	66
62	North Carolina	93
65	East Tenn. St.	73
77	South Carolina St.	79
51	South Carolina	71
51	Louisville	66
84	Liberty ⊠	77
60	Coastal Caro. ⊠	68
64	High Point	90
42	Winthrop	61
77	Radford	67
97	VMI ⊠	102
53	Charleston So. ⊠	40
65	Liberty	80
69	Winthrop ⊠	88
78	Brevard ⊠	70
88	VMI	102
67	High Point ⊠	69
78	Radford	68
82	Coastal Caro.	77
73	Charleston So.	56
77	Coastal Caro.	60
60	Winthrop	79

Nickname: Bulldogs
Colors: Royal Blue & White
Arena: Charlie Justice Center
Capacity: 1,100; Year Built: 1963
AD: Janet Cone
SID: Mike Gore

N.C. CENTRAL
Durham, NC 27707 II

Coach: Henry Dickerson, Charleston (W.V.) 1973

2006-07 RESULTS (13-15)

95	Columbus St. ⊠	82
67	Barton ⊠	65

47	East Caro.	68
67	St. Paul's	70
66	Elizabeth City St.	93
77	Augusta St. ⊠	76
66	Shaw ⊠	49
66	North Georgia †	58
63	Columbus St.	74
68	Fayetteville St.	71
64	Bowie St.	85
58	Shaw	54
61	St. Augustine's ⊠	63
75	Livingstone ⊠	64
67	Virginia St.	91
64	St. Augustine's †	75
55	Johnson C. Smith ⊠	60
66	Virginia St. ⊠	65
60	Fayetteville St. ⊠	67
53	Virginia Union ⊠	62
59	Livingstone	51
77	Elizabeth City St. ⊠	71
80	Bowie St. ⊠	75
56	Virginia Union	63
86	St. Paul's ⊠	70
54	Johnson C. Smith	61
75	St. Paul's †	74
68	Virginia Union †	79

Nickname: Eagles
Colors: Maroon & Gray
Arena: McLendon-McDougald Gym
  Capacity: 3,000; Year Built: 1955
AD: William Hayes
SID: Kyle Serba

UNC GREENSBORO
Greensboro, NC 27402-6170.........I

Coach: Mike Dement, East Caro. 1976

2006-07 RESULTS (16-14)

80	Marshall	82
56	Penn St.	69
48	Duke	75
64	East Caro. ⊠	72
79	Gardner-Webb	67
77	Wofford	54
64	Hampton	71
63	Davidson ⊠	66
91	Furman	86
79	St. Peter's ⊠	58
74	Delaware ⊠	64
68	Ga. Southern	47
93	North Carolina St.	95
54	Western Caro.	57
72	Elon	68
51	Virginia Tech ⊠	74
67	Chattanooga ⊠	57
80	Appalachian St. ⊠	76
47	Citadel	44
69	Furman ⊠	54
65	Ga. Southern ⊠	62
65	Davidson	75
75	Wofford	80
59	Col. of Charleston ⊠	81
86	Elon ⊠	73
79	Western Caro. ⊠	68
73	UNC Wilmington ⊠	66
66	Appalachian St.	80
68	Chattanooga	61
71	Furman †	73

Nickname: Spartans
Colors: Gold, White & Navy
Arena: Michael B. Fleming Gym
  Capacity: 2,320; Year Built: 1989
AD: Nelson E. Bobb
SID: Mike Hirschman

UNC PEMBROKE
Pembroke, NC 28372-1510...........II

Coach: Jason Tinsley, Northwestern St. 1989

2006-07 RESULTS (6-22)

66	St. Andrews ⊠	76
72	Lees-McRae †	76

66	King (Tenn.) †	79
64	Fayetteville St. ⊠	74
61	Queens (N.C.)	69
53	Ouachita Baptist †	82
60	Fayetteville St.	78
64	Chowan	61
57	Shaw	72
52	Lincoln Memorial ⊠	64
64	Chowan ⊠	76
69	North Georgia ⊠	56
54	Columbus St. ⊠	69
70	S.C.-Aiken ⊠	45
37	GCSU	66
77	North Georgia	70
39	Lander ⊠	56
54	Clayton St. ⊠	64
51	S.C.-Aiken	62
62	Armstrong Atlantic	60
54	Lander	62
51	Ga. Southwestern ⊠	48
48	Francis Marion ⊠	52
47	S.C. Upstate	64
57	Augusta St.	80
70	Francis Marion	75
52	S.C. Upstate ⊠	69
53	GCSU †	68

Nickname: Braves
Colors: Black & Gold
Arena: English E. Jones Center
  Capacity: 3,000; Year Built: 1972
AD: Dan Kenney
SID: Matt Pellegrin

NORTH CAROLINA ST.
Raleigh, NC 27695-7001 I

Coach: Sidney Lowe, North Carolina St. 1983

2006-07 RESULTS (20-16)

92	Wofford ⊠	88
63	Delaware St. ⊠	43
78	Valparaiso ⊠	64
88	Gardner-Webb ⊠	76
74	Michigan ⊠	67
62	Virginia	67
60	West Virginia †	71
74	Savannah St. ⊠	53
80	Mt. St. Mary's ⊠	65
75	Alabama ⊠	82
71	Cincinnati	80
64	East Caro. ⊠	57
72	UNC Wilmington ⊠	51
95	UNC Greensboro ⊠	93
58	Boston College ⊠	74
76	Clemson ⊠	87
88	Wake Forest ⊠	74
56	Duke ⊠	79
58	Virginia ⊠	71
70	Virginia Tech	59
83	North Carolina ⊠	79
65	Georgia Tech	74
65	Miami (Fla.) ⊠	80
70	Maryland ⊠	85
81	Virginia Tech ⊠	56
64	North Carolina	83
52	Florida St.	78
73	Wake Forest ⊠	66
59	Maryland	79
85	Duke †	80
79	Virginia †	71
72	Virginia Tech †	64
80	North Carolina †	89
63	Drexel	56
69	Marist ⊠	62
66	West Virginia	71

Nickname: Wolfpack
Colors: Red & White
Arena: RBC Center
  Capacity: 19,722; Year Built: 1999
AD: Lee G. Fowler
SID: Annabelle Vaughan

N.C. WESLEYAN
Rocky Mount, NC 27804 III

Coach: John Thompson, UNC Greensboro 1984

2006-07 RESULTS (12-15)

88	LaGrange †	110
81	Oglethorpe	99
79	Mary Washington ⊠	85
92	John Jay †	73
81	Southern Vt. †	75
114	Roanoke Bible ⊠	56
78	York (N.Y.) ⊠	70
57	Piedmont ⊠	78
69	Hampden-Sydney ⊠	81
45	Warner Southern †	82
73	Flagler	83
116	Fla. Christian	87
87	Shenandoah ⊠	79
92	Chris. Newport ⊠	85
80	Greensboro	91
88	Methodist ⊠	86
72	Averett ⊠	81
79	Ferrum	83
83	Shenandoah	78
102	Chris. Newport	96
62	Greensboro	78
73	Methodist	79
73	Ferrum ⊠	86
53	Averett ⊠	70
71	Chris. Newport	69
84	Greensboro †	76
105	Averett †	108

Nickname: Battling Bishops
Colors: Navy Blue & Vega Gold
Arena: Everett Gymnasium
  Capacity: 1,200; Year Built: 1960
AD: John M. Thompson
SID: Rikki C. Rich

UNC WILMINGTON
Wilmington, NC 28403-3297 I

Coach: Benny Moss, Charlotte 1992

2006-07 RESULTS (7-22)

88	Belmont †	83
75	Tennessee †	87
94	Campbell	100
70	Col. of Charleston	91
67	Colorado ⊠	55
51	Northeastern	58
59	East Caro. ⊠	44
62	Missouri St. ⊠	78
74	Toledo	77
51	North Carolina St.	72
69	Hofstra ⊠	80
55	Drexel	69
34	George Mason ⊠	55
80	James Madison ⊠	66
54	Georgia St. ⊠	59
65	VCU	74
61	Towson	75
50	Drexel ⊠	66
70	Old Dominion ⊠	86
65	George Mason ⊠	58
60	Georgia St.	72
67	William & Mary	61
69	Delaware	78
55	William & Mary ⊠	61
68	VCU ⊠	78
66	UNC Greensboro	73
65	Hofstra	68
75	Delaware ⊠	66
52	Towson †	67

Nickname: Seahawks
Colors: Teal, Navy & Gold
Arena: Trask Coliseum
  Capacity: 6,100; Year Built: 1977
AD: Kelly Landry Mehrtens
SID: Joe Browning

NORTH CENTRAL (ILL.)
Naperville, IL 60566-7063.............III

Coach: Todd Raridon, Hastings 1980

2006-07 RESULTS (16-10)

97	East-West U. ⊠	58
63	Bluffton †	49
85	Franklin ⊠	61
69	Aurora ⊠	85
64	Harris-Stowe †	73
85	Robert Morris-S'fiel †	75
74	Benedictine (Ill.)	54
53	Lincoln (Pa.) †	75
66	Gwynedd-Mercy †	44
69	Albion	58
58	Judson (Ill.)	49
52	Wheaton (Ill.)	47
68	North Park ⊠	77
79	Millikin	72
69	Carthage ⊠	80
59	Augustana (Ill.) ⊠	60
84	Elmhurst	98
79	Wheaton (Ill.) ⊠	68
51	Ill. Wesleyan	65
82	Millikin ⊠	76
68	North Park	70
62	Carthage	60
89	Elmhurst ⊠	74
85	Augustana (Ill.) ⊠	81
77	Ill. Wesleyan ⊠	70
67	Augustana (Ill.)	74

Nickname: Cardinals
Colors: Cardinal & White
Arena: Gregory Arena
  Capacity: 3,000; Year Built: 1931
AD: James L. Miller
SID: Josh Hendricks

NORTH DAKOTA
Grand Forks, ND 58202 II

Coach: Brian Jones, UNI 1994

2006-07 RESULTS (11-17)

75	Minn.-Crookston	62
72	Concordia-St. Paul †	76
63	Minn. St. Moorhead	70
84	Northern St. ⊠	88
71	Wayne St. (Neb.) †	66
69	Southwest Minn. St.	78
68	Mary ⊠	57
82	Mayville St. ⊠	75
94	Bemidji St. ⊠	49
90	Dickinson St. ⊠	75
67	Mary	69
85	Minot St. ⊠	67
79	Bemidji St.	56
72	Western Ore.	74
62	Central Wash. †	67
90	St. Cloud St. ⊠	92
91	Minn. St. Mankato ⊠	92
54	South Dakota	70
75	Neb.-Omaha ⊠	73
65	Minn. St. Mankato	71
59	Augustana (S.D.)	67
75	St. Cloud St.	72
68	Augustana (S.D.) ⊠	66
68	Minn. Duluth ⊠	73
68	South Dakota ⊠	69
50	Neb.-Omaha	52
67	Minn. Duluth	91
63	Minn. Duluth	85

Nickname: Fighting Sioux
Colors: Kelly Green & White
Arena: Betty Engelstad Sioux Center
  Capacity: 3,064; Year Built: 2004
AD: Thomas Buning
SID: Jayson Hajdu

RESULTS

NORTH DAKOTA ST.
Fargo, ND 58105-5600 II

Coach: Tim Miles, Mary 1989

2006-07 RESULTS (20-8)

91	Idaho	76
49	Minnesota	63
81	Texas Tech	85
60	Furman ⊠	58
85	Green Bay ⊠	73
57	Princeton †	50
64	Marquette	60
81	Kansas St. ⊠	83
79	Idaho ⊠	59
80	Colorado St.	82
72	Southwest Minn. St. ⊠	68
98	Mayville St. ⊠	60
54	Iowa St.	67
66	Eastern Mich.	74
89	Valley City St. ⊠	50
88	Mary ⊠	47
87	Winston-Salem	63
88	Tex.-Pan American ⊠	58
61	Utah Valley St. ⊠	53
78	South Dakota St.	60
69	IPFW	72
80	NJIT	57
64	Utah Valley St.	66
74	Tex.-Pan American	63
83	Winston-Salem ⊠	68
86	South Dakota St. ⊠	69
104	NJIT ⊠	52
73	IPFW ⊠	57

Nickname: Bison
Colors: Yellow and Green
Arena: Bison Sports Arena
   Capacity: 6,000; Year Built: 1970
AD: Gene Taylor
SID: Ryan Perreault

NORTH FLA.
Jacksonville, FL 32224-2645 II

Coach: Matt Kilcullen, Lehman 1976

2006-07 RESULTS (3-26)

53	St. John's (N.Y.)	74
50	Loyola (Md.) †	65
40	Florida	86
77	Concordia (N.Y.) ⊠	72
44	Fla. Atlantic	59
39	Northwestern	40
32	Belmont	87
54	Lipscomb	68
44	William & Mary	61
61	Binghamton ⊠	79
65	Florida A&M ⊠	66
70	Skidmore ⊠	43
48	Campbell ⊠	78
52	Gardner-Webb ⊠	72
60	Jacksonville ⊠	64
58	East Tenn. St.	77
57	Kennesaw St. ⊠	77
60	Stetson ⊠	63
58	Mercer ⊠	77
49	Campbell	54
46	Gardner-Webb	72
47	Savannah St.	49
61	Jacksonville	75
66	Kennesaw St. ⊠	68
51	East Tenn. St. ⊠	56
63	Stetson	74
59	Mercer	69
73	Lipscomb ⊠	64
54	Belmont ⊠	74

Nickname: Ospreys
Colors: Navy Blue & Gray
Arena: UNF Arena
   Capacity: 5,800; Year Built: 1993
AD: Richard E. Gropper
SID: Tom Strother

NORTH GEORGIA
Dahlonega, GA 30597 II

Coach: Chris Faulkner, North Ga. 1993

2006-07 RESULTS (9-21)

62	Southern Ind. †	85
76	Alas. Fairbanks †	79
87	Pace †	105
66	West Ga. ⊠	73
100	Reinhardt ⊠	75
107	Carver Bible ⊠	68
76	Valdosta St.	71
71	West Ala. †	61
68	West Ga.	83
58	N.C. Central †	66
78	St. Augustine's †	81
56	UNC Pembroke	69
70	Armstrong Atlantic	78
63	Lander ⊠	92
64	Ga. Southwestern ⊠	78
70	UNC Pembroke ⊠	77
56	S.C. Upstate	74
58	Augusta St. ⊠	75
64	Lander	73
77	Columbus St.	84
61	S.C. Upstate ⊠	76
63	GCSU	86
69	S.C.-Aiken ⊠	72
64	Francis Marion	61
61	Clayton St. ⊠	59
70	S.C.-Aiken	67
78	Francis Marion ⊠	75
79	Dist. Columbia †	71
62	Fla. Gulf Coast	99
66	Ga. Southwestern †	76

Nickname: Saints
Colors: Royal blue & white
Arena: Memorial Hall
Capacity: 2,500
AD: Randy Dunn
SID: Travis Jarome

NORTH GREENVILLE
Tigerville, SC 29688 II

Coach: Chad Lister, Furman 1995

2006-07 RESULTS (16-13)

82	Wingate ⊠	103
86	Warren Wilson ⊠	37
58	Presbyterian	81
81	Allen ⊠	73
67	Mars Hill ⊠	79
72	Virginia Intermont ⊠	69
67	Carson-Newman	79
47	Coker	73
81	Limestone	86
69	Anderson (S.C.)	59
96	Atlanta Christian ⊠	62
80	Virginia Intermont	67
79	Limestone ⊠	90
65	Carson-Newman ⊠	98
87	Belmont Abbey ⊠	80
83	Brevard	66
74	Morris	88
65	Lincoln Memorial	66
73	Allen	66
62	Anderson (S.C.) ⊠	54
82	Lees-McRae ⊠	71
77	Wingate	103
107	Morris ⊠	92
68	Brevard ⊠	72
92	Warren Wilson	40
74	Mars Hill	73
93	Lincoln Memorial ⊠	90
75	Pensacola Christian †	71
62	Emmanuel (Ga.)	71

Nickname: Crusaders
Colors: Red, Black, and White
Arena: Hayes Gymnasium
   Capacity: 1,800; Year Built: 1950
AD: Jan McDonald
SID: Rhett Burns

NORTH PARK
Chicago, IL 60625-4895 III

Coach: Paul Brenegan, Loras 1995

2006-07 RESULTS (13-12)

80	Mt. St. Joseph	82
69	Kalamazoo †	64
68	Concordia (Ill.)	31
62	Illinois Col.	66
65	Robert Morris-S'fiel ⊠	64
75	Eureka	66
87	Loras ⊠	69
91	Rockford ⊠	88
74	Judson (Ill.)	57
57	Lake Forest †	56
56	Coe †	70
48	Augustana (Ill.)	62
73	Millikin	65
77	North Central (Ill.)	68
60	Wheaton (Ill.)	73
76	Elmhurst	79
90	Ill. Wesleyan	81
62	Carthage ⊠	64
76	Millikin	72
56	Augustana (Ill.) ⊠	71
73	Wheaton (Ill.)	85
70	North Central (Ill.) ⊠	68
80	Elmhurst	83
79	Carthage	85
80	Ill. Wesleyan ⊠	81

Nickname: Vikings
Colors: Blue & Gold
Arena: North Park Gymnasium
   Capacity: 1,300; Year Built: 1958
AD: Jack Surridge
SID: Sara Carlson

NORTH TEXAS
Denton, TX 76207 I

Coach: Johnny Jones, LSU 1985

2006-07 RESULTS (23-11)

85	Cameron ⊠	47
90	Charlotte	72
81	Texas-Arlington ⊠	83
71	Rice	69
65	Tulsa	63
95	Texas St. ⊠	77
57	Nebraska	76
76	Stephen F. Austin	70
74	Nicholls St.	71
93	New Orleans	97
86	Western Ky.	85
94	Jarvis Christian ⊠	70
93	Belhaven ⊠	66
91	Denver ⊠	79
75	Ark.-Little Rock	86
60	Arkansas St.	84
73	La.-Lafayette ⊠	72
66	Florida Int'l.	67
76	Fla. Atlantic ⊠	59
66	Middle Tenn. ⊠	53
89	South Ala.	90
98	Troy ⊠	57
74	Western Ky. ⊠	70
62	New Orleans ⊠	64
62	La.-Monroe	66
78	Denver	65
74	Ark.-Little Rock ⊠	69
71	Arkansas St. ⊠	74
72	La.-Lafayette	70
93	La.-Lafayette ⊠	78
77	La.-Monroe †	71
59	Middle Tenn. †	52
83	Arkansas St. †	75
58	Memphis †	73

Nickname: Mean Green
Colors: Green & White
Arena: Super Pit
   Capacity: 10,032; Year Built: 1973
AD: Rick Villarreal
SID: Stephen Howard

NORTHEASTERN
Boston, MA 02115 I

Coach: Bill Coen, Hamilton 1983

2006-07 RESULTS (13-19)

58	Syracuse	81
52	Pittsburgh	78
52	Oakland †	67
56	Massachusetts †	79
73	Boston U. ⊠	54
69	Rider	70
58	UNC Wilmington ⊠	51
53	Connecticut	81
51	New Hampshire ⊠	41
51	Detroit	60
41	Louisville	61
82	Boston College	87
67	Old Dominion ⊠	73
57	William & Mary	60
44	VCU	64
84	Georgia St. ⊠	69
84	Hofstra	74
41	Drexel	67
53	George Mason	78
67	James Madison ⊠	51
73	Delaware	64
59	Drexel ⊠	68
61	Towson	74
66	Hofstra	82
65	Towson ⊠	55
67	James Madison	64
65	Georgia St.	71
71	Maine ⊠	61
70	Delaware	61
73	George Mason ⊠	50
77	Delaware †	67
50	Drexel †	64

Nickname: Huskies
Colors: Red & Black
Arena: Matthews Arena
   Capacity: 6,000; Year Built: 1910
AD: David O'Brien
SID: Mark Harris

NORTHEASTERN ST.
Tahlequah, OK 74464-2399 II

Coach: Larry Gipson, Heidelberg 1974

2006-07 RESULTS (10-16)

70	Emporia St. ⊠	75
58	Emporia St.	70
73	Mo. Western St. †	74
44	John Brown ⊠	48
43	Tex. A&M-Kingsville	55
83	Arkansas Tech ⊠	79
69	Mo. Southern St.	77
66	Abilene Christian ⊠	65
62	Angelo St. ⊠	67
79	Haskell ⊠	57
63	Eastern N.M.	58
57	West Tex. A&M	66
76	Rhema	51
55	Midwestern St. ⊠	64
59	Tex. A&M-Commerce ⊠	63
59	Central Okla.	75
84	Cameron ⊠	72
67	Southwestern Okla.	69
75	East Central ⊠	69
52	Southeastern Okla.	69
75	Central Okla. ⊠	84
67	Tex. A&M-Commerce	76
73	Cameron	63
81	Southwestern Okla. ⊠	73
70	East Central	56
56	Southeastern Okla. ⊠	72

Nickname: Redmen
Colors: Green & White
Arena: Dobbins Fieldhouse
   Capacity: 1,200; Year Built: 1954
AD: Eddie Griffin
SID: Scott Pettus

NORTHERN ARIZ.

Flagstaff, AZ 86011-5400 I

Coach: Mike Adras, UC Santa Barbara 1983

2006-07 RESULTS (18-12)

57	Kansas	91
75	Arizona St.	71
79	Arizona	101
85	Mont. St.-Northern ⊠	62
104	Mississippi Val. ⊠	77
73	San Francisco	82
53	UNLV †	93
84	San Francisco ⊠	62
106	Haskell ⊠	72
86	Pepperdine	101
60	Cal Poly	82
96	Sacramento St. ⊠	82
73	Weber St. ⊠	81
85	Portland St. ⊠	78
109	Eastern Wash. ⊠	101
86	Northern Colo.	88
94	Sacramento St.	71
91	Eastern Wash.	80
78	Portland St.	83
71	Montana ⊠	74
86	Montana St. ⊠	76
102	Idaho St.	98
79	Weber St.	86
73	Idaho St. ⊠	63
78	San Jose St. ⊠	67
88	Montana	81
92	Montana St.	84
89	Northern Colo. ⊠	77
78	Montana †	71
80	Weber St.	88

Nickname: Lumberjacks
Colors: Blue & Gold & Sage
Arena: Walkup Skydome
  Capacity: 7,000; Year Built: 1977
AD: James E. Fallis
SID: Steve Shaff

NORTHERN COLO.

Greeley, CO 80639 II

Coach: Tad Boyle, Kansas 1985

2006-07 RESULTS (4-24)

42	Ball St.	81
58	Purdue	90
91	UC-Colo. Springs ⊠	96
68	Denver	74
89	Colo. Christian ⊠	68
67	Oregon St. ⊠	69
51	Arizona St.	66
86	Colorado	88
66	Colorado St.	75
74	Denver ⊠	59
53	Bowling Green	63
61	Eastern Mich.	71
60	Weber St. ⊠	61
70	Sacramento St. ⊠	74
87	Eastern Wash. ⊠	88
66	Portland St. ⊠	79
88	Northern Ariz. ⊠	86
60	Idaho St.	70
71	Portland St.	86
79	Eastern Wash.	91
57	Montana St. ⊠	58
51	Montana ⊠	68
84	Sacramento St.	81
65	Weber St.	76
55	Idaho St. ⊠	66
66	Montana St.	89
64	Montana	85
77	Northern Ariz.	89

Nickname: Bears
Colors: Blue & Gold
Arena: Butler Hancock Sports Pavilion
  Capacity: 4,500; Year Built: 1975
AD: Jay Hinrichs
SID: Kyle Schwartz

NORTHERN ILL.

De Kalb, IL 60115-2854 I

Coach: Rob Judson, Illinois 1980

2006-07 RESULTS (7-23)

84	St. Mary's (Minn.) ⊠	69
87	Duquesne	82
85	Duquesne ⊠	74
62	Winthrop	72
48	Ill.-Chicago ⊠	71
70	Ga. Southern †	72
81	Troy †	84
52	Michigan	67
53	Lamar	74
78	Stephen F. Austin	86
63	Marist	67
59	Bucknell †	77
70	Western Mich. ⊠	68
62	Eastern Mich.	63
64	Central Mich. ⊠	67
60	Ball St.	71
60	Toledo	76
64	Akron ⊠	87
49	Kent St. ⊠	68
59	Miami (Ohio)	62
74	Buffalo	80
73	Bowling Green ⊠	51
81	Ohio	74
55	Ball St. ⊠	57
76	Green Bay ⊠	82
83	Toledo ⊠	86
64	Central Mich.	71
54	Western Mich.	68
76	Eastern Mich. ⊠	69
62	Western Mich. †	67

Nickname: Huskies
Colors: Cardinal & Black
Arena: Convocation Center
  Capacity: 9,100; Year Built: 2002
AD: James Phillips
SID: Matt Brendich

UNI

Cedar Falls, IA 50614 I

Coach: Ben Jacobson, North Dakota 1994

2006-07 RESULTS (18-13)

68	Nicholls St. †	63
83	Pepperdine †	58
61	Washington	70
69	Milwaukee ⊠	58
69	South Dakota St. ⊠	56
70	Iowa St. ⊠	57
57	Bucknell	48
57	Iowa	55
85	UMKC ⊠	53
67	Loyola (Ill.)	76
83	Wartburg ⊠	61
76	Bradley ⊠	65
63	Wichita St.	59
64	Evansville ⊠	61
66	Southern Ill.	61
64	Illinois St.	67
54	Creighton ⊠	62
75	Missouri St.	65
74	Indiana St. ⊠	64
54	Southern Ill.	56
61	Drake	74
61	Wichita St. ⊠	67
79	Evansville	71
46	Indiana St.	59
59	Drake ⊠	67
58	Missouri St. ⊠	62
55	Creighton	66
64	Nevada	79
79	Bradley	70
71	Illinois St. ⊠	66
48	Bradley †	51

Nickname: Panthers
Colors: Purple & Old Gold
Arena: McLeod Center
  Capacity: 7,018; Year Built: 2006
AD: Rick Hartzell
SID: Josh Lehman

NORTHERN KY.

Highland Heights, KY 41099 II

Coach: Dave Bezold, Viterbo 1990

2006-07 RESULTS (24-9)

73	Ferris St. ⊠	59
75	Wayne St. (Mich.) ⊠	69
66	Bellarmine	78
86	Thomas More ⊠	61
68	Quincy ⊠	70
81	SIU Edwardsville ⊠	76
89	Tiffin ⊠	51
53	Findlay	59
94	Cincy-Clermont ⊠	58
100	North Ala.	94
73	Wis.-Parkside	80
72	Lewis	66
101	Ky. Christian ⊠	60
81	Mo.-Rolla ⊠	73
68	Mo.-St. Louis ⊠	53
76	Ky. Wesleyan	65
71	Southern Ind.	83
67	Indianapolis ⊠	62
85	St. Joseph's (Ind.) ⊠	60
69	Drury	78
87	Rockhurst	63
82	Lewis ⊠	66
70	Wis.-Parkside ⊠	66
67	Ky. Wesleyan ⊠	49
91	Bellarmine ⊠	82
65	St. Joseph's (Ind.)	69
68	Indianapolis	60
71	Rockhurst †	61
69	Drury †	62
61	Southern Ind.	63
73	Drury †	68
60	Findlay	56
42	Grand Valley St. †	66

Nickname: Norse
Colors: Gold, Black & White
Arena: Regents Hall
  Capacity: 1,685; Year Built: 1972
AD: Jane Meier
SID: Don Owen

NORTHERN MICH.

Marquette, MI 49855-5391 II

Coach: Dean Ellis, Northern Mich. 1983

2006-07 RESULTS (18-11)

59	Green Bay	76
71	Wayne St. (Mich.)	76
80	Minn. Duluth	77
86	Minn. St. Mankato †	88
69	Michigan Tech ⊠	78
56	Findlay	70
72	Saginaw Valley ⊠	71
73	St. Norbert ⊠	57
95	Wis.-Stout ⊠	71
82	Ashland ⊠	80
123	Finlandia ⊠	68
101	Wis.-Stevens Point ⊠	92
93	St. Cloud St.	91
75	Lake Superior St. ⊠	77
49	Grand Valley St.	87
64	Ferris St.	65
52	Grand Valley St. ⊠	63
65	Hillsdale	57
75	Wayne St. (Mich.)	55
69	Northwood (Mich.)	44
77	Saginaw Valley	55
82	Mercyhurst ⊠	69
80	Gannon ⊠	72
73	Lake Superior St.	64
81	Ferris St.	89
94	Northwood (Mich.) ⊠	80
56	Michigan Tech	34
77	Michigan Tech ⊠	54
87	Grand Valley St. †	88

Nickname: Wildcats
Colors: Old Gold & Olive Green
Arena: Berry Events Center
  Capacity: 4,000; Year Built: 1999
AD: Kenneth Godfrey
SID: Dave Faiella

NORTHERN ST.

Aberdeen, SD 57401 II

Coach: Don Meyer, Northern Colo. 1967

2006-07 RESULTS (21-8)

84	Mt. Marty ⊠	55
78	Midland Lutheran ⊠	67
72	Augustana (S.D.) ⊠	70
88	North Dakota	84
60	Northwest Mo. St. ⊠	88
73	Neb.-Kearney ⊠	84
62	Winona St.	90
77	Upper Iowa	71
82	Wayne St. (Neb.) ⊠	66
72	Southwest Minn. St. ⊠	75
78	Jamestown ⊠	64
76	Black Hills St. ⊠	48
69	Hastings ⊠	65
81	Minn. St. Moorhead ⊠	60
58	Concordia-St. Paul ⊠	76
84	Minn.-Crookston ⊠	60
87	Bemidji St. ⊠	51
60	Mary ⊠	57
66	Winona St. ⊠	76
82	Upper Iowa ⊠	59
68	Southwest Minn. St.	75
82	Wayne St. (Neb.)	68
72	Concordia-St. Paul ⊠	65
75	Minn. St. Moorhead ⊠	69
61	Bemidji St.	57
90	Minn.-Crookston	72
77	Mary	59
68	Minn. St. Moorhead ⊠	62
63	Southwest Minn. St. †	82

Nickname: Wolves
Colors: Maroon & Gold
Arena: Wachs Arena
  Capacity: 8,057; Year Built: 1987
AD: Robert A. Olson
SID: Melissa Wolf

NORTHLAND

Ashland, WI 54806 III

Coach: Rob Robinson, Mt. Senario 1993

2006-07 RESULTS (9-16)

81	Northland Bapt.	76
72	Wis.-Superior	65
51	Wis.-Stout ⊠	78
61	Finlandia	73
46	Minn. Duluth	88
87	St. Scholastica	96
47	Wis.-Eau Claire ⊠	75
63	Milwaukee Engr.	71
74	Carthage	84
74	Crown (Minn.)	59
76	Northwestern (Minn.) ⊠	87
53	Minn.-Morris	99
62	Presentation	47
65	Bethany Lutheran	86
66	Martin Luther	73
79	Wis.-Superior ⊠	74
45	Martin Luther ⊠	76
53	Bethany Lutheran ⊠	81
70	Finlandia ⊠	56
38	Northwestern (Minn.)	72
83	Crown (Minn.) ⊠	58
74	Northland Bapt. ⊠	73
67	Presentation ⊠	80
57	Minn.-Morris ⊠	65
75	St. Scholastica ⊠	71

Nickname: Lumberjacks
Colors: Navy, Orange & White
Arena: Kendrigan Gymnasium
  Capacity: 1,200; Year Built: 1964
AD: Steve Wammer
SID: Eric Grice

RESULTS

NORTHWEST MO. ST.
Maryville, MO 64468-6001 II

Coach: Steve Tappmeyer, Southeast Mo. St. 1979

2006-07 RESULTS (24-7)
86	Upper Iowa ⊠	41
75	Lincoln (Mo.) ⊠	46
74	Graceland (Iowa) ⊠	54
88	Northern St.	60
57	Mary †	65
111	Principia	36
77	St. Mary (Kan.)	36
81	Southwest Baptist	80
59	Metro St. †	53
70	Midwestern St. †	72
72	Fort Hays St.	54
78	Mo. Western St. ⊠	72
69	Washburn	58
57	Mo. Southern St.	59
69	Pittsburg St. ⊠	64
70	Truman ⊠	52
55	Central Mo.	69
89	Emporia St.	72
68	Southwest Baptist ⊠	63
63	Emporia St. ⊠	58
82	Central Mo. ⊠	64
64	Truman	50
56	Pittsburg St.	74
87	Washburn ⊠	85
75	Mo. Southern St. ⊠	60
69	Mo. Western St.	61
66	Fort Hays St.	40
89	Mo. Southern St. †	56
70	Pittsburg St. †	76
74	Pittsburg St. †	53
61	Central Mo.	72

Nickname: Bearcats
Colors: Green & White
Arena: Bearcat Arena
  Capacity: 2,500; Year Built: 1955
AD: Bob Boerigter
SID: Chad Walller

NORTHWEST NAZARENE
Nampa, ID 83686 II

Coach: Tim Hills, Corban 1968

2006-07 RESULTS (10-17)
63	Colorado Mines	75
85	Mesa St. †	91
63	Eastern Ore. ⊠	69
61	Pacific (Ore.) ⊠	53
79	Alderson-Broaddus ⊠	91
88	Mont. St.-Billings ⊠	74
67	Dixie St. †	68
82	Westminster (Utah)	83
109	Warner Pacific ⊠	76
70	Mont. St.-Billings	50
90	Mont. St.-Billings	89
63	Seattle ⊠	76
95	Western Wash. ⊠	72
60	Alas. Fairbanks	79
57	Alas. Anchorage	60
80	Seattle Pacific ⊠	108
74	Western Ore.	70
79	St. Martin's	94
70	Seattle Pacific	88
53	Central Wash.	83
75	Alas. Anchorage ⊠	89
88	St. Martin's ⊠	78
85	Western Ore. ⊠	69
82	Western Wash.	93
63	Seattle	67
77	Alas. Fairbanks ⊠	67
91	Central Wash. ⊠	105

Nickname: Crusaders
Colors: Red and Black
Arena: Montgomery Fieldhouse
  Capacity: 3,500; Year Built: 1971
AD: Rich Sanders
SID: Craig Stensgaard

NORTHWESTERN
Evanston, IL 60208 I

Coach: Bill Carmody, Union (N.Y.) 1975

2006-07 RESULTS (13-18)
61	Cornell ⊠	64
49	DePaul ⊠	39
53	Stanford	58
64	Brown ⊠	40
40	North Fla. ⊠	39
61	Miami (Fla.) ⊠	59
77	Western Mich. ⊠	75
41	Wheaton (Ill.) ⊠	39
65	Tennessee Tech †	66
62	P.R.-Mayaguez †	55
77	Utah †	44
66	Loyola (Md.) ⊠	60
85	Northwestern St. ⊠	59
57	Penn St.	83
46	Michigan ⊠	58
45	Michigan St.	66
50	Wisconsin ⊠	56
41	Ohio St.	73
55	Minnesota ⊠	40
50	Ohio St. ⊠	59
55	Minnesota	62
52	Wisconsin	69
43	Illinois ⊠	58
53	Penn St. ⊠	51
58	Iowa ⊠	66
37	Illinois	48
67	Tex.-Pan American ⊠	56
68	Purdue ⊠	75
65	Indiana ⊠	69
50	Purdue	73
57	Michigan St. †	62

Nickname: Wildcats
Colors: Purple & White
Arena: Welsh-Ryan Arena
  Capacity: 8,117; Year Built: 1952
AD: Mark Murphy
SID: Adam Widman

NORTHWESTERN (MINN.)
St. Paul, MN 55113 III

Coach: Tim Grosz, Northwestern (Minn.) 1992

2006-07 RESULTS (22-9)
99	North Central (Minn. ⊠	81
65	Mayville St. ⊠	83
85	Macalester ⊠	70
79	Hamline ⊠	78
81	Hannibal-La Grange †	69
91	Trinity Int'l	75
74	Luther ⊠	62
76	Crown (Minn.) ⊠	56
91	North Central (Minn.)	46
91	Augsburg	77
82	Gordon	87
73	Keene St.	82
93	St. Scholastica ⊠	82
87	Northland	76
72	Martin Luther ⊠	69
92	Bethany Lutheran ⊠	72
80	Presentation ⊠	57
72	Minn.-Morris ⊠	62
78	Minn.-Morris ⊠	54
56	Presentation	58
72	Northland ⊠	38
83	St. Scholastica ⊠	95
69	Bethany Lutheran	59
75	Martin Luther	70
81	Crown (Minn.)	57
75	Martin Luther ⊠	65
90	St. Scholastica ⊠	92
95	Bethel (Ind.) ⊠	96
73	Dallas Baptist †	68
72	Grace (Ind.) †	90
70	Emmanuel (Ga.) †	75

Nickname: Eagles
Colors: Purple, Gold, White
Arena: Ericksen Center
  Capacity: 1,272; Year Built: 1996

AD: Matt Hill
SID: Corey Borchardt

NORTHWESTERN ST.
Natchitoches, LA 71497-0003 I

Coach: Mike McConathy, Louisiana Tech 1977

2006-07 RESULTS (17-15)
88	Utah St. ⊠	71
76	Oklahoma St.	79
87	Louisville	100
84	Henderson St. ⊠	64
71	New Orleans	67
89	Centenary (La.) ⊠	86
67	Marquette	83
51	Princeton †	53
64	Southern U. ⊠	57
78	Hawaii	89
67	DePaul	97
59	Northwestern	85
81	Texas St.	85
78	Texas-Arlington	65
57	A&M-Corpus Christi ⊠	69
82	UTSA ⊠	62
98	McNeese St. ⊠	90
81	Lamar	68
98	Nicholls St.	88
98	Southeastern La. ⊠	91
78	Central Ark. ⊠	66
80	Sam Houston St. ⊠	90
67	Stephen F. Austin	57
81	McNeese St.	83
84	Tennessee Tech	85
92	Nicholls St. ⊠	93
71	Southeastern La.	65
89	Lamar ⊠	82
86	Central Ark	92
85	Stephen F. Austin †	76
78	Lamar †	65
78	A&M-Corpus Christi †	81

Nickname: Demons
Colors: Purple & White with Orange trim
Arena: Prather Coliseum
  Capacity: 4,300; Year Built: 1963
AD: Gregory S. Burke
SID: Doug Ireland

NORTHWOOD (MICH.)
Midland, MI 48640-2398 II

Coach: Bob Taylor, Arkansas Tech 1980

2006-07 RESULTS (9-18)
58	Aquinas ⊠	73
53	Lewis	72
63	Ferris St. ⊠	69
53	Grand Valley St. ⊠	72
52	Michigan Tech	70
52	Lake Superior St.	50
87	Marygrove ⊠	49
89	Slippery Rock †	87
43	Mercyhurst	72
79	Alma ⊠	67
84	St. Joseph's (Ind.) ⊠	83
57	Hillsdale ⊠	66
60	Wayne St. (Mich.) ⊠	69
74	Mercyhurst	66
60	Gannon ⊠	52
77	Ashland	85
59	Findlay	74
44	Northern Mich. ⊠	69
57	Michigan Tech ⊠	66
79	Rochester College ⊠	63
79	Ferris St.	71
49	Grand Valley St	74
65	Saginaw Valley ⊠	74
57	Hillsdale	75
80	Northern Mich.	94
60	Lake Superior St. ⊠	64
81	Saginaw Valley	102

Nickname: Timberwolves
Colors: Columbia Blue & White
Arena: E.W. Bennett Sports Center

Capacity: 1,500; Year Built: 1979
AD: Pat Riepma
SID: Travis McCurdy

NORWICH
Northfield, VT 05663 III

Coach: Paul Booth, St. Joseph (Vt.) 1983

2006-07 RESULTS (13-12)
76	New England †	59
67	Hamilton	75
55	Plattsburgh St.	72
36	Western New Eng. ⊠	53
70	Lyndon St. ⊠	62
64	Babson ⊠	71
86	Southern Vt. ⊠	90
78	Albertus Magnus	63
62	Johnson & Wales (RI)	64
86	Southern Vt.	65
62	Rivier ⊠	68
47	Western New Eng.	56
86	Daniel Webster ⊠	52
77	Emerson	76
70	Albertus Magnus ⊠	67
76	Suffolk	74
61	Middlebury ⊠	57
78	Rivier	82
67	Emmanuel (Mass.) ⊠	66
74	Daniel Webster	57
68	Emmanuel (Mass.)	67
65	Emerson ⊠	76
59	Johnson & Wales (RI) ⊠	62
87	Suffolk ⊠	79
55	Emmanuel (Mass.) ⊠	60

Nickname: Cadets
Colors: Maroon & Gold
Arena: Andrews Hall
  Capacity: 1,500; Year Built: 1980
AD: Anthony A. Mariano
SID: Scott C. Miller

NOTRE DAME
Notre Dame, IN 46556 I

Coach: Mike Brey, George Washington 1982

2006-07 RESULTS (24-8)
92	IPFW ⊠	49
69	Butler †	71
92	Lafayette †	60
74	Citadel ⊠	50
93	Lehigh ⊠	57
90	Winston-Salem ⊠	45
81	Maryland †	74
99	Alabama ⊠	85
94	Elon ⊠	63
86	Portland ⊠	69
88	Army ⊠	47
101	Rider ⊠	51
95	Stony Brook ⊠	66
78	Louisville ⊠	62
48	Georgetown	66
61	West Virginia ⊠	58
88	Seton Hall ⊠	76
87	Villanova ⊠	102
82	South Fla. ⊠	58
68	St. John's (N.Y.)	71
66	Villanova ⊠	63
103	Syracuse	91
63	South Fla.	69
66	DePaul	67
81	Providence ⊠	78
76	Cincinnati	64
78	DePaul ⊠	54
85	Marquette ⊠	73
73	Rutgers	66
89	Syracuse †	83
82	Georgetown †	84
64	Winthrop †	74

Nickname: Fighting Irish
Colors: Blue & Gold
Arena: Joyce Center
  Capacity: 11,418; Year Built: 1968

AD: Kevin White
SID: Bernadette Cafarelli

NOTRE DAME DE NAMUR
Belmont, CA 94002-1997 II

Coach: George Puou, San Jose St. 1987

2006-07 RESULTS (9-18)
61	San Fran. St.	53
59	Occidental †	66
69	UC Santa Cruz †	58
84	Western Wash.	70
62	St. Martin's	56
63	Fresno Pacific ☒	58
62	Humboldt St.	76
71	Western Ore. †	80
65	Menlo	67
62	BYU-Hawaii	71
65	BYU-Hawaii	85
60	Hawaii Pacific	71
62	Chaminade ☒	64
70	Chaminade ☒	75
70	Hawaii-Hilo ☒	78
77	Grand Canyon ☒	83
49	Grand Canyon ☒	51
64	Dixie St.	63
71	Hawaii Pacific ☒	55
55	Hawaii Pacific	59
62	BYU-Hawaii ☒	81
73	Hawaii-Hilo	69
60	Hawaii-Hilo	71
48	Chaminade	78
65	Dixie St. ☒	51
62	Grand Canyon	82
68	Grand Canyon	80

Nickname: Argonauts
Colors: Vegas gold, white & navy blue
Arena: Gleason Center
Capacity: 900
AD: Joshua Doody
SID: Scott Kimmelman

NOVA SOUTHEASTERN
Fort Lauderdale, FL 33314 II

Coach: Gary Tuell, Louisville 1973

2006-07 RESULTS (13-15)
60	Ala.-Huntsville	79
108	North Ala. ☒	107
96	Valdosta St. ☒	82
66	Henderson St. †	59
61	West Fla.	77
60	St. Leo	52
91	West Fla. ☒	69
73	Ala.-Huntsville ☒	83
66	Valdosta St.	97
76	Fla. Southern ☒	72
67	Rollins	69
69	Barry ☒	63
61	Eckerd ☒	76
56	Lynn ☒	61
65	Florida Tech	59
59	Fla. Gulf Coast	70
72	Tampa ☒	80
50	Barry	61
73	Fla. Southern	68
79	Rollins ☒	80
55	St. Leo ☒	54
57	Eckerd ☒	81
66	Lynn	62
59	Florida Tech	63
75	Fla. Gulf Coast ☒	85
73	Tampa	64
71	Tampa †	55
49	Rollins †	62

Nickname: Sharks
Colors: Navy Blue & Gray
Arena: University Center
Capacity: 5,750; Year Built: 2006
AD: Michael Mominey
SID: Robert Prior

NYACK
Nyack, NY 10960-3698 II

Coach: John D. Jones, Liberty 1989

2006-07 RESULTS (9-18)
44	St. Rose	71
81	Assumption ☒	64
62	Molloy ☒	78
65	Post ☒	70
67	Dominican (N.Y.)	79
75	Phila. Sciences ☒	67
48	Holy Family	61
67	Rollins	81
70	Southern Conn. St. †	72
50	Le Moyne ☒	69
52	Goldey-Beacom ☒	64
59	Philadelphia U.	68
85	Columbia Union ☒	71
106	Wilmington (Del.) ☒	85
56	Caldwell ☒	67
67	Felician	79
60	Phila. Sciences	59
73	Post	85
62	Holy Family ☒	68
78	Bloomfield ☒	67
82	Goldey-Beacom	66
68	Dominican (N.Y.) ☒	56
62	Philadelphia U. ☒	73
82	Felician ☒	73
54	Caldwell	73
69	Bloomfield	78
70	Wilmington (Del.)	76

Nickname: Warriors
Colors: Crimson, Grey, Navy Blue
Arena: Bowman Center
Capacity: 1,300; Year Built: 1974
AD: Keith Davie
SID: Josh Thompson

OAKLAND
Rochester, MI 48309-4401 I

Coach: Greg Kampe, Bowling Green 1978

2006-07 RESULTS (19-14)
81	Defiance ☒	42
74	Green Bay ☒	57
56	Massachusetts †	65
67	Northeastern †	52
55	Pittsburgh	66
67	Duquesne	53
53	Michigan St.	71
61	Cincinnati	68
76	Milwaukee ☒	70
66	Eastern Mich.	54
46	Miami (Ohio)	72
57	Arkansas	91
53	UCLA	74
62	Marquette	80
88	Toledo ☒	78
62	IUPUI ☒	57
78	Chicago St. ☒	79
81	Valparaiso	76
79	Western Ill.	52
77	Southern Utah ☒	69
78	UMKC ☒	60
63	Oral Roberts	73
82	Centenary (La.)	74
70	IUPUI	60
63	Western Ill. ☒	64
64	Valparaiso ☒	61
76	UMKC	80
85	Southern Utah	87
70	Centenary (La.) ☒	63
85	Oral Roberts ☒	84
74	Western Ill. †	57
83	UMKC †	79
67	Oral Roberts †	71

Nickname: Golden Grizzlies
Colors: Black and Gold
Arena: Athletics Center 'O'Rena
Capacity: 4,000; Year Built: 1998
AD: Tracy Huth
SID: Phil Hess

OAKLAND CITY
Oakland City, IN 47660-1099 II

Coach: Mike Sandifar, Okla. Panhandle 1971

2006-07 RESULTS (16-12)
132	Ind.-East ☒	58
69	BYU-Hawaii	93
56	BYU-Hawaii	97
84	Upper Iowa ☒	83
52	Indiana St.	66
116	Great Lake Christian ☒	68
68	Mid-Continent ☒	59
90	Ohio Valley ☒	86
97	St. Louis Christian ☒	60
97	Boyce	43
62	Mo.-Rolla	78
70	Upper Iowa	74
59	Central St. (Ohio)	80
78	Robert Morris-S'fiel ☒	74
90	Logan Chiropractic	39
66	Ala.-Huntsville	82
63	Mo.-Rolla ☒	59
57	SIU Edwardsville	74
112	Boyce ☒	53
95	Ohio St.-Marion ☒	51
95	St. Louis Christian	93
92	Calvary Bible ☒	50
72	Central St. (Ohio) ☒	74
78	Ala.-Huntsville	77
125	Messenger	49
84	Bethel (Ind.) ☒	91
71	Mid-Continent	73
82	Dallas Baptist ☒	93

Nickname: Mighty Oaks
Colors: Navy & White
Arena: Johnson Center
Capacity: 1,600; Year Built: 1987
AD: Mike Sandifar
SID: Dave Terrell

OBERLIN
Oberlin, OH 44074 III

Coach: Isaiah Cavaco, Yale 2001

2006-07 RESULTS (5-20)
66	Brockport St.	78
60	St. Lawrence †	80
66	Baldwin-Wallace	81
52	Wash. & Lee	65
78	Case Reserve ☒	64
52	Wabash	50
76	Wooster	95
71	Hiram ☒	74
65	Wilmington (Ohio)	76
40	Adrian	77
65	Carnegie Mellon ☒	91
41	Wittenberg	71
72	Anderson (Ind.) ☒	73
48	Denison	75
63	Kenyon	62
68	Allegheny	93
59	Earlham	76
59	Ohio Wesleyan ☒	96
61	Wabash	66
82	Denison ☒	76
74	Hiram	82
69	Allegheny ☒	74
66	Kenyon	73
59	Ohio Wesleyan	96
79	Earlham ☒	76

Nickname: Yeomen
Colors: Crimson & Gold
Arena: Philips Gymnasium
Capacity: 1,800; Year Built: 1971
AD: Joe Karlgaard
SID: Zachary Pretzer

OCCIDENTAL
Los Angeles, CA 90041 III

Coach: Brian Newhall, Occidental 1983

2006-07 RESULTS (19-6)
63	St. Thomas (Minn.) †	72
76	La Sierra ☒	70
66	Notre Dame de Namur †	59
71	Cal St. Stanislaus	75
62	Cal Poly	81
70	La Sierra	55
67	Chapman ☒	62
92	Wis. Lutheran ☒	65
78	Williams ☒	65
71	Robert Morris-S'fiel ☒	65
103	Caltech ☒	40
71	Claremont-M-S ☒	56
70	Pomona-Pitzer ☒	54
68	Cal Lutheran	56
106	Redlands ☒	109
70	La Verne	49
82	Whittier ☒	60
108	Caltech	31
51	Claremont-M-S	68
76	Pomona-Pitzer	59
41	Cal Lutheran ☒	40
116	Redlands	106
85	La Verne ☒	54
63	Whittier	61
51	Mississippi Col.	68

Nickname: Tigers
Colors: Orange & Black
Arena: Rush Gymnasium
Capacity: 1,800; Year Built: 1967
AD: Dixon Farmer
SID: Andrew Holmes

OGLETHORPE
Atlanta, GA 30319-2797 III

Coach: Philip Ponder, LaGrange 1995

2006-07 RESULTS (14-12)
98	Carver Bible ☒	72
99	N.C. Wesleyan ☒	81
88	Maryville (Tenn.) †	92
87	LaGrange †	83
73	Emory	77
77	Sewanee	82
95	Piedmont ☒	90
63	Huntingdon	59
87	Piedmont	79
57	Centre ☒	76
70	DePauw ☒	76
76	Millsaps	78
92	Rhodes	68
90	LaGrange	95
92	Sewanee ☒	75
80	Maryville (Tenn.) ☒	84
80	Southwestern (Tex.)	75
81	Trinity (Tex.)	75
92	Austin ☒	80
81	Hendrix ☒	67
90	Emory ☒	73
74	Millsaps ☒	78
94	Rhodes ☒	86
68	Centre	96
71	DePauw	90
49	Trinity (Tex.) †	50

Nickname: Stormy Petrels
Colors: Black & Gold
Arena: Dorough Fieldhouse
Capacity: 2,000; Year Built: 1962
AD: Jay Gardiner
SID: Jim Owen

OHIO
Athens, OH 45701 I

Coach: Tim O'Shea, Boston College 1984

2006-07 RESULTS (19-13)

83	Marist ⊠	66
73	Yale ⊠	65
66	Samford	80
84	Marshall ⊠	78
77	St. Bonaventure	72
71	Louisville	74
91	Bellarmine †	74
79	St. Joseph's †	72
74	Davidson †	83
95	N.C. A&T †	83
97	Rhode Island ⊠	69
79	Cincinnati †	66
60	Marshall	70
77	Akron ⊠	72
67	Bowling Green ⊠	49
65	Kent St.	67
67	Buffalo ⊠	51
69	Miami (Ohio) ⊠	72
67	Eastern Mich. ⊠	61
57	Ball St.	69
91	Toledo ⊠	80
74	Central Mich.	73
78	Western Mich.	73
74	Northern Ill. ⊠	81
48	Akron	79
72	New Mexico St.	77
88	Bowling Green	63
71	Kent St. ⊠	73
52	Miami (Ohio) ⊠	45
65	Buffalo	84
69	Bowling Green †	59
51	Miami (Ohio) †	70

Nickname: Bobcats
Colors: Hunter Green & White
Arena: Convocation Center
  Capacity: 13,080; Year Built: 1968
AD: Kirby Hocutt
SID: Jason Cunningham

OHIO NORTHERN
Ada, OH 45810 III

Coach: Jeff Coleman, Ohio Northern 1990

2006-07 RESULTS (18-7)

74	DeSales †	57
76	Elizabethtown	60
74	Johnson & Wales (FL) †	60
80	Marietta ⊠	50
75	Heidelberg	70
77	Baldwin-Wallace ⊠	94
64	Mount Union	51
68	Wittenberg ⊠	51
91	Wooster	84
73	Wis.-La Crosse †	70
69	Muskingum	57
57	Capital ⊠	68
63	Wilmington (Ohio)	62
61	John Carroll	63
79	Otterbein ⊠	70
68	Marietta	72
83	Heidelberg ⊠	80
83	Baldwin-Wallace	74
66	Otterbein	63
67	John Carroll ⊠	79
75	Wilmington (Ohio) ⊠	53
70	Capital	74
63	Muskingum ⊠	57
74	Mount Union ⊠	59
51	Otterbein ⊠	52

Nickname: Polar Bears
Colors: Burnt Orange & Black
Arena: ONU Sports Center
  Capacity: 3,200; Year Built: 1975
AD: Thomas E. Simmons
SID: Tim Glon

OHIO ST.
Columbus, OH 43210 I

Coach: Thad Matta, Butler 1990

2006-07 RESULTS (35-4)

107	VMI ⊠	69
87	Loyola (Ill.) ⊠	75
81	Kent St. ⊠	59
74	Eastern Ky. ⊠	45
82	San Francisco ⊠	60
91	Youngstown St. †	57
89	North Carolina	98
78	Valparaiso ⊠	58
78	Cleveland St. ⊠	57
72	Cincinnati †	50
75	Iowa St. ⊠	56
60	Florida	86
91	Coppin St. ⊠	54
74	Indiana ⊠	67
62	Illinois	44
69	Wisconsin	72
68	Tennessee ⊠	66
73	Northwestern ⊠	41
82	Iowa ⊠	63
59	Northwestern	50
66	Michigan St. ⊠	64
78	Purdue	60
63	Michigan St.	54
76	Michigan	63
63	Purdue ⊠	56
64	Penn St.	62
85	Minnesota	67
68	Penn St. ⊠	60
49	Wisconsin ⊠	48
65	Michigan	61
72	Michigan †	62
63	Purdue †	52
66	Wisconsin †	49
78	Central Conn. St. †	57
78	Xavier †	71
85	Tennessee †	84
92	Memphis †	76
67	Georgetown †	60
75	Florida †	84

Nickname: Buckeyes
Colors: Scarlet & Gray
Arena: Value City Arena
  Capacity: 18,500; Year Built: 1998
AD: Eugene Smith
SID: Dan Wallenberg

OHIO VALLEY
Vienna, WV 26105 II

Coach: Bill McGee, Lubbock Chrst. 1982

2006-07 RESULTS (8-20)

94	Mount Olive	101
91	Coker †	83
82	Mercyhurst ⊠	87
79	Shippensburg ⊠	69
48	High Point	93
106	Slippery Rock ⊠	97
73	Shippensburg	103
86	Oakland City	90
65	Campbell	107
76	Shepherd ⊠	99
84	West Liberty St.	110
83	Wheeling Jesuit	101
89	West Va. Wesleyan ⊠	79
98	Glenville St. ⊠	87
83	Salem Int'l	100
79	Concord ⊠	77
85	Davis & Elkins	79
77	Wheeling Jesuit ⊠	106
71	Alderson-Broaddus	98
89	Fairmont St.	83
88	West Liberty St. ⊠	102
71	Charleston (W.V.)	83
62	Bluefield St. ⊠	73
66	Salem Int'l ⊠	95
63	Fairmont St.	81
104	West Virginia St.	122
72	Shepherd	87
74	Shepherd	75

Nickname: Fighting Scots
Colors: Royal Blue, White, and Red
Arena: Snyder Activity Center
  Capacity: 1,000; Year Built: 1993
AD: Ron Pavan
SID: Darren Waldo

OHIO WESLEYAN
Delaware, OH 43015 III

Coach: Mike DeWitt, Ohio Wesleyan 1987

2006-07 RESULTS (18-10)

96	D'Youville †	31
84	Penn St.-Behrend	64
90	Wash. & Jeff. ⊠	64
87	Ill. Wesleyan †	74
79	DePauw	85
81	Capital	71
90	Hiram ⊠	49
70	Allegheny	73
60	Wilmington (Ohio) ⊠	63
79	Aquinas †	80
86	Notre Dame (Ohio) †	76
72	Denison	50
53	Kenyon ⊠	47
74	Wabash	50
65	Earlham	68
70	Wittenberg ⊠	48
54	Wooster ⊠	61
96	Oberlin	59
92	Hiram	86
52	Wabash	54
87	Allegheny ⊠	58
64	Wittenberg	71
82	Earlham ⊠	70
96	Oberlin ⊠	59
89	Wooster	95
60	Kenyon ⊠	54
57	Wittenberg †	52
51	Wooster	86

Nickname: Battling Bishops
Colors: Red & Black
Arena: Branch Rickey Arena
  Capacity: 2,300; Year Built: 1976
AD: Roger Ingles
SID: Mark Beckenbach

OKLAHOMA
Norman, OK 73019 I

Coach: Jeff Capel III, Duke 1997

2006-07 RESULTS (16-15)

99	Norfolk St. ⊠	36
74	Liberty ⊠	48
65	Memphis †	77
71	Purdue †	74
72	Chaminade †	57
63	TCU ⊠	35
51	Villanova ⊠	67
64	Coppin St. ⊠	47
89	Texas-Arlington ⊠	60
58	Tulsa †	48
69	SMU ⊠	42
55	Alabama	70
54	Texas Tech	68
78	Colorado ⊠	54
69	Texas	80
70	Nebraska ⊠	53
91	Baylor ⊠	51
61	Oklahoma St.	66
61	Texas A&M	70
81	Longwood ⊠	40
75	Texas Tech ⊠	61
67	Oklahoma St. ⊠	60
68	Baylor	64
51	Iowa St.	58
49	Texas A&M ⊠	56
68	Missouri	72
58	Texas ⊠	68
65	Kansas ⊠	67
61	Kansas St.	72
68	Iowa St. †	63
47	Kansas †	64

Nickname: Sooners
Colors: Crimson & Cream
Arena: Lloyd Noble Center
  Capacity: 12,000; Year Built: 1975
AD: Joseph R. Castiglione
SID: Mike Houck

OKLA. PANHANDLE
Goodwell, OK 73939 II

Coach: Curt Connor, Loras 1995

2006-07 RESULTS (7-20)

77	N.M. Highlands ⊠	59
63	Midwestern St. ⊠	82
58	Cameron ⊠	67
41	Oral Roberts	91
67	Angelo St. ⊠	70
64	Western St.	74
71	UC-Colo. Springs †	95
53	Eastern N.M. ⊠	81
79	Johnson & Wales (CO)	67
54	Mont. St.-Billings	65
53	St. Mary's (Tex.)	63
69	Incarnate Word	76
73	Midwestern St.	89
69	Mont. St.-Billings	64
62	Mont. St.-Billings ⊠	48
75	Lincoln (Mo.) ⊠	57
62	Tex. Permian Basin	66
52	Dallas Baptist	73
51	Tex. A&M Int'l ⊠	59
50	St. Edward's †	66
91	Tex. Permian Basin ⊠	69
67	Dallas Baptist ⊠	68
66	Tex. A&M Int'l	76
63	St. Edward's	62
72	Lincoln (Mo.)	87
55	St. Mary's (Tex.) ⊠	57
57	Incarnate Word ⊠	76

Nickname: Aggies
Colors: Crimson, and Royal Blue
Arena: Carl Williams Field House
  Capacity: 2,200; Year Built: 1958
AD: Jerry Olson
SID: Scott Puryear

OKLAHOMA ST.
Stillwater, OK 74078-5070 I

Coach: Sean Sutton, Oklahoma St. 1992

2006-07 RESULTS (22-13)

95	Fla. Atlantic ⊠	50
79	Northwestern St. ⊠	76
86	Texas Southern ⊠	65
86	Sam Houston St. ⊠	67
75	Southern U. ⊠	59
66	Auburn †	65
73	Missouri St. †	70
95	A&M-Corpus Christi ⊠	73
90	Pepperdine ⊠	74
72	Syracuse †	68
75	Ball St. †	56
77	Tennessee †	79
95	Pittsburgh †	89
84	UTSA ⊠	47
129	Southwestern Okla. ⊠	77
81	Baylor ⊠	77
57	Kansas	87
105	Texas ⊠	103
49	Texas A&M	67
66	Oklahoma	61
62	Iowa St. ⊠	50
77	Colorado	89
60	Oklahoma	67
93	Texas Tech ⊠	91
54	Texas	83
64	Missouri	75
46	Texas A&M ⊠	66
57	Texas Tech	59
84	Kansas St. ⊠	70
82	Baylor	86
73	Nebraska	85
54	Nebraska †	39
57	Texas A&M †	56

(Oklahoma St. continued)
64	Texas †	69
64	Marist ⊠	67

Nickname: Cowboys
Colors: Orange & Black
Arena: Gallagher-Iba Arena
 Capacity: 13,611; Year Built: 1938
AD: Mike Holder
SID: Mike Noteware

OLD DOMINION
Norfolk, VA 23529-0197 I

Coach: Blaine Taylor, Montana 1982
2006-07 RESULTS (24-9)
54	Monmouth ⊠	40
69	Arkansas St. ⊠	61
70	Clemson ⊠	74
70	Fla. Atlantic ⊠	55
75	Georgetown	62
69	Richmond ⊠	52
71	Marist	84
70	James Madison ⊠	57
55	Virginia Tech	72
74	South Carolina St. ⊠	57
56	UAB ⊠	42
65	Winthrop ⊠	71
73	Northeastern	67
65	George Mason ⊠	63
58	Hofstra	70
83	Delaware ⊠	48
84	Drexel ⊠	57
65	James Madison	72
75	VCU	80
59	William & Mary ⊠	44
86	UNC Wilmington	70
92	Georgia St. ⊠	57
62	Drexel	52
66	George Mason	56
68	Georgia St.	55
79	VCU ⊠	63
96	Hofstra ⊠	82
73	Toledo	70
79	Towson ⊠	65
62	William & Mary	57
58	Towson †	55
63	George Mason †	79
46	Butler †	57

Nickname: Monarchs
Colors: Slate Blue, Sky Blue, & Silver
Arena: Ted Constant Convocation Ctr.
 Capacity: 8,424; Year Built: 2002
AD: Jim Jarrett
SID: Carol Hudson

OLD WESTBURY
Old Westbury, NY 11568-0210 III

Coach: Bernard Tomlin, Hofstra 1976
2006-07 RESULTS (18-11)
50	Long Island	105
92	Purchase St. ⊠	62
73	Stevens Institute ⊠	70
91	Merchant Marine	96
71	Centenary (N.J.) ⊠	63
82	Nazareth	91
55	New York U.	85
71	Baruch †	60
61	Maryland Bible †	44
56	Villa Julie	55
80	New Paltz St.	83
85	Mt. St. Mary (N.Y.)	75
93	St. Joseph's (L.I.)	79
75	Manhattanville ⊠	73
62	Yeshiva	70
92	Farmingdale St.	69
87	Mt. St. Vincent ⊠	72
83	Maritime (N.Y.) ⊠	57
67	Merchant Marine ⊠	71
88	Stevens Institute	95
84	St. Joseph's (L.I.) ⊠	67
64	Eastern Conn. St.	78
75	Yeshiva ⊠	60
108	Mt. St. Vincent	93

(Old Westbury continued)
105	Centenary (N.J.)	71
78	Merchant Marine ⊠	70
83	Stevens Institute	80
68	Manhattanville	87
73	Richard Stockton ⊠	78

Nickname: Panthers
Colors: Forest Green & White
Arena: Clark Athletic Center
 Capacity: 2,500; Year Built: 1981
AD: Bernard Tomlin
SID: Elizabeth Papetti Reilly

OLIVET
Olivet, MI 49076................................III

Coach: Kurt Soderberg, Wis.-Stevens Point 1993
2006-07 RESULTS (5-20)
45	Concordia (Mich.) ⊠	60
75	Andrews ⊠	62
67	Saginaw Valley ⊠	81
71	Baldwin-Wallace	74
68	Madonna ⊠	72
55	Defiance	61
63	Carthage †	82
72	Bridgewater (Va.) †	67
67	Westminster (Pa.) †	80
76	Lynchburg †	80
86	Alma ⊠	70
70	Hope	99
68	Tri-State	73
66	Adrian ⊠	69
58	Calvin	74
63	Kalamazoo ⊠	60
43	Albion	73
55	Alma	50
57	Hope ⊠	79
62	Tri-State ⊠	63
44	Adrian	63
43	Calvin	90
69	Kalamazoo	77
54	Albion ⊠	68
39	Calvin	69

Nickname: Comets
Colors: Red & White
Arena: Upton Center
 Capacity: 1,500; Year Built: 1981
AD: Thomas Shaw
SID: Geoffrey Henson

ONEONTA ST.
Oneonta, NY 13820-4015............. III

Coach: Vincent Medici, Cortland St. 1987
2006-07 RESULTS (11-15)
55	Averett †	71
62	Denison †	77
74	Cortland St. ⊠	67
79	Buffalo St. ⊠	72
56	Fredonia St. ⊠	51
72	Cazenovia	75
49	Hartwick ⊠	57
57	Dana †	60
62	Simon's Rock †	82
67	St. Joseph (Vt.) ⊠	60
60	Utica	67
58	Plattsburgh St.	56
56	Potsdam St.	62
74	SUNYIT	71
68	Oswego St. ⊠	67
58	Brockport St. ⊠	60
71	Brockport St.	103
72	Geneseo St.	49
68	Ithaca ⊠	62
75	New Paltz St.	57
55	Cortland St.	59
74	SUNYIT ⊠	79
59	Oswego St.	88
79	New Paltz St. ⊠	69
59	Potsdam St. ⊠	61
73	SUNYIT	90

Nickname: Red Dragons
Colors: Red & White
Arena: Dewar Arena
 Capacity: 3,500; Year Built: 1999
AD: Barton R. Ingersoll
SID: Geoff Hassard

ORAL ROBERTS
Tulsa, OK 74171 I

Coach: Scott Sutton, Oklahoma St. 1994
2006-07 RESULTS (23-11)
65	Loyola Marymount	68
78	Kansas	71
54	La.-Lafayette ⊠	51
91	Okla. Panhandle ⊠	41
57	Tulsa	75
59	Akron ⊠	61
88	Lamar ⊠	63
58	Georgetown	73
72	Chattanooga	76
69	Montana ⊠	58
56	Arkansas	68
76	Seton Hall †	74
62	BYU	72
90	Liberty †	58
65	Western Ill. ⊠	46
75	Valparaiso ⊠	60
69	Southern Utah	61
75	UMKC	68
59	Chicago St. ⊠	53
89	Centenary (La.)	66
73	Oakland ⊠	63
77	IUPUI ⊠	66
67	Valparaiso	70
67	Western Ill.	60
74	UMKC ⊠	68
79	Southern Utah ⊠	57
85	Centenary (La.) ⊠	80
65	Utah St. ⊠	71
83	IUPUI	73
84	Oakland	85
79	Centenary (La.) †	59
75	IUPUI †	54
71	Oakland †	67
54	Washington St. †	70

Nickname: Golden Eagles
Colors: Gold, Navy Blue & White
Arena: Mabee Center
 Capacity: 10,575; Year Built: 1972
AD: R. Michael Carter
SID: Cris Belvin

OREGON
Eugene, OR 97401 I

Coach: Ernie Kent, Oregon 1977
2006-07 RESULTS (29-8)
77	Lehigh ⊠	65
84	Cal St. Northridge ⊠	73
116	Portland St. ⊠	68
85	UC Irvine ⊠	42
79	Rice	73
57	Georgetown	50
68	Nebraska ⊠	56
92	Bethune-Cookman ⊠	64
100	Eastern Wash. ⊠	74
84	Idaho St. ⊠	55
84	Mercer ⊠	64
76	Portland ⊠	49
76	Oregon St.	73
82	Southern California ⊠	84
68	UCLA	66
60	Arizona St.	55
79	Arizona	77
66	Stanford ⊠	59
92	California ⊠	84
77	Washington	89
77	Washington St.	74
57	UCLA	69
68	Southern California	71
55	Arizona St. ⊠	51
74	Arizona ⊠	77

(Oregon continued)
61	California	63
69	Stanford	88
64	Washington St. ⊠	59
93	Washington ⊠	85
70	Oregon St. ⊠	49
69	Arizona †	50
81	California †	63
81	Southern California †	57
58	Miami (Ohio) †	56
75	Winthrop †	61
76	UNLV †	72
77	Florida †	85

Nickname: Ducks
Colors: Green & Yellow
Arena: McArthur Court
 Capacity: 9,087; Year Built: 1927
AD: William Moos
SID: Greg Walker

OREGON ST.
Corvallis, OR 97331 I

Coach: Jay John, Arizona 1981
2006-07 RESULTS (11-21)
65	Portland ⊠	48
63	Southeastern La. ⊠	65
78	Cal Poly ⊠	65
47	Nevada ⊠	75
41	Hawaii ⊠	85
69	Northern Colo. ⊠	67
72	Montana St.	63
69	Fresno St. ⊠	74
72	Bethune-Cookman ⊠	49
71	Western Ore. ⊠	58
53	LSU	60
84	Howard ⊠	67
93	Mercer ⊠	62
73	Oregon ⊠	76
56	UCLA ⊠	71
46	Southern California ⊠	91
72	Arizona	83
67	Arizona St.	59
74	California ⊠	77
56	Stanford ⊠	67
55	Washington St.	70
74	Washington	91
56	Southern California	73
35	UCLA	82
66	Arizona ⊠	72
59	Arizona St. ⊠	55
55	Stanford	70
80	California	84
73	Washington ⊠	65
54	Washington St. ⊠	58
49	Oregon	70
51	California †	70

Nickname: Beavers
Colors: Orange & Black
Arena: Gill Coliseum
 Capacity: 10,400; Year Built: 1949
AD: Bob DeCarolis
SID: Roger Horne

OSWEGO ST.
Oswego, NY 13126.......................... III

Coach: Kevin Broderick, Nazareth 1989
2006-07 RESULTS (17-13)
114	Cazenovia ⊠	60
76	Lehman ⊠	54
76	Morrisville St. ⊠	59
70	Geneseo St.	82
85	SUNYIT ⊠	57
81	Nazareth	73
82	Greensboro †	85
85	Chris. Newport	87
62	Clarkson ⊠	64
76	St. Lawrence	80
75	Plattsburgh St. ⊠	73
64	Fredonia St.	62
76	Buffalo St.	81
102	Brockport St. ⊠	89
67	Oneonta St.	68

398

2006-07 RESULTS

56	Cortland St.	51
62	Utica	63
82	Cortland St. ⊠	64
72	Potsdam St.	83
76	Brockport St.	91
67	Geneseo St. ⊠	60
92	New Paltz St. ⊠	87
88	Oneonta St. ⊠	59
77	Plattsburgh St.	78
77	Buffalo St.	69
61	Geneseo St. ⊠	51
73	Plattsburgh St. †	89
74	Rochester Inst. ⊠	63
91	SUNYIT †	84
65	Vassar	66

Nickname: Lakers
Colors: Hunter Green and Golden Yellow
Arena: Max Ziel Gymnasium
    Capacity: 3,500; Year Built: 1968
AD: Timothy Hale
SID: Joe Gladziszewski

OTTERBEIN
Westerville, OH 43081-2006......... III

Coach: Dick Reynolds, Otterbein 1965

2006-07 RESULTS (16-11)

56	Gettysburg	55
57	Richard Stockton †	64
58	Maryville (Tenn.)	55
78	Fisk	73
77	John Carroll	86
61	Marietta	55
95	Muskingum ⊠	84
59	Capital	77
72	Wittenberg ⊠	79
83	Kalamazoo ⊠	63
81	Maryville (Tenn.) ⊠	84
76	Wilmington (Ohio) ⊠	67
77	Heidelberg ⊠	95
83	Baldwin-Wallace	74
77	Mount Union ⊠	61
70	Ohio Northern	79
68	John Carroll ⊠	70
78	Marietta	69
80	Muskingum	79
63	Ohio Northern ⊠	66
78	Mount Union	68
76	Baldwin-Wallace ⊠	84
77	Heidelberg	74
52	Wilmington (Ohio)	49
73	Capital ⊠	69
52	Ohio Northern	51
49	Capital	69

Nickname: Cardinals
Colors: Tan & Cardinal
Arena: The Rike Center
    Capacity: 3,100; Year Built: 1974
AD: Richard E. Reynolds
SID: Ed Syguda

OUACHITA BAPTIST
Arkadelphia, AR 71998-0001 II

Coach: Charlie Schaef, Texas Tech 1993

2006-07 RESULTS (14-14)

89	Ozarks (Mo.) ⊠	56
118	Ecclesia	61
85	Southeastern Okla.	96
75	Southwestern Okla. †	88
65	West Tex. A&M	83
63	Tusculum †	65
82	UNC Pembroke †	53
77	Southeastern Okla. ⊠	93
94	North Ala. ⊠	98
90	Central Baptist ⊠	80
64	North Ala.	78
60	Delta St.	80
113	Champion Bapt. ⊠	22
77	Ark.-Monticello	78
77	Harding	76
68	Christian Bros. ⊠	72
59	Southern Ark.	50

65	Henderson St.	62
81	Arkansas Tech ⊠	74
92	Delta St. ⊠	81
82	Rhema ⊠	75
73	Ark.-Monticello ⊠	55
68	Harding	77
69	Christian Bros.	84
68	Southern Ark. ⊠	75
90	Henderson St. ⊠	80
77	Arkansas Tech	70
72	West Ga. †	86

Nickname: Tigers
Colors: Purple & Gold
Arena: Vining Arena
    Capacity: 2,500; Year Built: 1966
AD: David R. Sharp
SID: Ben Cutrell

OZARKS (ARK.)
Clarksville, AR 72830-2880........... III

Coach: Matt O'Connor, Davidson 1991

2006-07 RESULTS (8-17)

69	Austin	74
85	Dallas †	86
83	Rust ⊠	81
86	Howard Payne ⊠	74
75	Sul Ross St. ⊠	70
84	Schreiner	97
67	Texas Lutheran	58
79	Hardin-Simmons ⊠	86
67	Hendrix ⊠	73
98	Concordia (Tex.)	85
56	Mary Hardin-Baylor	90
69	McMurry ⊠	75
64	East Tex. Baptist	79
84	LeTourneau	86
68	Louisiana Col. ⊠	71
47	Mississippi Col. ⊠	65
64	Texas-Dallas ⊠	78
66	Texas-Tyler ⊠	57
58	Central Ark.	75
56	Texas-Dallas	76
66	Texas-Tyler	63
70	Louisiana Col.	80
63	Mississippi Col.	89
84	East Tex. Baptist ⊠	60
53	LeTourneau ⊠	77

Nickname: Eagles
Colors: Purple & Gold
Arena: Mabee Gym
    Capacity: 2,500; Year Built: 1958
AD: Jimmy Clark
SID: Josh Peppas

PACE
Pleasantville, NY 10570-2799 II

Coach: Jim Harter, Delaware 1982

2006-07 RESULTS (20-13)

91	Alas. Fairbanks †	96
72	Southern Ind. †	101
105	North Georgia †	87
81	Mercy	61
87	American Int'l	75
75	St. Michael's ⊠	76
84	Franklin Pierce ⊠	87
82	Southern N.H.	66
62	St. Rose	83
97	Post ⊠	65
96	Concordia (N.Y.)	109
63	Le Moyne	80
87	St. Anselm ⊠	61
88	Felician	58
67	Adelphi ⊠	70
70	Assumption	63
99	Merrimack	94
84	Southern Conn. St.	82
72	Bryant	80
75	Mass.-Lowell ⊠	65
71	St. Rose	69
62	Bentley ⊠	65
99	Stonehill	72

72	Franklin Pierce	53
67	St. Anselm	66
64	Le Moyne ⊠	63
85	Southern N.H. ⊠	65
88	Southern Conn. St. ⊠	82
72	St. Michael's	91
74	American Int'l ⊠	64
79	Le Moyne	70
81	St. Rose	82
71	St. Rose †	87

Nickname: Setters
Colors: Navy & Gold
Arena: Goldstein Athletics Center
    Capacity: 2,400; Year Built: 2002
AD: Joseph F. O'Donnell
SID: TBA

PACIFIC
Stockton, CA 95211............................ I

Coach: Bob Thomason, Pacific 1971

2006-07 RESULTS (12-19)

75	Cal St. Bakersfield ⊠	67
74	New Mexico St.	76
71	UMKC †	70
85	Loyola Marymount †	88
60	Hawaii †	71
79	San Francisco ⊠	72
62	Texas A&M	74
72	Sacramento St.	74
49	Santa Clara ⊠	67
60	St. Louis ⊠	67
53	Nevada	60
47	Wisconsin	83
68	Cal St. Northridge ⊠	64
62	UC Riverside	49
70	Cal St. Fullerton ⊠	76
42	UC Irvine ⊠	67
79	UC Davis	71
66	Cal Poly ⊠	43
62	UC Santa Barbara ⊠	70
89	UC Irvine	82
64	Long Beach St.	92
77	Cal St. Fullerton ⊠	82
86	UC Riverside ⊠	66
78	Montana	77
65	UC Davis ⊠	58
73	Cal St. Northridge	76
76	Long Beach St. ⊠	82
49	UC Santa Barbara	64
70	Cal Poly	82
71	Cal St. Northridge †	54
92	Cal St. Fullerton †	100

Nickname: Tigers
Colors: Orange & Black
Arena: A.G. Spanos Center
    Capacity: 6,150; Year Built: 1981
AD: Lynn King
SID: Mike Millerick

PACIFIC (ORE.)
Forest Grove, OR 97116-1797 III

Coach: Jason Lowery, Pomona-Pitzer 1997

2006-07 RESULTS (12-13)

58	Evergreen St. ⊠	74
58	Northwest Chrst. ⊠	62
53	Northwest Nazarene	61
111	Multnomah Bible ⊠	71
57	Whitworth	62
65	Whitman	46
79	Cascade ⊠	67
66	Cal Lutheran	57
98	Caltech †	57
55	La Sierra	73
62	Willamette	66
77	Puget Sound ⊠	71
80	Lewis & Clark ⊠	75
64	George Fox ⊠	57
53	Linfield	61
67	Pacific Lutheran	69
69	Whitworth	77

83	Whitman ⊠	69
69	Willamette ⊠	60
79	Puget Sound	85
54	Lewis & Clark	80
59	George Fox	68
61	Northwest Chrst.	64
54	Linfield	50
89	Pacific Lutheran ⊠	77

Nickname: Boxers
Colors: Red, Black & White
Arena: Pacific Athletic Center
    Capacity: 2,500; Year Built: 1970
AD: Ken Schumann
SID: Blake Timm

PACIFIC LUTHERAN
Tacoma, WA 98447-0003 III

Coach: Steve Dickerson, Washington St. 1969

2006-07 RESULTS (9-14)

80	Menlo †	74
84	UC Santa Cruz †	79
85	Linfield ⊠	79
90	Willamette ⊠	84
57	Portland St.	107
56	Northwest (Wash.)	85
75	Evergreen St. ⊠	80
65	Concordia (Ore.)	88
105	Puget Sound Chrst. ⊠	62
96	Puget Sound	108
76	Lewis & Clark	102
100	Whitman	96
56	Whitworth	80
68	George Fox ⊠	77
69	Pacific (Ore.) ⊠	67
73	Linfield	80
67	Willamette	90
86	Puget Sound	89
55	Lewis & Clark ⊠	59
71	Whitman ⊠	70
63	Whitworth ⊠	65
78	George Fox	66
77	Pacific (Ore.)	89

Nickname: Lutes
Colors: Black & Gold
Arena: Olson Auditorium
    Capacity: 3,200; Year Built: 1969
AD: Laurie Turner
SID: Nick Dawson

PAINE
Augusta, GA 30901-3182 II

Coach: Ron Spry, Campbellsville 1975

2006-07 RESULTS (17-10)

75	Claflin	68
60	Augusta St. ⊠	78
69	Kentucky St.	59
70	Lane	66
59	Augusta St.	87
93	LeMoyne-Owen	79
74	Miles	84
53	Clark Atlanta ⊠	41
72	Morehouse ⊠	60
93	Kentucky St. ⊠	80
57	Lane	77
49	Fort Valley St.	65
64	Albany St. (Ga.)	62
76	Morehouse	71
63	LeMoyne-Owen ⊠	65
79	Miles	48
60	Benedict	53
50	Stillman ⊠	48
81	Tuskegee ⊠	67
59	Clark Atlanta	53
78	Claflin	66
59	Benedict ⊠	71
42	Stillman	37
79	Tuskegee	53
74	Fort Valley St. ⊠	78
67	Albany St. (Ga.) ⊠	71
82	Kentucky St. †	88

Nickname: Lions
Colors: Purple & White
Arena: Randall Carter Gymnasium
 Capacity: 1,200; Year Built: 1952
AD: Ronnie O. Spry
SID: Kimberly May

PENN
Philadelphia, PA 19104-6322 I

Coach: Glen Miller, Connecticut 1986

2006-07 RESULTS (22-9)
66	UTEP †	69
60	Syracuse	78
86	St. Francis (N.Y.) †	56
97	Fla. Gulf Coast ⊠	74
68	Drexel ⊠	49
80	Monmouth ⊠	66
89	Villanova ⊠	99
79	Navy	58
60	Fordham ⊠	77
90	Ill.-Chicago ⊠	78
85	Seton Hall	94
64	North Carolina	102
66	Elon	64
74	Cornell	56
69	Columbia	43
93	La Salle	92
76	Temple ⊠	74
74	St. Joseph's	84
77	Brown ⊠	61
68	Yale	77
73	Dartmouth ⊠	53
67	Harvard ⊠	53
48	Princeton	35
73	Columbia ⊠	54
83	Cornell ⊠	71
83	Harvard	67
80	Dartmouth	78
86	Yale ⊠	58
67	Brown	64
64	Princeton	48
52	Texas A&M †	68

Nickname: Quakers
Colors: Red & Blue
Arena: The Palestra
 Capacity: 8,722; Year Built: 1927
AD: Steve Bilsky
SID: Mike Mahoney

PENN ST.
University Park, PA 16802 I

Coach: Ed DeChellis, Penn St. 1982

2006-07 RESULTS (11-19)
63	Morehead St. ⊠	46
69	UNC Greensboro ⊠	56
51	Stony Brook ⊠	59
63	Bucknell ⊠	60
65	St. Joseph's ⊠	61
73	Georgia Tech	77
80	Morgan St. ⊠	71
56	Hartford ⊠	55
59	Seton Hall	69
66	Long Island ⊠	45
66	Southeastern La. ⊠	69
75	Maine ⊠	42
129	VMI ⊠	111
83	Northwestern ⊠	57
74	Purdue	64
74	Indiana ⊠	84
57	Michigan	77
64	Michigan St. ⊠	91
63	Iowa	79
60	Minnesota ⊠	65
59	Purdue ⊠	69
58	Wisconsin ⊠	71
51	Northwestern	53
62	Ohio St. ⊠	64
49	Wisconsin	75
90	Ohio St.	68
50	Illinois ⊠	68
74	Iowa ⊠	72
63	Indiana	94

60	Illinois †	66

Nickname: Nittany Lions
Colors: Blue & White
Arena: Bryce Jordan Center
 Capacity: 15,261; Year Built: 1996
AD: Timothy M. Curley
SID: Brian Siegrist

PENN ST.-ALTOONA
Altoona, PA 16601-3760 III

Coach: Alan Seretti, Allegheny 1999

2006-07 RESULTS (10-16)
87	Bethany (W.V.) †	91
65	Franciscan †	76
59	Grove City	69
46	La Roche ⊠	48
73	Hilbert ⊠	53
63	Pitt.-Bradford	75
68	Lake Erie	86
64	Bethany (W.V.) ⊠	86
95	Lincoln (Pa.) ⊠	86
46	Heidelberg	68
56	Penn St.-Behrend	65
65	Frostburg St.	73
55	Medaille	57
90	Mt. Aloysius ⊠	81
88	Pitt.-Greensburg	76
75	Hilbert	73
59	La Roche	50
66	Lake Erie ⊠	94
88	Washington Bible ⊠	36
77	Pitt.-Bradford ⊠	56
61	Penn St.-Behrend	77
76	Frostburg St. ⊠	73
76	Medaille ⊠	77
69	Pitt.-Greensburg ⊠	68
68	Mt. Aloysius	77
49	Pitt.-Bradford	61

Nickname: Lions
Colors: Navy Blue & White
Arena: Adler Athletic Complex
 Capacity: 800; Year Built: 1972
AD: Fredina M. Ingold
SID: Brent Baird

PENN ST.-BEHREND
Erie, PA 16563-0101 III

Coach: Dave Niland, Le Moyne 1989

2006-07 RESULTS (21-8)
65	Elmira ⊠	50
64	Ohio Wesleyan ⊠	84
55	Allegheny	56
73	Mt. Aloysius ⊠	59
69	Frostburg St.	56
59	Hilbert	39
73	Pitt.-Greensburg ⊠	61
55	Westminster (Pa.)	73
48	Lebanon Valley †	56
64	St. John's (Minn.) †	59
65	Penn St.-Altoona	56
65	Medaille ⊠	54
74	La Roche ⊠	56
69	Pitt.-Bradford	64
51	Lake Erie ⊠	63
67	Frostburg St. ⊠	43
104	Mt. Aloysius	75
88	Pitt.-Greensburg	60
65	Hilbert ⊠	50
77	Penn St.-Altoona	61
66	Medaille	46
61	La Roche	71
66	Lake Erie	60
55	Pitt.-Bradford	53
63	Pitt.-Bradford †	39
58	Lake Erie	59
76	Grove City ⊠	46
77	Juniata †	69
63	DeSales	72

Nickname: Behrend Lions
Colors: Blue & White
Arena: Athletics & Recreation Cn

Capacity: 1,600; Year Built: 2000
AD: Brian Streeter
SID: Paul Benim

PENN ST.-BERKS
Reading, PA 19610-6009 III

Coach: Scott Yarnell, Alvernia 1990

2006-07 RESULTS (8-18)
59	Randolph-Macon †	106
53	John Jay †	71
63	Cabrini	79
56	West Chester	92
75	Purchase St.	76
76	Keystone ⊠	79
62	Keuka	80
59	Kutztown ⊠	96
60	Alvernia	94
66	Gallaudet ⊠	78
59	Chestnut Hill ⊠	88
69	D'Youville ⊠	66
75	Villa Julie ⊠	84
73	Phila. Biblical ⊠	67
74	Polytechnic (N.Y.)	61
89	Cazenovia	96
70	DeSales ⊠	99
79	Chestnut Hill ⊠	76
84	Bard	70
56	Villa Julie	78
72	Lancaster Bible ⊠	73
57	Baptist Bible (Pa.)	86
92	Polytechnic (N.Y.) ⊠	73
84	Phila. Biblical	79
71	Purchase St. ⊠	58
64	Chestnut Hill	89

Nickname: Nittany Lions
Colors: Blue & White
Arena: Beaver Community Center
 Capacity: 550; Year Built: 1980
AD: William Sutherland
SID: Kate Corcoran

PEPPERDINE
Malibu, CA 90263 I

Coach: Vance Walberg, Cal St. Bakersfield 1978

2006-07 RESULTS (8-23)
91	Washington	99
58	UNI †	83
98	Nicholls St. †	83
92	Cal St. Northridge	95
80	UC Santa Barbara ⊠	89
66	UC Irvine	68
74	Oklahoma St.	90
78	Colorado	72
90	Long Beach St.	95
81	Cal St. Fullerton ⊠	83
76	Cal St. Bakersfield ⊠	82
101	Northern Ariz. ⊠	86
66	Connecticut	88
90	Binghamton †	83
96	New Mexico	101
87	Manhattan ⊠	89
69	Portland	73
52	Gonzaga	69
67	San Diego ⊠	71
71	San Francisco ⊠	72
57	Loyola Marymount	55
68	St. Mary's (Cal.)	66
55	Santa Clara	77
57	Gonzaga ⊠	82
76	Portland ⊠	87
70	San Francisco	82
85	San Diego	97
95	Loyola Marymount ⊠	88
72	St. Mary's (Cal.) ⊠	97
89	Santa Clara ⊠	82
82	San Diego †	95

Nickname: Waves
Colors: Blue & Orange
Arena: Firestone Fieldhouse
 Capacity: 3,104; Year Built: 1973

AD: John G. Watson
SID: Al Barba

PFEIFFER
Misenheimer, NC 28109-0960 II

Coach: Dave Davis, Warren Wilson 1983

2006-07 RESULTS (17-11)
108	Allen ⊠	73
103	Mount Olive ⊠	97
102	King (Tenn.) ⊠	90
88	Lees-McRae ⊠	75
96	Belmont Abbey ⊠	71
88	Coker	86
112	Davis & Elkins ⊠	102
112	Glenville St.	105
94	Fairmont St. †	104
119	Columbia Union	111
97	Barton	122
83	Erskine ⊠	80
106	Queens (N.C.)	88
110	Lees-McRae	98
87	Anderson (S.C.)	80
101	St. Andrews ⊠	106
78	Limestone	80
107	Belmont Abbey	110
104	Mount Olive	110
89	Queens (N.C.) ⊠	101
91	Limestone ⊠	97
82	Coker ⊠	71
100	St. Andrews	70
105	Lees-McRae ⊠	77
77	Anderson (S.C.) ⊠	66
99	Barton ⊠	114
76	Erskine	88
77	Limestone	98

Nickname: Falcons
Colors: Black & Gold
Arena: Merner Gymnasium
 Capacity: 2,500; Year Built: 1971
AD: Robert Stewart
SID: Chris Potter

PHILA. BIBLICAL
Langhorne, PA 19047-2990 III

Coach: Dick Beach, King's (N.Y.) 1971

2006-07 RESULTS (9-17)
71	Moody Bible	64
57	Hannibal-La Grange †	67
76	Gordon ⊠	79
58	Rowan	76
69	Keuka ⊠	78
61	Polytechnic (N.Y.)	54
75	Widener	71
43	Messiah	78
66	Swarthmore ⊠	77
73	D'Youville	58
78	Purchase St. ⊠	67
63	Cazenovia ⊠	78
72	Chestnut Hill	75
67	Penn St.-Berks ⊠	73
66	Villa Julie	86
60	Polytechnic (N.Y.) ⊠	68
94	Bard	86
73	Purchase St.	70
63	Baptist Bible (Pa.) ⊠	86
60	Chestnut Hill	63
57	Montclair St. ⊠	87
57	Keystone	54
54	Villa Julie ⊠	82
67	Lancaster Bible	61
79	Penn St.-Berks	84
68	Villa Julie	83

Nickname: Crimson Eagles
Colors: Crimson & Black & White
Arena: Mason Activity Center
 Capacity: 800; Year Built: 1992
AD: Drew Watson
SID: Julie Brubaker

PHILA. SCIENCES
Philadelphia, PA 19104-4495 II

Coach: David Pauley, Temple 1979
2006-07 RESULTS (14-15)
62	West Chester ⊠	68
66	Wilmington (Del.)	53
53	Kutztown ⊠	55
67	Nyack ⊠	75
76	Goldey-Beacom ⊠	67
39	Holy Family ⊠	49
65	Caldwell ⊠	52
73	Bloomfield	69
64	Chestnut Hill ⊠	53
94	East Stroudsburg ⊠	98
64	Post ⊠	57
49	Dominican (N.Y.) ⊠	60
74	Penn St.-Abington	61
83	Felician ⊠	53
56	Philadelphia U.	51
59	Nyack ⊠	60
68	Wilmington (Del.) ⊠	57
65	Caldwell	75
55	Goldey-Beacom	68
63	Post	72
58	Holy Family	61
67	Bloomfield ⊠	76
68	Dominican (N.Y.)	75
74	Philadelphia U. ⊠	61
71	Bridgeport ⊠	82
83	Felician	73
55	Holy Family ⊠	50
62	Post †	55
60	Caldwell †	61

Nickname: Devils
Colors: Cardinal & Silver
Arena: Robert "Bobby" Morgan Arena
 Capacity: 1,000; Year Built: 2003
AD: Robert C. Morgan
SID: Bob Heller

PHILADELPHIA U.
Philadelphia, PA 19144-5497 II

Coach: Herb Magee, Philadelphia U. 1963
2006-07 RESULTS (20-10)
85	Bryant ⊠	63
75	Chestnut Hill ⊠	63
55	St. Thomas Aquinas ⊠	52
65	Holy Family ⊠	61
66	Felician	69
78	Wilmington (Del.) ⊠	49
102	Bloomfield	69
62	Post ⊠	61
63	American Int'l	57
69	Southern N.H. ⊠	55
62	St. Rose ⊠	63
90	Goldey-Beacom ⊠	67
62	Adelphi	66
68	Nyack ⊠	59
68	Caldwell	67
77	Dominican (N.Y.) ⊠	57
51	Phila. Sciences ⊠	56
79	Felician	67
63	Holy Family	56
67	Post	83
65	Wilmington (Del.) ⊠	60
90	Bloomfield ⊠	64
55	Goldey-Beacom	72
73	Nyack	62
61	Phila. Sciences	74
57	Caldwell ⊠	53
36	Dominican (N.Y.)	51
71	Dominican (N.Y.) ⊠	67
64	Caldwell †	73
65	Bridgeport †	67

Nickname: Rams
Colors: Maroon & Grey
Arena: Bucky Harris Gym
 Capacity: 1,000; Year Built: 1960
AD: Thomas R. Shirley Jr.
SID: Tony Berich

PIEDMONT
Demorest, GA 30535 III

Coach: Lee Glenn, Methodist 2000
2006-07 RESULTS (13-13)
71	Greensboro †	81
64	Ferrum	70
87	Methodist ⊠	73
68	Southern Tech	72
95	Wesley †	89
78	N.C. Wesleyan	57
90	Oglethorpe	95
97	Rust †	90
67	Averett †	73
79	Oglethorpe ⊠	87
93	Pensacola Christian ⊠	80
84	Maryville (Tenn.) ⊠	87
74	Huntingdon	63
74	Chris. Newport	72
55	Methodist	71
98	Atlanta Christian ⊠	65
66	LaGrange	71
95	Sewanee	92
98	Southeastern Bible ⊠	69
117	Toccoa Falls ⊠	74
80	LaGrange	87
96	Huntingdon ⊠	77
78	Maryville (Tenn.)	101
114	Southeastern Bible	83
75	Pensacola Christian	83
97	LaGrange	102

Nickname: Lions
Colors: Green & Gold
Arena: Johnny Mize Center
 Capacity: 5,000; Year Built: 2000
AD: John Dzik
SID: Richard Dombrowsky

PITTSBURG ST.
Pittsburg, KS 66762 II

Coach: Gene Iba, Tulsa 1963
2006-07 RESULTS (18-13)
73	West Tex. A&M †	59
81	Central Bible (Mo.) †	36
81	Evangel	66
53	Colorado Mines ⊠	39
72	Cameron	87
65	Avila	47
82	Rhema ⊠	49
67	Central Mo.	87
71	Midwestern St. †	74
77	Southeastern Okla. †	72
68	Truman	63
84	Mo. Southern St. ⊠	71
77	Emporia St. ⊠	86
84	Southwest Baptist	87
64	Northwest Mo. St.	69
69	Mo. Western St. ⊠	71
84	Washburn	79
75	Fort Hays St. ⊠	77
59	Central Mo. ⊠	81
56	Fort Hays St.	55
72	Washburn ⊠	61
64	Mo. Western St.	73
74	Northwest Mo. St. ⊠	56
91	Emporia St.	88
51	Southwest Baptist ⊠	58
72	Mo. Southern St.	67
68	Truman	65
73	Southwest Baptist †	70
76	Northwest Mo. St. †	70
56	Central Mo. †	59
53	Northwest Mo. St. †	74

Nickname: Gorillas
Colors: Crimson & Gold
Arena: John Lance Arena
 Capacity: 6,500; Year Built: 1971
AD: Charles Broyles
SID: Dan Wilkes

PITTSBURGH
Pittsburgh, PA 15260 I

Coach: Jamie Dixon, TCU 1987
2006-07 RESULTS (29-8)
86	Western Mich. †	67
67	Delaware St. ⊠	50
78	Northeastern ⊠	52
85	Massachusetts ⊠	68
66	Oakland ⊠	55
88	Florida St. ⊠	66
67	Robert Morris ⊠	53
74	Auburn	66
73	Duquesne ⊠	56
70	Buffalo	67
75	Wisconsin	89
89	Oklahoma St. †	95
84	Dayton ⊠	54
77	Florida A&M ⊠	51
74	Syracuse	66
69	South Fla. ⊠	48
59	DePaul	49
74	Georgetown ⊠	69
63	Connecticut ⊠	54
74	Marquette ⊠	77
67	Cincinnati	51
72	St. John's (N.Y.) ⊠	46
65	Villanova	59
60	West Virginia	47
74	Providence ⊠	68
53	Louisville ⊠	66
65	Washington ⊠	61
71	Seton Hall	68
53	Georgetown	61
80	West Virginia ⊠	66
71	Marquette	75
89	Marquette †	79
65	Louisville †	59
42	Georgetown †	65
79	Wright St. †	58
84	VCU †	79
55	UCLA †	64

Nickname: Panthers
Colors: Gold & Blue
Arena: Petersen Events Center
 Capacity: 12,508; Year Built: 2003
AD: Jeffrey Long
SID: Greg Hotchkiss

PITT.-BRADFORD
Bradford, PA 16701-2898 III

Coach: Andy Moore, Mansfield 1986
2006-07 RESULTS (14-13)
72	St. Lawrence †	79
80	Brockport St.	105
86	Westminster (Pa.)	82
80	Elmira ⊠	70
66	Medaille ⊠	57
66	La Roche	62
66	Fredonia St.	57
75	Penn St.-Altoona ⊠	63
99	Mt. Aloysius ⊠	91
61	Nazareth	81
57	Geneseo St. ⊠	77
52	Frostburg St.	54
52	Lake Erie	69
85	Pitt.-Greensburg ⊠	69
64	Penn St.-Behrend ⊠	69
75	Hilbert	73
85	La Roche ⊠	73
66	Medaille	69
108	Mt. Aloysius	90
56	Penn St.-Altoona	77
56	Frostburg St. ⊠	63
64	Lake Erie ⊠	93
70	Pitt.-Greensburg	57
67	Hilbert †	59
53	Penn St.-Behrend	55
61	Penn St.-Altoona †	49
39	Penn St.-Behrend †	63

Nickname: Panthers
Colors: Navy & Gold

Arena: Pitt Bradford Sport & Fitness Center
 Capacity: 1,100; Year Built: 2002
AD: Lori Mazza
SID: Greg Clark

PITT.-GREENSBURG
Greensburg, PA 15601-5898 III

Coach: Marcus Kahn, Redlands 1997
2006-07 RESULTS (3-22)
88	Dickinson	100
72	Messiah †	92
70	Bethany (W.V.) ⊠	90
52	Indiana (Pa.)	85
79	Frostburg St.	89
58	Lake Erie ⊠	97
96	Mt. Aloysius ⊠	84
61	Penn St.-Behrend	73
94	Westminster (Pa.)	99
71	Trinity (Tex.) †	82
34	Southwestern (Tex.)	76
74	Medaille ⊠	71
77	Hilbert ⊠	84
69	Pitt.-Bradford	85
86	La Roche	87
76	Penn St.-Altoona ⊠	88
86	Lake Erie	98
73	Frostburg St. ⊠	75
60	Penn St.-Behrend ⊠	88
86	Mt. Aloysius	106
77	Medaille	80
91	Hilbert	94
57	Pitt.-Bradford ⊠	70
68	Penn St.-Altoona	69
82	La Roche	67

Nickname: Bobcats
Colors: Navy Blue & Gold
Arena: Chambers Hall
 Capacity: 500; Year Built: 1989
AD: Dick William Hack
SID: Kevin Conlon

PITT.-JOHNSTOWN
Johnstown, PA 15904-2990 II

Coach: Bob Rukavina, Indiana (Pa.) 1985
2006-07 RESULTS (21-9)
82	Columbia Union	65
88	Wheeling Jesuit ⊠	93
96	West Liberty St. ⊠	87
86	West Virginia St. ⊠	79
86	Lock Haven †	71
68	Gannon	73
86	West Va. Wesleyan	67
94	Penn St.-Fayette ⊠	36
73	Seton Hill †	64
69	East Stroudsburg	62
94	West Liberty St. †	101
71	Wheeling Jesuit	73
69	Shippensburg	78
89	Indiana (Pa.) ⊠	61
100	Concord ⊠	88
72	Penn St.-New Kens. ⊠	63
62	West Chester	64
71	Dist. Columbia	70
86	Mansfield	82
101	Columbia Union ⊠	61
82	Penn St.-McKeesport ⊠	41
72	Indiana (Pa.)	63
61	California (Pa.)	67
82	Dist. Columbia ⊠	73
88	Bloomsburg ⊠	82
69	Mansfield ⊠	80
70	Lock Haven	71
61	Ga. Southwestern †	70
86	Palm Beach Atl. †	65
82	Dist. Columbia †	71

Nickname: Mountain Cats
Colors: Vegas Gold & Navy Blue
Arena: Sports Center
 Capacity: 2,400; Year Built: 1976

AD: Michael F. Castner
SID: Chris Caputo

PLATTSBURGH ST.
Plattsburgh, NY 12901 III

Coach: Tom Curle, Plattsburgh St. 1981

2006-07 RESULTS (21-9)
52	Connecticut Col. †	55
73	Penn St.-Abington †	68
72	Norwich ⊠	55
59	St. Lawrence	71
72	Brockport St. ⊠	74
65	Geneseo St. ⊠	59
73	Clarkson ⊠	63
62	Kean †	67
86	Colby †	70
73	Oswego St.	75
56	Oneonta St.	58
86	New Paltz St.	66
73	Fredonia St.	64
90	Buffalo St.	84
89	Potsdam St.	88
78	Buffalo St. ⊠	66
69	Fredonia St. ⊠	55
91	SUNYIT	76
62	Cortland St.	55
86	Middlebury ⊠	69
74	Geneseo St.	80
60	Morrisville St.	57
78	Oswego St. ⊠	77
84	SUNYIT	89
71	New Paltz St.	66
82	Buffalo St. ⊠	72
89	Oswego St. †	73
80	Brockport St.	75
61	Rochester (N.Y.) †	60
87	St. John Fisher	95

Nickname: Cardinals
Colors: Cardinal Red & White
Arena: Memorial Hall Gymnasium
 Capacity: 1,400; Year Built: 1961
AD: Bruce Delventhal
SID: Patrick Stewart

PLYMOUTH ST.
Plymouth, NH 03264-1595 III

Coach: John Scheinman, Marist 1984

2006-07 RESULTS (10-16)
82	Centenary (N.J.) ⊠	67
86	Wheaton (Mass.) ⊠	78
88	Castleton	87
86	Colby-Sawyer †	77
70	Salem St.	87
81	Western Conn. St. ⊠	84
74	Rivier ⊠	56
73	Bridgewater St.	82
89	Rhode Island Col. ⊠	91
77	Tufts	87
92	Johnson & Wales (RI) ⊠	86
64	Bowdoin ⊠	65
51	Mass.-Dartmouth	64
87	Me.-Farmington ⊠	64
90	Mass.-Boston	97
52	Eastern Conn. St. ⊠	51
74	Southern Me.	81
71	Western Conn. St.	76
57	Keene St. ⊠	58
52	Rhode Island Col.	67
69	Mass.-Dartmouth ⊠	71
68	Southern Me. ⊠	60
96	Mass.-Boston ⊠	67
73	Keene St.	88
80	Eastern Conn. St.	87
86	Keene St.	98

Nickname: Panthers
Colors: Green & White
Arena: Foley Gymnasium
 Capacity: 2,000; Year Built: 1969
AD: John P. Clark
SID: Kent Cherrington

POLYTECHNIC (N.Y.)
Brooklyn, NY 11201 III

Coach: Daniel Nigro, St. Francis (N.Y.) 1995

2006-07 RESULTS (4-20)
55	Thomas (Me.) †	58
63	City Tech †	66
70	Pratt ⊠	49
61	Baruch ⊠	79
64	D'Youville ⊠	69
54	Phila. Biblical ⊠	61
84	Cazenovia	80
53	New York U. ⊠	77
57	Bard ⊠	73
47	Yeshiva	66
49	Purchase St.	62
60	Chestnut Hill ⊠	74
61	Penn St.-Berks ⊠	74
68	Phila. Biblical	60
65	Baptist Bible (Pa.)	80
86	Villa Julie	95
74	St. Joseph's (L.I.) ⊠	103
67	Keystone ⊠	85
75	Purchase St. ⊠	73
65	Villa Julie ⊠	90
54	Keuka	82
73	Penn St.-Berks	92
69	St. Joseph's (Brkln) ⊠	86
65	Chestnut Hill	86

Nickname: Blue Jays
Colors: Blue & Gray
Arena: Joseph J. & Violet J. Jacobs Building
 Capacity: 327; Year Built: 2002
AD: Maureen Braziel
SID: Robert Zieg

POMONA-PITZER
Claremont, CA 91711-6346 III

Coach: Charles Katsiaficas, Tufts 1984

2006-07 RESULTS (16-8)
71	Vanguard	56
83	Hope Int'l †	82
80	Willamette †	68
89	Worcester St. †	61
65	Washington-St. Louis	81
84	La Sierra ⊠	66
89	Biola ⊠	95
77	Wooster	97
58	Westmont	72
94	La Sierra	81
110	Redlands	116
98	Caltech	55
54	Occidental ⊠	70
79	Whittier ⊠	71
66	Cal Lutheran	68
66	Claremont-M-S	62
77	La Verne ⊠	61
113	Redlands ⊠	102
97	Caltech ⊠	50
59	Occidental	76
80	Whittier	68
69	Cal Lutheran ⊠	64
61	Claremont-M-S ⊠	47
77	La Verne	72

Nickname: Sagehens
Colors: Blue, Orange & White
Arena: Voelkel Gymnasium
 Capacity: 1,500; Year Built: 1989
AD: Charles C. Katsiaficas
SID: Ben Belletto

PORTLAND
Portland, OR 97203-5798 I

Coach: Eric Reveno, Stanford 1989

2006-07 RESULTS (9-23)
48	Oregon St.	65
53	Cal Poly †	56

55	Southeastern La. †	63
59	Montana St. ⊠	53
76	UC Davis ⊠	72
50	BYU	79
53	Portland St.	69
50	Washington St.	62
67	UC Santa Barbara ⊠	75
56	Weber St.	72
66	Eastern Wash. ⊠	87
51	Weber St.	68
69	Notre Dame	86
61	Montana	58
49	Oregon	76
74	Lewis & Clark ⊠	64
73	Pepperdine	69
81	Loyola Marymount ⊠	65
57	St. Mary's (Cal.)	73
41	Santa Clara	57
68	Gonzaga ⊠	80
70	San Diego ⊠	74
65	San Francisco ⊠	66
59	Loyola Marymount	74
87	Pepperdine	76
53	Santa Clara	76
55	St. Mary's (Cal.) ⊠	47
67	Gonzaga	87
76	San Diego	82
67	San Francisco	70
55	Loyola Marymount ⊠	41
47	St. Mary's (Cal.) ⊠	87

Nickname: Pilots
Colors: Purple & White
Arena: Chiles Center
 Capacity: 4,852; Year Built: 1984
AD: Lawrence Williams
SID: Jason Brough

PORTLAND ST.
Portland, OR 97207-0751 I

Coach: Ken Bone, Seattle Pacific 1983

2006-07 RESULTS (19-13)
65	Cal St. Northridge †	90
94	Lehigh †	90
68	Oregon	116
71	Arizona St.	67
95	Evergreen St. ⊠	76
69	Portland ⊠	53
51	Gonzaga	69
71	Utah Valley St. ⊠	69
107	Pacific Lutheran ⊠	57
72	San Jose St.	63
73	Washington	105
93	UC Davis ⊠	61
78	Howard ⊠	49
74	Montana	80
79	Montana St. ⊠	65
78	Northern Ariz.	85
79	Northern Colo.	66
65	Weber St.	75
70	Eastern Wash. ⊠	88
86	Northern Colo. ⊠	71
83	Northern Ariz. ⊠	78
93	Sacramento St.	97
67	Idaho St.	65
70	Montana	68
71	Montana St.	79
62	Weber St. ⊠	64
92	Eastern Wash.	86
87	Cal Poly	92
100	Sacramento St. ⊠	73
70	Idaho St. ⊠	63
96	Montana St. ⊠	71
74	Weber St.	77

Nickname: Vikings
Colors: Green, White & Silver
Arena: Peter W. Stott Center
 Capacity: 1,500; Year Built: 1967
AD: Teri Mariani
SID: Mike Lund

POST
Waterbury, CT 06723 II

Coach: Mike Donnelly, Sacred Heart 1997

2006-07 RESULTS (17-12)
61	Merrimack ⊠	52
67	Bridgeport	70
70	Mass.-Lowell †	75
71	Molloy	74
70	Nyack ⊠	65
83	Felician ⊠	78
63	Holy Family	75
65	Pace	97
61	Philadelphia U. ⊠	62
73	C.W. Post	85
83	New Haven ⊠	61
57	Phila. Sciences	64
59	Goldey-Beacom ⊠	58
63	Wilmington (Del.)	62
96	Bloomfield ⊠	95
61	Caldwell	53
67	Holy Family ⊠	65
89	Dominican (N.Y.) ⊠	54
85	Nyack ⊠	73
83	Philadelphia U. ⊠	67
89	Felician	92
72	Phila. Sciences ⊠	63
59	Goldey-Beacom	68
73	Caldwell ⊠	56
100	Wilmington (Del.) ⊠	88
79	Bloomfield	85
74	Dominican (N.Y.)	73
78	Felician	71
55	Phila. Sciences †	62

Nickname: Eagles
Colors: Hunter, Black & White
Arena: Drubner Center
 Capacity: 350; Year Built: 1972
AD: Anthony Fallacaro
SID: Patrick Moran

POTSDAM ST.
Potsdam, NY 13676-0000 III

Coach: Sherry Dobbs, Plattsburgh St. 1998

2006-07 RESULTS (9-16)
82	Green Mountain ⊠	57
55	Clarkson ⊠	58
67	New York U.	77
63	Clarkson	74
64	Geneseo St. ⊠	67
98	Brockport St. ⊠	95
60	St. Lawrence ⊠	76
68	Alfred ⊠	62
78	Ithaca ⊠	91
71	Westfield St. †	76
85	Framingham St. †	66
88	SUNYIT	76
61	New Paltz St. ⊠	73
62	Oneonta St. ⊠	56
94	Buffalo St.	76
53	Fredonia St.	63
88	Plattsburgh St. ⊠	89
83	Oswego St. ⊠	72
74	Cortland St.	89
79	SUNYIT	90
75	Brockport St.	92
59	Geneseo St.	85
65	Cortland St.	67
66	New Paltz St.	75
61	Oneonta St.	59

Nickname: Bears
Colors: Maroon & Gray
Arena: Maxcy Hall
 Capacity: 3,600; Year Built: 1972
AD: James Zalacca
SID: Boyd Jones

PRAIRIE VIEW
Prairie View, TX 77446-0519 I

Coach: Byron Rimm II, Cal St. L.A. 1999

2006-07 RESULTS (8-22)
49	Texas A&M	81
61	S'western Assemblies ⊠	57
48	Ball St.	65
33	Florida	94
49	Tennessee St. †	60
66	Chattanooga †	79
54	Houston	101
51	SMU	68
54	Tulsa	83
65	Rice	82
61	Baylor	103
64	Alcorn St.	71
58	Southern U.	63
67	Texas Southern ⊠	71
89	Huston-Tillotson ⊠	70
52	Grambling ⊠	66
62	Jackson St. ⊠	74
61	Mississippi Val.	64
56	Ark.-Pine Bluff	61
50	Alabama St. ⊠	47
60	Alabama A&M ⊠	58
66	Texas Southern	65
73	Grambling	87
67	Jackson St.	79
47	Mississippi Val. ⊠	45
67	Ark.-Pine Bluff ⊠	70
74	Alabama St.	60
66	Alabama A&M	86
78	Alcorn St. ⊠	73
51	Southern U. ⊠	66

Nickname: Panthers
Colors: Purple & Gold
Arena: William J. Nicks Building
  Capacity: 5,000; Year Built: 1968
AD: Charles McClelland
SID: Harlan Robinson

PRESBYTERIAN
Clinton, SC 29325-2998 II

Coach: Gregg Nibert, Marietta 1979

2006-07 RESULTS (20-9)
69	Lander ⊠	63
81	North Greenville ⊠	58
60	Lander	59
86	Allen ⊠	54
51	Winthrop	76
71	GCSU ⊠	58
64	S.C. Upstate	68
77	GCSU	88
64	Erskine ⊠	59
66	Fla. Southern	67
82	Montevallo †	72
61	Tusculum	59
65	Mars Hill ⊠	42
61	Lenoir-Rhyne	75
57	Lincoln Memorial ⊠	74
69	Catawba ⊠	56
70	Wingate	84
59	Carson-Newman	51
70	Newberry ⊠	43
66	Mars Hill	63
75	Lenoir-Rhyne ⊠	72
73	Lincoln Memorial	57
88	Wingate ⊠	77
77	Carson-Newman ⊠	72
53	Tusculum ⊠	50
60	Newberry	29
57	Catawba	63
56	Newberry ⊠	48
64	Wingate †	73

Nickname: Blue Hose
Colors: Blue & Garnet
Arena: Ross E. Templeton Center
  Capacity: 2,500; Year Built: 1975
AD: William B. Carlton
SID: Brian Hand

PRESENTATION
Aberdeen, SD 57401 III

Coach: Brad Vanden Boogaard, Wis.-
  Parkside 1999

2006-07 RESULTS (9-15)
74	Trinity Bible (N.D.)	57
86	Minot St. ⊠	81
72	Augsburg	93
50	Viterbo	62
83	Minn.-Morris ⊠	69
50	Chaminade	92
63	Central (Iowa) †	68
69	Hastings ⊠	80
66	Mt. Marty ⊠	68
44	Valley City St. ⊠	67
62	Martin Luther	69
68	Bethany Lutheran ⊠	65
63	St. Scholastica ⊠	77
47	Northland ⊠	62
93	Trinity Bible (N.D.) ⊠	75
57	Northwestern (Minn.)	80
61	Crown (Minn.) ⊠	43
73	Crown (Minn.) ⊠	52
58	Northwestern (Minn.) ⊠	56
56	Bethany Lutheran ⊠	67
66	Martin Luther ⊠	86
80	Northland	67
59	St. Scholastica	72
59	Minn.-Morris	73

Nickname: Saints
Colors: Old gold & hunter green
Arena: Stode Activity Center
Capacity: 1,400
AD: Jim Zimmerman
SID: To be named

PRINCETON
Princeton, NJ 08544 I

Coach: Joe Scott, Princeton 1987

2006-07 RESULTS (11-17)
57	Loyola (Ill.) †	68
73	VMI †	68
56	Alabama A&M †	39
57	Manhattan	45
44	Lafayette	42
50	North Dakota St. †	57
53	Northwestern St. †	51
44	Lehigh ⊠	43
47	Rutgers ⊠	53
61	Marshall ⊠	45
48	South Carolina	54
57	Iona	46
51	Rice ⊠	28
56	Columbia	64
35	Cornell	55
41	Seton Hall	79
35	Yale	43
48	Brown	63
74	Harvard ⊠	68
44	Dartmouth ⊠	45
35	Penn	48
50	Cornell ⊠	57
54	Columbia ⊠	49
43	Dartmouth	53
43	Harvard	50
55	Brown ⊠	64
51	Yale ⊠	52
48	Penn ⊠	64

Nickname: Tigers
Colors: Orange & Black
Arena: Jadwin Gymnasium
  Capacity: 6,854; Year Built: 1969
AD: Gary D. Walters
SID: David Rosenfeld

PRINCIPIA
Elsah, IL 62028-9799 III

Coach: Garry Sprague, Principia 1986

2006-07 RESULTS (1-22)
60	St. Louis Pharmacy	68
50	Hendrix	97
50	Austin †	89
36	Northwest Mo. St.	111
52	Wheaton (Ill.)	112
48	Westminster (Mo.)	72
58	Greenville	91
72	MacMurray	83
52	Fontbonne ⊠	69
64	Blackburn	75
87	Lincoln Christian ⊠	53
63	Webster	82
56	Eureka ⊠	72
61	Maryville (Mo.)	78
64	Westminster (Mo.) ⊠	72
67	MacMurray ⊠	95
89	Greenville ⊠	96
53	Blackburn ⊠	77
53	Fontbonne	94
55	Maryville (Mo.) ⊠	75
68	Lincoln Christian	93
61	Webster ⊠	78
78	Eureka	84

Nickname: Panthers
Colors: Gold & Blue
Arena: Hay Field House
  Capacity: 1,000; Year Built: 1967
AD: Lenore Suarez
SID: Brian Peticolas

PROVIDENCE
Providence, RI 02918 I

Coach: Tim Welsh, Potsdam St. 1984

2006-07 RESULTS (18-13)
96	Fairleigh Dickinson ⊠	71
41	Brown ⊠	51
73	Boston College ⊠	64
86	George Washington ⊠	67
81	Columbia ⊠	55
95	Rhode Island ⊠	66
67	Fairfield ⊠	50
67	Florida	85
94	Maine ⊠	79
77	Holy Cross ⊠	68
101	Harvard ⊠	92
62	Florida St. †	92
107	Longwood ⊠	69
74	Marquette ⊠	59
91	Seton Hall ⊠	69
63	Louisville	78
68	Seton Hall	69
78	Rutgers ⊠	63
73	Villanova ⊠	82
84	Connecticut	72
62	Marquette	69
71	Cincinnati ⊠	70
68	Pittsburgh	74
78	Notre Dame	81
71	St. John's (N.Y.) ⊠	69
64	West Virginia ⊠	61
67	Syracuse ⊠	71
77	South Fla.	72
64	St. John's (N.Y.)	77
79	West Virginia †	92
78	Bradley	90

Nickname: Friars
Colors: Black, White & Silver
Arena: Dunkin' Donuts Center
  Capacity: 12,993; Year Built: 1972
AD: Robert Driscoll
SID: Arthur Parks

PUGET SOUND
Tacoma, WA 98416-9710 III

Coach: Justin Lunt, Pacific Lutheran
  2003

2006-07 RESULTS (18-7)
124	UC Santa Cruz ⊠	86
130	Menlo	102
98	Northwest Chrst.	91
102	Warner Pacific	109
140	Willamette ⊠	137
92	George Fox ⊠	79
114	Puget Sound Chrst. ⊠	56
114	La Verne	104
106	Whittier	88
117	Chapman	111
108	Pacific Lutheran	96
71	Pacific (Ore.)	77
77	Whitworth	72
102	Whitman	88
94	Lewis & Clark ⊠	88
70	Linfield ⊠	64
108	Willamette	119
63	George Fox	75
89	Pacific Lutheran ⊠	86
85	Pacific (Ore.) ⊠	79
95	Whitworth ⊠	90
99	Whitman ⊠	106
86	Lewis & Clark	98
83	Linfield	76
60	Lewis & Clark	66

Nickname: Loggers
Colors: Maroon & White
Arena: Memorial Fieldhouse
  Capacity: 4,000; Year Built: 1949
AD: Amy E. Hackett
SID: Chris Thompson

PURCHASE ST.
Purchase, NY 10577-1400 III

Coach: Denny Carroll, Dayton 1971

2006-07 RESULTS (5-20)
58	Lehman †	70
80	Cazenovia †	87
89	Pratt	58
62	Old Westbury	92
103	Cazenovia ⊠	106
76	Penn St.-Berks	75
66	Eastern Conn. St.	93
70	Brooklyn ⊠	71
40	Army	101
58	Vassar	85
67	Phila. Biblical	78
75	Bard	74
57	Baptist Bible (Pa.) ⊠	82
62	Polytechnic (N.Y.) ⊠	49
67	Villa Julie ⊠	81
44	Chestnut Hill	72
46	Keystone	65
70	Phila. Biblical ⊠	73
59	Keuka ⊠	70
73	Polytechnic (N.Y.)	75
68	D'Youville	66
54	Morrisville St.	69
72	Chestnut Hill ⊠	89
68	Villa Julie	98
58	Penn St.-Berks	71

Nickname: Panthers
Colors: Royal blue, white & orange
Arena: PC Arena-Field House
Capacity: 1,500
AD: Ernie Palmieri
SID: To be named

PURDUE
West Lafayette, IN 47907-1031 I

Coach: Matt Painter, Purdue 1993

2006-07 RESULTS (22-12)
90	Northern Colo. ⊠	58
82	Western Caro. ⊠	57

(continued, first column — Purdue)

61	Georgia Tech †	79
74	Oklahoma †	71
81	DePaul †	73
61	Virginia ⊠	59
62	Delaware St. ⊠	40
78	Loyola (Ill.) ⊠	62
79	Missouri ⊠	62
65	Butler †	68
95	Wagner ⊠	56
79	A&M-Corpus Christi ⊠	61
70	Indiana St. ⊠	89
102	Southeast Mo. St. ⊠	65
59	Minnesota	65
64	Penn St. ⊠	60
58	Indiana	85
67	Michigan ⊠	53
64	Wisconsin	69
55	Michigan	71
64	Illinois ⊠	47
60	Ohio St. ⊠	78
69	Penn St.	59
62	Michigan St. ⊠	38
56	Ohio St.	63
81	Indiana ⊠	68
59	Iowa	78
75	Northwestern	68
66	Minnesota ⊠	47
73	Northwestern ⊠	50
74	Iowa †	55
52	Ohio St. †	63
72	Arizona †	63
67	Florida †	74

Nickname: Boilermakers
Colors: Old Gold & Black
Arena: Mackey Arena
 Capacity: 14,123; Year Built: 1967
AD: Morgan J. Burke
SID: Elliot Bloom

QUEENS (N.Y.)
Flushing, NY 11367 II

Coach: Kyrk Peponakis, St. John's (N.Y.) 1988

2006-07 RESULTS (14-14)

102	Felician	90
66	St. Anselm ⊠	83
65	St. Thomas Aquinas	75
84	New Haven ⊠	67
75	Mass.-Lowell	96
76	Molloy	64
82	C.W. Post ⊠	72
80	Northwood (Fla.) ⊠	91
87	Bloomfield †	69
59	Dominican (N.Y.)	54
67	Bridgeport	83
50	Adelphi ⊠	64
57	Dominican (N.Y.) ⊠	66
73	NYIT ⊠	71
65	Concordia (N.Y.)	67
85	Dowling ⊠	62
76	Mercy	60
95	St. Thomas Aquinas ⊠	75
65	New Haven	73
74	C.W. Post	83
94	Molloy ⊠	103
86	Bridgeport ⊠	72
84	Adelphi	96
87	NYIT	96
88	Concordia (N.Y.) ⊠	74
97	Dowling	77
72	Mercy ⊠	61
79	Adelphi	85

Nickname: Knights
Colors: Blue & Silver
Arena: Fitzgerald Gymnasium
 Capacity: 3,000; Year Built: 1958
AD: Richard Wettan
SID: Neal Kaufer

QUEENS (N.C.)
Charlotte, NC 28274 II

Coach: Brian Good, Wisconsin 1993

2006-07 RESULTS (20-10)

97	Concord †	95
61	Shaw †	50
86	Erskine	85
69	UNC Pembroke ⊠	61
82	Tusculum	70
66	Augusta St.	78
68	Wingate ⊠	74
82	Augusta St. ⊠	97
69	Limestone ⊠	67
72	Coker	58
96	Mount Olive ⊠	91
75	Anderson (S.C.) ⊠	37
88	Pfeiffer ⊠	106
94	Barton	101
88	Lees-McRae	77
70	Belmont Abbey ⊠	68
78	St. Andrews ⊠	64
61	Coker ⊠	53
73	St. Andrews	89
101	Pfeiffer	89
59	Anderson (S.C.)	49
66	Limestone	63
72	Lees-McRae ⊠	58
87	Barton ⊠	95
71	Mount Olive	95
64	Erskine ⊠	55
84	Belmont Abbey ⊠	69
85	Erskine ⊠	76
86	Mount Olive †	93
76	Barton	85

Nickname: Royals
Colors: Navy Blue and Gold
Arena: Ovens Athletic Center
 Capacity: 900; Year Built: 1989
AD: Jeannie King
SID: Cherie Swarthout

QUINCY
Quincy, IL 62301-2699 II

Coach: Marty Bell, South Carolina 1985

2006-07 RESULTS (20-10)

75	Hannibal-La Grange ⊠	44
104	Grand View ⊠	67
82	Truman	76
89	South Dakota †	79
62	Neb.-Omaha	58
70	Northern Ky.	68
67	Bellarmine	81
79	Lewis ⊠	64
82	Wis.-Parkside ⊠	72
90	Gannon ⊠	61
64	Henderson St.	67
88	Truman ⊠	78
76	Mo.-St. Louis	69
86	Mo.-Rolla	79
81	Ky. Wesleyan ⊠	72
76	Southern Ind. ⊠	74
63	Indianapolis	68
63	St. Joseph's (Ind.)	67
74	Rockhurst ⊠	67
78	Drury †	74
67	SIU Edwardsville ⊠	55
61	Rockhurst	72
69	Drury	76
71	SIU Edwardsville	76
65	Southern Ind.	87
80	Mo.-St. Louis ⊠	70
92	Mo.-Rolla ⊠	83
79	St. Joseph's (Ind.) †	62
57	Southern Ind.	76
75	Grand Valley St. †	85

Nickname: Hawks
Colors: Brown, White & Gold
Arena: Pepsi Arena
 Capacity: 2,000; Year Built: 1950
AD: Patrick Atwell
SID: Brian Lovellette

QUINNIPIAC
Hamden, CT 06518-1940 I

Coach: Joe DeSantis, Fairfield 1979

2006-07 RESULTS (14-15)

46	Connecticut	53
92	Concordia (N.Y.) ⊠	77
71	Lehigh ⊠	55
59	New Hampshire ⊠	64
71	Colgate	80
74	Brown	80
73	Mt. St. Mary's	78
75	Fairleigh Dickinson ⊠	80
53	Dartmouth	56
87	Vermont ⊠	101
66	Fordham	67
68	Robert Morris	86
89	St. Francis (Pa.)	82
80	Wagner	72
71	Monmouth ⊠	51
74	St. Francis (N.Y.) ⊠	72
64	Fairleigh Dickinson	63
73	Long Island ⊠	71
54	Central Conn. St. ⊠	65
73	St. Francis (N.Y.)	70
70	Mt. St. Mary's ⊠	62
79	Sacred Heart ⊠	75
71	Central Conn. St.	94
70	Long Island	68
72	St. Francis (Pa.) ⊠	73
81	Robert Morris ⊠	75
84	Sacred Heart	87
78	Fairleigh Dickinson ⊠	77
69	Sacred Heart	83

Nickname: Bobcats
Colors: Blue & Gold
Arena: Burt Kahn Court-Athletic Center
 Capacity: 2,000; Year Built: 1969
AD: Jack McDonald
SID: Tom Wilkins

RADFORD
Radford, VA 24142 I

Coach: Byron Samuels, UNC Asheville 1986

2006-07 RESULTS (8-22)

60	Milwaukee	72
63	UAB †	76
67	Washington St. †	84
72	Western Ill. †	75
77	Alcorn St. †	49
59	Air Force	83
87	Campbell ⊠	80
67	Richmond	50
89	West Va. Wesleyan ⊠	64
60	George Mason ⊠	62
94	Shenandoah ⊠	63
88	Campbell	101
51	East Tenn. St.	71
46	Col. of Charleston	68
64	IUPUI †	67
74	High Point	81
66	Liberty	80
80	Coastal Caro. ⊠	76
61	Charleston So. ⊠	53
67	UNC Asheville ⊠	77
59	Winthrop ⊠	62
94	VMI	103
65	High Point ⊠	75
70	Charleston So.	84
67	Coastal Caro.	85
58	Winthrop	77
114	VMI ⊠	107
68	UNC Asheville	78
48	Liberty ⊠	64
73	High Point	90

Nickname: Highlanders
Colors: Red, White, Green & Blue
Arena: Donald N. Dedmon Center
 Capacity: 5,000; Year Built: 1981
AD: Greig W. Denny
SID: Drew Dickerson

RAMAPO
Mahwah, NJ 07430-1680 III

Coach: Chuck McBreen, Towson 1988

2006-07 RESULTS (22-8)

76	Yeshiva ⊠	65
70	Farmingdale St. ⊠	65
74	John Jay	59
77	Richard Stockton ⊠	75
91	City Tech	73
87	Kean	97
83	Rowan ⊠	73
91	Lincoln (Pa.) ⊠	75
90	Baruch	59
80	Roanoke †	63
71	Simpson †	86
60	Baldwin-Wallace †	72
91	Rutgers-Newark ⊠	90
72	Wm. Paterson ⊠	69
81	York (N.Y.) ⊠	62
77	Montclair St.	74
95	Medgar Evers ⊠	62
66	New Jersey City	73
71	Rutgers-Camden	67
72	Lincoln (Pa.)	73
74	TCNJ	55
91	Rutgers-Newark	75
67	Wm. Paterson ⊠	64
68	Montclair St. ⊠	71
64	New Jersey City ⊠	79
77	TCNJ ⊠	61
92	Rowan	84
83	New Jersey City	81
77	York (N.Y.) ⊠	68
61	Stevens Institute ⊠	69

Nickname: Roadrunners
Colors: Maroon, Black & White
Arena: Bradley Center
 Capacity: 1,500; Year Built: 2004
AD: Michael J. Ricciardi
SID: Rachel Pinton

RANDOLPH-MACON
Ashland, VA 23005 III

Coach: Mike Rhoades, Lebanon Valley 1995

2006-07 RESULTS (14-12)

106	Penn St.-Berks †	59
81	Lycoming	66
77	Chris. Newport	84
63	Wash. & Lee ⊠	58
67	Roanoke ⊠	62
70	Lynchburg	78
77	East. Mennonite	80
69	Methodist ⊠	76
84	Union (N.Y.) ⊠	54
70	Alfred †	59
68	Wis.-Platteville ⊠	64
73	Guilford ⊠	80
105	Emory & Henry ⊠	113
60	Hampden-Sydney ⊠	59
64	Bridgewater (Va.) ⊠	63
60	Va. Wesleyan	65
65	Guilford	65
106	Emory & Henry	102
70	Lynchburg ⊠	66
64	Wash. & Lee	63
78	Roanoke	55
63	Bridgewater (Va.) ⊠	65
69	Va. Wesleyan ⊠	77
73	East. Mennonite ⊠	48
53	Hampden-Sydney	82
58	Roanoke	79

Nickname: Yellow Jackets
Colors: Lemon & Black
Arena: Crenshaw Gymnasium
 Capacity: 1,300; Year Built: 1963
AD: Denis Kanach
SID: Chris Kilcoyne

REDLANDS

Redlands, CA 92373-0999............III

Coach: Gary Smith, Redlands 1964

2006-07 RESULTS (17-7)

152 West Coast Baptist ⊠....................98
105 Biola..138
131 UC Santa Cruz ⊠............................110
123 Cal St. East Bay ⊠........................115
110 Chapman ⊠......................................107
130 La Sierra ⊠......................................116
123 Hope Int'l..127
105 Cal St. L.A. ⊠....................................129
153 Whitman ⊠..149
151 Pacific Union ⊠................................120
116 Pomona-Pitzer ⊠..............................110
85 Cal Lutheran ⊠..................................129
98 Claremont-M-S......................................94
116 La Verne ⊠..104
109 Occidental..106
132 Whittier..122
121 Caltech ⊠...59
102 Pomona-Pitzer....................................113
90 Cal Lutheran..97
94 Claremont-M-S ⊠..................................86
97 La Verne..93
106 Occidental ⊠......................................116
136 Whittier ⊠..129
125 Caltech..43

Nickname: Bulldogs
Colors: Maroon & Gray
Arena: Currier Gym
Capacity: 1,200; Year Built: 1929
AD: Jeffrey Martinez
SID: Rachel J. Roche

REGIS (COLO.)

Denver, CO 80221-1099.................II

Coach: Lonnie Porter, Adams St. 1965

2006-07 RESULTS (9-17)

84 Johnson & Wales (CO) ⊠............76
72 Angelo St. ⊠......................................66
51 Seattle ⊠..54
67 Neb.-Omaha †....................................69
67 Minn. Duluth †....................................61
83 Colorado Col. ⊠................................66
60 Adams St..59
64 Colorado St.-Pueblo..........................75
67 Western St. ⊠....................................72
71 Johnson & Wales (CO)......................53
64 N.M. Highlands....................................67
37 Western N.M...62
55 Mesa St. ⊠..63
71 Fort Lewis ⊠......................................79
56 Neb.-Kearney......................................73
67 Chadron St...77
70 Metro St. ⊠..90
48 Colo. Christian ⊠................................61
71 UC-Colo. Springs................................65
49 Colorado Mines....................................71
37 Colo. Christian....................................59
61 Metro St...86
78 UC-Colo. Springs ⊠............................75
55 Colorado Mines ⊠..............................81
81 Chadron St. ⊠....................................72
72 Neb.-Kearney ⊠..................................85

Nickname: Rangers
Colors: Navy Blue & Gold
Arena: Regis University Fieldhouse
Capacity: 2,500; Year Built: 1959
AD: Barbara J. Schroeder
SID: Jake Strait

RENSSELAER

Troy, NY 12180-3590.......................III

Coach: Mike Griffin, Columbia 1965

2006-07 RESULTS (13-13)

60 Muhlenberg..62
57 Arcadia †..55
83 Mt. St. Mary (N.Y.) ⊠........................71
64 Williams..57
69 Middlebury..64
55 Connecticut Col. ⊠............................59
89 Morrisville St. ⊠..................................59
78 Wentworth Inst. ⊠..............................57
69 Stevens Institute ⊠............................74
48 Cortland St...65
74 Southern Vt. ⊠....................................62
76 Union (N.Y.) ⊠....................................79
62 Skidmore ⊠..50
51 Vassar..63
67 Clarkson..49
65 St. Lawrence..71
58 Hamilton ⊠..64
64 Hobart ⊠..58
70 St. Lawrence ⊠....................................75
77 Clarkson ⊠..57
67 Skidmore..53
74 Union (N.Y.)..68
66 Vassar ⊠..74
62 Hobart..69
64 Hamilton..86
69 Ithaca..80

Nickname: Red Hawks
Colors: Cherry & White
Arena: Robison Gymnasium
Capacity: 1,500; Year Built: 1920
AD: Kevin Beattie
SID: Kevin Beattie

RHODE ISLAND

Kingston, RI 02881-1303.................I

Coach: Jim Baron, St. Bonaventure 1977

2006-07 RESULTS (19-14)

86 Stonehill ⊠..62
99 Houston ⊠..102
78 Troy †..84
77 Alas. Fairbanks..................................73
92 Centenary (La.) †................................82
68 Boston College....................................86
85 Iona ⊠..60
66 Providence..95
72 Brown ⊠..68
85 Utah ⊠..84
81 DePaul ⊠..89
65 Boston U. ⊠..51
69 Ohio..97
69 Kansas..80
69 La Salle ⊠..66
75 Dayton ⊠..74
58 St. Louis..62
86 St. Joseph's..81
89 St. Bonaventure ⊠..............................78
85 Temple..77
75 Massachusetts ⊠................................72
78 George Washington ⊠........................82
45 Fordham..44
55 Massachusetts....................................77
111 Duquesne..87
83 St. Louis ⊠..67
86 Charlotte ⊠..69
72 Xavier..98
62 Fordham ⊠..71
69 Richmond..71
73 Fordham †..69
79 Xavier †..71
69 George Washington †..........................78

Nickname: Rams
Colors: Light & Dark Blue & White
Arena: Ryan Center
Capacity: 7,800; Year Built: 2002
AD: Thomas P. McElroy
SID: Tim Volkmann

RHODE ISLAND COL.

Providence, RI 02908.......................III

Coach: Bob Walsh, Hamilton 1994

2006-07 RESULTS (27-4)

73 Endicott †..59
95 Tufts..84
74 Fitchburg St. ⊠....................................63
78 Keene St. ⊠..82
82 Johnson & Wales (RI)........................53
84 Salve Regina..78
91 Plymouth St..89
76 Coast Guard..71
73 Springfield ⊠..65
88 Bridgewater St. ⊠................................80
87 Eastern Conn. St..................................79
67 Southern Me. ⊠..................................58
85 Framingham St....................................60
86 Mass.-Boston ⊠..................................77
85 Western Conn. St. ⊠..........................61
81 Keene St..92
78 Mass.-Dartmouth................................71
67 Plymouth St. ⊠....................................52
48 Amherst ⊠..62
84 Eastern Conn. St. ⊠............................62
76 Western Conn. St................................66
74 Southern Me..56
87 Mass.-Dartmouth ⊠............................77
90 Mass.-Boston..72
72 Southern Me. ⊠..................................69
76 Mass.-Dartmouth ⊠............................68
87 Keene St. ⊠..75
64 Coast Guard ⊠....................................60
70 Brandeis ⊠..67
75 Keene St. †..73
69 Amherst..81

Nickname: Anchormen
Colors: Gold, White & Burgundy
Arena: Intercollegiate Athletic
Capacity: 8,000; Year Built: 1995
AD: Donald E. Tencher
SID: Scott Gibbons

RHODES

Memphis, TN 38112-1690............III

Coach: Herb Hilgeman, Miami (Ohio) 1972

2006-07 RESULTS (8-15)

74 Westminster (Mo.) ⊠........................77
74 Rhema ⊠..62
57 Dallas ⊠..69
72 Wesley (Miss.) ⊠................................65
72 Rust ⊠..74
67 Trinity (Tex.)..65
55 Southwestern (Tex.)............................68
55 Rust..66
50 Huntingdon..49
59 Huntingdon ⊠......................................50
67 Millsaps ⊠..84
81 Dallas..53
56 Sewanee ⊠..77
68 Oglethorpe ⊠......................................92
68 Hendrix..70
71 Austin..67
65 DePauw ⊠..78
52 Centre ⊠..77
79 Trinity (Tex.) ⊠....................................83
61 Southwestern (Tex.) ⊠........................54
52 Sewanee..59
86 Oglethorpe..94
82 Millsaps..88

Nickname: Lynx
Colors: Red, Black & White
Arena: Mallory Gym
Capacity: 2,000
AD: Mike Clary
SID: Rob Sabau

RICE

Houston, TX 77251-1892.................I

Coach: Willis Wilson, Rice 1982

2006-07 RESULTS (16-16)

118 Paul Quinn ⊠......................................66
50 Gonzaga †..88
70 Colorado St. †......................................61
69 North Texas ⊠......................................71
73 Oregon ⊠..79
64 Utah..80
80 Tex. Permian Basin ⊠..........................46
83 Lamar ⊠..71
82 Prairie View ⊠....................................65
85 Belmont †..87
67 Western Caro. †..................................62
69 Vanderbilt ⊠..74
28 Princeton..51
75 Tulane ⊠..70
64 East Caro..47
76 Houston ⊠..71
67 UCF..72
73 UTEP ⊠..67
55 Tulane..75
63 Houston..70
83 East Caro. ⊠..74
70 Southern Miss. ⊠................................55
63 SMU..60
73 UAB..84
63 UCF ⊠..74
63 Memphis..99
75 SMU ⊠..66
64 Marshall..69
65 Tulsa ⊠..73
77 UTEP †..74
53 UCF †..51
62 Houston †..77

Nickname: Owls
Colors: Blue & Gray
Arena: Autry Court
Capacity: 5,000; Year Built: 1950
AD: Christopher M. DelConte
SID: Jay Jameson

RICHARD STOCKTON

Pomona, NJ 08240-0195...............III

Coach: Gerry Matthews, Kean 1965

2006-07 RESULTS (19-10)

85 Wesley †..72
64 Otterbein †..57
84 Delaware Valley ⊠..............................70
75 Ramapo..77
68 Rutgers-Newark ⊠..............................75
79 Rutgers-Camden..................................55
68 Neumann †..65
49 Messiah..55
42 Monmouth..75
51 Wis.-Platteville †..................................64
59 Alfred †..51
68 Gwynedd-Mercy..................................57
57 Averett †..51
65 York (Pa.)..63
66 TCNJ ⊠..57
91 Kean..82
83 Lincoln (Pa.) ⊠....................................69
53 New Jersey City..................................64
93 Rowan ⊠..83
78 Montclair St..84
80 Rutgers-Camden ⊠..............................50
66 Wm. Paterson ⊠..................................48
66 TCNJ..58
96 Kean ⊠..89
69 Rowan..80
76 Rutgers-Newark ⊠..............................84
78 Old Westbury..73
80 New Jersey City..................................69
55 New York U..58

Nickname: Ospreys
Colors: Black & White
Arena: Sports Center
Capacity: 3,000; Year Built: 2000
AD: G. Larry James
SID: Chris Rollman

RICHMOND

Richmond, VA 23173-1903............I

Coach: Chris Mooney, Princeton 1994

2006-07 RESULTS (8-22)

71 East Caro. ⊠......................................67
61 American ⊠..50
83 Longwood ⊠..72
52 Old Dominion......................................69
50 Radford ⊠..67

73	Marist ⊠	80
56	South Fla.	46
54	VCU ⊠	68
84	VMI ⊠	93
59	Wake Forest	72
63	Tulane ⊠	75
53	William & Mary	61
53	Virginia Tech	65
55	Fordham ⊠	58
71	St. Bonaventure	66
51	Charlotte ⊠	66
58	George Washington ⊠	63
54	Dayton	72
56	La Salle	79
53	St. Bonaventure ⊠	61
59	Temple ⊠	80
56	Massachusetts	72
46	Charlotte	61
69	Duquesne ⊠	66
50	Xavier	71
49	George Washington	68
78	St. Joseph's ⊠	68
68	St. Louis	78
71	Rhode Island ⊠	69
61	Fordham †	63

Nickname: Spiders
Colors: Red & Blue
Arena: Robins Center
Capacity: 9,071; Year Built: 1972
AD: Jim Miller
SID: Mark Kwolek

RIDER
Lawrenceville, NJ 08648-3099....... I

Coach: Tommy Dempsey, Susquehanna 1997

2006-07 RESULTS (16-15)
52	NJIT	63
66	Boston U.	60
77	Delaware	67
70	Northeastern ⊠	69
89	Drexel ⊠	81
66	Monmouth ⊠	67
79	Binghamton	65
69	Iona ⊠	55
79	Siena	87
61	Villanova	108
74	Fairleigh Dickinson	72
51	Notre Dame	101
58	Fairfield	55
55	Marist	71
75	St. Peter's ⊠	67
64	Fairfield	63
79	Niagara	80
75	Manhattan	86
73	Loyola (Md.) ⊠	78
84	Siena ⊠	78
54	St. Peter's	53
57	Iona	69
78	Marist ⊠	79
75	Manhattan ⊠	68
98	Canisius	88
73	Loyola (Md.)	95
51	Murray St. ⊠	58
81	Canisius	72
77	Niagara	89
77	Iona †	62
52	Niagara †	77

Nickname: Broncs
Colors: Cranberry & White
Arena: Alumni Gymnasium
Capacity: 1,650; Year Built: 1959
AD: Donald P. Harnum
SID: Bud Focht

RIPON
Ripon, WI 54971....................... III

Coach: Bob Gillespie, Lewis 1971

2006-07 RESULTS (13-10)
80	Buena Vista †	85
76	Viterbo †	65

76	Wis.-Stevens Point	90
62	Wis.-La Crosse	78
89	Knox ⊠	75
67	St. Norbert	65
80	Hardin-Simmons †	69
72	Mary Hardin-Baylor	86
72	Illinois Col. ⊠	70
60	Lawrence ⊠	56
73	Lake Forest	72
79	Monmouth (Ill.)	80
118	Grinnell	120
49	Lake Forest ⊠	62
80	Carroll (Wis.) ⊠	76
81	Beloit	77
71	St. Norbert ⊠	53
91	Illinois Col.	77
76	Knox	66
57	Lawrence	72
75	Carroll (Wis.)	89
82	Beloit ⊠	60
79	Carroll (Wis.) †	92

Nickname: Red Hawks
Colors: Red & White
Arena: Storzer Center
Capacity: 2,500; Year Built: 1967
AD: Robert G. Gillespie
SID: Patricia A. Malizia

RIVIER
Nashua, NH 03060-5086............... III

Coach: Dave Morissette, Plymouth St. 1994

2006-07 RESULTS (20-9)
94	Johnson St. ⊠	74
51	Anna Maria	49
84	New England Col.	69
55	Johnson & Wales (RI) ⊠	68
56	Plymouth St.	74
65	Mount Ida ⊠	64
66	Suffolk ⊠	74
84	Staten Island	74
44	Wheaton (Ill.) †	60
69	Emerson	66
68	Norwich	62
74	Johnson & Wales (RI)	63
64	Western New Eng. ⊠	60
67	Emmanuel (Mass.) ⊠	69
84	Southern Vt.	78
100	Daniel Webster ⊠	74
90	Suffolk	92
87	Albertus Magnus ⊠	82
81	Emerson ⊠	78
82	Norwich ⊠	78
47	Western New Eng.	70
74	Emmanuel (Mass.)	75
87	Southern Vt. ⊠	86
80	Daniel Webster	71
78	Albertus Magnus	75
88	Johnson & Wales (RI) ⊠	76
94	Suffolk ⊠	82
59	Emmanuel (Mass.) ⊠	57
47	Keene St.	81

Nickname: Raiders
Colors: Blue & Gray
Arena: Muldoon Fitness Center
Capacity: 300; Year Built: 1984
AD: Joanne Merrill
SID: Joanne Merrill

ROANOKE
Salem, VA 24153....................... III

Coach: Page Moir, Virginia Tech 1984

2006-07 RESULTS (17-11)
83	Sewanee ⊠	81
75	Robert Morris-Chi. ⊠	79
34	Va. Wesleyan	67
62	Randolph-Macon	67
92	Emory & Henry	101
67	Guilford	77
63	Ramapo †	80
48	Mount Union †	50

69	Colorado Col. †	40
89	Chestnut Hill ⊠	65
60	Drew ⊠	48
68	Wash. & Lee ⊠	64
78	East. Mennonite	58
72	Guilford ⊠	68
91	Lynchburg ⊠	34
62	Hampden-Sydney ⊠	65
64	Bridgewater (Va.) ⊠	59
70	Wash. & Lee	64
112	Emory & Henry	107
48	Va. Wesleyan ⊠	62
55	Randolph-Macon ⊠	78
69	Lynchburg	56
80	Hampden-Sydney	79
60	Bridgewater (Va.)	43
79	East. Mennonite ⊠	65
79	Randolph-Macon ⊠	58
87	Bridgewater (Va.) ⊠	62
62	Hampden-Sydney ⊠	77

Nickname: Maroons
Colors: Maroon & Gray
Arena: Bast Center
Capacity: 2,000; Year Built: 1982
AD: M. Scott Allison
SID: Chris Cummings

ROBERT MORRIS
Moon Township, PA 15108-1189 . I

Coach: Mark Schmidt, Boston College

2006-07 RESULTS (17-11)
96	Florida Int'l ⊠	72
73	Marshall	69
77	New Hampshire ⊠	64
55	Maine	43
53	Pittsburgh	67
73	Duquesne ⊠	72
74	Sacred Heart	90
60	Wagner	72
79	Youngstown St. ⊠	78
81	Canisius	77
83	Goucher ⊠	38
86	Quinnipiac ⊠	68
64	Central Conn. St. ⊠	48
56	Long Island	59
70	Fairleigh Dickinson ⊠	66
82	Sacred Heart ⊠	84
81	Mt. St. Mary's ⊠	78
94	St. Francis (Pa.)	75
68	Monmouth	76
79	Fairleigh Dickinson ⊠	84
76	St. Francis (Pa.) ⊠	68
65	Mt. St. Mary's	60
97	St. Francis (N.Y.) ⊠	102
71	Wagner ⊠	63
86	Central Conn. St.	88
75	Quinnipiac	81
90	Long Island ⊠	74
61	Mt. St. Mary's ⊠	78

Nickname: Colonials
Colors: Blue & White with Red
Arena: Charles L. Sewall Center
Capacity: 3,056; Year Built: 1985
AD: Craig Coleman
SID: Jim Duzyk

ROCHESTER (N.Y.)
Rochester, NY 14627-0296........... III

Coach: Mike Neer, Wash. & Lee 1970

2006-07 RESULTS (18-8)
81	Ithaca ⊠	72
62	Lake Erie ⊠	73
74	Nazareth ⊠	71
76	Wash. & Jeff. ⊠	44
88	Buffalo St. ⊠	57
60	Carnegie Mellon	51
80	Hobart ⊠	63
67	St. John Fisher	69
60	Rochester Inst. ⊠	54
83	Brandeis ⊠	65
61	New York U. ⊠	70

70	Nazareth †	57
82	St. John Fisher †	53
80	Geneseo St. †	53
59	Washington-St. Louis	68
74	Chicago ⊠	81
84	Case Reserve ⊠	43
84	Emory ⊠	75
81	Emory	65
67	Case Reserve	56
58	New York U.	53
66	Brandeis	73
73	Chicago ⊠	76
66	Washington-St. Louis ⊠	61
72	Carnegie Mellon ⊠	60
60	Plattsburgh St. †	61

Nickname: Yellowjackets
Colors: Yellow & Blue
Arena: Louis Alexander Palestra
Capacity: 1,889; Year Built: 1930
AD: George VanderZwaag
SID: Dennis O'Donnell

ROCHESTER INST.
Rochester, NY 14623-5603........... III

Coach: Bob McVean, Brockport St. 1969

2006-07 RESULTS (14-13)
86	D'Youville	46
51	Clarkson	62
54	St. Lawrence	57
67	Hobart ⊠	48
57	Houghton ⊠	49
64	York (N.Y.) ⊠	60
63	Cortland St.	62
54	Rochester (N.Y.)	60
59	St. John Fisher ⊠	65
60	Alfred ⊠	69
68	St. John Fisher ⊠	75
82	Nazareth †	76
54	Roberts Wesleyan †	61
82	Elmira	70
90	Ithaca	84
86	Nazareth	79
77	Utica ⊠	91
82	Hartwick ⊠	86
77	Alfred	64
70	St. John Fisher	68
69	Nazareth ⊠	60
69	Hartwick	73
66	Utica	61
74	Ithaca ⊠	83
73	Elmira ⊠	63
58	St. John Fisher	67
63	Oswego St.	74

Nickname: Tigers
Colors: Burnt Umber, Orange & White
Arena: Clark Memorial Gymnasium
Capacity: 2,200; Year Built: 1968
AD: Louis W. Spiotti Jr.
SID: Steve Jaynes

ROCKFORD
Rockford, IL 61108-2393.............. III

Coach: Ryan Rebsom, Montana Western 1998

2006-07 RESULTS (3-22)
68	Wis. Lutheran	77
59	Elmhurst ⊠	78
66	Milwaukee Engr.	70
54	Benedictine (Ill.)	74
88	North Park	91
64	Lakeland ⊠	108
67	Maranatha Baptist	56
44	Augustana (Ill.)	78
33	Transylvania †	77
52	Westminster (Utah) †	51
66	MacMurray	94
57	Concordia (Wis.)	68
55	Marian (Wis.) ⊠	74
50	Edgewood	69
67	Dominican (Ill.) ⊠	89
69	Concordia (Ill.) ⊠	68

RESULTS

47	Aurora (Wis.)	90
64	Concordia (Wis.) ⊠	71
57	Benedictine (Ill.) ⊠	64
57	Lakeland	90
53	Wis. Lutheran ⊠	83
61	Marian (Wis.)	86
65	Dominican (Ill.)	92
77	Aurora ⊠	97
59	Edgewood ⊠	71

Nickname: Regents
Colors: Purple, White
Arena: Seaver Center
  Capacity: 1,100; Year Built: 1964
AD: Hank Espensen
SID: Cory Espensen

ROCKHURST
Kansas City, MO 64110-2561 II

Coach: Bill O'Connor, St. Benedict 1972

2006-07 RESULTS (17-12)

67	St. Cloud St.	77
76	Neb.-Omaha †	63
69	William Jewell ⊠	57
66	St. Mary (Kan.)	40
79	Southwest Baptist ⊠	53
64	Mo. Southern St.	49
54	Wis.-Parkside	60
61	Lewis	71
82	Mo.-Rolla ⊠	76
82	Mo.-St. Louis	83
77	St. Mary (Kan.) ⊠	48
64	Southern Ind.	79
67	Ky. Wesleyan	61
63	Indianapolis	46
94	St. Joseph's (Ind.) ⊠	77
67	Park ⊠	68
78	Drury	70
67	Quincy	74
65	SIU Edwardsville	72
75	Bellarmine ⊠	72
63	Northern Ky. ⊠	87
72	Quincy ⊠	61
70	SIU Edwardsville ⊠	64
80	Mo.-Rolla	58
76	Mo.-St. Louis	67
60	Drury ⊠	69
75	Southern Ind.	63
61	Northern Ky. †	71
78	Southern Ind. †	84

Nickname: Hawks
Colors: Blue & White
Arena: Mason-Halpin Field House
  Capacity: 1,500; Year Built: 1938
AD: Rebecca Morrisey
SID: John Dodderidge

ROGER WILLIAMS
Bristol, RI 02809 III

Coach: Mike Tully, Clark (Mass.) 1991

2006-07 RESULTS (15-11)

82	Me.-Fort Kent ⊠	43
85	Salem St.	73
92	Johnson & Wales (RI) ⊠	78
57	Coast Guard	68
72	Colby-Sawyer ⊠	51
65	Curry	50
61	Mass.-Dartmouth	72
60	Connecticut Col.	65
77	Gordon	67
82	Nichols ⊠	49
84	Eastern Nazarene	47
89	Anna Maria	49
73	Wesleyan (Conn.) ⊠	62
67	Curry ⊠	69
61	New England	57
50	Salve Regina	56
95	New England Col.	85
74	Salve Regina ⊠	67
58	Endicott	62
64	Wentworth Inst.	74
74	Anna Maria ⊠	57

63	Eastern Nazarene ⊠	71
60	Nichols	65
83	Wheaton (Mass.)	73
78	Wentworth Inst. ⊠	81
65	St. Joseph's (Me.)	70

Nickname: Hawks
Colors: Blue & Gold
Arena: Campus Recreation Center
  Capacity: 1,200; Year Built: 2003
AD: George Kolb
SID: Dave Kemmy

ROLLINS
Winter Park, FL 32789 II

Coach: Tom Klusman, Rollins 1976

2006-07 RESULTS (25-7)

80	UCF	83
95	Flagler ⊠	81
83	P.R.-Mayaguez ⊠	56
76	Warner Southern ⊠	65
87	Southeastern (Fla.) ⊠	62
71	Tampa	80
105	Webber Int'l ⊠	79
88	Seattle Pacific †	75
74	Central Mo. †	81
81	Nyack ⊠	67
82	Ga. Southwestern ⊠	72
79	Palm Beach Atl. ⊠	77
69	Nova Southeastern ⊠	67
70	Fla. Southern	59
68	Lynn	52
70	St. Leo ⊠	57
73	Eckerd ⊠	66
87	Florida Tech	74
63	Barry ⊠	38
71	Fla. Southern ⊠	69
80	Nova Southeastern	79
60	Tampa ⊠	67
93	Lynn ⊠	71
81	St. Leo	63
57	Eckerd	62
70	Florida Tech ⊠	68
76	Barry	47
80	Florida Tech †	65
62	Nova Southeastern †	49
52	Eckerd †	67
61	Valdosta St. †	60
76	Eckerd †	85

Nickname: Tars
Colors: Blue & Gold
Arena: Alfond Sports Center
  Capacity: 2,500; Year Built: 2000
AD: Pennie Parker
SID: Nate Weyant

ROSE-HULMAN
Terre Haute, IN 47803 III

Coach: Jim Shaw, Indiana 1982

2006-07 RESULTS (9-16)

57	Wabash	50
61	Aurora †	66
74	Blackburn	57
63	Anderson (Ind.)	50
71	Hanover	72
50	Franklin ⊠	58
49	Bluffton ⊠	54
80	Fontbonne ⊠	78
62	Earlham	70
70	Cincinnati-Clermont ⊠	60
53	Tri-State ⊠	60
49	Robert Morris-S'fiel	67
39	Defiance	60
66	Transylvania	82
61	Mt. St. Joseph ⊠	77
50	Manchester ⊠	47
43	DePauw	58
61	Hanover ⊠	56
71	Anderson (Ind.) ⊠	59
53	Bluffton	62
51	Franklin	68
58	Transylvania ⊠	62
46	Mt. St. Joseph	67

52	Defiance ⊠	61
68	Manchester	56

Nickname: Fightin' Engineers
Colors: Old Rose & White
Arena: Hulbert Arena
  Capacity: 2,000; Year Built: 1997
AD: Jeffrey Jenkins
SID: Kevin Lanke

ROWAN
Glassboro, NJ 08028-1701 III

Coach: Joe Cassidy, St. Joseph's 1974

2006-07 RESULTS (20-6)

68	McMurry †	63
68	Johns Hopkins	70
93	Medgar Evers	73
76	Phila. Biblical ⊠	58
73	Ramapo	83
86	Newport News ⊠	76
95	Penn St.-Delaware ⊠	66
72	Cabrini ⊠	50
92	Gwynedd-Mercy ⊠	76
79	Chestnut Hill	61
79	Neumann	68
70	Rutgers-Camden ⊠	60
68	TCNJ	59
82	Penn St.-Abington	69
93	Kean	87
66	Wm. Paterson	68
83	Richard Stockton	93
82	New Jersey City ⊠	95
88	Rutgers-Newark ⊠	80
76	Valley Forge Chrst. ⊠	56
78	Montclair St. ⊠	68
85	Rutgers-Camden	65
81	TCNJ ⊠	61
88	Kean	68
80	Richard Stockton ⊠	69
84	Ramapo	92

Nickname: Profs
Colors: Brown & Gold
Arena: Esby Gym
  Capacity: 1,500; Year Built: 1963
AD: Joy L. Solomen
SID: Sheila Stevenson

RUST
Holly Springs, MS 38635 III

Coach: Rodney Stennis, Rust 1969

2006-07 RESULTS (11-14)

69	Millsaps	79
64	Hendrix	61
81	Ozarks (Ark.)	83
74	Rhodes	72
71	Hendrix	76
78	Maryville (Tenn.) ⊠	92
44	Southern Ark.	71
66	Rhodes ⊠	55
90	Piedmont †	97
61	Averett †	79
70	Belhaven	68
55	Dallas †	59
67	Huntingdon	51
92	Millsaps ⊠	70
69	LaGrange	75
62	Philander Smith	86
80	Oakwood ⊠	81
100	Knoxville ⊠	66
86	Fisk ⊠	81
73	LeMoyne-Owen	89
77	Philander Smith	64
59	Oakwood	69
92	Fisk	66
82	Knoxville	81
69	Maryville (Tenn.)	88

Nickname: Bearcats
Colors: Blue & White
Arena: McMillan Multipurpose Ctr
  Capacity: 2,000; Year Built: 1971
AD: Ishmell H. Edwards
SID: To be named

RUTGERS
New Brunswick, NJ 08903 ....

Coach: Fred Hill Jr., Monclair St. 1981

2006-07 RESULTS (10-19)

41	Kansas St. ⊠	55
82	St. Thomas Aquinas ⊠	41
70	Jackson St. ⊠	71
72	Bradley †	101
44	Miami (Ohio) †	57
54	Temple	77
75	Nebraska ⊠	73
55	New Hampshire ⊠	48
53	Princeton	47
66	Iona ⊠	51
67	Lehigh ⊠	61
48	North Carolina	87
75	South Carolina St. ⊠	68
72	Seton Hall	77
54	Cincinnati	42
58	Syracuse ⊠	68
37	DePaul	60
54	Georgetown ⊠	68
63	Providence	78
40	South Fla.	62
74	Seton Hall ⊠	70
83	West Virginia ⊠	89
50	Connecticut	61
47	Marquette	67
73	Cincinnati ⊠	69
55	St. John's (N.Y.)	60
55	Connecticut ⊠	65
51	Villanova	74
66	Notre Dame ⊠	73

Nickname: Scarlet Knights
Colors: Scarlet
Arena: Louis Brown Athletic Center
  Capacity: 8,000; Year Built: 1977
AD: Robert E. Mulcahy III
SID: John Wooding

RUTGERS-CAMDEN
Camden, NJ 08102 III

Coach: Brian Wischusen, Boston
College 1997

2006-07 RESULTS (6-19)

55	Alvernia	74
53	Curry †	51
93	Valley Forge Chrst.	77
89	Albany Pharmacy †	68
55	Keystone	47
55	Richard Stockton ⊠	79
35	Wm. Paterson ⊠	82
64	Baptist Bible (Pa.) ⊠	71
62	Montclair St.	81
70	Elizabethtown ⊠	75
51	Juniata	94
55	Widener ⊠	68
46	Keystone †	50
62	Lincoln (Pa.)	96
60	Rowan	70
62	TCNJ	65
65	Rutgers-Newark ⊠	61
49	Kean	80
67	Ramapo ⊠	71
50	Richard Stockton	80
46	New Jersey City	69
53	Eastern	66
65	Rowan ⊠	85
56	TCNJ	70
86	Kean ⊠	77

Nickname: Scarlet Raptors
Colors: Scarlet & Silver
Arena: Rutgers Camden Gymnasium
  Capacity: 2,100; Year Built: 1973
AD: Jeffrey L. Dean
SID: Mike Ballard

RUTGERS-NEWARK
Newark, NJ 07102 III

Coach: Joe Loughran, American Int'l 1993

2006-07 RESULTS (18-11)
79	Penn St.-Abington ⊠	73
64	Connecticut Col. ⊠	63
75	CCNY ⊠	66
80	York (N.Y.) ⊠	74
75	Richard Stockton	68
77	New Jersey City ⊠	72
70	Medgar Evers	56
93	Farmingdale St. ⊠	87
67	Hunter ⊠	65
79	Manhattanville	84
73	Elizabethtown †	87
76	Methodist †	72
90	Ramapo	91
73	City Tech	66
69	Wm. Paterson ⊠	62
61	Rutgers-Camden	65
61	John Jay	47
77	Montclair St.	76
76	TCNJ ⊠	52
80	Rowan	88
56	New Jersey City	77
95	Kean ⊠	93
75	Ramapo	91
61	Wm. Paterson	66
71	Montclair St. ⊠	78
84	Richard Stockton	76
69	New Jersey City	79
82	Farmingdale St. ⊠	73
72	New York U.	82

Nickname: Scarlet Raiders
Colors: Scarlet & Black
Arena: The Golden Dome
Capacity: 2,000; Year Built: 1977
AD: Mark Griffin
SID: John Stallings

SACRAMENTO ST.
Sacramento, CA 95819-6099 I

Coach: Jerome Jenkins, Regis 1990

2006-07 RESULTS (10-19)
107	Bethany (Cal.) ⊠	73
56	New Mexico	92
64	San Francisco ⊠	89
74	Denver	53
74	Washington	83
93	San Jose Christian ⊠	58
100	UC Davis ⊠	77
69	Illinois St.	86
69	Louisville	99
74	Pacific ⊠	72
55	Long Beach St.	76
66	Boise St.	99
82	Northern Ariz.	96
74	Northern Colo.	70
80	Montana ⊠	72
58	Idaho St. ⊠	73
68	Weber St.	88
71	Northern Ariz. ⊠	94
65	Cal Poly	74
85	Eastern Wash. ⊠	100
97	Portland St. ⊠	93
81	Northern Colo. ⊠	84
62	Idaho St.	85
69	Montana	76
59	Montana St.	74
90	Montana St. ⊠	82
73	Portland St.	100
72	Eastern Wash.	80
105	Weber St. ⊠	83

Nickname: Hornets
Colors: Green & Gold
Arena: Hornets Nest
Capacity: 1,200; Year Built: 1951
AD: Terry L. Wanless
SID: Ryan Bjork

SACRED HEART
Fairfield, CT 06825-1000 I

Coach: Dave Bike, Sacred Heart 1969

2006-07 RESULTS (18-14)
68	Fordham	70
81	North Carolina †	103
68	Iona †	61
63	Lehigh	72
90	Albany (N.Y.) ⊠	71
46	Connecticut	89
71	Columbia	76
90	Yale ⊠	80
90	Robert Morris ⊠	74
103	St. Francis (Pa.) ⊠	91
68	Boston College	101
95	Harvard	75
58	Army	59
63	St. Francis (N.Y.)	58
80	Mt. St. Mary's	91
74	Monmouth ⊠	57
84	Robert Morris	82
72	St. Francis (Pa.)	64
96	Central Conn. St.	103
88	Fairleigh Dickinson ⊠	91
80	Long Island ⊠	72
76	Wagner	80
75	Quinnipiac	79
81	Wagner ⊠	79
66	Central Conn. St. ⊠	80
79	Mt. St. Mary's ⊠	51
86	Fairleigh Dickinson	82
82	Monmouth	75
87	Quinnipiac ⊠	84
100	Wagner ⊠	68
83	Quinnipiac ⊠	69
70	Central Conn. St.	74

Nickname: Pioneers
Colors: Red & White
Arena: William H. Pitt Center
Capacity: 2,000; Year Built: 1997
AD: C. Donald Cook
SID: Gene Gumbs

SAGINAW VALLEY
University Center, MI 48710-0001 .. II

Coach: Jamie Matthews, Ball St. 1993

2006-07 RESULTS (11-14)
81	Central St. (Ohio) ⊠	75
81	Olivet	67
72	Hillsdale	81
72	Grand Valley St.	71
64	Ferris St.	62
71	Northern Mich.	72
56	Michigan Tech	64
64	Wis.-Parkside ⊠	81
62	Indianapolis	73
80	Ky. Wesleyan	86
60	Hillsdale	68
77	Rochester College ⊠	71
71	Gannon	63
71	Mercyhurst ⊠	68
60	Findlay	77
68	Ashland	79
44	Michigan Tech ⊠	50
55	Northern Mich. ⊠	77
73	Ferris St. ⊠	84
90	Lake Superior St. ⊠	78
74	Northwood (Mich.)	65
63	Lake Superior St.	60
66	Wayne St. (Mich.)	82
71	Grand Valley St. ⊠	76
102	Northwood (Mich.) ⊠	81

Nickname: Cardinals
Colors: Red, White & Blue
Arena: James O'Neill Jr. Arena
Capacity: 4,000; Year Built: 1989
AD: Mike E. Watson
SID: Ryan Thompson

ST. ANDREWS
Laurinburg, NC 28352-5598 II

Coach: Billy Lee, Atlanta Christian 1971

2006-07 RESULTS (11-17)
70	Mars Hill ⊠	55
76	UNC Pembroke	66
55	Barton ⊠	68
67	Wingate	87
71	Mount Olive	87
52	Erskine ⊠	67
58	N.C. A&T	92
84	St. Paul's ⊠	83
54	Coastal Caro.	74
46	Mars Hill	73
48	Anderson (S.C.)	69
58	Limestone ⊠	60
66	Belmont Abbey ⊠	63
75	Lees-McRae	71
77	Coker ⊠	67
106	Pfeiffer	101
64	Queens (N.C.)	78
79	Anderson (S.C.) ⊠	49
89	Queens (N.C.) ⊠	73
88	Barton	99
64	Limestone	89
80	Mount Olive ⊠	83
53	Erskine	64
70	Pfeiffer ⊠	100
78	Belmont Abbey	82
75	Lees-McRae ⊠	53
74	Coker	61
59	Coker ⊠	66

Nickname: Knights
Colors: Royal Blue & White
Arena: Harris Court
Capacity: 1,400; Year Built: 1967
AD: Howard Reichner
SID: Kevin Buczek

ST. ANSELM
Manchester, NH 03102-1310 II

Coach: Keith Dickson, New Hampshire 1979

2006-07 RESULTS (15-14)
85	Southern Conn. St. ⊠	61
62	C.W. Post	79
85	NYIT †	75
80	Bryant	84
62	Assumption ⊠	65
83	Queens (N.Y.)	66
84	Le Moyne	81
78	Southern N.H.	52
80	St. Thomas Aquinas ⊠	51
70	Caldwell ⊠	56
61	Pace	87
76	Franklin Pierce ⊠	73
81	Stonehill	90
67	Mass.-Lowell	61
62	St. Rose ⊠	83
60	Southern N.H. ⊠	64
80	St. Michael's ⊠	64
45	Bentley	74
75	American Int'l ⊠	63
71	Merrimack	83
69	Assumption	66
71	Bryant ⊠	70
66	Pace ⊠	67
61	Franklin Pierce	62
61	St. Rose	75
66	Le Moyne ⊠	49
70	Stonehill ⊠	81
66	Franklin Pierce	65
43	Bentley	77

Nickname: Hawks
Colors: Blue & White
Arena: Stoutenburgh Gymnasium
Capacity: 1,600; Year Built: 1961
AD: Edward Cannon
SID: Ken Johnson, Jr.

ST. AUGUSTINE'S
Raleigh, NC 27610-2298 II

Coach: Thomas Hargrove, St. Augustine's 1965

2006-07 RESULTS (19-9)
102	Barton †	106
71	Columbus St. †	50
62	Virginia Union ⊠	64
77	St. Paul's ⊠	71
62	Virginia St.	63
87	Bowie St.	80
51	Tarleton St.	70
72	Angelo St.	69
80	Columbus St.	73
81	North Georgia †	78
84	Shaw †	76
71	St. Paul's	70
76	Livingstone	73
63	N.C. Central	61
84	Elizabeth City St.	74
85	Shaw ⊠	58
76	Johnson C. Smith	80
75	N.C. Central †	64
76	Virginia St. ⊠	70
76	Virginia Union	69
104	Bowie St. ⊠	116
60	Fayetteville St.	61
73	Johnson C. Smith ⊠	82
78	Elizabeth City St. ⊠	72
74	Livingstone ⊠	47
81	Fayetteville St. ⊠	66
61	Fayetteville St. †	60
53	Virginia Union †	55

Nickname: Falcons
Colors: Blue & White
Arena: Emery Gymnasium
Capacity: 750; Year Built: 1962
AD: George Williams
SID: Anthony Jeffries

ST. BONAVENTURE
St. Bonaventure, NY 14778 I

Coach: Anthony Solomon, Virginia 1987

2006-07 RESULTS (7-22)
95	Chicago St. †	98
68	Alcorn St. †	59
69	Central Ark. ⊠	64
54	St. Francis (Pa.)	76
60	Central Conn. St.	57
63	Niagara ⊠	74
46	Boston U. ⊠	74
72	Ohio ⊠	77
57	Wright St. ⊠	59
56	Albany (N.Y.)	71
74	Hampton ⊠	89
71	Canisius ⊠	80
70	Syracuse	82
74	St. Louis	69
66	Richmond ⊠	71
63	George Washington	80
78	Rhode Island	89
87	La Salle ⊠	73
66	Xavier ⊠	92
61	Richmond	53
61	Fordham	67
92	Duquesne ⊠	111
70	Temple	109
62	Dayton ⊠	69
68	St. Joseph's ⊠	76
44	Massachusetts	83
97	Duquesne	94
60	Fordham ⊠	91
53	Charlotte	74

Nickname: Bonnies
Colors: Brown & White
Arena: Reilly Center
Capacity: 5,780; Year Built: 1966
AD: Steve Watson
SID: Steve Mest

ST. CLOUD ST.
St. Cloud, MN 56301-4498 II

Coach: Kevin Schlagel, St. Cloud St. 1976

2006-07 RESULTS (19-11)
77	Rockhurst ⊠	67
77	Mary ⊠	86
76	Concordia-St. Paul ⊠	50
68	Minn. St. Moorhead ⊠	66
80	Bemidji St.	50
75	Dakota St. ⊠	39
77	Upper Iowa	60
90	St. John's (Minn.)	78
76	Southwest Minn. St. ⊠	73
65	Wayne St. (Neb.) ⊠	52
77	Bowie St.	84
99	Columbia Union	73
83	Minn.-Crookston	57
91	Northern Mich. ⊠	93
92	North Dakota	90
86	Minn. Duluth	79
73	Minn. St. Mankato ⊠	83
81	Augustana (S.D.)	76
67	Sioux Falls	75
88	Minn. Duluth ⊠	69
76	Neb.-Omaha ⊠	67
72	North Dakota ⊠	75
68	Minn. St. Mankato	96
75	Neb.-Omaha	62
63	South Dakota	91
85	Augustana (S.D.) ⊠	80
83	South Dakota ⊠	90
63	Neb.-Omaha ⊠	52
73	Minn. St. Mankato	78
73	Winona St.	100

Nickname: Huskies
Colors: Cardinal Red & Black
Arena: Halenbeck Hall
    Capacity: 6,900; Year Built: 1965
AD: Morris Kurtz
SID: Anne Abicht

ST. EDWARD'S
Austin, TX 78704 II

Coach: Ryan Marks, Southern California 1993

2006-07 RESULTS (24-6)
89	Harding ⊠	91
71	Ala.-Huntsville ⊠	61
105	Concordia (Tex.) ⊠	89
65	Abilene Christian ⊠	60
86	Newman †	74
68	Harris-Stowe †	56
104	Huston-Tillotson ⊠	74
87	Schreiner ⊠	46
67	East Central	71
61	Abilene Christian	72
58	Tex. A&M Int'l	51
88	Dallas Baptist	83
91	Lincoln (Mo.)	60
56	Mont. St.-Billings	60
91	Mont. St.-Billings	60
64	Incarnate Word ⊠	60
54	St. Mary's (Tex.) ⊠	47
85	Tex. Permian Basin	84
66	Okla. Panhandle	50
94	Tex. A&M Int'l ⊠	83
78	Dallas Baptist	67
62	Okla. Panhandle ⊠	63
80	Tex. Permian Basin ⊠	61
66	Incarnate Word	61
62	St. Mary's (Tex.)	55
83	Lincoln (Mo.) ⊠	64
84	Mont. St.-Billings ⊠	67
73	Dallas Baptist †	64
85	Incarnate Word †	73
39	Central Mo.	76

Nickname: Hilltoppers
Colors: Navy & White
Arena: Recreation & Convocation Center
    Capacity: 2,500; Year Built: 1989
AD: Debora Taylor
SID: Naveen Boppana

ST. FRANCIS (PA.)
Loretto, PA 15940-0600 I

Coach: Bobby Jones, Western Ky. 1984

2006-07 RESULTS (8-21)
94	Lock Haven ⊠	60
76	St. Bonaventure ⊠	54
60	La Salle ⊠	69
69	Howard	75
56	Bucknell ⊠	60
67	Liberty	84
54	St. Francis (N.Y.)	50
91	Sacred Heart	103
70	Liberty ⊠	56
44	Akron	79
71	Duquesne ⊠	72
43	Georgia Tech	87
63	American	73
61	Central Conn. St. ⊠	80
82	Quinnipiac ⊠	89
84	Fairleigh Dickinson	91
60	Long Island	72
63	Mt. St. Mary's ⊠	67
64	Sacred Heart ⊠	72
75	Robert Morris ⊠	94
66	Monmouth	71
67	Wagner	83
68	Robert Morris	76
43	Mt. St. Mary's	58
81	St. Francis (N.Y.) ⊠	74
54	Wagner ⊠	57
73	Quinnipiac	72
72	Long Island ⊠	56
73	Monmouth	62

Nickname: Red Flash
Colors: Red & White
Arena: Maurice Stokes Athletic Center
    Capacity: 3,500; Year Built: 1972
AD: Robert S. Krimmel
SID: Pat Farabaugh

ST. FRANCIS (N.Y.)
Brooklyn Heights, NY 11201-4398
I

Coach: Brian Nash, Keene St. 1992

2006-07 RESULTS (9-22)
51	Syracuse	83
52	UTEP †	54
56	Penn †	86
60	Maine	79
49	Massachusetts	63
49	Fordham	76
64	Central Conn. St.	77
64	Fairfield	68
42	St. John's (N.Y.)	59
50	St. Francis (Pa.)	54
64	Hofstra	67
52	Hartford	58
76	Manhattan ⊠	73
67	Columbia ⊠	58
58	Sacred Heart ⊠	63
68	Long Island	52
54	Mt. St. Mary's ⊠	72
66	Wagner ⊠	73
72	Quinnipiac	74
66	Wagner	51
69	Monmouth ⊠	57
61	Central Conn. St. ⊠	69
70	Quinnipiac ⊠	73
60	Monmouth	69
71	Fairleigh Dickinson	69
79	Long Island ⊠	82
74	St. Francis (Pa.)	81
102	Robert Morris	97
56	Mt. St. Mary's ⊠	55
72	Fairleigh Dickinson ⊠	69
61	Central Conn. St.	79

Nickname: Terriers
Colors: Red & Blue
Arena: Pope Physical Education Center
    Capacity: 1,200; Year Built: 1971
AD: Irma Garcia
SID: Caitlin Howe

ST. JOHN FISHER
Rochester, NY 14618 III

Coach: Rob Kornaker, Alfred

2006-07 RESULTS (24-6)
86	Brockport St. ⊠	97
74	D'Youville	41
85	Morrisville St. ⊠	67
69	Rochester (N.Y.) ⊠	67
63	Geneseo St. ⊠	62
82	Cortland St. †	76
77	York (Pa.)	63
64	Hobart	43
65	Rochester Inst.	59
73	Nazareth	63
75	Rochester Inst.	68
53	Rochester (N.Y.) †	82
85	Brockport St. †	81
65	Hartwick	48
54	Utica	62
50	Alfred	51
91	Elmira ⊠	61
88	Ithaca ⊠	59
69	Nazareth ⊠	61
68	Rochester Inst. ⊠	70
81	Alfred ⊠	41
111	Elmira	99
86	Elmira	60
79	Utica ⊠	66
73	Hartwick ⊠	49
67	Rochester Inst.	58
78	Utica ⊠	73
98	Wentworth Inst. ⊠	72
95	Plattsburgh St. ⊠	87
91	Brockport St. ⊠	105

Nickname: Cardinals
Colors: Cardinal & Gold
Arena: Manning-Napier Varsity Gym
    Capacity: 1,200; Year Built: 1963
AD: Bob Ward
SID: Norm Kieffer

ST. JOHN'S (MINN.)
Collegeville, MN 56321 III

Coach: Jim Smith, Marquette 1956

2006-07 RESULTS (21-8)
100	Minn.-Morris ⊠	77
85	Concordia-M'head ⊠	79
91	St. Mary's (Minn.) ⊠	77
73	Carleton	71
63	Gust. Adolphus	54
78	St. Cloud St. ⊠	90
74	Minn.-Morris	56
49	Ursinus †	73
59	Penn St.-Behrend †	64
81	Bethel (Minn.) ⊠	77
82	St. Olaf	66
74	Macalester	68
75	Augsburg	65
92	Hamline	83
64	St. Thomas (Minn.) ⊠	59
78	Concordia-M'head	72
63	St. Mary's (Minn.)	66
65	Carleton	66
100	Gust. Adolphus ⊠	66
71	Bethel (Minn.)	83
70	St. Olaf	69
96	Macalester ⊠	76
67	Augsburg ⊠	54
97	Hamline ⊠	61
59	St. Thomas (Minn.)	74
87	Gust. Adolphus	65
49	St. Thomas (Minn.)	75
85	Loras ⊠	82
76	Wis.-Stevens Point	93

Nickname: Johnnies
Colors: Cardinal & Blue
Arena: Sexton Arena
    Capacity: 2,964; Year Built: 1974
AD: Tom Stock
SID: Ryan Klinkner

ST. JOHN'S (N.Y.)
Queens, NY 11439 I

Coach: Norm Roberts, Queens (N.Y.) 1987

2006-07 RESULTS (16-15)
74	North Fla. ⊠	53
72	Navy ⊠	49
60	Maryland †	92
76	Texas †	77
65	Illinois St. ⊠	78
64	Long Island ⊠	46
78	UMBC ⊠	57
59	St. Francis (N.Y.) ⊠	42
86	Niagara	64
68	NJIT ⊠	50
76	Columbia ⊠	70
45	Boston U. ⊠	44
51	Hofstra ⊠	63
64	DePaul ⊠	53
46	West Virginia ⊠	73
63	Seton Hall	79
59	Connecticut ⊠	68
63	DePaul	71
64	Syracuse ⊠	60
71	Notre Dame ⊠	68
46	Pittsburgh	72
48	Georgetown ⊠	72
73	Cincinnati	64
66	South Fla. ⊠	62
74	Syracuse	76
60	Rutgers ⊠	55
66	Providence	71
48	Louisville	67
50	Duke ⊠	67
77	Providence ⊠	64
67	Marquette †	76

Nickname: Red Storm
Colors: Red & White
Arena: Carnesecca Arena
    Capacity: 6,008; Year Built: 1961
AD: Chris Monasch
SID: Mark Fratto

ST. JOSEPH'S (IND.)
Rensselaer, IN 47978 II

Coach: Richard Davis, Ashland 2001

2006-07 RESULTS (16-12)
68	Winona St.	90
89	Ashland ⊠	73
83	Trinity Christian ⊠	70
80	Mo.-Rolla	73
86	Southern Ind. ⊠	96
69	Ky. Wesleyan ⊠	74
77	Purdue-North Cent. ⊠	69
48	Michigan Tech	62
75	Lake Superior St.	72
83	Northwood (Mich.)	84
86	Ferris St.	69
64	Indianapolis ⊠	61
69	Drury	81
77	Rockhurst	94
57	SIU Edwardsville ⊠	46
67	Quincy ⊠	63
64	Bellarmine	73
60	Northern Ky.	85
63	Wis.-Parkside ⊠	61
82	Lewis ⊠	74
80	Ky. Wesleyan ⊠	88
80	Mo.-St. Louis	67
70	Lewis	87
70	Wis.-Parkside	100
82	Indianapolis	56
69	Northern Ky. ⊠	65
81	Bellarmine ⊠	74
62	Quincy †	79

Nickname: Pumas
Colors: Cardinal & Purple
Arena: Richard F. Scharf Alumni Fieldhouse
    Capacity: 2,000; Year Built: 1941
AD: Bill Massoels
SID: Clark Teuscher

ST. JOSEPH'S (L.I.)
Patchogue, NY 11772-2603..........III

Coach: John Mateyko, American Int'l 1981

2006-07 RESULTS (17-10)
65	CCNY ⊠	74
82	Medgar Evers ⊠	71
86	Mt. St. Mary (N.Y.) ⊠	72
69	York (N.Y.) ⊠	76
78	City Tech	65
88	Lehman ⊠	52
74	SUNYIT †	75
88	Buena Vista †	77
89	Merchant Marine ⊠	72
78	Stevens Institute	88
91	Centenary (N.J.) ⊠	61
79	Old Westbury	93
64	Farmingdale St. ⊠	81
100	Mt. St. Vincent	82
106	Maritime (N.Y.)	94
66	Yeshiva	49
84	Manhattanville	81
103	Polytechnic (N.Y.)	74
92	Mt. St. Mary (N.Y.)	77
67	Old Westbury	84
70	Stevens Institute ⊠	86
76	Mt. St. Vincent ⊠	61
71	Hunter ⊠	43
60	Yeshiva ⊠	42
91	Merchant Marine	81
72	Farmingdale St.	74
68	New York U.	87

Nickname: Golden Eagles
Colors: Blue & Gold
Arena: Danzi Athletic Center
Capacity: 1,500; Year Built: 1996
AD: Donald L. Lizak
SID: Frank Flandina

ST. JOSEPH'S (ME.)
Standish, ME 04084-5263..............III

Coach: Rob Sanicola, St. Joseph's (Me.) 1999

2006-07 RESULTS (22-8)
49	Bridgewater St.	66
82	Me.-Machias †	69
64	Me.-Farmington ⊠	41
67	Husson	80
87	Me.-Presque Isle	60
71	Me.-Fort Kent	42
82	Framingham St. ⊠	69
55	Me.-Farmington	61
73	Husson ⊠	53
61	Colby ⊠	73
71	York (N.Y.)	69
84	Briarcliffe (N.Y.) ⊠	51
85	Thomas (Me.)	66
80	Bates ⊠	89
84	Maine Maritime	60
89	Lyndon St. ⊠	62
80	Southern Me.	58
91	Thomas (Me.) ⊠	41
72	Me.-Machias	67
81	New England †	64
82	Newbury ⊠	65
83	Bowdoin	87
99	Me.-Fort Kent ⊠	82
90	Me.-Presque Isle ⊠	43
68	Newbury	74
83	Mitchell ⊠	71
89	Lincoln (Pa.) ⊠	80
70	Roger Williams ⊠	65
76	Curry ⊠	67
62	Western New Eng.	68

Nickname: Monks
Colors: Royal Blue & White
Arena: Harold Alfond Center
Capacity: 1,320; Year Built: 1999
AD: Brian Curtin
SID: Deb Readon

ST. JOSEPH'S
Philadelphia, PA 19131-1395.........I

Coach: Phil Martelli, Widener 1976

2006-07 RESULTS (18-14)
63	Fairfield ⊠	47
81	Lafayette	73
63	Bucknell ⊠	53
61	Penn St.	65
55	Boston U. ⊠	39
56	Drexel	72
75	Bellarmine †	63
64	Louisville	74
72	Ohio †	79
55	St. Mary's (Cal.) ⊠	51
63	Hofstra †	65
58	Boston U. †	53
89	Duquesne ⊠	41
75	Charlotte	70
80	Temple	67
81	Rhode Island ⊠	86
55	Fordham	56
82	Xavier ⊠	74
65	George Washington	74
84	Penn ⊠	74
62	St. Louis	73
71	Dayton ⊠	65
39	Villanova	56
72	La Salle	50
62	George Washington ⊠	56
76	St. Bonaventure	68
92	Temple ⊠	76
68	Richmond	78
62	Xavier	72
67	Massachusetts ⊠	71
66	Temple †	62
48	George Washington †	58

Nickname: Hawks
Colors: Crimson & Gray
Arena: Alumni Memorial Fieldhouse
Capacity: 3,200; Year Built: 1949
AD: Don DiJulia
SID: Marie Wozniak

ST. LAWRENCE
Canton, NY 13617.............................III

Coach: Chris Downs, Oneonta St. 1991

2006-07 RESULTS (23-6)
79	Pitt.-Bradford †	72
80	Oberlin †	60
80	Middlebury ⊠	64
71	Plattsburgh St. ⊠	59
91	Elmira ⊠	67
57	Rochester Inst. ⊠	54
76	Potsdam St.	60
76	Ithaca ⊠	63
74	Alfred ⊠	65
80	Oswego St. ⊠	76
72	Brockport St.	102
66	Hobart	57
74	Hamilton ⊠	81
73	Clarkson ⊠	59
71	Vassar ⊠	74
71	Rensselaer ⊠	65
71	Skidmore ⊠	55
76	Union (N.Y.) ⊠	49
74	Clarkson ⊠	48
75	Rensselaer	70
83	Vassar	81
68	Hamilton ⊠	76
68	Hobart ⊠	70
86	Union (N.Y.)	73
79	Skidmore	55
72	Vassar †	67
65	Hamilton	64
85	Elms ⊠	79
49	Brockport St. ⊠	74

Nickname: Saints
Colors: Scarlet & Brown
Arena: Burkman Gymnasium
Capacity: 1,500; Year Built: 1970
AD: Margaret F. Strait
SID: Wally Johnson

ST. LEO
Saint Leo, FL 33574 II

Coach: Mike Madagan, Northern Ill. 1988

2006-07 RESULTS (13-15)
65	Colo. Christian †	93
60	Metro St.	85
82	Flagler	79
84	Southeastern (Fla.) ⊠	55
71	West Fla.	74
63	Henderson St. †	75
88	Warner Southern ⊠	61
52	Nova Southeastern ⊠	60
79	Palm Beach Atl.	71
80	Flagler ⊠	74
70	Tampa	58
72	Palm Beach Atl. ⊠	66
75	Eckerd ⊠	80
73	Florida Tech ⊠	70
57	Rollins	70
68	Barry	74
102	Fla. Southern ⊠	95
64	Lynn ⊠	62
52	Eckerd	66
55	Tampa ⊠	68
92	Florida Col. ⊠	56
54	Nova Southeastern	55
77	Florida Tech	71
63	Rollins ⊠	81
71	Barry ⊠	73
69	Fla. Southern	92
73	Lynn	68
45	Eckerd †	76

Nickname: Lions
Colors: Forest Green & Gold
Arena: Marion Bowman Center
Capacity: 1,500; Year Built: 1970
AD: Francis X. Reidy
SID: Eddie Kenny

ST. LOUIS
St. Louis, MO 63103...........................I

Coach: Brad Soderberg, Wis.-Stevens Point 1985

2006-07 RESULTS (20-13)
79	Quincy ⊠	55
87	Louisiana Tech †	65
82	Lamar †	69
33	Texas A&M	69
81	Houston ⊠	78
67	Loyola (Ill.) ⊠	64
56	Southern Ill.	65
71	Western Ill. ⊠	61
67	Pacific	60
77	Tenn.-Martin ⊠	53
51	Missouri St. ⊠	50
48	North Carolina ⊠	69
59	Mississippi ⊠	56
69	St. Bonaventure	74
63	Duquesne ⊠	73
62	Rhode Island ⊠	58
76	Xavier ⊠	65
79	Temple	85
68	Fordham	77
76	Charlotte ⊠	63
58	Houston	59
73	St. Joseph's	62
63	George Washington ⊠	53
57	Xavier	76
67	Rhode Island	83
59	La Salle ⊠	55
66	Dayton ⊠	56
50	Massachusetts	53
78	Richmond ⊠	68
64	Dayton	65
78	Duquesne †	77
74	Massachusetts †	71
40	George Washington †	60

Nickname: Billikens
Colors: Blue & White
Arena: Savvis Center
Capacity: 20,000; Year Built: 1994

AD: Cheryl L. Levick
SID: Doug McIlhagga

ST. MARTIN'S
Lacey, WA 98503...............................II

Coach: Keith Cooper, Seattle Pacific 1986

2006-07 RESULTS (10-17)
79	Ashland †	92
76	Sonoma St. †	75
60	Grand Canyon †	80
83	Northwest (Wash.) †	91
60	Hawaii Pacific	65
73	Chaminade	92
56	Notre Dame de Namur ⊠	62
86	Sonoma St.	93
83	Cal St. Monterey Bay †	87
93	Warner Pacific	84
78	George Fox ⊠	67
74	Western Ore. ⊠	73
84	Central Wash.	73
74	Seattle	64
76	Alas. Anchorage ⊠	74
89	Alas. Fairbanks ⊠	84
90	Seattle Pacific	100
94	Northwest Nazarene ⊠	79
67	Alas. Fairbanks	75
76	Alas. Anchorage	93
67	Western Wash. ⊠	64
85	Central Wash. ⊠	103
78	Northwest Nazarene	88
91	Seattle Pacific ⊠	99
72	Seattle ⊠	85
83	Western Ore.	94
69	Western Wash.	86

Nickname: Saints
Colors: Red & White
Arena: Saint Martin's Pavilion
Capacity: 4,300; Year Built: 1965
AD: Bob Grisham
SID: Tiffany N. Darling

ST. MARY'S (CAL.)
Moraga, CA 94575...............................I

Coach: Randy Bennett, UC San Diego 1986

2006-07 RESULTS (17-15)
71	Seattle Pacific ⊠	60
73	San Diego St. ⊠	74
62	Murray St. ⊠	44
89	Cal St. Monterey Bay ⊠	41
63	Southern California	69
74	TCU ⊠	53
59	Cal Poly	72
78	San Jose St. ⊠	60
82	Seton Hall	93
65	Cal St. Bakersfield ⊠	57
58	Nevada	76
73	Connecticut	89
51	St. Joseph's	55
61	Southern Ill. ⊠	66
93	Western Caro. ⊠	82
71	Belmont	60
69	Santa Clara	76
73	Portland	57
80	Gonzaga ⊠	75
71	San Francisco	64
85	San Diego	78
66	Pepperdine ⊠	68
69	Loyola Marymount ⊠	54
57	Santa Clara ⊠	63
72	San Diego ⊠	76
49	Gonzaga	60
47	Portland	55
92	San Francisco ⊠	83
97	Pepperdine	72
63	Loyola Marymount	47
87	Portland †	47
47	Santa Clara †	63

Nickname: Gaels
Colors: Navy Blue & Red

Arena: McKeon Pavilion
Capacity: 3,500; Year Built: 1978
AD: Mark Orr
SID: Rich Davi

ST. MARY'S (MD.)
St. Mary's City, MD 20686 III

Coach: Chris Harney, St. Mary's (Md.) 1997

2006-07 RESULTS (16-11)

60	Johns Hopkins ⊠	78
84	Frostburg St. †	68
61	Hood †	70
62	Catholic	67
52	Marymount (Va.) ⊠	64
70	Hood	99
79	Baruch	72
74	Washington (Md.) ⊠	62
64	TCNJ	63
73	TCNJ †	93
86	Immaculata †	67
75	York (Pa.)	81
77	Salisbury ⊠	76
68	Gallaudet	61
78	Mary Washington ⊠	75
86	Goucher	80
73	Catholic	75
80	Marymount (Va.)	89
87	Hood ⊠	81
95	York (Pa.) ⊠	85
77	Salisbury	84
85	Gallaudet ⊠	64
74	McDaniel	66
76	Mary Washington	64
87	Goucher ⊠	73
89	Marymount (Va.)	76
76	Hood	92

Nickname: Seahawks
Colors: Navy Blue & Old Gold
Arena: Athletics and Recreation Center Arena
Capacity: 1,200; Year Built: 2005
AD: Scott Devine
SID: Shawne McCoy

ST. MARY'S (MINN.)
Winona, MN 55987-1399..............III

Coach: Mike Trewick, St. John's (Minn.) 1993

2006-07 RESULTS (8-16)

54	Winona St.	98
65	Wis.-Eau Claire ⊠	78
43	St. Thomas (Minn.)	87
77	St. John's (Minn.)	91
81	Macalester ⊠	73
89	Hamline	87
57	Minn. St. Mankato	79
76	Neb. Wesleyan ⊠	61
54	St. Olaf ⊠	67
70	Gust. Adolphus ⊠	77
49	Carleton	77
73	Augsburg ⊠	83
58	Bethel (Minn.) ⊠	71
79	Concordia-M'head	67
46	St. Thomas (Minn.) ⊠	73
66	St. John's (Minn.) ⊠	63
60	Macalester	49
84	Hamline ⊠	70
57	St. Olaf	63
61	Gust. Adolphus	72
43	Carleton ⊠	66
80	Augsburg	68
57	Bethel (Minn.)	103
61	Concordia-M'head ⊠	70

Nickname: Cardinals
Colors: Red & White
Arena: St. Mary's Fieldhouse
Capacity: 3,500; Year Built: 1965
AD: Nikki Fennern
SID: Donny Nadeau

ST. MARY'S (TEX.)
San Antonio, TX 78228-8572 II

Coach: Jim Zeleznak, St. Mary's (Tex.)

2006-07 RESULTS (16-12)

59	Tex. A&M-Kingsville	72
79	Sul Ross St. ⊠	52
58	Tarleton St.	60
87	Dillard ⊠	59
67	Tex. A&M-Commerce ⊠	63
65	Tex. A&M-Kingsville ⊠	78
64	Mont. St.-Billings ⊠	52
68	Abilene Christian ⊠	70
66	Mo. Western St.	75
47	Fort Hays St. ⊠	49
73	Tarleton St. ⊠	69
63	Okla. Panhandle ⊠	53
76	Tex. Permian Basin ⊠	50
85	Dallas Baptist ⊠	80
94	Incarnate Word ⊠	96
63	Tex. A&M Int'l ⊠	48
47	St. Edward's	54
67	Mont. St.-Billings	51
69	Lincoln (Mo.)	67
68	Incarnate Word	70
70	Mont. St.-Billings	62
87	Lincoln (Mo.) ⊠	52
79	Dallas Baptist	74
77	Tex. A&M Int'l ⊠	63
55	St. Edward's ⊠	62
57	Okla. Panhandle	55
67	Tex. Permian Basin	79
65	Incarnate Word †	68

Nickname: Rattlers
Colors: Blue & Gold
Arena: Bill Greehey Arena
Capacity: 3,500; Year Built: 2000
AD: Charlie Migl
SID: Derek Smolik

ST. MICHAEL'S
Colchester, VT 05439 II

Coach: Tom O'Shea, Vermont 1986

2006-07 RESULTS (16-13)

63	Franklin Pierce ⊠	74
91	New Haven ⊠	79
78	Mass.-Lowell ⊠	75
76	Pace	75
88	Merrimack	79
94	Southern Conn. St. ⊠	82
60	American Int'l	66
75	Le Moyne ⊠	73
74	Bentley	78
60	St. Rose ⊠	73
79	Adelphi †	78
83	Felician †	90
71	Southern N.H.	66
92	Stonehill ⊠	76
81	St. Thomas Aquinas	60
87	Assumption ⊠	76
64	St. Anselm	80
67	Merrimack ⊠	62
69	Mass.-Lowell	65
75	American Int'l ⊠	76
75	Le Moyne	86
64	St. Rose	77
59	Bentley ⊠	83
75	Southern Conn. St.	77
74	Bryant ⊠	68
91	Pace ⊠	72
83	Franklin Pierce	86
68	Assumption ⊠	60
62	St. Rose	76

Nickname: Purple Knights
Colors: Purple & Gold
Arena: Ross Sports Center
Capacity: 2,500; Year Built: 1974
AD: Geraldine Knortz
SID: Seth Cole

ST. NORBERT
De Pere, WI 54115 III

Coach: Gary Grzesk, Green Bay 1996

2006-07 RESULTS (9-13)

57	Augustana (Ill.)	78
54	Elmhurst ⊠	56
74	Knox ⊠	61
122	Grinnell ⊠	97
65	Ripon ⊠	67
57	Northern Mich.	73
52	Wis.-Oshkosh	64
47	Centre	59
79	Geneva †	69
54	Beloit	61
55	Carroll (Wis.) ⊠	69
54	Illinois Col.	51
52	Lake Forest	51
68	Monmouth (Ill.) ⊠	56
75	Illinois Col. ⊠	69
49	Lawrence	55
53	Ripon	71
58	Knox	49
66	Grinnell	93
76	Beloit ⊠	47
70	Carroll (Wis.)	77
57	Lawrence ⊠	71

Nickname: Green Knights
Colors: Dartmouth Green & Old Gold
Arena: Schuldes Sports Center
Capacity: 2,000; Year Built: 1979
AD: Timothy A. Bald
SID: Dan Lukes

ST. OLAF
Northfield, MN 55057-1098..........III

Coach: Dan Kosmoski, Minnesota 1980

2006-07 RESULTS (13-14)

55	Southwest Minn. St.	67
57	Luther ⊠	60
75	Crown (Minn.) ⊠	48
69	Martin Luther	59
51	St. Thomas (Minn.)	83
76	Concordia-M'head ⊠	68
59	Augsburg ⊠	69
67	Hamline ⊠	73
82	Neb. Wesleyan ⊠	63
67	St. Mary's (Minn.)	54
66	St. John's (Minn.)	82
75	Bethel (Minn.) ⊠	65
65	Macalester	68
67	Carleton ⊠	51
57	Gust. Adolphus ⊠	60
66	Hamline	70
53	St. Thomas (Minn.) ⊠	78
63	Concordia-M'head	56
90	Augsburg	74
63	St. Mary's (Minn.) ⊠	57
69	St. John's (Minn.) ⊠	70
76	Bethel (Minn.)	85
61	Macalester ⊠	58
59	Carleton	75
58	Gust. Adolphus	52
81	Bethel (Minn.)	79
61	St. Thomas (Minn.)	77

Nickname: Oles
Colors: Black & Old Gold
Arena: Skoglund Athletic Center
Capacity: 3,000; Year Built: 1968
AD: Matt McDonald
SID: Le Ann Finger

ST. PAUL'S
Lawrenceville, VA 23868 II

Coach: Edward Joyner, Fla. Memorial 1974

2006-07 RESULTS (11-17)

78	West Virginia St. †	103
78	Bluefield St. †	56
93	Columbia Union	85

70	N.C. Central ⊠	67
71	St. Augustine's ⊠	77
75	Bowie St. ⊠	111
83	St. Andrews	84
92	Apprentice	98
112	Columbia Union ⊠	77
70	St. Augustine's ⊠	71
84	Virginia Union ⊠	113
90	Fayetteville St.	98
94	Apprentice ⊠	76
75	Johnson C. Smith ⊠	77
97	Shaw ⊠	82
82	Elizabeth City St.	91
89	Fayetteville St. ⊠	77
95	Livingstone	80
94	Virginia St. ⊠	92
77	Shaw	82
81	Johnson C. Smith	91
103	Elizabeth City St. ⊠	111
99	Livingstone ⊠	90
77	Virginia Union	90
106	Bowie St.	95
70	N.C. Central	86
74	Virginia St.	97
74	N.C. Central †	75

Nickname: Tigers
Colors: Black & Orange
Arena: Taylor-Whitehead Gym
Capacity: 1,500; Year Built: 1965
AD: LeRoy Bacote
SID: Tiffani Sykes

ST. PETER'S
Jersey City, NJ 07306 I

Coach: John Dunne, Ithaca 1992

2006-07 RESULTS (5-25)

67	UMBC ⊠	56
60	Kennesaw St. †	67
75	NJIT †	57
65	Fairleigh Dickinson ⊠	72
50	Monmouth	51
60	Seton Hall	80
69	Lafayette ⊠	72
66	Loyola (Md.) ⊠	55
70	Marist ⊠	89
58	UNC Greensboro	79
63	Florida St.	76
61	Long Island ⊠	72
55	Niagara	88
61	Canisius	64
67	Rider	75
47	Canisius ⊠	68
66	Manhattan ⊠	71
55	Loyola (Md.) ⊠	62
58	Marist	67
58	Fairfield	66
53	Rider ⊠	54
50	Siena	66
51	Manhattan	58
59	Niagara ⊠	63
65	Siena ⊠	82
59	Iona ⊠	52
58	Tenn.-Martin	59
54	Iona	52
60	Fairfield ⊠	63
48	Canisius †	62

Nickname: Peacocks
Colors: Blue & White
Arena: Yanitelli Center
Capacity: 3,200; Year Built: 1975
AD: William A. Stein
SID: Dan Drutz

ST. ROSE
Albany, NY 12203.............................II

Coach: Brian Beaury, St. Rose 1982

2006-07 RESULTS (22-10)

71	Nyack ⊠	44
84	Le Moyne	77
74	American Int'l ⊠	59
72	Southern N.H. ⊠	70
87	Merrimack	70

64	Bridgeport	68
83	Pace ⊠	62
66	Stonehill	69
70	Franklin Pierce	61
80	Southern Conn. St.	66
73	St. Michael's	60
88	Holy Family	73
63	Philadelphia U.	62
69	Mass.-Lowell ⊠	55
71	Bryant	72
83	St. Anselm	62
88	Merrimack ⊠	66
69	Pace	71
54	Bentley	65
69	Le Moyne ⊠	57
66	Franklin Pierce	61
86	Southern Conn. St. ⊠	78
77	St. Michael's	64
59	Southern N.H.	68
79	Assumption	83
75	St. Anselm	61
62	American Int'l	69
76	St. Michael's	62
82	Pace	81
61	Bentley	71
87	Pace †	71
62	Bryant †	65

Nickname: Golden Knights
Colors: Gold, White & Black
Arena: Daniel P. Nolan Gymnasium
 Capacity: 1,000; Year Built: 2004
AD: Catherine C. Haker
SID: David Alexander

ST. SCHOLASTICA
Duluth, MN 55811-4199 III

Coach: David Staniger, St. Scholastica
1989

2006-07 RESULTS (14-13)

72	Neb. Wesleyan †	73
79	Wis.-Superior	72
68	Minn. Duluth	78
79	Neb. Wesleyan	89
86	Peru St. †	92
67	Wis.-Superior ⊠	70
95	Augsburg ⊠	79
96	Northland ⊠	87
60	Wis.-Eau Claire	72
81	Hamline	85
76	St. Thomas (Minn.) †	82
93	North Central (Minn. †	73
82	Northwestern (Minn.) ⊠	93
103	Crown (Minn.) ⊠	53
77	Presentation	63
74	Minn.-Morris	69
68	Martin Luther	70
60	Bethany Lutheran	68
76	Bethany Lutheran ⊠	82
82	Martin Luther ⊠	71
85	Crown (Minn.)	75
95	Northwestern (Minn.)	83
91	Minn.-Morris ⊠	81
72	Presentation ⊠	59
71	Northland	75
72	Bethany Lutheran †	70
92	Northwestern (Minn.)	90

Nickname: Saints
Colors: Blue & Gold
Arena: Reif Center
 Capacity: 1,500; Year Built: 1975
AD: Tony Barrett
SID: Gregg Petcoff

ST. THOMAS (MINN.)
St. Paul, MN 55105 III

Coach: Steve Fritz, St. Thomas (Minn.)
1971

2006-07 RESULTS (24-4)

72	Occidental †	63
60	La Verne	46
87	St. Mary's (Minn.) ⊠	43

83	St. Olaf ⊠	51
81	Hamline	66
77	Macalester ⊠	72
54	Wis.-La Crosse ⊠	62
82	St. Scholastica †	76
87	Wis.-River Falls	84
64	Carleton	62
91	Bethel (Minn.)	86
80	Augsburg ⊠	63
74	Gust. Adolphus ⊠	57
68	Concordia-M'head	65
59	St. John's (Minn.)	64
73	St. Mary's (Minn.)	46
78	St. Olaf	53
90	Hamline ⊠	71
87	Macalester	55
51	Carleton	41
89	Bethel (Minn.) ⊠	67
80	Augsburg	75
74	Gust. Adolphus	80
77	Concordia-M'head ⊠	57
74	St. John's (Minn.)	59
77	St. Olaf ⊠	61
75	St. John's (Minn.)	49
80	Carroll (Wis.) ⊠	86

Nickname: Tommies
Colors: Purple & Grey
Arena: Schoenecker Arena
 Capacity: 2,200; Year Built: 1982
AD: Stephen J. Fritz
SID: Gene McGivern

ST. THOMAS AQUINAS
Sparkill, NY 10976 II

Coach: Dennis O'Donnell, St. John's
(N.Y.) 1980

2006-07 RESULTS (11-17)

44	Stonehill ⊠	80
41	Rutgers	82
52	Philadelphia U.	55
59	Concordia (N.Y.) ⊠	63
75	Queens (N.Y.) ⊠	65
51	NYIT	59
64	Adelphi ⊠	54
51	St. Anselm	80
59	Ala.-Huntsville †	89
59	West Fla.	63
60	Bridgeport ⊠	69
60	St. Michael's ⊠	81
54	Dowling	67
65	C.W. Post ⊠	60
65	Mercy	51
65	New Haven ⊠	54
62	Concordia (N.Y.)	52
64	Molloy	72
75	Queens (N.Y.)	95
47	NYIT ⊠	61
61	Adelphi	54
57	Bridgeport	53
68	Dowling ⊠	61
56	C.W. Post	65
63	Mercy ⊠	53
71	Molloy ⊠	60
53	New Haven	61
55	C.W. Post	58

Nickname: Spartans
Colors: Maroon & Gold
Arena: Aquinas Hall
Capacity: 800
AD: Gerald Oswald
SID: Mike McManus

ST. VINCENT
Latrobe, PA 15650-2690 III

Coach: D.P. Harris

2006-07 RESULTS (14-11)

64	Washington (Md.) †	30
66	Kean †	82
80	Point Park †	84
96	Penn St.-Fayette †	59
65	Penn St.-DuBois ⊠	56

98	Franciscan ⊠	47
65	Penn St.-Beaver ⊠	54
67	Thomas More ⊠	61
73	Franciscan	61
80	Lake Erie ⊠	88
68	Wash. & Jeff.	76
89	Westminster (Pa.) ⊠	93
62	Grove City	63
84	Penn St.-DuBois	70
72	Thiel	55
87	Waynesburg ⊠	78
105	Bethany (W.V.) ⊠	107
58	Thomas More	47
86	Westminster (Pa.)	94
92	Ohio-Eastern ⊠	63
83	Wash. & Jeff. ⊠	88
77	Thiel ⊠	63
84	Grove City ⊠	74
73	Bethany (W.V.)	76
74	Waynesburg	82

Nickname: Bearcats
Colors: Green & gold
Arena: Maggs PA Center
Capacity: 2,000
AD: Kristen Zawacki
SID: To be named

SALEM INT'L
Salem, WV 26426 II

Coach: Clark Maloney, Mid-America
Naz. 1990

2006-07 RESULTS (15-12)

73	Bowie St.	90
76	Cheyney †	72
77	S.C. Upstate †	79
87	Shaw †	73
90	Lincoln (Pa.) ⊠	79
50	Dist. Columbia ⊠	67
74	Dist. Columbia	87
72	Wheeling Jesuit ⊠	97
76	Shepherd ⊠	87
77	Charleston (W.V.)	72
68	Fairmont St.	66
79	West Liberty St. ⊠	85
100	Ohio Valley	83
72	Alderson-Broaddus	92
75	West Va. Wesleyan ⊠	68
85	West Virginia St.	89
68	Davis & Elkins	65
77	Glenville St. ⊠	66
101	Fairmont St. ⊠	91
89	West Liberty St	101
97	Concord ⊠	82
95	Ohio Valley	66
77	Bluefield St. ⊠	67
63	Shepherd	71
81	Wheeling Jesuit	77
73	Davis & Elkins	44
69	Concord †	71

Nickname: Tigers
Colors: Kelly Green, Black & White
Arena: T. Edward Davis Gym
Capacity: 1,620
AD: Clark Maloney
SID: Patrick McGinnis

SALEM ST.
Salem, MA 01970 III

Coach: Sean Doherty, Worcester St.
1993

2006-07 RESULTS (24-3)

74	Bowdoin †	64
73	Roger Williams	85
87	WPI ⊠	78
87	Plymouth St. ⊠	70
73	Newbury ⊠	61
97	Mass.-Boston	74
76	Gordon	70
87	Wesleyan (Conn.) ⊠	62
65	Wheaton (Mass.) ⊠	75
78	Lasell	71

81	Fitchburg St.	73
75	Westfield St. ⊠	59
68	Emmanuel (Mass.)	62
115	Framingham St.	96
81	Mass. Liberal Arts	62
87	Bridgewater St. ⊠	72
74	Worcester St.	59
70	Mass.-Dartmouth	68
83	Fitchburg St. ⊠	62
76	Westfield St.	67
115	Framingham St. ⊠	98
95	Mass. Liberal Arts ⊠	62
81	Bridgewater St.	72
78	Worcester St. ⊠	72
74	Worcester St. ⊠	63
72	Westfield St. ⊠	62
75	Keene St. ⊠	76

Nickname: Vikings
Colors: Orange & Blue
Arena: O'Keefe Sports Center
 Capacity: 2,200; Year Built: 1976
AD: Timothy Shea
SID: Thomas Roundy

SALISBURY
Salisbury, MD 21801-6860 III

Coach: Steve Holmes, Plattsburgh St.
1983

2006-07 RESULTS (12-14)

95	Waynesburg †	81
97	Mt. Aloysius	76
84	Villa Julie ⊠	83
57	McDaniel †	53
60	Johns Hopkins †	71
64	Va. Wesleyan	73
93	York (Pa.) ⊠	81
73	Goucher	67
74	Gallaudet	60
78	Washington (Md.) ⊠	65
71	Montclair St. †	78
54	Drew †	67
73	Mary Washington ⊠	68
76	St. Mary's (Md.)	77
58	Catholic ⊠	62
65	Marymount (Va.)	76
74	Hood ⊠	80
74	York (Pa.)	84
80	Goucher ⊠	65
71	Gallaudet ⊠	59
56	Mary Washington	57
84	St. Mary's (Md.) ⊠	77
72	Catholic	74
122	Marymount (Va.) ⊠	126
83	Hood	100
59	Catholic	79

Nickname: Sea Gulls
Colors: Maroon and Gold
Arena: Maggs Center
 Capacity: 2,200; Year Built: 1977
AD: Michael Vienna
SID: Sam Atkinson

SALVE REGINA
Newport, RI 02840-4192 III

Coach: Sean Foster, Salve Regina 1997

2006-07 RESULTS (13-13)

81	Me.-Machias †	61
62	Bridgewater St.	75
86	Mitchell	59
77	Wheaton (Mass.) ⊠	83
67	Johnson & Wales (RI)	49
81	Anna Maria ⊠	64
78	Rhode Island Col. ⊠	84
76	Connecticut Col.	70
71	Worcester St. ⊠	65
53	Colby-Sawyer	69
72	Curry ⊠	69
51	Gordon ⊠	68
65	Nichols ⊠	77
77	Curry	84
56	Roger Williams ⊠	50

55	New England	58
67	Roger Williams	74
81	Eastern Nazarene	63
89	New England Col. ⊠	61
81	Wesleyan (Conn.) ⊠	87
74	Nichols	76
67	Wentworth Inst. ⊠	58
71	Anna Maria	60
76	Eastern Nazarene ⊠	57
67	Endicott	68
56	Gordon	63

Nickname: Seahawks
Colors: Blue, Green & White
Arena: Rodgers Recreation Center
  Capacity: 550; Year Built: 2000
AD: Del Malloy
SID: Ed Habershaw

SAM HOUSTON ST.
Huntsville, TX 77341 I

Coach: Bob Marlin, Mississippi St. 1981

2006-07 RESULTS (21-10)

64	Texas Tech	79
94	Tex. A&M Int'l ⊠	45
67	Oklahoma St.	86
95	Louisiana Col. ⊠	31
72	East Tenn. St. †	61
62	Delaware St. †	55
86	Southern Miss.	94
81	Alcorn St.	78
92	Loyola Marymount ⊠	77
62	UC Irvine	70
61	UCLA	75
89	Milwaukee ⊠	73
86	McMurry ⊠	55
69	Southeastern La.	45
81	Nicholls St.	61
58	McNeese St. ⊠	59
88	Lamar ⊠	52
55	Stephen F. Austin	52
65	Texas-Arlington	78
88	Texas St. ⊠	74
76	UTSA ⊠	64
84	A&M-Corpus Christi	79
90	Northwestern St.	80
81	Central Ark. ⊠	68
63	Stephen F. Austin ⊠	51
60	Fresno St.	78
92	Texas-Arlington ⊠	78
97	Texas St.	83
73	UTSA	61
68	A&M-Corpus Christi ⊠	85
98	Lamar †	99

Nickname: Bearkats
Colors: Orange & White
Arena: Johnson Coliseum
  Capacity: 6,110; Year Built: 1976
AD: Bobby Williams
SID: Paul Ridings

SAMFORD
Birmingham, AL 35229 I

Coach: Jimmy Tillette, Holy Cross 1975

2006-07 RESULTS (16-16)

54	Florida	79
83	Tenn. Temple ⊠	59
62	Towson	69
57	Arizona	86
80	Ohio	66
54	South Ala.	59
54	Jacksonville St.	53
65	Southeast Mo. St.	64
55	Murray St.	44
64	Mississippi Val. †	59
50	Wright St. †	61
45	LSU	60
68	Tennessee Tech	65
55	Tenn.-Martin ⊠	41
64	Jacksonville St. ⊠	63
41	Tennessee St.	59
59	Tennessee Tech	73

66	Morehead St. ⊠	53
55	Eastern Ky. ⊠	46
71	Tenn.-Martin	66
48	Austin Peay	66
51	Murray St. ⊠	57
70	Tennessee St. ⊠	60
53	Eastern Ill.	48
50	Austin Peay ⊠	52
38	Eastern Ky.	46
58	Morehead St.	71
65	Evansville	69
67	Southeast Mo. St. ⊠	70
71	Eastern Ill. ⊠	45
70	Murray St.	60
55	Austin Peay †	65

Nickname: Bulldogs
Colors: Red & Blue
Arena: Seibert Hall
  Capacity: 4,000; Year Built: 1957
AD: Bob Roller
SID: Zac Schrieber

SAN DIEGO
San Diego, CA 92110-2492 I

Coach: Brad Holland, UCLA 1979

2006-07 RESULTS (18-14)

62	Stephen F. Austin	71
74	UC San Diego ⊠	69
74	Pt. Loma Nazarene ⊠	51
55	Loyola (Ill.)	69
49	UTSA	64
76	San Diego St. ⊠	79
67	Central Mich.	66
92	Cal St. Bakersfield ⊠	72
78	Eastern Mich. †	76
72	California	67
81	Campbell ⊠	69
81	Furman ⊠	70
81	UC Santa Barbara ⊠	63
65	Fresno St.	68
100	San Francisco	103
78	UC Riverside ⊠	62
71	Pepperdine	67
79	Loyola Marymount	74
47	Santa Clara	61
78	St. Mary's (Cal.) ⊠	85
74	Portland	70
82	Gonzaga	91
88	San Francisco ⊠	98
76	St. Mary's (Cal.)	72
66	Loyola Marymount ⊠	71
97	Pepperdine ⊠	85
72	Santa Clara	80
82	Portland ⊠	76
64	Gonzaga ⊠	74
95	Pepperdine †	82
77	San Francisco †	75
70	Gonzaga †	88

Nickname: Toreros
Colors: Columbia Blue, Navy & White
Arena: Jenny Craig Pavilion
  Capacity: 5,100; Year Built: 2000
AD: Ky Snyder
SID: Ted Gosen

SAN DIEGO ST.
San Diego, CA 92182 I

Coach: Steve Fisher, Illinois St. 1967

2006-07 RESULTS (22-11)

87	Murray St. †	84
74	St. Mary's (Cal.)	73
76	Seattle Pacific †	73
84	UC San Diego ⊠	48
86	California ⊠	79
79	UC Riverside ⊠	45
76	UC Santa Barbara	72
79	San Diego	76
73	Western Mich.	84
48	Arizona	69
119	Campbell ⊠	82
74	Loyola Marymount ⊠	63

54	Washington St. †	64
78	Lafayette ⊠	68
65	Wyoming ⊠	66
58	BYU	80
81	Colorado St. ⊠	76
73	New Mexico ⊠	68
51	Air Force	56
61	UNLV	68
63	Utah ⊠	53
76	TCU	71
62	Air Force ⊠	41
81	Colorado St.	66
67	UNLV ⊠	52
71	Wyoming	80
81	New Mexico	74
86	BYU ⊠	74
68	Utah	74
56	TCU ⊠	51
64	Colorado St. †	69
74	Missouri St.	70
64	Syracuse	80

Nickname: Aztecs
Colors: Scarlet & Black
Arena: Cox Arena
  Capacity: 12,414; Year Built: 1997
AD: Jeffrey W. Schemmel
SID: Mike May

SAN FRANCISCO
San Francisco, CA 94117-1080 I

Coach: Jessie Evans, Eastern Mich. 1972

2006-07 RESULTS (13-18)

87	Sonoma St. ⊠	73
89	Sacramento St. ⊠	64
66	Fresno St. ⊠	86
60	Ohio St.	82
88	UNLV	96
82	Northern Ariz. ⊠	73
72	Pacific	79
71	Southeastern La. †	56
78	New Mexico St.	89
62	Northern Ariz.	84
69	UC Santa Barbara ⊠	74
85	Hawaii	89
81	Wyoming †	84
59	Valparaiso †	64
63	Louisville	76
103	San Diego ⊠	100
68	Loyola Marymount ⊠	61
72	Pepperdine	71
64	St. Mary's (Cal.) ⊠	71
58	Santa Clara ⊠	61
56	Gonzaga	72
66	Portland	65
98	San Diego	88
62	Santa Clara	74
82	Pepperdine ⊠	70
76	Loyola Marymount ⊠	69
76	UC Irvine	62
83	St. Mary's (Cal.)	92
79	Gonzaga ⊠	86
70	Portland ⊠	67
75	San Diego †	77

Nickname: Dons
Colors: Green & Gold
Arena: War Memorial Gymnasium
  Capacity: 5,300; Year Built: 1958
AD: Debra Gore-Mann
SID: Peter Simon

SAN FRAN. ST.
San Francisco, CA 94132 II

Coach: Bill Treseler, California 1982

2006-07 RESULTS (6-21)

79	Pacific Union ⊠	65
53	Notre Dame de Namur ⊠	61
97	Cal St. East Bay ⊠	74
64	Cal St. Bakersfield ⊠	80
72	Cal St. L.A. ⊠	82
86	Walla Walla	64
67	Whitman	63

86	Cal St. Monterey Bay	82
60	Cal Poly Pomona ⊠	66
60	Cal St. San B'dino ⊠	73
82	Humboldt St.	101
43	Sonoma St.	54
56	Cal St. Chico	66
72	Cal St. Stanislaus	95
58	UC San Diego ⊠	63
51	Cal St. Dom. Hills ⊠	79
79	Cal St. L.A.	76
42	Cal St. Bakersfield	68
74	Cal St. Monterey Bay ⊠	75
55	Cal St. San B'dino	86
63	Cal Poly Pomona	79
56	Sonoma St. ⊠	61
62	Humboldt St. ⊠	94
92	Cal St. Stanislaus ⊠	97
66	Cal St. Chico ⊠	82
51	Cal St. Dom. Hills ⊠	91
47	UC San Diego	73

Nickname: Gators
Colors: Purple & Gold
Arena: SFSU Main Gym
  Capacity: 2,000; Year Built: 1949
AD: Michael J. Simpson
SID: Joe Danahey

SAN JOSE ST.
San Jose, CA 95192 I

Coach: George Nessman, California 1981

2006-07 RESULTS (5-25)

67	UC Santa Barbara	75
52	Stanford	73
67	Long Beach St. †	86
52	Arizona St.	64
53	Santa Clara	71
60	St. Mary's (Cal.)	78
80	Cal Poly ⊠	63
69	BYU	81
63	Portland St. ⊠	72
67	Long Beach St. ⊠	76
77	Cal St. Fullerton	104
51	Duke	70
56	Louisiana Tech	92
68	New Mexico St.	74
63	Nevada ⊠	72
64	Fresno St. ⊠	61
56	Utah St. ⊠	57
64	Fresno St.	67
52	Hawaii	72
78	New Mexico St. ⊠	85
68	Idaho	66
57	Utah St.	66
53	Louisiana Tech ⊠	50
64	Boise St. ⊠	65
60	Nevada	68
67	Northern Ariz.	78
64	Boise St.	83
55	Hawaii ⊠	67
62	Idaho ⊠	57
49	Idaho †	50

Nickname: Spartans
Colors: Gold, White & Blue
Arena: The Event Center
  Capacity: 5,000; Year Built: 1989
AD: Thomas Bowen
SID: Lawrence Fan

SANTA CLARA
Santa Clara, CA 95053 I

Coach: Dick Davey, Pacific 1964

2006-07 RESULTS (21-10)

83	Holy Names ⊠	51
83	Utah ⊠	72
48	California	73
70	Nevada ⊠	53
71	San Jose St. ⊠	53
68	Hawaii ⊠	59
71	Alabama St. †	45
51	Missouri St.	78

67	Pacific	49
91	Eastern Wash. ⊠	68
62	Stanford	46
60	Kentucky	74
77	Utah St. ⊠	75
53	Colgate ⊠	39
48	Air Force	78
76	St. Mary's (Cal.) ⊠	69
69	Gonzaga	77
57	Portland ⊠	41
61	San Diego	47
61	San Francisco	58
71	Loyola Marymount ⊠	74
77	Pepperdine	55
63	St. Mary's (Cal.)	57
74	San Francisco ⊠	62
76	Portland	53
84	Gonzaga	73
80	San Diego ⊠	72
66	Loyola Marymount	67
82	Pepperdine	89
63	St. Mary's (Cal.) †	47
68	Gonzaga †	77

Nickname: Broncos
Colors: Red (PMS 202) & White
Arena: Leavey Center
Capacity: 4,500; Year Built: 1975
AD: Daniel P. Coonan
SID: Jed Mettee

SAVANNAH ST.
Savannah, GA 31404 I

Coach: Horace Broadnax, Georgetown 1986

2006-07 RESULTS (12-18)

66	Clark Atlanta ⊠	59
67	Jacksonville ⊠	64
71	Mercer ⊠	61
68	SCAD ⊠	35
57	Southeastern (Fla.) ⊠	37
34	Illinois	81
71	Jackson St. †	72
65	Florida A&M †	74
49	Massachusetts ⊠	72
60	Georgia St.	70
45	Southern Miss.	61
53	North Carolina St.	74
59	Iowa St.	70
41	West Virginia	76
45	Louisville	71
52	Bethune-Cookman ⊠	49
46	Stetson ⊠	58
51	Marquette	69
53	Nebraska	81
54	Southern Miss. ⊠	52
56	Coastal Caro.	83
65	Longwood	59
64	Mercer	68
49	North Fla. ⊠	47
66	Coastal Caro. ⊠	65
49	High Point ⊠	70
74	Stetson	88
67	Allen ⊠	52
42	Bethune-Cookman	47
74	Longwood ⊠	72

Nickname: Tigers
Colors: Reflex Blue & Orange
Arena: Wiley Gym
Capacity: 2,100; Year Built: 1964
AD: Robert 'Tony' O'Neal
SID: Opio Mashariki

SCHREINER
Kerrville, TX 78028 III

Coach: Thirman Dimery, Schreiner 1993

2006-07 RESULTS (6-19)

75	Southwestern (Tex.) ⊠	76
68	Trinity (Tex.)	77
54	Stephen F. Austin	99
95	Texas-Dallas	103
75	Texas-Tyler	86

97	Ozarks (Ark.) ⊠	84
65	Texas Lutheran	71
46	St. Edward's	87
79	Louisiana Col.	62
69	Mississippi Col.	83
83	East Tex. Baptist ⊠	78
75	LeTourneau	89
67	Texas Lutheran	70
88	Howard Payne ⊠	82
86	Sul Ross St. ⊠	79
74	Hardin-Simmons	89
71	McMurry	90
85	Concordia (Tex.) ⊠	91
90	Mary Hardin-Baylor	101
82	Concordia (Tex.)	77
83	Mary Hardin-Baylor ⊠	91
64	Hardin-Simmons ⊠	86
83	McMurry	96
97	Howard Payne	99
65	Sul Ross St.	67

Nickname: Mountaineers
Colors: Maroon & White
Arena: Edington Center
Capacity: 3,000; Year Built: 1984
AD: Ronald Macosko
SID: Jeanette McKinney

SCRANTON
Scranton, PA 18510 III

Coach: Carl Danzig, Baker 1987

2006-07 RESULTS (19-7)

57	Misericordia	48
61	Catholic	71
69	King's (Pa.)	75
78	FDU-Florham ⊠	70
71	TCNJ ⊠	49
62	Clarkson ⊠	38
72	Moravian ⊠	59
89	Cabrini	60
70	Denison †	53
79	Manhattanville †	66
85	Hartwick	61
104	Pratt ⊠	46
66	Susquehanna ⊠	79
83	Lycoming ⊠	72
55	Drew	34
70	Wilkes ⊠	47
78	DeSales	70
84	Delaware Valley	68
65	Drew ⊠	51
72	King's (Pa.) ⊠	75
71	FDU-Florham	79
81	Wilkes	65
90	Delaware Valley ⊠	59
65	Lycoming	58
70	DeSales	75
60	DeSales ⊠	62

Nickname: Royals
Colors: Purple & White
Arena: John Long Center
Capacity: 2,800; Year Built: 1968
AD: Toby Lovecchio
SID: Kevin Southard

SEATTLE
Seattle, WA 98122-1090 II

Coach: Joe Callero, Central Wash. 1986

2006-07 RESULTS (20-9)

68	Sonoma St. ⊠	55
91	Ashland ⊠	81
76	Metro St.	84
83	Colo. Christian	79
54	Regis (Colo.)	51
80	Hawaii-Hilo ⊠	63
76	BYU-Hawaii	65
53	Hawaii Pacific	50
47	Cal St. Chico	75
87	Dixie St. †	70
61	Cheyney †	79
76	Northwest Nazarene	63
80	Western Wash. ⊠	86

64	St. Martin's ⊠	74
75	Central Wash.	71
86	Seattle Pacific ⊠	68
56	Alas. Fairbanks ⊠	57
65	Alas. Anchorage ⊠	64
74	Seattle Pacific	98
67	Western Ore. ⊠	69
76	Western Wash. ⊠	61
69	Alas. Anchorage	66
50	Alas. Fairbanks	48
85	St. Martin's	72
67	Northwest Nazarene ⊠	63
88	Central Wash. ⊠	73
82	Western Ore.	68
69	Cal Poly Pomona †	55
66	Cal St. San B'dino †	72

Nickname: Redhawks
Colors: Scarlet & White
Arena: Connolly Center
Capacity: 1,000; Year Built: 1969
AD: Bill J. Hogan
SID: Jason Behenna

SEATTLE PACIFIC
Seattle, WA 98119-1997 II

Coach: Jeff Hironaka, Eastern Ore. 1980

2006-07 RESULTS (18-10)

85	Cal St. L.A. ⊠	67
84	Cal Poly Pomona ⊠	71
52	UC San Diego †	62
84	Cal St. Dom. Hills †	65
98	BYU-Hawaii	93
66	Cal St. San B'dino	86
60	Central Mo. †	71
75	Rollins †	88
82	Dixie St.	76
75	Cheyney ⊠	71
71	Dixie St. ⊠	67
68	Alas. Anchorage	65
78	Alas. Fairbanks	90
86	Western Ore. ⊠	74
80	Western Wash. ⊠	65
108	Northwest Nazarene	80
68	Seattle	86
100	St. Martin's ⊠	90
91	Central Wash.	98
88	Northwest Nazarene ⊠	70
98	Seattle	74
73	Central Wash.	80
72	Western Ore.	61
99	St. Martin's	91
70	Alas. Fairbanks ⊠	75
89	Alas. Anchorage ⊠	80
70	Western Wash.	64
65	Grand Canyon †	87

Nickname: Falcons
Colors: Maroon & White
Arena: Brougham Pavilion
Capacity: 2,650; Year Built: 1953
AD: Tom Box
SID: Frank MacDonald

SETON HALL
South Orange, NJ 07079 I

Coach: Bobby Gonzalez, Buffalo St. 1986

2006-07 RESULTS (13-16)

91	Caldwell ⊠	52
71	Fairleigh Dickinson ⊠	76
83	Morgan St.	63
80	St. Peter's ⊠	60
93	St. Mary's (Cal.) ⊠	82
83	Monmouth ⊠	49
69	Penn St. ⊠	59
61	Virginia Tech †	80
94	Penn ⊠	85
74	Oral Roberts †	76
85	Liberty †	81
68	BYU	77
77	Rutgers ⊠	72
69	Providence	91

79	St. John's (N.Y.) ⊠	63
76	Notre Dame	88
69	Providence ⊠	68
58	Georgetown ⊠	74
76	Marquette	89
70	Rutgers	74
79	Princeton	41
70	West Virginia ⊠	81
69	Villanova ⊠	78
55	Connecticut	67
71	West Virginia	81
68	Pittsburgh ⊠	71
89	South Fla. ⊠	76
67	Cincinnati	70
71	Louisville	86

Nickname: Pirates
Colors: Blue & White
Arena: Continental Airlines Arena
Capacity: 20,029; Year Built: 1981
AD: Joseph A. Quinlan, Jr.
SID: Jeff Andriesse

SETON HILL
Greensburg, PA 15601 II

Coach: Bobby Gonzalez, Buffalo St. 1986

2006-07 RESULTS (15-11)

100	Penn St.-Fayette ⊠	55
54	Bloomsburg †	64
79	Millersville	89
102	Penn St.-Fayette	57
76	Wingate	82
76	West Virginia St. †	79
64	Pitt.-Johnstown †	73
94	Penn St.-Harrisburg †	75
109	Lincoln (Pa.) †	99
94	Western Conn. St. †	70
76	Daemen ⊠	67
66	Point Park	85
72	Geneva ⊠	70
86	Franciscan	71
58	Roberts Wesleyan ⊠	63
81	Houghton ⊠	72
77	Notre Dame (Ohio)	75
92	Flagler	78
86	Flagler	87
95	Myers ⊠	93
75	Daemen	80
76	Geneva	79
71	Roberts Wesleyan	55
70	Houghton	65
75	Point Park ⊠	81
78	Franciscan	73

Nickname: Griffins
Colors: Crimson & vegas gold
Arena: McKenna Center
Capacity: 1,400; Year Built: 2005
AD: Chris Snyder
SID: Jason Greene

SEWANEE
Sewanee, TN 37383-1000 III

Coach: Joe Thoni, Sewanee 1979

2006-07 RESULTS (6-19)

81	Roanoke	83
78	Guilford †	91
69	LaGrange	73
61	Emory ⊠	78
82	Oglethorpe ⊠	77
62	Emory	91
47	Maryville (Tenn.)	64
54	Keene St. †	67
61	Babson †	73
77	DePauw ⊠	70
68	Centre ⊠	80
77	Rhodes	56
69	Millsaps	77
74	Huntingdon ⊠	61
75	Oglethorpe	92
92	Piedmont ⊠	95
78	Trinity (Tex.)	92

60	Southwestern (Tex.)	62
66	Hendrix ☒	81
70	Austin ☒	58
59	Rhodes ☒	52
80	Millsaps ☒	93
82	DePauw	94
54	Centre	73
72	DePauw †	84

Nickname: Tigers
Colors: Purple & White
Arena: Juhan Gymnasium
 Capacity: 1,000; Year Built: 1955
AD: Mark Webb
SID: B.B. Branton

SHAW
Raleigh, NC 27601 II

Coach: Robert Brickey, Duke 1990

2006-07 RESULTS (3-25)

79	Belmont Abbey	76
50	Queens (N.C.) †	61
55	Fayetteville St.	76
73	Salem Int'l †	87
65	Johnson C. Smith.	80
45	Cheyney †	72
49	N.C. Central	66
72	UNC Pembroke ☒	57
44	Lynn	72
56	Claflin	60
76	St. Augustine's †	84
78	Elizabeth City St. ☒	99
54	N.C. Central ☒	58
64	Bowie St.	92
71	Virginia St. ☒	83
58	St. Augustine's ☒	85
82	St. Paul's	97
56	Fayetteville St. ☒	68
67	Livingstone	72
48	Virginia Union ☒	69
66	Elizabeth City St.	73
82	St. Paul's ☒	77
68	Bowie St. ☒	86
77	Virginia Union	86
78	Johnson C. Smith ☒	94
58	Virginia St.	79
69	Livingstone ☒	72
65	Bowie St. †	82

Nickname: Bears
Colors: Garnet & White
Arena: Spaulding Gym
 Capacity: 1,200; Year Built: 1946
AD: Alfonza L. Carter
SID: Maurice Williams

SHENANDOAH
Winchester, VA 22601 III

Coach: Robert Harris, Shenandoah 1991

2006-07 RESULTS (7-18)

83	East. Mennonite ☒	81
60	Longwood	88
65	Frostburg St.	74
64	Southern Va.	56
63	Radford	94
78	Mary Washington ☒	72
58	Guilford	70
58	Lycoming	67
70	Hampden-Sydney	69
94	Albright †	92
68	Davis & Elkins ☒	65
81	Chris. Newport ☒	84
79	N.C. Wesleyan	87
64	Md.-East. Shore	88
86	Averett ☒	82
71	Ferrum	75
52	Greensboro	65
78	Methodist	89
75	Chris. Newport	85
78	N.C. Wesleyan ☒	83
52	Ferrum	68
57	Averett	60

67	Greensboro ☒	77
73	Methodist ☒	74
75	Greensboro	86

Nickname: Hornets
Colors: Red, White & Midnight Blue
Arena: Shingleton Gymnasium
 Capacity: 680; Year Built: 1969
AD: John Hill
SID: Scott Musa

SHEPHERD
Shepherdstown, WV 25443-3210 II

Coach: Ken Tyler, William & Mary 1987

2006-07 RESULTS (16-13)

98	Columbia Union ☒	78
64	California (Pa.) ☒	60
60	Shippensburg ☒	51
79	Lock Haven	81
74	Davis & Elkins	64
114	Valley Forge Chrst. ☒	52
97	Penn St.-York ☒	48
64	Central Wash. †	84
81	Western Ore.	84
102	Penn St.-Fayette ☒	44
99	Ohio Valley	76
87	Salem Int'l	76
86	West Liberty St. ☒	97
85	Wheeling Jesuit ☒	99
66	Fairmont St.	58
70	Charleston (W.V.) ☒	73
80	West Virginia St. ☒	93
78	Concord	81
80	Bluefield St.	60
94	Glenville St. ☒	62
89	West Va. Wesleyan ☒	51
74	Alderson-Broaddus	92
79	Fairmont St. ☒	83
70	West Liberty St.	74
58	Wheeling Jesuit	85
71	Salem Int'l ☒	63
87	Ohio Valley ☒	72
75	Ohio Valley ☒	74
63	West Liberty St. †	73

Nickname: Rams
Colors: Blue & Gold
Arena: Butcher Athletic Center
 Capacity: 3,500; Year Built: 1989
AD: Karl Wolf
SID: Chip Ransom

SHIPPENSBURG
Shippensburg, PA 17257 II

Coach: Dave Springer, Ohio 1984

2006-07 RESULTS (17-14)

73	South Dakota †	78
60	S.C.-Aiken †	63
66	Wis.-Parkside †	73
69	Millersville ☒	67
62	Alderson-Broaddus †	61
86	Bloomfield †	68
51	Shepherd	60
69	Ohio Valley	79
64	Kutztown	69
46	East Stroudsburg	54
103	Ohio Valley ☒	73
70	Bloomfield ☒	54
95	Mansfield ☒	64
72	Neumann	50
78	Pitt.-Johnstown ☒	69
64	West Chester	70
59	Millersville	65
51	Edinboro	76
71	Cheyney ☒	57
75	Lock Haven	52
64	Clarion ☒	49
63	California (Pa.)	75
61	Slippery Rock ☒	59
70	Indiana (Pa.) ☒	50
69	Edinboro ☒	54
76	Lock Haven ☒	61
63	Clarion	64

62	Slippery Rock	48
51	California (Pa.) ☒	71
72	Indiana (Pa.)	51
60	Edinboro	67

Nickname: Red Raiders
Colors: Red and Blue
Arena: Heiges Field House
 Capacity: 2,768; Year Built: 1970
AD: Roberta Page
SID: Jason Eichelberger

SIENA
Loudonville, NY 12211-1462 I

Coach: Fran McCaffery, Penn 1982

2006-07 RESULTS (20-12)

72	Stanford	92
57	Holy Cross	65
83	Dartmouth	69
64	NJIT	40
80	Hofstra ☒	84
76	Albany (N.Y.) ☒	75
81	Niagara ☒	69
87	Rider ☒	79
64	Buffalo	69
81	Tennessee St. ☒	69
75	Maryland	94
78	Canisius	60
92	Niagara	81
87	Loyola (Md.) ☒	94
70	Canisius ☒	48
75	Marist	84
67	Fairfield	72
80	Manhattan	69
87	NJIT ☒	63
78	Rider	84
71	Loyola (Md.)	72
61	Iona ☒	60
66	St. Peter's ☒	50
71	Iona	53
82	St. Peter's	65
69	Fairfield	64
77	James Madison ☒	66
78	Manhattan ☒	61
88	Marist	98
75	Manhattan †	72
86	Marist †	78
79	Niagara †	83

Nickname: Saints
Colors: Green & Gold
Arena: Pepsi Arena
 Capacity: 15,500; Year Built: 1990
AD: John M. D'Argenio
SID: Jason Rich

SIMPSON
Indianola, IA 50125 III

Coach: Bruce Wilson, Simpson 1976

2006-07 RESULTS (18-9)

82	Elmhurst ☒	71
87	Grand View ☒	80
68	Loras ☒	84
53	Augustana (Ill.) ☒	55
73	Iowa Wesleyan	60
127	Grinnell	139
68	Neb. Wesleyan	66
80	Mount Union †	76
86	Ramapo †	71
69	Edgewood †	50
66	Buena Vista	81
68	Dubuque	81
72	Wartburg ☒	64
51	Luther	50
83	Central (Iowa)	65
68	Coe ☒	76
80	Cornell College ☒	60
59	Wartburg	71
74	Central (Iowa) ☒	57
66	Luther ☒	53
58	Loras	70
92	Cornell College	78
68	Buena Vista ☒	59

78	Coe	73
84	Dubuque ☒	58
95	Central (Iowa) ☒	87
52	Loras	69

Nickname: Storm
Colors: Red & Gold
Arena: Cowles Fieldhouse
 Capacity: 3,000; Year Built: 1976
AD: John Sirianni
SID: Matt Turk

SKIDMORE
Saratoga Springs, NY 12866 III

Coach: John Quattrocchi, Albany (N.Y.) 1973

2006-07 RESULTS (2-22)

56	Hartwick ☒	62
87	St. Joseph (Vt.) ☒	91
65	Williams ☒	96
55	Utica ☒	69
64	Westfield St.	79
86	Lyndon St. ☒	64
43	North Fla.	70
55	Stetson	85
65	Middlebury	81
60	Union (N.Y.) ☒	67
47	Vassar	75
50	Rensselaer	62
54	Hobart	69
88	Hamilton ☒	84
68	Castleton ☒	75
55	St. Lawrence	65
60	Clarkson	75
54	Union (N.Y.)	94
47	Hamilton	78
53	Hobart	65
53	Rensselaer ☒	67
60	Vassar ☒	78
67	Clarkson ☒	79
55	St. Lawrence ☒	79

Nickname: Thoroughbreds
Colors: Green, White & Gold
Arena: Sports & Recreation Center
 Capacity: 1,500; Year Built: 1982
AD: Gail Cummings-Danson
SID: Bill Jones

SLIPPERY ROCK
Slippery Rock, PA 16057 II

Coach: Jamal Palmer, Millersville 1999

2006-07 RESULTS (5-22)

57	Youngstown St.	95
82	Glenville St.	84
71	Ashland	97
79	West Va. Wesleyan	60
96	West Chester ☒	89
65	Millersville ☒	81
97	Ohio Valley	106
87	Northwood (Mich.) †	89
76	Columbia Union †	65
88	Kutztown ☒	95
54	East Stroudsburg ☒	68
61	Mercyhurst	86
50	Cheyney	70
79	Lock Haven ☒	60
60	Bloomsburg	62
92	Mansfield	96
59	Edinboro	87
69	Indiana (Pa.) ☒	76
59	Shippensburg	61
56	California (Pa.)	79
57	Clarion ☒	70
76	Lock Haven	62
64	Edinboro ☒	76
44	Indiana (Pa.)	47
48	Shippensburg ☒	62
63	California (Pa.) ☒	65
59	Clarion	76

Nickname: The Rock
Colors: Green & White
Arena: Morrow Field House

Capacity: 3,000; Year Built: 1962
AD: Paul A. Lueken
SID: Bob McComas

SONOMA ST.
Rohnert Park, CA 94928-3609 II

Coach: Pat Fuscaldo, San Fran. St. 1983

2006-07 RESULTS (15-11)
55	Seattle	68
75	St. Martin's †	76
71	Cal Poly Pomona	77
55	Cal St. San B'dino	75
93	St. Martin's ⊠	86
64	Chaminade ⊠	71
57	Humboldt St. ⊠	72
78	Humboldt St.	90
68	Cal St. Dom. Hills ⊠	62
65	UC San Diego	70
105	Cal St. Monterey Bay ⊠	93
54	San Fran. St. ⊠	43
65	Cal St. Bakersfield	58
74	Cal St. L.A.	69
76	Cal St. Chico ⊠	67
85	Cal St. Stanislaus	87
52	Cal St. San B'dino ⊠	74
65	Cal Poly Pomona ⊠	43
76	UC San Diego	90
57	Cal St. Dom. Hills	79
61	San Fran. St.	56
77	Cal St. Monterey Bay	74
75	Cal St. L.A. ⊠	53
58	Cal St. Bakersfield ⊠	53
77	Cal St. Stanislaus	62
71	Cal St. Chico	55

Nickname: Seawolves
Colors: Navy, Blue & White
Arena: Seawolf Gymnasium
Capacity: 1,800; Year Built: 1968
AD: William J. Fusco
SID: Brandon Bronzan

SOUTH ALA.
Mobile, AL 36688 I

Coach: John Pelphrey, Kentucky 1992

2006-07 RESULTS (20-12)
67	UC Irvine †	63
63	Fresno St.	73
76	Winston-Salem †	58
70	Morehead St. ⊠	55
91	West Fla. ⊠	71
64	Bowling Green	65
59	Samford ⊠	54
71	Auburn	82
46	Mississippi St.	84
72	Mississippi ⊠	82
80	Texas Col.	56
51	Western Ky.	73
91	Arkansas St.	78
51	Middle Tenn. ⊠	59
69	Florida Int'l ⊠	52
101	Fla. Atlantic ⊠	76
75	Troy	64
68	Ark.-Little Rock ⊠	54
73	La.-Lafayette	69
70	Denver	64
64	La.-Monroe ⊠	57
90	North Texas ⊠	89
76	New Orleans	58
61	Middle Tenn.	38
73	Western Ky. ⊠	71
85	Arkansas St. ⊠	67
66	Houston	61
67	Florida Int'l	69
69	Fla. Atlantic	79
88	Troy ⊠	92
60	Middle Tenn. †	63
73	Syracuse	79

Nickname: Jaguars
Colors: Red, White and Blue
Arena: Mitchell Center
Capacity: 10,000; Year Built: 1999

AD: Joseph E. Gottfried
SID: Kit Strief

SOUTH CAROLINA
Columbia, SC 29208 I

Coach: Dave Odom, Guilford 1965

2006-07 RESULTS (14-16)
55	South Carolina St. ⊠	52
52	UC Irvine	67
80	Southern California	74
75	Lipscomb ⊠	68
74	Citadel	59
53	Clemson ⊠	74
67	Col. of Charleston ⊠	55
64	Baylor	59
54	Princeton ⊠	48
71	UNC Asheville ⊠	51
80	Jacksonville	73
67	Western Caro. ⊠	53
54	Kansas	70
56	Georgia	80
50	Florida ⊠	84
49	Kentucky ⊠	87
61	Tennessee	64
66	Arkansas	60
66	Mississippi St.	63
75	Auburn ⊠	80
61	Alabama	64
89	Kentucky	95
54	Georgia ⊠	73
68	Vanderbilt	78
81	Tennessee ⊠	64
49	Florida	63
76	Mississippi ⊠	63
90	Vanderbilt ⊠	99
52	LSU	61
52	Arkansas †	82

Nickname: Gamecocks
Colors: Garnet & Black
Arena: The Colonial Center
Capacity: 18,000; Year Built: 2002
AD: Eric C. Hyman
SID: Michelle Schmitt

S.C.-AIKEN
Aiken, SC 29801 II

Coach: Vince Alexander, Okla. Baptist 1989

2006-07 RESULTS (9-22)
63	Wis.-Parkside †	79
63	Shippensburg †	60
69	South Dakota †	77
91	Morris ⊠	73
73	Anderson (S.C.) ⊠	63
82	GCSU	96
88	Mars Hill ⊠	77
72	Mars Hill	74
92	Allen ⊠	60
54	Furman	79
61	Tusculum ⊠	65
52	Limestone	78
72	S.C. Upstate ⊠	69
70	Augusta St. ⊠	89
45	UNC Pembroke	70
71	Columbus St.	83
78	Francis Marion	85
81	GCSU ⊠	93
65	Allen	53
62	UNC Pembroke ⊠	51
73	Clayton St.	89
68	Francis Marion ⊠	72
56	Armstrong Atlantic ⊠	85
72	North Georgia	69
62	Lander ⊠	80
57	Erskine ⊠	75
57	S.C. Upstate	75
49	Ga. Southwestern	70
67	North Georgia ⊠	70
59	Lander	70
58	Columbus St. †	66

Nickname: Pacers
Colors: Cardinal, Navy, and White
Arena: The Courthouse
Capacity: 2,500; Year Built: 1977
AD: Douglas R. Warrick
SID: Brad Fields

SOUTH CAROLINA ST.
Orangeburg, SC 29117-0001 I

Coach: Jamal Brown, South Carolina St. 1996

2006-07 RESULTS (13-17)
52	South Carolina	55
69	South Fla.	82
60	Georgia	105
74	Jacksonville	87
55	Dayton	67
77	N.C. A&T ⊠	67
87	VMI	99
81	Coastal Caro. ⊠	80
57	Old Dominion	74
79	UNC Asheville ⊠	77
68	Rutgers	75
53	Delaware St. ⊠	59
51	Howard ⊠	45
61	Md.-East. Shore ⊠	49
58	Florida A&M	73
68	Bethune-Cookman	56
62	Morgan St.	65
67	Coppin St.	70
74	Hampton ⊠	63
56	Norfolk St. ⊠	62
65	Howard	58
77	Md.-East. Shore	74
69	Florida A&M ⊠	72
44	Bethune-Cookman ⊠	46
70	Morgan St. ⊠	56
76	Coppin St. ⊠	65
61	Hampton	60
65	Norfolk St.	70
89	Winston-Salem ⊠	82
64	Morgan St. †	66

Nickname: Bulldogs
Colors: Garnet & Blue
Arena: SHM Memorial Center
Capacity: 3,200; Year Built: 1968
AD: Charlene M. Johnson
SID: Bill Hamilton

S.C. UPSTATE
Spartanburg, SC 29303-4999 II

Coach: Eddie Payne, Wake Forest 1973

2006-07 RESULTS (17-11)
73	Bellarmine ⊠	82
64	Newberry ⊠	61
78	Catawba	69
79	Salem Int'l †	77
82	Fayetteville St.	64
82	Mars Hill	66
88	West Virginia St. †	96
69	Wingate	90
68	Presbyterian ⊠	64
73	Mars Hill	70
87	Catawba ⊠	75
69	S.C.-Aiken	72
57	Ga. Southwestern ⊠	43
65	Francis Marion	48
69	Augusta St.	86
74	North Georgia	56
68	Columbus St. ⊠	63
62	Francis Marion	66
62	GCSU	66
76	North Georgia	61
49	Clayton St. ⊠	74
65	Lander	59
64	UNC Pembroke ⊠	47
75	S.C.-Aiken ⊠	57
61	Armstrong Atlantic	68
66	Lander ⊠	67
69	UNC Pembroke	52
43	Clayton St. †	63

Nickname: Spartans
Colors: Green, White & Black
Arena: G.B. Hodge Center
Capacity: 1,535; Year Built: 1973
AD: H. Michael Hall
SID: Bill English

SOUTH DAKOTA
Vermillion, SD 57069-2390 II

Coach: David Boots, Augsburg 1979

2006-07 RESULTS (23-7)
78	Shippensburg †	73
75	Wis.-Parkside †	86
77	S.C.-Aiken †	69
86	Wayne St. (Neb.) ⊠	90
78	Southwest Minn. St. ⊠	68
79	Quincy †	89
84	Chadron St. †	75
68	Chadron St.	73
82	Morningside ⊠	60
73	Valley City St. ⊠	54
75	South Dak. Tech ⊠	59
75	Minn. St. Moorhead ⊠	63
62	Upper Iowa †	51
98	Illinois Tech †	38
82	Jamestown	54
69	Augustana (S.D.) ⊠	57
70	North Dakota ⊠	54
93	Neb.-Omaha	78
68	Minn. Duluth	62
87	Minn. St. Mankato	91
86	Neb.-Omaha ⊠	67
85	Minn. St. Mankato ⊠	75
91	St. Cloud St. ⊠	63
69	North Dakota	68
75	Minn. Duluth ⊠	83
86	Augustana (S.D.)	71
90	St. Cloud St.	83
60	Minn. Duluth	56
97	Minn. St. Mankato ⊠	86
88	Neb.-Kearney †	95

Nickname: Coyotes
Colors: Red & White
Arena: DakotaDome
Capacity: 10,000; Year Built: 1979
AD: Joel Nielsen
SID: Shane Drahota

SOUTH DAKOTA ST.
Brookings, SD 57007 II

Coach: Scott Nagy, Delta St. 1988

2006-07 RESULTS (6-24)
50	Kent St. †	105
66	Alabama A&M †	70
89	VMI †	104
66	Idaho ⊠	74
58	Milwaukee	75
56	UNI	69
84	Arkansas St. ⊠	78
50	Utah St. ⊠	56
67	Denver	56
53	Minnesota	77
47	Montana	87
48	Green Bay	80
79	UMKC	71
65	Montana St. ⊠	62
67	Idaho	72
61	UCF ⊠	72
47	Butler	62
61	Cal St. Northridge	72
54	Utah Valley St. ⊠	66
82	Tex.-Pan American ⊠	67
56	Middle Tenn. ⊠	57
60	North Dakota St. ⊠	78
62	NJIT	67
52	IPFW	68
50	Tex.-Pan American	63
56	Utah Valley St.	83
63	Cal St. Northridge ⊠	64
69	North Dakota St.	86
72	IPFW ⊠	83
71	NJIT ⊠	61

Nickname: Jackrabbits
Colors: Yellow & Blue
Arena: Frost Arena
  Capacity: 8,000; Year Built: 1973
AD: Fred M. Oien
SID: Jason Hove

SOUTH FLA.
Tampa, FL 33620 I

Coach: Robert McCullum, Birmingham-So. 1976

2006-07 RESULTS (12-18)
77	Buffalo ⊠	61
82	South Carolina St. ⊠	69
79	Florida Int'l ⊠	50
77	Stetson ⊠	72
46	Richmond ⊠	56
63	Winston-Salem	43
65	East Caro.	52
87	Norfolk St. †	56
63	A&M-Corpus Christi †	69
59	UNLV	74
69	Missouri St. ⊠	81
62	UAB	78
75	Wake Forest †	67
82	Bethune-Cookman ⊠	49
50	Connecticut	69
48	Pittsburgh	69
55	Louisville ⊠	81
74	Cincinnati ⊠	59
58	West Virginia	69
58	Notre Dame	82
62	Rutgers ⊠	40
68	Marquette ⊠	70
69	Notre Dame ⊠	63
62	St. John's (N.Y.)	66
63	Louisville.	83
53	Syracuse ⊠	70
62	DePaul ⊠	75
76	Seton Hall	89
72	Providence ⊠	77
54	DePaul	70

Nickname: Bulls
Colors: Green & Gold
Arena: Sun Dome
  Capacity: 10,411; Year Built: 1979
AD: Doug Woolard
SID: Scott Kuykendall

SOUTHEAST MO. ST.
Cape Girardeau, MO 63701-4799 I

Coach: Scott Edgar, Pitt.-Johnstown 1978

2006-07 RESULTS (11-20)
52	Arkansas	92
51	Drake †	78
51	Centenary (La.) †	83
69	Alas. Fairbanks	66
78	UC Riverside ⊠	75
45	Evansville	65
65	IPFW ⊠	84
81	Tenn.-Martin ⊠	79
72	Tennessee St.	75
76	Tennessee Tech	91
67	Jacksonville St. ⊠	70
64	Samford ⊠	65
71	Iowa St.	87
65	Purdue	102
88	Eastern Ky.	74
80	Eastern Ill. ⊠	65
96	Murray St.	85
67	Austin Peay	68
92	Tennessee St. ⊠	78
80	Tennessee Tech ⊠	87
61	Morehead St.	59
67	Murray St. ⊠	85
73	Austin Peay ⊠	75
73	Tenn.-Martin	69
81	Morehead St. ⊠	78
61	Eastern Ky. ⊠	66
69	Eastern Ill.	77
56	Louisiana Tech ⊠	72

70	Samford	67
72	Jacksonville St.	78
60	Tennessee Tech	88

Nickname: Redhawks
Colors: Red & Black
Arena: Show Me Center
  Capacity: 7,000; Year Built: 1987
AD: Donald L. Kaverman
SID: Ron Hines

SOUTHEASTERN LA.
Hammond, LA 70402 I

Coach: Jim Yarbrough, Florida St. 1987

2006-07 RESULTS (16-14)
76	Cal Poly †	69
65	Oregon St.	63
63	Portland †	55
73	William Carey	50
84	Troy	86
73	Jackson St.	81
56	San Francisco †	71
59	Chicago St. †	44
62	Florida St.	88
70	Southern U.	59
69	Penn St.	66
90	Millsaps ⊠	67
61	Minnesota	63
45	Sam Houston St. ⊠	69
49	Stephen F. Austin	66
78	Texas St. ⊠	70
73	Texas-Arlington ⊠	69
75	Nicholls St. ⊠	69
74	Central Ark.	66
91	Northwestern St.	98
69	McNeese St. ⊠	64
73	Lamar ⊠	64
64	UTSA	57
74	A&M-Corpus Christi	80
72	Nicholls St.	74
66	Central Ark. ⊠	63
65	Northwestern St. ⊠	71
45	McNeese St.	63
64	Lamar	83
72	A&M-Corpus Christi †	80

Nickname: Lions
Colors: Green & Gold
Arena: University Center
  Capacity: 7,500; Year Built: 1982
AD: Dennis Roland
SID: Matt Sullivan

SOUTHEASTERN OKLA.
Durant, OK 74701-0609 II

Coach: Tony Robinson, Southeastern Okla. 1976

2006-07 RESULTS (27-5)
94	Southwestern Christ. ⊠	62
96	Ouachita Baptist ⊠	85
84	Okla. Sci. & Arts	61
92	Midwestern St.	70
93	Ouachita Baptist	77
81	Okla. Christian	74
80	Tex. A&M-Kingsville ⊠	62
84	Okla. Sci. & Arts ⊠	74
84	Fort Hays St. †	68
72	Pittsburg St. †	77
72	Angelo St.	63
77	Abilene Christian	66
58	Tarleton St.	68
85	West Tex. A&M ⊠	75
91	Cameron	82
89	Southwestern Okla. ⊠	74
74	East Central	60
90	Tex. A&M-Commerce	71
87	Central Okla.	69
69	Northeastern St. ⊠	52
108	Cameron ⊠	93
93	Southwestern Okla.	79
83	East Central	78
86	Tex. A&M-Commerce ⊠	82
88	Central Okla. ⊠	94

72	Northeastern St.	56
88	Tex. A&M-Kingsville ⊠	72
83	West Tex. A&M †	76
80	Midwestern St.	89
79	Emporia St. †	66
88	Midwestern St. †	77
54	Central Mo.	67

Nickname: Savage Storm
Colors: Blue & Gold
Arena: Bloomer Sullivan Gym
  Capacity: 2,000; Year Built: 1956
AD: Jeff Hale
SID: Trey Reed

SOUTHERN ARK.
Magnolia, AR 71754-0000 II

Coach: Eric Bozeman, Arkansas Tech 1981

2006-07 RESULTS (11-16)
64	Miles †	72
75	Clark Atlanta †	62
70	North Ala.	94
67	Dallas Baptist ⊠	72
89	Champion Bapt. ⊠	35
71	Rust	44
58	Dallas Baptist	65
56	Tulsa	88
81	Central Baptist ⊠	46
79	North Ala. ⊠	64
64	Armstrong Atlantic	74
40	GCSU †	50
86	Ecclesia ⊠	75
51	Christian Bros. ⊠	71
48	Henderson St. ⊠	56
68	Arkansas Tech	63
61	Delta St.	66
50	Ouachita Baptist ⊠	59
55	Harding	65
65	Ark.-Monticello ⊠	48
49	Christian Bros.	69
41	Henderson St.	72
71	Arkansas Tech ⊠	62
65	Delta St. ⊠	63
75	Ouachita Baptist	68
61	Harding ⊠	64
65	Ark.-Monticello	76

Nickname: Muleriders
Colors: Royal Blue & Old Gold
Arena: W.T. Watson Athletic Cent
  Capacity: 2,000; Year Built: 1962
AD: Jay Adcox
SID: Houston Taylor

SOUTHERN CALIFORNIA
Los Angeles, CA 90089-0602 I

Coach: Tim Floyd, Louisiana Tech 1977

2006-07 RESULTS (25-12)
74	South Carolina ⊠	80
69	St. Mary's (Cal.) ⊠	63
74	Citadel ⊠	58
79	Long Beach St. ⊠	61
63	Mississippi Val. ⊠	39
67	Loyola Marymount ⊠	50
62	Kansas	72
74	George Washington †	65
88	Bethune-Cookman ⊠	36
70	Charleston So. ⊠	58
83	Longwood ⊠	53
55	Kansas St. †	68
60	Wichita St. †	56
86	Washington	79
55	Washington St. ⊠	58
84	Oregon	82
91	Oregon St.	46
64	UCLA ⊠	65
80	Arizona	73
58	Arizona St. ⊠	49
50	Stanford	65
76	California	73
73	Oregon St. ⊠	56
71	Oregon	68

65	UCLA	70
80	Arizona	75
58	Arizona St.	68
69	Stanford	65
84	California ⊠	66
70	Washington.	85
86	Washington St.	88
83	Stanford †	79
70	Washington St. †	61
57	Oregon †	81
77	Arkansas †	60
87	Texas †	68
64	North Carolina †	74

Nickname: Trojans
Colors: Cardinal & Gold
Arena: Galen Center
  Capacity: 10,258; Year Built: 2006
AD: Michael Garrett
SID: Tim Tessalone

SOUTHERN CONN. ST.
New Haven, CT 06515 II

Coach: Jerry DeGregorio, St. John's (N.Y.) 1988

2006-07 RESULTS (7-20)
61	St. Anselm	85
61	Bentley	78
77	Merrimack	84
64	Le Moyne	60
82	St. Michael's	94
72	Mass.-Lowell ⊠	69
81	American Int'l ⊠	89
66	St. Rose ⊠	80
48	C.W. Post ⊠	56
72	Ga. Southwestern †	74
72	Nyack †	70
58	Bentley ⊠	81
79	Franklin Pierce	87
82	Pace †	84
60	Le Moyne	89
69	American Int'l.	75
74	Concordia (N.Y.) ⊠	56
75	Assumption	78
76	Stonehill ⊠	73
54	Southern N.H.	62
78	St. Rose	86
73	Merrimack ⊠	57
77	St. Michael's ⊠	75
69	Dominican (N.Y.)	84
82	Pace	88
72	Bryant ⊠	78
76	Mass.-Lowell	92

Nickname: Owls
Colors: Blue & White
Arena: James W. Moore Fieldhouse
  Capacity: 2,800; Year Built: 1973
AD: Patricia D. Nicol
SID: Richard Leddy

SIU EDWARDSVILLE
Edwardsville, IL 62026-1129 II

Coach: Marty Simmons, Evansville 1987

2006-07 RESULTS (15-12)
58	Bradley	74
63	Harris-Stowe ⊠	56
103	Robert Morris-Chi. ⊠	69
52	Ferris St.	57
54	Bellarmine	44
76	Northern Ky.	81
80	Central Bible (Mo.) ⊠	40
66	Wis.-Parkside	62
65	Lewis ⊠	46
80	Ky. Wesleyan	81
80	Illinois Tech ⊠	47
60	Mo.-Rolla	43
70	Mo.-St. Louis	68
54	Southern Ind.	46
64	Ky. Wesleyan ⊠	47
46	St. Joseph's (Ind.)	57
67	Indianapolis	69
57	Drury ⊠	60

72	Rockhurst ⊠	65
74	Oakland City ⊠	57
55	Quincy	67
71	Drury	79
64	Rockhurst	70
76	Quincy ⊠	71
54	Southern Ind.	73
72	Mo.-Rolla	58
92	Mo.-St. Louis ⊠	63

Nickname: Cougars
Colors: Red & White
Arena: Sam Vadalabene Center
  Capacity: 4,000; Year Built: 1984
AD: Bradley Hewitt
SID: Eric Hess

SOUTHERN ILL.
Carbondale, IL 62901-6620 I

Coach: Chris Lowery, Southern Ill. 1995

2006-07 RESULTS (29-7)

59	Washington-St. Louis ⊠	28
62	Murray St. ⊠	46
53	Arkansas †	61
69	Minnesota †	53
69	Virginia Tech †	64
50	Louisiana Tech	36
65	St. Louis ⊠	56
75	Western Ky.	70
47	Indiana	57
74	Central Mich. ⊠	61
66	St. Mary's (Cal.)	61
68	Illinois St.	49
73	Wichita St. ⊠	68
59	Drake	54
61	UNI	66
46	Bradley	48
76	Missouri St. ⊠	56
72	Drake	62
68	Evansville	75
58	Creighton	57
56	UNI ⊠	54
73	Illinois St.	62
61	Indiana St. ⊠	48
54	Wichita St.	46
60	Bradley ⊠	50
72	Creighton ⊠	68
51	Missouri St.	47
68	Butler	64
58	Indiana St.	50
76	Evansville ⊠	69
71	Drake †	59
53	Bradley †	51
61	Creighton †	67
61	Holy Cross †	51
63	Virginia Tech †	48
58	Kansas †	61

Nickname: Salukis
Colors: Maroon & White
Arena: The SIU Arena
  Capacity: 10,014; Year Built: 1964
AD: Mario Moccia
SID: Tom Weber

SOUTHERN IND.
Evansville, IN 47712-3534 II

Coach: Rick Herdes, Graceland (Iowa) 1980

2006-07 RESULTS (29-6)

85	North Georgia †	62
101	Pace †	72
94	Alas. Fairbanks †	73
81	Wayne St. (Mich.) ⊠	64
87	Tiffin ⊠	53
125	Judson (Ill.) ⊠	68
105	Ill.-Springfield ⊠	71
84	Ky. Wesleyan ⊠	69
96	St. Joseph's (Ind.)	86
55	Indianapolis	56
108	Glenville St. ⊠	80
78	Wayne St. (Mich.)	69
91	Ferris St. †	76

117	Harris-Stowe ⊠	78
79	Rockhurst ⊠	64
89	Drury	70
63	SIU Edwardsville ⊠	54
74	Quincy	76
88	Bellarmine ⊠	80
83	Northern Ky. ⊠	71
82	Lewis	68
75	Wis.-Parkside	80
83	Mo.-St. Louis ⊠	61
98	Mo.-Rolla ⊠	80
72	Mo.-St. Louis	59
80	Mo.-Rolla	64
73	SIU Edwardsville ⊠	54
87	Quincy ⊠	65
63	Rockhurst	75
72	Drury	77
57	Lewis ⊠	45
76	Quincy ⊠	57
63	Northern Ky. ⊠	61
84	Rockhurst †	78
83	Grand Valley St. †	90

Nickname: Screaming Eagles
Colors: Red, White & Blue
Arena: Physical Activities Center
  Capacity: 2,500; Year Built: 1980
AD: Jon Mark Hall
SID: Ray Simmons

SOUTHERN ME.
Gorham, ME 04038 III

Coach: Karl Henrikson, Southern Me. 1979

2006-07 RESULTS (6-20)

70	Lyndon St. †	54
70	Me.-Farmington †	65
55	Bates	78
36	Bowdoin	68
70	Mass.-Dartmouth ⊠	75
57	Colby	83
70	Eastern Conn. St. ⊠	74
83	New England	51
66	Me.-Farmington ⊠	53
59	Colby †	78
73	Husson †	77
59	Western Conn. St.	68
58	Rhode Island Col.	67
56	Keene St. ⊠	81
81	Plymouth St. ⊠	74
62	Mass.-Dartmouth	64
73	Mass.-Boston	60
72	Eastern Conn. St.	73
58	St. Joseph's (Me.) ⊠	80
82	Western Conn. St. ⊠	87
60	Plymouth St.	68
56	Rhode Island Col. ⊠	74
61	Mass.-Boston	96
62	Husson ⊠	72
65	Keene St.	79
69	Rhode Island Col.	72

Nickname: Huskies
Colors: Blue, Gold & White
Arena: Warren G. Hill Gymnasium
  Capacity: 1,400; Year Built: 1963
AD: Albert D. Bean Jr.
SID: B.L. Efring

SMU
Dallas, TX 75275.................................. I

Coach: Matt Doherty, North Carolina 1984

2006-07 RESULTS (14-17)

57	Illinois St. †	55
70	McNeese St. †	54
52	Florida St.	59
53	Dayton ⊠	48
99	La.-Monroe ⊠	66
76	Paul Quinn ⊠	54
79	Texas Col. ⊠	63
68	Prairie View ⊠	51
68	Centenary (La.)	40

64	TCU	62
42	Oklahoma	69
76	N.C. A&T ⊠	80
84	Tex.-Pan American ⊠	71
60	Brown ⊠	56
56	Southern Miss. ⊠	57
67	Houston	82
56	UCF	64
67	UTEP ⊠	72
55	Tulane	53
66	Tulsa	70
60	UAB	56
52	Memphis	88
49	Houston ⊠	64
60	Rice ⊠	63
49	Marshall	52
65	East Caro. ⊠	42
56	UTEP	85
66	Rice	75
60	Tulsa ⊠	67
61	Memphis ⊠	64
52	Southern Miss. †	59

Nickname: Mustangs
Colors: Red & Blue
Arena: Moody Coliseum
  Capacity: 8,998; Year Built: 1956
AD: Steven Orsini
SID: Brad Sutton

SOUTHERN MISS.
Hattiesburg, MS 39406-0001 I

Coach: Larry Eustachy, Long Beach St. 1979

2006-07 RESULTS (20-11)

63	Belhaven ⊠	38
77	Tenn.-Martin ⊠	67
80	Alabama St. ⊠	43
113	Spring Hill ⊠	57
94	Sam Houston St. ⊠	86
61	Savannah St. ⊠	45
70	Southern-N.O. ⊠	45
64	Alabama †	77
80	Reinhardt ⊠	56
73	Bradley	83
58	McNeese St. ⊠	41
56	Auburn ⊠	54
52	Savannah St.	54
57	SMU	56
62	Memphis ⊠	75
50	UTEP ⊠	68
57	UAB	55
83	East Caro. ⊠	72
64	Memphis	67
87	UTEP ⊠	78
64	Tulane ⊠	79
55	Rice	70
70	Tulsa ⊠	65
80	East Caro.	42
74	Houston ⊠	69
56	UCF	59
72	Tulane	77
76	UAB ⊠	68
83	Marshall ⊠	73
59	SMU †	52
59	Houston †	62

Nickname: Golden Eagles
Colors: Black & Gold
Arena: Reed Green Coliseum
  Capacity: 8,095; Year Built: 1965
AD: Richard C. Giannini
SID: Jack Dugggan

SOUTHERN N.H.
Manchester, NH 03106-1045 II

Coach: Stan Spirou, Keene St. 1974

2006-07 RESULTS (6-21)

75	Stonehill	78
69	Le Moyne	84
70	St. Rose	72
66	Pace ⊠	82
52	St. Anselm ⊠	78
89	American Int'l ⊠	75

46	Bryant	76
72	Franklin Pierce	73
69	Assumption	84
55	Philadelphia U.	69
50	Holy Family †	62
66	St. Michael's †	71
64	Bentley	84
68	Bridgeport ⊠	74
64	St. Anselm	60
46	Franklin Pierce ⊠	57
60	Bryant ⊠	67
65	Merrimack	78
62	Southern Conn. St. ⊠	54
62	NYIT	65
63	Mass.-Lowell	68
79	Assumption ⊠	68
68	St. Rose ⊠	59
65	Pace	85
61	Stonehill ⊠	71
86	New Haven	71
53	Le Moyne ⊠	59

Nickname: Penmen
Colors: Blue & Gold
Arena: SNHU Fieldhouse
  Capacity: 2,000; Year Built: 1980
AD: Joseph R. Polak
SID: Tom McDermott

SOUTHERN U.
Baton Rouge, LA 70813.................... I

Coach: Rob Spivery, Ashland 1972

2006-07 RESULTS (10-21)

37	Georgia	97
39	Wisconsin	92
59	Oklahoma St.	75
63	Delaware St. †	65
52	East Tenn. St. †	66
27	Florida	83
64	Stephen F. Austin ⊠	73
57	Northwestern St.	64
66	Louisiana Tech	74
59	Southeastern La. ⊠	70
62	Louisiana Tech ⊠	47
58	Missouri	87
64	Texas Southern ⊠	65
63	Prairie View ⊠	58
67	Grambling	70
73	Jackson St.	62
47	Ark.-Pine Bluff ⊠	54
72	Mississippi Val. ⊠	64
44	Alabama St.	49
63	Alabama A&M	68
73	Alcorn St.	85
76	Grambling ⊠	43
57	Jackson St. ⊠	64
58	Ark.-Pine Bluff	73
63	Mississippi Val.	62
58	Alabama St. ⊠	71
62	Alabama A&M ⊠	60
61	Alcorn St. ⊠	56
64	Texas Southern	55
66	Prairie View	51
65	Jackson St. †	74

Nickname: Jaguars
Colors: Columbia Blue & Gold
Arena: F.G. Clark Center
  Capacity: 7,500; Year Built: 1976
AD: Greg LaFleur
SID: Kevin Manns

SOUTHERN UTAH
Cedar City, UT 84720 I

Coach: Bill Evans, Southern Utah 1972

2006-07 RESULTS (16-14)

76	Utah	73
74	Denver	68
68	Boise St.	77
67	Idaho ⊠	50
61	BYU	80
73	Denver ⊠	63
68	Utah Valley St. ⊠	60

RESULTS

72	Idaho	50
72	Washington	87
75	Weber St. ⊠	63
74	Texas A&M Int'l ⊠	48
57	Weber St.	59
55	Utah Valley St.	64
84	Chicago St. ⊠	66
66	Western St. ⊠	55
62	UMKC	66
61	Oral Roberts ⊠	69
78	Centenary (La.) ⊠	57
69	Oakland	77
56	IUPUI	53
68	Western Ill. ⊠	65
76	Valparaiso ⊠	60
66	UMKC ⊠	59
63	Centenary (La.)	70
57	Oral Roberts	79
74	IUPUI ⊠	75
87	Oakland ⊠	85
48	Valparaiso	75
48	Western Ill.	51
59	IUPUI †	71

Nickname: Thunderbirds
Colors: Scarlet & White
Arena: Centrum
  Capacity: 5,300; Year Built: 1985
AD: Ken Beazer
SID: Neil Gardner

SOUTHERN VT.
Bennington, VT 05201-9983 III

Coach: Michael McDonough, Notre Dame

2006-07 RESULTS (7-14)

79	Williams	81
51	Bates †	77
73	Green Mountain	57
75	Gallaudet	73
75	N.C. Wesleyan †	81
69	Emerson	91
76	Middlebury	100
90	Norwich	86
75	Johnson & Wales (RI) ⊠	67
62	Rensselaer	74
65	Norwich ⊠	86
88	Suffolk	64
92	Albertus Magnus	83
78	Rivier ⊠	84
67	Amherst	111
63	Johnson & Wales (RI)	70
92	Daniel Webster	93
78	Albertus Magnus ⊠	74
86	Rivier	87
68	Emmanuel (Mass.)	76
54	Western New Eng.	92

Nickname: Mountaineers
Colors: Green, White & Gold
Arena: Field House
  Capacity: 300; Year Built: 1991
AD: Matthew Couloute, Jr.
SID: Ken Norris

SOUTHWEST BAPTIST
Bolivar, MO 65613 II

Coach: Jeff Guiot, Pittsburg St. 1987

2006-07 RESULTS (16-12)

79	Drury ⊠	80
113	Mo. Baptist ⊠	84
97	Park †	85
53	Rockhurst	79
98	Ark.-Monticello	73
100	Newman ⊠	66
104	Harris-Stowe ⊠	56
80	Northwest Mo. St. ⊠	81
59	Henderson St. †	74
92	Gannon †	80
84	Emporia St.	93
66	Central Mo. ⊠	77
69	Fort Hays St.	59
87	Pittsburg St. ⊠	84

76	Washburn	69
68	Truman ⊠	81
84	Mo. Southern St. ⊠	77
81	Mo. Western St.	66
63	Northwest Mo. St.	68
95	Mo. Western St. ⊠	75
53	Truman	60
79	Washburn ⊠	72
87	Mo. Southern St.	77
64	Fort Hays St. ⊠	74
58	Pittsburg St.	51
59	Central Mo.	69
108	Emporia St. ⊠	89
70	Pittsburg St. †	73

Nickname: Bearcats
Colors: Purple & White
Arena: Meyer Sports Center
  Capacity: 3,000; Year Built: 2005
AD: Brent Good
SID: Adam Ledyard

SOUTHWEST MINN. ST.
Marshall, MN 56258 II

Coach: Greg Stemen, Valley City St. 1988

2006-07 RESULTS (20-10)

67	St. Olaf	55
68	South Dakota	78
75	Dakota St. ⊠	61
78	North Dakota ⊠	69
66	Minn.-Crookston ⊠	50
87	Bemidji St. ⊠	45
64	Mary	56
75	Northern St.	72
73	St. Cloud St.	76
50	Minn. St. Mankato ⊠	55
68	North Dakota St.	72
69	Minn. Duluth	56
61	Augustana (S.D.)	66
88	Upper Iowa ⊠	60
71	Winona St. ⊠	76
69	Wayne St. (Neb.) ⊠	68
70	Concordia-St. Paul	64
56	Minn. St. Moorhead	58
63	Bemidji St.	54
81	Minn.-Crookston	60
75	Northern St. ⊠	68
58	Mary ⊠	41
59	Winona St.	68
70	Upper Iowa	44
70	Wayne St. (Neb.)	74
75	Minn. St. Moorhead ⊠	64
59	Concordia-St. Paul ⊠	45
86	Bemidji St. ⊠	43
82	Northern St. †	63
70	Winona St.	80

Nickname: Mustangs
Colors: Brown & Gold
Arena: R/A Facility
  Capacity: 4,000; Year Built: 1996
AD: Chris Hmielewski
SID: Kelly Loft

SOUTHWESTERN (TEX.)
Georgetown, TX 78627-0770 III

Coach: Bill Raleigh, Muhlenberg 1988

2006-07 RESULTS (11-15)

76	Schreiner	75
75	Texas Lutheran ⊠	72
58	Hardin-Simmons ⊠	56
75	FDU-Florham †	84
74	Chicago †	62
46	Dallas	58
68	Millsaps ⊠	70
68	Rhodes ⊠	55
48	Texas A&M Int'l ⊠	63
53	Swarthmore	55
76	Pitt.-Greensburg ⊠	34
66	Mary Hardin-Baylor	72
52	Austin	33
57	Hendrix	43

53	Trinity (Tex.)	62
38	Centre	55
51	DePauw	59
75	Oglethorpe ⊠	80
62	Sewanee ⊠	60
65	Millsaps	71
54	Rhodes	61
63	Trinity (Tex.) ⊠	67
77	Dallas ⊠	75
68	Austin ⊠	64
64	Hendrix ⊠	68
43	Centre †	63

Nickname: Pirates
Colors: Black & Gold
Arena: Corbin J. Robertson Center
  Capacity: 1,800; Year Built: 1995
AD: Glada C. Munt
SID: Jeff Sutton

SOUTHWESTERN OKLA.
Weatherford, OK 73096 II

Coach: Todd Thurman, Southern Nazarene

2006-07 RESULTS (17-10)

85	Arkansas Tech ⊠	72
93	Okla. Sci. & Arts ⊠	79
88	Ouachita Baptist †	75
84	Adams St. †	69
80	Eastern N.M.	65
84	West Tex. A&M	81
82	Okla. Sci. & Arts.	81
114	Midwestern St. ⊠	99
83	Mo. Southern St. ⊠	67
138	Southwestern Christ.	67
77	Oklahoma	129
77	Tex. A&M-Kingsville	88
104	Tarleton St. ⊠	80
91	Abilene Christian ⊠	84
88	East Central ⊠	72
74	Southeastern Okla.	89
77	Central Okla.	83
69	Northeastern St. ⊠	67
100	Cameron	101
110	Tex. A&M-Commerce ⊠	102
101	East Central	102
79	Southeastern Okla. ⊠	93
80	Central Okla. ⊠	79
73	Northeastern St.	81
95	Cameron ⊠	73
93	Tex. A&M-Commerce	102
67	Midwestern St.	90

Nickname: Bulldogs
Colors: Navy Blue & White
Arena: Rankin Williams Fieldhouse
  Capacity: 2,400; Year Built: 1957
AD: Cecil Perkins
SID: Justin Tinder

SPRINGFIELD
Springfield, MA 01109-3797 III

Coach: Charlie Brock, Springfield 1976

2006-07 RESULTS (12-14)

77	Colby-Sawyer †	53
63	Brandeis	90
76	Curry ⊠	67
61	Tufts	77
72	Westfield St. †	75
52	Amherst	91
76	Trinity (Conn.) ⊠	72
65	Williams	67
56	Connecticut Col.	69
65	Rhode Island Col.	73
64	Colby ⊠	48
76	Kean ⊠	73
57	MIT	56
75	WPI ⊠	82
79	Keene St.	84
67	Coast Guard	60
70	Wheaton (Mass.) ⊠	58
56	WPI	76
64	Babson	58

89	Clark (Mass.) ⊠	83
67	Coast Guard ⊠	77
68	MIT ⊠	71
71	Wheaton (Mass.)	69
72	Clark (Mass.)	73
70	Babson ⊠	67
54	Wheaton (Mass.) ⊠	61

Nickname: The Pride
Colors: Maroon & White
Arena: Blake Arena
  Capacity: 2,000; Year Built: 1981
AD: Cathie Schweitzer
SID: Steve Raczynski

STANFORD
Stanford, CA 94305-2060 I

Coach: Trent Johnson, Boise St. 1983

2006-07 RESULTS (18-13)

92	Siena ⊠	72
73	San Jose St. ⊠	52
45	Air Force ⊠	79
58	Northwestern ⊠	53
82	Denver ⊠	39
84	UC Davis ⊠	72
70	Texas Tech †	59
46	Santa Clara ⊠	62
69	Fresno St.	67
71	Arizona St. ⊠	60
75	Arizona	89
63	California ⊠	67
76	Virginia	75
78	Washington	77
71	Washington St. ⊠	68
59	Oregon	66
67	Oregon St.	56
65	Southern California ⊠	50
75	UCLA ⊠	68
86	Gonzaga ⊠	90
90	California	71
45	Washington St.	58
52	Washington	64
70	Oregon St. ⊠	55
88	Oregon ⊠	69
65	Southern California	69
61	UCLA	75
63	Arizona St. ⊠	53
80	Arizona ⊠	85
79	Southern California †	83
58	Louisville †	78

Nickname: Cardinal
Colors: Cardinal & White
Arena: Maples Pavilion
  Capacity: 7,391; Year Built: 1968
AD: Robert A. Bowlsby
SID: Aimee Dombroski

STATEN ISLAND
Staten Island, NY 10314 III

Coach: Anthony Petosa, Staten Island 1986

2006-07 RESULTS (15-13)

77	New Jersey City †	90
83	Emmanuel (Mass.)	77
68	FDU-Florham ⊠	85
66	Montclair St. ⊠	64
73	City Tech ⊠	49
85	Brooklyn	72
77	Farmingdale St. ⊠	81
67	Merchant Marine	70
74	Rivier	84
84	Nazareth ⊠	75
80	Medgar Evers	78
57	York (N.Y.)	69
77	Stevens Institute ⊠	95
68	Hunter ⊠	69
67	Kean	89
64	Baruch	77
64	CCNY	58
52	Drew	57
58	City Tech ⊠	70
76	Medgar Evers ⊠	70

70	Lehman ⊠	64
99	Brooklyn ⊠	84
74	York (N.Y.) ⊠	58
79	John Jay	76
88	St. Joseph's (Brkln) ⊠	72
62	Lehman †	55
68	Baruch †	59
54	York (N.Y.) †	56

Nickname: Dolphins
Colors: Blue and Maroon
Arena: Sports & Recreation Center
 Capacity: 1,200; Year Built: 1995
AD: Jason S. Fein
SID: David Pizzuto

STEPHEN F. AUSTIN
Nacogdoches, TX 75962 I

Coach: Danny Kaspar, North Texas 1978
2006-07 RESULTS (15-14)
71	San Diego ⊠	62
53	TCU	59
59	Arkansas	70
99	Schreiner ⊠	54
56	Missouri	85
85	Texas Col.	52
73	Southern U.	64
70	North Texas ⊠	76
80	La.-Lafayette ⊠	42
44	Tex.-Pan American	46
86	Northern Ill. ⊠	78
89	Howard Payne ⊠	63
61	Nicholls St. ⊠	55
66	Southeastern La. ⊠	49
73	Lamar	72
67	McNeese St.	53
52	Sam Houston St. ⊠	55
82	Texas St.	62
65	Texas-Arlington ⊠	54
62	A&M-Corpus Christi ⊠	70
45	UTSA ⊠	48
60	Central Ark.	54
57	Northwestern St. ⊠	67
51	Sam Houston St.	63
78	Texas St. ⊠	75
62	Texas-Arlington	69
65	A&M-Corpus Christi	69
49	UTSA ⊠	54
76	Northwestern St. †	85

Nickname: Lumberjacks
Colors: Purple & White
Arena: William Johnson Coliseum
 Capacity: 7,200; Year Built: 1974
AD: Robert Hill
SID: Brian Ross

STETSON
DeLand, FL 32720 I

Coach: Derek Waugh, Furman 1993
2006-07 RESULTS (11-20)
68	Army †	80
72	N.C. A&T †	69
45	Missouri	66
60	UCF	73
80	Palm Beach Atl. ⊠	63
72	South Fla.	77
61	Kennesaw St. ⊠	56
61	East Tenn. St. ⊠	75
63	Florida St. ⊠	82
64	Miami (Fla.)	89
67	Florida	88
58	Savannah St.	46
85	Skidmore ⊠	55
63	Mercer	84
68	Lipscomb	79
71	Belmont	73
64	Gardner-Webb ⊠	77
82	Campbell ⊠	73
63	North Fla.	60
63	Jacksonville	69
66	Mercer ⊠	78
58	Belmont ⊠	62

69	Lipscomb ⊠	67
82	Campbell	104
48	Gardner-Webb ⊠	73
88	Savannah St. ⊠	74
74	North Fla. ⊠	63
62	Jacksonville ⊠	57
49	East Tenn. St. ⊠	84
67	Kennesaw St. ⊠	72
61	East Tenn. St.	77

Nickname: Hatters
Colors: Green & White
Arena: Edmunds Center
 Capacity: 5,000; Year Built: 1974
AD: Jeff Altier
SID: Brian Petrotta

STEVENS INSTITUTE
Hoboken, NJ 07030-5991 III

Coach: Josh Loeffler, Swarthmore 2003
2006-07 RESULTS (23-7)
59	Arcadia †	54
73	Muhlenberg	66
65	FDU-Florham	77
79	CCNY ⊠	65
70	Old Westbury	73
67	New York U.	76
89	Maritime (N.Y.)	61
86	Mt. St. Mary (N.Y.) ⊠	55
74	Rensselaer	69
92	Tufts	71
95	Staten Island	77
88	St. Joseph's (L.I.) ⊠	78
79	Manhattanville	85
83	Mt. St. Vincent ⊠	59
53	Yeshiva	49
95	Hunter	80
108	Centenary (N.J.) ⊠	70
85	Merchant Marine	74
85	Farmingdale St. ⊠	81
68	Maritime (N.Y.) ⊠	55
95	Old Westbury ⊠	88
91	Mt. St. Vincent	76
86	St. Joseph's (L.I.)	70
92	Merchant Marine ⊠	86
77	Mt. St. Mary (N.Y.)	95
87	Yeshiva ⊠	51
80	Old Westbury ⊠	83
68	WPI †	57
69	Ramapo	61
74	Amherst	97

Nickname: Ducks
Colors: Red & Gray
Arena: Canavan Arena
 Capacity: 1,500; Year Built: 1994
AD: Russell B. Rogers
SID: Brian Granata

STILLMAN
Tuscaloosa, AL 35403 II

Coach: Tim Waller, Western Mich. 1979
2006-07 RESULTS (15-13)
60	Montevallo ⊠	71
65	Southern-N.O. ⊠	63
64	Alabama A&M	65
74	Clark Atlanta ⊠	58
64	Morehouse ⊠	52
61	Miles ⊠	78
74	Tuskegee	72
64	Albany St. (Ga.)	56
54	Fort Valley St.	52
80	LeMoyne-Owen ⊠	66
63	Fla. Gulf Coast	88
70	Tuskegee ⊠	67
64	LeMoyne-Owen	76
62	Miles	65
75	Morehouse	71
48	Clark Atlanta	41
65	Lane ⊠	59
69	Kentucky St. ⊠	67
48	Paine	50
50	Benedict	59

50	Albany St. (Ga.) ⊠	45
47	Fort Valley St. ⊠	62
37	Paine ⊠	42
61	Benedict ⊠	64
44	Claflin ⊠	43
60	Kentucky St. ⊠	57
55	Lane	69
58	Albany St. (Ga.) †	64

Nickname: Tigers
Colors: Navy Blue & Vegas Gold
Arena: Birthright
 Capacity: 1,000; Year Built: 1954
AD: Greg Thompson/Curtis Williams
SID: Wesley Peterson

STONEHILL
Easton, MA 02357 II

Coach: David McLaughlin, Colby 1997
2006-07 RESULTS (16-12)
80	St. Thomas Aquinas	44
78	Southern N.H. ⊠	75
72	Mercy †	55
74	Mass.-Lowell ⊠	75
70	Franklin Pierce †	78
69	Assumption	56
69	St. Rose ⊠	66
72	Bentley ⊠	80
77	Bryant ⊠	59
72	Merrimack	71
60	Dominican (N.Y.) ⊠	42
90	Molloy ⊠	78
91	Dowling	79
90	St. Anselm ⊠	81
76	St. Michael's	92
68	Merrimack ⊠	56
55	Bryant	70
58	American Int'l	63
72	Franklin Pierce ⊠	71
73	Southern Conn. St.	76
72	Pace ⊠	99
69	Le Moyne ⊠	74
68	Mass.-Lowell	72
51	Bentley	68
71	Southern N.H.	61
83	Assumption ⊠	81
81	St. Anselm	70
54	Le Moyne †	61

Nickname: Skyhawks
Colors: Purple & White
Arena: Merkert Gymnasium
 Capacity: 2,200; Year Built: 1973
AD: Paula Sullivan
SID: Jim Seavey

STONY BROOK
Stony Brook, NY 11794.....................I

Coach: Steve Pikiell, Connecticut 1990
2006-07 RESULTS (9-20)
65	Colgate	59
72	Cornell	76
59	Penn St.	51
76	Navy ⊠	87
54	Columbia	41
58	Md.-East. Shore ⊠	64
44	Villanova	72
57	Hofstra ⊠	73
65	NJIT	61
50	Dartmouth	71
82	Fairleigh Dickinson ⊠	58
66	Notre Dame	95
69	Vermont	80
53	UMBC ⊠	72
67	Binghamton ⊠	55
47	Hartford	50
61	Albany (N.Y.)	66
68	Boston U. ⊠	62
56	New Hampshire	69
66	Maine ⊠	74
61	Vermont ⊠	71
65	Binghamton	66
56	UMBC	39

44	Hartford ⊠	59
55	Boston U. ⊠	68
67	New Hampshire ⊠	49
46	Albany (N.Y.) ⊠	66
61	Maine	63
47	Hartford †	49

Nickname: Seawolves
Colors: Scarlet, Blue & Gray
Arena: USB Sports Complex
 Capacity: 4,103; Year Built: 1990
AD: James Fiore
SID: Rob Emmerich

SUFFOLK
Boston, MA 02114 III

Coach: Adam Nelson, Boston College
1996
2006-07 RESULTS (9-18)
58	Wesleyan (Conn.) †	79
91	Fitchburg St. †	89
60	Brandeis	87
81	MIT ⊠	94
63	Mass.-Boston	77
85	Emmanuel (Mass.) ⊠	78
61	Westfield St.	86
76	Western Conn. St.	88
74	Rivier	66
55	Western New Eng.	78
64	Southern Vt.	88
70	Emmanuel (Mass.)	96
87	Albertus Magnus	63
97	Johnson & Wales (RI)	91
88	Daniel Webster	89
72	Emerson ⊠	77
92	Rivier ⊠	90
74	Norwich ⊠	76
69	Western New Eng. ⊠	87
90	Lesley ⊠	93
88	Albertus Magnus	97
99	Johnson & Wales (RI) ⊠	94
95	Daniel Webster ⊠	58
67	Emerson	86
79	Norwich	87
80	Emerson	75
82	Rivier	94

Nickname: Rams
Colors: Blue & Gold
Arena: Regan Gymnasium
 Capacity: 150; Year Built: 1991
AD: James E. Nelson
SID: Brenda K. Laymance

SUL ROSS ST.
Alpine, TX 79832 III

Coach: Greg Wright, Texas A&M 1993
2006-07 RESULTS (8-16)
52	St. Mary's (Tex.)	79
67	Tex. Permian Basin ⊠	77
70	Ozarks (Ark.)	75
77	LeTourneau ⊠	63
70	East Tex. Baptist ⊠	62
62	Howard Payne ⊠	58
66	Texas-Dallas	81
57	Texas-Tyler	65
68	Lubbock Chrst.	87
39	Mississippi Col. ⊠	69
63	Louisiana Col. ⊠	57
70	Texas Lutheran	66
79	Schreiner	86
59	Howard Payne	91
62	Concordia (Tex.) ⊠	85
52	Mary Hardin-Baylor ⊠	64
59	McMurry	90
58	Hardin-Simmons	84
55	McMurry ⊠	69
53	Hardin-Simmons ⊠	49
55	Mary Hardin-Baylor	77
67	Concordia (Tex.)	99
68	Texas Lutheran ⊠	66
67	Schreiner ⊠	65

Nickname: Lobos
Colors: Scarlet & Gray
Arena: Pete P. Gallego Center
  Capacity: 3,100; Year Built: 2001
AD: Kay Whitley
SID: Travis Hendryx

SUSQUEHANNA
Selinsgrove, PA 17870-1025 III

Coach: Frank Marcinek, Penn St. 1981

2006-07 RESULTS (16-10)

105	Adelphi ⊠	60
98	King's (Pa.) ⊠	97
95	Marywood	57
79	Elizabethtown	84
82	Moravian ⊠	73
86	Wilkes ⊠	87
70	Misericordia	68
78	Lycoming ⊠	54
69	York (Pa.)	84
77	Cortland St. †	60
76	Catholic	78
74	Morrisville St. †	56
79	Scranton	66
63	Juniata ⊠	61
63	Widener	78
52	Messiah	55
78	Lebanon Valley ⊠	66
90	Albright	77
74	Widener ⊠	61
74	Elizabethtown ⊠	84
76	Moravian	70
53	Messiah	68
69	Albright ⊠	62
67	Juniata	82
74	Lebanon Valley	69
64	Juniata	76

Nickname: Crusaders
Colors: Orange & Maroon
Arena: O.W. Houts Gymnasium
  Capacity: 1,800; Year Built: 1976
AD: Pamela Samuelson
SID: Jim Miller

SWARTHMORE
Swarthmore, PA 19081-1397 III

Coach: Lee Wimberly, Stanford 1968

2006-07 RESULTS (11-14)

46	Wittenberg †	57
65	Trinity (Conn.) ⊠	76
75	Arcadia ⊠	66
57	Johns Hopkins	73
33	Lehigh	96
73	Frank. & Marsh. ⊠	64
69	Muhlenberg ⊠	73
73	Ursinus	77
55	Southwestern (Tex.)	53
41	Trinity (Tex.) †	57
77	Phila. Biblical	66
61	Dickinson	67
66	McDaniel	63
49	Gettysburg ⊠	52
73	Frank. & Marsh.	71
51	Haverford ⊠	50
67	Ursinus ⊠	70
83	Washington (Md.)	78
66	Dickinson ⊠	60
59	Johns Hopkins ⊠	63
85	McDaniel ⊠	75
65	Muhlenberg	78
49	Gettysburg	60
67	Washington (Md.) ⊠	57
78	Haverford	84

Nickname: Garnet Tide
Colors: Garnet, Gray & White
Arena: Tarble Pavillion
  Capacity: 1,800; Year Built: 1978
AD: Adam Hertz
SID: Mark Duzenski

SYRACUSE
Syracuse, NY 13244-5020 I

Coach: Jim Boeheim, Syracuse 1966

2006-07 RESULTS (24-11)

83	St. Francis (N.Y.) ⊠	51
78	Penn ⊠	60
83	UTEP	69
81	Northeastern ⊠	58
79	Charlotte ⊠	67
81	Canisius	71
72	Holy Cross ⊠	64
61	Wichita St. ⊠	64
68	Oklahoma St. †	72
79	Colgate ⊠	52
94	Baylor ⊠	71
79	Drexel ⊠	84
85	Hofstra ⊠	60
82	St. Bonaventure ⊠	70
66	Pittsburgh ⊠	74
70	Marquette ⊠	58
68	Rutgers ⊠	58
75	Villanova ⊠	64
77	Cincinnati ⊠	76
60	St. John's (N.Y.)	64
71	Louisville ⊠	76
91	Notre Dame ⊠	103
75	DePaul ⊠	69
60	Connecticut	67
76	St. John's (N.Y.) ⊠	74
70	South Fla.	53
73	Connecticut ⊠	63
71	Providence	67
72	Georgetown ⊠	58
75	Villanova	78
78	Connecticut †	65
83	Notre Dame †	89
79	South Ala. ⊠	73
80	San Diego St. ⊠	64
70	Clemson	74

Nickname: Orange
Colors: Orange
Arena: Carrier Dome
  Capacity: 33,000; Year Built: 1980
AD: Daryl J. Gross
SID: Pete Moore

TAMPA
Tampa, FL 33606-1490 II

Coach: Richard Schmidt, Western Ky. 1964

2006-07 RESULTS (15-14)

73	Palm Beach Atl.	69
76	Goldey-Beacom ⊠	70
72	West Ga. ⊠	75
67	West Fla.	52
76	P.R.-Mayaguez †	65
60	Fla. Memorial †	49
80	Rollins ⊠	71
58	West Fla.	61
82	West Virginia St. ⊠	90
64	Southeastern (Fla.) ⊠	50
67	Fayetteville St. ⊠	75
84	Fontbonne ⊠	71
58	St. Leo ⊠	70
55	Barry	60
52	Florida Tech ⊠	63
71	Palm Beach Atl. ⊠	63
73	Fla. Southern	81
61	Lynn ⊠	62
53	Eckerd	74
80	Nova Southeastern	72
63	Florida Tech	47
68	St. Leo	55
55	Barry ⊠	65
67	Rollins	60
68	Fla. Southern ⊠	63
60	Lynn	59
54	Eckerd ⊠	96
64	Nova Southeastern ⊠	73
55	Nova Southeastern †	71

Nickname: Spartans
Colors: Scarlet, Gold & Black

Arena: Martinez Sports Center
  Capacity: 3,432; Year Built: 1984
AD: Larry Marfise
SID: Tom Kolbe

TARLETON ST.
Stephenville, TX 76402 II

Coach: Lonn Reisman, Pittsburg St. 1977

2006-07 RESULTS (18-10)

68	LeTourneau ⊠	51
86	Cal St. Chico ⊠	63
85	Findlay ⊠	82
60	St. Mary's (Tex.) ⊠	58
80	Hillsdale Baptist ⊠	40
63	East Central ⊠	55
69	Cameron ⊠	71
70	St. Augustine's ⊠	51
107	Tex. Permian Basin ⊠	59
69	St. Mary's (Tex.)	73
104	Tex. A&M-Commerce ⊠	91
80	Southwestern Okla.	104
68	Southeastern Okla. ⊠	58
54	Central Okla.	71
88	Rhema ⊠	42
62	West Tex. A&M	69
77	Eastern N.M. ⊠	72
59	Midwestern St. ⊠	72
81	Angelo St.	78
87	Abilene Christian ⊠	67
58	Tex. A&M-Kingsville ⊠	55
76	Angelo St. ⊠	73
81	Abilene Christian	80
70	Midwestern St.	76
71	Tex. A&M-Kingsville ⊠	66
63	West Tex. A&M ⊠	69
74	Eastern N.M.	77
67	Central Okla.	92

Nickname: Texans
Colors: Purple & White
Arena: Wisdom Gymnasium
  Capacity: 3,212; Year Built: 1970
AD: Lonn Reisman
SID: Joey Roberts

TEMPLE
Philadelphia, PA 19122 I

Coach: Fran Dunphy, La Salle 1970

2006-07 RESULTS (12-18)

54	Kent St.	63
62	Buffalo ⊠	64
77	Rutgers ⊠	54
74	Long Beach St. ⊠	49
76	Western Mich. ⊠	71
71	Cincinnati †	80
75	Towson	70
75	Ball St.	70
54	Drexel ⊠	69
96	Lafayette ⊠	73
65	Villanova	83
55	Duke	73
68	Xavier	76
67	St. Joseph's ⊠	80
77	Massachusetts	88
85	St. Louis	79
77	Rhode Island ⊠	85
74	Penn	76
92	Duquesne	96
80	Richmond	59
89	La Salle ⊠	64
109	St. Bonaventure ⊠	70
98	Massachusetts ⊠	89
72	La Salle	77
72	George Washington	84
76	St. Joseph's	92
81	Charlotte ⊠	69
65	Dayton ⊠	73
73	Fordham	80
62	St. Joseph's †	66

Nickname: Owls
Colors: Cherry & White

Arena: Liacouras Center
  Capacity: 10,206; Year Built: 1997
AD: William Bradshaw
SID: Larry Dougherty

TENNESSEE
Knoxville, TN 37996 I

Coach: Bruce Pearl, Boston College 1982

2006-07 RESULTS (24-11)

83	Middle Tenn. ⊠	52
78	Fordham †	71
87	UNC Wilmington †	75
99	Coppin St. ⊠	65
44	Butler †	56
87	North Carolina †	101
77	La.-Lafayette	67
89	Murray St. ⊠	64
76	Memphis ⊠	58
93	Western Ky. ⊠	79
79	Oklahoma St. †	77
111	Texas ⊠	105
101	Tennessee Tech ⊠	77
93	East Tenn. ⊠	88
92	Mississippi St. ⊠	84
81	Vanderbilt	82
66	Ohio St.	68
80	Auburn	83
64	South Carolina ⊠	61
69	Mississippi	83
57	Kentucky	76
82	Georgia ⊠	71
78	Florida	94
70	LSU ⊠	67
84	Vanderbilt ⊠	57
89	Kentucky ⊠	85
64	South Carolina	81
69	Alabama ⊠	66
83	Arkansas	72
86	Florida ⊠	76
71	Georgia	65
67	LSU †	76
121	Long Beach St. †	86
77	Virginia †	74
84	Ohio St. †	85

Nickname: Volunteers
Colors: Orange & White
Arena: Thompson-Boling Arena
  Capacity: 24,535; Year Built: 1987
AD: Michael Hamilton
SID: Craig Pinkerton

TENNESSEE ST.
Nashville, TN 37209-1561 I

Coach: Cy Alexander, Catawba 1975

2006-07 RESULTS (12-20)

69	Western Ky.	87
54	Kansas	89
60	Prairie View †	49
49	Towson †	47
60	Alabama	78
56	Middle Tenn.	89
75	Southeast Mo. St. ⊠	72
59	Eastern Ill. ⊠	56
59	Auburn	86
67	Ball St. ⊠	60
60	Siena	81
60	Morehead St.	62
83	Murray St. ⊠	86
65	Tenn.-Martin	73
59	Samford	41
83	Jacksonville St. ⊠	74
85	Fisk ⊠	52
78	Southeast Mo. St.	92
61	Eastern Ill.	58
63	Eastern Ky.	62
67	Tennessee Tech ⊠	73
64	Jacksonville St.	72
60	Samford	70
53	Austin Peay	62
74	Tenn.-Martin ⊠	76
66	Tennessee Tech	86

44	Austin Peay ⊠	89
64	Murray St.	60
60	Loyola (Md.) ⊠	62
62	Morehead St.	46
53	Eastern Ky. ⊠	65
84	Austin Peay	89

Nickname: Tigers
Colors: Royal Blue & White
Arena: Gentry Center Complex
　Capacity: 10,500; Year Built: 1980
AD: Teresa Phillips
SID: Wallace Dooley

TENNESSEE TECH
Cookeville, TN 38505-0001 I

Coach: Mike Sutton, East Caro. 1978

2006-07 RESULTS (19-13)

110	Bluefield Col. ⊠	69
79	Kansas St.	101
77	Mississippi	86
78	Milwaukee	68
86	Bradley	84
70	Austin Peay	77
69	Eastern Ill. ⊠	74
91	Southeast Mo. St. ⊠	76
66	Northwestern †	65
62	Vanderbilt †	75
66	UCF †	73
77	Tennessee	101
65	Samford	68
75	Eastern Ky. ⊠	53
71	Morehead St.	82
75	Jacksonville St. ⊠	71
73	Samford ⊠	59
76	Eastern Ill.	64
87	Southeast Mo. St.	80
63	Murray St. ⊠	52
73	Tennessee St.	67
65	Morehead St. ⊠	52
82	Tenn.-Martin ⊠	74
90	Eastern Ky.	92
71	Jacksonville St.	72
86	Tennessee St. ⊠	66
65	Tenn.-Martin	61
85	Northwestern St. ⊠	84
73	Austin Peay ⊠	72
56	Murray St.	60
88	Southeast Mo. St. ⊠	60
54	Eastern Ky. †	57

Nickname: Golden Eagles
Colors: Purple & Gold
Arena: Eblen Center
　Capacity: 10,150; Year Built: 1977
AD: Mark Wilson
SID: Robert Schabert

TENN.-MARTIN
Martin, TN 38238-5021 I

Coach: Bret Campbell, Valdosta St. 1983

2006-07 RESULTS (8-23)

64	High Point †	61
49	Cincinnati	67
81	Howard †	86
67	Southern Miss.	77
63	Arkansas St. ⊠	68
56	Ark.-Little Rock	58
57	Evansville	75
79	Southeast Mo. St.	81
70	Freed-Hardeman ⊠	58
70	Jacksonville St.	69
53	St. Louis	77
55	Morehead St. ⊠	56
69	Eastern Ky. ⊠	82
53	Hawaii	66
61	Austin Peay	74
41	Samford	55
73	Tennessee St. ⊠	65
67	Eastern Ill. ⊠	43
48	Morehead St.	70
60	Austin Peay ⊠	75

65	Murray St.	78
66	Samford ⊠	71
83	Jacksonville St. ⊠	60
57	Eastern Ky.	94
74	Tennessee Tech	82
69	Southeast Mo. St. ⊠	73
76	Tennessee St.	74
59	Eastern Ill.	74
61	Tennessee Tech ⊠	65
59	St. Peter's ⊠	58
52	Murray St.	74

Nickname: Skyhawks
Colors: Blue and Orange
Arena: Skyhawk Arena
　Capacity: 6,700; Year Built: 1978
AD: Phil Dane
SID: Joe Lofaro

TEXAS
Austin, TX 78712 I

Coach: Rick Barnes, Lenoir-Rhyne 1977

2006-07 RESULTS (25-10)

103	Alcorn St. ⊠	44
92	Chicago St. ⊠	66
61	Michigan St. †	63
77	St. John's (N.Y.) †	76
91	Nicholls St. ⊠	60
90	Texas Southern ⊠	50
77	Gonzaga †	87
76	LSU †	75
96	Texas St. ⊠	70
80	Arkansas ⊠	76
105	Tennessee	111
76	Centenary (La.) ⊠	66
84	Texas-Arlington ⊠	52
102	Colorado	78
88	Missouri ⊠	68
80	Oklahoma ⊠	69
103	Oklahoma St.	105
69	Villanova	76
62	Nebraska	61
84	Baylor ⊠	79
76	Texas Tech	64
72	Kansas St. ⊠	73
82	Texas A&M	100
77	Iowa St. ⊠	68
83	Oklahoma St. ⊠	54
68	Baylor	67
80	Texas Tech ⊠	51
68	Oklahoma	58
98	Texas A&M ⊠	96
86	Kansas	90
74	Baylor †	69
69	Oklahoma St. †	64
84	Kansas †	88
79	New Mexico St. †	67
68	Southern California †	87

Nickname: Longhorns
Colors: Burnt Orange & White
Arena: Frank Erwin Center
　Capacity: 16,755; Year Built: 1977
AD: DeLoss Dodds
SID: Scott McConnell

TEXAS A&M
College Station, TX 77843-1228 ... I

Coach: Billy Gillispie, Texas St. 1983

2006-07 RESULTS (27-7)

81	Prairie View ⊠	49
94	Lamar ⊠	60
75	Louisiana Tech ⊠	59
69	St. Louis ⊠	33
74	Idaho St. ⊠	44
75	Ark.-Little Rock ⊠	35
74	Pacific ⊠	62
52	LSU	64
62	UCLA †	65
84	Fordham †	61
97	Jacksonville ⊠	58
87	Auburn	58
101	Grambling ⊠	27

71	Winthrop ⊠	51
69	Kansas St. ⊠	65
61	Baylor	51
87	Colorado	69
67	Oklahoma St. ⊠	49
68	Texas Tech	70
70	Oklahoma ⊠	61
73	Iowa St. ⊠	49
69	Kansas	66
100	Texas ⊠	82
66	Nebraska	55
75	Texas Tech ⊠	77
56	Oklahoma	49
66	Oklahoma St.	46
97	Baylor ⊠	87
96	Texas	98
94	Missouri ⊠	78
56	Oklahoma St. †	57
68	Penn †	52
72	Louisville †	69
64	Memphis †	65

Nickname: Aggies
Colors: Maroon & White
Arena: Reed Arena
　Capacity: 12,500; Year Built: 1998
AD: Bill Byrne
SID: Colin Killian

TEX. A&M-COMMERCE
Commerce, TX 75428 II

Coach: Sam Walker, Sam Houston St. 1991

2006-07 RESULTS (14-14)

85	Paul Quinn ⊠	60
72	Findlay †	89
89	Cal St. Chico †	66
92	Texas Col. ⊠	67
89	Paul Quinn †	65
63	St. Mary's (Tex.)	67
81	Angelo St.	75
84	Abilene Christian	88
64	West Tex. A&M ⊠	65
77	Eastern N.M. ⊠	68
80	Colorado Mines	84
76	Metro St.	92
91	Tarleton St.	104
84	Midwestern St.	101
78	Tex. A&M-Kingsville ⊠	63
63	Northeastern St.	59
71	East Central	74
71	Southeastern Okla. ⊠	90
64	Central Okla. ⊠	63
102	Cameron ⊠	83
102	Southwestern Okla.	110
106	Central Okla.	111
76	Northeastern St. ⊠	67
78	East Central	64
82	Southeastern Okla.	86
92	Cameron	81
102	Southwestern Okla.	93
80	West Tex. A&M	82

Nickname: Lions
Colors: Blue & Gold
Arena: A&M-C Field House
　Capacity: 5,000; Year Built: 1950
AD: James Johnson
SID: Danny Kambel

A&M-CORPUS CHRISTI
Corpus Christi, TX 78412 I

Coach: Ronnie Arrow, Texas St. 1969

2006-07 RESULTS (26-7)

90	Texas Col. ⊠	53
71	Monmouth ⊠	54
82	Detroit	73
73	Oklahoma	95
72	Mississippi St.	96
87	Huston-Tillotson ⊠	59
57	UNLV	67
69	South Fla. †	63
98	Norfolk St. †	82

61	Purdue ⊠	79
75	Howard ⊠	57
71	Brown ⊠	57
81	Kent St. ⊠	73
74	McNeese St. ⊠	62
69	Northwestern St.	57
85	Central Ark. ⊠	73
90	Texas St. ⊠	42
89	Texas-Arlington ⊠	63
78	UTSA	63
70	Stephen F. Austin ⊠	62
79	Sam Houston St. ⊠	84
107	Nicholls St. ⊠	91
80	Southeastern La. ⊠	74
99	Texas St.	89
91	Texas-Arlington ⊠	72
77	Lamar	78
75	UTSA	59
69	Stephen F. Austin ⊠	65
85	Sam Houston St.	68
80	Southeastern La. †	72
87	McNeese St. †	66
81	Northwestern St. †	78
63	Wisconsin †	76

Nickname: Islanders
Colors: Blue, Green & White
Arena: American Bank Center
　Capacity: 9,000; Year Built: 2004
AD: Brian Teter
SID: Craig Merriman

TEX. A&M-KINGSVILLE
Kingsville, TX 78363 II

Coach: Pete Peterson, Southwestern (Kan.) 1979

2006-07 RESULTS (19-9)

72	St. Mary's (Tex.) ⊠	59
97	Texas Col. ⊠	70
67	Incarnate Word	63
78	St. Mary's (Tex.)	65
55	Northeastern St. ⊠	43
72	Central Okla. ⊠	62
76	East Central	73
62	Southeastern Okla.	80
83	Incarnate Word ⊠	73
103	Huston-Tillotson ⊠	62
88	Paul Quinn ⊠	65
88	Southwestern Okla. ⊠	77
87	Cameron ⊠	70
93	Dixie St. ⊠	72
63	Tex. A&M-Commerce ⊠	78
73	Midwestern St. ⊠	76
57	Angelo St.	81
85	Abilene Christian	74
63	West Tex. A&M ⊠	65
85	Eastern N.M. ⊠	84
55	Tarleton St.	58
67	West Tex. A&M	76
78	Eastern N.M.	76
66	Tarleton St.	71
82	Midwestern St.	79
85	Angelo St. ⊠	61
92	Abilene Christian ⊠	87
72	Southeastern Okla.	88

Nickname: Javelinas
Colors: Blue & Gold
Arena: Steinke PE Center
　Capacity: 4,000; Year Built: 1970
AD: Jill Willson
SID: Sean Johnson

TEXAS-ARLINGTON
Arlington, TX 76019 I

Coach: Scott Cross, Texas-Arlington 1998

2006-07 RESULTS (13-17)

87	Texas-Tyler ⊠	59
83	North Texas	81
89	TCU	97
76	Tex.-Pan American ⊠	69
73	Tex.-Pan American	74

61 Illinois St. ...86
57 Western Ill. ...74
60 Oklahoma ...89
78 UC Riverside ...77
81 Texas Southern ...95
76 Texas-Dallas ⊠ ...78
52 Texas ...84
66 Central Ark. ⊠ ...60
65 Northwestern St. ⊠ ...78
81 Nicholls St. ...83
69 Southeastern La. ...73
63 A&M-Corpus Christi ⊠ ...89
64 UTSA ...72
78 Sam Houston St. ⊠ ...65
54 Stephen F. Austin ...65
105 Austin ⊠ ...63
110 Texas St. ...103
76 Lamar ...74
52 McNeese St. ...46
81 UTSA ⊠ ...52
72 A&M-Corpus Christi ...91
78 Sam Houston St. ...92
69 Stephen F. Austin ⊠ ...62
93 Texas St. ⊠ ...84
76 McNeese St. † ...77

Nickname: Mavericks
Colors: Royal Blue & White
Arena: Texas Hall
  Capacity: 4,200; Year Built: 1965
AD: Peter D. Carlon
SID: Bill Petitt

TCU

Fort Worth, TX 76129-0001 I

Coach: Neil Dougherty, Cameron 1984

2006-07 RESULTS (13-17)

72 Centenary (La.) ⊠ ...66
59 Stephen F. Austin ⊠ ...53
97 Texas-Arlington ⊠ ...89
53 St. Mary's (Cal.) ...74
64 Grambling ...46
60 Texas Tech ⊠ ...70
35 Oklahoma ...63
62 UTSA ...46
53 Tulane ⊠ ...51
73 Ark.-Pine Bluff ⊠ ...57
62 SMU ...64
63 UTSA ⊠ ...51
64 New Mexico ⊠ ...52
71 Utah ...68
65 BYU ...89
54 Colorado St. ⊠ ...66
66 UNLV ...75
39 Air Force ...72
56 Wyoming ...71
71 San Diego St. ⊠ ...76
65 Utah ⊠ ...70
67 UNLV ...82
72 BYU ⊠ ...85
66 Colorado St. ...82
58 New Mexico ...74
71 Air Force ⊠ ...66
77 Wyoming ⊠ ...58
51 San Diego St. ...56
62 New Mexico † ...54
64 BYU † ...77

Nickname: Horned Frogs
Colors: Purple & White
Arena: Daniel-Meyer Coliseum
  Capacity: 7,201; Year Built: 1961
AD: Danny Morrison
SID: Drew Harris

TEXAS-DALLAS

Richardson, TX 75083-0688 III

Coach: Terry Butterfield, Eckerd 1979

2006-07 RESULTS (18-8)

90 Dallas † ...56
83 Austin ...64
81 S'western Aly God ...70
103 Schreiner ⊠ ...95

82 Texas Lutheran ⊠ ...66
78 Mary Hardin-Baylor ...70
118 Concordia (Tex.) ...112
61 Austin ⊠ ...52
81 Sul Ross St. ⊠ ...66
85 Howard Payne ...71
78 Texas-Arlington ...76
56 Hardin-Simmons ...75
57 McMurry ...81
54 Mississippi Col. ...66
42 Louisiana Col. ...64
77 East Tex. Baptist ...81
54 LeTourneau ...40
77 Texas-Tyler ⊠ ...52
78 Ozarks (Ark.) ...64
76 Ozarks (Ark.) ⊠ ...56
60 Texas-Tyler ...47
85 East Tex. Baptist ...76
54 LeTourneau ...58
67 Mississippi Col. ⊠ ...70
72 Louisiana Col. ⊠ ...57
70 McMurry † ...71

Nickname: Comets
Colors: Forest Green & Orange
Arena: UTD Activity Center
  Capacity: 2,500; Year Built: 1998
AD: Chris C. Gage
SID: Bruce Unrue

UTEP

El Paso, TX 79968 I

Coach: Tony Barbee, Massachusetts 1993

2006-07 RESULTS (14-17)

69 Penn † ...66
54 St. Francis (N.Y.) † ...52
69 Syracuse ...83
80 UC Davis ...76
77 Texas Tech ⊠ ...94
82 Chicago St. ⊠ ...86
87 New Mexico ...63
69 New Mexico St. ...71
79 Ark.-Pine Bluff ⊠ ...51
62 New Mexico St. ⊠ ...68
108 Texas St. ...60
97 Jackson St. ⊠ ...100
92 Toledo ...71
95 UC Riverside ⊠ ...55
76 UAB ⊠ ...63
88 Marshall ⊠ ...64
79 Tulsa ...86
68 Southern Miss. ⊠ ...50
72 SMU ...67
67 Rice ...73
64 UCF ⊠ ...67
78 Southern Miss. ...87
79 Houston ⊠ ...71
67 Tulane ...92
64 UAB ...73
51 Tulsa ⊠ ...66
85 SMU ⊠ ...56
78 East Caro. ...79
67 Memphis ⊠ ...78
67 Houston ...74
74 Rice † ...77

Nickname: Miners
Colors: Dark Blue, Orange & Silver
Arena: Don Haskins Center
  Capacity: 11,500; Year Built: 1977
AD: Bob Stull
SID: Jeff Darby

TEXAS LUTHERAN

Seguin, TX 78155-5999 III

Coach: Tom Oswald, UTSA 1996

2006-07 RESULTS (4-20)

57 Trinity (Tex.) ⊠ ...65
72 Southwestern (Tex.) ...75
55 Texas-Tyler ...48
66 Texas-Dallas ...82
49 Tex. A&M Int'l ...67

58 Ozarks (Ark.) ⊠ ...67
71 Schreiner ⊠ ...65
68 Louisiana Col. ...80
53 Mississippi Col. ...77
63 LeTourneau ⊠ ...69
66 East Tex. Baptist ⊠ ...50
70 Schreiner ...67
66 Sul Ross St. ⊠ ...70
85 Howard Payne ⊠ ...100
64 McMurry ...69
60 Hardin-Simmons ...66
68 Mary Hardin-Baylor ⊠ ...75
70 Concordia (Tex.) ⊠ ...82
51 Mary Hardin-Baylor ...71
79 Concordia (Tex.) ⊠ ...93
58 McMurry ⊠ ...77
66 Hardin-Simmons ⊠ ...70
66 Sul Ross St. ...68
72 Howard Payne ...87

Nickname: Bulldogs
Colors: Black & Gold
Arena: Memorial Gym
  Capacity: 1,500; Year Built: 1952
AD: Bill Miller
SID: Tim Clark

TEX.-PAN AMERICAN

Edinburg, TX 78541 I

Coach: Tom Schuberth, Mississippi St. 1982

2006-07 RESULTS (14-15)

76 Incarnate Word ⊠ ...55
64 UTSA † ...54
102 Huston-Tillotson ⊠ ...49
77 Texas St. ⊠ ...64
69 Texas-Arlington ...76
74 Texas-Arlington ⊠ ...73
46 Iowa ...62
63 La Salle † ...64
58 Air Force ...70
74 Texas St. ...84
46 Stephen F. Austin ⊠ ...44
69 UTSA ⊠ ...64
70 James Madison † ...57
62 UCF ...88
71 SMU ...84
64 Tulsa ...72
91 Tex. Permian Basin ⊠ ...51
85 Texas A&M Int'l ⊠ ...57
58 North Dakota St. ...88
67 South Dakota St. ...82
77 IPFW ⊠ ...61
72 NJIT ⊠ ...60
76 Utah Valley St. ⊠ ...81
63 South Dakota St. ⊠ ...50
63 North Dakota St. ⊠ ...74
56 Northwestern ...67
64 IPFW ...82
70 NJIT ...58
57 Utah Valley St. ...66

Nickname: Broncs
Colors: Forest Green, Orange & White
Arena: UTPA Fieldhouse
  Capacity: 4,000; Year Built: 1969
AD: Scott Street
SID: Joe Monaco

UTSA

San Antonio, TX 78249-0691 I

Coach: Brooks Thompson, Oklahoma St. 2001

2006-07 RESULTS (7-22)

50 Tex. A&M Int'l ⊠ ...46
54 Tex.-Pan American † ...64
44 Washington St. ...67
48 Gonzaga ...92
63 Cal St. Fullerton ⊠ ...67
64 San Diego ⊠ ...49
55 Henderson St. ⊠ ...36
67 Cal St. Fullerton ...76
46 TCU ⊠ ...62

64 Texas Wesleyan ⊠ ...60
64 Tex.-Pan American ...69
51 TCU ...63
47 Oklahoma St. ...84
59 Lamar ⊠ ...71
49 Central Ark. ...59
62 Northwestern St. ...82
63 Texas St. ...67
72 Texas-Arlington ⊠ ...64
63 A&M-Corpus Christi ⊠ ...78
64 Sam Houston St. ...76
48 Stephen F. Austin ⊠ ...45
57 Southeastern La. ...64
54 Nicholls St. ⊠ ...65
52 Texas-Arlington ...81
65 Texas St. ⊠ ...77
57 McNeese St. ...63
59 A&M-Corpus Christi ...75
61 Sam Houston St. ⊠ ...73
54 Stephen F. Austin ...49

Nickname: Roadrunners
Colors: Orange, Navy Blue & White
Arena: Convocation Center
  Capacity: 4,500; Year Built: 1971
AD: Lynn Hickey
SID: Kyle Stephens

TEXAS SOUTHERN

Houston, TX 77004 I

Coach: Ronnie Courtney, McMurry 1981

2006-07 RESULTS (14-17)

64 Lamar ...72
65 Oklahoma St. ...86
50 Baylor ...74
66 Huston-Tillotson ⊠ ...62
44 Alabama ...74
50 Texas ...90
76 Paul Quinn ⊠ ...68
55 Connecticut ...106
95 Texas-Arlington ⊠ ...81
63 Iowa ...90
76 Angelo St. ⊠ ...57
65 Southern U. ...64
72 Alcorn St. ...69
71 Prairie View ...67
62 Jackson St. ⊠ ...73
55 Grambling ⊠ ...47
58 Ark.-Pine Bluff ...56
54 Mississippi Val. ...64
68 Alabama A&M ⊠ ...66
61 Alabama St. ...78
65 Prairie View ⊠ ...66
90 Jackson St. ...83
76 Grambling ...68
83 Ark.-Pine Bluff ⊠ ...80
47 Mississippi Val. ...63
73 Alabama A&M ...79
67 Alabama St. ...72
55 Southern U. ⊠ ...64
67 Alcorn St. ⊠ ...70
74 Alcorn St. † ...64
50 Mississippi Val. † ...54

Nickname: Tigers
Colors: Maroon & Gray
Arena: Health & Physical Education Arena
  Capacity: 8,100; Year Built: 1988
AD: Alois S. Blackwell
SID: Rodney Bush

TEXAS ST.

San Marcos, TX 78666-4615 I

Coach: Doug Davalos, Houston 1994

2006-07 RESULTS (9-20)

106 Dallas Baptist ...93
85 Centenary (La.) ...91
64 Tex.-Pan American ...77
77 Ark.-Little Rock ⊠ ...83
77 North Texas ...95
77 Alcorn St. ⊠ ...71

64	Baylor	89
84	Tex.-Pan American ⊠	74
102	Tex. Permian Basin ⊠	92
70	Texas	96
60	UTEP	108
97	Tex. A&M Int'l ⊠	78
81	Centenary (La.)	82
85	Northwestern St. ⊠	81
93	Central Ark. ⊠	80
70	Southeastern La.	78
67	Nicholls St.	82
42	A&M-Corpus Christi	90
67	UTSA ⊠	63
62	Stephen F. Austin	82
74	Sam Houston St.	88
103	Texas-Arlington ⊠	110
65	McNeese St. ⊠	67
69	Lamar	96
89	A&M-Corpus Christi ⊠	99
77	UTSA	65
75	Stephen F. Austin	78
83	Sam Houston St. ⊠	97
84	Texas-Arlington	93

Nickname: Bobcats
Colors: Maroon & Gold
Arena: Strahan Coliseum
  Capacity: 7,200; Year Built: 1979
AD: Larry Teis
SID: Ron Mears

TEXAS TECH
Lubbock, TX 79409-3021 I

Coach: Bob Knight, Ohio St. 1962

2006-07 RESULTS (21-13)

79	Sam Houston St. ⊠	64
86	Gardner-Webb ⊠	74
93	Ark.-Little Rock ⊠	59
85	North Dakota St. ⊠	81
72	Marquette †	87
53	Air Force †	67
94	UTEP	77
70	TCU	60
59	Stanford †	70
66	Louisiana Tech	59
98	Centenary (La.) ⊠	64
71	Arkansas †	56
72	Bucknell ⊠	60
66	UNLV ⊠	74
70	New Mexico ⊠	68
68	Oklahoma ⊠	54
62	Kansas St.	52
70	Baylor	73
69	Kansas ⊠	64
70	Texas A&M ⊠	68
58	Missouri	71
64	Texas ⊠	76
61	Oklahoma	75
59	Nebraska ⊠	61
91	Oklahoma St.	93
77	Texas A&M	75
95	Colorado ⊠	74
51	Texas	80
59	Oklahoma St. ⊠	57
85	Baylor ⊠	74
63	Iowa St.	61
81	Colorado †	71
45	Kansas St. †	66
75	Boston College †	84

Nickname: Red Raiders
Colors: Scarlet & Black
Arena: United Spirit Arena
  Capacity: 15,098; Year Built: 1999
AD: Gerald L. Myers
SID: Randy Farley

TEXAS-TYLER
Tyler, TX 75799 III

Coach: Matt Wallis, Austin

2006-07 RESULTS (6-18)

76	Jarvis Christian ⊠	83
48	Texas Lutheran ⊠	55

86	Schreiner ⊠	75
81	Mary Hardin-Baylor	84
112	Concordia (Tex.)	122
52	New Orleans	76
67	Howard Payne ⊠	78
65	Sul Ross St. ⊠	57
68	Jarvis Christian	82
74	McMurry	89
70	Hardin-Simmons	77
62	Louisiana Col.	79
45	Mississippi Col.	66
70	LeTourneau ⊠	67
66	East Tex. Baptist ⊠	62
52	Texas-Dallas	77
57	Ozarks (Ark.)	66
87	Dallas ⊠	78
63	Ozarks (Ark.)	66
47	Texas-Dallas ⊠	60
54	LeTourneau	57
83	East Tex. Baptist	85
68	Louisiana Col. ⊠	47
37	Mississippi Col. ⊠	61

Nickname: Patriots
Colors: Orange & navy
Arena: Herrington Patriot Center
Capacity: 2,500
AD: Howard Patterson
SID: To be named

THIEL
Greenville, PA 16125 III

Coach: Tim Loomis, Lock Haven 1975

2006-07 RESULTS (5-20)

59	Marietta †	75
66	Case Reserve	62
70	La Roche	75
43	Muskingum	67
77	Lancaster Bible	66
76	Bethany (W.V.)	78
42	Allegheny	49
63	Hiram ⊠	62
59	Ind.-Southeast †	83
71	York (N.Y.) †	83
64	Waynesburg	60
71	Grove City ⊠	57
45	Thomas More	59
55	St. Vincent ⊠	72
74	Wash. & Jeff.	82
56	Penn St.-Beaver	68
66	Westminster (Pa.) ⊠	78
72	Bethany (W.V.) ⊠	75
56	Grove City	65
61	Waynesburg ⊠	78
63	St. Vincent	77
64	Thomas More ⊠	71
74	Westminster (Pa.)	92
51	Wash. & Jeff. ⊠	58
80	Bethany (W.V.)	94

Nickname: Tomcats
Colors: Navy Blue & Old Gold
Arena: Rissell-Beeghly Gymnasium
  Capacity: 1,000; Year Built: 1968
AD: Roseanne Gill-Jacobson
SID: Kevin Fenstermacher

THOMAS (ME.)
Waterville, ME 04901 III

Coach: T.J. Maines, Colby 1995

2006-07 RESULTS (5-20)

58	Polytechnic (N.Y.) †	55
64	Amherst	98
63	Bowdoin ⊠	84
58	Me.-Farmington	76
80	New England Col.	96
54	Bates ⊠	76
84	Unity ⊠	70
79	Me.-Fort Kent ⊠	85
94	Mitchell †	96
56	St. Joseph's (Brkln) †	74
66	St. Joseph's (Me.) ⊠	85
73	Becker	60

60	Elms	78
35	Husson ⊠	79
73	Johnson St. ⊠	63
54	Castleton	70
48	Me.-Farmington ⊠	80
49	Maine Maritime	57
70	Lesley	72
41	St. Joseph's (Me.)	91
53	Husson	88
80	Mount Ida ⊠	74
51	Maine Maritime ⊠	78
71	Mount Ida	90
46	Lasell	89

Nickname: Terriers
Colors: Black & Red
Arena: P.E. Center
Capacity: 1,000
AD: Heidi Bernier
SID: To be named

THOMAS MORE
Crestview Hills, KY 41017-3495... III

Coach: John Ellenwood, Wooster 2000

2006-07 RESULTS (3-23)

48	Defiance	76
59	Anderson (Ind.) †	76
68	Mt. St. Joseph ⊠	74
61	Northern Ky.	86
57	Wilmington (Ohio) ⊠	77
64	Transylvania	100
61	St. Vincent	67
72	Transylvania ⊠	77
56	Centre ⊠	76
66	Cincinnati-Clermont ⊠	88
47	Westmont	77
50	Johns Hopkins †	72
79	Westminster (Pa.)	89
64	Bethany (W.V.) ⊠	70
59	Thiel	45
53	Wash. & Jeff.	69
48	Grove City	49
70	Waynesburg ⊠	66
47	St. Vincent ⊠	58
65	Bethany (W.V.)	74
63	Westminster (Pa.) †	76
67	Wash. & Jeff.	93
71	Thiel	64
77	Waynesburg	89
65	Grove City	101
49	Wash. & Jeff.	67

Nickname: Saints
Colors: Royal Blue, White & Silver
Arena: Connor Convocation Center
  Capacity: 1,200; Year Built: 1989
AD: Terry Connor
SID: J. Ameer Rasheed

TIFFIN
Tiffin, OH 44883-2161 II

Coach: Rodney Martin, Tiffin 1993

2006-07 RESULTS (5-22)

71	Central St. (Ohio)	85
53	Southern Ind.	87
35	Akron	97
54	Walsh ⊠	63
60	Ohio Dominican	70
59	Mt. Vernon (D.C.) ⊠	90
51	Northern Ky.	89
59	Shawnee St.	76
70	Myers ⊠	75
60	Ashland	76
58	Hillsdale ⊠	76
61	Findlay	100
50	Wilberforce	78
78	Cedarville ⊠	71
71	Urbana	80
55	Mt. Vernon (D.C.)	78
72	Malone ⊠	63
64	Wilberforce ⊠	60
48	Central St. (Ohio) ⊠	66
38	Shawnee St.	53

50	Walsh	63
73	Rio Grande	86
66	Urbana ⊠	61
67	Ohio Dominican ⊠	76
61	Cedarville	88
65	Malone	84
82	Rio Grande ⊠	79

Nickname: Dragons
Colors: Green & Gold
Arena: Gillmor Student Center
Capacity: 1,500
AD: Ian S. Day
SID: Shane O'Donnell

TOLEDO
Toledo, OH 43606 I

Coach: Stan Joplin, Toledo 1979

2006-07 RESULTS (19-13)

66	Missouri St.	79
65	Iowa †	78
75	Middle Tenn. †	69
60	VCU †	59
52	Drexel	57
93	Vanderbilt	98
58	Kansas †	68
77	UNC Wilmington ⊠	74
73	Detroit ⊠	63
52	Drake †	70
71	UTEP	92
78	Oakland	88
62	Ball St.	60
65	Central Mich.	60
80	Western Mich. ⊠	68
66	Eastern Mich.	56
76	Northern Ill. ⊠	60
78	Buffalo	62
61	Miami (Ohio) ⊠	56
80	Ohio	91
64	Bowling Green ⊠	48
60	Kent St.	64
68	Akron	65
68	Eastern Mich. ⊠	56
70	Old Dominion ⊠	73
86	Northern Ill.	83
79	Western Mich.	75
71	Ball St. ⊠	61
77	Central Mich. ⊠	57
62	Eastern Mich. †	54
53	Miami (Ohio) †	58
61	Florida St.	77

Nickname: Rockets
Colors: Blue & Gold
Arena: John F. Savage Hall
  Capacity: 9,000; Year Built: 1976
AD: Michael E. O'Brien
SID: Steve Easton

TOWSON
Towson, MD 21252-0001 I

Coach: Pat Kennedy, King's (Pa.) 1975

2006-07 RESULTS (15-17)

78	Hartford ⊠	64
69	Samford ⊠	62
61	Kansas	87
72	Western Ky.	95
56	Chattanooga †	55
47	Tennessee St. †	49
67	Vermont ⊠	54
73	William & Mary	60
70	Temple ⊠	75
41	Georgetown	69
80	Winston-Salem ⊠	59
80	VCU ⊠	84
81	Georgia St.	87
75	Delaware	68
44	George Mason ⊠	73
77	VCU	85
70	Loyola (Md.)	62
74	Hofstra	79
75	UNC Wilmington ⊠	61
85	Delaware ⊠	63

60	Hofstra ⊠	64
69	James Madison	60
74	Northeastern ⊠	61
56	Drexel	66
55	Northeastern	65
92	Georgia St.	65
76	James Madison ⊠	62
63	Bucknell	73
65	Old Dominion	79
68	Drexel	77
67	UNC Wilmington †	52
55	Old Dominion †	58

Nickname: Tigers
Colors: Gold, White & Black
Arena: Towson Center
   Capacity: 5,000; Year Built: 1976
AD: Michael J. Hermann
SID: Peter Schlehr

TRANSYLVANIA
Lexington, KY 40508-1797 III

Coach: Brian Lane, Transylvania 1990

2006-07 RESULTS (19-9)

77	Webster ⊠	61
85	Maryville (Mo.) ⊠	70
59	Wittenberg	66
73	Mt. St. Joseph	75
100	Thomas More ⊠	64
91	Anderson (Ind.) ⊠	86
86	Manchester	74
77	Thomas More	72
81	Maryville (Tenn.) ⊠	70
54	Centre	56
77	Rockford †	33
58	Westminster (Utah) †	57
92	Bluffton	95
82	Rose-Hulman ⊠	66
85	Franklin	84
74	Defiance ⊠	50
70	Hanover ⊠	71
84	Mt. St. Joseph ⊠	69
75	Manchester ⊠	91
61	Anderson (Ind.)	64
62	Rose-Hulman	58
66	Franklin ⊠	76
75	Bluffton ⊠	65
64	Hanover	47
61	Defiance	58
78	Bluffton †	66
77	Defiance †	64
66	Wooster	92

Nickname: Pioneers
Colors: Crimson & White
Arena: Clive M. Beck Center
   Capacity: 1,200; Year Built: 2002
AD: Jack Ebel
SID: Glenn Osborne

TRI-STATE
Angola, IN 46703 III

Coach: Rob Harmon, Ball St. 1991

2006-07 RESULTS (16-10)

73	Marygrove ⊠	60
78	Taylor (Ind.) ⊠	73
62	Manchester	67
77	Davenport ⊠	68
71	Berea †	68
55	Marian (Ind.)	65
60	Rose-Hulman	53
50	Wis.-Oshkosh †	80
70	Concordia (Neb.) †	72
70	Clarke	60
64	Calvin	80
74	Albion ⊠	66
73	Olivet ⊠	68
69	Kalamazoo ⊠	68
89	Alma ⊠	81
75	Adrian ⊠	59
57	Hope	101
68	Calvin ⊠	58
59	Albion	69

63	Olivet	62
75	Kalamazoo ⊠	53
62	Alma	76
70	Adrian ⊠	62
59	Hope ⊠	78
60	Kalamazoo ⊠	47
66	Calvin †	82

Nickname: Thunder
Colors: Royal blue & white
Arena: Hershey Hall
   Capacity: 4,500; Year Built: 1970
AD: David Anspaugh
SID: Melissa Cope

TRINITY (CONN.)
Hartford, CT 06106 III

Coach: Stan Ogrodnik, Providence
1963

2006-07 RESULTS (21-5)

78	Haverford	50
76	Swarthmore	65
72	Eastern Conn. St. ⊠	55
71	Babson	68
66	Western Conn. St.	50
104	Curry	87
82	Lasell ⊠	63
72	Springfield	76
93	Villa Julie ⊠	74
84	Ursinus ⊠	80
100	Framingham St. ⊠	61
77	Westfield St. ⊠	64
68	Bates	63
85	Tufts	102
65	Williams	62
82	Middlebury ⊠	67
106	Fisher ⊠	58
69	Bowdoin	75
77	Colby	68
95	Wesleyan (Conn.) ⊠	57
62	Connecticut Col. ⊠	47
72	Clark (Mass.)	70
62	Amherst	59
77	Bowdoin ⊠	67
89	Williams †	91
70	Brandeis †	77

Nickname: Bantams
Colors: Blue & Gold
Arena: Oosting Gym
   Capacity: 2,000; Year Built: 1963
AD: Richard J. Hazelton
SID: David Kingsley

TRINITY (TEX.)
San Antonio, TX 78212-7200 III

Coach: Pat Cunningham, Kalamazoo
1974

2006-07 RESULTS (16-12)

65	Texas Lutheran	57
77	Schreiner	68
49	Mary Hardin-Baylor	63
57	Chicago ⊠	60
66	FDU-Florham ⊠	71
65	Rhodes	67
57	Millsaps ⊠	53
62	McMurry	75
67	Hardin-Simmons	60
82	Pitt.-Greensburg †	71
57	Swarthmore †	41
54	Amherst ⊠	66
45	Hendrix	63
64	Austin	45
62	Southwestern (Tex.) ⊠	53
51	DePauw	66
52	Centre	61
92	Sewanee ⊠	78
75	Oglethorpe ⊠	81
83	Rhodes	79
54	Millsaps	53
67	Southwestern (Tex.)	63
68	Dallas	65
54	Hendrix ⊠	70

64	Austin ⊠	48
50	Oglethorpe †	49
77	DePauw †	72
57	Centre †	72

Nickname: Tigers
Colors: Maroon & White
Arena: Earl C. Sams Gymnasium
   Capacity: 1,850; Year Built: 1992
AD: Robert C. King
SID: Justin Parker

TROY
Troy, AL 36082 I

Coach: Don Maestri, Southern Miss.
1969

2006-07 RESULTS (13-17)

68	Auburn	71
87	Loyola (La.) ⊠	52
84	Rhode Island †	78
61	Weber St. †	66
80	Drake †	75
86	Southeastern La. ⊠	84
56	Alabama St.	63
69	Bowling Green	71
90	Drake	102
84	Northern Ill. †	81
87	Fla. Atlantic	91
64	Florida Int'l	67
55	Georgia Tech	85
82	Ark.-Little Rock ⊠	70
78	Western Ky.	82
71	Middle Tenn.	57
64	South Ala. ⊠	75
87	Arkansas St. ⊠	79
85	New Orleans ⊠	86
62	La.-Lafayette	69
66	Denver ⊠	63
78	La.-Monroe	91
57	North Texas	98
92	Fla. Atlantic ⊠	87
56	Florida Int'l	51
71	Ark.-Little Rock	79
74	Western Ky. ⊠	75
73	Middle Tenn. †	70
92	South Ala.	88
64	Middle Tenn. ⊠	72

Nickname: Trojans
Colors: Cardinal, Silver & Black
Arena: Trojan Arena
   Capacity: 4,000; Year Built: 1964
AD: Steve Dennis
SID: Jim Stephan

TRUMAN
Kirksville, MO 63501-4221 II

Coach: Jack Schrader, Arizona St. 1975

2006-07 RESULTS (16-13)

73	Cent. Christian (Mo) ⊠	26
67	Armstrong Atlantic †	70
76	Mo.-Rolla †	62
76	Quincy	82
87	Culver-Stockton ⊠	76
75	Hannibal-La Grange ⊠	69
60	Vennard ⊠	28
70	Mo. Southern St.	53
75	Robert Morris-S'fiel	67
78	Quincy	88
63	Pittsburg St.	68
70	Fort Hays St. ⊠	59
74	Mo. Western St.	60
60	Emporia St. ⊠	63
60	Washburn ⊠	45
52	Northwest Mo. St.	70
81	Southwest Baptist	68
64	Central Mo. ⊠	77
76	Mo. Southern St. ⊠	68
47	Central Mo.	66
60	Southwest Baptist ⊠	53
50	Northwest Mo. St. ⊠	64
58	Washburn	68
64	Mo. Western St. ⊠	68

64	Fort Hays St. ⊠	59
88	Emporia St.	78
65	Pittsburg St. ⊠	68
88	Emporia St. †	75
68	Central Mo. †	72

Nickname: Bulldogs
Colors: Purple & White
Arena: Pershing
   Capacity: 3,000; Year Built: 1959
AD: Jerry Wollmering
SID: Kevin White

TUFTS
Medford, MA 02155 III

Coach: Robert Sheldon, St. Lawrence
1977

2006-07 RESULTS (15-10)

85	Lasell ⊠	80
84	Rhode Island Col. ⊠	95
70	Western New Eng.	62
89	Brandeis	99
77	Springfield ⊠	61
88	MIT	81
118	Keene St. ⊠	109
87	Clark (Mass.)	79
87	Plymouth St. ⊠	77
57	Wm. Paterson	79
71	Stevens Institute	92
92	Amherst	96
102	Trinity (Conn.) ⊠	85
82	Mass.-Dartmouth	79
44	Bates	72
89	Wheaton (Mass.) ⊠	74
63	Connecticut Col.	56
94	Wesleyan (Conn.)	69
76	Babson	84
91	Middlebury	102
82	Williams	65
94	Bowdoin ⊠	84
84	Colby ⊠	89
93	Mass.-Boston ⊠	76
72	Williams	84

Nickname: Jumbos
Colors: Brown & Blue
Arena: Cousens Gym
   Capacity: 1,000; Year Built: 1932
AD: Bill Gehling
SID: Paul Sweeney

TULANE
New Orleans, LA 70118-0000 I

Coach: Dave Dickerson, Maryland 1989

2006-07 RESULTS (17-13)

37	Butler ⊠	77
78	New Orleans ⊠	64
75	Charleston So. ⊠	69
66	Loyola (La.) ⊠	53
47	Indiana ⊠	59
80	Huston-Tillotson ⊠	54
67	LSU ⊠	74
80	Buffalo ⊠	63
51	TCU	53
70	Ark.-Pine Bluff ⊠	68
75	Richmond	63
77	New Orleans	84
70	Rice	75
60	UAB ⊠	67
65	East Caro.	56
73	Marshall ⊠	79
53	SMU	55
75	Rice ⊠	79
78	Tulsa ⊠	79
79	Southern Miss.	64
92	UTEP	67
51	Memphis	95
86	UCF ⊠	80
73	Marshall	65
70	Houston	78
77	Southern Miss. ⊠	72
88	East Caro. ⊠	72
76	UAB	74

58 Tulsa †....56
49 Memphis....71

Nickname: Green Wave
Colors: Olive Green & Sky Blue
Arena: Avron B. Fogelman Arena
Capacity: 3,600; Year Built: 1933
AD: Rick Dickson
SID: Roger Dunaway

TULSA

Tulsa, OK 74104-3189....I

Coach: Doug Wojcik, Navy 1987

2006-07 RESULTS (20-11)

88 St. Gregory's ⊠....64
66 Ark.-Little Rock ⊠....60
63 North Texas....65
91 Cal St. Northridge ⊠....70
75 Oral Roberts ⊠....57
78 Lamar ⊠....64
79 Jackson St. ⊠....54
88 Southern Ark. ⊠....56
83 Prairie View ⊠....54
48 Oklahoma †....58
66 Eastern Mich. ⊠....48
59 Arkansas....68
72 Tex.-Pan American ⊠....64
67 East Caro. ⊠....49
86 UTEP ⊠....79
53 Marshall....65
67 Houston ⊠....69
59 Memphis....72
70 SMU ⊠....66
79 Tulane....78
53 UCF....63
63 Marshall ⊠....60
65 Southern Miss.....70
52 Memphis ⊠....69
66 UTEP....51
57 UAB ⊠....62
66 UCF ⊠....64
67 SMU....60
73 Rice....65
65 East Caro. †....50
56 Tulane †....58

Nickname: Golden Hurricane
Colors: Old Gold, Royal Blue & Crimson
Arena: Donald W. Reynolds Center
Capacity: 8,355; Year Built: 1998
AD: Lawrence R. Cunningham
SID: Don Tomkalski

TUSCULUM

Greeneville, TN 37743....II

Coach: Jim Boone, West Virginia St. 1981

2006-07 RESULTS (13-15)

88 Brevard....64
78 Bluefield Col. ⊠....61
80 Concord ⊠....67
65 Ouachita Baptist †....63
70 Queens (N.C.)....82
81 Glenville St. ⊠....68
66 UNC Asheville....84
61 Concord....68
65 S.C.-Aiken....61
57 King (Tenn.) ⊠....55
59 Presbyterian ⊠....61
62 Lenoir-Rhyne ⊠....72
63 Lincoln Memorial....67
50 Catawba....53
67 Brevard ⊠....68
81 Carson-Newman....73
76 Newberry ⊠....64
72 Wingate ⊠....82
64 Mars Hill....67
66 Lenoir-Rhyne....78
61 Lincoln Memorial ⊠....58
46 Catawba ⊠....60
58 Wingate....65
86 Carson-Newman ⊠....74
64 Newberry....42
50 Presbyterian....53
79 Mars Hill ⊠....48
56 Wingate....66

Nickname: Pioneers
Colors: Black & Orange
Arena: Pioneer Arena
Capacity: 2,000; Year Built: 1998
AD: To be named
SID: Dom Donnelly

TUSKEGEE

Tuskegee, AL 36088....II

Coach: Leon Douglas, Alabama 1976

2006-07 RESULTS (6-22)

69 Montevallo....103
77 Alabama St.....80
65 Clark Atlanta ⊠....56
57 Alabama A&M....59
72 Fla. Gulf Coast....91
74 Southern-N.O. ⊠....78
72 Stillman ⊠....74
57 Fort Valley St.....59
71 Albany St. (Ga.)....96
64 Miles ⊠....78
65 LeMoyne-Owen ⊠....78
67 Stillman....70
72 Miles....71
64 LeMoyne-Owen....71
66 Clark Atlanta....53
67 Morehouse....78
51 Kentucky St. ⊠....70
79 Lane ⊠....76
70 Benedict....72
67 Paine....81
61 Fort Valley St. ⊠....60
64 Albany St. (Ga.) ⊠....85
72 Benedict ⊠....76
53 Paine ⊠....79
66 Morehouse ⊠....70
67 Lane....80
79 Kentucky St.....72
85 Kentucky St. †....101

Nickname: Golden Tigers
Colors: Crimson & Old Gold
Arena: James Center Arena
Capacity: 5,000; Year Built: 1987
AD: Emmett L. Taylor
SID: Arnold Houston

UCLA

Los Angeles, CA 90095-1405....I

Coach: Ben Howland, Weber St. 1979

2006-07 RESULTS (30-6)

82 BYU ⊠....69
88 Chaminade †....63
73 Kentucky †....68
88 Georgia Tech †....73
88 Long Beach St. ⊠....58
61 UC Riverside ⊠....38
78 Cal St. Fullerton ⊠....54
65 Texas A&M †....62
74 Oakland ⊠....53
75 Sam Houston St. ⊠....61
92 Michigan ⊠....55
55 Washington St. ⊠....52
96 Washington ⊠....74
71 Oregon St.....56
66 Oregon....68
65 Southern California....64
60 Arizona St. ⊠....50
73 Arizona ⊠....69
62 California....46
68 Stanford....75
69 Oregon ⊠....57
82 Oregon St. ⊠....35
70 Southern California ⊠....65
65 West Virginia....70
67 Arizona St.....61
81 Arizona....66
85 California ⊠....75
75 Stanford ⊠....61
53 Washington St.....45
51 Washington....61
69 California †....76
70 Weber St. †....42
54 Indiana †....49
64 Pittsburgh †....55
68 Kansas †....55
66 Florida †....76

Nickname: Bruins
Colors: Blue & Gold
Arena: Pauley Pavilion
Capacity: 12,819; Year Built: 1965
AD: Daniel G. Guerrero
SID: Marc Dellins

UNION (N.Y.)

Schenectady, NY 12308....III

Coach: Bob Montana, Brockport St. 1972

2006-07 RESULTS (11-14)

90 City Tech ⊠....65
56 Lasell....77
70 Middlebury ⊠....76
63 Williams ⊠....73
76 Lehman ⊠....62
64 Wagner....105
49 Gettysburg †....64
54 Randolph-Macon....84
82 Mt. St. Vincent ⊠....74
66 Bates ⊠....81
67 Skidmore....60
79 Rensselaer....76
90 Vassar....85
59 Hamilton ⊠....79
85 Hobart ⊠....72
75 Clarkson....71
49 St. Lawrence....76
94 Skidmore ⊠....54
86 Hobart....68
58 Hamilton....63
54 Vassar ⊠....58
68 Rensselaer ⊠....74
73 St. Lawrence ⊠....86
74 Clarkson ⊠....69
62 Hamilton....74

Nickname: Dutchmen
Colors: Garnet
Arena: Viniar Sports Center
Capacity: 1,500; Year Built: 2004
AD: James McLaughlin
SID: Eric McDowell

UPPER IOWA

Fayette, IA 52142....II

Coach: Brian Dolan, William Jewell 1998

2006-07 RESULTS (3-25)

41 Northwest Mo. St.....86
67 Lincoln (Mo.) †....68
40 Grand Valley St.....74
83 Oakland City....84
47 Minn. St. Mankato....65
67 Mary ⊠....59
71 Northern St. ⊠....77
60 St. Cloud St. ⊠....77
62 Winona St. ⊠....80
51 South Dakota †....62
59 Augustana (S.D.)....81
74 Oakland City ⊠....70
60 Southwest Minn. St.....88
62 Wayne St. (Neb.)....75
52 Minn. St. Moorhead ⊠....74
44 Concordia-St. Paul ⊠....77
75 Minn.-Crookston....61
51 Bemidji St.....53
76 Mary....82
59 Northern St.....82
70 Winona St.....81
72 Wayne St. (Neb.) ⊠....84
44 Southwest Minn. St. ⊠....70
63 Concordia-St. Paul....77
59 Minn. St. Moorhead....72
59 Bemidji St. ⊠....60
62 Minn.-Crookston ⊠....73
63 Winona St.....94

Nickname: Peacocks
Colors: Peacock Blue & White
Arena: Dorman Memorial Gym
Capacity: 2,000; Year Built: 1963
AD: Gil Cloud
SID: Howie Thompson

URSINUS

Collegeville, PA 19426-1000....III

Coach: Kevin Small, St. Joseph's 1991

2006-07 RESULTS (16-10)

60 Lebanon Valley....51
77 Washington (Md.)....69
75 McDaniel ⊠....76
65 Gettysburg....60
53 Drew....50
77 Swarthmore ⊠....73
52 Wilkes †....72
50 King's (Pa.)....76
73 St. John's (Minn.) †....49
65 Lawrence †....70
80 Trinity (Conn.)....84
64 Frank. & Marsh. ⊠....52
80 Dickinson....71
50 Johns Hopkins ⊠....66
89 Muhlenberg....49
70 Swarthmore....67
70 Haverford ⊠....53
75 Frank. & Marsh.....69
82 McDaniel....68
75 Washington (Md.) ⊠....59
100 Dickinson ⊠....80
85 Gettysburg ⊠....73
68 Johns Hopkins....74
74 Haverford....75
68 Muhlenberg ⊠....76
69 Haverford †....70

Nickname: Bears
Colors: Red, Old Gold & Black
Arena: D.L. Helfferich Hall
Capacity: 2,500; Year Built: 1972
AD: Brian Thomas
SID: Jill Yamma

UTAH

Salt Lake City, UT 84112-9008....I

Coach: Ray Giacoletti, Minot St. 1985

2006-07 RESULTS (11-19)

73 Southern Utah ⊠....76
72 Santa Clara....83
59 Colorado ⊠....60
80 Rice ⊠....64
67 Weber St. ⊠....55
69 Washington St. ⊠....55
57 Utah St.....60
84 Rhode Island....85
77 Cal Poly ⊠....58
61 UCF †....67
94 Virginia †....70
44 Northwestern †....77
58 Albany (N.Y.) ⊠....59
94 UNLV....97
68 TCU ⊠....71
57 Colorado St.....73
82 New Mexico....86
85 Air Force ⊠....79
62 Wyoming....60
53 San Diego St.....63
66 BYU ⊠....76
70 TCU....65
82 Colorado St. ⊠....77
43 Air Force....69
57 UNLV ⊠....70
78 Wyoming....86
93 New Mexico ⊠....91
74 San Diego St. ⊠....68
62 BYU....85

54	UNLV	80

Nickname: Utes
Colors: Crimson & White
Arena: Jon M. Huntsman Center
  Capacity: 15,000; Year Built: 1969
AD: Christopher Hill
SID: Mike Lageschulte

UTAH ST.
Logan, UT 84322-7400 I

Coach: Stew Morrill, Gonzaga 1974

2006-07 RESULTS (23-12)

71	Northwestern St.	88
77	Centenary (La.) †	71
92	Drake †	74
68	Weber St. †	55
77	Weber St. ⊠	68
56	South Dakota St.	50
83	Idaho St. ⊠	46
60	Utah ⊠	57
69	Utah Valley St.	65
62	BYU	75
77	IPFW ⊠	63
75	Santa Clara	77
65	Cal St. Bakersfield ⊠	49
66	Boise St.	77
70	Fresno St.	79
81	Utah Valley St. ⊠	70
69	Louisiana Tech ⊠	49
74	Idaho ⊠	56
80	Boise St. ⊠	79
57	San Jose St.	56
62	Nevada	79
61	Hawaii	69
66	San Jose St. ⊠	57
75	New Mexico St. ⊠	63
75	Idaho	66
58	Hawaii ⊠	50
71	Oral Roberts	65
73	New Mexico St.	76
71	Louisiana Tech	84
79	Nevada ⊠	77
66	Fresno St. ⊠	71
73	Hawaii †	70
79	Nevada †	77
70	New Mexico St.	72
58	Michigan	68

Nickname: Aggies
Colors: Navy Blue & White
Arena: Dee Glen Smith Spectrum
  Capacity: 10,270; Year Built: 1970
AD: Randy Spetman
SID: Doug Hoffman

UTAH VALLEY ST.
Orem, UT 84058.................................. I

Coach: Dick Hunsaker, Weber St. 1977

2006-07 RESULTS (22-7)

69	Montana St. ⊠	37
74	Montana ⊠	57
47	California	60
65	Great Falls ⊠	47
77	Western Ill.	75
60	Southern Utah	68
69	Portland St.	71
91	UMKC	79
65	Utah St. ⊠	69
60	Montana St.	53
62	Idaho St.	76
64	Southern Utah ⊠	55
73	Albany (N.Y.) ⊠	66
74	UMKC ⊠	59
57	UC Davis	38
70	Utah St.	81
80	Longwood ⊠	52
95	Johnson & Wales (CO) ⊠	55
66	South Dakota St.	54
53	North Dakota St.	61
86	NJIT	55
96	IPFW ⊠	66
88	UC Davis ⊠	59

81	Tex.-Pan American	76
66	North Dakota St. ⊠	64
83	South Dakota St. ⊠	56
72	IPFW	63
77	NJIT	47
66	Tex.-Pan American ⊠	57

Nickname: Lakers
Colors: Blue, black & white
AD: Mike Jacobsen
SID: To be named

UTICA
Utica, NY 13502-4892..................... III

Coach: Andrew Goodemote, Albany
(N.Y.) 1990

2006-07 RESULTS (19-7)

104	Paul Smith ⊠	37
99	SUNYIT	82
79	Cazenovia ⊠	54
64	Hamilton	68
69	Skidmore	55
72	Cortland St.	58
99	SUNYIT	76
48	Clarkson	59
72	Hartwick	54
67	Oneonta St. ⊠	60
83	Elmira	64
85	Ithaca	63
60	Alfred ⊠	51
62	St. John Fisher ⊠	54
63	Oswego St. ⊠	62
91	Rochester Inst.	77
73	Nazareth	72
71	Hartwick	59
68	Ithaca ⊠	70
72	Elmira ⊠	49
65	Nazareth ⊠	45
61	Rochester Inst. ⊠	66
66	St. John Fisher	79
61	Alfred	62
72	Ithaca †	56
73	St. John Fisher	78

Nickname: Pioneers
Colors: Blue & Orange
Arena: Clark Athletic Center
  Capacity: 2,200; Year Built: 1970
AD: James A. Spartano
SID: Gil Burgmaster

VALDOSTA ST.
Valdosta, GA 31698.......................... II

Coach: Mike Helfer, Capital 1989

2006-07 RESULTS (20-9)

130	Carver Bible ⊠	62
74	Georgia	105
111	Albany St. (Ga.) ⊠	81
82	Barry †	76
82	Nova Southeastern	96
71	North Georgia ⊠	76
66	Ga. Southwestern ⊠	59
104	LaGrange ⊠	77
63	Columbus St. †	61
108	P.R.-Rio Piedras †	74
77	Fla. Gulf Coast	67
89	Florida Tech ⊠	66
97	Nova Southeastern ⊠	66
102	Webber Int'l ⊠	58
85	West Ga. ⊠	82
63	North Ala.	77
73	Ala.-Huntsville	59
81	West Ala.	70
68	Montevallo ⊠	81
70	West Fla.	62
70	Ala.-Huntsville ⊠	51
73	North Ala. ⊠	65
69	West Ga.	91
114	Palm Beach Atl. †	70
57	West Ala. ⊠	50
77	Montevallo	89
98	West Fla. ⊠	92
72	Harding †	73

60	Rollins †	61

Nickname: Blazers
Colors: Red & Black
Arena: The Complex
  Capacity: 5,350; Year Built: 1982
AD: Herb F. Reinhard III
SID: Shawn Reed

VALPARAISO
Valparaiso, IN 46383-6493............... I

Coach: Homer Drew, William Jewell
1966

2006-07 RESULTS (16-15)

84	Calumet Col. ⊠	65
75	IPFW	67
70	Niagara	58
64	North Carolina St.	78
62	Marquette ⊠	65
47	Butler ⊠	60
58	Ohio St.	78
64	Evansville	69
40	Ball St.	61
43	Creighton †	68
62	Charlotte †	74
64	San Francisco †	59
67	Chicago St. ⊠	64
66	Centenary (La.)	62
60	Oral Roberts	75
76	Oakland ⊠	81
69	IUPUI ⊠	55
78	Western Ill.	60
59	IPFW ⊠	45
56	UMKC	52
60	Southern Utah	76
70	Oral Roberts ⊠	67
68	Centenary (La.) ⊠	50
91	Chicago St.	76
54	IUPUI	68
61	Oakland	64
80	Western Ill. ⊠	56
80	Western Mich.	89
75	Southern Utah ⊠	48
77	UMKC ⊠	61
76	UMKC †	84

Nickname: Crusaders
Colors: Brown & Gold
Arena: Athletics-Recreation Center
  Capacity: 5,000; Year Built: 1984
AD: Mark LaBarbera
SID: Andy Viano

VANDERBILT
Nashville, TN 37212........................... I

Coach: Kevin Stallings, Purdue 1982

2006-07 RESULTS (22-12)

70	Georgetown ⊠	86
78	Wake Forest	88
81	Elon ⊠	70
62	Furman ⊠	70
98	Toledo ⊠	93
104	East Tenn. St. ⊠	62
59	Lipscomb ⊠	50
73	Georgia Tech ⊠	64
76	Nicholls St. ⊠	40
102	P.R.-Mayaguez †	59
75	Tennessee Tech †	62
79	Appalachian St. †	87
86	Alabama A&M ⊠	47
74	Rice	69
65	Auburn	68
82	Tennessee ⊠	81
73	Georgia	85
94	Alabama ⊠	73
72	Kentucky	67
64	LSU	53
85	Mississippi ⊠	80
66	Florida	74
66	Georgia ⊠	61
57	Tennessee	84
78	South Carolina ⊠	68
83	Florida ⊠	70

70	Mississippi St.	83
67	Kentucky ⊠	65
99	South Carolina	90
67	Arkansas ⊠	82
71	Arkansas †	72
77	George Washington †	44
78	Washington St. †	74
65	Georgetown †	66

Nickname: Commodores
Colors: Black & Gold
Arena: Memorial Gymnasium
  Capacity: 14,316; Year Built: 1952
AD: David Williams II
SID: Rod Williamson

VASSAR
Poughkeepsie, NY 12604-0750... III

Coach: Mike Dutton, New Hampshire
1981

2006-07 RESULTS (18-10)

74	Washington-St. Louis †	79
72	Babson	84
82	Delaware Valley ⊠	58
69	Manhattanville	78
77	New Paltz St. ⊠	72
72	Mt. St. Mary (N.Y.) ⊠	60
63	Drew	58
85	Purchase St. ⊠	58
65	Hartwick ⊠	59
75	Skidmore	47
85	Union (N.Y.) ⊠	90
63	Rensselaer ⊠	51
74	St. Lawrence	71
70	Clarkson	62
85	City Tech	77
66	Hobart ⊠	49
76	Hamilton ⊠	82
53	Clarkson ⊠	57
81	St. Lawrence ⊠	83
58	Union (N.Y.)	54
78	Skidmore	60
74	Rensselaer	66
70	Hamilton	85
78	Hobart	85
67	St. Lawrence †	72
80	Hilbert ⊠	63
84	Ithaca ⊠	76
66	Oswego St. ⊠	65

Nickname: Brewers
Colors: Burgundy & Gray
Arena: Athletic & Fitness Facility
  Capacity: 850; Year Built: 2000
AD: Sharon Beverly
SID: Robin Jonathan Deutsch

VERMONT
Burlington, VT 05405....................... I

Coach: Mike Lonergan, Catholic 1988

2006-07 RESULTS (25-8)

82	New Orleans †	65
63	Maryland	81
77	Boston College	63
46	Drexel ⊠	59
46	Michigan St.	66
77	Wagner	67
54	Towson	67
57	Delaware	55
63	Iona ⊠	50
76	Harvard ⊠	84
73	Dartmouth ⊠	62
101	Quinnipiac	87
55	Central Conn. St.	69
80	Stony Brook ⊠	69
62	New Hampshire	60
83	UMBC	69
75	Albany (N.Y.) ⊠	66
64	Maine ⊠	69
64	Binghamton	61
76	Hartford	63
71	Stony Brook	61
82	New Hampshire ⊠	79

72	Boston U. ⊠	63
66	UMBC ⊠	57
67	Albany (N.Y.) ⊠	63
90	Maine	75
71	Binghamton ⊠	61
57	Boston U.	55
90	Hartford ⊠	73
81	Hartford †	62
72	UMBC †	63
59	Albany (N.Y.) ⊠	60
57	Kansas St.	59

Nickname: Catamounts
Colors: Green & Gold
Arena: Roy L. Patrick Gymnasium
　　Capacity: 3,266; Year Built: 1963
AD: Robert Corran
SID: Ben Dickie

VILLA JULIE
Stevenson, MD 21153-9999 III

Coach: Brett Adams, York (Pa.) 1989

2006-07 RESULTS (20-8)

71	York (Pa.)	69
83	Salisbury	84
72	Hood †	83
64	Frostburg St. †	58
95	Bard ⊠	60
79	Chestnut Hill ⊠	69
69	Baptist Bible (Pa.) ⊠	81
67	Catholic	77
74	Trinity (Conn.)	93
63	Lebanon Valley ⊠	62
55	Old Westbury ⊠	56
70	Chestnut Hill	76
81	Keystone ⊠	64
84	Penn St.-Berks	75
81	Purchase St.	67
86	Phila. Biblical ⊠	66
84	Keuka	71
93	Cazenovia	75
95	Polytechnic (N.Y.) ⊠	86
81	D'Youville ⊠	50
78	Penn St.-Berks ⊠	56
90	Polytechnic (N.Y.)	65
82	Phila. Biblical	54
98	Purchase St. ⊠	68
83	Phila. Biblical ⊠	68
95	Keuka ⊠	73
94	Chestnut Hill ⊠	92
72	Johns Hopkins	84

Nickname: Mustangs
Colors: Green, Black & White
Arena: Villa Julie Student Union
　　Capacity: 1,200; Year Built: 1997
AD: Brett C. Adams
SID: Jeb Barber

VILLANOVA
Villanova, PA 19085-1674 I

Coach: Jay Wright, Bucknell 1983

2006-07 RESULTS (22-11)

97	Northwood (Mich.)	60
81	Col. of Charleston †	68
66	Xavier †	71
89	Iowa †	60
70	Navy ⊠	61
72	Stony Brook	44
99	Penn	89
67	Oklahoma	51
76	Drexel ⊠	81
108	Rider ⊠	61
64	La Salle	51
83	Temple ⊠	65
56	West Virginia	67
65	DePaul ⊠	73
56	Georgetown	52
64	Syracuse	75
102	Notre Dame ⊠	87
76	Texas ⊠	69
82	Providence	73
63	Notre Dame	66

59	Pittsburgh ⊠	65
57	Louisville ⊠	53
56	St. Joseph's ⊠	39
78	Seton Hall	69
64	Cincinnati ⊠	48
55	Georgetown ⊠	58
67	Marquette	80
74	Rutgers ⊠	51
78	Connecticut	74
78	Syracuse ⊠	75
75	DePaul †	67
57	Georgetown †	62
58	Kentucky †	67

Nickname: Wildcats
Colors: Blue & White
Arena: Pavilion
　　Capacity: 6,500; Year Built: 1986
AD: Vincent Nicastro
SID: Mike Sheridan

VIRGINIA
Charlottesville, VA 22904-4821 I

Coach: Dave Leitao, Northeastern 1983

2006-07 RESULTS (21-11)

93	Arizona ⊠	90
85	Morgan St. ⊠	66
81	UNC Asheville ⊠	64
104	Md.-East. Shore ⊠	63
59	Purdue	61
67	North Carolina St. ⊠	62
91	Hampton ⊠	69
69	Appalachian St. †	80
70	Utah †	94
59	P.R.-Mayaguez †	52
91	American †	70
108	Gonzaga ⊠	87
75	Stanford ⊠	76
69	North Carolina	79
73	Boston College	78
103	Maryland ⊠	91
88	Wake Forest ⊠	76
71	North Carolina St.	58
64	Clemson	63
68	Duke ⊠	66
81	Miami (Fla.) ⊠	70
69	Maryland	65
57	Virginia Tech	84
90	Longwood ⊠	49
73	Florida St. ⊠	70
60	Miami (Fla.)	68
75	Georgia Tech ⊠	69
69	Virginia Tech ⊠	56
72	Wake Forest	78
71	North Carolina St. †	79
84	Albany (N.Y.) †	57
74	Tennessee †	77

Nickname: Cavaliers
Colors: Orange & Blue
Arena: John Paul Jones Arena
　　Capacity: 15,219; Year Built: 2006
AD: Craig K. Littlepage
SID: Rich Murray

VCU
Richmond, VA 23284-3013 I

Coach: Anthony Grant, Dayton 1987

2006-07 RESULTS (28-7)

75	Longwood	63
67	Xavier †	70
71	Col. of Charleston †	59
59	Toledo †	60
74	Hampton ⊠	51
91	Elon	49
102	Houston ⊠	84
75	Albany (N.Y.)	57
68	Richmond	54
53	UAB ⊠	44
79	Delaware ⊠	60
70	Appalachian St. ⊠	73
84	Towson	80
77	James Madison ⊠	61

64	Northeastern ⊠	44
88	William & Mary	77
85	Towson ⊠	77
74	UNC Wilmington ⊠	65
80	Old Dominion ⊠	75
75	George Mason ⊠	62
75	Drexel ⊠	68
90	William & Mary ⊠	68
68	Hofstra	79
100	Georgia St. ⊠	71
63	George Mason	49
63	Old Dominion	79
78	UNC Wilmington	68
64	Bradley †	73
83	James Madison ⊠	72
72	Georgia St.	70
73	Georgia St. †	60
63	Drexel †	56
65	George Mason †	59
79	Duke †	77
79	Pittsburgh †	84

Nickname: Rams
Colors: Black & Gold
Arena: Alltel Pavilion at the Stuart C. Siegel Center
　　Capacity: 7,500; Year Built: 1999
AD: Norwood Teague
SID: Phil Stanton

VMI
Lexington, VA 24450-0304 I

Coach: Duggar Baucom, Charlotte 1995

2006-07 RESULTS (14-19)

69	Ohio St.	107
68	Princeton †	73
104	South Dakota St. †	89
156	Virginia Intermont ⊠	95
144	Southern Va.	127
87	James Madison	89
111	Howard	116
72	Army	79
94	Cornell †	99
85	Jacksonville St. †	87
135	Lees-McRae ⊠	75
103	Mercer ⊠	105
99	South Carolina St. ⊠	87
93	Richmond	84
111	Penn St.	129
76	Winthrop	108
104	High Point ⊠	115
116	Charleston So. ⊠	83
97	Coastal Caro. ⊠	99
125	Bridgewater (Va.) ⊠	95
102	UNC Asheville	97
103	Radford ⊠	94
117	Liberty	122
96	Winthrop ⊠	109
99	Coastal Caro.	108
105	Charleston So.	97
102	UNC Asheville ⊠	88
107	Radford	114
108	Liberty ⊠	118
92	High Point	109
79	Liberty	78
91	High Point †	81
81	Winthrop	84

Nickname: Keydets
Colors: Red, White, Yellow
Arena: Cameron Hall
　　Capacity: 5,029; Year Built: 1981
AD: Donald T. White
SID: Wade Branner

VIRGINIA ST.
Petersburg, VA 23806-0001 II

Coach: Tony Collins, Virginia St. 1978

2006-07 RESULTS (20-8)

73	Columbus St. ⊠	83
81	Chowan	79
68	Johnson C. Smith	59

63	St. Augustine's ⊠	62
80	Columbus St.	96
66	Ga. Southwestern	42
73	Cheyney	67
74	Claflin	65
85	Alderson-Broaddus ⊠	77
71	Fayetteville St.	57
84	Bowie St. ⊠	76
79	Livingstone ⊠	55
71	Virginia Union ⊠	76
83	Shaw	71
94	Elizabeth City St. ⊠	87
91	N.C. Central ⊠	67
66	Livingstone	57
70	St. Augustine's	76
65	N.C. Central	66
92	St. Paul's	94
74	Johnson C. Smith ⊠	66
51	Virginia Union	69
84	Fayetteville St. ⊠	62
83	Elizabeth City St. ⊠	76
79	Shaw ⊠	58
97	St. Paul's ⊠	74
75	Bowie St.	69
55	Elizabeth City St. †	57

Nickname: Trojans
Colors: Orange & Navy Blue
Arena: Daniel Gymnasium
　　Capacity: 3,454; Year Built: 1965
AD: Peggy L. Davis
SID: Jim Junot

VIRGINIA TECH
Blacksburg, VA 24061 I

Coach: Seth Greenberg, Fairleigh Dickinson 1978

2006-07 RESULTS (22-12)

94	Coppin St. ⊠	43
95	West Fla. ⊠	47
68	Western Mich. †	71
77	Montana †	56
64	Southern Ill. †	69
69	Iowa ⊠	65
62	George Washington †	63
72	Old Dominion ⊠	55
69	Appalachian St. ⊠	37
63	Wake Forest ⊠	60
80	Seton Hall †	61
94	Campbell ⊠	70
58	Marshall	59
65	Richmond ⊠	53
69	Duke	67
74	UNC Greensboro	51
94	North Carolina ⊠	88
73	Florida St.	82
67	Maryland ⊠	64
92	Miami (Fla.)	85
73	Georgia Tech	65
59	North Carolina St. ⊠	70
59	Boston College	80
84	Virginia ⊠	57
81	North Carolina	80
56	North Carolina St.	81
79	Boston College ⊠	62
73	Miami (Fla.) ⊠	57
56	Virginia	69
74	Clemson ⊠	75
71	Wake Forest †	52
64	North Carolina St. †	72
54	Illinois †	52
48	Southern Ill. †	63

Nickname: Hokies
Colors: Burnt Orange & Chicago Maroon
Arena: Cassell Coliseum
　　Capacity: 9,847; Year Built: 1961
AD: James C. Weaver
SID: Bill Dyer

VIRGINIA UNION
Richmond, VA 23220-1790 II

Coach: Dave Robbins, Catawba 1966

2006-07 RESULTS (23-6)

64	St. Augustine's	62
87	Bowie St. †	42
77	Fayetteville St.	68
100	Knoxville	41
55	Livingstone ⊠	48
70	Johnson C. Smith	79
85	Fayetteville St. ⊠	54
86	Dist. Columbia ⊠	72
113	St. Paul's	84
76	Virginia St.	71
74	Dist. Columbia	69
70	Bowie St.	92
79	Johnson C. Smith ⊠	82
73	Elizabeth City St. ⊠	70
69	Shaw	48
69	St. Augustine's ⊠	76
67	Livingstone	52
62	N.C. Central	53
69	Virginia St. ⊠	51
86	Shaw ⊠	77
90	St. Paul's ⊠	77
63	N.C. Central ⊠	56
95	Elizabeth City St.	94
79	N.C. Central †	68
55	St. Augustine's †	53
60	Elizabeth City St. †	63
74	Lander †	68
71	Clayton St. †	70
56	Wingate †	73

Nickname: Panthers
Colors: Steel & Maroon
Arena: Barco-Stevens Hall
   Capacity: 2,200; Year Built: 1939
AD: Michael Bailey
SID: Jim Junot

VA. WESLEYAN
Norfolk, VA 23502-5599 III

Coach: David Macedo, Wilkes 1996

2006-07 RESULTS (28-5)

72	Chris. Newport ⊠	71
73	Averett	81
73	Salisbury	64
67	Roanoke ⊠	34
74	Wash. & Lee ⊠	50
82	Bridgewater (Va.)	57
78	Hampden-Sydney	60
85	Apprentice	67
62	Mary Hardin-Baylor	63
67	Hardin-Simmons †	61
84	Methodist	49
128	Emory & Henry ⊠	84
75	Guilford ⊠	55
79	Lynchburg	57
85	East. Mennonite	56
65	Randolph-Macon ⊠	60
75	Hampden-Sydney ⊠	49
101	Emory & Henry	124
72	Guilford	69
85	Bridgewater (Va.) ⊠	46
62	Roanoke	48
61	Wash. & Lee	49
87	East. Mennonite ⊠	60
77	Randolph-Macon	69
90	Lynchburg ⊠	73
82	Wash. & Lee †	48
67	Hampden-Sydney †	70
63	Averett ⊠	60
61	Hampden-Sydney ⊠	51
81	Mississippi Col. ⊠	55
81	Guilford ⊠	71
67	Washington-St. Louis †	65
67	Amherst †	80

Nickname: Blue Marlins
Colors: Navy Blue & Silver
Arena: Batten Center
   Capacity: 1,400; Year Built: 2002
AD: To be named
SID: Joe Wasiluk

WABASH
Crawfordsville, IN 47933 III

Coach: Mac Petty, Tennessee 1968

2006-07 RESULTS (11-16)

50	Rose-Hulman ⊠	57
56	Ind.-South Bend ⊠	44
85	Hanover ⊠	90
82	DePauw	92
50	Oberlin	52
83	UC Clermont ⊠	51
60	Olivet Nazarene ⊠	75
62	Denison	56
58	Franklin	82
89	Lakeland †	71
68	Franklin	80
69	Allegheny	72
80	Hiram	83
50	Ohio Wesleyan ⊠	74
52	Wooster	96
73	Earlham ⊠	57
51	Wittenberg ⊠	64
66	Oberlin ⊠	61
54	Ohio Wesleyan	52
63	Denison	52
70	Earlham	72
63	Wooster ⊠	68
59	Wittenberg	82
77	Kenyon ⊠	74
87	Allegheny	84
80	Wooster	92
87	Kenyon	81

Nickname: Little Giants
Colors: Scarlet
Arena: Chadwick Court
   Capacity: 1,636; Year Built: 1917
AD: Vernon H. Mummert
SID: Brent Harris

WAGNER
Staten Island, NY 10301-4495 I

Coach: Mike Deane, Potsdam St. 1974

2006-07 RESULTS (11-19)

70	Lafayette ⊠	76
60	Manhattan	63
82	Md.-East. Shore	76
53	William & Mary	77
69	Vermont ⊠	77
61	Brown ⊠	66
72	Yale ⊠	65
44	Columbia	70
72	Robert Morris ⊠	60
105	Union (N.Y.) ⊠	64
56	Purdue	95
86	Indiana St.	92
58	Monmouth	69
95	Fairleigh Dickinson	96
72	Quinnipiac ⊠	80
73	St. Francis (N.Y.)	66
51	St. Francis (N.Y.) ⊠	66
88	Long Island	74
70	Mt. St. Mary's ⊠	80
83	St. Francis (Pa.) ⊠	67
80	Long Island	77
80	Sacred Heart ⊠	76
63	Monmouth ⊠	70
79	Sacred Heart	81
57	St. Francis (Pa.)	54
63	Robert Morris	71
77	Mt. St. Mary's ⊠	82
91	Fairleigh Dickinson ⊠	63
54	Central Conn. St.	79
68	Sacred Heart	100

Nickname: Seahawks
Colors: Green & White
Arena: Spiro Sports Center
   Capacity: 2,100; Year Built: 1999
AD: Walt Hameline
SID: Todd Vatter

WAKE FOREST
Winston-Salem, NC 27109 I

Coach: Skip Prosser, Merchant Marine 1972

2006-07 RESULTS (15-16)

91	James Madison ⊠	82
86	Bucknell ⊠	83
73	Elon ⊠	48
88	Vanderbilt ⊠	78
88	Appalachian St. ⊠	78
58	Air Force †	94
86	Georgia ⊠	87
63	DePaul	78
60	Virginia Tech	63
92	Gardner-Webb ⊠	60
72	Richmond ⊠	59
67	South Fla. †	75
81	East Caro. ⊠	65
59	Miami (Fla.)	58
85	Boston College ⊠	95
74	North Carolina St. ⊠	88
40	Duke	62
76	Virginia	88
60	North Carolina ⊠	88
66	Florida St.	74
85	Georgia Tech ⊠	75
72	Maryland ⊠	79
87	Winston-Salem ⊠	71
67	North Carolina	104
67	Clemson ⊠	65
74	Miami (Fla.) ⊠	69
61	Georgia Tech	75
66	North Carolina St.	73
78	Virginia	72
114	Georgia Tech †	112
52	Virginia Tech †	71

Nickname: Demon Deacons
Colors: Old Gold & Black
Arena: Lawrence Joel Coliseum
   Capacity: 14,665; Year Built: 1989
AD: Ronald D. Wellman
SID: Dean Buchan

WARTBURG
Waverly, IA 50677-1003 III

Coach: Dick Peth, Iowa 1981

2006-07 RESULTS (11-15)

77	Colorado St.-Pueblo	84
78	Colorado Col. †	58
97	Peru St. †	53
81	Neb. Wesleyan	58
88	Coe	92
82	Clarke	70
77	Augustana (Ill.)	92
61	UNI	83
88	Finlandia †	63
75	Wis.-Eau Claire	70
69	Central (Iowa) ⊠	83
56	Luther	70
64	Simpson	72
80	Cornell College	89
70	Buena Vista ⊠	84
61	Loras	62
64	Luther	55
71	Simpson ⊠	59
65	Dubuque	74
77	Buena Vista	90
60	Coe ⊠	82
69	Dubuque ⊠	63
71	Loras ⊠	59
73	Central (Iowa)	88
89	Cornell College ⊠	68
69	Coe	83

Nickname: Knights
Colors: Orange & Black
Arena: Knights Gym
   Capacity: 1,800; Year Built: 1949
AD: Rick Willis
SID: Mark Adkins

WASHBURN
Topeka, KS 66621 II

Coach: Bob Chipman, Kansas St. 1973

2006-07 RESULTS (8-19)

77	Kan. Wesleyan ⊠	72
69	Fort Hays St. †	70
63	Eastern N.M.	55
55	UNLV	83
64	Cameron	60
72	Central Okla.	82
77	Mo. Western St. ⊠	76
65	Cameron	73
61	Lynn	68
63	Barry †	47
50	Central Mo.	67
77	Emporia St.	80
58	Northwest Mo. St. ⊠	69
69	Fort Hays St. ⊠	57
45	Truman	60
69	Southwest Baptist ⊠	76
79	Pittsburg St.	84
57	Mo. Southern St.	68
77	Mo. Western St.	62
70	Mo. Southern St. ⊠	79
61	Pittsburg St.	72
72	Southwest Baptist	79
68	Truman ⊠	58
85	Northwest Mo. St.	87
74	Emporia St.	88
57	Fort Hays St.	58
62	Central Mo. ⊠	78

Nickname: Ichabods
Colors: Yale Blue & White
Arena: Lee Arena
   Capacity: 3,904; Year Built: 1984
AD: Loren Ferre'
SID: Jeremy Wangler

WASHINGTON
Seattle, WA 98195 I

Coach: Lorenzo Romar, Cincinnati 1992

2006-07 RESULTS (19-13)

99	Pepperdine ⊠	91
102	Nicholls St. ⊠	74
70	UNI ⊠	61
83	Sacramento St. ⊠	74
90	Eastern Wash. ⊠	83
87	Idaho ⊠	66
87	Southern Utah ⊠	72
77	Gonzaga	97
105	Portland St. ⊠	73
88	LSU	72
80	Weber St. ⊠	51
79	Southern California	86
74	UCLA	96
87	Arizona ⊠	96
64	Arizona St. ⊠	53
77	Stanford	78
69	California	77
47	Washington St. ⊠	75
89	Oregon ⊠	77
91	Oregon St. ⊠	74
66	Arizona St.	61
54	Arizona	84
79	California ⊠	71
64	Stanford ⊠	52
61	Washington St. ⊠	65
61	Pittsburgh	65
65	Oregon St.	73
85	Oregon	93
85	Southern California ⊠	70
61	UCLA ⊠	51
59	Arizona St. †	51
64	Washington St. †	74

Nickname: Huskies
Colors: Purple & Gold
Arena: Bank of America Arena
   Capacity: 10,000; Year Built: 1927
AD: Todd Turner
SID: Dan Lepse

WASH. & JEFF.
Washington, PA 15301-4801 III

Coach: Glenn Gutierrez, West Liberty St. 1985

2006-07 RESULTS (14-14)
66	Carnegie Mellon ⊠	77
75	Allegheny	81
64	Ohio Wesleyan	90
44	Rochester (N.Y.)	76
71	Buffalo St. †	83
58	Kenyon ⊠	69
66	Case Reserve	76
71	Denison ⊠	49
73	Westminster (Pa.)	88
67	Defiance	72
57	Manchester ⊠	59
62	Earlham ⊠	60
76	St. Vincent ⊠	68
77	Waynesburg ⊠	64
73	Bethany (W.V.)	82
69	Thomas More ⊠	53
82	Thiel ⊠	74
59	Grove City	74
89	Westminster (Pa.) ⊠	87
85	Waynesburg	63
88	St. Vincent	83
93	Thomas More	67
76	Bethany (W.V.) ⊠	79
87	Grove City ⊠	84
58	Thiel	51
67	Thomas More ⊠	49
78	Bethany (W.V.)	75
58	Grove City ⊠	60

Nickname: Presidents
Colors: Red & Black
Arena: Henry Memorial Center
    Capacity: 2,000; Year Built: 1970
AD: Bill Dukett
SID: Scott McGuinness

WASH. & LEE
Lexington, VA 24450 III

Coach: Adam Hutchinson, Amherst 1993

2006-07 RESULTS (11-14)
82	Denison ⊠	71
56	Averett ⊠	79
78	Dickinson	65
65	Oberlin ⊠	52
58	Randolph-Macon	63
50	Va. Wesleyan	74
81	East. Mennonite ⊠	77
75	Merchant Marine ⊠	53
69	Emory ⊠	57
64	Roanoke	68
81	Bridgewater (Va.)	74
98	Emory & Henry ⊠	96
58	Hampden-Sydney	66
84	Lynchburg	67
86	East. Mennonite	62
64	Roanoke ⊠	70
61	Guilford ⊠	62
63	Randolph-Macon ⊠	64
49	Va. Wesleyan ⊠	61
95	Emory & Henry	100
60	Hampden-Sydney ⊠	71
74	Lynchburg ⊠	56
77	Guilford	95
46	Bridgewater (Va.) ⊠	48
48	Va. Wesleyan †	82

Nickname: Generals
Colors: Royal Blue & White
Arena: Warner Center
    Capacity: 2,500; Year Built: 1972
AD: George C. O'Connell Jr.
SID: Brian Laubscher

WASHINGTON (MD.)
Chestertown, MD 21620-1197 III

Coach: Rob Nugent, Mass. Liberal Arts 1997

2006-07 RESULTS (4-20)
30	St. Vincent †	64
79	Manhattanville	94
69	Ursinus ⊠	77
73	Dickinson ⊠	71
61	Haverford	72
61	Muhlenberg	87
62	St. Mary's (Md.)	74
61	Keystone ⊠	55
37	Navy	83
65	Salisbury	78
72	Johns Hopkins	77
55	Gettysburg ⊠	70
54	Frank. & Marsh. ⊠	80
56	Dickinson	59
71	Muhlenberg ⊠	65
78	Swarthmore ⊠	83
54	Johns Hopkins ⊠	72
59	Ursinus	75
51	Gettysburg	88
69	McDaniel	79
61	Haverford ⊠	65
64	Frank. & Marsh.	90
57	Swarthmore	67
88	McDaniel ⊠	84

Nickname: Shoremen
Colors: Maroon & Black
Arena: Frank C. Russell Gymnasium at Cain Athletic Center
    Capacity: 1,200; Year Built: 1957
AD: Bryan Matthews
SID: Phil Ticknor

WASHINGTON-ST. LOUIS
St. Louis, MO 63130-4899 III

Coach: Mark Edwards, Washington-St. Louis 1969

2006-07 RESULTS (25-5)
79	Vassar †	74
79	Colby †	71
78	Blackburn ⊠	43
73	Augustana (Ill.) ⊠	75
87	Luther ⊠	71
81	Pomona-Pitzer ⊠	65
75	Ill. Wesleyan ⊠	63
101	Maryville (Mo.) ⊠	67
83	Fontbonne ⊠	68
81	Webster ⊠	65
70	Chicago	59
73	Case Reserve	56
78	Emory	73
68	Rochester (N.Y.) ⊠	59
73	Carnegie Mellon ⊠	49
68	Brandeis ⊠	64
79	New York U. ⊠	78
57	New York U.	73
75	Brandeis	81
74	Emory ⊠	62
86	Case Reserve ⊠	65
94	Carnegie Mellon	73
61	Rochester (N.Y.)	66
79	Chicago ⊠	74
77	Fontbonne	58
63	Whitworth †	61
78	Wis.-Stevens Point	66
58	Hope †	55
65	Va. Wesleyan †	67
92	Wooster †	84

Nickname: Bears
Colors: Red & Green
Arena: WU Field House
    Capacity: 3,000; Year Built: 1984
AD: John M. Schael
SID: Chris Mitchell

WASHINGTON ST.
Pullman, WA 99164-1602 I

Coach: Tony Bennett, Green Bay 1992

2006-07 RESULTS (26-8)
71	UAB †	60
74	Milwaukee	54
84	Radford †	67
67	UTSA	44
66	Idaho St. ⊠	60
65	Boise St. ⊠	63
62	Portland	50
55	Utah	69
77	Gonzaga ⊠	67
66	Idaho	54
69	Cal St. Northridge ⊠	50
64	San Diego St. †	54
52	UCLA	55
58	Southern California	55
75	Arizona St. ⊠	55
77	Arizona ⊠	73
73	California	56
68	Stanford	71
75	Washington	47
70	Oregon St. ⊠	55
74	Oregon ⊠	77
72	Arizona	66
48	Arizona St	47
58	Stanford ⊠	45
59	California ⊠	46
65	Washington	61
59	Oregon	64
58	Oregon St.	54
45	UCLA ⊠	53
88	Southern California ⊠	86
74	Washington †	64
61	Southern California †	70
70	Oral Roberts †	54
74	Vanderbilt †	78

Nickname: Cougars
Colors: Crimson & Gray
Arena: Friel Court
    Capacity: 11,566; Year Built: 1973
AD: James Sterk
SID: Craig Lawson

WAYNE ST. (MICH.)
Detroit, MI 48202-3489 II

Coach: David Greer, Bowling Green 1983

2006-07 RESULTS (13-13)
64	Southern Ind.	81
51	Christian Bros. †	66
69	Northern Ky.	75
76	Northern Mich. ⊠	71
72	Clarion ⊠	59
70	Gannon ⊠	67
57	Mercyhurst ⊠	65
73	Hillsdale ⊠	69
69	Southern Ind. ⊠	78
73	Indianapolis ⊠	65
52	Clarion	44
69	Northwood (Mich.) ⊠	60
71	Ashland	92
52	Findlay	68
80	Michigan Tech ⊠	74
55	Northern Mich. ⊠	75
44	Grand Valley St.	54
77	Lake Superior St.	54
56	Findlay ⊠	72
84	Ashland ⊠	65
57	Mercyhurst	67
71	Gannon	66
89	Ferris St. ⊠	78
82	Saginaw Valley ⊠	66
83	Hillsdale	88
54	Mercyhurst	59

Nickname: Warriors
Colors: Green & Gold
Arena: Matthaei Building
    Capacity: 2,000; Year Built: 1966
AD: Robert Fournier
SID: Jeff Weiss

WAYNE ST. (NEB.)
Wayne, NE 68787-1172 II

Coach: Rico Burkett, North Dakota 1993

2006-07 RESULTS (15-13)
81	York (Neb.) ⊠	70
90	South Dakota	86
66	North Dakota †	71
74	Dakota St. †	71
77	Neb.-Kearney ⊠	80
81	Bemidji St. ⊠	68
96	Minn.-Crookston ⊠	89
66	Northern St. ⊠	82
84	Mary	71
52	St. Cloud St. ⊠	65
55	Augustana (S.D.) ⊠	64
70	Mt. Marty ⊠	67
74	Winona St. ⊠	107
75	Upper Iowa ⊠	62
90	Morningside ⊠	84
68	Southwest Minn. St.	69
91	Minn. St. Moorhead	88
66	Concordia-St. Paul	77
82	Minn.-Crookston	80
59	Bemidji St.	66
75	Mary ⊠	65
68	Northern St. ⊠	82
84	Upper Iowa ⊠	72
72	Winona St.	80
74	Southwest Minn. St. ⊠	70
72	Concordia-St. Paul ⊠	80
65	Minn. St. Moorhead ⊠	62
61	Concordia-St. Paul	77

Nickname: Wildcats
Colors: Black & Gold
Arena: Rice Auditorium
    Capacity: 2,500; Year Built: 1960
AD: Eric Schoh
SID: Mike Grosz

WAYNESBURG
Waynesburg, PA 15370 III

Coach: Frank Ferraro, Duquesne 1975

2006-07 RESULTS (12-13)
81	Salisbury †	95
91	Gallaudet †	89
80	Southern Va.	91
93	Franciscan	71
69	Juniata ⊠	66
89	Grove City	82
83	La Roche ⊠	69
97	Frostburg St. ⊠	72
60	Thiel ⊠	64
64	Wash. & Jeff.	77
78	Penn St.-New Kens. ⊠	75
90	Westminster (Pa.) ⊠	92
54	Hood	77
80	Bethany (W.V.) ⊠	102
88	Franciscan ⊠	70
78	St. Vincent	87
66	Thomas More	70
75	Grove City ⊠	68
63	Wash. & Jeff. ⊠	85
78	Thiel	61
68	Bethany (W.V.)	80
82	Westminster (Pa.)	84
89	Thomas More ⊠	77
82	St. Vincent ⊠	74
60	Grove City	89

Nickname: Yellow Jackets
Colors: Orange & Black
Arena: Marisa Field House
    Capacity: 1,350; Year Built: 1985
AD: Rudy Marisa
SID: Matthew Kifer

RESULTS

WEBER ST.
Ogden, UT 84408-2701 I

Coach: Randy Rahe, Buena Vista 1982

2006-07 RESULTS (20-12)

83	Colo. Christian ⊠	57
71	Alas. Fairbanks	66
66	Troy †	61
55	Utah St. †	68
81	Montana Tech ⊠	53
68	Utah St.	77
55	Utah	67
69	BYU ⊠	73
72	Portland	56
63	Southern Utah	75
68	Portland	51
59	Southern Utah ⊠	57
51	Washington	80
61	Northern Colo.	60
81	Northern Ariz.	73
55	Idaho St. ⊠	58
84	Montana St.	63
75	Portland St.	65
88	Sacramento St. ⊠	68
48	Montana St.	63
86	Montana	90
71	Idaho St.	58
93	Eastern Wash. ⊠	84
76	Northern Colo. ⊠	65
86	Northern Ariz. ⊠	79
74	Eastern Wash.	89
64	Portland St.	62
73	Montana	67
83	Sacramento St.	105
77	Portland St. ⊠	74
88	Northern Ariz. ⊠	80
42	UCLA †	70

Nickname: Wildcats
Colors: Royal Purple & White
Arena: Dee Events Center
　Capacity: 12,000; Year Built: 1977
AD: Jerry Graybeal
SID: Brad Larsen

WEBSTER
St. Louis, MO 63119 III

Coach: Chris Bunch, Lincoln Memorial 1988

2006-07 RESULTS (16-10)

61	Transylvania	77
84	Hanover †	82
79	Milwaukee Engr. ⊠	82
73	Reinhardt ⊠	74
84	Fisk ⊠	60
68	Millikin	83
83	Maryville (Mo.) ⊠	67
66	MacMurray ⊠	71
65	Washington-St. Louis ⊠	81
65	Lincoln Christian	63
60	Westminster (Mo.)	61
62	Eureka ⊠	57
70	Blackburn	71
93	Greenville ⊠	76
89	Fontbonne	78
82	Principia ⊠	63
87	MacMurray	75
69	Maryville (Mo.)	66
86	Westminster (Mo.) ⊠	73
83	Lincoln Christian ⊠	72
80	Greenville	85
76	Eureka	68
84	Blackburn	75
86	Fontbonne ⊠	79
78	Principia	61
62	Fontbonne ⊠	67

Nickname: Gorloks
Colors: Gold, Navy Blue & White
Arena: Grant Gym
　Capacity: 800; Year Built: 1992
AD: Thomas Hart
SID: Merry Graf

WENTWORTH INST.
Boston, MA 02115 III

Coach: Tom Devitt, Boston College 1993

2006-07 RESULTS (17-12)

69	Wm. Paterson †	84
61	Hunter †	70
77	Mount Ida	61
90	Becker ⊠	75
62	Gordon	79
69	Colby-Sawyer	81
58	Coast Guard †	56
57	Rensselaer	78
55	FDU-Florham †	84
86	Mass. Liberal Arts †	74
67	New England Col.	66
72	New England	66
79	Nichols ⊠	64
76	Gordon ⊠	63
91	Anna Maria ⊠	84
66	Newbury ⊠	55
68	Endicott	83
63	Colby-Sawyer ⊠	68
73	Endicott ⊠	71
75	New England	62
74	Roger Williams ⊠	64
58	Salve Regina	67
87	New England Col. ⊠	75
74	Curry	79
76	Eastern Nazarene	87
81	Roger Williams	78
69	Gordon	68
98	Curry ⊠	90
72	St. John Fisher	98

Nickname: Leopards
Colors: Black & Gold
Arena: Tansey Gymnasium
　Capacity: 1,000; Year Built: 1970
AD: Lee Conrad
SID: Bill Gorman

WESLEY
Dover, DE 19901-3875 III

Coach: Jerry Kobasa, Delaware St. 1972

2006-07 RESULTS (11-15)

72	Richard Stockton †	85
67	Gettysburg	77
69	Neumann ⊠	80
89	Piedmont †	95
54	York (N.Y.) †	64
72	Cabrini ⊠	70
65	Alvernia	80
73	Gallaudet ⊠	61
84	Dickinson ⊠	59
74	Chris. Newport	78
81	Eastern	76
80	Marywood ⊠	77
87	Gwynedd-Mercy	88
64	Misericordia	83
78	Eastern ⊠	75
66	Immaculata	75
69	Alvernia ⊠	79
62	Neumann	82
80	Cabrini	57
79	Marywood	74
73	Arcadia ⊠	69
65	Immaculata	74
62	Arcadia	56
65	Gwynedd-Mercy ⊠	72
75	Misericordia ⊠	65
62	Immaculata	77

Nickname: Wolverines
Colors: Navy, Columbia and White
Arena: Jim and Shirley Wentworth Gymnasium
　Capacity: 400; Year Built: 1962
AD: Michael Drass
SID: John Davis

WESLEYAN (CONN.)
Middletown, CT 06459 III

Coach: Gerry McDowell, Colby 1976

2006-07 RESULTS (7-16)

79	Suffolk †	58
77	Mass.-Dartmouth	84
80	Williams	69
75	Eastern Conn. St.	85
83	CCNY ⊠	86
76	Hamilton	79
69	Emmanuel (Mass.)	63
98	Albertus Magnus ⊠	71
62	Salem St.	87
82	Fitchburg St. †	83
87	Nichols	90
52	Amherst ⊠	76
62	Connecticut Col. ⊠	61
62	Roger Williams	73
55	Colby	75
63	Bowdoin	61
56	Bates	59
69	Tufts ⊠	94
57	Trinity (Conn.)	95
56	Amherst	81
87	Salve Regina	81
58	Middlebury ⊠	64
65	Williams ⊠	80

Nickname: Cardinals
Colors: Red & Black
Arena: Silloway Gymnasium
　Capacity: 1,200; Year Built: 2004
AD: John Biddiscombe
SID: Brian Katten

WEST ALA.
Livingston, AL 35470 II

Coach: Rick Reedy, Flagler 1977

2006-07 RESULTS (10-17)

80	Southern-N.O. ⊠	68
49	Henderson St.	57
75	Dillard	67
66	Fla. Gulf Coast	77
58	P.R.-Bayamon †	63
65	Palm Beach Atl. †	62
42	Claflin	48
64	Ga. Southwestern †	73
61	North Georgia †	71
89	Dillard	79
81	Clark Atlanta ⊠	58
68	Delta St. ⊠	75
56	Delta St.	67
58	Ala.-Huntsville ⊠	80
79	North Ala. ⊠	69
75	West Ga.	77
70	Valdosta St. ⊠	81
82	West Fla. ⊠	72
58	Claflin	57
75	Montevallo	83
71	Concordia-Selma ⊠	49
76	West Ga. ⊠	72
85	North Ala.	109
78	Ala.-Huntsville	93
50	Valdosta St.	57
81	West Fla.	85
62	Montevallo	93

Nickname: Tigers
Colors: Red and White
Arena: Pruitt Hall
　Capacity: 1,500; Year Built: 1962
AD: E.J. Brophy
SID: Jason Hughes

WEST CHESTER
West Chester, PA 19383 II

Coach: Dick DeLaney, West Chester 1969

2006-07 RESULTS (13-14)

79	Wilmington (Del.)	57
84	Bloomfield ⊠	68
68	Alderson-Broaddus ⊠	73
68	Phila. Sciences	62
92	Penn St.-Berks ⊠	56
89	Slippery Rock	96
67	Edinboro	75
65	California (Pa.)	66
70	Shippensburg ⊠	64
80	Lock Haven ⊠	86
97	Kutztown	93
70	Indiana (Pa.) ⊠	64
73	Clarion	61
64	Pitt.-Johnstown ⊠	62
77	East Stroudsburg	78
59	Cheyney	65
74	Mansfield ⊠	65
85	Bloomsburg	82
72	Millersville ⊠	64
86	Kutztown ⊠	88
61	Dist. Columbia ⊠	71
67	East Stroudsburg ⊠	79
59	Cheyney	58
71	Mansfield	85
79	Dist. Columbia	87
69	Bloomsburg ⊠	75
81	Millersville	90

Nickname: Golden Rams
Colors: Purple & Gold
Arena: Hollinger Field House
　Capacity: 2,500; Year Built: 1949
AD: Edward Matejkovic
SID: Tom DiCamillo

WEST FLA.
Pensacola, FL 32514 II

Coach: Don Hogan, South Ala. 1981

2006-07 RESULTS (10-17)

86	P.R.-Mayaguez †	54
52	Tampa	67
71	South Ala.	91
85	William Carey ⊠	69
63	Dillard ⊠	64
74	St. Leo ⊠	71
77	Nova Southeastern ⊠	61
61	Tampa ⊠	58
69	Nova Southeastern	91
70	Northwood (Fla.)	73
87	Loyola (La.) ⊠	75
63	St. Thomas Aquinas ⊠	59
78	West Ga. ⊠	71
74	Ala.-Huntsville	80
60	North Ala.	89
72	Montevallo	90
62	Valdosta St. ⊠	70
62	Claflin ⊠	65
78	North Ala. ⊠	82
61	Ala.-Huntsville ⊠	80
73	William Carey.	87
82	Palm Beach Atl. ⊠	60
59	West Ga.	87
63	Montevallo ⊠	101
85	West Ala. ⊠	81
92	Valdosta St.	98

Nickname: Argonauts
Colors: Blue & Green
Arena: UWF Field House
　Capacity: 3,000; Year Built: 1969
AD: Richard C. Berg
SID: Jake Fish

WEST GA.
Carrollton, GA 30118 II

Coach: Ed Murphy, Hardin-Simmons 1964

2006-07 RESULTS (14-15)

73	North Georgia	66
87	Eckerd †	90
75	Tampa	72
108	Carver Bible ⊠	60
79	Columbus St.	84
71	GCSU †	84

82	Ark.-Monticello	72
69	Clayton St.	70
83	North Georgia ⊠	68
65	Delta St.	80
54	Clayton St. ⊠	62
77	Ark.-Monticello ⊠	70
71	West Fla.	78
82	Valdosta St.	85
84	Montevallo ⊠	98
77	West Ala. ⊠	75
81	North Ala. ⊠	73
78	Ala.-Huntsville ⊠	85
90	Palm Beach Atl	84
62	Fla. Gulf Coast	78
61	Montevallo	77
72	West Ala.	76
91	Valdosta St. ⊠	69
87	West Fla. ⊠	59
59	Ala.-Huntsville	72
84	North Ala.	80
106	Allen ⊠	82
86	Ouachita Baptist †	72
62	Montevallo †	78

Nickname: Wolves
Colors: Blue & Red
Arena: HPE Building
   Capacity: 2,800; Year Built: 1965
AD: Edward G. Murphy
SID: Mitch Gray

WEST LIBERTY ST.
West Liberty, WV 26074 II

Coach: Jim Crutchfield, West Virginia 1978

2006-07 RESULTS (25-5)

141	Ohio-Eastern ⊠	76
99	Dist. Columbia †	95
87	Pitt.-Johnstown	96
114	West Va. Wesleyan ⊠	78
110	Bethany (W.V.) ⊠	87
82	Wheeling Jesuit ⊠	101
107	Glenville St.	89
103	Mont. St.-Billings	85
101	Pitt.-Johnstown †	94
101	Mansfield †	90
99	West Va. Wesleyan	74
110	Ohio Valley ⊠	84
97	Shepherd	86
113	Davis & Elkins ⊠	80
85	Salem Int'l	79
116	West Virginia St.	108
95	Wheeling Jesuit	86
77	Charleston (W.V.)	72
91	Fairmont St. ⊠	73
100	Concord	90
115	Bluefield St. ⊠	81
102	Ohio Valley	88
101	Salem Int'l ⊠	89
74	Shepherd ⊠	70
83	Alderson-Broaddus ⊠	88
100	Wheeling Jesuit	93
118	Fairmont St.	102
73	Shepherd †	63
89	West Virginia St. †	107
79	California (Pa.) †	82

Nickname: Hilltoppers
Colors: Black & Gold
Arena: ASRC
   Capacity: 1,200; Year Built: 2000
AD: James W. Watson
SID: Lynn Ullom

WEST TEX. A&M
Canyon, TX 79016-0999 II

Coach: Rick Cooper, Wayland Baptist 1981

2006-07 RESULTS (18-11)

59	Pittsburg St. †	73
70	Mo. Southern St.	75
62	Adams St. ⊠	69
83	Ouachita Baptist ⊠	65

83	N.M. Highlands	64
84	Cameron ⊠	90
81	Southwestern Okla. ⊠	84
92	Lubbock Chrst.	84
65	Tex. A&M-Commerce	64
80	Wayland Baptist	66
78	Central Okla. ⊠	68
66	Northeastern St.	57
75	Southeastern Okla.	85
84	Angelo St.	94
78	Abilene Christian ⊠	69
92	N.M. Highlands ⊠	63
69	Tarleton St. ⊠	62
81	Midwestern St.	90
87	Eastern N.M.	72
65	Tex. A&M-Kingsville	63
91	Eastern N.M. ⊠	79
76	Tex. A&M-Kingsville ⊠	67
86	Angelo St. ⊠	56
80	Abilene Christian	68
69	Tarleton St.	63
55	Midwestern St. ⊠	61
82	Tex. A&M-Commerce ⊠	80
76	Southeastern Okla. †	83
81	Midwestern St. †	86

Nickname: Buffaloes
Colors: Maroon & White
Arena: First United Bank Center
   Capacity: 4,800; Year Built: 2001
AD: Michael McBroom
SID: Adam Quisenberry

WEST VIRGINIA
Morgantown, WV 26507 I

Coach: John Beilein, Wheeling Jesuit 1975

2006-07 RESULTS (27-9)

50	Mt. St. Mary's ⊠	42
87	Slippery Rock ⊠	37
66	Canisius ⊠	43
73	Montana †	56
79	Western Mich. †	54
64	Arkansas †	71
71	North Carolina St. †	60
85	Duquesne	54
76	Savannah St. ⊠	41
63	Citadel	36
95	Md.-East. Shore ⊠	49
81	Connecticut ⊠	71
67	Villanova ⊠	56
73	St. John's (N.Y.) ⊠	46
58	Notre Dame	61
63	Marquette	81
69	South Fla. ⊠	58
83	Cincinnati	96
77	Marshall †	63
64	DePaul ⊠	52
89	Rutgers	83
81	Seton Hall	70
47	Pittsburgh ⊠	60
70	UCLA ⊠	65
53	Georgetown	71
81	Seton Hall ⊠	71
61	Providence	64
66	Pittsburgh	80
79	Cincinnati ⊠	65
92	Providence †	79
71	Louisville †	82
74	Delaware St. ⊠	50
90	Massachusetts ⊠	77
71	North Carolina St. ⊠	66
63	Mississippi St. †	62
78	Clemson †	73

Nickname: Mountaineers
Colors: Old Gold & Blue
Arena: WVU Coliseum
   Capacity: 14,000; Year Built: 1970
AD: Ed Pastilong
SID: Bryan Messerly

WEST VIRGINIA ST.
Institute, WV 25112-1000 II

Coach: Bryan Poore, West Virginia St. 1987

2006-07 RESULTS (26-7)

103	St. Paul's †	78
95	Johnson C. Smith.	86
79	Pitt.-Johnstown	86
96	S.C. Upstate †	88
79	Seton Hill †	76
90	Tampa	82
81	Fla. Southern	71
94	Mount Olive ⊠	93
80	West Va. Tech ⊠	74
70	Fairmont St.	73
60	Davis & Elkins	47
98	Bluefield St. ⊠	75
102	Concord	96
92	Charleston (W.V.)	80
108	West Liberty St. ⊠	116
93	Shepherd	80
82	Alderson-Broaddus	105
89	Salem Int'l ⊠	85
87	West Va. Wesleyan	85
87	Wheeling Jesuit ⊠	84
107	Glenville St.	92
77	Alderson-Broaddus ⊠	80
103	Bluefield St.	78
84	Concord	85
86	Davis & Elkins ⊠	68
122	Ohio Valley ⊠	104
82	Charleston (W.V.) ⊠	68
103	West Va. Wesleyan ⊠	69
87	Bluefield St. †	61
107	West Liberty St. †	89
80	Alderson-Broaddus †	79
91	Alderson-Broaddus †	75
85	Barton	86

Nickname: Yellow Jackets
Colors: Old Gold & Black
Arena: Fleming Hall
   Capacity: 1,800; Year Built: 1942
AD: Robert Parker
SID: Sean McAndrews

WEST VA. WESLEYAN
Buckhannon, WV 26201 II

Coach: Bill Lilly, Glenville St. 1982

2006-07 RESULTS (3-25)

61	Edinboro	57
70	Glenville St. †	74
64	Fairmont St.	81
78	West Liberty St.	114
78	Ashland	87
67	Pitt.-Johnstown ⊠	86
60	Slippery Rock ⊠	79
64	Radford	89
60	Wofford	94
74	West Liberty St. ⊠	99
92	Glenville St. ⊠	89
60	Alderson-Broaddus	84
79	Ohio Valley	89
74	Wheeling Jesuit ⊠	91
53	Bluefield St.	57
73	Davis & Elkins ⊠	59
68	Salem Int'l	75
79	Concord	97
85	West Virginia St. ⊠	87
51	Shepherd	89
63	Glenville St.	70
77	Bluefield St. ⊠	79
78	Charleston (W.V.) ⊠	85
64	Fairmont St.	77
58	Davis & Elkins	62
81	Concord ⊠	101
65	Alderson-Broaddus ⊠	82
69	West Virginia St.	103

Nickname: Bobcats
Colors: Orange & Black
Arena: Rockefeller Center
   Capacity: 3,200; Year Built: 1974
AD: George A. Klebez
SID: Hailey Noble

WESTERN CARO.
Cullowhee, NC 28723 I

Coach: Larry Hunter, Ohio 1971

2006-07 RESULTS (11-20)

61	UNC Asheville	46
57	Purdue	82
105	Atlanta Christian ⊠	40
117	Toccoa Falls ⊠	58
81	Wofford	75
61	Xavier	95
73	Gardner-Webb	74
55	Dayton	66
82	Citadel ⊠	63
75	Col. of Charleston ⊠	82
60	Clemson	103
82	St. Mary's (Cal.)	93
62	Rice †	67
53	South Carolina	67
57	UNC Greensboro ⊠	54
73	Chattanooga	67
91	Appalachian St.	100
87	Furman	79
64	Elon ⊠	77
59	Davidson	79
77	Wofford ⊠	74
78	Citadel	68
64	Col. of Charleston	76
69	Ga. Southern ⊠	57
72	Chattanooga ⊠	75
68	UNC Greensboro	79
59	Davidson ⊠	92
65	Appalachian St. ⊠	76
65	Elon	74
69	Elon †	65
59	Appalachian St. †	78

Nickname: Catamounts
Colors: Purple & Gold
Arena: Ramsey Center
   Capacity: 7,826; Year Built: 1986
AD: Chip Smith
SID: Mike Cawood

WESTERN CONN. ST.
Danbury, CT 06810 III

Coach: Bob Campbell, Connecticut 1972

2006-07 RESULTS (14-12)

93	Albertus Magnus ⊠	54
102	Me.-Presque Isle ⊠	69
95	Mount Ida ⊠	70
50	Trinity (Conn.) ⊠	66
84	Plymouth St.	81
73	Manhattanville ⊠	94
88	Suffolk ⊠	76
82	Mass.-Boston	80
79	Lasell ⊠	90
79	Westfield St.	71
69	Frank. & Marsh.	68
70	Seton Hill †	94
68	Southern Me. ⊠	59
88	Keene St.	101
67	Mass.-Dartmouth	64
61	Rhode Island Col.	85
76	Plymouth St. ⊠	71
63	Eastern Conn. St. ⊠	52
90	Mass.-Boston	99
76	Bridgewater St.	82
87	Southern Me.	82
66	Rhode Island Col. ⊠	76
77	Keene St. ⊠	84
63	Eastern Conn. St.	79
74	Mass.-Dartmouth ⊠	64
82	Mass.-Boston ⊠	88

Nickname: Colonials
Colors: Dark Blue, Metallic Copper & White
Arena: Stephen Feldman Arena
   Capacity: 2,100; Year Built: 1994
AD: Edward Farrington
SID: Scott Ames

RESULTS

WESTERN ILL.
Macomb, IL 61455 I

Coach: Derek Thomas, Mo.-St. Louis 1989

2006-07 RESULTS (7-23)
72	Upper Iowa ⊠	64
75	Radford †	72
60	Florida Int'l.	62
95	IPFW ⊠	97
75	Utah Valley St. ⊠	77
56	Morehead St. ⊠	57
74	Texas-Arlington ⊠	57
40	Indiana	92
61	St. Louis	71
74	Culver-Stockton ⊠	48
56	Eastern Ill.	76
59	Brown †	63
67	Howard †	68
46	Oral Roberts	65
58	Centenary (La.)	64
77	IPFW	79
55	IUPUI	68
52	Oakland ⊠	79
60	Valparaiso ⊠	78
72	Chicago St. ⊠	82
65	Southern Utah	68
89	UMKC	95
45	Centenary (La.) ⊠	42
60	Oral Roberts ⊠	67
64	Oakland	63
47	IUPUI	69
56	Valparaiso	80
54	UMKC ⊠	89
51	Southern Utah ⊠	48
57	Oakland †	74

Nickname: Leathernecks
Colors: Purple & Gold
Arena: Western Hall
 Capacity: 5,139; Year Built: 1964
AD: Tim Van Alstine
SID: Russell Houghtaling

WESTERN KY.
Bowling Green, KY 42101-3576.... I

Coach: Darrin Horn, Western Ky. 1995
2006-07 RESULTS (22-11)
96	Kennesaw St.	55
70	Georgia	67
87	Tennessee St. ⊠	69
95	Towson ⊠	72
68	Florida †	101
76	Ball St. †	66
69	UAB ⊠	54
78	Eastern Ky. ⊠	55
81	Montana	65
70	Southern Ill. ⊠	75
79	Tennessee	93
85	North Texas ⊠	86
73	South Ala. ⊠	51
73	Middle Tenn.	64
93	Fla. Atlantic	83
82	Troy ⊠	78
71	Nebraska	82
86	Florida Int'l.	74
82	La.-Lafayette ⊠	72
69	Ark.-Little Rock	71
73	New Orleans ⊠	70
75	Arkansas St.	76
77	Denver	67
103	La.-Monroe ⊠	96
70	North Texas	74
71	South Ala.	73
65	Middle Tenn. ⊠	53
73	Fla. Atlantic ⊠	78
75	Troy	74
74	Ky. Wesleyan ⊠	67
82	Florida Int'l ⊠	64
86	Fla. Atlantic †	81
73	Arkansas St. †	80

Nickname: Hilltoppers
Colors: Red & White
Arena: E.A. Diddle Arena
 Capacity: 7,326; Year Built: 1963
AD: Camden Wood Selig
SID: Brian Fremund

WESTERN MICH.
Kalamazoo, MI 49008 I

Coach: Steve Hawkins, South Ala. 1987
2006-07 RESULTS (16-16)
67	Pittsburgh †	86
71	Indiana St.	73
69	Detroit ⊠	67
71	Virginia Tech †	68
54	West Virginia †	79
78	Marist †	89
84	San Diego St. ⊠	73
71	Temple	76
75	Northwestern	77
65	Illinois St.	57
69	Indiana	77
64	Davidson	71
83	Culver-Stockton ⊠	52
68	Northern Ill.	70
74	Ball St. ⊠	61
68	Toledo	80
86	Central Mich. ⊠	76
84	Eastern Mich. ⊠	80
72	Bowling Green	63
36	Akron	69
85	Buffalo ⊠	64
59	Miami (Ohio)	62
73	Ohio	78
79	Kent St. ⊠	57
66	Central Mich.	71
89	Valparaiso	80
80	Eastern Mich.	61
75	Toledo ⊠	79
68	Northern Ill. ⊠	54
71	Ball St.	67
67	Northern Ill. †	62
66	Kent St. †	75

Nickname: Broncos
Colors: Brown & Gold
Arena: University Arena
 Capacity: 5,421; Year Built: 1957
AD: Kathy Beauregard
SID: Matt Holmes

WESTERN NEW ENG.
Springfield, MA 01119 III

Coach: Mike Theulen, Keene St. 1980
2006-07 RESULTS (22-8)
59	Bates †	66
55	Williams	70
62	Tufts ⊠	70
53	Norwich	36
56	Amherst	92
75	Westfield St. †	73
61	MIT ⊠	52
70	Curry ⊠	53
61	Emmanuel (Mass.) ⊠	57
61	Nichols	66
78	Suffolk ⊠	55
86	Daniel Webster	68
56	Norwich ⊠	47
60	Rivier	64
51	Emerson	53
60	Johnson & Wales (RI) ⊠	55
72	Albertus Magnus	55
71	Emmanuel (Mass.)	67
87	Suffolk	69
80	Daniel Webster ⊠	46
70	Rivier ⊠	47
68	Emerson ⊠	46
69	Johnson & Wales (RI)	64
69	Albertus Magnus ⊠	54
92	Southern Vt. ⊠	54
81	Daniel Webster ⊠	50
62	Emmanuel (Mass.) ⊠	71
74	Castleton ⊠	58
74	Endicott ⊠	57
68	St. Joseph's (Me.) ⊠	62

WESTERN N.M.
Silver City, NM 88062 II

Coach: Mark Coleman, St. Lawrence 1983
2006-07 RESULTS (12-15)
82	Grand Canyon ⊠	75
90	Tex. Permian Basin ⊠	84
83	Hawaii-Hilo	70
77	Fort Lewis †	79
62	Hawaii-Hilo	78
63	Grand Canyon	79
62	Neb.-Kearney ⊠	76
97	Chadron St. ⊠	84
50	Colorado Mines	79
76	New Mexico St. ⊠	100
108	S'western (Ariz.) ⊠	63
89	UC-Colo. Springs ⊠	65
62	Regis (Colo.)	37
68	Colo. Christian	71
67	Metro St.	78
65	Adams St.	79
63	Colorado St.-Pueblo	73
69	Fort Lewis	63
67	Mesa St. ⊠	71
57	N.M. Highlands ⊠	52
74	Western St. ⊠	82
63	Mesa St.	62
65	Fort Lewis	77
90	N.M. Highlands	83
76	Western St. ⊠	61
75	Colorado St.-Pueblo ⊠	62
73	Adams St. ⊠	82

Nickname: Mustangs
Colors: Purple & Gold
Arena: Mustang Field House
 Capacity: 2,000; Year Built: 1957
AD: Scott Woodard
SID: Kent Beatty

WESTERN ORE.
Monmouth, OR 97361-1394 II

Coach: Craig Stanger, BYU 1992
2006-07 RESULTS (10-17)
54	Cal St. Chico	83
82	Humboldt St. †	89
97	Corban	96
58	Oregon St.	71
69	Southern Ore.	84
122	Cal St. Monterey Bay †	126
80	Notre Dame de Namur †	71
94	Willamette ⊠	57
40	BYU	102
74	North Dakota ⊠	72
84	Shepherd ⊠	81
94	Western Wash.	97
73	St. Martin's	74
74	Seattle Pacific	86
65	Central Wash.	70
79	Alas. Fairbanks ⊠	64
49	Alas. Anchorage ⊠	70
70	Northwest Nazarene ⊠	74
81	Alas. Anchorage	73
76	Alas. Fairbanks	79
69	Seattle	67
61	Seattle Pacific ⊠	72
68	Central Wash. ⊠	69
69	Northwest Nazarene	85
93	Western Wash. ⊠	91
94	St. Martin's ⊠	83
68	Seattle ⊠	82

Nickname: Wolves
Colors: Crimson Red & White
Arena: Physical Education Building
 Capacity: 2,473; Year Built: 1972

Nickname: Golden Bears
Colors: Royal Blue & Gold
Arena: Alumni Healthful Living Center
 Capacity: 2,000; Year Built: 1993
AD: Michael Theulen
SID: Ken Cerino

AD: Jon Carey
SID: Russ Blunck

WESTERN ST.
Gunnison, CO 81231 II

Coach: Al Sokaitis, Mass. Liberal Arts 1976
2006-07 RESULTS (12-15)
66	Eastern N.M.	64
57	Fort Hays St. †	62
72	Johnson & Wales (CO)	63
74	Okla. Panhandle ⊠	64
57	Minn. St. Mankato ⊠	74
61	Colorado Mines ⊠	46
90	Johnson & Wales (CO) ⊠	50
72	Regis (Colo.)	67
71	UC-Colo. Springs	84
55	Southern Utah	66
71	Metro St. ⊠	81
62	Colo. Christian ⊠	55
60	Colorado Col. ⊠	38
67	Neb.-Kearney	84
69	Chadron St.	70
66	Mesa St.	85
67	Fort Lewis	79
42	Colorado St.-Pueblo ⊠	71
51	Adams St. ⊠	64
82	Western N.M. ⊠	74
63	N.M. Highlands ⊠	71
62	Colorado St.-Pueblo	64
77	Adams St.	70
67	N.M. Highlands	51
61	Western N.M.	76
103	Fort Lewis ⊠	95
71	Mesa St. ⊠	78

Nickname: Mountaineers
Colors: Crimson & Slate
Arena: Paul Wright Gymnasium
 Capacity: 1,800; Year Built: 1951
AD: Greg Waggoner
SID: Bobby Heiken

WESTERN WASH.
Bellingham, WA 98225 II

Coach: Brad Jackson, Washington St. 1975
2006-07 RESULTS (11-15)
89	Multnomah Bible ⊠	47
66	Cal Poly Pomona †	75
67	Cal St. L.A. †	66
96	Northwest (Wash.) ⊠	88
77	Grand Canyon ⊠	67
75	Hawaii-Hilo ⊠	67
70	Notre Dame de Namur ⊠	84
64	Cal Poly Pomona	67
67	Cal St. San B'dino †	86
90	Dixie St. ⊠	72
97	Western Ore. ⊠	94
72	Northwest Nazarene	95
86	Seattle	80
65	Seattle Pacific	80
79	Central Wash. ⊠	77
72	Alas. Anchorage ⊠	92
64	Alas. Fairbanks ⊠	73
68	Central Wash.	82
64	St. Martin's	67
61	Seattle ⊠	76
62	Alas. Fairbanks	84
61	Alas. Anchorage	77
93	Northwest Nazarene ⊠	82
91	Western Ore.	93
64	Seattle Pacific ⊠	70
86	St. Martin's ⊠	69

Nickname: Vikings
Colors: Blue, Silver & White
Arena: Sam Carver Gymnasium
 Capacity: 2,534; Year Built: 1961
AD: Lynda Goodrich
SID: Paul Madison

WESTFIELD ST.
Westfield, MA 01086-1630 III

Coach: Rich Sutter, St. Bonaventure 1984

2006-07 RESULTS (17-11)
98	Briar Cliff (Iowa) †	50
82	Mt. St. Mary (N.Y.)	69
84	Elms	75
84	Nichols	77
75	Springfield †	72
73	Western New Eng. †	75
86	Suffolk	61
79	Skidmore	64
92	Lesley ⊠	84
71	Western Conn. St. ⊠	79
76	Potsdam St. †	71
64	Trinity (Conn.)	77
58	Bridgewater St.	73
75	Worcester St. ⊠	65
59	Salem St.	75
65	Fisher	81
82	Fitchburg St. ⊠	68
82	Framingham St. ⊠	79
95	Mass. Liberal Arts	67
74	Bridgewater St. ⊠	75
67	Worcester St.	76
67	Salem St. ⊠	76
53	Fitchburg St.	58
93	Framingham St.	75
101	Mass. Liberal Arts ⊠	91
98	Framingham St.	83
59	Bridgewater St. †	49
62	Salem St.	72

Nickname: Owls
Colors: Blue & White
Arena: Woodward Center
   Capacity: 1,100; Year Built: 2004
AD: Richard Lenfest/Vicky Carwein
SID: Mickey Curtis

WESTMINSTER (MO.)
Fulton, MO 65251-1299 III

Coach: Matt Mitchell, Arkansas 1987

2006-07 RESULTS (15-9)
77	Rhodes	74
60	Hendrix †	59
66	Central (Iowa) ⊠	64
40	Central Mo.	77
72	Principia ⊠	48
56	Illinois Col.	59
85	Baptist Bible (Mo.) ⊠	41
70	MacMurray ⊠	73
61	Webster ⊠	60
85	Lincoln Christian ⊠	64
76	Eureka ⊠	67
58	Fontbonne	76
55	Maryville (Mo.) ⊠	58
48	Blackburn	62
75	Greenville ⊠	67
72	Principia	64
73	Webster	86
95	MacMurray ⊠	85
53	Fontbonne ⊠	79
75	Lincoln Christian	63
81	Eureka	64
91	Maryville (Mo.)	75
65	Blackburn ⊠	62
77	Greenville	85

Nickname: Blue Jays
Colors: Blue & White
Arena: Westminster Gym
   Capacity: 1,000; Year Built: 1928
AD: Matt Mitchell
SID: To be named

WESTMINSTER (PA.)
New Wilmington, PA 16172 III

Coach: Larry Ondako, Westminster (Pa.) 1993

2006-07 RESULTS (18-9)
83	Lynchburg ⊠	101
84	Hampden-Sydney ⊠	93
82	Pitt.-Bradford ⊠	86
92	La Roche	89
80	Geneva	83
102	Allegheny ⊠	97
88	Wash. & Jeff. ⊠	73
73	Penn St.-Behrend ⊠	55
99	Pitt.-Greensburg ⊠	94
90	Hanover	116
80	Olivet †	67
98	Marietta	73
89	Thomas More ⊠	79
93	St. Vincent	89
92	Waynesburg	90
91	Grove City ⊠	101
96	Bethany (W.V.) ⊠	82
78	Thiel	66
87	Wash. & Jeff.	89
94	St. Vincent	86
76	Thomas More	63
71	Grove City	59
84	Waynesburg ⊠	82
92	Thiel ⊠	74
102	Bethany (W.V.) ⊠	90
67	Grove City ⊠	86
83	John Carroll	87

Nickname: Titans
Colors: Blue & White
Arena: Buzz Ridl Gymnasium
   Capacity: 2,300; Year Built: 1950
AD: James E. Dafler
SID: Justin Zackal

WHEATON (ILL.)
Wheaton, IL 60187-5593 III

Coach: Bill Harris, Gordon 1970

2006-07 RESULTS (17-9)
81	Franklin ⊠	78
67	Whitworth ⊠	70
70	Benedictine (Ill.) ⊠	58
77	Chicago	81
73	Calvin †	62
73	Hope †	70
112	Principia ⊠	52
39	Northwestern ⊠	41
93	Nazareth †	89
60	Rivier †	44
75	Baruch	66
47	North Central (Ill.) ⊠	52
69	Augustana (Ill.) ⊠	75
73	North Park ⊠	60
79	Ill. Wesleyan ⊠	65
77	Elmhurst ⊠	74
71	Millikin	57
68	North Central (Ill.)	79
71	Carthage ⊠	67
85	North Park ⊠	73
60	Augustana (Ill.)	63
93	Ill. Wesleyan	84
83	Millikin ⊠	72
74	Elmhurst	80
61	Carthage	59
82	Elmhurst †	85

Nickname: Thunder
Colors: Orange & Blue
Arena: King Arena
   Capacity: 2,650; Year Built: 2000
AD: Tony Ladd
SID: Brett Marhanka

WHEATON (MASS.)
Norton, MA 02766 III

Coach: Brian Walmsley, Bentley 1988

2006-07 RESULTS (11-15)
88	Husson †	82
78	Plymouth St.	86
83	Salve Regina	77
81	Emerson	76
77	Bridgewater St. ⊠	88
74	Connecticut Col.	77
67	Endicott	64
71	Fitchburg St. †	67
75	Salem St.	65
67	Babson	75
56	Coast Guard	69
96	Clark (Mass.) ⊠	89
53	MIT	65
74	Fitchburg St. ⊠	63
58	Springfield	70
60	Coast Guard ⊠	59
74	Tufts	89
64	WPI ⊠	67
71	MIT ⊠	52
71	Clark (Mass.)	75
72	Babson ⊠	82
69	Springfield ⊠	71
57	WPI	73
73	Roger Williams ⊠	83
61	Springfield	54
60	Coast Guard †	62

Nickname: Lyons
Colors: Royal & White
Arena: Emerson Gymnasium
   Capacity: 1,000; Year Built: 1991
AD: Chad Yowell
SID: Scott Dietz

WHEELING JESUIT
Wheeling, WV 26003-6295 II

Coach: Jay DeFruscio, Ursinus 1982

2006-07 RESULTS (18-10)
93	Pitt.-Johnstown	88
63	Dist. Columbia †	66
113	Ohio-Eastern †	40
101	West Liberty St.	82
73	Indiana (Pa.) ⊠	53
65	California (Pa.)	88
104	Mansfield ⊠	81
73	Pitt.-Johnstown ⊠	71
106	Ohio-Eastern ⊠	53
97	Salem Int'l	72
95	Fairmont St. ⊠	68
101	Ohio Valley ⊠	83
99	Shepherd	85
91	West Va. Wesleyan	74
65	Alderson-Broaddus ⊠	72
86	West Liberty St.	95
93	Glenville St.	78
106	Ohio Valley	77
74	Bluefield St. ⊠	65
80	Concord	83
84	West Virginia St.	87
76	Fairmont St.	81
76	Davis & Elkins ⊠	68
75	Charleston (W.V.)	69
85	Shepherd ⊠	58
93	West Liberty St. ⊠	100
77	Salem Int'l ⊠	81
69	Bluefield St. †	71

Nickname: Cardinals
Colors: Red & Gold
Arena: Alma McDonough Center
   Capacity: 2,200; Year Built: 1990
AD: Jay De Fruscio
SID: Chris Kreger

WHITMAN
Walla Walla, WA 99362 III

Coach: Skip Molitor, Gonzaga 1974

2006-07 RESULTS (9-16)
71	Corban	85
69	Lewis & Clark ⊠	72
46	Pacific (Ore.) ⊠	65
77	Eastern Ore.	86
63	San Fran. St. ⊠	67
85	Warner Pacific ⊠	92
71	Biola ⊠	69
79	West Coast Chrst.	75
62	La Sierra	59
149	Redlands	153
63	George Fox	77
90	Linfield	88
101	Walla Walla ⊠	63
96	Pacific Lutheran ⊠	100
88	Puget Sound ⊠	102
59	Whitworth	62
80	Willamette	89
84	Lewis & Clark	103
69	Pacific (Ore.)	83
69	George Fox ⊠	59
60	Linfield ⊠	57
70	Pacific Lutheran	71
106	Puget Sound	99
72	Whitworth ⊠	84
81	Willamette ⊠	70

Nickname: Missionaries
Colors: Blue & Gold
Arena: Sherwood Center
   Capacity: 2,000; Year Built: 1968
AD: Dean Snider
SID: Dave Holden

WHITTIER
Whittier, CA 90608-0634 III

Coach: Rock Carter, Whittier 1989

2006-07 RESULTS (9-16)
60	Chapman	57
72	Whitworth †	81
78	La Sierra ⊠	62
100	LIFE Pacific †	64
62	Chapman †	94
88	Cal St. East Bay †	71
84	West Coast Baptist ⊠	77
83	La Sierra ⊠	75
88	Puget Sound ⊠	106
61	Anderson (Ind.) ⊠	75
65	Chapman ⊠	66
49	Cal Lutheran	64
63	La Verne	67
96	Caltech ⊠	41
71	Pomona-Pitzer	79
75	Claremont-M-S ⊠	65
122	Redlands ⊠	132
60	Occidental	82
67	Cal Lutheran ⊠	76
63	La Verne ⊠	67
71	Caltech	38
68	Pomona-Pitzer ⊠	80
38	Claremont-M-S	64
129	Redlands ⊠	136
61	Occidental ⊠	63

Nickname: Poets
Colors: Purple & Gold
Arena: Graham Athletics Center
   Capacity: 2,200; Year Built: 1979
AD: Robert Coleman
SID: Mike Kennett

WHITWORTH
Spokane, WA 99251-2501 III

Coach: Jim Hayford, Azusa Pacific 1989

2006-07 RESULTS (24-4)
95	Eastern †	67
70	Wheaton (Ill.)	67

68	Bethany Lutheran †	56
68	Cal Lutheran †	55
81	Whittier †	72
83	Caltech †	30
95	Walla Walla ⊠	75
62	Pacific (Ore.) ⊠	57
82	Lewis & Clark ⊠	73
76	UC Santa Cruz	52
89	UC Santa Cruz	44
77	Linfield	64
83	George Fox	53
72	Puget Sound ⊠	77
80	Pacific Lutheran ⊠	56
62	Whitman ⊠	59
79	Willamette	66
77	Pacific (Ore.)	69
60	Lewis & Clark	66
71	Linfield ⊠	58
90	George Fox ⊠	64
90	Puget Sound	95
65	Pacific Lutheran	63
84	Whitman	72
81	Willamette ⊠	66
69	Lewis & Clark ⊠	62
62	DePauw †	59
61	Washington-St. Louis	63

Nickname: Pirates
Colors: Crimson & Black
Arena: Whitworth Field House
  Capacity: 1,600; Year Built: 1960
AD: Scott McQuilkin
SID: Steve Flegel

WICHITA ST.
Wichita, KS 67260 I

Coach: Mark Turgeon, Kansas 1987

2006-07 RESULTS (17-14)

71	Rockhurst ⊠	47
76	Chicago St. ⊠	64
72	George Mason	66
57	LSU	53
85	UMKC ⊠	55
64	Syracuse	61
83	Wyoming †	69
102	Md.-East. Shore ⊠	46
74	Kennesaw St. ⊠	65
68	New Mexico †	71
56	Southern California †	60
59	UNI ⊠	63
68	Southern Ill.	73
84	Bradley ⊠	63
87	Missouri St.	95
63	Indiana St.	68
69	Evansville ⊠	56
62	Creighton ⊠	59
75	Illinois St.	83
63	Bradley	78
82	Drake ⊠	77
66	Evansville	61
67	UNI	61
46	Southern Ill. ⊠	54
61	Indiana St. ⊠	45
69	Illinois St. ⊠	64
58	Drake	62
58	Appalachian St. ⊠	60
65	Missouri St. ⊠	71
54	Creighton	71
64	Missouri St. †	67

Nickname: Shockers
Colors: Yellow & Black
Arena: Charles Koch Arena
  Capacity: 10,478; Year Built: 2003
AD: Jim Schaus
SID: Larry Rankin

WIDENER
Chester, PA 19013-5792 III

Coach: Chris Carideo, Widener 1996

2006-07 RESULTS (15-13)

91	Lincoln (Pa.) †	98
44	Frank. & Marsh.	71

81	Chestnut Hill ⊠	58
81	King's (Pa.)	94
78	Moravian	65
69	Juniata	59
87	Immaculata	78
71	Phila. Biblical ⊠	75
61	Cabrini	46
75	Maryland Bible ⊠	46
70	Eastern ⊠	76
68	Rutgers-Camden ⊠	55
57	Albright ⊠	55
78	Susquehanna ⊠	63
71	Lebanon Valley ⊠	58
61	Messiah ⊠	74
70	Elizabethtown ⊠	65
61	Susquehanna	74
78	Lebanon Valley	87
62	Juniata ⊠	71
66	Albright	70
69	Elizabethtown ⊠	53
102	Moravian ⊠	108
59	Messiah	75
91	Messiah	84
63	Juniata	60
76	King's (Pa.)	63
70	Amherst	87

Nickname: Pride
Colors: Blue & Gold
Arena: Schwartz Center
  Capacity: 1,500; Year Built: 1971
AD: Jack Shafer
SID: Derek Crudele

WILKES
Wilkes-Barre, PA 18766 III

Coach: Jerry Rickrode, Skidmore 1985

2006-07 RESULTS (12-11)

78	Immaculata ⊠	72
65	Lycoming ⊠	48
66	Delaware Valley	77
87	Susquehanna	86
65	Clarkson ⊠	75
88	Penn St.-Harrisburg	53
83	Kean ⊠	73
72	Ursinus †	52
75	Misericordia †	73
100	Marywood ⊠	63
83	Baptist Bible (Pa.) ⊠	67
55	King's (Pa.)	76
58	DeSales ⊠	68
47	Scranton	70
49	Drew	58
63	FDU-Florham	70
51	DeSales	75
52	Lycoming	78
62	Delaware Valley ⊠	53
65	Scranton ⊠	81
78	FDU-Florham	89
66	King's (Pa.) ⊠	58
62	Drew ⊠	50

Nickname: Colonels
Colors: Blue & Gold
Arena: Arnaud Marts Sports Center
  Capacity: 3,500; Year Built: 1988
AD: Addy Malatesta
SID: John Seitzinger

WILLAMETTE
Salem, OR 97301-3931 III

Coach: Gordie James, Cal Poly Pomona 1964

2006-07 RESULTS (10-15)

77	Albertson	116
84	Eastern Ore. †	81
50	Claremont-M-S	60
68	Pomona-Pitzer †	80
137	Puget Sound	140
84	Pacific Lutheran	90
96	Concordia (Ore.) ⊠	93
66	Southern Ore. ⊠	51
57	Western Ore.	94

85	Cal Lutheran	72
64	Bethany (Kan.) †	79
66	Pacific (Ore.) ⊠	62
66	Lewis & Clark ⊠	76
52	George Fox	72
80	Linfield ⊠	68
66	Whitworth ⊠	79
89	Whitman ⊠	80
119	Puget Sound ⊠	108
90	Pacific Lutheran ⊠	67
60	Pacific (Ore.)	69
55	Lewis & Clark	60
84	George Fox ⊠	79
80	Linfield	83
66	Whitworth	81
70	Whitman	81

Nickname: Bearcats
Colors: Cardinal & Old Gold
Arena: Cone Fieldhouse
  Capacity: 2,600; Year Built: 1974
AD: Mark Majeski
SID: Cliff Voliva

WILLIAM & MARY
Williamsburg, VA 23187 I

Coach: Tony Shaver, North Carolina 1976

2006-07 RESULTS (15-15)

60	Kansas St.	70
77	Wagner ⊠	53
57	Holy Cross	66
63	Navy	79
59	Jacksonville St. ⊠	56
73	Cornell ⊠	68
60	Towson ⊠	73
61	North Fla. ⊠	44
70	UMBC ⊠	58
72	Hampton ⊠	67
61	Richmond ⊠	53
67	George Mason	63
60	Northeastern ⊠	57
57	Georgia St.	43
77	VCU ⊠	88
62	Delaware	77
63	George Mason ⊠	76
69	Hofstra	77
44	Old Dominion	59
81	Georgia St. ⊠	65
68	VCU	90
65	James Madison ⊠	62
61	UNC Wilmington ⊠	67
71	James Madison	56
61	UNC Wilmington	55
60	Drexel ⊠	47
45	Fairfield	61
57	Drexel	64
57	Old Dominion ⊠	62
68	Georgia St. †	70

Nickname: Tribe
Colors: Green, Gold & Silver
Arena: Kaplan Arena at William and Mary Hall
  Capacity: 8,600; Year Built: 1970
AD: Edward C. Driscoll Jr.
SID: Kris Sears

WM. PATERSON
Wayne, NJ 07470-2152 III

Coach: Jose Rebimbas, Seton Hall 1990

2006-07 RESULTS (15-10)

84	Wentworth Inst. †	69
55	Drew	37
78	City Tech ⊠	52
56	York (N.Y.)	65
63	Lehman	43
77	John Jay	45
66	Montclair St. ⊠	50
82	Rutgers-Camden	35
70	FDU-Florham	57
65	Seton Hall	83
63	CCNY	51

79	Tufts ⊠	57
66	Manhattanville	67
42	New Jersey City	56
69	Ramapo ⊠	72
70	Baruch ⊠	51
62	Rutgers-Newark ⊠	69
68	Rowan ⊠	66
53	TCNJ	56
77	Kean ⊠	73
48	Montclair St.	45
48	Richard Stockton	66
60	New Jersey City ⊠	71
64	Ramapo	67
66	Rutgers-Newark ⊠	61

Nickname: Pioneers
Colors: Orange & Black
Arena: Rec Center
  Capacity: 4,000; Year Built: 1984
AD: Sabrina Grant
SID: Brian Falzarano

WILLIAMS
Williamstown, MA 01267 III

Coach: David Paulsen, Williams 1987

2006-07 RESULTS (16-12)

81	Southern Vt. ⊠	79
70	Western New Eng. ⊠	55
69	Wesleyan (Conn.) ⊠	80
57	Rensselaer ⊠	64
56	Framingham St.	61
69	Montclair St. †	79
96	Skidmore	65
73	Union (N.Y.)	63
67	Springfield	65
74	Caltech	54
65	Occidental	78
45	Amherst ⊠	64
69	Bowdoin ⊠	64
62	Colby ⊠	55
60	Lasell	86
62	Trinity (Conn.)	65
51	Amherst	72
63	Hamilton ⊠	61
86	Middlebury	79
85	Keene St.	92
67	Bates ⊠	54
65	Tufts ⊠	82
61	Connecticut Col.	55
80	Wesleyan (Conn.)	65
84	Tufts ⊠	72
91	Trinity (Conn.) †	89
70	Amherst	69
66	Brockport St. †	74

Nickname: Ephs
Colors: Purple
Arena: Chandler Gymnasium
  Capacity: 1,564; Year Built: 1988
AD: Lisa M. Melendy
SID: Dick Quinn

WILMINGTON (DEL.)
New Castle, DE 19720 I

Coach: Kevin Welch, Bucknell 2004

2006-07 RESULTS (1-26)

57	West Chester ⊠	79
74	Millersville	113
61	Bloomsburg †	84
84	Kutztown ⊠	90
63	NYIT ⊠	81
53	Phila. Sciences ⊠	66
49	Philadelphia U.	78
77	Dominican (N.Y.) ⊠	85
76	Caldwell	83
76	Barry †	102
68	Lynn	115
62	Felician	63
62	Post ⊠	63
85	Nyack	106
80	Holy Family	89
85	Bloomfield	96
60	Caldwell ⊠	68

79	Goldey-Beacom ⊠	85
57	Phila. Sciences	68
69	Dominican (N.Y.)	87
60	Philadelphia U.	65
80	Felician	92
79	Bloomfield ⊠	80
88	Post	100
45	Holy Family ⊠	73
49	Goldey-Beacom ⊠	54
76	Nyack ⊠	70

Nickname: Wildcats
Colors: Forest Green & White
Arena: Pratt Center
   Capacity: 500; Year Built: 1986
AD: Frank Aiello
SID: Erin T. Harvey

WILMINGTON (OHIO)
Wilmington, OH 45177.................III

Coach: Scott Reule, Wilmington (Ohio) 2001

2006-07 RESULTS (13-13)

67	Anderson (Ind.) †	69
75	Defiance	65
75	UC Clermont ⊠	61
77	Thomas More	57
78	Heidelberg ⊠	90
76	Capital	83
75	Marietta	64
76	Oberlin ⊠	65
85	John Carroll ⊠	72
63	Ohio Wesleyan	60
60	Mt. St. Joseph	73
67	Otterbein	76
80	Mount Union	60
62	Ohio Northern ⊠	63
95	Baldwin-Wallace	88
65	Muskingum ⊠	55
89	Heidelberg	71
65	Capital ⊠	73
67	Marietta ⊠	64
67	Muskingum	71
75	Baldwin-Wallace ⊠	68
53	Ohio Northern	75
73	Mount Union ⊠	96
49	Otterbein ⊠	52
78	John Carroll	94
88	John Carroll	102

Nickname: Quakers
Colors: Green & White
Arena: Hermann Court
   Capacity: 3,000; Year Built: 1966
AD: Terry A. Rupert
SID: Jeff Hibbs

WINGATE
Wingate, NC 28174 II

Coach: Parker Laketa, Kansas St. 1986

2006-07 RESULTS (25-9)

103	North Greenville	82
61	Lander ⊠	74
87	St. Andrews ⊠	67
83	Anderson (S.C.) ⊠	61
82	Seton Hill ⊠	76
90	S.C. Upstate ⊠	69
92	Anderson (S.C.)	71
74	Queens (N.C.)	68
78	Winona St. †	91
67	Drury †	81
79	Newberry	89
77	Lincoln Memorial	71
90	Catawba ⊠	81
87	Carson-Newman ⊠	74
84	Presbyterian	70
75	Mars Hill	70
82	Tusculum	72
67	Lenoir-Rhyne	79
89	Lincoln Memorial ⊠	86
105	Catawba	108
103	North Greenville ⊠	77
65	Tusculum ⊠	58

77	Presbyterian	88
96	Mars Hill	79
84	Newberry ⊠	87
81	Lenoir-Rhyne ⊠	67
122	Carson-Newman ⊠	116
66	Tusculum ⊠	56
73	Presbyterian †	64
97	Catawba †	82
72	Armstrong Atlantic †	68
79	Augusta ⊠	78
73	Virginia Union †	56
73	Cal St. San B'dino †	100

Nickname: Bulldogs
Colors: Navy Blue & Old Gold
Arena: Cuddy Arena
   Capacity: 2,300; Year Built: 1986
AD: Steve Poston
SID: David Sherwood

WINONA ST.
Winona, MN 55987-5838.................II

Coach: Mike Leaf, St. Mary's (Minn.) 1983

2006-07 RESULTS (35-1)

88	Bethany Lutheran ⊠	79
90	St. Joseph's (Ind.) ⊠	68
98	St. Mary's (Minn.) ⊠	54
90	Northern St. ⊠	62
77	Mary ⊠	57
119	North Central (Minn. ⊠	38
80	Upper Iowa	62
84	Minn. Duluth	74
91	Wingate †	78
81	Hillsdale †	67
92	Wis.-Parkside ⊠	76
107	Wayne St. (Neb.)	74
76	Southwest Minn. St.	71
86	Concordia-St. Paul ⊠	83
69	Minn. St. Moorhead ⊠	66
82	Bemidji St.	37
93	Minn.-Crookston	79
76	Northern St.	66
80	Mary	63
79	Clarke ⊠	52
81	Upper Iowa ⊠	70
68	Southwest Minn. St. ⊠	59
80	Wayne St. (Neb.) ⊠	72
89	Minn. St. Moorhead	56
87	Concordia-St. Paul	68
104	Minn.-Crookston ⊠	66
76	Bemidji St. ⊠	60
94	Upper Iowa	63
87	Concordia-St. Paul ⊠	71
80	Southwest Minn. St. ⊠	70
100	St. Cloud St. ⊠	73
81	Neb.-Kearney ⊠	70
89	Minn. St. Mankato ⊠	76
64	Bentley †	51
90	Central Mo. †	85
75	Barton †	77

Nickname: Warriors
Colors: Purple & White
Arena: McCown Gymnasium
   Capacity: 3,500; Year Built: 1973
AD: Larry Holstad
SID: Michael Herzberg

WINSTON-SALEM
Winston-Salem, NC 27110 II

Coach: Bobby Collins, Eastern Ky. 1991

2006-07 RESULTS (5-24)

63	Fresno St.	85
41	UC Irvine †	53
58	South Ala. †	76
67	Anderson (S.C.) ⊠	44
62	Auburn	95
87	Georgia St.	94
56	Coppin St.	81
41	Ga. Southern	70
46	Lipscomb	62
45	Notre Dame	90

49	Ga. Southern ⊠	59
43	South Fla. ⊠	63
67	Akron	79
32	Georgetown	76
43	Kansas	94
53	UAB	84
59	Towson	80
46	Georgia Tech	97
50	Morgan St.	53
77	Ferrum	56
81	Norfolk St.	71
63	North Dakota St. ⊠	87
56	Bethune-Cookman	48
68	Florida A&M	83
71	Wake Forest	87
77	Columbia Union ⊠	61
63	Alabama A&M	79
68	North Dakota St. ⊠	83
82	South Carolina St.	89

Nickname: Rams
Colors: Scarlet & White
Arena: C.E. Gaines Center
   Capacity: 3,100; Year Built: 1978
AD: Percy Caldwell
SID: Chris Zona

WINTHROP
Rock Hill, SC 29733 I

Coach: Gregg Marshall, Randolph-Macon 1985

2006-07 RESULTS (29-5)

89	North Greenville ⊠	46
57	Iona †	38
66	North Carolina †	73
74	Mississippi St.	63
60	Maryland	71
90	Virginia Intermont ⊠	46
76	Presbyterian ⊠	51
72	Northern Ill.	62
79	Wisconsin	82
80	Limestone ⊠	46
74	Mt. St. Mary's ⊠	59
69	East Caro.	50
71	Old Dominion	65
51	Texas A&M	71
108	VMI ⊠	76
75	Charleston So.	52
68	Liberty	40
61	UNC Asheville ⊠	42
62	Radford	59
64	High Point	63
65	Coastal Caro. ⊠	63
109	VMI	96
88	UNC Asheville	69
80	Liberty ⊠	76
77	Radford ⊠	58
78	Charleston So. ⊠	54
77	Missouri St.	66
72	High Point ⊠	60
83	Coastal Caro.	69
72	Charleston So. ⊠	42
79	UNC Asheville †	60
84	VMI ⊠	81
74	Notre Dame †	64
61	Oregon †	75

Nickname: Eagles
Colors: Garnet & Gold
Arena: Winthrop Coliseum
   Capacity: 6,100; Year Built: 1982
AD: Thomas N. Hickman
SID: Jack Frost

WISCONSIN
Madison, WI 53711 I

Coach: Bo Ryan, Wilkes 1969

2006-07 RESULTS (30-6)

72	Mercer ⊠	48
79	Green Bay ⊠	62
92	Southern U. ⊠	39
64	Delaware St. ⊠	52
64	Missouri St. †	66

77	Auburn †	63
81	Florida St. ⊠	66
79	Florida Int'l ⊠	63
82	Winthrop ⊠	79
70	Marquette	66
68	Milwaukee ⊠	49
89	Pittsburgh ⊠	75
83	Pacific ⊠	47
98	Gardner-Webb ⊠	40
64	Georgia	54
68	Minnesota ⊠	45
72	Ohio St. ⊠	69
56	Northwestern	50
69	Purdue ⊠	64
71	Illinois	64
71	Michigan ⊠	58
57	Iowa	46
66	Indiana	71
69	Northwestern ⊠	52
71	Penn St.	58
74	Iowa ⊠	62
75	Minnesota	62
75	Penn St. ⊠	49
55	Michigan St.	64
48	Ohio St.	49
52	Michigan St. ⊠	50
70	Michigan St. †	57
53	Illinois †	41
49	Ohio St. †	66
76	A&M-Corpus Christi †	63
68	UNLV †	74

Nickname: Badgers
Colors: Cardinal & White
Arena: Kohl Center
   Capacity: 17,142; Year Built: 1998
AD: Barry Alvarez
SID: Brian Lucas

WIS. LUTHERAN
Milwaukee, WI 53226 III

Coach: Skip Noon, Martin Luther 1986

2006-07 RESULTS (15-11)

62	Coe	93
94	Cornell College	87
77	Rockford ⊠	68
75	Lawrence †	89
90	Voorhees †	95
91	Dominican (Ill.)	85
91	Aurora	100
102	Northland Bapt. ⊠	53
90	Concordia (Ill.)	83
94	Concordia (Wis.) ⊠	90
65	Occidental	92
117	Caltech	57
71	Benedictine (Ill.) ⊠	72
63	Lakeland	80
63	Marian (Wis.) ⊠	81
105	Maranatha Baptist	48
62	Dominican (Ill.) ⊠	66
90	Edgewood	96
87	Aurora ⊠	82
98	Concordia (Ill.) ⊠	74
83	Rockford	53
100	Concordia (Wis.)	76
84	Benedictine (Ill.)	62
87	Lakeland ⊠	81
89	Maranatha Baptist ⊠	60
50	Lakeland ⊠	51

Nickname: Warriors
Colors: Forest Green & White
Arena: The REX
   Capacity: 2,500; Year Built: 1992
AD: Edward Noon
SID: Adam Heinzen

WIS.-EAU CLAIRE
Eau Claire, WI 54702-4004............. III

Coach: Terry Gibbons, Wis.-Oshkosh 1983

2006-07 RESULTS (10-16)
69	Alma †	61
59	Manchester	68
78	St. Mary's (Minn.)	65
42	Wis.-Stout	65
44	Wis.-La Crosse	60
63	Wis.-River Falls ⊠	62
75	Northland	47
72	St. Scholastica ⊠	60
90	Finlandia	57
73	Marian (Wis.)	54
70	Wartburg ⊠	75
61	Wis.-Whitewater ⊠	81
55	Wis.-Oshkosh	80
43	Wis.-Stevens Point ⊠	77
47	Wis.-Platteville ⊠	53
72	Wis.-Superior	65
65	Wis.-La Crosse ⊠	47
69	Wis.-Stout ⊠	80
58	Wis.-Platteville	61
61	Wis.-Stevens Point	90
75	Finlandia ⊠	69
66	Wis.-River Falls	68
54	Wis.-Oshkosh ⊠	77
56	Wis.-Superior ⊠	58
72	Wis.-Whitewater	73
55	Wis.-Stevens Point	89

Nickname: Blugolds
Colors: Navy Blue & Old Gold
Arena: W.L. Zorn Arena
   Capacity: 2,450; Year Built: 1952
AD: Scott Kilgallon
SID: Tim Petermann

GREEN BAY
Green Bay, WI 54311-7001 I

Coach: Tod Kowalczyk, Minn.-Duluth 1989

2006-07 RESULTS (18-15)
57	Oakland	74
62	Wisconsin	79
76	Northern Mich. ⊠	59
61	Eastern Ill.	63
73	North Dakota St.	85
76	Fairleigh Dickinson	67
52	Loyola (Ill.)	71
89	Central Mich. ⊠	71
92	Chicago St. ⊠	81
80	South Dakota St. ⊠	48
64	Michigan St.	76
90	Jacksonville ⊠	67
62	Michigan Tech ⊠	50
65	Bowling Green ⊠	62
42	Detroit ⊠	60
65	Cleveland St. ⊠	53
59	Youngstown St.	49
67	Wright St.	78
59	Butler	80
77	Ill.-Chicago ⊠	57
73	Milwaukee	67
54	Wright St. ⊠	65
72	Detroit	76
79	Cleveland St.	66
55	Youngstown St. ⊠	46
52	Loyola (Ill.) ⊠	69
65	Ill.-Chicago	55
82	Northern Ill.	76
58	Butler ⊠	68
73	Milwaukee ⊠	74
78	Cleveland St. ⊠	59
72	Youngstown St. †	55
51	Wright St.	67

Nickname: Phoenix
Colors: Green, White & Red
Arena: Resch Center
   Capacity: 9,729; Year Built: 2002
AD: Ken Bothof
SID: Nick Brilowski

WIS.-LA CROSSE
La Crosse, WI 54601 III

Coach: Ken Koelbl, Viterbo 1990

2006-07 RESULTS (19-8)
74	Loras	82
71	Viterbo ⊠	45
91	Lakeland ⊠	81
78	Ripon ⊠	62
57	Wis.-Whitewater	53
60	Wis.-Eau Claire ⊠	44
69	Wis.-Platteville	56
64	Wis.-Stevens Point	67
64	Carleton	75
62	St. Thomas (Minn.)	54
87	Calvin †	77
70	Ohio Northern †	73
57	Wis.-Stout	42
48	Wis.-Oshkosh ⊠	47
77	Wis.-Superior	65
72	Wis.-River Falls	81
47	Wis.-Eau Claire	65
67	Wis.-Whitewater ⊠	49
90	Wis.-Superior ⊠	67
73	Wis.-Oshkosh	62
65	Wis.-Stevens Point ⊠	68
54	Wis.-Platteville ⊠	32
80	Wis.-River Falls ⊠	63
69	Wis.-Stout	58
63	Wis.-Stout ⊠	58
66	Wis.-Oshkosh ⊠	61
68	Wis.-Stevens Point	83

Nickname: Eagles
Colors: Maroon & Gray
Arena: Mitchell Hall
   Capacity: 2,880; Year Built: 1964
AD: Joe Baker
SID: David Johnson

MILWAUKEE
Milwaukee, WI 53211 I

Coach: Rob Jeter, Wis.-Platteville 1991

2006-07 RESULTS (9-22)
72	Radford ⊠	60
54	Washington St. ⊠	74
60	UAB ⊠	75
59	Michigan	66
58	UNI	69
75	South Dakota St. ⊠	58
68	Tennessee Tech ⊠	78
61	Central Mich.	76
70	Oakland	76
60	Missouri St.	79
65	Youngstown St. ⊠	68
49	Wisconsin	68
73	Sam Houston St.	89
75	Wyoming ⊠	73
50	Butler ⊠	55
65	Detroit ⊠	64
74	Loyola (Ill.)	87
60	Cleveland St.	48
63	Youngstown St.	81
76	Ill.-Chicago ⊠	65
73	Wright St. ⊠	69
84	Detroit	91
67	Green Bay	73
57	Cleveland St. ⊠	56
47	Butler	66
50	Wright St.	76
56	Loyola (Ill.) ⊠	66
76	Drake	84
59	Ill.-Chicago	72
74	Green Bay	73
77	Ill.-Chicago	83

Nickname: Panthers
Colors: Black & Gold
Arena: Klotsche Center
   Capacity: 5,000; Year Built: 1977
AD: Bud K. Haidet
SID: Kevin O'Connor

WIS.-OSHKOSH
Oshkosh, WI 54901-8683 III

Coach: Ted Van Dellen, Wis.-Oshkosh 1978

2006-07 RESULTS (21-6)
82	Edgewood	56
76	Wis.-Stevens Point ⊠	89
76	Wis.-Superior ⊠	44
52	Elmhurst	55
64	Wis.-Stout	50
64	St. Norbert ⊠	52
88	Lawrence ⊠	75
78	Carroll (Wis.) ⊠	59
80	Tri-State †	50
75	Cardinal Stritch †	64
78	Mt. Mercy †	67
79	Wis.-Platteville ⊠	58
123	Grinnell ⊠	105
80	Wis.-Eau Claire ⊠	55
47	Wis.-La Crosse	48
69	Wis.-River Falls	66
65	Wis.-Whitewater ⊠	60
79	Wis.-Superior	53
72	Wis.-Stevens Point	55
90	Wis.-River Falls ⊠	67
62	Wis.-La Crosse ⊠	73
79	Wis.-Stout ⊠	61
77	Wis.-Eau Claire	54
71	Wis.-Whitewater	88
67	Wis.-Platteville	51
83	Wis.-River Falls ⊠	65
61	Wis.-La Crosse	66

Nickname: Titans
Colors: Black, Gold & White
Arena: Kolf Sports Center
   Capacity: 5,800; Year Built: 1971
AD: Allen F. Ackerman
SID: Kennan Timm

WIS.-PARKSIDE
Kenosha, WI 53141-2000 II

Coach: Luke Reigel, Wis.-Platteville 1997

2006-07 RESULTS (19-13)
79	S.C.-Aiken †	63
86	South Dakota †	75
73	Shippensburg †	66
69	Michigan Tech	80
82	Lake Superior St. †	65
92	Central St. (Ohio) ⊠	78
60	Rockhurst ⊠	54
75	Drury ⊠	84
62	SIU Edwardsville	66
72	Quincy	82
81	Saginaw Valley ⊠	64
94	Illinois Tech ⊠	59
111	Grace (Ind.) ⊠	60
76	Winona St.	92
80	Northern Ky. ⊠	73
93	Bellarmine ⊠	76
97	Cardinal Stritch ⊠	78
84	Lewis ⊠	62
92	Mo.-Rolla	97
74	Mo.-St. Louis	77
73	Ky. Wesleyan ⊠	72
80	Southern Ind. ⊠	75
61	St. Joseph's (Ind.)	63
72	Indianapolis	67
63	Bellarmine	71
66	Northern Ky.	70
89	Indianapolis ⊠	80
100	St. Joseph's (Ind.) ⊠	70
70	Lewis	69
73	Ky. Wesleyan	75
75	Drury †	88
60	Findlay	74

Nickname: Rangers
Colors: Green, White & Black
Arena: DeSimone Gymnasium
   Capacity: 2,120; Year Built: 1970
AD: David C. Williams
SID: Steve Kratochvil

WIS.-PLATTEVILLE
Platteville, WI 53818-3099 III

Coach: Paul Combs, Ripon 1993

2006-07 RESULTS (13-12)
75	Viterbo ⊠	60
78	Buena Vista ⊠	65
66	Dubuque †	61
81	Loras †	73
58	Wis.-Stout ⊠	52
56	Wis.-La Crosse ⊠	69
70	Wis.-River Falls	66
74	Robert Morris-S'fiel	82
64	Richard Stockton †	51
64	Randolph-Macon	68
58	Wis.-Oshkosh	79
67	Wis.-Superior	69
66	Wis.-Whitewater	63
53	Wis.-Eau Claire	47
68	Wis.-Stevens Point ⊠	73
56	Wis.-Stout	38
71	Clarke	74
61	Wis.-Eau Claire ⊠	58
52	Wis.-Whitewater ⊠	67
65	Wis.-River Falls ⊠	61
32	Wis.-La Crosse	54
72	Wis.-Superior	58
58	Wis.-Stevens Point	69
51	Wis.-Oshkosh ⊠	67
57	Wis.-Whitewater	58

Nickname: Pioneers
Colors: Blue & Orange
Arena: Williams Fieldhouse
   Capacity: 2,300; Year Built: 1962
AD: Mark Molesworth
SID: Paul Erickson

WIS.-RIVER FALLS
River Falls, WI 54022........................ III

Coach: Jeff Berkhof, Wis.-River Falls 1994

2006-07 RESULTS (10-16)
99	William Penn †	91
77	Bethel (Minn.)	107
73	Macalester ⊠	87
90	Wis.-Superior	65
73	Wis.-Stevens Point ⊠	81
62	Wis.-Eau Claire	63
66	Wis.-Platteville ⊠	70
96	Bethany Lutheran ⊠	74
97	Crown (Minn.)	57
72	Concordia-St. Paul	105
110	North Cent. (Minn.) ⊠	66
84	St. Thomas (Minn.) ⊠	87
93	Finlandia	54
86	Wis.-Whitewater	91
76	Wis.-Stout ⊠	62
66	Wis.-Oshkosh ⊠	90
81	Wis.-La Crosse ⊠	72
61	Wis.-Stevens Point	106
76	Wis.-Superior ⊠	68
67	Wis.-Oshkosh	90
78	Wis.-Stout	84
61	Wis.-Platteville	65
68	Wis.-Eau Claire ⊠	66
72	Wis.-Whitewater ⊠	93
63	Wis.-La Crosse	80
65	Wis.-Oshkosh	83

Nickname: Falcons
Colors: Red & White
Arena: Karges Center
   Capacity: 2,000; Year Built: 1958
AD: Richard H. Bowen
SID: Jim Thies

WIS.-STEVENS POINT
Stevens Point, WI 54481.................III

Coach: Bob Semling, Wis.-Eau Claire 1981

2006-07 RESULTS (26-3)

93	Carroll (Wis.)	75
70	Lawrence	67
90	Ripon ⊠	76
89	Wis.-Oshkosh	76
81	Wis.-River Falls	73
75	Wis.-Whitewater	73
67	Wis.-La Crosse ⊠	64
69	Edgewood ⊠	47
75	Viterbo	49
92	Northern Mich.	101
71	Augustana (Ill.) ⊠	68
101	Wis.-Superior ⊠	45
80	Wis.-Stout	50
97	Lakeland ⊠	59
77	Wis.-Eau Claire	43
73	Wis.-Platteville	68
106	Wis.-River Falls ⊠	61
55	Wis.-Oshkosh ⊠	72
90	Wis.-Eau Claire ⊠	61
68	Wis.-La Crosse	65
83	Wis.-Whitewater ⊠	80
73	Wis.-Stout ⊠	72
69	Wis.-Platteville ⊠	58
103	Wis.-Superior	64
89	Wis.-Eau Claire	55
94	Wis.-Whitewater ⊠	69
83	Wis.-La Crosse ⊠	68
93	St. John's (Minn.) ⊠	76
66	Washington-St. Louis ⊠	78

Nickname: Pointers
Colors: Purple & Gold
Arena: Quandt Fieldhouse
    Capacity: 3,281; Year Built: 1969
AD: Frank O'Brien
SID: Jim Strick

WIS.-STOUT
Menomonie, WI 54751-0790 III

Coach: Ed Andrist, Wis.-Stout 1976

2006-07 RESULTS (12-13)

67	Bemidji St.	49
78	Northland	51
65	Wis.-Eau Claire ⊠	42
52	Wis.-Platteville	58
76	Wis.-Superior ⊠	61
50	Wis.-Oshkosh ⊠	64
73	Finlandia	58
71	Northern Mich.	95
57	Buena Vista †	56
79	SUNYIT †	62
59	Viterbo	55
76	Jamestown ⊠	68
42	Wis.-La Crosse	57
50	Wis.-Stevens Point ⊠	80
62	Wis.-River Falls	76
66	Wis.-Whitewater	79
38	Wis.-Platteville ⊠	56
80	Wis.-Eau Claire	69
59	Wis.-Whitewater ⊠	65
84	Wis.-River Falls ⊠	78
61	Wis.-Oshkosh	79
89	Wis.-Superior	74
72	Wis.-Stevens Point	73
58	Wis.-La Crosse ⊠	69
58	Wis.-La Crosse	63

Nickname: Blue Devils
Colors: Navy & White
Arena: Johnson Fieldhouse
    Capacity: 1,800; Year Built: 1965
AD: Steve Terry
SID: Layne Pitt

WIS.-SUPERIOR
Superior, WI 54880-4500 III

Coach: David Buchanan, Wis.-La Crosse 1995

2006-07 RESULTS (7-18)

86	Finlandia ⊠	88
72	St. Scholastica ⊠	79
65	Northland ⊠	72
65	Wis.-River Falls ⊠	90
70	St. Scholastica	67
44	Wis.-Oshkosh ⊠	76
61	Wis.-Stout	76
71	Wis.-Whitewater ⊠	82
72	Crown (Minn.)	64
75	Bemidji St.	69
45	Wis.-Stevens Point	101
69	Wis.-Platteville	67
83	Finlandia ⊠	71
65	Wis.-La Crosse ⊠	77
65	Wis.-Eau Claire ⊠	72
53	Wis.-Oshkosh ⊠	79
96	North Cent. (Minn.)	80
68	Wis.-River Falls	76
67	Wis.-La Crosse	90
74	Northland	79
56	Wis.-Whitewater	98
74	Wis.-Stout ⊠	89
58	Wis.-Platteville ⊠	72
58	Wis.-Eau Claire	56
64	Wis.-Stevens Point ⊠	103

Nickname: Yellowjackets
Colors: Gold, Black, & White
Arena: Gates Fieldhouse
    Capacity: 2,500; Year Built: 1966
AD: Steven E. Nelson
SID: Dan Laughlin

WIS.-WHITEWATER
Whitewater, WI 53190 III

Coach: Pat Miller, Wis.-Whitewater 1989

2006-07 RESULTS (18-9)

85	Martin Luther ⊠	61
68	Ill. Wesleyan ⊠	69
74	Marian (Wis.)	70
76	Beloit	51
53	Wis.-La Crosse ⊠	57
73	Wis.-Stevens Point	75
82	Wis.-Superior	71
126	Grinnell †	90
91	Elmhurst	98
93	Carroll (Wis.) ⊠	81
81	Wis.-Eau Claire	61
91	Wis.-River Falls ⊠	86
92	Maranatha Baptist ⊠	27
63	Wis.-Platteville ⊠	66
79	Wis.-Stout ⊠	66
60	Wis.-Oshkosh	65
95	Milwaukee Engr.	62
49	Wis.-La Crosse	67
65	Wis.-Stout	59
67	Wis.-Platteville	52
98	Wis.-Superior	56
80	Wis.-Stevens Point ⊠	83
93	Wis.-River Falls	72
88	Wis.-Oshkosh ⊠	71
73	Wis.-Eau Claire ⊠	72
58	Wis.-Platteville ⊠	57
69	Wis.-Stevens Point	94

Nickname: Warhawks
Colors: Purple & White
Arena: Williams Center
    Capacity: 3,000; Year Built: 1967
AD: Paul Plinske
SID: Tom Fick

WITTENBERG
Springfield, OH 45504.....................III

Coach: Bill L. Brown, Wittenberg 1973

2006-07 RESULTS (22-5)

57	Swarthmore †	46
68	Haverford †	53
73	Capital	68
66	Transylvania ⊠	59
100	Denison	85
66	Cedarville ⊠	61
65	Wooster ⊠	68
51	Ohio Northern	68
79	Otterbein	72
69	York (N.Y.)	62
78	Ind.-Southeast ⊠	47
72	Kenyon	67
71	Oberlin ⊠	41
71	Earlham	60
72	Hiram	50
48	Ohio Wesleyan	70
83	Allegheny ⊠	51
64	Wabash	51
87	Denison ⊠	65
87	Earlham ⊠	40
74	Wooster	71
71	Ohio Wesleyan ⊠	64
78	Hiram ⊠	41
82	Wabash ⊠	59
57	Allegheny	62
72	Hiram ⊠	49
52	Ohio Wesleyan †	57

Nickname: Tigers
Colors: Red & White
Arena: Health, PE & Rec Center
    Capacity: 3,000; Year Built: 1982
AD: Garnett Purnell
SID: Ryan Maurer

WOFFORD
Spartanburg, SC 29303-3663.........I

Coach: Mike Young, Emory & Henry 1986

2006-07 RESULTS (10-20)

88	North Carolina St.	92
74	Erskine ⊠	58
96	Union (N.Y.) ⊠	84
82	Jacksonville St.	80
91	Cincinnati	90
74	James Madison	78
54	UNC Greensboro	77
75	Western Caro. ⊠	81
49	Michigan	83
66	Clemson	90
76	Auburn	86
69	Elon	79
62	Charlotte	83
94	West Va. Wesleyan ⊠	60
71	Citadel ⊠	74
78	Ga. Southern	83
78	Davidson ⊠	83
65	Furman	68
66	Chattanooga	63
75	Col. of Charleston	77
74	Western Caro.	77
71	Elon ⊠	64
80	UNC Greensboro ⊠	75
52	Appalachian St.	72
61	Citadel	49
58	Col. of Charleston ⊠	71
73	Davidson	80
46	Ga. Southern ⊠	68
76	Furman ⊠	67
55	Chattanooga †	64

Nickname: Terriers
Colors: Old Gold & Black
Arena: Benjamin Johnson Arena
    Capacity: 3,500; Year Built: 1981
AD: Richard Johnson
SID: Steve Shutt

WOOSTER
Wooster, OH 44691 III

Coach: Steve Moore, Wittenberg 1974

2006-07 RESULTS (29-5)

128	Cabrini ⊠	71
85	Mount Union ⊠	60
85	Walsh	68
80	Georgetown (Ky.) ⊠	73
84	Earlham ⊠	62
95	Oberlin ⊠	76
68	Wittenberg	65
104	Cedarville ⊠	95
97	Pomona-Pitzer	77
89	Cal Baptist	94
84	Ohio Northern ⊠	91
98	Calvin ⊠	82
96	Denison ⊠	67
97	Allegheny	87
96	Wabash ⊠	52
111	Hiram	57
61	Ohio Wesleyan	54
89	Kenyon ⊠	54
64	Earlham	51
109	Allegheny ⊠	71
71	Wittenberg ⊠	74
90	Hiram ⊠	73
68	Wabash	63
87	Kenyon	62
95	Ohio Wesleyan ⊠	89
94	Earlham ⊠	76
92	Wabash ⊠	80
86	Ohio Wesleyan ⊠	51
92	Transylvania ⊠	66
73	Centre ⊠	56
83	John Carroll †	73
94	Brockport St. †	87
60	Amherst †	67
84	Washington-St. Louis †	92

Nickname: Fighting Scots
Colors: Black & Old Gold
Arena: Timken Gymnasium
    Capacity: 3,400; Year Built: 1968
AD: Keith D. Beckett
SID: Hugh Howard

WPI
Worcester, MA 01609 III

Coach: Chris Bartley, Mass.-Lowell 1994

2006-07 RESULTS (22-4)

86	Becker	53
83	Nichols †	64
75	Bridgewater St.	61
78	Salem St.	87
83	Elms ⊠	65
74	Fitchburg St.	54
81	Endicott ⊠	70
83	Case Reserve †	72
74	Milwaukee Engr.	71
75	Lasell ⊠	64
82	Springfield	75
59	Babson ⊠	53
77	Clark (Mass.)	61
64	MIT	43
76	Springfield ⊠	56
76	Coast Guard ⊠	68
67	Wheaton (Mass.)	64
77	Clark (Mass.) ⊠	53
69	Babson	79
89	Mass.-Boston ⊠	67
68	MIT ⊠	47
73	Wheaton (Mass.) ⊠	57
67	Coast Guard	57
66	MIT ⊠	49
66	Coast Guard ⊠	71
57	Stevens Institute †	68

Nickname: Engineers
Colors: Crimson & Gray
Arena: Harrington Auditorium
    Capacity: 3,000; Year Built: 1967
AD: Dana L. Harmon
SID: Rusty Eggen

RESULTS

438

2006-07 RESULTS

WORCESTER ST.
Worcester, MA 01602-2597..........III

Coach: Dave Lindberg, Worcester St. 1991

2006-07 RESULTS (11-16)
65	Nichols †	91
79	Becker	55
64	Mass.-Dartmouth	90
68	Clark (Mass.)	85
61	Pomona-Pitzer †	89
59	Luther †	56
81	Nichols ⊠	76
42	Amherst ⊠	70
65	Salve Regina	71
77	Becker ⊠	40
67	Fitchburg St. ⊠	72
65	Anna Maria ⊠	60
65	Westfield St.	75
91	Framingham St. ⊠	73
70	Newbury ⊠	77
77	Mass. Liberal Arts ⊠	67
53	Bridgewater St.	62
53	Elms	75
59	Salem St. ⊠	74
52	Fitchburg St.	67
76	Westfield St. ⊠	67
89	Framingham St.	84
87	Mass. Liberal Arts	69
71	Bridgewater St. ⊠	79
72	Salem St.	78
81	Fitchburg St.	72
63	Salem St.	74

Nickname: Lancers
Colors: Royal Blue & Gold
Arena: Lancer Gymnasium
 Capacity: 1,200; Year Built: 1953
AD: Susan E. Chapman
SID: John Meany

WRIGHT ST.
Dayton, OH 45435-0001 I

Coach: Brad Brownell, DePauw 1991

2006-07 RESULTS (23-10)
57	Miami (Ohio)	56
63	Coastal Caro.	70
70	Chicago St.	86
50	Detroit ⊠	49
49	Bradley	88
59	St. Bonaventure	57
72	Marshall	79
56	Bowling Green ⊠	59
63	Marist ⊠	53
63	Chicago St. ⊠	62
45	LSU	71
61	Samford †	50
55	Mississippi Val. †	54
72	IPFW ⊠	58
76	Ill.-Chicago ⊠	62
42	Butler	73
81	Loyola (Ill.) ⊠	55
78	Green Bay ⊠	67
78	Cleveland St.	67
69	Milwaukee	73
62	Youngstown St. ⊠	49
59	Loyola (Ill.)	47
65	Green Bay	54
66	Detroit	59
76	Milwaukee ⊠	50
74	Ill.-Chicago	64
77	Butler ⊠	65
68	Cleveland St. ⊠	55
77	Cal St. Fullerton ⊠	62
57	Youngstown St.	72
67	Green Bay ⊠	51
60	Butler ⊠	55
58	Pittsburgh †	79

Nickname: Raiders
Colors: Green & Gold
Arena: Ervin J. Nutter Center
 Capacity: 11,019; Year Built: 1990
AD: Michael J. Cusack
SID: Robert J. Noss

WYOMING
Laramie, WY 82071-3414...............I

Coach: Steve McClain, Chadron St. 1984

2006-07 RESULTS (17-15)
94	Boise St. ⊠	79
76	Montana ⊠	71
93	UAB ⊠	87
71	UAB	92
76	Colorado	73
78	Colorado Mines ⊠	67
73	Montana St. †	62
91	Denver ⊠	59
69	Wichita St. †	83
69	Lamar ⊠	64
58	Nebraska †	73
84	San Francisco †	81
78	Charlotte †	79
73	Milwaukee	75
66	San Diego St.	65
86	UNLV ⊠	76
56	Air Force ⊠	58
81	BYU	89
60	Utah	62
75	Colorado St. ⊠	70
71	TCU	56
83	New Mexico	91
43	Air Force	88
73	BYU ⊠	77
70	UNLV	80
80	San Diego St. ⊠	71
86	Utah ⊠	78
68	Colorado St.	86
58	TCU	77
76	New Mexico ⊠	67
67	Air Force †	62
84	BYU †	96

Nickname: Cowboys
Colors: Brown & Gold
Arena: Arena-Auditorium
 Capacity: 15,000; Year Built: 1982
AD: Tom Burman
SID: Tim Harkins

XAVIER
Cincinnati, OH 45207-7530 I

Coach: Sean Miller, Pittsburgh 1992

2006-07 RESULTS (25-9)
79	Coastal Caro. ⊠	46
70	VCU †	67
71	Villanova †	66
56	Alabama †	63
86	American ⊠	68
68	Miami (Ohio) ⊠	53
95	Western Caro. ⊠	61
88	Detroit ⊠	55
67	Creighton	73
57	Cincinnati	67
76	Arizona St. ⊠	58
67	Bucknell ⊠	68
65	Illinois †	59
76	Kansas St. †	66
76	Temple ⊠	68
71	Fordham	56
65	St. Louis	76
83	Massachusetts ⊠	77
74	St. Joseph's	82
92	St. Bonaventure ⊠	66
83	Dayton ⊠	67
91	Duquesne ⊠	93
91	Charlotte ⊠	57
76	St. Louis ⊠	57
87	George Washington	58
71	Richmond	50
98	Rhode Island ⊠	72
75	Dayton	67
72	St. Joseph's ⊠	62
76	La Salle	65
72	Dayton †	51
71	Rhode Island †	79
79	BYU †	77
71	Ohio St. †	78

Nickname: Musketeers
Colors: Blue, Gray & White
Arena: Cintas Center
 Capacity: 10,250; Year Built: 2000
AD: Mike Bobinski
SID: Tom Eiser

YALE
New Haven, CT 06520-8216..........I

Coach: James Jones, Albany (N.Y.) 1986

2006-07 RESULTS (14-13)
98	Allegheny ⊠	55
65	Ohio	73
62	Dayton	73
57	Bucknell †	72
58	Holy Cross †	63
65	Wagner	72
80	Sacred Heart	90
70	American	53
65	Hartford ⊠	66
69	Massachusetts	78
74	Navy	59
56	Boston College	72
74	Longwood ⊠	62
56	Brown	42
71	Brown ⊠	76
88	Harvard	78
71	Dartmouth	64
43	Princeton	35
77	Penn ⊠	68
85	Columbia	71
59	Cornell	60
69	Dartmouth ⊠	64
86	Harvard ⊠	71
68	Cornell ⊠	55
64	Columbia ⊠	82
58	Penn	86
52	Princeton	51

Nickname: Elis, Bulldogs
Colors: Yale Blue & White
Arena: John J. Lee Ampitheater
 Capacity: 3,100; Year Built: 1932
AD: Thomas A. Beckett
SID: Tim Bennett

YESHIVA
New York, NY 10033-3201.............III

Coach: Jonathan Halpert, Yeshiva 1966

2006-07 RESULTS (15-11)
65	Ramapo	76
71	Berkeley †	45
64	Baruch	74
64	Manhattanville	72
88	Mt. St. Vincent	78
55	Farmingdale St. ⊠	57
61	Maritime (N.Y.) ⊠	49
68	Lehman	44
84	Medgar Evers ⊠	70
101	CCNY ⊠	98
54	Dallas	46
66	Polytechnic (N.Y.) ⊠	47
49	Stevens Institute ⊠	53
70	Old Westbury ⊠	62
59	Brooklyn	54
70	Merchant Marine	60
49	St. Joseph's (L.I.)	66
68	Mt. St. Mary (N.Y.) ⊠	57
60	Farmingdale St.	64
65	Mt. St. Vincent ⊠	51
56	Manhattanville ⊠	62
87	Centenary (N.J.)	66
60	Old Westbury	75
42	St. Joseph's (L.I.) ⊠	60
84	Maritime (N.Y.)	69
51	Stevens Institute	87

Nickname: Maccabees
Colors: Royal Blue & White
Arena: Max Stern Athletic Center
 Capacity: 1,100; Year Built: 1985
AD: Joe Bednarsh
SID: Michael Gurock

YORK (N.Y.)
Jamaica, NY 11451 III

Coach: Ronald St. John, York (N.Y.) 1980

2006-07 RESULTS (18-11)
98	Chris. Newport	92
65	Wm. Paterson ⊠	56
36	New York U. ⊠	56
74	Rutgers-Newark	80
70	N.C. Wesleyan	78
64	Wesley †	54
89	Brooklyn ⊠	67
69	Medgar Evers ⊠	58
76	St. Joseph's (L.I.)	69
60	Rochester Inst.	64
62	Wittenberg	69
83	Thiel †	71
69	St. Joseph's (Me.) ⊠	71
69	Staten Island ⊠	57
78	Baruch	64
76	Lehman	63
86	City Tech ⊠	67
62	Ramapo	81
65	CCNY ⊠	50
72	John Jay	75
74	Brooklyn	56
92	Hunter ⊠	73
90	Medgar Evers	80
58	Staten Island	74
79	City Tech	82
81	Hunter †	62
65	CCNY	62
56	Staten Island †	54
68	Ramapo	77

Nickname: Cardinals
Colors: Red & White
Arena: Health & P.E. Complex
 Capacity: 1,200; Year Built: 1990
AD: Ronald St. John
SID: Jessica Cherry

YORK (PA.)
York, PA 17405-7199......................III

Coach: Jeff Gamber, Millersville 1968

2006-07 RESULTS (16-10)
69	Villa Julie ⊠	71
58	Gettysburg	42
72	Albright ⊠	70
69	Goucher	55
81	Salisbury	93
96	Gallaudet ⊠	79
52	Mary Washington ⊠	55
70	Juniata ⊠	57
84	Susquehanna ⊠	69
63	St. John Fisher ⊠	77
91	King's (Pa.) ⊠	87
75	Hobart ⊠	70
63	Richard Stockton ⊠	65
81	St. Mary's (Md.) ⊠	75
61	Catholic	63
96	Marymount (Va.) ⊠	75
78	Hood	80
91	Goucher ⊠	78
84	Salisbury ⊠	74
78	Gallaudet	73
90	Mary Washington	75
85	St. Mary's (Md.)	95
67	Catholic	63
94	Marymount (Va.)	82
71	Hood ⊠	78
76	Mary Washington ⊠	78

Nickname: Spartans
Colors: Kelly Green & White
Arena: Charles Wolf Gymnasium
 Capacity: 1,712; Year Built: 2006
AD: Sean Sullivan
SID: Scott Guise

YOUNGSTOWN ST.
Youngstown, OH 44555-0001 I

Coach: Jerry Slocum, King's (N.Y.) 1975

2006-07 RESULTS (14-17)
74	Central Mich. †	50
61	Michigan St.	86
75	Duquesne	81
95	Slippery Rock ⊠	57
56	Michigan	65
57	Ohio St. †	91
59	Canisius ⊠	71
64	Ill.-Chicago	80
70	Lock Haven ⊠	36
68	Milwaukee	65
78	Robert Morris	79
78	James Madison	58
62	Kent St.	58
76	Loyola (Ill.) ⊠	71
61	Akron ⊠	70
51	Detroit	66
49	Green Bay ⊠	59
81	Milwaukee ⊠	63
39	Butler	67
68	Cleveland St. ⊠	63
49	Wright St.	62
68	Loyola (Ill.)	80
58	Butler ⊠	71
92	Ill.-Chicago ⊠	87
46	Green Bay	55
82	Detroit ⊠	70
66	Eastern Ky. ⊠	61
72	Wright St. ⊠	57
55	Cleveland St.	68
82	Detroit ⊠	80
55	Green Bay †	72

Nickname: Penguins
Colors: Red & White
Arena: Beeghly Center
   Capacity: 6,400; Year Built: 1972
AD: Ron Strollo
SID: Trevor Parks